U0901227

中华人民共和国进出口税则
（法律文本）

Customs Tariff of Import and Export of the People's Republic of China
（The Legal Texts）

（2016）

（Enforced from January 1，2016）

国务院关税税则委员会办公室
中华人民共和国财政部关税司 编

Compiled by the Office of Customs Tariff Commission of the State Council
Tariff Policy Department of Ministry of Finance P.R.C.

中国财政经济出版社
China Financial & Economic Publishing House

图书在版编目（CIP）数据

中华人民共和国进出口税则：法律文本=Customs tariff of import and export of the People's Republic of China. 2016：汉英对照/国务院关税税则委员会办公室，中华人民共和国财政部关税司编. —北京：中国财政经济出版社，2016. 1

ISBN 978-7-5095-6623-7

Ⅰ. ①中… Ⅱ. ①国… ②中… Ⅲ. ①进出口贸易-关税-税则-中国-2016-汉、英 Ⅳ. ①D922.221

中国版本图书馆 CIP 数据核字（2016）第 018647 号

中国财政经济出版社 出版

URL：http://www.cfeph.cn

E-mail：cfeph@cfeph.cn

社址:北京海淀区阜成路甲 28 号 邮政编码：100142

发行处电话：88190406 财经书店电话：64033436

北京富生印刷厂印刷 各地新华书店经销

889×1194 毫米 16 开 77 印张 2 593 000 字

2016 年 1 月第 1 版 2016 年 1 月北京第 1 次印刷

定价：280.00 元

ISBN 978-7-5095-6623-7/D・0412

（图书出现印装问题，本社负责调换）

反盗版举报热线：88190492、88190446

使用说明

Explanation of Customs Tariff of Import and Export of the People's Republic of China

《中华人民共和国进出口税则》是《中华人民共和国进出口关税条例》(以下简称“《条例》”)的组成部分，主要包括进口税则、出口税则、本国子目注释等。

Customs Tariff of Import and Export of the People's Republic of China, which mainly comprises *Import Tariff*, *Export Tariff*, and Domestic Heading Explanation Notes, is a component part of *Regulations of the People's Republic of China on Import and Export Duties* (hereinafter referred to as " *Regulations*").

一、进口税则

I. Import Tariff

进口税则商品分类目录采用《商品名称及编码协调制度》。进口税则税目税率表设置税则号列、货品名称、最惠国税率、协定税率、特惠税率、普通税率等栏目。

The Harmonized Commodity Description and Coding System are introduced into the goods classification of the *Import Tariff*. The columns in the schedule of the *Import Tariff* are composed of tariff line, article description, Most Favored Nation (MFN) tariff rate, Agreement tariff rate, special preferential tariff rate, and general tariff rate.

（一）最惠国税率

(i) Most Favored Nation (MFN) Tariff Rates

根据《条例》规定，原产于共同适用最惠国待遇条款的世界贸易组织成员的进口货物，原产于与中华人民共和国签订含有相互给予最惠国待遇条款的双边贸易协定的国家或者地区的进口货物，以及原产于中华人民共和国境内的进口货物，适用最惠国税率。

According to the *Regulations*, the MFN tariff rates shall apply to the import goods originating in the members of the World Trade Organization providing that the MFN treatment is reciprocal between the People's Republic of China and these members, and the import goods originating in the countries and regions with which the People's Republic of China has concluded bilateral agreements that comprises reciprocal tariff preference clauses, and the import goods originating in the customs territory of the People's Republic of China.

以从价方式计征关税的最惠国税率，在最惠国税率栏中直接列明；以其他方式计征关税的最惠国税率在最惠国税率栏脚注中列明。

Ad valorem rates of the MFN tariffs are described in the column of the MFN tariff rate, the MFN tariff rates which in the form other than ad valorem rates are described in the footnotes.

非全税目信息技术产品的最惠国税率在最惠国税率栏中列明；其税则号列前标注“ex”，表示适用该税率的应税货物以货品名称栏中的描述为准。

The MFN tariff rates on Specific Information Technology Products are described in the column of the MFN tariff rate. The tariff lines prefixed by "ex" indicate their MFN tariff rates apply to the import goods that conform to the respective article description.

（二）协定税率

(ii) Agreement Tariff Rates

根据《条例》规定，原产于与中华人民共和国签订含有关税优惠条款的区域性贸易协定的国家或者地区的进口货物，适用协定税率。

According to the *Regulations*, the agreement tariff rates shall apply to the import goods originating in the countries and regions with which the People's Republic of China has concluded a regional trade agreement that comprises preferential tariff clauses.

根据《亚太贸易协定》及相关协议，对原产于大韩民国、斯里兰卡民主社会主义共和国、孟加拉人民共和国、印度共和国、老挝人民民主共和国的部分进口货物，实施协定税率。

According to *Asia Pacific Trade Agreement* and relevant agreements, the agreement tariff rates shall apply to certain import goods originating in the Republic of Korea, the Democratic Socialist Republic of Sri Lanka, the People's Republic of Bangladesh, the Republic of India, and the Lao People's Democratic Republic.

根据《中华人民共和国与东盟全面经济合作框架协议》及相关协议，对原产于文莱达鲁萨兰国、柬埔寨王国、印度尼西亚共和国、老挝人民民主共和国、马来西亚、缅甸联邦、菲律宾共和国、新加坡共和国、泰王国、越南社会主义共和国的部分进口货物，实施协定税率。

According to *Framework Agreement on Comprehensive Economic Co-Operation between China and ASEAN* and relevant agreements, the agreement tariff rates shall apply to certain import goods originating in Negara Brunei Darussalam, the Kingdom of Cambodia, the Republic of Indonesia, the Lao People's Democratic Republic, Malaysia, the Union of Myanmar, the Republic of the Philippines, the Republic of Singapore, the Kingdom of Thailand, and the Socialist Republic of Viet Nam.

根据《中华人民共和国政府与智利共和国政

According to *Free Trade Agreement between the Government of the*

府自由贸易协定》及相关协议，对原产于智利共和国的部分进口货物，实施协定税率。

People's Republic of China and the Government of the Republic of Chile and relevant agreements, the agreement tariff rates shall apply to certain import goods originating in the Republic of Chile.

根据《中华人民共和国政府与巴基斯坦伊斯兰共和国政府自由贸易协定》及相关协议，对原产于巴基斯坦伊斯兰共和国的部分进口货物，实施协定税率。

According to *Free Trade Agreement between the Government of the People's Republic of China and the Government of the Islamic Republic of Pakistan* and relevant agreements, the agreement tariff rates shall apply to certain import goods originating in the Islamic Republic of Pakistan.

根据《中华人民共和国政府与新西兰政府自由贸易协定》及相关协议，对原产于新西兰的部分进口货物，实施协定税率。

According to *Free Trade Agreement between the Government of the People's Republic of China and the Government of New Zealand* and relevant agreements, the agreement tariff rates shall apply to certain import goods originating in New Zealand.

根据《中华人民共和国政府与新加坡共和国政府自由贸易协定》及相关协议，对原产于新加坡共和国的部分进口货物，实施协定税率。

According to *Free Trade Agreement between the Government of the People's Republic of China and the Government of the Republic of Singapore* and relevant agreements, the agreement tariff rates shall apply to certain import goods originating in the Republic of Singapore.

根据《中华人民共和国政府与秘鲁共和国政府自由贸易协定》及相关协议，对原产于秘鲁共和国的部分进口货物，实施协定税率。

According to *Free Trade Agreement between the Government of the People's Republic of China and the Government of the Republic of Peru* and relevant agreements, the agreement tariff rates shall apply to certain import goods originating in the Republic of Peru.

根据《中华人民共和国政府与哥斯达黎加共和国政府自由贸易协定》及相关协议，对原产于哥斯达黎加共和国的部分进口货物，实施协定税率。

According to *Free Trade Agreement between the Government of the People's Republic of China and the Government of the Republic of Costa Rica* and relevant agreements, the agreement tariff rates shall apply to certain import goods originating in the Republic of Costa Rica.

根据《中华人民共和国政府与瑞士联邦政府自由贸易协定》及相关协议，对原产于瑞士联邦的部分进口货物，实施协定税率。

According to *Free Trade Agreement between the Government of the People's Republic of China and the Government of the Swiss Confederation* and relevant agreements, the agreement tariff rates shall apply to certain import goods originating in the Swiss Confederation.

根据《中华人民共和国政府与冰岛共和国政府自由贸易协定》及相关协议，对原产于冰岛共和国的部分进口货物，实施协定税率。

According to *Free Trade Agreement between the Government of the People's Republic of China and the Government of the Republic of Iceland* and relevant agreements, the agreement tariff rates shall apply to certain import goods originating in the Republic of Iceland.

根据《中华人民共和国政府与大韩民国政府自由贸易协定》及相关协议，对原产于大韩民国的部分进口货物，实施协定税率。

According to *Free Trade Agreement between the Government of the People's Republic of China and the Government of the Republic of Korea* and relevant agreements, the agreement tariff rates shall apply to certain import goods originating in the Republic of Iceland.

根据《中华人民共和国政府与澳大利亚政府自由贸易协定》及相关协议，对原产于澳大利亚的部分进口货物，实施协定税率。

According to *Free Trade Agreement between the Government of Australia and the Government of the People's Republic of China* and relevant agreements, the agreement tariff rates shall apply to certain import goods originating in the Republic of Iceland.

根据《内地与香港关于建立更紧密经贸关系的安排》、《内地与澳门关于建立更紧密经贸关系的安排》及相关协议，对原产于香港、澳门已完成原产地标准核准的进口货物，实施零关税。

According to *Mainland /Hong Kong Closer Economic Partnership Arrangement* and *Mainland / Macao Closer Economic Partnership Arrangement* and relevant agreements, the zero tariff rates shall apply to the import goods conforming to the approved rules of origin and originating in the Hong Kong Special Administrative Region, China and the Macao Special Administrative Region, China.

根据《海峡两岸经济合作框架协议》，对原产于台湾地区的部分进口货物，实施协定税率。

According to *Cross-Straits Economic Cooperation Framework Agreement*, the agreement tariff rates shall apply to certain import goods originating in Taiwan, China.

协定税率及其适用国别或地区在协定税率栏中标示，其中以从价以外方式计征关税的协定税率见脚注。国别或地区代码表附后。

The agreement tariff rates which in the form of ad valorem and specific rates and their applicable countries and regions are indicated in the column of the Agreement Tariff Rate. The agreement tariff rates which in the form other than ad valorem rates are described in the footnotes. The table of codes of countries and regions is attached.

（三）特惠税率

根据《条例》规定，原产于与中华人民共和国签订含有特殊关税优惠条款的贸易协定的国家或者地区的进口货物，适用特惠税率。

根据中华人民共和国政府与有关国家政府间换文协议，对原产于老挝人民民主共和国、孟加拉人民共和国、柬埔寨王国、缅甸联邦、埃塞俄比亚联邦民主共和国、安哥拉共和国、贝宁共和国、布隆迪共和国、赤道几内亚共和国、多哥共和国、厄立特里亚国、刚果民主共和国、吉布提共和国、几内亚共和国、几内亚比绍共和国、科摩罗联盟、莱索托王国、利比里亚共和国、卢旺达共和国、马达加斯加共和国、马里共和国、马拉维共和国、毛里塔尼亚伊斯兰共和国、莫桑比克共和国、尼日尔共和国、塞拉利昂共和国、塞内加尔共和国、苏丹共和国、南苏丹共和国、索马里联邦共和国、坦桑尼亚联合共和国、乌干达共和国、赞比亚共和国、乍得共和国、中非共和国、阿富汗伊斯兰共和国、尼泊尔联邦民主共和国、东帝汶民主共和国、萨摩亚独立国、瓦努阿图共和国、也门共和国的部分进口货物，实施特惠税率。

特惠税率及其适用国别或地区在特惠税率栏中标示，其中以从价以外方式计征关税的特惠税率见脚注。国别或地区代码表附后。

（四）普通税率

根据《条例》规定，原产于除适用最惠国税率、协定税率、特惠税率国家或地区以外的国家或者地区的进口货物，以及原产地不明的进口货物，适用普通税率。

以从价方式计征关税的普通税率，在进口税则普通税率栏中直接列明；以其他方式计征关税的普通税率在普通税率栏脚注中列明。

（五）配额税率

根据《条例》规定，按照国家规定实行关税配额管理的进口货物，关税配额内的，适用关税配额税率。

根据《中华人民共和国政府与澳大利亚政府自由贸易协定》，对原产于澳大利亚的部分产品，适用国别配额税率。

根据《中华人民共和国政府与新西兰政府自

(iii) Special Preferential Tariff Rates

According to the *Regulations*, the special preferential tariff rates shall apply to the import goods originating in countries and regions with which the People's Republic of China has concluded a trade agreement that comprises special preferential tariff clauses.

According to the Exchange Letter between the government of the People's Republic of China and the related governments, the special preferential tariff rates shall apply to certain import goods originating in the Lao People's Democratic Republic, the People's Republic of Bangladesh, the Kingdom of Cambodia, the Union of Myanmar, The Federal Democratic Republic of Ethiopia, The Republic of Angola, The Republic of Benin, The Republic of Burundi, The Republic of Equatorial Guinea, The Republic of Togo, The State of Eritrea The Democratic Republic of Congo, The Republic of Djibouti, The Republic of Guinea, The Republic of Guinea-Bissau, Union of Comoros, The Kingdom of Lesotho, The Republic Of Liberia, The Republic of Rwanda, The Republic of Madagascar, The Republic of Mali, The Republic of Malawi, The Islamic Republic of Mauritania, The Republic of Mozambique, The Republic of Niger, The Republic of Sierra Leone, The Republic of Senegal, The Republic of the Sudan, The Republic of the South Sudan, The Federal Republic of Somalia, The United Republic of Tanzania, The Republic of Uganda, The Republic of Zambia, The Republic of Chad, The Central African Republic, The Islamic Republic of Afghanistan, The Federal Democratic Republic of Nepal, Democratic Republic of Timor-Leste, The Independent State of Samoa, The Republic of Vanuatu, The Republic of Yemen.

The special preferential tariff rates which in the form of ad valorem and specific rates and their applicable countries and regions are indicated in the column of the Special Preferential Tariff Rate. The special preferential tariff rates which in the form other than ad valorem rates are described in the footnotes. The table of codes of countries and regions is attached.

(iv) General Tariff Rates

The general tariff rates shall apply to the import goods with undetermined origins and originating in the countries and regions that are not applicable to the MFN tariff rates, agreement tariff rates, or special preferential tariff rates.

The general tariff rates which in the form of ad valorem rates are de 是 cribed in the column of the General Tariff Rate. The general tariff rates which in the form other than ad valorem rates are described in the footnotes.

(v) Tariff Quota Rates

According to the *Regulations*, Where the quantity of import goods that are subject to tariff quota administration in accordance with the provisions of the State is within the tariff quota, the tariff quota rates shall apply.

According to *Free Trade Agreement between the Government of Australia and the Government of the People's Republic of China* and, the country-specific quota rates shall apply to certain import goods originating in Australia .

According to *Free Trade Agreement between the Government of the People's Republic of China and the Government of New Zealand*, the

由贸易协定》，对原产于新西兰的部分产品，适用国别配额税率。

country-specific quota rates shall apply to certain import goods originating in New Zealand.

关税配额税率在最惠国税率栏的脚注中列明。

All the tariff quota rates are described in the footnotes other than in the column of the MFN tariff rate.

（六）暂定税率

(vi) Interim Tariff Rates

根据《条例》规定，适用最惠国税率、协定税率、特惠税率、关税配额税率的进口货物在一定期限内可以实行暂定税率。

According to the *Regulations*, the import goods that are applicable to the MFN tariff rates, agreement tariff rates, special preferential tariff rates, and tariff quota rates may apply to the interim tariff rates within a specific time limit.

适用最惠国税率的进口货物有暂定税率的，应当适用暂定税率；适用协定税率、特惠税率的进口货物有暂定税率的，应当从低适用税率；适用关税配额税率的进口货物有暂定税率的，应当适用暂定税率。适用普通税率的进口货物，不适用暂定税率。

Where there are interim tariff rates on import goods to which the MFN tariff rates are applicable, such interim tariff rates shall apply; where there are interim tariff rates on import goods to which the agreement tariff rates or the special tariff rates are applicable, the lower tariff rates shall apply; where there are interim tariff rates on import goods to which the tariff quota rates are applicable, such interim tariff rates shall apply. Interim tariff rates shall not apply to the import goods to which the general tariff rates are applicable.

1．最惠国暂定税率

1. MFN Interim Tariff Rates

最惠国暂定税率在最惠国税率栏中以前置“△”标示（如“△8”表示该税目最惠国暂定税率为8%）。以从价以外方式计征关税的最惠国暂定税率见脚注。税则号列前标注“ex”，表示适用该税率的应税进口货物应在该税号范围内，以具体描述为准。

The MFN Interim Tariff rates are indicated with the fore mark of “△” in the column of the MFN tariff rate (for example, “△8” indicates that the MFN interim tariff rate on the respective tariff line is 8%). The MFN interim tariff rates which in the form other than ad valorem rates are described in the footnotes. The tariff lines prefixed by “ex” indicate their MFN interim tariff rates apply to the import goods that conform to the respective article description in these tariff lines.

2．关税配额暂定税率

2. Interim Tariff Quota Rates

关税配额暂定税率在最惠国税率栏的脚注中列明。

The interim tariff quota rates are described in the footnotes other than in the column of the MFN tariff rate.

二、出口税则

II. Export Tariff

出口税则的商品分类目录与进口税则相同。出口税则设置税则号列、货品名称、出口税率等栏目。

The goods classification of the *Export Tariff* is consistent with the *Import Tariff*. The columns in the schedule of the *Export Tariff* are composed of tariff line, article description, and export tariff rate.

根据《条例》规定，对出口货物在一定期限内可以实行暂定税率；适用出口税率的出口货物有暂定税率的，应当适用暂定税率。

According to the *Regulations*, interim tariff rates may apply to export goods within a specific time limit. Where there are interim tariff rates on export goods to which the export tariff rates are applicable, such interim tariff rates shall apply.

出口商品暂定税率见出口商品暂定税率表。税则号列前标注“ex”，表示适用该税率的应税出口货物应在该税号范围内，以具体描述为准。

Interim tariff rates of the export goods refer to the “Table of Interim Tariff Rate on Export Goods”. The tariff lines prefixed by “ex” indicate their export tariff rates apply to the export goods that conform to the respective article description in these tariff lines.

三、关税减免

III. Tariff Reduction and Exemption

特定地区、特定企业或者特定用途的进出口货物减征或者免征关税的，以及其他依法减征或者免征关税的，按照国务院的有关规定执行。

Tariff reduction or exemption granted to import and export goods of special areas, special enterprises or for special uses, as well as other temporary tariff reduction or exemption, shall be governed by the relevant provisions of the State Council.

四、计量单位

IV. Abbreviations and Symbols

税率计量单位代码如下。

The abbreviations and symbols used in the *Import Tariff* and the *Export Tariff* are listed in the following table.

计量单位代码	计量单位中文名称
￥	人民币元
kg	千克
ton	公吨
L	公升
m²	平方米
set	台、套
$	美元

abbreviation or symbol	unit
￥	Renminbi
kg	kilogram
ton	metric ton
L	liter
m²	square meter
set	set
$	US Dollar

五、本国子目注释

本国子目注释是国务院关税税则委员会对进口税则、出口税则解释的一部分。

六、文本效力

进出口税则内容以中文文本为准；英文译文仅供参考，不具法律效力。

七、附录

为查阅方便，在附录中收集整理了进口商品从量税、复合税税目税率表，关税配额商品税目税率表和《条例》(中英文文本)等。

V. Domestic Heading Explanation Notes

Domestic heading explanation notes, which explained by Customs Tariff Commission of the State Council, are the component parts of the *Import Tariff* and the *Export Tariff*.

VI. Force of the Text

The Chinese version of the *Import Tariff* and the *Export Tariff* is authentic. The English version is for reference only.

VII. Appendix

The appendix embodies the Table of Specific Rate and Compound Rate on Import Goods, the Table of Tariff Quota Rate on Import Goods, and both Chinese and English versions of the *Regulations* etc.

国别或地区代码表

序号	中文简称	英文代码	国家（组）及地区名称	包括国家或地区
适用协定税率				
1	亚太	AP	亚太贸易协定国家	大韩民国、斯里兰卡民主社会主义共和国、孟加拉人民共和国、印度共和国、老挝人民民主共和国
2	东盟	AS	东盟协定国家	文莱达鲁萨兰国、柬埔寨王国、印度尼西亚共和国、老挝人民民主共和国、马来西亚、缅甸联邦、菲律宾共和国、新加坡共和国、泰王国和越南社会主义共和国
3	新加坡	SG	新加坡共和国	新加坡共和国
4	巴	PK	巴基斯坦伊斯兰共和国	巴基斯坦伊斯兰共和国
5	智利	CL	智利共和国	智利共和国
6	新西兰	NZ	新西兰	新西兰
7	秘鲁	PE	秘鲁共和国	秘鲁共和国
8	哥	CR	哥斯达黎加共和国	哥斯达黎加共和国
9	瑞士	CH	瑞士联邦	瑞士联邦
10	冰岛	IS	冰岛共和国	冰岛共和国
11	韩国	KR	大韩民国	大韩民国

续表

序号	中文简称	英文代码	国家（组）及地区名称	包括国家或地区
12	澳	AU	澳大利亚	澳大利亚
13	香港	HK	香港特别行政区	香港特别行政区
14	澳门	MO	澳门特别行政区	澳门特别行政区
15	台湾	TW	台湾地区	台湾地区
适用特惠税率				
16	亚太	AP	亚太贸易协定的 2 个国家	孟加拉人民共和国、老挝人民民主共和国
17	受惠国	LD	埃塞俄比亚联邦民主共和国等 40 个最不发达国家	埃塞俄比亚联邦民主共和国、布隆迪共和国、赤道几内亚共和国、刚果民主共和国、吉布提共和国、几内亚共和国、几内亚比绍共和国、莱索托王国、马达加斯加共和国、马拉维共和国、马里共和国、莫桑比克共和国、南苏丹共和国、塞拉利昂共和国、塞内加尔共和国、苏丹共和国、索马里联邦共和国、坦桑尼亚联合共和国、乌干达共和国、乍得共和国、中非共和国、阿富汗伊斯兰共和国、也门共和国、瓦努阿图共和国、安哥拉共和国、多哥共和国、科摩罗联盟、利比里亚共和国、尼日尔共和国、赞比亚共和国、尼泊尔联邦民主共和国、毛里塔尼亚伊斯兰共和国、卢旺达共和国、贝宁共和国、厄立特里亚国、东帝汶民主共和国、柬埔寨王国、缅甸联邦共和国、萨摩亚独立国、孟加拉人民共和国
18	受惠国$_1$	LD_1	埃塞俄比亚联邦民主共和国等 39 个最不发达国家	埃塞俄比亚联邦民主共和国、布隆迪共和国、赤道几内亚共和国、刚果民主共和国、吉布提共和国、几内亚共和国、几内亚比绍共和国、莱索托王国、马达加斯加共和国、马拉维共和国、马里共和国、莫桑比克共和国、南苏丹共和国、塞拉利昂共和国、塞内加尔共和国、苏丹共和国、索马里联邦共和国、坦桑尼亚联合共和国、乌干达共和国、乍得共和国、中非共和国、阿富汗伊斯兰共和国、也门共和国、瓦努阿图共和国、安哥拉共和国、多哥共和国、科摩罗联盟、利比里亚共和国、尼日尔共和国、赞比亚共和国、尼泊尔联邦民主共和国、毛里塔尼亚伊斯兰共和国、卢旺达共和国、贝宁共和国、厄立特里亚国、东帝汶民主共和国、柬埔寨王国、缅甸联邦共和国、萨摩亚独立国
19	受惠国$_2$	LD_2	埃塞俄比亚联邦民主共和国等 33 个最不发达国家	埃塞俄比亚联邦民主共和国、布隆迪共和国、赤道几内亚共和国、刚果民主共和国、吉布提共和国、几内亚共和国、几内亚比绍共和国、莱索托王国、马达加斯加共和国、马拉维共和国、马里共和国、莫桑比克共和国、南苏丹共和国、塞拉利昂共和国、塞内加尔共和国、苏丹共和国、索马里联邦共和国、坦桑尼亚联合共和国、乌干达共和国、乍得共和国、中非共和国、阿富汗伊斯兰共和国、也门共和国、瓦努阿图共和国、安哥拉共和国、多哥共和国、科摩罗联盟、利比里亚共和国、尼日尔共和国、赞比亚共和国、尼泊尔联邦民主共和国、毛里塔尼亚伊斯兰共和国、卢旺达共和国
20	柬埔寨	KH	柬埔寨王国	柬埔寨王国
21	缅甸	MM	缅甸联邦	缅甸联邦
22	老挝	LA	老挝人民民主共和国	老挝人民民主共和国

Table of Codes of Countries and Regions

No.	Code	Countries (Group) or Regions	Relevant Countries and Regions
the agreement tariff rates			
1	AP	Countries under Asia Pacific Trade Agreement	Republic of Korea, Democratic Socialist Republic of Sri Lanka, People's Republic of Bangladesh, Republic of India, Lao People's Democratic Republic
2	AS	Members of ASEAN	Negara Brunei Darussalam, Kingdom of Cambodia, Republic of Indonesia, Lao People's Democratic Republic, Malaysia, Union of Myanmar, Republic of Philippines, Republic of Singapore, Kingdom of Thailand, Socialist Republic of Viet Nam
3	SG	Republic of Singapore	Republic of Singapore
4	PK	Islamic Republic of Pakistan	Islamic Republic of Pakistan
5	CL	Republic of Chile	Republic of Chile
6	NZ	New Zealand	New Zealand
7	PE	Republic of Peru	Republic of Peru
8	CR	Republic of Costa Rica	Republic of Costa Rica
9	CH	Swiss Confederation	Swiss Confederation
10	IS	Republic of Iceland	Republic of Iceland
11	KR	Republic of Korea	Republic of Korea
12	AU	Australia	Australia
13	HK	Hong Kong Special Administrative Region, China	Hong Kong Special Administrative Region, China
14	MO	Macao Special Administrative Region, China	Macao Special Administrative Region, China
15	TW	Taiwan, China	Taiwan, China
the special preferential tariff rates			
16	AP	Two countries of APTA	People's Republic of Bangladesh, Lao People's Democratic Republic
17	LD	40 Least Developing Countries	The Federal Democratic Republic of Ethiopia, The Republic of Burundi, The Republic of Angola, The Republic of Benin, The Republic of Togo, The State of Eritrea, The Democratic Republic of Congo, The Republic of Djibouti, The Republic of Guinea, The Republic of Guinea-Bissau, Union of Comoros, The Kingdom of Lesotho, The Republic of Liberia, The Republic of Rwanda, The Republic of Madagascar, The Republic of Mali, The Republic of Malawi, The Republic of Mozambique, The Republic of Sierra Leone, The Republic of Senegal, The Republic of the Sudan, The Republic of the South Sudan, The United Republic of Tanzania, The Republic of Uganda, The Republic of Zambia, The Republic of Chad, The Central African Republic, The Republic of Niger，The Islamic Republic of Afghanistan, The Federal Democratic Republic of Nepal, Democratic Republic of Timor-Leste, The Independent State of Samoa, The Republic of Vanuatu, The Republic of Yemen，Kingdom of Cambodia，Union of Myanmar, The People's Republic of Bangladesh, The Republic of Equatorial Guinea, The Islamic Republic of Mauritania, The Federal Republic of Somalia

续表

No.	Code	Countries (Group) or Regions	Relevant Countries and Regions
18	LD_1	39 Least Developing Countries	The Federal Democratic Republic of Ethiopia, The Republic of Burundi, The Republic of Angola, The Republic of Benin, The Republic of Togo, The State of Eritrea, The Democratic Republic of Congo, The Republic of Djibouti, The Republic of Guinea, The Republic of Guinea-Bissau, Union of Comoros, The Kingdom of Lesotho, The Republic of Liberia, The Republic of Rwanda, The Republic of Madagascar, The Republic of Mali, The Republic of Malawi, The Republic of Mozambique, The Republic of Sierra Leone, The Republic of Senegal, The Republic of the Sudan, The Republic of the South Sudan, The United Republic of Tanzania, The Republic of Uganda, The Republic of Zambia, The Republic of Chad, The Central African Republic, The Republic of Niger，The Islamic Republic of Afghanistan, The Federal Democratic Republic of Nepal, Democratic Republic of Timor-Leste, The Independent State of Samoa, The Republic of Vanuatu, The Republic of Yemen，Kingdom of Cambodia，Union of Myanmar，The Republic of Equatorial Guinea, The Islamic Republic of Mauritania, The Federal Republic of Somalia
19	LD_2	33 Least Developing Countries	The Federal Democratic Republic of Ethiopia, The Republic of Burundi, The Republic of Angola, The Republic of Togo, The Democratic Republic of Congo, The Republic of Djibouti, The Republic of Guinea, The Republic of Guinea-Bissau, Union of Comoros, The Kingdom of Lesotho, The Republic of Liberia, The Republic of Rwanda, The Republic of Madagascar, The Republic of Mali, The Republic of Malawi, The Republic of Mozambique, The Republic of Sierra Leone, The Republic of Senegal, The Republic of the Sudan, The Republic of the South Sudan, The United Republic of Tanzania, The Republic of Uganda, The Republic of Zambia, The Republic of Chad, The Central African Republic, The Republic of Niger，The Islamic Republic of Afghanistan, The Federal Democratic Republic of Nepal, The Republic of Vanuatu, The Republic of Yemen，The Republic of Equatorial Guinea, The Islamic Republic of Mauritania, The Federal Republic of Somalia
20	KH	Kingdom of Cambodia	Kingdom of Cambodia
21	MM	Union of Myanmar	Union of Myanmar
22	LA	Lao People's Democratic Republic	Lao People's Democratic Republic

总 目 录

Contents

中华人民共和国进口税则

（2016 年 1 月 1 日起实施）

Customs Tariff of Import of the People's Republic of China

(Enforced from January 1, 2016)

进口税则目录 Index of Import Tariff

归类总规则

GENERAL RULES FOR THE INTERPRETATION OF THE HARMONIZED SYSTEM

货品在本税则目录上的归类，应遵循以下原则：

Classification of goods in the Nomenclature shall be governed by the following Rules:

规则一　类、章及分章的标题，仅为查找方便而设；具有法律效力的归类，应按税目条文和有关类注或章注确定，如税目、类注或章注无其他规定，按以下规则确定。

1. The titles of Sections, Chapters and sub-Chapters are provided for ease of reference only; for legal purposes, classification shall be determined according to the terms of the headings and any relative Section or Chapter Notes and provided such headings or Notes do not otherwise require, according to the following provisions.

规则二　（一）税目所列货品，应视为包括该项货品的不完整品或未制成品，只要在进口或出口时该项不完整品或未制成品具有完整品或制成品的基本特征；还应视为包括该项货品的完整品或制成品（或按本款可作为完整品或制成品归类的货品）在进口或出口时的未组装件或拆散件。

2. (a) Any reference in a heading to an article shall be taken to include a reference to that article incomplete or unfinished, provided that, as presented, the incomplete or unfinished article has the essential character of the complete or finished article. It shall also be taken to include a reference to that article complete or finished(or falling to be classified as complete or finished by virtue of this Rule), presented unassembled or disassembled.

（二）税目中所列材料或物质，应视为包括该种材料或物质与其他材料或物质混合或组合的物品。税目所列某种材料或物质构成的货品，应视为包括全部或部分由该种材料或物质构成的货品。由一种以上材料或物质构成的货品，应按规则三归类。

(b) Any reference in a heading to a material or substance shall be taken to include a reference to mixtures or combinations of that material or substance with other materials or substances. Any reference to goods of a given material or substance shall be taken to include a reference to goods consisting wholly or partly of such material or substance. The classification of goods consisting of more than one material or substance shall be according to the principles of Rule 3.

规则三　当货品按规则二（二）或由于其他原因看起来可归入两个或两个以上税目时，应按以下规则归类：

3. When by application of Rule 2(b) or for any other reason, goods are, prima facie, classifiable under two or more headings, classification shall be effected as follows:

（一）列名比较具体的税目，优先于列名一般的税目。但是，如果两个或两个以上税目都仅述及混合或组合货品所含的某部分材料或物质，或零售的成套货品中的某些货品，即使其中某个税目对该货品描述得更为全面、详细，这些货品在有关税目的列名应视为同样具体。

(a) The heading which provides the most specific description shall be preferred to headings providing a more general description. However, when two or more headings each refer to part only of the materials or substances contained in mixed or composite goods or to part only of the items in a set put up for retail sale, those heading are to be regarded as equally specific in relation to those goods, even if one of them gives a more complete or precise description of the goods.

（二）混合物、不同材料构成或不同部件组成的组合物以及零售的成套货品，如果不能按照规则三（一）归类时，在本款可适用的条件下，应按构成货品基本特征的材料或部件归类。

(b) Mixtures, composite goods consisting of different materials or made up of different components, and goods put up in sets for retail sale, which cannot be classified by reference to Rule 3(a), shall be classified as they consisted of the material or component which gives them their essential character, insofar as this criterion is applicable.

（三）货品不能按照规则三（一）或（二）归类时，应按号列顺序归入其可归入的最末一个税目。

(c) When goods cannot be classified by reference to Rule 3(a) or Rule 3(b), they shall be classified under the heading which occurs last in numerical order among those which equally merit consideration.

规则四　根据上述规则无法归类的货品，应归入与其最相类似的货品的税目。

4. Goods which cannot be classified in accordance with the above Rules shall be classified under the heading appropriate to the goods to which they are most akin.

规则五　除上述规则外，本规则适用于下列货品的归类：

（一）制成特殊形状仅适用于盛装某个或某套物品并适合长期使用的照像机套、乐器盒、枪套、绘图仪器盒、项链盒及类似容器，如果与所装物品同时进口或出口，并通常与所装物品一同出售的，应与所装物品一并归类。但本款不适用于本身构成整个货品基本特征的容器。

（二）除规则五（一）规定的以外，与所装货品同时进口或出口的包装材料或包装容器，如果通常是用来包装这类货品的，应与所装货品一并归类。但明显可重复使用的包装材料和包装容器可不受本款限制。

5. In addition to the foregoing Rules, the following Rules shall apply in respect of the goods referred to therein:

(a) Camera cases, musical instrument cases, gun cases, drawing instrument cases, necklace cases and similar containers, specially shaped or fitted to contain a specific article or set of articles, suitable for long term use and presented with the articles for which they are intended, shall be classified with such articles when of a kind normally sold therewith. This Rule does not, however, apply to containers which give the whole its essential character.

(b) Subject to the provisions of Rule 5(a) above, packing materials and packing containers presented with the goods there in shall be classified with the goods if they are of a kind normally used for packing such goods. However, this provision is not binding when such packing materials or packing containers are clearly suitable for repetitive use.

规则六　货品在某一税目项下各子目的法定归类，应按子目条文或有关的子目注释以及以上各条规则来确定，但子目的比较只能在同一数级上进行。除本税则目录条文另有规定的以外，有关的类注、章注也适用于本规则。

6. For legal purposes, the classification of goods in the subheadings of a heading shall be determined according to the terms of those sub-headings and any related Subheading Notes and, mutatis mutandis, to the above Rules, on the understanding that only subheadings at the same level are comparable. For the purposes of this Rule the relative Section and Chapter Notes also apply, unless the context otherwise requires.

第一类

活动物；动物产品

注释：

一、本类所称的各属种动物，除条文另有规定的以外，均包括其幼仔在内。

二、除条文另有规定的以外，本目录所称干的产品，均包括经脱水、蒸发或冷冻干燥的产品。

第一章
活 动 物

注释：

本章包括所有活动物，但下列各项除外：

一、税号 03.01、03.06、03.07 或 03.08 的鱼、甲壳动物、软体动物及其他水生无脊椎动物；

二、税号 30.02 的培养微生物及其他产品；

三、税号 95.08 的动物。

SECTION I

LIVE ANIMALS; ANIMAL PRODUCTS

Notes:

1. Any reference in this Section to a particular genus or species of an animal, except where the context otherwise requires, includes a reference to the young of that genus or species.
2. Except where the context otherwise requires, throughout the Nomenclature any reference to "dried" products also covers products which have been dehydrated, evaporated or freeze-dried.

Chapter 1
Live animals

Notes:

This Chapter covers all live animals except:

1. Fish and crustaceans, molluscs and other aquatic invertebrates, of heading No.03.01, 03.06, 03.07 or 03.08;
2. Cultures of micro-organisms and other products of heading No.30.02; and
3. Animals of heading No.95.08.

序号 No.	税则号列 Tariff Line	中文货品名称 Article Description in Chinese	最惠国税率 MFN(%)	协定税率 Agreement(%)	特惠税率 SP(%)	普通税率 Gen(%)	英文货品名称 Article Description
	01.01	**马、驴、骡：**					**Live horses, asses, mules and hinnies:**
		-马：					-Horses:
1	0101.2100	--改良种用	0		0 受惠国LD	0	--Pure-bred breeding
2	0101.2900	--其他	10	0 冰岛IS,东盟AS,哥CR,新西兰NZ,智利CL 3 秘鲁PE 4 瑞士CH 5 巴PK 6 澳AU 8 韩国KR	0 受惠国LD	30	--Other
		-驴：					-Asses:
3	0101.3010	---改良种用	0		0 受惠国LD	0	---Pure-bred breeding
4	0101.3090	---其他	10	0 冰岛IS,东盟AS,哥CR,新西兰NZ,智利CL 3 秘鲁PE 4 瑞士CH 5 巴PK 6 澳AU 8 韩国KR	0 受惠国LD	30	---Other
5	0101.9000	-其他	10	0 冰岛IS,东盟AS,哥CR,新西兰NZ,智利CL 3 秘鲁PE 4 瑞士CH 5 巴PK 6 澳AU 8 韩国KR	0 受惠国LD	30	-Other
	01.02	**牛：**					**Live bovine animals:**
		-家牛：					-Cattle:
6	0102.2100	--改良种用	0		0 受惠国LD	0	--Pure-bred breeding
7	0102.2900	--其他	10	0 冰岛IS,东盟AS,哥CR,新西兰NZ,智利CL 3 秘鲁PE 4 瑞士CH 5 巴PK 6 澳AU 8 韩国KR	0 柬埔寨KH,老挝LA,缅甸MM,受惠国LD	30	--Other
		-水牛：					-Buffalo:

序号 No.	税则号列 Tariff Line	中文货品名称 Article Description in Chinese	最惠国税率 MFN(%)	协定税率 Agreement(%)	特惠税率 SP(%)	普通税率 Gen(%)	英文货品名称 Article Description
8	0102.3100	--改良种用	0		0 受惠国LD	0	--Pure-bred breeding
9	0102.3900	--其他	10	0 冰岛IS,东盟AS,哥CR,新西兰NZ,智利CL 3 秘鲁PE 4 瑞士CH 5 巴PK 6 澳AU 8 韩国KR	0 柬埔寨KH,老挝LA,缅甸MM,受惠国LD	30	--Other
		-其他:					-Other:
10	0102.9010	---改良种用	0		0 受惠国LD	0	---Pure-bred breeding
11	0102.9090	---其他	10	0 冰岛IS,东盟AS,哥CR,新西兰NZ,智利CL 3 秘鲁PE 4 瑞士CH 5 巴PK 6 澳AU 8 韩国KR	0 柬埔寨KH,老挝LA,缅甸MM,受惠国LD	30	---Other
	01.03	**猪:**					**Live swine:**
12	0103.1000	-改良种用	0		0 受惠国LD	0	-Pure-bred breeding
		-其他:					-Other:
		--重量在50公斤以下:					--Weighing less than 50kg:
13	0103.9110	---重量在10公斤以下	10	0 冰岛IS,东盟AS,哥CR,秘鲁PE,新西兰NZ,智利CL 4 瑞士CH 5 巴PK 6 澳AU 8 韩国KR	0 柬埔寨KH,缅甸MM,受惠国LD	50	---Weighing less than 10kg
14	0103.9120	---重量在10公斤及以上，但在50公斤以下	10	0 冰岛IS,东盟AS,哥CR,秘鲁PE,新西兰NZ,智利CL 4 瑞士CH 5 巴PK 6 澳AU 8 韩国KR	0 柬埔寨KH,缅甸MM,受惠国LD	50	---Weighing 10kg or more, but less than 50kg
15	0103.9200	--重量在50公斤及以上	10	0 冰岛IS,东盟AS,哥CR,秘鲁PE,新西兰NZ,智利CL 4 瑞士CH 5 巴PK 6 澳AU 8 韩国KR	0 柬埔寨KH,老挝LA,缅甸MM,受惠国LD	50	--Weighing 50kg or more
	01.04	**绵羊、山羊:**					**Live sheep and goats:**
		-绵羊:					-Sheep:
16	0104.1010	---改良种用	0		0 受惠国LD	0	---Pure-bred breeding
17	0104.1090	---其他	10	0 冰岛IS,东盟AS,哥CR,秘鲁PE,新西兰NZ,智利CL 4 瑞士CH 5 巴PK 6 澳AU 8 韩国KR	0 受惠国LD	50	---Other
		-山羊:					-Goats:
18	0104.2010	---改良种用	0		0 受惠国LD	0	---Pure-bred breeding
19	0104.2090	---其他	10	0 冰岛IS,东盟AS,哥CR,秘鲁PE,新西兰NZ,智利CL 4 瑞士CH 5 巴PK 6 澳AU 8 韩国KR	0 受惠国LD	50	---Other
	01.05	**家禽，即鸡、鸭、鹅、火鸡及珍珠鸡:**					**Live poultry, that is to say, fowls of the species *Gallus domesticus*, ducks, geese, turkeys and guinea fowls:**

序号 No.	税则号列 Tariff Line	中文货品名称 Article Description in Chinese	最惠国税率 MFN(%)	协定税率 Agreement(%)	特惠税率 SP(%)	普通税率 Gen(%)	英文货品名称 Article Description
		-重量不超过185克：					-Weighing not more than 185g:
		--鸡：					--Fowls of the species *Gallus domesticus*:
20	0105.1110	---改良种用	0		0 受惠国LD	0	---Pure-bred breeding
21	0105.1190	---其他	10	0 冰岛IS,东盟AS,哥CR,新西兰NZ,智利CL 3 秘鲁PE 4 瑞士CH 5 巴PK 6 澳AU 8 韩国KR	0 老挝LA,缅甸MM,受惠国LD	50	---Other
		--火鸡：					--Turkeys:
22	0105.1210	---改良种用	0		0 受惠国LD	0	---Pure-bred breeding
23	0105.1290	---其他	10	0 冰岛IS,东盟AS,哥CR,新西兰NZ,智利CL 3 秘鲁PE 4 瑞士CH 5 巴PK 6 澳AU 8 韩国KR	0 受惠国LD	50	---Other
		--鸭：					--Ducks:
24	0105.1310	---改良种用	0		0 受惠国LD	0	---Pure-bred breeding
25	0105.1390	---其他	10	0 冰岛IS,东盟AS,哥CR,秘鲁PE,新西兰NZ,智利CL 4 瑞士CH 5 巴PK 6 澳AU 8 韩国KR	0 老挝LA,受惠国LD	50	---Other
		--鹅：					--Geese:
26	0105.1410	---改良种用	0		0 受惠国LD	0	---Pure-bred breeding
27	0105.1490	---其他	10	0 冰岛IS,东盟AS,哥CR,秘鲁PE,新西兰NZ,智利CL 4 瑞士CH 5 巴PK 6 澳AU 8 韩国KR	0 老挝LA,受惠国LD	50	---Other
		--珍珠鸡：					--Guinea fowls:
28	0105.1510	改良种用	0		0 受惠国LD	0	---Pure-bred breeding
29	0105.1590	---其他	10	0 冰岛IS,东盟AS,哥CR,秘鲁PE,新西兰NZ,智利CL 4 瑞士CH 5 巴PK 6 澳AU 8 韩国KR	0 老挝LA,受惠国LD	50	---Other
		-其他：					-Other:
		--鸡：					--Fowls of the species *Gallus domesticus*:
30	0105.9410	---改良种用	0		0 受惠国LD	0	---Pure-bred breeding
31	0105.9490	---其他	10	0 冰岛IS,东盟AS,哥CR,秘鲁PE,新西兰NZ,智利CL 4 瑞士CH 5 巴PK 6 澳AU 8 韩国KR	0 受惠国LD	50	---Other
		--其他：					--Other:
32	0105.9910	---改良种用	0		0 受惠国LD	0	---Pure-bred breeding
		---其他：					---Other:

序号 No.	税则号列 Tariff Line	中文货品名称 Article Description in Chinese	最惠国税率 MFN(%)	协定税率 Agreement(%)	特惠税率 SP(%)	普通税率 Gen(%)	英文货品名称 Article Description
33	0105.9991	----鸭	10	0 冰岛IS,东盟AS,哥CR,秘鲁PE,新西兰NZ,智利CL 4 瑞士CH 5 巴PK 6 澳AU 8 韩国KR	0 受惠国LD	50	----Ducks
34	0105.9992	----鹅	10	0 冰岛IS,东盟AS,哥CR,秘鲁PE,新西兰NZ,智利CL 4 瑞士CH 5 巴PK 6 澳AU 8 韩国KR	0 受惠国LD	50	----Geese
35	0105.9993	----珍珠鸡	10	0 冰岛IS,东盟AS,哥CR,秘鲁PE,新西兰NZ,智利CL 4 瑞士CH 5 巴PK 6 澳AU 8 韩国KR	0 受惠国LD	50	----Guinea fowls
36	0105.9994	----火鸡	10	0 冰岛IS,东盟AS,哥CR,秘鲁PE,新西兰NZ,智利CL 4 瑞士CH 5 巴PK 6 澳AU 8 韩国KR	0 受惠国LD	50	----Turkeys
	01.06	**其他活动物:**					**Other live animals:**
		-哺乳动物:					-Mammals:
		--灵长目:					--Primates:
37	0106.1110	---改良种用	0		0 受惠国LD	0	---Pure-bred breeding
38	0106.1190	---其他	10	0 冰岛IS,东盟AS,哥CR,秘鲁PE,新西兰NZ,智利CL 4 瑞士CH 5 巴PK 6 澳AU 8 韩国KR	0 受惠国LD	50	---Other
		--鲸、海豚及鼠海豚（鲸目哺乳动物）；海牛及儒艮（海牛目哺乳动物）；海豹、海狮及海象（鳍足亚目哺乳动物）:					--Whales, dolphins and porpoises (mammals of the order Cetacea) ; manatees and dugongs (mammals of the order Sirenia) ; seals, sea lions and walruses (mammals of the suborder Pinnipedia) :
		---鲸、海豚及鼠海豚(鲸目哺乳动物);海牛及儒艮（海牛目哺乳动物）:					---Whales, dolphins and porpoises (mammals of the order Cetacea) ; manatees and dugongs (mammals of the order Sirenia) :
39	0106.1211	----改良种用	10△0	0 冰岛IS,东盟AS,哥CR,秘鲁PE,新西兰NZ,智利CL 4 瑞士CH 5 巴PK 6 澳AU,韩国KR	0 受惠国LD	50	----Pure-bred breeding
40	0106.1219	----其他	10	0 冰岛IS,东盟AS,哥CR,秘鲁PE,新西兰NZ,智利CL 4 瑞士CH 5 巴PK 6 澳AU 8 韩国KR	0 受惠国LD	50	----Other

序号 No.	税则号列 Tariff Line	中文货品名称 Article Description in Chinese	最惠国税率 MFN(%)	协定税率 Agreement(%)	特惠税率 SP(%)	普通税率 Gen(%)	英文货品名称 Article Description
		---海豹、海狮及海象(鳍足亚目哺乳动物):					---Seals, sea lions and walruses (mammals of the suborder Pinnipedia) :
41	0106.1221	----改良种用	0		0 受惠国LD	0	----Pure-bred breeding
42	0106.1229	----其他	10	0 冰岛IS,东盟AS,哥CR,新西兰NZ,智利CL 3 秘鲁PE 4 瑞士CH 5 巴PK 6 澳AU 8 韩国KR	0 受惠国LD	50	----Other
		--骆驼及其他骆驼科动物:					--Camels and other camelids (Camelidae) :
43	0106.1310	---改良种用	0		0 受惠国LD	0	---Pure-bred breeding
44	0106.1390	---其他	10	0 冰岛IS,东盟AS,哥CR,新西兰NZ,智利CL 3 秘鲁PE 4 瑞士CH 5 巴PK 6 澳AU 8 韩国KR	0 受惠国LD	50	---Other
		--家兔及野兔:					--Rabbits and hares:
45	0106.1410	---改良种用	0		0 受惠国LD	0	---Pure-bred breeding
46	0106.1490	---其他	10	0 冰岛IS,东盟AS,哥CR,新西兰NZ,智利CL 3 秘鲁PE 4 瑞士CH 5 巴PK 6 澳AU 8 韩国KR	0 受惠国LD	50	---Other
		--其他:					--Other:
47	0106.1910	---改良种用	0		0 受惠国LD	0	---Pure-bred breeding
48	0106.1990	---其他	10	0 冰岛IS,东盟AS,哥CR,新西兰NZ,智利CL 3 秘鲁PE 4 瑞士CH 5 巴PK 6 澳AU 8 韩国KR	0 受惠国LD	50	---Other
		-爬行动物(包括蛇及龟鳖):					-Reptiles (including snakes and turtles) :
		---改良种用:					---Pure-bred breeding:
49	0106.2011	----鳄鱼苗	0		0 受惠国LD	0	----Crocodiles for cultivation
50	0106.2019	----其他	0		0 受惠国LD	0	----Other
51	0106.2020	---食用	10	0 冰岛IS,东盟AS,哥CR,秘鲁PE,新西兰NZ,智利CL 4 瑞士CH 5 巴PK 6 澳AU 8 韩国KR	0 缅甸MM,受惠国LD	50	---For human consumption
52	0106.2090	---其他	10	0 冰岛IS,东盟AS,哥CR,秘鲁PE,新西兰NZ,智利CL 4 瑞士CH 5 巴PK 6 澳AU 8 韩国KR	0 受惠国LD	50	---Other
		-鸟:					-Birds:
		--猛禽:					--Birds of prey:
53	0106.3110	---改良种用	0		0 受惠国LD	0	---Pure-bred breeding

序号 No.	税则号列 Tariff Line	中文货品名称 Article Description in Chinese	最惠国税率 MFN(%)	协定税率 Agreement(%)	特惠税率 SP(%)	普通税率 Gen(%)	英文货品名称 Article Description
54	0106.3190	---其他	10	0 冰岛IS,东盟AS,哥CR,秘鲁PE,新西兰NZ,智利CL 4 瑞士CH 5 巴PK 6 澳AU 8 韩国KR	0 受惠国LD	50	---Other
		--鹦形目（包括普通鹦鹉、长尾鹦鹉、金刚鹦鹉及美冠鹦鹉）:					--Psittaciformes (including parrots, parakeets, macaws and cockatoos) :
55	0106.3210	---改良种用	0		0 受惠国LD	0	---Pure-bred breeding
56	0106.3290	---其他	10	0 冰岛IS,东盟AS,哥CR,秘鲁PE,新西兰NZ,智利CL 4 瑞士CH 5 巴PK 6 澳AU 8 韩国KR	0 受惠国LD	50	---Other
		--鸵鸟；鸸鹋:					--Ostriches; emus (*Dromaius novaehollandiae*) :
57	0106.3310	---改良种用	0		0 受惠国LD	0	---Pure-bred breeding
58	0106.3390	---其他	10	0 冰岛IS,东盟AS,哥CR,秘鲁PE,新西兰NZ,智利CL 4 瑞士CH 5 巴PK 6 澳AU 8 韩国KR	0 受惠国LD	50	---Other
		--其他:					--Other:
59	0106.3910	---改良种用	0		0 受惠国LD	0	---Pure-bred breeding
		---食用:					---For human consumption:
60	0106.3921	----乳鸽	10	0 冰岛IS,东盟AS,哥CR,秘鲁PE,新西兰NZ,智利CL 4 瑞士CH 5 巴PK 6 澳AU 8 韩国KR	0 缅甸MM,受惠国LD	50	----Squabs
61	0106.3923	----野鸭	10	0 冰岛IS,东盟AS,哥CR,秘鲁PE,新西兰NZ,智利CL 4 瑞士CH 5 巴PK 6 澳AU 8 韩国KR	0 缅甸MM,受惠国LD	50	----Teals
62	0106.3929	----其他	10	0 冰岛IS,东盟AS,哥CR,秘鲁PE,新西兰NZ,智利CL 4 瑞士CH 5 巴PK 6 澳AU 8 韩国KR	0 缅甸MM,受惠国LD	50	----Other
63	0106.3990	---其他	10	0 冰岛IS,东盟AS,哥CR,秘鲁PE,新西兰NZ,智利CL 4 瑞士CH 5 巴PK 6 澳AU 8 韩国KR	0 受惠国LD	50	---Other
		-昆虫:					-Insects:
		--蜂:					--Bees:
64	0106.4110	---改良种用	0		0 受惠国LD	0	---Pure-bred breeding

序号 No.	税则号列 Tariff Line	中文货品名称 Article Description in Chinese	最惠国税率 MFN(%)	协定税率 Agreement(%)	特惠税率 SP(%)	普通税率 Gen(%)	英文货品名称 Article Description
65	0106.4190	---其他	10	0 冰岛IS,东盟AS,哥CR,新西兰NZ,智利CL 3 秘鲁PE 4 瑞士CH 5 巴PK 6 澳AU,韩国KR 9 亚太AP	0 受惠国LD	50	---Other
		--其他:					--Other:
66	0106.4910	---改良种用	0		0 受惠国LD	0	---Pure-bred breeding
67	0106.4990	---其他	10	0 冰岛IS,东盟AS,哥CR,新西兰NZ,智利CL 3 秘鲁PE 4 瑞士CH 5 巴PK 6 澳AU,韩国KR 9 亚太AP	0 受惠国LD	50	---Other
		-其他:					-Other:
		---改良种用:					---Pure-bred breeding:
68	0106.9011	----蛙苗	0		0 受惠国LD	0	----Tadpole and young frogs
69	0106.9019	----其他	0		0 受惠国LD	0	----Other
70	0106.9090	---其他	10	0 冰岛IS,东盟AS,哥CR,新西兰NZ,智利CL 3 秘鲁PE 4 瑞士CH 5 巴PK 6 澳AU 8 韩国KR 9 亚太AP	0 受惠国LD	50	---Other

第二章
肉及食用杂碎

Chapter 2
Meat and edible meat offal

注释:

本章不包括:

一、税号 02.01 至 02.08 或 02.10 的不适合供人食用的产品;

二、动物的肠、膀胱、胃(税号 05.04)或动物血(税号 05.11、30.02);

三、税号 02.09 所列产品以外的动物脂肪(第十五章)。

Notes:

This Chapter does not cover:

1. Products of the kinds described in headings No.02.01 to 02.08 or 02.10, unfit or unsuitable for human consumption;
2. Guts, bladders or stomachs of animals (heading No.05.04) or animal blood (heading No.05.11 or 30.02); or
3. Animal fat, other than products of heading No.02.09 (Chapter15).

序号 No.	税则号列 Tariff Line	中文货品名称 Article Description in Chinese	最惠国税率 MFN(%)	协定税率 Agreement(%)	特惠税率 SP(%)	普通税率 Gen(%)	英文货品名称 Article Description
	02.01	**鲜、冷牛肉:**					**Meat of bovine animals, fresh or chilled:**
71	0201.1000	-整头及半头	20	0 冰岛IS,东盟AS,新西兰NZ,智利CL 10.7 秘鲁PE 12 哥CR 14 瑞士CH 16 澳AU 17.3 韩国KR	0 柬埔寨KH,老挝LA,受惠国LD	70	-Carcasses and half-carcasses
72	0201.2000	-带骨肉	12	0 冰岛IS,东盟AS,新西兰NZ,智利CL 6 巴PK 7.1 秘鲁PE 7.2 哥CR 8.4 瑞士CH 9.6 澳AU 10.4 韩国KR	0 柬埔寨KH,老挝LA,受惠国LD	70	-Other cuts with bone in
73	0201.3000	-去骨肉	12	0 冰岛IS,东盟AS,新西兰NZ,智利CL 6 巴PK 7.1 秘鲁PE 7.2 哥CR 8.4 瑞士CH 9.6 澳AU 10.4 韩国KR	0 柬埔寨KH,受惠国LD	70	-Boneless
	02.02	**冻牛肉:**					**Meat of bovine animals, frozen:**
74	0202.1000	-整头及半头	25	0 冰岛IS,东盟AS,哥CR,新西兰NZ,智利CL 13.3 秘鲁PE 17.5 瑞士CH 20 澳AU 22.5 韩国KR	0 柬埔寨KH,老挝LA,受惠国LD	70	-Carcasses and half-carcasses
75	0202.2000	-带骨肉	12	0 冰岛IS,东盟AS,哥CR,新西兰NZ,智利CL 6 巴PK 7.1 秘鲁PE 8.4 瑞士CH 9.6 澳AU 10.4 韩国KR	0 柬埔寨KH,老挝LA,受惠国LD	70	-Other cuts with bone in
76	0202.3000	-去骨肉	12	0 冰岛IS,东盟AS,哥CR,新西兰NZ,智利CL 6 巴PK 7.1 秘鲁PE 8.4 瑞士CH 9.6 澳AU 10.4 韩国KR	0 柬埔寨KH,受惠国LD	70	-Boneless
	02.03	**鲜、冷、冻猪肉:**					**Meat of swine, fresh, chilled or frozen:**
		-鲜或冷的:					-Fresh or chilled:
		--整头及半头:					--Carcases and half-carcases:

序号 No.	税则号列 Tariff Line	中文货品名称 Article Description in Chinese	最惠国税率 MFN(%)	协定税率 Agreement(%)	特惠税率 SP(%)	普通税率 Gen(%)	英文货品名称 Article Description
77	0203.1110	---乳猪	20	0 冰岛IS,东盟AS,哥CR,新西兰NZ,智利CL 6 秘鲁PE 12 澳AU 14 瑞士CH 17.3 韩国KR	0 柬埔寨KH,老挝LA,受惠国LD	70	---Sucking pig
78	0203.1190	---其他	20	0 冰岛IS,东盟AS,哥CR,秘鲁PE,新西兰NZ,智利CL 12 澳AU 14 瑞士CH 17.3 韩国KR	0 柬埔寨KH,老挝LA,受惠国LD	70	---Other
79	0203.1200	--带骨的前腿、后腿及其肉块	20	0 冰岛IS,东盟AS,哥CR,新西兰NZ,智利CL 6 秘鲁PE 12 澳AU 14 瑞士CH 17.3 韩国KR	0 柬埔寨KH,老挝LA,受惠国LD	70	--Hams, shoulders and cuts thereof, with bone in
80	0203.1900	--其他	20	0 冰岛IS,东盟AS,哥CR,秘鲁PE,新西兰NZ,智利CL 12 澳AU 14 瑞士CH 17.3 韩国KR	0 柬埔寨KH,老挝LA,受惠国LD	70	--Other
		-冻的:					-Frozen:
		--整头及半头:					--Carcases and half-carcases:
81	0203.2110	---乳猪	12	0 冰岛IS,东盟AS,哥CR,新西兰NZ,智利CL 3.6 秘鲁PE 6 巴PK 7.2 澳AU 8.4 瑞士CH 9.6 韩国KR	0 柬埔寨KH,老挝LA,受惠国LD	70	---Sucking pig
82	0203.2190	---其他	12	0 冰岛IS,东盟AS,哥CR,新西兰NZ,智利CL 3.6 秘鲁PE 6 巴PK 7.2 澳AU 8.4 瑞士CH 9.6 韩国KR	0 柬埔寨KH,老挝LA,受惠国LD	70	---Other
83	0203.2200	--带骨的前腿、后腿及其肉块	12	0 冰岛IS,东盟AS,哥CR,秘鲁PE,新西兰NZ,智利CL 6 巴PK 7.2 澳AU 8.4 瑞士CH 9.6 韩国KR	0 柬埔寨KH,老挝LA,受惠国LD	70	--Hams, shoulders and cuts thereof, with bone in
84	0203.2900	--其他	12	0 冰岛IS,东盟AS,哥CR,新西兰NZ,智利CL 6 巴PK 6.4 秘鲁PE 7.2 澳AU 8.4 瑞士CH 9.6 韩国KR	0 柬埔寨KH,受惠国LD	70	--Other
	02.04	**鲜、冷、冻绵羊肉或山羊肉:**					**Meat of sheep or goats, fresh, chilled or frozen:**
85	0204.1000	-鲜或冷的整头及半头羔羊	15	0 冰岛IS,东盟AS,新西兰NZ,智利CL 8 秘鲁PE 9 哥CR 10.5 瑞士CH 11.7 澳AU 12 巴PK,韩国KR	0 受惠国$_1$LD$_1$	70	-Carcasses and half-carcasses of lamb, fresh or chilled
		-其他鲜或冷的绵羊肉:					-Other meat of sheep, fresh or chilled:

序号 No.	税则号列 Tariff Line	中文货品名称 Article Description in Chinese	最惠国税率 MFN(%)	协定税率 Agreement(%)	特惠税率 SP(%)	普通税率 Gen(%)	英文货品名称 Article Description
86	0204.2100	--整头及半头	23	0 冰岛IS,东盟AS,新西兰NZ,智利CL 12.3 秘鲁PE 13.8 哥CR 16.1 瑞士CH 17.9 澳AU 20.7 韩国KR	0 受惠国$_1$LD$_1$	70	--Carcasses and half-carcasses
87	0204.2200	--带骨肉	15	0 冰岛IS,东盟AS,新西兰NZ,智利CL 8 秘鲁PE 9 哥CR 10.5 瑞士CH 11.7 澳AU 12 巴PK,韩国KR	0 受惠国$_1$LD$_1$	70	--Other cuts with bone in
88	0204.2300	--去骨肉	15	0 冰岛IS,东盟AS,新西兰NZ,智利CL 6.2 秘鲁PE 9 哥CR 10.5 瑞士CH 11.7 澳AU 12 巴PK,韩国KR	0 受惠国$_1$LD$_1$	70	--Boneless
89	0204.3000	-冻的整头及半头羔羊	15	0 冰岛IS,东盟AS,新西兰NZ,智利CL 8.8 秘鲁PE 9 哥CR 10.5 瑞士CH 11.7 澳AU 12 巴PK,韩国KR	0 受惠国$_1$LD$_1$	70	-Carcasses and half-carcasses of lamb, frozen
		-其他冻的绵羊肉:					-Other meat of sheep, frozen:
90	0204.4100	--整头及半头	23	0 冰岛IS,东盟AS,新西兰NZ,智利CL 13.5 秘鲁PE 13.8 哥CR 16.1 瑞士CH 17.9 澳AU 20.7 韩国KR	0 受惠国$_1$LD$_1$	70	--Carcasses and half-carcasses
91	0204.4200	--带骨肉	12	0 冰岛IS,东盟AS,新西兰NZ,智利CL 6 巴PK 7.1 秘鲁PE 7.2 哥CR 8.4 瑞士CH 9.3 澳AU 9.6 韩国KR	0 受惠国$_1$LD$_1$	70	--Other cuts with bone in
92	0204.4300	--去骨肉	15	0 冰岛IS,东盟AS,新西兰NZ,智利CL 8.8 秘鲁PE 9 哥CR 10.5 瑞士CH 11.7 澳AU 12 巴PK,韩国KR	0 受惠国$_1$LD$_1$	70	--Boneless
93	0204.5000	-山羊肉	20	0 冰岛IS,东盟AS,新西兰NZ,智利CL 8.3 秘鲁PE 12 哥CR 14 瑞士CH 15.6 澳AU 17.3 韩国KR	0 受惠国$_1$LD$_1$	70	-Meat of goats
	02.05	**鲜、冷、冻马、驴、骡肉**					**Meat of horses, asses, mules or hinnies, fresh, chilled or frozen**

序号 No.	税则号列 Tariff Line	中文货品名称 Article Description in Chinese	最惠国税率 MFN(%)	协定税率 Agreement(%)	特惠税率 SP(%)	普通税率 Gen(%)	英文货品名称 Article Description
94	0205.0000	鲜、冷、冻马、驴、骡肉	20	0 冰岛IS,东盟AS,哥CR,新西兰NZ,智利CL 6 秘鲁PE 12 澳AU 14 瑞士CH 17.3 韩国KR	0 受惠国$_1$LD$_1$	70	Meat of horses, asses, mules or hinnies, fresh, chilled or frozen
	02.06	**鲜、冷、冻牛、猪、绵羊、山羊、马、驴、骡的食用杂碎:**					**Edible offal of bovine animals, swine, sheep, goats, horses, asses, mules or hinnies, fresh, chilled or frozen:**
95	0206.1000	-鲜、冷牛杂碎	12	0 冰岛IS,东盟AS,哥CR,新西兰NZ,智利CL 5 秘鲁PE 6 巴PK 7.2 澳AU 8.4 瑞士CH 9.6 韩国KR	0 柬埔寨KH,老挝LA,受惠国LD	70	-Of bovine animals, fresh or chilled
		-冻牛杂碎:					-Of bovine animals, frozen:
96	0206.2100	--舌	12	0 冰岛IS,东盟AS,哥CR,新西兰NZ,智利CL 3.6 秘鲁PE 6 巴PK 7.2 澳AU 8.4 瑞士CH 9.6 韩国KR	0 柬埔寨KH,老挝LA,受惠国LD	70	--Tongues
97	0206.2200	--肝	12	0 冰岛IS,东盟AS,哥CR,秘鲁PE,新西兰NZ,智利CL 6 巴PK 7.2 澳AU 8.4 瑞士CH 9.6 韩国KR	0 柬埔寨KH,老挝LA,受惠国LD	70	--Livers
98	0206.2900	--其他	12	0 冰岛IS,东盟AS,哥CR,新西兰NZ,智利CL 3.6 秘鲁PE 6 巴PK 8.4 瑞士CH 9 澳AU 9.6 韩国KR	0 柬埔寨KH,老挝LA,受惠国LD	70	--Other
99	0206.3000	-鲜、冷猪杂碎	20	0 冰岛IS,东盟AS,哥CR,新西兰NZ,智利CL 6 秘鲁PE 12 澳AU 14 瑞士CH 17.3 韩国KR	0 柬埔寨KH,老挝LA,缅甸MM,受惠国LD	70	-Of swine, fresh of chilled
		-冻猪杂碎:					-Of swine, frozen:
100	0206.4100	--肝	20	0 冰岛IS,东盟AS,哥CR,新西兰NZ,智利CL 6 秘鲁PE 12 澳AU 14 瑞士CH 17.3 韩国KR	0 柬埔寨KH,老挝LA,受惠国LD	70	--Livers
101	0206.4900	--其他	12	0 冰岛IS,东盟AS,哥CR,新西兰NZ,智利CL 3.6 秘鲁PE 6 巴PK 7.2 澳AU 8.4 瑞士CH 9.6 韩国KR	0 柬埔寨KH,老挝LA,受惠国LD	70	--Other
102	0206.8000	-其他鲜或冷杂碎	20	0 冰岛IS,东盟AS,哥CR,新西兰NZ,智利CL 8.3 秘鲁PE 14 瑞士CH 16 澳AU 17.3 韩国KR	0 柬埔寨KH,受惠国LD	70	-Other, fresh or chilled

序号 No.	税则号列 Tariff Line	中文货品名称 Article Description in Chinese	最惠国税率 MFN(%)	协定税率 Agreement(%)	特惠税率 SP(%)	普通税率 Gen(%)	英文货品名称 Article Description
103	0206.9000	-其他冻杂碎	18	0 冰岛IS,东盟AS,哥CR,新西兰NZ,智利CL 10.6 秘鲁PE 12.6 瑞士CH 13.5 澳AU 14.4 巴PK 15.6 韩国KR	0 柬埔寨KH,受惠国LD	70	-Other, frozen
	02.07	**税号01.05所列家禽的鲜、冷、冻肉及食用杂碎:**					**Meat and edible offal, of the poultry of heading 0105, fresh, chilled or frozen:**
		-鸡:					-Of fowls of the species *Gallus domesticus*:
104	0207.1100	--整只，鲜或冷的	20	0 冰岛IS,东盟AS,哥CR,秘鲁PE,新西兰NZ,智利CL 12 澳AU 14 瑞士CH 17.3 韩国KR	0 柬埔寨KH,老挝LA,缅甸MM,受惠国LD	70	--Not cut in pieces, fresh or chilled
105	0207.1200	--整只，冻的	①	0 冰岛IS,东盟AS,哥CR,新西兰NZ,智利CL 6 秘鲁PE 12 澳AU 14 瑞士CH ③ 韩国KR	0 柬埔寨KH,老挝LA,缅甸MM,受惠国LD	②	--Not cut in pieces, frozen
		--块及杂碎，鲜或冷的:					--Cuts and offal, fresh or chilled:
		---块:					---Cut:
106	0207.1311	----带骨的	20	0 冰岛IS,东盟AS,哥CR,秘鲁PE,新西兰NZ,智利CL 12 澳AU 14 瑞士CH 17.3 韩国KR	0 柬埔寨KH,老挝LA,缅甸MM,受惠国LD	70	----With bone
107	0207.1319	----其他	20	0 冰岛IS,东盟AS,哥CR,秘鲁PE,新西兰NZ,智利CL 12 澳AU 14 瑞士CH 17.3 韩国KR	0 柬埔寨KH,老挝LA,缅甸MM,受惠国LD	70	----Other
		---杂碎:					---Offal:
108	0207.1321	----翼（不包括翼尖）	20	0 冰岛IS,东盟AS,哥CR,秘鲁PE,新西兰NZ,智利CL 12 澳AU 14 瑞士CH 17.3 韩国KR	0 柬埔寨KH,老挝LA,缅甸MM,受惠国LD	70	----Midjoint wing
109	0207.1329	----其他	20	0 冰岛IS,东盟AS,哥CR,秘鲁PE,新西兰NZ,智利CL 12 澳AU 14 瑞士CH 17.3 韩国KR	0 柬埔寨KH,老挝LA,缅甸MM,受惠国LD	70	----Other
		--块及杂碎，冻的:					--Cuts and offal, frozen:
		---块:					---Cut:

①**最惠国税率**: 1.3 元/千克
MFN Tariff: 1.3¥/kg

②**普通税率**: 5.6 元/千克
General Duty: 5.6¥/kg

③**协定税率**: 1.1 元/千克
Agreement Import Tariff: 1.1¥/kg

序号 No.	税则号列 Tariff Line	中文货品名称 Article Description in Chinese	最惠国税率 MFN(%)	协定税率 Agreement(%)	特惠税率 SP(%)	普通税率 Gen(%)	英文货品名称 Article Description
110	0207.1411	----带骨的	①	0 冰岛IS,东盟AS,哥CR,秘鲁PE,新西兰NZ,智利CL 4 瑞士CH 6 澳AU ③ 巴PK ④ 韩国KR	0 柬埔寨KH,老挝LA,缅甸MM,受惠国LD	②	----With bone
111	0207.1419	----其他	⑤	0 冰岛IS,东盟AS,哥CR,新西兰NZ,智利CL 3 秘鲁PE 4 瑞士CH 6 澳AU ⑦ 巴PK ⑧ 韩国KR	0 柬埔寨KH,老挝LA,缅甸MM,受惠国LD	⑥	----Other
		---杂碎:					---Offal:
112	0207.1421	----翼（不包括翼尖）	⑨	0 冰岛IS,东盟AS,哥CR,秘鲁PE,新西兰NZ,智利CL 4 瑞士CH 6 澳AU ⑪ 巴PK ⑫ 韩国KR	0 柬埔寨KH,老挝LA,缅甸MM,受惠国LD	⑩	----Midjoint wing
113	0207.1422	----鸡爪	⑬	0 冰岛IS,东盟AS,哥CR,新西兰NZ,智利CL 3 秘鲁PE 4 瑞士CH 6 澳AU ⑮ 巴PK ⑯ 韩国KR	0 柬埔寨KH,老挝LA,缅甸MM,受惠国LD	⑭	----Chicken claw

①**最惠国税率**: 0.6 元/千克
MFN Tariff: 0.6¥/kg
②**普通税率**: 4.2 元/千克
General Duty: 4.2¥/kg
③**协定税率**: 0.3 元/千克
Agreement Import Tariff: 0.3¥/kg
④**协定税率**: 0.4 元/千克
Agreement Import Tariff: 0.4¥/kg
⑤**最惠国税率**: 0.7 元/千克
MFN Tariff: 0.7¥/kg
⑥**普通税率**: 9.5 元/千克
General Duty: 9.5¥/kg
⑦**协定税率**: 0.35 元/千克
Agreement Import Tariff: 0.35¥/kg
⑧**协定税率**: 0.5 元/千克
Agreement Import Tariff: 0.5¥/kg
⑨**最惠国税率**: 0.8 元/千克
MFN Tariff: 0.8¥/kg
⑩**普通税率**: 8.1 元/千克
General Duty: 8.1¥/kg
⑪**协定税率**: 0.4 元/千克
Agreement Import Tariff: 0.4¥/kg
⑫**协定税率**: 0.6 元/千克
Agreement Import Tariff: 0.6¥/kg
⑬**最惠国税率**: 0.5 元/千克
MFN Tariff: 0.5¥/kg
⑭**普通税率**: 3.2 元/千克
General Duty: 3.2¥/kg
⑮**协定税率**: 0.25 元/千克
Agreement Import Tariff: 0.25¥/kg
⑯**协定税率**: 0.4 元/千克
Agreement Import Tariff: 0.4¥/kg

序号 No.	税则号列 Tariff Line	中文货品名称 Article Description in Chinese	最惠国税率 MFN(%)	协定税率 Agreement(%)	特惠税率 SP(%)	普通税率 Gen(%)	英文货品名称 Article Description
114	0207.1429	----其他	①	0 冰岛IS,东盟AS,哥CR,新西兰NZ,智利CL 3 秘鲁PE 4 瑞士CH 6 澳AU ③ 巴PK ④ 韩国KR	0 柬埔寨KH,老挝LA,缅甸MM,受惠国LD	②	----Other
		-火鸡:					-Of turkeys:
115	0207.2400	--整只，鲜或冷的	20	0 冰岛IS,东盟AS,哥CR,秘鲁PE,新西兰NZ,智利CL 12 澳AU 14 瑞士CH 17.3 韩国KR	0 老挝LA,受惠国LD	70	--Not cut in pieces, fresh or chilled
116	0207.2500	--整只，冻的	20	0 冰岛IS,东盟AS,哥CR,新西兰NZ,智利CL 6 秘鲁PE 12 澳AU 14 瑞士CH 17.3 韩国KR	0 老挝LA,受惠国LD	70	--Not cut in pieces, frozen
117	0207.2600	--块及杂碎，鲜或冷的	20	0 冰岛IS,东盟AS,哥CR,秘鲁PE,新西兰NZ,智利CL 12 澳AU 14 瑞士CH 17.3 韩国KR	0 老挝LA,受惠国LD	70	--Cuts and offal, fresh or chilled
118	0207.2700	--块及杂碎，冻的	10	0 冰岛IS,东盟AS,哥CR,新西兰NZ,智利CL 3 秘鲁PE 4 瑞士CH 5 巴PK 6 澳AU 8 韩国KR	0 老挝LA,受惠国LD	70	--Cuts and offal, frozen
		-鸭:					-Of ducks:
119	0207.4100	--整只，鲜或冷的	20	0 冰岛IS,东盟AS,哥CR,新西兰NZ,智利CL 6 秘鲁PE 12 澳AU 14 瑞士CH 17.3 韩国KR	0 柬埔寨KH,老挝LA,缅甸MM,受惠国LD	70	--Not cut in pieces, fresh or chilled
120	0207.4200	--整只，冻的	20	0 冰岛IS,东盟AS,哥CR,新西兰NZ,智利CL 6 秘鲁PE 12 澳AU 14 瑞士CH 17.3 韩国KR	0 柬埔寨KH,老挝LA,缅甸MM,受惠国LD	70	--Not cut in pieces, frozen
121	0207.4300	--肥肝，鲜或冷的	20	0 冰岛IS,东盟AS,哥CR,新西兰NZ,智利CL 6 秘鲁PE 12 澳AU 14 瑞士CH 17.3 韩国KR	0 柬埔寨KH,老挝LA,受惠国LD	70	--Fatty livers, fresh or chilled

①**最惠国税率**: 0.5 元/千克
MFN Tariff: 0.5¥/kg
②**普通税率**: 3.2 元/千克
General Duty: 3.2¥/kg
③**协定税率**: 0.25 元/千克
Agreement Import Tariff: 0.25¥/kg
④**协定税率**: 0.4 元/千克
Agreement Import Tariff: 0.4¥/kg

序号 No.	税则号列 Tariff Line	中文货品名称 Article Description in Chinese	最惠国税率 MFN(%)	协定税率 Agreement(%)	特惠税率 SP(%)	普通税率 Gen(%)	英文货品名称 Article Description
122	0207.4400	--其他，鲜或冷的	20	0 冰岛IS,东盟AS,哥CR,新西兰NZ,智利CL 6 秘鲁PE 12 澳AU 14 瑞士CH 17.3 韩国KR	0 柬埔寨KH,老挝LA,缅甸MM,受惠国LD	70	--Other, fresh or chilled
123	0207.4500	--其他，冻的	20	0 冰岛IS,东盟AS,哥CR,新西兰NZ,智利CL 6 秘鲁PE 12 澳AU 14 瑞士CH 18 韩国KR	0 柬埔寨KH,老挝LA,缅甸MM,受惠国LD	70	--Other, frozen
		-鹅:					-Of geese:
124	0207.5100	--整只，鲜或冷的	20	0 冰岛IS,东盟AS,哥CR,新西兰NZ,智利CL 6 秘鲁PE 12 澳AU 14 瑞士CH 17.3 韩国KR	0 柬埔寨KH,老挝LA,缅甸MM,受惠国LD	70	--Not cut in pieces, fresh or chilled
125	0207.5200	--整只，冻的	20	0 冰岛IS,东盟AS,哥CR,新西兰NZ,智利CL 6 秘鲁PE 12 澳AU 14 瑞士CH 17.3 韩国KR	0 柬埔寨KH,老挝LA,缅甸MM,受惠国LD	70	--Not cut in pieces, frozen
126	0207.5300	--肥肝，鲜或冷的	20	0 冰岛IS,东盟AS,哥CR,新西兰NZ,智利CL 6 秘鲁PE 12 澳AU 14 瑞士CH 17.3 韩国KR	0 柬埔寨KH,老挝LA,受惠国LD	70	--Fatty livers, fresh or chilled
127	0207.5400	--其他，鲜或冷的	20	0 冰岛IS,东盟AS,哥CR,新西兰NZ,智利CL 6 秘鲁PE 12 澳AU 14 瑞士CH 17.3 韩国KR	0 柬埔寨KH,老挝LA,缅甸MM,受惠国LD	70	--Other, fresh or chilled
128	0207.5500	--其他，冻的	20	0 冰岛IS,东盟AS,哥CR,新西兰NZ,智利CL 6 秘鲁PE 12 澳AU 14 瑞士CH 17.3 韩国KR	0 柬埔寨KH,老挝LA,缅甸MM,受惠国LD	70	--Other, frozen
129	0207.6000	-珍珠鸡	20	0 冰岛IS,东盟AS,哥CR,新西兰NZ,智利CL 6 秘鲁PE 12 澳AU 14 瑞士CH 17.3 韩国KR	0 柬埔寨KH,老挝LA,受惠国LD	70	-Of guinea fowls
	02.08	**其他鲜、冷、冻肉及食用杂碎:**					**Other meat and edible meat offal, fresh, chilled or frozen:**
		-家兔或野兔的:					-Of rabbits or hares:
130	0208.1010	---鲜、冷兔肉，兔头除外	20	0 冰岛IS,东盟AS,哥CR,新西兰NZ,智利CL 6 秘鲁PE 12 澳AU 14 瑞士CH 17.3 韩国KR	0 受惠国$_1$LD$_1$	70	---Meat of rabbits, fresh or chilled, excluding head
131	0208.1020	---冻兔肉，兔头除外	20	0 冰岛IS,东盟AS,哥CR,新西兰NZ,智利CL 6 秘鲁PE 12 澳AU 14 瑞士CH 17.3 韩国KR	0 受惠国$_1$LD$_1$	70	---Meat of rabbits, frozen, excluding head

序号 No.	税则号列 Tariff Line	中文货品名称 Article Description in Chinese	最惠国税率 MFN(%)	协定税率 Agreement(%)	特惠税率 SP(%)	普通税率 Gen(%)	英文货品名称 Article Description
132	0208.1090	---其他	20	0 冰岛IS,东盟AS,哥CR,新西兰NZ,智利CL 6 秘鲁PE 12 澳AU 14 瑞士CH 17.3 韩国KR	0 受惠国$_1$LD$_1$	70	---Other
133	0208.3000	-灵长目的	23	0 冰岛IS,东盟AS,哥CR,新西兰NZ,智利CL 6.9 秘鲁PE 13.8 澳AU 16.1 瑞士CH 18.4 韩国KR	0 受惠国$_1$LD$_1$	70	-Of primates
134	0208.4000	-鲸、海豚及鼠海豚（鲸目哺乳动物）的；海牛及儒艮（海牛目哺乳动物）的；海豹、海狮及海象（鳍足亚目哺乳动物）的	23	0 冰岛IS,东盟AS,哥CR,新西兰NZ,智利CL 6.9 秘鲁PE 13.8 澳AU 16.1 瑞士CH 18.4 韩国KR	0 受惠国$_1$LD$_1$	70	-Of whales, dolphins and porpoises (mammals of the order Cetacea) ; manatees and dugongs (mammals of the order Sirenia) ; seals, sea lions and walruses (mammals of the suborder Pinnipedia)
135	0208.5000	-爬行动物（包括蛇及龟鳖）的	23	0 冰岛IS,东盟AS,哥CR,新西兰NZ,智利CL 6.9 秘鲁PE 13.8 澳AU 16.1 瑞士CH 18.4 韩国KR	0 受惠国$_1$LD$_1$	70	-Of reptiles (including snakes and turtles)
136	0208.6000	-骆驼及其他骆驼科动物的	23	0 冰岛IS,东盟AS,哥CR,新西兰NZ,智利CL 6.9 秘鲁PE 13.8 澳AU 16.1 瑞士CH 18.4 韩国KR	0 受惠国$_1$LD$_1$	70	-Of camels and other camelids (Camelidae)
		-其他：					-Other:
137	0208.9010	---乳鸽的	20	0 冰岛IS,东盟AS,哥CR,新西兰NZ,智利CL 6 秘鲁PE 12 澳AU 14 瑞士CH 17.3 韩国KR	0 受惠国$_1$LD$_1$	70	---Squabs
138	0208.9090	---其他	23	0 冰岛IS,东盟AS,哥CR,新西兰NZ,智利CL 6.9 秘鲁PE 13.8 澳AU 16.1 瑞士CH 20.7 韩国KR	0 受惠国$_1$LD$_1$	70	---Other
	02.09	**未炼制或用其他方法提取的不带瘦肉的肥猪肉、猪脂肪及家禽脂肪，鲜、冷、冻、干、熏、盐腌或盐渍的：**					**Pig fat, free of lean meat, and poultry fat, not rendered or otherwise extracted, fresh, chilled, frozen, salted, in brine, dried or smoked:**
139	0209.1000	-猪的	20	0 冰岛IS,东盟AS,哥CR,新西兰NZ,智利CL 6 秘鲁PE 12 澳AU 14 瑞士CH 17.3 韩国KR	0 受惠国$_1$LD$_1$	70	-Of pigs
140	0209.9000	-其他	20	0 冰岛IS,东盟AS,哥CR,新西兰NZ,智利CL 6 秘鲁PE 12 澳AU 14 瑞士CH 17.3 韩国KR	0 受惠国$_1$LD$_1$	70	-Other
	02.10	**肉及食用杂碎，干、熏、盐腌或盐渍的；可供食用的肉或杂碎的细粉、粗粉：**					**Meat and edible meat offal, salted, in brine, dried or smoked; edible flours and meals of meat or meat offal:**
		-猪肉：					-Meat of swine:

序号 No.	税则号列 Tariff Line	中文货品名称 Article Description in Chinese	最惠国税率 MFN(%)	协定税率 Agreement(%)	特惠税率 SP(%)	普通税率 Gen(%)	英文货品名称 Article Description
		--带骨的前腿、后腿及其肉块：					--Hams, shoulders and cuts thereof, with bone in:
141	0210.1110	---带骨的腿	25	0 冰岛IS,东盟AS,哥CR,秘鲁PE,新西兰NZ,智利CL 15 澳AU 22.5 韩国KR	0 柬埔寨KH,老挝LA,受惠国LD	80	---Hams and shoulders, with bone in
142	0210.1190	---其他	25	0 冰岛IS,东盟AS,哥CR,秘鲁PE,新西兰NZ,智利CL 15 澳AU 22.5 韩国KR	0 柬埔寨KH,老挝LA,受惠国LD	80	---Other
143	0210.1200	--腹肉（五花肉）	25	0 冰岛IS,东盟AS,哥CR,秘鲁PE,新西兰NZ,智利CL 15 澳AU 22.5 韩国KR	0 柬埔寨KH,老挝LA,受惠国LD	80	--Bellies (streaky) and cuts thereof
144	0210.1900	--其他	25	0 冰岛IS,东盟AS,哥CR,新西兰NZ,智利CL 7.5 秘鲁PE 15 澳AU 22.5 韩国KR	0 柬埔寨KH,缅甸MM,受惠国LD	80	--Other
145	0210.2000	-牛肉	25	0 冰岛IS,东盟AS,哥CR,新西兰NZ,智利CL 7.5 秘鲁PE 10 瑞士CH 20 澳AU 22.5 韩国KR	0 柬埔寨KH,老挝LA,受惠国LD	80	-Meat of bovine animals
		-其他，包括可供食用的肉或杂碎的细粉、粗粉：					-Other, including edible flours and meals of meat or meat offal:
146	0210.9100	--灵长目的	25	0 冰岛IS,东盟AS,哥CR,新西兰NZ,智利CL 7.5 秘鲁PE 15 澳AU 17.5 瑞士CH 20 韩国KR	0 柬埔寨KH,老挝LA,受惠国LD	80	--Of primates
147	0210.9200	--鲸、海豚及鼠海豚（鲸目哺乳动物）的；海牛及儒艮（海牛目哺乳动物）的；海豹、海狮及海象（鳍足亚目哺乳动物）的	25	0 冰岛IS,东盟AS,哥CR,新西兰NZ,智利CL 7.5 秘鲁PE 15 澳AU 17.5 瑞士CH 20 韩国KR	0 柬埔寨KH,老挝LA,受惠国LD	80	--Of whales, dolphins and porpoises (mammals of the order Cetacea) ; of manatees and dugongs (mammals of the order Sirenia) ; seals, sea lions and walruses (mammals of the suborder Pinnipedia)
148	0210.9300	--爬行动物（包括蛇及龟鳖）的	25	0 冰岛IS,东盟AS,哥CR,新西兰NZ,智利CL 7.5 秘鲁PE 15 澳AU 17.5 瑞士CH 20 韩国KR	0 柬埔寨KH,老挝LA,受惠国LD	80	--Of reptiles (including snakes and turtles)
149	0210.9900	--其他	25	0 冰岛IS,东盟AS,哥CR,新西兰NZ,智利CL 7.5 秘鲁PE 15 澳AU 17.5 瑞士CH 22.5 韩国KR	0 柬埔寨KH,老挝LA,受惠国LD	80	--Other

第三章
鱼、甲壳动物、软体动物及
其他水生无脊椎动物

注释：

一、本章不包括：

（一）税目 01.06 的哺乳动物；

（二）税目 01.06 的哺乳动物的肉（税目 02.08 或 02.10）；

（三）因品种或鲜度不适合供人食用的死鱼（包括鱼肝及鱼卵）、死甲壳动物、死软体动物及其他死水生无脊椎动物（第五章）；不适合供人食用的鱼、甲壳动物、软体动物、其他水生无脊椎动物的粉、粒（税号 23.01）；

（四）鲟鱼子酱及用鱼卵制成的鲟鱼子酱代用品（税号 16.04）。

二、本章所称“团粒”，是指直接挤压或加入少量粘合剂制成的粒状产品。

Chapter 3
Fish and crustaceans, molluscs and other aquatic invertebrates

Notes:

1. This Chapter does not cover:
   (a) Mammals of heading No.01.06;
   (b) Meat of mammals of heading No.01.06 (heading No.02.08 or 02.10);
   (c) Fish (including livers and roes thereof) or crustaceans, molluscs or other aquatic invertebrates, dead and unfit or unsuitable for human consumption by reason of either their species or their condition (Chapter 5); flours, meals or pellets of fish or of crustaceans, molluscs or other aquatic invertebrates, unfit for human consumption (heading No.23.01) ; or
   (d) Caviar or caviar substitutes prepared from fish eggs (heading No.16.04).
2. In this Chapterthe term “pellets” means products which have been agglomerated either directly by compression or by the addition of a small quantity of binder.

序号 No.	税则号列 Tariff Line	中文货品名称 Article Description in Chinese	最惠国税率 MFN(%)	协定税率 Agreement(%)	特惠税率 SP(%)	普通税率 Gen(%)	英文货品名称 Article Description
	03.01	活鱼：					Live fish:
		-观赏鱼：					-Ornamental fish:
150	0301.1100	--淡水鱼	17.5	0 冰岛IS,东盟AS,秘鲁PE,香港HK,新西兰NZ,智利CL 7 哥CR 10.5 澳AU 12.3 瑞士CH 14 巴PK 15.1 韩国KR	0 受惠国LD	80	--Freshwater
151	0301.1900	--其他	17.5	0 冰岛IS,东盟AS,秘鲁PE,香港HK,新西兰NZ,智利CL 7 哥CR 10.5 澳AU 12.3 瑞士CH 14 巴PK 15.1 韩国KR	0 受惠国LD	80	--Other
		-其他活鱼：					-Other live fish:
		--鳟鱼（河鳟、虹鳟、克拉克大麻哈鱼、阿瓜大麻哈鱼、吉雨大麻哈鱼、亚利桑那大麻哈鱼、金腹大麻哈鱼）：					--Trout (*Salmo trutta, Oncorhynchus mykiss, Oncorhynchus clarki, Oncorhynchus aguabonita, Oncorhynchus gilae, Oncorhynchus apache* and *Oncorhynchus chrysogaster*) :
152	0301.9110	---鱼苗	0		0 受惠国LD	0	---Fry
153	0301.9190	---其他	10.5	0 冰岛IS,东盟AS,秘鲁PE,新西兰NZ,智利CL 4.2 哥CR 5 巴PK 6.3 澳AU 7.4 瑞士CH 8 亚太AP 8.4 韩国KR	0 受惠国LD	40	---Other
		--鳗鱼（鳗鲡属）：					--Eels (*Anguilla* spp.) :
154	0301.9210	---鱼苗	0		0 受惠国LD	0	---Fry

序号 No.	税则号列 Tariff Line	中文货品名称 Article Description in Chinese	最惠国税率 MFN(%)	协定税率 Agreement(%)	特惠税率 SP(%)	普通税率 Gen(%)	英文货品名称 Article Description
155	0301.9290	---其他	10	0 冰岛IS,东盟AS,秘鲁PE,新西兰NZ,智利CL 4 哥CR,瑞士CH 5 巴PK 6 澳AU 6.7 亚太AP 8 韩国KR	0 柬埔寨KH,缅甸MM,受惠国LD	40	---Other
		--鲤科鱼（西鲤、黑鲫、草鱼、鲢属、鲮属、青鱼）：					--Carp (*Cyprinus carpio*, *Carassius carassius*, *Ctenopharyngodon idellus*, *Hypophthalmichthys* spp., *Cirrhinus* spp., *Mylopharyngodon piceus*) :
156	0301.9310	---鱼苗	0		0 受惠国LD	0	---Fry
157	0301.9390	---其他	10.5	0 冰岛IS,东盟AS,秘鲁PE,新西兰NZ,智利CL 4.2 哥CR 5 巴PK 6.3 澳AU 7.4 瑞士CH 8 亚太AP 8.4 韩国KR	0 柬埔寨KH,缅甸MM,受惠国LD	40	---Other
		--大西洋及太平洋蓝鳍金枪鱼：					--Atlantic and Pacific bluefin tuna (*Thunnus thynnus*, *Thunnus orientalis*) :
158	0301.9410	---鱼苗	0		0 受惠国LD	0	---Fry
		---其他：					---Other:
159	0301.9491	----大西洋蓝鳍金枪鱼	10.5	0 冰岛IS,东盟AS,秘鲁PE,香港HK,新西兰NZ,智利CL 4.2 哥CR 5 巴PK 6.3 澳AU 7.4 瑞士CH 8 亚太AP 8.4 韩国KR	0 柬埔寨KH,缅甸MM,受惠国LD	40	----Atlantic bluefin tunas (*Thunnus thynnus*)
160	0301.9492	----太平洋蓝鳍金枪鱼	10.5	0 冰岛IS,东盟AS,台湾TW,香港HK,新西兰NZ,智利CL 3.2 秘鲁PE 4.2 哥CR 5 巴PK 6.3 澳AU 7.4 瑞士CH 8 亚太AP 8.4 韩国KR	0 柬埔寨KH,缅甸MM,受惠国LD	40	----Pacific bluefin tunas (*Thunnus orientalis*)
		--南方蓝鳍金枪鱼：					--Southern bluefin tuna (*Thunnus maccoyii*) :
161	0301.9510	---鱼苗	0		0 受惠国LD	0	---Fry
162	0301.9590	---其他	10.5	0 冰岛IS,东盟AS,秘鲁PE,香港HK,新西兰NZ,智利CL 4.2 哥CR 5 巴PK 6.3 澳AU 7.4 瑞士CH 8 亚太AP 8.4 韩国KR	0 柬埔寨KH,缅甸MM,受惠国LD	40	---Other
		--其他：					--Other:
		---鱼苗：					---Fry:
163	0301.9911	----鲈鱼	0		0 受惠国LD	0	----Of perches
164	0301.9912	----鲟鱼	0		0 受惠国LD	0	----Of sturgeon
165	0301.9919	----其他	0		0 受惠国LD	0	----Other
		---其他：					---Other:

序号 No.	税则号列 Tariff Line	中文货品名称 Article Description in Chinese	最惠国税率 MFN(%)	协定税率 Agreement(%)	特惠税率 SP(%)	普通税率 Gen(%)	英文货品名称 Article Description
166	0301.9991	----罗非鱼	10.5	0 冰岛IS,东盟AS,香港HK,新西兰NZ,智利CL 3.2 秘鲁PE 4.2 哥CR 5 巴PK 6.3 澳AU 7.4 瑞士CH 8.4 韩国KR	0 柬埔寨KH,缅甸MM,受惠国LD	40	----Tilapia
167	0301.9992	----鲀	10.5	0 冰岛IS,东盟AS,秘鲁PE,香港HK,新西兰NZ,智利CL 4.2 哥CR 5 巴PK 6.3 澳AU 7.4 瑞士CH 8 亚太AP 8.4 韩国KR	0 柬埔寨KH,缅甸MM,受惠国LD	40	----Puffer fish
168	0301.9993	----其他鲤科鱼	10.5	0 冰岛IS,东盟AS,秘鲁PE,新西兰NZ,智利CL 4.2 哥CR 5 巴PK 6.3 澳AU 7.4 瑞士CH 8 亚太AP 8.4 韩国KR	0 柬埔寨KH,缅甸MM,受惠国LD	40	----Other carp
169	0301.9999	----其他	10.5	0 冰岛IS,东盟AS,台湾TW,香港HK,新西兰NZ,智利CL 3.2 秘鲁PE 4.2 哥CR 5 巴PK 6.3 澳AU 7.4 瑞士CH 8 亚太AP 8.4 韩国KR	0 柬埔寨KH,缅甸MM,受惠国LD	40	----Other
	03.02	**鲜、冷鱼，但税号03.04的鱼片及其他鱼肉除外：**					**Fish, fresh or chilled, excluding fish fillets and other fish meat of heading 03.04:**
		-鲑科鱼，但鱼肝及鱼卵除外：					-Salmonidae, excluding livers and roes:
170	0302.1100	--鳟鱼（河鳟、虹鳟、克拉克大麻哈鱼、阿瓜大麻哈鱼、吉雨大麻哈鱼、亚利桑那大麻哈鱼、金腹大麻哈鱼）	12	0 冰岛IS,东盟AS,新西兰NZ,智利CL 3.6 秘鲁PE 4.8 哥CR 6 巴PK 7.2 澳AU 8.4 瑞士CH 9.6 韩国KR	0 受惠国LD	40	--Trout (*Salmo trutta*, *Oncorhynchus mykiss*, *Oncorhynchus clarki*, *Oncorhynchus aguabonita*, *Oncorhynchus gilae*, *Oncorhynchus apache* and *Oncorhynchus chrysogaster*)
171	0302.1300	--大麻哈鱼〔红大麻哈鱼、细磷大麻哈鱼、大麻哈鱼（种）、大鳞大麻哈鱼、银大麻哈鱼、马苏大麻哈鱼、玫瑰大麻哈鱼〕	10	0 冰岛IS,东盟AS,新西兰NZ,智利CL 3 秘鲁PE 4 哥CR,瑞士CH 5 巴PK 6 澳AU 8 韩国KR	0 受惠国LD	40	--Pacific salmon (*Oncorhynchus nerka*, *Oncorhynchus gorbuscha*, *Oncorhynchus keta*, *Oncorhynchus tschawytscha*, *Oncorhynchus kisutch*, *Oncorhynchus masou* and *Oncorhynchus rhodurus*)
		--大西洋鲑鱼及多瑙哲罗鱼：					--Atlantic salmon (*Salmo salar*) and Danube salmon (*Hucho hucho*) :
172	0302.1410	---大西洋鲑鱼	10	0 冰岛IS,东盟AS,新西兰NZ,智利CL 3 秘鲁PE 4 哥CR,瑞士CH 5 巴PK 6 澳AU 8 韩国KR	0 受惠国LD	40	---Atlantic salmon (*Salmo salar*)

序号 No.	税则号列 Tariff Line	中文货品名称 Article Description in Chinese	最惠国税率 MFN(%)	协定税率 Agreement(%)	特惠税率 SP(%)	普通税率 Gen(%)	英文货品名称 Article Description
173	0302.1420	---多瑙哲罗鱼	10	0 冰岛IS,东盟AS,新西兰NZ,智利CL 3 秘鲁PE 4 哥CR,瑞士CH 5 巴PK 6 澳AU 8 韩国KR	0 受惠国LD	40	---Danube salmon (*Hucho hucho*)
174	0302.1900	--其他	12	0 冰岛IS,东盟AS,秘鲁PE,新西兰NZ,智利CL 4.8 哥CR 5 巴PK 7.2 澳AU 8 亚太AP 8.4 瑞士CH 9.6 韩国KR	0 受惠国LD	40	--Other
		-比目鱼，但鱼肝及鱼卵除外：					-Flat fish (Pleuronectidae, Bothidae, Cynoglossidae, Soleidae, Scophthalmidae and Citharidae) , excluding livers and roes:
175	0302.2100	--庸鲽鱼	12	0 冰岛IS,东盟AS,秘鲁PE,新西兰NZ,智利CL 4.8 哥CR 5 巴PK 7.2 澳AU 8.4 瑞士CH 9 亚太AP 9.6 韩国KR	0 受惠国LD	40	--Halibut (*Reinhardtius hippoglossoides*, *Hippoglossus hippoglossus*, *Hippoglossus stenolepis*)
176	0302.2200	--鲽鱼	12	0 冰岛IS,东盟AS,秘鲁PE,新西兰NZ,智利CL 4.8 哥CR 5 巴PK 7.2 澳AU 8.4 瑞士CH 9 亚太AP 9.6 韩国KR	0 受惠国LD	40	--Plaice (Pleuronectes platessa)
177	0302.2300	--鳎鱼	12	0 冰岛IS,东盟AS,秘鲁PE,新西兰NZ,智利CL 4.8 哥CR 5 巴PK 7.2 澳AU 8.4 瑞士CH 9 亚太AP 9.6 韩国KR	0 受惠国LD	40	--Sole (Solea spp.)
178	0302.2400	--大菱鲆（瘤棘鲆）	12	0 冰岛IS,东盟AS,新西兰NZ,智利CL 3.6 秘鲁PE 4.8 哥CR 5 巴PK 6 亚太AP 7.2 澳AU 8.4 瑞士CH 9.6 韩国KR	0 柬埔寨KH,受惠国LD	40	--Turbots (Psetta maxima, Scophthalmidae)
179	0302.2900	--其他	12	0 冰岛IS,东盟AS,新西兰NZ,智利CL 3.6 秘鲁PE 4.8 哥CR 5 巴PK 6 亚太AP 7.2 澳AU 8.4 瑞士CH 9.6 韩国KR	0 柬埔寨KH,受惠国LD	40	--Other

序号 No.	税则号列 Tariff Line	中文货品名称 Article Description in Chinese	最惠国税率 MFN(%)	协定税率 Agreement(%)	特惠税率 SP(%)	普通税率 Gen(%)	英文货品名称 Article Description
		-金枪鱼(金枪鱼属)、鲣鱼或狐鲣(鲣)，但鱼肝及鱼卵除外：					-Tuna (of the genus *Thunnus*) , skipjack or stripe-bellied bonito (*Euthynnus* (*Katsuwonus*) *pelamis*) , excluding livers and roes:
180	0302.3100	--长鳍金枪鱼	12	0 冰岛IS,东盟AS,新西兰NZ,智利CL 3.6 秘鲁PE 4.8 哥CR 5 巴PK 7.2 澳AU 8.4 瑞士CH 9 亚太AP 9.6 韩国KR	0 柬埔寨KH,受惠国LD	40	--Albacore or longfinned tunas (*Thunnus alalunga*)
181	0302.3200	--黄鳍金枪鱼	12	0 冰岛IS,东盟AS,秘鲁PE,香港HK,新西兰NZ,智利CL 4.8 哥CR 5 巴PK 7.2 澳AU 8.4 瑞士CH 9 亚太AP 9.6 韩国KR	0 受惠国LD	40	--Yellowfin tunas (*Thunnus albacares*)
182	0302.3300	--鲣鱼或狐鲣	12	0 冰岛IS,东盟AS,秘鲁PE,新西兰NZ,智利CL 4.8 哥CR 5 巴PK 7.2 澳AU 8 亚太AP 8.4 瑞士CH 9.6 韩国KR	0 受惠国LD	40	--Skipjack or stripe-bellied bonito
183	0302.3400	--大眼金枪鱼	12	0 冰岛IS,东盟AS,秘鲁PE,新西兰NZ,智利CL 4.8 哥CR 6 巴PK 7.2 澳AU 8.4 瑞士CH 9.6 韩国KR	0 柬埔寨KH,缅甸MM,受惠国LD	40	--Bigeye tunas (*Thunnus* obesus)
		--大西洋及太平洋蓝鳍金枪鱼：					--Atlantic and Pacific bluefin tuna (*Thunnus thynnus*, *Thunnus orientalis*) :
184	0302.3510	---大西洋蓝鳍金枪鱼	12	0 冰岛IS,东盟AS,秘鲁PE,新西兰NZ,智利CL 4.8 哥CR 6 巴PK 7.2 澳AU 8.4 瑞士CH 9.6 韩国KR	0 柬埔寨KH,缅甸MM,受惠国LD	40	---Atlantic bluefin tunas (*Thunnus thynnus*)
185	0302.3520	---太平洋蓝鳍金枪鱼	12	0 冰岛IS,东盟AS,秘鲁PE,新西兰NZ,智利CL 4.8 哥CR 5 巴PK 7.2 澳AU 8 亚太AP 8.4 瑞士CH 9.6 韩国KR	0 柬埔寨KH,缅甸MM,受惠国LD	40	---Pacific bluefin tunas (*Thunnus orientlis*)
186	0302.3600	--南方蓝鳍金枪鱼	12	0 冰岛IS,东盟AS,秘鲁PE,新西兰NZ,智利CL 4.8 哥CR 6 巴PK 7.2 澳AU 8.4 瑞士CH 9.6 韩国KR	0 柬埔寨KH,缅甸MM,受惠国LD	40	--Southern bluefin tunas (*Thunnus maccoyii*)

序号 No.	税则号列 Tariff Line	中文货品名称 Article Description in Chinese	最惠国税率 MFN(%)	协定税率 Agreement(%)	特惠税率 SP(%)	普通税率 Gen(%)	英文货品名称 Article Description
187	0302.3900	--其他	12	0 冰岛IS,东盟AS,秘鲁PE,新西兰NZ,智利CL 4.8 哥CR 5 巴PK 7.2 澳AU 8 亚太AP 8.4 瑞士CH 9.6 韩国KR	0 柬埔寨KH,缅甸MM,受惠国LD	40	--Other
		-鲱鱼(大西洋鲱鱼、太平洋鲱鱼)、鳀鱼(鳀属)、沙丁鱼(沙丁鱼、沙瑙鱼属)、小沙丁鱼属、黍鲱或西鲱、鲭鱼〔大西洋鲭、澳洲鲭(鲐)、日本鲭(鲐)〕、对称竹荚鱼、新西兰竹荚鱼及竹荚鱼(竹荚鱼属)、军曹鱼及剑鱼,但鱼肝及鱼卵除外:					-Herring (*Clupea harengus*, *Clupea pallasii*) , anchovies (*Engraulis* spp.) , sardines (*Sardina pilchardus*, *Sardinops* spp.) , sardinella (*Sardinella* spp.) , brisling or sprats (*Sprattus sprattus*) , mackerel (*Scomber scombrus*, *Scomber australasicus*, *Scomber japonicus*) , jack and horse mackerel (*Trachurus* spp.) , cobia (*Rachycentron canadum*) and swordfish (*Xiphias gladius*) , excluding livers and roes:
188	0302.4100	--鲱鱼(大西洋鲱鱼、太平洋鲱鱼)	12	0 冰岛IS,东盟AS,秘鲁PE,新西兰NZ,智利CL 4.8 哥CR 5 巴PK 7.2 澳AU 8 亚太AP 8.4 瑞士CH 9.6 韩国KR	0 受惠国LD	40	--Herrings (*Clupea harengus*, *Clupea pallasii*)
189	0302.4200	--鳀鱼(鳀属)	12	0 冰岛IS,东盟AS,秘鲁PE,台湾TW,香港HK,新西兰NZ,智利CL 4.8 哥CR 5 巴PK 7.2 澳AU 8 亚太AP 8.4 瑞士CH 9.6 韩国KR	0 柬埔寨KH,缅甸MM,受惠国LD	40	--Anchovies (*Engraulis spp.*)
190	0302.4300	--沙丁鱼(沙丁鱼、沙瑙鱼属)、小沙丁鱼属、黍鲱或西鲱	12	0 冰岛IS,东盟AS,秘鲁PE,新西兰NZ,智利CL 4.8 哥CR 5 巴PK 7.2 澳AU 8 亚太AP 8.4 瑞士CH 9.6 韩国KR	0 受惠国LD	40	--Sardines (*Sardina pilchardus*, *Sardinops spp.*) , *sardinella* (*Sardinella spp.*) , brisling or sprats (*Sprattus sprattus*)
191	0302.4400	--鲭鱼〔大西洋鲭、澳洲鲭(鲐)、日本鲭(鲐)〕	12	0 冰岛IS,东盟AS,秘鲁PE,新西兰NZ,智利CL 4.8 哥CR 5 巴PK 7.2 澳AU 8 亚太AP 8.4 瑞士CH 9.6 韩国KR	0 受惠国LD	40	--Mackerel (*Scomber scombrus*, *Scomber australasicus*, *Scomberjaponicus*)
192	0302.4500	--对称竹荚鱼、新西兰竹荚鱼及竹荚鱼(竹荚鱼属)	12	0 冰岛IS,东盟AS,秘鲁PE,台湾TW,香港HK,新西兰NZ,智利CL 4.8 哥CR 5 巴PK 7.2 澳AU 8 亚太AP 8.4 瑞士CH 9.6 韩国KR	0 柬埔寨KH,缅甸MM,受惠国LD	40	--Jack and horse mackerel (*Trachurus spp.*)

序号 No.	税则号列 Tariff Line	中文货品名称 Article Description in Chinese	最惠国税率 MFN(%)	协定税率 Agreement(%)	特惠税率 SP(%)	普通税率 Gen(%)	英文货品名称 Article Description
193	0302.4600	--军曹鱼	12	0 冰岛IS,东盟AS,秘鲁PE,台湾TW,香港HK,新西兰NZ,智利CL 4.8 哥CR 5 巴PK 7.2 澳AU 8 亚太AP 8.4 瑞士CH 9.6 韩国KR	0 柬埔寨KH,缅甸MM,受惠国LD	40	--Cobia (*Rachycentron canadum*)
194	0302.4700	--剑鱼	12	0 冰岛IS,东盟AS,秘鲁PE,香港HK,新西兰NZ,智利CL 4.8 哥CR 5 巴PK 7.2 澳AU 8 亚太AP 8.4 瑞士CH 9.6 韩国KR	0 受惠国LD	40	--Swordfish (*Xiphias gladius*)
		-犀鳕科、多丝真鳕科、鳕科、长尾鳕科、黑鳕科、无须鳕科、深海鳕科及南极鳕科鱼，但鱼肝及鱼卵除外：					-Fish of the families Bregmacerotidae, Euclichthyidae, Gadidae, Macrouridae, Melanonidae, Merlucciidae, Moridae and Muraenolepididae, excluding livers and roes:
195	0302.5100	--鳕鱼(大西洋鳕鱼、格陵兰鳕鱼、太平洋鳕鱼)	12	0 冰岛IS,东盟AS,秘鲁PE,新西兰NZ,智利CL 4.8 哥CR 5 巴PK 7.2 澳AU 8 亚太AP 8.4 瑞士CH 9.6 韩国KR	0 受惠国LD	40	--Cod (Gadus morhua, Gadus ogac, Gadus macrocephalus)
196	0302.5200	--黑线鳕鱼（黑线鳕）	12	0 冰岛IS,东盟AS,秘鲁PE,新西兰NZ,智利CL 4.8 哥CR 5 巴PK 7.2 澳AU 8 亚太AP 8.4 瑞士CH 9.6 韩国KR	0 受惠国LD	40	--Haddock (Melanogrammus aeglefinus)
197	0302.5300	--绿青鳕鱼	12	0 冰岛IS,东盟AS,秘鲁PE,新西兰NZ,智利CL 4.8 哥CR 5 巴PK 7.2 澳AU 8 亚太AP 8.4 瑞士CH 9.6 韩国KR	0 受惠国LD	40	--Coalfish (Pollachius virens)
198	0302.5400	--狗鳕鱼(无须鳕属、长鳍鳕属)	12	0 冰岛IS,东盟AS,秘鲁PE,台湾TW,香港HK,新西兰NZ,智利CL 4.8 哥CR 5 巴PK 7.2 澳AU 8 亚太AP 8.4 瑞士CH 9.6 韩国KR	0 柬埔寨KH,缅甸MM,受惠国LD	40	--Hake (Merluccius spp., Urophycis spp.)

序号 No.	税则号列 Tariff Line	中文货品名称 Article Description in Chinese	最惠国税率 MFN(%)	协定税率 Agreement(%)	特惠税率 SP(%)	普通税率 Gen(%)	英文货品名称 Article Description
199	0302.5500	--狭鳕鱼	12	0 冰岛IS,东盟AS,秘鲁PE,台湾TW,香港HK,新西兰NZ,智利CL 4.8 哥CR 5 巴PK 7.2 澳AU 8 亚太AP 8.4 瑞士CH 9.6 韩国KR	0 柬埔寨KH,缅甸MM,受惠国LD	40	--Alaska Pollack (Theraga chalcogramma)
200	0302.5600	--蓝鳕鱼（小鳍鳕、南蓝鳕）	12	0 冰岛IS,东盟AS,秘鲁PE,台湾TW,香港HK,新西兰NZ,智利CL 4.8 哥CR 5 巴PK 7.2 澳AU 8 亚太AP 8.4 瑞士CH 9.6 韩国KR	0 柬埔寨KH,缅甸MM,受惠国LD	40	--Blue whitings (Micromesistius poutassou, Micromesistiusaustralis)
201	0302.5900	--其他	12	0 冰岛IS,东盟AS,秘鲁PE,台湾TW,香港HK,新西兰NZ,智利CL 4.8 哥CR 5 巴PK 7.2 澳AU 8 亚太AP 8.4 瑞士CH 9.6 韩国KR	0 柬埔寨KH,缅甸MM,受惠国LD	40	--Other
		-罗非鱼（口孵非鲫属）、鲶鱼（(鱼芒)鲶属、鲶属、胡鲶属、真鮰属）、鲤科鱼（西鲤、黑鲫、草鱼、鲢属、鲮属、青鱼）、鳗鱼（鳗鲡属）、尼罗河鲈鱼（尼罗尖吻鲈）及黑鱼（鳢属），但鱼肝及鱼卵除外：					-Tilapia (*Oreochromis* spp.) , catfish (*Pangasius* spp., *Silurus* spp., *Clarias* spp., *Ictalurus* spp.) , carp (*Cyprinus carpio*, *Carassius carassius*, *Ctenopharyngodon idellus*, *Hypophthalmichthys* spp., *Cirrhinus* spp., *Mylopharyngodon piceus*) , eels (*Anguilla* spp.) , Nile perch (*Lates niloticus*) and snakeheads (*Channa* spp.) , excluding livers and roes:
202	0302.7100	--罗非鱼（口孵非鲫属）	12	0 冰岛IS,东盟AS,新西兰NZ,智利CL 3.6 秘鲁PE 4.8 哥CR 6 巴PK 7.2 澳AU 8.4 瑞士CH 9.6 韩国KR	0 柬埔寨KH,缅甸MM,受惠国LD	40	--Tilapias (*Oreochromis* spp.)
203	0302.7200	--鲶鱼（(鱼芒)鲶属、鲶属、胡鲶属、真鮰属）	12	0 冰岛IS,东盟AS,秘鲁PE,台湾TW,香港HK,新西兰NZ,智利CL 4.8 哥CR 5 巴PK 7.2 澳AU 8 亚太AP 8.4 瑞士CH 9.6 韩国KR	0 柬埔寨KH,缅甸MM,受惠国LD	40	--Catfish (Pangasius spp., Silurus spp., Clarias spp., Ictalurus spp.)
204	0302.7300	--鲤科鱼（西鲤、黑鲫、草鱼、鲢属、鲮属、青鱼）	12	0 冰岛IS,东盟AS,秘鲁PE,台湾TW,香港HK,新西兰NZ,智利CL 4.8 哥CR 5 巴PK 7.2 澳AU 8 亚太AP 8.4 瑞士CH 9.6 韩国KR	0 柬埔寨KH,缅甸MM,受惠国LD	40	--Carp (Cyprinus carpio, Carassius carassius, Ctenopharyngodon idellus, Hypophthalmichthys spp., Cirrhinus spp., Mylopharyngodon piceus)

序号 No.	税则号列 Tariff Line	中文货品名称 Article Description in Chinese	最惠国税率 MFN(%)	协定税率 Agreement(%)	特惠税率 SP(%)	普通税率 Gen(%)	英文货品名称 Article Description
205	0302.7400	--鳗鱼（鳗鲡属）	12	0 冰岛IS,东盟AS,秘鲁PE,香港HK,新西兰NZ,智利CL 4.8 哥CR 5 巴PK 7.2 澳AU 8 亚太AP 8.4 瑞士CH 9.6 韩国KR	0 缅甸MM,受惠国LD	40	--Eels (*Anguilla spp.*)
206	0302.7900	--其他	12	0 冰岛IS,东盟AS,秘鲁PE,台湾TW,香港HK,新西兰NZ,智利CL 4.8 哥CR 5 巴PK 7.2 澳AU 8 亚太AP 8.4 瑞士CH 9.6 韩国KR	0 柬埔寨KH,缅甸MM,受惠国LD	40	--Other
		-其他鱼，但鱼肝及鱼卵除外：					-Other fish, excluding livers and roes:
207	0302.8100	--角鲨及其他鲨鱼	12	0 冰岛IS,东盟AS,香港HK,新西兰NZ,智利CL 3.6 秘鲁PE 4.8 哥CR 5 巴PK 7.2 澳AU 8.4 瑞士CH 9 亚太AP 9.6 韩国KR	0 受惠国LD	40	--Dogfish and other sharks
208	0302.8200	--魟鱼及鳐鱼（鳐科）	12	0 冰岛IS,东盟AS,秘鲁PE,台湾TW,香港HK,新西兰NZ,智利CL 4.8 哥CR 5 巴PK 7.2 澳AU 8 亚太AP 8.4 瑞士CH 9.6 韩国KR	0 柬埔寨KH,缅甸MM,受惠国LD	40	--Rays and skates (Rajidae)
209	0302.8300	--南极犬牙鱼（南极犬牙鱼属）	12	0 冰岛IS,东盟AS,秘鲁PE,香港HK,新西兰NZ,智利CL 4.8 哥CR 5 巴PK 7.2 澳AU 8 亚太AP 8.4 瑞士CH 9.6 韩国KR	0 柬埔寨KH,缅甸MM,受惠国LD	40	--Toothfish (Dissostichus spp.)
210	0302.8400	--尖吻鲈鱼(舌齿鲈属)	12	0 冰岛IS,东盟AS,秘鲁PE,台湾TW,香港HK,新西兰NZ,智利CL 4.8 哥CR 5 巴PK 7.2 澳AU 8 亚太AP 8.4 瑞士CH 9.6 韩国KR	0 柬埔寨KH,缅甸MM,受惠国LD	40	--Seabass (Dicentrarchus spp.)
211	0302.8500	--菱羊鲷(鲷科)	12	0 冰岛IS,东盟AS,秘鲁PE,台湾TW,香港HK,新西兰NZ,智利CL 4.8 哥CR 5 巴PK 7.2 澳AU 8 亚太AP 8.4 瑞士CH 9.6 韩国KR	0 柬埔寨KH,缅甸MM,受惠国LD	40	--Seabream (Sparidae)

序号 No.	税则号列 Tariff Line	中文货品名称 Article Description in Chinese	最惠国税率 MFN(%)	协定税率 Agreement(%)	特惠税率 SP(%)	普通税率 Gen(%)	英文货品名称 Article Description
		--其他:					--Other:
212	0302.8910	---带鱼	12	0 冰岛IS,东盟AS,香港HK,新西兰NZ,智利CL 3.6 秘鲁PE 4.8 哥CR 7.2 澳AU 8 巴PK,亚太AP 8.4 瑞士CH 9.6 韩国KR	0 受惠国LD	40	---Scabber fish (Trichurius)
213	0302.8920	---黄鱼	12	0 冰岛IS,东盟AS,香港HK,新西兰NZ,智利CL 3.6 秘鲁PE 4.8 哥CR 5 巴PK 7.2 澳AU 8 亚太AP 8.4 瑞士CH 9.6 韩国KR	0 受惠国LD	40	---Yellow croaker (Pseudosicaena)
214	0302.8930	---鲳鱼	12	0 冰岛IS,东盟AS,香港HK,新西兰NZ,智利CL 3.6 秘鲁PE 4.8 哥CR 5 巴PK 7.2 澳AU 8 亚太AP 8.4 瑞士CH 9.6 韩国KR	0 受惠国LD	40	---Butterfish (Pamus)
215	0302.8940	---鲀	12	0 冰岛IS,东盟AS,香港HK,新西兰NZ,智利CL 3.6 秘鲁PE 4.8 哥CR 5 巴PK 7.2 澳AU 8 亚太AP 8.4 瑞士CH 9.6 韩国KR	0 柬埔寨KH,缅甸MM,受惠国LD	40	---Puffer fish
216	0302.8990	---其他	12	0 冰岛IS,东盟AS,秘鲁PE,台湾TW,香港HK,新西兰NZ,智利CL 4.8 哥CR 5 巴PK 7.2 澳AU 8 亚太AP 8.4 瑞士CH 9.6 韩国KR	0 柬埔寨KH,缅甸MM,受惠国LD	40	---Other
217	0302.9000	-鱼肝及鱼卵	12	0 冰岛IS,东盟AS,秘鲁PE,新西兰NZ,智利CL 4.8 哥CR 6 巴PK 7.2 澳AU 8.4 瑞士CH 9.6 韩国KR	0 柬埔寨KH,受惠国LD	50	-Livers and roes
	03.03	**冻鱼，但税号03.04的鱼片及其他鱼肉除外：**					**Fish, frozen, excluding fish fillets and other fish meat of heading 0304:**
		-鲑科鱼，但鱼肝及鱼卵除外：					-Salmonidae, excluding livers and roes:
218	0303.1100	--红大麻哈鱼	10	0 冰岛IS,东盟AS,新西兰NZ,智利CL 3 秘鲁PE 4 哥CR,瑞士CH 5 巴PK 6 澳AU 6.7 亚太AP 8 韩国KR	0 柬埔寨KH,受惠国LD	40	--Sockeye salmon (red salmon) (*Oncorhynchus nerka*)

序号 No.	税则号列 Tariff Line	中文货品名称 Article Description in Chinese	最惠国税率 MFN(%)	协定税率 Agreement(%)	特惠税率 SP(%)	普通税率 Gen(%)	英文货品名称 Article Description
219	0303.1200	--其他大麻哈鱼〔细磷大麻哈鱼、大麻哈鱼（种）、大鳞大麻哈鱼、银大麻哈鱼、马苏大麻哈鱼、玫瑰大麻哈鱼〕	10	0 冰岛IS,东盟AS,新西兰NZ,智利CL 3 秘鲁PE 4 哥CR,瑞士CH 5 巴PK 6 澳AU 6.7 亚太AP 8 韩国KR	0 柬埔寨KH,受惠国LD	40	--Other Pacific salmon (*Oncorhynchus gorbuscha, Oncorhynchus keta, Oncorhynchus tschawytscha, Oncorhynchus kisutch, Oncorhynchus masou and Oncorhynchus rhodurus*)
220	0303.1300	--大西洋鲑鱼及多瑙哲罗鱼	10	0 冰岛IS,东盟AS,新西兰NZ,智利CL 3 秘鲁PE 4 哥CR,瑞士CH 5 巴PK 6 澳AU 8 韩国KR	0 受惠国LD	40	--Atlantic salmon (*Salmo salar*) and Danube salmon (*Hucho hucho*)
221	0303.1400	--鳟鱼(河鳟、虹鳟、克拉克大麻哈鱼、阿瓜大麻哈鱼、吉雨大麻哈鱼、亚利桑那大麻哈鱼、金腹大麻哈鱼)	12	0 冰岛IS,东盟AS,新西兰NZ,智利CL 3.6 秘鲁PE 4.8 哥CR 6 巴PK 7.2 澳AU 8.4 瑞士CH 9.6 韩国KR	0 受惠国LD	40	--Trout (*Salmo trutta, Oncorhynchus mykiss, Oncorhynchus clarki, Oncorhynchus aguabonita, Oncorhynchus gilae, Oncorhynchus apache* and *Oncorhynchus chrysogaster*)
222	0303.1900	--其他	10	0 冰岛IS,东盟AS,秘鲁PE,新西兰NZ,智利CL 4 哥CR,瑞士CH 5 巴PK 6 澳AU 6.7 亚太AP 8 韩国KR	0 受惠国LD	40	--Other
		-罗非鱼（口孵非鲫属）、鲶鱼（(鱼芒)鲶属、鲶属、胡鲶属、真鮰属）、鲤科鱼（西鲤、黑鲫、草鱼、鲢属、鲮属、青鱼）、鳗鱼（鳗鲡属）、尼罗河鲈鱼（尼罗尖吻鲈）及黑鱼（鳢属），但鱼肝及鱼卵除外：					-Tilapia (*Oreochromis spp.*), catfish (*Pangasius* spp., *Silurus* spp., *Clarias* spp., *Ictalurus* spp.), carp (*Cyprinus carpio, Carassius carassius, Ctenopharyngodon idellus, Hypophthalmichthys* spp., *Cirrhinus* spp., *Mylopharyngodon piceus*), eels (*Anguilla* spp.), Nile perch (*Lates niloticus*) and snakeheads (*Channa* spp.), excluding livers and roes:
223	0303.2300	--罗非鱼（口孵非鲫属）	10	0 冰岛IS,东盟AS,新西兰NZ,智利CL 3 秘鲁PE 4 哥CR,瑞士CH 5 巴PK,亚太AP 6 澳AU 8 韩国KR	0 柬埔寨KH,缅甸MM,受惠国LD,亚太AP	40	--Tilapias (*Oreochromis spp.*)
224	0303.2400	--鲶鱼（(鱼芒)鲶属、鲶属、胡鲶属、真鮰属）	10	0 冰岛IS,东盟AS,台湾TW,香港HK,新西兰NZ,智利CL 1.2 秘鲁PE 4 哥CR,瑞士CH 5 巴PK,亚太AP 6 澳AU,韩国KR	0 柬埔寨KH,缅甸MM,受惠国LD,亚太AP	40	--Catfish (*Pangasius spp., Silurus spp., Clarias spp., Ictalurus spp.*)
225	0303.2500	--鲤科鱼（西鲤、黑鲫、草鱼、鲢属、鲮属、青鱼）	10	0 冰岛IS,东盟AS,台湾TW,香港HK,新西兰NZ,智利CL 1.2 秘鲁PE 4 哥CR,瑞士CH 5 巴PK,亚太AP 6 澳AU,韩国KR	0 柬埔寨KH,缅甸MM,受惠国LD,亚太AP	40	--Carp (*Cyprinus carpio, Carassius carassius, Ctenopharyngodon idellus, Hypophthalmichthys spp., Cirrhinus spp., Mylopharyngodon piceus*)

序号 No.	税则号列 Tariff Line	中文货品名称 Article Description in Chinese	最惠国税率 MFN(%)	协定税率 Agreement(%)	特惠税率 SP(%)	普通税率 Gen(%)	英文货品名称 Article Description
226	0303.2600	--鳗鱼（鳗鲡属）	12	0 冰岛IS,东盟AS,香港HK,新西兰NZ,智利CL 3.6 秘鲁PE 4.8 哥CR 7.2 澳AU 8 巴PK,亚太AP 8.4 瑞士CH 9.6 韩国KR	0 受惠国LD	40	--Eels (*Anguilla spp.*)
227	0303.2900	--其他	10	0 冰岛IS,东盟AS,台湾TW,香港HK,新西兰NZ,智利CL 1.2 秘鲁PE 4 哥CR,瑞士CH 5 巴PK,亚太AP 6 澳AU,韩国KR	0 柬埔寨KH,缅甸MM,受惠国LD,亚太AP	40	--Other
		-比目鱼（鲽科、鲆科、舌鳎科、鳎科、菱鲆科、刺鲆科），但鱼肝及鱼卵除外：					-Flat fish (Pleuronectidae, Bothidae, Cynoglossidae, Soleidae, Scophthalmidae and Citharidae) , excluding livers and roes:
		--庸鲽鱼：					--Halibut (*Reinhardtius hippoglossoides*, *Hippoglossus hippoglossus*, *Hippoglossus stenolepis*) :
228	0303.3110	---格陵兰庸鲽鱼	10Δ5	0 冰岛IS,东盟AS,秘鲁PE,香港HK,新西兰NZ,智利CL 4 哥CR,瑞士CH 5 巴PK 6 澳AU 6.7 亚太AP 8 韩国KR	0 受惠国LD	40	---Greenland halibut
229	0303.3190	---其他	10	0 东盟AS,秘鲁PE,香港HK,新西兰NZ,智利CL 4 哥CR,瑞士CH 5 巴PK,冰岛IS 6 澳AU 6.7 亚太AP 8 韩国KR	0 受惠国LD	40	---Other
230	0303.3200	--鲽鱼	12Δ2	0 东盟AS,秘鲁PE,新西兰NZ,智利CL 4.8 哥CR 6 冰岛IS 7.2 澳AU 8 巴PK,亚太AP 8.4 瑞士CH 9.6 韩国KR	0 受惠国LD	40	--Plaice (Pleuronectes platessa)
231	0303.3300	--鳎鱼	12	0 冰岛IS,东盟AS,秘鲁PE,新西兰NZ,智利CL 4.8 哥CR 7.2 澳AU 8 巴PK,亚太AP 8.4 瑞士CH 9.6 韩国KR	0 受惠国LD	40	--Sole (Solea spp.)
232	0303.3400	--大菱鲆（瘤棘鲆）	10	0 冰岛IS,东盟AS,新西兰NZ,智利CL 3 秘鲁PE 4 哥CR,瑞士CH 6 澳AU 8 巴PK,韩国KR,亚太AP	0 受惠国LD	40	--Turbots (Psetta maxima, Scophthalmidae)

序号 No.	税则号列 Tariff Line	中文货品名称 Article Description in Chinese	最惠国税率 MFN(%)	协定税率 Agreement(%)	特惠税率 SP(%)	普通税率 Gen(%)	英文货品名称 Article Description
233	0303.3900	--其他	10	0 东盟AS,新西兰NZ,智利CL 3 秘鲁PE 4 哥CR,瑞士CH 5 冰岛IS 6 澳AU 8 巴PK,韩国KR,亚太AP	0 受惠国LD	40	--Other
		-金枪鱼(金枪鱼属)、鲣鱼或狐鲣(鲣),但鱼肝及鱼卵除外:					-Tuna (of the genus *Thunnus*), skipjack or stripe-bellied bonito (*Euthynnus* (*Katsuwonus*) *pelamis*), excluding livers and roes:
234	0303.4100	--长鳍金枪鱼	12	0 冰岛IS,东盟AS,秘鲁PE,新西兰NZ,智利CL 4.8 哥CR 5 巴PK 7.2 澳AU 8.4 瑞士CH 9 亚太AP 9.6 韩国KR	0 受惠国LD	40	--Albacore or longfinned tunas (*Thunnus alalunga*)
235	0303.4200	--黄鳍金枪鱼	12	0 冰岛IS,东盟AS,秘鲁PE,新西兰NZ,智利CL 4.8 哥CR 5 巴PK 7.2 澳AU 8.4 瑞士CH 9 亚太AP 9.6 韩国KR	0 受惠国LD	40	--Yellowfin tunas (*Thunnus albacares*)
236	0303.4300	--鲣鱼	12	0 冰岛IS,东盟AS,秘鲁PE,新西兰NZ,智利CL 4.8 哥CR 5 巴PK 7.2 澳AU 8.4 瑞士CH 9 亚太AP 10.8 韩国KR	0 受惠国LD	40	--Skipjack or stripe-bellied bonito
237	0303.4400	--大眼金枪鱼	12	0 冰岛IS,东盟AS,秘鲁PE,香港HK,新西兰NZ,智利CL 4.8 哥CR 6 巴PK 7.2 澳AU 8.4 瑞士CH 9.6 韩国KR	0 柬埔寨KH,缅甸MM,受惠国LD	40	--Bigeye tunas (*Thunnus* obesus)
		--大西洋及太平洋蓝鳍金枪鱼:					--Atlantic and Pacific bluefin tuna (*Thunnus thynnus*, *Thunnus orientalis*):
238	0303.4510	---大西洋蓝鳍金枪鱼	12	0 冰岛IS,东盟AS,秘鲁PE,新西兰NZ,智利CL 4.8 哥CR 6 巴PK 7.2 澳AU 8.4 瑞士CH 9.6 韩国KR	0 柬埔寨KH,缅甸MM,受惠国LD	40	---Atlantic bluefin tunas (*Thunnus thynnus*)
239	0303.4520	---太平洋蓝鳍金枪鱼	12	0 冰岛IS,东盟AS,秘鲁PE,新西兰NZ,智利CL 4.8 哥CR 5 巴PK 7.2 澳AU 8.4 瑞士CH 9 亚太AP 9.6 韩国KR	0 柬埔寨KH,缅甸MM,受惠国LD	40	---Pacific bluefin tunas (*Thunnus orientalis*)

序号 No.	税则号列 Tariff Line	中文货品名称 Article Description in Chinese	最惠国税率 MFN(%)	协定税率 Agreement(%)	特惠税率 SP(%)	普通税率 Gen(%)	英文货品名称 Article Description
240	0303.4600	--南方蓝鳍金枪鱼	12	0 冰岛IS,东盟AS,秘鲁PE,新西兰NZ,智利CL 4.8 哥CR 6 巴PK 7.2 澳AU 8.4 瑞士CH 9.6 韩国KR	0 柬埔寨KH,缅甸MM,受惠国LD	40	--Southern bluefin tunas (*Thunnus maccoyii*)
241	0303.4900	--其他	12	0 冰岛IS,东盟AS,秘鲁PE,新西兰NZ,智利CL 4.8 哥CR 5 巴PK 7.2 澳AU 8.4 瑞士CH 9 亚太AP 9.6 韩国KR	0 柬埔寨KH,缅甸MM,受惠国LD	40	--Other
		-鲱鱼（大西洋鲱鱼、太平洋鲱鱼）、沙丁鱼（沙丁鱼、沙瑙鱼属）、小沙丁鱼属、黍鲱或西鲱、鲭鱼〔大西洋鲭、澳洲鲭（鲐）、日本鲭（鲐）〕、对称竹荚鱼、新西兰竹荚鱼及竹荚鱼（竹荚鱼属）、军曹鱼及剑鱼，但鱼肝及鱼卵除外：					-Herring (*Clupea harengus*, *Clupea pallasii*) , sardines (*Sardina pilchardus*, *Sardinops* spp.) , sardinella (*Sardinella* spp.) , brisling or sprats (*Sprattus sprattus*) , mackerel (*Scomber scombrus*, *Scomber australasicus*, *Scomber japonicus*) , jack and horse mackerel (*Trachurus* spp.) , cobia (*Rachycentron canadum*) and swordfish (*Xiphias gladius*) , excluding livers and roes:
242	0303.5100	--鲱鱼（大西洋鲱鱼、太平洋鲱鱼）	10Δ2	0 冰岛IS,东盟AS,秘鲁PE,新西兰NZ,智利CL 4 哥CR,瑞士CH 5 巴PK 6 澳AU 6.7 亚太AP 8 韩国KR	0 受惠国LD	40	--Herrings (*Clupea harengus, Clupea pallasii*)
243	0303.5300	--沙丁鱼（沙丁鱼、沙瑙鱼属）、小沙丁鱼属、黍鲱或西鲱	12	0 冰岛IS,东盟AS,新西兰NZ,智利CL 3.6 秘鲁PE 4.8 哥CR 5 巴PK 7.2 澳AU 8 亚太AP 8.4 瑞士CII 9.6 韩国KR	0 受惠国LD	40	--Sardines (Sardina pilchardus, Sardinops spp.) , sardinella (*Sardinella spp.*) , brisling or sprats (*Sprattus sprattus*)
244	0303.5400	--鲭鱼〔大西洋鲭、澳洲鲭（鲐）、日本鲭（鲐）〕	10	0 冰岛IS,东盟AS,新西兰NZ,智利CL 1.2 秘鲁PE 4 哥CR,瑞士CH 6 澳AU 6.7 巴PK,亚太AP 8 韩国KR	0 受惠国LD	40	--Mackerel (*Scomber scombrus, Scomber australasicus, Scomberjaponicus*)
245	0303.5500	--对称竹荚鱼、新西兰竹荚鱼及竹荚鱼（竹荚鱼属）	10	0 冰岛IS,东盟AS,台湾TW,香港HK,新西兰NZ,智利CL 1.2 秘鲁PE 4 哥CR,瑞士CH 5 巴PK,亚太AP 6 澳AU,韩国KR	0 柬埔寨KH,缅甸MM,受惠国LD,亚太AP	40	--Jack and horse mackerel (*Trachurus spp.*)
246	0303.5600	--军曹鱼	10	0 冰岛IS,东盟AS,台湾TW,香港HK,新西兰NZ,智利CL 1.2 秘鲁PE 4 哥CR,瑞士CH 5 巴PK,亚太AP 6 澳AU,韩国KR	0 柬埔寨KH,缅甸MM,受惠国LD,亚太AP	40	--Cobia (*Rachycentron canadum*)

序号 No.	税则号列 Tariff Line	中文货品名称 Article Description in Chinese	最惠国税率 MFN(%)	协定税率 Agreement(%)	特惠税率 SP(%)	普通税率 Gen(%)	英文货品名称 Article Description
247	0303.5700	--剑鱼	10	0 冰岛IS,东盟AS,秘鲁PE,香港HK,新西兰NZ,智利CL 4 哥CR,瑞士CH 5 巴PK,亚太AP 6 澳AU 8 韩国KR	0 受惠国LD,亚太AP	40	--Swordfish (*Xiphias gladius*)
		-犀鳕科、多丝真鳕科、鳕科、长尾鳕科、黑鳕科、无须鳕科、深海鳕科及南极鳕科鱼，但鱼肝及鱼卵除外：					-Fish of the families Bregmacerotidae, Euclichthyidae, Gadidae, Macrouridae, Melanonidae, Merlucciidae, Moridae and Muraenolepididae, excluding livers and roes:
248	0303.6300	--鳕鱼(大西洋鳕鱼、格陵兰鳕鱼、太平洋鳕鱼)	10Δ2	0 东盟AS,秘鲁PE,新西兰NZ,智利CL 4 哥CR,瑞士CH 5 巴PK,冰岛IS 6 澳AU 6.7 亚太AP 8 韩国KR	0 受惠国LD	40	--Cod (Gadus morhua, Gadus ogac, Gadus macrocephalus)
249	0303.6400	--黑线鳕鱼（黑线鳕）	12	0 东盟AS,秘鲁PE,新西兰NZ,智利CL 4.8 哥CR 5 巴PK 6 冰岛IS 7.2 澳AU 8 亚太AP 8.4 瑞士CH 9.6 韩国KR	0 受惠国LD	40	--Haddock (Melanogrammus aeglefinus)
250	0303.6500	--绿青鳕鱼	12	0 冰岛IS,东盟AS,秘鲁PE,新西兰NZ,智利CL 4.8 哥CR 5 巴PK 7.2 澳AU 8 亚太AP 8.4 瑞士CH 9.6 韩国KR	0 受惠国LD	40	--Coalfish (Pollachius virens)
251	0303.6600	--狗鳕鱼(无须鳕属、长鳍鳕属)	12	0 冰岛IS,东盟AS,新西兰NZ,智利CL 3.6 秘鲁PE 4.8 哥CR 6 巴PK 7.2 澳AU 8.4 瑞士CH 9.6 韩国KR	0 受惠国LD	40	--Hake (Merluccius spp., Urophycis spp.)
252	0303.6700	--狭鳕鱼	10	0 冰岛IS,东盟AS,台湾TW,香港HK,新西兰NZ,智利CL 1.2 秘鲁PE 4 哥CR,瑞士CH 5 巴PK,亚太AP 6 澳AU 8 韩国KR	0 柬埔寨KH,缅甸MM,受惠国LD,亚太AP	40	--Alaska Pollack (Theraga chalcogramma)
253	0303.6800	--蓝鳕鱼（小鳍鳕、南蓝鳕）	10	0 冰岛IS,东盟AS,台湾TW,香港HK,新西兰NZ,智利CL 1.2 秘鲁PE 4 哥CR,瑞士CH 5 巴PK,亚太AP 6 澳AU,韩国KR	0 柬埔寨KH,缅甸MM,受惠国LD,亚太AP	40	--Blue whitings (Micromesistius poutassou, Micromesistiusaustralis)

序号 No.	税则号列 Tariff Line	中文货品名称 Article Description in Chinese	最惠国税率 MFN(%)	协定税率 Agreement(%)	特惠税率 SP(%)	普通税率 Gen(%)	英文货品名称 Article Description
254	0303.6900	--其他	10	0 冰岛IS,东盟AS,台湾TW,香港HK,新西兰NZ,智利CL 1.2 秘鲁PE 4 哥CR,瑞士CH 5 巴PK,亚太AP 6 澳AU,韩国KR	0 柬埔寨KH,缅甸MM,受惠国LD,亚太AP	40	--Other
		-其他鱼，但鱼肝及鱼卵除外：					-Other fish, excluding livers and roes:
255	0303.8100	--角鲨及其他鲨鱼	12	0 冰岛IS,东盟AS,新西兰NZ,智利CL 3.6 秘鲁PE 4.8 哥CR 7.2 澳AU 8.4 瑞士CH 9 巴PK,亚太AP 9.6 韩国KR	0 受惠国LD	40	--Dogfish and other sharks
256	0303.8200	--魟鱼及鳐鱼（鳐科）	10	0 冰岛IS,东盟AS,台湾TW,香港HK,新西兰NZ,智利CL 1.2 秘鲁PE 4 哥CR,瑞士CH 5 巴PK,亚太AP 6 澳AU,韩国KR	0 柬埔寨KH,缅甸MM,受惠国LD,亚太AP	40	--Rays and skates (Rajidae)
257	0303.8300	--南极犬牙鱼（南极犬牙鱼属）	10	0 冰岛IS,东盟AS,秘鲁PE,香港HK,新西兰NZ,智利CL 4 哥CR,瑞士CH 5 巴PK,亚太AP 6 澳AU 8 韩国KR	0 柬埔寨KH,缅甸MM,受惠国LD,亚太AP	40	--Toothfish (Dissostichus spp.)
258	0303.8400	--尖吻鲈鱼（舌齿鲈属）	12	0 冰岛IS,东盟AS,秘鲁PE,香港HK,新西兰NZ,智利CL 4.8 哥CR 5 巴PK 7.2 澳AU 8 亚太AP 8.4 瑞士CH 9.6 韩国KR	0 受惠国LD	40	--Seabass (Dicentrarchus spp.)
		--其他：					--Other:
259	0303.8910	---带鱼	10Δ5	0 东盟AS,香港HK,新西兰NZ,智利CL 3 秘鲁PE 4 哥CR,瑞士CH 5 巴PK,亚太AP 6 澳AU 7.3 冰岛IS 8 韩国KR	0 柬埔寨KH,缅甸MM,受惠国LD,亚太AP	40	---Scabber fish (Trichurius)
260	0303.8920	---黄鱼	10	0 冰岛IS,东盟AS,香港HK,新西兰NZ,智利CL 3 秘鲁PE 4 哥CR,瑞士CH 5 巴PK,亚太AP 6 澳AU 8 韩国KR	0 柬埔寨KH,缅甸MM,受惠国LD,亚太AP	40	---Yellow croaker (Pseudosicaena)
261	0303.8930	---鲳鱼	10	0 冰岛IS,东盟AS,香港HK,新西兰NZ,智利CL 3 秘鲁PE 4 哥CR,瑞士CH 5 巴PK,亚太AP 6 澳AU 8 韩国KR	0 柬埔寨KH,缅甸MM,受惠国LD,亚太AP	40	---Butterfish (Pamus)

序号 No.	税则号列 Tariff Line	中文货品名称 Article Description in Chinese	最惠国税率 MFN(%)	协定税率 Agreement(%)	特惠税率 SP(%)	普通税率 Gen(%)	英文货品名称 Article Description
262	0303.8990	---其他	10	0 冰岛IS,东盟AS,台湾TW,香港HK,新西兰NZ,智利CL 1.2 秘鲁PE 4 哥CR,瑞士CH 5 巴PK,亚太AP 6 澳AU 8.6 韩国KR	0 柬埔寨KH,缅甸MM,受惠国LD,亚太AP	40	---Other
263	0303.9000	-鱼肝及鱼卵	10	0 东盟AS,新西兰NZ,智利CL 4 哥CR,瑞士CH 5 巴PK,冰岛IS 6 澳AU 8 韩国KR 9 亚太AP	0 受惠国LD	50	-Livers and roes
	03.04	**鲜、冷、冻鱼片及其他鱼肉（不论是否绞碎）：**					**Fish fillets and other fish meat (whether or not minced) , fresh, chilled or frozen:**
		-鲜或冷的罗非鱼（口孵非鲫属）、鲶鱼（(鱼芒)鲶属、鲶属、胡鲶属、真鮰属）、鲤科鱼（西鲤、黑鲫、草鱼、鲢属、鲮属、青鱼）、鳗鱼（鳗鲡属）、尼罗河鲈鱼（尼罗尖吻鲈）及黑鱼（鳢属）的鱼片：					-Fresh or chilled fillets of tilapia (*Oreochromis spp.*) , catfish (*Pangasius spp., Silurus spp., Clarias spp., Ictalurus spp.*) , carp (*Cyprinus carpio, Carassius carassius, Ctenopharyngodon idellus, Hypophthalmichthys spp., Cirrhinus spp., Mylopharyngodon piceus*) , eels (*Anguilla spp.*) , Nile perch (*Lates niloticus*) and snakeheads (*Channa spp.*) :
264	0304.3100	--罗非鱼（口孵非鲫属）	12	0 冰岛IS,东盟AS,哥CR,香港HK,新西兰NZ,智利CL 3.6 秘鲁PE 5 巴PK 7.2 澳AU 8.4 瑞士CH 9 亚太AP 9.6 韩国KR	0 缅甸MM,受惠国LD	70	--Tilapias (*Oreochromis spp.*)
265	0304.3200	--鲶鱼（(鱼芒)鲶属、鲶属、胡鲶属、真鮰属）	12	0 冰岛IS,东盟AS,哥CR,香港HK,新西兰NZ,智利CL 3.6 秘鲁PE 5 巴PK 7.2 澳AU 8.4 瑞士CH 9 亚太AP 9.6 韩国KR	0 缅甸MM,受惠国LD	70	--Catfish (*Pangasius spp., Silurus spp., Clarias spp., Ictalurus spp.*)
266	0304.3300	--尼罗河鲈鱼（尼罗尖吻鲈）	12	0 冰岛IS,东盟AS,哥CR,香港HK,新西兰NZ,智利CL 3.6 秘鲁PE 5 巴PK 7.2 澳AU 8.4 瑞士CH 9 亚太AP 9.6 韩国KR	0 缅甸MM,受惠国LD	70	--Nile Perch (*Lates niloticus*)
267	0304.3900	--其他	12	0 冰岛IS,东盟AS,哥CR,香港HK,新西兰NZ,智利CL 3.6 秘鲁PE 5 巴PK 7.2 澳AU 8.4 瑞士CH 9 亚太AP 9.6 韩国KR	0 缅甸MM,受惠国LD	70	--Other

序号 No.	税则号列 Tariff Line	中文货品名称 Article Description in Chinese	最惠国税率 MFN(%)	协定税率 Agreement(%)	特惠税率 SP(%)	普通税率 Gen(%)	英文货品名称 Article Description
		-鲜或冷的其他鱼片：					-Fresh or chilled fillets of other fish:
268	0304.4100	--大麻哈鱼〔红大麻哈鱼、细磷大麻哈鱼、大麻哈鱼（种）、大鳞大麻哈鱼、银大麻哈鱼、马苏大麻哈鱼、玫瑰大麻哈鱼〕、大西洋鲑鱼及多瑙哲罗鱼	12	0 冰岛IS,东盟AS,哥CR,香港HK,新西兰NZ,智利CL 3.6 秘鲁PE 5 巴PK 7.2 澳AU 8.4 瑞士CH 9 亚太AP 9.6 韩国KR	0 缅甸MM,受惠国LD	70	--Pacific salmon (*Oncorhynchus nerka, Oncorhynchus gorbuscha, Oncorhynchus keta, Oncorhynchus tschawytscha, Oncorhynchus kisutch, Oncorhynchus masou and Oncorhynchus rhodurus*), Atlantic salmon (*Salmo salar*) and Danube salmon (*Hucho hucho*)
269	0304.4200	--鳟鱼（河鳟、虹鳟、克拉克大麻哈鱼、阿瓜大麻哈鱼、吉雨大麻哈鱼、亚利桑那大麻哈鱼、金腹大麻哈鱼）	12	0 冰岛IS,东盟AS,哥CR,香港HK,新西兰NZ,智利CL 3.6 秘鲁PE 5 巴PK 7.2 澳AU 8.4 瑞士CH 9 亚太AP 9.6 韩国KR	0 缅甸MM,受惠国LD	70	--Trout (*Salmo trutta, Oncorhynchus mykiss, Oncorhynchus clarki, Oncorhynchus aguabonita, Oncorhynchus gilae, Oncorhynchus apache* and *Oncorhynchus chrysogaster*)
270	0304.4300	--比目鱼（鲽科、鲆科、舌鳎科、鳎科、菱鲆科、刺鲆科）	12	0 冰岛IS,东盟AS,哥CR,香港HK,新西兰NZ,智利CL 3.6 秘鲁PE 5 巴PK 7.2 澳AU 8.4 瑞士CH 9 亚太AP 9.6 韩国KR	0 缅甸MM,受惠国LD	70	--Flat fish (Pleuronectidae, Bothidae, Cynoglossidae, Soleidae, Scophthalmidae and Citharidae)
271	0304.4400	--犀鳕科、多丝真鳕科、鳕科、长尾鳕科、黑鳕科、无须鳕科、深海鳕科及南极鳕科鱼	12	0 冰岛IS,东盟AS,哥CR,香港HK,新西兰NZ,智利CL 3.6 秘鲁PE 5 巴PK 7.2 澳AU 8.4 瑞士CH 9 亚太AP 9.6 韩国KR	0 缅甸MM,受惠国LD	70	--Fish of the families Bregmacerotidae, Euclichthyidae, Gadidae, Macrouridae, Melanonidae, Merlucciidae, Moridae and Muraenolepididae
272	0304.4500	--剑鱼	12	0 冰岛IS,东盟AS,哥CR,秘鲁PE,香港HK,新西兰NZ,智利CL 5 巴PK 7.2 澳AU 8.4 瑞士CH 9 亚太AP 9.6 韩国KR	0 缅甸MM,受惠国LD	70	--Swordfish (*Xiphias gladius*)
273	0304.4600	--南极犬牙鱼（南极犬牙鱼属）	12	0 冰岛IS,东盟AS,哥CR,秘鲁PE,香港HK,新西兰NZ,智利CL 5 巴PK 7.2 澳AU 8.4 瑞士CH 9 亚太AP 9.6 韩国KR	0 缅甸MM,受惠国LD	70	--Toothfish (Dissostichus spp.)
274	0304.4900	--其他	12	0 冰岛IS,东盟AS,哥CR,香港HK,新西兰NZ,智利CL 3.6 秘鲁PE 5 巴PK 7.2 澳AU 8.4 瑞士CH 9 亚太AP 9.6 韩国KR	0 缅甸MM,受惠国LD	70	--Other
		-其他，鲜或冷的：					-Other, fresh or chilled:

序号 No.	税则号列 Tariff Line	中文货品名称 Article Description in Chinese	最惠国税率 MFN(%)	协定税率 Agreement(%)	特惠税率 SP(%)	普通税率 Gen(%)	英文货品名称 Article Description
275	0304.5100	--罗非鱼（口孵非鲫属）、鲶鱼（(鱼芒)鲶属、鲶属、胡鲶属、真鮰属）、鲤科鱼（西鲤、黑鲫、草鱼、鲢属、鲮属、青鱼）、鳗鱼（鳗鲡属）、尼罗河鲈鱼（尼罗尖吻鲈）及黑鱼（醴属）	12	0 冰岛IS,东盟AS,哥CR,香港HK,新西兰NZ,智利CL 3.6 秘鲁PE 5 巴PK 7.2 澳AU 8.4 瑞士CH 9 亚太AP 9.6 韩国KR	0 缅甸MM,受惠国LD	70	--Tilapias (*Oreochromis spp.*) , catfish (*Pangasius spp., Silurus spp., Clarias spp., Ictalurus spp.*) , carp (*Cyprinus carpio, Carassius carassius, Ctenopharyngodon idellus, Hypophthalmichthys spp., Cirrhinus spp., Mylopharyngodon piceus*) , eels (*Anguilla spp.*) , Nile perch (*Lates niloticus*) and snakeheads (*Channa spp.*)
276	0304.5200	--鲑科鱼	12	0 冰岛IS,东盟AS,哥CR,香港HK,新西兰NZ,智利CL 3.6 秘鲁PE 5 巴PK 7.2 澳AU 8.4 瑞士CH 9 亚太AP 9.6 韩国KR	0 缅甸MM,受惠国LD	70	--Salmonidae
277	0304.5300	--犀鳕科、多丝真鳕科、鳕科、长尾鳕科、黑鳕科、无须鳕科、深海鳕科及南极鳕科鱼	12	0 冰岛IS,东盟AS,哥CR,香港HK,新西兰NZ,智利CL 3.6 秘鲁PE 5 巴PK 7.2 澳AU 8.4 瑞士CH 9 亚太AP 9.6 韩国KR	0 缅甸MM,受惠国LD	70	--Fish of the families Bregmacerotidae, Euclichthyidae, Gadidae, Macrouridae, Melanonidae, Merlucciidae, Moridae and Muraenolepididae
278	0304.5400	--剑鱼	12	0 冰岛IS,东盟AS,哥CR,秘鲁PE,香港HK,新西兰NZ,智利CL 5 巴PK 7.2 澳AU 8.4 瑞士CH 9 亚太AP 9.6 韩国KR	0 缅甸MM,受惠国LD	70	--Swordfish (*Xiphias gladius*)
279	0304.5500	--南极犬牙鱼（南极犬牙鱼属）	12	0 冰岛IS,东盟AS,哥CR,秘鲁PE,香港HK,新西兰NZ,智利CL 5 巴PK 7.2 澳AU 8.4 瑞士CH 9 亚太AP 9.6 韩国KR	0 缅甸MM,受惠国LD	70	--Toothfish (Dissostichus spp.)
280	0304.5900	--其他	12	0 冰岛IS,东盟AS,哥CR,香港HK,新西兰NZ,智利CL 3.6 秘鲁PE 5 巴PK 7.2 澳AU 8.4 瑞士CH 9 亚太AP 9.6 韩国KR	0 缅甸MM,受惠国LD	70	--Other
		-冻的罗非鱼（口孵非鲫属）、鲶鱼（(鱼芒)鲶属、鲶属、胡鲶属、真鮰属）、鲤科鱼（西鲤、黑鲫、草鱼、鲢属、鲮属、青鱼）、鳗鱼（鳗鲡属）、尼罗河鲈鱼（尼罗尖吻鲈）及黑鱼（鳢属）的鱼片：					-Frozen fillets of tilapia (*Oreochromis* spp.) , catfish (*Pangasius* spp., *Silurus* spp., *Clarias* spp., *Ictalurus* spp.) , carp (*Cyprinus carpio*, *Carassius carassius*, *Ctenopharyngodon idellus*, *Hypophthalmichthys* spp., *Cirrhinus* spp., *Mylopharyngodon piceus*) , eels (*Anguilla* spp.) , Nile perch (*Lates niloticus*) and snakeheads (*Channa* spp.) :

序号 No.	税则号列 Tariff Line	中文货品名称 Article Description in Chinese	最惠国税率 MFN(%)	协定税率 Agreement(%)	特惠税率 SP(%)	普通税率 Gen(%)	英文货品名称 Article Description
281	0304.6100	--罗非鱼（口孵非鲫属）	10	0 冰岛IS,东盟AS,哥CR,秘鲁PE,香港HK,新西兰NZ,智利CL 4 瑞士CH 5 巴PK 6 澳AU 8 韩国KR	0 柬埔寨KH,缅甸MM,受惠国LD	70	--Tilapias (*Oreochromis spp.*)
		--鲶鱼（(鱼芒)鲶属、鲶属、胡鲶属、真鮰属）:					--Catfish (*Pangasius spp.*, *Silurus spp.*, *Clarias spp.*, *Ictalurus spp.*) :
		---叉尾鮰鱼（真鮰属）:					---Of *Ictalurus spp.*:
282	0304.6211	----斑点叉尾鮰鱼	10	0 冰岛IS,东盟AS,哥CR,秘鲁PE,香港HK,新西兰NZ,智利CL 4 瑞士CH 5 巴PK 6 澳AU 8 韩国KR	0 受惠国LD	70	----Channel catfish (*Ictalurus punctatus*)
283	0304.6219	----其他	10	0 冰岛IS,东盟AS,哥CR,秘鲁PE,香港HK,新西兰NZ,智利CL 4 瑞士CH 5 巴PK 6 澳AU 8 韩国KR	0 受惠国LD	70	----Other
284	0304.6290	---其他	10	0 冰岛IS,东盟AS,哥CR,台湾TW,香港HK,新西兰NZ,智利CL 1.2 秘鲁PE 4 瑞士CH 5 巴PK 6 澳AU 8 韩国KR	0 柬埔寨KH,缅甸MM,受惠国LD	70	---Other
285	0304.6300	--尼罗河鲈鱼（尼罗尖吻鲈）	10	0 冰岛IS,东盟AS,哥CR,台湾TW,香港HK,新西兰NZ,智利CL 1.2 秘鲁PE 4 瑞士CH 5 巴PK 6 澳AU 8 韩国KR	0 柬埔寨KH,缅甸MM,受惠国LD	70	--Nile Perch (*Lates niloticus*)
286	0304.6900	--其他	10	0 冰岛IS,东盟AS,哥CR,台湾TW,香港HK,新西兰NZ,智利CL 1.2 秘鲁PE 4 瑞士CH 5 巴PK 6 澳AU 8 韩国KR	0 柬埔寨KH,缅甸MM,受惠国LD	70	--Other
		-冻的犀鳕科、多丝真鳕科、鳕科、长尾鳕科、黑鳕科、无须鳕科、深海鳕科及南极鳕科鱼的鱼片:					-Frozen fillets of fish of the families Bregmacerotidae, Euclichthyidae, Gadidae, Macrouridae, Melanonidae, Merlucciidae, Moridae and Muraenolepididae:
287	0304.7100	--鳕鱼(大西洋鳕鱼、格陵兰鳕鱼、太平洋鳕鱼)	10	0 冰岛IS,东盟AS,哥CR,台湾TW,香港HK,新西兰NZ,智利CL 1.2 秘鲁PE 4 瑞士CH 5 巴PK 6 澳AU 8 韩国KR	0 柬埔寨KH,缅甸MM,受惠国LD	70	--Cod (Gadus morhua, Gadus ogac, Gadus macrocephalus)

序号 No.	税则号列 Tariff Line	中文货品名称 Article Description in Chinese	最惠国税率 MFN(%)	协定税率 Agreement(%)		特惠税率 SP(%)		普通税率 Gen(%)	英文货品名称 Article Description
288	0304.7200	--黑线鳕鱼（黑线鳕）	10	0 1.2 4 5 6 8	冰岛IS,东盟AS,哥CR,台湾TW,香港HK,新西兰NZ,智利CL 秘鲁PE 瑞士CH 巴PK 澳AU 韩国KR	0	柬埔寨KH,缅甸MM,受惠国LD	70	--Haddock (Melanogrammus aeglefinus)
289	0304.7300	--绿青鳕鱼	10	0 1.2 4 5 6 8	冰岛IS,东盟AS,哥CR,台湾TW,香港HK,新西兰NZ,智利CL 秘鲁PE 瑞士CH 巴PK 澳AU 韩国KR	0	柬埔寨KH,缅甸MM,受惠国LD	70	--Coalfish (Pollachius virens)
290	0304.7400	--狗鳕鱼(无须鳕属、长鳍鳕属)	10	0 1.2 4 5 6 8	冰岛IS,东盟AS,哥CR,台湾TW,香港HK,新西兰NZ,智利CL 秘鲁PE 瑞士CH 巴PK 澳AU 韩国KR	0	柬埔寨KH,缅甸MM,受惠国LD	70	--Hake (Merluccius spp., Urophycis spp.)
291	0304.7500	--狭鳕鱼	10	0 1.2 4 5 6 8	冰岛IS,东盟AS,哥CR,台湾TW,香港HK,新西兰NZ,智利CL 秘鲁PE 瑞士CH 巴PK 澳AU 韩国KR	0	柬埔寨KH,缅甸MM,受惠国LD	70	--Alaska Pollack (Theraga chalcogramma)
292	0304.7900	--其他	10	0 1.2 4 5 6 8	冰岛IS,东盟AS,哥CR,台湾TW,香港HK,新西兰NZ,智利CL 秘鲁PE 瑞士CH 巴PK 澳AU 韩国KR	0	柬埔寨KH,缅甸MM,受惠国LD	70	--Other
		-其他冻鱼片:							-Frozen fillets of other fish:
293	0304.8100	--大麻哈鱼〔红大麻哈鱼、细磷大麻哈鱼、大麻哈鱼（种）、大鳞大麻哈鱼、银大麻哈鱼、马苏大麻哈鱼、玫瑰大麻哈鱼〕、大西洋鲑鱼及多瑙哲罗鱼	10	0 1.2 4 5 6 8	冰岛IS,东盟AS,哥CR,台湾TW,香港HK,新西兰NZ,智利CL 秘鲁PE 瑞士CH 巴PK 澳AU 韩国KR	0	柬埔寨KH,缅甸MM,受惠国LD	70	--Pacific salmon (*Oncorhynchus nerka, Oncorhynchus gorbuscha, Oncorhynchus keta, Oncorhynchus tschawytscha, Oncorhynchus kisutch, Oncorhynchus masou* and *Oncorhynchus rhodurus*) , Atlantic salmon (*Salmo salar*) and Danube salmon (*Hucho hucho*)
294	0304.8200	--鳟鱼(河鳟、虹鳟、克拉克大麻哈鱼、阿瓜大麻哈鱼、吉雨大麻哈鱼、亚利桑那大麻哈鱼、金腹大麻哈鱼)	10	0 1.2 4 5 6 8	冰岛IS,东盟AS,哥CR,台湾TW,香港HK,新西兰NZ,智利CL 秘鲁PE 瑞士CH 巴PK 澳AU 韩国KR	0	柬埔寨KH,缅甸MM,受惠国LD	70	--Trout (*Salmo trutta, Oncorhynchus mykiss, Oncorhynchus clarki, Oncorhynchus aguabonita, Oncorhynchus gilae, Oncorhynchus apache* and *Oncorhynchus chrysogaster*)

序号 No.	税则号列 Tariff Line	中文货品名称 Article Description in Chinese	最惠国税率 MFN(%)	协定税率 Agreement(%)	特惠税率 SP(%)	普通税率 Gen(%)	英文货品名称 Article Description
295	0304.8300	--比目鱼（鲽科、鲆科、舌鳎科、鳎科、菱鲆科、刺鲆科）	10	0 冰岛IS,东盟AS,哥CR,台湾TW,香港HK,新西兰NZ,智利CL 1.2 秘鲁PE 4 瑞士CH 5 巴PK 6 澳AU 8 韩国KR	0 柬埔寨KH,缅甸MM,受惠国LD	70	--Flat fish (Pleuronectidae, Bothidae, Cynoglossidae, Soleidae, Scophthalmidae and Citharidae)
296	0304.8400	--剑鱼	10	0 冰岛IS,东盟AS,哥CR,秘鲁PE,香港HK,新西兰NZ,智利CL 4 瑞士CH 5 巴PK 6 澳AU 8 韩国KR	0 柬埔寨KH,缅甸MM,受惠国LD	70	--Swordfish (*Xiphias gladius*)
297	0304.8500	--南极犬牙鱼(南极犬牙鱼属)	10	0 冰岛IS,东盟AS,哥CR,秘鲁PE,香港HK,新西兰NZ,智利CL 4 瑞士CH 5 巴PK 6 澳AU 8 韩国KR	0 柬埔寨KH,缅甸MM,受惠国LD	70	--Toothfish (Dissostichus spp.)
298	0304.8600	--鲱鱼（大西洋鲱鱼、太平洋鲱鱼）	10	0 冰岛IS,东盟AS,哥CR,台湾TW,香港HK,新西兰NZ,智利CL 1.2 秘鲁PE 4 瑞士CH 5 巴PK 6 澳AU 8 韩国KR	0 柬埔寨KH,缅甸MM,受惠国LD	70	--Herrings (*Clupea harengus, Clupea pallasii*)
299	0304.8700	--金枪鱼(金枪鱼属)、鲣鱼或狐鲣(鲣)	10	0 冰岛IS,东盟AS,哥CR,台湾TW,香港HK,新西兰NZ,智利CL 1.2 秘鲁PE 4 瑞士CH 5 巴PK 6 澳AU 8 韩国KR	0 柬埔寨KH,缅甸MM,受惠国LD	70	--Tunas (of the genus *Thunnus*) , skipjack or stripe-bellied bonito (Euthynnus (Katsuwonus) pelamis)
300	0304.8900	--其他	10	0 冰岛IS,东盟AS,哥CR,台湾TW,香港HK,新西兰NZ,智利CL 1.2 秘鲁PE 4 瑞士CH 5 巴PK 6 澳AU 8 韩国KR	0 柬埔寨KH,缅甸MM,受惠国LD	70	--Other
		-其他，冻的：					-Other, frozen:
301	0304.9100	--剑鱼	10	0 冰岛IS,东盟AS,哥CR,秘鲁PE,新西兰NZ,智利CL 4 瑞士CH 5 巴PK 6 澳AU 8 韩国KR	0 缅甸MM,受惠国LD,亚太AP	70	--Swordfish (*Xiphias gladius*)
302	0304.9200	--南极犬牙鱼(南极犬牙鱼属)	10	0 冰岛IS,东盟AS,哥CR,秘鲁PE,新西兰NZ,智利CL 4 瑞士CH 5 巴PK 6 澳AU 8 韩国KR	0 缅甸MM,受惠国LD,亚太AP	70	--Toothfish (Dissostichus spp.)

序号 No.	税则号列 Tariff Line	中文货品名称 Article Description in Chinese	最惠国税率 MFN(%)	协定税率 Agreement(%)	特惠税率 SP(%)	普通税率 Gen(%)	英文货品名称 Article Description
303	0304.9300	--罗非鱼（口孵非鲫属）、鲶鱼（(鱼芒)鲶属、鲶属、胡鲶属、真鮰属）、鲤科鱼（西鲤、黑鲫、草鱼、鲢属、鲮属、青鱼）、鳗鱼（鳗鲡属）、尼罗河鲈鱼（尼罗尖吻鲈）及黑鱼（鳢属）	10	0 冰岛IS,东盟AS,哥CR,秘鲁PE,新西兰NZ,智利CL 4 瑞士CH 5 巴PK 6 澳AU 8 韩国KR	0 缅甸MM,受惠国LD,亚太AP	70	--Tilapias (*Oreochromis spp.*) , catfish (*Pangasius spp., Silurus spp., Clarias spp., ctalurus spp.*) , carp (*Cyprinus carpio, Carassius carassius, Ctenopharyngodon idellus, Hypophthalmichthys spp., Cirrhinus spp., Mylopharyngodon piceus*) , eels (*Anguilla spp.*) , Nile perch (*Lates niloticus*) and snakeheads (*Channa spp.*)
304	0304.9400	--狭鳕鱼	10	0 冰岛IS,东盟AS,哥CR,秘鲁PE,新西兰NZ,智利CL 4 瑞士CH 5 巴PK 6 澳AU 8 韩国KR	0 缅甸MM,受惠国LD,亚太AP	70	--Alaska Pollack (Theraga chalcogramma)
305	0304.9500	--犀鳕科、多丝真鳕科、鳕科、长尾鳕科、黑鳕科、无须鳕科、深海鳕科及南极鳕科鱼，狭鳕鱼除外	10	0 冰岛IS,东盟AS,哥CR,秘鲁PE,新西兰NZ,智利CL 4 瑞士CH 5 巴PK 6 澳AU 8 韩国KR	0 缅甸MM,受惠国LD,亚太AP	70	--Fish of the families Bregmacerotidae, Euclichthyidae, Gadidae, Macrouridae, Melanonidae, Merlucciidae, Moridae and Muraenolepididae, other than Alaska Pollack (Theraga halcogramma)
306	0304.9900	--其他	10	0 冰岛IS,东盟AS,哥CR,秘鲁PE,新西兰NZ,智利CL 4 瑞士CH 5 巴PK 6 澳AU 8 韩国KR	0 缅甸MM,受惠国LD,亚太AP	70	--Other
	03.05	**干、盐腌或盐渍的鱼；熏鱼，不论在熏制前或熏制过程中是否烹煮；适合供人食用的鱼的细粉、粗粉及团粒：**					**Fish, dried, salted or in brine; smoked fish, whether or not cooked before or during the smoking process; flours, meals and pellets of fish, fit for human consumption:**
307	0305.1000	-适合供人食用的鱼的细粉、粗粉及团粒	10	0 澳门MO,冰岛IS,东盟AS,哥CR,秘鲁PE,新西兰NZ,智利CL 4 瑞士CH 5 巴PK 6 澳AU 8 韩国KR	0 受惠国LD	80	-Flours, meals and pellets of fish, fit for human consumption
308	0305.2000	-干、熏、盐腌或盐渍的鱼肝及鱼卵	10	0 冰岛IS,东盟AS,新西兰NZ,智利CL 4 哥CR 5 巴PK 6 澳AU 8 韩国KR	0 受惠国LD	80	-Livers and roes, dried, smoked, salted or in brine
		-干、盐腌或盐渍的鱼片，但熏制的除外：					-Fish fillets, dried, salted or in brine, but not smoked:
309	0305.3100	--罗非鱼（口孵非鲫属）、鲶鱼（(鱼芒)鲶属、鲶属、胡鲶属、真鮰属）、鲤科鱼（西鲤、黑鲫、草鱼、鲢属、鲮属、青鱼）、鳗鱼（鳗鲡属）、尼罗河鲈鱼（尼罗尖吻鲈）及黑鱼（鳢属）	10	0 澳门MO,冰岛IS,东盟AS,哥CR,香港HK,新西兰NZ,智利CL 3 秘鲁PE 5 巴PK 6 澳AU 7.8 亚太AP 8 韩国KR	0 缅甸MM,受惠国LD,亚太AP	80	--Tilapias (*Oreochromis spp.*) , catfish (*Pangasius spp., Silurus spp., Clarias spp., Ictalurus spp.*) , carp (*Cyprinus carpio, Carassius carassius, Ctenopharyngodon idellus, Hypophthalmichthys spp., Cirrhinus spp., Mylopharyngodon piceus*) , eels (*Anguilla spp.*) , Nile perch (*Lates niloticus*) and snakeheads (*Channa spp.*)

序号 No.	税则号列 Tariff Line	中文货品名称 Article Description in Chinese	最惠国税率 MFN(%)	协定税率 Agreement(%)	特惠税率 SP(%)	普通税率 Gen(%)	英文货品名称 Article Description
310	0305.3200	--犀鳕科、多丝真鳕科、鳕科、长尾鳕科、黑鳕科、无须鳕科、深海鳕科及南极鳕科鱼	10	0 澳门MO,冰岛IS,东盟AS,哥CR,香港HK,新西兰NZ,智利CL 3 秘鲁PE 5 巴PK 6 澳AU 7.8 亚太AP 8 韩国KR	0 缅甸MM,受惠国LD,亚太AP	80	--Fish of the families Bregmacerotidae, Euclichthyidae, Gadidae, Macrouridae, Melanonidae, Merlucciidae, Moridae and Muraenolepididae
311	0305.3900	--其他	10	0 澳门MO,冰岛IS,东盟AS,哥CR,香港HK,新西兰NZ,智利CL 3 秘鲁PE 5 巴PK 6 澳AU 7.8 亚太AP 8 韩国KR	0 缅甸MM,受惠国LD,亚太AP	80	--Other
		-熏鱼，包括鱼片，但食用杂碎除外：					-Smoked fish, including fillets, other than edible fish offal:
		--大麻哈鱼〔红大麻哈鱼、细磷大麻哈鱼、大麻哈鱼（种）、大鳞大麻哈鱼、银大麻哈鱼、马苏大麻哈鱼、玫瑰大麻哈鱼〕、大西洋鲑鱼及多瑙哲罗鱼：					--Pacific salmon (*Oncorhynchus nerka, Oncorhynchus gorbuscha, Oncorhynchus keta, Oncorhynchus tschawytscha, Oncorhynchus kisutch, Oncorhynchus masou* and *Oncorhynchus rhodurus*), Atlantic salmon (*Salmo salar*) and Danube salmon (*Hucho hucho*):
312	0305.4110	---大西洋鲑鱼	14	0 冰岛IS,东盟AS,哥CR,秘鲁PE,香港HK,新西兰NZ,智利CL 7 巴PK 8.4 澳AU 11.2 韩国KR	0 受惠国$_1$LD$_1$	80	---Atlantic salmon
313	0305.4120	---大马哈鱼及多瑙哲罗鱼	14	0 冰岛IS,东盟AS,哥CR,秘鲁PE,新西兰NZ,智利CL 8.4 澳AU 11.2 巴PK,韩国KR	0 受惠国$_1$LD$_1$	80	---Pacific salmon and Danube salmon
314	0305.4200	--鲱鱼（大西洋鲱鱼、太平洋鲱鱼）	16	0 冰岛IS,东盟AS,哥CR,秘鲁PE,新西兰NZ,智利CL 9.6 澳AU 12.8 巴PK 13.8 韩国KR	0 受惠国$_1$LD$_1$	80	--Herrings (*Clupea harengus, Clupea pallasii*)
315	0305.4300	--鳟鱼(河鳟、虹鳟、克拉克大麻哈鱼、阿瓜大麻哈鱼、吉雨大麻哈鱼、亚利桑那大麻哈鱼、金腹大麻哈鱼)	14	0 澳门MO,冰岛IS,东盟AS,哥CR,新西兰NZ,智利CL 4.2 秘鲁PE 8.4 澳AU 11.2 巴PK,韩国KR	0 缅甸MM,受惠国LD,亚太AP	80	--Trout (*Salmo trutta, Oncorhynchus mykiss, Oncorhynchus clarki, Oncorhynchus aguabonita, Oncorhynchus gilae, Oncorhynchus apache* and *Oncorhynchus chrysogaster*)
316	0305.4400	--罗非鱼（口孵非鲫属）、鲶鱼（(鱼芒)鲶属、鲶属、胡鲶属、真鮰属）、鲤科鱼（西鲤、黑鲫、草鱼、鲢属、鲮属、青鱼）、鳗鱼（鳗鲡属）、尼罗河鲈鱼（尼罗尖吻鲈）及黑鱼（鳢属）	14	0 澳门MO,冰岛IS,东盟AS,哥CR,新西兰NZ,智利CL 4.2 秘鲁PE 8.4 澳AU 11.2 巴PK,韩国KR	0 缅甸MM,受惠国LD,亚太AP	80	--Tilapias (*Oreochromis spp.*), catfish (*Pangasius spp., Silurus spp., Clarias spp., Ictalurus spp.*), carp (*Cyprinus carpio, Carassius carassius, Ctenopharyngodon idellus, Hypophthalmichthys spp., Cirrhinus spp., Mylopharyngodon piceus*), eels (*Anguilla spp.*), Nile perch (*Lates niloticus*) and snakeheads (*Channa spp.*)

序号 No.	税则号列 Tariff Line	中文货品名称 Article Description in Chinese	最惠国税率 MFN(%)	协定税率 Agreement(%)	特惠税率 SP(%)	普通税率 Gen(%)	英文货品名称 Article Description
317	0305.4900	--其他	14	0 澳门MO,冰岛IS,东盟AS,哥CR,新西兰NZ,智利CL 4.2 秘鲁PE 8.4 澳AU 11.2 巴PK,韩国KR	0 缅甸MM,受惠国LD,亚太AP	80	--Other
		-干鱼（不包括食用杂碎），不论是否盐腌，但熏制的除外：					-Dried fish, other than edible fish offal, whether or not salted but not smoked:
318	0305.5100	--鳕鱼	16	0 澳门MO,冰岛IS,东盟AS,哥CR,秘鲁PE,新西兰NZ,智利CL 9.6 澳AU 11.2 瑞士CH 12.8 巴PK 13.8 韩国KR	0 受惠国$_1$LD$_1$	80	--Cod (Gadus morhua, Gadus ogac, Gadus macrocephalus)
		--其他：					--Other:
319	0305.5910	---海龙、海马	2	0 澳AU,巴PK,冰岛IS,东盟AS,哥CR,韩国KR,秘鲁PE,瑞士CH,新西兰NZ,智利CL	0 柬埔寨KH,缅甸MM,受惠国LD,亚太AP	20	---Pipefish and hippocampi
320	0305.5990	---其他	16	0 澳门MO,冰岛IS,东盟AS,香港HK,新西兰NZ,智利CL 4.8 秘鲁PE 6.4 哥CR 9.6 澳AU 11.2 瑞士CH 13.8 韩国KR	0 缅甸MM,受惠国LD,亚太AP	80	---Other
		-盐腌及盐渍的鱼（不包括食用杂碎），但干或熏制的除外：					-Fish, salted but not dried or smoked and fish in brine, other than edible fish offal:
321	0305.6100	--鲱鱼（大西洋鲱鱼、太平洋鲱鱼）	16	0 冰岛IS,东盟AS,哥CR,秘鲁PE,新西兰NZ,智利CL 8 巴PK 9.6 澳AU 11.1 亚太AP 11.2 瑞士CH 13.8 韩国KR	0 受惠国$_1$LD$_1$	80	--Herrings (*Clupea harengus, Clupea pallasii*)
322	0305.6200	--鳕鱼(大西洋鳕鱼、格陵兰鳕鱼、太平洋鳕鱼)	16	0 澳门MO,冰岛IS,东盟AS,哥CR,秘鲁PE,新西兰NZ,智利CL 8 巴PK 9.6 澳AU 11.2 瑞士CH 12 亚太AP 13.8 韩国KR	0 受惠国LD	80	--Cod (Gadus morhua, Gadus ogac, Gadus Macrocephalus)
323	0305.6300	--鳀鱼	16	0 冰岛IS,东盟AS,哥CR,新西兰NZ,智利CL 4.8 秘鲁PE 8 巴PK 9.6 澳AU 11.2 瑞士CH 12 亚太AP 13.8 韩国KR	0 受惠国$_1$LD$_1$	80	--Anchovies (Engraul is spp.)

序号 No.	税则号列 Tariff Line	中文货品名称 Article Description in Chinese	最惠国税率 MFN(%)	协定税率 Agreement(%)	特惠税率 SP(%)	普通税率 Gen(%)	英文货品名称 Article Description
324	0305.6400	--罗非鱼（口孵非鲫属）、鲶鱼（(鱼芒)鲶属、鲶属、胡鲶属、真鮰属）、鲤科鱼（西鲤、黑鲫、草鱼、鲢属、鲮属、青鱼）、鳗鱼（鳗鲡属）、尼罗河鲈鱼（尼罗尖吻鲈）及黑鱼（鳢属）	16	0 冰岛IS,东盟AS,哥CR,香港HK,新西兰NZ,智利CL 4.8 秘鲁PE 9.6 澳AU 11.2 瑞士CH 12.8 巴PK 13.8 韩国KR	0 缅甸MM,受惠国LD,亚太AP	80	--Tilapias (*Oreochromis spp.*), catfish (*Pangasius spp., Silurus spp., Clarias spp., Ictalurus spp.*), carp (*Cyprinus carpio, Carassius carassius, Ctenopharyngodon idellus, Hypophthalmichthys spp., Cirrhinus spp., Mylopharyngodon piceus*), eels (*Anguilla spp.*), Nile perch (*Lates niloticus*) and snakeheads (*Channa spp.*)
		--其他：					--Other:
325	0305.6910	---带鱼	16	0 冰岛IS,东盟AS,哥CR,香港HK,新西兰NZ,智利CL 4.8 秘鲁PE 9.6 澳AU 11.2 瑞士CH 12.8 巴PK 13.8 韩国KR	0 缅甸MM,受惠国LD,亚太AP	80	---Scabber fish (Trichuri us)
326	0305.6920	---黄鱼	16	0 冰岛IS,东盟AS,哥CR,香港HK,新西兰NZ,智利CL 4.8 秘鲁PE 9.6 澳AU 11.2 瑞士CH 12.8 巴PK 13.8 韩国KR	0 缅甸MM,受惠国LD,亚太AP	80	---Yellow croaker (Pseudosicaena)
327	0305.6930	---鲳鱼	16	0 冰岛IS,东盟AS,哥CR,香港HK,新西兰NZ,智利CL 4.8 秘鲁PE 9.6 澳AU 11.2 瑞士CH 12.8 巴PK 13.8 韩国KR	0 缅甸MM,受惠国LD,亚太AP	80	---Butterfish (Pampus)
328	0305.6990	---其他	16	0 冰岛IS,东盟AS,哥CR,香港HK,新西兰NZ,智利CL 4.8 秘鲁PE 9.6 澳AU 11.2 瑞士CH 12.8 巴PK 13.8 韩国KR	0 缅甸MM,受惠国LD,亚太AP	80	---Other
		-鱼鳍、鱼头、鱼尾、鱼鳔及其他可食用杂碎：					-Fish fins, heads, tails, maws and other edible fish offal:
329	0305.7100	--鲨鱼翅	15	0 澳门MO,冰岛IS,东盟AS,新西兰NZ,智利CL 4.5 秘鲁PE 6 哥CR 10.5 瑞士CH	0 柬埔寨KH,缅甸MM,受惠国LD,亚太AP	80	--Shark fins
330	0305.7200	--鱼头、鱼尾、鱼鳔	16	0 冰岛IS,东盟AS,哥CR,秘鲁PE,新西兰NZ,智利CL 9.6 澳AU 12.8 巴PK 13.8 韩国KR	0 受惠国$_1$LD$_1$	80	--Fish heads, tails and maws
331	0305.7900	--其他	16	0 冰岛IS,东盟AS,哥CR,秘鲁PE,新西兰NZ,智利CL 9.6 澳AU 12.8 巴PK 13.8 韩国KR	0 受惠国$_1$LD$_1$	80	--Other

序号 No.	税则号列 Tariff Line	中文货品名称 Article Description in Chinese	最惠国税率 MFN(%)	协定税率 Agreement(%)	特惠税率 SP(%)	普通税率 Gen(%)	英文货品名称 Article Description
	03.06	带壳或去壳的甲壳动物，活、鲜、冷、冻、干、盐腌或盐渍的；熏制的带壳或去壳甲壳动物，不论在熏制前或熏制过程中是否烹煮；蒸过或用水煮过的带壳甲壳动物，不论是否冷、冻、干、盐腌或盐渍的；适合供人食用的甲壳动物的细粉、粗粉及团粒：					**Crustaceans, whether in shell or not, live, fresh, chilled, frozen, dried, salted or in brine; smoked crustaceans, whether in shell or not, whether or not cooked before or during the smoking process; crustaceans, in shell, cooked by steaming or by boiling in water, whether or not chilled, frozen, dried, salted or in brine; flours, meals and pellets of crustaceans, fit for human consumption:**
		-冻的：					-Frozen:
332	0306.1100	--岩礁虾和其他龙虾（真龙虾属、龙虾属、岩龙虾属）	10	0 冰岛IS,东盟AS,哥CR,秘鲁PE,新西兰NZ,智利CL 4 瑞士CH 5 巴PK 6 澳AU 8 韩国KR	0 柬埔寨KH,缅甸MM,受惠国LD	70	--Rock lobster and other sea crawfish (*Palinurus spp., Paniliruspp., Jasus spp.*)
333	0306.1200	--螯龙虾（螯龙虾属）	10	0 冰岛IS,东盟AS,哥CR,秘鲁PE,新西兰NZ,智利CL 4 瑞士CH 5 巴PK 6 澳AU 7.2 亚太AP 8 韩国KR	0 柬埔寨KH,受惠国LD	70	--Lobsters (*Homarus spp.*)
		--蟹：					--Crabs:
334	0306.1410	---梭子蟹	10	0 冰岛IS,东盟AS,哥CR,新西兰NZ,智利CL 3 秘鲁PE 4 瑞士CH 5 巴PK 6 澳AU 8 韩国KR	0 柬埔寨KH,缅甸MM,受惠国LD,亚太AP	70	---Swimming crab
335	0306.1490	---其他	10	0 冰岛IS,东盟AS,哥CR,新西兰NZ,智利CL 3 秘鲁PE 4 瑞士CH 5 巴PK 6 澳AU 8.6 韩国KR	0 柬埔寨KH,缅甸MM,受惠国LD,亚太AP	70	---Other
336	0306.1500	--挪威海螯虾	16	0 冰岛IS,东盟AS,哥CR,新西兰NZ,智利CL 4.8 秘鲁PE 9.6 澳AU 11.2 瑞士CH 12.8 巴PK 13.8 韩国KR	0 柬埔寨KH,受惠国LD	70	--Norway lobsters (*Nephrops norvegicus*)
		--冷水小虾及对虾（长额虾属、褐虾）：					--Cold-water shrimps and prawns (*Pandalus spp., Crangon crangon*) :
		---冷水小虾：					---Cold-water shrimps:
337	0306.1611	----虾仁	8	0 巴PK,冰岛IS,东盟AS,哥CR,秘鲁PE,香港HK,新西兰NZ,智利CL 3.2 瑞士CH 4 亚太AP 4.8 澳AU,韩国KR	0 柬埔寨KH,缅甸MM,受惠国LD	70	----Shelled
338	0306.1612	----其他，北方长额虾	5	0 澳AU,巴PK,冰岛IS,东盟AS,哥CR,韩国KR,秘鲁PE,瑞士CH,香港HK,新西兰NZ,智利CL 2.5 亚太AP	0 柬埔寨KH,缅甸MM,受惠国LD	70	----Other, Northem pandalus (*Pandalus*)

序号 No.	税则号列 Tariff Line	中文货品名称 Article Description in Chinese	最惠国税率 MFN(%)	协定税率 Agreement(%)	特惠税率 SP(%)	普通税率 Gen(%)	英文货品名称 Article Description
339	0306.1619	----其他	5	0 澳AU,巴PK,东盟AS,哥CR,韩国KR,秘鲁PE,瑞士CH,香港HK,新西兰NZ,智利CL 2.5 冰岛IS,亚太AP	0 柬埔寨KH,缅甸MM,受惠国LD	70	----Other
		---冷水对虾:					---Cold-water prawns:
340	0306.1621	----虾仁	8	0 巴PK,冰岛IS,东盟AS,哥CR,秘鲁PE,香港HK,新西兰NZ,智利CL 3.2 瑞士CH 4 亚太AP 4.8 澳AU,韩国KR	0 柬埔寨KH,缅甸MM,受惠国LD	70	----Shelled
341	0306.1629	----其他	5	0 澳AU,巴PK,冰岛IS,东盟AS,哥CR,韩国KR,秘鲁PE,瑞士CH,香港HK,新西兰NZ,智利CL 2.5 亚太AP	0 柬埔寨KH,缅甸MM,受惠国LD	70	----Other
		--其他小虾及对虾:					--Other shrimps and prawns:
		---小虾:					---Shrimps:
342	0306.1711	----虾仁	8	0 巴PK,冰岛IS,东盟AS,哥CR,秘鲁PE,香港HK,新西兰NZ,智利CL 3.2 瑞士CH 4 亚太AP 4.8 澳AU,韩国KR	0 柬埔寨KH,缅甸MM,受惠国LD	70	----Shelled
343	0306.1719	----其他	5	0 澳AU,巴PK,东盟AS,哥CR,韩国KR,秘鲁PE,瑞士CH,香港HK,新西兰NZ,智利CL 2.5 冰岛IS,亚太AP	0 柬埔寨KH,缅甸MM,受惠国LD	70	----Other
		---对虾:					---Prawns:
344	0306.1721	----虾仁	8	0 巴PK,冰岛IS,东盟AS,哥CR,秘鲁PE,香港HK,新西兰NZ,智利CL 3.2 瑞士CH 4 亚太AP 4.8 澳AU,韩国KR	0 柬埔寨KH,缅甸MM,受惠国LD	70	----Shelled
345	0306.1729	----其他	5	0 澳AU,巴PK,冰岛IS,东盟AS,哥CR,韩国KR,秘鲁PE,瑞士CH,香港HK,新西兰NZ,智利CL 2.5 亚太AP	0 柬埔寨KH,缅甸MM,受惠国LD	70	----Other
		--其他，包括适合供人食用的甲壳动物的细粉、粗粉及团粒:					--Other, including flours, meals and pellets of crustaceans, fit for human consumption:
		---淡水小龙虾:					---Freshwater crawfish:
346	0306.1911	----虾仁	16	0 冰岛IS,东盟AS,哥CR,秘鲁PE,新西兰NZ,智利CL 9.6 澳AU 11.2 瑞士CH 12.8 巴PK 13.8 韩国KR	0 柬埔寨KH,受惠国LD	70	----Shelled
347	0306.1919	----其他	16	0 冰岛IS,东盟AS,哥CR,秘鲁PE,新西兰NZ,智利CL 9.6 澳AU 11.2 瑞士CH 12.8 巴PK 13.8 韩国KR	0 柬埔寨KH,受惠国LD	70	----Other

序号 No.	税则号列 Tariff Line	中文货品名称 Article Description in Chinese	最惠国税率 MFN(%)	协定税率 Agreement(%)	特惠税率 SP(%)	普通税率 Gen(%)	英文货品名称 Article Description
348	0306.1990	---其他	16	0 冰岛IS,东盟AS,哥CR,新西兰NZ,智利CL 4.8 秘鲁PE 9.6 澳AU 11.2 瑞士CH 12.8 巴PK 13.8 韩国KR	0 柬埔寨KH,受惠国LD	70	---Other
		-未冻的:					-Not frozen:
		--岩礁虾和其他龙虾(真龙虾属、龙虾属、岩龙虾属):					--Rock lobster and other sea crawfish (*Palinurus* spp., *Panulirus* spp., *Jasus* spp.) :
349	0306.2110	---种苗	0		0 受惠国LD	0	---For cultivation
350	0306.2190	---其他	15∆10	0 冰岛IS,东盟AS,哥CR,秘鲁PE,香港HK,新西兰NZ,智利CL 9 澳AU 10.5 瑞士CH 12 韩国KR	0 柬埔寨KH,缅甸MM,受惠国LD	70	---Other
		--螯龙虾(螯龙虾属):					--Lobsters (*Homarus* spp.) :
351	0306.2210	---种苗	0		0 受惠国LD	0	---For cultivation
352	0306.2290	---其他	15∆10	0 冰岛IS,东盟AS,哥CR,秘鲁PE,香港HK,新西兰NZ,智利CL 9 澳AU 10.5 瑞士CH 12 巴PK,韩国KR	0 柬埔寨KH,缅甸MM,受惠国LD	70	---Other
		--蟹:					--Crabs:
353	0306.2410	---种苗	0		0 受惠国LD	0	---For cultivation
		---其他:					---Other:
354	0306.2491	----中华绒螯蟹	14	0 冰岛IS,东盟AS,哥CR,秘鲁PE,新西兰NZ,智利CL 7 巴PK 8.4 澳AU 9.8 瑞士CH 11.2 韩国KR	0 柬埔寨KH,受惠国LD	70	----Freshwater crabs, live
355	0306.2492	----梭子蟹	14	0 冰岛IS,东盟AS,哥CR,香港HK,新西兰NZ,智利CL 4.2 秘鲁PE 8.4 澳AU 9.8 瑞士CH 11.2 巴PK,韩国KR	0 柬埔寨KH,受惠国LD	70	----Swimming crab
356	0306.2499	----其他	14	0 冰岛IS,东盟AS,哥CR,香港HK,新西兰NZ,智利CL 4.2 秘鲁PE 8.4 澳AU 9.8 瑞士CH 11.2 韩国KR	0 柬埔寨KH,受惠国LD	70	----Other
		--挪威海螯虾:					--Norway lobsters (*Nephrops norvegicus*) :
357	0306.2510	---种苗	0		0 受惠国LD	0	---For cultivation
358	0306.2590	---其他	14	0 冰岛IS,东盟AS,哥CR,秘鲁PE,香港HK,新西兰NZ,智利CL 8.4 澳AU 9.8 瑞士CH 11.2 巴PK,韩国KR	0 柬埔寨KH,缅甸MM,受惠国LD	70	---Other
		--冷水小虾及对虾(长额虾属、褐虾):					--Cold-water shrimps and prawns (*Pandalus spp., Crangon crangon*) :
359	0306.2610	---种苗	0		0 受惠国LD	0	---For cultivation

序号 No.	税则号列 Tariff Line	中文货品名称 Article Description in Chinese	最惠国税率 MFN(%)	协定税率 Agreement(%)	特惠税率 SP(%)	普通税率 Gen(%)	英文货品名称 Article Description
360	0306.2620	---鲜、冷对虾	15	0 冰岛IS,东盟AS,哥CR,秘鲁PE,香港HK,新西兰NZ,智利CL 9 澳AU 10.5 瑞士CH 12 巴PK,韩国KR	0 柬埔寨KH,缅甸MM,受惠国LD	70	---Prawns, fresh or chilled
361	0306.2690	---其他	12	0 冰岛IS,东盟AS,哥CR,秘鲁PE,香港HK,新西兰NZ,智利CL 6 巴PK 7.2 澳AU 8.4 瑞士CH 9.6 韩国KR	0 柬埔寨KH,缅甸MM,受惠国LD	70	---Other
		--其他小虾及对虾:					--Other shrimps and prawns:
362	0306.2710	---种苗	0		0 受惠国LD	0	---For cultivation
363	0306.2720	---鲜、冷对虾	15	0 冰岛IS,东盟AS,哥CR,秘鲁PE,香港HK,新西兰NZ,智利CL 9 澳AU 10.5 瑞士CH 12 巴PK,韩国KR	0 柬埔寨KH,缅甸MM,受惠国LD	70	---Prawns, fresh or chilled
364	0306.2790	---其他	12	0 冰岛IS,东盟AS,哥CR,秘鲁PE,香港HK,新西兰NZ,智利CL 6 巴PK 7.2 澳AU 8.4 瑞士CH 9.6 韩国KR	0 柬埔寨KH,缅甸MM,受惠国LD	70	---Other
		--其他，包括适合供人食用的甲壳动物的细粉、粗粉及团粒:					--Other, including flours, meals and pellets of crustaceans, fit for human consumption:
365	0306.2910	---种苗	0		0 受惠国LD	0	---For cultivation
366	0306.2990	---其他	14	0 冰岛IS,东盟AS,哥CR,秘鲁PE,香港HK,新西兰NZ,智利CL 8.4 澳AU 9.8 瑞士CH 11.2 巴PK,韩国KR	0 柬埔寨KH,缅甸MM,受惠国LD	70	---Other
	03.07	**带壳或去壳的软体动物，活、鲜、冷、冻、干、盐腌或盐渍的；熏制的带壳或去壳软体动物，不论在熏制前或熏制过程中是否烹煮；适合供人食用的软体动物的细粉、粗粉及团粒：**					**Molluscs, whether in shell or not, live, fresh, chilled, frozen, dried, salted or in brine; smoked molluscs, whether in shell or not, whether or not cooked before or during the smoking process; flours, meals and pellets of molluscs, fit for human consumption:**
		-牡蛎（蚝）:					-Oysters:
		--活、鲜或冷的:					--Live, fresh or chilled:
367	0307.1110	---种苗	0		0 受惠国LD	0	---For cultivation
368	0307.1190	---其他	14	0 冰岛IS,东盟AS,哥CR,香港HK,新西兰NZ,智利CL 4.2 秘鲁PE 8.4 澳AU 9.8 瑞士CH 11.2 巴PK,韩国KR	0 缅甸MM,受惠国LD	70	---Other
369	0307.1900	--其他	14	0 冰岛IS,东盟AS,哥CR,香港HK,新西兰NZ,智利CL 4.2 秘鲁PE 8.4 澳AU 9.8 瑞士CH 11.2 巴PK,韩国KR	0 缅甸MM,受惠国LD	70	--Other

序号 No.	税则号列 Tariff Line	中文货品名称 Article Description in Chinese	最惠国税率 MFN(%)	协定税率 Agreement(%)	特惠税率 SP(%)	普通税率 Gen(%)	英文货品名称 Article Description
		-扇贝，包括海扇：					-Scallops, including queen scallops, of the genera *Pecten*, *Chlamys* or *Placopecten*:
		--活、鲜或冷的：					--Live, fresh or chilled:
370	0307.2110	---种苗	0		0 受惠国LD	0	---For cultivation
371	0307.2190	---其他	14	0 冰岛IS,东盟AS,哥CR,香港HK,新西兰NZ,智利CL 4.2 秘鲁PE 8.4 澳AU 9.8 瑞士CH 11.2 巴PK,韩国KR	0 缅甸MM,受惠国LD	70	---Other
372	0307.2900	--其他	14	0 冰岛IS,东盟AS,哥CR,新西兰NZ,智利CL 1.8 秘鲁PE 8.4 澳AU 9.8 瑞士CH 11.2 巴PK,韩国KR	0 缅甸MM,受惠国LD	80	--Other
		-贻贝：					-Mussels (*Mytilus spp., Perna spp.*) :
		--活、鲜或冷的：					--Live, fresh or chilled:
373	0307.3110	---种苗	0		0 受惠国LD	0	---For cultivation
374	0307.3190	---其他	14	0 冰岛IS,东盟AS,哥CR,秘鲁PE,香港HK,新西兰NZ,智利CL 8.4 澳AU 9.8 瑞士CH 11.2 巴PK,韩国KR	0 柬埔寨KH,缅甸MM,受惠国LD	70	---Other
375	0307.3900	--其他	14	0 冰岛IS,东盟AS,哥CR,新西兰NZ,智利CL 4.2 秘鲁PE 7 巴PK 8.4 澳AU 9.8 瑞士CH,亚太AP 11.2 韩国KR	0 柬埔寨KH,缅甸MM,受惠国LD	70	--Other
		-墨鱼及鱿鱼：					-Cuttle fish (*Sepia officinalis*, *Rossia macrosoma*, *Sepiola* spp.) and squid (*Ommastrephes* spp., *Loligo* spp., *Nototodarus* spp., *Sepioteuthis* spp.) :
		--活、鲜或冷的：					--Live, fresh or chilled:
376	0307.4110	---种苗	0		0 受惠国LD	0	---For cultivation
377	0307.4190	---其他	12	0 冰岛IS,东盟AS,哥CR,香港HK,新西兰NZ,智利CL 3.6 秘鲁PE 6 巴PK 7.2 澳AU 8.4 瑞士CH 9.6 韩国KR	0 柬埔寨KH,缅甸MM,受惠国LD	70	---Other
378	0307.4900	--其他	12	0 澳门MO,冰岛IS,东盟AS,哥CR,香港HK,新西兰NZ,智利CL 3.6 秘鲁PE 7.2 澳AU 8.4 瑞士CH 10 巴PK,亚太AP 10.8 韩国KR	0 柬埔寨KH,缅甸MM,受惠国LD	70	--Other
		-章鱼：					-Octopus (*Octopus spp.*) :

序号 No.	税则号列 Tariff Line	中文货品名称 Article Description in Chinese	最惠国税率 MFN(%)	协定税率 Agreement(%)	特惠税率 SP(%)	普通税率 Gen(%)	英文货品名称 Article Description
379	0307.5100	--活、鲜或冷的	17	0 冰岛IS,东盟AS,哥CR,香港HK,新西兰NZ,智利CL 5.1 秘鲁PE 10.2 澳AU 11.9 瑞士CH 13.6 巴PK 14.7 韩国KR	0 受惠国$_1$LD$_1$	70	--Live, fresh or chilled
380	0307.5900	--其他	17	0 澳门MO,冰岛IS,东盟AS,哥CR,香港HK,新西兰NZ,智利CL 5.1 秘鲁PE 10.2 澳AU 11.9 瑞士CH 13.6 巴PK 14.7 韩国KR	0 受惠国LD	70	--Other
		-蜗牛及螺，海螺除外：					-Snails, other than sea snails:
381	0307.6010	---种苗	0		0 受惠国LD	0	---For cultivation
382	0307.6090	---其他	14	0 冰岛IS,东盟AS,哥CR,秘鲁PE,新西兰NZ,智利CL 8.4 澳AU 9.8 瑞士CH 11.2 巴PK,韩国KR	0 柬埔寨KH,受惠国LD	70	---Other
		-蛤、鸟蛤及舟贝(蚶科、北极蛤科、鸟蛤科、斧蛤科、缝栖蛤科、蛤蜊科、中带蛤科、海螂科、双带蛤科、截蛏科、竹蛏科、砗磲科、帘蛤科)：					-Clams, cockles and ark shells (families Arcidae, Arcticidae, Cardiidae, Donacidae, Hiatellidae, Mactridae, Mesodesmatidae, Myidae, Semelidae, Solecurtidae, Solenidae, Tridacnidae and Veneridae) :
		--活、鲜或冷的：					--Live, fresh or chilled:
383	0307.7110	---种苗	0		0 受惠国LD	0	---For cultivation
		---其他：					---Other:
384	0307.7191	----蛤	14	0 冰岛IS,东盟AS,哥CR,秘鲁PE,香港HK,新西兰NZ,智利CL 8.4 澳AU 9.8 瑞士CH 11.2 巴PK,韩国KR	0 受惠国$_1$LD$_1$	70	----Clams
385	0307.7199	----其他	14	0 冰岛IS,东盟AS,哥CR,香港HK,新西兰NZ,智利CL 4.2 秘鲁PE 8.4 澳AU 9.8 瑞士CH 11.2 巴PK,韩国KR	0 柬埔寨KH,缅甸MM,受惠国LD	70	----Other
		--其他：					--Other:
386	0307.7910	---蛤	10	0 冰岛IS,东盟AS,哥CR,新西兰NZ,智利CL 4 瑞士CH 6 澳AU 8 韩国KR	0 受惠国LD	70	---Clams
387	0307.7990	---其他	10	0 澳门MO,冰岛IS,东盟AS,哥CR,新西兰NZ,智利CL 3 秘鲁PE 4 瑞士CH 6 澳AU 8.6 韩国KR	0 柬埔寨KH,缅甸MM,受惠国LD	70	---Other
		-鲍鱼（鲍属)：					-Abalone (*Haliotis spp.*) :
		--活、鲜或冷的：					--Live, fresh or chilled:
388	0307.8110	---种苗	0		0 受惠国LD	0	---For cultivation

序号 No.	税则号列 Tariff Line	中文货品名称 Article Description in Chinese	最惠国税率 MFN(%)	协定税率 Agreement(%)		特惠税率 SP(%)		普通税率 Gen(%)	英文货品名称 Article Description
389	0307.8190	---其他	14	0 4.2 8.4 9.8 11.2	冰岛IS,东盟AS,哥CR,香港HK,新西兰NZ,智利CL 秘鲁PE 澳AU 瑞士CH 巴PK,韩国KR	0	柬埔寨KH,缅甸MM,受惠国LD	80	---Other
390	0307.8900	--其他	10	0 4 5 6 8	澳门MO,冰岛IS,东盟AS,哥CR,香港HK,新西兰NZ,智利CL 瑞士CH 巴PK 澳AU 韩国KR	0	柬埔寨KH,缅甸MM,受惠国LD	80	--Other
		-其他,包括适合供人食用的细粉、粗粉及团粒:							-Other, including flours, meals and pellets, fit for human consumption:
		--活、鲜或冷的:							--Live, fresh or chilled:
391	0307.9110	---种苗	0			0	受惠国LD	0	---For cultivation
392	0307.9190	---其他	14	0 4.2 8.4 9.8 11.2	冰岛IS,东盟AS,哥CR,香港HK,新西兰NZ,智利CL 秘鲁PE 澳AU 瑞士CH 巴PK,韩国KR	0	柬埔寨KH,缅甸MM,受惠国LD	70	---Other
	ex03079190	活、鲜或冷的象拔蚌	Δ10						Panopea abrupta, live, fresh or chilled
393	0307.9900	--其他	10	0 3 4 6 9	澳门MO,冰岛IS,东盟AS,哥CR,新西兰NZ,智利CL 秘鲁PE 瑞士CH 澳AU 韩国KR	0	柬埔寨KH,缅甸MM,受惠国LD	70	--Other
	03.08	**不属于甲壳动物及软体动物的水生无脊椎动物,活、鲜、冷、冻、干、盐腌或盐渍的;熏制的不属于甲壳动物及软体动物的水生无脊椎动物,不论在熏制前或熏制过程中是否烹煮;适合供人食用的不属于甲壳动物及软体动物的水生无脊椎动物的细粉、粗粉及团粒:**							**Aquatic invertebrates other than crustaceans and molluscs, live, fresh, chilled, frozen, dried, salted or in brine; smoked aquatic invertebrates other than crustaceans and molluscs, whether or not cooked before or during the smoking process; flours, meals and pellets of aquatic invertebrates other than crustaceans and molluscs, fit for human consumption:**
		-海参(仿刺参、海参纲):							-Sea cucumbers (*Stichopus japonicus*, Holothurioidea) :
		--活、鲜或冷的:							--Live, fresh or chilled:
394	0308.1110	---种苗	0			0	受惠国LD	0	---For cultivation
395	0308.1190	---其他	14	0 4.2 8.4 9.8 11.2	冰岛IS,东盟AS,哥CR,香港HK,新西兰NZ,智利CL 秘鲁PE 澳AU 瑞士CH 巴PK,韩国KR	0	柬埔寨KH,缅甸MM,受惠国LD	70	---Other
396	0308.1900	--其他	10	0 3 4 5 6 8	东盟AS,哥CR,新西兰NZ,智利CL 秘鲁PE 瑞士CH 冰岛IS 澳AU 韩国KR	0	柬埔寨KH,缅甸MM,受惠国LD	80	--Other

序号 No.	税则号列 Tariff Line	中文货品名称 Article Description in Chinese	最惠国税率 MFN(%)	协定税率 Agreement(%)	特惠税率 SP(%)	普通税率 Gen(%)	英文货品名称 Article Description
		-海胆(球海胆属、拟球海胆、智利海胆、食用正海胆):					-Sea urchins (*Strongylocentrotus spp.*, *Paracentrotus lividus*, *Loxechinus albus*, *Echichinus esculentus*) :
		--活、鲜或冷的:					--Live, fresh or chilled:
397	0308.2110	---种苗	0		0 受惠国LD	0	---For cultivation
398	0308.2190	---其他	14	0 冰岛IS,东盟AS,哥CR,香港HK,新西兰NZ,智利CL 4.2 秘鲁PE 8.4 澳AU 9.8 瑞士CH 11.2 巴PK,韩国KR	0 柬埔寨KH,缅甸MM,受惠国LD	70	---Other
399	0308.2900	--其他	10	0 澳门MO,冰岛IS,东盟AS,哥CR,新西兰NZ,智利CL 3 秘鲁PE 4 瑞士CH 6 澳AU 8.6 韩国KR	0 柬埔寨KH,缅甸MM,受惠国LD	70	--Other
		-海蜇(海蜇属):					-Jellyfish (*Rhopilema spp.*) :
		---活、鲜或冷的:					---Live, fresh or chilled:
400	0308.3011	----种苗	0		0 受惠国LD	0	----For cultivation
401	0308.3019	----其他	14	0 冰岛IS,东盟AS,哥CR,香港HK,新西兰NZ,智利CL 4.2 秘鲁PE 8.4 澳AU 9.8 瑞士CH 11.2 巴PK,韩国KR	0 柬埔寨KH,缅甸MM,受惠国LD	70	----Other
402	0308.3090	---其他	10	0 澳门MO,冰岛IS,东盟AS,哥CR,新西兰NZ,智利CL 3 秘鲁PE 4 瑞士CH 6 澳AU 8.6 韩国KR	0 柬埔寨KH,缅甸MM,受惠国LD	70	---Other
		-其他:					-Other:
		---活、鲜或冷的:					---Live, fresh or chilled:
403	0308.9011	----种苗	0		0 受惠国LD	0	----For cultivation
404	0308.9012	----其他沙蚕	14	0 冰岛IS,东盟AS,哥CR,香港HK,新西兰NZ,智利CL 4.2 秘鲁PE 8.4 澳AU 9.8 瑞士CH 11.2 巴PK,韩国KR	0 柬埔寨KH,缅甸MM,受惠国LD	70	----Clamworm
405	0308.9019	----其他	14	0 冰岛IS,东盟AS,哥CR,香港HK,新西兰NZ,智利CL 4.2 秘鲁PE 8.4 澳AU 9.8 瑞士CH 11.2 巴PK,韩国KR	0 柬埔寨KH,缅甸MM,受惠国LD	70	----Other
406	0308.9090	---其他	10	0 澳门MO,冰岛IS,东盟AS,哥CR,新西兰NZ,智利CL 3 秘鲁PE 4 瑞士CH 6 澳AU 8.6 韩国KR	0 柬埔寨KH,缅甸MM,受惠国LD	70	---Other

第四章
乳品；蛋品；天然蜂蜜；其他食用动物产品

Chapter 4
Dairy produce; birds' eggs; natural honey; edible products of animal origin, not elsewhere specified or included

注释：

一、所称“乳”，是指全脂乳及半脱脂或全脱脂的乳。

二、税号 04.05 所称：

（一）“黄油”，仅指从乳中提取的天然黄油、乳清黄油及调制黄油（新鲜、加盐或酸败的，包括罐装黄油），按重量计乳脂含量在 80%及以上，但不超过 95%，乳的无脂固形物最大含量不超过 2%，以及水的最大含量不超过 16%。黄油中不含添加的乳化剂，但可含有氯化钠、食用色素、中和盐及无害乳酸菌的培养物。

（二）“乳酱”是一种油包水型可涂抹的乳状物，乳脂是该制品所含的唯一脂肪，按重量计其含量在 39%及以上，但小于 80%。

三、乳清经浓缩并加入乳或乳脂制成的产品，若同时具有下列三种特性，则视为乳酪归入税号 04.06：

（一）按干重计乳脂含量在 5%及以上的；

（二）按重量计干质成分至少为 70%，但不超过 85%的；

（三）已成形或可以成形的。

四、本章不包括：

（一）按重量计乳糖含量（以干燥无水乳糖计）超过 95%的乳清制品（税号 17.02）；

（二）白蛋白（包括按重量计干质成分的乳清蛋白含量超过 80%的两种或两种以上的乳清蛋白浓缩物）（税号 35.02）及球蛋白（税号 35.04）。

Notes:

1. The expression “milk” means full cream milk or partially or completely skimmed milk.

2. For the purposes of heading No.04.05:

(a) The term “butter” means natural butter, whey butter or recombined butter(fresh, salted or rancid, including canned butter)derived exclusively from milk, with a milkfat content of 80% or more but not more than 95% by weight, a maximum milk solids-not-rat content of 2% by weight and a maximum water content of 16% by weight. Butter does not contain emulsifiers, but may contain sodium chloride, food colours, neutralizing salts and cultures of harmless lactic-acid-pro-ducing bacteria.

(b) The expression “dairy spreads” means a spreadable emulsion of the water-in-oil type, containing milkfat as the only fat in the product, with a milkfat content of 39%or more but less than 80% by weight.

3. Products obtained by the concentration of whey and with the addition of milk or milkfat are to be classified as cheese in heading No.04.06 provided that they have the three following characteristics:

(a) A milkfat content, by weight of the dry matter,of5%or more;

(b) A dry matter content, by weight, of at least 70% but not exceeding 85%; and

(c) They are moulded or capable of being moulded.

4. This Chapter does not cover:

(a) Products obtained from whey, containing by weight more than 95% lactose, expressed as anhydrous lactose calculated on the dry matter(heading No.17.02); or

(b) Albumins(including concentrates of two or more whey proteins, containing by weight more than 80% whey proteins, calculated on the dry matter) (heading No.35.02) or globulins (heading No.35.04).

子目注释：

一、子目号 0404.10 所称“改性乳清”，是指由乳清成分构成的制品，即全部或部分去除乳糖、蛋白或矿物质的乳清、加入天然乳清成分的乳清及由混入天然乳清成分制成的产品。

Subheading Notes:

1. For the purpose of subheading No.0404.10, the expression “modified whey” means products consisting of whey constituents, that is, whey from which all or part of the lactose, proteins or minerals have been removed, whey to which natural whey constituents have been added and products obtained by mixing natural whey constituents.

二、子目号0405.10所称“黄油”，不包括脱水黄油及印度酥油（子目号0405.90）。

2. For the purposes of subheading No.0405.10 the term “butter” does not include dehydrated butter or ghee (subheading No.0405.90).

序号 No.	税则号列 Tariff Line	中文货品名称 Article Description in Chinese	最惠国税率 MFN(%)	协定税率 Agreement(%)	特惠税率 SP(%)	普通税率 Gen(%)	英文货品名称 Article Description
	04.01	**未浓缩及未加糖或其他甜物质的乳及奶油：**					**Milk and cream, not concentrated nor containing added sugar or other sweetening matter:**
407	0401.1000	-按重量计脂肪含量不超过1%	15	0 澳门MO,冰岛IS,东盟AS,新西兰NZ,智利CL 4.5 秘鲁PE 9 哥CR 10.5 瑞士CH 12 澳AU,巴PK	0 受惠国LD	40	-Of a fat content, by weight, not exceeding 1%
408	0401.2000	-按重量计脂肪含量超过1%，但不超过6%	15	0 澳门MO,冰岛IS,东盟AS,香港HK,智利CL 1.5 新西兰NZ 4.5 秘鲁PE 9 哥CR 10.5 瑞士CH 12 澳AU,巴PK	0 受惠国LD	40	-Of a fat content, by weight, exceeding 1% but not exceeding 6%
409	0401.4000	-按重量计脂肪含量超过6%，但不超过10%	15	0 澳门MO,冰岛IS,东盟AS,智利CL 1.5 新西兰NZ 4.5 秘鲁PE 9 哥CR 10.5 瑞士CH 12 澳AU,巴PK	0 受惠国LD	40	-Of a fat content, by weight, exceeding 6% but not exceeding 10%
410	0401.5000	-按重量计脂肪含量超过10%	15	0 澳门MO,冰岛IS,东盟AS,智利CL 1.5 新西兰NZ 4.5 秘鲁PE 9 哥CR 10.5 瑞士CH 12 澳AU,巴PK	0 受惠国LD	40	-Of a fat content, by weight, exceeding 10%
	04.02	**浓缩、加糖或其他甜物质的乳及奶油：**					**Milk and cream, concentrated or containing added sugar or other sweetening matter:**
411	0402.1000	-粉状、粒状或其他固体形状，按重量计脂肪含量不超过1.5%	10	0 澳门MO,冰岛IS,东盟AS,香港HK,智利CL 2.5 新西兰NZ 4 瑞士CH 5 巴PK 5.9 秘鲁PE 6 哥CR 7 亚太AP 8.3 澳AU	0 受惠国LD	40	-In powder, granules or other solid forms, of a fat content, by weight, not exceeding 1.5%
		-粉状、粒状或其他固体形状，按重量计脂肪含量超过1.5%：					-In powder, granules or other solid forms, of a fat content, by weight, exceeding 1.5 %:
412	0402.2100	--未加糖或其他甜物质	10	0 澳门MO,冰岛IS,东盟AS,香港HK,智利CL 2.5 新西兰NZ 5.9 秘鲁PE 6 哥CR 7 巴PK,亚太AP 8.3 澳AU	0 受惠国LD	40	--Not containing added sugar or other sweetening matter

序号 No.	税则号列 Tariff Line	中文货品名称 Article Description in Chinese	最惠国税率 MFN(%)	协定税率 Agreement(%)	特惠税率 SP(%)	普通税率 Gen(%)	英文货品名称 Article Description
413	0402.2900	--其他	10	0 澳门MO,冰岛IS,东盟AS,香港HK,智利CL 2.5 新西兰NZ 4 瑞士CH 5 巴PK 5.9 秘鲁PE 6 哥CR 8.3 澳AU	0 受惠国LD	40	--Other
		-其他:					-Other:
414	0402.9100	--未加糖或其他甜物质	10	0 澳门MO,冰岛IS,东盟AS,香港HK,智利CL 2.5 新西兰NZ 3 秘鲁PE 5 巴PK 6 哥CR 8.3 澳AU	0 受惠国LD	90	--Not containing added sugar or other sweetening matter
415	0402.9900	--其他	10	0 冰岛IS,东盟AS,新西兰NZ,智利CL 5 巴PK 5.9 秘鲁PE 6 哥CR 8.3 澳AU	0 受惠国LD	90	--Other
	04.03	**酪乳、结块的乳及奶油、酸乳、酸乳酒及其他发酵或酸化的乳和奶油,不论是否浓缩、加糖、加其他甜物质、加香料、加水果、加坚果或加可可:**					**Buttermilk, curdled milk and cream, yogurt, kephir and other fermented or acidified milk and cream, whether or not concentrated or containing added sugar or other sweetening matter or flavoured or containing added fruit, nuts or cocoa:**
416	0403.1000	-酸乳	10	0 澳门MO,冰岛IS,东盟AS,香港HK,新西兰NZ,智利CL 3 秘鲁PE 5 巴PK 6 哥CR 7.5 瑞士CH 8 澳AU	0 受惠国LD	90	-Yogurt
417	0403.9000	-其他	20	0 澳门MO,冰岛IS,东盟AS,香港HK,新西兰NZ,智利CL 6 秘鲁PE 12 哥CR 16 澳AU	0 受惠国$_1$LD$_1$	90	-Other
	04.04	**乳清,不论是否浓缩、加糖或其他甜物质;其他税号未列名的含天然乳的产品,不论是否加糖或其他甜物质:**					**Whey, whether or not concentrated or containing added sugar or other sweetening matter; products consisting of natural milk constituents, whether or not containing added sugar or other sweetening matter, not elsewhere specified or included:**
418	0404.1000	-乳清及改性乳清,不论是否浓缩、加糖或其他甜物质	6Δ2	0 冰岛IS,东盟AS,秘鲁PE,新西兰NZ,智利CL 3.6 澳AU,哥CR 5 巴PK 5.2 韩国KR	0 受惠国$_1$LD$_1$	30	-Whey and modified whey, whether or not concentrated or containing added sugar or other sweetening matter
419	0404.9000	-其他	20	0 冰岛IS,东盟AS,新西兰NZ,智利CL 6 秘鲁PE 12 哥CR 16 澳AU 17.3 韩国KR	0 受惠国$_1$LD$_1$	90	-Other

序号 No.	税则号列 Tariff Line	中文货品名称 Article Description in Chinese	最惠国税率 MFN(%)	协定税率 Agreement(%)	特惠税率 SP(%)	普通税率 Gen(%)	英文货品名称 Article Description
	04.05	黄油及其他从乳中提取的脂和油；乳酱：					**Butter and other fats and oils derived from milk; dairy spreads:**
420	0405.1000	-黄油	10	0 冰岛IS,东盟AS,智利CL 1 新西兰NZ 3 秘鲁PE 4 瑞士CH 5 巴PK 6 哥CR 8 澳AU 8.6 韩国KR	0 受惠国LD	90	-Butter
421	0405.2000	-乳酱	10	0 澳门MO,冰岛IS,东盟AS,秘鲁PE,新西兰NZ,智利CL 4 瑞士CH 5 巴PK 6 澳AU,哥CR 8.1 亚太AP 8.6 韩国KR	0 受惠国LD	90	-Dairy spreads
422	0405.9000	-其他	10	0 冰岛IS,东盟AS,智利CL 1 新西兰NZ 3 秘鲁PE 5 巴PK 6 哥CR 8 澳AU 8.6 韩国KR	0 受惠国LD	90	-Other
	04.06	乳酪及凝乳：					**Cheese and curd:**
423	0406.1000	-鲜乳酪（未熟化或未固化的），包括乳清乳酪；凝乳	12	0 澳门MO,冰岛IS,东盟AS,香港HK,智利CL 1.2 新西兰NZ 3.6 秘鲁PE 6 巴PK 7.2 哥CR 8.6 瑞士CH 9.6 澳AU 10.4 韩国KR	0 受惠国LD	90	-Fresh (unripened or uncured) cheese, including whey cheese, and curd
424	0406.2000	-各种磨碎或粉化的乳酪	12	0 冰岛IS,东盟AS,香港HK,新西兰NZ,智利CL 6 巴PK 6.4 秘鲁PE 7.2 哥CR 8.6 瑞士CH 9.6 澳AU 10.4 韩国KR	0 受惠国$_2$LD$_2$	90	-Grated or powdered cheese, of all kinds
425	0406.3000	-经加工的乳酪，但磨碎或粉化的除外	12	0 冰岛IS,东盟AS,智利CL 1.2 新西兰NZ 6 巴PK 6.4 秘鲁PE 7.2 哥CR 8.6 瑞士CH 9.6 澳AU 10.4 韩国KR	0 受惠国$_1$LD$_1$	90	-Processed cheese, not grated or powdered
426	0406.4000	-蓝纹乳酪和娄地青霉生产的带有纹理的其他乳酪	15	0 冰岛IS,东盟AS,新西兰NZ,智利CL 4.5 秘鲁PE 9 澳AU,哥CR 12 巴PK 13 韩国KR	0 受惠国$_1$LD$_1$	90	-Blue-veined cheese and other cheese containing veins produced by Penicillium roqueforti

序号 No.	税则号列 Tariff Line	中文货品名称 Article Description in Chinese	最惠国税率 MFN(%)	协定税率 Agreement(%)	特惠税率 SP(%)	普通税率 Gen(%)	英文货品名称 Article Description
427	0406.9000	-其他酪	12	0 冰岛IS,东盟AS,智利CL 1.2 新西兰NZ 3.6 秘鲁PE 6 巴PK 7.2 哥CR 8.6 瑞士CH 9.6 澳AU 10.4 韩国KR	0 受惠国LD	90	-Other cheese
	04.07	**带壳禽蛋，鲜、腌制或煮过的：**					**Birds' eggs, in shell, fresh, preserved or cooked:**
		-孵化用受精禽蛋：					-Fertilised eggs for incubation:
428	0407.1100	--鸡的	0		0 受惠国LD	0	--Of fowls of the species *Gallus domesticus*
429	0407.1900	--其他	0		0 受惠国LD	0	--Other
		-其他鲜蛋：					-Other fresh eggs:
430	0407.2100	--鸡的	20	0 冰岛IS,东盟AS,哥CR,新西兰NZ,智利CL 6 秘鲁PE 12 澳AU 14 瑞士CH 17.3 韩国KR	0 柬埔寨KH,缅甸MM,受惠国LD	80	--Of hens
431	0407.2900	--其他	20	0 冰岛IS,东盟AS,哥CR,新西兰NZ,智利CL 6 秘鲁PE 12 澳AU 14 瑞士CH 17.3 韩国KR	0 柬埔寨KH,缅甸MM,受惠国LD	80	--Other
		-其他：					-Other:
432	0407.9010	---咸蛋	20	0 冰岛IS,东盟AS,哥CR,秘鲁PE,新西兰NZ,智利CL 12 澳AU 14 瑞士CH 17.3 韩国KR	0 缅甸MM,受惠国LD	90	---Salted egg
433	0407.9020	---皮蛋	20	0 冰岛IS,东盟AS,哥CR,秘鲁PE,新西兰NZ,智利CL 12 澳AU 14 瑞士CH 17.3 韩国KR	0 受惠国$_1$LD$_1$	90	---Preserved egg
434	0407.9090	---其他	20	0 冰岛IS,东盟AS,哥CR,秘鲁PE,新西兰NZ,智利CL 12 澳AU 14 瑞士CH 17.3 韩国KR	0 受惠国$_1$LD$_1$	90	---Other
	04.08	**去壳禽蛋及蛋黄，鲜、干、冻、蒸过或水煮、制成型或用其他方法保藏的，不论是否加糖或其他甜物质：**					**Birds' eggs, not in shell, and egg yolks, fresh, dried, cooked by steaming or by boiling in water, moulded, frozen or otherwise preserved, whether or not containing added sugar or other sweetening matter:**
		-蛋黄：					-Egg yolks:
435	0408.1100	--干的	20	0 冰岛IS,东盟AS,哥CR,新西兰NZ,智利CL 6 秘鲁PE 12 澳AU 14 瑞士CH 17.3 韩国KR	0 受惠国$_1$LD$_1$	90	--Dried

序号 No.	税则号列 Tariff Line	中文货品名称 Article Description in Chinese	最惠国税率 MFN(%)	协定税率 Agreement(%)	特惠税率 SP(%)	普通税率 Gen(%)	英文货品名称 Article Description
436	0408.1900	--其他	20	0 冰岛IS,东盟AS,哥CR,新西兰NZ,智利CL 6 秘鲁PE 12 澳AU 14 瑞士CH 17.3 韩国KR	0 受惠国$_1$LD$_1$	90	--Other
		-其他:					-Other:
437	0408.9100	--干的	20	0 冰岛IS,东盟AS,哥CR,新西兰NZ,智利CL 6 秘鲁PE 12 澳AU 14 瑞士CH 17.3 韩国KR	0 受惠国$_1$LD$_1$	90	--Dried
438	0408.9900	--其他	20	0 冰岛IS,东盟AS,哥CR,香港HK,新西兰NZ,智利CL 6 秘鲁PE 12 澳AU 14 瑞士CH 17.3 韩国KR	0 受惠国$_1$LD$_1$	90	--Other
	04.09	**天然蜂蜜**					**Natural honey**
439	0409.0000	天然蜂蜜	15	0 澳门MO,冰岛IS,东盟AS,哥CR,新西兰NZ,智利CL 4.5 秘鲁PE 9 澳AU 10.5 瑞士CH 12 巴PK 13 韩国KR	0 柬埔寨KH,老挝LA,受惠国LD	80	Natural honey
	04.10	**其他税号未列名的食用动物产品:**					**Edible products of animal origin, not elsewhere specified or included:**
440	0410.0010	---燕窝	25	0 澳门MO,冰岛IS,东盟AS,哥CR,香港HK,新西兰NZ,智利CL 7.5 秘鲁PE 15 澳AU 17.5 瑞士CH 20 韩国KR	0 柬埔寨KH,缅甸MM,受惠国LD	80	---Salanganes nests
		---蜂产品:					---Bee products:
441	0410.0041	----鲜蜂王浆	15	0 冰岛IS,东盟AS,哥CR,新西兰NZ,智利CL 4.5 秘鲁PE 9 澳AU 10.5 瑞士CH 12 巴PK,韩国KR	0 受惠国$_1$LD$_1$	70	----Pure royal jelley
442	0410.0042	----鲜蜂王浆粉	15	0 冰岛IS,东盟AS,哥CR,新西兰NZ,智利CL 4.5 秘鲁PE 9 澳AU 10.5 瑞士CH 12 巴PK,韩国KR	0 受惠国$_1$LD$_1$	70	----Pure royal jelley, in powder
443	0410.0043	----蜂花粉	20	0 冰岛IS,东盟AS,哥CR,新西兰NZ,智利CL 6 秘鲁PE 12 澳AU 14 瑞士CH 17.3 韩国KR	0 受惠国$_1$LD$_1$	70	----Bee pollen

序号 No.	税则号列 Tariff Line	中文货品名称 Article Description in Chinese	最惠国税率 MFN(%)	协定税率 Agreement(%)	特惠税率 SP(%)	普通税率 Gen(%)	英文货品名称 Article Description
444	0410.0049	----其他	20	0 冰岛IS,东盟AS,哥CR,新西兰NZ,智利CL 6 秘鲁PE 12 澳AU 14 瑞士CH 17.3 韩国KR	0 受惠国$_1$LD$_1$	70	----Other
445	0410.0090	---其他	20	0 冰岛IS,东盟AS,哥CR,台湾TW,新西兰NZ,智利CL 6 秘鲁PE 12 澳AU 14 瑞士CH 17.3 韩国KR	0 缅甸MM,受惠国LD	70	---Other

第五章
其他动物产品

Chapter 5
Products of animal origin, not elsewhere specified or included

注释：

一、本章不包括：

（一）食用产品（整个或切块的动物肠、膀胱和胃以及液态或干制的动物血除外）；

（二）生皮或毛皮（第四十一章、第四十三章），但税号 05.05 的货品及税号 05.11 的生皮或毛皮的边角废料仍归入本章；

（三）马毛及废马毛以外的动物纺织原料（第十一类）；

（四）供制帚、制刷用的成束、成簇的材料（税号 96.03）。

二、仅按长度而未按发根和发梢整理的人发，视为未加工品，归入税号 05.01。

三、本目录所称"兽牙"，是指象、河马、海象、一角鲸和野猪的长牙、犀角及其他动物的牙齿。

四、本目录所称"马毛"，是指马科、牛科动物的鬃毛和尾毛。

Notes:

1. This Chapter does not cover:
   (a) Edible products (other than guts, bladders and stomachs of animals, whole and pieces thereof, and animal blood, liquid or dried);
   (b) Hides or skins (including furskins) other than goods of heading No.05.05and parings and similar waste of raw hides or skins of heading No.05.11 (Chapter 41 or 43);
   (c) Animal textile materials, other than horsehair and horsehair waste (SectionⅪ) ;or
   (d) Prepared knots or tufts for broom or brush making (heading No.96.03).
2. For the purposes of heading No.05.01, the sorting of human hair by length (provided the root ends and tip ends respectively are not arranged together) shall be deemed not to constitute orking.
3. Throughout the Nomenclature, elephant, hippopotamus, walrus, narwhal and wild boar tusks, rhinoceros horns and the teeth of all animals are regarded as "ivory".
4. Throughout the Nomenclature, the expression "horsehair" means hair of the manes or tails of equine or bovine animals.

序号 No.	税则号列 Tariff Line	中文货品名称 Article Description in Chinese	最惠国税率 MFN(%)	协定税率 Agreement(%)	特惠税率 SP(%)	普通税率 Gen(%)	英文货品名称 Article Description
	05.01	**未经加工的人发，不论是否洗涤；废人发**					**Human hair, unworked, whether or not washed or scoured; waste of human hair**
446	0501.0000	未经加工的人发，不论是否洗涤；废人发	15	0 冰岛IS,东盟AS,哥CR,新西兰NZ,智利CL 4.5 秘鲁PE 9 澳AU 10.5 瑞士CH 12 巴PK,韩国KR	0 受惠国$_1$LD$_1$	90	Human hair, unworked, whether or not washed or scoured; waste of human hair
	05.02	**猪鬃、猪毛；獾毛及其他制刷用兽毛；上述鬃毛的废料：**					**Pigs', hogs' or boars' bristles and hair; badger hair and other brush making hair; waste of such bristles or hair:**
		-猪鬃、猪毛及其废料：					-Pigs', hogs' or boars' bristles and hair and waste thereof:
447	0502.1010	---猪鬃	20	0 冰岛IS,东盟AS,哥CR,新西兰NZ,智利CL 6 秘鲁PE 12 澳AU 14 瑞士CH 17.3 韩国KR	0 受惠国$_1$LD$_1$	90	---Bristles
448	0502.1020	---猪毛	20	0 冰岛IS,东盟AS,哥CR,新西兰NZ,智利CL 6 秘鲁PE 12 澳AU 14 瑞士CH 17.3 韩国KR	0 受惠国$_1$LD$_1$	90	---Hair
449	0502.1030	---废料	20	0 冰岛IS,东盟AS,哥CR,新西兰NZ,智利CL 6 秘鲁PE 12 澳AU 14 瑞士CH 17.3 韩国KR	0 受惠国$_1$LD$_1$	90	---Waste
		-其他：					-Other:

序号 No.	税则号列 Tariff Line	中文货品名称 Article Description in Chinese	最惠国税率 MFN(%)	协定税率 Agreement(%)	特惠税率 SP(%)	普通税率 Gen(%)	英文货品名称 Article Description
		---獾毛及其他制刷用兽毛：					---Badger hair and other brush making hair:
450	0502.9011	----山羊毛	20	0 冰岛IS,东盟AS,哥CR,新西兰NZ,智利CL 6 秘鲁PE 12 澳AU 14 瑞士CH 17.3 韩国KR	0 受惠国$_1$LD$_1$	90	----Goat hair
451	0502.9012	----黄鼠狼尾毛	20	0 冰岛IS,东盟AS,哥CR,新西兰NZ,智利CL 6 秘鲁PE 12 澳AU 14 瑞士CH 17.3 韩国KR	0 受惠国$_1$LD$_1$	90	----Weasel tail hair
452	0502.9019	----其他	20	0 冰岛IS,东盟AS,哥CR,新西兰NZ,智利CL 6 秘鲁PE 12 澳AU 14 瑞士CH 17.3 韩国KR	0 受惠国$_1$LD$_1$	90	----Other
453	0502.9020	---废料	20	0 冰岛IS,东盟AS,哥CR,新西兰NZ,智利CL 6 秘鲁PE 12 澳AU 14 瑞士CH 17.3 韩国KR	0 受惠国$_1$LD$_1$	90	---Waste
	05.04	**整个或切块的动物（鱼除外）的肠、膀胱及胃，鲜、冷、冻、干、熏、盐腌或盐渍的：**					**Guts, bladders and stomachs of animals (other than fish), whole and pieces thereof, fresh, chilled, frozen, salted, in brine, dried or smoked:**
		---肠衣：					---Casings:
454	0504.0011	----盐渍猪肠衣（猪大肠头除外）	20	0 冰岛IS,东盟AS,哥CR,新西兰NZ,智利CL 6 秘鲁PE 8 瑞士CH 10 巴PK,亚太AP 12 澳AU 17.3 韩国KR	0 受惠国$_1$LD$_1$	90	----Hog casings, salted
455	0504.0012	----盐渍绵羊肠衣	18	0 冰岛IS,东盟AS,哥CR,新西兰NZ,智利CL 5.4 秘鲁PE 9 巴PK,亚太AP 10.8 澳AU 12.6 瑞士CH 15.6 韩国KR	0 受惠国$_1$LD$_1$	90	----Sheep casings, salted
456	0504.0013	----盐渍山羊肠衣	18	0 冰岛IS,东盟AS,哥CR,新西兰NZ,智利CL 5.4 秘鲁PE 9 巴PK,亚太AP 10.8 澳AU 12.6 瑞士CH 15.6 韩国KR	0 受惠国$_1$LD$_1$	90	----Goat casings, salted
457	0504.0014	----盐渍猪大肠头	20	0 冰岛IS,东盟AS,哥CR,新西兰NZ,智利CL 6 秘鲁PE 10 巴PK,亚太AP 12 澳AU 14 瑞士CH 17.3 韩国KR	0 受惠国$_1$LD$_1$	90	----Hog fat-ends, salted

序号 No.	税则号列 Tariff Line	中文货品名称 Article Description in Chinese	最惠国税率 MFN(%)	协定税率 Agreement(%)	特惠税率 SP(%)	普通税率 Gen(%)	英文货品名称 Article Description
458	0504.0019	----其他	18	0 冰岛IS,东盟AS,哥CR,新西兰NZ,智利CL 5.4 秘鲁PE 9 巴PK,亚太AP 10.8 澳AU 12.6 瑞士CH 15.6 韩国KR	0 受惠国$_1$LD$_1$	90	----Other
		---胃:					---Gizzard:
459	0504.0021	----冷、冻的鸡胗	①	0 冰岛IS,东盟AS,哥CR,新西兰NZ,智利CL 6 秘鲁PE 12 澳AU 14 瑞士CH ③ 巴PK,亚太AP ④ 韩国KR	0 受惠国$_1$LD$_1$	②	----Cold, frozen gizzard
460	0504.0029	----其他	20	0 冰岛IS,东盟AS,哥CR,新西兰NZ,智利CL 6 秘鲁PE 10 巴PK,亚太AP 12 澳AU 14 瑞士CH 17.3 韩国KR	0 受惠国LD	90	----Other
461	0504.0090	---其他	20	0 冰岛IS,东盟AS,哥CR,新西兰NZ,智利CL 6 秘鲁PE 8 瑞士CH 10 巴PK,亚太AP 12 澳AU 17.3 韩国KR	0 受惠国$_1$LD$_1$	80	---Other
	05.05	**带有羽毛或羽绒的鸟皮及鸟体其他部分；羽毛及不完整羽毛（不论是否修边）、羽绒，仅经洗涤、消毒或为了保藏而作过处理，但未经进一步加工；羽毛或不完整羽毛的粉末及废料：**					**Skins and other parts of birds, with their feathers or down, feathers and parts of feathers (whether or not with trimmed edges) and down, not further worked than cleaned, disinfected or treated for preservation; powder and waste of feathers or parts of feathers:**
462	0505.1000	-填充用羽毛，羽绒	10Δ2	0 冰岛IS,东盟AS,哥CR,秘鲁PE,新西兰NZ,智利CL 4 瑞士CH 5 巴PK 6 澳AU 7.5 亚太AP 8 韩国KR	0 受惠国LD	100	-Feathers of a kind used for stuffing; down
		-其他:					-Other:
463	0505.9010	---羽毛或不完整羽毛的粉末及废料	10	0 冰岛IS,东盟AS,哥CR,秘鲁PE,新西兰NZ,智利CL 4 瑞士CH 5 巴PK 6 澳AU 8 韩国KR	0 受惠国LD	35	---Powder and waste of feathers or parts of feathers

①**最惠国税率**: 1.3 元/千克
MFN Tariff: 1.3¥/kg
②**普通税率**: 7.7 元/千克
General Duty: 7.7¥/kg
③**协定税率**: 0.65 元/千克
Agreement Import Tariff: 0.65¥/kg
④**协定税率**: 1.1 元/千克
Agreement Import Tariff: 1.1¥/kg

序号 No.	税则号列 Tariff Line	中文货品名称 Article Description in Chinese	最惠国税率 MFN(%)	协定税率 Agreement(%)	特惠税率 SP(%)	普通税率 Gen(%)	英文货品名称 Article Description
464	0505.9090	---其他	10	0 冰岛IS,东盟AS,哥CR,秘鲁PE,新西兰NZ,智利CL 4 瑞士CH 5 巴PK 6 澳AU 8 韩国KR	0 受惠国LD	90	---Other
	05.06	**骨及角柱，未经加工或经脱脂、简单整理（但未切割成形）、酸处理或脱胶；上述产品的粉末及废料：**					**Bones and horn-cores, unworked, defatted, simply prepared (but not cut to shape), treated with acid or degelatinised; powder and waste of these products:**
465	0506.1000	-经酸处理的骨胶原及骨	12	0 冰岛IS,东盟AS,哥CR,秘鲁PE,新西兰NZ,智利CL 6 巴PK 7.2 澳AU 8.4 瑞士CH 9.6 韩国KR	0 老挝LA,受惠国LD	50	-Ossein and bones treated with acid
		-其他：					-Other:
		---骨粉、骨废料：					---Powder and waste of bones:
466	0506.9011	----含牛羊成分的	12	0 冰岛IS,东盟AS,哥CR,新西兰NZ,智利CL 3.6 秘鲁PE 6 巴PK 7.2 澳AU 8.4 瑞士CH 9.6 韩国KR	0 老挝LA,受惠国LD	35	----Of bovine and sheep
467	0506.9019	----其他	12	0 冰岛IS,东盟AS,哥CR,新西兰NZ,智利CL 3.6 秘鲁PE 6 巴PK 7.2 澳AU 8.4 瑞士CH 9.6 韩国KR	0 老挝LA,受惠国LD	35	----Other
468	0506.9090	---其他	12	0 澳门MO,冰岛IS,东盟AS,新西兰NZ,智利CL 3.6 秘鲁PE 4.8 哥CR 6 巴PK 7.2 澳AU 8.4 瑞士CH 9.6 韩国KR	0 老挝LA,受惠国LD	50	---Other
	05.07	**兽牙、龟壳、鲸须、鲸须毛、角、鹿角、蹄、甲、爪及喙，未经加工或仅简单整理但未切割成形；上述产品的粉末及废料：**					**Ivory, tortoiseshell, whalebone and whalebone hair, horns, antlers, hooves, nails, claws and beaks, unworked or simply prepared but not cut to shape; powder and waste of these products:**
469	0507.1000	-兽牙；兽牙粉末及废料	10	0 冰岛IS,东盟AS,哥CR,秘鲁PE,新西兰NZ,智利CL 4 瑞士CH 5 巴PK 6 澳AU 8 韩国KR	0 受惠国LD	30	-Ivory; ivory powder and waste
		-其他：					-Other:
470	0507.9010	---羚羊角及其粉末和废料	3	0 澳AU,巴PK,冰岛IS,东盟AS,哥CR,韩国KR,秘鲁PE,瑞士CH,新西兰NZ,智利CL	0 受惠国LD	14	---Antelope horns and powder or waste thereof

序号 No.	税则号列 Tariff Line	中文货品名称 Article Description in Chinese	最惠国税率 MFN(%)	协定税率 Agreement(%)	特惠税率 SP(%)	普通税率 Gen(%)	英文货品名称 Article Description
471	0507.9020	---鹿茸及其粉末	11	0 冰岛IS,东盟AS,哥CR,秘鲁PE,新西兰NZ,智利CL 5 巴PK 6.6 澳AU 7.7 瑞士CH 8.8 韩国KR	0 受惠国LD	30	---Pilose antlers and powder thereof
472	0507.9090	---其他	10	0 冰岛IS,东盟AS,哥CR,秘鲁PE,新西兰NZ,智利CL 4 瑞士CH 5 巴PK 6 澳AU 8 韩国KR	0 受惠国LD	50	---Other
	05.08	**珊瑚及类似品，未经加工或仅简单整理但未经进一步加工；软体动物壳、甲壳动物壳、棘皮动物壳、墨鱼骨，未经加工或仅简单整理但未切割成形，上述壳、骨的粉末及废料：**					**Coral and similar materials, unworked or simply prepared but not otherwise worked; shells of molluscs, crustaceans or echinoderms and cuttle-bone, unworked or simply prepared but not cut to shape, powder and waste thereof:**
473	0508.0010	---粉末及废料	12	0 冰岛IS,东盟AS,哥CR,香港HK,新西兰NZ,智利CL 3.6 秘鲁PE 7.2 澳AU 8.4 瑞士CH 9.6 韩国KR	0 受惠国LD	35	---Powder and waste
474	0508.0090	---其他	12	0 冰岛IS,东盟AS,哥CR,香港HK,新西兰NZ,智利CL 3.6 秘鲁PE 6 巴PK 7.2 澳AU 8.4 瑞士CH 9.6 韩国KR	0 受惠国LD	50	---Other
	05.10	**龙涎香、海狸香、灵猫香及麝香；斑蝥；胆汁，不论是否干制；供配制药用的腺体及其他动物产品，鲜、冷、冻或用其他方法暂时保藏的：**					**Ambergris, castoreum, civet and musk; cantharides; bile, whether or not dried; glands and other animal products used in the preparation of pharmaceutical products, fresh, chilled, frozen or otherwise provisionally preserved:**
475	0510.0010	---黄药	3	0 澳AU,巴PK,冰岛IS,东盟AS,哥CR,韩国KR,秘鲁PE,瑞士CH,新西兰NZ,智利CL	0 受惠国LD	14	---Bezoar
476	0510.0020	---龙涎香、海狸香、灵猫香	7	0 冰岛IS,东盟AS,哥CR,韩国KR,秘鲁PE,新西兰NZ,智利CL 2.8 瑞士CH 4.2 澳AU 5 巴PK	0 受惠国$_1$LD$_1$	50	---Ambergris, castoreum and civet
477	0510.0030	---麝香	7	0 冰岛IS,东盟AS,哥CR,韩国KR,秘鲁PE,新西兰NZ,智利CL 2.8 瑞士CH 4.2 澳AU 5 巴PK	0 受惠国$_1$LD$_1$	20	---Musk

序号 No.	税则号列 Tariff Line	中文货品名称 Article Description in Chinese	最惠国税率 MFN(%)	协定税率 Agreement(%)	特惠税率 SP(%)	普通税率 Gen(%)	英文货品名称 Article Description
478	0510.0040	---斑蝥	7	0 冰岛IS,东盟AS,哥CR,韩国KR,秘鲁PE,新西兰NZ,智利CL 2.8 瑞士CH 4.2 澳AU 5 巴PK	0 受惠国LD	50	---Cantharides
479	0510.0090	---其他	6	0 冰岛IS,东盟AS,哥CR,韩国KR,秘鲁PE,新西兰NZ,智利CL 2.4 瑞士CH 3.6 澳AU 5 巴PK	0 受惠国LD	20	---Other
	05.11	**其他税号未列名的动物产品；不适合供人食用的第一章或第三章的死动物：**					**Animal products not elsewhere specified or included; dead animals of Chapter 1 or 3, unfit for human consumption:**
480	0511.1000	-牛的精液	0		0 受惠国LD	0	-Bovine semen
		-其他：					-Other:
		--鱼、甲壳动物、软体动物、其他水生无脊椎动物的产品；第三章的死动物：					--Products of fish or crustaceans, molluscs or other aquatic invertebrates; dead animals of Chapter 3:
		---鱼的：					---Fish:
481	0511.9111	----受精鱼卵	12Δ0	0 冰岛IS,东盟AS,哥CR,秘鲁PE,新西兰NZ,智利CL 6 巴PK 7.2 澳AU,韩国KR 8.4 瑞士CH	0 受惠国LD	35	----Fertilized fish eggs
482	0511.9119	----其他	12	0 东盟AS,哥CR,新西兰NZ,智利CL 3.6 秘鲁PE 7.2 澳AU 8.4 瑞士CH 8.7 冰岛IS 9.6 韩国KR	0 受惠国LD	35	----Other
483	0511.9190	---其他	12	0 冰岛IS,东盟AS,哥CR,新西兰NZ,智利CL 3.6 秘鲁PE 6 巴PK 7.2 澳AU 8.4 瑞士CH 9.6 韩国KR	0 受惠国LD	35	---Other
		--其他：					--Other:
484	0511.9910	---动物精液（牛的精液除外）	0		0 受惠国LD	0	---Animal semen, other than bovine semen
485	0511.9920	---动物胚胎	0		0 受惠国LD	0	---Animal embryo
486	0511.9930	---蚕种	0		0 受惠国LD	0	---Silkworm graine
487	0511.9940	---马毛及废马毛，不论是否制成有或无衬垫的毛片	15	0 冰岛IS,东盟AS,哥CR,新西兰NZ,智利CL 4.5 秘鲁PE 9 澳AU 10.5 瑞士CH 12 巴PK,韩国KR	0 受惠国$_1$LD$_1$	90	---Horsehair and horsehair waste, whether or not put up as a layer with or without supporting material
488	0511.9990	---其他	12	0 冰岛IS,东盟AS,哥CR,新西兰NZ,智利CL 3.6 秘鲁PE 6 巴PK 7.2 澳AU 8.4 瑞士CH 9.6 韩国KR	0 受惠国LD	35	---Other

第二类

SECTION II

植物产品

VEGETABLE PRODUCTS

注释:

本类所称“团粒”，是指直接挤压或加入按重量计比例不超过3%的粘合剂制成的粒状产品。

Note:

In this Section the term “pellets” means products which have been agglomerated either directly by compression or by the addition of a binder in a proportion not exceeding 3% by weight.

第六章
活树及其他活植物;
鳞茎、根及类似品;
插花及装饰用簇叶

Chapter 6
Live trees and other plants;
Bulbs, roots and the like;
cut flowers and ornamental foliage

注释:

一、除税号06.01的菊苣植物及其根以外，本章包括通常由苗圃或花店供应为种植或装饰用的活树及其他货品(包括植物秧苗);但不包括马铃薯、洋葱、青葱、大蒜及其他第七章的产品。

二、税号06.03、06.04的各种货品，包括全部或部分用这些货品制成的花束、花篮、花圈及类似品，不论是否有其他材料制成的附件。但这些货品不包括税号97.01的拼贴画或类似的装饰板。

Notes:

1. Subject to the second part of heading No.06.01this Chapter covers only live trees and goods (including seeding vegetables) of a kind commonly supplied by nursery gardeners or florists for planting or for ornamental use; nevertheless it does not include potatoes, onions, shallots, garlic or other products of Chapter 7.
2. Any reference in heading No.06.03 or 06.04 to goods of any kind shall be construed as including a reference to bouquets, floral baskets, wreaths and similar articles made wholly or partly of goods of that kind, account not being taken of accessories of other materials. However, these headings do not include collages or similar decorative plaques of heading No.97.01.

序号 No.	税则号列 Tariff Line	中文货品名称 Article Description in Chinese	最惠国税率 MFN(%)	协定税率 Agreement(%)	特惠税率 SP(%)	普通税率 Gen(%)	英文货品名称 Article Description
	06.01	**鳞茎、块茎、块根、球茎、根颈及根茎，休眠、生长或开花的；菊苣植物及其根，但税号12.12的根除外：**					**Bulbs, tubers, tuberous roots, corms, crowns and rhizomes, dormant, in growth or in flower; chicory plants and roots other than roots of heading 1212:**
		-休眠的鳞茎、块茎、块根、球茎、根颈及根茎：					-Bulbs, tubers, tuberous roots, corms, crowns and rhizomes, dormant:
489	0601.1010	---番红花球茎	4	0 澳AU,巴PK,冰岛IS,东盟AS,哥CR,韩国KR,秘鲁PE,瑞士CH,新西兰NZ,智利CL 2 亚太AP	0 老挝LA,受惠国LD	14	---Stigma croci corms
		---百合球茎：					---Lily corms:
490	0601.1021	----种用	0		0 受惠国LD	0	----Seed
491	0601.1029	----其他	5	0 澳AU,巴PK,冰岛IS,东盟AS,哥CR,韩国KR,秘鲁PE,瑞士CH,新西兰NZ,智利CL 2.5 亚太AP	0 老挝LA,受惠国LD	40	----Other
		---其他：					---Other:
492	0601.1091	----种用	0		0 受惠国LD	0	----Seed
493	0601.1099	----其他	5	0 澳AU,巴PK,冰岛IS,东盟AS,哥CR,韩国KR,秘鲁PE,瑞士CH,新西兰NZ,智利CL 2.5 亚太AP	0 老挝LA,受惠国LD	40	----Others

序号 No.	税则号列 Tariff Line	中文货品名称 Article Description in Chinese	最惠国税率 MFN(%)	协定税率 Agreement(%)	特惠税率 SP(%)	普通税率 Gen(%)	英文货品名称 Article Description
494	0601.2000	-生长或开花的鳞茎、块茎、块根、球茎、根颈及根茎；菊苣植物及其根	15	0 冰岛IS,东盟AS,哥CR,新西兰NZ,智利CL 4.5 秘鲁PE 7.5 巴PK,亚太AP 9 澳AU 10.5 瑞士CH 12 韩国KR	0 受惠国$_1$LD$_1$	80	-Bulbs, tubers, tuberous roots, corms, crowns and rhizomes, in growth or in flower; chicory plants and roots
	06.02	**其他活植物(包括其根)、插枝及接穗；蘑菇菌丝：**					**Other live plants (including their roots) , cuttings and slips; mushroom spawn:**
495	0602.1000	-无根插枝及接穗	0		0 受惠国LD	0	-Unrooted cuttings and slips
		-食用水果或食用坚果的树、灌木，不论是否嫁接：					-Trees, shrubs and bushes, grafted or not, of kinds which bear edible fruit or nuts:
496	0602.2010	---种用苗木	0		0 受惠国LD	0	---Seedlings
497	0602.2090	---其他	10	0 冰岛IS,东盟AS,哥CR,新西兰NZ,智利CL 3 秘鲁PE 4 瑞士CH 5 巴PK,亚太AP 6 澳AU 8 韩国KR	0 受惠国LD	80	---Other
		-杜鹃，不论是否嫁接：					-Rhododendrons and azaleas, grafted or not:
498	0602.3010	---种用	0		0 受惠国LD	0	---Seedlings
499	0602.3090	---其他	15	0 冰岛IS,东盟AS,哥CR,新西兰NZ,智利CL 4.5 秘鲁PE 9 澳AU 10.5 瑞士CH 12 巴PK,韩国KR	0 受惠国$_1$LD$_1$	80	---Other
		-玫瑰，不论是否嫁接：					-Roses, grafted or not:
500	0602.4010	---种用	0		0 受惠国LD	0	---Seedlings
501	0602.4090	---其他	15	0 冰岛IS,东盟AS,哥CR,新西兰NZ,智利CL 4.5 秘鲁PE 9 澳AU 10.5 瑞士CH 12 巴PK,韩国KR	0 受惠国$_1$LD$_1$	80	---Other
		-其他：					-Other:
502	0602.9010	---蘑菇菌丝	0		0 受惠国LD	0	---Mushroom spawn
		---其他：					---Other:
503	0602.9091	----种用苗木	0		0 受惠国LD	0	----Seedlings
504	0602.9092	----兰花	10	0 冰岛IS,东盟AS,哥CR,新西兰NZ,智利CL 3 秘鲁PE 4 瑞士CH 5 巴PK 6 澳AU 8 韩国KR	0 受惠国LD	80	----Orchid
505	0602.9093	----菊花	10	0 冰岛IS,东盟AS,哥CR,新西兰NZ,智利CL 3 秘鲁PE 4 瑞士CH 5 巴PK 6 澳AU 8 韩国KR	0 受惠国LD	80	----Chrysathemum
506	0602.9094	----百合	10	0 冰岛IS,东盟AS,哥CR,新西兰NZ,智利CL 3 秘鲁PE 4 瑞士CH 5 巴PK 6 澳AU 8 韩国KR	0 受惠国LD	80	----Lily

序号 No.	税则号列 Tariff Line	中文货品名称 Article Description in Chinese	最惠国税率 MFN(%)	协定税率 Agreement(%)	特惠税率 SP(%)	普通税率 Gen(%)	英文货品名称 Article Description
507	0602.9095	----康乃馨	10	0 冰岛IS,东盟AS,哥CR,新西兰NZ,智利CL 3 秘鲁PE 4 瑞士CH 5 巴PK 6 澳AU 8 韩国KR	0 受惠国LD	80	----Carnation
508	0602.9099	----其他	10	0 冰岛IS,东盟AS,哥CR,新西兰NZ,智利CL 3 秘鲁PE 4 瑞士CH 5 巴PK,亚太AP 6 澳AU 8 韩国KR	0 受惠国LD	80	----Other
	06.03	**制花束或装饰用的插花及花蕾，鲜、干、染色、漂白、浸渍或用其他方法处理的：**					**Cut flowers and flower buds of a kind suitable for bouquets or for ornamental purposes, fresh, dried, dyed, bleached, impregnated or otherwise prepared:**
		-鲜的：					-Fresh:
509	0603.1100	--玫瑰	10	0 冰岛IS,东盟AS,哥CR,秘鲁PE,新西兰NZ,智利CL 4 瑞士CH 5 巴PK,亚太AP 6 澳AU 8 韩国KR	0 老挝LA,受惠国LD	100	--Roses
510	0603.1200	--康乃馨	10	0 冰岛IS,东盟AS,哥CR,秘鲁PE,新西兰NZ,智利CL 4 瑞士CH 5 巴PK,亚太AP 6 澳AU 8 韩国KR	0 老挝LA,受惠国LD	100	--Carnations
511	0603.1300	--兰花	10	0 冰岛IS,东盟AS,哥CR,秘鲁PE,台湾TW,新西兰NZ,智利CL 4 瑞士CH 5 巴PK,亚太AP 6 澳AU 8 韩国KR	0 老挝LA,受惠国LD	100	--Orchids
512	0603.1400	--菊花	10	0 冰岛IS,东盟AS,哥CR,秘鲁PE,新西兰NZ,智利CL 4 瑞士CH 5 巴PK,亚太AP 6 澳AU 8 韩国KR	0 老挝LA,受惠国LD	100	--Chrysanthemums
513	0603.1500	--百合花（百合属）	10	0 冰岛IS,东盟AS,哥CR,秘鲁PE,新西兰NZ,智利CL 4 瑞士CH 5 巴PK,亚太AP 6 澳AU 8 韩国KR	0 老挝LA,受惠国LD	100	--Lilies (Lilium spp.)
514	0603.1900	--其他	10	0 冰岛IS,东盟AS,哥CR,秘鲁PE,新西兰NZ,智利CL 4 瑞士CH 5 巴PK,亚太AP 6 澳AU 8 韩国KR	0 老挝LA,受惠国LD	100	--Other

序号 No.	税则号列 Tariff Line	中文货品名称 Article Description in Chinese	最惠国税率 MFN(%)	协定税率 Agreement(%)	特惠税率 SP(%)	普通税率 Gen(%)	英文货品名称 Article Description
515	0603.9000	-其他	23	0 冰岛IS,东盟AS,哥CR,香港HK,新西兰NZ,智利CL 6.9 秘鲁PE 11.5 巴PK,亚太AP 13.8 澳AU 16.1 瑞士CH 20.7 韩国KR	0 老挝LA,受惠国LD	100	-Other
	06.04	**制花束或装饰用的不带花及花蕾的植物枝、叶或其他部分、草、苔藓及地衣，鲜、干、染色、漂白、浸渍或用其他方法处理的：**					**Foliage, branches and other parts of plants, without flowers or flower buds, and grasses, mosses and lichens, being goods of a kind suitable for bouquets or for ornamental purposes, fresh, dried, dyed, bleached, impregnated or otherwise prepared:**
		-鲜的：					-Fresh:
516	0604.2010	---苔藓及地衣	23	0 冰岛IS,东盟AS,哥CR,新西兰NZ,智利CL 6.9 秘鲁PE 13.8 澳AU 16.1 瑞士CH 18.4 韩国KR	0 受惠国$_1$LD$_1$	100	---Mosses and lichens
517	0604.2090	---其他	10	0 冰岛IS,东盟AS,哥CR,新西兰NZ,智利CL 3 秘鲁PE 4 瑞士CH 5 巴PK 6 澳AU 8 韩国KR	0 受惠国LD	100	---Other
		-其他：					-Other:
518	0604.9010	---苔藓及地衣	23	0 冰岛IS,东盟AS,哥CR,新西兰NZ,智利CL 6.9 秘鲁PE 13.8 澳AU 16.1 瑞士CH 18.4 韩国KR	0 受惠国$_1$LD$_1$	100	---Mosses and lichens
519	0604.9090	---其他	10	0 冰岛IS,东盟AS,哥CR,秘鲁PE,香港HK,新西兰NZ,智利CL 4 瑞士CH 5 巴PK 6 澳AU 8 韩国KR	0 受惠国LD	100	---Other

第七章

食用蔬菜、根及块茎

注释:

一、本章不包括税号 12.14 的草料。

二、税号 07.09、07.10、07.11 及 07.12 所称"蔬菜",包括食用的蘑菇、块菌、油橄榄、刺山柑、菜葫芦、南瓜、茄子、甜玉米、辣椒、茴香菜、欧芹、细叶芹、龙蒿、水芹、甜茉乔栾那。

三、税号 07.12 包括干制的归入税号 07.01 至 07.11 的各种蔬菜,但下列各项除外:

(一)作蔬菜用的脱荚干豆(税号 07.13);

(二)税号 11.02 至 11.04 所列形状的甜玉米;

(三)马铃薯细粉、粗粉、粉末、粉片、颗粒及团粒(税号 11.05);

(四)用税号 07.13 的干豆制成的细粉、粗粉及粉末(税号 11.06)。

四、本章不包括辣椒干及辣椒粉(税号 09.04)。

Chapter 7

Edible vegetables and certain roots and tubers

Notes:

1.This Chapter does not cover forage products of heading No.12.14.

2. In headings No.07.09,07.10,07.11 and 07.12 the word "vegetables" includes edible mushrooms, truffles, olives, capers, marrows, pumpkins, aubergines, sweet corn (*Zea may svar.saccharata*), fruits of the genus *Capsicum* or of the genus *Pimenta*, fennel, parsley, chervil, tarragon, cress and sweet marjoram (*Majorana hortensis or Origanum majorana*).

3. Heading No.07.12 covers all dried vegetables of the kinds falling in headings No.07.01 to 07.11, other than:

(a) dried leguminous vegetables, shelled (heading No.07.13);

(b) sweet corn in the forms specified in headings No.11.02 to 11.04;

(c) flour, meal, powder, flakes, granules and pellets of potatoes (heading No.11.05);

(d) flour, meal and powder of the dried leguminous vegetables of heading No.07.13 (heading No.11.06).

4. However, dried or crushed or ground fruits of the genus *Capsicum* or of the genus *Pimenta* are excluded from this *Chapter* (heading No.09.04).

序号 No.	税则号列 Tariff Line	中文货品名称 Article Description in Chinese	最惠国税率 MFN(%)	协定税率 Agreement(%)	特惠税率 SP(%)	普通税率 Gen(%)	英文货品名称 Article Description
	07.01	**鲜或冷藏的马铃薯:**					**Potatoes, fresh or chilled:**
520	0701.1000	-种用	13	0 东盟AS,哥CR,秘鲁PE,新西兰NZ,智利CL 6.5 巴PK 7.8 澳AU 9.1 瑞士CH 10.4 韩国KR	0 受惠国LD	70	-Seeds
521	0701.9000	-其他	13	0 冰岛IS,东盟AS,哥CR,秘鲁PE,新西兰NZ,智利CL 5 巴PK 7.8 澳AU 9 亚太AP 9.1 瑞士CH 10.4 韩国KR	0 柬埔寨KH,受惠国LD	70	-Other
	07.02	**鲜或冷藏的番茄**					**Tomatoes, fresh or chilled**
522	0702.0000	鲜或冷藏的番茄	13	0 冰岛IS,东盟AS,哥CR,秘鲁PE,新西兰NZ,智利CL 6.5 巴PK 7.8 澳AU 9.1 瑞士CH 10.4 韩国KR	0 受惠国LD	70	Tomatoes, fresh or chilled
	07.03	**鲜或冷藏的洋葱、青葱、大蒜、韭葱及其他葱属蔬菜:**					**Onions, shallots, garlic, leeks and other alliaceous vegetables, fresh or chilled:**
		-洋葱及青葱:					-Onions and shallots:
523	0703.1010	---洋葱	13	0 冰岛IS,东盟AS,哥CR,秘鲁PE,新西兰NZ,智利CL 5 巴PK 6.5 亚太AP 7.8 澳AU 9.1 瑞士CH 10.4 韩国KR	0 柬埔寨KH,缅甸MM,受惠国LD	70	---Onions

序号 No.	税则号列 Tariff Line	中文货品名称 Article Description in Chinese	最惠国税率 MFN(%)	协定税率 Agreement(%)	特惠税率 SP(%)	普通税率 Gen(%)	英文货品名称 Article Description
524	0703.1020	---青葱	13	0 冰岛IS,东盟AS,哥CR,秘鲁PE,新西兰NZ,智利CL 5 巴PK 6.5 亚太AP 7.8 澳AU 9.1 瑞士CH 10.4 韩国KR	0 柬埔寨KH,缅甸MM,受惠国LD	70	---Shallots
		-大蒜:					-Garlic:
525	0703.2010	---蒜头	13	0 巴PK,冰岛IS,东盟AS,哥CR,秘鲁PE,新西兰NZ,智利CL 6.5 亚太AP 7.8 澳AU 9.1 瑞士CH 10.4 韩国KR	0 受惠国$_1$LD$_1$	70	---Garlic bulbs
526	0703.2020	---蒜苔及蒜苗(青蒜)	13	0 巴PK,冰岛IS,东盟AS,哥CR,秘鲁PE,新西兰NZ,智利CL 6.5 亚太AP 7.8 澳AU 9.1 瑞士CH 10.4 韩国KR	0 受惠国$_1$LD$_1$	70	---Garlic stems, garlic seedlings
527	0703.2090	---其他	13	0 巴PK,冰岛IS,东盟AS,哥CR,秘鲁PE,新西兰NZ,智利CL 6.5 亚太AP 7.8 澳AU 9.1 瑞士CH 10.4 韩国KR	0 受惠国$_1$LD$_1$	70	---Other
		-韭葱及其他葱属蔬菜:					-Leeks and other alliaceous vegetables:
528	0703.9010	---韭葱	13	0 冰岛IS,东盟AS,哥CR,秘鲁PE,新西兰NZ,智利CL 6.5 巴PK 7.8 澳AU 9.1 瑞士CH 10.4 韩国KR	0 柬埔寨KH,受惠国LD	70	---Leeks
529	0703.9020	---大葱	13	0 冰岛IS,东盟AS,哥CR,秘鲁PE,新西兰NZ,智利CL 6.5 巴PK 7.8 澳AU 9.1 瑞士CH 10.4 韩国KR	0 柬埔寨KH,受惠国LD	70	---Scallion
530	0703.9090	---其他	13	0 冰岛IS,东盟AS,哥CR,秘鲁PE,新西兰NZ,智利CL 6.5 巴PK 7.8 澳AU 9.1 瑞士CH 10.4 韩国KR	0 柬埔寨KH,受惠国LD	70	---Other
	07.04	**鲜或冷藏的卷心菜、菜花、球茎甘蓝、羽衣甘蓝及类似的食用芥菜类蔬菜:**					**Cabbages, cauliflowers, kohlrabi, kale and similar edible brassicas, fresh or chilled:**
531	0704.1000	-菜花及硬花甘蓝	10	0 东盟AS,哥CR,秘鲁PE,新西兰NZ,智利CL 4 瑞士CH 5 巴PK 6 澳AU 8 韩国KR	0 受惠国LD	70	-Cauliflowers and headed broccoli

序号 No.	税则号列 Tariff Line	中文货品名称 Article Description in Chinese	最惠国税率 MFN(%)	协定税率 Agreement(%)	特惠税率 SP(%)	普通税率 Gen(%)	英文货品名称 Article Description
532	0704.2000	-抱子甘蓝	13	0 冰岛IS,东盟AS,哥CR,秘鲁PE,新西兰NZ,智利CL 6.5 巴PK 7.8 澳AU 9.1 瑞士CH 10.4 韩国KR	0 受惠国$_1$LD$_1$	70	-Brussels sprouts
		-其他:					-Other:
533	0704.9010	---卷心菜	13	0 冰岛IS,东盟AS,哥CR,秘鲁PE,新西兰NZ,智利CL 6.5 巴PK 7.8 澳AU 9.1 瑞士CH 10.4 韩国KR	0 老挝LA,受惠国LD	70	---Cabbage (Brassica oleracea var. capitata)
534	0704.9020	---西兰花	13	0 冰岛IS,东盟AS,哥CR,秘鲁PE,新西兰NZ,智利CL 6.5 巴PK 7.8 澳AU 9.1 瑞士CH 10.4 韩国KR	0 老挝LA,受惠国LD	70	---Cabbage (Brassica oleracea var. italica)
535	0704.9090	---其他	13	0 冰岛IS,东盟AS,哥CR,秘鲁PE,新西兰NZ,智利CL 6.5 巴PK 7.8 澳AU 9.1 瑞士CH 10.4 韩国KR	0 老挝LA,受惠国LD	70	---Other
	07.05	**鲜或冷藏的莴苣及菊苣:**					**Lettuce (*Lactuca sativa*) and chicory (*Cichorium spp.*) , fresh or chilled:**
		-莴苣:					-Lettuce:
536	0705.1100	--结球莴苣（包心生菜）	10	0 巴PK,冰岛IS,东盟AS,哥CR,秘鲁PE,新西兰NZ,智利CL 4 瑞士CH 6 澳AU 8 韩国KR	0 受惠国LD	70	--Cabbage lettuce (head lettuce)
537	0705.1900	--其他	10	0 巴PK,冰岛IS,东盟AS,哥CR,秘鲁PE,新西兰NZ,智利CL 4 瑞士CH 6 澳AU 8 韩国KR	0 受惠国LD	70	--Other
		-菊苣:					-Chicory:
538	0705.2100	--维特罗夫菊苣	13	0 巴PK,冰岛IS,东盟AS,哥CR,秘鲁PE,新西兰NZ,智利CL 7.8 澳AU 9.1 瑞士CH 10.4 韩国KR	0 受惠国$_1$LD$_1$	70	--Witloof chicory (*Cichoriym intybus var. foliosum*)
539	0705.2900	--其他	13	0 巴PK,冰岛IS,东盟AS,哥CR,秘鲁PE,新西兰NZ,智利CL 7.8 澳AU 9.1 瑞士CH 10.4 韩国KR	0 受惠国$_1$LD$_1$	70	--Other
	07.06	**鲜或冷藏的胡萝卜、萝卜、色拉甜菜根、婆罗门参、块根芹、小萝卜及类似的食用根茎:**					**Carrots, turnips, salad beetroot, salsify, celeriac, radishes and similar edible roots, fresh or chilled:**

序号 No.	税则号列 Tariff Line	中文货品名称 Article Description in Chinese	最惠国税率 MFN(%)	协定税率 Agreement(%)	特惠税率 SP(%)	普通税率 Gen(%)	英文货品名称 Article Description
540	0706.1000	-胡萝卜及萝卜	13	0 东盟AS,哥CR,秘鲁PE,新西兰NZ,智利CL 6.5 巴PK 7.8 澳AU 9.1 瑞士CH 10.4 韩国KR	0 受惠国$_1$LD$_1$	70	-Carrots and turnips
541	0706.9000	-其他	13	0 冰岛IS,东盟AS,哥CR,秘鲁PE,新西兰NZ,智利CL 6.5 巴PK 7.8 澳AU 9.1 瑞士CH 10.4 韩国KR	0 受惠国$_1$LD$_1$	70	-Other
	07.07	**鲜或冷藏的黄瓜及小黄瓜**					**Cucumbers and gherkins, fresh or chilled**
542	0707.0000	鲜或冷藏的黄瓜及小黄瓜	13	0 冰岛IS,东盟AS,哥CR,秘鲁PE,新西兰NZ,智利CL 5 巴PK 6.5 亚太AP 7.8 澳AU 9.1 瑞士CH 10.4 韩国KR	0 柬埔寨KH,受惠国LD	70	Cucumbers and gherkins, fresh or chilled
	07.08	**鲜或冷藏的豆类蔬菜，不论是否脱荚：**					**Leguminous vegetables, shelled or unshelled, fresh or chilled:**
543	0708.1000	-豌豆	13	0 巴PK,冰岛IS,东盟AS,哥CR,秘鲁PE,新西兰NZ,智利CL 6.5 亚太AP 7.8 澳AU 9.1 瑞士CH 10.4 韩国KR	0 柬埔寨KH,受惠国LD	70	-Peas (*Pisum sativum*)
544	0708.2000	-豇豆及菜豆	13	0 巴PK,冰岛IS,东盟AS,哥CR,秘鲁PE,新西兰NZ,智利CL 6.5 亚太AP 7.8 澳AU 9.1 瑞士CH 10.4 韩国KR	0 柬埔寨KH,老挝LA,受惠国LD	70	-Beans (*Vigna spp., Phaseolus spp.*)
545	0708.9000	-其他豆类蔬菜	13	0 巴PK,冰岛IS,东盟AS,哥CR,秘鲁PE,新西兰NZ,智利CL 6.5 亚太AP 7.8 澳AU 9.1 瑞士CH 10.4 韩国KR	0 柬埔寨KH,受惠国LD	70	-Other leguminous vegetables
	07.09	**鲜或冷藏的其他蔬菜：**					**Other vegetables, fresh or chilled:**
546	0709.2000	-芦笋	13	0 巴PK,冰岛IS,东盟AS,哥CR,秘鲁PE,新西兰NZ,智利CL 6.5 亚太AP 7.8 澳AU 9.1 瑞士CH 10.4 韩国KR	0 受惠国LD	70	-Asparagus
547	0709.3000	-茄子	13	0 巴PK,冰岛IS,东盟AS,哥CR,秘鲁PE,新西兰NZ,智利CL 6.5 亚太AP 7.8 澳AU 9.1 瑞士CH 10.4 韩国KR	0 受惠国LD	70	-Aubergines (egg-plants)

序号 No.	税则号列 Tariff Line	中文货品名称 Article Description in Chinese	最惠国税率 MFN(%)	协定税率 Agreement(%)	特惠税率 SP(%)	普通税率 Gen(%)	英文货品名称 Article Description
548	0709.4000	-芹菜，但块根芹除外	10	0 巴PK,冰岛IS,东盟AS,哥CR,秘鲁PE,新西兰NZ,智利CL 4 瑞士CH 6 澳AU 8 韩国KR	0 受惠国LD	70	-Celery other than celeriac
		-蘑菇及块菌：					-Mushrooms and truffles:
549	0709.5100	--伞菌属蘑菇	13	0 巴PK,冰岛IS,东盟AS,哥CR,秘鲁PE,香港HK,新西兰NZ,智利CL 7.8 澳AU 9.1 瑞士CH 10.4 韩国KR	0 柬埔寨KH,受惠国LD	90	--Mushrooms of the genus Agaricus
		--其他：					--Other:
550	0709.5910	---松茸	13	0 巴PK,冰岛IS,东盟AS,哥CR,秘鲁PE,新西兰NZ,智利CL 7.8 澳AU 9.1 瑞士CH 10.4 韩国KR	0 柬埔寨KH,受惠国LD	90	---Sungmo
551	0709.5920	---香菇	13	0 巴PK,冰岛IS,东盟AS,哥CR,秘鲁PE,新西兰NZ,智利CL 7.8 澳AU 9.1 瑞士CH 10.4 韩国KR	0 柬埔寨KH,受惠国LD	90	---Shiitake
552	0709.5930	---金针菇	13	0 巴PK,冰岛IS,东盟AS,哥CR,秘鲁PE,台湾TW,新西兰NZ,智利CL 7.8 澳AU 9.1 瑞士CH 10.4 韩国KR	0 柬埔寨KH,受惠国LD	90	---Winter mushroom
553	0709.5940	---草菇	13	0 巴PK,冰岛IS,东盟AS,哥CR,秘鲁PE,新西兰NZ,智利CL 7.8 澳AU 9.1 瑞士CH 10.4 韩国KR	0 柬埔寨KH,受惠国LD	90	---Paddy Straw mushroom
554	0709.5950	---口蘑	13	0 巴PK,冰岛IS,东盟AS,哥CR,秘鲁PE,新西兰NZ,智利CL 7.8 澳AU 9.1 瑞士CH 10.4 韩国KR	0 柬埔寨KH,受惠国LD	90	---Tricholoma mongolicum Imai
555	0709.5960	---块菌	13	0 巴PK,冰岛IS,东盟AS,哥CR,秘鲁PE,新西兰NZ,智利CL 7.8 澳AU 9.1 瑞士CH 10.4 韩国KR	0 受惠国$_1$LD$_1$	90	---Truffle
556	0709.5990	---其他	13	0 巴PK,冰岛IS,东盟AS,哥CR,秘鲁PE,新西兰NZ,智利CL 7.8 澳AU 9.1 瑞士CH 10.4 韩国KR	0 柬埔寨KH,受惠国LD	90	---Other
557	0709.6000	-辣椒，包括甜椒	13	0 巴PK,冰岛IS,东盟AS,哥CR,秘鲁PE,新西兰NZ,智利CL 6.5 亚太AP 7.8 澳AU 9.1 瑞士CH 10.4 韩国KR	0 柬埔寨KH,受惠国LD	70	-Fruits of the genus *Capsicum* or of the genus *Pimenta*

序号 No.	税则号列 Tariff Line	中文货品名称 Article Description in Chinese	最惠国税率 MFN(%)	协定税率 Agreement(%)	特惠税率 SP(%)	普通税率 Gen(%)	英文货品名称 Article Description
558	0709.7000	-菠菜	13	0 巴PK,冰岛IS,东盟AS,哥CR,秘鲁PE,香港HK,新西兰NZ,智利CL 7.8 澳AU 9.1 瑞士CH 10.4 韩国KR	0 受惠国LD	70	-Spinach, New Zealand spinach and orache spinach (garden spinach)
		-其他:					-Other:
559	0709.9100	--洋蓟	13	0 巴PK,冰岛IS,东盟AS,哥CR,秘鲁PE,香港HK,新西兰NZ,智利CL 7.8 澳AU 9.1 瑞士CH 10.4 韩国KR	0 柬埔寨KH,受惠国LD	70	--Globe artichokes
560	0709.9200	--油橄榄	13	0 巴PK,冰岛IS,东盟AS,哥CR,秘鲁PE,香港HK,新西兰NZ,智利CL 7.8 澳AU 9.1 瑞士CH 10.4 韩国KR	0 柬埔寨KH,受惠国LD	70	--Olives
561	0709.9300	--南瓜、笋瓜及瓠瓜（南瓜属）	13	0 巴PK,冰岛IS,东盟AS,哥CR,秘鲁PE,香港HK,新西兰NZ,智利CL 7.8 澳AU 9.1 瑞士CH 10.4 韩国KR	0 柬埔寨KH,受惠国LD	70	--Pumpkins, squash and gourds (Cucurbita spp.)
		--其他:					--Other:
562	0709.9910	---竹笋	13	0 巴PK,冰岛IS,东盟AS,哥CR,秘鲁PE,新西兰NZ,智利CL 7.8 澳AU 9.1 瑞士CH 10.4 韩国KR	0 柬埔寨KH,老挝LA,受惠国LD	70	---Bamboo shoots
563	0709.9990	---其他	13	0 巴PK,冰岛IS,东盟AS,哥CR,秘鲁PE,香港HK,新西兰NZ,智利CL 7.8 澳AU 9.1 瑞士CH 10.4 韩国KR	0 柬埔寨KH,受惠国LD	70	---Other
	07.10	**冷冻蔬菜（不论是否蒸煮）:**					**Vegetables (uncooked or cooked by steaming or boiling in water), frozen:**
564	0710.1000	-马铃薯	13	0 东盟AS,哥CR,秘鲁PE,新西兰NZ,智利CL 6.5 巴PK 7.8 澳AU 9.1 瑞士CH 10.4 韩国KR	0 受惠国$_1$LD$_1$	70	-Potatoes
		-豆类蔬菜，不论是否脱荚:					-Leguminous vegetables, shelled or unshelled:
565	0710.2100	--豌豆	13	0 冰岛IS,东盟AS,哥CR,秘鲁PE,新西兰NZ,智利CL 6.5 巴PK 7.8 澳AU 9.1 瑞士CH 10.4 韩国KR	0 受惠国$_1$LD$_1$	70	--Peas (*Pisum sativum*)
		--豇豆及菜豆:					--Beans (*Vigna* spp., *Phaseolus* spp.):
566	0710.2210	---红小豆（赤豆）	13	0 冰岛IS,东盟AS,哥CR,秘鲁PE,新西兰NZ,智利CL 6.5 巴PK 7.8 澳AU 9.1 瑞士CH 10.4 韩国KR	0 柬埔寨KH,受惠国LD	70	---Adzuki beans

序号 No.	税则号列 Tariff Line	中文货品名称 Article Description in Chinese	最惠国税率 MFN(%)	协定税率 Agreement(%)	特惠税率 SP(%)	普通税率 Gen(%)	英文货品名称 Article Description
567	0710.2290	---其他	13	0 冰岛IS,东盟AS,哥CR,秘鲁PE,新西兰NZ,智利CL 6.5 巴PK 7.8 澳AU 9.1 瑞士CH 10.4 韩国KR	0 柬埔寨KH,受惠国LD	70	---Other
568	0710.2900	--其他	13	0 冰岛IS,东盟AS,哥CR,秘鲁PE,新西兰NZ,智利CL 6.5 巴PK 7.8 澳AU 9.1 瑞士CH 10.4 韩国KR	0 柬埔寨KH,受惠国LD	70	--Other
569	0710.3000	-菠菜	13	0 冰岛IS,东盟AS,哥CR,秘鲁PE,新西兰NZ,智利CL 6.5 巴PK 7.8 澳AU 9.1 瑞士CH 10.4 韩国KR	0 受惠国$_1$LD$_1$	70	-Spinach, New Zealand spinach and orache spinach (garden spinach)
570	0710.4000	-甜玉米	10	0 冰岛IS,东盟AS,哥CR,秘鲁PE,新西兰NZ,智利CL 4 瑞士CH 5 巴PK 6 澳AU 8 韩国KR	0 受惠国LD	70	-Sweet corn
		-其他蔬菜:					-Other vegetables:
571	0710.8010	---松茸	13	0 冰岛IS,东盟AS,哥CR,秘鲁PE,新西兰NZ,智利CL 6.5 巴PK 7.8 澳AU 9.1 瑞士CH 10.4 韩国KR	0 柬埔寨KH,受惠国LD	70	---Sungmo
572	0710.8020	---蒜苔及蒜苗（青蒜）	13	0 冰岛IS,东盟AS,哥CR,秘鲁PE,新西兰NZ,智利CL 6.5 巴PK 7.8 澳AU 9.1 瑞士CH 10.4 韩国KR	0 柬埔寨KH,受惠国LD	70	---Garlic stems, garlic seedlings
573	0710.8030	---蒜头	13	0 冰岛IS,东盟AS,哥CR,秘鲁PE,新西兰NZ,智利CL 6.5 巴PK 7.8 澳AU 9.1 瑞士CH 10.4 韩国KR	0 柬埔寨KH,受惠国LD	70	---Garlic bulbs
574	0710.8040	---牛肝菌	13	0 冰岛IS,东盟AS,哥CR,秘鲁PE,新西兰NZ,智利CL 6.5 巴PK 7.8 澳AU 9.1 瑞士CH 10.4 韩国KR	0 柬埔寨KH,受惠国LD	70	---Boletus (Porcini)
575	0710.8090	---其他	13	0 冰岛IS,东盟AS,哥CR,秘鲁PE,新西兰NZ,智利CL 6.5 巴PK 7.8 澳AU 9.1 瑞士CH 10.4 韩国KR	0 柬埔寨KH,受惠国LD	70	---Other

序号 No.	税则号列 Tariff Line	中文货品名称 Article Description in Chinese	最惠国税率 MFN(%)	协定税率 Agreement(%)	特惠税率 SP(%)	普通税率 Gen(%)	英文货品名称 Article Description
576	0710.9000	-什锦蔬菜	10	0 冰岛IS,东盟AS,哥CR,秘鲁PE,新西兰NZ,智利CL 4 瑞士CH 5 巴PK 6 澳AU 8 韩国KR	0 柬埔寨KH,受惠国LD	70	-Mixtures of vegetables
	07.11	**暂时保藏（例如，使用二氧化硫气体、盐水、亚硫酸水或其他防腐液）的蔬菜，但不适于直接食用的：**					**Vegetables provisionally preserved (for example, by sulphur dioxide gas, in brine, in sulphur water or in other preservative solutions) , but unsuitable in that state for immediate consumption:**
577	0711.2000	-油橄榄	13	0 巴PK,冰岛IS,东盟AS,哥CR,秘鲁PE,新西兰NZ,智利CL 7.8 澳AU 9.1 瑞士CH 10.4 韩国KR	0 受惠国$_1$LD$_1$	70	-Olives
578	0711.4000	-黄瓜及小黄瓜	13	0 巴PK,冰岛IS,东盟AS,哥CR,秘鲁PE,新西兰NZ,智利CL 7.8 澳AU 9.1 瑞士CH 10.4 韩国KR	0 受惠国$_1$LD$_1$	70	-Cucumbers and gherkins
		-蘑菇及块菌：					-Mushrooms and truffles:
		--伞菌属蘑菇：					--Mushrooms of the genus *Agaricus*:
		---盐水的：					---In brine:
579	0711.5112	----白蘑菇	13	0 巴PK,冰岛IS,东盟AS,哥CR,秘鲁PE,新西兰NZ,智利CL 7.8 澳AU 9.1 瑞士CH 10.4 韩国KR	0 受惠国$_1$LD$_1$	90	----White mushroom
580	0711.5119	----其他	13	0 巴PK,冰岛IS,东盟AS,哥CR,秘鲁PE,新西兰NZ,智利CL 7.8 澳AU 9.1 瑞士CH 10.4 韩国KR	0 受惠国$_1$LD$_1$	90	----Other
581	0711.5190	---其他	13	0 巴PK,冰岛IS,东盟AS,哥CR,秘鲁PE,新西兰NZ,智利CL 7.8 澳AU 9.1 瑞士CH 10.4 韩国KR	0 受惠国$_1$LD$_1$	90	---Other
		--其他：					--Other:
		---盐水的：					---In brine:
582	0711.5911	----松茸	13	0 巴PK,冰岛IS,东盟AS,哥CR,秘鲁PE,新西兰NZ,智利CL 7.8 澳AU 9.1 瑞士CH 10.4 韩国KR	0 受惠国$_1$LD$_1$	90	----Sungmo
583	0711.5919	----其他	13	0 巴PK,冰岛IS,东盟AS,哥CR,秘鲁PE,新西兰NZ,智利CL 7.8 澳AU 9.1 瑞士CH 10.4 韩国KR	0 受惠国$_1$LD$_1$	90	----Other

序号 No.	税则号列 Tariff Line	中文货品名称 Article Description in Chinese	最惠国税率 MFN(%)	协定税率 Agreement(%)	特惠税率 SP(%)	普通税率 Gen(%)	英文货品名称 Article Description
584	0711.5990	---其他	13	0 巴PK,冰岛IS,东盟AS,哥CR,秘鲁PE,新西兰NZ,智利CL 7.8 澳AU 9.1 瑞士CH 10.4 韩国KR	0 受惠国$_1$$LD_1$	90	---Other
		-其他蔬菜；什锦蔬菜：					-Other vegetables; mixtures of vegetables:
		---盐水的：					---In brine:
585	0711.9031	----竹笋	13	0 巴PK,冰岛IS,东盟AS,哥CR,秘鲁PE,新西兰NZ,智利CL 6.5 亚太AP 7.8 澳AU 9.1 瑞士CH 10.4 韩国KR	0 受惠国$_1$$LD_1$	70	----Bamboo shoots
586	0711.9034	----大蒜	13	0 巴PK,冰岛IS,东盟AS,哥CR,秘鲁PE,新西兰NZ,智利CL 6.5 亚太AP 7.8 澳AU 9.1 瑞士CH 10.4 韩国KR	0 受惠国$_1$$LD_1$	70	----Garlic
587	0711.9039	----其他	13	0 巴PK,冰岛IS,东盟AS,哥CR,秘鲁PE,新西兰NZ,智利CL 6.5 亚太AP 7.8 澳AU 9.1 瑞士CH 10.4 韩国KR	0 受惠国$_1$$LD_1$	70	----Other
588	0711.9090	---其他	13	0 巴PK,冰岛IS,东盟AS,哥CR,秘鲁PE,新西兰NZ,智利CL 6.5 亚太AP 7.8 澳AU 9.1 瑞士CH 10.4 韩国KR	0 受惠国$_1$$LD_1$	90	---Other
	07.12	**干蔬菜，整个、切块、切片、破碎或制成粉状，但未经进一步加工的：**					**Dried vegetables, whole, cut, sliced, broken or in powder, but not further prepared:**
589	0712.2000	-洋葱	13	0 冰岛IS,东盟AS,哥CR,秘鲁PE,新西兰NZ,智利CL 6.5 巴PK 7.8 澳AU 9.1 瑞士CH 10.4 韩国KR	0 受惠国LD	80	-Onions
		-蘑菇、木耳、银耳及块菌：					-Mushrooms, wood ears (*Auricularia* spp.) , jelly fungi (*Tremella* spp.) and truffles:
590	0712.3100	--伞菌属蘑菇	13	0 冰岛IS,东盟AS,哥CR,秘鲁PE,新西兰NZ,智利CL 5 巴PK 7.8 澳AU 9 亚太AP 9.1 瑞士CH 10.4 韩国KR	0 受惠国LD	80	--Mushrooms of the genus Agaricus
591	0712.3200	--木耳	13	0 冰岛IS,东盟AS,哥CR,秘鲁PE,新西兰NZ,智利CL 6.5 巴PK 7.8 澳AU 9.1 瑞士CH 10.4 韩国KR	0 受惠国$_1$$LD_1$	100	--Wood ears (*Auricularia spp.*)

序号 No.	税则号列 Tariff Line	中文货品名称 Article Description in Chinese	最惠国税率 MFN(%)	协定税率 Agreement(%)	特惠税率 SP(%)	普通税率 Gen(%)	英文货品名称 Article Description
592	0712.3300	--银耳	13	0 冰岛IS,东盟AS,哥CR,秘鲁PE,新西兰NZ,智利CL 6.5 巴PK 7.8 澳AU 9.1 瑞士CH 10.4 韩国KR	0 受惠国$_1$LD$_1$	90	--Jelly fungi (*Tremella spp.*)
		--其他:					--Other:
593	0712.3910	---香菇	13	0 冰岛IS,东盟AS,哥CR,秘鲁PE,新西兰NZ,智利CL 5 巴PK 7.8 澳AU 9 亚太AP 9.1 瑞士CH 10.4 韩国KR	0 受惠国$_1$LD$_1$	100	---Shiitake
594	0712.3920	---金针菇	13	0 冰岛IS,东盟AS,哥CR,秘鲁PE,新西兰NZ,智利CL 5 巴PK 7.8 澳AU 9 亚太AP 9.1 瑞士CH 10.4 韩国KR	0 受惠国$_1$LD$_1$	100	---Winter mushroom
595	0712.3930	---草菇	13	0 冰岛IS,东盟AS,哥CR,秘鲁PE,新西兰NZ,智利CL 5 巴PK 7.8 澳AU 9 亚太AP 9.1 瑞士CH 10.4 韩国KR	0 受惠国$_1$LD$_1$	100	---Paddy straw mushroom
596	0712.3940	---口蘑	13	0 冰岛IS,东盟AS,哥CR,秘鲁PE,新西兰NZ,智利CL 5 巴PK 7.8 澳AU 9 亚太AP 9.1 瑞士CH 10.4 韩国KR	0 受惠国$_1$LD$_1$	100	---Tricholoma mongolicum Imai
597	0712.3950	---牛肝菌	13	0 冰岛IS,东盟AS,哥CR,秘鲁PE,新西兰NZ,智利CL 5 巴PK 7.8 澳AU 9 亚太AP 9.1 瑞士CH 10.4 韩国KR	0 受惠国$_1$LD$_1$	100	---Boletus; Porcini
598	0712.3990	---其他	13	0 冰岛IS,东盟AS,哥CR,秘鲁PE,新西兰NZ,智利CL 7.8 澳AU 9 巴PK,亚太AP 9.1 瑞士CH 10.4 韩国KR	0 受惠国$_1$LD$_1$	100	---Other
		-其他蔬菜；什锦蔬菜:					-Other vegetables; mixtures of vegetables:
599	0712.9010	---笋干丝	13	0 冰岛IS,东盟AS,哥CR,秘鲁PE,新西兰NZ,智利CL 6.5 巴PK 7.8 澳AU 9.1 瑞士CH 10.4 韩国KR	0 受惠国LD	80	---Bamboo shoots

序号 No.	税则号列 Tariff Line	中文货品名称 Article Description in Chinese	最惠国税率 MFN(%)	协定税率 Agreement(%)	特惠税率 SP(%)	普通税率 Gen(%)	英文货品名称 Article Description
600	0712.9020	---紫萁（薇菜干）	13	0 冰岛IS,东盟AS,哥CR,秘鲁PE,新西兰NZ,智利CL 6.5 巴PK 7.8 澳AU 9.1 瑞士CH 10.4 韩国KR	0 受惠国$_1$LD$_1$	80	---Osmund
601	0712.9030	---金针菜（黄花菜）	13	0 冰岛IS,东盟AS,哥CR,秘鲁PE,新西兰NZ,智利CL 6.5 巴PK 7.8 澳AU 9.1 瑞士CH 10.4 韩国KR	0 受惠国$_1$LD$_1$	80	---Day lily flowers
602	0712.9040	---蕨菜	13	0 冰岛IS,东盟AS,哥CR,秘鲁PE,新西兰NZ,智利CL 6.5 巴PK 7.8 澳AU 9.1 瑞士CH 10.4 韩国KR	0 受惠国$_1$LD$_1$	80	---Wild brake
603	0712.9050	---大蒜	13	0 冰岛IS,东盟AS,哥CR,秘鲁PE,新西兰NZ,智利CL 6.5 巴PK 7.8 澳AU 9.1 瑞士CH 10.4 韩国KR	0 受惠国$_1$LD$_1$	80	---Garlic
		---其他：					---Other:
604	0712.9091	----辣根	13	0 冰岛IS,东盟AS,哥CR,秘鲁PE,新西兰NZ,智利CL 6.5 巴PK 7.8 澳AU 9.1 瑞士CH 10.4 韩国KR	0 受惠国LD	80	----Horseradish
605	0712.9099	----其他	13	0 冰岛IS,东盟AS,哥CR,秘鲁PE,新西兰NZ,智利CL 6.5 巴PK 7.8 澳AU 9.1 瑞士CH 10.4 韩国KR	0 受惠国LD	80	----Other
	07.13	**脱荚的干豆，不论是否去皮或分瓣：**					**Dried leguminous vegetables, shelled, whether or not skinned or split:**
		-豌豆：					-Peas (*Pisum sativum*) :
606	0713.1010	---种用	0		0 受惠国LD	0	---Seed
607	0713.1090	---其他	5	0 澳AU,巴PK,冰岛IS,东盟AS,哥CR,韩国KR,秘鲁PE,瑞士CH,新西兰NZ,智利CL	0 受惠国LD	20	---Other
		-鹰嘴豆：					-Chickpeas (garbanzos) :
608	0713.2010	---种用	0		0 受惠国LD	0	---Seed
609	0713.2090	---其他	7	0 冰岛IS,东盟AS,哥CR,韩国KR,秘鲁PE,新西兰NZ,智利CL 2.8 瑞士CH 4.2 澳AU 5 巴PK	0 受惠国LD	20	---Other
		-豇豆属及菜豆属：					-Beans (*Vigna* spp., *Phaseolus* spp.) :
		--绿豆：					--Beans of the species *Vigna mungo* (L.) Hepper or *Vigna radiata* (L.) Wilczek:
610	0713.3110	---种用	0		0 受惠国LD	0	---Seed

序号 No.	税则号列 Tariff Line	中文货品名称 Article Description in Chinese	最惠国税率 MFN(%)	协定税率 Agreement(%)		特惠税率 SP(%)		普通税率 Gen(%)	英文货品名称 Article Description
611	0713.3190	---其他	3	0 1.5	澳AU,巴PK,冰岛IS,东盟AS,哥CR,韩国KR,秘鲁PE,瑞士CH,新西兰NZ,智利CL 亚太AP	0	柬埔寨KH,缅甸MM,受惠国LD	11	---Other
		--红小豆（赤豆）:							--Small red (Adzuki) beans (*Phaseolus* or *Vigna angularis*) :
612	0713.3210	---种用	0			0	受惠国LD	0	---Seed
613	0713.3290	---其他	3	0	澳AU,巴PK,冰岛IS,东盟AS,哥CR,韩国KR,秘鲁PE,瑞士CH,新西兰NZ,智利CL	0	柬埔寨KH,受惠国LD	14	---Other
		--芸豆:							--Kidney beans, including white pea beans (*Phaseolus vulgaris*) :
614	0713.3310	---种用	0			0	受惠国LD	0	---Seed
615	0713.3390	---其他	7.5	0 3 4.5 5	冰岛IS,东盟AS,哥CR,韩国KR,秘鲁PE,新西兰NZ,智利CL 瑞士CH 澳AU 巴PK	0	柬埔寨KH,受惠国LD	20	---Other
616	0713.3400	--巴姆巴拉豆	7	0 2.8 3.5 4.2	巴PK,冰岛IS,东盟AS,哥CR,韩国KR,秘鲁PE,新西兰NZ,智利CL 瑞士CH 亚太AP 澳AU	0	柬埔寨KH,受惠国LD	20	--Bambara beans (*Vigna* subterranea or Voandzeia subterranea)
617	0713.3500	--牛豆(豇豆)	7	0 2.8 3.5 4.2	巴PK,冰岛IS,东盟AS,哥CR,韩国KR,秘鲁PE,新西兰NZ,智利CL 瑞士CH 亚太AP 澳AU	0	柬埔寨KH,受惠国LD	20	--Cow peas (*Vigna* unguiculata)
618	0713.3900	--其他	7	0 2.8 3.5 4.2	巴PK,冰岛IS,东盟AS,哥CR,韩国KR,秘鲁PE,新西兰NZ,智利CL 瑞士CH 亚太AP 澳AU	0	柬埔寨KH,受惠国LD	20	--Other
		-扁豆:							-Lentils:
619	0713.4010	---种用	0			0	受惠国LD	0	---Seed
620	0713.4090	---其他	7	0 2.8 4.2 5	冰岛IS,东盟AS,哥CR,韩国KR,秘鲁PE,新西兰NZ,智利CL 瑞士CH 澳AU 巴PK	0	受惠国LD	20	---Other
		-蚕豆:							-Broad beans (*Vicia faba* var. *major*) and horse beans (*Vicia faba* var. *equina*, *Vicia faba* var. *minor*) :
621	0713.5010	---种用	0			0	受惠国LD	0	---Seed
622	0713.5090	---其他	7	0 2.8 4.2 5	冰岛IS,东盟AS,哥CR,韩国KR,秘鲁PE,新西兰NZ,智利CL 瑞士CH 澳AU 巴PK	0	受惠国LD	20	---Other
		-木豆（木豆属）:							-Pigeon peas (*Cajanus cajan*) :
623	0713.6010	---种用	0			0	受惠国LD	0	---Seed
624	0713.6090	---其他	7	0 2.8 4.2 5	冰岛IS,东盟AS,哥CR,韩国KR,秘鲁PE,新西兰NZ,智利CL 瑞士CH 澳AU 巴PK	0	受惠国LD	20	---Other

序号 No.	税则号列 Tariff Line	中文货品名称 Article Description in Chinese	最惠国税率 MFN(%)	协定税率 Agreement(%)	特惠税率 SP(%)	普通税率 Gen(%)	英文货品名称 Article Description
		-其他:					-Other:
625	0713.9010	---种用干豆	0		0 受惠国LD	0	---Seed
626	0713.9090	---其他	7	0 冰岛IS,东盟AS,哥CR,韩国KR,秘鲁PE,新西兰NZ,智利CL 2.8 瑞士CH 4.2 澳AU 5 巴PK	0 受惠国LD	20	---Other
	07.14	**鲜、冷、冻或干的木薯、竹芋、兰科植物块茎、菊芋、甘薯及含有高淀粉或菊粉的类似根茎,不论是否切片或制成团粒;西谷茎髓:**					**Manioc, arrowroot, salep, Jerusalem artichokes, sweet potatoes and similar roots and tubers with high starch or inulin content, fresh, chilled, frozen or dried, whether or not sliced or in the form of pellets; sago pith:**
		-木薯:					-Manioc (cassava) :
627	0714.1010	---鲜的	10	0 冰岛IS,东盟AS,哥CR,秘鲁PE,新西兰NZ,智利CL 4 瑞士CH 5 巴PK 6 澳AU,韩国KR	0 柬埔寨KH,老挝LA,受惠国LD	30	---Fresh
628	0714.1020	---干的	5	0 澳AU,巴PK,冰岛IS,东盟AS,哥CR,韩国KR,秘鲁PE,瑞士CH,新西兰NZ,智利CL	0 柬埔寨KH,老挝LA,受惠国LD	30	---Dried
629	0714.1030	---冷或冻的	10	0 冰岛IS,东盟AS,哥CR,秘鲁PE,新西兰NZ,智利CL 4 瑞士CH 5 巴PK 6 澳AU 8 韩国KR	0 柬埔寨KH,老挝LA,受惠国LD	80	---Chilled or frozen
		-甘薯:					-Sweet potatoes:
		---鲜的:					---Fresh:
630	0714.2011	----种用	0		0 柬埔寨KH,老挝LA,受惠国LD	50	----For cultivation
631	0714.2019	----其他	13	0 冰岛IS,东盟AS,哥CR,秘鲁PE,新西兰NZ,智利CL 5 巴PK 6.5 亚太AP 7.8 澳AU 9.1 瑞士CH 10.4 韩国KR	0 柬埔寨KH,老挝LA,受惠国LD	50	----Other
632	0714.2020	---干的	13	0 冰岛IS,东盟AS,哥CR,秘鲁PE,新西兰NZ,智利CL 5 巴PK 6.5 亚太AP 7.8 澳AU 9.1 瑞士CH 10.4 韩国KR	0 柬埔寨KH,老挝LA,受惠国LD	50	---Dried
633	0714.2030	---冷或冻的	13	0 冰岛IS,东盟AS,哥CR,秘鲁PE,新西兰NZ,智利CL 5 巴PK 6.5 亚太AP 7.8 澳AU 9.1 瑞士CH 10.4 韩国KR	0 柬埔寨KH,老挝LA,受惠国LD	80	---Chilled or frozen

序号 No.	税则号列 Tariff Line	中文货品名称 Article Description in Chinese	最惠国税率 MFN(%)	协定税率 Agreement(%)	特惠税率 SP(%)	普通税率 Gen(%)	英文货品名称 Article Description
634	0714.3000	-山药	13	0 冰岛IS,东盟AS,哥CR,秘鲁PE,新西兰NZ,智利CL 5 巴PK 6.5 亚太AP 7.8 澳AU 9.1 瑞士CH 10.4 韩国KR	0 柬埔寨KH,老挝LA,受惠国LD	50	-Yams (Dioscorea spp.)
635	0714.4000	-芋头(芋属)	13	0 冰岛IS,东盟AS,哥CR,秘鲁PE,新西兰NZ,智利CL 5 巴PK 6.5 亚太AP 7.8 澳AU 9.1 瑞士CH 10.4 韩国KR	0 受惠国$_1$LD$_1$	50	-Taro (Colocasia spp.)
636	0714.5000	-箭叶黄体芋(黄肉芋属)	13	0 冰岛IS,东盟AS,哥CR,秘鲁PE,新西兰NZ,智利CL 5 巴PK 6.5 亚太AP 7.8 澳AU 9.1 瑞士CH 10.4 韩国KR	0 柬埔寨KH,老挝LA,受惠国LD	50	-Yautia (Xanthosoma spp.)
		-其他:					-Other:
637	0714.9010	---荸荠	13	0 冰岛IS,东盟AS,哥CR,秘鲁PE,新西兰NZ,智利CL 5 巴PK 6.5 亚太AP 7.8 澳AU 9.1 瑞士CH 10.4 韩国KR	0 柬埔寨KH,老挝LA,受惠国LD	50	---Water chestnut
		---藕:					---Lotus (Nelumbo nucifera) rootstock:
638	0714.9021	----种用	0		0 受惠国LD	0	----For cultivation
639	0714.9029	----其他	13	0 冰岛IS,东盟AS,哥CR,秘鲁PE,新西兰NZ,智利CL 5 巴PK 6.5 亚太AP 7.8 澳AU 9.1 瑞士CH 10.4 韩国KR	0 柬埔寨KH,老挝LA,受惠国LD	50	----Other
640	0714.9090	---其他	13	0 冰岛IS,东盟AS,哥CR,秘鲁PE,新西兰NZ,智利CL 5 巴PK 6.5 亚太AP 7.8 澳AU 9.1 瑞士CH 10.4 韩国KR	0 柬埔寨KH,老挝LA,受惠国LD	50	---Other

第八章
食用水果及坚果；
柑橘属水果或甜瓜的果皮

Chapter 8
Edible fruit and nuts;
peel of citrus fruit or melons

注释：

一、本章不包括非供食用的坚果或水果。

二、冷藏的水果和坚果应按相应的鲜果税号归类。

三、本章的干果可以部分复水或为下列目的进行其他处理：

（一） 为保藏或保持其稳定性（例如，经适度热处理或硫化处理、添加山梨酸或山梨酸钾）；

（二） 为改进或保持其外观（例如，添加植物油或少量葡萄糖浆）。

但必须保持干果的特征。

Notes:

1. This Chapter does not cover inedible nuts or fruits.
2. Chilled fruits and nuts are to be classified in the same headings as the corresponding fresh fruits and nuts.
3. Dried fruit or dried nuts of this Chapter may be partially rehydrated, or treated for the following purposes:
   (a) For additional preservation or stabilization (for example, by moderate heat treatment, sulphuring, the addition of sorbic acid or potassium sorbate):
   (b) To improve or maintain their appearance (for example, by the addition of vegetable oil or small quantities of glucose syrup).

Provided that they retain the character of dried fruit or dried nuts.

序号 No.	税则号列 Tariff Line	中文货品名称 Article Description in Chinese	最惠国税率 MFN(%)	协定税率 Agreement(%)	特惠税率 SP(%)	普通税率 Gen(%)	英文货品名称 Article Description
	08.01	**鲜或干的椰子、巴西果及腰果，不论是否去壳或去皮：**					**Coconuts, Brazil nuts and cashew nuts, fresh or dried, whether or not shelled or peeled:**
		-椰子：					-Coconuts:
641	0801.1100	--干的	12	0 澳门MO,冰岛IS,东盟AS,秘鲁PE,新西兰NZ,智利CL 5 巴PK 6 亚太AP 7.2 澳AU,哥CR,韩国KR 8.4 瑞士CH	0 柬埔寨KH,受惠国LD	80	--Desiccated
642	0801.1200	--未去内壳（内果皮）	12	0 冰岛IS,东盟AS,秘鲁PE,新西兰NZ,智利CL 5 巴PK 6 亚太AP 7.2 澳AU,哥CR,韩国KR 8.4 瑞士CH	0 柬埔寨KH,受惠国LD	80	--In the inner shell (endocarp)
		--其他：					--Other:
643	0801.1910	---种用	0		0 受惠国LD	0	---Seedlings
644	0801.1990	---其他	12	0 冰岛IS,东盟AS,秘鲁PE,新西兰NZ,智利CL 5 巴PK 6 亚太AP 7.2 澳AU,哥CR,韩国KR 8.4 瑞士CH	0 柬埔寨KH,受惠国LD	80	---Other
		-巴西果：					-Brazil nuts:
645	0801.2100	--未去壳	10	0 澳门MO,冰岛IS,东盟AS,秘鲁PE,新西兰NZ,智利CL 4 瑞士CH 5 巴PK 6 澳AU,哥CR,韩国KR	0 受惠国LD	80	--In shell
646	0801.2200	--去壳	10	0 澳门MO,冰岛IS,东盟AS,秘鲁PE,新西兰NZ,智利CL 4 瑞士CH 5 巴PK 6 澳AU,哥CR,韩国KR	0 受惠国LD	80	--Shelled
		-腰果：					-Cashew nuts:

序号 No.	税则号列 Tariff Line	中文货品名称 Article Description in Chinese	最惠国税率 MFN(%)	协定税率 Agreement(%)	特惠税率 SP(%)	普通税率 Gen(%)	英文货品名称 Article Description
647	0801.3100	--未去壳	20∆10	0 澳门MO,冰岛IS,东盟AS,新西兰NZ,智利CL 6 秘鲁PE 12 澳AU,哥CR 14 瑞士CH 16 韩国KR	0 柬埔寨KH,受惠国LD	70	--In shell
648	0801.3200	--去壳	10	0 澳门MO,冰岛IS,东盟AS,秘鲁PE,新西兰NZ,智利CL 4 瑞士CH 5 巴PK 6 澳AU,哥CR 8 韩国KR	0 柬埔寨KH,缅甸MM,受惠国LD	70	--Shelled
	08.02	**鲜或干的其他坚果，不论是否去壳或去皮：**					**Other nuts, fresh or dried, whether or not shelled or peeled:**
		-扁桃仁：					-Almonds:
649	0802.1100	--未去壳	24∆10	0 澳门MO,冰岛IS,东盟AS,新西兰NZ,智利CL 7.2 秘鲁PE 14.4 澳AU,哥CR 16.8 瑞士CH 19.2 韩国KR	0 受惠国1LD1	70	--In shell
650	0802.1200	--去壳	10	0 澳门MO,冰岛IS,东盟AS,新西兰NZ,智利CL 3 秘鲁PE 4 瑞士CH 5 巴PK 6 澳AU,哥CR 8 韩国KR	0 受惠国LD	70	--Shelled
		-榛子：					-Hazelnuts or filberts (*Corylus* spp.) :
651	0802.2100	--未去壳	25	0 澳门MO,冰岛IS,东盟AS,新西兰NZ,智利CL 7.5 秘鲁PE 15 澳AU,哥CR 17.5 瑞士CH 22.5 韩国KR	0 受惠国1LD1	70	--In shell
652	0802.2200	--去壳	10	0 澳门MO,冰岛IS,东盟AS,秘鲁PE,新西兰NZ,智利CL 4 瑞士CH 5 巴PK 6 澳AU,哥CR 8 韩国KR	0 受惠国LD	70	--Shelled
		-核桃：					-Walnuts:
653	0802.3100	--未去壳	25	0 澳门MO,冰岛IS,东盟AS,新西兰NZ,智利CL 7.5 秘鲁PE 15 澳AU,哥CR 17.5 瑞士CH 22.5 韩国KR	0 受惠国1LD1	70	--In shell
654	0802.3200	--去壳	20	0 澳门MO,冰岛IS,东盟AS,新西兰NZ,智利CL 6 秘鲁PE 12 澳AU,哥CR 14 瑞士CH 17.3 韩国KR	0 受惠国1LD1	70	--Shelled
		-栗子：					-Chestnuts (*Castanea* spp.) :
		--未去壳：					--In shell:
655	0802.4110	---板栗	25	0 澳门MO,冰岛IS,东盟AS,新西兰NZ,智利CL 7.5 秘鲁PE 15 澳AU,哥CR 17.5 瑞士CH	0 受惠国1LD1	70	---Chestnuts (*Castanea spp.*)

序号 No.	税则号列 Tariff Line	中文货品名称 Article Description in Chinese	最惠国税率 MFN(%)	协定税率 Agreement(%)	特惠税率 SP(%)	普通税率 Gen(%)	英文货品名称 Article Description
656	0802.4190	---其他	25Δ20	0 澳门MO,冰岛IS,东盟AS,新西兰NZ,智利CL 7.5 秘鲁PE 15 澳AU,哥CR 17.5 瑞士CH 22.5 韩国KR	0 受惠国$_1$LD$_1$	70	---Other
		--去壳:					--Shelled:
657	0802.4210	---板栗	25	0 澳门MO,冰岛IS,东盟AS,新西兰NZ,智利CL 7.5 秘鲁PE 15 澳AU,哥CR 17.5 瑞士CH 22.5 韩国KR	0 受惠国$_1$LD$_1$	70	---Chestnuts (*Castanea spp.*)
658	0802.4290	---其他	25Δ20	0 澳门MO,冰岛IS,东盟AS,新西兰NZ,智利CL 7.5 秘鲁PE 15 澳AU,哥CR 17.5 瑞士CH 22.5 韩国KR	0 受惠国$_1$LD$_1$	70	---Other
		-阿月浑子果（开心果）:					-Pistachios:
659	0802.5100	--未去壳	10Δ5	0 澳门MO,冰岛IS,东盟AS,秘鲁PE,新西兰NZ,智利CL 4 瑞士CH 5 巴PK 6 澳AU,哥CR 8 韩国KR	0 受惠国$_1$LD$_1$	70	--In shell
660	0802.5200	--去壳	10Δ5	0 澳门MO,冰岛IS,东盟AS,秘鲁PE,新西兰NZ,智利CL 4 瑞士CH 5 巴PK 6 澳AU,哥CR 8 韩国KR	0 受惠国$_1$LD$_1$	70	--Shelled
		-马卡达姆坚果（夏威夷果）:					-Macadamia nuts:
		--未去壳:					--In shell:
661	0802.6110	---种用	0		0 受惠国LD	70	---For cultivation
662	0802.6190	---其他	24Δ19	0 澳门MO,冰岛IS,东盟AS,新西兰NZ,智利CL 7.2 秘鲁PE 14.4 澳AU,哥CR 16.8 瑞士CH 19.2 韩国KR	0 受惠国$_1$LD$_1$	70	---Other
663	0802.6200	--去壳	24Δ19	0 澳门MO,冰岛IS,东盟AS,新西兰NZ,智利CL 7.2 秘鲁PE 14.4 澳AU,哥CR 16.8 瑞士CH 19.2 韩国KR	0 受惠国$_1$LD$_1$	70	--Shelled
664	0802.7000	-可乐果(可乐果属)	24	0 澳门MO,冰岛IS,东盟AS,新西兰NZ,智利CL 7.2 秘鲁PE 14.4 澳AU,哥CR 16.8 瑞士CH 21.6 韩国KR	0 受惠国$_1$LD$_1$	70	-Kola nuts (Cola spp.)
665	0802.8000	-槟榔果	10	0 澳门MO,冰岛IS,东盟AS,秘鲁PE,新西兰NZ,智利CL 4 瑞士CH 5 巴PK,亚太AP 6 澳AU,哥CR 8 韩国KR	0 受惠国LD	30	-Areca nuts
		-其他:					-Other:

序号 No.	税则号列 Tariff Line	中文货品名称 Article Description in Chinese	最惠国税率 MFN(%)	协定税率 Agreement(%)	特惠税率 SP(%)	普通税率 Gen(%)	英文货品名称 Article Description
666	0802.9020	---白果	25Δ20	0 澳门MO,冰岛IS,东盟AS,新西兰NZ,智利CL 7.5 秘鲁PE 15 澳AU,哥CR 17.5 瑞士CH 22.5 韩国KR	0 受惠国$_1$LD$_1$	70	---Gingko nuts
667	0802.9030	---松子仁	25	0 澳门MO,冰岛IS,东盟AS,新西兰NZ,智利CL 7.5 秘鲁PE 15 澳AU,哥CR 17.5 瑞士CH 22.5 韩国KR	0 受惠国$_1$LD$_1$	70	---Pine-nuts, shelled
668	0802.9090	---其他	24	0 澳门MO,冰岛IS,东盟AS,新西兰NZ,智利CL 7.2 秘鲁PE 14.4 澳AU,哥CR 16.8 瑞士CH 21.6 韩国KR	0 受惠国$_1$LD$_1$	70	---Other
	ex08029090	碧根果	Δ10				Pecan
	08.03	**鲜或干的香蕉，包括芭蕉:**					**Bananas, including plantains, fresh or dried:**
669	0803.1000	-芭蕉	10	0 澳门MO,冰岛IS,东盟AS,台湾TW,新西兰NZ,智利CL 3 秘鲁PE 4 瑞士CH 5 巴PK 6 澳AU,哥CR 6.9 亚太AP 8 韩国KR	0 柬埔寨KH,老挝LA,受惠国LD	40	-Plantains
670	0803.9000	-其他	10	0 澳门MO,冰岛IS,东盟AS,台湾TW,新西兰NZ,智利CL 3 秘鲁PE 4 瑞士CH 5 巴PK 6 澳AU,哥CR 6.9 亚太AP 8 韩国KR	0 柬埔寨KH,老挝LA,受惠国LD	40	-Other
	08.04	**鲜或干的椰枣、无花果、菠萝、鳄梨、番石榴、芒果及山竹果:**					**Dates, figs, pineapples, avocados, guavas, mangoes and mangosteens, fresh or dried:**
671	0804.1000	-椰枣	15	0 澳门MO,巴PK,冰岛IS,东盟AS,新西兰NZ,智利CL 4.5 秘鲁PE 9 澳AU,哥CR 10.5 瑞士CH 12 韩国KR	0 受惠国$_1$LD$_1$	40	-Dates
672	0804.2000	-无花果	30	0 澳门MO,巴PK,冰岛IS,东盟AS,新西兰NZ,智利CL 9 秘鲁PE 18 澳AU,哥CR 21.6 瑞士CH 27 韩国KR	0 受惠国$_1$LD$_1$	70	-Figs
673	0804.3000	-菠萝	12	0 澳门MO,巴PK,冰岛IS,东盟AS,秘鲁PE,香港HK,新西兰NZ,智利CL 7.2 澳AU,哥CR 7.9 亚太AP 8.4 瑞士CH 9.6 韩国KR	0 柬埔寨KH,受惠国LD	80	-Pineapples

序号 No.	税则号列 Tariff Line	中文货品名称 Article Description in Chinese	最惠国税率 MFN(%)	协定税率 Agreement(%)	特惠税率 SP(%)	普通税率 Gen(%)	英文货品名称 Article Description
674	0804.4000	-鳄梨	25Δ10	0 澳门MO,巴PK,冰岛IS,东盟AS,秘鲁PE,新西兰NZ,智利CL 12.5 亚太AP 15 澳AU,哥CR 17.5 瑞士CH 22.5 韩国KR	0 柬埔寨KH,受惠国LD	80	-Avocados
		-番石榴、芒果及山竹果:					-Guavas, mangoes and mangosteens:
675	0804.5010	---番石榴	15	0 澳门MO,巴PK,冰岛IS,东盟AS,新西兰NZ,智利CL 4.5 秘鲁PE 7.5 亚太AP 9 澳AU,哥CR 10.5 瑞士CH 12 韩国KR	0 受惠国$_1$LD$_1$	80	---Guavas
676	0804.5020	---芒果	15	0 澳门MO,巴PK,冰岛IS,东盟AS,秘鲁PE,新西兰NZ,智利CL 9 澳AU,哥CR 10.5 瑞士CH 10.6 亚太AP 12 韩国KR	0 受惠国LD	80	---Mangoes
677	0804.5030	---山竹果	15	0 澳门MO,巴PK,冰岛IS,东盟AS,秘鲁PE,新西兰NZ,智利CL 7.5 亚太AP 9 澳AU,哥CR 10.5 瑞士CH 12 韩国KR	0 受惠国$_1$LD$_1$	80	---Mangosteens
	08.05	**鲜或干的柑橘属水果:**					**Citrus fruit, fresh or dried:**
678	0805.1000	-橙	11	0 澳门MO,巴PK,冰岛IS,东盟AS,台湾TW,新西兰NZ,智利CL 1.4 秘鲁PE 6.6 哥CR 7.7 瑞士CH 8.6 澳AU 8.8 韩国KR	0 受惠国LD	100	-Oranges
		-柑橘;杂交柑橘:					-Mandarins (including tangerines and satsumas) ; clementines, wilkings and similar citrus hybrids:
679	0805.2010	---蕉柑	12	0 澳门MO,巴PK,冰岛IS,东盟AS,新西兰NZ,智利CL 3.6 秘鲁PE 7.2 哥CR 8.4 瑞士CH 9.3 澳AU 9.6 韩国KR	0 受惠国$_1$LD$_1$	100	---Chiao-Kan
680	0805.2020	---阔叶柑橘	12	0 澳门MO,巴PK,冰岛IS,东盟AS,新西兰NZ,智利CL 3.6 秘鲁PE 7.2 哥CR 8.4 瑞士CH 9.3 澳AU 9.6 韩国KR	0 受惠国$_1$LD$_1$	100	---Latifolia Citrus

序号 No.	税则号列 Tariff Line	中文货品名称 Article Description in Chinese	最惠国税率 MFN(%)	协定税率 Agreement(%)		特惠税率 SP(%)		普通税率 Gen(%)	英文货品名称 Article Description
681	0805.2090	---其他	12	0	澳门MO,巴PK,冰岛IS,东盟AS,新西兰NZ,智利CL	0	受惠国$_1$LD$_1$	100	---Other
				1.5	秘鲁PE				
				7.2	哥CR				
				8.4	瑞士CH				
				9.3	澳AU				
				9.6	韩国KR				
682	0805.4000	-葡萄柚，包括柚	12	0	澳门MO,巴PK,冰岛IS,东盟AS,香港HK,新西兰NZ,智利CL	0	受惠国LD	100	-Grapefruit, including pomelos
				3.6	秘鲁PE				
				7.2	哥CR				
				8.4	瑞士CH				
				9.3	澳AU				
				9.6	韩国KR				
683	0805.5000	-柠檬及酸橙	11	0	澳门MO,巴PK,冰岛IS,东盟AS,台湾TW,新西兰NZ,智利CL	0	受惠国LD	100	-Lemons (Citrus limon, Citrus limonum) and limes (Citrus aurantifolia)
				1.4	秘鲁PE				
				5.5	亚太AP				
				6.6	哥CR				
				7.7	瑞士CH				
				8.6	澳AU				
				8.8	韩国KR				
684	0805.9000	-其他	30	0	澳门MO,巴PK,冰岛IS,东盟AS,秘鲁PE,新西兰NZ,智利CL	0	受惠国$_1$LD$_1$	100	-Other
				15	亚太AP				
				18	哥CR				
				21.6	瑞士CH				
				23.3	澳AU				
				27	韩国KR				
	08.06	**鲜或干的葡萄：**							**Grapes, fresh or dried:**
685	0806.1000	-鲜的	13	0	冰岛IS,东盟AS,哥CR,秘鲁PE,新西兰NZ,智利CL	0	受惠国$_1$LD$_1$	80	-Fresh
				6.5	巴PK				
				7.8	澳AU				
				9.1	瑞士CH				
				10.4	韩国KR				
686	0806.2000	-干的	10	0	澳门MO,冰岛IS,东盟AS,哥CR,新西兰NZ,智利CL	0	受惠国$_1$LD$_1$	80	-Dried
				3	秘鲁PE				
				4	瑞士CH				
				5	巴PK				
				6	澳AU				
				8	韩国KR				
	08.07	**鲜的甜瓜（包括西瓜）及木瓜：**							**Melons (including watermelons) and papaws (papayas) , fresh:**
		-甜瓜，包括西瓜：							-Melons (including watermelons) :
687	0807.1100	--西瓜	25	0	冰岛IS,东盟AS,哥CR,新西兰NZ,智利CL	0	受惠国$_2$LD$_2$	70	--Watermelons
				7.5	秘鲁PE				
				12.5	巴PK,亚太AP				
				15	澳AU				
				17.5	瑞士CH				
				22.5	韩国KR				
		--其他：							--Other:

序号 No.	税则号列 Tariff Line	中文货品名称 Article Description in Chinese	最惠国税率 MFN(%)	协定税率 Agreement(%)	特惠税率 SP(%)	普通税率 Gen(%)	英文货品名称 Article Description
688	0807.1910	---哈蜜瓜	12	0 冰岛IS,东盟AS,哥CR,秘鲁PE,台湾TW,新西兰NZ,智利CL 5 巴PK 6 亚太AP 7.2 澳AU 8.4 瑞士CH 9.6 韩国KR	0 受惠国LD	70	---Hami melons
689	0807.1920	---罗马甜瓜及加勒比甜瓜	12	0 冰岛IS,东盟AS,哥CR,新西兰NZ,智利CL 3.6 秘鲁PE 5 巴PK 6 亚太AP 7.2 澳AU 8.4 瑞士CH 9.6 韩国KR	0 受惠国LD	70	---Cantaloupe and Galia melons
690	0807.1990	---其他	12	0 冰岛IS,东盟AS,新西兰NZ,智利CL 3.6 秘鲁PE 4.8 哥CR 5 巴PK 6 亚太AP 7.2 澳AU 8.4 瑞士CH 9.6 韩国KR	0 受惠国LD	70	---Other
691	0807.2000	-木瓜	25	0 冰岛IS,东盟AS,哥CR,新西兰NZ,智利CL 7.5 秘鲁PE 15 澳AU 17.5 瑞士CH 20 韩国KR	0 柬埔寨KH,受惠国LD	70	-Papaws (papayas)
	08.08	**鲜的苹果、梨及榅桲:**					**Apples, pears and quinces, fresh:**
692	0808.1000	-苹果	10	0 冰岛IS,东盟AS,哥CR,新西兰NZ,智利CL 3 秘鲁PE 4 瑞士CH 5 巴PK 6 澳AU 8 韩国KR	0 受惠国LD	100	-Apples
		-梨:					-Pears:
693	0808.3010	---鸭梨及雪梨	12	0 冰岛IS,东盟AS,哥CR,新西兰NZ,智利CL 3.6 秘鲁PE 5 巴PK 7.2 澳AU 8.4 瑞士CH 9.6 韩国KR 10 亚太AP	0 受惠国$_1$LD$_1$	100	---Ya pears, Hsueh pears
694	0808.3020	---香梨	12	0 冰岛IS,东盟AS,哥CR,新西兰NZ,智利CL 3.6 秘鲁PE 5 巴PK 7.2 澳AU 8.4 瑞士CH 9.6 韩国KR 10 亚太AP	0 受惠国$_1$LD$_1$	100	---Xiang pears
695	0808.3090	---其他	10	0 冰岛IS,东盟AS,哥CR,新西兰NZ,智利CL 3 秘鲁PE 4 瑞士CH 5 巴PK 6 澳AU 8 韩国KR	0 受惠国$_1$LD$_1$	100	---Other

序号 No.	税则号列 Tariff Line	中文货品名称 Article Description in Chinese	最惠国税率 MFN(%)	协定税率 Agreement(%)	特惠税率 SP(%)	普通税率 Gen(%)	英文货品名称 Article Description
696	0808.4000	-榅桲	16	0 冰岛IS,东盟AS,哥CR,新西兰NZ,智利CL 4.8 秘鲁PE 9.6 澳AU 11.2 瑞士CH 12.8 巴PK 13.8 韩国KR	0 受惠国$_1$LD$_1$	100	-Quinces
	08.09	**鲜的杏、樱桃、桃（包括油桃）、梅及李：**					**Apricots, cherries, peaches (including nectarines) , plums and sloes, fresh:**
697	0809.1000	-杏	25	0 冰岛IS,东盟AS,哥CR,新西兰NZ,智利CL 7.5 秘鲁PE 15 澳AU 17.5 瑞士CH 22.5 韩国KR	0 受惠国$_1$LD$_1$	70	-Apricots
		-樱桃：					-Cherries:
698	0809.2100	--欧洲酸樱桃	10	0 冰岛IS,东盟AS,哥CR,新西兰NZ,智利CL 3 秘鲁PE 4 瑞士CH 5 巴PK 6 澳AU 8 韩国KR	0 受惠国LD	70	--Sour cherries (Prunus cerasus)
699	0809.2900	--其他	10	0 冰岛IS,东盟AS,哥CR,新西兰NZ,智利CL 3 秘鲁PE 4 瑞士CH 5 巴PK 6 澳AU 8 韩国KR	0 受惠国LD	70	--Other
700	0809.3000	-桃，包括油桃	10	0 冰岛IS,东盟AS,哥CR,新西兰NZ,智利CL 3 秘鲁PE 4 瑞士CH 5 巴PK 6 澳AU 8 韩国KR	0 受惠国LD	70	-Peaches, including nectarines
701	0809.4000	-梅及李	10	0 冰岛IS,东盟AS,哥CR,新西兰NZ,智利CL 3 秘鲁PE 4 瑞士CH 5 巴PK 6 澳AU 8 韩国KR	0 受惠国$_1$LD$_1$	70	-Plums and sloes
	08.10	**其他鲜果：**					**Other fruit, fresh:**
702	0810.1000	-草莓	14	0 冰岛IS,东盟AS,哥CR,秘鲁PE,新西兰NZ,智利CL 8.4 澳AU 9.8 瑞士CH 11.2 韩国KR	0 受惠国LD	80	-Strawberries
703	0810.2000	-木莓、黑莓、桑椹及罗甘莓	25	0 冰岛IS,东盟AS,哥CR,新西兰NZ,智利CL 7.5 秘鲁PE 15 澳AU 17.5 瑞士CH 22.5 韩国KR	0 受惠国$_1$LD$_1$	80	-Raspberries, blackberries, mulberries and loganberries
704	0810.3000	-黑、白或红的穗醋栗（加仑子）及醋栗	25	0 冰岛IS,东盟AS,哥CR,新西兰NZ,智利CL 7.5 秘鲁PE 15 澳AU 17.5 瑞士CH 22.5 韩国KR	0 受惠国$_1$LD$_1$	80	-Black, white or red currants and gooseberries

序号 No.	税则号列 Tariff Line	中文货品名称 Article Description in Chinese	最惠国税率 MFN(%)	协定税率 Agreement(%)	特惠税率 SP(%)	普通税率 Gen(%)	英文货品名称 Article Description
705	0810.4000	-蔓越桔及越桔	30	0 冰岛IS,东盟AS,哥CR,秘鲁PE,新西兰NZ,智利CL 18 澳AU 21.6 瑞士CH 27 韩国KR	0 受惠国$_2$LD$_2$	80	-Cranberries, bilberries and other fruits of the genus Vaccinium
706	0810.5000	-猕猴桃	20	0 冰岛IS,东盟AS,哥CR,新西兰NZ,智利CL 6 秘鲁PE 12 澳AU 14 瑞士CH 16 巴PK 16.5 亚太AP 17.3 韩国KR	0 受惠国$_1$LD$_1$	80	-Kiwifruit
707	0810.6000	-榴莲	20	0 冰岛IS,东盟AS,哥CR,新西兰NZ,智利CL 6 秘鲁PE 12 澳AU 14 瑞士CH 16 韩国KR	0 柬埔寨KH,受惠国LD	80	-Durian
708	0810.7000	-柿子	20	0 冰岛IS,东盟AS,哥CR,秘鲁PE,香港HK,新西兰NZ,智利CL 12 澳AU 14 瑞士CH 16 巴PK 16.4 亚太AP 17.3 韩国KR	0 受惠国$_1$LD$_1$	80	-Persimmons
		-其他:					-Other:
709	0810.9010	---荔枝	30	0 冰岛IS,东盟AS,哥CR,新西兰NZ,智利CL 9 秘鲁PE 18 澳AU 20 巴PK,亚太AP 21.6 瑞士CH 27 韩国KR	0 受惠国$_1$LD$_1$	80	---Lychee
710	0810.9030	---龙眼	12	0 冰岛IS,东盟AS,哥CR,秘鲁PE,新西兰NZ,智利CL 6 巴PK 7.2 澳AU 8.4 瑞士CH 9.6 韩国KR	0 柬埔寨KH,受惠国LD	80	---Longan
711	0810.9040	---红毛丹	20	0 冰岛IS,东盟AS,哥CR,新西兰NZ,智利CL 6 秘鲁PE 12 澳AU 14 瑞士CH 16 韩国KR	0 受惠国$_1$LD$_1$	80	---Rambutan
712	0810.9050	---番荔枝	20	0 冰岛IS,东盟AS,哥CR,秘鲁PE,新西兰NZ,智利CL 12 澳AU 14 瑞士CH 16 韩国KR	0 受惠国$_1$LD$_1$	80	---Sugar apple
713	0810.9060	---杨桃	20	0 冰岛IS,东盟AS,哥CR,秘鲁PE,新西兰NZ,智利CL 12 澳AU 14 瑞士CH 17.3 韩国KR	0 受惠国$_1$LD$_1$	80	---Carambola

序号 No.	税则号列 Tariff Line	中文货品名称 Article Description in Chinese	最惠国税率 MFN(%)	协定税率 Agreement(%)	特惠税率 SP(%)	普通税率 Gen(%)	英文货品名称 Article Description
714	0810.9070	---莲雾	20	0 冰岛IS,东盟AS,哥CR,新西兰NZ,智利CL 6 秘鲁PE 12 澳AU 14 瑞士CH 16 巴PK,韩国KR 16.4 亚太AP	0 受惠国$_1$LD$_1$	80	---Wax apple
715	0810.9080	---火龙果	20	0 冰岛IS,东盟AS,哥CR,台湾TW,新西兰NZ,智利CL 6 秘鲁PE 12 澳AU 14 瑞士CH 16 巴PK,韩国KR 16.4 亚太AP	0 受惠国$_1$LD$_1$	80	---Dragon fruit
716	0810.9090	---其他	20	0 冰岛IS,东盟AS,哥CR,秘鲁PE,香港HK,新西兰NZ,智利CL 12 澳AU 14 瑞士CH 16 巴PK 16.4 亚太AP 17.3 韩国KR	0 受惠国$_1$LD$_1$	80	---Other
	08.11	**冷冻水果及坚果，不论是否蒸煮、加糖或其他甜物质：**					**Fruit and nuts, uncooked or cooked by steaming or boiling in water, frozen, whether or not containing added sugar or other sweetening matter:**
717	0811.1000	-草莓	30	0 冰岛IS,东盟AS,哥CR,新西兰NZ,智利CL 9 秘鲁PE 18 澳AU 27 韩国KR	0 受惠国$_1$LD$_1$	80	-Strawberries
718	0811.2000	-木莓、黑莓、桑椹、罗甘莓、黑、白或红的穗醋栗（加仑子）及醋栗	30	0 冰岛IS,东盟AS,哥CR,新西兰NZ,智利CL 9 秘鲁PE 18 澳AU 27 韩国KR	0 受惠国$_1$LD$_1$	80	-Raspberries, blackberries, mulberries, loganberries, black, white or red cur-rants and gooseberries
		-其他：					-Other:
719	0811.9010	---栗子，未去壳	30	0 冰岛IS,东盟AS,哥CR,新西兰NZ,智利CL 9 秘鲁PE 18 澳AU 27 韩国KR	0 受惠国$_1$LD$_1$	80	---Chestnuts, in shell
720	0811.9090	---其他	30	0 冰岛IS,东盟AS,哥CR,新西兰NZ,智利CL 9 秘鲁PE 18 澳AU 27 韩国KR	0 受惠国$_2$LD$_2$	80	---Other
	08.12	**暂时保藏（例如，使用二氧化硫气体、盐水、亚硫酸水或其他防腐液）的水果及坚果，但不适于直接食用的：**					**Fruit and nuts, provisionally preserved (for example, by sulphur dioxide gas, in brine, in sulphur water or in other preservative solutions) , but unsuitable in that state for immediate consumption:**
721	0812.1000	-樱桃	30	0 冰岛IS,东盟AS,哥CR,新西兰NZ,智利CL 9 秘鲁PE 18 澳AU 27 韩国KR	0 受惠国$_2$LD$_2$	80	-Cherries

序号 No.	税则号列 Tariff Line	中文货品名称 Article Description in Chinese	最惠国税率 MFN(%)	协定税率 Agreement(%)	特惠税率 SP(%)	普通税率 Gen(%)	英文货品名称 Article Description
722	0812.9000	-其他	25	0 冰岛IS,东盟AS,哥CR,新西兰NZ,智利CL 8 秘鲁PE 15 澳AU 17.5 瑞士CH 22.5 韩国KR	0 受惠国$_1$LD$_1$	80	-Other
	08.13	**税号08.01至08.06以外的干果；本章的什锦坚果或干果：**					**Fruit, dried, other than that of headings 0801 to 0806; mixtures of nuts or dried fruits of this chapter:**
723	0813.1000	-杏	25	0 澳门MO,冰岛IS,东盟AS,哥CR,新西兰NZ,智利CL 7.5 秘鲁PE 15 澳AU 17.5 瑞士CH 22.5 韩国KR	0 受惠国$_1$LD$_1$	70	-Apricots
724	0813.2000	-梅及李	25	0 澳门MO,冰岛IS,东盟AS,哥CR,新西兰NZ,智利CL 7.5 秘鲁PE 15 澳AU 17.5 瑞士CH 22.5 韩国KR	0 受惠国$_1$LD$_1$	70	-Prunes
725	0813.3000	-苹果	25	0 澳门MO,冰岛IS,东盟AS,哥CR,新西兰NZ,智利CL 7.5 秘鲁PE 15 澳AU 17.5 瑞士CH 22.5 韩国KR	0 受惠国$_1$LD$_1$	70	-Apples
		-其他干果：					-Other fruit:
726	0813.4010	---龙眼干、肉	20	0 澳门MO,冰岛IS,东盟AS,哥CR,新西兰NZ,智利CL 6 秘鲁PE 12 澳AU 14 瑞士CH 16 韩国KR	0 柬埔寨KH,受惠国LD	70	---Longans and longan pulps
727	0813.4020	---柿饼	25	0 澳门MO,冰岛IS,东盟AS,哥CR,新西兰NZ,智利CL 7.5 秘鲁PE 15 澳AU 17.5 瑞士CH 22.5 韩国KR	0 柬埔寨KH,受惠国LD	70	---Persimmons
728	0813.4030	---红枣	25	0 澳门MO,冰岛IS,东盟AS,哥CR,新西兰NZ,智利CL 7.5 秘鲁PE 15 澳AU 17.5 瑞士CH 22.5 韩国KR	0 柬埔寨KH,受惠国LD	70	---Red jujubes
729	0813.4040	---荔枝干	25	0 澳门MO,冰岛IS,东盟AS,哥CR,新西兰NZ,智利CL 7.5 秘鲁PE 15 澳AU 17.5 瑞士CH 20 韩国KR	0 柬埔寨KH,受惠国LD	70	---Preserved litchi

序号 No.	税则号列 Tariff Line	中文货品名称 Article Description in Chinese	最惠国税率 MFN(%)	协定税率 Agreement(%)	特惠税率 SP(%)	普通税率 Gen(%)	英文货品名称 Article Description
730	0813.4090	---其他	25	0 澳门MO,冰岛IS,东盟AS,哥CR,新西兰NZ,智利CL 7.5 秘鲁PE 15 澳AU 17.5 瑞士CH 22.5 韩国KR	0 柬埔寨KH,受惠国LD	70	---Other
731	0813.5000	-本章的什锦坚果或干果	18	0 澳门MO,冰岛IS,东盟AS,哥CR,新西兰NZ,智利CL 5.4 秘鲁PE 10.8 澳AU 12.6 瑞士CH 14.4 巴PK 15.6 韩国KR	0 受惠国$_1$LD$_1$	70	-Mixtures of nuts or dried fruits of this Chapter
	08.14	**柑橘属水果或甜瓜（包括西瓜）的果皮，鲜、冻、干或用盐水、亚硫酸水或其他防腐液暂时保藏的**					**Peel of citrus fruit or melons (including watermelons) , fresh, frozen, dried or provisionally preserved in brine, in sulphur water or in other preservative solutions**
732	0814.0000	柑橘属水果或甜瓜（包括西瓜）的果皮，鲜、冻、干或用盐水、亚硫酸水或其他防腐液暂时保藏的	25	0 澳门MO,冰岛IS,东盟AS,哥CR,新西兰NZ,智利CL 7.5 秘鲁PE 15 澳AU 17.5 瑞士CH 22.5 韩国KR	0 受惠国$_1$LD$_1$	70	Peel of citrus fruit or melons (including watermelons) , fresh, frozen, dried or provisionally preserved in brine, in sulphur water or in other preservative solutions

第九章
咖啡、茶、马黛茶及调味香料

注释：

一、税号 09.04 至 09.10 所列产品的混合物，应按下列规定归类：

（一）同一税号的两种或两种以上产品的混合物仍应归入该税号；

（二）不同税号的两种或两种以上产品的混合物应归入税号 09.10。

税号 09.04 至 09.10 的产品（或上述（一）或（二）项的混合物）如添加了其他物质，只要所得的混合物保持了原产品的基本特性，其归类应不受影响。基本特性已经改变的，则不应归入本章；构成混合调味品的，应归入税号 21.03。

二、本章不包括荜澄茄椒或税号 12.11 的其他产品。

Chapter 9
Coffee, tea, mate and spices

Notes:

1. Mixtures of the products of headings No.09.04 to 09.10 are to be classified as follows:

(a) Mixtures of two or more of the products of the same heading are to be classified in that heading;

(b) Mixtures of two or more of the products of different headings are to beclassified in heading No.09.10.

The addition of other substances to the products of headings No.09.04 to 09.10 (or to the mixtures referred to in paragraph (a) or (b) above) shall not affect their classification provided the resulting mixtures retain the essential character of the goods of those headings. Otherwise such mixtures are notclassifiedin this Chapter; those constituting mixed condiments or mixed seasonings are classified in heading No.21.03.

2. This Chapter does not cover Cubeb pepper (Piper cubeba) or other products of heading No.12.11.

序号 No.	税则号列 Tariff Line	中文货品名称 Article Description in Chinese	最惠国税率 MFN(%)	协定税率 Agreement(%)	特惠税率 SP(%)	普通税率 Gen(%)	英文货品名称 Article Description
	09.01	**咖啡，不论是否焙炒或浸除咖啡碱；咖啡豆荚及咖啡豆皮；含咖啡的咖啡代用品：**					**Coffee, whether or not roasted or decaffeinated; coffee husks and skins; coffee substitutes containing coffee in any proportion:**
		-未焙炒的咖啡：					-Coffee, not roasted:
733	0901.1100	--未浸除咖啡碱	8	0 冰岛IS,新西兰NZ,智利CL 3.2 哥CR,瑞士CH 4.8 澳AU,韩国KR	0 柬埔寨KH,老挝LA,受惠国LD	50	--Not decaffeinated
734	0901.1200	--已浸除咖啡碱	8	0 冰岛IS,新西兰NZ,智利CL 3.2 瑞士CH 4.8 澳AU,韩国KR	0 柬埔寨KH,老挝LA,受惠国LD	50	--Decaffeinated
		-已焙炒的咖啡：					-Coffee, roasted:
735	0901.2100	--未浸除咖啡碱	15	0 澳门MO,冰岛IS,香港HK,新西兰NZ,智利CL 6 哥CR 9 澳AU 12 韩国KR 12.3 瑞士CH	0 柬埔寨KH,老挝LA,受惠国LD	80	--Not decaffeinated
736	0901.2200	--已浸除咖啡碱	15	0 澳门MO,冰岛IS,东盟AS,新西兰NZ,智利CL 9 澳AU 10.5 瑞士CH 12 巴PK,韩国KR	0 柬埔寨KH,老挝LA,受惠国LD	80	--Decaffeinated
		-其他：					-Other:
737	0901.9010	---咖啡豆荚及咖啡豆皮	10	0 冰岛IS,东盟AS,哥CR,秘鲁PE,新加坡SG,新西兰NZ,智利CL 4 瑞士CH 5 巴PK 6 澳AU 8 韩国KR	0 柬埔寨KH,老挝LA,受惠国LD	30	---Coffee husks and skins
738	0901.9020	---含咖啡的咖啡代用品	30	0 澳门MO,冰岛IS,东盟AS,新加坡SG,新西兰NZ,智利CL 18 澳AU 27 韩国KR	0 柬埔寨KH,老挝LA,受惠国LD	80	---Coffee substitutes containing coffee
	09.02	**茶，不论是否加香料：**					**Tea, whether or not flavoured:**

序号 No.	税则号列 Tariff Line	中文货品名称 Article Description in Chinese	最惠国税率 MFN(%)	协定税率 Agreement(%)	特惠税率 SP(%)	普通税率 Gen(%)	英文货品名称 Article Description
		-绿茶（未发酵），内包装每件净重不超过3公斤：					-Green tea (not fermented) in immediate packings of a content not exceeding 3kg:
739	0902.1010	---花茶	15	0 澳门MO,冰岛IS,东盟AS,哥CR,新加坡SG,新西兰NZ,智利CL 4.5 秘鲁PE 7.5 巴PK,亚太AP 9 澳AU 10.5 瑞士CH 12 韩国KR	0 受惠国$_1$LD$_1$	100	---Flavoured
740	0902.1090	---其他	15	0 澳门MO,冰岛IS,东盟AS,哥CR,台湾TW,新加坡SG,新西兰NZ,智利CL 4.5 秘鲁PE 7.5 巴PK,亚太AP 9 澳AU 10.5 瑞士CH 12 韩国KR	0 受惠国LD	100	---Other
		-其他绿茶（未发酵）：					-Other green tea (not fermented) :
741	0902.2010	---花茶	15	0 澳门MO,冰岛IS,东盟AS,哥CR,新加坡SG,新西兰NZ,智利CL 4.5 秘鲁PE 7.5 巴PK,亚太AP 9 澳AU 10.5 瑞士CH 12 韩国KR	0 受惠国$_1$LD$_1$	100	---Flavoured
742	0902.2090	---其他	15	0 澳门MO,冰岛IS,东盟AS,哥CR,台湾TW,新加坡SG,新西兰NZ,智利CL 4.5 秘鲁PE 7.5 巴PK,亚太AP 9 澳AU 10.5 瑞士CH 12 韩国KR	0 受惠国LD	100	---Other
		-红茶（已发酵）及半发酵茶，内包装每件净重不超过3公斤：					-Black tea (fermented) and partly fermented tea, in immediate packings of a content not exceeding 3kg:
743	0902.3010	---乌龙茶	15	0 澳门MO,冰岛IS,东盟AS,哥CR,台湾TW,香港HK,新加坡SG,新西兰NZ,智利CL 4.5 秘鲁PE 7.5 巴PK,亚太AP 9 澳AU 10.5 瑞士CH 12 韩国KR	0 受惠国$_1$LD$_1$	100	---Oolong tea
744	0902.3020	---普洱茶	15	0 澳门MO,冰岛IS,东盟AS,哥CR,香港HK,新加坡SG,新西兰NZ,智利CL 4.5 秘鲁PE 7.5 巴PK,亚太AP 9 澳AU 10.5 瑞士CH 12 韩国KR	0 受惠国$_1$LD$_1$	100	---Pu-er tea

序号 No.	税则号列 Tariff Line	中文货品名称 Article Description in Chinese	最惠国税率 MFN(%)	协定税率 Agreement(%)	特惠税率 SP(%)	普通税率 Gen(%)	英文货品名称 Article Description
745	0902.3090	---其他	15	0 澳门MO,冰岛IS,东盟AS,哥CR,台湾TW,香港HK,新加坡SG,新西兰NZ,智利CL 4.5 秘鲁PE 7.5 巴PK,亚太AP 9 澳AU 10.5 瑞士CH 12 韩国KR	0 受惠国LD	100	---Other
		-其他红茶（已发酵）及半发酵茶：					-Other black tea (fermented) and other partly fermented tea:
746	0902.4010	---乌龙茶	15	0 澳门MO,冰岛IS,东盟AS,哥CR,台湾TW,香港HK,新加坡SG,新西兰NZ,智利CL 4.5 秘鲁PE 7.5 巴PK,亚太AP 9 澳AU 10.5 瑞士CH 12 韩国KR	0 柬埔寨KH,老挝LA,缅甸MM,受惠国LD	100	---Oolong tea
747	0902.4020	---普洱茶	15	0 澳门MO,冰岛IS,东盟AS,哥CR,香港HK,新加坡SG,新西兰NZ,智利CL 4.5 秘鲁PE 7.5 巴PK,亚太AP 9 澳AU 10.5 瑞士CH 12 韩国KR	0 柬埔寨KH,老挝LA,缅甸MM,受惠国LD	100	---Pu-er tea
748	0902.4090	---其他	15	0 澳门MO,冰岛IS,东盟AS,哥CR,台湾TW,香港HK,新加坡SG,新西兰NZ,智利CL 4.5 秘鲁PE 7.5 巴PK,亚太AP 9 澳AU 10.5 瑞士CH 12 韩国KR	0 柬埔寨KH,老挝LA,缅甸MM,受惠国LD	100	---Other
	09.03	**马黛茶**					**Maté**
749	0903.0000	马黛茶	10	0 冰岛IS,东盟AS,哥CR,秘鲁PE,新加坡SG,新西兰NZ,智利CL 4 瑞士CH 5 巴PK 6 澳AU 8 韩国KR	0 受惠国LD	100	Mate
	09.04	**胡椒；辣椒干及辣椒粉：**					**Pepper of the genus *Piper*; dried or crushed or ground fruit of the genus *Capsicum* or of the genus *Pimenta*:**
		-胡椒：					-Pepper:
750	0904.1100	--未磨	20	0 冰岛IS,哥CR,新西兰NZ,智利CL 6 秘鲁PE 12 澳AU 14 瑞士CH 17.3 韩国KR	0 受惠国$_1$LD$_1$	70	--Neither crushed nor ground
751	0904.1200	--已磨	20	0 冰岛IS,哥CR,香港HK,新西兰NZ,智利CL 6 秘鲁PE 10 巴PK,亚太AP 12 澳AU 14 瑞士CH 17.3 韩国KR	0 受惠国$_1$LD$_1$	70	--Crushed or ground
		-辣椒：					-Fruit of the genus *Capsicum* or of the genus *Pimenta*:

序号 No.	税则号列 Tariff Line	中文货品名称 Article Description in Chinese	最惠国税率 MFN(%)	协定税率 Agreement(%)	特惠税率 SP(%)	普通税率 Gen(%)	英文货品名称 Article Description
752	0904.2100	--干，未磨	20	0 冰岛IS,东盟AS,哥CR,秘鲁PE,香港HK,新加坡SG,新西兰NZ,智利CL 10 巴PK,亚太AP 12 澳AU 14 瑞士CH 17.3 韩国KR	0 受惠国$_1$LD$_1$	70	--Dried, neither crushed nor ground
753	0904.2200	--已磨	20	0 冰岛IS,东盟AS,哥CR,秘鲁PE,香港HK,新加坡SG,新西兰NZ,智利CL 10 巴PK,亚太AP 12 澳AU 14 瑞士CH 17.3 韩国KR	0 受惠国$_1$LD$_1$	70	--Crushed or ground
	09.05	香子兰豆：					**Vanilla:**
754	0905.1000	-未磨	15	0 冰岛IS,东盟AS,哥CR,新加坡SG,新西兰NZ,智利CL 4.5 秘鲁PE 9 澳AU 10.5 瑞士CH 12 巴PK,韩国KR	0 受惠国LD	50	-Neither crushed nor ground
755	0905.2000	-已磨	15	0 冰岛IS,东盟AS,哥CR,新加坡SG,新西兰NZ,智利CL 4.5 秘鲁PE 9 澳AU 10.5 瑞士CH 12 巴PK,韩国KR	0 受惠国LD	50	-Crushed or ground
	09.06	**肉桂及肉桂花：**					**Cinnamon and cinnamon-tree flowers:**
		-未磨：					-Neither crushed nor ground:
756	0906.1100	--锡兰肉桂	5	0 澳AU,巴PK,冰岛IS,东盟AS,哥CR,韩国KR,秘鲁PE,瑞士CH,新西兰NZ,智利CL	0 受惠国LD	50	--Cinnamon (Cinnamomum zeylanicum blume)
757	0906.1900	--其他	5	0 澳AU,巴PK,冰岛IS,东盟AS,哥CR,韩国KR,秘鲁PE,瑞士CH,新西兰NZ,智利CL	0 受惠国LD	50	--Other
758	0906.2000	-已磨	15	0 冰岛IS,东盟AS,哥CR,香港HK,新加坡SG,新西兰NZ,智利CL 4.5 秘鲁PE 9 澳AU 10.5 瑞士CH 12 巴PK,韩国KR	0 受惠国$_1$LD$_1$	50	-Crushed or ground
	09.07	丁香（母丁香、公丁香及丁香梗）：					**Cloves (whole fruit, cloves and stems) :**
759	0907.1000	-未磨	3	0 澳AU,巴PK,冰岛IS,东盟AS,哥CR,韩国KR,秘鲁PE,瑞士CH,新西兰NZ,智利CL	0 柬埔寨KH,受惠国LD	14	-Neither crushed nor ground
760	0907.2000	-已磨	3	0 澳AU,巴PK,冰岛IS,东盟AS,哥CR,韩国KR,秘鲁PE,瑞士CH,新西兰NZ,智利CL	0 柬埔寨KH,受惠国LD	14	-Crushed or ground
	09.08	**肉豆蔻、肉豆蔻衣及豆蔻：**					**Nutmeg, mace and cardamoms:**
		-肉豆蔻：					-Nutmeg:

序号 No.	税则号列 Tariff Line	中文货品名称 Article Description in Chinese	最惠国税率 MFN(%)	协定税率 Agreement(%)	特惠税率 SP(%)	普通税率 Gen(%)	英文货品名称 Article Description
761	0908.1100	--未磨	8	0 冰岛IS,东盟AS,哥CR,秘鲁PE,新西兰NZ,智利CL 3.2 瑞士CH 4.8 澳AU,韩国KR 5 巴PK	0 柬埔寨KH,老挝LA,受惠国LD	30	--Neither crushed nor ground
762	0908.1200	--已磨	8	0 冰岛IS,东盟AS,哥CR,秘鲁PE,新西兰NZ,智利CL 3.2 瑞士CH 4.8 澳AU,韩国KR 5 巴PK	0 柬埔寨KH,老挝LA,受惠国LD	30	--Crushed or ground
		-肉豆蔻衣:					-Mace:
763	0908.2100	--未磨	8	0 冰岛IS,东盟AS,哥CR,秘鲁PE,新西兰NZ,智利CL 3.2 瑞士CH 4.8 澳AU,韩国KR 5 巴PK	0 柬埔寨KH,老挝LA,受惠国LD	30	--Neither crushed nor ground
764	0908.2200	--已磨	8	0 冰岛IS,东盟AS,哥CR,秘鲁PE,新西兰NZ,智利CL 3.2 瑞士CH 4.8 澳AU,韩国KR 5 巴PK	0 柬埔寨KH,老挝LA,受惠国LD	30	--Crushed or ground
		-豆蔻:					-Cardamoms:
765	0908.3100	--未磨	3	0 澳AU,巴PK,冰岛IS,东盟AS,哥CR,韩国KR,秘鲁PE,瑞士CH,新西兰NZ,智利CL	0 柬埔寨KH,老挝LA,受惠国LD	14	--Neither crushed nor ground
766	0908.3200	--已磨	3	0 澳AU,巴PK,冰岛IS,东盟AS,哥CR,韩国KR,秘鲁PE,瑞士CH,新西兰NZ,智利CL	0 柬埔寨KH,老挝LA,受惠国LD	14	--Crushed or ground
	09.09	**茴芹子、八角茴香、小茴香子、芫荽子、枯茗子及黄蒿子；杜松果:**					**Seeds of anise, badian, fennel, coriander, cumin or caraway; juniper berries:**
		-芫荽子:					-Seeds of coriander:
767	0909.2100	--未磨	15	0 冰岛IS,东盟AS,哥CR,新加坡SG,新西兰NZ,智利CL 4.5 秘鲁PE 9 澳AU 10.5 瑞士CH 12 巴PK,韩国KR	0 受惠国$_1$LD$_1$	50	--Neither crushed nor ground
768	0909.2200	--已磨	15	0 冰岛IS,东盟AS,哥CR,新加坡SG,新西兰NZ,智利CL 4.5 秘鲁PE 9 澳AU 10.5 瑞士CH 12 巴PK,韩国KR	0 受惠国$_1$LD$_1$	50	--Crushed or ground
		-枯茗子:					-Seeds of cumin:
769	0909.3100	--未磨	15	0 冰岛IS,东盟AS,哥CR,新加坡SG,新西兰NZ,智利CL 4.5 秘鲁PE 7.5 巴PK,亚太AP 9 澳AU 10.5 瑞士CH 12 韩国KR	0 受惠国$_1$LD$_1$	50	--Neither crushed nor ground

序号 No.	税则号列 Tariff Line	中文货品名称 Article Description in Chinese	最惠国税率 MFN(%)	协定税率 Agreement(%)		特惠税率 SP(%)	普通税率 Gen(%)	英文货品名称 Article Description
770	0909.3200	--已磨	15	0 4.5 7.5 9 10.5 12	冰岛IS,东盟AS,哥CR,新加坡SG,新西兰NZ,智利CL 秘鲁PE 巴PK,亚太AP 澳AU 瑞士CH 韩国KR	0 受惠国$_1$LD$_1$	50	--Crushed or ground
		-茴芹子或八角茴香、蒿子或小茴香子；杜松果：						-Seeds of anise, badian, caraway or fennel; juniper berries:
		--未磨：						--Neither crushed nor ground:
771	0909.6110	---八角茴香	20	0 6 12 14 17.3	冰岛IS,东盟AS,哥CR,新加坡SG,新西兰NZ,智利CL 秘鲁PE 澳AU 瑞士CH 韩国KR	0 受惠国$_1$LD$_1$	90	---Star aniseed
772	0909.6190	---其他	15	0 4.5 9 10.5 12	冰岛IS,东盟AS,哥CR,新加坡SG,新西兰NZ,智利CL 秘鲁PE 澳AU 瑞士CH 巴PK,韩国KR	0 受惠国$_1$LD$_1$	50	---Other
		--已磨：						--Crushed or ground:
773	0909.6210	---八角茴香	20	0 6 12 14 17.3	冰岛IS,东盟AS,哥CR,新加坡SG,新西兰NZ,智利CL 秘鲁PE 澳AU 瑞士CH 韩国KR	0 受惠国$_1$LD$_1$	90	---Star aniseed
774	0909.6290	---其他	15	0 4.5 9 10.5 12	冰岛IS,东盟AS,哥CR,新加坡SG,新西兰NZ,智利CL 秘鲁PE 澳AU 瑞士CH 巴PK,韩国KR	0 受惠国$_1$LD$_1$	50	---Other
	09.10	**姜、番红花、姜黄、麝香草、月桂叶、咖喱及其他调味香料：**						**Ginger, saffron, turmeric (curcuma) , thyme, bay leaves, curry and other spices:**
		-姜：						-Ginger:
775	0910.1100	--未磨	15	0 4.5 7.5 9 10.5 12	冰岛IS,东盟AS,哥CR,新加坡SG,新西兰NZ,智利CL 秘鲁PE 巴PK,亚太AP 澳AU 瑞士CH 韩国KR	0 柬埔寨KH,老挝LA,受惠国LD	50	--Neither crushed nor ground
776	0910.1200	--已磨	15	0 4.5 7.5 9 10.5 12	冰岛IS,东盟AS,哥CR,新加坡SG,新西兰NZ,智利CL 秘鲁PE 巴PK,亚太AP 澳AU 瑞士CH 韩国KR	0 柬埔寨KH,老挝LA,受惠国LD	50	--Crushed or ground
777	0910.2000	-番红花	2	0	澳AU,巴PK,冰岛IS,东盟AS,哥CR,韩国KR,秘鲁PE,瑞士CH,新西兰NZ,智利CL	0 受惠国LD	14	-Saffron

序号 No.	税则号列 Tariff Line	中文货品名称 Article Description in Chinese	最惠国税率 MFN(%)	协定税率 Agreement(%)	特惠税率 SP(%)	普通税率 Gen(%)	英文货品名称 Article Description
778	0910.3000	-姜黄	15	0 冰岛IS,东盟AS,哥CR,香港HK,新加坡SG,新西兰NZ,智利CL 4.5 秘鲁PE 7.5 巴PK,亚太AP 9 澳AU 10.5 瑞士CH 12 韩国KR	0 柬埔寨KH,受惠国LD	50	-Turmeric (curcuma)
		-其他调味香料:					-Other spices:
779	0910.9100	--本章注释一(二)所述的混合物	15	0 澳门MO,冰岛IS,东盟AS,哥CR,香港HK,新加坡SG,新西兰NZ,智利CL 4.5 秘鲁PE 7.5 巴PK,亚太AP 9 澳AU 10.5 瑞士CH 12 韩国KR	0 受惠国LD	50	--Mixtures referred to in Note1 (b) to this Chapter
780	0910.9900	--其他	15	0 冰岛IS,东盟AS,哥CR,香港HK,新加坡SG,新西兰NZ,智利CL 4.5 秘鲁PE 9 澳AU 10.5 瑞士CH 12 巴PK,韩国KR	0 受惠国LD	50	--Other

第十章
谷物

注释：

一、

（一）本章各税号所列产品必须带有谷粒，不论是否成穗或带杆。

（二）本章不包括已去壳或经其他加工的谷物。但去壳、碾磨、磨光、上光、半熟或破碎的稻米仍应归入税号10.06。

二、税号10.05不包括甜玉米（第七章）。

子目注释：

所称“硬粒小麦”，是指硬粒小麦属的小麦及以该属具有相同染色体数目（28）的小麦种间杂交所得的小麦。

Chapter 10
Cereals

Notes:

1.

(a) The products specified in the headings of this Chapter are tobe classified in those headings only if grains are present, whether or not in the ear or on the stalk.

(b) This Chapter does not cover grains which have been hulled or otherwise worked. However, rice, husked, milled, polished, glazed, parboiled or broken remains classified in heading No.10.06.

2. Heading No.10.05 does not cover sweet corn (Chapter 7).

Subheading Note:

The term “durum wheat” means wheat of the *Triticum durum* species and the hybrids derived from the inter-specific crossing of *Triticum durum* which have the same number (28) of chromosomes as that species.

序号 No.	税则号列 Tariff Line	中文货品名称 Article Description in Chinese	最惠国税率 MFN(%)	协定税率 Agreement(%)	特惠税率 SP(%)	普通税率 Gen(%)	英文货品名称 Article Description
	10.01	小麦及混合麦：					**Wheat and meslin:**
		-硬粒小麦：					-Durum wheat:
781	1001.1100	--种用	65①	20 东盟AS		180	--Seed
782	1001.1900	--其他	65②	20 东盟AS		180	--Other
		-其他：					-Other:
783	1001.9100	--种用	65③	20 东盟AS		180	--Seed
784	1001.9900	--其他	65④	20 东盟AS		180	--Other
	10.02	**黑麦：**					**Rye:**
785	1002.1000	-种用	0		0 受惠国LD	0	-Seed
786	1002.9000	-其他	3	0 澳AU,巴PK,冰岛IS,东盟AS,哥CR,韩国KR,秘鲁PE,瑞士CH,新西兰NZ,智利CL	0 受惠国LD	8	-Other
	10.03	大麦：					**Barley:**
787	1003.1000	-种用	0		0 受惠国LD	160	-Seed
788	1003.9000	-其他	3	0 澳AU,巴PK,冰岛IS,东盟AS,哥CR,韩国KR,秘鲁PE,瑞士CH,新西兰NZ,亚太AP,智利CL	0 受惠国LD	160	-Other
	10.04	**燕麦：**					**Oats:**
789	1004.1000	-种用	0		0 受惠国LD	0	-Seed
790	1004.9000	-其他	2	0 澳AU,巴PK,冰岛IS,东盟AS,哥CR,韩国KR,秘鲁PE,瑞士CH,新西兰NZ,智利CL	0 受惠国LD	8	-Other
	10.05	玉米：					**Maize (corn) :**
791	1005.1000	-种用	20⑤			180	-Seed
792	1005.9000	-其他	65⑥	50 东盟AS		180	-Other
	10.06	稻谷、大米：					**Rice:**

①配额税率: 1
In-quota Tariff: 1
②配额税率: 1
In-quota Tariff: 1
③配额税率: 1
In-quota Tariff: 1
④配额税率: 1
In-quota Tariff: 1
⑤配额税率: 1
In-quota Tariff: 1
⑥配额税率: 1
In-quota Tariff: 1

序号 No.	税则号列 Tariff Line	中文货品名称 Article Description in Chinese	最惠国税率 MFN(%)	协定税率 Agreement(%)	特惠税率 SP(%)	普通税率 Gen(%)	英文货品名称 Article Description
		-稻谷:					-Rice in the husk (paddy or rough) :
		---种用:					---Seed:
793	1006.1011	----籼米	65①	50 东盟AS		180	----Long grain
794	1006.1019	----其他	65②	20 东盟AS		180	----Other
		---其他:					---Other:
795	1006.1091	----籼米	65③	50 东盟AS		180	----Long grain
796	1006.1099	----其他	65④	20 东盟AS		180	----Other
		-糙米:					-Husked (brown) rice:
797	1006.2010	---籼米	65⑤	50 东盟AS		180	---Long grain
798	1006.2090	---其他	65⑥	20 东盟AS		180	---Other
		-精米，不论是否磨光或上光:					-Semi-milled or wholly milled rice, whether or not polished or glazed:
799	1006.3010	---籼米	65⑦	50 东盟AS		180	---Long grain
800	1006.3090	---其他	65⑧	20 东盟AS		180	---Other
		-碎米:					-Broken rice:
801	1006.4010	---籼米	65⑨	20 东盟AS		180	---Long grain
802	1006.4090	---其他	65⑩	20 东盟AS		180	---Other
	10.07	**食用高粱:**					**Grain sorghum:**
803	1007.1000	-种用	0		0 受惠国LD	0	-Seed
804	1007.9000	-其他	2	0 澳AU,巴PK,冰岛IS,东盟AS,哥CR,韩国KR,秘鲁PE,瑞士CH,新西兰NZ,智利CL	0 受惠国$_1$LD$_1$	8	-Other
	10.08	**荞麦、谷子及加那利草子；其他谷物:**					**Buckwheat, millet and canary seed; other cereals:**
805	1008.1000	-荞麦	2	0 澳AU,巴PK,冰岛IS,东盟AS,哥CR,韩国KR,秘鲁PE,瑞士CH,新西兰NZ,智利CL	0 受惠国LD	8	-Buckwheat
		-谷子:					-Millet:
806	1008.2100	--种用	2	0 澳AU,巴PK,冰岛IS,东盟AS,哥CR,韩国KR,秘鲁PE,瑞士CH,新西兰NZ,智利CL	0 老挝LA,受惠国LD	8	--Seed
807	1008.2900	--其他	2	0 澳AU,巴PK,冰岛IS,东盟AS,哥CR,韩国KR,秘鲁PE,瑞士CH,新西兰NZ,智利CL	0 老挝LA,受惠国LD	8	--Other
808	1008.3000	-加那利草子	2	0 澳AU,巴PK,冰岛IS,东盟AS,哥CR,韩国KR,秘鲁PE,瑞士CH,新西兰NZ,智利CL	0 老挝LA,受惠国LD	8	-Canary seeds
		-直长马唐（马唐属）:					-Fonio (*Digitaria* spp.) :

①配额税率: 1
In-quota Tariff: 1

②配额税率: 1
In-quota Tariff: 1

③配额税率: 1
In-quota Tariff: 1

④配额税率: 1
In-quota Tariff: 1

⑤配额税率: 1
In-quota Tariff: 1

⑥配额税率: 1
In-quota Tariff: 1

⑦配额税率: 1
In-quota Tariff: 1

⑧配额税率: 1
In-quota Tariff: 1

⑨配额税率: 1
In-quota Tariff: 1

⑩配额税率: 1
In-quota Tariff: 1

序号 No.	税则号列 Tariff Line	中文货品名称 Article Description in Chinese	最惠国税率 MFN(%)	协定税率 Agreement(%)		特惠税率 SP(%)		普通税率 Gen(%)	英文货品名称 Article Description
809	1008.4010	---种用	0			0	受惠国LD	0	---Seed
810	1008.4090	---其他	3	0	澳AU,巴PK,冰岛IS,东盟AS,哥CR,韩国KR,秘鲁PE,瑞士CH,新西兰NZ,智利CL	0	老挝LA,受惠国LD	8	---Other
		-昆诺阿藜:							-Quinoa (*Chenopodium quinoa*) :
811	1008.5010	---种用	0			0	受惠国LD	0	---Seed
812	1008.5090	---其他	3	0	澳AU,巴PK,冰岛IS,东盟AS,哥CR,韩国KR,秘鲁PE,瑞士CH,新西兰NZ,智利CL	0	老挝LA,受惠国LD	8	---Other
		-黑小麦:							-Triticale:
813	1008.6010	---种用	0			0	受惠国LD	0	---Seed
814	1008.6090	---其他	3	0	澳AU,巴PK,冰岛IS,东盟AS,哥CR,韩国KR,秘鲁PE,瑞士CH,新西兰NZ,智利CL	0	老挝LA,受惠国LD	8	---Other
		-其他谷物:							-Other cereals:
815	1008.9010	---种用	0			0	受惠国LD	0	---Seed
816	1008.9090	---其他	3	0	澳AU,巴PK,冰岛IS,东盟AS,哥CR,韩国KR,秘鲁PE,瑞士CH,新西兰NZ,智利CL	0	老挝LA,受惠国LD	8	---Other

第十一章

制粉工业产品；麦芽；淀粉；菊粉；面筋

注释：

一、本章不包括：

（一）作为咖啡代用品的焙制麦芽（税号 09.01 或 21.01）；

（二）税号 19.01 的经制作的细粉、粗粒、粗粉或淀粉；

（三）税号 19.04 的玉米片及其他产品；

（四）税号 20.01、20.04 或 20.05 的经制作或保藏的蔬菜；

（五）药品（第三十章）；

（六）具有芳香料制品或化妆盥洗品性质的淀粉（第三十三章）。

二、

（一）下表所列谷物碾磨产品按干制品重量计如果同时符合以下两个条件，应归入本章；但是，整粒、滚压、制片或磨碎的谷物胚芽均应归入税目 11.04：

1. 淀粉含量（按修订的尤艾斯旋光法测定）超过表列第（2）栏的比例；

2. 灰分含量（除去任何添加的矿物质）不超过表列第（3）栏的比例。

否则，应归入税号 23.02。

（二）符合上述规定归入本章的产品，如果用表列第（4）或第（5）栏规定孔径的金属丝网筛过筛，其通过率按重量计不低于表列比例的，应归入税号 11.01 或 11.02。

否则，应归入税号 11.03 或 11.04。

三、税号 11.03 所称"粗粒"及"粗粉"，是指谷物经碾碎所得的下列产品：

（一）玉米产品，用 2 毫米孔径的金属丝网筛过筛，通过率按重量计不低于 95%的；

（二）其他谷物产品，用 1.25 毫米孔径的金属丝网筛过筛，通过率按重量计不低于 95%的。

Chapter 11

Products of the milling industry; malt; starches; inulin; wheat gluten

Notes:

1.This Chapter does not cover:

(a) Roasted malt put up as coffee substitutes (heading No.09.01 or 21.01);

(b) Prepared flours, groats, meals or starches of heading No.19.01;

(c) Corn flakes or other products of heading No.19.04;

(d) Vegetables, prepared or preserved, of heading No.20.01, 20.04 or 20.05;

(e) Pharmaceutical products (Chapter 30); or

(f) Starches having the character of perfumery, cosmetic or toilet preparations (Chapter 33).

2.

(A) Products from the milling of the cereals listed in the table below fall in this Chapter if they have, by weight on the dry product (However, germ of cereals, whole, rolled, flaked or ground is always classified in heading No.11.04):

(a) a starch content (determined by the modified Ewers polarimetric method) exceeding that indicated in Column (2); and

(b) an ash content (after deduction of any added minerals) not exceeding that indicated in Column (3).

Otherwise, they fall in heading No.23.02.

(B) Products falling in this Chapter under the above provisions shall be classified in heading No.11.01 or 11.02 if the percentage passing through a woven metal wire cloth sieve with the aperture indicated in Column (4) or (5) is not less, by weight, than that shown against the cereal concerned.

Otherwise, they fall in heading No.11.03 or 11.04.

3. For the purposes of heading No.11.03, the terms "groats" and "meal" mean products obtained by the fragmentation of cereal grains, of which:

(a) in the case of maize (corn) products,at least 95% by weight passes through a woven metal wire cloth sieve with an aperture of 2mm;

(b) in the case of other cereal products, at least 95% by weight passes through a woven metal wire cloth sieve with an aperture of 1.25mm.

序号 No.	税则号列 Tariff Line	中文货品名称 Article Description in Chinese	最惠国税率 MFN(%)	协定税率 Agreement(%)		特惠税率 SP(%)		普通税率 Gen(%)	英文货品名称 Article Description
	11.01	**小麦或混合麦的细粉**							**Wheat or meslin flour**
817	1101.0000	小麦或混合麦的细粉	65①	50	东盟AS			130	Wheat or maslin flour
	11.02	**其他谷物细粉，但小麦或混合麦的细粉除外：**							**Cereal flours other than of wheat or meslin:**
818	1102.2000	-玉米细粉	40②					130	-Maize (corn) flour
		-其他：							-Other:
		---大米细粉：							---Rice flour:
819	1102.9011	----籼米的	40③					130	----Of long grain
820	1102.9019	----其他	40④	20	东盟AS			130	----Other
821	1102.9090	---其他	5	0	澳AU,巴PK,冰岛IS,东盟AS,哥CR,韩国KR,秘鲁PE,瑞士CH,新西兰NZ,智利CL	0	柬埔寨KH,受惠国LD	14	---Other
	11.03	**谷物的粗粒、粗粉及团粒：**							**Cereal groats, meal and pellets:**
		-粗粒及粗粉：							-Groats and meal:
822	1103.1100	--小麦的	65⑤	50	东盟AS			130	--Of wheat
823	1103.1300	--玉米的	65⑥	50	东盟AS			130	--Of maize (corn)
		--其他：							--Of other cereals:
824	1103.1910	---燕麦的	5	0	澳AU,巴PK,冰岛IS,东盟AS,哥CR,韩国KR,秘鲁PE,瑞士CH,新西兰NZ,智利CL	0	受惠国LD	14	---Of oats
		---大米的：							---Of rice:
825	1103.1921	----籼米的	10⑦					70	----Of long grain
826	1103.1929	----其他	10⑧					70	----Other
827	1103.1990	---其他	5	0	澳AU,巴PK,冰岛IS,东盟AS,哥CR,韩国KR,秘鲁PE,瑞士CH,新西兰NZ,智利CL	0	柬埔寨KH,受惠国LD	14	---Other
		-团粒：							-Pellets:
828	1103.2010	---小麦的	65⑨	50	东盟AS			180	---Of wheat
829	1103.2090	---其他	20	0	冰岛IS,东盟AS,哥CR,新加坡SG,新西兰NZ,智利CL	0	受惠国$_1$LD$_1$	50	---Of other cereals
				6	秘鲁PE				
				12	澳AU				
				14	瑞士CH				
				17.3	韩国KR				
	11.04	**经其他加工的谷物（例如，去壳、滚压、制片、制成粒状、切片或粗磨），但税号10.06的稻谷、大米除外；谷物胚芽，整粒、滚压、制片或磨碎的：**							**Cereal grains otherwise worked (for example, hulled, rolled, flaked, pearled, sliced or kibbled) , except rice of heading 1006; germ of cereals, whole, rolled, flaked or ground:**
		-滚压或制片的谷物：							-Rolled or flaked grains:

①配额税率：6
In-quota Tariff: 6
②配额税率：9
In-quota Tariff: 9
③配额税率：9
In-quota Tariff: 9
④配额税率：9
In-quota Tariff: 9
⑤配额税率：9
In-quota Tariff: 9
⑥配额税率：9
In-quota Tariff: 9
⑦配额税率：9
In-quota Tariff: 9
⑧配额税率：9
In-quota Tariff: 9
⑨配额税率：10
In-quota Tariff: 10

序号 No.	税则号列 Tariff Line	中文货品名称 Article Description in Chinese	最惠国税率 MFN(%)	协定税率 Agreement(%)	特惠税率 SP(%)	普通税率 Gen(%)	英文货品名称 Article Description
830	1104.1200	--燕麦的	20	0 冰岛IS,东盟AS,哥CR,新加坡SG,新西兰NZ,智利CL 6 秘鲁PE 12 澳AU 14 瑞士CH 17.3 韩国KR	0 受惠国$_1$LD$_1$	50	--Of oats
		--其他:					--Of other cereals:
831	1104.1910	---大麦的	20	0 冰岛IS,东盟AS,哥CR,新加坡SG,新西兰NZ,智利CL 6 秘鲁PE 12 澳AU 14 瑞士CH 17.3 韩国KR	0 受惠国$_1$LD$_1$	50	---Of barley
832	1104.1990	---其他	20	0 冰岛IS,东盟AS,哥CR,新加坡SG,新西兰NZ,智利CL 6 秘鲁PE 12 澳AU 14 瑞士CH 17.3 韩国KR	0 受惠国$_1$LD$_1$	50	---Other
		-经其他加工的谷物（例如，去壳、制成粒状、切片或粗磨）:					-Other worked grains (for example, hulled, pearled, sliced or kibbled) :
833	1104.2200	--燕麦的	20	0 冰岛IS,东盟AS,哥CR,新加坡SG,新西兰NZ,智利CL 6 秘鲁PE 12 澳AU 14 瑞士CH 17.3 韩国KR	0 受惠国$_1$LD$_1$	50	--Of oats
834	1104.2300	--玉米的	65①	50 东盟AS		180	--Of maize (corn)
		--其他:					--Of other cereals:
835	1104.2910	---大麦的	65	0 东盟AS,哥CR,新加坡SG,新西兰NZ,智利CL 19.5 秘鲁PE 39 澳AU	0 受惠国$_1$LD$_1$	114	---Of barley
836	1104.2990	---其他	20	0 冰岛IS,东盟AS,哥CR,新加坡SG,新西兰NZ,智利CL 6 秘鲁PE 12 澳AU 14 瑞士CH 17.3 韩国KR	0 受惠国$_1$LD$_1$	50	---Other
837	1104.3000	-谷物胚芽，整粒、滚压、制片或磨碎的	20	0 冰岛IS,东盟AS,哥CR,新加坡SG,新西兰NZ,智利CL 6 秘鲁PE 12 澳AU 14 瑞士CH 17.3 韩国KR	0 受惠国$_1$LD$_1$	50	-Germ of cereals, whole, rolled, flaked or ground
	11.05	**马铃薯的细粉、粗粉、粉末、粉片、颗粒及团粒:**					**Flour, meal, powder, flakes, granules and pellets of potatoes:**
838	1105.1000	-细粉、粗粉及粉末	15	0 冰岛IS,东盟AS,哥CR,秘鲁PE,新加坡SG,新西兰NZ,智利CL 9 澳AU 10.5 瑞士CH 12 巴PK,韩国KR	0 受惠国$_1$LD$_1$	50	-Flour, meal and powder

①配额税率: 10
In-quota Tariff: 10

序号 No.	税则号列 Tariff Line	中文货品名称 Article Description in Chinese	最惠国税率 MFN(%)	协定税率 Agreement(%)	特惠税率 SP(%)	普通税率 Gen(%)	英文货品名称 Article Description
839	1105.2000	-粉片、颗粒及团粒	15	0 冰岛IS,东盟AS,哥CR,新加坡SG,新西兰NZ,智利CL 4.5 秘鲁PE 9 澳AU 10.5 瑞士CH 12 巴PK,韩国KR	0 受惠国$_1$LD$_1$	50	-Flakes, granules and pellets
	11.06	**用税号07.13的干豆或税号07.14的西谷茎髓及植物根茎、块茎制成的细粉、粗粉及粉末；用第八章的产品制成的细粉、粗粉及粉末：**					**Flour, meal and powder of the dried leguminous vegetables of heading 0713, of sago or of roots or tubers of heading 0714 or of the products of Chapter 8:**
840	1106.1000	-用税号07. 13的干豆制成的	10	0 冰岛IS,东盟AS,哥CR,秘鲁PE,新加坡SG,新西兰NZ,智利CL 4 瑞士CH 6 澳AU 8 韩国KR	0 柬埔寨KH,受惠国LD	30	-Of the dried leguminous vegetables of heading No.07.13
841	1106.2000	-用税号07. 14的西谷茎髓及植物根茎、块茎制成的	20	0 冰岛IS,东盟AS,哥CR,秘鲁PE,新加坡SG,新西兰NZ,智利CL 12 澳AU 14 瑞士CH 17.3 韩国KR	0 柬埔寨KH,老挝LA,缅甸MM,受惠国LD	50	-Of sago or of roots or tubers of head-ing No.07.14
842	1106.3000	-用第八章的产品制成的	20	0 冰岛IS,东盟AS,哥CR,新加坡SG,新西兰NZ,智利CL 6 秘鲁PE 10 巴PK,亚太AP 12 澳AU 14 瑞士CH 17.3 韩国KR	0 受惠国$_1$LD$_1$	80	-Of the products of Chapter 8
	11.07	**麦芽，不论是否焙制：**					**Malt, whether or not roasted:**
843	1107.1000	-未焙制	10	0 冰岛IS,东盟AS,哥CR,新加坡SG,新西兰NZ,智利CL 3 秘鲁PE 4 瑞士CH 5 巴PK 6 澳AU 8 韩国KR	0 受惠国$_1$LD$_1$	50	-Not roasted
844	1107.2000	-已焙制	10	0 冰岛IS,东盟AS,哥CR,新加坡SG,新西兰NZ,智利CL 3 秘鲁PE 4 瑞士CH 5 巴PK 6 澳AU 8 韩国KR	0 受惠国$_1$LD$_1$	50	-Roasted
	11.08	**淀粉；菊粉：**					**Starches; inulin:**
		-淀粉：					-Starches:
845	1108.1100	--小麦淀粉	20	0 冰岛IS,东盟AS,哥CR,新加坡SG,新西兰NZ,智利CL 6 秘鲁PE 12 澳AU 14 瑞士CH 17.3 韩国KR	0 受惠国$_1$LD$_1$	50	--Wheat starch
846	1108.1200	--玉米淀粉	20	0 冰岛IS,东盟AS,哥CR,秘鲁PE,新加坡SG,新西兰NZ,智利CL 12 澳AU 14 瑞士CH 17.3 韩国KR	0 受惠国$_1$LD$_1$	50	--Maize (corn) starch

序号 No.	税则号列 Tariff Line	中文货品名称 Article Description in Chinese	最惠国税率 MFN(%)	协定税率 Agreement(%)	特惠税率 SP(%)	普通税率 Gen(%)	英文货品名称 Article Description
847	1108.1300	--马铃薯淀粉	15	0 冰岛IS,东盟AS,哥CR,新加坡SG,新西兰NZ,智利CL 4.5 秘鲁PE 9 澳AU 10.5 瑞士CH 12 巴PK,韩国KR	0 受惠国$_1$LD$_1$	50	--Potato starch
848	1108.1400	--木薯淀粉	10	0 冰岛IS,东盟AS,哥CR,秘鲁PE,新加坡SG,新西兰NZ,智利CL 4 瑞士CH 5 巴PK 6 澳AU 8 韩国KR	0 受惠国LD	50	--Manioc (cassava) starch
849	1108.1900	--其他	20	0 冰岛IS,东盟AS,哥CR,新加坡SG,新西兰NZ,智利CL 6 秘鲁PE 12 澳AU 14 瑞士CH 17.3 韩国KR	0 受惠国$_1$LD$_1$	50	--Other starches
850	1108.2000	-菊粉	20	0 冰岛IS,东盟AS,哥CR,新加坡SG,新西兰NZ,智利CL 6 秘鲁PE 12 澳AU 14 瑞士CH 16 韩国KR	0 受惠国$_1$LD$_1$	50	-Inulin
	11.09	**面筋，不论是否干制**					**Wheat gluten, whether or not dried**
851	1109.0000	面筋，不论是否干制	18	0 冰岛IS,东盟AS,哥CR,新加坡SG,新西兰NZ,智利CL 5.4 秘鲁PE 10.8 澳AU 12.6 瑞士CH 14.4 巴PK 15.6 韩国KR	0 受惠国$_1$LD$_1$	80	Wheat gluten, whether or not dried

第十二章
含油子仁及果实；项子仁及果实；工业用或药用植物；稻草、秸秆及饲料

注释：

一、税号 12.07 主要包括棕榈果及棕榈仁、棉子、蓖麻子、芝麻、芥子、红花子、罂粟子、牛油树果。但不包括税号 08.01 或 08.02 的产品及油橄榄（第七章或第二十章）。

二、税号 12.08 不仅包括未脱脂的细粉和粗粉，而且包括部分或全部脱脂以及用其本身的油料全部或部分复脂的细粉和粗粉。但不包括税号 23.04 至 23.06 的残渣。

三、甜菜子、草子及其他草本植物种子、观赏用花的种子、蔬菜种子、林木种子、果树种子、巢菜子（蚕豆除外）、羽扇豆属植物种子，可一律视为种植用种子，归入税号 12.09。

但下列各项即使作种子用，也不归入税号 12.09：

（一）豆类蔬菜或甜玉米（第七章）；
（二）第九章的调味香料及其他产品；
（三）谷物（第十章）；
（四）税号 12.01 至 12.07 或 12.11 的产品。

四、税号 12.11 主要包括下列植物或这些植物的某部分：罗勒、琉璃苣、人参、海索草、甘草、薄荷、迷迭香、芸香、鼠尾草及苦艾。但税号 12.11 不包括：
（一）第三十章的药品；
（二）第三十三章的芳香料制品及化妆盥洗品；
（三）税号 38.08 的杀虫剂、杀菌剂、除草剂、消毒剂及类似产品。

五、税号 12.12 的“海草及其他藻类”不包括：

（一）税号 21.02 的已死的单细胞微生物；
（二）税号 30.02 的培养微生物；
（三）税号 31.01 或 31.05 的肥料。

子目注释：

子目 1205.10 所称“低芥子酸油菜子”，是指所获取的固定油中芥子酸含量按重量计低于 2%，以及所得的固体成分每克葡萄糖苷酸（酯）含量低于 30 微摩尔的油菜子。

Chapter 12
Oil seeds and oleaginous fruits; miscellaneous grains, seeds and fruit; industrial or medicinal plants; straw and fodder

Notes:

1. Heading No.12.07 applies, *inter alia*, to palm nuts and kernels, cotton seeds, castor oil seeds, sesamum seeds, mustard seeds, safflower seeds, poppy seeds and shea nuts (karite nuts). It does not apply to products of heading No.08.01 or 08.02 or to olives (Chapter 7 or Chapter 20).

2. Heading No.12.08 applies not only to non-defatted flours and meals but also to flours and meals which have been defatted or partially defatted and wholly or partially refatted with their original oils. It does not, however, apply to residues of headings No.23.04 to 23.06.

3. For the purposes of heading No.12.09, beet seeds, grass and other herbage seeds, seeds of ornamental flowers, vegetable seeds, seeds of forest trees, seeds of fruit trees, seeds of vetches(other than those of the species Vicia faba) or of lupines are to be regarded as “seeds of a kind used for sowing”.
Heading No.12.09 does not, however, apply to the following even if for sowing:
(a) Laguminous vegetables or sweet corn (Chapter 7);
(b) Spices or other products of Chapter 9;
(c) Cereals (Chapter 10); or
(d) Products of headings No.12.01 to 12.07 or 12.11.

4. Heading No.12.11 applies, inter alia, to the following plants or parts thereof: Basil, borage, ginseng, hyssop, liquorice, all species of mint, rosemary, rue, sage and wormwood. Heading No.12.11does not, however, apply to:
(a)Medicaments of Chapter 30;
(b)Perfumery, cosmetic or toilet preparations of Chapter 33; or
(c)Insecticides, fungicides, herbicides, disinfectants or similar products of heading No.38.08.

5. For the purposes of heading No.12.12, the term “seaweeds and other algae” does not include:
(a) Dead singlecell micro-organisms of heading No.21.02;
(b) Cultures of micro-organisms of heading No.30.02; or
(c) Fertillizers of heading No.31.01 or 31.05.

Subheading Note:

For the purposes of subheading No.1205.10, the expression “low erucic acid rape or colza seeds” means rape of colza seeds yielding a fixed oil which has an erucic acid content of less than 2% by weight and yielding a solid component which contains less than 30 micromoles of glucosinolates per gram.

序号 No.	税则号列 Tariff Line	中文货品名称 Article Description in Chinese	最惠国税率 MFN(%)	协定税率 Agreement(%)	特惠税率 SP(%)	普通税率 Gen(%)	英文货品名称 Article Description
	12.01	**大豆，不论是否破碎：**					**Soya beans, whether or not broken:**
852	1201.1000	-种用	0		0 受惠国LD	180	-Seed
		-其他：					-Other:
853	1201.9010	---黄大豆	3	0 巴PK,冰岛IS,东盟AS,哥CR,韩国KR,秘鲁PE,瑞士CH,新西兰NZ,亚太AP,智利CL	0 柬埔寨KH,老挝LA,受惠国LD	180	---Yellow soya beans
854	1201.9020	---黑大豆	3	0 巴PK,冰岛IS,东盟AS,哥CR,韩国KR,秘鲁PE,瑞士CH,新西兰NZ,亚太AP,智利CL	0 柬埔寨KH,老挝LA,受惠国LD	180	---Black soya beans
855	1201.9030	---青大豆	3	0 巴PK,冰岛IS,东盟AS,哥CR,韩国KR,秘鲁PE,瑞士CH,新西兰NZ,亚太AP,智利CL	0 柬埔寨KH,老挝LA,受惠国LD	180	---Green soya beans
856	1201.9090	---其他	3	0 巴PK,冰岛IS,东盟AS,哥CR,韩国KR,秘鲁PE,瑞士CH,新西兰NZ,亚太AP,智利CL	0 受惠国LD	180	---Other
	12.02	**未焙炒或未烹煮的花生，不论是否去壳或破碎：**					**Groundnuts, not roasted or otherwise cooked, whether or not shelled or broken:**
857	1202.3000	-种用	0		0 受惠国LD	0	-Seed
		-其他：					-Other:
858	1202.4100	--未去壳	15	0 冰岛IS,东盟AS,哥CR,新加坡SG,新西兰NZ,智利CL 4.5 秘鲁PE 9 澳AU 10.5 瑞士CH 12 巴PK,韩国KR	0 老挝LA,受惠国LD	70	--In shell
859	1202.4200	--去壳，不论是否破碎	15	0 冰岛IS,东盟AS,哥CR,新加坡SG,新西兰NZ,智利CL 4.5 秘鲁PE 9 澳AU 10.5 瑞士CH 12 巴PK,韩国KR	0 老挝LA,受惠国LD	70	--Shelled, whether or not broken
	12.03	**干椰子肉**					**Copra**
860	1203.0000	干椰子肉	15	0 冰岛IS,东盟AS,哥CR,新加坡SG,新西兰NZ,智利CL 4.5 秘鲁PE 7.5 巴PK,亚太AP 9 澳AU 10.5 瑞士CH 12 韩国KR	0 柬埔寨KH,受惠国LD	30	Copra
	12.04	**亚麻子，不论是否破碎**					**Linseed, whether or not broken**
861	1204.0000	亚麻子，不论是否破碎	15	0 冰岛IS,东盟AS,哥CR,新加坡SG,新西兰NZ,智利CL 4.5 秘鲁PE 9 澳AU 10.5 瑞士CH 12 巴PK,韩国KR	0 受惠国$_1$LD$_1$	70	Linseed, whether or not broken
	12.05	**油菜子，不论是否破碎：**					**Rape or colza seeds, whether or not broken:**
		-低芥子酸油菜籽：					-Low erucic acid rape or colza seeds:
862	1205.1010	---种用	0		0 受惠国LD	80	---Seed
863	1205.1090	---其他	9	0 巴PK,冰岛IS,东盟AS,哥CR,秘鲁PE,新西兰NZ,亚太AP,智利CL 3.6 瑞士CH 5.4 韩国KR	0 受惠国$_1$LD$_1$	80	---Other

序号 No.	税则号列 Tariff Line	中文货品名称 Article Description in Chinese	最惠国税率 MFN(%)	协定税率 Agreement(%)	特惠税率 SP(%)	普通税率 Gen(%)	英文货品名称 Article Description
		-其他：					-Other:
864	1205.9010	---种用	0		0 受惠国LD	80	---Seed
865	1205.9090	---其他	9	0 巴PK,冰岛IS,东盟AS,哥CR,秘鲁PE,新西兰NZ,亚太AP,智利CL 3.6 瑞士CH 5.4 韩国KR	0 受惠国$_1$LD$_1$	80	---Other
	12.06	**葵花子，不论是否破碎：**					**Sunflower seeds, whether or not broken:**
866	1206.0010	---种用	0		0 受惠国LD	0	---Seed
867	1206.0090	---其他	15	0 冰岛IS,东盟AS,哥CR,新加坡SG,新西兰NZ,智利CL 4.5 秘鲁PE 9 澳AU 10.5 瑞士CH 12 巴PK,韩国KR	0 受惠国$_1$LD$_1$	70	---Other
	12.07	**其他含油子仁及果实，不论是否破碎：**					**Other oil seeds and oleaginous fruits, whether or not broken:**
		-棕榈果及棕榈仁：					-Palm nuts and kernels:
868	1207.1010	---种用	0		0 受惠国LD	0	---Seed
869	1207.1090	---其他	10	0 冰岛IS,东盟AS,哥CR,秘鲁PE,新加坡SG,新西兰NZ,智利CL 4 瑞士CH 5 巴PK 6 澳AU 8 韩国KR	0 柬埔寨KH,受惠国LD	70	---Other
		-棉子：					-Cotton seeds:
870	1207.2100	--种用	0		0 受惠国LD	0	--Seed
871	1207.2900	--其他	15	0 冰岛IS,东盟AS,哥CR,新加坡SG,新西兰NZ,智利CL 4.5 秘鲁PE 9 澳AU 10.5 瑞士CH 12 巴PK,韩国KR	0 受惠国$_1$LD$_1$	70	--Other
		-蓖麻子：					-Castor oil seeds:
872	1207.3010	---种用	0		0 受惠国LD	0	---Seed
873	1207.3090	---其他	15	0 冰岛IS,东盟AS,哥CR,新加坡SG,新西兰NZ,智利CL 4.5 秘鲁PE 9 澳AU 10.5 瑞士CH 12 韩国KR	0 柬埔寨KH,老挝LA,缅甸MM,受惠国LD	70	---Other
		-芝麻：					-Sesamum seeds:
874	1207.4010	---种用	0		0 受惠国LD	0	---Seed
875	1207.4090	---其他	10	0 冰岛IS,东盟AS,哥CR,秘鲁PE,新加坡SG,新西兰NZ,智利CL 4 瑞士CH 6 澳AU 8 韩国KR 9 巴PK,亚太AP	0 柬埔寨KH,老挝LA,缅甸MM,受惠国LD	70	---Other
		-芥子：					-Mustard seeds:
876	1207.5010	---种用	0		0 受惠国LD	0	---Seed
877	1207.5090	---其他	15	0 冰岛IS,东盟AS,哥CR,新加坡SG,新西兰NZ,智利CL 4.5 秘鲁PE 9 澳AU 10.5 瑞士CH 12 巴PK,韩国KR	0 受惠国$_1$LD$_1$	70	---Other

序号 No.	税则号列 Tariff Line	中文货品名称 Article Description in Chinese	最惠国税率 MFN(%)	协定税率 Agreement(%)	特惠税率 SP(%)	普通税率 Gen(%)	英文货品名称 Article Description
		-红花子：					-Safflower (*Carthamus tinctorius*) seeds:
878	1207.6010	---种用	0		0 受惠国LD	0	---Seed
879	1207.6090	---其他	20	0 冰岛IS,东盟AS,哥CR,新加坡SG,新西兰NZ,智利CL 6 秘鲁PE 12 澳AU 14 瑞士CH 17.3 韩国KR	0 受惠国$_1$LD$_1$	70	---Other
		-甜瓜的子：					-Melon seeds:
880	1207.7010	---种用	0		0 受惠国LD	0	---Seed
		---其他：					---Other:
881	1207.7091	----黑瓜子	20	0 冰岛IS,东盟AS,哥CR,新加坡SG,新西兰NZ,智利CL 6 秘鲁PE 12 澳AU 14 瑞士CH 17.3 韩国KR	0 受惠国$_1$LD$_1$	80	----Black watermelon seeds
882	1207.7092	----红瓜子	20	0 冰岛IS,东盟AS,哥CR,新加坡SG,新西兰NZ,智利CL 6 秘鲁PE 12 澳AU 14 瑞士CH 17.3 韩国KR	0 受惠国$_1$LD$_1$	80	----Red watermelon seeds
883	1207.7099	----其他	30	0 冰岛IS,东盟AS,哥CR,新西兰NZ,智利CL 9 秘鲁PE 18 澳AU 27 韩国KR	0 受惠国LD	70	----Other
		-其他：					-Other:
884	1207.9100	--罂粟子	20	0 冰岛IS,东盟AS,哥CR,新加坡SG,新西兰NZ,智利CL 6 秘鲁PE 12 澳AU 14 瑞士CH 17.3 韩国KR	0 受惠国$_1$LD$_1$	70	--Poppy seeds
		--其他：					--Other:
885	1207.9910	---种用	0		0 受惠国LD	0	---Seed
		---其他：					---Other:
886	1207.9991	----牛油树果	20	0 冰岛IS,东盟AS,哥CR,新加坡SG,新西兰NZ,智利CL 6 秘鲁PE 12 澳AU 14 瑞士CH 17.3 韩国KR	0 缅甸MM,受惠国LD	70	----Shea nuts (karite nuts)
887	1207.9999	----其他	10	0 冰岛IS,东盟AS,哥CR,新加坡SG,新西兰NZ,智利CL 3 秘鲁PE 4 瑞士CH 5 巴PK 6 澳AU 8 韩国KR	0 柬埔寨KH,老挝LA,缅甸MM,受惠国LD	70	----Other
	12.08	**含油子仁或果实的细粉及粗粉，但芥子粉除外：**					**Flours and meals of oil seeds or oleaginous fruits, other than those of mustard:**
888	1208.1000	-大豆粉	9	0 冰岛IS,东盟AS,哥CR,秘鲁PE,新西兰NZ,智利CL 3.6 瑞士CH 5 巴PK 5.4 澳AU,韩国KR	0 柬埔寨KH,受惠国LD	70	-Of soya beans

序号 No.	税则号列 Tariff Line	中文货品名称 Article Description in Chinese	最惠国税率 MFN(%)	协定税率 Agreement(%)	特惠税率 SP(%)	普通税率 Gen(%)	英文货品名称 Article Description
889	1208.9000	-其他	15	0 冰岛IS,东盟AS,哥CR,香港HK,新加坡SG,新西兰NZ,智利CL 4.5 秘鲁PE 9 澳AU 10.5 瑞士CH 12 巴PK,韩国KR	0 柬埔寨KH,受惠国LD	80	-Other
	12.09	**种植用的种子、果实及孢子：**					**Seeds, fruit and spores, of a kind used for sowing:**
890	1209.1000	-糖甜菜子	0		0 受惠国LD	0	-Sugar beet seeds
		-饲料植物种子：					-Seeds of forage plants:
891	1209.2100	--紫苜蓿子	0		0 受惠国LD	0	--Lucerne (alfalfa) seeds
892	1209.2200	--三叶草子	0		0 受惠国LD	0	--Clover (Trifolium spp.) seeds
893	1209.2300	--羊茅子	0		0 受惠国LD	0	--Fescue seeds
894	1209.2400	--草地早熟禾子	0		0 受惠国LD	0	--Kentucky blue grass (Poa pratensis L.) seeds
895	1209.2500	--黑麦草种子	0		0 受惠国LD	0	--Rye grass (Lolium multiflorum Lam., Lolium perenne L.) seeds
		--其他：					--Other:
896	1209.2910	---甜菜籽，糖甜菜籽除外	0		0 受惠国LD	0	---Sugar beet seed
897	1209.2990	---其他	0		0 受惠国LD	0	---Other
898	1209.3000	-草本花卉植物种子	0		0 受惠国LD	0	-Seeds of herbaceous plants cultivated principally for their flowers
		-其他：					-Other:
899	1209.9100	--蔬菜种子	0		0 受惠国LD	0	--Vegetable seeds
900	1209.9900	--其他	0		0 受惠国LD	0	--Other
	12.10	**鲜或干的啤酒花，不论是否研磨或制成团粒；蛇麻腺：**					**Hop cones, fresh or dried, whethr or not ground, powdered or in the form of pellets; lupulin:**
901	1210.1000	-啤酒花，未经研磨也未制成团粒	20	0 冰岛IS,东盟AS,哥CR,新加坡SG,新西兰NZ,智利CL 6 秘鲁PE 12 澳AU 14 瑞士CH 17.3 韩国KR	0 受惠国$_1$LD$_1$	50	-Hop cones, neither ground nor powdered nor in the form of pellets
902	1210.2000	-啤酒花，经研磨或制成团粒；蛇麻腺	10	0 冰岛IS,东盟AS,哥CR,秘鲁PE,新加坡SG,新西兰NZ,智利CL 4 瑞士CH 5 巴PK 6 澳AU 8 韩国KR	0 受惠国LD	50	-Hop cones, ground, powdered or in the form of pellets; lupulin
	12.11	**主要用作香料、药料、杀虫、杀菌或类似用途的植物或这些植物的某部分（包括子仁及果实），鲜或干的，不论是否切割、压碎或研磨成粉：**					**Plants and parts of plants (including seeds and fruits) , of a kind used primarily in perfumery, in pharmacy or for insecticidal, fungicidal or similar purposes, fresh or dried, whether or not cut, crushed or powdered:**
		-人参：					-Ginseng roots:
903	1211.2010	---西洋参	7.5	0 澳门MO,冰岛IS,东盟AS,哥CR,韩国KR,秘鲁PE,香港HK,新加坡SG,新西兰NZ,智利CL 3 瑞士CH 4.5 澳AU 5 巴PK	0 受惠国LD	70	---American ginseng

序号 No.	税则号列 Tariff Line	中文货品名称 Article Description in Chinese	最惠国税率 MFN(%)	协定税率 Agreement(%)	特惠税率 SP(%)	普通税率 Gen(%)	英文货品名称 Article Description
904	1211.2020	---野山参(西洋参除外)	20	0 冰岛IS,东盟AS,哥CR,新加坡SG,新西兰NZ,智利CL 6 秘鲁PE 12 澳AU 14 瑞士CH 16 巴PK 16.4 亚太AP 17.3 韩国KR	0 受惠国$_1$LD$_1$	90	---Wild ginseng (other than American ginseng)
		---其他:					---Other:
905	1211.2091	----鲜的	20	0 冰岛IS,东盟AS,哥CR,香港HK,新加坡SG,新西兰NZ,智利CL 6 秘鲁PE 12 澳AU 14 瑞士CH 17.3 韩国KR	0 受惠国$_1$LD$_1$	50	----Fresh
906	1211.2099	----其他	20	0 冰岛IS,东盟AS,哥CR,香港HK,新加坡SG,新西兰NZ,智利CL 6 秘鲁PE 12 澳AU 14 瑞士CH	0 受惠国$_1$LD$_1$	50	----Other
907	1211.3000	-古柯叶	9	0 冰岛IS,东盟AS,哥CR,秘鲁PE,新西兰NZ,智利CL 3.6 瑞士CH 5 巴PK 5.4 澳AU,韩国KR	0 柬埔寨KH,受惠国LD	50	-Coca leaf
908	1211.4000	-罂粟杆	9	0 冰岛IS,东盟AS,哥CR,秘鲁PE,新西兰NZ,智利CL 3.6 瑞士CH 5 巴PK 5.4 澳AU,韩国KR	0 柬埔寨KH,受惠国LD	50	-Poppy straw
		-其他:					-Other:
		---主要用作药料的植物及其某部分:					---Of a kind used primarily in pharmacy:
909	1211.9011	----当归	6	0 巴PK,冰岛IS,东盟AS,哥CR,韩国KR,秘鲁PE,新西兰NZ,智利CL 2.4 瑞士CH 3 亚太AP 3.6 澳AU	0 柬埔寨KH,受惠国LD	30	----Radix angelicae sinensis
910	1211.9012	----三七(田七)	6	0 巴PK,冰岛IS,东盟AS,哥CR,韩国KR,秘鲁PE,新西兰NZ,智利CL 2.4 瑞士CH 3 亚太AP 3.6 澳AU	0 柬埔寨KH,受惠国LD	20	----Radix pseudoginseng
911	1211.9013	----党参	6	0 巴PK,冰岛IS,东盟AS,哥CR,韩国KR,秘鲁PE,新西兰NZ,智利CL 2.4 瑞士CH 3 亚太AP 3.6 澳AU	0 受惠国LD	20	----Radix codonopsitis
912	1211.9014	----黄连	6	0 巴PK,冰岛IS,东盟AS,哥CR,韩国KR,秘鲁PE,新西兰NZ,智利CL 2.4 瑞士CH 3 亚太AP 3.6 澳AU	0 受惠国LD	20	----Rhizoma coptidis

序号 No.	税则号列 Tariff Line	中文货品名称 Article Description in Chinese	最惠国税率 MFN(%)	协定税率 Agreement(%)		特惠税率 SP(%)		普通税率 Gen(%)	英文货品名称 Article Description
913	1211.9015	----菊花	6	0 2.4 3 3.6	巴PK,冰岛IS,东盟AS,哥CR,韩国KR,秘鲁PE,新西兰NZ,智利CL 瑞士CH 亚太AP 澳AU	0	柬埔寨KH,受惠国LD	20	----Flos chrysanthemi
914	1211.9016	----冬虫夏草	6	0 2.4 3 3.6	澳门MO,巴PK,冰岛IS,东盟AS,哥CR,韩国KR,秘鲁PE,新西兰NZ,智利CL 瑞士CH 亚太AP 澳AU	0	柬埔寨KH,受惠国LD	20	----Cordyceps sinensis
915	1211.9017	----贝母	6	0 2.4 3 3.6	巴PK,冰岛IS,东盟AS,哥CR,韩国KR,秘鲁PE,新西兰NZ,智利CL 瑞士CH 亚太AP 澳AU	0	柬埔寨KH,受惠国LD	20	----Bulbs fritillariae thunbergii
916	1211.9018	----川芎	6	0 2.4 3 3.6	巴PK,冰岛IS,东盟AS,哥CR,韩国KR,秘鲁PE,新西兰NZ,智利CL 瑞士CH 亚太AP 澳AU	0	柬埔寨KH,受惠国LD	20	----Rhizoma ligustici
917	1211.9019	----半夏	6	0 2.4 3 3.6	巴PK,冰岛IS,东盟AS,哥CR,韩国KR,秘鲁PE,新西兰NZ,智利CL 瑞士CH 亚太AP 澳AU	0	柬埔寨KH,受惠国LD	20	----Rhizoma pinelliae
918	1211.9021	----白芍	6	0 2.4 3 3.6	巴PK,冰岛IS,东盟AS,哥CR,韩国KR,秘鲁PE,新西兰NZ,智利CL 瑞士CH 亚太AP 澳AU	0	柬埔寨KH,受惠国LD	20	----Radix p aeoniae lactiflorae
919	1211.9022	----天麻	6	0 2.4 3 3.6	巴PK,冰岛IS,东盟AS,哥CR,韩国KR,秘鲁PE,新西兰NZ,智利CL 瑞士CH 亚太AP 澳AU	0	柬埔寨KH,受惠国LD	20	----Rhizoma gastrodiae
920	1211.9023	----黄芪	6	0 2.4 3 3.6	巴PK,冰岛IS,东盟AS,哥CR,韩国KR,秘鲁PE,新西兰NZ,智利CL 瑞士CH 亚太AP 澳AU	0	柬埔寨KH,受惠国LD	30	----Radix astragali
921	1211.9024	----大黄、籽黄	6	0 2.4 3 3.6	巴PK,冰岛IS,东盟AS,哥CR,韩国KR,秘鲁PE,新西兰NZ,智利CL 瑞士CH 亚太AP 澳AU	0	柬埔寨KH,受惠国LD	20	----Rhubarb
922	1211.9025	----白术	6	0 2.4 3 3.6	巴PK,冰岛IS,东盟AS,哥CR,韩国KR,秘鲁PE,新西兰NZ,智利CL 瑞士CH 亚太AP 澳AU	0	柬埔寨KH,受惠国LD	20	----Rhizoma atractylodis macrocephalae

序号 No.	税则号列 Tariff Line	中文货品名称 Article Description in Chinese	最惠国税率 MFN(%)	协定税率 Agreement(%)	特惠税率 SP(%)	普通税率 Gen(%)	英文货品名称 Article Description
923	1211.9026	----地黄	6	0 巴PK,冰岛IS,东盟AS,哥CR,韩国KR,秘鲁PE,新西兰NZ,智利CL 2.4 瑞士CH 3 亚太AP 3.6 澳AU	0 柬埔寨KH,受惠国LD	20	----Radix rehmanniae
924	1211.9027	----槐米	6	0 巴PK,冰岛IS,东盟AS,哥CR,韩国KR,秘鲁PE,新西兰NZ,智利CL 2.4 瑞士CH 3 亚太AP 3.6 澳AU	0 柬埔寨KH,受惠国LD	20	----Flos sophorae
925	1211.9028	----杜仲	6	0 巴PK,冰岛IS,东盟AS,哥CR,韩国KR,秘鲁PE,新西兰NZ,智利CL 2.4 瑞士CH 3 亚太AP 3.6 澳AU	0 柬埔寨KH,受惠国LD	20	----Cortex eucommiae
926	1211.9029	----茯苓	6	0 巴PK,冰岛IS,东盟AS,哥CR,韩国KR,秘鲁PE,新西兰NZ,智利CL 2.4 瑞士CH 3 亚太AP 3.6 澳AU	0 柬埔寨KH,老挝LA,缅甸MM,受惠国LD	20	----Poria
927	1211.9031	----枸杞	6	0 巴PK,冰岛IS,东盟AS,哥CR,韩国KR,秘鲁PE,新西兰NZ,智利CL 2.4 瑞士CH 3 亚太AP 3.6 澳AU	0 柬埔寨KH,受惠国LD	30	----Fructus lycii
928	1211.9032	----大海子	6	0 巴PK,冰岛IS,东盟AS,哥CR,韩国KR,秘鲁PE,新西兰NZ,智利CL 2.4 瑞士CH 3 亚太AP 3.6 澳AU	0 柬埔寨KH,受惠国LD	20	----Bantaroi seeds
929	1211.9033	----沉香	3	0 澳AU,巴PK,冰岛IS,东盟AS,哥CR,韩国KR,秘鲁PE,瑞士CH,新西兰NZ,智利CL 1.5 亚太AP	0 柬埔寨KH,受惠国LD	20	----Aloes wood
930	1211.9034	----沙参	6	0 巴PK,冰岛IS,东盟AS,哥CR,韩国KR,秘鲁PE,新西兰NZ,智利CL 2.4 瑞士CH 3 亚太AP 3.6 澳AU	0 柬埔寨KH,受惠国LD	20	----Adenophora axilliflora
931	1211.9035	----青蒿	6	0 冰岛IS,东盟AS,哥CR,韩国KR,秘鲁PE,新西兰NZ,智利CL 2.4 瑞士CH 3.6 澳AU 5 巴PK	0 柬埔寨KH,受惠国LD	20	----Southernwood
932	1211.9036	----甘草	6△0	0 冰岛IS,东盟AS,哥CR,韩国KR,秘鲁PE,新西兰NZ,智利CL 2.4 瑞士CH 3.6 澳AU 5 巴PK	0 受惠国LD	30	----Liquorice roots
933	1211.9037	----黄芩	6	0 巴PK,冰岛IS,东盟AS,哥CR,韩国KR,秘鲁PE,新西兰NZ,智利CL 2.4 瑞士CH 3 亚太AP 3.6 澳AU	0 柬埔寨KH,老挝LA,缅甸MM,受惠国LD	20	----Radix scutellariae

序号 No.	税则号列 Tariff Line	中文货品名称 Article Description in Chinese	最惠国税率 MFN(%)	协定税率 Agreement(%)		特惠税率 SP(%)		普通税率 Gen(%)	英文货品名称 Article Description
934	1211.9038	----椴树(欧椴)花及叶	6	0 2.4 3 3.6	巴PK,冰岛IS,东盟AS,哥CR,韩国KR,秘鲁PE,新西兰NZ,智利CL 瑞士CH 亚太AP 澳AU	0	柬埔寨KH,老挝LA,缅甸MM,受惠国LD	20	----Flowers and leaves of Linden (*tilia europaea*)
935	1211.9039	----其他	6	0 2.4 3 3.6	巴PK,冰岛IS,东盟AS,哥CR,韩国KR,秘鲁PE,新西兰NZ,智利CL 瑞士CH 亚太AP 澳AU	0	柬埔寨KH,老挝LA,缅甸MM,受惠国LD	20	----Other
936	1211.9050	---主要用作香料的植物及其某部分	8	0 3.2 4 4.8	巴PK,冰岛IS,东盟AS,哥CR,秘鲁PE,新西兰NZ,智利CL 瑞士CH 亚太AP 澳AU,韩国KR	0	柬埔寨KH,受惠国LD	50	---Of a kind used primarily in perfumery
		---其他:							---Other:
937	1211.9091	----鱼藤根、除虫菊	3	0 1.5	澳AU,巴PK,冰岛IS,东盟AS,哥CR,韩国KR,秘鲁PE,瑞士CH,新西兰NZ,智利CL 亚太AP	0	柬埔寨KH,受惠国LD	11	----Derris roots and pyrethrum
938	1211.9099	----其他	9	0 3.6 4.5 5.4	冰岛IS,东盟AS,哥CR,秘鲁PE,新西兰NZ,智利CL 瑞士CH 巴PK,亚太AP 澳AU,韩国KR	0	柬埔寨KH,受惠国LD	30	----Other
	12.12	**鲜、冷、冻或干的刺槐豆、海草及其他藻类、甜菜及甘蔗，不论是否碾磨；主要供人食用的其他税号未列名的果核、果仁及植物产品(包括未焙制的菊苣根)：**							**Locust beans, seaweeds and other algae, sugar beet and sugar cane, fresh, chilled, frozen or dried, whether or not ground; fruit stones and kernels and other vegetable products (including unroasted chicory roots of the variety *Cichorium intybus sativum*) of a kind used primarily for human consumption, not elsewhere specified or included:**
		-海草及其他藻类:							-Seaweeds and other algae:
		--适合供人食用的:							--Fit for human consumption:
939	1212.2110	---海带	20	0 6 10 12 14 17.3	冰岛IS,东盟AS,哥CR,新加坡SG,新西兰NZ,智利CL 秘鲁PE 巴PK,亚太AP 澳AU 瑞士CH 韩国KR	0	受惠国$_1$LD$_1$	70	---Sea tangle
940	1212.2120	---发菜	20	0 6 10 12 14 17.3	冰岛IS,东盟AS,哥CR,新加坡SG,新西兰NZ,智利CL 秘鲁PE 巴PK,亚太AP 澳AU 瑞士CH 韩国KR	0	受惠国$_1$LD$_1$	70	---Blackmoss
		---裙带菜:							---Pinnatifida:

序号 No.	税则号列 Tariff Line	中文货品名称 Article Description in Chinese	最惠国税率 MFN(%)	协定税率 Agreement(%)	特惠税率 SP(%)	普通税率 Gen(%)	英文货品名称 Article Description
941	1212.2131	----干的	15	0 冰岛IS,东盟AS,哥CR,新加坡SG,新西兰NZ,智利CL 6.2 秘鲁PE 7.5 巴PK,亚太AP 9 澳AU 10.5 瑞士CH 12 韩国KR	0 受惠国$_1$LD$_1$	70	----Dried
942	1212.2132	----鲜的	15	0 冰岛IS,东盟AS,哥CR,新加坡SG,新西兰NZ,智利CL 6.2 秘鲁PE 7.5 巴PK,亚太AP 9 澳AU 10.5 瑞士CH 12 韩国KR	0 受惠国$_1$LD$_1$	70	----Fresh
943	1212.2139	----其他	15	0 冰岛IS,东盟AS,哥CR,新加坡SG,新西兰NZ,智利CL 6.2 秘鲁PE 7.5 巴PK,亚太AP 9 澳AU 10.5 瑞士CH 12 韩国KR	0 受惠国$_1$LD$_1$	70	----Other
		---紫菜:					---Laver:
944	1212.2141	----干的	15	0 冰岛IS,东盟AS,哥CR,新加坡SG,新西兰NZ,智利CL 6.2 秘鲁PE 7.5 巴PK,亚太AP 9 澳AU 10.5 瑞士CH 12 韩国KR	0 受惠国$_1$LD$_1$	70	----Dried
945	1212.2142	----鲜的	15	0 冰岛IS,东盟AS,哥CR,新加坡SG,新西兰NZ,智利CL 6.2 秘鲁PE 7.5 巴PK,亚太AP 9 澳AU 10.5 瑞士CH 12 韩国KR	0 受惠国$_1$LD$_1$	70	----Fresh
946	1212.2149	----其他	15	0 冰岛IS,东盟AS,哥CR,新加坡SG,新西兰NZ,智利CL 6.2 秘鲁PE 7.5 巴PK,亚太AP 9 澳AU 10.5 瑞士CH 12 韩国KR	0 受惠国$_1$LD$_1$	70	----Other
		---麒麟菜:					---Eucheuma:
947	1212.2161	----干的	15	0 冰岛IS,东盟AS,哥CR,新西兰NZ,智利CL 6.2 秘鲁PE 7.5 巴PK,亚太AP 9 澳AU 10.5 瑞士CH 12 韩国KR	0 受惠国LD	70	----Dried
948	1212.2169	----其他	15	0 冰岛IS,东盟AS,哥CR,新西兰NZ,智利CL 6.2 秘鲁PE 7.5 巴PK,亚太AP 9 澳AU 10.5 瑞士CH 12 韩国KR	0 受惠国$_1$LD$_1$	70	----Other
		---江蓠:					---Gracilaria:

序号 No.	税则号列 Tariff Line	中文货品名称 Article Description in Chinese	最惠国税率 MFN(%)	协定税率 Agreement(%)	特惠税率 SP(%)	普通税率 Gen(%)	英文货品名称 Article Description
949	1212.2171	----干的	15	0 冰岛IS,东盟AS,哥CR,新西兰NZ,智利CL 6.2 秘鲁PE 7.5 巴PK,亚太AP 9 澳AU 10.5 瑞士CH 12 韩国KR	0 受惠国$_1$LD$_1$	70	----Dried
950	1212.2179	----其他	15	0 冰岛IS,东盟AS,哥CR,新西兰NZ,智利CL 6.2 秘鲁PE 7.5 巴PK,亚太AP 9 澳AU 10.5 瑞士CH 12 韩国KR	0 受惠国$_1$LD$_1$	70	----Other
951	1212.2190	---其他	15Δ2	0 冰岛IS,东盟AS,哥CR,新加坡SG,新西兰NZ,智利CL 6.2 秘鲁PE 7.5 巴PK,亚太AP 9 澳AU 10.5 瑞士CH 12 韩国KR	0 受惠国LD	70	---Other
		--其他:					--Other:
952	1212.2910	---马尾藻	15Δ2	0 冰岛IS,东盟AS,哥CR,新加坡SG,新西兰NZ,智利CL 6.2 秘鲁PE 7.5 巴PK,亚太AP 9 澳AU,韩国KR 10.5 瑞士CH	0 受惠国LD	70	---Sargassum
953	1212.2990	---其他	15Δ2	0 冰岛IS,东盟AS,哥CR,新加坡SG,新西兰NZ,智利CL 6.2 秘鲁PE 7.5 巴PK,亚太AP 9 澳AU,韩国KR 10.5 瑞士CH	0 受惠国LD	70	---Other
		-其他:					-Other:
954	1212.9100	--甜菜	20	0 冰岛IS,东盟AS,哥CR,新加坡SG,新西兰NZ,智利CL 6 秘鲁PE 12 澳AU 14 瑞士CH 17.3 韩国KR	0 受惠国$_1$LD$_1$	70	--Sugar beet
955	1212.9200	--刺槐豆	20	0 冰岛IS,东盟AS,哥CR,新加坡SG,新西兰NZ,智利CL 6 秘鲁PE 10 巴PK,亚太AP 12 澳AU 14 瑞士CH 17.3 韩国KR	0 受惠国$_1$LD$_1$	70	--Locust beans (carob)
956	1212.9300	--甘蔗	20	0 冰岛IS,东盟AS,哥CR,新西兰NZ,智利CL 6 秘鲁PE 12 澳AU 14 瑞士CH 16 韩国KR	0 柬埔寨KH,老挝LA,缅甸MM,受惠国LD	70	--Sugar cane
957	1212.9400	--菊苣根	20	0 冰岛IS,东盟AS,哥CR,新西兰NZ,智利CL 9 秘鲁PE 12 澳AU 17.3 韩国KR	0 受惠国LD	70	--Chicory roots
		--其他:					--Other:

序号 No.	税则号列 Tariff Line	中文货品名称 Article Description in Chinese	最惠国税率 MFN(%)	协定税率 Agreement(%)	特惠税率 SP(%)	普通税率 Gen(%)	英文货品名称 Article Description
		---杏、桃（包括油桃）、梅或李的核及核仁：					---Apricot, peach (including nectarine) or plum stones and kernels:
958	1212.9911	----苦杏仁	20	0 冰岛IS,东盟AS,哥CR,新加坡SG,新西兰NZ,智利CL 6 秘鲁PE 12 澳AU 14 瑞士CH 17.3 韩国KR	0 受惠国$_1$LD$_1$	80	----Bitter
959	1212.9912	----甜杏仁	20	0 冰岛IS,东盟AS,哥CR,香港HK,新加坡SG,新西兰NZ,智利CL 6 秘鲁PE 12 澳AU 14 瑞士CH 17.3 韩国KR	0 受惠国$_1$LD$_1$	80	----Sweet
960	1212.9919	----其他	20	0 冰岛IS,东盟AS,哥CR,新加坡SG,新西兰NZ,智利CL 6 秘鲁PE 12 澳AU 14 瑞士CH 17.3 韩国KR	0 受惠国$_1$LD$_1$	80	----Other
		---其他：					---Other:
961	1212.9993	----白瓜子	20	0 冰岛IS,东盟AS,哥CR,新加坡SG,新西兰NZ,智利CL 6 秘鲁PE 12 澳AU 14 瑞士CH 17.3 韩国KR	0 受惠国$_1$LD$_1$	80	----Pumpkin seeds
962	1212.9994	----莲子	20	0 冰岛IS,东盟AS,哥CR,新加坡SG,新西兰NZ,智利CL 6 秘鲁PE 12 澳AU 14 瑞士CH 17.3 韩国KR	0 受惠国$_1$LD$_1$	80	----Lotus seeds (Semen Nelumbinis)
963	1212.9996	----甜叶菊叶	30	0 冰岛IS,东盟AS,哥CR,新加坡SG,新西兰NZ,智利CL 9 秘鲁PE 18 澳AU	0 受惠国LD	70	----Leaves of stevia
964	1212.9999	----其他	30	0 冰岛IS,东盟AS,哥CR,新加坡SG,新西兰NZ,智利CL 9 秘鲁PE 18 澳AU	0 受惠国LD	70	----Other
	12.13	**未经处理的谷类植物的茎、秆及谷壳，不论是否碎、碾磨、挤压或制成团粒：**					**Cereal straw and husks, unprepared, whether or not chopped, ground, pressed or in the form of pellets:**
965	1213.0010	---未经处理的稻草的茎、杆	12	0 冰岛IS,东盟AS,哥CR,秘鲁PE,新加坡SG,新西兰NZ,智利CL 6 巴PK 7.2 澳AU 8.4 瑞士CH 9.6 韩国KR	0 柬埔寨KH,受惠国LD	35	---Cereal straw, unprepared

序号 No.	税则号列 Tariff Line	中文货品名称 Article Description in Chinese	最惠国税率 MFN(%)	协定税率 Agreement(%)		特惠税率 SP(%)		普通税率 Gen(%)	英文货品名称 Article Description
966	1213.0090	---其他	12	0 6 7.2 8.4 9.6	冰岛IS,东盟AS,哥CR,秘鲁PE,新加坡SG,新西兰NZ,智利CL 巴PK 澳AU 瑞士CH 韩国KR	0	柬埔寨KH,受惠国LD	35	---Other
	12.14	**芜菁甘蓝、饲料甜菜、饲料用根、干草、紫苜蓿、三叶草、驴喜豆、饲料羽衣甘蓝、羽扇豆、巢菜及类似饲料，不论是否制成团粒：**							**Swedes, mangolds, fodder roots, hay, lucerne (alfalfa) , clover, sainfoin, forage kale, lupines, vetches and similar forage products, whether or not in the form of pellets:**
967	1214.1000	-紫苜蓿粗粉及团粒	5	0	澳AU,巴PK,冰岛IS,东盟AS,哥CR,韩国KR,秘鲁PE,瑞士CH,新西兰NZ,智利CL	0	柬埔寨KH,受惠国LD	35	-Lucerne (alfalfa) meal and pellets
968	1214.9000	-其他	9	0 3.6 5 5.4	冰岛IS,东盟AS,哥CR,秘鲁PE,新西兰NZ,智利CL 瑞士CH 巴PK 澳AU,韩国KR	0	柬埔寨KH,受惠国LD	35	-Other
	ex12149000	以除紫苜蓿外的禾本科和豆科为主的多种混合天然饲草	Δ4						Mixed non-artificial forage grass majorly composed of poaceae and fabaceae other than lucerne
	ex12149000	其他紫苜蓿（粗粉及团粒除外）	Δ7						Other lucerne (alfalfa) , excluding meal and pellets

第十三章
虫胶；树胶、树脂及其他植物液、汁

Chapter 13
Lac; gums, resins and other vegetable saps and extracts

注释：

税号 13.02 主要包括甘草、除虫菊、啤酒花、芦荟的浸膏及鸦片，但不包括：

一、按重量计蔗糖含量在10%以上或制成糖食的甘草浸膏（税号 17.04）；

二、麦芽膏（税号 19.01）；

三、咖啡精、茶精、马黛茶精（税号 21.01）；

四、构成含酒精饮料的植物汁、液（第二十二章）；

五、樟脑、甘草甜及税号 29.14 或 29.38 的其他产品；

六、罂粟杆浓缩物，按重量计生物碱含量不低于 50%（税目 29.39）；

七、税号 30.03 或 30.04 的药品及税号 30.06 的血型试剂；

八、鞣料或染料的浸膏（税号 32.01 或 32.03）；

九、精油、浸膏、净油、香膏、提取的油树脂或精油的水馏液及水溶液；饮料制造业用的以芳香物质为基料的制剂（第三十三章）；

十、天然橡胶、巴拉塔胶、古塔波胶、银胶菊胶、糖胶树胶或类似的天然树胶（税号 40.01）。

Notes:

Heading No.13.02 applies, inter alia, to liquorice extract and extract of pyrethrum, extract of hops, extract of aloes and opium. The heading does not apply to:

1. Liquorice extract containing more than 10% by weight of sucrose or put up as confectionery (heading No.17.04);
2. Malt extract (heading No.19.01);
3. Extracts of coffee, tea or mate (heading No.21.01);
4. Vegetable saps or extracts constituting alcoholic beverages (Chapter 22);
5. Camphor, glycyrrhizin or other products of heading No.29.14 or 29.38;
6. Concentrates of poppy straw containing not less than 50% by weight of alkaloids (heading 29.39);.
7. Medicaments of heading No.30.03 or 30.04 or blood-grouping reagents (heading No.30.06);
8. Tanning or dyeing extracts (heading No.32.01 or 32.03);
9. Essential oils, concretes, absolutes, resinoids, extracted oleoresins, aqueous distillates or aqueous solutions of essential oils or preparations based on odoriferous substances of a kind used for the manufacture of beverages (Chapter 33); or
10. Natural rubber, balata, guttapercha, guayule, chicle or similar natural gums (heading No.40.01).

本国注释：

子目号 1302.1100 的鸦片，我国禁止进口。

National note:

Opium of Subheading No.1302.1100 is subject to import ban.

序号 No.	税则号列 Tariff Line	中文货品名称 Article Description in Chinese	最惠国税率 MFN(%)	协定税率 Agreement(%)	特惠税率 SP(%)	普通税率 Gen(%)	英文货品名称 Article Description
	13.01	**虫胶；天然树胶、树脂、树胶脂及油树脂（例如，香树脂）：**					**Lac; natural gums, resins, gum-resins and oleoresins (for example, balsams) :**
969	1301.2000	-阿拉伯胶	15	0 巴PK,冰岛IS,东盟AS,哥CR,秘鲁PE,新加坡SG,新西兰NZ,智利CL 9 澳AU 10.5 瑞士CH 12 韩国KR	0 受惠国LD	40	-Gum Arabic
		-其他：					-Other:
970	1301.9010	---胶黄耆树胶（卡喇杆胶）	15	0 巴PK,冰岛IS,东盟AS,哥CR,秘鲁PE,新加坡SG,新西兰NZ,智利CL 9 澳AU 10.5 瑞士CH 12 韩国KR	0 受惠国$_1$LD$_1$	40	---Gum tragacanth
971	1301.9020	---乳香、没药及血竭	3	0 澳AU,巴PK,冰岛IS,东盟AS,哥CR,韩国KR,秘鲁PE,瑞士CH,新西兰NZ,智利CL	0 受惠国LD	17	---Olibanum, myrrh and dragon' s blood

序号 No.	税则号列 Tariff Line	中文货品名称 Article Description in Chinese	最惠国税率 MFN(%)	协定税率 Agreement(%)	特惠税率 SP(%)	普通税率 Gen(%)	英文货品名称 Article Description
972	1301.9030	---阿魏	3	0 澳AU,巴PK,冰岛IS,东盟AS,哥CR,韩国KR,秘鲁PE,瑞士CH,新西兰NZ,智利CL	0 受惠国LD	17	---Asafoetida
973	1301.9040	---松脂	15	0 巴PK,冰岛IS,东盟AS,哥CR,秘鲁PE,新加坡SG,新西兰NZ,智利CL 9 澳AU 10.5 瑞士CH 12 韩国KR	0 受惠国LD	45	---Pine-resin
974	1301.9090	---其他	15	0 巴PK,冰岛IS,东盟AS,哥CR,秘鲁PE,新加坡SG,新西兰NZ,智利CL 9 澳AU 10.5 瑞士CH 12 韩国KR	0 受惠国LD	45	---Other
	13.02	**植物液汁及浸膏；果胶、果胶酸盐及果胶酸酯；从植物产品制得的琼脂、其他胶液及增稠剂，不论是否改性：**					**Vegetable saps and extracts; pectic substances, pectinates and pectates; agar-agar and other mucilages and thickeners, whether or not modified, derived from vegetable products:**
		-植物液汁及浸膏：					-Vegetable saps and extracts:
975	1302.1100	--鸦片	0		0 受惠国LD	0	--Opium
976	1302.1200	--甘草的	6Δ0	0 冰岛IS,东盟AS,哥CR,韩国KR,秘鲁PE,新西兰NZ,智利CL 2.4 瑞士CH 3.6 澳AU 5 巴PK	0 受惠国LD	20	--Of liquorice
977	1302.1300	--啤酒花的	10	0 冰岛IS,东盟AS,哥CR,秘鲁PE,新加坡SG,新西兰NZ,智利CL 4 瑞士CH 5 巴PK 6 澳AU 8 韩国KR	0 受惠国LD	80	--Of hops
		--其他：					--Other:
978	1302.1910	---生漆	20	0 冰岛IS,东盟AS,哥CR,新加坡SG,新西兰NZ,智利CL 6 秘鲁PE 12 澳AU 14 瑞士CH 17.3 韩国KR	0 受惠国$_1$LD$_1$	90	---Crude lacquer
979	1302.1920	---印楝素	3	0 澳AU,巴PK,冰岛IS,东盟AS,哥CR,韩国KR,秘鲁PE,瑞士CH,新西兰NZ,智利CL	0 受惠国LD	11	---Azadirachtin
980	1302.1930	---除虫菊的或含鱼藤酮植物根茎的	3	0 澳AU,巴PK,冰岛IS,东盟AS,哥CR,韩国KR,秘鲁PE,瑞士CH,新西兰NZ,智利CL	0 受惠国LD	11	---Of pyrethrum or of the roots of plants containing rotenone
981	1302.1940	---银杏的	20	0 冰岛IS,东盟AS,哥CR,新加坡SG,新西兰NZ,智利CL 6 秘鲁PE 8 瑞士CH 12 澳AU 15 巴PK,亚太AP 17.3 韩国KR	0 受惠国$_1$LD$_1$	80	---Ginkgo biloba

序号 No.	税则号列 Tariff Line	中文货品名称 Article Description in Chinese	最惠国税率 MFN(%)	协定税率 Agreement(%)	特惠税率 SP(%)	普通税率 Gen(%)	英文货品名称 Article Description
982	1302.1990	---其他	20	0 冰岛IS,东盟AS,哥CR,新加坡SG,新西兰NZ,智利CL 6 秘鲁PE 8 瑞士CH 12 澳AU 15 巴PK,亚太AP 17.3 韩国KR	0 受惠国$_1$LD$_1$	80	---Other
983	1302.2000	-果胶、果胶酸盐及果胶酸酯	20	0 冰岛IS,东盟AS,哥CR,新加坡SG,新西兰NZ,智利CL 6 秘鲁PE 12 澳AU 14 瑞士CH 17.3 韩国KR	0 受惠国$_1$LD$_1$	80	-Pectic substances, pectinates and pectates
		-从植物产品制得的胶液及增稠剂，不论是否改性：					-Mucilages and thickeners, whether or not modified, derived from vegetable products:
984	1302.3100	--琼脂	10	0 冰岛IS,东盟AS,哥CR,新加坡SG,新西兰NZ,智利CL 3 秘鲁PE 4 瑞士CH 5 巴PK 6 澳AU 8 韩国KR	0 受惠国LD	80	--Agar-agar
985	1302.3200	--从刺槐豆、刺槐豆子或瓜尔豆制得的胶液及增稠剂，不论是否改性	15	0 巴PK,冰岛IS,东盟AS,哥CR,新加坡SG,新西兰NZ,智利CL 4.5 秘鲁PE 9 澳AU 10 亚太AP 10.5 瑞士CH 12 韩国KR	0 受惠国$_1$LD$_1$	80	--Mucilages and thickeners, whether or not modified, derived from locust beans locust bean seeds or guar seeds
		--其他：					--Other:
		---海草及其他藻类制品：					---Mucilages and thickeners, whether or not modified, derived from seaweeds and other algae:
986	1302.3911	----卡拉胶	15	0 冰岛IS,东盟AS,哥CR,新加坡SG,新西兰NZ,智利CL 4.5 秘鲁PE 9 澳AU 10.5 瑞士CH 12 巴PK,韩国KR	0 受惠国$_1$LD$_1$	80	----Carrageenan
987	1302.3912	----褐藻胶	15	0 冰岛IS,东盟AS,哥CR,新加坡SG,新西兰NZ,智利CL 4.5 秘鲁PE 9 澳AU 10.5 瑞士CH 12 巴PK,韩国KR	0 受惠国$_1$LD$_1$	80	----Algin
988	1302.3919	----其他	15	0 冰岛IS,东盟AS,哥CR,新加坡SG,新西兰NZ,智利CL 8.8 秘鲁PE 9 澳AU 10.5 瑞士CH 12 巴PK,韩国KR	0 受惠国$_1$LD$_1$	80	----Other

序号 No.	税则号列 Tariff Line	中文货品名称 Article Description in Chinese	最惠国税率 MFN(%)	协定税率 Agreement(%)	特惠税率 SP(%)	普通税率 Gen(%)	英文货品名称 Article Description
989	1302.3990	---其他	15	0 冰岛IS,东盟AS,哥CR,新加坡SG,新西兰NZ,智利CL 6.2 秘鲁PE 9 澳AU 10.5 瑞士CH 12 巴PK,韩国KR	0 受惠国$_1$LD$_1$	80	---Other

第十四章
编结用植物材料；
其他植物产品

Chapter14
Vegetable plaiting materials; vegetable products not elsewhere specified or included

注释：

一、本章不包括归入第十一类的下列产品：

主要供纺织用的植物材料或植物纤维，不论其加工程度如何；或经过处理使其只能作为纺织原料用的其他植物材料。

二、税号14.01主要包括竹（不论是否劈开、纵锯、切段、圆端、漂白、磨光、染色或进行不燃处理）、劈开的柳条、芦苇及类似品和藤心、藤丝、藤片。但不包括木片条（税号44.04）。

三、税号14.04不包括木丝（税号44.05）及供制帚、制刷用成束、成簇的材料（税号96.03）。

Notes:

1.This Chapter does not cover the following products which are to be classified in Section XI:

Vegetable materials or fibres of vegetable materials of a kind used primarily in the manufacture of textiles, however prepared, or other vegetable materials which have undergone treatment so as to render them suitable for use only as textile materials.

2. Heading No.14.01 applies, inter alia, to bamboos (whether or not split, sawn lengthwise, cut to length, rounded at the ends, bleached, rendered non-in-flammable, polished or dyed), split osier, reeds and the like, to rattan cores andto drawn or split rattans. The heading does not apply to chipwood (heading No.44.04).

3. Heading No.14.04 does not apply to wood wool (heading No.44.05) and prepared knots or tufts for broom or brush making (heading No.96.03).

序号 No.	税则号列 Tariff Line	中文货品名称 Article Description in Chinese	最惠国税率 MFN(%)	协定税率 Agreement(%)	特惠税率 SP(%)	普通税率 Gen(%)	英文货品名称 Article Description
	14.01	**主要作编结用的植物材料（例如，竹、藤、芦苇、灯芯草、柳条、酒椰叶，已净、漂白或染色的谷类植物的茎秆，椴树皮）：**					**Vegetable materials of a kind used primarily for plaiting (for example, bamboos, rattans, reeds, rushes, osier, raffia, cleaned, bleached or dyed cereal straw, and lime bark) :**
990	1401.1000	-竹	10	0 冰岛IS,东盟AS,哥CR,秘鲁PE,新加坡SG,新西兰NZ,智利CL 4 瑞士CH 5 巴PK 6 澳AU 8 韩国KR	0 柬埔寨KH,老挝LA,受惠国LD	70	-Bamboos
991	1401.2000	-藤	10	0 冰岛IS,东盟AS,哥CR,秘鲁PE,新加坡SG,新西兰NZ,智利CL 4 瑞士CH 5 巴PK 6 澳AU 8 韩国KR	0 柬埔寨KH,老挝LA,受惠国LD	35	-Rattans
		-其他：					-Other:
992	1401.9010	---谷类植物的茎秆（麦秸除外）	10	0 冰岛IS,东盟AS,哥CR,新加坡SG,新西兰NZ,智利CL 3 秘鲁PE 4 瑞士CH 5 巴PK 6 澳AU 8 韩国KR	0 柬埔寨KH,受惠国LD	70	---Cereal straw (other than wheat straw)
993	1401.9020	---芦苇	10	0 冰岛IS,东盟AS,哥CR,秘鲁PE,新加坡SG,新西兰NZ,智利CL 4 瑞士CH 5 巴PK 6 澳AU 8 韩国KR	0 柬埔寨KH,受惠国LD	70	---Reeds
		---灯芯草属：					---Rushes:

序号 No.	税则号列 Tariff Line	中文货品名称 Article Description in Chinese	最惠国税率 MFN(%)	协定税率 Agreement(%)	特惠税率 SP(%)	普通税率 Gen(%)	英文货品名称 Article Description
994	1401.9031	----蔺草	10	0 冰岛IS,东盟AS,哥CR,秘鲁PE,新加坡SG,新西兰NZ,智利CL 4 瑞士CH 5 巴PK 6 澳AU 8 韩国KR	0 柬埔寨KH,受惠国LD	70	----Juncaceae
995	1401.9039	----其他	10	0 冰岛IS,东盟AS,哥CR,秘鲁PE,新加坡SG,新西兰NZ,智利CL 4 瑞士CH 5 巴PK 6 澳AU 8 韩国KR	0 柬埔寨KH,受惠国LD	70	----Other
996	1401.9090	---其他	10	0 冰岛IS,东盟AS,哥CR,新加坡SG,新西兰NZ,智利CL 3 秘鲁PE 4 瑞士CH 5 巴PK 6 澳AU 8 韩国KR	0 柬埔寨KH,受惠国LD	70	---Other
	14.04	**其他税号未列名的植物产品:**					**Vegetable products not elsewhere specified or included:**
997	1404.2000	-棉短绒	4	0 澳AU,巴PK,冰岛IS,东盟AS,哥CR,韩国KR,秘鲁PE,瑞士CH,新西兰NZ,智利CL	0 受惠国LD	30	-Cotton linters
		-其他:					-Other:
998	1404.9010	---主要供染料、鞣料用的植物原料	5	0 澳AU,巴PK,冰岛IS,东盟AS,哥CR,韩国KR,瑞士CH,新西兰NZ,智利CL 2.1 秘鲁PE 4.3 亚太AP	0 受惠国LD	45	---Raw vegetable materials of a kind used primarily in dyeing or tanning
999	1404.9090	---其他	15	0 冰岛IS,东盟AS,哥CR,秘鲁PE,新加坡SG,新西兰NZ,智利CL 9 澳AU 10.5 瑞士CH 12 韩国KR	0 受惠国LD	70	---Other

第三类
动、植物油、脂及其分解产品；精制的食用油脂；动、植物蜡

SECTION Ⅲ
ANIMAL OR VEGETABLE FATS AND OILS ANDTHEIR CLEAVAGE PRODUCTS; PREPARED EDIBLE FATS; ANIMAL OR VEGETABLE WAXES

第十五章
动、植物油、脂及其分解产品；精制的食用油脂；动、植物蜡

Chapter 15
Animal or vegetable fats and oils and their cleavage products; prepared edible fats; animal or vegetable waxes

注释：

一、本章不包括：

（一）税号 02.09 的猪脂肪及家禽脂肪；

（二）可可脂、可可油（税号 18.04）；

（三）按重量计税号 04.05 所列产品的含量超过 15% 的食品（通常归入第二十一章）；

（四）税号 23.01 的油渣或税号 23.04 至 23.06 的残渣；

（五）第六类的脂肪酸、精制蜡、药品、油漆、清漆、肥皂、芳香料制品、化妆盥洗品、磺化油及其他货品；

（六）从油类提取的油膏（税号 40.02）。

二、税号 15.09 不包括用溶剂提取的橄榄油（税号 15.10）。

三、税号 15.18 不包括变性的油、脂及其分离品，这些货品应归入其相应的未变性油、脂及其分离品的税号。

四、皂料、油脚、硬脂沥青、甘油沥青及羊毛脂残渣，归入税号 15.22。

Notes:

1. This Chapter does not cover:

(a) Pig fat or poultry fat of heading No.02.09;

(b) Cocoa butter, fat or oil (heading No.18.04);

(c) Edible preparations containing by weight more than 15% of the products of heading No.04.05 (generally Chapter 21);

(d) Greaves (heading No.23.01) or residues of headings No.23.04 to 23.06;

(e) Fatty acids, prepared waxes, medicaments, paints, varnishes, soap, perfumery, cosmetic or toilet preparations, sulphonated oils or other goods of Section Ⅵ;or

(f) Factice derived from oils (heading No.40.02).

2. Heading No.15.09 does not apply to oils obtained from olives by solvent extraction (heading No.15.10).

3. Heading No.15.18 does not cover fats or oils or their fractions, merely denatured, which are to be classified in the heading appropriate to the corresponding undenatured fats and oils and their fractions.

4. Soap-stocks, oil foots and dregs, stearin pitch, glycerol pitch and wool grease residues fall in heading No.15.22.

子目注释：

子目 1514.11 及 1514.19 所称“低芥子酸菜子油”，是指按重量计芥子酸含量低于 2%的固定油。

Subheading Note:

For the purposes of subheadings 1514.11 and 1514.19, the expression “low erucic acid rape of colza oil” means the fixed oil which has an erucic acid content of less than 2% by weight.

序号 No.	税则号列 Tariff Line	中文货品名称 Article Description in Chinese	最惠国税率 MFN(%)	协定税率 Agreement(%)	特惠税率 SP(%)	普通税率 Gen(%)	英文货品名称 Article Description
	15.01	**猪脂肪（包括已炼制的猪油）及家禽脂肪，但税号02.09及15.03的货品除外：**					**Pig fat (including lard) and poultry fat, other than that of heading 0209 or 1503:**
1000	1501.1000	-猪油	10	0 澳门MO,冰岛IS,东盟AS,哥CR,秘鲁PE,香港HK,新加坡SG,新西兰NZ,智利CL 4 瑞士CH 6 澳AU 8 韩国KR	0 受惠国LD	35	-Lard

序号 No.	税则号列 Tariff Line	中文货品名称 Article Description in Chinese	最惠国税率 MFN(%)	协定税率 Agreement(%)	特惠税率 SP(%)	普通税率 Gen(%)	英文货品名称 Article Description
1001	1501.2000	-其他猪脂肪	10	0 澳门MO,冰岛IS,东盟AS,哥CR,秘鲁PE,香港HK,新加坡SG,新西兰NZ,智利CL 4 瑞士CH 6 澳AU 8 韩国KR	0 受惠国LD	35	-Other pig fat
1002	1501.9000	-其他	10	0 澳门MO,冰岛IS,东盟AS,哥CR,秘鲁PE,香港HK,新加坡SG,新西兰NZ,智利CL 4 瑞士CH 6 澳AU 8 韩国KR	0 受惠国LD	35	-Other
	15.02	**牛、羊脂肪，但税号15.03的货品除外：**					**Fats of bovine animals, sheep or goats, other than those of heading 1503:**
1003	1502.1000	-牛、羊油脂	8Δ2	0 澳门MO,巴PK,冰岛IS,东盟AS,哥CR,秘鲁PE,新西兰NZ,亚太AP,智利CL 3.2 瑞士CH 4.8 澳AU,韩国KR	0 受惠国LD	30	-Tallow
1004	1502.9000	-其他	8Δ4	0 澳门MO,巴PK,冰岛IS,东盟AS,哥CR,秘鲁PE,新西兰NZ,亚太AP,智利CL 3.2 瑞士CH 4.8 澳AU,韩国KR	0 受惠国LD	70	-Other
	15.03	**猪油硬脂、液体猪油、油硬脂、食用或非食用脂油，未经乳化、混合或其他方法制作**					**Lard stearin, lard oil, oleostearin, oleo-oil and tallow oil, not emulsified or mixed or otherwise prepared**
1005	1503.0000	猪油硬脂、液体猪油、油硬脂、食用或非食用脂油，未经乳化、混合或其他方法制作	10	0 澳门MO,冰岛IS,东盟AS,哥CR,秘鲁PE,新加坡SG,新西兰NZ,智利CL 4 瑞士CH 6 澳AU 8 韩国KR	0 受惠国LD	30	Lard stearin, lard oil, oleostearin, oleooil and tallow oil, not emulsified or mixed or otherwise prepared
	15.04	**鱼或海生哺乳动物的油、脂及其分离品，不论是否精制，但未经化学改性：**					**Fats and oils and their fractions, of fish or marine mammals, whether or not refined, but not chemically modified:**
1006	1504.1000	-鱼肝油及其分离品	12	0 澳门MO,冰岛IS,东盟AS,哥CR,秘鲁PE,新加坡SG,新西兰NZ,智利CL 7.2 澳AU 8.4 瑞士CH 9.6 韩国KR	0 受惠国$_1$LD$_1$	30	-Fish-liver oils and their fractions
1007	1504.2000	-除鱼肝油以外的鱼油、脂及其分离品	12	0 澳门MO,冰岛IS,东盟AS,哥CR,新加坡SG,新西兰NZ,智利CL 1.5 秘鲁PE 7.2 澳AU 8.6 瑞士CH 9.6 韩国KR	0 受惠国$_1$LD$_1$	50	-Fats and oils and their fractions, of fish, other than liver oils
1008	1504.3000	-海生哺乳动物的油、脂及其分离品	14.4	0 澳门MO,冰岛IS,东盟AS,哥CR,秘鲁PE,新加坡SG,新西兰NZ,智利CL 8.6 澳AU 10 瑞士CH 11.5 韩国KR	0 受惠国$_1$LD$_1$	50	-Fats and oils and their fractions of marine mammals

序号 No.	税则号列 Tariff Line	中文货品名称 Article Description in Chinese	最惠国税率 MFN(%)	协定税率 Agreement(%)	特惠税率 SP(%)	普通税率 Gen(%)	英文货品名称 Article Description
	15.05	**羊毛脂及从羊毛脂制得的脂肪物质（包括纯净的羊毛脂）**					**Wool grease and fatty substances derived therefrom (including lanolin)**
1009	1505.0000	羊毛脂及从羊毛脂制得的脂肪物质（包括纯净的羊毛脂）	20	0 冰岛IS,东盟AS,哥CR,新加坡SG,新西兰NZ,智利CL 6 秘鲁PE 12 澳AU 14 瑞士CH 17.3 韩国KR	0 受惠国$_1$LD$_1$	70	Wool grease and fatty substances derived therefrom (including lanolin)
	15.06	**其他动物油、脂及其分离品，不论是否精制，但未经化学改性**					**Other animal fats and oils and their fractions, whether or not refined, but not chemically modified**
1010	1506.0000	其他动物油、脂及其分离品，不论是否精制，但未经化学改性	20	0 澳门MO,冰岛IS,东盟AS,哥CR,新加坡SG,新西兰NZ,智利CL 6 秘鲁PE 12 澳AU 14 瑞士CH 17.3 韩国KR	0 受惠国$_1$LD$_1$	70	Other animal fats and oils and their fractions, whether or not refined, but not chemically modified
	15.07	**豆油及其分离品，不论是否精制，但未经化学改性：**					**Soya-bean oil and its fractions, whether or not refined, but not chemically modified:**
1011	1507.1000	-初榨的，不论是否脱胶	9			190	-Crude oil whether or not degummed
1012	1507.9000	-其他	9			190	-Other
	15.08	**花生油及其分离品，不论是否精制，但未经化学改性：**					**Groundnut oil and its fractions, whether or not refined, but not chemically modified:**
1013	1508.1000	-初榨的	10	0 东盟AS,新加坡SG		100	-Crude oil
1014	1508.9000	-其他	10	0 东盟AS,新加坡SG		100	-Other
	15.09	**油橄榄油及其分离品，不论是否精制，但未经化学改性：**					**Olive oil and its fractions, whether or not refined, but not chemically modified:**
1015	1509.1000	-初榨的	10	0 澳门MO,冰岛IS,东盟AS,哥CR,新加坡SG,新西兰NZ,智利CL 3 秘鲁PE 4 瑞士CH 8 韩国KR	0 受惠国$_1$LD$_1$	30	-Virgin
1016	1509.9000	-其他	10	0 澳门MO,冰岛IS,东盟AS,哥CR,秘鲁PE,香港HK,新加坡SG,新西兰NZ,智利CL 4 瑞士CH 8 韩国KR	0 受惠国$_1$LD$_1$	30	-Other
	15.10	**其他橄榄油及其分离品，不论是否精制，但未经化学改性，包括掺有税号15.09的油或分离品的混合物**					**Other oils and their fractions, obtained solely from olives, whether or not refined, but not chemically modified, including blends of these oils or fractions with oils or fractions of heading No.15.09**
1017	1510.0000	其他橄榄油及其分离品，不论是否精制，但未经化学改性，包括掺有税号15.09的油或分离品的混合物	10	0 澳门MO,冰岛IS,东盟AS,哥CR,秘鲁PE,新加坡SG,新西兰NZ,智利CL 4 瑞士CH 8 韩国KR	0 受惠国$_1$LD$_1$	30	Other oils and their fractions, obtained solely from olives, whether or not refined, but not chemically modified, including blends of these oils or fractions with oils or fractions of heading No.15.09
	15.11	**棕榈油及其分离品，不论是否精制，但未经化学改性：**					**Palm oil and its fractions, whether or not refined, but not chemically modified:**
1018	1511.1000	-初榨的	9			60	-Crude oil
		-其他：					-Other:

序号 No.	税则号列 Tariff Line	中文货品名称 Article Description in Chinese	最惠国税率 MFN(%)	协定税率 Agreement(%)		特惠税率 SP(%)		普通税率 Gen(%)	英文货品名称 Article Description
1019	1511.9010	---棕榈液油（熔点19～24度）	9					60	---Palm olein
1020	1511.9020	---棕榈硬脂（熔点44～56度）	8					60	---Palm stearin
	ex15119020	固态棕榈硬脂（50度≤熔点≤56度）	Δ2						Solid palm stearin (melting point no less than 50 centigrade and no more than 56 centigrade)
1021	1511.9090	---其他	9					60	---Other
	15.12	**葵花油、红花油或棉子油及其分离品，不论是否精制，但未经化学改性：**							**Sunflower-seed, safflower or cotton-seed oil and fractions thereof, whether or not refined, but not chemically modified:**
		-葵花油或红花油及其分离品：							-Sunflower-seed or safflower oil and fractions thereof:
1022	1512.1100	--初榨的	9	0	澳门MO,东盟AS			160	--Crude oil
1023	1512.1900	--其他	9	0	澳门MO,东盟AS			160	--Other
		-棉子油及其分离品：							-Cotton-seed oil and its fractions:
1024	1512.2100	--初榨的，不论是否去除棉子酚	10	0	澳门MO,东盟AS,新加坡SG			70	--Crude oil, whether or not gossypol has been removed
1025	1512.2900	--其他	10	0	澳门MO,东盟AS,新加坡SG			70	--Other
	15.13	**椰子油、棕榈仁油或巴巴苏棕榈果油及其分离品，不论是否精制，但未经化学改性：**							**Coconut (copra) , palm kernel or babassu oil and fractions thereof, whether or not refined, but not chemically modified:**
		-椰子油及其分离品：							-Coconut (copra) oil and its fractions:
1026	1513.1100	--初榨的	9	0 3.6 4.5 5.4	澳门MO,冰岛IS,东盟AS,哥CR,秘鲁PE,新西兰NZ,智利CL 瑞士CH 巴PK,亚太AP 韩国KR	0	受惠国$_1$LD$_1$	40	--Crude oil
1027	1513.1900	--其他	9	0 3.6 4.5 5.4	澳门MO,冰岛IS,东盟AS,哥CR,秘鲁PE,新西兰NZ,智利CL 瑞士CH 巴PK,亚太AP 韩国KR	0	受惠国LD	40	--Other
		-棕榈仁油或巴巴苏棕榈果油及其分离品：							-Palm kernel or babassu oil and fractions thereof:
1028	1513.2100	--初榨的	9	0 3.6 5.4	澳门MO,冰岛IS,东盟AS,哥CR,秘鲁PE,新西兰NZ,智利CL 瑞士CH 韩国KR	0	受惠国$_1$LD$_1$	40	--Crude oil
1029	1513.2900	--其他	9	0 3.6 5.4	澳门MO,冰岛IS,东盟AS,哥CR,秘鲁PE,新西兰NZ,智利CL 瑞士CH 韩国KR	0	受惠国$_1$LD$_1$	40	--Other
	15.14	**菜子油或芥子油及其分离品，不论是否精制，但未经化学改性：**							**Rape, colza or mustard oil and fractions thereof, whether or not refined, but not chemically modified:**
		-低芥子酸菜子油及其分离品：							-Low-erucic-acid rape or colza oil and its fractions:
1030	1514.1100	--初榨的	9					170	--Crude oil
1031	1514.1900	--其他	9					170	--Other
		-其他：							-Other:
		--初榨的：							--Crude oil:
1032	1514.9110	---菜子油	9					170	---Rape oil
1033	1514.9190	---芥子油	9					170	---Mustard oil
1034	1514.9900	--其他	9					170	--Other

序号 No.	税则号列 Tariff Line	中文货品名称 Article Description in Chinese	最惠国税率 MFN(%)	协定税率 Agreement(%)	特惠税率 SP(%)	普通税率 Gen(%)	英文货品名称 Article Description
	15.15	其他固定植物油、脂（包括希蒙得木油）及其分离品，不论是否精制，但未经化学改性：					**Other fixed vegetable fats and oils (including jojoba oil) and their fractions, whether or not refined, but not chemically modified:**
		-亚麻子油及其分离品：					-Linseed oil and its fractions:
1035	1515.1100	--初榨的	15	0 澳门MO,冰岛IS,东盟AS,哥CR,新加坡SG新西兰NZ,智利CL 4.5 秘鲁PE 10.5 瑞士CH 12 韩国KR	0 受惠国$_1$LD$_1$	30	--Crude oil
1036	1515.1900	--其他	15	0 澳门MO,冰岛IS,东盟AS,哥CR,新加坡SG新西兰NZ,智利CL 4.5 秘鲁PE 10.5 瑞士CH 12 韩国KR	0 受惠国$_1$LD$_1$	30	--Other
		-玉米油及其分离品：					-Maize (corn) oil and its fractions:
1037	1515.2100	--初榨的	10	0 澳门MO,东盟AS,新加坡SG	0 柬埔寨KH,老挝LA,受惠国LD	160	--Crude oil
1038	1515.2900	--其他	10	0 澳门MO,东盟AS,新加坡SG	0 柬埔寨KH,老挝LA,受惠国LD	160	--Other
1039	1515.3000	-蓖麻油及其分离品	10	0 澳门MO,冰岛IS,东盟AS,哥CR,秘鲁PE,新加坡SG新西兰NZ,智利CL 4 瑞士CH 6 澳AU 8 韩国KR	0 柬埔寨KH,老挝LA,受惠国LD	70	-Castor oil and its fractions
1040	1515.5000	-芝麻油及其分离品	12	0 澳门MO,冰岛IS,东盟AS,哥CR,秘鲁PE,新加坡SG新西兰NZ,智利CL 7.2 澳AU 8.4 瑞士CH 9.6 韩国KR	0 柬埔寨KH,老挝LA,受惠国LD	20	-Sesame oil and its fractions
		其他：					-Other:
1041	1515.9010	---希蒙得木油及其分离品	20	0 澳门MO,冰岛IS,东盟AS,哥CR,新加坡SG新西兰NZ,智利CL 12 澳AU 14 瑞士CH 17.3 韩国KR	0 柬埔寨KH,受惠国LD	70	---Jojoba oil and its fractions
1042	1515.9020	---印楝油及其分离品	20	0 澳门MO,冰岛IS,东盟AS,哥CR,新加坡SG新西兰NZ,智利CL 12 澳AU 14 瑞士CH 17.3 韩国KR	0 受惠国$_1$LD$_1$	70	---Neem oil and its fractions
1043	1515.9030	---桐油及其分离品	20	0 澳门MO,冰岛IS,东盟AS,哥CR,新加坡SG新西兰NZ,智利CL 12 澳AU 14 瑞士CH 17.3 韩国KR	0 柬埔寨KH,受惠国LD	70	---Tung oil and its fractions
1044	1515.9090	---其他	20	0 澳门MO,冰岛IS,东盟AS,哥CR,新加坡SG新西兰NZ,智利CL 12 澳AU 14 瑞士CH	0 柬埔寨KH,老挝LA,缅甸MM,受惠国LD	70	---Other

序号 No.	税则号列 Tariff Line	中文货品名称 Article Description in Chinese	最惠国税率 MFN(%)	协定税率 Agreement(%)	特惠税率 SP(%)	普通税率 Gen(%)	英文货品名称 Article Description
	15.16	**动、植物油、脂及其分离品，全部或部分氢化、相互酯化、再酯化或反油酸化，不论是否精制，但未经进一步加工：**					**Animal or vegetable fats and oils and their fractions, partly or wholly hydrogenated, inter-esterified, re-esterified or elaidinised, whether or not refined, but not further prepared:**
1045	1516.1000	-动物油、脂及其分离品	5	0 澳AU,澳门MO,冰岛IS,东盟AS,哥CR,韩国KR,秘鲁PE,瑞士CH,新西兰NZ,智利CL	0 受惠国LD	70	-Animal fats and oils and fractions thereof
1046	1516.2000	-植物油、脂及其分离品	25	0 澳门MO,冰岛IS,东盟AS,哥CR,新西兰NZ,智利CL 7.5 秘鲁PE 15 澳AU	0 受惠国$_1$LD$_1$	70	-Vegetable fats and oils and fractions thereof
	15.17	**人造黄油；本章各种动、植物油、脂及其分离品混合制成的食用油、脂或制品，但税号15.16的食用油、脂及其分离品除外：**					**Margarine; edible mixtures or preparations of animal or vegetable fats or oils or of fractions of different fats or oils of this chapter, other than edible fats or oils or their fractions of heading 1516:**
1047	1517.1000	-人造黄油，但不包括液态的	30	0 澳门MO,东盟AS,哥CR,新加坡SG,新西兰NZ,智利CL 18 澳AU		80	-Margarine, excluding liquid margarine
		-其他：					-Other:
1048	1517.9010	---起酥油	25	0 澳门MO,冰岛IS,东盟AS,哥CR,香港HK,新西兰NZ,智利CL 7.5 秘鲁PE 15 澳AU 17.5 瑞士CH	0 受惠国$_1$LD$_1$	70	---Shortening
1049	1517.9090	---其他	25	0 澳门MO,冰岛IS,东盟AS,哥CR,香港HK,新西兰NZ,智利CL 7.5 秘鲁PE 18 瑞士CH	0 受惠国$_1$LD$_1$	70	---Other
	15.18	**动、植物油、脂及其分离品，经过熟炼、氧化、脱水、硫化、吹制或在真空、惰性气体中加热聚合及用其他化学方法改性的，但税号15.16的产品除外；本章各种油、脂及其分离品混合制成的其他税号未列名的非食用油、脂或制品**					**Animal or vegetable fats and oils and their fractions, boiled, oxidised, dehydrated, sulphurised, blown, polymerised by heat in vacuum or in inert gas or otherwise chemically modified, excluding those of heading 1516; inedible mixtures or preparations of animal or vegetable fats or oils or of fractions of different fats or oils of this chapter, not elsewhere specified or included**
1050	1518.0000	动、植物油、脂及其分离品，经过熟炼、氧化、脱水、硫化、吹制或在真空、惰性气体中加热聚合及用其他化学方法改性的，但税号15.16的产品除外；本章各种油、脂及其分离品混合制成的其他税号未列名的非食用油、脂或制品	10	0 澳门MO,冰岛IS,东盟AS,哥CR,新加坡SG,新西兰NZ,智利CL 3 秘鲁PE 4 瑞士CH 9 韩国KR	0 受惠国LD	70	Animal or vegetable fats and oils and fractions thereof, boiled, oxidized, dehydrated, sulphurized, blown, polymerized by heat in vacuum or in inert gas or otherwise chemically modified, excluding those of heading No.15.16; inedible mixtures or preparations of animal or vegetable fats or oils or of fractions of different fats or oils of this Chapter, not elsewhere specified or included
	15.20	**粗甘油；甘油水及甘油碱液**					**Glycerol, crude; glycerol waters and glycerol lyes**

序号 No.	税则号列 Tariff Line	中文货品名称 Article Description in Chinese	最惠国税率 MFN(%)	协定税率 Agreement(%)	特惠税率 SP(%)	普通税率 Gen(%)	英文货品名称 Article Description
1051	1520.0000	粗甘油；甘油水及甘油碱液	20Δ6	0 澳门MO,冰岛IS,东盟AS,哥CR,香港HK,新加坡SG,新西兰NZ,智利CL 6 秘鲁PE 12 澳AU 14 瑞士CH 17.3 韩国KR	0 受惠国$_1$LD$_1$	50	Glycerol, crude; glycerol waters and glycerol lyes
	15.21	**植物蜡（甘油三酯除外）、蜂蜡、其他虫蜡及鲸蜡，不论是否精制或着色：**					**Vegetable waxes (other than triglycerides) , beeswax, other insect waxes and spermaceti, whether or not refined or coloured:**
1052	1521.1000	-植物蜡	20	0 冰岛IS,东盟AS,哥CR,新加坡SG,新西兰NZ,智利CL 6 秘鲁PE 12 澳AU 14 瑞士CH 17.3 韩国KR	0 受惠国$_1$LD$_1$	80	-Vegetable waxes
		-其他：					-Other:
1053	1521.9010	---蜂蜡	20	0 冰岛IS,东盟AS,哥CR,新加坡SG,新西兰NZ,智利CL 6 秘鲁PE 12 澳AU 14 瑞士CH 17.3 韩国KR	0 受惠国$_1$LD$_1$	80	---Beeswax
1054	1521.9090	---其他	20	0 冰岛IS,东盟AS,哥CR,新加坡SG,新西兰NZ,智利CL 6 秘鲁PE 12 澳AU 14 瑞士CH 17.3 韩国KR	0 受惠国$_1$LD$_1$	80	---Other
	15.22	**油鞣回收脂；加工处理油脂物质及动、植物蜡所剩的残渣**					**Degras; residues resulting from the treatment of fatty substances or animal or vegetable waxes**
1055	1522.0000	油鞣回收脂；加工处理油脂物质及动、植物蜡所剩的残渣	20	0 冰岛IS,东盟AS,哥CR,新加坡SG,新西兰NZ,智利CL 6 秘鲁PE 12 澳AU 14 瑞士CH 17.3 韩国KR	0 受惠国$_1$LD$_1$	50	Degras; residues resulting from the treatment of fatty substances of animal or vegetable waxes

第四类
食品；饮料、酒及醋；烟草、烟草及烟草代用品的制品

SECTION Ⅳ
PREPARED FOODSTUFFS; BEVERAGES, SPIRITS AND VINEGAR;TOBACCO AND MANUFACTURED TOBACCO SUBSTITUTES

注释：

本类所称“团粒”，是指直接挤压或加入按重量计比例不超过3%的粘合剂制成的粒状产品。

Note:

In this Section the term“pellets”means products which have been agglomerated either directly by compression or by the addition of a binder in a proportion not exceeding 3% by weight.

第十六章
肉、鱼、甲壳动物、软体动物及其他水生无脊椎动物的制品

Chapter 16
Preparations of meat, of fish or of crustaceans, molluscs or other aquatic invertebrates

注释：

一、本章不包括用第二章、第三章及税号05.04所列方法制作或保藏的肉、食用杂碎、鱼、甲壳动物、软体动物或其他水生无脊椎动物。

二、本章的食品按重量计必须含有20%以上的香肠、肉、食用杂碎、动物血、鱼、甲壳动物、软体动物或其他水生无脊椎动物及其混合物。对于含有两种或两种以上前述产品的食品，则应按其中重量最大的产品归入第十六章的相应税号。但本条规定不适用于税号19.02的包馅食品和税号21.03及21.04的食品。

Notes:

1. This Chapter does not cover meat, meat offal, fish, crustaceans, molluscs or other aquatic invertebrates, prepared or preserved by the processes specified in Chapter2 or 3 or heading No.05.04.
2. Food preparations fall in this Chapter provided that they contain more than 20% by weight of sausage, meat, meat offal, blood, fish or crustaceans, molluscs or other aquatic invertebrates, or any combination thereof. In cases where the preparation contains two or more of the products mentioned above, it is classified in the heading of Chapter16corresponding to the component or components which predominate by weight. These provisions do not apply to the stuffed products of heading No.19.02 or to the preparations of heading No.21.03 or 21.04.

子目注释：

一、子目号1602.10的“均化食品”，是指用肉、食用杂碎或动物血经精细均化制成供婴幼儿食用或营养用的零售包装食品（每件净重不超过250克）。为了调味、保藏或其他目的，均化食品中可以加入少量其他配料，还可以含有少量可见的肉粒或食用杂碎粒。归类时该子目优先于税号16.02的其他子目。

二、税号16.04或16.05项下各子目所列的是鱼、甲壳动物、软体动物及其他水生无脊椎动物的俗名，它们与第三章中相同名称的鱼、甲壳动物、软体动物及其他水生无脊椎动物种类范围相同。

Subheading Notes:

1. For the purposes of subheading No.1602.10, the expression “homogenized preparations” means preparations of meat, meat offal or blood, finely homogenized, put up for retail sale as infant food or for dietetic purposes, in containers of a net weight content not exceeding 250g. For the application of this definition no account is to be taken of small quantities of any ingredients which may have been added to the preparation for seasoning, preservation or other purposes. These preparations may contain a small quantity of visible pieces of meat or meat offal. This subheading takes precedence over all other subheadings of heading No.16.02.
2. The fish, crustaceans, mollusks and other aquatic invertebrates specified in the subheahings of heading No.16.04 or 16.05 under their common names only, are of the same species as those mentioned in Chapter 3 under the same name.

序号 No.	税则号列 Tariff Line	中文货品名称 Article Description in Chinese	最惠国税率 MFN(%)	协定税率 Agreement(%)	特惠税率 SP(%)	普通税率 Gen(%)	英文货品名称 Article Description
	16.01	**肉、食用杂碎或动物血制成的香肠及类似产品；用香肠制成的食品：**					**Sausages and similar products, of meat, meat offal or blood; food preparations based on these products:**
1056	1601.0010	---用天然肠衣做外包装的香肠及类似产品	15	0 澳门MO,冰岛IS,东盟AS,哥CR,香港HK,新加坡SG,新西兰NZ,智利CL 4.5 秘鲁PE 9 澳AU 10.5 瑞士CH 12 巴PK,韩国KR	0 受惠国$_1$LD$_1$	90	---Sausages and similar products coated with natural casings
1057	1601.0020	---其他香肠及类似产品	15	0 澳门MO,冰岛IS,东盟AS,哥CR,香港HK,新加坡SG,新西兰NZ,智利CL 4.5 秘鲁PE 9 澳AU 10.5 瑞士CH 12 巴PK,韩国KR	0 受惠国$_1$LD$_1$	90	---Other sausages and similar products
1058	1601.0030	---用香肠制成的食品	15	0 澳门MO,冰岛IS,东盟AS,哥CR,新加坡SG,新西兰NZ,智利CL 4.5 秘鲁PE 9 澳AU 10.5 瑞士CH 12 巴PK,韩国KR	0 受惠国$_1$LD$_1$	90	---Sausage based food products
	16.02	**其他方法制作或保藏的肉、食用杂碎或动物血：**					**Other prepared or preserved meat, meat offal or blood:**
1059	1602.1000	-均化食品	15	0 冰岛IS,东盟AS,哥CR,新加坡SG,新西兰NZ,智利CL 4.5 秘鲁PE 9 澳AU 10.5 瑞士CH 12 巴PK,韩国KR	0 受惠国$_1$LD$_1$	90	-Homogenized preparations
1060	1602.2000	-动物肝	15	0 冰岛IS,东盟AS,哥CR,香港HK,新加坡SG,新西兰NZ,智利CL 4.5 秘鲁PE 9 澳AU 10.5 瑞士CH 12 巴PK,韩国KR	0 受惠国$_1$LD$_1$	90	-Of liver of any animal
		-税号01. 05的家禽的：					-Of poultry of heading 0105:
1061	1602.3100	--火鸡的	15	0 冰岛IS,东盟AS,哥CR,新加坡SG,新西兰NZ,智利CL 4.5 秘鲁PE 9 澳AU 10.5 瑞士CH 12 巴PK,韩国KR	0 受惠国$_1$LD$_1$	90	--Of turkeys
		--鸡的：					--Of fowls of the species *Gallus domesticus*:
1062	1602.3210	---罐头	15	0 澳门MO,冰岛IS,东盟AS,哥CR,新加坡SG,新西兰NZ,智利CL 4.5 秘鲁PE 9 澳AU 10.5 瑞士CH 12 巴PK,韩国KR	0 受惠国$_1$LD$_1$	90	---In airtight containers
		---其他：					---Other:

序号 No.	税则号列 Tariff Line	中文货品名称 Article Description in Chinese	最惠国税率 MFN(%)	协定税率 Agreement(%)	特惠税率 SP(%)	普通税率 Gen(%)	英文货品名称 Article Description
1063	1602.3291	----鸡胸肉	15	0 冰岛IS,东盟AS,哥CR,香港HK,新加坡SG,新西兰NZ,智利CL 4.5 秘鲁PE 9 澳AU 10.5 瑞士CH 12 巴PK,韩国KR	0 受惠国$_1$LD$_1$	90	----Chicken breast filets
1064	1602.3292	----鸡腿肉	15	0 冰岛IS,东盟AS,哥CR,香港HK,新加坡SG,新西兰NZ,智利CL 4.5 秘鲁PE 9 澳AU 10.5 瑞士CH 12 巴PK,韩国KR	0 受惠国$_1$LD$_1$	90	----Chicken leg meat
1065	1602.3299	----其他	15	0 澳门MO,冰岛IS,东盟AS,哥CR,香港HK,新加坡SG,新西兰NZ,智利CL 4.5 秘鲁PE 9 澳AU 10.5 瑞士CH 12 巴PK,韩国KR	0 受惠国$_1$LD$_1$	90	----Other
		--其他:					--Other:
1066	1602.3910	---罐头	15	0 澳门MO,冰岛IS,东盟AS,哥CR,新加坡SG,新西兰NZ,智利CL 4.5 秘鲁PE 9 澳AU 10.5 瑞士CH 12 巴PK,韩国KR	0 受惠国$_1$LD$_1$	90	---In airtight containers
		---其他:					---Other:
1067	1602.3991	----鸭的	15	0 冰岛IS,东盟AS,哥CR,香港HK,新加坡SG,新西兰NZ,智利CL 4.5 秘鲁PE 9 澳AU 10.5 瑞士CH 12 巴PK,韩国KR	0 受惠国$_1$LD$_1$	90	----Of duck
1068	1602.3999	----其他	15	0 澳门MO,冰岛IS,东盟AS,哥CR,新加坡SG,新西兰NZ,智利CL 4.5 秘鲁PE 9 澳AU 10.5 瑞士CH 12 巴PK,韩国KR	0 受惠国$_1$LD$_1$	90	----Other
		-猪的:					-Of swine:
1069	1602.4100	--后腿及其肉块	15	0 澳门MO,冰岛IS,东盟AS,哥CR,新加坡SG,新西兰NZ,智利CL 4.5 秘鲁PE 9 澳AU 10.5 瑞士CH 12 巴PK,韩国KR	0 受惠国$_1$LD$_1$	90	--Hams and cuts thereof
1070	1602.4200	--前腿及其肉块	15	0 澳门MO,冰岛IS,东盟AS,哥CR,新加坡SG,新西兰NZ,智利CL 4.5 秘鲁PE 9 澳AU 10.5 瑞士CH 12 巴PK,韩国KR	0 受惠国$_1$LD$_1$	90	--Shoulders and cuts thereof
		--其他，包括混合的肉:					--Other, including mixtures:

序号 No.	税则号列 Tariff Line	中文货品名称 Article Description in Chinese	最惠国税率 MFN(%)	协定税率 Agreement(%)	特惠税率 SP(%)	普通税率 Gen(%)	英文货品名称 Article Description
1071	1602.4910	---罐头	15	0 澳门MO,冰岛IS,东盟AS,哥CR,新加坡SG,新西兰NZ,智利CL 4.5 秘鲁PE 9 澳AU 10.5 瑞士CH 12 巴PK,韩国KR	0 受惠国$_1$LD$_1$	90	---In airtight containers
1072	1602.4990	---其他	15	0 澳门MO,冰岛IS,东盟AS,哥CR,香港HK,新加坡SG,新西兰NZ,智利CL 4.5 秘鲁PE 9 澳AU 10.5 瑞士CH 12 巴PK,韩国KR	0 受惠国$_1$LD$_1$	90	---Other
		-牛的:					-Of bovine animals:
1073	1602.5010	---罐头	12	0 澳门MO,冰岛IS,东盟AS,哥CR,香港HK,新加坡SG,新西兰NZ,智利CL 3.6 秘鲁PE 6 巴PK 7.2 澳AU 8.4 瑞士CH 9.6 韩国KR	0 受惠国$_1$LD$_1$	90	---In airtight containers
1074	1602.5090	---其他	12	0 澳门MO,冰岛IS,东盟AS,哥CR,香港HK,新加坡SG,新西兰NZ,智利CL 3.6 秘鲁PE 6 巴PK 7.2 澳AU 8.4 瑞士CH 9.6 韩国KR	0 受惠国$_1$LD$_1$	90	---Other
		-其他，包括动物血的食品:					-Other, including preparations of blood of any animal:
1075	1602.9010	---罐头	15	0 澳门MO,冰岛IS,东盟AS,哥CR,新加坡SG,新西兰NZ,智利CL 4.5 秘鲁PE 9 澳AU 10.5 瑞士CH 12 巴PK,韩国KR	0 受惠国$_1$LD$_1$	90	---In airtight containers
1076	1602.9090	---其他	15	0 澳门MO,冰岛IS,东盟AS,哥CR,新加坡SG,新西兰NZ,智利CL 4.5 秘鲁PE 9 澳AU 10.5 瑞士CH 12 巴PK,韩国KR	0 受惠国$_1$LD$_1$	90	---Other
	16.03	**肉、鱼、甲壳动物、软体动物或其他水生无脊椎动物的精及汁**					**Extracts and juices of meat, fish or crustaceans, molluscs or other aquatic invertebrates**
1077	1603.0000	肉、鱼、甲壳动物、软体动物或其他水生无脊椎动物的精及汁	23	0 冰岛IS,东盟AS,哥CR,香港HK,新加坡SG,新西兰NZ,智利CL 6.9 秘鲁PE 13.8 澳AU 16.1 瑞士CH 20.7 韩国KR	0 受惠国$_1$LD$_1$	90	Extracts and juices of meat, fish or crustaceans, molluscs or other aquatic invertebrates
	16.04	**制作或保藏的鱼；鲟鱼子酱及鱼卵制的鲟鱼子酱代用品:**					**Prepared or preserved fish; caviar and caviar substitutes prepared from fish eggs:**
		-鱼，整条或切块，但未绞碎:					-Fish, whole or in pieces, but not minced:
		--鲑鱼:					--Salmon:

序号 No.	税则号列 Tariff Line	中文货品名称 Article Description in Chinese	最惠国税率 MFN(%)	协定税率 Agreement(%)	特惠税率 SP(%)	普通税率 Gen(%)	英文货品名称 Article Description
1078	1604.1110	---大西洋鲑鱼	12	0 冰岛IS,东盟AS,哥CR,香港HK,新加坡SG,新西兰NZ,智利CL 6 巴PK 7.2 澳AU 9.6 韩国KR	0 受惠国$_1$LD$_1$	90	---Atalantic salmon
1079	1604.1190	---其他	12	0 冰岛IS,东盟AS,哥CR,新加坡SG,新西兰NZ,智利CL 6 巴PK 7.2 澳AU 9.6 韩国KR	0 受惠国$_1$LD$_1$	90	---Other
1080	1604.1200	--鲱鱼	12	0 冰岛IS,东盟AS,哥CR,秘鲁PE,新加坡SG,新西兰NZ,智利CL 6 巴PK 7.2 澳AU 8.4 瑞士CH 9.6 韩国KR	0 受惠国$_1$LD$_1$	90	--Herrings
1081	1604.1300	--沙丁鱼、小沙丁鱼属、黍鲱或西鲱	5	0 澳AU,澳门MO,巴PK,冰岛IS,东盟AS,哥CR,韩国KR,瑞士CH,新西兰NZ,智利CL 0.6 秘鲁PE	0 柬埔寨KH,受惠国LD	90	--Sardines, sardinella and brisling or sprats
1082	1604.1400	--金枪鱼、鲣鱼及狐鲣（狐鲣属）	5	0 澳AU,巴PK,冰岛IS,东盟AS,哥CR,韩国KR,秘鲁PE,瑞士CH,香港HK,新西兰NZ,智利CL	0 柬埔寨KH,受惠国LD	90	--Tunas, skipjack and bonito (Sarda spp.)
1083	1604.1500	--鲭鱼	12	0 冰岛IS,东盟AS,哥CR,新加坡SG,新西兰NZ,智利CL 1.5 秘鲁PE 6 巴PK 7.2 澳AU 8.4 瑞士CH 9.6 韩国KR	0 受惠国$_1$LD$_1$	90	--Mackerel
1084	1604.1600	--鳀鱼	12	0 冰岛IS,东盟AS,哥CR,新加坡SG,新西兰NZ,智利CL 1.5 秘鲁PE 6 巴PK 7.2 澳AU 8.4 瑞士CH 9.6 韩国KR	0 受惠国$_1$LD$_1$	90	--Anchovies
1085	1604.1700	--鳗鱼	12	0 冰岛IS,东盟AS,哥CR,香港HK,新加坡SG,新西兰NZ,智利CL 5 巴PK 7.2 澳AU 8.4 瑞士CH 9.6 韩国KR 9.9 亚太AP	0 受惠国LD	90	--Eels
		--其他：					--Other:
1086	1604.1920	---罗非鱼	12	0 冰岛IS,东盟AS,哥CR,香港HK,新加坡SG,新西兰NZ,智利CL 6 巴PK 7.2 澳AU 8.4 瑞士CH 9.6 韩国KR	0 受惠国$_1$LD$_1$	90	---Tilapia
		---叉尾鮰鱼：					---Of *Ictalurus*:

序号 No.	税则号列 Tariff Line	中文货品名称 Article Description in Chinese	最惠国税率 MFN(%)	协定税率 Agreement(%)	特惠税率 SP(%)	普通税率 Gen(%)	英文货品名称 Article Description
1087	1604.1931	----斑点叉尾鮰鱼	12	0 冰岛IS,东盟AS,哥CR,香港HK,新加坡SG,新西兰NZ,智利CL 5 巴PK 7.2 澳AU 8.4 瑞士CH 9.6 韩国KR 9.9 亚太AP	0 受惠国LD	90	----Channel catfish (*Ictalurus punctatus*)
1088	1604.1939	----其他	12	0 冰岛IS,东盟AS,哥CR,香港HK,新加坡SG,新西兰NZ,智利CL 5 巴PK 7.2 澳AU 8.4 瑞士CH 9.6 韩国KR 9.9 亚太AP	0 受惠国LD	90	----Other
1089	1604.1990	---其他	12	0 澳门MO,冰岛IS,东盟AS,哥CR,香港HK,新加坡SG,新西兰NZ,智利CL 5 巴PK 7.2 澳AU 8.4 瑞士CH 9.6 韩国KR 9.9 亚太AP	0 受惠国LD	90	---Other
		-其他制作或保藏的鱼:					-Other prepared or preserved fish:
		---罐头:					---In airtight containers:
1090	1604.2011	----鱼翅	12	0 澳门MO,冰岛IS,东盟AS,哥CR,香港HK,新加坡SG,新西兰NZ,智利CL 3.6 秘鲁PE 5 巴PK 8.4 瑞士CH 9.9 亚太AP	0 受惠国$_1$LD$_1$	90	----Shark fin
1091	1604.2019	----其他	12	0 澳门MO,冰岛IS,东盟AS,哥CR,香港HK,新加坡SG,新西兰NZ,智利CL 3.6 秘鲁PE 5 巴PK 7.2 澳AU 8.4 瑞士CH 9.6 韩国KR 9.9 亚太AP	0 受惠国$_1$LD$_1$	90	----Other
		---其他:					---Other:
1092	1604.2091	----鱼翅	12	0 澳门MO,冰岛IS,东盟AS,哥CR,香港HK,新加坡SG,新西兰NZ,智利CL 3.6 秘鲁PE 5 巴PK 8.4 瑞士CH 9.9 亚太AP	0 受惠国$_1$LD$_1$	90	----Shark fin
1093	1604.2099	----其他	12	0 澳门MO,冰岛IS,东盟AS,哥CR,香港HK,新加坡SG,新西兰NZ,智利CL 3.6 秘鲁PE 5 巴PK 7.2 澳AU 8.4 瑞士CH 9.6 韩国KR 9.9 亚太AP	0 受惠国$_1$LD$_1$	90	----Other
		-鲟鱼子酱及鲟鱼子酱代用品:					-Caviar and caviar substitutes:

序号 No.	税则号列 Tariff Line	中文货品名称 Article Description in Chinese	最惠国税率 MFN(%)	协定税率 Agreement(%)	特惠税率 SP(%)	普通税率 Gen(%)	英文货品名称 Article Description
1094	1604.3100	--鲟鱼子酱	12	0 冰岛IS,东盟AS,哥CR,秘鲁PE,新加坡SG,新西兰NZ,智利CL 6 巴PK 7.2 澳AU 8.4 瑞士CH 9.6 韩国KR	0 受惠国$_1$LD$_1$	90	--Caviar
1095	1604.3200	--鲟鱼子酱代用品	12	0 冰岛IS,东盟AS,哥CR,秘鲁PE,新加坡SG,新西兰NZ,智利CL 6 巴PK 7.2 澳AU 8.4 瑞士CH 9.6 韩国KR	0 受惠国$_1$LD$_1$	90	--Caviar substitutes
	16.05	**制作或保藏的甲壳动物、软体动物及其他水生无脊椎动物:**					**Crustaceans, molluscs and other aquatic invertebrates, prepared or preserved:**
1096	1605.1000	-蟹	5	0 澳AU,巴PK,冰岛IS,东盟AS,哥CR,韩国KR,秘鲁PE,瑞士CH,香港HK,新西兰NZ,智利CL	0 受惠国LD	90	-Crab
		-小虾及对虾:					-Shrimps and prawns:
1097	1605.2100	--非密封包装	5	0 澳AU,巴PK,冰岛IS,东盟AS,哥CR,韩国KR,秘鲁PE,瑞士CH,香港HK,新西兰NZ,智利CL	0 柬埔寨KH,受惠国LD	90	--Not in airtight container
1098	1605.2900	--其他	5	0 澳AU,巴PK,冰岛IS,东盟AS,哥CR,韩国KR,秘鲁PE,瑞士CH,香港HK,新西兰NZ,智利CL	0 柬埔寨KH,受惠国LD	90	--Other
1099	1605.3000	-龙虾	5	0 澳AU,巴PK,冰岛IS,东盟AS,哥CR,韩国KR,秘鲁PE,瑞士CH,香港HK,新西兰NZ,智利CL	0 柬埔寨KH,受惠国LD	90	-Lobster
		-其他甲壳动物:					-Other crustaceans:
		---淡水小龙虾:					---Freshwater crawfish:
1100	1605.4011	----虾仁	5	0 澳AU,巴PK,冰岛IS,东盟AS,哥CR,韩国KR,秘鲁PE,瑞士CH,新西兰NZ,智利CL	0 柬埔寨KH,受惠国LD	90	----Shelled
1101	1605.4019	----其他	5	0 澳AU,巴PK,冰岛IS,东盟AS,哥CR,韩国KR,秘鲁PE,瑞士CH,新西兰NZ,智利CL	0 柬埔寨KH,受惠国LD	90	----Other
1102	1605.4090	---其他	5	0 澳AU,澳门MO,巴PK,冰岛IS,东盟AS,哥CR,韩国KR,秘鲁PE,瑞士CH,新西兰NZ,智利CL	0 柬埔寨KH,受惠国LD	90	---Other
		-软体动物:					-Molluscs:
1103	1605.5100	--牡蛎(蚝)	5	0 澳AU,澳门MO,巴PK,冰岛IS,东盟AS,哥CR,韩国KR,瑞士CH,香港HK,新西兰NZ,智利CL 0.6 秘鲁PE 3.9 亚太AP	0 受惠国LD	90	--Oysters
1104	1605.5200	--扇贝,包括海扇	5	0 澳AU,澳门MO,巴PK,冰岛IS,东盟AS,哥CR,韩国KR,瑞士CH,香港HK,新西兰NZ,智利CL 0.6 秘鲁PE 3.9 亚太AP	0 受惠国LD	90	--Scallops, including queen scallops

序号 No.	税则号列 Tariff Line	中文货品名称 Article Description in Chinese	最惠国税率 MFN(%)	协定税率 Agreement(%)	特惠税率 SP(%)	普通税率 Gen(%)	英文货品名称 Article Description
1105	1605.5300	--贻贝	5	0 澳AU,澳门MO,巴PK,冰岛IS,东盟AS,哥CR,韩国KR,瑞士CH,香港HK,新西兰NZ,智利CL 0.6 秘鲁PE 3.9 亚太AP	0 受惠国LD	90	--Mussels
1106	1605.5400	--墨鱼及鱿鱼	5	0 澳AU,澳门MO,巴PK,冰岛IS,东盟AS,哥CR,韩国KR,瑞士CH,香港HK,新西兰NZ,智利CL 0.6 秘鲁PE 3.9 亚太AP	0 受惠国LD	90	--Cuttle fish and squid
1107	1605.5500	--章鱼	5	0 澳AU,澳门MO,巴PK,冰岛IS,东盟AS,哥CR,韩国KR,瑞士CH,香港HK,新西兰NZ,智利CL 0.6 秘鲁PE 3.9 亚太AP	0 受惠国LD	90	--Octopus
		--蛤、鸟蛤及舟贝:					--Clams, cockles and arkshells:
1108	1605.5610	---蛤	5	0 澳AU,巴PK,冰岛IS,东盟AS,哥CR,韩国KR,瑞士CH,香港HK,新西兰NZ,智利CL 3.9 亚太AP	0 受惠国LD	90	---Clams
1109	1605.5620	---鸟蛤及舟贝	5	0 澳AU,澳门MO,巴PK,冰岛IS,东盟AS,哥CR,韩国KR,瑞士CH,香港HK,新西兰NZ,智利CL 0.6 秘鲁PE 3.9 亚太AP	0 受惠国LD	90	---Cockles and arkshells
1110	1605.5700	--鲍鱼	5	0 澳AU,澳门MO,巴PK,冰岛IS,东盟AS,哥CR,韩国KR,瑞士CH,香港HK,新西兰NZ,智利CL 0.6 秘鲁PE 3.9 亚太AP	0 受惠国LD	90	--Abalone
1111	1605.5800	--蜗牛及螺，海螺除外	5	0 澳AU,澳门MO,巴PK,冰岛IS,东盟AS,哥CR,韩国KR,瑞士CH,香港HK,新西兰NZ,智利CL 0.6 秘鲁PE 3.9 亚太AP	0 受惠国LD	90	--Snails, other than sea snails
1112	1605.5900	--其他	5	0 澳AU,澳门MO,巴PK,冰岛IS,东盟AS,哥CR,韩国KR,瑞士CH,香港HK,新西兰NZ,智利CL 0.6 秘鲁PE 3.9 亚太AP	0 受惠国LD	90	--Other
		-其他水生无脊椎动物:					-Other aquatic invertebrates:
1113	1605.6100	--海参	5	0 澳AU,澳门MO,巴PK,冰岛IS,东盟AS,哥CR,韩国KR,瑞士CH,香港HK,新西兰NZ,智利CL 0.6 秘鲁PE 3.9 亚太AP	0 受惠国LD	90	--Sea cucumbers
1114	1605.6200	--海胆	5	0 澳AU,澳门MO,巴PK,冰岛IS,东盟AS,哥CR,韩国KR,瑞士CH,香港HK,新西兰NZ,智利CL 0.6 秘鲁PE 3.9 亚太AP	0 受惠国LD	90	--Sea urchins

序号 No.	税则号列 Tariff Line	中文货品名称 Article Description in Chinese	最惠国税率 MFN(%)	协定税率 Agreement(%)		特惠税率 SP(%)		普通税率 Gen(%)	英文货品名称 Article Description
1115	1605.6300	--海蜇	15	0 9 10.5 12	冰岛IS,东盟AS,哥CR, 香港HK,新加坡SG,新 西兰NZ,智利CL 澳AU 瑞士CH 巴PK,韩国KR	0	受惠国LD	90	--Jellyfish
1116	1605.6900	--其他	5	0 0.6 3.9	澳AU,澳门MO,巴PK, 冰岛IS,东盟AS,哥CR, 韩国KR,瑞士CH,香港 HK,新西兰NZ,智利CL 秘鲁PE 亚太AP	0	受惠国LD	90	--Other

第十七章
糖及糖食

注释：

本章不包括：

一、含有可可的糖食（税号 18.06）；

二、税号 29.40 的化学纯糖（蔗糖、乳糖、麦芽糖、葡萄糖及果糖除外）及其他产品；

三、第三十章的药品及其他产品。

子目注释：

一、子目号 1701.12、1701.13 及 1701.14 所称“原糖”，是指按重量计干燥状态的蔗糖含量对应的旋光读数低于 99.5° 的糖。

二、子目 1701.13 仅包括非离心甘蔗糖，其按重量计干燥状态的蔗糖含量对应的旋光读数不低于 69° 但低于 93°。该产品仅含肉眼不可见的不规则形状天然他形微晶，外被糖蜜残余及其他甘蔗成分。

Chapter 17
Sugars and sugar confectionery

Notes:

This Chapter does not cover:

1. Sugar confectionery containing cocoa (heading No.18.06);
2. Chemically pure sugars (other than sucrose, lactose, maltose, glucose and fructose) or other products of heading No.29.40; or
3. Medicaments or other products of Chapter 30.

Subheading Notes:

1. For the purposes of subheadings No.1701.12, 1701.13 and 1701.14, “raw sugar” means sugar whose content of sucrose by weight, in the dry state, corresponds to a polarimeter reading of less than 99.5°.
2. Subheading No.1701.13 covers only cane sugar obtained without centrifugation, whose content of sucrose by weight, in the dry state, corresponds to a polarimeter reading of 69° or more but less than 93°. The product contains only natural anhedral microcrystals, of irregular shape, not visible to the naked eye, which are surrounded by residues of molasses and other constituents of sugar cane.

序号 No.	税则号列 Tariff Line	中文货品名称 Article Description in Chinese	最惠国税率 MFN(%)	协定税率 Agreement(%)	特惠税率 SP(%)	普通税率 Gen(%)	英文货品名称 Article Description
	17.01	**固体甘蔗糖、甜菜糖及化学纯蔗糖：**					**Cane or beet sugar and chemically pure sucrose, in solid form:**
		-未加香料或着色剂的原糖：					-Raw sugar not containing added flavouring or colouring matter:
1117	1701.1200	--甜菜糖	50①			125	--Beet sugar
1118	1701.1300	--本章子目注释二所述的甘蔗糖	50②			125	--Cane sugar specified in Subheading Note 2 to this Chapter
1119	1701.1400	--其他甘蔗糖	50③			125	--Other cane sugar
		-其他：					-Other:
1120	1701.9100	--加有香料或着色剂	50④			125	--Containing added flavouring or colouring matter
		--其他：					--Other:
1121	1701.9910	---砂糖	50⑤			125	---Granulated sugar
1122	1701.9920	---绵白糖	50⑥			125	---Superfine sugar
1123	1701.9990	---其他	50⑦			125	---Other
	17.02	**其他固体糖，包括化学纯乳糖、麦芽糖、葡萄糖及果糖；未加香料或着色剂的糖浆；人造蜜，不论是否掺有天然蜂蜜；焦糖：**					**Other sugars, including chemically pure lactose, maltose, glucose and fructose, in solid form; sugar syrups not containing added flavouring or colouring matter; artificial honey, whether or not mixed with natural honey; caramel:**

①配额税率：15
In-quota Tariff: 15

②配额税率：15
In-quota Tariff: 15

③配额税率：15
In-quota Tariff: 15

④配额税率：15
In-quota Tariff: 15

⑤配额税率：15
In-quota Tariff: 15

⑥配额税率：15
In-quota Tariff: 15

⑦配额税率：15
In-quota Tariff: 15

序号 No.	税则号列 Tariff Line	中文货品名称 Article Description in Chinese	最惠国税率 MFN(%)	协定税率 Agreement(%)	特惠税率 SP(%)	普通税率 Gen(%)	英文货品名称 Article Description
		-乳糖及乳糖浆:					-Lactose and lactose syrup:
1124	1702.1100	--按重量计干燥无水乳糖含量在99%及以上	10	0 澳门MO,东盟AS,哥CR,秘鲁PE,新加坡SG,新西兰NZ,智利CL 4 瑞士CH 5 巴PK 6 澳AU 8 韩国KR	0 受惠国LD	80	--Containing by weight 99% or more lactose, expressed as anhydrous lactose, calculated on the dry matter
1125	1702.1900	--其他	10	0 澳门MO,东盟AS,哥CR,秘鲁PE,新加坡SG,新西兰NZ,智利CL 4 瑞士CH 5 巴PK 6 澳AU 8 韩国KR	0 受惠国LD	80	--Other
1126	1702.2000	-槭糖及槭糖浆	30	0 澳门MO,东盟AS,哥CR,新加坡SG,新西兰NZ,智利CL 9 秘鲁PE 18 澳AU 27 韩国KR	0 受惠国$_2$LD$_2$	80	-Maple sugar and maple syrup
1127	1702.3000	-葡萄糖及葡萄糖浆，不含果糖或按重量计干燥状态的果糖含量在20%以下	30	0 澳门MO,东盟AS,哥CR,香港HK,新加坡SG,新西兰NZ,智利CL 9 秘鲁PE 18 澳AU	0 受惠国$_2$LD$_2$	80	-Glucose and glucose syrup, not containing fructose or containing in the dry state less than 20% by weight of fructose
1128	1702.4000	-葡萄糖及葡萄糖浆，按重量计干燥状态的果糖含量在20%及以上，但在50%以下	30	0 澳门MO,东盟AS,哥CR,新加坡SG,新西兰NZ,智利CL 9 秘鲁PE 18 澳AU	0 受惠国$_2$LD$_2$	80	-Glucose and glucose syrup, containing in the dry state at least 20% but less than 50% by weight of fructose
1129	1702.5000	-化学纯果糖	30	0 澳门MO,冰岛IS,东盟AS,哥CR,新加坡SG,新西兰NZ,智利CL 9 秘鲁PE 18 澳AU	0 受惠国$_2$LD$_2$	80	-Chemically pure fructose
1130	1702.6000	-其他果糖及果糖浆，按重量计干燥状态的果糖含量在50%以上	30	0 澳门MO,冰岛IS,东盟AS,哥CR,新加坡SG,新西兰NZ,智利CL 9 秘鲁PE 18 澳AU	0 受惠国$_2$LD$_2$	80	-Other fructose and fructose syrup, containing in the dry state more than 50% by weight of fructose
1131	1702.9000	-其他，包括转化糖	30	0 澳门MO,冰岛IS,东盟AS,哥CR,香港HK,新加坡SG,新西兰NZ,智利CL 17.6 秘鲁PE 18 澳AU 21.6 瑞士CH	0 受惠国LD	80	-Other, including invert sugar
	17.03	**制糖后所剩的糖蜜:**					**Molasses resulting from the extraction or refining of sugar:**
1132	1703.1000	-甘蔗糖蜜	8	0 冰岛IS,东盟AS,哥CR,秘鲁PE,新西兰NZ,智利CL 3.2 瑞士CH 4.8 澳AU,韩国KR 5 巴PK	0 受惠国LD	50	-Cane molasses
1133	1703.9000	-其他	8	0 冰岛IS,东盟AS,哥CR,秘鲁PE,新西兰NZ,智利CL 3.2 瑞士CH 4.8 澳AU,韩国KR 5 巴PK	0 受惠国LD	50	-Other
	17.04	**不含可可的糖食(包括白巧克力):**					**Sugar confectionery (including white chocolate) , not containing cocoa:**

序号 No.	税则号列 Tariff Line	中文货品名称 Article Description in Chinese	最惠国税率 MFN(%)	协定税率 Agreement(%)	特惠税率 SP(%)	普通税率 Gen(%)	英文货品名称 Article Description
1134	1704.1000	-口香糖，不论是否裹糖	12	0 冰岛IS,东盟AS,哥CR,香港HK,新加坡SG,新西兰NZ,智利CL 5 巴PK 7.1 秘鲁PE 7.2 澳AU 8.4 瑞士CH 9.5 亚太AP	0 受惠国LD	50	-Chewing gum, whether or not sugarcoated
1135	1704.9000	-其他	10	0 澳门MO,冰岛IS,东盟AS,哥CR,瑞士CH,香港HK,新加坡SG,新西兰NZ,智利CL 3 秘鲁PE 6 澳AU 8.2 巴PK,亚太AP 9 韩国KR	0 受惠国LD	50	-Other

第十八章
可可及可可制品

Chapter 18
Cocoa and cocoa preparations

注释：

一、本章不包括税号 04.03、19.01、19.04、19.05、21.05、22.02、22.08、30.03、30.04 的制品。

二、税号 18.06 包括含有可可的糖食及注释一以外的其他含可可的食品。

Notes:

1. This Chapter does not cover the preparations of heading No.04.03, 19.01, 19.04, 19.05, 21.05, 22.02, 22.08, 30.03 or 30.04.
2. Heading No.18.06 includes sugar confectionery containing cocoa and, subject to Note 1 to this Chapter, other food preparations containing cocoa.

序号 No.	税则号列 Tariff Line	中文货品名称 Article Description in Chinese	最惠国税率 MFN(%)	协定税率 Agreement(%)	特惠税率 SP(%)	普通税率 Gen(%)	英文货品名称 Article Description
	18.01	**整颗或破碎的可可豆，生的或焙炒的**					**Cocoa beans, whole or broken, raw or roasted**
1136	1801.0000	整颗或破碎的可可豆，生的或焙炒的	8Δ2	0 冰岛IS,东盟AS,哥CR,秘鲁PE,新西兰NZ,智利CL 3.2 瑞士CH 4.8 澳AU,韩国KR 5 巴PK	0 受惠国LD	30	Cocoa beans, whole or broken, raw or roasted
	18.02	**可可荚、壳、皮及废料**					**Cocoa shells, husks, skins and other cocoa waste**
1137	1802.0000	可可荚、壳、皮及废料	10	0 冰岛IS,东盟AS,哥CR,秘鲁PE,新加坡SG,新西兰NZ,智利CL 4 瑞士CH 5 巴PK 6 澳AU 8 韩国KR	0 受惠国LD	30	Cocoa shells, husks, skins and other cocoa waste
	18.03	**可可膏，不论是否脱脂：**					**Cocoa paste, whether or not defatted:**
1138	1803.1000	-未脱脂	10	0 冰岛IS,东盟AS,哥CR,秘鲁PE,新西兰NZ,智利CL 4 瑞士CH 5 巴PK 6 澳AU 8 韩国KR	0 受惠国$_{1}$LD$_{1}$	30	-Not defatted
1139	1803.2000	-全脱脂或部分脱脂	10	0 冰岛IS,东盟AS,哥CR,秘鲁PE,新西兰NZ,智利CL 4 瑞士CH 5 巴PK 6 澳AU 8 韩国KR	0 受惠国$_{1}$LD$_{1}$	30	-Wholly or partly defatted
	18.04	**可可脂、可可油**					**Cocoa butter, fat and oil**
1140	1804.0000	可可脂、可可油	22	0 冰岛IS,东盟AS,哥CR,新西兰NZ,智利CL 6.6 秘鲁PE 13.2 澳AU 15.4 瑞士CH 19.8 韩国KR	0 受惠国LD	70	Cocoa butter, fat and oil
	18.05	**未加糖或其他甜物质的可可粉**					**Cocoa powder, not containing added sugar or other sweetening matter**
1141	1805.0000	未加糖或其他甜物质的可可粉	15	0 冰岛IS,东盟AS,哥CR,新西兰NZ,智利CL 4.5 秘鲁PE 9 澳AU 10.5 瑞士CH 12 巴PK,韩国KR	0 受惠国$_{1}$LD$_{1}$	40	Cocoa powder, not containing added sugar or other sweetening matter
	18.06	**巧克力及其他含可可的食品：**					**Chocolate and other food preparations containing cocoa:**

序号 No.	税则号列 Tariff Line	中文货品名称 Article Description in Chinese	最惠国税率 MFN(%)	协定税率 Agreement(%)	特惠税率 SP(%)	普通税率 Gen(%)	英文货品名称 Article Description
1142	1806.1000	-加糖或其他甜物质的可可粉	10	0 冰岛IS,东盟AS,哥CR,新西兰NZ,智利CL 3 秘鲁PE 4 瑞士CH 5 巴PK 6 澳AU 8 韩国KR	0 受惠国$_1$LD$_1$	50	-Cocoa powder, containing added sugar or other sweetening matter
1143	1806.2000	-其他重量超过2公斤的块状或条状含可可食品，或液状、膏状、粉状、粒状或其他散装形状的含可可食品，容器包装或内包装每件净重超过2公斤的	10	0 澳门MO,冰岛IS,东盟AS,哥CR,瑞士CH,香港HK,新加坡SG,新西兰NZ,智利CL 3 秘鲁PE 5 巴PK 6 澳AU 7.7 亚太AP 8 韩国KR	0 受惠国$_1$LD$_1$	50	-Other preparations in blocks, slabs or bars weighing more than 2kg or in liquid, paste, powder, granular or other bulk form in containers or immediate packings, of a content exceeding 2kg
		-其他块状或条状的含可可食品:					-Other, in blocks, slabs or bars:
1144	1806.3100	--夹心	8	0 澳门MO,冰岛IS,东盟AS,哥CR,秘鲁PE,香港HK,新西兰NZ,智利CL 3.2 瑞士CH 4.8 澳AU 5 巴PK 6.4 亚太AP 6.9 韩国KR	0 受惠国LD	50	--Filled
1145	1806.3200	--不夹心	10	0 澳门MO,冰岛IS,东盟AS,哥CR,瑞士CH,香港HK,新加坡SG,新西兰NZ,智利CL 3 秘鲁PE 5 巴PK 6 澳AU 7.7 亚太AP 8.6 韩国KR	0 受惠国$_1$LD$_1$	50	--Not filled
1146	1806.9000	-其他	8	0 澳门MO,冰岛IS,东盟AS,哥CR,秘鲁PE,香港HK,新西兰NZ,智利CL 4.8 澳AU 5 巴PK 5.6 瑞士CH 6.4 亚太AP 6.9 韩国KR	0 受惠国LD	50	-Other

第十九章
谷物、粮食粉、淀粉或乳的制品；糕饼点心

Chapter 19
Preparations of cereals, flour, starch or milk; pastry cook's products

注释：

一、本章不包括：

（一）按重量计含香肠、肉、食用杂碎、动物血、鱼、甲壳动物，软体动物、其他水生无脊椎动物及其混合物超过20%的食品（第十六章），但税号19.02的包馅食品除外；

（二）用粮食粉或淀粉制的专作动物饲料用的饼干及其他制品（税号23.09）；

（三）第三十章的药品及其他产品。

二、税目19.01所称：

（一）"粗粒"是指第十一章谷物的粗粒；

（二）"细粉"及"粗粉"，是指：

1. 第十一章谷物的细粉及粗粉；
2. 其他章植物的细粉、粗粉及粉末，但不包括干蔬菜、马铃薯和干豆类的细粉、粗粉及粉末（应分别归入税目07.12、11.05和11.06）。

三、税号19.04不包括按重量计全脱脂可可含量超过6%或用巧克力完全包裹的食品以及税号18.06的其他含可可食品（税号18.06）。

四、税号19.04所称"其他方法制作的"，是指制作或加工程度超过第十章或第十一章各税号或注释所规定范围的。

Notes:

1. This Chapter does not cover:

(a) Except in the case of stuffed products of heading No.19.02, food preparations containing more than 20% by weight of sausage, meat, meat offal, blood, fish or crustaceans, mollusks or other aquatic invertebrates, or any combination thereof (Chapter 16) ;

(b) Biscuits or other articles made from flour or from starch, specially prepared for use in animal feeding (heading No.23.09) ; or

(c) Medicaments or other products of Chapter 30.

2. For the purposes of heading No.19.01:

(a) The term "groats" means cereal groats of Chapter11;

(b) The terms "flour" and "meal" mean:

(1) Cereal flour and meal of Chapter11; and

(2) Flour, meal and powder of vegetable origin of any Chapter, other than flour, meal or powder of dried vegetables (headingNo.07.12), ofpotatoes (heading No.11.05) or of dried leguminous vegetables (heading No.11.06).

3. Heading No.19.04 does not cover preparations containing more than 6% by weight of cocoa calculated on a totally defatted basis or completely coated with chocolate or other food preparations containing cocoa (heading No.18.06) .

4. For the purposes of heading No.19.04, the expression "otherwise prepared" means prepared or processed to an extent beyond that provided for in the headings of or Notes to Chapter10 or Chapter 11.

序号 No.	税则号列 Tariff Line	中文货品名称 Article Description in Chinese	最惠国税率 MFN(%)	协定税率 Agreement(%)	特惠税率 SP(%)	普通税率 Gen(%)	英文货品名称 Article Description
	19.01	**麦精；细粉、粗粒、粗粉、淀粉或麦精制的其他税目未列名的食品，不含可可或按重量计全脱脂可可含量低于40%；税目04.01至04.04所列货品制的其他税目未列名的食品，不含可可或按重量计全脱脂可可含量低于5%：**					**Malt extract; food preparations of flour, groats, meal, starch or malt extract, not containing cocoa or containing less than 40 % by weight of cocoa calculated on a totally defatted basis, not elsewhere specified or included; food preparations of goods of headings 0401 to 0404, not containing cocoa or containing less than 5 % by weight of cocoa calculated on a totally defatted basis, not elsewhere specified or included:**
		-供婴幼儿食用的零售包装食品：					-Preparations for infant use, put up for retail sale:
1147	1901.1010	---配方奶粉	15Δ5	0 澳门MO,冰岛IS,东盟AS,哥CR,新加坡SG,新西兰NZ,智利CL 4.5 秘鲁PE 9 澳AU 10.5 瑞士CH 12 巴PK	0 受惠国$_1$LD$_1$	40	---Formula milk powder

序号 No.	税则号列 Tariff Line	中文货品名称 Article Description in Chinese	最惠国税率 MFN(%)	协定税率 Agreement(%)	特惠税率 SP(%)	普通税率 Gen(%)	英文货品名称 Article Description
1148	1901.1090	---其他	15∆5	0 澳门MO,冰岛IS,东盟AS,哥CR,新加坡SG,新西兰NZ,智利CL 4.5 秘鲁PE 9 澳AU 10.5 瑞士CH 12 巴PK	0 受惠国$_1$LD$_1$	40	---Other
1149	1901.2000	-供烘焙税号19.05所列面包糕饼用的调制品及面团	25	0 澳门MO,冰岛IS,东盟AS,哥CR,香港HK,新加坡SG,新西兰NZ,智利CL 7.5 秘鲁PE 15 澳AU 17.5 瑞士CH 22.5 韩国KR	0 受惠国$_1$LD$_1$	80	-Mixes and doughs for the preparation of bakers' wares of heading No.19.05
1150	1901.9000	-其他	10∆5	0 澳门MO,冰岛IS,东盟AS,哥CR,香港HK,新加坡SG,新西兰NZ,智利CL 3 秘鲁PE 4 瑞士CH 5 巴PK 6 澳AU 8.6 韩国KR	0 受惠国$_1$LD$_1$	80	-Other
	19.02	**面食，不论是否煮熟、包馅（肉馅或其他馅）或其他方法制作，例如，通心粉、面条、汤团、馄饨、饺子、奶油面卷；古斯古斯面食，不论是否制作：**					**Pasta, whether or not cooked or stuffed (with meat or other substances) or otherwise prepared, such as spaghetti, macaroni, noodles, lasagne, gnocchi, ravioli, cannelloni; couscous, whether or not prepared:**
		-生的面食，未包馅或未经其他方法制作：					-Uncooked pasta, not stuffed or otherwise prepared:
1151	1902.1100	--含蛋	15	0 澳门MO,东盟AS,哥CR,香港HK,新加坡SG,新西兰NZ,智利CL 4.5 秘鲁PE 9 澳AU 10.5 瑞士CH 12 巴PK,韩国KR	0 受惠国LD	80	--Containing eggs
1152	1902.1900	--其他	15	0 澳门MO,东盟AS,哥CR,香港HK,新加坡SG,新西兰NZ,智利CL 4.5 秘鲁PE 9 澳AU 10.5 瑞士CH 12 巴PK 13 韩国KR	0 受惠国LD	80	--Other
1153	1902.2000	-包馅面食，不论是否烹煮或经其他方法制作	15	0 澳门MO,冰岛IS,东盟AS,哥CR,香港HK,新加坡SG,新西兰NZ,智利CL 4.5 秘鲁PE 9 澳AU 12 巴PK 13 韩国KR	0 受惠国LD	80	-Stuffed pasta, whether or not cooked or otherwise prepared
		-其他面食：					-Other pasta:
1154	1902.3010	---米粉干	15	0 澳门MO,冰岛IS,东盟AS,哥CR,新加坡SG,新西兰NZ,智利CL 4.5 秘鲁PE 9 澳AU 10.5 瑞士CH 12 巴PK,韩国KR	0 受惠国$_1$LD$_1$	80	---Rice vermicelli, cooked

序号 No.	税则号列 Tariff Line	中文货品名称 Article Description in Chinese	最惠国税率 MFN(%)	协定税率 Agreement(%)	特惠税率 SP(%)	普通税率 Gen(%)	英文货品名称 Article Description
1155	1902.3020	---粉丝	15	0 澳门MO,冰岛IS,东盟AS,哥CR,新加坡SG,新西兰NZ,智利CL 4.5 秘鲁PE 9 澳AU 10.5 瑞士CH 12 巴PK,韩国KR	0 受惠国$_1$LD$_1$	80	---Bean vermicelli, cooked
1156	1902.3030	---即食或快熟面条	15	0 澳门MO,冰岛IS,东盟AS,哥CR,香港HK,新加坡SG,新西兰NZ,智利CL 4.5 秘鲁PE 7.5 巴PK 9 澳AU 10.5 瑞士CH 13.1 亚太AP 13.5 韩国KR	0 受惠国LD	80	---Instant noodle
1157	1902.3090	---其他	15	0 澳门MO,冰岛IS,东盟AS,哥CR,香港HK,新加坡SG,新西兰NZ,智利CL 4.5 秘鲁PE 7.5 巴PK 9 澳AU 13 韩国KR 13.1 亚太AP	0 受惠国$_1$LD$_1$	80	---Other
1158	1902.4000	-古斯古斯面食	25	0 澳门MO,冰岛IS,东盟AS,哥CR,新加坡SG,新西兰NZ,智利CL 7.5 秘鲁PE 15 澳AU 17.5 瑞士CH 22.5 韩国KR	0 受惠国$_1$LD$_1$	80	-Couscous
	19.03	**珍粉及淀粉制成的珍粉代用品，片、粒、珠、粉或类似形状的**					**Tapioca and substitutes therefor prepared from starch, in the form of flakes, grains, pearls, siftings or similar forms**
1159	1903.0000	珍粉及淀粉制成的珍粉代用品，片、粒、珠、粉或类似形状的	15	0 澳门MO,冰岛IS,东盟AS,哥CR,新加坡SG,新西兰NZ,智利CL 4.5 秘鲁PE 9 澳AU 10.5 瑞士CH 12 巴PK,韩国KR	0 受惠国LD	80	Tapioca and substitutes therefor prepared from starch, in the form of flakes, grains, pearls, siftings or in similar forms
	19.04	**谷物或谷物产品经膨化或烘炒制成的食品（例如，玉米片）；其他税号未列名的预煮或经其他方法制作的谷粒（玉米除外）、谷物片或经其他加工的谷粒（细粉及粗粉除外）：**					**Prepared foods obtained by the swelling or roasting of cereals or cereal products (for example, corn flakes) ; cereals (other than maize (corn)) in grain form or in the form of flakes or other worked grains (except flour, groats and meal) , pre-cooked or otherwise prepared, not elsewhere specified or included:**
1160	1904.1000	-谷物或谷物产品经膨化或烘炒制成的食品	25	0 澳门MO,冰岛IS,东盟AS,哥CR,新加坡SG,新西兰NZ,智利CL 7.5 秘鲁PE 15 澳AU 18.8 瑞士CH 22.5 韩国KR	0 受惠国$_1$LD$_1$	80	-Prepared foods obtained by the swelling or roasting of cereals or cereal products

序号 No.	税则号列 Tariff Line	中文货品名称 Article Description in Chinese	最惠国税率 MFN(%)	协定税率 Agreement(%)	特惠税率 SP(%)	普通税率 Gen(%)	英文货品名称 Article Description
1161	1904.2000	-未烘炒谷物片制成的食品及未烘炒的谷物片与烘炒的谷物片或膨化的谷物混合制成的食品	30	0 冰岛IS,东盟AS,哥CR,香港HK,新加坡SG,新西兰NZ,智利CL 12 瑞士CH 16 秘鲁PE 18 澳AU 27 韩国KR	0 受惠国$_2$LD$_2$	80	-Prepared foods obtained from unroasted cereal flakes or from mixtures of unroasted cereal flakes and roasted cereal flakes or swelled cereals
1162	1904.3000	-碾碎的干小麦	30	0 澳门MO,冰岛IS,东盟AS,哥CR,新加坡SG,新西兰NZ,智利CL 16 秘鲁PE 18 澳AU 27 韩国KR	0 受惠国$_2$LD$_2$	80	-Bulgur wheet
1163	1904.9000	-其他	30	0 澳门MO,冰岛IS,东盟AS,哥CR,香港HK,新加坡SG,新西兰NZ,智利CL 12 瑞士CH 12.5 秘鲁PE 18 澳AU 27 韩国KR	0 受惠国$_2$LD$_2$	80	-Other
	19.05	**面包、糕点、饼干及其他烘焙糕饼，不论是否含可可；圣餐饼、装药空囊、封缄、糯米纸及类似制品：**					**Bread, pastry, cakes, biscuits and other bakers' wares, whether or not containing cocoa; communion wafers, empty cachets of a kind suitable for pharmaceutical use, sealing wafers, rice paper and similar products:**
1164	1905.1000	-黑麦脆面包片	20	0 澳门MO,冰岛IS,东盟AS,哥CR,新加坡SG,新西兰NZ,智利CL 6 秘鲁PE 12 澳AU 14 瑞士CH 17.3 韩国KR	0 受惠国$_1$LD$_1$	80	-Crispbread
1165	1905.2000	-姜饼及类似品	20	0 澳门MO,冰岛IS,东盟AS,哥CR,新加坡SG,新西兰NZ,智利CL 6 秘鲁PE 12 澳AU 14 瑞士CH 17.3 韩国KR	0 受惠国$_1$LD$_1$	80	-Gingerbread and the like
		-甜饼干；华夫饼干及圣餐饼：					-Sweet biscuits; waffles and wafers:
1166	1905.3100	--甜饼干	15	0 澳门MO,冰岛IS,东盟AS,哥CR,香港HK,新加坡SG,新西兰NZ,智利CL 4.5 秘鲁PE 9 澳AU 11.3 瑞士CH 12.4 巴PK,亚太AP 13 韩国KR	0 受惠国LD 7.5 亚太AP	80	--Sweet biscuits
1167	1905.3200	--华夫饼干及圣餐饼	15	0 澳门MO,冰岛IS,东盟AS,哥CR,瑞士CH,香港HK,新加坡SG,新西兰NZ,智利CL 4.5 秘鲁PE 7.5 巴PK 9 澳AU 12.4 亚太AP 13 韩国KR	0 受惠国LD 7.5 亚太AP	80	--Waffles and wafers

序号 No.	税则号列 Tariff Line	中文货品名称 Article Description in Chinese	最惠国税率 MFN(%)	协定税率 Agreement(%)	特惠税率 SP(%)	普通税率 Gen(%)	英文货品名称 Article Description
1168	1905.4000	-面包干、吐司及类似的烤面包	20	0 澳门MO,东盟AS,哥CR,新加坡SG,新西兰NZ,智利CL 6 秘鲁PE 12 澳AU 14 瑞士CH 17.3 韩国KR	0 受惠国$_1$LD$_1$	80	-Rusks, toasted bread and similar toasted products
1169	1905.9000	-其他	20	0 澳门MO,冰岛IS,东盟AS,哥CR,香港HK,新加坡SG,新西兰NZ,智利CL 6 秘鲁PE 12 澳AU 14 瑞士CH 16 巴PK 17.1 亚太AP 18 韩国KR	0 受惠国$_1$LD$_1$ 10 亚太AP	80	-Other

第二十章
蔬菜、水果、坚果或植物其他部分的制品

注释:

一、本章不包括:

（一）用第七章、第八章或第十一章所列方法制作或保藏的蔬菜、水果或坚果;

（二）按重量计含香肠、肉、食用杂碎、动物血、鱼、甲壳动物、软体动物、其他水生无脊椎动物及其混合物超过 20%的食品（第十六章);

（三）税号 19.05 的烘焙糕饼及其他制品;

（四）税号 21.04 的均化混合食品。

二、税号 20.07 及 20.08 不包括制成糖食的果冻、果膏、糖衣杏仁或类似品(税号 17.04)及巧克力糖食(税号 18.06)。

三、税号 20.01、20.04 及 20.05 仅酌情包括用本章注释一（一）以外的方法制作或保藏的第七章或税号 11.05、11.06 的产品（第八章产品的细粉、粗粉除外）。

四、干重量在 7%及以上的番茄汁归入税号 20.02。

五、税目 20.07 所称“烹煮的”是指，在常压或减压下，通过减少水分或其他方法增加产品粘稠度的热处理。

六、税号 20.09 所称“未发酵及未加酒精的水果汁”，是指按容量计酒精浓度（标准见第二十二章注释二）不超过 0.5%的水果汁。

子目注释:

一、子目号 2005.10 所称“均化蔬菜”，是指蔬菜经精细均化制成供婴幼儿食用或营养用的零售包装食品（每件净重不超过 250 克)。为了调味、保藏或其他目的，均化蔬菜中可以加入少量其他配料，还可以含有少量可见的蔬菜粒。归类时，子目号 2005.10 优先于税号 20.05 的其他子目。

Chapter 20
Preparations of vegetables, fruit, nuts or other parts of plants

Notes:

1. This Chapter does not cover:

(a) Vegetables, fruit or nuts, prepared or preserved by the processes specified in Chapter 7, 8 or 11;

(b) Food preparations containing more than 20% by weight of sausage, meat, meat offal, blood, fish or crustaceans, molluscs or other aquatic invertebrates, or any combination thereof (Chapter16); or

(c) Bakers' wares and other products of heading 19.05; or

(d) Homogenized composite food preparations of heading No.21.04.

2. Headings No.20.07 and 20.08 do not apply to fruit jellies, fruit pastes, sugar-coated almonds or the like in the form of sugar confectionery (heading No.17.04) or chocolate confectionery (heading No.18.06) .

3. Headings No.20.01, 20.04 and 20.05 cover, as the case may be, only those products of Chapter 7 or of heading No.11.05 or 11.06 (other than flour, meal and powder of the products of Chapter 8) which have been prepared or preserved by processes other than those referred to in Note 1(a).

4. Tomato juice, the dry weight content of which is 7% or more, is to be classified in heading No.20.02.

5. For the purposes of heading No.20.07, the expression "obtained by cooking" means obtained by heat treatment at atmospheric pressure or under reduced pressure to increase the viscosity of a product through reduction of water content or other means.

6. For the purposes of heading No.20.09, the expression "juices, unfermented and not containing added spirit" means juices of an alcoholic strength by volume (see Note 2 to Chapter 22) not exceeding 0.5% vol.

Subheading Notes:

1. For the purposes of subheading No.2005.10, the expression "homogenized vegetables" means preparations of vegetables, finely homogenized, put up for retail sale as infant food or for dietetic purposes, in containers of a net weight content not exceeding 250g. For the application of this definition no account is to be taken of small quantities of any ingredients which may have been added to the preparation for seasoning, preparation or other purposes. These preparations may contain a small quantity of visible pieces of vegetables. Subheading No.2005.10 takes precedence over all other subheadings of heading No.20.05.

二、子目号 2007.10 所称“均化食品”，是指果实经精细均化制成供婴幼儿食用或营养用的零售包装食品（每件净重不超过 250 克）。为了调味、保藏或其他目的，均化食品中可以加入少量其他配料，还可以含有少量可见的果粒。归类时，子目号 2007.10 优先于税号 20.07 的其他子目。

2. For the purposes of subheading No.2007.10, the expression "homogenized preparations" means preparations of fruit, finely homogenized, put up for retail sale as infant food or for dietetic purposes, in containers of a net weight content not exceeding 250g. For the application of this definition no account is to be taken of small quantities of any ingredients which may have been added to the preparation for seasoning, preservation or other purposes. These preparations may contain a small quantity of visible pieces of fruit. Subheading No.2007.10 takes precedence over all other subheadings of heading No.20.07.

三、子目 2009.12、2009.12、2009.31、2009.41、2009.61 及 2009.71 所称“白利糖度值”，是指直接从白利糖度计读取的度数或在 20℃时从折射计读取的以蔗糖百分比含量计的折射率，在其他温度下读取的数值应折算为 20℃时的折射率。

3. For the purposes of subheadings No.2009.12, 2009.21, 2009.31, 2009.41, 2009.61 and 2009.71, the expression "Brix value" means the direct reading of degrees Brix obtained from a Brix hydrometer of refractive index expressed in terms of percentage sucrose content obtained from a refractometer, at a temperature of 20℃ or corrected for 20℃ if the reading is made at a different temperature.

序号 No.	税则号列 Tariff Line	中文货品名称 Article Description in Chinese	最惠国税率 MFN(%)	协定税率 Agreement(%)	特惠税率 SP(%)	普通税率 Gen(%)	英文货品名称 Article Description
	20.01	**蔬菜、水果、坚果及植物的其他食用部分，用醋或醋酸制作或保藏的：**					**Vegetables, fruit, nuts and other edible parts of plants, prepared or preserved by vinegar or acetic acid:**
1170	2001.1000	-黄瓜及小黄瓜	25	0 冰岛IS,东盟AS,哥CR,新加坡SG,新西兰NZ,智利CL 7.5 秘鲁PE 15 澳AU 17.5 瑞士CH 22.5 韩国KR	0 受惠国$_1$LD$_1$	70	-Cucumbers and gherkins
		-其他：					-Other:
1171	2001.9010	---大蒜	25	0 冰岛IS,东盟AS,哥CR,新加坡SG,新西兰NZ,智利CL 7.5 秘鲁PE 15 澳AU 17.5 瑞士CH 22.5 韩国KR	0 受惠国$_1$LD$_1$ 12.5 亚太AP	70	---Garlic
1172	2001.9090	---其他	25	0 澳门MO,冰岛IS,东盟AS,哥CR,新加坡SG,新西兰NZ,智利CL 7.5 秘鲁PE 15 澳AU 17.5 瑞士CH 22.5 韩国KR	0 受惠国$_1$LD$_1$ 12.5 亚太AP	70	---Other
	20.02	**番茄，用醋或醋酸以外的其他方法制作或保藏的：**					**Tomatoes prepared or preserved otherwise than by vinegar or acetic acid:**
		-番茄，整个或切片：					-Tomatoes, whole or in pieces:

序号 No.	税则号列 Tariff Line	中文货品名称 Article Description in Chinese	最惠国税率 MFN(%)	协定税率 Agreement(%)	特惠税率 SP(%)	普通税率 Gen(%)	英文货品名称 Article Description
1173	2002.1010	---罐头	19	0 澳门MO,冰岛IS,东盟AS,哥CR,新加坡SG,新西兰NZ,智利CL 5.7 秘鲁PE 11.4 澳AU 13.3 瑞士CH 16.4 韩国KR	0 受惠国$_1$LD$_1$	80	---In airtight containers
1174	2002.1090	---其他	25	0 冰岛IS,东盟AS,哥CR,新加坡SG,新西兰NZ,智利CL 7.5 秘鲁PE 15 澳AU 17.5 瑞士CH 22.5 韩国KR	0 受惠国$_1$LD$_1$	70	---Other
		-其他:					-Other:
		---番茄酱罐头:					---Tomato paste, in airtight containers:
1175	2002.9011	----重量不超过5kg的番茄酱罐头	20	0 澳门MO,冰岛IS,东盟AS,哥CR,秘鲁PE,新加坡SG,新西兰NZ,智利CL 12 澳AU 14 瑞士CH 17.3 韩国KR	0 受惠国$_1$LD$_1$	80	----Tomato paste, in airtight containers, weighing not more than 5kg
1176	2002.9019	----重量大于5kg的番茄酱罐头	20	0 澳门MO,冰岛IS,东盟AS,哥CR,秘鲁PE,新加坡SG,新西兰NZ,智利CL 12 澳AU 14 瑞士CH 16 韩国KR	0 受惠国$_1$LD$_1$	80	----Tomato paste, in airtight containers, weighing more than 5kg
1177	2002.9090	---其他	18	0 澳门MO,冰岛IS,东盟AS,哥CR,秘鲁PE,新加坡SG,新西兰NZ,智利CL 10.8 澳AU 12.6 瑞士CH 14.4 巴PK 15.6 韩国KR	0 受惠国$_1$LD$_1$	70	---Other
	20.03	**蘑菇及块菌,用醋或醋酸以外的其他方法制作或保藏的:**					**Mushrooms and truffles, prepared or preserved otherwise than by vinegar or acetic acid:**
		-伞菌属蘑菇:					-Mushrooms of the genus *Agaricus*:
		---罐头:					---In airtight containers:
1178	2003.1011	----小白蘑菇	25	0 澳门MO,冰岛IS,东盟AS,哥CR,新加坡SG,新西兰NZ,智利CL 7.5 秘鲁PE 15 澳AU 17.5 瑞士CH 20 韩国KR	0 受惠国$_1$LD$_1$	90	----Small white agaric
1179	2003.1019	----其他	25	0 澳门MO,冰岛IS,东盟AS,哥CR,新加坡SG,新西兰NZ,智利CL 7.5 秘鲁PE 15 澳AU 17.5 瑞士CH 20 韩国KR	0 受惠国$_1$LD$_1$	90	----Other
1180	2003.1090	---其他	25	0 澳门MO,冰岛IS,东盟AS,哥CR,新加坡SG,新西兰NZ,智利CL 7.5 秘鲁PE 15 澳AU 17.5 瑞士CH 20 韩国KR	0 受惠国$_1$LD$_1$	90	---Other

序号 No.	税则号列 Tariff Line	中文货品名称 Article Description in Chinese	最惠国税率 MFN(%)	协定税率 Agreement(%)	特惠税率 SP(%)	普通税率 Gen(%)	英文货品名称 Article Description
		-其他:					-Other:
1181	2003.9010	---罐头	25	0 澳门MO,冰岛IS,东盟AS,哥CR,新加坡SG,新西兰NZ,智利CL 7.5 秘鲁PE 15 澳AU 17.5 瑞士CH 20 韩国KR	0 受惠国$_1$LD$_1$	90	---In airtight containers
1182	2003.9090	---其他	25	0 澳门MO,冰岛IS,东盟AS,哥CR,新加坡SG,新西兰NZ,智利CL 7.5 秘鲁PE 15 澳AU 17.5 瑞士CH 20 韩国KR	0 受惠国$_1$LD$_1$	90	---Other
	20.04	**其他冷冻蔬菜,用醋或醋酸以外的其他方法制作或保藏的,但税号20.06的产品除外:**					**Other vegetables prepared or preserved otherwise than by vinegar or acetic acid, frozen, other than products of heading 2006:**
1183	2004.1000	-马铃薯	13	0 东盟AS,哥CR,新加坡SG,新西兰NZ,智利CL 3.9 秘鲁PE 6.5 巴PK 7.8 澳AU 9.1 瑞士CH 10.4 韩国KR	0 受惠国LD	70	-Potatoes
1184	2004.9000	-其他蔬菜及什锦蔬菜	25	0 冰岛IS,东盟AS,哥CR,新加坡SG,新西兰NZ,智利CL 7.5 秘鲁PE 15 澳AU 17.5 瑞士CH 20 韩国KR	0 受惠国$_1$LD$_1$	70	-Other vegetables and mixtures of vegetables
	20.05	**其他未冷冻蔬菜,用醋或醋酸以外的其他方法制作或保藏的,但税号20.06的产品除外:**					**Other vegetables prepared or preserved otherwise than by vinegar or acetic acid, not frozen, other than products of heading 2006:**
1185	2005.1000	-均化蔬菜	25	0 冰岛IS,东盟AS,哥CR,新加坡SG,新西兰NZ,智利CL 7.5 秘鲁PE 15 澳AU 17.5 瑞士CH 20 韩国KR	0 受惠国$_1$LD$_1$	70	-Homogenized vegetables
1186	2005.2000	-马铃薯	15	0 东盟AS,哥CR,香港HK,新加坡SG,新西兰NZ,智利CL 4.5 秘鲁PE 9 澳AU 10.5 瑞士CH 12 巴PK,韩国KR	0 受惠国$_1$LD$_1$	70	-Potatoes
1187	2005.4000	-豌豆	25	0 冰岛IS,东盟AS,哥CR,新加坡SG,新西兰NZ,智利CL 7.5 秘鲁PE 15 澳AU 17.5 瑞士CH 20 韩国KR	0 受惠国$_1$LD$_1$	70	-Peas (Pisum sativum)
		-豇豆及菜豆:					-Beans (*Vigna* spp., *Phaseolus* spp.) :
		--脱荚的:					--Beans, shelled:
		---罐头:					---In airtight containers:

序号 No.	税则号列 Tariff Line	中文货品名称 Article Description in Chinese	最惠国税率 MFN(%)	协定税率 Agreement(%)	特惠税率 SP(%)	普通税率 Gen(%)	英文货品名称 Article Description
1188	2005.5111	----赤豆馅	25	0 澳门MO,冰岛IS,东盟AS,哥CR,香港HK,新加坡SG,新西兰NZ,智利CL 7.5 秘鲁PE 15 澳AU 17.5 瑞士CH 20 韩国KR	0 受惠国$_1$LD$_1$	80	----Red bean paste
1189	2005.5119	----其他	25	0 澳门MO,冰岛IS,东盟AS,哥CR,香港HK,新加坡SG,新西兰NZ,智利CL 7.5 秘鲁PE 15 澳AU 17.5 瑞士CH 22.5 韩国KR	0 受惠国$_1$LD$_1$	80	----Other
		---其他:					---Other:
1190	2005.5191	----赤豆馅	25	0 冰岛IS,东盟AS,哥CR,新加坡SG,新西兰NZ,智利CL 7.5 秘鲁PE 15 澳AU 17.5 瑞士CH 20 韩国KR	0 受惠国$_1$LD$_1$	70	----Red bean paste
1191	2005.5199	----其他	25	0 东盟AS,哥CR,香港HK,新加坡SG,新西兰NZ,智利CL 7.5 秘鲁PE 15 澳AU 17.5 瑞士CH 22.5 韩国KR	0 受惠国$_1$LD$_1$	70	----Other
		--其他:					--Other:
1192	2005.5910	---罐头	25	0 澳门MO,东盟AS,哥CR,新加坡SG,新西兰NZ,智利CL 7.5 秘鲁PE 15 澳AU 17.5 瑞士CH 20 韩国KR	0 受惠国$_1$LD$_1$	80	---In airtight containers
1193	2005.5990	---其他	25	0 东盟AS,哥CR,新加坡SG,新西兰NZ,智利CL 7.5 秘鲁PE 15 澳AU 17.5 瑞士CH 20 韩国KR	0 受惠国$_1$LD$_1$	70	---Other
		-芦笋:					-Asparagus:
1194	2005.6010	---罐头	25	0 澳门MO,东盟AS,哥CR,新加坡SG,新西兰NZ,智利CL 7.5 秘鲁PE 15 澳AU 17.5 瑞士CH 20 韩国KR	0 受惠国$_1$LD$_1$	80	---In airtight containers
1195	2005.6090	---其他	25	0 冰岛IS,东盟AS,哥CR,新加坡SG,新西兰NZ,智利CL 7.5 秘鲁PE 15 澳AU 17.5 瑞士CH 20 韩国KR	0 受惠国$_1$LD$_1$	70	---Other

序号 No.	税则号列 Tariff Line	中文货品名称 Article Description in Chinese	最惠国税率 MFN(%)	协定税率 Agreement(%)	特惠税率 SP(%)	普通税率 Gen(%)	英文货品名称 Article Description
1196	2005.7000	-油橄榄	10	0 冰岛IS,东盟AS,哥CR,新加坡SG,新西兰NZ,智利CL 3 秘鲁PE 4 瑞士CH 5 巴PK 6 澳AU 8 韩国KR	0 受惠国$_1$LD$_1$	70	-Olives
1197	2005.8000	-甜玉米	10	0 冰岛IS,东盟AS,哥CR,秘鲁PE,新加坡SG,新西兰NZ,智利CL 4 瑞士CH 5 巴PK 6 澳AU 8 韩国KR	0 受惠国$_1$LD$_1$	80	-Sweet corn (Zea mays var.saccharata)
		-其他蔬菜及什锦蔬菜:					-Other vegetables and mixtures of vegetables:
		--竹笋:					--Bamboo shoots:
1198	2005.9110	---竹笋罐头	25	0 澳门MO,冰岛IS,东盟AS,哥CR,新加坡SG,新西兰NZ,智利CL 7.5 秘鲁PE 15 澳AU 17.5 瑞士CH 20 韩国KR	0 受惠国$_1$LD$_1$	80	---In airtight containers
1199	2005.9190	---其他	25	0 冰岛IS,东盟AS,哥CR,新加坡SG,新西兰NZ,智利CL 7.5 秘鲁PE 15 澳AU 17.5 瑞士CH 20 韩国KR	0 受惠国$_1$LD$_1$	70	---Other
		--其他:					--Other:
1200	2005.9920	---蚕豆罐头	25	0 澳门MO,冰岛IS,东盟AS,哥CR,新加坡SG,新西兰NZ,智利CL 7.5 秘鲁PE 15 澳AU 17.5 瑞士CH 20 韩国KR	0 受惠国$_1$LD$_1$	80	---Broad beans, in airtight containers
1201	2005.9940	---榨菜	25	0 冰岛IS,东盟AS,哥CR,新加坡SG,新西兰NZ,智利CL 7.5 秘鲁PE 15 澳AU 17.5 瑞士CH 20 韩国KR	0 受惠国$_1$LD$_1$	70	---Hot pickled mustard tubers
1202	2005.9950	---咸蕨菜	25	0 冰岛IS,东盟AS,哥CR,新加坡SG,新西兰NZ,智利CL 7.5 秘鲁PE 15 澳AU 17.5 瑞士CH 20 韩国KR	0 受惠国$_1$LD$_1$	70	---Chueh tsai (fiddle-head) , salted
1203	2005.9960	---咸藠头	25	0 冰岛IS,东盟AS,哥CR,新加坡SG,新西兰NZ,智利CL 7.5 秘鲁PE 15 澳AU 17.5 瑞士CH 20 韩国KR	0 受惠国$_1$LD$_1$	70	---Scallion, salted
		---其他:					---Other:

序号 No.	税则号列 Tariff Line	中文货品名称 Article Description in Chinese	最惠国税率 MFN(%)	协定税率 Agreement(%)	特惠税率 SP(%)	普通税率 Gen(%)	英文货品名称 Article Description
1204	2005.9991	----罐头	25	0 澳门MO,冰岛IS,东盟AS,哥CR,秘鲁PE,新加坡SG,新西兰NZ,智利CL 15 澳AU 17.5 瑞士CH 22.5 韩国KR	0 受惠国$_1$LD$_1$	70	----In airtight containers
1205	2005.9999	----其他	25	0 冰岛IS,东盟AS,哥CR,秘鲁PE,新加坡SG,新西兰NZ,智利CL 15 澳AU 18 瑞士CH 22.5 韩国KR	0 受惠国$_1$LD$_1$	70	----Other
	20.06	**糖渍蔬菜、水果、坚果、果皮及植物的其他部分（沥干、糖渍或裹糖的）：**					**Vegetables, fruit, nuts, fruit-peel and other parts of plants, preserved by sugar (drained, glacé or crystallised) :**
1206	2006.0010	---蜜枣	30	0 冰岛IS,东盟AS,哥CR,香港HK,新加坡SG,新西兰NZ,智利CL 9 秘鲁PE 18 澳AU 27 韩国KR	0 缅甸MM,受惠国LD	90	---Preserved jujubes
1207	2006.0020	---橄榄	30	0 冰岛IS,东盟AS,哥CR,香港HK,新加坡SG,新西兰NZ,智利CL 17.6 秘鲁PE 18 澳AU 27 韩国KR	0 缅甸MM,受惠国LD	90	---Preserved olives
1208	2006.0090	---其他	30	0 澳门MO,冰岛IS,东盟AS,哥CR,瑞士CH,香港HK,新加坡SG,新西兰NZ,智利CL 17.6 秘鲁PE 18 澳AU 27 韩国KR	0 缅甸MM,受惠国LD	90	---Other
	20.07	**烹煮的果酱、果冻、柑橘酱、果泥及果膏，不论是否加糖或其他甜物质：**					**Jams, fruit jellies, marmalades, fruit or nut purée and fruit or nut pastes, obtained by cooking, whether or not containing added sugar or other sweetening matter:**
1209	2007.1000	-均化食品	30	0 冰岛IS,东盟AS,哥CR,新加坡SG,新西兰NZ,智利CL 12 瑞士CH 17.6 秘鲁PE 18 澳AU 27 韩国KR	0 受惠国$_2$LD$_2$	80	-Homogenized preparations
		-其他：					-Other:
1210	2007.9100	--柑橘属水果的	30	0 澳门MO,冰岛IS,东盟AS,哥CR,瑞士CH,新加坡SG,新西兰NZ,智利CL 9 秘鲁PE 18 澳AU 27 韩国KR	0 缅甸MM,受惠国LD	80	--Citrus fruit
		--其他：					--Other:
1211	2007.9910	---罐头	5	0 澳AU,澳门MO,巴PK,冰岛IS,东盟AS,哥CR,韩国KR,瑞士CH,新西兰NZ,智利CL 1.5 秘鲁PE	0 受惠国LD 2.5 亚太AP	80	---In airtight containers

序号 No.	税则号列 Tariff Line	中文货品名称 Article Description in Chinese	最惠国税率 MFN(%)	协定税率 Agreement(%)	特惠税率 SP(%)	普通税率 Gen(%)	英文货品名称 Article Description
1212	2007.9990	---其他	5	0 澳AU,澳门MO,巴PK,冰岛IS,东盟AS,韩国KR,新西兰NZ,智利CL 1.5 秘鲁PE 2 瑞士CH 3 哥CR	0 受惠国LD 2.5 亚太AP	80	---Other
	20.08	**用其他方法制作或保藏的其他税号未列名水果、坚果及植物的其他食用部分，不论是否加酒、加糖或其他甜物质：**					**Fruit, nuts and other edible parts of plants, otherwise prepared or preserved, whether or not containing added sugar or other sweetening matter or spirit, not elsewhere specified or included:**
		-坚果、花生及其他子仁，不论是否混合：					-Nuts, groundnuts and other seeds, whether or not mixed together:
		--花生：					--Groundnuts:
1213	2008.1110	---花生米罐头	30	0 澳门MO,冰岛IS,东盟AS,哥CR,香港HK,新加坡SG,新西兰NZ,智利CL 18 澳AU 27 韩国KR	0 受惠国$_2$LD$_2$	90	---Ground-nut kernels, in airtight containers
1214	2008.1120	---烘焙花生	30	0 澳门MO,冰岛IS,东盟AS,哥CR,香港HK,新加坡SG,新西兰NZ,智利CL 18 澳AU 27 韩国KR	0 柬埔寨KH,受惠国LD	80	---Roasted ground-nuts
1215	2008.1130	---花生酱	30	0 冰岛IS,东盟AS,哥CR,新加坡SG,新西兰NZ,智利CL 18 澳AU 27 韩国KR	0 受惠国$_2$LD$_2$	90	---Ground_nut butter
1216	2008.1190	---其他	30	0 澳门MO,冰岛IS,东盟AS,哥CR,香港HK,新加坡SG,新西兰NZ,智利CL 18 澳AU 27 韩国KR	0 受惠国$_2$LD$_2$	80	---Other
		--其他，包括什锦坚果及其他子仁：					--Other, including mixtures:
1217	2008.1910	---核桃仁罐头	20	0 澳门MO,冰岛IS,东盟AS,哥CR,香港HK,新加坡SG,新西兰NZ,智利CL 6 秘鲁PE 10 巴PK,亚太AP 12 澳AU 14 瑞士CH 17.3 韩国KR	0 柬埔寨KH,老挝LA,受惠国LD	90	---Walnut meats, in airtight containers
1218	2008.1920	---其他果仁罐头	13	0 澳门MO,冰岛IS,东盟AS,哥CR,香港HK,新加坡SG,新西兰NZ,智利CL 3.9 秘鲁PE 5 巴PK 6.5 亚太AP 7.8 澳AU 9.1 瑞士CH 10.4 韩国KR	0 柬埔寨KH,老挝LA,受惠国LD	90	---Other nuts, in airtight containers
		---其他：					---Other:

序号 No.	税则号列 Tariff Line	中文货品名称 Article Description in Chinese	最惠国税率 MFN(%)	协定税率 Agreement(%)	特惠税率 SP(%)	普通税率 Gen(%)	英文货品名称 Article Description
1219	2008.1991	----栗仁	10	0 澳门MO,冰岛IS,东盟AS,哥CR,香港HK,新加坡SG,新西兰NZ,智利CL 3 秘鲁PE 5 巴PK,亚太AP 6 澳AU 7.2 瑞士CH 8 韩国KR	0 柬埔寨KH,老挝LA,受惠国LD	80	----Chestnut seed
1220	2008.1992	----芝麻	10	0 澳门MO,东盟AS,哥CR,秘鲁PE,香港HK,新加坡SG,新西兰NZ,智利CL 4 瑞士CH 5 巴PK,亚太AP 6 澳AU 8 韩国KR	0 受惠国$_1$LD$_1$	80	----Sesames
1221	2008.1999	----其他	10	0 澳门MO,冰岛IS,东盟AS,哥CR,香港HK,新加坡SG,新西兰NZ,智利CL 3 秘鲁PE 4 瑞士CH 5 巴PK,亚太AP 6 澳AU 8 韩国KR	0 柬埔寨KH,老挝LA,受惠国LD	80	----Other
		-菠萝:					-Pineapples:
1222	2008.2010	---罐头	15	0 澳门MO,冰岛IS,新西兰NZ,智利CL 4.5 秘鲁PE 9 澳AU,哥CR 10.5 瑞士CH 12 韩国KR	0 老挝LA,受惠国LD	90	---In airtight containers
1223	2008.2090	---其他	15	0 冰岛IS,新西兰NZ,智利CL 4.5 秘鲁PE 9 澳AU,哥CR 10.5 瑞士CH 12 韩国KR	0 老挝LA,受惠国LD	80	---Other
		-柑橘属水果:					-Citrus fruit:
1224	2008.3010	---罐头	20	0 澳门MO,冰岛IS,东盟AS,秘鲁PE,新加坡SG,新西兰NZ,智利CL 12 澳AU,哥CR 14 瑞士CH 17.3 韩国KR	0 老挝LA,受惠国LD	90	---In airtight containers
1225	2008.3090	---其他	20	0 冰岛IS,东盟AS,哥CR,秘鲁PE,香港HK,新加坡SG,新西兰NZ,智利CL 12 澳AU 14 瑞士CH 18 韩国KR	0 老挝LA,受惠国LD	80	---Other
		-梨:					-Pears:
1226	2008.4010	---罐头	20	0 澳门MO,冰岛IS,东盟AS,哥CR,新加坡SG,新西兰NZ,智利CL 6 秘鲁PE 12 澳AU 14 瑞士CH 17.3 韩国KR	0 老挝LA,受惠国LD	90	---In airtight containers

序号 No.	税则号列 Tariff Line	中文货品名称 Article Description in Chinese	最惠国税率 MFN(%)	协定税率 Agreement(%)	特惠税率 SP(%)	普通税率 Gen(%)	英文货品名称 Article Description
1227	2008.4090	---其他	20	0 冰岛IS,东盟AS,哥CR,新加坡SG,新西兰NZ,智利CL 6 秘鲁PE 12 澳AU 14 瑞士CH 17.3 韩国KR	0 老挝LA,受惠国LD	80	---Other
1228	2008.5000	-杏	20	0 冰岛IS,东盟AS,哥CR,新加坡SG,新西兰NZ,智利CL 6 秘鲁PE 12 澳AU 14 瑞士CH 17.3 韩国KR	0 受惠国$_1$LD$_1$	90	-Apricots
		-樱桃:					-Cherries:
1229	2008.6010	---罐头	20	0 冰岛IS,东盟AS,哥CR,新加坡SG,新西兰NZ,智利CL 6 秘鲁PE 12 澳AU 14 瑞士CH 17.3 韩国KR	0 受惠国$_1$LD$_1$	90	---In airtight containers
1230	2008.6090	---其他	20	0 冰岛IS,东盟AS,哥CR,新加坡SG,新西兰NZ,智利CL 6 秘鲁PE 12 澳AU 14 瑞士CH 17.3 韩国KR	0 受惠国$_1$LD$_1$	90	---Other
		-桃:					-Peaches, including nectarines:
1231	2008.7010	---罐头	10	0 澳门MO,冰岛IS,东盟AS,哥CR,新加坡SG,新西兰NZ,智利CL 3 秘鲁PE 4 瑞士CH 5 巴PK 6 澳AU 8 韩国KR	0 老挝LA,受惠国LD	90	---In airtight containers
1232	2008.7090	---其他	20	0 冰岛IS,东盟AS,哥CR,香港HK,新加坡SG,新西兰NZ,智利CL 6 秘鲁PE 12 澳AU 14 瑞士CH 17.3 韩国KR	0 老挝LA,受惠国LD	80	---Other
1233	2008.8000	-草莓	15	0 冰岛IS,东盟AS,哥CR,新加坡SG,新西兰NZ,智利CL 4.5 秘鲁PE 9 澳AU 10.5 瑞士CH 12 巴PK,韩国KR	0 受惠国$_1$LD$_1$	90	-Strawberries
		-其他，包括子目号2008. 19以外的什锦果实:					-Other, including mixtures other than those of subheading 200819:
1234	2008.9100	--棕榈芯	5	0 澳AU,巴PK,冰岛IS,东盟AS,哥CR,韩国KR,秘鲁PE,瑞士CH,新西兰NZ,智利CL	0 柬埔寨KH,受惠国LD	80	--Palm hearts

序号 No.	税则号列 Tariff Line	中文货品名称 Article Description in Chinese	最惠国税率 MFN(%)	协定税率 Agreement(%)	特惠税率 SP(%)	普通税率 Gen(%)	英文货品名称 Article Description
1235	2008.9300	--蔓越橘(大果蔓越橘、小果蔓越橘、越橘)	15	0 澳门MO,冰岛IS,东盟AS,哥CR,香港HK,新加坡SG,新西兰NZ,智利CL 4.5 秘鲁PE 6 瑞士CH 9 澳AU 12 巴PK,韩国KR	0 柬埔寨KH,受惠国LD	80	--Cranberries (Vaccinium macrocarpon, Vaccinium oxycoccos, Vaccinium vitis-idaea)
1236	2008.9700	--什锦果实	10	0 澳门MO,冰岛IS,东盟AS,哥CR,新加坡SG,新西兰NZ,智利CL 3 秘鲁PE 4 瑞士CH 5 巴PK 6 澳AU 8 韩国KR	0 柬埔寨KH,受惠国LD	80	--Mixtures
		--其他:					--Other:
1237	2008.9910	---荔枝罐头	20	0 澳门MO,冰岛IS,东盟AS,哥CR,香港HK,新加坡SG,新西兰NZ,智利CL 6 秘鲁PE 12 澳AU 14 瑞士CH 17.3 韩国KR	0 受惠国$_1$LD$_1$	90	---Lychee can
1238	2008.9920	---龙眼罐头	15	0 澳门MO,冰岛IS,哥CR,香港HK,新西兰NZ,智利CL 4.5 秘鲁PE 9 澳AU 10.5 瑞士CH 12 韩国KR	0 柬埔寨KH,受惠国LD	80	---Longan can
		---海草及其他藻类制品:					---Seaweed and otheralga product:
1239	2008.9931	----调味紫菜	15	0 澳门MO,冰岛IS,东盟AS,哥CR,香港HK,新加坡SG,新西兰NZ,智利CL 4.5 秘鲁PE 9 澳AU 10.5 瑞士CH 13.5 韩国KR	0 柬埔寨KH,受惠国LD	90	----Seasoned laver
1240	2008.9932	----盐腌海带	15	0 澳门MO,冰岛IS,东盟AS,哥CR,香港HK,新西兰NZ,智利CL 4.5 秘鲁PE 9 澳AU 10.5 瑞士CH 12 巴PK,韩国KR	0 柬埔寨KH,受惠国LD	80	----Salted sea tangle
1241	2008.9933	----盐腌裙带菜	15	0 澳门MO,冰岛IS,东盟AS,哥CR,香港HK,新西兰NZ,智利CL 4.5 秘鲁PE 9 澳AU 10.5 瑞士CH 12 巴PK,韩国KR	0 柬埔寨KH,受惠国LD	80	----Salted undaria pinnatifida
1242	2008.9939	----其他	15	0 澳门MO,冰岛IS,东盟AS,哥CR,香港HK,新西兰NZ,智利CL 4.5 秘鲁PE 9 澳AU 10.5 瑞士CH 12 巴PK,韩国KR	0 柬埔寨KH,受惠国LD	80	----Other

序号 No.	税则号列 Tariff Line	中文货品名称 Article Description in Chinese	最惠国税率 MFN(%)	协定税率 Agreement(%)	特惠税率 SP(%)	普通税率 Gen(%)	英文货品名称 Article Description
1243	2008.9940	---清水荸荠（马蹄）罐头	25	0 澳门MO,冰岛IS,东盟AS,哥CR,新加坡SG,新西兰NZ,智利CL 7.5 秘鲁PE 15 澳AU 17.5 瑞士CH 20 韩国KR	0 受惠国$_1$LD$_1$	80	---Water chestnut (*Eleocharis dulcis*) , in airtight containers
1244	2008.9990	---其他	15	0 澳门MO,冰岛IS,东盟AS,哥CR,香港HK,新加坡SG,新西兰NZ,智利CL 4.5 秘鲁PE 6 瑞士CH 9 澳AU 12 巴PK,韩国KR	0 柬埔寨KH,受惠国LD	80	---Other
	20.09	**未发酵及未加酒精的水果汁（包括酿酒葡萄汁）、蔬菜汁，不论是否加糖或其他甜物质：**					**Fruit juices (including grape must) and vegetable juices, unfermented and not containing added spirit, whether or not containing added sugar or other sweetening matter:**
		-橙汁：					-Orange juice:
1245	2009.1100	--冷冻的	7.5	0 澳门MO,冰岛IS,东盟AS,哥CR,香港HK,新西兰NZ,智利CL 2.2 秘鲁PE 3 瑞士CH 4.5 韩国KR 5 巴PK 5.6 澳AU	0 柬埔寨KH,老挝LA,受惠国LD	90	--Frozen
1246	2009.1200	--非冷冻的，白利糖度值不超过20	30	0 澳门MO,冰岛IS,东盟AS,瑞士CH,香港HK,新加坡SG,新西兰NZ,智利CL 9 秘鲁PE 22.5 澳AU 27 韩国KR	0 柬埔寨KH,老挝LA,受惠国LD	90	--Not frozen, of a Brix value not exceeding 20
1247	2009.1900	--其他	30	0 澳门MO,冰岛IS,东盟AS,新加坡SG,新西兰NZ,智利CL 9 秘鲁PE 22.5 澳AU 27 韩国KR	0 柬埔寨KH,老挝LA,受惠国LD	90	--Other
		-葡萄柚（包括柚）汁：					-Grapefruit (including pomelo) juice:
1248	2009.2100	--白利糖度值不超过20的	15	0 澳门MO,冰岛IS,东盟AS,哥CR,秘鲁PE,香港HK,新加坡SG,新西兰NZ,智利CL 9 澳AU 10.5 瑞士CH 12 巴PK,韩国KR	0 老挝LA,受惠国LD	90	--Of a Brix value not exceeding 20
1249	2009.2900	--其他	15	0 澳门MO,冰岛IS,东盟AS,哥CR,秘鲁PE,新加坡SG,新西兰NZ,智利CL 9 澳AU 10.5 瑞士CH 12 巴PK,韩国KR	0 老挝LA,受惠国LD	90	--Other
		-其他未混合的柑橘属水果汁：					-Juice of any other single citrus fruit:
		--白利糖度值不超过20的：					--Of a Brix value not exceeding 20:

序号 No.	税则号列 Tariff Line	中文货品名称 Article Description in Chinese	最惠国税率 MFN(%)	协定税率 Agreement(%)	特惠税率 SP(%)	普通税率 Gen(%)	英文货品名称 Article Description
1250	2009.3110	---柠檬汁	18	0 澳门MO,冰岛IS,东盟AS,哥CR,香港HK,新加坡SG,新西兰NZ,智利CL	0 柬埔寨KH,受惠国LD	90	---Lemon juice
				5.4 秘鲁PE	9 亚太AP		
				10.8 澳AU			
				12.6 瑞士CH			
				14.4 巴PK			
				15.6 韩国KR			
				16.8 亚太AP			
1251	2009.3190	---其他	18	0 澳门MO,冰岛IS,东盟AS,哥CR,香港HK,新加坡SG,新西兰NZ,智利CL	0 柬埔寨KH,受惠国LD	90	---Other
				5.4 秘鲁PE	9 亚太AP		
				10.8 澳AU			
				12.6 瑞士CH			
				14.4 巴PK			
				15.6 韩国KR			
				16.8 亚太AP			
		--其他：					--Other:
1252	2009.3910	---柠檬汁	18	0 澳门MO,冰岛IS,东盟AS,哥CR,秘鲁PE,新加坡SG,新西兰NZ,智利CL	0 柬埔寨KH,受惠国LD	90	---Lemon juice
				10.8 澳AU	9 亚太AP		
				12.6 瑞士CH			
				14.4 巴PK			
				15.6 韩国KR			
				16.8 亚太AP			
1253	2009.3990	---其他	18	0 澳门MO,冰岛IS,东盟AS,哥CR,秘鲁PE,新加坡SG,新西兰NZ,智利CL	0 柬埔寨KH,受惠国LD	90	---Other
				10.8 澳AU	9 亚太AP		
				12.6 瑞士CH			
				14.4 巴PK			
				15.6 韩国KR			
				16.8 亚太AP			
		-菠萝汁：					-Pineapple juice:
1254	2009.4100	--白利糖度值不超过20	10	0 澳门MO,冰岛IS,哥CR,秘鲁PE,香港HK,新西兰NZ,智利CL	0 柬埔寨KH,老挝LA,受惠国LD	90	--Of a Brix value not exceeding 20
				4 瑞士CH			
				6 澳AU			
				8 韩国KR			
1255	2009.4900	--其他	10	0 澳门MO,冰岛IS,哥CR,秘鲁PE,新西兰NZ,智利CL	0 柬埔寨KH,老挝LA,受惠国LD	90	--Other
				4 瑞士CH			
				6 澳AU			
				8 韩国KR			
1256	2009.5000	-番茄汁	30	0 澳门MO,冰岛IS,东盟AS,哥CR,新加坡SG,新西兰NZ,智利CL	0 老挝LA,受惠国LD	80	-Tomato juice
				9 秘鲁PE	15 亚太AP		
				18 澳AU			
				27 韩国KR			
		-葡萄汁，包括酿酒葡萄汁：					-Grape juice (including grape must) :

序号 No.	税则号列 Tariff Line	中文货品名称 Article Description in Chinese	最惠国税率 MFN(%)	协定税率 Agreement(%)	特惠税率 SP(%)	普通税率 Gen(%)	英文货品名称 Article Description
1257	2009.6100	--白利糖度值不超过30的	20	0 澳门MO,冰岛IS,东盟AS,哥CR,香港HK,新加坡SG,新西兰NZ,智利CL 8.3 秘鲁PE 12 澳AU 14 瑞士CH 17.3 韩国KR	0 受惠国$_1$LD$_1$	90	--Of a Brix value not exceeding 30
1258	2009.6900	--其他	20	0 澳门MO,冰岛IS,东盟AS,哥CR,新加坡SG,新西兰NZ,智利CL 8.3 秘鲁PE 12 澳AU 14 瑞士CH 17.3 韩国KR	0 受惠国$_1$LD$_1$	90	--Other
		-苹果汁:					-Apple juice:
1259	2009.7100	--白利糖度值不超过20的	20	0 澳门MO,冰岛IS,东盟AS,哥CR,秘鲁PE,香港HK,新加坡SG,新西兰NZ,智利CL 12 澳AU 14 瑞士CH 17.3 韩国KR	0 受惠国$_1$LD$_1$	90	--Of a Brix value not exceeding 20
1260	2009.7900	--其他	20	0 澳门MO,冰岛IS,东盟AS,哥CR,新加坡SG,新西兰NZ,智利CL 6 秘鲁PE 12 澳AU 14 瑞士CH 17.3 韩国KR	0 受惠国$_1$LD$_1$	90	--Other
		-其他未混合的水果汁或蔬菜汁:					-Juice of any other single fruit or vegetable:
1261	2009.8100	--蔓越橘汁(大果蔓越橘、小果蔓越橘、越橘)	20	0 澳门MO,冰岛IS,东盟AS,哥CR,香港HK,新加坡SG,新西兰NZ,智利CL 6 秘鲁PE 10 巴PK,亚太AP 12 澳AU 14 瑞士CH 17.3 韩国KR	0 老挝LA,缅甸MM,受惠国LD	90	--Cranberry (Vaccinium macrocarpon, Vaccinium oxycoccos, Vaccinium vitis-idaea) juice
		--其他:					--Other:
		---水果汁:					---Fruit juice:
1262	2009.8912	----芒果汁	20	0 澳门MO,冰岛IS,东盟AS,哥CR,香港HK,新加坡SG,新西兰NZ,智利CL 6 秘鲁PE 12 澳AU 14 瑞士CH 16 巴PK 17.3 韩国KR 17.4 亚太AP	0 老挝LA,缅甸MM,受惠国LD	90	----Mango juice
1263	2009.8913	----西番莲果汁	20	0 澳门MO,冰岛IS,东盟AS,哥CR,香港HK,新加坡SG,新西兰NZ,智利CL 6 秘鲁PE 12 澳AU 14 瑞士CH 16 巴PK 17.3 韩国KR 17.4 亚太AP	0 老挝LA,缅甸MM,受惠国LD	90	----Passion-fruit juice

序号 No.	税则号列 Tariff Line	中文货品名称 Article Description in Chinese	最惠国税率 MFN(%)	协定税率 Agreement(%)	特惠税率 SP(%)	普通税率 Gen(%)	英文货品名称 Article Description
1264	2009.8914	----番石榴果汁	20	0 澳门MO,冰岛IS,东盟AS,哥CR,香港HK,新加坡SG,新西兰NZ,智利CL 6 秘鲁PE 12 澳AU 14 瑞士CH 16 巴PK 17.3 韩国KR 17.4 亚太AP	0 老挝LA,缅甸MM,受惠国LD	90	----Guva juice
1265	2009.8915	----梨汁	20	0 澳门MO,冰岛IS,东盟AS,哥CR,香港HK,新加坡SG,新西兰NZ,智利CL 6 秘鲁PE 10 巴PK,亚太AP 12 澳AU 14 瑞士CH 17.3 韩国KR	0 老挝LA,缅甸MM,受惠国LD	90	----Pear juice
1266	2009.8919	----其他	20	0 澳门MO,冰岛IS,东盟AS,哥CR,香港HK,新加坡SG,新西兰NZ,智利CL 6 秘鲁PE 10 巴PK,亚太AP 12 澳AU 14 瑞士CH 17.3 韩国KR	0 老挝LA,缅甸MM,受惠国LD	90	----Other
1267	2009.8920	---蔬菜汁	20	0 澳门MO,冰岛IS,东盟AS,哥CR,香港HK,新加坡SG,新西兰NZ,智利CL 6 秘鲁PE 10 巴PK,亚太AP 12 澳AU 14 瑞士CH 17.3 韩国KR	0 缅甸MM,受惠国LD	80	---Vegetable juice
		-混合汁:					-Mixtures of juices:
1268	2009.9010	---水果汁	20	0 澳门MO,冰岛IS,东盟AS,哥CR,秘鲁PE,香港HK,新加坡SG,新西兰NZ,智利CL 12 澳AU 14 瑞士CH 16 巴PK 17.3 韩国KR 17.4 亚太AP	0 柬埔寨KH,老挝LA,受惠国LD 10 亚太AP	90	---Of fruit juices
1269	2009.9090	---其他	20	0 澳门MO,冰岛IS,东盟AS,哥CR,秘鲁PE,香港HK,新加坡SG,新西兰NZ,智利CL 12 澳AU 14 瑞士CH 17.3 韩国KR	0 柬埔寨KH,老挝LA,受惠国LD 10 亚太AP	80	---Other

第二十一章
杂项食品

注释：

一、本章不包括：

（一）税号 07.12 的什锦蔬菜；

（二）含咖啡的焙炒咖啡代用品（税号 09.01）；

（三）加香料的茶（税号 09.02）；

（四）税号 09.04 至 09.10 的调味香料或其他产品；

（五）按重量计含香肠、肉、食用杂碎、动物血、鱼、甲壳动物、软体动物、其他水生无脊椎动物及其混合物超过 20%的食品（第十六章），但税号 21.03 或 21.04 的产品除外；

（六）税号 30.03 或 30.04 的药用酵母及其他产品；

（七）税号 35.07 的酶制品。

二、上述注释一（二）所述咖啡代用品的精汁归入税号 21.01。

三、税号 21.04 所称"均化混合食品"，是指两种或两种以上的基本配料，例如，肉、鱼、蔬菜或果实等，经精细均化制成供婴幼儿食用或营养用的零售包装食品（每件净重不超过 250 克）。为了调味、保藏或其他目的，可以加入少量其他配料，还可以含有少量可见的小块配料。

Chapter 21
Miscellaneous edible preparations

Notes:

1. This Chapter does not cover:

(a) Mixed vegetables of heading No.07.12;

(b) Roasted coffee substitutes containing coffee in any proportion (heading No.09.01) ;

(c) Flavoured tea (heading No.09.02) ;

(d) Spices or other products of headings No.09.04 to 09.10;

(e) Food preparations, other than the products described in heading No.21.03 or 21.04, containing more than 20% by weight of sausage, meat, meat offal, blood, fish or crustaceans, molluscs or other aquatic invertebrates, or any combination thereof (Chapter16) ;

(f) Yeast put up as a medicament or other products of heading No.30.03 or 30.04; or

(g) Prepared enzymes of heading No.35.07.

2. Extracts of the substitutes referred to in Note 1(b) above are to be classified in heading No.21.01.

3. For the purposes of heading No.21.04, the expression " homogenized composite food preparations " means preparations consisting of a finely homogenized mixture of two or more basic ingredients such as meat, fish, vegetables, fruit or nuts, put up for retail sale as infant food or for dietetic purposes, in containers of a net weight content not exceeding 250g. For the application of this definition, no account is to be taken of small quantities of any ingredients which may be added to the mixture for seasoning, preservation or other purposes.Such preparations may contain a small quantity of visible pieces of ingredients.

序号 No.	税则号列 Tariff Line	中文货品名称 Article Description in Chinese	最惠国税率 MFN(%)	协定税率 Agreement(%)	特惠税率 SP(%)	普通税率 Gen(%)	英文货品名称 Article Description
	21.01	咖啡、茶、马黛茶的浓缩精汁及以其为基本成分或以咖啡、茶、马黛茶为基本成分的制品；烘焙菊苣和其他烘焙咖啡代用品及其浓缩精汁：					**Extracts, essences and concentrates, of coffee, tea or maté and preparations with a basis of these products or with a basis of coffee, tea or maté; roasted chicory and other roasted coffee substitutes, and extracts, essences and concentrates thereof:**
		-咖啡浓缩精汁及以其为基本成分或以咖啡为基本成分的制品：					-Extracts, essences and concentrates, of coffee, and preparations with a basis of these extracts, essences or concentrates or with a basis of coffee:

序号 No.	税则号列 Tariff Line	中文货品名称 Article Description in Chinese	最惠国税率 MFN(%)	协定税率 Agreement(%)	特惠税率 SP(%)	普通税率 Gen(%)	英文货品名称 Article Description
1270	2101.1100	--浓缩精汁	17	0 澳门MO,冰岛IS,东盟AS,哥CR,香港HK,新加坡SG,新西兰NZ,智利CL 10.2 澳AU 13.6 巴PK 14.7 韩国KR	0 受惠国LD	130	--Extracts, essences and concentrates
1271	2101.1200	--以浓缩精汁或咖啡为基本成分的制品	30	0 澳门MO,冰岛IS,东盟AS,哥CR,香港HK,新加坡SG,新西兰NZ,智利CL 18 澳AU 27 韩国KR	0 受惠国$_2$LD$_2$	130	--Preparations with a basis of extracts, essences or concentrates or with a basis of coffee
1272	2101.2000	-茶、马黛茶浓缩精汁及以其为基本成分或以茶、马黛茶为基本成分的制品	32	0 澳门MO,冰岛IS,东盟AS,哥CR,香港HK,新加坡SG,新西兰NZ,智利CL 9.6 秘鲁PE 12.8 瑞士CH 16 巴PK,亚太AP 19.2 澳AU	0 受惠国$_1$LD$_1$	130	-Extracts, essences and concentrates, of tea or maté, and preparations with a basis of these extracts, essences or concentrates or with a basis of tea or mate
1273	2101.3000	-烘焙菊苣和其他烘焙咖啡代用品及其浓缩精汁	32	0 东盟AS,哥CR,新加坡SG,新西兰NZ,智利CL 19.2 澳AU 28.8 韩国KR	0 受惠国$_1$LD$_1$	130	-Roasted chicory and other roasted coffee substitutes, and extracts, essences and concentrates thereof
	21.02	**酵母（活性或非活性）；已死的其他单细胞微生物（不包括税号30.02的疫苗）；发酵粉：**					**Yeasts (active or inactive) ; other single-cell micro-organisms, dead (but not including vaccines of heading 3002) ; prepared baking powders:**
1274	2102.1000	-活性酵母	25	0 澳门MO,冰岛IS,东盟AS,哥CR,香港HK,新加坡SG,新西兰NZ,智利CL 7.5 秘鲁PE 10 瑞士CH 15 澳AU 22.5 韩国KR	0 受惠国$_1$LD$_1$	80	-Active yeasts
1275	2102.2000	-非活性酵母；已死的其他单细胞微生物	25	0 澳门MO,冰岛IS,东盟AS,哥CR,新加坡SG,新西兰NZ,智利CL 7.5 秘鲁PE 10 瑞士CH 15 澳AU 22.5 韩国KR	0 受惠国$_1$LD$_1$	70	-Inactive yeasts; other single-cell micro-rganisms, dead
1276	2102.3000	-发酵粉	25	0 澳门MO,冰岛IS,东盟AS,哥CR,新加坡SG,新西兰NZ,智利CL 7.5 秘鲁PE 15 澳AU 22.5 韩国KR	0 受惠国$_1$LD$_1$	70	-Prepared baking powders
	21.03	**调味汁及其制品；混合调味品；芥子粉及其调制品：**					**Sauces and preparations therefor; mixed condiments and mixed seasonings; mustard flour and meal and prepared mustard:**
1277	2103.1000	-酱油	28∆15	0 澳门MO,冰岛IS,东盟AS,哥CR,香港HK,新加坡SG,新西兰NZ,智利CL 8.4 秘鲁PE 16.8 澳AU 19.6 瑞士CH 25.2 韩国KR	0 柬埔寨KH,受惠国LD	90	-Soya sauce

序号 No.	税则号列 Tariff Line	中文货品名称 Article Description in Chinese	最惠国税率 MFN(%)	协定税率 Agreement(%)	特惠税率 SP(%)	普通税率 Gen(%)	英文货品名称 Article Description
1278	2103.2000	-番茄沙司及其他番茄调味汁	15	0 澳门MO,东盟AS,哥CR,香港HK,新加坡SG,新西兰NZ,智利CL 4.5 秘鲁PE 9 澳AU 10.5 瑞士CH 12 巴PK,韩国KR	0 柬埔寨KH,受惠国LD	90	-Tomato ketchup and other tomato sauces
1279	2103.3000	-芥子粉及其调制品	15	0 澳门MO,东盟AS,哥CR,新加坡SG,新西兰NZ,智利CL 4.5 秘鲁PE 9 澳AU 10.5 瑞士CH 12 巴PK,韩国KR	0 柬埔寨KH,受惠国LD	70	-Mustard flour and meal and prepared mustard
		-其他:					-Other:
1280	2103.9010	---味精	21	0 澳门MO,冰岛IS,东盟AS,哥CR,香港HK,新加坡SG,新西兰NZ,智利CL 6.3 秘鲁PE 12.6 澳AU 14.7 瑞士CH 18.2 巴PK,亚太AP 18.9 韩国KR	0 受惠国$_1$LD$_1$	130	---Gourmet powder
1281	2103.9020	---别特酒(Aromaticbitters),按体积计酒精含量44.2%～49.2%,按重量计含1.5%～6%的香料、各种配料以及4%～10%的糖	21	0 澳门MO,冰岛IS,东盟AS,哥CR,香港HK,新加坡SG,新西兰NZ,智利CL 12.4 秘鲁PE 12.6 澳AU 14.7 瑞士CH 18.9 韩国KR	0 受惠国$_1$LD$_1$	90	---Aromatic bitters, 44.2%～49.2% of which is alcoholic strength by volume, 1.5%～6% of which is spiles and various ingredients by weight and 4%～10% of which is sugar by weight
1282	2103.9090	---其他	21	0 澳门MO,冰岛IS,东盟AS,哥CR,香港HK,新加坡SG,新西兰NZ,智利CL 8.8 秘鲁PE 12.6 澳AU 15.8 瑞士CH 18.4 巴PK,亚太AP 18.9 韩国KR	0 受惠国LD	90	---Other
	21.04	**汤料及其制品;均化混合食品:**					**Soups and broths and preparations therefor; homogenised composite food preparations:**
1283	2104.1000	-汤料及其制品	15	0 澳门MO,冰岛IS,东盟AS,哥CR,香港HK,新加坡SG,新西兰NZ,智利CL 4.5 秘鲁PE 9 澳AU 10.5 瑞士CH 12 巴PK,韩国KR	0 受惠国$_1$LD$_1$	90	-Soups and broths and preparations therefor
1284	2104.2000	-均化混合食品	32	0 澳门MO,东盟AS,哥CR,新加坡SG,新西兰NZ,智利CL 9.6 秘鲁PE 19.2 澳AU 28.8 韩国KR	0 受惠国$_1$LD$_1$	90	-Homogenized composite food preparations
	21.05	**冰淇淋及其他冰制食品,不论是否含可可**					**Ice cream and other edible ice, whether or not containing cocoa**

序号 No.	税则号列 Tariff Line	中文货品名称 Article Description in Chinese	最惠国税率 MFN(%)	协定税率 Agreement(%)	特惠税率 SP(%)	普通税率 Gen(%)	英文货品名称 Article Description
1285	2105.0000	冰淇淋及其他冰制食品，不论是否含可可	19	0 澳门MO,冰岛IS,东盟AS,哥CR,瑞士CH,香港HK,新加坡SG,新西兰NZ,智利CL 5.7 秘鲁PE 11.4 澳AU	0 受惠国$_1$LD$_1$	90	Ice cream and other edible ice, whether or not containing cocoa
	21.06	**其他税号未列名的食品：**					**Food preparations not elsewhere specified or included:**
1286	2106.1000	-浓缩蛋白质及人造蛋白物质	10	0 澳门MO,冰岛IS,东盟AS,哥CR,新加坡SG,新西兰NZ,智利CL 3 秘鲁PE 4 瑞士CH 5 巴PK 6 澳AU 8 韩国KR	0 受惠国$_1$LD$_1$	90	-Protein concentrates and textured protein substances
		-其他：					-Other:
1287	2106.9010	---制造碳酸饮料的浓缩物	35	0 澳门MO,冰岛IS,东盟AS,哥CR,香港HK,新加坡SG,新西兰NZ,智利CL 10.5 秘鲁PE 21 澳AU 31.5 韩国KR	0 受惠国$_1$LD$_1$	100	---Beverage bases
1288	2106.9020	---制造饮料用的复合酒精制品	20	0 澳门MO,冰岛IS,东盟AS,哥CR,香港HK,新加坡SG,新西兰NZ,智利CL 6 秘鲁PE 12 澳AU 14 瑞士CH 17.3 韩国KR	0 受惠国$_1$LD$_1$	180	---Compound alcoholic preparations of a kind used for the manufacture of beverages
1289	2106.9030	---蜂王浆制剂	3	0 澳AU,澳门MO,巴PK,冰岛IS,东盟AS,哥CR,韩国KR,秘鲁PE,瑞士CH,香港HK,新西兰NZ,智利CL	0 老挝LA,受惠国LD	80	---Royal jelly, put up as tonic essences
1290	2106.9040	---椰子汁	10	0 澳门MO,冰岛IS,哥CR,香港HK,新西兰NZ,智利CL 3 秘鲁PE 4 瑞士CH 6 澳AU 8 韩国KR 9 巴PK,亚太AP	0 老挝LA,缅甸MM,受惠国LD	90	---Coconut juice
1291	2106.9050	---海豹油胶囊	20	0 澳门MO,冰岛IS,东盟AS,哥CR,香港HK,新加坡SG,新西兰NZ,智利CL 6 秘鲁PE 12 澳AU 15 瑞士CH 18.4 巴PK,亚太AP 19.3 韩国KR	0 受惠国$_1$LD$_1$	90	---Seal-oil capsule
1292	2106.9090	---其他	20	0 澳门MO,冰岛IS,东盟AS,哥CR,香港HK,新加坡SG,新西兰NZ,智利CL 6 秘鲁PE 12 澳AU 15 瑞士CH 18.4 巴PK,亚太AP 19.3 韩国KR	0 受惠国$_1$LD$_1$	90	---Other
	ex21069090	乳蛋白部分水解配方、乳蛋白深度水解配方、氨基酸配方、无乳糖配方特殊婴幼儿奶粉	Δ5				Partial hydrolyzed, extensively hydrolyzed milk protein, amino acid based, and lactose-free inftant formula milk powder

第二十二章
饮料、酒及醋

注释:

一、本章不包括:

（一）本章的产品（税号 22.09 的货品除外）经配制后，用于烹饪而不适于作为饮料的制品（通常归入税号 21.03）;

（二）海水（税号 25.01）;

（三）蒸馏水、导电水及类似的纯净水（税号 28.53）;

（四）按重量计浓度超过 10%的醋酸（税号 29.15）;

（五）税号 30.03 或 30.04 的药品;

（六）芳香料制品及盥洗品（第三十三章）。

二、本章及第二十章和第二十一章所称“按容量计酒精浓度”，应是温度在 20℃时测得的浓度。

三、税号 22.02 所称“无酒精饮料”，是指按容量计酒精浓度不超过 0.5%的饮料。含酒精饮料应分别归入税号 22.03 至 22.06 或税号 22.08。

子目注释:

子目号 2204.10 所称“汽酒”，是指温度在 20℃时装在密封容器中超过大气压力 3 巴及以上的酒。

Chapter 22
Beverages, spirits and vinegar

Notes:

1. This Chapter does not cover:

(a) Products of this Chapter (other than those of heading No.22.09) prepared for culinary purposes and thereby rendered unsuitable for consumption as beverages (generally heading No.21.03) ;

(b) Sea water (heading No.25.01) ;

(c) Distilled or conductivity water or water of similar purity (heading No. 28.53) ;

(d) Acetic acid of a concentration exceeding 10% by weight of acetic acid (heading No.29.15) ;

(e) Medicaments of heading No.30.03 or 30.04; or

(f) Perfumery or toilet preparations (Chapter 33) .

2. For the purposes of this Chapter and of Chapter 20 and 21, the “alcoholic strength by volume” shall be determined at a temperature of 20℃.

3. For the purposes of heading No.22.02, the term “non-alcoholic beverages” means beverages of an alcoholic strength by volume not exceeding 0.5% vol. Alcoholic beverages are classified in headings No.22.03 to 22.06 or heading No.22.08 as appropriate.

Subheading Note:

For the purposes of subheading No.2204.10, the expression “sparkling wine” means wine which, when kept at a temperature of 20℃ in closed containers, has an excess pressure of not less than 3 bars.

序号 No.	税则号列 Tariff Line	中文货品名称 Article Description in Chinese	最惠国税率 MFN(%)	协定税率 Agreement(%)	特惠税率 SP(%)	普通税率 Gen(%)	英文货品名称 Article Description
	22.01	未加糖或其他甜物质及未加味的水，包括天然或人造矿泉水及汽水；冰及雪：					**Waters, including natural or artificial mineral waters and aerated waters, not containing added sugar or other sweetening matter nor flavoured; ice and snow:**
		-矿泉水及汽水：					-Mineral waters and aerated waters:
1293	2201.1010	---矿泉水	20	0 澳门MO,冰岛IS,东盟AS,哥CR,香港HK,新加坡SG,新西兰NZ,智利CL 6 秘鲁PE 12 澳AU 14 瑞士CH 18 韩国KR	0 受惠国LD	90	---Mineral waters

序号 No.	税则号列 Tariff Line	中文货品名称 Article Description in Chinese	最惠国税率 MFN(%)	协定税率 Agreement(%)	特惠税率 SP(%)	普通税率 Gen(%)	英文货品名称 Article Description
1294	2201.1020	---汽水	20	0 澳门MO,冰岛IS,东盟AS,哥CR,新加坡SG,新西兰NZ,智利CL 6 秘鲁PE 12 澳AU 14 瑞士CH 17.3 韩国KR	0 受惠国LD	90	---Aerated waters
		-其他:					-Other:
		---天然水:					---Natural waters:
1295	2201.9011	----已包装	10	0 澳门MO,冰岛IS,东盟AS,哥CR,秘鲁PE,香港HK,新加坡SG,新西兰NZ,智利CL 4 瑞士CH 5 巴PK 6 澳AU 8 韩国KR	0 受惠国$_1$LD$_1$	30	----Packed
1296	2201.9019	----其他	10	0 澳门MO,冰岛IS,东盟AS,哥CR,秘鲁PE,香港HK,新加坡SG,新西兰NZ,智利CL 4 瑞士CH 5 巴PK 6 澳AU 8 韩国KR	0 受惠国$_1$LD$_1$	30	----Not packed
1297	2201.9090	---其他	10	0 冰岛IS,东盟AS,哥CR,秘鲁PE,香港HK,新加坡SG,新西兰NZ,智利CL 4 瑞士CH 5 巴PK 6 澳AU 8 韩国KR	0 受惠国$_1$LD$_1$	30	---Other
	22.02	**加味、加糖或其他甜物质的水，包括矿泉水及汽水，其他无酒精饮料，但不包括税号20.09的水果汁或蔬菜汁：**					**Waters, including mineral waters and aerated waters, containing added sugar or other sweetening matter or flavoured, and other non-alcoholic beverages, not including fruit or vegetable juices of heading 2009:**
1298	2202.1000	加味、加糖或其他甜物质的水，包括矿泉水及汽水	20	0 澳门MO,冰岛IS,东盟AS,哥CR,香港HK,新加坡SG,新西兰NZ,智利CL 6 秘鲁PE 12 澳AU 14 瑞士CH 18 韩国KR	0 受惠国$_1$LD$_1$	100	-Waters, including mineral waters and aerated waters, containing added sugar or other sweetening matter or flavoured
1299	2202.9000	-其他	35	0 澳门MO,冰岛IS,东盟AS,哥CR,香港HK,新加坡SG,新西兰NZ,智利CL 10.5 秘鲁PE 21 澳AU 26.3 瑞士CH 29.5 巴PK,亚太AP 31.5 韩国KR	0 受惠国LD	100	-Other
	22.03	**麦芽酿造的啤酒**					**Beer made from malt**
1300	2203.0000	麦芽酿造的啤酒	0		0 受惠国LD	①	Beer made from malt
	22.04	**鲜葡萄酿造的酒，包括加酒精的；税号20.09以外的酿酒葡萄汁：**					**Wine of fresh grapes, including fortified wines; grape must other than that of heading 2009:**

①普通税率: 7.5 元/升
General Duty: 7.5¥/L

序号 No.	税则号列 Tariff Line	中文货品名称 Article Description in Chinese	最惠国税率 MFN(%)	协定税率 Agreement(%)	特惠税率 SP(%)	普通税率 Gen(%)	英文货品名称 Article Description
1301	2204.1000	-汽酒	14	0 澳门MO,冰岛IS,东盟AS,哥CR,新加坡SG,新西兰NZ,智利CL 4.2 秘鲁PE 8.4 澳AU 9.8 瑞士CH 11.2 巴PK,韩国KR	0 受惠国$_1$LD$_1$	180	-Sparkling wine
		-其他酒；加酒精抑制发酵的酿酒葡萄汁：					-Other wine; grape must with fermentation prevented or arrested by the addition of alcohol:
1302	2204.2100	--装入2升及以下容器的	14	0 澳门MO,冰岛IS,东盟AS,哥CR,香港HK,新加坡SG,新西兰NZ,智利CL 7.5 秘鲁PE 8.4 澳AU 9.8 瑞士CH 11.2 巴PK,韩国KR	0 受惠国$_1$LD$_1$	180	--In containers holding 2L or less
1303	2204.2900	--其他	20	0 冰岛IS,东盟AS,哥CR,新加坡SG,新西兰NZ,智利CL 10.7 秘鲁PE 12 澳AU 14 瑞士CH 17.3 韩国KR	0 受惠国$_1$LD$_1$	180	--Other
1304	2204.3000	-其他酿酒葡萄汁	30	0 冰岛IS,东盟AS,哥CR,新加坡SG,新西兰NZ,智利CL 12.5 秘鲁PE 18 澳AU 27 韩国KR		90	-Other grape must
	22.05	**味美思酒及其他加植物或香料的用鲜葡萄酿造的酒：**					**Vermouth and other wine of fresh grapes flavoured with plants or aromatic substances:**
1305	2205.1000	-装入2升及以下容器的	65	0 东盟AS,哥CR,新加坡SG,新西兰NZ,智利CL 27.1 秘鲁PE 39 澳AU 58.5 韩国KR		180	-In containers holding 2L or less
1306	2205.9000	-其他	65	0 东盟AS,哥CR,新加坡SG,新西兰NZ,智利CL 27.1 秘鲁PE 39 澳AU 58.5 韩国KR		180	-Other
	22.06	**其他发酵饮料（例如，苹果酒、梨酒、蜂蜜酒）；其他税号未列名的发酵饮料的混合物及发酵饮料与无酒精饮料的混合物：**					**Other fermented beverages (for example, cider, perry, mead) ; mixtures of fermented beverages and mixtures of fermented beverages and non-alcoholic beverages, not elsewhere specified or included:**
1307	2206.0010	---黄酒	40	0 澳门MO,冰岛IS,东盟AS,哥CR,香港HK,新加坡SG,新西兰NZ,智利CL 13.4 秘鲁PE 24 澳AU 36 韩国KR	0 受惠国$_1$LD$_1$	180	---Chinese rice wine
1308	2206.0090	---其他	40	0 澳门MO,冰岛IS,东盟AS,哥CR,香港HK,新加坡SG,新西兰NZ,智利CL 13.4 秘鲁PE 24 澳AU 36 韩国KR	0 受惠国$_1$LD$_1$	180	---Other

序号 No.	税则号列 Tariff Line	中文货品名称 Article Description in Chinese	最惠国税率 MFN(%)	协定税率 Agreement(%)	特惠税率 SP(%)	普通税率 Gen(%)	英文货品名称 Article Description
	22.07	**未改性乙醇，按容量计酒精浓度在80%及以上；任何浓度的改性乙醇及其他酒精：**					**Undenatured ethyl alcohol of an alcoholic strength by volume of 80 % vol or higher; ethyl alcohol and other spirits, denatured, of any strength:**
1309	2207.1000	-未改性乙醇，按容量计酒精浓度在80%及以上	40	0 澳门MO,巴PK,冰岛IS,东盟AS,哥CR,新加坡SG,新西兰NZ,智利CL 12 秘鲁PE 24 澳AU 36 韩国KR	0 受惠国$_1$LD$_1$	100	-Undenatured ethyl alcohol of an alcoholic strength by volume of 80% vol or higher
1310	2207.2000	-任何浓度的改性乙醇及其他酒精	30Δ5	0 巴PK,冰岛IS,东盟AS,哥CR,秘鲁PE,新加坡SG,新西兰NZ,智利CL 18 澳AU 27 韩国KR	0 受惠国$_1$LD$_1$	80	-Ethyl alcohol and other spirits, denatured, of any strength
	22.08	**未改性乙醇，按容量计酒精浓度在80%以下；蒸馏酒、利口酒及其他酒精饮料：**					**Undenatured ethyl alcohol of an alcoholic strength by volume of less than 80% vol; spirits, liqueurs and other spirituous beverages:**
1311	2208.2000	-蒸馏葡萄酒制得的烈性酒	10	0 冰岛IS,东盟AS,哥CR,新加坡SG,新西兰NZ,智利CL 3 秘鲁PE 4 瑞士CH 5 巴PK 6 澳AU 8 韩国KR	0 受惠国LD	180	-Spirits obtained by distilling grape wine or grape marc
1312	2208.3000	-威士忌酒	10	0 冰岛IS,东盟AS,哥CR,新加坡SG,新西兰NZ,智利CL 3 秘鲁PE 4 瑞士CH 5 巴PK 6 澳AU 8 韩国KR	0 受惠国LD	180	-Whiskies
1313	2208.4000	-朗姆酒及蒸馏已发酵甘蔗产品制得的其他烈性酒	10	0 冰岛IS,东盟AS,哥CR,秘鲁PE,新加坡SG,新西兰NZ,智利CL 4 瑞士CH 5 巴PK 6 澳AU 8 韩国KR	0 受惠国LD	180	-Rum and other spirit obtained by distilling fermented sugarcane products
1314	2208.5000	-杜松子酒	10	0 东盟AS,哥CR,秘鲁PE,新加坡SG,新西兰NZ,智利CL 4 瑞士CH 5 巴PK 6 澳AU 8 韩国KR	0 受惠国LD	180	-Gin and geneva
1315	2208.6000	-伏特加酒	10	0 东盟AS,哥CR,秘鲁PE,新加坡SG,新西兰NZ,智利CL 4 瑞士CH 5 巴PK 6 澳AU 8 韩国KR 8.8 亚太AP	0 受惠国LD	180	-Vodka

序号 No.	税则号列 Tariff Line	中文货品名称 Article Description in Chinese	最惠国税率 MFN(%)	协定税率 Agreement(%)	特惠税率 SP(%)	普通税率 Gen(%)	英文货品名称 Article Description
1316	2208.7000	-利口酒及柯迪尔酒	10	0 冰岛IS,东盟AS,哥CR,香港HK,新加坡SG,新西兰NZ,智利CL 3 秘鲁PE 4 瑞士CH 5 巴PK 6 澳AU 8 韩国KR 8.8 亚太AP	0 受惠国LD	180	-Liqueurs and cordials
		-其他:					-Other:
1317	2208.9010	---龙舌兰酒	10	0 冰岛IS,东盟AS,哥CR,秘鲁PE,新加坡SG,新西兰NZ,智利CL 4 瑞士CH 5 巴PK 6 澳AU 8 韩国KR 8.8 亚太AP	0 受惠国$_1$LD$_1$	180	---Tequila, Mezcal
1318	2208.9020	---白酒	10	0 澳门MO,冰岛IS,东盟AS,哥CR,新加坡SG,新西兰NZ,智利CL 3 秘鲁PE 4 瑞士CH 5 巴PK 6 澳AU 8 韩国KR 8.8 亚太AP	0 受惠国LD	180	---Chinese spirits
1319	2208.9090	---其他	10	0 澳门MO,冰岛IS,东盟AS,哥CR,新加坡SG,新西兰NZ,智利CL 3 秘鲁PE 4 瑞士CH 5 巴PK 6 澳AU 8.8 亚太AP 9 韩国KR	0 受惠国LD	180	---Other
	22.09	**醋及用醋酸制得的醋代用品**					**Vinegar and substitutes for vinegar obtained from acetic acid**
1320	2209.0000	醋及用醋酸制得的醋代用品	20∆15	0 澳门MO,冰岛IS,东盟AS,哥CR,香港HK,新加坡SG,新西兰NZ,智利CL 6 秘鲁PE 12 澳AU 14 瑞士CH 17.3 韩国KR	0 受惠国$_1$LD$_1$	70	Vinegar and substitutes for vinegar obtained from acetic acid

第二十三章
食品工业的残渣及废料；配制的动物饲料

注释：

税号 23.09 包括其他税号未列号的配制动物饲料，这些饲料是由动、植物原料加工而成的，并且已改变了原料的基本特性，但加工过程中的植物废料、植物残渣及副产品除外。

子目注释：

子目 2306.41 所称“低芥子酸油菜子”，是指第十二章子目注释一所定义的油菜子。

Chapter 23
Residues and waste from the food industries; prepared animal fodder

Note:

Heading No.23.09 includes products of a kind used in animal feeding, not elsewhere specified or included, obtained by processing vegetable or animal materials to such an extent that they have lost the essential characteristics of the original material, other than vegetable waste, vegetable residues and by-products of such processing.

Subheading Note:

For the purposes of subheading No.2306.41, the expression “low erucic acid rape or colza seeds” means seeds as defined in Subheading Note 1 to Chapter 12.

序号 No.	税则号列 Tariff Line	中文货品名称 Article Description in Chinese	最惠国税率 MFN(%)	协定税率 Agreement(%)		特惠税率 SP(%)		普通税率 Gen(%)	英文货品名称 Article Description
	23.01	不适于供人食用的肉、杂碎、鱼、甲壳动物、软体动物或其他水生无脊椎动物的渣粉及团粒；油渣：							**Flours, meals and pellets, of meat or meat offal, of fish or of crustaceans, molluscs or other aquatic invertebrates, unfit for human consumption; greaves:**
		-肉、杂碎的渣粉及团粒；油渣：							-Flours, meals and pellets, of meat or meat offal; greaves:
		---肉骨粉：							---Flours and meals, of meat bones:
1321	2301.1011	----含牛羊成分的	2	0	澳AU,巴PK,冰岛IS,东盟AS,哥CR,韩国KR,秘鲁PE,瑞士CH,新西兰NZ,智利CL	0	受惠国LD	11	----Of bovine and sheep
1322	2301.1019	----其他	2	0	澳AU,巴PK,冰岛IS,东盟AS,哥CR,韩国KR,秘鲁PE,瑞士CH,新西兰NZ,智利CL	0	受惠国LD	11	----Other
1323	2301.1020	---油渣	5	0	澳AU,巴PK,冰岛IS,东盟AS,哥CR,韩国KR,秘鲁PE,瑞士CH,香港HK,新西兰NZ,智利CL	0	受惠国LD	50	---Greaves
1324	2301.1090	---其他	5	0	澳AU,巴PK,冰岛IS,东盟AS,哥CR,韩国KR,秘鲁PE,瑞士CH,新西兰NZ,智利CL	0	受惠国LD	30	---Other
		-鱼、甲壳动物、软体动物或其他水生无脊椎动物的渣粉及团粒：							-Flours, meals and pellets, of fish or of crustaceans, molluscs or other aquatic invertebrates:
1325	2301.2010	---饲料用鱼粉	2	0 .8	澳AU,巴PK,冰岛IS,东盟AS,韩国KR,秘鲁PE,瑞士CH,香港HK,新西兰NZ,亚太AP,智利CL 哥CR	0	受惠国LD	11	---Flours and meals of fish, of a kind used in animal feeding
1326	2301.2090	---其他	5	0 0.6	澳AU,巴PK,冰岛IS,东盟AS,哥CR,韩国KR,瑞士CH,香港HK,新西兰NZ,亚太AP,智利CL 秘鲁PE	0	受惠国LD	30	---Other
	23.02	谷物或豆类植物在筛、碾或其他加工过程中所产生的糠、麸及其他残渣，不论是否制成团粒：							**Bran, sharps and other residues, whether or not in the form of pellets, derived from the sifting, milling or other working of cereals or of leguminous plants:**
1327	2302.1000	-玉米的	5	0	澳AU,巴PK,冰岛IS,东盟AS,哥CR,韩国KR,秘鲁PE,瑞士CH,新西兰NZ,智利CL	0	受惠国LD	30	-Of maize (corn)

序号 No.	税则号列 Tariff Line	中文货品名称 Article Description in Chinese	最惠国税率 MFN(%)	协定税率 Agreement(%)		特惠税率 SP(%)		普通税率 Gen(%)	英文货品名称 Article Description
1328	2302.3000	-小麦的	3	0	澳AU,巴PK,冰岛IS,东盟AS,哥CR,韩国KR,秘鲁PE,瑞士CH,新西兰NZ,智利CL	0	受惠国LD	30	-Of wheat
1329	2302.4000	-其他谷物的	5	0	澳AU,巴PK,冰岛IS,东盟AS,哥CR,韩国KR,秘鲁PE,瑞士CH,新西兰NZ,智利CL	0	受惠国LD	30	-Of other cereals
1330	2302.5000	-豆类植物的	5	0	澳AU,巴PK,冰岛IS,东盟AS,哥CR,韩国KR,秘鲁PE,瑞士CH,香港HK,新西兰NZ,智利CL	0	受惠国LD	30	-Of leguminous plants
	23.03	**制造淀粉过程中的残渣及类似的残渣，甜菜渣、甘蔗渣及制糖过程中的其他残渣，酿造及蒸馏过程中的糟粕及残渣，不论是否制成团粒：**							**Residues of starch manufacture and similar residues, beet-pulp, bagasse and other waste of sugar manufacture, brewing or distilling dregs and waste, whether or not in the form of pellets:**
1331	2303.1000	-制造淀粉过程中的残渣及类似的残渣	5	0	澳AU,巴PK,冰岛IS,东盟AS,哥CR,韩国KR,秘鲁PE,瑞士CH,新西兰NZ,智利CL	0	受惠国LD	30	-Residues of starch manufacture and similar residues
1332	2303.2000	-甜菜渣、甘蔗渣及制糖过程中的其他残渣	5	0	澳AU,巴PK,冰岛IS,东盟AS,哥CR,韩国KR,秘鲁PE,瑞士CH,新西兰NZ,智利CL	0	受惠国LD	30	-Beet-pulp, bagasses and other waste of sugar manufacture
1333	2303.3000	-酿造及蒸馏过程中的糟粕及残渣	5	0	澳AU,巴PK,冰岛IS,东盟AS,哥CR,韩国KR,秘鲁PE,瑞士CH,新西兰NZ,智利CL	0	受惠国LD	30	-Brewing or distilling dregs and waste
	23.04	**提炼豆油所得的油渣饼及其他固体残渣，不论是否碾磨或制成团粒：**							**Oilcake and other solid residues, whether or not ground or in the form of pellets, resulting from the extraction of soya-bean oil:**
1334	2304.0010	---油渣饼	5	0 3	巴PK,冰岛IS,东盟AS,哥CR,韩国KR,秘鲁PE,瑞士CH,新西兰NZ,亚太AP,智利CL 澳AU	0	受惠国LD	30	---Oil-cake
1335	2304.0090	---其他	5	0 3	巴PK,冰岛IS,东盟AS,哥CR,韩国KR,秘鲁PE,瑞士CH,新西兰NZ,亚太AP,智利CL 澳AU	0	受惠国LD	30	---Other
	23.05	**提炼花生油所得的油渣饼及其他固体残渣，不论是否碾磨或制成团粒**							**Oilcake and other solid residues, whether or not ground or in the form of pellets, resulting from the extraction of groundnut oil**
1336	2305.0000	提炼花生油所得的油渣饼及其他固体残渣，不论是否碾磨或制成团粒	5	0 3	巴PK,冰岛IS,东盟AS,哥CR,韩国KR,秘鲁PE,瑞士CH,新西兰NZ,智利CL 澳AU	0	受惠国LD	30	Oil-cake and other solid residues, whether or not ground or in the form of pellets, resulting from the extraction of groundnut oil
	23.06	**税号23.04或23.05以外的提炼植物油脂所得的油渣饼及其他固体残渣，不论是否碾磨或制成团粒：**							**Oilcake and other solid residues, whether or not ground or in the form of pellets, resulting from the extraction of vegetable fats or oils, other than those of heading 2304 or 2305:**
1337	2306.1000	-棉子的	5	0	澳AU,巴PK,冰岛IS,东盟AS,哥CR,韩国KR,秘鲁PE,瑞士CH,新西兰NZ,智利CL	0	受惠国LD	30	-Of cotton seeds

序号 No.	税则号列 Tariff Line	中文货品名称 Article Description in Chinese	最惠国税率 MFN(%)	协定税率 Agreement(%)	特惠税率 SP(%)	普通税率 Gen(%)	英文货品名称 Article Description
1338	2306.2000	-亚麻子的	5	0 澳AU,巴PK,冰岛IS,东盟AS,哥CR,韩国KR,秘鲁PE,瑞士CH,新西兰NZ,智利CL	0 老挝LA,受惠国LD	30	-Of linseed
1339	2306.3000	-葵花子的	5	0 巴PK,冰岛IS,东盟AS,哥CR,韩国KR,秘鲁PE,瑞士CH,新西兰NZ,智利CL 3 澳AU	0 受惠国LD	30	-Of sunflower seeds
		-油菜子的:					-Of rape or colza seeds:
1340	2306.4100	--低芥子酸的	5	0 巴PK,冰岛IS,东盟AS,哥CR,韩国KR,秘鲁PE,瑞士CH,新西兰NZ,智利CL 3 澳AU	0 受惠国$_1$LD$_1$	30	--Of low erucic acid rape or colza seeds
1341	2306.4900	--其他	5	0 巴PK,冰岛IS,东盟AS,哥CR,韩国KR,秘鲁PE,瑞士CH,新西兰NZ,智利CL 3 澳AU	0 受惠国$_1$LD$_1$	30	--Other
1342	2306.5000	-椰子或干椰肉的	5	0 澳AU,巴PK,冰岛IS,东盟AS,哥CR,韩国KR,秘鲁PE,瑞士CH,新西兰NZ,智利CL 2.5 亚太AP	0 柬埔寨KH,受惠国LD	30	-Of coconut or copra
1343	2306.6000	-棕榈果或棕榈仁的	5	0 巴PK,冰岛IS,东盟AS,哥CR,韩国KR,秘鲁PE,瑞士CH,新西兰NZ,智利CL 3 澳AU	0 柬埔寨KH,受惠国LD	30	-Of palm nuts or kernels
1344	2306.9000	-其他	5	0 巴PK,冰岛IS,东盟AS,哥CR,韩国KR,秘鲁PE,瑞士CH,新西兰NZ,智利CL 3 澳AU	0 老挝LA,受惠国LD	30	-Other
	23.07	**葡萄酒渣;粗酒石**					**Wine lees; argol**
1345	2307.0000	葡萄酒渣;粗酒石	5	0 澳AU,巴PK,冰岛IS,东盟AS,哥CR,韩国KR,秘鲁PE,瑞士CH,新西兰NZ,智利CL	0 受惠国LD	30	Wine lees; argol
	23.08	**动物饲料用的其他税号未列名的植物原料、废料、残渣及副产品,不论是否制成团粒**					**Vegetable materials and vegetable waste, vegetable residues and by-products, whether or not in the form of pellets, of a kind used in animal feeding, not elsewhere specified or included**
1346	2308.0000	动物饲料用的其他税号未列名的植物原料、废料、残渣及副产品,不论是否制成团粒	5	0 澳AU,巴PK,冰岛IS,东盟AS,哥CR,韩国KR,秘鲁PE,瑞士CH,新西兰NZ,智利CL	0 受惠国$_1$LD$_1$	35	Vegetable materials and vegetable waste, vegetable residues and by-products, whether or not in the form of pellets, of a kind used in animal feeding, not elsewhere specified or included
	23.09	**配制的动物饲料:**					**Preparations of a kind used in animal feeding:**
		-零售包装的狗食或猫食:					-Dog or cat food, put up for retail sale:
1347	2309.1010	---罐头	15	0 澳门MO,冰岛IS,东盟AS,哥CR,香港HK,新加坡SG,新西兰NZ,智利CL 4.5 秘鲁PE 9 澳AU 10.5 瑞士CH 12 巴PK,韩国KR	0 受惠国$_1$LD$_1$	90	---In airtight containers

序号 No.	税则号列 Tariff Line	中文货品名称 Article Description in Chinese	最惠国税率 MFN(%)	协定税率 Agreement(%)	特惠税率 SP(%)	普通税率 Gen(%)	英文货品名称 Article Description
1348	2309.1090	---其他	15	0 澳门MO,冰岛IS,东盟AS,哥CR,香港HK,新加坡SG,新西兰NZ,智利CL 4.5 秘鲁PE 9 澳AU 10.5 瑞士CH 12 巴PK,韩国KR	0 受惠国$_1$LD$_1$	90	---Other
		-其他:					-Other:
1349	2309.9010	---制成的饲料添加剂	5	0 澳AU,巴PK,冰岛IS,东盟AS,哥CR,韩国KR,香港HK,新西兰NZ,智利CL 1.5 秘鲁PE 2 瑞士CH 2.5 亚太AP	0 受惠国LD	14	---Preparations for use in making the complete feeds or supplementary feeds
1350	2309.9090	---其他	6.5Δ4	0 澳门MO,巴PK,冰岛IS,东盟AS,哥CR,香港HK,新西兰NZ,智利CL 2 秘鲁PE 2.6 瑞士CH 3.3 亚太AP 3.9 澳AU 5.2 韩国KR	0 受惠国LD	14	---Other

第二十四章
烟草及烟草
代用品的制品

Chapter 24
Tobacco and manufactured tobacco substitutes

注释：

本章不包括药用卷烟（第三十章）。

子目注释：

子目 2403.11 所称“水烟料”，是指由烟草和甘油混合而成用水烟筒吸用的烟草，不论是否含有芳香油及提取物、糖蜜或糖，也不论是否用水果调味，但供在水烟筒中吸用的非烟草产品不归入该子目。

Note:

This Chapter does not cover medicinal cigarettes (Chapter 30).

Subheading note:

For the purposes of subheading 2403.11, the expression “water pipe tobacco” means tobacco intended for smoking in a water pipe and which consists of a mixture of tobacco and glycerol, whether or not containing aromatic oils and extracts, molasses or sugar, and whether or not flavoured with fruit. However, tobacco-free products intended for smoking in a water pipe are excluded from this subheading.

序号 No.	税则号列 Tariff Line	中文货品名称 Article Description in Chinese	最惠国税率 MFN(%)	协定税率 Agreement(%)	特惠税率 SP(%)	普通税率 Gen(%)	英文货品名称 Article Description
	24.01	**烟草；烟草废料：**					**Unmanufactured tobacco; tobacco refuse:**
		-未去梗的烟草：					-Tobacco, not stemmed/stripped:
1351	2401.1010	---烤烟	10	0 新西兰NZ,智利CL 9.4 巴PK,亚太AP		70	---Flue-cured
1352	2401.1090	---其他	10	0 新西兰NZ,智利CL		70	---Other
		-部分或全部去梗的烟草：					-Tobacco, partly or wholly stemmed/stripped:
1353	2401.2010	---烤烟	10	0 新西兰NZ,智利CL		70	---Flue-cured
1354	2401.2090	---其他	10	0 新西兰NZ,智利CL		70	---Other
1355	2401.3000	-烟草废料	10	0 新西兰NZ,智利CL 3 秘鲁PE	0 受惠国LD	70	-Tobacco refuse
	24.02	**烟草或烟草代用品制成的雪茄烟及卷烟：**					**Cigars, cheroots, cigarillos and cigarettes, of tobacco or of tobacco substitutes:**
1356	2402.1000	-烟草制的雪茄烟	25	0 新西兰NZ,智利CL		180	-Cigars, cheroots and cigarillos, containing tobacco
1357	2402.2000	-烟草制的卷烟	25	0 新西兰NZ,智利CL		180	-Cigarettes containing tobacco
1358	2402.9000	-其他	25	0 新西兰NZ,智利CL		180	-Other
	24.03	**其他烟草及烟草代用品的制品；“均化”或“再造”烟草；烟草精汁：**					**Other manufactured tobacco and manufactured tobacco substitutes; ‘homogenised’ or ‘reconstituted’ tobacco; tobacco extracts and essences:**
		-供吸用的烟草，不论是否含有任何比例的烟草代用品：					-Smoking tobacco, whether or not containing tobacco substitutes in any proportion:
1359	2403.1100	--本章子目注释所述的水烟料	57	0 新西兰NZ,智利CL 50 巴PK,东盟AS,亚太AP		180	--Water pipe tobacco specified in Subheading Note 1 to this Chapter
1360	2403.1900	--其他	57	0 新西兰NZ,智利CL 50 巴PK,东盟AS,亚太AP		180	--Other
		-其他：					-Other:
1361	2403.9100	--“均化”或“再造”烟草	57	0 新西兰NZ,智利CL 50 东盟AS		180	--“Homogenized” or “reconstituted” tobacco
	ex24039100	再造烟草	Δ40				Reconstituted tobacco
1362	2403.9900	--其他	57	0 新西兰NZ,智利CL 50 东盟AS		180	--Other

第五类
矿 产 品

SECTION V
MINERAL PRODUCTS

第二十五章
盐；硫磺；泥土及石料；石膏料、石灰及水泥

Chapter 25
Salt; sulphur; earths and stone; plastering materials, lime and cement

注释：

一、除条文及注释四另有规定的以外，本章各税号只包括原产状态的矿产品，或只经过洗涤（包括用化学物质清除杂质而未改变产品结构的）、破碎、磨碎、研粉、淘洗、筛分以及用浮选、磁选和其他机械物理方法（不包括结晶法）精选过的货品，但不得经过焙烧、煅烧、混合或超过税目所列的加工范围。

本章产品可含有添加的抗尘剂，但所加剂料并不使原产品改变其一般用途而适合于某些特殊用途。

二、本章不包括：

（一）升华硫磺、沉淀硫磺及胶态硫磺（税号28.02）；

（二）土色料，按重量计三氧化二铁含量在70%及以上（税号28.21）；

（三）第三十章的药品及其他产品；

（四）芳香料制品及化妆盥洗品（第三十三章）；

（五）长方砌石、路缘石、扁平石（税号68.01）、镶嵌石或类似石料（税号68.02）及铺屋顶、饰墙面或防潮用的板岩（税号68.03）；

（六）宝石或半宝石（税号71.02或71.03）；

（七）每颗重量不低于2.5克的氯化钠或氧化镁培养晶体（光学元件除外）（税号38.24）；氯化钠或氧化镁制的光学元件（税号90.01）；

（八）台球用粉块（税号95.04）；

（九）书写或绘画用粉笔及裁缝划粉（税号96.09）。

三、既可归入税号25.17又可归入本章其他税号的产品，应归入税号25.17。

四、税号25.30主要包括：未膨胀的蛭石、珍珠岩及绿泥石；不论是否煅烧或混合的土色料；天然云母氧化铁；海泡石（不论是否磨光成块）；琥珀；模制后未经进一步加工的片、条、杆或类似形状的粘聚海泡石及粘聚琥珀；黑玉；菱锶矿（不论是否煅烧），但不包括氧化锶；破碎陶器；砖或混凝土的碎块。

Notes:

1. Except where their context or Note 4 to this Chapter otherwise requires, the headings of this Chapter cover only products which are in the crude state or which have been washed (even with chemical substances eliminating the impurities without changing the structure of the product), crushed, ground, powdered, levigated, sifted, screened, concentrated by flotation, magnetic separation or other mechanical or physical processes (except crystallization), but not products which have been roasted, calcined, obtained by mixing or subjected to processing be yond that mentioned in each heading.

   The products of this Chapter may contain an added antidusting agent, provided that such addition does not render the product particularly suitable for specific use rather than for general use.

2. This Chapter does not cover:

   (a) Sublimed sulphur, precipitated sulphur or colloidal sulphur (heading No.28.02);

   (b) Earth colours containing 70% or more by weight of combined iron evaluated as Fe_2O_3(heading No.28.21);

   (c) Medicaments or other products of Chapter 30;

   (d) Perfumery, cosmetic or toilet preparations (Chapter 33);

   (e) Setts, curbstones or flagstones (heading No.68.01); mosaic cubes or the like (heading No.68.02); roofing, facing or damp course slates (heading No.68.03);

   (f) Precious or semi-precious stones (heading No.71.02 or 71.03);

   (g)Cultured crystals (other than optical elements) weighing not less than 2.5g each, of sodium chloride or of magnesium oxide, of heading No.38.24;optical elements of sodium chloride or of magnesium oxide (heading No.90.01);

   (h) Billiard chalks (heading No.95.04); or

   (i) Writing or drawing chalks or tailors′ chalks (heading No, 96.09).

3. Any products classifiable in heading No.25.17 and any other heading of this Chapter are to be classified in heading No.25.17.

4. Heading No.25.30 applies, *inter alia*, to: vermiculite, perlite and chlorites, unexpanded; earth colours, whether or not calcined or mixed together; natural micaceous iron oxides; meerschaum (whether or not in polished pieces); amber; agglomerated meerschaum and agglomerated amber, in plates, rods, sticks or similar forms, not worked after moulding; jet; strontianite (whether or not calcined), other than strontium oxide; broken pieces of pottery, brick or concrete.

序号 No.	税则号列 Tariff Line	中文货品名称 Article Description in Chinese	最惠国税率 MFN(%)	协定税率 Agreement(%)	特惠税率 SP(%)	普通税率 Gen(%)	英文货品名称 Article Description
	25.01	盐（包括精制盐及变性盐）及纯氯化钠，不论是否为水溶液，也不论是否添加抗结块剂或松散剂；海水：					**Salt (including table salt and denatured salt) and pure sodium chloride, whether or not in aqueous solution or containing added anti-caking or free-flowing agents; sea water:**

序号 No.	税则号列 Tariff Line	中文货品名称 Article Description in Chinese	最惠国税率 MFN(%)	协定税率 Agreement(%)	特惠税率 SP(%)	普通税率 Gen(%)	英文货品名称 Article Description
		---盐:					---Salt:
1363	2501.0011	----食用盐	0		0 受惠国LD	0	----Edible salt
1364	2501.0019	----其他	0		0 受惠国LD	0	----Other
1365	2501.0020	---纯氯化钠	3	0 澳AU,巴PK,冰岛IS,东盟AS,哥CR,韩国KR,秘鲁PE,瑞士CH,新西兰NZ,智利CL	0 老挝LA,受惠国LD	35	---Pure sodium chloride
1366	2501.0030	---海水	0		0 受惠国LD	0	---Sea water
	25.02	**未焙烧的黄铁矿**					**Unroasted iron pyrites**
1367	2502.0000	未焙烧的黄铁矿	3Δ1	0 澳AU,巴PK,冰岛IS,东盟AS,哥CR,韩国KR,秘鲁PE,瑞士CH,新西兰NZ,智利CL	0 受惠国LD	20	Unroasted iron pyrite
	25.03	**各种硫磺，但升华硫磺、沉淀硫磺及胶态硫磺除外**					**Sulphur of all kinds, other than sublimed sulphur, precipitated sulphur and colloidal sulphur**
1368	2503.0000	各种硫磺，但升华硫磺、沉淀硫磺及胶态硫磺除外	3Δ1	0 澳AU,巴PK,冰岛IS,东盟AS,哥CR,韩国KR,秘鲁PE,瑞士CH,新西兰NZ,智利CL	0 受惠国$_1$LD$_1$	17	Sulphur of all kinds, other than sublimed sulphur, precipitated sulphur and colloidal sulphur
	25.04	**天然石墨:**					**Natural graphite:**
		-粉末或粉片:					-In powder or in flakes:
1369	2504.1010	---磷片	3Δ1	0 澳AU,巴PK,冰岛IS,东盟AS,哥CR,韩国KR,秘鲁PE,新西兰NZ,智利CL 2.1 瑞士CH	0 受惠国LD	30	---In flakes
		---其他:					---Other:
1370	2504.1091	----球化石墨	3	0 澳AU,巴PK,冰岛IS,东盟AS,哥CR,韩国KR,秘鲁PE,瑞士CH,新西兰NZ,智利CL	0 受惠国LD	30	----Spherical Graphite
1371	2504.1099	----其他	3	0 澳AU,巴PK,冰岛IS,东盟AS,哥CR,韩国KR,秘鲁PE,瑞士CH,新西兰NZ,智利CL	0 受惠国LD	30	----Other
1372	2504.9000	-其他	3	0 澳AU,巴PK,冰岛IS,东盟AS,哥CR,韩国KR,秘鲁PE,瑞士CH,新西兰NZ,智利CL	0 受惠国LD	30	-Other
	25.05	**各种天然砂，不论是否着色，但第二十六章的含金属矿砂除外：**					**Natural sands of all kinds, whether or not coloured, other than metal-bearing sands of Chapter 26:**
1373	2505.1000	-硅砂及石英砂	3Δ1	0 澳AU,巴PK,冰岛IS,东盟AS,哥CR,秘鲁PE,瑞士CH,新西兰NZ,智利CL 1.8 韩国KR	0 受惠国LD	40	-Silica sands and quartz sands
1374	2505.9000	-其他	3Δ1	0 澳AU,巴PK,冰岛IS,东盟AS,哥CR,韩国KR,秘鲁PE,瑞士CH,新西兰NZ,智利CL	0 受惠国LD	40	-Other
	25.06	**石英（天然砂除外）；石英岩，不论是否粗加修整或仅用锯或其他方法切割成矩形（包括正方形）的板、块：**					**Quartz (other than natural sands) ; quartzite, whether or not roughly trimmed or merely cut, by sawing or otherwise, into blocks or slabs of a rectangular (including square) shape:**
1375	2506.1000	-石英	3Δ1	0 澳AU,巴PK,冰岛IS,东盟AS,哥CR,韩国KR,秘鲁PE,瑞士CH,新西兰NZ,智利CL	0 受惠国LD	40	-Quartz

序号 No.	税则号列 Tariff Line	中文货品名称 Article Description in Chinese	最惠国税率 MFN(%)	协定税率 Agreement(%)		特惠税率 SP(%)		普通税率 Gen(%)	英文货品名称 Article Description
1376	2506.2000	-石英岩	3∆1	0	澳AU,巴PK,冰岛IS,东盟AS,哥CR,韩国KR,秘鲁PE,瑞士CH,新西兰NZ,智利CL	0	受惠国LD	40	-Quartzite
	25.07	**高岭土及类似土，不论是否煅烧：**							**Kaolin and other kaolinic clays, whether or not calcined:**
1377	2507.0010	---高岭土	3∆1	0	澳AU,巴PK,冰岛IS,东盟AS,哥CR,韩国KR,秘鲁PE,瑞士CH,新西兰NZ,智利CL	0	受惠国LD	50	---Kaolin
1378	2507.0090	---其他	3∆1	0	澳AU,巴PK,冰岛IS,东盟AS,哥CR,韩国KR,秘鲁PE,瑞士CH,新西兰NZ,智利CL	0	受惠国LD	50	---Other
	25.08	**其他粘土（不包括税号68.06的膨胀粘土）、红柱石、蓝晶石及硅线石，不论是否煅烧;富铝红柱石;火泥及第纳斯土：**							**Other clays (not including expanded clays of heading 6806) , andalusite, kyanite and sillimanite, whether or not calcined; mullite; chamotte or dinas earths:**
1379	2508.1000	-膨润土	3	0	澳AU,巴PK,冰岛IS,东盟AS,哥CR,韩国KR,秘鲁PE,瑞士CH,新西兰NZ,智利CL	0	受惠国LD	50	-Bentonite
1380	2508.3000	-耐火粘土	3∆1	0	澳AU,巴PK,冰岛IS,东盟AS,哥CR,韩国KR,秘鲁PE,瑞士CH,新西兰NZ,智利CL	0	受惠国LD	20	-Fire-clay
1381	2508.4000	-其他粘土	3	0	澳AU,巴PK,冰岛IS,东盟AS,哥CR,韩国KR,秘鲁PE,瑞士CH,新西兰NZ,智利CL	0	受惠国LD	50	-Other clays
1382	2508.5000	-红柱石、蓝晶石及硅线石	3	0	澳AU,巴PK,冰岛IS,东盟AS,哥CR,韩国KR,秘鲁PE,瑞士CH,新西兰NZ,智利CL	0	受惠国LD	40	-Andalusite, kyanite and sillimanite
1383	2508.6000	-富铝红柱石	3	0	澳AU,巴PK,冰岛IS,东盟AS,哥CR,韩国KR,秘鲁PE,瑞士CH,新西兰NZ,智利CL	0	受惠国LD	40	-Mullite
1384	2508.7000	-火泥及第纳斯土	3	0 2.1	澳AU,巴PK,冰岛IS,东盟AS,哥CR,韩国KR,秘鲁PE,新西兰NZ,智利CL 瑞士CH	0	受惠国LD	20	-Chamotte or dinas earths
	25.09	**白垩**							**Chalk**
1385	2509.0000	白垩	3	0	澳AU,巴PK,冰岛IS,东盟AS,哥CR,韩国KR,秘鲁PE,瑞士CH,新西兰NZ,智利CL	0	受惠国LD	45	Chalk
	25.10	**天然磷酸钙、天然磷酸铝钙及磷酸盐白垩：**							**Natural calcium phosphates, natural aluminium calcium phosphates and phosphatic chalk:**
		-未碾磨：							-Unground:
1386	2510.1010	---磷灰石	3∆0	0	澳AU,巴PK,冰岛IS,东盟AS,哥CR,韩国KR,秘鲁PE,瑞士CH,新西兰NZ,智利CL	0	受惠国LD	11	---Apatite
1387	2510.1090	---其他	3	0	澳AU,巴PK,冰岛IS,东盟AS,哥CR,韩国KR,秘鲁PE,瑞士CH,新西兰NZ,智利CL	0	受惠国LD	20	---Other
		-已碾磨：							-Ground:
1388	2510.2010	---磷灰石	3∆0	0	澳AU,巴PK,冰岛IS,东盟AS,哥CR,韩国KR,秘鲁PE,瑞士CH,新西兰NZ,智利CL	0	受惠国LD	11	---Apatite

序号 No.	税则号列 Tariff Line	中文货品名称 Article Description in Chinese	最惠国税率 MFN(%)	协定税率 Agreement(%)		特惠税率 SP(%)		普通税率 Gen(%)	英文货品名称 Article Description
1389	2510.2090	---其他	3	0	澳AU,巴PK,冰岛IS,东盟AS,哥CR,韩国KR,秘鲁PE,瑞士CH,新西兰NZ,智利CL	0	受惠国LD	20	---Other
	25.11	**天然硫酸钡（重晶石）；天然碳酸钡（毒重石），不论是否煅烧，但税号28.16的氧化钡除外：**							**Natural barium sulphate (barytes) ; natural barium carbonate (witherite) , whether or not calcined, other than barium oxide of heading 2816:**
1390	2511.1000	-天然硫酸钡（重晶石）	3	0	澳AU,巴PK,冰岛IS,东盟AS,哥CR,韩国KR,秘鲁PE,瑞士CH,新西兰NZ,智利CL	0	受惠国$_1$LD$_1$	45	-Natural barium sulphate (barytes)
1391	2511.2000	-天然碳酸钡（毒重石）	3	0	澳AU,巴PK,冰岛IS,东盟AS,哥CR,韩国KR,秘鲁PE,瑞士CH,新西兰NZ,智利CL	0	受惠国$_1$LD$_1$	45	-Natural barium carbonate (witherite)
	25.12	**硅质化石粗粉（例如各种硅藻土）及类似的硅质土，不论是否煅烧，其表观比重不超过1：**							**Siliceous fossil meals (for example, kieselguhr, tripolite and diatomite) and similar siliceous earths, whether or not calcined, of an apparent specific gravity of 1 or less:**
1392	2512.0010	---硅藻土	3	0	澳AU,巴PK,冰岛IS,东盟AS,哥CR,韩国KR,秘鲁PE,瑞士CH,新西兰NZ,智利CL	0	受惠国LD	40	---Kieselguhr
1393	2512.0090	---其他	3	0	澳AU,巴PK,冰岛IS,东盟AS,哥CR,韩国KR,秘鲁PE,瑞士CH,新西兰NZ,智利CL	0	受惠国LD	40	---Other
	25.13	**浮石;刚玉岩;天然刚玉砂;天然石榴石及其他天然磨料，不论是否热处理：**							**Pumice stone; emery; natural corundum, natural garnet and other natural abrasives, whether or not heat-treated:**
1394	2513.1000	-浮石	3	0	澳AU,巴PK,冰岛IS,东盟AS,哥CR,韩国KR,秘鲁PE,瑞士CH,新西兰NZ,智利CL	0	受惠国LD	35	-Pumice stone
1395	2513.2000	-刚玉岩、天然刚玉砂、天然石榴石及其他天然磨料	3	0	澳AU,巴PK,冰岛IS,东盟AS,哥CR,韩国KR,秘鲁PE,瑞士CH,新西兰NZ,智利CL	0	受惠国LD	17	-Emery, natural corundum, natural garnet and other natural abrasives
	25.14	**板岩，不论是否粗加修整或仅用锯或其他方法切割成矩形（包括正方形）的板、块**							**Slate, whether or not roughly trimmed or merely cut, by sawing or otherwise, into blocks or slabs of a rectangular (including square) shape**
1396	2514.0000	板岩，不论是否粗加修整或仅用锯或其他方法切割成矩形（包括正方形）的板、块	3	0	澳AU,巴PK,冰岛IS,东盟AS,哥CR,韩国KR,秘鲁PE,瑞士CH,新西兰NZ,智利CL	0	受惠国LD	50	Slate, whether or not roughly trimmed or merely cut, by sawing or otherwise, into blocks or slabs of a rectangular (including square) shape
	25.15	**大理石、石灰华及其他石灰质碑用或建筑用石，表观比重为2.5及以上，蜡石，不论是否粗加修整或仅用锯或其他方法切割成矩形（包括正方形）的板、块：**							**Marble, travertine, ecaussine and other calcareous monumental or building stone of an apparent specific gravity of 2, 5 or more, and alabaster, whether or not roughly trimmed or merely cut, by sawing or otherwise, into blocks or slabs of a rectangular (including square) shape:**
		-大理石及石灰华：							-Marble and travertine:

序号 No.	税则号列 Tariff Line	中文货品名称 Article Description in Chinese	最惠国税率 MFN(%)	协定税率 Agreement(%)	特惠税率 SP(%)	普通税率 Gen(%)	英文货品名称 Article Description
1397	2515.1100	--原状或粗加修整	4∆0	0 澳AU,巴PK,冰岛IS,东盟AS,哥CR,韩国KR,秘鲁PE,瑞士CH,新西兰NZ,智利CL	0 受惠国LD	80	--Crude or roughly trimmed
1398	2515.1200	--用锯或其他方法切割成矩形，包括正方形	4∆0	0 澳AU,巴PK,冰岛IS,东盟AS,哥CR,韩国KR,秘鲁PE,瑞士CH,新西兰NZ,智利CL	0 受惠国LD	80	--Merely cut, by sawing or otherwise, into blocks or slabs of a rectangular (including square) shape
1399	2515.2000	-其他石灰质碑用或建筑用石蜡石	3∆0	0 澳AU,巴PK,冰岛IS,东盟AS,哥CR,韩国KR,秘鲁PE,瑞士CH,新西兰NZ,智利CL	0 受惠国LD	50	-Ecaussine and other calcareous monumental or building stone; alabaster
	25.16	**花岗岩、斑岩、玄武岩、砂岩以及其他碑用或建筑用石，不论是否粗加修整或仅用锯或其他方法切割成矩形（包括正方形）的板、块：**					**Granite, porphyry, basalt, sandstone and other monumental or building stone, whether or not roughly trimmed or merely cut, by sawing or otherwise, into blocks or slabs of a rectangular (including square) shape:**
		-花岗岩：					-Granite:
1400	2516.1100	--原状或粗加修整	4∆0	0 澳AU,巴PK,冰岛IS,东盟AS,哥CR,韩国KR,秘鲁PE,瑞士CH,新西兰NZ,智利CL 2 亚太AP	0 受惠国LD	50	--Crude or roughly trimmed
1401	2516.1200	--仅用锯或其他方法切割成矩形，包括正方形	4∆0	0 澳AU,巴PK,冰岛IS,东盟AS,哥CR,韩国KR,秘鲁PE,瑞士CH,新西兰NZ,智利CL 2 亚太AP	0 受惠国LD	50	--Merely cut, by sawing or otherwise, into blocks or slabs of a rectangular (including square) shape
1402	2516.2000	-砂岩	3∆0	0 澳AU,巴PK,冰岛IS,东盟AS,哥CR,韩国KR,秘鲁PE,瑞士CH,新西兰NZ,智利CL 2.1 亚太AP	0 受惠国LD	50	-Sandstone
1403	2516.9000	-其他碑用或建筑用石	3∆0	0 澳AU,巴PK,冰岛IS,东盟AS,哥CR,韩国KR,秘鲁PE,瑞士CH,新西兰NZ,智利CL 2.1 亚太AP	0 受惠国LD	50	-Other monumental or building stone
	25.17	**通常作混凝土粒料、铺路、铁道路基或其他路基用的卵石、砾石及碎石，圆石子及燧石，不论是否热处理;矿渣、浮渣及类似的工业残渣，不论是否混有本税号第一部分所列的材料;沥青碎石;税号25.15、25.16所列各种石料的碎粒、碎屑及粉末，不论是否热处理：**					**Pebbles, gravel, broken or crushed stone, of a kind commonly used for concrete aggregates, for road metalling or for railway or other ballast, shingle and flint, whether or not heat-treated; macadam of slag, dross or similar industrial waste, whether or not incorporating the materials cited in the first part of the heading; tarred macadam; granules, chippings and powder, of stones of heading 2515 or 2516, whether or not heat-treated:**
1404	2517.1000	-通常作混凝土粒料、铺路、铁道路基或其他路基用的卵石、砾石及碎石，圆石子及燧石，不论是否热处理	4	0 澳AU,巴PK,冰岛IS,东盟AS,哥CR,韩国KR,秘鲁PE,瑞士CH,新西兰NZ,智利CL	0 受惠国LD	50	-Pebbles, gravel, broken or crushed stone, of a kind commonly used for concrete aggregates, for road metalling or for railway or other ballast, shingle and flint, whether or not bead-treated
1405	2517.2000	-矿渣、浮渣及类似的工业残渣，不论是否混有子目号2517. 10所列的材料	3	0 澳AU,巴PK,冰岛IS,东盟AS,哥CR,韩国KR,秘鲁PE,瑞士CH,新西兰NZ,智利CL	0 受惠国LD	50	-Macadam of slag, dross or similar industrial waste, whether or not incorporating the materials cited in subheading No.2517.10

序号 No.	税则号列 Tariff Line	中文货品名称 Article Description in Chinese	最惠国税率 MFN(%)	协定税率 Agreement(%)	特惠税率 SP(%)	普通税率 Gen(%)	英文货品名称 Article Description
1406	2517.3000	-沥青碎石	3	0 澳AU,巴PK,冰岛IS,东盟AS,哥CR,韩国KR,秘鲁PE,瑞士CH,新西兰NZ,智利CL	0 受惠国LD	50	-Tarred macadam
		-税号25.15及25.16所列各种石料的碎粒、碎屑及粉末，不论是否热处理：					-Granules, chippings and powder, of stones of heading 2515 or 2516, whether or not heat-treated:
1407	2517.4100	--大理石的	3	0 澳AU,巴PK,冰岛IS,东盟AS,哥CR,韩国KR,秘鲁PE,瑞士CH,新西兰NZ,智利CL	0 受惠国LD	50	--Of marble
1408	2517.4900	--其他	3	0 澳AU,巴PK,冰岛IS,东盟AS,哥CR,韩国KR,秘鲁PE,瑞士CH,新西兰NZ,智利CL	0 受惠国LD	50	--Other
	25.18	**白云石，不论是否煅烧或烧结、粗加修整或仅用锯或其他方法切割成矩形（包括正方形）的板、块；夯混白云石：**					**Dolomite, whether or not calcined or sintered, including dolomite roughly trimmed or merely cut, by sawing or otherwise, into blocks or slabs of a rectangular (including square) shape; dolomite ramming mix:**
1409	2518.1000	-未煅烧或烧结的白云石	3Δ0	0 澳AU,巴PK,冰岛IS,东盟AS,哥CR,韩国KR,秘鲁PE,瑞士CH,新西兰NZ,智利CL	0 受惠国LD	40	-Dolomite, not calcinecd or sintered
1410	2518.2000	-已煅烧或烧结的白云石	3Δ0	0 澳AU,巴PK,冰岛IS,东盟AS,哥CR,韩国KR,秘鲁PE,瑞士CH,新西兰NZ,智利CL	0 受惠国LD	40	-Calcined or sintered dolomite
1411	2518.3000	-夯混白云石	3Δ0	0 澳AU,巴PK,冰岛IS,东盟AS,哥CR,韩国KR,秘鲁PE,瑞士CH,新西兰NZ,智利CL	0 受惠国LD	40	-Dolomite ramming mix
	25.19	**天然碳酸镁（菱镁矿）；熔凝镁氧矿;烧结镁氧矿，不论烧结前是否加入少量其他氧化物;其他氧化镁，不论是否纯净：**					**Natural magnesium carbonate (magnesite) ; fused magnesia; dead-burned (sintered) magnesia, whether or not containing small quantities of other oxides added before sintering; other magnesium oxide, whether or not pure:**
1412	2519.1000	-天然碳酸镁（菱镁矿）	3Δ1	0 澳AU,巴PK,冰岛IS,东盟AS,哥CR,韩国KR,秘鲁PE,瑞士CH,新西兰NZ,智利CL	0 受惠国LD	40	-Natural magnesium carbonate (magnesite)
		-其他：					-Other:
1413	2519.9010	---熔凝镁氧矿	3Δ1	0 澳AU,巴PK,冰岛IS,东盟AS,哥CR,韩国KR,秘鲁PE,瑞士CH,新西兰NZ,智利CL	0 受惠国LD	40	---Fused magnesia
1414	2519.9020	---烧结镁氧矿（重烧镁）	3Δ1	0 澳AU,巴PK,冰岛IS,东盟AS,哥CR,韩国KR,秘鲁PE,瑞士CH,新西兰NZ,智利CL	0 受惠国LD	40	---Dead-burned (sintered) magnesia
1415	2519.9030	---碱烧镁（轻烧镁）	3Δ1	0 澳AU,巴PK,冰岛IS,东盟AS,哥CR,韩国KR,秘鲁PE,瑞士CH,新西兰NZ,智利CL	0 受惠国LD	40	---Light-burned magnesia
		---其他：					---Other:
1416	2519.9091	----化学纯氧化镁	3	0 澳AU,巴PK,冰岛IS,东盟AS,哥CR,韩国KR,秘鲁PE,瑞士CH,新西兰NZ,智利CL	0 受惠国LD	35	----Magnesium oxide, chemically pure

序号 No.	税则号列 Tariff Line	中文货品名称 Article Description in Chinese	最惠国税率 MFN(%)	协定税率 Agreement(%)		特惠税率 SP(%)		普通税率 Gen(%)	英文货品名称 Article Description
1417	2519.9099	----其他	3	0	澳AU,巴PK,冰岛IS,东盟AS,哥CR,韩国KR,秘鲁PE,瑞士CH,新西兰NZ,智利CL	0	受惠国LD	40	----Other
	ex25199099	其他氧化镁含量在70%（含70%）以上的矿产品	Δ1						Other mineral substances, containing MgO 70% or more
	25.20	**生石膏;硬石膏;熟石膏（由煅烧的生石膏或硫酸钙构成），不论是否着色，也不论是否带有少量促凝剂或缓凝剂:**							**Gypsum; anhydrite; plasters (consisting of calcined gypsum or calcium sulphate) whether or not coloured, with or without small quantities of accelerators or retarders:**
1418	2520.1000	-生石膏;硬石膏	5	0	澳AU,巴PK,冰岛IS,东盟AS,哥CR,韩国KR,秘鲁PE,瑞士CH,香港HK,新西兰NZ,智利CL	0	老挝LA,受惠国LD	80	-Gypsum; anhydrite
		-熟石膏:							-Plasters:
1419	2520.2010	---牙科用	5	0 3	澳AU,巴PK,冰岛IS,东盟AS,哥CR,秘鲁PE,瑞士CH,新西兰NZ,智利CL 韩国KR	0	老挝LA,受惠国LD	40	---For dental use
1420	2520.2090	---其他	5	0 4	澳AU,巴PK,冰岛IS,东盟AS,哥CR,秘鲁PE,瑞士CH,新西兰NZ,智利CL 韩国KR	0	老挝LA,受惠国LD	80	---Other
	25.21	**石灰石助熔剂;通常用于制造石灰或水泥的石灰石及其他钙质石**							**Limestone flux; limestone and other calcareous stone, of a kind used for the manufacture of lime or cement**
1421	2521.0000	石灰石助熔剂;通常用于制造石灰或水泥的石灰石及其他钙质石	5	0 2.5	澳AU,巴PK,东盟AS,哥CR,韩国KR,秘鲁PE,瑞士CH,香港HK,新西兰NZ,智利CL 冰岛IS	0	受惠国LD	50	Limestone flux; limestone and other calcareous stone, of a kind used for the manufacture of lime or cement
	25.22	**生石灰、熟石灰及水硬石灰，但税号28.25的氧化钙及氢氧化钙除外:**							**Quicklime, slaked lime and hydraulic lime, other than calcium oxide and hydroxide of heading 2825:**
1422	2522.1000	-生石灰	5	0	澳AU,巴PK,冰岛IS,东盟AS,哥CR,韩国KR,秘鲁PE,瑞士CH,新西兰NZ,智利CL	0	受惠国LD	80	-Quicklime
1423	2522.2000	-熟石灰	5	0	澳AU,巴PK,冰岛IS,东盟AS,哥CR,韩国KR,秘鲁PE,瑞士CH,新西兰NZ,智利CL	0	受惠国LD	80	-Slaked lime
1424	2522.3000	-水硬石灰	5	0 3	澳AU,巴PK,冰岛IS,东盟AS,哥CR,秘鲁PE,瑞士CH,新西兰NZ,智利CL 韩国KR	0	受惠国LD	80	-Hydraulic lime
	25.23	**硅酸盐水泥、矾土水泥、矿渣水泥、富硫酸盐水泥及类似的水凝水泥，不论是否着色，包括水泥熟料:**							**Portland cement, aluminous cement, slag cement, supersulphate cement and similar hydraulic cements, whether or not coloured or in the form of clinkers:**
1425	2523.1000	-水泥熟料	8	0 3.2 4.8 5	冰岛IS,东盟AS,哥CR,秘鲁PE,台湾TW,香港HK,新西兰NZ,智利CL 瑞士CH 澳AU,韩国KR 巴PK	0	受惠国LD	30	-Cement clinkers
		-硅酸盐水泥:							-Portland cement:

序号 No.	税则号列 Tariff Line	中文货品名称 Article Description in Chinese	最惠国税率 MFN(%)	协定税率 Agreement(%)	特惠税率 SP(%)	普通税率 Gen(%)	英文货品名称 Article Description
1426	2523.2100	--白水泥，不论是否人工着色	6	0 巴PK,冰岛IS,东盟AS,哥CR,韩国KR,秘鲁PE,台湾TW,新西兰NZ,智利CL 2.4 瑞士CH 3.6 澳AU 4.5 亚太AP	0 受惠国LD	30	--White cement, whether or not artificially coloured
1427	2523.2900	--其他	8	0 澳门MO,冰岛IS,东盟AS,哥CR,秘鲁PE,台湾TW,香港HK,新西兰NZ,智利CL 3.2 瑞士CH 4.8 澳AU,韩国KR 5 巴PK 6 亚太AP	0 受惠国LD	30	--Other
1428	2523.3000	-矾土水泥	6	0 冰岛IS,东盟AS,哥CR,韩国KR,秘鲁PE,新西兰NZ,智利CL 2.4 瑞士CH 3.6 澳AU 5 巴PK	0 受惠国LD	30	-Aluminous cement
1429	2523.9000	-其他水凝水泥	8	0 冰岛IS,东盟AS,哥CR,秘鲁PE,新西兰NZ,智利CL 3.2 瑞士CH 4.8 澳AU,韩国KR 5 巴PK	0 受惠国LD	30	-Other hydraulic cements
	25.24	**石棉：**					**Asbestos:**
1430	2524.1000	-青石棉	5	0 澳AU,巴PK,冰岛IS,东盟AS,哥CR,秘鲁PE,瑞士CH,新西兰NZ,智利CL 3 韩国KR	0 受惠国$_1$LD$_1$	30	-Crocidlite
		-其他：					-Other:
1431	2524.9010	---长纤维石棉	5	0 澳AU,巴PK,冰岛IS,东盟AS,哥CR,秘鲁PE,瑞士CH,新西兰NZ,智利CL 3 韩国KR	0 受惠国$_1$LD$_1$	30	---Of long staple
1432	2524.9090	---其他	5	0 澳AU,巴PK,冰岛IS,东盟AS,哥CR,秘鲁PE,瑞士CH,新西兰NZ,智利CL 3 韩国KR	0 受惠国$_1$LD$_1$	35	---Other
	25.25	**云母，包括云母片;云母废料：**					**Mica, including splittings; mica waste:**
1433	2525.1000	-原状云母及劈开的云母片	5Δ1	0 澳AU,巴PK,冰岛IS,东盟AS,哥CR,韩国KR,秘鲁PE,瑞士CH,新西兰NZ,智利CL	0 受惠国LD	30	-Crude mica and mica rifted into sheets or splittings
1434	2525.2000	-云母粉	5	0 澳AU,巴PK,冰岛IS,东盟AS,哥CR,韩国KR,秘鲁PE,瑞士CH,新西兰NZ,智利CL	0 受惠国LD	30	-Mica powder
1435	2525.3000	-云母废料	5	0 澳AU,巴PK,冰岛IS,东盟AS,哥CR,秘鲁PE,瑞士CH,新西兰NZ,智利CL 3 韩国KR	0 受惠国LD	30	-Mica waste
	25.26	**天然冻石，不论是否粗加修整或仅用锯或其他方法切割成矩形（包括正方形）的板、块;滑石：**					**Natural steatite, whether or not roughly trimmed or merely cut, by sawing or otherwise, into blocks or slabs of a rectangular (including square) shape; talc:**
		-未破碎及未研粉：					-Not crushed, not powdered:

序号 No.	税则号列 Tariff Line	中文货品名称 Article Description in Chinese	最惠国税率 MFN(%)	协定税率 Agreement(%)		特惠税率 SP(%)		普通税率 Gen(%)	英文货品名称 Article Description
1436	2526.1010	---冻石	3	0	澳AU,巴PK,冰岛IS,东盟AS,哥CR,韩国KR,秘鲁PE,瑞士CH,新西兰NZ,智利CL	0	受惠国LD	50	---Natural steatite
1437	2526.1020	---滑石	3Δ1	0	澳AU,巴PK,冰岛IS,东盟AS,哥CR,韩国KR,秘鲁PE,瑞士CH,新西兰NZ,智利CL	0	受惠国LD	50	---Talc
		-已破碎或已研粉:							-Crushed or powdered:
1438	2526.2010	---冻石	3	0	澳AU,巴PK,冰岛IS,东盟AS,哥CR,韩国KR,秘鲁PE,瑞士CH,新西兰NZ,智利CL	0	受惠国LD	50	---Natural steatite
1439	2526.2020	---滑石	3Δ1	0	澳AU,巴PK,冰岛IS,东盟AS,哥CR,秘鲁PE,瑞士CH,新西兰NZ,智利CL	0	受惠国LD	50	---Talc
				1.8	韩国KR				
	25.28	**天然硼酸盐及其精矿(不论是否煅烧),但不包括从天然盐水析离的硼酸盐;天然粗硼酸,含硼酸干重不超过85%:**							**Natural borates and concentrates thereof (whether or not calcined) , but not including borates separated from natural brine; natural boric acid containing not more than 85% of H_3BO_3 calculated on the dry weight:**
1440	2528.0010	---天然硼砂及其精矿(不论是否煅烧)	3Δ0	0	澳AU,巴PK,冰岛IS,东盟AS,哥CR,韩国KR,秘鲁PE,瑞士CH,新西兰NZ,智利CL	0	受惠国LD	30	---Natural sodium borates and concentrates thereof (whether or not calcined)
1441	2528.0090	---其他	5Δ0	0	澳AU,巴PK,冰岛IS,东盟AS,哥CR,韩国KR,瑞士CH,新西兰NZ,智利CL	0	受惠国LD	30	---Other
				1.5	秘鲁PE				
	25.29	**长石;白榴石;霞石及霞石正长岩;萤石(氟石):**							**Feldspar; leucite; nepheline and nepheline syenite; fluorspar:**
1442	2529.1000	-长石	3Δ1	0	澳AU,巴PK,冰岛IS,东盟AS,哥CR,韩国KR,秘鲁PE,瑞士CH,新西兰NZ,智利CL	0	受惠国LD	50	-Feldspar
		-萤石:							-Fluorspar:
1443	2529.2100	--按重量计氟化钙含量在97%及以下	3	0	澳AU,巴PK,冰岛IS,东盟AS,哥CR,韩国KR,秘鲁PE,瑞士CH,新西兰NZ,智利CL	0	受惠国LD	50	--Containing by weight 97% or less of calcium fluoride
1444	2529.2200	--按重量计氟化钙含量在97%以上	3	0	澳AU,巴PK,冰岛IS,东盟AS,哥CR,韩国KR,秘鲁PE,瑞士CH,新西兰NZ,智利CL	0	受惠国LD	50	--Containing by weight more than 97% of calcium fluoride
1445	2529.3000	-白榴石;霞石及霞石正长岩	5	0	澳AU,巴PK,冰岛IS,东盟AS,哥CR,秘鲁PE,瑞士CH,新西兰NZ,智利CL	0	受惠国LD	50	-Leucite; nepheline and nepheline syenite
				3	韩国KR				
	25.30	**其他税号未列名的矿产品:**							**Mineral substances not elsewhere specified or included:**
		-未膨胀的蛭石、珍珠岩及绿泥石:							-Vermiculite, perlite and chlorites, unexpanded:
1446	2530.1010	---绿泥石	5	0	澳AU,巴PK,冰岛IS,东盟AS,哥CR,秘鲁PE,瑞士CH,新西兰NZ,智利CL	0	受惠国LD	30	---Chlorites
				3	韩国KR				

序号 No.	税则号列 Tariff Line	中文货品名称 Article Description in Chinese	最惠国税率 MFN(%)	协定税率 Agreement(%)		特惠税率 SP(%)		普通税率 Gen(%)	英文货品名称 Article Description
1447	2530.1020	---未膨胀的蛭石和珍珠岩	5	0	澳AU,巴PK,冰岛IS,东盟AS,哥CR,韩国KR,秘鲁PE,瑞士CH,新西兰NZ,智利CL	0	受惠国LD	30	---Vermiculite, perlite unexpanded
1448	2530.2000	-硫镁矾矿及泻盐矿（天然硫酸镁）	3	0	澳AU,巴PK,冰岛IS,东盟AS,哥CR,韩国KR,秘鲁PE,瑞士CH,新西兰NZ,智利CL	0	受惠国LD	30	-Kieserite, epsomite (natural magnesium sulphates)
		-其他：							-Other:
1449	2530.9010	---矿物性药材	3	0	澳AU,巴PK,冰岛IS,东盟AS,哥CR,韩国KR,秘鲁PE,瑞士CH,新西兰NZ,智利CL	0	受惠国LD	30	---Mineral medicinal substances
1450	2530.9020	---稀土金属矿	0			0	受惠国LD	0	---Ores of rare earth metals
		---其他：							---Other:
1451	2530.9091	----硅灰石	3	0	澳AU,巴PK,冰岛IS,东盟AS,哥CR,韩国KR,秘鲁PE,瑞士CH,新西兰NZ,智利CL	0	受惠国LD	50	----Wollastonite
1452	2530.9099	----其他	3	0	澳AU,巴PK,东盟AS,哥CR,韩国KR,秘鲁PE,瑞士CH,新西兰NZ,智利CL	0	受惠国LD	50	----Other
	ex25309099	锂辉石矿	Δ0						Spodumene
	ex25309099	天青石	Δ1						Celesite
	ex25309099	废镁砖	Δ1						Waste magnesia brick
	ex25309099	未煅烧的水镁石	Δ1						Brucite

第二十六章
矿砂、矿渣及矿灰

注释：

一、本章不包括：

（一）铺路用的矿渣及类似的工业废渣（税号 25.17）；

（二）天然碳酸镁（菱镁矿），不论是否煅烧（税号 25.19）；

（三）储油罐的淤渣，主要成分为税号 27.10 项下的油品；

（四）第三十一章的碱性熔渣；

（五）矿物棉（税号 68.06）；

（六）贵金属或包贵金属的废碎料；主要用于回收贵金属的含贵金属或贵金属化合物的其他废碎料（税号 71.12）；

（七）通过熔炼所产生的铜锍、镍锍或钴锍（第十五类）。

二、税号 26.01 至 26.17 所称"矿砂"，是指冶金工业中提炼汞、税号 28.44 的金属以及第十四类、第十五类金属的矿物，即使这些矿物不用于冶金工业，也包括在内。但税号 26.01 至 26.17 不包括不是以冶金工业正常加工方法处理的各种矿物。

三、税号 26.20 只适用于：（一）在工业上提炼金属或作为生产金属化合物基本原料的矿渣、矿灰及残渣，但焚化城市垃圾所产生的灰、渣除外（税目 26.21）；（二）含有砷的矿渣、矿灰及残渣，不论其是否含有金属，用于提取或生产砷、金属及其化合物。

子目注释：

一、子目 2620.21 所称"含铅汽油的淤渣及含铅抗震化合物的淤渣"，是指取自含铅汽油及含铅抗震化合物（例如，四乙铅）储罐的淤渣，主要含有铅、铅化合物以及铁的氧化物。

二、含有砷、汞、铊及其混合物的矿渣、矿灰及残渣，用于提取或生产砷、汞、铊及其化合物，归入子目 2620.60。

Chapter 26
Ores, slag and ash

Notes:

1. This Chapter does not cover:

(a) Slag or similar industrial waste prepared as macadam (heading No.25.17);

(b) Natural magnesium carbonate (magnesite) , whether or not calcined (heading No.25.19) ;

(c) Sludges from the storage tanks of petroleum oils, consisting mainly of such oils(heading 27.10) ;

(d) Basic slag of Chapter 31;

(e) Slag wool, rock wool or similar mineral wools (heading No.68.06) ;

(f) Waste or scrap of precious metal or of metal clad with precious metal; other waste or scrap containing precious metal or precious metal compounds, of a kind used principally for the recovery of precious metal (heading No.71.12) ; or

(g) Copper, nickel or cobalt mattes produced by any process of smelting (Section XV) .

2. For the purposes of headings Nos.26.01 to 26.17, the term "ores" means minerals of mineralogical species actually used in the metallurgical industry for the extraction of mercury, of the metals of heading No.28.44 or of the metals of Section XIV or XV, even if they are intended for non-metallurgical purposes. Headings Nos.26.01 to 26.17 do not, however, include minerals which have been submitted to processes not normal to the metallurgical industry.

3. Heading No.26.20 applies only to: (a) Slag, ash and residues of a kind used in industry either for the extraction of metals or as a basis for the manufacture of chemical compounds of metals, excluding ash and residues from the incineration of municipul waste (hending 26.21); and (b) Slag, ash and residues containing arsenic, whether or not containing metals, of a kind used either for the extraction of arsenic or metals or for the manufacture of their chemical compounds.

Subheading Notes:

1. For the purposes of subheading 2620.21, "leaded gasoline sludges and leaded anti-knock compound sludges" mean sludges obtained from storage tanks of leaded gasoline and leaded anti-knock compounds (for example, tetraethyl lead), and consisting essentially of lead, lead compounds and iron oxide.

2. Slag, ash and residues containing arsenic, mercury, thallium or their mixtures, of a kind used for the extraction of arsenic or those metals classified in subheading 2620.60.

序号 No.	税则号列 Tariff Line	中文货品名称 Article Description in Chinese	最惠国税率 MFN(%)	协定税率 Agreement(%)	特惠税率 SP(%)	普通税率 Gen(%)	英文货品名称 Article Description
	26.01	铁矿砂及其精矿，包括焙烧黄铁矿：					**Iron ores and concentrates, including roasted iron pyrites:**
		-铁矿砂及其精矿，但焙烧黄铁矿除外：					-Iron ores and concentrates, other than roasted iron pyrites:
		--未烧结：					--Non-agglomerated:
1453	2601.1110	---平均粒度小于0.8毫米的	0		0 受惠国LD	0	---Of a granularity less than 0.8mm

序号 No.	税则号列 Tariff Line	中文货品名称 Article Description in Chinese	最惠国税率 MFN(%)	协定税率 Agreement(%)	特惠税率 SP(%)	普通税率 Gen(%)	英文货品名称 Article Description
1454	2601.1120	---平均粒度不小于0.8毫米，但不大于6.3毫米的	0		0 受惠国LD	0	---Of a granularity of 0.8mm or more, but not exceeding 6.3mm
1455	2601.1190	---其他	0		0 受惠国LD	0	---Other
1456	2601.1200	--已烧结	0		0 受惠国LD	0	--Agglomerated
1457	2601.2000	-焙烧黄铁矿	0		0 受惠国LD	0	-Roasted iron pyrites
	26.02	**锰矿砂及其精矿，包括以干重计含锰量在20%及以上的锰铁矿及其精矿**					**Manganese ores and concentrates, including ferruginous manganese ores and concentrates with a manganese content of 20% or more, calculated on the dry weight**
1458	2602.0000	锰矿砂及其精矿，包括以干重计含锰量在20%及以上的锰铁矿及其精矿	0		0 受惠国LD	0	Manganese ores and concentrates, including ferruginous manganese ores and concentrates with a manganese content of 20% or more, calculated on the dry weight
	26.03	**铜矿砂及其精矿**					**Copper ores and concentrates**
1459	2603.0000	铜矿砂及其精矿	0		0 受惠国LD	0	Copper ores and concentrates
	26.04	**镍矿砂及其精矿**					**Nickel ores and concentrates**
1460	2604.0000	镍矿砂及其精矿	0		0 受惠国LD	0	Nickel ores and concentrates
	26.05	**钴矿砂及其精矿**					**Cobalt ores and concentrates**
1461	2605.0000	钴矿砂及其精矿	0		0 受惠国LD	0	Cobalt ores and concentrates
	26.06	**铝矿砂及其精矿**					**Aluminium ores and concentrates**
1462	2606.0000	铝矿砂及其精矿	0		0 受惠国LD	0	Aluminium ores and concentrate
	26.07	**铅矿砂及其精矿**					**Lead ores and concentrates**
1463	2607.0000	铅矿砂及其精矿	0		0 受惠国LD	0	Lead ores and concentrates
	26.08	**锌矿砂及其精矿**					**Zinc ores and concentrates**
1464	2608.0000	锌矿砂及其精矿	0		0 受惠国LD	0	Zinc ores and concentrates
	26.09	**锡矿砂及其精矿**					**Tin ores and concentrates**
1465	2609.0000	锡矿砂及其精矿	0		0 受惠国LD	0	Tin ores and concentrates
	26.10	**铬矿砂及其精矿**					**Chromium ores and concentrates**
1466	2610.0000	铬矿砂及其精矿	0		0 受惠国LD	0	Chromium ores and concentrates
	26.11	**钨矿砂及其精矿**					**Tungsten ores and concentrates**
1467	2611.0000	钨矿砂及其精矿	0		0 受惠国LD	0	Tungsten ores and concentrates
	26.12	**铀或钍矿砂及其精矿：**					**Uranium or thorium ores and concentrates:**
1468	2612.1000	-铀矿砂及其精矿	0		0 受惠国LD	0	-Uranium ores and concentrates
1469	2612.2000	-钍矿砂及其精矿	0		0 受惠国LD	0	-Thorium ores and concentrates
	26.13	**钼矿砂及其精矿：**					**Molybdenum ores and concentrates:**
1470	2613.1000	-已焙烧	0		0 受惠国LD	0	-Roasted
1471	2613.9000	-其他	0		0 受惠国LD	0	-Other
	26.14	**钛矿砂及其精矿**					**Titanium ores and concentrates**
1472	2614.0000	钛矿砂及其精矿	0		0 受惠国LD	0	Titanium ores and concentrates
	26.15	**铌、钽、钒或锆矿砂及其精矿：**					**Niobium, tantalum, vanadium or zirconium ores and concentrates:**
1473	2615.1000	-锆矿砂及其精矿	0		0 受惠国LD	0	-Zirconium ores and concentrates
		-其他：					-Other:
1474	2615.9010	---水合钽铌原料（钽铌矿富集物）	0		0 受惠国LD	0	--- (Hydrated Tantalum/Niobium materials or enriched materials from Tantalum/ Niobium Ore)
1475	2615.9090	---其他	0		0 受惠国LD	0	---Other
	26.16	**贵金属矿砂及其精矿：**					**Precious-metal ores and concentrates:**
1476	2616.1000	-银矿砂及其精矿	0		0 受惠国LD	0	-Silver ores and concentrates
1477	2616.9000	-其他	0		0 受惠国LD	0	-Other
	26.17	**其他矿砂及其精矿：**					**Other ores and concentrates:**
		-锑矿砂及其精矿：					-Antimony ores and concentrates:
1478	2617.1010	---生锑（锑精矿，选矿产品）	0		0 受惠国LD	0	---Crude antimony (Antimony concentrates which are mineral products)
1479	2617.1090	---其他	0		0 受惠国LD	0	---Other

序号 No.	税则号列 Tariff Line	中文货品名称 Article Description in Chinese	最惠国税率 MFN(%)	协定税率 Agreement(%)		特惠税率 SP(%)		普通税率 Gen(%)	英文货品名称 Article Description
		-其他：							-Other:
1480	2617.9010	---朱砂（辰砂）	3	0	澳AU,巴PK,冰岛IS,东盟AS,哥CR,韩国KR,秘鲁PE,瑞士CH,新西兰NZ,智利CL	0	受惠国LD	14	---Cinnabar
1481	2617.9090	---其他	0			0	受惠国LD	0	---Other
	26.18	**冶炼钢铁所产生的粒状熔渣（熔渣砂）：**							**Granulated slag (slag sand) from the manufacture of iron or steel:**
1482	2618.0010	---主要含锰	4	0	澳AU,巴PK,冰岛IS,东盟AS,哥CR,韩国KR,秘鲁PE,瑞士CH,新西兰NZ,智利CL	0	受惠国$_1$LD$_1$	35	---Containing mainly Manganese
	ex26180010	冶炼钢铁产生的锰渣，含锰量大于25%	Δ1						Granulated slag from the manufacture of iron or steel, containing manganese more than 25%
1483	2618.0090	---其他	4	0	澳AU,巴PK,冰岛IS,东盟AS,哥CR,韩国KR,秘鲁PE,瑞士CH,新西兰NZ,智利CL	0	受惠国$_1$LD$_1$	35	---Other
	26.19	**冶炼钢铁所产生的熔渣、浮渣（粒状熔渣除外）、氧化皮及其他废料**							**Slag, dross (other than granulated slag) , scalings and other waste from the manufacture of iron or steel**
1484	2619.0000	冶炼钢铁所产生的熔渣、浮渣（粒状熔渣除外）、氧化皮及其他废料	4	0	澳AU,巴PK,冰岛IS,东盟AS,哥CR,韩国KR,秘鲁PE,瑞士CH,新西兰NZ,智利CL	0	受惠国$_1$LD$_1$	35	Slag, dross (other than granulated slag) , scalings and other waste from the manufacture of iron or steel
	ex26190000	冶炼钢铁产生的熔渣、浮渣、氧化皮及其他废料，五氧化二钒含量大于20%	Δ1						Slag, dross scalings and other from manufacture of iron or steel, containing V_2O_5>20%
	26.20	**含有金属、砷及其化合物的矿渣、矿灰及残渣（冶炼钢铁所产生的灰、渣除外）：**							**Slag, ash and residues (other than from the manufacture of iron or steel) containing metals, arsenic or their compounds:**
		-主要含锌：							-Containing mainly zinc:
1485	2620.1100	--含硬锌	4	0	澳AU,巴PK,冰岛IS,东盟AS,哥CR,韩国KR,秘鲁PE,瑞士CH,新西兰NZ,智利CL	0	受惠国LD	35	--Hard zinc spelter
1486	2620.1900	--其他	4	0	澳AU,巴PK,冰岛IS,东盟AS,哥CR,韩国KR,秘鲁PE,瑞士CH,新西兰NZ,智利CL	0	受惠国LD	35	--Other
		-主要含铅：							-Containing mainly lead:
1487	2620.2100	--含铅汽油的淤渣及含铅抗震化合物的淤渣	4	0	澳AU,巴PK,冰岛IS,东盟AS,哥CR,韩国KR,秘鲁PE,瑞士CH,新西兰NZ,智利CL	0	受惠国LD	35	--Leaded gasoline sludges and leaded anti-knock compound sludges
1488	2620.2900	--其他	4	0	澳AU,巴PK,冰岛IS,东盟AS,哥CR,韩国KR,秘鲁PE,瑞士CH,新西兰NZ,智利CL	0	受惠国LD	35	--Other
1489	2620.3000	-主要含铜	4	0	澳AU,巴PK,冰岛IS,东盟AS,哥CR,韩国KR,秘鲁PE,瑞士CH,新西兰NZ,智利CL	0	受惠国LD	35	-Containing mainly copper
1490	2620.4000	-主要含铝	4	0	澳AU,巴PK,冰岛IS,东盟AS,哥CR,韩国KR,秘鲁PE,瑞士CH,新西兰NZ,智利CL	0	受惠国LD	35	-Containing mainly aluminium

序号 No.	税则号列 Tariff Line	中文货品名称 Article Description in Chinese	最惠国税率 MFN(%)	协定税率 Agreement(%)		特惠税率 SP(%)		普通税率 Gen(%)	英文货品名称 Article Description
1491	2620.6000	-含砷、汞、铊及其混合物，用于提取或生产砷、汞、铊及其化合物	4	0	澳AU,巴PK,冰岛IS,东盟AS,哥CR,韩国KR,秘鲁PE,瑞士CH,新西兰NZ,智利CL	0	受惠国LD	35	-Containing arsenic, mercury, thallium or their mixtures, of a kind used for the extraction of arsenic or those metals or for the manufacture of their chemical compounds.
		-其他:							-Other:
1492	2620.9100	--含锑、铍、镉、铬及其混合物	4	0	澳AU,巴PK,冰岛IS,东盟AS,哥CR,韩国KR,秘鲁PE,瑞士CH,新西兰NZ,智利CL	0	受惠国LD	35	--Containing antimony, beryllium, cadmium, chromium or their mixtures
		--其他:							--Other:
1493	2620.9910	---主要含钨	4	0	澳AU,巴PK,冰岛IS,东盟AS,哥CR,韩国KR,秘鲁PE,瑞士CH,新西兰NZ,智利CL	0	受惠国LD	35	---Containing mainly tungsten
1494	2620.9990	---其他	4	0	澳AU,巴PK,冰岛IS,东盟AS,哥CR,韩国KR,秘鲁PE,瑞士CH,新西兰NZ,智利CL	0	受惠国LD	35	---Other
	ex26209990	含其他金属及化合物的矿灰及残渣，五氧化二钒含量大于20%	Δ1						Ash and residues containing V_2O_5>20%
	26.21	**其他矿渣及矿灰，包括海藻灰（海草灰）；焚化城市垃圾所产生的灰、渣:**							**Other slag and ash, including seaweed ash (kelp) ; ash and residues from the incineration of municipal waste:**
1495	2621.1000	-焚化城市垃圾所产生的灰、渣	4	0	澳AU,巴PK,冰岛IS,东盟AS,哥CR,秘鲁PE,瑞士CH,新西兰NZ,智利CL	0	受惠国LD	35	-Ash and residues from the incineration of municipal waste
1496	2621.9000	-其他	4	0	澳AU,巴PK,冰岛IS,东盟AS,哥CR,韩国KR,秘鲁PE,瑞士CH,香港HK,新西兰NZ,智利CL	0	受惠国LD	35	-Other

第二十七章
矿物燃料、矿物油及其蒸馏产品；沥青物质；矿物蜡

注释：

一、本章不包括：

（一）单独的已有化学定义的有机化合物，但纯甲烷及纯丙烷应归入税号 27.11；

（二）税号 30.03 及 30.04 的药品；

（三）税号 33.01、33.02 及 38.05 的不饱和烃混合物。

二、税号 27.10 所称“石油及从沥青矿物提取的油类”，不仅包括石油、从沥青矿物提取的油及类似油，还包括那些用任何方法提取的主要含有不饱和烃混合物的油，但其非芳族成分的重量必须超过芳族成分。然而，它不包括温度在 300℃时，压力转为 1013 毫巴后减压蒸馏出的液体合成聚烯烃以体积计小于 60%的货品（第三十九章）。

三、税目 27.10 所称“废油”，是指主要含石油及从沥青矿物提取的油类（参见本章注释二）的废油，不论其是否与水混合。它们包括：

（一）不再适于作为原产品使用的废油（例如，用过的润滑油、液压油及变压器油）；

（二）石油储罐的淤渣油，主要含有石油及高浓度的在生产原产品时使用的添加剂（例如，化学品）；

（三）水乳浊液状或与水混合的废油，例如，浮油、清洗油罐所得的油或机械加工中已用过的切削油。

子目注释：

一、子目号 2701.11 所称“无烟煤”，是指含挥发物（以干燥、无矿物质计）不超过 14%的煤。

二、子目号 2701.12 所称“烟煤”，是指含挥发物（以干燥、无矿物质计）超过 14%，并且热值（以潮湿、无矿物质计）等于或大于 5833 大卡/公斤的煤。

三、子目号 2707.10、2707.20、2707.30 及 2707.40 所称“粗苯”、“粗甲苯”、“粗二甲苯”、“萘”，是分别指按重量计苯、甲苯、二甲苯、萘的含量在 50%以上的产品。

四、子目 2710.12 所称“轻油及其制品”，是指温度在 210℃时以体积计馏出量（包括损耗）在 90%及以上的产品（以美国标准试验法 D86 为准）。

Chapter 27
Mineral fuels, mineral oils and products of their distillation; bituminous substances; mineral waxes

Notes:

1. This Chapter does not cover:

(a) Separate chemically defined organic compounds, other than pure methane and propane which are to be classified in heading No.27.11;

(b) Medicaments of heading No.30.03 or 30.04; or

(c) Mixed unsaturated hydrocarbons of heading No.33.01, 33.02 or 38.05.

2. References in heading No.27.10 to “petroleum oils and oils obtained from bituminous minerals” include not only petroleum oils and oils obtained from bituminous minerals but also similar oils, as well as those consisting mainly of mixed unsaturated hydrocarbons, obtained by any process, provided that the weight of the non-aromatic constituents exceeds that of the aromatic constituents. However, the references do not include liquid synthetic polyolefins of which less than 60% by volume distils at 300℃, after conversion to 1,013 millibars when a reduced-pressure distillation method is used (Chapter 39).

3. For the purposes of heading 27.10,“waste oils” means waste containing mainly petroleum oils and oils obtained from bituminous minerals(as described in Note 2 to this Chapter) , whether or not mixed with water. These include:

(a) Such oils no longer fit for use as primary products(for example, used lubricating oils, used hydraulic oils and used transformer oils) ;

(b) Sludge oils from the storage tanks of petroleum oils, mainly containing such oils and a high concentration of additives(for example, chemicals) used in the manufacture of the primary products;and

(c) Such oils in the form of emulsions in water or mixtures with water, such as those resulting from oil spills, storage tank washings, or from the use of cutting oils for machining operations.

Subheading Notes:

1. For the purposes of subheading No.2701.11,“anthracite” means coal having a volatile matter limit(on a dry, mineral-matter-free basis) not exceeding14%.

2. For the purposes of subheading No.2701.12, “bituminous coal” means coal having a volatile matter limit (on a dry, mineral-matter-free basis) exceeding 14% and a calorific value limit (on a moist, mineral-matter-free basis) equal to or greater than 5,833 kcal/kg.

3. For the purposes of subheadings 2707.10, 2707.20, 2707.30 and 2707.40, the terms “benzole (benzene)”, “toluole (toluene)” , “xylole (xylenes)” , “naphthalene” and “phenols” apply to products which contain more than 50% by weight of benzene, toluene, xylene or naphthalene, respectively.

4. For the purposes of subheading 2710.12, “light oils and preparations” are those of which 90% or more by volume (including losses) distil at 210℃(ASTMD 86 me-

五、税目 27.10 所称“生物柴油”，是指从动植物油脂（不论是否使用过）得到的用作燃料的脂肪酸单烷基酯。

thod).

5. For the purposes of the subheadings of heading 27.10, the term “biodiesel” means mono-alkyl esters of fatty acids of a kind used as a fuel, derived fromanimal or vegetable fats and oils whether or not used.

序号 No.	税则号列 Tariff Line	中文货品名称 Article Description in Chinese	最惠国税率 MFN(%)	协定税率 Agreement(%)	特惠税率 SP(%)	普通税率 Gen(%)	英文货品名称 Article Description
	27.01	**煤;煤砖、煤球及用煤制成的类似固体燃料:**					**Coal; briquettes, ovoids and similar solid fuels manufactured from coal:**
		-煤，不论是否粉化，但未制成型:					-Coal, whether or not pulverised, but not agglomerated:
1497	2701.1100	--无烟煤	3	0 澳AU,巴PK,冰岛IS,东盟AS,哥CR,韩国KR,秘鲁PE,瑞士CH,新西兰NZ,智利CL	0 老挝LA,受惠国LD	20	--Anthracite
		--烟煤:					--Bituminous coal:
1498	2701.1210	---炼焦煤	3	0 澳AU,巴PK,冰岛IS,东盟AS,哥CR,韩国KR,秘鲁PE,瑞士CH,新西兰NZ,智利CL	0 老挝LA,受惠国LD	20	---Coking coal
1499	2701.1290	---其他	6	0 冰岛IS,东盟AS,哥CR,韩国KR,秘鲁PE,新西兰NZ,智利CL 2 澳AU 2.4 瑞士CH 5 巴PK	0 老挝LA,受惠国LD	20	---Other
1500	2701.1900	--其他煤	5	0 澳AU,巴PK,冰岛IS,东盟AS,哥CR,韩国KR,秘鲁PE,瑞士CH,新西兰NZ,智利CL 3.5 亚太AP	0 老挝LA,受惠国LD	20	--Other coal
1501	2701.2000	-煤砖、煤球及用煤制成的类似固体燃料	5	0 澳AU,巴PK,冰岛IS,东盟AS,哥CR,韩国KR,秘鲁PE,瑞士CH,新西兰NZ,智利CL	0 老挝LA,受惠国LD	50	-Briquettes, ovoids and similar solid fuels manufactured from coal
	27.02	**褐煤，不论是否制成型，但不包括黑玉:**					**Lignite, whether or not agglomerated, excluding jet:**
1502	2702.1000	-褐煤，不论是否粉化，但未制成型	3	0 澳AU,巴PK,冰岛IS,东盟AS,哥CR,韩国KR,秘鲁PE,瑞士CH,新西兰NZ,智利CL	0 受惠国LD	20	-Lignite, whether or not pulverized, but not agglomerated
1503	2702.2000	-制成型的褐煤	3	0 澳AU,巴PK,冰岛IS,东盟AS,哥CR,韩国KR,秘鲁PE,瑞士CH,新西兰NZ,智利CL	0 受惠国LD	20	-Agglomerated ignite
	27.03	**泥煤(包括肥料用泥煤)，不论是否制成型**					**Peat (including peat litter), whether or not agglomerated**
1504	2703.0000	泥煤(包括肥料用泥煤)，不论是否制成型	5	0 澳AU,巴PK,冰岛IS,东盟AS,哥CR,韩国KR,秘鲁PE,瑞士CH,新西兰NZ,智利CL	0 受惠国$_1$LD$_1$	20	Peat (including peat litter), whether or not agglomerated
	27.04	**煤、褐煤或泥煤制成的焦炭及半焦炭，不论是否制成型;甑炭:**					**Coke and semi-coke of coal, of lignite or of peat, whether or not agglomerated; retort carbon:**
1505	2704.0010	---焦炭及半焦炭	5Δ0	0 澳AU,巴PK,冰岛IS,东盟AS,哥CR,韩国KR,秘鲁PE,瑞士CH,新西兰NZ,智利CL 2.5 亚太AP	0 受惠国$_1$LD$_1$	11	---Coke and semi-coke
1506	2704.0090	---其他	5Δ0	0 澳AU,巴PK,冰岛IS,东盟AS,哥CR,韩国KR,秘鲁PE,瑞士CH,新西兰NZ,智利CL 2.5 亚太AP	0 受惠国$_1$LD$_1$	11	---Other

序号 No.	税则号列 Tariff Line	中文货品名称 Article Description in Chinese	最惠国税率 MFN(%)	协定税率 Agreement(%)	特惠税率 SP(%)	普通税率 Gen(%)	英文货品名称 Article Description
	27.05	煤气、水煤气、炉煤气及类似气体，但石油气及其他烃类气除外					**Coal gas, water gas, producer gas and similar gases, other than petroleum gases and other gaseous hydrocarbons**
1507	2705.0000	煤气、水煤气、炉煤气及类似气体，但石油气及其他烃类气除外	5∆1	0 澳AU,巴PK,冰岛IS,东盟AS,哥CR,韩国KR,秘鲁PE,瑞士CH,新西兰NZ,智利CL	0 受惠国$_1$LD$_1$	20	Coal gas, water gas, producer gas and similar gases, other than petroleum gases and other gaseous hydrocarbons
	27.06	从煤、褐煤或泥煤蒸馏所得的焦油及其他矿物焦油，不论是否脱水或部分蒸馏，包括再造焦油					**Tar distilled from coal, from lignite or from peat, and other mineral tars, whether or not dehydrated or partially distilled, including reconstituted tars**
1508	2706.0000	从煤、褐煤或泥煤蒸馏所得的焦油及其他矿物焦油，不论是否脱水或部分蒸馏，包括再造焦油	6∆1	0 冰岛IS,东盟AS,哥CR,韩国KR,秘鲁PE,新西兰NZ,智利CL 2.4 瑞士CH 3.6 澳AU 5 巴PK	0 受惠国$_1$LD$_1$	30	Tar distilled from coal, from lignite or from peat, and other mineral tars, whether or not dehydrated or partially distilled, including reconstituted tars
	27.07	蒸馏高温煤焦油所得的油类及其他产品；芳族成分重量超过非芳族成分的类似产品：					**Oils and other products of the distillation of high temperature coal tar; similar products in which the weight of the aromatic constituents exceeds that of the non-aromatic constituents:**
1509	2707.1000	-粗苯	6	0 冰岛IS,东盟AS,哥CR,秘鲁PE,新西兰NZ,智利CL 2.4 瑞士CH 3.6 澳AU 5 巴PK 5.2 韩国KR	0 受惠国LD	20	-Benzole
1510	2707.2000	-粗甲苯	6	0 冰岛IS,东盟AS,哥CR,秘鲁PE,新西兰NZ,智利CL 2.4 瑞士CH 3.6 澳AU,韩国KR 5 巴PK	0 受惠国LD	30	-Toluole
1511	2707.3000	-粗二甲苯	6∆2	0 冰岛IS,东盟AS,哥CR,秘鲁PE,新西兰NZ,智利CL 2.4 瑞士CH 3.6 澳AU 5 巴PK 5.2 韩国KR	0 受惠国LD	20	-Xylole
1512	2707.4000	-萘	7	0 冰岛IS,东盟AS,哥CR,秘鲁PE,新西兰NZ,智利CL 2.8 瑞士CH 4.2 澳AU 5 巴PK 6 韩国KR,亚太AP	0 受惠国LD	30	-Naphthalene
1513	2707.5000	-其他芳烃混合物，温度在250℃时馏出物以体积计（包括损耗）在65%及以上（以美国标准试验法D86为准）	7	0 冰岛IS,东盟AS,哥CR,秘鲁PE,新西兰NZ,智利CL 2.8 瑞士CH 4.2 澳AU 5 巴PK 6 韩国KR	0 受惠国LD	30	-Other aromatic hydrocarbon mixtures of which 65% or more by volume (including losses) distils at 250℃ by the ASTM D86 method
		-其他：					-Other:

序号 No.	税则号列 Tariff Line	中文货品名称 Article Description in Chinese	最惠国税率 MFN(%)	协定税率 Agreement(%)	特惠税率 SP(%)	普通税率 Gen(%)	英文货品名称 Article Description
1514	2707.9100	--杂酚油	7	0 冰岛IS,东盟AS,哥CR,秘鲁PE,新西兰NZ,智利CL 2.8 瑞士CH 4.2 澳AU 5 巴PK 5.6 韩国KR	0 受惠国LD	30	--Creosote oils
		--其他:					--Other:
1515	2707.9910	---酚	7	0 冰岛IS,东盟AS,哥CR,秘鲁PE,新西兰NZ,智利CL 2.8 瑞士CH 4.2 澳AU,韩国KR 5 巴PK	0 受惠国LD	30	---Phenols
1516	2707.9990	---其他	7	0 冰岛IS,东盟AS,哥CR,秘鲁PE,新西兰NZ,智利CL 2.8 瑞士CH 4.2 澳AU 5 巴PK 6 韩国KR	0 受惠国LD	30	---Other
	27.08	**从煤焦油或其他矿物焦油所得的沥青及沥青焦:**					**Pitch and pitch coke, obtained from coal tar or from other mineral tars:**
1517	2708.1000	-沥青	7	0 冰岛IS,东盟AS,哥CR,秘鲁PE,新西兰NZ,智利CL 2.8 瑞士CH 4.2 澳AU,韩国KR 5 巴PK	0 受惠国$_1$LD$_1$	35	-Pitch
1518	2708.2000	-沥青焦	6	0 冰岛IS,东盟AS,哥CR,秘鲁PE,新西兰NZ,智利CL 2.4 瑞士CH 3.6 澳AU 4.8 韩国KR 5 巴PK	0 受惠国$_1$LD$_1$	11	-Pitch coke
	ex27082000	针状沥青焦	Δ3				Needle Pitch coke
	27.09	**石油原油及从沥青矿物提取的原油**					**Petroleum oils and oils obtained from bituminous minerals, crude**
1519	2709.0000	石油原油及从沥青矿物提取的原油	0		0 受惠国LD	①	Petroleum oils and oils obtained from bituminous minerals, crude
	27.10	**石油及从沥青矿物提取的油类，但原油除外;以上述油为基本成分(按重量计不低于70%)的其他税号未列名制品;废油:**					**Petroleum oils and oils obtained from bituminous minerals, other than crude; preparations not elsewhere specified or included, containing by weight 70% or more of petroleum oils or of oils obtained from bituminous minerals, these oils being the basic constituents of the preparations; waste oils:**

①普通税率: 85 元/吨
General Duty: 85¥/T

序号 No.	税则号列 Tariff Line	中文货品名称 Article Description in Chinese	最惠国税率 MFN(%)	协定税率 Agreement(%)	特惠税率 SP(%)	普通税率 Gen(%)	英文货品名称 Article Description
		-石油及从沥青矿物提取的油类（但原油除外）以及以上述油为基本成分（按重量计不低于70%）的其他税目未列名制品，不含有生物柴油，但废油除外：					-Petroleum oils and oils obtained from bituminous minerals (other than crude) and preparations not elsewhere specified or included, containing by weight 70% or more of petroleum oils or of oils obtained from bituminous minerals, these oils being the basic constituents of the preparations, other than those containing biodiesel and other than waste oils:
		--轻油及其制品：					--Light oils and preparations:
1520	2710.1210	---车用汽油及航空汽油	5Δ1	0 澳AU,巴PK,冰岛IS,东盟AS,哥CR,瑞士CH,新加坡SG,新西兰NZ,智利CL 4.3 韩国KR	0 受惠国$_1$LD$_1$	14	---Motor gasoline, aviation gasoline
1521	2710.1220	---石脑油	6Δ0	0 巴PK,冰岛IS,东盟AS,哥CR,新加坡SG,新西兰NZ,智利CL 2.4 瑞士CH 3.6 澳AU 5.2 韩国KR 5.4 亚太AP	0 受惠国$_1$LD$_1$	20	---Naphtha
1522	2710.1230	---橡胶溶剂油，油漆溶剂油、抽提溶剂油	6	0 冰岛IS,哥CR,新西兰NZ,智利CL 2.4 瑞士CH 3.6 澳AU 5.2 韩国KR	0 受惠国$_2$LD$_2$	30	---Rubber solvent, paint solvent, extractive solvent
		---其他：					---Other:
1523	2710.1291	----壬烯	9	0 冰岛IS,哥CR,新西兰NZ,智利CL 3.6 瑞士CH 5.4 澳AU 7.8 韩国KR	0 受惠国$_2$LD$_2$	20	----Nonene
	ex27101291	壬烯(碳九混合异构体含量高于90%)	Δ4				Nonene (C9 >90%)
1524	2710.1299	----其他	9	0 冰岛IS,哥CR,新西兰NZ,智利CL 3.6 瑞士CH 5.4 澳AU 7.8 韩国KR	0 受惠国$_2$LD$_2$	20	----Other
	ex27101299	异戊烯同分异构体混合物	Δ5				ISO pentene
		--其他：					--Other:
		---煤油馏分：					---Kerosene distillages:
1525	2710.1911	----航空煤油	9Δ0	0 冰岛IS,东盟AS,哥CR,韩国KR,秘鲁PE,台湾TW,新加坡SG,新西兰NZ,智利CL 3.6 瑞士CH 5 巴PK 5.4 澳AU	0 受惠国$_1$LD$_1$	14	----Aviation kerosene
1526	2710.1912	----灯用煤油	9	0 冰岛IS,哥CR,新西兰NZ,智利CL 2.7 秘鲁PE 3.6 瑞士CH 5.4 澳AU 7.8 韩国KR	0 受惠国$_2$LD$_2$	14	----Lamp-kerosene

序号 No.	税则号列 Tariff Line	中文货品名称 Article Description in Chinese	最惠国税率 MFN(%)	协定税率 Agreement(%)	特惠税率 SP(%)	普通税率 Gen(%)	英文货品名称 Article Description
1527	2710.1919	----其他	6	0 冰岛IS,东盟AS,哥CR,韩国KR,秘鲁PE,台湾TW,新加坡SG,新西兰NZ,智利CL 2.4 瑞士CH 3.6 澳AU 5 巴PK	0 受惠国$_1$LD$_1$	20	----Other
	ex27101919	正构烷烃(C9～C13)	Δ2				n-Alkanes (C9～C13)
		---柴油及其他燃料油:					---Diesel oils and other fuel oils:
1528	2710.1922	----5～7号燃料油	6Δ1	0 冰岛IS,东盟AS,哥CR,秘鲁PE,新加坡SG,新西兰NZ,智利CL 2.4 瑞士CH 3.6 澳AU,韩国KR 5 巴PK	0 受惠国$_1$LD$_1$	20	----Fuel oils No.5～No.7
1529	2710.1923	----柴油	6Δ1	0 冰岛IS,哥CR,新西兰NZ,智利CL 1.8 秘鲁PE 2.4 瑞士CH 3.6 澳AU 5.2 韩国KR		11	----Diesel oil
1530	2710.1929	----其他	6	0 澳门MO,冰岛IS,东盟AS,哥CR,新加坡SG,新西兰NZ,智利CL 1.8 秘鲁PE 2.4 瑞士CH 3.6 澳AU 5 巴PK 5.2 韩国KR	0 受惠国$_2$LD$_2$	20	----Other
	ex27101929	350度以下馏出物体积百分比小于20%，550度以下馏出物体积百分比大于80%的蜡油	Δ0				Paraffin oils: 350°C distillage<20%, 550°C distillage>80%
		---润滑油、润滑脂及其他重油:					---Lubricating oils, lubricating greases and other heavy oils:
1531	2710.1991	----润滑油	6	0 澳门MO,巴PK,冰岛IS,东盟AS,哥CR,秘鲁PE,香港HK,新西兰NZ,智利CL 2.4 瑞士CH 3.6 澳AU 5.2 韩国KR 5.4 亚太AP	0 受惠国LD	17	----Lubricating grease
1532	2710.1992	----润滑脂	6	0 巴PK,冰岛IS,东盟AS,哥CR,秘鲁PE,新西兰NZ,智利CL 2.4 瑞士CH 3.6 澳AU 5.2 韩国KR 5.4 亚太AP	0 受惠国$_1$LD$_1$	17	----Lubricating oils
1533	2710.1993	----润滑油基础油	6	0 冰岛IS,东盟AS,哥CR,秘鲁PE,台湾TW,新西兰NZ,智利CL 2.4 瑞士CH 3.6 澳AU 5 巴PK 5.2 韩国KR	0 受惠国$_1$LD$_1$	17	----Basic oils for lubricating oils
1534	2710.1994	----液体石蜡和重质液体石蜡	6	0 巴PK,冰岛IS,东盟AS,哥CR,韩国KR,秘鲁PE,台湾TW,新西兰NZ,智利CL 2.4 瑞士CH 3.6 澳AU 5.4 亚太AP	0 受惠国$_1$LD$_1$	20	----Liquid paraffin and heavy liquid paraffin

序号 No.	税则号列 Tariff Line	中文货品名称 Article Description in Chinese	最惠国税率 MFN(%)	协定税率 Agreement(%)	特惠税率 SP(%)	普通税率 Gen(%)	英文货品名称 Article Description
1535	2710.1999	----其他	6	0 冰岛IS,东盟AS,哥CR,秘鲁PE,香港HK,新西兰NZ,智利CL 2.4 瑞士CH 3.6 澳AU 5 巴PK 5.4 韩国KR	0 受惠国$_1$LD$_1$	20	----Other
1536	2710.2000	-石油及从沥青矿物提取的油类（但原油除外）以及以上述油为基本成分（按重量计不低于70%）的其他税目未列名制品，含有生物柴油，但废油除外	6	0 巴PK,冰岛IS,东盟AS,哥CR,瑞士CH,台湾TW,新加坡SG,新西兰NZ,智利CL 3.6 澳AU 5.2 韩国KR	0 受惠国$_1$LD$_1$	20	-Petroleum oils and oils obtained from bituminous minerals (other than crude) and preparations not elsewhere specified or included, containing by weight 70% or more of petroleum oils or of oils obtained from bituminous minerals, these oils being the basic constituents of the preparations, containing biodiesel, other than waste oils
		-废油：					-Waste oils:
1537	2710.9100	--含多氯联苯（PCBs）、多氯三联（PCTs）或多溴联苯（PBBs）的	6	0 冰岛IS,东盟AS,哥CR,秘鲁PE,新西兰NZ,智利CL 2.4 瑞士CH 3.6 澳AU 5 巴PK	0 受惠国$_1$LD$_1$	20	--Containing poly chlorinated biphenyls (PCBs), polychlorinated terphenyls (PCTs) or polybrominated biphenyls (PBBs)
1538	2710.9900	--其他	6	0 冰岛IS,东盟AS,哥CR,秘鲁PE,新西兰NZ,智利CL 2.4 瑞士CH 3.6 澳AU,韩国KR 5 巴PK	0 受惠国$_1$LD$_1$	20	--Other
	27.11	石油气及其他烃类气：					**Petroleum gases and other gaseous hydrocarbons:**
		-液化的：					-Liquefied:
1539	2711.1100	--天然气	0		0 受惠国LD	20	--Natural gas
1540	2711.1200	--丙烷	5Δ1	0 澳AU,巴PK,冰岛IS,东盟AS,哥CR,秘鲁PE,瑞士CH,新西兰NZ,智利CL 3 韩国KR 3.5 亚太AP	0 受惠国$_1$LD$_1$	20	--Propane
		--丁烷：					--Butanes:
1541	2711.1310	---直接灌注香烟打火机及类似打火器用，其包装容器的容积超过300立方厘米	11	0 冰岛IS,东盟AS,哥CR,秘鲁PE,新加坡SG,新西兰NZ,智利CL 5 巴PK 6.6 澳AU 7.7 瑞士CH 8.8 韩国KR	0 受惠国$_1$LD$_1$	80	---Liquid or liquefied-gas fuels in containers of a kind used for filling or refilling cigarette or similar lighters and of a capacity exceeding 300cm^3
1542	2711.1390	---其他	5Δ1	0 澳AU,巴PK,冰岛IS,东盟AS,哥CR,瑞士CH,新西兰NZ,智利CL 1.5 秘鲁PE 4 韩国KR	0 受惠国$_2$LD$_2$	20	---Other
1543	2711.1400	--乙烯、丙烯、丁烯及丁二烯	5	0 澳AU,巴PK,冰岛IS,东盟AS,哥CR,秘鲁PE,瑞士CH,新西兰NZ,智利CL 4.3 韩国KR	0 受惠国$_1$LD$_1$	20	--Ethylene, propylene, butylene and butadiene
		--其他：					--Other:

序号 No.	税则号列 Tariff Line	中文货品名称 Article Description in Chinese	最惠国税率 MFN(%)	协定税率 Agreement(%)	特惠税率 SP(%)	普通税率 Gen(%)	英文货品名称 Article Description
1544	2711.1910	---直接灌注香烟打火机及类似打火器用的燃料，其包装容器的容积超过300立方厘米	10	0 冰岛IS,东盟AS,哥CR,秘鲁PE,新西兰NZ,智利CL 4 瑞士CH 5 巴PK 6 澳AU 7 亚太AP 8 韩国KR	0 受惠国$_1$LD$_1$	80	---Liquid or liquefied-gas fuels in containers of a kind used for filling or refilling cigarette or similar lighters and of a capacity exceeding 300cm^3
1545	2711.1990	---其他	3	0 澳AU,巴PK,冰岛IS,东盟AS,哥CR,瑞士CH,新西兰NZ,智利CL 0.9 秘鲁PE 1.8 韩国KR 2.1 亚太AP	0 受惠国$_2$LD$_2$	20	---Other
		-气态的：					-In gaseous state:
1546	2711.2100	--天然气	0		0 受惠国LD	20	--Natural gas
1547	2711.2900	--其他	6	0 冰岛IS,东盟AS,哥CR,秘鲁PE,新西兰NZ,智利CL 2.4 瑞士CH 3.6 澳AU,韩国KR 5 巴PK	0 受惠国$_1$LD$_1$	20	--Other
	27.12	**凡士林;石蜡、微晶石蜡、疏松石蜡、地蜡、褐煤蜡、泥煤蜡、其他矿物蜡及用合成或其他方法制得的类似产品，不论是否着色：**					**Petroleum jelly; paraffin wax, microcrystalline petroleum wax, slack wax, ozokerite, lignite wax, peat wax, other mineral waxes, and similar products obtained by synthesis or by other processes, whether or not coloured:**
1548	2712.1000	-凡士林	8	0 冰岛IS,东盟AS,哥CR,秘鲁PE,新西兰NZ,智利CL 3.2 瑞士CH 4.8 澳AU,韩国KR 5 巴PK	0 受惠国LD	45	-Petroleum jelly
1549	2712.2000	-石蜡，按重量计含油量小于0. 75%	8	0 冰岛IS,东盟AS,哥CR,秘鲁PE,新西兰NZ,智利CL 3.2 瑞士CH 4.8 澳AU 5 巴PK 6.4 韩国KR	0 受惠国LD	45	-Paraffin wax containing by weight less than 0.75% of oil
		-其他：					-Other:
1550	2712.9010	---微晶石蜡	8	0 冰岛IS,东盟AS,哥CR,秘鲁PE,新西兰NZ,智利CL 3.2 瑞士CH 4.8 澳AU 5 巴PK 6.4 韩国KR	0 受惠国LD	45	---Microcrystalline petroleum wax
1551	2712.9090	---其他	8	0 冰岛IS,东盟AS,哥CR,秘鲁PE,新西兰NZ,智利CL 3.2 瑞士CH 4.8 澳AU 5 巴PK 6.4 韩国KR	0 受惠国LD	45	---Other
	27.13	**石油焦、石油沥青及其他石油或从沥青矿物提取的油类的残渣：**					**Petroleum coke, petroleum bitumen and other residues of petroleum oils or of oils obtained from bituminous minerals:**
		-石油焦：					-Petroleum coke:
		--未煅烧：					--Not calcined:

序号 No.	税则号列 Tariff Line	中文货品名称 Article Description in Chinese	最惠国税率 MFN(%)	协定税率 Agreement(%)		特惠税率 SP(%)		普通税率 Gen(%)	英文货品名称 Article Description
1552	2713.1110	---硫的重量百分比小于3%的	3	0	澳AU,巴PK,冰岛IS,东盟AS,哥CR,秘鲁PE,瑞士CH,新西兰NZ,智利CL	0	受惠国LD	11	---Containing by weight less than 3% of Sulphur
				2.6	韩国KR				
1553	2713.1190	---其他	3	0	澳AU,巴PK,冰岛IS,东盟AS,哥CR,秘鲁PE,瑞士CH,新西兰NZ,智利CL	0	受惠国LD	11	---Other
				2.6	韩国KR				
		--已煅烧:							--Calcined:
1554	2713.1210	---硫的重量百分比小于0.8%的	3	0	澳AU,巴PK,冰岛IS,东盟AS,哥CR,秘鲁PE,瑞士CH,新西兰NZ,智利CL	0	受惠国LD	11	---Containing by weight less than 0.8% of Sulphur
				2.6	韩国KR				
1555	2713.1290	---其他	3	0	澳AU,巴PK,冰岛IS,东盟AS,哥CR,秘鲁PE,瑞士CH,新西兰NZ,智利CL	0	受惠国LD	11	---Other
				2.6	韩国KR				
1556	2713.2000	-石油沥青	8	0	冰岛IS,东盟AS,哥CR,秘鲁PE,新西兰NZ,智利CL	0	受惠国LD	35	-Petroleum bitumen
				3.2	瑞士CH				
				4.8	澳AU				
				5	巴PK				
				5.6	亚太AP				
				6.9	韩国KR				
1557	2713.9000	-其他石油或从沥青矿物提取的油类的残渣	6	0	冰岛IS,东盟AS,哥CR,秘鲁PE,新西兰NZ,智利CL	0	受惠国LD	35	-Other residues of petroleum oils or of oils obtained from bituminous minerals
				2.4	瑞士CH				
				3.6	澳AU,韩国KR				
				5	巴PK				
	27.14	**天然沥青(地沥青)、沥青页岩、油页岩及焦油砂;沥青岩:**							**Bitumen and asphalt, natural; bituminous or oil-shale and tar sands; asphaltites and asphaltic rocks:**
1558	2714.1000	-沥青页岩、油页岩及焦油砂	6	0	冰岛IS,东盟AS,哥CR,秘鲁PE,新西兰NZ,智利CL	0	受惠国LD	20	-Bituminous or oil shale and tar sands
				2.4	瑞士CH				
				3.6	澳AU,韩国KR				
				5	巴PK				
		-其他:							-Other:
1559	2714.9010	---天然沥青(地沥青)	8Δ4	0	冰岛IS,东盟AS,哥CR,秘鲁PE,新西兰NZ,智利CL	0	受惠国LD	35	---Natural bitumen and asphalt
				3.2	瑞士CH				
				4.8	澳AU				
				5	巴PK				
				6.9	韩国KR				
1560	2714.9020	---乳化沥青	0			0	受惠国LD	20	---Emulsified bitumen and asphalt
1561	2714.9090	---其他	3	0	澳AU,巴PK,冰岛IS,东盟AS,哥CR,韩国KR,秘鲁PE,瑞士CH,新西兰NZ,智利CL	0	受惠国LD	20	---Other
	27.15	**以天然沥青(地沥青)、石油沥青、矿物焦油或矿物焦油沥青为基本成分的沥青混合物(例如,沥青胶粘剂、稀释沥青)**							**Bituminous mixtures based on natural asphalt, on natural bitumen, on petroleum bitumen, on mineral tar or on mineral tar pitch (for example, bituminous mastics, cut-backs)**

序号 No.	税则号列 Tariff Line	中文货品名称 Article Description in Chinese	最惠国税率 MFN(%)	协定税率 Agreement(%)	特惠税率 SP(%)	普通税率 Gen(%)	英文货品名称 Article Description
1562	2715.0000	以天然沥青（地沥青）、石油沥青、矿物焦油或矿物焦油沥青为基本成分的沥青混合物（例如，沥青胶粘剂、稀释沥青）	8	0 澳门MO,冰岛IS,东盟AS,哥CR,秘鲁PE,新西兰NZ,智利CL 3.2 瑞士CH 4.8 澳AU 5 巴PK 6.4 韩国KR	0 受惠国LD	35	Bituminous mixtures based on natural asphalt, on natural bitumen, on petroleum bitumen, on mineral tar or on mineral tar pitch (for example, bituminous mastics, cut-backs)
	27.16	**电力**					**Electrical energy**
1563	2716.0000	电力	0		0 受惠国LD	8	Electrical energy

第六类
化学工业及其相关工业的产品

SECTION Ⅵ
PRODUCTS OF THE CHEMICAL OR ALLIED INDUSTRIES

注释:

一、

（一）凡符合税号 28.44 或 28.45 规定的货品（放射性矿砂除外），应分别归入以上税号而不归入本目录的其他税号；

（二）除上述（一）款另有规定的以外，凡符合税号 28.43、28.46 或 28.52 规定的货品，应分别归入这两个税号而不归入本类的其他税号。

二、除上述注释一另有规定的以外，凡由于按一定剂量或作为零售包装而可归入税号 30.04、30.05、30.06、32.12、33.03、33.04、33.05、33.06、33.07、35.06、37.07 或 38.08 的货品，应分别归入以上税号，而不归入本目录的其他税号。

三、由两种或两种以上单独成分配套的货品，其部分或全部成分属于本类范围以内，混合后则构成第六类或第七类的货品，应按混合后产品归入相应的税号，但其组成成分必须同时符合下列条件：

（一）其包装形式足以表明这些成分不需经过改装就可一起使用的；

（二）一起进口或出口的；

（三）这些成分的属性及相互比例足以表明是相互配用的。

Notes:

1. (a) Goods (other than radioactive ores) answering to a description in heading No.28.44 or 28.45 are to be classified in those headings and in no other heading of the Nomenclature;

(b) Subject to paragraph (A) above, goods answering to a description in heading No.28.43 , 28.46 or 28.52 are to be classified in those headings and in no other heading of this Section.

2. Subject to Note 1 above, goods classifiable in heading No.30.04, 30.05, 30.06, 32.12, 33.03, 33.04, 33.05, 33.06, 33.07, 35.06, 37.07, or 38.08 by reason of being put up in measured doses or for retail sale are to be classified in those headings and in no other headings of the Nomenclature.

3. Goods put up in sets consisting of two or more separate constituents, some or all of which fall in this Section and are intended to be mixed together to obtain a product of Section Ⅵ or Ⅶ, are to be classified in the heading appropriate to that product, provided that the constituents are:

(a) having regard to the manner in which they are put up, clearly identifiable as being intended to be used together without first being repacked;

(b) presented together; and

(c) identifiable, whether by their nature or by the relative proportions in which they are present, as being complementary one to another.

第二十八章
无机化学品；贵金属、稀土金属、放射性元素及其同位素的有机及无机化合物

Chapter 28
Inorganic chemicals; organic or inorganic compounds of precious metals, of rare-earth metals of radioactive elements or of isotopes

注释:

一、除条文另有规定的以外，本章各税号只适用于：

（一）单独的化学元素及单独的已有化学定义的化合物，不论是否含有杂质；

（二）上述（一）款产品的水溶液；

（三）溶于其他溶剂的上述（一）款产品，但该产品处于溶液状态只是为了安全或运输所采取的正常必要方法，其所用溶剂并不使该产品改变其一般用途而适合于某些特殊用途；

（四）为了保存或运输需要，加入稳定剂（包括抗

Notes:

1. Except where the context otherwise requires, the headings of this Chapter apply only to:

(a) Separate chemical elements and separate chemically defined compounds, whether or not containing impurities;

(b) The products mentioned in (a) above dissolved in water;

(c) The products mentioned in (a) above dissolved in other solvents, provided that the solution constitutes a normal and necessary method of putting up these products adopted solely for reasons of safety or for transport, and that the solvent does not render the product particularly suitable for specific use rather than for general use;

(d) The products mentioned in (a), (b) or (c) above with

结块剂）的上述（一）、（二）、（三）款产品；

（五）为了便于识别或安全起见，加入抗尘剂或着色剂的上述（一）、（二）、（三）、（四）款产品，但所加剂料并不使原产品改变其一般用途而适合于某些特殊用途。

二、除以有机物质稳定的连二亚硫酸盐及次硫酸盐（税号28.31），无机碱的碳酸盐及过碳酸盐（税号28.36），无机碱的氰化物、氧氰化物及氰络合物（税号28.37），无机碱的雷酸盐、氰酸盐及硫氰酸盐（税号28.42），税号28.43至28.46及28.52的有机产品，以及碳化物（税号28.49）之外，本章仅包括下列碳化合物：

（一）碳的氧化物，氰化氢及雷酸、异氰酸、硫氰酸及其他简单或络合氰酸（税号28.11）；

（二）碳的卤氧化物（税号28.12）；

（三）二硫化碳（税号28.13）；

（四）硫代碳酸盐、硒代碳酸盐、碲代碳酸盐、硒代氰酸盐、碲代氰酸盐、四氰硫基二氨基络酸盐及其他无机碱络合氰酸盐（税号28.42）；

（五）用尿素固化的过氧化氢（税号28.47）、氧硫化碳、硫代羰基卤化物、氰、卤化氰、氨基氰及其金属衍生物（税号28.53），不论是否纯净，但氰氨化钙除外（第三十一章）。

三、除第六类注释一另有规定的以外，本章不包括：

（一）氯化钠或氧化镁（不论是否纯净）及第五类的其他产品；

（二）上述注释二所述以外的有机——无机化合物；

（三）第三十一章注释二、三、四或五所述的产品；

（四）税号32.06的用作发光剂的无机产品；税目32.07的搪瓷玻璃料及其他玻璃，呈粉、粒或粉片状的；

（五）人造石墨（税号38.01）；税号38.13的灭火器的装配药及已装药的灭火弹；税号38.24的零售包装的除墨剂；税号38.24的每颗重量不少于2.5克的碱金属或碱土金属卤化物的培养晶体（光学元件除外）；

（六）宝石或半宝石（天然、合成或再造）及这些宝石、半宝石的粉末（税号71.02至71.05），第七十一章的贵金属及贵金属合金；

an added stabilizer(including an anti-caking agent necessary for their preservation or transport;

(e) The products mentioned in (a), (b), (c) or (d) above with an added antidusting agent or a colouring substance added to facilitate their identification or for safety reasons, provided that the additions do not render the product particularly suitable for specific use rather than for general use.

2. In addition to dithionites and sulphoxylates, stabilized with organic substances (heading No.28.31), carbonates and peroxocarbonates of inorganic bases (heading No.28.36), cyanides, cyanide oxides and complex cyanides of inorganic bases (heading No.28.37), fulminates, cyanates and thiocyanates, of inorganic bases (heading No.28.42), organic products included in headings No.28.43 to 28.46 and 28.52 and carbides (heading No.28.49), only the following compounds of carbon are to the classified in this Chapter:

(a) Oxides of carbon, hydrogen cyanide and fulminic, isocyanic, thiocyanic and other simple or complex cyanogen acids (heading No.28.11) ;

(b) Halide oxides of carbon (heading No.28.12) ;

(c) Carbon disulphide (heading No.28.13) ;

(d) Thiocarbonates, selenocarbonates, tellurocarbonates, selenocyanates, tellurocyanates, tetrathiocyanato diamminochromates (reineckates) and other complex cyanates, of inorganic bases (heading No.28.42) ;

(e) Hydrogen peroxide, soildified with urea (heading No. 28.47), carbon oxysulphide, thiocarbonyl halides, cyanogen, cyanogen halides and cyanamide and its metal derivatives (heading No.28.53) other than calcium cyanamide, whether or not pure (Chapter 31) .

3. Subject to the provisions of Note 1 to SectionⅥ, this Chapter does not cover:

(a) Sodium chloride or magnesium oxide, whether or not pure, or other products of SectionⅤ;

(b) Organo-inorganic compounds other than those mentioned in Note 2 above;

(c) Products mentioned in Note 2, 3, 4 or 5 to Chapter 31;

(d) Inorganic products of a kind used as luminophores, of heading No.32.06; glass frit and other glass in the form of powder, granules or flakes, of heading 32.07;

(e) Artificial graphite (heading No.38.01) ; products put up as charges for fire-extinguishers or put up in fire-extinguishing grenades, of heading No.38.13; ink removers put up in packings for retail sale, of heading No.38.24, cultured crystals (other than optical elements) weighing not less than 2.5g each, of the halides of the alkali or alkaline-earth metals, of heading No.38.24;

(f) Precious or semi-precious stones (natural, synthetic or reconstructed) or dust or powder of such stones (headings Nos.71.02 to 71.05) , or precious metals or precious metal alloys of Chapter 71;

（七）第十五类的金属（不论是否纯净）、金属合金或金属陶瓷，包括硬质合金（与金属烧结的金属碳化物）；

（八）光学元件，例如用碱金属或碱土金属卤化物制成的（税号90.01）。

四、由本章第二分章的非金属酸和第四分章的金属酸所构成的已有化学定义的络酸，应归入税号28.11。

五、税号28.26至28.42只适用于金属盐、铵盐及过氧酸盐。除条文另有规定的以外，复盐及络盐应归入税号28.42。

六、税号28.44只适用于:

（一）锝（原子序数43）、钷（原子序数61）、钋（原子序数84）及原子序数大于84的所有化学元素;

（二）天然或人造放射性同位素（包括第十四类及第十五类的贵金属和贱金属的放射性同位素），不论是否混合;

（三）上述元素或同位素的无机或有机化合物，不论是否已有化学定义或是否混合;

（四）含有上述元素或同位素及其无机或有机化合物并且具有某种放射性强度超过 74 贝克勒尔/克（0.002 微居里/克）的合金、分散体（包括金属陶瓷）、陶瓷产品及混合物;

（五）核反应堆已耗尽（已辐照）的燃料元件 （释热元件）;

（六）放射性的残渣，不论是否有用。

税号 28.44、28.45 及本注释所称“同位素”，是指:

1.单独的核素，但不包括自然界中以单一同位素状态存在的核素;

2.同一元素的同位素混合物，其中一种或几种同位素已被浓缩，即人工地改变了该元素同位素的自然构成。

七、税号 28.48 包括按重量计含磷量超过 15%的磷化铜（磷铜）。

八、经掺杂用于电子工业的化学元素（例如，硅、硒），如果拉制后未经加工或呈圆筒形、棒形，应归入本章；如果已切成圆片、薄片或类似形状，则归入税号 38.18。

(g) The metals, whether or not pure, metal alloys or cermets, including sintered metal carbides (metal carbides sintered with a metal) , of Section ⅩⅤ; or

(h) Optical elements, for example, of the halides of the alkali or alkaline-earth metals (heading No.90.01) .

4. Chemically defined complex acids consisting of a non-metalacid of sub-Chapter Ⅱ and a metal acid of sub-Chapter Ⅳare to be lassified in heading No.28.11.

5. Headings Nos.28.26 to 28.42 apply only to metal or ammonium salts or peroxysalts. Except where the context otherwise requires, double or complex salts are to be classified in heading No.28.42.

6. Heading No.28.44 applies only to:

(a) Technetium (atomic No.43), promethium (atomic No.61), polonium (atomic No.84) and all elements with an atomic number greater than 84;

(b) Natural or artificial radioactive isotopes (including those of the precious metals or of the base metals of Sections ⅩⅣ and ⅩⅤ), whether or not mixed together;

(c) Compounds, inorganic or organic, of these elements or isotopes, whether or not chemically defined, whether or not mixed together;

(d) Alloys, dispersions (including cermets), ceramic products and mixtures containing these elements or istopes or inorganic or organic compounds thereof and having a specific radioactivity exceeding 74 Bq/g (0.002 μCi/g) ;

(e) Spent (irradiated) fuel elements (cartridges) of nuclear reactors;

(f) Radioactive residues whether or not usable. The term “isotopes”, for the purposes of this Note and of the wording of headings Nos.28.44 and 28.45, refers to:

-individual nuclides, excluding, however, those existing in nature in the monoisotopic state;

-mixtures of isotopes of one and the same element, enriched in one or several of the said isotopes, that is, elements of which the natural isotopic composition has been artificially modified.

7. Heading No.28.48 includes copper phosphide (phosphor copper) containing more than 15% by weight of phosphorus.

8. Chemical elements (for example, silicon and selenium) doped for use in electronics are to be classified in this Chapter, provided that they are in forms unworked as drawn, or in the form of cylinders or rods. When cut in the form of discs, wafers or similar forms, they fall in heading No.38.18.

子目注释:

子目 2852.10 所称“已有化学定义”是指符合第二十八章注释一(一)至（五）或第二十九章注释一（一）至（八）规定的汞的无机或有机化合物。

Subheading Notes:

For the purposes of subheading 2852.10, the expression “chemicallydefined” means all organic or inorganic compounds of mercury meeting the requirements of paragraphs (a) to (e) of Note 1 to Chapter 28 or paragraphs (a) to (h) of Note 1 to Chapter 29.

序号 No.	税则号列 Tariff Line	中文货品名称 Article Description in Chinese	最惠国税率 MFN(%)	协定税率 Agreement(%)	特惠税率 SP(%)	普通税率 Gen(%)	英文货品名称 Article Description
		第一分章化学元素					I. CHEMICAL ELEMENTS
	28.01	**氟、氯、溴及碘:**					**Fluorine, chlorine, bromine and iodine:**
1564	2801.1000	-氯	5.5	0 澳AU,冰岛IS,东盟AS,哥CR,秘鲁PE,新西兰NZ,智利CL 2.2 瑞士CH 3.3 韩国KR 5 巴PK	0 受惠国$_1$LD$_1$	80	-Chlorine
1565	2801.2000	-碘	5.5	0 澳AU,冰岛IS,东盟AS,哥CR,新西兰NZ 2.2 瑞士CH 3.3 韩国KR 5 巴PK	0 受惠国$_1$LD$_1$	30	-Iodine
		氟;溴:					-Fluorine; bromine:
1566	2801.3010	---氟	5.5	0 澳AU,巴PK,冰岛IS,东盟AS,哥CR,秘鲁PE,新西兰NZ,智利CL 2.2 瑞士CH 3.3 韩国KR	0 受惠国$_1$LD$_1$	30	---Fluorine
1567	2801.3020	---溴	5.5Δ1	0 澳AU,巴PK,冰岛IS,东盟AS,哥CR,韩国KR,秘鲁PE,新西兰NZ,智利CL 2.2 瑞士CH	0 受惠国$_1$LD$_1$	30	---Bromine
	28.02	**升华硫磺、沉淀硫磺;胶态硫磺**					**Sulphur, sublimed or precipitated; colloidal sulphur**
1568	2802.0000	升华硫磺、沉淀硫磺;胶态硫磺	5.5Δ1	0 澳AU,巴PK,冰岛IS,东盟AS,哥CR,秘鲁PE,新西兰NZ,智利CL 2.2 瑞士CH 3.3 韩国KR	0 受惠国$_1$LD$_1$	17	Sulphur, sublimed or precipitated; colloidal sulphur
	28.03	**碳(碳黑及其他税号未列名的其他形态的碳)**					**Carbon (carbon blacks and other forms of carbon not elsewhere specified or included)**
1569	2803.0000	碳(碳黑及其他税号未列名的其他形态的碳)	5.5	0 澳AU,巴PK,东盟AS,哥CR,秘鲁PE,台湾TW,香港HK,新西兰NZ,智利CL 2.2 瑞士CH 4.4 亚太AP 4.7 韩国KR	0 受惠国LD	35	Carbon (carbon blacks and other forms of carbon not elsewhere specified or included)
	28.04	**氢、稀有气体及其他非金属:**					**Hydrogen, rare gases and other non-metals:**
1570	2804.1000	-氢	5.5	0 澳AU,巴PK,冰岛IS,东盟AS,哥CR,秘鲁PE,香港HK,新西兰NZ,智利CL 2.2 瑞士CH 4.4 韩国KR	0 受惠国LD	30	-Hydrogen
		-稀有气体:					-Rare gases:
1571	2804.2100	--氩	5.5	0 澳AU,冰岛IS,东盟AS,哥CR,秘鲁PE,香港HK,新西兰NZ,智利CL 2.2 瑞士CH 3.3 韩国KR 5 巴PK	0 受惠国LD	30	--Argon
1572	2804.2900	--其他	5.5	0 澳AU,冰岛IS,东盟AS,哥CR,秘鲁PE,香港HK,新西兰NZ,智利CL 2.2 瑞士CH 3.3 韩国KR 5 巴PK	0 受惠国LD	30	--Other

序号 No.	税则号列 Tariff Line	中文货品名称 Article Description in Chinese	最惠国税率 MFN(%)	协定税率 Agreement(%)	特惠税率 SP(%)	普通税率 Gen(%)	英文货品名称 Article Description
1573	2804.3000	-氮	5.5	0 澳AU,冰岛IS,东盟AS,哥CR,秘鲁PE,香港HK,新西兰NZ,智利CL 2.2 瑞士CH 3.3 韩国KR 5 巴PK	0 受惠国LD	30	-Nitrogen
1574	2804.4000	-氧	5.5	0 澳AU,冰岛IS,东盟AS,哥CR,秘鲁PE,香港HK,新西兰NZ,智利CL 2.2 瑞士CH 3.3 韩国KR 5 巴PK	0 受惠国LD	80	-Oxygen
1575	2804.5000	-硼；碲	5.5	0 澳AU,巴PK,冰岛IS,东盟AS,哥CR,韩国KR,秘鲁PE,新西兰NZ,智利CL 2.2 瑞士CH	0 受惠国LD	17	-Boron; tellurium
	ex28045000	碲	Δ0				Polysilicon
		-硅：					-Silicon:
		--按重量计含硅量不少于99.99%：					--Containing by weight not less than 99.99 % of silicon:
		---经掺杂用于电子工业的直径在7.5厘米及以上的单晶硅棒：					---Monocrystals doped for use in electronics, in the form of cylinders or rods, 7.5cm or more in diameter:
1576	2804.6117	----直径在30厘米及以上的	4	0 澳AU,巴PK,冰岛IS,东盟AS,哥CR,韩国KR,秘鲁PE,瑞士CH,新西兰NZ,智利CL	0 受惠国LD	11	----30cm or more in diameter
1577	2804.6119	----其他	4	0 澳AU,巴PK,冰岛IS,东盟AS,哥CR,秘鲁PE,瑞士CH,新西兰NZ,智利CL	0 受惠国LD	11	----Other
1578	2804.6120	---经掺杂用于电子工业的其他单晶硅棒	4	0 澳AU,巴PK,冰岛IS,东盟AS,哥CR,韩国KR,秘鲁PE,瑞士CH,新西兰NZ,智利CL	0 受惠国LD	17	---Other monocrystals doped for use in electronics, in the form of cylinders or rods
1579	2804.6190	---其他	4	0 澳AU,巴PK,冰岛IS,东盟AS,哥CR,秘鲁PE,新西兰NZ,智利CL 1.6 瑞士CH 3.4 韩国KR	0 受惠国LD	30	---Other
1580	2804.6900	--其他	4	0 澳AU,巴PK,冰岛IS,东盟AS,哥CR,秘鲁PE,瑞士CH,新西兰NZ,智利CL 2.4 韩国KR	0 受惠国LD	30	--Other
		-磷：					-Phosphorus:
1581	2804.7010	---黄磷（白磷）	5.5	0 澳AU,巴PK,冰岛IS,东盟AS,哥CR,秘鲁PE,新西兰NZ,智利CL 2.2 瑞士CH 3.3 韩国KR	0 受惠国LD	30	---Yellow phosphorus (white phosphorus)
1582	2804.7090	---其他	5.5	0 澳AU,巴PK,冰岛IS,东盟AS,哥CR,秘鲁PE,新西兰NZ,智利CL 2.2 瑞士CH 4.4 韩国KR	0 受惠国LD	30	---Other
1583	2804.8000	-砷	5.5	0 澳AU,巴PK,冰岛IS,东盟AS,哥CR,秘鲁PE,新西兰NZ,智利CL 2.2 瑞士CH 3.3 韩国KR	0 受惠国LD	30	-Arsenic
		-硒：					-Selenium:

序号 No.	税则号列 Tariff Line	中文货品名称 Article Description in Chinese	最惠国税率 MFN(%)	协定税率 Agreement(%)	特惠税率 SP(%)	普通税率 Gen(%)	英文货品名称 Article Description
1584	2804.9010	---经掺杂用于电子工业的晶体棒	4	0 澳AU,巴PK,冰岛IS,东盟AS,哥CR,韩国KR,瑞士CH,新西兰NZ,智利CL 1.2 秘鲁PE	0 受惠国LD	17	---Crystals doped for use in electronics, in the form of cylinders or rods
1585	2804.9090	---其他	5.5Δ0	0 澳AU,巴PK,冰岛IS,东盟AS,哥CR,韩国KR,新西兰NZ,智利CL 2.2 瑞士CH 3.5 秘鲁PE	0 受惠国$_1$LD$_1$	30	---Other
	28.05	**碱金属、碱土金属;稀土金属、钪及钇，不论是否相互混合或相互熔合;汞:**					**Alkali or alkaline-earth metals; rare-earth metals, scandium and yttrium, whether or not intermixed or interalloyed; mercury:**
		-碱金属及碱土金属:					-Alkali or alkaline-earth metals:
1586	2805.1100	--钠	5.5	0 澳AU,巴PK,冰岛IS,东盟AS,哥CR,韩国KR,秘鲁PE,新西兰NZ,智利CL 2.2 瑞士CH	0 受惠国$_1$LD$_1$	30	--Sodium
1587	2805.1200	--钙	5.5Δ1	0 澳AU,巴PK,冰岛IS,东盟AS,哥CR,韩国KR,秘鲁PE,新西兰NZ,智利CL 2.2 瑞士CH	0 受惠国$_1$LD$_1$	30	--Calcium
		--其他:					--Other:
1588	2805.1910	---锂	5.5Δ1	0 澳AU,巴PK,冰岛IS,东盟AS,哥CR,韩国KR,秘鲁PE,新西兰NZ,智利CL 2.2 瑞士CH	0 受惠国$_1$LD$_1$	30	---Lithium
1589	2805.1990	---其他	5.5Δ1	0 澳AU,巴PK,冰岛IS,东盟AS,哥CR,韩国KR,秘鲁PE,新西兰NZ,智利CL 2.2 瑞士CH	0 受惠国$_1$LD$_1$	30	---Other
		-稀土金属、钪及钇，不论是否相互混合或相互熔合:					-Rare-earth metals, scandium and yttrium, whether or not intermixed or interalloyed:
		---稀土金属、钪及钇，未相互混合或相互熔合:					---Not intermixed or interalloyed:
1590	2805.3011	----钕	5.5Δ0	0 澳AU,巴PK,冰岛IS,东盟AS,哥CR,韩国KR,秘鲁PE,新西兰NZ,智利CL 2.2 瑞士CH	0 受惠国$_1$LD$_1$	30	----Neodymium
1591	2805.3012	----镝	5.5Δ0	0 澳AU,巴PK,冰岛IS,东盟AS,哥CR,韩国KR,秘鲁PE,新西兰NZ,智利CL 2.2 瑞士CH	0 受惠国$_1$LD$_1$	30	----Dysprosium
1592	2805.3013	----铽	5.5Δ0	0 澳AU,巴PK,冰岛IS,东盟AS,哥CR,韩国KR,秘鲁PE,新西兰NZ,智利CL 2.2 瑞士CH	0 受惠国$_1$LD$_1$	30	----Terbium
1593	2805.3014	----镧	5.5Δ0	0 澳AU,巴PK,冰岛IS,东盟AS,哥CR,韩国KR,秘鲁PE,新西兰NZ,智利CL 2.2 瑞士CH	0 受惠国$_1$LD$_1$	30	----Lanthanum

序号 No.	税则号列 Tariff Line	中文货品名称 Article Description in Chinese	最惠国税率 MFN(%)	协定税率 Agreement(%)	特惠税率 SP(%)	普通税率 Gen(%)	英文货品名称 Article Description
1594	2805.3015	----铈	5.5∆0	0 澳AU,巴PK,冰岛IS,东盟AS,哥CR,韩国KR,秘鲁PE,新西兰NZ,智利CL 2.2 瑞士CH	0 受惠国$_1$LD$_1$	30	----Cerium
1595	2805.3016	----镨	5.5∆0	0 澳AU,巴PK,冰岛IS,东盟AS,哥CR,韩国KR,秘鲁PE,新西兰NZ,智利CL 2.2 瑞士CH	0 受惠国$_1$LD$_1$	30	----Praseodymium
1596	2805.3017	----钇	5.5∆0	0 澳AU,巴PK,冰岛IS,东盟AS,哥CR,韩国KR,秘鲁PE,新西兰NZ,智利CL 2.2 瑞士CH	0 受惠国$_1$LD$_1$	30	----Yttrium
1597	2805.3019	----其他	5.5∆0	0 澳AU,巴PK,冰岛IS,东盟AS,哥CR,韩国KR,秘鲁PE,新西兰NZ,智利CL 2.2 瑞士CH	0 受惠国$_1$LD$_1$	30	----Other
		---稀土金属、钪及钇，相互混合或相互熔合：					---Intermixed or interalloyed:
1598	2805.3021	----电池级	5.5∆0	0 澳AU,巴PK,冰岛IS,东盟AS,哥CR,韩国KR,秘鲁PE,新西兰NZ,智利CL 2.2 瑞士CH	0 受惠国$_1$LD$_1$	30	----Battery grade
1599	2805.3029	----其他	5.5∆0	0 澳AU,巴PK,冰岛IS,东盟AS,哥CR,韩国KR,秘鲁PE,新西兰NZ,智利CL 2.2 瑞士CH	0 受惠国$_1$LD$_1$	30	----Other
1600	2805.4000	-汞	5.5	0 澳AU,巴PK,冰岛IS,东盟AS,哥CR,秘鲁PE,新西兰NZ,智利CL 2.2 瑞士CH 3.3 韩国KR	0 受惠国$_1$LD$_1$	17	-Mercury
		第二分章无机酸及非金属无机氧化物					II. INORGANIC ACIDS AND INORGANIC OXYGEN COMPOUNDS OF NON-METALS
	28.06	**氯化氢（盐酸）;氯磺酸:**					**Hydrogen chloride (hydrochloric acid) ; chlorosulphuric acid:**
1601	2806.1000	-氯化氢（盐酸）	5.5	0 澳AU,冰岛IS,东盟AS,哥CR,秘鲁PE,新西兰NZ,智利CL 2.2 瑞士CH 3.3 韩国KR 5 巴PK	0 受惠国$_1$LD$_1$	80	-Hydrogen chloride (hydrochloric acid)
1602	2806.2000	-氯磺酸	5.5	0 澳AU,巴PK,冰岛IS,东盟AS,哥CR,秘鲁PE,新西兰NZ,智利CL 2.2 瑞士CH 3.3 韩国KR	0 受惠国$_1$LD$_1$	40	-Chlorosulphuric acid
	28.07	**硫酸;发烟硫酸**					**Sulphuric acid; oleum**
1603	2807.0000	硫酸;发烟硫酸	5.5∆1	0 澳AU,冰岛IS,东盟AS,哥CR,秘鲁PE,新西兰NZ,智利CL 2.2 瑞士CH 3.3 韩国KR 5 巴PK	0 受惠国$_1$LD$_1$	35	Sulphuric acid; oleum
	28.08	**硝酸;磺硝酸**					**Nitric acid; sulphonitric acids**

序号 No.	税则号列 Tariff Line	中文货品名称 Article Description in Chinese	最惠国税率 MFN(%)	协定税率 Agreement(%)	特惠税率 SP(%)	普通税率 Gen(%)	英文货品名称 Article Description
1604	2808.0000	硝酸;磺硝酸	5.5	0 澳AU,冰岛IS,东盟AS,哥CR,秘鲁PE,新西兰NZ,智利CL 2.2 瑞士CH 3.3 韩国KR 5 巴PK	0 受惠国$_1$LD$_1$	40	Nitric acid; sulphonitric acids
	28.09	**五氧化二磷;磷酸;多磷酸,不论是否已有化学定义:**					**Diphosphorus pentaoxide; phosphoric acid; polyphosphoric acids, whether or not chemically defined:**
1605	2809.1000	-五氧化二磷	1	0 澳AU,巴PK,冰岛IS,东盟AS,哥CR,韩国KR,秘鲁PE,瑞士CH,新西兰NZ,智利CL	0 受惠国$_1$LD$_1$	8	-Diphosphorus pentaoxide
		-磷酸及多磷酸:					-Phosphoric acid and polyphosphoric acids:
		---磷酸及偏磷酸、焦磷酸:					---Phosphoric acid, metaphosphoric acid and pyrophosphoric acid:
1606	2809.2011	----食品级磷酸	1	0 澳AU,巴PK,冰岛IS,东盟AS,哥CR,韩国KR,秘鲁PE,瑞士CH,新西兰NZ,智利CL	0 受惠国$_1$LD$_1$	8	----Phosphoric acid, food grade
1607	2809.2019	----其他	1	0 澳AU,巴PK,冰岛IS,东盟AS,哥CR,秘鲁PE,瑞士CH,新西兰NZ,智利CL 0.8 韩国KR	0 受惠国$_1$LD$_1$	8	----Other
1608	2809.2090	---其他	5.5	0 澳AU,冰岛IS,东盟AS,哥CR,秘鲁PE,新西兰NZ,智利CL 2.2 瑞士CH 3.3 韩国KR 5 巴PK	0 受惠国$_1$LD$_1$	35	---Other
	28.10	**硼的氧化物;硼酸:**					**Oxides of boron; boric acids:**
1609	2810.0010	---硼的氧化物	5.5	0 澳AU,巴PK,冰岛IS,东盟AS,哥CR,新西兰NZ,智利CL 1.6 秘鲁PE 2.2 瑞士CH 3.3 韩国KR	0 受惠国$_1$LD$_1$	30	---Oxides of boron
1610	2810.0020	---硼酸	5.5	0 澳AU,巴PK,冰岛IS,东盟AS,哥CR,新西兰NZ,智利CL 1.6 秘鲁PE 2.2 瑞士CH 3.3 韩国KR	0 受惠国$_1$LD$_1$	30	---Boric acids
	28.11	**其他无机酸及非金属无机氧化物:**					**Other inorganic acids and other inorganic oxygen compounds of non-metals:**
		-其他无机酸:					-Other inorganic acids:
1611	2811.1100	--氟化氢(氢氟酸)	5.5	0 澳AU,巴PK,冰岛IS,东盟AS,哥CR,秘鲁PE,新西兰NZ,智利CL 2.2 瑞士CH 3.3 韩国KR	0 受惠国LD	35	--Hydrofluoric acid
		--其他:					--Other:
1612	2811.1910	---氢氰酸	5.5	0 澳AU,巴PK,冰岛IS,东盟AS,哥CR,秘鲁PE,新西兰NZ,智利CL 2.2 瑞士CH 3.3 韩国KR	0 受惠国LD	35	---Hydrocyanic acid

序号 No.	税则号列 Tariff Line	中文货品名称 Article Description in Chinese	最惠国税率 MFN(%)	协定税率 Agreement(%)	特惠税率 SP(%)	普通税率 Gen(%)	英文货品名称 Article Description
1613	2811.1920	---硒化氢	5.5	0 澳AU,冰岛IS,东盟AS,哥CR,秘鲁PE,新西兰NZ,智利CL 2.2 瑞士CH 4.4 韩国KR 5 巴PK	0 受惠国LD	35	---Hydrogen selenide
1614	2811.1990	---其他	5.5	0 澳AU,冰岛IS,东盟AS,哥CR,秘鲁PE,新西兰NZ,智利CL 2.2 瑞士CH 4.4 韩国KR 5 巴PK	0 受惠国LD	35	---Other
		-其他非金属无机氧化物:					-Other inorganic oxygen compounds of non-metals:
1615	2811.2100	--二氧化碳	5.5	0 澳AU,冰岛IS,东盟AS,哥CR,秘鲁PE,香港HK,新西兰NZ,智利CL 2.2 瑞士CH 3.3 韩国KR 5 巴PK	0 受惠国LD	30	--Carbon dioxide
		--二氧化硅:					--Silicon dioxide:
1616	2811.2210	---硅胶	5.5	0 澳AU,澳门MO,冰岛IS,东盟AS,哥CR,秘鲁PE,新西兰NZ,智利CL 2.2 瑞士CH 3.3 韩国KR 5 巴PK	0 受惠国LD	30	---Silica gel
1617	2811.2290	---其他	5.5	0 澳AU,澳门MO,冰岛IS,东盟AS,哥CR,秘鲁PE,新西兰NZ,智利CL 2.2 瑞士CH 3.3 韩国KR 5 巴PK	0 受惠国LD	30	---Other
1618	2811.2900	--其他	5.5	0 澳AU,冰岛IS,东盟AS,哥CR,秘鲁PE,香港HK,新西兰NZ,智利CL 2.2 瑞士CH 3.3 韩国KR 5 巴PK	0 受惠国LD	30	--Other
		第三分章非金属卤化物及硫化物					III. HALOGEN OR SULPHUR COMPOUNDS OF NON-METALS
	28.12	**非金属卤化物及卤氧化物:**					**Halides and halide oxides of non-metals:**
		-氯化物及氯氧化物:					-Chlorides and chloride oxides:
1619	2812.1010	---氯化亚砜	5.5Δ2	0 澳AU,冰岛IS,东盟AS,哥CR,韩国KR,秘鲁PE,新西兰NZ,智利CL 2.2 瑞士CH 5 巴PK	0 受惠国$_1$LD$_1$	30	---Sulphoxide chloride
1620	2812.1020	---氧氯化磷(磷酰氯;三氯氧磷)	5.5	0 澳AU,冰岛IS,东盟AS,哥CR,秘鲁PE,新西兰NZ,智利CL 2.2 瑞士CH 3.3 韩国KR 5 巴PK	0 受惠国$_1$LD$_1$	30	---Phosphorus oxychloride (phosphoryl monochloride, phosphorus oxytrichloride)
1621	2812.1030	---碳酰二氯(光气)	5.5	0 澳AU,巴PK,冰岛IS,东盟AS,哥CR,秘鲁PE,新西兰NZ,智利CL 2.2 瑞士CH 3.3 韩国KR	0 受惠国$_1$LD$_1$	30	---Carbonyl dichloride (phosgene)
		---非金属氯化物:					---Other chlorides of non-metals:

序号 No.	税则号列 Tariff Line	中文货品名称 Article Description in Chinese	最惠国税率 MFN(%)	协定税率 Agreement(%)	特惠税率 SP(%)	普通税率 Gen(%)	英文货品名称 Article Description
1622	2812.1041	----一氯化硫（氯化硫）	5.5	0 澳AU,巴PK,冰岛IS,东盟AS,哥CR,秘鲁PE,新西兰NZ,智利CL 2.2 瑞士CH 3.3 韩国KR	0 受惠国$_1$LD$_1$	30	----Sulfur monochloride
1623	2812.1042	----二氯化硫	5.5	0 澳AU,巴PK,冰岛IS,东盟AS,哥CR,秘鲁PE,新西兰NZ,智利CL 2.2 瑞士CH 3.3 韩国KR	0 受惠国$_1$LD$_1$	30	----Sulfur dichloride
1624	2812.1043	----三氯化磷	5.5	0 澳AU,巴PK,冰岛IS,东盟AS,哥CR,秘鲁PE,新西兰NZ,智利CL 2.2 瑞士CH 3.3 韩国KR	0 受惠国$_1$LD$_1$	30	----Phosphorus trichloride
1625	2812.1044	----三氯化砷	5.5	0 澳AU,巴PK,冰岛IS,东盟AS,哥CR,秘鲁PE,新西兰NZ,智利CL 2.2 瑞士CH 3.3 韩国KR	0 受惠国$_1$LD$_1$	30	----Arsenic trichloride
1626	2812.1045	----五氯化磷	5.5	0 澳AU,巴PK,冰岛IS,东盟AS,哥CR,秘鲁PE,新西兰NZ,智利CL 2.2 瑞士CH 3.3 韩国KR	0 受惠国$_1$LD$_1$	30	----Phosphorus pentachloride
1627	2812.1049	----其他	5.5	0 澳AU,冰岛IS,东盟AS,哥CR,秘鲁PE,新西兰NZ,智利CL 2.2 瑞士CH 3.3 韩国KR 5 巴PK	0 受惠国$_1$LD$_1$	30	----Other
1628	2812.1090	---其他	5.5	0 澳AU,巴PK,冰岛IS,东盟AS,哥CR,秘鲁PE,新西兰NZ,智利CL 2.2 瑞士CH 3.3 韩国KR	0 受惠国$_1$LD$_1$	30	---Other
		-其他:					-Other:
		---氟化物及氟氧化物:					---Fluorid and oxyfluoride:
1629	2812.9011	----三氟化氮	5.5	0 澳AU,巴PK,冰岛IS,东盟AS,哥CR,秘鲁PE,新西兰NZ,智利CL 2.2 瑞士CH 4.7 韩国KR	0 受惠国$_1$LD$_1$	30	----Nitrogen trifluoride
1630	2812.9019	----其他	5.5	0 澳AU,巴PK,冰岛IS,东盟AS,哥CR,秘鲁PE,新西兰NZ,智利CL 2.2 瑞士CH 3.3 韩国KR	0 受惠国$_1$LD$_1$	30	----Other
1631	2812.9090	---其他	5.5	0 澳AU,巴PK,冰岛IS,东盟AS,哥CR,秘鲁PE,新西兰NZ,智利CL 2.2 瑞士CH 4.4 韩国KR	0 受惠国$_1$LD$_1$	30	---Other
	28.13	**非金属硫化物;商品三硫化二磷:**					**Sulphides of non-metals; commercial phosphorus trisulphide:**
1632	2813.1000	-二硫化碳	5.5	0 澳AU,巴PK,冰岛IS,东盟AS,哥CR,秘鲁PE,香港HK,新西兰NZ,智利CL 2.2 瑞士CH 3.3 韩国KR	0 受惠国$_1$LD$_1$	30	-Carbon disulphide

序号 No.	税则号列 Tariff Line	中文货品名称 Article Description in Chinese	最惠国税率 MFN(%)	协定税率 Agreement(%)	特惠税率 SP(%)	普通税率 Gen(%)	英文货品名称 Article Description
1633	2813.9000	-其他	5.5	0 澳AU,巴PK,冰岛IS,东盟AS,哥CR,秘鲁PE,新西兰NZ,智利CL 2.2 瑞士CH 3.3 韩国KR	0 受惠国$_1$LD$_1$	30	-Other
		第四分章无机碱和金属氧化物、氢氧化物及过氧化物					IV. INORGANIC BASES AND OXIDES, HYDROXIDES AND PEROXIDES OF METALS
	28.14	**氨及氨水:**					**Ammonia, anhydrous or in aqueous solution:**
1634	2814.1000	-氨	5.5Δ0	0 澳AU,巴PK,冰岛IS,东盟AS,哥CR,秘鲁PE,新西兰NZ,智利CL 2.2 瑞士CH 3.3 韩国KR	0 受惠国LD	35	-Anhydrous ammonia
1635	2814.2000	-氨水	5.5Δ0	0 澳AU,巴PK,冰岛IS,东盟AS,哥CR,韩国KR,秘鲁PE,新西兰NZ,智利CL 2.2 瑞士CH	0 受惠国LD	35	-Ammonia in aqueous solution
	28.15	**氢氧化钠(烧碱);氢氧化钾(苛性钾);过氧化钠及过氧化钾:**					**Sodium hydroxide (caustic soda) ; potassium hydroxide (caustic potash) ; peroxides of sodium or potassium:**
		-氢氧化钠(烧碱):					-Sodium hydroxide (caustic soda) :
1636	2815.1100	--固体	10	0 冰岛IS,哥CR,秘鲁PE,新西兰NZ,智利CL 4 瑞士CH 6 澳AU 7 巴PK,亚太AP 8 韩国KR	0 受惠国LD	35	--Solid
1637	2815.1200	--水溶液(氢氧化钠浓溶液及液体烧碱)	8	0 冰岛IS,哥CR,秘鲁PE,新西兰NZ,智利CL 3.2 瑞士CH 4.8 澳AU 5.6 巴PK,亚太AP 6.4 韩国KR	0 受惠国LD	35	--In aqueous solution (soda lye or liquid soda)
1638	2815.2000	-氢氧化钾(苛性钾)	5.5	0 澳AU,冰岛IS,东盟AS,哥CR,秘鲁PE,新西兰NZ,智利CL 2.2 瑞士CH 3.3 韩国KR 5 巴PK	0 受惠国LD	30	-Potassium hydroxide (caustic potash)
1639	2815.3000	-过氧化钠及过氧化钾	5.5	0 澳AU,巴PK,冰岛IS,东盟AS,哥CR,秘鲁PE,新西兰NZ,智利CL 2.2 瑞士CH 3.3 韩国KR	0 受惠国LD	30	-Peroxides of sodium or potassium
	28.16	**氢氧化镁及过氧化镁;锶或钡的氧化物、氢氧化物及过氧化物:**					**Hydroxide and peroxide of magnesium; oxides, hydroxides and peroxides, of strontium or barium:**
1640	2816.1000	-氢氧化镁及过氧化镁	5.5	0 澳AU,冰岛IS,东盟AS,哥CR,秘鲁PE,新西兰NZ,智利CL 2.2 瑞士CH 4.4 韩国KR 5 巴PK	0 受惠国$_1$LD$_1$	30	-Hydroxide and peroxide of magnesium
1641	2816.4000	-锶或钡的氧化物、氢氧化物及过氧化物	5.5Δ2	0 澳AU,冰岛IS,东盟AS,哥CR,韩国KR,秘鲁PE,新西兰NZ,智利CL 2.2 瑞士CH 5 巴PK	0 受惠国$_1$LD$_1$	30	-Oxides, hydroxides and peroxides, of strontium or barium
	28.17	**氧化锌及过氧化锌:**					**Zinc oxide; zinc peroxide:**

序号 No.	税则号列 Tariff Line	中文货品名称 Article Description in Chinese	最惠国税率 MFN(%)	协定税率 Agreement(%)	特惠税率 SP(%)	普通税率 Gen(%)	英文货品名称 Article Description
1642	2817.0010	---氧化锌	5.5	0 澳AU,巴PK,冰岛IS,东盟AS,哥CR,新西兰NZ,智利CL 0.7 秘鲁PE 2.2 瑞士CH 3.3 韩国KR	0 受惠国LD	40	---Zinc oxide
1643	2817.0090	---过氧化锌	5.5	0 澳AU,巴PK,冰岛IS,东盟AS,哥CR,新西兰NZ,智利CL 1.6 秘鲁PE 2.2 瑞士CH 3.3 韩国KR	0 受惠国LD	30	---Zinc peroxide
	28.18	**人造刚玉，不论是否已有化学定义;氧化铝;氢氧化铝:**					**Artificial corundum, whether or not chemically defined; aluminium oxide; aluminium hydroxide:**
		-人造刚玉，不论是否已有化学定义:					-Artificial corundum, whether or not chemically defined:
1644	2818.1010	---棕刚玉	5.5	0 澳AU,巴PK,冰岛IS,东盟AS,哥CR,秘鲁PE,新西兰NZ,智利CL 2.2 瑞士CH 4.4 韩国KR	0 受惠国LD	20	---Brown corundum
1645	2818.1090	---其他	5.5	0 澳AU,巴PK,冰岛IS,东盟AS,哥CR,秘鲁PE,新西兰NZ,智利CL 2.2 瑞士CH 3.3 韩国KR	0 受惠国LD	20	---Other
1646	2818.2000	-氧化铝，但人造刚玉除外	8Δ0	0 澳AU,冰岛IS,东盟AS,哥CR,秘鲁PE,新加坡SG,新西兰NZ,智利CL 3.2 瑞士CH 4.8 韩国KR 5 巴PK	0 受惠国LD	30	-Aluminium oxide, other than artificial corundum
1647	2818.3000	-氢氧化铝	5.5	0 澳AU,巴PK,冰岛IS,东盟AS,哥CR,秘鲁PE,新西兰NZ,智利CL 2.2 瑞士CH 3.3 韩国KR	0 受惠国LD	30	-Aluminium hydroxide
	28.19	**铬的氧化物及氢氧化物:**					**Chromium oxides and hydroxides:**
1648	2819.1000	-三氧化铬	5.5	0 澳AU,巴PK,冰岛IS,东盟AS,哥CR,秘鲁PE,新西兰NZ,智利CL 2.2 瑞士CH 4.4 韩国KR	0 受惠国LD	20	-Chromium trioxide
1649	2819.9000	-其他	5.5	0 澳AU,巴PK,冰岛IS,东盟AS,哥CR,秘鲁PE,新西兰NZ,智利CL 2.2 瑞士CH 3.3 韩国KR	0 受惠国LD	30	-Other
	28.20	**锰的氧化物:**					**Manganese oxide:**
1650	2820.1000	-二氧化锰	5.5	0 澳AU,巴PK,冰岛IS,东盟AS,哥CR,秘鲁PE,新西兰NZ,智利CL 2.2 瑞士CH 3.3 韩国KR	0 受惠国LD	40	-Manganese dioxide
1651	2820.9000	-其他	5.5	0 澳AU,巴PK,冰岛IS,东盟AS,哥CR,秘鲁PE,新西兰NZ,智利CL 2.2 瑞士CH 3.3 韩国KR	0 受惠国LD	30	-Other
	28.21	**铁的氧化物及氢氧化物;土色料，按重量计三氧化二铁含量在70%及以上:**					**Iron oxides and hydroxides; earth colours containing 70% or more by weight of combined iron evaluated as Fe_2O_3:**

序号 No.	税则号列 Tariff Line	中文货品名称 Article Description in Chinese	最惠国税率 MFN(%)	协定税率 Agreement(%)	特惠税率 SP(%)	普通税率 Gen(%)	英文货品名称 Article Description
1652	2821.1000	-铁的氧化物及氢氧化物	5.5	0 澳AU,巴PK,冰岛IS,东盟AS,哥CR,秘鲁PE,新西兰NZ,智利CL 2.2 瑞士CH 4.7 韩国KR	0 受惠国LD	30	-Iron oxides and hydroxides
1653	2821.2000	-土色料	5.5	0 澳AU,巴PK,冰岛IS,东盟AS,哥CR,秘鲁PE,新西兰NZ,智利CL 2.2 瑞士CH 4.4 韩国KR	0 受惠国LD	45	-Earth colours
	28.22	**钴的氧化物及氢氧化物;商品氧化钴:**					**Cobalt oxides and hydroxides; commercial cobalt oxides:**
1654	2822.0010	---四氧化三钴	5.5Δ2	0 澳AU,巴PK,冰岛IS,东盟AS,哥CR,韩国KR,秘鲁PE,新西兰NZ,智利CL 2.2 瑞士CH	0 受惠国$_1$LD$_1$	30	---Cobalt tetroxide
1655	2822.0090	---其他	5.5Δ2	0 澳AU,巴PK,冰岛IS,东盟AS,哥CR,秘鲁PE,新西兰NZ,智利CL 2.2 瑞士CH 3.3 韩国KR	0 受惠国$_1$LD$_1$	30	---Other
	28.23	**钛的氧化物**					**Titanium oxides**
1656	2823.0000	钛的氧化物	5.5	0 澳AU,巴PK,冰岛IS,东盟AS,哥CR,秘鲁PE,新西兰NZ,智利CL 2.2 瑞士CH 3.3 韩国KR	0 受惠国$_1$LD$_1$	30	Titanium oxides
	28.24	**铅的氧化物;铅丹及铅橙:**					**Lead oxides; red lead and orange lead:**
1657	2824.1000	-一氧化铅（铅黄、黄丹）	5.5	0 澳AU,巴PK,冰岛IS,东盟AS,哥CR,秘鲁PE,新西兰NZ,智利CL 2.2 瑞士CH 3.3 韩国KR	0 受惠国$_1$LD$_1$	30	-Lead monoxide (litharge, massicot)
		-其他:					-Other:
1658	2824.9010	---铅丹及铅橙	5.5	0 澳AU,巴PK,冰岛IS,东盟AS,哥CR,秘鲁PE,新西兰NZ,智利CL 2.2 瑞士CH 3.3 韩国KR	0 受惠国$_1$LD$_1$	45	---Red lead and orange lead
1659	2824.9090	---其他	5.5	0 澳AU,巴PK,冰岛IS,东盟AS,哥CR,秘鲁PE,新西兰NZ,智利CL 2.2 瑞士CH 3.3 韩国KR	0 受惠国$_1$LD$_1$	30	---Other
	28.25	**肼（联氨）、胲（羟胺）及其无机盐;其他无机碱;其他金属氧化物、氢氧化物及过氧化物:**					**Hydrazine and hydroxylamine and their inorganic salts; other inorganic bases; other metal oxides, hydroxides and peroxides:**
		-肼（联氨）、胲（羟胺）及其无机盐:					-Hydrazine and hydroxylamine and their inorganic salts:
1660	2825.1010	---水合肼	5.5	0 澳AU,巴PK,冰岛IS,东盟AS,哥CR,秘鲁PE,新西兰NZ,智利CL 2.2 瑞士CH 4.4 韩国KR	0 受惠国LD	30	---Hydrazine hydrate
1661	2825.1020	---硫酸羟胺	5.5	0 澳AU,冰岛IS,东盟AS,哥CR,秘鲁PE,新西兰NZ,智利CL 2.2 瑞士CH 4.4 韩国KR 5 巴PK	0 受惠国LD	30	---Hydroxyamine sulfate

序号 No.	税则号列 Tariff Line	中文货品名称 Article Description in Chinese	最惠国税率 MFN(%)	协定税率 Agreement(%)	特惠税率 SP(%)	普通税率 Gen(%)	英文货品名称 Article Description
1662	2825.1090	---其他	5.5	0 澳AU,冰岛IS,东盟AS,哥CR,秘鲁PE,新西兰NZ,智利CL 2.2 瑞士CH 3.3 韩国KR 5 巴PK	0 受惠国LD	30	---Other
		-锂的氧化物及氢氧化物:					-Lithium oxide and hydroxide:
1663	2825.2010	---氢氧化锂	5.5	0 澳AU,巴PK,冰岛IS,东盟AS,哥CR,秘鲁PE,新西兰NZ,智利CL 2.2 瑞士CH 3.3 韩国KR	0 受惠国LD	30	---Lithium hydroxide
1664	2825.2090	---其他	5.5	0 澳AU,巴PK,冰岛IS,东盟AS,哥CR,秘鲁PE,新西兰NZ,智利CL 2.2 瑞士CH 3.3 韩国KR	0 受惠国LD	30	---Other
		-钒的氧化物及氢氧化物:					-Vanadium oxides and hydroxides:
1665	2825.3010	---五氧化二钒	5.5	0 澳AU,巴PK,冰岛IS,东盟AS,哥CR,秘鲁PE,新西兰NZ,智利CL 2.2 瑞士CH 4.4 韩国KR	0 受惠国LD	30	---Divanadium pentaoxide
1666	2825.3090	---其他	5.5	0 澳AU,巴PK,冰岛IS,东盟AS,哥CR,秘鲁PE,新西兰NZ,智利CL 2.2 瑞士CH 3.3 韩国KR	0 受惠国LD	30	---Other
1667	2825.4000	-镍的氧化物及氢氧化物	5.5Δ2	0 澳AU,巴PK,冰岛IS,东盟AS,哥CR,秘鲁PE,新西兰NZ,智利CL 2.2 瑞士CH 3.3 韩国KR	0 受惠国LD	30	-Nickel oxides and hydroxides
1668	2825.5000	-铜的氧化物及氢氧化物	5.5	0 澳AU,巴PK,冰岛IS,东盟AS,哥CR,秘鲁PE,新西兰NZ,智利CL 2.2 瑞士CH 3.3 韩国KR	0 受惠国LD	30	-Copper oxides and hydroxides
1669	2825.6000	-锗的氧化物及二氧化锆	5.5	0 澳AU,巴PK,冰岛IS,东盟AS,哥CR,秘鲁PE,新西兰NZ,智利CL 2.2 瑞士CH 3.3 韩国KR	0 受惠国LD	30	-Germanium oxides and zirconium dioxide
1670	2825.7000	-钼的氧化物及氢氧化物	5.5	0 澳AU,巴PK,冰岛IS,东盟AS,哥CR,新西兰NZ,智利CL 2.2 瑞士CH 3.3 韩国KR	0 受惠国LD	30	-Molybdenum oxides and hydroxides
1671	2825.8000	-锑的氧化物	5.5	0 澳AU,巴PK,冰岛IS,东盟AS,哥CR,秘鲁PE,新西兰NZ,智利CL 2.2 瑞士CH 3.3 韩国KR	0 受惠国LD	30	-Antimony oxides
		-其他:					-Other:
		---钨的氧化物及氢氧化物:					---Tungsten oxides and hydroxides:
1672	2825.9011	----钨酸	5.5	0 澳AU,巴PK,冰岛IS,东盟AS,哥CR,秘鲁PE,新西兰NZ,智利CL 2.2 瑞士CH 3.3 韩国KR	0 受惠国LD	30	----Tungstic acid

序号 No.	税则号列 Tariff Line	中文货品名称 Article Description in Chinese	最惠国税率 MFN(%)	协定税率 Agreement(%)	特惠税率 SP(%)	普通税率 Gen(%)	英文货品名称 Article Description
1673	2825.9012	----三氧化钨	5.5	0 澳AU,巴PK,冰岛IS,东盟AS,哥CR,秘鲁PE,新西兰NZ,智利CL 2.2 瑞士CH 3.3 韩国KR	0 受惠国LD	30	----Tungstic oxide
1674	2825.9019	----其他	5.5	0 澳AU,巴PK,冰岛IS,东盟AS,哥CR,秘鲁PE,新西兰NZ,智利CL 2.2 瑞士CH 3.3 韩国KR	0 受惠国LD	30	----Other
		---铋的氧化物及氢氧化物:					---Bismuth oxides and hydroxides:
1675	2825.9021	----三氧化二铋	5.5	0 澳AU,巴PK,冰岛IS,东盟AS,哥CR,秘鲁PE,新西兰NZ,智利CL 2.2 瑞士CH 3.3 韩国KR	0 受惠国LD	30	----Bismuth trioxide
1676	2825.9029	----其他	5.5	0 澳AU,巴PK,冰岛IS,东盟AS,哥CR,秘鲁PE,新西兰NZ,智利CL 2.2 瑞士CH 3.3 韩国KR	0 受惠国LD	30	----Other
		---锡的氧化物及氢氧化物:					---Tin oxides and hydroxides:
1677	2825.9031	----二氧化锡	5.5	0 澳AU,巴PK,冰岛IS,东盟AS,哥CR,秘鲁PE,新西兰NZ,智利CL 2.2 瑞士CH 3.3 韩国KR	0 受惠国LD	30	----Tin dioxide
1678	2825.9039	----其他	5.5	0 澳AU,巴PK,冰岛IS,东盟AS,哥CR,秘鲁PE,新西兰NZ,智利CL 2.2 瑞士CH 3.3 韩国KR	0 受惠国LD	30	----Other
		---铌的氧化物及氢氧化物:					---Niobium oxide and hydroxide:
1679	2825.9041	----一氧化铌	5.5	0 澳AU,巴PK,冰岛IS,东盟AS,哥CR,秘鲁PE,新西兰NZ,智利CL 2.2 瑞士CH 3.3 韩国KR	0 受惠国LD	30	----Columbium monoxide
1680	2825.9049	----其他	5.5	0 澳AU,巴PK,冰岛IS,东盟AS,哥CR,秘鲁PE,新西兰NZ,智利CL 2.2 瑞士CH 3.3 韩国KR	0 受惠国LD	30	----Other
1681	2825.9090	---其他	5.5	0 澳AU,巴PK,冰岛IS,东盟AS,哥CR,秘鲁PE,新西兰NZ,智利CL 2.2 瑞士CH 3.3 韩国KR	0 受惠国LD	30	---Other
		第五分章　无机酸盐、无机过氧酸盐及金属酸盐、金属过氧酸盐					V. SALTS AND PEROXYSALTS, OFINORGANIC ACIDS AND METALS
	28.26	**氟化物;氟硅酸盐、氟铝酸盐及其他氟络盐:**					**Fluorides; fluorosilicates, fluoroaluminates and other complex fluorine salts:**
		-氟化物:					-Fluorides:
		--氟化铝:					--Of aluminium:
1682	2826.1210	---无水氟化铝	5.5	0 澳AU,巴PK,冰岛IS,东盟AS,哥CR,秘鲁PE,新西兰NZ,智利CL 2.2 瑞士CH 3.3 韩国KR	0 受惠国LD	30	---Anhydrous fluorides of aluminium

序号 No.	税则号列 Tariff Line	中文货品名称 Article Description in Chinese	最惠国税率 MFN(%)	协定税率 Agreement(%)	特惠税率 SP(%)	普通税率 Gen(%)	英文货品名称 Article Description
1683	2826.1290	---其他	5.5	0 澳AU,巴PK,冰岛IS,东盟AS,哥CR,秘鲁PE,新西兰NZ,智利CL 2.2 瑞士CH 3.3 韩国KR	0 受惠国LD	30	---Other
		--其他:					--Other:
1684	2826.1910	---铵的氟化物	5.5	0 澳AU,巴PK,冰岛IS,东盟AS,哥CR,秘鲁PE,新西兰NZ,智利CL 2.2 瑞士CH 3.3 韩国KR	0 受惠国LD	30	---Of ammonium
1685	2826.1920	---钠的氟化物	5.5	0 澳AU,巴PK,冰岛IS,东盟AS,哥CR,秘鲁PE,新西兰NZ,智利CL 2.2 瑞士CH 3.3 韩国KR	0 受惠国LD	30	---Of sodium
1686	2826.1990	---其他	5.5	0 澳AU,冰岛IS,东盟AS,哥CR,秘鲁PE,新西兰NZ,智利CL 2.2 瑞士CH 3.3 韩国KR 5 巴PK	0 受惠国LD	30	---Other
1687	2826.3000	-六氟铝酸钠(人造冰晶石)	5.5	0 澳AU,巴PK,冰岛IS,东盟AS,哥CR,秘鲁PE,新西兰NZ,智利CL 2.2 瑞士CH 3.3 韩国KR	0 受惠国LD	30	-Sodium hexafluoroaluminate (synthetic cryolite)
		-其他:					-Other:
1688	2826.9010	---氟硅酸盐	5.5	0 澳AU,冰岛IS,东盟AS,哥CR,秘鲁PE,香港HK,新西兰NZ,智利CL 2.2 瑞士CH 4.4 韩国KR 5 巴PK	0 受惠国LD	30	---Fluorosilicates
1689	2826.9020	---六氟磷酸锂	5.5	0 澳AU,冰岛IS,东盟AS,哥CR,秘鲁PE,新西兰NZ,智利CL 2.2 瑞士CH 4.7 韩国KR 5 巴PK	0 受惠国LD	30	---Lithium hexafluorophate
1690	2826.9090	---其他	5.5	0 澳AU,冰岛IS,东盟AS,哥CR,秘鲁PE,新西兰NZ,智利CL 2.2 瑞士CH 4.7 韩国KR 5 巴PK	0 受惠国LD	30	---Other
	28.27	**氯化物、氯氧化物及氢氧基氯化物;溴化物及溴氧化物;碘化物及碘氧化物:**					**Chlorides, chloride oxides and chloride hydroxides; bromides and bromide oxides; iodides and iodide oxides:**
		-氯化铵:					-Ammonium chloride:
1691	2827.1010	---肥料用	4	0 澳AU,巴PK,冰岛IS,东盟AS,哥CR,韩国KR,秘鲁PE,瑞士CH,新西兰NZ,智利CL	0 受惠国LD	11	---For use as fertilizer
1692	2827.1090	---其他	5.5	0 澳AU,冰岛IS,东盟AS,哥CR,秘鲁PE,新西兰NZ,智利CL 2.2 瑞士CH 3.3 韩国KR 5 巴PK	0 受惠国LD	30	---Other

序号 No.	税则号列 Tariff Line	中文货品名称 Article Description in Chinese	最惠国税率 MFN(%)	协定税率 Agreement(%)	特惠税率 SP(%)	普通税率 Gen(%)	英文货品名称 Article Description
1693	2827.2000	-氯化钙	5.5	0 澳AU,冰岛IS,东盟AS,哥CR,秘鲁PE,新西兰NZ,智利CL 2.2 瑞士CH 3.3 韩国KR 5 巴PK	0 受惠国LD	50	-Calcium chloride
		-其他氯化物：					-Other chlorides:
1694	2827.3100	--氯化镁	5.5	0 澳AU,冰岛IS,东盟AS,哥CR,秘鲁PE,新西兰NZ,智利CL 2.2 瑞士CH 4.4 韩国KR 5 巴PK	0 受惠国LD	30	--Of magnesium
1695	2827.3200	--氯化铝	5.5	0 澳AU,冰岛IS,东盟AS,哥CR,秘鲁PE,新西兰NZ,智利CL 2.2 瑞士CH 3.3 韩国KR 5 巴PK	0 受惠国LD	30	--Of aluminium
1696	2827.3500	--氯化镍	5.5	0 澳AU,冰岛IS,东盟AS,哥CR,秘鲁PE,新西兰NZ,智利CL 2.2 瑞士CH 3.3 韩国KR 5 巴PK	0 受惠国LD	30	--Of nickel
		--其他：					--Other:
1697	2827.3910	---氯化锂	5.5	0 澳AU,巴PK,冰岛IS,东盟AS,哥CR,新西兰NZ,智利CL 2.2 瑞士CH 3.3 韩国KR 4.4 亚太AP	0 受惠国LD	30	---Lithium chloride
1698	2827.3920	---氯化钡	5.5	0 澳AU,巴PK,冰岛IS,东盟AS,哥CR,新西兰NZ,智利CL 3.3 韩国KR 4.4 亚太AP	0 受惠国LD	30	---Barium chloride
1699	2827.3930	---氯化钴	5.5	0 澳AU,巴PK,冰岛IS,东盟AS,哥CR,秘鲁PE,新西兰NZ,智利CL 2.2 瑞士CH 3.3 韩国KR 4.4 亚太AP	0 受惠国LD	30	---Cobalt chloride
1700	2827.3990	---其他	5.5	0 澳AU,巴PK,冰岛IS,东盟AS,哥CR,新西兰NZ,智利CL 2.2 瑞士CH 3.3 韩国KR 4.4 亚太AP	0 受惠国LD	30	---Other
		-氯氧化物及氢氧基氯化物：					-Chloride oxides and chloride hydroxides:
1701	2827.4100	--铜的氯氧化物及氢氧基氯化物	5.5	0 澳AU,巴PK,冰岛IS,东盟AS,哥CR,新西兰NZ,智利CL 1.6 秘鲁PE 2.2 瑞士CH 3.3 韩国KR	0 受惠国LD	30	--Of copper
		--其他：					--Other:
1702	2827.4910	---锆的氯氧化物及氢氧基氯化物	5.5	0 澳AU,冰岛IS,东盟AS,哥CR,秘鲁PE,新西兰NZ,智利CL 2.2 瑞士CH 3.3 韩国KR 5 巴PK	0 受惠国LD	30	---Of Zirconium

序号 No.	税则号列 Tariff Line	中文货品名称 Article Description in Chinese	最惠国税率 MFN(%)	协定税率 Agreement(%)	特惠税率 SP(%)	普通税率 Gen(%)	英文货品名称 Article Description
1703	2827.4990	---其他	5.5	0 澳AU,冰岛IS,东盟AS,哥CR,秘鲁PE,新西兰NZ,智利CL 2.2 瑞士CH 3.3 韩国KR 5 巴PK	0 受惠国LD	30	---Other
		-溴化物及溴氧化物:					-Bromides and bromide oxides:
1704	2827.5100	--溴化钠及溴化钾	5.5	0 澳AU,巴PK,冰岛IS,东盟AS,哥CR,秘鲁PE,新西兰NZ,智利CL 2.2 瑞士CH 3.3 韩国KR	0 受惠国LD	30	--Bromides of sodium or of potassium
1705	2827.5900	--其他	5.5	0 澳AU,冰岛IS,东盟AS,哥CR,秘鲁PE,新西兰NZ,智利CL 2.2 瑞士CH 4.4 韩国KR 5 巴PK	0 受惠国LD	30	--Other
1706	2827.6000	-碘化物及碘氧化物	5.5	0 澳AU,冰岛IS,东盟AS,哥CR,新西兰NZ,智利CL 2.2 瑞士CH 3.3 韩国KR 5 巴PK	0 受惠国LD	30	-Iodides and iodide oxides
	28.28	**次氯酸盐;商品次氯酸钙;亚氯酸盐;次溴酸盐:**					**Hypochlorites; commercial calcium hypochlorite; chlorites; hypobromites:**
1707	2828.1000	-商品次氯酸钙及其他钙的次氯酸盐	12	0 冰岛IS,东盟AS,哥CR,秘鲁PE,新加坡SG,新西兰NZ,智利CL 5 巴PK 7.2 澳AU 8.4 瑞士CH,亚太AP 9.6 韩国KR	0 受惠国$_1$LD$_1$	80	-Commercial calcium hypochlorite and other calcium hypochlorites
1708	2828.9000	-其他	5.5	0 澳AU,冰岛IS,东盟AS,哥CR,秘鲁PE,新西兰NZ,智利CL 2.2 瑞士CH 3.3 韩国KR 5 巴PK	0 受惠国$_1$LD$_1$	30	-Other
	28.29	**氯酸盐及高氯酸盐;溴酸盐及过溴酸盐;碘酸盐及高碘酸盐:**					**Chlorates and perchlorates; bromates and perbromates; iodates and periodates:**
		-氯酸盐:					-Chlorates:
1709	2829.1100	--氯酸钠	12	0 冰岛IS,东盟AS,哥CR,秘鲁PE,新加坡SG,新西兰NZ,智利CL 6 巴PK 7.2 澳AU 8.4 瑞士CH 9.6 韩国KR	0 受惠国$_1$LD$_1$	30	--Of sodium
		--其他:					--Other:
1710	2829.1910	---氯酸钾(洋硝)	5.5	0 澳AU,巴PK,冰岛IS,东盟AS,哥CR,秘鲁PE,新西兰NZ,智利CL 2.2 瑞士CH 3.3 韩国KR	0 受惠国$_1$LD$_1$	20	---Potassium chlorate
1711	2829.1990	---其他	5.5	0 澳AU,巴PK,冰岛IS,东盟AS,哥CR,秘鲁PE,新西兰NZ,智利CL 2.2 瑞士CH 3.3 韩国KR	0 受惠国$_1$LD$_1$	30	---Other

序号 No.	税则号列 Tariff Line	中文货品名称 Article Description in Chinese	最惠国税率 MFN(%)	协定税率 Agreement(%)	特惠税率 SP(%)	普通税率 Gen(%)	英文货品名称 Article Description
1712	2829.9000	-其他	5.5	0 澳AU,冰岛IS,东盟AS,哥CR,秘鲁PE,新西兰NZ,智利CL 2.2 瑞士CH 3.3 韩国KR 5 巴PK	0 受惠国$_1$LD$_1$	30	-Other
	28.30	**硫化物;多硫化物，无论是否已有化学定义:**					**Sulphides; polysulphides, whether or not chemically defined:**
		-钠的硫化物:					-Sodium sulphides:
1713	2830.1010	---硫化钠	5.5	0 澳AU,冰岛IS,东盟AS,哥CR,秘鲁PE,新西兰NZ,智利CL 2.2 瑞士CH 3.3 韩国KR 5 巴PK	0 受惠国LD	40	---Sodium sulphide
1714	2830.1090	---其他	5.5	0 澳AU,巴PK,冰岛IS,东盟AS,哥CR,秘鲁PE,新西兰NZ,智利CL 2.2 瑞士CH 3.3 韩国KR	0 受惠国LD	30	---Other
		-其他:					-Other:
1715	2830.9020	---硫化锑	5.5	0 澳AU,巴PK,冰岛IS,东盟AS,哥CR,秘鲁PE,新西兰NZ,智利CL 2.2 瑞士CH 3.3 韩国KR	0 受惠国LD	45	---Antimony sulphide
1716	2830.9030	---硫化钴	5.5	0 澳AU,巴PK,冰岛IS,东盟AS,哥CR,秘鲁PE,新西兰NZ,智利CL 2.2 瑞士CH 4.4 韩国KR	0 受惠国LD	30	---Cobalt sulphide
1717	2830.9090	---其他	5.5	0 澳AU,冰岛IS,东盟AS,哥CR,秘鲁PE,新西兰NZ,智利CL 2.2 瑞士CH 3.3 韩国KR 5 巴PK	0 受惠国LD	30	---Other
	28.31	**连二亚硫酸盐及次硫酸盐:**					**Dithionites and sulphoxylates:**
		-钠的连二亚硫酸盐及次硫酸盐:					-Of sodium:
1718	2831.1010	---钠的连亚二硫酸盐	5.5	0 澳AU,冰岛IS,东盟AS,哥CR,秘鲁PE,新西兰NZ,智利CL 2.2 瑞士CH 3.3 韩国KR 5 巴PK	0 受惠国$_1$LD$_1$	30	---Dithionites
1719	2831.1020	---钠的次硫酸盐	5.5	0 澳AU,冰岛IS,东盟AS,哥CR,秘鲁PE,新西兰NZ,智利CL 2.2 瑞士CH 3.3 韩国KR 5 巴PK	0 受惠国$_1$LD$_1$	30	---Sulphoxylates
1720	2831.9000	-其他	5.5	0 澳AU,冰岛IS,东盟AS,哥CR,秘鲁PE,新西兰NZ,智利CL 2.2 瑞士CH 3.3 韩国KR 5 巴PK	0 受惠国$_1$LD$_1$	30	-Other
	28.32	**亚硫酸盐;硫代硫酸盐:**					**Sulphites; thiosulphates:**

序号 No.	税则号列 Tariff Line	中文货品名称 Article Description in Chinese	最惠国税率 MFN(%)	协定税率 Agreement(%)	特惠税率 SP(%)	普通税率 Gen(%)	英文货品名称 Article Description
1721	2832.1000	-钠的亚硫酸盐	5.5	0 澳AU,冰岛IS,东盟AS,哥CR,秘鲁PE,新西兰NZ,智利CL 2.2 瑞士CH 3.3 韩国KR 5 巴PK	0 受惠国$_1$LD$_1$	30	-Sodium sulphites
1722	2832.2000	-其他亚硫酸盐	5.5	0 澳AU,巴PK,冰岛IS,东盟AS,哥CR,秘鲁PE,新西兰NZ,智利CL 2.2 瑞士CH 3.3 韩国KR	0 受惠国$_1$LD$_1$	30	-Other sulphites
1723	2832.3000	-硫代硫酸盐	5.5	0 澳AU,冰岛IS,东盟AS,哥CR,秘鲁PE,新西兰NZ,智利CL 2.2 瑞士CH 3.3 韩国KR 5 巴PK	0 受惠国$_1$LD$_1$	30	-Thiosulphates
	28.33	**硫酸盐;矾;过硫酸盐:**					**Sulphates; alums; peroxosulphates (persulphates) :**
		-钠的硫酸盐:					-Sodium sulphates:
1724	2833.1100	--硫酸钠	5.5	0 澳AU,冰岛IS,东盟AS,哥CR,韩国KR,秘鲁PE,新西兰NZ,智利CL 3.9 瑞士CH 5 巴PK	0 受惠国$_1$LD$_1$	40	--Disodium sulphate
1725	2833.1900	--其他	5.5	0 澳AU,冰岛IS,东盟AS,哥CR,秘鲁PE,新西兰NZ,智利CL 2.2 瑞士CH 3.3 韩国KR 5 巴PK	0 受惠国$_1$LD$_1$	30	--Other
		-其他硫酸盐:					-Other sulphates:
1726	2833.2100	--硫酸镁	5.5	0 澳AU,冰岛IS,东盟AS,哥CR,秘鲁PE,新西兰NZ,智利CL 2.2 瑞士CH 3.3 韩国KR 5 巴PK	0 受惠国LD	30	--Of magnesium
1727	2833.2200	--硫酸铝	5.5	0 澳AU,冰岛IS,东盟AS,哥CR,秘鲁PE,新西兰NZ,智利CL 2.2 瑞士CH 3.3 韩国KR 5 巴PK	0 受惠国LD	30	--Of aluminium
1728	2833.2400	--镍的硫酸盐	5.5	0 澳AU,冰岛IS,东盟AS,哥CR,秘鲁PE,新西兰NZ,智利CL 2.2 瑞士CH 3.3 韩国KR 5 巴PK	0 受惠国LD	30	--Of nickel
1729	2833.2500	--铜的硫酸盐	5.5	0 澳AU,冰岛IS,东盟AS,哥CR,秘鲁PE,新西兰NZ,智利CL 2.2 瑞士CH 3.3 韩国KR 5 巴PK	0 受惠国LD	30	--Of copper
1730	2833.2700	--硫酸钡	5.5	0 澳AU,冰岛IS,东盟AS,哥CR,秘鲁PE,新西兰NZ,智利CL 2.2 瑞士CH 4.4 韩国KR 5 巴PK	0 受惠国LD	30	--Of barium
		--其他:					--Other:

序号 No.	税则号列 Tariff Line	中文货品名称 Article Description in Chinese	最惠国税率 MFN(%)	协定税率 Agreement(%)	特惠税率 SP(%)	普通税率 Gen(%)	英文货品名称 Article Description
1731	2833.2910	---硫酸亚铁	5.5	0 澳AU,冰岛IS,东盟AS,哥CR,秘鲁PE,新西兰NZ,智利CL 2.2 瑞士CH 3.3 韩国KR 5 巴PK	0 受惠国LD	45	---Ferrous sulphate
1732	2833.2920	---铬的硫酸盐	5.5	0 澳AU,巴PK,冰岛IS,东盟AS,哥CR,秘鲁PE,新西兰NZ,智利CL 2.2 瑞士CH 3.3 韩国KR	0 受惠国LD	30	---Of chromium
1733	2833.2930	---硫酸锌	5.5	0 澳AU,冰岛IS,东盟AS,哥CR,秘鲁PE,新西兰NZ,智利CL 2.2 瑞士CH 4.4 韩国KR 5 巴PK	0 受惠国LD	30	---Of zinc
1734	2833.2990	---其他	5.5	0 澳AU,冰岛IS,东盟AS,哥CR,秘鲁PE,新西兰NZ,智利CL 3.3 韩国KR 3.9 瑞士CH 5 巴PK	0 受惠国LD	30	---Other
		-矾:					-Alums:
1735	2833.3010	---钾铝矾	5.5	0 澳AU,巴PK,冰岛IS,东盟AS,哥CR,秘鲁PE,新西兰NZ,智利CL 2.2 瑞士CH 4.4 韩国KR	0 受惠国LD	45	---Potassium aluminum sulfate
1736	2833.3090	---其他	5.5	0 澳AU,巴PK,冰岛IS,东盟AS,哥CR,秘鲁PE,新西兰NZ,智利CL 2.2 瑞士CH 4.4 韩国KR	0 受惠国LD	30	---Other
1737	2833.4000	-过硫酸盐	5.5	0 澳AU,冰岛IS,东盟AS,哥CR,秘鲁PE,新西兰NZ,智利CL 2.2 瑞士CH 4.4 韩国KR 5 巴PK	0 受惠国LD	30	-Peroxosulphates (persulphates)
	28.34	**亚硝酸盐;硝酸盐:**					**Nitrites; nitrates:**
1738	2834.1000	-亚硝酸盐	5.5	0 澳AU,冰岛IS,东盟AS,哥CR,秘鲁PE,新西兰NZ,智利CL 2.2 瑞士CH 3.3 韩国KR 5 巴PK	0 受惠国LD	30	-Nitrites
		-硝酸盐: --硝酸钾:					-Nitrates: --Of potassium:
1739	2834.2110	---肥料用	4∆1	0 澳AU,巴PK,冰岛IS,东盟AS,哥CR,韩国KR,秘鲁PE,瑞士CH,新西兰NZ,智利CL	0 受惠国LD	11	---For use as fertilizer
1740	2834.2190	---其他	5.5	0 澳AU,冰岛IS,东盟AS,哥CR,秘鲁PE,新西兰NZ,智利CL 2.2 瑞士CH 3.3 韩国KR 5 巴PK	0 受惠国LD	30	---Other
		--其他:					--Other:
1741	2834.2910	---硝酸钴	5.5	0 澳AU,巴PK,冰岛IS,东盟AS,哥CR,秘鲁PE,新西兰NZ,智利CL 2.2 瑞士CH 3.3 韩国KR	0 受惠国LD	30	---Of cobalt

序号 No.	税则号列 Tariff Line	中文货品名称 Article Description in Chinese	最惠国税率 MFN(%)	协定税率 Agreement(%)	特惠税率 SP(%)	普通税率 Gen(%)	英文货品名称 Article Description
1742	2834.2990	---其他	5.5	0 澳AU,冰岛IS,东盟AS,哥CR,秘鲁PE,新西兰NZ,智利CL 2.2 瑞士CH 3.3 韩国KR 5 巴PK	0 受惠国LD	30	---Other
	ex28342990	硝酸钡	Δ2				Barium nitrate
	28.35	**次磷酸盐、亚磷酸盐、磷酸盐及多磷酸盐，无论是否已有化学定义：**					**Phosphinates (hypophosphites), phosphonates (phosphites) and phosphates; polyphosphates, whether or not chemically defined:**
1743	2835.1000	-次磷酸盐及亚磷酸盐	5.5	0 澳AU,冰岛IS,东盟AS,哥CR,秘鲁PE,新西兰NZ,智利CL 2.2 瑞士CH 3.3 韩国KR 5 巴PK	0 受惠国LD	20	-Phosphinates (hypophosphites) and phosphonates (phosphites)
		-磷酸盐：					-Phosphates:
1744	2835.2200	--磷酸一钠及磷酸二钠	5.5	0 澳AU,冰岛IS,东盟AS,哥CR,秘鲁PE,新西兰NZ,智利CL 2.2 瑞士CH 4.4 韩国KR 5 巴PK	0 受惠国LD	20	--Of mono-or disodium
1745	2835.2400	--钾的磷酸盐	5.5	0 澳AU,冰岛IS,东盟AS,哥CR,秘鲁PE,新西兰NZ,智利CL 2.2 瑞士CH 3.3 韩国KR 5 巴PK	0 受惠国LD	20	--Of potassium
		--正磷酸氢钙（磷酸二钙）：					--Calcium hydrogenorthophosphate (‘dicalcium phosphate’):
1746	2835.2510	---饲料级的	5.5	0 澳AU,冰岛IS,东盟AS,哥CR,秘鲁PE,新西兰NZ,智利CL 2.2 瑞士CH 3.3 韩国KR 5 巴PK	0 受惠国LD	20	---Feed Grade
1747	2835.2520	---食品级的	5.5	0 澳AU,冰岛IS,东盟AS,哥CR,秘鲁PE,新西兰NZ,智利CL 2.2 瑞士CH 3.3 韩国KR 5 巴PK	0 受惠国LD	20	---Food Grade
1748	2835.2590	---其他	5.5	0 澳AU,冰岛IS,东盟AS,哥CR,秘鲁PE,新西兰NZ,智利CL 3.3 韩国KR 4 瑞士CH 5 巴PK	0 受惠国LD	20	---Other
1749	2835.2600	--其他磷酸钙	5.5	0 澳AU,冰岛IS,东盟AS,哥CR,秘鲁PE,新西兰NZ,智利CL 2.2 瑞士CH 4.4 韩国KR 5 巴PK	0 受惠国LD	20	--Other phosphates of calcium
		--其他：					--Other:
1750	2835.2910	---磷酸三钠	5.5	0 澳AU,冰岛IS,东盟AS,哥CR,秘鲁PE,新西兰NZ,智利CL 2.2 瑞士CH 3.3 韩国KR 5 巴PK	0 受惠国LD	20	---Of trisodium

序号 No.	税则号列 Tariff Line	中文货品名称 Article Description in Chinese	最惠国税率 MFN(%)	协定税率 Agreement(%)	特惠税率 SP(%)	普通税率 Gen(%)	英文货品名称 Article Description
1751	2835.2990	---其他	5.5	0 澳AU,冰岛IS,东盟AS,哥CR,秘鲁PE,新西兰NZ,智利CL 2.2 瑞士CH 4.4 韩国KR 5 巴PK	0 受惠国LD	20	---Other
		-多磷酸盐:					-Polyphosphates:
		--三磷酸钠（三聚磷酸钠）:					--Sodium triphosphate (sodium tripolyphosphate) :
1752	2835.3110	---食品级的	5.5	0 澳AU,冰岛IS,东盟AS,哥CR,秘鲁PE,新西兰NZ,智利CL 2.2 瑞士CH 3.3 韩国KR 5 巴PK	0 受惠国LD	20	---Food Grade
1753	2835.3190	---其他	5.5	0 澳AU,冰岛IS,东盟AS,哥CR,秘鲁PE,新西兰NZ,智利CL 2.2 瑞士CH 4.4 韩国KR 5 巴PK	0 受惠国LD	20	---Other
		--其他:					--Other:
		---六偏磷酸钠:					---Sodium Hexametaphosphate:
1754	2835.3911	----食品级的	5.5	0 澳AU,冰岛IS,东盟AS,哥CR,秘鲁PE,新西兰NZ,智利CL 2.2 瑞士CH 3.3 韩国KR 5 巴PK	0 受惠国LD	20	----Food Grade
1755	2835.3919	----其他	5.5	0 澳AU,冰岛IS,东盟AS,哥CR,秘鲁PE,新西兰NZ,智利CL 2.2 瑞士CH 4.4 韩国KR 5 巴PK	0 受惠国LD	20	----Other
1756	2835.3990	---其他	5.5	0 澳AU,东盟AS,哥CR,秘鲁PE,新西兰NZ,智利CL 2.2 瑞士CH 3.3 韩国KR 5 巴PK	0 受惠国LD	20	---Other
	28.36	**碳酸盐;过碳酸盐;含氨基甲酸铵的商品碳酸铵:**					**Carbonates; peroxocarbonates (percarbonates) ; commercial ammonium carbonate containing ammonium carbamate:**
1757	2836.2000	-碳酸钠（纯碱）	5.5	0 澳AU,冰岛IS,东盟AS,哥CR,秘鲁PE,新西兰NZ,智利CL 2.2 瑞士CH 3.3 韩国KR 5 巴PK	0 受惠国LD	35	-Disodium carbonate
1758	2836.3000	-碳酸氢钠（小苏打）	5.5	0 澳AU,冰岛IS,东盟AS,哥CR,秘鲁PE,新西兰NZ,智利CL 2.2 瑞士CH 4.4 韩国KR 5 巴PK	0 受惠国LD	45	-Sodium hydrogencarbonate (sodium bicar bonate)
1759	2836.4000	-钾的碳酸盐	5.5	0 澳AU,冰岛IS,东盟AS,哥CR,秘鲁PE,新西兰NZ,智利CL 2.2 瑞士CH 3.3 韩国KR 5 巴PK	0 受惠国LD	30	-Potassium carbonates

序号 No.	税则号列 Tariff Line	中文货品名称 Article Description in Chinese	最惠国税率 MFN(%)	协定税率 Agreement(%)	特惠税率 SP(%)	普通税率 Gen(%)	英文货品名称 Article Description
1760	2836.5000	-碳酸钙	5.5	0 澳AU,冰岛IS,东盟AS,哥CR,秘鲁PE,新西兰NZ,智利CL 2.2 瑞士CH 3.3 韩国KR 5 巴PK	0 受惠国LD	45	-Calcium carbonate
1761	2836.6000	-碳酸钡	5.5Δ1	0 澳AU,冰岛IS,东盟AS,哥CR,韩国KR,秘鲁PE,新西兰NZ,智利CL 2.2 瑞士CH 5 巴PK	0 受惠国LD	40	-Barium carbonate
		-其他:					-Other:
1762	2836.9100	--锂的碳酸盐	5.5Δ2	0 澳AU,冰岛IS,东盟AS,哥CR,新西兰NZ,智利CL 2.2 瑞士CH 3.3 韩国KR 5 巴PK	0 受惠国LD	30	--Lithium carbonates
1763	2836.9200	--锶的碳酸盐	5.5Δ2	0 澳AU,冰岛IS,东盟AS,哥CR,韩国KR,秘鲁PE,新西兰NZ,智利CL 2.2 瑞士CH 5 巴PK	0 受惠国LD	30	--Strontium carbonate
		--其他:					--Other:
1764	2836.9910	---碳酸镁	5.5	0 澳AU,冰岛IS,东盟AS,哥CR,秘鲁PE,新西兰NZ,智利CL 2.2 瑞士CH 4.4 韩国KR 5 巴PK	0 受惠国LD	45	---Magnesium carbonate
1765	2836.9930	---碳酸钴	5.5Δ2	0 澳AU,冰岛IS,东盟AS,哥CR,韩国KR,秘鲁PE,新西兰NZ,智利CL 2.2 瑞士CH 5 巴PK	0 受惠国LD	30	---Cobalt carbonate
1766	2836.9940	---商品碳酸铵及其他铵的碳酸盐	5.5	0 澳AU,巴PK,冰岛IS,东盟AS,哥CR,秘鲁PE,新西兰NZ,智利CL 2.2 瑞士CH 3.3 韩国KR	0 受惠国LD	30	---Commercial ammonium carbonate and other ammonium carbonates
1767	2836.9950	---碳酸锆	5.5	0 澳AU,冰岛IS,东盟AS,哥CR,秘鲁PE,新西兰NZ,智利CL 2.2 瑞士CH 3.3 韩国KR 5 巴PK	0 受惠国LD	30	---Zirconium carbonates
1768	2836.9990	---其他	5.5	0 澳AU,澳门MO,冰岛IS,东盟AS,哥CR,秘鲁PE,新西兰NZ,智利CL 2.2 瑞士CH 3.3 韩国KR 5 巴PK	0 受惠国LD	30	---Other
	28.37	**氰化物、氧氰化物及氰络合物:**					**Cyanides, cyanide oxides and complex cyanides:**
		-氰化物及氧氰化物:					-Cyanides and cyanide oxides:
		--氰化钠及氧氰化钠:					--Of sodium:
1769	2837.1110	---氰化钠	5.5	0 澳AU,巴PK,冰岛IS,东盟AS,哥CR,秘鲁PE,新西兰NZ,智利CL 2.2 瑞士CH 4.7 韩国KR	0 受惠国$_1$LD$_1$	20	---Sodium cyanide

序号 No.	税则号列 Tariff Line	中文货品名称 Article Description in Chinese	最惠国税率 MFN(%)	协定税率 Agreement(%)	特惠税率 SP(%)	普通税率 Gen(%)	英文货品名称 Article Description
1770	2837.1120	---氧氰化钠	5.5	0 澳AU,巴PK,冰岛IS,东盟AS,哥CR,秘鲁PE,新西兰NZ,智利CL 2.2 瑞士CH 3.3 韩国KR 5 亚太AP	0 受惠国$_1$LD$_1$	30	---Sodium cyanide oxide
		--其他:					--Other:
1771	2837.1910	---氰化钾	5.5	0 澳AU,巴PK,冰岛IS,东盟AS,哥CR,秘鲁PE,新西兰NZ,智利CL 2.2 瑞士CH 3.3 韩国KR	0 受惠国$_1$LD$_1$	20	---Potassium cyanide
1772	2837.1990	---其他	5.5	0 澳AU,巴PK,冰岛IS,东盟AS,哥CR,秘鲁PE,新西兰NZ,智利CL 2.2 瑞士CH 4.7 韩国KR	0 受惠国$_1$LD$_1$	30	---Other
1773	2837.2000	-氰络合物	5.5	0 澳AU,巴PK,冰岛IS,东盟AS,哥CR,秘鲁PE,新西兰NZ,智利CL 2.2 瑞士CH 3.3 韩国KR	0 受惠国$_1$LD$_1$	30	-Complex cyanides
	28.39	**硅酸盐;商品碱金属硅酸盐:**					**Silicates; commercial alkali metal silicates:**
		-钠盐:					-Of sodium:
1774	2839.1100	--偏硅酸钠	5.5	0 澳AU,冰岛IS,东盟AS,哥CR,秘鲁PE,新西兰NZ,智利CL 2.2 瑞士CH 4.4 韩国KR 5 巴PK	0 受惠国$_1$LD$_1$	40	--Sodium metasilicates
		--其他:					--Other:
1775	2839.1910	---硅酸钠	5.5	0 澳AU,冰岛IS,东盟AS,哥CR,秘鲁PE,新西兰NZ,智利CL 2.2 瑞士CH 4.4 韩国KR 5 巴PK	0 受惠国$_1$LD$_1$	30	---Sodium silicate
1776	2839.1990	---其他	5.5	0 澳AU,冰岛IS,东盟AS,哥CR,秘鲁PE,新西兰NZ,智利CL 2.2 瑞士CH 4.4 韩国KR 5 巴PK	0 受惠国$_1$LD$_1$	30	---Other
1777	2839.9000	-其他	5.5	0 澳AU,冰岛IS,东盟AS,哥CR,秘鲁PE,新西兰NZ,智利CL 3.3 韩国KR 3.9 瑞士CH 5 巴PK	0 受惠国$_1$LD$_1$	30	-Other
	ex28399000	锆的硅酸盐	Δ2				Ziconium silicate
	28.40	**硼酸盐及过硼酸盐:**					**Borates; peroxoborates (perborates) :**
		-四硼酸钠（精炼硼砂）:					-Disodium tetraborate (refined borax) :
1778	2840.1100	--无水四硼酸钠	5.5Δ2	0 澳AU,巴PK,冰岛IS,东盟AS,哥CR,韩国KR,秘鲁PE,新西兰NZ,智利CL 2.2 瑞士CH	0 受惠国$_1$LD$_1$	20	--Anhydrous
1779	2840.1900	--其他	5.5Δ2	0 澳AU,巴PK,冰岛IS,东盟AS,哥CR,韩国KR,秘鲁PE,新西兰NZ,智利CL 2.2 瑞士CH	0 受惠国$_1$LD$_1$	20	--Other

序号 No.	税则号列 Tariff Line	中文货品名称 Article Description in Chinese	最惠国税率 MFN(%)	协定税率 Agreement(%)	特惠税率 SP(%)	普通税率 Gen(%)	英文货品名称 Article Description
1780	2840.2000	-其他硼酸盐	5.5	0 澳AU,巴PK,冰岛IS,东盟AS,哥CR,秘鲁PE,新西兰NZ,智利CL 2.2 瑞士CH 4.4 韩国KR	0 受惠国$_1$LD$_1$	30	-Other borates
1781	2840.3000	-过硼酸盐	5.5	0 澳AU,巴PK,冰岛IS,东盟AS,哥CR,秘鲁PE,新西兰NZ,智利CL 2.2 瑞士CH 3.3 韩国KR	0 受惠国$_1$LD$_1$	30	-Peroxoborates (perborates)
	28.41	**金属酸盐及过金属酸盐:**					**Salts of oxometallic or peroxometallic acids:**
1782	2841.3000	-重铬酸钠	5.5	0 澳AU,巴PK,冰岛IS,东盟AS,哥CR,秘鲁PE,新西兰NZ,智利CL 2.2 瑞士CH 3.3 韩国KR	0 受惠国LD	20	-Sodium dichromate
1783	2841.5000	-其他铬酸盐及重铬酸盐;过铬酸盐	5.5	0 澳AU,冰岛IS,东盟AS,哥CR,秘鲁PE,新西兰NZ,智利CL 2.2 瑞士CH 3.3 韩国KR 5 巴PK	0 受惠国LD	30	-Other chromates and dichromates; peroxochromates
		-亚锰酸盐、锰酸盐及高锰酸盐:					-Manganites, manganates and permanganates:
1784	2841.6100	--高锰酸钾	5.5	0 澳AU,冰岛IS,东盟AS,哥CR,秘鲁PE,新西兰NZ,智利CL 2.2 瑞士CH 3.3 韩国KR 5 巴PK	0 受惠国LD	30	--Potassium permanganate
		--其他:					--Other:
1785	2841.6910	---锰酸锂	5.5	0 澳AU,巴PK,冰岛IS,东盟AS,哥CR,秘鲁PE,新西兰NZ,智利CL 2.2 瑞士CH 3.3 韩国KR	0 受惠国LD	30	---Lithium manganate
1786	2841.6990	---其他	5.5	0 澳AU,巴PK,冰岛IS,东盟AS,哥CR,秘鲁PE,新西兰NZ,智利CL 2.2 瑞士CH 3.3 韩国KR	0 受惠国LD	30	---Other
		-钼酸盐:					-Molybdates:
1787	2841.7010	---钼酸铵	5.5	0 澳AU,冰岛IS,东盟AS,哥CR,韩国KR,秘鲁PE,新西兰NZ,智利CL 2.2 瑞士CH 5 巴PK	0 受惠国LD	30	---Ammonium molybdates
1788	2841.7090	---其他	5.5	0 澳AU,冰岛IS,东盟AS,哥CR,秘鲁PE,新西兰NZ,智利CL 2.2 瑞士CH 3.3 韩国KR 5 巴PK	0 受惠国LD	30	---Other
		-钨酸盐:					-Tungstates (wolframates) :
1789	2841.8010	---仲钨酸铵	5.5	0 澳AU,巴PK,冰岛IS,东盟AS,哥CR,秘鲁PE,新西兰NZ,智利CL 2.2 瑞士CH 3.3 韩国KR	0 受惠国LD	30	---Ammonium paratungstate
1790	2841.8020	---钨酸钠	5.5	0 澳AU,巴PK,冰岛IS,东盟AS,哥CR,秘鲁PE,新西兰NZ,智利CL 2.2 瑞士CH 3.3 韩国KR	0 受惠国LD	30	---Sodium tungstate

序号 No.	税则号列 Tariff Line	中文货品名称 Article Description in Chinese	最惠国税率 MFN(%)	协定税率 Agreement(%)	特惠税率 SP(%)	普通税率 Gen(%)	英文货品名称 Article Description
1791	2841.8030	---钨酸钙	5.5	0 澳AU,巴PK,冰岛IS,东盟AS,哥CR,秘鲁PE,新西兰NZ,智利CL 2.2 瑞士CH 3.3 韩国KR	0 受惠国LD	30	---Calcium wolframate
1792	2841.8040	---偏钨酸铵	5.5	0 澳AU,巴PK,冰岛IS,东盟AS,哥CR,秘鲁PE,新西兰NZ,智利CL 2.2 瑞士CH 3.3 韩国KR	0 受惠国LD	30	---Ammonium metatungstate
1793	2841.8090	---其他	5.5	0 澳AU,巴PK,冰岛IS,东盟AS,哥CR,韩国KR,秘鲁PE,新西兰NZ,智利CL 2.2 瑞士CH	0 受惠国LD	30	---Other
1794	2841.9000	-其他	5.5	0 澳AU,冰岛IS,东盟AS,哥CR,秘鲁PE,新西兰NZ,智利CL 2.2 瑞士CH 4.4 韩国KR 5 巴PK	0 受惠国LD	30	-Other
	ex28419000	铼酸盐	Δ0				Rhenate
	ex28419000	钴酸锂	Δ2				Lithium cobaltate
	28.42	**其他无机酸盐及过氧酸盐（包括不论是否已有化学定义的硅铝酸盐），但迭氮化物除外：**					**Other salts of inorganic acids or peroxoacids (including aluminosilicates whether or not chemically defined) , other than azides:**
1795	2842.1000	-硅酸复盐及硅酸络盐，（包括不论是否已有化学定义的硅铝酸盐）	5.5	0 澳AU,冰岛IS,东盟AS,哥CR,秘鲁PE,香港HK,新西兰NZ,智利CL 3.3 韩国KR 4 瑞士CH 5 巴PK	0 受惠国$_1$LD$_1$	30	-Double or complex silicates, including aluminosilicates whether or not chemically defined
		-其他：					-Other:
		---雷酸盐、氰酸盐及硫氰酸盐：					---Fulminates, cyanates and thiocyanates:
1796	2842.9011	----硫氰酸钠	5.5	0 澳AU,冰岛IS,东盟AS,哥CR,秘鲁PE,新西兰NZ,智利CL 2.2 瑞士CH 3.3 韩国KR 5 巴PK	0 受惠国$_1$LD$_1$	30	----Sodium sulfocyanate
1797	2842.9019	----其他	5.5	0 澳AU,冰岛IS,东盟AS,哥CR,秘鲁PE,新西兰NZ,智利CL 2.2 瑞士CH 3.3 韩国KR 5 巴PK	0 受惠国$_1$LD$_1$	30	----Other
1798	2842.9020	---碲化镉	5.5	0 澳AU,冰岛IS,东盟AS,哥CR,秘鲁PE,新西兰NZ,智利CL 2.2 瑞士CH 3.3 韩国KR 5 巴PK	0 受惠国$_1$LD$_1$	30	---Cadmium telluride
1799	2842.9030	---锂镍钴锰氧化物	5.5	0 澳AU,冰岛IS,东盟AS,哥CR,秘鲁PE,新西兰NZ,智利CL 2.2 瑞士CH 3.3 韩国KR 5 巴PK	0 受惠国$_1$LD$_1$	30	---Lithium nickel cobalt manganese oxide

序号 No.	税则号列 Tariff Line	中文货品名称 Article Description in Chinese	最惠国税率 MFN(%)	协定税率 Agreement(%)		特惠税率 SP(%)	普通税率 Gen(%)	英文货品名称 Article Description
1800	2842.9040	---磷酸铁锂	5.5	0 2.2 4.4 5	澳AU,冰岛IS,东盟AS,哥CR,秘鲁PE,新西兰NZ,智利CL 瑞士CH 韩国KR 巴PK	0 受惠国$_1$LD$_1$	30	---Lithium iron phosphate
1801	2842.9050	---硒酸盐及亚硒酸盐	5.5	0 2.2 3.3 5	澳AU,冰岛IS,东盟AS,哥CR,秘鲁PE,新西兰NZ,智利CL 瑞士CH 韩国KR 巴PK	0 受惠国$_1$LD$_1$	30	---Selenate and selenite
1802	2842.9090	---其他	5.5	0 2.2 3.3 5	澳AU,冰岛IS,东盟AS,哥CR,秘鲁PE,新西兰NZ,智利CL 瑞士CH 韩国KR 巴PK	0 受惠国$_1$LD$_1$	30	---Other
		第六分章　杂项产品						VI. MISCELLANEOUS
	28.43	**胶态贵金属;贵金属的无机或有机化合物,不论是否已有化学定义;贵金属汞齐:**						**Colloidal precious metals; inorganic or organic compounds of precious metals, whether or not chemically defined; amalgams of precious metals:**
1803	2843.1000	-胶态贵金属	5.5	0 2.2 3.3	澳AU,巴PK,冰岛IS,东盟AS,哥CR,秘鲁PE,新西兰NZ,智利CL 瑞士CH 韩国KR	0 受惠国$_1$LD$_1$	30	-Colloidal precious metals
		-银化合物:						-Silver compounds:
1804	2843.2100	--硝酸银	5.5	0 2.2 3.3	澳AU,巴PK,冰岛IS,东盟AS,哥CR,秘鲁PE,香港HK,新西兰NZ,智利CL 瑞士CH 韩国KR	0 受惠国$_1$LD$_1$	30	--Silver nitrate
1805	2843.2900	--其他	5.5	0 2.2 3.3	澳AU,巴PK,冰岛IS,东盟AS,哥CR,秘鲁PE,香港HK,新西兰NZ,智利CL 瑞士CH 韩国KR	0 受惠国$_1$LD$_1$	30	--Other
1806	2843.3000	-金化合物	5.5	0 2.2 3.3	澳AU,巴PK,冰岛IS,东盟AS,哥CR,秘鲁PE,香港HK,新西兰NZ,智利CL 瑞士CH 韩国KR	0 受惠国$_1$LD$_1$	30	-Gold compounds
1807	2843.9000	-其他贵金属化合物;贵金属汞齐	5.5	0 3.3 5	澳AU,冰岛IS,东盟AS,哥CR,秘鲁PE,香港HK,新西兰NZ,智利CL 韩国KR 巴PK	0 受惠国$_1$LD$_1$	30	-Other compounds; amalgams
	28.44	**放射性化学元素及放射性同位素(包括可裂变或可转换的化学元素及同位素)及其化合物;含上述产品的混合物及残渣:**						**Radioactive chemical elements and radioactive isotopes (including the fissile or fertile chemical elements and isotopes) and their compounds; mixtures and residues containing these products:**
1808	2844.1000	-天然铀及其化合物;含天然铀或天然铀化合物的合金、分散体(包括金属陶瓷)、陶瓷产品及混合物	5.5	0 2.2 3.3	澳AU,巴PK,冰岛IS,东盟AS,哥CR,秘鲁PE,新西兰NZ,智利CL 瑞士CH 韩国KR	0 受惠国LD	30	-Natural uranium and its compounds; aloys, dispersions (including cermets), ceramic products and mixtures containing natural uranium or natural uranium compounds

序号 No.	税则号列 Tariff Line	中文货品名称 Article Description in Chinese	最惠国税率 MFN(%)	协定税率 Agreement(%)	特惠税率 SP(%)	普通税率 Gen(%)	英文货品名称 Article Description
	ex28441000	天然铀及其化合物	Δ0				Nature uranium and its compounds
1809	2844.2000	-U_{235}浓缩铀及其化合物；钚及其化合物；含U_{235}浓缩铀、钚或它们的化合物的合金、分散体（包括金属陶瓷）、陶瓷产品及混合物	5.5	0 澳AU,巴PK,冰岛IS,东盟AS,哥CR,秘鲁PE,新西兰NZ,智利CL 2.2 瑞士CH 3.3 韩国KR	0 受惠国LD	30	-Uranium enriched in U_{235} and its compounds; plutonium and its compounds; alloys dispersion (including cermets) , ceramic products and mixtures containing uranium enriched in U_{235}, plutonium or compounds of these products
	ex28442000	含U_{235}浓度低于5%的低浓铀及其化合物	Δ0				Uranium (including enriched U_{235} less than 5%) and its compounds
1810	2844.3000	-U_{235}贫化铀及其化合物；钍及其化合物；含U_{235}贫化铀、钍或它们的化合物的合金、分散体（包括金属陶瓷）、陶瓷产品及混合物	5.5	0 澳AU,巴PK,冰岛IS,东盟AS,哥CR,秘鲁PE,新西兰NZ,智利CL 2.2 瑞士CH 3.3 韩国KR	0 受惠国LD	30	-Uranium depleted in U_{235} and its compounds; thorium and its compounds; alloys, dispersions (including cermets) , ceramic products and mixtures containing uranium depleted in U_{235}, thorium or compounds of these products
		-除子目号2844.10、2844.20及2844.30以外的放射性元素、同位素及其化合物；含这些元素、同位素及其化合物的合金、分散体（包括金属陶瓷）、陶瓷产品及混合物：					-Radioactive elements and isotopes and compounds other than those of subheading 284410, 284420 or 284430; alloys, dispersions (including cermets) , ceramic products and mixtures containing these elements, isotopes or compounds; radioactive residues:
1811	2844.4010	---镭及镭盐	4	0 澳AU,巴PK,冰岛IS,东盟AS,哥CR,韩国KR,秘鲁PE,瑞士CH,新西兰NZ,智利CL	0 受惠国LD	14	---Radium and its salts
1812	2844.4020	---钴及钴盐	4	0 澳AU,巴PK,冰岛IS,东盟AS,哥CR,韩国KR,秘鲁PE,瑞士CH,新西兰NZ,智利CL	0 受惠国LD	14	---Cobalt and its salts
1813	2844.4090	---其他	5.5	0 澳AU,巴PK,冰岛IS,东盟AS,哥CR,秘鲁PE,新西兰NZ,智利CL 2.2 瑞士CH 3.3 韩国KR	0 受惠国LD	30	---Other
1814	2844.5000	-核反应堆已耗尽（已辐照）的燃料元件（释热元件）	5.5	0 澳AU,巴PK,冰岛IS,东盟AS,哥CR,秘鲁PE,新西兰NZ,智利CL 2.2 瑞士CH 3.3 韩国KR	0 受惠国$_1$LD$_1$	30	-Spent (irradiated) fuel elements (cartridges) of nuclear reactors
	28.45	**税号28.44以外的同位素；这些同位素的无机或有机化合物，不论是否已有化学定义：**					**Isotopes other than those of heading 2844; compounds, inorganic or organic, of such isotopes, whether or not chemically defined:**
1815	2845.1000	-重水（氧化氘）	5.5	0 澳AU,巴PK,冰岛IS,东盟AS,哥CR,秘鲁PE,新西兰NZ,智利CL 2.2 瑞士CH 3.3 韩国KR	0 受惠国$_1$LD$_1$	30	-Heavy water (deuterium oxide)
1816	2845.9000	-其他	5.5	0 澳AU,巴PK,冰岛IS,东盟AS,哥CR,秘鲁PE,新西兰NZ,智利CL 2.2 瑞士CH 3.3 韩国KR	0 受惠国$_1$LD$_1$	30	-Other
	28.46	**稀土金属、钇、钪及其混合物的无机或有机化合物：**					**Compounds, inorganic or organic, of rare-earth metals, of yttrium or of scandium or of mixtures of these metals:**
		-铈的化合物：					-Cerium compounds:

序号 No.	税则号列 Tariff Line	中文货品名称 Article Description in Chinese	最惠国税率 MFN(%)	协定税率 Agreement(%)	特惠税率 SP(%)	普通税率 Gen(%)	英文货品名称 Article Description
1817	2846.1010	---氧化铈	5.5Δ0	0 澳AU,巴PK,冰岛IS,东盟AS,哥CR,韩国KR,秘鲁PE,新西兰NZ,智利CL 2.2 瑞士CH 3.9 亚太AP	0 受惠国$_1$LD$_1$	30	---Cerium oxide
1818	2846.1020	---氢氧化铈	5.5Δ0	0 澳AU,巴PK,冰岛IS,东盟AS,哥CR,韩国KR,秘鲁PE,新西兰NZ,智利CL 2.2 瑞士CH 3.9 亚太AP	0 受惠国$_1$LD$_1$	30	---Cerium hydroxide
1819	2846.1030	---碳酸铈	5.5Δ0	0 澳AU,巴PK,冰岛IS,东盟AS,哥CR,韩国KR,秘鲁PE,新西兰NZ,智利CL 2.2 瑞士CH 3.9 亚太AP	0 受惠国$_1$LD$_1$	30	---Cerium carbonate
1820	2846.1090	---其他	5.5Δ0	0 澳AU,巴PK,冰岛IS,东盟AS,哥CR,韩国KR,秘鲁PE,新西兰NZ,智利CL 2.2 瑞士CH 3.9 亚太AP	0 受惠国$_1$LD$_1$	30	---Other
		-其他:					-Other:
		---氧化稀土（氧化铈除外）:					---Rare－earth oxides (other than cerium oxide) :
1821	2846.9011	----氧化钇	5.5Δ0	0 澳AU,巴PK,冰岛IS,东盟AS,哥CR,韩国KR,秘鲁PE,新西兰NZ,智利CL 2.2 瑞士CH	0 受惠国$_1$LD$_1$	30	----Yttrium oxide
1822	2846.9012	----氧化镧	5.5Δ0	0 澳AU,巴PK,冰岛IS,东盟AS,哥CR,韩国KR,秘鲁PE,新西兰NZ,智利CL 2.2 瑞士CH	0 受惠国$_1$LD$_1$	30	----Lanthanum oxide
1823	2846.9013	----氧化钕	5.5Δ0	0 澳AU,巴PK,冰岛IS,东盟AS,哥CR,韩国KR,秘鲁PE,新西兰NZ,智利CL 2.2 瑞士CH	0 受惠国$_1$LD$_1$	30	----Neodymium oxide
1824	2846.9014	----氧化铕	5.5Δ0	0 澳AU,巴PK,冰岛IS,东盟AS,哥CR,韩国KR,秘鲁PE,新西兰NZ,智利CL 2.2 瑞士CH	0 受惠国$_1$LD$_1$	30	----Europium oxide
1825	2846.9015	----氧化镝	5.5Δ0	0 澳AU,巴PK,冰岛IS,东盟AS,哥CR,韩国KR,秘鲁PE,新西兰NZ,智利CL 2.2 瑞士CH	0 受惠国$_1$LD$_1$	30	----Dysprosium oxide
1826	2846.9016	----氧化铽	5.5Δ0	0 澳AU,巴PK,冰岛IS,东盟AS,哥CR,韩国KR,秘鲁PE,新西兰NZ,智利CL 2.2 瑞士CH	0 受惠国$_1$LD$_1$	30	----Terbium oxide
1827	2846.9017	----氧化镨	5.5Δ0	0 澳AU,巴PK,冰岛IS,东盟AS,哥CR,韩国KR,秘鲁PE,新西兰NZ,智利CL 2.2 瑞士CH	0 受惠国$_1$LD$_1$	30	----Praseodymium oxide

序号 No.	税则号列 Tariff Line	中文货品名称 Article Description in Chinese	最惠国税率 MFN(%)	协定税率 Agreement(%)		特惠税率 SP(%)	普通税率 Gen(%)	英文货品名称 Article Description
1828	2846.9019	----其他	5.5△0	0 2.2	澳AU,巴PK,冰岛IS,东盟AS,哥CR,韩国KR,秘鲁PE,新西兰NZ,智利CL 瑞士CH	0 受惠国$_1$LD$_1$	30	----Other
		---氯化稀土:						---Rare－earth chlorides:
1829	2846.9021	----氯化铽	5.5△0	0 2.2	澳AU,巴PK,冰岛IS,东盟AS,哥CR,韩国KR,秘鲁PE,新西兰NZ,智利CL 瑞士CH	0 受惠国$_1$LD$_1$	30	----Terbium chlorinates
1830	2846.9022	----氯化镝	5.5△0	0 2.2	澳AU,巴PK,冰岛IS,东盟AS,哥CR,韩国KR,秘鲁PE,新西兰NZ,智利CL 瑞士CH	0 受惠国$_1$LD$_1$	30	----Dysprosium chlorinates
1831	2846.9023	----氯化镧	5.5△0	0 2.2	澳AU,巴PK,冰岛IS,东盟AS,哥CR,韩国KR,秘鲁PE,新西兰NZ,智利CL 瑞士CH	0 受惠国$_1$LD$_1$	30	----Lanthanum chlorinates
1832	2846.9024	----氯化钕	5.5△0	0 2.2	澳AU,巴PK,冰岛IS,东盟AS,哥CR,韩国KR,秘鲁PE,新西兰NZ,智利CL 瑞士CH	0 受惠国$_1$LD$_1$	30	----Neodymium chlorinates
1833	2846.9025	----氯化镨	5.5△0	0 2.2	澳AU,巴PK,冰岛IS,东盟AS,哥CR,韩国KR,秘鲁PE,新西兰NZ,智利CL 瑞士CH	0 受惠国$_1$LD$_1$	30	----Praseodymium chlorinates
1834	2846.9026	----氯化钇	5.5△0	0 2.2	澳AU,巴PK,冰岛IS,东盟AS,哥CR,韩国KR,秘鲁PE,新西兰NZ,智利CL 瑞士CH	0 受惠国$_1$LD$_1$	30	----Yttrium chlorinates
1835	2846.9028	----混合氯化稀土	5.5△0	0 2.2	澳AU,巴PK,冰岛IS,东盟AS,哥CR,韩国KR,秘鲁PE,新西兰NZ,智利CL 瑞士CH	0 受惠国$_1$LD$_1$	30	----Mixture of rareearth chlorides
1836	2846.9029	----其他	5.5△0	0 2.2	澳AU,巴PK,冰岛IS,东盟AS,哥CR,韩国KR,秘鲁PE,新西兰NZ,智利CL 瑞士CH	0 受惠国$_1$LD$_1$	30	----Other
		---氟化稀土:						---Rare-earth fluorides:
1837	2846.9031	----氟化铽	5.5△0	0 2.2	澳AU,巴PK,冰岛IS,东盟AS,哥CR,韩国KR,秘鲁PE,新西兰NZ,智利CL 瑞士CH	0 受惠国$_1$LD$_1$	30	----Terbium fluorides
1838	2846.9032	----氟化镝	5.5△0	0 2.2	澳AU,巴PK,冰岛IS,东盟AS,哥CR,韩国KR,秘鲁PE,新西兰NZ,智利CL 瑞士CH	0 受惠国$_1$LD$_1$	30	----Dysprosium fluorides
1839	2846.9033	----氟化镧	5.5△0	0 2.2	澳AU,巴PK,冰岛IS,东盟AS,哥CR,韩国KR,秘鲁PE,新西兰NZ,智利CL 瑞士CH	0 受惠国$_1$LD$_1$	30	----Lanthanum fluorides

序号 No.	税则号列 Tariff Line	中文货品名称 Article Description in Chinese	最惠国税率 MFN(%)	协定税率 Agreement(%)	特惠税率 SP(%)	普通税率 Gen(%)	英文货品名称 Article Description
1840	2846.9034	----氟化钕	5.5Δ0	0 澳AU,巴PK,冰岛IS,东盟AS,哥CR,韩国KR,秘鲁PE,新西兰NZ,智利CL 2.2 瑞士CH	0 受惠国$_1$LD$_1$	30	----Neodymium fluorides
1841	2846.9035	----氟化镨	5.5Δ0	0 澳AU,巴PK,冰岛IS,东盟AS,哥CR,韩国KR,秘鲁PE,新西兰NZ,智利CL 2.2 瑞士CH	0 受惠国$_1$LD$_1$	30	----Praseodymium fluorides
1842	2846.9036	----氟化钇	5.5Δ0	0 澳AU,巴PK,冰岛IS,东盟AS,哥CR,韩国KR,秘鲁PE,新西兰NZ,智利CL 2.2 瑞士CH	0 受惠国$_1$LD$_1$	30	----Yttrium fluorides
1843	2846.9039	----其他	5.5Δ0	0 澳AU,巴PK,冰岛IS,东盟AS,哥CR,韩国KR,秘鲁PE,新西兰NZ,智利CL 2.2 瑞士CH	0 受惠国$_1$LD$_1$	30	----Other
		---碳酸稀土:					---Rare-earth carbonate:
1844	2846.9041	----碳酸镧	5.5Δ0	0 澳AU,巴PK,冰岛IS,东盟AS,哥CR,韩国KR,秘鲁PE,新西兰NZ,智利CL 2.2 瑞士CH	0 受惠国$_1$LD$_1$	30	----Lanthanum carbonates
1845	2846.9042	----碳酸铽	5.5Δ0	0 澳AU,巴PK,冰岛IS,东盟AS,哥CR,韩国KR,秘鲁PE,新西兰NZ,智利CL 2.2 瑞士CH	0 受惠国$_1$LD$_1$	30	----Terbium carbonates
1846	2846.9043	----碳酸镝	5.5Δ0	0 澳AU,巴PK,冰岛IS,东盟AS,哥CR,韩国KR,秘鲁PE,新西兰NZ,智利CL 2.2 瑞士CH	0 受惠国$_1$LD$_1$	30	----Dysprosium carbonates
1847	2846.9044	----碳酸钕	5.5Δ0	0 澳AU,巴PK,冰岛IS,东盟AS,哥CR,韩国KR,秘鲁PE,新西兰NZ,智利CL 2.2 瑞士CH	0 受惠国$_1$LD$_1$	30	----Neodymium carbonates
1848	2846.9045	----碳酸镨	5.5Δ0	0 澳AU,巴PK,冰岛IS,东盟AS,哥CR,韩国KR,秘鲁PE,新西兰NZ,智利CL 2.2 瑞士CH	0 受惠国$_1$LD$_1$	30	----Praseodymium carbonates
1849	2846.9046	----碳酸钇	5.5Δ0	0 澳AU,巴PK,冰岛IS,东盟AS,哥CR,韩国KR,秘鲁PE,新西兰NZ,智利CL 2.2 瑞士CH	0 受惠国$_1$LD$_1$	30	----Yttrium carbonates
1850	2846.9048	----混合碳酸稀土	5.5Δ0	0 澳AU,巴PK,冰岛IS,东盟AS,哥CR,韩国KR,秘鲁PE,新西兰NZ,智利CL 2.2 瑞士CH	0 受惠国$_1$LD$_1$	30	----Mixture of rare－earth carbonate
1851	2846.9049	----其他	5.5Δ0	0 澳AU,巴PK,冰岛IS,东盟AS,哥CR,韩国KR,秘鲁PE,新西兰NZ,智利CL 2.2 瑞士CH	0 受惠国$_1$LD$_1$	30	----Other
		---其他:					---Other:

序号 No.	税则号列 Tariff Line	中文货品名称 Article Description in Chinese	最惠国税率 MFN(%)	协定税率 Agreement(%)	特惠税率 SP(%)	普通税率 Gen(%)	英文货品名称 Article Description
1852	2846.9091	----镧的其他化合物	5.5Δ0	0 澳AU,巴PK,冰岛IS,东盟AS,哥CR,韩国KR,秘鲁PE,新西兰NZ,智利CL 2.2 瑞士CH	0 受惠国$_1$LD$_1$	30	----Of Lanthanum
1853	2846.9092	----钕的其他化合物	5.5Δ0	0 澳AU,巴PK,冰岛IS,东盟AS,哥CR,韩国KR,秘鲁PE,新西兰NZ,智利CL 2.2 瑞士CH	0 受惠国$_1$LD$_1$	30	----Of Neodymium
1854	2846.9093	----铽的其他化合物	5.5Δ0	0 澳AU,巴PK,冰岛IS,东盟AS,哥CR,韩国KR,秘鲁PE,新西兰NZ,智利CL 2.2 瑞士CH	0 受惠国$_1$LD$_1$	30	----Of Terbium
1855	2846.9094	----镝的其他化合物	5.5Δ0	0 澳AU,巴PK,冰岛IS,东盟AS,哥CR,韩国KR,秘鲁PE,新西兰NZ,智利CL 2.2 瑞士CH	0 受惠国$_1$LD$_1$	30	----Of Dysprosium
1856	2846.9095	----镨的其他化合物	5.5Δ0	0 澳AU,巴PK,冰岛IS,东盟AS,哥CR,韩国KR,秘鲁PE,新西兰NZ,智利CL 2.2 瑞士CH	0 受惠国$_1$LD$_1$	30	----Of Praseodymium
1857	2846.9096	----钇的其他化合物	5.5Δ0	0 澳AU,巴PK,冰岛IS,东盟AS,哥CR,韩国KR,秘鲁PE,新西兰NZ,智利CL 2.2 瑞士CH	0 受惠国$_1$LD$_1$	30	----Of Yttrium
1858	2846.9099	----其他	5.5Δ0	0 澳AU,巴PK,冰岛IS,东盟AS,哥CR,韩国KR,秘鲁PE,新西兰NZ,智利CL 2.2 瑞士CH	0 受惠国$_1$LD$_1$	30	----Other
	28.47	**过氧化氢，不论是否用尿素固化**					**Hydrogen peroxide, whether or not solidified with urea**
1859	2847.0000	过氧化氢，不论是否用尿素固化	5.5	0 澳AU,冰岛IS,东盟AS,哥CR,秘鲁PE,新西兰NZ,智利CL 2.2 瑞士CH 4.7 韩国KR 5 巴PK	0 受惠国$_1$LD$_1$	30	Hydrogen peroxide, whether or not solidified with urea
	28.48	**磷化物，不论是否已有化学定义，但不包括磷铁**					**Phosphides, whether or not chemically defined, excluding ferrophosphorus**
1860	2848.0000	磷化物，不论是否已有化学定义，但不包括磷铁	5.5	0 澳AU,巴PK,冰岛IS,东盟AS,哥CR,秘鲁PE,新西兰NZ,智利CL 2.2 瑞士CH 4.4 韩国KR	0 受惠国$_1$LD$_1$	20	Phosphides, whether or not chemically defined, excluding ferrophophorus
	28.49	**碳化物，不论是否已有化学定义：**					**Carbides, whether or not chemically defined:**
1861	2849.1000	-碳化钙	5.5	0 澳AU,巴PK,冰岛IS,东盟AS,哥CR,秘鲁PE,新西兰NZ,智利CL 2.2 瑞士CH 3.3 韩国KR	0 受惠国$_1$LD$_1$	45	-Of calcium
1862	2849.2000	-碳化硅	5.5	0 澳AU,冰岛IS,东盟AS,哥CR,秘鲁PE,新西兰NZ,智利CL 2.2 瑞士CH 4.4 韩国KR 5 巴PK	0 受惠国$_1$LD$_1$	30	-Of silicon
		-其他：					-Other:

序号 No.	税则号列 Tariff Line	中文货品名称 Article Description in Chinese	最惠国税率 MFN(%)	协定税率 Agreement(%)	特惠税率 SP(%)	普通税率 Gen(%)	英文货品名称 Article Description
1863	2849.9010	---碳化硼	5.5	0 澳AU,巴PK,冰岛IS,东盟AS,哥CR,秘鲁PE,新西兰NZ,智利CL 2.2 瑞士CH 3.3 韩国KR	0 受惠国$_1$LD$_1$	30	---Of boron
1864	2849.9020	---碳化钨	5.5	0 澳AU,巴PK,冰岛IS,东盟AS,哥CR,秘鲁PE,新西兰NZ,智利CL 2.2 瑞士CH 3.3 韩国KR	0 受惠国$_1$LD$_1$	30	---Of tungsten
1865	2849.9090	---其他	5.5	0 澳AU,巴PK,冰岛IS,东盟AS,哥CR,秘鲁PE,新西兰NZ,智利CL 2.2 瑞士CH 3.3 韩国KR	0 受惠国$_1$LD$_1$	30	---Other
	28.50	**氢化物、氮化物、迭氮化物、硅化物及硼化物，不论是否已有化学定义，但可归入税号28.49的碳化物除外：**					**Hydrides, nitrides, azides, silicides and borides, whether or not chemically defined, other than compounds which are also carbides of heading No.28. 49:**
		---氮化物：					---Nitrides:
1866	2850.0011	----氮化锰	5.5	0 澳AU,巴PK,冰岛IS,东盟AS,哥CR,秘鲁PE,香港HK,新西兰NZ,智利CL 2.2 瑞士CH 3.3 韩国KR 3.9 亚太AP	0 受惠国$_1$LD$_1$	30	----Manganese nitride
1867	2850.0012	----氮化硼	5.5	0 澳AU,巴PK,冰岛IS,东盟AS,哥CR,秘鲁PE,香港HK,新西兰NZ,智利CL 2.2 瑞士CH 3.3 韩国KR 3.9 亚太AP	0 受惠国$_1$LD$_1$	30	----Boron nitride
1868	2850.0019	----其他	5.5	0 澳AU,巴PK,冰岛IS,东盟AS,哥CR,秘鲁PE,香港HK,新西兰NZ,智利CL 2.2 瑞士CH 3.3 韩国KR 3.9 亚太AP	0 受惠国$_1$LD$_1$	30	----Other
1869	2850.0090	---其他	5.5	0 澳AU,巴PK,冰岛IS,东盟AS,哥CR,秘鲁PE,香港HK,新西兰NZ,智利CL 2.2 瑞士CH 3.9 亚太AP 4.7 韩国KR	0 受惠国$_1$LD$_1$	30	---Other
	28.52	**汞的无机或有机化合物，不论是否已有化学定义，汞齐除外：**					**Inorganic or organic compounds of mercury, whether or not chemically defined, excluding amalgams:**
1870	2852.1000	-已有化学定义的	5.5	0 澳AU,巴PK,冰岛IS,东盟AS,哥CR,秘鲁PE,香港HK,新西兰NZ,智利CL 2.2 瑞士CH 3.3 韩国KR	0 受惠国$_1$LD$_1$	30	-Chemically defined
1871	2852.9000	-其他	5.5	0 澳AU,冰岛IS,东盟AS,哥CR,秘鲁PE,新西兰NZ,智利CL 2.2 瑞士CH 3.3 韩国KR 5 巴PK	0 受惠国LD	30	-Other

序号 No.	税则号列 Tariff Line	中文货品名称 Article Description in Chinese	最惠国税率 MFN(%)	协定税率 Agreement(%)	特惠税率 SP(%)	普通税率 Gen(%)	英文货品名称 Article Description
	28.53	其他无机化合物(包括蒸馏水、导电水及类似的纯净水);液态空气(不论是否除去稀有气体);压缩空气;汞齐,但贵金属汞齐除外:					**Other inorganic compounds (including distilled or conductivity water and water of similar purity) ; liquid air (whether or not rare gases have been removed) ; compressed air; amalgams, other than amalgams of precious metals:**
1872	2853.0010	---饮用蒸馏水	5.5	0 澳AU,澳门MO,巴PK,冰岛IS,东盟AS,哥CR,秘鲁PE,香港HK,新西兰NZ,智利CL 2.2 瑞士CH 3.3 韩国KR	0 受惠国$_1$LD$_1$	70	---Distilled water for human consumption
1873	2853.0020	---氯化氰	5.5	0 澳AU,巴PK,冰岛IS,东盟AS,哥CR,秘鲁PE,新西兰NZ,智利CL 2.2 瑞士CH 3.3 韩国KR	0 受惠国$_1$LD$_1$	30	---Chlorocyanogen, cyanogen chloride
1874	2853.0030	---镍钴锰氢氧化物	6.5	0 澳门MO,冰岛IS,东盟AS,哥CR,秘鲁PE,香港HK,新西兰NZ,智利CL 2.2 瑞士CH 3.9 澳AU,韩国KR 5 巴PK	0 受惠国$_1$LD$_1$	30	---Nickel cobalt manganese composite hydrogenoxide
1875	2853.0090	---其他	5.5	0 澳AU,澳门MO,冰岛IS,东盟AS,哥CR,秘鲁PE,香港HK,新西兰NZ,智利CL 2.2 瑞士CH 3.3 韩国KR 5 巴PK	0 受惠国$_1$LD$_1$	30	---Other

第二十九章
有机化学品

注释:

一、除条文另有规定的以外,本章各税号只适用于:

(一)单独的已有化学定义的有机化合物,不论是否含有杂质;

(二)同一有机化合物的两种或两种以上异构体的混合物(不论是否含有杂质),但无环烃异构体的混合物(立体异构体除外),不论是否饱和,应归入第二十七章;

(三)税号 29.36 至 29.39 的产品,税号 29.40 的糖醚、糖缩醛、糖酯及其盐类和税号 29.41 的产品,不论是否已有化学定义;

(四)上述(一)、(二)、(三)款产品的水溶液;

(五)溶于其他溶剂的上述(一)、(二)、(三)款的产品,但该产品处于溶液状态只是为了安全或运输所采取的正常必要方法,其所用溶剂并不使该产品改变其一般用途而适合于某些特殊用途;

(六)为了保存或运输的需要,加入稳定剂(包括抗结块剂)的上述(一)、(二)、(三)、(四)、(五)各款产品;

(七)为了便于识别或安全起见,加入抗尘剂、着色剂或气味剂的上述(一)、(二)、(三)、(四)、(五)、(六)各款产品,但所加剂料并不使原产品改变其一般用途而适合于某些特殊用途;

(八)为生产偶氮染料而稀释至标准浓度的下列产品:重氮盐,用于重氮盐、可重氮化的胺及其盐类的偶合剂。

二、本章不包括:

(一)税号 15.04 的货品及税号 15.20 的粗甘油;

(二)乙醇(税号 22.07 或 22.08);

(三)甲烷及丙烷(税号 27.11);

(四)第二十八章注释二所述的碳化合物;

(五)税目 30.02 的免疫制品

(六)尿素(税号 31.02 或 31.05);

(七)植物性或动物性着色料(税号 32.03)、合成有机着色料、用作萤光增白剂或发光体的合成有机产品(税号 32.04)及零售包装的染料或其他着色料(税号 32.12);

(八)酶(税号 35.07);

(九)聚乙醛、六亚甲基四胺(乌洛托品)及类似物质,制成片、条或类似形状作为燃料用的,以及包装容器的容积不超过 300 立方厘米的直接灌注香烟打火机及类似打火器用的液体燃料或液化气体燃料(税号 36.06);

(十)灭火器的装配药及已装药的灭火弹(税号 38.13);零售包装的除墨剂(税号 38.24);

Chapter 29
Organic chemicals

Notes:

1. Except where the context otherwise requires, the headings of this Chapter apply only to:

(a) Separate chemically defined organic compounds, whether or not containing impurities;

(b) Mixtures of two or more isomers of the same organic compound (whether or not containing impurities), except mixtures of acyclic hydrocarbon isomers (other than stereoisomers), whether or not saturated (Chapter 27) ;

(c) The products of headings 29.36 to 29.39 or the sugar ethers, sugar acetals and sugar esters, and their salts, of heading 29.40, or the products of heading 29.41, whether or not chemically defined;

(d) The products mentioned in (a), (b) or (c) above dissolved in water;

(e) The products mentioned in (a), (b) or (c) above dissolved in other slovents provided that the solution constitutes a normal and necessary method of putting up these products adopted solely for reasons of safety or for transport and that the solvent does not render the product particularly suitable for specific use rather than for general use;

(f) The products mentioned in (a), (b), (c), (d) or (e) above with an added stabilizer (including an anticaking agent) necessary for their preservation or transport;

(g) The products mentioned in (a), (b), (c), (d), (e) or (f) above with an added anti-dusting agent or a colouring or odoriferous substance added to facilitate their identification or for safety reasons, provided that the additions do not render the product particularly suitable for specific use rather than for general use;

(h) The following products, diluted to standard strengths, for the production of azo dyes:diazonium salts, couplers used for these salts and diazotisable amines and their salts.

2. This Chapter does not cover:

(a) Goods of heading No.15.04 or crude glycerol of heading No.15.20;

(b) Ethyl alcohol (heading No.22.07 or 22.08) ;

(c) Methane or propane (heading No.27.11) ;

(d) The compounds of carbon mentioned in Note 2 to Chapter 28;

(e) Immunological products of heading 30.02;

(f) Urea (heading No.31.02 or 31.05);

(g) Colouring matter of vegetable or animal origin (heading No.32.03), synthetic organic colouring matter, synthetic organic products of a kind used as fluores cent brightening agents or as luminophores (heading No.32.04) or dyes or other colouring matter put up in forms or packings for retail sale (heading No.32.12) ;

(h) Enzymes (heading No.35.07) ;

(i) Metaldehyde, hexamethylenetetramine or similar substances, put up in forms (for example, tablets, sticks or similar forms) for use as fuels, or liquid or liquefied_gas fuels in containers of a kind used for filling or refilling cigarette or similar lighters and of a capacity not exceeding300cm^3 (heading No.36.06) ;

(j) Products put up as charges for fire-extinguishers or put up in fire-extinguishing grenades,of heading No.38.13; ink removers put up in packings for retail sale,of

（十一）光学元件，例如用酒石酸乙二胺制成的（税号 90.01）。

三、可以归入本章两个或两个以上税号的货品，应归入有关税号中的最后一个税号。

四、税号 29.04 至 29.06、29.08 至 29.11 及 29.13 至 29.20 的卤化、磺化、硝化或亚硝化衍生物均包括复合衍生物，例如，卤磺化、卤硝化、磺硝化及卤磺硝化衍生物。

硝基及亚硝基不作为税号29.29的含氮基官能团。

税号 29.11、29.12、29.14、29.18 及 29.22 所称“含氧基”，仅限于税号 29.05 至 29.20 的各种含氧基（其特征为有机含氧基）。

五、

（一）本章第一分章至第七分章的酸基有机化合物与这些分章的有机化合物构成的酯应归入有关税号中的最后一个税号；

（二）乙醇与本章第一分章至第七分章的酸基有机化合物所构成的酯，应按有关酸基化合物归类。

（三）除第六类注释一及第二十八章注释二另有规定的以外：

1. 第一分章至第十分章及税号 29.42 的有机化合物的无机盐，例如，含酸基、酚基或烯醇基的化合物及有机碱的无机盐，应归入相应的有机化合物的税号；

2. 第一分章至第十分章及税号 29.42 的有机化合物之间生成的盐，应按生成该盐的碱或酸（包括酚基或烯醇基化合物）归入本章有关税号中的最后一个税号；

3. 除第十一分章或税目 29.41 的产品外，配位化合物应按该化合物所有金属键（金属-碳键除外）“断开”所形成的片段归入第二十九章有关税目中的最后一个税目。

（四）除乙醇外，金属醇化物应按相应的醇归类（税号 29.05）。

（五）羧酸酰卤化物应按相应的酸归类。

六、税号 29.30 及 29.31 的化合物是指有机化合物，其分子中除含氢、氧或氮原子外，还含有与碳原子直接连接的其他非金属或金属原子（例如，硫、砷或铅）。

税号 29.30（有机硫化合物）及税号 29.31（其他有机—无机化合物）不包括某些磺化或卤化衍生物（含复合衍生物）。这些衍生物分子中除氢、氧、氮之外，只有具有磺化或卤化衍生物（或复合衍生物）

heading No.38.24;or

(k) Optical elements, for example, of ethylenediamine tartrate (heading No.90.01).

3. Goods which could be included in two or more of the headings of this Chapter are to be classified in that one of those headings which occurs last in numerical order.

4. In headings Nos.29.04 to 29.06, 29.08 to 29.11 and 29.13 to 29.20, any reference to halogenated, sulphonated, nitrated or nitrosated derivatives includes a reference to compound derivatives, such as sulphohalogenated, nitrohalogenated, nitrosulphonated or nitrosulphohalogenated derivatives.

Nitro or nitroso groups are not to be taken as “nitrogenfunctions” for the purpose of heading No.29.29.

For the purposes of headings Nos.29.11, 29.12, 29.14, 29.18 and 29.22, “oxygen-function” is to be restricted to the functions (the characteristic organic oxygen-containing groups) referred to in headings Nos.29.05 to 29.20.

5.

(a) The esters of acid-function organic compounds of sub-Chapters Ⅰ to Ⅶ with organic compounds of these sub- Chapters are to be classified with that compound which is classified in the heading which occurs last in numerical order in these sub-Chapters.

(b) Esters of ethyl alcohol with acid-function organic compounds of sub-Chapters Ⅰ to Ⅶ are to be classified in the same heading as the corresponding acid-function compounds.

(c) Subject to Note 1 to Section Ⅵ and Note 2 to Chapter28:

(1) Inorganic salts of organic compounds such as acid, phenol or enol-function compounds or organic bases, of sub-Chapters Ⅰ to Ⅹ or heading No.29.42, are to be classified in the heading appropriate to the organic compound;

(2) Salts formed between organic compounds of sub-Chapters Ⅰ to Ⅹ or heading No.29.42 are to be classified in the heading appropriate to the base or to the acid (including phenol or enol-function compounds) from which they are formed, whichever occurs last in numerical order in the Chapter; and

(3) Co-ordination compounds, other than products classifiable in sub-Chapter XI or heading 29.41, are to be classified in the heading which occurs last in numerical order in Chapter 29, among those appropriate to the fragments formed by “cleaving” of all metal bonds, other than metalcarbon bonds.

(d) Metal alcoholates are to be classified in the same heading as the corresponding alcohols except in the case of ethanol (heading No.29.05) .

(e) Halides of carboxylic acids are to be classified in the same heading as the corresponding acids.

6. The compounds of headings Nos.29.30 and 29.31are organic compounds the molecules of which contain, in addition to atoms of hydrogen, oxygen or nitrogen, atoms of other non- metals of or metals (such as sulphur, arsenic or lead) directly linked to carbon atoms.

Heading No.29.30 (organo-sulphur compounds) and heading No.29.31 (other organo-inorganic compounds) do not include sulphonated or halogenated derivatives (in cluding compound derivatives) which, apart from

性质的硫原子或卤素原子与碳原子直接连接。

hydrogen, oxygen and nitrogen, only have directly linked to carbon the atoms of sulphur or of a halogen which give them their nature of sulphonated or halogenated derivatives (or compound derivatives) .

七、税号 29.32、29.33 及 29.34 不包括三节环环氧化物、过氧化酮、醛或硫醛的环聚合物、多元羧酸酐、多元醇或酚与多元酸构成的环酯及多元酸酰亚胺。

本条规定只适用于由本条所列环化功能形成环内杂原子的化合物。

7. Headings Nos.29.32, 29.33 and 29.34do not include epoxides with a three-membered ring, ketone peroxides, cyclic polymers of aldehydes or of thioaldehydes, anhydrides of polybasic carboxylic acids, cyclic esters of polyhydric alcohols or phenols with polybasic acids, and imides of polybasic acids.

These provisions apply only when the ring-position heteroatoms are those resulting solely form the cyclising function or functions here listed.

八、税目 29.37 所称:

（一）“激素”包括激素释放因子、激素刺激和释放因子、激素抑制剂以及激素抗体;

（二）“主要起激素作用”，不仅适用于激素衍生物以及主要起激素作用的结构类似物，也适用于在本税目所列产品合成过程中主要用作中间体的激素衍生物以及结构类似物。

8. For the purposes of heading29.37:

(a) the term“hormones”includes hormone-releasing or hormone-stimulating factors, hormone inhibitors and hormone antagonists (anti-hormones) ;

(b) the expression“used primarily as hormones”applies not only to hormone derivatives and structural analogues used primarily for their hormonal effect, but also to those derivatives and structural analogues used primarily as intermediates in the synthesis of products of this heading.

子目注释:

一、属于本章任一税号项下的一种（组）化合物的衍生物，如果该税号其他子目未明确将其包括在内，而且有关的子目中又无列名为“其他”的子目，则应与该种（组）化合物归入同一子目。

二、第二十九章注释三不适用于本章的子目。

Subheading Notes:

1. Within any one heading of this Chapter, derivatives of a chemical compound (or group of chemical compounds) are to be classified in the same subheading as that compound (or group of compounds) provided that they are not more specifically covered by any other subheading and that there is no residual subheading named “other” in the series of subheadings concerned.
2. Note 3 to Chapter 29 does not apply to the subheadings of this Chapter.

序号 No.	税则号列 Tariff Line	中文货品名称 Article Description in Chinese	最惠国税率 MFN(%)	协定税率 Agreement(%)		特惠税率 SP(%)	普通税率 Gen(%)	英文货品名称 Article Description
		第一分章　烃类及其卤化、磺化、硝化或亚硝化衍生物						I. HYDROCARBONS AND THEIR HALOGENATED, SULPHONAT-ED, NITRATED OR NITROSATED DERIVATIVES
	29.01	**无环烃:**						**Acyclic hydrocarbons:**
1876	2901.1000	饱和	2	0	澳AU,巴PK,冰岛IS,东盟AS,哥CR,韩国KR,秘鲁PE,瑞士CH,香港HK,新西兰NZ,智利CL	0 受惠国$_1$LD$_1$	30	-Saturated
		-不饱和:						-Unsaturated:
1877	2901.2100	--乙烯	2Δ1	0 1.6	澳AU,巴PK,冰岛IS,东盟AS,哥CR,秘鲁PE,瑞士CH,新西兰NZ,智利CL 韩国KR	0 受惠国$_1$LD$_1$	20	--Ethylene
1878	2901.2200	--丙烯	2Δ1	0 1.6	澳AU,巴PK,冰岛IS,东盟AS,哥CR,秘鲁PE,瑞士CH,台湾TW,新西兰NZ,智利CL 韩国KR	0 受惠国$_1$LD$_1$	20	--Propene (propylene)
		--丁烯及其异构体:						--Butene (butylene) and isomers thereof:
1879	2901.2310	---1-丁烯	2	0 1.6	澳AU,巴PK,冰岛IS,东盟AS,哥CR,秘鲁PE,瑞士CH,新西兰NZ,智利CL 韩国KR	0 受惠国$_1$LD$_1$	20	---1-butene

序号 No.	税则号列 Tariff Line	中文货品名称 Article Description in Chinese	最惠国税率 MFN(%)	协定税率 Agreement(%)	特惠税率 SP(%)	普通税率 Gen(%)	英文货品名称 Article Description
1880	2901.2320	---2-丁烯	2	0 澳AU,巴PK,冰岛IS,东盟AS,哥CR,韩国KR,秘鲁PE,瑞士CH,新西兰NZ,智利CL	0 受惠国$_1$LD$_1$	20	---2-butene
1881	2901.2330	---2-甲基丙稀	2	0 澳AU,巴PK,冰岛IS,东盟AS,哥CR,韩国KR,秘鲁PE,瑞士CH,新西兰NZ,智利CL	0 受惠国$_1$LD$_1$	20	---2-methyl-propene
		--1，3-丁二烯及异戊二烯：					--Buta-1, 3-diene and isoprene:
1882	2901.2410	---1, 3-丁二烯	2	0 澳AU,巴PK,冰岛IS,东盟AS,哥CR,秘鲁PE,瑞士CH,台湾TW,新西兰NZ,智利CL 1.6 韩国KR	0 受惠国$_1$LD$_1$	20	---Buta-1, 3-diene
1883	2901.2420	---异戊二烯	2	0 澳AU,巴PK,冰岛IS,东盟AS,哥CR,秘鲁PE,瑞士CH,台湾TW,新西兰NZ,智利CL 1.7 韩国KR	0 受惠国$_1$LD$_1$	20	---Isoprene
		--其他：					--Other:
1884	2901.2910	---异戊烯	2	0 澳AU,巴PK,冰岛IS,东盟AS,哥CR,韩国KR,秘鲁PE,瑞士CH,新西兰NZ,智利CL	0 受惠国$_1$LD$_1$	30	---Isopentene
1885	2901.2920	---乙炔	2	0 澳AU,巴PK,冰岛IS,东盟AS,哥CR,韩国KR,秘鲁PE,瑞士CH,新西兰NZ,智利CL	0 受惠国$_1$LD$_1$	45	---Acetylene
1886	2901.2990	---其他	2	0 澳AU,巴PK,东盟AS,哥CR,秘鲁PE,瑞士CH,新西兰NZ,智利CL 1 冰岛IS 1.6 韩国KR	0 受惠国$_1$LD$_1$	30	---Other
	29.02	**环烃：**					**Cyclic hydrocarbons:**
		-环烷烃、环烯及环萜烯：					-Cyclanes, cyclenes and cycloterpenes:
1887	2902.1100	--环己烷	2	0 澳AU,巴PK,冰岛IS,东盟AS,哥CR,韩国KR,秘鲁PE,瑞士CH,新西兰NZ,智利CL	0 受惠国$_1$LD$_1$	30	--Cyclohexane
		--其他：					--Other:
1888	2902.1910	---蒎烯	2	0 澳AU,巴PK,东盟AS,哥CR,韩国KR,秘鲁PE,瑞士CH,新西兰NZ,智利CL 1 冰岛IS	0 受惠国$_1$LD$_1$	30	---Pinene
1889	2902.1920	---4-烷基-4’-烷基双环己烷	2	0 澳AU,巴PK,东盟AS,哥CR,韩国KR,秘鲁PE,瑞士CH,新西兰NZ,智利CL 1 冰岛IS	0 受惠国$_1$LD$_1$	30	---4-alkyl-4' -alkyl-bicyclohexyl
1890	2902.1990	---其他	2	0 澳AU,巴PK,东盟AS,哥CR,韩国KR,秘鲁PE,瑞士CH,新西兰NZ,智利CL 1 冰岛IS	0 受惠国$_1$LD$_1$	30	---Other
1891	2902.2000	-苯	2	0 澳AU,巴PK,冰岛IS,东盟AS,哥CR,秘鲁PE,瑞士CH,新西兰NZ,智利CL 1.7 韩国KR	0 受惠国$_1$LD$_1$	20	-Benzene

序号 No.	税则号列 Tariff Line	中文货品名称 Article Description in Chinese	最惠国税率 MFN(%)	协定税率 Agreement(%)	特惠税率 SP(%)	普通税率 Gen(%)	英文货品名称 Article Description
1892	2902.3000	-甲苯	2	0 澳AU,巴PK,冰岛IS,东盟AS,哥CR,秘鲁PE,瑞士CH,新西兰NZ,智利CL 1.7 韩国KR	0 受惠国$_1$LD$_1$	30	-Toluene
		-二甲苯:					-Xylenes:
1893	2902.4100	--邻二甲苯	2	0 澳AU,巴PK,冰岛IS,东盟AS,哥CR,秘鲁PE,瑞士CH,台湾TW,新西兰NZ,智利CL 1.6 韩国KR	0 受惠国$_1$LD$_1$	20	--*o*-Xylene
1894	2902.4200	--间二甲苯	2	0 澳AU,巴PK,冰岛IS,东盟AS,哥CR,韩国KR,秘鲁PE,瑞士CH,台湾TW,新西兰NZ,智利CL	0 受惠国$_1$LD$_1$	20	--*m*-Xylene
1895	2902.4300	--对二甲苯	2	0 澳AU,巴PK,冰岛IS,东盟AS,哥CR,秘鲁PE,台湾TW,新西兰NZ,智利CL 1.4 瑞士CH	0 受惠国$_1$LD$_1$	20	--*p*-Xylene
1896	2902.4400	--混合二甲苯异构体	2	0 澳AU,巴PK,冰岛IS,东盟AS,哥CR,韩国KR,秘鲁PE,瑞士CH,台湾TW,新西兰NZ,智利CL	0 受惠国$_1$LD$_1$	20	--Mixed xylene isomers
1897	2902.5000	-苯乙烯	2	0 澳AU,巴PK,冰岛IS,哥CR,秘鲁PE,新西兰NZ,智利CL 1.4 瑞士CH,亚太AP 1.8 韩国KR		30	-Styrene
1898	2902.6000	-乙苯	2	0 澳AU,巴PK,冰岛IS,东盟AS,哥CR,秘鲁PE,瑞士CH,新西兰NZ,智利CL 1.6 韩国KR	0 受惠国$_1$LD$_1$	30	-Ethylbenzene
1899	2902.7000	-异丙基苯	2	0 澳AU,巴PK,冰岛IS,东盟AS,哥CR,韩国KR,秘鲁PE,瑞士CH,新西兰NZ,智利CL	0 受惠国$_1$LD$_1$	30	-Cumene
		-其他:					-Other:
1900	2902.9010	---四氢萘	2	0 澳AU,巴PK,冰岛IS,东盟AS,哥CR,韩国KR,秘鲁PE,瑞士CH,新西兰NZ,智利CL	0 受惠国$_1$LD$_1$	11	---Tetrahydronaphthalene (tetralin)
1901	2902.9020	---精萘	2	0 澳AU,巴PK,冰岛IS,东盟AS,哥CR,秘鲁PE,瑞士CH,新西兰NZ,智利CL 1.7 韩国KR	0 受惠国$_1$LD$_1$	35	---Naphthalene
1902	2902.9030	---十二烷基苯	2	0 澳AU,巴PK,冰岛IS,东盟AS,哥CR,秘鲁PE,瑞士CH,台湾TW,新西兰NZ,智利CL	0 受惠国$_1$LD$_1$	30	---Dodecylbenzene
1903	2902.9040	---4-(4'-烷基环己基)环己基乙烯	2	0 澳AU,巴PK,冰岛IS,东盟AS,哥CR,韩国KR,秘鲁PE,瑞士CH,新西兰NZ,智利CL	0 受惠国$_1$LD$_1$	30	---4- (4' -alkylcyclohexyl) cyclohexylethene
1904	2902.9090	---其他	2	0 澳AU,巴PK,冰岛IS,东盟AS,哥CR,韩国KR,秘鲁PE,瑞士CH,新西兰NZ,智利CL	0 受惠国$_1$LD$_1$	30	---Other
	29.03	**烃的卤化衍生物:**					**Halogenated derivatives of hydrocarbons:**
		-无环烃的饱和氯化衍生物:					-Saturated chlorinated derivatives of acyclic hydrocarbons:

序号 No.	税则号列 Tariff Line	中文货品名称 Article Description in Chinese	最惠国税率 MFN(%)	协定税率 Agreement(%)	特惠税率 SP(%)	普通税率 Gen(%)	英文货品名称 Article Description
1905	2903.1100	---一氯甲烷及氯乙烷	5.5	0 澳AU,巴PK,冰岛IS,东盟AS,哥CR,秘鲁PE,新西兰NZ,智利CL 2.2 瑞士CH 3.3 韩国KR	0 受惠国$_1$LD$_1$	30	--Chloromethane (methyl chloride) and chloroethane (ethyl chloride)
1906	2903.1200	--二氯甲烷	8	0 冰岛IS,东盟AS,哥CR,秘鲁PE,香港HK,新西兰NZ,智利CL 3.2 瑞士CH 4.8 澳AU 5 巴PK 6.9 韩国KR	0 受惠国$_1$LD$_1$	30	--Dichloromethane (methylene chloride)
1907	2903.1300	--氯仿（三氯甲烷）	10	0 冰岛IS,东盟AS,哥CR,秘鲁PE,台湾TW,香港HK,新西兰NZ,智利CL 4 瑞士CH 5 巴PK 6 澳AU 8 韩国KR 9 亚太AP	0 受惠国$_1$LD$_1$	30	--Chloroform (trichloromethane)
1908	2903.1400	--四氯化碳	8	0 冰岛IS,东盟AS,哥CR,秘鲁PE,新西兰NZ,智利CL 3.2 瑞士CH 4.8 澳AU,韩国KR 5 巴PK	0 受惠国$_1$LD$_1$	30	--Carbon tetrachloride
1909	2903.1500	--1，2-二氯乙烷（ISO）	5.5Δ1	0 澳AU,冰岛IS,哥CR,新西兰NZ,智利CL 2.2 瑞士CH 3.3 韩国KR	0 受惠国$_2$LD$_2$	30	--1, 2-Dichloroethane (ISO) (ethylene dichloride)
		--其他：					--Other:
1910	2903.1910	---1，1，1-三氯乙烷（甲基氯仿）	8	0 冰岛IS,东盟AS,哥CR,秘鲁PE,新西兰NZ,智利CL 3.2 瑞士CH 4.8 澳AU,韩国KR 5 巴PK	0 受惠国$_1$LD$_1$	30	---1, 1, 1-Trichloroethane (methylchloro form)
1911	2903.1990	---其他	5.5	0 澳AU,冰岛IS,东盟AS,哥CR,秘鲁PE,新西兰NZ,智利CL 2.2 瑞士CH 4.4 韩国KR 5 巴PK	0 受惠国$_1$LD$_1$	30	---Other
		-无环烃的不饱和氯化衍生物：					-Unsaturated chlorinated derivatives of acyclic hydrocarbons:
1912	2903.2100	--氯乙烯	5.5Δ1	0 澳AU,巴PK,冰岛IS,东盟AS,哥CR,韩国KR,秘鲁PE,台湾TW,新西兰NZ,智利CL 2.2 瑞士CH 3.9 亚太AP	0 受惠国$_1$LD$_1$	30	--Vinyl chloride (chloroethylene)
1913	2903.2200	--三氯乙烯	8	0 冰岛IS,东盟AS,哥CR,秘鲁PE,新西兰NZ,智利CL 3.2 瑞士CH 4.8 澳AU 5 巴PK 6.9 韩国KR	0 受惠国$_1$LD$_1$	30	--Trichloroethylene
1914	2903.2300	--四氯乙烯（全氯乙烯）	5.5	0 澳AU,巴PK,冰岛IS,东盟AS,哥CR,秘鲁PE,新西兰NZ,智利CL 2.2 瑞士CH 3.3 韩国KR	0 受惠国$_1$LD$_1$	30	--Tetrachloroethylene (perchloroethylene)
		--其他：					--Other:

序号 No.	税则号列 Tariff Line	中文货品名称 Article Description in Chinese	最惠国税率 MFN(%)	协定税率 Agreement(%)	特惠税率 SP(%)	普通税率 Gen(%)	英文货品名称 Article Description
1915	2903.2910	---3-氯-1-丙烯（氯丙烯）	5.5	0 澳AU,巴PK,冰岛IS,东盟AS,哥CR,秘鲁PE,新西兰NZ,智利CL 2.2 瑞士CH 3.3 韩国KR	0 受惠国$_1$LD$_1$	30	---3-Chloropropene
1916	2903.2990	---其他	5.5	0 澳AU,巴PK,冰岛IS,东盟AS,哥CR,秘鲁PE,新西兰NZ,智利CL 2.2 瑞士CH 3.3 韩国KR	0 受惠国$_1$LD$_1$	30	---Other
		-无环烃的氟化、溴化或碘化衍生物：					-Fluorinated, brominated or iodinated derivatives of acyclic hydrocarbons:
1917	2903.3100	--1，2-二溴乙烷（ISO）	5.5	0 澳AU,冰岛IS,东盟AS,哥CR,秘鲁PE,香港HK,新西兰NZ,智利CL 2.2 瑞士CH 3.3 韩国KR 5 巴PK	0 受惠国$_1$LD$_1$	30	--Ethylene dibromide (ISO)
		--其他：					--Other:
1918	2903.3910	---1，1，3，3，3-五氟-2-三氟甲基-1-丙烯（全氟异丁烯；八氟异丁烯）	5.5	0 澳AU,巴PK,冰岛IS,东盟AS,哥CR,秘鲁PE,新西兰NZ,智利CL 2.2 瑞士CH 3.3 韩国KR	0 受惠国$_1$LD$_1$	30	---1, 1, 3, 3, 3-Pentafluro–2-trifluromethyl-1-propene (Perfluor-olisobutylene, isobutylene octafluoride)
1919	2903.3990	---其他	5.5	0 澳AU,冰岛IS,东盟AS,哥CR,秘鲁PE,香港HK,新西兰NZ,智利CL 2.2 瑞士CH 3.3 韩国KR 5 巴PK	0 受惠国$_1$LD$_1$	30	---Other
		-含有两种或两种以上不同卤素的无环烃卤化衍生物：					-Halogenated derivatives of acyclic hydrocarbons containing two or more different halogens:
1920	2903.7100	--一氯二氟甲烷	5.5	0 澳AU,冰岛IS,东盟AS,哥CR,秘鲁PE,新西兰NZ,智利CL 2.2 瑞士CH 3.3 韩国KR 5 巴PK	0 受惠国$_1$LD$_1$	30	--Chlorodifluoromethane
1921	2903.7200	--二氯三氟乙烷	5.5	0 澳AU,冰岛IS,东盟AS,哥CR,秘鲁PE,新西兰NZ,智利CL 2.2 瑞士CH 3.3 韩国KR 5 巴PK	0 受惠国$_1$LD$_1$	30	--Dichlorotrifluoroethanes
1922	2903.7300	--二氯一氟乙烷	5.5	0 澳AU,冰岛IS,东盟AS,哥CR,秘鲁PE,新西兰NZ,智利CL 2.2 瑞士CH 3.3 韩国KR 5 巴PK	0 受惠国$_1$LD$_1$	30	--Dichlorofluoroethanes
1923	2903.7400	--一氯二氟乙烷	5.5	0 澳AU,冰岛IS,东盟AS,哥CR,秘鲁PE,新西兰NZ,智利CL 2.2 瑞士CH 3.3 韩国KR 5 巴PK	0 受惠国$_1$LD$_1$	30	--Chlorodifluoroethanes
1924	2903.7500	--二氯五氟丙烷	5.5	0 澳AU,冰岛IS,东盟AS,哥CR,秘鲁PE,新西兰NZ,智利CL 2.2 瑞士CH 3.3 韩国KR 5 巴PK	0 受惠国$_1$LD$_1$	30	--Dichloropentafluoropropanes

序号 No.	税则号列 Tariff Line	中文货品名称 Article Description in Chinese	最惠国税率 MFN(%)	协定税率 Agreement(%)	特惠税率 SP(%)	普通税率 Gen(%)	英文货品名称 Article Description
1925	2903.7600	--溴氯二氟甲烷、溴三氟甲烷及二溴四氟乙烷	5.5	0 澳AU,巴PK,冰岛IS,东盟AS,哥CR,秘鲁PE,新西兰NZ,智利CL 2.2 瑞士CH 3.3 韩国KR	0 受惠国$_1$LD$_1$	30	--Bromochlorodifluoromethane, bromotrifluoromethane and dibromotetrafluoroethanes
		--其他，仅含氟和氯的全卤化物:					--Other, perhalogenated only with fluorine and chlorine:
1926	2903.7710	---三氯氟甲烷	5.5	0 澳AU,冰岛IS,东盟AS,哥CR,秘鲁PE,新西兰NZ,智利CL 2.2 瑞士CH 3.3 韩国KR 5 巴PK	0 受惠国$_1$LD$_1$	30	---Trichlorofluoromethane
1927	2903.7720	---其他仅含氟和氯的甲烷、乙烷及丙烷的全卤化物	5.5	0 澳AU,巴PK,冰岛IS,东盟AS,哥CR,秘鲁PE,新西兰NZ,智利CL 2.2 瑞士CH 3.3 韩国KR	0 受惠国$_1$LD$_1$	30	---Other methane, ethane and propane perhalogenated derivatives only with fluorine and chlorinederivatives
1928	2903.7790	---其他	5.5	0 澳AU,冰岛IS,东盟AS,哥CR,秘鲁PE,新西兰NZ,智利CL 2.2 瑞士CH 4.4 韩国KR 5 巴PK	0 受惠国$_1$LD$_1$	30	---Other
1929	2903.7800	--其他全卤化衍生物	5.5	0 澳AU,巴PK,冰岛IS,东盟AS,哥CR,秘鲁PE,新西兰NZ,智利CL 2.2 瑞士CH 3.3 韩国KR	0 受惠国$_1$LD$_1$	30	--Other perhalogenated derivatives
		--其他:					--Other:
1930	2903.7910	---其他仅含氟和氯的甲烷、乙烷及丙烷的卤化衍生物	5.5	0 澳AU,冰岛IS,东盟AS,哥CR,秘鲁PE,新西兰NZ,智利CL 2.2 瑞士CH 3.3 韩国KR 5 巴PK	0 受惠国$_1$LD$_1$	30	---Other methane, ethane and propane halogenated derivatives only with fluorine and chlorine
1931	2903.7990	---其他	5.5	0 澳AU,巴PK,冰岛IS,东盟AS,哥CR,秘鲁PE,新西兰NZ,智利CL 2.2 瑞士CH 3.3 韩国KR	0 受惠国$_1$LD$_1$	30	---Other
		-环烷烃、环烯烃或环萜烯烃的卤化衍生物:					-Halogenated derivatives of cyclanic, cyclenic or cycloterpenic hydrocarbons:
1932	2903.8100	--1, 2, 3, 4, 5, 6-六氯环己烷〔六六六（ISO)〕，包括林丹（ISO，INN）	5.5	0 澳AU,巴PK,冰岛IS,东盟AS,哥CR,秘鲁PE,新西兰NZ,智利CL 2.2 瑞士CH 3.3 韩国KR	0 受惠国$_1$LD$_1$	30	--1, 2, 3, 4, 5, 6-Hexachlorocyclohexane (HCH (ISO)), including lindane (ISO, INN)
1933	2903.8200	--艾氏剂（ISO）、氯丹（ISO）及七氯（ISO）	5.5	0 澳AU,巴PK,冰岛IS,东盟AS,哥CR,秘鲁PE,新西兰NZ,智利CL 2.2 瑞士CH 3.3 韩国KR	0 受惠国$_1$LD$_1$	30	--Aldrin (ISO), chlordane (ISO) and heptachlor (ISO)
1934	2903.8900	--其他	5.5	0 澳AU,巴PK,冰岛IS,东盟AS,哥CR,秘鲁PE,新西兰NZ,智利CL 2.2 瑞士CH 3.3 韩国KR	0 受惠国$_1$LD$_1$	30	--Other
		-芳烃卤化衍生物:					-Halogenated derivatives of aromatic hydrocarbons:
		--氯苯、邻二氯苯及对二氯苯:					--Chlorobenzene, *o*-dichlorobenzene and *p*-dichlorobenzene:

序号 No.	税则号列 Tariff Line	中文货品名称 Article Description in Chinese	最惠国税率 MFN(%)	协定税率 Agreement(%)	特惠税率 SP(%)	普通税率 Gen(%)	英文货品名称 Article Description
1935	2903.9110	---邻二氯苯	5.5	0 澳AU,巴PK,冰岛IS,东盟AS,哥CR,秘鲁PE,新西兰NZ,智利CL 2.2 瑞士CH 4.4 韩国KR	0 受惠国$_1$LD$_1$	30	---O-Dichlorobenzene
1936	2903.9190	---其他	5.5	0 澳AU,冰岛IS,东盟AS,哥CR,秘鲁PE,新西兰NZ,智利CL 2.2 瑞士CH 3.3 韩国KR 5 巴PK	0 受惠国$_1$LD$_1$	30	---Other
1937	2903.9200	--六氯苯（ISO）及滴滴涕（ISO，INN）〔1，1，1-三氯-2，2-双（4-氯苯基）乙烷〕	5.5	0 澳AU,巴PK,冰岛IS,东盟AS,哥CR,秘鲁PE,新西兰NZ,智利CL 2.2 瑞士CH 3.3 韩国KR	0 受惠国$_1$LD$_1$	30	--Hexachlorobenzene (ISO) and DDT (ISO) (clofenotane (INN), 1, 1, 1-trichloro-2, 2-bis (p-chlorophenyl) ethane)
		--其他：					--Other:
1938	2903.9910	---对氯甲苯	5.5	0 澳AU,巴PK,冰岛IS,东盟AS,哥CR,秘鲁PE,新西兰NZ,智利CL 2.2 瑞士CH 3.3 韩国KR	0 受惠国$_1$LD$_1$	30	---P-Chlorotoluene
1939	2903.9920	---3，4-二氯三氟甲苯	5.5	0 澳AU,巴PK,冰岛IS,东盟AS,哥CR,秘鲁PE,新西兰NZ,智利CL 2.2 瑞士CH 3.3 韩国KR	0 受惠国$_1$LD$_1$	30	---3, 4-Dichlorotrifluoride toluene
1940	2903.9930	---4-(4-烷基苯基)-1-(4-烷基苯基)-2-氟苯	5.5	0 澳AU,冰岛IS,东盟AS,哥CR,秘鲁PE,新西兰NZ,智利CL 2.2 瑞士CH 3.3 韩国KR 5 巴PK	0 受惠国$_1$LD$_1$	30	---4- (4-alkylphenyl) -1-(4-alkylphenyl) -2-fluorobenzene
1941	2903.9990	---其他	5.5	0 澳AU,冰岛IS,东盟AS,哥CR,秘鲁PE,新西兰NZ,智利CL 2.2 瑞士CH 3.3 韩国KR 5 巴PK	0 受惠国$_1$LD$_1$	30	---Other
	29.04	**烃的磺化、硝化或亚硝化衍生物，不论是否卤化：**					**Sulphonated, nitrated or nitrosated derivatives of hydrocarbons, whether or not halogenated:**
1942	2904.1000	-仅含磺基的衍生物及其盐和乙酯	5.5	0 澳AU,冰岛IS,东盟AS,哥CR,秘鲁PE,香港HK,新西兰NZ,智利CL 2.2 瑞士CH 3.3 韩国KR 5 巴PK	0 受惠国$_1$LD$_1$	30	-Derivatives containing only sulpho groups, their salts and ethyl esters
		-仅含硝基或亚硝基的衍生物：					-Derivatives containing only nitro or only nitroso groups:
1943	2904.2010	---硝基苯	5.5	0 澳AU,巴PK,冰岛IS,东盟AS,哥CR,秘鲁PE,新西兰NZ,智利CL 2.2 瑞士CH 3.3 韩国KR	0 受惠国$_1$LD$_1$	20	---Nitrobenzene
1944	2904.2020	---硝基甲苯	5.5	0 澳AU,巴PK,冰岛IS,东盟AS,哥CR,秘鲁PE,新西兰NZ,智利CL 2.2 瑞士CH 3.3 韩国KR	0 受惠国$_1$LD$_1$	30	---Nitrotoluene and nitrochlorobenzene
1945	2904.2030	---二硝基甲苯	5.5	0 澳AU,巴PK,冰岛IS,东盟AS,哥CR,秘鲁PE,新西兰NZ,智利CL 2.2 瑞士CH 3.3 韩国KR	0 受惠国$_1$LD$_1$	20	---Dinitrotoluene and dinitrochlorobenzene

序号 No.	税则号列 Tariff Line	中文货品名称 Article Description in Chinese	最惠国税率 MFN(%)	协定税率 Agreement(%)	特惠税率 SP(%)	普通税率 Gen(%)	英文货品名称 Article Description
1946	2904.2040	---三硝基甲苯（TNT）	5.5	0 澳AU,巴PK,冰岛IS,东盟AS,哥CR,秘鲁PE,新西兰NZ,智利CL 2.2 瑞士CH 3.3 韩国KR	0 受惠国$_1$LD$_1$	40	---Trinitrotoluene
1947	2904.2090	---其他	5.5	0 澳AU,冰岛IS,东盟AS,哥CR,秘鲁PE,新西兰NZ,智利CL 2.2 瑞士CH 3.3 韩国KR 5 巴PK	0 受惠国$_1$LD$_1$	30	---Other
		-其他：					-Other:
		---硝基氯化苯：					---Nitrochlorobenzene:
1948	2904.9011	----邻硝基氯化苯	5.5	0 澳AU,巴PK,冰岛IS,东盟AS,哥CR,秘鲁PE,新西兰NZ,智利CL 2.2 瑞士CH 3.3 韩国KR	0 受惠国$_1$LD$_1$	30	----O-nitrochlorobenzene
1949	2904.9012	----间硝基氯化苯	5.5	0 澳AU,巴PK,冰岛IS,东盟AS,哥CR,秘鲁PE,新西兰NZ,智利CL 2.2 瑞士CH 3.3 韩国KR	0 受惠国$_1$LD$_1$	30	----M-nitrochlorobenzene
1950	2904.9013	----对硝基氯化苯	5.5	0 澳AU,巴PK,冰岛IS,东盟AS,哥CR,秘鲁PE,新西兰NZ,智利CL 2.2 瑞士CH 3.3 韩国KR	0 受惠国$_1$LD$_1$	30	----P-nitrochlorobenzene
1951	2904.9020	---二硝基氯化苯	5.5	0 澳AU,巴PK,冰岛IS,东盟AS,哥CR,秘鲁PE,新西兰NZ,智利CL 2.2 瑞士CH 3.3 韩国KR	0 受惠国$_1$LD$_1$	20	---Dinitrochlorobenzene
1952	2904.9030	---三氯硝基甲烷（氯化苦；硝基氯仿）	5.5	0 澳AU,巴PK,冰岛IS,东盟AS,哥CR,秘鲁PE,新西兰NZ,智利CL 2.2 瑞士CH 3.3 韩国KR	0 受惠国$_1$LD$_1$	30	---Trichloronitromethane (chloropicrin, nitrochloroform)
1953	2904.9090	---其他	5.5	0 澳AU,冰岛IS,东盟AS,哥CR,秘鲁PE,新西兰NZ,智利CL 2.2 瑞士CH 3.3 韩国KR 5 巴PK	0 受惠国$_1$LD$_1$	30	---Other
		第二分章　醇类及其卤化、磺化、硝化或亚硝化衍生物					II. ALCOHOLS AND THEIR HALOGENATED, SULPHONATED, NITRATED OR NITR-OSATED DERIVATIVES
	29.05	**无环醇及其卤化、磺化、硝化或亚硝化衍生物：**					**Acyclic alcohols and their halogenated, sulphonated, nitrated or nitrosated derivatives:**
		-饱和一元醇：					-Saturated monohydric alcohols:
1954	2905.1100	--甲醇	5.5	0 澳AU,澳门MO,巴PK,冰岛IS,东盟AS,哥CR,香港HK,新西兰NZ,智利CL 2.2 瑞士CH		30	--Methanol (methyl alcohol)
		--丙醇及异丙醇：					--Propan-1-ol (propyl alcohol) and propan-2-ol (isopropyl alcohol) :
1955	2905.1210	---丙醇	5.5∆3	0 澳AU,巴PK,冰岛IS,东盟AS,哥CR,秘鲁PE,新西兰NZ,智利CL 2.2 瑞士CH 4.7 韩国KR	0 受惠国$_1$LD$_1$	30	---Propan-1-ol (propyl alcohol)

序号 No.	税则号列 Tariff Line	中文货品名称 Article Description in Chinese	最惠国税率 MFN(%)	协定税率 Agreement(%)	特惠税率 SP(%)	普通税率 Gen(%)	英文货品名称 Article Description
1956	2905.1220	---异丙醇	5.5	0 澳AU,巴PK,冰岛IS,东盟AS,哥CR,秘鲁PE,台湾TW,新西兰NZ,智利CL 2.2 瑞士CH 4.7 韩国KR	0 受惠国$_1$LD$_1$	30	---Propan-2-ol (isopropyl alcohol)
1957	2905.1300	--正丁醇	5.5	0 澳AU,巴PK,冰岛IS,东盟AS,哥CR,秘鲁PE,台湾TW,新西兰NZ,智利CL 2.2 瑞士CH 4.7 韩国KR	0 受惠国$_1$LD$_1$	30	--Butan-1-ol (n-butyl alcohol)
		--其他丁醇:					--Other butanols:
1958	2905.1410	---异丁醇	5.5	0 澳AU,巴PK,冰岛IS,东盟AS,哥CR,秘鲁PE,台湾TW,新西兰NZ,智利CL 2.2 瑞士CH 4.7 韩国KR	0 受惠国$_1$LD$_1$	30	---Iso-butyl alcohol
1959	2905.1420	---仲丁醇	5.5	0 澳AU,巴PK,冰岛IS,东盟AS,哥CR,秘鲁PE,新西兰NZ,智利CL 2.2 瑞士CH 4.7 韩国KR	0 受惠国$_1$LD$_1$	30	---Sec-butyl alcohol
1960	2905.1430	---叔丁醇	5.5	0 澳AU,巴PK,冰岛IS,东盟AS,哥CR,秘鲁PE,新西兰NZ,智利CL 2.2 瑞士CH 4.7 韩国KR	0 受惠国$_1$LD$_1$	30	---Tert-butgl alcohol
		--辛醇及其异构体:					--Octanol (octyl alcohol) and isomers thereof:
1961	2905.1610	---正辛醇	5.5	0 澳AU,冰岛IS,东盟AS,哥CR,新西兰NZ,智利CL 2.2 瑞士CH 5 巴PK		30	---N-octyl alchol
1962	2905.1690	---其他	5.5	0 澳AU,冰岛IS,东盟AS,哥CR,新西兰NZ,智利CL 2.2 瑞士CH 5 巴PK		30	---Other
1963	2905.1700	--十二醇、十六醇及十八醇	7	0 冰岛IS,东盟AS,哥CR,秘鲁PE,新西兰NZ,智利CL 2.8 瑞士CH 4.2 澳AU 5 巴PK 6 韩国KR	0 受惠国$_1$LD$_1$	30	--Dodecan-1-ol (lauryl alcohol), hexade can-1-ol (cetyl alcohol) and octadecan-1-ol (stearyl alcohol)
		--其他:					--Other:
1964	2905.1910	---3，3-二甲基丁-2-醇（频哪基醇）	5.5	0 澳AU,巴PK,冰岛IS,东盟AS,哥CR,秘鲁PE,新西兰NZ,智利CL 2.2 瑞士CH 3.3 韩国KR	0 受惠国$_1$LD$_1$	30	---3, 3-Dimethyl-2-butanol (pinacolyl alcohol)
1965	2905.1990	---其他	5.5	0 澳AU,冰岛IS,东盟AS,哥CR,秘鲁PE,新西兰NZ,智利CL 3.3 韩国KR 3.9 瑞士CH 5 巴PK	0 受惠国$_1$LD$_1$	30	---Other
		-不饱和一元醇:					-Unsaturated monohydric alcohols:
		--无环萜烯醇:					--Acyclic terpene alcohols:

序号 No.	税则号列 Tariff Line	中文货品名称 Article Description in Chinese	最惠国税率 MFN(%)	协定税率 Agreement(%)	特惠税率 SP(%)	普通税率 Gen(%)	英文货品名称 Article Description
1966	2905.2210	---香叶醇、橙花醇（3，7-二甲基-2，6-辛二烯-1-醇）	5.5	0 澳AU,巴PK,冰岛IS,东盟AS,哥CR,秘鲁PE,新西兰NZ,智利CL 2.2 瑞士CH 3.3 韩国KR	0 受惠国$_1$LD$_1$	30	---Geraniol, nerol (cis-3, 7-Dimethyl-2, 6-octadien-1-ol)
1967	2905.2220	---香茅醇（3，7-二甲基-6-辛烯-1-醇）	5.5	0 澳AU,冰岛IS,东盟AS,哥CR,秘鲁PE,新西兰NZ,智利CL 2.2 瑞士CH 3.3 韩国KR 5 巴PK	0 受惠国$_1$LD$_1$	30	---Citronellol (3, 7-Dimethyl-6-octen -1-ol)
1968	2905.2230	---芳樟醇	5.5	0 澳AU,冰岛IS,东盟AS,哥CR,秘鲁PE,新西兰NZ,智利CL 3.3 韩国KR 5 巴PK	0 受惠国$_1$LD$_1$	30	---Linalool
1969	2905.2290	---其他	5.5	0 澳AU,冰岛IS,东盟AS,哥CR,秘鲁PE,新西兰NZ,智利CL 3.3 韩国KR 4 瑞士CH 5 巴PK	0 受惠国$_1$LD$_1$	30	---Other
1970	2905.2900	--其他	5.5	0 澳AU,冰岛IS,东盟AS,哥CR,秘鲁PE,新西兰NZ,智利CL 2.2 瑞士CH 3.3 韩国KR 5 巴PK	0 受惠国$_1$LD$_1$	30	--Other
		-二元醇：					-Diols:
1971	2905.3100	--1，2-乙二醇	5.5	0 澳AU,冰岛IS,哥CR,新西兰NZ,智利CL		30	--Ethylene glycol (ethanediol)
1972	2905.3200	--1，2-丙二醇	5.5Δ3	0 澳AU,冰岛IS,东盟AS,哥CR,秘鲁PE,新西兰NZ,智利CL 2.2 瑞士CH 4.4 韩国KR 5 巴PK	0 受惠国$_1$LD$_1$	30	--Propylene glycol (propane-1, 2-diol)
		--其他：					--Other:
1973	2905.3910	---2，5-二甲基已二醇	4	0 澳AU,巴PK,冰岛IS,东盟AS,哥CR,韩国KR,秘鲁PE,瑞士CH,新西兰NZ,智利CL	0 受惠国$_1$LD$_1$	11	---2, 5-dimethyl hexandiol
1974	2905.3990	---其他	5.5	0 澳AU,冰岛IS,东盟AS,哥CR,秘鲁PE,新西兰NZ,智利CL 2.2 瑞士CH 5 巴PK	0 受惠国$_1$LD$_1$	30	---Other
	ex29053990	1，3-丙二醇	Δ3				1, 3-dihydroxypropare
		-其他多元醇：					-Other polyhydric alcohols:
1975	2905.4100	--2-乙基-2-（羟甲基）丙烷-1，3-二醇（三羟甲基丙烷）	5.5	0 澳AU,巴PK,冰岛IS,东盟AS,哥CR,秘鲁PE,新西兰NZ,智利CL 2.2 瑞士CH 3.3 韩国KR	0 受惠国$_1$LD$_1$	30	--2-Ethyl-2- (hydroxymethyl) propane-1, 3-diol (trimethylolpropane)
1976	2905.4200	--季戊四醇	5.5	0 澳AU,冰岛IS,东盟AS,哥CR,秘鲁PE,新西兰NZ,智利CL 2.2 瑞士CH 4.4 韩国KR 5 巴PK	0 受惠国$_1$LD$_1$	30	--Pentaerythritol
1977	2905.4300	--甘露糖醇	8	0 冰岛IS,东盟AS,哥CR,秘鲁PE,新西兰NZ,智利CL 3.2 瑞士CH 4.8 澳AU,韩国KR 5 巴PK	0 受惠国LD	30	--Mannitol

序号 No.	税则号列 Tariff Line	中文货品名称 Article Description in Chinese	最惠国税率 MFN(%)	协定税率 Agreement(%)	特惠税率 SP(%)	普通税率 Gen(%)	英文货品名称 Article Description
1978	2905.4400	--山梨醇	14	0 冰岛IS,东盟AS,哥CR,秘鲁PE,新加坡SG,新西兰NZ,智利CL 8.4 澳AU 9.8 瑞士CH 11.2 巴PK,韩国KR	0 受惠国$_1$LD$_1$	40	--D-glucitol (sorbitol)
1979	2905.4500	--丙三醇（甘油）	14Δ3	0 澳门MO,冰岛IS,东盟AS,哥CR,秘鲁PE,新加坡SG,新西兰NZ,智利CL 7 巴PK 8.4 澳AU 9.8 瑞士CH 11.2 韩国KR,亚太AP	0 受惠国$_1$LD$_1$	50	--Glycerol
		--其他:					--Other:
1980	2905.4910	---木糖醇	5.5	0 澳AU,冰岛IS,东盟AS,哥CR,秘鲁PE,新西兰NZ,智利CL 2.2 瑞士CH 3.3 韩国KR 5 巴PK	0 受惠国$_1$LD$_1$	30	---Xylitol
1981	2905.4990	---其他	5.5	0 澳AU,冰岛IS,东盟AS,哥CR,秘鲁PE,新西兰NZ,智利CL 2.2 瑞士CH 3.3 韩国KR 5 巴PK	0 受惠国$_1$LD$_1$	30	---Other
		-无环醇的卤化、磺化、硝化或亚硝化衍生物:					-Halogenated, sulphonated, nitrated or nitrosated derivatives of acyclic alcohols:
1982	2905.5100	--乙氯维诺（INN）	5.5	0 澳AU,巴PK,冰岛IS,东盟AS,哥CR,秘鲁PE,新西兰NZ,智利CL 2.2 瑞士CH 3.3 韩国KR	0 受惠国$_1$LD$_1$	30	--Ethchlorvynol (INN)
1983	2905.5900	--其他	5.5	0 澳AU,冰岛IS,东盟AS,哥CR,秘鲁PE,新西兰NZ,智利CL 2.2 瑞士CH 4.4 韩国KR 5 巴PK	0 受惠国$_1$LD$_1$	30	--Other
	29.06	**环醇及其卤化、磺化、硝化或亚硝化衍生物:**					**Cyclic alcohols and their halogenated, sulphonated, nitrated or nitrosated derivatives:**
		-环烷醇、环烯醇及环萜烯醇:					-Cyclanic, cyclenic or cycloterpenic:
1984	2906.1100	--薄荷醇	5	0 澳AU,巴PK,冰岛IS,东盟AS,哥CR,秘鲁PE,瑞士CH,新西兰NZ,智利CL 3 韩国KR	0 受惠国$_1$LD$_1$	70	--Menthol
1985	2906.1200	--环己醇、甲基环己醇及二甲基环己醇	5.5	0 澳AU,冰岛IS,东盟AS,哥CR,秘鲁PE,新西兰NZ,智利CL 2.2 瑞士CH 3.3 韩国KR 5 巴PK	0 受惠国$_1$LD$_1$	30	--Cyclohexanol, methylcyclohexanols and dimethylcyclohexanols
		--固醇及肌醇:					--Sterols and inositols:
1986	2906.1310	---固醇	5.5Δ3	0 澳AU,巴PK,冰岛IS,东盟AS,哥CR,秘鲁PE,新西兰NZ,智利CL 2.2 瑞士CH 4.4 韩国KR	0 受惠国$_1$LD$_1$	30	---Sterol

序号 No.	税则号列 Tariff Line	中文货品名称 Article Description in Chinese	最惠国税率 MFN(%)	协定税率 Agreement(%)	特惠税率 SP(%)	普通税率 Gen(%)	英文货品名称 Article Description
1987	2906.1320	---肌醇	5.5	0 澳AU,冰岛IS,东盟AS,哥CR,秘鲁PE,新西兰NZ,智利CL 2.2 瑞士CH 3.3 韩国KR 5 巴PK	0 受惠国$_1$LD$_1$	30	---Inositol
		--其他:					--Other:
1988	2906.1910	---萜品醇	5.5	0 澳AU,冰岛IS,东盟AS,哥CR,秘鲁PE,新西兰NZ,智利CL 2.2 瑞士CH 3.3 韩国KR 5 巴PK	0 受惠国$_1$LD$_1$	30	---Terpineols
1989	2906.1990	---其他	5.5	0 澳AU,冰岛IS,东盟AS,哥CR,秘鲁PE,新西兰NZ,智利CL 3.3 韩国KR 5 巴PK	0 受惠国$_1$LD$_1$	30	---Other
		-芳香醇:					-Aromatic:
1990	2906.2100	--苄醇	5	0 澳AU,巴PK,冰岛IS,东盟AS,哥CR,秘鲁PE,瑞士CH,新西兰NZ,智利CL 3 韩国KR	0 受惠国$_1$LD$_1$	30	--Benzyl alcohol
		--其他:					--Other:
1991	2906.2910	---2-苯基乙醇	5.5	0 澳AU,冰岛IS,东盟AS,哥CR,秘鲁PE,新西兰NZ,智利CL 2.2 瑞士CH 3.3 韩国KR 5 巴PK	0 受惠国$_1$LD$_1$	30	---2-Phenyl ethyl alcohol
1992	2906.2990	---其他	5.5	0 澳AU,冰岛IS,东盟AS,哥CR,秘鲁PE,新西兰NZ,智利CL 4 瑞士CH 4.4 韩国KR 5 巴PK	0 受惠国$_1$LD$_1$	30	---Other
		第三分章　酚、酚醇及其卤化、磺化、硝化或亚硝化衍生物					III. PHENOLS, PHENOL-ALCOHOLS, AND THEIR HALOGENATED, SULPHONATED, NITRATED OR NITROSATED DERIVATIVES
	29.07	**酚;酚醇:**					**Phenols; phenol-alcohols:**
		-一元酚:					-Monophenols:
		--苯酚及其盐:					--Phenol (hydroxybenzene) and its salts:
1993	2907.1110	---苯酚	5.5	0 澳AU,巴PK,冰岛IS,东盟AS,哥CR,秘鲁PE,新西兰NZ,智利CL 2.2 瑞士CH	0 受惠国LD	30	---Phenol
1994	2907.1190	---其他	5.5	0 澳AU,巴PK,冰岛IS,东盟AS,哥CR,秘鲁PE,新西兰NZ,智利CL 3.9 瑞士CH	0 受惠国LD	30	---Other
		--甲酚及其盐:					--Cresols and their salts:
		---甲酚:					---Cresol:
1995	2907.1211	----间甲酚	5.5Δ3	0 澳AU,巴PK,冰岛IS,东盟AS,哥CR,秘鲁PE,新西兰NZ,智利CL 2.2 瑞士CH 3.3 韩国KR	0 受惠国LD	30	----*m*-Cresol

序号 No.	税则号列 Tariff Line	中文货品名称 Article Description in Chinese	最惠国税率 MFN(%)	协定税率 Agreement(%)	特惠税率 SP(%)	普通税率 Gen(%)	英文货品名称 Article Description
1996	2907.1212	----邻甲酚	5.5Δ3	0 澳AU,巴PK,冰岛IS,东盟AS,哥CR,秘鲁PE,新西兰NZ,智利CL 2.2 瑞士CH 3.3 韩国KR	0 受惠国LD	30	----*o*-Cresol
1997	2907.1219	----其他	5.5	0 澳AU,冰岛IS,东盟AS,哥CR,秘鲁PE,新西兰NZ,智利CL 2.2 瑞士CH 4.4 韩国KR 5 巴PK	0 受惠国LD	30	----Other
1998	2907.1290	---其他	5.5	0 澳AU,巴PK,冰岛IS,东盟AS,哥CR,秘鲁PE,新西兰NZ,智利CL 2.2 瑞士CH 3.3 韩国KR	0 受惠国LD	30	---Other
		--辛基酚、壬基酚及其异构体以及它们的盐:					--Octylphenol, nonylphenol and their isomers; salts thereof:
1999	2907.1310	---壬基酚	5.5	0 澳AU,巴PK,冰岛IS,东盟AS,哥CR,秘鲁PE,新西兰NZ,智利CL 2.2 瑞士CH	0 受惠国LD	30	---Nonylphenol
2000	2907.1390	---其他	5.5	0 澳AU,巴PK,冰岛IS,东盟AS,哥CR,秘鲁PE,新西兰NZ,智利CL 2.2 瑞士CH 4.7 韩国KR	0 受惠国LD	30	---Other
		--萘酚及其盐:					--Naphthols and their salts:
2001	2907.1510	---2-萘酚(β-萘酚)	5.5	0 澳AU,巴PK,冰岛IS,东盟AS,哥CR,秘鲁PE,新西兰NZ,智利CL 2.2 瑞士CH 3.3 韩国KR	0 受惠国LD	30	---2-Naphthols (β-naphthol)
2002	2907.1590	---其他	5.5	0 澳AU,冰岛IS,东盟AS,哥CR,秘鲁PE,新西兰NZ,智利CL 2.2 瑞士CH 3.3 韩国KR 5 巴PK	0 受惠国LD	30	---Other
		--其他:					--Other:
2003	2907.1910	---邻仲丁基酚、邻异丙基酚	4Δ2	0 澳AU,巴PK,冰岛IS,东盟AS,哥CR,韩国KR,秘鲁PE,新西兰NZ,智利CL 2.8 瑞士CH	0 受惠国LD	11	---O-Sec-butyl phenol, o isopropyl phenol
2004	2907.1990	---其他	5.5	0 澳AU,冰岛IS,东盟AS,哥CR,秘鲁PE,新西兰NZ,智利CL 3.3 韩国KR 3.9 瑞士CH 5 巴PK	0 受惠国LD	30	---Other
		-多元酚;酚醇:					-Polyphenols; phenol-alcohols:
2005	2907.2100	--间苯二酚及其盐	5.5	0 澳AU,冰岛IS,东盟AS,哥CR,秘鲁PE,新西兰NZ,智利CL 2.2 瑞士CH 4.4 韩国KR 5 巴PK	0 受惠国LD	30	--M-Dihydroxybenzene (resorcinol) and its salts
		--对苯二酚及其盐:					--Hydroquinone (quinol) and its salts:
2006	2907.2210	---对苯二酚	5.5	0 澳AU,冰岛IS,东盟AS,哥CR,秘鲁PE,新西兰NZ,智利CL 2.2 瑞士CH 3.3 韩国KR 5 巴PK	0 受惠国LD	30	---Hydroquinone

序号 No.	税则号列 Tariff Line	中文货品名称 Article Description in Chinese	最惠国税率 MFN(%)	协定税率 Agreement(%)	特惠税率 SP(%)	普通税率 Gen(%)	英文货品名称 Article Description
2007	2907.2290	---其他	5.5	0 澳AU,巴PK,冰岛IS,东盟AS,哥CR,秘鲁PE,新西兰NZ,智利CL 2.2 瑞士CH 3.3 韩国KR	0 受惠国LD	30	---Other
2008	2907.2300	--4，4′-异亚丙基联苯酚（双酚A，二苯基酚丙烷）及其盐	5.5	0 澳AU,冰岛IS,东盟AS,哥CR,秘鲁PE,新西兰NZ,智利CL 2.2 瑞士CH 5 巴PK	0 受惠国LD	30	--4, 4' -Isopropylidenediphenol (bisph-enol A, diphenylolpropane) and its salts
		--其他：					--Other:
2009	2907.2910	---邻苯二酚	4	0 澳AU,巴PK,冰岛IS,东盟AS,哥CR,秘鲁PE,瑞士CH,新西兰NZ,智利CL	0 受惠国LD	11	---O-Dihydroxybenzene (catechol, pyrocatechol)
2010	2907.2990	---其他	5.5	0 澳AU,冰岛IS,东盟AS,哥CR,秘鲁PE,新西兰NZ,智利CL 2.2 瑞士CH 4.7 韩国KR 5 巴PK	0 受惠国LD	30	---Other
	29.08	**酚及酚醇的卤化、磺化、硝化或亚硝化衍生物：**					**Halogenated, sulphonated, nitrated or nitrosated derivatives of phenols or phenol-alcohols:**
		-仅含卤素取代基的衍生物及其盐：					-Derivatives containing only halogen substituents and their salts:
2011	2908.1100	--五氯苯酚（ISO）	5.5	0 澳AU,冰岛IS,东盟AS,哥CR,秘鲁PE,新西兰NZ,智利CL 2.2 瑞士CH 3.3 韩国KR 5 巴PK	0 受惠国$_1$LD$_1$	30	--Pentachlorophenol (ISO)
		--其他：					--Other:
2012	2908.1910	---对氯苯酚	4	0 澳AU,巴PK,冰岛IS,东盟AS,哥CR,韩国KR,秘鲁PE,瑞士CH,新西兰NZ,智利CL	0 受惠国$_1$LD$_1$	11	---P-Chlorophenol
2013	2908.1990	---其他	5.5	0 澳AU,冰岛IS,东盟AS,哥CR,秘鲁PE,新西兰NZ,智利CL 2.2 瑞士CH 3.3 韩国KR 5 巴PK	0 受惠国$_1$LD$_1$	30	---Other
		-其他：					-Other:
2014	2908.9100	--地乐酚（ISO）及其盐	5.5	0 澳AU,冰岛IS,东盟AS,哥CR,秘鲁PE,新西兰NZ,智利CL 2.2 瑞士CH 3.3 韩国KR 5 巴PK	0 受惠国$_1$LD$_1$	30	--Dinoseb (ISO) and its salts
2015	2908.9200	--4，6-二硝基邻甲酚〔二硝酚（ISO）〕及其盐	5.5	0 澳AU,冰岛IS,东盟AS,哥CR,秘鲁PE,新西兰NZ,智利CL 2.2 瑞士CH 3.3 韩国KR 5 巴PK	0 受惠国$_1$LD$_1$	30	--4, 6-Dinitro-o-cresol (DNOC (ISO)) and its salts
		--其他：					--Other:
2016	2908.9910	---对硝基酚、对硝基酚钠	5.5	0 澳AU,巴PK,冰岛IS,东盟AS,哥CR,秘鲁PE,新西兰NZ,智利CL 2.2 瑞士CH 3.3 韩国KR	0 受惠国$_1$LD$_1$	30	---P-Nitrophenol, sodium p-nitro-phenolate

序号 No.	税则号列 Tariff Line	中文货品名称 Article Description in Chinese	最惠国税率 MFN(%)	协定税率 Agreement(%)	特惠税率 SP(%)	普通税率 Gen(%)	英文货品名称 Article Description
2017	2908.9990	---其他	5.5	0 澳AU,冰岛IS,东盟AS,哥CR,秘鲁PE,新西兰NZ,智利CL 2.2 瑞士CH 4.4 韩国KR 5 巴PK	0 受惠国$_1$LD$_1$	30	---Other
		第四分章　醚、过氧化醇、过氧化醚、过氧化酮、三节环环氧化物、缩醛及半缩醛及其卤化、磺化、硝化或亚硝化衍生物					IV. ETHERS, ALCOHOL PEROXIDES, ETHER PEROXIDES, KETONE PEROXIDES, EPOXIDES WITH A THREE-MEMBERED RING, ACETALS AND HEMIACETALS, AND THEIR HALOGENATED, SULPHONATED, NITRATED OR NITROSATED DERIVATIVES
	29.09	**醚、醚醇、醚酚、醚醇酚、过氧化醇、过氧化醚、过氧化酮(不论是否已有化学定义)及其卤化、磺化、硝化或亚硝化衍生物:**					**Ethers, ether-alcohols, ether-phenols, ether-alcohol-phenols, alcohol peroxides, ether peroxides, ketone peroxides (whether or not chemically defined) , and their halogenated, sulphonated, nitrated or nitrosated derivatives:**
		-无环醚及其卤化、磺化、硝化或亚硝化衍生物:					-Acyclic ethers and their halogenated, sulphonated, nitrated or nitrosated derivatives:
2018	2909.1100	--乙醚	5.5	0 澳AU,巴PK,冰岛IS,东盟AS,哥CR,秘鲁PE,新西兰NZ,智利CL 2.2 瑞士CH 3.3 韩国KR	0 受惠国LD	30	--Diethyl ether
		--其他:					--Other:
2019	2909.1910	---甲醚	5.5	0 澳AU,冰岛IS,东盟AS,哥CR,新西兰NZ,智利CL 2.2 瑞士CH 4.7 韩国KR 5 巴PK	0 受惠国$_2$LD$_2$	30	---Methyl ether
2020	2909.1990	---其他	5.5	0 澳AU,冰岛IS,东盟AS,哥CR,新西兰NZ,智利CL 2.2 瑞士CH 4.7 韩国KR 5 巴PK	0 受惠国$_2$LD$_2$	30	---Other
2021	2909.2000	-环烷醚、环烯醚或环萜烯醚及其卤化、磺化、硝化或亚硝化衍生物	5.5	0 澳AU,巴PK,冰岛IS,东盟AS,哥CR,秘鲁PE,新西兰NZ,智利CL 2.2 瑞士CH 3.3 韩国KR	0 受惠国LD	30	-Cyclanic, cyclenic or cycloterpenic ethers and their halogenated, sulphonated, nitrated or nitrosated derivatives
		-芳香醚及其卤化、磺化、硝化或亚硝化衍生物:					-Aromatic ethers and their halogenated, sulphonated, nitrated or nitrosated derivatives:
2022	2909.3010	---1-烷氧基-4-(4-乙烯基环己基)-2,3-二氟苯	5.5	0 澳AU,冰岛IS,东盟AS,哥CR,秘鲁PE,新西兰NZ,智利CL 2.2 瑞士CH 3.3 韩国KR 5 巴PK	0 受惠国LD	30	---1-alkoxy-4- (4-vinylcyclohexyl) -2, 3-difluoro benzene

序号 No.	税则号列 Tariff Line	中文货品名称 Article Description in Chinese	最惠国税率 MFN(%)	协定税率 Agreement(%)	特惠税率 SP(%)	普通税率 Gen(%)	英文货品名称 Article Description
2023	2909.3090	---其他	5.5	0 澳AU,冰岛IS,东盟AS,哥CR,秘鲁PE,新西兰NZ,智利CL 2.2 瑞士CH 3.3 韩国KR 5 巴PK	0 受惠国LD	30	---Other
		-醚醇及其卤化、磺化、硝化或亚硝化衍生物：					-Ether-alcohols and their halogenated, sulphonated, nitrated or nitrosated derivatives:
2024	2909.4100	--2，2′-氧联二乙醇（二甘醇）	5.5Δ3	0 澳AU,巴PK,冰岛IS,东盟AS,哥CR,韩国KR,台湾TW,新西兰NZ,智利CL 2.2 瑞士CH	0 受惠国$_2$LD$_2$	30	--2, 2' -Oxydiethanol (diethylene glycol, digol)
2025	2909.4300	--乙二醇或二甘醇的单丁醚	5.5	0 澳AU,澳门MO,冰岛IS,东盟AS,哥CR,韩国KR,秘鲁PE,台湾TW,新西兰NZ,智利CL 2.2 瑞士CH 5 巴PK	0 受惠国LD	30	--Monobutyl ethers of ethylene glycol or of diethylene glycol
2026	2909.4400	--乙二醇或二丁醇的其他单烷基醚	5.5	0 澳AU,冰岛IS,东盟AS,哥CR,秘鲁PE,新西兰NZ,智利CL 2.2 瑞士CH 4.7 韩国KR 5 巴PK	0 受惠国LD	30	--Other monoalkylethers of ethylene glycol or of diethylene glycol
		--其他：					--Other:
2027	2909.4910	---间苯氧基苄醇	4	0 澳AU,巴PK,冰岛IS,东盟AS,哥CR,韩国KR,秘鲁PE,瑞士CH,新西兰NZ,智利CL	0 受惠国LD	11	---M-Phenoxy benzalcohol
2028	2909.4990	---其他	5.5	0 澳AU,冰岛IS,东盟AS,哥CR,秘鲁PE,新西兰NZ,智利CL 2.2 瑞士CH 4.7 韩国KR 5 巴PK	0 受惠国LD	30	---Other
2029	2909.5000	-醚酚、醚醇酚及其卤化、磺化、硝化或亚硝化衍生物	5.5	0 澳AU,东盟AS,哥CR,秘鲁PE,新西兰NZ,智利CL 2.2 瑞士CH 4.7 韩国KR 5 巴PK	0 受惠国LD	30	-Ether-phenols, ether-alcohol-phen-ols and their halogenated, sulphonated, nitrated or nitrosated derivatives
2030	2909.6000	-过氧化醇、过氧化醚、过氧化酮及其卤化、磺化、硝化或亚硝化衍生物	5.5	0 澳AU,冰岛IS,东盟AS,哥CR,秘鲁PE,新西兰NZ,智利CL 2.2 瑞士CH 4.7 韩国KR 5 巴PK	0 受惠国LD	30	-Alcohol peroxides, ether peroxides, ketone peroxides and their halogenated, sulphonated, nitrated or nitrosated derivatives
	29.10	**三节环环氧化物、环氧醇、环氧酚、环氧醚及其卤化、磺化、硝化或亚硝化衍生物：**					**Epoxides, epoxyalcohols, epox-yphenols and epoxyethers, with a three-membered ring, and their halogenated, sulphonated, nitrated or nitrosated derivatives:**
2031	2910.1000	-环氧乙烷（氧化乙烯）	5.5	0 澳AU,巴PK,冰岛IS,东盟AS,哥CR,秘鲁PE,新西兰NZ,智利CL 2.2 瑞士CH 4.7 韩国KR	0 受惠国$_1$LD$_1$	30	-Oxirane (ethylene oxide)
2032	2910.2000	-甲基环氧乙烷（氧化丙烯）	5.5	0 澳AU,巴PK,冰岛IS,东盟AS,哥CR,秘鲁PE,新西兰NZ,智利CL 2.2 瑞士CH 4.7 韩国KR	0 受惠国$_1$LD$_1$	30	-Methyloxirane (propylene oxide)

序号 No.	税则号列 Tariff Line	中文货品名称 Article Description in Chinese	最惠国税率 MFN(%)	协定税率 Agreement(%)	特惠税率 SP(%)	普通税率 Gen(%)	英文货品名称 Article Description
2033	2910.3000	-1-氯-2,3-环氧丙烷（表氯醇）	5.5	0 澳AU,冰岛IS,东盟AS,哥CR,秘鲁PE,台湾TW,新西兰NZ,智利CL 2.2 瑞士CH 4.4 韩国KR 5 巴PK	0 受惠国$_1$LD$_1$	30	-1-Chloro-2, 3-epoxypropane (epichlorohydrin)
2034	2910.4000	-狄氏剂（ISO，INN）	5.5	0 澳AU,冰岛IS,东盟AS,哥CR,秘鲁PE,新西兰NZ,智利CL 2.2 瑞士CH 3.3 韩国KR 5 巴PK	0 受惠国$_1$LD$_1$	30	-Dieldrin (ISO, INN)
2035	2910.9000	-其他	5.5	0 澳AU,澳门MO,冰岛IS,东盟AS,哥CR,秘鲁PE,新西兰NZ,智利CL 3.3 韩国KR 4 瑞士CH 5 巴PK	0 受惠国$_1$LD$_1$	30	-Other
	29.11	**缩醛及半缩醛，不论是否含有其他含氧基，及其卤化、磺化、硝化或亚硝化衍生物**					**Acetals and hemiacetals, whether or not with other oxygen function, and their halogenated, sulphonated, nitrated or nitrosated derivatives**
2036	2911.0000	缩醛及半缩醛，不论是否含有其他含氧基，及其卤化、磺化、硝化或亚硝化衍生物	5.5	0 澳AU,冰岛IS,东盟AS,哥CR,秘鲁PE,新西兰NZ,智利CL 4 瑞士CH 4.4 韩国KR 5 巴PK	0 受惠国$_1$LD$_1$	30	Acetals and hemiacetals, whether or not with other oxygen function, and their halogenated, sulphonated, nitrated or nitrosated derivatives
		第五分章　醛基化合物					V. ALDEHYDE-FUNCTION COMPOUNDS
	29.12	**醛，不论是否含有其他含氧基；环聚醛；多聚甲醛：**					**Aldehydes, whether or not with other oxygen function; cyclic polymers of aldehydes; paraformaldehyde:**
		-不含其他含氧基的无环醛：					-Acyclic aldehydes without other oxygen function:
2037	2912.1100	--甲醛	5.5	0 澳AU,巴PK,冰岛IS,东盟AS,哥CR,秘鲁PE,新西兰NZ,智利CL 2.2 瑞士CH 3.3 韩国KR	0 受惠国$_1$LD$_1$	30	--Methanal (formaldehyde)
2038	2912.1200	--乙醛	5.5	0 澳AU,巴PK,冰岛IS,东盟AS,哥CR,秘鲁PE,新西兰NZ,智利CL 2.2 瑞士CH 3.3 韩国KR	0 受惠国$_1$LD$_1$	30	--Ethanal (acetaldehyde)
2039	2912.1900	--其他	5.5	0 澳AU,冰岛IS,东盟AS,哥CR,秘鲁PE,新西兰NZ,智利CL 3.9 瑞士CH 4.7 韩国KR 5 巴PK	0 受惠国$_1$LD$_1$	30	--Other
	ex29121900	乙二醛	Δ3				Glyoxal (Ethanedial)
		-不含其他含氧基的环醛：					-Cyclic aldehydes without other oxygen function:
2040	2912.2100	--苯甲醛	5.5	0 澳AU,冰岛IS,东盟AS,哥CR,秘鲁PE,新西兰NZ,智利CL 2.2 瑞士CH 3.3 韩国KR 5 巴PK	0 受惠国$_1$LD$_1$	30	--Benzaldehyde
		--其他：					--Other:

序号 No.	税则号列 Tariff Line	中文货品名称 Article Description in Chinese	最惠国税率 MFN(%)	协定税率 Agreement(%)	特惠税率 SP(%)	普通税率 Gen(%)	英文货品名称 Article Description
2041	2912.2910	---铃兰醛（对叔丁基-α-甲基-氧化肉桂醛）	5.5	0 澳AU,冰岛IS,东盟AS,哥CR,秘鲁PE,新西兰NZ,智利CL 2.2 瑞士CH 3.3 韩国KR 5 巴PK	0 受惠国$_1$LD$_1$	30	---Lilial (p-tert-butyl-α-methyl-oxocinnamaldehyde)
2042	2912.2990	---其他	5.5	0 澳AU,冰岛IS,东盟AS,哥CR,秘鲁PE,新西兰NZ,智利CL 3.3 韩国KR 4 瑞士CH 5 巴PK	0 受惠国$_1$LD$_1$	30	---Other
		-醛醇、醛醚、醛酚及含其他含氧基的醛：					-Aldehyde-alcohols, aldehyde-ethers, aldehyde-phenols and aldehydes with other oxygen function:
2043	2912.4100	--香草醛（3-甲氧基-4-羟基苯甲醛）	5.5	0 澳AU,冰岛IS,东盟AS,哥CR,秘鲁PE,新西兰NZ,智利CL 2.2 瑞士CH 3.3 韩国KR 5 巴PK	0 受惠国$_1$LD$_1$	30	--Vanillin (4-hydroxy-3-metho-xybenzaldehyde)
2044	2912.4200	--乙基香草醛（3-乙氧基-4-羟基苯甲醛）	5.5	0 澳AU,冰岛IS,东盟AS,哥CR,秘鲁PE,新西兰NZ,智利CL 2.2 瑞士CH 3.3 韩国KR 5 巴PK	0 受惠国$_1$LD$_1$	30	--Ethylvanillin (3-ethoxy-4-hydrox-yben-zaldehyde)
		--其他：					--Other:
2045	2912.4910	---醛醇	5.5	0 澳AU,冰岛IS,东盟AS,哥CR,秘鲁PE,新西兰NZ,智利CL 2.2 瑞士CH 3.3 韩国KR 5 巴PK	0 受惠国$_1$LD$_1$	30	---Aldehyde-alcohols
2046	2912.4990	---其他	5.5	0 澳AU,冰岛IS,东盟AS,哥CR,秘鲁PE,新西兰NZ,智利CL 2.2 瑞士CH 3.3 韩国KR 5 巴PK	0 受惠国$_1$LD$_1$	30	---Other
2047	2912.5000	-环聚醛	5.5	0 澳AU,巴PK,冰岛IS,东盟AS,哥CR,秘鲁PE,新西兰NZ,智利CL 4.7 韩国KR	0 受惠国$_1$LD$_1$	30	-Cyclic-polymers of aldehydes
2048	2912.6000	-多聚甲醛	5.5	0 澳AU,冰岛IS,东盟AS,哥CR,秘鲁PE,新西兰NZ,智利CL 2.2 瑞士CH 4.7 韩国KR 5 巴PK	0 受惠国$_1$LD$_1$	30	-Paraformaldehyde
	29.13	**税号29.12所列产品的卤化、磺化、硝化或亚硝化衍生物**					**Halogenated, sulphonated, nitrated or nitrosated derivatives of products of heading 2912**
2049	2913.0000	税号29.12所列产品的卤化、磺化、硝化或亚硝化衍生物	5.5	0 澳AU,冰岛IS,东盟AS,哥CR,秘鲁PE,新西兰NZ,智利CL 2.2 瑞士CH 3.3 韩国KR 5 巴PK	0 受惠国$_1$LD$_1$	30	Halogenated, sulphonated, nitrated or nitrosated derivatives of products of heading No.29.12
		第六分章　酮基化合物及醌基化合物					VI. KETONE-FUNCTION COMPOUNDS AND QUINONE-FUNCTION COMPOUNDS

序号 No.	税则号列 Tariff Line	中文货品名称 Article Description in Chinese	最惠国税率 MFN(%)	协定税率 Agreement(%)	特惠税率 SP(%)	普通税率 Gen(%)	英文货品名称 Article Description
	29.14	**酮及醌，不论是否含有其他含氧基，及其卤化、磺化、硝化或亚硝化衍生物：**					**Ketones and quinones, whether or not with other oxygen function, and their halogenated, sulphonated, nitrated or nitrosated derivatives:**
		-不含其他含氧基的无环酮：					-Acyclic ketones without other oxygen function:
2050	2914.1100	--丙酮	5.5	0 澳AU,巴PK,冰岛IS,东盟AS,哥CR,秘鲁PE,新西兰NZ,智利CL 2.2 瑞士CH	0 受惠国$_1$LD$_1$	20	--Acetone
2051	2914.1200	--丁酮［甲基乙基（甲）酮］	5.5	0 澳AU,澳门MO,巴PK,冰岛IS,东盟AS,哥CR,秘鲁PE,新西兰NZ,智利CL 2.2 瑞士CH	0 受惠国$_1$LD$_1$	30	--Butanone (methyl ethyl ketone)
2052	2914.1300	--4-甲基-2-戊酮［甲基异丁基（甲）酮］	5.5	0 澳AU,巴PK,冰岛IS,东盟AS,哥CR,秘鲁PE,新西兰NZ,智利CL 2.2 瑞士CH 4.7 韩国KR	0 受惠国$_1$LD$_1$	30	--4-Methyl-2-pentanone (isobutyl methyl ketone)
2053	2914.1900	--其他	5.5	0 澳AU,冰岛IS,东盟AS,哥CR,秘鲁PE,新西兰NZ,智利CL 2.2 瑞士CH 4.7 韩国KR 5 巴PK	0 受惠国$_1$LD$_1$	30	--Other
		-不含其他含氧基的环烷酮、环烯酮或环萜烯酮：					-Cyclanic, cyclenic or cycloterpenic ketones without other oxygen function:
2054	2914.2200	--环已酮及甲基环已酮	5.5	0 澳AU,巴PK,冰岛IS,东盟AS,哥CR,秘鲁PE,新西兰NZ,智利CL 2.2 瑞士CH 4.7 韩国KR	0 受惠国$_1$LD$_1$	30	--Cyclohexanone and methylcyclo-hexanone
2055	2914.2300	--芷香酮及甲基芷香酮	5.5	0 澳AU,巴PK,冰岛IS,东盟AS,哥CR,秘鲁PE,新西兰NZ,智利CL 3.3 韩国KR	0 受惠国$_1$LD$_1$	30	--Ionones and methylionones
		--其他：					--Other:
2056	2914.2910	---樟脑	5.5	0 澳AU,冰岛IS,东盟AS,哥CR,秘鲁PE,新西兰NZ,智利CL 2.2 瑞士CH 3.3 韩国KR 5 巴PK	0 受惠国$_1$LD$_1$	40	---Camphor
2057	2914.2990	---其他	5.5	0 澳AU,冰岛IS,东盟AS,哥CR,秘鲁PE,新西兰NZ,智利CL 4.4 韩国KR 5 巴PK	0 受惠国$_1$LD$_1$	30	---Other
		-不含其他含氧基的芳香酮：					-Aromatic ketones without other oxygen function:
2058	2914.3100	--苯丙酮（苯基丙-2-酮）	5.5	0 澳AU,巴PK,冰岛IS,东盟AS,哥CR,秘鲁PE,新西兰NZ,智利CL 2.2 瑞士CH 3.3 韩国KR	0 受惠国$_1$LD$_1$	30	--Propiophenone (phenyl-propan-2-one)
		--其他：					--Other:
2059	2914.3910	---苯乙酮	4	0 澳AU,巴PK,冰岛IS,东盟AS,哥CR,韩国KR,秘鲁PE,瑞士CH,新西兰NZ,智利CL	0 受惠国$_1$LD$_1$	11	---Acetophenone

序号 No.	税则号列 Tariff Line	中文货品名称 Article Description in Chinese	最惠国税率 MFN(%)	协定税率 Agreement(%)	特惠税率 SP(%)	普通税率 Gen(%)	英文货品名称 Article Description
2060	2914.3990	---其他	5.5	0 澳AU,冰岛IS,东盟AS,哥CR,秘鲁PE,新西兰NZ,智利CL 3.3 韩国KR 3.9 瑞士CH 5 巴PK	0 受惠国$_1$LD$_1$	30	---Other
2061	2914.4000	-酮醇及酮醛	5.5	0 澳AU,冰岛IS,东盟AS,哥CR,秘鲁PE,新西兰NZ,智利CL 3.3 韩国KR 3.9 瑞士CH 5 巴PK	0 受惠国$_1$LD$_1$	30	-Ketone-alcohols and ketonealde-hydes
		-酮酚及含有其他含氧基的酮:					-Ketone-phenols and ketones with other oxygen function:
		---酮酚:					---Ketene-alcohols:
2062	2914.5011	----覆盆子酮	5.5	0 澳AU,巴PK,冰岛IS,东盟AS,哥CR,秘鲁PE,新西兰NZ,智利CL 2.2 瑞士CH 3.3 韩国KR	0 受惠国$_1$LD$_1$	30	----Raspberry ketone
2063	2914.5019	----其他	5.5	0 澳AU,冰岛IS,东盟AS,哥CR,秘鲁PE,新西兰NZ,智利CL 3.3 韩国KR 3.9 瑞士CH 5 巴PK	0 受惠国$_1$LD$_1$	30	----Other
2064	2914.5020	---2-羟基-4-甲氧基二苯甲酮	5.5	0 澳AU,冰岛IS,东盟AS,哥CR,秘鲁PE,新西兰NZ,智利CL 2.2 瑞士CH 3.3 韩国KR 5 巴PK	0 受惠国$_1$LD$_1$	30	---2-hydroxy-4-methoxybenzophenone
2065	2914.5090	---其他	5.5	0 澳AU,冰岛IS,东盟AS,哥CR,秘鲁PE,新西兰NZ,智利CL 2.2 瑞士CH 4.4 韩国KR 5 巴PK	0 受惠国$_1$LD$_1$	30	---Other
		-醌:					-Quinones:
2066	2914.6100	--蒽醌	5.5	0 澳AU,冰岛IS,东盟AS,哥CR,秘鲁PE,新西兰NZ,智利CL 2.2 瑞士CH 4.4 韩国KR 5 巴PK	0 受惠国$_1$LD$_1$	30	--Anthraquinone
		--其他:					--Other:
2067	2914.6910	---辅酶Q10	5.5	0 澳AU,巴PK,冰岛IS,东盟AS,哥CR,秘鲁PE,新西兰NZ,智利CL 2.2 瑞士CH 4.4 韩国KR	0 受惠国$_1$LD$_1$	30	---Coenzyme Q10
2068	2914.6990	---其他	5.5	0 澳AU,巴PK,冰岛IS,东盟AS,哥CR,秘鲁PE,新西兰NZ,智利CL 2.2 瑞士CH 4.4 韩国KR	0 受惠国$_1$LD$_1$	30	---Other
2069	2914.7000	-卤化、磺化、硝化或亚硝化衍生物	5.5	0 澳AU,冰岛IS,东盟AS,哥CR,秘鲁PE,新西兰NZ,智利CL 4.4 韩国KR 5 巴PK	0 受惠国$_1$LD$_1$	30	-Halogenated, sulphonated, nitrated or nitrosated derivatives

序号 No.	税则号列 Tariff Line	中文货品名称 Article Description in Chinese	最惠国税率 MFN(%)	协定税率 Agreement(%)	特惠税率 SP(%)	普通税率 Gen(%)	英文货品名称 Article Description
		第七分章　羧酸及其酸酐、酰卤化物、过氧化物和过氧酸以及它们的卤化、磺化、硝化或亚硝化衍生物					VII. CARBOXYLIC ACIDS AND THEIR ANHYDRIDES, HALIDES, PEROXIDES AND PEROXYACIDS AND THEIR HALOGENATED, SULPHONATED, NITRATED OR NITROSATED DERIVATIVES
	29.15	**饱和无环一元羧酸及其酸酐、酰卤化物、过氧化物和过氧酸以及它们的卤化、磺化、硝化或亚硝化衍生物：**					**Saturated acyclic monocarboxylic acids and their anhydrides, halides, peroxides and peroxyacids; their halogenated, sulphonated, nitrated or nitrosated derivatives:**
		-甲酸及其盐和酯：					-Formic acid, its salts and esters:
2070	2915.1100	--甲酸	5.5	0 澳AU,冰岛IS,东盟AS,哥CR,秘鲁PE,新西兰NZ,智利CL 2.2 瑞士CH 4.4 韩国KR 5 巴PK	0 受惠国LD	40	--Formic acid
2071	2915.1200	--甲酸盐	5.5	0 澳AU,冰岛IS,东盟AS,哥CR,秘鲁PE,新西兰NZ,智利CL 2.2 瑞士CH 4.4 韩国KR 5 巴PK	0 受惠国LD	30	--Salts of formic acid
2072	2915.1300	--甲酸酯	5.5	0 澳AU,冰岛IS,东盟AS,哥CR,秘鲁PE,新西兰NZ,智利CL 2.2 瑞士CH 3.3 韩国KR 5 巴PK	0 受惠国LD	30	--Esters of formic acid
		-乙酸及其盐；乙酸酐：					-Acetic acid and its salts; acetic anhydride:
		--乙酸：					--Acetic acid:
		---冰乙酸：					---Acetic acid, glacial:
2073	2915.2111	----食品级的	5.5	0 澳AU,冰岛IS,东盟AS,哥CR,韩国KR,秘鲁PE,台湾TW,新西兰NZ,智利CL 2.2 瑞士CH 5 巴PK	0 受惠国LD	30	----Food grade
2074	2915.2119	----其他	5.5	0 澳AU,冰岛IS,东盟AS,哥CR,韩国KR,秘鲁PE,台湾TW,新西兰NZ,智利CL 2.2 瑞士CH 5 巴PK	0 受惠国LD	30	----Other
2075	2915.2190	---其他	5.5	0 澳AU,冰岛IS,东盟AS,哥CR,秘鲁PE,新西兰NZ,智利CL 2.2 瑞士CH 3.3 韩国KR 5 巴PK	0 受惠国LD	50	---Other
2076	2915.2400	--乙酸酐	5.5	0 澳AU,巴PK,冰岛IS,东盟AS,哥CR,秘鲁PE,新西兰NZ,智利CL 2.2 瑞士CH 3.3 韩国KR	0 受惠国LD	50	--Acetic anhydride
		--其他：					--Other:

序号 No.	税则号列 Tariff Line	中文货品名称 Article Description in Chinese	最惠国税率 MFN(%)	协定税率 Agreement(%)	特惠税率 SP(%)	普通税率 Gen(%)	英文货品名称 Article Description
2077	2915.2910	---乙酸钠	5.5	0 澳AU,冰岛IS,东盟AS,哥CR,秘鲁PE,新西兰NZ,智利CL 2.2 瑞士CH 3.3 韩国KR 5 巴PK	0 受惠国LD	50	---Sodium acetate
2078	2915.2990	---其他	5.5	0 澳AU,冰岛IS,东盟AS,哥CR,秘鲁PE,新西兰NZ,智利CL 2.2 瑞士CH 4.4 韩国KR 5 巴PK	0 受惠国LD	50	---Other
		-乙酸酯:					-Esters of acetic acid:
2079	2915.3100	--乙酸乙酯	5.5	0 澳AU,冰岛IS,东盟AS,哥CR,秘鲁PE,新西兰NZ,智利CL 2.2 瑞士CH 3.3 韩国KR 5 巴PK	0 受惠国LD	30	--Ethyl acetate
2080	2915.3200	--乙酸乙烯酯	5.5	0 澳AU,冰岛IS,东盟AS,哥CR,韩国KR,秘鲁PE,台湾TW,新西兰NZ,智利CL 2.2 瑞士CH 5 巴PK	0 受惠国LD	30	--Vinyl acetate
2081	2915.3300	--乙酸（正）丁酯	5.5	0 澳AU,巴PK,冰岛IS,东盟AS,哥CR,秘鲁PE,新西兰NZ,智利CL 2.2 瑞士CH 4.7 韩国KR	0 受惠国LD	30	--N-Butyl acetate
2082	2915.3600	--地乐酚（ISO）乙酸酯	5.5	0 澳AU,冰岛IS,东盟AS,哥CR,秘鲁PE,新西兰NZ,智利CL 2.2 瑞士CH 3.3 韩国KR 5 巴PK	0 受惠国LD	30	--Dinoseb (ISO) acetate
2083	2915.3900	--其他	5.5	0 澳AU,冰岛IS,东盟AS,哥CR,秘鲁PE,新西兰NZ,智利CL 3.9 瑞士CH 4.7 韩国KR 5 巴PK	0 受惠国LD	30	--Other
2084	2915.4000	-一氯代乙酸、二氯乙酸或三氯乙酸及其盐和酯	5.5	0 澳AU,冰岛IS,东盟AS,哥CR,秘鲁PE,新西兰NZ,智利CL 2.2 瑞士CH 3.3 韩国KR 5 巴PK	0 受惠国LD	30	-Mono-, di-or trichloroacetic acids, their salts and esters
		-丙酸及其盐和酯:					-Propionic acid, its salts and esters:
2085	2915.5010	---丙酸	5.5Δ3	0 澳AU,冰岛IS,东盟AS,哥CR,秘鲁PE,新西兰NZ,智利CL 2.2 瑞士CH 3.3 韩国KR 5 巴PK	0 受惠国LD	30	---Propionic acid
2086	2915.5090	---其他	5.5	0 澳AU,冰岛IS,东盟AS,哥CR,秘鲁PE,新西兰NZ,智利CL 2.2 瑞士CH 4.7 韩国KR 5 巴PK	0 受惠国LD	30	---Other

序号 No.	税则号列 Tariff Line	中文货品名称 Article Description in Chinese	最惠国税率 MFN(%)	协定税率 Agreement(%)	特惠税率 SP(%)	普通税率 Gen(%)	英文货品名称 Article Description
2087	2915.6000	-丁酸、戊酸及其盐和酯	5.5	0 澳AU,冰岛IS,东盟AS,哥CR,秘鲁PE,新西兰NZ,智利CL 2.2 瑞士CH 4.4 韩国KR 5 巴PK	0 受惠国LD	30	-Butanoic acids, pentanoic acids, their salts and esters
		-棕榈酸、硬脂酸及其盐和酯:					-Palmitic acid, stearic acid, their salts and esters:
2088	2915.7010	---硬脂酸	7	0 冰岛IS,东盟AS,哥CR,秘鲁PE,新西兰NZ,智利CL 2.8 瑞士CH 4.2 澳AU,韩国KR 5 巴PK	0 受惠国LD	50	---Stearic acid
2089	2915.7090	---其他	5.5	0 澳AU,冰岛IS,东盟AS,哥CR,秘鲁PE,新西兰NZ,智利CL 2.2 瑞士CH 4.7 韩国KR 5 巴PK	0 受惠国LD	30	---Other
2090	2915.9000	-其他	5.5	0 澳AU,澳门MO,冰岛IS,东盟AS,哥CR,秘鲁PE,新西兰NZ,智利CL 3.3 韩国KR 3.9 瑞士CH 5 巴PK	0 受惠国LD	30	-Other
	29.16	**不饱和无环一元羧酸、环一元羧酸及其酸酐、酰卤化物、过氧化物和过氧酸以及它们的卤化、磺化、硝化或亚硝化衍生物:**					**Unsaturated acyclic monocarboxylic acids, cyclic monocarboxylic acids, their anhydrides, halides, peroxides and peroxyacids; their halogenated, sulphonated, nitrated or nitrosated derivatives:**
		-不饱和无环一元羧酸及其酸酐、酰卤化物、过氧化物和过氧酸以及它们的衍生物:					-Unsaturated acyclic monocarboxylic acids, their anhydrides, halides, peroxides, peroxyacids and their derivatives:
2091	2916.1100	--丙烯酸及其盐	6.5	0 冰岛IS,东盟AS,哥CR,秘鲁PE,新西兰NZ,智利CL 2.6 瑞士CH 3.9 澳AU 5.6 韩国KR	0 受惠国$_1$LD$_1$	30	--Acrylic acid and its salts
		--丙烯酸酯:					--Esters of acrylic acid:
2092	2916.1210	---丙烯酸甲酯	6.5	0 冰岛IS,东盟AS,哥CR,秘鲁PE,新加坡SG,新西兰NZ,智利CL 3.9 澳AU 4.7 瑞士CH 5 巴PK 5.6 韩国KR	0 受惠国$_1$LD$_1$	30	---Methacylate
2093	2916.1220	---丙烯酸乙酯	6.5	0 冰岛IS,东盟AS,哥CR,秘鲁PE,新加坡SG,新西兰NZ,智利CL 2.6 瑞士CH 3.9 澳AU 5 巴PK 5.6 韩国KR	0 受惠国$_1$LD$_1$	30	---Ethyl Acrylate
2094	2916.1230	---丙烯酸丁酯	6.5	0 冰岛IS,东盟AS,哥CR,秘鲁PE,新加坡SG,新西兰NZ,智利CL 2.6 瑞士CH 3.9 澳AU 5 巴PK	0 受惠国$_1$LD$_1$	30	---N-Butyl Acrylate

序号 No.	税则号列 Tariff Line	中文货品名称 Article Description in Chinese	最惠国税率 MFN(%)	协定税率 Agreement(%)	特惠税率 SP(%)	普通税率 Gen(%)	英文货品名称 Article Description
2095	2916.1240	---丙烯酸异辛酯	6.5	0 冰岛IS,东盟AS,哥CR,秘鲁PE,新加坡SG,新西兰NZ,智利CL 2.6 瑞士CH 3.9 澳AU 5 巴PK 5.6 韩国KR	0 受惠国$_1$LD$_1$	30	---2-Ethylhexyl acrylate
2096	2916.1290	---其他	6.5	0 冰岛IS,东盟AS,哥CR,秘鲁PE,新加坡SG,新西兰NZ,智利CL 2.6 瑞士CH 3.9 澳AU 5 巴PK	0 受惠国$_1$LD$_1$	30	---Other
2097	2916.1300	--甲基丙烯酸及其盐	6.5	0 冰岛IS,东盟AS,哥CR,韩国KR,秘鲁PE,台湾TW,新西兰NZ,智利CL 2.6 瑞士CH 3.9 澳AU 5 巴PK	0 受惠国$_1$LD$_1$	80	--Methacrylic acid and its salts
2098	2916.1400	--甲基丙烯酸酯	6.5	0 冰岛IS,东盟AS,哥CR,韩国KR,秘鲁PE,台湾TW,新西兰NZ,智利CL 2.6 瑞士CH 3.9 澳AU 5 巴PK	0 受惠国$_1$LD$_1$	80	--Esters of methacrylic acid
2099	2916.1500	--油酸、亚油酸或亚麻酸及其盐和酯	6.5	0 冰岛IS,东盟AS,哥CR,秘鲁PE,香港HK,新西兰NZ,智利CL 2.6 瑞士CH 3.9 澳AU 5 巴PK 5.6 韩国KR	0 受惠国$_1$LD$_1$	30	--Oleic, linoleic or linolenic acids, their salts and esters
2100	2916.1600	--乐杀螨（ISO）	6.5	0 冰岛IS,东盟AS,哥CR,秘鲁PE,新西兰NZ,智利CL 2.6 瑞士CH 3.9 澳AU,韩国KR 5 巴PK	0 受惠国$_1$LD$_1$	30	--Binapacryl (ISO)
2101	2916.1900	--其他	6.5	0 冰岛IS,东盟AS,哥CR,秘鲁PE,新西兰NZ,智利CL 3.9 澳AU,韩国KR 5 巴PK	0 受惠国$_1$LD$_1$	30	--Other
		-环烷一元羧酸、环烯一元羧酸或环萜烯一元羧酸及其酸酐、酰卤化物、过氧化物和过氧酸以及它们的衍生物：					-Cyclanic, cyclenic or cycloterpenic monocarboxylic acids, their anhydrides, halides, peroxides, peroxyacids and their derivatives:
2102	2916.2010	---二溴菊酸、DV菊酸甲酯	4	0 澳AU,巴PK,冰岛IS,东盟AS,哥CR,韩国KR,秘鲁PE,瑞士CH,新西兰NZ,智利CL	0 受惠国$_1$LD$_1$	11	---Dibromochrysanthemicacid, DV chrysanthemimono carboxylate
2103	2916.2090	---其他	6.5	0 冰岛IS,东盟AS,哥CR,秘鲁PE,新西兰NZ,智利CL 3.9 澳AU,韩国KR 4.7 瑞士CH 5 巴PK	0 受惠国$_1$LD$_1$	30	---Other
		-芳香一元羧酸及其酸酐、酰卤化物、过氧化物和过氧酸以及它们的衍生物：					-Aromatic monocarboxylic acids, their anhydrides, halides, peroxides, peroxyacids and their derivatives:

序号 No.	税则号列 Tariff Line	中文货品名称 Article Description in Chinese	最惠国税率 MFN(%)	协定税率 Agreement(%)	特惠税率 SP(%)	普通税率 Gen(%)	英文货品名称 Article Description
2104	2916.3100	--苯甲酸及其盐和酯	6.5	0 冰岛IS,东盟AS,哥CR,秘鲁PE,新西兰NZ,智利CL 3.9 澳AU 5 巴PK 5.2 韩国KR	0 受惠国$_1$LD$_1$	30	--Benzoic acid, its salts and esters
2105	2916.3200	--过氧化苯甲酰及苯甲酰氯	6.5	0 冰岛IS,东盟AS,哥CR,秘鲁PE,新西兰NZ,智利CL 2.6 瑞士CH 3.9 澳AU 5 巴PK 5.2 韩国KR	0 受惠国$_1$LD$_1$	30	--Benzoyl peroxide and benzoyl chloride
2106	2916.3400	--苯乙酸及其盐	6.5	0 冰岛IS,东盟AS,哥CR,秘鲁PE,新西兰NZ,智利CL 3.9 澳AU,韩国KR 5 巴PK	0 受惠国$_1$LD$_1$	30	--Phenylacetic acid and its salts
		--其他:					--Other:
2107	2916.3910	---邻甲基苯甲酸	6.5	0 冰岛IS,东盟AS,哥CR,秘鲁PE,新西兰NZ,智利CL 2.6 瑞士CH 3.9 澳AU,韩国KR 5 巴PK	0 受惠国$_1$LD$_1$	30	---M-Methylbenzoic acid
2108	2916.3920	---布洛芬	6.5	0 冰岛IS,东盟AS,哥CR,秘鲁PE,新西兰NZ,智利CL 2.6 瑞士CH 3.9 澳AU,韩国KR 5 巴PK	0 受惠国$_1$LD$_1$	30	---Brufen (Ibuprofen)
2109	2916.3990	---其他	6.5	0 冰岛IS,东盟AS,哥CR,秘鲁PE,新西兰NZ,智利CL 3.9 澳AU,韩国KR 4.7 瑞士CH 5 巴PK	0 受惠国$_1$LD$_1$	30	---Other
	29.17	**多元羧酸及其酸酐、酰卤化物、过氧化物和过氧酸以及它们的卤化、磺化、硝化或亚硝化衍生物:**					**Polycarboxylic acids, their anhydrides, halides, peroxides and peroxyacids; their halogenated, sulphonated, nitrated or nitrosated derivatives:**
		-无环多元羧酸及其酸酐、酰卤化物、过氧化物和过氧酸以及它们的衍生物:					-Acyclic polycarboxylic acids, their anhydrides, halides, peroxides, peroxyacids and their derivatives:
		--草酸及其盐和酯:					--Oxalic acid, its salts and esters:
2110	2917.1110	---草酸	6.5	0 冰岛IS,东盟AS,哥CR,秘鲁PE,新西兰NZ,智利CL 2.6 瑞士CH 3.9 澳AU 5 巴PK 5.2 韩国KR	0 受惠国$_1$LD$_1$	40	---Oxalic acid
2111	2917.1120	---草酸钴	9	0 冰岛IS,东盟AS,哥CR,秘鲁PE,新西兰NZ,智利CL 3.6 瑞士CH 5 巴PK 5.4 澳AU,韩国KR	0 受惠国$_1$LD$_1$	30	---Cobalt oxalate

序号 No.	税则号列 Tariff Line	中文货品名称 Article Description in Chinese	最惠国税率 MFN(%)	协定税率 Agreement(%)	特惠税率 SP(%)	普通税率 Gen(%)	英文货品名称 Article Description
2112	2917.1190	---其他	6.5	0 冰岛IS,东盟AS,哥CR,秘鲁PE,新西兰NZ,智利CL 2.6 瑞士CH 3.9 澳AU 5 巴PK 5.2 韩国KR	0 受惠国$_1$LD$_1$	30	---Other
2113	2917.1200	--己二酸及其盐和酯	6.5	0 冰岛IS,东盟AS,哥CR,秘鲁PE,新西兰NZ,智利CL 2.6 瑞士CH 3.9 澳AU 5 巴PK	0 受惠国$_1$LD$_1$	30	--Adipic acid, its salts and esters
		--壬二酸、癸二酸及其盐和酯:					--Azelaic acid, sebacic acid, their salts and esters:
2114	2917.1310	---癸二酸及其盐和酯	6.5	0 冰岛IS,东盟AS,哥CR,秘鲁PE,新西兰NZ,智利CL 2.6 瑞士CH 3.9 澳AU 5 巴PK 5.6 韩国KR	0 受惠国$_1$LD$_1$	30	---Sebacic acid, its salts and esters
2115	2917.1390	---其他	6.5	0 冰岛IS,东盟AS,哥CR,秘鲁PE,新西兰NZ,智利CL 2.6 瑞士CH 3.9 澳AU,韩国KR 5 巴PK	0 受惠国$_1$LD$_1$	30	---Other
2116	2917.1400	--马来酐	6.5	0 冰岛IS,东盟AS,哥CR,秘鲁PE,新西兰NZ,智利CL 2.6 瑞士CH 3.9 澳AU 5 巴PK 5.2 韩国KR	0 受惠国$_1$LD$_1$	30	--Maleic anhydride
2117	2917.1900	--其他	6.5	0 澳门MO,冰岛IS,东盟AS,哥CR,秘鲁PE,新西兰NZ,智利CL 2.6 瑞士CH 3.9 澳AU,韩国KR 5 巴PK	0 受惠国$_1$LD$_1$	30	--Other
		-环烷多元羧酸、环烯多元羧酸、环萜烯多元羧酸及其酸酐、酰卤化物、过氧化物和过氧酸以及它们的衍生物:					-Cyclanic, cyclenic or cycloterpenic polycarboxylic acids, their anhydrides, halides, peroxides, peroxyacids and their derivatives:
2118	2917.2010	---四氢苯酐	4	0 澳AU,巴PK,冰岛IS,东盟AS,哥CR,秘鲁PE,瑞士CH,新西兰NZ,智利CL 3.4 韩国KR	0 受惠国$_1$LD$_1$	11	---Tetrahydro benzoic anhydride
2119	2917.2090	---其他	6.5	0 冰岛IS,东盟AS,哥CR,秘鲁PE,新西兰NZ,智利CL 2.6 瑞士CH 3.9 澳AU 5 巴PK 5.6 韩国KR	0 受惠国$_1$LD$_1$	30	---Other
		-芳香多元羧酸及其酸酐、酰卤化物、过氧化物和过氧酸以及它们的衍生物:					-Aromatic polycarboxylic acids, their anhydrides, halides, peroxides, peroxyacids and their derivatives:

序号 No.	税则号列 Tariff Line	中文货品名称 Article Description in Chinese	最惠国税率 MFN(%)	协定税率 Agreement(%)	特惠税率 SP(%)	普通税率 Gen(%)	英文货品名称 Article Description
2120	2917.3200	--邻苯二甲酸二辛酯	6.5	0 冰岛IS,东盟AS,哥CR,秘鲁PE,台湾TW,新西兰NZ,智利CL 2.6 瑞士CH 3.9 澳AU 5 巴PK	0 受惠国$_1$LD$_1$	30	--Dioctyl orthophthalates
2121	2917.3300	--邻苯二甲酸二壬酯及邻苯二甲酸二癸酯	6.5	0 冰岛IS,东盟AS,哥CR,韩国KR,秘鲁PE,台湾TW,新西兰NZ,智利CL 2.6 瑞士CH 3.9 澳AU 5 巴PK	0 受惠国$_1$LD$_1$	30	--Dinonyl or didecyl orthophthalates
		--其他邻苯二甲酸酯:					--Other esters of orthophthalic acid:
2122	2917.3410	---邻苯二甲酸二丁酯	6.5	0 冰岛IS,东盟AS,哥CR,秘鲁PE,新西兰NZ,智利CL 2.6 瑞士CH 3.9 澳AU 5 巴PK 5.2 韩国KR	0 受惠国$_1$LD$_1$	30	---Dibutyl orthophthalates
2123	2917.3490	---其他	6.5	0 冰岛IS,东盟AS,哥CR,韩国KR,秘鲁PE,台湾TW,新西兰NZ,智利CL 2.6 瑞士CH 3.9 澳AU 5 巴PK	0 受惠国$_1$LD$_1$	30	---Other
2124	2917.3500	--邻苯二甲酸酐	6.5	0 冰岛IS,东盟AS,哥CR,秘鲁PE,新西兰NZ,智利CL 2.6 瑞士CH 3.9 澳AU 5 巴PK	0 受惠国$_1$LD$_1$	30	--Phthalic anhydride
		--对苯二甲酸及其盐:					--Terephthalic acid and its salts:
		---对苯二甲酸:					---Terephthalic acid:
2125	2917.3611	----精对苯二甲酸	6.5	0 冰岛IS,东盟AS,哥CR,新加坡SG,新西兰NZ,智利CL 3.9 澳AU 4.7 瑞士CH 6 巴PK,亚太AP	0 受惠国$_1$LD$_1$	30	----Pure terephthalic acid
2126	2917.3619	----其他	6.5	0 冰岛IS,东盟AS,哥CR,秘鲁PE,新加坡SG,新西兰NZ,智利CL 3.9 澳AU 4.7 瑞士CH 6 巴PK,亚太AP	0 受惠国$_1$LD$_1$	30	----Other
2127	2917.3690	---其他	6.5	0 冰岛IS,东盟AS,哥CR,秘鲁PE,新西兰NZ,智利CL 2.6 瑞士CH 3.9 澳AU 5 巴PK	0 受惠国$_1$LD$_1$	30	---Other
2128	2917.3700	--对苯二甲酸二甲酯	6.5	0 冰岛IS,东盟AS,哥CR,秘鲁PE,新西兰NZ,智利CL 2.6 瑞士CH 3.9 澳AU 5 巴PK 5.6 韩国KR	0 受惠国$_1$LD$_1$	30	--Dimethyl terephthalate
		--其他:					--Other:

序号 No.	税则号列 Tariff Line	中文货品名称 Article Description in Chinese	最惠国税率 MFN(%)	协定税率 Agreement(%)	特惠税率 SP(%)	普通税率 Gen(%)	英文货品名称 Article Description
2129	2917.3910	---间苯二甲酸	6.5	0 冰岛IS,东盟AS,哥CR,秘鲁PE,新西兰NZ,智利CL 2.6 瑞士CH 3.9 澳AU 5 巴PK	0 受惠国$_1$LD$_1$	30	---Isophthalic acid
2130	2917.3990	---其他	6.5	0 冰岛IS,东盟AS,哥CR,秘鲁PE,新西兰NZ,智利CL 2.6 瑞士CH 3.9 澳AU 5 巴PK 5.6 韩国KR	0 受惠国$_1$LD$_1$	30	---Other
	29.18	**含附加含氧基的羧酸及其酸酐、酰卤化物、过氧化物和过氧酸以及它们的卤化、磺化、硝化或亚硝化衍生物：**					**Carboxylic acids with additional oxygen function and their anhydrides, halides, peroxides and peroxyacids; their halogenated, sulphonated, nitrated or nitrosated derivatives:**
		-含醇基但不含其他含氧基的羧酸及其酸酐、酰卤化物、过氧化物和过氧酸以及它们的衍生物：					-Carboxylic acids with alcohol function but without other oxygen function, their anhydrides, halides, peroxides, peroxyacids and their derivatives:
2131	2918.1100	--乳酸及其盐和酯	6.5	0 冰岛IS,东盟AS,哥CR,秘鲁PE,新西兰NZ,智利CL 2.6 瑞士CH 3.9 澳AU 5 巴PK 5.2 韩国KR	0 受惠国$_1$LD$_1$	30	--Lactic acid, its salts and esters
2132	2918.1200	--酒石酸	6.5	0 冰岛IS,东盟AS,哥CR,秘鲁PE,新西兰NZ,智利CL 2.6 瑞士CH 3.9 澳AU,韩国KR 5 巴PK	0 受惠国$_1$LD$_1$	35	--Tartaric acid
2133	2918.1300	--酒石酸盐及酒石酸酯	6.5	0 冰岛IS,东盟AS,哥CR,秘鲁PE,新西兰NZ,智利CL 2.6 瑞士CH 3.9 澳AU,韩国KR 5 巴PK	0 受惠国$_1$LD$_1$	30	--Salts and esters of tartaric acid
2134	2918.1400	--柠檬酸	6.5	0 冰岛IS,东盟AS,哥CR,秘鲁PE,新西兰NZ,智利CL 2.6 瑞士CH 3.9 澳AU 5 巴PK 5.2 韩国KR	0 受惠国$_1$LD$_1$	35	--Citric acid
2135	2918.1500	--柠檬酸盐及柠檬酸酯	6.5	0 冰岛IS,东盟AS,哥CR,秘鲁PE,新西兰NZ,智利CL 2.6 瑞士CH 3.9 澳AU,韩国KR 5 巴PK	0 受惠国$_1$LD$_1$	30	--Salts and esters of citric acid
2136	2918.1600	--葡糖酸及其盐和酯	6.5	0 冰岛IS,东盟AS,哥CR,秘鲁PE,新西兰NZ,智利CL 2.6 瑞士CH 3.9 澳AU,韩国KR 5 巴PK	0 受惠国$_1$LD$_1$	30	--Gluconic acid, its salts and esters

序号 No.	税则号列 Tariff Line	中文货品名称 Article Description in Chinese	最惠国税率 MFN(%)	协定税率 Agreement(%)	特惠税率 SP(%)	普通税率 Gen(%)	英文货品名称 Article Description
2137	2918.1800	--乙酯杀螨醇（ISO）	6.5	0 冰岛IS,东盟AS,哥CR,秘鲁PE,新西兰NZ,智利CL 2.6 瑞士CH 3.9 澳AU,韩国KR 5 巴PK	0 受惠国$_1$LD$_1$	30	--Chlorobenzilate (ISO)
		--其他：					--Other:
2138	2918.1910	---2，2-二苯基-2-羟基乙酸（二苯羟乙酸；二苯乙醇酸）	6.5	0 冰岛IS,东盟AS,哥CR,秘鲁PE,新西兰NZ,智利CL 2.6 瑞士CH 3.9 澳AU,韩国KR 5 巴PK	0 受惠国$_1$LD$_1$	30	---2, 2-Diphenyl-2-hydroxyacetic acid (ahydroxydiphenylacetic acid, benzilic acid)
2139	2918.1990	---其他	6.5	0 冰岛IS,东盟AS,哥CR,秘鲁PE,新西兰NZ,智利CL 2.6 瑞士CH 3.9 澳AU,韩国KR 5 巴PK	0 受惠国$_1$LD$_1$	30	---Other
		-含酚基但不含其他含氧基的羧酸及其酸酐、酰卤化物、过氧化物和过氧酸以及它们的衍生物：					-Carboxylic acids with phenol function but without other oxygen function, their anhydrides, halides, peroxides, peroxyacids and their derivatives:
		--水杨酸及其盐：					--Salicylic acid and its salts:
2140	2918.2110	---水杨酸、水杨酸钠	6.5	0 冰岛IS,东盟AS,哥CR,秘鲁PE,新西兰NZ,智利CL 3.9 澳AU 4.7 瑞士CH 5 巴PK 5.2 韩国KR	0 受惠国$_1$LD$_1$	20	---Salicylic acid and sodium salicylate
2141	2918.2190	---其他	6.5	0 冰岛IS,东盟AS,哥CR,秘鲁PE,新西兰NZ,智利CL 2.6 瑞士CH 3.9 澳AU,韩国KR 5 巴PK	0 受惠国$_1$LD$_1$	30	---Other
		--邻乙酰水杨酸及其盐和酯：					--*o*-Acetylsalicylic acid, its salts and esters:
2142	2918.2210	---邻乙酰水杨酸（阿斯匹林）	6	0 冰岛IS,东盟AS,哥CR,秘鲁PE,新西兰NZ,智利CL 2.4 瑞士CH 3.6 澳AU,韩国KR 5 巴PK	0 受惠国$_1$LD$_1$	20	---Acetylsalicylic acid
2143	2918.2290	---其他	6.5	0 冰岛IS,东盟AS,哥CR,秘鲁PE,新西兰NZ,智利CL 2.6 瑞士CH 3.9 澳AU,韩国KR 5 巴PK	0 受惠国$_1$LD$_1$	30	---Other
2144	2918.2300	--水杨酸的其他酯及其盐	6.5	0 冰岛IS,东盟AS,哥CR,秘鲁PE,新西兰NZ,智利CL 3.9 澳AU,韩国KR 5 巴PK	0 受惠国$_1$LD$_1$	30	--Other esters of salicylic acid and their salts
2145	2918.2900	--其他	6.5	0 澳门MO,冰岛IS,东盟AS,哥CR,秘鲁PE,新西兰NZ,智利CL 2.6 瑞士CH 3.9 澳AU 5 巴PK 5.6 韩国KR	0 受惠国$_1$LD$_1$	30	--Other

序号 No.	税则号列 Tariff Line	中文货品名称 Article Description in Chinese	最惠国税率 MFN(%)	协定税率 Agreement(%)	特惠税率 SP(%)	普通税率 Gen(%)	英文货品名称 Article Description
2146	2918.3000	-含醛基或酮基但不含其他含氧基的羧酸及其酸酐、酰卤化物、过氧化物和过氧酸以及它们的衍生物	6.5	0 冰岛IS,东盟AS,哥CR,秘鲁PE,新西兰NZ,智利CL 3.9 澳AU,韩国KR 4.7 瑞士CH 5 巴PK	0 受惠国$_1$LD$_1$	30	-Carboxylic acids with aldehyde or ketone function but without other oxygen function, their anhydrides, halides, peroxides, peroxyacids and their derivatives
		-其他:					-Other:
2147	2918.9100	--2，4，5-滴（ISO）（2，4，5-三氯苯氧基乙酸）及其盐或酯	6.5	0 冰岛IS,东盟AS,哥CR,秘鲁PE,新西兰NZ,智利CL 2.6 瑞士CH 3.9 澳AU,韩国KR 5 巴PK	0 受惠国$_1$LD$_1$	30	--2, 4, 5-T (ISO) (2, 4, 5-trichlorophenoxyacetic acid) , its salts and esters
2148	2918.9900	--其他	6.5	0 冰岛IS,东盟AS,哥CR,秘鲁PE,新西兰NZ,智利CL 3.9 澳AU,韩国KR 4.7 瑞士CH 5 巴PK	0 受惠国$_1$LD$_1$	30	--Other
		第八分章 非金属无机酸酯及其盐以及它们的卤化、磺化、硝化或亚硝化衍生物					VIII. ESTERS OF INORGANIC ACIDS OF NON-METALS AND THEIR SALTS, AND THEIR HALOGENATED, SULPHONATED, NITRATED OR NITROSATED DERIVATIVES
	29.19	**磷酸酯及其盐，包括乳磷酸盐，以及它们的卤化、磺化、硝化或亚硝化衍生物：**					**Phosphoric esters and their salts, including lactophosphates; their halogenated, sulphonated, nitrated or nitrosated derivatives:**
2149	2919.1000	-三（2，3-二溴丙基）磷酸酯	6.5	0 冰岛IS,东盟AS,哥CR,秘鲁PE,新西兰NZ,智利CL 2.6 瑞士CH 3.9 澳AU,韩国KR 5 巴PK	0 受惠国$_1$LD$_1$	30	-Tris (2, 3-dibromopropyl) phosphate
2150	2919.9000	-其他	6.5	0 冰岛IS,东盟AS,哥CR,秘鲁PE,新西兰NZ,智利CL 2.6 瑞士CH 3.9 澳AU,韩国KR 5 巴PK	0 受惠国$_1$LD$_1$	30	-Other
	29.20	**其他非金属无机酸酯（不包括卤化氢的酯）及其盐以及它们的卤化、磺化、硝化或亚硝化衍生物：**					**Esters of other inorganic acids of non-metals (excluding esters of hydrogen halides) and their salts; their haloge-nated, sulphonated, nitrated or nitrosated derivatives:**
		-硫代磷酸酯及其盐以及它们的卤化、磺化、硝化或亚硝化衍生物：					-Thiophosphoric esters (phosphorothioates) and their salts; their halogenated, sulphonated, nitrated or nitrosated derivatives:
2151	2920.1100	--对硫磷（ISO）及甲基对硫磷（ISO）	6.5	0 冰岛IS,东盟AS,哥CR,秘鲁PE,新西兰NZ,智利CL 2.6 瑞士CH 3.9 澳AU,韩国KR 5 巴PK	0 受惠国$_1$LD$_1$	30	--Parathion (ISO) and parathion-methyl (ISO) (methyl-parathion)
2152	2920.1900	--其他	6.5	0 冰岛IS,东盟AS,哥CR,秘鲁PE,新西兰NZ,智利CL 2.6 瑞士CH 3.9 澳AU,韩国KR 5 巴PK	0 受惠国$_1$LD$_1$	30	--Other

序号 No.	税则号列 Tariff Line	中文货品名称 Article Description in Chinese	最惠国税率 MFN(%)	协定税率 Agreement(%)	特惠税率 SP(%)	普通税率 Gen(%)	英文货品名称 Article Description
		-其他:					-Other:
		---亚磷酸酯:					---Phosphites:
2153	2920.9011	----亚磷酸三甲酯	6.5	0 冰岛IS,东盟AS,哥CR,秘鲁PE,新西兰NZ,智利CL 2.6 瑞士CH 3.9 澳AU,韩国KR 5 巴PK	0 受惠国$_1$LD$_1$	30	----Trimethyl phosphite
2154	2920.9012	----亚磷酸三乙酯	6.5	0 冰岛IS,东盟AS,哥CR,秘鲁PE,新西兰NZ,智利CL 2.6 瑞士CH 3.9 澳AU,韩国KR 5 巴PK	0 受惠国$_1$LD$_1$	30	----Trimethyl phosphite
2155	2920.9013	----亚磷酸二甲酯	6.5	0 冰岛IS,东盟AS,哥CR,秘鲁PE,新西兰NZ,智利CL 2.6 瑞士CH 3.9 澳AU,韩国KR 5 巴PK	0 受惠国$_1$LD$_1$	30	----Dimethyl phosphite
2156	2920.9014	----亚磷酸二乙酯	6.5	0 冰岛IS,东盟AS,哥CR,秘鲁PE,新西兰NZ,智利CL 2.6 瑞士CH 3.9 澳AU,韩国KR 5 巴PK	0 受惠国$_1$LD$_1$	30	----Diethyl phosphite
2157	2920.9019	----其他	6.5	0 冰岛IS,东盟AS,哥CR,秘鲁PE,新西兰NZ,智利CL 2.6 瑞士CH 3.9 澳AU,韩国KR 5 巴PK	0 受惠国$_1$LD$_1$	30	----Other
2158	2920.9090	---其他	6.5	0 冰岛IS,东盟AS,哥CR,秘鲁PE,新西兰NZ,智利CL 2.6 瑞士CH 3.9 澳AU,韩国KR 5 巴PK	0 受惠国$_1$LD$_1$	30	---Other
	ex29209090	碳酸二苯酯	Δ2				Diphenyl carbonate
		第九分章 含氮基化合物					IX. NITROGEN FUNCTION COMPOUNDS
	29.21	**氨基化合物:**					**Amine-function compounds:**
		-无环单胺及其衍生物以及它们的盐:					-Acyclic monoamines and their derivatives; salts thereof:
2159	2921.1100	--甲胺、二甲胺或三甲胺及其盐	6.5	0 冰岛IS,东盟AS,哥CR,秘鲁PE,新西兰NZ,智利CL 2.6 瑞士CH 3.9 澳AU,韩国KR 5 巴PK	0 受惠国$_1$LD$_1$	30	--Methylamine, di-or trimethylamine and their salts
		--其他:					--Other:
2160	2921.1910	---二正丙胺	4	0 澳AU,巴PK,冰岛IS,东盟AS,哥CR,韩国KR,秘鲁PE,瑞士CH,新西兰NZ,智利CL	0 受惠国$_1$LD$_1$	11	---Di-n-propylamine
2161	2921.1920	---异丙胺	6.5Δ2	0 冰岛IS,东盟AS,哥CR,韩国KR,秘鲁PE,新西兰NZ,智利CL 2.6 瑞士CH 3.9 澳AU 5 巴PK	0 受惠国$_1$LD$_1$	30	---Isopropyl amine

序号 No.	税则号列 Tariff Line	中文货品名称 Article Description in Chinese	最惠国税率 MFN(%)	协定税率 Agreement(%)	特惠税率 SP(%)	普通税率 Gen(%)	英文货品名称 Article Description
2162	2921.1930	---N，N—二（2-氯乙基）乙胺	6.5	0 冰岛IS,东盟AS,哥CR,秘鲁PE,新西兰NZ,智利CL 2.6 瑞士CH 3.9 澳AU,韩国KR 5 巴PK	0 受惠国$_1$LD$_1$	30	---N, N-Bis (2-chloroethyl) ethylamine
2163	2921.1940	---N，N—二（2-氯乙基）甲胺	6.5	0 冰岛IS,东盟AS,哥CR,秘鲁PE,新西兰NZ,智利CL 2.6 瑞士CH 3.9 澳AU,韩国KR 5 巴PK	0 受惠国$_1$LD$_1$	30	---N, N-Bis (2-chloroethyl) methylamine
2164	2921.1950	---三（2-氯乙基）胺	6.5	0 冰岛IS,东盟AS,哥CR,秘鲁PE,新西兰NZ,智利CL 2.6 瑞士CH 3.9 澳AU,韩国KR 5 巴PK	0 受惠国$_1$LD$_1$	30	---Tri- (2-chloroethyl) amine
2165	2921.1960	---二烷（甲、乙、正丙或异丙）氨基乙基-2-氯及其质子化盐	6.5	0 冰岛IS,东盟AS,哥CR,秘鲁PE,新西兰NZ,智利CL 2.6 瑞士CH 3.9 澳AU,韩国KR 5 巴PK	0 受惠国$_1$LD$_1$	30	---N, N-Dialkyl (Me, Et, n-Pr or i-Pr) aminoethyl-2-chlorides and corresponking protonated salts
2166	2921.1990	---其他	6.5	0 冰岛IS,东盟AS,哥CR,秘鲁PE,新西兰NZ,智利CL 2.6 瑞士CH 3.9 澳AU,韩国KR 5 巴PK	0 受惠国$_1$LD$_1$	30	---Other
		-无环多胺及其衍生物以及它们的盐： --乙二胺及其盐：					-Acyclic polyamines and their derivatives; salts thereof: --Ethylenediamine and its salts:
2167	2921.2110	---乙二胺	6.5	0 冰岛IS,东盟AS,哥CR,秘鲁PE,新西兰NZ,智利CL 2.6 瑞士CH 3.9 澳AU 5 巴PK 5.6 韩国KR	0 受惠国$_1$LD$_1$	30	---Ethylenediamine
2168	2921.2190	---其他	6.5	0 冰岛IS,东盟AS,哥CR,秘鲁PE,新西兰NZ,智利CL 3.9 澳AU 4.7 瑞士CH 5 巴PK 5.2 韩国KR	0 受惠国$_1$LD$_1$	30	---Other
		--六亚甲基二胺及其盐：					--Hexamethylenediamine and its salts:
2169	2921.2210	---己二酸己二胺盐（尼龙66盐）	6.5	0 冰岛IS,东盟AS,哥CR,秘鲁PE,新西兰NZ,智利CL 2.6 瑞士CH 3.9 澳AU,韩国KR 5 巴PK	0 受惠国$_1$LD$_1$	20	---Nylon-66salt
2170	2921.2290	---其他	6.5	0 冰岛IS,东盟AS,哥CR,秘鲁PE,新西兰NZ,智利CL 2.6 瑞士CH 3.9 澳AU 5 巴PK 5.2 韩国KR	0 受惠国$_1$LD$_1$	30	---Other

序号 No.	税则号列 Tariff Line	中文货品名称 Article Description in Chinese	最惠国税率 MFN(%)	协定税率 Agreement(%)	特惠税率 SP(%)	普通税率 Gen(%)	英文货品名称 Article Description
2171	2921.2900	--其他	6.5	0 冰岛IS,东盟AS,哥CR,秘鲁PE,新西兰NZ,智利CL 2.6 瑞士CH 3.9 澳AU 5 巴PK 5.2 韩国KR	0 受惠国$_1$LD$_1$	30	--Other
2172	2921.3000	-环烷单胺或多胺、环烯单胺或多胺、环萜烯单胺或多胺及其衍生物以及它们的盐	6.5	0 冰岛IS,东盟AS,哥CR,秘鲁PE,新西兰NZ,智利CL 2.6 瑞士CH 3.9 澳AU,韩国KR 5 巴PK	0 受惠国$_1$LD$_1$	30	-Cyclanic, cyclenic or cycloterpenic monoor polyamines, and their derivatives; salts thereof
		-芳香单胺及其衍生物以及它们的盐:					-Aromatic monoamines and their derivatives; salts thereof:
		--苯胺及其盐:					--Aniline and its salts:
2173	2921.4110	---苯胺	6.5	0 冰岛IS,东盟AS,哥CR,秘鲁PE,新西兰NZ,智利CL 2.6 瑞士CH 3.9 澳AU,韩国KR 5 巴PK	0 受惠国$_1$LD$_1$	20	---Aniline
2174	2921.4190	---其他	6.5	0 冰岛IS,东盟AS,哥CR,秘鲁PE,新西兰NZ,智利CL 3.9 澳AU,韩国KR 5 巴PK	0 受惠国$_1$LD$_1$	30	---Other
2175	2921.4200	--苯胺衍生物及其盐	6.5	0 冰岛IS,东盟AS,哥CR,秘鲁PE,新西兰NZ,智利CL 3.9 澳AU 5 巴PK 5.2 韩国KR	0 受惠国$_1$LD$_1$	30	--Aniline derivatives and their salts
2176	2921.4300	--甲苯胺及其衍生物以及它们的盐	6.5	0 冰岛IS,东盟AS,哥CR,秘鲁PE,新西兰NZ,智利CL 2.6 瑞士CH 3.9 澳AU 5 巴PK 5.6 韩国KR	0 受惠国$_1$LD$_1$	30	--Toluidines and their derivatives; salts thereof
2177	2921.4400	--二苯胺及其衍生物以及它们的盐	6.5	0 冰岛IS,东盟AS,哥CR,秘鲁PE,新西兰NZ,智利CL 3.9 澳AU 5 巴PK 5.2 韩国KR	0 受惠国$_1$LD$_1$	30	--Diphenylamine and its derivatives; salts thereof
2178	2921.4500	--1-萘胺（α-萘胺）、2-萘胺（β-萘胺）及其衍生物以及它们的盐	6.5	0 冰岛IS,东盟AS,哥CR,秘鲁PE,新西兰NZ,智利CL 3.9 澳AU,韩国KR 5 巴PK	0 受惠国$_1$LD$_1$	30	--1-Naphthylamine (α-naphthy-lamine), 2-naphthylamine (β-na-phthylamine) and their derivatives; salts thereof
2179	2921.4600	--安非他明（INN）、苄非他明（INN）、右苯丙胺（INN）、乙非他明、芬坎法明（INN）、利非他明、左苯丙胺（INN）、美芬雷司（INN）、苯丁胺（INN）以及它们的盐	6.5	0 冰岛IS,东盟AS,哥CR,秘鲁PE,新西兰NZ,智利CL 2.6 瑞士CH 3.9 澳AU,韩国KR 5 巴PK	0 受惠国$_1$LD$_1$	30	--Amfetamine (INN), benzfetamine (INN), dexamfetamine (INN), etilamfetamine (INN), fencamfamin (INN), lefetamine (INN), levamfetamine (INN), mefenorex (INN) and phentermine (INN); salts thereof
		--其他:					--Other:
2180	2921.4910	---对异丙基苯胺	4	0 澳AU,巴PK,冰岛IS,东盟AS,哥CR,韩国KR,秘鲁PE,瑞士CH,新西兰NZ,智利CL	0 受惠国$_1$LD$_1$	11	---P-Isopropyl-aniline

序号 No.	税则号列 Tariff Line	中文货品名称 Article Description in Chinese	最惠国税率 MFN(%)	协定税率 Agreement(%)	特惠税率 SP(%)	普通税率 Gen(%)	英文货品名称 Article Description
2181	2921.4920	---二甲基苯胺	6.5	0 冰岛IS,东盟AS,哥CR,秘鲁PE,新西兰NZ,智利CL 2.6 瑞士CH 3.9 澳AU 5 巴PK 5.2 韩国KR	0 受惠国$_1$LD$_1$	20	---Dimethylanilines
2182	2921.4930	---2，6-甲基乙基苯胺	4	0 澳AU,巴PK,冰岛IS,东盟AS,哥CR,韩国KR,秘鲁PE,瑞士CH,新西兰NZ,智利CL	0 受惠国$_1$LD$_1$	11	---2, 6-Methyl ethyl aniline
2183	2921.4940	---2，6-二乙基苯胺	6.5	0 冰岛IS,东盟AS,哥CR,秘鲁PE,新西兰NZ,智利CL 3.9 澳AU,韩国KR 5 巴PK	0 受惠国$_1$LD$_1$	20	---2, 6-Diethylaniline
2184	2921.4990	---其他	6.5	0 冰岛IS,东盟AS,哥CR,秘鲁PE,新西兰NZ,智利CL 3.9 澳AU,韩国KR 5 巴PK	0 受惠国$_1$LD$_1$	30	---Other
		-芳香多胺及其衍生物以及它们的盐：					-Aromatic polyamines and their derivatives; salts thereof:
		--邻-、间-、对-苯二胺、二氨基甲苯及其衍生物以及它们的盐：					--*o*-, *m*-, *p*-Phenylenediamine, diaminotoluenes, and their derivatives; salts thereof:
2185	2921.5110	---邻苯二胺	4	0 澳AU,巴PK,冰岛IS,东盟AS,哥CR,韩国KR,秘鲁PE,瑞士CH,新西兰NZ,智利CL	0 受惠国$_1$LD$_1$	11	---O-Phenylenediamine
2186	2921.5190	---其他	6.5	0 冰岛IS,东盟AS,哥CR,秘鲁PE,新西兰NZ,智利CL 2.6 瑞士CH 3.9 澳AU,韩国KR 5 巴PK	0 受惠国$_1$LD$_1$	30	---Other
2187	2921.5900	--其他	6.5	0 冰岛IS,东盟AS,哥CR,秘鲁PE,新西兰NZ,智利CL 3.9 澳AU 5 巴PK 5.2 韩国KR	0 受惠国$_1$LD$_1$	30	--Other
	29.22	**含氧基氨基化合物：**					**Oxygen-function amino-compounds:**
		-氨基醇（但含有一种以上含氧基的除外）及其醚和酯，以及它们的盐：					-Amino-alcohols, other than those containing more than one kind of oxygen function, their ethers and esters; salts thereof:
2188	2922.1100	--单乙醇胺及其盐	6.5	0 冰岛IS,东盟AS,哥CR,秘鲁PE,新西兰NZ,智利CL 2.6 瑞士CH 3.9 澳AU 5 巴PK	0 受惠国$_1$LD$_1$	30	--Monoethanolamine and its salts
2189	2922.1200	--二乙醇胺及其盐	6.5	0 冰岛IS,东盟AS,哥CR,秘鲁PE,新西兰NZ,智利CL 2.6 瑞士CH 3.9 澳AU 5 巴PK	0 受惠国$_1$LD$_1$	30	--Diethanolamine and its salts
		--三乙醇胺及其盐：					--Triethanolamine and its salts:

序号 No.	税则号列 Tariff Line	中文货品名称 Article Description in Chinese	最惠国税率 MFN(%)	协定税率 Agreement(%)	特惠税率 SP(%)	普通税率 Gen(%)	英文货品名称 Article Description
2190	2922.1310	---三乙醇胺	6.5	0 冰岛IS,东盟AS,哥CR,秘鲁PE,新西兰NZ,智利CL 2.6 瑞士CH 3.9 澳AU 5 巴PK 5.6 韩国KR	0 受惠国$_1$LD$_1$	30	---Triethanolamine
2191	2922.1320	---三乙醇胺盐	6.5	0 冰岛IS,东盟AS,哥CR,秘鲁PE,新西兰NZ,智利CL 2.6 瑞士CH 3.9 澳AU,韩国KR 5 巴PK	0 受惠国$_1$LD$_1$	30	---Salts of triethanolamine
2192	2922.1400	--右丙氧吩（INN）及其盐	6.5	0 冰岛IS,东盟AS,哥CR,秘鲁PE,新西兰NZ,智利CL 2.6 瑞士CH 3.9 澳AU,韩国KR 5 巴PK	0 受惠国$_1$LD$_1$	30	--Dextropropoxyphene (INN) and its saltsZ
		--其他：					--Other:
2193	2922.1910	---乙胺丁醇	6.5	0 冰岛IS,东盟AS,哥CR,秘鲁PE,新西兰NZ,智利CL 2.6 瑞士CH 3.9 澳AU,韩国KR 5 巴PK	0 受惠国$_1$LD$_1$	30	---Ethylamino butanol (Ethambutol)
		---二烷（甲、乙、正丙或异丙）氨基乙-2-醇及其质子化盐：					---N, N-Dialkyl- (Me, Et, n-Pr or i-Pr) aminoethane-2-ols and corresponding protonated salts:
2194	2922.1921	----二甲氨基乙醇及其质子化盐	6.5	0 冰岛IS,东盟AS,哥CR,秘鲁PE,新西兰NZ,智利CL 2.6 瑞士CH 3.9 澳AU,韩国KR 5 巴PK	0 受惠国$_1$LD$_1$	30	----N, N-Dimethylaminoethanol and corresponding protonated salts
2195	2922.1922	----二乙氨基乙醇及其质子化盐	6.5	0 冰岛IS,东盟AS,哥CR,秘鲁PE,新西兰NZ,智利CL 2.6 瑞士CH 3.9 澳AU,韩国KR 5 巴PK	0 受惠国$_1$LD$_1$	30	----N, N-Diethylaminoethanol and corresponding protonated salts
2196	2922.1929	----其他	6.5	0 冰岛IS,东盟AS,哥CR,秘鲁PE,新西兰NZ,智利CL 2.6 瑞士CH 3.9 澳AU,韩国KR 5 巴PK	0 受惠国$_1$LD$_1$	30	----Other
2197	2922.1930	---乙基二乙醇胺	6.5	0 冰岛IS,东盟AS,哥CR,秘鲁PE,新西兰NZ,智利CL 2.6 瑞士CH 3.9 澳AU,韩国KR 5 巴PK	0 受惠国$_1$LD$_1$	30	---Ethyldiethanolamine
2198	2922.1940	---甲基二乙醇胺	6.5	0 冰岛IS,东盟AS,哥CR,秘鲁PE,新西兰NZ,智利CL 2.6 瑞士CH 3.9 澳AU,韩国KR 5 巴PK	0 受惠国$_1$LD$_1$	30	---Methyldiethanolamine
2199	2922.1950	---本芴醇	6.5	0 冰岛IS,东盟AS,哥CR,秘鲁PE,新西兰NZ,智利CL 2.6 瑞士CH 3.9 澳AU,韩国KR 5 巴PK	0 受惠国$_1$LD$_1$	30	---Iumefantrine

序号 No.	税则号列 Tariff Line	中文货品名称 Article Description in Chinese	最惠国税率 MFN(%)	协定税率 Agreement(%)	特惠税率 SP(%)	普通税率 Gen(%)	英文货品名称 Article Description
2200	2922.1990	---其他	6.5	0 冰岛IS,东盟AS,哥CR,秘鲁PE,新西兰NZ,智利CL 2.6 瑞士CH 3.9 澳AU,韩国KR 5 巴PK	0 受惠国$_1$LD$_1$	30	---Other
		-氨基萘酚和其他氨基酚（但含有一种以上含氧基的除外）及其醚和酯，以及它们的盐：					-Amino-naphthols and other amino-phenols, other than those containing more than one kind of oxygen function, their ethers and esters; salts thereof:
2201	2922.2100	--氨基羟基萘磺酸及其盐	6.5	0 冰岛IS,东盟AS,哥CR,秘鲁PE,新西兰NZ,智利CL 2.6 瑞士CH 3.9 澳AU 5 巴PK 5.2 韩国KR	0 受惠国$_1$LD$_1$	30	--Aminohydroxynaphthalenesulphonic acid and their salts
		--其他：					--Other:
2202	2922.2910	---茴香胺、二茴香胺、氨基苯乙醚及其盐	6.5	0 冰岛IS,东盟AS,哥CR,秘鲁PE,新西兰NZ,智利CL 2.6 瑞士CH 3.9 澳AU 5 巴PK 5.2 韩国KR	0 受惠国$_1$LD$_1$	30	---Anisidine, dianisidine, phenetidine and their salts
2203	2922.2990	---其他	6.5	0 冰岛IS,东盟AS,哥CR,秘鲁PE,新西兰NZ,智利CL 2.6 瑞士CH 3.9 澳AU,韩国KR 5 巴PK	0 受惠国$_1$LD$_1$	30	---Other
		-氨基醛、氨基酮和氨基醌，但含有一种以上含氧基的除外，以及它们的盐：					-Amino-aldehydes, amino-ketones and amino-quinones, other than those containing more than one kind of oxygen function; salts thereof:
2204	2922.3100	--安非拉酮、美沙酮和去甲美沙酮以及它们的盐	6.5	0 冰岛IS,东盟AS,哥CR,秘鲁PE,新西兰NZ,智利CL 2.6 瑞士CH 3.9 澳AU,韩国KR 5 巴PK	0 受惠国$_1$LD$_1$	30	--Amfepramone (INN) , methadone (INN) and normethadone (INN) ; salts thereof
		--其他：					--Other:
2205	2922.3910	---4-甲基甲卡西酮	6.5	0 冰岛IS,东盟AS,哥CR,秘鲁PE,新西兰NZ,智利CL 2.6 瑞士CH 3.9 澳AU,韩国KR 5 巴PK	0 受惠国$_1$LD$_1$	30	---4-methyl-methcathinone
2206	2922.3990	---其他	6.5	0 冰岛IS,东盟AS,哥CR,秘鲁PE,新西兰NZ,智利CL 2.6 瑞士CH 3.9 澳AU,韩国KR 5 巴PK	0 受惠国$_1$LD$_1$	30	---Other
		-氨基酸及其酯，但含有一种以上含氧基的除外，以及它们的盐：					-Amino-acids, other than those containing more than one kind of oxygen function, and their esters; salts thereof:
		--赖氨酸及其酯以及它们的盐：					--Lysine and its esters; salts thereof:

序号 No.	税则号列 Tariff Line	中文货品名称 Article Description in Chinese	最惠国税率 MFN(%)	协定税率 Agreement(%)	特惠税率 SP(%)	普通税率 Gen(%)	英文货品名称 Article Description
2207	2922.4110	---赖氨酸	5	0 澳AU,巴PK,冰岛IS,东盟AS,哥CR,秘鲁PE,瑞士CH,新西兰NZ,智利CL 4.3 韩国KR	0 受惠国$_1$LD$_1$	20	---Lysine
2208	2922.4190	---其他	6Δ5	0 冰岛IS,东盟AS,哥CR,秘鲁PE,新西兰NZ,智利CL 2.4 瑞士CH 3.6 澳AU,韩国KR 5 巴PK	0 受惠国$_1$LD$_1$	30	---Other
		--谷氨酸及其盐:					--Glutamic acid and its salts:
2209	2922.4210	---谷氨酸	10Δ5	0 冰岛IS,东盟AS,哥CR,秘鲁PE,新加坡SG,新西兰NZ,智利CL 4 瑞士CH 5 巴PK 6 澳AU 8 韩国KR 8.6 亚太AP	0 受惠国$_1$LD$_1$	90	---Glutamic acid
2210	2922.4220	---谷氨酸钠	10	0 冰岛IS,东盟AS,哥CR,秘鲁PE,香港HK,新加坡SG,新西兰NZ,智利CL 4 瑞士CH 5 巴PK 6 澳AU 8 韩国KR	0 受惠国$_1$LD$_1$	130	---Sodium glutamate
2211	2922.4290	---其他	6.5	0 冰岛IS,东盟AS,哥CR,秘鲁PE,新西兰NZ,智利CL 2.6 瑞士CH 3.9 澳AU,韩国KR 5 巴PK	0 受惠国$_1$LD$_1$	30	---Other
		--氨基酸(但含有一种以上含氧基的除外)及其酯，以及它们的盐:					--Anthranilic acid and its salts:
2212	2922.4310	---邻氨基苯甲酸（氨茴酸）	6.5	0 冰岛IS,东盟AS,哥CR,秘鲁PE,新西兰NZ,智利CL 2.6 瑞士CH 3.9 澳AU,韩国KR 5 巴PK	0 受惠国$_1$LD$_1$	20	---Anthranilic acid
2213	2922.4390	---其他	6.5	0 冰岛IS,东盟AS,哥CR,秘鲁PE,新西兰NZ,智利CL 2.6 瑞士CH 3.9 澳AU,韩国KR 5 巴PK	0 受惠国$_1$LD$_1$	30	---Other
2214	2922.4400	--替利定（INN）及其盐	6.5	0 冰岛IS,东盟AS,哥CR,秘鲁PE,新西兰NZ,智利CL 2.6 瑞士CH 3.9 澳AU,韩国KR 5 巴PK	0 受惠国$_1$LD$_1$	30	--Tilidine (INN) and its salts
		--其他:					--Other:
		---其他氨基酸:					---Amino acids:
2215	2922.4911	----氨甲环酸	6.5	0 冰岛IS,东盟AS,哥CR,秘鲁PE,新西兰NZ,智利CL 2.6 瑞士CH 3.9 澳AU 5 巴PK 5.6 韩国KR	0 受惠国$_1$LD$_1$	20	----Tranexamic acid

序号 No.	税则号列 Tariff Line	中文货品名称 Article Description in Chinese	最惠国税率 MFN(%)	协定税率 Agreement(%)	特惠税率 SP(%)	普通税率 Gen(%)	英文货品名称 Article Description
2216	2922.4919	----其他	6.5	0 冰岛IS,东盟AS,哥CR,秘鲁PE,新西兰NZ,智利CL 2.6 瑞士CH 3.9 澳AU 5 巴PK 5.6 韩国KR	0 受惠国$_1$LD$_1$	20	----Other
	ex29224919	苏氨酸	Δ5				Threonine
		---其他:					---Other:
2217	2922.4991	----普鲁卡因	6	0 冰岛IS,东盟AS,哥CR,秘鲁PE,新西兰NZ,智利CL 2.4 瑞士CH 3.6 澳AU,韩国KR 5 巴PK	0 受惠国$_1$LD$_1$	20	----Procaine
2218	2922.4999	----其他	6.5	0 冰岛IS,东盟AS,哥CR,秘鲁PE,新西兰NZ,智利CL 2.6 瑞士CH 3.9 澳AU,韩国KR 5 巴PK	0 受惠国$_1$LD$_1$	30	----Other
		-氨基醇酚、氨基酸酚及其他含氧基氨基化合物:					-Amino-alcohol-phenols, amino-acid-phenols and other amino-compounds with oxygen function:
2219	2922.5010	---对羟基苯甘氨酸及其邓钾盐	6.5	0 冰岛IS,东盟AS,哥CR,秘鲁PE,新西兰NZ,智利CL 2.6 瑞士CH 3.9 澳AU,韩国KR 5 巴PK	0 受惠国$_1$LD$_1$	30	---Potassium-((3-ethoxy-1-methyl-3-oxoprop-1-enyl) amino) (4-hydroxyphenyl) acetate
2220	2922.5020	---莱克多巴胺和盐酸莱克多巴胺	6.5	0 冰岛IS,东盟AS,哥CR,秘鲁PE,新西兰NZ,智利CL 2.6 瑞士CH 3.9 澳AU 5 巴PK 5.6 韩国KR	0 受惠国$_1$LD$_1$	30	---Ractopamine; Ractopamine hydrochloride
2221	2922.5090	---其他	6.5	0 冰岛IS,东盟AS,哥CR,秘鲁PE,新西兰NZ,智利CL 2.6 瑞士CH 3.9 澳AU 5 巴PK 5.2 韩国KR	0 受惠国$_1$LD$_1$	30	---Other
	29.23	**季铵盐及季铵碱;卵磷脂及其他磷氨基类脂,无论是否已有化学定义:**					**Quaternary ammonium salts and hydroxides; lecithins and other phosphoaminolipids, whether or not chemically defined:**
2222	2923.1000	-胆碱及其盐	6.5	0 冰岛IS,东盟AS,哥CR,秘鲁PE,新西兰NZ,智利CL 2.6 瑞士CH 3.9 澳AU,韩国KR 5 巴PK	0 受惠国$_1$LD$_1$	30	-Choline and its salts
2223	2923.2000	-卵磷脂及其他磷氨基类脂	6.5	0 冰岛IS,东盟AS,哥CR,秘鲁PE,新西兰NZ,智利CL 2.6 瑞士CH 3.9 澳AU 5 巴PK 5.2 韩国KR	0 受惠国$_1$LD$_1$	30	-Lecithins and other phosphoamin-olipids

序号 No.	税则号列 Tariff Line	中文货品名称 Article Description in Chinese	最惠国税率 MFN(%)	协定税率 Agreement(%)	特惠税率 SP(%)	普通税率 Gen(%)	英文货品名称 Article Description
2224	2923.9000	-其他	6.5	0 冰岛IS,东盟AS,哥CR,秘鲁PE,新西兰NZ,智利CL 2.6 瑞士CH 3.9 澳AU,韩国KR 5 巴PK	0 受惠国$_1$LD$_1$	30	-Other
	29.24	**羧基酰胺基化合物;碳酸酰胺基化合物:**					**Carboxyamide-function compounds; amide-function compounds of carbonic acid:**
		-无环酰胺（包括无环氨基甲酸酯）及其衍生物以及它们的盐:					-Acyclic amides (including acyclic carbamates) and their derivatives; salts thereof:
2225	2924.1100	--甲丙氨酯（INN）	6.5	0 冰岛IS,东盟AS,哥CR,秘鲁PE,新西兰NZ,智利CL 2.6 瑞士CH 3.9 澳AU,韩国KR 5 巴PK	0 受惠国$_1$LD$_1$	30	--Meprobamate (INN)
2226	2924.1200	--氟乙酰胺（ISO）、久效磷（ISO）及磷胺（ISO）	6.5	0 冰岛IS,东盟AS,哥CR,秘鲁PE,新西兰NZ,智利CL 2.6 瑞士CH 3.9 澳AU,韩国KR 5 巴PK	0 受惠国$_1$LD$_1$	30	--Fluoroacetamide (ISO) , monocrotophos (ISO) and phosphamidon (ISO)
		--其他（INN）:					--Other:
2227	2924.1910	---二甲基甲酰胺	6.5	0 冰岛IS,东盟AS,哥CR,韩国KR,秘鲁PE,台湾TW,香港HK,新西兰NZ,智利CL 2.6 瑞士CH 3.9 澳AU 5 巴PK	0 受惠国$_1$LD$_1$	30	---N, N-dimethylformamide
2228	2924.1990	---其他	6.5	0 冰岛IS,东盟AS,哥CR,秘鲁PE,新西兰NZ,智利CL 2.6 瑞士CH 3.9 澳AU 5 巴PK 5.6 韩国KR	0 受惠国$_1$LD$_1$	30	---Other
		-环酰胺（包括环氨基甲酸酯）及其衍生物以及它们的盐:					-Cyclic amides (including cyclic carbamates) and their derivatives; salts thereof:
2229	2924.2100	--酰脲及其衍生物以及它们的盐	6.5	0 冰岛IS,东盟AS,哥CR,秘鲁PE,新西兰NZ,智利CL 2.6 瑞士CH 3.9 澳AU,韩国KR 5 巴PK	0 受惠国$_1$LD$_1$	30	--Ureides and their derivatives; salts thereof
2230	2924.2300	--2-乙酰氨基苯甲酸（N-乙酰邻氨基苯甲酸）及其盐	6.5	0 冰岛IS,东盟AS,哥CR,秘鲁PE,新西兰NZ,智利CL 3.9 澳AU,韩国KR 5 巴PK	0 受惠国$_1$LD$_1$	30	--2-Acetamidobenzoic acid (N-acety-lanthranilic acid) and its salts
2231	2924.2400	--炔已蚁胺（INN）	6.5	0 冰岛IS,东盟AS,哥CR,秘鲁PE,新西兰NZ,智利CL 2.6 瑞士CH 3.9 澳AU,韩国KR 5 巴PK	0 受惠国$_1$LD$_1$	30	--Ethinamate (INN)
		--其他:					--Other:
2232	2924.2910	---对乙酰氨基苯乙醚（非那西丁）	6	0 冰岛IS,东盟AS,哥CR,秘鲁PE,新西兰NZ,智利CL 2.4 瑞士CH 3.6 澳AU,韩国KR 5 巴PK	0 受惠国$_1$LD$_1$	30	---Phenacetin

序号 No.	税则号列 Tariff Line	中文货品名称 Article Description in Chinese	最惠国税率 MFN(%)	协定税率 Agreement(%)	特惠税率 SP(%)	普通税率 Gen(%)	英文货品名称 Article Description
2233	2924.2920	---对乙酰氨基酚（扑热息痛）	6	0 冰岛IS,东盟AS,哥CR,秘鲁PE,新西兰NZ,智利CL 2.4 瑞士CH 3.6 澳AU,韩国KR 5 巴PK	0 受惠国$_1$LD$_1$	30	---P-Acetaminophenol (paracetanol)
2234	2924.2930	---阿斯巴甜	6.5	0 澳门MO,冰岛IS,东盟AS,哥CR,秘鲁PE,新西兰NZ,智利CL 3.9 澳AU,韩国KR 4.6 瑞士CH 5 巴PK	0 受惠国$_1$LD$_1$	30	---Aspartame
2235	2924.2990	---其他	6.5	0 澳门MO,冰岛IS,东盟AS,哥CR,秘鲁PE,新西兰NZ,智利CL 3.9 澳AU,韩国KR 4.6 瑞士CH 5 巴PK	0 受惠国$_1$LD$_1$	30	---Other
	29.25	**羧基酰亚胺化合物(包括糖精及其盐)及亚胺基化合物:**					**Carboxyimide-function compounds (including saccharin and its salts) and imine-function compounds:**
		-酰亚胺及其衍生物以及它们的盐:					-Imides and their derivatives; salts thereof:
2236	2925.1100	--糖精及其盐	9	0 冰岛IS,东盟AS,哥CR,秘鲁PE,新西兰NZ,智利CL 3.6 瑞士CH 5 巴PK 5.4 澳AU 7.2 韩国KR	0 受惠国$_1$LD$_1$	90	--Saccharin and its salts
2237	2925.1200	--格鲁米特（INN）	6.5	0 冰岛IS,东盟AS,哥CR,秘鲁PE,新西兰NZ,智利CL 2.6 瑞士CH 3.9 澳AU,韩国KR 5 巴PK	0 受惠国$_1$LD$_1$	30	--Glutethimide (INN)
2238	2925.1900	--其他	6.5	0 冰岛IS,东盟AS,哥CR,秘鲁PE,新西兰NZ,智利CL 3.9 澳AU,韩国KR 4.7 瑞士CH 5 巴PK	0 受惠国$_1$LD$_1$	30	--Other
		-亚胺及其衍生物以及它们的盐:					-Imines and their derivatives; salts thereof:
2239	2925.2100	--杀虫脒（ISO）	6.5	0 冰岛IS,东盟AS,哥CR,秘鲁PE,新西兰NZ,智利CL 2.6 瑞士CH 3.9 澳AU,韩国KR 5 巴PK	0 受惠国$_1$LD$_1$	30	--Chlordimeform (ISO)
2240	2925.2900	--其他	6.5	0 冰岛IS,东盟AS,哥CR,秘鲁PE,新西兰NZ,智利CL 2.6 瑞士CH 3.9 澳AU,韩国KR 5 巴PK	0 受惠国$_1$LD$_1$	30	--Other
	29.26	**腈基化合物:**					**Nitrile-function compounds:**
2241	2926.1000	-丙烯腈	6.5Δ3	0 冰岛IS,哥CR,秘鲁PE,新西兰NZ,智利CL 2.6 瑞士CH 3.9 澳AU	0 受惠国$_1$LD$_1$	30	-Acrylonitrile

序号 No.	税则号列 Tariff Line	中文货品名称 Article Description in Chinese	最惠国税率 MFN(%)	协定税率 Agreement(%)	特惠税率 SP(%)	普通税率 Gen(%)	英文货品名称 Article Description
2242	2926.2000	-1-氰基胍（双氰胺）	6.5	0 冰岛IS,东盟AS,哥CR,秘鲁PE,新西兰NZ,智利CL 2.6 瑞士CH 3.9 澳AU 5 巴PK 5.2 韩国KR	0 受惠国$_1$LD$_1$	30	-1-cyanoguanidine (dicyandiamide)
2243	2926.3000	-芬普雷司（INN）及其盐；美沙酮中间体（4-氰基-2-二甲氨基-4，4-二苯基丁烷）	6.5	0 冰岛IS,东盟AS,哥CR,秘鲁PE,新西兰NZ,智利CL 2.6 瑞士CH 3.9 澳AU,韩国KR 5 巴PK	0 受惠国$_1$LD$_1$	30	-Fenproporex (INN) and its salts; methadone (INN) intermediate (4-cyano-2-dimethylamino-4, 4-diphenylbutane)
		-其他：					-Other:
2244	2926.9010	---对氯氰苄	4	0 澳AU,巴PK,冰岛IS,东盟AS,哥CR,韩国KR,秘鲁PE,瑞士CH,新西兰NZ,智利CL	0 受惠国$_1$LD$_1$	11	---P-Chlorobenzyl cyanide
2245	2926.9020	---间苯二甲腈	6.5	0 冰岛IS,东盟AS,哥CR,秘鲁PE,新西兰NZ,智利CL 2.6 瑞士CH 3.9 澳AU,韩国KR 5 巴PK	0 受惠国$_1$LD$_1$	30	---M-Phthalonitrile
2246	2926.9090	---其他	6.5	0 冰岛IS,东盟AS,哥CR,秘鲁PE,香港HK,新西兰NZ,智利CL 3.9 澳AU,韩国KR 4.6 瑞士CH 5 巴PK	0 受惠国$_1$LD$_1$	30	---Other
	ex29269090	己二腈	Δ1				Hexanedinitrile
	29.27	**重氮化合物、偶氮化合物及氧化偶氮化合物**					**Diazo-, azo- or azoxy-compounds**
2247	2927.0000	重氮化合物、偶氮化合物及氧化偶氮化合物	6.5	0 澳门MO,冰岛IS,东盟AS,哥CR,秘鲁PE,新西兰NZ,智利CL 2.6 瑞士CH 3.9 澳AU,韩国KR 5 巴PK	0 受惠国$_1$LD$_1$	30	Diazo-, azo-.or azoxy-compounds
	29.28	**肼（联氨）及胲（羟胺）的有机衍生物**					**Organic derivatives of hydrazine or of hydroxylamine**
2248	2928.0000	肼（联氨）及胲（羟胺）的有机衍生物	6.5	0 冰岛IS,东盟AS,哥CR,秘鲁PE,新西兰NZ,智利CL 2.6 瑞士CH 3.9 澳AU 5 巴PK 5.2 韩国KR	0 受惠国$_1$LD$_1$	20	Organic derivatives of hydrazine or of hydroxylamine
	29.29	**其他含氮基化合物：**					**Compounds with other nitrogen function:**
2249	2929.1010	---2，4-和2，6-甲苯二异氰酸酯混合物（甲苯二异氰酸酯TDI）	6.5	0 冰岛IS,东盟AS,哥CR,秘鲁PE,台湾TW,新西兰NZ,智利CL 2.6 瑞士CH 3.9 澳AU 5 巴PK 5.6 韩国KR	0 受惠国$_1$LD$_1$	30	---Toluene diisocyanate
2250	2929.1020	---二甲苯二异氰酸酯（TODI）	6.5	0 冰岛IS,东盟AS,哥CR,秘鲁PE,新西兰NZ,智利CL 3.9 澳AU,韩国KR 5 巴PK	0 受惠国$_1$LD$_1$	30	---O-Xylene diisocyanate

序号 No.	税则号列 Tariff Line	中文货品名称 Article Description in Chinese	最惠国税率 MFN(%)	协定税率 Agreement(%)	特惠税率 SP(%)	普通税率 Gen(%)	英文货品名称 Article Description
2251	2929.1030	---二苯基甲烷二异氰酸酯（纯MDI）	6.5	0 冰岛IS,东盟AS,哥CR,秘鲁PE,新西兰NZ,智利CL 3.9 澳AU 4.6 瑞士CH 5 巴PK	0 受惠国$_1$LD$_1$	30	---Diphenylmethane diisocyanate
2252	2929.1040	---六亚甲基二异氰酸酯	6.5	0 冰岛IS,东盟AS,哥CR,秘鲁PE,新西兰NZ,智利CL 2.6 瑞士CH 3.9 澳AU 5 巴PK 5.2 韩国KR	0 受惠国$_1$LD$_1$	30	---Hexamethelene diisocyanate
2253	2929.1090	---其他	6.5	0 冰岛IS,东盟AS,哥CR,秘鲁PE,新西兰NZ,智利CL 2.6 瑞士CH 3.9 澳AU,韩国KR 5 巴PK	0 受惠国$_1$LD$_1$	30	---Other
		-其他:					-Other:
2254	2929.9010	---环己基氨基磺酸钠（甜蜜素）	9	0 冰岛IS,东盟AS,哥CR,秘鲁PE,新西兰NZ,智利CL 3.6 瑞士CH 5 巴PK 5.4 澳AU,韩国KR	0 受惠国$_1$LD$_1$	90	---Sodium cyclamate
2255	2929.9020	---二烷（甲、乙、正丙或异丙）氨基膦酰二卤	6.5	0 冰岛IS,东盟AS,哥CR,秘鲁PE,新西兰NZ,智利CL 2.6 瑞士CH 3.9 澳AU,韩国KR 5 巴PK	0 受惠国$_1$LD$_1$	30	---N, N-Dialkyl (Me, Et, n-Pr or i-Pr) phosphoramidic dihalides
2256	2929.9030	---二烷（甲、乙、正丙或异丙）氨基膦酸二烷（甲、乙、正丙或异丙）酯	6.5	0 冰岛IS,东盟AS,哥CR,秘鲁PE,新西兰NZ,智利CL 2.6 瑞士CH 3.9 澳AU,韩国KR 5 巴PK	0 受惠国$_1$LD$_1$	30	---Dialkyl (Me, Et, n-Pr or i-Pr) N, Ndialkyl (Me, Et, n-Pr or i-Pr) -phosphoramidates
2257	2929.9040	---乙酰甲胺磷	6.5	0 冰岛IS,东盟AS,哥CR,秘鲁PE,新西兰NZ,智利CL 2.6 瑞士CH 3.9 澳AU,韩国KR 5 巴PK	0 受惠国$_1$LD$_1$	30	---Acephate
2258	2929.9090	---其他	6.5	0 冰岛IS,东盟AS,哥CR,秘鲁PE,新西兰NZ,智利CL 2.6 瑞士CH 3.9 澳AU 5 巴PK 5.6 韩国KR	0 受惠国$_1$LD$_1$	30	---Other
		第十分章　有机-无机化合物、杂环化合物、核酸及其盐以及磺（酰）胺					X. ORGANO-INORGANIC COMPOUNDS, HETEROCYCLIC COMPOUNDS, NUCLEIC ACIDS AND THEIR SALTS, AND SULPHONAMIDES
	29.30	**有机硫化合物:**					**Organo-sulphur compounds:**
2259	2930.2000	-硫代氨基甲酸盐（或酯）及二硫代氨基甲酸盐	6.5	0 冰岛IS,东盟AS,哥CR,秘鲁PE,新西兰NZ,智利CL 2.6 瑞士CH 3.9 澳AU,韩国KR 5 巴PK	0 受惠国$_1$LD$_1$	30	-Thiocarbamates and dithiocarba-mates

序号 No.	税则号列 Tariff Line	中文货品名称 Article Description in Chinese	最惠国税率 MFN(%)	协定税率 Agreement(%)	特惠税率 SP(%)	普通税率 Gen(%)	英文货品名称 Article Description
2260	2930.3000	-一硫化二烃氨基硫羰、二硫化二烃氨基硫羰及四硫化二烃氨基硫羰	6.5	0 冰岛IS,东盟AS,哥CR,秘鲁PE,新西兰NZ,智利CL 2.6 瑞士CH 3.9 澳AU,韩国KR 5 巴PK	0 受惠国$_1$LD$_1$	30	-Thiuram mono-, di or tetrasulphide
2261	2930.4000	-甲硫氨酸（蛋氨酸）	6.5Δ5	0 冰岛IS,东盟AS,哥CR,秘鲁PE,新西兰NZ,智利CL 2.6 瑞士CH 3.9 澳AU,韩国KR 5 巴PK	0 受惠国$_1$LD$_1$	30	-Methionine
2262	2930.5000	-敌菌丹（ISO）及甲胺磷（ISO）	6.5	0 冰岛IS,东盟AS,哥CR,秘鲁PE,新西兰NZ,智利CL 2.6 瑞士CH 3.9 澳AU,韩国KR 5 巴PK	0 受惠国$_1$LD$_1$	30	-Captafol (ISO) and methamidophos (ISO)
		-其他：					-Other:
2263	2930.9010	---双巯丙氨酸（胱氨酸）	6.5	0 冰岛IS,东盟AS,哥CR,秘鲁PE,新西兰NZ,智利CL 2.6 瑞士CH 3.9 澳AU,韩国KR 5 巴PK	0 受惠国$_1$LD$_1$	30	---Cystine
2264	2930.9020	---二硫代碳酸酯（或盐）［黄原酸酯（或盐）］	6.5	0 冰岛IS,东盟AS,哥CR,秘鲁PE,新西兰NZ,智利CL 2.6 瑞士CH 3.9 澳AU,韩国KR 5 巴PK	0 受惠国$_1$LD$_1$	30	---Dithiocarbonates (xanthates)
2265	2930.9090	---其他	6.5	0 冰岛IS,东盟AS,哥CR,秘鲁PE,香港HK,新西兰NZ,智利CL 2.6 瑞士CH 3.9 澳AU,韩国KR 5 巴PK	0 受惠国$_1$LD$_1$	30	---Other
	29.31	**其他有机-无机化合物：**					**Other organo-inorganic compounds:**
2266	2931.1000	-四甲基铅及四乙基铅	6.5	0 冰岛IS,东盟AS,哥CR,秘鲁PE,新西兰NZ,智利CL 2.6 瑞士CH 3.9 澳AU,韩国KR 5 巴PK	0 受惠国$_1$LD$_1$	30	-Tetramethyl lead and tetraethyl lead
2267	2931.2000	-三丁基锡化合物	6.5	0 冰岛IS,东盟AS,哥CR,秘鲁PE,新西兰NZ,智利CL 2.6 瑞士CH 3.9 澳AU,韩国KR 5 巴PK	0 受惠国$_1$LD$_1$	30	-Tributyltin compounds
		-其他：					-Other:
		---含有磷原子的：					---Containning phosphorus:
2268	2931.9011	----双甘膦	6.5	0 冰岛IS,东盟AS,哥CR,秘鲁PE,新西兰NZ,智利CL 2.6 瑞士CH 3.9 澳AU,韩国KR 5 巴PK	0 受惠国$_1$LD$_1$	30	----N- (Phosphonomethyl) iminodiaceticacid
2269	2931.9019	----其他	6.5	0 冰岛IS,东盟AS,哥CR,秘鲁PE,新西兰NZ,智利CL 2.6 瑞士CH 3.9 澳AU,韩国KR 5 巴PK	0 受惠国$_1$LD$_1$	30	----Other

序号 No.	税则号列 Tariff Line	中文货品名称 Article Description in Chinese	最惠国税率 MFN(%)	协定税率 Agreement(%)	特惠税率 SP(%)	普通税率 Gen(%)	英文货品名称 Article Description
2270	2931.9090	---其他	6.5	0 冰岛IS,东盟AS,哥CR,秘鲁PE,新西兰NZ,智利CL 2.6 瑞士CH 3.9 澳AU,韩国KR 5 巴PK	0 受惠国$_1$LD$_1$	30	---Other
	29.32	**仅含有氧杂原子的杂环化合物:** -结构上含有一个非稠合呋喃环(不论是否氢化)的化合物:					**Heterocyclic compounds with oxygen hetero-atom (s) only:** -Compounds containing an unfused furan ring (whether or not hydrogenated) in the structure:
2271	2932.1100	--四氢呋喃	6	0 冰岛IS,东盟AS,哥CR,韩国KR,秘鲁PE,台湾TW,香港HK,新西兰NZ,智利CL 2.4 瑞士CH 3.6 澳AU 5 巴PK	0 受惠国$_1$LD$_1$	20	--Tetrahydrofuran
2272	2932.1200	--2-糠醛	6	0 冰岛IS,东盟AS,哥CR,秘鲁PE,新西兰NZ,智利CL 2.4 瑞士CH 3.6 澳AU,韩国KR 5 巴PK	0 受惠国$_1$LD$_1$	20	--2-Furaldehyde (furfuraldehyde)
2273	2932.1300	--糠醇及四氢糠醇	6	0 冰岛IS,东盟AS,哥CR,秘鲁PE,新西兰NZ,智利CL 2.4 瑞士CH 3.6 澳AU,韩国KR 5 巴PK	0 受惠国$_1$LD$_1$	20	--Furfuryl alcohol and tetrahydrofur-furyl alcohol
2274	2932.1900	--其他	6.5	0 冰岛IS,东盟AS,哥CR,秘鲁PE,新西兰NZ,智利CL 3.9 澳AU,韩国KR 5 巴PK	0 受惠国$_1$LD$_1$	20	--Other
		-内酯:					-Lactones:
2275	2932.2010	---香豆素、甲基香豆素及乙基香豆素	6.5	0 冰岛IS,东盟AS,哥CR,秘鲁PE,新西兰NZ,智利CL 2.6 瑞士CH 3.9 澳AU,韩国KR 5 巴PK	0 受惠国$_1$LD$_1$	20	---Coumarin, methylcoumarins and ethylcoumarins
2276	2932.2090	---其他内酯	6.5	0 冰岛IS,东盟AS,哥CR,秘鲁PE,新西兰NZ,智利CL 3.9 澳AU,韩国KR 4.6 瑞士CH 5 巴PK	0 受惠国$_1$LD$_1$	20	---Other lactones
		-其他:					-Other:
2277	2932.9100	--4-丙烯基-1,2-亚甲二氧基苯(异黄樟脑)	6.5	0 冰岛IS,东盟AS,哥CR,秘鲁PE,新西兰NZ,智利CL 2.6 瑞士CH 3.9 澳AU,韩国KR 5 巴PK	0 受惠国$_1$LD$_1$	20	--Isosafrole
2278	2932.9200	--1-(1,3-苯并二口恶茂-5-基)丙烷-2-酮	6.5	0 冰岛IS,东盟AS,哥CR,秘鲁PE,新西兰NZ,智利CL 2.6 瑞士CH 3.9 澳AU,韩国KR 5 巴PK	0 受惠国$_1$LD$_1$	20	--1- (1, 3-Benzodioxol-5-yl) propan-2-one

序号 No.	税则号列 Tariff Line	中文货品名称 Article Description in Chinese	最惠国税率 MFN(%)	协定税率 Agreement(%)	特惠税率 SP(%)	普通税率 Gen(%)	英文货品名称 Article Description
2279	2932.9300	--3，4-亚甲二氧基苯甲醛（胡椒醛）	6.5	0 冰岛IS,东盟AS,哥CR,秘鲁PE,新西兰NZ,智利CL 2.6 瑞士CH 3.9 澳AU,韩国KR 5 巴PK	0 受惠国$_1$LD$_1$	20	--Piperonal
2280	2932.9400	--4-烯丙基-1，2-亚甲二氧基苯（黄樟脑）	6.5	0 冰岛IS,东盟AS,哥CR,秘鲁PE,新西兰NZ,智利CL 2.6 瑞士CH 3.9 澳AU,韩国KR 5 巴PK	0 受惠国$_1$LD$_1$	20	--Safrole
2281	2932.9500	--四氢大麻酚（所有的异构体）	6.5	0 冰岛IS,东盟AS,哥CR,秘鲁PE,新西兰NZ,智利CL 2.6 瑞士CH 3.9 澳AU,韩国KR 5 巴PK	0 受惠国$_1$LD$_1$	20	--Tetrahydrocannabinols (all isomers)
		--其他：					--Other:
2282	2932.9910	---7-羟基苯并呋喃（呋喃酚）	4	0 澳AU,巴PK,冰岛IS,东盟AS,哥CR,秘鲁PE,瑞士CH,新西兰NZ,智利CL 3.4 韩国KR	0 受惠国$_1$LD$_1$	11	---Furan phenol
2283	2932.9920	---2，2′-双甲氧羰基-4，4′-双甲氧基-5，6，5′，6′-双亚甲二氧基联苯（联苯双酯）	6.5	0 冰岛IS,东盟AS,哥CR,秘鲁PE,新西兰NZ,智利CL 2.6 瑞士CH 3.9 澳AU,韩国KR 5 巴PK	0 受惠国$_1$LD$_1$	20	---Bifendate
2284	2932.9930	---蒿甲醚	6.5	0 冰岛IS,东盟AS,哥CR,秘鲁PE,新西兰NZ,智利CL 3.9 澳AU,韩国KR 4.6 瑞士CH 5 巴PK	0 受惠国$_1$LD$_1$	20	---Artemether
2285	2932.9990	---其他	6.5	0 冰岛IS,东盟AS,哥CR,秘鲁PE,新西兰NZ,智利CL 3.9 澳AU,韩国KR 4.6 瑞士CH 5 巴PK	0 受惠国$_1$LD$_1$	20	---Other
	29.33	**仅含有氮杂原子的杂环化合物：**					**Heterocyclic compounds with nitrogen hetero-atom (s) only:**
		-结构上含有一个非稠合吡唑环（不论是否氢化）的化合物：					-Compounds containing an unfused pyrazole ring (whether or not hydrogenated) in the structure:
2286	2933.1100	--二甲基苯基吡唑酮（安替比林）及其衍生物	6.5	0 冰岛IS,东盟AS,哥CR,秘鲁PE,新西兰NZ,智利CL 2.6 瑞士CH 3.9 澳AU,韩国KR 5 巴PK 6 亚太AP	0 受惠国$_1$LD$_1$	20	--Phenazone (antipyrin) and its derivatives
		--其他：					--Other:
2287	2933.1920	---安乃近	6	0 冰岛IS,东盟AS,哥CR,秘鲁PE,新西兰NZ,智利CL 2.4 瑞士CH 3.6 澳AU,韩国KR 5 巴PK	0 受惠国$_1$LD$_1$	20	---Analgin

序号 No.	税则号列 Tariff Line	中文货品名称 Article Description in Chinese	最惠国税率 MFN(%)	协定税率 Agreement(%)	特惠税率 SP(%)	普通税率 Gen(%)	英文货品名称 Article Description
2288	2933.1990	---其他	6.5	0 冰岛IS,东盟AS,哥CR,秘鲁PE,新西兰NZ,智利CL 2.6 瑞士CH 3.9 澳AU,韩国KR 5 巴PK	0 受惠国$_1$LD$_1$	20	---Other
		-结构上含有一个非稠合咪唑环(不论是否氢化)的化合物:					-Compounds containing an unfused imidazole ring (whether or not hydrogenated) in the structure:
2289	2933.2100	--乙内酰脲及其衍生物	6.5	0 冰岛IS,东盟AS,哥CR,秘鲁PE,新西兰NZ,智利CL 2.6 瑞士CH 3.9 澳AU,韩国KR 5 巴PK	0 受惠国$_1$LD$_1$	30	--Hydantoin and its derivatives
2290	2933.2900	--其他	6.5	0 冰岛IS,东盟AS,哥CR,秘鲁PE,新西兰NZ,智利CL 3.9 澳AU 4.7 瑞士CH 5 巴PK 5.2 韩国KR	0 受惠国$_1$LD$_1$	20	--Other
		-结构上含有一个非稠合吡啶环(不论是否氢化)的化合物:					-Compounds containing an unfused pyridine ring (whether or not hydrogenated) in the structure:
2291	2933.3100	--吡啶及其盐	6	0 冰岛IS,东盟AS,哥CR,韩国KR,秘鲁PE,台湾TW,新西兰NZ,智利CL 2.4 瑞士CH 3.6 澳AU 5 巴PK	0 受惠国$_1$LD$_1$	20	--Pyridine and its salts
		--六氢吡啶(哌啶)及其盐:					--Piperidine and its salts:
2292	2933.3210	---六氢吡啶(哌啶)	4	0 澳AU,巴PK,冰岛IS,东盟AS,哥CR,韩国KR,秘鲁PE,瑞士CH,新西兰NZ,智利CL	0 受惠国$_1$LD$_1$	11	---Hexahydropyridine (piperidine)
2293	2933.3220	---六氢吡啶(哌啶)盐	6.5	0 冰岛IS,东盟AS,哥CR,秘鲁PE,新西兰NZ,智利CL 2.6 瑞士CH 3.9 澳AU,韩国KR 5 巴PK	0 受惠国$_1$LD$_1$	20	---Isoniazidum
2294	2933.3300	--阿芬太尼(INN),阿尼利定(INN),苯氰米特(INN),溴西泮(INN),地芬诺新(INN),地芬诺酯(INN),地匹哌酮(INN),芬太尼(INN),凯托米酮(INN),哌醋甲酯(INN),喷他左辛(INN),哌替啶(INN),哌替啶中间体A(INN),苯环利定(INN),苯哌利定(INN),哌苯甲醇(INN),哌氰米特(INN),哌丙吡胺(INN)和三甲利定(INN)以及它们的盐	6.5	0 冰岛IS,东盟AS,哥CR,秘鲁PE,新西兰NZ,智利CL 2.6 瑞士CH 3.9 澳AU 5 巴PK 5.6 韩国KR	0 受惠国$_1$LD$_1$	20	--Alfentanil (INN) , anil-eridine (INN) , bezitra-mide (INN) , bromaze-pam (INN) , difenoxin (INN) , diphenoxylate (INN) , dipipanone (INN) , fentanyl (INN) , ketobemidone (INN) , methylpheni-date (INN) , pentazo-cine (INN) , pethidine (INN) , intermediate A (INN) , phencyclidine (INN) (PCP) , phenop-eridine (INN) , piprad-rol (INN) , pipradrol (INN) , piritramide (INN) , propiram (INN) and trimeperidine (INN) , salts thereof
		--其他:					--Other:

序号 No.	税则号列 Tariff Line	中文货品名称 Article Description in Chinese	最惠国税率 MFN(%)	协定税率 Agreement(%)	特惠税率 SP(%)	普通税率 Gen(%)	英文货品名称 Article Description
2295	2933.3910	---二苯乙醇酸-3-奎宁环脂	6.5	0 冰岛IS,东盟AS,哥CR,秘鲁PE,新西兰NZ,智利CL 2.6 瑞士CH 3.9 澳AU,韩国KR 5 巴PK	0 受惠国$_1$LD$_1$	20	---Benzilic acid-3-quinuclidinate
2296	2933.3920	---奎宁坏-3-醇	6.5	0 冰岛IS,东盟AS,哥CR,秘鲁PE,新西兰NZ,智利CL 2.6 瑞士CH 3.9 澳AU,韩国KR 5 巴PK	0 受惠国$_1$LD$_1$	20	---Quinuclidine-3-ol
2297	2933.3990	---其他	6.5	0 冰岛IS,东盟AS,哥CR,秘鲁PE,新西兰NZ,智利CL 3.9 澳AU,韩国KR 4.6 瑞士CH 5 巴PK	0 受惠国$_1$LD$_1$	20	---Other
		-结构上含有一个喹啉或异喹啉环系（不论是否氢化）的化合物，但未经进一步稠合的：					-Compounds containing in the structure a quinoline or isoquinoline ring-system (whether or not hydrogenated) , not further fused:
2298	2933.4100	--左非诺（INN）及其盐	6.5	0 冰岛IS,东盟AS,哥CR,秘鲁PE,新西兰NZ,智利CL 2.6 瑞士CH 3.9 澳AU,韩国KR 5 巴PK	0 受惠国$_1$LD$_1$	20	--Levorpharol (INN) and its salts
2299	2933.4900	--其他	6.5	0 冰岛IS,东盟AS,哥CR,秘鲁PE,新西兰NZ,智利CL 2.6 瑞士CH 3.9 澳AU,韩国KR 5 巴PK	0 受惠国$_1$LD$_1$	20	--Other
		-结构上含有一个嘧啶环（不论是否氢化）或哌嗪环的化合物：					-Compounds containing a pyrimidine ring (whether or not hydrogenated) or piperazine ring in the structure:
2300	2933.5200	丙二酰脲（巴比土酸）及其盐	6.5	0 冰岛IS,东盟AS,哥CR,秘鲁PE,新西兰NZ,智利CL 2.6 瑞士CH 3.9 澳AU,韩国KR 5 巴PK	0 受惠国$_1$LD$_1$	20	--Malonylurea (barbituric acid) and its salts
2301	2933.5300	--阿洛巴比妥（INN），异戊巴比妥（INN），巴比妥（INN），布他比妥（INN），正丁巴比妥（INN），环己巴比妥（INN），甲苯巴比妥（INN），戊巴比妥（INN），苯巴比妥（INN），仲丁巴比妥（INN），司可巴比妥（INN），和乙烯比妥（INN）以及它们的盐	6.5	0 冰岛IS,东盟AS,哥CR,秘鲁PE,新西兰NZ,智利CL 2.6 瑞士CH 3.9 澳AU,韩国KR 5 巴PK	0 受惠国$_1$LD$_1$	20	--Allobarbital (INN) , amobarbital (INN) , barbital (INN) , butalbital (INN) , butobarbital, cyclobarbital (INN) , methylphenobarbital (INN) , pentobarbital (INN) , phenobarbital (INN) , secbutabarbital (INN) , seco-barbital (INN) and vinylbital (INN) ; salts thereof
2302	2933.5400	--其他丙二酰脲（巴比土酸）的衍生物以及它们的盐	6.5	0 冰岛IS,东盟AS,哥CR,秘鲁PE,新西兰NZ,智利CL 2.6 瑞士CH 3.9 澳AU,韩国KR 5 巴PK	0 受惠国$_1$LD$_1$	20	--Other derivatives of malonylurea (barbituric acid) ; salts thereof

序号 No.	税则号列 Tariff Line	中文货品名称 Article Description in Chinese	最惠国税率 MFN(%)	协定税率 Agreement(%)	特惠税率 SP(%)	普通税率 Gen(%)	英文货品名称 Article Description
2303	2933.5500	--氯普唑仑（INN），甲氯喹酮（INN），甲喹酮（INN）和齐培丙醇（INN）以及它们的盐	6.5	0 冰岛IS,东盟AS,哥CR,秘鲁PE,新西兰NZ,智利CL 2.6 瑞士CH 3.9 澳AU,韩国KR 5 巴PK	0 受惠国$_1$LD$_1$	20	--Loprazolam (INN), mecloqualone (INN), methaqualone (INN) and zipeprol (INN); salts thereof
		--其他:					--Other:
2304	2933.5910	---胞嘧啶	6.5	0 巴PK,冰岛IS,东盟AS,哥CR,秘鲁PE,新西兰NZ,智利CL 2.6 瑞士CH 3.9 澳AU,韩国KR 4.6 亚太AP	0 受惠国$_1$LD$_1$	20	---Cytosine
2305	2933.5920	---环丙氟哌酸	6.5	0 冰岛IS,东盟AS,哥CR,秘鲁PE,新西兰NZ,智利CL 2.6 瑞士CH 3.9 澳AU,韩国KR 5 巴PK 6 亚太AP	0 受惠国$_1$LD$_1$	20	---Ciprofloxacin
2306	2933.5990	---其他	6.5	0 巴PK,冰岛IS,东盟AS,哥CR,秘鲁PE,新西兰NZ,智利CL 3.9 澳AU,韩国KR 4.6 瑞士CH,亚太AP	0 受惠国$_1$LD$_1$	20	---Other
		-结构上含有一个非稠合三嗪环(不论是否氢化)的化合物:					-Compounds containing an unfused triazine ring (whether or not hydrogenated) in the structure:
2307	2933.6100	--三聚氰胺（蜜胺）	6.5	0 冰岛IS,东盟AS,哥CR,秘鲁PE,新西兰NZ,智利CL 2.6 瑞士CH 3.9 澳AU,韩国KR 5 巴PK	0 受惠国$_1$LD$_1$	20	--Melamine
		--其他:					--Other:
2308	2933.6910	---三聚氰氯	6	0 澳门MO,冰岛IS,东盟AS,哥CR,秘鲁PE,新西兰NZ,智利CL 2.4 瑞士CH 3.6 澳AU,韩国KR 5 巴PK	0 受惠国$_1$LD$_1$	20	---Cyanuric chloride
		---异氰脲酸氯化衍生物:					---Chloroisocyanurate:
2309	2933.6921	----二氯异氰脲酸	6.5	0 澳门MO,冰岛IS,东盟AS,哥CR,秘鲁PE,新西兰NZ,智利CL 2.6 瑞士CH 3.9 澳AU,韩国KR 5 巴PK	0 受惠国$_1$LD$_1$	20	----Dichloroisooyanurate acid
2310	2933.6922	----三氯异氰脲酸	6.5	0 澳门MO,冰岛IS,东盟AS,哥CR,秘鲁PE,新西兰NZ,智利CL 2.6 瑞士CH 3.9 澳AU,韩国KR 5 巴PK	0 受惠国$_1$LD$_1$	20	----Trichloroisocyanurate acid
2311	2933.6929	----其他	6.5	0 澳门MO,冰岛IS,东盟AS,哥CR,秘鲁PE,新西兰NZ,智利CL 2.6 瑞士CH 3.9 澳AU,韩国KR 5 巴PK	0 受惠国$_1$LD$_1$	20	----Other

序号 No.	税则号列 Tariff Line	中文货品名称 Article Description in Chinese	最惠国税率 MFN(%)	协定税率 Agreement(%)	特惠税率 SP(%)	普通税率 Gen(%)	英文货品名称 Article Description
2312	2933.6990	---其他	6.5	0 澳门MO,冰岛IS,东盟AS,哥CR,秘鲁PE,新西兰NZ,智利CL 2.6 瑞士CH 3.9 澳AU 5 巴PK 5.2 韩国KR	0 受惠国$_1$LD$_1$	20	---Other
		-内酰胺:					-Lactams:
2313	2933.7100	--6-己内酰胺	9	0 冰岛IS,哥CR,新西兰NZ,智利CL 3.6 瑞士CH 5.4 澳AU		35	--6-Hexanolactam (epsilon-caprola-ctam)
2314	2933.7200	--氯巴占（INN）和甲乙哌酮（INN）	9	0 冰岛IS,东盟AS,哥CR,秘鲁PE,新西兰NZ,智利CL 3.6 瑞士CH 5 巴PK 5.4 澳AU,韩国KR	0 受惠国$_1$LD$_1$	15	--Clobazam (INN) and methyprylon (INN)
2315	2933.7900	--其他内酰胺	9	0 冰岛IS,东盟AS,哥CR,秘鲁PE,新西兰NZ,智利CL 5 巴PK 5.4 澳AU,韩国KR	0 受惠国$_1$LD$_1$	20	--Other lactams
		-其他:					-Other:
2316	2933.9100	--阿普唑仑（INN），卡马西泮（INN），氯氮卓（INN），氯硝西泮（INN），氯拉卓酸，地洛西泮（INN），地西泮（INN），艾司唑仑（INN），氯氟卓乙酯（INN），氟地西泮（INN），氟硝西泮（INN），氟西泮（INN），哈拉西泮（INN），劳拉西泮（INN），氯甲西泮（INN），马吲哚（INN），美达西泮（INN），咪达唑仑（INN），硝甲西泮（INN），去甲西泮（INN），奥沙西泮（INN），匹那西泮（INN），普拉西泮（INN），吡咯戊酮（INN），替马西泮（INN），四氢西泮（INN）和三唑仑（INN）以及他们的盐	6.5	0 冰岛IS,东盟AS,哥CR,秘鲁PE,新西兰NZ,智利CL 2.6 瑞士CH 3.9 澳AU,韩国KR 5 巴PK	0 受惠国$_1$LD$_1$	20	--Alprazolam (INN) , camazepam (INN) , chlor-diazepoxide (INN) , clonazepam (INN) , clorazepate, delorazepam (INN) , diazepam (INN) , estazolam (INN) , ethyl loflazepate (INN) , fludi-azepam (INN) , fluni-trazepam (INN) , fluraze-pam (INN) , halazepam (INN) , lorazepam (INN) , lormetazepam (INN) , mazindol (INN) , madazepam (INN) , mi-dazolam (INN) , ni-metazepam (INN) , ni-trazepam (INN) nordaze-pam (INN) , oxazepam (INN) , pinazepam (INN) , prazepam (INN) , py-rovalerone (INN) , te-mazepam (INN) , tetraze-pam (INN) , and triazdam (INN) ; salts thereof
2317	2933.9900	--其他	6.5	0 冰岛IS,东盟AS,哥CR,秘鲁PE,新西兰NZ,智利CL 3.9 澳AU,韩国KR 4.7 瑞士CH 5 巴PK	0 受惠国$_1$LD$_1$	20	--Other
	ex29339900	阿托伐他汀钙	Δ4				Atorvatatin calcium
	29.34	**核酸及其盐;无论是否已有化学定义;其他杂环化合物:**					**Nucleic acids and their salts, whether or not chemically defined; other heterocyclic compounds:**
2318	2934.1000	-结构上含有一个非稠合噻唑环（不论是否氢化）的化合物	6.5	0 冰岛IS,东盟AS,哥CR,秘鲁PE,新西兰NZ,智利CL 2.6 瑞士CH 3.9 澳AU 5 巴PK 5.6 韩国KR	0 受惠国$_1$LD$_1$	20	-Compounds containing an unfused thiazole ring (whether or not hydrogenated) in the structure

序号 No.	税则号列 Tariff Line	中文货品名称 Article Description in Chinese	最惠国税率 MFN(%)	协定税率 Agreement(%)	特惠税率 SP(%)	普通税率 Gen(%)	英文货品名称 Article Description
2319	2934.2000	-结构上含有一个苯并噻唑环系(不论是否氢化)的化合物，但未经进一步稠合的	6.5	0 冰岛IS,东盟AS,哥CR,秘鲁PE,新西兰NZ,智利CL 2.6 瑞士CH 3.9 澳AU 5 巴PK 5.2 韩国KR	0 受惠国$_1$LD$_1$	20	-Compounds containing in the structure a benzothiazole ringsystem (whether or not hydrogenated) , not further fused
2320	2934.3000	-结构上含有一个吩噻嗪环系（不论是否氢化）的化合物，但未经进一步稠合的	6.5	0 冰岛IS,东盟AS,哥CR,秘鲁PE,新西兰NZ,智利CL 2.6 瑞士CH 3.9 澳AU,韩国KR 5 巴PK	0 受惠国$_1$LD$_1$	20	-Compounds containing in the struct-ure a phenothiazine ring-system (whether or not hydrogenated) , not further fused
		-其他：					-Other:
2321	2934.9100	--阿米雷司（INN），溴替唑仑（INN），氯噻西泮（INN），氯恶唑仑（INN），右吗拉胺（INN），卤恶唑仑（INN），凯他唑仑（INN），美索卡（INN），恶唑仑（INN），匹莫林（INN），苯巴曲嗪（INN），芬美曲嗪（INN）和舒芬太尼（INN）及它们的盐	6.5	0 冰岛IS,东盟AS,哥CR,秘鲁PE,新西兰NZ,智利CL 2.6 瑞士CH 3.9 澳AU,韩国KR 5 巴PK	0 受惠国$_1$LD$_1$	20	--Aminorex (INN) , brotizolam (INN) , clotiazepam (INN) , cloxazolam (INN) , dextromoramide (INN) , haloxazolam (INN) , ketazolam (INN) , mesocarb (INN) , oxazolam (INN) , pemoline (INN) , phendimetrazine (INN) , phenmetrazine (INN) and sufentanil (INN) ; salts thereof
		--其他：					--Other:
2322	2934.9910	---磺内酯及磺内酰胺	6.5	0 冰岛IS,东盟AS,哥CR,秘鲁PE,新西兰NZ,智利CL 2.6 瑞士CH 3.9 澳AU,韩国KR 5 巴PK	0 受惠国$_1$LD$_1$	30	---Sultones and sultams
2323	2934.9920	---呋喃唑酮	6	0 冰岛IS,东盟AS,哥CR,秘鲁PE,新西兰NZ,智利CL 3.6 澳AU,韩国KR 5 巴PK	0 受惠国$_1$LD$_1$	20	---Furazolidone
2324	2934.9930	---核酸及其盐	6.5	0 冰岛IS,东盟AS,哥CR,秘鲁PE,新西兰NZ,智利CL 2.6 瑞士CH 3.9 澳AU,韩国KR 5 巴PK	0 受惠国$_1$LD$_1$	35	---Nucleic acids and their salts
2325	2934.9940	---奈韦拉平、依发韦仑、利托那韦及它们的盐	6.5	0 冰岛IS,东盟AS,哥CR,秘鲁PE,新西兰NZ,智利CL 2.6 瑞士CH 3.9 澳AU,韩国KR 5 巴PK	0 受惠国$_1$LD$_1$	20	---Nevirapine, Efavirenz, Ritonavir and their salts
2326	2934.9950	---克拉维酸及其盐	6.5	0 冰岛IS,东盟AS,哥CR,秘鲁PE,新西兰NZ,智利CL 2.6 瑞士CH 3.9 澳AU,韩国KR 5 巴PK	0 受惠国$_1$LD$_1$	20	---Clavulante acid and its salt
2327	2934.9960	---7-苯乙酰氨基-3-氯甲基-4-头孢烷酸对甲氧基苄酯、7-氨基头孢烷酸、7-氨基脱乙酰氧基头孢烷酸	6	0 巴PK,冰岛IS,东盟AS,哥CR,秘鲁PE,新西兰NZ,智利CL 2.4 瑞士CH 3.6 澳AU,韩国KR 5 亚太AP	0 受惠国$_1$LD$_1$	20	---7-Phenylacetamido-3-(chloromethyl) -3-cephem-4-carboxylic acid p-methoxybenzyl ester、7-aminocephalosporianic acid、7-aminodeacetoxycefanoic acid

序号 No.	税则号列 Tariff Line	中文货品名称 Article Description in Chinese	最惠国税率 MFN(%)	协定税率 Agreement(%)	特惠税率 SP(%)	普通税率 Gen(%)	英文货品名称 Article Description
2328	2934.9990	---其他	6.5	0 冰岛IS,东盟AS,哥CR,秘鲁PE,新西兰NZ,智利CL 2.6 瑞士CH 3.9 澳AU,韩国KR 5 巴PK	0 受惠国$_1$LD$_1$	20	---Other
	29.35	**磺(酰)胺:**					**Sulphonamides:**
2329	2935.0010	---磺胺嘧啶	6.5	0 冰岛IS,东盟AS,哥CR,秘鲁PE,新西兰NZ,智利CL 2.6 瑞士CH 3.9 澳AU,韩国KR 5 巴PK	0 受惠国$_1$LD$_1$	35	---Sulphadiazine
2330	2935.0020	---磺胺双甲基嘧啶	6.5	0 冰岛IS,东盟AS,哥CR,秘鲁PE,新西兰NZ,智利CL 2.6 瑞士CH 3.9 澳AU,韩国KR 5 巴PK	0 受惠国$_1$LD$_1$	35	---Sulfadimidine
2331	2935.0030	---磺胺甲噁唑	6.5	0 冰岛IS,东盟AS,哥CR,秘鲁PE,新西兰NZ,智利CL 2.6 瑞士CH 3.9 澳AU,韩国KR 5 巴PK	0 受惠国$_1$LD$_1$	35	---Sulfamethoxazole
2332	2935.0090	---其他	6.5	0 冰岛IS,东盟AS,哥CR,秘鲁PE,新西兰NZ,智利CL 3.9 澳AU,韩国KR 4.7 瑞士CH 5 巴PK	0 受惠国$_1$LD$_1$	35	---Other
		第十一分章 维生素原、维生素及激素					XI. PROVITAMINS, VITAMINS AND HORMONES
	29.36	**天然或合成再制的维生素原和维生素(包括天然浓缩物)及其主要用作维生素的衍生物,上述产品的混合物,不论是否溶于溶剂:**					**Provitamins and vitamins, natural or reproduced by synthesis (including natural concentrates), derivatives thereof used primarily as vitamins, and intermixtures of the foregoing, whether or not in any solvent:**
		-未混合的维生素及其衍生物:					-Vitamins and their derivatives, unmixed:
2333	2936.2100	--维生素A及其衍生物	4	0 澳AU,澳门MO,巴PK,冰岛IS,东盟AS,哥CR,韩国KR,秘鲁PE,新西兰NZ,智利CL 2.9 瑞士CH	0 受惠国LD	20	--Vitamins A and their derivatives
2334	2936.2200	--维生素B_1及其衍生物	4	0 澳AU,澳门MO,巴PK,冰岛IS,东盟AS,哥CR,韩国KR,秘鲁PE,瑞士CH,新西兰NZ,智利CL	0 受惠国LD	20	--Vitamin B_1 and its derivatives
2335	2936.2300	--维生素B_2及其衍生物	4	0 澳AU,澳门MO,巴PK,冰岛IS,东盟AS,哥CR,秘鲁PE,瑞士CH,新西兰NZ,智利CL 2.4 韩国KR	0 受惠国LD	20	--Vitamin B_2 and its derivatives
2336	2936.2400	--D或DL-泛酸(维生素B_3或维生素B_5)及其衍生物	4	0 澳AU,澳门MO,巴PK,冰岛IS,东盟AS,哥CR,韩国KR,秘鲁PE,瑞士CH,新西兰NZ,智利CL	0 受惠国LD	20	--D-or DL-Pantothenic acid (Vitamin B_3 or Vitamin B_5) and its derivatives
2337	2936.2500	--维生素B_6及其衍生物	4	0 澳AU,澳门MO,巴PK,冰岛IS,东盟AS,哥CR,韩国KR,秘鲁PE,瑞士CH,新西兰NZ,智利CL	0 受惠国LD	20	--Vitamin B_6 and its derivatives

序号 No.	税则号列 Tariff Line	中文货品名称 Article Description in Chinese	最惠国税率 MFN(%)	协定税率 Agreement(%)		特惠税率 SP(%)		普通税率 Gen(%)	英文货品名称 Article Description
2338	2936.2600	--维生素B12及其衍生物	4	0 2.8	澳AU,澳门MO,巴PK,冰岛IS,东盟AS,哥CR,韩国KR,秘鲁PE,新西兰NZ,智利CL 瑞士CH	0	受惠国LD	20	--Vitamin B_{12} and its derivatives
2339	2936.2700	--维生素C及其衍生物	4	0	澳AU,澳门MO,巴PK,冰岛IS,东盟AS,哥CR,韩国KR,秘鲁PE,瑞士CH,新西兰NZ,智利CL	0	受惠国LD	20	--Vitamin C and its derivatives
2340	2936.2800	--维生素E及其衍生物	4	0 2.8	澳AU,澳门MO,巴PK,冰岛IS,东盟AS,哥CR,韩国KR,秘鲁PE,新西兰NZ,智利CL 瑞士CH	0	受惠国LD	20	--Vitamin E and its derivatives
2341	2936.2900	--其他维生素及其衍生物	4	0 2.8	澳AU,澳门MO,巴PK,冰岛IS,东盟AS,哥CR,韩国KR,秘鲁PE,新西兰NZ,智利CL 瑞士CH	0	受惠国LD	20	--Other vitamins and their deriv-atives
		-其他，包括天然浓缩物:							-Other, including natural concentrates:
2342	2936.9010	---维生素AD3	4	0	澳AU,澳门MO,巴PK,冰岛IS,东盟AS,哥CR,韩国KR,秘鲁PE,瑞士CH,新西兰NZ,智利CL	0	受惠国LD	20	---Vitamins AD_3
2343	2936.9090	---其他	4	0	澳AU,澳门MO,巴PK,冰岛IS,东盟AS,哥CR,韩国KR,秘鲁PE,瑞士CH,新西兰NZ,智利CL	0	受惠国LD	20	---Other
	29.37	**天然或合成再制的激素、前列腺素、血栓烷、血细胞三烯及其衍生物和结构类似物，包括主要用作激素的改性链多肽:**							**Hormones, prostaglandins, thromboxanes and leukotrienes, natural or reproduced by synthesis; derivatives and structural analogues thereof, including chain modified polypeptides, used primarily as hormones:**
		-多肽激素、蛋白激素、糖蛋白激素及其衍生物和结构类似物:							-Polypeptide hormones, protein hormones and glycoprotein hormones, their derivatives and structural analogues:
2344	2937.1100	--生长激素及其衍生物和结构类似物	4	0	澳AU,巴PK,冰岛IS,东盟AS,哥CR,韩国KR,秘鲁PE,瑞士CH,新西兰NZ,智利CL	0	受惠国1LD1	20	--Somatotropin, its derivatives and structural analogues
		--胰岛素及其盐:							--Insulin and its salts:
2345	2937.1210	---重组人胰岛素及其盐	4	0	澳AU,巴PK,冰岛IS,东盟AS,哥CR,韩国KR,秘鲁PE,瑞士CH,新西兰NZ,智利CL	0	受惠国1LD1	20	---Recombinant human insulin and its salts
2346	2937.1290	---其他	4	0	澳AU,巴PK,冰岛IS,东盟AS,哥CR,韩国KR,秘鲁PE,瑞士CH,新西兰NZ,智利CL	0	受惠国1LD1	20	---Other
2347	2937.1900	--其他	4	0 2.8	澳AU,巴PK,冰岛IS,东盟AS,哥CR,韩国KR,秘鲁PE,新西兰NZ,智利CL 瑞士CH	0	受惠国1LD1	20	--Other
		-甾族激素及其衍生物和结构类似物:							-Steroidal hormones, their derivatives and structural analogues:
2348	2937.2100	--可的松、氢化可的松、脱氢可的松及脱氢皮质醇	4	0	澳AU,巴PK,冰岛IS,东盟AS,哥CR,韩国KR,秘鲁PE,瑞士CH,新西兰NZ,智利CL	0	受惠国1LD1	20	--Cortisone, hydrocortisone, prednisone (dehydrocortisone) and prednisolone (dehydrocortisone)

序号 No.	税则号列 Tariff Line	中文货品名称 Article Description in Chinese	最惠国税率 MFN(%)	协定税率 Agreement(%)		特惠税率 SP(%)		普通税率 Gen(%)	英文货品名称 Article Description
		--皮质甾类激素的卤化衍生物:							--Halogenated derivatives of corticosteroidal hormones:
2349	2937.2210	---地塞米松	4	0	澳AU,巴PK,冰岛IS,东盟AS,哥CR,韩国KR,秘鲁PE,瑞士CH,新西兰NZ,智利CL	0	受惠国$_1$LD$_1$	30	---Dexamethasone
2350	2937.2290	---其他	4	0	澳AU,巴PK,冰岛IS,东盟AS,哥CR,韩国KR,秘鲁PE,瑞士CH,新西兰NZ,智利CL	0	受惠国$_1$LD$_1$	30	---Other
		--雌(甾)激素和孕激素:							--Oestrogens and progestogens:
		---动物源的:							---Of animals:
2351	2937.2311	----孕马结合雌激素	4	0	澳AU,巴PK,冰岛IS,东盟AS,哥CR,韩国KR,秘鲁PE,瑞士CH,新西兰NZ,智利CL	0	受惠国$_1$LD$_1$	30	----Pregnant mare congugated estrogens
2352	2937.2319	----其他	4	0	澳AU,巴PK,冰岛IS,东盟AS,哥CR,韩国KR,秘鲁PE,瑞士CH,新西兰NZ,智利CL	0	受惠国$_1$LD$_1$	30	----Other
2353	2937.2390	---其他	4	0	澳AU,巴PK,冰岛IS,东盟AS,哥CR,韩国KR,秘鲁PE,瑞士CH,新西兰NZ,智利CL	0	受惠国$_1$LD$_1$	30	---Other
2354	2937.2900	--其他	4	0	澳AU,巴PK,冰岛IS,东盟AS,哥CR,韩国KR,秘鲁PE,瑞士CH,新西兰NZ,智利CL	0	受惠国$_1$LD$_1$	30	--Other
2355	2937.5000	-前列腺素、血栓烷和白细胞三烯及其衍生物和结构类似物	4	0 2.4	澳AU,巴PK,冰岛IS,东盟AS,哥CR,秘鲁PE,瑞士CH,新西兰NZ,智利CL 韩国KR	0	受惠国$_1$LD$_1$	30	-Prostaglandins, thromboxanes and leukotrienes, their derivatives and structural analogues
2356	2937.9000	-其他	4	0	澳AU,巴PK,冰岛IS,东盟AS,哥CR,韩国KR,秘鲁PE,瑞士CH,新西兰NZ,智利CL	0	受惠国$_1$LD$_1$	30	-Other
		第十二分章　天然或合成再制的苷(配糖物)、植物碱及其盐、醚、酯和其他衍生物							XII. GLYCOSIDES AND VEGETABLE ALKALOIDS, NATURAL OR REPRODUCED BY SYNTHESIS, AND THEIR SALTS, ETHERS, ESTERS AND OTHER DERIVATIVES
	29.38	**天然或合成再制的苷(配糖物)及其盐、醚、酯和其他衍生物:**							**Glycosides, natural or reproduced by synthesis, and their salts, ethers, esters and other derivatives:**
2357	2938.1000	-芸香苷(芦丁)及其衍生物	6.5	0 2.6 3.9 5	冰岛IS,东盟AS,哥CR,秘鲁PE,新西兰NZ,智利CL 瑞士CH 澳AU,韩国KR 巴PK	0	受惠国$_1$LD$_1$	20	-Rutoside (rutin) and its derivatives
		-其他:							-Other:
2358	2938.9010	---齐多夫定、拉米夫定、司他夫定、地达诺新及它们的盐	6.5	0 2.6 3.9 5	冰岛IS,东盟AS,哥CR,秘鲁PE,新西兰NZ,智利CL 瑞士CH 澳AU,韩国KR 巴PK	0	受惠国$_1$LD$_1$	20	---Zidovudine, Lamivudine, Stavudine, Didanosine and their salts
2359	2938.9090	---其他	6.5	0 2.6 3.9 5	冰岛IS,东盟AS,哥CR,秘鲁PE,新西兰NZ,智利CL 瑞士CH 澳AU,韩国KR 巴PK	0	受惠国$_1$LD$_1$	20	---Other

序号 No.	税则号列 Tariff Line	中文货品名称 Article Description in Chinese	最惠国税率 MFN(%)	协定税率 Agreement(%)		特惠税率 SP(%)		普通税率 Gen(%)	英文货品名称 Article Description
	29.39	天然或合成再制的生物碱及其盐、醚、酯和其他衍生物:							**Vegetable alkaloids, natural or reproduced by synthesis, and their salts, ethers, esters and other derivatives:**
		-鸦片碱及其衍生物以及它们的盐:							-Alkaloids of opium and their derivatives; salts thereof:
2360	2939.1100	--罂粟杆浓缩物、丁丙诺啡(INN)、可待因、双氢可待因(INN)、乙基吗啡、埃托啡(INN)、海洛因、氢可酮(INN)、氢吗啡酮(INN)、吗啡、尼可吗啡(INN)、羟考酮(INN)、羟吗啡酮(INN)、福尔可定(INN)、醋氢可酮(INN)和蒂巴因,以及它们的盐	4	0	澳AU,巴PK,冰岛IS,东盟AS,哥CR,韩国KR,秘鲁PE,瑞士CH,新西兰NZ,智利CL	0	受惠国LD	50	--Concentrates of poppy straw; buprenorphine (INN) , codeine, dihydrocodeine (INN) , ethylmorphine, etorphine (INN) , heroin, hydrocodone (INN) , hydromorphone (INN) , morphine, nicomorphine (INN) , oxycodone (INN) , oxymorphone (INN) , pholcodine (INN) , thebacon (INN) and thebaine; salts thereof
2361	2939.1900	--其他	4	0	澳AU,巴PK,冰岛IS,东盟AS,哥CR,韩国KR,秘鲁PE,瑞士CH,新西兰NZ,智利CL	0	受惠国LD	50	--Other
2362	2939.2000	-金鸡纳生物碱及其衍生物以及它们的盐	4	0	澳AU,巴PK,冰岛IS,东盟AS,哥CR,韩国KR,秘鲁PE,瑞士CH,新西兰NZ,智利CL	0	受惠国LD	20	-Alkaloids of cinchona and their derivatives; salts thereof
2363	2939.3000	-咖啡因及其盐	4	0	澳AU,巴PK,冰岛IS,东盟AS,哥CR,韩国KR,秘鲁PE,瑞士CH,新西兰NZ,智利CL	0	受惠国LD	20	-Caffeine and its salts
		-麻黄碱类及其盐:							-Ephedrines and their salts:
2364	2939.4100	--麻黄碱及其盐	4	0	澳AU,巴PK,冰岛IS,东盟AS,哥CR,韩国KR,秘鲁PE,瑞士CH,新西兰NZ,智利CL	0	受惠国LD	20	--Ephedrine and its salts
2365	2939.4200	--假麻黄碱及其盐	4	0	澳AU,巴PK,冰岛IS,东盟AS,哥CR,韩国KR,秘鲁PE,瑞士CH,新西兰NZ,智利CL	0	受惠国LD	20	--Pseudoephedrine (INN) and its salts
2366	2939.4300	--d-去甲假麻黄碱(INN)及其盐	4	0	澳AU,巴PK,冰岛IS,东盟AS,哥CR,韩国KR,秘鲁PE,瑞士CH,新西兰NZ,智利CL	0	受惠国LD	20	--D-Norpseudoephedrine and its salts
2367	2939.4400	--去甲麻黄碱及其盐	4	0	澳AU,巴PK,冰岛IS,东盟AS,哥CR,韩国KR,秘鲁PE,瑞士CH,新西兰NZ,智利CL	0	受惠国LD	20	--Norephedrine and its salts
2368	2939.4900	--其他	4	0	澳AU,巴PK,冰岛IS,东盟AS,哥CR,韩国KR,秘鲁PE,瑞士CH,新西兰NZ,智利CL	0	受惠国LD	20	--Other
		-茶碱和氨茶碱及其衍生物以及它们的盐:							-Theophylline and aminophylline (theophylline-ethylenediamine) and their derivatives; salts thereof:
2369	2939.5100	--芬乙茶碱(INN)及其盐	4	0	澳AU,巴PK,冰岛IS,东盟AS,哥CR,韩国KR,秘鲁PE,瑞士CH,新西兰NZ,智利CL	0	受惠国LD	20	--Fenetylline (INN) and its salts
2370	2939.5900	--其他	4	0	澳AU,巴PK,冰岛IS,东盟AS,哥CR,韩国KR,秘鲁PE,瑞士CH,新西兰NZ,智利CL	0	受惠国LD	20	--Other
		-麦角生物碱及其衍生物以及它们的盐:							-Alkaloids of rye ergot and their derivatives; salts thereof:

序号 No.	税则号列 Tariff Line	中文货品名称 Article Description in Chinese	最惠国税率 MFN(%)	协定税率 Agreement(%)		特惠税率 SP(%)		普通税率 Gen(%)	英文货品名称 Article Description
2371	2939.6100	--麦角新碱及其盐	4	0	澳AU,巴PK,冰岛IS,东盟AS,哥CR,韩国KR,秘鲁PE,瑞士CH,新西兰NZ,智利CL	0	受惠国LD	20	--Ergometrine (INN) and its salts
2372	2939.6200	--麦角胺及其盐	4	0	澳AU,巴PK,冰岛IS,东盟AS,哥CR,韩国KR,秘鲁PE,瑞士CH,新西兰NZ,智利CL	0	受惠国LD	20	--Ergotamine (INN) and its salts
2373	2939.6300	--麦角酸及其盐	4	0	澳AU,巴PK,冰岛IS,东盟AS,哥CR,韩国KR,秘鲁PE,瑞士CH,新西兰NZ,智利CL	0	受惠国LD	20	--Lysergic acid and its salts
2374	2939.6900	--其他	4	0 2.8	澳AU,巴PK,冰岛IS,东盟AS,哥CR,韩国KR,秘鲁PE,新西兰NZ,智利CL 瑞士CH	0	受惠国LD	20	--Other
		--可卡因，芽子碱、左甲苯丙胺、去氧麻黄碱（INN），去氧麻黄碱外消旋体，它们的盐、酯及其他衍生物：							--Cocaine, ecgonine, levometamfetamine, metamfetamine (INN) , metamfetamine racemate; salts, esters and other derivatives thereof:
2375	2939.9110	---可卡因及其盐	4	0	澳AU,巴PK,冰岛IS,东盟AS,哥CR,韩国KR,秘鲁PE,瑞士CH,新西兰NZ,智利CL	0	受惠国LD	20	---Cocaine and its salts
2376	2939.9190	---其他	4	0	澳AU,巴PK,冰岛IS,东盟AS,哥CR,韩国KR,秘鲁PE,瑞士CH,新西兰NZ,智利CL	0	受惠国LD	20	---Other
		--其他：							--Other:
2377	2939.9910	---烟碱及其盐	4	0	澳AU,巴PK,冰岛IS,东盟AS,哥CR,韩国KR,秘鲁PE,瑞士CH,新西兰NZ,智利CL	0	受惠国LD	20	---Nicotine and its salts
2378	2939.9920	---番木鳖碱（士的年）及其盐	4	0	澳AU,巴PK,冰岛IS,东盟AS,哥CR,韩国KR,秘鲁PE,瑞士CH,新西兰NZ,智利CL	0	受惠国LD	17	---Strychnine and its salts
2379	2939.9990	---其他	4	0 2.8	澳AU,巴PK,冰岛IS,东盟AS,哥CR,韩国KR,秘鲁PE,新西兰NZ,智利CL 瑞士CH	0	受惠国LD	20	---Other
		第十三分章　其他有机化合物							XIII . OTHER ORGANIC COMPOUNDS
	29.40	**化学纯糖，但蔗糖、乳糖、麦芽糖、葡萄糖及果糖除外；糖醚、糖缩醛、糖酯及其盐，但不包括税号29.37、29.38及29.39的产品：**							**Sugars, chemically pure, other than sucrose, lactose, maltose, glucose and fructose; sugar ethers, sugar acetals and sugar esters, and their salts, other than products of heading No.29.37, 29.38 or 29.39:**
2380	2940.0010	---木糖	6	0 2.4 3.6 4.8 5	冰岛IS,东盟AS,哥CR,秘鲁PE,新西兰NZ,智利CL 瑞士CH 澳AU 韩国KR 巴PK	0	受惠国LD	30	---Wood sugar

序号 No.	税则号列 Tariff Line	中文货品名称 Article Description in Chinese	最惠国税率 MFN(%)	协定税率 Agreement(%)	特惠税率 SP(%)	普通税率 Gen(%)	英文货品名称 Article Description
2381	2940.0090	---其他	6	0 冰岛IS,东盟AS,哥CR,秘鲁PE,新西兰NZ,智利CL 2.4 瑞士CH 3.6 澳AU 4.8 韩国KR 5 巴PK	0 受惠国LD	30	---Other
	29.41	**抗菌素:**					**Antibiotics:**
		-青霉素和具有青霉烷酸结构的青霉素衍生物及其盐:					-Penicillins and their derivatives with a penicillanic acid structure; salts thereof:
		---氨苄青霉素及其盐:					---Ampicillin and its salts:
2382	2941.1011	----氨苄青霉素	6	0 巴PK,冰岛IS,东盟AS,哥CR,秘鲁PE,新西兰NZ,智利CL 2.4 瑞士CH 3.6 澳AU,韩国KR 5 亚太AP	0 受惠国LD	20	----Ampicillin
2383	2941.1012	----氨苄青霉素三水酸	6	0 巴PK,冰岛IS,东盟AS,哥CR,秘鲁PE,新西兰NZ,智利CL 2.4 瑞士CH 3.6 澳AU,韩国KR 5 亚太AP	0 受惠国LD	20	----Ampicillin trihydrate
2384	2941.1019	----其他	6	0 巴PK,冰岛IS,东盟AS,哥CR,秘鲁PE,新西兰NZ,智利CL 2.4 瑞士CH 3.6 澳AU,韩国KR 5 亚太AP	0 受惠国LD	20	----Other
		---其他:					---Other:
2385	2941.1091	----羟氨苄青霉素	4	0 澳AU,巴PK,冰岛IS,东盟AS,哥CR,韩国KR,秘鲁PE,瑞士CH,新西兰NZ,智利CL	0 受惠国LD	20	----Amoxycillin
2386	2941.1092	----羟氨苄青霉素三水酸	4	0 澳AU,巴PK,冰岛IS,东盟AS,哥CR,韩国KR,秘鲁PE,瑞士CH,新西兰NZ,智利CL	0 受惠国LD	20	----Amoxycillin trihydrate
2387	2941.1093	----6-氨基青霉烷酸（6APA）	4	0 澳AU,巴PK,冰岛IS,东盟AS,哥CR,韩国KR,秘鲁PE,瑞士CH,新西兰NZ,智利CL	0 受惠国LD	20	----6-Aminopenicillanic acid
2388	2941.1094	----青霉素V	4	0 澳AU,巴PK,冰岛IS,东盟AS,哥CR,韩国KR,秘鲁PE,瑞士CH,新西兰NZ,智利CL	0 受惠国LD	20	----Penicillin V
2389	2941.1095	----磺苄青霉素	4	0 澳AU,巴PK,冰岛IS,东盟AS,哥CR,韩国KR,秘鲁PE,瑞士CH,新西兰NZ,智利CL	0 受惠国LD	20	----Sulfobenzylpenicillin
2390	2941.1096	----邻氯青霉素	4	0 澳AU,巴PK,冰岛IS,东盟AS,哥CR,韩国KR,秘鲁PE,瑞士CH,新西兰NZ,智利CL	0 受惠国LD	20	----Cloxacillin
2391	2941.1099	----其他	4	0 澳AU,巴PK,冰岛IS,东盟AS,哥CR,韩国KR,秘鲁PE,瑞士CH,新西兰NZ,智利CL	0 受惠国LD	20	----Other
2392	2941.2000	-链霉素及其衍生物以及它们的盐	4	0 澳AU,巴PK,冰岛IS,东盟AS,哥CR,韩国KR,秘鲁PE,瑞士CH,新西兰NZ,智利CL	0 受惠国LD	20	-Streptomycins and their derivatives; salts thereof
		-四环素及其衍生物以及它们的盐:					-Tetracyclines and their derivatives; salts thereof:
		---四环素及其盐:					---Tetracyclines and their salts:

序号 No.	税则号列 Tariff Line	中文货品名称 Article Description in Chinese	最惠国税率 MFN(%)	协定税率 Agreement(%)	特惠税率 SP(%)	普通税率 Gen(%)	英文货品名称 Article Description
2393	2941.3011	----四环素	4	0 澳AU,澳门MO,巴PK,冰岛IS,东盟AS,哥CR,韩国KR,秘鲁PE,瑞士CH,新西兰NZ,智利CL	0 受惠国LD	20	----Tetracyclines
2394	2941.3012	----四环素盐	4	0 澳AU,澳门MO,巴PK,冰岛IS,东盟AS,哥CR,韩国KR,秘鲁PE,瑞士CH,新西兰NZ,智利CL	0 受惠国LD	20	----Salts of tetracyclines
2395	2941.3020	---四环素衍生物及其盐	4	0 澳AU,澳门MO,巴PK,冰岛IS,东盟AS,哥CR,韩国KR,秘鲁PE,瑞士CH,新西兰NZ,智利CL	0 受惠国LD	20	---Tetracyclines derivatives and their salts
2396	2941.4000	-氯霉素及其衍生物以及它们的盐	4	0 澳AU,巴PK,冰岛IS,东盟AS,哥CR,韩国KR,秘鲁PE,瑞士CH,新西兰NZ,智利CL	0 受惠国LD	20	-Chloramphenicol and its derivative-s; salts thereof
2397	2941.5000	-红霉素及其衍生物以及它们的盐	4	0 澳AU,澳门MO,巴PK,冰岛IS,东盟AS,哥CR,韩国KR,秘鲁PE,瑞士CH,新西兰NZ,智利CL	0 受惠国LD	20	-Erythromycin and its derivatives; salts thereof
		-其他:					-Other:
2398	2941.9010	---庆大霉素及其衍生物以及它们的盐	4	0 澳AU,巴PK,冰岛IS,东盟AS,哥CR,韩国KR,秘鲁PE,瑞士CH,新西兰NZ,智利CL	0 受惠国LD	20	---Gentamycin and its derivatives; salts thereof
2399	2941.9020	---卡那霉素及其衍生物以及它们的盐	4	0 澳AU,巴PK,冰岛IS,东盟AS,哥CR,韩国KR,秘鲁PE,瑞士CH,新西兰NZ,智利CL	0 受惠国LD	20	---Kanamycin and its derivatives; salts thereof
2400	2941.9030	---利福平及其衍生物以及它们的盐	4	0 澳AU,巴PK,冰岛IS,东盟AS,哥CR,韩国KR,秘鲁PE,瑞士CH,新西兰NZ,智利CL	0 受惠国LD	20	---Rifampicin (RFP) ; salts thereof
2401	2941.9040	---林可霉素及其衍生物以及它们的盐	4	0 澳AU,巴PK,冰岛IS,东盟AS,哥CR,韩国KR,秘鲁PE,瑞士CH,新西兰NZ,智利CL	0 受惠国LD	20	---Lincomycin and its derivatives; salts thereof
		---头孢菌素及其衍生物以及它们的盐:					---Cephar[illegible]in and its derivatives; salts th[illegible]of:
2402	2941.9052	----头孢氨苄及其盐	6	0 巴PK,冰岛IS,东盟AS,哥CR,秘鲁PE,新西兰NZ,智利CL 2.4 瑞士CH 3.6 澳AU,韩国KR 5 亚太AP	0 受惠国LD	20	----Cefalexin and its salts
2403	2941.9053	----头孢唑啉及其盐	6	0 巴PK,冰岛IS,东盟AS,哥CR,秘鲁PE,新西兰NZ,智利CL 2.4 瑞士CH 3.6 澳AU,韩国KR 5 亚太AP	0 受惠国LD	20	----Cefazolin and its salts
2404	2941.9054	----头孢拉啶及其盐	6	0 巴PK,冰岛IS,东盟AS,哥CR,秘鲁PE,新西兰NZ,智利CL 2.4 瑞士CH 3.6 澳AU,韩国KR 5 亚太AP	0 受惠国LD	20	----Cefradine and its salts
2405	2941.9055	----头孢三嗪（头孢曲松）及其盐	6	0 巴PK,冰岛IS,东盟AS,哥CR,秘鲁PE,新西兰NZ,智利CL 3.6 澳AU,韩国KR 4.3 瑞士CH 5 亚太AP	0 受惠国LD	20	----Ceftriaxone and its salts

序号 No.	税则号列 Tariff Line	中文货品名称 Article Description in Chinese	最惠国税率 MFN(%)	协定税率 Agreement(%)	特惠税率 SP(%)	普通税率 Gen(%)	英文货品名称 Article Description
2406	2941.9056	----头孢哌酮及其盐	6	0 巴PK,冰岛IS,东盟AS,哥CR,秘鲁PE,新西兰NZ,智利CL 2.4 瑞士CH 3.6 澳AU,韩国KR 5 亚太AP	0 受惠国LD	20	----Cefoperazone and its salts
2407	2941.9057	----头孢噻肟及其盐	6	0 巴PK,冰岛IS,东盟AS,哥CR,秘鲁PE,新西兰NZ,智利CL 2.4 瑞士CH 3.6 澳AU,韩国KR 5 亚太AP	0 受惠国LD	20	----Cefotaxime and its salts
2408	2941.9058	----头孢克罗及其盐	6	0 巴PK,冰岛IS,东盟AS,哥CR,秘鲁PE,新西兰NZ,智利CL 2.4 瑞士CH 3.6 澳AU,韩国KR 5 亚太AP	0 受惠国LD	20	----Cefaclor and its salts
2409	2941.9059	----其他	6	0 巴PK,冰岛IS,东盟AS,哥CR,秘鲁PE,新西兰NZ,智利CL 2.4 瑞士CH 3.6 澳AU 4.8 韩国KR 5 亚太AP	0 受惠国LD	20	----Other
2410	2941.9060	---麦迪霉素及其衍生物以及它们的盐	6	0 巴PK,冰岛IS,东盟AS,哥CR,秘鲁PE,新西兰NZ,智利CL 2.4 瑞士CH 3.6 澳AU,韩国KR 4.2 亚太AP	0 受惠国LD	20	---Midecamycin and its derivatives; salts thereof
2411	2941.9070	---乙酰螺旋霉素及其衍生物以及它们的盐	4	0 澳AU,巴PK,冰岛IS,东盟AS,哥CR,韩国KR,秘鲁PE,瑞士CH,新西兰NZ,智利CL	0 受惠国LD	20	---Acetyl-spiramycin and its deriva-tives; salts thereof
2412	2941.9090	---其他	6	0 巴PK,冰岛IS,东盟AS,哥CR,秘鲁PE,新西兰NZ,智利CL 2.4 瑞士CH 3.6 澳AU,韩国KR 5 亚太AP	0 受惠国LD	20	---Other
	29.42	**其他有机化合物**					**Other organic compounds**
2413	2942.0000	其他有机化合物	6.5	0 冰岛IS,东盟AS,哥CR,秘鲁PE,新西兰NZ,智利CL 2.6 瑞士CH 3.9 澳AU,韩国KR 5 巴PK	0 受惠国LD	30	Other organic compounds

第三十章
药　品

注释:

一、本章不包括:

（一）食品及饮料（例如，营养品、糖尿病食品、强化食品、保健食品、滋补饮料及矿泉水）（第四类），但不包括供静脉摄入用的滋养品;

（二）用于帮助吸烟者戒烟的制剂，例如片剂、咀嚼胶或透皮贴片（税目21.06或38.24）;

（二）经特殊煅烧或精细研磨的牙科用熟石膏（税号25.20）;

（三）适合医药用的精油水馏液及水溶液（税号33.01）;

（四）税号 33.03 至 33.07 的制品，不论是否具有治疗及预防疾病的作用;

（五）加有药料的肥皂及税号34.01的其他产品;

（六）以熟石膏为基本成分的牙科用制品（税号34.07）;

（七）不作治疗及预防疾病用的血清蛋白（税号35.02）。

二、税目 30.02 所称的“免疫制品”是指直接参与免疫过程调节的多肽及蛋白质（税目 29.37 的货品除外），例如单克隆抗体（MAB）、抗体片段、抗体偶联物及抗体片段偶联物、白介素、干扰素（IFN）、趋化因子及特定的肿瘤坏死因子（TNF）、生长因子（GF）、促红细胞生成素及集落刺激因子（CSF）。

三、税号30.03及30.04以及本章注释四（四）所述的非混合产品及混合产品，按下列规定处理:

（一）非混合产品:

1.溶于水的非混合产品;

2.第二十八章及第二十九章的所有货品;

3.税号13.02的单一植物浸膏，只经标定或溶于溶剂的。

（二）混合产品:

1.胶体溶液及悬浮液（胶态硫磺除外）;

2.从植物性混合物加工所得的植物浸膏;

Chapter 30
Pharmaceutical products

Notes:

1.This Chapter does not cover:

(a) Foods or beverages(such as dietetic, diabetic or fortified foods，food supplements，tonic beverages and mineral waters) other than nutritional preparations for intraverwas administration (SectionⅣ) ;

(b) Preparations, such as tablets, chewing gum or patches (transdermalsystems), intended to assist smokers to stop smoking (heading 21.06 or 38.24);

(c) Plasters specially calcined or finely ground for use in dentistry (heading No.25.20) ;

(d) Aqueous distillates or aqueous solutions of essential oils，suitable for medicinal uses (heading No.33.01) ;

(e) Preparations of headings Nos.33.03 to 33.07，even if they have therapeutic or prophylactic properties;

(f) Soap or other products of heading No.34.01 containing added medicaments;

(g) Preparations with a basis of plaster for use in dentistry (heading No.34.07) ; or

(h) Blood albumin not prepared for therapeutic or prophylactic uses (heading No.35.02) .

2.For the purposes of heading 30.02, the expression “immunological products” applies to peptides and proteins (other than goods of heading 29.37) whichare directly involved in the regulation of immunological processes, such asmonoclonal antibodies (MAB), antibody fragments, antibody conjugates andantibody fragment conjugates, interleukins, interferons (IFN), chemokinesand certain tumor necrosis factors (TNF), growth factors (GF), hematopoietins and colony stimulating factors (CSF).

3.For the purposes of headings Nos.30.03 and 30.04 and of Note4 (d) to this Chapter，the following are to be treated:

(a) As unmixed products:

(1) Unmixed products dissolved in water;

(2) All goods of Chapter 28 or 29;and

(3) Simple vegetable extracts of heading No.13.02，merely standardised or dissolved in any solvent;

(b) As products which have been mixed:

(1) Colloidal solutions and suspensions (other than colloidal sulphur) ;

(2) Vegetable extracts obtained by the treatment of mixtures of vegetable materials; and

3. 蒸发天然矿质水所得的盐及浓缩物。

(3) Salts and concentrates obtained by evaporating natural mineral waters.

四、税号30.06仅适用于下列物品（这些物品只能归入税号30.06而不得归入本目录其他税号）：

4.Heading No.30.06 applies only to the following，which are to be classified in that heading and in no other heading of the nomenclature:

（一）无菌外科肠线、类似的无菌缝合材料（包括外科或牙科用无菌可吸收缝线）及外伤创口闭合用的无菌粘合胶布；

(a)Sterile surgical catgut，similar sterile suture materials (including sterile absorbable surgical or dental yarns) and sterile tissue adhesives for surgical wound closure;

（二）无菌昆布及无菌昆布塞条；

(b)Sterile laminaria and sterile laminaria tents;

（三）外科或牙科用无菌吸收性止血材料；外科或牙科用无菌抗粘连阻隔材料，不论是否可吸收；

(c)Sterile absorbable surgical or dental haemostatics; sterile surgical or dental adhesion barriers, whether or not absorbable;

（四）用于病人的X光检查造影剂及其他诊断试剂，这些药剂是由单一产品配定剂量或由两种以上成分混合而成的；

(d)Opacifying preparations for X-ray examinations and diagnostic reagents designed to be administered to the patient，being unmixed products put up in measured doses or products consisting of two or more ingredients which have been mixed together for such uses;

（五）血型试剂；

(e) Blood-grouping reagents;

（六）牙科粘固剂及其他牙科填料；骨骼粘固剂；

(f) Dental cements and other dental fillings; bone reconstruction cements;

（七）急救药箱、药包；

(g) First-aid boxes and kits;

（八）以激素、税目29.37的其他产品或杀精子剂为基本成分的化学避孕药物；

(h) Chemical contraceptive preparations based on hormones，on other products or heading 29.37 or on spermicides.

（九）专用于人类或作兽药用的凝胶制品，作为外科手术或体检时躯体部位的润滑剂，或者作为躯体和医疗器械之间的偶合剂；

(i) Gel preparations designed to be used in human or veterinary medicine as a lubricant for parts of the body for surgical operations or physical examinations or as a coupling agent between the body and medical instruments;

（十）废药物即那些因超过有效保存期等原因而不适于作原用途的药品；

(j) Waste pharmaceuticals，that is，pharmaceutical products which are unfit for their original intended purpose due to，for example，expiry of shelf life; and

（十一）可确定用于造口术的用具，即裁切成型的结肠造口术、回肠造口术、尿道造口术用袋及其具有粘性的片或底盘。

(k) Appliances identifiable for ostomy use, that is, colostomy, ileostomy and urostomy pouches cut to shape and their adhesive wafers or faceplates.

序号 No.	税则号列 Tariff Line	中文货品名称 Article Description in Chinese	最惠国税率 MFN(%)	协定税率 Agreement(%)	特惠税率 SP(%)	普通税率 Gen(%)	英文货品名称 Article Description
	30.01	已干燥的器官疗法用腺体及其他器官，不论是否制成粉末；器官疗法用腺体、其他器官及其分泌物的提取物；肝素及其盐；其他供治疗或预防疾病用的其他税号未列名的人体或动物制品：					**Glands and other organs for organo-therapeutic uses, dried, whether or not powdered; extracts of glands or other organs or of their secretions for organo-therapeutic uses; heparin and its salts; other human or animal substances prepared for therapeutic or prophylactic uses, not elsewhere specified or included:**

序号 No.	税则号列 Tariff Line	中文货品名称 Article Description in Chinese	最惠国税率 MFN(%)	协定税率 Agreement(%)		特惠税率 SP(%)		普通税率 Gen(%)	英文货品名称 Article Description
2414	3001.2000	-腺体、其他器官及其分泌物的提取物	3	0	澳AU,巴PK,冰岛IS,东盟AS,哥CR,韩国KR,秘鲁PE,瑞士CH,新西兰NZ,智利CL	0	受惠国$_1$LD$_1$	30	-Extracts of glands or other organs or of their secretions
		-其他：							-Other:
2415	3001.9010	---肝素及其盐	3	0	澳AU,巴PK,冰岛IS,东盟AS,哥CR,韩国KR,秘鲁PE,瑞士CH,新西兰NZ,智利CL	0	受惠国$_1$LD$_1$	30	---Heparin and its salts
2416	3001.9090	---其他	3	0	澳AU,巴PK,冰岛IS,东盟AS,哥CR,韩国KR,秘鲁PE,瑞士CH,新西兰NZ,智利CL	0	受惠国$_1$LD$_1$	30	---Other
	30.02	**人血；治病、防病或诊断用的动物血制品；抗血清、其他血份及免疫制品，不论是否修饰或通过生物工艺加工制得；疫苗、毒素、培养微生物（不包括酵母）及类似产品：**							**Human blood; animal blood prepared for therapeutic, prophylactic or diagnostic uses; antisera, other blood fractions and immunological products, whether or not modified or obtained by means of biotechnological processes; vaccines, toxins, cultures of micro-organisms (excluding yeasts) and similar products:**
2417	3002.1000	-抗血清、其他血份及免疫制品，不论是否修饰或通过生物工艺加工制得	3Δ0	0 2.2	澳AU,巴PK,冰岛IS,东盟AS,哥CR,韩国KR,秘鲁PE,新西兰NZ,智利CL 瑞士CH	0	受惠国LD	20	-Antisera, other blood fractions and immunological products, whether or not modified or obtained by means of biotechnological processes
2418	3002.2000	-人用疫苗	3Δ0	0 2.1	澳AU,巴PK,冰岛IS,东盟AS,哥CR,韩国KR,秘鲁PE,新西兰NZ,智利CL 瑞士CH	0	受惠国LD	20	-Vaccines for human medicine
2419	3002.3000	-兽用疫苗	3	0	澳AU,巴PK,冰岛IS,东盟AS,哥CR,韩国KR,秘鲁PE,瑞士CH,新西兰NZ,智利CL	0	受惠国LD	20	-Vaccines for veterinary medicine
		-其他：							-Other:
2420	3002.9010	---石房蛤毒素	3	0	澳AU,巴PK,冰岛IS,东盟AS,哥CR,韩国KR,秘鲁PE,瑞士CH,新西兰NZ,智利CL	0	受惠国LD	20	---Saxitoxin
2421	3002.9020	---蓖麻毒素	3	0	澳AU,巴PK,冰岛IS,东盟AS,哥CR,韩国KR,秘鲁PE,瑞士CH,新西兰NZ,智利CL	0	受惠国LD	20	---Ricitoxin
2422	3002.9030	---细菌及病毒	3	0 2.1	澳AU,巴PK,冰岛IS,东盟AS,哥CR,韩国KR,秘鲁PE,新西兰NZ,智利CL 瑞士CH	0	受惠国LD	20	---Bacteria and Virus
2423	3002.9040	---遗传物质和基因修饰生物体	3Δ0	0	澳AU,巴PK,冰岛IS,东盟AS,哥CR,韩国KR,秘鲁PE,瑞士CH,新西兰NZ,智利CL	0	受惠国LD	20	---Genetics material and Gene modified Organism
2424	3002.9090	---其他	3Δ0	0	澳AU,巴PK,冰岛IS,东盟AS,哥CR,韩国KR,秘鲁PE,瑞士CH,香港HK,新西兰NZ,智利CL	0	受惠国LD	20	---Other

序号 No.	税则号列 Tariff Line	中文货品名称 Article Description in Chinese	最惠国税率 MFN(%)	协定税率 Agreement(%)	特惠税率 SP(%)	普通税率 Gen(%)	英文货品名称 Article Description
	30.03	**两种或两种以上成分混合而成的治病或防病用药品（不包括税号30.02、30.05或30.06的货品），未配定剂量或制成零售包装：**					**Medicaments (excluding goods of heading 3002, 3005 or 3006) consisting of two or more constituents which have been mixed together for therapeutic or prophylactic uses, not put up in measured doses or in forms or packings for retail sale:**
		-含有青霉素及具有青霉烷酸结构的青霉素衍生物或链霉素及其衍生物：					-Containing penicillins or derivatives thereof, with a penicillanic acid structure, or streptomycins or their derivatives:
		---青霉素：					---Containing penicillins:
2425	3003.1011	----氨苄青霉素	6	0 巴PK,冰岛IS,东盟AS,哥CR,秘鲁PE,新西兰NZ,智利CL 2.4 瑞士CH 3.6 澳AU,韩国KR 4.5 亚太AP	0 受惠国LD	30	----Ampicillin
2426	3003.1012	----羟氨苄青霉素	6	0 巴PK,冰岛IS,东盟AS,哥CR,秘鲁PE,新西兰NZ,智利CL 2.4 瑞士CH 3.6 澳AU,韩国KR 4.5 亚太AP	0 受惠国LD	30	----Amoxycillin
2427	3003.1013	----青霉素V	6	0 巴PK,冰岛IS,东盟AS,哥CR,秘鲁PE,新西兰NZ,智利CL 2.4 瑞士CH 3.6 澳AU,韩国KR 4.5 亚太AP	0 受惠国LD	30	----Penicillin V
2428	3003.1019	----其他	6	0 巴PK,冰岛IS,东盟AS,哥CR,秘鲁PE,新西兰NZ,智利CL 2.4 瑞士CH 3.6 澳AU,韩国KR 4.5 亚太AP	0 受惠国LD	30	----Other
2429	3003.1090	---其他	6	0 巴PK,冰岛IS,东盟AS,哥CR,秘鲁PE,新西兰NZ,智利CL 2.4 瑞士CH 3.6 澳AU,韩国KR 4.5 亚太AP	0 受惠国LD	30	---Other
		-含有其他抗菌素：					-Containing other antibiotics:
		---头孢菌素：					---Containing cephamycins:
2430	3003.2011	----头孢噻肟	6	0 巴PK,冰岛IS,东盟AS,哥CR,秘鲁PE,新西兰NZ,智利CL 2.4 瑞士CH 3.6 澳AU,韩国KR 5.4 亚太AP	0 受惠国LD	30	----Cefotaxime
2431	3003.2012	----头孢他啶	6	0 巴PK,冰岛IS,东盟AS,哥CR,秘鲁PE,新西兰NZ,智利CL 2.4 瑞士CH 3.6 澳AU,韩国KR 5.4 亚太AP	0 受惠国LD	30	----Ceftazidime
2432	3003.2013	----头孢西丁	6	0 巴PK,冰岛IS,东盟AS,哥CR,秘鲁PE,新西兰NZ,智利CL 2.4 瑞士CH 3.6 澳AU,韩国KR 5.4 亚太AP	0 受惠国LD	30	----Cefoxitin

序号 No.	税则号列 Tariff Line	中文货品名称 Article Description in Chinese	最惠国税率 MFN(%)	协定税率 Agreement(%)	特惠税率 SP(%)	普通税率 Gen(%)	英文货品名称 Article Description
2433	3003.2014	----头孢替唑	6	0 巴PK,冰岛IS,东盟AS,哥CR,秘鲁PE,新西兰NZ,智利CL 2.4 瑞士CH 3.6 澳AU,韩国KR 5.4 亚太AP	0 受惠国LD	30	----Ceftezole
2434	3003.2015	----头孢克罗	6	0 巴PK,冰岛IS,东盟AS,哥CR,秘鲁PE,新西兰NZ,智利CL 2.4 瑞士CH 3.6 澳AU,韩国KR 5.4 亚太AP	0 受惠国LD	30	----Cefaclor
2435	3003.2016	----头孢呋辛	6	0 巴PK,冰岛IS,东盟AS,哥CR,秘鲁PE,新西兰NZ,智利CL 2.4 瑞士CH 3.6 澳AU,韩国KR 5.4 亚太AP	0 受惠国LD	30	----Cefuroxime
2436	3003.2017	----头孢三嗪（头孢曲松）	6	0 巴PK,冰岛IS,东盟AS,哥CR,秘鲁PE,新西兰NZ,智利CL 2.4 瑞士CH 3.6 澳AU,韩国KR 5.4 亚太AP	0 受惠国LD	30	----Ceftriaxone
2437	3003.2018	----头孢哌酮	6	0 巴PK,冰岛IS,东盟AS,哥CR,秘鲁PE,新西兰NZ,智利CL 2.4 瑞士CH 3.6 澳AU,韩国KR 5.4 亚太AP	0 受惠国LD	30	----Cefoperazone
2438	3003.2019	----其他	6	0 巴PK,冰岛IS,东盟AS,哥CR,秘鲁PE,新西兰NZ,智利CL 2.4 瑞士CH 3.6 澳AU,韩国KR 5.4 亚太AP	0 受惠国LD	30	----Other
2439	3003.2090	---其他	6	0 巴PK,冰岛IS,东盟AS,哥CR,秘鲁PE,新西兰NZ,智利CL 2.4 瑞士CH 3.6 澳AU,韩国KR 4.2 亚太AP	0 受惠国LD	30	---Other
		-含有激素或税号29. 37的其他产品，但不含抗菌素：					-Containing hormones or other products of heading 2937 but not containing antibiotics:
2440	3003.3100	--含有胰岛素	5	0 澳AU,巴PK,冰岛IS,东盟AS,哥CR,秘鲁PE,瑞士CH,新西兰NZ,智利CL 3 韩国KR 3.5 亚太AP	0 受惠国LD	30	--Containing insulin
2441	3003.3900	--其他	6	0 巴PK,冰岛IS,东盟AS,哥CR,秘鲁PE,新西兰NZ,智利CL 2.4 瑞士CH 3.6 澳AU,韩国KR 4.2 亚太AP	0 受惠国LD	30	--Other
		-含有生物碱及其衍生物，但不含抗菌素及税号29. 37的激素或其他产品：					-Containing alkaloids or derivatives thereof but not containing hormones or other products of heading 2937 or antibiotics:

序号 No.	税则号列 Tariff Line	中文货品名称 Article Description in Chinese	最惠国税率 MFN(%)	协定税率 Agreement(%)	特惠税率 SP(%)	普通税率 Gen(%)	英文货品名称 Article Description
2442	3003.4010	---含有奎宁或其盐	5	0 澳AU,巴PK,冰岛IS,东盟AS,哥CR,秘鲁PE,瑞士CH,新西兰NZ,智利CL 3 韩国KR	0 受惠国LD	35	---Containing quinine or its salts
2443	3003.4090	---其他	5	0 澳AU,巴PK,冰岛IS,东盟AS,哥CR,秘鲁PE,瑞士CH,新西兰NZ,智利CL 3 韩国KR	0 受惠国LD	30	---Other
		-其他:					-Other:
2444	3003.9010	---含有磺胺类	6	0 澳门MO,巴PK,冰岛IS,东盟AS,哥CR,秘鲁PE,新西兰NZ,智利CL 2.4 瑞士CH 3.6 澳AU,韩国KR 4.2 亚太AP	0 受惠国LD	40	---Containing sulfa drugs
2445	3003.9020	---含有青蒿素及其衍生物	5	0 澳AU,澳门MO,巴PK,冰岛IS,东盟AS,哥CR,秘鲁PE,瑞士CH,新西兰NZ,智利CL 3 韩国KR	0 受惠国LD	30	---Containing artemisinins and their derivatives
2446	3003.9090	---其他	5	0 澳AU,澳门MO,巴PK,冰岛IS,东盟AS,哥CR,秘鲁PE,新西兰NZ,智利CL 3 韩国KR 3.6 瑞士CH	0 受惠国LD	30	---Other
	30.04	**由混合或非混合产品构成的治病或防病用药品（不包括税目30.02、30.05或30.06的货品），已配定剂量或（包括制成皮肤摄入形式的）制成零售包装：**					**Medicaments (excluding goods of heading 3002, 3005 or 3006) consisting of mixed or unmixed products for therapeutic or prophylactic uses, put up in measured doses (including those in the form of transdermal administration systems) or in forms or packings for retail sale:**
		-含有青霉素及具有青霉烷酸结构的青霉素衍生物或链霉素及其衍生物:					-Containing penicillins or derivatives thereof, with a penicillanic acid structure, or streptomycins or their derivatives:
		---青霉素:					---Containing penicillins:
2447	3004.1011	----氨苄青霉素制剂	6	0 澳门MO,巴PK,冰岛IS,东盟AS,哥CR,秘鲁PE,香港HK,新西兰NZ,智利CL 2.4 瑞士CH 3.6 澳AU,韩国KR 4.5 亚太AP	0 受惠国LD	30	----Ampicillin
2448	3004.1012	----羟氨苄青霉素制剂	6	0 澳门MO,巴PK,冰岛IS,东盟AS,哥CR,秘鲁PE,香港HK,新西兰NZ,智利CL 2.4 瑞士CH 3.6 澳AU,韩国KR 4.5 亚太AP	0 受惠国LD	30	----Amoxycillin
2449	3004.1013	----青霉素V制剂	6	0 澳门MO,巴PK,冰岛IS,东盟AS,哥CR,秘鲁PE,香港HK,新西兰NZ,智利CL 2.4 瑞士CH 3.6 澳AU,韩国KR 4.5 亚太AP	0 受惠国LD	30	----Penicillin V

序号 No.	税则号列 Tariff Line	中文货品名称 Article Description in Chinese	最惠国税率 MFN(%)	协定税率 Agreement(%)	特惠税率 SP(%)	普通税率 Gen(%)	英文货品名称 Article Description
2450	3004.1019	----其他	6	0 澳门MO,巴PK,冰岛IS,东盟AS,哥CR,秘鲁PE,香港HK,新西兰NZ,智利CL 2.4 瑞士CH 3.6 澳AU,韩国KR 4.5 亚太AP	0 受惠国LD	30	----Other
2451	3004.1090	---其他	6	0 澳门MO,巴PK,冰岛IS,东盟AS,哥CR,秘鲁PE,香港HK,新西兰NZ,智利CL 2.4 瑞士CH 3.6 澳AU,韩国KR 4.5 亚太AP	0 受惠国LD	30	---Other
		-含有其他抗菌素:					-Containing other antibiotics:
		---头孢菌素:					---Containing cephamycins:
2452	3004.2011	----头孢噻肟制剂	6	0 巴PK,冰岛IS,东盟AS,哥CR,秘鲁PE,香港HK,新西兰NZ,智利CL 2.4 瑞士CH 3.6 澳AU,韩国KR 5 亚太AP	0 受惠国LD	30	----Cefotaxime
2453	3004.2012	----头孢他啶制剂	6	0 巴PK,冰岛IS,东盟AS,哥CR,秘鲁PE,香港HK,新西兰NZ,智利CL 2.4 瑞士CH 3.6 澳AU,韩国KR 5 亚太AP	0 受惠国LD	30	----Ceftazidime
2454	3004.2013	----头孢西丁制剂	6	0 巴PK,冰岛IS,东盟AS,哥CR,秘鲁PE,香港HK,新西兰NZ,智利CL 2.4 瑞士CH 3.6 澳AU,韩国KR 5 亚太AP	0 受惠国LD	30	----Cefoxitin
2455	3004.2014	----头孢替唑制剂	6	0 巴PK,冰岛IS,东盟AS,哥CR,秘鲁PE,香港HK,新西兰NZ,智利CL 2.4 瑞士CH 3.6 澳AU,韩国KR 5 亚太AP	0 受惠国LD	30	----Ceftezole
2456	3004.2015	----头孢克罗制剂	6	0 巴PK,冰岛IS,东盟AS,哥CR,秘鲁PE,香港HK,新西兰NZ,智利CL 2.4 瑞士CH 3.6 澳AU,韩国KR 5 亚太AP	0 受惠国LD	30	----Cefaclor
2457	3004.2016	----头孢呋辛制剂	6	0 巴PK,冰岛IS,东盟AS,哥CR,秘鲁PE,香港HK,新西兰NZ,智利CL 2.4 瑞士CH 3.6 澳AU,韩国KR 5 亚太AP	0 受惠国LD	30	----Cefuroxime
2458	3004.2017	----头孢三嗪(头孢曲松)制剂	6	0 巴PK,冰岛IS,东盟AS,哥CR,秘鲁PE,香港HK,新西兰NZ,智利CL 2.4 瑞士CH 3.6 澳AU,韩国KR 5 亚太AP	0 受惠国LD	30	----Ceftriaxone
2459	3004.2018	----头孢哌酮制剂	6	0 巴PK,冰岛IS,东盟AS,哥CR,秘鲁PE,香港HK,新西兰NZ,智利CL 2.4 瑞士CH 3.6 澳AU,韩国KR 5 亚太AP	0 受惠国LD	30	----Cefoperazone

序号 No.	税则号列 Tariff Line	中文货品名称 Article Description in Chinese	最惠国税率 MFN(%)	协定税率 Agreement(%)	特惠税率 SP(%)	普通税率 Gen(%)	英文货品名称 Article Description
2460	3004.2019	----其他	6	0 巴PK,冰岛IS,东盟AS,哥CR,秘鲁PE,香港HK,新西兰NZ,智利CL 2.4 瑞士CH 3.6 澳AU 4.8 韩国KR 5 亚太AP	0 受惠国LD	30	----Other
2461	3004.2090	---其他	6	0 澳门MO,巴PK,冰岛IS,东盟AS,哥CR,秘鲁PE,香港HK,新西兰NZ,智利CL 3.6 澳AU,韩国KR 4.2 瑞士CH,亚太AP	0 受惠国LD	30	---Other
		-含有激素或税号29.37的其他产品，但不含抗菌素：					-Containing hormones or other products of heading 2937 but not containing antibiotics:
		--含有胰岛素：					--Containing insulin:
2462	3004.3110	---含有重组人胰岛素的	5	0 澳AU,巴PK,冰岛IS,东盟AS,哥CR,秘鲁PE,瑞士CH,新西兰NZ,智利CL 3 韩国KR 3.5 亚太AP	0 受惠国LD	30	---Containing Recombinant human insulin
2463	3004.3190	---其他	5	0 澳AU,巴PK,冰岛IS,东盟AS,哥CR,秘鲁PE,瑞士CH,新西兰NZ,智利CL 3 韩国KR 3.5 亚太AP	0 受惠国LD	30	---Other
2464	3004.3200	--含有皮质甾类激素及其衍生物或结构类似物	5	0 澳AU,巴PK,冰岛IS,东盟AS,哥CR,秘鲁PE,瑞士CH,香港HK,新西兰NZ,智利CL 3 韩国KR 3.5 亚太AP	0 受惠国LD	30	--Containing corticosteroid hormones, their derivatives or structural analogues
2465	3004.3900	--其他	5	0 澳AU,巴PK,冰岛IS,东盟AS,哥CR,秘鲁PE,香港HK,新西兰NZ,智利CL 3 韩国KR 3.5 瑞士CH,亚太AP	0 受惠国LD	30	--Other
		-含有生物碱及其衍生物，但不含抗菌素及税号29.37的激素或其他产品：					-Containing alkaloids or derivatives thereof but not containing hormones, other products of heading 2937 or antibiotics:
2466	3004.4010	---含有奎宁或其盐	5	0 澳AU,巴PK,冰岛IS,东盟AS,哥CR,秘鲁PE,瑞士CH,香港HK,新西兰NZ,智利CL 3 韩国KR 4 亚太AP	0 受惠国LD	35	---Containing quinine or its salts
2467	3004.4090	---其他	5	0 澳AU,巴PK,冰岛IS,东盟AS,哥CR,秘鲁PE,瑞士CH,香港HK,新西兰NZ,智利CL 3 韩国KR	0 受惠国LD	30	---Other
2468	3004.5000	-含有维生素或税号29.36所列产品的其他药品	6	0 澳门MO,巴PK,冰岛IS,东盟AS,哥CR,秘鲁PE,新西兰NZ,智利CL 2.4 瑞士CH 3.6 澳AU,韩国KR 5 亚太AP	0 受惠国LD	40	-Other medicaments containing vitamins or other products of heading No.29.36
		-其他：					-Other:

序号 No.	税则号列 Tariff Line	中文货品名称 Article Description in Chinese	最惠国税率 MFN(%)	协定税率 Agreement(%)	特惠税率 SP(%)	普通税率 Gen(%)	英文货品名称 Article Description
2469	3004.9010	---含有磺胺类	6	0 澳门MO,巴PK,冰岛IS,东盟AS,哥CR,秘鲁PE,香港HK,新西兰NZ,智利CL 2.4 瑞士CH 3.6 澳AU,韩国KR 4.2 亚太AP	0 受惠国LD	40	---Containing sulfa drugs
2470	3004.9020	---含有联苯双酯	4	0 澳AU,澳门MO,巴PK,冰岛IS,东盟AS,哥CR,韩国KR,秘鲁PE,瑞士CH,新西兰NZ,智利CL 2.8 亚太AP	0 受惠国LD	30	---Containing biphenyl dicarbxybte
		---中式成药:					---Medicaments of Chinese type:
2471	3004.9051	----中药酒	3	0 澳AU,澳门MO,巴PK,冰岛IS,东盟AS,哥CR,韩国KR,秘鲁PE,瑞士CH,香港HK,新西兰NZ,智利CL 2 亚太AP	0 受惠国LD	30	----Medicated liquors or wines
2472	3004.9052	----片仔癀	3	0 澳AU,澳门MO,巴PK,冰岛IS,东盟AS,哥CR,韩国KR,秘鲁PE,瑞士CH,香港HK,新西兰NZ,智利CL 2 亚太AP	0 受惠国LD	30	----Pien Tzu Huang
2473	3004.9053	----白药	3	0 澳AU,澳门MO,巴PK,冰岛IS,东盟AS,哥CR,韩国KR,秘鲁PE,瑞士CH,香港HK,新西兰NZ,智利CL 2 亚太AP	0 受惠国LD	30	----Bai Yao
2474	3004.9054	----清凉油	3	0 澳AU,澳门MO,巴PK,冰岛IS,东盟AS,哥CR,韩国KR,秘鲁PE,瑞士CH,香港HK,新西兰NZ,智利CL 2 亚太AP	0 受惠国LD	30	----Essential balm
2475	3004.9055	----安宫牛黄丸	3	0 澳AU,澳门MO,巴PK,冰岛IS,东盟AS,哥CR,韩国KR,秘鲁PE,瑞士CH,香港HK,新西兰NZ,智利CL 2 亚太AP	0 受惠国LD	30	----Angong niuhuang wan
2476	3004.9059	----其他	3	0 澳AU,澳门MO,巴PK,冰岛IS,东盟AS,哥CR,韩国KR,秘鲁PE,瑞士CH,香港HK,新西兰NZ,智利CL 2 亚太AP	0 受惠国LD	30	----Other
2477	3004.9060	---含有青蒿素及其衍生物	4	0 澳AU,澳门MO,巴PK,冰岛IS,东盟AS,哥CR,韩国KR,秘鲁PE,瑞士CH,香港HK,新西兰NZ,智利CL	0 受惠国LD	30	---Containing artemisinins and their derivatives
2478	3004.9090	---其他	4	0 澳AU,澳门MO,巴PK,冰岛IS,东盟AS,哥CR,韩国KR,秘鲁PE,香港HK,新西兰NZ,智利CL 2.8 瑞士CH,亚太AP	0 受惠国$_1$LD$_1$	30	---Other

序号 No.	税则号列 Tariff Line	中文货品名称 Article Description in Chinese	最惠国税率 MFN(%)	协定税率 Agreement(%)		特惠税率 SP(%)		普通税率 Gen(%)	英文货品名称 Article Description
	30.05	**软填料、纱布、绷带及类似物品（例如，敷料、橡皮膏、泥罨剂），经过药物浸涂或制成零售包装供医疗、外科、牙科或兽医用：**							**Wadding, gauze, bandages and similar articles (for example, dressings, adhesive plasters, poultices) , impregnated or coated with pharmaceutical substances or put up in forms or packings for retail sale for medical, surgical, dental or veterinary purposes:**
		-胶粘敷料及有胶粘涂层的其他物品：							-Adhesive dressings and other articles having an adhesive layer:
2479	3005.1010	---橡皮膏	5	0 3	澳AU,澳门MO,巴PK,冰岛IS,东盟AS,哥CR,秘鲁PE,瑞士CH,新西兰NZ,智利CL 韩国KR	0	受惠国LD	70	---Adhesive plasters
2480	3005.1090	---其他	5	0 3	澳AU,澳门MO,巴PK,东盟AS,哥CR,秘鲁PE,瑞士CH,新西兰NZ,智利CL 韩国KR	0	受惠国LD	35	---Other
		-其他：							-Other:
2481	3005.9010	---药棉、纱布、绷带	5	0 3	澳AU,巴PK,冰岛IS,东盟AS,哥CR,秘鲁PE,瑞士CH,香港HK,新西兰NZ,智利CL 韩国KR,亚太AP	0	受惠国LD	70	---Absorbent cotton, gauze, bandages
2482	3005.9090	---其他	5	0 3	澳AU,澳门MO,巴PK,东盟AS,哥CR,秘鲁PE,瑞士CH,香港HK,新西兰NZ,智利CL 韩国KR	0	受惠国LD	35	---Other
	30.06	**本章注释四所规定的医药用品：**							**Pharmaceutical goods specified in note 4 to this chapter:**
2483	3006.1000	-无菌外科肠线、类似的无菌缝合材料（包括外科或牙科用无菌可吸收缝线）及外伤创口闭合用的无菌粘合胶布；无菌昆布及无菌昆布塞条；外科或牙科用无菌吸收性止血材料；外科或牙科用无菌抗粘连阻隔材料，不论是否可吸收	5	0 2 3	澳AU,澳门MO,巴PK,冰岛IS,东盟AS,哥CR,秘鲁PE,香港HK,新西兰NZ,智利CL 瑞士CH 韩国KR	0	受惠国LD	30	-Sterile surgical catgut, similar sterile suture materials (including sterile absorbable surgical or dental yarns) and sterile tissue adhesives for surgical wound closure; sterile laminaria and sterile laminaria tents; sterile absorbable surgical or dental haemostatics; sterile surgical or dental adhesion barriers, whether or not absorbable
2484	3006.2000	-血型试剂	3	0 2.1	澳AU,巴PK,冰岛IS,东盟AS,哥CR,韩国KR,秘鲁PE,新西兰NZ,智利CL 瑞士CH	0	受惠国LD	20	-Blood-grouping reagents
2485	3006.3000	-X光检查造影剂；用于病人的诊断试剂	4	0 1.6	澳AU,巴PK,冰岛IS,东盟AS,哥CR,韩国KR,秘鲁PE,新西兰NZ,智利CL 瑞士CH	0	受惠国LD	30	-Opacifying preparations for X-ray examinations; diagnostic reagents designed to be administered to the patient
2486	3006.4000	-牙科粘固剂及其他牙科填料；骨骼粘固剂	5	0 2 4	澳AU,巴PK,冰岛IS,东盟AS,哥CR,秘鲁PE,新西兰NZ,智利CL 瑞士CH 韩国KR	0	受惠国LD	30	-Dental cements and other dental fillings; bone reconstruction cements
2487	3006.5000	-急救药箱、药包	5	0 3	澳AU,巴PK,冰岛IS,东盟AS,哥CR,秘鲁PE,瑞士CH,新西兰NZ,智利CL 韩国KR	0	受惠国LD	30	-First-aid boxes and kits

序号 No.	税则号列 Tariff Line	中文货品名称 Article Description in Chinese	最惠国税率 MFN(%)	协定税率 Agreement(%)		特惠税率 SP(%)	普通税率 Gen(%)	英文货品名称 Article Description
		-以激素、税目29.37的其他产品或杀精子剂为基本成分的化学避孕药物:						-Chemical contraceptive preparations based on hormones, on other products of heading 2937 or on spermicides:
2488	3006.6010	---以激素为基本成分的避孕药	0			0 受惠国LD	0	---Contraceptive preparations based on hormones
2489	3006.6090	---其他	0			0 受惠国LD	0	---Other
2490	3006.7000	-专用于人类或作兽药用的凝胶制品，作为外科手术或体检时躯体部位的润滑剂，或者作为躯体和医疗器械之间的偶合剂	6.5	0 2.6 3.9 5	冰岛IS,东盟AS,哥CR,秘鲁PE,香港HK,新西兰NZ,智利CL 瑞士CH 澳AU,韩国KR 巴PK	0 受惠国LD	30	-Gel preparations designed to be used in human or veterinary medicine as a lubricant for parts of the body for surgical operations or physical examinations or as a coupling agent between the body and medical instruments
		-其他:						-Other:
2491	3006.9100	--可确定用于造口术的用具	10	0 4 6 8 9.2	澳门MO,冰岛IS,东盟AS,哥CR,秘鲁PE,香港HK,新加坡SG,新西兰NZ,智利CL 瑞士CH 澳AU 韩国KR 巴PK,亚太AP	0 受惠国LD	80	--Appliances identifiable for ostomy use
2492	3006.9200	--废药物	5	0 3	澳AU,巴PK,冰岛IS,东盟AS,哥CR,秘鲁PE,瑞士CH,新西兰NZ,智利CL 韩国KR	0 受惠国LD	30	--Waste pharmaceuticals

第三十一章
肥料

注释:

一、本章不包括:

（一）税号05.11的动物血;

（二）单独的已有化学定义的化合物（符合下列注释二（一）、三（一）、四（一）或五所规定的化合物除外）;

（三）税号38.24的每颗重量不低于2.5克的氯化钾培养晶体（光学元件除外）; 氯化钾光学元件（税号90.01）。

二、税号31.02只适用于下列货品，但未制成税号31.05所述形状或包装:

（一）符合下列任何一条规定的货品:

1. 硝酸钠，不论是否纯净;
2. 硝酸铵，不论是否纯净;
3. 硫酸铵及硝酸铵的复盐，不论是否纯净;
4. 硫酸铵，不论是否纯净;
5. 硝酸钙及硝酸铵的复盐（不论是否纯净）或硝酸钙及硝酸铵的混合物;
6. 硝酸钙及硝酸镁的复盐（不论是否纯净）或硝酸钙及硝酸镁的混合物;
7. 氰氨化钙，不论是否纯净或用油处理;
8. 尿素，不论是否纯净。

（二）由上述（一）款任何货品相互混合的肥料。

（三）由氯化铵或上述（一）或（二）款任何货品与白垩、石膏或其他无肥效无机物混合而成的肥料。

（四）由上述（一）2或8项的货品或其混合物溶于水或液氨的液体肥料。

三、税号31.03只适用于下列货品，但未制成税号31.05所述形状或包装:

（一）符合下列任何一条规定的货品:

1. 碱性熔渣;
2. 税号25.10的天然磷酸盐，已焙烧或经过超出清除杂质范围的热处理;

Chapter 31
Fertilizers

Notes:

1. This Chapter does not cover:

(a) Animal blood of heading No.05.11;

(b) Separate chemically defined compounds (other than those answering to the descriptions in Note 2(a), 3(a), 4(a) or 5 below); or

(c) Cultured potassium chloride crystals (other than optical elements) weighing not less than 2.5g each, of heading No.38.24; optical elements of potassium chloride (heading No.90.01) .

2. Heading No.31.02 applies only to the following goods, provided that they are not put up in the forms or packages described in heading No.31.05:

(a) Goods which answer to one or other of the descriptions given below:

(1) Sodium nitrate, whether or not pure;

(2) Ammonium nitrate, whether or not pure;

(3) Double salts, whether or not pure, of ammonium sulphate and ammonium nitrate;

(4) Ammonium sulphate, whether or not pure;

(5) Double salts (whether or not pure) or mixtures of calcium nitrate and ammonium nitrate;

(6) Double salts (whether or not pure) or mixtures of calcium nitrate and magnesium nitrate;

(7) Calcium cyanamide, whether or not pure or treated with oil;

(8) Urea, whether or not pure.

(b) Fertilizers consisting of any of the goods described in (a) above mixed together.

(c) Fertilizers consisting of ammonium chloride or of any of the goods described in (a) or (b) above mixed with chalk, gypsum or other inorganic nonfertilizing substances.

(d) Liquid fertilizers consisting of the goods of subparagraph (a)(2) or (8) above, or of mixtures of those goods, in an aqueous or ammoniacal solution.

3. Heading No.31.03 applies only to the following goods, provided that they are not put up in the forms or packages described in heading No.31.05:

(a) Goods which answer to one or other of the descriptions given below:

(1) Basic slag;

(2) Natural phosphates of heading No.25.10, calcined or further heat-treated than for the removal of impurities;

3. 过磷酸钙（一过磷酸钙、二过磷酸钙或三过磷酸钙）；

4. 磷酸氢钙，按干燥无水产品重量计含氟量不低于0.2%。

（二）由上述（一）款的任何货品相互混合的肥料，不论含氟量多少。

（三）由上述（一）或（二）款的任何货品与白垩、石膏或其他无肥效无机物混合而成的肥料，不论含氟量多少。

四、税号31.04只适用于下列货品，但未制成税号31.05所述形状或包装：

（一）符合下列任何一条规定的货品：

1. 天然粗钾盐（例如，光卤石、钾盐镁矾及钾盐）；

2. 氯化钾，不论是否纯净，但上述注释一（三）所述的产品除外；

3. 硫酸钾，不论是否纯净；

4. 硫酸镁钾，不论是否纯净。

（二）由上述（一）款任何货品相互混合的肥料。

五、磷酸二氢铵及磷酸氢二铵（不论是否纯净）及其相互之间的混合物应归入税号31.05。

六、税号31.05所称“其他肥料”，仅适用于其基本成分至少含有氮、磷、钾中一种肥效元素的肥料用产品。

(3) Superphosphates (single, double or triple);

(4) Calcium hydrogenorthophosphate containing not less than 0.2% by weight of flourine calculated on the dry anhydrous product.

(b) Fertilizers consisting of any of the goods described in (a) above mixed together, but with no account being taken of the fluorine content limit.

(c) Fertilizers consisting of any of the goods described in (a) or (b) above, but with no account being taken of the fluorine content limit, mixed with chalk, gypsum or other inorganic non-fertilizing substances.

4. Heading No.31.04 applies only to the following goods, provided that they are not put up in the forms or packages described in heading No.31.05:

(a) Goods which answer to one or other of the descriptions given below:

(1) Crude natural potassium salts (for example, car-nallite, kainite and sylvite);

(2) Potassium chloride, whether or not pure, except as provided in Note1 (c) above;

(3) Potassium sulphate, whether or not pure;

(4) Magnesium potassium sulphate, whether or not pure.

(b) Fertilizers consisting of any of the goods described in (a) above mixed together.

5. Ammonium dihydrogenorthophosphate (monoammonium phosphate) and diammonium hydrogenorthophosphate (di-ammonium phosphate), whether or not pure, and intermixtures thereof, are to be classified in heading No.31.05.

6. For the purposes of heading No.31.05, the term “other fer-tilizers” applies only to products of a kind used as fertilizers and containing, as an essential constituent, at least one of the fertilizing elements nitrogen, phosphorus or potassium.

序号 No.	税则号列 Tariff Line	中文货品名称 Article Description in Chinese	最惠国税率 MFN(%)	协定税率 Agreement(%)	特惠税率 SP(%)	普通税率 Gen(%)	英文货品名称 Article Description
	31.01	**动物或植物肥料，不论是否相互混合或经化学处理；动植物产品经混合或化学处理制成的肥料：**					**Animal or vegetable fertilisers, whether or not mixed together or chemically treated; fertilisers produced by the mixing or chemical treatment of animal or vegetable products:**
		---未经化学处理：					---Not chemically treated:
2493	3101.0011	----鸟粪	3	0 澳AU,巴PK,冰岛IS,东盟AS,哥CR,韩国KR,秘鲁PE,瑞士CH,新西兰NZ,智利CL	0 受惠国LD	11	----Guano

序号 No.	税则号列 Tariff Line	中文货品名称 Article Description in Chinese	最惠国税率 MFN(%)	协定税率 Agreement(%)	特惠税率 SP(%)	普通税率 Gen(%)	英文货品名称 Article Description
2494	3101.0019	----其他	6.5	0 澳门MO,冰岛IS,东盟AS,哥CR,秘鲁PE,新西兰NZ,智利CL 2.6 瑞士CH 3.9 澳AU,韩国KR 5 巴PK	0 受惠国LD	30	----Other
2495	3101.0090	---其他	4	0 澳AU,巴PK,冰岛IS,东盟AS,哥CR,秘鲁PE,瑞士CH,香港HK,新西兰NZ,智利CL 3.4 韩国KR	0 受惠国LD	11	---Other
	31.02	**矿物氮肥及化学氮肥:**					**Mineral or chemical fertilisers, nitrogenous:**
2496	3102.1000	-尿素，不论是否水溶液	50①	0 香港HK 40 巴PK,亚太AP		150	-Urea, whether or not in aqueous solution
		-硫酸铵;硫酸铵和硝酸铵的复盐及混合物:					-Ammonium sulphate; double salts and mixtures of ammonium sulphate and ammonium nitrate:
2497	3102.2100	--硫酸铵	4	0 澳AU,巴PK,冰岛IS,东盟AS,哥CR,韩国KR,秘鲁PE,瑞士CH,新西兰NZ,智利CL	0 受惠国$_1$LD$_1$	11	--Ammonium sulphate
2498	3102.2900	--其他	4	0 澳AU,巴PK,冰岛IS,东盟AS,哥CR,韩国KR,秘鲁PE,瑞士CH,新西兰NZ,智利CL	0 受惠国$_1$LD$_1$	11	--Other
2499	3102.3000	-硝酸铵，不论是否水溶液	4	0 澳AU,巴PK,冰岛IS,东盟AS,哥CR,韩国KR,秘鲁PE,瑞士CH,新西兰NZ,智利CL	0 受惠国$_1$LD$_1$	11	-Ammonium nitrate, whether or not in aqueous solution
2500	3102.4000	-硝酸铵与碳酸钙或其他无肥效无机物的混合物	4	0 澳AU,巴PK,冰岛IS,东盟AS,哥CR,韩国KR,秘鲁PE,瑞士CH,新西兰NZ,智利CL	0 受惠国$_1$LD$_1$	11	-Mixtures of ammonium nitrate with calcium carbonate or other inorganic nonfertilizing substances
2501	3102.5000	-硝酸钠	4	0 澳AU,巴PK,冰岛IS,东盟AS,哥CR,韩国KR,秘鲁PE,瑞士CH,新西兰NZ,智利CL	0 受惠国$_1$LD$_1$	11	-Sodium nitrate
2502	3102.6000	-硝酸钙和硝酸铵的复盐及混合物	4	0 澳AU,巴PK,冰岛IS,东盟AS,哥CR,韩国KR,秘鲁PE,瑞士CH,新西兰NZ,智利CL	0 受惠国$_1$LD$_1$	11	-Double salts and mixtures of calcium nitrate and ammonium nitrate
2503	3102.8000	-尿素及硝酸铵混合物的水溶液或氨水溶液	4	0 澳AU,巴PK,冰岛IS,东盟AS,哥CR,韩国KR,秘鲁PE,瑞士CH,新西兰NZ,智利CL	0 受惠国$_1$LD$_1$	11	-Mixtures of urea and ammonium ni-trate in aqueous or ammoniacal solution
		-其他，包括上述子目未列名的混合物:					-Other, including mixtures not specified in the foregoing subheadings:
2504	3102.9010	---氰氨化钙	4	0 澳AU,巴PK,冰岛IS,东盟AS,哥CR,韩国KR,秘鲁PE,瑞士CH,新西兰NZ,智利CL	0 受惠国$_1$LD$_1$	11	---Calcium cyanamide
2505	3102.9090	---其他	4	0 澳AU,巴PK,冰岛IS,东盟AS,哥CR,韩国KR,秘鲁PE,瑞士CH,新西兰NZ,智利CL	0 受惠国$_1$LD$_1$	11	---Other
	31.03	**矿物磷肥及化学磷肥:**					**Mineral or chemical fertilisers, phosphatic:**
		-过磷酸钙:					-Superphosphates:

①**配额税率**: 4
In-quota Tariff: 4
暂定关税配额税率: 1
Interim In-quota Tariff: 1

序号 No.	税则号列 Tariff Line	中文货品名称 Article Description in Chinese	最惠国税率 MFN(%)	协定税率 Agreement(%)		特惠税率 SP(%)		普通税率 Gen(%)	英文货品名称 Article Description
2506	3103.1010	---重过磷酸钙	4Δ1	0	澳AU,巴PK,冰岛IS,东盟AS,哥CR,韩国KR,秘鲁PE,瑞士CH,新西兰NZ,智利CL	0	受惠国$_1$LD$_1$	11	---Triple superphosphates
2507	3103.1090	---其他	4Δ1	0	澳AU,巴PK,冰岛IS,东盟AS,哥CR,韩国KR,秘鲁PE,瑞士CH,新西兰NZ,智利CL	0	受惠国$_1$LD$_1$	11	---Other
2508	3103.9000	-其他	4Δ1	0	澳AU,巴PK,冰岛IS,东盟AS,哥CR,韩国KR,秘鲁PE,瑞士CH,新西兰NZ,智利CL	0	受惠国$_1$LD$_1$	11	-Other
	31.04	**矿物钾肥及化学钾肥:**							**Mineral or chemical fertilisers, potassic:**
		-氯化钾:							-Potassium chloride:
2509	3104.2020	---纯氯化钾	3	0	澳AU,巴PK,冰岛IS,东盟AS,哥CR,韩国KR,秘鲁PE,瑞士CH,新西兰NZ,智利CL	0	受惠国$_1$LD$_1$	11	---Pure
2510	3104.2090	---其他	3Δ1	0	澳AU,巴PK,冰岛IS,东盟AS,哥CR,韩国KR,秘鲁PE,瑞士CH,新西兰NZ,智利CL	0	受惠国$_1$LD$_1$	11	---Other
2511	3104.3000	-硫酸钾	3Δ1	0 2.6	澳AU,巴PK,冰岛IS,东盟AS,哥CR,秘鲁PE,瑞士CH,新西兰NZ,智利CL 韩国KR	0	受惠国$_1$LD$_1$	11	-Potassium sulphate
		-其他:							-Other:
2512	3104.9010	---光卤石、钾盐及其他天然粗钾盐	3Δ1	0	澳AU,巴PK,冰岛IS,东盟AS,哥CR,韩国KR,秘鲁PE,瑞士CH,新西兰NZ,智利CL	0	受惠国$_1$LD$_1$	11	---Carnallite, sylvite and other crude natural potassium salts
2513	3104.9090	---其他	3Δ1	0	澳AU,巴PK,冰岛IS,东盟AS,哥CR,韩国KR,秘鲁PE,瑞士CH,新西兰NZ,智利CL	0	受惠国$_1$LD$_1$	11	---Other
	31.05	**含氮、磷、钾中两种或三种肥效元素的矿物肥料或化学肥料;其他肥料;制成片及类似形状或每包毛重不超过10公斤的本章各项货品:**							**Mineral or chemical fertilisers containing two or three of the fertilising elements nitrogen, phosphorus and potassium; other fertilisers; goods of this chapter in tablets or similar forms or in packages of a gross weight not exceeding 10kg:**
2514	3105.1000	-制成片及类似形状或每包毛重不超过10公斤的本章各项货品	4Δ1	0	澳AU,巴PK,冰岛IS,东盟AS,哥CR,韩国KR,秘鲁PE,瑞士CH,香港HK,新西兰NZ,智利CL	0	受惠国$_1$LD$_1$	11	-Goods of this Chapter in tablets or similar forms or in packages of a gross weight not exceeding10kg
2515	3105.2000	-含氮、磷、钾三种肥效元素的矿物肥料或化学肥料	50①	0	香港HK			150	-Mineral or chemical fertilizers containing the three fertilizing elements nitrogen, phosphorus and potassium
2516	3105.3000	-磷酸氢二铵	50②					150	-Diammonium hy drogenorthophosphate (diammonium phosphate)

①**配额税率**: 4
In-quota Tariff: 4
暂定关税配额税率: 1
Interim In-quota Tariff: 1

②**配额税率**: 4
In-quota Tariff: 4
暂定关税配额税率: 1
Interim In-quota Tariff: 1

序号 No.	税则号列 Tariff Line	中文货品名称 Article Description in Chinese	最惠国税率 MFN(%)	协定税率 Agreement(%)		特惠税率 SP(%)		普通税率 Gen(%)	英文货品名称 Article Description
2517	3105.4000	-磷酸二氢铵及磷酸二氢铵与磷酸氢二铵的混合物	4△1	0	澳AU,巴PK,冰岛IS,东盟AS,哥CR,韩国KR,秘鲁PE,瑞士CH,新西兰NZ,智利CL	0	受惠国$_1$LD$_1$	11	-Ammonium dihydrogenorthophosphate (monoammonium phosphate) and mixtures thereof with diammonium hydrogenorthophosphate (diammonium phosphate)
		-其他含氮、磷两种肥效元素的矿物肥料或化学肥料:							-Other mineral or chemical fertilisers containing the two fertilising elements nitrogen and phosphorus:
2518	3105.5100	--含有硝酸盐及磷酸盐	4△1	0	澳AU,巴PK,冰岛IS,东盟AS,哥CR,韩国KR,秘鲁PE,瑞士CH,香港HK,新西兰NZ,智利CL	0	受惠国$_1$LD$_1$	11	--Containing nitrates and phosphates
2519	3105.5900	--其他	4△1	0	澳AU,巴PK,冰岛IS,东盟AS,哥CR,韩国KR,秘鲁PE,瑞士CH,新西兰NZ,智利CL	0	受惠国$_1$LD$_1$	11	--Other
2520	3105.6000	-含磷、钾两种肥效元素的矿物肥料或化学肥料	4△1	0	澳AU,巴PK,冰岛IS,东盟AS,哥CR,韩国KR,秘鲁PE,瑞士CH,香港HK,新西兰NZ,智利CL	0	受惠国$_1$LD$_1$	11	-Mineral or chemical fertilizers containing the two fertilizing elements phosphorus and potassium
2521	3105.9000	-其他	4△1	0	澳AU,巴PK,冰岛IS,东盟AS,哥CR,韩国KR,秘鲁PE,瑞士CH,香港HK,新西兰NZ,智利CL	0	受惠国$_1$LD$_1$	11	-Other

第三十二章
鞣料浸膏及染料浸膏；鞣酸及其衍生物；染料、颜料及其他着色料；油漆及清漆；油灰及其他类似胶粘剂；墨水、油墨

注释:

一、本章不包括:

（一）单独的已有化学定义的化学元素及化合物（税号32.03及32.04的货品、税号32.06的用作发光体的无机产品、税号32.07所述形状的熔融石英或其他熔融硅石制成的玻璃及税号32.12的零售形状或零售包装的染料及其他着色料除外）；

（二）税号29.36至29.39、29.41及35.01至35.04的鞣酸盐及其他鞣酸衍生物；

（三）沥青胶粘剂（税号27.15）。

二、税号 32.04 包括生产偶氮染料用的稳定重氮盐与偶合物的混合物。

三、税号32.03、32.04、32.05及32.06也包括以着色料为基本成分的制品（例如，税号32.06包括以税号25.30或第二十八章的颜料，金属粉片及金属粉末为基本成分的制品）。该制品是用作原材料着色剂的拼料。但以上税号不包括分散在非水介质中呈液状或浆状的制漆用颜料，例如，税号32.12的瓷漆及税号32.07、32.08、32.09、32.10、32.12、32.13及32.15的其他制品。

四、税号32.08包括由税号39.01至39.13所列产品溶于挥发性有机溶剂的溶液（胶棉除外），但溶剂重量必须超过溶液重量的50%。

五、本章所称“着色料”，不包括作为油漆填料的产品，不论这些产品能否用于水浆涂料的着色。

六、税号32.12所称“压印箔”，只包括用以压印诸如书本封面或帽带之类的薄片，这些薄片由以下材料构成:

（一）金属粉（包括贵金属粉）或颜料经胶水、明胶及其他粘合剂凝结而成的；

（二）金属（包括贵金属）或颜料沉积于任何材料衬片上的。

Chapter 32
Tanning or dyeing extracts; tannins and their derivatives; dyes, pigments and other colouring matter; paints and varnishes; putty and other mastics; inks

Notes:

1. This Chapter does not cover:

(a) Separate chemically defined elements or compounds (except those of heading No.32.03 or 32.04, inorganic products of a kind used as luminophores (heading No.32.06), glass obtained from fused quartz or other fused silica in the forms provided for in heading No.32.07, and also dyes and other colouring matter put up in forms or packings for retail sale, of heading No.32.12);

(b) Tannates or other tannin derivatives of products of headings Nos.29.36 to 29.39, 29.41 or 35.01 to 35.04; or

(c) Mastics of asphalt or other bituminous mastics (heading No.27.15).

2. Heading No.32.04 includes mixtures of stabilized diazonium salts and couplers for the production of azo dyes.

3. Headings Nos.32.03, 32.04, 32.05 and 32.06 apply also to preparations based on colouring matter (including, in the case of heading No.32.06, colouring pigments of heading No.25.30 or Chapter 28, metal flakes and metal powders), of a kind used for colouring any material or used as ingredi-ents in the manufacture of colouring preparations. The headings do not apply, however, to pigments dispersed in nonaqueous media, in liquid or paste form, of a kind used in the manufacture of paints, including enamels (heading No.32.12), or to other preparations of heading No.32.07, 32.08, 32.09, 32.10, 32.12, 32.13 or 32.15.

4. Heading No.32.08 includes solutions (other than collodions) consisting of any of the products specified in headings Nos.39.01 to 39.13in volatile organic solvents when the weight of the solvent exceeds 50% of the weight of the solution.

5. The expression "colouring matter" in this Chapter does not include products of a kind used as extenders in oil paints, whether or not they are also suitable for colouring distem pers.

6. The expression "stamping foils" in heading No.32.12 aplies only to thin sheets of a kind used for printing, for example, book covers or hat bands, and consisting of:

(a) Metallic powder(including powder of precious metal) or pigment, agglomerated with glue, gelatin or other binder; or

(b) Metal (including precious metal) or pigment, deposited on a supporting sheet of any material.

序号 No.	税则号列 Tariff Line	中文货品名称 Article Description in Chinese	最惠国税率 MFN(%)	协定税率 Agreement(%)	特惠税率 SP(%)	普通税率 Gen(%)	英文货品名称 Article Description
	32.01	**植物鞣料浸膏;鞣酸及其盐、醚、酯和其他衍生物:**					**Tanning extracts of vegetable origin; tannins and their salts, ethers, esters and other derivatives:**
2522	3201.1000	-坚木浸膏	5	0 澳AU,巴PK,冰岛IS,东盟AS,哥CR,秘鲁PE,瑞士CH,新西兰NZ,智利CL 3 韩国KR	0 受惠国$_1$LD$_1$	35	-Quebracho extract
2523	3201.2000	-荆树皮浸膏	6.5	0 冰岛IS,东盟AS,哥CR,秘鲁PE,新西兰NZ,智利CL 2.6 瑞士CH 3.9 澳AU,韩国KR 5 巴PK	0 受惠国$_1$LD$_1$	35	-Wattle extract
		-其他:					-Other:
2524	3201.9010	---其他鞣料浸膏	6.5	0 冰岛IS,东盟AS,哥CR,秘鲁PE,新西兰NZ,智利CL 2.6 瑞士CH 3.9 澳AU,韩国KR 5 巴PK	0 受惠国$_1$LD$_1$	40	---Other tanning extracts
2525	3201.9090	---其他	6.5	0 冰岛IS,东盟AS,哥CR,秘鲁PE,新西兰NZ,智利CL 2.6 瑞士CH 3.9 澳AU,韩国KR 5 巴PK	0 受惠国$_1$LD$_1$	35	---Other
	32.02	**有机合成鞣料;无机鞣料;鞣料制剂,不论是否含有天然鞣料;预鞣用酶制剂:**					**Synthetic organic tanning substances; inorganic tanning substances; tanning preparations, whether or not containing natural tanning substances; enzymatic preparations for pre-tanning:**
2526	3202.1000	-有机合成鞣料	6.5	0 冰岛IS,东盟AS,哥CR,秘鲁PE,香港HK,新西兰NZ,智利CL 2.6 瑞士CH 3.9 澳AU,韩国KR 5 巴PK	0 受惠国$_1$LD$_1$	35	-Synthetic organic tanning substances
2527	3202.9000	-其他	6.5	0 澳门MO,冰岛IS,东盟AS,哥CR,秘鲁PE,香港HK,新西兰NZ,智利CL 2.6 瑞士CH 3.9 澳AU,韩国KR 5 巴PK	0 受惠国$_1$LD$_1$	35	-Other
	ex32029000	无铬鞣剂	Δ3				Tanning agent, with out chromium
	32.03	**动植物质着色料(包括染料浸膏,但动物炭黑除外),不论是否已有化学定义;本章注释三所述的以动植物质着色料为基本成分的制品:**					**Colouring matter of vegetable or animal origin (including dyeing extracts but excluding animal black) , whether or not chemically defined; preparations as specified in note 3 to this chapter based on colouring matter of vegetable or animal origin:**
		---植物质着色料及以其为基本成分的制品:					---Colouring matter of vegetable origin and preparations based thereon:
2528	3203.0011	----天然靛蓝及以其为基本成分的制品	6.5	0 冰岛IS,东盟AS,哥CR,新西兰NZ,智利CL 2.6 瑞士CH 3.9 澳AU,韩国KR 4.1 秘鲁PE 5 巴PK	0 受惠国LD	80	----Natural indigo and preparations based thereon

序号 No.	税则号列 Tariff Line	中文货品名称 Article Description in Chinese	最惠国税率 MFN(%)	协定税率 Agreement(%)	特惠税率 SP(%)	普通税率 Gen(%)	英文货品名称 Article Description
2529	3203.0019	----其他	6.5	0 澳门MO,冰岛IS,东盟AS,哥CR,新西兰NZ,智利CL 2.6 瑞士CH 3.9 澳AU,韩国KR 4.1 秘鲁PE 5 巴PK	0 受惠国LD	45	----Other
2530	3203.0020	---动物质着色料及以其为基本成分的制品	6.5	0 冰岛IS,东盟AS,哥CR,新西兰NZ,智利CL 2.6 瑞士CH 3.9 澳AU,韩国KR 4.1 秘鲁PE 5 巴PK	0 受惠国LD	50	---Colouring matter of animal origin and preparations based thereon
	32.04	**有机合成着色料,不论是否已有化学定义;本章注释三所述的以有机合成着色料为基本成分的制品;用作荧光增白剂或发光体的有机合成产品,不论是否已有化学定义:**					**Synthetic organic colouring matter, whether or not chemically defined; preparations as specified in note 3 to this chapter based on synthetic organic colouring matter; synthetic organic products of a kind used as fluorescent brightening agents or as luminophores, whether or not chemically defined:**
		-有机合成着色料及本章注释三所述的以有机合成着色料为基本成分的制品:					-Synthetic organic colouring matter and preparations based thereon as specified in note 3 to this chapter:
2531	3204.1100	--分散染料及以其为基本成分的制品	6.5	0 巴PK,冰岛IS,东盟AS,哥CR,秘鲁PE,新西兰NZ,智利CL 3.9 澳AU,韩国KR 5.8 亚太AP	0 受惠国LD	35	--Disperse dyes and preparations based thereon
2532	3204.1200	--酸性染料(不论是否预金属络合)及以其为基本成分的制品;媒染染料及以其为基本成分的制品	6.5	0 巴PK,冰岛IS,东盟AS,哥CR,韩国KR,秘鲁PE,台湾TW,香港HK,新西兰NZ,智利CL 3.9 澳AU 4.7 瑞士CH 5.8 亚太AP	0 受惠国LD	35	--Acid dyes, whether or not premetallized, and preparations based there-on; mordant dyes and preparations based thereon
2533	3204.1300	--碱性染料及以其为基本成分的制品	6.5	0 巴PK,冰岛IS,东盟AS,哥CR,秘鲁PE,新西兰NZ,智利CL 2.6 瑞士CH 3.9 澳AU,韩国KR 6 亚太AP	0 受惠国LD	35	--Basic dyes and preparations based thereon
2534	3204.1400	--直接染料及以其为基本成分的制品	6.5	0 巴PK,冰岛IS,东盟AS,哥CR,韩国KR,秘鲁PE,台湾TW,新西兰NZ,智利CL 3.9 澳AU 4.6 瑞士CH 6 亚太AP	0 受惠国LD	35	--Direct dyes and preparations based thereon
		--瓮染料(包括颜料用的)及以其为基本成分的制品:					--Vat dyes (including those usable in that state as pigments) and preparations based thereon:
2535	3204.1510	---合成靛蓝(还原靛蓝)	6.5	0 巴PK,冰岛IS,东盟AS,哥CR,秘鲁PE,新西兰NZ,智利CL 2.6 瑞士CH 3.9 澳AU 5.2 韩国KR 6 亚太AP	0 受惠国LD	35	---Synthetic indigo (reductive indigo)

序号 No.	税则号列 Tariff Line	中文货品名称 Article Description in Chinese	最惠国税率 MFN(%)	协定税率 Agreement(%)	特惠税率 SP(%)	普通税率 Gen(%)	英文货品名称 Article Description
2536	3204.1590	---其他	6.5	0 巴PK,冰岛IS,东盟AS,哥CR,秘鲁PE,新西兰NZ,智利CL 2.6 瑞士CH 3.9 澳AU 5.2 韩国KR 6 亚太AP	0 受惠国LD	35	---Other
2537	3204.1600	--活性染料及以其为基本成分的制品	6.5	0 巴PK,冰岛IS,东盟AS,哥CR,韩国KR,秘鲁PE,台湾TW,香港HK,新西兰NZ,智利CL 3.9 澳AU 4.7 瑞士CH 5.8 亚太AP	0 受惠国LD	35	--Reactive dyes and preparations based thereon
2538	3204.1700	--颜料及以其为基本成分的制品	6.5	0 巴PK,冰岛IS,东盟AS,哥CR,韩国KR,秘鲁PE,台湾TW,香港HK,新西兰NZ,智利CL 3.9 澳AU 4.6 瑞士CH,亚太AP	0 受惠国LD	35	--Pigments and preparations based thereon
		--其他，包括由子目号3204.11至3204.19中两个或多个子目所列着色料组成的混合物：					--Other, including mixtures of colouring matter of two or more of the subheadings 320411 to 320419:
		---硫化染料及以其为基本成分的制品：					---Sulphur dyes and preparations based thereon:
2539	3204.1911	----硫化黑（硫化青）及以其为基本成分的制品	6.5	0 巴PK,冰岛IS,东盟AS,哥CR,秘鲁PE,新西兰NZ,智利CL 2.6 瑞士CH 3.9 澳AU 5.2 韩国KR 6 亚太AP	0 受惠国LD	35	----Sulphur black and preparations based thereon
2540	3204.1919	----其他	6.5	0 巴PK,冰岛IS,东盟AS,哥CR,秘鲁PE,新西兰NZ,智利CL 2.6 瑞士CH 3.9 澳AU 5.2 韩国KR 6 亚太AP	0 受惠国LD	35	----Other
2541	3204.1990	---其他	6.5	0 巴PK,冰岛IS,东盟AS,哥CR,韩国KR,秘鲁PE,台湾TW,新西兰NZ,智利CL 3.9 澳AU 6 亚太AP	0 受惠国LD	35	---Other
2542	3204.2000	-用作荧光增白剂的有机合成产品	6.5	0 巴PK,冰岛IS,东盟AS,哥CR,韩国KR,秘鲁PE,台湾TW,香港HK,新西兰NZ,智利CL 3.9 澳AU 4.7 瑞士CH 6 亚太AP	0 受惠国LD	40	-Synthetic organic products of a kind used as flourescent brightening agents
		-其他：					-Other:
2543	3204.9010	---生物染色剂及染料指示剂	6.5	0 巴PK,冰岛IS,东盟AS,哥CR,秘鲁PE,新西兰NZ,智利CL 3.9 澳AU,韩国KR 4.6 瑞士CH 6 亚太AP	0 受惠国LD	20	---Biological stains and dye indicators
2544	3204.9020	---胡萝卜素及类胡萝卜素	6.5	0 巴PK,冰岛IS,东盟AS,哥CR,秘鲁PE,新西兰NZ,智利CL 2.6 瑞士CH 3.9 澳AU,韩国KR 6 亚太AP	0 受惠国LD	20	---Carotene and carotenoid

序号 No.	税则号列 Tariff Line	中文货品名称 Article Description in Chinese	最惠国税率 MFN(%)	协定税率 Agreement(%)	特惠税率 SP(%)	普通税率 Gen(%)	英文货品名称 Article Description
2545	3204.9090	---其他	6.5	0 巴PK,冰岛IS,东盟AS,哥CR,秘鲁PE,新西兰NZ,智利CL 2.6 瑞士CH 3.9 澳AU,韩国KR 6 亚太AP	0 受惠国LD	40	---Other
	32.05	**色淀;本章注释三所述的以色淀为基本成分的制品**					**Colour lakes; preparations as specified in note 3 to this chapter based on colour lakes**
2546	3205.0000	色淀;本章注释三所述的以色淀为基本成分的制品	6.5	0 冰岛IS,东盟AS,哥CR,秘鲁PE,新西兰NZ,智利CL 2.6 瑞士CH 3.9 澳AU 5 巴PK 5.6 韩国KR	0 受惠国LD	35	Colour lakes; preparations as specified in Note 3 to this Chapter based on colour lakes
	32.06	**其他着色料;本章注释三所述的制品，但税号32.03、32.04及32.05的货品除外;用作发光体的无机产品，不论是否已有化学定义:**					**Other colouring matter; preparations as specified in note 3 to this chapter, other than those of heading 3203, 3204 or 3205; inorganic products of a kind used as luminophores, whether or not chemically defined:**
		-以二氧化钛为基本成分的颜料及制品:					-Pigments and preparations based on titanium dioxide:
		--以干物质计二氧化钛含量在80%及以上的:					--Containing 80% or more by weight of titanium dioxide calculated on the dry matter:
2547	3206.1110	---钛白粉	6.5	0 冰岛IS,东盟AS,哥CR,韩国KR,秘鲁PE,台湾TW,新西兰NZ,智利CL 2.6 瑞士CH 3.9 澳AU 5 巴PK	0 受惠国LD	30	---Titanium White
2548	3206.1190	---其他	6.5	0 冰岛IS,东盟AS,哥CR,秘鲁PE,新西兰NZ,智利CL 2.6 瑞士CH 3.9 澳AU,韩国KR 5 巴PK	0 受惠国LD	30	---Other
2549	3206.1900	--其他	10	0 冰岛IS,东盟AS,哥CR,秘鲁PE,台湾TW,香港HK,新加坡SG,新西兰NZ,智利CL 4 瑞士CH 5 巴PK 6 澳AU 8 韩国KR	0 受惠国LD	30	--Other
2550	3206.2000	-以铬化合物为基本成分的颜料及制品	6.5	0 冰岛IS,东盟AS,哥CR,秘鲁PE,新西兰NZ,智利CL 2.6 瑞士CH 3.9 澳AU,韩国KR 5 巴PK	0 受惠国LD	35	-Pigments and preparations based on chromium compounds
		-其他着色料及其他制品:					-Other colouring matter and other preparations:
2551	3206.4100	--群青及以其为基本成分的制品	6.5	0 冰岛IS,东盟AS,哥CR,秘鲁PE,新西兰NZ,智利CL 2.6 瑞士CH 3.9 澳AU,韩国KR 5 巴PK	0 受惠国LD	35	--Ultramarine and preparations based thereon
		--锌钡白及以硫化锌为基本成分的其他颜料和制品:					--Lithopone and other pigments and preparations based on zinc sulphide:

序号 No.	税则号列 Tariff Line	中文货品名称 Article Description in Chinese	最惠国税率 MFN(%)	协定税率 Agreement(%)	特惠税率 SP(%)	普通税率 Gen(%)	英文货品名称 Article Description
2552	3206.4210	---锌钡白	6.5	0 冰岛IS,东盟AS,哥CR,秘鲁PE,新西兰NZ,智利CL 2.6 瑞士CH 3.9 澳AU,韩国KR 5 巴PK	0 受惠国LD	30	---Lithopone
2553	3206.4290	---其他	6.5	0 冰岛IS,东盟AS,哥CR,秘鲁PE,新西兰NZ,智利CL 2.6 瑞士CH 3.9 澳AU 5 巴PK 5.2 韩国KR	0 受惠国LD	30	---Other
		--其他: ---以铋化合物为基本成分的颜料及制品:					--Other: ---Pigments and preparations based on Bismuth compounds:
2554	3206.4911	----以钒酸铋为基本成分的颜料及制品	6.5	0 巴PK,冰岛IS,东盟AS,哥CR,秘鲁PE,台湾TW,香港HK,新西兰NZ,智利CL 2.6 瑞士CH 3.3 亚太AP 3.9 澳AU 5.2 韩国KR	0 受惠国LD	35	----Pigments and preparations based on Bismuth vanadium tetraoxide
2555	3206.4919	----其他	6.5	0 巴PK,冰岛IS,东盟AS,哥CR,秘鲁PE,台湾TW,香港HK,新西兰NZ,智利CL 2.6 瑞士CH 3.3 亚太AP 3.9 澳AU 5.2 韩国KR	0 受惠国LD	35	----Other
2556	3206.4990	---其他	6.5	0 巴PK,冰岛IS,东盟AS,哥CR,秘鲁PE,台湾TW,香港HK,新西兰NZ,智利CL 2.6 瑞士CH 3.3 亚太AP 3.9 澳AU 5.2 韩国KR	0 受惠国LD	35	---Other
2557	3206.5000	-用作发光体的无机产品	6.5	0 冰岛IS,东盟AS,哥CR,秘鲁PE,新西兰NZ,智利CL 2.6 瑞士CH 3.9 澳AU 5 巴PK 5.2 韩国KR 5.9 亚太AP	0 受惠国LD	35	-Inorganic products of a kind used as luminophores
	32.07	**陶瓷、搪瓷及玻璃工业用的调制颜料、遮光剂、着色剂、珐琅和釉料、釉底料（泥釉）、光瓷釉以及类似产品;搪瓷玻璃料及其他玻璃，呈粉、粒或粉片状的:**					**Prepared pigments, prepared opacifiers and prepared colours, vitrifiable enamels and glazes, engobes (slips), liquid lustres and similar preparations, of a kind used in the ceramic, enamelling or glass industry; glass frit and other glass, in the form of powder, granules or flakes:**
2558	3207.1000	-调制颜料、遮光剂、着色剂及类似制品	5	0 澳AU,巴PK,冰岛IS,东盟AS,哥CR,秘鲁PE,瑞士CH,新西兰NZ,智利CL 4 韩国KR	0 受惠国LD	50	-Prepared pigments, prepared opacifiers, prepared colours and similar preparations

序号 No.	税则号列 Tariff Line	中文货品名称 Article Description in Chinese	最惠国税率 MFN(%)	协定税率 Agreement(%)	特惠税率 SP(%)	普通税率 Gen(%)	英文货品名称 Article Description
2559	3207.2000	-珐琅和釉料、釉底料（泥釉）及类似制品	5	0 澳AU,巴PK,冰岛IS,东盟AS,哥CR,秘鲁PE,瑞士CH,新西兰NZ,智利CL 4.3 韩国KR	0 受惠国LD	50	-Vitrifiable enamels and glazes, engobes (slips) and similar preparations
2560	3207.3000	-光瓷釉及类似制品	5	0 澳AU,巴PK,冰岛IS,东盟AS,哥CR,秘鲁PE,瑞士CH,新西兰NZ,智利CL 3 韩国KR	0 受惠国LD	50	-Liquid lustres and similar preparations
2561	3207.4000	-搪瓷玻璃料及其他玻璃，呈粉、粒或粉片状的	5	0 澳AU,巴PK,冰岛IS,东盟AS,哥CR,秘鲁PE,瑞士CH,新西兰NZ,智利CL 3 韩国KR	0 受惠国LD	50	-Glass frit and other glass, in the form of powder, granules or flakes
	32.08	**以合成聚合物或化学改性天然聚合物为基本成分的油漆及清漆（包括瓷漆及大漆），分散于或溶于非水介质的;本章注释四所述的溶液：**					**Paints and varnishes (including enamels and lacquers) based on synthetic polymers or chemically modified natural polymers, dispersed or dissolved in a non-aqueous medium; solutions as defined in note 4 to this chapter:**
2562	3208.1000	-以聚酯为基本成分	10	0 澳门MO,冰岛IS,东盟AS,哥CR,台湾TW,香港HK,新加坡SG,新西兰NZ,智利CL 3 秘鲁PE 4 瑞士CH 5 巴PK 6 澳AU 9 韩国KR,亚太AP	0 受惠国LD	50	-Based on polyesters
		-以丙烯酸聚合物或乙烯聚合物为基本成分：					-Based on acrylic or vinyl polymers:
2563	3208.2010	---以丙烯酸聚合物为基本成分	10	0 冰岛IS,东盟AS,哥CR,台湾TW,新加坡SG,新西兰NZ,智利CL 3 秘鲁PE 4 瑞士CH 5 巴PK 6 澳AU 9 韩国KR,亚太AP	0 受惠国$_1$LD$_1$	50	---Based on acrylic polymers
	ex32082010	分散于或溶于非水介质的光导纤维用涂料（主要成分为聚胺酯丙烯酸酯类化合物）	Δ6				Paint for optical fibers (based on polyaminate acrylate resin polymers) , dispersed or dissolved in a nonaqueous medium
2564	3208.2020	---以乙烯聚合物为基本成分	10	0 冰岛IS,东盟AS,哥CR,新西兰NZ,智利CL 3 秘鲁PE 4 瑞士CH 5 巴PK 6 澳AU 8 韩国KR 9 亚太AP	0 受惠国$_1$LD$_1$	50	---Based on vinyl polymers
		-其他：					-Other:
2565	3208.9010	---以聚胺酯类化合物为基本成分	10	0 冰岛IS,东盟AS,哥CR,新加坡SG,新西兰NZ,智利CL 3 秘鲁PE 4 瑞士CH 5 巴PK 6 澳AU 8 韩国KR 9 亚太AP	0 受惠国$_1$LD$_1$	50	---Based on polyurethane polymers

序号 No.	税则号列 Tariff Line	中文货品名称 Article Description in Chinese	最惠国税率 MFN(%)	协定税率 Agreement(%)	特惠税率 SP(%)	普通税率 Gen(%)	英文货品名称 Article Description
	ex32089010	光导纤维用涂料(主要成分为聚胺酯丙烯酸酯类化合物)	Δ6				Paint for optial fibers (based on polyaminate acrylate resin polymers)
2566	3208.9090	---其他	10	0 澳门MO,冰岛IS,东盟AS,哥CR,台湾TW,香港HK,新加坡SG,新西兰NZ,智利CL 3 秘鲁PE 5 巴PK 6 澳AU 7 瑞士CH 9 韩国KR,亚太AP	0 受惠国$_1$LD$_1$	50	---Other
	32.09	**以合成聚合物或化学改性天然聚合物为基本成分的油漆及清漆(包括瓷漆及大漆),分散于或溶于水介质的:**					**Paints and varnishes (including enamels and lacquers) based on synthetic polymers or chemically modified natural polymers, dispersed or dissolved in an aqueous medium:**
2567	3209.1000	-以丙烯酸聚合物或乙烯聚合物为基本成分	10	0 澳门MO,冰岛IS,东盟AS,哥CR,新加坡SG,新西兰NZ,智利CL 3 秘鲁PE 4 瑞士CH 5 巴PK 6 澳AU 8 韩国KR 9 亚太AP	0 受惠国LD	50	-Based on acrylic or vinyl polymers
		-其他:					-Other:
2568	3209.9010	---以环氧树脂为基本成分	10	0 冰岛IS,东盟AS,哥CR,秘鲁PE,台湾TW,新加坡SG,新西兰NZ,智利CL 4 瑞士CH 5 巴PK 6 澳AU 9 韩国KR	0 受惠国$_1$LD$_1$	50	---Based on epoxy resin
2569	3209.9020	---以氟树脂为基本成分	10	0 冰岛IS,东盟AS,哥CR,秘鲁PE,新加坡SG,新西兰NZ,智利CL 4 瑞士CH 5 巴PK 6 澳AU 8 韩国KR	0 受惠国$_1$LD$_1$	50	---Based on fluororesin
2570	3209.9090	---其他	10	0 冰岛IS,东盟AS,哥CR,秘鲁PE,台湾TW,香港HK,新加坡SG,新西兰NZ,智利CL 5 巴PK 6 澳AU 7 瑞士CH 9 韩国KR	0 受惠国$_1$LD$_1$	50	---Other
	32.10	**其他油漆及清漆(包括瓷漆、大漆及水浆涂料);加工皮革用的水性颜料**					**Other paints and varnishes (including enamels, lacquers and distempers) ; prepared water pigments of a kind used for finishing leather**
2571	3210.0000	其他油漆及清漆(包括瓷漆、大漆及水浆涂料);加工皮革用的水性颜料	10	0 澳门MO,冰岛IS,东盟AS,哥CR,台湾TW,香港HK,新加坡SG,新西兰NZ,智利CL 3 秘鲁PE 4 瑞士CH 5 巴PK 6 澳AU,韩国KR 9 亚太AP	0 受惠国LD	50	Other paints and varnishes (including enamels, lacquers and distempers) ; prepared water pigments of a kind used for finishing leather
	ex32100000	光导纤维用涂料	Δ6				Paint for optial fibers

序号 No.	税则号列 Tariff Line	中文货品名称 Article Description in Chinese	最惠国税率 MFN(%)	协定税率 Agreement(%)	特惠税率 SP(%)	普通税率 Gen(%)	英文货品名称 Article Description
	32.11	配制的催干剂					**Prepared driers**
2572	3211.0000	配制的催干剂	10	0 冰岛IS,东盟AS,哥CR,秘鲁PE,新加坡SG,新西兰NZ,智利CL 5 巴PK 6 澳AU 7 瑞士CH 8.6 韩国KR	0 受惠国$_{1}$LD$_{1}$	50	Prepared driers
	32.12	**制造油漆（含瓷漆）用的颜料（包括金属粉末或金属粉片），分散于非水介质中呈液状或浆状的;压印箔;零售形状及零售包装的染料或其他着色料:**					**Pigments (including metallic powders and flakes) dispersed in non-aqueous media, in liquid or paste form, of a kind used in the manufacture of paints (including enamels) ; stamping foils; dyes and other colouring matter put up in forms or packings for retail sale:**
2573	3212.1000	-压印箔	15	0 冰岛IS,东盟AS,哥CR,新加坡SG,新西兰NZ,智利CL 4.5 秘鲁PE 9 澳AU 10.5 瑞士CH 12 巴PK,韩国KR	0 受惠国$_{1}$LD$_{1}$	80	-Stamping foils
2574	3212.9000	-其他	10	0 冰岛IS,东盟AS,哥CR,秘鲁PE,新加坡SG,新西兰NZ,智利CL 4 瑞士CH 5 巴PK 6 澳AU 8 韩国KR	0 受惠国$_{1}$LD$_{1}$	50	-Other
	32.13	**艺术家、学生和广告美工用的颜料、调色料、文娱颜料及类似品，片状、管装、罐装、瓶装、扁盒装以及类似形状或包装的:**					**Artists' , students' or signboard painters' colours, modifying tints, amusement colours and the like, in tablets, tubes, jars, bottles, pans or in similar forms or packings:**
2575	3213.1000	-成套的颜料	10	0 冰岛IS,东盟AS,哥CR,新西兰NZ,智利CL 3 秘鲁PE 4 瑞士CH 5 巴PK 6 澳AU 8 韩国KR	0 受惠国$_{1}$LD$_{1}$	70	-Colours in sets
2576	3213.9000	-其他	10	0 冰岛IS,东盟AS,哥CR,秘鲁PE,新西兰NZ,智利CL 4 瑞士CH 5 巴PK 6 澳AU 8 韩国KR 9 亚太AP	0 受惠国LD	70	-Other
	32.14	**安装玻璃用油灰、接缝用油灰、树脂胶泥、嵌缝胶及其他类似胶粘剂;漆工用填料;非耐火涂面制剂，涂门面、内墙、地板、天花板等用:**					**Glaziers' putty, grafting putty, resin cements, caulking compounds and other mastics; painters' fillings; non-refractory surfacing preparations for façades, indoor walls, floors, ceilings or the like:**
		-安装玻璃用油灰、接缝用油灰、树脂胶泥、嵌缝胶及其他类似胶粘剂;漆工用填料:					-Glaziers' putty, grafting putty, resin cements, caulking compounds and other mastics; painters' fillings:

序号 No.	税则号列 Tariff Line	中文货品名称 Article Description in Chinese	最惠国税率 MFN(%)	协定税率 Agreement(%)	特惠税率 SP(%)	普通税率 Gen(%)	英文货品名称 Article Description
2577	3214.1010	---半导体器件封装材料	9	0 冰岛IS,东盟AS,哥CR,秘鲁PE,新西兰NZ,智利CL 3.6 瑞士CH 5 巴PK 5.4 澳AU	0 受惠国LD	70	---Encapsulation materials for semiconductor device
2578	3214.1090	---其他	9	0 冰岛IS,东盟AS,哥CR,秘鲁PE,新西兰NZ,智利CL 5 巴PK 5.4 澳AU,韩国KR 6.3 瑞士CH	0 受惠国LD	70	---Other
2579	3214.9000	-其他	9	0 冰岛IS,东盟AS,哥CR,秘鲁PE,香港HK,新西兰NZ,智利CL 3.6 瑞士CH 5 巴PK 5.4 澳AU 7.8 韩国KR	0 受惠国LD	70	-Other
	32.15	**印刷油墨、书写或绘图墨水及其他墨类，不论是否固体或浓缩：**					**Printing ink, writing or drawing ink and other inks, whether or not concentrated or solid:**
		-印刷油墨：					-Printing ink:
2580	3215.1100	--黑色	6.5	0 澳门MO,巴PK,冰岛IS,东盟AS,哥CR,秘鲁PE,香港HK,新西兰NZ,智利CL 2.6 瑞士CH 3.9 澳AU,韩国KR 4.6 亚太AP	0 受惠国LD	45	--Black
2581	3215.1900	--其他	6.5	0 澳门MO,巴PK,冰岛IS,东盟AS,哥CR,秘鲁PE,台湾TW,香港HK,新西兰NZ,智利CL 3.9 澳AU 4.6 瑞士CH,亚太AP 5.2 韩国KR	0 受惠国LD	45	--Other
		-其他：					-Other:
2582	3215.9010	---书写墨水	6.5	0 澳门MO,冰岛IS,东盟AS,哥CR,秘鲁PE,香港HK,新西兰NZ,智利CL 2.6 瑞士CH 3.9 澳AU,韩国KR 5 巴PK	0 受惠国LD	70	---Writing or drawing inks
2583	3215.9020	---水性喷墨墨水	10	0 澳门MO,冰岛IS,东盟AS,哥CR,秘鲁PE,香港HK,新加坡SG,新西兰NZ,智利CL 5 巴PK 6 澳AU,韩国KR 7 瑞士CH	0 受惠国LD	70	---Water based inkjet ink
2584	3215.9090	---其他	10	0 澳门MO,冰岛IS,东盟AS,哥CR,秘鲁PE,香港HK,新加坡SG,新西兰NZ,智利CL 5 巴PK 6 澳AU,韩国KR 7 瑞士CH	0 受惠国LD	70	---Other

第三十三章
精油及香膏；芳香料制品
及化妆盥洗品

注释:

一、本章不包括:

(一)税号13.01及13.02的天然油树脂及植物浸膏;

(二)税号34.01的肥皂及其他产品;

(三)税号38.05的脂松节油、木松节油和硫酸盐松节油及其他产品。

二、税号33.02所称“香料”，仅指税号33.01所列的物质、从这些物质离析出来的香料组分以及合成芳香剂。

三、税号33.03至33.07主要包括适合作这些税号所列用途的零售包装产品，不论其是否混合（精油水馏液及水溶液除外）。

四、税号33.07所称“芳香料制品及化妆盥洗品”，主要适用于下列产品:香袋;通过燃烧散发香气的制品;香纸及用化妆品浸渍或涂布的纸;隐形眼镜片或假眼用的溶液;用香水或化妆品浸渍、涂布、包覆的絮胎、毡呢及无纺织物;动物用盥洗品。

Chapter 33

Essential oils and resinoids;
perfumery, cosmetic or toilet preparations

Notes:

1. This Chapter does not cover:

(a) Natural oleoresins or vegetable extracts of heading No.13.01 or 13.02;

(b) Soap or other products of heading No.34.01;or

(c) Gum, wood or sulphate turpentine or other products of heading No.38.05.

2. The expression “odoriferous substances” in heading No.33.02 refers only to the substances of heading No.33.01, to odoriferous constituents isolated from those substances or to synthetic aromatics.

3. Headings Nos.33.03 to 33.07 apply, *inter alia*, to products, whether or not mixed (other than aqueous distillates and aqueous solutions of essential oils), suitable for use as goods of these headings and put up in packings of a kind sold by retail for such use.

4. The expression “perfumery, cosmetic or toilet preparations” in heading No.33.07 applies, *inter alia*, to the following products: scented sachets; odoriferous preparations which operate by burning; perfumed papers and papers impregnated or coated with cosmetics; contact lens or artificial eye solutions; wadding, felt and nonwovens, impregnated, coated or covered with perfume or cosmetics; animal toilet preparations.

序号 No.	税则号列 Tariff Line	中文货品名称 Article Description in Chinese	最惠国税率 MFN(%)	协定税率 Agreement(%)	特惠税率 SP(%)	普通税率 Gen(%)	英文货品名称 Article Description
	33.01	**精油（无萜或含萜），包括浸膏及净油;香膏;提取的油树脂;用花香吸取法或浸渍法制成的含浓缩精油的脂肪、固定油、蜡及类似品;精油脱萜时所得的萜烯副产品;精油水馏液及水溶液:**					**Essential oils (terpeneless or not), including concretes and absolutes; resinoids; extracted oleoresins; concentrates of essential oils in fats, in fixed oils, in waxes or the like, obtained by enfleurage or maceration; terpenic by-products of the deterpenation of essential oils; aqueous distillates and aqueous solutions of essential oils:**
		-柑桔属果实的精油:					-Essential oils of citrus fruit:
2585	3301.1200	--橙油	20	0 澳门MO,冰岛IS,东盟AS,哥CR,新加坡SG,新西兰NZ,智利CL 6 秘鲁PE 12 澳AU 15 瑞士CH 17.3 韩国KR	0 受惠国$_1$LD$_1$	80	--Of orange

序号 No.	税则号列 Tariff Line	中文货品名称 Article Description in Chinese	最惠国税率 MFN(%)	协定税率 Agreement(%)	特惠税率 SP(%)	普通税率 Gen(%)	英文货品名称 Article Description
2586	3301.1300	--柠檬油	20	0 澳门MO,冰岛IS,东盟AS,哥CR,秘鲁PE,新加坡SG,新西兰NZ,智利CL 8 瑞士CH 12 澳AU 17.3 韩国KR	0 受惠国LD	80	--Of lemon
		--其他:					--Other:
2587	3301.1910	---白柠檬油（酸橙油）	20	0 澳门MO,冰岛IS,东盟AS,哥CR,秘鲁PE,新加坡SG,新西兰NZ,智利CL 12 澳AU 14 瑞士CH 17.3 韩国KR	0 受惠国$_1$LD$_1$	80	---Of lime
2588	3301.1990	---其他	20	0 澳门MO,冰岛IS,东盟AS,哥CR,秘鲁PE,新加坡SG,新西兰NZ,智利CL 12 澳AU 14 瑞士CH 17.3 韩国KR	0 受惠国$_1$LD$_1$	80	---Other
		-非柑桔属果实的精油:					-Essential oils other than those of citrus fruit:
2589	3301.2400	--胡椒薄荷油	20	0 澳门MO,冰岛IS,东盟AS,哥CR,新加坡SG,新西兰NZ,智利CL 6 秘鲁PE 12 澳AU 14 瑞士CH 17.3 韩国KR	0 受惠国$_1$LD$_1$	90	--Of peppermint (Mentha piperita)
2590	3301.2500	--其他薄荷油	15Δ5	0 澳门MO,冰岛IS,东盟AS,哥CR,新加坡SG,新西兰NZ,智利CL 4.5 秘鲁PE 9 澳AU 10.5 瑞士CH 12 巴PK,韩国KR 14 亚太AP	0 受惠国LD	90	--Of other mints
		--其他:					--Other:
2591	3301.2910	---樟脑油	20	0 澳门MO,冰岛IS,东盟AS,哥CR,新加坡SG,新西兰NZ,智利CL 6 秘鲁PE 12 澳AU 14 瑞士CH 17.3 韩国KR	0 受惠国$_1$LD$_1$	90	---Of camphor
2592	3301.2920	---香茅油	15	0 澳门MO,冰岛IS,东盟AS,哥CR,新加坡SG,新西兰NZ,智利CL 4.5 秘鲁PE 9 澳AU 10.5 瑞士CH 12 巴PK,韩国KR	0 受惠国LD	70	---Of citronella
2593	3301.2930	---茴香油	20	0 澳门MO,冰岛IS,东盟AS,哥CR,新加坡SG,新西兰NZ,智利CL 6 秘鲁PE 12 澳AU 14 瑞士CH 17.3 韩国KR	0 受惠国$_1$LD$_1$	80	---Of aniseed

序号 No.	税则号列 Tariff Line	中文货品名称 Article Description in Chinese	最惠国税率 MFN(%)	协定税率 Agreement(%)	特惠税率 SP(%)	普通税率 Gen(%)	英文货品名称 Article Description
2594	3301.2940	---桂油	20	0 澳门MO,冰岛IS,东盟AS,哥CR,新加坡SG,新西兰NZ,智利CL 6 秘鲁PE 12 澳AU 14 瑞士CH 17.3 韩国KR	0 受惠国$_1$LD$_1$	80	---Of cassia
2595	3301.2950	---山苍子油	20	0 澳门MO,冰岛IS,东盟AS,哥CR,新加坡SG,新西兰NZ,智利CL 6 秘鲁PE 12 澳AU 14 瑞士CH 17.3 韩国KR	0 受惠国$_1$LD$_1$	80	---Of litsea cubeba
2596	3301.2960	---桉叶油	20	0 澳门MO,冰岛IS,东盟AS,哥CR,新加坡SG,新西兰NZ,智利CL 6 秘鲁PE 12 澳AU 14 瑞士CH 17.3 韩国KR	0 受惠国$_1$LD$_1$	80	---Of eucalyptus
		---其他:					---Other:
2597	3301.2991	----老鹳草油(香叶油)	20	0 澳门MO,冰岛IS,东盟AS,哥CR,新加坡SG,新西兰NZ,智利CL 6 秘鲁PE 12 澳AU 14 瑞士CH 17.3 韩国KR	0 受惠国$_1$LD$_1$	80	----Of geranium
2598	3301.2999	----其他	15	0 澳门MO,冰岛IS,东盟AS,哥CR,秘鲁PE,新加坡SG,新西兰NZ,智利CL 9 澳AU 10.5 瑞士CH 12 巴PK 13 韩国KR	0 受惠国LD	80	----Other
	ex33012999	黄樟油	Δ7				Sassafras oil
		-香膏:					-Resinoids:
2599	3301.3010	---鸢尾凝脂	20Δ10	0 澳门MO,冰岛IS,东盟AS,哥CR,新加坡SG,新西兰NZ,智利CL 6 秘鲁PE 12 澳AU 14 瑞士CH 17.3 韩国KR	0 受惠国$_1$LD$_1$	80	---Balsam of irises
2600	3301.3090	---其他	20	0 澳门MO,冰岛IS,东盟AS,哥CR,新加坡SG,新西兰NZ,智利CL 6 秘鲁PE 12 澳AU 14 瑞士CH 17.3 韩国KR	0 受惠国$_1$LD$_1$	80	---Other
		-其他:					-Other:
2601	3301.9010	---提取的油树脂	20	0 澳门MO,冰岛IS,东盟AS,哥CR,秘鲁PE,新加坡SG,新西兰NZ,智利CL 12 澳AU 14 瑞士CH 17.3 韩国KR 18 巴PK,亚太AP	0 受惠国$_1$LD$_1$	80	---Extracted oleoresins

序号 No.	税则号列 Tariff Line	中文货品名称 Article Description in Chinese	最惠国税率 MFN(%)	协定税率 Agreement(%)	特惠税率 SP(%)	普通税率 Gen(%)	英文货品名称 Article Description
2602	3301.9020	---柑桔属果实的精油脱萜的萜烯副产品	20	0 澳门MO,冰岛IS,东盟AS,哥CR,秘鲁PE,新加坡SG,新西兰NZ,智利CL 12 澳AU 14 瑞士CH 17.3 韩国KR 18 巴PK,亚太AP	0 受惠国$_1$LD$_1$	80	---Terpenic byproducts of the deterpenation of essential oils of citrus fruit
2603	3301.9090	---其他	20	0 澳门MO,冰岛IS,东盟AS,哥CR,秘鲁PE,新加坡SG,新西兰NZ,智利CL 12 澳AU 14 瑞士CH 17.3 韩国KR 18 巴PK,亚太AP	0 受惠国LD	80	---Other
	33.02	**工业原料用的混合香料以及以一种或多种香料为基本成分的混合物(包括酒精溶液);生产饮料用的以香料为基本成分的其他制品:**					**Mixtures of odoriferous substances and mixtures (including alcoholic solutions) with a basis of one or more of these substances, of a kind used as raw materials in industry; other preparations based on odoriferous substances, of a kind used for the manufacture of beverages:**
		-食品或饮料工业用:					-Of a kind used in the food or drink industries:
2604	3302.1010	---生产饮料用的以香料为基本成分的制品,按容量计酒精浓度不超过0.5%的	15	0 澳门MO,冰岛IS,东盟AS,哥CR,新加坡SG,新西兰NZ,智利CL 4.5 秘鲁PE 7.5 巴PK 9 澳AU 10.5 瑞士CH 12 韩国KR 12.8 亚太AP	0 受惠国$_1$LD$_1$	90	---Preparations based on odoriferous substances, of a kind used for the manufacture of beverages, alcoholic strength by volume not exceeding 0.5% vol.
2605	3302.1090	---其他	15	0 澳门MO,冰岛IS,东盟AS,哥CR,新加坡SG,新西兰NZ,智利CL 4.5 秘鲁PE 9 澳AU 10.5 瑞士CH 12 巴PK,韩国KR	0 受惠国LD	130	---Other
2606	3302.9000	-其他	10	0 澳门MO,冰岛IS,东盟AS,哥CR,香港HK,新加坡SG,新西兰NZ,智利CL 3 秘鲁PE 4 瑞士CH 5 巴PK 6 澳AU 8 韩国KR	0 受惠国LD	130	-Other
	33.03	**香水及花露水**					**Perfumes and toilet waters**
2607	3303.0000	香水及花露水	10	0 澳门MO,冰岛IS,东盟AS,哥CR,秘鲁PE,香港HK,新加坡SG,新西兰NZ,智利CL 4 瑞士CH 5 巴PK 6 澳AU 8.2 亚太AP	0 受惠国LD	150	Perfumes and toilet waters

序号 No.	税则号列 Tariff Line	中文货品名称 Article Description in Chinese	最惠国税率 MFN(%)	协定税率 Agreement(%)	特惠税率 SP(%)	普通税率 Gen(%)	英文货品名称 Article Description
	33.04	美容品或化妆品及护肤品（药品除外），包括防晒油或晒黑油;指（趾）甲化妆品:					**Beauty or make-up preparations and preparations for the care of the skin (other than medicaments) , including sunscreen or suntan preparations; manicure or pedicure preparations:**
2608	3304.1000	-唇用化妆品	10	0 澳门MO,冰岛IS,东盟AS,哥CR,秘鲁PE,香港HK,新加坡SG,新西兰NZ,智利CL 4 瑞士CH 5 巴PK 6 澳AU	0 受惠国$_1$LD$_1$	150	-Lip make-up preparations
2609	3304.2000	-眼用化妆品	10	0 澳门MO,冰岛IS,东盟AS,哥CR,秘鲁PE,香港HK,新加坡SG,新西兰NZ,智利CL 4 瑞士CH 5 巴PK 6 澳AU	0 受惠国$_1$LD$_1$	150	-Eye make-up preparations
2610	3304.3000	-指（趾）甲化妆品	15Δ10	0 澳门MO,冰岛IS,东盟AS,哥CR,香港HK,新加坡SG,新西兰NZ,智利CL 4.5 秘鲁PE 9 澳AU 10.5 瑞士CH 12 巴PK	0 受惠国$_1$LD$_1$	150	-Manicure or pedicure preparations
		-其他:					-Other:
2611	3304.9100	--粉,不论是否压紧	10	0 澳门MO,冰岛IS,东盟AS,哥CR,秘鲁PE,新加坡SG,新西兰NZ,智利CL 4 瑞士CH 5 巴PK 6 澳AU	0 受惠国$_1$LD$_1$	150	--Powdrs, whether or not compressed
2612	3304.9900	--其他	6.5	0 澳门MO,东盟AS,哥CR,秘鲁PE,香港HK,新加坡SG,新西兰NZ,智利CL 2.6 瑞士CH 3.3 冰岛IS 3.9 澳AU 5.2 巴PK 5.9 韩国KR	0 受惠国$_1$LD$_1$	150	--Other
	ex33049900	护肤品	Δ2				Skin care products
	33.05	**护发品:**					**Preparations for use on the hair:**
2613	3305.1000	-洗发剂（香波）	6.5	0 澳门MO,东盟AS,哥CR,秘鲁PE,香港HK,新加坡SG,新西兰NZ,智利CL 2.6 瑞士CH 3.9 澳AU 5 巴PK 5.4 亚太AP 5.5 韩国KR	0 受惠国LD	150	-Shampoos
2614	3305.2000	-烫发剂	15Δ10	0 澳门MO,冰岛IS,东盟AS,哥CR,新加坡SG,新西兰NZ,智利CL 4.5 秘鲁PE 9 澳AU 10.5 瑞士CH 12 巴PK	0 受惠国$_1$LD$_1$	150	-Preparations for permanent waving or straightening

序号 No.	税则号列 Tariff Line	中文货品名称 Article Description in Chinese	最惠国税率 MFN(%)	协定税率 Agreement(%)	特惠税率 SP(%)	普通税率 Gen(%)	英文货品名称 Article Description
2615	3305.3000	-定型剂	15Δ10	0 澳门MO,冰岛IS,东盟AS,哥CR,新加坡SG,新西兰NZ,智利CL 4.5 秘鲁PE 9 澳AU 10.5 瑞士CH 12 巴PK	0 受惠国$_1$LD$_1$	150	-Hair lacquers
2616	3305.9000	-其他	10	0 澳门MO,东盟AS,哥CR,秘鲁PE,香港HK,新加坡SG,新西兰NZ,智利CL 4 瑞士CH 5 巴PK 6 澳AU 8.5 亚太AP 8.6 韩国KR	0 受惠国LD	150	-Other
	33.06	**口腔及牙齿清洁剂,包括假牙模膏及粉;清洁牙缝用的纱线(牙线),单独零售包装的:**					**Preparations for oral or dental hygiene, including denture fixative pastes and powders; yarn used to clean between the teeth (dental floss), in individual retail packages:**
		-洁齿品:					-Dentifrices:
2617	3306.1010	---牙膏	10	0 澳门MO,冰岛IS,东盟AS,哥CR,秘鲁PE,香港HK,新加坡SG,新西兰NZ,智利CL 4 瑞士CH 5 巴PK 6 澳AU 7 亚太AP 8 韩国KR	0 受惠国LD	150	---Toothpastes
2618	3306.1090	---其他	10	0 冰岛IS,东盟AS,哥CR,秘鲁PE,新加坡SG,新西兰NZ,智利CL 4 瑞士CH 5 巴PK 6 澳AU 7 亚太AP 8 韩国KR	0 受惠国$_1$LD$_1$	150	---Other
2619	3306.2000	-清洁牙缝用的纱线(牙线)	10	0 冰岛IS,东盟AS,哥CR,秘鲁PE,新西兰NZ,智利CL 4 瑞士CH 5 巴PK 6 澳AU 8 韩国KR 9.2 亚太AP	0 受惠国$_1$LD$_1$	70	-Yarn used to clean between the teeth (dental floss)
2620	3306.9000	-其他	10	0 澳门MO,冰岛IS,东盟AS,哥CR,秘鲁PE,香港HK,新加坡SG,新西兰NZ,智利CL 4 瑞士CH 5 巴PK 6 澳AU 8 韩国KR	0 受惠国$_1$LD$_1$	70	-Other
	33.07	**剃须用制剂、人体除臭剂、沐浴用制剂、脱毛剂和其他税号未列名的芳香料制品及化妆盥洗品;室内除臭剂,不论是否加香水或消毒剂:**					**Pre-shave, shaving or aftershave preparations, personal deodorants, bath preparations, depilatories and other perfumery, cosmetic or toilet preparations, not elsewhere specified or included; prepared room deodorisers, whether or not perfumed or having disinfectant properties:**

序号 No.	税则号列 Tariff Line	中文货品名称 Article Description in Chinese	最惠国税率 MFN(%)	协定税率 Agreement(%)	特惠税率 SP(%)	普通税率 Gen(%)	英文货品名称 Article Description
2621	3307.1000	-剃须用制剂	10	0 冰岛IS,东盟AS,哥CR,秘鲁PE,新加坡SG,新西兰NZ,智利CL 4 瑞士CH 5 巴PK 6 澳AU 7 亚太AP	0 受惠国$_1$LD$_1$	150	-Pre-shave, shaving or after-shave preparations
2622	3307.2000	-人体除臭剂及止汗剂	10	0 澳门MO,冰岛IS,东盟AS,哥CR,秘鲁PE,新加坡SG,新西兰NZ,智利CL 4 瑞士CH 5 巴PK 6 澳AU 7 亚太AP	0 受惠国$_1$LD$_1$	150	-Personal deodorants and antiperspirants
2623	3307.3000	-香浴盐及其他沐浴用制剂	10	0 澳门MO,冰岛IS,东盟AS,哥CR,秘鲁PE,香港HK,新加坡SG,新西兰NZ,智利CL 4 瑞士CH 5 巴PK 6 澳AU 8.5 亚太AP 8.6 韩国KR	0 受惠国$_1$LD$_1$	150	-Perfumed bath salts and other bath preparations
		-室内散香或除臭制品，包括宗教仪式用的香：					-Preparations for perfuming or deodorising rooms, including odoriferous preparations used during religious rites:
2624	3307.4100	--神香及其他通过燃烧散发香气的制品	10	0 冰岛IS,东盟AS,哥CR,秘鲁PE,香港HK,新加坡SG,新西兰NZ,智利CL 4 瑞士CH 5 巴PK 6 澳AU 8 韩国KR	0 受惠国LD	150	--Agarbatti and other odoriferous preparations which operate by burning
2625	3307.4900	--其他	10	0 冰岛IS,东盟AS,哥CR,秘鲁PE,香港HK,新加坡SG,新西兰NZ,智利CL 4 瑞士CH 5 巴PK 6 澳AU 8 韩国KR	0 受惠国LD	150	--Other
2626	3307.9000	-其他	9	0 澳门MO,冰岛IS,东盟AS,哥CR,秘鲁PE,新西兰NZ,智利CL 3.6 瑞士CH 5 巴PK 5.4 澳AU 6.3 亚太AP 7.7 韩国KR	0 受惠国LD	150	-Other

第三十四章
肥皂、有机表面活性剂、洗涤剂、润滑剂、人造蜡、调制蜡、光洁剂、蜡烛及类似品、塑型用膏、“牙科用蜡”及牙科用熟石膏制剂

Chapter 34
Soap, organic surface-active agents, washing preparations, lubricating preparations, artificial waxes, prepared waxes, polishing or scouring preparations, candles and similar articles, modelling pastes, “dental waxes” and dental preparations with a basis of plaster

注释:

一、本章不包括:

（一）用作脱模剂的食用动植物油、脂混合物或制品（税号15.17）；

（二）单独的已有化学定义的化合物;

（三）含肥皂或其他有机表面活性剂的洗发剂、洁齿品、剃须膏及沐浴用制剂（税号33.05、33.06及33.07）。

二、税号34.01所称“肥皂”，只适用于水溶性肥皂。税号34.01的肥皂及其他产品可以含有添加料（例如，消毒剂、磨料粉、填料或药料）。含磨料粉的产品，只有条状、块状或模制形状可以归入税号34.01。其他形状的应作为“去污粉及类似品”归入税号34.05。

三、税号34.02所称“有机表面活性剂”，是指温度在20℃时与水混合配成0.5%浓度的水溶液，并在同样温度下搁置一小时后与下列规定相符的产品:

（一）成为透明或半透明的液体或稳定的乳浊液而未离析出不溶解物质;

（二）将水的表面张力减低到每厘米45达因及以下。

四、税号34.03所称“石油及从沥青矿物提取的油类”，适用于第二十七章注释二所规定的产品。

五、税号34.04所称“人造蜡及调制蜡”，仅适用于:

（一）用化学方法生产的具有蜡质特性的有机产品，不论是否为水溶性的;

（二）各种蜡混合制成的产品;

（三）以一种或几种蜡为基本原料并含有油脂、树脂、矿物质或其他原料的具有蜡质特性的产品。

本税号不包括:

（一）税号15.16、34.02或38.23的产品，不论是否具有蜡质特性;

（二）税号15.21的未混合的动物蜡或未混合的植物蜡，不论是否精制或着色;

Notes:

1. This Chapter does not cover:

(a) Edible mixtures or preparations of animal or vegetable fats or oils of a kind used as mould release preparations (heading No.15.17) ;

(b) Separate chemically defined compounds; or

(c) Shampoos, dentifrices, shaving creams and foams, or bath preparations, containing soap or other organic surface-active agents (heading No.33.05, 33.06 or 33.07) .

2. For the purposes of heading No.34.01, the expression “soap”applies only to soap soluble in water. Soap and the other products of heading No.34.01may contain added sub-stances (for example, disinfectants, abrasive powders, fillers or medicaments). Products containing abrasive powders remain classified in heading No.34.01only if in the form of bars, cakes or moulded pieces or shapes. In other forms they are to be classified in heading No.34.05 as “scouring powders and similar preparations”.

3. For the purposes of heading No.34.02, “organic surface active agents” are products which when mixed with water at a concentration of 0.5% at 20℃and left to stand for one hour at the same temperature:

(a) give a transparent or translucent liquid or stable emulsion without separation of insoluble matter; and

(b) reduce the surface tension of water to 4.5×10^{-2}N/m (45dyen/cm) orless.

4. In heading No.34.03 the expression “petroleum oils and oils obtained from bituminous minerals” applies to the products defined in Note 2 to Chapter 27.

5. In heading No.34.04, subject to the exclusions provided below, the expression “artificial waxes and prepared waxes” applies only to:

(a) Chemically produced organic products of a waxy cha-rac-ter, whether or not water-soluble;

(b) Products obtained by mixing different waxes;

(c) Products of a waxy character with a basis of one or morewaxes and containing fats, resins, mineral substances or other materials.

The heading does not apply to:

(a) Products of heading No.15.16, 34.02 or 38.23, even if having a waxy character;

(b) Unmixed animal waxes or unmixed vegetable waxes, whether or not refined or coloured, of heading No.15.21;

（三）税号27.12的矿物蜡或类似产品，不论是否相互混合或仅经着色；

（四）混合、分散或溶解于液体溶剂的蜡（税号34.05、38.09等）。

(c) Mineral waxes or similar products of heading No.27.12, whether or not intermixed or merely coloured; or

(d) Waxes mixed with, dispersed in or dissolved in a liquid medium (headings Nos.34.05, 38.09, etc.) .

序号 No.	税则号列 Tariff Line	中文货品名称 Article Description in Chinese	最惠国税率 MFN(%)	协定税率 Agreement(%)	特惠税率 SP(%)	普通税率 Gen(%)	英文货品名称 Article Description
	34.01	**肥皂;作肥皂用的有机表面活性产品及制品，条状、块状或模制形状的，不论是否含有肥皂;洁肤用的有机表面活性产品及制品，液状或膏状并制成零售包装的，不论是否含有肥皂;用肥皂或洗涤剂浸渍、涂面或包覆的纸、絮胎、毡呢及无纺织物:**					**Soap; organic surface-active products and preparations for use as soap, in the form of bars, cakes, moulded pieces or shapes, whether or not containing soap; organic surface-active products and preparations for washing the skin, in the form of liquid or cream and put up for retail sale, whether or not containing soap; paper, wadding, felt and nonwovens, impregnated, coated or covered with soap or detergent:**
		-肥皂及有机表面活性产品及制品，条状、块状或模制形状的，以及用肥皂或洗涤剂浸渍、涂面或包覆的纸、絮胎、毡呢及无纺织物:					-Soap and organic surface-active products and preparations, in the form of bars, cakes, moulded pieces or shapes, and paper, wadding, felt and nonwovens, impregnated, coated or covered with soap or detergent:
2627	3401.1100	--盥洗用（包括含有药物的产品）	10	0 澳门MO,冰岛IS,东盟AS,哥CR,秘鲁PE,香港HK,新加坡SG,新西兰NZ,智利CL 4 瑞士CH 6 澳AU 8 韩国KR 8.3 巴PK,亚太AP	0 受惠国LD,亚太AP	130	--For toilet use (including medicated products)
		--其他:					--Other:
2628	3401.1910	---洗衣皂	10	0 澳门MO,冰岛IS,东盟AS,哥CR,秘鲁PE,新加坡SG,新西兰NZ,智利CL 4 瑞士CH 5 巴PK 6 澳AU	0 受惠国LD	80	---Laundry soap
2629	3401.1990	---其他	15Δ10	0 冰岛IS,东盟AS,哥CR,新西兰NZ,智利CL 4.5 秘鲁PE 9 澳AU 10.5 瑞士CH 12 巴PK,韩国KR	0 受惠国$_1$LD$_1$	130	---Other
2630	3401.2000	-其他形状的肥皂	15Δ10	0 澳门MO,冰岛IS,东盟AS,哥CR,香港HK,新西兰NZ,智利CL 4.5 秘鲁PE 7.5 巴PK 9 澳AU 10.5 瑞士CH 12 韩国KR 12.4 亚太AP	0 受惠国LD,亚太AP	130	-Soap in other forms

序号 No.	税则号列 Tariff Line	中文货品名称 Article Description in Chinese	最惠国税率 MFN(%)	协定税率 Agreement(%)	特惠税率 SP(%)	普通税率 Gen(%)	英文货品名称 Article Description
2631	3401.3000	-洁肤用的有机表面活性产品及制品，液状或膏状并制成零售包装的，不论是否含有肥皂	10	0 澳门MO,冰岛IS,东盟AS,哥CR,秘鲁PE,新加坡SG,新西兰NZ,智利CL 4 瑞士CH 5 巴PK 6 澳AU 8 韩国KR	0 受惠国LD	130	-Organic surface-active products and preparations for washing the skin, in the form of liquid or cream and put up for retail sale, whether or not containing soap
	34.02	**有机表面活性剂（肥皂除外）；表面活性剂制品、洗涤剂（包括助洗剂）及清洁剂，不论是否含有肥皂，但税号34.01的产品除外：**					**Organic surface-active agents (other than soap) ; surface-active preparations, washing preparations (including auxiliary washing preparations) and cleaning preparations, whether or not containing soap, other than those of heading 3401:**
		-有机表面活性剂，不论是否零售包装：					-Organic surface-active agents, whether or not put up for retail sale:
2632	3402.1100	--阴离子型	6.5	0 澳门MO,冰岛IS,东盟AS,哥CR,秘鲁PE,香港HK,新西兰NZ,智利CL 2.6 瑞士CH 3.9 澳AU 5 巴PK 5.5 韩国KR 6 亚太AP	0 受惠国LD	30	--Anionic
2633	3402.1200	--阳离子型	6.5	0 澳门MO,冰岛IS,东盟AS,哥CR,秘鲁PE,香港HK,新西兰NZ,智利CL 2.6 瑞士CH 3.9 澳AU 5 巴PK 5.5 韩国KR 6 亚太AP	0 受惠国LD	30	--Cationic
2634	3402.1300	--非离子型	6.5	0 澳门MO,冰岛IS,东盟AS,哥CR,秘鲁PE,台湾TW,香港HK,新西兰NZ,智利CL 3.9 澳AU 4.6 瑞士CH 5 巴PK 5.6 韩国KR 5.9 亚太AP	0 受惠国LD	30	--Non-ionic
2635	3402.1900	--其他	6.5	0 澳门MO,冰岛IS,东盟AS,哥CR,秘鲁PE,新西兰NZ,智利CL 2.6 瑞士CH 3.9 澳AU 5 巴PK 5.5 韩国KR 6 亚太AP	0 受惠国LD	30	--Other
		-零售包装的制品：					-Preparations put up for retail sale:
2636	3402.2010	---合成洗涤粉	10	0 澳门MO,冰岛IS,东盟AS,哥CR,秘鲁PE,新加坡SG,新西兰NZ,智利CL 4 瑞士CH 5 巴PK 6 澳AU 8.5 亚太AP 8.6 韩国KR	0 受惠国$_1$LD$_1$	80	---Synthetic detergents in powder form

序号 No.	税则号列 Tariff Line	中文货品名称 Article Description in Chinese	最惠国税率 MFN(%)	协定税率 Agreement(%)	特惠税率 SP(%)	普通税率 Gen(%)	英文货品名称 Article Description
2637	3402.2090	---其他	10	0 澳门MO,冰岛IS,东盟AS,哥CR,秘鲁PE,香港HK,新加坡SG,新西兰NZ,智利CL 4 瑞士CH 5 巴PK 6 澳AU 8.5 亚太AP 8.6 韩国KR	0 受惠国$_1$LD$_1$	80	---Other
2638	3402.9000	-其他	9	0 澳门MO,冰岛IS,东盟AS,哥CR,秘鲁PE,香港HK,新加坡SG,新西兰NZ,智利CL 5 巴PK 5.4 澳AU,韩国KR 6.3 瑞士CH 7.8 亚太AP	0 受惠国LD	80	-Other
	ex34029000	十二烷基苯磺酸钙甲醇溶液(十二烷基苯磺酸钙含量应高于70%)	Δ7				Calcium dodecyl benzosulfonate methanol solution (Calcium dodecyl benzosulfonate content>70%)
	34.03	**润滑剂(包括以润滑剂为基本成分的切削油制剂、螺栓或螺母松开剂、防锈或防腐蚀制剂及脱模剂)及用于纺织材料、皮革、毛皮或其他材料油脂处理的制剂,但不包括以石油或从沥青矿物提取的油类为基本成分(按重量计不低于70%)的制剂:**					**Lubricating preparations (including cutting-oil preparations, bolt or nut release preparations, anti-rust or anti-corrosion preparations and mould-release preparations, based on lubricants) and preparations of a kind used for the oil or grease treatment of textile materials, leather, furskins or other materials, but excluding preparations containing, as basic constituents, 70% or more by weight of petroleum oils or of oils obtained from bituminous minerals:**
		-含有石油或从沥青矿物提取的油类:					-Containing petroleum oils or oils obtained from bituminous minerals:
2639	3403.1100	--处理纺织材料、皮革、毛皮或其他材料的制剂	10Δ8	0 冰岛IS,东盟AS,哥CR,秘鲁PE,香港HK,新加坡SG,新西兰NZ,智利CL 4 瑞士CH 5 巴PK 6 澳AU 8 韩国KR 9.5 亚太AP	0 受惠国$_1$LD$_1$	50	--Preparations for the treatment of textile materials, leather, furskins or other materials
2640	3403.1900	--其他	10Δ8	0 冰岛IS,东盟AS,哥CR,秘鲁PE,瑞士CH,香港HK,新加坡SG,新西兰NZ,智利CL 5 巴PK 6 澳AU,韩国KR	0 受惠国LD	50	--Other
		-其他:					-Other:
2641	3403.9100	--处理纺织材料、皮革、毛皮或其他材料的制剂	10Δ8	0 冰岛IS,东盟AS,哥CR,香港HK,新加坡SG,新西兰NZ,智利CL 3 秘鲁PE 4 瑞士CH 5 巴PK 6 澳AU,韩国KR	0 受惠国$_1$LD$_1$	50	--Preparations for the treatment of textile materials, leather, furskins or other materials

序号 No.	税则号列 Tariff Line	中文货品名称 Article Description in Chinese	最惠国税率 MFN(%)	协定税率 Agreement(%)	特惠税率 SP(%)	普通税率 Gen(%)	英文货品名称 Article Description
2642	3403.9900	--其他	10	0 澳门MO,冰岛IS,东盟AS,哥CR,新加坡SG,新西兰NZ,智利CL 3 秘鲁PE 5 巴PK 6 澳AU,韩国KR 7 瑞士CH	0 受惠国$_1$LD$_1$	50	--Other
	34.04	**人造蜡及调制蜡：**					**Artificial waxes and prepared waxes:**
2643	3404.2000	-聚氧乙烯（聚乙二醇）蜡	10	0 冰岛IS,东盟AS,哥CR,秘鲁PE,新西兰NZ,智利CL 4 瑞士CH 5 巴PK 6 澳AU	0 受惠国$_1$LD$_1$	70	-Of poly (oxyethylene) (polyethylene glycol)
2644	3404.9000	-其他	10	0 冰岛IS,东盟AS,哥CR,新西兰NZ,智利CL 3 秘鲁PE 4 瑞士CH 5 巴PK 6 澳AU,韩国KR	0 受惠国LD	70	-Other
	34.05	**鞋靴、家具、地板、车身、玻璃或金属用的光洁剂、擦洗膏、去污粉及类似制品（包括用这类制剂浸渍、涂面或包覆的纸、絮胎、毡呢、无纺织物、泡沫塑料或海绵橡胶），但不包括税号34.04的蜡：**					**Polishes and creams, for footwear, furniture, floors, coachwork, glass or metal, scouring pastes and powders and similar preparations (whether or not in the form of paper, wadding, felt, nonwovens, cellular plastics or cellular rubber, impregnated, coated or covered with such preparations) , excluding waxes of heading 3404:**
2645	3405.1000	-鞋靴或皮革用的上光剂及类似制品	10	0 冰岛IS,东盟AS,哥CR,香港HK,新加坡SG,新西兰NZ,智利CL 3 秘鲁PE 4 瑞士CH 5 巴PK 6 澳AU 8 韩国KR	0 受惠国$_1$LD$_1$	80	-Polishes, creams and similar preparations for footwear or leather
2646	3405.2000	-保养木制家具、地板或其他木制品用的上光剂及类似制品	10	0 冰岛IS,东盟AS,哥CR,香港HK,新加坡SG,新西兰NZ,智利CL 3 秘鲁PE 4 瑞士CH 5 巴PK 6 澳AU 8 韩国KR	0 受惠国$_1$LD$_1$	80	-Polishes, creams and similar preparations for the maintenance of wooden furniture, floors or other woodwork
2647	3405.3000	-车身用的上光剂及类似制品，但金属用的光洁剂除外	10	0 冰岛IS,东盟AS,哥CR,新加坡SG,新西兰NZ,智利CL 3 秘鲁PE 4 瑞士CH 5 巴PK 6 澳AU 8 韩国KR	0 受惠国$_1$LD$_1$	80	-Polishes and similar preparations for coachwork, other than metal polishes
2648	3405.4000	-擦洗膏、去污粉及类似制品	10	0 冰岛IS,东盟AS,哥CR,秘鲁PE,新西兰NZ,智利CL 4 瑞士CH 5 巴PK 6 澳AU 8 韩国KR	0 受惠国$_1$LD$_1$	80	-Scouring pastes and powders and other scouring preparations

序号 No.	税则号列 Tariff Line	中文货品名称 Article Description in Chinese	最惠国税率 MFN(%)	协定税率 Agreement(%)	特惠税率 SP(%)	普通税率 Gen(%)	英文货品名称 Article Description
2649	3405.9000	-其他	10	0 冰岛IS,东盟AS,哥CR,香港HK,新加坡SG,新西兰NZ,智利CL 3 秘鲁PE 4 瑞士CH 5 巴PK 6 澳AU,韩国KR 8.5 亚太AP	0 受惠国$_1$LD$_1$	80	-Other
	34.06	**各种蜡烛及类似品**					**Candles, tapers and the like**
2650	3406.0000	各种蜡烛及类似品	10	0 澳门MO,冰岛IS,东盟AS,哥CR,秘鲁PE,新加坡SG,新西兰NZ,智利CL 4 瑞士CH 5 巴PK 6 澳AU 8 韩国KR	0 受惠国$_1$LD$_1$	130	Candles, tapers and the like
	34.07	**塑型用膏，包括供儿童娱乐用的在内;通称为“牙科用蜡”或“牙科造形膏”的制品，成套、零售包装或制成片状、马蹄形、条状及类似形状的;以熟石膏（煅烧石膏或硫酸钙）为基本成分的牙科用其他制品:**					**Modelling pastes, including those put up for children' s amusement; preparations known as ' dental wax' or as ' dental impression compounds' , put up in sets, in packings for retail sale or in plates, horseshoe shapes, sticks or similar forms; other preparations for use in dentistry, with a basis of plaster (of calcined gypsum or calcium sulphate) :**
2651	3407.0010	---牙科用蜡及造型膏	6.5	0 冰岛IS,东盟AS,哥CR,秘鲁PE,新西兰NZ,智利CL 3.9 澳AU 4.6 瑞士CH 5 巴PK 5.2 韩国KR	0 受惠国LD	30	---Preparations of a kind known as“dental wax”or as“dental impression compounds”
2652	3407.0020	---以熟石膏为基本成分的牙科用其他制品	6.5	0 冰岛IS,东盟AS,哥CR,秘鲁PE,新西兰NZ,智利CL 2.6 瑞士CH 3.9 澳AU,韩国KR 5 巴PK	0 受惠国LD	40	---Other preparations for use in dentistry, with a basis of plaster
2653	3407.0090	---其他	10	0 冰岛IS,东盟AS,哥CR,秘鲁PE,新西兰NZ,智利CL 4 瑞士CH 5 巴PK 6 澳AU 8 韩国KR	0 受惠国$_1$LD$_1$	100	---Other

第三十五章
蛋白类物质；改性淀粉；胶；酶

Chapter 35
Albuminoidal substances; modified starches; glues; enzymes

注释:

一、本章不包括:

（一）酵母（税号21.02）；

（二）第三十章的血份（非治病、防病用的血清白蛋白除外）、药品及其他产品;

（三）预鞣用酶制剂（税号32.02）;

（四）第三十四章的加酶的浸透剂、洗涤剂及其他产品;

（五）硬化蛋白（税号39.13）;

（六）印刷工业用的明胶产品（第四十九章）。

二、税号35.05所称“糊精”，是指淀粉的降解产品，其还原糖含量以右旋糖的干重量计不超过10%。

如果还原糖含量超过10%，应归入税号17.02。

Notes:

1. This Chapter does not cover:
   (a) Yeasts (heading No.21.02);
   (b) Blood fractions (other than blood albumin not prepared for therapeutic or prophylactic uses)，medicaments or other products of Chapter 30;
   (c) Enzymatic preparations for pre-tanning (heading No.32.02) ;
   (d) Enzymatic soaking or washing preparations or other products of Chapter 34;
   (e) Hardened proteins (heading No.39.13); or
   (f) Gelatin products of the printing industry (Chapter49).
2. For the purposes of heading No.35.05，the term “dextrins” means starch degradation products with a reducing sugar content，expressed as dextrose on the dry substance，not exceeding 10%.

Such products with a reducing sugar content exceeding 10% fall in heading No.17.02.

序号 No.	税则号列 Tariff Line	中文货品名称 Article Description in Chinese	最惠国税率 MFN(%)	协定税率 Agreement(%)	特惠税率 SP(%)	普通税率 Gen(%)	英文货品名称 Article Description
	35.01	**酪蛋白、酪蛋白酸盐及其他酪蛋白衍生物;酪蛋白胶:**					**Casein, caseinates and other casein derivatives; casein glues:**
2654	3501.1000	-酪蛋白	10	0 冰岛IS,东盟AS,哥CR,秘鲁PE,新加坡SG,新西兰NZ,智利CL 4 瑞士CH 5 巴PK 6 澳AU 8 韩国KR	0 受惠国$_1$LD$_1$	35	-Casein
2655	3501.9000	-其他	10	0 冰岛IS,东盟AS,哥CR,新西兰NZ,智利CL 3 秘鲁PE 4 瑞士CH 5 巴PK 6 澳AU 8 韩国KR	0 受惠国$_1$LD$_1$	35	-Other
	35.02	**白蛋白(包括按重量计干质成分的乳清蛋白含量超过80%的两种或两种以上的乳清蛋白浓缩物)、白蛋白盐及其他白蛋白衍生物:**					**Albumins (including concentrates of two or more whey proteins, containing by weight more than 80% whey proteins, calculated on the dry matter) , albuminates and other albumin derivatives:**
		-卵清蛋白:					-Egg albumin:
2656	3502.1100	--干的	10	0 冰岛IS,东盟AS,哥CR,秘鲁PE,新西兰NZ,智利CL 4 瑞士CH 5 巴PK 6 澳AU 8 韩国KR	0 受惠国$_1$LD$_1$	80	--Dried

序号 No.	税则号列 Tariff Line	中文货品名称 Article Description in Chinese	最惠国税率 MFN(%)	协定税率 Agreement(%)	特惠税率 SP(%)	普通税率 Gen(%)	英文货品名称 Article Description
2657	3502.1900	--其他	10	0 冰岛IS,东盟AS,哥CR,秘鲁PE,新西兰NZ,智利CL 4 瑞士CH 5 巴PK 6 澳AU 8 韩国KR	0 受惠国$_1$LD$_1$	80	--Other
2658	3502.2000	-乳白蛋白，包括两种或两种以上的乳清蛋白浓缩物	10	0 冰岛IS,东盟AS,哥CR,秘鲁PE,新西兰NZ,智利CL 4 瑞士CH 5 巴PK 6 澳AU 8 韩国KR	0 受惠国$_1$LD$_1$	35	-Milk albumin, including concentrates of two or more whey proteins
2659	3502.9000	-其他	10	0 冰岛IS,东盟AS,哥CR,香港HK,新西兰NZ,智利CL 3 秘鲁PE 4 瑞士CH 5 巴PK 6 澳AU 8 韩国KR	0 受惠国$_1$LD$_1$	35	-Other
	35.03	**明胶（包括长方形、正方形明胶薄片，不论是否表面加工或着色）及其衍生物;鱼鳔胶;其他动物胶，但不包括税号35.01的酪蛋白胶:**					**Gelatin (including gelatin in rectangular (including square) sheets, whether or not surface-worked or coloured) and gelatin derivatives; isinglass; other glues of animal origin, excluding casein glues of heading 3501:**
2660	3503.0010	---明胶及其衍生物	12	0 冰岛IS,东盟AS,哥CR,秘鲁PE,新加坡SG,新西兰NZ,智利CL 6 巴PK 7.2 澳AU 8.4 瑞士CH 9.6 韩国KR	0 受惠国$_1$LD$_1$	35	---Gelatin and gelatin derivatives
	ex35030010	明胶	Δ5				Gelatin
2661	3503.0090	---其他	12	0 冰岛IS,东盟AS,哥CR,秘鲁PE,新加坡SG,新西兰NZ,智利CL 6 巴PK 7.2 澳AU 8.4 瑞士CH 9.6 韩国KR	0 受惠国$_1$LD$_1$	50	---Other
	35.04	**蛋白胨及其衍生物;其他税号未列名的蛋白质及其衍生物;皮粉，不论是否加入铬矾:**					**Peptones and their derivatives; other protein substances and their derivatives, not elsewhere specified or included; hide powder, whether or not chromed:**
2662	3504.0010	---蛋白胨	3	0 澳AU,澳门MO,巴PK,冰岛IS,东盟AS,哥CR,韩国KR,秘鲁PE,瑞士CH,新西兰NZ,智利CL	0 受惠国LD	11	---Peptones
2663	3504.0090	---其他	8	0 澳门MO,冰岛IS,东盟AS,哥CR,秘鲁PE,新西兰NZ,智利CL 3.2 瑞士CH 4.8 澳AU,韩国KR 5 巴PK	0 受惠国LD	35	---Other

序号 No.	税则号列 Tariff Line	中文货品名称 Article Description in Chinese	最惠国税率 MFN(%)	协定税率 Agreement(%)	特惠税率 SP(%)	普通税率 Gen(%)	英文货品名称 Article Description
	35.05	**糊精及其他改性淀粉(例如,预凝化淀粉或酯化淀粉);以淀粉、糊精或其他改性淀粉为基本成分的胶:**					**Dextrins and other modified starches (for example, pregelatinised or esterified starches) ; glues based on starches, or on dextrins or other modified starches:**
2664	3505.1000	-糊精及其他改性淀粉	12△6	0 澳门MO,冰岛IS,东盟AS,哥CR,香港HK,新加坡SG,新西兰NZ,智利CL 3.6 秘鲁PE 6 巴PK 7.2 澳AU 8.4 瑞士CH 9.6 韩国KR	0 受惠国$_1$LD$_1$	50	-Dextrins and other modified starches
2665	3505.2000	-胶	20	0 冰岛IS,东盟AS,哥CR,新加坡SG,新西兰NZ,智利CL 6 秘鲁PE 12 澳AU 14 瑞士CH 17.3 韩国KR	0 受惠国$_1$LD$_1$	50	-Glues
	35.06	**其他税号未列名的调制胶及其他调制粘合剂;适于作胶或粘合剂用的产品,零售包装每件净重不超过1公斤:**					**Prepared glues and other prepared adhesives, not elsewhere specified or included; products suitable for use as glues or adhesives, put up for retail sale as glues or adhesives, not exceeding a net weight of 1kg:**
2666	3506.1000	-适于作胶或粘合剂用的产品,零售包装每件净重不超过1公斤	10	0 东盟AS,哥CR,台湾TW,香港HK,新加坡SG,新西兰NZ,智利CL 3 秘鲁PE 5 巴PK 6 澳AU,韩国KR 7 瑞士CH 9.2 亚太AP	0 受惠国LD	90	-Products suitable for use as glues or adhesives, put up for retail sale as glues or adhesives, not exceeding a net weight, of 1kg
		-其他: --以橡胶或税目39.01至39.13的聚合物为基本成分的粘合剂:					-Other: --Adhesives based on polymers of headings 39.01 to 39.13 or on rubber:
2667	3506.9110	---以聚酰胺为基本成分的	10	0 澳门MO,冰岛IS,东盟AS,哥CR,台湾TW,香港HK,新加坡SG,新西兰NZ,智利CL 3 秘鲁PE 4 瑞士CH 5 巴PK 6 澳AU 7 亚太AP 8.6 韩国KR	0 受惠国LD	90	---Based on polyamide
2668	3506.9120	---以环氧树脂为基本成分的	10	0 澳门MO,冰岛IS,东盟AS,哥CR,台湾TW,香港HK,新加坡SG,新西兰NZ,智利CL 3 秘鲁PE 5 巴PK 6 澳AU 7 瑞士CH,亚太AP 9 韩国KR	0 受惠国LD	90	---Based on epoxy resin

序号 No.	税则号列 Tariff Line	中文货品名称 Article Description in Chinese	最惠国税率 MFN(%)	协定税率 Agreement(%)	特惠税率 SP(%)	普通税率 Gen(%)	英文货品名称 Article Description
2669	3506.9190	---其他	10	0 澳门MO,冰岛IS,东盟AS,哥CR,台湾TW,香港HK,新加坡SG,新西兰NZ,智利CL 3 秘鲁PE 5 巴PK 6 澳AU 7 瑞士CH,亚太AP 8 韩国KR	0 受惠国LD	90	---Other
2670	3506.9900	--其他	10	0 澳门MO,冰岛IS,东盟AS,哥CR,台湾TW,香港HK,新加坡SG,新西兰NZ,智利CL 3 秘鲁PE 5 巴PK 6 澳AU 7 瑞士CH 8.6 亚太AP 9 韩国KR	0 受惠国LD	90	--Other
	35.07	**酶;其他税号未列名的酶制品:**					**Enzymes; prepared enzymes not elsewhere specified or included:**
2671	3507.1000	-粗制凝乳酶及其浓缩物	6	0 冰岛IS,东盟AS,哥CR,秘鲁PE,新西兰NZ,智利CL 2.4 瑞士CH 3.6 澳AU,韩国KR 5 巴PK	0 受惠国LD	30	-Rennet and concentrates thereof
		-其他:					-Other:
2672	3507.9010	---碱性蛋白酶	6	0 冰岛IS,东盟AS,哥CR,秘鲁PE,新西兰NZ,智利CL 2.4 瑞士CH 3.6 澳AU 4.8 韩国KR 5 巴PK	0 受惠国LD	30	---Basic proteinase
2673	3507.9020	---碱性脂肪酶	6	0 冰岛IS,东盟AS,哥CR,秘鲁PE,新西兰NZ,智利CL 2.4 瑞士CH 3.6 澳AU 4.8 韩国KR 5 巴PK	0 受惠国LD	30	---Basic lipase
2674	3507.9090	---其他	6	0 澳门MO,冰岛IS,东盟AS,哥CR,秘鲁PE,新西兰NZ,智利CL 2.4 瑞士CH 3.6 澳AU,韩国KR 5 巴PK	0 受惠国LD	30	---Other

第三十六章
炸药；烟火制品；火柴；引火合金；易燃材料制品

注释：

一、本章不包括单独的已有化学定义的化合物，但下列注释二（一）、（二）所述物品除外。

二、税号36.06所称“易燃材料制品”，只适用于：

（一）聚乙醛、六甲撑四胺及类似物质，已制成片、棒或类似形状作燃料用的；以酒精为基本成分的固体或半固体燃料及类似的配制燃料；

（二）直接灌注香烟打火机及类似打火器用的液体燃料或液化气体燃料，其包装容器的容积不超过300立方厘米；

（三）树脂火炬、引火物及类似品。

Chapter 36
Explosives; pyrotechnic products; matches; pyrophoric alloys; certain combustible preparations

Notes:

1. This Chapter does not cover separate chemically defined compounds other than those described in Note 2 (a) or (b) below.
2. The expression “articles of combustible materials” in heading No.36.06 applies only to:

(a) Metaldehyde, hexamethylenetetramine and similar substances, put up in forms (for example，tablets, sticks or similar forms) for use as fuels; fuels with as basis of alcohol, and similar prepared fuels, in solid or semi-solid form;

(b) Liquid or liquefied-gas fuels in containers of a kind used for filling or refilling cigarette or similar lighters and of a capacity not exceeding 300 cm^3, and

(c) Resin torches，firelighters and the like.

序号 No.	税则号列 Tariff Line	中文货品名称 Article Description in Chinese	最惠国税率 MFN(%)	协定税率 Agreement(%)	特惠税率 SP(%)	普通税率 Gen(%)	英文货品名称 Article Description
	36.01	**发射药**					**Propellent powders**
2675	3601.0000	发射药	9	0 冰岛IS,东盟AS,哥CR,秘鲁PE,新西兰NZ,智利CL 3.6 瑞士CH 5 巴PK 5.4 澳AU,韩国KR	0 受惠国$_1$LD$_1$	50	Propellent powders
	36.02	**配制炸药，但发射药除外：**					**Prepared explosives, other than propellent powders:**
2676	3602.0010	---硝铵炸药	9	0 冰岛IS,东盟AS,哥CR,秘鲁PE,新西兰NZ,智利CL 3.6 瑞士CH 5 巴PK 5.4 澳AU,韩国KR	0 受惠国$_1$LD$_1$	50	---Based on ammonals nitrate
2677	3602.0090	---其他	9	0 冰岛IS,东盟AS,哥CR,秘鲁PE,新西兰NZ,智利CL 3.6 瑞士CH 5 巴PK 5.4 澳AU,韩国KR	0 受惠国$_1$LD$_1$	50	---Other
	36.03	**安全导火索;导爆索;火帽或雷管;引爆器;电雷管**					**Safety fuses; detonating fuses; percussion or detonating caps; igniters; electric detonators**
2678	3603.0000	安全导火索;导爆索;火帽或雷管;引爆器;电雷管	9	0 冰岛IS,东盟AS,哥CR,秘鲁PE,新西兰NZ,智利CL 3.6 瑞士CH 5 巴PK 5.4 澳AU,韩国KR	0 受惠国LD	50	Safety fuses; detonating fuses; percussion or detonating caps; igniters; electric detonators
	36.04	**烟花、爆竹、信号弹、降雨火箭、浓雾信号弹及其他烟火制品：**					**Fireworks, signalling flares, rain rockets, fog signals and other pyrotechnic articles:**
2679	3604.1000	-烟花、爆竹	6	0 冰岛IS,东盟AS,哥CR,秘鲁PE,新西兰NZ,智利CL 2.4 瑞士CH 3.6 澳AU,韩国KR 5 巴PK	0 受惠国$_1$LD$_1$	130	-Fireworks

序号 No.	税则号列 Tariff Line	中文货品名称 Article Description in Chinese	最惠国税率 MFN(%)	协定税率 Agreement(%)	特惠税率 SP(%)	普通税率 Gen(%)	英文货品名称 Article Description
2680	3604.9000	-其他	6	0 冰岛IS,东盟AS,哥CR,秘鲁PE,新西兰NZ,智利CL 2.4 瑞士CH 3.6 澳AU,韩国KR 5 巴PK	0 受惠国$_1$LD$_1$	100	-Other
	36.05	**火柴，但税号36.04的烟火制品除外**					**Matches, other than pyrotechnic articles of heading 3604**
2681	3605.0000	火柴，但税号36.04的烟火制品除外	6	0 冰岛IS,东盟AS,哥CR,秘鲁PE,新西兰NZ,智利CL 2.4 瑞士CH 3.6 澳AU,韩国KR 5 巴PK	0 受惠国LD	100	Matches, other than pyrotechnic articles of heading No.36.04
	36.06	**各种形状的铈铁及其他引火合金;本章注释二所述的易燃材料制品:**					**Ferro-cerium and other pyrophoric alloys in all forms; articles of combustible materials as specified in note 2 to this chapter:**
2682	3606.1000	-直接灌注香烟打火机及类似打火器用的液体燃料或液化气体燃料，其包装容器的容积不超过300立方厘米	10	0 冰岛IS,东盟AS,哥CR,秘鲁PE,香港HK,新西兰NZ,智利CL 4 瑞士CH 5 巴PK 6 澳AU 8 韩国KR	0 受惠国$_1$LD$_1$	80	-Liquid or liquefied-gas fuels in containers of a kind used for filling or refilling cigarette or similar lighters and of a capacity not exceeding 300cm^3
		-其他:					-Other:
		---铈铁及其他引火合金:					---Ferro-cerium and other pyrophoric alloys:
2683	3606.9011	----已切成形可直接使用	9	0 冰岛IS,东盟AS,哥CR,秘鲁PE,新西兰NZ,智利CL 3.6 瑞士CH 5 巴PK 5.4 澳AU,韩国KR	0 受惠国LD	80	----Cut to shape, for immediate use
2684	3606.9019	----其他	9	0 冰岛IS,东盟AS,哥CR,秘鲁PE,新西兰NZ,智利CL 3.6 瑞士CH 5 巴PK 5.4 澳AU,韩国KR	0 受惠国LD	50	----Other
2685	3606.9090	---其他	9	0 冰岛IS,东盟AS,哥CR,秘鲁PE,新西兰NZ,智利CL 3.6 瑞士CH 5 巴PK 5.4 澳AU,韩国KR	0 受惠国LD	80	---Other

第三十七章
照相及电影用品

注释:

一、本章不包括废碎料。

二、本章所称"摄影"，是指光或其他射线作用于感光面上直接或间接形成可见影像的过程。

Chapter 37
Photographic or cinematographic goods

Notes:

1. This Chapter does not cover waste or scrap.
2. In this Chapter the word "photographic" relates to the process by which visible images are formed, directly or indirectly, by the action of light or other forms of radiation on photosensitive surfaces.

序号 No.	税则号列 Tariff Line	中文货品名称 Article Description in Chinese	最惠国税率 MFN(%)	协定税率 Agreement(%)	特惠税率 SP(%)	普通税率 Gen(%)	英文货品名称 Article Description
	37.01	**未曝光的摄影感光硬片及平面软片，用纸、纸板及纺织物以外任何材料制成;未曝光的一次成像感光平片，不论是否分装:**					**Photographic plates and film in the flat, sensitised, unexposed, of any material other than paper, paperboard or textiles; instant print film in the flat, sensitised, unexposed, whether or not in packs:**
2686	3701.1000	-X光用	20Δ10	0 冰岛IS,哥CR,新西兰NZ,智利CL 6 秘鲁PE 12 澳AU 14 瑞士CH 18.4 韩国KR	0 受惠国$_1$LD$_1$	40	-For X-ray
2687	3701.2000	-一次成像平片	5	0 澳AU,巴PK,冰岛IS,东盟AS,哥CR,秘鲁PE,新西兰NZ,智利CL 3.6 瑞士CH 4 韩国KR	0 受惠国LD	40	-Instant print film
		-其他硬片及软片，任何一边超过255毫米:					-Other plates and film, with any side exceeding 255mm:
		---照相制版用:					---For preparing printing plates or cylinders:
2688	3701.3021	----激光照排片	10	0 澳门MO,冰岛IS,哥CR,秘鲁PE,新西兰NZ,智利CL 6 澳AU 7 瑞士CH ① 韩国KR	0 受惠国$_1$LD$_1$	50	----Laser phototypesetting film
2689	3701.3022	----PS版	10	0 澳门MO,冰岛IS,哥CR,秘鲁PE,新西兰NZ,智利CL 4 瑞士CH 6 澳AU ② 韩国KR	0 受惠国$_1$LD$_1$	50	----Precoated sensitized plate
2690	3701.3024	----CTP版	10	0 澳门MO,冰岛IS,东盟AS,哥CR,秘鲁PE,新西兰NZ,智利CL 4 瑞士CH 5 巴PK 6 澳AU ③ 韩国KR	0 受惠国$_1$LD$_1$	50	----CTP plate

①**协定税率**: 2.9 元/平方米
Agreement Import Tariff: 2.9¥/m^2

②**协定税率**: 6.4 元/平方米
Agreement Import Tariff: 6.4¥/m^2

③**协定税率**: 6.4 元/平方米
Agreement Import Tariff: 6.4¥/m^2

序号 No.	税则号列 Tariff Line	中文货品名称 Article Description in Chinese	最惠国税率 MFN(%)	协定税率 Agreement(%)	特惠税率 SP(%)	普通税率 Gen(%)	英文货品名称 Article Description
2691	3701.3025	----柔性印刷版	10	0 澳门MO,冰岛IS,哥CR,秘鲁PE,新西兰NZ,智利CL 6 澳AU 7 瑞士CH ① 韩国KR	0 受惠国$_1$LD$_1$	50	----Flexographic plate
	ex37013025	柔性印刷版（厚度小于3毫米的）	Δ5				Flexographic plate (Thickness<3mm)
2692	3701.3029	----其他	10	0 澳门MO,冰岛IS,哥CR,秘鲁PE,新西兰NZ,智利CL 6 澳AU 7 瑞士CH ② 韩国KR	0 受惠国$_1$LD$_1$	50	----Other
2693	3701.3090	---其他	20	0 冰岛IS,东盟AS,哥CR,新加坡SG,新西兰NZ,智利CL 6 秘鲁PE 12 澳AU 14 瑞士CH 17.3 韩国KR	0 受惠国$_1$LD$_1$	70	---Other
		-其他:					-Other:
2694	3701.9100	--彩色摄影用	22	0 冰岛IS,东盟AS,哥CR,新加坡SG,新西兰NZ,智利CL 6.6 秘鲁PE 13.2 澳AU 15.4 瑞士CH	0 受惠国$_1$LD$_1$	70	--For colour photography (polychrome)
		--其他:					--Other:
2695	3701.9920	---照相制版用	10	0 冰岛IS,东盟AS,哥CR,新西兰NZ,智利CL 3 秘鲁PE 4 瑞士CH 5 巴PK 6 澳AU 8 韩国KR	0 受惠国$_1$LD$_1$	40	---For preparing printing plates or cylinders
	ex37019920	石英玻璃基质的未曝光感光硬片	Δ5				Photographic plates and film, unexposed, quartz based
2696	3701.9990	---其他	25	0 冰岛IS,东盟AS,哥CR,新加坡SG,新西兰NZ,智利CL 7.5 秘鲁PE 15 澳AU 17.5 瑞士CH	0 受惠国$_1$LD$_1$	70	---Other
	37.02	**成卷的未曝光摄影感光胶片，用纸、纸板及纺织物以外任何材料制成;未曝光的一次成像感光卷片:**					**Photographic film in rolls, sensitised, unexposed, of any material other than paper, paperboard or textiles; instant print film in rolls, sensitised, unexposed:**
2697	3702.1000	-X光用	10	0 冰岛IS,哥CR,秘鲁PE,新西兰NZ,智利CL 4 瑞士CH 6 澳AU 8.6 韩国KR	0 受惠国$_1$LD$_1$	40	-For X-ray
		-无齿孔的其他胶片，宽度不超过105毫米:					-Other film, without perforations, of a width not exceeding 105mm:
		--彩色摄影用:					--For colour photography (polychrome) :

①协定税率: 12 元/平方米
Agreement Import Tariff: 12¥/m^2
②协定税率: 9 元/平方米
Agreement Import Tariff: 9¥/m^2

序号 No.	税则号列 Tariff Line	中文货品名称 Article Description in Chinese	最惠国税率 MFN(%)	协定税率 Agreement(%)	特惠税率 SP(%)	普通税率 Gen(%)	英文货品名称 Article Description
2698	3702.3110	---一次成像卷片	5	0 澳AU,巴PK,冰岛IS,东盟AS,哥CR,秘鲁PE,瑞士CH,新西兰NZ,智利CL 3 韩国KR	0 受惠国LD	40	---Instant print film
2699	3702.3190	---其他	①	0 冰岛IS,东盟AS,哥CR,新加坡SG,新西兰NZ,智利CL 12 秘鲁PE 24 澳AU	0 受惠国$_1$LD$_1$	②	---Other
		--其他涂卤化银乳液的:					--Other, with silver halide emulsion:
2700	3702.3210	---一次成像卷片	5	0 澳AU,巴PK,冰岛IS,东盟AS,哥CR,秘鲁PE,瑞士CH,新西兰NZ,智利CL 3 韩国KR	0 受惠国LD	40	---Instant print film
2701	3702.3220	---照相制版用	③	0 冰岛IS,东盟AS,哥CR,秘鲁PE,新西兰NZ,智利CL 4 瑞士CH 6 澳AU ⑤ 巴PK ⑥ 韩国KR	0 受惠国$_1$LD$_1$	④	---For preparing printing plates or cylinders
2702	3702.3290	---其他	⑦	0 冰岛IS,东盟AS,哥CR,新加坡SG,新西兰NZ,智利CL 6.6 秘鲁PE 13.2 澳AU 15.4 瑞士CH ⑨ 韩国KR	0 受惠国$_1$LD$_1$	⑧	---Other
		--其他:					--Other:
2703	3702.3920	---照相制版用	⑩	0 冰岛IS,东盟AS,哥CR,秘鲁PE,新西兰NZ,智利CL 4 瑞士CH 6 澳AU ⑫ 巴PK ⑬ 韩国KR	0 受惠国$_1$LD$_1$	⑪	---For preparing printing plates or cylinders

①**最惠国税率**: 67 元/平方米
MFN Tariff: 67¥/m^2
②**普通税率**: 433 元/平方米
General Duty: 433¥/m^2
③**最惠国税率**: 4.5 元/平方米
MFN Tariff: 4.5¥/m^2
④**普通税率**: 104 元/平方米
General Duty: 104¥/m^2
⑤**协定税率**: 2.25 元/平方米
Agreement Import Tariff: 2.25¥/m^2
⑥**协定税率**: 3.6 元/平方米
Agreement Import Tariff: 3.6¥/m^2
⑦**最惠国税率**: 21 元/平方米
MFN Tariff: 21¥/m^2
⑧**普通税率**: 202 元/平方米
General Duty: 202¥/m^2
⑨**协定税率**: 18.9 元/平方米
Agreement Import Tariff: 18.9¥/m^2
⑩**最惠国税率**: 12 元/平方米
MFN Tariff: 12¥/m^2
⑪**普通税率**: 104 元/平方米
General Duty: 104¥/m^2
⑫**协定税率**: 6 元/平方米
Agreement Import Tariff: 6¥/m^2
⑬**协定税率**: 9.6 元/平方米
Agreement Import Tariff: 9.6¥/m^2

序号 No.	税则号列 Tariff Line	中文货品名称 Article Description in Chinese	最惠国税率 MFN(%)	协定税率 Agreement(%)	特惠税率 SP(%)	普通税率 Gen(%)	英文货品名称 Article Description
2704	3702.3990	---其他	①	0 冰岛IS,东盟AS,哥CR,新加坡SG,新西兰NZ,智利CL 6.6 秘鲁PE 13.2 澳AU 15.4 瑞士CH ③ 韩国KR	0 受惠国$_1$LD$_1$	②	---Other
		-无齿孔的其他胶片，宽度超过105毫米:					-Other film, without perforations, of a width exceeding 105mm:
2705	3702.4100	--彩色摄影用，宽度超过610毫米，长度超过200米	④	0 冰岛IS,哥CR,新西兰NZ,智利CL 4.8 秘鲁PE 9.6 澳AU 11.2 瑞士CH	0 受惠国$_1$LD$_1$	⑤	--Of a width exceeding 610mm and of a length exceeding 200m, for colour photography (polychrome)
		--非彩色摄影用，宽度超过610毫米，长度超过200米:					--Of a width exceeding 610 mm and of a length exceeding 200m, other than for colour photography:
		---照相制版用:					---For preparing printing plates or cylinders:
2706	3702.4221	----印刷电路板制造用光致抗蚀干膜	⑥	0 冰岛IS,东盟AS,哥CR,秘鲁PE,新加坡SG,新西兰NZ,智利CL 4 瑞士CH 6 澳AU ⑧ 巴PK	0 受惠国$_1$LD$_1$	⑦	----Wide anticorrosive photographic plate for printed circuit processing
2707	3702.4229	----其他	⑨	0 冰岛IS,东盟AS,哥CR,秘鲁PE,新西兰NZ,智利CL 4 瑞士CH 6 澳AU ⑪ 巴PK ⑫ 韩国KR	0 受惠国$_1$LD$_1$	⑩	----Other
		---其他:					---Other:

①**最惠国税率**: 24 元/平方米
MFN Tariff: 24¥/m^2
②**普通税率**: 202 元/平方米
General Duty: 202¥/m^2
③**协定税率**: 21.6 元/平方米
Agreement Import Tariff: 21.6¥/m^2
④**最惠国税率**: 7.1 元/平方米
MFN Tariff: 7.1¥/m^2
⑤**普通税率**: 202 元/平方米
General Duty: 202¥/m^2
⑥**最惠国税率**: 0.6 元/平方米
MFN Tariff: 0.6¥/m^2
⑦**普通税率**: 110 元/平方米
General Duty: 110¥/m^2
⑧**协定税率**: 0.3 元/平方米
Agreement Import Tariff: 0.3¥/m^2
⑨**最惠国税率**: 1.6 元/平方米
MFN Tariff: 1.6¥/m^2
⑩**普通税率**: 110 元/平方米
General Duty: 110¥/m^2
⑪**协定税率**: 0.8 元/平方米
Agreement Import Tariff: 0.8¥/m^2
⑫**协定税率**: 1.2 元/平方米
Agreement Import Tariff: 1.2¥/m^2

序号 No.	税则号列 Tariff Line	中文货品名称 Article Description in Chinese	最惠国税率 MFN(%)	协定税率 Agreement(%)	特惠税率 SP(%)	普通税率 Gen(%)	英文货品名称 Article Description
2708	3702.4292	----红色或红外激光胶片	①	0 冰岛IS,东盟AS,哥CR,新加坡SG,新西兰NZ,智利CL 4.8 秘鲁PE 9.6 澳AU 11.2 瑞士CH ③ 韩国KR	0 受惠国$_1$LD$_1$	②	----Red or infra-red laser film
	ex37024292	红色或红外激光胶片，宽度>80cm，长度大于1000m	④				Red or infra-red laser film width>80cm, length>1000m
2709	3702.4299	----其他	⑤	0 冰岛IS,东盟AS,哥CR,新加坡SG,新西兰NZ,智利CL 4.8 秘鲁PE 9.6 澳AU 11.2 瑞士CH ⑦ 韩国KR	0 受惠国$_1$LD$_1$	⑥	----Other
		--宽度超过610毫米，长度不超过200米：					--Of a width exceeding 610mm and of a length not exceeding 200m:
		---照相制版用：					---For preparing printing plates or cylinders:
2710	3702.4321	----激光照排片	⑧	0 冰岛IS,东盟AS,哥CR,秘鲁PE,新西兰NZ,智利CL 4 瑞士CH 6 澳AU ⑩ 巴PK ⑪ 韩国KR	0 受惠国$_1$LD$_1$	⑨	----Laser phototypesetting film
2711	3702.4329	----其他	⑫	0 冰岛IS,东盟AS,哥CR,秘鲁PE,新西兰NZ,智利CL 4 瑞士CH 6 澳AU ⑭ 巴PK ⑮ 韩国KR	0 受惠国$_1$LD$_1$	⑬	----Other

①**最惠国税率**: 2.4 元/平方米
MFN Tariff: 2.4¥/m^2
②**普通税率**: 213 元/平方米
General Duty: 213¥/m^2
③**协定税率**: 1.9 元/平方米
Agreement Import Tariff: 1.9¥/m^2
④**暂定最惠国税率**: 1.05 元/平方米
Interim MFN Tariff: 1.05¥/m^2
⑤**最惠国税率**: 7 元/平方米
MFN Tariff: 7¥/m^2
⑥**普通税率**: 213 元/平方米
General Duty: 213¥/m^2
⑦**协定税率**: 5.6 元/平方米
Agreement Import Tariff: 5.6¥/m^2
⑧**最惠国税率**: 1.8 元/平方米
MFN Tariff: 1.8¥/m^2
⑨**普通税率**: 104 元/平方米
General Duty: 104¥/m^2
⑩**协定税率**: 0.9 元/平方米
Agreement Import Tariff: 0.9¥/m^2
⑪**协定税率**: 1.4 元/平方米
Agreement Import Tariff: 1.4¥/m^2
⑫**最惠国税率**: 3.7 元/平方米
MFN Tariff: 3.7¥/m^2
⑬**普通税率**: 104 元/平方米
General Duty: 104¥/m^2
⑭**协定税率**: 1.85 元/平方米
Agreement Import Tariff: 1.85¥/m^2
⑮**协定税率**: 2.9 元/平方米
Agreement Import Tariff: 2.9¥/m^2

序号 No.	税则号列 Tariff Line	中文货品名称 Article Description in Chinese	最惠国税率 MFN(%)	协定税率 Agreement(%)	特惠税率 SP(%)	普通税率 Gen(%)	英文货品名称 Article Description
2712	3702.4390	---其他	①	0 冰岛IS,东盟AS,哥CR,新加坡SG,新西兰NZ,智利CL 6 秘鲁PE 12 澳AU 14 瑞士CH ③ 韩国KR	0 受惠国$_1$LD$_1$	②	---Other
		--宽度超过105毫米，但不超过610毫米：					--Of a width exceeding 105 mm but not exceeding 610mm:
		---照相制版用：					---For preparing printing plates or cylinders:
2713	3702.4421	----激光照排片	④	0 冰岛IS,东盟AS,哥CR,秘鲁PE,新西兰NZ,智利CL 4 瑞士CH 6 澳AU ⑥ 巴PK ⑦ 韩国KR	0 受惠国$_1$LD$_1$	⑤	----Laser phototypesetting film
2714	3702.4422	----印刷电路板制造用光致抗蚀干膜	⑧	0 冰岛IS,东盟AS,哥CR,秘鲁PE,新西兰NZ,智利CL 4 瑞士CH 6 澳AU ⑩ 巴PK	0 受惠国$_1$LD$_1$	⑨	----Narrow anticorrosive photographic plate for printed circuit processing
2715	3702.4429	----其他	⑪	0 冰岛IS,东盟AS,哥CR,秘鲁PE,新西兰NZ,智利CL 4 瑞士CH 6 澳AU ⑬ 巴PK ⑭ 韩国KR	0 受惠国$_1$LD$_1$	⑫	----Other

①最惠国税率: 17 元/平方米
MFN Tariff: 17¥/m^2
②普通税率: 202 元/平方米
General Duty: 202¥/m^2
③协定税率: 14.7 元/平方米
Agreement Import Tariff: 14.7¥/m^2
④最惠国税率: 2.0 元/平方米
MFN Tariff: 2.0¥/m^2
⑤普通税率: 115 元/平方米
General Duty: 115¥/m^2
⑥协定税率: 1.0 元/平方米
Agreement Import Tariff: 1.0¥/m^2
⑦协定税率: 1.6 元/平方米
Agreement Import Tariff: 1.6¥/m^2
⑧最惠国税率: 0.9 元/平方米
MFN Tariff: 0.9¥/m^2
⑨普通税率: 115 元/平方米
General Duty: 115¥/m^2
⑩协定税率: 0.45 元/平方米
Agreement Import Tariff: 0.45¥/m^2
⑪最惠国税率: 2.9 元/平方米
MFN Tariff: 2.9¥/m^2
⑫普通税率: 115 元/平方米
General Duty: 115¥/m^2
⑬协定税率: 1.45 元/平方米
Agreement Import Tariff: 1.45¥/m^2
⑭协定税率: 2.3 元/平方米
Agreement Import Tariff: 2.3¥/m^2

序号 No.	税则号列 Tariff Line	中文货品名称 Article Description in Chinese	最惠国税率 MFN(%)	协定税率 Agreement(%)	特惠税率 SP(%)	普通税率 Gen(%)	英文货品名称 Article Description
2716	3702.4490	---其他	①	0 冰岛IS,东盟AS,哥CR,新加坡SG,新西兰NZ,智利CL 6 秘鲁PE 12 澳AU 14 瑞士CH ③ 韩国KR	0 受惠国$_1$LD$_1$	②	---Other
		-彩色摄影用的其他胶片:					-Other film, for colour photography (polychrome) :
2717	3702.5200	--宽度不超过16毫米	④	0 冰岛IS,东盟AS,哥CR,新加坡SG,新西兰NZ,智利CL 14.1 秘鲁PE 28.2 澳AU	0 受惠国$_1$LD$_1$	⑤	--Of a width not exceeding 16mm
2718	3702.5300	--幻灯片用，宽度超过16毫米，但不超过35毫米，长度不超过30米	⑥	0 冰岛IS,东盟AS,哥CR,香港HK,新加坡SG,新西兰NZ,智利CL 14.1 秘鲁PE 28.2 澳AU	0 受惠国$_1$LD$_1$	⑦	--Of a width exceeding16mm but not exceeding 35mm and of a length not exceeding 30m, for slides
		--非幻灯片用，宽度超过16毫米，但不超过35毫米，长度不超过30米:					--Of a width exceeding 16 mm but not exceeding 35mm and of a length not exceeding 30m, other than for slides:
2719	3702.5410	---宽度为35毫米，长度不超过2米	⑧	0 冰岛IS,哥CR,香港HK,新西兰NZ,智利CL 5.4 秘鲁PE 10.8 澳AU 12.6 瑞士CH ⑩ 韩国KR	0 受惠国$_1$LD$_1$	⑨	---Of a width 35mm and of a length not exceeding 2m
2720	3702.5490	---其他	⑪	0 冰岛IS,哥CR,香港HK,新西兰NZ,智利CL 5.4 秘鲁PE 10.8 澳AU 12.6 瑞士CH ⑬ 韩国KR	0 受惠国$_1$LD$_1$	⑫	---Other
		--宽度超过16毫米，但不超过35毫米，长度超过30米:					--Of a width exceeding 16mm but not exceeding 35mm and of a length exceeding 30m:

①**最惠国税率**: 27 元/平方米
MFN Tariff: 27¥/m^2
②**普通税率**: 202 元/平方米
General Duty: 202¥/m^2
③**协定税率**: 23.4 元/平方米
Agreement Import Tariff: 23.4¥/m^2
④**最惠国税率**: 95 元/平方米
MFN Tariff: 95¥/m^2
⑤**普通税率**: 433 元/平方米
General Duty: 433¥/m^2
⑥**最惠国税率**: 128 元/平方米
MFN Tariff: 128¥/m^2
⑦**普通税率**: 433 元/平方米
General Duty: 433¥/m^2
⑧**最惠国税率**: 22 元/平方米
MFN Tariff: 22¥/m^2
⑨**普通税率**: 433 元/平方米
General Duty: 433¥/m^2
⑩**协定税率**: 19 元/平方米
Agreement Import Tariff: 19¥/m^2
⑪**最惠国税率**: 24 元/平方米
MFN Tariff: 24¥/m^2
⑫**普通税率**: 433 元/平方米
General Duty: 433¥/m^2
⑬**协定税率**: 20.8 元/平方米
Agreement Import Tariff: 20.8¥/m^2

序号 No.	税则号列 Tariff Line	中文货品名称 Article Description in Chinese	最惠国税率 MFN(%)	协定税率 Agreement(%)	特惠税率 SP(%)	普通税率 Gen(%)	英文货品名称 Article Description
2721	3702.5520	---电影胶片	①	0 冰岛IS,哥CR,新西兰NZ,智利CL 7.8 秘鲁PE 15.6 澳AU 20 东盟AS	0 受惠国$_1$LD$_1$	②	---Cinematographic film
2722	3702.5590	---其他	③	0 冰岛IS,哥CR,新西兰NZ,智利CL 20 东盟AS 24 澳AU	0 受惠国$_1$LD$_2$	④	---Other
		--宽度超过35毫米:					--Of a width exceeding 35mm:
2723	3702.5620	---电影胶片	⑤	0 冰岛IS,东盟AS,哥CR,新加坡SG,新西兰NZ,智利CL 7.2 秘鲁PE 14.4 澳AU 16.8 瑞士CH ⑦ 韩国KR	0 受惠国$_1$LD$_1$	⑥	---Cinematographic film
2724	3702.5690	---其他	⑧	0 冰岛IS,东盟AS,哥CR,新加坡SG,新西兰NZ,智利CL 12 秘鲁PE 24 澳AU	0 受惠国$_1$LD$_1$	⑨	---Other
		-其他:					-Other:
2725	3702.9600	--宽度不超过35毫米，长度不超过30米	⑩	0 冰岛IS,哥CR,新西兰NZ,智利CL 6 秘鲁PE 12 澳AU 14 瑞士CH ⑫ 韩国KR	0 受惠国$_1$LD$_1$	⑪	--Of a width not exceeding 35mm and of a length not exceeding 30m
2726	3702.9700	--宽度不超过35毫米，长度超过30米	⑬	0 冰岛IS,哥CR,新西兰NZ,智利CL 5.4 秘鲁PE 10.8 澳AU 12.6 瑞士CH ⑮ 韩国KR ⑯ 巴PK	0 受惠国$_1$LD$_1$	⑭	--Of a width not exceeding 35mm and of a length exceeding 30m

①**最惠国税率**: 9 元/平方米
MFN Tariff: 9¥/m^2
②**普通税率**: 232 元/平方米
General Duty: 232¥/m^2
③**最惠国税率**: 27 元/平方米
MFN Tariff: 27¥/m^2
④**普通税率**: 433 元/平方米
General Duty: 433¥/m^2
⑤**最惠国税率**: 13 元/平方米
MFN Tariff: 13¥/m^2
⑥**普通税率**: 232 元/平方米
General Duty: 232¥/m^2
⑦**协定税率**: 11.7 元/平方米
Agreement Import Tariff: 11.7¥/m^2
⑧**最惠国税率**: 74 元/平方米
MFN Tariff: 74¥/m^2
⑨**普通税率**: 433 元/平方米
General Duty: 433¥/m^2
⑩**最惠国税率**: 21 元/平方米
MFN Tariff: 21¥/m^2
⑪**普通税率**: 210 元/平方米
General Duty: 210¥/m^2
⑫**协定税率**: 18.2 元/平方米
Agreement Import Tariff: 18.2¥/m^2
⑬**最惠国税率**: 9 元/平方米
MFN Tariff: 9¥/m^2
⑭**普通税率**: 210 元/平方米
General Duty: 210¥/m^2
⑮**协定税率**: 7.8 元/平方米
Agreement Import Tariff: 7.8¥/m^2
⑯**协定税率**: 9 元/平方米
Agreement Import Tariff: 9¥/m^2

序号 No.	税则号列 Tariff Line	中文货品名称 Article Description in Chinese	最惠国税率 MFN(%)	协定税率 Agreement(%)	特惠税率 SP(%)	普通税率 Gen(%)	英文货品名称 Article Description
2727	3702.9800	--宽度超过35毫米	①	0 冰岛IS,东盟AS,哥CR,新加坡SG,新西兰NZ,智利CL 5.4 秘鲁PE 10.8 澳AU 12.6 瑞士CH ③ 巴PK,韩国KR	0 受惠国$_1$LD$_1$	②	--Of a width exceeding 35mm
	37.03	**未曝光的摄影感光纸、纸板及纺织物:**					**Photographic paper, paperboard and textiles, sensitised, unexposed:**
		-成卷，宽度超过610毫米:					-In rolls of a width exceeding 610mm:
2728	3703.1010	---感光纸及纸板	18	0 冰岛IS,哥CR,新西兰NZ,智利CL 5.4 秘鲁PE 10.8 澳AU 12.6 瑞士CH 15.6 韩国KR	0 受惠国$_1$LD$_1$	100	---Photographic paper and paperboard
2729	3703.1090	---其他	18	0 冰岛IS,哥CR,新西兰NZ,智利CL 5.4 秘鲁PE 10.8 澳AU 12.6 瑞士CH 15.6 韩国KR	0 受惠国$_1$LD$_1$	70	---Other
		-其他，彩色摄影用:					-Other, for colour photography (polychrome) :
2730	3703.2010	---感光纸及纸板	35	0 冰岛IS,哥CR,香港HK,新西兰NZ,智利CL 20 东盟AS 21 澳AU	0 受惠国$_2$LD$_2$	100	---Photographic paper and paperboard
2731	3703.2090	---其他	18	0 冰岛IS,哥CR,香港HK,新西兰NZ,智利CL 5.4 秘鲁PE 10.8 澳AU 12.6 瑞士CH 15.6 韩国KR	0 受惠国$_1$LD$_1$	70	---Other
		-其他:					-Other:
2732	3703.9010	---感光纸及纸板	35	0 冰岛IS,哥CR,新西兰NZ,智利CL 20 东盟AS 21 澳AU	0 受惠国$_2$LD$_2$	100	---Photographic paper and paperboard
2733	3703.9090	---其他	18	0 冰岛IS,哥CR,新西兰NZ,智利CL 5.4 秘鲁PE 10.8 澳AU 12.6 瑞士CH 15.6 韩国KR	0 受惠国$_1$LD$_1$	70	---Other
	37.04	**已曝光未冲洗的摄影硬片、软片、纸、纸板及纺织物:**					**Photographic plates, film, paper, paperboard and textiles, exposed but not developed:**
2734	3704.0010	---电影胶片	6.5	0 冰岛IS,东盟AS,哥CR,秘鲁PE,新西兰NZ,智利CL 2.6 瑞士CH 3.9 澳AU,韩国KR 5 巴PK	0 受惠国$_1$LD$_1$	30	---Cinematographic film

①最惠国税率: 10 元/平方米
MFN Tariff: 10¥/m^2
②普通税率: 210 元/平方米
General Duty: 210¥/m^2
③协定税率: 8 元/平方米
Agreement Import Tariff: 8¥/m^2

序号 No.	税则号列 Tariff Line	中文货品名称 Article Description in Chinese	最惠国税率 MFN(%)	协定税率 Agreement(%)	特惠税率 SP(%)	普通税率 Gen(%)	英文货品名称 Article Description
2735	3704.0090	---其他	18	0 冰岛IS,东盟AS,哥CR,新加坡SG,新西兰NZ,智利CL 5.4 秘鲁PE 10.8 澳AU 12.6 瑞士CH 14.4 巴PK,韩国KR	0 受惠国1LD1	70	---Other
	37.05	**已曝光已冲洗的摄影硬片及软片，但电影胶片除外：**					**Photographic plates and film, exposed and developed, other than cinematographic film:**
2736	3705.1000	-供复制胶版用	18	0 冰岛IS,东盟AS,哥CR,新加坡SG,新西兰NZ,智利CL 5.4 秘鲁PE 10.8 澳AU 12.6 瑞士CH 14.4 巴PK,韩国KR	0 受惠国1LD1	70	-For offset reproduction
		-其他：					-Other:
2737	3705.9010	---教学专用幻灯片	0		0 受惠国LD	0	---Lantern slides, for educational use only
		---缩微胶片：					---Microfilms:
2738	3705.9021	----书籍、报刊的	0		0 受惠国LD	0	----For printed books and newspapers
2739	3705.9029	----其他	4	0 澳AU,巴PK,冰岛IS,东盟AS,哥CR,韩国KR,秘鲁PE,瑞士CH,新西兰NZ,智利CL	0 受惠国1LD1	14	----Other
2740	3705.9090	---其他	18	0 冰岛IS,东盟AS,哥CR,新加坡SG,新西兰NZ,智利CL 5.4 秘鲁PE 10.8 澳AU 12.6 瑞士CH 14.4 巴PK,韩国KR	0 受惠国1LD1	70	---Other
	37.06	**已曝光已冲洗的电影胶片，不论是否配有声道或仅有声道：**					**Cinematographic film, exposed and developed, whether or not incorporating soundtrack or consisting only of soundtrack:**
		-宽度在35毫米及以上：					-Of a width of 35mm or more:
2741	3706.1010	---教学专用	0		0 受惠国LD	0	---For educational use only
2742	3706.1090	---其他	5	0 澳AU,巴PK,冰岛IS,东盟AS,哥CR,秘鲁PE,瑞士CH,香港HK,新西兰NZ,智利CL 4.3 韩国KR	0 受惠国LD	14	---Other
		-其他：					-Other:
2743	3706.9010	---教学专用	0		0 受惠国LD	0	---For educational use only
2744	3706.9090	---其他	4	0 澳AU,巴PK,冰岛IS,东盟AS,哥CR,韩国KR,秘鲁PE,瑞士CH,香港HK,新西兰NZ,智利CL	0 受惠国LD	14	---Other
	37.07	**摄影用化学制剂（不包括上光漆、胶水、粘合剂及类似制剂）；摄影用未混合产品；定量包装或零售包装可立即使用的：**					**Chemical preparations for photographic uses (other than varnishes, glues, adhesives and similar preparations) ; unmixed products for photographic uses, put up in measured portions or put up for retail sale in a form ready for use:**
2745	3707.1000	-感光乳液	8	0 澳门MO,冰岛IS,东盟AS,哥CR,秘鲁PE,新西兰NZ,智利CL 4.8 澳AU 5 巴PK 5.6 瑞士CH 6.9 韩国KR	0 受惠国LD	35	-Sensitizing emulsions

序号 No.	税则号列 Tariff Line	中文货品名称 Article Description in Chinese	最惠国税率 MFN(%)	协定税率 Agreement(%)	特惠税率 SP(%)	普通税率 Gen(%)	英文货品名称 Article Description
	ex37071000	感光乳剂（不含银的）	Δ4				Sensitizing emulsions (without silver component)
		-其他：					-Other:
2746	3707.9010	---冲洗照相胶卷及相片用	16	0 冰岛IS,东盟AS,哥CR,香港HK,新加坡SG,新西兰NZ,智利CL 4.8 秘鲁PE 9.6 澳AU 11.2 瑞士CH 12.8 巴PK 13.8 韩国KR	0 受惠国$_1$LD$_1$	100	---For use in developing photographic film and photographs
2747	3707.9020	---复印机用	10Δ8	0 澳门MO,冰岛IS,东盟AS,哥CR,香港HK,新加坡SG,新西兰NZ,智利CL 3 秘鲁PE 4 瑞士CH 5 巴PK 6 澳AU 8 韩国KR	0 受惠国LD	45	---For use in photo-copying apparatus
2748	3707.9090	---其他	8	0 澳门MO,冰岛IS,东盟AS,哥CR,秘鲁PE,香港HK,新西兰NZ,智利CL 4.8 澳AU 5 巴PK 5.6 瑞士CH 6.4 韩国KR	0 受惠国LD	35	---Other

第三十八章 杂项化学产品

注释:

一、本章不包括:

（一）单独的已有化学定义的元素及化合物，但下列各项除外:

1. 人造石墨（税号38.01）;
2. 制成税号38.08所述的形状或包装的杀虫剂、杀鼠剂、杀菌剂、除草剂、抗萌剂、植物生长调节剂、消毒剂及类似产品;
3. 灭火器的装配药及已装药的灭火弹（税号38.13）;
4. 下列注释二所规定的检定参照物;
5. 下列注释三（一）及三（三）所规定的产品。

（二）配制食品用的与食物或其他营养物质混合的化学品（一般归入税号21.06）;

（三）符合第二十六章注释三（一）或三（二）的规定，含有金属，砷及其混合物的矿渣、矿灰及残渣（包括淤渣，但下水道淤泥除外）（税目26.20）;

（四）药品（税号30.03及30.04）;

（五）用于提取贱金属或生产贱金属化合物的废催化剂（税号26.20），主要用于回收贵金属的废催化剂（税号71.12），或某种形状（例如，精细粉末或纱网状）的金属或金属合金催化剂（第十四类或第十五类）。

二、

（一）税目38.22所称的“检定参照物”，是指附有证书的参照物，该证书标明了参照物属性的指标、确定这些指标的方法以及与每一指标相关的确定度，这些参照物适用于分析、校准和比较。

（二）除第二十八章和二十九章的产品外，检定参照物在本目录中应优先归入税目38.22。

三、税号38.24包括不归入本目录其他税号的下列货品:

（一）每颗重量不小于2.5克的氧化镁、碱金属或碱土金属卤化物制成的培养晶体（光学元件除外）;

（二）杂醇油;骨焦油;

（三）零售包装的除墨剂;

（四）零售包装的蜡纸改正液，其他改正液及改正带（税目96.12的产品除外）；以及

（五）可熔性陶瓷测温器（例如，塞格测温锥）。

Chapter 38 Miscellaneous chemical products

Notes:

1. This Chapter does not cover:

(a) Separate chemically defined elements or compounds with the exception of the following:

(1) Artificial graphite (heading No.38.01) ;

(2) Insecticides, rodenticides, fungicides, herbicides, anti-sprouting products and plant-growth regulators, disinfectants and similar products, put up as described in heading No.38.08;

(3) Products put up as charges for fire-extinguishers or put up in fire-extinguishing grenades (heading No.38.13) ;

(4) Certified reference materials specified in Note 2 below;

(5) Products specified in Note 3(a) or 3(c) below;

(b) Mixtures of chemicals with foodstuffs or other substances with nutritive value, of a kind used in the preparations of human foodstuffs (generally heading No.21.06) ;

(c) Slag, ash and residues (including sludges, other than sewage sludge), containing metals, arsenic or their mixtures and meeting the requirements of Note 3(a) or 3 (b) to Chapter 26 (heading 26.20) ;

(d) Medicaments (heading No.30.03 or 30.04) ;

(e) Spent catalysts of a kind used for the extraction of base metals or for the manufacture of chemical compounds of base metals (heading No.26.20), spent catalysts of a kind used princi pally for the recovery of precious metal (heading No.71.12) or catalysts consisting or metals of metal alloys in the form of, for example, finely divided powder or woven gauze (Section XIV or XV) .

2.

(a) For the purpose of heading 38.22, the expression “certified reference materials” means reference materials which are accompanied by a certificate which indicates the values of the certified properties, the methods used to determine these values and the degree of certainty associated with each value and which are suitable for analytical, calibrating or referenc ing purboses.

(b) With the exception of the products of Chapter 28 or 29, for the classification of certified reference materials, heading 38.22 shall take precedence over any other heading in the Nomenclature.”

3. Heading No.38.24 includes the following goods which are not to be classified in any other heading of the Nomenclature:

(a) Cultured crystals (other than optical elements) weighing not less than 2.5g each, of magnesium oxide or of the halides of the alkali or alkaline-earth metals;

(b) Fusel oil; Dippel s oil;

(c) Ink removers put up in packings for retail sale;

(d) Stencil correctors, other correcting fluids and correction tapes (other thanthose of heading 96.12), put up in packings for retail sale; and

(e) Ceramic firing testers, fusible (for example, Seger-cones).

四、本目录所称“城市垃圾”是指一种从家庭、宾馆、餐馆、医院、商店、办公室等收集来的废物、马路和人行道的垃圾以及建筑垃圾或废墟废物。城市垃圾通常含有大量各种各样的材料，例如，塑料、橡胶、木材、纸张、纺织品、玻璃、金属、食物、破碎家具和其他已损坏或被丢弃的物品，但不包括：

（一）已从垃圾中分拣出来的单独的材料或物品，例如，塑料、橡胶、木材、纸张、纺织品、玻璃、金属及电池的废品，这些材料或物品应归入本目录中适当税目；

（二）工业废物；

（三）在第三十章注释四（十）所规定的废药物；

（四）本章注释六（一）所规定的医疗废物。

五、税目38.25所称“下水道淤泥”，是指城市污水处理厂产生的淤渣，包括预处理的废物、洗涤污垢和性质不稳定的淤泥。但适合作为肥料用的性质稳定的淤泥除外（第三十一章）。

六、税目38.25所称“其他废物”适用于：

（一）医疗废物，即医学研究、诊断、治疗以及其他内科、外科、牙科或兽医治疗所产生的被污染的废物，通常含有病菌和药物，需作专门的处理（例如，脏的敷料、用过的手套和注射器）；

（二）废有机溶剂；

（三）废的金属酸洗液、液压油、制动油和防冻液；

（四）其他化学工业及相关工业的废物。

但不包括主要含有石油及从沥青矿物提取的油类的废油（税目27.10）。

七、税目38.26所称的“生物柴油”，是指从动植物油脂（不论是否使用过）得到的用作燃料的脂肪酸单烷基酯。

子目注释：

一、子目3808.50仅包括税目38.08的货品，含有一种或多种下列物质：艾氏剂（ISO）；乐杀螨（ISO）；毒杀芬（ISO）；敌菌丹（ISO）；氯丹（ISO）；杀虫脒（ISO）；乙酯杀螨醇（ISO）；滴滴涕（ISO，INN）〔1，1，1-三氯-2，2-双（4-氯苯基）乙烷〕；狄氏剂（ISO，INN）；4，6-二硝基邻甲酚（二硝酚（ISO））及其盐；地乐酚（ISO）及其盐或酯；1，2-二溴乙烷（ISO）；1，2-二氯乙烷（ISO）；氟乙酰胺（ISO）；七氯（ISO）；六氯苯（ISO）；1，2，3，4，5，6-六氯环己烷〔六六六（ISO）〕，包括林丹（ISO，INN）；汞化合物；甲胺磷（ISO）；久效磷（ISO）；环氧乙烷（氧化乙烯）；对硫磷（ISO）；甲基对硫磷（ISO）；五氯苯酚（ISO）及其盐或酯；磷胺（ISO）；2，4，5-涕（ISO）（2，4，5-

4. Throughout the Nomenclature, “municipal waste” means waste of a kind collected from households, hotels, res-tau-rants, hospitals, shops, offices, etc., road and pave-ment sweepings, as well as construction and demolition waste. Municipal waste generally contains a large variety of materials such as plastics, rubber, wood, paper, textiles, glass, metals, food materials, broken furniture and other damaged or discarded articles.The term “municipal waste”, however, does not cover:

(a) Individual materials or articles segregated from the waste, such as wastes of plastics, rubber, wood, paper, textiles, glass or metals and spent batteries which fall in their appropriate head ings of the Nomenclature;

(b) Industrial waste;

(c) Waste pharmaceuticals, as defined in Note 4(k) to Chapter 30; or

(d) Clinical waste, as defined in Note6(a) below.

5. For the purposes of heading 38.25, “sewage sludge” means sludge arising from urban effluent treatment plant and includes pretrea-tment waste, scourings and unstabilised sludge. Stabilised sludge when suitable for use as fertiliser is excluded (Chapter 31) .

6. For the purposes of heading38.25, the expression“other wastes” applies to:

(a) Clinical waste, that is, contaminated waste arising from medical research, diagnosis, treatment or other medical, surgical, dental or veterinary procedures, which often contain pathogens and pharmaceutical substances and require special disposal procedures (for example, soiled dressings, used gloves and used syringes) ;

(b) Waste organic solvents;

(c) Wastes of metal pickling liquors, hydraulic fluids, brake fluids and antifreezing fluids; and

(d) Other wastes from chemical or allied industries.

The expression “other wastes” does not, however, cover wastes which contain mainly petroleum oils or oils obtained from bituminous minerals (heading27.10) .

7. For the purposes of heading 38.26, the term “biodiesel” means mono-alkylesters of fatty acids of a kind used as a fuel, derived from animal orvegetable fats and oils whether or not used.

Subheading Notes:

1. Subheading 3808.50 covers only goods of heading 38.08, containing one ormore of the following substances : aldrin (ISO); binapacryl (ISO);camphechlor (ISO) (toxaphene); captafol (ISO); chlordane (ISO);chlordimeform (ISO); chlorobenzilate (ISO); DDT (ISO) (clofenotane (INN),1,1,1-trichloro-2,2-bis (p-chlorophenyl) ethane); dieldrin (ISO, INN); 4,6-dinitro-o-cresol (DNOC (ISO)) or its salts; dinoseb (ISO), its salts or itsesters; ethylene dibromide (ISO) (1,2-dibromoethane); ethylene dichloride(ISO) (1,2-dichloroethane); fluoroacetamide (ISO); heptachlor (ISO); hexachlorobenzene (ISO); 1,2,3,4,5,6-hexachlorocyclohexane (HCH (ISO)),including lindane (ISO, INN); mercury compounds; methamidophos (ISO); monocrotophos (ISO); oxirane (ethylenc oxide); para-

三氯苯氧基乙酸）及其盐或酯；三丁基锡化合物。

子目3808.50还包括含有苯菌灵（ISO）、克百威（ISO）及福美双（ISO）混合物的粉状制剂。

二、子目3825.41和3825.49所称“废有机溶剂”，是指主要含有有机溶剂的废物，不适合再作原产品使用，不论其是否用于回收溶剂。

thion (ISO); parathionmethyl(ISO) (methyl-parathion); pentachlorophenol (ISO), its salts or its esters; phosphamidon (ISO); 2,4,5-T (ISO) (2,4,5-trichlorophenoxyaceticacid), its salts or its esters; tributyltin compounds.

Subheading 3808.50 also covers dustable powder formulations containing amixture of benomyl (ISO), carbofuran (ISO) and thiram (ISO).

2. For the purposes of subheadings 3825.41 and 3825.49, “waste organic solvents”are wastes containing mainly organic solvents, not fit for further use as presented as primary products, whether or not intended for recovery of the solvents.

序号 No.	税则号列 Tariff Line	中文货品名称 Article Description in Chinese	最惠国税率 MFN(%)	协定税率 Agreement(%)	特惠税率 SP(%)	普通税率 Gen(%)	英文货品名称 Article Description
	38.01	**人造石墨;胶态或半胶态石墨;以石墨或其他碳为基本成分的糊状、块状、板状制品或其他半制品:**					**Artificial graphite; colloidal or semi-colloidal graphite; preparations based on graphite or other carbon in the form of pastes, blocks, plates or other semi-manufactures:**
2749	3801.1000	-人造石墨	6.5Δ3	0 冰岛IS,东盟AS,哥CR,秘鲁PE,香港HK,新西兰NZ,智利CL 3.9 澳AU 4.6 瑞士CH 5 巴PK 5.2 韩国KR	0 受惠国LD	30	-Artificial graphite
2750	3801.2000	-胶态或半胶态石墨	6.5	0 冰岛IS,东盟AS,哥CR,秘鲁PE,新西兰NZ,智利CL 2.6 瑞士CH 3.9 澳AU 5 巴PK 5.6 韩国KR	0 受惠国LD	30	-Colloidal or semi-colloidal graphite
2751	3801.3000	-电极用碳糊及炉衬用的类似糊	6.5	0 冰岛IS,东盟AS,哥CR,秘鲁PE,新西兰NZ,智利CL 3.9 澳AU,韩国KR 4.6 瑞士CH 5 巴PK	0 受惠国LD	35	-Carbonaceous pastes for electrodes and similar pastes for furnace linings
		-其他:					-Other:
2752	3801.9010	---表面处理的球化石墨	6.5	0 冰岛IS,东盟AS,哥CR,秘鲁PE,新西兰NZ,智利CL 2.6 瑞士CH 3.9 澳AU,韩国KR 5 巴PK	0 受惠国LD	35	---Surface modified spherical graphite
2753	3801.9090	---其他	6.5	0 冰岛IS,东盟AS,哥CR,秘鲁PE,新西兰NZ,智利CL 2.6 瑞士CH 3.9 澳AU,韩国KR 5 巴PK	0 受惠国LD	35	---Other
	38.02	**活性碳;活性天然矿产品;动物炭黑,包括废动物炭黑:**					**Activated carbon; activated natural mineral products; animal black, including spent animal black:**
		-活性碳:					-Activated carbon:
2754	3802.1010	---木质的	6.5	0 冰岛IS,东盟AS,哥CR,秘鲁PE,新西兰NZ,智利CL 2.6 瑞士CH 3.9 澳AU,韩国KR 5 巴PK 5.5 亚太AP	0 受惠国$_1$LD$_1$	20	---Of wood

序号 No.	税则号列 Tariff Line	中文货品名称 Article Description in Chinese	最惠国税率 MFN(%)	协定税率 Agreement(%)	特惠税率 SP(%)	普通税率 Gen(%)	英文货品名称 Article Description
2755	3802.1090	---其他	6.5	0 冰岛IS,东盟AS,哥CR,秘鲁PE,新西兰NZ,智利CL 2.6 瑞士CH 3.9 澳AU,韩国KR 5 巴PK 5.5 亚太AP	0 受惠国$_1$LD$_1$	20	---Other
2756	3802.9000	-其他	10	0 冰岛IS,东盟AS,哥CR,新加坡SG,新西兰NZ,智利CL 3 秘鲁PE 4 瑞士CH 5 巴PK 6 澳AU 8 韩国KR	0 受惠国$_1$LD$_1$	45	-Other
	38.03	**妥尔油，不论是否精炼**					**Tall oil, whether or not refined**
2757	3803.0000	妥尔油，不论是否精炼	6.5	0 冰岛IS,东盟AS,哥CR,秘鲁PE,新西兰NZ,智利CL 2.6 瑞士CH 3.9 澳AU,韩国KR 5 巴PK	0 受惠国LD	35	Tall oil, whether or not refined
	38.04	**木浆残余碱液，不论是否浓缩、脱糖或经化学处理，包括木素磺酸盐，但不包括税号38.03的妥尔油**					**Residual lyes from the manufacture of wood pulp, whether or not concentrated, desugared or chemically treated, including lignin sulphonates, but excluding tall oil of heading 3803**
2758	3804.0000	木浆残余碱液，不论是否浓缩、脱糖或经化学处理，包括木素磺酸盐，但不包括税号38.03的妥尔油	6.5	0 冰岛IS,东盟AS,哥CR,秘鲁PE,新西兰NZ,智利CL 2.6 瑞士CH 3.9 澳AU 5 巴PK 5.2 韩国KR	0 受惠国$_1$LD$_1$	35	Residual lyes from the manufacture of wood pulp, whether or not concentrated, desugared or chemically treated, including lignin sulphonates, but excluding tall oil of heading No.38.03
	38.05	**脂松节油、木松节油和硫酸盐松节油及其他萜烯油，用蒸馏或其他方法从针叶木制得;粗制二聚戊烯;亚硫酸盐松节油及其他粗制对异丙基苯甲烷;以a萜品醇为基本成分的松油:**					**Gum, wood or sulphate turpentine and other terpenic oils produced by the distillation or other treatment of coniferous woods; crude dipentene; sulphite turpentine and other crude para-cymene; pine oil containing alpha-terpineol as the main constituent:**
2759	3805.1000	-脂松节油、木松节油和硫酸盐松节油	6.5	0 冰岛IS,东盟AS,哥CR,秘鲁PE,新西兰NZ,智利CL 2.6 瑞士CH 3.9 澳AU,韩国KR 5 巴PK	0 受惠国LD	50	-Gum, wood or sulphate turpentine oils
		-其他:					-Other:
2760	3805.9010	---松油	6.5	0 冰岛IS,东盟AS,哥CR,秘鲁PE,新西兰NZ,智利CL 2.6 瑞士CH 3.9 澳AU,韩国KR 5 巴PK	0 受惠国LD	50	---Pine oil
2761	3805.9090	---其他	6.5	0 冰岛IS,东盟AS,哥CR,秘鲁PE,新西兰NZ,智利CL 2.6 瑞士CH 3.9 澳AU,韩国KR 5 巴PK	0 受惠国LD	50	---Other

序号 No.	税则号列 Tariff Line	中文货品名称 Article Description in Chinese	最惠国税率 MFN(%)	协定税率 Agreement(%)	特惠税率 SP(%)	普通税率 Gen(%)	英文货品名称 Article Description
	38.06	**松香和树脂酸及其衍生物;松香精及松香油;再熔胶:**					**Rosin and resin acids, and derivatives thereof; rosin spirit and rosin oils; run gums:**
		-松香及树脂酸:					-Rosin and resin acids:
2762	3806.1010	---松香	10	0 澳门MO,冰岛IS,东盟AS,哥CR,秘鲁PE,新加坡SG,新西兰NZ,智利CL 4 瑞士CH 5 巴PK 6 澳AU 8 韩国KR	0 受惠国$_1$LD$_1$	70	---Rosin
2763	3806.1020	---树脂酸	10	0 澳门MO,冰岛IS,东盟AS,哥CR,秘鲁PE,新西兰NZ,智利CL 4 瑞士CH 5 巴PK 6 澳AU 8 韩国KR	0 受惠国$_1$LD$_1$	70	---Resin acides
		-松香盐、树脂酸盐及松香或树脂酸衍生物的盐，但松香加合物的盐除外:					-Salts of rosin, of resin acids or of derivatives of rosin or resin acids, other than salts of rosin adducts:
2764	3806.2010	---松香盐及树脂酸盐	6.5	0 澳门MO,冰岛IS,东盟AS,哥CR,秘鲁PE,新西兰NZ,智利CL 2.6 瑞士CH 3.9 澳AU,韩国KR 5 巴PK	0 受惠国$_1$LD$_1$	40	---Salts of rosin, of resin acids
2765	3806.2090	---其他	6.5	0 澳门MO,冰岛IS,东盟AS,哥CR,秘鲁PE,新西兰NZ,智利CL 2.6 瑞士CH 3.9 澳AU,韩国KR 5 巴PK	0 受惠国$_1$LD$_1$	40	---Other
2766	3806.3000	-酯胶	6.5	0 澳门MO,冰岛IS,东盟AS,哥CR,秘鲁PE,新西兰NZ,智利CL 2.6 瑞士CH 3.9 澳AU,韩国KR 5 巴PK	0 受惠国$_1$LD$_1$	50	-Ester gums
2767	3806.9000	-其他	6.5	0 澳门MO,冰岛IS,东盟AS,哥CR,秘鲁PE,新西兰NZ,智利CL 2.6 瑞士CH 3.9 澳AU,韩国KR 5 巴PK	0 受惠国$_1$LD$_1$	40	-Other
	38.07	**木焦油;精制木焦油;木杂酚油;粗木精;植物沥青;以松香、树脂酸或植物沥青为基本成分的啤酒桶沥青及类似制品**					**Wood tar; wood tar oils; wood creosote; wood naphtha; vegetable pitch; brewers' pitch and similar preparations based on rosin, resin acids or on vegetable pitch**
2768	3807.0000	木焦油;精制木焦油;木杂酚油;粗木精;植物沥青;以松香、树脂酸或植物沥青为基本成分的啤酒桶沥青及类似制品	6.5	0 冰岛IS,东盟AS,哥CR,秘鲁PE,新西兰NZ,智利CL 2.6 瑞士CH 3.9 澳AU,韩国KR 5 巴PK	0 受惠国$_1$LD$_1$	35	Wood tar; wood tar oils; wood creosote; wood naphtha; vegetable pitch; brewers' pitch and similar preparations based on rosin, resin acids or on vegetable pitch

序号 No.	税则号列 Tariff Line	中文货品名称 Article Description in Chinese	最惠国税率 MFN(%)	协定税率 Agreement(%)	特惠税率 SP(%)	普通税率 Gen(%)	英文货品名称 Article Description
	38.08	杀虫剂、杀鼠剂、杀菌剂、除草剂、抗萌剂、植物生长调节剂、消毒剂及类似产品，零售形状、零售包装或制成制剂及成品（例如，经硫磺处理的带子、杀虫灯芯、蜡烛及捕蝇纸）：					**Insecticides, rodenticides, fungicides, herbicides, anti-sprouting products and plant-growth regulators, disinfectants and similar products, put up in forms or packings for retail sale or as preparations or articles (for example, sulphur-treated bands, wicks and candles, and fly-papers) :**
		-本章子目注释一所规定的货品：					-Goods specified in subheading note 1 to this chapter:
2769	3808.5010	---零售包装	9	0 冰岛IS,东盟AS,哥CR,秘鲁PE,香港HK,新西兰NZ,智利CL 3.6 瑞士CH 5 巴PK 5.4 澳AU,韩国KR	0 受惠国LD	35	---Put up for retail sale
2770	3808.5090	---其他	5	0 澳AU,冰岛IS,东盟AS,哥CR,秘鲁PE,瑞士CH,香港HK,新西兰NZ,智利CL 3 韩国KR	0 受惠国LD	11	---Other
		-其他：					-Other:
		--杀虫剂：					--Insecticides:
		---零售包装：					---Put up for retail sale:
2771	3808.9111	----蚊香	10	0 澳门MO,巴PK,冰岛IS,东盟AS,哥CR,秘鲁PE,新西兰NZ,亚太AP,智利CL 4 瑞士CH 6 澳AU,韩国KR	0 受惠国LD	80	----Mosquito smudges
2772	3808.9112	----生物杀虫剂	10	0 澳门MO,冰岛IS,东盟AS,哥CR,秘鲁PE,香港HK,新西兰NZ,智利CL 4 瑞士CH 5 巴PK 6 澳AU 7 亚太AP 8 韩国KR	0 受惠国LD	35	----Biological products
2773	3808.9119	----其他	10	0 澳门MO,冰岛IS,东盟AS,哥CR,秘鲁PE,香港HK,新西兰NZ,智利CL 4 瑞士CH 5 巴PK 6 澳AU 7 亚太AP 8 韩国KR	0 受惠国LD	35	----Other
2774	3808.9190	---其他	6	0 澳门MO,巴PK,冰岛IS,东盟AS,哥CR,秘鲁PE,香港HK,新西兰NZ,智利CL 3.6 澳AU,韩国KR 4.2 瑞士CH,亚太AP	0 受惠国LD	11	---Other
		--杀菌剂：					--Fungicides:
2775	3808.9210	---零售包装	9	0 冰岛IS,东盟AS,哥CR,秘鲁PE,香港HK,新西兰NZ,智利CL 5 巴PK 5.4 澳AU,韩国KR 6.3 瑞士CH	0 受惠国LD	35	---Put up for retail sale

序号 No.	税则号列 Tariff Line	中文货品名称 Article Description in Chinese	最惠国税率 MFN(%)	协定税率 Agreement(%)	特惠税率 SP(%)	普通税率 Gen(%)	英文货品名称 Article Description
2776	3808.9290	---其他	6	0 冰岛IS,东盟AS,哥CR,秘鲁PE,新西兰NZ,智利CL 3.6 澳AU,韩国KR 4.2 瑞士CH 5 巴PK	0 受惠国LD	11	---Other
		--除草剂、抗萌剂及植物生长调节剂:					--Herbicides, anti-sprouting products and plant-growth regulators:
		---除草剂:					---Herbicides:
2777	3808.9311	----零售包装	9	0 冰岛IS,东盟AS,哥CR,秘鲁PE,新西兰NZ,智利CL 3.6 瑞士CH 5 巴PK 5.4 澳AU,韩国KR	0 受惠国LD	35	----Put up for retai sale
2778	3808.9319	----其他	5	0 澳AU,巴PK,冰岛IS,东盟AS,哥CR,秘鲁PE,新西兰NZ,智利CL 3 韩国KR 3.5 瑞士CH 4.5 亚太AP	0 受惠国LD	11	----Other
		---其他:					---Other:
2779	3808.9391	----零售包装	9	0 冰岛IS,东盟AS,哥CR,秘鲁PE,新西兰NZ,智利CL 3.6 瑞士CH 5 巴PK 5.4 澳AU,韩国KR 8.3 亚太AP	0 受惠国LD	35	----Put up for retail sale
2780	3808.9399	----其他	6	0 冰岛IS,东盟AS,哥CR,秘鲁PE,新西兰NZ,智利CL 2.4 瑞士CH 3.6 澳AU,韩国KR 5 巴PK 5.5 亚太AP	0 受惠国LD	14	----Other
2781	3808.9400	--消毒剂	9	0 冰岛IS,东盟AS,哥CR,秘鲁PE,香港HK,新西兰NZ,智利CL 5 巴PK 5.4 澳AU,韩国KR 6.3 瑞士CH	0 受惠国LD	35	--Disinfectants
		--其他:					--Other:
2782	3808.9910	---零售包装	9	0 冰岛IS,东盟AS,哥CR,秘鲁PE,香港HK,新西兰NZ,智利CL 3.6 瑞士CH 5 巴PK 5.4 澳AU,韩国KR	0 受惠国LD	35	---Put up for retail sale
2783	3808.9990	---其他	9	0 澳门MO,冰岛IS,东盟AS,哥CR,秘鲁PE,新西兰NZ,智利CL 3.6 瑞士CH 5 巴PK 5.4 澳AU,韩国KR	0 受惠国LD	14	---Other
	38.09	纺织、造纸、制革及类似工业用的其他税号未列名的整理剂、染料加速着色或固色助剂及其他产品和制剂（例如，修整剂及媒染剂）:					**Finishing agents, dye carriers to accelerate the dyeing or fixing of dyestuffs and other products and preparations (for example, dressings and mordants), of a kind used in the textile, paper, leather or like industries, not elsewhere specified or included:**

序号 No.	税则号列 Tariff Line	中文货品名称 Article Description in Chinese	最惠国税率 MFN(%)	协定税率 Agreement(%)	特惠税率 SP(%)	普通税率 Gen(%)	英文货品名称 Article Description
2784	3809.1000	-以淀粉物质为基本成分	10	0 巴PK,冰岛IS,东盟AS,哥CR,秘鲁PE,新加坡SG,新西兰NZ,智利CL 4 瑞士CH 6 澳AU 8 韩国KR	0 受惠国LD	35	-With a basis of amylaceous substances
		-其他:					-Other:
2785	3809.9100	--纺织工业及类似工业用	6.5	0 巴PK,冰岛IS,东盟AS,哥CR,秘鲁PE,香港HK,新西兰NZ,智利CL 3.9 澳AU,韩国KR 4.6 瑞士CH 6 亚太AP	0 受惠国LD	35	--Of a kind used in the textile or like industries
2786	3809.9200	--造纸工业及类似工业用	6.5	0 巴PK,冰岛IS,东盟AS,哥CR,秘鲁PE,香港HK,新西兰NZ,智利CL 2.6 瑞士CH 3.9 澳AU 5.2 韩国KR	0 受惠国LD	35	--Of a kind used in the paper or like industries
2787	3809.9300	--制革工业及类似工业用	6.5	0 巴PK,冰岛IS,东盟AS,哥CR,秘鲁PE,香港HK,新西兰NZ,智利CL 2.6 瑞士CH 3.9 澳AU,韩国KR	0 受惠国LD	35	--Of a kind used in the leather or like industries
	38.10	**金属表面酸洗剂;焊接用的焊剂及其他辅助剂;金属及其他材料制成的焊粉或焊膏;作焊条芯子或焊条涂料用的制品:**					**Pickling preparations for metal surfaces; fluxes and other auxiliary preparations for soldering, brazing or welding; soldering, brazing or welding powders and pastes consisting of metal and other materials; preparations of a kind used as cores or coatings for welding electrodes or rods:**
2788	3810.1000	-金属表面酸洗剂;金属及其他材料制成的焊粉或焊膏	6.5	0 澳门MO,冰岛IS,东盟AS,哥CR,秘鲁PE,香港HK,新西兰NZ,智利CL 2.6 瑞士CH 3.9 澳AU 5 巴PK 5.6 韩国KR 6 亚太AP	0 受惠国LD	35	-Pickling preparations for metal surfaces; soldering, brazing or welding powders and pastes consisting of metal and other materials
2789	3810.9000	-其他	6.5	0 冰岛IS,东盟AS,哥CR,秘鲁PE,新西兰NZ,智利CL 2.6 瑞士CH 3.9 澳AU 5 巴PK 5.6 韩国KR	0 受惠国LD	35	-Other
	38.11	**抗震剂、抗氧剂、防胶剂、粘度改良剂、防腐蚀制剂及其他配制添加剂,用于矿物油(包括汽油)或与矿物油同样用途的其他液体:**					**Anti-knock preparations, oxidation inhibitors, gum inhibitors, viscosity improvers, anti-corrosive preparations and other prepared additives, for mineral oils (including gasoline) or for other liquids used for the same purposes as mineral oils:**
		-抗震剂:					-Anti-knock preparations:
2790	3811.1100	--以铅化合物为基本成分	6.5	0 冰岛IS,东盟AS,哥CR,秘鲁PE,新西兰NZ,智利CL 2.6 瑞士CH 3.9 澳AU,韩国KR 5 巴PK	0 受惠国$_1$LD$_1$	35	--Based on lead compounds

序号 No.	税则号列 Tariff Line	中文货品名称 Article Description in Chinese	最惠国税率 MFN(%)	协定税率 Agreement(%)	特惠税率 SP(%)	普通税率 Gen(%)	英文货品名称 Article Description
2791	3811.1900	--其他	6.5	0 冰岛IS,东盟AS,哥CR,秘鲁PE,新西兰NZ,智利CL 2.6 瑞士CH 3.9 澳AU,韩国KR 5 巴PK	0 受惠国$_1$LD$_1$	35	--Other
		-润滑油添加剂:					-Additives for lubricating oils:
2792	3811.2100	--含有石油或从沥青矿物提取的油类	6.5	0 冰岛IS,东盟AS,哥CR,秘鲁PE,新西兰NZ,智利CL 2.6 瑞士CH 3.9 澳AU,韩国KR 5 巴PK	0 受惠国$_1$LD$_1$	35	--Containing petroleum oils or oils obtained from bituminous minerals
2793	3811.2900	--其他	6.5	0 澳门MO,冰岛IS,东盟AS,哥CR,秘鲁PE,新西兰NZ,智利CL 2.6 瑞士CH 3.9 澳AU 5 巴PK 5.2 韩国KR 5.5 亚太AP	0 受惠国$_1$LD$_1$	35	--Other
2794	3811.9000	-其他	6.5	0 澳门MO,冰岛IS,东盟AS,哥CR,秘鲁PE,香港HK,新西兰NZ,智利CL 2.6 瑞士CH 3.9 澳AU,韩国KR 5 巴PK	0 受惠国$_1$LD$_1$	35	-Other
	38.12	**配制的橡胶促进剂;其他税号未列名的橡胶或塑料用复合增塑剂;橡胶或塑料用抗氧制剂及其他复合稳定剂:**					**Prepared rubber accelerators; compound plasticisers for rubber or plastics, not elsewhere specified or included; anti-oxidising preparations and other compound stabilisers for rubber or plastics:**
2795	3812.1000	-配制的橡胶促进剂	6	0 冰岛IS,东盟AS,哥CR,秘鲁PE,新西兰NZ,智利CL 2.4 瑞士CH 3.6 澳AU 5 巴PK 5.2 韩国KR	0 受惠国LD	20	-Prepared rubber accelerators
2796	3812.2000	-橡胶或塑料用复合增塑剂	6.5	0 冰岛IS,东盟AS,哥CR,秘鲁PE,新西兰NZ,智利CL 2.6 瑞士CH 3.9 澳AU 5 巴PK 5.6 韩国KR	0 受惠国LD	35	-Compound plasticizers for rubber or plastics
		-橡胶或塑料用抗氧制剂及其他复合稳定剂:					-Anti-oxidising preparations and other compound stabilisers for rubber or plastics:
2797	3812.3010	---橡胶防老剂	6	0 冰岛IS,东盟AS,哥CR,秘鲁PE,香港HK,新西兰NZ,智利CL 2.4 瑞士CH 3.6 澳AU 5 巴PK 5.2 韩国KR	0 受惠国LD	20	---Rubber antioxidants
2798	3812.3090	---其他	6.5	0 巴PK,冰岛IS,东盟AS,哥CR,秘鲁PE,香港HK,新西兰NZ,智利CL 3.9 澳AU,韩国KR 4.6 瑞士CH,亚太AP	0 受惠国LD	35	---Other
	38.13	**灭火器的装配药;已装药的灭火弹:**					**Preparations and charges for fire-extinguishers; charged fire-extinguishing grenades:**

序号 No.	税则号列 Tariff Line	中文货品名称 Article Description in Chinese	最惠国税率 MFN(%)	协定税率 Agreement(%)	特惠税率 SP(%)	普通税率 Gen(%)	英文货品名称 Article Description
2799	3813.0010	---灭火器的装配药	6.5	0 冰岛IS,东盟AS,哥CR,秘鲁PE,新西兰NZ,智利CL 2.6 瑞士CH 3.9 澳AU 5 巴PK 5.2 韩国KR	0 受惠国LD	35	---Preparations and charges for ire-extinguishers
2800	3813.0020	---已装药的灭火弹	10	0 冰岛IS,东盟AS,哥CR,秘鲁PE,新西兰NZ,智利CL 4 瑞士CH 5 巴PK 6 澳AU 8 韩国KR	0 受惠国LD	70	---Charged fire-extinguishing grenades
	38.14	**其他税号未列名的有机复合溶剂及稀释剂;除漆剂**					**Organic composite solvents and thinners, not elsewhere specified or included; prepared paint or varnish removers**
2801	3814.0000	其他税号未列名的有机复合溶剂及稀释剂;除漆剂	10	0 澳门MO,冰岛IS,东盟AS,哥CR,香港HK,新加坡SG,新西兰NZ,智利CL 3 秘鲁PE 5 巴PK 6 澳AU 7 瑞士CH 9 韩国KR,亚太AP	0 受惠国LD	50	Organic composite solvents and thinners, not elsewhere specified or included; prepared paint or varnish removers
	38.15	**其他税号未列名的反应引发剂、反应促进剂、催化剂:**					**Reaction initiators, reaction accelerators and catalytic preparations, not elsewhere specified or included:**
		-载体催化剂:					-Supported catalysts:
2802	3815.1100	--以镍及其化合物为活性物的	6.5	0 冰岛IS,东盟AS,哥CR,秘鲁PE,新西兰NZ,智利CL 2.6 瑞士CH 3.9 澳AU 5 巴PK 5.2 韩国KR	0 受惠国LD	35	--With nickel or nickel compounds as the active substance
2803	3815.1200	--以贵金属及其化合物为活性物的	6.5Δ4	0 冰岛IS,东盟AS,哥CR,秘鲁PE,香港HK,新西兰NZ,智利CL 2.6 瑞士CH 3.9 澳AU 5 巴PK 5.2 韩国KR	0 受惠国LD	35	--With precious metal or precious metal compounds as the active substance
2804	3815.1900	--其他	6.5	0 巴PK,冰岛IS,东盟AS,哥CR,秘鲁PE,新西兰NZ,智利CL 2.6 瑞士CH 3.9 澳AU,韩国KR 4.6 亚太AP	0 受惠国LD	35	--Other
2805	3815.9000	-其他	6.5	0 澳门MO,冰岛IS,东盟AS,哥CR,秘鲁PE,新西兰NZ,智利CL 3.9 澳AU,韩国KR 4.6 瑞士CH 5 巴PK 6 亚太AP	0 受惠国LD	35	-Other
	38.16	**耐火的水泥、灰泥、混凝土及类似耐火混合制品,但税号38.01的产品除外**					**Refractory cements, mortars, concretes and similar compositions, other than products of heading 3801**

序号 No.	税则号列 Tariff Line	中文货品名称 Article Description in Chinese	最惠国税率 MFN(%)	协定税率 Agreement(%)	特惠税率 SP(%)	普通税率 Gen(%)	英文货品名称 Article Description
2806	3816.0000	耐火的水泥、灰泥、混凝土及类似耐火混合制品，但税号38.01的产品除外	6.5	0 冰岛IS,东盟AS,哥CR,秘鲁PE,新西兰NZ,智利CL 2.6 瑞士CH 3.9 澳AU,韩国KR 5 巴PK	0 受惠国$_1$LD$_1$	35	Refractory cements, mortars, concretes and similar compositions, other than products of heading No.38.01
	38.17	**混合烷基苯及混合烷基萘，但税号27.07及29.02的货品除外**					**Mixed alkylbenzenes and mixed alkylnaphthalenes, other than those of heading 2707 or 2902**
2807	3817.0000	混合烷基苯及混合烷基萘	6.5	0 冰岛IS,东盟AS,哥CR,秘鲁PE,台湾TW,新西兰NZ,智利CL 2.6 瑞士CH 3.9 澳AU 5 巴PK 5.6 韩国KR	0 受惠国LD	35	Mixed alkylbenzenes and alkylnaphthalenes38.18
	38.18	**经掺杂用于电子工业的化学元素，已切成圆片、薄片或类似形状;经掺杂用于电子工业的化合物:**					**Chemical elements doped for use in electronics, in the form of discs, wafers or similar forms; chemical compounds doped for use in electronics:**
		---直径在7.5厘米及以上的单晶硅切片:					---Monocrystalline sillicon, in the form of discs, wafers or similar form, 7.5cm or more in diameter:
2808	3818.0011	----直径在15.24厘米及以下的	0		0 受惠国LD	11	----Diameter not exceeding 15.24cm
2809	3818.0019	----其他	0		0 受惠国LD	11	----Other
2810	3818.0090	---其他	0		0 受惠国LD	17	---Other
	38.19	**闸用液压油及其他液压传动用液体，不含石油或从沥青矿物提取的油类，或者按重量计石油或从沥青矿物提取的油类含量低于70%**					**Hydraulic brake fluids and other prepared liquids for hydraulic transmission, not containing or containing less than 70% by weight of petroleum oils or oils obtained from bituminous minerals**
2811	3819.0000	闸用液压油及其他液压传动用液体，不含石油或从沥青矿物提取的油类，或者按重量计石油或从沥青矿物提取的油类含量低于70%	6.5	0 澳门MO,冰岛IS,东盟AS,哥CR,秘鲁PE,新西兰NZ,智利CL 2.6 瑞士CH 3.9 澳AU,韩国KR 5 巴PK	0 受惠国$_1$LD$_1$	35	Hydraulic brake fluids and other prepared liquids for hydraulic transmission, not containing or containing less than 70% by weight of petroleum oils or oils obtained from bituminous minerals
	38.20	**防冻剂及解冻剂**					**Anti-freezing preparations and prepared de-icing fluids**
2812	3820.0000	防冻剂及解冻剂	10	0 澳门MO,冰岛IS,东盟AS,哥CR,秘鲁PE,新加坡SG,新西兰NZ,智利CL 4 瑞士CH 5 巴PK 6 澳AU 8 韩国KR	0 受惠国LD	35	Anti-freezing preparations and prepared de-cing fluids
	38.21	**制成的供微生物（包括病毒及类似品）或植物、人体、动物细胞生长或维持用的培养基**					**Prepared culture media for the development or maintenance of micro-organisms (including viruses and the like) or of plant, human or animal cells**
2813	3821.0000	制成的供微生物（包括病毒及类似品）或植物、人体、动物细胞生长或维持用的培养基	3	0 澳AU,巴PK,冰岛IS,东盟AS,哥CR,秘鲁PE,瑞士CH,香港HK,新西兰NZ,智利CL 1.8 韩国KR	0 受惠国$_1$LD$_1$	11	Prepared culture media for the development or maintenance of micro-organisms (including viruses and the like) or of plant, human or animal cells

序号 No.	税则号列 Tariff Line	中文货品名称 Article Description in Chinese	最惠国税率 MFN(%)	协定税率 Agreement(%)	特惠税率 SP(%)	普通税率 Gen(%)	英文货品名称 Article Description
	38.22	**附于衬背上的诊断或实验用试剂及不论是否附于衬背上的诊断或实验用配制试剂，但税号30.02及30.06的货品除外;检定参照物:**					**Diagnostic or laboratory reagents on a backing, prepared diagnostic or laboratory reagents whether or not on a backing, other than those of heading 3002 or 3006; certified reference materials:**
2814	3822.0010	---附于衬背上的	4	0 澳AU,巴PK,东盟AS,哥CR,秘鲁PE,香港HK,新西兰NZ,智利CL 1.6 瑞士CH 2 冰岛IS 2.4 韩国KR	0 受惠国LD	35	---On a backing
2815	3822.0090	---其他	5	0 澳AU,巴PK,东盟AS,哥CR,秘鲁PE,香港HK,新西兰NZ,智利CL 2 瑞士CH 2.5 冰岛IS 3 韩国KR	0 受惠国LD	35	---Other
	38.23	**工业用单羧脂肪酸;精炼所得的酸性油;工业用脂肪醇:**					**Industrial monocarboxylic fatty acids; acid oils from refining; industrial fatty alcohols:**
		-工业用单羧脂肪酸;精炼所得的酸性油:					-Industrial monocarboxylic fatty acids; acid oils from refining:
2816	3823.1100	--硬脂酸	16	0 东盟AS,哥CR,新西兰NZ,智利CL 4.8 秘鲁PE 9.6 澳AU 11.2 瑞士CH 12.8 巴PK 13.8 韩国KR	0 受惠国$_1$LD$_1$	50	--Stearic acid
2817	3823.1200	--油酸	16Δ8	0 东盟AS,哥CR,香港HK,新加坡SG,新西兰NZ,智利CL 4.8 秘鲁PE 9.6 澳AU 11.2 瑞士CH 12.8 巴PK 13.8 韩国KR	0 受惠国$_1$LD$_1$	50	--Oleic acid
2818	3823.1300	--妥尔油脂肪酸	16	0 冰岛IS,东盟AS,哥CR,新加坡SG,新西兰NZ,智利CL 4.8 秘鲁PE 9.6 澳AU 11.2 瑞士CH 12.8 巴PK 13.8 韩国KR	0 受惠国$_1$LD$_1$	50	--Tall oil fatty acids
2819	3823.1900	--其他	16	0 澳门MO,冰岛IS,东盟AS,哥CR,香港HK,新加坡SG,新西兰NZ,智利CL 4.8 秘鲁PE 9.6 澳AU 11.2 瑞士CH 12.8 巴PK 13.8 韩国KR	0 受惠国$_1$LD$_1$	50	--Other
	ex38231900	植物酸性油	Δ5				Botanic acid oil
2820	3823.7000	-工业用脂肪醇	13Δ9	0 冰岛IS,东盟AS,哥CR,秘鲁PE,新加坡SG,新西兰NZ,智利CL 6.5 巴PK 7.8 澳AU 9.1 瑞士CH 11.2 韩国KR	0 受惠国$_1$LD$_1$	50	-Industrial fatty alcohols

序号 No.	税则号列 Tariff Line	中文货品名称 Article Description in Chinese	最惠国税率 MFN(%)	协定税率 Agreement(%)	特惠税率 SP(%)	普通税率 Gen(%)	英文货品名称 Article Description
	38.24	**铸模及铸芯用粘合剂;其他税号未列名的化学工业及其相关工业的化学产品及配制品(包括由天然产品混合组成的):**					**Prepared binders for foundry moulds or cores; chemical products and preparations of the chemical or allied industries (including those consisting of mixtures of natural products), not elsewhere specified or included:**
2821	3824.1000	-铸模及铸芯用粘合剂	6.5	0 冰岛IS,东盟AS,哥CR,秘鲁PE,新西兰NZ,智利CL 2.6 瑞士CH 3.9 澳AU 5 巴PK 5.2 韩国KR	0 受惠国LD	35	-Prepared binders for foundry moulds or cores
2822	3824.3000	-自身混合或与金属粘合剂混合的未烧结金属碳化物	6.5	0 冰岛IS,东盟AS,哥CR,秘鲁PE,新西兰NZ,智利CL 2.6 瑞士CH 3.9 澳AU,韩国KR 5 巴PK	0 受惠国LD	35	-Non-agglomerated metal carbides mixed together or with metallic binders
		-水泥、灰泥及混凝土用添加剂:					-Prepared additives for cements, mortars or concretes:
2823	3824.4010	---高效减水剂	6.5	0 冰岛IS,东盟AS,哥CR,秘鲁PE,香港HK,新西兰NZ,智利CL 2.6 瑞士CH 3.9 澳AU 5 巴PK 5.6 韩国KR	0 受惠国LD	35	---High efficiency water reducing admixture
2824	3824.4090	---其他	6.5	0 冰岛IS,东盟AS,哥CR,秘鲁PE,香港HK,新西兰NZ,智利CL 2.6 瑞士CH 3.9 澳AU,韩国KR 5 巴PK	0 受惠国LD	35	---Other
2825	3824.5000	-非耐火的灰泥及混凝土	6.5	0 澳门MO,冰岛IS,东盟AS,哥CR,秘鲁PE,香港HK,新西兰NZ,智利CL 2.6 瑞士CH 3.9 澳AU,韩国KR 5 巴PK	0 受惠国LD	35	-Non-refractory mortars and concretes
2826	3824.6000	-子目号2905.44以外的山梨醇	14	0 冰岛IS,东盟AS,哥CR,秘鲁PE,新加坡SG,新西兰NZ,智利CL 8.4 澳AU 9.8 瑞士CH 11.2 巴PK,韩国KR	0 受惠国$_1$LD$_1$	40	-Sorbitol other than that of subheading No.2905.44
		-含有甲烷、乙烷或丙烷的卤化衍生物的混合物::					-Mixtures containing halogenated derivatives of methane, ethane or propane:
2827	3824.7100	--含全氯氟烃(CFCs)的,不论是否含氢氯氟烃(HCFCs)、全氟烃(PFCs)或氢氟烃(HFCs)	6.5	0 澳门MO,冰岛IS,东盟AS,哥CR,秘鲁PE,香港HK,新西兰NZ,智利CL 2.6 瑞士CH 3.9 澳AU,韩国KR 5 巴PK	0 受惠国LD	35	--Containing chlorofluorocarbons (CFCs), whether or not containing hydrochlorofluorocarbons (HCFCs), perfluorocarbons (PFCs) orhydrofluorocarbons (HFCs)
2828	3824.7200	--含溴氯二氟甲烷、溴三氟甲烷或二溴四氟乙烷的	6.5	0 冰岛IS,东盟AS,哥CR,秘鲁PE,新西兰NZ,智利CL 2.6 瑞士CH 3.9 澳AU,韩国KR 5 巴PK	0 受惠国LD	35	--Containing bromochlorodifluoromethane, bromotrifluoromethane or dibromotetrafluoroethanes

序号 No.	税则号列 Tariff Line	中文货品名称 Article Description in Chinese	最惠国税率 MFN(%)	协定税率 Agreement(%)	特惠税率 SP(%)	普通税率 Gen(%)	英文货品名称 Article Description
2829	3824.7300	--含氢溴氟烃(HBFCs)的	6.5	0 澳门MO,冰岛IS,东盟AS,哥CR,秘鲁PE,香港HK,新西兰NZ,智利CL 2.6 瑞士CH 3.9 澳AU,韩国KR 5 巴PK	0 受惠国LD	35	--Containing hydrobromofluorocarbons (HBFCs)
2830	3824.7400	--含氢氯氟烃(HCFCs)的,不论是否含全氟烃(PFCs)或氢氟烃(HFCs)	6.5	0 澳门MO,冰岛IS,东盟AS,哥CR,秘鲁PE,香港HK,新西兰NZ,智利CL 2.6 瑞士CH 3.9 澳AU,韩国KR 5 巴PK	0 受惠国LD	35	--Containing hydrochlorofluorocarbons (HCFCs), whether or not containing perfluorocarbons (PFCs) or hydrofluorocarbons (HFCs), but not containing chlorofluorocarbons (CFCs)
2831	3824.7500	--含四氯化碳的	6.5	0 澳门MO,冰岛IS,东盟AS,哥CR,秘鲁PE,香港HK,新西兰NZ,智利CL 2.6 瑞士CH 3.9 澳AU,韩国KR 5 巴PK 6 亚太AP	0 受惠国LD	35	--Containing carbon tetrachloride
2832	3824.7600	--含1,1,1-三氯乙烷(甲基氯仿)的	6.5	0 澳门MO,冰岛IS,东盟AS,哥CR,秘鲁PE,香港HK,新西兰NZ,智利CL 2.6 瑞士CH 3.9 澳AU,韩国KR 5 巴PK 6 亚太AP	0 受惠国LD	35	--Containing 1, 1, 1-trichloroethane (methyl chloroform)
2833	3824.7700	--含溴化甲烷（甲基溴）或溴氯甲烷的	6.5	0 澳门MO,冰岛IS,东盟AS,哥CR,秘鲁PE,香港HK,新西兰NZ,智利CL 2.6 瑞士CH 3.9 澳AU,韩国KR 5 巴PK	0 受惠国LD	35	--Containing bromomethane (methyl bromide) or bromochloromethane
2834	3824.7800	--含全氟烃(PFCs)或氢氟烃(HFCs)的,但不含全氯氟烃(CFCs)或氢氯氟烃(HCFCs)的	6.5	0 澳门MO,冰岛IS,东盟AS,哥CR,秘鲁PE,香港HK,新西兰NZ,智利CL 2.6 瑞士CH 3.9 澳AU,韩国KR 5 巴PK 6 亚太AP	0 受惠国LD	35	--Containing perfluorocarbons (PFCs) or hydrofluorocarbons (HFCs), but not containing chlorofluorocarbons (CFCs) or hydrochlorofluorocarbons (HCFCs)
2835	3824.7900	--其他	6.5	0 澳门MO,冰岛IS,东盟AS,哥CR,秘鲁PE,香港HK,新西兰NZ,智利CL 2.6 瑞士CH 3.9 澳AU,韩国KR 5 巴PK	0 受惠国LD	35	--Other
		-含环氧乙烷（氧化乙烯）、多溴联苯（PBBs）、多氯联苯(PCBs)、多氯三联苯(PCTs)或三（2,3-二溴丙基）磷酸酯的混合物及制品:					-Mixtures and preparations containing oxirane (ethylene oxide), polybrominated biphenyls (PBBs), polychlorinated biphenyls (PCBs), polychlorinated terphenyls (PCTs) or tris (2, 3-dibromopropyl) phosphate:
2836	3824.8100	--含环氧乙烷（氧化乙烯）的	6.5	0 澳门MO,冰岛IS,东盟AS,哥CR,秘鲁PE,香港HK,新西兰NZ,智利CL 2.6 瑞士CH 3.9 澳AU,韩国KR 5 巴PK 6 亚太AP	0 受惠国LD	35	--Containing oxirane (ethylene oxide)

序号 No.	税则号列 Tariff Line	中文货品名称 Article Description in Chinese	最惠国税率 MFN(%)	协定税率 Agreement(%)	特惠税率 SP(%)	普通税率 Gen(%)	英文货品名称 Article Description
2837	3824.8200	--含多氯联苯(PCBs)、多氯三联苯(PCTs)或多溴联苯(PBBs)的	6.5	0 澳门MO,冰岛IS,东盟AS,哥CR,秘鲁PE,香港HK,新西兰NZ,智利CL 2.6 瑞士CH 3.9 澳AU,韩国KR 5 巴PK 6 亚太AP	0 受惠国LD	35	--Containing polychlorinated biphenyls (PCBs) , polychlorinated terphenyls (PCTs) or polybrominated biphenyls (PBBs)
2838	3824.8300	--含三(2,3-二溴丙基)磷酸酯的	6.5	0 澳门MO,冰岛IS,东盟AS,哥CR,秘鲁PE,香港HK,新西兰NZ,智利CL 2.6 瑞士CH 3.9 澳AU,韩国KR 5 巴PK 6 亚太AP	0 受惠国LD	35	--Containing tris (2, 3-dibromopropyl) phosphate
		-其他:					-Other:
2839	3824.9010	---杂醇油	6.5	0 冰岛IS,东盟AS,哥CR,秘鲁PE,新西兰NZ,智利CL 2.6 瑞士CH 3.9 澳AU 5 巴PK 5.2 韩国KR 5.5 亚太AP	0 受惠国LD	40	---Fusel oil
2840	3824.9020	---除墨剂、蜡纸改正液及类似品	9	0 冰岛IS,东盟AS,哥CR,秘鲁PE,新加坡SG,新西兰NZ,智利CL 3.6 瑞士CH 5 巴PK 5.4 澳AU,韩国KR 8.3 亚太AP	0 受惠国LD	80	---Ink-removers, stencil correctors and the like
2841	3824.9030	---增炭剂	6.5	0 冰岛IS,东盟AS,哥CR,秘鲁PE,新西兰NZ,智利CL 2.6 瑞士CH 3.9 澳AU,韩国KR 5 巴PK	0 受惠国LD	35	---Carburetant
		---其他:					---Other:
2842	3824.9091	----按重量计含滑石50%以上的混合物	6.5	0 澳门MO,冰岛IS,东盟AS,哥CR,秘鲁PE,香港HK,新西兰NZ,智利CL 2.6 瑞士CH 3.9 澳AU,韩国KR 5 巴PK 6 亚太AP	0 受惠国LD	35	----Mixture containing more than 50% Talc by weight
2843	3824.9092	----按重量计含氧化镁70%以上的混合物	6.5	0 澳门MO,冰岛IS,东盟AS,哥CR,秘鲁PE,香港HK,新西兰NZ,智利CL 2.6 瑞士CH 3.9 澳AU,韩国KR 5 巴PK 6 亚太AP	0 受惠国LD	35	----Mixture containing more than 70% Magnesium Oxide by weight
2844	3824.9093	----表层包覆钴化合物的氢氧化镍(掺杂碳)	6.5	0 澳门MO,冰岛IS,东盟AS,哥CR,秘鲁PE,香港HK,新西兰NZ,智利CL 3.9 澳AU 5 巴PK 5.6 韩国KR 6 亚太AP	0 受惠国LD	35	----Cobalt compound coated nickel hydroxide (mixed carbon)
2845	3824.9099	----其他	6.5	0 澳门MO,冰岛IS,东盟AS,哥CR,秘鲁PE,香港HK,新西兰NZ,智利CL 3.9 澳AU 5 巴PK 5.6 韩国KR 6 亚太AP	0 受惠国LD	35	----Other

序号 No.	税则号列 Tariff Line	中文货品名称 Article Description in Chinese	最惠国税率 MFN(%)	协定税率 Agreement(%)	特惠税率 SP(%)	普通税率 Gen(%)	英文货品名称 Article Description
	ex38249099	高钛渣（二氧化钛质量百分含量大于70％的）	Δ0				The Ag electrode paste, dieletric paste, barrier ribs paste phosphor paste used for the plasma display panel production
	ex38249099	按重量计氧化锌含量在50％及以上的混合物	Δ3				Mixture containing ZnO 50% or more
	38.25	**其他税目未列名的化学工业及其相关工业的副产品;城市垃圾;下水道淤泥;本章注释六所规定的其他废物:**					**Residual products of the chemical or allied industries, not elsewhere specified or included; municipal waste; sewage sludge; other wastes specified in note 6 to this chapter:**
2846	3825.1000	-城市垃圾	6.5	0 冰岛IS,东盟AS,哥CR,秘鲁PE,新西兰NZ,智利CL 2.6 瑞士CH 3.9 澳AU,韩国KR 5 巴PK	0 受惠国$_1$LD$_1$	35	-Municipal waste
2847	3825.2000	-下水道淤泥	6.5	0 冰岛IS,东盟AS,哥CR,秘鲁PE,新西兰NZ,智利CL 2.6 瑞士CH 3.9 澳AU,韩国KR 5 巴PK	0 受惠国$_1$LD$_1$	35	-Sewage sludge
2848	3825.3000	-医疗废物	6.5	0 冰岛IS,东盟AS,哥CR,秘鲁PE,新西兰NZ,智利CL 2.6 瑞士CH 3.9 澳AU,韩国KR 5 巴PK	0 受惠国$_1$LD$_1$	35	-Clinical waste
		-废有机溶剂:					-Waste organic solvents:
2849	3825.4100	--卤化物的	6.5	0 冰岛IS,东盟AS,哥CR,秘鲁PE,新西兰NZ,智利CL 2.6 瑞士CH 3.9 澳AU,韩国KR 5 巴PK	0 受惠国$_1$LD$_1$	35	--Halogenated
2850	3825.4900	--其他	6.5	0 冰岛IS,东盟AS,哥CR,秘鲁PE,新西兰NZ,智利CL 2.6 瑞士CH 3.9 澳AU,韩国KR 5 巴PK	0 受惠国$_1$LD$_1$	35	--Other
2851	3825.5000	-废的金属酸液、液压油、制动油及防冻液	6.5	0 冰岛IS,东盟AS,哥CR,秘鲁PE,新加坡SG,新西兰NZ,智利CL 2.6 瑞士CH 3.9 澳AU,韩国KR 5 巴PK	0 受惠国$_1$LD$_1$	35	-Wastes of metal pickling liguors, hyd-raulic fluids, brake fluids and anti freeze fluids
		-其他化学工业及相关工业的废物:					-Other wastes from chemical or allied industries:
2852	3825.6100	--主要含有有机成分的	6.5	0 冰岛IS,东盟AS,哥CR,秘鲁PE,新西兰NZ,智利CL 2.6 瑞士CH 3.9 澳AU,韩国KR 5 巴PK	0 受惠国$_1$LD$_1$	35	--Mainly containing organic constituents
2853	3825.6900	--其他	6.5	0 冰岛IS,东盟AS,哥CR,秘鲁PE,新西兰NZ,智利CL 2.6 瑞士CH 3.9 澳AU,韩国KR 5 巴PK	0 受惠国$_1$LD$_1$	35	--Other

序号 No.	税则号列 Tariff Line	中文货品名称 Article Description in Chinese	最惠国税率 MFN(%)	协定税率 Agreement(%)	特惠税率 SP(%)	普通税率 Gen(%)	英文货品名称 Article Description
2854	3825.9000	-其他	6.5	0 冰岛IS,东盟AS,哥CR,秘鲁PE,香港HK,新西兰NZ,智利CL 2.6 瑞士CH 3.9 澳AU,韩国KR 5 巴PK	0 受惠国$_1$LD$_1$	35	-Other
	38.26	**生物柴油及其混合物，不含或含有按重量计低于70%的石油或从沥青矿物提取的油类**					**Biodiesel and mixtures thereof, not containing or containing less than 70% by weight of petroleum oils or oils obtained from bituminous minerals**
2855	3826.0000	生物柴油及其混合物，不含或含有按重量计低于70%的石油或从沥青矿物提取的油类	6.5	0 澳门MO,冰岛IS,东盟AS,哥CR,秘鲁PE,香港HK,新西兰NZ,智利CL 3.9 澳AU 5 巴PK 5.6 韩国KR 6 亚太AP	0 受惠国LD	35	Biodiesel and mixtures thereof, not containing or containing less than 70% by weight of petroleum oils or oils obtained from bituminous minerals

第七类
塑料及其制品；
橡胶及其制品

SECTION Ⅶ
PLASTICS AND ARTICLES THEREOF; RUBBER AND ARTICLES THEREOF

注释：

一、由两种或两种以上单独成分配套的货品，其部分或全部成分属于本类范围以内，混合后则构成第六类或第七类的货品，应按混合后产品归入相应的税号，但其组成成分必须同时符合下列条件：

（一）其包装形式足以表明这些成分不需经过改装就可以一起使用的；

（二）一起进口或出口的；

（三）这些成分的属性及相互比例足以表明是相互配用的。

二、除税号 39.18 或 39.19 的货品外，印有花纹、文字、图画的塑料、橡胶及其制品，如果所印花纹、字画作为其主要用途，应归入第四十九章。

Notes:

1. Goods put up in sets consisting of two or more separate constituents, some or all of which fall in this Section and are intended to be mixed together to obtain a product of SectionⅥ orⅦ, are to be classified in the heading appropriate to that product, provided that the constituents are:

(a) having regard to the manner in which they are put up, clearly identifiable as being intended to be used together without first being repacked;

(b) presented together; and

(c) identifiable, whether by their nature or by the relative proportions inwhich they are present, as being complementary one to another.

2. Except for the goods of heading No.39.18 or 39.19, plastics, rubber, and articles thereof, printed with motifs, characters or pictorial representations, which are not merely incidental to the primary use of the goods, fall in Chapter 49.

第三十九章
塑料及其制品

Chapter 39
Plastics and articles thereof

注释：

一、本目录所称“塑料”，是指税号 39.01 至 39.14 的材料，这些材料能够在聚合时或聚合后在外力（一般是热力和压力，必要时加入溶剂或增塑剂）作用下通过模制、浇铸、挤压、滚轧或其他工序制成一定的形状，成形后除去外力，其形状仍保持不变。

本目录所称“塑料”，还应包括钢纸，但不包括第十一类的纺织材料。

二、本章不包括：

（一）税目 27.10 或 34.03 的润滑油；

（二）税号 27.12 或 34.04 的蜡；

（三）单独的已有化学定义的有机化合物（第二十九章）；

（四）肝素及其盐（税号 30.01）；

Notes:

1. Throughout the Nomenclature the expression “plastics” means those materials of headings Nos.39.01to 39.14 which are or have been capable, either at the moment of polymerization or at some subsequent stage, of being formed under external influence (usually heat and pressure, if necessary with a solvent or plasticizer) by moulding, casting, extruding, rolling or other process into shapes which are retained on the removal of the external influence.

Throughout the Nomenclature any reference to “plastics” also includes vulcanized fibre. The expression, however, does not apply to materials regarded as textile materials of SectionⅪ.

2. This Chapter does not cover:

(a) Lubricating preparations of heading 27.10 or 34.03;

(b) Waxes of heading No.27.12 or 34.04;

(c) Separate chemically defined organic compounds (Chapter 29) ;

(d) Heparin or its salts (heading No.30.01) ;

(五）税号 39.01 至 39.13 所列的任何产品溶于挥发性有机溶剂的溶液（胶棉除外），但溶剂的重量必须超过溶液重量的 50%（税号 32.08）；税号 32.12 的压印箔；

(e) Solutions (other than collodions) consisting of any of the products specified in headings Nos.39.01 to 39.13 in volatile organic solvents when the weight of the solvent exceeds 50% of the weight of the solution (heading No.32.08); stamping foils of heading No.32.12;

(六）有机表面活性剂或税号 34.02 的制剂；

(f) Organic surface-active agents or preparations of heading No.34.02;

(七）再熔胶及酯胶（税号 38.06）；

(g) Run gums or ester gums (heading No.38.06) ;

(八）配制的添加剂，用于矿物油（包括汽油）或与矿物油同样用途的其他液体（税目 38.11）；

(h) Prepared additives for mineral oils (including gasoline) or for other liquids used for the same purposes as mineral oils (heading 38.11);

(九）以第三十九章的聚乙二醇、聚硅氧烷或其他聚合物为基本成分的液压用液体（税目 38.19）；

(ij) Prepared hydraulic fluids based on polyglycols, silicones or other polymers of Chapter 39 (heading 38.19);

(十）附于塑料衬背上的诊断或实验用试剂（税号 38.22）；

(k) Diagnostic or laboratory reagents on a backing of plastics (heading No.38.22) ;

(十一）第四十章规定的合成橡胶及其制品；

(l) Synthetic rubber, as defined for the purposes of Chapter 40, or articles thereof;

(十二）鞍具及挽具（税号 42.01）；税号 42.02 的衣箱、提箱、手提包及其他容器；

(m) Sadlery or harness (heading No.42.01) or trunks, suitcases, handbags or other containers of heading No.42.02;

(十三）第四十六章的缏条、编结品及其他制品；

(n) Plaits, wickerwork or other articles of Chapter 46;

(十四）税号 48.14 的壁纸；

(o) Wall coverings of heading No.48.14;

(十五）第十一类的货品（纺织原料及纺织制品）；

(p) Goods of Section XI(textiles and textile articles) ;

(十六）第十二类的物品（例如，鞋靴、帽类、雨伞、阳伞、手杖、鞭子、马鞭及其零件）；

(q) Articles of Section XII(for example, footwear, headgear, umbrellas, sun umbrellas, walking • sticks, whips, riding-crops or parts thereof) ;

(十七）税号 71.17 的仿首饰；

(r) Imitation jewellery of heading No.71.17;

(十八）第十六类的物品（机器、机械器具或电气器具）；

(s) Articles of Section XIV (machines and mechanical or electrical appliances) ;

(十九）第十七类的航空器零件及车辆零件；

(t) Parts of aircraft or vehicles of Section XVII;

(二十）第九十章的物品（例如，光学元件、眼镜架及绘图仪器）；

(u) Articles of Chapter 90 (for example, optical elements, spectacle frames, drawing instruments) ;

(二十一）第九十一章的物品（例如，钟壳及表壳）；

(v) Articles of Chapter 91 (for example, clock or watch cases);

(二十二）第九十二章的物品（例如，乐器及其零件）；

(w) Articles of Chapter 92 (for example, musical instruments or parts thereof) ;

(二十三）第九十四章的物品（例如，家具、灯具、照明装置、灯箱及活动房屋）；

(x) Articles of Chapter 94 (for example, furniture, lamps and lighting fittings. illuminated signs, prefabricated buildings);

(二十四）第九十五章的物品（例如，玩具、游戏品及运动用品）；

(y) Articles of Chapter 95 (for example, toys, games, sports requisites) ;or

(二十五）第九十六章的物品（例如，刷子、钮扣、

(z) Articles of Chapter 96 (for example, brushes, buttons,

拉链、梳子、烟斗的嘴及柄、香烟嘴及类似品、保温瓶的零件及类似品、钢笔、活动铅笔)。

slide fasteners, combs, mouthpieces or stems for smoking pipes, cigaretteholders or the like, parts of vacuum flasks or the like, pens, propelling pencils).

三、税号 39.01 至 39.11 仅适用于化学合成的下列货品:

(一)温度在 300℃时,压力转为 1013 毫巴后减压蒸馏出的液体合成聚烯烃以体积计小于 60% 的货品(税号 39.01 及 39.02);

(二)非高度聚合的苯并呋喃—茚树脂(税号 39.11);

(三)平均至少有五个单体单元的其他合成聚合物;

(四)聚硅氧烷(税号 39.10);

(五)甲阶酚醛树脂(税号 39.09)及其他预聚物。

3. Headings Nos.39.01 to 39.11apply only to goods of a kind produced by chemical synthesis, falling in the following categories:

(a) Liquid synthetic polyolefins of which less than 60% by volume distils at 300℃, after conversion to 1013 millibars when a reduced-pressure distillation method is used (headings Nos. 39.01 and 39.02);

(b) Resins, not highly polymerized, of the coumarone-indene type (heading No.39.11);

(c) Other synthetic polymers with an average of at least 5 monomer units;

(d) Silicones (heading No.39.10);

(e) Resols (heading No.39.09) and other prepolymers.

四、所称"共聚物",包括在整个聚合物中按重量计没有一种单体单元的含量在 95%及以上的各种聚合物。

在本章中,除条文另有规定的以外,共聚物(包括共缩聚物、共加聚物、嵌段共聚物及接枝共聚物)及聚合物混合体应按聚合物中重量最大的那种共聚单体单元所构成的聚合物归入相应税号。在本注释中,归入同一税号的聚合物的共聚单体单元应作为一种单体单元对待。

如果没有任何一种共聚单体单元重量为最大,共聚物或聚合物混合体应按号列顺序归入其可归入的最末一个税号。

4. The expression"copolymers"covers all polymers in which no single monomer unit contributes 95% or more by weight to the total polymer content.

For the purposes of this Chapter, except where the context otherwise requires, copolymers (including copolycondensates, co polyaddition products, block copolymers and graft copolymers) and polymer blends are to be classified in the heading covering polymers of that comonomet unit which predominates by weight over every other single comonomer unit. For the purposes of this Note, constituent comonomer units of polymers falling in the same heading shall be taken together.

If no single comonomer unit predominates, copolymens or polymer blends, as the case may be, are to be classified in the heading which occurs last in numerical order among those which equally merit consideration.

五、化学改性聚合物,即聚合物主链上的支链通过化学反应发生了变化的聚合物,应按未改性的聚合物的相应税号归类。本规定不适用于接枝共聚物。

5. Chemically modified polymers, that is those in which only appendages to the main polymer chain have been changed by chemical reaction, are to be classified in the heading appropriate to the unmodified polymer. This provision does not apply to graft copolymers.

六、税号 39.01 至 39.14 所称"初级形状",只限于下列各种形状:

(一)液状及糊状,包括分散体(乳浊液及悬浮液)及溶液;

(二)不规则形状的块,团、粉(包括压型粉)、颗粒、粉片及类似的散装形状。

6. In headings Nos.39.01 to 39.04, the expression "primary forms" applies only to the following forms:

(a) Liquids and pastes, including dispersions (emulsions and suspensions) and solutions;

(b) Blocks of irregular shape, lumps, powders (including moulding powders), granules, flakes and similar bulk forms.

七、税号 39.15 不适用于已制成初级形状的单一的热

7. Heading No.39.15 does not apply to waste, parings and

塑材料废碎料及下脚料（税号 39.01 至 39.14）。

scrap of a single thermoplastic material, transformed into primary forms (headings Nos.39.01 to 39.14) .

八、税号 39.17 所称“管子”，是指通常用于输送或供给气体或液体的空心制品或半制品（例如，肋纹浇花软管、多孔管），还包括香肠用肠衣及其他扁平管。除肠衣及扁平管外，内截面如果不呈圆形、椭圆形、矩形（其长度不超过宽度的 1.5 倍）或正几何形，则不能视为管子，而应作为异型材。

8. For the purposes of heading No.39.17, the expression “tubes, pipes and hoses” means hollow products, whether semi-manufactures or finished products, of a kind generally used for conveying, conducting or distributing gases or liquids (for example, ribbed garden hose, perforated tubes). This expression also includes sausage casings and other layflat tubing.However, except for the last-mentioned, those having an internal cross-section other than round, oval, rectangular (in which the length does not exceed 1.5 times the width) or in the shape of a regular polygon are not to be regarded as tubes, pipes and hoses but as profile shapes.

九、税号 39.18 所称“塑料糊墙品”，适用于墙壁或天花板装饰用的宽度不小于 45 厘米的成卷产品，这类产品是将塑料牢固地附着在除纸张以外任何材料的衬背上，并且在塑料面起纹、压花、着色、印制图案或用其他方法装饰。

9. For the purposes of heading No.39.18, the expression “wall or ceiling coverings of plastics” applies to products in rolls, of a width not less than 45 cm, suitable for wall or ceiling decoration, consisting of plastics fixed permanently on a backing of any material other than paper, the layer of plastics (on the face side) being grained, embossed, coloured, design-printed or otherwise decorated.

十、税号 39.20 及 39.21 所称“板、片、膜、箔、扁条”，只适用于未切割或仅切割成矩形（包括正方形）（含切割后即可供使用的）;但未经进一步加工的板、片、膜、箔、扁条（第五十四章的物品除外）及正几何形块，不论是否经过印制或其他表面加工。

10. In headings Nos. 39.20 and 39.21, the expression“plates, sheets, film, foil and strip” applies only to plates, sheets, film, foil and strip (other than those of Chapter 54) and to blocks of regular geometric shape, whether or not printed or otherwise surface-woked, uncut or cut into rectangles (including squares) but not further worked (even if when so cut they become articles ready for use) .

十一、税号 39.25 只适用于第二分章以前各税号未包括的下列物品:

（一）容积超过 300 升的囤、柜（包括化粪池)、罐、桶及类似容器;

（二）用于地板、墙壁、隔墙、天花板或屋顶等方面的结构件;

（三）槽管及其附件;

（四）门、窗及其框架和门槛;

（五）阳台、栏杆、栅栏、栅门及类似品;

（六）窗板、百叶窗（包括威尼斯式百叶窗）或类似品及其零件、附件;

（七）商店、工棚、仓库等用的拼装式固定大型货架;

11. Heading No.39.25 applies only to the following articles, not being products covered by any of the earlier headings of sub-Chapter II:

(a) Reservoirs, tanks (including septic tanks) , vats and similar containers, of a capacity exceeding 300L;

(b) Structural elements used, for example, in floors, walls or partitions, ceilings or roofs;

(c) Gutters and fittings therefor;

(d) Doors, windows and their frames and thresholds for doors;

(e) Balconies, balustrades, fencing, gates and similar barriers;

(f)Shutters, blinds (including Venetian blinds) and similar articles and parts and fittings thereof;

(g) Large-scale shelving for assembly and permanent installation, for example, in shops, workshops, ware-

（八）建筑用的特色（例如，凹槽、圆顶及鸽棚式）装饰件；

（九）固定装于门窗、楼梯、墙壁或建筑物其他部位的附件及架座，例如，球形把手、拉手、挂钩、托架、毛巾架、开关板及其他护板。

houses;

(h) Ornamental architectural features, for example, flutings, cupolas, dovecotes; and

(i) Fittings and mountings intended for permanent installation in or on doors, windows, staircases, walls or other parts of buildings, for example, knobs, handles, hooks, brackets, towel rails, switch-plates and other protective plates.

子目注释：

属于本章任一税号项下的聚合物（包括共聚物）及化学改性聚合物应按下列规则归类：

一、在同级子目中有一个"其他"子目的：

（一）子目所列聚合物名称冠有"聚（多）"的（例如，聚乙烯及聚酰胺-6，6），是指列名的该种聚合物单体单元含量在整个聚合物中按重量计必须占95%及以上。

（二）子目号3901.30、3903.20、3903.30及3904.30所列的共聚物，如果该种共聚单体单元含量在整个聚合物中按重量计占95%及以上，即应归入上述子目。

（三）化学改性聚合物如未在其他子目具体列名，应归入列明为"其他"的子目内。

（四）不符合上述（一）、（二）、（三）款规定的聚合物，应按聚合物中重量最大的那种单体单元（与其他各种单一的共聚单体单元相比）所构成的聚合物归入该级其他相应子目。为此，归入同一子目的聚合物单体单元应作为一种单体单元对待。只有在同级子目中的聚合物共聚单体单元才可以进行比较。

二、在同级子目中没有"其他"子目的：

（一）聚合物应按聚合物中重量最大的那种单体单元（与其他各种单一的共聚单体单元相比）所构成的聚合物归入该级相应子目。为此，归入同一子目的聚合物单体单元应作为一种单体单元对待。只有在同级子目中的聚合物共聚单体

Subheading Notes:

1. Within any one heading of this Chapter, polymers (including copolymers) and chemically modified polymers are to be classified according to the following provisions:

(a) Where there is a subheading named "Other" in the same series:

(1) The designation in a subheading of a polymer by the prefix "poly" (for example, polyethylene and polyamide-6, 6) means that the constituent monomer unit or monomer units of the named polymer taken together must contribute 95% or more by weight of the total polymer content.

(2) The copolymers named in subheadings Nos.3901.30, 3903.20, 3903.30 and 3904.30 are to be classified in those subheadings, provided that the comonomer units of the named copolymers contribute 95% or more by weight of the total polymer content.

(3) Chemically modified polymers are to be classified in the subheading named "Other", provided that the chemically modified polymers are not more specifically covered by another subheading.

(4) Polymers not meeting (1), (2) or (3) above, are to be classified in the subheading, among the remaining subheadings in the series, covering polymers of that monomer unit which predominates by weight over every other single comonomer unit. For this purpose, constituent monomer units of polymers falling in the same subheading shall be taken together. Only the constituent comonomer units of the polymers in the series of subheadings under consideration are to be compared.

2. Where there is no subheading named "Other" in the same series:

(a) Polymers are to be classified in the subheading covering polymers of that monomer unit which predominates by weight over every other single comonomer unit. For this purpose, constituent monomer units of polymers falling in the same subheading shall be taken

单元才可以进行比较。

together. Only the constituent comonomer units of the polymers in the series under consideration are to be compared.

（二）化学改性聚合物应按相应的未改性聚合物的子目归类。聚合物混合体应按单体单元比例相等、种类相同的聚合物归入相应子目。

(b) Chemically modified polymers are to be classified in the subheading appropriate to the unmodified polymer.Polymer blends are to be classified in the same subheading as polymers of the same monomer units in the same proportions.

三、子目 3920.43 所称"增塑剂"，包括"次级增塑剂"。

3. For the purposes of subheading 3920.43, the term "plasticisers" includes "secondary plasticisers".

序号 No.	税则号列 Tariff Line	中文货品名称 Article Description in Chinese	最惠国税率 MFN(%)	协定税率 Agreement(%)	特惠税率 SP(%)	普通税率 Gen(%)	英文货品名称 Article Description
		第一分章初级形状					I.PRIMARY FORMS
	39.01	**初级形状的乙烯聚合物：**					**Polymers of ethylene, in primary forms:**
2856	3901.1000	-聚乙烯，比重小于0.94	6.5	0 澳门MO,冰岛IS,哥CR,香港HK,新西兰NZ,智利CL 3.9 澳AU 4.7 瑞士CH 6 巴PK,亚太AP 6.2 韩国KR		45	-Polyethylene having a specific gravity of less than 0.94
	ex39011000	比重小于0.94的聚乙烯（进口CIF价高于3800美元/吨）	Δ3				Polyethylene, gravity<0.94, (import CIF≥3800usd/t)
2857	3901.2000	-聚乙烯，比重在0.94及以上	6.5	0 澳门MO,冰岛IS,哥CR,香港HK,新西兰NZ,智利CL 3.9 澳AU 4.7 瑞士CH 6 巴PK,亚太AP 6.2 韩国KR		45	-Polyethylene having a specific gravity of 0.94 or more
	ex39012000	比重在0.94及以上的聚乙烯（进口CIF价高于3800美元/吨）	Δ3				Polyethylene, gravity≥0.94, (import CIF≥3800usd/t)
2858	3901.3000	-乙烯-乙酸乙烯酯共聚物	6.5	0 冰岛IS,东盟AS,哥CR,秘鲁PE,香港HK,新西兰NZ,智利CL 2.6 瑞士CH 3.9 澳AU 5 巴PK 6 亚太AP 6.2 韩国KR	0 受惠国$_1$LD$_1$	45	-Ethylene-vinyl acetate copolymers
		-其他：					-Other:
2859	3901.9010	---乙烯-丙烯共聚物（乙丙橡胶）	6.5	0 冰岛IS,东盟AS,哥CR,秘鲁PE,新加坡SG,新西兰NZ,智利CL 2.6 瑞士CH 3.9 澳AU 5 巴PK 5.6 韩国KR	0 受惠国$_1$LD$_1$	45	---Ethylene-propylene copolymers
2860	3901.9020	---线型低密度聚乙烯	6.5	0 冰岛IS,东盟AS,哥CR,新加坡SG,新西兰NZ,智利CL 3.9 澳AU 5 巴PK	0 受惠国LD	45	---Linearity low density polyethylene

序号 No.	税则号列 Tariff Line	中文货品名称 Article Description in Chinese	最惠国税率 MFN(%)	协定税率 Agreement(%)	特惠税率 SP(%)	普通税率 Gen(%)	英文货品名称 Article Description
2861	3901.9090	---其他	6.5	0 澳门MO,冰岛IS,东盟AS,哥CR,秘鲁PE,香港HK,新加坡SG,新西兰NZ,智利CL 2.6 瑞士CH 3.9 澳AU 5 巴PK 5.5 韩国KR 6.3 亚太AP	0 受惠国$_1$LD$_1$	45	---Other
	39.02	**初级形状的丙烯或其他烯烃聚合物:**					**Polymers of propylene or of other olefins, in primary forms:**
2862	3902.1000	-聚丙烯	6.5	0 澳门MO,冰岛IS,东盟AS,哥CR,香港HK,新加坡SG,新西兰NZ,智利CL 3.9 澳AU 4.7 瑞士CH 5 巴PK		45	-Polypropylene
	ex39021000	电工级初级形状聚丙烯树脂(灰分含量不大于30ppm)	Δ3				Electrotechonical polypropylene resin in primary forms (Ash content not more than 30ppm)
2863	3902.2000	-聚异丁烯	6.5	0 冰岛IS,东盟AS,哥CR,秘鲁PE,新西兰NZ,智利CL 2.6 瑞士CH 3.9 澳AU 5 巴PK	0 受惠国LD	45	-Polyisobutylene
		-丙烯共聚物:					-Propylene copolymers:
2864	3902.3010	---乙烯-丙烯共聚物(乙丙橡胶)	6.5	0 冰岛IS,东盟AS,哥CR,秘鲁PE,台湾TW,香港HK,新加坡SG,新西兰NZ,智利CL 2.6 瑞士CH 3.9 澳AU 5 巴PK 5.6 韩国KR 6 亚太AP	0 受惠国LD	45	---Ethylene-propylene copolymers
2865	3902.3090	---其他	6.5	0 冰岛IS,东盟AS,哥CR,秘鲁PE,香港HK,新加坡SG,新西兰NZ,智利CL 2.6 瑞士CH 3.9 澳AU 5 巴PK 6 亚太AP 6.2 韩国KR	0 受惠国LD	45	---Other
2866	3902.9000	-其他	6.5	0 冰岛IS,东盟AS,哥CR,秘鲁PE,台湾TW,新加坡SG,新西兰NZ,智利CL 2.6 瑞士CH 3.9 澳AU 5 巴PK	0 受惠国LD	45	-Other
	39.03	**初级形状的苯乙烯聚合物:**					**Polymers of styrene, in primary forms:**
		-聚苯乙烯:					-Polystyrene:
2867	3903.1100	--可发性的	6.5	0 冰岛IS,东盟AS,哥CR,秘鲁PE,新加坡SG,新西兰NZ,智利CL 2.6 瑞士CH 3.9 澳AU 5 巴PK 6 亚太AP 6.2 韩国KR	0 受惠国LD	45	--Expansible
		--其他:					--Other:

序号 No.	税则号列 Tariff Line	中文货品名称 Article Description in Chinese	最惠国税率 MFN(%)	协定税率 Agreement(%)	特惠税率 SP(%)	普通税率 Gen(%)	英文货品名称 Article Description
2868	3903.1910	---改性的	6.5	0 冰岛IS,东盟AS,哥CR,秘鲁PE,香港HK,新加坡SG,新西兰NZ,智利CL 2.6 瑞士CH 3.9 澳AU 5 巴PK 5.8 韩国KR 6 亚太AP	0 受惠国LD	45	---Modified
2869	3903.1990	---其他	6.5	0 冰岛IS,东盟AS,哥CR,秘鲁PE,香港HK,新加坡SG,新西兰NZ,智利CL 2.6 瑞士CH 3.9 澳AU 5 巴PK 5.8 韩国KR 6 亚太AP	0 受惠国LD	45	---Other
2870	3903.2000	-苯乙烯-丙烯腈（SAN）共聚物	12	0 冰岛IS,东盟AS,哥CR,秘鲁PE,台湾TW,新加坡SG,新西兰NZ,智利CL 6 巴PK 7.2 澳AU 8.4 瑞士CH 11 韩国KR	0 受惠国[1]LD[1]	45	-Styrene-acrylonitrile (SAN) copoly-mers
		-丙烯腈-丁二烯-苯乙烯（ABS）共聚物：					-Acrylonitrile-butadiene-styrene (ABS) copolymers:
2871	3903.3010	---改性的	6.5	0 澳门MO,冰岛IS,东盟AS,哥CR,秘鲁PE,香港HK,新加坡SG,新西兰NZ,智利CL 3.9 澳AU 4.7 瑞士CH 5 巴PK 5.8 韩国KR 6 亚太AP	0 受惠国LD	45	---Modified
2872	3903.3090	---其他	6.5	0 澳门MO,冰岛IS,东盟AS,哥CR,秘鲁PE,香港HK,新加坡SG,新西兰NZ,智利CL 3.9 澳AU 4.6 瑞士CH 5 巴PK 5.8 韩国KR 6 亚太AP	0 受惠国LD	45	---Other
2873	3903.9000	-其他	6.5	0 冰岛IS,东盟AS,哥CR,秘鲁PE,台湾TW,香港HK,新加坡SG,新西兰NZ,智利CL 2.6 瑞士CH 3.9 澳AU 5 巴PK 5.6 韩国KR 6 亚太AP	0 受惠国LD	45	-Other
	39.04	**初级形状的氯乙烯或其他卤化烯烃聚合物：**					**Polymers of vinyl chloride or of other halogenated olefins, in primary forms:**
		-聚氯乙烯，未掺其他物质：					-Poly (vinyl chloride) , not mixed with any other substances:

序号 No.	税则号列 Tariff Line	中文货品名称 Article Description in Chinese	最惠国税率 MFN(%)	协定税率 Agreement(%)	特惠税率 SP(%)	普通税率 Gen(%)	英文货品名称 Article Description
2874	3904.1010	---糊树脂	6.5	0 冰岛IS,东盟AS,哥CR,秘鲁PE,新加坡SG,新西兰NZ,智利CL 2.6 瑞士CH 3.9 澳AU 5.8 韩国KR 6 巴PK,亚太AP	0 受惠国LD	45	---Paste Poly (vinyl chloride)
2875	3904.1090	---其他	6.5	0 冰岛IS,东盟AS,哥CR,秘鲁PE,新加坡SG,新西兰NZ,智利CL 2.6 瑞士CH 3.9 澳AU 5.5 韩国KR 6 巴PK,亚太AP	0 受惠国LD	45	---Other
		-其他聚氯乙烯:					-Other poly (vinyl chloride) :
2876	3904.2100	--未塑化	6.5	0 冰岛IS,东盟AS,哥CR,秘鲁PE,香港HK,新加坡SG,新西兰NZ,智利CL 2.6 瑞士CH 3.9 澳AU 5 巴PK 5.8 韩国KR	0 受惠国LD	45	--Non-plasticized
2877	3904.2200	--已塑化	6.5	0 冰岛IS,东盟AS,哥CR,秘鲁PE,香港HK,新加坡SG,新西兰NZ,智利CL 2.6 瑞士CH 3.9 澳AU 5.8 韩国KR	0 受惠国LD	45	--Plasticized
2878	3904.3000	-氯乙烯-乙酸乙烯酯共聚物	9	0 冰岛IS,东盟AS,哥CR,秘鲁PE,新西兰NZ,智利CL 3.6 瑞士CH 5 巴PK 5.4 澳AU 7.8 韩国KR 8.6 亚太AP	0 受惠国LD	45	-Vinyl chloride-vinyl acetate copolymers
2879	3904.4000	-其他氯乙烯共聚物	12	0 冰岛IS,东盟AS,哥CR,新加坡SG,新西兰NZ,智利CL 3.6 秘鲁PE 6 巴PK 7.2 澳AU 8.4 瑞士CH 10.4 韩国KR 11.4 亚太AP	0 受惠国$_1$LD$_1$	45	-Other vinyl chloride copolymers
2880	3904.5000	-偏二氯乙烯聚合物	6.5	0 冰岛IS,东盟AS,哥CR,秘鲁PE,新西兰NZ,智利CL 2.6 瑞士CH 3.9 澳AU,韩国KR 5 巴PK	0 受惠国LD	45	-Vinylidene chloride polymers
		-氟聚合物:					-Fluoropolymers:
2881	3904.6100	--聚四氟乙烯	10	0 冰岛IS,东盟AS,哥CR,秘鲁PE,新加坡SG,新西兰NZ,智利CL 4 瑞士CH 5 巴PK 6 澳AU 8 韩国KR	0 受惠国LD	45	--Polytetrafl uoroethylene

序号 No.	税则号列 Tariff Line	中文货品名称 Article Description in Chinese	最惠国税率 MFN(%)	协定税率 Agreement(%)	特惠税率 SP(%)	普通税率 Gen(%)	英文货品名称 Article Description
2882	3904.6900	--其他	6.5	0 冰岛IS,东盟AS,哥CR,秘鲁PE,新西兰NZ,智利CL 2.6 瑞士CH 3.9 澳AU,韩国KR 5 巴PK	0 受惠国LD	45	--Other
2883	3904.9000	-其他	10	0 冰岛IS,东盟AS,哥CR,秘鲁PE,新西兰NZ,智利CL 4 瑞士CH 5 巴PK 6 澳AU 8.6 韩国KR	0 受惠国LD	45	-Other
	39.05	**初级形状的乙酸乙烯酯或其他乙烯酯聚合物;初级形状的其他乙烯基聚合物:**					**Polymers of vinyl acetate or of other vinyl esters, in primary forms; other vinyl polymers in primary forms:**
		-聚乙酸乙烯酯:					-Poly (vinyl acetate) :
2884	3905.1200	--水分散体	10	0 冰岛IS,东盟AS,哥CR,新加坡SG,新西兰NZ,智利CL 3 秘鲁PE 4 瑞士CH 6 澳AU 8.6 韩国KR	0 受惠国$_1$LD$_1$	45	--In aqueous dispersion
2885	3905.1900	--其他	10	0 冰岛IS,东盟AS,哥CR,秘鲁PE,新西兰NZ,智利CL 4 瑞士CH 5 巴PK 6 澳AU 8.6 韩国KR	0 受惠国$_1$LD$_1$	45	--Other
		-乙酸乙烯酯共聚物:					-Vinyl acetate copolymers:
2886	3905.2100	--水分散体	10	0 冰岛IS,东盟AS,哥CR,秘鲁PE,台湾TW,新加坡SG,新西兰NZ,智利CL 4 瑞士CH 5 巴PK 6 澳AU 8.6 韩国KR	0 受惠国$_1$LD$_1$	45	--In aqueous dispersion
2887	3905.2900	--其他	10	0 冰岛IS,东盟AS,哥CR,秘鲁PE,新加坡SG,新西兰NZ,智利CL 5 巴PK 6 澳AU 8.6 韩国KR	0 受惠国$_1$LD$_1$	45	--Other
2888	3905.3000	-聚乙烯醇，不论是否含有未水解的乙酸酯基	14	0 冰岛IS,东盟AS,哥CR,秘鲁PE,台湾TW,新加坡SG,新西兰NZ,智利CL 8.4 澳AU 9.8 瑞士CH 11.2 巴PK,韩国KR	0 受惠国$_1$LD$_1$	45	-Poly (vinyl alcohol) , whether or not containing unhydrolyzed acetate groups
		-其他:					-Other:
2889	3905.9100	--共聚物	10	0 冰岛IS,东盟AS,哥CR,秘鲁PE,新西兰NZ,智利CL 4 瑞士CH 5 巴PK 6 澳AU 8.6 韩国KR	0 受惠国$_1$LD$_1$	45	--Copolymers

序号 No.	税则号列 Tariff Line	中文货品名称 Article Description in Chinese	最惠国税率 MFN(%)	协定税率 Agreement(%)	特惠税率 SP(%)	普通税率 Gen(%)	英文货品名称 Article Description
2890	3905.9900	--其他	10	0 冰岛IS,东盟AS,哥CR,香港HK,新西兰NZ,智利CL 3 秘鲁PE 4 瑞士CH 6 澳AU 8.6 韩国KR	0 受惠国$_1$LD$_1$	45	--Other
	39.06	**初级形状的丙烯酸聚合物:**					**Acrylic polymers in primary forms:**
2891	3906.1000	-聚甲基丙烯酸甲酯	6.5	0 冰岛IS,东盟AS,哥CR,秘鲁PE,台湾TW,香港HK,新西兰NZ,智利CL 2.6 瑞士CH 3.9 澳AU 5 巴PK 6 亚太AP 6.2 韩国KR	0 受惠国LD	45	-Poly (methyl methacrylate)
		-其他:					-Other:
2892	3906.9010	---聚丙烯酰胺	6.5	0 冰岛IS,东盟AS,哥CR,秘鲁PE,台湾TW,香港HK,新西兰NZ,智利CL 2.6 瑞士CH 3.9 澳AU 5 巴PK 6 亚太AP 6.2 韩国KR	0 受惠国LD	45	---Polyacrylamide
2893	3906.9090	---其他	6.5	0 冰岛IS,东盟AS,哥CR,秘鲁PE,台湾TW,香港HK,新西兰NZ,智利CL 3.9 澳AU 4.6 瑞士CH 5 巴PK 5.2 韩国KR 6 亚太AP	0 受惠国LD	45	---Other
	ex39069090	丙烯酸钠聚合物	Δ3				Sodium acrylate polymer
	39.07	**初级形状的聚缩醛、其他聚醚及环氧树脂;初级形状的聚碳酸酯、醇酸树脂、聚烯丙基酯及其他聚酯:**					**Polyacetals, other polyethers and epoxide resins, in primary forms; polycarbonates, alkyd resins, polyallyl esters and other polyesters, in primary forms:**
		-聚缩醛:					-Polyacetals:
2894	3907.1010	---聚甲醛	6.5	0 冰岛IS,东盟AS,哥CR,秘鲁PE,台湾TW,香港HK,新加坡SG,新西兰NZ,智利CL 2.6 瑞士CH 3.9 澳AU 5 巴PK 5.6 韩国KR 6 亚太AP	0 受惠国LD	45	---Polyoxymethylene (POM)
2895	3907.1090	---其他	6.5	0 冰岛IS,东盟AS,哥CR,秘鲁PE,香港HK,新加坡SG,新西兰NZ,智利CL 2.6 瑞士CH 3.9 澳AU,韩国KR 5 巴PK 6 亚太AP	0 受惠国LD	45	---Other
		-其他聚醚:					-Other polyethers:

序号 No.	税则号列 Tariff Line	中文货品名称 Article Description in Chinese	最惠国税率 MFN(%)	协定税率 Agreement(%)	特惠税率 SP(%)	普通税率 Gen(%)	英文货品名称 Article Description
2896	3907.2010	---聚四亚甲基醚二醇	6.5Δ3	0 冰岛IS,东盟AS,哥CR,韩国KR,秘鲁PE,台湾TW,新加坡SG,新西兰NZ,智利CL 2.6 瑞士CH 3.9 澳AU 5 巴PK 6 亚太AP	0 受惠国LD	45	---Polvtetramethylene Ether Glycol
2897	3907.2090	---其他	6.5	0 冰岛IS,东盟AS,哥CR,秘鲁PE,新加坡SG,新西兰NZ,智利CL 3.9 澳AU 4.6 瑞士CH 5 巴PK 5.6 韩国KR 6 亚太AP	0 受惠国LD	45	---Other
2898	3907.3000	-环氧树脂	6.5	0 冰岛IS,东盟AS,哥CR,秘鲁PE,台湾TW,香港HK,新加坡SG,新西兰NZ,智利CL 3.9 澳AU 4.7 瑞士CH 5 巴PK 5.6 韩国KR 6 亚太AP	0 受惠国LD	45	-Epoxide resins
	ex39073000	溴的质量百分含量在18%及以上或进口CIF价格高于3800美元/吨的环氧树脂（如溶于溶剂，以纯环氧树脂折算溴的百分含量）	Δ4				Epoxyresins containing by weight more than 18% Bromine or import CIF>3800usd/t (base on pure epoxyresins if dissolved in solvent)
2899	3907.4000	-聚碳酸酯	6.5Δ3	0 冰岛IS,东盟AS,哥CR,秘鲁PE,台湾TW,香港HK,新西兰NZ,智利CL 3.9 澳AU 4.6 瑞士CH 5 巴PK 5.6 韩国KR 6.1 亚太AP	0 受惠国LD	45	-Polycarbonates
2900	3907.5000	-醇酸树脂	10	0 冰岛IS,东盟AS,哥CR,台湾TW,新加坡SG,新西兰NZ,智利CL 3 秘鲁PE 4 瑞士CH 5 巴PK 6 澳AU 8 韩国KR 9.5 亚太AP	0 受惠国LD	45	-Alkyd resins
		-聚对苯二甲酸乙二酯：					-Poly (ethylene terephthalate) :
		---切片：					---In the form of slices or chips:
2901	3907.6011	----高粘度	6.5	0 冰岛IS,哥CR,秘鲁PE,新西兰NZ,智利CL 2.6 瑞士CH 3.9 澳AU 5.8 韩国KR	0 受惠国LD	45	----High viscosity
2902	3907.6019	----其他	6.5	0 澳门MO,冰岛IS,哥CR,秘鲁PE,香港HK,新西兰NZ,智利CL 2.6 瑞士CH 3.9 澳AU 5.8 韩国KR	0 受惠国LD	45	----Other

序号 No.	税则号列 Tariff Line	中文货品名称 Article Description in Chinese	最惠国税率 MFN(%)	协定税率 Agreement(%)	特惠税率 SP(%)	普通税率 Gen(%)	英文货品名称 Article Description
2903	3907.6090	---其他	6.5	0 澳门MO,冰岛IS,东盟AS,哥CR,秘鲁PE,新西兰NZ,智利CL 2.6 瑞士CH 3.9 澳AU 5.6 韩国KR	0 受惠国LD	45	---Other
2904	3907.7000	-聚乳酸	6.5∆3	0 澳门MO,冰岛IS,东盟AS,哥CR,秘鲁PE,香港HK,新西兰NZ,智利CL 2.6 瑞士CH 3.9 澳AU,韩国KR 5 巴PK 6.2 亚太AP	0 受惠国LD	45	-Poly (lactic acid)
		-其他聚酯:					-Other polyesters:
2905	3907.9100	--不饱和	6.5	0 冰岛IS,东盟AS,哥CR,秘鲁PE,台湾TW,新加坡SG,新西兰NZ,智利CL 2.6 瑞士CH 3.9 澳AU 5 巴PK 5.2 韩国KR	0 受惠国LD	45	--Unsaturated
		--其他:					--Other:
2906	3907.9910	---聚对苯二甲酸丁二酯	6.5	0 澳门MO,冰岛IS,东盟AS,哥CR,秘鲁PE,香港HK,新西兰NZ,智利CL 2.6 瑞士CH 3.9 澳AU 5 巴PK 5.6 韩国KR 6.2 亚太AP	0 受惠国LD	45	---Polybutylene terephthalate
		---其他:					---Other:
2907	3907.9991	----聚对苯二甲酸-己二醇-丁二醇酯	6.5	0 澳门MO,冰岛IS,东盟AS,哥CR,韩国KR,秘鲁PE,台湾TW,香港HK,新西兰NZ,智利CL 2.6 瑞士CH 3.9 澳AU 5 巴PK 6.2 亚太AP	0 受惠国LD	45	----Poly (butylene adipata-co-terephthalate)
2908	3907.9999	----其他	6.5	0 澳门MO,冰岛IS,东盟AS,哥CR,韩国KR,秘鲁PE,台湾TW,香港HK,新西兰NZ,智利CL 2.6 瑞士CH 3.9 澳AU 5 巴PK 6.2 亚太AP	0 受惠国LD	45	----Other
	39.08	**初级形状的聚酰胺:**					**Polyamides in primary forms:**
		-聚酰胺-6、-11、-12、-6，6、-6，9、-6，10或-6，12:					-Polyamide-6, -11, -12, -6, 6, -6, 9, -6, 10 or -6, 12:
		--切片:					--In the form of slices or chips:
2909	3908.1011	----聚酰胺-6，6切片	6.5	0 冰岛IS,东盟AS,哥CR,秘鲁PE,香港HK,新加坡SG,新西兰NZ,智利CL 3.9 澳AU 4.6 瑞士CH 5 巴PK	0 受惠国LD	45	----Of polyamide-6, 6

序号 No.	税则号列 Tariff Line	中文货品名称 Article Description in Chinese	最惠国税率 MFN(%)	协定税率 Agreement(%)	特惠税率 SP(%)	普通税率 Gen(%)	英文货品名称 Article Description
2910	3908.1012	----聚酰胺-6切片	6.5	0 冰岛IS,东盟AS,哥CR,秘鲁PE,香港HK,新加坡SG,新西兰NZ,智利CL 3.9 澳AU 4.7 瑞士CH 5 巴PK	0 受惠国LD	45	----Of polyamide-6
2911	3908.1019	----其他	6.5	0 冰岛IS,东盟AS,哥CR,秘鲁PE,香港HK,新加坡SG,新西兰NZ,智利CL 3.9 澳AU 4.7 瑞士CH 5 巴PK	0 受惠国LD	45	----Other
2912	3908.1090	---其他	6.5	0 冰岛IS,东盟AS,哥CR,秘鲁PE,香港HK,新西兰NZ,智利CL 3.9 澳AU 4.6 瑞士CH 5 巴PK	0 受惠国LD	45	---Other
		-其他:					-Other:
2913	3908.9010	---芳香族聚酰胺及其共聚物	10	0 冰岛IS,东盟AS,哥CR,秘鲁PE,香港HK,新加坡SG,新西兰NZ,智利CL 5 巴PK 6 澳AU	0 受惠国LD	45	---Aromatic polyamide and copolymers
2914	3908.9020	---半芳香族聚酰胺及其共聚物	10	0 冰岛IS,东盟AS,哥CR,秘鲁PE,香港HK,新加坡SG,新西兰NZ,智利CL 5 巴PK 6 澳AU	0 受惠国LD	45	---Semi-aromatic polyamide and copolymers
2915	3908.9090	---其他	10	0 冰岛IS,东盟AS,哥CR,秘鲁PE,香港HK,新加坡SG,新西兰NZ,智利CL 5 巴PK 6 澳AU	0 受惠国LD	45	---Other
	39.09	**初级形状的氨基树脂、酚醛树脂及聚氨酯类:**					**Amino-resins, phenolic resins and polyurethanes, in primary forms:**
2916	3909.1000	-尿素树脂;硫尿树脂	6.5	0 冰岛IS,东盟AS,哥CR,韩国KR,秘鲁PE,台湾TW,新西兰NZ,智利CL 2.6 瑞士CH 3.9 澳AU 5 巴PK 6.1 亚太AP	0 受惠国LD	45	-Urea resins; thiourea resins
2917	3909.2000	-蜜胺树脂	6.5	0 冰岛IS,东盟AS,哥CR,韩国KR,秘鲁PE,台湾TW,新西兰NZ,智利CL 2.6 瑞士CH 3.9 澳AU 5 巴PK 6.1 亚太AP	0 受惠国LD	45	-Melamine resins
		-其他氨基树脂:					-Other amino-resins:
2918	3909.3010	---聚（亚甲基苯基异氰酸酯）（聚合MDI或粗MDI）	6.5	0 冰岛IS,东盟AS,哥CR,秘鲁PE,香港HK,新加坡SG,新西兰NZ,智利CL 2.6 瑞士CH 3.9 澳AU 5 巴PK 5.6 韩国KR 6 亚太AP	0 受惠国LD	35	---Poly (methylene phenyl isocyanate)

序号 No.	税则号列 Tariff Line	中文货品名称 Article Description in Chinese	最惠国税率 MFN(%)	协定税率 Agreement(%)	特惠税率 SP(%)	普通税率 Gen(%)	英文货品名称 Article Description
2919	3909.3090	---其他	6.5	0 冰岛IS,东盟AS,哥CR,韩国KR,秘鲁PE,台湾TW,新加坡SG,新西兰NZ,智利CL 2.6 瑞士CH 3.9 澳AU 5 巴PK	0 受惠国LD	45	---Other
2920	3909.4000	-酚醛树脂	6.5	0 冰岛IS,东盟AS,哥CR,秘鲁PE,台湾TW,新西兰NZ,智利CL 2.6 瑞士CH 3.9 澳AU 5 巴PK 5.2 韩国KR 6.1 亚太AP	0 受惠国LD	45	-Phenolic resins
2921	3909.5000	-聚氨基甲酸酯	6.5	0 澳门MO,冰岛IS,东盟AS,哥CR,韩国KR,秘鲁PE,台湾TW,香港HK,新加坡SG,新西兰NZ,智利CL 2.6 瑞士CH 3.9 澳AU 5 巴PK 6 亚太AP	0 受惠国LD	45	-Polyurethanes
	39.10	**初级形状的聚硅氧烷**					**Silicones in primary forms**
2922	3910.0000	初级形状的聚硅氧烷	6.5	0 冰岛IS,东盟AS,哥CR,秘鲁PE,台湾TW,香港HK,新西兰NZ,智利CL 2.6 瑞士CH 3.9 澳AU 5 巴PK 5.2 韩国KR 6.1 亚太AP	0 受惠国LD	45	Silicones in primary forms
	39.11	**初级形状的石油树脂、苯并呋喃—茚树脂、多萜树脂、多硫化物、聚砜及本章注释三所规定的其他税号未列名产品:**					**Petroleum resins, coumarone-indene resins, polyterpenes, polysulphides, polysulphones and other products specified in note 3 to this chapter, not elsewhere specified or included, in primary forms:**
2923	3911.1000	-石油树脂、苯并呋喃树脂、茚树脂、苯并呋喃茚树脂及多萜树脂	6.5	0 冰岛IS,东盟AS,哥CR,秘鲁PE,台湾TW,新西兰NZ,智利CL 2.6 瑞士CH 3.9 澳AU 5 巴PK 5.6 韩国KR 6.1 亚太AP	0 受惠国LD	45	-Petroleum resins, coumarone, indene or coumarone-indene resins and polyterpenes
2924	3911.9000	-其他	6.5	0 冰岛IS,东盟AS,哥CR,秘鲁PE,新西兰NZ,智利CL 2.6 瑞士CH 3.9 澳AU,韩国KR 5 巴PK	0 受惠国LD	45	-Other
	ex39119000	偏苯三酸酐和异氰酸预缩聚物	Δ3				Precondensed polymer of modified trihydroxy acetate
	ex39119000	芳基酸与芳基胺预缩聚物	Δ3				Precondensed polymer of modified trihydroxy acetate
	ex39119000	改性三羟乙基脲酸酯类预缩聚物	Δ3				Precondensed polymer of modified trihydroxy acetate
	39.12	**初级形状的其他税号未列名的纤维素及其化学衍生物:**					**Cellulose and its chemical derivatives, not elsewhere specified or included, in primary forms:**
		-乙酸纤维素:					-Cellulose acetates:

序号 No.	税则号列 Tariff Line	中文货品名称 Article Description in Chinese	最惠国税率 MFN(%)	协定税率 Agreement(%)	特惠税率 SP(%)	普通税率 Gen(%)	英文货品名称 Article Description
2925	3912.1100	--未塑化	6.5	0 冰岛IS,东盟AS,哥CR,秘鲁PE,新西兰NZ,智利CL 2.6 瑞士CH 3.9 澳AU 5 巴PK 5.2 韩国KR	0 受惠国$_1$LD$_1$	40	--Non-plasticized
2926	3912.1200	--已塑化	6.5	0 冰岛IS,东盟AS,哥CR,秘鲁PE,新西兰NZ,智利CL 2.6 瑞士CH 3.9 澳AU,韩国KR 5 巴PK	0 受惠国$_1$LD$_1$	40	---Plasticized
2927	3912.2000	-硝酸纤维素(包括胶棉)	6.5	0 冰岛IS,东盟AS,哥CR,秘鲁PE,新西兰NZ,智利CL 2.6 瑞士CH 3.9 澳AU,韩国KR 5 巴PK	0 受惠国$_1$LD$_1$	45	-Cellulose nitrates (including collodions)
		-纤维素醚:					-Cellulose ethers:
2928	3912.3100	--羧甲基纤维素及其盐	6.5	0 冰岛IS,东盟AS,哥CR,秘鲁PE,新西兰NZ,智利CL 2.6 瑞士CH 3.9 澳AU,韩国KR 5 巴PK	0 受惠国$_1$LD$_1$	45	--Carboxymethylcellulose and its salts
2929	3912.3900	--其他	6.5	0 冰岛IS,东盟AS,哥CR,秘鲁PE,新西兰NZ,智利CL 2.6 瑞士CH 3.9 澳AU,韩国KR 5 巴PK	0 受惠国$_1$LD$_1$	45	--Other
2930	3912.9000	-其他	6.5	0 冰岛IS,东盟AS,哥CR,秘鲁PE,香港HK,新西兰NZ,智利CL 2.6 瑞士CH 3.9 澳AU,韩国KR 5 巴PK	0 受惠国$_1$LD$_1$	45	-Other
	39.13	**初级形状的其他税号未列名的天然聚合物(例如藻酸)及改性天然聚合物(例如,硬化蛋白、天然橡胶的化学衍生物):**					**Natural polymers (for example, alginic acid) and modified natural polymers (for example, hardened proteins, chemical derivatives of natural rubber), not elsewhere specified or included, in primary forms:**
2931	3913.1000	-藻酸及其盐和酯	10	0 冰岛IS,东盟AS,哥CR,新加坡SG,新西兰NZ,智利CL 4 瑞士CH 5 巴PK 6 澳AU 8 韩国KR	0 受惠国LD	45	-Alginic acid, its salts and esters
2932	3913.9000	-其他	6.5	0 东盟AS,哥CR,秘鲁PE,新西兰NZ,智利CL 2.6 瑞士CH 3.3 冰岛IS 3.9 澳AU,韩国KR 5 巴PK	0 受惠国LD	50	-Other
	39.14	**初级形状的离子交换剂,以税号39.01至39.13的聚合物为基本成分的**					**Ion-exchangers based on polymers of headings 3901 to 3913, in primary forms**
2933	3914.0000	初级形状的离子交换剂,以税号39.01至39.13的聚合物为基本成分的	6.5	0 东盟AS,哥CR,秘鲁PE,新西兰NZ,智利CL 2.6 瑞士CH 3.9 澳AU,韩国KR 5 巴PK	0 受惠国LD	45	Ion-exchangers based on polymers of headings Nos.39.01 to 39.13, in primary forms

序号 No.	税则号列 Tariff Line	中文货品名称 Article Description in Chinese	最惠国税率 MFN(%)	协定税率 Agreement(%)	特惠税率 SP(%)	普通税率 Gen(%)	英文货品名称 Article Description
		第二分章废碎料及下脚料;半制品;制成品					II.WASTE, PARINGS AND SCRAP; SEMI MANUFACTURES; ARTICLES
	39.15	**塑料的废碎料及下脚料:**					**Waste, parings and scrap, of plastics:**
2934	3915.1000	-乙烯聚合物的	6.5	0 澳门MO,冰岛IS,东盟AS,哥CR,秘鲁PE,香港HK,新加坡SG,新西兰NZ,智利CL 2.6 瑞士CH 3.9 澳AU 5 巴PK 5.6 韩国KR	0 受惠国LD	50	-Of polymers of ethylene
2935	3915.2000	-苯乙烯聚合物的	6.5	0 澳门MO,冰岛IS,东盟AS,哥CR,秘鲁PE,香港HK,新加坡SG,新西兰NZ,智利CL 2.6 瑞士CH 3.9 澳AU 5 巴PK 5.6 韩国KR	0 受惠国LD	50	-Of polymers of styrene
2936	3915.3000	-氯乙烯聚合物的	6.5	0 澳门MO,冰岛IS,东盟AS,哥CR,秘鲁PE,香港HK,新加坡SG,新西兰NZ,智利CL 2.6 瑞士CH 3.9 澳AU 5 巴PK 5.6 韩国KR	0 受惠国LD	50	-Of polymers of vinyl chloride
		-其他塑料的:					-Of other plastics:
2937	3915.9010	---聚对苯二甲酸乙二酯的	6.5	0 澳门MO,冰岛IS,东盟AS,哥CR,秘鲁PE,香港HK,新加坡SG,新西兰NZ,智利CL 3.9 澳AU 4.6 瑞士CH 5 巴PK 5.6 韩国KR	0 受惠国LD	50	---Of pdyethylene glycol tevephthalate
2938	3915.9090	---其他	6.5	0 澳门MO,冰岛IS,东盟AS,哥CR,秘鲁PE,香港HK,新加坡SG,新西兰NZ,智利CL 3.9 澳AU 4.6 瑞士CH 5 巴PK 5.6 韩国KR	0 受惠国LD	50	---Other
	39.16	**塑料制的单丝(截面直径超过1毫米)、条、杆、型材及异型材,不论是否经表面加工,但未经其他加工:**					**Monofilament of which any cross-sectional dimension exceeds 1 mm, rods, sticks and profile shapes, whether or not surface-worked but not otherwise worked, of plastics:**
2939	3916.1000	-乙烯聚合物制	10	0 冰岛IS,东盟AS,哥CR,新加坡SG,新西兰NZ,智利CL 3 秘鲁PE 4 瑞士CH 5 巴PK 6 澳AU 8 韩国KR	0 受惠国$_1$LD$_1$	45	-Of polymers of ethylene
		-氯乙烯聚合物制:					-Of polymers of vinyl chloride:

序号 No.	税则号列 Tariff Line	中文货品名称 Article Description in Chinese	最惠国税率 MFN(%)	协定税率 Agreement(%)	特惠税率 SP(%)	普通税率 Gen(%)	英文货品名称 Article Description
2940	3916.2010	---异型材	10	0 冰岛IS,东盟AS,哥CR,秘鲁PE,新西兰NZ,智利CL 4 瑞士CH 5 巴PK 6 澳AU 7 亚太AP 8 韩国KR	0 受惠国$_1$LD$_1$	45	---Profile shapes
2941	3916.2090	---其他	10	0 冰岛IS,东盟AS,哥CR,秘鲁PE,新西兰NZ,智利CL 4 瑞士CH 5 巴PK 6 澳AU 7 亚太AP 8 韩国KR	0 受惠国$_1$LD$_1$	45	---Other
		-其他塑料制:					-Of other plastics:
2942	3916.9010	---聚酰胺制	10	0 冰岛IS,东盟AS,哥CR,秘鲁PE,香港HK,新加坡SG,新西兰NZ,智利CL 4 瑞士CH 5 巴PK 6 澳AU 8 韩国KR	0 受惠国$_1$LD$_1$	45	---Of polyamides
2943	3916.9090	---其他	10	0 冰岛IS,东盟AS,哥CR,秘鲁PE,新加坡SG,新西兰NZ,智利CL 4 瑞士CH 5 巴PK 6 澳AU 8 韩国KR	0 受惠国$_1$LD$_1$	45	---Other
	39.17	**塑料制的管子及其附件（例如，接头、肘管、法兰）:**					**Tubes, pipes and hoses, and fittings therefor (for example, joints, elbows, flanges), of plastics:**
2944	3917.1000	-硬化蛋白或纤维素材料制的人造肠衣（香肠用肠衣）	10	0 冰岛IS,东盟AS,哥CR,秘鲁PE,新西兰NZ,智利CL 4 瑞士CH 5 巴PK 6 澳AU 8 韩国KR	0 受惠国$_1$LD$_1$	50	-Artificial guts (sausage casings) of hardened protein or of cellulosic materials
		-硬管:					-Tubes, pipes and hoses, rigid:
2945	3917.2100	--乙烯聚合物制	10	0 冰岛IS,东盟AS,哥CR,新加坡SG,新西兰NZ,智利CL 3 秘鲁PE 4 瑞士CH 5 巴PK 6 澳AU 8 韩国KR	0 受惠国LD	45	--Of polymers of ethylene
2946	3917.2200	--丙烯聚合物制	10	0 冰岛IS,东盟AS,哥CR,秘鲁PE,新西兰NZ,智利CL 4 瑞士CH 5 巴PK 6 澳AU 8 韩国KR	0 受惠国LD	45	--Of polymers of propylene

序号 No.	税则号列 Tariff Line	中文货品名称 Article Description in Chinese	最惠国税率 MFN(%)	协定税率 Agreement(%)	特惠税率 SP(%)	普通税率 Gen(%)	英文货品名称 Article Description
2947	3917.2300	--氯乙烯聚合物制	10	0 冰岛IS,东盟AS,哥CR,香港HK,新加坡SG,新西兰NZ,智利CL 3 秘鲁PE 4 瑞士CH 5 巴PK 6 澳AU 8 韩国KR	0 受惠国LD	45	--Of polymers of vinyl chloride
2948	3917.2900	--其他塑料制	10	0 冰岛IS,东盟AS,哥CR,秘鲁PE,新加坡SG,新西兰NZ,智利CL 5 巴PK 6 澳AU 7 瑞士CH 8 韩国KR	0 受惠国LD	45	--Of other plastics
		-其他管:					-Other tubes, pipes and hoses:
2949	3917.3100	--软管，最小爆破压力为27.6兆帕斯卡	10	0 冰岛IS,东盟AS,哥CR,秘鲁PE,香港HK,新加坡SG,新西兰NZ,智利CL 4 瑞士CH 5 巴PK 6 澳AU,韩国KR 7 亚太AP	0 受惠国LD	45	--Flexible tubes, pipes and hoses, having a minimum burst pressure of 27.6Mpa
2950	3917.3200	--其他未装有附件的管子，未经加强也未与其他材料合制	6.5	0 巴PK,冰岛IS,东盟AS,哥CR,秘鲁PE,新西兰NZ,智利CL 3.9 澳AU,韩国KR 4.6 瑞士CH,亚太AP	0 受惠国LD	45	--Other, not reinforced or otherwise combined with other materials, without fittings
2951	3917.3300	--其他装有附件的管子，未经加强也未与其他材料合制	6.5	0 巴PK,冰岛IS,东盟AS,哥CR,秘鲁PE,新西兰NZ,智利CL 2.6 瑞士CH 3.9 澳AU,韩国KR 4.6 亚太AP	0 受惠国LD	45	--Other, not reinforced or otherwise combined with other materials, with fittings
2952	3917.3900	--其他	6.5	0 冰岛IS,东盟AS,哥CR,秘鲁PE,新加坡SG,新西兰NZ,智利CL 2.6 瑞士CH 3.9 澳AU 4.5 巴PK,亚太AP 5.6 韩国KR	0 受惠国LD	45	--Other
2953	3917.4000	-管子附件	10	0 冰岛IS,东盟AS,哥CR,新加坡SG,新西兰NZ,智利CL 3 秘鲁PE 5 巴PK 6 澳AU,韩国KR 7 瑞士CH,亚太AP	0 受惠国LD	45	-Fittings
	39.18	**块状或成卷的塑料铺地制品，不论是否胶粘;本章注释九所规定的塑料糊墙品:**					**Floor coverings of plastics, whether or not self-adhesive, in rolls or in the form of tiles; wall or ceiling coverings of plastics, as defined in note 9 to this chapter:**
		-氯乙烯聚合物制:					-Of polymers of vinyl chloride:
2954	3918.1010	---糊墙品	10	0 冰岛IS,东盟AS,哥CR,新西兰NZ,智利CL 3 秘鲁PE 4 瑞士CH 5 巴PK 6 澳AU 8 韩国KR	0 受惠国$_1$LD$_1$	45	---Wall or ceiling coverings

序号 No.	税则号列 Tariff Line	中文货品名称 Article Description in Chinese	最惠国税率 MFN(%)	协定税率 Agreement(%)	特惠税率 SP(%)	普通税率 Gen(%)	英文货品名称 Article Description
2955	3918.1090	---其他	10	0 冰岛IS,东盟AS,哥CR,新西兰NZ,智利CL 3 秘鲁PE 5 巴PK 6 澳AU 7 瑞士CH	0 受惠国1LD1	45	---Other
		-其他塑料制:					-Of other plastics:
2956	3918.9010	---糊墙品	10	0 冰岛IS,东盟AS,哥CR,秘鲁PE,香港HK,新西兰NZ,智利CL 4 瑞士CH 5 巴PK 6 澳AU 8 韩国KR	0 受惠国1LD1	45	---Wall or ceiling coverings
2957	3918.9090	---其他	10	0 冰岛IS,东盟AS,哥CR,秘鲁PE,香港HK,新西兰NZ,智利CL 4 瑞士CH 5 巴PK 6 澳AU 8 韩国KR	0 受惠国1LD1	45	---Other
	39.19	**自粘的塑料板、片、膜、箔、带、扁条及其他扁平形状材料，不论是否成卷：**					**Self-adhesive plates, sheets, film, foil, tape, strip and other flat shapes, of plastics, whether or not in rolls:**
		-成卷，宽度不超过20厘米：					-In rolls of a width not exceeding 20cm:
2958	3919.1010	---丙烯酸树脂类为基本成分	6.5	0 冰岛IS,东盟AS,哥CR,秘鲁PE,新西兰NZ,智利CL 2.6 瑞士CH 3.9 澳AU,韩国KR 5 巴PK	0 受惠国LD	45	---Based on acrylic resin
		---其他：					---Other:
2959	3919.1091	----胶囊型反光膜	6.5	0 冰岛IS,东盟AS,哥CR,秘鲁PE,新西兰NZ,智利CL 2.6 瑞士CH 3.9 澳AU,韩国KR 5 巴PK	0 受惠国LD	45	----Encapsulant reflective film
2960	3919.1099	----其他	6.5	0 冰岛IS,东盟AS,哥CR,秘鲁PE,台湾TW,新西兰NZ,智利CL 3.9 澳AU 4.6 瑞士CH 5 巴PK	0 受惠国LD	45	----Other
		-其他：					-Other:
2961	3919.9010	---胶囊型反光膜	6.5	0 巴PK,冰岛IS,东盟AS,哥CR,秘鲁PE,香港HK,新西兰NZ,智利CL 2.6 瑞士CH 3.9 澳AU 4.6 亚太AP 5.6 韩国KR	0 受惠国LD	45	---Encapsulant reflective film
2962	3919.9090	---其他	6.5	0 巴PK,冰岛IS,东盟AS,哥CR,秘鲁PE,台湾TW,香港HK,新西兰NZ,智利CL 2.6 瑞士CH 3.9 澳AU 4.6 亚太AP 5.6 韩国KR	0 受惠国LD	45	---Other

序号 No.	税则号列 Tariff Line	中文货品名称 Article Description in Chinese	最惠国税率 MFN(%)	协定税率 Agreement(%)	特惠税率 SP(%)	普通税率 Gen(%)	英文货品名称 Article Description
	39.20	**其他非泡沫塑料的板、片、膜、箔及扁条，未用其他材料强化、层压、支撑或用类似方法合制：**					**Other plates, sheets, film, foil and strip, of plastics, non-cellular and not reinforced, laminated, supported or similarly combined with other materials:**
		-乙烯聚合物制：					-Of polymers of ethylene:
2963	3920.1010	---乙烯聚合物制电池隔膜	6.5Δ3	0 巴PK,冰岛IS,东盟AS,哥CR,秘鲁PE,香港HK,新西兰NZ,智利CL 2.6 瑞士CH 3.9 澳AU 4.6 亚太AP 5.2 韩国KR	0 受惠国LD	45	---Battery separator, of polymers of ethylene
2964	3920.1090	---其他	6.5	0 澳门MO,巴PK,冰岛IS,东盟AS,哥CR,秘鲁PE,台湾TW,香港HK,新西兰NZ,智利CL 3.9 澳AU 4.6 瑞士CH,亚太AP 5.6 韩国KR	0 受惠国LD	45	---Other
		-丙烯聚合物制：					-Of polymers of propylene:
2965	3920.2010	---丙烯聚合物制电池隔膜	6.5	0 冰岛IS,东盟AS,哥CR,秘鲁PE,香港HK,新西兰NZ,智利CL 2.6 瑞士CH 3.9 澳AU 5 巴PK	0 受惠国LD	45	---Battery separator, of polymers of propylene
2966	3920.2090	---其他	6.5	0 澳门MO,冰岛IS,东盟AS,哥CR,秘鲁PE,台湾TW,香港HK,新西兰NZ,智利CL 3.9 澳AU 4.6 瑞士CH 5 巴PK 5.2 韩国KR	0 受惠国LD	45	---Other
2967	3920.3000	-苯乙烯聚合物制	6.5	0 巴PK,冰岛IS,东盟AS,哥CR,秘鲁PE,台湾TW,香港HK,新西兰NZ,智利CL 2.6 瑞士CH 3.9 澳AU 4.6 亚太AP 5.2 韩国KR	0 受惠国LD	45	-Of polymers of styrene
		-氯乙烯聚合物制：					-Of polymers of vinyl chloride:
2968	3920.4300	--按重量计增塑剂含量不小于6%	6.5	0 冰岛IS,东盟AS,哥CR,秘鲁PE,台湾TW,香港HK,新加坡SG,新西兰NZ,智利CL 2.6 瑞士CH 3.9 澳AU 4.5 巴PK,亚太AP 5.2 韩国KR	0 受惠国LD	45	--Containing by weight not less than 6% of pleasticisers
2969	3920.4900	--其他	6.5	0 澳门MO,冰岛IS,东盟AS,哥CR,秘鲁PE,台湾TW,香港HK,新西兰NZ,智利CL 3.9 澳AU 4.5 巴PK,亚太AP 4.6 瑞士CH 5.6 韩国KR	0 受惠国LD	45	--Other
		-丙烯酸聚合物制：					-Of acrylic polymers:

序号 No.	税则号列 Tariff Line	中文货品名称 Article Description in Chinese	最惠国税率 MFN(%)	协定税率 Agreement(%)	特惠税率 SP(%)	普通税率 Gen(%)	英文货品名称 Article Description
2970	3920.5100	--聚甲基丙烯酸甲酯制	6.5	0 巴PK,冰岛IS,东盟AS,哥CR,秘鲁PE,台湾TW,新西兰NZ,智利CL 2.6 瑞士CH 3.9 澳AU 4.6 亚太AP 5.2 韩国KR	0 受惠国LD	45	--Of poly (methyl methacrylate)
2971	3920.5900	--其他	6.5	0 冰岛IS,东盟AS,哥CR,秘鲁PE,新西兰NZ,智利CL 2.6 瑞士CH 3.9 澳AU 5 巴PK 5.6 韩国KR	0 受惠国LD	45	--Other
		-聚碳酸酯、醇酸树脂、聚烯丙酯或其他聚酯制:					-Of polycarbonates, alkyd resins, polyallyl esters or other polyesters:
2972	3920.6100	--聚碳酸酯制	6.5	0 巴PK,冰岛IS,东盟AS,哥CR,秘鲁PE,台湾TW,新西兰NZ,智利CL 2.6 瑞士CH 3.9 澳AU 4.6 亚太AP 5.6 韩国KR	0 受惠国LD	45	--Of polycarbonates
2973	3920.6200	--聚对苯二甲酸乙二酯制	6.5	0 澳门MO,巴PK,冰岛IS,东盟AS,哥CR,秘鲁PE,台湾TW,香港HK,新西兰NZ,智利CL 2.6 瑞士CH 3.9 澳AU 4.6 亚太AP 5.6 韩国KR	0 受惠国LD	45	--Of poly (ethylene terephthalate)
2974	3920.6300	--不饱和聚酯制	10	0 冰岛IS,东盟AS,哥CR,秘鲁PE,新西兰NZ,智利CL 4 瑞士CH 5 巴PK 6 澳AU 8 韩国KR	0 受惠国LD	45	--Of unsaturated polyesters
2975	3920.6900	--其他聚酯制	10	0 冰岛IS,东盟AS,哥CR,台湾TW,新加坡SG,新西兰NZ,智利CL 3 秘鲁PE 4 瑞士CH 5 巴PK 6 澳AU 9 韩国KR,亚太AP	0 受惠国LD	45	--Of other polyesters
		-纤维素及其化学衍生物制:					-Of cellulose or its chemical derivatives:
2976	3920.7100	--再生纤维素制	6.5	0 冰岛IS,东盟AS,哥CR,秘鲁PE,新西兰NZ,智利CL 2.6 瑞士CH 3.9 澳AU 5 巴PK 5.2 韩国KR	0 受惠国LD	45	--Of regenerated cellulose
2977	3920.7300	--乙酸纤维素制	6.5	0 冰岛IS,东盟AS,哥CR,秘鲁PE,香港HK,新西兰NZ,智利CL 2.6 瑞士CH 3.9 澳AU,韩国KR 5 巴PK	0 受惠国LD	45	--Of cellulose acetate

序号 No.	税则号列 Tariff Line	中文货品名称 Article Description in Chinese	最惠国税率 MFN(%)	协定税率 Agreement(%)	特惠税率 SP(%)	普通税率 Gen(%)	英文货品名称 Article Description
2978	3920.7900	--其他纤维素衍生物制	10	0 冰岛IS,东盟AS,哥CR,秘鲁PE,新西兰NZ,智利CL 4 瑞士CH 5 巴PK 6 澳AU 8 韩国KR	0 受惠国LD	45	--Of other cellulose derivatives
		-其他塑料制:					-Of other plastics:
2979	3920.9100	--聚乙烯醇缩丁醛制	6.5	0 冰岛IS,东盟AS,哥CR,秘鲁PE,新西兰NZ,智利CL 2.6 瑞士CH 3.9 澳AU 5 巴PK 5.6 韩国KR	0 受惠国LD	45	--Of poly (vinyl butyral)
	ex39209100	聚乙烯醇缩丁醛膜(厚度不超过3毫米)	Δ3				Polyvinyl butyral membrane (Thickness≤3mm)
2980	3920.9200	--聚酰胺制	10	0 冰岛IS,东盟AS,哥CR,秘鲁PE,新加坡SG,新西兰NZ,智利CL 4 瑞士CH 5 巴PK 6 澳AU,韩国KR	0 受惠国LD	45	--Of polyamides
2981	3920.9300	--氨基树脂制	6.5	0 冰岛IS,东盟AS,哥CR,秘鲁PE,新西兰NZ,智利CL 2.6 瑞士CH 3.9 澳AU,韩国KR 5 巴PK	0 受惠国LD	45	--Of amino-resins
2982	3920.9400	--酚醛树脂制	10	0 冰岛IS,东盟AS,哥CR,秘鲁PE,新加坡SG,新西兰NZ,智利CL 4 瑞士CH 5 巴PK 6 澳AU 7 亚太AP 8 韩国KR	0 受惠国LD	45	--Of phenolic resins
		--其他塑料制:					--Of other plastics:
2983	3920.9910	---聚四氟乙烯制	6.5	0 冰岛IS,东盟AS,哥CR,秘鲁PE,新西兰NZ,智利CL 2.6 瑞士CH 3.9 澳AU 5 巴PK 5.6 韩国KR	0 受惠国LD	45	---Of polytetrafluoroethylene
2984	3920.9990	---其他塑料制	6.5	0 冰岛IS,东盟AS,哥CR,秘鲁PE,台湾TW,香港HK,新西兰NZ,智利CL 2.6 瑞士CH 3.9 澳AU 5 巴PK 5.2 韩国KR	0 受惠国LD	45	---Of other plastics
	ex39209990	聚酰亚胺膜(厚度不超过0.03毫米)	Δ3				Membrane of polyimide (thickness ≤0.03mm)
	39.21	**其他塑料板、片、膜、箔、扁条:**					**Other plates, sheets, film, foil and strip, of plastics:**
		-泡沫塑料的:					-Cellular:
2985	3921.1100	--苯乙烯聚合物制	10	0 冰岛IS,东盟AS,哥CR,秘鲁PE,新西兰NZ,智利CL 4 瑞士CH 5 巴PK 6 澳AU 8 韩国KR 9 亚太AP	0 受惠国LD	45	--Of polymers of styrene
		--氯乙烯聚合物制:					--Of polymers of vinyl chloride:

序号 No.	税则号列 Tariff Line	中文货品名称 Article Description in Chinese	最惠国税率 MFN(%)	协定税率 Agreement(%)	特惠税率 SP(%)	普通税率 Gen(%)	英文货品名称 Article Description
2986	3921.1210	---人造革及合成革	9	0 冰岛IS,东盟AS,哥CR,秘鲁PE,台湾TW,香港HK,新加坡SG,新西兰NZ,智利CL 3.6 瑞士CH 5 巴PK 5.4 澳AU 7.8 韩国KR	0 受惠国LD	70	---Combined with textile fabrics
2987	3921.1290	---其他	6.5	0 冰岛IS,东盟AS,哥CR,秘鲁PE,香港HK,新西兰NZ,智利CL 3.9 澳AU,韩国KR 4.6 瑞士CH 5 巴PK	0 受惠国LD	45	---Other
		--氨酯聚合物制:					--Of polyurethanes:
2988	3921.1310	---人造革及合成革	9	0 冰岛IS,东盟AS,哥CR,秘鲁PE,台湾TW,香港HK,新加坡SG,新西兰NZ,智利CL 3.6 瑞士CH 5 巴PK 5.4 澳AU 6.3 亚太AP 7.8 韩国KR	0 受惠国LD	70	---Combined with textile fabrics
2989	3921.1390	---其他	6.5	0 巴PK,冰岛IS,东盟AS,哥CR,秘鲁PE,香港HK,新西兰NZ,智利CL 2.6 瑞士CH 3.9 澳AU 4.6 亚太AP 5.2 韩国KR	0 受惠国LD	45	---Other
2990	3921.1400	--再生纤维素制	10	0 冰岛IS,东盟AS,哥CR,秘鲁PE,新西兰NZ,智利CL 4 瑞士CH 5 巴PK 6 澳AU 8 韩国KR	0 受惠国LD	45	--Of regenerated cellulose
		--其他塑料制:					--Of other plastics:
2991	3921.1910	---人造革及合成革	9	0 冰岛IS,东盟AS,哥CR,秘鲁PE,新西兰NZ,智利CL 3.6 瑞士CH 5 巴PK 5.4 澳AU 6.3 亚太AP 7.8 韩国KR	0 受惠国LD	45	---Combined with textile fabrics
2992	3921.1990	---其他	6.5	0 巴PK,冰岛IS,东盟AS,哥CR,秘鲁PE,台湾TW,新西兰NZ,智利CL 3.9 澳AU 4.6 瑞士CH,亚太AP 5.6 韩国KR	0 受惠国LD	45	---Other
		-其他:					-Other:
2993	3921.9020	---聚乙烯嵌有玻璃纤维的板、片	6.5	0 巴PK,冰岛IS,东盟AS,哥CR,秘鲁PE,香港HK,新西兰NZ,智利CL 3.9 澳AU,韩国KR 4.6 瑞士CH,亚太AP	0 受惠国LD	45	---Plates, sheets of polyethylene with glass fibres
2994	3921.9030	---聚异丁烯为基本成分的附有人造毛毡的板、片、卷材	6.5	0 巴PK,冰岛IS,东盟AS,哥CR,秘鲁PE,香港HK,新西兰NZ,智利CL 2.6 瑞士CH 3.9 澳AU 4.6 亚太AP 5.2 韩国KR	0 受惠国LD	45	---Plates, sheets, coils of polyisobutylene with man-made felt

序号 No.	税则号列 Tariff Line	中文货品名称 Article Description in Chinese	最惠国税率 MFN(%)	协定税率 Agreement(%)		特惠税率 SP(%)		普通税率 Gen(%)	英文货品名称 Article Description
2995	3921.9090	---其他	6.5	0 3.9 4.6 5.6	巴PK,冰岛IS,东盟AS,哥CR,秘鲁PE,台湾TW,香港HK,新西兰NZ,智利CL 澳AU 瑞士CH,亚太AP 韩国KR	0	受惠国LD	45	---Other
	ex39219090	离子交换膜	Δ5						Ion exchange membrane
	39.22	**塑料浴缸、淋浴盘、洗涤槽、盥洗盆、坐浴盆、便盆、马桶座圈及盖、抽水箱及类似卫生洁具:**							**Baths, shower-baths, sinks, washbasins, bidets, lavatory pans, seats and covers, flushing cisterns and similar sanitary ware, of plastics:**
2996	3922.1000	-浴缸、淋浴盘、洗涤槽及盥洗盆	10	0 4 5 6 8	澳门MO,冰岛IS,东盟AS,哥CR,秘鲁PE,新西兰NZ,智利CL 瑞士CH 巴PK 澳AU 韩国KR	0	老挝LA,受惠国LD	80	-Baths, shower-baths, sinks and washbasins
2997	3922.2000	-马桶座圈及盖	10	0 3 4 5 6 8	澳门MO,冰岛IS,东盟AS,哥CR,新西兰NZ,智利CL 秘鲁PE 瑞士CH 巴PK 澳AU 韩国KR	0	老挝LA,受惠国LD	80	-Lavatory seats and covers
2998	3922.9000	-其他	10	0 4 5 6 8	冰岛IS,东盟AS,哥CR,秘鲁PE,新西兰NZ,智利CL 瑞士CH 巴PK 澳AU 韩国KR	0	受惠国LD	80	-Other
	39.23	**供运输或包装货物用的塑料制品;塑料制的塞子、盖子及类似品:**							**Articles for the conveyance or packing of goods, of plastics; stoppers, lids, caps and other closures, of plastics:**
2999	3923.1000	-盒、箱(包括板条箱)及类似品	10	0 3 4 5 6 7 9	澳门MO,冰岛IS,东盟AS,哥CR,台湾TW,香港HK,新加坡SG,新西兰NZ,智利CL 秘鲁PE 瑞士CH 巴PK 澳AU 亚太AP 韩国KR	0	受惠国LD	80	-Boxes, cases, crates and similar articles
		-袋及包(包括锥形的):							-Sacks and bags (including cones) :
3000	3923.2100	--乙烯聚合物制	10	0 3 4 5 6	澳门MO,冰岛IS,东盟AS,哥CR,香港HK,新加坡SG,新西兰NZ,智利CL 秘鲁PE 瑞士CH 巴PK 澳AU,韩国KR	0	受惠国$_1$LD$_1$	80	--Of polymers of ethylene

序号 No.	税则号列 Tariff Line	中文货品名称 Article Description in Chinese	最惠国税率 MFN(%)	协定税率 Agreement(%)	特惠税率 SP(%)	普通税率 Gen(%)	英文货品名称 Article Description
3001	3923.2900	--其他塑料制	10	0 澳门MO,冰岛IS,东盟AS,哥CR,香港HK,新加坡SG,新西兰NZ,智利CL 3 秘鲁PE 4 瑞士CH 5 巴PK 6 澳AU 8.6 韩国KR	0 受惠国LD	80	--Of other plastics
3002	3923.3000	-坛、瓶及类似品	6.5	0 冰岛IS,东盟AS,哥CR,香港HK,新加坡SG,新西兰NZ,智利CL 2.6 瑞士CH 3.9 澳AU 5 巴PK 5.6 韩国KR	0 受惠国LD	80	-Carboys, bottles, flasks and similar articles
3003	3923.4000	-卷轴、纡子、筒管及类似品	10	0 冰岛IS,东盟AS,哥CR,秘鲁PE,新加坡SG,新西兰NZ,智利CL 4 瑞士CH 5 巴PK 6 澳AU 7 亚太AP 8.6 韩国KR	0 受惠国$_1$LD$_1$	35	-Spools, cops, bobbins and similar supports
3004	3923.5000	-塞子、盖子及类似品	10	0 冰岛IS,东盟AS,哥CR,台湾TW,香港HK,新加坡SG,新西兰NZ,智利CL 3 秘鲁PE 5 巴PK 6 澳AU 7 瑞士CH 8 韩国KR	0 受惠国LD	80	-Stoppers, lids, caps and other closures
3005	3923.9000	-其他	10	0 澳门MO,冰岛IS,东盟AS,哥CR,台湾TW,香港HK,新加坡SG,新西兰NZ,智利CL 3 秘鲁PE 4 瑞士CH 5 巴PK 6 澳AU 7 亚太AP 9 韩国KR	0 受惠国$_1$LD$_1$	80	-Other
	39.24	**塑料制的餐具、厨房用具、其他家庭用具及卫生或盥洗用具:**					**Tableware, kitchenware, other household articles and hygienic or toilet articles, of plastics:**
3006	3924.1000	-餐具及厨房用具	10	0 澳门MO,冰岛IS,东盟AS,哥CR,香港HK,新加坡SG,新西兰NZ,智利CL 3 秘鲁PE 4 瑞士CH 5 巴PK 6 澳AU 8.6 韩国KR	0 受惠国LD,亚太AP	80	-Tableware and kitchenware
3007	3924.9000	-其他	10	0 澳门MO,冰岛IS,东盟AS,哥CR,香港HK,新加坡SG,新西兰NZ,智利CL 3 秘鲁PE 4 瑞士CH 5 巴PK 6 澳AU 8 韩国KR	0 受惠国LD	80	-Other
	39.25	**其他税号未列名的建筑用塑料制品:**					**Builders' ware of plastics, not elsewhere specified or included:**

序号 No.	税则号列 Tariff Line	中文货品名称 Article Description in Chinese	最惠国税率 MFN(%)	协定税率 Agreement(%)	特惠税率 SP(%)	普通税率 Gen(%)	英文货品名称 Article Description
3008	3925.1000	-囤、柜、罐、桶及类似容器，容积超过300升	10	0 冰岛IS,东盟AS,哥CR,新西兰NZ,智利CL 3 秘鲁PE 4 瑞士CH 5 巴PK 6 澳AU 8 韩国KR	0 受惠国LD	80	-Reservoirs, tanks, vats and similar containers, of a capacity exceeding 300L
3009	3925.2000	-门、窗及其框架、门槛	10	0 冰岛IS,东盟AS,哥CR,新西兰NZ,智利CL 3 秘鲁PE 4 瑞士CH 5 巴PK 6 澳AU 7 亚太AP 8 韩国KR	0 受惠国$_1$LD$_1$	80	-Doors, windows and their frames and thresholds for doors
3010	3925.3000	-窗板、百叶窗（包括威尼斯式百叶窗）或类似制品及其零件	10	0 冰岛IS,东盟AS,哥CR,秘鲁PE,新西兰NZ,智利CL 4 瑞士CH 5 巴PK 6 澳AU 8 韩国KR	0 受惠国$_1$LD$_1$	80	-Shutters, blinds (including Venetian blinds) and similar articles and parts thereof
3011	3925.9000	-其他	10	0 冰岛IS,东盟AS,哥CR,香港HK,新西兰NZ,智利CL 3 秘鲁PE 5 巴PK 6 澳AU 7.2 瑞士CH 8 韩国KR	0 受惠国$_1$LD$_1$	80	-Other
	39.26	**其他塑料制品及税号39.01至39.14所列其他材料的制品：**					**Other articles of plastics and articles of other materials of headings 3901 to 3914:**
3012	3926.1000	-办公室或学校用品	10	0 冰岛IS,东盟AS,哥CR,秘鲁PE,新加坡SG,新西兰NZ,智利CL 4 瑞士CH 5 巴PK 6 澳AU 8 韩国KR	0 受惠国LD	80	-Office or school supplies
		-衣服及衣着附件（包括分指手套、连指手套及露指手套）：					-Articles of apparel and clothing accessories (including gloves, mittens and mitts) :
		---手套（包括分指手套、连指手套及露指手套）：					---Gloves, mittens and mitts:
3013	3926.2011	----聚氯乙稀制	10	0 冰岛IS,东盟AS,哥CR,秘鲁PE,香港HK,新加坡SG,新西兰NZ,智利CL 4 瑞士CH 6 澳AU 8 韩国KR	0 受惠国$_1$LD$_1$	90	----Of Poly (vinyl chloride)
3014	3926.2019	----其他	10	0 冰岛IS,东盟AS,哥CR,秘鲁PE,香港HK,新加坡SG,新西兰NZ,智利CL 4 瑞士CH 6 澳AU 8 韩国KR	0 受惠国$_1$LD$_1$	90	----Other

序号 No.	税则号列 Tariff Line	中文货品名称 Article Description in Chinese	最惠国税率 MFN(%)	协定税率 Agreement(%)	特惠税率 SP(%)	普通税率 Gen(%)	英文货品名称 Article Description
3015	3926.2090	---其他	10	0 冰岛IS,东盟AS,哥CR,秘鲁PE,香港HK,新加坡SG,新西兰NZ,智利CL 4 瑞士CH 6 澳AU 8 韩国KR	0 受惠国LD	90	---Other
3016	3926.3000	-家具、车厢或类似品的附件	10	0 冰岛IS,东盟AS,哥CR,新加坡SG,新西兰NZ,智利CL 3 秘鲁PE 4 瑞士CH 5 巴PK 6 澳AU 8.6 韩国KR	0 受惠国LD	80	-Fittings for furniture, coachwork or the like
3017	3926.4000	-小雕塑品及其他装饰品	10	0 冰岛IS,东盟AS,哥CR,秘鲁PE,新西兰NZ,智利CL 4 瑞士CH 5 巴PK 6 澳AU 8 韩国KR 8.3 亚太AP	0 受惠国LD	100	-Statuettes and other ornamental articles
		-其他:					-Other:
3018	3926.9010	---机器及仪器用零件	10	0 澳门MO,冰岛IS,东盟AS,哥CR,台湾TW,香港HK,新加坡SG,新西兰NZ,智利CL 3 秘鲁PE 5 巴PK 6 澳AU 7 瑞士CH 8 韩国KR 9 亚太AP	0 受惠国LD	35	---Of a kind for used in machines or instruments
3019	3926.9090	---其他	10	0 澳门MO,冰岛IS,东盟AS,哥CR,台湾TW,香港HK,新加坡SG,新西兰NZ,智利CL 3 秘鲁PE 6 澳AU 7 瑞士CH 8 韩国KR 9.2 巴PK,亚太AP	0 受惠国LD	80	---Other

第四十章
橡胶及其制品

注释:

一、除条文另有规定的以外，本目录所称“橡胶”，是指不论是否硫化或硬化的下列产品: 天然橡胶、巴拉塔胶、古塔波胶、银胶菊胶、糖胶树胶及类似的天然树胶、合成橡胶、从油类中提取的油膏以及上述物品的再生品。

二、本章不包括:

（一）第十一类的货品（纺织原料及纺织制品）;

（二）第六十四章的鞋靴及其零件;

（三）第六十五章的帽类及其零件（包括游泳帽）;

（四）第十六类的硬质橡胶制的机械器具、电气器具及其零件（包括各种电气用品）;

（五）第九十章、第九十二章、第九十四章或第九十六章的物品;

（六）第九十五章的物品（运动用分指手套、连指手套、露指手套及税号 40.11 至 40.13 的制品除外）。

三、税号 40.01 至 40.03 及 40.05 所称“初级形状”，只限于下列形状:

（一）液状及糊状，包括胶乳（不论是否预硫化）及其他分散体和溶液;

（二）不规则形状的块、团、包、粉、粒、碎屑及类似的散装形状。

四、本章注释一和税号40.02所称“合成橡胶”，适用于:

（一）不饱和合成物质，即用硫磺硫化能使其不可逆地变为非热塑物质，这种物质能在温度 18℃至 29℃之间被拉长到其原长度的三倍而不致断裂，拉长到原长度的两倍时，在五分钟内能回复到不超过原长度的一倍半。为了进行上述试验，可以加入交联所需的硫化活化剂或促进剂；也允许含有注释五（二）2 及 3 所述的物质。但不能加入非交联所需的物质，例如，增量剂、增塑剂及填料;

（二）聚硫橡胶（TM）;

（三）与塑料接枝共聚或混合而改性的天然橡胶、解聚天然橡胶以及不饱和合成物质与饱和合成高聚物的混合物，但这些产品必须符合以上（一）款关于硫化、延伸及回复的要求。

Chapter 40
Rubber and articles thereof

Notes:

1. Except where the context otherwise requires, throughout the Nomenclature the expression “rubber” means the following products, whether or not vulcanized or hard: natural rubber, balata, gutta-percha, guayule, chicle and similar natural gums, synthetic rubber, factice derived from oils, and such substances reclaimed.

2. This Chapter does not cover:

(a) Goods of Section XI(texitils and textile articles) ;

(b) Footwear or parts thereof of Chapter 64;

(c) Headgear or parts thereof (including bathing caps) of Chapter 65 ;

(d) Mechanical or electrical appliances or parts thereof of Section XVI(including electrical goods of all kinds) , of hard rubber;

(e) Articles of Chapter 90, 92, 94 or 96; or

(f) Articles of Chapter 95 (other than sports gloves, mittens and mitts and articles of headings Nos.40.11 to 40.13) .

3. In headings Nos.40.01 to 40.03 and 40.05, the expression “primary forms” applies only to the following forms:

(a) Liquids and pastes (including latex, whether or not pre-vulcanized, and other dispersions and solutions) ;

(b) Blocks of irregular shape, lumps, bales, powders, granules, crumbs and similar bulk forms.

4. In Note 1 to this Chapter and in heading No. 40.02, the expression “synthetic rubber” applies to:

(a) Unsaturated synthetic substances which can be irreversibly transformed by vulcanization with sulphur into non-thermoplastic substances which, at a temperature between18℃ and 29℃, will not break on being extended to three times their original length and will return, after being extended to twice their original length, within a period of five minutes, to a length not greater than one and a half times their original length. For the purposes of this test, substances necessary for the cross-linking, such as vulcanizing activators or accelerators, may be added; the presence of substances as provided for by Note 5 (b) (2) and (3) is also permitted. However, the presence of any substances not necessary for the cross-linking, such as extenders, plasticizers and fillers, is not permitted;

(b) Thioplasts (TM); and

(c) Natural rubber modified by grafting or mixing with plastics, depolymerized natural rubber, mixtures of unsaturated synthetic substances with saturated synthetic high polymers provided that all the above-mentioned products comply with the requirements concerning vulcanization, elongation and recovery in(a) above.

五、

（一）税号 40.01 及 40.02 不适用于任何凝结前或凝结后与下列物质相混合的橡胶或橡胶混合物：

1. 硫化剂、促进剂、防焦剂或活性剂（为制造预硫胶乳所加入的除外）；

2. 颜料或其他着色料，但仅为易于识别而加入的除外；

3. 增塑剂或增量剂（用油增量的橡胶中所加的矿物油除外）、填料、增强剂、有机溶剂或其他物质，但以下（二）款所述的除外。

（二）含有下列物质的橡胶或橡胶混合物，只要仍具有原料的基本特性，应归入税号40.01或40.02：

1. 乳化剂或防粘剂；

2. 少量的乳化剂分解产品；

3. 微量的下列物质：热敏剂（一般为制造热敏胶乳用）、阳离子表面活性剂（一般为制造阳性胶乳用）、抗氧剂、凝固剂、碎裂剂、抗冻剂、胶溶剂、保存剂、稳定剂、粘度控制剂或类似的特殊用途添加剂。

六、税号40.04所称“废碎料及下脚料”，是指在橡胶或橡胶制品生产或加工过程中由于切割、磨损或其他原因所造成没有使用价值的废橡胶及下脚料。

七、全部用硫化橡胶制成的线，其任一截面的尺寸超过 5 毫米的，应作为带、杆或型材及异型材归入税号 40.08。

八、税号 40.10 包括用橡胶浸渍、涂布、包覆或层压的织物制成的或用橡胶浸渍、涂布、包覆或套裹的纱线或绳制成的传动带、输送带。

九、税号40.01、40.02、40.03、40.05及40.08所称“板”、“片”、“带”，仅指未切割或只简单切割成矩形（包括正方形）的板、片、带及正几何形块，不论是否具有成品的特征，也不论是否经过印制或其他表面加工，但未切割成其他形状或进一步加工。

税号40.08所称“杆”或“型材及异型材”，仅指不论是否切割成一定长度或表面加工，但未经进一步加工的该类产品。

5.

(a) Headings Nos. 40.01 and 40.02 do not apply to any rubber or mixture of rubbers which has been compounded, before or after coagulation, with:

(1) vulcanizing agents, accelerators, retarders or activators (other than those added for the preparation of pre-vulcanized rubber latex) ;

(2) pigments or other colouring matter, other than those added solely for the purpose of identification;

(3) plasticizers or extenders (except mineral oil in the case of oil-extended rubber), fillers, reinforcing agents, organic solvents or any other substances, except those permitted under (b).

(b) The presence of the following substances in any rubber or mixture of rubbers shall not affect its classification in heading No.40.01 or 40.02, as the case may be, provided that such rubber or mixture of rubbers retains its essential character as a raw material:

(1) emulsifiers or anti-tack agents;

(2) small amounts of breakdown products of emulsifiers;

(3) very small amounts of the following:heat-sensitive agents (generally for obtaining thermosensitive rubber latexes), cationic surface-active agents (generally for obtaining electro-positive rubber latexes), antioxidants, coagulants, crumbling agents, freeze- resisting agents, peptizers, preservatives, stabilizers, viscosity-control agents, or similar special-purpose additives.

6. For the purposes ofheadingNo.40.04, the expression “waste, parings and scrap” means rubber waste, parings and scrap from the manufacture or working of rubber and rubber goods definitely not usable as such because of cuttingup, wear or other reasons.

7. Thread wholly of vulcanized rubber, of which any cross-sectional dimension exceeds 5mm, is to be classified as strip, rods or profile shapes, of heading No.40.08.

8. Heading No. 40.10 includes conveyor or transmission belts or belting of textile fabric impregnated, coated, covered or laminated with rubber or made from textile yarn or cord impregnated, coated, covered or sheathed with rubber.

9. In headings Nos.40.01, 40.02, 40.03, 40.05, and 40.08, the expressions “plates”, “sheets” and “strip” apply only to plates, sheets and strip and to blocks of regular geometric shape, uncut or simply cut to rectangular (including square) shape, whether or not having the character of articles and whether or not printed or otherwise surface-worked, but not otherwise cut to shape or further worked.

In heading No.40.08 the expressions “rods” and “profile shapes” apply only to such products, whether or not cut to length or surface-worked but not otherwise worked.

序号 No.	税则号列 Tariff Line	中文货品名称 Article Description in Chinese	最惠国税率 MFN(%)	协定税率 Agreement(%)	特惠税率 SP(%)	普通税率 Gen(%)	英文货品名称 Article Description
	40.01	**天然橡胶、巴拉塔胶、古塔波胶、银胶菊胶、糖胶树胶及类似的天然树胶，初级形状或板、片、带：**					**Natural rubber, balata, gutta-percha, guayule, chicle and similar natural gums, in primary forms or in plates, sheets or strip:**
3020	4001.1000	-天然胶乳，不论是否预硫化	20①	0 冰岛IS,哥CR,新西兰NZ,智利CL 12 澳AU 14 瑞士CH 17.3 韩国KR		40	-Natural rubber latex, whether or not prevulcanized
		-其他形状的天然橡胶：					-Natural rubber in other forms:
3021	4001.2100	--烟胶片	20②	0 冰岛IS,哥CR,新西兰NZ,智利CL 12 澳AU 14 瑞士CH 17 巴PK,亚太AP 17.3 韩国KR		40	--Smoked sheets
3022	4001.2200	--技术分类天然橡胶（TSNR）	20③	0 冰岛IS,哥CR,新西兰NZ,智利CL 12 澳AU 14 瑞士CH		40	--Technically specified natural rubber (TSNR)
3023	4001.2900	--其他	20	0 冰岛IS,哥CR,新西兰NZ,智利CL 12 澳AU 14 瑞士CH 17 巴PK,亚太AP		40	--Other
3024	4001.3000	-巴拉塔胶、古塔波胶、银胶菊胶、糖胶树胶及类似的天然树胶	20	0 冰岛IS,东盟AS,哥CR,新加坡SG,新西兰NZ,智利CL 6 秘鲁PE 12 澳AU 14 瑞士CH 17.3 韩国KR	0 受惠国$_1$LD$_1$	40	-Balata, gutta-percha, guayule, chicle and similar natural gums
	40.02	**合成橡胶及从油类提取的油膏，初级形状或板、片、带；税号40.01所列产品与本税号所列产品的混合物，初级形状或板、片、带：**					**Synthetic rubber and factice derived from oils, in primary forms or in plates, sheets or strip; mixtures of any product of heading 4001 with any product of this heading, in primary forms or in plates, sheets or strip:**
		-丁苯橡胶（SBR）；羧基丁苯橡胶（XSBR）：					-Styrene-butadiene rubber (SBR) ; carboxylated styrene-butadiene rubber (XSBR) :
		--胶乳：					--Latex:
3025	4002.1110	---羧基丁苯橡胶	7.5	0 冰岛IS,东盟AS,哥CR,秘鲁PE,香港HK,新西兰NZ,智利CL 3 瑞士CH 4.5 澳AU 5 巴PK 6.5 韩国KR	0 受惠国LD	14	---Carboxylated styrene-butadiene rubber (XSBR)

①暂定最惠国税率: 10%或 900 元/吨:两者从低
Interim MFN Tariff: 10% or 900¥/T: the less
②暂定最惠国税率: 20%或 1500 元/吨:两者从低
Interim MFN Tariff: 20% or 1500¥/T: the less
③暂定最惠国税率: 20%或 1500 元/吨:两者从低
Interim MFN Tariff: 20% or 1500¥/T: the less

序号 No.	税则号列 Tariff Line	中文货品名称 Article Description in Chinese	最惠国税率 MFN(%)	协定税率 Agreement(%)	特惠税率 SP(%)	普通税率 Gen(%)	英文货品名称 Article Description
3026	4002.1190	---其他	7.5	0 冰岛IS,东盟AS,哥CR,秘鲁PE,香港HK,新西兰NZ,智利CL 3 瑞士CH 4.5 澳AU 5 巴PK 6.5 韩国KR	0 受惠国LD	14	---Other
		--其他:					--Other:
		---初级形状的:					---In primary forms:
3027	4002.1911	----未经任何加工的丁苯橡胶(溶聚的除外)	7.5	0 冰岛IS,东盟AS,哥CR,秘鲁PE,香港HK,新西兰NZ,智利CL 3 瑞士CH 4.5 澳AU 5 巴PK 6.5 韩国KR	0 受惠国LD	14	----SBR, except for SSBR, not worked
3028	4002.1912	----充油丁苯橡胶(溶聚的除外)	7.5	0 冰岛IS,东盟AS,哥CR,秘鲁PE,香港HK,新西兰NZ,智利CL 3 瑞士CH 4.5 澳AU 5 巴PK 6.5 韩国KR	0 受惠国LD	14	----SBR, except for SSBR, oil-filled
3029	4002.1913	----热塑丁苯橡胶	7.5	0 冰岛IS,东盟AS,哥CR,秘鲁PE,香港HK,新西兰NZ,智利CL 3 瑞士CH 4.5 澳AU 5 巴PK 6.5 韩国KR	0 受惠国LD	14	----SBR, thermo-plasticated
3030	4002.1914	----充油热塑丁苯橡胶	7.5	0 冰岛IS,东盟AS,哥CR,秘鲁PE,香港HK,新西兰NZ,智利CL 3 瑞士CH 4.5 澳AU 5 巴PK 6.5 韩国KR	0 受惠国LD	14	----SBR, oil-filled and thermo-plasticated
3031	4002.1915	----未经任何加工的溶聚丁苯橡胶	7.5	0 冰岛IS,东盟AS,哥CR,秘鲁PE,香港HK,新西兰NZ,智利CL 3 瑞士CH 4.5 澳AU 5 巴PK 6.5 韩国KR	0 受惠国LD	14	----SSBR, not worked
3032	4002.1916	----充油溶聚丁苯橡胶	7.5	0 冰岛IS,东盟AS,哥CR,秘鲁PE,香港HK,新西兰NZ,智利CL 3 瑞士CH 4.5 澳AU 5 巴PK 6.5 韩国KR	0 受惠国LD	14	----SSBR, oil-filled
3033	4002.1919	----其他	7.5	0 冰岛IS,哥CR,秘鲁PE,香港HK,新西兰NZ,智利CL 3 瑞士CH 4.5 澳AU 6.5 韩国KR	0 受惠国LD	14	----Other
3034	4002.1990	---其他	7.5	0 冰岛IS,东盟AS,哥CR,秘鲁PE,香港HK,新西兰NZ,智利CL 3 瑞士CH 4.5 澳AU 5 巴PK 6.5 韩国KR 7.1 亚太AP	0 受惠国LD	35	---Other

序号 No.	税则号列 Tariff Line	中文货品名称 Article Description in Chinese	最惠国税率 MFN(%)	协定税率 Agreement(%)	特惠税率 SP(%)	普通税率 Gen(%)	英文货品名称 Article Description
		-丁二烯橡胶（BR）:					-Butadiene rubber (BR) :
3035	4002.2010	---初级形状的	7.5	0 冰岛IS,东盟AS,哥CR,秘鲁PE,新西兰NZ,智利CL 3 瑞士CH 4.5 澳AU 5 巴PK 6.5 韩国KR	0 受惠国LD	14	---In primary forms
3036	4002.2090	---其他	7.5	0 冰岛IS,东盟AS,哥CR,秘鲁PE,新西兰NZ,智利CL 3 瑞士CH 4.5 澳AU 5 巴PK 6.5 韩国KR 7 亚太AP	0 受惠国LD	35	---Other
		-异丁烯-异戊二烯（丁基）橡胶（IIR）;卤代丁基橡胶（CIIR或BIIR）:					-Isobutene-isoprene (butyl) rubber (IIR) ; halo-isobutene-isoprene rubber (CIIR or BIIR) :
		--异丁烯-异戊二烯（丁基）橡胶（IIR）:					--Isobutene-isoprene (butyl) rubber (IIR) :
3037	4002.3110	---初级形状的	6	0 冰岛IS,东盟AS,哥CR,秘鲁PE,新西兰NZ,智利CL 2.4 瑞士CH 3.6 澳AU 5 巴PK 5.2 韩国KR 5.6 亚太AP	0 受惠国LD	14	---In primary forms
3038	4002.3190	---其他	7.5	0 冰岛IS,东盟AS,哥CR,秘鲁PE,新西兰NZ,智利CL 3 瑞士CH 4.5 澳AU 5 巴PK 6.5 韩国KR 7.1 亚太AP	0 受惠国LD	35	---Other
		--其他:					--Other:
3039	4002.3910	---初级形状的	7.5	0 冰岛IS,东盟AS,哥CR,秘鲁PE,新西兰NZ,智利CL 3 瑞士CH 4.5 澳AU 5 巴PK 6.5 韩国KR	0 受惠国LD	14	---In pimary forms
3040	4002.3990	---其他	7.5	0 冰岛IS,东盟AS,哥CR,秘鲁PE,新西兰NZ,智利CL 3 瑞士CH 4.5 澳AU 5 巴PK 6.5 韩国KR 7.1 亚太AP	0 受惠国LD	35	---Other
		-氯丁二烯（氯丁）橡胶（CR）:					-Chloroprene (chlorobutadiene) rubber (CR) :
3041	4002.4100	--胶乳	7.5	0 冰岛IS,东盟AS,哥CR,秘鲁PE,新西兰NZ,智利CL 3 瑞士CH 4.5 澳AU,韩国KR 5 巴PK 7.1 亚太AP	0 受惠国LD	14	--Latex
		--其他:					--Other:

序号 No.	税则号列 Tariff Line	中文货品名称 Article Description in Chinese	最惠国税率 MFN(%)	协定税率 Agreement(%)	特惠税率 SP(%)	普通税率 Gen(%)	英文货品名称 Article Description
3042	4002.4910	---初级形状的	7.5	0 冰岛IS,东盟AS,哥CR,秘鲁PE,新西兰NZ,智利CL 3 瑞士CH 4.5 澳AU 5 巴PK	0 受惠国LD	14	---In primary forms
3043	4002.4990	---其他	7.5	0 冰岛IS,东盟AS,哥CR,秘鲁PE,新西兰NZ,智利CL 3 瑞士CH 4.5 澳AU 5 巴PK 6.5 韩国KR 7.1 亚太AP	0 受惠国LD	35	---Other
		-丁腈橡胶（NBR）:					-Acrylonitrile-butadiene rubber (NBR) :
3044	4002.5100	--胶乳	7.5	0 冰岛IS,东盟AS,哥CR,秘鲁PE,新西兰NZ,智利CL 3 瑞士CH 4.5 澳AU 5 巴PK 6.5 韩国KR 7.1 亚太AP	0 受惠国LD	14	--Latex
		--其他:					--Other:
3045	4002.5910	---初级形状的	7.5	0 冰岛IS,东盟AS,哥CR,秘鲁PE,新西兰NZ,智利CL 3 瑞士CH 4.5 澳AU 5 巴PK 6.5 韩国KR	0 受惠国LD	14	---In primary forms
3046	4002.5990	---其他	7.5	0 冰岛IS,东盟AS,哥CR,秘鲁PE,新西兰NZ,智利CL 3 瑞士CH 4.5 澳AU 5 巴PK 6.5 韩国KR	0 受惠国LD	35	---Other
		-异戊二烯橡胶（IR）:					-Isoprene rubber (IR) :
3047	4002.6010	---初级形状的	3	0 澳AU,巴PK,冰岛IS,东盟AS,哥CR,秘鲁PE,瑞士CH,新西兰NZ,智利CL 2.6 韩国KR	0 受惠国LD	14	---In primary forms
3048	4002.6090	---其他	5	0 澳AU,巴PK,冰岛IS,东盟AS,哥CR,秘鲁PE,瑞士CH,新西兰NZ,智利CL 4.3 韩国KR 4.5 亚太AP	0 受惠国LD	35	---Other
		-乙丙非共轭二烯橡胶（EPDM）:					-Ethylene-propylene-non-conjugated diene rubber (EPDM) :
3049	4002.7010	---初级形状的	7.5	0 冰岛IS,东盟AS,哥CR,秘鲁PE,新西兰NZ,智利CL 3 瑞士CH 4.5 澳AU 5 巴PK 6.5 韩国KR	0 受惠国LD	14	---In primary forms

序号 No.	税则号列 Tariff Line	中文货品名称 Article Description in Chinese	最惠国税率 MFN(%)	协定税率 Agreement(%)	特惠税率 SP(%)	普通税率 Gen(%)	英文货品名称 Article Description
3050	4002.7090	---其他	7.5	0 冰岛IS,东盟AS,哥CR,秘鲁PE,新西兰NZ,智利CL 3 瑞士CH 4.5 澳AU 5 巴PK 6.5 韩国KR 7.1 亚太AP	0 受惠国LD	35	---Other
3051	4002.8000	-税号40.01所列产品与本税号所列产品的混合物	7.5	0 冰岛IS,东盟AS,哥CR,秘鲁PE,新西兰NZ,智利CL 3 瑞士CH 4.5 澳AU 5 巴PK 6.5 韩国KR	0 受惠国LD	35	-Mixtures of any product of heading No. 40.01 with any product of this heading
		-其他:					-Other:
3052	4002.9100	--胶乳	7.5	0 冰岛IS,东盟AS,哥CR,秘鲁PE,新西兰NZ,智利CL 3 瑞士CH 4.5 澳AU 5 巴PK 6.5 韩国KR	0 受惠国LD	14	--Latex
		--其他:					--Other:
		---其他合成橡胶:					---Other synthetic rubber:
3053	4002.9911	----初级形状的	7.5	0 冰岛IS,东盟AS,哥CR,秘鲁PE,台湾TW,香港HK,新西兰NZ,智利CL 3 瑞士CH 4.5 澳AU 5 巴PK 6.5 韩国KR	0 受惠国LD	14	----In primary forms
3054	4002.9919	----其他	7.5	0 冰岛IS,东盟AS,哥CR,秘鲁PE,香港HK,新西兰NZ,智利CL 3 瑞士CH 4.5 澳AU 5 巴PK 6.5 韩国KR	0 受惠国LD	35	----Other
3055	4002.9990	---其他	4	0 澳AU,巴PK,冰岛IS,东盟AS,哥CR,韩国KR,秘鲁PE,瑞士CH,新西兰NZ,智利CL	0 受惠国LD	14	---Other
	40.03	**再生橡胶，初级形状或板、片、带**					**Reclaimed rubber in primary forms or in plates, sheets or strip**
3056	4003.0000	再生橡胶，初级形状或板、片、带	8	0 冰岛IS,东盟AS,哥CR,秘鲁PE,香港HK,新西兰NZ,智利CL 3.2 瑞士CH 4.8 澳AU 5 巴PK 6.9 韩国KR	0 受惠国LD	30	Reclaimed rubber in primary forms or in plates, sheets or strip
	40.04	**橡胶（硬质橡胶的除外）的废碎料、下脚料及其粉、粒**					**Waste, parings and scrap of rubber (other than hard rubber) and powders and granules obtained therefrom**
3057	4004.0000	橡胶（硬质橡胶的除外）的废碎料、下脚料及其粉、粒	8	0 冰岛IS,东盟AS,哥CR,秘鲁PE,新西兰NZ,智利CL 3.2 瑞士CH 4.8 澳AU,韩国KR 5 巴PK 7.6 亚太AP	0 受惠国$_1$LD$_1$	30	Waste, parings and scrap of rubber (other than hard rubber) and powders and granules obtained therefrom
	40.05	**未硫化的复合橡胶，初级形状或板、片、带:**					**Compounded rubber, unvulcanised, in primary forms or in plates, sheets or strip:**

序号 No.	税则号列 Tariff Line	中文货品名称 Article Description in Chinese	最惠国税率 MFN(%)	协定税率 Agreement(%)	特惠税率 SP(%)	普通税率 Gen(%)	英文货品名称 Article Description
3058	4005.1000	-与碳黑或硅石混合	8	0 澳门MO,冰岛IS,东盟AS,哥CR,秘鲁PE,新西兰NZ,智利CL 3.2 瑞士CH 4.8 澳AU 5 巴PK 6.9 韩国KR	0 受惠国LD	35	-Compounded with carbon black or silica
3059	4005.2000	-溶液;子目号4005.10以外的分散体	8	0 冰岛IS,东盟AS,哥CR,秘鲁PE,新西兰NZ,智利CL 3.2 瑞士CH 4.8 澳AU 5 巴PK 6.9 韩国KR	0 受惠国LD	35	-Solutions; dispersions other than those of subheading No.4005.10
		-其他:					-Other:
3060	4005.9100	--板、片、带	8	0 冰岛IS,东盟AS,哥CR,秘鲁PE,新西兰NZ,智利CL 3.2 瑞士CH 4.8 澳AU,韩国KR 5 巴PK	0 受惠国LD	35	--Plates, sheets and strip
3061	4005.9900	--其他	8	0 冰岛IS,东盟AS,哥CR,秘鲁PE,香港HK,新西兰NZ,智利CL 3.2 瑞士CH 4.8 澳AU 5 巴PK 6.9 韩国KR	0 受惠国LD	35	--Other
	40.06	**其他形状(例如,杆、管或型材及异型材)的未硫化橡胶及未硫化橡胶制品(例如,盘、环):**					**Other forms (for example, rods, tubes and profile shapes) and articles (for example, discs and rings), of unvulcanised rubber:**
3062	4006.1000	-轮胎翻新用胎面补料胎条	8	0 冰岛IS,东盟AS,哥CR,秘鲁PE,新西兰NZ,智利CL 3.2 瑞士CH 4.8 澳AU,韩国KR 5 巴PK	0 受惠国LD	35	-Camel-back strips for retreading rubber tyres
		其他:					-Other:
3063	4006.9010	---其他形状的未硫化橡胶	8	0 冰岛IS,东盟AS,哥CR,秘鲁PE,新西兰NZ,智利CL 3.2 瑞士CH 4.8 澳AU 5 巴PK 6.4 韩国KR	0 受惠国LD	35	---Other forms of unvulcanized rubber
3064	4006.9020	---未硫化橡胶制品	14	0 冰岛IS,东盟AS,哥CR,秘鲁PE,新加坡SG,新西兰NZ,智利CL 8.4 澳AU 9.8 瑞士CH 11.2 巴PK,韩国KR	0 受惠国$_1$LD$_1$	80	---Articles of unvulcanized rubber
	40.07	**硫化橡胶线及绳**					**Vulcanised rubber thread and cord**
3065	4007.0000	硫化橡胶线及绳	14	0 冰岛IS,东盟AS,哥CR,秘鲁PE,香港HK,新加坡SG,新西兰NZ,智利CL 8.4 澳AU 9.8 瑞士CH 11.2 巴PK,韩国KR	0 受惠国$_1$LD$_1$	80	Vulcanized rubber thread and cord
	40.08	**硫化橡胶(硬质橡胶除外)制的板、片、带、杆或型材及异型材:**					**Plates, sheets, strip, rods and profile shapes, of vulcanised rubber other than hard rubber:**
		-海绵橡胶制:					-Of cellular rubber:

序号 No.	税则号列 Tariff Line	中文货品名称 Article Description in Chinese	最惠国税率 MFN(%)	协定税率 Agreement(%)	特惠税率 SP(%)	普通税率 Gen(%)	英文货品名称 Article Description
3066	4008.1100	--板、片、带	8	0 冰岛IS,东盟AS,哥CR,秘鲁PE,新西兰NZ,智利CL 3.2 瑞士CH 4.8 澳AU 5 巴PK 6.9 韩国KR	0 受惠国LD	35	--Plates, sheets and strip
3067	4008.1900	--其他	8	0 冰岛IS,东盟AS,哥CR,秘鲁PE,新西兰NZ,智利CL 3.2 瑞士CH 4.8 澳AU,韩国KR 5 巴PK	0 受惠国LD	35	--Other
		-非海绵橡胶制:					-Of non-cellular rubber:
3068	4008.2100	--板、片、带	8	0 冰岛IS,东盟AS,哥CR,秘鲁PE,新西兰NZ,智利CL 3.2 瑞士CH 4.8 澳AU,韩国KR 5 巴PK	0 受惠国LD	35	--Plates, sheets and strip
3069	4008.2900	--其他	8	0 冰岛IS,东盟AS,哥CR,秘鲁PE,新西兰NZ,智利CL 3.2 瑞士CH 4.8 澳AU,韩国KR 5 巴PK	0 受惠国LD	35	--Other
	40.09	**硫化橡胶（硬质橡胶除外）制的管子，不论是否装有附件（例如，接头、肘管、法兰）：**					**Tubes, pipes and hoses, of vulcanised rubber other than hard rubber, with or without their fittings (for example, joints, elbows, flanges) :**
		-未经加强或未与其他材料合制:					-Not reinforced or otherwise combined with other materials:
3070	4009.1100	--未装有附件	10.5	0 冰岛IS,东盟AS,哥CR,秘鲁PE,新加坡SG,新西兰NZ,智利CL 5 巴PK 6.3 澳AU 7.4 瑞士CH 8.4 韩国KR	0 受惠国$_1$LD$_1$	40	--Without fittings
3071	4009.1200	--装有附件	10	0 冰岛IS,东盟AS,哥CR,秘鲁PE,新西兰NZ,智利CL 4 瑞士CH 5 巴PK 6 澳AU 8 韩国KR	0 受惠国$_1$LD$_1$	40	--With fittings
		-用金属加强或只与金属合制:					-Reinforced or otherwise combined only with metal:
3072	4009.2100	--未装有附件	10.5	0 冰岛IS,东盟AS,哥CR,新加坡SG,新西兰NZ,智利CL 3.2 秘鲁PE 5 巴PK 6.3 澳AU 7.4 瑞士CH 8.4 韩国KR	0 受惠国$_1$LD$_1$	40	--Without fittings
3073	4009.2200	--装有附件	10	0 冰岛IS,东盟AS,哥CR,秘鲁PE,新加坡SG,新西兰NZ,智利CL 4 瑞士CH 5 巴PK 6 澳AU 8 韩国KR	0 受惠国$_1$LD$_1$	40	--With fittings

序号 No.	税则号列 Tariff Line	中文货品名称 Article Description in Chinese	最惠国税率 MFN(%)	协定税率 Agreement(%)	特惠税率 SP(%)	普通税率 Gen(%)	英文货品名称 Article Description
		-用纺织材料加强或只与纺织材料合制:					-Reinforced or otherwise combined only with textile materials:
3074	4009.3100	--未装有附件	10.5	0 冰岛IS,东盟AS,哥CR,新加坡SG,新西兰NZ,智利CL 3.2 秘鲁PE 5 巴PK 6.3 澳AU 7.4 瑞士CH 9.4 韩国KR	0 受惠国$_1$LD$_1$	40	--Without fittings
3075	4009.3200	--装有附件	10	0 冰岛IS,东盟AS,哥CR,秘鲁PE,新西兰NZ,智利CL 4 瑞士CH 5 巴PK 6 澳AU 8 韩国KR	0 受惠国$_1$LD$_1$	40	--With fittings
		-用其他材料加强或与其他材料合制:					-Reinforced or otherwise combined with other materials:
3076	4009.4100	--未装有附件	10.5	0 冰岛IS,东盟AS,哥CR,新加坡SG,新西兰NZ,智利CL 3.2 秘鲁PE 5 巴PK 6.3 澳AU 7.4 瑞士CH 8.4 韩国KR	0 受惠国$_1$LD$_1$	40	--Without fittings
3077	4009.4200	--装有附件	10	0 冰岛IS,东盟AS,哥CR,新加坡SG,新西兰NZ,智利CL 3 秘鲁PE 4 瑞士CH 5 巴PK 6 澳AU 8 韩国KR	0 受惠国$_1$LD$_1$	40	--With fittings
	40.10	**硫化橡胶制的传动带或输送带及带料:**					**Conveyor or transmission belts or bel-ting, of vulcanized rubber:**
		-输送带及带料:					-Conveyor belts or belting:
3078	4010.1100	--仅用金属加强的	10	0 冰岛IS,东盟AS,哥CR,香港HK,新西兰NZ,智利CL 3 秘鲁PE 5 巴PK 6 澳AU 7.5 瑞士CH 8 韩国KR	0 受惠国$_1$LD$_1$	35	--Reinforced only with metal
3079	4010.1200	--仅用纺织材料加强的	10	0 冰岛IS,东盟AS,哥CR,瑞士CH,新西兰NZ,智利CL 3 秘鲁PE 5 巴PK 6 澳AU 8 韩国KR	0 受惠国$_1$LD$_1$	35	--Reinforced only with textile materials
3080	4010.1900	--其他	10	0 冰岛IS,东盟AS,哥CR,瑞士CH,新西兰NZ,智利CL 3 秘鲁PE 5 巴PK 6 澳AU 8 韩国KR	0 受惠国$_1$LD$_1$	35	--Other
		-传动带及带料:					-Transmission belts or belting:

序号 No.	税则号列 Tariff Line	中文货品名称 Article Description in Chinese	最惠国税率 MFN(%)	协定税率 Agreement(%)	特惠税率 SP(%)	普通税率 Gen(%)	英文货品名称 Article Description
3081	4010.3100	--梯形截面的环形传动带（三角带），V形肋状的，外周长超过60厘米，但不超过180厘米	8	0 冰岛IS,东盟AS,哥CR,秘鲁PE,新西兰NZ,智利CL 3.2 瑞士CH 4.8 澳AU,韩国KR 5 巴PK	0 受惠国LD	35	--Endless transmission belts of trapezoidal cross-section (V-belts) , V-ribbed, of a circumference exceeding 60cm but not exceeding 180cm
3082	4010.3200	--梯形截面的环形传动带（三角带），外周长超过60厘米，但不超过180厘米，V形肋状的除外	8	0 冰岛IS,东盟AS,哥CR,秘鲁PE,新西兰NZ,智利CL 3.2 瑞士CH 4.8 澳AU,韩国KR 5 巴PK	0 受惠国LD	35	--Endless transmission belts of trapezoidal cross-section (V-belts) , other than V-ribbed, of an outside circumference exceeding 60cm but not exceeding 180cm
3083	4010.3300	--梯形截面的环形传动带（三角带），V形肋状的，外周长超过180厘米，但不超过240厘米	8	0 冰岛IS,东盟AS,哥CR,秘鲁PE,新西兰NZ,智利CL 3.2 瑞士CH 4.8 澳AU,韩国KR 5 巴PK	0 受惠国LD	35	--Endless transmission belts of trapezoidal cross-section (V-belts) , V-ribbed, of an outside circumference exceeding 180cm but not exceeding 240cm
3084	4010.3400	--梯形截面的环形传动带（三角带），外周长超过180厘米，但不超过240厘米，V形肋状的除外	8	0 冰岛IS,东盟AS,哥CR,秘鲁PE,新西兰NZ,智利CL 3.2 瑞士CH 4.8 澳AU,韩国KR 5 巴PK	0 受惠国LD	35	--Endless transmission belts of trapezoidal cross-section (V-belts) , Vribbed, of an outside circumference exceeding 180cm but not exceeding 240cm
3085	4010.3500	--环形同步带，外周长超过60厘米，但不超过150厘米	10	0 冰岛IS,东盟AS,哥CR,秘鲁PE,新加坡SG,新西兰NZ,智利CL 4 瑞士CH 5 巴PK 6 澳AU 8 韩国KR	0 受惠国$_1$LD$_1$	35	--Endless transmission belts of trapezoidal cross-section (V-belts) , other than Vribbed, of an outside circumference exceeding 60cm but not exceeding 150cm
3086	4010.3600	--环形同步带，外周长超过150厘米，但不超过198厘米	10	0 冰岛IS,东盟AS,哥CR,秘鲁PE,新西兰NZ,智利CL 4 瑞士CH 5 巴PK 6 澳AU 8 韩国KR	0 受惠国$_1$LD$_1$	35	--Endless synchronous belts, of an outside circumference exceeding 150cm but not exceeding 198cm
3087	4010.3900	--其他	8	0 冰岛IS,东盟AS,哥CR,秘鲁PE,瑞士CH,新西兰NZ,智利CL 4.8 澳AU,韩国KR 5 巴PK 7.6 亚太AP	0 受惠国LD	35	--Other
	40.11	**新的充气橡胶轮胎：**					**New pneumatic tyres, of rubber:**
3088	4011.1000	-机动小客车（包括旅行小客车及赛车）用	10	0 冰岛IS,东盟AS,哥CR,台湾TW,新加坡SG,新西兰NZ,智利CL 4 瑞士CH 5 巴PK 6 澳AU 8.6 韩国KR 9.4 亚太AP	0 受惠国LD	50	-Of a kind used on motor cars (including station wagons and racing cars)
3089	4011.2000	-客运机动车辆或货运机动车辆用	10	0 冰岛IS,东盟AS,哥CR,台湾TW,新加坡SG,新西兰NZ,智利CL 3 秘鲁PE 4 瑞士CH 5 巴PK 6 澳AU 8.6 韩国KR 9.4 亚太AP	0 受惠国$_1$LD$_1$	50	-Of a kind used on buses or lorries
	ex40112000	断面宽度30英寸及以上的轮胎	Δ8				Tyres, having a fracture surface of a width of 30 inches or more

序号 No.	税则号列 Tariff Line	中文货品名称 Article Description in Chinese	最惠国税率 MFN(%)	协定税率 Agreement(%)	特惠税率 SP(%)	普通税率 Gen(%)	英文货品名称 Article Description
3090	4011.3000	-航空器用	1	0 澳AU,巴PK,冰岛IS,东盟AS,哥CR,韩国KR,秘鲁PE,瑞士CH,新西兰NZ,智利CL	0 受惠国LD	11	-Of a kind used on aircraft
3091	4011.4000	-摩托车用	15	0 冰岛IS,东盟AS,哥CR,台湾TW,新加坡SG,新西兰NZ,智利CL 4.5 秘鲁PE 9 澳AU 10.5 瑞士CH 12 巴PK 13 韩国KR	0 受惠国$_1$LD$_1$	80	-Of a kind used on motorcycles
3092	4011.5000	-自行车用	20	0 冰岛IS,东盟AS,哥CR,台湾TW,新加坡SG,新西兰NZ,智利CL 6 秘鲁PE 12 澳AU 14 瑞士CH 17.3 韩国KR	0 受惠国$_1$LD$_1$	80	-Of a kind used on bicycles
		-其他，人字形胎面或类似胎面的：					-Other, having a ' herring-bone' or similar tread:
3093	4011.6100	--农业或林业车辆及机器用	17.5	0 冰岛IS,东盟AS,哥CR,台湾TW,新加坡SG,新西兰NZ,智利CL 5.2 秘鲁PE 10.5 澳AU 12.3 瑞士CH 14 巴PK,韩国KR	0 受惠国$_1$LD$_1$	50	--Of a kind used on agricultural or forestry vehicles and machines
	ex40116100	断面宽度24英寸及以上的轮胎	Δ8				Tyres, having a fracture surface of a width of 24 inches or more
3094	4011.6200	--建筑业或工业搬运车辆及机器用，辋圈尺寸不超过61厘米	17.5	0 冰岛IS,东盟AS,哥CR,新加坡SG,新西兰NZ,智利CL 5.2 秘鲁PE 10.5 澳AU 12.3 瑞士CH 14 巴PK,韩国KR	0 受惠国$_1$LD$_1$	50	--Of a kind used on construction or industrial handling vehicles and machines and having a rim size not exceeding 61cm
3095	4011.6300	--建筑业或工业搬运车辆及机器用，辋圈尺寸超过61厘米	17.5	0 冰岛IS,东盟AS,哥CR,新加坡SG,新西兰NZ,智利CL 5.2 秘鲁PE 10.5 澳AU 12.3 瑞士CH 14 巴PK,韩国KR	0 受惠国$_1$LD$_1$	50	--Of a kind used on construction or industrial handling vehicles and machines and having a rim size exceeding 61cm
	ex40116300	断面宽度24英寸及以上的轮胎	Δ8				Tyres, having a fracture surface of a width of 24 inches or more
3096	4011.6900	--其他	17.5	0 冰岛IS,东盟AS,哥CR,台湾TW,新加坡SG,新西兰NZ,智利CL 5.2 秘鲁PE 10.5 澳AU 12.3 瑞士CH 14 巴PK,韩国KR	0 受惠国$_1$LD$_1$	50	--Other
	ex40116900	断面宽度30英寸及以上的轮胎	Δ8				Tyres, having a fracture surface of a width of 30 inches or more
		-其他：					-Other:
3097	4011.9200	--农业或林业车辆及机器用	25	0 冰岛IS,东盟AS,哥CR,台湾TW,新加坡SG,新西兰NZ,智利CL 15 澳AU 22.5 韩国KR	0 受惠国LD	50	--Of a kind used on agricultural or forestry vehicles and machines
3098	4011.9300	--建筑业或工业搬运车辆及机器用，辋圈尺寸不超过61厘米	25	0 冰岛IS,东盟AS,哥CR,新加坡SG,新西兰NZ,智利CL 15 澳AU 22.5 韩国KR	0 受惠国$_2$LD$_2$	50	--Of a kind used on construction or industrial handling vehicles and machines and having a rim size not exceeding 61cm

序号 No.	税则号列 Tariff Line	中文货品名称 Article Description in Chinese	最惠国税率 MFN(%)	协定税率 Agreement(%)	特惠税率 SP(%)	普通税率 Gen(%)	英文货品名称 Article Description
3099	4011.9400	--建筑业或工业搬运车辆及机器用，辋圈尺寸超过61厘米	25	0 冰岛IS,东盟AS,哥CR,新加坡SG,新西兰NZ,智利CL 15 澳AU 22.5 韩国KR	0 受惠国$_2$LD$_2$	50	--Of a kind used on construction or industrial handling vehicles and machines and having a rim size exceeding 61cm
	ex40119400	断面宽度24英寸及以上的轮胎	Δ8				Tyres, having a fracture surface of a width of 24 inches or more
3100	4011.9900	--其他	25	0 冰岛IS,东盟AS,哥CR,新加坡SG,新西兰NZ,智利CL 15 澳AU 22.5 韩国KR	0 受惠国$_2$LD$_2$	50	--Other
	ex40119900	断面宽度30英寸及以上的轮胎	Δ8				Tyres, having a fracture surface of a width of 30 inches or more
	40.12	**翻新的或旧的充气橡胶轮胎;实心或半实心橡胶轮胎、橡胶胎面及橡胶轮胎衬带:**					**Retreaded or used pneumatic tyres of rubber; solid or cushion tyres, tyre treads and tyre flaps, of rubber:**
		-翻新轮胎:					-Retreaded tyres:
3101	4012.1100	--机动小客车(包括旅行小客车及赛车)用	20	0 冰岛IS,东盟AS,哥CR,新加坡SG,新西兰NZ,智利CL 6 秘鲁PE 12 澳AU 14 瑞士CH 17.3 韩国KR	0 受惠国$_1$LD$_1$	50	--Of a kind used on motor cars, (including station wagons and racing cars)
3102	4012.1200	--机动大客车或货运机动车辆用	20	0 冰岛IS,东盟AS,哥CR,香港HK,新加坡SG,新西兰NZ,智利CL 6 秘鲁PE 12 澳AU 14 瑞士CH 17.3 韩国KR	0 受惠国$_1$LD$_1$	50	--Of a kind used on buses or corries
3103	4012.1300	--航空器用	20Δ4	0 冰岛IS,东盟AS,哥CR,香港HK,新加坡SG,新西兰NZ,智利CL 6 秘鲁PE 12 澳AU 14 瑞士CH 17.3 韩国KR	0 受惠国$_1$LD$_1$	50	--Of a kind used on aircraft
3104	4012.1900	--其他	20	0 冰岛IS,东盟AS,哥CR,新加坡SG,新西兰NZ,智利CL 6 秘鲁PE 12 澳AU 14 瑞士CH 17.3 韩国KR	0 受惠国$_1$LD$_1$	50	--Other
		-旧的充气轮胎:					-Used pneumatic tyres:
3105	4012.2010	---汽车用	25	0 冰岛IS,东盟AS,哥CR,香港HK,新加坡SG,新西兰NZ,智利CL 15 澳AU 22.5 韩国KR		50	---Of a kind used on motor cars, buses or lorries
3106	4012.2090	---其他	25	0 冰岛IS,东盟AS,哥CR,香港HK,新加坡SG,新西兰NZ,智利CL 15 澳AU 22.5 韩国KR		80	---Other
		-其他:					-Other:
3107	4012.9010	---航空器用	3	0 澳AU,巴PK,冰岛IS,东盟AS,哥CR,韩国KR,秘鲁PE,瑞士CH,新西兰NZ,智利CL	0 受惠国$_1$LD$_1$	11	---Of a kind used on aircraft

序号 No.	税则号列 Tariff Line	中文货品名称 Article Description in Chinese	最惠国税率 MFN(%)	协定税率 Agreement(%)	特惠税率 SP(%)	普通税率 Gen(%)	英文货品名称 Article Description
3108	4012.9020	---汽车用	22	0 冰岛IS,东盟AS,哥CR,新加坡SG,新西兰NZ,智利CL 6.6 秘鲁PE 13.2 澳AU 15.4 瑞士CH 19.8 韩国KR	0 受惠国$_1$LD$_1$	50	---Of a kind used on motor cars, buses or lorries
3109	4012.9090	---其他	22	0 冰岛IS,东盟AS,哥CR,新加坡SG,新西兰NZ,智利CL 6.6 秘鲁PE 13.2 澳AU 15.4 瑞士CH 19.8 韩国KR	0 受惠国$_1$LD$_1$	50	---Other
	40.13	橡胶内胎：					**Inner tubes, of rubber:**
3110	4013.1000	-机动小客车（包括旅行小客车及赛车）、客运机动车辆或货运机动车辆用	15	0 冰岛IS,东盟AS,哥CR,新加坡SG,新西兰NZ,智利CL 4.5 秘鲁PE 7.5 巴PK 9 澳AU 10.5 瑞士CH 13 韩国KR,亚太AP	0 受惠国$_1$LD$_1$	50	-Of a kind used on motor cars (including station wagons and racing cars), buses or lorries
3111	4013.2000	-自行车用	15	0 冰岛IS,东盟AS,哥CR,新加坡SG,新西兰NZ,智利CL 4.5 秘鲁PE 9 澳AU 10.5 瑞士CH 12 巴PK,韩国KR	0 受惠国$_1$LD$_1$	80	-Of a kind used on bicycles
		-其他：					-Other:
3112	4013.9010	---航空器用	3	0 澳AU,巴PK,冰岛IS,东盟AS,哥CR,韩国KR,秘鲁PE,瑞士CH,新西兰NZ,智利CL	0 受惠国LD	11	---Of a kind used on aircraft
3113	4013.9090	---其他	15	0 冰岛IS,东盟AS,哥CR,新加坡SG,新西兰NZ,智利CL 4.5 秘鲁PE 9 澳AU 10.5 瑞士CH 12 巴PK,韩国KR	0 受惠国$_1$LD$_1$	50	Other
	40.14	硫化橡胶（硬质橡胶除外）制的卫生及医疗用品（包括奶嘴），不论是否装有硬质橡胶制的附件：					**Hygienic or pharmaceutical articles (including teats), of vulcanised rubber other than hard rubber, with or without fittings of hard rubber:**
3114	4014.1000	-避孕套	0		0 受惠国LD	0	-Sheath contraceptives
3115	4014.9000	-其他	17.5	0 澳门MO,冰岛IS,东盟AS,哥CR,新加坡SG,新西兰NZ,智利CL 5.2 秘鲁PE 10.5 澳AU 12.3 瑞士CH 14 巴PK,韩国KR	0 受惠国$_1$LD$_1$	50	-Other
	40.15	硫化橡胶（硬质橡胶除外）制的衣着用品及附件（包括手套）：					**Articles of apparel and clothing accessories (including gloves, mittens and mitts), for all purposes, of vulcanised rubber other than hard rubber:**
		-手套：					-Gloves, mittens and mitts:

序号 No.	税则号列 Tariff Line	中文货品名称 Article Description in Chinese	最惠国税率 MFN(%)	协定税率 Agreement(%)	特惠税率 SP(%)	普通税率 Gen(%)	英文货品名称 Article Description
3116	4015.1100	--外科用	8	0 冰岛IS,东盟AS,哥CR,秘鲁PE,新西兰NZ,智利CL 3.2 瑞士CH 4.8 澳AU,韩国KR 5 巴PK	0 受惠国LD	30	--Surgical
3117	4015.1900	--其他	18	0 冰岛IS,东盟AS,哥CR,新加坡SG,新西兰NZ,智利CL 5.4 秘鲁PE 10.8 澳AU 12.6 瑞士CH 14.4 韩国KR	0 受惠国LD	80	--Other
		-其他:					-Other:
3118	4015.9010	---医疗用	8	0 东盟AS,哥CR,秘鲁PE,新西兰NZ,智利CL 3.2 瑞士CH 4.8 澳AU,韩国KR 5 巴PK	0 受惠国LD	30	---For medical purpose
3119	4015.9090	---其他	15	0 冰岛IS,东盟AS,哥CR,新加坡SG,新西兰NZ,智利CL 4.5 秘鲁PE 9 澳AU 10.5 瑞士CH 12 韩国KR	0 受惠国$_1$LD$_1$	90	---Other
	40.16	**硫化橡胶(硬质橡胶除外)的其他制品:**					**Other articles of vulcanised rubber other than hard rubber:**
		-海绵橡胶制:					-Of cellular rubber:
3120	4016.1010	---机器及仪器用零件	8	0 冰岛IS,东盟AS,哥CR,秘鲁PE,新西兰NZ,智利CL 3.2 瑞士CH 4.8 澳AU 5 巴PK 6.9 韩国KR	0 受惠国LD	30	---Of a kind used in machines or instruments
3121	4016.1090	---其他	15	0 冰岛IS,东盟AS,哥CR,新加坡SG,新西兰NZ,智利CL 4.5 秘鲁PE 9 澳AU 10.5 瑞士CH 12 巴PK,韩国KR	0 受惠国$_1$LD$_1$	80	---Other
		-其他:					-Other:
3122	4016.9100	--铺地制品及门垫	18	0 冰岛IS,东盟AS,哥CR,香港HK,新加坡SG,新西兰NZ,智利CL 5.4 秘鲁PE 10.8 澳AU 12.6 瑞士CH 14.4 韩国KR	0 受惠国$_1$LD$_1$	80	--Floor coverings and mats
3123	4016.9200	--橡皮擦	18	0 冰岛IS,东盟AS,哥CR,新西兰NZ,智利CL 5.4 秘鲁PE 10.8 澳AU 12.6 瑞士CH 14.4 韩国KR	0 受惠国$_1$LD$_1$	80	--Erasers
		--垫片、垫圈及其他密封垫:					--Gaskets, washers and other seals:
3124	4016.9310	---机器及仪器用	8	0 冰岛IS,东盟AS,哥CR,秘鲁PE,香港HK,新西兰NZ,智利CL 4.8 澳AU,韩国KR 5 巴PK 5.6 瑞士CH	0 受惠国LD	30	---Of a kind used in machines or instruments

序号 No.	税则号列 Tariff Line	中文货品名称 Article Description in Chinese	最惠国税率 MFN(%)	协定税率 Agreement(%)	特惠税率 SP(%)	普通税率 Gen(%)	英文货品名称 Article Description
3125	4016.9390	---其他	15	0 冰岛IS,东盟AS,哥CR,香港HK,新加坡SG,新西兰NZ,智利CL 4.5 秘鲁PE 9 澳AU,韩国KR 10.5 瑞士CH	0 受惠国LD	80	---Other
3126	4016.9400	--船舶或码头的碰垫，不论是否可充气	18	0 冰岛IS,东盟AS,哥CR,新加坡SG,新西兰NZ,智利CL 5.4 秘鲁PE 10.8 澳AU 12.6 瑞士CH 14.4 韩国KR	0 受惠国$_1$LD$_1$	80	--Boat or dock fenders, whether or not inflatable
3127	4016.9500	--其他可充气制品	18	0 澳门MO,冰岛IS,东盟AS,哥CR,新加坡SG,新西兰NZ,智利CL 5.4 秘鲁PE 10.8 澳AU 12.6 瑞士CH 14.4 韩国KR	0 受惠国$_1$LD$_1$	80	--Other inflatable articles
	ex40169500	液压隔离式蓄能器用胶囊	Δ9				Hydraulic pressure-insulation type accumulator bladder
		--其他:					--Other:
3128	4016.9910	---机器及仪器用零件	8	0 澳门MO,冰岛IS,东盟AS,哥CR,秘鲁PE,新西兰NZ,智利CL 4.8 澳AU 5 巴PK 5.6 瑞士CH 6.9 韩国KR 7.6 亚太AP	0 受惠国LD	30	---Of a kind used in machines or instr-uments
	ex40169910	奶衬	Δ4				Liner
3129	4016.9990	---其他	10	0 澳门MO,冰岛IS,东盟AS,哥CR,新加坡SG,新西兰NZ,智利CL 3 秘鲁PE 5 巴PK 6 澳AU 7 瑞士CH 8 韩国KR 9.5 亚太AP	0 受惠国LD	80	---Other
	ex40169990	动车组用胶囊、外风挡板	Δ5				Locomotive fording intercar barrier, gangway bellows
	40.17	**各种形状的硬质橡胶(例如纯硬质胶)，包括废碎料;硬质橡胶制品:**					**Hard rubber (for example, ebonite) in all forms, including waste and scrap; articles of hard rubber:**
3130	4017.0010	---各种形状的硬质橡胶，包括废碎料	8	0 澳门MO,冰岛IS,东盟AS,哥CR,秘鲁PE,新西兰NZ,智利CL 3.2 瑞士CH 4.8 澳AU 5 巴PK 6.4 韩国KR	0 受惠国$_1$LD$_1$	35	---Hard rubber in all forms, including waste and scrap
3131	4017.0020	---硬质橡胶制品	15	0 澳门MO,冰岛IS,东盟AS,哥CR,新加坡SG,新西兰NZ,智利CL 4.5 秘鲁PE 9 澳AU 10.5 瑞士CH 12 巴PK,韩国KR	0 受惠国$_1$LD$_1$	90	---Articles of hard rubber

第八类
生皮、皮革、毛皮及其制品；鞍具及挽具；旅行用品、手提包及类似容器；动物肠线（蚕胶丝除外）制品

SECTION Ⅷ
RAW HIDES AND SKINS, LEATHER, FURSKINS AND ARTICLES THEREOF; SADDLERY AND HARNESS; TRAVEL GOODS, HANDBAGS AND SIMILAR CONTAINERS; ARTICLES OF ANIMAL GUT (OTHER THAN SILK-WORM GUT)

第四十一章
生皮（毛皮除外）及皮革

Chapter 41
Raw hides and skins (other than furskins) and leather

注释：

一、本章不包括：

（一）生皮的边角废料（税号05.11）；

（二）税号05.05或67.01的带羽毛或羽绒的整张或部分鸟皮；

（三）带毛生皮或已鞣的带毛皮张（第四十三章）：但下列动物的带毛生皮应归入第四十一章，牛（包括水牛）、马、绵羊及羔羊（不包括阿斯特拉罕、喀拉科尔、波斯羔羊或类似羔羊、印度、中国或蒙古羔羊）、山羊或小山羊（不包括也门或蒙古山羊及小山羊）、猪（包括西藏）、小羚羊、瞪羚、骆驼（包括单峰骆驼）、驯鹿、麋、鹿、狍或狗。

二、

（一）税目41.04至41.06不包括经退鞣（包括预鞣）加工的皮（酌情归入税目41.01至41.03）；

（二）税目41.04至41.06所称“坯革”包括在干燥前经复鞣、染色或加油（加脂）的皮。

三、本目录所称“再生皮革”，仅指税号41.15的皮革。

Notes:

1.This Chapter does not cover:

(a) Parings or similar waste, of raw hides or skins (heading No.05.11);

(b) Birdskins or parts of birdskins, with their feathers or down, of heading No.05.05 or 67.01; or

(c) Hides or skins, with the hair or wool on, raw, tanned or dressed (Chapter43); the following are, however, to be classified in Chapter41, namely, raw hides and skins with the hair or wool on, of bovine animals (including buffalo), of equine animals, of sheep or lambs (except Astrakhan, Broadtail, Caracul, Persian or similar lambs, Indian, Chinese, Mongolian or Tibetan lambs), of goats or kids (except Yemen, Mongolian or Tibetan goats and kids), of swine (including peccary), of chamois, of gazelle, of camels (including dromedaries), of reindeer, of elk, of deer, of roebucks or of dogs.

2.

(a) Headings 41.04 to 41.06 do not cover hides and skins which have undergone a tanning (including pre-tanning) process which is reversible (headings 41.01 to 41.03, as the case may be);

(b) For the purposes of headings 41.04 to 41.06, the term “crust” includes hides and skins that have been retanned, coloured or fat-liquored (stuffed) prior to drying.

3. Throughout the Nomenclature the expression “composition leather” means only substances of the kind referred to in heading No.41.15.

序号 No.	税则号列 Tariff Line	中文货品名称 Article Description in Chinese	最惠国税率 MFN(%)	协定税率 Agreement(%)	特惠税率 SP(%)	普通税率 Gen(%)	英文货品名称 Article Description
	41.01	生牛皮（包括水牛皮）、生马皮（鲜的、盐腌的、干的、石灰浸渍的、浸酸的或以其他方法保藏，但未鞣制、未经羊皮纸化处理或进一步加工的），不论是否去毛或剖层：					**Raw hides and skins of bovine (including buffalo) or equine animals (fresh, or salted, dried, limed, pickled or otherwise preserved, but not tanned, parchment-dressed or further prepared), whether or not dehaired or split:**
		-未剖层的整张皮，完全干燥的每张重量不超过8千克，干盐腌的不超过10千克，鲜的、湿盐腌的或以其他方法保藏的不超过16千克：					-Whole hides and skins, unsplit, of a weight per skin not exceeding 8 kg when simply dried, 10 kg when dry-salted, or 16 kg when fresh, wet-salted or otherwise preserved:
		---牛皮：					---Of bovine animals:

序号 No.	税则号列 Tariff Line	中文货品名称 Article Description in Chinese	最惠国税率 MFN(%)	协定税率 Agreement(%)	特惠税率 SP(%)	普通税率 Gen(%)	英文货品名称 Article Description
3132	4101.2011	----经退鞣处理的	8	0 冰岛IS,东盟AS,哥CR,秘鲁PE,香港HK,新西兰NZ,智利CL 3.2 瑞士CH 4.8 韩国KR 5 巴PK 6 澳AU,亚太AP	0 受惠国LD	17	----Have undergone a reversible tanning process
3133	4101.2019	----其他	5	0 巴PK,冰岛IS,东盟AS,哥CR,韩国KR,秘鲁PE,瑞士CH,香港HK,新西兰NZ,智利CL 3.8 澳AU	0 柬埔寨KH,老挝LA,受惠国LD	17	----Other
3134	4101.2020	---马皮	5	0 巴PK,冰岛IS,东盟AS,韩国KR,秘鲁PE,瑞士CH,香港HK,新西兰NZ,智利CL 1.7 澳AU 2 哥CR	0 柬埔寨KH,老挝LA,受惠国LD	30	---Of equine animals
		-整张皮，重量超过16千克：					-Whole hides and skins, of a weight exceeding 16kg:
		---牛皮：					---Of bovine animals:
3135	4101.5011	----经退鞣处理的	8.4	0 冰岛IS,东盟AS,哥CR,秘鲁PE,新西兰NZ,智利CL 3.36 瑞士CH 5 巴PK,韩国KR 6.3 澳AU 7 亚太AP	0 受惠国LD	17	----Have undergone a reversible tanning process
3136	4101.5019	----其他	5	0 巴PK,冰岛IS,东盟AS,哥CR,韩国KR,秘鲁PE,瑞士CH,新西兰NZ,智利CL 3.8 澳AU	0 柬埔寨KH,老挝LA,受惠国LD	17	----Other
3137	4101.5020	---马皮	5	0 巴PK,冰岛IS,东盟AS,韩国KR,秘鲁PE,瑞士CH,新西兰NZ,智利CL 2 哥CR 3 澳AU	0 柬埔寨KH,老挝LA,受惠国LD	30	---Of equine animals
		-其他，包括整张或半张的背皮及腹皮：					-Other, including butts, bends and bellies:
		---牛皮：					---Of bovine animals:
3138	4101.9011	----经退鞣处理的	8.4	0 冰岛IS,东盟AS,哥CR,秘鲁PE,新西兰NZ,智利CL 3.36 瑞士CH 5 巴PK,韩国KR 6.3 澳AU 7 亚太AP	0 受惠国LD	17	----Have undergone a reversible tanning process
3139	4101.9019	----其他	5	0 巴PK,冰岛IS,东盟AS,哥CR,韩国KR,秘鲁PE,瑞士CH,新西兰NZ,智利CL 3.8 澳AU	0 柬埔寨KH,老挝LA,受惠国LD	17	----Other
3140	4101.9020	---马皮	5	0 巴PK,冰岛IS,东盟AS,韩国KR,秘鲁PE,瑞士CH,新西兰NZ,智利CL 2 哥CR 3 澳AU	0 柬埔寨KH,老挝LA,受惠国LD	30	---Of equine animals

序号 No.	税则号列 Tariff Line	中文货品名称 Article Description in Chinese	最惠国税率 MFN(%)	协定税率 Agreement(%)	特惠税率 SP(%)	普通税率 Gen(%)	英文货品名称 Article Description
	41.02	绵羊或羔羊生皮（鲜的、盐腌的、干的、石灰浸渍的、浸酸的或经其他方法保藏，但未鞣制、未经羊皮纸化处理或进一步加工的），不论是否带毛或剖层，但本章注释一(三)所述不包括的生皮除外：					**Raw skins of sheep or lambs (fresh, or salted, dried, limed, pickled or otherwise preserved, but not tanned, parchment-dressed or further prepared) , whether or not with wool on or split, other than those excluded by note 1 (c) to this chapter:**
3141	4102.1000	-带毛	7	0 冰岛IS,东盟AS,韩国KR,新西兰NZ,智利CL 2.8 哥CR,瑞士CH 4.2 澳AU 5 巴PK	0 受惠国LD	30	-With wool on
		-不带毛：					-Without wool on:
		--浸酸的：					--Pickled:
3142	4102.2110	---经退鞣处理的	14	0 冰岛IS,东盟AS,新加坡SG,新西兰NZ,智利CL 5.6 哥CR 9.8 瑞士CH 10.5 澳AU 11.2 巴PK,韩国KR	0 受惠国$_1$LD$_1$	30	---Have undergone a reversible tanning process
3143	4102.2190	---其他	9	0 冰岛IS,东盟AS,秘鲁PE,新西兰NZ,智利CL 3.6 哥CR,瑞士CH 5 巴PK 5.4 韩国KR 6.8 澳AU 8 亚太AP	0 受惠国LD	30	---Other
		--其他：					--Other:
3144	4102.2910	---经退鞣处理的	14	0 冰岛IS,东盟AS,秘鲁PE,新加坡SG,新西兰NZ,智利CL 5.6 哥CR 7 巴PK 9.8 瑞士CH 10.5 澳AU 11.2 韩国KR	0 受惠国$_1$LD$_1$	30	---Have undergone a reversible tanning process
3145	4102.2990	---其他	7	0 冰岛IS,东盟AS,韩国KR,秘鲁PE,新西兰NZ,智利CL 2.8 哥CR,瑞士CH 5 巴PK 5.3 澳AU 6 亚太AP	0 受惠国LD	30	---Other
	41.03	其他生皮(鲜的、盐腌的、干的、石灰浸渍的、浸酸的或以其他方法保藏，但未鞣制、未经羊皮纸化处理或进一步加工的)，不论是否去毛或剖层，但本章注释一（二）或（三）所述不包括的生皮除外：					**Other raw hides and skins (fresh, or salted, dried, limed, pickled or otherwise preserved, but not tanned, parchment-dressed or further prepared) , whether or not dehaired or split, other than those excluded by note 1 (b) or 1 (c) to this chapter:**
3146	4103.2000	-爬行动物皮	9	0 冰岛IS,东盟AS,秘鲁PE,新西兰NZ,智利CL 3.6 哥CR,瑞士CH 5 巴PK 5.4 韩国KR 6.8 澳AU	0 受惠国LD	30	-Of reptiles
3147	4103.3000	-猪皮	9	0 冰岛IS,东盟AS,秘鲁PE,新西兰NZ,智利CL 3.6 哥CR,瑞士CH 5 巴PK 5.4 澳AU,韩国KR	0 缅甸MM,受惠国LD	30	-Of swine
		-其他：					-Other:

序号 No.	税则号列 Tariff Line	中文货品名称 Article Description in Chinese	最惠国税率 MFN(%)	协定税率 Agreement(%)	特惠税率 SP(%)	普通税率 Gen(%)	英文货品名称 Article Description
		---山羊板皮:					---Dried hides and skins of goats:
3148	4103.9011	----经退鞣处理的	14	0 冰岛IS,东盟AS,秘鲁PE,新加坡SG,新西兰NZ,智利CL 5.6 哥CR 7 巴PK 9.8 瑞士CH 10.5 澳AU 11.2 韩国KR	0 受惠国$_1$LD$_1$	35	----Have undergone a reversible tanning process
3149	4103.9019	----其他	9	0 冰岛IS,东盟AS,秘鲁PE,新西兰NZ,智利CL 3.6 哥CR,瑞士CH 5 巴PK 5.4 韩国KR 6 澳AU	0 受惠国LD	35	----Other
		---其他山羊或小山羊皮:					---Other hides and skins of goats or of kids:
3150	4103.9021	----经退鞣处理的	14	0 冰岛IS,东盟AS,秘鲁PE,新加坡SG,新西兰NZ,智利CL 5.6 哥CR 7 巴PK 9.8 瑞士CH 10.5 澳AU 11.2 韩国KR	0 受惠国$_1$LD$_1$	30	----Have undergone a reversible tanning process
3151	4103.9029	----其他	9	0 冰岛IS,东盟AS,秘鲁PE,新西兰NZ,智利CL 3.6 哥CR,瑞士CH 5 巴PK 5.4 韩国KR 6 澳AU	0 受惠国LD	30	----Other
3152	4103.9090	---其他	9	0 冰岛IS,东盟AS,秘鲁PE,香港HK,新西兰NZ,智利CL 3.6 哥CR,瑞士CH 5 巴PK 5.4 澳AU,韩国KR	0 缅甸MM,受惠国LD	30	---Other
	41.04	**经鞣制的不带毛牛皮(包括水牛皮)、马皮及其坯革,不论是否剖层,但未经进一步加工:**					**Tanned or crust hides and skins of bovine (including buffalo) or equine animals, without hair on, whether or not split, but not further prepared:**
		-湿革(包括蓝湿皮):					-In the wet state (including wet-blue):
		--全粒面未剖层革;粒面剖层革:					--Full grains, unsplit; grain splits:
		---牛皮:					---Of bovine animals:
3153	4104.1111	----蓝湿的	7△3	0 巴PK,冰岛IS,东盟AS,秘鲁PE,新西兰NZ,智利CL 2.8 哥CR,瑞士CH 3.5 亚太AP 4.2 澳AU,韩国KR	0 受惠国LD 1.4 亚太AP	17	----Wet-blue
3154	4104.1119	----其他	8	0 巴PK,冰岛IS,东盟AS,秘鲁PE,香港HK,新西兰NZ,智利CL 3.2 哥CR,瑞士CH 4 亚太AP 4.8 澳AU,韩国KR	0 受惠国LD 2 亚太AP	35	----Other
3155	4104.1120	---马皮	5	0 澳AU,巴PK,冰岛IS,东盟AS,秘鲁PE,瑞士CH,香港HK,新西兰NZ,智利CL 2 哥CR 2.5 亚太AP 3 韩国KR	0 受惠国LD 2 亚太AP	35	---Of equine animals

序号 No.	税则号列 Tariff Line	中文货品名称 Article Description in Chinese	最惠国税率 MFN(%)	协定税率 Agreement(%)	特惠税率 SP(%)	普通税率 Gen(%)	英文货品名称 Article Description
		--其他:					--Other:
		---牛皮:					---Of bovine animals:
3156	4104.1911	----蓝湿的	6Δ3	0 冰岛IS,东盟AS,秘鲁PE,新西兰NZ,智利CL 2.4 瑞士CH 2.8 哥CR 3 巴PK,亚太AP 3.6 澳AU,韩国KR	0 受惠国LD 1.4 亚太AP	17	----Wet-blue
3157	4104.1919	----其他	7	0 巴PK,冰岛IS,东盟AS,秘鲁PE,香港HK,新西兰NZ,智利CL 2.8 哥CR,瑞士CH 3.5 亚太AP 4.2 澳AU,韩国KR	0 受惠国LD 1.8 亚太AP	35	----Other
3158	4104.1920	---马皮	7Δ5	0 巴PK,冰岛IS,东盟AS,秘鲁PE,香港HK,新西兰NZ,智利CL 2.8 哥CR,瑞士CH 3.5 亚太AP 4.2 澳AU,韩国KR	0 受惠国LD 2.1 亚太AP	35	---Of equine animals
		-干革(坯革):					-In the dry state (crust) :
3159	4104.4100	--全粒面未剖层革粒面剖层革的	5Δ3	0 澳AU,巴PK,冰岛IS,东盟AS,秘鲁PE,瑞士CH,香港HK,新西兰NZ,智利CL 2 哥CR 3 韩国KR 3.5 亚太AP	0 受惠国LD 2 亚太AP	35	--Full grain, unsplit; grain splits
		--其他:					--Other:
3160	4104.4910	---机器带用牛、马皮革	5	0 澳AU,巴PK,冰岛IS,东盟AS,秘鲁PE,瑞士CH,新西兰NZ,智利CL 2 哥CR 3 韩国KR 3.5 亚太AP	0 受惠国LD,亚太AP	20	---For machinery belting
3161	4104.4990	---其他	7	0 冰岛IS,东盟AS,秘鲁PE,香港HK,新西兰NZ,智利CL 2.8 哥CR,瑞士CH 4.2 澳AU 4.9 巴PK,亚太AP 6 韩国KR	0 受惠国LD 2.1 亚太AP	35	---Other
	41.05	**经鞣制的不带毛绵羊或者羔羊皮及其坯革,不论是否剖层,但未经进一步加工:**					**Tanned or crust skins of sheep or lambs, without wool on, whether or not split, but not further prepared:**
		-湿革(包括蓝湿皮):					-In the wet state (including wet-blue) :
3162	4105.1010	---蓝湿的	14Δ10	0 冰岛IS,东盟AS,新加坡SG,新西兰NZ,智利CL 5 巴PK 5.6 哥CR 7 亚太AP 8.4 澳AU 9.8 瑞士CH 11.2 韩国KR	0 受惠国LD 2.1 亚太AP	50	---Wet-blue
3163	4105.1090	---其他	10	0 冰岛IS,东盟AS,秘鲁PE,新西兰NZ,智利CL 4 哥CR,瑞士CH 5 巴PK,亚太AP 6 澳AU 8 韩国KR	0 受惠国LD 2 亚太AP	50	---Other

序号 No.	税则号列 Tariff Line	中文货品名称 Article Description in Chinese	最惠国税率 MFN(%)	协定税率 Agreement(%)	特惠税率 SP(%)	普通税率 Gen(%)	英文货品名称 Article Description
3164	4105.3000	-干革（坯革）	8	0 冰岛IS,东盟AS,秘鲁PE,新西兰NZ,智利CL 3.2 哥CR,瑞士CH 4.8 澳AU 5.6 巴PK,亚太AP 6.4 韩国KR	0 受惠国LD 4.8 亚太AP	50	-In the dry state (crust)
	41.06	**经鞣制的其他不带毛动物皮及其坯革，不论是否剖层，但未经进一步加工：**					**Tanned or crust hides and skins of other animals, without wool or hair on, whether or not split, but not further prepared:**
		-山羊或小山羊的：					-Of goats or kids:
3165	4106.2100	--湿革（包括蓝湿皮）	14	0 冰岛IS,东盟AS,秘鲁PE,新加坡SG,新西兰NZ,智利CL 5.6 哥CR 8.4 澳AU 9.8 瑞士CH 11.2 韩国KR 12 巴PK,亚太AP	0 受惠国LD 2.1 亚太AP	50	--In the wet state (including wet-blue)
	ex41062100	蓝湿山羊皮	Δ10				Goat skin leather, in the wet-blue state, without hair on, but not further prepared, whether or not split
3166	4106.2200	--干革（坯革）	14	0 冰岛IS,东盟AS,新加坡SG,新西兰NZ,智利CL 5.6 哥CR 8.4 澳AU 9.8 巴PK,瑞士CH,亚太AP 11.2 韩国KR	0 受惠国LD 8.4 亚太AP	50	--In the dry state (crust)
		-猪的：					-Of swine:
		--湿革（包括蓝湿皮）：					--In the wet state (including wet-blue) :
3167	4106.3110	---蓝湿的	14Δ10	0 冰岛IS,东盟AS,秘鲁PE,新加坡SG,新西兰NZ,智利CL 5.6 哥CR 8.4 澳AU 9.8 瑞士CH 11.2 巴PK,韩国KR	0 受惠国$_1$LD$_1$ 4.2 亚太AP	50	---Wet-blue
3168	4106.3190	---其他	14	0 冰岛IS,东盟AS,秘鲁PE,新加坡SG,新西兰NZ,智利CL 5.6 哥CR 7 巴PK 8.4 澳AU 9.8 瑞士CH 11.2 韩国KR	0 受惠国$_1$LD$_1$ 4.2 亚太AP	50	---Other
3169	4106.3200	--干革（坯革）	14	0 冰岛IS,东盟AS,秘鲁PE,新加坡SG,新西兰NZ,智利CL 5.6 哥CR 8.4 澳AU 9.8 瑞士CH 11.2 巴PK,韩国KR	0 受惠国$_1$LD$_1$ 4.2 亚太AP	50	--In the dry state (crust)
3170	4106.4000	-爬行动物的	14	0 冰岛IS,东盟AS,秘鲁PE,新加坡SG,新西兰NZ,智利CL 5.6 哥CR 7 巴PK 8.4 澳AU 9.8 瑞士CH 11.2 韩国KR	0 受惠国LD,亚太AP	50	-Of reptiles
		-其他：					-Other:

序号 No.	税则号列 Tariff Line	中文货品名称 Article Description in Chinese	最惠国税率 MFN(%)	协定税率 Agreement(%)	特惠税率 SP(%)	普通税率 Gen(%)	英文货品名称 Article Description
3171	4106.9100	--湿革（包括蓝湿皮）	14	0 冰岛IS,东盟AS,秘鲁PE,新加坡SG,新西兰NZ,智利CL 5.6 哥CR 8.4 澳AU 9.8 瑞士CH 11.2 巴PK,韩国KR	0 受惠国LD,亚太AP	50	--In the wet state (including wet-blue)
3172	4106.9200	--干革（坯革）	14	0 冰岛IS,东盟AS,秘鲁PE,新加坡SG,新西兰NZ,智利CL 5.6 哥CR 8.4 澳AU 9.8 瑞士CH 11.2 巴PK,韩国KR	0 受惠国LD,亚太AP	50	--In the dry state (crust)
	41.07	**经鞣制或半硝处理后进一步加工的不带毛的牛皮革（包括水牛皮革）及马皮革，包括羊皮纸化处理的皮革，不论是否剖层，但税目41.14皮革除外：**					**Leather further prepared after tanning or crusting, including parchment-dressed leather, of bovine (including buffalo) or equine animals, without hair on, whether or not split, other than leather of heading 4114:**
		-整张的：					-Whole hides and skins:
		--全粒面未剖层革：					--Full grains, unsplit:
3173	4107.1110	---牛皮	8	0 冰岛IS,东盟AS,香港HK,新西兰NZ,智利CL 3.2 哥CR,瑞士CH 4.8 澳AU 6.9 韩国KR		50	---Of bovine animals
3174	4107.1120	---马皮	5	0 澳AU,巴PK,冰岛IS,东盟AS,秘鲁PE,瑞士CH,香港HK,新西兰NZ,智利CL 2 哥CR 3 韩国KR	0 受惠国LD	50	---Of equine animals
		--粒面剖层革：					--Grain splits:
3175	4107.1210	---牛皮	8Δ6	0 冰岛IS,东盟AS,香港HK,新西兰NZ,智利CL 3.2 哥CR,瑞士CH 4.8 澳AU 6.4 韩国KR		50	---Of bovine animals
3176	4107.1220	---马皮	5	0 澳AU,巴PK,冰岛IS,东盟AS,秘鲁PE,瑞士CH,香港HK,新西兰NZ,智利CL 2 哥CR 3 韩国KR	0 受惠国LD	50	---Of equine animals
		--其他：					--Other:
3177	4107.1910	---机器带用	5	0 澳AU,巴PK,冰岛IS,东盟AS,秘鲁PE,瑞士CH,新西兰NZ,智利CL 2 哥CR 4 韩国KR	0 受惠国LD	50	---For machinery belting
3178	4107.1990	---其他	7	0 冰岛IS,东盟AS,香港HK,新西兰NZ,智利CL 2.8 哥CR,瑞士CH 4.2 澳AU,韩国KR		50	---Other
		-其他，包括半张的：					-Other, including sides:
3179	4107.9100	--全粒面未剖层革	5	0 澳AU,巴PK,冰岛IS,东盟AS,秘鲁PE,瑞士CH,新西兰NZ,智利CL 2 哥CR 4 韩国KR	0 受惠国LD	50	--Full grains, un split

序号 No.	税则号列 Tariff Line	中文货品名称 Article Description in Chinese	最惠国税率 MFN(%)	协定税率 Agreement(%)	特惠税率 SP(%)	普通税率 Gen(%)	英文货品名称 Article Description
3180	4107.9200	--粒面剖层革	5	0 澳AU,冰岛IS,东盟AS,秘鲁PE,新西兰NZ,智利CL 2 哥CR,瑞士CH 4.3 韩国KR	0 受惠国LD	50	--Grain splits
		--其他:					--Other:
3181	4107.9910	---机器带用	5	0 澳AU,巴PK,冰岛IS,东盟AS,秘鲁PE,瑞士CH,新西兰NZ,智利CL 2 哥CR 3 韩国KR	0 受惠国LD	50	---For machinery belting
3182	4107.9990	---其他	7	0 冰岛IS,东盟AS,秘鲁PE,香港HK,新西兰NZ,智利CL 2.8 哥CR,瑞士CH 4.2 澳AU 6 韩国KR	0 受惠国LD	50	---Other
	41.12	**经鞣制或半硝处理后进一步加工的不带毛的绵羊或羔羊皮革,包括羊皮纸化处理的,不论是否剖层,但税目41.14的皮革除外**					**Leather further prepared after tanning or crusting, including parchment-dressed leather, of sheep or lamb, without wool on, whether or not split, other than leather of heading 4114**
3183	4112.0000	经鞣制或半硝处理后进一步加工的不带毛的绵羊或羔羊皮革,包括羊皮纸化处理的,不论是否剖层,但税目41.14的皮革除外	8	0 冰岛IS,东盟AS,秘鲁PE,香港HK,新西兰NZ,智利CL 3.2 哥CR,瑞士CH 4.8 澳AU 5.6 巴PK,亚太AP 6.9 韩国KR	0 受惠国LD	50	Leather further prepared after tanning or crusting, including parchment dressed leather, of sheep or lamb, without wool on, whether or not split, other than leather of heading 4114
	41.13	**经鞣制或半硝处理后进一步加工的不带毛的其他动物皮革,包括羊皮纸化处理的,不论是否剖层,但税目的41.14的皮革除外:**					**Leather further prepared after tanning or crusting, including parchment-dressed leather, of other animals, without wool or hair on, whether or not split, other than leather of heading 4114:**
3184	4113.1000	-山羊或小山羊皮的	14	0 东盟AS,香港HK,新加坡SG,新西兰NZ,智利CL 5.6 哥CR 8.4 澳AU 9.8 巴PK,瑞士CH,亚太AP 11.2 韩国KR	0 受惠国LD	50	-Of goats or kids
3185	4113.2000	-猪皮的	14	0 冰岛IS,东盟AS,秘鲁PE,香港HK,新加坡SG,新西兰NZ,智利CL 5.6 哥CR 8.4 澳AU 9.8 瑞士CH 11.2 韩国KR	0 受惠国$_1$LD$_1$	50	-Of swine
3186	4113.3000	-爬行动物皮的	14	0 东盟AS,秘鲁PE,新加坡SG,新西兰NZ,智利CL 5.6 哥CR 8.4 澳AU 9.8 瑞士CH 11.2 巴PK,韩国KR	0 受惠国LD	50	-Of reptiles
3187	4113.9000	-其他	14	0 东盟AS,秘鲁PE,新加坡SG,新西兰NZ,智利CL 5.6 哥CR 7 冰岛IS 8.4 澳AU 9.8 瑞士CH 11.2 韩国KR	0 受惠国LD	50	-Other

序号 No.	税则号列 Tariff Line	中文货品名称 Article Description in Chinese	最惠国税率 MFN(%)	协定税率 Agreement(%)	特惠税率 SP(%)	普通税率 Gen(%)	英文货品名称 Article Description
	41.14	**油鞣皮革(包括结合鞣制的油鞣皮革);漆皮及层压漆皮;镀金属皮革:**					**Chamois (including combination chamois) leather; patent leather and patent laminated leather; metallised leather:**
3188	4114.1000	-油鞣皮革(包括结合鞣制的油鞣皮革)	14	0 冰岛IS,东盟AS,新加坡SG,新西兰NZ,智利CL 4.2 秘鲁PE 5.6 哥CR 8.4 澳AU 9.8 瑞士CH 11.2 韩国KR	0 受惠国$_1$LD$_1$	50	-Chamois (including combination chamois) leather
3189	4114.2000	-漆皮及层压漆皮;镀金属皮革	10	0 冰岛IS,东盟AS,新加坡SG,新西兰NZ,智利CL 4 哥CR,瑞士CH 6 澳AU 9 巴PK,韩国KR,亚太AP		50	-Patent leather and patent laminated leather; metallised leather
	41.15	**以皮革或皮革纤维为基本成分的再生皮革,成块、成张或成条的,不论是否成卷;皮革或再生皮革的边角废料;不适宜作皮革制品用;皮革粉末:**					**Composition leather with a basis of leather or leather fibre, in slabs, sheets or strip, whether or not in rolls; parings and other waste of leather or of composition leather, not suitable for the manufacture of leather articles; leather dust, powder and flour:**
3190	4115.1000	-以皮革或皮革纤维为基本成分的再生皮革,成块、成张或成条,不论是否成卷	14	0 冰岛IS,东盟AS,新加坡SG,新西兰NZ,智利CL 5.6 哥CR 8.4 澳AU 9.8 瑞士CH 11.2 韩国KR		50	-Composition leather with a basis of leather or leather fibre, in slabs, sheets or strip, whether or not in rolls
3191	4115.2000	-皮革或再生皮革的边角废料,不适宜作皮革制品用;皮革粉末	14	0 冰岛IS,东盟AS,秘鲁PE,新加坡SG,新西兰NZ,智利CL 5.6 哥CR 8.4 澳AU 9.8 瑞士CH 11.2 韩国KR	0 受惠国$_1$LD$_1$ 4.2 亚太AP	50	-Parings and other waste of leather or of composition leather, not suitable for the manufacture of leather articles; leather dust, powder and flour

第四十二章
皮革制品；鞍具及挽具；旅行用品、手提包及类似容器；动物肠线（蚕胶丝除外）制品

注释：

一、本章所称的“皮革”包括油鞣皮革（包括结合鞣制的油鞣皮革）、漆皮、层压漆皮和镀金属皮革。

二、本章不包括：

（一）外科用无菌肠线或类似的无菌缝合材料（税号30.06）；

（二）以毛皮或人造毛皮衬里或作面（仅饰边的除外）的衣服及衣着附件（分指手套、连指手套及露指手套除外）（税目43.03或43.04）；

（三）网线袋及类似品（税号56.08）；

（四）第六十四章的物品；

（五）第六十五章的帽类及其零件；

（六）税号66.02的鞭子、马鞭或其他物品；

（七）袖扣、手镯或其他仿首饰（税号71.17）；

（八）单独进口或出口的挽具附件或装饰物，例如，马镫、马嚼子、马铃铛及类似品、带扣（一般归入第十五类）；

（九）弦线、鼓面皮或类似品及其他乐器零件（税号92.09）；

（十）第九十四章的物品（例如，家具、灯具及照明装置）；

（十一）第九十五章的物品（例如，玩具、游戏品及运动用品）；

（十二）税号96.06的钮扣、揿扣、钮扣芯或这些物品的其他零件、钮扣坯。

三、（一）除上述注释一所规定的以外，税号42.02也不包括：

1. 非供长期使用的带把手塑料薄膜袋，不论是否印制（税号39.23）；

2. 编结材料制品（税号46.02）。

（二）税号42.02及42.03的制品，如果装有用贵金属、包贵金属、天然或养殖珍珠、宝石或半宝石（天然、合成或再造）制的零件，即使这些零件不是仅作为小配件或小饰物的，只要其未构成物品的基本特征，仍应归入上述税号。但如果这些零件已构成物品的基本特征，则应归入第七十一章。

Chapter 42
Articles of leather; saddlery and harness; travel goods, handbags and similar containers; articles of animal gut (other than silk-worm gut)

Notes:

1. For the purposes of this Chapter, the term “leather” includes chamois (including combination chamois) leather, patent leather, patent laminatedleather and metallised leather.

2. This Chapter does not cover:

(a) Sterile surgical catgut or similar sterile suture materials (heading No. 30.06);

(b) Articles of apparel or clothing accessories (except gloves, mittens and mitts), lined with furskin or artificial fur or to which furskin or artificial fur is attached on the outside except as mere trimming (heading No. 43.03 or 43.04);

(c) Made up articles of netting (heading No.56.08);

(d) Articles of Chapter 64;

(e) Headgear or parts thereof of Chapter 65;

(f) Whips, riding-crops or other articles of heading No.66.02;

(g) Cuff-links, bracelets or other imitation jewellery (heading No.71.17);

(h) Fittings or trimmings for harness, such as stirrups, bits, horse brasses and buckles, separately presented (generally Section XV);

(i) Strings, skins for drums or the like, or other parts of musical instruments (heading No.92.09);

(j) Articles of Chapter 94 (for example, furniture, lamps and lighting fittings);

(k) Articles of Chapter 95 (for example, toys, games, sports requisites); or

(l) Buttons, press-fasteners, snap-fasteners, press-studs, button moulds or other parts of these articles, button blanks, of heading No. 96.06.

3. (a) In addition to the provisions ofNote 1 above, heading No.42.02 does not cover:

(1) Bags made of sheeting of plastics, whether or not printed, with handles, not designed for prolonged use (heading No.39.23);

(2) Articles of plaiting materials (heading No.46.02).

(b) Articles of headings Nos. 42.02 and 42.03 which have parts of precious metal or metal clad with precious metal, of natural or cultured pearls, of precious or semi-precious stones (natural, synthetic or reconstructed) remain classified in those headings even if such parts constitute more than minor fittings or minor ornamentation, provided that these parts do not give the articles their essential character. If, on the other hand, the parts give the articles their essential character, the articles are to be classified in Chapter 71.

四、税号 42.03 所称“衣服及衣着附件”，主要包括分指手套、连指手套及露指手套（包括运动及防护手套）、围裙及其他防护用衣着、裤吊带、腰带、子弹带及腕带，但不包括表带（税目 91.13）。

4. For the purpose of heading No. 42.03, the expression “articles of apparel and clothing accessories” applies, *inter alia*, to gloves, mittens and mitts (including those for sport or for protection) , aprons and other protective clothing, braces, belts, bandoliers and wrist straps, but excluding watch straps (heading No. 91.13) .

序号 No.	税则号列 Tariff Line	中文货品名称 Article Description in Chinese	最惠国税率 MFN(%)	协定税率 Agreement(%)	特惠税率 SP(%)	普通税率 Gen(%)	英文货品名称 Article Description
	42.01	各种材料制成的鞍具及挽具（包括缰绳、挽绳、护膝垫、口套、鞍褥、马褡裢、狗外套及类似品），适合各种动物用					**Saddlery and harness for any animal (including traces, leads, knee pads, muzzles, saddle-cloths, saddlebags, dog coats and the like) , of any material**
3192	4201.0000	各种材料制成的鞍具及挽具（包括缰绳、挽绳、护膝垫、口套、鞍褥、马褡裢、狗外套及类似品），适合各种动物用	20	0 澳门MO,冰岛IS,东盟AS,哥CR,新加坡SG,新西兰NZ,智利CL 6 秘鲁PE 10 巴PK 12 澳AU,亚太AP 14 瑞士CH 17.3 韩国KR	0 受惠国LD 8 亚太AP	100	Saddlery and harness for any animal (including traces, leads, knee pads, muzzles, saddle cloths, saddle bags, dog coats and the like) , of any material
	42.02	衣箱、提箱、小手袋、公文箱、公文包、书包、眼镜盒、望远镜盒、照相机套、乐器盒、枪套及类似容器;旅行包、食品或饮料保温包、化妆包、帆布包、手提包、购物袋、钱夹、钱包、地图盒、烟盒、烟袋、工具包、运动包、瓶盒、首饰盒、粉盒、刀叉餐具盒及类似容器，用皮革或再生皮革、塑料片、纺织材料、钢纸或纸板制成，或者全部或主要用上述材料或纸包覆制成:					**Trunks, suitcases, vanity cases, executive-cases, briefcases, school satchels, spectacle cases, binocular cases, camera cases, musical instrument cases, gun cases, holsters and similar containers; travelling-bags, insulated food or beverages bags, toilet bags, rucksacks, handbags, shopping-bags, wallets, purses, map-cases, cigarette-cases, tobacco-pouches, tool bags, sports bags, bottle-cases, jewellery boxes, powder boxes, cutlery cases and similar containers, of leather or of composition leather, of sheeting of plastics, of textile materials, of vulcanised fibre or of paperboard, or wholly or mainly covered with such materials or with paper:**
		-衣箱、提箱、小手袋、公文箱、公文包、书包及类似容器:					-Trunks, suitcases, vanity cases, executive-cases, briefcases, school satchels and similar containers:
		--以皮革或再生皮革作面:					--With outer surface of leather or of composition leather:
3193	4202.1110	---衣箱	15Δ10	0 冰岛IS,东盟AS,哥CR,新加坡SG,新西兰NZ,智利CL 4.5 秘鲁PE 9 澳AU 10.5 瑞士CH 12 巴PK,韩国KR	0 受惠国$_1$LD$_1$ 8.3 亚太AP	100	---Trunks and suit-cases

序号 No.	税则号列 Tariff Line	中文货品名称 Article Description in Chinese	最惠国税率 MFN(%)	协定税率 Agreement(%)	特惠税率 SP(%)	普通税率 Gen(%)	英文货品名称 Article Description
3194	4202.1190	---其他	10	0 冰岛IS,东盟AS,哥CR,秘鲁PE,新西兰NZ,智利CL 5 巴PK 6 澳AU 7 瑞士CH 8 韩国KR	0 受惠国LD 8 亚太AP	100	---Other
		--以塑料或纺织材料作面:					--With outer surface of plastics or of textile materials:
3195	4202.1210	---衣箱	20△10	0 冰岛IS,东盟AS,哥CR,台湾TW,新加坡SG,新西兰NZ,智利CL 6 秘鲁PE 12 澳AU 14 瑞士CH 16 巴PK 17 亚太AP 17.3 韩国KR	0 受惠国$_1$LD$_1$	100	---Trunks and suit-cases
3196	4202.1290	---其他	20	0 澳门MO,冰岛IS,东盟AS,哥CR,台湾TW,新加坡SG,新西兰NZ,智利CL 6 秘鲁PE 12 澳AU 14 瑞士CH 16 巴PK,韩国KR 17 亚太AP	0 受惠国LD	100	---Other
3197	4202.1900	--其他	20	0 冰岛IS,东盟AS,哥CR,台湾TW,新加坡SG,新西兰NZ,智利CL 6 秘鲁PE 12 澳AU 14 瑞士CH 17.3 韩国KR	0 受惠国LD 8 亚太AP	100	--Other
		-手提包，不论是否有背带，包括无把手的:					-Handbags, whether or not with shoulder strap, including those without handle:
3198	4202.2100	--以皮革或再生皮革作面	10	0 澳门MO,冰岛IS,东盟AS,哥CR,香港HK,新西兰NZ,智利CL 3 秘鲁PE 5 巴PK 6 澳AU 6.9 亚太AP 7 瑞士CH 8 韩国KR	0 受惠国LD	100	--With outer surface of leather or composition leather
3199	4202.2200	--以塑料片或纺织材料作面	10	0 澳门MO,冰岛IS,东盟AS,哥CR,台湾TW,新加坡SG,新西兰NZ,智利CL 3 秘鲁PE 5 巴PK 6 澳AU 7 瑞士CH 8 韩国KR 8.2 亚太AP	0 受惠国LD	100	--With outer surface of plastic sheeting or of textile materials
3200	4202.2900	--其他	20△10	0 澳门MO,冰岛IS,东盟AS,哥CR,新加坡SG,新西兰NZ,智利CL 6 秘鲁PE 12 澳AU 14 巴PK,瑞士CH,亚太AP 17.3 韩国KR	0 受惠国$_1$LD$_1$ 8 亚太AP	100	--Other
		-通常置于口袋或手提包内的物品:					-Articles of a kind normally carried in the pocket or in the handbag:

序号 No.	税则号列 Tariff Line	中文货品名称 Article Description in Chinese	最惠国税率 MFN(%)	协定税率 Agreement(%)	特惠税率 SP(%)	普通税率 Gen(%)	英文货品名称 Article Description
3201	4202.3100	--以皮革或再生皮革作面	10	0 澳门MO,冰岛IS,东盟AS,哥CR,秘鲁PE,新西兰NZ,智利CL 5 巴PK 6 澳AU 6.9 亚太AP 7 瑞士CH 8 韩国KR	0 受惠国LD	100	--With outer surface of leather or composition leather
3202	4202.3200	--以塑料片或纺织材料作面	20	0 澳门MO,冰岛IS,东盟AS,哥CR,新加坡SG,新西兰NZ,智利CL 6 秘鲁PE 12 澳AU 14 巴PK,瑞士CH,亚太AP 16 韩国KR	0 受惠国LD	100	--With outer surface of plastic sheeting or of textile materials
3203	4202.3900	--其他	20	0 冰岛IS,东盟AS,哥CR,新加坡SG,新西兰NZ,智利CL 6 秘鲁PE 12 澳AU 14 巴PK,瑞士CH,亚太AP 17.3 韩国KR	0 受惠国$_1$LD$_1$ 8 亚太AP	100	--Other
		-其他:					-Other:
3204	4202.9100	--以皮革或再生皮革作面	10	0 澳门MO,冰岛IS,东盟AS,哥CR,秘鲁PE,新西兰NZ,智利CL 5 巴PK 6 澳AU 7 瑞士CH 8 韩国KR 8.5 亚太AP	0 受惠国LD	100	--With outer surface of leather or composition leather
3205	4202.9200	--以塑料片或纺织材料作面	10	0 澳门MO,冰岛IS,东盟AS,哥CR,香港HK,新加坡SG,新西兰NZ,智利CL 3 秘鲁PE 4 瑞士CH 5 巴PK 6 澳AU 8 韩国KR 8.5 亚太AP	0 受惠国LD	100	--With outer surface of plastic sheeting or of textile materials
3206	4202.9900	--其他	20	0 澳门MO,冰岛IS,东盟AS,哥CR,新加坡SG,新西兰NZ,智利CL 6 秘鲁PE 12 澳AU 14.4 瑞士CH 17.3 韩国KR	0 受惠国$_1$LD$_1$	100	--Other
	42.03	**皮革或再生皮革制的衣服及衣着附件:**					**Articles of apparel and clothing accessories, of leather or of composition leather:**
3207	4203.1000	-衣服	10	0 澳门MO,巴PK,冰岛IS,东盟AS,哥CR,香港HK,新西兰NZ,智利CL 3 秘鲁PE 4 瑞士CH 6 澳AU,韩国KR	0 受惠国LD 8 亚太AP	100	-Articles of apparel
		-手套，包括连指或露指的:					-Gloves, mittens and mitts:
3208	4203.2100	--专供运动用	20	0 澳门MO,巴PK,东盟AS,哥CR,香港HK,新加坡SG,新西兰NZ,智利CL 6 秘鲁PE 12 澳AU 14 瑞士CH,亚太AP 17.3 韩国KR	0 受惠国$_1$LD$_1$	100	--Specially designed for use in sports
		--其他:					--Other:

序号 No.	税则号列 Tariff Line	中文货品名称 Article Description in Chinese	最惠国税率 MFN(%)	协定税率 Agreement(%)	特惠税率 SP(%)	普通税率 Gen(%)	英文货品名称 Article Description
3209	4203.2910	---劳保手套	20	0 澳门MO,巴PK,东盟AS,哥CR,香港HK,新加坡SG,新西兰NZ,智利CL 6 秘鲁PE 12 澳AU 14 瑞士CH 17.3 韩国KR	0 受惠国$_1$LD$_1$ 8 亚太AP	100	---Working gloves
3210	4203.2990	---其他	20	0 澳门MO,巴PK,东盟AS,哥CR,香港HK,新加坡SG,新西兰NZ,智利CL 6 秘鲁PE 12 澳AU 14 瑞士CH 17.3 韩国KR	0 受惠国$_1$LD$_1$ 8 亚太AP	100	---Other
		-腰带及子弹带:					-Belts and bandoliers:
3211	4203.3010	---腰带	10	0 澳门MO,巴PK,冰岛IS,东盟AS,哥CR,香港HK,新西兰NZ,智利CL 3 秘鲁PE 4 瑞士CH 6 澳AU 8 韩国KR	0 受惠国LD 8 亚太AP	100	---Belts
3212	4203.3020	---子弹带	10	0 巴PK,冰岛IS,东盟AS,哥CR,香港HK,新西兰NZ,智利CL 3 秘鲁PE 4 瑞士CH 6 澳AU 8 韩国KR	0 受惠国LD 8 亚太AP	100	---Bandoliers
3213	4203.4000	-其他衣着附件	20	0 澳门MO,巴PK,东盟AS,哥CR,香港HK,新加坡SG,新西兰NZ,智利CL 6 秘鲁PE 12 澳AU 14 瑞士CH 17.3 韩国KR	0 受惠国$_1$LD$_1$ 8 亚太AP	100	-Other clothing accessories
	42.05	**皮革或再生皮革的其他制品:**					**Other articles of leather or of composition leather:**
3214	4205.0010	---座套	12	0 冰岛IS,东盟AS,哥CR,秘鲁PE,香港HK,新加坡SG,新西兰NZ,智利CL 6 巴PK 7.2 澳AU 8.4 瑞士CH	0 受惠国LD 7.8 亚太AP	100	---Cover of seat
3215	4205.0020	---机器、机械器具或其他专门技术用途的	8	0 冰岛IS,东盟AS,哥CR,秘鲁PE,新西兰NZ,智利CL 4.8 澳AU 5 巴PK 5.8 瑞士CH 6.4 韩国KR	0 受惠国LD	35	---Of a kind used in machinery or mechanical appliances or for other technical uses
3216	4205.0090	---其他	12	0 冰岛IS,东盟AS,哥CR,香港HK,新加坡SG,新西兰NZ,智利CL 3.6 秘鲁PE 6 巴PK 7.2 澳AU 8.4 瑞士CH 10.4 韩国KR	0 受惠国LD 7.8 亚太AP	100	---Other
	42.06	**肠线(蚕胶丝除外)、肠膜、膀胱或筋腱制品**					**Articles of gut (other than silkworm gut) , of goldbeater' s skin, of bladders or of tendons**
3217	4206.0000	肠线(蚕胶丝除外)、肠膜、膀胱或筋腱制品	20	0 冰岛IS,东盟AS,哥CR,新加坡SG,新西兰NZ,智利CL 6 秘鲁PE 12 澳AU 14 瑞士CH 17.3 韩国KR	0 受惠国$_1$LD$_1$	90	Articles of gut (other than silk-worm gut) , of goldbeater' s skin, of bladders or of tendons

第四十三章
毛皮、人造毛皮及其制品

Chapter 43
Furskins and artificial fur; manufactures thereof

注释:

一、本目录所称"毛皮",是指已鞣的各种动物的带毛毛皮,但不包括税号43.01的生毛皮。

二、本章不包括:

(一)带羽毛或羽绒的整张或部分鸟皮(税号05.05或67.01);

(二)第四十一章的带毛生皮该章注释一(三);

(三)用皮革与毛皮或用皮革与人造毛皮制成的分指手套、连指手套及露指手套(税目42.03);

(四)第六十四章的物品;

(五)第六十五章的帽类及其零件;

(六)第九十五章的物品(例如,玩具、游戏品及运动用品)。

三、税号43.03包括加有其他材料缝合的毛皮和毛皮部分品,以及缝合成衣服、衣服部分品、衣着附件或其他制品的毛皮和毛皮部分品。

四、以毛皮或人造毛皮衬里或作面(仅饰边的除外)的衣服及衣着附件(不包括注释二所述的货品),应分别归入税号43.03或43.04,但毛皮或人造毛皮仅作为装饰的除外。

五、本目录所称"人造毛皮",是指以毛、发或其他纤维粘附或缝合于皮革、织物或其他材料之上而构成的仿毛皮,但不包括以机织或针织方法制得的仿毛皮(一般应归入税号58.01或60.01)。

Notes:

1. Throughout the Nomenclature references to "furskins", other than to raw furskins of heading No. 43.01, apply to hides or skins of all animals which have been tanned or dressed with the hair or wool on.

2. This Chapter does not cover:

(a) Birdskins or parts of birdskins, with their feathers or down (heading No. 05.05 or 67.01);

(b) Raw hides or skins, with the hair or wool on, of Chapter41 (see Note 1 (c) to that Chapter);

(c) Gloves, mittens and mitts consisting of leather and furskin or of leather and artificial fur (heading No. 42.03);

(d) Articles of Chapter 64;

(e) Headgear or parts thereof of Chapter 65; or

(f) Articles of Chapter 95 (for example, toys, games, sports requisites).

3. Heading No.43.03 includes furskins and parts thereof, assembled with the addition of other materials, and furskins and parts thereof, sewn together in the form of garments or parts or accessories of garments or in the form of other articles.

4. Articles of apparel and clothing accessories (except those excluded by Note 2) lined with furskin or artificial fur or to which furskin or artificial fur is attached on the outside except as mere trimming are to be classified in heading No.43.03 or 43.04as the case may be.

5. Throughout the Nomenclature the expression "artificial-fur" means any imitation of furskin consisting of wool, hair or other fibres gummed or sewn on to leather, woven fabric or other materials, but does not includeimitation furskins obtained by weaving or knitting (generally, heading No. 58.01 or 60.01) .

序号 No.	税则号列 Tariff Line	中文货品名称 Article Description in Chinese	最惠国税率 MFN(%)	协定税率 Agreement(%)	特惠税率 SP(%)	普通税率 Gen(%)	英文货品名称 Article Description
	43.01	生毛皮(包括适合加工皮货用的头、尾、爪及其他块、片),但税号41.01、41.02或41.03的生皮除外:					**Raw furskins (including heads, tails, paws and other pieces or cuttings, suitable for furriers' use) , other than raw hides and skins of heading 4101, 4102 or 4103:**
3218	4301.1000	-整张水貂皮,不论是否带头、尾或爪	15Δ10	0 冰岛IS,东盟AS,哥CR,香港HK,新加坡SG,新西兰NZ,智利CL 4.5 秘鲁PE 9 澳AU 10.5 瑞士CH 12 巴PK,韩国KR	0 受惠国$_1$LD$_1$	100	-Of mink, whole, with or without head, tail or paws

序号 No.	税则号列 Tariff Line	中文货品名称 Article Description in Chinese	最惠国税率 MFN(%)	协定税率 Agreement(%)	特惠税率 SP(%)	普通税率 Gen(%)	英文货品名称 Article Description
3219	4301.3000	-下列羔羊的整张毛皮，不论是否带头、尾或爪：阿斯特拉罕、喀拉科尔、波斯羔羊及类似羔羊、印度、中国或蒙古羔羊	20	0 冰岛IS,东盟AS,哥CR,香港HK,新加坡SG,新西兰NZ,智利CL 6 秘鲁PE 12 澳AU 14 瑞士CH 17.3 韩国KR	0 受惠国$_1$LD$_1$	90	-Of lamb, the following: Astrakhan, Broadtail, Caracul, Persian and similar lamb, Indian, Chinese, Mongolian or Tibetan lamb, whole, with or without head, tail or paws
3220	4301.6000	-整张狐皮，不论是否带头、尾或爪	20Δ15	0 冰岛IS,东盟AS,哥CR,香港HK,新加坡SG,新西兰NZ,智利CL 6 秘鲁PE 12 澳AU 14 瑞士CH 17.3 韩国KR	0 受惠国$_1$LD$_1$	100	-Of fox, whole, with or without head, tail or paws
		-整张的其他毛皮，不论是否带头、尾或爪：					-Other furskins, whole, with or without head, tail or paws:
3221	4301.8010	---整张兔皮，不论是否带头、尾或爪	20	0 冰岛IS,东盟AS,哥CR,香港HK,新加坡SG,新西兰NZ,智利CL 6 秘鲁PE 12 澳AU 14 瑞士CH 17.3 韩国KR	0 受惠国$_1$LD$_1$	90	---Of rabbit or hare, whole, with or without head, tail or paws
3222	4301.8090	---其他	20	0 冰岛IS,东盟AS,哥CR,香港HK,新加坡SG,新西兰NZ,智利CL 6 秘鲁PE 12 澳AU 14 瑞士CH 17.3 韩国KR	0 受惠国$_1$LD$_1$	90	---Other
		-适合加工皮货用的头、尾、爪及其他块、片：					-Heads, tails, paws and other pieces or cuttings, suitable for furriers' use:
3223	4301.9010	---黄鼠狼尾	20	0 冰岛IS,东盟AS,哥CR,香港HK,新加坡SG,新西兰NZ,智利CL 6 秘鲁PE 12 澳AU 14 瑞士CH 17.3 韩国KR	0 受惠国$_1$LD$_1$	50	---Weasel tails
3224	4301.9090	---其他	20	0 冰岛IS,东盟AS,哥CR,香港HK,新加坡SG,新西兰NZ,智利CL 6 秘鲁PE 12 澳AU 14 瑞士CH 17.3 韩国KR	0 受惠国$_1$LD$_1$	90	---Other
	43.02	**未缝制或已缝制（不加其他材料）的已鞣毛皮（包括头、尾、爪及其他块、片），但税号43.03的货品除外：**					**Tanned or dressed furskins (including heads, tails, paws and other pieces or cuttings), unassembled, or assembled (without the addition of other materials) other than those of heading 4303:**
		-未缝制的整张毛皮，不论是否带头、尾或爪：					-Whole skins, with or without head, tail or paws, not assembled:
3225	4302.1100	--水貂皮	12	0 冰岛IS,东盟AS,哥CR,秘鲁PE,香港HK,新加坡SG,新西兰NZ,智利CL 6 巴PK 7.2 澳AU 8.4 瑞士CH 9.6 韩国KR	0 受惠国$_1$LD$_1$	130	--Of mink
		--其他：					--Other:

序号 No.	税则号列 Tariff Line	中文货品名称 Article Description in Chinese	最惠国税率 MFN(%)	协定税率 Agreement(%)	特惠税率 SP(%)	普通税率 Gen(%)	英文货品名称 Article Description
3226	4302.1910	---灰鼠皮、白鼬皮、其他貂皮、狐皮、水獭皮、旱獭皮及猞猁皮	10	0 冰岛IS,东盟AS,哥CR,秘鲁PE,香港HK,新西兰NZ,智利CL 4 瑞士CH 5 巴PK 6 澳AU 8 韩国KR	0 受惠国$_1$LD$_1$	130	---Of gray squirrel, ermine, other marten, fox, otter, marmot and lynx
3227	4302.1920	---兔皮	10	0 冰岛IS,东盟AS,哥CR,秘鲁PE,香港HK,新西兰NZ,智利CL 4 瑞士CH 5 巴PK 6 澳AU 8 韩国KR	0 受惠国LD	100	---Of rabbit or hare
3228	4302.1930	---下列羔羊皮:阿斯特拉罕、喀拉科尔、波斯羔羊及类似羔羊、印度、中国或蒙古羔羊	20	0 东盟AS,哥CR,香港HK,新加坡SG,新西兰NZ,智利CL 6 秘鲁PE 12 澳AU 14 瑞士CH 17.3 韩国KR	0 受惠国LD	100	---Of lamb, the following: Astrakhan, Broadtail, Caracul, Persian and similar lamb, Indian, Chinese (including Tibetan) or Mongolian lamb
3229	4302.1990	---其他	10	0 冰岛IS,东盟AS,哥CR,秘鲁PE,香港HK,新西兰NZ,智利CL 4 瑞士CH 6 澳AU 8 韩国KR	0 受惠国LD	100	---Other
3230	4302.2000	-未缝制的头、尾、爪及其他块、片	20	0 冰岛IS,东盟AS,哥CR,香港HK,新加坡SG,新西兰NZ,智利CL 6 秘鲁PE 12 澳AU 14 瑞士CH 17.3 韩国KR	0 受惠国$_1$LD$_1$	100	-Heads, tails, paws and other pieces or cuttings, not assembled
		-已缝制的整张毛皮及其块、片:					-Whole skins and pieces or cuttings thereof, assembled:
3231	4302.3010	---灰鼠、白鼬、貂、狐、水獭、旱獭及猞猁的整张毛皮及其块、片	20	0 冰岛IS,东盟AS,哥CR,香港HK,新加坡SG,新西兰NZ,智利CL 6 秘鲁PE 12 澳AU 14 瑞士CH 17.3 韩国KR	0 受惠国$_1$LD$_1$	130	---Of grey squirrel, ermine, other marten, fox, otter, marmot and lynx
3232	4302.3090	---其他	20	0 东盟AS,哥CR,香港HK,新加坡SG,新西兰NZ,智利CL 6 秘鲁PE 12 澳AU 14 瑞士CH 17.3 韩国KR	0 受惠国$_1$LD$_1$	100	---Other
	43.03	**毛皮制的衣服、衣着附件及其他物品:**					**Articles of apparel, clothing accessories and other articles of furskin:**
		-衣服及衣着附件:					-Articles of apparel and clothing accessories:
3233	4303.1010	---毛皮衣服	23Δ10	0 东盟AS,哥CR,香港HK,新加坡SG,新西兰NZ,智利CL 6.9 秘鲁PE 13.8 澳AU 16.1 瑞士CH 20.7 韩国KR	0 受惠国$_1$LD$_1$ 10.4 亚太AP	150	---Articles of appare

序号 No.	税则号列 Tariff Line	中文货品名称 Article Description in Chinese	最惠国税率 MFN(%)	协定税率 Agreement(%)	特惠税率 SP(%)	普通税率 Gen(%)	英文货品名称 Article Description
3234	4303.1020	---毛皮衣着附件	18	0 东盟AS,哥CR,香港HK,新加坡SG,新西兰NZ,智利CL 5.4 秘鲁PE 10.8 澳AU 12.6 瑞士CH 14.4 韩国KR	0 受惠国$_1$LD$_1$ 9.9 亚太AP	150	---Clothing accessories
3235	4303.9000	-其他	18	0 东盟AS,哥CR,秘鲁PE,香港HK,新加坡SG,新西兰NZ,智利CL 10.8 澳AU 12.6 瑞士CH 14.4 巴PK,韩国KR	0 受惠国$_1$LD$_1$ 9.9 亚太AP	150	-Other
	43.04	**人造毛皮及其制品:**					**Artificial fur and articles thereof:**
3236	4304.0010	---人造毛皮	18	0 东盟AS,哥CR,香港HK,新加坡SG,新西兰NZ,智利CL 5.4 秘鲁PE 10.8 澳AU 12.6 瑞士CH 14.4 韩国KR	0 受惠国$_1$LD$_1$ 10.8 亚太AP	130	---Artificial fur
3237	4304.0020	---人造毛皮制品	18	0 东盟AS,哥CR,香港HK,新加坡SG,新西兰NZ,智利CL 5.4 秘鲁PE 10.8 澳AU 12.6 瑞士CH 14.4 巴PK,韩国KR	0 受惠国$_1$LD$_1$ 10.8 亚太AP	150	---Articles of artificial fur

第九类
木及木制品；木炭；软木及软木制品；稻草、秸秆、针茅或其他编结材料制品；篮筐及柳条编结品

SECTION Ⅸ
WOOD AND ARTICLES OF WOOD; WOOD CHARCOAL; CORK AND ARTICLES OF CORK; MANUFACTURES OF STRAW, OF ESPARTO OR OF OTHER PLAITING MATERIALS; BASKETWARE AND WICKERWORK

第四十四章
木及木制品；木炭

Chapter 44
Wood and articles of wood; wood charcoal

注释：

一、本章不包括：

（一）主要作香料、药料、杀虫、杀菌或类似用途的木片、刨花、碎木、木粒或木粉（税号 12.11）；

（二）竹或主要作编结用的其他木质材料，未经加工、劈开、纵锯或切段（税号 14.01）；

（三）主要作染料或鞣料用的木片、刨花、木粒或木粉（税号 14.04）；

（四）活性炭（税号 38.02）；

（五）税号 42.02 的物品；

（六）第四十六章的货品；

（七）第六十四章的鞋靴及其零件；

（八）第六十六章的货品（例如，伞、手杖及其零件）；

（九）税号 68.08 的货品；

（十）税号 71.17 的仿首饰；

（十一）第十六类或第十七类的货品（例如，机器零件，机器及器具的箱、罩、壳，车辆部件）；

（十二）第十八类的货品（例如，钟壳、乐器及其零件）；

（十三）火器的零件（税号 93.05）；

（十四）第九十四章的物品（例如，家具、灯具及照明器具、活动房屋）；

（十五）第九十五章的物品（例如，玩具、游戏品及运动用品）；

（十六）第九十六章的物品（例如，烟斗及其零件、钮扣、铅笔），但税号 96.03 所列物品的木身及木柄除外；

（十七）第九十七章的物品（例如艺术品）。

二、本章所称“强化木”，是指经过化学或物理方法处理

Notes:

1. This Chapter does not cover:

(a) Wood, in chips, in shavings, crushed, ground or powdered, of a kind used primarily in perfumery, in pharmacy, or for insecticidal, fungicidal or similar purposes (heading No.12.11);

(b) Bamboos or other materials of a woody nature of a kind used primarily for plaiting, in the rough, whether or not split, sawn lengthwise or cut to length (heading No.14.01);

(c) Wood, in chips, in shavings, ground or powdered, of a kind used primarily in dyeing or in tanning (heading No.14.04);

(d) Activated charcoal (heading No.38.02);

(e) Articles of heading No.42.02;

(f) Goods of Chapter 46;

(g) Footwear or parts thereof of Chapter 64;

(h) Goods of Chapter 66 (for example, umbrellas and walking-sticks and parts thereof);

(i) Goods of heading No.68.08;

(j) Imitation jewellery of heading No.71.17;

(k) Goods of Section Ⅹ Ⅵ or Section Ⅹ Ⅶ (for example, machine parts, cases, covers, cabinets for machines and apparatus and wheel wrights' wares);

(l) Goods of Section Ⅹ Ⅷ (for example, clock cases and musical instruments and parts thereof）;

(m) Parts of firearms (heading No.93.05);

(n) Articles of Chapter 94 (for example, furniture, lamps and lighting fittings, prefabricated buildings);

(o) Articles of Chapter 95 (for example, toys, games, sports requisites);

(p) Articles of Chapter 96 (for example, smoking pipes and parts thereof, buttons, pencils）excluding bodies and handles, of wood, for articles of heading No.96.03;

(q) Articles, of Chapter 97 (for example, works of art).

2. In this Chapter, the expression “densified wood” means wood

（对于多层粘合木材，其处理应超出一般粘合需要），从而增加了密度或硬度并改善了机械强度、抗化学或抗电性能的木材。

which has been subjected to chemical or physical treatment (being, in the case of layers bonded together, treatment in excess of that needed to ensure a good bond), and which has thereby acquired increased density or hardness together with improved mechanical strength or resistance to chemical or electrical agencies.

三、税号 44.14 至 44.21 适用于木质碎料板或类似木质材料板、纤维板、层压板或强化木的制品。

3. Headings No. 44.14 to 44.21 apply to articles of the respective descriptions of particle board or similar board, fibreboard, laminated wood or densified wood as they apply to such articles of wood.

四、税号 44.10、44.11 或 44.12 的产品，可以加工成税号 44.09 所述的各种形状，也可以加工成弯曲、瓦楞、多孔或其他形状（正方形或矩形除外），以及经其他任何加工，但未具有其他税号所列制品的特性。

4. Products of heading No.44.10, 44.11 or 44.12 may be worked to form the shapes provided for in respect of the goods of heading No.44.09, curved, corrugated, perforated, cut or formed to shapes other than square or rectangular or submitted to any other operation provided it does not give them the character of articles of other headings.

五、税号 44.17 不包括装有第八十二章注释一所述材料制成的刀片、工作刃、工作面或其他工作部件的工具。

5. Heading No.44.17 does not apply to tools in which the blade, working edge, working surface or other working part is formed by any of the materials specified in Note 1 to Chapter 82.

六、除上述注释一及其他条文另有规定的以外，本章税目中所称"木"，也包括竹及其他木质材料。

6. Subject to Note1above and except where the context otherwise requires, any reference to "wood" in a heading of this Chapter applies also to bamboos and other materials of a woody nature.

子目注释：

Subheading Notes:

一、子目 4401.31 所称"木屑棒"是指由木材加工业、家具制造业及其他木材加工活动中产生的副产品（例如刨花、锯木及碎木片）直接压制而成或加入按重量计不超过 3%的粘合剂后粘聚而成的产品。此类产品呈圆柱状，其直径不超过 25mm，长度不超过 100mm。

1. For the purposes of subheading 4401.31, the expression "wood pellets" means by-products such as cutter shavings, sawdust or chips, of themechanical wood processing industry, furniture-making industry or otherwood transformation activities, which have been agglomerated either directlyby compression or by the addition of a binder in a proportion not exceeding3% by weight. Such pellets are cylindrical, with a diameter not exceeding25 mm and a length not exceeding 100 mm.

二、子目号 4403.41 至 4403.49、4407.21 至 4407.29、4408.31 至 4408.39 及 4412.31 所称"热带木"，是指下列木材：

2. For the purposes of subheadings No.4403.41to4403.49, 4407.21 to 4407.29, 4408.31 to 4408.39 and 4412.31, the expression "tropical wood" means one of the following types of wood:

大叶帽柱木、非洲桃花心木、西非红豆木、箭毒木、阿兰木、圭亚那苦油楝木、非洲甘比山榄木、杜楝木、非洲栎柞木、婆罗双木、美洲轻木、白驼峰楝木、黑驼

Abura, Acajou d'Afrique, Afrormosia, Ako, Alan, Andiroba, Aningré, Avodiré, Azobé, Balau, Balsa, Bossé clair, Bossé foncé, Cativo, Cedro, Dabema, Dark Red Meranti,

峰楝木、卡蒂沃木、雪松木、西非褐红椴木、深红色红柳桉木，非洲核桃楝木、阿夫苏木、象牙海岸榄仁木、破布木、吉贝木、丝棉木、乔状黄牛木、安哥拉丛花木、巴西胡桃木、皮蚁木、伊罗科木、拟爱神木、夹竹桃木、巴西红木、绒根木、龙脑香木、开姆帕斯木、羯布罗香木、康多非洲楝木、象牙海岸褐红椴木、象牙海岸翼梧桐木、浅红色红柳桉木、非洲榄仁木、南美樟木、圭亚那铁线子木、西印度桃花心木、猴子果木、肖氏夸利亚木、曼孙梧桐木、马来蝴蝶木、巴栲红柳桉木、粗轴坡垒木、印茄木、斯温漆木、异翅香木、非洲梨木、非洲银叶木、胶木、非洲白梧桐木、加蓬榄木、蓖麻木、爱里古夷苏木、奥文科尔木、中非蜡烛木、紫檀木、人面子木、危地马拉黑黄檀木、印度黑黄檀木、巴西黑黄檀木、巴西柚、巴西花梨木、白坚木、鸡骨常山木、印马四出香木、大沃契希亚木、东西亚棱柱木、萨撇列木、萌生木棉木、苏帕楠木、西波木、苏古皮拉木、红椿木、圭亚那考拉玉蕊木、柚木、安哥拉香桃花心木、非洲阿勃木、南美肉豆蔻木、白柳桉木、白色红柳桉木、白色柳桉木、黄色红柳桉木。

Dibétou, Doussié, Framiré, Freijo, Fromager, Fuma, Geronggang, Ilomba, Imb uia, Ipé, Iroko, Jaboty, Jelutong, Jequitiba, Jongkong, Kapur, Kempas, Keruing, Kosipo, Kotib,KotoLight Red Meranti, Limba, Louroé, Macaranduba, Mahogany, Makor,Mandioqueira, Mansonia, Mengkulang, Meranti Bakau, Merawan, Merbau, Merpauh, Mersawa, Moabi, Niangon, Nyatoh, Obeche, Okoum, Onzabili, Orey, Ovengkol, Ozigo, Padauk, Paldao, Palissandre de Guatemala, Palissandre de Para, Palissandre de Rio, Palissandre de Rose, Pau Amarelo, Pau Marfim, Pulai, Punah, Quaruba, Ramin, Sapelli, Saqui-Saqui, Sepetir, Sipo, Sucupira, Suren, Tauari, Teak, Tiama, Tola, Virola, White Lauan, White Meranti, White Seraya, Yellow Meranti.

序号 No.	税则号列 Tariff Line	中文货品名称 Article Description in Chinese	最惠国税率 MFN(%)	协定税率 Agreement(%)	特惠税率 SP(%)	普通税率 Gen(%)	英文货品名称 Article Description
	44.01	薪柴（圆木段、块、枝、成捆或类似形状）；木片或木粒；锯末、木废料及碎片，不论是否粘结成圆木段、块、片或类似形状：					**Fuel wood, in logs, in billets, in twigs, in faggots or in similar forms; wood in chips or particles; sawdust and wood waste and scrap, whether or not agglomerated in logs, briquettes, pellets or similar forms:**
3238	4401.1000	-薪柴（圆木段、块、枝、成捆或类似形状）	0		0 受惠国LD	70	-Fuel wood, in logs, in billets, in twigs, in faggots or in similar forms
		-木片或木粒：					-Wood in chips or particles:
3239	4401.2100	--针叶木	0		0 受惠国LD	8	--Coniferous
3240	4401.2200	--非针叶木	0		0 受惠国LD	8	--Non-coniferous
		-锯末、木废料及碎片，不论是否粘结成圆木段、块、片或类似形状：					-Sawdust and wood waste and scrap, whether or not agglomerated in logs, briquettes, pellets or similar forms:
3241	4401.3100	--木屑棒	0		0 受惠国LD	8	--Wood pellets
3242	4401.3900	--其他	0		0 受惠国LD	8	--Other
	44.02	木炭（包括果壳炭及果核炭），不论是否结块：					**Wood charcoal (including shell or nut charcoal) , whether or not agglomerated:**
3243	4402.1000	-竹的	10.5	0 冰岛IS,东盟AS,哥CR,秘鲁PE,新加坡SG,新西兰NZ,智利CL 5 巴PK 6.3 澳AU 7.4 瑞士CH 8.4 韩国KR	0 受惠国$_1$LD$_1$	70	-Of bamboo

序号 No.	税则号列 Tariff Line	中文货品名称 Article Description in Chinese	最惠国税率 MFN(%)	协定税率 Agreement(%)	特惠税率 SP(%)	普通税率 Gen(%)	英文货品名称 Article Description
3244	4402.9000	-其他	10.5	0 冰岛IS,东盟AS,哥CR,秘鲁PE,新加坡SG,新西兰NZ,智利CL 5 巴PK 6.3 澳AU 7.4 瑞士CH 8.4 韩国KR	0 受惠国[1]LD[1]	70	-Other
	44.03	**原木，不论是否去皮、去边材或粗锯成方：**					**Wood in the rough, whether or not stripped of bark or sapwood, or roughly squared:**
3245	4403.1000	-用油漆、着色剂、杂酚油或其他防腐剂处理	0		0 受惠国LD	8	-Treated with paint, stains, creosote or other preservatives
		-其他针叶木：					-Other, coniferous:
3246	4403.2010	---红松和樟子松	0		0 受惠国LD	8	---Korean pine and Mongolian scotch pine
3247	4403.2020	---白松（云杉和冷杉）	0		0 受惠国LD	8	---White pine (spruce and fir)
3248	4403.2030	---辐射松	0		0 受惠国LD	8	---Radiata pine
3249	4403.2040	---落叶松	0		0 受惠国LD	8	---Larch
3250	4403.2050	---花旗松	0		0 受惠国LD	8	---Douglas fir
3251	4403.2090	---其他	0		0 受惠国LD	8	---Other
		-其他本章子目注释二所列的热带木：					-Other, of tropical wood specified in subheading note 2 to this chapter:
3252	4403.4100	--深红色红柳安木、浅红色红柳安木及巴栲红柳安木	0		0 受惠国LD	8	--Dark Red Meranti, Light Red Meranti and Meranti Bakau
		--其他（本章子目注释所列热带非针叶木）：					--Other:
3253	4403.4910	---柚木	0		0 受惠国LD	35	---Teak
3254	4403.4920	---奥克曼（奥克榄）	0		0 受惠国LD	35	---Okoume (Aukoumed Klaineana)
3255	4403.4930	---龙脑香木（克隆）	0		0 受惠国LD	35	---Dipterocarpus spp. Keruing
3256	4403.4940	---山樟（香木）	0		0 受惠国LD	35	---Kapur (Dryobalanops spp.)
3257	4403.4950	---印加木（波罗格）	0		0 受惠国LD	35	---Intsia spp. (Mengaris)
3258	4403.4960	---大干巴豆（门格里斯或康派斯	0		0 受惠国LD	35	---Koompassia spp. (Mengaris or Kempas)
3259	4403.4970	---异翅香木	0		0 受惠国LD	35	---Anisopter spp.
3260	4403.4990	---其他	0		0 受惠国LD	8	---Other
		-其他：					-Other:
3261	4403.9100	--栎木（橡木）	0		0 受惠国LD	8	--Of oak (Quercus spp.)
3262	4403.9200	--山毛榉木	0		0 受惠国LD	8	--Of beech (Fagus spp.)
		--其他：					--Other:
3263	4403.9910	---楠木	0		0 受惠国LD	35	---Of nan mu (Phoebe)
3264	4403.9920	---樟木	0		0 受惠国LD	35	---Of camphor wood
3265	4403.9930	---红木	0		0 受惠国LD	35	---Of rosewood
3266	4403.9940	---泡桐木	0		0 受惠国LD	8	---Of Kiri (Paulownia)
3267	4403.9950	---水曲柳	0		0 受惠国LD	8	---Ash
3268	4403.9960	---北美硬阔叶木（包括樱桃木、黑胡桃木、枫木）	0		0 受惠国LD	8	---North American hard wood (including cherry, walnut, and maple)
3269	4403.9980	---其他未列名的温带非针叶木	0		0 受惠国LD	8	---Other temperate non-coniferous not specified
3270	4403.9990	---其他	0		0 受惠国LD	8	---Other
	44.04	**箍木;木劈条;已削尖但未经纵锯的木桩;粗加修整但未经车圆、弯曲或其他方式加工的木棒，适合制手杖、伞柄、工具把柄及类似品;木片条及类似品:**					**Hoopwood; split poles; piles, pickets and stakes of wood, pointed but not sawn lengthwise; wooden sticks, roughly trimmed but not turned, bent or otherwise worked, suitable for the manufacture of walking sticks, umbrellas, tool handles or the like; chipwood and the like:**

序号 No.	税则号列 Tariff Line	中文货品名称 Article Description in Chinese	最惠国税率 MFN(%)	协定税率 Agreement(%)	特惠税率 SP(%)	普通税率 Gen(%)	英文货品名称 Article Description
3271	4404.1000	-针叶木的	8	0 冰岛IS,东盟AS,哥CR,秘鲁PE,新加坡SG,新西兰NZ,智利CL 3.2 瑞士CH 4.8 澳AU,韩国KR 5 巴PK	0 受惠国$_1$LD$_1$	50	-Coniferous
3272	4404.2000	-非针叶木的	8	0 冰岛IS,东盟AS,哥CR,秘鲁PE,新加坡SG,新西兰NZ,智利CL 3.2 瑞士CH 4.8 澳AU,韩国KR 5 巴PK	0 受惠国$_1$LD$_1$	50	-Non-coniferous
	44.05	**木丝;木粉**					**Wood wool; wood flour**
3273	4405.0000	木丝;木粉	8	0 冰岛IS,东盟AS,哥CR,秘鲁PE,新加坡SG,新西兰NZ,智利CL 3.2 瑞士CH 4.8 澳AU,韩国KR 5 巴PK	0 受惠国LD	40	Wood wool; wood flour
	44.06	**铁道及电车道枕木:**					**Railway or tramway sleepers (cross-ties) of wood:**
3274	4406.1000	-未浸渍	0		0 受惠国LD	14	-Not impregnated
3275	4406.9000	-其他	0		0 受惠国LD	14	-Other
	44.07	**经纵锯、纵切、刨切或旋切的木材，不论是否刨平、砂光或指榫接合，厚度超过6毫米:**					**Wood sawn or chipped lengthwise, sliced or peeled, whether or not planed, sanded or end-jointed, of a thickness exceeding 6mm:**
		-针叶木:					-Coniferous:
3276	4407.1010	---红松和樟子松	0		0 受惠国LD	14	---Korean pine and Mongolian scotch pine
3277	4407.1020	---白松（云杉和冷杉）	0		0 受惠国LD	14	---White pine (spruce and fir)
3278	4407.1030	---辐射松	0		0 受惠国LD	14	---Rediata pine
3279	4407.1040	---花旗松	0		0 受惠国LD	14	---Douglas fir
3280	4407.1090	---其他	0		0 受惠国LD	14	---Other
		-本章子目注释二所列的热带木:					-Of tropical wood specified in subheading note 2 to this chapter:
3281	4407.2100	--美洲桃花心木	0		0 受惠国LD	14	--Mahogany (Swietenia spp.)
3282	4407.2200	--苏里南肉豆蔻木、美洲桃花心木、巴西胡桃木及美洲轻木	0		0 受惠国LD	14	--Virola, Imbuia and Balsa
3283	4407.2500	--深红色红柳安木、浅红色红柳安木及巴栲红柳安木	0		0 受惠国LD	14	--Dark Red Meranti, Light Red Meranti and Meranti Bakau
3284	4407.2600	--白柳安木、白色红柳安木、白色柳安木、黄色红柳安木及阿兰木	0		0 受惠国LD	14	--White Lauan, White Meranti, White Seraya, Yellow Meranti and Alan
3285	4407.2700	--沙比利	0		0 受惠国LD	40	--Sapelli
3286	4407.2800	--伊罗科木	0		0 受惠国LD	14	--Iroko
		--其他:					--Other:
3287	4407.2910	---柚木	0		0 受惠国LD	40	---Teak
3288	4407.2920	---非洲桃花心木	0		0 受惠国LD	40	---Acajou
3289	4407.2930	---波罗格	0		0 受惠国LD	40	---Merban
3290	4407.2990	---其他	0		0 受惠国LD	14	---Other
		-其他:					-Other:
3291	4407.9100	--栎木（橡木）	0		0 受惠国LD	14	--Of oak (Quercus spp.)
3292	4407.9200	--山毛榉木	0		0 受惠国LD	14	--Of beech (Fagus spp.)
3293	4407.9300	--枫木	0		0 受惠国LD	14	--Of maple (Acer spp.)
3294	4407.9400	--樱桃木	0		0 受惠国LD	14	--Of cherry (Prunus spp.)
3295	4407.9500	--白蜡木	0		0 受惠国LD	14	--Of ash (Fraxinus spp.)
		--其他:					--Other:
3296	4407.9910	---樟木、楠木、红木	0		0 受惠国LD	40	---Of camphor-wood, nanmu or rosewood
3297	4407.9920	---泡桐木	0		0 受惠国LD	14	---Of Paulownia
3298	4407.9930	---北美硬阔叶材（含黑胡桃木）	0		0 受惠国LD	14	---North American hard wood (including walnut)

序号 No.	税则号列 Tariff Line	中文货品名称 Article Description in Chinese	最惠国税率 MFN(%)	协定税率 Agreement(%)	特惠税率 SP(%)	普通税率 Gen(%)	英文货品名称 Article Description
3299	4407.9980	---其他温带非针叶木厚板材	0		0 受惠国LD	14	---Other temperate non-coniferous wood
3300	4407.9990	---其他	0		0 受惠国LD	14	---Other
	44.08	**饰面用单板（包括刨切积层木获得的单板）、制胶合板或似多层板用单板以及其他经纵锯、刨切或旋切的木材，不论是否刨平、砂光、拼接或端部接合，厚度不超过6毫米：**					**Sheets for veneering (including those obtained by slicing laminated wood) , for plywood or for similar laminated wood and other wood, sawn lengthwise, sliced or peeled, whether or not planed, sanded, spliced or end-jointed, of a thickness not exceeding 6mm:**
		-针叶木的：					-Coniferous:
		---饰面用单板：					---Veneer sheets:
3301	4408.1011	----用胶合板等多层板制的	8	0 冰岛IS,哥CR,秘鲁PE,新西兰NZ,智利CL 3.2 瑞士CH 4.8 澳AU 6.9 韩国KR	0 受惠国$_2$LD$_2$	40	----Of laminated plywood
3302	4408.1019	----其他	4	0 澳AU,巴PK,冰岛IS,东盟AS,哥CR,韩国KR,秘鲁PE,瑞士CH,新加坡SG,新西兰NZ,智利CL	0 受惠国$_1$LD$_1$	40	----Other
3303	4408.1020	---制胶合板用单板	4	0 澳AU,巴PK,冰岛IS,东盟AS,哥CR,韩国KR,秘鲁PE,瑞士CH,新加坡SG,新西兰NZ,智利CL	0 受惠国$_1$LD$_1$	17	---Sheets for plywood
3304	4408.1090	---其他	4	0 澳AU,巴PK,冰岛IS,东盟AS,哥CR,韩国KR,秘鲁PE,瑞士CH,新加坡SG,新西兰NZ,智利CL	0 受惠国$_1$LD$_1$	30	---Other
		-本章子目注释二所列的热带木：					-Of tropical wood specified in subheading note 2 to this chapter:
		--深红色红柳安木、浅红色红柳安木及巴栲红柳安木：					--Dark red meranti, light red meranti and meranti bakau:
		---饰面用单板：					---Veneer sheets:
3305	4408.3111	----用胶合板等多层板制的	10	0 冰岛IS,哥CR,秘鲁PE,新西兰NZ,智利CL 4 瑞士CH 6 澳AU 8.6 韩国KR	0 受惠国$_2$LD$_2$	40	----Of laminated plywood
3306	4408.3119	----其他	4	0 澳AU,巴PK,冰岛IS,东盟AS,哥CR,韩国KR,秘鲁PE,瑞士CH,新加坡SG,新西兰NZ,智利CL	0 受惠国$_1$LD$_1$	40	----Other
3307	4408.3120	---制胶合板用单板	4	0 澳AU,巴PK,冰岛IS,东盟AS,哥CR,韩国KR,秘鲁PE,瑞士CH,新加坡SG,新西兰NZ,智利CL	0 受惠国$_1$LD$_1$	17	---Sheets for plywood
3308	4408.3190	---其他	4	0 澳AU,巴PK,冰岛IS,东盟AS,哥CR,韩国KR,秘鲁PE,瑞士CH,新加坡SG,新西兰NZ,智利CL	0 受惠国$_1$LD$_1$	30	---Other
		--其他：					--Other:
		---饰面用单板：					---Veneer sheets:
3309	4408.3911	----用胶合板等多层板制的	10	0 冰岛IS,哥CR,秘鲁PE,新西兰NZ,智利CL 4 瑞士CH 6 澳AU 8.6 韩国KR	0 受惠国$_2$LD$_2$	40	----Of laminated plywood
3310	4408.3919	----其他	4	0 澳AU,巴PK,冰岛IS,东盟AS,哥CR,韩国KR,秘鲁PE,瑞士CH,新加坡SG,新西兰NZ,智利CL	0 受惠国$_1$LD$_1$	40	----Other

序号 No.	税则号列 Tariff Line	中文货品名称 Article Description in Chinese	最惠国税率 MFN(%)	协定税率 Agreement(%)	特惠税率 SP(%)	普通税率 Gen(%)	英文货品名称 Article Description
3311	4408.3920	---制胶合板用单板	4	0 澳AU,巴PK,冰岛IS,东盟AS,哥CR,韩国KR,秘鲁PE,瑞士CH,新加坡SG,新西兰NZ,智利CL	0 受惠国$_1$LD$_1$	17	---Sheets for plywood
3312	4408.3990	---其他	4	0 澳AU,巴PK,冰岛IS,东盟AS,哥CR,韩国KR,秘鲁PE,瑞士CH,新加坡SG,新西兰NZ,智利CL	0 受惠国$_1$LD$_1$	30	---Other
		-其他：					-Other:
		---饰面用单板：					---Veneer sheets:
3313	4408.9011	----用胶合板等多层板制的	4	0 澳AU,冰岛IS,哥CR,秘鲁PE,瑞士CH,新西兰NZ,智利CL 3.4 韩国KR	0 受惠国$_2$LD$_2$	40	----Of laminated plywood
3314	4408.9012	----温带非针叶木制	3Δ1	0 澳AU,巴PK,冰岛IS,东盟AS,哥CR,韩国KR,秘鲁PE,瑞士CH,新加坡SG,新西兰NZ,智利CL	0 受惠国$_1$LD$_1$	40	----Of temperate non-coniferous wood
3315	4408.9013	----竹制	4	0 澳AU,冰岛IS,哥CR,秘鲁PE,瑞士CH,新西兰NZ,智利CL 3.4 韩国KR	0 受惠国$_2$LD$_2$	40	----Of bamboo
3316	4408.9019	----其他	3	0 澳AU,巴PK,冰岛IS,东盟AS,哥CR,秘鲁PE,瑞士CH,新加坡SG,新西兰NZ,智利CL 1.8 韩国KR	0 受惠国$_1$LD$_1$	40	----Other
	ex44089019	家具饰面单板	Δ1				Veneer sheets for furniture
		---胶合板用单板：					---Sheets for plywood:
3317	4408.9021	----温带非针叶木制	3	0 澳AU,巴PK,冰岛IS,东盟AS,哥CR,韩国KR,秘鲁PE,瑞士CH,新加坡SG,新西兰NZ,智利CL	0 受惠国$_1$LD$_1$	17	----Of temperate non-coniferous wood
3318	4408.9029	----其他	3	0 澳AU,巴PK,冰岛IS,东盟AS,哥CR,韩国KR,秘鲁PE,瑞士CH,新加坡SG,新西兰NZ,智利CL	0 受惠国$_1$LD$_1$	17	----Other
	ex44089029	胶合板用旋切单板	Δ1				Peeled sheets for plywood
		---其他：					---Other:
3319	4408.9091	----温带非针叶木制	3	0 澳AU,巴PK,冰岛IS,东盟AS,哥CR,韩国KR,秘鲁PE,瑞士CH,新加坡SG,新西兰NZ,智利CL	0 受惠国$_1$LD$_1$	30	----Of temperate non-coniferous wood
3320	4408.9099	----其他	3	0 澳AU,巴PK,冰岛IS,东盟AS,哥CR,韩国KR,秘鲁PE,瑞士CH,新加坡SG,新西兰NZ,智利CL	0 受惠国$_1$LD$_1$	30	----Other
	44.09	**任何一边端或面制成连续形状（舌榫、槽榫、半槽榫、斜角、V形接头、珠榫、缘饰、刨圆及类似形状）的木材（包括未装拼的拼花地板用板条及缘板），不论是否刨平、砂光或端部接合：**					**Wood (including strips and friezes for parquet flooring, not assembled) continuously shaped (tongued, grooved, rebated, chamfered, V-jointed, beaded, moulded, rounded or the like) along any of its edges, ends or faces, whether or not planed, sanded or end-jointed:**
		-针叶木：					-Coniferous:
3321	4409.1010	---地板条（块）	7.5	0 冰岛IS,东盟AS,哥CR,秘鲁PE,新加坡SG,新西兰NZ,智利CL 3 瑞士CH 4.5 澳AU 5 巴PK 6 韩国KR	0 受惠国LD	50	---Floor board strips

序号 No.	税则号列 Tariff Line	中文货品名称 Article Description in Chinese	最惠国税率 MFN(%)	协定税率 Agreement(%)	特惠税率 SP(%)	普通税率 Gen(%)	英文货品名称 Article Description
3322	4409.1090	---其他	7.5	0 冰岛IS,东盟AS,哥CR,秘鲁PE,新加坡SG,新西兰NZ,智利CL 3 瑞士CH 4.5 澳AU,韩国KR 5 巴PK	0 受惠国LD	50	---Other
		-非针叶木:					-Non-coniferous:
		--竹的:					--Of bamboo:
3323	4409.2110	---地板条(块)	4	0 澳AU,巴PK,冰岛IS,东盟AS,哥CR,韩国KR,秘鲁PE,瑞士CH,新加坡SG,新西兰NZ,智利CL	0 受惠国LD	50	---Floor board strips
3324	4409.2190	---其他	4	0 澳AU,巴PK,冰岛IS,东盟AS,哥CR,韩国KR,秘鲁PE,瑞士CH,新加坡SG,新西兰NZ,智利CL	0 受惠国LD	50	---Other
		--其他:					--Other:
3325	4409.2910	---地板条(块)	4	0 澳AU,巴PK,冰岛IS,东盟AS,哥CR,韩国KR,秘鲁PE,瑞士CH,新加坡SG,新西兰NZ,智利CL	0 受惠国LD	50	---Floor board strips
3326	4409.2990	---其他	4	0 澳AU,巴PK,冰岛IS,东盟AS,哥CR,韩国KR,秘鲁PE,瑞士CH,新加坡SG,新西兰NZ,智利CL	0 受惠国$_1$LD$_1$	50	---Other
	44.10	**木质碎料板及其他类似木质材料板,(例如,定向板及华夫板),不论是否用树脂或其他有机粘合剂粘合:**					**Particle board and similar board of wood or other ligneous materials (for example, oriented strand board and waferboabd) , whether or not agglomerated with resins or other organic binding substances:**
		-木制:					-Of wood:
3327	4410.1100	--碎料板	4	0 瑞士CH,新西兰NZ		40	--Particle board
3328	4410.1200	--定向刨花板	4	0 瑞士CH,新西兰NZ		40	--Oriented standard board (OSB)
3329	4410.1900	--其他	4	1.6 瑞士CH,新西兰NZ		40	--Other
		-其他:					-Other:
		---碎料板:					---Particle board:
3330	4410.9011	----麦稻秸秆制	7.5			40	----Particle board of wheat/rice straw
3331	4410.9019	----其他	7.5			40	----Other
3332	4410.9090	---其他	7.5			40	---Other
	44.11	**木纤维板或其他木质材料纤维板,不论是否用树脂或其他有机粘合剂粘合:**					**Fibreboard of wood or other ligneous materials, whether or not bonded with resins or other organic substances:**
		-中密度纤维板:					-Medium density fibreboard (MDF) :
		--厚度不超过5毫米:					--Of a thickness not exceeding 5mm:
		---密度超过每立方厘米0.8克:					---Of a density exceeding 0.8 g/cm^3:
3333	4411.1211	----未经机械加工或盖面的	4	0 瑞士CH,新西兰NZ 3.4 韩国KR		40	----Not mechanically worked or surface covered
3334	4411.1219	----其他	7.5	3 瑞士CH,新西兰NZ 4.5 韩国KR		40	----Other
		---密度超过每立方厘米0.5克,但未超过每立方厘米0.8克:					---Of a density exceeding 0.5 g/cm^3 but not exceeding 0.8 g/cm^3:
3335	4411.1221	----辐射松制的	4	0 澳AU,瑞士CH,新西兰NZ 3.4 韩国KR	0 受惠国$_2$LD$_2$	40	----Of radiata pine
3336	4411.1229	----其他	4	0 瑞士CH,新西兰NZ 3.4 韩国KR		40	----Other
		---其他:					---Other:

序号 No.	税则号列 Tariff Line	中文货品名称 Article Description in Chinese	最惠国税率 MFN(%)	协定税率 Agreement(%)	特惠税率 SP(%)	普通税率 Gen(%)	英文货品名称 Article Description
3337	4411.1291	----未经机械加工或盖面的	7.5	3 瑞士CH,新西兰NZ 6.5 韩国KR		40	----Not mechanically worked or surface covered
3338	4411.1299	----其他	4	0 瑞士CH,新西兰NZ 3.4 韩国KR		40	----Other
		--厚度超过5毫米但未超过9毫米:					--Of a thickness exceeding 5mm but not exceeding 9mm:
		---密度超过每立方厘米0.8克:					---Of a density exceeding 0.8g/cm^3:
3339	4411.1311	----未经机械加工或盖面的	4	0 瑞士CH,新西兰NZ		40	----Not mechanically worked or surface covered
3340	4411.1319	----其他	7.5	5.4 瑞士CH,新西兰NZ		40	----Other
		---密度超过每立方厘米0.5克，但未超过每立方厘米0.8克:					---Of a density exceeding 0.5g/cm^3 but not exceeding 0.8g/cm^3:
3341	4411.1321	----辐射松制的	4	0 澳AU,瑞士CH,新西兰NZ	0 受惠国$_2$LD$_2$	40	----Of radiata pine
3342	4411.1329	----其他	4	0 瑞士CH,新西兰NZ		40	----Other
		---其他:					---Other:
3343	4411.1391	----未经机械加工或盖面的	7.5	3 瑞士CH,新西兰NZ		40	----Not mechanically worked or surface covered
3344	4411.1399	----其他	4	0 瑞士CH,新西兰NZ 3.4 韩国KR		40	----Other
		--厚度超过9毫米:					--Of a thickness exceeding 9mm:
		---密度超过每立方厘米0.8克:					---Of a density exceeding 0.8g/cm^3:
3345	4411.1411	----未经机械加工或盖面的	4	0 瑞士CH,新西兰NZ 3.4 韩国KR		40	----Not mechanically worked or surface covered
3346	4411.1419	----其他	7.5	5.4 瑞士CH,新西兰NZ 6.5 韩国KR		40	----Other
		---密度超过每立方厘米0.5克，但未超过每立方厘米0.8克:					---Of a density exceeding 0.5g/cm^3 but not exceeding 0.8g/cm^3:
3347	4411.1421	----辐射松制的	4	0 澳AU,瑞士CH,新西兰NZ 3.4 韩国KR	0 受惠国$_2$LD$_2$	40	----Of radiata pine
3348	4411.1429	----其他	4	0 瑞士CH,新西兰NZ 3.4 韩国KR		40	----Other
		---其他:					---Other:
3349	4411.1491	----未经机械加工或盖面的	7.5	3 瑞士CH,新西兰NZ 6.5 韩国KR		40	----Not mechanically worked or surface covered
3350	4411.1499	----其他	4	0 瑞士CH,新西兰NZ 3.4 韩国KR		40	----Other
		-其他:					-Other:
		--密度超过每立方厘米0.8克:					--Of a density exceeding 0.8g/cm^3:
3351	4411.9210	---未经机械加工或盖面的	4	0 瑞士CH,新西兰NZ 3.4 韩国KR		40	---Not mechanically worked or surface covered
3352	4411.9290	---其他	7.5	3 瑞士CH,新西兰NZ 6.5 韩国KR		40	---Other
		--密度超过每立方厘米0.5克，但未超过每立方厘米0.8克:					--Of a density exceeding 0.5g/cm^3 but not exceeding 0.8g/cm^3:
3353	4411.9310	---辐射松制的	4	0 澳AU,瑞士CH,新西兰NZ	0 受惠国$_2$LD$_2$	40	---Of radiata pine
3354	4411.9390	---其他	4	0 瑞士CH,新西兰NZ		40	---Other
		--密度未超过每立方厘米0.5克:					--Of a density not exceeding 0.5g/cm^3:
3355	4411.9410	---密度超过每立方厘米0.35克，但未超过每立方厘米0.5克	7.5	3 瑞士CH,新西兰NZ 6.5 韩国KR		40	---Of a density exceeding 0.35g/cm^3 but not exceeding 0.5g/cm^3
		---密度未超过每立方厘米0.35克:					---Of a density not exceeding 0.35g/cm^3:
3356	4411.9421	----未经机械加工或盖面的	7.5	3 瑞士CH,新西兰NZ 6.5 韩国KR		40	----Not mechanically worked or surface covered
3357	4411.9429	----其他	4	0 瑞士CH,新西兰NZ 3.4 韩国KR		40	----Other

序号 No.	税则号列 Tariff Line	中文货品名称 Article Description in Chinese	最惠国税率 MFN(%)	协定税率 Agreement(%)	特惠税率 SP(%)	普通税率 Gen(%)	英文货品名称 Article Description
	44.12	胶合板、单板饰面板及类似的多层板：					**Plywood, veneered panels and similar laminated wood:**
		-竹制的：					-Of bamboo:
		---仅由薄板制的胶合板，每层厚度不超过6毫米：					---Plywood consisting solely of sheets, each ply not exceeding 6mm:
3358	4412.1011	----至少有一表层是本章子目注释二所列的热带木	12	0 冰岛IS,哥CR,秘鲁PE,新西兰NZ,智利CL 7.2 澳AU 8.4 瑞士CH 10.4 韩国KR	0 受惠国$_2$LD$_2$	30	----With at least one outer ply of tropical wood specified in Subheading Note 2 to this Chapter
3359	4412.1019	----其他	4	0 瑞士CH,新西兰NZ 3.4 韩国KR		30	----Other
3360	4412.1020	---其他，至少有一表层是非针叶木	10	0 哥CR,秘鲁PE,新西兰NZ 4 瑞士CH 5 巴PK 6 澳AU 8.6 韩国KR	0 受惠国$_2$LD$_2$	30	---Other, with at least one outer ply of nonconiferous wood
		---其他：					---Other:
3361	4412.1091	----至少有一层是本章子目注释二所列的热带木	8	3.2 瑞士CH,新西兰NZ 6.9 韩国KR		30	----With at least one ply of tropical wood specified in Subheading Note 2 to this Chapter
3362	4412.1092	----其他，至少含有一层木碎料板	10	4 瑞士CH,新西兰NZ 8.6 韩国KR		30	----Other, containing at least one layer of particle board
3363	4412.1099	----其他	4	0 澳AU,巴PK,冰岛IS,东盟AS,哥CR,韩国KR,秘鲁PE,瑞士CH,新加坡SG,新西兰NZ,智利CL	0 受惠国LD	30	----Other
		-其他仅由薄木板制的胶合板（竹制除外），每层厚度不超过6毫米：					-Other plywood consisting solely of sheets of wood (other than bamboo), each ply not exceeding 6mm thickness:
3364	4412.3100	--至少有一表层是本章子目注释二所列的热带木	12	0 冰岛IS,哥CR,秘鲁PE,新西兰NZ,智利CL 7.2 澳AU 8.4 瑞士CH 10.4 韩国KR	0 受惠国$_2$LD$_2$	30	--With at least one outer ply of tropical wood specified in Subheading Note 2 to this Chapter
		--其他，至少有一表层是非针叶木：					--Other, with at least one outer ply of non-coniferous wood:
3365	4412.3210	---至少有一表层是温带非针叶木	4	0 瑞士CH,新西兰NZ 3.4 韩国KR		30	---Other, with at least one outer ply of temperate nonconiferous wood
3366	4412.3290	---其他	4	0 瑞士CH,新西兰NZ 3.4 韩国KR		30	---Other
3367	4412.3900	--其他	4	0 澳AU,巴PK,冰岛IS,东盟AS,哥CR,韩国KR,秘鲁PE,瑞士CH,新加坡SG,新西兰NZ,智利CL	0 受惠国LD	30	--Other
		-其他：					-Other:
		--木块芯胶合板，侧板条芯胶合板及板条芯胶合板：					--Blockboard, laminboard and battenboard:
3368	4412.9410	---至少有一表层是非针叶木	10	4 瑞士CH,新西兰NZ 5 巴PK 8.6 韩国KR		30	---With at least one outer ply of nonconiferous wood
		---其他：					---Other:
3369	4412.9491	----至少有一层是本章子目注释二所列的热带木	8	3.2 瑞士CH,新西兰NZ 6.9 韩国KR		30	----With at least one ply of tropical wood specified in Subheading Note 2 to this Chapter
3370	4412.9492	----其他，至少含有一层木碎料板	10	4 瑞士CH,新西兰NZ 8.6 韩国KR		30	----Other, containing at least one layer of particle board
3371	4412.9499	----其他	4	0 澳AU,巴PK,冰岛IS,东盟AS,哥CR,韩国KR,秘鲁PE,瑞士CH,新加坡SG,新西兰NZ,智利CL	0 受惠国LD	30	----Other

序号 No.	税则号列 Tariff Line	中文货品名称 Article Description in Chinese	最惠国税率 MFN(%)	协定税率 Agreement(%)	特惠税率 SP(%)	普通税率 Gen(%)	英文货品名称 Article Description
		--其他:					--Other:
3372	4412.9910	---至少有一表层是非针叶木	10	4 瑞士CH,新西兰NZ 5 巴PK 8.6 韩国KR		30	---With at least one outer ply of nonconiferous wood
		---其他:					---Other:
3373	4412.9991	----至少有一层是本章子目注释二所列的热带木	8	3.2 瑞士CH,新西兰NZ 6.9 韩国KR		30	----With at least one ply of tropical wood specified in Subheading Note 2 to this Chapter
3374	4412.9992	----其他，至少含有一层木碎料板	10	4 瑞士CH,新西兰NZ 8.6 韩国KR		30	----Other, containing at least one layer of particle board
3375	4412.9999	----其他	4	0 澳AU,巴PK,冰岛IS,东盟AS,哥CR,韩国KR,秘鲁PE,瑞士CH,新加坡SG,新西兰NZ,智利CL	0 受惠国$_1$LD$_1$	30	----Other
	44.13	**强化木，成块、板、条或异型的**					**Densified wood, in blocks, plates, strips or profile shapes**
3376	4413.0000	强化木，成块、板、条或异型的	6	0 冰岛IS,东盟AS,哥CR,秘鲁PE,新加坡SG,新西兰NZ,智利CL 2.4 瑞士CH 3.6 澳AU 4.8 韩国KR 5 巴PK	0 受惠国LD	20	Densified wood, in blocks, plates, strips or profile shapes
	44.14	**木制的画框、相框、镜框及类似品：**					**Wooden frames for paintings, photographs, mirrors or similar objects:**
3377	4414.0010	---辐射松制的	20	0 新西兰NZ 12 澳AU	0 受惠国$_2$LD$_2$	100	---Of radiata pine
3378	4414.0090	---其他	20			100	---Other
	44.15	**包装木箱、木盒、板条箱、圆桶及类似的包装容器；木制电缆卷筒；木托板、箱形托盘及其他装载用木板；木制的托盘护框：**					**Packing cases, boxes, crates, drums and similar packings, of wood; cable-drums of wood; pallets, box pallets and other load boards, of wood; pallet collars of wood:**
3379	4415.1000	-箱、盒、板条箱、圆桶及类似的包装容器；电缆卷筒	7.5	0 冰岛IS,东盟AS,哥CR,秘鲁PE,新加坡SG,新西兰NZ,智利CL 3 瑞士CH 4.5 澳AU 5 巴PK 6 韩国KR	0 受惠国LD	80	-Cases, boxes, crates, drums and similar packing; cable-drums
		-木托板、箱形托盘及其他装载用木板；木制的托盘护框：					-Pallets, box pallets and other load boards; pallet collars:
3380	4415.2010	---辐射松制的	7.5	0 新西兰NZ 4.5 澳AU	0 受惠国$_2$LD$_2$	80	---Of radiata pine
3381	4415.2090	---其他	7.5			80	---Other
	44.16	**木制大桶、琵琶桶、盆和其他木制箍桶及其零件，包括桶板：**					**Casks, barrels, vats, tubs and other coopers' products and parts thereof, of wood, including staves:**
3382	4416.0010	---辐射松制的	16	0 新西兰NZ 9.6 澳AU	0 受惠国$_2$LD$_2$	80	---Of radiata pine
3383	4416.0090	---其他	16			80	---Other
	44.17	**木制的工具、工具支架、工具柄、扫帚及刷子的身及柄；木制鞋靴楦及楦头：**					**Tools, tool bodies, tool handles, broom or brush bodies and handles, of wood; boot or shoe lasts and trees, of wood:**
3384	4417.0010	---辐射松制的	16	0 新西兰NZ 9.6 澳AU	0 受惠国$_2$LD$_2$	80	---Of radiata pine
3385	4417.0090	---其他	16			80	---Other
	44.18	**建筑用木工制品，包括蜂窝结构木镶板、已装拼的拼花地板、木瓦及盖屋板：**					**Builders' joinery and carpentry of wood, including cellular wood panels, assembled flooring panels, shingles and shakes:**

序号 No.	税则号列 Tariff Line	中文货品名称 Article Description in Chinese	最惠国税率 MFN(%)	协定税率 Agreement(%)	特惠税率 SP(%)	普通税率 Gen(%)	英文货品名称 Article Description
		-窗、法兰西式（落地）窗及其框架：					-Windows, French windows and their frames:
3386	4418.1010	---辐射松制的	4	0 澳AU,新西兰NZ	0 受惠国$_2$LD$_2$	70	---Of radiata pine
3387	4418.1090	---其他	4	0 澳门MO	0 受惠国$_2$LD$_2$	70	---Other
3388	4418.2000	-门及其框架和门槛	4	0 澳AU,澳门MO,巴PK,冰岛IS,东盟AS,哥CR,韩国KR,秘鲁PE,瑞士CH,新加坡SG,新西兰NZ,智利CL	0 受惠国LD	70	-Doors and their frames and thresholds
3389	4418.4000	-水泥构件的模板	4	0 澳AU,巴PK,冰岛IS,东盟AS,哥CR,韩国KR,秘鲁PE,瑞士CH,新西兰NZ,智利CL	0 受惠国LD	70	-Shuttering for concrete constructional work
3390	4418.5000	-木瓦及盖屋板	7.5	0 冰岛IS,东盟AS,哥CR,秘鲁PE,新西兰NZ,智利CL 3 瑞士CH 4.5 澳AU,韩国KR 5 巴PK	0 受惠国LD	70	-Shingles and shakes
3391	4418.6000	-柱和梁	4	0 澳AU,巴PK,冰岛IS,东盟AS,哥CR,韩国KR,秘鲁PE,瑞士CH,新加坡SG,新西兰NZ,智利CL	0 受惠国LD	70	-Posts and beams
		-已装拼的地板：					-Assembled flooring panels:
3392	4418.7100	--马赛克地板用	4	0 澳AU,巴PK,冰岛IS,东盟AS,哥CR,韩国KR,秘鲁PE,瑞士CH,新加坡SG,新西兰NZ,智利CL	0 受惠国LD	70	--For mosaic floors
		--其他，多层的：					--Other, multilayer:
3393	4418.7210	---竹制	4	0 澳AU,巴PK,冰岛IS,东盟AS,哥CR,韩国KR,秘鲁PE,瑞士CH,新加坡SG,新西兰NZ,智利CL	0 受惠国$_1$LD$_1$	70	---Of Bamboos
3394	4418.7290	---其他	4	0 澳AU,巴PK,冰岛IS,东盟AS,哥CR,韩国KR,秘鲁PE,瑞士CH,新加坡SG,新西兰NZ,智利CL	0 受惠国$_1$LD$_1$	70	---Other
		其他：					--Other:
3395	4418.7910	---竹制	4	0 澳AU,巴PK,冰岛IS,东盟AS,哥CR,韩国KR,秘鲁PE,瑞士CH,新加坡SG,新西兰NZ,智利CL	0 受惠国$_1$LD$_1$	70	---Of Bamboos
3396	4418.7990	---其他	4	0 澳AU,巴PK,冰岛IS,东盟AS,哥CR,韩国KR,秘鲁PE,瑞士CH,新加坡SG,新西兰NZ,智利CL	0 受惠国$_1$LD$_1$	70	---Other
		-其他：					-Other:
3397	4418.9010	---竹制	4	0 澳AU,巴PK,冰岛IS,东盟AS,哥CR,韩国KR,秘鲁PE,瑞士CH,新加坡SG,新西兰NZ,智利CL	0 受惠国LD	70	---Of bamboo
3398	4418.9090	---其他	4	0 澳AU,巴PK,冰岛IS,东盟AS,哥CR,韩国KR,秘鲁PE,瑞士CH,新加坡SG,新西兰NZ,智利CL	0 受惠国LD	70	---Other
	44.19	木制餐具及厨房用具：					**Tableware and kitchenware, of wood:**
		---一次性筷子：					---One-time chopsticks:
3399	4419.0031	----木制	0		0 受惠国LD	100	----Of wood
3400	4419.0032	----竹制	0		0 受惠国LD	100	----Of bamboos
		---其他：					---Other:
3401	4419.0091	----竹制	0		0 受惠国LD	100	----Of Bamboos
3402	4419.0099	----其他	0		0 受惠国LD	100	----Other

序号 No.	税则号列 Tariff Line	中文货品名称 Article Description in Chinese	最惠国税率 MFN(%)	协定税率 Agreement(%)	特惠税率 SP(%)	普通税率 Gen(%)	英文货品名称 Article Description
	44.20	**镶嵌木（包括细工镶嵌木）;装珠宝或刀具用的木制盒子和小匣子及类似品;木制小雕像及其他装饰品;第九十四章以外的木制家具:**					**Wood marquetry and inlaid wood; caskets and cases for jewellery or cutlery, and similar articles, of wood; statuettes and other ornaments, of wood; wooden articles or furniture not falling in Chapter 94:**
		-木制小雕像及其他装饰品:					-Statuettes and other ornaments, of wood:
		---木刻及竹刻:					---Wood or bamboo carvings:
3403	4420.1011	----木刻	0		0 受惠国LD	100	----Wood carvings
3404	4420.1012	----竹刻	0		0 受惠国LD	100	----Bamboo carvings
3405	4420.1020	---木扇	0		0 受惠国LD	100	---Wooden fans
3406	4420.1090	---其他	0		0 受惠国LD	100	---Other
		-其他:					-Other:
3407	4420.9010	---镶嵌木	0		0 受惠国LD	45	---Wood marquetry and inlaid wood
3408	4420.9090	---其他	0		0 受惠国LD	100	---Other
	44.21	**其他木制品:**					**Other articles of wood:**
3409	4421.1000	-衣架	0		0 受惠国LD	90	-Clothes hangers
		-其他:					-Other:
3410	4421.9010	---卷轴、纡子、筒管、缝纫用线轴及类似品	0		0 受惠国LD	35	---Spools, cops, bobbins, sewing thread reels and the like
		---圆签、圆棒、冰果棒、压舌片及类似一次性制品:					---Round picks and sticks, sticks for icesucker, spatulas and similar one time articles:
3411	4421.9021	----木制	0		0 受惠国LD	35	----Of wood
3412	4421.9022	----竹制	0		0 受惠国LD	35	----Of bamboos
3413	4421.9090	---其他	0		0 受惠国LD	90	---Other

第四十五章
软木及软木制品

注释：

本章不包括：

一、第六十四章的鞋靴及其零件；

二、第六十五章的帽类及其零件；

三、第九十五章的物品（例如，玩具、游戏品及运动用品）。

Chapter 45
Cork and articles of cork

Notes:

This Chapter does not cover:

(a) Footwear or parts of footwear of Chapter 64;

(b) Headgear or parts of headgear of Chapter 65; or

(c) Articles of Chapter 95 (or example, toys, games, sports requisites).

序号 No.	税则号列 Tariff Line	中文货品名称 Article Description in Chinese	最惠国税率 MFN(%)	协定税率 Agreement(%)	特惠税率 SP(%)	普通税率 Gen(%)	英文货品名称 Article Description
	45.01	**未加工或简单加工的天然软木；软木废料；碎的、粒状的或粉状的软木：**					**Natural cork, raw or simply prepared; waste cork; crushed, granulated or ground cork:**
3414	4501.1000	-未加工或简单加工的天然软木	6Δ1	0 冰岛IS,东盟AS,哥CR,韩国KR,秘鲁PE,新西兰NZ,智利CL 2.4 瑞士CH 3.6 澳AU 5 巴PK	0 受惠国$_1$LD$_1$	17	-Natural cork, raw or simply prepared
		-其他：					-Other:
3415	4501.9010	---软木废料	0		0 受惠国LD	17	---Waste cork
3416	4501.9020	---碎的、粉粒状的或粉状的软木（软木碎、软木粒或软木粉）	0		0 受惠国LD	17	---Crushed, granulated or ground cork
	45.02	**天然软木，除去表皮或粗切成方形，或成长方块、正方块、板、片或条状（包括作塞子用的方块坯料）**					**Natural cork, debacked or roughly squared, or in rectangular (including square) blocks, plates, sheets or strip (including sharp-edged blanks for corks or stoppers)**
3417	4502.0000	天然软木，除去表皮或粗切成方形，或成长方块、正方块、板、片或条状（包括作塞子用的方块坯料）	8	0 冰岛IS,东盟AS,哥CR,秘鲁PE,新西兰NZ,智利CL 3.2 瑞士CH 4.8 澳AU,韩国KR 5 巴PK	0 受惠国LD	30	Natural cork, debarked or roughly squared, or in rectangular (including square) blocks, plates, sheets or strip (including sharp-edged blanks for corks or stoppers)
	45.03	**天然软木制品：**					**Articles of natural cork:**
3418	4503.1000	-塞子	8	0 冰岛IS,东盟AS,哥CR,秘鲁PE,新西兰NZ,智利CL 3.2 瑞士CH 4.8 澳AU,韩国KR 5 巴PK	0 受惠国LD	50	-Corks and stoppers
3419	4503.9000	-其他	10.5	0 冰岛IS,东盟AS,哥CR,秘鲁PE,新加坡SG,新西兰NZ,智利CL 5 巴PK 6.3 澳AU 7.4 瑞士CH 8.4 韩国KR	0 受惠国LD	50	-Other
	45.04	**压制软木（不论是否使用粘合剂压成）及其制品：**					**Agglomerated cork (with or without a binding substance) and articles of agglomerated cork:**
3420	4504.1000	-块、板、片及条；任何形状的砖、瓦；实心圆柱体，包括圆片	8.4	0 冰岛IS,东盟AS,哥CR,秘鲁PE,新西兰NZ,智利CL 3.36 瑞士CH 5 澳AU,巴PK 6.7 韩国KR	0 受惠国LD	30	-Blocks, plates, sheets and strip; tiles of any shape; solid cylinders, including discs
3421	4504.9000	-其他	0		0 受惠国LD	50	-Other

第四十六章
稻草、秸秆、针茅或其他编结材料制品；篮筐及柳条编结品

Chapter 46
Manufactures of straw, of esparto or of other plaiting materials; basketware and wickerwork

注释：

一、本章所称"编结材料"，是指其状态或形状适于编结、交织或类似加工的材料，包括稻草、秸秆、柳条、竹、藤、灯芯草、芦苇、木片条、其他植物材料扁条（例如，树皮条、狭叶、酒椰叶纤维或其他从阔叶获取的条）、未纺的天然纺织纤维、塑料单丝及扁条、纸带，但不包括皮革、再生皮革、毡呢或无纺织物的扁条、人发、马毛、纺织粗纱或纱线以及第五十四章的单丝和扁条。

二、本章不包括：

（一）税号48.14的壁纸；

（二）不论是否编结而成的线、绳、索、缆（税号56.07）；

（三）第六十四章和第六十五章的鞋靴、帽类及其零件；

（四）编结而成的车辆或车身（第八十七章）；

（五）第九十四章的物品（例如，家具、灯具及照明装置）。

三、税号46.01所称"平行连结的成片编结材料、缏条或类似的编结材料产品"，是指编结材料、缏条及类似的编结材料产品平行排列连结成片的制品，其连结材料不论是否为纺制的纺织材料。

Notes:

1. In this Chapter the expression "plaiting materials" means materi-als in astate or form suitable for plaiting, interlacing or similar processes; it includes straw, osier or willow, bamboos, rattans, rushes, reeds, strips of wood, strips of other vegetable material (for example, strips of bark, narrow leaves and raffia or other strips obtained from broad leaves), unspun natural textile fibres, monofilament and strip and the like of plastics and strips of paper, but not strips of leather or composition leather or of felt or nonwovens, human hair, horsehair, textile rovings or yarns, or monofilament and strip and the like of Chapter 54.
2. This Chapter does not cover:
(a) Wall coverings of heading No.48.14;
(b) Twine, cordage, ropes or cables, plaited or not (heading No.56.07);
(c) Footwear or headgear or parts thereof of Chapter 64 or 65;
(d) Vehicles or bodies for vehicles of basketware (Chapter 87); or
(e) Articles of Chapter 94 (for example, furniture, lamps and lighting fittings).
3. For the purposes of heading No.46.01, the expression "plaiting materials, plaits and similar products of plaiting materials, bound together in parallel strands" means plaiting materials, plaits and similar products of plaiting materials, placed side by side and bound together, in the form of sheets, whether or not the binding materials are to spun textile materials.

序号 No.	税则号列 Tariff Line	中文货品名称 Article Description in Chinese	最惠国税率 MFN(%)	协定税率 Agreement(%)	特惠税率 SP(%)	普通税率 Gen(%)	英文货品名称 Article Description
	46.01	用编结材料编成的缏条及类似产品，不论是否缝合成宽条；平行连结或编结的成片材料、缏条或类似的编结材料产品，不论是否制成品（例如，席子、席料、帘子）：					**Plaits and similar products of plaiting materials, whether or not assembled into strips; plaiting materials, plaits and similar products of plaiting materials, bound together in parallel strands or woven, in sheet form, whether or not being finished articles (for example, mats, matting, screens) :**
		-植物材料制的席子、席料及帘子：					-Mats, matting and screens of vegetable materials:
3422	4601.2100	--竹制的	9	0 澳门MO,冰岛IS,东盟AS,哥CR,秘鲁PE,新西兰NZ,智利CL 3.6 瑞士CH 5 巴PK 5.4 澳AU,韩国KR	0 老挝LA,受惠国LD	90	--Of bamboo
3423	4601.2200	--藤制的	9	0 澳门MO,冰岛IS,东盟AS,哥CR,秘鲁PE,新西兰NZ,智利CL 3.6 瑞士CH 5 巴PK 5.4 澳AU,韩国KR	0 老挝LA,受惠国LD	100	--Of rattan

序号 No.	税则号列 Tariff Line	中文货品名称 Article Description in Chinese	最惠国税率 MFN(%)	协定税率 Agreement(%)	特惠税率 SP(%)	普通税率 Gen(%)	英文货品名称 Article Description
		--其他:					--Other:
		---草制的:					---Of grass or straw:
3424	4601.2911	----灯心草属材料制的	9	0 澳门MO,冰岛IS,东盟AS,哥CR,秘鲁PE,新西兰NZ,智利CL 3.6 瑞士CH 5 巴PK 5.4 澳AU,韩国KR	0 老挝LA,受惠国LD	90	----Of rush
3425	4601.2919	----其他	9	0 冰岛IS,东盟AS,哥CR,秘鲁PE,新西兰NZ,智利CL 3.6 瑞士CH 5 巴PK 5.4 澳AU,韩国KR	0 老挝LA,受惠国LD	90	----Other
		---芦苇制的:					---Of reed:
3426	4601.2921	----苇帘	9	0 冰岛IS,东盟AS,哥CR,秘鲁PE,新西兰NZ,智利CL 3.6 瑞士CH 5 巴PK 5.4 澳AU,韩国KR	0 老挝LA,受惠国LD	90	----Screens of reed
3427	4601.2929	----其他	9	0 冰岛IS,东盟AS,哥CR,秘鲁PE,新西兰NZ,智利CL 3.6 瑞士CH 5 巴PK 5.4 澳AU,韩国KR	0 老挝LA,受惠国LD	90	----Other
3428	4601.2990	---其他	9	0 冰岛IS,东盟AS,哥CR,秘鲁PE,新西兰NZ,智利CL 3.6 瑞士CH 5 巴PK 5.4 澳AU,韩国KR	0 老挝LA,受惠国LD	90	---Other
		-其他:					-Other:
		--竹制的:					--Of bamboo:
3429	4601.9210	---鞭条及类似产品，不论是否缝合成宽条	9	0 澳门MO,冰岛IS,东盟AS,哥CR,秘鲁PE,新西兰NZ,智利CL 3.6 瑞士CH 5 巴PK 5.4 澳AU,韩国KR	0 老挝LA,受惠国LD	100	---Plaits and similar products of plaiting materials, whether or not assembled into strips
3430	4601.9290	---其他	9	0 澳门MO,冰岛IS,东盟AS,哥CR,秘鲁PE,新西兰NZ,智利CL 3.6 瑞士CH 5 巴PK 5.4 澳AU,韩国KR	0 受惠国LD	90	---Other
		--藤制的:					--Of rattan:
3431	4601.9310	---鞭条及类似产品，不论是否缝合成宽条	9	0 澳门MO,冰岛IS,东盟AS,哥CR,秘鲁PE,新西兰NZ,智利CL 3.6 瑞士CH 5 巴PK 5.4 澳AU,韩国KR	0 老挝LA,受惠国LD	100	---Plaits and similar products of plaiting materials, whether or not assembled into strips
3432	4601.9390	---其他	9	0 澳门MO,冰岛IS,东盟AS,哥CR,新西兰NZ,智利CL 3.6 瑞士CH 5 巴PK 5.4 澳AU,韩国KR	0 受惠国$_2$LD$_2$	90	---Other
		--其他植物材料制:					--Of other vegetable materials:
		---稻草制的:					---Of straw:

序号 No.	税则号列 Tariff Line	中文货品名称 Article Description in Chinese	最惠国税率 MFN(%)	协定税率 Agreement(%)	特惠税率 SP(%)	普通税率 Gen(%)	英文货品名称 Article Description
3433	4601.9411	----缏条（绳）	10	0 冰岛IS,东盟AS,哥CR,秘鲁PE,新西兰NZ,智利CL 4 瑞士CH 5 巴PK 6 澳AU 8 韩国KR	0 受惠国$_1$LD$_1$	90	----Plaits
3434	4601.9419	----其他	10	0 冰岛IS,东盟AS,哥CR,秘鲁PE,新西兰NZ,智利CL 4 瑞士CH 5 巴PK 6 澳AU 8 韩国KR	0 受惠国$_1$LD$_1$	90	----Other
		---其他：					---Other:
3435	4601.9491	----鞭条及类似产品，不论是否缝合成宽条	9	0 冰岛IS,东盟AS,哥CR,秘鲁PE,新西兰NZ,智利CL 3.6 瑞士CH 5 巴PK 5.4 澳AU,韩国KR	0 老挝LA,受惠国LD	100	----Plaits and similar products of plaiting materials, whether or not assembled into strips
3436	4601.9499	----其他	9	0 冰岛IS,东盟AS,哥CR,秘鲁PE,新西兰NZ,智利CL 3.6 瑞士CH 5 巴PK 5.4 澳AU,韩国KR	0 受惠国LD	90	----Other
		--其他：					--Other:
3437	4601.9910	---鞭条及类似产品，不论是否缝合成宽条	9	0 冰岛IS,东盟AS,哥CR,秘鲁PE,新西兰NZ,智利CL 3.6 瑞士CH 5 巴PK 5.4 澳AU,韩国KR	0 老挝LA,受惠国LD	90	---Plaits and similar products of plaiting materials, whether or not assembled into strips
3438	4601.9990	---其他	9	0 冰岛IS,东盟AS,哥CR,秘鲁PE,新西兰NZ,智利CL 3.6 瑞士CH 5 巴PK 5.4 澳AU 7.2 韩国KR	0 受惠国$_1$LD$_1$	90	---Other
	46.02	**用编结材料直接编成或用税号46.01所列货品制成的篮筐、柳条编结品及其他制品;丝瓜络制品：**					**Basketwork, wickerwork and other articles, made directly to shape from plaiting materials or made up from goods of heading 4601; articles of loofah:**
		-植物材料制：					-Of vegetable materials:
3439	4602.1100	--竹制的	9	0 冰岛IS,东盟AS,哥CR,秘鲁PE,新西兰NZ,智利CL 3.6 瑞士CH 5 巴PK 5.4 澳AU,韩国KR	0 柬埔寨KH,受惠国LD	100	--Of bamboo
3440	4602.1200	--藤制的	9	0 冰岛IS,东盟AS,哥CR,新西兰NZ,智利CL 3.6 瑞士CH 5 巴PK 5.4 澳AU,韩国KR	0 柬埔寨KH,受惠国LD	100	--Of rattan
		--其他：					--Other:
3441	4602.1910	---草制的	9	0 冰岛IS,东盟AS,哥CR,秘鲁PE,新西兰NZ,智利CL 3.6 瑞士CH 5 巴PK 5.4 澳AU,韩国KR	0 柬埔寨KH,受惠国LD	100	---Of grass or straw

序号 No.	税则号列 Tariff Line	中文货品名称 Article Description in Chinese	最惠国税率 MFN(%)	协定税率 Agreement(%)		特惠税率 SP(%)		普通税率 Gen(%)	英文货品名称 Article Description
3442	4602.1920	---玉米皮制的	9	0 3.6 5 5.4	冰岛IS,东盟AS,哥CR,秘鲁PE,新西兰NZ,智利CL 瑞士CH 巴PK 澳AU,韩国KR	0	柬埔寨KH,受惠国LD	100	---Of maize-shuck
3443	4602.1930	---柳条制的	9	0 3.6 5 5.4	冰岛IS,东盟AS,哥CR,秘鲁PE,新西兰NZ,智利CL 瑞士CH 巴PK 澳AU,韩国KR	0	柬埔寨KH,受惠国LD	100	---Of osier
3444	4602.1990	---其他	9	0 3.6 5 5.4	冰岛IS,东盟AS,哥CR,新西兰NZ,智利CL 瑞士CH 巴PK 澳AU,韩国KR	0	柬埔寨KH,受惠国LD	100	---Other
3445	4602.9000	-其他	9	0 3.6 5 5.4 8	澳门MO,冰岛IS,东盟AS,哥CR,秘鲁PE,新西兰NZ,智利CL 瑞士CH 巴PK 澳AU,韩国KR 亚太AP	0	柬埔寨KH,受惠国LD	100	-Other

第十类
木浆及其他纤维状纤维素浆、回收（废碎）纸或纸板；纸、纸板及其制品

SECTION X
PULP OF WOOD OR OF OTHER FIBROUS CELLULOSIC MATERIAL; RECOVERED（WASTE AND SCRAP）PAPER OR PAPERBOARD; PAPER AND PAPERBOARD AND ARTICLES THEREOF

第四十七章
木浆及其他纤维状纤维素浆；回收（废碎）纸或纸板

Chapter 47
Pulp of wood or of other fibrous cellulosic material; recovered (waste and scrap) paper or paperboard

注释:

税号47.02所称“化学木浆，溶解级”，是指温度在20℃时浸入含18%氢氧化钠的苛性碱溶液内，一小时后，按重量计含有92%及以上的不溶级分的碱木浆或硫酸盐木浆，或者含有88%及以上的不溶级分的亚硫酸盐木浆。对于亚硫酸盐木浆，按重量计灰分含量不得超过0.15%。

Notes:

For the purposes of heading No.47.02, the expression “chemical wood pulp，dissolving grades” means chemical wood pulp having by weight an insoluble fraction of 92% or more for soda or sulphate wood pulp of 88% or more for sulphite wood pulp after one hour in a caustic soda solution containing 18% sodium bydroxide (NaOH) at 20℃, and for sulphite wood pulp an ash content that does not exceed 0.15% by weight.

序号 No.	税则号列 Tariff Line	中文货品名称 Article Description in Chinese	最惠国税率 MFN(%)	协定税率 Agreement(%)	特惠税率 SP(%)	普通税率 Gen(%)	英文货品名称 Article Description
	47.01	**机械木浆**					**Mechanical wood pulp**
3446	4701.0000	机械木浆	0		0 受惠国LD	8	Mechanical wood pulp
	47.02	**化学木浆，溶解级**					**Chemical wood pulp, dissolving grades**
3447	4702.0000	化学木浆，溶解级	0		0 受惠国LD	8	Chemical wood pulp, dissolving grades
	47.03	**碱木浆或硫酸盐木浆，但溶解级的除外：**					**Chemical wood pulp, soda or sulphate, other than dissolving grades:**
		-未漂白：					-Unbleached:
3448	4703.1100	--针叶木的	0		0 受惠国LD	8	--Coniferous
3449	4703.1900	--非针叶木的	0		0 受惠国LD	8	--Non-coniferous
		-半漂白或漂白：					-Semi-bleached or bleached:
3450	4703.2100	--针叶木的	0		0 受惠国LD	8	--Coniferous
3451	4703.2900	--非针叶木的	0		0 受惠国LD	8	--Non-coniferous
	47.04	**亚硫酸盐木浆，但溶解级的除外：**					**Chemical wood pulp, sulphite, other than dissolving grades:**
		-未漂白：					-Unbleached:
3452	4704.1100	--针叶木的	0		0 受惠国LD	8	--Coniferous
3453	4704.1900	--非针叶木的	0		0 受惠国LD	8	--Non-coniferous
		-半漂白或漂白：					-Semi-bleached or bleached:
3454	4704.2100	--针叶木的	0		0 受惠国LD	8	--Coniferous
3455	4704.2900	--非针叶木的	0		0 受惠国LD	8	--Non-coniferous
	47.05	**用机械与化学联合制浆法制得的木浆**					**Wood pulp obtained by a combination of mechanical and chemical pulping processes**
3456	4705.0000	用机械与化学联合制浆法制得的木浆	0		0 受惠国LD	8	Wood pulp obtained by a combination of mechanical and chemical pulping proce-sses
	47.06	**从回收（废碎）纸或纸板提取的纤维浆或其他纤维状纤维素浆：**					**Pulps of fibres derived from recovered (waste and scrap) paper or paperboard or of other fibrous cellulosic material:**
3457	4706.1000	-棉短绒纸浆	0		0 受惠国LD	8	-Cotton linters pulp

序号 No.	税则号列 Tariff Line	中文货品名称 Article Description in Chinese	最惠国税率 MFN(%)	协定税率 Agreement(%)	特惠税率 SP(%)	普通税率 Gen(%)	英文货品名称 Article Description
3458	4706.2000	-从回收（废碎）纸或纸板提取的纤维浆	0		0 受惠国LD	8	-Pulps of fibres derived from recovered (waste and scrap) paper or paperboard
3459	4706.3000	-其他，竹浆	0		0 受惠国LD	8	-Other, of bamboo
		-其他：					-Other:
3460	4706.9100	--机械浆	0		0 受惠国LD	8	--Mechanical
3461	4706.9200	--化学浆	0		0 受惠国LD	8	--Chemical
3462	4706.9300	--用机械和化学联合法制得的浆	0		0 受惠国LD	8	--Obtained by a combination of mechanical and chemical processes
	47.07	**回收（废碎）纸或纸板：**					**Recovered (waste and scrap) paper or paperboard:**
3463	4707.1000	-未漂白的牛皮纸或纸板及瓦楞纸或纸板	0		0 受惠国LD	8	-Unbleached kraft paper or paperboard or of corrugated paper or paperboard
3464	4707.2000	-主要由漂白化学木浆制成未经本体染色的其他纸和纸板	0		0 受惠国LD	8	-Other paper or paperboard made mainly of bleached chemical pulp, not coloured in the mass
3465	4707.3000	-主要由机械浆制成的纸或纸板（例如，报纸、杂志及类似印刷品）	0		0 受惠国LD	8	-Paper or paperboard made mainly of mechanical pulp (for example, news-papers, journals and similar printed matter)
3466	4707.9000	-其他，包括未分选的废碎品	0		0 受惠国LD	8	-Other, including unsorted waste and scrap

第四十八章
纸及纸板；纸浆、纸或纸板制品

注释：

一、除条文另有规定的以外，本章所称“纸”包括“纸板”（不论其厚度或每平方米重量如何）。

二、本章不包括：

（一）第三十章的物品；

（二）税号32.12的压印箔；

（三）香纸及用化妆品浸渍或涂布的纸（第三十三章）；

（四）用肥皂或洗涤剂浸渍、覆盖或涂布的纸或纤维素絮纸（税号34.01）和用光洁剂、擦光膏及类似制剂浸渍、覆盖或涂布的纸或纤维素絮纸（税号34.05）；

（五）税号37.01至37.04的感光纸或感光纸板；

（六）用诊断或实验用试剂浸渍的纸（税号38.22）；

（七）第三十九章的用纸强化的层压塑料板，用塑料覆盖或涂布的单层纸或纸板（塑料部分占总厚度的一半以上），以及上述材料的制品，但税号48.14的壁纸除外；

（八）税号42.02的物品（例如旅行用品）；

（九）第四十六章的物品（编结材料制品）；

（十）纸纱线或纸纱线纺织物（第十一类）；

（十一）第六十四章或第六十五章的物品；

（十二）税号68.05的砂纸或税号68.14的用纸或纸板衬底的云母（但涂布云母粉的纸及纸板归入本章）；

（十三）用纸或纸板衬底的金属箔（通常为第十四类或第十五类）；

（十四）税号92.09的制品；

（十五）第九十五章的物品（例如，玩具、游戏品及运动用品）；或

（十六）第九十六章的物品（例如，钮扣，卫生巾（护垫）及止血塞、婴儿尿布及尿布衬里）。

三、除注释七另有规定的以外，税号48.01至48.05包括经砑光、高度砑光、釉光或类似处理、仿水印、表面施胶的纸及纸板；同时还包括用各种方法本体着色或染成斑纹的纸、纸板、纤维素絮纸及纤维素纤维网纸。除税号48.03另有规定的以外，上述税号不适用于经过其他方法加工的纸、纸板、纤维素絮纸或纤维素纤维网纸。

四、本章所称“新闻纸”，是指所含用机械或化学—机械方法制得的木纤维不少于全部纤维重量的50%的未经涂布的报刊用纸，未施胶或微施胶，每面的粗糙度[帕克印刷面粗糙度(1兆帕)]超过2.5微米，每平方米重量不小于40克，但不超过65克。

Chapter 48
Paper and paperboard; articles of paper pulp, of paper or of paperboard

Notes:

1. For the purposes of this Chapter, except where the context Otherwise requires, a reference to “paper” includes references to paperboard (irrespective of thickness or weight per m^2).

2. This Chapter does not cover:

(a) Articles of Chapter 30;

(b) Stamping foils of heading No. 32.12;

(c) Perfumed papers or papers impregnated or coated with cosmetics (Chapter 33);

(d) Paper or cellulose wadding impregnated, coated or covered with soap or detergent (heading No.34.01), or with polishes, creams or similar preparations (heading No.34.05);

(e) Sensitized paper or paperboard of headings Nos.37.01 to 37.04;

(f) Paper impregnated with diagnostic or laboratory reagents (heading No.38.22);

(g) Paper-reinforced stratified sheeting of plastics, or one layer of paper or paperboard coated or covered with a layer of plastics, the latter constituting more than half the total thickness, or articles of such materials, other than wall coverings of heading No.48.14 (Chapter 39);

(h) Articles of heading No.42.02 (for example, travel goods);

(i) Articles of Chapter 46 (manufactures of plaiting material);

(j) Paper yarn or textile articles of paper yarn (Section Ⅺ);

(k) Articles of Chapter 64 or Chapter 65;

(l) Abrasive paper or paperboard (heading No. 68.05) or paper-or paperboard-backed mica (heading No.68.14) (paper and paperboard coated with mica powder are, however, to be classified in this Chapter);

(m) Metal foil backed with paper or paperboard (generally Section ⅩⅣ on ⅩⅤ);

(n) Articles of heading No.92.09;

(o) Articles of Chapter 95 (for example, toys, games, sports requisites) ; or

(p) Articles of Chapter 96 (for example, buttons, sanitary towels (pads) and tampons, napkins (diapers) and napkin liners for babies).

3. Subject to the provisions of Note 7, headings Nos.48.01 to 48.05 include paper and paperboard which have been subjected to calendering, super-calendering, glazing or similar finishing, false watermarking or surface sizing, and also paper, paperboard, cellulose wadding and webs of cellulose fibres, colouredor marbled throughout the mass by any method. Except where heading No.48.03 otherwise requires, these headings do not apply to paper, paperboard, cellulose wadding or webs of cellulose fibres which have been otherwise processed.

4. In this Chapter the expression “newsprint” means uncoated paper of a kind used for the printing of newspapers, of which not less than 50% by weight of the total fibre content consists of wood fibres obtained by a mechanical or chemi-mechanical process, unsized or very lightly sized, having a surface roughness Parker Print Surf (1Mpa) on each side

五、税目48.02所称“书写、印刷或类似用途的纸及纸板”及“未打孔的穿孔卡片纸及穿孔纸带纸”，是指主要用漂白纸浆或用机械或化学—机械方法制得的纸浆制成的纸及纸板，并且符合下列任一标准:

每平方米重量不超过150克的纸或纸板:

（一）用机械或化学—机械方法制得的纤维含量在10%及以上，并且

1.每平方米重量不超过80克;或

2.本体着色;

（二）灰分含量在8%以上，并且

1.每平方米重量不超过80克;或

2.本体着色;

（三）灰分含量在3%以上，亮度在60%及以上;

（四）灰分含量在3%以上，但不超过8%，亮度低于60%，耐破指数等于或小于2.5千帕斯卡·平方米/克;

（五）灰分含量在3%及以下，亮度在60%及以上，耐破指数等于或小于2.5千帕斯卡·平方米/克。

每平方米重量超过150克的纸或纸板:

（一）本体着色;或

（二）亮度在60%及以上，并且

1.厚度在225微米及以下;或

2.厚度在225微米以上，但不超过508微米，灰分含量在3%以上;

（三）亮度低于60%，厚度不超过254微米，灰分含量在8%以上。

税目48.02不包括滤纸及纸板（含茶袋纸）或毡纸及纸板。

六、本章所称“牛皮纸及纸板”，是指所含用硫酸盐法或烧碱法制得的纤维不少于全部纤维重量的80%的纸及纸板。

七、除税目条文另有规定的以外，符合税目48.01至48.11中两个或两个以上税号所规定的纸、纸板、纤维素絮纸及纤维素纤维网纸，应按号列顺序归入有关税号中的最末一个税号。

八、税号48.01及48.03至48.09仅适用于下列规格的纸、纸板、纤维素絮纸及纤维素纤维网纸:

（一）成条或成卷，宽度超过36厘米;

（二）成张矩形（包括正方形），一边超过36厘米，另一边超过15厘米(以未折叠计)。

九、税号48.14所称“壁纸及类似品”，仅限于:

（一）适合作墙壁或天花板装饰用的成卷纸张，宽度不小于45厘米，但不超过160厘米:

1.起纹、压花、染面、印有图案或经其他

exceeding 2.5 micrometres (microns), weighing not less than $40g/m^2$ and not more than $65g/m^2$.

5. For the purposes of heading 48.02, the expressions “paper and paperboard, of a kind used for writing, printing or other graphic purposes” and “non perforated punch-cards and punch tape paper” mean paper and paperboard made mainly from bleached pulp or from pulp obtained by a mechanical or chemi-mechanical process and satisfying any of the following criteria:

For paper or paperboard weighing not more than $150g/m^2$:

(a) containing 10% or more of fibres obtained by a mechanical or chemi-mechanical process, and

(1) weighing not more than $80g/m^2$, or

(2) coloured throughout the mass; or

(b) containing more than 8% ash, and

(1) weighing not more than $80g/m^2$, or

(2) coloured throughout the mass; or

(c) containing more than 3% ash and having a brightness of 60% or more; or

(d) containing more than 3% but not more than 8% ash, having a brightness less than 60%, and a burst index equal to or less than $2.5kPa/m^2/g$; or

(e) containing 3% ash or less, having a brightness of 60% or more and a burst index equal to or less than $2.5kPa \cdot m^2/g$.

For paper or paperboard weighing more than $150g/m^2$:

(a) coloured throughout the mass; or

(b) having a brightness of60% or more, and

①a caliper of225 micrometres (microns) or less, or

②a caliper more than 225 micrometres (microns) but not more than 508 micrometres (microns) and an ash content more than 3%; or

(c) having a brightness of less than 60% a caliper of 254 micrometres (microns) or less and an ash content more than 8%.

Heading No.48.02 does not, however, cover filter paper and paperboard (including tea-bag paper) or felt paper or paperboard.

6. In this Chapter “kraft paper and paperboard” means paper and paperboard of which not less than 80%by weight of the total fibre content consists offibres obtained by the chemical sulphate or soda processes.

7. Except where the terms of the headings otherwise require, paper, paperboard, cellulose wadding and webs of cellulose fibres ans-wering to a description in two or more of the headings Nos. 48.01 to 48.11 are to be classified under that one of such headings which occurs last in numerical order in the Nomenclature.

8. Headings Nos. 48.01 and 48.03 to 48.09 apply only to paper, paperboard, cellulose wadding and webs of cellulose fibres:

(a) in strips or rolls of width exceeding 36cm; or

(b) in rectangular (including square) sheets with one side exceeding 36cm and the other side exceeding 15cm in the unfolded state.

9. For the purposes of heading No.48.14, the expression “wallpaper and similar wall coverings” applies only to:

(a) Paper in rolls, of a width of not less than 45cm and not more than 160cm, suitable for wall or ceiling decoration:

(1) Grained, embossed, surface-coloured, design-printed or

装饰的（例如起绒），不论是否用透明的防护塑料涂布或覆盖；

2. 表面饰有木粒或草粒而凹凸不平的；

3. 表面用塑料涂布或覆盖并起纹、压花、染面、印有图案或经其他装饰的；

4. 表面用不论是否平行连结或编织的编结材料覆盖的。

（二）适于装饰墙壁或天花板用的经上述加工的纸边及纸条，不论是否成卷。

（三）由几幅拼成的壁纸，成卷或成张，贴到墙上可组成印刷的风景或图案。

既可作铺地制品，也可作壁纸的以纸或纸板为底的产品，应归入税号48.23。

十、税号48.20不包括切成一定尺寸的活页纸张或卡片，不论是否印制、压花、打孔。

十一、税号48.23主要适用于提花机或类似机器用的穿孔纸或卡片，以及纸花边。

十二、除税号48.14及48.21的货品外，印有图案、文字或图画的纸、纸板、纤维素絮纸及其制品，如果所印图案、文字或图画作为其主要用途，应归入第四十九章。

子目注释：

一、子目号4804.11及4804.19所称“牛皮挂面纸”，是指所含用硫酸盐法或烧碱法制得的木纤维不少于全部纤维重量的80%的成卷机器上光或研光纸及纸板，每平方米重量超过115克，并且最低缪伦耐破度符合下表所示（其他重量的耐破度可参照下表换算）：

重量（克/平方米）	最低耐破度（千帕斯卡）
115	393
125	417
200	637
300	824
400	961

二、子目号4804.21及4804.29所称“袋用牛皮纸”，是指所含用硫酸盐法或烧碱法制得的木纤维不少于全部纤维重量的 80%的成卷机器上光纸，每平方米重量不小于60克，但不超过115克，并且符合下列一种规格：

（一）缪伦耐破指数不小于3.7千帕斯卡·平方米/克，并且横向伸长率大于4.5%，纵向伸长率大于2%。

（二）至少能达到下表所示的最小撕裂度和抗张强度（其他重量的可参照下表换算）：

otherwise surface-decorated (e.g., with textile flock), whether or not coated or covered with transparent protective plastics;

(2) With an uneven surface resulting from the incorporation of particles of wood, straw, etc.;

(3) Coated or covered on the face side with plastics, the layer of plastics being grained, embossed, coloured, design-printed or otherwise decorated; or

(4) Covered on the face side with plaiting material, whether or not bound together in parallel strands or woven.

(b) Borders and friezes, of paper, treated as above, whether or not in rolls, suitable for wall or ceiling decoration.

(c) Wall coverings of paper made up of several panels, in rolls or sheets, printed so as to make up a scene, design or motif when applied to a wall.

Products on a base of paper or paperboard, suitable for use both as floor coverings and as wall coverings, are to be classified in heading No. 48.23.

10. Heading No. 48.20 does not cover loose sheets or cards, cut to size, whether or not printed, embossed or perforated.

11. Heading No. 48.23 applies, *inter alia*, to perforated paper or paperboard cards for Jacquard or similar machines and paper lace.

12. Except for the goods of heading No.48.14or48.21, paper, paperboard, cellulose wadding and articles thereof, printed with motifs, characters or pictorial representations, which are not merely incidental to the primary use of the goods, fallin Chapter 49.

Subheading Notes:

1. For the purposes of subheadings Nos.4804.11 and 4804.19. “kraftliner” means machine-finished or machine-glazed paper and paperboard, of which not less than 80% by weight ofthe total fibre content consists of wood fibres obtained by the chemical sulphate or soda processes, in rolls, weighing more than 115g/m^2 and having a minimum Mullen bursting strength as indicated in the following table or the linearly interpolated or extrapolated equi-valent for any other weight:

Weight (g /m^2)	**Minimum Mullen bursting strength (kPa)**
115	393
125	417
200	637
300	824
400	961

2. For the purposes of subheadings Nos. 4804.21 and 4804.29, “sack kraft paper” means machine-finished paper, of which not less than 80% by weight of the total fibre content consists of fibres obtained by the chemical sulphate or soda processes, in rolls, weighing not less than 60g/m^2 but not more than 115g/m^2 and meeting one of the following setsofspecifications:

(a) Having a Mullen burst index of not less than 3.7kPa • m^2/g and a stretch factor of more than 4.5% in the cross direction and of more than 2% in the machine direction.

(b) Having minima for tear and tensile as indicated in the following table or the linearly interpolated equivalent for any other eight:

重量 克/平方米	最小撕裂度 毫牛顿		最小抗张强度千牛顿/米	
	纵向	纵向加横向	横向	纵向加横向
60	700	1510	1.9	6
70	830	1790	2.3	7.2
80	965	2070	2.8	8.3
100	1230	2635	3.7	10.6
115	1425	3060	4.4	12.3

三、子目号4805.11所称“半化学的瓦楞纸”，是指所含用机械和化学联合法制得的未漂白硬木纤维不少于全部纤维重量的65%的成卷纸张，并且在温度为23℃和相对湿度为50%时，经过30分钟的瓦楞芯纸平压强度测定（CMT30），抗压强度超过1.8牛顿/克/平方米。

四、子目4805.12包括主要用机械和化学联合法制得的草浆制成的成卷纸张，每平方米重量在130克及以上，并且在温度为23℃和相对湿度为50%时，经过30分钟瓦楞芯纸平压强度测定（CMT30），抗压强度超过1.4牛顿/克/平方米。

五、子目4805.24及4805.25包括全部或主要用回收（废碎）纸及纸板制得的纸浆制成的纸及纸板，强韧箱纸板也可以有一面用染色纸或由漂白或未漂白的非再生浆制得的纸做表层，这些产品缪伦耐破指数不小于2千帕斯卡·平方米/克。

六、子目号4805.30所称“亚硫酸盐包装纸”，是指所含用亚硫酸盐法制得的木纤维超过全部纤维重量的40%的机器研光纸，灰分含量不超过8%，并且缪伦耐破指数不小于1.47千帕斯卡·平方米/克。

七、子目号4810.22所称“轻质涂布纸”，是指双面涂布纸，其每平方米总重量不超过72克，每面每平方米的涂层重量不超过15克，原纸中所含用机械方法制得的木纤维不少于全部纤维重量的50%。

Weight g/m^2	Minimum tear mN		Minimum tensile kN/m	
	Machine direction	Machine direction plus cross direction	Cross direction	Machine direction plus cross direction
60	700	1510	1.9	6
70	830	1790	2.3	7.2
80	965	2070	2.8	8.3
100	1230	2635	3.7	10.6
115	1425	3060	4.4	12.3

3. For the purposes of subheading No.4805.11, “semi-chemical fluting paper” means paper, in rolls, of which not less than 65% by weight of the total fibre content consists of unbleached hardwood fibres obtained bya combination of mechanical and chemical pulping processes, and having a CMT 30 (Corrugated Medium Test with 30 minutes of conditioning) crush resistance exceeding 1.8 newtons/g/m^2 at 50% relative humidity, at 23℃.

4. Subheading 4805.12 covers paper, in rolls, made mainly of straw pulp obtained by acombination of mechanical and chemical processes, weighing 130g/m^2 or more, and having a CMT30 (Corrugated Medium Test with 30 minutes of conditioning) crush resistance exceeding 1.4 newtons/g/m^2 at 50% relative humidity, at 23℃.

5. Subheadings 4805.24 and 4805.25 cover paper and paperboard made wholly or mainly of pulp of recovered (waste and scrap) paper or paperboard. Testliner may also have a surface layer of dyed paper or of paper made of bleached or unbleached non- recovered pulp. These products have a Mullen burst index of not less than 2kPa • m^2 /g.

6. For the purposes of subheading No.4805.30, “sulphite wrapping paper” means machine-glazed paper, of which more than 40% by weight of the total fibre content consists of wood fibres obtained by the chemical sulpohite process, having an ash content not exceeding 8% and having a Mullen burst index of not less than 1.47kPa • m^2 /g.

7. For the purposes of subheading No.4810.22, “lightweight coated paper” means paper, coated on both sides, of a total weight not exceeding 72g/m^2, with a coating weight not exceeding 15g/m^2 per side, on a base of which not less than 50% by weight of the total fibre content consists of wood fibres obtained by a mechanical process.

序号 No.	税则号列 Tariff Line	中文货品名称 Article Description in Chinese	最惠国税率 MFN(%)	协定税率 Agreement(%)	特惠税率 SP(%)	普通税率 Gen(%)	英文货品名称 Article Description
	48.01	成卷或成张的新闻纸					**Newsprint, in rolls or sheets**
3467	4801.0000	成卷或成张的新闻纸	5			30	Newsprint, in rolls or sheets
	48.02	书写、印刷或类似用途的未经涂布的纸及纸板、未打孔的穿孔卡片纸及穿孔纸带纸、成卷或成张矩形（包括正方形），任何尺寸，但税目48.01或48.03的纸除外;手工制纸及纸板:					**Uncoated paper and paperboard, of a kind used for writing, printing or other graphic purposes, and non-perforated punchcards and punch-tape paper, in rolls or rectangular (including square) sheets, of any size, other than paper of heading 4801 or 4803; handmade paper and paperboard:**
		-手工制纸及纸板:					-Handmade paper and paperboard:
3468	4802.1010	---宣纸	7.5			70	---Xuan paper
3469	4802.1090	---其他	7.5			70	---Other

序号 No.	税则号列 Tariff Line	中文货品名称 Article Description in Chinese	最惠国税率 MFN(%)	协定税率 Agreement(%)	特惠税率 SP(%)	普通税率 Gen(%)	英文货品名称 Article Description
		-光敏、热敏、电敏纸及纸板的原纸和原纸板：					-Paper and paperboard of a kind used as a base for photosensitive, heat-sensitive or electrosensitive paper or paperboard:
3470	4802.2010	---照相原纸	7.5Δ5	0 香港HK	0 受惠国$_2$LD$_2$	40	---Photo poper bese
3471	4802.2090	---其他	7.5	0 香港HK	0 受惠国$_2$LD$_2$	40	---Other
3472	4802.4000	-壁纸原纸	7.5	0 香港HK	0 受惠国$_2$LD$_2$	40	-Wallpaper base
		-其他纸及纸板，不含用机械或化学—机械方法制得的纤维或所含前述纤维不超过全部纤维重量的10%：					-Other paper and paperboard, not containing fibres obtained by a mechanical or chemi-mechanical process or of which not more than 10 % by weight of the total fibre content consists of such fibres:
3473	4802.5400	--每平方米重量小于40克	7.5	0 香港HK	0 受惠国$_2$LD$_2$	30	--Weighing less than 40g/m^2
3474	4802.5500	--每平方米重量在40克及以上，但不超过150克，成卷	5	0 香港HK	0 受惠国$_2$LD$_2$	30	--Weighing 40g/m^2 or more but not more than 150g/m^2, in rolls
3475	4802.5600	--每平方米重量在40克及以上，但不超过150克，一边不越过435毫米，另一边不超过297毫米（以未折叠计）成张的	5	0 香港HK	0 受惠国$_2$LD$_2$	30	--Weighing 40g/m^2 or more but not more than 150g/m^2, in sheets with one side not exceeding 435mm and the other side not exceeding 297mm in the unfolded state
3476	4802.5700	--其他，每平方米重量在40克及以上，但不超过150克	5	0 香港HK	0 受惠国$_2$LD$_2$	30	--Other, weighing 40g/m^2 or more but not more than 150g/m^2
3477	4802.5800	--每平方米重量超过150克	5	0 香港HK	0 受惠国$_2$LD$_2$	30	--Weighing more than 150g/m^2
		-其他纸及纸板，所含用机械或化学—机械方法制得的纤维超过全部纤维重量的10%：					-Other paper and paperboard, of which more than 10% by weight of the total fibre content consists of fibres obtained by a mechanical or chemi-mechanical process:
		--成卷的：					--In rolls:
3478	4802.6110	---新闻纸	7.5			30	---Newsprint
3479	4802.6190	---其他	5	0 香港HK	0 受惠国$_2$LD$_2$	30	---Other
3480	4802.6200	--成张的，一边不超过435毫米，另一边不超过297毫米（以未折叠计）	5	0 香港HK	0 受惠国$_2$LD$_2$	30	--In sheets with one side not exceeding 435mm and the other side not exceeding 297mm in the unfolded state
		--其他：					--Other:
3481	4802.6910	---新闻纸	7.5			30	---Newsprint
3482	4802.6990	---其他	5	0 香港HK	0 受惠国$_2$LD$_2$	30	---Other
	48.03	**卫生纸、面巾纸、餐巾纸以及家庭或卫生用的类似纸、纤维素絮纸和纤维素纤维网纸，不论是否起纹、压花、打孔、染面、饰面或印花，成卷或成张的**					**Toilet or facial tissue stock, towel or napkin stock and similar paper of a kind used for household or sanitary purposes, cellulose wadding and webs of cellulose fibres, whether or not creped, crinkled, embossed, perforated, surface-coloured, surface-decorated or printed, in rolls or sheets**
3483	4803.0000	卫生纸、面巾纸、餐巾纸以及家庭或卫生用的类似纸、纤维素絮纸和纤维素纤维网纸，不论是否起纹、压花、打孔、染面、饰面或印花，成卷或成张的	7.5			40	Toilet or facial tissue stock, towel or napkin stock and similar paper of a kind used for household or sanitary purposes, cellulose wadding and webs of cellulose fibres, whether or not creped, crinkled, embossed, perforated, surface-coloured, surface-decorated or printed, in rolls or sheets

序号 No.	税则号列 Tariff Line	中文货品名称 Article Description in Chinese	最惠国税率 MFN(%)	协定税率 Agreement(%)	特惠税率 SP(%)	普通税率 Gen(%)	英文货品名称 Article Description
	48.04	**成卷或成张的未经涂布的牛皮纸及纸板，但不包括税号48.02或48.03的货品：**					**Uncoated kraft paper and paperboard, in rolls or sheets, other than that of heading 4802 or 4803:**
		-牛皮挂面纸：					-Kraftliner:
3484	4804.1100	--未漂白	5			30	--Unbleached
3485	4804.1900	--其他	5			30	--Other
		-袋用牛皮纸：					-Sack kraft paper:
3486	4804.2100	--未漂白	5			30	--Unbleached
3487	4804.2900	--其他	5			30	--Other
		-其他牛皮纸及纸板，每平方米重量不超过150克：					-Other kraft paper and paperboard weighing 150 g/m^2 or less:
3488	4804.3100	--未漂白	2			30	--Unbleached
3489	4804.3900	--其他	2			30	--Other
		-其他牛皮纸及纸板，每平方米重量超过150克，但小于225克：					-Other kraft paper and paperboard weighing more than $150g/m^2$ but less than $225g/m^2$:
3490	4804.4100	--未漂白	2			30	--Unbleached
3491	4804.4200	--本体均匀漂白，所含用化学方法制得的木纤维超过全部纤维重量的95%	5			30	--Bleached uniformly throughout the mass and of which more than 95% by weight of the total fibre content consists of wood fibres obtained by a chemical process
3492	4804.4900	--其他	2			30	--Other
		-其他牛皮纸及纸板，每平方米重量在225克及以上：					-Other kraft paper and paperboard weighing $225g/m^2$ or more:
3493	4804.5100	--未漂白	2			30	--Unbleached
3494	4804.5200	--本体均匀漂白，所含用化学方法制得的木纤维超过全部纤维重量的95%	5			30	--Bleached uniformly throughout the mass and of which more than 95% by weight of the total fibre content consists of wood fibres obtained by a chemical process
3495	4804.5900	--其他	2			30	--Other
	48.05	**成卷或成张的其他未经涂布的纸及纸板，加工程度不超过本章注释三所列范围：**					**Other uncoated paper and paperboard, in rolls or sheets, not further worked or processed than as specified in note 3 to this chapter:**
		-瓦楞原纸：					-Fluting paper:
3496	4805.1100	--半化学的瓦楞原纸	7.5	0 香港HK	0 受惠国$_2$LD$_2$	30	--Semi-chemical fluting paper
3497	4805.1200	--草浆瓦楞原纸	7.5	0 香港HK	0 受惠国$_2$LD$_2$	30	--Straw fluting paper
3498	4805.1900	--其他	7.5	0 香港HK	0 受惠国$_2$LD$_2$	30	--Other
		-强韧箱纸板（再生挂面纸板）：					-Testliner (recycled liner board) :
3499	4805.2400	--每平方米重量在150克及以下	7.5	0 香港HK	0 受惠国$_2$LD$_2$	30	--Weighing $150g/m^2$ or less
3500	4805.2500	--每平方米重量超过150克	7.5	0 香港HK	0 受惠国$_2$LD$_2$	30	--Weighing more than $150g/m^2$
3501	4805.3000	-亚硫酸盐包装纸	7.5			30	-Sulphite wrapping paper
3502	4805.4000	-滤纸及纸板	7.5			30	-Filter paper and paperboard
3503	4805.5000	-毡纸及纸板	7.5			30	-Felt paper and paperboard
		-其他：					-Other:
		--每平方米重量在150克及以下：					--Weighing $150g/m^2$ or less:
3504	4805.9110	---电解电容器原纸	7.5	0 香港HK	0 受惠国$_2$LD$_2$	30	---Paper for electrolytic capacitor
3505	4805.9190	---其他	7.5	0 香港HK	0 受惠国$_2$LD$_2$	30	---Other
3506	4805.9200	--每平方米重量超过150克，但小于225克	7.5			30	--Weighing more than $150g/m^2$ but less than $225g/m^2$
3507	4805.9300	--每平方米重量在225克及以上	7.5	0 香港HK	0 受惠国$_2$LD$_2$	30	--Weighing $225g/m^2$ or more

序号 No.	税则号列 Tariff Line	中文货品名称 Article Description in Chinese	最惠国税率 MFN(%)	协定税率 Agreement(%)	特惠税率 SP(%)	普通税率 Gen(%)	英文货品名称 Article Description
	48.06	**成卷或成张的植物羊皮纸、防油纸、描图纸、半透明纸及其他高光泽透明或半透明纸：**					**Vegetable parchment, greaseproof papers, tracing papers and glassine and other glazed transparent or translucent papers, in rolls or sheets:**
3508	4806.1000	-植物羊皮纸	7.5			40	-Vegetable parchment
3509	4806.2000	-防油纸	7.5			40	-Greaseproof papers
3510	4806.3000	-描图纸	7.5			30	-Tracing papers
3511	4806.4000	-高光泽透明或半透明纸	7.5Δ5			40	-Glassine and other glazed transparent or translucent papers
	48.07	**成卷或成张的复合纸及纸板（用粘合剂粘合各层纸或纸板制成），未经表面涂布或未浸渍，不论内层是否有加强材料**					**Composite paper and paperboard (made by sticking flat layers of paper or paperboard together with an adhesive) , not surface-coated or impregnated, whether or not internally reinforced, in rolls or sheets**
3512	4807.0000	成卷或成张的复合纸及纸板（用粘合剂粘合各层纸或纸板制成），未经表面涂布或未浸渍，不论内层是否有加强材料	7.5Δ5			40	Composite paper and paperboard (made by sticking flat layers of paper or paperboard together with an adhesive) , not surface-coated or impregnated, whether or not internally reinforced, in rolls or sheets.
	48.08	**成卷或成张的瓦楞纸及纸板（不论是否与平面纸胶合）、皱纹纸及纸板、压纹纸及纸板、穿孔纸及纸板，但税号48.03的纸除外：**					**Paper and paperboard, corrugated (with or without glued flat surface sheets) , creped, crinkled, embossed or perforated, in rolls or sheets, other than paper of the kind described in heading 4803:**
3513	4808.1000	-瓦楞纸及纸板，不论是否穿孔	7.5	5.4 瑞士CH,新西兰NZ		30	-Corrugated paper and paperboard, whether or not perforated
3514	4808.4000	-皱纹牛皮纸，不论是否压花或穿孔	7.5			40	-Kraft paper, creped or crinkled, whether or not embossed or perforated
3515	4808.9000	-其他	7.5			40	-Other
	48.09	**复写纸、自印复写纸及其他拷贝或转印纸（包括涂布或浸渍的油印蜡纸或胶印版纸），不论是否印制，成卷或成张的：**					**Carbon paper, self-copy paper and other copying or transfer papers (including coated or impregnated paper for duplicator stencils or offset plates) , whether or not printed, in rolls or sheets:**
3516	4809.2000	-自印复写纸	7.5			40	-Self-copy paper
3517	4809.9000	-其他	7.5			40	-Other
	48.10	**成卷或成张矩形（包括正方形）的任何尺寸的单面或双面涂布高岭土或其他无机物质（不论是否加粘合剂）的纸及纸板，未涂布其他涂料，不论是否染面、饰面或印花：**					**Paper and paperboard, coated on one or both sides with kaolin (China clay) or other inorganic substances, with or without a binder, and with no other coating, whether or not surface-coloured, surface-decorated or printed, in rolls or rectangular (including square) sheets, of any size:**
		-书写、印刷或类似用途的纸及纸板，不含用机械或化学—机械方法制得的纤维或所含前述纤维不超过全部纤维重量的10%：					-Paper and paperboard of a kind used for writing, printing or other graphic purposes, not containing fibres obtained by a mechanical or chemi-mechanical process or of which not more than 10% by weight of the total fibre content consists of such fibres:
3518	4810.1300	--成卷的	5	0 香港HK	0 受惠国$_2$LD$_2$	40	--In rolls

序号 No.	税则号列 Tariff Line	中文货品名称 Article Description in Chinese	最惠国税率 MFN(%)	协定税率 Agreement(%)	特惠税率 SP(%)	普通税率 Gen(%)	英文货品名称 Article Description
3519	4810.1400	--成张的，一边不超过435毫米，另一边不超过297毫米（以未折叠计）	5	0 香港HK	0 受惠国$_2$LD$_2$	40	--In sheets with one side not exceeding 435mm and the other side not exceeding 297mm in the unfolded state
3520	4810.1900	--其他	5	0 香港HK	0 受惠国$_2$LD$_2$	40	--Other
		-书写、印刷或类似用途的纸及纸板，所含用机械或化学—机械方法制得的纤维超过全部纤维重量的10%：					-Paper and paperboard of a kind used for writing, printing or other graphic purposes, of which more than 10% by weight of the total fibre content consists of fibres obtained by a mechanical or chemi-mechanical process:
3521	4810.2200	--轻质涂布纸	5			40	--Light-weight coated paper
3522	4810.2900	--其他	5	0 香港HK	0 受惠国$_2$LD$_2$	40	--Other
		-牛皮纸及纸板，但书写、印刷或类似用途的除外：					-Kraft paper and paperboard, other than that of a kind used for writing, printing or other graphic purposes:
3523	4810.3100	--本体均匀漂白，所含用化学方法制得的木纤维超过全部纤维重量的95%，每平方米重量不超过150克	5	0 澳门MO,香港HK	0 受惠国$_2$LD$_2$	40	--Bleached uniformly throughout the mass and of which more than 95% by weight of the total fibre content consists of wood fibres obtained by a chemical process, and weighing 150g/m^2 or less
3524	4810.3200	--本体均匀漂白，所含用化学方法制得的木纤维超过全部纤维重量的95%，每平方米重量超过150克	5	0 澳门MO,香港HK	0 受惠国$_2$LD$_2$	40	--Bleached uniformly throughout the mass and of which more than 95% by weight of the total fibre content consists of wood fibres obtained by a chemical process, and weighing more than 150g/m^2
3525	4810.3900	--其他	5	0 澳门MO,香港HK	0 受惠国$_2$LD$_2$	40	--Other
		-其他纸及纸板：					-Other paper and paperboard:
3526	4810.9200	--多层的	5	0 澳门MO,香港HK	0 受惠国$_2$LD$_2$	40	--Multi-ply
3527	4810.9900	--其他	7.5	0 澳门MO,香港HK	0 受惠国$_2$LD$_2$	40	--Other
	48.11	**成卷或成张矩形（包括正方形）的任何尺寸的经涂布、浸渍、覆盖、染面、饰面或印花的纸、纸板、纤维素絮纸及纤维素纤维网纸，但税目48.03、48.09或48.10的货品除外：**					**Paper, paperboard, cellulose wadding and webs of cellulose fibres, coated, impregnated, covered, surface-coloured, surface-decorated or printed, in rolls or rectangular (including square) sheets, of any size, other than goods of the kind described in heading 4803, 4809 or 4810:**
3528	4811.1000	-焦油纸及纸板、沥青纸及纸板	7.5	0 澳门MO,香港HK	0 受惠国$_2$LD$_2$	40	-Tarred, bituminised or asphalted paper and paperboard
		-胶粘纸及纸板：					-Gummed or adhesive paper and paperboard:
3529	4811.4100	--自粘的	7.5	0 澳门MO,香港HK	0 受惠国$_2$LD$_2$	40	--Self-adhesive
3530	4811.4900	--其他	7.5	0 澳门MO,香港HK	0 受惠国$_2$LD$_2$	40	--Other
		-用塑料（不包括粘合剂）涂布、浸渍或覆盖的纸及纸板：					-Paper and paperboard, coated, impregnated or covered with plastics (excluding adhesives) :
		--漂白的，每平方米重量超过150克：					--Bleached, weighing more than 150g/m^2:
3531	4811.5110	---彩色相纸用双面涂塑纸	7.5Δ1	0 澳门MO,香港HK	0 受惠国$_2$LD$_2$	40	---Paper coated on both sides with plastics for colour photography
		---其他：					---Other:
3532	4811.5191	----纸塑铝复合材料	7.5	0 澳门MO,香港HK	0 受惠国$_2$LD$_2$	40	----Paper-aluminum-plastic materials

序号 No.	税则号列 Tariff Line	中文货品名称 Article Description in Chinese	最惠国税率 MFN(%)	协定税率 Agreement(%)		特惠税率 SP(%)		普通税率 Gen(%)	英文货品名称 Article Description
3533	4811.5199	----其他	7.5	0	澳门MO,香港HK	0	受惠国$_2$LD$_2$	40	----Other
		--其他:							--Other:
3534	4811.5910	---绝缘纸及纸板	7.5	0	澳门MO,香港HK	0	受惠国$_2$LD$_2$	30	---Insulating paper and paperboard
		---其他:							---Other:
3535	4811.5991	----镀铝的	7.5	0	澳门MO,香港HK	0	受惠国$_2$LD$_2$	40	----Aluminized
3536	4811.5999	----其他	7.5	0	澳门MO,香港HK	0	受惠国$_2$LD$_2$	40	----Other
		-用蜡、石蜡、硬脂精、油或甘油涂布、浸渍、覆盖的纸及纸板:							-Paper and paperboard, coated, impregnated or covered with wax, paraffin wax, stearin, oil or glycerol:
3537	4811.6010	---绝缘纸及纸板	7.5	0	澳门MO,香港HK	0	受惠国$_2$LD$_2$	30	---Insulating paper and paperboard
3538	4811.6090	---其他	7.5	0	澳门MO,香港HK	0	受惠国$_2$LD$_2$	40	---Other
3539	4811.9000	-其他纸、纸板、纤维素絮纸及纤维素纤维网纸	7.5	0	澳门MO,香港HK	0	受惠国$_2$LD$_2$	40	-Other paper, paperboard, cellulose wadding and webs of cellulose fibres
	48.12	**纸浆制的滤块、滤板及滤片**							**Filter blocks, slabs and plates, of paper pulp**
3540	4812.0000	纸浆制的滤块、滤板及滤片	7.5					40	Filter blocks, slabs and plates, of paper pulp
	48.13	**烟卷纸,不论是否切成一定尺寸、成小本或管状:**							**Cigarette paper, whether or not cut to size or in the form of booklets or tubes:**
3541	4813.1000	-成小本或管状	7.5					100	-In the form of booklets or tubes
3542	4813.2000	-宽度不超过5厘米成卷的	7.5					100	-In rolls of a width not exceeding 5cm
3543	4813.9000	-其他	7.5					100	-Other
	48.14	**壁纸及类似品;窗用透明纸:**							**Wallpaper and similar wallcoverings; window transparencies of paper:**
3544	4814.2000	-用塑料涂面或盖面的壁纸及类似品，起纹、压花、着色、印刷图案或经其他装饰	7.5					50	-Wallpaper and similar wall coverings, consisting of paper coated or covered, on the face side, with a grained, embossed, coloured, design-printed or otherwise decorated layer of plastics
3545	4814.9000	-其他	7.5					50	-Other
	48.16	**复写纸、自印复写纸及其他拷贝或转印纸(不包括税号48.09的纸)、油印蜡纸或胶印版纸,不论是否盒装:**							**Carbon paper, self-copy paper and other copying or transfer papers (other than those of heading 4809) , duplicator stencils and offset plates, of paper, whether or not put up in boxes:**
3546	4816.2000	-自印复写纸	7.5					70	-Self-copy paper
		-其他:							-Other:
3547	4816.9010	---热敏转印纸	7.5					40	---Heat transfer paper
3548	4816.9090	---其他	7.5					70	---Other
	48.17	**纸或纸板制的信封、封缄信片、素色明信片及通信卡片;纸或纸板制的盒子、袋子及夹子，内装各种纸制文具:**							**Envelopes, letter cards, plain postcards and correspondence cards, of paper or paperboard; boxes, pouches, wallets and writing compendiums, of paper or paperboard, containing an assortment of paper stationery:**
3549	4817.1000	-信封	7.5					80	-Envelopes
3550	4817.2000	-封缄信片、素色明信片及通信卡片	7.5					80	-Letter cards, plain postcards and correspondence cards
3551	4817.3000	-纸或纸板制的盒子、袋子及夹子，内装各种纸制文具	7.5					80	-Boxes, pouches, wallets and writing compendiums, of paper or paperboard, containing an assortment of paper stationery

序号 No.	税则号列 Tariff Line	中文货品名称 Article Description in Chinese	最惠国税率 MFN(%)	协定税率 Agreement(%)	特惠税率 SP(%)	普通税率 Gen(%)	英文货品名称 Article Description
	48.18	**卫生纸及类似纸，家庭或卫生用纤维素絮纸及纤维素纤维网纸，成卷宽度不超过36厘米或切成一定尺寸或形状的;纸浆、纸、纤维素絮纸或纤维素纤维网纸制的手帕、面巾、台布、餐巾、床单及类似的家庭、卫生或医院用品、衣服及衣着附件:**					**Toilet paper and similar paper, cellulose wadding or webs of cellulose fibres, of a kind used for household or sanitary purposes, in rolls of a width not exceeding 36 cm, or cut to size or shape; handkerchiefs, cleansing tissues, towels, tablecloths, serviettes, bedsheets and similar household, sanitary or hospital articles, articles of apparel and clothing accessories, of paper pulp, paper, cellulose wadding or webs of cellulose fibres:**
3552	4818.1000	-卫生纸	7.5			80	-Toilet paper
3553	4818.2000	-纸手帕及纸面巾	7.5			90	-Handkerchiefs, cleansing or facial tissues and towels
3554	4818.3000	-纸台布及纸餐巾	7.5			90	-Tablecloths and serviettes
3555	4818.5000	-衣服及衣着附件	7.5	0 冰岛IS,东盟AS,哥CR,秘鲁PE,新西兰NZ,智利CL 3 瑞士CH 4.5 澳AU,韩国KR 5 巴PK	0 受惠国LD	90	-Articles of apparel and clothing accessories
3556	4818.9000	-其他	7.5			90	-Other
	48.19	**纸、纸板、纤维素絮纸或纤维素纤维网纸制的箱、盒、匣、袋及其他包装容器;纸或纸板制的卷宗盒、信件盘及类似品，供办公室、商店及类似场所使用的:**					**Cartons, boxes, cases, bags and other packing containers, of paper, paperboard, cellulose wadding or webs of cellulose fibres; box files, letter trays, and similar articles, of paper or paperboard, of a kind used in offices, shops or the like:**
3557	4819.1000	-瓦楞纸或纸板制的箱、盒、匣	5	0 澳门MO,香港HK	0 受惠国$_2$LD$_2$	80	-Cartons, boxes and cases, of corrugated paper or paperboard
3558	4819.2000	-非瓦楞纸或纸板制的可折叠箱、盒、匣	5	0 澳门MO,香港HK	0 受惠国$_2$LD$_2$	80	-Folding cartons, boxes and cases, of non-corrugated paper or paperboard
3559	4819.3000	-底宽40厘米及以上的纸袋	7.5	0 冰岛IS,东盟AS,哥CR,秘鲁PE,新加坡SG,新西兰NZ,智利CL 3 瑞士CH 4.5 澳AU,韩国KR 5 巴PK	0 受惠国LD	80	-Sacks and bags, having a base of a width of 40cm or more
3560	4819.4000	-其他纸袋，包括锥形袋	7.5			80	-Other sacks and bags, including cones
3561	4819.5000	-其他包装容器，包括唱片套	7.5			80	-Other packing containers, including record sleeves
3562	4819.6000	-办公室、商店及类似场所使用的卷宗盒、信件盘、存储盒及类似品	7.5			80	-Box files, letter trays, storage boxes and similar articles, of a kind used in offices, shops or the like
	48.20	**纸或纸板制的登记本、账本、笔记本、定货本、收据本、信笺本、记事本、日记本及类似品、练习本、吸墨纸本、活动封面（活页及非活页）、文件夹、卷宗皮、多联商业表格纸、页间夹有复写纸的本及其他文具用品;纸或纸板制的样品簿、粘贴簿及书籍封面:**					**Registers, account books, note books, order books, receipt books, letter pads, memorandum pads, diaries and similar articles, exercise books, blotting-pads, binders (loose-leaf or other) , folders, file covers, manifold business forms, interleaved carbon sets and other articles of stationery, of paper or paperboard; albums for samples or for collections and book covers, of paper or paperboard:**

序号 No.	税则号列 Tariff Line	中文货品名称 Article Description in Chinese	最惠国税率 MFN(%)	协定税率 Agreement(%)	特惠税率 SP(%)	普通税率 Gen(%)	英文货品名称 Article Description
3563	4820.1000	-登记本、账本、笔记本、定货本、收据本、信笺本、记事本、日记本及类似品	7.5			80	-Registers, account books, note nooks, order books, receipt books, letter pads, memorandum pads, diaries and similar articles
3564	4820.2000	-练习本	7.5			80	-Exercise books
3565	4820.3000	-活动封面（书籍封面除外）、文件夹及卷宗皮	7.5			80	-Binders (other than book covers) , folders and file covers
3566	4820.4000	-多联商业表格纸、页间夹有复写纸的本	7.5	0 冰岛IS,东盟AS,哥CR,秘鲁PE,新西兰NZ,智利CL 3 瑞士CH 4.5 澳AU 5 巴PK 6 韩国KR	0 受惠国LD	80	-Manifold business forms and interleaved carbon sets
3567	4820.5000	-样品簿及粘贴簿	7.5			80	-Albums for samples or for collections
3568	4820.9000	-其他	7.5			80	-Other
	48.21	**纸或纸板制的各种标签，不论是否印制：**					**Paper or paperboard labels of all kinds, whether or not printed:**
3569	4821.1000	-印制	7.5	0 澳门MO,香港HK	0 受惠国$_2$LD$_2$	50	-Printed
3570	4821.9000	-其他	7.5			50	-Other
	48.22	**纸浆、纸或纸板（不论是否穿孔或硬化）制的筒管、卷轴、纡子及类似品：**					**Bobbins, spools, cops and similar supports, of paper pulp, paper or paperboard (whether or not perforated or hardened) :**
3571	4822.1000	-纺织纱线用	7.5			35	-Of a kind used for winding textile yarn
3572	4822.9000	-其他	7.5			70	-Other
	48.23	**切成一定尺寸或形状的其他纸、纸板、纤维素絮纸及纤维素纤维网纸;纸浆、纸、纸板、纤维素絮纸及纤维素纤维网纸制的其他物品：**					**Other paper, paperboard, cellulose wadding and webs of cellulose fibres, cut to size or shape; other articles of paper pulp, paper, paperboard, cellulose wadding or webs of cellulose fibres:**
3573	4823.2000	-滤纸及纸板	7.5			30	-Filter paper and paperboard
3574	4823.4000	-已印制的自动记录器用打印纸卷、纸张及纸盘	7.5			30	-Rolls, sheets and dials, printed for self-recording apparatus
		-纸或纸板制的盘、碟、盆、杯及类似品：					-Trays, dishes, plates, cups and the like, of paper or paperboard:
3575	4823.6100	--竹浆纸制	7.5	0 冰岛IS,东盟AS,哥CR,秘鲁PE,新西兰NZ,智利CL 3 瑞士CH 4.5 澳AU,韩国KR 5 巴PK	0 受惠国LD	90	--Of bamboo
		--其他：					--Other:
3576	4823.6910	---非木植物浆制	7.5	0 冰岛IS,东盟AS,哥CR,秘鲁PE,新西兰NZ,智利CL 3 瑞士CH 4.5 澳AU 5 巴PK 6 韩国KR	0 受惠国LD	90	---Other than those of wood
3577	4823.6990	---其他	7.5	0 冰岛IS,东盟AS,哥CR,秘鲁PE,新西兰NZ,智利CL 3 瑞士CH 4.5 澳AU 5 巴PK 6 韩国KR	0 受惠国LD	90	---Other
3578	4823.7000	-压制或模制纸浆制品	7.5			90	-Moulded or pressed articles of paper pulp
		-其他：					-Other:

序号 No.	税则号列 Tariff Line	中文货品名称 Article Description in Chinese	最惠国税率 MFN(%)	协定税率 Agreement(%)	特惠税率 SP(%)	普通税率 Gen(%)	英文货品名称 Article Description
3579	4823.9010	---以纸或纸板为底制成的铺地制品	7.5	3 瑞士CH,新西兰NZ 6.5 韩国KR		90	---Floor coverings on a base of paper or of paperboard
3580	4823.9020	---神纸及类似用品	7.5	0 冰岛IS,东盟AS,哥CR,秘鲁PE,新西兰NZ,智利CL 3 瑞士CH 4.5 澳AU,韩国KR 5 巴PK	0 受惠国LD	180	---Joss paper and the like
3581	4823.9030	---纸扇	7.5	0 冰岛IS,东盟AS,哥CR,秘鲁PE,新西兰NZ,智利CL 3 瑞士CH 4.5 澳AU,韩国KR 5 巴PK	0 受惠国LD	90	---Paper fans
3582	4823.9090	---其他	7.5	0 澳门MO,香港HK	0 受惠国$_2$LD$_2$	90	---Other

第四十九章
书籍、报纸、印刷图画及其他印刷品；手稿、打字稿及设计图纸

Chapter 49
Printed books, newspapers, pictures and other products of the printing industry; manuscripts, typescripts and plans

注释：

一、本章不包括：

（一）透明基的照相负片或正片（第三十七章）；

（二）立体地图、设计图表或地球仪、天体仪，不论是否印刷（税号 90.23）；

（三）第九十五章的扑克牌或其他物品；

（四）雕版画、印刷画、石印画的原本（税号 97.02），税号 97.04 的邮票、印花税票、纪念封、首日封、邮政信笺及类似品，以及第九十七章的超过一百年的古物或其他物品。

二、第四十九章所称“印刷”，也包括用胶版复印机、油印机印制，在自动数据处理设备控制下打印绘制，压印、冲印、感光复印、热敏复印或打字。

三、用纸以外材料装订成册的报纸、杂志和期刊，以及一期以上装订在同一封面里的成套报纸、杂志和期刊，应归入税号 49.01，不论是否有广告材料。

四、税号 49.01 还包括：

（一）附有说明文字，每页编有号数以便装订成一册或几册的整集印刷复制品，例如，美术作品、绘画；

（二）随同成册书籍的图画附刊；

（三）供装订书籍或小册子用的散页、集页或书帖形式的印刷品，已构成一部作品的全部或部分。

但没有说明文字的印刷图画或图解，不论是否散页或书帖形式，应归入税号 49.11。

五、除本章注释三另有规定的以外，税号 49.01 不包括主要作广告用的出版物（例如，小册子，散页印刷品、商业目录、同业公会出版的年鉴、旅游宣传品），这类出版物应归入税号 49.11。

六、税号 49.03 所称“儿童图画书”，是指以图画为主、文字为辅，供儿童阅览的书籍。

Notes:

1. This Chapter does not cover:

(a) Photographic negatives or positives on transparent bases (Chapter 37);

(b) Maps, plans or globes, in relief, whether or not printed (heading No.90.23);

(c) Playing cards or other goods of Chapter 95; or

(d) Original engravings, prints or lithographs (heading No.97.02), postage or revenue stamps, stamp-postmarks, first-day covers, postal stationery or the like of heading No.97.04, antiques of an age exceeding one hundred years or other articles of Chapter 97.

2. For the purposes of Chapter 49, the term “printed” also means reproduced by means of a duplicating machine, produced under the control of an automatic data processing machine, embossed, photographed, photocopied, thermo-copied or typewritten.

3. Newspapers, journals and periodicals which are bound otherwise than in paper, and sets of newspapers, journals or periodicals comprising more than one number under a single cover are to be classified in heading No.49.01, whether or not containing advertising material.

4. Heading No.49.01 also covers:

(a) A collection of printed reproductions of, for example, works of art or drawings, with a relative text, put up with numbered pages in a form suitable for binding into one or more volumes;

(b) A pictorial supplement accompanying, and subsidiary to, a bound volume; and

(c) Printed parts of books or booklets, in the form of assembled or separate sheets or signatures, constituting the whole or a part of a complete work and designed for binding.

However, printed pictures or illustrations not bearing a text, whether in the form of signatures or separate sheets, fall in heading No.49.11.

5. Subject to Note 3 to this Chapter, heading No.49.01 does not cover publications which are essentially devoted to advertising (for example, brochures, pamphlets, leaflets, trade catalogues, year books published by trade associations, tourist propaganda). Such publications are to be classified in heading No.49.11.

6. For the purposes of heading No.49.03, the expression “children’s picture books” means books for children in which the pictures form the principal interest and the text is subsidiary.

序号 No.	税则号列 Tariff Line	中文货品名称 Article Description in Chinese	最惠国税率 MFN(%)	协定税率 Agreement(%)	特惠税率 SP(%)	普通税率 Gen(%)	英文货品名称 Article Description
	49.01	书籍、小册子、散页印刷品及类似印刷品，不论是否单张：					**Printed books, brochures, leaflets and similar printed matter, whether or not in single sheets:**

序号 No.	税则号列 Tariff Line	中文货品名称 Article Description in Chinese	最惠国税率 MFN(%)	协定税率 Agreement(%)	特惠税率 SP(%)	普通税率 Gen(%)	英文货品名称 Article Description
3583	4901.1000	-单张的，不论是否折叠	0		0 受惠国LD	0	-In single sheets, whether or not folded
		-其他：					-Other:
3584	4901.9100	--字典或百科全书及其连续出版的分册	0		0 受惠国LD	0	--Dictionaries and encyclopaedias, and serial instalments thereof
3585	4901.9900	--其他	0		0 受惠国LD	0	--Other
	49.02	**报纸、杂志及期刊，不论有无插图或广告材料：**					**Newspapers, journals and periodicals, whether or not illustrated or containing advertising material:**
3586	4902.1000	-每周至少出版四次	0		0 受惠国LD	0	-Appearing at least four times a week
3587	4902.9000	-其他	0		0 受惠国LD	0	-Other
	49.03	**儿童图画书、绘画或涂色书**					**Children' s picture, drawing or colouring books**
3588	4903.0000	儿童图画书、绘画或涂色书	0		0 受惠国LD	0	Children' s picture, drawing or colouring books
	49.04	**乐谱原稿或印本，不论是否装订或印有插图**					**Music, printed or in manuscript, whether or not bound or illustrated**
3589	4904.0000	乐谱原稿或印本，不论是否装订或印有插图	0		0 受惠国LD	0	Music, printed or in manuscript, whether or not bound or illustrated
	49.05	**各种印刷的地图、水道图及类似图表，包括地图册、挂图、地形图及地球仪、天体仪：**					**Maps and hydrographic or similar charts of all kinds, including atlases, wall maps, topographical plans and globes, printed:**
3590	4905.1000	-地球仪、天体仪	0		0 受惠国LD	0	-Globes
		-其他：					-Other:
3591	4905.9100	--成册的	0		0 受惠国LD	0	--In book form
3592	4905.9900	--其他	0		0 受惠国LD	0	--Other
	49.06	**手绘的建筑、工程、工业、商业、地形或类似用途的设计图纸原稿;手稿;用感兴纸照相复印或用复写纸誊写的上述物品复制件**					**Plans and drawings for architectural, engineering, industrial, commercial, topographical or similar purposes, being originals drawn by hand; handwritten texts; photographic reproductions on sensitised paper and carbon copies of the foregoing**
3593	4906.0000	手绘的建筑、工程、工业、商业、地形或类似用途的设计图纸原稿;手稿;用感兴纸照相复印或用复写纸誊写的上述物品复制件	0		0 受惠国LD	0	Plans and drawings for architectural, engineering, industrial, commercial topographical or similar purposes, being originals drawn by hand; hand-written text; photographic reproductions on sensitized paper and carbon copies of the foregoing
	49.07	**在承认或将承认其面值的国家流通或新发行并且未经使用的邮票、印花税票及类似票证;印有邮票或印花税票的纸品;钞票;空白支票;股票、债券及类似所有权凭证：**					**Unused postage, revenue or similar stamps of current or new issue in the country in which they have, or will have, a recognised face value; stamp-impressed paper; banknotes; cheque forms; stock, share or bond certificates and similar documents of title:**
3594	4907.0010	---邮票	7.5	3 瑞士CH,新西兰NZ 6.5 韩国KR	0 受惠国$_1$LD$_1$	50	---Postage
3595	4907.0020	---钞票	0		0 受惠国LD	50	---Banknotes
3596	4907.0030	---证券凭证	0		0 受惠国LD	50	---Documents of title
3597	4907.0090	---其他	7.5	3 瑞士CH,新西兰NZ 6.5 韩国KR	0 受惠国$_1$LD$_1$	50	---Other

序号 No.	税则号列 Tariff Line	中文货品名称 Article Description in Chinese	最惠国税率 MFN(%)	协定税率 Agreement(%)	特惠税率 SP(%)	普通税率 Gen(%)	英文货品名称 Article Description
	ex49070090	特许权使用凭证（包括软件升级许可证、软件用户许可证等。但游戏软件升级许可证、游戏软件用户许可证除外）	Δ0				Certificate of Franchise license inculding software upgrade license, software user license, etc.Excluding game software upgrade license, software user license
	49.08	**转印贴花纸（移画印花法用图案纸）：**					**Transfers (decalcomanias) :**
3598	4908.1000	-釉转印贴花纸（移画印花法用图案纸）	7.5	3 瑞士CH,新西兰NZ 6.5 韩国KR	0 受惠国$_1$LD$_1$	50	-Transfers (decalcomanias) , vitrifiable
3599	4908.9000	-其他	7.5	0 香港HK 3 瑞士CH,新西兰NZ 6.5 韩国KR	0 受惠国$_1$LD$_1$	50	-Other
	49.09	**印刷或有图画的明信片；印有个人问候、祝贺、通告的卡片，不论是否有图画、带信封或饰边：**					**Printed or illustrated postcards; printed cards bearing personal greetings, messages or announcements, whether or not illustrated, with or without envelopes or trimmings:**
3600	4909.0010	---印刷或有图画的明信片	7.5	3 瑞士CH,新西兰NZ 6.5 韩国KR	0 受惠国$_1$LD$_1$	50	---Printed or illustrated postcards
3601	4909.0090	---其他	7.5	3 瑞士CH,新西兰NZ 6.5 韩国KR	0 受惠国$_1$LD$_1$	50	---Other
	49.10	**印刷的各种日历，包括日历芯**					**Calendars of any kind, printed, including calendar blocks**
3602	4910.0000	印刷的各种日历，包括日历芯	7.5	5.3 瑞士CH,新西兰NZ 6.5 韩国KR	0 受惠国LD	50	Calendars of any kind, printed, including calendar blocks
	49.11	**其他印刷品，包括印刷的图片及照片：**					**Other printed matter, including printed pictures and photographs:**
		-商业广告品、商品目录及类似印刷品：					-Trade advertising material, commercial catalogues and the like:
3603	4911.1010	---无商业价值的	0		0 受惠国LD	0	---No commercial value
3604	4911.1090	---其他	7.5	0 香港HK 5.3 瑞士CH,新西兰NZ 6.5 韩国KR	0 受惠国$_1$LD$_1$	50	---Other
		-其他：					-Other:
3605	4911.9100	--图片、设计图样及照片	7.5	3 瑞士CH,新西兰NZ 6.5 韩国KR	0 受惠国$_1$LD$_1$	50	--Pictures, designs and photographs
		--其他：					--Other:
3606	4911.9910	---纸质的	7.5	0 冰岛IS,香港HK 5.4 瑞士CH,新西兰NZ 6.5 韩国KR	0 受惠国$_1$LD$_1$	50	---Papery
3607	4911.9990	---其他	7.5	0 冰岛IS,香港HK 5.4 瑞士CH,新西兰NZ 6.5 韩国KR	0 受惠国$_1$LD$_1$	50	---Other

第十一类
纺织原料及纺织制品

注释:

一、本类不包括:

（一）制刷用的动物鬃、毛（税号 05.02）；马毛及废马毛（税号 05.11）；

（二）人发及人发制品（税号 05.01、67.03 或 67.04），但通常用于榨油机或类似机器的滤布除外（税号 59.11）；

（三）第十四章的棉短绒或其他植物材料；

（四）税号 25.24 的石棉、税号 68.12 或 68.13 的石棉制品或其他产品；

（五）税号 30.05 或 30.06 的物品；税号 33.06 的用于清洁牙缝的纱线（牙线），单独零售包装的；

（六）税号 37.01 至 37.04 的感光布；

（七）截面尺寸超过 1 毫米的塑料单丝和表面宽度超过 5 毫米的塑料扁条及类似品（例如人造草）（第三十九章），以及上述单丝或扁条的缏条、织物、篮筐或柳条编结品（第四十六章）；

（八）第三十九章的用塑料浸渍、涂布、包覆或层压的机织物、针织物或钩编织物、毡呢或无纺织物及其制品；

（九）第四十章的用橡胶浸渍、涂布、包覆或层压的机织物、针织物或钩编织物、毡呢或无纺织物及其制品；

（十）带毛皮张（第四十一章或第四十三章）、税号 43.03 或 43.04 的毛皮制品、人造毛皮及其制品；

（十一）税号 42.01 或 42.02 的用纺织材料制成的物品；

（十二）第四十八章的产品或物品（例如纤维素絮纸）；

（十三）第六十四章的鞋靴及其零件、护腿、裹腿及类似品；

（十四）第六十五章的发网、其他帽类及其零件；

（十五）第六十七章的货品；

（十六）涂有研磨料的纺织材料（税号 68.05）以及税号 68.15 的碳纤维及其制品；

（十七）玻璃纤维及其制品，但可见底布的玻璃线刺绣品除外（第七十章）；

（十八）第九十四章的物品（例如，家具、寝具、灯具及照明装置）；

（十九）第九十五章的物品（例如，玩具、游戏品、运动用品及网具）；

（二十）第九十六章的物品（例如，刷子、旅行用成套缝纫用具、拉链、打字机色带、卫生巾（护垫）及止血塞、婴儿尿布及尿布衬里）；或

（二十一）第九十七章的物品。

二、

（一）可归入第五十章至第五十五章及税号 58.09 或 59.02 的由两种或两种以上纺织材料混合制成的

SECTION XI
TEXTILES AND TEXTILE ARTICLES

Notes:

1.This Section does not cover:

(a) Animal brush-making bristles or hair (heading No.05.02); horsehair or horsehair waste (heading No. 05.11) ;

(b) Human hair or articles of human hair (heading No. 05.01, 67.03 or 67.04) , except straining cloth of a kind commonly used in oil presses or the like (heading No.59.11) ;

(c) Cotton linters or other vegetable materials of Chapter 14;

(d) Asbestos of heading No.25.24 or articles of asbestos or other products of heading No.68.12or68.13;

(e) Articles of heading No.30.05 or 30.06; yarn used to clean between the teeth (dental floss), in individual retail packages, of heading No.33.06;

(f) Sensitized textiles of headings No.37.01 to 37.04;

(g) Monofilament of which any cross-sectional dimension exceeds 1mm or strip or the like (for example, artificial straw) of an apparent width exceeding 5mm, of plastics (Chapter 39), or plaits or fabrics or other basketware or wickerwork of such monofi- lament or strip (Chapter 46) ;

(h) Woven, knitted or crocheted fabrics, felt or nonwovens, impregnated, coated, covered or laminated with plastics, or articles thereof, of Chapter 39;

(i) Woven, knitted or crocheted fabrics, felt or nonwovens, impregnated, coated, covered or laminated with rubber, or articles thereof, of Chapter 40;

(j) Hides or skins with their hair or wool on (Chapter41 or 43) or artcles of furskin, artificial fur or articles thereof, of heading No.43.03 or 43.04;

(k) Articles of textile materials of heading No.42.01 or 42.02;

(l) Products or articles of Chapter 48 (for example, cellulose wadding) ;

(m) Footwear or parts of footwear, gaiters or leggings or similar articles of Chapter64;

(n) Hair-nets or other headgear or parts thereof of Chapter 65;

(o) Goods of Chapter 67;

(p) Abrasive-coated textile material (Heading No.68.05) and also carbon fibres or articles of carbon fibres of heading No.68.15;

(q) Glass fibres or articles of glass fibres, other than embroi-dery with glass thread on a visible ground of fabric (Chapter 70) ;

(r) Articles of Chapter 94 (for example, furniture, bedding, lamps and lighting fittings) ;

(s) Articles of Chapter 95 (for example, toys games, sports requisites and nets) ;

(t) Articles of Chapter 96 (for example, brushes, travel sets for sewing, slide fasteners, typewriter ribbons, sanitary towels (pads) and tampons, napkins(diapers) and napkin liners for babies) ;or

(u) Articles of Chapter 97.

2.

(a) Goods classifiable in Chapters50 to 55or in heading No.58.09or59.02and of a mixture of two or more

货品，应按其中重量最大的那种纺织材料归类。

当没有一种纺织材料重量较大时，应按可归入的有关税号中最后一个税号所列的纺织材料归类。

（二）应用上述规定时：

1. 马毛粗松螺旋花线（税号51.10）和含金属纱线（税号56.05）均应作为一种单一的纺织材料，其重量应为它们在纱线中的合计重量；在机织物的归类中，金属线应作为一种纺织材料；

2. 在选择合适的税号时，应首先确定章，然后再确定该章的有关税号，至于不归入该章的其他材料可不予考虑；

3. 当归入第五十四章及第五十五章的货品与其他章的货品进行比较时，应将这两章作为一个单一的章对待；

4. 同一章或同一税号所列各种不同的纺织材料应作为单一的纺织材料对待。

（三）上述（一）、（二）两款规定亦适用于以下注释三、四、五或六所述纱线。

三、

（一）本类的纱线（单纱、多股纱线或缆线）除下列（二）款另有规定的以外，凡符合以下规格的应作为“线、绳、索、缆”：

1. 丝或绢丝纱线，细度在20000分特以上；

2. 化学纤维纱线（包括第五十四章的用两根及以上单丝纺成的纱线），细度在10000分特以上；

3. 大麻或亚麻纱线：

（1）加光或上光的，细度在1429分特及以上；

（2）未加光或上光的，细度在20000分特以上；

4. 三股或三股以上的椰壳纤维纱线；

5. 其他植物纤维纱线，细度在20000分特以上；

6. 用金属线加强的纱线。

（二）下列各项不按上述（一）款规定办理：

1. 羊毛或其他动物毛纱线及纸纱线，但用金属线加强的纱线除外；

2. 第五十五章的化学纤维长丝丝束以及第五十四章的未加捻或捻度每米少于5转的复丝纱线；

3. 税号50.06的蚕胶丝及第五十四章的单丝；

4. 税号56.05的含金属纱线；但用金属线加强的纱线按上述（一）款6项规定办理；

textile materials are to be classified as if consisting wholly of that one textile material which predominates by weight over any other single textile material.

When no one textile material predominates by weight, the goods are to be classified as if consisting wholly of that one textile material which is covered by the heading which occurs last in numerical order among those which equally merit consideration.

(b) For the purposes of the above rule:

(1) Gimped horsehair yarn (heading No.51.10) and metallized yarn (heading No.56.05) are to be treated as a single textile material the weight of which is to be taken as the aggregate of the weights of its components; for the classification of woven fabrics, metal thread is to be regarded as a textile material;

(2) The choice of appropriate heading shall be effected by determining first the Chapter and then the applicable heading within that Chapter, disregarding any materials not classified in that Chapter;

(3) When both Chapters 54 and 55 are involved with any other Chapter, Chapters 54and55are to be treated as a single Chapter;

(4) Where a Chapter or a heading refers to goods of different textile materials, such materials are to be treated as a single textile material.

(c) The provisions of paragraphs (A) and (B) above apply also to the yarns referred to in Notes3, 4, 5 or 6 below.

3.

(A) For the purposes of this Section, and subject to the exceptions in paragraph(B) below, yarns (single, multiple (folded) or cabled) of the following descriptions are to be treated as “twine, cordage, ropes and cables”:

(a) Of silk or waste silk, measuring more than 20000decitex;

(b) Of man-made fibres (including yarn of two or more monofilaments of Chapter 54), measuring more than10000 decitex;

(c) Of true hemp or flax:

(i) Polished or glazed, measuring 1429 decitex or more; or

(ii) Not polished or glzed, measuring more than 20000 decitex;

(d) Of coir, consisting of three or more plies;

(e) Of other vegetable fibres, measuring more than20000 decitex, or

(f) Reinforced with metal thread.

(B) Exceptions:

(a) Yarn of wool or other animal hair and paper yarn, other than yarn, rein forced with metal thread;

(b) Man-made filament tow of Chapter 55 and multifilament yarn without twist or with a twist of less than5turns per metre of Chapter54;

(c) Silk worm gut of heading No.50.06, and monofilaments of Chapter 54;

(d) Metallized yarn of Heading No.56.05; yarn reinforced with metal thread is subject to para-

5. 税号 56.06 的绳绒线、粗松螺旋花线及纵行起圈纱线。

四、

（一）除下列（二）款另有规定的以外，第五十章、第五十一章、第五十二章、第五十四章和第五十五章所称“供零售用”纱线，是指以下列方式包装的纱线（单纱、股纱线或缆线）：

1. 绕于纸板、线轴、纱管或类似芯子上，其重量（含线芯）符合下列规定：

（1）丝、绢丝或化学纤维长丝纱线，不超过 85 克；

（2）其他纱线，不超过 125 克。

2. 绕成团、绞或束，其重量符合下列规定：

（1）细度在 3000 分特以下的化学纤维长丝纱线，丝或绢丝纱线，不超过 85 克；

（2）细度在 2000 分特以下的任何其他纱线，不超过 125 克；

（3）其他纱线，不超过 500 克。

3. 绕成绞或束，每绞或每束中有若干用线分开的小绞或小束，每小绞或小束的重量相等，并且符合下列规定：

（1）丝、绢丝或化学纤维长丝纱线，不超过 85 克；

（2）其他纱线，不超过 125 克。

（二）下列各项不按上述（一）款规定办理：

1. 各种纺织材料制的单纱，但下列两种除外：

（1）未漂白的羊毛或动物细毛单纱；

（2）漂白、染色或印色的羊毛或动物细毛单纱，细度在 5000 分特以上。

2. 未漂白的多股纱线或缆线：

（1）丝或绢丝制的，不论何种包装；

（2）除羊毛或动物细毛外其他纺织材料制，成绞或成束的。

3. 漂白、染色或印色丝或绢丝制的多股纱线或缆线，细度在 133 分特及以下；

4. 任何纺织材料制的单纱、多股纱线或缆线：

（1）交叉绕成绞或束的；

（2）绕于纱芯上或以其他方式卷绕，明显用于纺织工业的（例如，绕于纱管、加捻管、纬纱管、锥形筒管或锭子上的或者绕成蚕茧状以供绣花机使用的纱线）。

五、税号 52.04、54.01 及 55.08 所称“缝纫线”，是指下列多股纱线或缆线：

（一）绕于芯子（例如，线轴、纱管）上，重量（包括纱芯）不超过 1000 克；

（二）作为缝纫线上过浆的；

（三）终捻为反手（Z）捻的。

六、本类所称“高强力纱”，是指断裂强度大于下列标准的纱线：

graph (A) (f) above; and

(e) Chenille, yarn, gimped yarn and loop wale-yarn of heading No.56.06.

4.

(A) For the purposes of Chapters 50, 51, 52, 54 and 55, the expression “put up for retail sale” in relation to yarn means, subject to the exceptions in paragraph(B) below, yarn (single, multiple (folded) or cabled) put up:

(a) On cards, reels, tubes or similar supports, of a weight (including support) not exceeding:

(i) 85g in the case of silk, waste silk or manmade filament yarn; or

(ii) 125g in other cases;

(b) In balls, hanks or skeins of a weight not exceeding:

(i) 85g in the case of man-made filament yarn of less than 3000 decitex, silk or silk waste;

(ii) 125g in the case of all other yarns of less than 2000 decitex;or

(iii) 500g in other cases.

(c) In hanks or skeins comprising several smaller hanks or skeins separated by dividing threads which render them independent one of the other, each of uniform weight not exceeding:

(i) 85g in the case of silk, waste silk or manmade filament yarn;or

(ii) 125g in other cases.

(B) Exceptions:

(a) Single yarn of any textile material, except:

(i) Single yarn of wool or fine animal hair, unbleached; and;

(ii) Single yarn of wool or fine animal hair, bleached, dyed or printed, measuring more than5000decitex;

(b) Multiple (folded) or cabled yarn, unbleached:

(i) Of silk or waste silk, however put up; or

(ii) Of other textile material except wool or fine animal hair, in hanks or skeins;

(c) Multiple (folded) or cabled yarn of silk or waste silk, bleached, dyed or printed, measuring 133 decitex or less; and

(d) Single, multiple (folded) or cabled yarn of any textile material:

(i) In cross-reeled hanks or skeins;or

(ii) Put up on supports or in some other manner indicating its use in the textile industry (for example, on cops, twisting mill tubes, pirns, conical bobbins or spindles, or reeled in the form of cocoons for embroidery looms) .

5. For the purposes of headings Nos.52.04, 54.01 and 55.08 the expression “sewing thread” means multiple (folded) or cabled yarn:

(a) Put up on supports (for example, reels, tubes) of a weight (including support) not exceeding 1000g;

(b) Dressed for use as sewing thread; and

(c) With a final “Z” twist.

6. For the purposes of this Section, the expression “high tenacity yarn” means yarn having a tenacity, expressed in cN/tex

尼龙、其他聚酰胺或聚酯制的单纱——60 厘牛顿/特克斯;
尼龙、其他聚酰胺或聚酯制的多股纱线或缆线——53 厘牛顿/特克斯;
粘胶纤维制的单纱、多股纱线或缆线——27 厘牛顿/特克斯。

七、本类所称“制成的”,是指:

(一)裁剪成除正方形或长方形以外的其他形状的;

(二)呈制成状态,无需缝纫或其他进一步加工(或仅需剪断分隔联线)即可使用的(例如,某些抹布、毛巾、台布、方披巾、毯子);

(三)裁剪成一定尺寸,至少有一边为带有可见的锥形或压平形的热封边,其余各边经本注释其他各项所述加工,但不包括为防止剪边脱纱而用热切法或其他简单方法处理的织物;

(四)已缝边或滚边,或者在任一边带有结制的流苏,但不包括为防止剪边脱纱而锁边或用其他简单方法处理的织物;

(五)裁剪成一定尺寸并经抽纱加工的;

(六)缝合、胶合或用其他方法拼合而成的(将两段或两段以上同样料子的织物首尾连接而成的匹头,以及由两层或两层以上的织物,不论中间有无胎料,层迭而成的匹头除外);

(七)针织或钩编成一定形状,不论进口或出口时是单件还是以若干件相连成幅的。

八、对于第五十章至第六十章:

(一)第五十章至第五十五章和第六十章,以及除条文另有规定以外的第五十六章至第五十九章,不适用于上述注释七所规定的制成货品;

(二)第五十章至第五十五章及第六十章不包括第五十六章至第五十九章的货品。

九、第五十章至第五十五章的机织物包括由若干层平行纱线以锐角或直角相互层迭,在纱线交叉点用粘合剂或以热粘合法粘合而成的织物。

十、用纺织材料和橡胶线制成的弹性产品归入本类。

十一、本类所称“浸渍”,包括“浸泡”。

十二、本类所称“聚酰胺”,包括“芳族聚酰胺”。

十三、本类及本目录所称“弹性纱线”是指合成纤维纺织材料制成的长丝纱线(包括单丝,变形纱线除外)。这些纱线可拉伸至原长的三倍而不断裂,并可在拉伸至原长两倍后五分钟内回复到不超过原长度的一倍半。

(centinewtons per tex), greater than the following:

Single yarn of nylon or other polyamides, or of polyesters 60c N/tex;
Multiple (folded) or cabled yarn of nylon or other polyamides, or of polyesters 53cN/tex;
Single, multiple (folded) or cabled yarn of viscose rayon 27c N/tex.

7. For the purposes of this Section, the expression “made up” means:

(a) Cut otherwise than into squares or rectangles;

(b) Produced in the finished state, ready for use (or merely needing separation by cutting dividing threads) without sewing or other working (for example, certain dusters, towels, table cloths, scarf squares, blankets);

(c) Cut to size and with at least one heat-sealed edge with a visibly tapered orcompressed border and the other edges treated as described in any othersubparagraph of this Note, but excluding fabrics the cut edges of which havebeen prevented from unravelling by hot cutting or by other simple means;

(d) Hemmed or with rolled edges, or with a knotted fringe at any of the edges, but excluding fabrics the cut deges of which have been prevented from unravelling by whipping or by other simple means;

(e) Cut to size and having undergone a process of drawn thread work;

(f) Assembled by sewing, gumming or otherwise (other than piece goods consisting of two or more lengths of identical material joined end to end and piece goods composed of two or more textiles assembled in layers, whether or not padded);

(g) Knitted or crocheted to shape, whether presented as separate items or in the form of a number of items in the length.

8. For the purposes of Chapters50to60:

(a) Chapters 50 to 55 and 60 and, except where the context otherwise requires, Chapters 56 to 59 do not apply to goods made up within the meaning of Note7 above; and;

(b) Chapters 50 to55 and 60 do not apply to goods of Chapters 56 to 59.

9. The woven fabrics of Chapters 50 to 55 include fabrics consisting of layers of parallel textile yarns superimposed on each other at acute or right angles. These layers are bonded at the intersections of the yarns by an adhesive or by thermal bonding;

10. Elastic products consisting of textile materials combined with rubber threads are classified in this Section.

11. For the purposes of this Section, the expression “impregnated” includes “dipped”.

12. For the purposes of this Section, the expression “polyamides” includes “aramides”.

13. For the purposes of this Section and, where applicable, throughout the nomenclature, the expression “elastomeric yarn” means filament yarn, including monofilament, of synthetic textile material, other than textured yarn, which does not break on being extended to three times

十四、除条文另有规定的以外，各种服装即使成套包装供零售用，也应按各自税号分别归类。本注释所称“纺织服装”，是指税号 61.01 至 61.14 及税号 62.01 至 62.11 所列的各种服装。

子目注释:

一、本类及本目录所用有关名词解释如下:

（一）未漂白纱线:

1. 带有纤维自然色泽并且未经漂染（不论是否整体染色）或印色的纱线;

2. 从回收纤维制得，色泽未定的纱线（本色纱）。

这种纱线可用无色浆料或易褪色染料（可轻易地用肥皂洗去）处理，如果是化学纤维纱线，则整体用消光剂（例如二氧化钛）进行处理。

（二）漂白纱线:

1. 经漂白加工、用漂白纤维制得或经染白（除条文另有规定的以外）（不论是否整体染色）及用白浆料处理的纱线;

2. 用未漂白纤维和漂白纤维混纺制得的纱线;

3. 用未漂白纱和漂白纱纺成多股纱线或缆线。

（三）着色（染色或印色）纱线:

1. 染成彩色（不论是否整体染色，但白色或易褪色除外）或印色的纱线，以及用染色或印色纤维纺制的纱线;

2. 用各色染色纤维混合纺制或用未漂白或漂白纤维与着色纤维混合制得的纱线（夹色纱或混色纱），以及用一种或几种颜色间隔印色而获得点纹印迹的纱线;

3. 用已经印色的纱条或粗纱纺制的纱线;

4. 用未漂白纱和漂白纱与着色纱纺成的多股纱线或缆线。

上述定义作相应调整后适用于第五十四章的单丝、扁条或类似产品。

（四）未漂白机织物:

用未漂白纱线织成后未经漂白、染色或印花的机织物。这类织物可用无色浆料或易褪色染料处理。

（五）漂白机织物:

its original length and which returns, after being extended to twice its original length, within a period of five minutes, to a length not greater than one and a half times its original length.

14. Unless the context otherwise requires, textile garments of different headings are to be classified in their own headings even if put up in sets for retail sale. For the purposes of this Note, the expression“textile garments” means garments of headings Nos.61.01 to 61.14 and heading Nos.62.01 to 62.11.

Subheading Notes:

1. In the Section , where applicable, throughout the Nomenclature, the following expressions have the meanings hereby assigned to them:

(a) Unbleached yarn

Yarn which:

(1) has the natural colour of its constituent fibres and has not been bleached, dyed (whether or not in the mass) or printed; or

(2) is of indeterminate colour (“grey yarn”) , manufactured from garnetted stock.

Such yarn may have been treated with a colourless dressing or fugitive dye (which disappears after simple washing with soap) and, in the case of man-made fibres, treated in the mass with delustring agent (for example, titanium dioxide) .

(b) Bleached yarn

Yarn which:

(1) has undergone a bleaching process, is made of bleached fibres or, unless the context otherwise requires, has been dyed white (whether or not in the mass) or treated with a white dressing;

(2) consists of a mixture of unbleached and bleached fibres;or

(3) is multiple (folded) or cabled and consists of unbleached and bleached yarns.

(c) Coloured (dyed or printed) yarn

Yarn which:

(1) is dyed (whether or not in the mass) other than white or in a fugitive colour, or printed, or made from dyed or printed fibres;

(2) consists of a mixture of dyed fibres of different colours or of a mixture of unbleached or bleached fibres with coloured fibres (marl or mixture yarns), or is printed in one or more colours at intervals to give the impression of dots;

(3) is obtained from slivers or rovings which have been printed; or

(4) is multiple (folded) or cabled and consists of unbleached or bleached yarn and coloured yarn.

The above definitions also apply, *mutatis mutandis*, to monofilament and to strip or the like of Chapter54.

(d) Unbleached woven fabric:

Woven fabric made from unbleached yarn and which has not been bleached, dyed or printed.Such fabric may have treated with a colourless dressing or a fugitive dye.

(e) Bleached woven fabric

Woven fabric which:

1. 经漂白、染白或用白浆料处理（除条文另有规定的以外）的成匹机织物；

2. 用漂白纱线织成的机织物；

3. 用未漂白纱线和漂白纱线织成的机织物；

（六）染色机织物：

1. 除条文另有规定的以外，染成白色以外的其他单一颜色或用白色以外的其他有色整理剂处理的成匹机织物；

2. 用单一颜色的着色纱线织成的机织物。

（七）色织机织物：

除印花机织物以外的下列机织物：

1. 用各种不同颜色纱线或同一颜色不同深浅（纤维的自然色彩除外）纱线织成的机织物；

2. 用未漂白或漂白与着色纱线织成的机织物；

3. 用夹色纱线或混色纱线织成的机织物。

不论何种情况，布边或布头的纱线均可忽略不计。

（八）印花机织物：

成匹印花的机织物，不论是否用各色纱线织成。用刷子或喷枪，经转印纸转印、植绒或蜡防印花等方法印成花纹图案的机织物亦可视为印花机织物。

上述各类纱线或织物如经丝光工艺处理并不影响其归类。上述（四）至（八）的定义在作必要修改后适用于针织或钩编织物。

（九）平纹组织：

每根纬纱在并排的经纱间上下交错而过，而每根经纱也在并排的纬纱间上下交错而过的织物组织。

二、

（一）含有两种或两种以上纺织材料的第五十六章至第六十三章的产品，应根据本类注释二对第五十章至第五十五章或税目 58.09 的此类纺织材料产品归类的规定来确定归类。

（二）运用本条规定时：

1. 应酌情考虑按归类总规则第三条来确定归类；

2. 对由底布和绒面或毛圈面构成的纺织品，在归类时可不考虑底布的属性；

3. 对税号 58.10 的刺绣品及其制品，归类时应只考虑底布的属性，但不见底布的刺绣品及其制品应根据绣线的属性确定归类。

(1) has been bleached or, unless the context otherwise requires, dyed white or treated with a white dressing, in the piece;

(2) consists of bleached yarn; or

(3) consists of unbleached and bleached yarn.

(f) Dyed woven fabric

Woven fabric which:

(1) is dyed a single uniform colour other than white (unless the context otherwise requires) or has been treated with a coloured finish other than white (unless the context otherwise requires), in the piece; or

(2) consists of coloured yarn of a single uniform colour.

(g) Woven fabric of yarns of different colours:

Woven fabric (other than printed woven fabric) which:

(1) consists of yarns of different colours or yarns of different shades of the same colour (other than the natural colour of the constituent fibres) ;

(2) consists of unbleached or bleached yarn and coloured yarn; or

(3) consists of marl or mixture yarns.

(In all cases, the yarn used in selvedges and piece ends is not taken into consideration.)

(h) Printed woven fabric:

Woven fabric which has been printed in the piece, whether or not made from yarns of differenent colours.

(The following are also regarded as printed woven fabrics: woven fabrics bearing designs made, for example, with a brush or spray gun, by means of transfer paper, by flocking or by the batik process.)

The process of mercerization does not affect the classification of yarns or fabrics withinthe above categories.

The definitions at (d) to (h) above apply, *mutatis mutandis*, or to knitted crocheted fabrics.

(i) Plain weave:

A fabric construction in which each yarn of the weft passes alternately over and under successive yarns of the warp and each yarn of the warp passes alternately over and under successive yarns of the weft.

2.

(a) Products of Chapters 56 to 63 containing two or more textile materials are to be regarded as consisting wholly of that textile material which would be selected under Note2to this Section for the classification of the product of Chapters 50 to 55 or of heading 58.09 consisting of the same textile materials.

(b) For the application of this rule:

(1) where appropriate, only the part which determines the classification under interpretative Rule3shall be taken into account;

(2) in the case of textile products consisting of a ground fabric and a pile or looped surface, no account shall be taken of the ground fabric;

(3) in the case of embroidery of heading No.58.10 and goods thereof, only the ground fabric shall be taken into account. However, embroidery without visible ground, and goods thereof, shall be classified with reference to the embroidering threads alone.

第五十章
蚕丝

Chapter 50
SILK

序号 No.	税则号列 Tariff Line	中文货品名称 Article Description in Chinese	最惠国税率 MFN(%)	协定税率 Agreement(%)	特惠税率 SP(%)	普通税率 Gen(%)	英文货品名称 Article Description
	50.01	**适于缫丝的蚕茧：**					**Silkworm cocoons suitable for reeling:**
3608	5001.0010	---适于缫丝的桑蚕茧	6	0 冰岛IS,东盟AS,哥CR,韩国KR,秘鲁PE,新西兰NZ,智利CL 2.4 瑞士CH 3.6 澳AU 5 巴PK	0 受惠国LD	70	---Bombyx mori cocoons (Mulberry feeding silk-worm cocoons)
3609	5001.0090	---其他	6	0 冰岛IS,东盟AS,哥CR,韩国KR,秘鲁PE,新西兰NZ,智利CL 2.4 瑞士CH 3.6 澳AU 5 巴PK	0 受惠国LD	70	---Other
	50.02	**生丝（未加捻）：**					**Raw silk (not thrown) :**
		---桑蚕丝：					---Steam filature silk:
3610	5002.0011	----厂丝	9	0 冰岛IS,东盟AS,哥CR,秘鲁PE,新西兰NZ,智利CL 3.6 瑞士CH 5 巴PK 5.4 澳AU,韩国KR	0 受惠国LD	80	----Plant reeled (filature silk)
3611	5002.0012	----土丝	9	0 冰岛IS,东盟AS,哥CR,秘鲁PE,新西兰NZ,智利CL 3.6 瑞士CH 5 巴PK 5.4 澳AU,韩国KR	0 受惠国LD	80	----Home reeled
3612	5002.0013	----双宫丝	9	0 冰岛IS,东盟AS,哥CR,秘鲁PE,新西兰NZ,智利CL 3.6 瑞士CH 5 巴PK 5.4 澳AU,韩国KR	0 受惠国LD	80	----Doupion
3613	5002.0019	----其他	9	0 冰岛IS,东盟AS,哥CR,秘鲁PE,新西兰NZ,智利CL 3.6 瑞士CH 5 巴PK 5.4 澳AU,韩国KR	0 受惠国LD	80	----Other
3614	5002.0020	---柞蚕丝	9	0 冰岛IS,东盟AS,哥CR,秘鲁PE,新西兰NZ,智利CL 3.6 瑞士CH 5 巴PK 5.4 澳AU,韩国KR	0 受惠国LD	80	---Tussah silk
3615	5002.0090	---其他	9	0 冰岛IS,东盟AS,哥CR,秘鲁PE,新西兰NZ,智利CL 3.6 瑞士CH 5 巴PK 5.4 澳AU,韩国KR	0 受惠国LD	80	---Other
	50.03	**废丝（包括不适于缫丝的蚕茧、废纱及回收纤维）：**					**Silk waste (including cocoons unsuitable for reeling, yarn waste and garnetted stock) :**
		---未梳：					---Not carded or combed:

序号 No.	税则号列 Tariff Line	中文货品名称 Article Description in Chinese	最惠国税率 MFN(%)	协定税率 Agreement(%)	特惠税率 SP(%)	普通税率 Gen(%)	英文货品名称 Article Description
3616	5003.0011	----下茧、茧衣、长吐、滞头	9	0 冰岛IS,东盟AS,哥CR,秘鲁PE,新西兰NZ,智利CL 3.6 瑞士CH 5 巴PK 5.4 澳AU,韩国KR	0 受惠国LD	70	----Inferior cocoon (cocoon unsuitable for reeling) , blaze, frison and frigon (knub from reeling)
3617	5003.0012	----回收纤维	9	0 冰岛IS,东盟AS,哥CR,秘鲁PE,新西兰NZ,智利CL 3.6 瑞士CH 5 巴PK 5.4 澳AU,韩国KR	0 受惠国LD	70	----Garnetted stock
3618	5003.0019	----其他	9	0 冰岛IS,东盟AS,哥CR,秘鲁PE,新西兰NZ,智利CL 3.6 瑞士CH 5 巴PK 5.4 澳AU,韩国KR	0 受惠国LD	70	----Other
		---其他:					---Other:
3619	5003.0091	----绵球	9	0 冰岛IS,东盟AS,哥CR,秘鲁PE,新西兰NZ,智利CL 3.6 瑞士CH 5 巴PK 5.4 澳AU,韩国KR	0 受惠国LD	70	----Silk tops
3620	5003.0099	----其他	9	0 冰岛IS,东盟AS,哥CR,秘鲁PE,新西兰NZ,智利CL 3.6 瑞士CH 5 巴PK 5.4 澳AU,韩国KR	0 受惠国LD	70	----Other
	50.04	**丝纱线(绢纺纱线除外),非供零售用**					**Silk yarn (other than yarn spun from silk waste) not put up for retail sale**
3621	5004.0000	丝纱线(绢纺纱线除外),非供零售用	6	0 澳门MO,冰岛IS,东盟AS,哥CR,韩国KR,秘鲁PE,新西兰NZ,智利CL 2.4 瑞士CH 3.6 澳AU 5 巴PK	0 受惠国LD	90	Silk yarn (other than yarn spun from silk waste) not put up for retail sale
	50.05	**绢纺纱线,非供零售用:**					**Yarn spun from silk waste, not put up for retail sale:**
3622	5005.0010	---细丝纱线	6	0 澳门MO,冰岛IS,东盟AS,哥CR,韩国KR,秘鲁PE,新西兰NZ,智利CL 2.4 瑞士CH 3.6 澳AU 5 巴PK	0 受惠国LD	90	---Spun from noil
3623	5005.0090	---其他	6	0 澳门MO,冰岛IS,东盟AS,哥CR,韩国KR,秘鲁PE,新西兰NZ,智利CL 2.4 瑞士CH 3.6 澳AU 5 巴PK	0 受惠国LD	90	---Other
	50.06	**丝纱线及绢纺纱线,供零售用;蚕胶丝**					**Silk yarn and yarn spun from silk waste, put up for retail sale; silkworm gut**
3624	5006.0000	丝纱线及绢纺纱线,供零售用;蚕胶丝	6	0 澳门MO,冰岛IS,东盟AS,哥CR,韩国KR,秘鲁PE,新西兰NZ,智利CL 2.4 瑞士CH 3.6 澳AU 5 巴PK	0 受惠国LD	100	Silk yarn and yarn spun from silk waste, put up for retail sale; silk-worm gut
	50.07	**丝或绢丝机织物:**					**Woven fabrics of silk or of silk waste:**
		-细丝机织物:					-Fabrics of noil silk:

序号 No.	税则号列 Tariff Line	中文货品名称 Article Description in Chinese	最惠国税率 MFN(%)	协定税率 Agreement(%)	特惠税率 SP(%)	普通税率 Gen(%)	英文货品名称 Article Description
3625	5007.1010	---未漂白(包括未练白或练白)或漂白	10	0 冰岛IS,东盟AS,哥CR,秘鲁PE,新西兰NZ,智利CL 4 瑞士CH 5 巴PK 6 澳AU,韩国KR	0 老挝LA,受惠国LD	130	---Unbleaded (unscoured or scoured) or bleached
3626	5007.1090	---其他	10	0 冰岛IS,东盟AS,哥CR,秘鲁PE,新西兰NZ,智利CL 4 瑞士CH 5 巴PK 6 澳AU,韩国KR	0 老挝LA,受惠国LD	130	---Other
		-其他机织物,按重量计丝或绢丝(细丝除外)含量在85%及以上:					-Other fabrics, containing 85% or more by weight of silk or of silk waste other than noil silk:
		---桑蚕丝机织物:					---Of Bombyx mori silk:
3627	5007.2011	----未漂白(包括未练白或练白)或漂白	10	0 冰岛IS,东盟AS,哥CR,秘鲁PE,新西兰NZ,智利CL 4 瑞士CH 5 巴PK 6 澳AU,韩国KR 9 亚太AP	0 老挝LA,受惠国LD	130	----Unbleached (unscoured or scoured) or bleached
3628	5007.2019	----其他	10	0 冰岛IS,东盟AS,哥CR,秘鲁PE,香港HK,新西兰NZ,智利CL 4 瑞士CH 5 巴PK 6 澳AU 8.6 韩国KR 9 亚太AP	0 老挝LA,受惠国LD	130	----Other
		---柞蚕丝机织物:					---Of tussah silk:
3629	5007.2021	----未漂白(包括未练白或练白)或漂白	10	0 冰岛IS,东盟AS,哥CR,秘鲁PE,新西兰NZ,智利CL 4 瑞士CH 5 巴PK 6 澳AU,韩国KR 9 亚太AP	0 老挝LA,受惠国LD	130	----Unbleached (unscoured or scoured) or bleached
3630	5007.2029	----其他	10	0 冰岛IS,东盟AS,哥CR,秘鲁PE,新西兰NZ,智利CL 4 瑞士CH 5 巴PK 6 澳AU,韩国KR 9 亚太AP	0 老挝LA,受惠国LD	130	----Other
		---绢丝机织物:					---Of silk waste other than noil silk:
3631	5007.2031	----未漂白(包括未练白或练白)或漂白	10	0 冰岛IS,东盟AS,哥CR,秘鲁PE,新西兰NZ,智利CL 4 瑞士CH 5 巴PK 6 澳AU,韩国KR 9 亚太AP	0 老挝LA,受惠国LD	130	----Unbleached (unscoured or scoured) or bleached
3632	5007.2039	----其他	10	0 冰岛IS,东盟AS,哥CR,秘鲁PE,新西兰NZ,智利CL 4 瑞士CH 5 巴PK 6 澳AU,韩国KR 9 亚太AP	0 老挝LA,受惠国LD	130	----Other

序号 No.	税则号列 Tariff Line	中文货品名称 Article Description in Chinese	最惠国税率 MFN(%)	协定税率 Agreement(%)	特惠税率 SP(%)	普通税率 Gen(%)	英文货品名称 Article Description
3633	5007.2090	---其他	10	0 冰岛IS,东盟AS,哥CR,秘鲁PE,新西兰NZ,智利CL 4 瑞士CH 5 巴PK 6 澳AU,韩国KR 9 亚太AP	0 老挝LA,受惠国LD	130	---Other
		-其他机织物:					-Other fabrics:
3634	5007.9010	---未漂白（包括未练白或练白）或漂白	10	0 冰岛IS,东盟AS,哥CR,秘鲁PE,新西兰NZ,智利CL 4 瑞士CH 5 巴PK 6 澳AU,韩国KR 8.5 亚太AP	0 老挝LA,受惠国LD	130	---Unbleached (unscoured or scoured) or bleached
3635	5007.9090	---其他	10	0 冰岛IS,东盟AS,哥CR,新西兰NZ,智利CL 3 秘鲁PE 4 瑞士CH 5 巴PK 6 澳AU,韩国KR 8.5 亚太AP	0 老挝LA,受惠国LD	130	---Other

第五十一章
羊毛、动物细毛或粗毛；
马毛纱线及其机织物

注释：

本目录所称：

一、“羊毛”，是指绵羊或羔羊身上长的天然纤维；

二、“动物细毛”，是指下列动物的毛:羊驼、美洲驼、驼马、骆驼（包括单峰骆驼）、牦牛、安哥拉山羊、西藏山羊、喀什米尔山羊及类似山羊（普通山羊除外）、家兔（包括安哥拉兔）、野兔、海狸、河狸鼠或麝鼠；

三、“动物粗毛”，是指以上未提及的其他动物的毛，但不包括制刷用鬃、毛（税目05.02）以及马毛（税目05.11）。

Chapter 51
Wool, fine or coarse animal hair; horsehair yarn and woven fabric

Note:

Throughout the Nomenclature:

1. “Wool” means the natural fibre grown by sheep or lambs;
2. “Fine animal hair” means the hair of alpaca, llama, vicuna, camel (including dromedary), yak, Angora, Tibetan, Kashmir or similar goats (but not common goats), rabbit (including Angora rabbit), hare, beaver, nutria or muskrat;
3. “Coarse animal hair” means the hair of animals not mentioned above, excluding brush-making hair and bristles (heading No.05.02) and horsehair (heading No.05.11).

序号 No.	税则号列 Tariff Line	中文货品名称 Article Description in Chinese	最惠国税率 MFN(%)	协定税率 Agreement(%)	特惠税率 SP(%)	普通税率 Gen(%)	英文货品名称 Article Description
	51.01	**未梳的羊毛：**					**Wool, not carded or combed:**
		-含脂羊毛，包括剪前水洗毛：					-Greasy, including fleece-washed wool:
3636	5101.1100	--剪羊毛	38①	② 澳AU,新西兰NZ 20 东盟AS		50	--Shorn wool
3637	5101.1900	--其他	38③	④ 澳AU,新西兰NZ 20 东盟AS		50	--Other
		-脱脂羊毛，未碳化：					-Degreased, not carbonised:
3638	5101.2100	--剪羊毛	38⑤	⑥ 澳AU,新西兰NZ 20 东盟AS		50	--Shorn wool
3639	5101.2900	--其他	38⑦	⑧ 澳AU,新西兰NZ 20 东盟AS		50	--Other
3640	5101.3000	-碳化羊毛	38⑨	⑩ 澳AU,澳门MO,新西兰NZ 20 东盟AS		50	-Carbonized
	51.02	**未梳的动物细毛或粗毛：**					**Fine or coarse animal hair, not carded or combed:**
		-细毛：					-Fine animal hair:
3641	5102.1100	--喀什米尔山羊的	9	0 冰岛IS,东盟AS,哥CR,秘鲁PE,新西兰NZ,智利CL 3.6 瑞士CH 5 巴PK 5.4 澳AU,韩国KR	0 受惠国LD	45	--Of kashmir (cashmere) goats
		--其他：					--Other:

①配额税率: 1
In-quota Tariff: 1
②国别配额税率: 0
Country Specific TRQ rate: 0
③配额税率: 1
In-quota Tariff: 1
④国别配额税率: 0
Country Specific TRQ rate: 0
⑤配额税率: 1
In-quota Tariff: 1
⑥国别配额税率: 0
Country Specific TRQ rate: 0
⑦配额税率: 1
In-quota Tariff: 1
⑧国别配额税率: 0
Country Specific TRQ rate: 0
⑨配额税率: 1
In-quota Tariff: 1
⑩国别配额税率: 0
Country Specific TRQ rate: 0

序号 No.	税则号列 Tariff Line	中 文 货 品 名 称 Article Description in Chinese	最惠国税率 MFN(%)	协 定 税 率 Agreement(%)	特惠税率 SP(%)	普通税率 Gen(%)	英 文 货 品 名 称 Article Description
3642	5102.1910	---兔毛	9	0 冰岛IS,东盟AS,哥CR,秘鲁PE,新西兰NZ,智利CL 3.6 瑞士CH 5 巴PK 5.4 澳AU,韩国KR	0 受惠国LD	50	---Of rabbit and hare
3643	5102.1920	---其他山羊绒	9	0 冰岛IS,东盟AS,哥CR,秘鲁PE,新西兰NZ,智利CL 3.6 瑞士CH 5 巴PK 5.4 澳AU,韩国KR	0 受惠国LD	45	---Of other goats
3644	5102.1930	---骆驼毛、骆驼绒	9	0 冰岛IS,东盟AS,哥CR,秘鲁PE,新西兰NZ,智利CL 3.6 瑞士CH 5 巴PK 5.4 澳AU,韩国KR	0 受惠国LD	45	---Of camel
3645	5102.1990	---其他	9	0 冰岛IS,东盟AS,哥CR,秘鲁PE,新西兰NZ,智利CL 3.6 瑞士CH 5 巴PK 5.4 澳AU,韩国KR	0 受惠国$_1$LD$_1$	45	---Other
3646	5102.2000	-粗毛	9	0 冰岛IS,东盟AS,哥CR,秘鲁PE,新西兰NZ,智利CL 3.6 瑞士CH 5 巴PK 5.4 澳AU,韩国KR	0 受惠国LD	50	-Coarse animal hair
	51.03	**羊毛或动物细毛或粗毛的废料，包括废纱线，但不包括回收纤维：**					**Waste of wool or of fine or coarse animal hair, including yarn waste but excluding garnetted stock:**
		-羊毛或动物细毛的落毛：					-Noils of wool or of fine animal hair:
3647	5103.1010	---羊毛落毛	38①	② 澳AU,新西兰NZ 20 东盟AS		50	---Of wool
3648	5103.1090	---其他	9	0 冰岛IS,东盟AS,哥CR,秘鲁PE,新西兰NZ,智利CL 3.6 瑞士CH 5 巴PK 5.4 澳AU,韩国KR	0 受惠国LD	50	---Other
		-羊毛或动物细毛的其他废料：					-Other waste of wool or of fine animal hair:
3649	5103.2010	---羊毛废料	13.5	0 冰岛IS,东盟AS,哥CR,新加坡SG,新西兰NZ,智利CL 4 秘鲁PE 6.8 巴PK 8.1 澳AU 9.5 瑞士CH 10.8 韩国KR	0 受惠国$_1$LD$_1$	20	---Of wool
3650	5103.2090	---其他	9	0 冰岛IS,东盟AS,哥CR,秘鲁PE,新西兰NZ,智利CL 3.6 瑞士CH 5 巴PK 5.4 澳AU,韩国KR	0 受惠国$_1$LD$_1$	50	---Other

①**配额税率**: 1
In-quota Tariff: 1
②**国别配额税率**: 0
Country Specific TRQ rate: 0

序号 No.	税则号列 Tariff Line	中文货品名称 Article Description in Chinese	最惠国税率 MFN(%)	协定税率 Agreement(%)	特惠税率 SP(%)	普通税率 Gen(%)	英文货品名称 Article Description
3651	5103.3000	-动物粗毛废料	9	0 冰岛IS,东盟AS,哥CR,秘鲁PE,新西兰NZ,智利CL 3.6 瑞士CH 5 巴PK 5.4 澳AU,韩国KR	0 受惠国LD	50	-Waste of coarse animal hair
	51.04	**羊毛或动物细毛或粗毛的回收纤维:**					**Garnetted stock of wool or of fine or coarse animal hair:**
3652	5104.0010	---羊毛的回收纤维	15	0 冰岛IS,东盟AS,哥CR,新加坡SG,新西兰NZ,智利CL 4.5 秘鲁PE 9 澳AU 10.5 瑞士CH 12 巴PK,韩国KR	0 受惠国$_1$LD$_1$	20	---Of wool
3653	5104.0090	---其他	5	0 澳AU,巴PK,冰岛IS,东盟AS,哥CR,韩国KR,秘鲁PE,瑞士CH,新西兰NZ,智利CL	0 受惠国LD	50	---Other
	51.05	**已梳的羊毛及动物细毛或粗毛(包括精梳片毛):**					**Wool and fine or coarse animal hair, carded or combed (including combed wool in fragments) :**
3654	5105.1000	-粗梳羊毛	38①	② 新西兰NZ		50	-Carded wool
		-羊毛条及其他精梳羊毛:					-Wool tops and other combed wool:
3655	5105.2100	--精梳片毛	38③	④ 新西兰NZ		50	--Combed wool in fragments
3656	5105.2900	--其他	38⑤	⑥ 新西兰NZ		50	--Other
		-已梳动物细毛:					-Fine animal hair, carded or combed:
3657	5105.3100	--喀什米尔山羊的	5	0 澳AU,巴PK,冰岛IS,东盟AS,哥CR,韩国KR,秘鲁PE,瑞士CH,新西兰NZ,智利CL	0 受惠国LD	50	--Of kashmir (cashmere) goats
		--其他:					--Other:
3658	5105.3910	---兔毛	5	0 澳AU,巴PK,冰岛IS,东盟AS,哥CR,韩国KR,瑞士CH,新西兰NZ,智利CL	0 受惠国LD	70	---Of rabbit or hare
		---其他山羊绒:					---Of other goats:
3659	5105.3921	----无毛山羊绒	5	0 澳AU,巴PK,冰岛IS,东盟AS,哥CR,韩国KR,瑞士CH,新西兰NZ,智利CL	0 受惠国LD	50	----Dehaired goats wool
3660	5105.3929	----其他	5	0 澳AU,巴PK,冰岛IS,东盟AS,哥CR,韩国KR,瑞士CH,新西兰NZ,智利CL	0 受惠国LD	50	----Other
3661	5105.3990	---其他	5	0 澳AU,巴PK,冰岛IS,东盟AS,哥CR,韩国KR,瑞士CH,新西兰NZ,智利CL	0 受惠国$_1$LD$_1$	50	---Other

①**配额税率**: 3
In-quota Tariff: 3
②**新西兰配额税率**: 0
Country Specific TRQ rate for New Zealand: 0
③**配额税率**: 3
In-quota Tariff: 3
④**新西兰配额税率**: 0
Country Specific TRQ rate for New Zealand: 0
⑤**配额税率**: 3
In-quota Tariff: 3
⑥**新西兰配额税率**: 0
Country Specific TRQ rate for New Zealand: 0

序号 No.	税则号列 Tariff Line	中文货品名称 Article Description in Chinese	最惠国税率 MFN(%)	协定税率 Agreement(%)		特惠税率 SP(%)		普通税率 Gen(%)	英文货品名称 Article Description
3662	5105.4000	-已梳动物粗毛	5	0	澳AU,巴PK,冰岛IS,东盟AS,哥CR,韩国KR,瑞士CH,新西兰NZ,智利CL	0	受惠国LD	50	-Coarse animal hair, carded or combed
	51.06	**粗梳羊毛纱线，非供零售用：**							**Yarn of carded wool, not put up for retail sale:**
3663	5106.1000	-按重量计羊毛含量在85%及以上	5	0	澳AU,澳门MO,巴PK,冰岛IS,东盟AS,哥CR,韩国KR,秘鲁PE,瑞士CH,香港HK,新西兰NZ,智利CL	0	受惠国LD	70	-Containing 85% or more by weight of wool
3664	5106.2000	-按重量计羊毛含量在85%以下	5	0	澳AU,澳门MO,巴PK,冰岛IS,东盟AS,哥CR,韩国KR,秘鲁PE,瑞士CH,香港HK,新西兰NZ,智利CL	0	受惠国LD	70	-Containing less than 85% by weight of wool
	51.07	**精梳羊毛纱线，非供零售用：**							**Yarn of combed wool, not put up for retail sale:**
3665	5107.1000	-按重量计羊毛含量在85%及以上	5	0 2.5	澳AU,澳门MO,巴PK,东盟AS,哥CR,韩国KR,秘鲁PE,瑞士CH,香港HK,新西兰NZ,智利CL 亚太AP	0	受惠国LD	70	-Containing 85% or more by weight of wool
3666	5107.2000	-按重量计羊毛含量在85%以下	5	0	澳AU,澳门MO,巴PK,冰岛IS,东盟AS,哥CR,韩国KR,秘鲁PE,瑞士CH,新西兰NZ,智利CL	0	受惠国LD	70	-Containing less than 85% by weight of wool
	51.08	**动物细毛（粗梳或精梳）纱线，非供零售用：**							**Yarn of fine animal hair (carded or combed) , not put up for retail sale:**
		-粗梳：							-Carded:
		---按重量计动物细毛含量在85%及以上的：							---Containing 85% or more by weight of fine animal hair:
3667	5108.1011	----山羊绒的	5	0 4.3	澳AU,澳门MO,巴PK,冰岛IS,东盟AS,哥CR,韩国KR,秘鲁PE,瑞士CH,新西兰NZ,智利CL 亚太AP	0	受惠国LD	70	----Of cashmere
3668	5108.1019	----其他	5	0 4.3	澳AU,澳门MO,巴PK,冰岛IS,东盟AS,哥CR,韩国KR,秘鲁PE,瑞士CH,新西兰NZ,智利CL 亚太AP	0	受惠国LD	70	----Other
3669	5108.1090	---其他	5	0 4.3	澳AU,澳门MO,巴PK,冰岛IS,东盟AS,哥CR,韩国KR,秘鲁PE,瑞士CH,新西兰NZ,智利CL 亚太AP	0	受惠国LD	70	---Other
		-精梳：							-Combed:
		---按重量计动物细毛含量在85%及以上的：							---Containing 85% or more by weight of fine animal hair:
3670	5108.2011	----山羊绒的	5	0	澳AU,澳门MO,巴PK,冰岛IS,东盟AS,哥CR,韩国KR,瑞士CH,新西兰NZ,智利CL	0	受惠国LD	70	----Of cashmere
3671	5108.2019	----其他	5	0	澳AU,澳门MO,巴PK,冰岛IS,东盟AS,哥CR,韩国KR,瑞士CH,新西兰NZ,智利CL	0	受惠国LD	70	----Other
3672	5108.2090	---其他	5	0	澳AU,澳门MO,巴PK,冰岛IS,东盟AS,哥CR,韩国KR,瑞士CH,新西兰NZ,智利CL	0	受惠国LD	70	---Other
	51.09	**羊毛或动物细毛的纱线，供零售用：**							**Yarn of wool or of fine animal hair, put up for retail sale:**

序号 No.	税则号列 Tariff Line	中文货品名称 Article Description in Chinese	最惠国税率 MFN(%)	协定税率 Agreement(%)	特惠税率 SP(%)	普通税率 Gen(%)	英文货品名称 Article Description
		-按重量计羊毛或动物细毛含量在85%及以上:					-Containing 85% or more by weight of wool or of fine animal hair:
		---动物细毛的:					---Of fine animal hair:
3673	5109.1011	----山羊绒的	6	0 冰岛IS,东盟AS,哥CR,韩国KR,秘鲁PE,新西兰NZ,智利CL 2.4 瑞士CH 3.6 澳AU 5 巴PK	0 受惠国LD	80	----Of cashmere
3674	5109.1019	----其他	6	0 澳门MO,冰岛IS,东盟AS,哥CR,韩国KR,秘鲁PE,新西兰NZ,智利CL 2.4 瑞士CH 3.6 澳AU 5 巴PK	0 受惠国LD	80	----Other
3675	5109.1090	---其他	6	0 澳门MO,冰岛IS,东盟AS,哥CR,韩国KR,秘鲁PE,新西兰NZ,智利CL 2.4 瑞士CH 3.6 澳AU 5 巴PK	0 受惠国LD	80	---Other
		-其他:					-Other:
		---动物细毛的:					---Of fine animal hair:
3676	5109.9011	----山羊绒的	6	0 澳门MO,冰岛IS,东盟AS,哥CR,韩国KR,新西兰NZ,智利CL 2.4 瑞士CH 3.6 澳AU 5 巴PK	0 受惠国LD	80	----Of cashmere
3677	5109.9019	----其他	6	0 澳门MO,冰岛IS,东盟AS,哥CR,韩国KR,新西兰NZ,智利CL 2.4 瑞士CH 3.6 澳AU 5 巴PK	0 受惠国LD	80	----Other
3678	5109.9090	---其他	6	0 澳门MO,冰岛IS,东盟AS,哥CR,韩国KR,新西兰NZ,智利CL 2.4 瑞士CH 3.6 澳AU 5 巴PK	0 受惠国LD	80	---Other
	51.10	**动物粗毛或马毛的纱线（包括马毛粗松螺旋花线），不论是否供零售用**					**Yarn of coarse animal hair or of horsehair (including gimped horsehair yarn) , whether or not put up for retail sale**
3679	5110.0000	动物粗毛或马毛的纱线（包括马毛粗松螺旋花线），不论是否供零售用	6	0 澳门MO,冰岛IS,东盟AS,哥CR,韩国KR,秘鲁PE,新西兰NZ,智利CL 2.4 瑞士CH 3.6 澳AU 5 巴PK	0 受惠国LD	70	Yarn of coarse animal hair or of horsehair (including gimped horsehair yarn) , whether or not put up for retail sale
	51.11	**粗梳羊毛或粗梳动物细毛的机织物:**					**Woven fabrics of carded wool or of carded fine animal hair:**
		-按重量计羊毛或动物细毛含量在85%及以上:					-Containing 85% or more by weight of wool or of fine animal hair:
		--每平方米重量不超过300克:					--Of a weight not exceeding 300 g/m^2:
		---动物细毛的:					---Of fine animal hair:

序号 No.	税则号列 Tariff Line	中文货品名称 Article Description in Chinese	最惠国税率 MFN(%)	协定税率 Agreement(%)	特惠税率 SP(%)	普通税率 Gen(%)	英文货品名称 Article Description
3680	5111.1111	----山羊绒的	10	0 冰岛IS,东盟AS,哥CR,秘鲁PE,新加坡SG,新西兰NZ,智利CL 4 瑞士CH 5 巴PK 6 澳AU,韩国KR 8.5 亚太AP	0 受惠国$_1$LD$_1$	130	----Of cashmere
3681	5111.1119	----其他	10	0 冰岛IS,东盟AS,哥CR,秘鲁PE,新加坡SG,新西兰NZ,智利CL 4 瑞士CH 5 巴PK 6 澳AU,韩国KR 8.5 亚太AP	0 受惠国$_1$LD$_1$	130	----Other
3682	5111.1190	---其他	10	0 澳门MO,冰岛IS,东盟AS,哥CR,新加坡SG,新西兰NZ,智利CL 3 秘鲁PE 4 瑞士CH 5 巴PK 6 澳AU,韩国KR 8.5 亚太AP	0 受惠国$_1$LD$_1$	130	---Other
		--其他:					--Other:
		---动物细毛的:					---Of fine animal hair:
3683	5111.1911	----山羊绒的	10	0 冰岛IS,东盟AS,哥CR,秘鲁PE,新加坡SG,新西兰NZ,智利CL 4 瑞士CH 5 巴PK 6 澳AU,韩国KR 8.5 亚太AP	0 受惠国$_1$LD$_1$	130	----Of cashmere
3684	5111.1919	----其他	10	0 冰岛IS,东盟AS,哥CR,秘鲁PE,新加坡SG,新西兰NZ,智利CL 4 瑞士CH 5 巴PK 6 澳AU,韩国KR 8.5 亚太AP	0 受惠国$_1$LD$_1$	130	----Other
3685	5111.1990	---其他	10	0 冰岛IS,东盟AS,哥CR,新加坡SG,新西兰NZ,智利CL 3 秘鲁PE 4 瑞士CH 5 巴PK 6 澳AU,韩国KR 8.5 亚太AP	0 受惠国$_1$LD$_1$	130	---Other
3686	5111.2000	-其他，主要或仅与化学纤维长丝混纺	10	0 冰岛IS,东盟AS,哥CR,秘鲁PE,新加坡SG,新西兰NZ,智利CL 4 瑞士CH 5 巴PK 6 澳AU,韩国KR	0 受惠国$_1$LD$_1$	130	-Other, mixed mainly or solely with manmade filaments
3687	5111.3000	-其他，主要或仅与化学纤维短纤混纺	10	0 冰岛IS,东盟AS,哥CR,秘鲁PE,新加坡SG,新西兰NZ,智利CL 4 瑞士CH 5 巴PK 6 澳AU,韩国KR 8.5 亚太AP	0 受惠国$_1$LD$_1$	130	-Other, mixed mainly or solely with manmade staple fibres
3688	5111.9000	-其他	10	0 东盟AS,哥CR,秘鲁PE,新加坡SG,新西兰NZ,智利CL 4 瑞士CH 5 巴PK 6 澳AU,韩国KR	0 受惠国$_1$LD$_1$	130	-Other

序号 No.	税则号列 Tariff Line	中文货品名称 Article Description in Chinese	最惠国税率 MFN(%)	协定税率 Agreement(%)	特惠税率 SP(%)	普通税率 Gen(%)	英文货品名称 Article Description
	51.12	**精梳羊毛或精梳动物细毛的机织物:**					**Woven fabrics of combed wool or of combed fine animal hair:**
		-按重量计羊毛或动物细毛含量在85%及以上:					-Containing 85% or more by weight of wool or of fine animal hair:
3689	5112.1100	--每平方米重量不超过200克	10	0 澳门MO,冰岛IS,东盟AS,哥CR,香港HK,新加坡SG,新西兰NZ,智利CL 3 秘鲁PE 4 瑞士CH 5 巴PK,亚太AP 6 澳AU,韩国KR	0 受惠国LD	130	--Of a weight not exceeding 200g/m^2
3690	5112.1900	--其他	10	0 澳门MO,冰岛IS,东盟AS,哥CR,香港HK,新加坡SG,新西兰NZ,智利CL 3 秘鲁PE 4 瑞士CH 5 巴PK,亚太AP 6 澳AU,韩国KR	0 柬埔寨KH,老挝LA,缅甸MM,受惠国LD	130	--Other
3691	5112.2000	-其他，主要或仅与化学纤维长丝混纺	10	0 澳门MO,冰岛IS,东盟AS,哥CR,秘鲁PE,新加坡SG,新西兰NZ,智利CL 4 瑞士CH 5 巴PK 6 澳AU,韩国KR	0 受惠国LD	130	-Other, mixed mainly or solely with manmade filaments
3692	5112.3000	-其他，主要或仅与化学纤维短纤混纺	10	0 澳门MO,冰岛IS,东盟AS,哥CR,秘鲁PE,新加坡SG,新西兰NZ,智利CL 4 瑞士CH 5 巴PK 6 澳AU,韩国KR	0 受惠国LD	130	-Other, mixed mainly or solely with manmade staple fibres
3693	5112.9000	-其他	10	0 澳门MO,冰岛IS,东盟AS,哥CR,新加坡SG,新西兰NZ,智利CL 3 秘鲁PE 4 瑞士CH 5 巴PK 6 澳AU,韩国KR	0 受惠国LD	130	-Other
	51.13	**动物粗毛或马毛的机织物**					**Woven fabrics of coarse animal hair or of horsehair**
3694	5113.0000	动物粗毛或马毛的机织物	10	0 澳门MO,冰岛IS,东盟AS,哥CR,秘鲁PE,新加坡SG,新西兰NZ,智利CL 4 瑞士CH 5 巴PK 6 澳AU,韩国KR	0 受惠国LD	130	Woven fabrics of coarse animal hair or of horsehair

第五十二章
棉花

Chapter 52
Cotton

子目注释：

子目号 5209.42 及 5211.42 所称"粗斜纹布（劳动布）"，是指用不同颜色的纱线织成的三线或四线斜纹织物，包括破斜纹组织的织物，这种织物以经纱为面，经纱染成一种相同的颜色，纬纱未漂白或经漂白、染成灰色或比经纱稍浅的颜色。

Subheading Note:

For the purposes of subheadings Nos.5209.42 and 5211.42, the expression "denim" means fabrics of yarns of different colours, of 3-thread or 4-thread twill, including broken twill, warp faced, the warp yarns of which are of one and the same colour and the weft yarns of which are unbleached, bleached, dyed grey or coloured a lighter shade of the colour of the warp yarns.

序号 No.	税则号列 Tariff Line	中文货品名称 Article Description in Chinese	最惠国税率 MFN(%)	协定税率 Agreement(%)	特惠税率 SP(%)	普通税率 Gen(%)	英文货品名称 Article Description
	52.01	**未梳的棉花**					**Cotton, not carded or combed**
3695	5201.0000	未梳的棉花	40①	20 东盟AS		125	Cotton, not carded or combed
	52.02	**废棉（包括废棉纱线及回收纤维）：**					**Cotton waste (including yarn waste and garnetted stock) :**
3696	5202.1000	-废棉纱线（包括废棉线）	10	0 冰岛IS,东盟AS,哥CR,新加坡SG,新西兰NZ,智利CL 3 秘鲁PE 4 瑞士CH 6 澳AU 8 韩国KR	0 受惠国$_1$LD$_1$	30	-Yarn waste (including thread waste)
		-其他：					-Other:
3697	5202.9100	--回收纤维	10	0 冰岛IS,东盟AS,哥CR,秘鲁PE,香港HK,新加坡SG,新西兰NZ,智利CL 4 瑞士CH 6 澳AU,韩国KR	0 受惠国LD	30	--Garnetted stock
3698	5202.9900	--其他	10	0 冰岛IS,东盟AS,哥CR,新加坡SG,新西兰NZ,智利CL 4 瑞士CH 6 澳AU 8 韩国KR		30	--Other
	52.03	**已梳的棉花**					**Cotton, carded or combed**
3699	5203.0000	已梳的棉花	40②			125	Cotton, carded or combed
	52.04	**棉制缝纫线，不论是否供零售用：**					**Cotton sewing thread, whether or not put up for retail sale:**
		-非供零售用：					-Not put up for retail sale:
3700	5204.1100	--按重量计含棉量在85%及以上	5	0 澳AU,澳门MO,冰岛IS,东盟AS,哥CR,韩国KR,秘鲁PE,瑞士CH,新西兰NZ,智利CL	0 老挝LA,受惠国LD	40	--Containing 85% or more by weight of cotton
3701	5204.1900	--其他	5	0 澳AU,澳门MO,冰岛IS,东盟AS,哥CR,韩国KR,秘鲁PE,瑞士CH,新西兰NZ,智利CL	0 受惠国LD	40	--Other
3702	5204.2000	-供零售用	5	0 澳AU,澳门MO,冰岛IS,东盟AS,哥CR,韩国KR,秘鲁PE,瑞士CH,新西兰NZ,智利CL	0 老挝LA,受惠国LD	50	-Put up for retail sale

①**配额税率**: 1
In-quota Tariff: 1

暂定最惠国税率：对配额外进口的一定数量棉花,适用滑准税形式暂定关税,具体方式如下：

1.当进口棉花完税价格（Pi）高于或等于 15.000 元/千克时,暂定从量税率为 0.570 元/千克；

2.当进口棉花完税价格（Pi）低于 15.000 元/千克时，暂定从价税率（Ri）按下式计算：Ri=9.337/Pi +2.77%×Pi -1 (Ri≤40%)。

Interim MFN Tariff: The following Sliding-Scale Interim Tariff(SIT) should be applied on certain amount of out-quota imported cotton.

Price≥15.000￥/kg:SIT Specific Rate=0.570￥/kg;

Price<15.000￥/kg:SIT ad valorem Rate=9.337/Price +2.77%×Price -1.

SIT ad valorem rate ≤40%, round up to 3rd digit.

②**配额税率**: 1
In-quota Tariff: 1

序号 No.	税则号列 Tariff Line	中文货品名称 Article Description in Chinese	最惠国税率 MFN(%)	协定税率 Agreement(%)	特惠税率 SP(%)	普通税率 Gen(%)	英文货品名称 Article Description
	52.05	**棉纱线（缝纫线除外），按重量计含棉量在85%及以上，非供零售用：**					**Cotton yarn (other than sewing thread), containing 85% or more by weight of cotton, not put up for retail sale:**
		-未精梳纤维纺制的单纱：					-Single yarn, of uncombed fibres:
3703	5205.1100	--细度在714.29分特及以上（不超过14公支）	5	0 澳门MO,冰岛IS,东盟AS,哥CR,秘鲁PE,瑞士CH,台湾TW,香港HK,新西兰NZ,智利CL 3.5 巴PK,亚太AP 3.9 澳AU 4.3 韩国KR	0 柬埔寨KH,老挝LA,缅甸MM,受惠国LD	40	--Measuring 714.29 decitex or more (not exceeding 14 metric number)
3704	5205.1200	--细度在714.29分特以下，但不细于232.56分特（超过14公支，但不超过43公支）	5	0 冰岛IS,东盟AS,哥CR,秘鲁PE,瑞士CH,台湾TW,香港HK,新西兰NZ,智利CL 3.5 巴PK,亚太AP 3.9 澳AU 4.3 韩国KR	0 柬埔寨KH,老挝LA,缅甸MM,受惠国LD	40	--Measuring less than 714.29 decitex but not less than 232.56 decitex (exceeding 14 metric number but not exceeding 43 metric number)
3705	5205.1300	--细度在232.56分特以下，但不细于192.31分特（超过43公支，但不超过52公支）	5	0 冰岛IS,东盟AS,哥CR,秘鲁PE,瑞士CH,香港HK,新西兰NZ,智利CL 3.5 巴PK,亚太AP 3.9 澳AU 4.3 韩国KR	0 受惠国LD	40	--Measuring less than 232.56 decitex but not less than 192.31 decitex (exceeding 43 metric number but not exceeding 52 metric number)
3706	5205.1400	--细度在192.31分特以下，但不细于125分特（超过52公支，但不超过80公支）	5	0 冰岛IS,东盟AS,哥CR,秘鲁PE,瑞士CH,香港HK,新西兰NZ,智利CL 3.5 巴PK,亚太AP 3.9 澳AU 4.4 韩国KR	0 老挝LA,缅甸MM,受惠国LD	40	--Measuring less than 192.31 decitex but not less than 125 decitex (exceeding 52 metric number but not exceeding 80 metric number)
3707	5205.1500	--细度在125分特以下（超过80公支）	5	0 冰岛IS,东盟AS,哥CR,秘鲁PE,瑞士CH,新西兰NZ,智利CL 3.5 巴PK,亚太AP 3.9 澳AU 4.3 韩国KR	0 受惠国LD	40	--Measuring less than 125 decitex (exceeding 80 metric number)
		-精梳纤维纺制的单纱：					-Single yarn, of combed fibres:
3708	5205.2100	--细度在714.29分特及以上（不超过14公支）	5	0 冰岛IS,东盟AS,哥CR,秘鲁PE,瑞士CH,香港HK,新西兰NZ,智利CL 3.5 巴PK,亚太AP 3.9 澳AU 4.3 韩国KR	0 缅甸MM,受惠国LD	40	--Measuring 714.29 decitex or more (not exceeding 14 metric number)
3709	5205.2200	--细度在714.29分特以下，但不细于232.56分特（超过14公支，但不超过43公支）	5	0 冰岛IS,东盟AS,哥CR,秘鲁PE,瑞士CH,香港HK,新西兰NZ,智利CL 3.5 巴PK,亚太AP 3.9 澳AU 4.3 韩国KR	0 受惠国LD	40	--Measuring less than 714.29 decitex but not less than 232.56 decitex (exceeding 14 metric number but not exceeding 43 metric number)
3710	5205.2300	--细度在232.56分特以下，但不细于192.31分特（超过43公支，但不超过52公支）	5	0 冰岛IS,东盟AS,哥CR,秘鲁PE,瑞士CH,香港HK,新西兰NZ,智利CL 3.5 巴PK,亚太AP 3.9 澳AU 4 韩国KR	0 受惠国LD	40	--Measuring less than 232.56 decitex but not less than 192.31 decitex (exceeding 43 metric number but not exceeding 52 metric number)
3711	5205.2400	--细度在192.31分特以下，但不细于125分特（超过52公支，但不超过80公支）	5	0 冰岛IS,东盟AS,哥CR,秘鲁PE,瑞士CH,香港HK,新西兰NZ,智利CL 3.5 巴PK,亚太AP 3.9 澳AU 4 韩国KR	0 老挝LA,缅甸MM,受惠国LD	40	--Measuring less than 192.31 decitex but not less than 125 decitex (exceeding 52 metric number but not exceeding 80 metric number)

序号 No.	税则号列 Tariff Line	中文货品名称 Article Description in Chinese	最惠国税率 MFN(%)	协定税率 Agreement(%)	特惠税率 SP(%)	普通税率 Gen(%)	英文货品名称 Article Description
3712	5205.2600	--细度在125分特以下，但不细于106.38分特（超过80公支，但不超过94公支）	5	0 冰岛IS,东盟AS,哥CR,秘鲁PE,瑞士CH,香港HK,新西兰NZ,智利CL 3.9 澳AU 4.3 韩国KR	0 受惠国LD	40	--Measuring less than 125 decitex but not less than 106.38 decitex (exceeding 80 metric number but not exceeding 94 metric number)
3713	5205.2700	--细度在106.38分特以下，但不细于83.33分特（超过94公支，但不超过120公支）	5	0 冰岛IS,东盟AS,哥CR,秘鲁PE,瑞士CH,香港HK,新西兰NZ,智利CL 3.9 澳AU 4.3 韩国KR	0 受惠国LD	40	--Measuring less than 106.38 decitex but not less than 83.33 decitex (exceeding 94 metric number but not exceeding 120 metric number)
3714	5205.2800	--细度在83.33分特以下（超过120公支）	5	0 冰岛IS,东盟AS,哥CR,秘鲁PE,瑞士CH,香港HK,新西兰NZ,智利CL 3.9 澳AU 4.3 韩国KR	0 受惠国LD	40	--Measuring less than 83.33 decitex (exceeding 120 metric number)
		-未精梳纤维纺制的多股纱线或缆线：					-Multiple (folded) or cabled yarn, of uncombed fibres:
3715	5205.3100	--每根单纱细度在714.29分特及以上（每根单纱不超过14公支）	5	0 澳门MO,冰岛IS,东盟AS,哥CR,瑞士CH,香港HK,新西兰NZ,智利CL 3.9 澳AU 4.3 韩国KR 4.5 巴PK,亚太AP		40	--Measuring per single yarn 714.29 decitex or more (not exceeding 14 metric number per single yarn)
3716	5205.3200	--每根单纱细度在714.29分特以下，但不细于232.56分特（每根单纱超过14公支，但不超过43公支）	5	0 澳门MO,冰岛IS,东盟AS,哥CR,秘鲁PE,瑞士CH,香港HK,新西兰NZ,智利CL 3.5 巴PK,亚太AP 3.9 澳AU 4.3 韩国KR	0 受惠国LD	40	--Measuring per single yarn less than 714.29 decitex but not less than 232.56 decitex (exceeding 14 metric number but not exceeding 43 metric number per single yarn)
3717	5205.3300	--每根单纱细度在232.56分特以下，但不细于192.31分特（每根单纱超过43公支，但不超过52公支）	5	0 澳门MO,冰岛IS,东盟AS,哥CR,秘鲁PE,瑞士CH,香港HK,新西兰NZ,智利CL 3.9 澳AU 4.3 韩国KR	0 受惠国LD	40	--Measuring per single yarn less than 232.56 decitex but not less than 192.31 decitex (exceeding 43 metric number but not exceeding 52 metric number per single yarn)
3718	5205.3400	--每根单纱细度在192.31分特以下，但不细于125分特（每根单纱超过52公支，但不超过80公支）	5	0 澳门MO,冰岛IS,东盟AS,哥CR,秘鲁PE,瑞士CH,香港HK,新西兰NZ,智利CL 3.9 澳AU 4.3 韩国KR	0 受惠国LD	40	--Measuring per single yarn less than 192.31 decitex but not less than 125 decitex (exceeding 52 metric number but not exceeding 80 metric number per single yarn)
3719	5205.3500	--每根单纱细度在125分特以下（每根单纱超过80公支）	5	0 澳门MO,冰岛IS,东盟AS,哥CR,秘鲁PE,瑞士CH,新西兰NZ,智利CL 3.9 澳AU 4.3 韩国KR	0 受惠国LD	40	--Measuring per single yarn less than 125 decitex (exceeding 80 metric number per single yarn)
		-精梳纤维纺制的多股纱线或缆线：					-Multiple (folded) or cabled yarn, of combed fibres:
3720	5205.4100	--每根单纱细度在714.29分特及以上（每根单纱不超过14公支）	5	0 澳门MO,冰岛IS,东盟AS,哥CR,瑞士CH,香港HK,新西兰NZ,智利CL 3.9 澳AU 4.3 韩国KR 4.5 巴PK,亚太AP	0 受惠国$_1$LD$_1$	40	--Measuring per single yarn 714.29 decitex or more (not exceeding 14 metric number per single yarn)
3721	5205.4200	--每根单纱细度在714.29分特以下，但不细于232.56分特（每根单纱超过14公支，但不超过43公支）	5	0 澳门MO,冰岛IS,哥CR,秘鲁PE,香港HK,新西兰NZ,智利CL 2 瑞士CH 3.5 巴PK,亚太AP 3.9 澳AU 4.4 韩国KR	0 受惠国LD	40	--Measuring per single yarn less than 714.29 decitex but not less than 232.56 decitex (exceeding 14 metric number but not exceeding 43 metric number per single yarn)

序号 No.	税则号列 Tariff Line	中文货品名称 Article Description in Chinese	最惠国税率 MFN(%)	协定税率 Agreement(%)	特惠税率 SP(%)	普通税率 Gen(%)	英文货品名称 Article Description
3722	5205.4300	--每根单纱细度在232.56分特以下，但不细于192.31分特（每根单纱超过43公支，但不超过52公支）	5	0 澳门MO,冰岛IS,东盟AS,哥CR,瑞士CH,香港HK,新西兰NZ,智利CL 3.9 澳AU 4.3 韩国KR	0 受惠国LD	40	--Measuring per singleyarn less than 232.56 decitex but not less than 192.31 decitex (exceeding 43 metric number but not exceeding 52 metric number per single yarn)
3723	5205.4400	--每根单纱细度在192.31分特以下，但不细于125分特（每根单纱超过52公支，但不超过80公支）	5	0 澳门MO,冰岛IS,东盟AS,哥CR,秘鲁PE,瑞士CH,香港HK,新西兰NZ,智利CL 3.9 澳AU 4.3 韩国KR	0 受惠国LD	40	--Measuring per single yarn less than 192.31 decitex but not less than 125 decitex (exceeding 52 metric number but not exceeding 80 metric number per single yarn)
3724	5205.4600	--每根单纱细度在125分特以下，但不细于106.38分特（每根单纱超过80公支，但不超过94公支）	5	0 澳门MO,冰岛IS,东盟AS,哥CR,秘鲁PE,瑞士CH,香港HK,新西兰NZ,智利CL 3.9 澳AU 4.3 韩国KR 4.5 巴PK,亚太AP	0 受惠国LD	40	--Measuring per single yarn less than 125 decitex but not less than 106.38 decitex (exceeding 80 metric number but not exceeding 94 metric number per single yarn)
3725	5205.4700	--每根单纱细度在106.38分特以下，但不细于83.33分特（每根单纱超过94公支，但不超过120公支）	5	0 澳门MO,冰岛IS,东盟AS,哥CR,秘鲁PE,瑞士CH,香港HK,新西兰NZ,智利CL 3.9 澳AU 4.3 韩国KR 4.5 巴PK,亚太AP	0 受惠国LD	40	--Measuring per single yarn less than 106.38 decitex but not less than 83.33 decitex (exceeding 94 metric number but not exceeding 120 metric number per single yarn)
3726	5205.4800	--每根单纱细度在83.33分特以下（每根单纱超过120公支）	5	0 澳门MO,冰岛IS,东盟AS,哥CR,秘鲁PE,瑞士CH,香港HK,新西兰NZ,智利CL 3.9 澳AU 4.3 韩国KR 4.5 巴PK,亚太AP	0 受惠国LD	40	--Measuring per single yarn less than 83.33 decitex (exceeding 120 metric number per single yarn)
	52.06	**棉纱线（缝纫线除外），按重量计含棉量在85%以下，非供零售用：**					**Cotton yarn (other than sewing thread) , containing less than 85% by weight of cotton, not put up for retail sale:**
		-未精梳纤维纺制的单纱：					-Single yarn, of uncombed fibres:
3727	5206.1100	--细度在714.29分特及以上（不超过14公支）	5	0 澳门MO,冰岛IS,东盟AS,哥CR,瑞士CH,香港HK,新西兰NZ,智利CL 3.5 巴PK,亚太AP 3.9 澳AU 4.3 韩国KR		40	Measuring 714.29 decitex or more (not exceeding 14 metric number)
3728	5206.1200	--细度在714.29分特以下，但不细于232.56分特（超过14公支，但不超过43公支）	5	0 澳门MO,冰岛IS,东盟AS,哥CR,秘鲁PE,瑞士CH,台湾TW,香港HK,新西兰NZ,智利CL 3.5 巴PK,亚太AP 3.9 澳AU 4.3 韩国KR	0 受惠国$_1$LD$_1$	40	--Measuring less than 714.29 decitex but not less than 232.56 decitex (exceeding 14 metric number but not exceeding 43 metric number)
3729	5206.1300	--细度在232.56分特以下，但不细于192.31分特（超过43公支，但不超过52公支）	5	0 澳门MO,冰岛IS,东盟AS,哥CR,秘鲁PE,瑞士CH,香港HK,新西兰NZ,智利CL 3.9 澳AU 4.3 韩国KR	0 受惠国LD	40	--Measuring less than 232.56 decitex but not less than 192.31 decitex (exceeding 43 metric number but not exceeding 52 metric number)
3730	5206.1400	--细度在192.31分特以下，但不细于125分特（超过52公支，但不超过80公支）	5	0 澳门MO,冰岛IS,东盟AS,哥CR,秘鲁PE,瑞士CH,香港HK,新西兰NZ,智利CL 3.9 澳AU 4.3 韩国KR	0 受惠国LD	40	--Measuring less than 192.31 decitex but not less than 125 decitex (exceeding 52 metric number but not exceeding 80 metric number)

序号 No.	税则号列 Tariff Line	中文货品名称 Article Description in Chinese	最惠国税率 MFN(%)	协定税率 Agreement(%)	特惠税率 SP(%)	普通税率 Gen(%)	英文货品名称 Article Description
3731	5206.1500	--细度在125分特以下（超过80公支）	5	0 澳门MO,冰岛IS,东盟AS,哥CR,秘鲁PE,瑞士CH,香港HK,新西兰NZ,智利CL 3.5 巴PK,亚太AP 3.9 澳AU 4.3 韩国KR	0 受惠国LD	40	--Measuring less than 125 decitex (exceeding 80 metric number)
		-精梳纤维纺制的单纱:					-Single yarn, of combed fibres:
3732	5206.2100	--细度在714.29分特及以上（不超过14公支）	5	0 澳门MO,冰岛IS,东盟AS,哥CR,秘鲁PE,瑞士CH,香港HK,新西兰NZ,智利CL 3.9 澳AU 4.3 韩国KR 4.5 巴PK,亚太AP	0 受惠国$_1$LD$_1$	40	--Measuring 714.29 decitex or more (not exceeding 14 metric number)
3733	5206.2200	--细度在714.29分特以下，但不细于232.56分特（超过14公支，但不超过43公支）	5	0 澳门MO,冰岛IS,东盟AS,哥CR,秘鲁PE,瑞士CH,台湾TW,香港HK,新西兰NZ,智利CL 3.9 澳AU 4.3 韩国KR	0 受惠国$_1$LD$_1$	40	--Measuring less than 714.29 decitex but not less than 232.56 decitex (exceeding 14 metric number but not exceeding 43 metric number)
3734	5206.2300	--细度在232.56分特以下，但不细于192.31分特（超过43公支，但不超过52公支）	5	0 澳门MO,冰岛IS,东盟AS,哥CR,秘鲁PE,瑞士CH,香港HK,新西兰NZ,智利CL 3.9 澳AU 4.3 韩国KR	0 受惠国LD	40	--Measuring less than 232.56 decitex but not less than 192.31 decite (exceeding 43 metric number but not exceeding 52 metric number)
3735	5206.2400	--细度在192.31分特以下，但不细于125分特（超过52公支，但不超过80公支）	5	0 澳门MO,冰岛IS,东盟AS,哥CR,秘鲁PE,瑞士CH,台湾TW,香港HK,新西兰NZ,智利CL 3.9 澳AU 4.3 韩国KR	0 受惠国LD	40	--Measuring less than 192.31 decitex but not less than 125 decitex (exceeding 52 metric number but not exceeding 80 metric number)
3736	5206.2500	--细度在125分特以下（超过80公支）	5	0 澳门MO,冰岛IS,东盟AS,哥CR,秘鲁PE,瑞士CH,香港HK,新西兰NZ,智利CL 3.9 澳AU 4.3 韩国KR	0 受惠国LD	40	--Measuring less than 125 decitex (exceeding 80 metric number)
		-未精梳纤维纺制的多股纱线或缆线:					-Multiple (folded) or cabled yarn, of uncombed fibres:
3737	5206.3100	--每根单纱细度在714.29分特及以上（每根单纱不超过14公支）	5	0 澳门MO,冰岛IS,东盟AS,哥CR,秘鲁PE,瑞士CH,香港HK,新西兰NZ,智利CL 3.9 澳AU 4.3 韩国KR	0 受惠国$_1$LD$_1$	40	--Measuring per single yarn 714.29 decitex or more (not exceeding 14 metric number per single yarn)
3738	5206.3200	--每根单纱细度在714.29分特以下，但不细于232.56分特（每根单纱超过14公支，但不超过43公支）	5	0 澳门MO,冰岛IS,东盟AS,哥CR,秘鲁PE,瑞士CH,香港HK,新西兰NZ,智利CL 3.9 澳AU 4.3 韩国KR	0 受惠国$_1$LD$_1$	40	--Measuring per single yarn less than 714.29 decitex but not less than 232.56 decitex (exceeding 14 metric number but not exceeding 43 metric number per single yarn)
3739	5206.3300	--每根单纱细度在232.56分特以下，但不细于192.31分特（每根单纱超过43公支，但不超过52公支）	5	0 澳门MO,冰岛IS,东盟AS,哥CR,秘鲁PE,瑞士CH,香港HK,新西兰NZ,智利CL 3.9 澳AU 4.3 韩国KR	0 受惠国LD	40	--Measuring per single yarn less than 232.56 decitex but not less than 192.31 decitex (exceeding 43 metric number but not exceeding 52 metric number per single yarn)
3740	5206.3400	--每根单纱细度在192.31分特以下，但不细于125分特（每根单纱超过52公支，但不超过80公支）	5	0 澳门MO,冰岛IS,东盟AS,哥CR,秘鲁PE,瑞士CH,香港HK,新西兰NZ,智利CL 3.9 澳AU 4.3 韩国KR	0 受惠国LD	40	--Measuring per single yarn less than 192.31 decitex but not less than 125 decitex (exceeding 52 metric number but not exceeding 80 metric number per single yarn)

序号 No.	税则号列 Tariff Line	中文货品名称 Article Description in Chinese	最惠国税率 MFN(%)	协定税率 Agreement(%)	特惠税率 SP(%)	普通税率 Gen(%)	英文货品名称 Article Description
3741	5206.3500	--每根单纱细度在125分特以下（每根单纱超过80公支）	5	0 澳门MO,冰岛IS,东盟AS,哥CR,秘鲁PE,瑞士CH,香港HK,新西兰NZ,智利CL 3.9 澳AU 4.3 韩国KR	0 受惠国LD	40	--Measuring per single yarn less than 125 decitex (exceeding 80 metric number per single yarn)
		-精梳纤维纺制的多股纱线或缆线：					-Multiple (folded) or cabled yarn, of combed fibres:
3742	5206.4100	--每根单纱细度在714.29分特及以上（每根单纱不超过14公支）	5	0 澳门MO,冰岛IS,东盟AS,哥CR,秘鲁PE,瑞士CH,香港HK,新西兰NZ,智利CL 3.9 澳AU 4.3 韩国KR	0 受惠国$_1$LD$_1$	40	--Measuring per single yarn 714.29 decitex or more (not exceeding 14 metric number per single yarn)
3743	5206.4200	--每根单纱细度在714.29分特以下，但不细于232.56分特（每根单纱超过14公支，但不超过43公支）	5	0 澳门MO,冰岛IS,东盟AS,哥CR,秘鲁PE,瑞士CH,香港HK,新西兰NZ,智利CL 3.9 澳AU 4.3 韩国KR	0 受惠国$_1$LD$_1$	40	--Measuring per single yarn less than 714.29 decitex but not less than 232.56 decitex (exceeding 14 metric number but not exceeding 43 metric number per single yarn)
3744	5206.4300	--每根单纱细度在232.56分特以下，但不细于192.31分特（每根单纱超过43公支，但不超过52公支）	5	0 澳门MO,冰岛IS,东盟AS,哥CR,秘鲁PE,瑞士CH,香港HK,新西兰NZ,智利CL 3.9 澳AU 4.3 韩国KR	0 受惠国LD	40	--Measuring per single yarn less than 232.56 decitex but not less then 192.31 decitex (exceeding 43 metric number but not exceeding 52 metric number per single yarn)
3745	5206.4400	--每根单纱细度在192.31分特以下，但不细于125分特（每根单纱超过52公支，但不超过80公支）	5	0 澳门MO,冰岛IS,东盟AS,哥CR,秘鲁PE,瑞士CH,香港HK,新西兰NZ,智利CL 3.9 澳AU 4.3 韩国KR	0 受惠国LD	40	--Measuring per single yarn less than 192.31 decitex but not less than 125 decitex (exceeding 52 metric number but not exceeding 80 metric number per single yarn)
3746	5206.4500	--每根单纱细度在125分特以下（每根单纱超过80公支）	5	0 澳门MO,冰岛IS,东盟AS,哥CR,秘鲁PE,瑞士CH,香港HK,新西兰NZ,智利CL 3.9 澳AU 4.3 韩国KR	0 受惠国LD	40	--Measuring per single yarn less than 125 decitex (exceeding 80 metric number per single yarn)
	52.07	**棉纱线（缝纫线除外），供零售用：**					**Cotton yarn (other than sewing thread) put up for retail sale:**
3747	5207.1000	-按重量计含棉量在85%及以上	6	0 澳门MO,冰岛IS,东盟AS,哥CR,韩国KR,秘鲁PE,新西兰NZ,智利CL 2.4 瑞士CH 3.6 澳AU 5 巴PK,亚太AP	0 受惠国$_1$LD$_1$	50	-Containing 85% or more by weight of cotton
3748	5207.9000	-其他	6	0 澳门MO,冰岛IS,东盟AS,哥CR,韩国KR,秘鲁PE,新西兰NZ,智利CL 2.4 瑞士CH 3.6 澳AU 5 巴PK	0 受惠国LD	50	-Other
	52.08	**棉机织物，按重量计含棉量在85%及以上，每平方米重量不超过200克：**					**Woven fabrics of cotton, containing 85% or more by weight of cotton, weighing not more than 200 g/m^2:**
		-未漂白：					-Unbleached:
3749	5208.1100	--平纹机织物，每平方米重量不超过100克	10	0 巴PK,冰岛IS,东盟AS,哥CR,秘鲁PE,香港HK,新西兰NZ,智利CL 4 瑞士CH 6 澳AU,韩国KR	0 受惠国$_1$LD$_1$	70	--Plain weave, weighing not more than 100g/m^2

序号 No.	税则号列 Tariff Line	中文货品名称 Article Description in Chinese	最惠国税率 MFN(%)	协定税率 Agreement(%)	特惠税率 SP(%)	普通税率 Gen(%)	英文货品名称 Article Description
3750	5208.1200	--平纹机织物，每平方米重量超过100克	10	0 巴PK,冰岛IS,东盟AS,哥CR,秘鲁PE,香港HK,新加坡SG,新西兰NZ,智利CL 4 瑞士CH 6 澳AU,韩国KR	0 受惠国$_1$LD$_1$	70	--Plain weave, weighing more than $100g/m^2$
3751	5208.1300	--三线或四线斜纹机织物，包括双面斜纹机织物	10	0 巴PK,冰岛IS,东盟AS,哥CR,秘鲁PE,香港HK,新西兰NZ,智利CL 4 瑞士CH 6 澳AU 8 韩国KR 8.5 亚太AP	0 受惠国$_1$LD$_1$	70	--3-thread or 4-thread twill, including cross twill
3752	5208.1900	--其他机织物	10	0 巴PK,冰岛IS,东盟AS,哥CR,秘鲁PE,香港HK,新加坡SG,新西兰NZ,智利CL 4 瑞士CH 6 澳AU,韩国KR	0 受惠国$_1$LD$_1$	70	--Other fabrics
		-漂白:					-Bleached:
3753	5208.2100	--平纹机织物，每平方米重量不超过100克	10	0 巴PK,冰岛IS,东盟AS,哥CR,秘鲁PE,香港HK,新西兰NZ,智利CL 4 瑞士CH 6 澳AU,韩国KR	0 受惠国$_1$LD$_1$	70	--Plain weave, weighing not more than $100g/m^2$
3754	5208.2200	--平纹机织物，每平方米重量超过100克	10	0 巴PK,冰岛IS,东盟AS,哥CR,秘鲁PE,香港HK,新加坡SG,新西兰NZ,智利CL 4 瑞士CH 6 澳AU,韩国KR	0 柬埔寨KH,老挝LA,缅甸MM,受惠国LD	70	--Plain weave, weighing more than $100g/m^2$
3755	5208.2300	--三线或四线斜纹机织物，包括双面斜纹机织物	12	0 巴PK,冰岛IS,东盟AS,哥CR,秘鲁PE,香港HK,新加坡SG,新西兰NZ,智利CL 7.2 澳AU,韩国KR 8.6 瑞士CH	0 受惠国$_1$LD$_1$	70	--3-thread or 4-thread twill, icluding cross twill
3756	5208.2900	--其他机织物	10	0 巴PK,冰岛IS,东盟AS,哥CR,秘鲁PE,香港HK,新西兰NZ,智利CL 4 瑞士CH 6 澳AU,韩国KR	0 受惠国$_1$LD$_1$	70	--Other fabrics
		-染色:					-Dyed:
3757	5208.3100	--平纹机织物，每平方米重量不超过100克	10	0 巴PK,冰岛IS,东盟AS,哥CR,秘鲁PE,台湾TW,香港HK,新西兰NZ,智利CL 4 瑞士CH 6 澳AU,韩国KR	0 受惠国LD	70	--Plain weave, weighing not more than $100g/m^2$
3758	5208.3200	--平纹机织物，每平方米重量超过100克	10	0 巴PK,冰岛IS,东盟AS,哥CR,秘鲁PE,台湾TW,香港HK,新加坡SG,新西兰NZ,智利CL 4 瑞士CH 6 澳AU,韩国KR 8.5 亚太AP	0 受惠国LD	70	--Plain weave, weighing more than $100g/m^2$
3759	5208.3300	--三线或四线斜纹机织物，包括双面斜纹机织物	10	0 巴PK,冰岛IS,东盟AS,哥CR,秘鲁PE,香港HK,新西兰NZ,智利CL 4 瑞士CH 6 澳AU,韩国KR 8.5 亚太AP	0 柬埔寨KH,老挝LA,缅甸MM,受惠国LD	70	--3-thread or 4-thread twill, including cross twill

序号 No.	税则号列 Tariff Line	中文货品名称 Article Description in Chinese	最惠国税率 MFN(%)	协定税率 Agreement(%)	特惠税率 SP(%)	普通税率 Gen(%)	英文货品名称 Article Description
3760	5208.3900	--其他机织物	10	0 巴PK,冰岛IS,东盟AS,哥CR,秘鲁PE,台湾TW,香港HK,新加坡SG,新西兰NZ,智利CL 4 瑞士CH 6 澳AU,韩国KR 8.5 亚太AP	0 受惠国LD	70	--Other fabrics
		-色织:					-Of yarns of different colours:
3761	5208.4100	--平纹机织物，每平方米重量不超过100克	10	0 巴PK,冰岛IS,东盟AS,哥CR,秘鲁PE,香港HK,新加坡SG,新西兰NZ,智利CL 6 澳AU,韩国KR 7 瑞士CH	0 受惠国$_1$LD$_1$	70	--Plain weave, weighing not more than 100g/m^2
3762	5208.4200	--平纹机织物，每平方米重量超过100克	10	0 巴PK,冰岛IS,东盟AS,哥CR,秘鲁PE,台湾TW,香港HK,新加坡SG,新西兰NZ,智利CL 6 澳AU,韩国KR 7 瑞士CH,亚太AP	0 受惠国LD	70	--Plain weave, weighing more than 100g/m^2
3763	5208.4300	--三线或四线斜纹机织物，包括双面斜纹机织物	10	0 巴PK,冰岛IS,东盟AS,哥CR,秘鲁PE,香港HK,新西兰NZ,智利CL 6 澳AU,韩国KR 7 瑞士CH	0 受惠国$_1$LD$_1$	70	--3-thread or 4-thread twill, including cross twill
3764	5208.4900	--其他机织物	10	0 巴PK,冰岛IS,东盟AS,哥CR,秘鲁PE,香港HK,新加坡SG,新西兰NZ,智利CL 4 瑞士CH 6 澳AU,韩国KR 9 亚太AP	0 柬埔寨KH,老挝LA,缅甸MM,受惠国LD	70	--Other fabrics
		-印花:					-Printed:
3765	5208.5100	--平纹机织物，每平方米重量不超过100克	10	0 巴PK,冰岛IS,东盟AS,哥CR,秘鲁PE,香港HK,新西兰NZ,智利CL 4 瑞士CH 6 澳AU,韩国KR	0 受惠国LD	70	--Plain weave, weighing not more than 100g/m^2
3766	5208.5200	--平纹机织物，每平方米重量超过100克	10	0 巴PK,冰岛IS,东盟AS,哥CR,秘鲁PE,香港HK,新加坡SG,新西兰NZ,智利CL 4 瑞士CH 6 澳AU 8.5 亚太AP 9 韩国KR	0 受惠国LD	70	--Plain weave, weighing more than 100g/m^2
		--其他机织物:					--Other fabrics:
3767	5208.5910	---三线或四线斜纹机织物，包括双面斜纹机织物	10	0 巴PK,冰岛IS,东盟AS,哥CR,秘鲁PE,香港HK,新西兰NZ,智利CL 4 瑞士CH 6 澳AU,韩国KR	0 受惠国$_1$LD$_1$	70	---3-thread or 4-thread twill, including cross twill
3768	5208.5990	---其他	10	0 巴PK,冰岛IS,东盟AS,哥CR,秘鲁PE,台湾TW,新西兰NZ,智利CL 4 瑞士CH 6 澳AU,韩国KR 8.5 亚太AP	0 受惠国$_1$LD$_1$	70	---Other
	52.09	**棉机织物，按重量计含棉量在85%及以上，每平方米重量超过200克:**					**Woven fabrics of cotton, containing 85% or more by weight of cotton, weighing more than 200g/m^2:**
		-未漂白:					-Unbleached:

序号 No.	税则号列 Tariff Line	中文货品名称 Article Description in Chinese	最惠国税率 MFN(%)	协定税率 Agreement(%)	特惠税率 SP(%)	普通税率 Gen(%)	英文货品名称 Article Description
3769	5209.1100	--平纹机织物	10	0 巴PK,冰岛IS,哥CR,香港HK,新西兰NZ,智利CL 4 瑞士CH 6 澳AU 9 韩国KR	0 受惠国LD	70	--Plain weave
3770	5209.1200	--三线或四线斜纹机织物，包括双面斜纹机织物	10	0 巴PK,冰岛IS,东盟AS,哥CR,秘鲁PE,香港HK,新加坡SG,新西兰NZ,智利CL 4 瑞士CH 6 澳AU,韩国KR 7 亚太AP	0 受惠国$_1$LD$_1$	70	--3-thread or 4-thread twill, including cross twill
3771	5209.1900	--其他机织物	10	0 巴PK,冰岛IS,东盟AS,哥CR,秘鲁PE,香港HK,新加坡SG,新西兰NZ,智利CL 4 瑞士CH 6 澳AU,韩国KR	0 受惠国LD	70	--Other fabrics
		-漂白:					-Bleached:
3772	5209.2100	--平纹机织物	12	0 巴PK,冰岛IS,东盟AS,哥CR,秘鲁PE,香港HK,新加坡SG,新西兰NZ,智利CL 7.2 澳AU,韩国KR 8.4 瑞士CH	0 受惠国LD	70	--Plain weave
3773	5209.2200	--三线或四线斜纹机织物，包括双面斜纹机织物	12	0 巴PK,冰岛IS,东盟AS,哥CR,秘鲁PE,香港HK,新加坡SG,新西兰NZ,智利CL 7.2 澳AU,韩国KR 8.4 瑞士CH	0 受惠国$_1$LD$_1$	70	--3-thread or 4-thread twill, including cross twill
3774	5209.2900	--其他机织物	12	0 巴PK,冰岛IS,东盟AS,哥CR,秘鲁PE,香港HK,新加坡SG,新西兰NZ,智利CL 7.2 澳AU,韩国KR 8.4 瑞士CH	0 受惠国$_1$LD$_1$	70	--Other fabrics
		-染色:					-Dyed:
3775	5209.3100	--平纹机织物	10	0 巴PK,冰岛IS,东盟AS,哥CR,秘鲁PE,台湾TW,香港HK,新加坡SG,新西兰NZ,智利CL 4 瑞士CH 6 澳AU,韩国KR 8.5 亚太AP	0 柬埔寨KH,老挝LA,缅甸MM,受惠国LD	70	--Plain weave
3776	5209.3200	--三线或四线斜纹机织物，包括双面斜纹机织物	10	0 巴PK,冰岛IS,东盟AS,哥CR,秘鲁PE,台湾TW,香港HK,新加坡SG,新西兰NZ,智利CL 4 瑞士CH 6 澳AU,韩国KR 8.5 亚太AP	0 柬埔寨KH,老挝LA,缅甸MM,受惠国LD	70	--3-thread or 4-thread twill, including cross twill
3777	5209.3900	--其他机织物	10	0 巴PK,冰岛IS,东盟AS,哥CR,秘鲁PE,台湾TW,香港HK,新加坡SG,新西兰NZ,智利CL 4 瑞士CH 6 澳AU,韩国KR 8.5 亚太AP	0 柬埔寨KH,老挝LA,缅甸MM,受惠国LD	70	--Other fabrics
		-色织:					-Of yarns of different colours:

序号 No.	税则号列 Tariff Line	中文货品名称 Article Description in Chinese	最惠国税率 MFN(%)	协定税率 Agreement(%)	特惠税率 SP(%)	普通税率 Gen(%)	英文货品名称 Article Description
3778	5209.4100	--平纹机织物	10	0 巴PK,冰岛IS,东盟AS,哥CR,秘鲁PE,台湾TW,香港HK,新加坡SG,新西兰NZ,智利CL 4 瑞士CH 6 澳AU,韩国KR	0 受惠国$_1$LD$_1$	70	--Plain weave
3779	5209.4200	--粗斜纹布（劳动布）	10	0 澳门MO,巴PK,冰岛IS,东盟AS,哥CR,秘鲁PE,台湾TW,香港HK,新加坡SG,新西兰NZ,智利CL 4 瑞士CH 6 澳AU,韩国KR 8.5 亚太AP	0 柬埔寨KH,老挝LA,缅甸MM,受惠国LD	70	--Denim
3780	5209.4300	--其他三线或四线斜纹机织物，包括双面斜纹机织物	10	0 巴PK,冰岛IS,东盟AS,哥CR,秘鲁PE,香港HK,新西兰NZ,智利CL 4 瑞士CH 6 澳AU,韩国KR 9.3 亚太AP	0 受惠国$_1$LD$_1$	70	--Other coloured 3 or 4-thread twill, with≥85% cotton, >200g/m^2
3781	5209.4900	--其他机织物	10	0 巴PK,冰岛IS,东盟AS,哥CR,秘鲁PE,香港HK,新加坡SG,新西兰NZ,智利CL 4 瑞士CH 6 澳AU 8.6 韩国KR	0 受惠国$_1$LD$_1$	70	--Other fabrics
		-印花：					-Printed:
3782	5209.5100	--平纹机织物	10	0 巴PK,冰岛IS,东盟AS,哥CR,秘鲁PE,香港HK,新加坡SG,新西兰NZ,智利CL 4 瑞士CH 6 澳AU,韩国KR 9.3 亚太AP	0 受惠国LD	70	--Plain weave
3783	5209.5200	--三线或四线斜纹机织物，包括双面斜纹机织物	10	0 巴PK,冰岛IS,东盟AS,哥CR,秘鲁PE,香港HK,新西兰NZ,智利CL 4 瑞士CH 6 澳AU,韩国KR	0 受惠国$_1$LD$_1$	70	--3-thread or 4-thread twill, including cross twill
3784	5209.5900	--其他机织物	10	0 巴PK,冰岛IS,东盟AS,哥CR,秘鲁PE,香港HK,新西兰NZ,智利CL 4 瑞士CH 6 澳AU,韩国KR 8.5 亚太AP	0 受惠国LD	70	--Other fabrics
	52.10	**棉机织物，按重量计含棉量在85%以下，主要或仅与化学纤维混纺，每平方米重量不超过200克：**					**Woven fabrics of cotton, containing less than 85% by weight of cotton, mixed mainly or solely with man-made fibres, weighing not more than 200g/m^2:**
		-未漂白：					-Unbleached:
3785	5210.1100	--平纹机织物	12Δ6	0 巴PK,冰岛IS,东盟AS,哥CR,秘鲁PE,香港HK,新加坡SG,新西兰NZ,智利CL 7.2 澳AU,韩国KR 8.4 瑞士CH 10.2 亚太AP	0 受惠国LD	90	--Plain weave
		--其他机织物：					--Other fabrics:

序号 No.	税则号列 Tariff Line	中文货品名称 Article Description in Chinese	最惠国税率 MFN(%)	协定税率 Agreement(%)	特惠税率 SP(%)	普通税率 Gen(%)	英文货品名称 Article Description
3786	5210.1910	---三线或四线斜纹机织物，包括双面斜纹机织物	12	0 巴PK,冰岛IS,东盟AS,哥CR,秘鲁PE,香港HK,新加坡SG,新西兰NZ,智利CL 7.2 澳AU,韩国KR 8.4 瑞士CH	0 受惠国$_1$LD$_1$	90	---3-thread or 4-thread twill, including cross twill
3787	5210.1990	---其他	12Δ6	0 巴PK,冰岛IS,东盟AS,哥CR,秘鲁PE,香港HK,新加坡SG,新西兰NZ,智利CL 7.2 澳AU,韩国KR 8.4 瑞士CH	0 受惠国LD	90	---Other
		-漂白：					-Bleached:
3788	5210.2100	--平纹机织物	14	0 巴PK,冰岛IS,东盟AS,哥CR,秘鲁PE,香港HK,新加坡SG,新西兰NZ,智利CL 8.4 澳AU 9.8 瑞士CH 11.2 韩国KR	0 受惠国LD	90	--Plain weave
		--其他机织物：					--Other fabrics:
3789	5210.2910	---三线或四线斜纹机织物，包括双面斜纹机织物	14	0 巴PK,冰岛IS,东盟AS,哥CR,秘鲁PE,香港HK,新加坡SG,新西兰NZ,智利CL 8.4 澳AU 9.8 瑞士CH 11.2 韩国KR	0 受惠国$_1$LD$_1$	90	---3-thread or 4-thread twill, including cross twill
3790	5210.2990	---其他	14	0 巴PK,冰岛IS,东盟AS,哥CR,秘鲁PE,新加坡SG,新西兰NZ,智利CL 8.4 澳AU 9.8 瑞士CH 11.2 韩国KR	0 受惠国$_1$LD$_1$	90	---Other
		-染色：					-Dyed:
3791	5210.3100	--平纹机织物	10	0 巴PK,冰岛IS,东盟AS,哥CR,秘鲁PE,台湾TW,香港HK,新加坡SG,新西兰NZ,智利CL 4 瑞士CH 6 澳AU 8.5 亚太AP 9 韩国KR	0 受惠国LD	90	--Plain weave
3792	5210.3200	--三线或四线斜纹机织物，包括双面斜纹机织物	10	0 巴PK,冰岛IS,东盟AS,哥CR,秘鲁PE,香港HK,新加坡SG,新西兰NZ,智利CL 4 瑞士CH 6 澳AU,韩国KR 8.5 亚太AP	0 受惠国$_1$LD$_1$	90	--3-thread or 4-thread twill, including cross twill
3793	5210.3900	--其他机织物	10	0 巴PK,冰岛IS,东盟AS,哥CR,台湾TW,香港HK,新加坡SG,新西兰NZ,智利CL 3 秘鲁PE 4 瑞士CH 6 澳AU 8.5 亚太AP 8.6 韩国KR	0 受惠国$_1$LD$_1$	90	--Other fabrics
		-色织：					-Of yarns of different colours:
3794	5210.4100	--平纹机织物	10	0 巴PK,冰岛IS,东盟AS,哥CR,秘鲁PE,台湾TW,香港HK,新加坡SG,新西兰NZ,智利CL 4 瑞士CH 6 澳AU,韩国KR	0 受惠国$_1$LD$_1$	90	--Plain weave

序号 No.	税则号列 Tariff Line	中文货品名称 Article Description in Chinese	最惠国税率 MFN(%)	协定税率 Agreement(%)	特惠税率 SP(%)	普通税率 Gen(%)	英文货品名称 Article Description
		--其他机织物:					--Other fabrics:
3795	5210.4910	---三线或四线斜纹机织物，包括双面斜纹机织物	10	0 巴PK,冰岛IS,东盟AS,哥CR,秘鲁PE,香港HK,新加坡SG,新西兰NZ,智利CL 4 瑞士CH 6 澳AU,韩国KR	0 受惠国$_1$LD$_1$	90	---3-thread or 4-thread twill, including cross twill
3796	5210.4990	---其他	10	0 巴PK,冰岛IS,东盟AS,哥CR,秘鲁PE,台湾TW,香港HK,新加坡SG,新西兰NZ,智利CL 4 瑞士CH 6 澳AU,韩国KR	0 受惠国LD	90	---Other
		-印花:					-Printed:
3797	5210.5100	--平纹机织物	10	0 巴PK,冰岛IS,东盟AS,哥CR,秘鲁PE,新西兰NZ,智利CL 4 瑞士CH 6 澳AU,韩国KR	0 受惠国LD	90	--Plain weave
		--其他机织物:					--Other fabrics:
3798	5210.5910	---三线或四线斜纹机织物，包括双面斜纹机织物	10	0 巴PK,冰岛IS,东盟AS,哥CR,秘鲁PE,新西兰NZ,智利CL 4 瑞士CH 6 澳AU,韩国KR	0 受惠国$_1$LD$_1$	90	---3-thread or 4-thread twill, including cross twill
3799	5210.5990	---其他机织物	10	0 巴PK,冰岛IS,东盟AS,哥CR,秘鲁PE,新西兰NZ,智利CL 4 瑞士CH 6 澳AU,韩国KR	0 受惠国LD	90	---Other fabrics
	52.11	**棉机织物，按重量计含棉量在85%以下，主要或仅与化学纤维混纺，每平方米重量超过200克:**					**Woven fabrics of cotton, containing less than 85% by weight of cotton, mixed mainly or solely with man-made fibres, weighing more than 200g/m^2:**
		-未漂白:					-Unbleached:
3800	5211.1100	--平纹机织物	12Δ6	0 巴PK,冰岛IS,东盟AS,哥CR,秘鲁PE,香港HK,新加坡SG,新西兰NZ,智利CL 7.2 澳AU 8.4 瑞士CH 10.4 韩国KR	0 受惠国LD	90	--Plain weave
3801	5211.1200	--三线或四线斜纹机织物，包括双面斜纹机织物	12Δ6	0 巴PK,冰岛IS,东盟AS,哥CR,秘鲁PE,香港HK,新加坡SG,新西兰NZ,智利CL 7.2 澳AU,韩国KR 8.4 瑞士CH	0 受惠国LD	90	--3-thread or 4-thread twill, including cross twill
3802	5211.1900	--其他机织物	12	0 巴PK,冰岛IS,东盟AS,哥CR,秘鲁PE,香港HK,新加坡SG,新西兰NZ,智利CL 7.2 澳AU,韩国KR 8.4 瑞士CH	0 受惠国LD	90	--Other fabrics
3803	5211.2000	-漂白	14	0 巴PK,冰岛IS,东盟AS,哥CR,秘鲁PE,香港HK,新加坡SG,新西兰NZ,智利CL 8.4 澳AU 9.8 瑞士CH 11.2 韩国KR	0 受惠国$_1$LD$_1$	90	-Bleached
		-染色:					-Dyed:

序号 No.	税则号列 Tariff Line	中文货品名称 Article Description in Chinese	最惠国税率 MFN(%)	协定税率 Agreement(%)		特惠税率 SP(%)		普通税率 Gen(%)	英文货品名称 Article Description
3804	5211.3100	--平纹机织物	10	0	巴PK,冰岛IS,东盟AS,哥CR,秘鲁PE,香港HK,新加坡SG,新西兰NZ,智利CL	0	受惠国LD	90	--Plain weave
				4	瑞士CH				
				6	澳AU				
				8.5	亚太AP				
				9.4	韩国KR				
3805	5211.3200	--三线或四线斜纹机织物，包括双面斜纹机织物	10	0	巴PK,冰岛IS,东盟AS,哥CR,秘鲁PE,香港HK,新加坡SG,新西兰NZ,智利CL	0	受惠国$_1$LD$_1$	90	--3-thread or 4-thread twill, including cross twill
				4	瑞士CH				
				6	澳AU,韩国KR				
				8.5	亚太AP				
3806	5211.3900	--其他机织物	10	0	巴PK,冰岛IS,东盟AS,哥CR,台湾TW,香港HK,新加坡SG,新西兰NZ,智利CL	0	受惠国LD	90	--Other fabrics
				3	秘鲁PE				
				4	瑞士CH				
				6	澳AU				
				8.5	亚太AP				
				8.6	韩国KR				
		-色织：							-Of yarns of different colours:
3807	5211.4100	--平纹机织物	10	0	巴PK,冰岛IS,东盟AS,哥CR,秘鲁PE,香港HK,新西兰NZ,智利CL	0	受惠国$_1$LD$_1$	90	--Plain weave
				4	瑞士CH				
				6	澳AU,韩国KR				
3808	5211.4200	--粗斜纹布（劳动布）	10	0	巴PK,冰岛IS,东盟AS,哥CR,秘鲁PE,香港HK,新加坡SG,新西兰NZ,智利CL	0	受惠国$_1$LD$_1$	90	--Denim
				4	瑞士CH				
				6	澳AU,韩国KR				
3809	5211.4300	--其他三线或四线斜纹机织物，包括双面斜纹机织物	10	0	巴PK,冰岛IS,东盟AS,哥CR,秘鲁PE,香港HK,新西兰NZ,智利CL	0	受惠国$_1$LD$_1$	90	--Other coloured 3 or 4-thread twill, containing less than 85% of cotton by weight, more than 200g/m^2
				4	瑞士CH				
				6	澳AU,韩国KR				
3810	5211.4900	--其他机织物	10	0	巴PK,冰岛IS,东盟AS,哥CR,秘鲁PE,新加坡SG,新西兰NZ,智利CL	0	受惠国$_1$LD$_1$	90	--Other fabrics
				4	瑞士CH				
				6	澳AU				
				8.6	韩国KR				
		-印花：							-Printed:
3811	5211.5100	--平纹机织物	10	0	巴PK,冰岛IS,东盟AS,哥CR,秘鲁PE,新西兰NZ,智利CL	0	受惠国$_1$LD$_1$	90	--Plain weave
				4	瑞士CH				
				6	澳AU,韩国KR				
3812	5211.5200	--三线或四线斜纹机织物，包括双面斜纹机织物	10	0	巴PK,冰岛IS,东盟AS,哥CR,秘鲁PE,新西兰NZ,智利CL	0	受惠国$_1$LD$_1$	90	--3-thread or 4-thread twill, including cross twill
				4	瑞士CH				
				6	澳AU,韩国KR				
3813	5211.5900	--其他机织物	10	0	巴PK,冰岛IS,东盟AS,哥CR,秘鲁PE,新西兰NZ,智利CL	0	受惠国$_1$LD$_1$	90	--Other fabrics
				4	瑞士CH				
				6	澳AU,韩国KR				
				8.5	亚太AP				
	52.12	**其他棉机织物：**							**Other woven fabrics of cotton:**

序号 No.	税则号列 Tariff Line	中文货品名称 Article Description in Chinese	最惠国税率 MFN(%)	协定税率 Agreement(%)	特惠税率 SP(%)	普通税率 Gen(%)	英文货品名称 Article Description
		-每平方米重量不超过200克：					-Weighing not more than 200 g/m^2:
3814	5212.1100	--未漂白	12	0 巴PK,冰岛IS,东盟AS,哥CR,秘鲁PE,香港HK,新加坡SG,新西兰NZ,智利CL 7.2 澳AU,韩国KR 8.4 瑞士CH	0 受惠国LD	80	--Unbleached
3815	5212.1200	--漂白	14	0 巴PK,冰岛IS,东盟AS,哥CR,秘鲁PE,香港HK,新加坡SG,新西兰NZ,智利CL 8.4 澳AU 9.8 瑞士CH 11.2 韩国KR	0 受惠国$_1$LD$_1$	80	--Bleached
3816	5212.1300	--染色	10	0 巴PK,冰岛IS,东盟AS,哥CR,秘鲁PE,香港HK,新西兰NZ,智利CL 4 瑞士CH 6 澳AU,韩国KR	0 受惠国$_1$LD$_1$	80	--Dyed
3817	5212.1400	--色织	10	0 巴PK,冰岛IS,东盟AS,哥CR,秘鲁PE,新西兰NZ,智利CL 4 瑞士CH 6 澳AU,韩国KR	0 受惠国$_1$LD$_1$	80	--Of yarns of different colours
3818	5212.1500	--印花	10	0 巴PK,冰岛IS,东盟AS,哥CR,秘鲁PE,新西兰NZ,智利CL 4 瑞士CH 6 澳AU,韩国KR	0 受惠国$_1$LD$_1$	80	--Printed
		-每平方米重量超过200克：					-Weighing more than 200g/m^2:
3819	5212.2100	--未漂白	12Δ6	0 巴PK,冰岛IS,东盟AS,哥CR,秘鲁PE,香港HK,新加坡SG,新西兰NZ,智利CL 7.2 澳AU,韩国KR 8.4 瑞士CH	0 受惠国LD	80	--Unbleached
3820	5212.2200	--漂白	14	0 巴PK,冰岛IS,东盟AS,哥CR,秘鲁PE,香港HK,新加坡SG,新西兰NZ,智利CL 8.4 澳AU 9.8 瑞士CH 11.2 韩国KR	0 受惠国$_1$LD$_1$	80	--Bleached
3821	5212.2300	--染色	10	0 巴PK,冰岛IS,东盟AS,哥CR,秘鲁PE,香港HK,新西兰NZ,智利CL 4 瑞士CH 6 澳AU,韩国KR	0 受惠国$_1$LD$_1$	80	--Dyed
3822	5212.2400	--色织	10	0 巴PK,冰岛IS,东盟AS,哥CR,秘鲁PE,新西兰NZ,智利CL 4 瑞士CH 6 澳AU,韩国KR	0 受惠国$_1$LD$_1$	80	--Of yarns of different colours
3823	5212.2500	--印花	10	0 巴PK,冰岛IS,东盟AS,哥CR,秘鲁PE,新西兰NZ,智利CL 4 瑞士CH 6 澳AU,韩国KR	0 受惠国LD	80	--Printed

第五十三章
其他植物纺织纤维；纸纱线及其机织物

Chapter 53
Other vegetable textile fibres; paper yarn and woven fabrics of paper yarn

序号 No.	税则号列 Tariff Line	中文货品名称 Article Description in Chinese	最惠国税率 MFN(%)	协定税率 Agreement(%)	特惠税率 SP(%)	普通税率 Gen(%)	英文货品名称 Article Description
	53.01	亚麻，生的或经加工但未纺制的；亚麻短纤及废麻（包括废麻纱线及回收纤维）：					**Flax, raw or processed but not spun; flax tow and waste (including yarn waste and garnetted stock) :**
3824	5301.1000	-生的或经沤制的亚麻	6	0 冰岛IS,东盟AS,哥CR,韩国KR,秘鲁PE,新西兰NZ,智利CL 2.4 瑞士CH 3.6 澳AU 5 巴PK	0 受惠国LD	30	-Flax, raw or retted
		-破开、打成、栉梳或经其他加工但未纺制的亚麻：					-Flax, broken, scutched, hackled or otherwise processed, but not spun:
3825	5301.2100	--破开的或打成的	6Δ1	0 冰岛IS,东盟AS,哥CR,韩国KR,秘鲁PE,新西兰NZ,智利CL 2.4 瑞士CH 3.6 澳AU 5 巴PK	0 受惠国LD	30	--Broken or scutched
3826	5301.2900	--其他	6	0 冰岛IS,东盟AS,哥CR,韩国KR,秘鲁PE,新西兰NZ,智利CL 2.4 瑞士CH 3.6 澳AU 5 巴PK	0 受惠国LD	30	--Other
3827	5301.3000	-亚麻短纤及废麻	6Δ1	0 冰岛IS,东盟AS,哥CR,韩国KR,秘鲁PE,新西兰NZ,智利CL 2.4 瑞士CH 3.6 澳AU 5 巴PK	0 受惠国LD	30	-Flax tow and waste
	53.02	大麻，生的或经加工但未纺制的；大麻短纤及废麻（包括废麻纱线及回收纤维）：					**True hemp (*Cannabis sativa L.*), raw or processed but not spun; tow and waste of true hemp (including yarn waste and garnetted stock) :**
3828	5302.1000	-生的或经沤制的大麻	6	0 冰岛IS,东盟AS,哥CR,韩国KR,秘鲁PE,新西兰NZ,智利CL 2.4 瑞士CH 3.6 澳AU 5 巴PK	0 受惠国LD	30	-True hemp, raw or retted
3829	5302.9000	-其他	6	0 冰岛IS,东盟AS,哥CR,韩国KR,秘鲁PE,新西兰NZ,智利CL 2.4 瑞士CH 3.6 澳AU 5 巴PK	0 受惠国LD	30	-Other
	53.03	**黄麻及其他纺织用韧皮纤维（不包括亚麻、大麻及苎麻），生的或经加工但未纺制的；上述纤维的短纤及废麻（包括废纱线及回收纤维）：**					**Jute and other textile bast fibres (excluding flax, true hemp and ramie), raw or processed but not spun; tow and waste of these fibres (including yarn waste and garnetted stock) :**
3830	5303.1000	-生的或经沤制的黄麻及其他纺织用韧皮纤维	5	0 澳AU,巴PK,冰岛IS,东盟AS,哥CR,韩国KR,秘鲁PE,瑞士CH,新西兰NZ,智利CL	0 柬埔寨KH,老挝LA,缅甸MM,受惠国LD,亚太AP	20	-Jute and other textile bast fibres, raw or retted

序号 No.	税则号列 Tariff Line	中文货品名称 Article Description in Chinese	最惠国税率 MFN(%)	协定税率 Agreement(%)	特惠税率 SP(%)	普通税率 Gen(%)	英文货品名称 Article Description
3831	5303.9000	-其他	5	0 澳AU,巴PK,冰岛IS,东盟AS,哥CR,韩国KR,秘鲁PE,瑞士CH,新西兰NZ,智利CL	0 柬埔寨KH,老挝LA,缅甸MM,受惠国LD	30	-Other
	53.05	**椰壳纤维、蕉麻（马尼拉麻）、苎麻及其他税号未列名的纺织用植物纤维，生的或经加工但未纺制的；上述纤维的短纤、落麻及废料（包括废纱线及回收纤维）：**					**Coconut, abaca (Manila hemp or *Musa textilis Nee*) , ramie and other vegetable textile fibres, not elsewhere specified or included, raw or processed but not spun; tow, noils and waste of these fibres (including yarn waste and garnetted stock) :**
		---苎麻：					---Ramie:
3832	5305.0011	----生的	5	0 澳AU,巴PK,冰岛IS,东盟AS,哥CR,韩国KR,秘鲁PE,瑞士CH,新西兰NZ,智利CL	0 受惠国LD	30	----Raw
3833	5305.0012	----经加工但未纺制的	5	0 澳AU,巴PK,冰岛IS,东盟AS,哥CR,韩国KR,秘鲁PE,瑞士CH,新西兰NZ,智利CL	0 受惠国LD	30	----Processed but not spun
3834	5305.0013	----短纤及废料	5	0 澳AU,巴PK,冰岛IS,东盟AS,哥CR,韩国KR,秘鲁PE,瑞士CH,新西兰NZ,智利CL	0 受惠国LD	30	----Fibres and weste
3835	5305.0019	----其他	5	0 澳AU,巴PK,冰岛IS,东盟AS,哥CR,韩国KR,秘鲁PE,瑞士CH,新西兰NZ,智利CL	0 受惠国LD	20	----Other
3836	5305.0020	---蕉麻	3	0 澳AU,巴PK,冰岛IS,东盟AS,哥CR,韩国KR,秘鲁PE,瑞士CH,新西兰NZ,智利CL	0 受惠国LD	20	---Abaca
		---其他：					---Other:
3837	5305.0091	----西沙尔麻及其他纺织用龙舌兰类纤维	5	0 澳AU,巴PK,冰岛IS,东盟AS,哥CR,韩国KR,秘鲁PE,瑞士CH,新西兰NZ,智利CL	0 受惠国LD	30	----Sisal and other textile fabrics of the genus Agave
3838	5305.0092	----椰壳纤维	5	0 澳AU,巴PK,冰岛IS,东盟AS,哥CR,韩国KR,秘鲁PE,瑞士CH,新西兰NZ,智利CL 4 亚太AP	0 柬埔寨KH,老挝LA,缅甸MM,受惠国LD	30	----Coconut fabrics
3839	5305.0099	----其他	5	0 澳AU,巴PK,冰岛IS,东盟AS,哥CR,韩国KR,秘鲁PE,瑞士CH,新西兰NZ,智利CL	0 受惠国LD	30	----Other
	53.06	**亚麻纱线：**					**Flax yarn:**
3840	5306.1000	-单纱	6	0 澳门MO,冰岛IS,东盟AS,哥CR,韩国KR,秘鲁PE,香港HK,新西兰NZ,智利CL 2.4 瑞士CH 3.6 澳AU 5 巴PK	0 受惠国LD	50	-Single
3841	5306.2000	-多股纱线或缆线	10Δ5	0 澳门MO,冰岛IS,东盟AS,哥CR,秘鲁PE,香港HK,新西兰NZ,智利CL 4 瑞士CH 5 巴PK 6 澳AU,韩国KR	0 受惠国LD	50	-Multiple (folded) or cabled
	53.07	**黄麻纱线或税号53.03的其他纺织用韧皮纤维纱线：**					**Yarn of jute or of other textile bast fibres of heading 5303:**

序号 No.	税则号列 Tariff Line	中文货品名称 Article Description in Chinese	最惠国税率 MFN(%)	协定税率 Agreement(%)	特惠税率 SP(%)	普通税率 Gen(%)	英文货品名称 Article Description
3842	5307.1000	-单纱	6	0 澳门MO,冰岛IS,东盟AS,哥CR,韩国KR,秘鲁PE,新西兰NZ,智利CL 2.4 瑞士CH 3.6 澳AU 5 巴PK	0 柬埔寨KH,受惠国LD 3 亚太AP	35	-Single
3843	5307.2000	-多股纱线或缆线	6	0 澳门MO,冰岛IS,东盟AS,哥CR,韩国KR,秘鲁PE,新西兰NZ,智利CL 2.4 瑞士CH 3.6 澳AU 5 巴PK	0 柬埔寨KH,受惠国LD 3 亚太AP	35	-Multiple (folded) or cabled
	53.08	**其他植物纺织纤维纱线;纸纱线:**					**Yarn of other vegetable textile fibres; paper yarn:**
3844	5308.1000	-椰壳纤维纱线	6	0 澳门MO,冰岛IS,东盟AS,哥CR,韩国KR,秘鲁PE,新西兰NZ,智利CL 2.4 瑞士CH 3.6 澳AU 5 巴PK	0 受惠国LD	45	-Coir yarn
3845	5308.2000	-大麻纱线	6	0 澳门MO,冰岛IS,东盟AS,哥CR,韩国KR,秘鲁PE,新西兰NZ,智利CL 2.4 瑞士CH 3.6 澳AU 5 巴PK	0 受惠国LD	45	-True hemp yarn
		-其他: ---苎麻纱线:					-Other: ---Ramie yarn:
3846	5308.9011	----按重量计苎麻含量在85%及以上的未漂白或漂白纱线	6	0 澳门MO,冰岛IS,东盟AS,哥CR,韩国KR,秘鲁PE,新西兰NZ,智利CL 2.4 瑞士CH 3.6 澳AU 5 巴PK	0 受惠国LD	50	----Containing 85% or more by weight of ramie, unbleached or bleached yarn
3847	5308.9012	----按重量计苎麻含量在85%及以上的色纱线	6	0 澳门MO,冰岛IS,东盟AS,哥CR,韩国KR,秘鲁PE,新西兰NZ,智利CL 2.4 瑞士CH 3.6 澳AU 5 巴PK	0 受惠国LD	50	----Containing 85% or more by weight of ramie, coloured yarn
3848	5308.9013	----按重量计苎麻含量在85%以下的未漂白或漂白纱线	6	0 澳门MO,冰岛IS,东盟AS,哥CR,韩国KR,秘鲁PE,新西兰NZ,智利CL 2.4 瑞士CH 3.6 澳AU 5 巴PK	0 受惠国LD	50	----Containing less than 85% by weight of ramie, unbleached or bleached yarn
3849	5308.9014	----按重量计苎麻含量在85%以下的色纱线	6	0 澳门MO,冰岛IS,东盟AS,哥CR,韩国KR,秘鲁PE,新西兰NZ,智利CL 2.4 瑞士CH 3.6 澳AU 5 巴PK	0 受惠国LD	50	----Containing less than 85% by weight of ramie, coloured yarn
		---其他:					---Other:
3850	5308.9091	----纸纱线	6	0 澳门MO,冰岛IS,东盟AS,哥CR,韩国KR,秘鲁PE,新西兰NZ,智利CL 2.4 瑞士CH 3.6 澳AU 5 巴PK	0 受惠国LD	70	----Paper yarn
3851	5308.9099	----其他	6	0 澳门MO,冰岛IS,东盟AS,哥CR,韩国KR,秘鲁PE,新西兰NZ,智利CL 2.4 瑞士CH 3.6 澳AU 5 巴PK	0 受惠国LD	45	----Other
	53.09	**亚麻机织物:**					**Woven fabrics of flax:**

序号 No.	税则号列 Tariff Line	中文货品名称 Article Description in Chinese	最惠国税率 MFN(%)	协定税率 Agreement(%)	特惠税率 SP(%)	普通税率 Gen(%)	英文货品名称 Article Description
		-按重量计亚麻含量在85%及以上：					-Containing 85 % or more by weight of flax:
		--未漂白或漂白：					--Unbleached or bleached:
3852	5309.1110	---未漂白	10	0 巴PK,冰岛IS,东盟AS,哥CR,秘鲁PE,新西兰NZ,智利CL 4 瑞士CH 6 澳AU,韩国KR	0 受惠国LD	80	---Unbleached
3853	5309.1120	---漂白	10	0 巴PK,冰岛IS,东盟AS,哥CR,秘鲁PE,新西兰NZ,智利CL 4 瑞士CH 6 澳AU,韩国KR	0 受惠国LD	80	---Bleached
3854	5309.1900	--其他	10	0 巴PK,冰岛IS,东盟AS,哥CR,秘鲁PE,香港HK,新西兰NZ,智利CL 4 瑞士CH 6 澳AU,韩国KR 9.3 亚太AP	0 受惠国LD	80	--Other
		-按重量计亚麻含量在85%以下：					-Containing less than 85% by weight of flax:
		--未漂白或漂白：					--Unbleached or bleached:
3855	5309.2110	---未漂白	10	0 澳门MO,巴PK,冰岛IS,东盟AS,哥CR,秘鲁PE,新西兰NZ,智利CL 4 瑞士CH 6 澳AU,韩国KR	0 受惠国LD	80	---Unbleached
3856	5309.2120	---漂白	10	0 澳门MO,巴PK,冰岛IS,东盟AS,哥CR,秘鲁PE,新西兰NZ,智利CL 4 瑞士CH 6 澳AU,韩国KR	0 受惠国LD	80	---Bleached
3857	5309.2900	--其他	10	0 澳门MO,巴PK,冰岛IS,东盟AS,哥CR,秘鲁PE,香港HK,新西兰NZ,智利CL 4 瑞士CH 6 澳AU,韩国KR 8.5 亚太AP	0 受惠国LD	80	--Other
	53.10	**黄麻或税号53.03的其他纺织用韧皮纤维机织物：**					**Woven fabrics of jute or of other textilebast fibres of heading No.53.03:**
3858	5310.1000	-未漂白	10	0 冰岛IS,东盟AS,哥CR,秘鲁PE,新西兰NZ,智利CL 4 瑞士CH 5 巴PK 6 澳AU,韩国KR	0 柬埔寨KH,受惠国LD 5 亚太AP	40	-Unbleached
3859	5310.9000	-其他	10	0 冰岛IS,东盟AS,哥CR,秘鲁PE,新西兰NZ,智利CL 4 瑞士CH 5 巴PK 6 澳AU,韩国KR	0 柬埔寨KH,受惠国LD 5 亚太AP	40	-Other
	53.11	**其他纺织用植物纤维机织物；纸纱线机织物：**					**Woven fabrics of other vegetable textile fibres; woven fabrics of paper yarn:**
		---苎麻的：					---Of ramie:
3860	5311.0012	----按重量计苎麻含量在85%及以上的未漂白机织物	10	0 澳门MO,冰岛IS,东盟AS,哥CR,秘鲁PE,新西兰NZ,智利CL 4 瑞士CH 5 巴PK 6 澳AU,韩国KR	0 受惠国LD	80	----Containing 85% or more by weight of ramie, unbleached woven fabrics

序号 No.	税则号列 Tariff Line	中文货品名称 Article Description in Chinese	最惠国税率 MFN(%)	协定税率 Agreement(%)	特惠税率 SP(%)	普通税率 Gen(%)	英文货品名称 Article Description
3861	5311.0013	----按重量计苎麻含量在85%及以上的其他机织物	12	0 澳门MO,冰岛IS,东盟AS,哥CR,秘鲁PE,新加坡SG,新西兰NZ,智利CL 6 巴PK 7.2 澳AU,韩国KR 8.4 瑞士CH	0 受惠国LD	80	----Containing 85% or more by weight of ramie, other woven fabrics
3862	5311.0014	----按重量计苎麻含量在85%以下的未漂白机织物	10	0 冰岛IS,东盟AS,哥CR,秘鲁PE,新西兰NZ,智利CL 4 瑞士CH 5 巴PK 6 澳AU,韩国KR	0 受惠国LD	80	----Containing less than 85% by weight of ramie, unbleached woven fabrics
3863	5311.0015	----按重量计苎麻含量在85%以下的其他机织物	12	0 澳门MO,冰岛IS,东盟AS,哥CR,秘鲁PE,新加坡SG,新西兰NZ,智利CL 6 巴PK 7.2 澳AU,韩国KR 8.4 瑞士CH	0 受惠国$_1$LD$_1$	80	----Containing less than 85% by weight of ramie, other woven fabrics
3864	5311.0020	---纸纱线的	10	0 冰岛IS,东盟AS,哥CR,秘鲁PE,新西兰NZ,智利CL 4 瑞士CH 5 巴PK 6 澳AU,韩国KR	0 受惠国LD	90	---Of paper yarn
3865	5311.0030	---大麻的	10	0 冰岛IS,东盟AS,哥CR,秘鲁PE,新西兰NZ,智利CL 4 瑞士CH 5 巴PK 6 澳AU,韩国KR 9.3 亚太AP	0 受惠国LD	50	---Of true hemp
3866	5311.0090	---其他	10	0 冰岛IS,东盟AS,哥CR,秘鲁PE,新西兰NZ,智利CL 4 瑞士CH 5 巴PK 6 澳AU,韩国KR 9.3 亚太AP	0 受惠国LD	50	---Other

第五十四章
化学纤维长丝

注释：

一、本目录所称“化学纤维”，是指通过下列任一方法加工制得的有机聚合物的短纤或长丝：

（一）将有机单体物质加以聚合而制成聚合物，例如，聚酰胺、聚酯、聚烯烃、聚氨基甲酸酯；或通过上述加工将聚合物经化学改性制得（例如，聚乙酸乙烯酯水解得的聚乙烯醇）；或

（二）将天然有机聚合物（例如，纤维素）溶解或经化学处理制成聚合物，例如，铜铵纤维或粘胶纤维；或将天然有机聚合物（例如，纤维素、酪蛋白及其他蛋白质、或藻酸）经化学改性制成聚合物，例如醋酸纤维素纤维或藻酸盐纤维。

对于化学纤维，所称“合成”，是指（一）款所述的纤维;所称“人造”，是指（二）款所述的纤维。税目54.04或54.05的扁条及类似品不视作化学纤维。

对于纺织材料，所称“化学纤维”、“合成纤维”及“人造纤维”，其含义应与上述解释相同。

二、税号54.02及54.03不适用于第五十五章的合成纤维或人造纤维的长丝丝束。

Chapter 54
Man-made filaments; strip and the like of man made textile materials

Notes:

1. Throughout the Nomenclature，the term “man-made fibres” means staple fibres and filaments of organic polymers produced by manufacturing processes, either:

(a) By polymerisation of organic monomers toproduce polymers such as polyamides, polyesters, polyolefins or polyurethanes, or bychemical modification of polymers produced by this process (for example, poly (vinyl alcohol) prepared by the hydrolysis of poly (vinyl acetate); or

(b) By dissolution or chemical treatment of natural organic polymers (for example, cellulose) toproduce polymers such as cuprammonium rayon (cupro) or viscose rayon, or by chemical modification of natural organic polymers (for example, cellulose, casein and other proteins, oralginic acid), to produce polymers such as cellulose acetate or alginates.

The terms “synthetic” and “artificial”, used in relation to fibres, mean: synthetic: fibres as defined at (a); artificial: fibres as defined at (b). Strip and the like ofheading 54.04 or 54.05 are not considered to be manmade fibres.

The terms “man-made”, “synthetic” and “artificial” shall have the same meanings when used in relation to “textile materials”.

2. Headings Nos.54.02 and 54.03 do not apply to synthetic or artificial filament tow of Chapter 55.

序号 No.	税则号列 Tariff Line	中文货品名称 Article Description in Chinese	最惠国税率 MFN(%)	协定税率 Agreement(%)	特惠税率 SP(%)	普通税率 Gen(%)	英文货品名称 Article Description
	54.01	**化学纤维长丝纺制的缝纫线，不论是否供零售用：**					**Sewing thread of man-made filaments, whether or not put up for retail sale:**
		-合成纤维长丝纺制.					-Of synthetic filaments:
3867	5401.1010	非供零售用	5	0 澳AU,澳门MO,巴PK,冰岛IS,东盟AS,哥CR,秘鲁PE,台湾TW,香港HK,新西兰NZ,智利CL 2 瑞士CH 4.3 韩国KR	0 受惠国LD	70	---Not put up for retail sale
3868	5401.1020	---供零售用	5	0 澳AU,巴PK,冰岛IS,东盟AS,哥CR,韩国KR,秘鲁PE,瑞士CH,新西兰NZ,智利CL	0 受惠国LD	90	---Put up for retail sale
		-人造纤维长丝纺制:					-Of artificial filaments:
3869	5401.2010	---非供零售用	5	0 澳AU,巴PK,冰岛IS,东盟AS,哥CR,韩国KR,秘鲁PE,瑞士CH,新西兰NZ,智利CL	0 受惠国LD	35	---Not put up for retail sale
3870	5401.2020	---供零售用	5	0 澳AU,巴PK,冰岛IS,东盟AS,哥CR,韩国KR,秘鲁PE,瑞士CH,新西兰NZ,智利CL	0 受惠国LD	90	---Put up for retail sale
	54.02	**合成纤维长丝纱线（缝纫线除外），非供零售用，包括细度在67分特以下的合成纤维单丝：**					**Synthetic filament yarn (other than sewing thread) , not put up for retail sale, including synthetic monofilament of less than 67 decitex:**
		-尼龙或其他聚酰胺纺制的高强力纱：					-High-tenacity yarn of nylon or other polyamides:
		--芳香族聚酰胺纺制:					--Of aramids:

序号 No.	税则号列 Tariff Line	中文货品名称 Article Description in Chinese	最惠国税率 MFN(%)	协定税率 Agreement(%)	特惠税率 SP(%)	普通税率 Gen(%)	英文货品名称 Article Description
3871	5402.1110	---聚间苯二甲酰间苯二胺纺制	5	0 澳AU,澳门MO,巴PK,冰岛IS,东盟AS,哥CR,秘鲁PE,瑞士CH,新西兰NZ,智利CL 4.3 韩国KR	0 受惠国LD	70	---Of polyisophthaloyl metaphenylene diamine
3872	5402.1120	---聚对苯二甲酰对苯二胺纺制	5	0 澳AU,澳门MO,巴PK,冰岛IS,东盟AS,哥CR,秘鲁PE,瑞士CH,新西兰NZ,智利CL 4.3 韩国KR	0 受惠国LD	70	---Of polyisophthaloyl paraphenylene diamine
3873	5402.1190	---其他	5	0 澳AU,澳门MO,巴PK,冰岛IS,东盟AS,哥CR,秘鲁PE,瑞士CH,新西兰NZ,智利CL 4.3 韩国KR	0 受惠国LD	70	---Other
		--其他：					--Other:
3874	5402.1910	---聚酰胺-6（尼龙-6）纺制	5	0 澳AU,澳门MO,巴PK,冰岛IS,东盟AS,哥CR,秘鲁PE,瑞士CH,新西兰NZ,智利CL	0 受惠国LD	70	---Of nylon-6
3875	5402.1920	---聚酰胺-6，6（尼龙-6，6）纺制	5	0 澳AU,澳门MO,巴PK,冰岛IS,东盟AS,哥CR,秘鲁PE,瑞士CH,新西兰NZ,智利CL	0 受惠国LD	70	---Of nylon-6, 6
3876	5402.1990	---其他	5	0 澳AU,澳门MO,巴PK,冰岛IS,东盟AS,哥CR,秘鲁PE,瑞士CH,新西兰NZ,智利CL 4.3 韩国KR	0 受惠国LD	70	---Other
3877	5402.2000	-聚酯高强力纱	5	0 澳AU,澳门MO,巴PK,冰岛IS,东盟AS,哥CR,秘鲁PE,台湾TW,新西兰NZ,智利CL 2 瑞士CH 4.3 韩国KR	0 受惠国LD	70	-High tenacity yarn of polyesters
		-变形纱线：					-Textured yarn:
		--尼龙或其他聚酰胺纺制，每根单纱细度不超过50特：					--Of nylon or other polyamides, measuring per single yarn not more than 50 tex:
		---弹力丝：					---Elastic filament:
3878	5402.3111	----聚酰胺-6（尼龙-6）纺制	5	0 澳AU,澳门MO,巴PK,冰岛IS,东盟AS,哥CR,秘鲁PE,瑞士CH,香港HK,新西兰NZ,智利CL	0 受惠国LD	80	----Of nylon-6
3879	5402.3112	----聚酰胺-6，6（尼龙-6，6）纺制	5	0 澳AU,澳门MO,巴PK,冰岛IS,东盟AS,哥CR,秘鲁PE,瑞士CH,香港HK,新西兰NZ,智利CL	0 受惠国LD	80	----Of nylon-6, 6
3880	5402.3113	----芳香族聚酰胺纺制	5	0 澳AU,澳门MO,巴PK,冰岛IS,东盟AS,哥CR,秘鲁PE,瑞士CH,香港HK,新西兰NZ,智利CL	0 受惠国LD	80	----Of aramides
3881	5402.3119	----其他	5	0 澳AU,澳门MO,巴PK,冰岛IS,东盟AS,哥CR,秘鲁PE,瑞士CH,香港HK,新西兰NZ,智利CL 4.3 韩国KR	0 受惠国LD	80	----Other
3882	5402.3190	---其他	5	0 澳AU,澳门MO,巴PK,冰岛IS,东盟AS,哥CR,秘鲁PE,瑞士CH,香港HK,新西兰NZ,智利CL 4.3 韩国KR	0 受惠国LD	70	---Other
		--尼龙或其他聚酰胺纺制，每根单纱细度超过50特：					--Of nylon or other polyamides, measuring per single yarn more than 50 tex:
		---弹力丝：					---Elastic filament:

序号 No.	税则号列 Tariff Line	中文货品名称 Article Description in Chinese	最惠国税率 MFN(%)	协定税率 Agreement(%)	特惠税率 SP(%)	普通税率 Gen(%)	英文货品名称 Article Description
3883	5402.3211	----聚酰胺-6（尼龙-6）纺制	5	0 澳AU,澳门MO,巴PK,冰岛IS,东盟AS,哥CR,秘鲁PE,瑞士CH,香港HK,新西兰NZ,智利CL	0 受惠国LD	80	----Of nylon-6
3884	5402.3212	----聚酰胺-6，6（尼龙-6，6）纺制	5	0 澳AU,澳门MO,巴PK,冰岛IS,东盟AS,哥CR,秘鲁PE,瑞士CH,香港HK,新西兰NZ,智利CL	0 受惠国LD	80	----Of nylon-6, 6
3885	5402.3213	----芳香族聚酰胺纺制	5	0 澳AU,澳门MO,巴PK,冰岛IS,东盟AS,哥CR,秘鲁PE,瑞士CH,香港HK,新西兰NZ,智利CL 4.3 韩国KR	0 受惠国LD	80	----Of aramids
3886	5402.3219	----其他	5	0 澳AU,澳门MO,巴PK,冰岛IS,东盟AS,哥CR,秘鲁PE,瑞士CH,香港HK,新西兰NZ,智利CL	0 受惠国LD	80	----Other
3887	5402.3290	---其他	5	0 澳AU,澳门MO,巴PK,冰岛IS,东盟AS,哥CR,秘鲁PE,瑞士CH,香港HK,新西兰NZ,智利CL 4.3 韩国KR 4.5 亚太AP	0 受惠国LD	70	---Other
		--聚酯纺制：					--Of polyesters:
3888	5402.3310	---弹力丝	5	0 澳AU,澳门MO,巴PK,冰岛IS,东盟AS,哥CR,韩国KR,秘鲁PE,瑞士CH,台湾TW,新西兰NZ,智利CL	0 受惠国LD	90	---Elastic filament
3889	5402.3390	---其他	5	0 澳AU,澳门MO,巴PK,冰岛IS,哥CR,秘鲁PE,瑞士CH,新西兰NZ,智利CL 4 韩国KR	0 受惠国LD	70	---Other
3890	5402.3400	--聚丙烯纱线	5	0 澳AU,澳门MO,巴PK,冰岛IS,东盟AS,哥CR,秘鲁PE,瑞士CH,新西兰NZ,智利CL 4 韩国KR	0 受惠国LD	70	--Of polypropylene
3891	5402.3900	其他	5	0 澳AU,澳门MO,巴PK,冰岛IS,东盟AS,哥CR,秘鲁PE,瑞士CH,新西兰NZ,智利CL 4 韩国KR	0 受惠国LD	70	--Other
		-其他单纱，未加捻或捻度每米不超过50转：					-Other yarn, single, untwisted or with a twist not exceeding 50 turns per metre:
		--弹性纱线：					--Elastomeric:
3892	5402.4410	---氨纶纱线	5	0 澳AU,澳门MO,巴PK,冰岛IS,东盟AS,哥CR,秘鲁PE,瑞士CH,新西兰NZ,智利CL	0 受惠国LD	70	---Of polyurethane
3893	5402.4490	---其他	5	0 澳AU,澳门MO,巴PK,冰岛IS,东盟AS,哥CR,韩国KR,秘鲁PE,瑞士CH,香港HK,新西兰NZ,智利CL 4.7 亚太AP	0 受惠国LD	70	---Other
		--其他，尼龙或其他聚酰胺纱线：					--Other, of nylon or other polyamides:
3894	5402.4510	---聚酰胺-6（尼龙-6）制	5	0 澳AU,澳门MO,巴PK,冰岛IS,东盟AS,哥CR,秘鲁PE,瑞士CH,新西兰NZ,智利CL 4.3 韩国KR 4.7 亚太AP	0 受惠国LD	70	---Of nylon-6

序号 No.	税则号列 Tariff Line	中文货品名称 Article Description in Chinese	最惠国税率 MFN(%)	协定税率 Agreement(%)	特惠税率 SP(%)	普通税率 Gen(%)	英文货品名称 Article Description
3895	5402.4520	---聚酰胺-6,6(尼龙-6,6)制	5	0 澳AU,澳门MO,巴PK,冰岛IS,东盟AS,哥CR,秘鲁PE,瑞士CH,新西兰NZ,智利CL 4.3 韩国KR 4.7 亚太AP	0 受惠国LD	70	---Of nylon-6, 6
3896	5402.4530	---芳香族聚酰胺制	5	0 澳AU,澳门MO,巴PK,冰岛IS,东盟AS,哥CR,秘鲁PE,瑞士CH,新西兰NZ,智利CL 4.3 韩国KR 4.7 亚太AP	0 受惠国LD	70	---Of aramids
3897	5402.4590	---其他	5	0 澳AU,澳门MO,巴PK,冰岛IS,东盟AS,哥CR,秘鲁PE,瑞士CH,新西兰NZ,智利CL 4.3 韩国KR 4.7 亚太AP	0 受惠国LD	70	---Other
3898	5402.4600	--其他，部分定向聚酯纱线	5	0 澳AU,澳门MO,巴PK,冰岛IS,哥CR,秘鲁PE,瑞士CH,新西兰NZ,智利CL 4 韩国KR	0 受惠国LD	70	--Other, of polyesters, partially oriented
3899	5402.4700	--其他，聚酯纱线	5	0 澳AU,澳门MO,巴PK,冰岛IS,哥CR,秘鲁PE,新西兰NZ,智利CL 3.5 瑞士CH 4.3 韩国KR 4.7 亚太AP	0 受惠国LD	70	--Other, of polyesters
3900	5402.4800	--其他，聚丙烯纱线	5	0 澳AU,澳门MO,巴PK,冰岛IS,东盟AS,哥CR,韩国KR,秘鲁PE,瑞士CH,新西兰NZ,智利CL	0 受惠国LD	70	--Other , of polypropylene
		--其他:					--Other:
3901	5402.4910	---断裂强度大于等于22cN/dtex,且初始模量大于等于750cN/dtex的聚乙烯纱线	5	0 澳AU,澳门MO,巴PK,冰岛IS,东盟AS,哥CR,秘鲁PE,瑞士CH,新西兰NZ,智利CL	0 受惠国LD	70	---Of polyethylene, breaking strengths≥22cN/dtex, initial modulus≥750cN/dtex
3902	5402.4990	---其他	5	0 澳AU,澳门MO,巴PK,冰岛IS,东盟AS,哥CR,秘鲁PE,瑞士CH,新西兰NZ,智利CL	0 受惠国LD	70	---Other
		-其他单纱，捻度每米超过50转:					-Other yarn, single, with a twist exceeding 50 turns per metre:
		--尼龙或其他聚酰胺纱线:					--Of nylon or other polyamides:
3903	5402.5110	---聚酰胺-6（尼龙-6）制	5	0 澳AU,澳门MO,巴PK,冰岛IS,哥CR,秘鲁PE,瑞士CH,新西兰NZ,智利CL	0 受惠国LD	70	---Of nylon-6
3904	5402.5120	---聚酰胺-6,6(尼龙-6,6）制	5	0 澳AU,澳门MO,巴PK,冰岛IS,东盟AS,哥CR,秘鲁PE,瑞士CH,新西兰NZ,智利CL	0 受惠国LD	70	---Of nylon-6, 6
3905	5402.5130	---芳香族聚酰胺制	5	0 澳AU,澳门MO,巴PK,冰岛IS,东盟AS,哥CR,秘鲁PE,瑞士CH,新西兰NZ,智利CL 4.3 韩国KR	0 受惠国LD	70	---Of aramides
3906	5402.5190	---其他	5	0 澳AU,澳门MO,巴PK,冰岛IS,东盟AS,哥CR,秘鲁PE,瑞士CH,新西兰NZ,智利CL 4.3 韩国KR	0 受惠国LD	70	---Other

序号 No.	税则号列 Tariff Line	中文货品名称 Article Description in Chinese	最惠国税率 MFN(%)	协定税率 Agreement(%)		特惠税率 SP(%)	普通税率 Gen(%)	英文货品名称 Article Description
3907	5402.5200	--聚酯纱线	5	0 4 4.3	澳AU,澳门MO,巴PK,冰岛IS,哥CR,秘鲁PE,瑞士CH,新西兰NZ,智利CL 韩国KR 亚太AP	0 受惠国LD	70	--Of polyesters
		--其他:						--Other:
3908	5402.5910	---聚丙烯纱线	5	0	澳AU,澳门MO,巴PK,冰岛IS,东盟AS,哥CR,韩国KR,秘鲁PE,瑞士CH,新西兰NZ,智利CL	0 受惠国LD	70	---Of polypropylene
3909	5402.5920	---断裂强度大于等于22cN/dtex,且初始模量大于等于750cN/dtex的聚乙烯纱线	5	0	澳AU,澳门MO,巴PK,冰岛IS,东盟AS,哥CR,韩国KR,秘鲁PE,瑞士CH,新西兰NZ,智利CL	0 受惠国LD	70	---Of polyethylene, breaking strengths≥22cN/dtex, initial modulus≥750cN/dtex
3910	5402.5990	---其他	5	0	澳AU,澳门MO,巴PK,冰岛IS,东盟AS,哥CR,韩国KR,秘鲁PE,瑞士CH,新西兰NZ,智利CL	0 受惠国LD	70	---Other
		-其他纱线(多股纱线或缆线):						-Other yarn, multiple (folded) or cabled:
		--尼龙或其他聚酰胺纺制:						--Of nylon or other polyamides:
3911	5402.6110	---聚酰胺-6(尼龙-6)制	5	0 4.3	澳AU,澳门MO,巴PK,冰岛IS,东盟AS,哥CR,秘鲁PE,瑞士CH,新西兰NZ,智利CL 韩国KR	0 受惠国LD	70	---Of nylon-6
3912	5402.6120	---聚酰胺-6,6(尼龙-6,6)制	5	0 4.3	澳AU,澳门MO,巴PK,冰岛IS,东盟AS,哥CR,秘鲁PE,瑞士CH,新西兰NZ,智利CL 韩国KR	0 受惠国LD	70	---Of nylon-6, 6
3913	5402.6130	---芳香族聚酰胺制	5	0 4.3	澳AU,澳门MO,巴PK,冰岛IS,东盟AS,哥CR,秘鲁PE,瑞士CH,新西兰NZ,智利CL 韩国KR	0 受惠国LD	70	---Of aramides
3914	5402.6190	---其他	5	0 3	澳AU,澳门MO,巴PK,冰岛IS,东盟AS,哥CR,秘鲁PE,瑞士CH,新西兰NZ,智利CL 韩国KR	0 受惠国LD	70	---Other
3915	5402.6200	--聚酯纺制	5	0 3	澳AU,澳门MO,巴PK,冰岛IS,东盟AS,哥CR,秘鲁PE,瑞士CH,台湾TW,新西兰NZ,智利CL 韩国KR	0 受惠国LD	70	--Of polyesters
		--其他:						--Other:
3916	5402.6910	---聚丙烯纱线	5	0 4.3	澳AU,澳门MO,巴PK,冰岛IS,东盟AS,哥CR,秘鲁PE,瑞士CH,新西兰NZ,智利CL 韩国KR	0 受惠国LD	70	---Of polypropylene
3917	5402.6920	---氨纶纱线	5	0	澳AU,澳门MO,巴PK,冰岛IS,东盟AS,哥CR,秘鲁PE,瑞士CH,新西兰NZ,智利CL	0 受惠国LD	70	---Of polyurethane
3918	5402.6990	---其他	5	0 4	澳AU,澳门MO,巴PK,冰岛IS,东盟AS,哥CR,秘鲁PE,瑞士CH,新西兰NZ,智利CL 韩国KR	0 受惠国LD	70	---Other

序号 No.	税则号列 Tariff Line	中文货品名称 Article Description in Chinese	最惠国税率 MFN(%)	协定税率 Agreement(%)	特惠税率 SP(%)	普通税率 Gen(%)	英文货品名称 Article Description
	54.03	**人造纤维长丝纱线（缝纫线除外），非供零售用，包括细度在67分特以下的人造纤维单丝：**					**Artificial filament yarn (other than sewing thread), not put up for retail sale, including artificial monofilament of less than 67 decitex:**
3919	5403.1000	-粘胶纤维纺制的高强力纱	5	0 澳AU,澳门MO,巴PK,冰岛IS,东盟AS,哥CR,韩国KR,秘鲁PE,瑞士CH,新西兰NZ,智利CL	0 受惠国LD	35	-High tenacity yarn of viscose rayon
		-其他单纱：					-Other yarn, single:
		--粘胶纤维纺制，未加捻或捻度每米不超过120转：					--Of viscose rayon, untwisted or with a twist not exceeding 120 turns per metre:
3920	5403.3110	---竹制	5	0 澳AU,澳门MO,巴PK,冰岛IS,东盟AS,哥CR,韩国KR,秘鲁PE,瑞士CH,新西兰NZ,智利CL	0 受惠国LD	35	---Of bamboo
3921	5403.3190	---其他	5	0 澳AU,澳门MO,巴PK,冰岛IS,东盟AS,哥CR,韩国KR,秘鲁PE,瑞士CH,新西兰NZ,智利CL	0 受惠国LD	35	---Other
		--粘胶纤维纺制，捻度每米超过120转：					--Of viscose rayon, with a twist exceeding 120 turns per metre:
3922	5403.3210	---竹制	5	0 澳AU,澳门MO,巴PK,冰岛IS,东盟AS,哥CR,韩国KR,秘鲁PE,瑞士CH,新西兰NZ,智利CL	0 受惠国LD	35	---Of bamboo
3923	5403.3290	---其他	5	0 澳AU,澳门MO,巴PK,冰岛IS,东盟AS,哥CR,韩国KR,秘鲁PE,瑞士CH,新西兰NZ,智利CL	0 受惠国LD	35	---Other
		--醋酸纤维纺制：					--Of cellulose acetate:
3924	5403.3310	---二醋酸纤维纺制	5	0 澳AU,澳门MO,巴PK,冰岛IS,东盟AS,哥CR,韩国KR,秘鲁PE,瑞士CH,新西兰NZ,智利CL	0 受惠国LD	40	---Of cellulose diacetate
3925	5403.3390	---其他	5	0 澳AU,澳门MO,巴PK,冰岛IS,东盟AS,哥CR,韩国KR,秘鲁PE,瑞士CH,新西兰NZ,智利CL	0 受惠国LD	35	---Other
3926	5403.3900	--其他	5	0 澳AU,澳门MO,巴PK,冰岛IS,东盟AS,哥CR,韩国KR,秘鲁PE,瑞士CH,新西兰NZ,智利CL	0 受惠国LD	35	--Other
		-其他纱线（多股纱线或缆线）：					-Other yarn, multiple (folded) or cabled:
3927	5403.4100	--粘胶纤维纺制	5	0 澳AU,澳门MO,巴PK,冰岛IS,东盟AS,哥CR,韩国KR,秘鲁PE,瑞士CH,新西兰NZ,智利CL	0 受惠国LD	35	--Of viscose rayon
3928	5403.4200	--醋酸纤维纺制	5	0 澳AU,澳门MO,巴PK,冰岛IS,东盟AS,哥CR,韩国KR,秘鲁PE,瑞士CH,新西兰NZ,智利CL	0 受惠国LD	35	--Of cellulose acetate
3929	5403.4900	--其他	5	0 澳AU,澳门MO,巴PK,冰岛IS,东盟AS,哥CR,韩国KR,秘鲁PE,瑞士CH,新西兰NZ,智利CL	0 受惠国LD	35	--Other
	54.04	**截面尺寸不超过1毫米，细度在67分特及以上的合成纤维单丝；表观宽度不超过5毫米的合成纤维纺织材料制扁条及类似品（例如人造草）：**					**Synthetic monofilament of 67 decitex or more and of which no cross-sectional dimension exceeds 1mm; strip and the like (for example, artificial straw), of synthetic textile materials, of an apparent width not exceeding 5mm:**
		-单丝：					-Monofilament:

序号 No.	税则号列 Tariff Line	中文货品名称 Article Description in Chinese	最惠国税率 MFN(%)	协定税率 Agreement(%)	特惠税率 SP(%)	普通税率 Gen(%)	英文货品名称 Article Description
3930	5404.1100	--弹性	5	0 澳AU,巴PK,冰岛IS,东盟AS,哥CR,秘鲁PE,瑞士CH,香港HK,新西兰NZ,智利CL 4.3 韩国KR	0 受惠国LD	80	--Elastomeric
3931	5404.1200	--其他，聚丙烯制	5	0 澳AU,巴PK,冰岛IS,东盟AS,哥CR,韩国KR,秘鲁PE,瑞士CH,香港HK,新西兰NZ,智利CL	0 受惠国LD	80	--Other, of polypropylene
3932	5404.1900	--其他	5	0 澳AU,巴PK,冰岛IS,东盟AS,哥CR,秘鲁PE,香港HK,新西兰NZ,智利CL 2 瑞士CH 4 韩国KR	0 受惠国LD	80	--Other
3933	5404.9000	-其他	5	0 澳AU,澳门MO,巴PK,冰岛IS,东盟AS,哥CR,秘鲁PE,瑞士CH,新西兰NZ,智利CL 4 韩国KR	0 受惠国LD	80	-Other
	54.05	**截面尺寸不超过1毫米，细度在67分特及以上的人造纤维单丝;表观宽度不超过5毫米的人造纤维纺织材料制扁条及类似品（例如人造草）**					**Artificial monofilament of 67 decitex or more and of which no cross-sectional dimension exceeds 1mm; strip and the like (for example, artificial straw) , of artificial textile materials, of an apparent width not exceeding 5mm**
3934	5405.0000	截面尺寸不超过1毫米，细度在67分特及以上的人造纤维单丝;表观宽度不超过5毫米的人造纤维纺织材料制扁条及类似品（例如人造草）	5	0 澳AU,澳门MO,巴PK,冰岛IS,东盟AS,哥CR,韩国KR,秘鲁PE,瑞士CH,新西兰NZ,智利CL	0 受惠国LD	80	Artificial monofilament of 67 decitex or more and of which no cross-sectional dimension exceeds 1mm; strip and the like (for example, artificial straw) of artificial textile materials of an apparent width not exceeding 5mm
	54.06	**化学纤维长丝纱线（缝纫线除外），供零售用：**					**Man-made filament yarn (other than sewing thread) , put up for retail sale:**
3935	5406.0010	---合成纤维长丝纱线	5	0 澳AU,澳门MO,巴PK,冰岛IS,东盟AS,哥CR,韩国KR,秘鲁PE,瑞士CH,新西兰NZ,智利CL	0 受惠国LD	90	---Synthetic filament yarn
3936	5406.0020	---人造纤维长丝纱线	5	0 澳AU,澳门MO,巴PK,冰岛IS,东盟AS,哥CR,韩国KR,秘鲁PE,瑞士CH,新西兰NZ,智利CL	0 受惠国LD	90	---Artificial filament yarn
	54.07	**合成纤维长丝纱线的机织物，包括税号54.04所列材料的机织物：**					**Woven fabrics of synthetic filament yarn, including woven fabrics obtained from materials of heading 5404:**
		-尼龙或其他聚酰胺高强力纱、聚酯高强力纱纺制的机织物：					-Woven fabrics obtained from high-tenacity yarn of nylon or other polyamides or of polyesters:
3937	5407.1010	---尼龙或其他聚酰胺高强力纱纺制	10	0 巴PK,冰岛IS,东盟AS,哥CR,秘鲁PE,台湾TW,香港HK,新加坡SG,新西兰NZ,智利CL 4 瑞士CH 6 澳AU,韩国KR	0 受惠国$_1$LD$_1$	130	---Of nylon or other polyamides
3938	5407.1020	---聚酯高强力纱纺制	10	0 巴PK,冰岛IS,东盟AS,哥CR,秘鲁PE,台湾TW,新加坡SG,新西兰NZ,智利CL 4 瑞士CH 6 澳AU,韩国KR	0 受惠国$_1$LD$_1$	130	---Of polyesters

序号 No.	税则号列 Tariff Line	中文货品名称 Article Description in Chinese	最惠国税率 MFN(%)	协定税率 Agreement(%)	特惠税率 SP(%)	普通税率 Gen(%)	英文货品名称 Article Description
3939	5407.2000	-扁条及类似品的机织物	10	0 巴PK,冰岛IS,东盟AS,哥CR,秘鲁PE,新加坡SG,新西兰NZ,智利CL 4 瑞士CH 6 澳AU 9 韩国KR	0 受惠国$_1$LD$_1$	130	-Woven fabrics obtained from strip or the like
3940	5407.3000	-第十一类注释九所列的机织物	10	0 巴PK,冰岛IS,东盟AS,哥CR,秘鲁PE,新加坡SG,新西兰NZ,智利CL 4 瑞士CH 6 澳AU,韩国KR	0 受惠国$_1$LD$_1$	130	-Fabrics specified in Note 9 to Section XI
		-其他机织物，按重量计尼龙或其他聚酰胺长丝含量在85%及以上：					-Other woven fabrics, containing 85 % or more by weight of filaments of nylon or other polyamides:
3941	5407.4100	--未漂白或漂白	10	0 巴PK,冰岛IS,东盟AS,哥CR,秘鲁PE,台湾TW,香港HK,新加坡SG,新西兰NZ,智利CL 4 瑞士CH 6 澳AU,韩国KR	0 受惠国$_1$LD$_1$	130	--Unbleached or bleached
3942	5407.4200	--染色	10	0 澳门MO,巴PK,冰岛IS,东盟AS,哥CR,秘鲁PE,台湾TW,香港HK,新加坡SG,新西兰NZ,智利CL 4 瑞士CH 6 澳AU 9 韩国KR 9.5 亚太AP	0 柬埔寨KH,老挝LA,缅甸MM,受惠国LD	130	--Dyed
3943	5407.4300	--色织	10	0 巴PK,冰岛IS,东盟AS,哥CR,秘鲁PE,台湾TW,香港HK,新加坡SG,新西兰NZ,智利CL 4 瑞士CH 6 澳AU,韩国KR 7 亚太AP	0 受惠国$_1$LD$_1$	130	--Of yarns of different colours
3944	5407.4400	--印花	10	0 巴PK,冰岛IS,东盟AS,哥CR,秘鲁PE,新加坡SG,新西兰NZ,智利CL 4 瑞士CH 6 澳AU 9 韩国KR	0 受惠国$_1$LD$_1$	130	--Printed
		-其他机织物，按重量计聚酯变形长丝含量在85%及以上：					-Other woven fabrics, containing 85% or more by weight of textured polyester filaments:
3945	5407.5100	--未漂白或漂白	10	0 巴PK,冰岛IS,东盟AS,哥CR,秘鲁PE,台湾TW,新加坡SG,新西兰NZ,智利CL 4 瑞士CH 6 澳AU,韩国KR 7 亚太AP	0 受惠国$_1$LD$_1$	130	--Unbleached or bleached
3946	5407.5200	--染色	10	0 巴PK,冰岛IS,东盟AS,哥CR,秘鲁PE,台湾TW,香港HK,新加坡SG,新西兰NZ,智利CL 4 瑞士CH 6 澳AU 9 韩国KR 9.5 亚太AP	0 柬埔寨KH,老挝LA,缅甸MM,受惠国LD	130	--Dyed

序号 No.	税则号列 Tariff Line	中文货品名称 Article Description in Chinese	最惠国税率 MFN(%)	协定税率 Agreement(%)	特惠税率 SP(%)	普通税率 Gen(%)	英文货品名称 Article Description
3947	5407.5300	--色织	10	0 巴PK,冰岛IS,东盟AS,哥CR,秘鲁PE,台湾TW,新加坡SG,新西兰NZ,智利CL 4 瑞士CH 6 澳AU,韩国KR	0 受惠国$_1$LD$_1$	130	--Of yarns of different colours
3948	5407.5400	--印花	10	0 巴PK,冰岛IS,东盟AS,哥CR,秘鲁PE,台湾TW,新加坡SG,新西兰NZ,智利CL 4 瑞士CH 6 澳AU 8.6 韩国KR	0 受惠国$_1$LD$_1$	130	--Printed
		-其他机织物，按重量计聚酯长丝含量在85%及以上：					-Other woven fabrics, containing 85% or more by weight of polyester filaments:
3949	5407.6100	--按重量计聚酯非变形长丝含量在85%及以上	10	0 澳门MO,巴PK,冰岛IS,东盟AS,哥CR,秘鲁PE,台湾TW,香港HK,新加坡SG,新西兰NZ,智利CL 4 瑞士CH 6 澳AU 9 韩国KR 9.5 亚太AP	0 受惠国LD	130	--Containing 85% or more by weight of nontextured polyester filaments
3950	5407.6900	--其他	10	0 巴PK,冰岛IS,东盟AS,哥CR,秘鲁PE,台湾TW,新加坡SG,新西兰NZ,智利CL 4 瑞士CH 6 澳AU 9 韩国KR 9.5 亚太AP	0 受惠国LD	130	--Other
		-其他机织物，按重量计其他合成纤维长丝含量在85%及以上：					-Other woven fabrics, containing 85% or more by weight of synthetic filaments:
3951	5407.7100	--未漂白或漂白	10	0 巴PK,冰岛IS,东盟AS,哥CR,秘鲁PE,台湾TW,香港HK,新加坡SG,新西兰NZ,智利CL 4 瑞士CH 6 澳AU,韩国KR 8.8 亚太AP	0 受惠国$_1$LD$_1$	130	--Unbleached or bleached
3952	5407.7200	--染色	10	0 巴PK,冰岛IS,东盟AS,哥CR,秘鲁PE,台湾TW,香港HK,新加坡SG,新西兰NZ,智利CL 4 瑞士CH 6 澳AU 9 韩国KR 9.5 亚太AP	0 柬埔寨KH,老挝LA,缅甸MM,受惠国LD	130	--Dyed
3953	5407.7300	--色织	10	0 巴PK,冰岛IS,东盟AS,哥CR,秘鲁PE,新加坡SG,新西兰NZ,智利CL 4 瑞士CH 6 澳AU 9 韩国KR	0 受惠国$_1$LD$_1$	130	--Of yarns of different colours
3954	5407.7400	--印花	10	0 巴PK,冰岛IS,东盟AS,哥CR,秘鲁PE,新加坡SG,新西兰NZ,智利CL 4 瑞士CH 6 澳AU,韩国KR 9.5 亚太AP	0 受惠国$_1$LD$_1$	130	--Printed

序号 No.	税则号列 Tariff Line	中文货品名称 Article Description in Chinese	最惠国税率 MFN(%)	协定税率 Agreement(%)	特惠税率 SP(%)	普通税率 Gen(%)	英文货品名称 Article Description
		-其他机织物，按重量计其他合成纤维长丝含量在85%以下，主要或仅与棉混纺：					-Other woven fabrics, containing less than 85 % by weight of synthetic filaments, mixed mainly or solely with cotton:
3955	5407.8100	--未漂白或漂白	10	0 巴PK,冰岛IS,东盟AS,哥CR,秘鲁PE,香港HK,新加坡SG,新西兰NZ,智利CL 4 瑞士CH 6 澳AU,韩国KR	0 受惠国$_1$LD$_1$	130	--Unbleached or bleached
3956	5407.8200	--染色	10	0 巴PK,冰岛IS,东盟AS,哥CR,秘鲁PE,台湾TW,香港HK,新加坡SG,新西兰NZ,智利CL 4 瑞士CH 6 澳AU 9 韩国KR	0 受惠国LD	130	--Dyed
3957	5407.8300	--色织	10	0 巴PK,冰岛IS,东盟AS,哥CR,秘鲁PE,台湾TW,新加坡SG,新西兰NZ,智利CL 4 瑞士CH 6 澳AU,韩国KR	0 受惠国$_1$LD$_1$	130	--Of yarns of different colours
3958	5407.8400	--印花	10	0 巴PK,冰岛IS,东盟AS,哥CR,秘鲁PE,新加坡SG,新西兰NZ,智利CL 4 瑞士CH 6 澳AU,韩国KR	0 受惠国$_1$LD$_1$	130	--Printed
		-其他机织物：					-Other woven fabrics:
3959	5407.9100	--未漂白或漂白	10	0 巴PK,冰岛IS,东盟AS,哥CR,秘鲁PE,香港HK,新加坡SG,新西兰NZ,智利CL 4 瑞士CH 6 澳AU 9 韩国KR	0 受惠国$_1$LD$_1$	130	--Unbleached or bleached
3960	5407.9200	--染色	10	0 巴PK,冰岛IS,东盟AS,哥CR,秘鲁PE,台湾TW,香港HK,新加坡SG,新西兰NZ,智利CL 4 瑞士CH 6 澳AU 9 韩国KR	0 柬埔寨KH,老挝LA,缅甸MM,受惠国LD	130	--Dyed
3961	5407.9300	--色织	10	0 巴PK,冰岛IS,东盟AS,哥CR,秘鲁PE,台湾TW,新加坡SG,新西兰NZ,智利CL 4 瑞士CH 6 澳AU,韩国KR	0 受惠国$_1$LD$_1$	130	--Of yarns of different colours
3962	5407.9400	--印花	10	0 巴PK,冰岛IS,东盟AS,哥CR,秘鲁PE,新加坡SG,新西兰NZ,智利CL 4 瑞士CH 6 澳AU,韩国KR	0 受惠国$_1$LD$_1$	130	--Printed
	54.08	**人造纤维长丝纱线的机织物，包括税号54.05所列材料的机织物：**					**Woven fabrics of artificial filament yarn, including woven fabrics obtained from materials of heading 5405:**
3963	5408.1000	-粘胶纤维高强力纱的机织物	10	0 巴PK,冰岛IS,东盟AS,哥CR,秘鲁PE,新加坡SG,新西兰NZ,智利CL 4 瑞士CH 6 澳AU,韩国KR	0 受惠国$_1$LD$_1$	130	-Woven fabrics obtained from high tenacity yarn of viscose rayon

序号 No.	税则号列 Tariff Line	中文货品名称 Article Description in Chinese	最惠国税率 MFN(%)	协定税率 Agreement(%)	特惠税率 SP(%)	普通税率 Gen(%)	英文货品名称 Article Description
		-其他机织物，按重量计人造纤维长丝、扁条或类似品含量在85%及以上：					-Other woven fabrics, containing 85 % or more by weight of artificial filament or strip or the like:
		--未漂白或漂白：					--Unbleached or bleached:
3964	5408.2110	---粘胶纤维制	12	0 巴PK,冰岛IS,东盟AS,哥CR,秘鲁PE,新加坡SG,新西兰NZ,智利CL 7.2 澳AU,韩国KR 8.4 瑞士CH	0 受惠国$_1$$LD_1$	130	---Of yarns of viscose rayon
3965	5408.2120	---醋纤纤维制	12	0 巴PK,冰岛IS,东盟AS,哥CR,秘鲁PE,新加坡SG,新西兰NZ,智利CL 7.2 澳AU 8.4 瑞士CH 10.8 韩国KR	0 受惠国$_1$$LD_1$	130	---Of yarns of cellulose acetate
3966	5408.2190	---其他	12	0 巴PK,冰岛IS,东盟AS,哥CR,秘鲁PE,新加坡SG,新西兰NZ,智利CL 7.2 澳AU,韩国KR 8.4 瑞士CH	0 受惠国$_1$$LD_1$	130	---Other
		--染色：					--Dyed:
3967	5408.2210	---粘胶纤维制	10	0 巴PK,冰岛IS,东盟AS,哥CR,秘鲁PE,香港HK,新加坡SG,新西兰NZ,智利CL 4 瑞士CH 6 澳AU,韩国KR	0 受惠国$_1$$LD_1$	130	---Of yarns of viscose rayon
3968	5408.2220	---醋纤纤维制	10	0 巴PK,冰岛IS,东盟AS,哥CR,秘鲁PE,台湾TW,香港HK,新加坡SG,新西兰NZ,智利CL 4 瑞士CH 6 澳AU,韩国KR	0 受惠国$_1$$LD_1$	130	---Of yarns of cellulose acetate
3969	5408.2290	---其他	10	0 巴PK,冰岛IS,东盟AS,哥CR,秘鲁PE,台湾TW,香港HK,新加坡SG,新西兰NZ,智利CL 4 瑞士CH 6 澳AU,韩国KR	0 受惠国$_1$$LD_1$	130	---Other
		--色织：					--Of yarns of different colours:
3970	5408.2310	---粘胶纤维制	10	0 巴PK,冰岛IS,东盟AS,哥CR,秘鲁PE,新加坡SG,新西兰NZ,智利CL 4 瑞士CH 6 澳AU,韩国KR	0 受惠国$_1$$LD_1$	130	---Of yarns of viscose rayon
3971	5408.2320	---醋纤纤维制	10	0 巴PK,冰岛IS,东盟AS,哥CR,秘鲁PE,新加坡SG,新西兰NZ,智利CL 4 瑞士CH 6 澳AU,韩国KR	0 受惠国$_1$$LD_1$	130	---Of yarns of cellulose acetate
3972	5408.2390	---其他	10	0 巴PK,冰岛IS,东盟AS,哥CR,秘鲁PE,台湾TW,新加坡SG,新西兰NZ,智利CL 4 瑞士CH 6 澳AU,韩国KR	0 受惠国$_1$$LD_1$	130	---Other
		--印花：					--Printed:
3973	5408.2410	---粘胶纤维制	10	0 巴PK,冰岛IS,东盟AS,哥CR,秘鲁PE,香港HK,新加坡SG,新西兰NZ,智利CL 4 瑞士CH 6 澳AU,韩国KR	0 受惠国$_1$$LD_1$	130	---Of yarns of viscose rayon

序号 No.	税则号列 Tariff Line	中文货品名称 Article Description in Chinese	最惠国税率 MFN(%)	协定税率 Agreement(%)	特惠税率 SP(%)	普通税率 Gen(%)	英文货品名称 Article Description
3974	5408.2420	---醋纤纤维制	10	0 巴PK,冰岛IS,东盟AS,哥CR,秘鲁PE,香港HK,新加坡SG,新西兰NZ,智利CL 4 瑞士CH 6 澳AU,韩国KR	0 受惠国$_1$LD$_1$	130	---Of yarns of cellulose acetate
3975	5408.2490	---其他	10	0 巴PK,冰岛IS,东盟AS,哥CR,秘鲁PE,香港HK,新加坡SG,新西兰NZ,智利CL 4 瑞士CH 6 澳AU,韩国KR	0 受惠国$_1$LD$_1$	130	---Other
		-其他机织物:					-Other woven fabrics:
3976	5408.3100	--未漂白或漂白	10	0 巴PK,冰岛IS,东盟AS,哥CR,秘鲁PE,新加坡SG,新西兰NZ,智利CL 4 瑞士CH 6 澳AU,韩国KR	0 受惠国$_1$LD$_1$	130	--Unbleached or bleached
3977	5408.3200	--染色	10	0 巴PK,冰岛IS,东盟AS,哥CR,秘鲁PE,台湾TW,新加坡SG,新西兰NZ,智利CL 4 瑞士CH 6 澳AU 8.6 韩国KR 9.5 亚太AP	0 受惠国LD	130	--Dyed
3978	5408.3300	--色织	10	0 巴PK,冰岛IS,东盟AS,哥CR,秘鲁PE,新加坡SG,新西兰NZ,智利CL 4 瑞士CH 6 澳AU,韩国KR	0 受惠国$_1$LD$_1$	130	--Of yarns of different colours
3979	5408.3400	--印花	10	0 巴PK,冰岛IS,东盟AS,哥CR,秘鲁PE,新加坡SG,新西兰NZ,智利CL 4 瑞士CH 6 澳AU,韩国KR	0 受惠国$_1$LD$_1$	130	--Printed

第五十五章
化学纤维短纤

注释：

税号 55.01 和 55.02 仅适用于每根与丝束长度相等的平行化学纤维长丝丝束。前述丝束应同时符合下列规格：

一、丝束长度超过 2 米；
二、捻度每米少于 5 转；
三、每根长丝细度在 67 分特以下；
四、合成纤维长丝丝束，须经拉伸处理，即本身不能被拉伸至超过本身长度的一倍；
五、丝束总细度大于 20000 分特。

丝束长度不超过 2 米的归入税号 55.03 或 55.04。

Chapter 55
Man-made staple fibres

Notes:

Headings Nos.55.01 and 55.02 apply only to man-made filament tow, consisting of parallel filaments of a uniform length equal to the length of the tow, meeting the following specifications:

1. Length of tow exceeding 2m;
2. Twist less than 5 turns per metre;
3. Measuring per filament less than 67 decitex;
4. Synthetic filament tow only: the tow must be drawn, that is to say, be incapable of being stretched by more than 100% of its length;
5. Total measurement of tow more than 20000 decitex.

Tow of a length not exceeding 2m is to be classified in heading No.55.03 or 55.04.

序号 No.	税则号列 Tariff Line	中文货品名称 Article Description in Chinese	最惠国税率 MFN(%)	协定税率 Agreement(%)	特惠税率 SP(%)	普通税率 Gen(%)	英文货品名称 Article Description
	55.01	合成纤维长丝丝束：					Synthetic filament tow:
3980	5501.1000	-尼龙或其他聚酰胺制	5	0 澳AU,巴PK,冰岛IS,东盟AS,哥CR,韩国KR,秘鲁PE,瑞士CH,新西兰NZ,智利CL	0 受惠国LD	70	-Of nylon or other polyamides
3981	5501.2000	-聚酯制	5	0 澳AU,巴PK,冰岛IS,哥CR,秘鲁PE,瑞士CH,新西兰NZ,智利CL 4 韩国KR	0 受惠国LD	70	-Of polyesters
3982	5501.3000	-聚丙烯腈或变性聚丙烯腈制	5	0 澳AU,巴PK,冰岛IS,哥CR,瑞士CH,新西兰NZ,智利CL 4.3 韩国KR 4.5 亚太AP	0 受惠国LD	35	-Acrylic or modacrylic
3983	5501.4000	-聚丙烯制	5	0 澳AU,巴PK,冰岛IS,东盟AS,哥CR,韩国KR,秘鲁PE,瑞士CH,香港HK,新西兰NZ,智利CL	0 受惠国LD	70	-Of polypropylene
3984	5501.9000	-其他	5	0 澳AU,巴PK,冰岛IS,东盟AS,哥CR,秘鲁PE,瑞士CH,香港HK,新西兰NZ,智利CL 4 韩国KR	0 受惠国LD	70	-Other
	55.02	人造纤维长丝丝束：					Artificial filament tow:
3985	5502.0010	---二醋酸纤维丝束	3	0 澳AU,巴PK,冰岛IS,东盟AS,哥CR,韩国KR,秘鲁PE,瑞士CH,新西兰NZ,智利CL 2.1 亚太AP	0 受惠国LD	40	---Cellulose diacetate filament tow
3986	5502.0090	---其他	5	0 澳AU,巴PK,冰岛IS,东盟AS,哥CR,秘鲁PE,瑞士CH,新西兰NZ,智利CL 3.5 亚太AP 4.3 韩国KR	0 受惠国LD	35	---Other
	55.03	合成纤维短纤，未梳或未经其他纺前加工：					Synthetic staple fibres, not carded, combed or otherwise processed for spinning:
		-尼龙或其他聚酰胺制：					-Of nylon or other polyamides:
		--芳族聚酰胺纺制：					--Of aramids:

序号 No.	税则号列 Tariff Line	中文货品名称 Article Description in Chinese	最惠国税率 MFN(%)	协定税率 Agreement(%)	特惠税率 SP(%)	普通税率 Gen(%)	英文货品名称 Article Description
3987	5503.1110	---聚间苯二甲酰间苯二胺纺制	5	0 澳AU,巴PK,冰岛IS,东盟AS,哥CR,秘鲁PE,瑞士CH,新西兰NZ,智利CL	0 受惠国LD	70	---Of polyisophthaloyl metaphenylene diamine
3988	5503.1120	---聚对苯二甲酰对苯二胺纺制	5	0 澳AU,巴PK,冰岛IS,东盟AS,哥CR,秘鲁PE,瑞士CH,新西兰NZ,智利CL	0 受惠国LD	70	---Of polyisophthaloyl paraphenylene diamine
3989	5503.1190	---其他	5	0 澳AU,巴PK,冰岛IS,东盟AS,哥CR,秘鲁PE,新西兰NZ,智利CL 3.5 瑞士CH	0 受惠国LD	70	---Other
3990	5503.1900	--其他	5	0 澳AU,巴PK,冰岛IS,东盟AS,哥CR,秘鲁PE,新西兰NZ,智利CL 3.5 瑞士CH 4 韩国KR	0 受惠国LD	70	--Other
3991	5503.2000	-聚酯制	5	0 澳AU,巴PK,冰岛IS,哥CR,秘鲁PE,瑞士CH,新西兰NZ,智利CL 4.3 韩国KR 4.5 亚太AP	0 受惠国LD	70	-Of polyesters
3992	5503.3000	-聚丙烯腈或变性聚丙烯腈制	5	0 澳AU,巴PK,冰岛IS,哥CR,秘鲁PE,瑞士CH,新西兰NZ,智利CL 4 韩国KR 4.5 亚太AP	0 受惠国LD	35	-Acrylic or modacrylic
3993	5503.4000	-聚丙烯制	5	0 澳AU,巴PK,冰岛IS,东盟AS,哥CR,秘鲁PE,瑞士CH,新西兰NZ,智利CL 4 韩国KR	0 受惠国LD	70	-Of polypropylene
		-其他:					-Other:
3994	5503.9010	---聚苯硫醚制	5	0 澳AU,巴PK,冰岛IS,东盟AS,哥CR,秘鲁PE,瑞士CH,台湾TW,新西兰NZ,智利CL 4 韩国KR	0 受惠国LD	70	---Of polyphenylene sulfide
3995	5503.9090	---其他	5	0 澳AU,巴PK,冰岛IS,东盟AS,哥CR,韩国KR,秘鲁PE,瑞士CH,台湾TW,新西兰NZ,智利CL	0 受惠国LD	70	---Other
	55.04	**人造纤维短纤,未梳或未经其他纺前加工:**					**Artificial staple fibres, not carded, combed or otherwise processed for spinning:**
		-粘胶纤维制:					-Of viscose rayon:
3996	5504.1010	---竹制	5	0 澳AU,巴PK,冰岛IS,东盟AS,哥CR,韩国KR,秘鲁PE,瑞士CH,新西兰NZ,智利CL	0 受惠国LD	35	---Of bamboo
		---木制:					---Of wood:
3997	5504.1021	----阻燃的	5	0 澳AU,巴PK,冰岛IS,东盟AS,哥CR,秘鲁PE,瑞士CH,新西兰NZ,智利CL 4 韩国KR	0 受惠国LD	35	----Flame retardant
3998	5504.1029	----其他	5	0 澳AU,巴PK,冰岛IS,东盟AS,哥CR,秘鲁PE,瑞士CH,新西兰NZ,智利CL 4 韩国KR	0 受惠国LD	35	----Other
3999	5504.1090	---其他	5	0 澳AU,巴PK,冰岛IS,东盟AS,哥CR,秘鲁PE,瑞士CH,新西兰NZ,智利CL 4 韩国KR	0 受惠国LD	35	---Other

序号 No.	税则号列 Tariff Line	中文货品名称 Article Description in Chinese	最惠国税率 MFN(%)	协定税率 Agreement(%)		特惠税率 SP(%)		普通税率 Gen(%)	英文货品名称 Article Description
4000	5504.9000	-其他	5	0	澳AU,巴PK,冰岛IS,东盟AS,哥CR,韩国KR,秘鲁PE,瑞士CH,台湾TW,新西兰NZ,智利CL	0	受惠国LD	35	-Other
	55.05	**化学纤维废料（包括落绵、废纱及回收纤维）：**							**Waste (including noils, yarn waste and garnetted stock) of man-made fibres:**
4001	5505.1000	-合成纤维的	5	0 4	澳AU,巴PK,冰岛IS,东盟AS,哥CR,秘鲁PE,瑞士CH,新西兰NZ,智利CL 韩国KR	0	受惠国LD	70	-Of synthetic fibres
4002	5505.2000	-人造纤维的	5	0 4	澳AU,巴PK,冰岛IS,东盟AS,哥CR,秘鲁PE,瑞士CH,香港HK,新西兰NZ,智利CL 韩国KR	0	受惠国LD	70	-Of artificial fibres
	55.06	**合成纤维短纤，已梳或经其他纺前加工：**							**Synthetic staple fibres, carded, combed or otherwise processed for spinning:**
		-尼龙或其他聚酰胺制：							-Of nylon or other polyamides:
		---芳族聚酰胺纺制：							---Of aramids:
4003	5506.1011	----聚间苯二甲酰间苯二胺纺制	5	0	澳AU,巴PK,冰岛IS,东盟AS,哥CR,秘鲁PE,瑞士CH,新西兰NZ,智利CL	0	受惠国LD	70	----Of polyisophthaloyl metaphenylene diamine
4004	5506.1012	----聚对苯二甲酰对苯二胺纺制	5	0	澳AU,巴PK,冰岛IS,东盟AS,哥CR,秘鲁PE,瑞士CH,新西兰NZ,智利CL	0	受惠国LD	70	----Of polyisophthaloyl paraphenylene diamine
4005	5506.1019	----其他	5	0 4.3	澳AU,巴PK,冰岛IS,东盟AS,哥CR,秘鲁PE,瑞士CH,新西兰NZ,智利CL 韩国KR	0	受惠国LD	70	----Other
4006	5506.1090	---其他	5	0 3	澳AU,巴PK,冰岛IS,东盟AS,哥CR,秘鲁PE,瑞士CH,新西兰NZ,智利CL 韩国KR	0	受惠国LD	70	---Other
4007	5506.2000	-聚酯制	5	0 4 4.5	澳AU,冰岛IS,哥CR,秘鲁PE,瑞士CH,新西兰NZ,智利CL 韩国KR 巴PK,亚太AP	0	受惠国LD	70	-Of polyesters
4008	5506.3000	-聚丙烯腈或变性聚丙烯腈制	5	0 4 4.5	澳AU,冰岛IS,哥CR,秘鲁PE,瑞士CH,新西兰NZ,智利CL 韩国KR 巴PK,亚太AP	0	受惠国LD	35	-Acrylic or modacrylic
		-其他：							-Other:
4009	5506.9010	---聚苯硫醚制	5	0 4.3	澳AU,巴PK,冰岛IS,东盟AS,哥CR,秘鲁PE,瑞士CH,新西兰NZ,智利CL 韩国KR	0	受惠国LD	70	---Of polyphenylene sulfide
4010	5506.9090	---其他	5	0 4.3	澳AU,巴PK,冰岛IS,东盟AS,哥CR,秘鲁PE,瑞士CH,新西兰NZ,智利CL 韩国KR	0	受惠国LD	70	---Other
	55.07	**人造纤维短纤，已梳或经其他纺前加工**							**Artificial staple fibres, carded, combed or otherwise processed for spinning**

序号 No.	税则号列 Tariff Line	中文货品名称 Article Description in Chinese	最惠国税率 MFN(%)	协定税率 Agreement(%)		特惠税率 SP(%)		普通税率 Gen(%)	英文货品名称 Article Description
4011	5507.0000	人造纤维短纤，已梳或经其他纺前加工	5	0	澳AU,巴PK,冰岛IS,东盟AS,哥CR,韩国KR,秘鲁PE,瑞士CH,新西兰NZ,智利CL	0	受惠国LD	35	Artificial staple fibres, carded, combed or otherwise processed for spinning
	55.08	**化学纤维短纤纺制的缝纫线，不论是否供零售用：**							**Sewing thread of man-made staple fibres, whether or not put up for retail sale:**
4012	5508.1000	-合成纤维短纤纺制	5	0 4.5	澳AU,澳门MO,巴PK,冰岛IS,东盟AS,哥CR,韩国KR,秘鲁PE,瑞士CH,香港HK,新西兰NZ,智利CL 亚太AP	0	受惠国LD	90	-Of synthetic staple fibres
4013	5508.2000	-人造纤维短纤纺制	5	0	澳AU,巴PK,冰岛IS,东盟AS,哥CR,韩国KR,秘鲁PE,瑞士CH,新西兰NZ,智利CL	0	受惠国LD	70	-Of artificial staple fibres
	55.09	**合成纤维短纤纺制的纱线（缝纫线除外），非供零售用：**							**Yarn (other than sewing thread) of synthetic staple fibres, not put up for retail sale:**
		-按重量计尼龙或其他聚酰胺短纤含量在85%及以上：							-Containing 85% or more by weight of staple fibres of nylon or other polyamides:
4014	5509.1100	--单纱	5	0	澳AU,澳门MO,巴PK,冰岛IS,东盟AS,哥CR,韩国KR,秘鲁PE,瑞士CH,香港HK,新西兰NZ,智利CL	0	受惠国LD	90	--Single yarn
4015	5509.1200	--多股纱线或缆线	5	0	澳AU,澳门MO,巴PK,冰岛IS,东盟AS,哥CR,韩国KR,秘鲁PE,瑞士CH,香港HK,新西兰NZ,智利CL	0	受惠国LD	90	--Multiple (folded) or cabled yarn
		-按重量计聚酯短纤含量在85%及以上：							-Containing 85% or more by weight of polyester staple fibres:
4016	5509.2100	--单纱	5	0	澳AU,澳门MO,巴PK,冰岛IS,东盟AS,哥CR,韩国KR,秘鲁PE,瑞士CH,香港HK,新西兰NZ,智利CL	0	受惠国LD	90	--Single yarn
4017	5509.2200	--多股纱线或缆线	5	0	澳AU,澳门MO,巴PK,冰岛IS,东盟AS,哥CR,韩国KR,秘鲁PE,瑞士CH,香港HK,新西兰NZ,智利CL	0	受惠国LD	90	--Multiple (folded) or cabled yarn
		-按重量计聚丙烯腈或变性聚丙烯腈短纤含量在85%及以上：							-Containing 85% or more by weight of acrylic or modacrylic staple fibres:
4018	5509.3100	--单纱	5	0	澳AU,澳门MO,巴PK,冰岛IS,东盟AS,哥CR,韩国KR,秘鲁PE,瑞士CH,香港HK,新西兰NZ,智利CL	0	受惠国LD	90	--Single yarn
4019	5509.3200	--多股纱线或缆线	5	0 4.8	澳AU,澳门MO,巴PK,冰岛IS,东盟AS,哥CR,韩国KR,秘鲁PE,瑞士CH,台湾TW,香港HK,新西兰NZ,智利CL 亚太AP	0	受惠国LD	90	--Multiple (folded) or cabled yarn
		-其他纱线，按重量计合成纤维短纤含量在85%及以上：							-Other yarn, containing 85% or more by weight of synthetic staple fibres:
4020	5509.4100	--单纱	5	0	澳AU,澳门MO,巴PK,冰岛IS,东盟AS,哥CR,韩国KR,秘鲁PE,瑞士CH,香港HK,新西兰NZ,智利CL	0	受惠国LD	90	--Single yarn

序号 No.	税则号列 Tariff Line	中文货品名称 Article Description in Chinese	最惠国税率 MFN(%)	协定税率 Agreement(%)		特惠税率 SP(%)		普通税率 Gen(%)	英文货品名称 Article Description
4021	5509.4200	--多股纱线或缆线	5	0 4	澳AU,澳门MO,巴PK,冰岛IS,东盟AS,哥CR,秘鲁PE,瑞士CH,香港HK,新西兰NZ,智利CL 韩国KR	0	受惠国LD	90	--Multiple (folded) or cabled yarn
		-其他聚酯短纤纺制的纱线：							-Other yarn, of polyester staple fibres:
4022	5509.5100	--主要或仅与人造纤维短纤混纺	5	0 4	澳AU,澳门MO,巴PK,冰岛IS,东盟AS,哥CR,秘鲁PE,瑞士CH,香港HK,新西兰NZ,智利CL 韩国KR	0	受惠国LD	90	--Mixed mainly or solely with artificial staple fibres
4023	5509.5200	--主要或仅与羊毛或动物细毛混纺	5	0	澳AU,澳门MO,巴PK,冰岛IS,东盟AS,哥CR,韩国KR,秘鲁PE,瑞士CH,香港HK,新西兰NZ,智利CL	0	受惠国LD	90	--Mixed mainly or solely with wool or fine animal hair
4024	5509.5300	--主要或仅与棉混纺	5	0 3.5	澳AU,澳门MO,巴PK,冰岛IS,东盟AS,哥CR,韩国KR,秘鲁PE,瑞士CH,台湾TW,香港HK,新西兰NZ,智利CL 亚太AP	0	受惠国LD	90	--Mixed maninly or solely with cotton
4025	5509.5900	--其他	5	0	澳AU,澳门MO,巴PK,冰岛IS,东盟AS,哥CR,韩国KR,秘鲁PE,瑞士CH,香港HK,新西兰NZ,智利CL	0	受惠国LD	90	--Other
		-其他聚丙烯腈或变性聚丙烯腈短纤纺制的纱线：							-Other yarn, of acrylic or modacrylic staple fibres:
4026	5509.6100	--主要或仅与羊毛或动物细毛混纺	5	0	澳AU,澳门MO,巴PK,冰岛IS,东盟AS,哥CR,韩国KR,秘鲁PE,瑞士CH,香港HK,新西兰NZ,智利CL	0	受惠国LD	90	--Mixed mainly or solely with wool or fine animal hair
4027	5509.6200	--主要或仅与棉混纺	5	0 4.8	澳AU,澳门MO,巴PK,冰岛IS,东盟AS,哥CR,韩国KR,秘鲁PE,瑞士CH,香港HK,新西兰NZ,智利CL 亚太AP	0	受惠国LD	90	--Mixed mainly or solely with cotton
4028	5509.6900	其他	5	0	澳AU,澳门MO,巴PK,冰岛IS,东盟AS,哥CR,韩国KR,秘鲁PE,瑞士CH,香港HK,新西兰NZ,智利CL	0	受惠国LD	90	--Other
		-其他纱线：							-Other yarn:
4029	5509.9100	--主要或仅与羊毛或动物细毛混纺	5	0 3	澳AU,澳门MO,巴PK,东盟AS,哥CR,秘鲁PE,瑞士CH,香港HK,新西兰NZ,智利CL 韩国KR	0	受惠国LD	90	--Mixed nainly or solely with wool or fine animal hair
4030	5509.9200	--主要或仅与棉混纺	5	0	澳AU,澳门MO,巴PK,冰岛IS,东盟AS,哥CR,韩国KR,秘鲁PE,瑞士CH,台湾TW,香港HK,新西兰NZ,智利CL	0	受惠国LD	90	--Mixed mainly or solely with cotton
4031	5509.9900	--其他	5	0	澳AU,澳门MO,巴PK,冰岛IS,东盟AS,哥CR,韩国KR,秘鲁PE,瑞士CH,香港HK,新西兰NZ,智利CL	0	受惠国LD	90	--Other
	55.10	**人造纤维短纤纺制的纱线（缝纫线除外），非供零售用：**							**Yarn (other than sewing thread) of artificial staple fibres, not put up for retail sale:**

序号 No.	税则号列 Tariff Line	中文货品名称 Article Description in Chinese	最惠国税率 MFN(%)	协定税率 Agreement(%)	特惠税率 SP(%)	普通税率 Gen(%)	英文货品名称 Article Description
		-按重量计人造纤维短纤含量在85%及以上:					-Containing 85 % or more by weight of artificial staple fibres:
4032	5510.1100	--单纱	5	0 澳AU,澳门MO,巴PK,冰岛IS,东盟AS,哥CR,秘鲁PE,瑞士CH,台湾TW,香港HK,新西兰NZ,智利CL 4.3 韩国KR 4.5 亚太AP	0 受惠国LD	70	--Single yarn
4033	5510.1200	--多股纱线或缆线	5	0 澳AU,澳门MO,巴PK,冰岛IS,东盟AS,哥CR,秘鲁PE,瑞士CH,台湾TW,香港HK,新西兰NZ,智利CL 4.3 韩国KR	0 受惠国LD	70	--Multiple (folded) or cabled yarn
4034	5510.2000	-其他纱线，主要或仅与羊毛或动物细毛混纺	5	0 澳AU,澳门MO,巴PK,冰岛IS,东盟AS,哥CR,韩国KR,秘鲁PE,瑞士CH,香港HK,新西兰NZ,智利CL	0 受惠国LD	70	-Other yarn, mixed mainly or solely with wool or fine animal hair
4035	5510.3000	-其他纱线，主要或仅与棉混纺	5	0 澳AU,澳门MO,巴PK,冰岛IS,东盟AS,哥CR,韩国KR,秘鲁PE,瑞士CH,台湾TW,香港HK,新西兰NZ,智利CL 3.5 亚太AP	0 受惠国LD	70	-Other yarn, mixed mainly or solely with cotton
4036	5510.9000	-其他	5	0 澳AU,澳门MO,巴PK,冰岛IS,东盟AS,哥CR,秘鲁PE,瑞士CH,香港HK,新西兰NZ,智利CL 4 韩国KR 4.5 亚太AP	0 受惠国LD	70	-Other yarn
	55.11	**化学纤维短纤纺制的纱线（缝纫线除外），供零售用:**					**Yarn (other than sewing thread) of man-made staple fibres, put up for retail sale:**
4037	5511.1000	-按重量计合成纤维短纤含量在85%及以上	5	0 澳AU,巴PK,冰岛IS,东盟AS,哥CR,韩国KR,秘鲁PE,瑞士CH,新西兰NZ,智利CL	0 受惠国LD	90	-Of synthetic staple fibres, containing 85% or more by weight of such fibres
4038	5511.2000	-按重量计合成纤维短纤含量在85%以下	5	0 澳AU,巴PK,冰岛IS,东盟AS,哥CR,韩国KR,秘鲁PE,瑞士CH,新西兰NZ,智利CL	0 受惠国LD	90	-Of synthetic staple fibres, containing less than 85% by weight of such fibres
4039	5511.3000	-人造纤维短纤纺制	5	0 澳AU,巴PK,冰岛IS,东盟AS,哥CR,韩国KR,秘鲁PE,瑞士CH,新西兰NZ,智利CL	0 受惠国LD	90	-Of artificial staple fibres
	55.12	**合成纤维短纤纺制的机织物，按重量计合成纤维短纤含量在85%及以上:**					**Woven fabrics of synthetic staple fibres, containing 85% or more by weight of synthetic staple fibres:**
		-按重量计聚酯短纤含量在85%及以上:					-Containing 85% or more by weight of polyester staple fibres:
4040	5512.1100	--未漂白或漂白	15	0 巴PK,冰岛IS,东盟AS,哥CR,台湾TW,新加坡SG,新西兰NZ,智利CL 5.4 秘鲁PE 9 澳AU 10.5 瑞士CH,亚太AP 12 韩国KR	0 受惠国LD	130	--Unbleached or bleached

序号 No.	税则号列 Tariff Line	中文货品名称 Article Description in Chinese	最惠国税率 MFN(%)	协定税率 Agreement(%)	特惠税率 SP(%)	普通税率 Gen(%)	英文货品名称 Article Description
4041	5512.1900	--其他	10	0 巴PK,冰岛IS,东盟AS,哥CR,台湾TW,香港HK,新加坡SG,新西兰NZ,智利CL 3 秘鲁PE 4 瑞士CH 6 澳AU 9 韩国KR	0 受惠国LD	130	--Other
		-按重量计聚丙烯腈或变性聚丙烯腈短纤含量在85%及以上:					-Containing 85% or more by weight of acrylic or modacrylic staple fibres:
4042	5512.2100	--未漂白或漂白	13	0 巴PK,冰岛IS,东盟AS,哥CR,秘鲁PE,新加坡SG,新西兰NZ,智利CL 7.8 澳AU 9.1 瑞士CH 10.4 韩国KR	0 受惠国LD	130	--Unbleached or bleached
4043	5512.2900	--其他	10	0 巴PK,冰岛IS,东盟AS,哥CR,秘鲁PE,新加坡SG,新西兰NZ,智利CL 4 瑞士CH 6 澳AU,韩国KR 9.3 亚太AP	0 受惠国$_1$LD$_1$	130	--Other
		-其他:					-Other:
4044	5512.9100	--未漂白或漂白	18	0 巴PK,冰岛IS,东盟AS,哥CR,新加坡SG,新西兰NZ,智利CL 5.4 秘鲁PE 10.8 澳AU 12.6 瑞士CH 14.4 韩国KR	0 受惠国$_1$LD$_1$	130	--Unbleached or bleached
4045	5512.9900	--其他	10	0 澳门MO,巴PK,冰岛IS,东盟AS,哥CR,秘鲁PE,台湾TW,香港HK,新加坡SG,新西兰NZ,智利CL 4 瑞士CH 6 澳AU 8.6 韩国KR	0 柬埔寨KH,老挝LA,缅甸MM,受惠国LD	130	--Other
	55.13	**合成纤维短纤纺制的机织物，按重量计合成纤维短纤含量在85%以下，主要或仅与棉混纺，每平方米重量不超过170克：**					**Woven fabrics of synthetic staple fibres, containing less than 85% by weight of such fibres, mixed mainly or solely with cotton, of a weight not exceeding 170g/m^2:**
		-未漂白或漂白:					-Unbleached or bleached:
		--聚酯短纤纺制的平纹机织物:					--Of polyester staple fibres, plain weave:
4046	5513.1110	---未漂白	16	0 巴PK,冰岛IS,东盟AS,哥CR,香港HK,新加坡SG,新西兰NZ,智利CL 4.8 秘鲁PE 9.6 澳AU 11.2 瑞士CH 12.8 韩国KR	0 受惠国$_1$LD$_1$	130	---Unbleached
4047	5513.1120	---漂白	15	0 巴PK,冰岛IS,东盟AS,哥CR,香港HK,新加坡SG,新西兰NZ,智利CL 4.5 秘鲁PE 9 澳AU 10.5 瑞士CH 12 韩国KR	0 受惠国$_1$LD$_1$	130	---Bleached
		--聚酯短纤纺制的三线或四线斜纹机织物，包括双面斜纹机织物:					--3-thread or 4-thread twill, including cross twill, of polyester staple fibres:

序号 No.	税则号列 Tariff Line	中文货品名称 Article Description in Chinese	最惠国税率 MFN(%)	协定税率 Agreement(%)	特惠税率 SP(%)	普通税率 Gen(%)	英文货品名称 Article Description
4048	5513.1210	---未漂白	16	0 巴PK,冰岛IS,东盟AS,哥CR,香港HK,新加坡SG,新西兰NZ,智利CL 4.8 秘鲁PE 9.6 澳AU 11.2 瑞士CH 12.8 韩国KR	0 受惠国$_1$LD$_1$	130	---Unbleached
4049	5513.1220	---漂白	18	0 巴PK,冰岛IS,东盟AS,哥CR,香港HK,新加坡SG,新西兰NZ,智利CL 5.4 秘鲁PE 10.8 澳AU 12.6 瑞士CH 14.4 韩国KR	0 受惠国$_1$LD$_1$	130	---Bleached
		--其他聚酯短纤纺制的机织物：					--Other woven fabrics of polyester staple fibres:
4050	5513.1310	---未漂白	16	0 巴PK,冰岛IS,东盟AS,哥CR,新加坡SG,新西兰NZ,智利CL 4.8 秘鲁PE 9.6 澳AU 11.2 瑞士CH 12.8 韩国KR	0 受惠国$_1$LD$_1$	130	---Unbleached
4051	5513.1320	---漂白	18	0 巴PK,冰岛IS,东盟AS,哥CR,新加坡SG,新西兰NZ,智利CL 5.4 秘鲁PE 10.8 澳AU 12.6 瑞士CH 14.4 韩国KR	0 受惠国$_1$LD$_1$	130	---Bleached
4052	5513.1900	--其他机织物	18	0 巴PK,冰岛IS,东盟AS,哥CR,新加坡SG,新西兰NZ,智利CL 5.4 秘鲁PE 10.8 澳AU 12.6 瑞士CH 14.4 韩国KR	0 受惠国$_1$LD$_1$	130	--Other woven fabrics
		-染色：					-Dyed:
4053	5513.2100	--聚酯短纤纺制的平纹机织物	10	0 澳门MO,巴PK,冰岛IS,东盟AS,哥CR,秘鲁PE,台湾TW,香港HK,新加坡SG,新西兰NZ,智利CL 4 瑞士CH 6 澳AU,韩国KR 9.1 亚太AP	0 受惠国$_1$LD$_1$	130	--Of polyester staple fibres, plain weave
		--其他聚酯短纤纺制的机织物：					--Other woven fabrics of polyester staple fibres:
4054	5513.2310	---聚酯短纤纺制的三线或四线斜纹机织物，包括双面斜纹机织物	10	0 巴PK,冰岛IS,东盟AS,哥CR,秘鲁PE,香港HK,新加坡SG,新西兰NZ,智利CL 4 瑞士CH 6 澳AU,韩国KR	0 受惠国$_1$LD$_1$	130	---3-thread or 4-thread twill, including crosstwill, of polyester staple fibres
4055	5513.2390	---其他	10	0 巴PK,冰岛IS,东盟AS,哥CR,秘鲁PE,新加坡SG,新西兰NZ,智利CL 4 瑞士CH 6 澳AU 8 韩国KR	0 受惠国$_1$LD$_1$	130	---Other
4056	5513.2900	--其他机织物	10	0 巴PK,冰岛IS,东盟AS,哥CR,秘鲁PE,新加坡SG,新西兰NZ,智利CL 4 瑞士CH 6 澳AU,韩国KR	0 受惠国LD	130	--Other woven fabrics
		-色织：					-Of yarns of different colours:

序号 No.	税则号列 Tariff Line	中文货品名称 Article Description in Chinese	最惠国税率 MFN(%)	协定税率 Agreement(%)	特惠税率 SP(%)	普通税率 Gen(%)	英文货品名称 Article Description
4057	5513.3100	--聚酯短纤纺制的平纹机织物	10	0 巴PK,冰岛IS,东盟AS,哥CR,秘鲁PE,香港HK,新加坡SG,新西兰NZ,智利CL 4 瑞士CH 6 澳AU,韩国KR	0 受惠国$_1$LD$_1$	130	--Of polyester staple fibres, plain weave
		--其他机织物：					--Other woven fabrics:
4058	5513.3910	---聚酯短纤纺制的三线或四线斜纹机织物，包括双面斜纹机织物	10	0 巴PK,冰岛IS,东盟AS,哥CR,秘鲁PE,香港HK,新加坡SG,新西兰NZ,智利CL 4 瑞士CH 6 澳AU,韩国KR 8.8 亚太AP	0 受惠国$_1$LD$_1$	130	---3-thread or 4-thread twill, including cross twill, of polyester staple fibres
4059	5513.3920	---其他聚酯短纤纺制的机织物	10	0 巴PK,冰岛IS,东盟AS,哥CR,秘鲁PE,香港HK,新加坡SG,新西兰NZ,智利CL 4 瑞士CH 6 澳AU,韩国KR	0 受惠国$_1$LD$_1$	130	---Other woven fabrics of polyester staple fibres
4060	5513.3990	---其他机织物	10	0 巴PK,冰岛IS,东盟AS,哥CR,秘鲁PE,新加坡SG,新西兰NZ,智利CL 4 瑞士CH 6 澳AU,韩国KR	0 受惠国$_1$LD$_1$	130	---Other woven fabrics
		-印花：					-Printed:
4061	5513.4100	--聚酯短纤纺制的平纹机织物	10	0 巴PK,冰岛IS,东盟AS,哥CR,秘鲁PE,新加坡SG,新西兰NZ,智利CL 4 瑞士CH 6 澳AU,韩国KR	0 柬埔寨KH,老挝LA,缅甸MM,受惠国LD	130	--Of polyester staple fibres, plain weave
		--其他机织物：					--Other woven fabrics:
4062	5513.4910	---聚酯短纤纺制的三线或四线斜纹机织物，包括双面斜纹机织物	10	0 巴PK,冰岛IS,东盟AS,哥CR,秘鲁PE,新加坡SG,新西兰NZ,智利CL 4 瑞士CH 6 澳AU,韩国KR	0 受惠国$_1$LD$_1$	130	---3-thread or 4-thread twill, including cross twill, of polyester staple fibres
4063	5513.4920	---其他聚酯短纤纺制的机织物	10	0 巴PK,冰岛IS,东盟AS,哥CR,秘鲁PE,新加坡SG,新西兰NZ,智利CL 4 瑞士CH 6 澳AU,韩国KR	0 受惠国$_1$LD$_1$	130	---Other woven fabrics of polyester staple fibres
4064	5513.4990	---其他	10	0 巴PK,冰岛IS,东盟AS,哥CR,秘鲁PE,新加坡SG,新西兰NZ,智利CL 4 瑞士CH 6 澳AU,韩国KR	0 受惠国$_1$LD$_1$	130	---Other
	55.14	**合成纤维短纤纺制的机织物，按重量计合成纤维短纤含量在85%以下，主要或仅与棉混纺，每平方米重量超过170克：**					**Woven fabrics of synthetic staple fibres, containing less than 85% by weight of such fibres, mixed mainly or solely with cotton, of a weight exceeding 170g/m^2:**
		-未漂白或漂白：					-Unbleached or bleached:
		--聚酯短纤纺制的平纹机织物：					--Of polyester staple fibres, plain weave:
4065	5514.1110	---未漂白	16	0 巴PK,冰岛IS,东盟AS,哥CR,新加坡SG,新西兰NZ,智利CL 4.8 秘鲁PE 9.6 澳AU 11.2 瑞士CH 12.8 韩国KR 14.4 亚太AP	0 受惠国$_1$LD$_1$	130	---Unbleached

序号 No.	税则号列 Tariff Line	中文货品名称 Article Description in Chinese	最惠国税率 MFN(%)	协定税率 Agreement(%)	特惠税率 SP(%)	普通税率 Gen(%)	英文货品名称 Article Description
4066	5514.1120	---漂白	18	0 巴PK,冰岛IS,东盟AS,哥CR,新加坡SG,新西兰NZ,智利CL 5.4 秘鲁PE 10.8 澳AU 12.6 瑞士CH 14.4 韩国KR	0 受惠国$_1$LD$_1$	130	---Bleached
		--聚酯短纤纺制的三线或四线斜纹机织物，包括双面斜纹机织物：					--3-thread or 4-thread twill, including cross twill, of polyester staple fibres:
4067	5514.1210	---未漂白	16	0 巴PK,冰岛IS,东盟AS,哥CR,香港HK,新加坡SG,新西兰NZ,智利CL 4.8 秘鲁PE 9.6 澳AU 11.2 瑞士CH 12.8 韩国KR	0 受惠国$_1$LD$_1$	130	---Unbleached
4068	5514.1220	---漂白	18	0 巴PK,冰岛IS,东盟AS,哥CR,香港HK,新加坡SG,新西兰NZ,智利CL 5.4 秘鲁PE 10.8 澳AU 12.6 瑞士CH 14.4 韩国KR	0 受惠国$_1$LD$_1$	130	---Bleached
		--其他机织物：					--Other woven fabrics:
		---聚酯短纤纺制的机织物：					---Other woven fabrics of polyester staple fibres:
4069	5514.1911	----未漂白	16	0 巴PK,冰岛IS,东盟AS,哥CR,新加坡SG,新西兰NZ,智利CL 4.8 秘鲁PE 9.6 澳AU 11.2 瑞士CH 12.8 韩国KR	0 受惠国$_1$LD$_1$	130	----Unbleached
4070	5514.1912	----漂白	18	0 巴PK,冰岛IS,东盟AS,哥CR,新加坡SG,新西兰NZ,智利CL 5.4 秘鲁PE 10.8 澳AU 12.6 瑞士CH 14.4 韩国KR	0 受惠国$_1$LD$_1$	130	----Bleached
4071	5514.1990	---其他	16	0 巴PK,冰岛IS,东盟AS,哥CR,新加坡SG,新西兰NZ,智利CL 4.8 秘鲁PE 9.6 澳AU 11.2 瑞士CH 12.8 韩国KR 15.2 亚太AP	0 受惠国$_1$LD$_1$	130	---Other
		-染色：					-Dyed:
4072	5514.2100	--聚酯短纤纺制的平纹机织物	10	0 巴PK,冰岛IS,东盟AS,哥CR,秘鲁PE,香港HK,新加坡SG,新西兰NZ,智利CL 4 瑞士CH 6 澳AU,韩国KR	0 受惠国$_1$LD$_1$	130	--Of polyester staple fibres, plain weave
4073	5514.2200	--聚酯短纤纺制的三线或四线斜纹机织物，包括双面斜纹机织物	10	0 巴PK,冰岛IS,东盟AS,哥CR,秘鲁PE,香港HK,新加坡SG,新西兰NZ,智利CL 4 瑞士CH 6 澳AU,韩国KR	0 受惠国$_1$LD$_1$	130	--3-thread or 4-thread twill, including cross twill, of polyester staple fibres

序号 No.	税则号列 Tariff Line	中文货品名称 Article Description in Chinese	最惠国税率 MFN(%)	协定税率 Agreement(%)	特惠税率 SP(%)	普通税率 Gen(%)	英文货品名称 Article Description
4074	5514.2300	--其他聚酯短纤纺制的机织物	10	0 巴PK,冰岛IS,东盟AS,哥CR,秘鲁PE,新加坡SG,新西兰NZ,智利CL 4 瑞士CH 6 澳AU,韩国KR	0 柬埔寨KH,老挝LA,缅甸MM,受惠国LD	130	--Other woven fabrics of polyester staple fibres
4075	5514.2900	--其他机织物	10	0 巴PK,冰岛IS,东盟AS,哥CR,秘鲁PE,新加坡SG,新西兰NZ,智利CL 4 瑞士CH 6 澳AU,韩国KR	0 受惠国LD	130	--Other woven fabrics
		-色织:					-Of yarns of different colours:
4076	5514.3010	---聚酯短纤纺制的平纹机织物	10	0 巴PK,冰岛IS,东盟AS,哥CR,秘鲁PE,香港HK,新加坡SG,新西兰NZ,智利CL 4 瑞士CH 6 澳AU,韩国KR	0 受惠国$_1$LD$_1$	130	---Of polyester staple fibres, plain weave
4077	5514.3020	---聚酯短纤纺制的三线或四线斜纹机织物,包括双面斜纹机织物	10	0 巴PK,冰岛IS,东盟AS,哥CR,秘鲁PE,香港HK,新加坡SG,新西兰NZ,智利CL 4 瑞士CH 6 澳AU,韩国KR	0 受惠国$_1$LD$_1$	130	---3-thread or 4-thread twill, including cross twill, of polyester staple fibres
4078	5514.3030	---其他聚酯短纤纺制的机织物	10	0 巴PK,冰岛IS,东盟AS,哥CR,秘鲁PE,新加坡SG,新西兰NZ,智利CL 4 瑞士CH 6 澳AU,韩国KR	0 受惠国$_1$LD$_1$	130	---Other woven fabrics of polyester staple fibres
4079	5514.3090	---其他机织物	10	0 巴PK,冰岛IS,东盟AS,哥CR,秘鲁PE,新加坡SG,新西兰NZ,智利CL 4 瑞士CH 6 澳AU,韩国KR	0 受惠国$_1$LD$_1$	130	---Other woven fabrics
		-印花:					-Printed:
4080	5514.4100	--聚酯短纤纺制的平纹机织物	10	0 巴PK,冰岛IS,东盟AS,哥CR,秘鲁PE,新加坡SG,新西兰NZ,智利CL 4 瑞士CH 6 澳AU,韩国KR	0 受惠国$_1$LD$_1$	130	--Of polyester staple fibres, plain weave
4081	5514.4200	--聚酯短纤纺制的三线或四线斜纹机织物,包括双面斜纹机织物	10	0 巴PK,冰岛IS,东盟AS,哥CR,秘鲁PE,新加坡SG,新西兰NZ,智利CL 4 瑞士CH 6 澳AU,韩国KR	0 受惠国$_1$LD$_1$	130	--3-thread or 4-thread twill, including cross twill, of polyester staple fibres
4082	5514.4300	--其他聚酯短纤纺制的机织物	10	0 巴PK,冰岛IS,东盟AS,哥CR,秘鲁PE,新加坡SG,新西兰NZ,智利CL 4 瑞士CH 6 澳AU,韩国KR	0 受惠国$_1$LD$_1$	130	--Other woven fabrics of polyester staple fibres
4083	5514.4900	--其他机织物	10	0 巴PK,冰岛IS,东盟AS,哥CR,秘鲁PE,新加坡SG,新西兰NZ,智利CL 4 瑞士CH 6 澳AU,韩国KR	0 受惠国$_1$LD$_1$	130	--Other woven fabrics
	55.15	**合成纤维短纤纺制的其他机织物:**					**Other woven fabrics of synthetic staple fibres:**
		-聚酯短纤纺制:					-Of polyester staple fibres:
4084	5515.1100	--主要或仅与粘胶纤维短纤混纺	10	0 巴PK,冰岛IS,东盟AS,哥CR,秘鲁PE,台湾TW,新加坡SG,新西兰NZ,智利CL 4 瑞士CH 6 澳AU,韩国KR 8.8 亚太AP	0 受惠国$_1$LD$_1$	130	--Mixed mainly or solely with viscose rayon staple fibres

序号 No.	税则号列 Tariff Line	中文货品名称 Article Description in Chinese	最惠国税率 MFN(%)	协定税率 Agreement(%)	特惠税率 SP(%)	普通税率 Gen(%)	英文货品名称 Article Description
4085	5515.1200	--主要或仅与化学纤维长丝混纺	10	0 巴PK,冰岛IS,东盟AS,哥CR,秘鲁PE,台湾TW,新加坡SG,新西兰NZ,智利CL 4 瑞士CH 6 澳AU,韩国KR 9 亚太AP	0 受惠国$_1$LD$_1$	130	--Mixed mainly or solely with man-made filaments
4086	5515.1300	--主要或仅与羊毛或动物细毛混纺	10	0 巴PK,冰岛IS,东盟AS,哥CR,秘鲁PE,新加坡SG,新西兰NZ,智利CL 4 瑞士CH 6 澳AU,韩国KR	0 受惠国$_1$LD$_1$	130	--Mixed mainly or solely with wool or fine animal hair
4087	5515.1900	--其他	10	0 巴PK,冰岛IS,东盟AS,哥CR,秘鲁PE,新加坡SG,新西兰NZ,智利CL 4 瑞士CH 6 澳AU,韩国KR 9 亚太AP	0 受惠国$_1$LD$_1$	130	--Other
		-聚丙烯腈或变性聚丙烯腈短纤纺制:					-Of acrylic or modacrylic staple fibres:
4088	5515.2100	--主要或仅与化学纤维长丝混纺	10	0 巴PK,冰岛IS,东盟AS,哥CR,秘鲁PE,新加坡SG,新西兰NZ,智利CL 4 瑞士CH 6 澳AU,韩国KR	0 受惠国$_1$LD$_1$	130	--Mixed mainly or solely with man-made filaments
4089	5515.2200	--主要或仅与羊毛或动物细毛混纺	12	0 巴PK,冰岛IS,东盟AS,哥CR,秘鲁PE,新加坡SG,新西兰NZ,智利CL 7.2 澳AU,韩国KR 8.4 瑞士CH	0 受惠国LD	130	--Mixed mainly or solely with wool or fine animal hair
4090	5515.2900	--其他	10	0 巴PK,冰岛IS,东盟AS,哥CR,秘鲁PE,新加坡SG,新西兰NZ,智利CL 4 瑞士CH 6 澳AU,韩国KR	0 受惠国$_1$LD$_1$	130	--Other
		-其他机织物:					-Other woven fabrics:
4091	5515.9100	--主要或仅与化学纤维长丝混纺	10	0 巴PK,冰岛IS,东盟AS,哥CR,秘鲁PE,新加坡SG,新西兰NZ,智利CL 4 瑞士CH 6 澳AU,韩国KR	0 受惠国$_1$LD$_1$	130	--Mixed mainly or solely with man-made filaments
4092	5515.9900	--其他	10	0 巴PK,冰岛IS,东盟AS,哥CR,秘鲁PE,新加坡SG,新西兰NZ,智利CL 4 瑞士CH 6 澳AU,韩国KR 9 亚太AP	0 受惠国$_1$LD$_1$	130	--Other
	55.16	人造纤维短纤纺制的机织物:					**Woven fabrics of artificial staple fibres:**
		-按重量计人造纤维短纤含量在85%及以上:					-Containing 85% or more by weight of artificial staple fibres:
4093	5516.1100	--未漂白或漂白	12	0 巴PK,冰岛IS,东盟AS,哥CR,秘鲁PE,香港HK,新加坡SG,新西兰NZ,智利CL 7.2 澳AU,韩国KR 8.4 瑞士CH	0 受惠国LD	130	--Unbleached or bleached
4094	5516.1200	--染色	10	0 巴PK,冰岛IS,东盟AS,哥CR,秘鲁PE,台湾TW,香港HK,新加坡SG,新西兰NZ,智利CL 4 瑞士CH 6 澳AU,韩国KR	0 受惠国$_1$LD$_1$	130	--Dyed

序号 No.	税则号列 Tariff Line	中文货品名称 Article Description in Chinese	最惠国税率 MFN(%)	协定税率 Agreement(%)	特惠税率 SP(%)	普通税率 Gen(%)	英文货品名称 Article Description
4095	5516.1300	--色织	10	0 巴PK,冰岛IS,东盟AS,哥CR,秘鲁PE,香港HK,新加坡SG,新西兰NZ,智利CL 4 瑞士CH 6 澳AU,韩国KR	0 受惠国$_1$LD$_1$	130	--Of yarns of different colours
4096	5516.1400	--印花	10	0 巴PK,冰岛IS,东盟AS,哥CR,秘鲁PE,香港HK,新加坡SG,新西兰NZ,智利CL 4 瑞士CH 6 澳AU,韩国KR	0 受惠国$_1$LD$_1$	130	--Printed
		-按重量计人造纤维短纤含量在85%以下，主要或仅与化学纤维长丝混纺:					-Containing less than 85% by weight of artificial staple fibres, mixed mainly or solely with man-made filaments:
4097	5516.2100	--未漂白或漂白	12	0 巴PK,冰岛IS,东盟AS,哥CR,秘鲁PE,香港HK,新加坡SG,新西兰NZ,智利CL 7.2 澳AU,韩国KR 8.4 瑞士CH	0 受惠国$_1$LD$_1$	130	--Unbleached or bleached
4098	5516.2200	--染色	10	0 巴PK,冰岛IS,东盟AS,哥CR,秘鲁PE,台湾TW,香港HK,新加坡SG,新西兰NZ,智利CL 4 瑞士CH 6 澳AU 8.6 韩国KR 9.5 亚太AP	0 受惠国$_1$LD$_1$	130	--Dyed
4099	5516.2300	--色织	10	0 巴PK,冰岛IS,东盟AS,哥CR,秘鲁PE,香港HK,新加坡SG,新西兰NZ,智利CL 4 瑞士CH 6 澳AU,韩国KR	0 受惠国$_1$LD$_1$	130	--Of yarns of different colours
4100	5516.2400	--印花	10	0 巴PK,冰岛IS,东盟AS,哥CR,秘鲁PE,香港HK,新加坡SG,新西兰NZ,智利CL 4 瑞士CH 6 澳AU,韩国KR	0 受惠国$_1$LD$_1$	130	--Printed
		-按重量计人造纤维短纤含量在85%以下，主要或仅与羊毛或动物细毛混纺:					-Containing less than 85% by weight of artificial staple fibres, mixed mainly or solely with wool or fine animal hair:
4101	5516.3100	--未漂白或漂白	12	0 巴PK,冰岛IS,东盟AS,哥CR,秘鲁PE,香港HK,新加坡SG,新西兰NZ,智利CL 7.2 澳AU,韩国KR 8.4 瑞士CH	0 受惠国$_1$LD$_1$	130	--Unbleached or bleached
4102	5516.3200	--染色	10	0 巴PK,冰岛IS,东盟AS,哥CR,秘鲁PE,香港HK,新加坡SG,新西兰NZ,智利CL 4 瑞士CH 6 澳AU,韩国KR	0 受惠国$_1$LD$_1$	130	--Dyed
4103	5516.3300	--色织	10	0 巴PK,冰岛IS,东盟AS,哥CR,秘鲁PE,香港HK,新加坡SG,新西兰NZ,智利CL 4 瑞士CH 6 澳AU,韩国KR	0 受惠国$_1$LD$_1$	130	--Of yarns of different colours

序号 No.	税则号列 Tariff Line	中文货品名称 Article Description in Chinese	最惠国税率 MFN(%)	协定税率 Agreement(%)		特惠税率 SP(%)		普通税率 Gen(%)	英文货品名称 Article Description
4104	5516.3400	--印花	10	0 4 6	巴PK,冰岛IS,东盟AS,哥CR,秘鲁PE,香港HK,新加坡SG,新西兰NZ,智利CL 瑞士CH 澳AU,韩国KR	0	受惠国$_1$LD$_1$	130	--Printed
		-按重量计人造纤维短纤含量在85%以下，主要或仅与棉混纺：							-Containing less than 85% by weight of artificial staple fibres, mixed mainly or solely with cotton:
4105	5516.4100	--未漂白或漂白	12	0 7.2 8.4	巴PK,冰岛IS,东盟AS,哥CR,秘鲁PE,香港HK,新加坡SG,新西兰NZ,智利CL 澳AU,韩国KR 瑞士CH	0	受惠国$_1$LD$_1$	130	--Unbleached or bleached
4106	5516.4200	--染色	12	0 7.2 8.4	巴PK,冰岛IS,东盟AS,哥CR,秘鲁PE,香港HK,新加坡SG,新西兰NZ,智利CL 澳AU,韩国KR 瑞士CH	0	受惠国$_1$LD$_1$	130	--Dyed
4107	5516.4300	--色织	10	0 4 6	巴PK,冰岛IS,东盟AS,哥CR,秘鲁PE,香港HK,新加坡SG,新西兰NZ,智利CL 瑞士CH 澳AU,韩国KR	0	受惠国$_1$LD$_1$	130	--Of yarns of different colours
4108	5516.4400	--印花	10	0 4 6	巴PK,冰岛IS,东盟AS,哥CR,秘鲁PE,香港HK,新加坡SG,新西兰NZ,智利CL 瑞士CH 澳AU,韩国KR	0	受惠国$_1$LD$_1$	130	--Printed
		-其他：							-Other:
4109	5516.9100	--未漂白或漂白	12	0 7.2 8.4	巴PK,冰岛IS,东盟AS,哥CR,秘鲁PE,香港HK,新加坡SG,新西兰NZ,智利CL 澳AU,韩国KR 瑞士CH	0	受惠国$_1$LD$_1$	130	--Unbleached or bleached
4110	5516.9200	--染色	10	0 4 6 8.6	巴PK,冰岛IS,东盟AS,哥CR,秘鲁PE,香港HK,新加坡SG,新西兰NZ,智利CL 瑞士CH 澳AU 韩国KR	0	受惠国LD	130	--Dyed
4111	5516.9300	--色织	10	0 4 6	巴PK,冰岛IS,东盟AS,哥CR,秘鲁PE,香港HK,新加坡SG,新西兰NZ,智利CL 瑞士CH 澳AU,韩国KR	0	受惠国$_1$LD$_1$	130	--Of yarns of different colours
4112	5516.9400	--印花	10	0 4 6 9.4	巴PK,冰岛IS,东盟AS,哥CR,秘鲁PE,香港HK,新加坡SG,新西兰NZ,智利CL 瑞士CH 澳AU,韩国KR 亚太AP	0	受惠国$_1$LD$_1$	130	--Printed

第五十六章
絮胎、毡呢及无纺织物；特种纱线；线、绳、索、缆及其制品

注释：

一、本章不包括：

（一）用各种物质或制剂（例如，第三十三章的香水或化妆品、税号 34.01 的肥皂或洗涤剂、税号 34.05 的光洁剂及类似制剂、税号 38.09 的织物柔软剂）浸渍、涂布、包覆的絮胎、毡呢或无纺织物，其中的纺织材料仅作为承载介质；

（二）税号 58.11 的纺织产品；

（三）以毡呢或无纺织物为底的砂布及类似品（税号 68.05）；

（四）以毡呢或无纺织物为底的粘聚或复制云母（税号 68.14）；

（五）以毡呢或无纺织物为底的金属箔（通常为第十四类或第十五类）；或

（六）税目 96.19 的卫生巾（护垫）及止血塞、婴儿尿布及尿布衬里和类似品。

二、所称“毡呢”，包括针刺机制毡呢以及纤维本身通过缝编工序增强了抱合力的纺织纤维网状织物。

三、税号 56.02 及 56.03 分别包括用各种性质（紧密结构或泡沫状）的塑料或橡胶浸渍、涂布、包覆或层压的毡呢及无纺织物。

税号 56.03 还包括用塑料或橡胶作粘合材料的无纺织物。

但税号 56.02 及 56.03 不包括：

（一）用塑料或橡胶浸渍、涂布、包覆或层压，按重量计纺织材料含量在 50%及以下的毡呢或者完全嵌入塑料或橡胶之内的毡呢（第三十九章或第四十章）；

（二）完全嵌入塑料或橡胶之内的无纺织物，以及用肉眼可辨别出两面都用塑料或橡胶涂布、包覆的无纺织物，涂布或包覆所引起的颜色变化可不予考虑（第三十九章或第四十章）；

（三）与毡呢或无纺织物混制的泡沫塑料或海绵橡胶板、片或扁条，纺织材料仅在其中起增强作用（第三十九章或第四十章）。

四、税号 56.04 不包括用肉眼无法辨别出是否经过浸渍，涂布或包覆的纺织纱线或税号 54.04 或 54.05 的扁条及类似品（通常归入第五十章至第五十五章）；运用本条规定，可不考虑浸渍、涂布或包覆所引起的颜色变化。

Chapter 56
Wadding, felt and nonwovens; special yarns; twine, cordage, ropes and cables and articles thereof

Notes:

1.This Chapter does not cover:

(a) Wadding，felt or nonwovens，impregnated，coated or covered with substances or preparations (for example，pefumes or cosmetics of Chapter 33，soaps or detergents of heading No.34.01，polishes，creams or similar preparations of heading No.34.05，fabric softeners of heading No.38.09) where the textile material is present merely as a carrying medium;

(b) Textile products of heading No.58.11;

(c) Natural or artificial abrasive powder or grain，on a backing of felt or nonwovens (heading No.68.05);

(d) Agglomerated or reconstituted mica，on a backing of felt or nonwovens (heading No.68.14);

(e) Metalfoil on a backing of felt or nonwovens (Generelly Section XIV or Section XV); or

(f) Sanitary towels (pads) and tampons, napkins and napkin liners for babiesand similar articles of heading 96.19.

2. The term “felt” includes needleloom felt and fabrics consisting of a web of textile fibres the cohesion of which has been enhanced by a stitch-bonding process using fibres from the web itself.

3. Headings Nos.56.02 and 56.03 cover respectively felt and nonwovens，impregnated，coated，covered or laminated with plastics or rubber whatever the nature of these materials (compact or cellular).

Heading No.56.03 also includes nonwovens in which plastics or rubber forms the bonding substance.

Headings Nos.56.02 and 56.03 do not，however，cover:

(a) Felt impregnated，coated，covered or laminated with plastics or rubber，containing 50% or less by weight of textile material or felt completely embedded in plastics or rubber (Chapter 39 or 40);

(b) Nonwovens，either completely embedded in plastics or rubber，or entirely coated or covered on both sides with such materials，provided that such coating or covering can be seen with the naked eye with no account being taken of any resulting change of colour (Chapter 39 or 40);or

(c) Plates，sheets or strips of cellular plastics or cellular rubber combined with felt or nonwovens，where the textile material is present merely for reinforcing purposes (Chapter 39 or 40).

4. Heading No.56.04 does not cover textile yarn，or strip or the like of heading No.54.04 or 54.05，in which the impregnation，coating or covering cannot be seen with the naked eye (usually Chapters 50 to 55); for the purpose of this provision，no account should be taken of any resulting change of colour.

序号 No.	税则号列 Tariff Line	中文货品名称 Article Description in Chinese	最惠国税率 MFN(%)	协定税率 Agreement(%)	特惠税率 SP(%)	普通税率 Gen(%)	英文货品名称 Article Description
	56.01	纺织材料絮胎及其制品；长度不超过5毫米的纺织纤维（纤维屑）、纤维粉末及球结：					**Wadding of textile materials and articles thereof; textile fibres, not exceeding 5 mm in length (flock) , textile dust and mill neps:**
		-絮胎;其他絮胎制品：					-Wadding; other articles of wadding:
4113	5601.2100	--棉制	10	0 澳门MO,冰岛IS,东盟AS,哥CR,秘鲁PE,香港HK,新加坡SG,新西兰NZ,智利CL 4 瑞士CH 5 巴PK 6 澳AU,韩国KR	0 受惠国$_1$LD$_1$	50	--Of cotton
		--化学纤维制：					--Of man-made fibres:
4114	5601.2210	---卷烟滤嘴	12	0 冰岛IS,东盟AS,哥CR,秘鲁PE,新加坡SG,新西兰NZ,智利CL 6 巴PK 8.4 瑞士CH	0 受惠国$_1$LD$_1$	100	---Cigarette filter tips
4115	5601.2290	---其他	12	0 冰岛IS,东盟AS,哥CR,秘鲁PE,台湾TW,新加坡SG,新西兰NZ,智利CL 7.2 澳AU 8.4 瑞士CH 10.4 韩国KR	0 受惠国LD	100	---Other
4116	5601.2900	--其他	10	0 冰岛IS,东盟AS,哥CR,秘鲁PE,新加坡SG,新西兰NZ,智利CL 4 瑞士CH 5 巴PK 6 澳AU,韩国KR	0 受惠国LD	90	--Other
4117	5601.3000	-纤维屑、纤维粉末及球结	10	0 冰岛IS,东盟AS,哥CR,秘鲁PE,新加坡SG,新西兰NZ,智利CL 4 瑞士CH 5 巴PK 6 澳AU,韩国KR	0 受惠国$_1$LD$_1$	100	-Textile flock and dust and mill neps
	ex56013000	由两种或两种以上有机聚合物纺制的纤维（横截面为皮芯结构或并列结构或海岛结构），长度不超过5毫米	Δ5				of two or more kinds of polymers (with cross section of skin-core or juxtapose or island structure) , length not more than 5mm
	56.02	**毡呢，不论是否浸渍、涂布、包覆或层压：**					**Felt, whether or not impregnated, coated, covered or laminated:**
4118	5602.1000	-针刺机制毡呢及纤维缝编织物	10	0 冰岛IS,东盟AS,哥CR,秘鲁PE,新加坡SG,新西兰NZ,智利CL 4 瑞士CH 5 巴PK 6 澳AU,韩国KR	0 受惠国$_1$LD$_1$	100	-Needleloom felt and stitch-bonded fibre fabrics
		-其他毡呢，未浸渍、涂布、包覆或层压：					-Other felt, not impregnated, coated, covered or laminated:
4119	5602.2100	--羊毛或动物细毛制	10	0 冰岛IS,东盟AS,哥CR,秘鲁PE,新加坡SG,新西兰NZ,智利CL 4 瑞士CH 5 巴PK 6 澳AU,韩国KR	0 受惠国$_1$LD$_1$	100	--Of wool or fine animal hair

序号 No.	税则号列 Tariff Line	中文货品名称 Article Description in Chinese	最惠国税率 MFN(%)	协定税率 Agreement(%)	特惠税率 SP(%)	普通税率 Gen(%)	英文货品名称 Article Description
4120	5602.2900	--其他纺织材料制	10	0 冰岛IS,东盟AS,哥CR,秘鲁PE,新加坡SG,新西兰NZ,智利CL 4 瑞士CH 5 巴PK 6 澳AU,韩国KR	0 受惠国$_1$LD$_1$	100	--Of other textile materials
4121	5602.9000	-其他	10	0 冰岛IS,东盟AS,哥CR,秘鲁PE,新加坡SG,新西兰NZ,智利CL 4 瑞士CH 5 巴PK 6 澳AU,韩国KR	0 受惠国LD	100	-Other
	56.03	**无纺织物，不论是否浸渍、涂布、包覆或层压：**					**Nonwovens, whether or not impregnated, coated, covered or laminated:**
		-化学纤维长丝制：					-Of man-made filaments:
		--每平方米重量不超过25克：					--Weighing not more than 25g/m^2:
4122	5603.1110	---经浸渍、涂布、包覆或层压	10	0 巴PK,冰岛IS,东盟AS,哥CR,秘鲁PE,台湾TW,新加坡SG,新西兰NZ,智利CL 4 瑞士CH 6 澳AU,韩国KR 8.5 亚太AP	0 柬埔寨KH,老挝LA,缅甸MM,受惠国LD	70	---Impregnated, coated, covered or laminated
4123	5603.1190	---其他	10	0 巴PK,冰岛IS,东盟AS,哥CR,秘鲁PE,新加坡SG,新西兰NZ,智利CL 4 瑞士CH 6 澳AU 8 韩国KR 8.5 亚太AP	0 受惠国$_1$LD$_1$	130	---Other
		--每平方米重量超过25克，但不超过70克：					--Weighing more than 25g/m^2 but not more than 70g/m^2:
4124	5603.1210	---经浸渍、涂布、包覆或层压	10	0 澳门MO,巴PK,冰岛IS,东盟AS,哥CR,秘鲁PE,香港HK,新加坡SG,新西兰NZ,智利CL 4 瑞士CH 6 澳AU 8.5 亚太AP 8.6 韩国KR	0 柬埔寨KH,老挝LA,缅甸MM,受惠国LD	70	---Impregnated, coated, covered or laminated
4125	5603.1290	---其他	10	0 澳门MO,巴PK,冰岛IS,东盟AS,哥CR,秘鲁PE,台湾TW,香港HK,新加坡SG,新西兰NZ,智利CL 4 瑞士CH 6 澳AU,韩国KR	0 受惠国LD	130	---Other
		--每平方米重量超过70克，但不超过150克：					--Weighing more than 70g/m^2 but not more than 150g/m^2:
4126	5603.1310	---经浸渍、涂布、包覆或层压	10	0 澳门MO,巴PK,冰岛IS,东盟AS,哥CR,秘鲁PE,台湾TW,新加坡SG,新西兰NZ,智利CL 4 瑞士CH 6 澳AU,韩国KR 8.5 亚太AP	0 受惠国$_1$LD$_1$	70	---Impregnated, coated, covered or laminated
4127	5603.1390	---其他	10	0 澳门MO,巴PK,冰岛IS,东盟AS,哥CR,秘鲁PE,台湾TW,新加坡SG,新西兰NZ,智利CL 4 瑞士CH 6 澳AU,韩国KR	0 受惠国LD	130	---Other
		--每平方米重量超过150克：					--Weighing more than 150g/m^2:

序号 No.	税则号列 Tariff Line	中文货品名称 Article Description in Chinese	最惠国税率 MFN(%)	协定税率 Agreement(%)	特惠税率 SP(%)	普通税率 Gen(%)	英文货品名称 Article Description
4128	5603.1410	---经浸渍、涂布、包覆或层压	10	0 巴PK,冰岛IS,东盟AS,哥CR,秘鲁PE,台湾TW,新加坡SG,新西兰NZ,智利CL 4 瑞士CH 6 澳AU 8.5 亚太AP 8.6 韩国KR	0 受惠国$_1$LD$_1$	70	---Regnated, coated, covered or laminated
4129	5603.1490	---其他	10	0 巴PK,冰岛IS,东盟AS,哥CR,秘鲁PE,台湾TW,新加坡SG,新西兰NZ,智利CL 4 瑞士CH 6 澳AU,韩国KR 7 亚太AP	0 受惠国LD	130	---Other
		-其他:					-Other:
		--每平方米重量不超过25克:					--Weighing not more than 25g/m^2:
4130	5603.9110	---经浸渍、涂布、包覆或层压	10	0 巴PK,冰岛IS,东盟AS,哥CR,秘鲁PE,新加坡SG,新西兰NZ,智利CL 4 瑞士CH 6 澳AU 8 韩国KR 8.5 亚太AP	0 受惠国$_1$LD$_1$	70	---Impregnated, coated, covered or laminated
	ex56039110	乙烯聚合物制电池隔膜基布	Δ5				Base cloth for battery separator, of polymers of ethylene
4131	5603.9190	---其他	10	0 巴PK,冰岛IS,东盟AS,哥CR,秘鲁PE,新加坡SG,新西兰NZ,智利CL 4 瑞士CH 6 澳AU 8 韩国KR 8.5 亚太AP	0 受惠国$_1$LD$_1$	85	---Other
		--每平方米重量超过25克，但不超过70克:					--Weighing more than 25g/m^2 but not more than 70g/m^2:
4132	5603.9210	---经浸渍、涂布、包覆或层压	10	0 澳门MO,巴PK,冰岛IS,东盟AS,哥CR,秘鲁PE,香港HK,新加坡SG,新西兰NZ,智利CL 4 瑞士CH 6 澳AU 8 韩国KR 8.5 亚太AP	0 受惠国$_1$LD$_1$	70	---Impregnated, coated, covered or laminated
	ex56039210	乙烯聚合物制电池隔膜基布	Δ5				Base cloth for battery separator, of polymers of ethylene
4133	5603.9290	---其他	10	0 澳门MO,巴PK,冰岛IS,东盟AS,哥CR,秘鲁PE,台湾TW,香港HK,新西兰NZ,智利CL 4 瑞士CH 6 澳AU,韩国KR 9.3 亚太AP	0 柬埔寨KH,老挝LA,缅甸MM,受惠国LD	85	---Other
		--每平方米重量超过70克，但不超过150克:					--Weighing more than 70g/m^2 but not more than 150g/m^2:
4134	5603.9310	---经浸渍、涂布、包覆或层压	10	0 澳门MO,巴PK,冰岛IS,东盟AS,哥CR,秘鲁PE,香港HK,新加坡SG,新西兰NZ,智利CL 4 瑞士CH 6 澳AU 8 韩国KR 8.5 亚太AP	0 受惠国$_1$LD$_1$	70	---Impregnated, coated, covered or laminated
	ex56039310	乙烯聚合物制电池隔膜基布	Δ5				Base cloth for battery separator, of polymers of ethylene

序号 No.	税则号列 Tariff Line	中文货品名称 Article Description in Chinese	最惠国税率 MFN(%)	协定税率 Agreement(%)	特惠税率 SP(%)	普通税率 Gen(%)	英文货品名称 Article Description
4135	5603.9390	---其他	10	0 澳门MO,巴PK,冰岛IS,东盟AS,哥CR,秘鲁PE,台湾TW,香港HK,新加坡SG,新西兰NZ,智利CL 4 瑞士CH 6 澳AU,韩国KR 9.3 亚太AP	0 受惠国$_1$LD$_1$	85	---Other
		--每平方米重量超过150克：					--Weighing more than 150g/m^2:
4136	5603.9410	---经浸渍、涂布、包覆或层压	10	0 巴PK,冰岛IS,东盟AS,哥CR,秘鲁PE,台湾TW,香港HK,新加坡SG,新西兰NZ,智利CL 4 瑞士CH 6 澳AU,韩国KR 8.5 亚太AP	0 受惠国$_1$LD$_1$	70	---Impregnated, coated, covered or laminated
4137	5603.9490	---其他	10	0 巴PK,冰岛IS,东盟AS,哥CR,秘鲁PE,台湾TW,香港HK,新加坡SG,新西兰NZ,智利CL 4 瑞士CH 6 澳AU 8.6 韩国KR 9.3 亚太AP	0 柬埔寨KH,老挝LA,缅甸MM,受惠国LD	85	---Other
	56.04	**用纺织材料包覆的橡胶线及绳;用橡胶或塑料浸渍、涂布、包覆或套裹的纺织纱线及税号54.04或54.05的扁条及类似品：**					**Rubber thread and cord, textile covered; textile yarn, and strip and the like of heading 5404 or 5405, impregnated, coated, covered or sheathed with rubber or plastics:**
4138	5604.1000	-用纺织材料包覆的橡胶线及绳	5	0 澳AU,澳门MO,巴PK,冰岛IS,东盟AS,哥CR,秘鲁PE,瑞士CH,新西兰NZ,智利CL 3 韩国KR	0 柬埔寨KH,老挝LA,缅甸MM,受惠国LD	80	-Rubber thread and cord, textile covered
4139	5604.9000	-其他	5	0 澳AU,澳门MO,巴PK,冰岛IS,东盟AS,哥CR,秘鲁PE,瑞士CH,新西兰NZ,智利CL 4 韩国KR	0 受惠国LD	80	-Other
	56.05	**含金属纱线，不论是否螺旋花线，由纺织纱线或税号54.04或54.05的扁条及类似品与金属线、扁条或粉末混合制得或用金属包覆制得**					**Metallised yarn, whether or not gimped, being textile yarn, or strip or the like of heading 5404 or 5405, combined with metal in the form of thread, strip or powder or covered with metal**
4140	5605.0000	含金属纱线，不论是否螺旋花线，由纺织纱线或税号54.04或54.05的扁条及类似品与金属线、扁条或粉末混合制得或用金属包覆制得	5	0 澳AU,澳门MO,巴PK,冰岛IS,东盟AS,哥CR,韩国KR,秘鲁PE,瑞士CH,新西兰NZ,智利CL	0 受惠国LD	70	Metallzied yarn, whether or not gimped, being textile yarn, or strip or the like of heading No.54.04 or 54.05, combined with metal in the form of thread, strip or powder or covered with metal
	56.06	**粗松螺旋花线，税号54.04或54.05的扁条及类似品制的螺旋花线（税号56.05的货品及马毛粗松螺旋花线除外）;绳绒线（包括植绒绳绒线）;纵行起圈纱线**					**Gimped yarn, and strip and the like of heading 5404 or 5405, gimped (other than those of heading 5605 and gimped horsehair yarn) ; chenille yarn (including flock chenille yarn) ; loop wale-yarn**

序号 No.	税则号列 Tariff Line	中文货品名称 Article Description in Chinese	最惠国税率 MFN(%)	协定税率 Agreement(%)	特惠税率 SP(%)	普通税率 Gen(%)	英文货品名称 Article Description
4141	5606.0000	粗松螺旋花线，税号54.04或54.05的扁条及类似品制的螺旋花线（税号56.05的货品及马毛粗松螺旋花线除外）；绳绒线（包括植绒绳绒线）；纵行起圈纱线	5	0 澳AU,澳门MO,巴PK,冰岛IS,东盟AS,哥CR,韩国KR,秘鲁PE,瑞士CH,新西兰NZ,智利CL	0 受惠国LD	70	Gimped yarn, and strip and the like of heading No.54.04 or 54.05, gimped (other than those of heading No.56.05 and gimped horsehair yarn) ; chenille yarn (including flock chenille yarn) ; loop waleyarn
	56.07	**线、绳、索、缆，不论是否编织或编结而成，也不论是否用橡胶或塑料浸渍，涂布、包覆或套裹：**					**Twine, cordage, ropes and cables, whether or not plaited or braided and whether or not impregnated, coated, covered or sheathed with rubber or plastics:**
		-西沙尔麻或其他纺织用龙舌兰类纤维纺制：					-Of sisal or other textile fibres of the genus *Agave*:
4142	5607.2100	--包扎用绳	5	0 澳AU,澳门MO,巴PK,冰岛IS,东盟AS,哥CR,韩国KR,秘鲁PE,瑞士CH,新西兰NZ,智利CL	0 受惠国LD	50	--Binder or baler twine
4143	5607.2900	--其他	5	0 澳AU,澳门MO,巴PK,冰岛IS,东盟AS,哥CR,韩国KR,秘鲁PE,瑞士CH,新西兰NZ,智利CL	0 受惠国LD	50	--Other
		-聚乙烯或聚丙烯纺制：					-Of polyethylene or polypropylene:
4144	5607.4100	--包扎用绳	5	0 澳AU,澳门MO,巴PK,冰岛IS,东盟AS,哥CR,韩国KR,秘鲁PE,瑞士CH,新西兰NZ,智利CL	0 受惠国LD	100	--Binder or baler twine
4145	5607.4900	--其他	5	0 澳AU,澳门MO,巴PK,冰岛IS,东盟AS,哥CR,韩国KR,秘鲁PE,瑞士CH,新西兰NZ,智利CL	0 受惠国LD	100	--Other
4146	5607.5000	-其他合成纤维纺制	5	0 澳AU,澳门MO,巴PK,冰岛IS,东盟AS,哥CR,韩国KR,秘鲁PE,台湾TW,新西兰NZ,智利CL 2 瑞士CH	0 受惠国LD	100	-Of other synthetic fibres
		-其他：					-Other:
4147	5607.9010	---蕉麻（马尼拉麻）或其他硬质（叶）纤维纺制	5	0 澳AU,澳门MO,巴PK,冰岛IS,东盟AS,哥CR,韩国KR,秘鲁PE,瑞士CH,新西兰NZ,智利CL	0 受惠国LD	50	---Of abaca (Manila hemp or *Musa textilis* Nee) or other hard (leaf) fibres
4148	5607.9090	---其他	5	0 澳AU,澳门MO,巴PK,冰岛IS,东盟AS,哥CR,韩国KR,秘鲁PE,瑞士CH,新西兰NZ,智利CL	0 柬埔寨KH,老挝LA,缅甸MM,受惠国LD 2.5 亚太AP	100	---Other
	56.08	**线、绳或索结制的网料；纺织材料制成的渔网及其他网：**					**Knotted netting of twine, cordage or rope; made-up fishing nets and other made-up nets, of textile materials:**
		-化学纤维材料制：					-Of man-made textile materials:
4149	5608.1100	--制成的渔网	10	0 冰岛IS,东盟AS,哥CR,新西兰NZ,智利CL 3 秘鲁PE 4 瑞士CH 5 巴PK 6 澳AU,韩国KR	0 受惠国LD	50	--Made up fishing nets
4150	5608.1900	--其他	12	0 冰岛IS,东盟AS,哥CR,秘鲁PE,台湾TW,新加坡SG,新西兰NZ,智利CL 6 巴PK 7.2 澳AU,韩国KR 8.4 瑞士CH	0 受惠国$_{1}$,LD$_{1}$	100	--Other

序号 No.	税则号列 Tariff Line	中文货品名称 Article Description in Chinese	最惠国税率 MFN(%)	协定税率 Agreement(%)	特惠税率 SP(%)	普通税率 Gen(%)	英文货品名称 Article Description
4151	5608.9000	-其他	10	0 冰岛IS,东盟AS,哥CR,秘鲁PE,香港HK,新西兰NZ,智利CL 4 瑞士CH 5 巴PK 6 澳AU,韩国KR	0 受惠国LD	100	-Other
	56.09	**用纱线、税号54.04或54.05的扁条及类似品或线、绳、索、缆制成的其他税号未列名物品**					**Articles of yarn, strip or the like of heading 5404 or 5405, twine, cordage, rope or cables, not elsewhere specified or included**
4152	5609.0000	用纱线、税号54.04或54.05的扁条及类似品或线、绳、索、缆制成的其他税号未列名物品	10	0 冰岛IS,东盟AS,哥CR,秘鲁PE,新西兰NZ,智利CL 4 瑞士CH 5 巴PK 6 澳AU,韩国KR	0 受惠国LD,亚太AP	100	Articles of yarn, strip or the like of heading No.54.04 or 54.05, twine, cordage, rope or cables, not elsewhere specified or included

第五十七章
地毯及纺织材料的其他铺地制品

Chapter 57
Carpets and other textile floor coverings

注释：

一、本章所称“地毯及纺织材料的其他铺地制品”，是指使用时以纺织材料作面的铺地制品，也包括具有纺织材料铺地制品特征但作其他用途的物品。

二、本章不包括铺地制品衬垫。

Notes:

1. For the purposes of this Chapter, the term “carpets and other textilefloor coverings” means floor coverings in which textile materials serve as the exposed surface of the article when in use and includes articles having the characteristics of textile floor coverings but intended for use for other purposes.
2. This Chapter does not cover floor covering underlays.

序号 No.	税则号列 Tariff Line	中文货品名称 Article Description in Chinese	最惠国税率 MFN(%)	协定税率 Agreement(%)	特惠税率 SP(%)	普通税率 Gen(%)	英文货品名称 Article Description
	57.01	**结织栽绒地毯及纺织材料的其他结织栽绒铺地制品，不论是否制成的：**					**Carpets and other textile floor coverings, knotted, whether or not made up:**
4153	5701.1000	-羊毛或动物细毛制	14	0 冰岛IS,东盟AS,哥CR,秘鲁PE,新加坡SG,新西兰NZ,智利CL 8.4 澳AU 9.8 瑞士CH 11.2 韩国KR	0 受惠国LD	130	-Of wool or fine animal hair
		-其他纺织材料制：					-Of other textile materials:
4154	5701.9010	---化学纤维制	16	0 冰岛IS,东盟AS,哥CR,新加坡SG,新西兰NZ,智利CL 4.8 秘鲁PE 9.6 澳AU 11.2 瑞士CH 12.8 巴PK,韩国KR	0 受惠国LD	130	---Of man-made textile materials
4155	5701.9020	---丝制	14	0 冰岛IS,东盟AS,哥CR,秘鲁PE,新加坡SG,新西兰NZ,智利CL 7 巴PK 8.4 澳AU 9.8 瑞士CH 11.2 韩国KR	0 受惠国$_1$LD$_1$	100	---Of silk
4156	5701.9090	---其他	14	0 冰岛IS,东盟AS,哥CR,秘鲁PE,新加坡SG,新西兰NZ,智利CL 7 巴PK 8.4 澳AU 9.8 瑞士CH 11.2 韩国KR	0 受惠国$_1$LD$_1$	100	---Other
	57.02	**机织地毯及纺织材料的其他机织铺地制品，未簇绒或未植绒，不论是否制成的，包括“开来姆”、“苏麦克”、“卡拉马尼”及类似的手织地毯：**					**Carpets and other textile floor coverings, woven, not tufted or flocked, whether or not made up, including ' Kelem' , ' Schumacks' , ' Karamanie' and similar hand-woven rugs:**
4157	5702.1000	-“开来姆”、“苏麦克”、“卡拉马尼”及类似的手织地毯	14	0 巴PK,冰岛IS,东盟AS,哥CR,秘鲁PE,新加坡SG,新西兰NZ,智利CL 8.4 澳AU 9.8 瑞士CH 11.2 韩国KR	0 受惠国LD,亚太AP	130	-“Kelem”, “Schumacks”, “Karamanie”and similar hand-woven rugs
4158	5702.2000	-椰壳纤维制的铺地制品	14	0 巴PK,冰岛IS,东盟AS,哥CR,秘鲁PE,新加坡SG,新西兰NZ,智利CL 8.4 澳AU 9.8 瑞士CH 11.2 韩国KR	0 受惠国$_1$LD$_1$	100	-Floor coverings of coconut fibres (coir)
		-其他起绒结构的铺地制品，未制成的：					-Other, of pile construction, not made up:

序号 No.	税则号列 Tariff Line	中文货品名称 Article Description in Chinese	最惠国税率 MFN(%)	协定税率 Agreement(%)	特惠税率 SP(%)	普通税率 Gen(%)	英文货品名称 Article Description
4159	5702.3100	--羊毛或动物细毛制	10	0 巴PK,冰岛IS,东盟AS,哥CR,秘鲁PE,新加坡SG,新西兰NZ,智利CL 6 澳AU,韩国KR 7 瑞士CH	0 受惠国LD	130	--Of wool or fine animal hair
4160	5702.3200	--化学纤维制	16	0 巴PK,冰岛IS,东盟AS,哥CR,新加坡SG,新西兰NZ,智利CL 4.8 秘鲁PE 9.6 澳AU 11.2 瑞士CH 12.8 韩国KR	0 受惠国$_1$LD$_1$	130	--Of man-made textile materials
4161	5702.3900	--其他纺织材料制	14	0 巴PK,冰岛IS,东盟AS,哥CR,秘鲁PE,新加坡SG,新西兰NZ,智利CL 8.4 澳AU 9.8 瑞士CH 11.2 韩国KR	0 受惠国LD,亚太AP	100	--Of other textile materials
		-其他起绒结构的铺地制品，制成的：					-Other, of pile construction, made up:
4162	5702.4100	--羊毛或动物细毛制	10	0 巴PK,冰岛IS,东盟AS,哥CR,秘鲁PE,新加坡SG,新西兰NZ,智利CL 4 瑞士CH 6 澳AU,韩国KR	0 受惠国LD	130	--Of wool or fine animal hair
4163	5702.4200	--化学纤维制	10	0 巴PK,冰岛IS,东盟AS,哥CR,秘鲁PE,新加坡SG,新西兰NZ,智利CL 4 瑞士CH 6 澳AU,韩国KR	0 受惠国LD	130	--Of man-made textile materials
4164	5702.4900	--其他纺织材料制	14	0 巴PK,冰岛IS,东盟AS,哥CR,秘鲁PE,新加坡SG,新西兰NZ,智利CL 8.4 澳AU 9.3 亚太AP 9.8 瑞士CH 11.2 韩国KR	0 受惠国$_1$LD$_1$	100	--Of other textile materials
		-其他非起绒结构的铺地制品，未制成的：					-Other, not of pile construction, not made up:
4165	5702.5010	---羊毛或动物细毛制	14	0 巴PK,冰岛IS,东盟AS,哥CR,秘鲁PE,新加坡SG,新西兰NZ,智利CL 8.4 澳AU 9.8 瑞士CH 11.2 韩国KR	0 受惠国$_1$LD$_1$	130	---Of wool or fine animal hair
4166	5702.5020	---化学纤维制	16	0 巴PK,冰岛IS,东盟AS,哥CR,新加坡SG,新西兰NZ,智利CL 4.8 秘鲁PE 9.6 澳AU 11.2 瑞士CH 12.8 韩国KR	0 受惠国$_1$LD$_1$	130	---Of man-made textile materials
4167	5702.5090	---其他纺织材料制	14	0 巴PK,冰岛IS,东盟AS,哥CR,秘鲁PE,新加坡SG,新西兰NZ,智利CL 8.4 澳AU 9.8 瑞士CH 11.2 韩国KR	0 受惠国$_1$LD$_1$	100	---Of other textile materials
		-其他非起绒结构的铺地制品，制成的：					-Other, not of pile construction, made up:
4168	5702.9100	--羊毛或动物细毛制	14	0 巴PK,冰岛IS,东盟AS,哥CR,秘鲁PE,新加坡SG,新西兰NZ,智利CL 8.4 澳AU 9.8 瑞士CH 11.2 韩国KR	0 受惠国$_1$LD$_1$	130	--Of wool or fine animal hair

序号 No.	税则号列 Tariff Line	中文货品名称 Article Description in Chinese	最惠国税率 MFN(%)	协定税率 Agreement(%)	特惠税率 SP(%)	普通税率 Gen(%)	英文货品名称 Article Description
4169	5702.9200	--化学纤维制	16	0 巴PK,冰岛IS,东盟AS,哥CR,新加坡SG,新西兰NZ,智利CL 4.8 秘鲁PE 9.6 澳AU 11.2 瑞士CH 12.8 韩国KR	0 受惠国$_1$LD$_1$	130	--Of man-made textile materials
4170	5702.9900	--其他纺织材料制	14	0 巴PK,冰岛IS,东盟AS,哥CR,秘鲁PE,新加坡SG,新西兰NZ,智利CL 8.4 澳AU 9.8 瑞士CH 11.2 韩国KR	0 受惠国$_1$LD$_1$	100	--Of other textile materials
	57.03	**簇绒地毯及纺织材料的其他簇绒铺地制品，不论是否制成的：**					**Carpets and other textile floor coverings, tufted, whether or not made up:**
4171	5703.1000	-羊毛或动物细毛制	14	0 冰岛IS,东盟AS,哥CR,秘鲁PE,新加坡SG,新西兰NZ,智利CL 8.4 澳AU 9.8 瑞士CH 11.2 韩国KR	0 受惠国LD	130	-Of wool or fine animal hair
4172	5703.2000	-尼龙或其他聚酰胺制	10	0 冰岛IS,东盟AS,哥CR,秘鲁PE,新加坡SG,新西兰NZ,智利CL 4 瑞士CH 5 巴PK 6 澳AU 9 韩国KR	0 受惠国LD	130	-Of nylon or other polyamides
4173	5703.3000	-其他化学纤维制	10	0 冰岛IS,东盟AS,哥CR,秘鲁PE,新加坡SG,新西兰NZ,智利CL 4 瑞士CH 6 澳AU,韩国KR	0 受惠国LD	130	-Of other man-made textile materials
4174	5703.9000	-其他纺织材料制	14	0 冰岛IS,东盟AS,哥CR,秘鲁PE,新加坡SG,新西兰NZ,智利CL 8.4 澳AU 9.8 瑞士CH 11.2 巴PK,韩国KR	0 受惠国LD,亚太AP	100	-Of other textile materials
	57.04	**毡呢地毯及纺织材料的其他毡呢铺地制品，未簇绒或未植绒，不论是否制成的：**					**Carpets and other textile floor coverings, of felt, not tufted or flocked, whether or not made up:**
4175	5704.1000	-最大表面面积不超过0.3平方米	14	0 冰岛IS,东盟AS,哥CR,秘鲁PE,新加坡SG,新西兰NZ,智利CL 7 巴PK 8.4 澳AU 9.8 瑞士CH 11.2 韩国KR	0 受惠国$_1$LD$_1$	130	-Tiles, having a maximum surface area of $0.3m^2$
4176	5704.9000	-其他	10	0 冰岛IS,东盟AS,哥CR,秘鲁PE,新加坡SG,新西兰NZ,智利CL 4 瑞士CH 5 巴PK 6 澳AU,韩国KR	0 受惠国LD	130	-Other
	57.05	**其他地毯及纺织材料的其他铺地制品，不论是否制成的：**					**Other carpets and other textile floor coverings, whether or not made up:**
4177	5705.0010	---羊毛或动物细毛制	14	0 冰岛IS,东盟AS,哥CR,秘鲁PE,新加坡SG,新西兰NZ,智利CL 8.4 澳AU 9.8 瑞士CH 11.2 巴PK,韩国KR	0 受惠国LD,亚太AP	130	---Of wool or fine animal hair

序号 No.	税则号列 Tariff Line	中文货品名称 Article Description in Chinese	最惠国税率 MFN(%)	协定税率 Agreement(%)	特惠税率 SP(%)	普通税率 Gen(%)	英文货品名称 Article Description
4178	5705.0020	---化学纤维制	10	0 冰岛IS,东盟AS,哥CR,秘鲁PE,新加坡SG,新西兰NZ,智利CL 4 瑞士CH 5 巴PK 6 澳AU,韩国KR	0 受惠国LD,亚太AP	130	---Of man-made textile materials
4179	5705.0090	---其他纺织材料制	14	0 冰岛IS,东盟AS,哥CR,秘鲁PE,新加坡SG,新西兰NZ,智利CL 8.4 澳AU 9.8 瑞士CH 11.2 巴PK,韩国KR	0 受惠国LD,亚太AP	100	---Of other textile materialsr

第五十八章
特种机织物；簇绒织物；花边；
装饰毯；装饰带；刺绣品

注释：

一、本章不适用于经浸渍、涂布、包覆或层压的第五十九章注释一所述的纺织物或第五十九章的其他货品。

二、税号 58.01 也包括因未将浮纱割断而使表面无竖绒的纬起绒织物。

三、税号 58.03 所称“纱罗”，是指经线全部或部分由地经纱和绞经纱构成的织物，其中绞经纱绕地经纱半圈、一圈或几圈而形成圈状，纬纱从圈中穿过。

四、税号 58.04 不适用于税号 56.08 的线、绳、索结制的网状织物。

五、税号 58.06 所称“狭幅机织物”，是指：

（一）幅宽不超过 30 厘米的机织物，不论是否织成或从宽幅料剪成，但两侧必须有织成的、胶粘的或用其他方法制成的布边；

（二）压平宽度不超过 30 厘米的圆筒机织物；

（三）折边的斜裁滚条布，其未折边时的宽度不超过 30 厘米。

流苏状的狭幅织物归入税号 58.08。

六、税号 58.10 所称“刺绣品”，除了一般纺织材料绣线绣制的刺绣品外，还包括在可见底布上用金属线或玻璃线刺绣的刺绣品，也包括用珠片、饰珠、纺织材料或其他材料制的装饰用花纹图案所缝绣的贴花织物。但不包括手工针绣嵌花装饰毯（税号 58.05）。

七、除税号 58.09 的产品外，本章还包括金属线制 的用于衣着、装饰及类似用途的物品。

Chapter 58
Special woven fabrics; tufted textile fabrics; lace; tapestries; trimmings; embroidery

Notes:

1. This Chapter does not apply to textile fabrics referred to in Note 1 to Chapter 59，impregnated，coated，covered or laminated，or to other goods of Chapter 59.
2. Heading 58.01also includes woven weft pile fabrics which have not yet had the floats cut，at which stage they have no pile standing up.
3. For the purpose of heading 58.03，“gauze”means a fabric with a warp composed wholly or in part of standing or ground threads and crossing or doup threads which cross the standing or ground threads making a half turn，a complete turn or more to form loops through which weft threads pass.
4. Heading 58.04 does not apply to knotted net fabrics of twine，cordage or rope，of heading 56.08.
5. For the purposes of heading 58.06，the expression “narrow woven fabrics” means:

(a) Woven fabrics of a width not exceeding30cm，whether woven as such or cut from wider pieces，provided with selvedges (woven，gummed or otherwise made) on both edges;

(b) Tubular woven fabrics of a flattened width not exceeding 30cm; and

(c) Bias binding with folded edges，of a width when unfolded not exceeding30cm.

Narrow woven fabrics with woven fringes are to be classified in heading No.58.08.

6. In heading No.58.10，the expression“embroidery”means，*inter alia*，embroidery with metal or glass thread on a visible ground of textile fabric，and sewn applique work of sequins，beads or ornamental motifs of textile or other materials. The heading does not apply to needlework tapestry (heading 58.05).
7. In addition to the products of heading58.09，this Chapter also includes articles made of metal thread and of a kind used in apparel，as furnishing fabrics or for similar purposes.

序号 No.	税则号列 Tariff Line	中文货品名称 Article Description in Chinese	最惠国税率 MFN(%)	协定税率 Agreement(%)	特惠税率 SP(%)	普通税率 Gen(%)	英文货品名称 Article Description
	58.01	**起绒机织物及绳绒织物，但税号58.02或58.06的织物除外：**					**Woven pile fabrics and chenille fabrics, other than fabrics of heading 5802 or 5806:**
4180	5801.1000	-羊毛或动物细毛制	10	0 巴PK,冰岛IS,东盟AS,哥CR,秘鲁PE,新加坡SG,新西兰NZ,智利CL 4 瑞士CH 6 澳AU,韩国KR	0 受惠国LD	130	-Of wool or fine animal hair
		-棉制：					-Of cotton:
4181	5801.2100	--不割绒的纬起绒织物	12	0 巴PK,冰岛IS,东盟AS,哥CR,秘鲁PE,新加坡SG,新西兰NZ,智利CL 7.2 澳AU,韩国KR 8.4 瑞士CH	0 受惠国$_1$LD$_1$	70	--Uncut weft pile fabrics

序号 No.	税则号列 Tariff Line	中文货品名称 Article Description in Chinese	最惠国税率 MFN(%)	协定税率 Agreement(%)	特惠税率 SP(%)	普通税率 Gen(%)	英文货品名称 Article Description
4182	5801.2200	--割绒的灯芯绒	10	0 巴PK,冰岛IS,东盟AS,哥CR,秘鲁PE,台湾TW,香港HK,新西兰NZ,智利CL 4 瑞士CH 6 澳AU,韩国KR	0 受惠国LD	70	--Cut corduroy
4183	5801.2300	--其他纬起绒织物	10	0 巴PK,冰岛IS,东盟AS,哥CR,秘鲁PE,新西兰NZ,智利CL 4 瑞士CH 6 澳AU 8 韩国KR	0 受惠国LD	70	--Other weft pile fabrics
4184	5801.2600	--绳绒织物	10	0 巴PK,冰岛IS,东盟AS,哥CR,秘鲁PE,新西兰NZ,智利CL 4 瑞士CH 6 澳AU,韩国KR	0 受惠国LD	70	--Chenille fabrics
		--经起绒织物:					--Warp pile fabrics:
4185	5801.2710	---不割绒的（棱纹绸）	10	0 巴PK,冰岛IS,东盟AS,哥CR,秘鲁PE,新西兰NZ,智利CL 4 瑞士CH 6 澳AU,韩国KR	0 受惠国LD	70	---Èpinglè (uncut)
4186	5801.2720	---割绒的	10	0 巴PK,冰岛IS,东盟AS,哥CR,秘鲁PE,香港HK,新西兰NZ,智利CL 4 瑞士CH 6 澳AU,韩国KR	0 受惠国LD	70	---Cut
		-化学纤维制:					-Of man-made fibres:
4187	5801.3100	--不割绒的纬起绒织物	10	0 巴PK,冰岛IS,东盟AS,哥CR,秘鲁PE,新加坡SG,新西兰NZ,智利CL 4 瑞士CH 6 澳AU 8.6 韩国KR	0 受惠国LD	130	--Uncut weft pile fabrics
4188	5801.3200	--割绒的灯芯绒	10	0 巴PK,冰岛IS,东盟AS,哥CR,秘鲁PE,新加坡SG,新西兰NZ,智利CL 4 瑞士CH 6 澳AU,韩国KR	0 受惠国LD	130	--Cut corduroy
4189	5801.3300	--其他纬起绒织物	10	0 巴PK,冰岛IS,东盟AS,哥CR,秘鲁PE,台湾TW,新加坡SG,新西兰NZ,智利CL 4 瑞士CH 6 澳AU,韩国KR	0 柬埔寨KH,老挝LA,缅甸MM,受惠国LD	130	--Other weft pile fabrics
4190	5801.3600	--绳绒织物	10	0 巴PK,冰岛IS,东盟AS,哥CR,秘鲁PE,新加坡SG,新西兰NZ,智利CL 4 瑞士CH 6 澳AU,韩国KR	0 受惠国LD	130	--Chenille fabrics
		--经起绒织物:					--Warp pile fabrics:
4191	5801.3710	---不割绒的（棱纹绸）	10	0 巴PK,冰岛IS,东盟AS,哥CR,秘鲁PE,新加坡SG,新西兰NZ,智利CL 4 瑞士CH 6 澳AU,韩国KR	0 受惠国LD	130	---Èpinglè (uncut)
4192	5801.3720	---割绒的	10	0 巴PK,冰岛IS,东盟AS,哥CR,秘鲁PE,新加坡SG,新西兰NZ,智利CL 4 瑞士CH 6 澳AU,韩国KR	0 受惠国LD	130	---Cut
		-其他纺织材料制:					-Of other textile materials:

序号 No.	税则号列 Tariff Line	中文货品名称 Article Description in Chinese	最惠国税率 MFN(%)	协定税率 Agreement(%)	特惠税率 SP(%)	普通税率 Gen(%)	英文货品名称 Article Description
4193	5801.9010	---丝及绢丝制	10	0 巴PK,冰岛IS,东盟AS,哥CR,秘鲁PE,新加坡SG,新西兰NZ,智利CL 4 瑞士CH 6 澳AU,韩国KR	0 受惠国LD	130	---Of silk or silk waste
4194	5801.9090	---其他	10	0 巴PK,冰岛IS,东盟AS,哥CR,秘鲁PE,新加坡SG,新西兰NZ,智利CL 4 瑞士CH 6 澳AU,韩国KR	0 受惠国LD	80	---Other
	58.02	**毛巾织物及类似的毛圈机织物，但税号58.06的狭幅织物除外；簇绒织物，但税号57.03的产品除外：**					**Terry towelling and similar woven terry fabrics, other than narrow fabrics of heading 5806; tufted textile fabrics, other than products of heading 5703:**
		-棉制毛巾织物及类似毛圈机织物：					-Terry towelling and similar woven terry fabrics, of cotton:
4195	5802.1100	--未漂白	12	0 澳门MO,巴PK,冰岛IS,东盟AS,哥CR,秘鲁PE,新加坡SG,新西兰NZ,智利CL 7.2 澳AU,韩国KR 8.4 瑞士CH	0 受惠国LD,亚太AP	70	--Unbleached
4196	5802.1900	--其他	10	0 澳门MO,巴PK,冰岛IS,东盟AS,哥CR,秘鲁PE,新西兰NZ,智利CL 4 瑞士CH 6 澳AU,韩国KR	0 受惠国LD	70	--Other
		-其他纺织材料制的毛巾织物及类似的毛圈机织物：					-Terry towelling and similar woven terry fabrics, of other textile materials:
4197	5802.2010	---丝及绢丝制	12	0 澳门MO,巴PK,冰岛IS,东盟AS,哥CR,秘鲁PE,新加坡SG,新西兰NZ,智利CL 7.2 澳AU,韩国KR 8.4 瑞士CH	0 受惠国LD,亚太AP	130	---Of silk or silk waste
4198	5802.2020	---羊毛或动物细毛制	12	0 澳门MO,巴PK,冰岛IS,东盟AS,哥CR,秘鲁PE,新加坡SG,新西兰NZ,智利CL 7.2 澳AU,韩国KR 8.4 瑞士CH	0 受惠国LD,亚太AP	130	---Of wool or fine animal hair
4199	5802.2030	---化学纤维制	14	0 澳门MO,巴PK,冰岛IS,东盟AS,哥CR,秘鲁PE,新加坡SG,新西兰NZ,智利CL 8.4 澳AU 9.8 瑞士CH 11.2 韩国KR	0 受惠国LD,亚太AP	130	---Of man-made fibres
4200	5802.2090	---其他	12	0 澳门MO,巴PK,冰岛IS,东盟AS,哥CR,秘鲁PE,新加坡SG,新西兰NZ,智利CL 7.2 澳AU,韩国KR 8.4 瑞士CH	0 受惠国LD,亚太AP	80	---Other
		-簇绒织物：					-Tufted textile fabrics:
4201	5802.3010	---丝及绢丝制	10	0 巴PK,冰岛IS,东盟AS,哥CR,秘鲁PE,新加坡SG,新西兰NZ,智利CL 4 瑞士CH 6 澳AU,韩国KR	0 受惠国LD	130	---Of silk or silk waste

序号 No.	税则号列 Tariff Line	中文货品名称 Article Description in Chinese	最惠国税率 MFN(%)	协定税率 Agreement(%)	特惠税率 SP(%)	普通税率 Gen(%)	英文货品名称 Article Description
4202	5802.3020	---羊毛或动物细毛制	10	0 巴PK,冰岛IS,东盟AS,哥CR,秘鲁PE,新加坡SG,新西兰NZ,智利CL 4 瑞士CH 6 澳AU,韩国KR	0 受惠国LD	130	---Of wool or fine animal hair
4203	5802.3030	---棉或麻制	10	0 巴PK,冰岛IS,东盟AS,哥CR,秘鲁PE,新西兰NZ,智利CL 4 瑞士CH 6 澳AU,韩国KR	0 受惠国LD	70	---Of cotton or bast fibre
4204	5802.3040	---化学纤维制	10	0 巴PK,冰岛IS,东盟AS,哥CR,新加坡SG,新西兰NZ,智利CL 3 秘鲁PE 4 瑞士CH 6 澳AU,韩国KR	0 受惠国LD	130	---Of manmade fibres
4205	5802.3090	---其他纺织材料制	10	0 巴PK,冰岛IS,东盟AS,哥CR,秘鲁PE,新加坡SG,新西兰NZ,智利CL 4 瑞士CH 6 澳AU,韩国KR	0 受惠国LD	80	---Of other textile materials
	58.03	**纱罗，但税号58.06的狭幅织物除外：**					**Gauze, other than narrow fabrics of heading 5806:**
4206	5803.0010	---棉制	10	0 冰岛IS,东盟AS,哥CR,秘鲁PE,新西兰NZ,智利CL 4 瑞士CH 5 巴PK 6 澳AU,韩国KR	0 受惠国LD	70	---Of cotton
4207	5803.0020	---丝及绢丝制	10	0 冰岛IS,东盟AS,哥CR,秘鲁PE,新加坡SG,新西兰NZ,智利CL 4 瑞士CH 5 巴PK 6 澳AU,韩国KR	0 受惠国LD	130	---Of silk or silk waste
4208	5803.0030	---化学纤维制	10	0 冰岛IS,东盟AS,哥CR,秘鲁PE,新加坡SG,新西兰NZ,智利CL 4 瑞士CH 5 巴PK 6 澳AU,韩国KR	0 受惠国LD	130	---Of man-made fibres
4209	5803.0090	---其他纺织材料制	10	0 冰岛IS,东盟AS,哥CR,秘鲁PE,新加坡SG,新西兰NZ,智利CL 4 瑞士CH 5 巴PK 6 澳AU,韩国KR	0 受惠国LD	80	---Of other textile materials
	58.04	**网眼薄纱及其他网眼织物，但不包括机织物、针织物或钩编织物;成卷、成条或成小块图案的花边，但税号60.02的织物除外：**					**Tulles and other net fabrics, not including woven, knitted or crocheted fabrics; lace in the piece, in strips or in motifs, other than fabrics of headings 6002 to 6006:**
		-网眼薄纱及其他网眼织物：					-Tulles and other net fabrics:
4210	5804.1010	---丝及绢丝制	10	0 冰岛IS,东盟AS,哥CR,秘鲁PE,新加坡SG,新西兰NZ,智利CL 4 瑞士CH 5 巴PK 6 澳AU,韩国KR 7 亚太AP	0 受惠国LD	130	---Of silk or silk waste

序号 No.	税则号列 Tariff Line	中文货品名称 Article Description in Chinese	最惠国税率 MFN(%)	协定税率 Agreement(%)	特惠税率 SP(%)	普通税率 Gen(%)	英文货品名称 Article Description
4211	5804.1020	---棉制	10	0 冰岛IS,东盟AS,哥CR,秘鲁PE,新西兰NZ,智利CL 5 巴PK 6 澳AU,韩国KR 7 亚太AP 7.2 瑞士CH	0 受惠国LD	70	---Of cotton
4212	5804.1030	---化学纤维制	12	0 冰岛IS,东盟AS,哥CR,秘鲁PE,台湾TW,新加坡SG,新西兰NZ,智利CL 5 巴PK 7.2 澳AU 8.4 瑞士CH,亚太AP 10.8 韩国KR	0 柬埔寨KH,老挝LA,缅甸MM,受惠国LD	130	---Of man-made fibres
4213	5804.1090	---其他纺织材料制	10	0 冰岛IS,东盟AS,哥CR,秘鲁PE,台湾TW,新加坡SG,新西兰NZ,智利CL 4 瑞士CH 5 巴PK 6 澳AU,韩国KR 7 亚太AP	0 受惠国LD	90	---Of other textile materials
		-机制花边:					-Mechanically made lace:
4214	5804.2100	--化学纤维制	10	0 澳门MO,冰岛IS,东盟AS,哥CR,秘鲁PE,台湾TW,香港HK,新加坡SG,新西兰NZ,智利CL 4 瑞士CH 5 巴PK 6 澳AU,韩国KR	0 受惠国LD	130	--Of man-made fibres
		--其他纺织材料制:					--Of other textile materials:
4215	5804.2910	---丝及绢丝制	10	0 冰岛IS,东盟AS,哥CR,秘鲁PE,新加坡SG,新西兰NZ,智利CL 4 瑞士CH 5 巴PK 6 澳AU,韩国KR	0 受惠国LD	130	---Of silk or silk waste
4216	5804.2920	---棉制	10	0 冰岛IS,东盟AS,哥CR,秘鲁PE,新西兰NZ,智利CL 4 瑞士CH 5 巴PK 6 澳AU,韩国KR	0 柬埔寨KH,老挝LA,缅甸MM,受惠国LD	70	---Of cotton
4217	5804.2990	---其他	10	0 冰岛IS,东盟AS,哥CR,秘鲁PE,新加坡SG,新西兰NZ,智利CL 4 瑞士CH 5 巴PK 6 澳AU,韩国KR	0 受惠国LD	90	---Other
4218	5804.3000	-手工制花边	10	0 冰岛IS,东盟AS,哥CR,秘鲁PE,新加坡SG,新西兰NZ,智利CL 4 瑞士CH 5 巴PK 6 澳AU,韩国KR	0 受惠国LD	100	-Hand-made lace
	58.05	**"哥白林"、"弗朗德"、"奥步生"、"波威"及类似式样的手织装饰毯，以及手工针绣嵌花装饰毯（例如，小针脚或十字绣），不论是否制成的：**					**Hand-woven tapestries of the type Gobelins, Flanders, Aubusson, Beauvais and the like, and needle-worked tapestries (for example, petit point, cross stitch) , whether or not made up:**

序号 No.	税则号列 Tariff Line	中文货品名称 Article Description in Chinese	最惠国税率 MFN(%)	协定税率 Agreement(%)	特惠税率 SP(%)	普通税率 Gen(%)	英文货品名称 Article Description
4219	5805.0010	---手工针绣嵌花装饰毯	12	0 冰岛IS,东盟AS,哥CR,秘鲁PE,新加坡SG,新西兰NZ,智利CL 6 巴PK 7.2 澳AU,韩国KR 8.4 瑞士CH	0 受惠国LD	130	---Needleworked tapestries
4220	5805.0090	---其他	12	0 冰岛IS,东盟AS,哥CR,秘鲁PE,新加坡SG,新西兰NZ,智利CL 6 巴PK 7.2 澳AU,韩国KR 8.4 瑞士CH	0 受惠国LD	130	---Other
	58.06	**狭幅机织物，但税号58.07的货品除外;用粘合剂粘合制成的有经纱而无纬纱的狭幅织物(包扎匹头用带):**					**Narrow woven fabrics, other than goods of heading 5807; narrow fabrics consisting of warp without weft assembled by means of an adhesive (bolducs) :**
		-起绒机织物（包括毛巾织物及类似的毛圈织物）及绳绒织物:					-Woven pile fabrics (including terry towelling and similar terry fabrics) and chenille fabrics:
4221	5806.1010	---棉或麻制	10	0 冰岛IS,东盟AS,哥CR,秘鲁PE,新西兰NZ,智利CL 4 瑞士CH 5 巴PK 6 澳AU,韩国KR	0 受惠国LD	70	---Of cotton or bast fibres
4222	5806.1090	---其他纺织材料制	10	0 冰岛IS,东盟AS,哥CR,秘鲁PE,台湾TW,新加坡SG,新西兰NZ,智利CL 4 瑞士CH 5 巴PK 6 澳AU,韩国KR 9.1 亚太AP	0 柬埔寨KH,老挝LA,缅甸MM,受惠国LD	80	---Of other textile materials
4223	5806.2000	-按重量计弹性纱线或橡胶线含量在5%及以上的其他机织物	10	0 澳门MO,冰岛IS,东盟AS,哥CR,秘鲁PE,台湾TW,香港HK,新加坡SG,新西兰NZ,智利CL 4 瑞士CH 5 巴PK 6 澳AU,韩国KR	0 柬埔寨KH,老挝LA,缅甸MM,受惠国LD	100	-Other woven fabrics, containing by weight 5% or more of elastomeric yarn or rubber thread
		-其他机织物:					-Other woven fabrics:
4224	5806.3100	--棉制	10	0 冰岛IS,东盟AS,哥CR,秘鲁PE,新西兰NZ,智利CL 4 瑞士CH 5 巴PK 6 澳AU,韩国KR	0 柬埔寨KH,老挝LA,缅甸MM,受惠国LD	70	--Of cotton
4225	5806.3200	--化学纤维制	10	0 澳门MO,冰岛IS,东盟AS,哥CR,秘鲁PE,台湾TW,新加坡SG,新西兰NZ,智利CL 4 瑞士CH 5 巴PK 6 澳AU,韩国KR 7 亚太AP	0 柬埔寨KH,老挝LA,缅甸MM,受惠国LD	130	--Of man-made fibres
		--其他纺织材料制:					--Of other textile materials:
4226	5806.3910	---丝及绢丝制	10	0 冰岛IS,东盟AS,哥CR,秘鲁PE,新加坡SG,新西兰NZ,智利CL 4 瑞士CH 5 巴PK 6 澳AU,韩国KR	0 受惠国LD	130	---Of silk or silk waste

序号 No.	税则号列 Tariff Line	中文货品名称 Article Description in Chinese	最惠国税率 MFN(%)	协定税率 Agreement(%)	特惠税率 SP(%)	普通税率 Gen(%)	英文货品名称 Article Description
4227	5806.3920	---羊毛或动物细毛制	10	0 冰岛IS,东盟AS,哥CR,秘鲁PE,新加坡SG,新西兰NZ,智利CL 4 瑞士CH 5 巴PK 6 澳AU,韩国KR	0 受惠国LD	130	---Of wool or fine animal hair
4228	5806.3990	---其他	10	0 冰岛IS,东盟AS,哥CR,秘鲁PE,新加坡SG,新西兰NZ,智利CL 4 瑞士CH 5 巴PK 6 澳AU,韩国KR	0 受惠国LD	80	---Other
		-用粘合剂粘合制成的有经纱而无纬纱的织物(包扎匹头用带):					-Fabrics consisting of warp without weft assembled by means of an adhesive (bolducs) :
4229	5806.4010	---棉或麻制	10	0 冰岛IS,东盟AS,哥CR,秘鲁PE,新西兰NZ,智利CL 4 瑞士CH 5 巴PK 6 澳AU,韩国KR	0 受惠国LD	70	---Of cotton or bast fibres
4230	5806.4090	---其他纺织材料制	10	0 冰岛IS,东盟AS,哥CR,秘鲁PE,新加坡SG,新西兰NZ,智利CL 4 瑞士CH 5 巴PK 6 澳AU,韩国KR	0 受惠国LD	80	---Of other textile materials
	58.07	**非绣制的纺织材料制标签、徽章及类似品,成匹、成条或裁成一定形状或尺寸:**					**Labels, badges and similar articles of textile materials, in the piece, in strips or cut to shape or size, not embroidered:**
4231	5807.1000	-机织	10	0 澳门MO,冰岛IS,东盟AS,哥CR,台湾TW,香港HK,新加坡SG,新西兰NZ,智利CL 3 秘鲁PE 4 瑞士CH 6 澳AU,韩国KR 8.5 巴PK,亚太AP	0 柬埔寨KH,老挝LA,缅甸MM,受惠国LD	100	-Woven
4232	5807.9000	-其他	10	0 冰岛IS,东盟AS,哥CR,秘鲁PE,新加坡SG,新西兰NZ,智利CL 4 瑞士CH 5 巴PK 6 澳AU,韩国KR	0 受惠国LD	100	-Other
	58.08	**成匹的编带;非绣制的成匹装饰带,但针织或钩编的除外;流苏、绒球及类似品:**					**Braids in the piece; ornamental trimmings in the piece, without embroidery, other than knitted or crocheted; tassels, pompons and similar articles:**
4233	5808.1000	-成匹的编带	10	0 澳门MO,冰岛IS,东盟AS,哥CR,秘鲁PE,新加坡SG,新西兰NZ,智利CL 4 瑞士CH 6 澳AU,韩国KR	0 受惠国LD	100	-Braids in the piece
4234	5808.9000	-其他	10	0 澳门MO,冰岛IS,东盟AS,哥CR,秘鲁PE,新加坡SG,新西兰NZ,智利CL 4 瑞士CH 5 巴PK 6 澳AU,韩国KR	0 柬埔寨KH,老挝LA,缅甸MM,受惠国LD	100	-Other

序号 No.	税则号列 Tariff Line	中文货品名称 Article Description in Chinese	最惠国税率 MFN(%)	协定税率 Agreement(%)	特惠税率 SP(%)	普通税率 Gen(%)	英文货品名称 Article Description
	58.09	**其他税号未列名的金属线机织物及税号56.05所列含金属纱线的机织物，用于衣着、装饰及类似用途：**					**Woven fabrics of metal thread and woven fabrics of metallised yarn of heading 5605, of a kind used in apparel, as furnishing fabrics or for similar purposes, not elsewhere specified or included:**
4235	5809.0010	---与棉混制	10	0 冰岛IS,东盟AS,哥CR,秘鲁PE,新加坡SG,新西兰NZ,智利CL 4 瑞士CH 5 巴PK 6 澳AU,韩国KR	0 受惠国LD	90	---Combined with cotton
4236	5809.0020	---与化学纤维混制	10	0 冰岛IS,东盟AS,哥CR,秘鲁PE,新加坡SG,新西兰NZ,智利CL 4 瑞士CH 5 巴PK 6 澳AU,韩国KR	0 受惠国LD	130	---Combined with manmade fibres
4237	5809.0090	---其他	10	0 冰岛IS,东盟AS,哥CR,秘鲁PE,新加坡SG,新西兰NZ,智利CL 4 瑞士CH 5 巴PK 6 澳AU,韩国KR	0 受惠国LD	100	---Other
	58.10	**成匹、成条或成小块图案的刺绣品：**					**Embroidery in the piece, in strips or in motifs:**
4238	5810.1000	-不见底布的刺绣品	10	0 冰岛IS,东盟AS,哥CR,秘鲁PE,新加坡SG,新西兰NZ,智利CL 4 瑞士CH 5 巴PK 6 澳AU,韩国KR	0 受惠国LD	130	-Embroidery without visible ground
		-其他刺绣品：					-Other embroidery:
4239	5810.9100	--棉制	10	0 冰岛IS,东盟AS,哥CR,新加坡SG,新西兰NZ,智利CL 3 秘鲁PE 4 瑞士CH 6 澳AU,韩国KR	0 受惠国LD	130	--Of cotton
4240	5810.9200	--化学纤维制	10	0 冰岛IS,东盟AS,哥CR,秘鲁PE,台湾TW,新加坡SG,新西兰NZ,智利CL 4 瑞士CH 5 巴PK 6 澳AU 8.6 韩国KR	0 受惠国LD	130	--Of man-made fibres
4241	5810.9900	--其他纺织材料制	10	0 冰岛IS,东盟AS,哥CR,秘鲁PE,新加坡SG,新西兰NZ,智利CL 4 瑞士CH 5 巴PK 6 澳AU,韩国KR	0 受惠国LD	130	--Of other textile materials
	58.11	**用一层或几层纺织材料与胎料经绗缝或其他方法组合制成的被褥状纺织品，但税号58.10的刺绣品除外：**					**Quilted textile products in the piece, composed of one or more layers of textile materials assembled with padding by stitching or otherwise, other than embroidery of heading 5810:**
4242	5811.0010	---丝及绢丝制	10	0 巴PK,冰岛IS,东盟AS,哥CR,秘鲁PE,新加坡SG,新西兰NZ,智利CL 4 瑞士CH 6 澳AU,韩国KR	0 受惠国LD	130	---Of silk or silk waste

序号 No.	税则号列 Tariff Line	中文货品名称 Article Description in Chinese	最惠国税率 MFN(%)	协定税率 Agreement(%)	特惠税率 SP(%)	普通税率 Gen(%)	英文货品名称 Article Description
4243	5811.0020	---羊毛或动物细毛制	10	0 巴PK,冰岛IS,东盟AS,哥CR,秘鲁PE,新加坡SG,新西兰NZ,智利CL 4 瑞士CH 6 澳AU,韩国KR	0 受惠国LD	130	---Of wool or fine animal hair
4244	5811.0030	---棉制	10	0 巴PK,冰岛IS,东盟AS,哥CR,秘鲁PE,新西兰NZ,智利CL 4 瑞士CH 6 澳AU,韩国KR	0 受惠国LD	80	---Of cotton
4245	5811.0040	---化学纤维制	12	0 巴PK,冰岛IS,东盟AS,哥CR,秘鲁PE,新加坡SG,新西兰NZ,智利CL 7.2 澳AU 8.4 瑞士CH 10.8 韩国KR	0 受惠国LD	130	---Of man-made fibres
4246	5811.0090	---其他纺织材料制	10	0 巴PK,冰岛IS,东盟AS,哥CR,秘鲁PE,新加坡SG,新西兰NZ,智利CL 4 瑞士CH 6 澳AU,韩国KR	0 受惠国LD	90	---Of other textile materials

第五十九章
浸渍、涂布、包覆或层压的纺织物；工业用纺织制品

注释：

一、除条文另有规定的以外，本章所称"纺织物"，仅适用于第五十章至第五十五章、税号 58.03 及 58.06 的机织物、税号 58.08 的成匹编带和装饰带及税号 60.02 至 60.06 的针织物或钩编织物。

二、税号 59.03 适用于：

（一）用塑料浸渍、涂布、包覆或层压的纺织物，不论每平方米重量多少以及塑料的性质如何（紧密结构或泡沫状的），但下列各项除外：

1. 用肉眼无法辨别出是否经过浸渍、涂布、包覆或层压的织物（通常归入第五十章至第五十五章、第五十八章或第六十章），但由于浸渍、涂布、包覆或层压所引起的颜色变化可不予考虑；
2. 温度在 15℃至 30℃时，用手工将其绕于直径 7 毫米的圆柱体上会发生断裂的产品（通常归入第三十九章）；
3. 纺织物完全嵌入塑料内或在其两面均用塑料完全包覆或涂布，而这种包覆或涂布用肉眼是能够辨别出的产品（但由于包覆或涂布所引起的颜色变化可不予考虑）(第三十九章)；
4. 用塑料部分涂布或包覆并由此而形成图案的织物（通常归入第五十章至第五十五章、第五十八章或第六十章）；
5. 与纺织物混制而其中纺织物仅起增强作用的泡沫塑料板、片或带（第三十九章）；
6. 税号 58.11 的纺织品。

（二）由税号 56.04 的用塑料浸渍、涂布、包覆或套裹的纱线、扁条或类似品制成的织物。

三、税号 59.05 所称"糊墙织物"，是指以纺织材料作面，固定在一衬背上或在背面进行处理（浸渍或涂布以便于裱糊），适于装饰墙壁或天花板，且宽度不小于 45 厘米的成卷产品。

但本税号不适用于以纺织纤维屑或粉末直接粘于纸上（税号 48.14）或布底上（通常归入税号 59.07）的糊墙物品。

四、税号 59.06 所称"用橡胶处理的纺织物"是指：

Chapter 59
Impregnated, coated, covered or laminated textile fabrics; textile articles of a kind suitable for industrial use

Notes:

1. Except where the context otherwise requires, for the purposes of this Chapter the expression "textile fabrics" applies only to the woven fabrics of Chapters 50 to 55 and headings Nos.58.03 and 58.06, the braids and ornamental trimmings in the piece of heading No.58.08and the knitted or crocheted fabrics of headings No.60.02 to 60.06.
2. Heading No.59.03 applies to:
   (a) Textile fabrics, impregnated, coated, covered or laminated with plastics, whatever the weight per square metre and whatever the nature of the plastic material (compact or cellular), other than:
   (1) Fabrics in which the impregnation, coating, or covering cannot be seen with the naked eye (usually Chapters 50 to 55, 58 or 60); for the purpose of this provision, no account should be taken of any resulting change of colour;
   (2) Products which cannot, without fracturing, be bent manually around a cylinder of a diameter of 7mm, at a temperature between15℃ and 30℃ (usually Chapter39);
   (3) Products in which the textile fabric is either completely embedded in plastics or entirely coated or covered on both sides with such materal, provided that such coating or covering can be seen with the naked eye with no account being taken of any resulting change of colour (Chapter 39);
   (4) Fabrics partially coated or partially covered with plastics and bearing designs resulting from these treatments (usually Chapters 50 to 55, 58 or 60);
   (5) Plates, sheets of strip of cellular plastics, combined with textile fabric, where the textile fabric is present merely for reinforcing purposes (Chapter 39); or
   (6) Textile products of heading No.58.11;
   (b) Fabrics made from yarn, strip or the like, impregnated, coated, covered or sheathed with plastics, of heading No.56.04.
3. For the purposes of heading No.59.05, the expression "textile wall coverings" applies to products in rolls, of a width of not less than45cm, suitable for wall or ceiling decoration, consisting of a textile surface which has beenfixed on a backing or has been treated on the back (impregnated or coated to permit pasting).
   This heading does not, however, apply to wall coverings consisting of textile flock or dust fixed directly on backing of paper (heading No.48.14) or on a textile backing (generally heading No.59.07).
4. For the purposes of heading No.59.06, the expression

（一）用橡胶浸渍、涂布、包覆或层压的纺织物：

1. 每平方米重量不超过1500克；
2. 每平方米重量超过1500克，按重量计纺织材料含量在50%以上；

（二）由税号56.04的用橡胶浸渍、涂布、包覆或套裹的纱线、扁条或类似品制成的织物；

（三）平行纺织纱线经橡胶粘合的织物，不论每平方米重量多少。

但本税号不包括与纺织物混制而其中纺织物仅起增强作用的海绵橡胶板、片或带（第四十章），也不包括税号58.11的纺织品。

五、税号59.07不适用于：

（一）用肉眼无法辨别出是否经过浸渍、涂布或包覆的织物（通常归入第五十章至第五十五章、第五十八章或第六十章），但由于浸渍、涂布或包覆所引起的颜色变化可不予考虑；

（二）绘有图画的织物（作为舞台、摄影布景或类似品的已绘制的画布除外）；

（三）用短绒、粉末、软木粉或类似品部分覆面并由此而形成图案的织物，但仿绒织物仍归入本税号；

（四）以淀粉或类似物质为基本成分的普通浆料上浆整理的织物；

（五）以纺织物为底的木饰面板（税号44.08）；

（六）以纺织物为底的砂布及类似品（税号68.05）；

（七）以纺织物为底的粘聚或复制云母片（税号68.14）；

（八）以纺织物为底的金属箔（通常为第十四类或第十五类）。

六、税号59.10不适用于：

（一）厚度小于3毫米的纺织材料制传动带或输送带；

（二）用橡胶浸渍、涂布、包覆或层压的织物制成的或用橡胶浸渍、涂布、包覆或套裹的纱线或绳制成的传动带及运输带（税号40.10）。

七、税号59.11适用于下列不能归入第十一类其他税号的货品：

（一）下列成匹的、裁成一定长度或仅裁成矩形（包括正方形）的纺织产品（具有税号59.08至59.10所列产品特征的产品除外）：

1. 用橡胶、皮革或其他材料涂布、包覆或层压

"rubberized textile fabrics" means:

(a) Textile fabrics impregnated, coated, covered or laminated with rubber:

(Ⅰ) Weighing not more than1500g/m^2;or

(Ⅱ) Weighing more than1500g/m^2 and containing more than 50% by weight of textile material;

(b) Fabrics made from yarn, strip or the like, impregnated, coated, covered or sheathed with rubber, of heading No.56.04; and

(c) Fabrics composed of parallel textile yarns agglomerated with rubber, irrespective of their weight per square metre.

This heading does not, however, apply to plates, sheets or strip of cellular rubber, combined with textile fabric, where the textile fabric is present merely for reinforcing purposes (Chapter 40), or textile products of heading No.58.11.

5. Heading No.59.07does not apply to:

(a) Fabrics in which the impregnation, coating or covering cannot be seen with the naked eye (usually Chapters50 to 55, 58 or 60); for the purpose of this provision, no account should be taken of any resulting change of colour;

(b) Fabrics painted with designs (other than painted canvas being theatrical scenery, studio backcloths or the like);

(c) Fabrics partially covered with flock, dust, powdered cork or the like and bearing designs resulting from these treatments; however, imitation pile fabrics remain classified in this heading;

(d) Fabrics finished with normal dressings having a basis of amylaceous or similar substances;

(e) Wood veneered on a backing of textile fabrics (heading No.44.08);

(f) Natural or artificial abrasive powder or grain, on a backing of textile fabrics (heading No.68.05);

(g) Agglomerated or reconstituted mica, on a backing of fextile fabrics (heading No.68.14);or

(h) Metal foil on a backing of textile fabrics (Generally Section XIV or Section XV).

6. Heading No.59.10does not apply to:

(a) Transmission or conveyor belting, of textile material, of a thickness of less than 3mm; or

(b) Transmission or conveyor belts or belting of textile fabric impregnated, coated, covered or laminated with rubber or made from textile yarn or cord impregnated, coated, covered or sheathed with rubber (heading No.40.10).

7. Heading No.59.11 applies to the following goods, which do not fall in any other heading of SectionXI:

(a) Textile products in the piece, cut to length or simply cut to rectangular (including square) shape (other than those having the character of the products of headings No.59.08 to 59.10), the following only:

(1) Textile fabrics, felt and feltlined woven fabrics,

的作针布用的纺织物、毡呢及毡呢衬里机织物，以及其他专门技术用途的类似织物，包括用橡胶浸渍的用于包覆纺缍（织轴）的狭幅丝绒织物；

2. 筛布；

3. 用于榨油机器或类似机器的纺织材料制或人发制滤布；

4. 用多股经纱或纬纱平织而成的纺织物，不论是否毡化、浸渍或涂布，通常用于机械或其他专门技术用途；

5. 专门技术用途的增强纺织物；

6. 工业上作填塞或润滑材料的线绳、编带及类似品，不论是否涂布、浸渍或用金属加强。

（二）专门技术用途的纺织制品（税号 59.08 至 59.10 的货品除外），例如，造纸机器或类似机器（如制浆机或制石棉水泥的机器）用的环状或装有联接装置的纺织物或毡呢、密封垫、垫圈、抛光盘及其他机器零件。

coated，covered or laminated with rubber，leather or other material，of a kind used for card clothing，and similar fabrics of a kind used for other technical purposes，including narrow fabrics made of velvet impregnated with rubber，for covering weaving spindles (weaving beams);

(2) Bolting cloth；

(3) Straining cloth of a kind used in oil presses or the like，of textile material or of human hair;

(4) Flat woven textile fabrics with multiple warp or weft，whether or not felted，impregnated or coated，of a kind used in machinery or for other technical purposes;

(5) Textile fabrics reinforced with metal，of a kind used for technical purposes;

(6) Cords，braids and the like，whether or not coated，impregnated or reinforced with metal，of a kind used in industry as packing or lubricating materials.

(b) Textile articles（other than those of headings Nos.59.08 to 59.10）of a kind used for technical purposes，for example，textile fabrics and felts，endless or fitted with linking devicse，of a kind used in paper-making or similar machines（for example，for pulp or asbestos-cement），gaskets，washers，polishing discs and other machinery parts.

序号 No.	税则号列 Tariff Line	中文货品名称 Article Description in Chinese	最惠国税率 MFN(%)	协定税率 Agreement(%)	特惠税率 SP(%)	普通税率 Gen(%)	英文货品名称 Article Description
	59.01	**用胶或淀粉物质涂布的纺织物，作书籍封面及类似用途的；描图布；制成的油画布；作帽里的硬衬布及类似硬挺纺织物：**					**Textile fabrics coated with gum or amylaceous substances, of a kind used for the outer covers of books or the like; tracing cloth; prepared painting canvas; buckram and similar stiffened textile fabrics of a kind used for hat foundations:**
		-用胶或淀粉物质涂布的纺织物，作书籍封面及类似用途的：					-Textile fabrics coated with gum or amylaceous substances, of a kind used for the outer covers of books or the like:
4247	5901.1010	---棉或麻制	10	0 冰岛IS,东盟AS,哥CR,秘鲁PE,新加坡SG,新西兰NZ,智利CL 4 瑞士CH 5 巴PK 6 澳AU 8 韩国KR	0 受惠国LD	80	---Of cotton or bast fibres
4248	5901.1020	---化学纤维制	10	0 冰岛IS,东盟AS,哥CR,秘鲁PE,新加坡SG,新西兰NZ,智利CL 4 瑞士CH 5 巴PK 6 澳AU,韩国KR	0 受惠国LD	130	---Of man-made fibres
4249	5901.1090	---其他	10	0 冰岛IS,东盟AS,哥CR,秘鲁PE,新加坡SG,新西兰NZ,智利CL 4 瑞士CH 5 巴PK 6 澳AU,韩国KR	0 受惠国LD	100	---Other
		-其他：					-Other:

序号 No.	税则号列 Tariff Line	中文货品名称 Article Description in Chinese	最惠国税率 MFN(%)	协定税率 Agreement(%)	特惠税率 SP(%)	普通税率 Gen(%)	英文货品名称 Article Description
4250	5901.9010	---制成的油画布	10	0 冰岛IS,东盟AS,哥CR,秘鲁PE,新西兰NZ,智利CL 4 瑞士CH 5 巴PK 6 澳AU,韩国KR	0 受惠国LD	50	---Prepared painting canvas
		---其他:					---Other:
4251	5901.9091	----棉或麻制	10	0 冰岛IS,东盟AS,哥CR,秘鲁PE,新西兰NZ,智利CL 4 瑞士CH 5 巴PK 6 澳AU,韩国KR	0 柬埔寨KH,老挝LA,缅甸MM,受惠国LD	80	----Of cotton or bast fibres
4252	5901.9092	----化学纤维制	10	0 冰岛IS,东盟AS,哥CR,秘鲁PE,新西兰NZ,智利CL 4 瑞士CH 5 巴PK 6 澳AU,韩国KR	0 受惠国LD	130	----Of man-made fibres
4253	5901.9099	----其他	10	0 冰岛IS,东盟AS,哥CR,秘鲁PE,新西兰NZ,智利CL 4 瑞士CH 5 巴PK 6 澳AU,韩国KR	0 受惠国LD	100	----Other
	59.02	**尼龙或其他聚酰胺，聚酯或粘胶纤维高强力纱制的帘子布：**					**Tyre cord fabric of high-tenacity yarn of nylon or other polyamides, polyesters or viscose rayon:**
		-尼龙或其他聚酰胺制：					-Of nylon or other polyamides:
4254	5902.1010	---聚酰胺-6（尼龙-6）制	10	0 冰岛IS,东盟AS,哥CR,秘鲁PE,新加坡SG,新西兰NZ,智利CL 4 瑞士CH 5 巴PK 6 澳AU 8.6 韩国KR 9 亚太AP	0 受惠国LD	40	---Of nylon-6
4255	5902.1020	---聚酰胺-6，6（尼龙-6，6）制	10	0 冰岛IS,东盟AS,哥CR,秘鲁PE,新加坡SG,新西兰NZ,智利CL 4 瑞士CH 5 巴PK 6 澳AU 8.6 韩国KR 9 亚太AP	0 受惠国LD	40	---Of nylon-6, 6
4256	5902.1090	---其他	10	0 冰岛IS,东盟AS,哥CR,秘鲁PE,新加坡SG,新西兰NZ,智利CL 4 瑞士CH 5 巴PK 6 澳AU 8 韩国KR 9 亚太AP	0 受惠国LD	40	---Other
4257	5902.2000	-聚酯制	10	0 冰岛IS,东盟AS,哥CR,秘鲁PE,新加坡SG,新西兰NZ,智利CL 4 瑞士CH 5 巴PK 6 澳AU 9 韩国KR,亚太AP	0 受惠国LD	40	-Of polyesters

序号 No.	税则号列 Tariff Line	中文货品名称 Article Description in Chinese	最惠国税率 MFN(%)	协定税率 Agreement(%)	特惠税率 SP(%)	普通税率 Gen(%)	英文货品名称 Article Description
4258	5902.9000	-其他	10	0 冰岛IS,东盟AS,哥CR,秘鲁PE,新西兰NZ,智利CL 5 巴PK 6 澳AU,韩国KR 7 瑞士CH	0 受惠国LD	40	-Other
	59.03	**用塑料浸渍、涂布、包覆或层压的纺织物，但税号59.02的货品除外：**					**Textile fabrics impregnated, coated, covered or laminated with plastics, other than those of heading 5902:**
		-用聚氯乙烯浸渍、涂布、包覆或层压的：					-With poly (vinyl chloride) :
4259	5903.1010	---绝缘布或带	10	0 冰岛IS,东盟AS,哥CR,秘鲁PE,新西兰NZ,智利CL 4 瑞士CH 5 巴PK 6 澳AU,韩国KR 8.5 亚太AP	0 受惠国LD	40	---Insulating cloth or tape
4260	5903.1020	---人造革	10	0 冰岛IS,东盟AS,哥CR,秘鲁PE,台湾TW,香港HK,新加坡SG,新西兰NZ,智利CL 4 瑞士CH 5 巴PK 6 澳AU 8.5 亚太AP 9 韩国KR	0 受惠国LD	70	---Imitation leather
4261	5903.1090	---其他	10	0 冰岛IS,东盟AS,哥CR,秘鲁PE,台湾TW,香港HK,新加坡SG,新西兰NZ,智利CL 4 瑞士CH 5 巴PK 6 澳AU 8.5 亚太AP 9 韩国KR	0 受惠国LD	90	---Other
		-用聚氨基甲酸酯浸渍、涂布、包覆或层压的：					-With polyurethane.
4262	5903.2010	---绝缘布或带	10	0 冰岛IS,东盟AS,哥CR,秘鲁PE,新西兰NZ,智利CL 4 瑞士CH 5 巴PK 6 澳AU,韩国KR 8.5 亚太AP	0 受惠国LD	40	---Insulating cloth or tape
4263	5903.2020	---人造革	10	0 冰岛IS,东盟AS,哥CR,秘鲁PE,台湾TW,新加坡SG,新西兰NZ,智利CL 4 瑞士CH 5 巴PK 6 澳AU 8.5 亚太AP 9 韩国KR	0 受惠国LD	70	---Imitation leather
4264	5903.2090	---其他	10	0 冰岛IS,东盟AS,哥CR,秘鲁PE,台湾TW,香港HK,新加坡SG,新西兰NZ,智利CL 4 瑞士CH 6 澳AU 8.5 巴PK,亚太AP 9 韩国KR	0 受惠国LD	90	---Other
		-其他：					-Other:

序号 No.	税则号列 Tariff Line	中文货品名称 Article Description in Chinese	最惠国税率 MFN(%)	协定税率 Agreement(%)	特惠税率 SP(%)	普通税率 Gen(%)	英文货品名称 Article Description
4265	5903.9010	---绝缘布或带	10	0 冰岛IS,东盟AS,哥CR,秘鲁PE,新西兰NZ,智利CL 5 巴PK 6 澳AU,韩国KR 7 瑞士CH 8.5 亚太AP	0 受惠国LD	40	---Insulating cloth or tape
4266	5903.9020	---人造革	10	0 冰岛IS,东盟AS,哥CR,秘鲁PE,台湾TW,新加坡SG,新西兰NZ,智利CL 4 瑞士CH 5 巴PK 6 澳AU 8.5 亚太AP 8.6 韩国KR	0 受惠国LD	70	---Imitation leather
4267	5903.9090	---其他	10	0 冰岛IS,东盟AS,哥CR,秘鲁PE,台湾TW,香港HK,新加坡SG,新西兰NZ,智利CL 4 瑞士CH 6 澳AU 8.5 巴PK,亚太AP 9 韩国KR	0 柬埔寨KH,老挝LA,缅甸MM,受惠国LD	90	---Other
	59.04	**列诺伦（亚麻油地毡），不论是否剪切成形;以织物为底布经涂布或覆面的铺地制品，不论是否剪切成形：**					**Linoleum, whether or not cut to shape; floor coverings consisting of a coating or covering applied on a textile backing, whether or not cut to shape:**
4268	5904.1000	-列诺伦（亚麻油地毡）	14	0 冰岛IS,东盟AS,哥CR,秘鲁PE,新加坡SG,新西兰NZ,智利CL 8.4 澳AU 9.8 瑞士CH 11.2 巴PK,韩国KR	0 受惠国$_1$LD$_1$	90	-Linoleum
4269	5904.9000	-其他	14	0 冰岛IS,东盟AS,哥CR,秘鲁PE,新加坡SG,新西兰NZ,智利CL 7 巴PK 8.4 澳AU 9.8 瑞士CH 11.2 韩国KR	0 受惠国$_1$LD$_1$	90	-Other
	59.05	**糊墙织物**					**Textile wall coverings**
4270	5905.0000	糊墙织物	10	0 冰岛IS,东盟AS,哥CR,秘鲁PE,新加坡SG,新西兰NZ,智利CL 4 瑞士CH 5 巴PK 6 澳AU,韩国KR	0 受惠国LD	80	Textile wall coverings
	59.06	**用橡胶处理的纺织物，但税号59.02的货品除外：**					**Rubberised textile fabrics, other than those of heading 5902:**
		-宽度不超过20厘米的胶粘带：					-Adhesive tape of a width not exceeding 20cm:
4271	5906.1010	---绝缘带	10	0 冰岛IS,东盟AS,哥CR,秘鲁PE,新西兰NZ,智利CL 4 瑞士CH 5 巴PK 6 澳AU,韩国KR	0 受惠国LD	40	---Insulating tape
4272	5906.1090	---其他	10	0 东盟AS,哥CR,秘鲁PE,新加坡SG,新西兰NZ,智利CL 4 瑞士CH 5 巴PK 6 澳AU,韩国KR	0 受惠国LD	100	---Other
		-其他：					-Other:

序号 No.	税则号列 Tariff Line	中文货品名称 Article Description in Chinese	最惠国税率 MFN(%)	协定税率 Agreement(%)	特惠税率 SP(%)	普通税率 Gen(%)	英文货品名称 Article Description
4273	5906.9100	--针织或钩编的	10	0 冰岛IS,东盟AS,哥CR,秘鲁PE,台湾TW,新加坡SG,新西兰NZ,智利CL 4 瑞士CH 5 巴PK 6 澳AU,韩国KR	0 受惠国LD	130	--Knitted or crocheted
		--其他:					--Other:
4274	5906.9910	---绝缘布或带	10	0 冰岛IS,东盟AS,哥CR,秘鲁PE,新西兰NZ,智利CL 4 瑞士CH 5 巴PK 6 澳AU,韩国KR	0 受惠国LD	40	---Insulating cloth or tape
4275	5906.9990	---其他	10	0 冰岛IS,东盟AS,哥CR,秘鲁PE,台湾TW,新加坡SG,新西兰NZ,智利CL 4 瑞士CH 5 巴PK 6 澳AU,韩国KR	0 受惠国LD	100	---Other
	59.07	**用其他材料浸渍、涂布或包覆的纺织物;作舞台、摄影布景或类似用途的已绘制画布:**					**Textile fabrics otherwise impregnated, coated or covered; painted canvas being theatrical scenery, studio backcloths or the like:**
4276	5907.0010	---绝缘布或带	10	0 冰岛IS,东盟AS,哥CR,秘鲁PE,新西兰NZ,智利CL 5 巴PK 6 澳AU,韩国KR 7 瑞士CH 8.5 亚太AP	0 受惠国LD	40	---Insulating cloth or tape
4277	5907.0020	---已绘制画布	10	0 冰岛IS,东盟AS,哥CR,秘鲁PE,香港HK,新西兰NZ,智利CL 4 瑞士CH 5 巴PK 6 澳AU,韩国KR 8.5 亚太AP	0 受惠国LD	50	---Painted canvas
4278	5907.0090	---其他	10	0 冰岛IS,东盟AS,哥CR,秘鲁PE,新加坡SG,新西兰NZ,智利CL 4 瑞士CH 5 巴PK 6 澳AU 8.5 亚太AP 9 韩国KR	0 受惠国LD	100	---Other
	59.08	**用纺织材料机织、编结或针织而成的灯芯、炉芯、打火机芯、烛芯或类似品;煤气灯纱筒及纱罩,不论是否浸渍**					**Textile wicks, woven, plaited or knitted, for lamps, stoves, lighters, candles or the like; incandescent gas mantles and tubular knitted gas-mantle fabric therefor, whether or not impregnated**
4279	5908.0000	用纺织材料机织、编结或针织而成的灯芯、炉芯、打火机芯、烛芯或类似品;煤气灯纱筒及纱罩,不论是否浸渍	10	0 冰岛IS,东盟AS,哥CR,秘鲁PE,新西兰NZ,智利CL 4 瑞士CH 5 巴PK 6 澳AU,韩国KR	0 受惠国LD	70	Textile wicks, woven, plaited or knitted, for lamps, stoves, lighters, candles or the like; incandescent gas mantles and tubular knitted gas mantle fbric therefor, whether or not impregnated
	59.09	**纺织材料制的水龙软管及类似的管子,不论有无其他材料作衬里、护套或附件**					**Textile hosepiping and similar textile tubing, with or without lining, armour or accessories of other materials**

序号 No.	税则号列 Tariff Line	中文货品名称 Article Description in Chinese	最惠国税率 MFN(%)	协定税率 Agreement(%)	特惠税率 SP(%)	普通税率 Gen(%)	英文货品名称 Article Description
4280	5909.0000	纺织材料制的水龙软管及类似的管子，不论有无其他材料作衬里、护套或附件	8	0 澳门MO,冰岛IS,东盟AS,哥CR,秘鲁PE,新西兰NZ,智利CL 3.2 瑞士CH 4.8 澳AU,韩国KR 5 巴PK	0 受惠国LD	35	Textile hosepiping and similar textile tubing, with or without lining, armour or accessories of other materials
	59.10	**纺织材料制的传动带或输送带及带料，不论是否用塑料浸渍、涂布、包覆或压层，也不论是否用金属或其他材料加强**					**Transmission or conveyor belts or belting, of textile material, whether or not impregnated, coated, covered or laminated with plastics, or reinforced with metal or other material**
4281	5910.0000	纺织材料制的传动带或输送带及带料，不论是否用塑料浸渍、涂布、包覆或压层，也不论是否用金属或其他材料加强	8	0 冰岛IS,东盟AS,哥CR,秘鲁PE,台湾TW,新西兰NZ,智利CL 3.2 瑞士CH 4.8 澳AU,韩国KR 5 巴PK	0 受惠国LD	35	Transmission or conveyor belts or belting, of textile material, whether or not impregnated, coated, covered or laminated with plastics, or reinforced with metal or other material
	59.11	**本章注释七所规定的作专门技术用途的纺织产品及制品：**					**Textile products and articles, for technical uses, specified in note 7 to this chapter:**
		-用橡胶、皮革或其他材料涂布、包覆或层压的作针布用的纺织物、毡呢及毡呢衬里机织物，以及作专门技术用途的类似织物，包括用橡胶浸渍的、用于包覆纺绖（织轴）的狭幅丝绒织物：					-Textile fabrics, felt and felt-lined woven fabrics, coated, covered or laminated with rubber, leather or other material, of a kind used for card clothing, and similar fabrics of a kind used for other technical purposes, including narrow fabrics made of velvet impregnated with rubber, for covering weaving spindles (weaving beams) :
4282	5911.1010	---用橡胶浸渍的、用于包覆纺绖（织轴）的狭幅丝绒织物	8	0 冰岛IS,东盟AS,哥CR,秘鲁PE,新西兰NZ,智利CL 3.2 瑞士CH 4.8 澳AU,韩国KR 5 巴PK 7.2 亚太AP	0 受惠国LD	75	---Narrow fabrics made of velvet impregnated with rubber, for covering weaving spindles (weaving beams)
4283	5911.1090	---其他	8	0 冰岛IS,东盟AS,哥CR,秘鲁PE,新西兰NZ,智利CL 3.2 瑞士CH 4.8 澳AU,韩国KR 5 巴PK	0 受惠国LD	35	---Other
4284	5911.2000	-筛布，不论是否制成的	8	0 冰岛IS,东盟AS,哥CR,秘鲁PE,瑞士CH,新西兰NZ,智利CL 4.8 澳AU,韩国KR 5 巴PK	0 受惠国LD	35	-Bolting cloth, whether or not made up
		-环状或装有联接装置的纺织物及毡呢，用于造纸机器或类似机器（例如，制浆机或制石棉水泥的机器）：					-Textile fabrics and felts, endless or fitted with linking devices, of a kind used in paper-making or similar machines (for example, for pulp or asbestos-cement) :
4285	5911.3100	--每平方米重量在650克以下	8	0 冰岛IS,东盟AS,哥CR,秘鲁PE,新西兰NZ,智利CL 3.2 瑞士CH 4.8 澳AU,韩国KR 5 巴PK	0 受惠国LD	35	--Weighing less than $650g/m^2$

序号 No.	税则号列 Tariff Line	中文货品名称 Article Description in Chinese	最惠国税率 MFN(%)	协定税率 Agreement(%)	特惠税率 SP(%)	普通税率 Gen(%)	英文货品名称 Article Description
4286	5911.3200	--每平方米重量在650克及以上	8	0 冰岛IS,东盟AS,哥CR,秘鲁PE,新西兰NZ,智利CL 4.8 澳AU,韩国KR 5 巴PK 5.6 瑞士CH	0 受惠国LD	35	--Weighing 650g/m^2 or more
4287	5911.4000	-用于榨油机器或类似机器的滤布，包括人发制滤布	8	0 冰岛IS,东盟AS,哥CR,秘鲁PE,新西兰NZ,智利CL 3.2 瑞士CH 4.8 澳AU,韩国KR 5 巴PK	0 受惠国LD	35	-Straining cloth of a kind used in oil presses or the like, including that of human hair
4288	5911.9000	-其他	8	0 冰岛IS,东盟AS,哥CR,秘鲁PE,新西兰NZ,智利CL 3.2 瑞士CH 4.8 澳AU 5 巴PK	0 受惠国LD	35	-Other

第六十章

针织物及钩编织物

注释：

一、本章不包括：

（一）税号58.04的钩编花边；

（二）税号58.07的针织或钩编的标签、徽章及类似品；

（三）第五十九章的经浸渍、涂布、包覆或层压的针织物及钩编织物。但经浸渍、涂布、包覆或层压的起绒针织物及起绒钩编织物仍归入税号60.01。

二、本章还包括用金属线制的用于衣着、装饰或类似用途的织物。

三、本目录所称"针织物"，包括由纺织纱线用链式针法构成的缝编织物。

Chapter 60

Knitted or crocheted fabrics

Notes:

1. This Chapter does not cover:

(a) Crochet lace of heading No.58.04;

(b) Labels, badges or similar articles, knitted or crocheted, of heading No.58.07; or

(c) Knitted or crocheted fabrics, impregnated, coated, covered or laminated, of Chapter 59.However, knitted or crocheted plie fabrics, impregnated, coated, covered or laminated, remain classified in heading No.60.01.

2. This Chapter also includes fabrics made of metal thread and of a kind used in apparel, as furnishing fabrics or for similar purposes.

3. Throughout the Nomenclature any reference to "knitted" goods includes a reference to stitch-bonded goods in which the chain stitches are formed of textile yarn.

序号 No.	税则号列 Tariff Line	中文货品名称 Article Description in Chinese	最惠国税率 MFN(%)	协定税率 Agreement(%)	特惠税率 SP(%)	普通税率 Gen(%)	英文货品名称 Article Description
	60.01	**针织或钩编的起绒织物，包括"长毛绒"织物及毛圈织物：**					**Pile fabrics, including ' long pile' fabrics and terry fabrics, knitted or crocheted:**
4289	6001.1000	-"长毛绒"织物	10	0 巴PK,冰岛IS,东盟AS,哥CR,秘鲁PE,新加坡SG,新西兰NZ,智利CL 4 瑞士CH 6 澳AU 8.5 亚太AP 8.6 韩国KR	0 受惠国LD	130	-"Long pile"fabrics
		-毛圈绒头织物：					-Looped pile fabrics:
4290	6001.2100	--棉制	10	0 巴PK,冰岛IS,东盟AS,哥CR,秘鲁PE,新西兰NZ,智利CL 4 瑞士CH 6 澳AU,韩国KR 8.5 亚太AP	0 受惠国LD	70	--Of cotton
4291	6001.2200	--化学纤维制	10	0 巴PK,冰岛IS,东盟AS,哥CR,秘鲁PE,新加坡SG,新西兰NZ,智利CL 4 瑞士CH 6 澳AU,韩国KR 8.5 亚太AP	0 受惠国LD	130	--Of man-made fibres
4292	6001.2900	--其他纺织材料制	12	0 巴PK,冰岛IS,东盟AS,哥CR,秘鲁PE,新加坡SG,新西兰NZ,智利CL 7.2 澳AU,韩国KR 8.4 瑞士CH	0 受惠国$_1$LD$_1$	130	--Of other textile materials
		-其他：					-Other:
4293	6001.9100	--棉制	10	0 巴PK,冰岛IS,东盟AS,哥CR,秘鲁PE,新西兰NZ,智利CL 4 瑞士CH 6 澳AU,韩国KR 7 亚太AP	0 受惠国LD	70	--Of cotton

序号 No.	税则号列 Tariff Line	中文货品名称 Article Description in Chinese	最惠国税率 MFN(%)	协定税率 Agreement(%)	特惠税率 SP(%)	普通税率 Gen(%)	英文货品名称 Article Description
4294	6001.9200	--化学纤维制	10	0 澳门MO,巴PK,冰岛IS,东盟AS,哥CR,秘鲁PE,台湾TW,香港HK,新加坡SG,新西兰NZ,智利CL 4 瑞士CH 6 澳AU 8.5 亚太AP 9 韩国KR	0 受惠国LD	130	--Of man-made fibres
4295	6001.9900	--其他纺织材料制	12	0 巴PK,冰岛IS,东盟AS,哥CR,秘鲁PE,新加坡SG,新西兰NZ,智利CL 7.2 澳AU,韩国KR 8.4 瑞士CH	0 受惠国$_1$LD$_1$	130	--Of other textile materials
	60.02	**宽度不超过30厘米，按重量计弹性纱线或橡胶线含量在5%及以上的针织物或钩编织物，但税目60.01的货品除外：**					**Knitted or crocheted fabrics of a width not exceeding 30cm, containing by weight 5% or more of elastomeric yarn or rubber thread, other than those of heading 6001:**
		-按重量计弹性纱线含量在5%及以上，但不含橡胶线：					-Containing by weight 5% or more of elastomeric yarn, but not containing rubber thread:
4296	6002.4010	---棉制	10	0 巴PK,冰岛IS,东盟AS,哥CR,秘鲁PE,新西兰NZ,智利CL 4 瑞士CH 6 澳AU,韩国KR 8.5 亚太AP	0 受惠国LD	70	---Of cotton
4297	6002.4020	---丝及绢丝制	10	0 巴PK,冰岛IS,东盟AS,哥CR,秘鲁PE,新加坡SG,新西兰NZ,智利CL 4 瑞士CH 6 澳AU,韩国KR 8.5 亚太AP	0 受惠国LD	130	---Of silk or silk waste
4298	6002.4030	---合成纤维制	10	0 巴PK,冰岛IS,东盟AS,哥CR,秘鲁PE,新加坡SG,新西兰NZ,智利CL 4 瑞士CH 6 澳AU,韩国KR	0 受惠国LD	130	---Of synthetic fibres
4299	6002.4040	---人造纤维制	10	0 巴PK,冰岛IS,东盟AS,哥CR,秘鲁PE,新加坡SG,新西兰NZ,智利CL 4 瑞士CH 6 澳AU,韩国KR	0 受惠国LD	130	---Of artificial fibres
4300	6002.4090	---其他	10	0 巴PK,冰岛IS,东盟AS,哥CR,秘鲁PE,新加坡SG,新西兰NZ,智利CL 4 瑞士CH 6 澳AU,韩国KR 7 亚太AP	0 受惠国LD	130	---Other
		-其他：					-Other:
4301	6002.9010	---棉制	10	0 巴PK,冰岛IS,东盟AS,哥CR,秘鲁PE,新西兰NZ,智利CL 4 瑞士CH 6 澳AU,韩国KR 8.5 亚太AP	0 柬埔寨KH,老挝LA,缅甸MM,受惠国LD	70	---Of cotton
4302	6002.9020	---丝及绢丝制	10	0 巴PK,冰岛IS,东盟AS,哥CR,秘鲁PE,新加坡SG,新西兰NZ,智利CL 4 瑞士CH 6 澳AU,韩国KR 8.5 亚太AP	0 受惠国LD	130	---Of silk or silk waste

序号 No.	税则号列 Tariff Line	中文货品名称 Article Description in Chinese	最惠国税率 MFN(%)	协定税率 Agreement(%)	特惠税率 SP(%)	普通税率 Gen(%)	英文货品名称 Article Description
4303	6002.9030	---合成纤维制	10	0 巴PK,冰岛IS,东盟AS,哥CR,秘鲁PE,新加坡SG,新西兰NZ,智利CL 4 瑞士CH 5 亚太AP 6 澳AU 8.6 韩国KR	0 柬埔寨KH,老挝LA,缅甸MM,受惠国LD	130	---Of synthetic fibres
4304	6002.9040	---人造纤维制	10	0 巴PK,冰岛IS,东盟AS,哥CR,秘鲁PE,新加坡SG,新西兰NZ,智利CL 4 瑞士CH 5 亚太AP 6 澳AU,韩国KR	0 受惠国LD	130	---Of artificial fibres
4305	6002.9090	---其他	10	0 巴PK,冰岛IS,东盟AS,哥CR,秘鲁PE,新加坡SG,新西兰NZ,智利CL 4 瑞士CH 6 澳AU,韩国KR 8.5 亚太AP	0 受惠国LD	130	---Other
	60.03	**宽度不超过30厘米的针织或钩编织物，但税目60.01或60.02的货品除外：**					**Knitted or crocheted fabrics of a width not exceeding 30cm, other than those of heading 6001 or 6002:**
4306	6003.1000	-羊毛或动物细毛制	10	0 巴PK,冰岛IS,东盟AS,哥CR,秘鲁PE,新加坡SG,新西兰NZ,智利CL 4 瑞士CH 6 澳AU,韩国KR	0 受惠国LD	130	-Of wool or fine animal hair
4307	6003.2000	-棉制	10	0 巴PK,冰岛IS,东盟AS,哥CR,秘鲁PE,新西兰NZ,智利CL 4 瑞士CH 6 澳AU,韩国KR	0 受惠国LD	70	-Of cotton
4308	6003.3000	-合成纤维制	10	0 巴PK,冰岛IS,东盟AS,哥CR,秘鲁PE,新加坡SG,新西兰NZ,智利CL 4 瑞士CH 6 澳AU,韩国KR 9.4 亚太AP	0 受惠国LD	130	-Of synthetic fibres
4309	6003.4000	-人造纤维制	10	0 巴PK,冰岛IS,东盟AS,哥CR,秘鲁PE,新加坡SG,新西兰NZ,智利CL 4 瑞士CH 6 澳AU,韩国KR 9.4 亚太AP	0 受惠国LD	130	-Of artificial fibres
4310	6003.9000	-其他	10	0 巴PK,冰岛IS,东盟AS,哥CR,秘鲁PE,新加坡SG,新西兰NZ,智利CL 4 瑞士CH 6 澳AU,韩国KR	0 受惠国LD	130	-Other
	60.04	**宽度超过30厘米，按重量计弹性纱线或橡胶线含量在5%及以上的针织物或钩编织物，但税目60.01的货品除外：**					**Knitted or crocheted fabrics of a width exceeding 30cm, containing by weight 5% or more of elastomeric yarn or rubber thread, other than those of heading 6001:**
		-按重量计弹性纱线含量在5%及以上，但不含橡胶线：					-Containing by weight 5% or more of elastomeric yarn, but not containing rubber thread:
4311	6004.1010	---棉制	10	0 巴PK,冰岛IS,东盟AS,哥CR,秘鲁PE,香港HK,新加坡SG,新西兰NZ,智利CL 4 瑞士CH 6 澳AU,韩国KR 7 亚太AP	0 柬埔寨KH,老挝LA,缅甸MM,受惠国LD	70	---Of cotton

序号 No.	税则号列 Tariff Line	中文货品名称 Article Description in Chinese	最惠国税率 MFN(%)	协定税率 Agreement(%)	特惠税率 SP(%)	普通税率 Gen(%)	英文货品名称 Article Description
4312	6004.1020	---丝及绢丝制	10	0 巴PK,冰岛IS,东盟AS,哥CR,秘鲁PE,新加坡SG,新西兰NZ,智利CL 4 瑞士CH 6 澳AU,韩国KR 8.5 亚太AP	0 受惠国LD	130	---Of silk or silk waste
4313	6004.1030	---合成纤维制	10	0 澳门MO,巴PK,冰岛IS,东盟AS,哥CR,秘鲁PE,台湾TW,香港HK,新加坡SG,新西兰NZ,智利CL 4 瑞士CH 6 澳AU 9 韩国KR	0 受惠国LD	130	---Of synthetic fibres
4314	6004.1040	---人造纤维制	10	0 澳门MO,巴PK,冰岛IS,东盟AS,哥CR,秘鲁PE,香港HK,新加坡SG,新西兰NZ,智利CL 4 瑞士CH 6 澳AU 8.6 韩国KR	0 受惠国LD	130	---Of artificial fibres
4315	6004.1090	---其他	10	0 澳门MO,巴PK,冰岛IS,东盟AS,哥CR,秘鲁PE,台湾TW,香港HK,新加坡SG,新西兰NZ,智利CL 4 瑞士CH 6 澳AU,韩国KR 8.5 亚太AP	0 受惠国LD	130	---Other
		-其他:					-Other:
4316	6004.9010	---棉制	10	0 巴PK,冰岛IS,东盟AS,哥CR,秘鲁PE,香港HK,新西兰NZ,智利CL 4 瑞士CH 6 澳AU,韩国KR 8.5 亚太AP	0 受惠国LD	70	---Of cotton
4317	6004.9020	---丝及绢丝制	10	0 巴PK,冰岛IS,东盟AS,哥CR,秘鲁PE,新加坡SG,新西兰NZ,智利CL 4 瑞士CH 6 澳AU,韩国KR 8.5 亚太AP	0 受惠国LD	130	---Of silk or silk waste
4318	6004.9030	---合成纤维制	10	0 澳门MO,巴PK,冰岛IS,东盟AS,哥CR,秘鲁PE,台湾TW,香港HK,新加坡SG,新西兰NZ,智利CL 4 瑞士CH 6 澳AU 9 韩国KR	0 受惠国LD	130	---Of synthetic fibres
4319	6004.9040	---人造纤维制	10	0 澳门MO,巴PK,冰岛IS,东盟AS,哥CR,秘鲁PE,香港HK,新加坡SG,新西兰NZ,智利CL 4 瑞士CH 6 澳AU,韩国KR	0 受惠国LD	130	---Of artificial fibres
4320	6004.9090	---其他	10	0 澳门MO,巴PK,冰岛IS,东盟AS,哥CR,秘鲁PE,台湾TW,香港HK,新加坡SG,新西兰NZ,智利CL 4 瑞士CH 6 澳AU,韩国KR 7 亚太AP	0 受惠国LD	130	---Other

序号 No.	税则号列 Tariff Line	中文货品名称 Article Description in Chinese	最惠国税率 MFN(%)	协定税率 Agreement(%)	特惠税率 SP(%)	普通税率 Gen(%)	英文货品名称 Article Description
	60.05	**经编织物(包括由花边针织机织成的),但税目60.01至60.04的货品除外:**					**Warp knit fabrics (including those made on galloon knitting machines), other than those of headings 6001 to 6004:**
		-棉制:					-Of cotton:
4321	6005.2100	--未漂白或漂白	10	0 巴PK,冰岛IS,东盟AS,哥CR,秘鲁PE,香港HK,新西兰NZ,智利CL 4 瑞士CH 6 澳AU,韩国KR	0 受惠国LD	70	--Unbleached or bleached
4322	6005.2200	--染色	10	0 巴PK,冰岛IS,东盟AS,哥CR,秘鲁PE,香港HK,新西兰NZ,智利CL 4 瑞士CH 6 澳AU,韩国KR	0 受惠国LD	70	--Dyed
4323	6005.2300	--色织	10	0 巴PK,冰岛IS,东盟AS,哥CR,秘鲁PE,香港HK,新西兰NZ,智利CL 4 瑞士CH 6 澳AU,韩国KR	0 受惠国LD	70	--Of yarns of different colours
4324	6005.2400	--印花	10	0 巴PK,冰岛IS,东盟AS,哥CR,秘鲁PE,香港HK,新西兰NZ,智利CL 4 瑞士CH 6 澳AU,韩国KR	0 受惠国LD	70	--Printed
		-合成纤维制:					-Of synthetic fibres:
4325	6005.3100	--未漂白或漂白	10	0 巴PK,冰岛IS,东盟AS,哥CR,秘鲁PE,台湾TW,新加坡SG,新西兰NZ,智利CL 4 瑞士CH 6 澳AU,韩国KR 8.5 亚太AP	0 受惠国LD	130	--Unbleached or bleached
4326	6005.3200	--染色	10	0 巴PK,冰岛IS,东盟AS,哥CR,秘鲁PE,台湾TW,新加坡SG,新西兰NZ,智利CL 4 瑞士CH 6 澳AU 8.5 亚太AP 9 韩国KR	0 柬埔寨KH,老挝LA,缅甸MM,受惠国LD	130	--Dyed
4327	6005.3300	--色织	10	0 巴PK,冰岛IS,东盟AS,哥CR,秘鲁PE,新加坡SG,新西兰NZ,智利CL 4 瑞士CH 6 澳AU,韩国KR 8.5 亚太AP	0 受惠国LD	130	--Of yarns of different colours
4328	6005.3400	--印花	10	0 巴PK,冰岛IS,东盟AS,哥CR,秘鲁PE,新加坡SG,新西兰NZ,智利CL 4 瑞士CH 6 澳AU,韩国KR 8.5 亚太AP	0 受惠国LD	130	--Printed
		-人造纤维制:					-Of artificial fibres:
4329	6005.4100	--未漂白或漂白	10	0 巴PK,冰岛IS,东盟AS,哥CR,秘鲁PE,新加坡SG,新西兰NZ,智利CL 4 瑞士CH 6 澳AU,韩国KR 8.5 亚太AP	0 受惠国LD	130	--Unbleached or bleached
4330	6005.4200	--染色	10	0 巴PK,冰岛IS,东盟AS,哥CR,秘鲁PE,新加坡SG,新西兰NZ,智利CL 4 瑞士CH 6 澳AU,韩国KR 8.5 亚太AP	0 受惠国LD	130	--Dyed

序号 No.	税则号列 Tariff Line	中文货品名称 Article Description in Chinese	最惠国税率 MFN(%)	协定税率 Agreement(%)	特惠税率 SP(%)	普通税率 Gen(%)	英文货品名称 Article Description
4331	6005.4300	--色织	10	0 巴PK,冰岛IS,东盟AS,哥CR,秘鲁PE,新加坡SG,新西兰NZ,智利CL 4 瑞士CH 6 澳AU,韩国KR 8.5 亚太AP	0 受惠国LD	130	--Of yarns of different colours
4332	6005.4400	--印花	10	0 巴PK,冰岛IS,东盟AS,哥CR,秘鲁PE,新加坡SG,新西兰NZ,智利CL 4 瑞士CH 6 澳AU,韩国KR 8.5 亚太AP	0 受惠国LD	130	--Printed
		-其他:					-Other:
4333	6005.9010	---羊毛或动物细毛制	12	0 巴PK,冰岛IS,东盟AS,哥CR,秘鲁PE,新加坡SG,新西兰NZ,智利CL 7.2 澳AU,韩国KR 8.4 瑞士CH	0 受惠国$_1$LD$_1$	130	---Of wool or fine animal hair
4334	6005.9090	---其他	12	0 巴PK,冰岛IS,东盟AS,哥CR,秘鲁PE,新加坡SG,新西兰NZ,智利CL 7.2 澳AU,韩国KR 8.4 瑞士CH	0 受惠国$_1$LD$_1$	130	---Other
	60.06	**其他针织或钩编织物:**					**Other knitted or crocheted fabrics:**
4335	6006.1000	-羊毛或动物细毛制	12	0 巴PK,冰岛IS,东盟AS,哥CR,秘鲁PE,新加坡SG,新西兰NZ,智利CL 7.2 澳AU,韩国KR 8.4 瑞士CH	0 受惠国$_1$LD$_1$	130	-Of wool or fine animal hair
		-棉制:					-Of cotton:
4336	6006.2100	--未漂白或漂白	10	0 澳门MO,巴PK,冰岛IS,东盟AS,哥CR,秘鲁PE,香港HK,新西兰NZ,智利CL 4 瑞士CH 6 澳AU 7 亚太AP 8.6 韩国KR	0 受惠国LD	70	--Unbleached or bleached
4337	6006.2200	--染色	10	0 澳门MO,巴PK,冰岛IS,东盟AS,哥CR,秘鲁PE,香港HK,新加坡SG,新西兰NZ,智利CL 4 瑞士CH 6 澳AU,韩国KR 8.5 亚太AP	0 柬埔寨KH,老挝LA,缅甸MM,受惠国LD	70	--Dyed
4338	6006.2300	--色织	10	0 澳门MO,巴PK,冰岛IS,东盟AS,哥CR,秘鲁PE,香港HK,新加坡SG,新西兰NZ,智利CL 4 瑞士CH 6 澳AU,韩国KR 7 亚太AP	0 柬埔寨KH,老挝LA,缅甸MM,受惠国LD	70	--Of yarns of different colours
4339	6006.2400	--印花	10	0 澳门MO,巴PK,冰岛IS,东盟AS,哥CR,秘鲁PE,台湾TW,香港HK,新西兰NZ,智利CL 4 瑞士CH 6 澳AU,韩国KR 8.5 亚太AP	0 受惠国LD	70	--Printed
		-合成纤维制:					-Of synthetic fibres:

序号 No.	税则号列 Tariff Line	中文货品名称 Article Description in Chinese	最惠国税率 MFN(%)	协定税率 Agreement(%)	特惠税率 SP(%)	普通税率 Gen(%)	英文货品名称 Article Description
4340	6006.3100	--未漂白或漂白	10	0 澳门MO,巴PK,冰岛IS,东盟AS,哥CR,秘鲁PE,台湾TW,香港HK,新加坡SG,新西兰NZ,智利CL 4 瑞士CH 6 澳AU,韩国KR 8.5 亚太AP	0 受惠国LD	130	--Unbleached or bleached
4341	6006.3200	--染色	10	0 澳门MO,巴PK,冰岛IS,东盟AS,哥CR,秘鲁PE,台湾TW,香港HK,新加坡SG,新西兰NZ,智利CL 4 瑞士CH 6 澳AU 8.5 亚太AP 9 韩国KR	0 受惠国LD	130	--Dyed
4342	6006.3300	--色织	10	0 澳门MO,巴PK,冰岛IS,东盟AS,哥CR,秘鲁PE,台湾TW,香港HK,新加坡SG,新西兰NZ,智利CL 4 瑞士CH 6 澳AU 8.5 亚太AP 9 韩国KR	0 受惠国LD	130	--Of yarns of different colours
4343	6006.3400	--印花	10	0 澳门MO,巴PK,冰岛IS,东盟AS,哥CR,秘鲁PE,台湾TW,香港HK,新加坡SG,新西兰NZ,智利CL 4 瑞士CH 6 澳AU 8.5 亚太AP 9 韩国KR	0 受惠国LD	130	--Printed
		-人造纤维制:					-Of artificial fibres:
4344	6006.4100	--未漂白或漂白	10	0 澳门MO,巴PK,冰岛IS,东盟AS,哥CR,秘鲁PE,香港HK,新加坡SG,新西兰NZ,智利CL 4 瑞士CH 6 澳AU,韩国KR 8.5 亚太AP	0 受惠国LD	130	--Unbleached or bleached
4345	6006.4200	--染色	10	0 澳门MO,巴PK,冰岛IS,东盟AS,哥CR,秘鲁PE,台湾TW,香港HK,新加坡SG,新西兰NZ,智利CL 4 瑞士CH 6 澳AU 8.5 亚太AP 8.6 韩国KR	0 受惠国LD	130	--Dyed
4346	6006.4300	--色织	10	0 澳门MO,巴PK,冰岛IS,东盟AS,哥CR,秘鲁PE,香港HK,新加坡SG,新西兰NZ,智利CL 4 瑞士CH 6 澳AU,韩国KR 8.5 亚太AP	0 受惠国LD	130	--Of yarns of different colours

序号 No.	税则号列 Tariff Line	中文货品名称 Article Description in Chinese	最惠国税率 MFN(%)	协定税率 Agreement(%)	特惠税率 SP(%)	普通税率 Gen(%)	英文货品名称 Article Description
4347	6006.4400	--印花	10	0 澳门MO,巴PK,冰岛IS,东盟AS,哥CR,秘鲁PE,香港HK,新加坡SG,新西兰NZ,智利CL 4 瑞士CH 6 澳AU,韩国KR 8.5 亚太AP	0 受惠国LD	130	--Printed
4348	6006.9000	-其他	12	0 巴PK,冰岛IS,东盟AS,哥CR,秘鲁PE,新加坡SG,新西兰NZ,智利CL 7.2 澳AU,韩国KR 8.4 瑞士CH 10.2 亚太AP	0 受惠国$_1$LD$_1$	130	-Other

第六十一章
针织或钩编的服装及衣着附件

注释：

一、本章仅适用于制成的针织品或钩编织品。

二、本章不包括：

（一）税号 62.12 的货品；

（二）税号 63.09 的旧衣着或其他旧物品；

（三）矫形器具、外科手术带、疝气带及类似品（税号 90.21）。

三、税号 61.03 及 61.04 所称：

（一）"西服套装"，是指面料用相同的织物制成的两件套或三件套的下列成套服装：

一件人体上半身穿着的外套或短上衣，除袖子外，其面料数为四片或四片以上；也可附带一件西服背心，这件背心的前片面料应与套装其他各件的面料相同，后片面料则应与外套或短上衣的衬里料相同；

以及一件人体下半身穿着的服装，即不带背带或护胸的长裤、马裤、短裤（游泳裤除外）、裙子或裙裤。西服套装各件面料质地、颜色及构成必须相同，其款式也必须相同，尺寸大小还须相互般配，但可以用不同织物滚边（缝口上缝入长条织物）。

如果数件人体下半身穿着的服装同时进口或出口（例如，两条长裤、长裤与短裤、裙子或裙裤与长裤），构成西服套装下装的应是一条长裤，而对于女式西服套装，则应是一条裙子或裙裤，其他服装应分别归类。

所称"西服套装"，包括不论是否完全符合上述条件的下列配套服装：

1. 常礼服，由一件后襟下垂并下端开圆弧形叉的素色短上衣和一条条纹长裤组成；

2. 晚礼服（燕尾服），一般用黑色织物制成，上衣前襟较短且不闭合，背后有燕尾；

3. 无燕尾套装夜礼服，其中上衣款式与普通上衣相似（可以更为显露衬衣前胸），但有光

Chapter 61
Articles of apparel and clothing accessories, knitted or crocheted

Notes:

1. This Chapter applies only to made up knitted or crocheted articles.
2. This Chapter does not cover:
   (a) Goods of heading No.62.12;
   (b) Worn clothing or other worn articles of heading No.63.09; or
   (c) Orthopaedic appliances, surgical belts, trusses or the like (heaing No.90.21).
3. For the purposes of headings Nos.61.03 and 61.04:
   (a) The term "suit" means a set of garments composed of two or three pieces made up, in respect of their outer surface, in identical fabric and comprising:

   -One suit coat or jacket the outer shell of which, exclusive of sleeves, consists of four or more panels, designed to cover the upper part of the body, possibly with a tailored waistcoat in addition whose front panel is made from the same fabric as the outer shell of the other components of the set and whose rear panel is made from the same fabric as the lining of the suit coat or jacket; and

   -One garment designed to cover the lower part of the body and consisting of trousers, breeches or shorts (other than swimwear), a skirt or a divided skirt, having neither braces nor bibs.All of the components of a suit must be of the same fabric construction,colour and composition; they must alsobe of the same style and of corresponding or compatible size.However, these components may have piping (a strip of fabric sewn into the seam) in a different fabric.

   If several separate components to cover the lower part of the body are presented together（for example, two pairs of trousers or trousers and shorts, or a skirt or divided skirt and trousers）, the constituent lower part shall be one pair of trousers or, in the case of women's or girls' suits, the skirt or divided skirt, the other garments being considered separately.

   The term "suit" includes the following sets of garments, whether or not they fulfill all the above conditions:

   (1) morning dress, comprising a plain jacket (cutaway) with rounded tails hanging well down at the back and striped trousers;

   (2) evening dress (tailcoat), generally made of black fabric, the jacket of which is relatively short at the front, does not close and has narrow skirts cut in at the hips and hanging down behind;

   (3) dinner jacket suits, in which the jacket is similar in style to an ordinary jacket (though perhaps re-

滑丝质或仿丝质的翻领。

（二）"便服套装"，是指面料相同并作零售包装的下列成套服装（西服套装及税号 61.07、61.08 或 61.09 的物品除外）：

一件人体上半身穿着的服装，但套衫及背心除外，因为套衫可在两件套服装中作为内衣，背心也可作为内衣；

以及一件或两件不同的人体下半身穿着的服装，即长裤、护胸背带工装裤、马裤、短裤（游泳裤除外）、裙子或裙裤。

便服套装各件面料质地、款式、颜色及构成必须相同；尺寸大小也须相互般配。所称"便服套装"，不包括税号 61.12 的运动服及滑雪服。

四、税号 61.05 及 61.06 不包括在腰围以下有口袋的服装、带有罗纹腰带及以其他方式收紧下摆的服装或其织物至少在 10 厘米 × 10 厘米的面积内沿各方向的直线长度上平均每厘米少于 10 针的服装。税号 61.05 不包括无袖服装。

五、税号 61.09 不包括带有束带、罗纹腰带或其他方式收紧下摆的服装。

六、对于税号 61.11：

（一）所称"婴儿服装及衣着附件"，是指用于身高不超过 86 厘米幼儿的服装；

（二）既可归入税号 61.11，也可归入本章其他税号的物品，应归入税号 61.11。

七、税号 61.12 所称"滑雪服"，是指从整个外观和织物质地来看，主要在滑雪（速度滑雪或高山滑雪）时穿着的下列服装或成套服装：

（一）"滑雪连身服"，即上下身连在一起的单件服装；除袖子和领子外，滑雪连身服可有口袋或脚带；或

（二）"滑雪套装"即由两件或三件构成一套并作零售包装的下列服装：

一件用一条拉链扣合的带风帽的厚夹克、防风衣、防风短上衣或类似的服装，可以附带

vealing more of the shirt front), but has shiny silk or imitation silk lapels.

(b) The term "ensemble" means a set of garments (other than suits and articles of heading No.61.07, 61.08 or 61.09), composed of several pieces made up in identical fabric, put up for retail sale, and comprising:

-One garment designed to cover the upper part of the body, with the exception of pullovers which may form a sceond upper garment in the sole context of twin sets, and of waistcoats which may also form a second upper garment; and

-One or two different garments, designed to cover the lower part of the body and consisting of trousers, bib and brace overalls, breeches, shorts (other than swimwear), a skirt or a divided skirt.

All of the components of an ensemble must be of the same fabric construction, style, colour and composition; they also must be of corresponding or compatible size.The term "ensemble" does not apply to track suits or ski suits, of heading No.61.12.

4. Headings Nos.61.05 and 61.06 do not cover garments with pockets below the waist, with a ribbed waistband or other means of tightening at the bottom of the garment, or garments having an average of less than 10 stitches per linear centimetre in each direction counted on an area measuring at least 10cm × 10cm.Heading No.61.05 does not cover sleeveless garments.

5. Heading No.61.09 does not cover garments with a drawstring, a ribbed waistband or other means of tightening at the bottom of the garment.

6. For the purposes of heading No.61.11:

(a) The expression "babies' garments and clothing accessories" means articles for young children of a body height not exceeding 86cm;

(b) Articles which are, *prima facie*, classifiable both in heading No.61.11 and in other headings of this Chapter are to be classified in heading No.61.11.

7. For the purposes of heading No.61.12, "ski suits" means garments or sets of garments which, by their general appearance and texture, are identifiable as intended to be worn principally for sking (cross-country or alpine).They consist either of:

(a) a "ski overall", that is, a one-piece garment designed to cover the upper and the lower parts of the body; in addition to sleeves and a collar the ski overall may have pockets or footstraps; or

(b) a "ski ensemble", that is, a set of garments composed of two or three pieces, put up for retail sale and comprising:

-one garment such as an anorak, wind cheater, wind-jacket or similar article, closed by a slide fastener

一件背心；

以及一条不论是否过腰的长裤、一条马裤或一条护胸背带工装裤。

“滑雪套装”也可由一件类似以上（一）款所述的连身服和一件可套在连身服外面的有胎料背心组成。

“滑雪套装”各件颜色可以不同，但面料质地、款式及构成必须相同；尺寸大小也须相互般配。

八、既可归入税号 61.13，也可归入本章其他税号的服装，除税号 61.11 所列的仍归入该税号外，其余的应一律归入税号 61.13。

九、本章的服装，凡门襟为左压右的，应视为男式；右压左的，应视为女式。但本规定不适用于其式样已明显为男式或女式的服装。无法区别是男式还是女式的服装，应按女式服装归入有关税号。

十、本章物品可用金属线制成。

(zipper), possibly with a waistcoat in addition; and

-one pair of trousers whether or not extending above waist-level, one pair of breeches or one bib and brace overall.

The “ski ensemble” may also consist of an overall similar to the one mentioned in paragraph (a) above and a type of padded, sleeveless jacket worn over the overall.

All the components of a “ski ensemble” must be made up in afabric of the same texture, style and composition whether or not of the same colour; they also must be of corresponding or compatible size.

8. Garments which are, *prima facie*, classifiable both in heading No.61.13 and in other headings of this Chapter, excluding heading No.61.11, are to be classified in heading No.61.13.

9. Garments of this Chapter desinged for left over right closure at the front shall be regarded as men's or boys' garments, and those designed for right over left closure at the front as women's or girls' garments. These provisions do not apply where the cut of the garment clearly indicates that it is designed for one or other of the sexes.

Garments which cannot be identified as either men's or boys' garments or as women's or girls' garments are to be classified in the headings covering women or girls garments.

10. Articles of this Chapter may be made of metal thread.

序号 No.	税则号列 Tariff Line	中文货品名称 Article Description in Chinese	最惠国税率 MFN(%)	协定税率 Agreement(%)	特惠税率 SP(%)	普通税率 Gen(%)	英文货品名称 Article Description
	61.01	**针织或钩编的男式大衣、短大衣、斗篷、短斗篷、带风帽的防寒短上衣(包括滑雪短上衣)、防风衣、防风短上衣及类似品，但税号61.03的货品除外：**					**Men' s or boys' overcoats, car coats, capes, cloaks, anoraks (including ski jackets) , windcheaters, wind-jackets and similar articles, knitted or crocheted, other than those of heading 6103:**
4349	6101.2000	-棉制	17.5	0 澳门MO,冰岛IS,东盟AS,哥CR,香港HK,新加坡SG,新西兰NZ,智利CL 5.2 秘鲁PE 10.5 澳AU 12.3 瑞士CH 14 巴PK,韩国KR,亚太AP	0 受惠国LD	90	-Of cotton
4350	6101.3000	-化学纤维制	17.5	0 澳门MO,冰岛IS,东盟AS,哥CR,香港HK,新加坡SG,新西兰NZ,智利CL 5.2 秘鲁PE 8.8 巴PK 10.5 澳AU 12.3 瑞士CH,亚太AP 14 韩国KR	0 受惠国LD	130	-Of man-made fibres
		-其他纺织材料制：					-Of other textile materials:

序号 No.	税则号列 Tariff Line	中文货品名称 Article Description in Chinese	最惠国税率 MFN(%)	协定税率 Agreement(%)	特惠税率 SP(%)	普通税率 Gen(%)	英文货品名称 Article Description
4351	6101.9010	----羊毛或动物细毛制	25△13	0 澳门MO,冰岛IS,东盟AS,哥CR,香港HK,新加坡SG,新西兰NZ,智利CL 7.5 秘鲁PE 15 澳AU 17.5 瑞士CH 18 巴PK,亚太AP 22.5 韩国KR	0 受惠国$_1$LD$_1$	130	---Of wool or fine animal hair
4352	6101.9090	----其他	17.5	0 澳门MO,冰岛IS,东盟AS,哥CR,香港HK,新加坡SG,新西兰NZ,智利CL 5.2 秘鲁PE 8.8 巴PK 10.5 澳AU 12.3 瑞士CH,亚太AP 14 韩国KR	0 受惠国$_1$LD$_1$	130	---Other
	61.02	**针织或钩编的女式大衣、短大衣、斗篷、短斗篷、带风帽的防寒短上衣(包括滑雪短上衣)、防风衣、防风短上衣及类似品,但税号61.04的货品除外:**					**Women' s or girls' overcoats, car coats, capes, cloaks, anoraks (including ski jackets), windcheaters, wind-jackets and similar articles, knitted or crocheted, other than those of heading 6104:**
4353	6102.1000	-羊毛或动物细毛制	25△13	0 澳门MO,冰岛IS,东盟AS,哥CR,香港HK,新加坡SG,新西兰NZ,智利CL 7.5 秘鲁PE 15 澳AU 17.5 瑞士CH 18 巴PK,亚太AP 22.5 韩国KR	0 受惠国$_1$LD$_1$	130	-Of wool or fine animal hair
4354	6102.2000	-棉制	17.5	0 澳门MO,冰岛IS,东盟AS,哥CR,香港HK,新加坡SG,新西兰NZ,智利CL 10.5 澳AU 12.3 瑞士CH 14 巴PK,韩国KR,亚太AP	0 受惠国LD	90	-Of cotton
4355	6102.3000	-化学纤维制	17.5	0 澳门MO,冰岛IS,东盟AS,哥CR,香港HK,新加坡SG,新西兰NZ,智利CL 5.2 秘鲁PE 8.8 巴PK 10.5 澳AU 12.3 瑞士CH,亚太AP 14 韩国KR	0 受惠国LD	130	-Of man-made fibres
4356	6102.9000	-其他纺织材料制	20	0 澳门MO,冰岛IS,东盟AS,哥CR,香港HK,新加坡SG,新西兰NZ,智利CL 6 秘鲁PE 10 巴PK 12 澳AU 13.8 亚太AP 14 瑞士CH 17.3 韩国KR	0 受惠国$_1$LD$_1$	130	-Of other textile materials
	61.03	**针织或钩编的男式西服套装、便服套装、上衣、长裤、护胸背带工装裤、马裤及短裤(游泳裤除外):**					**Men' s or boys' suits, ensembles, jackets, blazers, trousers, bib and brace overalls, breeches and shorts (other than swimwear), knitted or crocheted:**
		-西服套装:					-Suits:

序号 No.	税则号列 Tariff Line	中文货品名称 Article Description in Chinese	最惠国税率 MFN(%)	协定税率 Agreement(%)	特惠税率 SP(%)	普通税率 Gen(%)	英文货品名称 Article Description
4357	6103.1010	---羊毛或动物细毛制	25	0 澳门MO,冰岛IS,东盟AS,哥CR,香港HK,新加坡SG,新西兰NZ,智利CL 7.5 秘鲁PE 15 澳AU 17.5 瑞士CH 18 巴PK,亚太AP 22.5 韩国KR	0 受惠国$_1$LD$_1$	130	---Of wool or fine animal hair
4358	6103.1020	---合成纤维制	25	0 澳门MO,冰岛IS,东盟AS,哥CR,香港HK,新加坡SG,新西兰NZ,智利CL 7.5 秘鲁PE 15 澳AU 17.5 瑞士CH 18 巴PK,亚太AP 22.5 韩国KR	0 受惠国$_1$LD$_1$	130	---Of synthetic fibres
4359	6103.1090	---其他纺织材料制	17.5	0 澳门MO,冰岛IS,东盟AS,哥CR,香港HK,新加坡SG,新西兰NZ,智利CL 5.2 秘鲁PE 8.8 巴PK 10.5 澳AU 12.3 瑞士CH,亚太AP 14 韩国KR	0 老挝LA,受惠国LD	130	---Of other textile materials
		-便服套装:					-Ensembles:
4360	6103.2200	--棉制	20	0 澳门MO,冰岛IS,东盟AS,哥CR,香港HK,新加坡SG,新西兰NZ,智利CL 6 秘鲁PE 12 澳AU 14 瑞士CH 14.8 巴PK,亚太AP 17.3 韩国KR	0 老挝LA,受惠国LD	90	--Of cotton
4361	6103.2300	--合成纤维制	25	0 澳门MO,冰岛IS,东盟AS,哥CR,香港HK,新加坡SG,新西兰NZ,智利CL 7.5 秘鲁PE 15 澳AU 17.5 瑞士CH 18 巴PK,亚太AP 22.5 韩国KR	0 受惠国$_1$LD$_1$	130	--Of synthetic fibres
		--其他纺织材料制:					--Of other textile materials:
4362	6103.2910	---羊毛或动物细毛制	25	0 澳门MO,冰岛IS,东盟AS,哥CR,香港HK,新加坡SG,新西兰NZ,智利CL 7.5 秘鲁PE 15 澳AU 17.5 瑞士CH 18 巴PK,亚太AP 22.5 韩国KR	0 受惠国$_1$LD$_1$	130	---Of wool or fine animal hair
4363	6103.2990	---其他	25	0 澳门MO,冰岛IS,东盟AS,哥CR,新加坡SG,新西兰NZ,智利CL 7.5 秘鲁PE 15 澳AU 17.5 瑞士CH 18 巴PK,亚太AP 22.5 韩国KR	0 老挝LA,受惠国LD	130	---Other
		-上衣:					-Jackets and blazers:

序号 No.	税则号列 Tariff Line	中文货品名称 Article Description in Chinese	最惠国税率 MFN(%)	协定税率 Agreement(%)	特惠税率 SP(%)	普通税率 Gen(%)	英文货品名称 Article Description
4364	6103.3100	--羊毛或动物细毛制	16	0 澳门MO,冰岛IS,东盟AS,哥CR,香港HK,新加坡SG,新西兰NZ,智利CL 4.8 秘鲁PE 8 巴PK 9.6 澳AU 11.2 瑞士CH 11.7 亚太AP 12.8 韩国KR	0 受惠国$_1$LD$_1$	130	--Of wool or fine animal hair
4365	6103.3200	--棉制	16	0 澳门MO,冰岛IS,东盟AS,哥CR,香港HK,新加坡SG,新西兰NZ,智利CL 4.8 秘鲁PE 8 巴PK 9.6 澳AU 11.2 瑞士CH 12 亚太AP 12.8 韩国KR	0 柬埔寨KH,老挝LA,缅甸MM,受惠国LD	90	--Of cotton
4366	6103.3300	--合成纤维制	19	0 澳门MO,冰岛IS,东盟AS,哥CR,香港HK,新加坡SG,新西兰NZ,智利CL 5.7 秘鲁PE 9.5 巴PK 11.4 澳AU 13.3 瑞士CH 13.6 亚太AP 15.2 韩国KR	0 柬埔寨KH,受惠国LD	130	--Of synthetic fibres
4367	6103.3900	--其他纺织材料制	16	0 澳门MO,冰岛IS,东盟AS,哥CR,香港HK,新加坡SG,新西兰NZ,智利CL 4.8 秘鲁PE 8 巴PK 9.6 澳AU 11.2 瑞士CH 11.7 亚太AP 12.8 韩国KR	0 柬埔寨KH,老挝LA,受惠国LD	130	--Of other textile materials
		-长裤、护胸背带工装裤、马裤及短裤:					-Trousers, bib and brace overalls, breeches and shorts:
4368	6103.4100	--羊毛或动物细毛制	16	0 澳门MO,冰岛IS,东盟AS,哥CR,香港HK,新加坡SG,新西兰NZ,智利CL 4.8 秘鲁PE 8 巴PK 9.6 澳AU 11.2 瑞士CH 11.7 亚太AP 12.8 韩国KR	0 受惠国LD,亚太AP	130	--Of wool or fine animal hair
4369	6103.4200	--棉制	16	0 澳门MO,冰岛IS,东盟AS,哥CR,香港HK,新加坡SG,新西兰NZ,智利CL 4.8 秘鲁PE 8 巴PK 9.6 澳AU 11.2 瑞士CH 12.8 韩国KR 13.6 亚太AP	0 柬埔寨KH,老挝LA,缅甸MM,受惠国LD 6.4 亚太AP	90	--Of cotton

序号 No.	税则号列 Tariff Line	中文货品名称 Article Description in Chinese	最惠国税率 MFN(%)	协定税率 Agreement(%)	特惠税率 SP(%)	普通税率 Gen(%)	英文货品名称 Article Description
4370	6103.4300	--合成纤维制	17.5	0 澳门MO,冰岛IS,东盟AS,哥CR,香港HK,新加坡SG,新西兰NZ,智利CL 5.2 秘鲁PE 8.8 巴PK 10.5 澳AU 12.3 瑞士CH,亚太AP 14 韩国KR	0 柬埔寨KH,受惠国LD,亚太AP	130	--Of synthetic fibres
4371	6103.4900	--其他纺织材料制	16	0 澳门MO,冰岛IS,东盟AS,哥CR,香港HK,新加坡SG,新西兰NZ,智利CL 4.8 秘鲁PE 8 巴PK 9.6 澳AU 11.2 瑞士CH 11.7 亚太AP 12.8 韩国KR	0 柬埔寨KH,老挝LA,受惠国LD,亚太AP	130	--Of other textile materials
	61.04	**针织或钩编的女式西服套装、便服套装、上衣、连衣裙、裙子、裙裤、长裤、护胸背带工装裤、马裤及短裤(游泳服除外):**					**Women' s or girls' suits, ensembles, jackets, blazers, dresses, skirts, divided skirts, trousers, bib and brace overalls, breeches and shorts (other than swimwear) , knitted or crocheted:**
		-西服套装:					-Suits:
4372	6104.1300	--合成纤维制	25	0 澳门MO,冰岛IS,东盟AS,哥CR,香港HK,新加坡SG,新西兰NZ,智利CL 7.5 秘鲁PE 15 澳AU 17.5 瑞士CH 18 巴PK,亚太AP 22.5 韩国KR	0 受惠国$_1$LD$_1$	130	--Of synthetic fibres
		--其他纺织材料制:					--Of other textile materials:
4373	6104.1910	---羊毛或动物细毛制	17.5	0 澳门MO,冰岛IS,东盟AS,哥CR,香港HK,新加坡SG,新西兰NZ,智利CL 5.2 秘鲁PE 8.8 巴PK 10.5 澳AU 12.3 瑞士CH,亚太AP 14 韩国KR	0 受惠国LD	130	---Of wool or fine animal hair
4374	6104.1920	---棉制	17.5	0 澳门MO,冰岛IS,东盟AS,哥CR,香港HK,新加坡SG,新西兰NZ,智利CL 5.2 秘鲁PE 10.5 澳AU 12.3 瑞士CH 14 巴PK,韩国KR,亚太AP	0 老挝LA,受惠国LD	90	---Of cotton
4375	6104.1990	---其他	17.5	0 澳门MO,冰岛IS,东盟AS,哥CR,香港HK,新加坡SG,新西兰NZ,智利CL 5.2 秘鲁PE 8.8 巴PK 10.5 澳AU 12.3 瑞士CH,亚太AP 14 韩国KR	0 老挝LA,受惠国LD	130	---Other
		-便服套装:					-Ensembles:

序号 No.	税则号列 Tariff Line	中文货品名称 Article Description in Chinese	最惠国税率 MFN(%)	协定税率 Agreement(%)	特惠税率 SP(%)	普通税率 Gen(%)	英文货品名称 Article Description
4376	6104.2200	--棉制	17.5	0 澳门MO,冰岛IS,东盟AS,哥CR,香港HK,新加坡SG,新西兰NZ,智利CL 5.2 秘鲁PE 10.5 澳AU 12.3 瑞士CH 14 巴PK,韩国KR,亚太AP	0 老挝LA,受惠国LD	90	--Of cotton
4377	6104.2300	--合成纤维制	25	0 澳门MO,冰岛IS,东盟AS,哥CR,香港HK,新加坡SG,新西兰NZ,智利CL 7.5 秘鲁PE 15 澳AU 17.5 瑞士CH 18 巴PK,亚太AP 22.5 韩国KR	0 受惠国$_1$LD$_1$	130	--Of synthetic fibres
		--其他纺织材料制:					--Of other textile materials:
4378	6104.2910	---羊毛或动物细毛制	17.5	0 澳门MO,冰岛IS,东盟AS,哥CR,香港HK,新加坡SG,新西兰NZ,智利CL 5.2 秘鲁PE 8.8 巴PK 10.5 澳AU 12.3 瑞士CH,亚太AP 14 韩国KR	0 受惠国$_1$LD$_1$	130	---Of wool or fine animal hair
4379	6104.2990	---其他纺织材料制	15	0 澳门MO,冰岛IS,东盟AS,哥CR,香港HK,新加坡SG,新西兰NZ,智利CL 4.5 秘鲁PE 7.5 巴PK 9 澳AU 10.4 亚人AP 10.5 瑞十CH 12 韩国KR	0 受惠国LD	130	---Other
		-上衣:					-Jackets and blazers:
4380	6104.3100	--羊毛或动物细毛制	16	0 澳门MO,冰岛IS,东盟AS,哥CR,香港HK,新加坡SG,新西兰NZ,智利CL 4.8 秘鲁PE 8 巴PK 9.6 澳AU 11.2 瑞士CH 11.7 亚太AP 12.8 韩国KR	0 受惠国LD	130	--Of wool or fine animal hair
4381	6104.3200	--棉制	16	0 澳门MO,冰岛IS,东盟AS,哥CR,香港HK,新加坡SG,新西兰NZ,智利CL 4.8 秘鲁PE 9.6 澳AU 11.2 瑞士CH 12.8 韩国KR 13.6 巴PK,亚太AP	0 柬埔寨KH,老挝LA,缅甸MM,受惠国LD	90	--Of cotton

序号 No.	税则号列 Tariff Line	中文货品名称 Article Description in Chinese	最惠国税率 MFN(%)	协定税率 Agreement(%)	特惠税率 SP(%)	普通税率 Gen(%)	英文货品名称 Article Description
4382	6104.3300	--合成纤维制	19	0 澳门MO,冰岛IS,东盟AS,哥CR,香港HK,新加坡SG,新西兰NZ,智利CL 5.7 秘鲁PE 9.5 巴PK 11.4 澳AU 13.3 瑞士CH 13.6 亚太AP 15.2 韩国KR	0 柬埔寨KH,受惠国LD	130	--Of synthetic fibres
4383	6104.3900	--其他纺织材料制	16	0 澳门MO,冰岛IS,东盟AS,哥CR,香港HK,新加坡SG,新西兰NZ,智利CL 4.8 秘鲁PE 8 巴PK 9.6 澳AU 11.2 瑞士CH 11.7 亚太AP 12.8 韩国KR	0 柬埔寨KH,受惠国LD	130	--Of other textile materials
		-连衣裙:					-Dresses:
4384	6104.4100	--羊毛或动物细毛制	16	0 澳门MO,冰岛IS,东盟AS,哥CR,香港HK,新加坡SG,新西兰NZ,智利CL 4.8 秘鲁PE 8 巴PK 9.6 澳AU 11.2 瑞士CH 11.7 亚太AP 12.8 韩国KR	0 受惠国$_1$LD$_1$	130	--Of wool or fine animal hair
4385	6104.4200	--棉制	16	0 澳门MO,冰岛IS,东盟AS,哥CR,香港HK,新加坡SG,新西兰NZ,智利CL 4.8 秘鲁PE 8 巴PK 9.6 澳AU 11.2 瑞士CH 12.8 韩国KR 13.6 亚太AP	0 受惠国LD	90	--Of cotton
4386	6104.4300	--合成纤维制	17.5	0 澳门MO,冰岛IS,东盟AS,哥CR,香港HK,新加坡SG,新西兰NZ,智利CL 5.2 秘鲁PE 8.8 巴PK 10.5 澳AU 12.3 瑞士CH,亚太AP 14 韩国KR	0 柬埔寨KH,受惠国LD	130	--Of synthetic fibres
4387	6104.4400	--人造纤维制	16	0 澳门MO,冰岛IS,东盟AS,哥CR,香港HK,新加坡SG,新西兰NZ,智利CL 4.8 秘鲁PE 8 巴PK 9.6 澳AU 11.2 瑞士CH 11.7 亚太AP 12.8 韩国KR	0 柬埔寨KH,受惠国LD	130	--Of artificial fibres

序号 No.	税则号列 Tariff Line	中文货品名称 Article Description in Chinese	最惠国税率 MFN(%)	协定税率 Agreement(%)	特惠税率 SP(%)	普通税率 Gen(%)	英文货品名称 Article Description
4388	6104.4900	--其他纺织材料制	16	0 澳门MO,冰岛IS,东盟AS,哥CR,香港HK,新加坡SG,新西兰NZ,智利CL 4.8 秘鲁PE 8 巴PK 9.6 澳AU 11.2 瑞士CH 11.7 亚太AP 12.8 韩国KR	0 柬埔寨KH,受惠国LD	130	--Of other textile materials
		-裙子及裙裤:					-Skirts and divided skirts:
4389	6104.5100	--羊毛或动物细毛制	14	0 澳门MO,冰岛IS,东盟AS,哥CR,秘鲁PE,香港HK,新加坡SG,新西兰NZ,智利CL 7 巴PK 8.4 澳AU 9.8 瑞士CH 10.8 亚太AP 11.2 韩国KR	0 受惠国$_1$LD$_1$	130	--Of wool or fine animal hair
4390	6104.5200	--棉制	14	0 澳门MO,冰岛IS,东盟AS,哥CR,秘鲁PE,香港HK,新加坡SG,新西兰NZ,智利CL 7 巴PK 8.4 澳AU 9.8 瑞士CH 10.3 亚太AP 11.2 韩国KR	0 受惠国LD	90	--Of cotton
4391	6104.5300	--合成纤维制	16	0 澳门MO,冰岛IS,东盟AS,哥CR,香港HK,新加坡SG,新西兰NZ,智利CL 4.8 秘鲁PE 8 巴PK 9.6 澳AU 11.2 瑞士CH 11.7 亚太AP 12.8 韩国KR	0 柬埔寨KH,受惠国LD	130	--Of synthetic fibres
4392	6104.5900	--其他纺织材料制	14	0 澳门MO,冰岛IS,东盟AS,哥CR,秘鲁PE,香港HK,新加坡SG,新西兰NZ,智利CL 7 巴PK 8.4 澳AU 9.8 瑞士CH 10.8 亚太AP 11.2 韩国KR	0 柬埔寨KH,老挝LA,缅甸MM,受惠国LD	130	--Of other textile materials
		-长裤、护胸背带工装裤、马裤及短裤:					-Trousers, bib and brace overalls, breeches and shorts:
4393	6104.6100	--羊毛或动物细毛制	16	0 澳门MO,冰岛IS,东盟AS,哥CR,香港HK,新加坡SG,新西兰NZ,智利CL 4.8 秘鲁PE 8 巴PK 9.6 澳AU 11.2 瑞士CH 11.7 亚太AP 12.8 韩国KR	0 受惠国LD	130	--Of wool or fine animal hair

序号 No.	税则号列 Tariff Line	中文货品名称 Article Description in Chinese	最惠国税率 MFN(%)	协定税率 Agreement(%)	特惠税率 SP(%)	普通税率 Gen(%)	英文货品名称 Article Description
4394	6104.6200	--棉制	16	0 澳门MO,冰岛IS,东盟AS,哥CR,香港HK,新加坡SG,新西兰NZ,智利CL 4.8 秘鲁PE 8 巴PK 9.6 澳AU 11.2 瑞士CH 12.8 韩国KR 13.6 亚太AP	0 受惠国LD 6.4 亚太AP	90	--Of cotton
4395	6104.6300	--合成纤维制	17.5	0 澳门MO,冰岛IS,东盟AS,哥CR,香港HK,新加坡SG,新西兰NZ,智利CL 5.2 秘鲁PE 8.8 巴PK 10.5 澳AU 12.3 瑞士CH,亚太AP 14 韩国KR	0 受惠国LD	130	--Of synthetic fibres
4396	6104.6900	--其他纺织材料制	16	0 澳门MO,冰岛IS,东盟AS,哥CR,香港HK,新加坡SG,新西兰NZ,智利CL 4.8 秘鲁PE 8 巴PK 9.6 澳AU 11.2 瑞士CH 12 亚太AP 12.8 韩国KR	0 受惠国LD,亚太AP	130	--Of other textile materials
	61.05	**针织或钩编的男衬衫:**					**Men' s or boys' shirts, knitted or crocheted:**
4397	6105.1000	-棉制	16	0 澳门MO,冰岛IS,东盟AS,哥CR,台湾TW,香港HK,新加坡SG,新西兰NZ,智利CL 9.6 澳AU 11.2 瑞士CH 12.8 韩国KR 13.6 巴PK,亚太AP	0 柬埔寨KH,老挝LA,缅甸MM,受惠国LD 11.2 亚太AP	90	-Of cotton
4398	6105.2000	-化学纤维制	17.5	0 澳门MO,冰岛IS,东盟AS,哥CR,香港HK,新加坡SG,新西兰NZ,智利CL 5.2 秘鲁PE 8.8 巴PK 10.5 澳AU 12.3 瑞士CH,亚太AP 14 韩国KR	0 受惠国LD,亚太AP	130	-Of man-made fibres
4399	6105.9000	-其他纺织材料制	16	0 澳门MO,冰岛IS,东盟AS,哥CR,香港HK,新加坡SG,新西兰NZ,智利CL 4.8 秘鲁PE 8 巴PK 9.6 澳AU 11.2 瑞士CH 11.7 亚太AP 12.8 韩国KR	0 受惠国LD,亚太AP	130	-Of other textile materials
	61.06	**针织或钩编的女衬衫:**					**Women' s or girls' blouses, shirts and shirt-blouses, knitted or crocheted:**

序号 No.	税则号列 Tariff Line	中文货品名称 Article Description in Chinese	最惠国税率 MFN(%)	协定税率 Agreement(%)	特惠税率 SP(%)	普通税率 Gen(%)	英文货品名称 Article Description
4400	6106.1000	-棉制	16	0 澳门MO,冰岛IS,东盟AS,哥CR,香港HK,新加坡SG,新西兰NZ,智利CL 4.8 秘鲁PE 8 巴PK 9.6 澳AU 11.2 瑞士CH 12.8 韩国KR 13.6 亚太AP	0 柬埔寨KH,老挝LA,缅甸MM,受惠国LD 6.4 亚太AP	90	-Of cotton
4401	6106.2000	-化学纤维制	17.5	0 澳门MO,冰岛IS,东盟AS,哥CR,香港HK,新加坡SG,新西兰NZ,智利CL 5.2 秘鲁PE 8.8 巴PK 10.5 澳AU 12.3 瑞士CH,亚太AP 14 韩国KR	0 受惠国LD,亚太AP	130	-Of man-made fibres
4402	6106.9000	-其他纺织材料制	16	0 澳门MO,冰岛IS,东盟AS,哥CR,台湾TW,香港HK,新加坡SG,新西兰NZ,智利CL 4.8 秘鲁PE 8 巴PK 9.6 澳AU 11.2 瑞士CH 11.7 亚太AP 12.8 韩国KR	0 受惠国LD,亚太AP	130	-Of other textile materials
	61.07	**针织或钩编的男式内裤、三角裤、长睡衣、睡衣裤、浴衣、晨衣及类似品:**					**Men' s or boys' underpants, briefs, nightshirts, pyjamas, bathrobes, dressing gowns and similar articles, knitted or crocheted:**
		-内裤及三角裤:					-Underpants and briefs:
4403	6107.1100	--棉制	14	0 澳门MO,冰岛IS,东盟AS,哥CR,香港HK,新加坡SG,新西兰NZ,智利CL 4.2 秘鲁PE 8.4 澳AU 9.8 瑞士CH 11.2 巴PK,韩国KR	0 柬埔寨KH,老挝LA,缅甸MM,受惠国LD 5.6 亚太AP	90	--Of cotton
4404	6107.1200	--化学纤维制	16	0 澳门MO,冰岛IS,东盟AS,哥CR,香港HK,新加坡SG,新西兰NZ,智利CL 4.8 秘鲁PE 8 巴PK 9.6 澳AU 10.9 亚太AP 11.2 瑞士CH 12.8 韩国KR	0 受惠国$_1$LD$_1$	130	--Of man-made fibres
		--其他纺织材料制:					--Of other textile materials:
4405	6107.1910	---丝及绢丝制	14	0 澳门MO,冰岛IS,东盟AS,哥CR,秘鲁PE,香港HK,新加坡SG,新西兰NZ,智利CL 7 巴PK 8.4 澳AU 9.3 亚太AP 9.8 瑞士CH 11.2 韩国KR	0 受惠国$_1$LD$_1$	130	---Of silk or silk waste

序号 No.	税则号列 Tariff Line	中文货品名称 Article Description in Chinese	最惠国税率 MFN(%)	协定税率 Agreement(%)	特惠税率 SP(%)	普通税率 Gen(%)	英文货品名称 Article Description
4406	6107.1990	---其他	14	0 澳门MO,冰岛IS,东盟AS,哥CR,秘鲁PE,香港HK,新加坡SG,新西兰NZ,智利CL 7 巴PK 8.4 澳AU 9.3 亚太AP 9.8 瑞士CH 11.2 韩国KR	0 受惠国$_1$LD$_1$	130	---Other
		-长睡衣及睡衣裤:					-Nightshirts and pyjamas:
4407	6107.2100	--棉制	14	0 澳门MO,冰岛IS,东盟AS,哥CR,香港HK,新加坡SG,新西兰NZ,智利CL 8.4 澳AU 9.8 瑞士CH 11.2 巴PK,韩国KR	0 柬埔寨KH,老挝LA,缅甸MM,受惠国LD 5.6 亚太AP	90	--Of cotton
4408	6107.2200	--化学纤维制	16	0 澳门MO,冰岛IS,东盟AS,哥CR,香港HK,新加坡SG,新西兰NZ,智利CL 4.8 秘鲁PE 8 巴PK 9.6 澳AU 10.9 亚太AP 11.2 瑞士CH 12.8 韩国KR	0 受惠国LD,亚太AP	130	--Of man-made fibres
		--其他纺织材料制:					--Of other textile materials:
4409	6107.2910	---丝及绢丝制	14	0 冰岛IS,东盟AS,哥CR,秘鲁PE,香港HK,新加坡SG,新西兰NZ,智利CL 7 巴PK 8.4 澳AU 9.3 亚太AP 9.8 瑞士CH 11.2 韩国KR	0 受惠国LD,亚太AP	130	---Of silk or silk waste
4410	6107.2990	---其他	14	0 冰岛IS,东盟AS,哥CR,秘鲁PE,香港HK,新加坡SG,新西兰NZ,智利CL 7 巴PK 8.4 澳AU 9.3 亚太AP 9.8 瑞士CH 11.2 韩国KR	0 柬埔寨KH,老挝LA,缅甸MM,受惠国LD,亚太AP	130	---Other
		-其他:					-Other:
4411	6107.9100	--棉制	14	0 冰岛IS,东盟AS,哥CR,秘鲁PE,香港HK,新加坡SG,新西兰NZ,智利CL 7 巴PK 8.4 澳AU 9.8 瑞士CH 11.2 韩国KR	0 受惠国$_1$LD$_1$	90	--Of cotton
		--其他纺织材料制:					--Of other textile materials:
4412	6107.9910	---化学纤维制	16	0 冰岛IS,东盟AS,哥CR,香港HK,新加坡SG,新西兰NZ,智利CL 4.8 秘鲁PE 8 巴PK 9.6 澳AU 10.9 亚太AP 11.2 瑞士CH 12.8 韩国KR	0 受惠国$_1$LD$_1$	130	---Of man-made fibres

序号 No.	税则号列 Tariff Line	中文货品名称 Article Description in Chinese	最惠国税率 MFN(%)	协定税率 Agreement(%)	特惠税率 SP(%)	普通税率 Gen(%)	英文货品名称 Article Description
4413	6107.9990	---其他	14	0 冰岛IS,东盟AS,哥CR,秘鲁PE,新加坡SG,新西兰NZ,智利CL 7 巴PK 8.4 澳AU 9.3 亚太AP 9.8 瑞士CH 11.2 韩国KR	0 受惠国$_1$LD$_1$	130	---Other
	61.08	**针织或钩编的女式长衬裙、衬裙、三角裤、短衬裤、睡衣、睡衣裤、浴衣、晨衣及类似品:**					**Women' s or girls' slips, petticoats, briefs, panties, nightdresses, pyjamas, négligés, bathrobes, dressing gowns and similar articles, knitted or crocheted:**
		-长衬裙及衬裙:					-Slips and petticoats:
4414	6108.1100	--化学纤维制	16	0 冰岛IS,东盟AS,哥CR,香港HK,新加坡SG,新西兰NZ,智利CL 4.8 秘鲁PE 8 巴PK 9.6 澳AU 10.9 亚太AP 11.2 瑞士CH 12.8 韩国KR	0 受惠国$_1$LD$_1$	130	--Of man-made fibres
		--其他纺织材料制:					--Of other textile materials:
4415	6108.1910	---棉制	14	0 冰岛IS,东盟AS,哥CR,秘鲁PE,香港HK,新加坡SG,新西兰NZ,智利CL 7 巴PK 8.4 澳AU 9.8 瑞士CH 11.2 韩国KR	0 受惠国LD	90	---Of cotton
4416	6108.1920	---丝及绢丝制	14	0 冰岛IS,东盟AS,哥CR,秘鲁PE,香港HK,新加坡SG,新西兰NZ,智利CL 7 巴PK 8.4 澳AU 9.8 瑞士CH 11.2 韩国KR	0 受惠国$_1$LD$_1$	130	---Of silk or silk waste
4417	6108.1990	---其他	14	0 冰岛IS,东盟AS,哥CR,秘鲁PE,香港HK,新加坡SG,新西兰NZ,智利CL 7 巴PK 8.4 澳AU 9.3 亚太AP 9.8 瑞士CH 11.2 韩国KR	0 受惠国$_1$LD$_1$	130	---Other
		-三角裤及短衬裤:					-Briefs and panties:
4418	6108.2100	--棉制	14	0 澳门MO,冰岛IS,东盟AS,哥CR,秘鲁PE,香港HK,新加坡SG,新西兰NZ,智利CL 8.4 澳AU 9.8 瑞士CH 11.2 巴PK,韩国KR	0 柬埔寨KH,老挝LA,缅甸MM,受惠国LD	90	--Of cotton

序号 No.	税则号列 Tariff Line	中文货品名称 Article Description in Chinese	最惠国税率 MFN(%)	协定税率 Agreement(%)	特惠税率 SP(%)	普通税率 Gen(%)	英文货品名称 Article Description
4419	6108.2200	--化学纤维制	16	0 澳门MO,冰岛IS,东盟AS,哥CR,香港HK,新加坡SG,新西兰NZ,智利CL 4.8 秘鲁PE 8 巴PK 9.6 澳AU 10.9 亚太AP 11.2 瑞士CH 12.8 韩国KR	0 受惠国LD	130	--Of man-made fibres
		--其他纺织材料制:					--Of other textile materials:
4420	6108.2910	---丝及绢丝制	14	0 澳门MO,冰岛IS,东盟AS,哥CR,秘鲁PE,香港HK,新加坡SG,新西兰NZ,智利CL 7 巴PK 8.4 澳AU 9.3 亚太AP 9.8 瑞士CH 11.2 韩国KR	0 受惠国$_{1}$LD$_{1}$	130	---Of silk or silk waste
4421	6108.2990	---其他	14	0 澳门MO,冰岛IS,东盟AS,哥CR,秘鲁PE,香港HK,新加坡SG,新西兰NZ,智利CL 7 巴PK 8.4 澳AU 9.3 亚太AP 9.8 瑞士CH 11.2 韩国KR	0 受惠国$_{1}$LD$_{1}$	130	---Other
		-睡衣及睡衣裤:					-Nightdresses and pyjamas:
4422	6108.3100	--棉制	14	0 澳门MO,冰岛IS,东盟AS,哥CR,香港HK,新加坡SG,新西兰NZ,智利CL 4.2 秘鲁PE 8.4 澳AU 9.8 瑞士CH 11.2 巴PK,韩国KR	0 柬埔寨KH,老挝LA,缅甸MM,受惠国LD 5.6 亚太AP	90	--Of cotton
4423	6108.3200	--化学纤维制	16	0 澳门MO,冰岛IS,东盟AS,哥CR,香港HK,新加坡SG,新西兰NZ,智利CL 4.8 秘鲁PE 8 巴PK 9.6 澳AU 10.9 亚太AP 11.2 瑞士CH 12.8 韩国KR	0 受惠国LD,亚太AP	130	--Of man-made fibres
		--其他纺织材料制:					--Of other textile materials:
4424	6108.3910	---丝及绢丝制	14	0 冰岛IS,东盟AS,哥CR,秘鲁PE,香港HK,新加坡SG,新西兰NZ,智利CL 7 巴PK 8.4 澳AU 9.3 亚太AP 9.8 瑞士CH 11.2 韩国KR	0 受惠国LD,亚太AP	130	---Of silk or silk waste

序号 No.	税则号列 Tariff Line	中文货品名称 Article Description in Chinese	最惠国税率 MFN(%)	协定税率 Agreement(%)	特惠税率 SP(%)	普通税率 Gen(%)	英文货品名称 Article Description
4425	6108.3990	---其他	14	0 冰岛IS,东盟AS,哥CR,秘鲁PE,香港HK,新加坡SG,新西兰NZ,智利CL 7 巴PK 8.4 澳AU 9.3 亚太AP 9.8 瑞士CH 11.2 韩国KR	0 受惠国LD,亚太AP	130	---Other
		-其他:					-Other:
4426	6108.9100	--棉制	14	0 澳门MO,冰岛IS,东盟AS,哥CR,香港HK,新加坡SG,新西兰NZ,智利CL 4.2 秘鲁PE 8.4 澳AU 9.8 瑞士CH 11.2 巴PK,韩国KR	0 柬埔寨KH,老挝LA,缅甸MM,受惠国LD	90	--Of cotton
4427	6108.9200	--化学纤维制	16	0 澳门MO,冰岛IS,东盟AS,哥CR,香港HK,新加坡SG,新西兰NZ,智利CL 4.8 秘鲁PE 8 巴PK 9.6 澳AU 10.9 亚太AP 11.2 瑞士CH 12.8 韩国KR	0 受惠国LD	130	--Of man-made fibres
4428	6108.9900	--其他纺织材料制	14	0 澳门MO,冰岛IS,东盟AS,哥CR,秘鲁PE,香港HK,新加坡SG,新西兰NZ,智利CL 7 巴PK 8.4 澳AU 9.3 亚太AP 9.8 瑞士CH 11.2 韩国KR	0 受惠国[1]LD[1]	130	--Of other textile materials
	61.09	**针织或钩编的T恤衫、汗衫及其他背心:**					**T-shirts, singlets and other vests, knitted or crocheted:**
4429	6109.1000	-棉制	14	0 澳门MO,冰岛IS,东盟AS,哥CR,香港HK,新加坡SG,新西兰NZ,智利CL 4.2 秘鲁PE 8.4 澳AU,韩国KR 9.4 巴PK,亚太AP 9.8 瑞士CH	0 柬埔寨KH,老挝LA,缅甸MM,受惠国LD	90	-Of cotton
		-其他纺织材料制:					-Of other textile materials:
4430	6109.9010	---丝及绢丝制	14	0 澳门MO,冰岛IS,东盟AS,哥CR,秘鲁PE,香港HK,新加坡SG,新西兰NZ,智利CL 7 巴PK 8.4 澳AU 9.3 亚太AP 9.8 瑞士CH 11.2 韩国KR	0 受惠国LD,亚太AP	130	---Of silk or silk waste
4431	6109.9090	---其他	14	0 澳门MO,冰岛IS,东盟AS,哥CR,香港HK,新加坡SG,新西兰NZ,智利CL 4.2 秘鲁PE 8.4 澳AU 9.3 巴PK,亚太AP 9.8 瑞士CH 11.2 韩国KR	0 柬埔寨KH,老挝LA,缅甸MM,受惠国LD,亚太AP	130	---Other

序号 No.	税则号列 Tariff Line	中文货品名称 Article Description in Chinese	最惠国税率 MFN(%)	协定税率 Agreement(%)	特惠税率 SP(%)	普通税率 Gen(%)	英文货品名称 Article Description
	61.10	针织或钩编的套头衫、开襟衫、背心及类似品：					**Jerseys, pullovers, cardigans, waistcoats and similar articles, knitted or crocheted:**
		-羊毛或动物细毛制：					-Of wool or fine animal hair:
4432	6110.1100	--羊毛制	14	0 澳门MO,巴PK,冰岛IS,东盟AS,哥CR,台湾TW,香港HK,新加坡SG,新西兰NZ,智利CL 4.2 秘鲁PE 8.4 澳AU,韩国KR 9.3 亚太AP 9.8 瑞士CH	0 柬埔寨KH,老挝LA,缅甸MM,受惠国LD,亚太AP	130	--Of wool
4433	6110.1200	--喀什米尔山羊细毛制	14∆7	0 澳门MO,巴PK,冰岛IS,东盟AS,哥CR,秘鲁PE,香港HK,新加坡SG,新西兰NZ,智利CL 8.4 澳AU 9.3 亚太AP 9.8 瑞士CH 11.2 韩国KR	0 受惠国LD	130	--Of kashmir (cashmere) goats
		--其他：					--Other:
4434	6110.1910	---其他山羊细毛制	14	0 澳门MO,巴PK,冰岛IS,东盟AS,哥CR,秘鲁PE,香港HK,新加坡SG,新西兰NZ,智利CL 8.4 澳AU 9.3 亚太AP 9.8 瑞士CH 11.2 韩国KR	0 受惠国LD	130	---Of other goats
4435	6110.1920	---兔毛制	14	0 澳门MO,巴PK,冰岛IS,东盟AS,哥CR,秘鲁PE,香港HK,新加坡SG,新西兰NZ,智利CL 8.4 澳AU 9.3 亚太AP 9.8 瑞士CH 11.2 韩国KR	0 受惠国$_1$LD$_1$	130	---Of rabbit and hare
4436	6110.1990	---其他	14	0 澳门MO,巴PK,冰岛IS,东盟AS,哥CR,香港HK,新加坡SG,新西兰NZ,智利CL 4.2 秘鲁PE 8.4 澳AU 9.3 亚太AP 9.8 瑞士CH 11.2 韩国KR	0 受惠国LD	130	---Other
4437	6110.2000	-棉制	14	0 澳门MO,巴PK,冰岛IS,东盟AS,哥CR,台湾TW,香港HK,新加坡SG,新西兰NZ,智利CL 4.2 秘鲁PE 8.4 澳AU 9.8 瑞士CH 11 亚太AP 11.2 韩国KR	0 柬埔寨KH,老挝LA,缅甸MM,受惠国LD 5.6 亚太AP	90	-Of cotton
4438	6110.3000	-化学纤维制	16	0 澳门MO,巴PK,冰岛IS,东盟AS,哥CR,台湾TW,香港HK,新加坡SG,新西兰NZ,智利CL 4.8 秘鲁PE 9.6 澳AU 10.9 亚太AP 11.2 瑞士CH 13.8 韩国KR	0 受惠国LD,亚太AP	130	-Of man-made fibres
		-其他纺织材料制：					-Of other textile materials:

序号 No.	税则号列 Tariff Line	中文货品名称 Article Description in Chinese	最惠国税率 MFN(%)	协定税率 Agreement(%)	特惠税率 SP(%)	普通税率 Gen(%)	英文货品名称 Article Description
4439	6110.9010	---丝及绢丝制	14	0 澳门MO,巴PK,冰岛IS,东盟AS,哥CR,秘鲁PE,香港HK,新加坡SG,新西兰NZ,智利CL 8.4 澳AU 9.3 亚太AP 9.8 瑞士CH 11.2 韩国KR	0 受惠国LD,亚太AP	130	---Of silk or silk waste
4440	6110.9090	---其他	14	0 澳门MO,巴PK,冰岛IS,东盟AS,哥CR,香港HK,新加坡SG,新西兰NZ,智利CL 4.2 秘鲁PE 8.4 澳AU 9.3 亚太AP 9.8 瑞士CH 11.2 韩国KR	0 受惠国LD,亚太AP	130	---Other
	61.11	**针织或钩编的婴儿服装及衣着附件:**					**Babies' garments and clothing accessories, knitted or crocheted:**
4441	6111.2000	-棉制	14	0 澳门MO,冰岛IS,东盟AS,哥CR,秘鲁PE,香港HK,新加坡SG,新西兰NZ,智利CL 8.4 澳AU 9.8 瑞士CH 11.2 巴PK,韩国KR	0 受惠国LD	90	-Of cotton
4442	6111.3000	-合成纤维制	16	0 澳门MO,冰岛IS,东盟AS,哥CR,香港HK,新加坡SG,新西兰NZ,智利CL 4.8 秘鲁PE 8 巴PK 9.6 澳AU 10.9 亚太AP 11.2 瑞士CH 12.8 韩国KR	0 受惠国LD	130	-Of synthetic fibres
		-其他纺织材料制:					-Of other textile materials:
4443	6111.9010	---羊毛或动物细毛制	14	0 澳门MO,冰岛IS,东盟AS,哥CR,秘鲁PE,香港HK,新加坡SG,新西兰NZ,智利CL 7 巴PK 8.4 澳AU 9.3 亚太AP 9.8 瑞士CH 11.2 韩国KR	0 受惠国LD	130	---Of wool or fine animal hair
4444	6111.9090	---其他	14	0 澳门MO,冰岛IS,东盟AS,哥CR,香港HK,新加坡SG,新西兰NZ,智利CL 4.2 秘鲁PE 7 巴PK 8.4 澳AU 9.3 亚太AP 9.8 瑞士CH 11.2 韩国KR	0 受惠国LD	130	---Other
	61.12	**针织或钩编的运动服、滑雪服及游泳服:**					**Tracksuits, ski suits and swimwear, knitted or crocheted:**
		-运动服:					-Tracksuits:

序号 No.	税则号列 Tariff Line	中文货品名称 Article Description in Chinese	最惠国税率 MFN(%)	协定税率 Agreement(%)	特惠税率 SP(%)	普通税率 Gen(%)	英文货品名称 Article Description
4445	6112.1100	--棉制	16	0 澳门MO,冰岛IS,东盟AS,哥CR,香港HK,新加坡SG,新西兰NZ,智利CL 4.8 秘鲁PE 8 巴PK 9.6 澳AU 11.2 瑞士CH 12.8 韩国KR 13.6 亚太AP	0 受惠国$_1$LD$_1$	90	--Of cotton
4446	6112.1200	--合成纤维制	17.5	0 澳门MO,冰岛IS,东盟AS,哥CR,香港HK,新加坡SG,新西兰NZ,智利CL 5.2 秘鲁PE 8.8 巴PK 10.5 澳AU 12.3 瑞士CH,亚太AP 14 韩国KR	0 受惠国LD	130	--Of synthetic fibres
4447	6112.1900	--其他纺织材料制	16	0 澳门MO,冰岛IS,东盟AS,哥CR,香港HK,新加坡SG,新西兰NZ,智利CL 4.8 秘鲁PE 8 巴PK 9.6 澳AU 11.2 瑞士CH 11.7 亚太AP 12.8 韩国KR	0 受惠国$_1$LD$_1$	130	--Of other textile materials
		-滑雪服:					-Ski suits:
4448	6112.2010	---棉制	16	0 冰岛IS,东盟AS,哥CR,新加坡SG,新西兰NZ,智利CL 4.8 秘鲁PE 8 巴PK 9.6 澳AU 11.2 瑞士CH 12.8 韩国KR 13.6 亚太AP	0 受惠国LD	90	---Of cotton
4449	6112.2090	---其他	19	0 冰岛IS,东盟AS,哥CR,新加坡SG,新西兰NZ,智利CL 5.7 秘鲁PE 9.5 巴PK 11.4 澳AU 13.3 瑞士CH 13.6 亚太AP 15.2 韩国KR	0 受惠国$_1$LD$_1$	130	---Other
		-男式游泳服:					-Men' s or boys' swimwear:
4450	6112.3100	--合成纤维制	17.5	0 冰岛IS,东盟AS,哥CR,香港HK,新加坡SG,新西兰NZ,智利CL 5.2 秘鲁PE 8.8 巴PK 10.5 澳AU 12.3 瑞士CH,亚太AP 14 韩国KR	0 受惠国$_1$LD$_1$	130	--Of synthetic fibres

序号 No.	税则号列 Tariff Line	中文货品名称 Article Description in Chinese	最惠国税率 MFN(%)	协定税率 Agreement(%)	特惠税率 SP(%)	普通税率 Gen(%)	英文货品名称 Article Description
4451	6112.3900	--其他纺织材料制	16	0 冰岛IS,东盟AS,哥CR,香港HK,新加坡SG,新西兰NZ,智利CL 4.8 秘鲁PE 8 巴PK 9.6 澳AU 11.2 瑞士CH 11.7 亚太AP 12.8 韩国KR	0 受惠国$_1$LD$_1$	130	--Of other textile materials
		-女式游泳服:					-Women' s or girls' swimwear:
4452	6112.4100	--合成纤维制	17.5	0 冰岛IS,东盟AS,哥CR,台湾TW,香港HK,新加坡SG,新西兰NZ,智利CL 5.2 秘鲁PE 8.8 巴PK 10.5 澳AU 12.3 瑞士CH,亚太AP 14 韩国KR	0 受惠国$_1$LD$_1$	130	--Of synthetic fibres
4453	6112.4900	--其他纺织材料制	16	0 冰岛IS,东盟AS,哥CR,香港HK,新加坡SG,新西兰NZ,智利CL 4.8 秘鲁PE 8 巴PK 9.6 澳AU 11.2 瑞士CH 11.7 亚太AP 12.8 韩国KR	0 受惠国$_1$LD$_1$	130	--Of other textile materials
	61.13	**用税号59.03、59.06或59.07的针织物或钩编织物制成的服装**					**Garments, made up of knitted or crocheted fabrics of heading 5903, 5906 or 5907**
4454	6113.0000	用税号59.03、59.06或59.07的针织物或钩编织物制成的服装	16	0 澳门MO,冰岛IS,东盟AS,哥CR,香港HK,新加坡SG,新西兰NZ,智利CL 4.8 秘鲁PE 8 巴PK 9.6 澳AU 11.2 瑞士CH 11.7 亚太AP 12.8 韩国KR	0 受惠国LD,亚太AP	130	Garments, made up of knitted or crocheted fabrics of heading No.59.03, 59.06 or 59.07
	61.14	**针织或钩编的其他服装:**					**Other garments, knitted or crocheted:**
4455	6114.2000	-棉制	16	0 澳门MO,冰岛IS,东盟AS,哥CR,香港HK,新加坡SG,新西兰NZ,智利CL 9.6 澳AU 11.2 瑞士CH 12.8 巴PK,韩国KR	0 受惠国LD 6.4 亚太AP	90	-Of cotton
4456	6114.3000	-化学纤维制	17.5	0 澳门MO,冰岛IS,东盟AS,哥CR,香港HK,新加坡SG,新西兰NZ,智利CL 5.2 秘鲁PE 10.5 澳AU 12.3 瑞士CH 14 巴PK,韩国KR	0 受惠国LD	130	-Of man-made fibres
		-其他纺织材料制:					-Of other textile materials:
4457	6114.9010	---羊毛或动物细毛制	16	0 冰岛IS,东盟AS,哥CR,香港HK,新加坡SG,新西兰NZ,智利CL 4.8 秘鲁PE 9.6 澳AU 11.2 瑞士CH 12.8 巴PK,韩国KR	0 受惠国$_1$LD$_1$	130	---Of wool or fine animal hair

序号 No.	税则号列 Tariff Line	中文货品名称 Article Description in Chinese	最惠国税率 MFN(%)	协定税率 Agreement(%)	特惠税率 SP(%)	普通税率 Gen(%)	英文货品名称 Article Description
4458	6114.9090	---其他	16	0 冰岛IS,东盟AS,哥CR,香港HK,新加坡SG,新西兰NZ,智利CL 4.8 秘鲁PE 9.6 澳AU 11.2 瑞士CH 12.8 巴PK,韩国KR	0 受惠国$_1$LD$_1$	130	---Other
	61.15	**针织或钩编的连裤袜、紧身裤袜、长统袜、短袜及其他袜类，包括用以治疗静脉曲张的长统袜和无外绱鞋底的鞋类：**					**Pantyhose, tights, stockings, socks and other hosiery, including graduated compression hosiery (for example, stockings for varicose veins) and footwear without applied soles, knitted or crocheted:**
4459	6115.1000	-渐紧压袜类（例如，用以治疗静脉曲张的长统袜）	16	0 冰岛IS,东盟AS,哥CR,香港HK,新加坡SG,新西兰NZ,智利CL 4.8 秘鲁PE 8 巴PK 9.3 亚太AP 9.6 澳AU 11.5 瑞士CH 12.8 韩国KR	0 受惠国$_1$LD$_1$	130	-Stockings, gradually press tighted (including stockings for varicose veins and footwear without applied soles)
		-其他连裤袜及紧身裤袜：					-Other pantyhose and tights:
4460	6115.2100	--每根单丝细度在67分特以下的合成纤维制	16	0 澳门MO,冰岛IS,东盟AS,哥CR,香港HK,新加坡SG,新西兰NZ,智利CL 4.8 秘鲁PE 9.6 澳AU 11.2 瑞士CH 12.8 巴PK,韩国KR 14.4 亚太AP	0 受惠国$_1$LD$_1$	130	--Of synthetic fibres, measuring per single yarn less than 67 decitex
4461	6115.2200	--每根单丝细度在67分特及以上的合成纤维制	16	0 澳门MO,冰岛IS,东盟AS,哥CR,台湾TW,新加坡SG,新西兰NZ,智利CL 4.8 秘鲁PE 8 巴PK 9.6 澳AU 10.9 亚太AP 11.2 瑞士CH 12.8 韩国KR	0 受惠国$_1$LD$_1$	130	--Of synthetic fibres, measuring per single yarn 67 decitex or more
		--其他纺织材料制：					--Of other textile materials:
4462	6115.2910	---棉制	14	0 澳门MO,冰岛IS,东盟AS,哥CR,秘鲁PE,新加坡SG,新西兰NZ,智利CL 8.4 澳AU 9.8 瑞士CH 11.2 巴PK,韩国KR	0 受惠国LD	90	---Cotton
4463	6115.2990	---其他	14	0 澳门MO,冰岛IS,东盟AS,哥CR,秘鲁PE,台湾TW,新加坡SG,新西兰NZ,智利CL 7 巴PK 8.4 澳AU 9.3 亚太AP 9.8 瑞士CH 11.2 韩国KR	0 受惠国$_1$LD$_1$	130	---Other

序号 No.	税则号列 Tariff Line	中文货品名称 Article Description in Chinese	最惠国税率 MFN(%)	协定税率 Agreement(%)	特惠税率 SP(%)	普通税率 Gen(%)	英文货品名称 Article Description
4464	6115.3000	-女式长统袜及中统袜，每根单丝细度在67分特以下	14	0 冰岛IS,东盟AS,哥CR,秘鲁PE,新加坡SG,新西兰NZ,智利CL 7 巴PK 8.4 澳AU 9.3 亚太AP 9.8 瑞士CH 11.2 韩国KR	0 受惠国LD,亚太AP	130	-Women's full-length or knee-length hosiery, measuring per single yarn less than 67 decitex
		-其他：					-Other:
4465	6115.9400	--羊毛或动物细毛制	14	0 冰岛IS,东盟AS,哥CR,秘鲁PE,香港HK,新加坡SG,新西兰NZ,智利CL 8.4 澳AU 9.8 瑞士CH 11.2 巴PK,韩国KR	0 受惠国$_1$LD$_1$	130	--Of wool or fine animal hair
4466	6115.9500	--棉制	14	0 冰岛IS,东盟AS,哥CR,香港HK,新加坡SG,新西兰NZ,智利CL 4.2 秘鲁PE 8.4 澳AU 9.8 瑞士CH 11.2 巴PK,韩国KR	0 受惠国LD	90	--Of cotton
4467	6115.9600	--合成纤维制	16	0 冰岛IS,东盟AS,哥CR,香港HK,新加坡SG,新西兰NZ,智利CL 4.8 秘鲁PE 8 巴PK 9.6 澳AU 10.9 亚太AP 11.2 瑞士CH 12.8 韩国KR	0 受惠国LD	130	--Of synthetic fibres
4468	6115.9900	--其他纺织材料制	14	0 冰岛IS,东盟AS,哥CR,秘鲁PE,台湾TW,香港HK,新加坡SG,新西兰NZ,智利CL 7 巴PK 8.4 澳AU 9.3 亚太AP 9.8 瑞士CH 11.2 韩国KR	0 受惠国$_1$LD$_1$	130	--Of other textile materials
	61.16	**针织或钩编的分指手套、连指手套及露指手套：**					**Gloves, mittens and mitts, knitted or crocheted:**
4469	6116.1000	-用塑料或橡胶浸渍、涂布或包覆的	14	0 冰岛IS,东盟AS,哥CR,秘鲁PE,香港HK,新加坡SG,新西兰NZ,智利CL 8.4 澳AU 9.8 瑞士CH 11.2 韩国KR	0 受惠国LD	130	-Gloves impregnated, coated or covered with plastics or rubber
		-其他：					-Other:
4470	6116.9100	--羊毛或动物细毛制	14	0 冰岛IS,东盟AS,哥CR,秘鲁PE,香港HK,新加坡SG,新西兰NZ,智利CL 7 巴PK 8.4 澳AU 9.8 瑞士CH 11.2 韩国KR	0 受惠国LD	130	--Of wool of fine animal hair
4471	6116.9200	--棉制	14	0 澳门MO,冰岛IS,东盟AS,哥CR,秘鲁PE,香港HK,新加坡SG,新西兰NZ,智利CL 8.4 澳AU 9.8 瑞士CH 11.2 韩国KR	0 受惠国$_1$LD$_1$	90	--Of cotton

序号 No.	税则号列 Tariff Line	中文货品名称 Article Description in Chinese	最惠国税率 MFN(%)	协定税率 Agreement(%)	特惠税率 SP(%)	普通税率 Gen(%)	英文货品名称 Article Description
4472	6116.9300	--合成纤维制	16	0 澳门MO,冰岛IS,东盟AS,哥CR,香港HK,新加坡SG,新西兰NZ,智利CL 4.8 秘鲁PE 8 巴PK 9.6 澳AU 10.9 亚太AP 11.2 瑞士CH 12.8 韩国KR	0 受惠国LD	130	--Of synthetic fibres
4473	6116.9900	--其他纺织材料制	14	0 冰岛IS,东盟AS,哥CR,香港HK,新加坡SG,新西兰NZ,智利CL 4.2 秘鲁PE 8.4 澳AU 9.3 巴PK,亚太AP 9.8 瑞士CH 11.2 韩国KR	0 受惠国LD	130	--Of other textile materials
	61.17	**其他制成的针织或钩编的衣着附件;服装或衣着附件的针织或钩编的零件:**					**Other made-up clothing accessories, knitted or crocheted; knitted or crocheted parts of garments or of clothing accessories:**
		-披巾、头巾、围巾、披纱、面纱及类似品:					-Shawls, scarves, mufflers, mantillas, veils and the like:
		---动物细毛制:					---Of fine animal hair:
4474	6117.1011	----山羊绒制	14	0 巴PK,冰岛IS,东盟AS,哥CR,香港HK,新加坡SG,新西兰NZ,智利CL 4.2 秘鲁PE 8.4 澳AU 9.3 亚太AP 9.8 瑞士CH 11.2 韩国KR	0 受惠国LD	130	----Of cashmere
4475	6117.1019	----其他	14	0 巴PK,冰岛IS,东盟AS,哥CR,香港HK,新加坡SG,新西兰NZ,智利CL 4.2 秘鲁PE 8.4 澳AU 9.3 亚太AP 9.8 瑞士CH 11.2 韩国KR	0 受惠国LD	130	----Other
4476	6117.1020	---羊毛制	14	0 巴PK,冰岛IS,东盟AS,哥CR,香港HK,新加坡SG,新西兰NZ,智利CL 4.2 秘鲁PE 8.4 澳AU 9.3 亚太AP 9.8 瑞士CH 11.2 韩国KR	0 受惠国LD	130	---Of wool
4477	6117.1090	---其他	14	0 巴PK,冰岛IS,东盟AS,哥CR,香港HK,新加坡SG,新西兰NZ,智利CL 4.2 秘鲁PE 8.4 澳AU 9.3 亚太AP 9.8 瑞士CH 11.2 韩国KR	0 受惠国LD	130	---Other
		-其他附件:					-Other accessories:

序号 No.	税则号列 Tariff Line	中文货品名称 Article Description in Chinese	最惠国税率 MFN(%)	协定税率 Agreement(%)	特惠税率 SP(%)	普通税率 Gen(%)	英文货品名称 Article Description
4478	6117.8010	----领带及领结	14	0 巴PK,冰岛IS,东盟AS,哥CR,秘鲁PE,台湾TW,香港HK,新加坡SG,新西兰NZ,智利CL 8.4 澳AU 9.3 亚太AP 9.8 瑞士CH 11.2 韩国KR	0 受惠国LD	130	---Ties, bow ties and cravats
4479	6117.8090	----其他	14	0 巴PK,冰岛IS,东盟AS,哥CR,台湾TW,香港HK,新加坡SG,新西兰NZ,智利CL 4.2 秘鲁PE 8.4 澳AU 9.3 亚太AP 9.8 瑞士CH 11.2 韩国KR	0 受惠国LD	130	---Other
4480	6117.9000	-零件	14	0 澳门MO,巴PK,冰岛IS,东盟AS,哥CR,秘鲁PE,台湾TW,香港HK,新加坡SG,新西兰NZ,智利CL 7 亚太AP 8.4 澳AU 9.8 瑞士CH 11.2 韩国KR	0 受惠国LD	130	-Parts

第六十二章
非针织或非钩编的服装及衣着附件

注释：

一、本章仅适用于除絮胎以外任何纺织物的制成品，但不适用于针织品或钩编织品（税号 62.12 的除外）。

二、本章不包括：

（一）税号 63.09 的旧衣着或其他旧物品；

（二）矫形器具、外科手术带、疝气带及类似品（税号 90.21）。

三、税号 62.03 及 62.04 所称：

（一）"西服套装"，是指面料用相同的织物制成的两件套或三件套的下列成套服装：

一件人体上半身穿着的外套或短上衣，除袖子外，其面料数为四片或四片以上；也可附带一件西服背心，这件背心的前片面料应与套装其他各件的面料相同，后片料则应与外套或短上衣的衬里料相同；

以及一件人体下半身穿着的服装，即不带背带或护胸的长裤、马裤、短裤（游泳裤除外）、裙子或裙裤。

西服套装各件面料质地、颜色及构成必须相同，其款式也必须相同，尺寸大小还须相互般配，但可以用不同织物滚边（缝口上缝入长条织物）。

如果数件人体下半身穿着的服装同时进口或出口（例如，两条长裤、长裤与短裤、裙子或裙裤与长裤），构成西服套装下装的应是一条长裤，而对于女式西服套装，则应是一条裙子或裙裤，其他服装应分别归类。

所称"西服套装"，包括不论是否完全符合上述条件的下列配套服装：

1. 常礼服，由一件后襟下垂并下端开圆弧形叉的素色短上衣和一条条纹长裤组成；

2. 晚礼服（燕尾服），一般用黑色织物制成，上衣前襟较短且不闭合，背后有燕尾；

3. 无燕尾套装夜礼服，其中上衣款式与普通上衣相似（可以更为显露衬衣前胸），但有光滑丝质或仿丝质的翻领。

（二）"便服套装"，是指面料相同并作零售包装的下列成套服装（西服套装及税号 62.07 或 62.08 的物品除外）：

一件人体上半身穿着的服装，但背心除外，

Chapter 62
Articles of apparel and clothing accessories, not knitted or crocheted

Notes:

1. This Chapter applies only to made up articles of any textile fabric other than wadding, excluding knitted or rocheted articles (other than those of heading No.62.12).

2. This Chapter does not cover:

(a) Worn clothing or other worn articles of heading No.63. 09; or

(b) Orthopaedic appliances, surgical belts, trusses or the like (heading No.90.21).

3. For the purposes of headings Nos.62.03 and 62.04:

(a) The term "suit" means a set of garments composed of two or three pieces made up in respect of their outer surface, in identical fabric and comprising:

-one suit coat or jacket theouter shell of which, exclusive of sleeves, consists of four or more panels, designed to cover the upper part of the body, possibly with a tailored waistcoat in addition whose front panel is made from the same fabric as the lining of the suit coat or jacket; and

-one garment designed to cover the lower part of the body and consisting of trousers, breeches or shorts (other than swimwear), a skirt or a divided skirt, having neither braces nor bibs.

All of the components of a "suit" must be of the same fabricconstruction, colour and composition; they must also be of the same style and of corresponding or compatible size.However, these components may have piping (a strip of fabric sewn into the seam) in a different fabric.

If several separate components to cover the lower part of the body are presented together (for example, two pairs of trousers or trousers and shorts, or a skirt or divided skirt and trousers), the constituent lower part shall be the trousers, or, in the case of women's or girls'suits, the skirt or divided skirt, the other garments being considered separately.

The term "suit" includes the following sets of garments, whether or not they fulfil all the above conditions:

(1) morning dress, comprising a plain jacket (cutaway) with rounded tails hanging well down at the back and striped trousers;

(2) evening dress (tailcoat), generally made of black cloth, the jacket of which is relatively short at the front, does not close and has narrow skirts cut in at the hips and hanging down behind;

(3) dinner jacket suits, in which the jacket is similar in style to an ordinary jacket (though perhaps revealing more of the shirt front), but has shiny silk or imitation silk lapels.

(b) The term "ensemble" means a set of garments (other than suits and articles of heading No.62.07 or 62.08) composed of several pieces made up in identical fabric, put up for retail sale, and comprising:

-one garment designed to cover the upper part of the

因为背心可作为内衣;

以及一件或两件不同的人体下半身穿着的服装，即长裤、护胸背带工装裤、马裤、短裤（泳裤除外）、裙子或裙裤。

便服套装各件面料质地、款式、颜色及构成必须相同;尺寸大小也须相互般配。所称“便服套装”，不包括税号 62.11 的运动服及滑雪服。

四、对于税号 62.09:

（一）所称“婴儿服装及衣着附件”，是指用于身高不超过 86 厘米幼儿的服装;

（二）既可归入税号 62.09，也可归入本章其他税号的物品，应归入税号 62.09;

五、既可归入税号 62.10，也可归入本章其他税号的服装，除税号 62.09 所列的仍归入该税号外，其余的应一律归入税号 62.10。

六、税号 62.11 所称“滑雪服”，是指从整个外观和织物质地来看，主要在滑雪（速度滑雪和高山滑雪）时穿着的下列服装或成套服装:

（一）“滑雪连身服”，即上下身连在一起的单件服装;除袖子和领子外，滑雪连身服可有口袋或脚带;或

（二）“滑雪套装”，即由两件或三件构成一套并作零售包装的下列服装:

一件用一条拉链扣合的带风帽的厚夹克、防风衣、防风短上衣或类似的服装，可以附带一件背心;

以及一条不论是否过腰的长裤、一条马裤或一条护胸背带工装裤。

“滑雪套装”也可由一件类似以上（一）款所述的连身服和一件可套在连身服外面的有胎料背心组成。

“滑雪套装”各件颜色可以不同，但面料质地、款式及构成必须相同;尺寸大小也须相互般配。

七、正方形或近似正方形的围巾及围巾式样的物品，如果每边均不超过 60 厘米，应作为手帕归类（税号 62.13）。任何一边超过 60 厘米的手帕，应归入税号 62.14。

八、本章的服装，凡门襟为左压右的，应视为男式;右压左的，应视为女式。但本规定不适用于其式样已明显为男式或女式的服装。无法区别是男式还是女式的服装，应按女式服装归入有关税号。

body，with the exception of waistcoats which may also form a second upper garment，and

-one or two different garments，designed to cover the lower part of the body and consisting of trousers，bib and brace overalls，breeches，shorts（other than swimwear），a skirt or a divided skirt.

All of the components of an ensemble must be of the same fabric construction，style，colour and composition; they also must be of corresponding or compatible size. The term “ensemble” does not apply to track suits or ski suits，of heading No. 62.11.

4. For the purposes of heading No.62.09:

(a) The expression “babies' garments and clothing accessories” means articles for young children of a body height not exceeding 86cm;

(b) Articles which are，*prima facie*，classifiable both in heading No.62.09 and in other headings of this Chapter are to be classified in heading No.62.09.

5.Garments which are，*prima facie*，classifiable both in heading No.62.10 and in other headings of this Chapter，excluding heading No.62.09，are to be classified in heading No.62.10.

6.For the purposes of heading No.62.11，“ski suits” means garments or sets of garments which，by their general appearance and texture，are identifiable as intended to be worn principally for skiing (cross-country or alpine).They consist either of:

(a) a “ski overall”，that is，a one-piece garment designed to cover the upper and the lower parts of the body; in addition to sleeves and a collar the skioverall may have pockets or footstraps; or

(b) a “ski ensemble”，that is，a set of garments composed of two or three pieces，put up for retail sale and comprising:

-one garment such as an anorak，wind-cheater，wind-jacket or similar article，closed by a slide fastener (zipper)，possibly with a waistcoat in addition，and

-one pair of trousers whether or not extending above waist-level，one pair of breeches or one bib and brace overall.

The “ski ensemble” may also consist of an overall similar to the one mentioned in paragraph (a) above and a type of padded，sleeveless jacket worn over the overall.

All the components of a “ski ensemble” must be made up in a fabric of the same texture，style and composition whether or not of the same colour; they also must be of corresponding or compatible size.

7. Scarves and articles of the scarf type，square or approximately square，of which no side exceeds60cm，are to be classified as handkerchiefs (heading No.62.13). Handkerchiefs of which any side exceeds 60cm are to be classified in heading No.62.14.

8. Garments of this Chapter designed for left over right closure at the front shall be regarded as men's or boys' garments，and those designed for right over left closure at the front as women's or girls' garments. These provisions do not apply where the cut of the garment clearly indicates

that it is designed for other of sexes.

Garments which cannot be identified as either men's or boys' garments or as women's or girls' garments are to be classified in the headings concerning women s or girls garments.

九、本章物品可用金属线制成。

9. Articles of this chapter may be made of metal thread.

序号 No.	税则号列 Tariff Line	中文货品名称 Article Description in Chinese	最惠国税率 MFN(%)	协定税率 Agreement(%)	特惠税率 SP(%)	普通税率 Gen(%)	英文货品名称 Article Description
	62.01	**男式大衣、短大衣、斗篷、短斗篷、带风帽的防寒短上衣(包括滑雪短上衣)、防风衣、防风短上衣及类似品,但税号62.03的货品除外:**					**Men' s or boys' overcoats, car coats, capes, cloaks, anoraks (including ski jackets) , windcheaters, wind-jackets and similar articles, other than those of heading 6203:**
		-大衣、雨衣、短大衣、斗篷、短斗篷及类似品:					-Overcoats, raincoats, car coats, capes, cloaks and similar articles:
4481	6201.1100	--羊毛或动物细毛制	16Δ8	0 澳门MO,冰岛IS,东盟AS,哥CR,香港HK,新加坡SG,新西兰NZ,智利CL 4.8 秘鲁PE 8 巴PK 9.6 澳AU 11.2 瑞士CH 11.7 亚太AP 12.8 韩国KR	0 受惠国LD	130	--Of wool or fine animal hair
		--棉制:					--Of cotton:
4482	6201.1210	---羽绒服	16	0 澳门MO,冰岛IS,东盟AS,哥CR,香港HK,新加坡SG,新西兰NZ,智利CL 4.8 秘鲁PE 9.6 澳AU 11.2 瑞士CH 12.8 巴PK,韩国KR	0 受惠国$_1$LD$_1$	90	---Padded with feathers or down
4483	6201.1290	---其他	16Δ8	0 澳门MO,冰岛IS,东盟AS,哥CR,香港HK,新加坡SG,新西兰NZ,智利CL 4.8 秘鲁PE 9.6 澳AU 11.2 瑞士CH 12.8 巴PK,韩国KR	0 受惠国LD	90	---Other
		--化学纤维制:					--Of man-made fibres:
4484	6201.1310	---羽绒服	17.5	0 澳门MO,冰岛IS,东盟AS,哥CR,香港HK,新加坡SG,新西兰NZ,智利CL 5.2 秘鲁PE 8.8 巴PK 10.5 澳AU 12.3 瑞士CH,亚太AP 14 韩国KR	0 受惠国LD	130	---Padded with feathers or down
4485	6201.1390	---其他	17.5	0 澳门MO,冰岛IS,东盟AS,哥CR,香港HK,新加坡SG,新西兰NZ,智利CL 5.2 秘鲁PE 8.8 巴PK 10.5 澳AU 12.3 瑞士CH,亚太AP 14 韩国KR	0 受惠国LD	130	---Other

序号 No.	税则号列 Tariff Line	中文货品名称 Article Description in Chinese	最惠国税率 MFN(%)	协定税率 Agreement(%)	特惠税率 SP(%)	普通税率 Gen(%)	英文货品名称 Article Description
4486	6201.1900	--其他纺织材料制	16	0 澳门MO,冰岛IS,东盟AS,哥CR,香港HK,新加坡SG,新西兰NZ,智利CL 4.8 秘鲁PE 8 巴PK 9.6 澳AU 11.2 瑞士CH 11.7 亚太AP 12.8 韩国KR	0 受惠国LD	100	--Of other textile materials
		-其他:					-Other:
4487	6201.9100	--羊毛或动物细毛制	16	0 澳门MO,冰岛IS,东盟AS,哥CR,香港HK,新加坡SG,新西兰NZ,智利CL 4.8 秘鲁PE 8 巴PK 9.6 澳AU 11.2 瑞士CH 11.7 亚太AP 12.8 韩国KR	0 受惠国LD	130	--Of wool or fine animal hair
		--棉制:					--Of cotton:
4488	6201.9210	---羽绒服	16	0 澳门MO,冰岛IS,东盟AS,哥CR,香港HK,新加坡SG,新西兰NZ,智利CL 4.8 秘鲁PE 9.6 澳AU 11.2 瑞士CH 12.8 巴PK,韩国KR	0 受惠国LD	90	---Padded with feathers or down
4489	6201.9290	---其他	16	0 澳门MO,冰岛IS,东盟AS,哥CR,香港HK,新加坡SG,新西兰NZ,智利CL 4.8 秘鲁PE 9.6 澳AU 11.2 瑞士CH 12.8 巴PK,韩国KR	0 柬埔寨KH,老挝LA,缅甸MM,受惠国LD	90	---Other
		--化学纤维制:					--Of man-made fibres:
4490	6201.9310	---羽绒服	17.5	0 澳门MO,冰岛IS,东盟AS,哥CR,香港HK,新加坡SG,新西兰NZ,智利CL 5.2 秘鲁PE 8.8 巴PK 10.5 澳AU 12.3 瑞士CH,亚太AP 14 韩国KR	0 受惠国LD	130	---Padded with feathers or down
4491	6201.9390	---其他	17.5	0 澳门MO,冰岛IS,东盟AS,哥CR,香港HK,新加坡SG,新西兰NZ,智利CL 5.2 秘鲁PE 8.8 巴PK 10.5 澳AU 12.3 瑞士CH,亚太AP 14 韩国KR	0 受惠国LD	130	---Other

序号 No.	税则号列 Tariff Line	中文货品名称 Article Description in Chinese	最惠国税率 MFN(%)	协定税率 Agreement(%)	特惠税率 SP(%)	普通税率 Gen(%)	英文货品名称 Article Description
4492	6201.9900	--其他纺织材料制	16	0 澳门MO,冰岛IS,东盟AS,哥CR,香港HK,新加坡SG,新西兰NZ,智利CL 4.8 秘鲁PE 8 巴PK 9.6 澳AU 11.2 瑞士CH 11.7 亚太AP 12.8 韩国KR	0 缅甸MM,受惠国LD	100	--Of other textile materials
	62.02	**女式大衣、短大衣、斗篷、短斗篷、带风帽的防寒短上衣(包括滑雪短上衣)、防风衣、防风短上衣及类似品，但税号62.04的货品除外：**					**Women' s or girls' overcoats, car coats, capes, cloaks, anoraks (including ski jackets) , windcheaters, wind-jackets and similar articles, other than those of heading 6204:**
		-大衣、雨衣、短大衣、斗篷、短斗篷及类似品:					-Overcoats, raincoats, car coats, capes, cloaks and similar articles:
4493	6202.1100	--羊毛或动物细毛制	16Δ8	0 澳门MO,冰岛IS,东盟AS,哥CR,香港HK,新加坡SG,新西兰NZ,智利CL 4.8 秘鲁PE 8 巴PK 9.6 澳AU 11.2 瑞士CH 11.7 亚太AP 12.8 韩国KR	0 受惠国LD	130	--Of wool or fine animal hair
		--棉制:					--Of cotton:
4494	6202.1210	---羽绒服	16	0 澳门MO,冰岛IS,东盟AS,哥CR,香港HK,新加坡SG,新西兰NZ,智利CL 4.8 秘鲁PE 9.6 澳AU 11.2 瑞士CH 12.8 巴PK,韩国KR	0 受惠国$_1$LD$_1$	90	---Padded with feathers or down
4495	6202.1290	---其他	16Δ8	0 澳门MO,冰岛IS,东盟AS,哥CR,香港HK,新加坡SG,新西兰NZ,智利CL 4.8 秘鲁PE 9.6 澳AU 11.2 瑞士CH 12.8 巴PK,韩国KR	0 受惠国LD	90	---Other
		--化学纤维制:					--Of man-made fibres:
4496	6202.1310	---羽绒服	19	0 澳门MO,冰岛IS,东盟AS,哥CR,香港HK,新加坡SG,新西兰NZ,智利CL 5.7 秘鲁PE 9.5 巴PK 11.4 澳AU 13.3 瑞士CH 13.6 亚太AP 15.2 韩国KR	0 受惠国LD	130	---Padded with feathers or down
4497	6202.1390	---其他	19	0 澳门MO,冰岛IS,东盟AS,哥CR,香港HK,新加坡SG,新西兰NZ,智利CL 5.7 秘鲁PE 9.5 巴PK 11.4 澳AU 13.3 瑞士CH 13.6 亚太AP 15.2 韩国KR	0 受惠国LD	130	---Other

序号 No.	税则号列 Tariff Line	中文货品名称 Article Description in Chinese	最惠国税率 MFN(%)	协定税率 Agreement(%)	特惠税率 SP(%)	普通税率 Gen(%)	英文货品名称 Article Description
4498	6202.1900	--其他纺织材料制	16	0 澳门MO,冰岛IS,东盟AS,哥CR,香港HK,新加坡SG,新西兰NZ,智利CL 4.8 秘鲁PE 8 巴PK 9.6 澳AU 11.2 瑞士CH 11.7 亚太AP 12.8 韩国KR	0 受惠国LD	100	--Of other textile materials
		-其他:					-Other:
4499	6202.9100	--羊毛或动物细毛制	16	0 澳门MO,冰岛IS,东盟AS,哥CR,香港HK,新加坡SG,新西兰NZ,智利CL 4.8 秘鲁PE 8 巴PK 9.6 澳AU 11.2 瑞士CH 11.7 亚太AP 12.8 韩国KR	0 受惠国$_1$LD$_1$	130	--Of wool or fine animal hair
		--棉制:					--Of cotton:
4500	6202.9210	---羽绒服	16	0 澳门MO,冰岛IS,东盟AS,哥CR,香港HK,新加坡SG,新西兰NZ,智利CL 4.8 秘鲁PE 9.6 澳AU 11.2 瑞士CH 12.8 巴PK,韩国KR	0 受惠国$_1$LD$_1$	90	---Padded with feathers or down
4501	6202.9290	---其他	16	0 澳门MO,冰岛IS,东盟AS,哥CR,香港HK,新加坡SG,新西兰NZ,智利CL 4.8 秘鲁PE 9.6 澳AU 11.2 瑞士CH 12.8 巴PK,韩国KR	0 受惠国LD	90	---Other
		--化学纤维制:					--Of man-made fibres:
4502	6202.9310	---羽绒服	17.5	0 澳门MO,冰岛IS,东盟AS,哥CR,香港HK,新加坡SG,新西兰NZ,智利CL 5.2 秘鲁PE 8.8 巴PK 10.5 澳AU 12.3 瑞士CH,亚太AP 14 韩国KR	0 受惠国LD	130	---Padded with feathers or down
4503	6202.9390	---其他	17.5	0 澳门MO,冰岛IS,东盟AS,哥CR,香港HK,新加坡SG,新西兰NZ,智利CL 5.2 秘鲁PE 8.8 巴PK 10.5 澳AU 12.3 瑞士CH,亚太AP 14 韩国KR	0 受惠国LD	130	---Other

序号 No.	税则号列 Tariff Line	中文货品名称 Article Description in Chinese	最惠国税率 MFN(%)	协定税率 Agreement(%)	特惠税率 SP(%)	普通税率 Gen(%)	英文货品名称 Article Description
4504	6202.9900	--其他纺织材料制	16	0 澳门MO,冰岛IS,东盟AS,哥CR,香港HK,新加坡SG,新西兰NZ,智利CL 4.8 秘鲁PE 8 巴PK 9.6 澳AU 11.2 瑞士CH 11.7 亚太AP 12.8 韩国KR	0 受惠国LD	100	--Of other textile materials
	62.03	**男式西服套装、便服套装、上衣、长裤、护胸背带工装裤、马裤及短裤（游泳裤除外）：**					**Men' s or boys' suits, ensembles, jackets, blazers, trousers, bib and brace overalls, breeches and shorts (other than swimwear) :**
		-西服套装:					-Suits:
4505	6203.1100	--羊毛或动物细毛制	17.5Δ10	0 澳门MO,冰岛IS,东盟AS,哥CR,瑞士CH,香港HK,新加坡SG,新西兰NZ,智利CL 5.2 秘鲁PE 8.8 巴PK 10.5 澳AU 12.3 亚太AP 14 韩国KR	0 受惠国LD	130	--Of wool or fine animal hair
4506	6203.1200	--合成纤维制	17.5	0 澳门MO,冰岛IS,东盟AS,哥CR,香港HK,新加坡SG,新西兰NZ,智利CL 5.2 秘鲁PE 8.8 巴PK 10.5 澳AU 12.3 瑞士CH,亚太AP 14 韩国KR	0 受惠国LD	130	--Of synthetic fibres
		--其他纺织材料制:					--Of other textile materials:
4507	6203.1910	---丝及绢丝制	17.5	0 澳门MO,冰岛IS,东盟AS,哥CR,香港HK,新加坡SG,新西兰NZ,智利CL 5.2 秘鲁PE 8.8 巴PK 10.5 澳AU 12.3 瑞士CH,亚太AP 14 韩国KR	0 受惠国$_1$LD$_1$	100	---Of silk or silk waste
4508	6203.1990	---其他	17.5	0 澳门MO,冰岛IS,东盟AS,哥CR,香港HK,新加坡SG,新西兰NZ,智利CL 5.2 秘鲁PE 8.8 巴PK 10.5 澳AU 12.3 亚太AP 12.6 瑞士CH 14 韩国KR	0 受惠国$_1$LD$_1$	100	---Other
		-便服套装:					-Ensembles:
4509	6203.2200	--棉制	17.5	0 澳门MO,冰岛IS,东盟AS,哥CR,香港HK,新加坡SG,新西兰NZ,智利CL 5.2 秘鲁PE 10.5 澳AU 12.3 瑞士CH 14 巴PK,韩国KR	0 受惠国LD	90	--Of cotton

序号 No.	税则号列 Tariff Line	中文货品名称 Article Description in Chinese	最惠国税率 MFN(%)	协定税率 Agreement(%)	特惠税率 SP(%)	普通税率 Gen(%)	英文货品名称 Article Description
4510	6203.2300	--合成纤维制	17.5	0 澳门MO,冰岛IS,东盟AS,哥CR,香港HK,新加坡SG,新西兰NZ,智利CL 5.2 秘鲁PE 8.8 巴PK 10.5 澳AU 12.3 瑞士CH,亚太AP 14 韩国KR	0 受惠国LD	130	--Of synthetic fibres
		--其他纺织材料制:					--Of other textile materials:
4511	6203.2910	---丝及绢丝制	17.5	0 澳门MO,冰岛IS,东盟AS,哥CR,新加坡SG,新西兰NZ,智利CL 5.2 秘鲁PE 8.8 巴PK 10.5 澳AU 12.3 瑞士CH,亚太AP 14 韩国KR	0 受惠国$_1$LD$_1$	130	---Of silk or silk waste
4512	6203.2920	---羊毛或动物细毛制	17.5	0 澳门MO,冰岛IS,东盟AS,哥CR,香港HK,新加坡SG,新西兰NZ,智利CL 5.2 秘鲁PE 8.8 巴PK 10.5 澳AU 12.3 瑞士CH,亚太AP 14 韩国KR	0 受惠国$_1$LD$_1$	130	---Of wool or fine animal hair
4513	6203.2990	---其他	17.5	0 澳门MO,冰岛IS,东盟AS,哥CR,香港HK,新加坡SG,新西兰NZ,智利CL 5.2 秘鲁PE 8.8 巴PK 10.5 澳AU 12.3 瑞士CH,亚太AP 14 韩国KR	0 受惠国$_1$LD$_1$	100	---Other
		-上衣:					-Jackets and blazers:
4514	6203.3100	--羊毛或动物细毛制	16Δ8	0 澳门MO,冰岛IS,东盟AS,哥CR,香港HK,新加坡SG,新西兰NZ,智利CL 4.8 秘鲁PE 8 巴PK 9.6 澳AU 11.2 瑞士CH 11.7 亚太AP 12.8 韩国KR	0 柬埔寨KH,老挝LA,缅甸MM,受惠国LD 9.6 亚太AP	130	--Of wool or fine animal hair
4515	6203.3200	--棉制	16	0 澳门MO,冰岛IS,东盟AS,哥CR,香港HK,新加坡SG,新西兰NZ,智利CL 4.8 秘鲁PE 9.6 澳AU 11.2 瑞士CH 12.8 巴PK,韩国KR 14.4 亚太AP	0 柬埔寨KH,老挝LA,缅甸MM,受惠国LD 11.2 亚太AP	90	--Of cotton
4516	6203.3300	--合成纤维制	17.5	0 澳门MO,冰岛IS,东盟AS,哥CR,香港HK,新加坡SG,新西兰NZ,智利CL 5.2 秘鲁PE 8.8 巴PK 10.5 澳AU,韩国KR 12.3 瑞士CH,亚太AP	0 受惠国LD	130	--Of synthetic fibres
		--其他纺织材料制:					--Of other textile materials:

序号 No.	税则号列 Tariff Line	中文货品名称 Article Description in Chinese	最惠国税率 MFN(%)	协定税率 Agreement(%)	特惠税率 SP(%)	普通税率 Gen(%)	英文货品名称 Article Description
4517	6203.3910	---丝及绢丝制	16	0 澳门MO,冰岛IS,东盟AS,哥CR,香港HK,新加坡SG,新西兰NZ,智利CL 4.8 秘鲁PE 8 巴PK 9.6 澳AU 11.2 瑞士CH 11.7 亚太AP 12.8 韩国KR	0 受惠国LD 9.6 亚太AP	130	---Of silk or silk waste
4518	6203.3990	---其他	16	0 澳门MO,冰岛IS,东盟AS,哥CR,香港HK,新加坡SG,新西兰NZ,智利CL 4.8 秘鲁PE 8 巴PK 9.6 澳AU 11.2 瑞士CH 11.7 亚太AP 12.8 韩国KR	0 受惠国LD 9.6 亚太AP	100	---Other
		-长裤、护胸背带工装裤、马裤及短裤:					-Trousers, bib and brace overalls, breeches and shorts:
4519	6203.4100	--羊毛或动物细毛制	16	0 澳门MO,冰岛IS,东盟AS,哥CR,瑞士CH,香港HK,新加坡SG,新西兰NZ,智利CL 4.8 秘鲁PE 8 巴PK 9.6 澳AU 11.7 亚太AP 12.8 韩国KR	0 受惠国LD,亚太AP	130	--Of wool or fine animal hair
		--棉制:					--Of cotton:
4520	6203.4210	---阿拉伯裤	16	0 澳门MO,冰岛IS,东盟AS,哥CR,香港HK,新加坡SG,新西兰NZ,智利CL 4.8 秘鲁PE 8 巴PK 9.6 澳AU 11.2 瑞士CH 12.8 韩国KR 12.9 亚太AP	0 受惠国$_1$LD$_1$ 11.2 亚太AP	90	---Arabian trousers
4521	6203.4290	---其他	16	0 澳门MO,冰岛IS,东盟AS,哥CR,香港HK,新加坡SG,新西兰NZ,智利CL 4.8 秘鲁PE 8 巴PK 9.6 澳AU 11.2 瑞士CH 12.8 韩国KR 12.9 亚太AP	0 柬埔寨KH,老挝LA,缅甸MM,受惠国LD 11.2 亚太AP	90	---Other
		--合成纤维制:					--Of synthetic fibres:
4522	6203.4310	---阿拉伯裤	17.5	0 澳门MO,冰岛IS,东盟AS,哥CR,香港HK,新加坡SG,新西兰NZ,智利CL 5.2 秘鲁PE 8.8 巴PK 10.5 澳AU 12.3 瑞士CH 13.1 亚太AP 14 韩国KR	0 受惠国$_1$LD$_1$	130	---Arabian trousers

序号 No.	税则号列 Tariff Line	中文货品名称 Article Description in Chinese	最惠国税率 MFN(%)	协定税率 Agreement(%)	特惠税率 SP(%)	普通税率 Gen(%)	英文货品名称 Article Description
4523	6203.4390	---其他	17.5	0 澳门MO,冰岛IS,东盟AS,哥CR,香港HK,新加坡SG,新西兰NZ,智利CL 5.2 秘鲁PE 8.8 巴PK 10.5 澳AU 12.3 瑞士CH 13.1 亚太AP 14 韩国KR	0 受惠国LD	130	---Other
		--其他纺织材料制:					--Of other textile materials:
4524	6203.4910	---阿拉伯裤	16	0 澳门MO,冰岛IS,东盟AS,哥CR,香港HK,新加坡SG,新西兰NZ,智利CL 4.8 秘鲁PE 8 巴PK 9.6 澳AU 11.2 瑞士CH 11.7 亚太AP 12.8 韩国KR	0 受惠国LD,亚太AP	100	---Arabian trousers
4525	6203.4990	---其他	16	0 澳门MO,冰岛IS,东盟AS,哥CR,香港HK,新加坡SG,新西兰NZ,智利CL 4.8 秘鲁PE 8 巴PK 9.6 澳AU 11.2 瑞士CH 11.7 亚太AP 12.8 韩国KR	0 受惠国LD,亚太AP	100	---Other
	62.04	**女式西服套装、便服套装、上衣、连衣裙、裙子、裙裤、长裤、护胸背带工装裤、马裤及短裤(游泳服除外):**					**Women' s or girls' suits, ensembles, jackets, blazers, dresses, skirts, divided skirts, trousers, bib and brace overalls, breeches and shorts (other than swimwear) :**
		-西服套装:					-Suits:
4526	6204.1100	--羊毛或动物细毛制	17.5Δ10	0 澳门MO,冰岛IS,东盟AS,哥CR,香港HK,新加坡SG,新西兰NZ,智利CL 5.2 秘鲁PE 8.8 巴PK 10.5 澳AU 12.3 瑞士CH,亚太AP 14 韩国KR	0 受惠国$_1$LD$_1$	130	--Of wool or fine animal hair
4527	6204.1200	--棉制	17.5	0 澳门MO,冰岛IS,东盟AS,哥CR,香港HK,新加坡SG,新西兰NZ,智利CL 5.2 秘鲁PE 10.5 澳AU 12.3 瑞士CH 14 巴PK,韩国KR	0 受惠国$_1$LD$_1$	90	--Of cotton
4528	6204.1300	--合成纤维制	17.5	0 澳门MO,冰岛IS,东盟AS,哥CR,香港HK,新加坡SG,新西兰NZ,智利CL 5.2 秘鲁PE 8.8 巴PK 10.5 澳AU 12.3 瑞士CH,亚太AP 14 韩国KR	0 受惠国$_1$LD$_1$	130	--Of synthetic fibres
		--其他纺织材料制:					--Of other textile materials:

序号 No.	税则号列 Tariff Line	中文货品名称 Article Description in Chinese	最惠国税率 MFN(%)	协定税率 Agreement(%)	特惠税率 SP(%)	普通税率 Gen(%)	英文货品名称 Article Description
4529	6204.1910	---丝及绢丝制	17.5	0 澳门MO,冰岛IS,东盟AS,哥CR,香港HK,新加坡SG,新西兰NZ,智利CL 5.2 秘鲁PE 8.8 巴PK 10.5 澳AU 12.3 瑞士CH,亚太AP 14 韩国KR	0 受惠国$_1$LD$_1$	100	---Of silk or silk waste
4530	6204.1990	---其他	17.5	0 澳门MO,冰岛IS,东盟AS,哥CR,香港HK,新加坡SG,新西兰NZ,智利CL 5.2 秘鲁PE 8.8 巴PK 10.5 澳AU 12.3 瑞士CH,亚太AP 14 韩国KR	0 受惠国$_1$LD$_1$	100	---Other
		-便服套装:					-Ensembles:
4531	6204.2100	--羊毛或动物细毛制	17.5	0 澳门MO,冰岛IS,东盟AS,哥CR,香港HK,新加坡SG,新西兰NZ,智利CL 5.2 秘鲁PE 8.8 巴PK 10.5 澳AU 12.3 瑞士CH,亚太AP 14 韩国KR	0 受惠国$_1$LD$_1$	130	--Of wool or fine animal hair
4532	6204.2200	--棉制	17.5	0 澳门MO,冰岛IS,东盟AS,哥CR,香港HK,新加坡SG,新西兰NZ,智利CL 5.2 秘鲁PE 10.5 澳AU 12.3 瑞士CH 14 巴PK,韩国KR	0 受惠国$_1$LD$_1$	90	--Of cotton
4533	6204.2300	--合成纤维制	20	0 澳门MO,冰岛IS,东盟AS,哥CR,香港HK,新加坡SG,新西兰NZ,智利CL 6 秘鲁PE 10 巴PK 12 澳AU 13.8 亚太AP 14 瑞士CH 17.3 韩国KR	0 受惠国$_1$LD$_1$	130	--Of synthetic fibres
		--其他纺织材料制:					--Of other textile materials:
4534	6204.2910	---丝及绢丝制	20	0 澳门MO,冰岛IS,东盟AS,哥CR,新加坡SG,新西兰NZ,智利CL 6 秘鲁PE 10 巴PK 12 澳AU 13.8 亚太AP 14 瑞士CH 17.3 韩国KR	0 受惠国$_1$LD$_1$	130	---Of silk or silk waste
4535	6204.2990	---其他	14	0 澳门MO,冰岛IS,东盟AS,哥CR,秘鲁PE,香港HK,新加坡SG,新西兰NZ,智利CL 7 巴PK 8.4 澳AU 9.8 瑞士CH 9.9 亚太AP 11.2 韩国KR	0 受惠国$_1$LD$_1$	100	---Other

序号 No.	税则号列 Tariff Line	中文货品名称 Article Description in Chinese	最惠国税率 MFN(%)	协定税率 Agreement(%)	特惠税率 SP(%)	普通税率 Gen(%)	英文货品名称 Article Description
		-上衣:					-Jackets and blazers:
4536	6204.3100	--羊毛或动物细毛制	16Δ8	0 澳门MO,冰岛IS,东盟AS,哥CR,香港HK,新加坡SG,新西兰NZ,智利CL 4.8 秘鲁PE 8 巴PK 9.6 澳AU 11.2 瑞士CH 11.7 亚太AP 12.8 韩国KR	0 受惠国LD	130	--Of wool or fine animal hair
4537	6204.3200	--棉制	16	0 澳门MO,冰岛IS,东盟AS,哥CR,香港HK,新加坡SG,新西兰NZ,智利CL 4.8 秘鲁PE 9.6 澳AU 11.2 瑞士CH 12.8 巴PK,韩国KR	0 柬埔寨KH,老挝LA,缅甸MM,受惠国LD 6.4 亚太AP	90	--Of cotton
4538	6204.3300	--合成纤维制	17.5	0 澳门MO,冰岛IS,东盟AS,哥CR,香港HK,新加坡SG,新西兰NZ,智利CL 5.2 秘鲁PE 8.8 巴PK 10.5 澳AU 12.3 瑞士CH,亚太AP 15.1 韩国KR	0 受惠国LD,亚太AP	130	--Of synthetic fibres
		--其他纺织材料制:					--Of other textile materials:
4539	6204.3910	---丝及绢丝制	16	0 澳门MO,冰岛IS,东盟AS,哥CR,香港HK,新加坡SG,新西兰NZ,智利CL 4.8 秘鲁PE 8 巴PK 9.6 澳AU 11.2 瑞士CH 11.7 亚太AP 12.8 韩国KR	0 受惠国LD,亚太AP	130	---Of silk or silk waste
4540	6204.3990	---其他	16	0 澳门MO,冰岛IS,东盟AS,哥CR,香港HK,新加坡SG,新西兰NZ,智利CL 4.8 秘鲁PE 8 巴PK 9.6 澳AU 11.2 瑞士CH 11.7 亚太AP 12.8 韩国KR	0 受惠国LD,亚太AP	100	---Other
		-连衣裙:					-Dresses:
4541	6204.4100	--羊毛或动物细毛制	16	0 澳门MO,冰岛IS,东盟AS,哥CR,香港HK,新加坡SG,新西兰NZ,智利CL 4.8 秘鲁PE 8 巴PK 9.6 澳AU 11.2 瑞士CH 11.7 亚太AP 12.8 韩国KR	0 受惠国LD	130	--Of wool or fine animal hair

序号 No.	税则号列 Tariff Line	中文货品名称 Article Description in Chinese	最惠国税率 MFN(%)	协定税率 Agreement(%)	特惠税率 SP(%)	普通税率 Gen(%)	英文货品名称 Article Description
4542	6204.4200	--棉制	16	0 澳门MO,冰岛IS,东盟AS,哥CR,香港HK,新加坡SG,新西兰NZ,智利CL 4.8 秘鲁PE 9.6 澳AU 11.2 瑞士CH 12.8 巴PK,韩国KR	0 柬埔寨KH,老挝LA,缅甸MM,受惠国LD	90	--Of cotton
4543	6204.4300	--合成纤维制	17.5	0 澳门MO,冰岛IS,东盟AS,哥CR,香港HK,新加坡SG,新西兰NZ,智利CL 5.2 秘鲁PE 8.8 巴PK 10.5 澳AU 12.3 瑞士CH,亚太AP 15.1 韩国KR	0 受惠国LD	130	--Of synthetic fibres
4544	6204.4400	--人造纤维制	16	0 澳门MO,冰岛IS,东盟AS,哥CR,香港HK,新加坡SG,新西兰NZ,智利CL 4.8 秘鲁PE 8 巴PK 9.6 澳AU 11.2 瑞士CH 11.7 亚太AP 12.8 韩国KR	0 受惠国LD	130	--Of artificial fibres
		--其他纺织材料制:					--Of other textile materials:
4545	6204.4910	---丝及绢丝制	16	0 澳门MO,冰岛IS,东盟AS,哥CR,香港HK,新加坡SG,新西兰NZ,智利CL 4.8 秘鲁PE 8 巴PK 9.6 澳AU 11.2 瑞士CH 11.7 亚太AP 12.8 韩国KR	0 受惠国LD	130	---Of silk or silk waste
4546	6204.4990	---其他	16	0 澳门MO,冰岛IS,东盟AS,哥CR,香港HK,新加坡SG,新西兰NZ,智利CL 4.8 秘鲁PE 8 巴PK 9.6 澳AU 11.2 瑞士CH 11.7 亚太AP 12.8 韩国KR	0 受惠国LD	100	---Other
		-裙子及裙裤:					-Skirts and divided skirts:
4547	6204.5100	--羊毛或动物细毛制	14	0 澳门MO,冰岛IS,东盟AS,哥CR,秘鲁PE,香港HK,新加坡SG,新西兰NZ,智利CL 7 巴PK 8.4 澳AU 9.3 亚太AP 9.8 瑞士CH 11.2 韩国KR	0 受惠国LD	130	--Of wool or fine animal hair
4548	6204.5200	--棉制	14	0 澳门MO,冰岛IS,东盟AS,哥CR,秘鲁PE,香港HK,新加坡SG,新西兰NZ,智利CL 8.4 澳AU 9.8 瑞士CH 11.2 巴PK,韩国KR	0 受惠国LD	90	--Of cotton

序号 No.	税则号列 Tariff Line	中文货品名称 Article Description in Chinese	最惠国税率 MFN(%)	协定税率 Agreement(%)	特惠税率 SP(%)	普通税率 Gen(%)	英文货品名称 Article Description
4549	6204.5300	--合成纤维制	16	0 澳门MO,冰岛IS,东盟AS,哥CR,香港HK,新加坡SG,新西兰NZ,智利CL 4.8 秘鲁PE 8 巴PK 9.6 澳AU 11.2 瑞士CH 11.7 亚太AP 12.8 韩国KR	0 受惠国LD	130	--Of synthetic fibres
		--其他纺织材料制:					--Of other textile materials:
4550	6204.5910	---丝及绢丝制	14	0 澳门MO,冰岛IS,东盟AS,哥CR,秘鲁PE,香港HK,新加坡SG,新西兰NZ,智利CL 7 巴PK 8.4 澳AU 9.3 亚太AP 9.8 瑞士CH 11.2 韩国KR	0 受惠国LD	130	---Of silk or silk waste
4551	6204.5990	---其他	14	0 澳门MO,冰岛IS,东盟AS,哥CR,香港HK,新加坡SG,新西兰NZ,智利CL 4.2 秘鲁PE 7 巴PK 8.4 澳AU 9.3 亚太AP 9.8 瑞士CH 11.2 韩国KR	0 受惠国LD	100	---Other
		-长裤、护胸背带工装裤、马裤及短裤:					-Trousers, bib and brace overalls, breeches and shorts:
4552	6204.6100	--羊毛或动物细毛制	16	0 澳门MO,冰岛IS,东盟AS,哥CR,香港HK,新加坡SG,新西兰NZ,智利CL 4.8 秘鲁PE 8 巴PK 9.6 澳AU 11.2 瑞士CH 11.7 亚太AP 12.8 韩国KR	0 受惠国LD	130	--Of wool or fine animal hair
4553	6204.6200	--棉制	16	0 澳门MO,冰岛IS,东盟AS,哥CR,香港HK,新加坡SG,新西兰NZ,智利CL 4.8 秘鲁PE 9.6 澳AU,韩国KR 11.2 瑞士CH 12.8 巴PK 14.4 亚太AP	0 柬埔寨KH,老挝LA,缅甸MM,受惠国LD 11.2 亚太AP	90	--Of cotton
4554	6204.6300	--合成纤维制	17.5	0 澳门MO,冰岛IS,东盟AS,哥CR,香港HK,新加坡SG,新西兰NZ,智利CL 5.2 秘鲁PE 8.8 巴PK 10.5 澳AU 12.3 瑞士CH,亚太AP 14 韩国KR	0 受惠国LD	130	--Of synthetic fibres

序号 No.	税则号列 Tariff Line	中文货品名称 Article Description in Chinese	最惠国税率 MFN(%)	协定税率 Agreement(%)	特惠税率 SP(%)	普通税率 Gen(%)	英文货品名称 Article Description
4555	6204.6900	--其他纺织材料制	16	0 澳门MO,冰岛IS,东盟AS,哥CR,香港HK,新加坡SG,新西兰NZ,智利CL 4.8 秘鲁PE 8 巴PK 9.6 澳AU 11.2 瑞士CH 12 亚太AP 12.8 韩国KR	0 受惠国LD	100	--Of other textile materials
	62.05	**男衬衫:**					**Men' s or boys' shirts:**
4556	6205.2000	-棉制	16	0 澳门MO,冰岛IS,东盟AS,哥CR,香港HK,新加坡SG,新西兰NZ,智利CL 4.8 秘鲁PE 8 巴PK,亚太AP 9.6 澳AU 11.2 瑞士CH 12.8 韩国KR	0 柬埔寨KH,老挝LA,缅甸MM,受惠国LD 6.4 亚太AP	90	-Of cotton
4557	6205.3000	-化学纤维制	16	0 澳门MO,冰岛IS,东盟AS,哥CR,香港HK,新加坡SG,新西兰NZ,智利CL 4.8 秘鲁PE 8 巴PK 9.6 澳AU 11.2 瑞士CH 11.7 亚太AP 12.8 韩国KR	0 受惠国LD,亚太AP	130	-Of man-made fibres
4558	6205.9010	---丝及绢丝制	16	0 澳门MO,冰岛IS,东盟AS,哥CR,香港HK,新加坡SG,新西兰NZ,智利CL 4.8 秘鲁PE 8 巴PK 9.6 澳AU 11.2 瑞士CH 11.7 亚太AP 12.8 韩国KR	0 受惠国LD,亚太AP	130	---Of silk or silk waste
4559	6205.9020	---羊毛或动物细毛制	16	0 澳门MO,冰岛IS,东盟AS,哥CR,香港HK,新加坡SG,新西兰NZ,智利CL 4.8 秘鲁PE 8 巴PK 9.6 澳AU 11.2 瑞士CH 11.7 亚太AP 12.8 韩国KR	0 受惠国LD,亚太AP	100	---Of wool or fine animal hair
4560	6205.9090	---其他	16	0 澳门MO,冰岛IS,东盟AS,哥CR,香港HK,新加坡SG,新西兰NZ,智利CL 4.8 秘鲁PE 8 巴PK 9.6 澳AU 11.2 瑞士CH 11.7 亚太AP 12.8 韩国KR	0 受惠国LD,亚太AP	100	---Other
	62.06	**女衬衫:**					**Women' s or girls' blouses, shirts and shirt-blouses:**

序号 No.	税则号列 Tariff Line	中文货品名称 Article Description in Chinese	最惠国税率 MFN(%)	协定税率 Agreement(%)	特惠税率 SP(%)	普通税率 Gen(%)	英文货品名称 Article Description
4561	6206.1000	-丝及绢丝制	16	0 澳门MO,冰岛IS,东盟AS,哥CR,香港HK,新加坡SG,新西兰NZ,智利CL 4.8 秘鲁PE 8 巴PK 9.6 澳AU 11.2 瑞士CH 11.7 亚太AP 12.8 韩国KR	0 受惠国LD	130	-Of silk or silk waste
4562	6206.2000	-羊毛或动物细毛制	16	0 澳门MO,冰岛IS,东盟AS,哥CR,香港HK,新加坡SG,新西兰NZ,智利CL 4.8 秘鲁PE 8 巴PK 9.6 澳AU 11.2 瑞士CH 11.7 亚太AP 12.8 韩国KR	0 受惠国$_1$LD$_1$	130	-Of wool or fine animal hair
4563	6206.3000	-棉制	16	0 澳门MO,冰岛IS,东盟AS,哥CR,香港HK,新加坡SG,新西兰NZ,智利CL 4.8 秘鲁PE 8 巴PK 9.6 澳AU 11.2 瑞士CH 12.8 韩国KR 13.6 亚太AP	0 柬埔寨KH,老挝LA,缅甸MM,受惠国LD 6.4 亚太AP	90	-Of cotton
4564	6206.4000	-化学纤维制	17.5	0 澳门MO,冰岛IS,东盟AS,哥CR,香港HK,新加坡SG,新西兰NZ,智利CL 5.2 秘鲁PE 8.8 巴PK 10.5 澳AU 12.3 瑞士CH,亚太AP 14 韩国KR	0 受惠国LD	130	-Of man-made fibres
4565	6206.9000	-其他纺织材料制	16	0 澳门MO,冰岛IS,东盟AS,哥CR,香港HK,新加坡SG,新西兰NZ,智利CL 4.8 秘鲁PE 8 巴PK 9.6 澳AU 11.2 瑞士CH 11.7 亚太AP 12.8 韩国KR	0 受惠国LD,亚太AP	100	-Of other textile materials
	62.07	**男式背心及其他内衣、内裤、三角裤、长睡衣、睡衣裤、浴衣、晨衣及类似品：**					**Men' s or boys' singlets and other vests, underpants, briefs, nightshirts, pyjamas, bathrobes, dressing gowns and similar articles:**
		-内裤及三角裤：					-Underpants and briefs:
4566	6207.1100	--棉制	14	0 澳门MO,冰岛IS,东盟AS,哥CR,香港HK,新加坡SG,新西兰NZ,智利CL 4.2 秘鲁PE 7 巴PK 8.4 澳AU 9.8 瑞士CH 10.3 亚太AP 11.2 韩国KR	0 受惠国LD	90	--Of cotton
		--其他纺织材料制：					--Of other textile materials:

序号 No.	税则号列 Tariff Line	中文货品名称 Article Description in Chinese	最惠国税率 MFN(%)	协定税率 Agreement(%)	特惠税率 SP(%)	普通税率 Gen(%)	英文货品名称 Article Description
4567	6207.1910	---丝及绢丝制	14	0 澳门MO,冰岛IS,东盟AS,哥CR,秘鲁PE,香港HK,新加坡SG,新西兰NZ,智利CL 7 巴PK 8.4 澳AU 9.8 瑞士CH 11.2 韩国KR	0 受惠国$_1$LD$_1$	130	---Of silk or silk waste
4568	6207.1920	---化学纤维制	16	0 澳门MO,冰岛IS,东盟AS,哥CR,香港HK,新加坡SG,新西兰NZ,智利CL 4.8 秘鲁PE 9.6 澳AU 11.2 瑞士CH 12.8 巴PK,韩国KR	0 受惠国$_1$LD$_1$	130	---Of man-made fibres
4569	6207.1990	---其他	14	0 澳门MO,冰岛IS,东盟AS,哥CR,秘鲁PE,香港HK,新加坡SG,新西兰NZ,智利CL 7 巴PK 8.4 澳AU 9.8 瑞士CH 11.2 韩国KR	0 受惠国$_1$LD$_1$	100	---Other
		-长睡衣及睡衣裤:					-Nightshirts and pyjamas:
4570	6207.2100	--棉制	14	0 澳门MO,冰岛IS,东盟AS,哥CR,秘鲁PE,香港HK,新加坡SG,新西兰NZ,智利CL 8.4 澳AU 9.8 瑞士CH 11.2 巴PK,韩国KR	0 柬埔寨KH,老挝LA,缅甸MM,受惠国LD	90	--Of cotton
4571	6207.2200	--化学纤维制	16	0 澳门MO,冰岛IS,东盟AS,哥CR,香港HK,新加坡SG,新西兰NZ,智利CL 4.8 秘鲁PE 9.6 澳AU 11.2 瑞士CH 12.8 巴PK,韩国KR	0 受惠国$_1$LD$_1$	130	--Of man-made fibres
		--其他纺织材料制:					--Of other textile materials:
4572	6207.2910	---丝及绢丝制	14	0 冰岛IS,东盟AS,哥CR,秘鲁PE,新加坡SG,新西兰NZ,智利CL 7 巴PK 8.4 澳AU 9.8 瑞士CH 11.2 韩国KR	0 受惠国$_1$LD$_1$	130	---Of silk or silk waste
4573	6207.2990	---其他	14	0 冰岛IS,东盟AS,哥CR,秘鲁PE,新加坡SG,新西兰NZ,智利CL 7 巴PK 8.4 澳AU 9.8 瑞士CH 11.2 韩国KR	0 柬埔寨KH,老挝LA,缅甸MM,受惠国LD	100	---Other
		-其他:					-Other:
4574	6207.9100	--棉制	14	0 澳门MO,冰岛IS,东盟AS,哥CR,秘鲁PE,香港HK,新加坡SG,新西兰NZ,智利CL 8.4 澳AU 9.8 瑞士CH 11.2 巴PK,韩国KR	0 受惠国LD	90	--Of cotton
		--其他纺织材料制:					--Of other textile materials:

序号 No.	税则号列 Tariff Line	中文货品名称 Article Description in Chinese	最惠国税率 MFN(%)	协定税率 Agreement(%)	特惠税率 SP(%)	普通税率 Gen(%)	英文货品名称 Article Description
4575	6207.9910	---丝及绢丝制	14	0 澳门MO,冰岛IS,东盟AS,哥CR,秘鲁PE,香港HK,新加坡SG,新西兰NZ,智利CL 7 巴PK 8.4 澳AU 9.8 瑞士CH 11.2 韩国KR 12.6 亚太AP	0 受惠国$_1$LD$_1$	130	---Of silk or silk waste
4576	6207.9920	---化学纤维制	16	0 澳门MO,冰岛IS,东盟AS,哥CR,香港HK,新加坡SG,新西兰NZ,智利CL 4.8 秘鲁PE 9.6 澳AU 11.2 瑞士CH 12.8 巴PK,韩国KR	0 受惠国LD	130	---Of man-made fibres
4577	6207.9990	---其他	14	0 澳门MO,冰岛IS,东盟AS,哥CR,秘鲁PE,香港HK,新加坡SG,新西兰NZ,智利CL 7 巴PK 8.4 澳AU 9.8 瑞士CH 11.2 韩国KR 12.6 亚太AP	0 受惠国LD	100	---Other
	62.08	**女式背心及其他内衣、长衬裙、衬裙、三角裤、短衬裤、睡衣、睡衣裤、浴衣、晨衣及类似品:**					**Women' s or girls' singlets and other vests, slips, petticoats, briefs, panties, nightdresses, pyjamas, négligés, bathrobes, dressing gowns and similar articles:**
		-长衬裙及衬裙:					-Slips and petticoats:
4578	6208.1100	--化学纤维制	16	0 冰岛IS,东盟AS,哥CR,香港HK,新加坡SG,新西兰NZ,智利CL 4.8 秘鲁PE 9.6 澳AU 11.2 瑞士CH 12.8 巴PK,韩国KR	0 受惠国$_1$LD$_1$	130	--Of man-made fibresr
		--其他纺织材料制:					--Of other textile materials:
4579	6208.1910	---丝及绢丝制	14	0 冰岛IS,东盟AS,哥CR,秘鲁PE,香港HK,新加坡SG,新西兰NZ,智利CL 7 巴PK 8.4 澳AU 9.8 瑞士CH 11.2 韩国KR	0 受惠国$_1$LD$_1$	130	---Of silk or silk waste
4580	6208.1920	---棉制	14	0 冰岛IS,东盟AS,哥CR,秘鲁PE,香港HK,新加坡SG,新西兰NZ,智利CL 7 巴PK 8.4 澳AU 9.8 瑞士CH 11.2 韩国KR	0 受惠国LD	90	---Of cotton
4581	6208.1990	---其他	14	0 冰岛IS,东盟AS,哥CR,秘鲁PE,香港HK,新加坡SG,新西兰NZ,智利CL 7 巴PK 8.4 澳AU 9.8 瑞士CH 11.2 韩国KR	0 受惠国$_1$LD$_1$	100	---Other
		-睡衣及睡衣裤:					-Nightdresses and pyjamas:

序号 No.	税则号列 Tariff Line	中文货品名称 Article Description in Chinese	最惠国税率 MFN(%)	协定税率 Agreement(%)	特惠税率 SP(%)	普通税率 Gen(%)	英文货品名称 Article Description
4582	6208.2100	--棉制	14	0 澳门MO,冰岛IS,东盟AS,哥CR,秘鲁PE,香港HK,新加坡SG,新西兰NZ,智利CL 7 巴PK 8.4 澳AU 9.8 瑞士CH 10.3 亚太AP 11.2 韩国KR	0 柬埔寨KH,老挝LA,缅甸MM,受惠国LD	90	--Of cotton
4583	6208.2200	--化学纤维制	16	0 澳门MO,冰岛IS,东盟AS,哥CR,香港HK,新加坡SG,新西兰NZ,智利CL 4.8 秘鲁PE 9.6 澳AU 11.2 瑞士CH 12.8 巴PK,韩国KR	0 柬埔寨KH,老挝LA,缅甸MM,受惠国LD	130	--Of man-made fibres
		--其他纺织材料制:					--Of other textile materials:
4584	6208.2910	---丝及绢丝制	14	0 冰岛IS,东盟AS,哥CR,秘鲁PE,香港HK,新加坡SG,新西兰NZ,智利CL 7 巴PK 8.4 澳AU 9.8 瑞士CH 11.2 韩国KR	0 受惠国$_1$LD$_1$	130	---Of silk or silk waste
4585	6208.2990	---其他	14	0 冰岛IS,东盟AS,哥CR,秘鲁PE,香港HK,新加坡SG,新西兰NZ,智利CL 7 巴PK 8.4 澳AU 9.8 瑞士CH 11.2 韩国KR	0 受惠国$_1$LD$_1$	100	---Other
		-其他:					-Other:
4586	6208.9100	--棉制	14	0 澳门MO,冰岛IS,东盟AS,哥CR,香港HK,新加坡SG,新西兰NZ,智利CL 4.2 秘鲁PE 8.4 澳AU 9.8 瑞士CH 11.2 巴PK,韩国KR	0 柬埔寨KH,老挝LA,缅甸MM,受惠国LD	90	--Of cotton
4587	6208.9200	--化学纤维制	16	0 澳门MO,冰岛IS,东盟AS,哥CR,台湾TW,香港HK,新加坡SG,新西兰NZ,智利CL 4.8 秘鲁PE 9.6 澳AU 11.2 瑞士CH 12.8 巴PK,韩国KR	0 柬埔寨KH,老挝LA,缅甸MM,受惠国LD	130	--Of man-made fibres
		--其他纺织材料制:					--Of other textile materials:
4588	6208.9910	---丝及绢丝制	14	0 澳门MO,冰岛IS,东盟AS,哥CR,秘鲁PE,香港HK,新加坡SG,新西兰NZ,智利CL 7 巴PK 8.4 澳AU 9.8 瑞士CH 11.2 韩国KR 12.6 亚太AP	0 受惠国$_1$LD$_1$	130	---Of silk or silk waste

序号 No.	税则号列 Tariff Line	中文货品名称 Article Description in Chinese	最惠国税率 MFN(%)	协定税率 Agreement(%)	特惠税率 SP(%)	普通税率 Gen(%)	英文货品名称 Article Description
4589	6208.9990	---其他	14	0 澳门MO,冰岛IS,东盟AS,哥CR,秘鲁PE,香港HK,新加坡SG,新西兰NZ,智利CL 7 巴PK 8.4 澳AU 9.8 瑞士CH 11.2 韩国KR 12.6 亚太AP	0 受惠国LD	100	---Other
	62.09	**婴儿服装及衣着附件:**					**Babies' garments and clothing accessories:**
4590	6209.2000	-棉制	14	0 澳门MO,冰岛IS,东盟AS,哥CR,秘鲁PE,香港HK,新加坡SG,新西兰NZ,智利CL 7 巴PK 8.4 澳AU 9.8 瑞士CH 11.2 韩国KR	0 受惠国LD	90	-Of cotton
4591	6209.3000	-合成纤维制	16	0 澳门MO,冰岛IS,东盟AS,哥CR,香港HK,新加坡SG,新西兰NZ,智利CL 4.8 秘鲁PE 9.6 澳AU 11.2 瑞士CH 12.8 巴PK,韩国KR	0 受惠国LD	130	-Of synthetic fibres
		-其他纺织材料制:					-Of other textile materials:
4592	6209.9010	---羊毛或动物细毛制	14	0 澳门MO,冰岛IS,东盟AS,哥CR,秘鲁PE,香港HK,新加坡SG,新西兰NZ,智利CL 7 巴PK 8.4 澳AU 9.8 瑞士CH 11.2 韩国KR	0 受惠国$_1$LD$_1$	130	---Of wool or fine animal hair
4593	6209.9090	---其他	14	0 澳门MO,冰岛IS,东盟AS,哥CR,秘鲁PE,香港HK,新加坡SG,新西兰NZ,智利CL 7 巴PK 8.4 澳AU 9.8 瑞士CH 11.2 韩国KR	0 受惠国$_1$LD$_1$	100	---Other
	62.10	**用税号56.02、56.03、59.03、59.06或59.07的织物制成的服装:**					**Garments, made up of fabrics of heading No.56.02, 56.03, 59.03, 59.06 or 59.07:**
		-用税号56.02或56.03的织物制成的服装:					-Of fabrics of heading 5602 or 5603:
4594	6210.1010	---羊毛或动物细毛制	16	0 澳门MO,冰岛IS,东盟AS,哥CR,香港HK,新加坡SG,新西兰NZ,智利CL 4.8 秘鲁PE 8 巴PK 9.6 澳AU 11.2 瑞士CH 11.7 亚太AP 12.8 韩国KR	0 受惠国LD,亚太AP	130	---Of wool or fine animal hair

序号 No.	税则号列 Tariff Line	中文货品名称 Article Description in Chinese	最惠国税率 MFN(%)	协定税率 Agreement(%)	特惠税率 SP(%)	普通税率 Gen(%)	英文货品名称 Article Description
4595	6210.1020	---棉或麻制	16	0 澳门MO,冰岛IS,东盟AS,哥CR,香港HK,新加坡SG,新西兰NZ,智利CL 4.8 秘鲁PE 9.6 澳AU 11.2 瑞士CH 12.8 巴PK,韩国KR	0 受惠国$_1$LD$_1$ 6.4 亚太AP	90	---Of cotton or bast fibres
4596	6210.1030	---化学纤维制	17.5	0 澳门MO,冰岛IS,东盟AS,哥CR,香港HK,新加坡SG,新西兰NZ,智利CL 5.2 秘鲁PE 8.8 巴PK 10.5 澳AU 12.3 瑞士CH,亚太AP 14 韩国KR	0 受惠国LD,亚太AP	130	---Of manmade fibres
4597	6210.1090	---其他纺织材料制	16	0 澳门MO,冰岛IS,东盟AS,哥CR,香港HK,新加坡SG,新西兰NZ,智利CL 4.8 秘鲁PE 9.6 澳AU 11.2 瑞士CH 12.8 巴PK,韩国KR	0 受惠国LD,亚太AP	100	---Of other textile materials
4598	6210.2000	-子目号6201. 11至6201. 19所列类型的其他服装	16	0 澳门MO,冰岛IS,东盟AS,哥CR,香港HK,新加坡SG,新西兰NZ,智利CL 4.8 秘鲁PE 8 巴PK 9.6 澳AU 11.2 瑞士CH 11.7 亚太AP 12.8 韩国KR	0 受惠国LD,亚太AP	100	-Other garments, of the type described in subheadings 6201.11 to 6201.19
4599	6210.3000	-子目号6202. 11至6202. 19所列类型的其他服装	16	0 澳门MO,冰岛IS,东盟AS,哥CR,香港HK,新加坡SG,新西兰NZ,智利CL 4.8 秘鲁PE 8 巴PK 9.6 澳AU 11.2 瑞士CH 11.7 亚太AP 12.8 韩国KR	0 受惠国LD	100	-Other garments, of the type described in subheadings 6202.11 to 6202.19
4600	6210.4000	-其他男式服装	16	0 澳门MO,冰岛IS,东盟AS,哥CR,香港HK,新加坡SG,新西兰NZ,智利CL 4.8 秘鲁PE 8 巴PK 9.6 澳AU 11.2 瑞士CH 11.7 亚太AP 12.8 韩国KR	0 受惠国LD,亚太AP	100	-Other men' s or boys' garments
4601	6210.5000	-其他女式服装	16	0 澳门MO,冰岛IS,东盟AS,哥CR,香港HK,新加坡SG,新西兰NZ,智利CL 4.8 秘鲁PE 8 巴PK 9.6 澳AU 11.2 瑞士CH 11.7 亚太AP 12.8 韩国KR	0 受惠国LD,亚太AP	100	-Other women' s or girls' garments

序号 No.	税则号列 Tariff Line	中文货品名称 Article Description in Chinese	最惠国税率 MFN(%)	协定税率 Agreement(%)	特惠税率 SP(%)	普通税率 Gen(%)	英文货品名称 Article Description
	62.11	运动服、滑雪服及游泳服;其他服装:					**Tracksuits, ski suits and swimwear; other garments:**
		-游泳服:					-Swimwear:
4602	6211.1100	--男式	16	0 澳门MO,冰岛IS,东盟AS,哥CR,香港HK,新加坡SG,新西兰NZ,智利CL 4.8 秘鲁PE 8 巴PK 9.6 澳AU 11.2 瑞士CH 11.7 亚太AP 12.8 韩国KR	0 受惠国$_1$LD$_1$	130	--Men' s or boys'
4603	6211.1200	--女式	16	0 冰岛IS,东盟AS,哥CR,香港HK,新加坡SG,新西兰NZ,智利CL 4.8 秘鲁PE 8 巴PK 9.6 澳AU 11.2 瑞士CH 11.7 亚太AP 12.8 韩国KR	0 受惠国LD	130	--Women' s or girls'
		-滑雪服:					-Ski suits:
4604	6211.2010	---棉制	16	0 冰岛IS,东盟AS,哥CR,香港HK,新加坡SG,新西兰NZ,智利CL 4.8 秘鲁PE 9.6 澳AU 11.2 瑞士CH 12.8 巴PK,韩国KR	0 受惠国LD	90	---Of cotton
4605	6211.2090	---其他纺织材料制	19	0 冰岛IS,东盟AS,哥CR,香港HK,新加坡SG,新西兰NZ,智利CL 5.7 秘鲁PE 9.5 巴PK 11.4 澳AU 13.3 瑞士CH 13.6 亚太AP 15.2 韩国KR	0 受惠国$_1$LD$_1$	130	---Of other textile materials
		-其他男式服装:					-Other garments, men' s or boys' :
		--棉制:					--Of cotton:
4606	6211.3210	---阿拉伯袍	16	0 冰岛IS,东盟AS,哥CR,香港HK,新加坡SG,新西兰NZ,智利CL 4.8 秘鲁PE 9.6 澳AU 11.2 瑞士CH 12.8 巴PK,韩国KR	0 受惠国$_1$LD$_1$	90	---Arabian robes
4607	6211.3220	---运动服	16	0 澳门MO,冰岛IS,东盟AS,哥CR,香港HK,新加坡SG,新西兰NZ,智利CL 4.8 秘鲁PE 9.6 澳AU 11.2 瑞士CH 12.8 韩国KR	0 受惠国LD	90	---Sports wear
4608	6211.3290	---其他	16	0 澳门MO,冰岛IS,东盟AS,哥CR,香港HK,新加坡SG,新西兰NZ,智利CL 4.8 秘鲁PE 9.6 澳AU 11.2 瑞士CH 12.8 韩国KR	0 受惠国LD	90	---Other
		--化学纤维制:					--Of man-made fibres:

序号 No.	税则号列 Tariff Line	中文货品名称 Article Description in Chinese	最惠国税率 MFN(%)	协定税率 Agreement(%)	特惠税率 SP(%)	普通税率 Gen(%)	英文货品名称 Article Description
4609	6211.3310	---阿拉伯袍	17.5	0 冰岛IS,东盟AS,哥CR,香港HK,新加坡SG,新西兰NZ,智利CL 5.2 秘鲁PE 8.8 巴PK 10.5 澳AU 12.3 瑞士CH,亚太AP 14 韩国KR	0 受惠国$_1$LD$_1$	130	---Arabian robes
4610	6211.3320	---运动服	18	0 澳门MO,冰岛IS,东盟AS,哥CR,香港HK,新加坡SG,新西兰NZ,智利CL 5.4 秘鲁PE 10.8 澳AU 12.3 巴PK,亚太AP 12.6 瑞士CH 14.4 韩国KR	0 受惠国LD	130	---Sports wear
4611	6211.3390	---其他	17.5	0 澳门MO,冰岛IS,东盟AS,哥CR,香港HK,新加坡SG,新西兰NZ,智利CL 5.2 秘鲁PE 10.5 澳AU 12.3 巴PK,瑞士CH,亚太AP 14 韩国KR	0 受惠国LD	130	---Other
		--其他纺织材料制:					--Of other textile materials:
4612	6211.3910	---丝及绢丝制	16	0 澳门MO,冰岛IS,东盟AS,哥CR,香港HK,新加坡SG,新西兰NZ,智利CL 4.8 秘鲁PE 8 巴PK 9.6 澳AU 11.2 瑞士CH 11.7 亚太AP 12.8 韩国KR	0 受惠国$_1$LD$_1$	130	---Of silk or silk waste
4613	6211.3920	---羊毛或动物细毛制	16	0 澳门MO,冰岛IS,东盟AS,哥CR,香港HK,新加坡SG,新西兰NZ,智利CL 4.8 秘鲁PE 8 巴PK 9.6 澳AU 11.2 瑞士CH 11.7 亚太AP 12.8 韩国KR	0 受惠国$_1$LD$_1$	130	---Of wool or fine animal hair
4614	6211.3990	---其他	16	0 澳门MO,冰岛IS,东盟AS,哥CR,香港HK,新加坡SG,新西兰NZ,智利CL 4.8 秘鲁PE 8 巴PK 9.6 澳AU 11.2 瑞士CH 11.7 亚太AP 12.8 韩国KR	0 受惠国$_1$LD$_1$	100	---Other
		-其他女式服装:					-Other garments, women' s or girls' :
		--棉制:					--Of cotton:

序号 No.	税则号列 Tariff Line	中文货品名称 Article Description in Chinese	最惠国税率 MFN(%)	协定税率 Agreement(%)	特惠税率 SP(%)	普通税率 Gen(%)	英文货品名称 Article Description
4615	6211.4210	---运动服	16	0 澳门MO,冰岛IS,东盟AS,哥CR,香港HK,新加坡SG,新西兰NZ,智利CL 4.8 秘鲁PE 9.6 澳AU 11.2 瑞士CH 12.8 巴PK,韩国KR	0 受惠国LD	90	---Sports wear
4616	6211.4290	---其他	16	0 澳门MO,冰岛IS,东盟AS,哥CR,香港HK,新加坡SG,新西兰NZ,智利CL 4.8 秘鲁PE 9.6 澳AU 11.2 瑞士CH 12.8 巴PK,韩国KR	0 受惠国LD	90	---Other
		--化学纤维制:					--Of man-made fibres:
4617	6211.4310	---运动服	17.5	0 澳门MO,冰岛IS,东盟AS,哥CR,香港HK,新加坡SG,新西兰NZ,智利CL 5.2 秘鲁PE 8.8 巴PK 10.5 澳AU 12.3 瑞士CH,亚太AP 14 韩国KR	0 受惠国LD	130	---Sports wear
4618	6211.4390	---其他	17.5	0 澳门MO,冰岛IS,东盟AS,哥CR,香港HK,新加坡SG,新西兰NZ,智利CL 5.2 秘鲁PE 8.8 巴PK 10.5 澳AU 12.3 瑞士CH,亚太AP 14 韩国KR	0 受惠国LD	130	---Other
		--其他纺织材料制:					--Of other textile materials:
4619	6211.4910	---丝及绢丝制	16	0 澳门MO,冰岛IS,东盟AS,哥CR,香港HK,新加坡SG,新西兰NZ,智利CL 4.8 秘鲁PE 8 巴PK 9.6 澳AU 11.2 瑞士CH 11.7 亚太AP 12.8 韩国KR	0 受惠国LD	130	---Of silk or silk waste
4620	6211.4990	---其他	16	0 澳门MO,冰岛IS,东盟AS,哥CR,香港HK,新加坡SG,新西兰NZ,智利CL 4.8 秘鲁PE 8 巴PK 9.6 澳AU 11.2 瑞士CH 11.7 亚太AP 12.8 韩国KR	0 受惠国LD	100	---Other
	62.12	**胸罩、束腰带、紧身胸衣、吊裤带、吊袜带、束袜带和类似品及其零件,不论是否针织或钩编的:**					**Brassières, girdles, corsets, braces, suspenders, garters and similar articles and parts thereof, whether or not knitted or crocheted:**
		-胸罩:					-Brassières:

序号 No.	税则号列 Tariff Line	中文货品名称 Article Description in Chinese	最惠国税率 MFN(%)	协定税率 Agreement(%)	特惠税率 SP(%)	普通税率 Gen(%)	英文货品名称 Article Description
4621	6212.1010	---化学纤维制	16	0 澳门MO,冰岛IS,东盟AS,哥CR,台湾TW,香港HK,新加坡SG,新西兰NZ,智利CL 4.8 秘鲁PE 9.6 澳AU 11.2 瑞士CH 12.8 巴PK,韩国KR 14.4 亚太AP	0 柬埔寨KH,老挝LA,缅甸MM,受惠国LD	130	---Of man-made fibres
4622	6212.1090	---其他纺织材料制	14	0 澳门MO,冰岛IS,东盟AS,哥CR,秘鲁PE,台湾TW,香港HK,新加坡SG,新西兰NZ,智利CL 7 巴PK 8.4 澳AU 9.8 瑞士CH 11.2 韩国KR 12.6 亚太AP	0 受惠国LD	100	---Of other textile materials
		-束腰带及腹带:					-Girdles and panty girdles:
4623	6212.2010	---化学纤维制	16	0 澳门MO,冰岛IS,东盟AS,哥CR,台湾TW,香港HK,新加坡SG,新西兰NZ,智利CL 4.8 秘鲁PE 9.6 澳AU 11.2 瑞士CH 12.8 巴PK,韩国KR	0 受惠国$_1$LD$_1$	130	---Of man-made fibres
4624	6212.2090	---其他纺织材料制	14	0 澳门MO,冰岛IS,东盟AS,哥CR,秘鲁PE,台湾TW,香港HK,新加坡SG,新西兰NZ,智利CL 8.4 澳AU 9.8 瑞士CH 11.2 巴PK,韩国KR	0 受惠国LD	100	---Of other textile materials
		-束腰胸衣:					-Corselettes:
4625	6212.3010	---化学纤维制	16	0 澳门MO,冰岛IS,东盟AS,哥CR,香港HK,新加坡SG,新西兰NZ,智利CL 4.8 秘鲁PE 9.6 澳AU 11.2 瑞士CH 12.8 巴PK,韩国KR	0 受惠国$_1$LD$_1$	130	---Of man-made fibres
4626	6212.3090	---其他纺织材料制	14	0 澳门MO,冰岛IS,东盟AS,哥CR,秘鲁PE,香港HK,新加坡SG,新西兰NZ,智利CL 7 巴PK 8.4 澳AU 9.8 瑞士CH 11.2 韩国KR	0 受惠国LD	100	---Of other textile materials
		-其他:					-Other:
4627	6212.9010	---化学纤维制	16	0 澳门MO,冰岛IS,东盟AS,哥CR,台湾TW,香港HK,新加坡SG,新西兰NZ,智利CL 4.8 秘鲁PE 9.6 澳AU 11.2 瑞士CH 12.8 巴PK,韩国KR 14.4 亚太AP	0 受惠国$_1$LD$_1$	130	---Of man-made fibres

序号 No.	税则号列 Tariff Line	中文货品名称 Article Description in Chinese	最惠国税率 MFN(%)	协定税率 Agreement(%)	特惠税率 SP(%)	普通税率 Gen(%)	英文货品名称 Article Description
4628	6212.9090	---其他纺织材料制	14	0 澳门MO,冰岛IS,东盟AS,哥CR,秘鲁PE,台湾TW,香港HK,新加坡SG,新西兰NZ,智利CL 7 巴PK 8.4 澳AU 9.8 瑞士CH 11.2 韩国KR 12.6 亚太AP	0 受惠国$_1$LD$_1$	100	---Of other textile materials
	62.13	**手帕:**					**Handkerchiefs:**
		-棉制:					-Of cotton:
4629	6213.2010	---刺绣的	14	0 冰岛IS,东盟AS,哥CR,秘鲁PE,香港HK,新加坡SG,新西兰NZ,智利CL 7 巴PK 8.4 澳AU 9.8 瑞士CH 11.2 韩国KR	0 老挝LA,受惠国LD	90	---Embroidered
4630	6213.2090	---其他	14	0 冰岛IS,东盟AS,哥CR,秘鲁PE,香港HK,新加坡SG,新西兰NZ,智利CL 8.4 澳AU 9.8 瑞士CH 11.2 巴PK,韩国KR	0 老挝LA,受惠国LD	90	---Other
		-其他纺织材料制:					-Of other textile materials:
4631	6213.9020	---刺绣的	14	0 冰岛IS,东盟AS,哥CR,秘鲁PE,新加坡SG,新西兰NZ,智利CL 7 巴PK 8.4 澳AU 9.8 瑞士CH 11.2 韩国KR	0 老挝LA,受惠国LD	100	---Embroidered
4632	6213.9090	---其他	14	0 冰岛IS,东盟AS,哥CR,秘鲁PE,香港HK,新加坡SG,新西兰NZ,智利CL 7 巴PK 8.4 澳AU 9.8 瑞士CH 11.2 韩国KR	0 老挝LA,受惠国LD	100	---Other
	62.14	**披巾、领巾、围巾、披纱、面纱及类似品:**					**Shawls, scarves, mufflers, mantillas, veils and the like:**
4633	6214.1000	-丝或绢丝制	14Δ8	0 冰岛IS,东盟AS,哥CR,秘鲁PE,香港HK,新加坡SG,新西兰NZ,智利CL 8.4 澳AU 9.8 瑞士CH 11.2 巴PK,韩国KR	0 受惠国LD	130	-Of silk or silk waste
		-羊毛或动物细毛制:					-Of wool or fine animal hair:
4634	6214.2010	---羊毛制	14Δ8	0 冰岛IS,东盟AS,哥CR,香港HK,新加坡SG,新西兰NZ,智利CL 4.2 秘鲁PE 8.4 澳AU 9.8 瑞士CH 11.2 巴PK,韩国KR	0 受惠国LD	130	---Of wool
4635	6214.2020	---山羊绒制	14Δ8	0 冰岛IS,东盟AS,哥CR,香港HK,新加坡SG,新西兰NZ,智利CL 4.2 秘鲁PE 8.4 澳AU 9.8 瑞士CH 11.2 巴PK,韩国KR	0 受惠国LD	130	---Of cashmere

序号 No.	税则号列 Tariff Line	中文货品名称 Article Description in Chinese	最惠国税率 MFN(%)	协定税率 Agreement(%)	特惠税率 SP(%)	普通税率 Gen(%)	英文货品名称 Article Description
4636	6214.2090	---其他	14	0 冰岛IS,东盟AS,哥CR,香港HK,新加坡SG,新西兰NZ,智利CL 4.2 秘鲁PE 8.4 澳AU 9.8 瑞士CH 11.2 巴PK,韩国KR	0 受惠国LD	130	---Other
4637	6214.3000	-合成纤维制	16	0 冰岛IS,东盟AS,哥CR,香港HK,新加坡SG,新西兰NZ,智利CL 4.8 秘鲁PE 9.6 澳AU 11.2 瑞士CH 12.8 巴PK,韩国KR	0 受惠国LD	130	-Of synthetic fibres
4638	6214.4000	-人造纤维制	14	0 冰岛IS,东盟AS,哥CR,秘鲁PE,香港HK,新加坡SG,新西兰NZ,智利CL 8.4 澳AU 9.8 瑞士CH 11.2 巴PK,韩国KR	0 受惠国LD	130	-Of artificial fibres
4639	6214.9000	-其他纺织材料制	14	0 冰岛IS,东盟AS,哥CR,秘鲁PE,香港HK,新加坡SG,新西兰NZ,智利CL 8.4 澳AU 9.8 瑞士CH 11.2 巴PK,韩国KR	0 受惠国LD	100	-Of other textile materials
	62.15	**领带及领结:**					**Ties, bow ties and cravats:**
4640	6215.1000	-丝或绢丝制	14	0 冰岛IS,东盟AS,哥CR,秘鲁PE,香港HK,新加坡SG,新西兰NZ,智利CL 8.4 澳AU 9.8 瑞士CH 11.2 巴PK,韩国KR	0 受惠国LD	130	-Of silk or silk waste
4641	6215.2000	-化学纤维制	16	0 冰岛IS,东盟AS,哥CR,香港HK,新加坡SG,新西兰NZ,智利CL 4.8 秘鲁PE 9.6 澳AU 11.2 瑞士CH 12.8 巴PK,韩国KR 14.4 亚太AP	0 受惠国LD	130	-Of man-made fibres
4642	6215.9000	-其他纺织材料制	14	0 冰岛IS,东盟AS,哥CR,秘鲁PE,香港HK,新加坡SG,新西兰NZ,智利CL 7 巴PK 8.4 澳AU 9.8 瑞士CH 11.2 韩国KR	0 受惠国LD	100	-Of other textile materials
	62.16	**分指手套、连指手套及露指手套**					**Gloves, mittens and mitts**
4643	6216.0000	分指手套、连指手套及露指手套	14	0 澳门MO,冰岛IS,东盟AS,哥CR,秘鲁PE,香港HK,新加坡SG,新西兰NZ,智利CL 8.4 澳AU 9.8 瑞士CH 11.2 韩国KR	0 受惠国LD	100	Gloves, mittens and mitts
	62.17	**其他制成的衣着附件;服装或衣着附件的零件,但税号62.12的货品除外:**					**Other made-up clothing accessories; parts of garments or of clothing accessories, other than those of heading 6212:**
		-附件:					-Accessories:

序号 No.	税则号列 Tariff Line	中文货品名称 Article Description in Chinese	最惠国税率 MFN(%)	协定税率 Agreement(%)	特惠税率 SP(%)	普通税率 Gen(%)	英文货品名称 Article Description
4644	6217.1010	---袜子及袜套	14	0 冰岛IS,东盟AS,哥CR,秘鲁PE,台湾TW,新加坡SG,新西兰NZ,智利CL 7 巴PK 8.4 澳AU 9.8 瑞士CH 11.2 韩国KR 12.2 亚太AP	0 受惠国[1]LD[1]	130	---Stocking, socks and sockettes
4645	6217.1020	---和服腰带	14	0 冰岛IS,东盟AS,哥CR,秘鲁PE,台湾TW,香港HK,新加坡SG,新西兰NZ,智利CL 7 巴PK 8.4 澳AU 9.8 瑞士CH 11.2 韩国KR 12.2 亚太AP	0 受惠国LD	100	---Kimono belts
4646	6217.1090	---其他	14	0 冰岛IS,东盟AS,哥CR,秘鲁PE,台湾TW,香港HK,新加坡SG,新西兰NZ,智利CL 8.4 澳AU 9.8 瑞士CH 11.2 韩国KR 12.2 巴PK,亚太AP	0 柬埔寨KH,老挝LA,缅甸MM,受惠国LD	100	---Other
4647	6217.9000	-零件	14	0 澳门MO,冰岛IS,东盟AS,哥CR,秘鲁PE,台湾TW,香港HK,新加坡SG,新西兰NZ,智利CL 8.4 澳AU 9.8 瑞士CH 12.1 韩国KR 12.6 巴PK,亚太AP	0 柬埔寨KH,老挝LA,缅甸MM,受惠国LD	100	-Parts

第六十三章

其他纺织制成品；成套物品；旧衣着及旧纺织品；碎织物

注释:

一、第一分章仅适用于各种纺织物制成的物品。

二、第一分章不包括:

(一)第五十六章至第六十二章的货品;

(二)税号 63.09 的旧衣着或其他旧物品。

三、税号 63.09 仅适用于下列货品:

(一)纺织材料制品:

1. 衣着和衣着附件及其零件;

2. 毯子及旅行毯;

3. 床上、餐桌、盥洗及厨房用的织物制品;

4. 装饰用织物制品，但税号 57.01 至 57.05 的地毯及税号 58.05 的装饰毯除外。

(二)用石棉以外其他任何材料制成的鞋帽类。

上述物品只有同时符合下列两个条件才能归入本税号:

1. 必须明显看得出穿用过;

2. 必须以散装、捆装、袋装或类似的大包装形式进口或出口。

Chapter63

Other made up textile articles; sets; worn clothing and worn textile articles; rags

Notes:

1.Sub-Chapter1applies only to made up articles，of any textile fabric.

2.Sub-Chapter1does not cover:

(a) Goods of Chapters 56 to 62; or

(b) Worn clothing or other worn articles of heading No.63.09.

3.Heading No.63.09 applies only to the following goods:

(a) Articles of textile materials:

(1) Clothing and clothing accessories，and parts thereof;

(2) Blankets and travelling rugs;

(3) Bed linen，table linen，toilet lined and kitchen linen;

(4) Furnishing articles，other than carpets of headings Nos. 57.01 to 57.05 and tapestries of heading No.58.05.

(b) Footwear and headgear of any material other than asbestos.

In order to be classified in this heading, the articles mentioned above must comply with both of the following requirements:

(1) they must show signs of appreciable wear; and

(2) they must be presented in bulk or in bales，sacks or similar packings.

序号 No.	税则号列 Tariff Line	中文货品名称 Article Description in Chinese	最惠国税率 MFN(%)	协定税率 Agreement(%)	特惠税率 SP(%)	普通税率 Gen(%)	英文货品名称 Article Description
		第一分章　其他纺织制成品					I.OTHER MADE UP TEXTILE ARTICLES
	63.01	**毯子及旅行毯:**					**Blankets and travelling rugs:**
4648	6301.1000	-电暖毯	16	0 冰岛IS,东盟AS,哥CR,新加坡SG,新西兰NZ,智利CL 4.8 秘鲁PE 9.6 澳AU 11.2 瑞士CH 12.8 巴PK,韩国KR	0 受惠国$_1$LD$_1$	100	-Electric blankets
4649	6301.2000	-羊毛或动物细毛制的毯子（电暖毯除外）及旅行毯	16Δ8	0 澳门MO,冰岛IS,东盟AS,哥CR,新加坡SG,新西兰NZ,智利CL 4.8 秘鲁PE 9.6 澳AU 11.2 瑞士CH 12.8 巴PK,韩国KR	0 受惠国LD	130	-Blankets (other than electric blankets) and travelling rugs, of wool or of fine animal hair
4650	6301.3000	-棉制的毯子（电暖毯除外）及旅行毯	16	0 澳门MO,冰岛IS,东盟AS,哥CR,新加坡SG,新西兰NZ,智利CL 4.8 秘鲁PE 9.6 澳AU 11.2 瑞士CH 12.8 巴PK,韩国KR	0 受惠国LD	90	-Blankets (other than electric blankets) and travelling rugs, of cotton

序号 No.	税则号列 Tariff Line	中文货品名称 Article Description in Chinese	最惠国税率 MFN(%)	协定税率 Agreement(%)	特惠税率 SP(%)	普通税率 Gen(%)	英文货品名称 Article Description
4651	6301.4000	-合成纤维制的毯子（电暖毯除外）及旅行毯	17.5	0 澳门MO,冰岛IS,东盟AS,哥CR,新加坡SG,新西兰NZ,智利CL 5.2 秘鲁PE 10.5 澳AU 12.3 瑞士CH 14 巴PK,韩国KR	0 受惠国LD	130	-Blankets (other than electric blankets) and travelling rugs, of synthetic fibres
4652	6301.9000	-其他毯子及旅行毯	16	0 澳门MO,冰岛IS,东盟AS,哥CR,台湾TW,新加坡SG,新西兰NZ,智利CL 4.8 秘鲁PE 9.6 澳AU 11.2 瑞士CH 12.8 巴PK,韩国KR	0 受惠国LD	90	-Other blankets and travelling rugs
	63.02	**床上、餐桌、盥洗及厨房用的织物制品：**					**Bedlinen, table linen, toilet linen and kitchen linen:**
		-针织或钩编的床上用织物制品：					-Bedlinen, knitted or crocheted:
4653	6302.1010	---棉制	14	0 巴PK,冰岛IS,东盟AS,哥CR,秘鲁PE,新加坡SG,新西兰NZ,智利CL 8.4 澳AU 9.8 瑞士CH 11.2 韩国KR	0 受惠国LD	90	---Of cotton
4654	6302.1090	---其他纺织材料制	14	0 巴PK,冰岛IS,东盟AS,哥CR,秘鲁PE,新加坡SG,新西兰NZ,智利CL 8.4 澳AU 9.8 瑞士CH 11.2 韩国KR	0 受惠国$_1$LD$_1$	130	---Other
		-其他印花的床上用织物制品：					-Other bedlinen, printed:
		--棉制：					--Of cotton:
4655	6302.2110	---床单	14	0 巴PK,冰岛IS,东盟AS,哥CR,秘鲁PE,新加坡SG,新西兰NZ,智利CL 8.4 澳AU 10 瑞士CH 11.2 韩国KR	0 受惠国LD	90	---Bed sheets
4656	6302.2190	---其他	14	0 巴PK,冰岛IS,东盟AS,哥CR,秘鲁PE,新加坡SG,新西兰NZ,智利CL 8.4 澳AU 9.8 瑞士CH 11.2 韩国KR	0 受惠国LD	90	---Other
		--化学纤维制：					--Of man-made fibres:
4657	6302.2210	---床单	16	0 巴PK,冰岛IS,东盟AS,哥CR,新加坡SG,新西兰NZ,智利CL 4.8 秘鲁PE 9.6 澳AU 11.2 瑞士CH 12.8 韩国KR	0 受惠国LD	130	---Bed sheets
4658	6302.2290	---其他	16	0 巴PK,冰岛IS,东盟AS,哥CR,新加坡SG,新西兰NZ,智利CL 4.8 秘鲁PE 9.6 澳AU 11.2 瑞士CH 12.8 韩国KR	0 受惠国LD	130	---Other
		--其他纺织材料制：					--Of other textile materials:

序号 No.	税则号列 Tariff Line	中文货品名称 Article Description in Chinese	最惠国税率 MFN(%)	协定税率 Agreement(%)	特惠税率 SP(%)	普通税率 Gen(%)	英文货品名称 Article Description
4659	6302.2910	---丝及绢丝制	14	0 巴PK,冰岛IS,东盟AS,哥CR,秘鲁PE,新加坡SG,新西兰NZ,智利CL 8.4 澳AU 9.8 瑞士CH 11.2 韩国KR	0 受惠国$_1$LD$_1$	130	---Of silk or silk waste
4660	6302.2920	---麻制	14	0 巴PK,冰岛IS,东盟AS,哥CR,秘鲁PE,新加坡SG,新西兰NZ,智利CL 8.4 澳AU 9.8 瑞士CH 11.2 韩国KR	0 受惠国$_1$LD$_1$	90	---Of bast fibres
4661	6302.2990	---其他	14	0 巴PK,冰岛IS,东盟AS,哥CR,秘鲁PE,新加坡SG,新西兰NZ,智利CL 8.4 澳AU 9.8 瑞士CH 11.2 韩国KR	0 受惠国$_1$LD$_1$	100	---Other
		-其他床上用织物制品：					-Other bedlinen:
		--棉制：					--Of cotton:
4662	6302.3110	---刺绣的	14	0 巴PK,冰岛IS,东盟AS,哥CR,秘鲁PE,新加坡SG,新西兰NZ,智利CL 8.4 澳AU 9.8 瑞士CH 11.2 韩国KR	0 受惠国LD	90	---Embroidered
		---其他：					---Other:
4663	6302.3191	----床单	14	0 巴PK,冰岛IS,东盟AS,哥CR,秘鲁PE,新加坡SG,新西兰NZ,智利CL 8.4 澳AU 9.8 瑞士CH 11.2 韩国KR	0 受惠国LD	90	----Bed sheets
4664	6302.3192	----毛巾被	14	0 巴PK,冰岛IS,东盟AS,哥CR,秘鲁PE,新加坡SG,新西兰NZ,智利CL 8.4 澳AU 9.8 瑞士CH 11.2 韩国KR	0 受惠国$_1$LD$_1$	90	----Towelling coverlets
4665	6302.3199	----其他	14	0 巴PK,冰岛IS,东盟AS,哥CR,秘鲁PE,新加坡SG,新西兰NZ,智利CL 8.4 澳AU 9.8 瑞士CH 11.2 韩国KR	0 受惠国LD	90	----Other
		--化学纤维制：					--Of man-made fibres:
4666	6302.3210	---刺绣的	16	0 巴PK,冰岛IS,东盟AS,哥CR,新加坡SG,新西兰NZ,智利CL 4.8 秘鲁PE 9.6 澳AU 11.2 瑞士CH 12.8 韩国KR	0 受惠国LD	130	---Embroidered
4667	6302.3290	---其他	16	0 巴PK,冰岛IS,东盟AS,哥CR,新加坡SG,新西兰NZ,智利CL 4.8 秘鲁PE 9.6 澳AU 11.2 瑞士CH 12.8 韩国KR	0 受惠国LD	130	---Other
		--其他纺织材料制：					--Of other textile materials:

序号 No.	税则号列 Tariff Line	中文货品名称 Article Description in Chinese	最惠国税率 MFN(%)	协定税率 Agreement(%)	特惠税率 SP(%)	普通税率 Gen(%)	英文货品名称 Article Description
4668	6302.3910	---丝及绢丝制	14	0 巴PK,冰岛IS,东盟AS,哥CR,秘鲁PE,新加坡SG,新西兰NZ,智利CL 8.4 澳AU 9.8 瑞士CH 11.2 韩国KR	0 受惠国$_1$LD$_1$	130	---Of silk or silk waste
		---麻制:					---Of bast fibres:
4669	6302.3921	----刺绣的	14	0 巴PK,冰岛IS,东盟AS,哥CR,秘鲁PE,新加坡SG,新西兰NZ,智利CL 8.4 澳AU 9.8 瑞士CH 11.2 韩国KR	0 受惠国$_1$LD$_1$	90	----Embroidered
4670	6302.3929	----其他	14	0 巴PK,冰岛IS,东盟AS,哥CR,秘鲁PE,新加坡SG,新西兰NZ,智利CL 8.4 澳AU 9.8 瑞士CH 11.2 韩国KR	0 受惠国$_1$LD$_1$	90	----Other
		---其他:					---Other:
4671	6302.3991	----刺绣的	14	0 巴PK,冰岛IS,东盟AS,哥CR,秘鲁PE,新加坡SG,新西兰NZ,智利CL 8.4 澳AU 9.8 瑞士CH 11.2 韩国KR	0 受惠国$_1$LD$_1$	100	----Embroidered
4672	6302.3999	----其他	14	0 巴PK,冰岛IS,东盟AS,哥CR,秘鲁PE,新加坡SG,新西兰NZ,智利CL 8.4 澳AU 9.8 瑞士CH 11.2 韩国KR	0 受惠国LD	100	----Other
		-针织或钩编的餐桌用织物制品:					-Table linen, knitted or crocheted:
4673	6302.4010	---手工制	14	0 巴PK,冰岛IS,东盟AS,哥CR,秘鲁PE,新加坡SG,新西兰NZ,智利CL 8.4 澳AU 9.8 瑞士CH 11.2 韩国KR	0 受惠国$_1$LD$_1$	100	---Hand-worked
4674	6302.4090	---其他	14	0 巴PK,冰岛IS,东盟AS,哥CR,秘鲁PE,新加坡SG,新西兰NZ,智利CL 8.4 澳AU 9.8 瑞士CH 11.2 韩国KR	0 受惠国LD	100	---Other
		-其他餐桌用织物制品:					-Other table linen:
		--棉制:					--Of cotton:
4675	6302.5110	---刺绣的	14	0 巴PK,冰岛IS,东盟AS,哥CR,秘鲁PE,香港HK,新加坡SG,新西兰NZ,智利CL 8.4 澳AU 9.8 瑞士CH 11.2 韩国KR	0 受惠国$_1$LD$_1$	90	---Embroidered
4676	6302.5190	---其他	14	0 澳门MO,巴PK,冰岛IS,东盟AS,哥CR,秘鲁PE,香港HK,新加坡SG,新西兰NZ,智利CL 8.4 澳AU 9.8 瑞士CH 11.2 韩国KR	0 受惠国LD	90	---Other
		--化学纤维制:					--Of man-made fibres:

序号 No.	税则号列 Tariff Line	中文货品名称 Article Description in Chinese	最惠国税率 MFN(%)	协定税率 Agreement(%)	特惠税率 SP(%)	普通税率 Gen(%)	英文货品名称 Article Description
4677	6302.5310	---刺绣的	14	0 巴PK,冰岛IS,东盟AS,哥CR,秘鲁PE,新加坡SG,新西兰NZ,智利CL 8.4 澳AU 9.8 瑞士CH 11.2 韩国KR	0 受惠国$_1$LD$_1$	130	---Embroidered
4678	6302.5390	---其他	16	0 巴PK,冰岛IS,东盟AS,哥CR,新加坡SG,新西兰NZ,智利CL 4.8 秘鲁PE 9.6 澳AU 11.2 瑞士CH 12.8 韩国KR	0 受惠国LD	130	---Other
		--其他纺织材料制:					--Of other textile materials:
		---亚麻制:					---Of flax:
4679	6302.5911	----刺绣的	14	0 巴PK,冰岛IS,东盟AS,哥CR,秘鲁PE,新加坡SG,新西兰NZ,智利CL 8.4 澳AU 9.8 瑞士CH 11.2 韩国KR	0 受惠国$_1$LD$_1$	90	----Embroidered
4680	6302.5919	----其他	14	0 巴PK,冰岛IS,东盟AS,哥CR,秘鲁PE,新加坡SG,新西兰NZ,智利CL 8.4 澳AU 9.8 瑞士CH 11.2 韩国KR	0 受惠国$_1$LD$_1$	90	----Other
4681	6302.5990	---其他	14	0 巴PK,冰岛IS,东盟AS,哥CR,秘鲁PE,新加坡SG,新西兰NZ,智利CL 8.4 澳AU 9.8 瑞士CH 11.2 韩国KR	0 受惠国$_1$LD$_1$	100	---Other
		-盥洗及厨房用棉制毛巾织物或类似的毛圈织物的制品:					-Toilet linen and kitchen linen, of terry towelling or similar terry fabrics, of cotton:
4682	6302.6010	---浴巾	14	0 巴PK,冰岛IS,东盟AS,哥CR,秘鲁PE,台湾TW,新加坡SG,新西兰NZ,智利CL 8.4 澳AU 9.8 瑞士CH 11.2 韩国KR	0 受惠国LD	90	---Bath towels
4683	6302.6090	---其他	14	0 巴PK,冰岛IS,东盟AS,哥CR,秘鲁PE,台湾TW,新加坡SG,新西兰NZ,智利CL 8.4 澳AU 9.8 瑞士CH 11.2 韩国KR	0 受惠国LD	90	---Other
		-其他:					-Other:
4684	6302.9100	--棉制	14	0 巴PK,冰岛IS,东盟AS,哥CR,秘鲁PE,新加坡SG,新西兰NZ,智利CL 8.4 澳AU 9.8 瑞士CH 11.2 韩国KR	0 受惠国LD	90	--Of cotton
4685	6302.9300	--化学纤维制	16	0 巴PK,冰岛IS,东盟AS,哥CR,香港HK,新加坡SG,新西兰NZ,智利CL 4.8 秘鲁PE 9.6 澳AU 11.2 瑞士CH 12.8 韩国KR	0 受惠国$_1$LD$_1$	130	--Of man-made fibres
		--其他纺织材料制:					--Of other textile materials:

序号 No.	税则号列 Tariff Line	中文货品名称 Article Description in Chinese	最惠国税率 MFN(%)	协定税率 Agreement(%)	特惠税率 SP(%)	普通税率 Gen(%)	英文货品名称 Article Description
4686	6302.9910	---亚麻制	14	0 巴PK,冰岛IS,东盟AS,哥CR,秘鲁PE,新加坡SG,新西兰NZ,智利CL 8.4 澳AU 9.8 瑞士CH 11.2 韩国KR	0 受惠国$_1$LD$_1$	90	---Of flax
4687	6302.9990	---其他	14	0 巴PK,冰岛IS,东盟AS,哥CR,秘鲁PE,新加坡SG,新西兰NZ,智利CL 8.4 澳AU 9.8 瑞士CH 11.2 韩国KR	0 受惠国$_1$LD$_1$	100	---Other
	63.03	**窗帘(包括帷帘)及帐幔;帘帷或床帷:**					**Curtains (including drapes) and interior blinds; curtain or bed valances:**
		-针织或钩编的:					-Knitted or crocheted:
		--合成纤维制:					--Of synthetic fibres:
4688	6303.1210	---针织的	16	0 巴PK,冰岛IS,东盟AS,哥CR,新加坡SG,新西兰NZ,智利CL 4.8 秘鲁PE 9.6 澳AU 11.2 瑞士CH 12.8 韩国KR	0 受惠国$_1$LD$_1$	130	---Knitted
4689	6303.1220	---钩编的	16	0 巴PK,冰岛IS,东盟AS,哥CR,新加坡SG,新西兰NZ,智利CL 4.8 秘鲁PE 9.6 澳AU 11.2 瑞士CH 12.8 韩国KR	0 受惠国$_1$LD$_1$	130	---Crocheted
		--其他纺织材料制:					--Of other textile materials:
		---棉制:					---Of cotton:
4690	6303.1931	----针织的	14	0 巴PK,冰岛IS,东盟AS,哥CR,秘鲁PE,新加坡SG,新西兰NZ,智利CL 8.4 澳AU 9.8 瑞士CH 11.2 韩国KR	0 受惠国LD	90	----Knitted
4691	6303.1932	----钩编的	14	0 巴PK,冰岛IS,东盟AS,哥CR,秘鲁PE,新加坡SG,新西兰NZ,智利CL 8.4 澳AU 9.8 瑞士CH 11.2 韩国KR	0 受惠国$_1$LD$_1$	90	----Crocheted
		---其他:					---Other:
4692	6303.1991	----针织的	14	0 巴PK,冰岛IS,东盟AS,哥CR,秘鲁PE,新加坡SG,新西兰NZ,智利CL 8.4 澳AU 9.8 瑞士CH 11.2 韩国KR	0 受惠国$_1$LD$_1$	130	----Knitted
4693	6303.1992	----钩编的	14	0 巴PK,冰岛IS,东盟AS,哥CR,秘鲁PE,新加坡SG,新西兰NZ,智利CL 8.4 澳AU 9.8 瑞士CH 11.2 韩国KR	0 受惠国$_1$LD$_1$	130	----Crocheted
		-其他:					-Other:
4694	6303.9100	--棉制	14	0 巴PK,冰岛IS,东盟AS,哥CR,秘鲁PE,新加坡SG,新西兰NZ,智利CL 8.4 澳AU 9.8 瑞士CH 11.2 韩国KR	0 受惠国LD	90	--Of cotton

序号 No.	税则号列 Tariff Line	中文货品名称 Article Description in Chinese	最惠国税率 MFN(%)	协定税率 Agreement(%)	特惠税率 SP(%)	普通税率 Gen(%)	英文货品名称 Article Description
4695	6303.9200	--合成纤维制	16	0 巴PK,冰岛IS,东盟AS,哥CR,香港HK,新加坡SG,新西兰NZ,智利CL 4.8 秘鲁PE 9.6 澳AU 11.2 瑞士CH 12.8 韩国KR	0 受惠国LD	130	--Of synthetic fibres
4696	6303.9900	--其他纺织材料制	14	0 巴PK,冰岛IS,东盟AS,哥CR,秘鲁PE,新加坡SG,新西兰NZ,智利CL 8.4 澳AU 9.8 瑞士CH 11.2 韩国KR	0 受惠国LD	100	--Of other textile materials
	63.04	**其他装饰用织物制品，但税号94.04的货品除外：**					**Other furnishing articles, excluding those of heading 9404:**
		-床罩：					-Bedspreads:
		--针织或钩编的：					--Knitted or crocheted:
		---针织的：					---Knitted:
4697	6304.1121	----手工制	14	0 澳门MO,冰岛IS,东盟AS,哥CR,秘鲁PE,新加坡SG,新西兰NZ,智利CL 7 巴PK 8.4 澳AU 9.8 瑞士CH 11.2 韩国KR	0 受惠国$_1$LD$_1$	100	----Hand-worked
4698	6304.1129	----其他	14	0 澳门MO,冰岛IS,东盟AS,哥CR,秘鲁PE,新加坡SG,新西兰NZ,智利CL 7 巴PK 8.4 澳AU 9.8 瑞士CH 11.2 韩国KR	0 受惠国$_1$LD$_1$	100	----Other
		---钩编的：					---Crocheted:
4699	6304.1131	----手工制	14	0 冰岛IS,东盟AS,哥CR,秘鲁PE,新加坡SG,新西兰NZ,智利CL 7 巴PK 8.4 澳AU 9.8 瑞士CH 11.2 韩国KR	0 受惠国LD	100	----Hand-worked
4700	6304.1139	----其他	14	0 冰岛IS,东盟AS,哥CR,秘鲁PE,新加坡SG,新西兰NZ,智利CL 7 巴PK 8.4 澳AU 9.8 瑞士CH 11.2 韩国KR	0 受惠国LD	100	----Other
		--其他：					--Other:
4701	6304.1910	---丝及绢丝制	14	0 冰岛IS,东盟AS,哥CR,秘鲁PE,新加坡SG,新西兰NZ,智利CL 7 巴PK 8.4 澳AU 9.8 瑞士CH 11.2 韩国KR	0 受惠国$_1$LD$_1$	130	---Of silk or silk waste
		---棉或麻制：					---Of cotton or bast fibres:
4702	6304.1921	----刺绣的	14	0 冰岛IS,东盟AS,哥CR,秘鲁PE,新加坡SG,新西兰NZ,智利CL 7 巴PK 8.4 澳AU 9.8 瑞士CH 11.2 韩国KR	0 受惠国$_1$LD$_1$	90	----Embroidered

序号 No.	税则号列 Tariff Line	中文货品名称 Article Description in Chinese	最惠国税率 MFN(%)	协定税率 Agreement(%)	特惠税率 SP(%)	普通税率 Gen(%)	英文货品名称 Article Description
4703	6304.1929	----其他	14	0 冰岛IS,东盟AS,哥CR,秘鲁PE,新加坡SG,新西兰NZ,智利CL 8.4 澳AU 9.8 瑞士CH 11.2 韩国KR	0 受惠国LD	90	----Other
		---化学纤维制:					---Of man-made fibres:
4704	6304.1931	----刺绣的	16	0 冰岛IS,东盟AS,哥CR,新加坡SG,新西兰NZ,智利CL 4.8 秘鲁PE 9.6 澳AU 11.2 瑞士CH 12.8 巴PK,韩国KR	0 受惠国$_1$LD$_1$	130	----Embroidered
4705	6304.1939	----其他	16	0 冰岛IS,东盟AS,哥CR,新加坡SG,新西兰NZ,智利CL 4.8 秘鲁PE 9.6 澳AU 11.2 瑞士CH 12.8 巴PK,韩国KR	0 受惠国$_1$LD$_1$	130	----Other
		---其他纺织材料制:					---Of other textile materials:
4706	6304.1991	----刺绣的	14	0 冰岛IS,东盟AS,哥CR,秘鲁PE,新加坡SG,新西兰NZ,智利CL 7 巴PK 8.4 澳AU 9.8 瑞士CH 11.2 韩国KR	0 受惠国$_1$LD$_1$	100	----Embroidered
4707	6304.1999	----其他	14	0 冰岛IS,东盟AS,哥CR,秘鲁PE,新加坡SG,新西兰NZ,智利CL 7 巴PK 8.4 澳AU 9.8 瑞士CH 11.2 韩国KR	0 受惠国$_1$LD$_1$	100	----Other
		-其他:					-Other:
		--针织或钩编的:					--Knitted or crocheted:
		---针织的:					---Knitted:
4708	6304.9121	----手工制	14	0 冰岛IS,东盟AS,哥CR,秘鲁PE,新加坡SG,新西兰NZ,智利CL 7 巴PK 8.4 澳AU 9.8 瑞士CH 11.2 韩国KR	0 受惠国LD	100	----Hand-worked
4709	6304.9129	----其他	14	0 澳门MO,冰岛IS,东盟AS,哥CR,秘鲁PE,新加坡SG,新西兰NZ,智利CL 7 巴PK 8.4 澳AU 9.8 瑞士CH 11.2 韩国KR	0 受惠国LD	100	----Other
		---钩编的:					---Crocheted:
4710	6304.9131	----手工制	14	0 冰岛IS,东盟AS,哥CR,秘鲁PE,新加坡SG,新西兰NZ,智利CL 8.4 澳AU 9.8 瑞士CH 11.2 巴PK,韩国KR	0 受惠国$_1$LD$_1$	100	----Hand-worked

序号 No.	税则号列 Tariff Line	中文货品名称 Article Description in Chinese	最惠国税率 MFN(%)	协定税率 Agreement(%)	特惠税率 SP(%)	普通税率 Gen(%)	英文货品名称 Article Description
4711	6304.9139	----其他	14	0 冰岛IS,东盟AS,哥CR,秘鲁PE,新加坡SG,新西兰NZ,智利CL 7 巴PK 8.4 澳AU 9.8 瑞士CH 11.2 韩国KR	0 受惠国$_1$LD$_1$	100	----Other
		--非针织或非钩编的，棉制:					--Not knitted or crocheted, of cotton:
4712	6304.9210	---刺绣的	14	0 冰岛IS,东盟AS,哥CR,秘鲁PE,新加坡SG,新西兰NZ,智利CL 7 巴PK 8.4 澳AU 9.8 瑞士CH 11.2 韩国KR	0 受惠国$_1$LD$_1$	90	---Embroidered
4713	6304.9290	---其他	14	0 冰岛IS,东盟AS,哥CR,秘鲁PE,新加坡SG,新西兰NZ,智利CL 8.4 澳AU 9.8 瑞士CH 11.2 巴PK,韩国KR	0 受惠国LD	90	---Other
		--非针织或非钩编的，合成纤维制:					--Not knitted or crocheted, of synthetic fibres:
4714	6304.9310	---刺绣的	16	0 冰岛IS,东盟AS,哥CR,新加坡SG,新西兰NZ,智利CL 4.8 秘鲁PE 9.6 澳AU 11.2 瑞士CH 12.8 巴PK,韩国KR	0 受惠国$_1$LD$_1$	130	---Embroidered
4715	6304.9390	---其他	16	0 冰岛IS,东盟AS,哥CR,新加坡SG,新西兰NZ,智利CL 4.8 秘鲁PE 9.6 澳AU 11.2 瑞士CH 12.8 巴PK,韩国KR	0 受惠国LD	130	---Other
		--非针织或非钩编的，其他纺织材料制:					--Not knitted or crocheted, of other textile materials:
4716	6304.9910	---丝及绢丝制	14	0 冰岛IS,东盟AS,哥CR,秘鲁PE,新加坡SG,新西兰NZ,智利CL 7 巴PK 8.4 澳AU 9.8 瑞士CH 11.2 韩国KR	0 受惠国LD	130	---Of silk or silk waste
		---麻制:					---Of bast fibres:
4717	6304.9921	----刺绣的	14	0 冰岛IS,东盟AS,哥CR,秘鲁PE,新加坡SG,新西兰NZ,智利CL 7 巴PK 8.4 澳AU 9.8 瑞士CH 11.2 韩国KR	0 受惠国$_1$LD$_1$	90	----Embroidered
4718	6304.9929	----其他	14	0 冰岛IS,东盟AS,哥CR,秘鲁PE,新加坡SG,新西兰NZ,智利CL 7 巴PK 8.4 澳AU 9.8 瑞士CH 11.2 韩国KR	0 受惠国$_1$LD$_1$	90	----Other

序号 No.	税则号列 Tariff Line	中文货品名称 Article Description in Chinese	最惠国税率 MFN(%)	协定税率 Agreement(%)	特惠税率 SP(%)	普通税率 Gen(%)	英文货品名称 Article Description
4719	6304.9990	---其他	14	0 冰岛IS,东盟AS,哥CR,秘鲁PE,新加坡SG,新西兰NZ,智利CL 7 巴PK 8.4 澳AU 9.8 瑞士CH 11.2 韩国KR	0 受惠国LD	100	---Other
	63.05	**货物包装用袋:**					**Sacks and bags, of a kind used for the packing of goods:**
4720	6305.1000	-黄麻或税号53.03的其他韧皮纺织纤维制	10	0 冰岛IS,东盟AS,哥CR,秘鲁PE,新西兰NZ,智利CL 4 瑞士CH 5 巴PK 6 澳AU,韩国KR	0 受惠国LD,亚太AP	40	-Of jute or of other textile bast fibres of heading No.53.03
4721	6305.2000	-棉制	16	0 冰岛IS,东盟AS,哥CR,新加坡SG,新西兰NZ,智利CL 4.8 秘鲁PE 9.6 澳AU 11.2 瑞士CH 12.8 巴PK,韩国KR	0 受惠国LD	90	-Of cotton
		-化学纤维材料制:					-Of man-made textile materials:
4722	6305.3200	--散装货物储运软袋	16	0 冰岛IS,东盟AS,哥CR,新加坡SG,新西兰NZ,智利CL 4.8 秘鲁PE 9.6 澳AU 11.2 瑞士CH 12.8 巴PK,韩国KR	0 受惠国LD	100	--Flexible intermediate bulk containers
4723	6305.3300	--其他，聚乙烯、聚丙烯扁条或类似材料制	16	0 冰岛IS,东盟AS,哥CR,新加坡SG,新西兰NZ,智利CL 4.8 秘鲁PE 8 巴PK 9.6 澳AU 11.2 瑞士CH 12.8 韩国KR 13.6 亚太AP	0 受惠国$_1$LD$_1$	100	--Other, of polyethylene or polypropy lene strip or the like
4724	6305.3900	其他	16	0 冰岛IS,东盟AS,哥CR,新加坡SG,新西兰NZ,智利CL 4.8 秘鲁PE 9.6 澳AU 11.2 瑞士CH 12.8 巴PK,韩国KR	0 受惠国$_1$LD$_1$	100	--Other
4725	6305.9000	-其他纺织材料制	14	0 冰岛IS,东盟AS,哥CR,秘鲁PE,新加坡SG,新西兰NZ,智利CL 8.4 澳AU 9.8 瑞士CH 11.2 巴PK,韩国KR	0 受惠国LD	90	-Of other textile materials
	63.06	**油苫布、天篷及遮阳篷;帐篷;风帆;野营用品:**					**Tarpaulins, awnings and sunblinds; tents; sails for boats, sailboards or landcraft; camping goods:**
		-油苫布、天篷及遮阳篷:					-Tarpaulins, awnings and sunblinds:
4726	6306.1200	--合成纤维制	16	0 巴PK,冰岛IS,东盟AS,哥CR,新加坡SG,新西兰NZ,智利CL 4.8 秘鲁PE 9.6 澳AU 11.2 瑞士CH 12.8 韩国KR	0 受惠国$_1$LD$_1$	130	--Of synthetic fibres
		--其他纺织材料制:					--Of other textile materials:

序号 No.	税则号列 Tariff Line	中文货品名称 Article Description in Chinese	最惠国税率 MFN(%)	协定税率 Agreement(%)	特惠税率 SP(%)	普通税率 Gen(%)	英文货品名称 Article Description
4727	6306.1910	---麻制	14	0 巴PK,冰岛IS,东盟AS,哥CR,秘鲁PE,新加坡SG,新西兰NZ,智利CL 8.4 澳AU 9.8 瑞士CH 11.2 韩国KR	0 受惠国$_1$LD$_1$	80	---Of bast fibres
4728	6306.1920	---棉制	14	0 巴PK,冰岛IS,东盟AS,哥CR,秘鲁PE,新加坡SG,新西兰NZ,智利CL 8.4 澳AU 9.8 瑞士CH 11.2 韩国KR	0 受惠国$_1$LD$_1$	80	---Of cotton
4729	6306.1990	---其他	14	0 巴PK,冰岛IS,东盟AS,哥CR,秘鲁PE,新加坡SG,新西兰NZ,智利CL 8.4 澳AU 9.8 瑞士CH 11.2 韩国KR	0 受惠国$_1$LD$_1$	100	---Other
		-帐篷:					-Tents:
4730	6306.2200	--合成纤维制	16	0 巴PK,冰岛IS,东盟AS,哥CR,新加坡SG,新西兰NZ,智利CL 4.8 秘鲁PE 9.6 澳AU 11.2 瑞士CH 12.8 韩国KR	0 受惠国LD	130	--Of synthetic fibres
		--其他纺织材料制:					--Of other textile materials:
4731	6306.2910	---棉制	14	0 巴PK,冰岛IS,东盟AS,哥CR,秘鲁PE,新加坡SG,新西兰NZ,智利CL 8.4 澳AU 9.8 瑞士CH 11.2 韩国KR	0 受惠国$_1$LD$_1$	80	---Of cotton
4732	6306.2990	---其他	14	0 巴PK,冰岛IS,东盟AS,哥CR,秘鲁PE,新加坡SG,新西兰NZ,智利CL 8.4 澳AU 9.8 瑞士CH 11.2 韩国KR	0 受惠国LD	100	---Other
		-风帆:					-Sails:
4733	6306.3010	---合成纤维制	16	0 巴PK,冰岛IS,东盟AS,哥CR,香港HK,新加坡SG,新西兰NZ,智利CL 4.8 秘鲁PE 9.6 澳AU 11.2 瑞士CH 12.8 韩国KR	0 受惠国$_1$LD$_1$	130	---Of synthetic fibres
4734	6306.3090	---其他纺织材料制	14	0 巴PK,冰岛IS,东盟AS,哥CR,秘鲁PE,新加坡SG,新西兰NZ,智利CL 8.4 澳AU 9.8 瑞士CH 11.2 韩国KR	0 受惠国$_1$LD$_1$	100	---Of other textile materials
		-充气褥垫:					-Pneumatic mattresses:
4735	6306.4010	---棉制	14	0 巴PK,冰岛IS,东盟AS,哥CR,秘鲁PE,新加坡SG,新西兰NZ,智利CL 8.4 澳AU 9.8 瑞士CH 11.2 韩国KR	0 受惠国$_1$LD$_1$	80	---Of cotton

序号 No.	税则号列 Tariff Line	中文货品名称 Article Description in Chinese	最惠国税率 MFN(%)	协定税率 Agreement(%)	特惠税率 SP(%)	普通税率 Gen(%)	英文货品名称 Article Description
4736	6306.4020	---化学纤维制	16	0 巴PK,冰岛IS,东盟AS,哥CR,新加坡SG,新西兰NZ,智利CL 4.8 秘鲁PE 9.6 澳AU 11.2 瑞士CH 12.8 韩国KR	0 受惠国LD	130	---Of man-made fibres
4737	6306.4090	---其他纺织材料制	14	0 巴PK,冰岛IS,东盟AS,哥CR,秘鲁PE,新加坡SG,新西兰NZ,智利CL 8.4 澳AU 9.8 瑞士CH 11.2 韩国KR	0 受惠国$_1$LD$_1$	100	---Of other textile materials
		-其他:					-Other:
4738	6306.9010	---棉制	14	0 巴PK,冰岛IS,东盟AS,哥CR,秘鲁PE,新加坡SG,新西兰NZ,智利CL 8.4 澳AU 9.8 瑞士CH 11.2 韩国KR	0 受惠国LD	80	---Of cotton
4739	6306.9020	---麻制	14	0 巴PK,冰岛IS,东盟AS,哥CR,秘鲁PE,新加坡SG,新西兰NZ,智利CL 8.4 澳AU 9.8 瑞士CH 11.2 韩国KR	0 受惠国$_1$LD$_1$	80	---Of bast fibres
4740	6306.9030	---化学纤维制	16	0 巴PK,冰岛IS,东盟AS,哥CR,新加坡SG,新西兰NZ,智利CL 4.8 秘鲁PE 9.6 澳AU 11.2 瑞士CH 12.8 韩国KR	0 受惠国$_1$LD$_1$	130	---Of man-made fibres
4741	6306.9090	---其他	14	0 巴PK,冰岛IS,东盟AS,哥CR,秘鲁PE,新加坡SG,新西兰NZ,智利CL 8.4 澳AU 9.8 瑞士CH 11.2 韩国KR	0 受惠国$_1$LD$_1$	100	---Other
	63.07	**其他制成品,包括服装裁剪样:**					**Other made-up articles, including dress patterns:**
4742	6307.1000	-擦地布、擦碗布、抹布及类似擦拭用布	14	0 冰岛IS,东盟AS,哥CR,秘鲁PE,台湾TW,新加坡SG,新西兰NZ,智利CL 7 巴PK 8.4 澳AU 9.8 瑞士CH 11.2 韩国KR 11.9 亚太AP	0 受惠国$_1$LD$_1$	130	-Floor-cloths, dish-cloths, dusters and similar cleaning cloths
4743	6307.2000	-救生衣及安全带	14	0 冰岛IS,东盟AS,哥CR,秘鲁PE,新加坡SG,新西兰NZ,智利CL 8.4 澳AU 9.8 瑞士CH 11.2 巴PK,韩国KR	0 受惠国LD	70	-Life-jackets and life-belts
4744	6307.9000	-其他	14	0 澳门MO,冰岛IS,东盟AS,哥CR,秘鲁PE,香港HK,新加坡SG,新西兰NZ,智利CL 8.4 澳AU 9.8 瑞士CH 11.2 巴PK 12.1 韩国KR	0 柬埔寨KH,老挝LA,缅甸MM,受惠国LD	100	-Other
		第二分章　成套物品					II.SETS

序号 No.	税则号列 Tariff Line	中文货品名称 Article Description in Chinese	最惠国税率 MFN(%)	协定税率 Agreement(%)	特惠税率 SP(%)	普通税率 Gen(%)	英文货品名称 Article Description
	63.08	由机织物及纱线构成的零售包装成套物品，不论是否带附件，用以制作小地毯、装饰毯、绣花台布、餐巾或类似的纺织物品					**Sets consisting of woven fabric and yarn, whether or not with accessories, for making up into rugs, tapestries, embroidered tablecloths or serviettes, or similar textile articles, put up in packings for retail sale**
4745	6308.0000	由机织物及纱线构成的零售包装成套物品，不论是否带附件，用以制作小地毯、装饰毯、绣花台布、餐巾或类似的纺织物品	14	0 冰岛IS,东盟AS,哥CR,秘鲁PE,新加坡SG,新西兰NZ,智利CL 7 巴PK 8.4 澳AU 9.8 瑞士CH 11.2 韩国KR	0 受惠国$_1$LD$_1$	130	Sets consisting of woven fabric and yarn, whether or not with accessories, for making up into rugs, tapestries, embroidered table cloths or serviettes, or similar textile articles, put up in packings for retail sale
		第三分章　旧衣着及旧纺织品；碎织物					III. WORN CLOTHING AND WORN TEXTILE ARTICLES; RAGS
	63.09	**旧衣物**					**Worn clothing and other worn articles**
4746	6309.0000	旧衣物	14	0 冰岛IS,东盟AS,哥CR,秘鲁PE,新加坡SG,新西兰NZ,智利CL 7 巴PK 8.4 澳AU 9.8 瑞士CH 11.2 韩国KR	0 受惠国$_1$LD$_1$	130	Worn clothing and other worn articles
	63.10	**纺织材料的新的或旧的碎织物及废线、绳、索、缆及其制品：**					**Used or new rags, scrap twine, cordage, rope and cables and worn out articles of twine, cordage, rope or cables, of textile materials:**
4747	6310.1000	-经分拣的	14	0 冰岛IS,东盟AS,哥CR,秘鲁PE,新加坡SG,新西兰NZ,智利CL 8.4 澳AU 9.8 瑞士CH 11.2 巴PK,韩国KR	0 受惠国LD	50	-Sorted
4748	6310.9000	-其他	14	0 冰岛IS,东盟AS,哥CR,秘鲁PE,新加坡SG,新西兰NZ,智利CL 8.4 澳AU 9.8 瑞士CH 11.2 韩国KR	0 柬埔寨KH,老挝LA,缅甸MM,受惠国LD	50	-Other

第十二类
鞋、帽、伞、杖、鞭及其零件；已加工的羽毛及其制品；人造花；人发制品

SECTION XII
FOOTWEAR, HEADGEAR, UMBRELLAS, SUN UMBRELLAS, WALKING-STICKS, SEAT-STICKS, WHIPS, RIDING-CROPS AND PARTS THEREOF; PREPARED FEATHERS AND ARTICLES MADE THEREWITH; ARTIFICIAL FLOWERS; ARTICLES OF HUMAN HAIR

第六十四章
鞋靴、护腿和类似品及其零件

注释：

一、本章不包括：

（一）易损材料（例如，纸、塑料薄膜）制的无外绱鞋底的一次性鞋靴罩或套，这些产品应按其构成材料归类；

（二）纺织材料制的鞋靴，没有用粘、缝或其他方法将外底固定或安装在鞋面上的（第十一类）；

（三）税号63.09的旧鞋靴；

（四）石棉制品（税号68.12）；

（五）矫形鞋靴或其他矫形器具及其零件（税号90.21）；

（六）玩具鞋及装有冰刀或轮子的滑冰鞋；护胫或类似的运动防护服装（第九十五章）。

二、税号64.06所称“零件”，不包括鞋钉、护鞋铁掌、鞋眼、鞋钩、鞋扣、饰物、编带、鞋带、绒球或其他装饰带（应分别归入相应税号）及税号96.06的钮扣或其他货品。

三、本章所称：

（一）“橡胶”及“塑料”，包括能用肉眼辨出其外表有一层橡胶或塑料的机织物或其他纺织产品，运用本款时，橡胶或塑料仅引起颜色变化的不计在内。

（二）“皮革”，是指税号41.07及41.12至41.14的货品。

四、除本章注释三另有规定的以外：

（一）鞋面的材料应以占表面面积最大的那种材料为准，计算表面面积可不考虑附件及加固件，例如，护踝、裹边、饰物、扣子、拉襻、鞋眼或类似附属件；

（二）外底的主要材料应以与地面接触最广的那种材料为准，计算接触面时可不考虑鞋底钉、铁掌或类似附属件。

子目注释：

子目号6402.12、6402.19、6403.12、6403.19及6404.11所称“运动鞋靴”，仅适用于：

Chapter 64
Footwear, gaiters and the like; parts of such articles

Notes:

1. This Chapter does not cover :

(a) Disposable foot or shoe coverings of flimsy material (for example, paper, sheeting of plastics) without applied soles. These products are classified according to their constituent material;

(b) Footwear of textile material, without an outer sole glued, sewn or otherwise affixed or applied to the upper (Section XI);

(c) Worn footwear of heading No.63.09;

(d) Articles of asbestos (heading No.68.12);

(e) Orthopaedic footwear or other orthopaedic appliances, or parts thereof (heading No.90.21); or

(f) Toy footwear or skating boots with ice or roller skates attached; shin guards or similar protective sportswear (Chapter 95).

2. For the purposes of heading No.64.06, the term "parts" does not include pegs, protectors, eyelets, hooks, buckles, ornaments, braid, laces, pompons or other trimmings (which are to be classified in their appropriate headings) or buttons or other goods of heading No.96.06.

3. For the purposes of this Chapter:

(a) the terms "rubber" and "plastics" include woven fabrics or other textile products with an external layer of rubber or plastics being visible to the naked eye; for the purpose of this provision, no account should be taken of any resulting change of colour; and

(b) the term "leather" refers to the goods of headings 41.07 and 41.12 to 41.14.

4. Subject to Note3 to this Chapter:

(a) the material of the upper shall be taken to be the constituent material having the greatest external surface area, no account being taken of accessories or reinforcements such as ankle patches, edging, ornamentation, buckles, tabs, eyelet stays or similar attachments;

(b) the constituent material of the outer sole shall be taken to be the material having the greatest surface area in contact with the ground, no account being taken of accessories or reinforcements such as spikes, bars, nails, protectors or similar attachments.

Subheading Notes:

For the purposes of subheadings Nos.6402.12, 6402.19, 6403.12, 6403.19 and 6404.11, the expression "sports foot-

一、带有或可装鞋底钉、止滑柱、夹钳、马蹄掌或类似品的体育专用鞋靴；

二、滑冰靴、滑雪靴及越野滑雪用鞋靴、滑雪板靴、角力靴、拳击靴及赛车鞋。

wear” applies only to:

1. footwear which is designed for a sporting activity and has, or has provision for the attachment of, spikes, sprigs, stops, clips, bars or the like;
2. skating boots, ski-boots and cross-country ski footwear, snow-board boots, wrestling boots, boxing boots and cycling shoes.

序号 No.	税则号列 Tariff Line	中文货品名称 Article Description in Chinese	最惠国税率 MFN(%)	协定税率 Agreement(%)	特惠税率 SP(%)	普通税率 Gen(%)	英文货品名称 Article Description
	64.01	**橡胶或塑料制外底及鞋面的防水鞋靴，其鞋面不是用缝、铆、钉、旋、塞或类似方法固定在鞋底上的：**					**Waterproof footwear with outer soles and uppers of rubber or of plastics, the uppers of which are neither fixed to the sole nor assembled by stitching, riveting, nailing, screwing, plugging or similar processes:**
		-装有金属防护鞋头的鞋靴：					-Footwear incorporating a protective metal toecap:
4749	6401.1010	---橡胶制鞋面的	24	0 冰岛IS,东盟AS,哥CR,新加坡SG,新西兰NZ,智利CL 7.2 秘鲁PE 12 巴PK,亚太AP 14.4 澳AU 16.8 瑞士CH 21.6 韩国KR	0 受惠国$_1$LD$_1$	100	---With uppers of rubber
4750	6401.1090	---塑料制鞋面的	24	0 冰岛IS,东盟AS,哥CR,新加坡SG,新西兰NZ,智利CL 7.2 秘鲁PE 12 巴PK,亚太AP 14.4 澳AU 16.8 瑞士CH 21.6 韩国KR	0 受惠国$_1$LD$_1$	100	---With uppers of plastics
		-其他鞋靴：					-Other footwear:
		--中、短统靴（过踝但未到膝）：					--Covering the ankle but not covering the knee:
4751	6401.9210	---橡胶制鞋面的	24	0 冰岛IS,东盟AS,哥CR,新加坡SG,新西兰NZ,智利CL 7.2 秘鲁PE 12 巴PK,亚太AP 14.4 澳AU 16.8 瑞士CH 21.6 韩国KR	0 受惠国$_1$LD$_1$	100	---With uppers of rubber
4752	6401.9290	---塑料制鞋面的	24	0 冰岛IS,东盟AS,哥CR,新加坡SG,新西兰NZ,智利CL 7.2 秘鲁PE 12 巴PK,亚太AP 14.4 澳AU 16.8 瑞士CH 21.6 韩国KR	0 受惠国$_1$LD$_1$	100	---With uppers of plastics
4753	6401.9900	--其他	24	0 冰岛IS,东盟AS,哥CR,新加坡SG,新西兰NZ,智利CL 7.2 秘鲁PE 12 巴PK,亚太AP 14.4 澳AU 16.8 瑞士CH 21.6 韩国KR	0 受惠国$_1$LD$_1$	100	--Other
	64.02	**橡胶或塑料制外底及鞋面的其他鞋靴：**					**Other footwear with outer soles and uppers of rubber or plastics:**
		-运动鞋靴：					-Sports footwear:

序号 No.	税则号列 Tariff Line	中文货品名称 Article Description in Chinese	最惠国税率 MFN(%)	协定税率 Agreement(%)	特惠税率 SP(%)	普通税率 Gen(%)	英文货品名称 Article Description
4754	6402.1200	--滑雪靴、越野滑雪鞋靴及滑雪板靴	10	0 冰岛IS,东盟AS,哥CR,秘鲁PE,新西兰NZ,智利CL 4 瑞士CH 5 巴PK,亚太AP 6 澳AU 8 韩国KR	0 受惠国LD	100	--Ski-boots, cross-country ski footwear and snowboard boots
4755	6402.1900	--其他	24	0 冰岛IS,东盟AS,哥CR,新加坡SG,新西兰NZ,智利CL 7.2 秘鲁PE 12 巴PK,亚太AP 14.4 澳AU 16.8 瑞士CH 21.6 韩国KR	0 受惠国$_1$LD$_1$	100	--Other
4756	6402.2000	-用栓塞方法将鞋面条带装配在鞋底上的鞋	24	0 冰岛IS,东盟AS,哥CR,新加坡SG,新西兰NZ,智利CL 7.2 秘鲁PE 12 巴PK,亚太AP 14.4 澳AU 16.8 瑞士CH 21.6 韩国KR	0 受惠国$_1$LD$_1$	100	-Footwear with uppe r straps or thongs assembled to the sole by means of plugs
		-其他鞋靴:					-Other footwear:
4757	6402.9100	--短统靴（过踝）	24Δ12	0 澳门MO,冰岛IS,东盟AS,哥CR,新加坡SG,新西兰NZ,智利CL 7.2 秘鲁PE 12 巴PK,亚太AP 14.4 澳AU 16.8 瑞士CH 21.6 韩国KR	0 受惠国$_1$LD$_1$	100	--Covering the ankle
		--其他:					--Other:
4758	6402.9910	---橡胶制鞋面的	24Δ12	0 澳门MO,冰岛IS,东盟AS,哥CR,新加坡SG,新西兰NZ,智利CL 7.2 秘鲁PE 12 巴PK,亚太AP 14.4 澳AU 16.8 瑞士CH 21.6 韩国KR	0 受惠国LD	100	---With uppers of rubber
		---塑料制鞋面的:					---With uppers of plastics:
4759	6402.9921	----以机织物或其他纺织材料作衬底的	24	0 澳门MO,冰岛IS,东盟AS,哥CR,新加坡SG,新西兰NZ,智利CL 7.2 秘鲁PE 12 巴PK,亚太AP 14.4 澳AU 16.8 瑞士CH 21.6 韩国KR	0 受惠国LD	100	----Woven fabrics or other textile products as substrate
4760	6402.9929	----其他	24	0 澳门MO,冰岛IS,东盟AS,哥CR,新加坡SG,新西兰NZ,智利CL 7.2 秘鲁PE 12 巴PK,亚太AP 14.4 澳AU 16.8 瑞士CH 21.6 韩国KR	0 受惠国LD	100	----Other
	64.03	**橡胶、塑料、皮革或再生皮革制外底，皮革制鞋面的鞋靴:**					**Footwear with outer soles of rubber, plastics, leather or composition leather and uppers of leather:**
		-运动鞋靴:					-Sports footwear:

序号 No.	税则号列 Tariff Line	中文货品名称 Article Description in Chinese	最惠国税率 MFN(%)	协定税率 Agreement(%)	特惠税率 SP(%)	普通税率 Gen(%)	英文货品名称 Article Description
4761	6403.1200	--滑雪靴、越野滑雪鞋靴及滑雪板靴	24	0 冰岛IS,东盟AS,哥CR,新加坡SG,新西兰NZ,智利CL 7.2 秘鲁PE 14.4 澳AU 16.8 瑞士CH 21.6 韩国KR	0 柬埔寨KH,受惠国LD	100	--Ski-boots, cross-country ski footwear and snowboard boots
4762	6403.1900	--其他	15	0 澳门MO,冰岛IS,东盟AS,哥CR,新加坡SG,新西兰NZ,智利CL 4.5 秘鲁PE 9 澳AU 10.5 瑞士CH 12 巴PK,韩国KR	0 柬埔寨KH,受惠国LD	100	--Other
4763	6403.2000	-皮革制外底，由交叉于脚背并绕大脚趾的皮革条带构成鞋面的鞋	24	0 澳门MO,冰岛IS,东盟AS,哥CR,新加坡SG,新西兰NZ,智利CL 7.2 秘鲁PE 14.4 澳AU 16.8 瑞士CH 21.6 韩国KR	0 柬埔寨KH,受惠国LD	100	-Footwear with outer soles of leather, and uppers which consist of leather straps across the instep and around the big toe
4764	6403.4000	-装有金属防护鞋头的其他鞋靴	24	0 冰岛IS,东盟AS,哥CR,新加坡SG,新西兰NZ,智利CL 7.2 秘鲁PE 14.4 澳AU 16.8 瑞士CH 21.6 韩国KR	0 柬埔寨KH,受惠国LD	100	-Other footwear, incorporating a protective metal toe-cap
		-皮革制外底的其他鞋靴：					-Other footwear with outer soles of leather:
		--短统靴（过踝）：					--Covering the ankle:
		---过脚踝但低于小腿的短统靴，按内底长度分类：					---No part of the calf, with insoles of a length:
4765	6403.5111	----小于24厘米的	10	0 澳门MO,冰岛IS,东盟AS,哥CR,秘鲁PE,新西兰NZ,智利CL 4 瑞士CH 5 巴PK 6 澳AU 8 韩国KR	0 柬埔寨KH,受惠国LD	100	----Of less than 24cm
4766	6403.5119	----其他	10	0 冰岛IS,东盟AS,哥CR,秘鲁PE,新西兰NZ,智利CL 4 瑞士CH 5 巴PK 6 澳AU 8 韩国KR	0 柬埔寨KH,受惠国LD	100	----Other
		---其他，按内底长度分类：					---Other, with insoles of a length:
4767	6403.5191	----小于24厘米的	10	0 冰岛IS,东盟AS,哥CR,秘鲁PE,新西兰NZ,智利CL 4 瑞士CH 5 巴PK 6 澳AU 8 韩国KR	0 柬埔寨KH,受惠国LD	100	----Of less than 24cm
4768	6403.5199	----其他	10	0 冰岛IS,东盟AS,哥CR,秘鲁PE,新西兰NZ,智利CL 4 瑞士CH 5 巴PK 6 澳AU 8 韩国KR	0 柬埔寨KH,受惠国LD	100	----Other

序号 No.	税则号列 Tariff Line	中文货品名称 Article Description in Chinese	最惠国税率 MFN(%)	协定税率 Agreement(%)	特惠税率 SP(%)	普通税率 Gen(%)	英文货品名称 Article Description
4769	6403.5900	--其他	10	0 澳门MO,冰岛IS,东盟AS,哥CR,新西兰NZ,智利CL 3 秘鲁PE 5 巴PK 6 澳AU 7 瑞士CH 8 韩国KR	0 柬埔寨KH,受惠国LD	100	--Other
		-其他鞋靴:					-Other footwear:
		--短统靴（过踝）:					--Covering the ankle:
		---过脚踝但低于小腿的短统靴，按内底长度分类:					---No part of the calf, with insoles of a length:
4770	6403.9111	----小于24厘米的	10	0 澳门MO,冰岛IS,东盟AS,哥CR,秘鲁PE,新加坡SG,新西兰NZ,智利CL 5 巴PK 6 澳AU 7 瑞士CH 8 韩国KR	0 柬埔寨KH,受惠国LD	100	----Of less than 24cm
4771	6403.9119	----其他	10	0 澳门MO,冰岛IS,东盟AS,哥CR,秘鲁PE,新加坡SG,新西兰NZ,智利CL 4 瑞士CH 5 巴PK 6 澳AU 8 韩国KR	0 柬埔寨KH,受惠国LD	100	----Other
		---其他，按内底长度分类:					---Other, with insoles of a length:
4772	6403.9191	----小于24厘米的	10	0 澳门MO,冰岛IS,东盟AS,哥CR,秘鲁PE,新加坡SG,新西兰NZ,智利CL 4 瑞士CH 5 巴PK 6 澳AU 8 韩国KR	0 柬埔寨KH,受惠国LD	100	----Of less than 24cm
4773	6403.9199	----其他	10	0 澳门MO,冰岛IS,东盟AS,哥CR,秘鲁PE,新加坡SG,新西兰NZ,智利CL 4 瑞士CH 5 巴PK 6 澳AU 8 韩国KR	0 柬埔寨KH,受惠国LD	100	----Other
4774	6403.9900	--其他	10	0 澳门MO,冰岛IS,东盟AS,哥CR,秘鲁PE,新加坡SG,新西兰NZ,智利CL 5 巴PK 6 澳AU 7 瑞士CH 8 韩国KR 8.5 亚太AP	0 柬埔寨KH,受惠国LD	100	--Other
	64.04	**橡胶、塑料、皮革或再生皮革制外底，用纺织材料制鞋面的鞋靴:**					**Footwear with outer soles of rubber, plastics, leather or composition leather and uppers of textile materials:**
		-橡胶或塑料制外底的鞋靴:					-Footwear with outer soles of rubber or plastics:

序号 No.	税则号列 Tariff Line	中文货品名称 Article Description in Chinese	最惠国税率 MFN(%)	协定税率 Agreement(%)	特惠税率 SP(%)	普通税率 Gen(%)	英文货品名称 Article Description
4775	6404.1100	--运动鞋靴;网球鞋、篮球鞋、体操鞋、训练鞋及类似鞋	24Δ12	0 澳门MO,冰岛IS,东盟AS,哥CR,新加坡SG,新西兰NZ,智利CL 7.2 秘鲁PE 12 巴PK,亚太AP 14.4 澳AU 16.8 瑞士CH 21.6 韩国KR	0 受惠国$_1$LD$_1$	100	--Sports footwear, tennis shoes, basketba-ll shoes, gym shoes, training shoes and the like
		--其他:					--Other:
4776	6404.1910	---拖鞋	24	0 澳门MO,冰岛IS,东盟AS,哥CR,新加坡SG,新西兰NZ,智利CL 7.2 秘鲁PE 12 巴PK,亚太AP 14.4 澳AU 16.8 瑞士CH 21.6 韩国KR	0 受惠国$_1$LD$_1$	100	---Slippers
4777	6404.1990	---其他	24	0 澳门MO,冰岛IS,东盟AS,哥CR,新加坡SG,新西兰NZ,智利CL 7.2 秘鲁PE 12 巴PK,亚太AP 14.4 澳AU 16.8 瑞士CH 21.6 韩国KR	0 受惠国$_1$LD$_1$	100	---Other
		-皮革或再生皮革制外底的鞋靴:					-Footwear with outer soles of leather or composition leather:
4778	6404.2010	---拖鞋	24	0 冰岛IS,东盟AS,哥CR,新加坡SG,新西兰NZ,智利CL 7.2 秘鲁PE 12 巴PK,亚太AP 14.4 澳AU 16.8 瑞士CH 21.6 韩国KR	0 受惠国$_1$LD$_1$	100	---Slippers
4779	6404.2090	---其他	24	0 冰岛IS,东盟AS,哥CR,新加坡SG,新西兰NZ,智利CL 7.2 秘鲁PE 12 巴PK,亚太AP 14.4 澳AU 16.8 瑞士CH 21.6 韩国KR	0 受惠国$_1$LD$_1$	100	---Other
	64.05	**其他鞋靴:**					**Other footwear:**
		-皮革或再生皮革制鞋面的:					-With uppers of leather or composition leather:
4780	6405.1010	---橡胶、塑料、皮革及再生皮革制外底的	24Δ12	0 冰岛IS,东盟AS,哥CR,新加坡SG,新西兰NZ,智利CL 7.2 秘鲁PE 12 巴PK,亚太AP 14.4 澳AU 16.8 瑞士CH 21.6 韩国KR	0 受惠国$_1$LD$_1$	100	---With outer soles of rubber, plastics, leather or composition leather
4781	6405.1090	---其他材料制外底的	24Δ12	0 冰岛IS,东盟AS,哥CR,新加坡SG,新西兰NZ,智利CL 7.2 秘鲁PE 12 巴PK,亚太AP 14.4 澳AU 16.8 瑞士CH 21.6 韩国KR	0 受惠国$_1$LD$_1$	100	---With outer soles of other materials

序号 No.	税则号列 Tariff Line	中文货品名称 Article Description in Chinese	最惠国税率 MFN(%)	协定税率 Agreement(%)	特惠税率 SP(%)	普通税率 Gen(%)	英文货品名称 Article Description
4782	6405.2000	-纺织材料制鞋面的	22Δ12	0 冰岛IS,东盟AS,哥CR,新加坡SG,新西兰NZ,智利CL 6.6 秘鲁PE 11 巴PK,亚太AP 13.2 澳AU 15.4 瑞士CH 19.8 韩国KR	0 受惠国$_1$LD$_1$	100	-With uppers of textile material
		-其他:					-Other:
4783	6405.9010	---橡胶、塑料、皮革及再生皮革制外底的	15	0 冰岛IS,东盟AS,哥CR,新加坡SG,新西兰NZ,智利CL 4.5 秘鲁PE 7.5 巴PK 9 澳AU 10.5 瑞士CH,亚太AP 12 韩国KR	0 受惠国$_1$LD$_1$	100	---With outer soles of rubber, plastics, leather or composition leather
4784	6405.9090	---其他材料制外底的	15	0 冰岛IS,东盟AS,哥CR,新加坡SG,新西兰NZ,智利CL 4.5 秘鲁PE 7.5 巴PK 9 澳AU 10.5 瑞士CH,亚太AP 12 韩国KR	0 受惠国$_1$LD$_1$	100	---With outer soles of other materials
	64.06	**鞋靴零件(包括鞋面,不论是否带有除外底以外的其他鞋底);活动式鞋内底、跟垫及类似品;护腿、裹腿和类似品及其零件:**					**Parts of footwear (including uppers whether or not attached to soles other than outer soles) ; removable insoles, heel cushions and similar articles; gaiters, leggings and similar articles, and parts thereof:**
4785	6406.1000	-鞋面及其零件,但硬衬除外	15	0 冰岛IS,东盟AS,哥CR,台湾TW,新加坡SG,新西兰NZ,智利CL 4.5 秘鲁PE 7.5 巴PK 9 澳AU 10.5 瑞士CH 13.2 亚太AP 13.5 韩国KR	0 受惠国$_1$LD$_1$	90	-Uppers and parts thereof, other than stiffeners
		-橡胶或塑料制的外底及鞋跟:					-Outer soles and heels, of rubber or plastics:
4786	6406.2010	---橡胶制的	15	0 冰岛IS,东盟AS,哥CR,台湾TW,新加坡SG,新西兰NZ,智利CL 4.5 秘鲁PE 9 澳AU 10.5 瑞士CH 12 巴PK,韩国KR	0 受惠国LD	90	---Of rubber
4787	6406.2020	---塑料制的	15	0 冰岛IS,东盟AS,哥CR,新加坡SG,新西兰NZ,智利CL 4.5 秘鲁PE 9 澳AU 10.5 瑞士CH 12 巴PK,韩国KR	0 受惠国LD	90	---Of plastics
		-其他:					-Other:
4788	6406.9010	---木制	15	0 冰岛IS,东盟AS,哥CR,新加坡SG,新西兰NZ,智利CL 4.5 秘鲁PE 7.5 巴PK 9 澳AU 10.5 瑞士CH,亚太AP 12 韩国KR	0 受惠国$_1$LD$_1$	90	---Of wood

序号 No.	税则号列 Tariff Line	中文货品名称 Article Description in Chinese	最惠国税率 MFN(%)	协定税率 Agreement(%)	特惠税率 SP(%)	普通税率 Gen(%)	英文货品名称 Article Description
		---其他材料制:					---Of other materials:
4789	6406.9091	----活动式鞋内底、跟垫及类似品	15	0 澳门MO,冰岛IS,东盟AS,哥CR,台湾TW,香港HK,新加坡SG,新西兰NZ,智利CL 4.5 秘鲁PE 7.5 巴PK 9 澳AU 10.5 瑞士CH,亚太AP 13.5 韩国KR	0 受惠国$_1$LD$_1$	90	----Non-wood removable insoles, heel cushions and similar articles
4790	6406.9092	----护腿、裹腿和类似品及其零件	15	0 澳门MO,冰岛IS,东盟AS,哥CR,台湾TW,香港HK,新加坡SG,新西兰NZ,智利CL 4.5 秘鲁PE 7.5 巴PK 9 澳AU 10.5 瑞士CH,亚太AP 13.5 韩国KR	0 受惠国$_1$LD$_1$	90	----Non-wood gaiters, leggings and similar articles, and parts thereof
4791	6406.9099	----其他	15	0 澳门MO,冰岛IS,东盟AS,哥CR,台湾TW,香港HK,新加坡SG,新西兰NZ,智利CL 4.5 秘鲁PE 7.5 巴PK 9 澳AU 10.5 瑞士CH,亚太AP 13.5 韩国KR	0 受惠国$_1$LD$_1$	90	----Of other materials

第六十五章

帽类及其零件

Chapter 65

Headgear and parts thereof

注释：

一、本章不包括：

（一）税号 63.09 的旧帽类；

（二）石棉制帽类（税号 68.12）；

（三）第九十五章的玩偶帽、其他玩具帽或狂欢节用品。

二、税号 65.02 不包括缝制的帽坯，但仅将条带缝成螺旋形的除外。

Notes:

1. This Chapter does not cover:

(a) Worn headgear of heading No.63.09;

(b) Asbestos headgear (Heading No.68.12); or

(c) Dolls' hats, other toy hats or carnival articles of Chapter 95.

2. Heading No.65.02 does not cover hat-shapes made by sewing, other than those obtained simply by sewing strips in spirals.

序号 No.	税则号列 Tariff Line	中文货品名称 Article Description in Chinese	最惠国税率 MFN(%)	协定税率 Agreement(%)	特惠税率 SP(%)	普通税率 Gen(%)	英文货品名称 Article Description
	65.01	**毡呢制的帽坯、帽身及帽兜，未楦制成形，也未加帽边；毡呢制的圆帽片及制帽用的毡呢筒（包括裁开的毡呢筒）**					**Hat-forms, hat bodies and hoods of felt, neither blocked to shape nor with made brims; plateaux and manchons (including slit manchons), of felt**
4792	6501.0000	毡呢制的帽坯、帽身及帽兜，未楦制成形，也未加帽边；毡呢制的圆帽片及制帽用的毡呢筒（包括裁开的毡呢筒）	22	0 冰岛IS,东盟AS,哥CR,新加坡SG,新西兰NZ,智利CL 6.6 秘鲁PE 13.2 澳AU 15.4 瑞士CH 19.8 韩国KR	0 受惠国$_1$LD$_1$	100	Hat-forms, hat bodies and hoods of felt, neither blocked to shape nor with made brims; plateaux and manchons (including slit manchons) , of felt
	65.02	**编结的帽坯或用任何材料的条带拼制而成的帽坯，未楦制成形，也未加帽边、衬里或装饰物**					**Hat-shapes, plaited or made by assembling strips of any material, neither blocked to shape, nor with made brims, nor lined, nor trimmed**
4793	6502.0000	编结的帽坯或用任何材料的条带拼制而成的帽坯，未楦制成形，也未加帽边、衬里或装饰物	20	0 冰岛IS,东盟AS,哥CR,新加坡SG,新西兰NZ,智利CL 6 秘鲁PE 12 澳AU 14 瑞士CH 17.3 韩国KR	0 受惠国$_1$LD$_1$	100	Hat-shapes, plaited or made by assembling strips of any material, neither blocked to shape, nor with made brims, nor lined, nor trimmed
	65.04	**编结帽或用任何材料的条带拼制而成的帽类，不论有无衬里或装饰物**					**Hats and other headgear, plaited or made by assembling strips of any material, whether or not lined or trimmed**
4794	6504.0000	编结帽或用任何材料的条带拼制而成的帽类，不论有无衬里或装饰物	20	0 冰岛IS,东盟AS,哥CR,新加坡SG,新西兰NZ,智利CL 6 秘鲁PE 12 澳AU 14 瑞士CH 17.3 韩国KR	0 受惠国$_1$LD$_1$	130	Hats and other headgear, plaited or made by assembling strips of any material, whether or not lined or trimmed
	65.05	**针织或钩编的帽类，用成匹的花边、毡呢或其他纺织物（条带除外）制成的帽类，不论有无衬里或装饰物；任何材料制的发网，不论有无衬里或装饰物：**					**Hats and other headgear, knitted or crocheted, or made up from lace, felt or other textile fabric, in the piece (but not in strips) , whether or not lined or trimmed; hairnets of any material, whether or not lined or trimmed:**

序号 No.	税则号列 Tariff Line	中文货品名称 Article Description in Chinese	最惠国税率 MFN(%)	协定税率 Agreement(%)	特惠税率 SP(%)	普通税率 Gen(%)	英文货品名称 Article Description
4795	6505.0010	---发网	10	0 冰岛IS,东盟AS,哥CR,秘鲁PE,新西兰NZ,智利CL 4 瑞士CH 5 巴PK 6 澳AU 8 韩国KR	0 受惠国LD	130	---Hair-nets
4796	6505.0020	---钩编的帽类	20	0 冰岛IS,东盟AS,哥CR,新加坡SG,新西兰NZ,智利CL 6 秘鲁PE 12 澳AU 14 瑞士CH 17.3 韩国KR 19 巴PK,亚太AP	0 受惠国LD	130	---Hats and other headgear, knitted or crocheted
		---其他:					---Other:
4797	6505.0091	----用税号65.01的帽身、帽兜或圆帽片制成的毡呢帽类，不论有无衬里或装饰物	22	0 冰岛IS,东盟AS,哥CR,新加坡SG,新西兰NZ,智利CL 6.6 秘鲁PE 13.2 澳AU 15.4 瑞士CH 19.8 韩国KR	0 受惠国$_1$LD$_1$	130	----Felt hats and other felt headgear, made from the hat bodies, hoods or plateaux of heading No.65.01, whether or not lined or trimmed
4798	6505.0099	----其他	20	0 澳门MO,冰岛IS,东盟AS,哥CR,新加坡SG,新西兰NZ,智利CL 6 秘鲁PE 12 澳AU 14 瑞士CH 16 韩国KR 19 巴PK,亚太AP	0 受惠国LD	130	----Other
	65.06	**其他帽类，不论有无衬里或装饰物:**					**Other headgear, whether or not lined or trimmed:**
4799	6506.1000	-安全帽	10	0 冰岛IS,东盟AS,哥CR,秘鲁PE,新西兰NZ,智利CL 4 瑞士CH 5 巴PK 6 澳AU 8 韩国KR	0 受惠国$_1$LD$_1$	100	-Safety headgear
		-其他:					-Other:
4800	6506.9100	--橡胶或塑料制	10	0 冰岛IS,东盟AS,哥CR,秘鲁PE,新西兰NZ,智利CL 4 瑞士CH 5 巴PK 6 澳AU 8 韩国KR	0 受惠国$_1$LD$_1$	100	--Of rubber or of plastics
		--其他材料制:					--Of other materials:
4801	6506.9910	---皮革制	10	0 冰岛IS,东盟AS,哥CR,秘鲁PE,新西兰NZ,智利CL 4 瑞士CH 5 巴PK 6 澳AU 8 韩国KR	0 受惠国$_1$LD$_1$	130	---Of leather
4802	6506.9920	---毛皮制	10	0 冰岛IS,东盟AS,哥CR,秘鲁PE,香港HK,新西兰NZ,智利CL 4 瑞士CH 5 巴PK 6 澳AU 8 韩国KR	0 受惠国LD	130	---Of furskin

序号 No.	税则号列 Tariff Line	中文货品名称 Article Description in Chinese	最惠国税率 MFN(%)	协定税率 Agreement(%)	特惠税率 SP(%)	普通税率 Gen(%)	英文货品名称 Article Description
4803	6506.9990	---其他	24	0 冰岛IS,东盟AS,哥CR,新加坡SG,新西兰NZ,智利CL 7.2 秘鲁PE 14.4 澳AU 16.8 瑞士CH 21.6 韩国KR	0 受惠国LD	100	---Other
	65.07	**帽圈、帽衬、帽套、帽帮、帽骨架、帽舌及帽颏带**					**Headbands, linings, covers, hat foundations, hat frames, peaks and chinstraps, for headgear**
4804	6507.0000	帽圈、帽衬、帽套、帽帮、帽骨架、帽舌及帽颏带	24	0 澳门MO,冰岛IS,东盟AS,哥CR,新加坡SG,新西兰NZ,智利CL 7.2 秘鲁PE 14.4 澳AU 16.8 瑞士CH 21.6 韩国KR	0 受惠国$_1$LD$_1$	100	Head-bands, linings, covers, hat foundations, hat frames, peaks and chinstraps, for headgear

第六十六章
雨伞、阳伞、手杖、鞭子、马鞭及其零件

Chapter 66
Umbrellas, sun umbrellas, walking-sticks, seat-sticks, whips, riding-crops and parts thereof

注释：

一、本章不包括：

（一）丈量用杖及类似品（税号 90.17）；

（二）火器手杖、刀剑手杖、灌铅手杖及类似品（第九十三章）；

（三）第九十五章的货品（例如，玩具雨伞、玩具阳伞）。

二、税号 66.03 不包括纺织材料制的零件、附件及装饰品或者任何材料制的罩套、流苏、鞭梢、伞套及类似品。此类货品即使与税号 66.01 或 66.02 的物品一同进口或出口，只要未装配在一起，则不应视为上述税号所列物品的组成零件，而应分别归入各有关税号。

Notes:

1. This Chapter does not cover:

(a) Measure walking-sticks or the like (heading No.90.17);

(b) Firearm-sticks，sword-sticks，loaded walking-sticks or the like (Chapter 93); or

(c) Goods of Chapter 95 (for example, toy umbrellas, toy sun umbrellas).

2. Heading No.66.03 does not cover parts，trimmings or accessories of textile material，or covers，tassels，thongs，umbrella cases or the like，of any material. Such goods presented with，but not fitted to，articles of heading No.66.01 or 66.02 are to be classified separately and not to be treated as forming part of those articles.

序号 No.	税则号列 Tariff Line	中文货品名称 Article Description in Chinese	最惠国税率 MFN(%)	协定税率 Agreement(%)	特惠税率 SP(%)	普通税率 Gen(%)	英文货品名称 Article Description
	66.01	**雨伞及阳伞（包括手杖伞、庭园用伞及类似伞）：**					**Umbrellas and sun umbrellas (including walking-stick umbrellas, garden umbrellas and similar umbrellas) :**
4805	6601.1000	-庭园用伞及类似伞	14	0 冰岛IS,东盟AS,哥CR,秘鲁PE,新加坡SG,新西兰NZ,智利CL 7 巴PK 8.4 澳AU 9.8 瑞士CH 11.2 韩国KR	0 受惠国$_1$LD$_1$	130	-Garden or similar umbrellas
		-其他：					-Other:
4806	6601.9100	--折叠伞	10	0 冰岛IS,东盟AS,哥CR,秘鲁PE,新西兰NZ,智利CL 4 瑞士CH 5 巴PK 6 澳AU 8 韩国KR	0 受惠国LD	130	--Having a telescopic shaft
4807	6601.9900	--其他	10	0 冰岛IS,东盟AS,哥CR,秘鲁PE,新西兰NZ,智利CL 4 瑞士CH 5 巴PK 6 澳AU 8 韩国KR	0 受惠国$_1$LD$_1$	130	--Other
	66.02	**手杖、带座手杖、鞭子、马鞭及类似品**					**Walking sticks, seat-sticks, whips, riding-crops and the like**
4808	6602.0000	手杖、带座手杖、鞭子、马鞭及类似品	10	0 冰岛IS,东盟AS,哥CR,秘鲁PE,新西兰NZ,智利CL 4 瑞士CH 5 巴PK 6 澳AU 8 韩国KR	0 受惠国$_1$LD$_1$	130	Walking-sticks, seat-sticks, whips, riding-crops and the like
	66.03	**税号66.01或66.02所列物品的零件及装饰品：**					**Parts, trimmings and accessories of articles of heading 6601 or 6602:**

序号 No.	税则号列 Tariff Line	中文货品名称 Article Description in Chinese	最惠国税率 MFN(%)	协定税率 Agreement(%)	特惠税率 SP(%)	普通税率 Gen(%)	英文货品名称 Article Description
4809	6603.2000	-伞骨，包括装在伞柄上的伞骨	14	0 冰岛IS,东盟AS,哥CR,秘鲁PE,新加坡SG,新西兰NZ,智利CL 8.4 澳AU 9.8 瑞士CH 11.2 巴PK,韩国KR	0 受惠国$_1$LD$_1$	130	-Umbrella frames, including frames mounted on shafts (sticks)
4810	6603.9000	-其他	14	0 冰岛IS,东盟AS,哥CR,秘鲁PE,新加坡SG,新西兰NZ,智利CL 8.4 澳AU 9.8 瑞士CH 11.2 巴PK,韩国KR	0 受惠国LD	130	-Other

第六十七章
已加工羽毛、羽绒及其制品；人造花；人发制品

Chapter 67
Prepared feathers and down and articles made of feathers or of down; artificial flowers; articles of human hair

注释：

一、本章不包括：

（一）人发制滤布（税号59.11）；

（二）花边、刺绣品或其他纺织物制成的花卉图案（第十一类）；

（三）鞋靴（第六十四章）；

（四）帽类及发网（第六十五章）；

（五）玩具、运动用品或狂欢节用品（第九十五章）；

（六）羽毛掸帚、粉扑及人发制的筛子（第九十六章）。

二、税号67.01不包括：

（一）羽毛或羽绒仅在其中作为填充料的物品（例如税号94.04的寝具）；

（二）羽毛或羽绒仅作为饰物或填充料的衣服或衣着附件；

（三）税号67.02的人造花、叶及其部分品，以及它们的制成品。

三、税号67.02不包括：

（一）玻璃制品（第七十章）；

（二）用陶器、石料、金属、木料或其他材料经模铸、锻造、雕刻、冲压或其他方法整件制成形的人造花、叶或果实；用捆扎、胶粘及类似方法以外的其他方法将部分品组合而成的上述制品。

Notes:

1. This Chapter does not cover:

(a) Straining cloth of human hair (heading No.59.11);

(b) Floral motifs of lace, of embroidery or other textile fabric (Section XI);

(c) Footwear (Chapter64);

(d) Headgear or hair-nets (Chapter65);

(e) Toys, sports requisites or carnival articles (Chapter95); or

(f) Feather dusters, powder-puffs or hair sieves (Chapter 96).

2. Heading No.67.01does not cover:

(a) Articles in which feathers or down constitute only filling or padding (for example, bedding of heading No.94.04);

(b) Articles of apparel or clothing accessories in which feathers or down constitute no more than mere trimming or padding; or

(c) Artificial flowers or foliage or parts thereof or made up articles of heading No.67.02.

3. Heading No.67.02does not cover:

(a) Articles of glass (Chapter70); or

(b) Artificial flowers, foliage or fruit of pottery, stone, metal, wood or other materials, obtained in one piece by moulding, forging, carving, stamping or other process, or consisting of parts assembled otherwise than by binding, glueing, fitting into one another or similar methods.

序号 No.	税则号列 Tariff Line	中文货品名称 Article Description in Chinese	最惠国税率 MFN(%)	协定税率 Agreement(%)	特惠税率 SP(%)	普通税率 Gen(%)	英文货品名称 Article Description
	67.01	**带羽毛或羽绒的鸟皮及鸟体其他部分、羽毛、部分羽毛、羽绒及其制品（税号05.05的货品和经加工的羽管及羽轴除外）**					**Skins and other parts of birds with their feathers or down, feathers, parts of feathers, down and articles thereof (other than goods of heading 0505 and worked quills and scapes)**
4811	6701.0000	带羽毛或羽绒的鸟皮及鸟体其他部分、羽毛、部分羽毛、羽绒及其制品（税号05.05的货品和经加工的羽管及羽轴除外）	20	0 澳门MO,冰岛IS,东盟AS,哥CR,新加坡SG,新西兰NZ,智利CL 6 秘鲁PE 12 澳AU 14 瑞士CH 17.3 韩国KR	0 受惠国$_1$LD$_1$	130	Skins and other parts of birds with their feathers or down, feathers, parts of feathers, down and articles thereof (other than goods of heading No.05.05 and worked quills and scapes)
	67.02	**人造花、叶、果实及其零件;用人造花、叶或果实制成的物品：**					**Artificial flowers, foliage and fruit and parts thereof; articles made of artificial flowers, foliage or fruit:**

序号 No.	税则号列 Tariff Line	中文货品名称 Article Description in Chinese	最惠国税率 MFN(%)	协定税率 Agreement(%)	特惠税率 SP(%)	普通税率 Gen(%)	英文货品名称 Article Description
4812	6702.1000	-塑料制	20	0 冰岛IS,东盟AS,哥CR,新加坡SG,新西兰NZ,智利CL 6 秘鲁PE 12 澳AU 14 瑞士CH 17.3 韩国KR	0 受惠国$_1$LD$_1$	130	-Of plastics
		-其他材料制:					-Of other materials:
4813	6702.9010	---羽毛制	20	0 冰岛IS,东盟AS,哥CR,新加坡SG,新西兰NZ,智利CL 6 秘鲁PE 12 澳AU 14 瑞士CH 17.3 韩国KR	0 受惠国$_1$LD$_1$	130	---Of feathers or down
4814	6702.9020	---丝及绢丝制	24	0 冰岛IS,东盟AS,哥CR,新加坡SG,新西兰NZ,智利CL 7.2 秘鲁PE 14.4 澳AU 16.8 瑞士CH 21.6 韩国KR	0 受惠国$_1$LD$_1$	130	---Of silk or silk waste
4815	6702.9030	---化学纤维制	24	0 冰岛IS,东盟AS,哥CR,新加坡SG,新西兰NZ,智利CL 7.2 秘鲁PE 14.4 澳AU 16.8 瑞士CH 21.6 韩国KR	0 受惠国$_1$LD$_1$	130	---Of man-made fibres
4816	6702.9090	---其他	20	0 冰岛IS,东盟AS,哥CR,新加坡SG,新西兰NZ,智利CL 6 秘鲁PE 12 澳AU 14 瑞士CH 17.3 韩国KR	0 受惠国$_1$LD$_1$	130	---Other
	67.03	**经梳理、稀疏、脱色或其他方法加工的人发;作假发及类似品用的羊毛、其他动物毛或其他纺织材料**					**Human hair, dressed, thinned, bleached or otherwise worked; wool or other animal hair or other textile materials, prepared for use in making wigs or the like**
4817	6703.0000	经梳理、稀疏、脱色或其他方法加工的人发;作假发及类似品用的羊毛、其他动物毛或其他纺织材料	20	0 冰岛IS,东盟AS,哥CR,新加坡SG,新西兰NZ,智利CL 6 秘鲁PE 12 澳AU 14 瑞士CH 16 韩国KR 18 巴PK,亚太AP	0 受惠国$_1$LD$_1$	100	Human hair, dressed, thinned, bleached or otherwise worked; wool or other animal hair or other textile materials, prepared for use in making wigs or the like
	67.04	**人发、动物毛或纺织材料制的假发、假胡须、假眉毛、假睫毛及类似品;其他税号未列名的人发制品:**					**Wigs, false beards, eyebrows and eyelashes, switches and the like, of human or animal hair or of textile materials; articles of human hair not elsewhere specified or included:**
		-合成纤维纺织材料制:					-Of synthetic textile materials:
4818	6704.1100	--整头假发	25	0 冰岛IS,东盟AS,哥CR,新加坡SG,新西兰NZ,智利CL 7.5 秘鲁PE 15 澳AU 18 瑞士CH 22.5 韩国KR	0 受惠国LD	130	--Complete wigs

序号 No.	税则号列 Tariff Line	中文货品名称 Article Description in Chinese	最惠国税率 MFN(%)	协定税率 Agreement(%)	特惠税率 SP(%)	普通税率 Gen(%)	英文货品名称 Article Description
4819	6704.1900	--其他	25	0 澳门MO,冰岛IS,东盟AS,哥CR,新加坡SG,新西兰NZ,智利CL 7.5 秘鲁PE 15 澳AU 18 瑞士CH 22.5 韩国KR	0 受惠国LD	130	--Other
4820	6704.2000	-人发制	15	0 澳门MO,冰岛IS,东盟AS,哥CR,新加坡SG,新西兰NZ,智利CL 4.5 秘鲁PE 9 澳AU 10.5 瑞士CH 12 巴PK,韩国KR	0 受惠国LD	130	-Of human hair
4821	6704.9000	-其他材料制	25	0 澳门MO,冰岛IS,东盟AS,哥CR,新加坡SG,新西兰NZ,智利CL 7.5 秘鲁PE 15 澳AU 18 瑞士CH 22.5 韩国KR	0 受惠国LD	130	-Of other materials

第十三类
石料、石膏、水泥、石棉、云母及类似材料的制品；陶瓷产品；玻璃及其制品

SECTION XIII
ARTICLES OF STONE, PLASTER, CEMENT, ASBESTOS, MICA OR SIMILAR MATERIALS; CERAMIC PRODUCTS; GLASS AND GLASSWARE

第六十八章
石料、石膏、水泥、石棉、云母及类似材料的制品

注释：

一、本章不包括：

（一）第二十五章的货品；

（二）税号48.10或48.11的经涂布、浸渍或覆盖的纸及纸板（例如，用云母粉或石墨涂布的纸及纸板、沥青纸及纸板）；

（三）第五十六章或第五十九章的经涂布、浸渍或包覆的纺织物（例如，用云母粉、沥青涂布或包覆的织物）；

（四）第七十一章的物品；

（五）第八十二章的工具及其零件；

（六）税号84.42的印刷用石板；

（七）绝缘子（税号85.46）或绝缘材料制的零件（税号85.47）；

（八）牙科用磨锉（税号90.18）；

（九）第九十一章的物品（例如，钟及钟壳）；

（十）第九十四章的物品（例如，家具、灯具及照明装置、活动房屋）；

（十一）第九十五章的物品（例如，玩具、游戏品及运动用品）；

（十二）用第九十六章注释二（二）所述材料制成的税号96.02的物品或税号96.06的物品（例如钮扣）、税号96.09的物品（例如石笔）或税号96.10的物品（例如绘画石板）；

（十三）第九十七章的物品（例如艺术品）。

二、税号68.02所称“已加工的碑石或建筑用石”，不仅适用于已加工的税号25.15、25.16的各种石料，也适用于所有经类似加工的其他天然石料（例如，石英岩、燧石、白云石及冻石），但不适用于板岩。

Chapter 68
Articles of stone, plaster, cement, asbestos, mica or similar materials

Notes:

1. This Chapter does not cover :

(a) Goods of Chapter 25;

(b) Coated, impregnated or covered paper and paperboard of heading No.48.10or48.11 (for example, paper and paperboard coated with mica powder or graphite, bituminised or asphalted paper and paperboard);

(c) Coated, impregnated or covered textile fabric of Chapter 56 or 59 (for example, fabric coated or covered with mica powder, bituminised or asphalted fabric);

(d) Articles of Chapter 71;

(e) Tools or parts of tools, of Chapter 82;

(f) Lithographic stones of heading No.84.42;

(g) Electrical insulators (heading No.85.46) or fittings of insulating material of heading No.85.47;

(h) Dental burrs (heading No.90.18);

(i) Articles of Chapter 91 (for example, clocks and clock cases);

(j) Articles of Chapter 94 (for example, furniture, lamps and lighting fittings, prefabricated buildings);

(k) Articles of Chapter 95 (for example, toys, games and sports requisites);

(l) Articles of heading No.96.02, if made of materials specified in Note 2 (b) to Chapter 96, or of heading No.96.06 (for example, buttons) , No.96.09 (for example, slate pencils) or No.96.10 (for example, drawing slates);or

(m) Articles of Chapter 97 (for example, works of art) .

2. In heading No.68.02, the expression “worked monumental or building stone” applies not only to the varieties of stone referred to in heading No.25.15 or 25.16, but also to all other natural stone (for example, quartzite, flint, dolomite and steatite) similarly worked; it does not, however, apply to slate.

序号 No.	税则号列 Tariff Line	中文货品名称 Article Description in Chinese	最惠国税率 MFN(%)	协定税率 Agreement(%)	特惠税率 SP(%)	普通税率 Gen(%)	英文货品名称 Article Description
	68.01	天然石料（不包括板岩）制的长方砌石、路缘石、扁平石					**Setts, curbstones and flagstones, of natural stone (except slate)**

序号 No.	税则号列 Tariff Line	中文货品名称 Article Description in Chinese	最惠国税率 MFN(%)	协定税率 Agreement(%)	特惠税率 SP(%)	普通税率 Gen(%)	英文货品名称 Article Description
4822	6801.0000	天然石料（不包括板岩）制的长方砌石、路缘石、扁平石	12	0 澳门MO,冰岛IS,东盟AS,哥CR,秘鲁PE,新加坡SG,新西兰NZ,智利CL 6 巴PK 7.2 澳AU 8.4 瑞士CH 9.6 韩国KR	0 受惠国$_1$LD$_1$	70	Setts, curbstones and flagstones, of natural stone (except slate)
	68.02	**已加工的碑石或建筑用石（不包括板岩）及其制品，但税号68.01的货品除外;天然石料（包括板岩）制的镶嵌石（马赛克）及类似品，不论是否有衬背;天然石料（包括板岩）制的人工染色石粒、石片及石粉：**					**Worked monumental or building stone (except slate) and articles thereof, other than goods of heading 6801; mosaic cubes and the like, of natural stone (including slate) , whether or not on a backing; artificially coloured granules, chippings and powder, of natural stone (including slate) :**
		-砖、瓦、方块及类似品，不论是否为矩形（包括正方形），其最大表面积以可置入边长小于7厘米的方格为限;人工染色的石粒、石片及石粉：					-Tiles, cubes and similar articles, whether or not rectangular (including square) , the largest surface area of which is capable of being enclosed in a square the side of which is less than 7cm; artificially coloured granules, chippings and powder:
4823	6802.1010	---大理石	24	0 澳门MO,巴PK,冰岛IS,东盟AS,哥CR,秘鲁PE,香港HK,新加坡SG,新西兰NZ,智利CL 14.4 澳AU 16.8 瑞士CH 19.2 亚太AP 21.6 韩国KR	0 受惠国LD	90	---Marble
4824	6802.1090	---其他	20	0 澳门MO,巴PK,冰岛IS,东盟AS,哥CR,秘鲁PE,香港HK,新加坡SG,新西兰NZ,智利CL 12 澳AU 14 瑞士CH 16 亚太AP 17.3 韩国KR	0 受惠国$_1$LD$_1$	90	---Other
		-简单切削或锯开并具有一个平面的其他碑石或建筑用石及其制品：					-Other monumental or building stone and articles thereof, simply cut or sawn, with a flat or even surface:
		--大理石、石灰华及蜡石：					--Marble, travertine and alabaster:
4825	6802.2110	---大理石	10	0 澳门MO,巴PK,冰岛IS,东盟AS,哥CR,秘鲁PE,新西兰NZ,智利CL 4 瑞士CH 6 澳AU 8 韩国KR	0 受惠国LD	90	---Marble
4826	6802.2120	---石灰华	24	0 澳门MO,巴PK,冰岛IS,东盟AS,哥CR,秘鲁PE,新加坡SG,新西兰NZ,智利CL 14.4 澳AU 16.8 瑞士CH 21.6 韩国KR	0 受惠国$_1$LD$_1$	90	---Travertine

序号 No.	税则号列 Tariff Line	中文货品名称 Article Description in Chinese	最惠国税率 MFN(%)	协定税率 Agreement(%)	特惠税率 SP(%)	普通税率 Gen(%)	英文货品名称 Article Description
4827	6802.2190	---其他	24	0 巴PK,冰岛IS,东盟AS,哥CR,秘鲁PE,新加坡SG,新西兰NZ,智利CL 14.4 澳AU 16.8 瑞士CH 21.6 韩国KR	0 受惠国$_1$LD$_1$	90	---Other
4828	6802.2300	--花岗岩	10	0 澳门MO,巴PK,冰岛IS,东盟AS,哥CR,秘鲁PE,新西兰NZ,智利CL 4 瑞士CH 6 澳AU 8 韩国KR 9.2 亚太AP	0 受惠国LD	90	--Granite
		--其他石:					--Other stone:
4829	6802.2910	---其他石灰石	24	0 澳门MO,巴PK,冰岛IS,东盟AS,哥CR,新加坡SG,新西兰NZ,智利CL 7.2 秘鲁PE 14.4 澳AU 16.8 瑞士CH 21.6 韩国KR	0 受惠国$_1$LD$_1$	90	---Other calcareous stone
4830	6802.2990	---其他	15	0 澳门MO,巴PK,冰岛IS,东盟AS,哥CR,新加坡SG,新西兰NZ,智利CL 4.5 秘鲁PE 9 澳AU 10.5 瑞士CH 12 韩国KR	0 受惠国LD	90	---Other
		-其他:					-Other:
		--大理石、石灰华及蜡石:					--Marble, travertine and alabaster:
4831	6802.9110	---石刻	24	0 澳门MO,巴PK,冰岛IS,东盟AS,哥CR,秘鲁PE,新加坡SG,新西兰NZ,智利CL 14.4 澳AU 16.8 瑞士CH 21.6 韩国KR	0 受惠国$_1$LD$_1$	90	---Carvings
4832	6802.9190	---其他	10	0 澳门MO,巴PK,冰岛IS,东盟AS,哥CR,秘鲁PE,香港HK,新西兰NZ,智利CL 4 瑞士CH 6 澳AU 8 韩国KR	0 受惠国LD	90	---Other
		--其他石灰石:					--Other calcareous stone:
4833	6802.9210	---石刻	24	0 澳门MO,巴PK,冰岛IS,东盟AS,哥CR,新加坡SG,新西兰NZ,智利CL 7.2 秘鲁PE 14.4 澳AU 16.8 瑞士CH 21.6 韩国KR	0 受惠国$_1$LD$_1$	90	---Carvings
4834	6802.9290	---其他	10	0 澳门MO,巴PK,冰岛IS,东盟AS,哥CR,香港HK,新西兰NZ,智利CL 3 秘鲁PE 4 瑞士CH 6 澳AU 8 韩国KR	0 受惠国LD	90	---Other
		--花岗岩:					--Granite:
		---石刻:					---Carvings:

序号 No.	税则号列 Tariff Line	中文货品名称 Article Description in Chinese	最惠国税率 MFN(%)	协定税率 Agreement(%)	特惠税率 SP(%)	普通税率 Gen(%)	英文货品名称 Article Description
4835	6802.9311	----墓碑石	24	0 澳门MO,巴PK,冰岛IS,东盟AS,哥CR,新加坡SG,新西兰NZ,智利CL 7.2 秘鲁PE 14.4 澳AU 16.8 瑞士CH 21.6 韩国KR	0 受惠国$_1$LD$_1$	90	----Tombstone
4836	6802.9319	----其他	24	0 澳门MO,巴PK,冰岛IS,东盟AS,哥CR,香港HK,新加坡SG,新西兰NZ,智利CL 7.2 秘鲁PE 14.4 澳AU 16.8 瑞士CH 21.6 韩国KR	0 受惠国$_1$LD$_1$	90	----Other
4837	6802.9390	---其他	10	0 澳门MO,巴PK,冰岛IS,东盟AS,哥CR,秘鲁PE,新西兰NZ,智利CL 4 瑞士CH 6 澳AU 8 韩国KR 9.2 亚太AP	0 受惠国LD	90	---Other
		--其他石:					--Other stone:
4838	6802.9910	---石刻	24	0 澳门MO,巴PK,冰岛IS,东盟AS,哥CR,秘鲁PE,新加坡SG,新西兰NZ,智利CL 14.4 澳AU 16.8 瑞士CH 21.6 韩国KR	0 受惠国$_1$LD$_1$	90	---Carvings
4839	6802.9990	---其他	24	0 澳门MO,巴PK,冰岛IS,东盟AS,哥CR,秘鲁PE,香港HK,新加坡SG,新西兰NZ,智利CL 14.4 澳AU 16.8 瑞士CH 21.6 韩国KR	0 受惠国LD	90	---Other
	68.03	**已加工的板岩及板岩或粘聚板岩的制品:**					**Worked slate and articles of slate or of agglomerated slate:**
4840	6803.0010	---板岩制	20	0 澳门MO,冰岛IS,东盟AS,哥CR,新加坡SG,新西兰NZ,智利CL 6 秘鲁PE 12 澳AU 14 瑞士CH 17.3 韩国KR	0 受惠国$_1$LD$_1$	80	---Of slate
4841	6803.0090	---其他	20	0 冰岛IS,东盟AS,哥CR,新加坡SG,新西兰NZ,智利CL 6 秘鲁PE 12 澳AU 14 瑞士CH 17.3 韩国KR	0 受惠国$_1$LD$_1$	80	---Other
	68.04	**未装支架的石磨、石碾、砂轮和类似品及其零件，用于研磨、磨刃、抛光、整形或切割，以及手用磨石、抛光石及其零件，用天然石料、粘聚的天然磨料、人造磨料或陶瓷制成，不论是否装有由其他材料制成的零件:**					**Millstones, grindstones, grinding wheels and the like, without frameworks, for grinding, sharpening, polishing, trueing or cutting, hand sharpening or polishing stones, and parts thereof, of natural stone, of agglomerated natural or artificial abrasives, or of ceramics, with or without parts of other materials:**

序号 No.	税则号列 Tariff Line	中文货品名称 Article Description in Chinese	最惠国税率 MFN(%)	协定税率 Agreement(%)	特惠税率 SP(%)	普通税率 Gen(%)	英文货品名称 Article Description
4842	6804.1000	-碾磨或磨浆用石磨、石碾	8	0 冰岛IS,东盟AS,哥CR,秘鲁PE,新西兰NZ,智利CL 3.2 瑞士CH 4.8 澳AU,韩国KR 5 巴PK	0 受惠国LD	40	-Millstones and grindstones for milling, grinding or pulping
		-其他石磨、石碾、砂轮及类似品:					-Other millstones, grindstones, grinding wheels and the like:
		--粘聚合成或天然金刚石制:					--Of agglomerated synthetic or natural diamond:
4843	6804.2110	---砂轮	8	0 冰岛IS,东盟AS,哥CR,秘鲁PE,香港HK,新西兰NZ,智利CL 4.8 澳AU 5 巴PK 5.6 瑞士CH 6.4 韩国KR	0 受惠国LD	17	---Grinding wheel
4844	6804.2190	---其他	8	0 冰岛IS,东盟AS,哥CR,秘鲁PE,香港HK,新西兰NZ,智利CL 4.8 澳AU 5 巴PK 5.6 瑞士CH 6.4 韩国KR	0 受惠国LD	17	---Other
		--其他粘聚磨料制或陶瓷制:					--Of other agglomerated abrasives or of ceramics:
4845	6804.2210	---砂轮	8	0 冰岛IS,东盟AS,哥CR,秘鲁PE,香港HK,新西兰NZ,智利CL 4.8 澳AU,韩国KR 5 巴PK 5.6 瑞士CH	0 受惠国LD	17	---Grinding wheels
4846	6804.2290	---其他	8	0 冰岛IS,东盟AS,哥CR,秘鲁PE,香港HK,新西兰NZ,智利CL 3.2 瑞士CH 4.8 澳AU,韩国KR 5 巴PK	0 受惠国LD	40	---Other
		--天然石料制:					--Of natural stone:
4847	6804.2310	---砂轮	8	0 冰岛IS,东盟AS,哥CR,秘鲁PE,新西兰NZ,智利CL 3.2 瑞士CH 4.8 澳AU,韩国KR 5 巴PK	0 受惠国LD	17	---Grinding wheels
4848	6804.2390	---其他	8	0 冰岛IS,东盟AS,哥CR,秘鲁PE,新西兰NZ,智利CL 3.2 瑞士CH 4.8 澳AU 5 巴PK 6.4 韩国KR	0 受惠国LD	40	---Other
		-手用磨石及抛光石:					-Hand sharpening or polishing stones:
4849	6804.3010	---琢磨油石	8	0 冰岛IS,东盟AS,哥CR,秘鲁PE,新西兰NZ,智利CL 3.2 瑞士CH 4.8 澳AU,韩国KR 5 巴PK 6.4 亚太AP	0 受惠国LD	17	---Oilstones

序号 No.	税则号列 Tariff Line	中文货品名称 Article Description in Chinese	最惠国税率 MFN(%)	协定税率 Agreement(%)	特惠税率 SP(%)	普通税率 Gen(%)	英文货品名称 Article Description
4850	6804.3090	---其他	8	0 冰岛IS,东盟AS,哥CR,秘鲁PE,新西兰NZ,智利CL 3.2 瑞士CH 4.8 澳AU 5 巴PK 6.4 韩国KR,亚太AP	0 受惠国LD	40	---Other
	68.05	**砂布、砂纸及以其他材料为底的类似品,不论是否裁切、缝合或用其他方法加工成形:**					**Natural or artificial abrasive powder or grain, on a base of textile material, of paper, of paperboard or of other materials, whether or not cut to shape or sewn or otherwise made up:**
4851	6805.1000	-砂布	8	0 冰岛IS,东盟AS,哥CR,秘鲁PE,新西兰NZ,智利CL 4.8 澳AU 5 巴PK 5.6 瑞士CH 6.9 韩国KR	0 受惠国LD	40	-On a base of woven textile fabric only
4852	6805.2000	-砂纸	8	0 冰岛IS,东盟AS,哥CR,秘鲁PE,新西兰NZ,智利CL 4.8 澳AU 5 巴PK 5.6 瑞士CH 6.4 韩国KR	0 受惠国LD	40	-On a base of paper or paperboard only
4853	6805.3000	-其他	8	0 冰岛IS,东盟AS,哥CR,秘鲁PE,新西兰NZ,智利CL 3.2 瑞士CH 4.8 澳AU 5 巴PK 6.4 韩国KR	0 受惠国LD	40	-On a base of other materials
	68.06	**矿渣棉、岩石棉及类似的矿质棉;页状蛭石、膨胀粘土、泡沫矿渣及类似的膨胀矿物材料;具有隔热、隔音或吸音性能的矿物材料的混合物及制品,但税号68.11、68.12或第六十九章的货品除外:**					**Slag-wool, rock-wool and similar mineral wools; exfoliated vermiculite, expanded clays, foamed slag and similar expanded mineral materials; mixtures and articles of heat-insulating, sound-insulating or sound-absorbing mineral materials, other than those of heading 6811 or 6812 or of Chapter 69:**
		-矿渣棉、岩石棉及类似的矿质棉(包括其相互混合物),块状、成片或成卷:					-Slag wool, rock wool and similar mineral wools (including intermixtures thereof) , in bulk, sheets or rolls:
4854	6806.1010	---硅酸铝纤维及其制品	10.5	0 冰岛IS,东盟AS,哥CR,秘鲁PE,新加坡SG,新西兰NZ,智利CL 5 巴PK 6.3 澳AU 7.4 瑞士CH 8.4 韩国KR	0 受惠国LD	40	---Aluminium silicate fibre and its products
4855	6806.1090	---其他	10.5	0 冰岛IS,东盟AS,哥CR,秘鲁PE,新加坡SG,新西兰NZ,智利CL 5 巴PK 6.3 澳AU 7.4 瑞士CH 8.4 韩国KR	0 受惠国LD	40	---Other
	ex68061090	矿物纤维,渣球含量小于5%	Δ5				Mineral fiber, of a shot content less than 5%

序号 No.	税则号列 Tariff Line	中文货品名称 Article Description in Chinese	最惠国税率 MFN(%)	协定税率 Agreement(%)	特惠税率 SP(%)	普通税率 Gen(%)	英文货品名称 Article Description
4856	6806.2000	-页状蛭石、膨胀粘土、泡沫矿渣及类似的膨胀矿物材料（包括其相互混合物）	10.5	0 冰岛IS,东盟AS,哥CR,秘鲁PE,新加坡SG,新西兰NZ,智利CL 5 巴PK 6.3 澳AU 7.4 瑞士CH 8.4 韩国KR	0 受惠国LD	40	-Exfoliated vermiculite, expanded clays, foamed slag and similar expanded mineral materials (including intermixtures thereof)
4857	6806.9000	-其他	10	0 冰岛IS,东盟AS,哥CR,秘鲁PE,新西兰NZ,智利CL 4 瑞士CH 5 巴PK 6 澳AU 8.6 韩国KR	0 受惠国LD	50	-Other
	68.07	**沥青或类似原料（例如，石油沥青或煤焦油沥青）的制品：**					**Articles of asphalt or of similar material (for example, petroleum bitumen or coal tar pitch) :**
4858	6807.1000	-成卷	12	0 冰岛IS,东盟AS,哥CR,秘鲁PE,新加坡SG,新西兰NZ,智利CL 6 巴PK 7.2 澳AU 8.4 瑞士CH 9.6 韩国KR	0 受惠国$_1$LD$_1$	50	-In rolls
4859	6807.9000	-其他	12	0 冰岛IS,东盟AS,哥CR,秘鲁PE,新加坡SG,新西兰NZ,智利CL 5 巴PK 7.2 澳AU 8.4 瑞士CH 9.6 韩国KR,亚太AP	0 受惠国$_1$LD$_1$	50	-Other
	68.08	**镶板、平板、瓦、砖及类似品，用水泥、石膏及其他矿物粘合材料粘合植物纤维、稻草、刨花、木片屑、木粉、锯末或木废料制成**					**Panels, boards, tiles, blocks and similar articles of vegetable fibre, of straw or of shavings, chips, particles, sawdust or other waste of wood, agglomerated with cement, plaster or other mineral binders**
4860	6808.0000	镶板、平板、瓦、砖及类似品，用水泥、石膏及其他矿物粘合材料粘合植物纤维、稻草、刨花、木片屑、木粉、锯末或木废料制成	10.5	0 冰岛IS,东盟AS,哥CR,秘鲁PE,新加坡SG,新西兰NZ,智利CL 5 巴PK 6.3 澳AU 7.4 瑞士CH 8.4 韩国KR	0 受惠国$_1$LD$_1$	40	Panels, boards, tiles, blocks and similar articles of vegetable fibre, of straw or of shavings, chips, particles, sawdust or other waste, of wood, agglomerated with cement, plaster or other mineral binders
	68.09	**石膏制品及以石膏为基本成分的混合材料制品：**					**Articles of plaster or of compositions based on plaster:**
		-未经装饰的板、片、砖、瓦及类似品：					-Boards, sheets, panels, tiles and similar articles, not ornamented:
4861	6809.1100	--仅用纸、纸板贴面或加强的	28	0 冰岛IS,东盟AS,哥CR,新加坡SG,新西兰NZ,智利CL 8.4 秘鲁PE 16.8 澳AU 19.6 瑞士CH	0 受惠国$_1$LD$_1$	100	--Faced or reinforced with paper or paper board only
4862	6809.1900	--其他	25	0 澳门MO,冰岛IS,东盟AS,哥CR,新加坡SG,新西兰NZ,智利CL 7.5 秘鲁PE 15 澳AU 22.5 韩国KR	0 受惠国$_1$LD$_1$	100	--Other

序号 No.	税则号列 Tariff Line	中文货品名称 Article Description in Chinese	最惠国税率 MFN(%)	协定税率 Agreement(%)	特惠税率 SP(%)	普通税率 Gen(%)	英文货品名称 Article Description
4863	6809.9000	-其他制品	25	0 冰岛IS,东盟AS,哥CR,新加坡SG,新西兰NZ,智利CL 7.5 秘鲁PE 15 澳AU 22.5 韩国KR	0 受惠国$_1$LD$_1$	100	-Other articles
	68.10	**水泥、混凝土或人造石制品，不论是否加强：**					**Articles of cement, of concrete or of artificial stone, whether or not reinforced:**
		-砖、瓦、扁平石及类似品：					-Tiles, flagstones, bricks and similar articles:
4864	6810.1100	--建筑用砖及石砌块	10.5	0 冰岛IS,东盟AS,哥CR,秘鲁PE,香港HK,新加坡SG,新西兰NZ,智利CL 5 巴PK 6.3 澳AU 7.4 瑞士CH 8.4 韩国KR,亚太AP	0 受惠国LD	40	--Building blocks and bricks
		--其他：					--Other:
4865	6810.1910	---人造石制	10.5	0 澳门MO,冰岛IS,东盟AS,哥CR,秘鲁PE,新加坡SG,新西兰NZ,智利CL 5 巴PK 6.3 澳AU 7.4 瑞士CH 8.4 韩国KR,亚太AP	0 受惠国LD	70	---Of artificial stone
4866	6810.1990	---其他	10.5	0 冰岛IS,东盟AS,哥CR,秘鲁PE,新加坡SG,新西兰NZ,智利CL 5 巴PK 6.3 澳AU 7.4 瑞士CH 8.4 韩国KR,亚太AP	0 受惠国LD	70	---Other
		-其他制品：					-Other articles:
		--建筑或土木工程用的预制结构件：					--Prefabricated structural components for building or civil engineering:
4867	6810.9110	---钢筋混凝土和预应力混凝土管、杆、板、桩等	10.5	0 冰岛IS,东盟AS,哥CR,秘鲁PE,香港HK,新加坡SG,新西兰NZ,智利CL 5 巴PK 6.3 澳AU 7.4 瑞士CH 8.4 韩国KR	0 受惠国LD	40	---Reinforced concrete and prestressed concrete tubes, pipes, rods, plates, piles and similar articles
4868	6810.9190	---其他	10.5	0 澳门MO,冰岛IS,东盟AS,哥CR,秘鲁PE,香港HK,新加坡SG,新西兰NZ,智利CL 5 巴PK 6.3 澳AU 7.4 瑞士CH 8.4 韩国KR	0 受惠国LD	40	---Other
		--其他：					--Other:
4869	6810.9910	---铁道用水泥枕	8	0 冰岛IS,东盟AS,哥CR,秘鲁PE,新西兰NZ,智利CL 3.2 瑞士CH 4.8 澳AU,韩国KR 5 巴PK	0 受惠国LD	14	---Railway sleepers of concrete

序号 No.	税则号列 Tariff Line	中文货品名称 Article Description in Chinese	最惠国税率 MFN(%)	协定税率 Agreement(%)	特惠税率 SP(%)	普通税率 Gen(%)	英文货品名称 Article Description
4870	6810.9990	---其他	10.5	0 冰岛IS,东盟AS,哥CR,秘鲁PE,新加坡SG,新西兰NZ,智利CL 5 巴PK 6.3 澳AU 7.4 瑞士CH 8.4 韩国KR	0 受惠国LD	70	---Other
	68.11	**石棉水泥、纤维素水泥或类似材料的制品:**					**Articles of asbestos-cement, of cellulose fibre-cement or the like:**
		-含石棉的:					-Containing asbestos:
4871	6811.4010	---瓦楞板	5	0 澳AU,巴PK,冰岛IS,东盟AS,哥CR,秘鲁PE,瑞士CH,新西兰NZ,智利CL 3 韩国KR	0 受惠国$_1$LD$_1$	40	---Corrugated sheets
4872	6811.4020	---其他片、板、砖、瓦及类似制品	10.5	0 冰岛IS,东盟AS,哥CR,秘鲁PE,新加坡SG,新西兰NZ,智利CL 5 巴PK 6.3 澳AU 7.4 瑞士CH 8.4 韩国KR	0 受惠国$_1$LD$_1$	40	---Other sheets, panels, tiles and similar articles
4873	6811.4030	---管子及管子附件	8	0 冰岛IS,东盟AS,哥CR,秘鲁PE,新西兰NZ,智利CL 3.2 瑞士CH 4.8 澳AU,韩国KR 5 巴PK	0 受惠国$_1$LD$_1$	40	---Tubes, pipes and tube or pipe fittings
4874	6811.4090	---其他制品	8.4	0 冰岛IS,东盟AS,哥CR,秘鲁PE,新西兰NZ,智利CL 3.36 瑞士CH 5 澳AU,巴PK 6.7 韩国KR	0 受惠国$_1$LD$_1$	40	---Other articles
		-不含石棉的:					-Not containing asbestos:
4875	6811.8100	--瓦楞板	5	0 澳AU,巴PK,冰岛IS,东盟AS,哥CR,秘鲁PE,瑞士CH,新西兰NZ,智利CL 3 韩国KR	0 受惠国$_1$LD$_1$	40	--Corrugated sheets
4876	6811.8200	--其他片、板、砖、瓦及类似制品	10.5	0 冰岛IS,东盟AS,哥CR,秘鲁PE,新加坡SG,新西兰NZ,智利CL 5 巴PK 6.3 澳AU 7.6 瑞士CH 8.4 韩国KR	0 受惠国$_1$LD$_1$	40	--Other sheets, panels, tiles and similar articles
		--其他制品:					--Other articles:
4877	6811.8910	---管子及管子附件	8	0 冰岛IS,东盟AS,哥CR,秘鲁PE,新西兰NZ,智利CL 3.2 瑞士CH 4.8 澳AU,韩国KR 5 巴PK	0 受惠国$_1$LD$_1$	40	---Tubes, pipes and tube or pipe fittings
4878	6811.8990	---其他制品	8.4	0 冰岛IS,东盟AS,哥CR,秘鲁PE,新西兰NZ,智利CL 3.36 瑞士CH 5 澳AU,巴PK,韩国KR	0 受惠国$_1$LD$_1$	40	---Other articles

序号 No.	税则号列 Tariff Line	中文货品名称 Article Description in Chinese	最惠国税率 MFN(%)	协定税率 Agreement(%)	特惠税率 SP(%)	普通税率 Gen(%)	英文货品名称 Article Description
	68.12	**已加工的石棉纤维;以石棉为基本成分或以石棉和碳酸镁为基本成分的混合物;上述混合物或石棉的制品（例如，纱线、机织物、服装、帽类、鞋靴、衬垫），不论是否加强，但税号68.11或68.13的货品除外:**					**Fabricated asbestos fibres; mixtures with a basis of asbestos or with a basis of asbestos and magnesium carbonate; articles of such mixtures or of asbestos (for example, thread, woven fabric, clothing, headgear, footwear, gaskets) , whether or not reinforced, other than goods of heading 6811 or 6813:**
4879	6812.8000	-青石棉的	10.5	0 冰岛IS,东盟AS,哥CR,秘鲁PE,新加坡SG,新西兰NZ,智利CL 5 巴PK 6.3 澳AU 7.4 瑞士CH 8.4 韩国KR	0 受惠国LD	40	-Of crocidolite
		-其他:					-Other:
4880	6812.9100	--服装、衣着附件、帽类及鞋靴	10.5	0 冰岛IS,东盟AS,哥CR,秘鲁PE,新加坡SG,新西兰NZ,智利CL 5 巴PK 6.3 澳AU 7.4 瑞士CH 8.4 韩国KR	0 受惠国LD	40	--Clothing, clothing accessories, footwear and headgear
4881	6812.9200	--纸、麻丝板及毡子	10.5	0 冰岛IS,东盟AS,哥CR,秘鲁PE,新加坡SG,新西兰NZ,智利CL 5 巴PK 6.3 澳AU 7.4 瑞士CH 8.4 韩国KR	0 受惠国LD	40	--Paper, millboard and felt
4882	6812.9300	--成片或成卷的压缩石棉纤维接合材料	10.5	0 冰岛IS,东盟AS,哥CR,秘鲁PE,新加坡SG,新西兰NZ,智利CL 5 巴PK 6.3 澳AU 7.4 瑞士CH 8.4 韩国KR	0 受惠国LD	40	--Compressed asbestos fibre jointing, in sheets or rolls
4883	6812.9900	--其他	10	0 冰岛IS,东盟AS,哥CR,秘鲁PE,新西兰NZ,智利CL 4 瑞士CH 5 巴PK 6 澳AU 8 韩国KR	0 受惠国LD	40	--Other
	68.13	**以石棉、其他矿物质或纤维素为基本成分的未装配摩擦材料及其制品（例如，片、卷、带、盘、圈、垫及扇形），适于作制动器、离合器及类似品，不论是否与织物或其他材料结合而成:**					**Friction material and articles thereof (for example, sheets, rolls, strips, segments, discs, washers, pads) , not mounted, for brakes, for clutches or the like, with a basis of asbestos, of other mineral substances or of cellulose, whether or not combined with textile or other materials:**
		-含石棉的:					-Containing asbestos:
4884	6813.2010	---闸衬、闸垫	10	0 冰岛IS,东盟AS,哥CR,秘鲁PE,新西兰NZ,智利CL 4 瑞士CH 5 巴PK 6 澳AU 8 韩国KR	0 受惠国LD	40	---Brake linings and pads

序号 No.	税则号列 Tariff Line	中文货品名称 Article Description in Chinese	最惠国税率 MFN(%)	协定税率 Agreement(%)	特惠税率 SP(%)	普通税率 Gen(%)	英文货品名称 Article Description
4885	6813.2090	---其他	12	0 冰岛IS,东盟AS,哥CR,秘鲁PE,新加坡SG,新西兰NZ,智利CL 6 巴PK 7.2 澳AU 8.4 瑞士CH 9.6 韩国KR	0 受惠国$_1$LD$_1$	40	---Other
		-不含石棉的：					-Not containing asbestos:
4886	6813.8100	--闸衬、闸垫	10	0 冰岛IS,东盟AS,哥CR,秘鲁PE,新西兰NZ,智利CL 4 瑞士CH 5 巴PK 6 澳AU 8 韩国KR	0 受惠国LD	40	--Brake linings and pads
4887	6813.8900	--其他	12	0 冰岛IS,东盟AS,哥CR,秘鲁PE,新加坡SG,新西兰NZ,智利CL 6 巴PK 7.2 澳AU 8.4 瑞士CH 9.6 韩国KR	0 受惠国$_1$LD$_1$	40	--Other
	68.14	**已加工的云母及其制品，包括粘聚或复制的云母，不论是否附于纸、纸板或其他材料上：**					**Worked mica and articles of mica, including agglomerated or reconstituted mica, whether or not on a support of paper, paperboard or other materials:**
4888	6814.1000	-粘聚或复制云母制的板、片、带，不论是否附于其他材料上	10.5	0 冰岛IS,东盟AS,哥CR,秘鲁PE,瑞士CH,新加坡SG,新西兰NZ,智利CL 5 巴PK 6.3 澳AU 8.4 韩国KR	0 受惠国LD	35	-Plates, sheets and strips of agglomerated or reconstituted mica, whether or not on a support
4889	6814.9000	-其他	10.5	0 冰岛IS,东盟AS,哥CR,秘鲁PE,新加坡SG,新西兰NZ,智利CL 5 巴PK 6.3 澳AU 7.4 瑞士CH 8.4 韩国KR	0 受惠国LD	35	-Other
	68.15	**其他税号未列名的石制品及其他矿物制品（包括碳纤维及其制品和泥煤制品）：**					**Articles of stone or of other mineral substances (including carbon fibres, articles of carbon fibres and articles of peat) , not elsewhere specified or included:**
4890	6815.1000	-非电器用的石墨或其他碳精制品	15	0 冰岛IS,东盟AS,哥CR,新加坡SG,新西兰NZ,智利CL 4.5 秘鲁PE 9 澳AU 10.5 瑞士CH 12 巴PK	0 受惠国LD	70	-Non-electrical articles of graphite or other carbon
4891	6815.2000	-泥煤制品	15	0 冰岛IS,东盟AS,哥CR,新加坡SG,新西兰NZ,智利CL 4.5 秘鲁PE 9 澳AU 10.5 瑞士CH 12 巴PK,韩国KR	0 受惠国$_1$LD$_1$	70	-Articles of peat
		-其他制品：					-Other articles:

序号 No.	税则号列 Tariff Line	中文货品名称 Article Description in Chinese	最惠国税率 MFN(%)	协定税率 Agreement(%)	特惠税率 SP(%)	普通税率 Gen(%)	英文货品名称 Article Description
4892	6815.9100	--含有菱镁矿、白云石或铬铁矿的	15	0 冰岛IS,东盟AS,哥CR,新加坡SG,新西兰NZ,智利CL 4.5 秘鲁PE 9 澳AU 10.5 瑞士CH 12 巴PK,韩国KR	0 受惠国$_1$LD$_1$	70	--Containing magnesite, dolomite or chromite
		--其他:					--Other:
4893	6815.9920	---碳纤维	17.5	0 冰岛IS,东盟AS,哥CR,新加坡SG,新西兰NZ,智利CL 5.2 秘鲁PE 10.5 澳AU 12.3 瑞士CH	0 受惠国LD	70	---Carbon fibres
		---碳纤维制品:					---Articles of carbon fibres:
4894	6815.9931	----碳布	17.5	0 冰岛IS,东盟AS,哥CR,新加坡SG,新西兰NZ,智利CL 5.2 秘鲁PE 10.5 澳AU 12.3 瑞士CH	0 受惠国LD	70	----Carbon fibre fabric
4895	6815.9932	----碳纤维预浸料	17.5	0 冰岛IS,东盟AS,哥CR,新加坡SG,新西兰NZ,智利CL 5.2 秘鲁PE 10.5 澳AU 12.3 瑞士CH	0 受惠国LD	70	----Carbon fibre prepreg
4896	6815.9939	----其他	17.5	0 冰岛IS,东盟AS,哥CR,新加坡SG,新西兰NZ,智利CL 5.2 秘鲁PE 10.5 澳AU 12.3 瑞士CH	0 受惠国LD	70	----Other
4897	6815.9940	---玄武岩纤维及其制品	17.5	0 冰岛IS,东盟AS,哥CR,新加坡SG,新西兰NZ,智利CL 5.2 秘鲁PE 10.5 澳AU 12.3 瑞士CH 14 韩国KR	0 受惠国LD	70	---Basalt fiber and its product
4898	6815.9990	---其他	17.5	0 冰岛IS,东盟AS,哥CR,新加坡SG,新西兰NZ,智利CL 5.2 秘鲁PE 10.5 澳AU 12.3 瑞士CH 14 韩国KR	0 受惠国LD	70	---Other

第六十九章

陶瓷产品

注释：

一、本章仅适用于成形后经过烧制的陶瓷产品。税号 69.04 至 69.14 仅适用于不能归入税号 69.01 至 69.03 的产品。

二、本章不包括：

（一）税号 28.44 的产品；

（二）税号 68.04 的物品；

（三）第七十一章的物品（例如，仿首饰）；

（四）税号 81.13 的金属陶瓷；

（五）第八十二章的物品；

（六）绝缘子（税号 85.46）或绝缘材料制的零件（税号 85.47）；

（七）假牙（税号 90.21）；

（八）第九十一章的物品（例如，钟及钟壳）；

（九）第九十四章的物品（例如，家具、灯具及照明装置、活动房屋）；

（十）第九十五章的物品（例如，玩具、游戏品及运动用品）；

（十一）税号 96.06 的物品（例如，钮扣）或税号 96.14 的物品（例如，烟斗）；

（十二）第九十七章的物品（例如，艺术品）。

Chapter 69

Ceramic products

Notes:

1.This Chapter applies only to ceramic products which have been fired after shaping. Headings Nos.69.04 to 69.14 apply only to such products other than those classifiable in headings Nos.69.01 to 69.03.

2.This Chapter does not cover:

(a) Products of heading No.28.44;

(b) Articles of heading No.68.04;

(c) Articles of Chapter 71 (for example, imitation jewellery);

(d) Cermets of heading No.81.13;

(e) Articles of Chapter 82;

(f) Electrical insulators (heading No.85.46) or fittings of insulating material of heading No.85.47;

(g) Artificial teeth (heading No.90.21);

(h) Articles of Chapter 91 (for example, clocks and clock cases);

(i) Articles of Chapter 94 (for example, furniture, lamps and lighting fittings, prefabricated buildings);

(j) Articles of Chapter 95 (for example, toys, games and sports requisites);

(k) Articles of heading No.96.06 (for example, buttons) or of heading No.96.14 (for example, smoking pipes); or

(l) Articles of Chapter 97 (for example, works of art).

序号 No.	税则号列 Tariff Line	中文货品名称 Article Description in Chinese	最惠国税率 MFN(%)	协定税率 Agreement(%)	特惠税率 SP(%)	普通税率 Gen(%)	英文货品名称 Article Description
		第一分章　硅化石粉或类似硅土及耐火材料制品					I. GOODS OF SILICEOUS FOSSIL MEALS OR OF SIMILAR SILICEOUS EARTHS, AND REFRACTORY GOODS
	69.01	**硅质化石粉（例如各种硅藻土）或类似硅土制的砖、块、瓦及其他陶瓷制品**					**Bricks, blocks, tiles and other ceramic goods of siliceous fossil meals (for example, kieselguhr, tripolite or diatomite) or of similar siliceous earths**
4899	6901.0000	硅质化石粉（例如各种硅藻土）或类似硅土制的砖、块、瓦及其他陶瓷制品	8	0 冰岛IS,东盟AS,哥CR,秘鲁PE,新西兰NZ,智利CL 3.2 瑞士CH 4.8 澳AU,韩国KR 5 巴PK 6.4 亚太AP	0 受惠国$_1$LD$_1$	50	Bricks, blocks, tiles and other ceramic goods of siliceous fossil meals (for example, kieselguhr, tripolite or diatomite) or of similar siliceous earths
	69.02	**耐火砖、块、瓦及类似耐火陶瓷建材制品，但硅质化石粉及类似硅土制的除外：**					**Refractory bricks, blocks, tiles and similar refractory ceramic constructional goods, other than those of siliceous fossil meals or similar siliceous earths:**
4900	6902.1000	-单独或同时含有按重量计超过50%的镁、钙或铬（分别以氧化镁、氧化钙及三氧化二铬的含量计）	8	0 冰岛IS,东盟AS,哥CR,秘鲁PE,新西兰NZ,智利CL 3.2 瑞士CH 4.8 澳AU,韩国KR 5 巴PK	0 受惠国LD	30	-Containing by weight, singly or together, more than 50% of the elements Mg, Ca or Cr, expressed as MgO, CaO or Cr_2O_3

序号 No.	税则号列 Tariff Line	中文货品名称 Article Description in Chinese	最惠国税率 MFN(%)	协定税率 Agreement(%)	特惠税率 SP(%)	普通税率 Gen(%)	英文货品名称 Article Description
4901	6902.2000	-含有按重量计超过50%的三氧化二铝、二氧化硅或其混合物或化合物	8	0 冰岛IS,东盟AS,哥CR,秘鲁PE,新西兰NZ,智利CL 4.8 澳AU,韩国KR 5 巴PK 5.6 瑞士CH	0 受惠国LD	30	-Containing by weight more than 50% of alumina (Al_2O_3) , of silica (SiO_2) or of a mixture or compound of these products
4902	6902.9000	-其他	8	0 冰岛IS,东盟AS,哥CR,秘鲁PE,新西兰NZ,智利CL 3.2 瑞士CH 4.8 澳AU 5 巴PK 6.4 韩国KR	0 受惠国LD	30	-Other
	69.03	**其他耐火陶瓷制品（例如，甑、坩埚、马弗罩、喷管、栓塞、支架、烤钵、管子、护套及棒条），但硅质化石粉及类似硅土制的除外：**					**Other refractory ceramic goods (for example, retorts, crucibles, muffles, nozzles, plugs, supports, cupels, tubes, pipes, sheaths and rods) , other than those of siliceous fossil meals or of similar siliceous earths:**
4903	6903.1000	-含有按重量计超过50%的石墨、其他碳或其混合物	8	0 冰岛IS,东盟AS,哥CR,秘鲁PE,新西兰NZ,智利CL 3.2 瑞士CH 4.8 澳AU 5 巴PK 6.4 韩国KR	0 老挝LA,受惠国LD	20	-Containing by weight more than 50% of graphite or other carbon or of a mixture of these products
4904	6903.2000	-含有按重量计超过50%的三氧化二铝或三氧化二铝和二氧化硅的混合物或化合物	8	0 冰岛IS,东盟AS,哥CR,秘鲁PE,新西兰NZ,智利CL 3.2 瑞士CH 4.8 澳AU,韩国KR 5 巴PK	0 老挝LA,受惠国LD	20	-Containing by weight more than 50% of alumina (Al_2O_3) or of a mixture of compound of alumina and of silica (SiO_2)
4905	6903.9000	-其他	8	0 冰岛IS,东盟AS,哥CR,秘鲁PE,新西兰NZ,智利CL 3.2 瑞士CH 4.8 澳AU,韩国KR 5 巴PK	0 老挝LA,受惠国LD	20	-Other
		第二分章　其他陶瓷产品					II. OTHER CERAMIC PRODUCTS
	69.04	**陶瓷制建筑用砖、铺地砖、支撑或填充用砖及类似品：**					**Ceramic building bricks, flooring blocks, support or filler tiles and the like:**
4906	6904.1000	-建筑用砖	15	0 冰岛IS,东盟AS,哥CR,新加坡SG,新西兰NZ,智利CL 4.5 秘鲁PE 9 澳AU 10.5 瑞士CH 12 巴PK,韩国KR	0 受惠国LD	90	-Building bricks
4907	6904.9000	-其他	24.5	0 冰岛IS,东盟AS,哥CR,新加坡SG,新西兰NZ,智利CL 7.4 秘鲁PE 14.7 澳AU 17.2 瑞士CH 22 韩国KR	0 受惠国$_1$LD$_1$	90	-Other
	69.05	**屋顶瓦、烟囱罩、通风帽、烟囱衬壁、建筑装饰物及其他建筑用陶瓷制品：**					**Roofing tiles, chimney pots, cowls, chimney liners, architectural ornaments and other ceramic constructional goods:**

序号 No.	税则号列 Tariff Line	中文货品名称 Article Description in Chinese	最惠国税率 MFN(%)	协定税率 Agreement(%)	特惠税率 SP(%)	普通税率 Gen(%)	英文货品名称 Article Description
4908	6905.1000	-屋顶瓦	24.5Δ15	0 冰岛IS,东盟AS,哥CR,新加坡SG,新西兰NZ,智利CL 7.4 秘鲁PE 14.7 澳AU 17.2 瑞士CH 22 韩国KR	0 受惠国$_1$LD$_1$	90	-Roofing tiles
4909	6905.9000	-其他	24.5	0 冰岛IS,东盟AS,哥CR,新加坡SG,新西兰NZ,智利CL 7.4 秘鲁PE 14.7 澳AU 17.2 瑞士CH 22 韩国KR	0 受惠国$_1$LD$_1$	90	-Other
	69.06	**陶瓷套管、导管、槽管及管子附件**					**Ceramic pipes, conduits, guttering and pipe fittings**
4910	6906.0000	陶瓷套管、导管、槽管及管子附件	15Δ10	0 冰岛IS,东盟AS,哥CR,新加坡SG,新西兰NZ,智利CL 4.5 秘鲁PE 9 澳AU 10.5 瑞士CH 12 巴PK,韩国KR	0 受惠国$_1$LD$_1$	90	Ceramic pipes, conduits, guttering and pipe fittings
	69.07	**未上釉的陶瓷贴面砖、铺面砖，包括炉面砖及墙面砖;未上釉的陶瓷镶嵌砖（马赛克）及类似品，不论是否有衬背:**					**Unglazed ceramic flags and paving, hearth or wall tiles; unglazed ceramic mosaic cubes and the like, whether or not on a backing:**
4911	6907.1000	-砖、瓦、块及类似品，不论是否矩形，其最大表面积以可置入边长小于7厘米的方格为限	24.5	0 冰岛IS,东盟AS,哥CR,新加坡SG,新西兰NZ,智利CL 7.4 秘鲁PE 14.7 澳AU 17.2 瑞士CH 22 韩国KR	0 受惠国$_1$LD$_1$	90	-Tiles, cubes and similar articles, whether or not rectangular, the largest surface area of which is capable of being enclosed in a square the side of which is less than 7cm
4912	6907.9000	-其他	12	0 冰岛IS,东盟AS,哥CR,秘鲁PE,新加坡SG,新西兰NZ,智利CL 6 巴PK 7.2 澳AU 8.4 瑞士CH 9.6 韩国KR	0 受惠国$_1$LD$_1$	90	-Other
	69.08	**上釉的陶瓷贴面砖、铺面砖，包括炉面砖及墙面砖;上釉的陶瓷镶嵌砖（马赛克）及类似品，不论是否有衬背:**					**Glazed ceramic flags and paving, hearth or wall tiles; glazed ceramic mosaic cubes and the like, whether or not on a backing:**
4913	6908.1000	-砖、瓦、块及类似品，不论是否矩形，其最大表面积以可置入边长小于7厘米的方格为限	12	0 冰岛IS,东盟AS,哥CR,秘鲁PE,新加坡SG,新西兰NZ,智利CL 5 巴PK 7.2 澳AU 8.4 瑞士CH 9.6 韩国KR 10.4 亚太AP	0 受惠国$_1$LD$_1$	100	-Tiles, cubes and similar articles, whether or not rectangular, the largest surface area of which is capable of being enclosed in a square the side of which is less than 7cm
4914	6908.9000	-其他	12	0 冰岛IS,东盟AS,哥CR,秘鲁PE,新加坡SG,新西兰NZ,智利CL 6 巴PK 7.2 澳AU 8.4 瑞士CH 9.6 韩国KR	0 受惠国$_1$LD$_1$	100	-Other

序号 No.	税则号列 Tariff Line	中文货品名称 Article Description in Chinese	最惠国税率 MFN(%)	协定税率 Agreement(%)	特惠税率 SP(%)	普通税率 Gen(%)	英文货品名称 Article Description
	69.09	**实验室、化学或其他专门技术用途的陶瓷器;农业用陶瓷槽、缸及类似容器;通常供运输及盛装货物用的陶瓷罐、坛及类似品:**					**Ceramic wares for laboratory, chemical or other technical uses; ceramic troughs, tubs and similar receptacles of a kind used in agriculture; ceramic pots, jars and similar articles of a kind used for the conveyance or packing of goods:**
		-实验室、化学或其他专门技术用途的陶瓷器:					-Ceramic wares for laboratory, chemical or other technical uses:
4915	6909.1100	--瓷制	8	0 冰岛IS,东盟AS,哥CR,秘鲁PE,新西兰NZ,智利CL 3.2 瑞士CH 4.8 澳AU,韩国KR 5 巴PK	0 受惠国LD	30	--Of porcelain or china
4916	6909.1200	--莫氏硬度为9或以上的物品	8	0 冰岛IS,东盟AS,哥CR,秘鲁PE,新西兰NZ,智利CL 3.2 瑞士CH 4.8 澳AU,韩国KR 5 巴PK	0 受惠国LD	30	--Articles having a hardness equivalent to 9 or more on the Mohs scale
4917	6909.1900	--其他	8	0 冰岛IS,东盟AS,哥CR,秘鲁PE,瑞士CH,新西兰NZ,智利CL 4.8 澳AU,韩国KR 5 巴PK	0 受惠国LD	30	--Other
4918	6909.9000	-其他	21Δ15	0 冰岛IS,东盟AS,哥CR,新加坡SG,新西兰NZ,智利CL 6.3 秘鲁PE 12.6 澳AU 14.7 瑞士CH 18.9 韩国KR	0 受惠国$_1$LD$_1$	90	-Other
	69.10	**陶瓷洗涤槽、脸盆、脸盆座、浴缸、坐浴盆、抽水马桶、水箱、小便池及类似的固定卫生设备:**					**Ceramic sinks, wash basins, wash basin pedestals, baths, bidets, water closet pans, flushing cisterns, urinals and similar sanitary fixtures:**
4919	6910.1000	-瓷制	10	0 冰岛IS,东盟AS,哥CR,秘鲁PE,新加坡SG,新西兰NZ,智利CL 4 瑞士CH 5 巴PK 6 澳AU 8 韩国KR 9 亚太AP	0 受惠国LD	100	-Of porcelain or china
4920	6910.9000	-其他	10	0 冰岛IS,东盟AS,哥CR,秘鲁PE,新加坡SG,新西兰NZ,智利CL 4 瑞士CH 5 巴PK 6 澳AU 8 韩国KR	0 受惠国LD	100	-Other
	69.11	**瓷餐具、厨房器具及其他家用或盥洗用瓷器:**					**Tableware, kitchenware, other household articles and toilet articles, of porcelain or china:**
		-餐具及厨房器具:					-Tableware and kitchenware:
		---餐具:					---Tableware:

序号 No.	税则号列 Tariff Line	中文货品名称 Article Description in Chinese	最惠国税率 MFN(%)	协定税率 Agreement(%)	特惠税率 SP(%)	普通税率 Gen(%)	英文货品名称 Article Description
4921	6911.1011	----骨瓷	12∆8	0 冰岛IS,东盟AS,哥CR,秘鲁PE,新加坡SG,新西兰NZ,智利CL 5 巴PK 7.2 澳AU 8.4 瑞士CH 9.6 韩国KR 10 亚太AP	0 受惠国LD	100	----Bone porcelain
4922	6911.1019	----其他	12∆8	0 冰岛IS,东盟AS,哥CR,秘鲁PE,新加坡SG,新西兰NZ,智利CL 5 巴PK 7.2 澳AU 8.4 瑞士CH 9.6 韩国KR 10 亚太AP	0 受惠国LD	100	----Other
		---厨房器具:					---Kitchenware:
4923	6911.1021	----刀具	15∆10	0 冰岛IS,东盟AS,哥CR,新加坡SG,新西兰NZ,智利CL 4.5 秘鲁PE 7.5 巴PK 9 澳AU 10.5 瑞士CH 12 韩国KR 12.5 亚太AP	0 受惠国$_1$LD$_1$	100	----Knife
4924	6911.1029	----其他	15∆10	0 冰岛IS,东盟AS,哥CR,新加坡SG,新西兰NZ,智利CL 4.5 秘鲁PE 7.5 巴PK 9 澳AU 10.5 瑞士CH 12 韩国KR 12.5 亚太AP	0 受惠国$_1$LD$_1$	100	----Other
4925	6911.9000	-其他	24.5	0 冰岛IS,东盟AS,哥CR,新加坡SG,新西兰NZ,智利CL 7.4 秘鲁PE 14.7 澳AU 17.2 瑞士CH 20 巴PK,亚太AP 22 韩国KR	0 受惠国$_1$LD$_1$	100	-Other
	69.12	**陶餐具、厨房器具及其他家用或盥洗用陶器:**					**Ceramic tableware, kitchenware, other household articles and toilet articles, other than of porcelain or china:**
4926	6912.0010	---餐具	15∆10	0 冰岛IS,东盟AS,哥CR,新加坡SG,新西兰NZ,智利CL 4.5 秘鲁PE 9 澳AU 10.5 瑞士CH 12 巴PK,韩国KR	0 受惠国LD	100	---Tableware
4927	6912.0090	---其他	15∆10	0 冰岛IS,东盟AS,哥CR,新加坡SG,新西兰NZ,智利CL 4.5 秘鲁PE 9 澳AU 10.5 瑞士CH 12 巴PK,韩国KR	0 受惠国$_1$LD$_1$	100	---Other
	69.13	**塑像及其他装饰用陶瓷制品:**					**Statuettes and other ornamental ceramic articles:**

序号 No.	税则号列 Tariff Line	中文货品名称 Article Description in Chinese	最惠国税率 MFN(%)	协定税率 Agreement(%)	特惠税率 SP(%)	普通税率 Gen(%)	英文货品名称 Article Description
4928	6913.1000	-瓷制	15	0 冰岛IS,东盟AS,哥CR,新加坡SG,新西兰NZ,智利CL 4.5 秘鲁PE 9 澳AU 10.5 瑞士CH 12 巴PK,韩国KR	0 受惠国LD	100	-Of porcelain or china
4929	6913.9000	-其他	15	0 冰岛IS,东盟AS,哥CR,新加坡SG,新西兰NZ,智利CL 4.5 秘鲁PE 9 澳AU 10.5 瑞士CH 12 巴PK,韩国KR	0 受惠国LD	100	-Other
	69.14	**其他陶瓷制品:**					**Other ceramic articles:**
4930	6914.1000	-瓷制	24.5	0 冰岛IS,东盟AS,哥CR,新加坡SG,新西兰NZ,智利CL 7.4 秘鲁PE 14.7 澳AU 17.2 瑞士CH 22 韩国KR	0 受惠国$_1$LD$_1$	100	-Of porcelain or china
4931	6914.9000	-其他	10	0 冰岛IS,东盟AS,哥CR,秘鲁PE,新加坡SG,新西兰NZ,智利CL 5 巴PK 6 澳AU 7 瑞士CH 8.6 韩国KR	0 受惠国LD	100	-Other

第七十章
玻璃及其制品

注释：

一、本章不包括：

（一）税号 32.07 的货品（例如，珐琅和釉料、搪瓷玻璃料及其他玻璃粉、粒或粉片）；

（二）第七十一章的物品（例如，仿首饰）；

（三）税号 85.44 的光缆、税号 85.46 的绝缘子或税号 85.47 所列绝缘材料制的零件；

（四）光导纤维、经光学加工的光学元件、注射用针管、假眼、温度计、气压计、液体比重计或第九十章的其他物品；

（五）有永久固定电光源的灯具及照明装置、灯箱标志或名牌和类似品及其零件（税号 94.05）；

（六）玩具、游戏品、运动用品、圣诞树装饰品及第九十五章的其他物品（供玩偶或第九十五章其他物品用的无机械装置的玻璃假眼除外）；

（七）钮扣、保温瓶、香水喷雾器和类似的喷雾器及第九十六章的其他物品。

二、对于税号 70.03、70.04 及 70.05：

（一）玻璃在退火前的各种处理都不视为“已加工”；

（二）玻璃切割成一定形状并不影响其作为板片归类；

（三）所称“吸收、反射或非反射层”，是指极薄的金属或化合物（例如，金属氧化物）镀层，该镀层可以吸收红外线等光线或可以提高玻璃的反射性能，同时仍然使玻璃具有一定程度的透明性或半透明性；或者该镀层可以防止光线在玻璃表面的反射。

三、税号 70.06 所述产品，不论是否具有制成品的特性仍归入该税号。

四、税号 70.19 所称“玻璃棉”，是指：

（一）按重量计二氧化硅的含量在 60%及以上的矿质棉；

（二）按重量计二氧化硅的含量在 60%以下，但碱性氧化物（氧化钾或氧化钠）的含量在 5%以上或氧化硼的含量在 2%以上的矿质棉。

不符合上述规定的矿质棉归入税号 68.06。

五、本目录所称“玻璃”，包括熔融石英及其他熔融硅石。

子目注释：

子目号 7013.22、7013.33、7013.41 及 7013.91 所称“铅晶质玻璃”，仅指按重量计氧化铅含量不低于 24%的玻璃。

Chapter 70
Glass and glassware

Notes:

1. This Chapter does not cover:
   (a) Goods of heading No.32.07 (for example, vitrifiable enamels and glazes, glass frit, other glass in the form of powder, granules or flakes);
   (b) Articles of Chapter 71 (for example, imitation jewellery);
   (c) Optical fibre cables (heading No.85.44), electrical insulators (heading No.85.46) or fitting of insulating material of heading No.85.47;
   (d) Optical fibres, optically worked optical elements, hypodermic syringes, artificial eyes, thermometers, barometers, hydrometers or other articles of Chapter 90;
   (e) Lamps or lighting fittings, illuminated signs, illuminated nameplates or the like, having a permanently fixed light source, or parts thereof of heading No.94.05;
   (f) Toys, games, sports requisites, Christmas tree ornaments or other articles of Chapter 95 (excluding glass eyes without mechanisms for dolls or for other articles of Chapter 95); or
   (g) Buttons, fitted vacuum flasks, scent or similar sprays or other articles of Chapter 96.
2. For the purposes of headings Nos.70.03, 70.04 and 70.05:
   (a) glass is not regarded as “worked” by reason of any process it has undergone before annealing;
   (b) cutting to shape does not affect the classification of glass in sheets;
   (c) the expression “absorbent, reflecting or nonreflecting layer” means a microscopically thin coating of metal or of a chemical compound (for example, metal oxide) which absorbs, for example, infrared light or improves the reflecting qualities of the glass while still allowing it to retain a degree of transparency or translucency; or which prevents light from being reflected on the surface of the glass.
3. The products referred to in heading No.70.06 remain classified in that heading whether or not they have the character of articles.
4. For the purposes of heading No.70.19, the expression “glass wool” means:
   (a) Mineral wools with a silica (SiO_2) content not less than 60% by weight;
   (b) Mineral wools with a silica (SiO_2) content less than 60% but with an alkaline oxide (K_2O or Na_2O) content exceeding 5% by weight or a boric oxide (B_2O_3) content exceeding 2% by weight.

Mineral wools which do not comply with the above specifications fall in heading No.68.06.

5. Throughout the Nomenclature, the expression “glass” includes fused quartz and other fused silica.

Subheading Note:

For the purposes of subheadings Nos.7013.22, 7013.33, 7013.41 and 7013.91, the expression “lead crystal” means only glass having a minimum lead monoxide (PbO) content by weight of 24%.

序号 No.	税则号列 Tariff Line	中文货品名称 Article Description in Chinese	最惠国税率 MFN(%)	协定税率 Agreement(%)	特惠税率 SP(%)	普通税率 Gen(%)	英文货品名称 Article Description
	70.01	碎玻璃及废玻璃;玻璃块料					**Cullet and other waste and scrap of glass; glass in the mass**
4932	7001.0000	碎玻璃及废玻璃;玻璃块料	12	0 冰岛IS,东盟AS,哥CR,秘鲁PE,新加坡SG,新西兰NZ,智利CL 6 巴PK 7.2 澳AU 8.4 瑞士CH 9.6 韩国KR	0 受惠国$_1$LD$_1$	50	Cullet and other waste and scrap of glass; glass in the mass
	70.02	未加工的玻璃球、棒及管(税号70.18的微型玻璃球除外):					**Glass in balls (other than microspheres of heading 7018), rods or tubes, unworked:**
4933	7002.1000	-玻璃球	12	0 冰岛IS,东盟AS,哥CR,秘鲁PE,新加坡SG,新西兰NZ,智利CL 6 巴PK 7.2 澳AU 8.4 瑞士CH 9.6 韩国KR	0 受惠国$_1$LD$_1$	50	-Balls
		-玻璃棒:					-Rods:
4934	7002.2010	---光导纤维预制棒	6	0 冰岛IS,东盟AS,哥CR,秘鲁PE,新西兰NZ,智利CL 2.4 瑞士CH 3.6 澳AU,韩国KR 5 巴PK	0 受惠国$_1$LD$_1$	50	---Preformed bars for drawing optical fibre
4935	7002.2090	---其他	12	0 冰岛IS,东盟AS,哥CR,秘鲁PE,新加坡SG,新西兰NZ,智利CL 6 巴PK 7.2 澳AU 8.4 瑞士CH 9.6 韩国KR	0 受惠国$_1$LD$_1$	50	---Other
		-玻璃管:					-Tubes:
		--熔融石英或其他熔融硅石制:					--Of fused quartz or other fused silica:
4936	7002.3110	---光导纤维用波导级石英玻璃管	5Δ1	0 澳AU,巴PK,冰岛IS,东盟AS,哥CR,秘鲁PE,瑞士CH,新西兰NZ,智利CL 3 韩国KR	0 受惠国$_1$LD$_1$	17	---Waveguide quartz tubes for optical fibres use
4937	7002.3190	---其他	14	0 冰岛IS,东盟AS,哥CR,秘鲁PE,新加坡SG,新西兰NZ,智利CL 8.4 澳AU 9.8 瑞士CH 11.2 巴PK,韩国KR	0 受惠国$_1$LD$_1$	50	---Other
4938	7002.3200	--温度在0℃至300℃时线膨胀系数不超过5×10^{-6}/开尔文的其他玻璃制	12	0 冰岛IS,东盟AS,哥CR,秘鲁PE,新加坡SG,新西兰NZ,智利CL 6 巴PK 7.2 澳AU 8.4 瑞士CH 9.6 韩国KR	0 受惠国$_1$LD$_1$	50	--Of other glass having a linear coefficient of expansion not exceeding 5×10^{-6} per Kelvin within a tempera-ture range of 0℃ to 300℃
4939	7002.3900	--其他	12	0 冰岛IS,东盟AS,哥CR,秘鲁PE,新加坡SG,新西兰NZ,智利CL 6 巴PK 7.2 澳AU 8.4 瑞士CH 9.6 韩国KR	0 受惠国$_1$LD$_1$	50	--Other

序号 No.	税则号列 Tariff Line	中文货品名称 Article Description in Chinese	最惠国税率 MFN(%)	协定税率 Agreement(%)	特惠税率 SP(%)	普通税率 Gen(%)	英文货品名称 Article Description
	ex70023900	光通信用微光组件的玻璃毛细管、定位管（外径小于3毫米）	Δ3				Micro capillary and galass tube for optical communication (out diameter < 3mm)
	70.03	**铸制或轧制玻璃板、片或型材及异型材，不论是否有吸收、反射或非反射层，但未经其他加工：**					**Cast glass and rolled glass, in sheets or profiles, whether or not having an absorbent, reflecting or non-reflecting layer, but not otherwise worked:**
		-非夹丝玻璃板、片：					-Non-wired sheets:
4940	7003.1200	--整块着色、不透明、镶色或具有吸收、反射或非反射层的	15	0 冰岛IS,东盟AS,哥CR,新加坡SG,新西兰NZ,智利CL 4.5 秘鲁PE 9 澳AU 10.5 瑞士CH 12 巴PK,韩国KR	0 受惠国$_1$LD$_1$	50	--Coloured throughout the mass (body tinted) , opacified, flashed or having an absorbent, or nonreflecting reflecting layer, but not otherwise worked
4941	7003.1900	--其他	17.5	0 冰岛IS,东盟AS,哥CR,台湾TW,新加坡SG,新西兰NZ,智利CL 5.2 秘鲁PE 10.5 澳AU 12.3 瑞士CH 14 巴PK,韩国KR	0 受惠国$_1$LD$_1$	50	--Other
	ex70031900	液晶或有机发光二极管（OLED）显示屏用原板玻璃，包括保护屏用含碱玻璃	Δ3				Bare glass for liquid crystal or organic light emitting diode display, inculding the protective glass containing alkali
4942	7003.2000	-夹丝玻璃板、片	15	0 冰岛IS,东盟AS,哥CR,新加坡SG,新西兰NZ,智利CL 4.5 秘鲁PE 9 澳AU 10.5 瑞士CH 12 巴PK,韩国KR	0 受惠国$_1$LD$_1$	50	-Wired sheets
4943	7003.3000	-型材及异型材	15	0 冰岛IS,东盟AS,哥CR,新加坡SG,新西兰NZ,智利CL 4.5 秘鲁PE 9 澳AU 10.5 瑞士CH 12 巴PK,韩国KR	0 受惠国$_1$LD$_1$	50	-Profiles
	70.04	**拉制或吹制玻璃板、片，不论是否有吸收、反射或非反射层，但未经其他加工：**					**Drawn glass and blown glass, in sheets, whether or not having an absorbent, reflecting or non-reflecting layer, but not otherwise worked:**
4944	7004.2000	-整块着色、不透明、镶色或具有吸收、反射或非反射层的	17.5	0 冰岛IS,东盟AS,哥CR,新加坡SG,新西兰NZ,智利CL 5.2 秘鲁PE 10.5 澳AU 12.3 瑞士CH 14 巴PK,韩国KR	0 受惠国LD	50	-Glass, coloured throughout the mass (body tinted) , opacified, flashed or having an absorbent, reflecting or nonreflecting layer
4945	7004.9000	-其他玻璃	17.5	0 冰岛IS,东盟AS,哥CR,新加坡SG,新西兰NZ,智利CL 5.2 秘鲁PE 10.5 澳AU 12.3 瑞士CH 14 巴PK 15.7 韩国KR	0 受惠国$_1$LD$_1$	50	-Other glass
	ex70049000	光学平板玻璃，厚度0.7毫米以下	Δ9				Optical flat glass, of a thickness less than 0.7mm

序号 No.	税则号列 Tariff Line	中文货品名称 Article Description in Chinese	最惠国税率 MFN(%)	协定税率 Agreement(%)	特惠税率 SP(%)	普通税率 Gen(%)	英文货品名称 Article Description
	70.05	**浮法玻璃板、片及表面研磨或抛光玻璃板、片，不论是否有吸收、反射或非反射层，但未经其他加工：**					**Float glass and surface ground or polished glass, in sheets, whether or not having an absorbent, reflecting or non-reflecting layer, but not otherwise worked:**
4946	7005.1000	-具有吸收、反射或非反射层的非夹丝玻璃	15	0 冰岛IS,东盟AS,哥CR,新加坡SG,新西兰NZ,智利CL 4.5 秘鲁PE 9 澳AU 10.5 瑞士CH 12 巴PK,韩国KR	0 受惠国$_1$LD$_1$	50	-Non-wired glass, having an absorbent, reflecting or noon-reflecting layer
		-其他非夹丝玻璃：					-Other non-wired glass:
4947	7005.2100	--整块着色、不透明、镶色或仅表面研磨的	15	0 冰岛IS,东盟AS,哥CR,新加坡SG,新西兰NZ,智利CL 4.5 秘鲁PE 9 澳AU 10.5 瑞士CH 12 巴PK,韩国KR	0 受惠国$_1$LD$_1$	50	--Coloured throughout the mass (body tinted) , opacified, flashed or merely surface ground
4948	7005.2900	--其他	15	0 冰岛IS,东盟AS,哥CR,新加坡SG,新西兰NZ,智利CL 4.5 秘鲁PE 9 澳AU 10.5 瑞士CH 12 巴PK,韩国KR	0 受惠国$_1$LD$_1$	50	--Other
	ex70052900	液晶或有机发光二极管（OLED）显示屏用原板玻璃，包括保护屏用含碱玻璃	Δ3				Float glass, for liquid crystal or organic light emitting diode display, inculding the protective glass containing alkali
4949	7005.3000	-夹丝玻璃	17.5	0 冰岛IS,东盟AS,哥CR,新加坡SG,新西兰NZ,智利CL 5.2 秘鲁PE 10.5 澳AU 12.3 瑞士CH 14 巴PK,韩国KR	0 受惠国$_1$LD$_1$	50	-Wired glass
	70.06	**经弯曲、磨边、镂刻、钻孔、涂珐琅或其他加工的税号70.03、70.04或70.05的玻璃，但未用其他材料镶框或装配**					**Glass of heading 7003, 7004 or 7005, bent, edge-worked, engraved, drilled, enamelled or otherwise worked, but not framed or fitted with other materials**
4950	7006.0000	经弯曲、磨边、镂刻、钻孔、涂珐琅或其他加工的税号70.03、70.04或70.05的玻璃，但未用其他材料镶框或装配	15	0 冰岛IS,东盟AS,哥CR,台湾TW,新加坡SG,新西兰NZ,智利CL 4.5 秘鲁PE 9 澳AU 10.5 瑞士CH 12 巴PK 13 韩国KR	0 受惠国$_1$LD$_1$	50	Glass of heading No.70.03, 70.04 or 70.05, bent, edge-worked, engraved, drilled, enamelled or otherwise worked, but not framed or fitted with other materials
	ex70060000	液晶玻璃基板,6代(1850毫米×1500毫米）以上，不含6代	Δ4				Glass parts for liquid crystal display, above the 6 generation (1850mm×1500mm)
	ex70060000	液晶玻璃基板,6代(1850毫米×1500毫米）及以下	Δ6				Glass parts for liquid crystal display, the 6 generation (1850mm×1500mm) and below
	70.07	**钢化或层压玻璃制的安全玻璃：**					**Safety glass, consisting of toughened (tempered) or laminated glass:**
		-钢化安全玻璃：					-Toughened (tempered) safety glass:

序号 No.	税则号列 Tariff Line	中文货品名称 Article Description in Chinese	最惠国税率 MFN(%)	协定税率 Agreement(%)	特惠税率 SP(%)	普通税率 Gen(%)	英文货品名称 Article Description
		--规格及形状适于安装在车辆、航空器、航天器及船舶上:					--Of size and shape suitable for incorporation in vehicles, aircraft, spacecraft or vessels:
4951	7007.1110	---航空器、航天器及船舶用	2	0 澳AU,巴PK,冰岛IS,东盟AS,哥CR,韩国KR,秘鲁PE,瑞士CH,香港HK,新西兰NZ,智利CL	0 受惠国LD	11	---For aircraft, spacecraft or vessels
	ex70071110	空载重量25吨及以上飞机的挡风玻璃	Δ1				Windshield for airplane unloaden weight ≥25t
4952	7007.1190	---其他	10	0 冰岛IS,东盟AS,哥CR,秘鲁PE,香港HK,新西兰NZ,智利CL 4 瑞士CH 5 巴PK 6 澳AU 8.6 韩国KR	0 受惠国LD	50	---Other
4953	7007.1900	--其他	14	0 冰岛IS,东盟AS,哥CR,秘鲁PE,新加坡SG,新西兰NZ,智利CL 8.4 澳AU 9.8 瑞士CH 11.2 巴PK,韩国KR	0 受惠国$_1$LD$_1$	50	--Other
		-层压安全玻璃:					-Laminated safety glass:
		--规格及形状适于安装在车辆、航空器、航天器及船舶上:					--Of size and shape suitable for incorporation in vehicles, aircraft, spacecraft or vessels:
4954	7007.2110	---航空器、航天器及船舶用	2	0 澳AU,巴PK,冰岛IS,东盟AS,哥CR,韩国KR,秘鲁PE,瑞士CH,新西兰NZ,智利CL	0 受惠国LD	11	---For aircraft, spacecraft or vessels
4955	7007.2190	---其他	20	0 冰岛IS,东盟AS,哥CR,新加坡SG,新西兰NZ,智利CL 6 秘鲁PE 12 澳AU 14 瑞士CH 18 韩国KR	0 受惠国LD	50	---Other
4956	7007.2900	--其他	14	0 冰岛IS,东盟AS,哥CR,秘鲁PE,新加坡SG,新西兰NZ,智利CL 8.4 澳AU 9.8 瑞士CH 11.2 巴PK,韩国KR	0 受惠国$_1$LD$_1$	50	--Other
	70.08	**多层隔温、隔音玻璃组件:**					**Multiple-walled insulating units of glass:**
4957	7008.0010	---中空或真空隔温、隔音玻璃	14	0 冰岛IS,东盟AS,哥CR,秘鲁PE,新加坡SG,新西兰NZ,智利CL 8.4 澳AU 9.8 瑞士CH 11.2 巴PK,韩国KR	0 受惠国$_1$LD$_1$	50	---Sealed or vacuum insulating glass
4958	7008.0090	---其他	14	0 澳门MO,冰岛IS,东盟AS,哥CR,秘鲁PE,新加坡SG,新西兰NZ,智利CL 8.4 澳AU 9.8 瑞士CH 11.2 巴PK,韩国KR	0 受惠国$_1$LD$_1$	50	---Other
	70.09	**玻璃镜(包括后视镜),不论是否镶框:**					**Glass mirrors, whether or not framed, including rear-view mirrors:**

序号 No.	税则号列 Tariff Line	中文货品名称 Article Description in Chinese	最惠国税率 MFN(%)	协定税率 Agreement(%)	特惠税率 SP(%)	普通税率 Gen(%)	英文货品名称 Article Description
4959	7009.1000	-车辆后视镜	10	0 冰岛IS,东盟AS,哥CR,秘鲁PE,台湾TW,新加坡SG,新西兰NZ,智利CL 4 瑞士CH 5 巴PK 6 澳AU 9 韩国KR	0 受惠国LD	100	-Rear-view mirrors for vehicles
		-其他:					-Other:
4960	7009.9100	--未镶框	21	0 冰岛IS,东盟AS,哥CR,新加坡SG,新西兰NZ,智利CL 6.3 秘鲁PE 12.6 澳AU 14.7 瑞士CH 18.9 韩国KR	0 受惠国$_1$LD$_1$	70	--Unframed
	ex70099100	槽式太阳能抛物面反射镜	Δ10				Parabolic trough in Solar Energy Generating Systems (SEGS)
4961	7009.9200	--已镶框	12	0 冰岛IS,东盟AS,哥CR,秘鲁PE,新加坡SG,新西兰NZ,智利CL 5 巴PK 7.2 澳AU 8.4 瑞士CH 9.6 韩国KR 10.8 亚太AP	0 受惠国LD	100	--Framed
	70.10	**玻璃制的坛、瓶、缸、罐、安瓿及其他容器,用于运输或盛装货物;玻璃制保藏罐;玻璃塞、盖及类似的封口器:**					**Carboys, bottles, flasks, jars, pots, phials, ampoules and other containers, of glass, of a kind used for the conveyance or packing of goods; preserving jars of glass; stoppers, lids and other closures, of glass:**
4962	7010.1000	-安瓿	14	0 冰岛IS,东盟AS,哥CR,秘鲁PE,新加坡SG,新西兰NZ,智利CL 8.4 澳AU 9.8 瑞士CH 11.2 巴PK,韩国KR	0 受惠国$_1$LD$_1$	50	-Ampoules
4963	7010.2000	-塞、盖及类似的封口器	14	0 冰岛IS,东盟AS,哥CR,秘鲁PE,新加坡SG,新西兰NZ,智利CL 8.4 澳AU 9.8 瑞士CH 11.2 巴PK,韩国KR	0 受惠国$_1$LD$_1$	50	-Stoppers, lids and other closures
		-其他:					-Other:
4964	7010.9010	---超过1升	14	0 冰岛IS,东盟AS,哥CR,秘鲁PE,新加坡SG,新西兰NZ,智利CL 8.4 澳AU 9.8 瑞士CH 11.2 巴PK,韩国KR	0 受惠国$_1$LD$_1$	50	---Exceeding 1L
4965	7010.9020	---超过0. 33升，但不超过1升	14	0 冰岛IS,东盟AS,哥CR,秘鲁PE,新加坡SG,新西兰NZ,智利CL 8.4 澳AU 9.8 瑞士CH 11.2 巴PK,韩国KR	0 受惠国$_1$LD$_1$	50	---Exceeding 0.33L but not exceeding 1L
4966	7010.9030	---超过0. 15升，但不超过0. 33升	14	0 冰岛IS,东盟AS,哥CR,秘鲁PE,新加坡SG,新西兰NZ,智利CL 8.4 澳AU 9.8 瑞士CH 11.2 巴PK,韩国KR	0 受惠国$_1$LD$_1$	50	---Exceeding 0.15L but not exceeding 0.33L

序号 No.	税则号列 Tariff Line	中文货品名称 Article Description in Chinese	最惠国税率 MFN(%)	协定税率 Agreement(%)	特惠税率 SP(%)	普通税率 Gen(%)	英文货品名称 Article Description
4967	7010.9090	---不超过0.15升	14	0 冰岛IS,东盟AS,哥CR,秘鲁PE,新加坡SG,新西兰NZ,智利CL 8.4 澳AU 9.8 瑞士CH 11.2 巴PK,韩国KR	0 受惠国LD	50	---Not exceeding 0.15L
	70.11	**制灯泡、阴极射线管及类似品用的未封口玻璃外壳(包括玻璃泡及管)及其玻璃零件,但未装有配件:**					**Glass envelopes (including bulbs and tubes), open, and glass parts thereof, without fittings, for electric lamps, cathode ray tubes or the like:**
4968	7011.1000	-电灯用	21	0 冰岛IS,东盟AS,哥CR,新加坡SG,新西兰NZ,智利CL 6.3 秘鲁PE 12.6 澳AU 14.7 瑞士CH 18.9 韩国KR	0 受惠国$_1$LD$_1$	80	-For electric lighting
		-阴极射线管用:					-For cathode ray tubes:
4969	7011.2010	---显像管玻壳及其零件	10	0 冰岛IS,东盟AS,哥CR,秘鲁PE,新西兰NZ,智利CL 4 瑞士CH 5 巴PK 6 澳AU 7 亚太AP 8 韩国KR	0 受惠国$_1$LD$_1$	35	---Glass envelopes for kinescope and glass parts there of
4970	7011.2090	---其他	10	0 冰岛IS,东盟AS,哥CR,秘鲁PE,新西兰NZ,智利CL 4 瑞士CH 5 巴PK 6 澳AU 7 亚太AP	0 受惠国$_1$LD$_1$	35	---Other
	ex70112090	显示管玻壳及其零件	Δ6				Glass envelopes and parts thereof for display tubes
		-其他:					-Other:
4971	7011.9010	---电子管用(阴极射线管用的除外)	8	0 冰岛IS,东盟AS,哥CR,秘鲁PE,新西兰NZ,智利CL 3.2 瑞士CH 4.8 澳AU,韩国KR 5 巴PK	0 受惠国$_1$LD$_1$	35	---For electronic tubes and valves (other than cathode-ray tubes)
4972	7011.9090	---其他	21	0 冰岛IS,东盟AS,哥CR,新加坡SG,新西兰NZ,智利CL 6.3 秘鲁PE 12.6 澳AU 14.7 瑞士CH 18.9 韩国KR	0 受惠国$_1$LD$_1$	80	---Other
	70.13	**玻璃器,供餐桌、厨房、盥洗室、办公室、室内装饰或类似用途(税号70.10或70.18的货品除外):**					**Glassware of a kind used for table, kitchen, toilet, office, indoor decoration or similar purposes (other than that of heading 7010 or 7018):**
4973	7013.1000	-玻璃陶瓷制	24.5	0 冰岛IS,东盟AS,哥CR,新加坡SG,新西兰NZ,智利CL 7.4 秘鲁PE 14.7 澳AU 17.2 瑞士CH 22 韩国KR	0 受惠国LD	100	-Of glass-ceramics
		-高脚杯,但玻璃陶瓷制的除外:					-Stemware drinking glasses, other than of glass ceramics:

序号 No.	税则号列 Tariff Line	中文货品名称 Article Description in Chinese	最惠国税率 MFN(%)	协定税率 Agreement(%)	特惠税率 SP(%)	普通税率 Gen(%)	英文货品名称 Article Description
4974	7013.2200	--铅晶质玻璃制	24.5Δ15	0 冰岛IS,东盟AS,哥CR,新加坡SG,新西兰NZ,智利CL 7.4 秘鲁PE 14.7 澳AU 17.2 瑞士CH 22 韩国KR	0 受惠国$_1$LD$_1$	100	--Of lead crystal
4975	7013.2800	--其他	8	0 冰岛IS,东盟AS,哥CR,秘鲁PE,新加坡SG,新西兰NZ,智利CL 3.2 瑞士CH 4.8 澳AU,韩国KR 5 巴PK	0 受惠国LD	100	--Other
		-其他杯子，但玻璃陶瓷制的除外：					-Other drinking glasses, other than of glass ceramics:
4976	7013.3300	--铅晶质玻璃制	24.5Δ15	0 冰岛IS,东盟AS,哥CR,新加坡SG,新西兰NZ,智利CL 7.4 秘鲁PE 14.7 澳AU 17.2 瑞士CH 22 韩国KR	0 受惠国$_1$LD$_1$	100	--Of lead crystal
4977	7013.3700	--其他	8	0 冰岛IS,东盟AS,哥CR,秘鲁PE,新加坡SG,新西兰NZ,智利CL 3.2 瑞士CH 4.8 澳AU,韩国KR 5 巴PK	0 受惠国LD	100	--Other
		-餐桌或厨房用玻璃器皿（不包括杯子），但玻璃陶瓷制的除外：					-Glassware of a kind used for table (other than drinking glasses) or kitchen purposes other than of glass ceramics:
4978	7013.4100	--铅晶质玻璃制	24.5Δ15	0 冰岛IS,东盟AS,哥CR,新加坡SG,新西兰NZ,智利CL 7.4 秘鲁PE 14.7 澳AU 17.2 瑞士CH 22 韩国KR	0 受惠国$_1$LD$_1$	100	--Of lead crystal
4979	7013.4200	--温度在0℃至300℃时线膨胀系数不超过5×10^{-6}/开尔文的其他玻璃制	10	0 冰岛IS,东盟AS,哥CR,秘鲁PE,新加坡SG,新西兰NZ,智利CL 4 瑞士CH 5 巴PK 6 澳AU 8 韩国KR	0 受惠国LD	100	--Of glass having a linear coefficient of expansion not exceeding 5×10^{-6} per Kelvin within a temperature range of 0℃ to 300℃
4980	7013.4900	--其他	10	0 冰岛IS,东盟AS,哥CR,秘鲁PE,新加坡SG,新西兰NZ,智利CL 4 瑞士CH 5 巴PK 6 澳AU 8 韩国KR	0 受惠国LD	100	--Other
		-其他玻璃器：					-Other glassware:
4981	7013.9100	--铅晶质玻璃制	10	0 冰岛IS,东盟AS,哥CR,秘鲁PE,新加坡SG,新西兰NZ,智利CL 4 瑞士CH 5 巴PK 6 澳AU 8 韩国KR	0 受惠国LD	100	--Of lead crystal

序号 No.	税则号列 Tariff Line	中文货品名称 Article Description in Chinese	最惠国税率 MFN(%)	协定税率 Agreement(%)	特惠税率 SP(%)	普通税率 Gen(%)	英文货品名称 Article Description
4982	7013.9900	--其他	10	0 冰岛IS,东盟AS,哥CR,秘鲁PE,新加坡SG,新西兰NZ,智利CL 4 瑞士CH 5 巴PK 6 澳AU 8 韩国KR	0 受惠国LD	100	--Other
	70.14	**未经光学加工的信号玻璃器及玻璃制光学元件(税号70.15的货品除外):**					**Signalling glassware and optical elements of glass (other than those of heading 7015) , not optically worked:**
4983	7014.0010	---光学仪器用光学元件毛坯	10	0 澳门MO,冰岛IS,东盟AS,哥CR,秘鲁PE,新加坡SG,新西兰NZ,智利CL 4 瑞士CH 5 巴PK 6 澳AU,韩国KR	0 受惠国LD	40	---Blanks of optical elements, for optical instruments
4984	7014.0090	---其他	17.5	0 冰岛IS,东盟AS,哥CR,新加坡SG,新西兰NZ,智利CL 5.2 秘鲁PE 10.5 澳AU 12.3 瑞士CH 14 巴PK,韩国KR	0 受惠国$_1$LD$_1$	80	---Other
	ex70140090	带有抗红外和防反射薄膜的滤波玻璃	Δ9				Wave-filter galss with anti-IR and anti-reflection film
	70.15	**钟表玻璃及类似玻璃、视力矫正或非视力矫正眼镜用玻璃,呈弧面、弯曲、凹形或类似形状但未经光学加工的;制造上述玻璃用的凹面圆形及扇形玻璃:**					**Clock or watch glasses and similar glasses, glasses for non-corrective or corrective spectacles, curved, bent, hollowed or the like, not optically worked; hollow glass spheres and their segments, for the manufacture of such glasses:**
		-视力矫正眼镜用玻璃:					-Glasses for corrective spectacles:
4985	7015.1010	---变色镜片坯件	21	0 冰岛IS,东盟AS,哥CR,新加坡SG,新西兰NZ,智利CL 6.3 秘鲁PE 12.6 澳AU 14.7 瑞士CH 18.2 韩国KR	0 受惠国$_1$LD$_1$	80	---Blanks for photochromic spectacles
4986	7015.1090	---其他	17.5	0 冰岛IS,东盟AS,哥CR,新加坡SG,新西兰NZ,智利CL 5.2 秘鲁PE 10.5 澳AU 12.3 瑞士CH 14 巴PK,韩国KR	0 受惠国$_1$LD$_1$	70	---Other
		-其他:					-Other:
4987	7015.9010	---钟表玻璃	17.5	0 冰岛IS,东盟AS,哥CR,新加坡SG,新西兰NZ,智利CL 5.2 秘鲁PE 10.5 澳AU 12.3 瑞士CH 14 巴PK,韩国KR	0 受惠国$_1$LD$_1$	70	---Clock and watch glasses
4988	7015.9020	---平光变色镜片坯件	18	0 冰岛IS,东盟AS,哥CR,新加坡SG,新西兰NZ,智利CL 5.4 秘鲁PE 10.8 澳AU 12.6 瑞士CH 14.4 巴PK,韩国KR	0 受惠国$_1$LD$_1$	80	---Blanks for plane photochromic spectacles

序号 No.	税则号列 Tariff Line	中文货品名称 Article Description in Chinese	最惠国税率 MFN(%)	协定税率 Agreement(%)	特惠税率 SP(%)	普通税率 Gen(%)	英文货品名称 Article Description
4989	7015.9090	---其他	12	0 冰岛IS,东盟AS,哥CR,秘鲁PE,新加坡SG,新西兰NZ,智利CL 6 巴PK 7.2 澳AU 8.6 瑞士CH 9.6 韩国KR	0 受惠国LD	80	---Other
	70.16	**建筑用压制或模制的铺面用玻璃块、砖、片、瓦及其他制品，不论是否夹丝;供镶嵌或类似装饰用的玻璃马赛克及其他小件玻璃品，不论是否有衬背;花饰铅条窗玻璃及类似品;多孔或泡沫玻璃块、板、片及类似品:**					**Paving blocks, slabs, bricks, squares, tiles and other articles of pressed or moulded glass, whether or not wired, of a kind used for building or construction purposes; glass cubes and other glass smallwares, whether or not on a backing, for mosaics or similar decorative purposes; leaded lights and the like; multicellular or foam glass in blocks, panels, plates, shells or similar forms:**
4990	7016.1000	-供镶嵌或类似装饰用的玻璃马赛克及其他小件玻璃品，不论是否有衬背	22	0 冰岛IS,东盟AS,哥CR,新加坡SG,新西兰NZ,智利CL 6.6 秘鲁PE 13.2 澳AU 15.4 瑞士CH 19.8 韩国KR	0 受惠国$_1$LD$_1$	100	-Glass cubes and other glass smallwares, whether or not on a backing, for mosaics or similar decorative purposes
		-其他:					-Other:
4991	7016.9010	---花饰铅条窗玻璃及类似品	24	0 冰岛IS,东盟AS,哥CR,新加坡SG,新西兰NZ,智利CL 7.2 秘鲁PE 14.4 澳AU 16.8 瑞士CH 21.6 韩国KR	0 受惠国$_1$LD$_1$	90	---Leaded lights and the like
4992	7016.9090	---其他	18	0 冰岛IS,东盟AS,哥CR,新加坡SG,新西兰NZ,智利CL 5.4 秘鲁PE 10.8 澳AU 12.6 瑞士CH 14.4 韩国KR	0 受惠国$_1$LD$_1$	90	---Other
	70.17	**实验室、卫生及配药用的玻璃器，不论有无刻度或标量:**					**Laboratory, hygienic or pharmaceutical glassware, whether or not graduated or calibrated:**
4993	7017.1000	-熔融石英或其他熔融硅石制	0		0 受惠国LD	30	-Of fused quartz or other fused silica
4994	7017.2000	-温度在0℃至300℃时线膨胀系数不超过5×10^{-6}/开尔文的其他玻璃制	8	0 冰岛IS,东盟AS,哥CR,秘鲁PE,新西兰NZ,智利CL 4.8 澳AU,韩国KR 5 巴PK 5.8 瑞士CH	0 受惠国LD	30	-Of other glass having a linear coefficient of expansion not exceeding 5×10^{-6} per Kelvin within a temperature range of 0℃ to 300℃
4995	7017.9000	-其他	8	0 冰岛IS,东盟AS,哥CR,秘鲁PE,新西兰NZ,智利CL 3.2 瑞士CH 4.8 澳AU 5 巴PK 6.4 韩国KR	0 受惠国LD	30	-Other

序号 No.	税则号列 Tariff Line	中文货品名称 Article Description in Chinese	最惠国税率 MFN(%)	协定税率 Agreement(%)	特惠税率 SP(%)	普通税率 Gen(%)	英文货品名称 Article Description
	70.18	**玻璃珠、仿珍珠、仿宝石或仿半宝石和类似小件玻璃品及其制品，但仿首饰除外；玻璃假眼，但医用假眼除外；灯工方法制作的玻璃塑像及其他玻璃装饰品，但仿首饰除外；直径不超过1毫米的微型玻璃球：**					**Glass beads, imitation pearls, imitation precious or semi-precious stones and similar glass smallwares, and articles thereof other than imitation jewellery; glass eyes other than prosthetic articles; statuettes and other ornaments of lamp-worked glass, other than imitation jewellery; glass microspheres not exceeding 1mm in diameter:**
4996	7018.1000	-玻璃珠、仿珍珠、仿宝石或仿半宝石及类似小件玻璃品	10	0 冰岛IS,东盟AS,哥CR,秘鲁PE,新加坡SG,新西兰NZ,智利CL 4 瑞士CH 5 巴PK 6 澳AU,韩国KR	0 受惠国LD	100	-Glass beads, imitation pearls, imitation precious or semiprecious stones and similar glass smallwares
4997	7018.2000	-直径不超过1毫米的微型玻璃球	20	0 冰岛IS,东盟AS,哥CR,新加坡SG,新西兰NZ,智利CL 6 秘鲁PE 12 澳AU 14 瑞士CH 17.3 韩国KR	0 受惠国$_1$LD$_1$	100	-Glass microspheres not exceeding1mm in diameter
	ex70182000	熔融球形二氧化硅微粉，直径小于等于100微米	Δ5.5				Fused spherical SiO_2, diameter not exceeding 100 micron
4998	7018.9000	-其他	20Δ10	0 冰岛IS,东盟AS,哥CR,新加坡SG,新西兰NZ,智利CL 6 秘鲁PE 12 澳AU 14 瑞士CH 17.3 韩国KR	0 受惠国$_1$LD$_1$	100	-Other
	70.19	**玻璃纤维（包括玻璃棉）及其制品（例如，玻璃纤维纱线及其织物）：**					**Glass fibres (including glass wool) and articles thereof (for example, yarn, woven fabrics):**
		-梳条、粗纱、纱线及短切纤维：					-Slivers, rovings, yarn and chopped strands:
4999	7019.1100	--长度不超过50毫米的短切纤维	12	0 冰岛IS,东盟AS,哥CR,秘鲁PE,台湾TW,新加坡SG,新西兰NZ,智利CL 6 巴PK 7.2 澳AU 8.4 瑞士CH 9.6 韩国KR	0 受惠国LD	50	--Chopped strands, of a length of not more than 50mm
5000	7019.1200	--粗纱	12	0 冰岛IS,东盟AS,哥CR,秘鲁PE,新加坡SG,新西兰NZ,智利CL 6 巴PK 7.2 澳AU 8.4 瑞士CH	0 受惠国LD	50	--Rovings
5001	7019.1900	--其他	10	0 澳门MO,冰岛IS,东盟AS,哥CR,秘鲁PE,台湾TW,新西兰NZ,智利CL 4 瑞士CH 5 巴PK 6 澳AU 8 韩国KR	0 受惠国LD	50	--Other
		-薄片（巴厘纱）、纤维网、席、垫、板及类似无纺产品：					-Thin sheets (voiles) , webs, mats, mattresses, boards and similar non-woven products:

序号 No.	税则号列 Tariff Line	中文货品名称 Article Description in Chinese	最惠国税率 MFN(%)	协定税率 Agreement(%)	特惠税率 SP(%)	普通税率 Gen(%)	英文货品名称 Article Description
5002	7019.3100	--席	5	0 澳AU,巴PK,冰岛IS,东盟AS,哥CR,秘鲁PE,瑞士CH,新西兰NZ,智利CL 3 韩国KR	0 受惠国LD	40	--Mats
5003	7019.3200	--薄片（巴厘纱）	14	0 冰岛IS,东盟AS,哥CR,秘鲁PE,新加坡SG,新西兰NZ,智利CL 8.4 澳AU 9.8 瑞士CH 11.2 巴PK,韩国KR	0 受惠国$_1$LD$_1$	40	--Thin sheets (voiles)
		--其他：					--Other:
5004	7019.3910	---垫	10.5	0 冰岛IS,东盟AS,哥CR,秘鲁PE,台湾TW,新加坡SG,新西兰NZ,智利CL 5 巴PK 6.3 澳AU 7.4 瑞士CH 8.4 韩国KR	0 受惠国LD	40	---Mattresses
5005	7019.3990	---其他	10.5	0 冰岛IS,东盟AS,哥CR,秘鲁PE,台湾TW,新加坡SG,新西兰NZ,智利CL 5 巴PK 6.3 澳AU 7.4 瑞士CH 8.4 韩国KR	0 受惠国LD	40	---Other
5006	7019.4000	-粗纱机织物	12	0 冰岛IS,东盟AS,哥CR,秘鲁PE,新加坡SG,新西兰NZ,智利CL 6 巴PK 7.2 澳AU 8.4 瑞士CH 9.6 韩国KR	0 受惠国LD	40	-Woven fabrics of rovings
		-其他机织物：					-Other woven fabrics:
5007	7019.5100	--宽度不超过30厘米的	12	0 冰岛IS,东盟AS,哥CR,秘鲁PE,香港HK,新加坡SG,新西兰NZ,智利CL 6 巴PK 7.2 澳AU 8.4 瑞士CH 9.6 韩国KR	0 受惠国LD	40	--Of a width not exceeding 30cm
5008	7019.5200	--宽度超过30厘米的长丝平纹织物，每平方米重量不超过250克，单根纱线细度不超过136特克斯	12	0 澳门MO,冰岛IS,东盟AS,哥CR,秘鲁PE,香港HK,新加坡SG,新西兰NZ,智利CL 6 巴PK 7.2 澳AU 8.4 瑞士CH	0 受惠国LD	40	--Of a width exceeding 30cm, plain weave, weighing less than 250g/m^2, of filaments measuring per single yarn not more than 136tex
	ex70195200	覆铜板用玻璃纤维长丝平纹布，开纤或每平方米重不超过180克	Δ10				Glass fiber colth, covered with copper foil, open filament fabric or weighting less than or equal to 180g/m^2
5009	7019.5900	--其他	12	0 澳门MO,冰岛IS,东盟AS,哥CR,秘鲁PE,香港HK,新加坡SG,新西兰NZ,智利CL 5 巴PK 7.2 澳AU 8.4 瑞士CH,亚太AP 10.3 韩国KR	0 受惠国LD	40	--Other
		-其他：					-Other:

序号 No.	税则号列 Tariff Line	中文货品名称 Article Description in Chinese	最惠国税率 MFN(%)	协定税率 Agreement(%)	特惠税率 SP(%)	普通税率 Gen(%)	英文货品名称 Article Description
5010	7019.9010	---玻璃棉及其制品	7	0 澳门MO,冰岛IS,东盟AS,哥CR,秘鲁PE,新西兰NZ,智利CL 2.8 瑞士CH 4.2 澳AU 5 巴PK 6 韩国KR	0 受惠国LD	40	---Glass wool and their product
		---玻璃纤维布浸胶制品:					---Glass fiber cloth dipped product:
5011	7019.9021	----每平方米重量小于450克	7	0 澳门MO,冰岛IS,东盟AS,哥CR,秘鲁PE,新西兰NZ,智利CL 2.8 瑞士CH 4.2 澳AU 5 巴PK 6 韩国KR	0 受惠国LD	40	----Weighting less than 450g/m^2
5012	7019.9029	----其他	7	0 澳门MO,冰岛IS,东盟AS,哥CR,秘鲁PE,新西兰NZ,智利CL 2.8 瑞士CH 4.2 澳AU 5 巴PK 6 韩国KR	0 受惠国LD	40	----Other
5013	7019.9090	---其他	7	0 澳门MO,冰岛IS,东盟AS,哥CR,秘鲁PE,新西兰NZ,智利CL 2.8 瑞士CH 4.2 澳AU 5 巴PK 6 韩国KR	0 受惠国LD	40	---Other
	70.20	**其他玻璃制品:**					**Other articles of glass:**
		---工业用:					---For technical use:
5014	7020.0011	----导电玻璃	10.5Δ7	0 冰岛IS,东盟AS,哥CR,秘鲁PE,香港HK,新加坡SG,新西兰NZ,智利CL 5 巴PK 6.3 澳AU 7.4 瑞士CH	0 受惠国LD	40	----Conductivity glass
5015	7020.0012	----绝缘子用玻璃伞盘	10.5	0 冰岛IS,东盟AS,哥CR,秘鲁PE,新加坡SG,新西兰NZ,智利CL 5 巴PK 6.3 澳AU 7.4 瑞士CH 8.4 韩国KR 9.5 亚太AP	0 受惠国LD	40	----Glass umbrella for insulator
5016	7020.0013	----熔融石英或其他熔融硅石制	10.5	0 冰岛IS,东盟AS,哥CR,秘鲁PE,新加坡SG,新西兰NZ,智利CL 5 巴PK 6.3 澳AU,韩国KR 7.4 瑞士CH 8.9 亚太AP	0 受惠国LD	40	----Of fused quartz or other fused silica
	ex70200013	用于插入熔化和氧化炉内以制备半导体晶片的石英反应管及夹持器	0				Quartz reactor tubes and holders designed for insertion into diffusion and oxidation furnaces for production of semiconductor wafers
5017	7020.0019	----其他	10.5	0 冰岛IS,东盟AS,哥CR,秘鲁PE,新加坡SG,新西兰NZ,智利CL 5 巴PK 6.3 澳AU,韩国KR 7.4 瑞士CH 8.9 亚太AP	0 受惠国LD	40	----Other

序号 No.	税则号列 Tariff Line	中文货品名称 Article Description in Chinese	最惠国税率 MFN(%)	协定税率 Agreement(%)	特惠税率 SP(%)	普通税率 Gen(%)	英文货品名称 Article Description
	ex70200019	用于插入熔化和氧化炉内以制备半导体晶片的石英反应管及夹持器	0				Quartz reactor tubes and holders designed for insertion into diffusion and oxidation furnaces for production of semiconductor wafers
		---其他:					---Other:
5018	7020.0091	----保温瓶或其他保温容器用的玻璃胆	21	0 冰岛IS,东盟AS,哥CR,香港HK,新加坡SG,新西兰NZ,智利CL 6.3 秘鲁PE 12.6 澳AU 14.7 瑞士CH 18.2 韩国KR	0 受惠国$_1$LD$_1$	100	----Glass inners for vacuum flasks or for other vacuum vessels
5019	7020.0099	----其他	15	0 冰岛IS,东盟AS,哥CR,香港HK,新加坡SG,新西兰NZ,智利CL 4.5 秘鲁PE 7.5 巴PK 9 澳AU 10.5 瑞士CH 12 韩国KR 12.8 亚太AP	0 受惠国LD	100	----Other
	ex70200099	石英玻璃，平整度小于等于1微米	Δ4				Quartz glass, of a flatness less than or equal to 1μm

第十四类
天然或养殖珍珠、宝石或半宝石、贵金属、包贵金属及其制品；仿首饰；硬币

SECTION XIV
NATURAL OR CULTURED PEARLS, PRECIOUS OR SEMI-PRECIOUS STONES, PRECIOUS METALS, METALS CLAD WITH PRECIOUS METAL, AND ARTICLES THEREOF; IMITATION JEWELLERY; COIN

第七十一章
天然或养殖珍珠、宝石或半宝石、贵金属、包贵金属及其制品；仿首饰；硬币

注释：

一、除第六类注释一（一）及下列各款另有规定的以外，凡制品的全部或部分由下列物品构成，均应归入本章：

（一）天然或养殖珍珠、宝石或半宝石（天然、合成或再造）；

（二）贵金属或包贵金属。

二、（一）税号 71.13、71.14 及 71.15 不包括带有贵金属或包贵金属制的小零件或小装饰品（例如，交织字母、套、圈、套环）的制品，上述注释一（二）也不适用于这类制品；

（二）税号 71.16 不包括含有贵金属或包贵金属（仅作为小零件或小装饰品的除外）的制品。

三、本章不包括：

（一）贵金属汞齐及胶态贵金属（税号 28.43）；

（二）第三十章的外科用无菌缝合材料、牙科填料或其他货品；

（三）第三十二章的货品（例如光瓷釉）；

（四）载体催化剂（税号 38.15）；

（五）第四十二章注释三（二）所述的税号 42.02 或 42.03 的物品；

（六）税号 43.03 或 43.04 的物品；

（七）第十一类的货品（纺织原料及纺织制品）；

（八）第六十四章或第六十五章的鞋靴、帽类及其他物品；

（九）第六十六章的伞、手杖及其他物品；

（十）税号 68.04 或 68.05 及第八十二章含有宝石或半宝石（天然或合成）粉末的研磨材料制品；第八十二章装有宝石或半宝石（天然、合成或再造）工作部件的器具；第十六类的机器、机械器具、电气设备及其零件。然而，完全以宝石或半宝石（天然、合成或再造）制成的物品及其零件，除未安装的唱针用已加工蓝宝石或钻石外（税号 85.22），其余仍应归入本章；

Chapter 71
Natural or cultured pearls, precious or semi-precious stones, precious metals, metals clad with precious metal, and articles thereof; imitation jewellery; coin

Notes:

1. Subject to Note1 (a) to SectionⅥ and except as provided below, all articles consisting wholly or partly:

(a) Of natural or cultured pearls or of precious or semi-precious stones (natural, synthetic or reconstructed); or

(b) Of precious metal or of metal clad with precious metal, are to be classified in this Chapter.

2. (a) Headings Nos.71.13, 71.14 and 71.15 do not cover articles in which precious metal or metal clad with precious metal is present as minor constituents only, such as minor fittings or minor ornamentation (for example, monograms, ferrules and rims), and paragraph (b) of the foregoing Note does not apply to such articles;

(b) Heading No.71.16does not cover articles containing precious metal or metal clad with precious metal (other than as minor constituents) .

3. This Chapter does not cover:

(a) Amalgams of precious metal, or colloidal precious metal (heading No.28.43);

(b) Sterile surgical suture materials, dental fillings or other goods of Chapter 30;

(c) Goods of Chapter 32 (for example, lustres);

(d) Supported catalysts (heading No.38.15);

(e) Articles of heading No.42.02 or 42.03 referred to in Note 3 (B) to Chapter 42;

(f) Articles of heading No.43.03 or 43.04;

(g) Goods of SectionⅪ (textiles and textile articles);

(h) Footwear, headgear or other articles of Chapter 64 or 65;

(i) Umbrellas, walking-sticks or other articles of Chapter 66;

(j) Abrasive goods of heading No.68.04 or 68.05 or Chapter 82, containing dust or powder of precious or semiprecious stones (natural or synthetic); articles of Chapter 82 with a working part of precious or semi-precious stones (natural, synthetic or reconsturcted); machinery, mechanical appliances or electrical goods, or parts thereof, of SectionⅩⅥ.However, articles and parts thereof, wholly of precious or semiprecious stones (natural, synthetic or reconstructed) remain

（十一）第九十章、第九十一章或第九十二章的物品（科学仪器、钟表及乐器）；

（十二）武器及其零件（第九十三章）；

（十三）第九十五章注释二所述物品；

（十四）根据第九十六章注释四应归入该章的物品；

（十五）雕塑品原件（税号 98.03）、收藏品（税号 98.05）或超过一百年的古物（税号 98.06）、但天然或养殖珍珠、宝石及半宝石除外。

classified in this Chapter, except unmounted worked sapphires and diamonds for styli (heading No.85.22);

(k) Articles of Chapter 90, 91 or 92 (scientific instruments, clocks and watches, musical instruments);

(l) Arms or parts thereof (Chapter 93);

(m) Articles covered by Note 2 to Chapter 95;

(n) Articles classified in Chapter 96 by virtue of Note 4 to that Chapter;

(o) Original sculptures or statuary (heading No.97.03), collectors pieces (heading No.97.05) or antiques of an age exceeding one hundred years (heading No.97.06), other than natural or cultured pearls or precious or semi-precious stones.

四、

（一）所称"贵金属"，是指银、金及铂。

（二）所称"铂"，是指铂、铱、锇、钯、铑及钌。

（三）所称"宝石或半宝石"，不包括第九十六章注释二（二）所述任何物质。

4.

(a) The expression "precious metal" means silver, gold and platinum;

(b) The expression "platinum" means platinum, iridium, osmium, palladium, rhodium and ruthenium;

(c) The expression "precious or semi-precious stones" does not include any of the substances specified in Note2 (b) to Chapter96.

五、含有贵金属的合金（包括烧结及化合的），只要其中任何一种贵金属的含量达到合金重量的 2%，即应视为本章的贵金属合金。贵金属合金应按下列规则归类：

（一）按重量计含铂量在 2%及以上的合金，应视为铂合金；

（二）按重量计含金量在 2%及以上，但不含铂或按重量计含铂量在 2%以下的合金，应视为金合金；

（三）按重量计含银量在 2%及以上的其他合金，应视为银合金。

5. For the purposes of this Chapter, any alloy (including a sintered mixture and an inter-metallic compound) containing precious metal is to be treated as an alloy of precious metal if any one precious metal constitutes as much as 2%, by weight, of the alloy. Alloys of precious metal are to be classified according to the following rules:

(a) An alloy containing 2% or more, by weight, of platinum is to be treated as an alloy of platinum;

(b) An alloy containing 2% or more, by weight, of gold but no platinum, or less than 2%, by weight, of platinum, is to be treated as an alloy of gold;

(c) Other alloys containing 2% or more, by weight, of silver are to be treated as alloys of silver.

六、除条文另有规定的以外，本目录所称贵金属应包括上述注释五所规定的贵金属合金，但不包括包贵金属或表面镀以贵金属的贱金属及非金属。

6. Except where the context otherwise requires, any reference in the Nomenclature to precious metal or to any particular precious metal includes a reference to alloys treated as alloys of precious metal or of the particular metal in accordance with the rules in Note 5 above, but not to metal clad with precious metal or to base metal or nonmetals plated with precious metal.

七、本目录所称"包贵金属"，是指以贱金属为底料，在其一面或多面用焊接、熔接、热轧或类似机械方法覆盖一层贵金属的材料。除条文另有规定的以外，也包括镶嵌贵金属的贱金属。

7. Throughout the Nomenclature the expression "metal clad with precious metal" means material made with a base of metal upon one or more surfaces of which there is affixed by soldering, brazing, welding, hot-rolling or similar mechanical means a covering of precious metal. Except where the context otherwise requires, the expression also covers base metal inlaid with precious metal.

八、除第六类注释一（一）另有规定的以外，凡符合税号 71.12 规定的货品，应归入该税号而不归入本目录的其他税号。

8. Subject to Note1 (a) to SectionⅥ, goods answering to a description in heading No.71.12 are to be classified in that heading and in no other heading of the Nomenclature.

九、税号 71.13 所称"首饰"，是指：

（一）个人用小饰物（不论是否镶嵌宝石）（例如，戒指、手镯、项圈、饰针、耳环、表链、表链饰物、垂饰、领带别针、袖扣、饰扣、宗教性或其他勋章及徽章）；

9. For the purposes of heading No.71.13, the expression "articles of jewellery" means:

(a) Any small objects of personal adornment (gem-set or not) (for example, rings, bracelets, necklaces, brooches, earrings, watch-chains, fobs, pendants, tie-pins, cufflinks, dress-studs, religious or other medals

（二）通常放置在衣袋、手提包或佩戴在身上的个人用品（例如，烟盒、鼻烟盒、口香丸和药丸盒、粉盒、链袋或念珠）。

这些物品可以和下列物品组合或镶嵌下列物品：例如，天然或养殖珍珠、宝石或半宝石、合成或再造的宝石或半宝石、玳瑁壳、珍珠母、兽牙、天然或再生琥珀、黑玉或珊瑚。

十、税号 71.14 所称“金银器”，包括装饰品、餐具、梳妆用具、吸烟用具及类似的家庭、办公室或宗教用的其他物品。

十一、税号 71.17 所称“仿首饰”，是指不含天然或养殖珍珠、宝石或半宝石（天然、合成或再造）及贵金属或包贵金属（仅作为镀层或小零件、小装饰品的除外）的上述注释九（一）所述的首饰（不包括税号 96.06 的钮扣及其他物品或税号 96.15 的梳子、发夹及类似品）。

and insignia); and

(b) Articles of personal use of a kind normally carried in the pocket, in the handbag or on the person (for example, cigar or cigarette cases, snuff boxes, cachou or pill boxes, cachou powder boxes, chain purses or prayer beads) .

These articles may be combined or set, for example, with natural or cultured pearls, precious or semi-precious stones, synthetic or reconstructed precious or semi-precious stones, tortoise shell, mother-of pearl, ivory, natural or reconstituted amber, jet or coral.

10. For the purposes of heading No.71.14, the expression “articles of goldsmiths or silversmiths wares” includes sucharticles as ornaments, tableware, toilet-ware, smokers requisites and other articles of household, office or religious use.

11. For the purposes of heading No.71.17, the expression “imitation jewellery” means articles of jewellery within the meaning of paragraph (a) of Note 9 above (but not including buttons or other articles of heading No.96.06, or dress-combs, hair-slides or the like, or hairpins, of heading No.96.15), not incorporating natural or cultured pearls, precious or semiprecious stones (natural, synthetic or reconstructed) nor (except as plating or as minor constituents) precious metal or metal clad with precious metal.

子目注释：

一、子目号 7106.10、7108.11、7110.11、7110.21、7110.31 及 7110.41 所称“粉末”，是指按重量计 90%及以上可从网眼孔径为 0.5 毫米的筛子通过的产品。

二、子目号 7110.11 及 7110.19 所称“铂”，可不受本章注释四（二）的规定约束，不包括铱、锇、钯、铑及钌。

三、对于税号 71.10 项下的子目所列合金的归类，按其所含铂、钯、铑、铱、锇或钌中重量最大的一种金属归类。

Subheading Notes:

1. For the purposes of subheadings Nos.7106.10, 7108.11, 7110.11, 7110.21, 7110.31 and 7110.41, the expressions “powder” and “in powder form” mean products of which 90% or more by weight passes through a sieve having a mesh aperture of 0.5mm.

2. Notwithstanding the provisions of Chapter Note4 (b) , for the purposes of subheadings Nos.7110.11 and 7110.19, the expression “platinum” does not include indium, osmium, palladium, rhodium or ruthenium.

3. For the classification of alloys in the subheadings of heading No.71.10, each alloy is to be classified with that metal, platinum, palladium, rhodium, iridium, osmium or ruthenium which predominates by weight over each other of these metals.

序号 No.	税则号列 Tariff Line	中文货品名称 Article Description in Chinese	最惠国税率 MFN(%)	协定税率 Agreement(%)	特惠税率 SP(%)	普通税率 Gen(%)	英文货品名称 Article Description
		第一分章　天然或养殖珍珠、宝石或半宝石					I. NATURAL OR CULTURED PEARLS AND PRECIOUS OR SEMI-PRECIOUS STONES
	71.01	**天然或养殖珍珠，不论是否加工或分级，但未成串或镶嵌；天然或养殖珍珠，为便于运输而暂穿成串：**					**Pearls, natural or cultured, whether or not worked or graded but not strung, mounted or set; pearls, natural or cultured, temporarily strung for convenience of transport:**
		-天然珍珠：					-Natural pearls:
		---未分级：					---Ungraded:

序号 No.	税则号列 Tariff Line	中文货品名称 Article Description in Chinese	最惠国税率 MFN(%)	协定税率 Agreement(%)	特惠税率 SP(%)	普通税率 Gen(%)	英文货品名称 Article Description
5020	7101.1011	----黑珍珠	21Δ0	0 冰岛IS,东盟AS,哥CR,新加坡SG,新西兰NZ,智利CL 6.3 秘鲁PE 12.6 澳AU 14.7 瑞士CH 18.2 韩国KR	0 受惠国$_1$LD$_1$	100	----Tahitian pearls
5021	7101.1019	----其他	21	0 冰岛IS,东盟AS,哥CR,新加坡SG,新西兰NZ,智利CL 6.3 秘鲁PE 12.6 澳AU 14.7 瑞士CH 18.2 韩国KR	0 受惠国$_1$LD$_1$	100	----Other
		---其他:					---Other:
5022	7101.1091	----黑珍珠	21Δ0	0 冰岛IS,东盟AS,哥CR,新加坡SG,新西兰NZ,智利CL 6.3 秘鲁PE 12.6 澳AU 14.7 瑞士CH 18.2 韩国KR	0 受惠国$_1$LD$_1$	130	----Tahitian pearls
5023	7101.1099	----其他	21	0 冰岛IS,东盟AS,哥CR,新加坡SG,新西兰NZ,智利CL 6.3 秘鲁PE 12.6 澳AU 14.7 瑞士CH 18.2 韩国KR	0 受惠国$_1$LD$_1$	130	----Other
		-养殖珍珠:					-Cultured pearls:
		--未加工:					--Unworked:
5024	7101.2110	---未分级	21	0 冰岛IS,东盟AS,哥CR,新加坡SG,新西兰NZ,智利CL 6.3 秘鲁PE 12.6 澳AU 14.7 瑞士CH 18.2 韩国KR	0 受惠国$_1$LD$_1$	100	---Ungraded
	ex71012110	养殖黑珍珠	Δ0				Cultured tahitian pearls
5025	7101.2190	---其他	21	0 冰岛IS,东盟AS,哥CR,新加坡SG,新西兰NZ,智利CL 6.3 秘鲁PE 12.6 澳AU 14.7 瑞士CH 18.2 韩国KR	0 受惠国$_1$LD$_1$	130	---Other
	ex71012190	养殖黑珍珠	Δ0				Cultured tahitian pearls
		--已加工:					--Worked:
5026	7101.2210	---未分级	21	0 冰岛IS,东盟AS,哥CR,新加坡SG,新西兰NZ,智利CL 6.3 秘鲁PE 12.6 澳AU 14.7 瑞士CH 18.9 韩国KR	0 受惠国$_1$LD$_1$	100	---Ungraded
	ex71012210	养殖黑珍珠	Δ0				Cultured tahitian pearls
5027	7101.2290	---其他	21	0 冰岛IS,东盟AS,哥CR,新加坡SG,新西兰NZ,智利CL 6.3 秘鲁PE 12.6 澳AU 14.7 瑞士CH 18.9 韩国KR	0 受惠国$_1$LD$_1$	130	---Other
	ex71012290	养殖黑珍珠	Δ0				Cultured tahitian pearls

序号 No.	税则号列 Tariff Line	中文货品名称 Article Description in Chinese	最惠国税率 MFN(%)	协定税率 Agreement(%)	特惠税率 SP(%)	普通税率 Gen(%)	英文货品名称 Article Description
	71.02	**钻石，不论是否加工，但未镶嵌：**					**Diamonds, whether or not worked, but not mounted or set:**
5028	7102.1000	-未分级	3	0 澳AU,巴PK,冰岛IS,东盟AS,哥CR,韩国KR,秘鲁PE,瑞士CH,新西兰NZ,智利CL	0 受惠国LD	14	-Unsorted
		-工业用：					-Industrial:
5029	7102.2100	--未加工或经简单锯开、劈开或粗磨	0		0 受惠国LD	14	--Unworked or simply sawn, cleaved or bruted
5030	7102.2900	--其他	0		0 受惠国LD	14	--Other
		-非工业用：					-Non-industrial:
5031	7102.3100	--未加工或经简单锯开、劈开或粗磨	3	0 澳AU,巴PK,冰岛IS,东盟AS,哥CR,韩国KR,秘鲁PE,香港HK,新西兰NZ,智利CL 2.1 瑞士CH	0 受惠国LD	14	--Unworked or simply sawn, cleaved or bruted
5032	7102.3900	--其他	8	0 巴PK,冰岛IS,东盟AS,哥CR,秘鲁PE,新西兰NZ,亚太AP,智利CL 4.8 澳AU,韩国KR 5.6 瑞士CH	0 受惠国LD	35	--Other
	71.03	**宝石（钻石除外）或半宝石，不论是否加工或分级，但未成串或镶嵌;未分级的宝石（钻石除外）或半宝石，为便于运输而暂穿成串：**					**Precious stones (other than diamonds) and semi-precious stones, whether or not worked or graded but not strung, mounted or set; ungraded precious stones (other than diamonds) and semi-precious stones, temporarily strung for convenience of transport:**
5033	7103.1000	-未加工或经简单锯开或粗制成形	3	0 澳AU,巴PK,冰岛IS,东盟AS,哥CR,秘鲁PE,瑞士CH,新西兰NZ,智利CL 1.8 韩国KR 2.8 亚太AP	0 老挝LA,受惠国LD	14	-Unworked or simply sawn or roughly shaped
		-经其他加工：					-Otherwise worked:
5034	7103.9100	--红宝石、蓝宝石、绿宝石	8	0 巴PK,冰岛IS,东盟AS,哥CR,秘鲁PE,新西兰NZ,智利CL 4 亚太AP 4.8 澳AU,韩国KR 5.6 瑞士CH	0 老挝LA,受惠国LD	35	--Rubies, sapphires and emeralds
		--其他：					--Other:
5035	7103.9910	---翡翠	8	0 巴PK,冰岛IS,东盟AS,哥CR,秘鲁PE,新西兰NZ,智利CL 3.2 瑞士CH 4 亚太AP 4.8 澳AU,韩国KR	0 受惠国LD	35	---Jadeite
5036	7103.9920	---水晶	8	0 巴PK,冰岛IS,东盟AS,哥CR,秘鲁PE,新西兰NZ,智利CL 4 亚太AP 4.8 澳AU 5.6 瑞士CH 6.4 韩国KR	0 受惠国LD	35	---Crystal
5037	7103.9930	---碧玺	8	0 巴PK,冰岛IS,东盟AS,哥CR,秘鲁PE,新西兰NZ,智利CL 4 亚太AP 4.8 澳AU 5.6 瑞士CH 6.4 韩国KR	0 受惠国LD	35	---Tourmaline

序号 No.	税则号列 Tariff Line	中文货品名称 Article Description in Chinese	最惠国税率 MFN(%)	协定税率 Agreement(%)	特惠税率 SP(%)	普通税率 Gen(%)	英文货品名称 Article Description
5038	7103.9940	---软玉	8	0 巴PK,冰岛IS,东盟AS,哥CR,秘鲁PE,新西兰NZ,智利CL 4 亚太AP 4.8 澳AU 5.6 瑞士CH 6.4 韩国KR	0 受惠国LD	35	---Nephrite
5039	7103.9990	---其他	8	0 巴PK,冰岛IS,东盟AS,哥CR,秘鲁PE,新西兰NZ,智利CL 4 亚太AP 4.8 澳AU 5.6 瑞士CH 6.4 韩国KR	0 受惠国LD	35	---Other
	71.04	**合成或再造的宝石或半宝石，不论是否加工或分级，但未成串或镶嵌的；未分级的合成或再造的宝石或半宝石，为便于运输而暂穿成串：**					**Synthetic or reconstructed precious or semi-precious stones, whether or not worked or graded but not strung, mounted or set; ungraded synthetic or reconstructed precious or semi-precious stones, temporarily strung for convenience of transport:**
5040	7104.1000	-压电石英	6	0 冰岛IS,东盟AS,哥CR,秘鲁PE,新西兰NZ,智利CL 2.4 瑞士CH 3.6 澳AU 5 巴PK	0 受惠国LD	14	-Piezo-electric quartz
		-其他，未加工或经简单锯开或粗制成形：					-Other, unworked or simply sawn or roughly shaped:
5041	7104.2010	---钻石	0		0 受惠国LD	14	---Diamonds
5042	7104.2090	---其他	0	0 香港HK	0 受惠国LD	14	---Other
		-其他：					-Other:
		---工业用：					---For technical use:
5043	7104.9011	----钻石	6	0 冰岛IS,东盟AS,哥CR,秘鲁PE,新西兰NZ,智利CL 2.4 瑞士CH 3.6 澳AU,韩国KR 5 巴PK	0 受惠国LD	14	----Diamonds
5044	7104.9012	----蓝宝石	6	0 冰岛IS,东盟AS,哥CR,秘鲁PE,香港HK,新西兰NZ,智利CL 2.4 瑞士CH 3.6 澳AU,韩国KR 5 巴PK	0 受惠国LD	14	----Sapphires
	ex71049012	蓝宝石衬底（由人造刚玉加工而成，厚度小于0.5毫米）	Δ1				Sapphire substrate (made of synthetic corundum, with thickness less than 0.5mm)
5045	7104.9019	----其他	6	0 冰岛IS,东盟AS,哥CR,秘鲁PE,新西兰NZ,智利CL 2.4 瑞士CH 3.6 澳AU 4.8 韩国KR 5 巴PK	0 受惠国LD	14	----Other
		---其他：					---Other:
5046	7104.9091	----钻石	8	0 冰岛IS,东盟AS,哥CR,秘鲁PE,新西兰NZ,智利CL 3.2 瑞士CH 4.8 澳AU,韩国KR 5 巴PK	0 受惠国LD	35	----Diamonds

序号 No.	税则号列 Tariff Line	中文货品名称 Article Description in Chinese	最惠国税率 MFN(%)	协定税率 Agreement(%)	特惠税率 SP(%)	普通税率 Gen(%)	英文货品名称 Article Description
5047	7104.9099	----其他	8	0 冰岛IS,东盟AS,哥CR,秘鲁PE,新西兰NZ,智利CL 3.2 瑞士CH 4.8 澳AU,韩国KR 5 巴PK	0 受惠国LD	35	----Other
	71.05	**天然或合成的宝石或半宝石的粉末:**					**Dust and powder of natural or synthetic precious or semi-precious stones:**
		-钻石的:					-Of diamonds:
5048	7105.1010	---天然的	0		0 受惠国LD	17	---Natural
5049	7105.1020	---人工合成的	0		0 受惠国LD	17	---Synthetic
5050	7105.9000	-其他	0		0 受惠国LD	17	-Other
		第二分章　贵金属及包贵金属					II. PRECIOUS METALS AND METALS CLAD WITH PRECIOUS METAL
	71.06	**银（包括镀金、镀铂的银），未锻造、半制成或粉末状:**					**Silver (including silver plated with gold or platinum) , unwrought or in semi-manufactured forms, or in powder form:**
		-其他:					-Powder:
		---银粉:					---Powder:
5051	7106.1011	----非片状粉末	0		0 受惠国LD	0	----Not Flake
5052	7106.1019	----平均粒径小于3微米	0		0 受惠国LD	0	----Average diameter less than 3micron
		---片状粉末:					---Flake:
5053	7106.1021	----平均粒径小于10微米	0		0 受惠国LD	0	----Average diameter less than10 micron
5054	7106.1029	----其他	0		0 受惠国LD	0	----Other
		-其他:					-Other:
		--未锻造:					--Unwrought:
5055	7106.9110	---纯度达99. 99%及以上	0		0 受惠国LD	0	---Of a purity of 99.99 percent or more
5056	7106.9190	---其他	0		0 受惠国LD	0	---Other
		--半制成:					--Semi-manufactured:
5057	7106.9210	---纯度达99. 99%及以上	0		0 受惠国LD	50	---Of a purity of 99.99 percent or more
5058	7106.9290	---其他	0		0 受惠国LD	50	---Other
	71.07	**以贱金属为底的包银材料**					**Base metals clad with silver, not further worked than semi-manufactured**
5059	7107.0000	以贱金属为底的包银材料	10.5	0 冰岛IS,东盟AS,哥CR,秘鲁PE,新加坡SG,新西兰NZ,智利CL 5 巴PK 6.3 澳AU 7.4 瑞士CH 8.4 韩国KR	0 老挝LA,受惠国LD	50	Base metals clad with silver, not further worked than semi-manufactured
	71.08	**金（包括镀铂的金），未锻造、半制成或粉末状:**					**Gold (including gold plated with platinum) , unwrought or in semi-manufactured forms, or in powder form:**
		-非货币用:					-Non-monetary:
5060	7108.1100	--金粉	0		0 受惠国LD	0	--Powder
5061	7108.1200	--其他未锻造形状	0		0 受惠国LD	0	--Other unwrought forms
5062	7108.1300	--其他半制成形状	0		0 老挝LA,受惠国LD	50	--Other semi-manufactured forms
5063	7108.2000	-货币用	0		0 受惠国LD	0	-Monetary
	71.09	**以贱金属或银为底的包金材料**					**Base metals or silver, clad with gold, not further worked than semi-manufactured**

序号 No.	税则号列 Tariff Line	中文货品名称 Article Description in Chinese	最惠国税率 MFN(%)	协定税率 Agreement(%)	特惠税率 SP(%)	普通税率 Gen(%)	英文货品名称 Article Description
5064	7109.0000	以贱金属或银为底的包金材料	10.5	0 冰岛IS,东盟AS,哥CR,秘鲁PE,新加坡SG,新西兰NZ,智利CL 5 巴PK 6.3 澳AU 7.4 瑞士CH 8.4 韩国KR	0 受惠国LD	50	Base metals or silver, clad with gold, not further worked than semi-manufactured
	71.10	**铂，未锻造、半制成或粉末状：**					**Platinum, unwrought or in semi-manufactured forms, or in powder form:**
		-铂：					-Platinum:
5065	7110.1100	--未锻造或粉末状	0		0 受惠国LD	0	--Unwrought or in powder form
		--其他：					--Other:
5066	7110.1910	---板、片	0		0 受惠国LD	0	---Plates and sheets
5067	7110.1990	---其他	3	0 澳AU,巴PK,冰岛IS,东盟AS,哥CR,韩国KR,秘鲁PE,瑞士CH,香港HK,新西兰NZ,智利CL	0 受惠国LD	11	---Other
		-钯：					-Palladium:
5068	7110.2100	--未锻造或粉末状	0		0 受惠国LD	10	--Unwrought or in powder form
		--其他：					--Other:
5069	7110.2910	---板、片	0		0 受惠国LD	0	---Plates and sheets
5070	7110.2990	---其他	3	0 澳AU,巴PK,冰岛IS,东盟AS,哥CR,韩国KR,秘鲁PE,瑞士CH,香港HK,新西兰NZ,智利CL	0 受惠国LD	11	---Other
		-铑：					-Rhodium:
5071	7110.3100	--未锻造或粉末状	0		0 受惠国LD	0	--Unwrought or in powder form
		--其他：					--Other:
5072	7110.3910	---板、片	0		0 受惠国LD	0	---Plates and sheets
5073	7110.3990	---其他	3	0 澳AU,巴PK,冰岛IS,东盟AS,哥CR,韩国KR,秘鲁PE,瑞士CH,新西兰NZ,智利CL	0 受惠国LD	11	---Other
		-铱、锇及钌：					-Iridium, osmium and ruthenium:
5074	7110.4100	--未锻造或粉末状	0		0 受惠国LD	0	--Unwrought or in powder form
		--其他：					--Other:
5075	7110.4910	---板、片	0		0 受惠国LD	0	---Plates and sheets
5076	7110.4990	---其他	3	0 澳AU,巴PK,冰岛IS,东盟AS,哥CR,韩国KR,秘鲁PE,瑞士CH,新西兰NZ,智利CL	0 受惠国LD	11	---Other
	71.11	**以贱金属、银或金为底的包铂材料**					**Base metals, silver or gold, clad with platinum, not further worked than semi-manufactured**
5077	7111.0000	以贱金属、银或金为底的包铂材料	3	0 澳AU,巴PK,冰岛IS,东盟AS,哥CR,韩国KR,秘鲁PE,瑞士CH,新西兰NZ,智利CL	0 受惠国[1]LD[1]	11	Base metals, silver or gold, clad with platinum, not further worked than semi-manufactured
	71.12	**贵金属或包贵金属的废碎料；含有贵金属或贵金属化合物的其他废碎料，主要用于回收贵金属：**					**Waste and scrap of precious metal or of metal clad with precious metal; other waste and scrap containing precious metal or precious-metal compounds, of a kind used principally for the recovery of precious metal:**
		-含有贵金属或金属化合物的灰：					-Ash containing precious metal or precious-metal compounds:
5078	7112.3010	---含有银或银化合物的	8	0 冰岛IS,东盟AS,哥CR,秘鲁PE,新西兰NZ,智利CL 3.2 瑞士CH 4.8 澳AU,韩国KR 5 巴PK	0 受惠国LD	50	---Of silver or silver compounds

序号 No.	税则号列 Tariff Line	中文货品名称 Article Description in Chinese	最惠国税率 MFN(%)	协定税率 Agreement(%)	特惠税率 SP(%)	普通税率 Gen(%)	英文货品名称 Article Description
5079	7112.3090	---其他	6	0 冰岛IS,东盟AS,哥CR,秘鲁PE,新西兰NZ,智利CL 2.4 瑞士CH 3.6 澳AU,韩国KR 5 巴PK	0 受惠国LD	50	---Other
		-其他：					-Other:
		--金及包金的废碎料，但含有其他贵金属的除外：					--Of gold, including metal clad with gold but excluding sweepings containing other precious metals:
5080	7112.9110	---金及包金的废碎料	0		0 受惠国LD	0	---Of gold or gold compounds
5081	7112.9120	---含有金或金化合物的废碎料	6	0 冰岛IS,东盟AS,哥CR,秘鲁PE,新西兰NZ,智利CL 2.4 瑞士CH 3.6 澳AU,韩国KR 5 巴PK	0 受惠国LD	35	---Waste and scrap with gold or gold compounds
		--铂及包铂的废碎料，但含有其他贵金属的除外：					--Of platinum, including metal clad with platinum but excluding sweepings containing other precious metals:
5082	7112.9210	---铂及包铂的废碎料	0		0 受惠国LD	0	---Of platinum
5083	7112.9220	---含有铂或铂化合物的废碎料	6	0 冰岛IS,东盟AS,哥CR,韩国KR,秘鲁PE,新西兰NZ,智利CL 2.4 瑞士CH 3.6 澳AU 5 巴PK	0 受惠国LD	35	---Wasted and scrap with plutinum
	ex71129220	铂含量在3%以上的其他含铂或铂化合物的废碎料	Δ0				Waste and scrap with plutinum containing by weight more than 3% plutinum
		--其他：					--Other:
5084	7112.9910	---含有银或银化合物的废碎料	8	0 冰岛IS,东盟AS,哥CR,秘鲁PE,新西兰NZ,智利CL 3.2 瑞士CH 4.8 澳AU,韩国KR 5 巴PK	0 受惠国LD	35	---Waste and scrap with silver or silver compounds
5085	7112.9920	---含有其他贵金属或贵金属化合物的废碎料	6	0 冰岛IS,东盟AS,哥CR,秘鲁PE,新西兰NZ,智利CL 2.4 瑞士CH 3.6 澳AU,韩国KR 5 巴PK	0 受惠国LD	35	---Waste and scrap with other precious metals
5086	7112.9990	---其他	0		0 受惠国LD	50	---Other
		第三分章 珠宝首饰、金银器及其他制品					III. JEWELLERY, GOLDSMITHS' AND SILVERSMITHS' WARES AND OTHER ARTICLES
	71.13	**贵金属或包贵金属制的首饰及其零件：**					**Articles of jewellery and parts thereof, of precious metal or of metal clad with precious metal:**
		-贵金属制，不论是否包、镀贵金属：					-Of precious metal whether or not plated or clad with precious metal:
		--银制，不论是否包、镀其他贵金属：					--Of silver, whether or not plated or clad with other precious metal:

序号 No.	税则号列 Tariff Line	中文货品名称 Article Description in Chinese	最惠国税率 MFN(%)	协定税率 Agreement(%)	特惠税率 SP(%)	普通税率 Gen(%)	英文货品名称 Article Description
5087	7113.1110	---镶嵌钻石的	20	0 澳门MO,冰岛IS,东盟AS,哥CR,香港HK,新加坡SG,新西兰NZ,智利CL 6 秘鲁PE 12 澳AU 14.4 瑞士CH 16 巴PK 16.5 亚太AP 17.3 韩国KR	0 受惠国$_1$LD$_1$	130	---Diamond mounted or set
5088	7113.1190	---其他	20	0 澳门MO,冰岛IS,东盟AS,哥CR,香港HK,新加坡SG,新西兰NZ,智利CL 6 秘鲁PE 8 瑞士CH 12 澳AU 16 巴PK 16.5 亚太AP 17.3 韩国KR	0 受惠国LD	130	---Other
		--其他贵金属制，不论是否包、镀贵金属：					--Of other precious metal, whether or not plated or clad with precious metal:
		---黄金制：					---Of gold:
5089	7113.1911	----镶嵌钻石的	20	0 澳门MO,冰岛IS,东盟AS,哥CR,香港HK,新加坡SG,新西兰NZ,智利CL 6 秘鲁PE 12 澳AU 14 巴PK,亚太AP 15 瑞士CH 17.3 韩国KR	0 受惠国$_1$LD$_1$	130	----Diamond mounted
5090	7113.1919	----其他	20	0 澳门MO,冰岛IS,东盟AS,哥CR,香港HK,新加坡SG,新西兰NZ,智利CL 6 秘鲁PE 8 瑞士CH 12 澳AU 16 巴PK,韩国KR,亚太AP	0 受惠国$_1$LD$_1$	130	----Other
		---铂制：					---Of platinum:
5091	7113.1921	----镶嵌钻石的	35	0 澳门MO,冰岛IS,东盟AS,哥CR,香港HK,新加坡SG,新西兰NZ,智利CL 10.5 秘鲁PE 21 澳AU 28 巴PK,亚太AP	0 受惠国$_1$LD$_1$	130	----Diamond mounted
5092	7113.1929	----其他	35	0 澳门MO,冰岛IS,东盟AS,哥CR,香港HK,新加坡SG,新西兰NZ,智利CL 10.5 秘鲁PE 14 瑞士CH 21 澳AU 28 巴PK,亚太AP	0 受惠国LD	130	----Other
		---其他：					---Other:
5093	7113.1991	----镶嵌钻石的	35	0 澳门MO,冰岛IS,东盟AS,哥CR,香港HK,新加坡SG,新西兰NZ,智利CL 10.5 秘鲁PE 21 澳AU 28 巴PK,亚太AP	0 受惠国$_1$LD$_1$	130	----Diamond mounted or set

序号 No.	税则号列 Tariff Line	中文货品名称 Article Description in Chinese	最惠国税率 MFN(%)	协定税率 Agreement(%)	特惠税率 SP(%)	普通税率 Gen(%)	英文货品名称 Article Description
5094	7113.1999	----其他	35	0 澳门MO,冰岛IS,东盟AS,哥CR,香港HK,新加坡SG,新西兰NZ,智利CL 10.5 秘鲁PE 14 瑞士CH 21 澳AU 28 巴PK,亚太AP	0 受惠国LD	130	----Other
		-以贱金属为底的包贵金属制:					-Of base metal clad with precious metal:
5095	7113.2010	---镶嵌钻石的	35	0 澳门MO,东盟AS,哥CR,香港HK,新加坡SG,新西兰NZ,智利CL 10.5 秘鲁PE 21 澳AU 25.2 瑞士CH 30 巴PK,亚太AP	0 受惠国1LD1	130	---Diamond mounted or set
5096	7113.2090	---其他	35	0 澳门MO,冰岛IS,东盟AS,哥CR,香港HK,新加坡SG,新西兰NZ,智利CL 10.5 秘鲁PE 21 澳AU 30 巴PK,亚太AP	0 受惠国1LD1	130	---Other
	71.14	**贵金属或包贵金属制的金银器及其零件:**					**Articles of goldsmiths' or silversmiths' wares and parts thereof, of precious metal or of metal clad with precious metal:**
		-贵金属制，不论是否包、镀贵金属:					-Of precious metal whether or not plated or clad with precious metal:
5097	7114.1100	--银制，不论是否包、镀其他贵金属	35	0 澳门MO,冰岛IS,东盟AS,哥CR,秘鲁PE,香港HK,新加坡SG,新西兰NZ,智利CL 14 瑞士CH 21 澳AU	0 受惠国LD	100	--Of silver, whether or not plated or clad with other precious metal
5098	7114.1900	--其他贵金属制，不论是否包、镀贵金属	35	0 澳门MO,冰岛IS,东盟AS,哥CR,香港HK,新加坡SG,新西兰NZ,智利CL 10.5 秘鲁PE 21 澳AU 26.3 瑞士CH	0 受惠国1LD1	100	--Of other precious metal, whether or not plated or clad with precious metal
5099	7114.2000	-以贱金属为底的包贵金属制	35	0 澳门MO,冰岛IS,东盟AS,哥CR,香港HK,新加坡SG,新西兰NZ,智利CL 10.5 秘鲁PE 21 澳AU 25.2 瑞士CH	0 受惠国LD	100	-Of base metal clad with precious metal
	71.15	**贵金属或包贵金属的其他制品:**					**Other articles of precious metal or of metal clad with precious metal:**
5100	7115.1000	-金属丝布或格栅形状的铂催化剂	3	0 澳AU,巴PK,冰岛IS,东盟AS,哥CR,韩国KR,秘鲁PE,瑞士CH,香港HK,新西兰NZ,智利CL	0 受惠国LD	11	-Catalysts in the form of wire cloth or grill, of platinum
		-其他:					-Other:
5101	7115.9010	---工业或实验室用	3Δ0	0 澳AU,澳门MO,巴PK,冰岛IS,东盟AS,哥CR,韩国KR,秘鲁PE,瑞士CH,香港HK,新西兰NZ,智利CL	0 受惠国LD	11	---For technical or laboratory use

序号 No.	税则号列 Tariff Line	中文货品名称 Article Description in Chinese	最惠国税率 MFN(%)	协定税率 Agreement(%)	特惠税率 SP(%)	普通税率 Gen(%)	英文货品名称 Article Description
5102	7115.9090	---其他	35	0 澳门MO,冰岛IS,东盟AS,哥CR,香港HK,新加坡SG,新西兰NZ,智利CL 10.5 秘鲁PE 21 澳AU	0 受惠国$_1$LD$_1$	100	---Other
	71.16	**用天然或养殖珍珠、宝石或半宝石（天然、合成或再造）制成的物品：**					**Articles of natural or cultured pearls, precious or semi-precious stones (natural, synthetic or reconstructed) :**
5103	7116.1000	-天然或养殖珍珠制	35	0 澳门MO,冰岛IS,东盟AS,哥CR,香港HK,新加坡SG,新西兰NZ,智利CL 10.5 秘鲁PE 21 澳AU 24.5 瑞士CH	0 受惠国$_1$LD$_1$	130	-Of natural or cultured pearls
5104	7116.2000	-宝石或半宝石（天然、合成或再造）制	35	0 澳门MO,冰岛IS,东盟AS,哥CR,香港HK,新加坡SG,新西兰NZ,智利CL 10.5 秘鲁PE 14 瑞士CH 21 澳AU	0 受惠国LD	130	-Of precious or semi-precious stones (natural, synthetic or reconstructed)
	71.17	**仿首饰：**					**Imitation jewellery:**
		-贱金属制，不论是否镀贵金属：					-Of base metal, whether or not plated with precious metal:
5105	7117.1100	--袖扣、饰扣	35	0 澳门MO,冰岛IS,东盟AS,哥CR,香港HK,新加坡SG,新西兰NZ,智利CL 10.5 秘鲁PE 21 澳AU 25.2 瑞士CH	0 受惠国$_1$LD$_1$	130	--Cuff-links and studs
5106	7117.1900	--其他	17	0 澳门MO,冰岛IS,东盟AS,哥CR,香港HK,新加坡SG,新西兰NZ,智利CL 5.1 秘鲁PE 10.2 澳AU 11.9 瑞士CH 13.6 巴PK,韩国KR 15.3 亚太AP	0 受惠国LD	130	--Other
5107	7117.9000	-其他	35	0 澳门MO,东盟AS,哥CR,香港HK,新加坡SG,新西兰NZ,智利CL 10.5 秘鲁PE 21 澳AU 30 巴PK,亚太AP 30.1 韩国KR	0 受惠国LD	130	-Other
	71.18	**硬币：**					**Coin:**
5108	7118.1000	-非法定货币的硬币（金币除外）	0		0 受惠国LD	0	-Coin (other than gold coin) , not being legal tender
5109	7118.9000	-其他	0		0 受惠国LD	0	-Other

第十五类
贱金属及其制品

注释：

一、本类不包括:

（一）以金属粉末为基本成分的调制油漆、油墨或其他产品（税号 32.07 至 32.10、32.12、32.13 或 32.15）;

（二）铈铁或其他引火合金（税号36.06）;

（三）税号65.06或65.07的帽类及其零件;

（四）税号66.03的伞骨及其他物品;

（五）第七十一章的货品（例如，贵金属合金、以贱金属为底的包贵金属、仿首饰）;

（六）第十六类的物品（机器、机械器具及电气设备）;

（七）已装配的铁路或电车轨道（税号86.08）或第十七类的其他物品（车辆、船舶、航空器）;

（八）第十八类的仪器及器具，包括钟表发条;

（九）做弹药用的铅弹（税号93.06）或第十九类的其他物品（武器、弹药）;

（十）第九十四章的物品（例如，家具、弹簧床垫、灯具及照明装置、发光标志、活动房屋）;

（十一）第九十五章的物品（例如，玩具、游戏品及运动用品）;

（十二）手用筛子、钮扣、钢笔、铅笔套、钢笔尖或第九十六章的其他物品（杂项制品）;

（十三）第九十七章的物品（例如，艺术品）。

二、本目录所称“通用零件”，是指:

（一）税号73.07、73.12、73.15、73.17或73.18的物品及其他贱金属制的类似品;

（二）贱金属制的弹簧及弹簧片，但钟表发条（税号91.14）除外;

（三）税号83.01、83.02、83.08、83.10的物品及税号83.06的贱金属制的框架及镜子。

第七十三章至第七十六章（税号 73.15 除外）及第七十八章至第八十二章所列货品的零件，不包括上述的通用零件。

除上段及第八十三章注释一另有规定的以外，第七十二章至第七十六章及第七十八章至第八十一章不包括第八十二章、第八十三章的物品。

三、本目录所称“贱金属”是指:铁及钢、铜、镍、铝、铅、锌、锡、钨、钼、钽、镁、钴、铋、镉、钛、锆、锑、锰、铍、铬、锗、钒、镓、铪、铟、铌（钶）、铼及铊。

四、本目录所称“金属陶瓷”是指金属与陶瓷成分以极细微粒不均匀结合而成的产品。“金属陶瓷”包括硬质合金（金属碳化物与金属烧结而成）。

五、合金的归类规则（第七十二章、第七十四章所规定的铁合金及母合金除外）:

SECTION XV
BASE METALS AND ARTICLES OF BASE METAL

Notes:

1. This Section does not cover:

(a) Prepared paints, inks or other products with a basis of metallic flakes or powder (headings Nos.32.07 to 32.10, 32.12, 32.13 or 32.15);

(b) Ferro-cerium or other pyrophoric alloys(heading No.36.06);

(c) Headgear or parts thereof of heading No.65.06 or 65.07;

(d) Umbrella frames or other articles of heading No.66.03;

(e) Goods of Chapter71 (for example, precious metal alloys, base metal clad with precious metal, imitation jewellery);

(f) Articles of Section XVI(machinery, mechanical appliances and electrical goods);

(g) Assembled railway or tramway track (heading No.86.08)or other articles of Section XVII(vehicles, ships and boats, aircraft);

(h) Instruments or apparatus of Section XVIII, including clock or watch springs;

(ij) Lead shot prepared for anmmunition(heading No.93.06) or other articles of Section XIX(arms and ammunition);

(k) Articles of Chapter 94 (for example, furniture, mattress supports, lamps and lighting fittings, illuminated signs, prefabricated buildings);

(l) Articles of Chapter95 (for example, toys, games, sports requisites);

(m) Hand sieves, buttons, pens, pencil-holders, pen nibs or other articles of Chapter 96 (miscellaneous manufactured articles); or

(n) Articles of Chapter 97 (for example, works of art).

2. Throughout the Nomenclature, the expression “parts of general use” means:

(a) Articles of heading No.73.07, 73.12, 73.15, 73.17 or 73.18 and similar articles of other base metal;

(b) Springs and leaves for springs, of base metal, other than clock or watch springs (heading No.91.14);

(c) Articles of headings No.83.01, 83.02, 83.08, 83.10 and frames and mirrors, of basc metal, of heading No.83.06.

In Chapters 73 to76 and 78 to 82 (but not in heading No.73.15) references to parts of goods do not include references to parts of general use as defined above.

subject to the preceding paragraph and to Note1to Chapter 83, the articles of Chapter 82 or 83 are excluded from Chapters 72 to 76 and 78 to 81.

3. Throughout the Nomenclature, the expression “base metals” means:iron and steel, copper, nickel, aluminium, lead, zinc, tin, tungsten (wolfram), molybdenum, tantalum, magnesium, cobalt, bismuth, cadmium, titanium, zirconium, antimony, manganese, beryllium, chromium, germanium, vanadium, gallium, hafnium, indium, niobium (columbium), rhenium and thallium.

4. Throughout the Nomenclature, the term “cermets” means products containing a microscopic heterogeneous combination of a metallic component and a ceramic component. The term “cermets” includes sintered metal carbides (metal carbides sintered with a metal).

5. Classification of alloys (other than ferro-alloys and master alloys as defined in Chapters 72 and 74):

（一） 贱金属的合金按其所含重量最大的金属归类；

（二） 由本类的贱金属和非本类的元素构成的合金，如果所含贱金属的总重量等于或超过所含其他元素的总重量，应作为本类贱金属合金归类；

（三）本类所称“合金”，包括金属粉末的烧结混合物、熔化而得的不均匀紧密混合物（金属陶瓷除外）及金属间化合物。

六、除条文另有规定的以外，本目录所称的贱金属包括贱金属合金，这类合金应按上述注释五的规则进行归类。

七、复合材料制品的归类规则：
除各税号另有规定的以外，贱金属制品（包括根据“归类总规则”作为贱金属制品的混合材料制品）如果含有两种或两种以上贱金属的，按其所含重量最大的贱金属的制品归类。为此：

（一）钢、铁或不同种类的钢铁，均视为一种金属；

（二）按照注释五的规定作为某一种金属归类的合金，应视为一种金属；

（三）税号81.13的金属陶瓷，应视为一种贱金属。

八、本类所用有关名词解释如下：

（一）废碎料
在金属生产或机械加工中产生的废料及碎屑以及因破裂、切断、磨损及其他原因而明显不能作为原物使用的金属货品。

（二）粉末
按重量计90%及以上可从网眼孔径为1毫米的筛子通过的产品。

(a) An alloy of base metals is to be classified as an alloy of the metal which predominates by weight over each of the other metals;

(b) An alloy composed of base metals of this Section and of elements not falling within this Section is to be treated as an alloy of base metals of this Section if the total weight of such metals equals or exceeds the total weight of the other elements present;

(c) In this Section the term “alloys” includes sintered mixtures of metal powders, heterogeneous intimate mixtures obtained by melting (other than cermets) and intermetallic compounds.

6. Unless the context otherwise requires, any reference in the Nomenclature to base metal includes a reference to alloys which, by virtue of Note5above, are to be classified as alloys of that metal.

7. Classification of composite articles:
Except where the headings otherwise require, articles of base metal (including articles of mixed materials treated as articles of base metal under the Interpretative Rules) containing two or more base metals are to be treated as articles of the base metal predominating by weight over each of the other metals.For this purpose:

(a) Iron and steel, or different kinds of iron or steel, are regarded as one and the same metal;

(b) An alloy is regarded as being entirely composed of that metal as an alloy of which, by virtue of Note5, it is classified;and

(c) A cermet of heading No.81.13is regarded as a single base metal.

8. In this Section, the following expressions have the meanings hereby assigned to them:

(a) Waste and scrap
Metal waste and scrap from the manufacture of mechanical working of metals, and metal goods definitely not usable as such because of breakage, cuttingup, wear or other reasons.

(b) Powders
Products of which90%or more by weight passes through a sieve having a mesh aperture of1mm.

第七十二章 钢铁

注释：

一、本章所述有关名词解释如下（本条注释（四）、（五）、（六）适用于本目录其他各章）：

（一）生铁：
无实用可锻性的铁碳合金，按重量计含碳量在2%以上并可含有一种或几种下列含量范围的其他元素：

铬不超过10%；
锰不超过6%；
磷不超过3%；
硅不超过8%；
其他元素合计不超过10%。

（二）镜铁：
按重量计含锰量在6%以上，但不超过30%的铁碳合金，其他方面符合上述（一）款所列标准。

（三）铁合金：

Chapter 72 Iron and steel

Notes:

1. In this Chapter and, in the case of Notes (d), (e) and (f) throughout the Nomenclature, the following expressions have the meanings hereby assigned to them:

(a) Pig iron:
Iron-carbon alloys not usefully malleable, containing more than 2% by weight of carbon and which may contain by weight one or more other elements within the following limits:
-not more than 10% of chromium;
-not more than 6% of manganese;
-not more than 3% of phosphorus;
-not more than 8% of silicon;
-a total of not more than 10% of other elements.

(b) Spiegeleisen:
Iron-carbon alloys containing by weight more than 6% but not more than 30% of manganese and otherwise conforming to the specification at (a) above.

(c) Ferro-alloys:

锭、块、团或类似初级形状、连续铸造而形成的各种形状及颗粒、粉末状的合金，不论是否烧结，通常用于其他合金生产过程中的添加剂或在黑色金属冶炼中作除氧剂、脱硫剂及类似用途，一般无实用可锻性，按重量计铁元素含量在4%及以上并含有下列一种或几种元素：

铬超过10%;
锰超过30%;
磷超过3%;
硅超过 8%;
除碳以外的其他元素，合计超过 10%，但最高含铜量不得超过 10%。

（四）钢：
除税号72.03以外的黑色金属材料（某些铸造而成的种类除外），具有实用可锻性，按重量计含碳量在2%及以下，但铬钢可具有较高的含碳量。

（五）不锈钢：
按重量计含碳量在 1.2%及以下，含铬量在10.5%及以上的合金钢，不论是否含有其他元素。

（六）其他合金钢：
不符合以上不锈钢定义的钢，含有一种或几种按重量计符合下列含量比例的元素：

铝0.3%及以上;
硼0.0008%及以上;
铬0.3%及以上;
钴0.3%及以上;
铜0.4%及以上;
铅0.4%及以上;
锰1.65%及以上;
钼0.08%及以上;
镍0.3%及以上;
铌0.06%及以上;
硅0.6%及以上;
钛0.05%及以上;
钨0.3%及以上;
钒0.1%及以上;
锆0.05%及以上;
其他元素（硫、磷、碳及氮除外）单项含量在0.1%及以上。

（七）供再熔的碎料钢铁锭：
粗铸成形无缩孔或冒口的锭块产品，表面有明显瑕疵，化学成分不同于生铁、镜铁及铁合金。

（八）颗粒：
按重量计不到 90%可从网眼孔径为 1 毫米的筛子通过，而 90%及以上可从网眼孔径为 5 毫米的筛子通过的产品。

（九）半制成品：
连续铸造的实心产品，不论是否初步热轧；其他实心产品，除经初步热轧或锻造粗制成形以外未经进一步加工，包括角材、型材及异型材的坯件。
本类产品不包括成卷的产品。

Alloys in pigs, blocks, lumps or similar primary forms, in forms obtained by continuous casting and also in granular or powder forms, whether or not agglomerated, commonly used as an additive in the manufacture of other alloys or as deoxidants, desulphurizing agents or for similar uses in ferrous metallurgy and generally not usefully malleable, containing by weight 4% or more of the element iron and one or more of the following:
-more than 10% of chromium;
-more than 30% of manganese;
-more than 3% of phosphorus;
-more than 8% of silicon;
-a total of more than 10% of other elements, excluding carbon, subject to a maximum content of 10% in the case of copper.

(d) Steel:
Ferrous materials other than those of heading No.72.03 which (with the exception of certain types produced in the form of castings) are usefully malleable and which contain by weight 2% or less of carbon. However, chromium steels may contain higher proportions of carbon.

(e) Stainless steel:
Alloy steels containing, by weight, 1.2% or less of carbon and 10.5% or more of chromium, with or without other elements.

(f) Other alloy steel:
Steels not complying with the definition of stainless steel and containing by weight one or more of the following elements in the proportion shown:
-0.3% or more of aluminium;
-0.0008% or more of boron;
-0.3% or more of chromium;
-0.3% or more of cobalt;
-0.4% or more of copper;
-0.4% or more of lead;
-1.65% or more of manganese;
-0.08% or more of molybdenum;
0.3% or more of nickel;
-0.06% or more of niobium;
-0.6% or more of silicon;
-0.05% or more of titanium;
-0.3% or more of tungsten(wolfram);
-0.1% or more of vanadium;
-0.05% or more of zirconium;
-0.1% or more of other elements (except sulphur, phosphorus, carbon and nitrogen), taken separately.

(g) Remelting scrap ingots of iron or steel:
Products roughly cast in the form of ingots without feeder-heads or hot tops, or of pigs, having obvious surface faults and not complying with the chemical composition of pig iron, spiegeleisen or ferro-alloys.

(h) Granules:
Products of which less than 90% by weight passes through a sieve with a mesh aperture of1mm and of which 90% or more by weight passes through a sieve with a mesh aperture of5mm.

(i) Semi-finished products:
Continuous cast products of solid section, whether or not subjected to primary hot-rolling; and Other products of solid section, which have not been further worked than subjected to primary hot-rolling or roughly shaped by forging, including blanks for angles, shapes or sections.

（十）平板轧材：

截面为矩形（正方形除外）并且不符合以上第（九）款所述定义的下列形状实心轧制产品：

1. 层叠的卷材；

2. 平直形状，其厚度如果在4.75毫米以下，则宽度至少是厚度的十倍；其厚度如果在4.75毫米及以上，其宽度应超过150毫米，并且至少应为厚度的两倍。

平板轧材包括直接轧制而成并有凸起式样（例如，凹槽、肋条形、格槽、珠粒、菱形）的产品以及穿孔、抛光或制成瓦楞形的产品，但不具有其他税号所列制品或产品的特征。

各种规格的平板轧材（矩形或正方形除外），但不具有其他税号所列制品或产品的特征，都应作为宽度为600毫米及以上的产品归类。

（十一）不规则盘绕的热轧条、杆：

经热轧不规则盘绕的实心产品，其截面为圆形、扇形、椭圆形、矩形（包括正方形）、三角形或其他外凸多边形（包括“扁圆形”及“变形矩形”，即相对两边为弧拱形，另外两边为等长平行直线形）。这类产品可带有在轧制过程中产生的凹痕、凸缘、槽沟或其他变形（钢筋）。

（十二）其他条、杆：

不符合上述（九）、（十）、（十一）款或“丝”定义的实心产品，其全长截面均为圆形、扇形、椭圆形、矩形（包括正方形）、三角形或其他外凸多边形（包括“扁圆形”及“变形矩形”，即相对两边为弧拱形，另两边为等长平行直线形）。这些产品可以：

1. 带有在轧制过程中产生的凹痕、凸缘、槽沟或其他变形（钢筋）；

2. 轧制后扭曲的。

（十三）角材、型材及异型材：

不符合上述（九）、（十）、（十一）、（十二）款或“丝”定义，但其全长截面均为同样形状的实心产品。

第七十二章不包括税号 73.01 或 73.02 的产品。

（十四）丝：

不符合平板轧材定义但全长截面均为同样形状的盘卷冷成形实心产品。

（十五）空心钻钢：

适合钻探用的各种截面的空心条、杆，其最大外形尺寸超过15毫米但不超过52毫米，最大内孔尺寸不超过最大外形尺寸的二分之一。不符合本定义的钢铁空心条、

These products are not presented in coils.

(j) Flat-rolled products:

Rolled products of solid rectangular(other than square) cross-section, which do not conform to the definition at (i) above in the form of:

(1)coils of successively superimposed layers; or

(2)straight lenghths, which if of a thickness less than 4.75mm are of a width measuring at least ten times the thickness or if of a thickness of 4.75mm or more are of a width which exceeds 150mm and measures at least twice the thickness.

Flat-rolled products include those with patterns in relief derived directly from rolling (for example, grooves, ribs, chequers, tears, buttons, lozenges) and those which have been perforated, corrugated or polished, provided that they do not thereby assume the character of articles or products of other headings.

Flat-rolled products of a shape other than rectangular or square, of any size, are to be classified as products of a width of 600mm or more, provided that they do not assume the character of articles or products of other headings.

(k)Bars and rods, hot-rolled, in irregularly wound coils:

Hot-rolled products in irregularly wound coils, which have a solid cross-section in the shape of circles, segments of circles, ovals, rectangles (including squares), triangles or other convex polygons (including "flattened circles" and modified rectangles of which two opposite sides are convex arcs, the other two sides being straight, of equal length and paralled). These products may have indentations, ribs, grooves or other deformations produced during the rolling process (reinforcing bars and rods).

(l)Other bars and rods:

Products which do not conform to any of the definitions at (i), (j) or (k) above or to the definition of wire, which have a uniform solid cross-section along their whole length in the shape of circles, segments of circles, ovals, rectangles (including squares), triangles or other convex polygons (including "flattened circles" and "modified rectangles", of which two opposite sides are convex arcs, the other two sides being straight, of equal length and parallel). These products may:

-have indentations, ribs, grooves or other deformations produced during the rolling process (reinforcing bars and rods);

-be twisted after rolling.

(m) Angles, shapes and sections:

Products having a uniform solid cross-section along their whole length which do not conform to any of the definitions at (i), (j), (k) or (l) above or to the definition of wire.

Chapter 72 does not include products of heading No.73.01 or 73.02.

(n)Wire:

Cold-formed products in coils, of any uniform solid cross-section along their whole length, which do not conform to the definition of flat-rolled products.

(o)Hollow drill bars and rods:

Hollow bars and rods of any cross-section, suitable for drills, of which the greatest external dimension of the cross-section exceeds 15mm but does not exceed 52mm, and of which the greatest internal dimension

杆应归入税号73.04。

does not exceed one half of the greatest external dimension. Hollow bars and rods of iron or steel not conforming to this definition are to be classified in heading No.73.04.

二、用一种黑色金属包覆不同种类的黑色金属，应按其中重量最大的材料归类。

2. Ferrous metals clad with another ferrous metal are to be classified as products of the ferrous metal predominating by weight.

三、用电解沉积法、压铸法或烧结法所得的钢铁产品，应按其形状、成分及外观归入本章类似热轧产品的相应税号。

3. Iron or steel products obtained by electrolytic deposition, by pressure casting or by sintering are to be classified, according to their form, their composition and their appearance, in the headings of this Chapter appropriate to similar hot-rolled products.

子目注释：

Subheading Notes:

一、本章所用有关名词解释如下：

1. In this Chapter the following expressions have the meanings hereby assigned to them:

（一）合金生铁：
按重量计含有一种或几种下列比例的元素的生铁：
铬0.2%以上；
铜0.3%以上；
镍0.3%以上；
0.1%以上的任何下列元素：
铝、钼、钛、钨、钒。

(a)Alloy pig iron:
Pig iron containing, by weight, one or more of the following elements in the specified proportions:
-more than 0.2% of chromiumi;
-more than 0.3% of copper;
-more than 0.3% of nickel;
-more than 0.1% of any of the following elements: aluminium, molybdenum, titanium, tungsten (wolfram),vanadium.

（二）非合金易切削钢：
按重量计含有一种或几种下列比例的元素的非合金钢：
硫0.08%及以上；
铅0.1%及以上；
硒0.05%以上；
碲0.01%以上；
铋0.05%以上。

(b)Non-alloy free-cutting steel:
Non-alloy steel containing, by weight, one or more of the following elements in the specified proportions:
-0.08% or more of sulphur
-0.1% or more of lead;
-more than 0.05% of selenium;
-more than 0.01% of tellurium;
-more than 0.05% of bismuth.

（三）硅电钢：
按重量计含硅量至少为0.6%但不超过6%，含碳量不超过0.08%的合金钢。这类钢还可含有按重量计不超过1%的铝，但所含其他元素的比例并不使其具有其他合金钢的特性。

(c)Silicon-electrical steel:
Alloy steels containing by weight at least 0.6% but notmore than 6% of silicon and not more than 0.08% of carbon. They may also contain by weight not more than 1% of aluminium but no other element in a proportion that would give the steel the characteristics of another alloy steel.

（四）高速钢：
不论是否含有其他元素，但至少含有按重量计合计含量在7%及以上的钼、钨、钒中两种元素的合金钢，按重量计其含碳量在0.6%及以上，含铬量在3%～6%。

(d)High speed steel:
Alloy steels containing, with or without other elements, at least two of the three elements molybdenum, tungsten and vanadium with a combined content by weight of 7% or more, 0.6% or more of carbon and 3% to 6% of chromium.

（五）硅锰钢：
按重量计同时含有下列元素的合金钢：
碳不超过0.7%；
锰0.5%及以上，但不超过1.9%；
硅0.6%及以上，但不超过2.3%；
所含其他元素的比例并不使其具有其他合金钢的特性。

(c)Silico-manganese steel:
Alloy steels containing by weight:
-not more than 0.7% of carbon;
-0.5% or more but not more than 1.9% of manganese; and
-0.6% or more but not more than 2.3% of silicon; but no other element in a proportion that would give the steel the characteristics of another alloy steel.

二、税号72.02项下的子目所列铁合金，应按照下列规则归类：
对于只有一种元素超出本章注释一（三）规定的最低百分比的铁合金，应作为二元合金归入相应的子目号。以此类推，如果有两种或三种合金元素超出了最低百分比的，则可分别作为三元或四元合金。

2. For the classification of ferroalloys in the subheadings of heading No.72.02 the following rule should be observed: A ferro-alloy is considered as binary and classified under the relevant subheading (if it exists) if only one of the alloy elements exceeds the minimum percentage laid down in Chapter Note1(c); by analogy, it is considered respectively as ternary or quaternary if two or three alloy elements exceed the minimum percentage.

在运用本规定时，本章注释一（三）所述的未列名的“其他元素”，按重量计单项含量必须超过10%。

For the application of this rule the unspecified “other elements” referred to in Chapter Note1(c) must each exceed 10% by weight.

序号 No.	税则号列 Tariff Line	中文货品名称 Article Description in Chinese	最惠国税率 MFN(%)	协定税率 Agreement(%)	特惠税率 SP(%)	普通税率 Gen(%)	英文货品名称 Article Description
		第一分章原料;粒状及粉状产品					I. PRIMARY ATERIALS; PRODUCTS IN GRANULAR OR POWDER FORM
	72.01	**生铁及镜铁，锭、块或其他初级形状：**					**Pig iron and spiegeleisen in pigs, blocks or other primary forms:**
5110	7201.1000	-非合金生铁，按重量计含磷量在0.5%及以下	1	0 澳AU,巴PK,冰岛IS,东盟AS,哥CR,韩国KR,秘鲁PE,瑞士CH,新西兰NZ,智利CL	0 受惠国LD	8	-Non-alloy pig iron containing by weight 0.5% or less of phosphorus
5111	7201.2000	-非合金生铁，按重量计含磷量在0.5%以上	1	0 澳AU,巴PK,冰岛IS,东盟AS,哥CR,韩国KR,秘鲁PE,瑞士CH,新西兰NZ,智利CL	0 受惠国LD	8	-Non-alloy pig iron containing by weight more than 0.5% of phosphorus
5112	7201.5000	-合金生铁;镜铁	1	0 澳AU,巴PK,冰岛IS,东盟AS,哥CR,韩国KR,秘鲁PE,瑞士CH,新西兰NZ,智利CL	0 受惠国LD	8	-Alloy pig iron; spiegeleisen
	72.02	**铁合金:**					**Ferro-alloys:**
		-锰铁:					-Ferro-manganese:
5113	7202.1100	--按重量计含碳量在2%以上	2	0 澳AU,巴PK,冰岛IS,东盟AS,哥CR,韩国KR,秘鲁PE,瑞士CH,新西兰NZ,智利CL	0 受惠国LD	11	--Containing by weight more than 2% of carbon
5114	7202.1900	--其他	2	0 澳AU,巴PK,冰岛IS,东盟AS,哥CR,韩国KR,秘鲁PE,瑞士CH,新西兰NZ,智利CL	0 受惠国LD	11	--Other
		-硅铁:					-Ferro-silicon:
5115	7202.2100	--按重量计含硅量55%以上	2	0 澳AU,巴PK,冰岛IS,东盟AS,哥CR,韩国KR,秘鲁PE,瑞士CH,新西兰NZ,智利CL	0 受惠国LD	11	--Containing by weight more than 55% of silicon
5116	7202.2900	--其他	2	0 澳AU,巴PK,冰岛IS,东盟AS,哥CR,韩国KR,秘鲁PE,瑞士CH,新西兰NZ,智利CL	0 受惠国LD	11	--Other
5117	7202.3000	-硅锰铁	2	0 澳AU,巴PK,冰岛IS,东盟AS,哥CR,韩国KR,秘鲁PE,瑞士CH,新西兰NZ,智利CL	0 受惠国LD	11	-Ferro-silico-manganese
		-铬铁:					-Ferro-chromium:
5118	7202.4100	--按重量计含碳量在4%以上	2△0	0 澳AU,巴PK,冰岛IS,东盟AS,哥CR,韩国KR,秘鲁PE,瑞士CH,新西兰NZ,智利CL	0 受惠国LD	8	--Containing by weight more than 4% of carbon
5119	7202.4900	--其他	2△1	0 澳AU,巴PK,冰岛IS,东盟AS,哥CR,韩国KR,秘鲁PE,瑞士CH,新西兰NZ,智利CL	0 受惠国LD	8	--Other
5120	7202.5000	-硅铬铁	2	0 澳AU,巴PK,冰岛IS,东盟AS,哥CR,韩国KR,秘鲁PE,瑞士CH,新西兰NZ,智利CL	0 受惠国LD	11	-Ferro-silico-chromium
5121	7202.6000	-镍铁	2△0	0 澳AU,巴PK,冰岛IS,东盟AS,哥CR,韩国KR,秘鲁PE,瑞士CH,新西兰NZ,智利CL	0 受惠国LD	11	-Ferro-nickel
5122	7202.7000	-钼铁	2△1	0 澳AU,巴PK,冰岛IS,东盟AS,哥CR,韩国KR,秘鲁PE,瑞士CH,新西兰NZ,智利CL	0 受惠国LD	11	-Ferro-molybdenum
		-钨铁及硅钨铁:					-Ferro-tungsten and ferro-silico-tungsten:
5123	7202.8010	---钨铁	2△1	0 澳AU,巴PK,冰岛IS,东盟AS,哥CR,韩国KR,秘鲁PE,瑞士CH,新西兰NZ,智利CL	0 受惠国LD	11	---Ferro-tungsten

序号 No.	税则号列 Tariff Line	中文货品名称 Article Description in Chinese	最惠国税率 MFN(%)	协定税率 Agreement(%)		特惠税率 SP(%)		普通税率 Gen(%)	英文货品名称 Article Description
5124	7202.8020	---硅钨铁	2	0	澳AU,巴PK,冰岛IS,东盟AS,哥CR,韩国KR,秘鲁PE,瑞士CH,新西兰NZ,智利CL	0	受惠国LD	11	---Ferro-silico-tungsten
		-其他:							-Other:
5125	7202.9100	--钛铁及硅钛铁	2	0	澳AU,巴PK,冰岛IS,东盟AS,哥CR,韩国KR,秘鲁PE,瑞士CH,新西兰NZ,智利CL	0	受惠国LD	11	--Ferro-titanium and ferrosilicotitanium
		--钒铁:							--Ferro-vanadium:
5126	7202.9210	---按重量计含钒量在75%及以上	9	0 3.6 5 5.4	冰岛IS,东盟AS,哥CR,秘鲁PE,新西兰NZ,智利CL 瑞士CH 巴PK 澳AU,韩国KR	0	受惠国LD	30	---Containing by weight more than 75% of ranadium
5127	7202.9290	---其他	9	0 3.6 5 5.4	冰岛IS,东盟AS,哥CR,秘鲁PE,新西兰NZ,智利CL 瑞士CH 巴PK 澳AU,韩国KR	0	受惠国LD	30	---Other
5128	7202.9300	--铌铁	2Δ1	0	澳AU,巴PK,冰岛IS,东盟AS,哥CR,韩国KR,秘鲁PE,瑞士CH,新西兰NZ,智利CL	0	受惠国LD	11	--Ferro-niobium
		--其他:							--Other:
		---钕铁硼合金:							---Neodynium-ferro-boron:
5129	7202.9911	----速凝永磁片	2	0	澳AU,巴PK,冰岛IS,东盟AS,哥CR,韩国KR,秘鲁PE,瑞士CH,新西兰NZ,智利CL	0	受惠国LD	11	----Permanent magnetic strip-casting flakes
5130	7202.9912	----磁粉	2	0	澳AU,巴PK,冰岛IS,东盟AS,哥CR,韩国KR,秘鲁PE,瑞士CH,新西兰NZ,智利CL	0	受惠国LD	11	----Magnetic powders
5131	7202.9919	----其他	2	0	澳AU,巴PK,冰岛IS,东盟AS,哥CR,韩国KR,秘鲁PE,瑞士CH,新西兰NZ,智利CL	0	受惠国LD	11	----Other
		---其他:							---Other:
5132	7202.9991	----按重量计稀土元素总含量在10%以上的	2	0	澳AU,巴PK,冰岛IS,东盟AS,哥CR,韩国KR,秘鲁PE,瑞士CH,新西兰NZ,智利CL	0	受惠国LD	11	----Containing by weight more than 10% of rare-earth elements
5133	7202.9999	----其他	2	0	澳AU,巴PK,冰岛IS,东盟AS,哥CR,韩国KR,秘鲁PE,瑞士CH,新西兰NZ,智利CL	0	受惠国LD	11	----Other
	72.03	**直接从铁矿还原所得的铁产品及其他海绵铁产品，块、团、团粒及类似形状;按重量计纯度在99.94%及以上的铁，块、团、团粒及类似形状:**							**Ferrous products obtained by direct reduction of iron ore and other spongy ferrous products, in lumps, pellets or similar forms; iron having a minimum purity by weight of 99.94%, in lumps, pellets or similar forms:**
5134	7203.1000	-直接从铁矿还原所得的铁产品	2	0	澳AU,巴PK,冰岛IS,东盟AS,哥CR,韩国KR,秘鲁PE,瑞士CH,新西兰NZ,智利CL	0	受惠国$_1$LD$_1$	8	-Ferrous products obtained by direct reduction of iron ore
	ex72031000	热压铁块	Δ0						Hot Briguetted Iron (HBI)
5135	7203.9000	-其他	2	0	澳AU,巴PK,冰岛IS,东盟AS,哥CR,韩国KR,秘鲁PE,瑞士CH,新西兰NZ,智利CL	0	受惠国$_1$LD$_1$	8	-Other

序号 No.	税则号列 Tariff Line	中文货品名称 Article Description in Chinese	最惠国税率 MFN(%)	协定税率 Agreement(%)	特惠税率 SP(%)	普通税率 Gen(%)	英文货品名称 Article Description
	72.04	**钢铁废碎料;供再熔的碎料钢铁锭:**					**Ferrous waste and scrap; remelting scrap ingots of iron or steel:**
5136	7204.1000	-铸铁废碎料	2Δ0	0 澳AU,巴PK,冰岛IS,东盟AS,哥CR,韩国KR,秘鲁PE,瑞士CH,新西兰NZ,智利CL	0 受惠国LD	8	-Waste and scrap of cast iron
		-合金钢废碎料:					-Waste and scrap of alloy steel:
5137	7204.2100	--不锈钢废碎料	0		0 受惠国LD	8	--Of stainless steel
5138	7204.2900	--其他	0		0 受惠国LD	8	--Other
5139	7204.3000	-镀锡钢铁废碎料	2Δ0	0 澳AU,巴PK,冰岛IS,东盟AS,哥CR,韩国KR,秘鲁PE,瑞士CH,新西兰NZ,智利CL	0 受惠国LD	8	-Waste and scrap of tinned iron or steel
		-其他废碎料:					-Other waste and scrap:
5140	7204.4100	--车、刨、铣、磨、锯、锉、剪、冲加工过程中产生的废料,不论是否成捆	2Δ0	0 澳AU,巴PK,冰岛IS,东盟AS,哥CR,秘鲁PE,瑞士CH,新西兰NZ,智利CL 1.6 韩国KR	0 受惠国LD	8	--Turnings, shavings, chips, milling waste, sawdust, filings, trimmings and stampings, whether or not in bundles
5141	7204.4900	--其他	0		0 受惠国LD	8	--Other
5142	7204.5000	-供再熔的碎料钢铁锭	0		0 受惠国LD	8	-Remelting scrap ingots
	72.05	**生铁、镜铁及钢铁的颗粒和粉末:**					**Granules and powders, of pig iron, spiegeleisen, iron or steel:**
5143	7205.1000	-颗粒	2	0 澳AU,巴PK,冰岛IS,东盟AS,哥CR,韩国KR,秘鲁PE,瑞士CH,新西兰NZ,智利CL	0 受惠国LD	30	-Granules
		-粉末:					-Powders:
5144	7205.2100	--合金钢的	2	0 澳AU,巴PK,冰岛IS,东盟AS,哥CR,韩国KR,秘鲁PE,瑞士CH,香港HK,新西兰NZ,智利CL	0 受惠国LD	17	--Of alloy steel
5145	7205.2900	--其他	2	0 澳AU,巴PK,冰岛IS,东盟AS,哥CR,秘鲁PE,瑞士CH,新西兰NZ,智利CL 1.6 韩国KR	0 受惠国LD	17	--Other
		第二分章铁及非合金钢					II. IRON AND NON-ALLOY STEEL
	72.06	**铁及非合金钢,锭状或其他初级形状(税号72.03的铁除外):**					**Iron and non-alloy steel in ingots or other primary forms (excluding iron of heading 7203) :**
5146	7206.1000	-锭状	2	0 澳AU,巴PK,冰岛IS,东盟AS,哥CR,韩国KR,秘鲁PE,瑞士CH,新西兰NZ,智利CL	0 受惠国$_1$LD$_1$	11	-Ingots
5147	7206.9000	-其他	2	0 澳AU,巴PK,冰岛IS,东盟AS,哥CR,韩国KR,秘鲁PE,瑞士CH,新西兰NZ,智利CL	0 受惠国$_1$LD$_1$	11	-Other
	72.07	**铁及非合金钢的半制成品:**					**Semi-finished products of iron or non-alloy steel:**
		-按重量计含碳量在0. 25%以下:					-Containing by weight less than 0.25% of carbon:
5148	7207.1100	--矩形(包括正方形)截面,宽度小于厚度的两倍	2	0 澳AU,巴PK,冰岛IS,东盟AS,哥CR,韩国KR,秘鲁PE,瑞士CH,新西兰NZ,智利CL	0 受惠国$_1$LD$_1$	11	--Of rectangular (including square) crosssection, the width measuring less than twice the thickness
5149	7207.1200	--其他矩形(正方形除外)截面的	2	0 澳AU,巴PK,冰岛IS,东盟AS,哥CR,韩国KR,秘鲁PE,瑞士CH,新西兰NZ,智利CL	0 受惠国$_1$LD$_1$	11	--Other, of rectangular (other than square) cross-section

序号 No.	税则号列 Tariff Line	中文货品名称 Article Description in Chinese	最惠国税率 MFN(%)	协定税率 Agreement(%)	特惠税率 SP(%)	普通税率 Gen(%)	英文货品名称 Article Description
5150	7207.1900	--其他	2	0 澳AU,巴PK,冰岛IS,东盟AS,哥CR,秘鲁PE,瑞士CH,新西兰NZ,智利CL 1.7 韩国KR	0 受惠国$_1$LD$_1$	11	--Other
5151	7207.2000	-按重量计含碳量在0.25%及以上	2	0 澳AU,巴PK,冰岛IS,东盟AS,哥CR,韩国KR,秘鲁PE,瑞士CH,新西兰NZ,智利CL	0 受惠国$_1$LD$_1$	11	-Containing by weight 0.25% or more of carbon
	72.08	**宽度在600毫米及以上的铁或非合金钢平板轧材，经热轧，但未经包覆、镀层或涂层：**					**Flat-rolled products of iron or non-alloy steel, of a width of 600mm or more, hot-rolled, not clad, plated or coated:**
5152	7208.1000	-除热轧外未经进一步加工的卷材，已轧压花纹	5	0 澳AU,巴PK,冰岛IS,东盟AS,哥CR,秘鲁PE,瑞士CH,新西兰NZ,智利CL 4 韩国KR	0 受惠国LD	14	-In coils, not further worked than hotrolled, with patterns in relief
		-其他经酸洗的卷材，除热轧外未经进一步加工：					-Other, in coils, not further worked than hot-rolled, pickled:
5153	7208.2500	--厚度在4.75毫米及以上	5	0 澳AU,巴PK,冰岛IS,东盟AS,哥CR,秘鲁PE,瑞士CH,新西兰NZ,智利CL	0 受惠国LD	14	--Of a thickness of 4.75mm or more
		--厚度在3毫米及以上，但小于4.75毫米：					--Of a thickness of 3mm or more but less than 4.75mm:
5154	7208.2610	---屈服强度大于355牛顿/平方毫米	5	0 澳AU,巴PK,冰岛IS,东盟AS,哥CR,秘鲁PE,瑞士CH,新西兰NZ,智利CL	0 受惠国LD	14	---Of a yield strength exceeding 355N/mm^2
5155	7208.2690	---其他	5	0 澳AU,巴PK,冰岛IS,东盟AS,哥CR,秘鲁PE,瑞士CH,新西兰NZ,智利CL	0 受惠国LD	14	---Other
		--厚度小于3毫米：					--Of a thickness of less than 3 mm:
5156	7208.2710	---厚度小于1.5毫米	5	0 澳AU,巴PK,冰岛IS,东盟AS,哥CR,秘鲁PE,瑞士CH,新西兰NZ,智利CL 4.3 韩国KR	0 受惠国LD	14	---Of a thickness of less than 1.5mm
5157	7208.2790	---其他	5	0 澳AU,巴PK,冰岛IS,东盟AS,哥CR,秘鲁PE,瑞士CH,台湾TW,新西兰NZ,智利CL	0 受惠国LD	14	---Other
		-其他卷材，除热轧外未经进一步加工：					-Other, in coils, not further worked than hot-rolled:
5158	7208.3600	--厚度超过10毫米	6	0 冰岛IS,东盟AS,哥CR,秘鲁PE,新西兰NZ,智利CL 2.4 瑞士CH 3.6 澳AU 4.8 韩国KR 5 巴PK	0 受惠国LD	14	--Of a thickness exceeding 10mm
5159	7208.3700	--厚度在4.75毫米及以上，但不超过10毫米	5	0 澳AU,巴PK,冰岛IS,东盟AS,哥CR,秘鲁PE,瑞士CH,新西兰NZ,智利CL 4 韩国KR	0 受惠国LD	14	--Of a thickness of 4.75mm or more but not exceeding 10mm
		--厚度在3毫米及以上，但小于4.75毫米：					--Of a thickness of 3mm or more but less than 4.75mm:
5160	7208.3810	---屈服强度大于355牛顿/平方毫米	5	0 澳AU,巴PK,冰岛IS,东盟AS,哥CR,秘鲁PE,瑞士CH,新西兰NZ,智利CL 4 韩国KR	0 受惠国LD	14	---Of a yield strength exceeding 355N/mm^2

序号 No.	税则号列 Tariff Line	中文货品名称 Article Description in Chinese	最惠国税率 MFN(%)	协定税率 Agreement(%)	特惠税率 SP(%)	普通税率 Gen(%)	英文货品名称 Article Description
5161	7208.3890	---其他	5	0 澳AU,巴PK,冰岛IS,东盟AS,哥CR,秘鲁PE,瑞士CH,台湾TW,新西兰NZ,智利CL 4 韩国KR	0 受惠国LD	14	---Other
		--厚度小于3毫米:					--Of a thickness of less than 3 mm:
5162	7208.3910	---厚度小于1.5毫米	3	0 澳AU,巴PK,冰岛IS,东盟AS,哥CR,秘鲁PE,瑞士CH,新西兰NZ,智利CL 2.4 韩国KR	0 受惠国LD	14	---Of a thickness of less than 1.5mm
5163	7208.3990	---其他	3	0 澳AU,巴PK,冰岛IS,东盟AS,哥CR,秘鲁PE,瑞士CH,台湾TW,新西兰NZ,智利CL 2.4 韩国KR	0 受惠国LD	14	---Other
5164	7208.4000	-已轧压花纹的非卷材，除热轧外未经进一步加工	6	0 冰岛IS,东盟AS,哥CR,秘鲁PE,新西兰NZ,智利CL 2.4 瑞士CH 3.6 澳AU 4.8 韩国KR 5 巴PK	0 受惠国LD	17	-Not in coils, not further worked than hotrolled, with patterns in relief
		-其他非卷材，除热轧外未经进一步加工:					-Other, not in coils, not further worked than hot-rolled:
		--厚度超过10毫米:					--Of a thickness exceeding 10mm:
5165	7208.5110	---厚度超过50毫米	6	0 冰岛IS,东盟AS,哥CR,秘鲁PE,新西兰NZ,智利CL 2.4 瑞士CH 3.6 澳AU 5 巴PK 5.2 韩国KR	0 受惠国LD	17	---Of a thickness exceeding 50mm
5166	7208.5120	---厚度在20毫米以上，但不超过50毫米	6	0 冰岛IS,东盟AS,哥CR,秘鲁PE,新西兰NZ,智利CL 2.4 瑞士CH 3.6 澳AU 5 巴PK 5.2 韩国KR	0 受惠国LD	17	---Of a thickness exceeding 20mm but not exceeding 50mm
5167	7208.5190	---其他	6	0 冰岛IS,东盟AS,哥CR,秘鲁PE,新西兰NZ,智利CL 2.4 瑞士CH 3.6 澳AU 4.8 韩国KR 5 巴PK	0 受惠国LD	17	---Other
5168	7208.5200	--厚度在4.75毫米及以上，但不超过10毫米	6	0 冰岛IS,东盟AS,哥CR,秘鲁PE,新西兰NZ,智利CL 2.4 瑞士CH 3.6 澳AU 4.8 韩国KR 5 巴PK	0 受惠国LD	17	--Of a thickness of 4.75mm or more but not exceeding10mm
		--厚度在3毫米及以上，但小于4.75毫米:					--Of a thickness of 3mm or more but less than 4.75mm:
5169	7208.5310	---屈服强度大于355牛顿/平方毫米	6	0 巴PK,冰岛IS,东盟AS,哥CR,秘鲁PE,新西兰NZ,智利CL 2.4 瑞士CH 3.6 澳AU 4.8 韩国KR 5.1 亚太AP	0 受惠国LD	17	---Of a yield strength exceeding 355N/mm^2

序号 No.	税则号列 Tariff Line	中文货品名称 Article Description in Chinese	最惠国税率 MFN(%)	协定税率 Agreement(%)	特惠税率 SP(%)	普通税率 Gen(%)	英文货品名称 Article Description
5170	7208.5390	---其他	6	0 巴PK,冰岛IS,东盟AS,哥CR,秘鲁PE,新西兰NZ,智利CL 2.4 瑞士CH 3.6 澳AU 4.8 韩国KR 5.1 亚太AP	0 受惠国LD	17	---Other
		--厚度小于3毫米:					--Of a thickness of less than 3 mm:
5171	7208.5410	---厚度小于1.5毫米	6	0 巴PK,冰岛IS,东盟AS,哥CR,秘鲁PE,新西兰NZ,智利CL 2.4 瑞士CH 3.6 澳AU,韩国KR 5.1 亚太AP	0 受惠国LD	17	---Of a thickness of less than 1.5mm
5172	7208.5490	---其他	6	0 巴PK,冰岛IS,东盟AS,哥CR,秘鲁PE,新西兰NZ,智利CL 2.4 瑞士CH 3.6 澳AU 5.1 亚太AP 5.2 韩国KR	0 受惠国LD	17	---Other
5173	7208.9000	-其他	6	0 冰岛IS,东盟AS,哥CR,秘鲁PE,新西兰NZ,智利CL 2.4 瑞士CH 3.6 澳AU 5 巴PK	0 受惠国LD	17	-Other
	72.09	**宽度在600毫米及以上的铁或非合金钢平板轧材,经冷轧,但未经包覆、镀层或涂层:**					**Flat-rolled products of iron or non-alloy steel, of a width of 600mm or more, cold-rolled (cold-reduced) , not clad, plated or coated:**
		-卷材,除冷轧外未经进一步加工:					-In coils, not further worked than cold-rolled (cold-reduced) :
		--厚度在3毫米及以上:					--Of a thickness of 3mm or more:
5174	7209.1510	---屈服强度大于355牛顿/平方毫米	6	0 冰岛IS,东盟AS,哥CR,秘鲁PE,新西兰NZ,智利CL 2.4 瑞士CH 3.6 澳AU 4.8 韩国KR 5 巴PK	0 受惠国LD	17	---Of a yield strength exceeding 355N/mm^2
5175	7209.1590	---其他	6	0 冰岛IS,东盟AS,哥CR,秘鲁PE,新西兰NZ,智利CL 2.4 瑞士CH 3.6 澳AU 4.8 韩国KR 5 巴PK	0 受惠国LD	17	---Other
		--厚度超过1毫米,但小于3毫米:					--Of a thickness exceeding 1mm but less than 3mm:
5176	7209.1610	---屈服强度大于275牛顿/平方毫米	6	0 巴PK,冰岛IS,东盟AS,哥CR,秘鲁PE,新西兰NZ,智利CL 2.4 瑞士CH 3.6 澳AU 4.2 亚太AP 4.8 韩国KR	0 受惠国LD	17	---Of a yield strength exceeding 275N/mm^2
5177	7209.1690	---其他	6	0 巴PK,冰岛IS,东盟AS,哥CR,秘鲁PE,台湾TW,新西兰NZ,智利CL 2.4 瑞士CH 3.6 澳AU 4.2 亚太AP 5.2 韩国KR	0 受惠国LD	17	---Other

序号 No.	税则号列 Tariff Line	中文货品名称 Article Description in Chinese	最惠国税率 MFN(%)	协定税率 Agreement(%)	特惠税率 SP(%)	普通税率 Gen(%)	英文货品名称 Article Description
		--厚度在0.5毫米及以上，但不超过1毫米：					--Of a thickness of 0.5mm or more but not exceeding 1mm:
5178	7209.1710	---屈服强度大于275牛顿/平方毫米	3	0 澳AU,巴PK,冰岛IS,东盟AS,哥CR,秘鲁PE,瑞士CH,新西兰NZ,智利CL 2.1 亚太AP 2.6 韩国KR	0 受惠国LD	17	---Of a yield strength exceeding 275N/mm^2
5179	7209.1790	---其他	3	0 澳AU,巴PK,冰岛IS,东盟AS,哥CR,秘鲁PE,瑞士CH,台湾TW,新西兰NZ,智利CL 2.1 亚太AP 2.4 韩国KR	0 受惠国LD	17	---Other
		--厚度小于0.5毫米：					--Of a thickness of less than 0.5mm:
5180	7209.1810	---厚度小于0.3毫米	6Δ4	0 巴PK,冰岛IS,东盟AS,哥CR,秘鲁PE,新西兰NZ,智利CL 2.4 瑞士CH 3.6 澳AU 4.2 亚太AP 5.2 韩国KR	0 受惠国LD	17	---Of a thickness less than 0.3mm
5181	7209.1890	---其他	6	0 巴PK,冰岛IS,东盟AS,哥CR,秘鲁PE,台湾TW,新西兰NZ,智利CL 2.4 瑞士CH 3.6 澳AU 4.2 亚太AP 5.2 韩国KR	0 受惠国LD	17	---Other
		-非卷材，除冷轧外未经进一步加工：					-Not in coils, not further worked than cold-rolled (cold-reduced) :
5182	7209.2500	--厚度在3毫米及以上	6	0 冰岛IS,东盟AS,哥CR,秘鲁PE,新西兰NZ,智利CL 2.4 瑞士CH 3.6 澳AU 4.8 韩国KR 5 巴PK	0 受惠国LD	17	--Of a thickness of 3mm or more
5183	7209.2600	--厚度超过1毫米，但小于3毫米	6	0 冰岛IS,东盟AS,哥CR,秘鲁PE,新西兰NZ,智利CL 2.4 瑞士CH 3.6 澳AU 5 巴PK	0 受惠国LD	17	--Of a thickness exceeding 1mm but less than 3mm
5184	7209.2700	--厚度在0.5毫米及以上，但不超过1毫米	6	0 巴PK,冰岛IS,东盟AS,哥CR,秘鲁PE,新西兰NZ,智利CL 2.4 瑞士CH 3.6 澳AU 4.2 亚太AP 5.2 韩国KR	0 受惠国LD	17	--Of a thickness of 0.5mm or more but not exceeding 1mm
5185	7209.2800	--厚度小于0.5毫米	6	0 冰岛IS,东盟AS,哥CR,秘鲁PE,新西兰NZ,智利CL 2.4 瑞士CH 3.6 澳AU 5 巴PK	0 受惠国LD	17	--Of a thickness of less than 0.5mm
5186	7209.9000	-其他	6	0 巴PK,冰岛IS,东盟AS,哥CR,秘鲁PE,新西兰NZ,智利CL 2.4 瑞士CH 3.6 澳AU 4.2 亚太AP 4.8 韩国KR	0 受惠国LD	17	-Other

序号 No.	税则号列 Tariff Line	中文货品名称 Article Description in Chinese	最惠国税率 MFN(%)	协定税率 Agreement(%)	特惠税率 SP(%)	普通税率 Gen(%)	英文货品名称 Article Description
	72.10	**宽度在600毫米及以上的铁或非合金钢平板轧材，经包覆、镀层或涂层：**					**Flat-rolled products of iron or non-alloy steel, of a width of 600mm of more, clad, plated or coated:**
		-镀或涂锡的：					-Plated or coated with tin:
5187	7210.1100	--厚度在0.5毫米及以上	10	0 冰岛IS,东盟AS,哥CR,秘鲁PE,新加坡SG,新西兰NZ,智利CL 4 瑞士CH 5 巴PK 6 澳AU 8 韩国KR	0 受惠国LD	20	--Of a thickness of 0.5mm or more
5188	7210.1200	--厚度小于0.5毫米	5	0 澳AU,巴PK,冰岛IS,东盟AS,哥CR,秘鲁PE,瑞士CH,新西兰NZ,智利CL	0 受惠国LD	20	--Of a thickness of less than 0.5mm
5189	7210.2000	-镀或涂铅的，包括镀铅锡钢板	4	0 澳AU,巴PK,冰岛IS,东盟AS,哥CR,秘鲁PE,瑞士CH,新西兰NZ,智利CL 2.4 韩国KR	0 受惠国LD	20	-Plated or coated with lead, including terneplate
5190	7210.3000	-电镀锌的	8	0 冰岛IS,东盟AS,哥CR,秘鲁PE,台湾TW,新西兰NZ,智利CL 3.2 瑞士CH 4.8 澳AU 5 巴PK	0 受惠国LD	20	-Electrolytically plated or coated with zinc
		-用其他方法镀或涂锌的：					-Otherwise plated or coated with zinc:
5191	7210.4100	--瓦楞形	8	0 冰岛IS,东盟AS,哥CR,秘鲁PE,新西兰NZ,智利CL 3.2 瑞士CH 4.8 澳AU,韩国KR 5 巴PK	0 受惠国LD	20	--Corrugated
5192	7210.4900	--其他	4	0 澳AU,巴PK,冰岛IS,东盟AS,哥CR,秘鲁PE,瑞士CH,台湾TW,新西兰NZ,智利CL	0 受惠国LD	20	--Other
5193	7210.5000	-镀或涂氧化铬或铬及氧化铬的	8	0 冰岛IS,东盟AS,哥CR,秘鲁PE,新西兰NZ,智利CL 3.2 瑞士CH 4.8 澳AU 5 巴PK 6.4 韩国KR	0 受惠国LD	20	-Plated or coated with chromium oxides or with chromium and chromium oxides
		-镀或涂铝的：					-Plated or coated with aluminium:
5194	7210.6100	--镀或涂铝锌合金的	8	0 冰岛IS,东盟AS,哥CR,秘鲁PE,新西兰NZ,智利CL 3.2 瑞士CH 4.8 澳AU 5 巴PK	0 受惠国LD	20	--Plated or coated with aluminium-zinc alloys
5195	7210.6900	--其他	8	0 冰岛IS,东盟AS,哥CR,秘鲁PE,新西兰NZ,智利CL 3.2 瑞士CH 4.8 澳AU 5 巴PK	0 受惠国LD	20	--Other
		-涂漆或涂塑的：					-Painted, varnished or coated with plastics:

序号 No.	税则号列 Tariff Line	中文货品名称 Article Description in Chinese	最惠国税率 MFN(%)	协定税率 Agreement(%)	特惠税率 SP(%)	普通税率 Gen(%)	英文货品名称 Article Description
5196	7210.7010	---厚度小于1.5毫米	4	0 澳AU,巴PK,冰岛IS,东盟AS,哥CR,秘鲁PE,香港HK,新西兰NZ,智利CL 1.6 瑞士CH 3.4 韩国KR	0 受惠国LD	20	---Of a thickness less than 1.5mm
5197	7210.7090	---其他	4	0 澳AU,巴PK,冰岛IS,东盟AS,哥CR,秘鲁PE,香港HK,新西兰NZ,智利CL 1.6 瑞士CH 3.4 韩国KR	0 受惠国LD	20	---Other
5198	7210.9000	-其他	8	0 冰岛IS,东盟AS,哥CR,秘鲁PE,新西兰NZ,智利CL 3.2 瑞士CH 4.8 澳AU 5 巴PK 6.9 韩国KR	0 受惠国LD	20	-Other
	72.11	**宽度小于600毫米的铁或非合金钢平板轧材，但未经包覆、镀层或涂层：**					**Flat-rolled products of iron or non-alloy steel, of a width of less than 600mm, not clad, plated or coated:**
		-除热轧外未经进一步加工：					-Not further worked than hot-rolled:
5199	7211.1300	--经四面轧制或在闭合匣内轧制的非卷材，宽度超过150毫米，厚度不小于4毫米，未轧压花纹	6	0 冰岛IS,东盟AS,哥CR,秘鲁PE,新西兰NZ,智利CL 2.4 瑞士CH 3.6 澳AU 4.8 韩国KR 5 巴PK	0 受惠国LD	30	--Rolled on four faces or in a closed box pass, of a width exceeding150mm and a thickness of not less than 4mm, not in coils and without patterns in relief
5200	7211.1400	--其他，厚度在4.75毫米及以上	6	0 冰岛IS,东盟AS,哥CR,秘鲁PE,新西兰NZ,智利CL 2.4 瑞士CH 3.6 澳AU 4.8 韩国KR 5 巴PK	0 受惠国LD	30	--Other, of a thickness of 4.75mm or more
5201	7211.1900	--其他	6	0 冰岛IS,东盟AS,哥CR,秘鲁PE,新西兰NZ,智利CL 2.4 瑞士CH 3.6 澳AU 5 巴PK 5.2 韩国KR	0 受惠国LD	30	--Other
		-除冷轧外未经进一步加工：					-Not further worked than cold-rolled (cold-reduced) :
5202	7211.2300	--按重量计含碳量低于0.25%	6	0 冰岛IS,东盟AS,哥CR,秘鲁PE,新西兰NZ,智利CL 2.4 瑞士CH 3.6 澳AU 5 巴PK 5.2 韩国KR	0 受惠国LD	30	--Containing by weight less than 0.25% of carbon
5203	7211.2900	--其他	6	0 冰岛IS,东盟AS,哥CR,秘鲁PE,新西兰NZ,智利CL 2.4 瑞士CH 3.6 澳AU 5 巴PK 5.2 韩国KR	0 受惠国LD	30	--Other

序号 No.	税则号列 Tariff Line	中文货品名称 Article Description in Chinese	最惠国税率 MFN(%)	协定税率 Agreement(%)	特惠税率 SP(%)	普通税率 Gen(%)	英文货品名称 Article Description
5204	7211.9000	-其他	6	0 冰岛IS,东盟AS,哥CR,秘鲁PE,新西兰NZ,智利CL 2.4 瑞士CH 3.6 澳AU 4.8 韩国KR 5 巴PK	0 受惠国LD	30	-Other
	72.12	**宽度小于600毫米的铁或非合金钢平板轧材，经包覆、镀层或涂层：**					**Flat-rolled products of iron or non-alloy steel, of a width of less than 600mm, clad, plated or coated:**
5205	7212.1000	-镀或涂锡的	5	0 澳AU,巴PK,冰岛IS,东盟AS,哥CR,秘鲁PE,瑞士CH,新西兰NZ,智利CL 4 韩国KR	0 受惠国LD	20	-Plated or coated with tin
5206	7212.2000	-电镀锌的	8	0 冰岛IS,东盟AS,哥CR,秘鲁PE,新西兰NZ,智利CL 3.2 瑞士CH 4.8 澳AU 5 巴PK 6.9 韩国KR	0 受惠国LD	20	-Electrolytically plated or coated with zinc
5207	7212.3000	-用其他方法镀或涂锌的	8	0 冰岛IS,东盟AS,哥CR,秘鲁PE,新西兰NZ,智利CL 3.2 瑞士CH 4.8 澳AU 5 巴PK 6.4 韩国KR	0 受惠国LD	20	-Otherwise plated or coated with zinc
5208	7212.4000	-涂漆或涂塑的	4	0 澳AU,巴PK,冰岛IS,东盟AS,哥CR,秘鲁PE,瑞士CH,香港HK,新西兰NZ,智利CL 3.4 韩国KR	0 受惠国LD	20	-Painted, varnished or coated with plastics
5209	7212.5000	-镀或涂其他材料的	8	0 冰岛IS,东盟AS,哥CR,秘鲁PE,新西兰NZ,智利CL 3.2 瑞士CH 4.8 澳AU 5 巴PK 6.9 韩国KR	0 受惠国LD	20	-Otherwise plated or coated
5210	7212.6000	-经包覆的	8	0 冰岛IS,东盟AS,哥CR,秘鲁PE,新西兰NZ,智利CL 3.2 瑞士CH 4.8 澳AU 5 巴PK 6.4 韩国KR	0 受惠国LD	20	-Clad
	72.13	**不规则盘卷的铁及非合金钢的热轧条、杆：**					**Bars and rods, hot-rolled, in irregularly wound coils, of iron or non-alloy steel:**
5211	7213.1000	-带有轧制过程中产生的凹痕、凸缘、槽沟及其他变形的	3	0 澳AU,巴PK,冰岛IS,东盟AS,哥CR,秘鲁PE,瑞士CH,新西兰NZ,智利CL 1.8 韩国KR	0 受惠国LD	20	-Containing indentations, ribs, grooves or other deformations produced during the rolling process
5212	7213.2000	-其他，易切削钢制	3	0 澳AU,巴PK,冰岛IS,东盟AS,哥CR,秘鲁PE,瑞士CH,新西兰NZ,智利CL 2.6 韩国KR	0 受惠国LD	20	-Other, of free-cutting steel
		-其他：					-Other:

序号 No.	税则号列 Tariff Line	中文货品名称 Article Description in Chinese	最惠国税率 MFN(%)	协定税率 Agreement(%)	特惠税率 SP(%)	普通税率 Gen(%)	英文货品名称 Article Description
5213	7213.9100	--直径小于14毫米圆形截面的	5	0 澳AU,巴PK,冰岛IS,东盟AS,哥CR,秘鲁PE,瑞士CH,新西兰NZ,智利CL 4 韩国KR 4.3 亚太AP	0 受惠国LD	20	--Of circular cross-section measuring less than 14mm in diameter
5214	7213.9900	--其他	5	0 澳AU,巴PK,冰岛IS,东盟AS,哥CR,秘鲁PE,瑞士CH,新西兰NZ,智利CL 4.3 韩国KR	0 受惠国LD	20	--Other
	72.14	**铁或非合金钢的其他条、杆，除锻造、热轧、热拉拔或热挤压外未经进一步加工，包括轧制后扭曲的：**					**Other bars and rods of iron or non-alloy steel, not further worked than forged, hot-rolled, hot-drawn or hot-extruded, but including those twisted after rolling:**
5215	7214.1000	-锻造的	7	0 冰岛IS,东盟AS,哥CR,秘鲁PE,新西兰NZ,智利CL 2.8 瑞士CH 4.2 澳AU 5 巴PK 5.6 韩国KR	0 受惠国LD	10	-Forged
5216	7214.2000	-带有轧制过程中产生的凹痕、凸缘、槽沟或其他变形以及轧制后扭曲的	3	0 澳AU,巴PK,冰岛IS,东盟AS,哥CR,韩国KR,秘鲁PE,瑞士CH,香港HK,新西兰NZ,亚太AP,智利CL	0 受惠国LD	20	-Containing indentations, ribs, grooves or other deformations produced during the rolling process or twisted after rolling
5217	7214.3000	-其他，易切削钢制	7	0 冰岛IS,东盟AS,哥CR,秘鲁PE,新西兰NZ,智利CL 2.8 瑞士CH 4.2 澳AU 5 巴PK 5.6 韩国KR	0 受惠国LD	20	-Other, of free-cutting steel
		-其他：					-Other:
5218	7214.9100	--矩形（正方形除外）截面的	3	0 澳AU,巴PK,冰岛IS,东盟AS,哥CR,韩国KR,秘鲁PE,瑞士CH,新西兰NZ,智利CL	0 受惠国LD	20	--Of rectangular cross section (other than square)
5219	7214.9900	--其他	3	0 澳AU,巴PK,冰岛IS,东盟AS,哥CR,秘鲁PE,瑞士CH,新西兰NZ,智利CL 1.8 韩国KR	0 受惠国LD	20	--Other
	72.15	**铁及非合金钢的其他条、杆：**					**Other bars and rods of iron or non-alloy steel:**
5220	7215.1000	-易切削钢制，除冷成形或冷加工外未经进一步加工	7	0 冰岛IS,东盟AS,哥CR,秘鲁PE,新西兰NZ,智利CL 4.2 澳AU 4.9 瑞士CH 5 巴PK 5.6 韩国KR	0 受惠国LD	20	-Of free-cutting steel, not further worked than cold-formed or cold-finished
5221	7215.5000	-其他，除冷成形或冷加工外未经进一步加工	7	0 冰岛IS,东盟AS,哥CR,秘鲁PE,新西兰NZ,智利CL 2.8 瑞士CH 4.2 澳AU 5 巴PK 6 韩国KR	0 受惠国LD	20	-Other, not further worked than cold-formed or cold-finished

序号 No.	税则号列 Tariff Line	中文货品名称 Article Description in Chinese	最惠国税率 MFN(%)	协定税率 Agreement(%)	特惠税率 SP(%)	普通税率 Gen(%)	英文货品名称 Article Description
5222	7215.9000	-其他	3	0 澳AU,巴PK,冰岛IS,东盟AS,哥CR,秘鲁PE,瑞士CH,新西兰NZ,智利CL 1.8 韩国KR	0 受惠国LD	20	-Other
	72.16	**铁或非合金钢的角材、型材及异型材：**					**Angles, shapes and sections of iron or non-alloy steel:**
		-槽钢、工字钢及H型钢，除热轧、热拉拔或热挤压外未经进一步加工，截面高度低于80毫米：					-U, I or H sections, not further worked than hot-rolled, hot-drawn or extruded, of a height of less than 80mm:
5223	7216.1010	---H型钢	3	0 澳AU,巴PK,冰岛IS,东盟AS,哥CR,韩国KR,秘鲁PE,瑞士CH,新西兰NZ,智利CL	0 受惠国LD	14	---H sections
5224	7216.1020	---工字钢	3	0 澳AU,巴PK,冰岛IS,东盟AS,哥CR,韩国KR,秘鲁PE,瑞士CH,新西兰NZ,智利CL	0 受惠国LD	14	---I sections
5225	7216.1090	---其他	3	0 澳AU,巴PK,冰岛IS,东盟AS,哥CR,韩国KR,秘鲁PE,瑞士CH,新西兰NZ,智利CL	0 受惠国LD	14	---Other
		-角钢及丁字钢，除热轧、热拉拔或热挤压外未经进一步加工，截面高度低于80毫米：					-L or T sections, not further worked than hot-rolled, hot-drawn or extruded, of a height of less than 80mm:
5226	7216.2100	--角钢	6	0 冰岛IS,东盟AS,哥CR,秘鲁PE,新西兰NZ,智利CL 2.4 瑞士CH 3.6 澳AU 4.8 韩国KR 5 巴PK	0 受惠国LD	17	--L sections
5227	7216.2200	--丁字钢	6	0 冰岛IS,东盟AS,哥CR,秘鲁PE,新西兰NZ,智利CL 2.4 瑞士CH 3.6 澳AU,韩国KR 5 巴PK	0 受惠国LD	14	--T sections
		-槽钢、工字钢及H型钢，除热轧、热拉拔或热挤压外未经进一步加工，截面高度在80毫米及以上：					-U, I or H sections, not further worked than hot-rolled, hot-drawn or extruded, of a height of 80mm or more:
5228	7216.3100	--槽钢	6	0 冰岛IS,东盟AS,哥CR,秘鲁PE,新西兰NZ,智利CL 2.4 瑞士CH 3.6 澳AU 4.8 韩国KR 5 巴PK	0 受惠国LD	14	--U sections
		--工字钢：					--I sections:
5229	7216.3210	---截面高度在200毫米以上	6	0 冰岛IS,东盟AS,哥CR,秘鲁PE,新西兰NZ,智利CL 2.4 瑞士CH 3.6 澳AU 4.8 韩国KR 5 巴PK	0 受惠国LD	14	---Of a height exceeding 200mm

序号 No.	税则号列 Tariff Line	中文货品名称 Article Description in Chinese	最惠国税率 MFN(%)	协定税率 Agreement(%)	特惠税率 SP(%)	普通税率 Gen(%)	英文货品名称 Article Description
5230	7216.3290	---其他	6	0 冰岛IS,东盟AS,哥CR,秘鲁PE,新西兰NZ,智利CL 2.4 瑞士CH 3.6 澳AU 4.8 韩国KR 5 巴PK	0 受惠国LD	14	---Other
		--H型钢:					--H sections:
		---截面高度在200毫米以上:					---Of a height exceeding 200mm:
5231	7216.3311	----截面高度在800毫米以上	6	0 冰岛IS,东盟AS,哥CR,秘鲁PE,新西兰NZ,智利CL 2.4 瑞士CH 3.6 澳AU,韩国KR 5 巴PK	0 受惠国LD	14	----Of a height exceeding 800mm
5232	7216.3319	----其他	6	0 冰岛IS,东盟AS,哥CR,秘鲁PE,新西兰NZ,智利CL 2.4 瑞士CH 3.6 澳AU 5 巴PK 5.2 韩国KR	0 受惠国LD	14	----Other
5233	7216.3390	---其他	6	0 冰岛IS,东盟AS,哥CR,秘鲁PE,新西兰NZ,智利CL 2.4 瑞士CH 3.6 澳AU 4.8 韩国KR 5 巴PK	0 受惠国LD	14	---Other
		-角钢及丁字钢,除热轧、热拉拔或热挤压外未经进一步加工,截面高度在80毫米及以上:					-L or T sections, not further worked than hot-rolled, hot-drawn or extruded, of a height of 80mm or more:
5234	7216.4010	---角钢	3	0 澳AU,巴PK,冰岛IS,东盟AS,哥CR,韩国KR,秘鲁PE,瑞士CH,新西兰NZ,智利CL	0 受惠国LD	17	---L sections
5235	7216.4020	---丁字钢	3	0 澳AU,巴PK,冰岛IS,东盟AS,哥CR,韩国KR,秘鲁PE,瑞士CH,新西兰NZ,智利CL	0 受惠国LD	14	---T sections
		-其他角材、型材及异型材,除热轧、热拉拔或热挤压外未经进一步加工:					-Other angles, shapes and sections, not further worked than hot-rolled, hot-drawn or extruded:
5236	7216.5010	---乙字钢	6	0 冰岛IS,东盟AS,哥CR,秘鲁PE,新西兰NZ,智利CL 2.4 瑞士CH 3.6 澳AU,韩国KR 5 巴PK	0 受惠国LD	14	---Z sections
5237	7216.5020	---球扁钢	3	0 澳AU,巴PK,冰岛IS,东盟AS,哥CR,韩国KR,秘鲁PE,瑞士CH,新西兰NZ,智利CL	0 受惠国LD	20	---Bulb flat steel
5238	7216.5090	---其他	3	0 澳AU,巴PK,冰岛IS,东盟AS,哥CR,秘鲁PE,瑞士CH,新西兰NZ,智利CL 1.8 韩国KR	0 受惠国LD	20	---Other
		-角材、型材及异型材,除冷成形或冷加工外未经进一步加工:					-Angles, shapes and sections, not further worked than cold-formed or cold-finished:

序号 No.	税则号列 Tariff Line	中文货品名称 Article Description in Chinese	最惠国税率 MFN(%)	协定税率 Agreement(%)		特惠税率 SP(%)		普通税率 Gen(%)	英文货品名称 Article Description
5239	7216.6100	--平板轧材制的	3	0	澳AU,巴PK,冰岛IS,东盟AS,哥CR,韩国KR,秘鲁PE,瑞士CH,新西兰NZ,智利CL	0	受惠国LD	20	--Obtained from flat-rolled products
5240	7216.6900	--其他	3	0	澳AU,巴PK,冰岛IS,东盟AS,哥CR,秘鲁PE,瑞士CH,新西兰NZ,智利CL	0	受惠国LD	20	--Other
				1.8	韩国KR				
		-其他:							-Other:
5241	7216.9100	--平板轧材经冷成形或冷加工制的	3	0	澳AU,巴PK,冰岛IS,东盟AS,哥CR,韩国KR,秘鲁PE,瑞士CH,新西兰NZ,智利CL	0	受惠国LD	20	--Cold-formed or cold-finished from flatrolled products
5242	7216.9900	--其他	3	0	澳AU,巴PK,冰岛IS,东盟AS,哥CR,韩国KR,秘鲁PE,瑞士CH,新西兰NZ,智利CL	0	受惠国LD	20	--Other
	72.17	**铁丝或非合金钢丝:**							**Wire of iron or non-alloy steel:**
5243	7217.1000	-未经镀或涂层，不论是否抛光	8	0	冰岛IS,东盟AS,哥CR,秘鲁PE,台湾TW,新西兰NZ,智利CL	0	受惠国LD	40	-Not plated or coated, whether or not polished
				3.2	瑞士CH				
				4.8	澳AU				
				5	巴PK				
5244	7217.2000	-镀或涂锌的	8	0	冰岛IS,东盟AS,哥CR,秘鲁PE,新西兰NZ,智利CL	0	受惠国LD	40	-Plated or coated with zinc
				3.2	瑞士CH				
				4.8	澳AU				
				5	巴PK				
				6.4	韩国KR				
		-镀或涂其他贱金属的:							-Plated or coated with other base metals:
5245	7217.3010	---镀或涂铜的	8	0	冰岛IS,东盟AS,哥CR,秘鲁PE,新西兰NZ,智利CL	0	受惠国LD	40	---Plated or coated with copper
				3.2	瑞士CH				
				4.8	澳AU				
				5	巴PK				
				6.4	亚太AP				
				7.3	韩国KR				
5246	7217.3090	---其他	8	0	冰岛IS,东盟AS,哥CR,秘鲁PE,新西兰NZ,智利CL	0	受惠国LD	40	---Other
				3.2	瑞士CH				
				4.8	澳AU				
				5	巴PK				
				6.4	亚太AP				
				6.9	韩国KR				
5247	7217.9000	-其他	8	0	冰岛IS,东盟AS,哥CR,秘鲁PE,香港HK,新西兰NZ,智利CL	0	受惠国LD	40	-Other
				3.2	瑞士CH				
				4.8	澳AU				
				5	巴PK				
				6.4	韩国KR				
		第三分章不锈钢							III. STAINLESS STEEL
	72.18	**不锈钢，锭状或其他初级形状;不锈钢半制成品:**							**Stainless steel in ingots or other primary forms; semi-finished products of stainless steel:**
5248	7218.1000	-锭状及其他初级形状	2	0	澳AU,巴PK,冰岛IS,东盟AS,哥CR,秘鲁PE,瑞士CH,新西兰NZ,智利CL	0	受惠国LD	11	-Ingots and other primary forms
				1.2	韩国KR				

序号 No.	税则号列 Tariff Line	中文货品名称 Article Description in Chinese	最惠国税率 MFN(%)	协定税率 Agreement(%)	特惠税率 SP(%)	普通税率 Gen(%)	英文货品名称 Article Description
		-其他：					-Other:
5249	7218.9100	--矩形（正方形除外）截面的	2	0 澳AU,巴PK,冰岛IS,东盟AS,哥CR,秘鲁PE,瑞士CH,新西兰NZ,智利CL 1.2 韩国KR	0 受惠国LD	11	--Of rectangular (other than square) crosssection
5250	7218.9900	--其他	2	0 澳AU,巴PK,冰岛IS,东盟AS,哥CR,秘鲁PE,瑞士CH,新西兰NZ,智利CL 1.2 韩国KR	0 受惠国LD	11	--Other
	72.19	**不锈钢平板轧材，宽度在600毫米及以上：**					**Flat-rolled products of stainless steel, of a width of 600mm or more:**
		-除热轧外未经进一步加工的卷材：					-Not further worked than hot-rolled, in coils:
5251	7219.1100	--厚度超过10毫米	4	0 澳AU,巴PK,冰岛IS,东盟AS,哥CR,秘鲁PE,瑞士CH,新西兰NZ,智利CL 2.4 韩国KR	0 受惠国LD	14	--Of a thickness exceeding 10mm
5252	7219.1200	--厚度在4.75毫米及以上，但不超过10毫米	4	0 澳AU,巴PK,冰岛IS,东盟AS,哥CR,秘鲁PE,瑞士CH,台湾TW,新西兰NZ,智利CL 3.2 韩国KR	0 受惠国LD	14	--Of a thickness of 4.75mm or more but not exceeding10mm
		--厚度在3毫米及以上，但小于4.75毫米：					--Of a thickness of 3 mm or more but less than 4.75mm:
		---未经酸洗的：					---Not acid Pickled:
5253	7219.1312	----按重量计含锰量在5.5%及以上的铬锰系不锈钢	4	0 澳AU,巴PK,冰岛IS,东盟AS,哥CR,秘鲁PE,瑞士CH,新西兰NZ,智利CL 2.4 韩国KR	0 受惠国LD	14	----Containing by weight no less than 5.5% of manganese of Ferro-chromium-manganese steel
5254	7219.1319	----其他	4	0 澳AU,巴PK,冰岛IS,东盟AS,哥CR,秘鲁PE,瑞士CH,台湾TW,新西兰NZ,智利CL 3.2 韩国KR	0 受惠国LD	14	----Other
		---经酸洗的：					---Acid pickled:
5255	7219.1322	----按重量计含锰量在5.5%及以上的铬锰系不锈钢	4	0 澳AU,巴PK,冰岛IS,东盟AS,哥CR,秘鲁PE,瑞士CH,新西兰NZ,智利CL 2.4 韩国KR	0 受惠国LD	14	----Containing by weight no less than 5.5% of manganese of Ferro-chromium-manganese steel
5256	7219.1329	----其他	4	0 澳AU,巴PK,冰岛IS,东盟AS,哥CR,秘鲁PE,瑞士CH,台湾TW,新西兰NZ,智利CL 3.2 韩国KR	0 受惠国LD	14	----Other
		--厚度小于3毫米：					--Of a thickness of less than 3mm:
		---未经酸洗的：					---Not acid Pickled:
5257	7219.1412	----按重量计含锰量在5.5%及以上的铬锰系不锈钢	4	0 澳AU,巴PK,冰岛IS,东盟AS,哥CR,韩国KR,秘鲁PE,瑞士CH,新西兰NZ,智利CL	0 受惠国LD	14	----Containing by weight no less than 5.5% of manganese of Ferro-chromium-manganese steel
5258	7219.1419	----其他	4	0 澳AU,巴PK,冰岛IS,东盟AS,哥CR,秘鲁PE,瑞士CH,新西兰NZ,智利CL 2.4 韩国KR	0 受惠国LD	14	----Other
		---经酸洗的：					---Acid pickled:
5259	7219.1422	----按重量计含锰量在5.5%及以上的铬锰系不锈钢	4	0 澳AU,巴PK,冰岛IS,东盟AS,哥CR,韩国KR,秘鲁PE,瑞士CH,新西兰NZ,智利CL	0 受惠国LD	14	----Containing by weight no less than 5.5% of manganese of Ferro-chromium-manganese steel

序号 No.	税则号列 Tariff Line	中文货品名称 Article Description in Chinese	最惠国税率 MFN(%)	协定税率 Agreement(%)	特惠税率 SP(%)	普通税率 Gen(%)	英文货品名称 Article Description
5260	7219.1429	-----其他	4	0 澳AU,巴PK,冰岛IS,东盟AS,哥CR,秘鲁PE,瑞士CH,新西兰NZ,智利CL 2.4 韩国KR	0 受惠国LD	14	----Other
		-除热轧外未经进一步加工的非卷材:					-Not further worked than hot-rolled, not in coils:
5261	7219.2100	--厚度超过10毫米	10	0 冰岛IS,东盟AS,哥CR,秘鲁PE,香港HK,新加坡SG,新西兰NZ,智利CL 4 瑞士CH 5 巴PK 6 澳AU 8.6 韩国KR 9.3 亚太AP	0 受惠国$_1$LD$_1$	40	--Of a thickness exceeding10mm
5262	7219.2200	--厚度在4.75毫米及以上，但不超过10毫米	10	0 冰岛IS,东盟AS,哥CR,香港HK,新加坡SG,新西兰NZ,智利CL 3 秘鲁PE 4 瑞士CH 5 巴PK 6 澳AU 9 韩国KR 9.3 亚太AP	0 受惠国$_1$LD$_1$	40	--Of a thickness of 4.75mm or more but not exceeding 10mm
5263	7219.2300	--厚度在3毫米及以上，但小于4.75毫米	10	0 冰岛IS,东盟AS,哥CR,秘鲁PE,台湾TW,新加坡SG,新西兰NZ,智利CL 4 瑞士CH 5 巴PK 6 澳AU 8.6 韩国KR 9.3 亚太AP	0 受惠国$_1$LD$_1$	40	--Of a thickness of 3mm or more but less than 4.75mm
		--厚度小于3毫米:					--Of a thickness of less than 3mm:
5264	7219.2410	---厚度超过1毫米但小于3毫米	10	0 冰岛IS,东盟AS,哥CR,秘鲁PE,台湾TW,新加坡SG,新西兰NZ,智利CL 4 瑞士CH 5 巴PK 6 澳AU 8.6 韩国KR 9.3 亚太AP	0 受惠国$_1$LD$_1$	40	---Of a thickness exceeding 1mm but less than 3mm
5265	7219.2420	---厚度在0.5毫米及以上，但不超过1毫米	10	0 冰岛IS,东盟AS,哥CR,秘鲁PE,新加坡SG,新西兰NZ,智利CL 4 瑞士CH 5 巴PK 6 澳AU 9 韩国KR 9.3 亚太AP	0 受惠国$_1$LD$_1$	40	---Of a thickness of 0.5mm or more but not exceeding 1mm
5266	7219.2430	---厚度小于0.5毫米	10	0 冰岛IS,东盟AS,哥CR,秘鲁PE,新加坡SG,新西兰NZ,智利CL 4 瑞士CH 5 巴PK 6 澳AU 8.6 韩国KR 9.3 亚太AP	0 受惠国$_1$LD$_1$	40	---Of a thickness of less than 0.5mm
		-除冷轧外未经进一步加工:					-Not further worked than cold-rolled (cold-reduced) :

序号 No.	税则号列 Tariff Line	中文货品名称 Article Description in Chinese	最惠国税率 MFN(%)	协定税率 Agreement(%)	特惠税率 SP(%)	普通税率 Gen(%)	英文货品名称 Article Description
5267	7219.3100	--厚度在4.75毫米及以上	10	0 冰岛IS,东盟AS,哥CR,台湾TW,新加坡SG,新西兰NZ,智利CL 3 秘鲁PE 4 瑞士CH 5 巴PK 6 澳AU 8 韩国KR	0 受惠国$_1$LD$_1$	40	--Of a thickness of 4.75mm or more
5268	7219.3200	--厚度在3毫米及以上，但小于4.75毫米	10	0 冰岛IS,东盟AS,哥CR,台湾TW,新加坡SG,新西兰NZ,智利CL 3 秘鲁PE 4 瑞士CH 5 巴PK 6 澳AU 8 韩国KR	0 受惠国$_1$LD$_1$	40	--Of a thickness of 3mm or more but less than 4.75mm
		--厚度超过1毫米，但小于3毫米：					--Of a thickness exceeding 1mm but less than 3mm:
5269	7219.3310	---按重量计含锰量在5.5%及以上的铬锰系不锈钢	10	0 冰岛IS,东盟AS,哥CR,台湾TW,香港HK,新加坡SG,新西兰NZ,智利CL 3 秘鲁PE 4 瑞士CH 5 巴PK 6 澳AU 8 韩国KR	0 受惠国$_1$LD$_1$	40	---Containing by weight no less than 5.5% of manganese of Terro-chromium manganese steel
5270	7219.3390	---其他	10	0 冰岛IS,东盟AS,哥CR,台湾TW,香港HK,新加坡SG,新西兰NZ,智利CL 3 秘鲁PE 4 瑞士CH 5 巴PK 6 澳AU 8.6 韩国KR	0 受惠国$_1$LD$_1$	40	---Other
5271	7219.3400	--厚度在0.5毫米及以上，但不超过1毫米	10	0 冰岛IS,东盟AS,哥CR,台湾TW,香港HK,新加坡SG,新西兰NZ,智利CL 3 秘鲁PE 4 瑞士CH 5 巴PK 6 澳AU 9 韩国KR	0 受惠国$_1$LD$_1$	40	--Of a thickness of 0.5mm or more but not exceeding 1mm
5272	7219.3500	--厚度小于0.5毫米	10	0 冰岛IS,东盟AS,哥CR,台湾TW,香港HK,新加坡SG,新西兰NZ,智利CL 3 秘鲁PE 4 瑞士CH 5 巴PK 6 澳AU 9 韩国KR	0 受惠国$_1$LD$_1$	40	--Of a thickness of less than 0.5mm
5273	7219.9000	-其他	10	0 冰岛IS,东盟AS,哥CR,秘鲁PE,台湾TW,新加坡SG,新西兰NZ,智利CL 4 瑞士CH 5 巴PK 6 澳AU 8 韩国KR	0 受惠国$_1$LD$_1$	40	-Other
	72.20	**不锈钢平板轧材，宽度小于600毫米：**					**Flat-rolled products stainless steel, of a width of less than 600mm:**

序号 No.	税则号列 Tariff Line	中文货品名称 Article Description in Chinese	最惠国税率 MFN(%)	协定税率 Agreement(%)	特惠税率 SP(%)	普通税率 Gen(%)	英文货品名称 Article Description
		-除热轧外未经进一步加工：					-Not further worked than hot-rolled:
5274	7220.1100	--厚度在4.75毫米及以上	10	0 冰岛IS,东盟AS,哥CR,秘鲁PE,香港HK,新加坡SG,新西兰NZ,智利CL 4 瑞士CH 5 巴PK 6 澳AU	0 受惠国$_1$LD$_1$	20	--Of a thickness of 4.75mm or more
5275	7220.1200	--厚度小于4.75毫米	10	0 冰岛IS,东盟AS,哥CR,秘鲁PE,新加坡SG,新西兰NZ,智利CL 4 瑞士CH 5 巴PK 6 澳AU 8 韩国KR	0 受惠国$_1$LD$_1$	20	--Of a thickness of less than 4.75mm
		-除冷轧外未经进一步加工：					-Not further worked than cold-rolled (cold-reduced) :
5276	7220.2020	---厚度在0.35毫米及以下	10	0 冰岛IS,东盟AS,哥CR,秘鲁PE,新加坡SG,新西兰NZ,智利CL 4 瑞士CH 5 巴PK 6 澳AU 8.6 韩国KR	0 受惠国$_1$LD$_1$	20	---Of a thickness of 0.35mm or less
5277	7220.2030	---厚度在0.35毫米以上但小于3毫米	10	0 冰岛IS,东盟AS,哥CR,秘鲁PE,新加坡SG,新西兰NZ,智利CL 4 瑞士CH 5 巴PK 6 澳AU 8.6 韩国KR	0 受惠国$_1$LD$_1$	20	---Of a thickness of more than 0.35mm but not exceeding 3mm
5278	7220.2040	---厚度在3毫米及以上	10	0 冰岛IS,东盟AS,哥CR,秘鲁PE,新加坡SG,新西兰NZ,智利CL 4 瑞士CH 5 巴PK 6 澳AU 8 韩国KR	0 受惠国$_1$LD$_1$	20	---Of a thickness of 3mm or more
5279	7220.9000	-其他	10	0 冰岛IS,东盟AS,哥CR,秘鲁PE,台湾TW,新加坡SG,新西兰NZ,智利CL 4 瑞士CH 5 巴PK 6 澳AU 8 韩国KR	0 受惠国$_1$LD$_1$	20	-Other
	72.21	**不规则盘卷的不锈钢热轧条、杆**					**Bars and rods, hot-rolled, in irregularly wound coils, of stainless steel**
5280	7221.0000	不规则盘卷的不锈钢热轧条、杆	10	0 冰岛IS,东盟AS,哥CR,秘鲁PE,新加坡SG,新西兰NZ,智利CL 4 瑞士CH 5 巴PK 6 澳AU 8 亚太AP 9.2 韩国KR	0 受惠国$_1$LD$_1$	20	Bars and rods, hot-rolled, in irregularly wound coils, of stainless steel
	72.22	**不锈钢其他条、杆;不锈钢角材、型材及异型材：**					**Other bars and rods of stainless steel; angles, shapes and sections of stainless steel:**
		-条、杆，除热轧、热拉拔或热挤压外未经进一步加工：					-Bars and rods, not further worked than hot-rolled, hot-drawn or extruded:

序号 No.	税则号列 Tariff Line	中文货品名称 Article Description in Chinese	最惠国税率 MFN(%)	协定税率 Agreement(%)	特惠税率 SP(%)	普通税率 Gen(%)	英文货品名称 Article Description
5281	7222.1100	--圆形截面的	10	0 冰岛IS,东盟AS,哥CR,秘鲁PE,新加坡SG,新西兰NZ,智利CL 4 瑞士CH 5 巴PK 6 澳AU 9 亚太AP 9.6 韩国KR	0 受惠国$_1$LD$_1$	40	--Of circular cross-section
5282	7222.1900	--其他	10	0 冰岛IS,东盟AS,哥CR,秘鲁PE,新加坡SG,新西兰NZ,智利CL 4 瑞士CH 5 巴PK 6 澳AU 9 亚太AP 9.6 韩国KR	0 受惠国$_1$LD$_1$	40	--Other
5283	7222.2000	-条、杆，除冷成形或冷加工外未经进一步加工	10	0 冰岛IS,东盟AS,哥CR,秘鲁PE,新加坡SG,新西兰NZ,智利CL 4 瑞士CH 5 巴PK 6 澳AU	0 受惠国$_1$LD$_1$	40	-Bars and rods, not further worked than cold-formed or cold-finished
5284	7222.3000	-其他条、杆	10	0 冰岛IS,东盟AS,哥CR,秘鲁PE,新加坡SG,新西兰NZ,智利CL 4 瑞士CH 5 巴PK 6 澳AU 8.9 亚太AP 9.6 韩国KR	0 受惠国$_1$LD$_1$	40	-Other bars and rods
5285	7222.4000	-角材、型材及异型材	10	0 冰岛IS,东盟AS,哥CR,秘鲁PE,新加坡SG,新西兰NZ,智利CL 4 瑞士CH 5 巴PK 6 澳AU	0 受惠国$_1$LD$_1$	17	-Angles, shapes and sections
	72.23	**不锈钢丝**					**Wire of stainless steel**
5286	7223.0000	不锈钢丝	10	0 冰岛IS,东盟AS,哥CR,秘鲁PE,香港HK,新加坡SG,新西兰NZ,智利CL 4 瑞士CH 5 巴PK 6 澳AU	0 受惠国LD	20	Wire of stainless steel
		第四分章其他合金钢;合金钢或非合金钢制的空心钻钢					IV. OTHER ALLOY STEEL; HOLLOW DRILL BARS AND RODS, OF ALLOY OR NON-ALLOY STEEL
	72.24	**其他合金钢，锭状或其他初级形状;其他合金钢制的半制成品:**					**Other alloy steel in ingots or other primary forms; semi-finished products of other alloy steel:**
5287	7224.1000	-锭状及其他初级形状	2	0 澳AU,巴PK,冰岛IS,东盟AS,哥CR,韩国KR,秘鲁PE,瑞士CH,新西兰NZ,智利CL	0 受惠国LD	11	-Ingots and other primary forms
		-其他:					-Other:
5288	7224.9010	---单件重量在10吨及以上的粗铸锻件坯	2	0 澳AU,巴PK,冰岛IS,东盟AS,哥CR,韩国KR,秘鲁PE,瑞士CH,新西兰NZ,智利CL	0 受惠国LD	11	---Raw casting forging stocks, individual piece weight of 10T or more
5289	7224.9090	---其他	2	0 澳AU,巴PK,冰岛IS,东盟AS,哥CR,韩国KR,秘鲁PE,瑞士CH,新西兰NZ,智利CL	0 受惠国LD	11	---Other

序号 No.	税则号列 Tariff Line	中文货品名称 Article Description in Chinese	最惠国税率 MFN(%)	协定税率 Agreement(%)	特惠税率 SP(%)	普通税率 Gen(%)	英文货品名称 Article Description
	72.25	**其他合金钢平板轧材，宽度在600毫米及以上：**					**Flat-rolled products of other alloy steel, of a width of 600mm or more:**
		-硅电钢制：					-Of silicon-electrical steel:
5290	7225.1100	--取向性硅电钢	3	0 澳AU,巴PK,冰岛IS,东盟AS,哥CR,秘鲁PE,瑞士CH,新西兰NZ,智利CL 2.1 亚太AP 2.6 韩国KR	0 受惠国LD	20	--Grain-oriented
5291	7225.1900	--其他	6	0 冰岛IS,东盟AS,哥CR,秘鲁PE,台湾TW,新西兰NZ,智利CL 2.4 瑞士CH 3.6 澳AU 5 巴PK	0 受惠国LD	20	--Other
5292	7225.3000	-其他卷材，除热轧外未经进一步加工	3	0 澳AU,巴PK,冰岛IS,东盟AS,哥CR,秘鲁PE,瑞士CH,新西兰NZ,智利CL	0 受惠国LD	14	-Other, not further worked than hot-rolled, in coils
		-其他非卷材，除热轧外未经进一步加工：					-Other, not further worked than hot-rolled, not in coils:
5293	7225.4010	---工具钢	3	0 澳AU,巴PK,冰岛IS,东盟AS,哥CR,秘鲁PE,瑞士CH,新西兰NZ,智利CL 1.8 韩国KR	0 受惠国LD	17	---Tool steel
		---其他：					---Other:
5294	7225.4091	----含硼合金钢	3	0 澳AU,巴PK,冰岛IS,东盟AS,哥CR,秘鲁PE,瑞士CH,新西兰NZ,智利CL 1.8 韩国KR	0 受惠国LD	17	----Boron steel
5295	7225.4099	----其他	3	0 澳AU,巴PK,冰岛IS,东盟AS,哥CR,秘鲁PE,瑞士CH,新西兰NZ,智利CL 1.8 韩国KR	0 受惠国LD	17	----Other
5296	7225.5000	-其他，除冷轧外未经进一步加工	3	0 澳AU,巴PK,冰岛IS,东盟AS,哥CR,秘鲁PE,瑞士CH,新西兰NZ,智利CL	0 受惠国LD	17	-Other, not further worked than cold-rolled (cold-reduced)
		-其他：					-Other:
5297	7225.9100	--电镀或涂锌的	7	0 冰岛IS,东盟AS,哥CR,秘鲁PE,新西兰NZ,智利CL 2.8 瑞士CH 4.2 澳AU 5 巴PK 5.6 韩国KR	0 受惠国LD	17	--Electrolytically plated or coated with zinc
5298	7225.9200	--用其他方法镀或涂锌的	7	0 冰岛IS,东盟AS,哥CR,秘鲁PE,新西兰NZ,智利CL 2.8 瑞士CH 4.2 澳AU 5 巴PK 6 韩国KR	0 受惠国LD	17	--Otherwise plated or coated with zinc
		--其他：					--Other:
5299	7225.9910	---高速钢制	3	0 澳AU,巴PK,冰岛IS,东盟AS,哥CR,秘鲁PE,瑞士CH,新西兰NZ,智利CL 1.8 韩国KR	0 受惠国LD	17	---Of high speed steel

序号 No.	税则号列 Tariff Line	中文货品名称 Article Description in Chinese	最惠国税率 MFN(%)	协定税率 Agreement(%)		特惠税率 SP(%)		普通税率 Gen(%)	英文货品名称 Article Description
5300	7225.9990	---其他	7	0 2.8 4.2 5 5.6	冰岛IS,东盟AS,哥CR,秘鲁PE,新西兰NZ,智利CL 瑞士CH 澳AU 巴PK 韩国KR	0	受惠国LD	17	---Other
	72.26	**其他合金钢平板轧材，宽度小于600毫米：**							**Flat-rolled products of other alloy steel, of a width of less than 600mm:**
		-硅电钢制：							-Of silicon-electrical steel:
5301	7226.1100	--取向性硅电钢	3	0	澳AU,巴PK,冰岛IS,东盟AS,哥CR,秘鲁PE,瑞士CH,新西兰NZ,智利CL	0	受惠国LD	20	--Grain-oriented
5302	7226.1900	--其他	3	0	澳AU,巴PK,冰岛IS,东盟AS,哥CR,秘鲁PE,瑞士CH,新西兰NZ,智利CL	0	受惠国LD	20	--Other
5303	7226.2000	-高速钢制	3	0 2.4	澳AU,巴PK,冰岛IS,东盟AS,哥CR,秘鲁PE,瑞士CH,新西兰NZ,智利CL 韩国KR	0	受惠国LD	20	-Of high speed steel
		-其他：							-Other:
		--除热轧外未经进一步加工：							--Not further worked than hot-rolled:
5304	7226.9110	---工具钢	3	0 2.4	澳AU,巴PK,冰岛IS,东盟AS,哥CR,秘鲁PE,瑞士CH,新西兰NZ,智利CL 韩国KR	0	受惠国LD	20	---Tool steel
		---其他：							---Other:
5305	7226.9191	----含硼合金钢	3	0 2.4	澳AU,巴PK,冰岛IS,东盟AS,哥CR,秘鲁PE,瑞士CH,新西兰NZ,智利CL 韩国KR	0	受惠国LD	20	----Boron steel
5306	7226.9199	----其他	3	0 2.4	澳AU,巴PK,冰岛IS,东盟AS,哥CR,秘鲁PE,瑞士CH,新西兰NZ,智利CL 韩国KR	0	受惠国LD	20	----Other
5307	7226.9200	--除冷轧外未经进一步加工	3	0 2.6	澳AU,巴PK,冰岛IS,东盟AS,哥CR,秘鲁PE,瑞士CH,新西兰NZ,智利CL 韩国KR	0	受惠国LD	20	--Not further worked than cold-rolled (cold-reduced)
		--其他：							--Other:
5308	7226.9910	---电镀或涂锌的	7	0 2.8 4.2 5 5.6	冰岛IS,东盟AS,哥CR,秘鲁PE,新西兰NZ,智利CL 瑞士CH 澳AU 巴PK 韩国KR	0	受惠国LD	20	---Electrolytically plated or coated with zinc
5309	7226.9920	---用其他方法镀或涂锌的	7	0 2.8 4.2 5 5.6	冰岛IS,东盟AS,哥CR,秘鲁PE,新西兰NZ,智利CL 瑞士CH 澳AU 巴PK 韩国KR	0	受惠国LD	20	---Otherwise plated or coated with zinc

序号 No.	税则号列 Tariff Line	中文货品名称 Article Description in Chinese	最惠国税率 MFN(%)	协定税率 Agreement(%)		特惠税率 SP(%)		普通税率 Gen(%)	英文货品名称 Article Description
5310	7226.9990	---其他	7	0 2.8 4.2 5 5.6	冰岛IS,东盟AS,哥CR,秘鲁PE,新西兰NZ,智利CL 瑞士CH 澳AU 巴PK 韩国KR	0	受惠国LD	20	---Other
	ex72269990	铁镍合金带材（生产集成电路框架用），宽度小于600毫米	Δ4						Fe-Ni alloy strip (production of the frame for electronic integrated circuits) , of a width less than 600mm
	72.27	**不规则盘卷的其他合金钢热轧条、杆：**							**Bars and rods, hot-rolled, in irregularly wound coils, of other alloy steel:**
5311	7227.1000	-高速钢制	3	0	澳AU,巴PK,冰岛IS,东盟AS,哥CR,韩国KR,秘鲁PE,瑞士CH,新西兰NZ,智利CL	0	受惠国LD	20	-Of high speed steel
5312	7227.2000	-硅锰钢制	6	0 2.4 3.6 5 5.2	冰岛IS,东盟AS,哥CR,秘鲁PE,新西兰NZ,智利CL 瑞士CH 澳AU 巴PK 韩国KR	0	受惠国LD	20	-Of silico-manganese steel
		-其他：							-Other:
5313	7227.9010	---含硼合金钢制	3	0	澳AU,巴PK,冰岛IS,东盟AS,哥CR,韩国KR,秘鲁PE,瑞士CH,新西兰NZ,智利CL	0	受惠国LD	20	---Of boron steel
5314	7227.9090	---其他	3	0	澳AU,巴PK,冰岛IS,东盟AS,哥CR,韩国KR,秘鲁PE,瑞士CH,新西兰NZ,智利CL	0	受惠国LD	20	---Other
	72.28	**其他合金钢条、杆;其他合金钢角材、型材及异型材;合金钢或非合金钢制的空心钻钢：**							**Other bars and rods of other alloy steel; angles, shapes and sections, of other alloy steel; hollow drill bars and rods, of alloy or non-alloy steel:**
5315	7228.1000	-高速钢条、杆	3	0 2.4	澳AU,巴PK,冰岛IS,东盟AS,哥CR,秘鲁PE,瑞士CH,新西兰NZ,智利CL 韩国KR	0	受惠国LD	20	-Bars and rods, of high speed steel
5316	7228.2000	-硅锰钢条、杆	6	0 2.4 3.6 4.8 5	冰岛IS,东盟AS,哥CR,秘鲁PE,新西兰NZ,智利CL 瑞士CH 澳AU 韩国KR 巴PK	0	受惠国LD	20	-Bars and rods, of silico-manganese steel
		-其他条、杆，除热轧、热拉拔或热挤压外未经进一步加工：							-Other bars and rods, not further worked than hot-crolled, hot-drawn or extruded:
5317	7228.3010	---含硼合金钢制	3	0 2.4	澳AU,巴PK,冰岛IS,东盟AS,哥CR,秘鲁PE,瑞士CH,新西兰NZ,智利CL 韩国KR	0	受惠国LD	20	---Of boron steel
5318	7228.3090	---其他	3	0 2.4	澳AU,巴PK,冰岛IS,东盟AS,哥CR,秘鲁PE,瑞士CH,新西兰NZ,智利CL 韩国KR	0	受惠国LD	20	---Other

序号 No.	税则号列 Tariff Line	中文货品名称 Article Description in Chinese	最惠国税率 MFN(%)	协定税率 Agreement(%)	特惠税率 SP(%)	普通税率 Gen(%)	英文货品名称 Article Description
5319	7228.4000	-其他条、杆，除锻造外未经进一步加工	3	0 澳AU,巴PK,冰岛IS,东盟AS,哥CR,秘鲁PE,瑞士CH,新西兰NZ,智利CL 2.4 韩国KR	0 受惠国LD	20	-Other bars and rods, not further worked than forged
5320	7228.5000	-其他条、杆，除冷成形或冷加工外未经进一步加工	3	0 澳AU,巴PK,冰岛IS,东盟AS,哥CR,秘鲁PE,瑞士CH,新西兰NZ,智利CL 2.4 韩国KR	0 受惠国LD	20	-Other bars and rods, not further worked than cold-formed of cold-finished
5321	7228.6000	-其他条、杆	3	0 澳AU,巴PK,冰岛IS,东盟AS,哥CR,秘鲁PE,瑞士CH,新西兰NZ,智利CL 2.4 韩国KR	0 受惠国LD	20	-Other bars and rods
		-角材、型材及异型材：					-Angles, shapes and sections:
5322	7228.7010	---履带板型钢	6	0 冰岛IS,东盟AS,哥CR,秘鲁PE,新西兰NZ,智利CL 2.4 瑞士CH 3.6 澳AU,韩国KR 5 巴PK	0 受惠国LD	17	---Shapes of crawler tread
5323	7228.7090	---其他	6	0 冰岛IS,东盟AS,哥CR,秘鲁PE,新西兰NZ,智利CL 2.4 瑞士CH 3.6 澳AU 4.8 韩国KR 5 巴PK	0 受惠国LD	17	---Other
5324	7228.8000	-空心钻钢	7	0 冰岛IS,东盟AS,哥CR,秘鲁PE,新西兰NZ,智利CL 2.8 瑞士CH 4.2 澳AU,韩国KR 5 巴PK	0 受惠国LD	35	-Hollow drill bars and rods
	72.29	**其他合金钢丝：**					**Wire of other alloy steel:**
5325	7229.2000	-硅锰钢制	7	0 冰岛IS,东盟AS,哥CR,秘鲁PE,新西兰NZ,智利CL 2.8 瑞士CH 4.2 澳AU 5 巴PK 6 韩国KR	0 受惠国$_1$LD$_1$	20	-Of silico-manganese steel
		-其他：					-Other:
5326	7229.9010	---高速钢制	3	0 澳AU,巴PK,冰岛IS,东盟AS,哥CR,秘鲁PE,瑞士CH,新西兰NZ,智利CL 2.4 韩国KR	0 受惠国$_1$LD$_1$	20	---Of high speed steel
5327	7229.9090	---其他	7	0 冰岛IS,东盟AS,哥CR,秘鲁PE,新西兰NZ,智利CL 2.8 瑞士CH 4.2 澳AU 5 巴PK	0 受惠国$_1$LD$_1$	20	---Other

第七十三章
钢铁制品

注释:

一、称"铸铁"，适用于经铸造而得的产品，按重量计其铁元素含量超过其他元素单项含量并与第七十二章注释一（四）所述的钢的化学成分不同。

二、本章所称"丝"，是指热或冷成形的任何截面形状的产品，但其截面尺寸均不超过16毫米。

Chapter 73
Articles of iron or steel

Notes:

1. In this Chapter the expression "cast iron" applies to products obtained by casting in which iron predominates by weight over each of the other elements and which do not comply with the chemical composition of steel as defined in Note1 (d) to Chapter 72.
2. In this Chapter the word "wire" means hot orcold-formed products of any cross-sectional shape, of which no cross-sectional dimension exceeds 16mm.

序号 No.	税则号列 Tariff Line	中文货品名称 Article Description in Chinese	最惠国税率 MFN(%)	协定税率 Agreement(%)	特惠税率 SP(%)	普通税率 Gen(%)	英文货品名称 Article Description
	73.01	**钢铁板桩，不论是否钻孔、打眼或组装;焊接的钢铁角材、型材及异型材:**					**Sheet piling of iron or steel, whether or not drilled, punched or made from assembled elements; welded angles, shapes and sections, of iron or steel:**
5328	7301.1000	-钢铁板桩	7	0 冰岛IS,东盟AS,哥CR,秘鲁PE,新西兰NZ,智利CL 2.8 瑞士CH 4.2 澳AU 5 巴PK 5.6 韩国KR 6.3 亚太AP	0 受惠国LD	20	-Sheet piling
5329	7301.2000	-角材、型材及异型材	7	0 冰岛IS,东盟AS,哥CR,秘鲁PE,新西兰NZ,智利CL 2.8 瑞士CH 4.2 澳AU 5 巴PK 5.6 韩国KR	0 受惠国LD	30	-Angles, shapes and sections
	73.02	**铁道及电车道铺轨用钢铁材料（钢轨、护轨、齿轨、道岔尖轨、辙叉、尖轨拉杆及其他叉道段体、轨枕、鱼尾板、轨座、轨座楔、钢轨垫板、钢轨夹、底板、固定板及其他专门用于连接或加固路轨的材料）:**					**Railway or tramway track construction material of iron or steel, the following: rails, check-rails and rack rails, switch blades, crossing frogs, point rods and other crossing pieces, sleepers (cross-ties) , fish-plates, chairs, chair wedges, sole plates (base plates) , rail clips, bedplates, ties and other material specialised for jointing or fixing rails:**
5330	7302.1000	-钢轨	6	0 冰岛IS,东盟AS,哥CR,秘鲁PE,新西兰NZ,智利CL 2.4 瑞士CH 3.6 澳AU 4.8 韩国KR 5 巴PK	0 受惠国LD	14	-Rails
5331	7302.3000	-道岔尖轨、辙叉、尖轨拉杆及其他叉道段体	8	0 冰岛IS,东盟AS,哥CR,秘鲁PE,新西兰NZ,智利CL 3.2 瑞士CH 4.8 澳AU,韩国KR 5 巴PK	0 受惠国LD	17	-Switch blades, crossing frogs, point rods and other crossing pieces

序号 No.	税则号列 Tariff Line	中文货品名称 Article Description in Chinese	最惠国税率 MFN(%)	协定税率 Agreement(%)	特惠税率 SP(%)	普通税率 Gen(%)	英文货品名称 Article Description
5332	7302.4000	-鱼尾板及钢轨垫板	7	0 冰岛IS,东盟AS,哥CR,秘鲁PE,新西兰NZ,智利CL 2.8 瑞士CH 4.2 澳AU 5 巴PK 5.6 韩国KR	0 受惠国LD	17	-Fish-plates and sole plates
		-其他:					-Other:
5333	7302.9010	---轨枕	6	0 巴PK,冰岛IS,东盟AS,哥CR,秘鲁PE,新西兰NZ,智利CL 2.4 瑞士CH 3.6 澳AU,韩国KR 5.1 亚太AP	0 受惠国LD	14	---Sleepers (cross-ties)
5334	7302.9090	---其他	7	0 冰岛IS,东盟AS,哥CR,秘鲁PE,新西兰NZ,智利CL 4.2 澳AU,韩国KR 4.9 瑞士CH 5 巴PK 6 亚太AP	0 受惠国LD	17	---Other
	73.03	**铸铁管及空心异型材:**					**Tubes, pipes and hollow profiles, of cast iron:**
5335	7303.0010	---内径在500毫米及以上的圆形截面管	4	0 澳AU,巴PK,冰岛IS,东盟AS,哥CR,韩国KR,秘鲁PE,瑞士CH,新西兰NZ,智利CL	0 受惠国LD	40	---Tubes and pipes of circular crosssection, of the internal diameter of 500mm or more
5336	7303.0090	---其他	4	0 澳AU,巴PK,冰岛IS,东盟AS,哥CR,秘鲁PE,瑞士CH,新西兰NZ,智利CL 2.4 韩国KR	0 受惠国LD	40	---Other
	73.04	**无缝钢铁管及空心异型材(铸铁的除外):**					**Tubes, pipes and hollow profiles, seamless, of iron (other than cast iron) or steel:**
		-石油或天然气管道管:					-Line pipe of a kind used for oil or gas pipelines:
		--不锈钢制:					--Of stainless steel:
5337	7304.1110	---外径大于等于215.9毫米,但不超过406.4毫米	5	0 澳AU,巴PK,冰岛IS,东盟AS,哥CR,秘鲁PE,瑞士CH,新西兰NZ,智利CL 4 韩国KR	0 受惠国LD	17	---Having an outside diameter of 215.9mm or more but not exceeding 406.4mm
5338	7304.1120	---外径超过114.3毫米,但小于215.9毫米	5	0 澳AU,巴PK,冰岛IS,东盟AS,哥CR,秘鲁PE,瑞士CH,新西兰NZ,智利CL 4 韩国KR	0 受惠国LD	17	---Having an outside diameter exceeding 114.3mm but less than 215.9mm
5339	7304.1130	---外径不超过114.3毫米	5	0 澳AU,巴PK,冰岛IS,东盟AS,哥CR,秘鲁PE,瑞士CH,新西兰NZ,智利CL 4 韩国KR	0 受惠国LD	17	---Having an outside diameter not exceeding 114.3mm
5340	7304.1190	---其他	5	0 澳AU,巴PK,冰岛IS,东盟AS,哥CR,秘鲁PE,瑞士CH,新西兰NZ,智利CL 3 韩国KR	0 受惠国LD	17	---Other
		--其他:					--Other:
5341	7304.1910	---外径大于等于215.9毫米,但不超过406.4毫米	5	0 澳AU,巴PK,冰岛IS,东盟AS,哥CR,秘鲁PE,瑞士CH,新西兰NZ,智利CL 4 韩国KR	0 受惠国LD	17	---Having an outside diameter of 215.9mm or more but not exceeding 406.4mm

序号 No.	税则号列 Tariff Line	中文货品名称 Article Description in Chinese	最惠国税率 MFN(%)	协定税率 Agreement(%)	特惠税率 SP(%)	普通税率 Gen(%)	英文货品名称 Article Description
5342	7304.1920	---外径超过114.3毫米，但小于215.9毫米	5	0 澳AU,巴PK,冰岛IS,东盟AS,哥CR,秘鲁PE,瑞士CH,新西兰NZ,智利CL 4 韩国KR	0 受惠国LD	17	---Having an outside diameter exceeding 114.3mm but less than 215.9mm
5343	7304.1930	---外径不超过114.3毫米	5	0 澳AU,巴PK,冰岛IS,东盟AS,哥CR,秘鲁PE,瑞士CH,新西兰NZ,智利CL 4 韩国KR	0 受惠国LD	17	---Having an outside diameter not exceeding 114.3mm
5344	7304.1990	---其他	5	0 澳AU,巴PK,冰岛IS,东盟AS,哥CR,秘鲁PE,瑞士CH,新西兰NZ,智利CL 3 韩国KR	0 受惠国LD	17	---Other
		-钻探石油及天然气用的套管、导管及钻管：					-Casing, tubing and drill pipe, of a kind used in drilling for oil or gas:
		--不锈钢制钻管：					--Drill pipe of stainless steel:
5345	7304.2210	---外径不超过168.3毫米	4	0 澳AU,巴PK,冰岛IS,东盟AS,哥CR,韩国KR,秘鲁PE,瑞士CH,新西兰NZ,智利CL	0 受惠国LD	17	---Having an outside diameter not exceeding 168.3mm
5346	7304.2290	---其他	4	0 澳AU,巴PK,冰岛IS,东盟AS,哥CR,韩国KR,秘鲁PE,瑞士CH,新西兰NZ,智利CL	0 受惠国LD	17	---Other
		--其他钻管：					--Other drill pipe:
5347	7304.2310	---外径不超过168.3毫米	4	0 澳AU,巴PK,冰岛IS,东盟AS,哥CR,韩国KR,秘鲁PE,瑞士CH,新西兰NZ,智利CL	0 受惠国LD	17	---Having an outside diameter not exceeding 168.3mm
5348	7304.2390	---其他	4	0 澳AU,巴PK,冰岛IS,东盟AS,哥CR,韩国KR,秘鲁PE,瑞士CH,新西兰NZ,智利CL	0 受惠国LD	17	---Other
5349	7304.2400	--其他不锈钢管	4	0 澳AU,巴PK,冰岛IS,东盟AS,哥CR,韩国KR,秘鲁PE,瑞士CH,新西兰NZ,智利CL 2 亚太AP	0 受惠国LD	17	--Other pipe, of stainless steel
		--其他：					--Other:
5350	7304.2910	---屈服强度小于552兆帕的	4	0 澳AU,巴PK,冰岛IS,东盟AS,哥CR,韩国KR,秘鲁PE,瑞士CH,新西兰NZ,智利CL 2 亚太AP	0 受惠国LD	17	---Of a yield strength less than 552MPa
5351	7304.2920	---屈服强度大于等于552兆帕，但小于758兆帕的	4	0 澳AU,巴PK,冰岛IS,东盟AS,哥CR,韩国KR,秘鲁PE,瑞士CH,新西兰NZ,智利CL 2 亚太AP	0 受惠国LD	17	---Of a yield strength of 552MPa or more but less than 758MPa
5352	7304.2930	---屈服强度大于等于758兆帕的	4	0 澳AU,巴PK,冰岛IS,东盟AS,哥CR,韩国KR,秘鲁PE,瑞士CH,新西兰NZ,智利CL 2 亚太AP	0 受惠国LD	17	---Of a yield strength of 758MPa or more
		-铁或非合金钢的其他圆形截面管：					-Other, of circular cross-section, of iron or non-alloy steel:
		--冷拔或冷轧的：					--Cold-drawn or cold-rolled (cold-reduced) :
5353	7304.3110	---锅炉管	4	0 澳AU,巴PK,冰岛IS,东盟AS,哥CR,韩国KR,秘鲁PE,瑞士CH,新西兰NZ,智利CL	0 受惠国LD	17	---Boiler tubes and pipes

序号 No.	税则号列 Tariff Line	中文货品名称 Article Description in Chinese	最惠国税率 MFN(%)	协定税率 Agreement(%)	特惠税率 SP(%)	普通税率 Gen(%)	英文货品名称 Article Description
5354	7304.3120	---地质钻管、套管	8	0 冰岛IS,东盟AS,哥CR,秘鲁PE,新西兰NZ,智利CL 3.2 瑞士CH 4.8 澳AU,韩国KR 5 巴PK	0 受惠国LD	17	---Geological casing and drill pipes
5355	7304.3190	---其他	4	0 澳AU,巴PK,冰岛IS,东盟AS,哥CR,秘鲁PE,新西兰NZ,智利CL 1.6 瑞士CH 2.4 韩国KR	0 受惠国LD	17	---Other
		--其他:					--Other:
5356	7304.3910	---锅炉管	4	0 澳AU,巴PK,冰岛IS,东盟AS,哥CR,韩国KR,秘鲁PE,瑞士CH,香港HK,新西兰NZ,智利CL	0 受惠国LD	17	---Boiler tubes and pipes
5357	7304.3920	---地质钻管、套管	5	0 澳AU,巴PK,冰岛IS,东盟AS,哥CR,秘鲁PE,瑞士CH,香港HK,新西兰NZ,智利CL 3 韩国KR	0 受惠国LD	17	---Geological casing and drill pipes
5358	7304.3990	---其他	4	0 澳AU,巴PK,冰岛IS,东盟AS,哥CR,秘鲁PE,瑞士CH,香港HK,新西兰NZ,智利CL 3.2 韩国KR	0 受惠国LD	17	---Other
		-不锈钢的其他圆形截面管:					-Other, of circular cross-section, of stainless steel:
		--冷拔或冷轧的:					--Cold-drawn or cold-rolled (cold-reduced) :
5359	7304.4110	---锅炉管	10	0 冰岛IS,东盟AS,哥CR,秘鲁PE,新加坡SG,新西兰NZ,智利CL 4 瑞士CH 5 巴PK 6 澳AU 8 韩国KR	0 受惠国$_1$LD$_1$	17	---Boiler tubes and pipes
5360	7304.4190	---其他	10	0 冰岛IS,东盟AS,哥CR,秘鲁PE,新加坡SG,新西兰NZ,智利CL 4 瑞士CH 5 巴PK 6 澳AU 9 韩国KR	0 受惠国$_1$LD$_1$	40	---Other
		--其他:					--Other:
5361	7304.4910	---锅炉管	10	0 冰岛IS,东盟AS,哥CR,秘鲁PE,新加坡SG,新西兰NZ,智利CL 4 瑞士CH 5 巴PK 6 澳AU 8 韩国KR	0 受惠国$_1$LD$_1$	17	---Boiler tubes and pipes
5362	7304.4990	---其他	10	0 冰岛IS,东盟AS,哥CR,秘鲁PE,新加坡SG,新西兰NZ,智利CL 4 瑞士CH 5 巴PK 6 澳AU 8 韩国KR	0 受惠国$_1$LD$_1$	40	---Other
		-其他合金钢的其他圆形截面管:					-Other, of circular cross-section, of other alloy steel:
		--冷拔或冷轧的:					--Cold-drawn or cold-rolled (cold-reduced) :

序号 No.	税则号列 Tariff Line	中文货品名称 Article Description in Chinese	最惠国税率 MFN(%)	协定税率 Agreement(%)		特惠税率 SP(%)		普通税率 Gen(%)	英文货品名称 Article Description
5363	7304.5110	----锅炉管	4	0	澳AU,巴PK,冰岛IS,东盟AS,哥CR,韩国KR,秘鲁PE,瑞士CH,新西兰NZ,智利CL	0	受惠国LD	17	---Boiler tubes and pipes
5364	7304.5120	----地质钻管、套管	4	0	澳AU,巴PK,冰岛IS,东盟AS,哥CR,韩国KR,秘鲁PE,瑞士CH,新西兰NZ,智利CL	0	受惠国LD	17	---Geological casing and drill pipes
5365	7304.5190	----其他	4	0 1.6	澳AU,巴PK,冰岛IS,东盟AS,哥CR,韩国KR,秘鲁PE,新西兰NZ,智利CL 瑞士CH	0	受惠国LD	17	---Other
		--其他：							--Other:
5366	7304.5910	----锅炉管	4	0	澳AU,巴PK,冰岛IS,东盟AS,哥CR,韩国KR,秘鲁PE,瑞士CH,新西兰NZ,智利CL	0	受惠国LD	17	---Boiler tubes and pipes
5367	7304.5920	----地质钻管、套管	4	0	澳AU,巴PK,冰岛IS,东盟AS,哥CR,韩国KR,秘鲁PE,瑞士CH,新西兰NZ,智利CL	0	受惠国LD	17	---Geological casing and drill pipes
5368	7304.5990	----其他	4	0 2.4	澳AU,巴PK,冰岛IS,东盟AS,哥CR,秘鲁PE,瑞士CH,新西兰NZ,智利CL 韩国KR	0	受惠国LD	17	---Other
5369	7304.9000	-其他	4	0 2.4	澳AU,巴PK,冰岛IS,东盟AS,哥CR,秘鲁PE,瑞士CH,新西兰NZ,智利CL 韩国KR	0	受惠国LD	17	-Other
	73.05	**其他圆形截面钢铁管（例如，焊、铆及用类似方法接合的管），外径超过406.4毫米：**							**Other tubes and pipes (for example, welded, riveted or similarly closed) , having circular cross-sections, the external diameter of which exceeds 406.4mm, of iron or steel:**
		-石油或天然气管道管：							-Line pipe of a kind used for oil or gas pipelines:
5370	7305.1100	--纵向埋弧焊接的	7	0 2.8 4.2 5 6	冰岛IS,东盟AS,哥CR,秘鲁PE,新西兰NZ,智利CL 瑞士CH 澳AU 巴PK 韩国KR	0	受惠国LD	17	--Longitudinally submerged arc welded
5371	7305.1200	--其他纵向焊接的	3	0 1.8	澳AU,巴PK,冰岛IS,东盟AS,哥CR,秘鲁PE,瑞士CH,新西兰NZ,智利CL 韩国KR	0	受惠国LD	17	--Other, longitudinally welded
5372	7305.1900	--其他	7	0 2.8 4.2 5	冰岛IS,东盟AS,哥CR,秘鲁PE,新西兰NZ,智利CL 瑞士CH 澳AU,韩国KR 巴PK	0	受惠国LD	17	--Other
5373	7305.2000	-钻探石油或天然气用套管	7	0 2.8 4.2 5	冰岛IS,东盟AS,哥CR,秘鲁PE,新西兰NZ,智利CL 瑞士CH 澳AU,韩国KR 巴PK	0	受惠国LD	17	-Casing of a kind used in drilling for oil or gas
		-其他焊接的：							-Other, welded:

序号 No.	税则号列 Tariff Line	中文货品名称 Article Description in Chinese	最惠国税率 MFN(%)	协定税率 Agreement(%)	特惠税率 SP(%)	普通税率 Gen(%)	英文货品名称 Article Description
5374	7305.3100	--纵向焊接的	6	0 冰岛IS,东盟AS,哥CR,秘鲁PE,新西兰NZ,智利CL 2.4 瑞士CH 3.6 澳AU 5 巴PK 5.2 韩国KR	0 受惠国LD	30	--Longitudinally welded
5375	7305.3900	--其他	6	0 冰岛IS,东盟AS,哥CR,秘鲁PE,新西兰NZ,智利CL 2.4 瑞士CH 3.6 澳AU 5 巴PK 5.2 韩国KR	0 受惠国LD	30	--Other
5376	7305.9000	-其他	6	0 冰岛IS,东盟AS,哥CR,秘鲁PE,新西兰NZ,智利CL 2.4 瑞士CH 3.6 澳AU,韩国KR 5 巴PK	0 受惠国LD	30	-Other
	73.06	**其他钢铁管及空心异型材（例如，辊缝、焊、铆及类似方法接合的）：**					**Other tubes, pipes and hollow profiles (for example, open seam or welded, riveted or similarly closed) , of iron or steel:**
		-石油及天然气管道管：					-Line pipe of a kind used for oil or gas pipelines:
5377	7306.1100	--不锈钢焊缝管	7	0 冰岛IS,东盟AS,哥CR,秘鲁PE,新西兰NZ,智利CL 2.8 瑞士CH 4.2 澳AU 5 巴PK 5.6 韩国KR	0 受惠国LD	17	--Welded, of stainless steel
5378	7306.1900	--其他	7	0 冰岛IS,东盟AS,哥CR,秘鲁PE,新西兰NZ,智利CL 2.8 瑞士CH 4.2 澳AU 5 巴PK 6 韩国KR	0 受惠国LD	17	--Welded, other
		-钻探石油及天然气用的套管及导管：					-Casing and tubing of a kind used in drilling for oil or gas:
5379	7306.2100	--不锈钢焊缝管	3	0 澳AU,巴PK,冰岛IS,东盟AS,哥CR,韩国KR,秘鲁PE,瑞士CH,新西兰NZ,智利CL	0 受惠国LD	17	--Welded, of stainless steel
5380	7306.2900	--其他	3	0 澳AU,巴PK,冰岛IS,东盟AS,哥CR,韩国KR,秘鲁PE,瑞士CH,新西兰NZ,智利CL	0 受惠国LD	17	--Welded, other
		-铁或非合金钢的其他圆形截面焊缝管：					-Other, welded, of circular cross-section, of iron or non-alloy steel:
		---外径不超过10毫米的：					---Having an outside diameter not exceeding 10mm:
5381	7306.3011	----壁厚在0. 7毫米及以下	3	0 澳AU,巴PK,冰岛IS,东盟AS,哥CR,秘鲁PE,瑞士CH,新西兰NZ,智利CL 1.8 韩国KR	0 受惠国LD	30	----Of a wall thickness of 0.7mm or less
5382	7306.3019	----其他	3	0 澳AU,巴PK,冰岛IS,东盟AS,哥CR,秘鲁PE,瑞士CH,新西兰NZ,智利CL 2.6 韩国KR	0 受惠国LD	30	----Other

序号 No.	税则号列 Tariff Line	中文货品名称 Article Description in Chinese	最惠国税率 MFN(%)	协定税率 Agreement(%)	特惠税率 SP(%)	普通税率 Gen(%)	英文货品名称 Article Description
5383	7306.3090	---其他	3	0 澳AU,巴PK,冰岛IS,东盟AS,哥CR,秘鲁PE,瑞士CH,新西兰NZ,智利CL 2.6 韩国KR	0 受惠国LD	30	---Other
5384	7306.4000	-不锈钢的其他圆形截面焊缝管	6	0 冰岛IS,东盟AS,哥CR,秘鲁PE,新西兰NZ,智利CL 2.4 瑞士CH 3.6 澳AU 5 巴PK	0 受惠国LD	30	-Other, welded, of circular cross-section, of stainless steel
5385	7306.5000	-其他合金钢的圆形截面焊缝管	3	0 澳AU,巴PK,冰岛IS,东盟AS,哥CR,秘鲁PE,瑞士CH,新西兰NZ,智利CL 2.6 韩国KR	0 受惠国LD	30	-Other, welded, of circular cross-section, of other alloy steel
		-非圆形截面的其他焊缝管:					-Other, welded, of non-circular cross-section:
5386	7306.6100	--矩形或正方形截面	3	0 澳AU,巴PK,冰岛IS,东盟AS,哥CR,秘鲁PE,瑞士CH,新西兰NZ,智利CL 1.8 韩国KR	0 受惠国LD	30	--Of square or rectangular cross-section
5387	7306.6900	--其他非圆形截面	3	0 澳AU,巴PK,冰岛IS,东盟AS,哥CR,秘鲁PE,瑞士CH,新西兰NZ,智利CL 2.6 韩国KR	0 受惠国LD	30	--Of other non-circular cross-section
5388	7306.9000	-其他	6	0 冰岛IS,东盟AS,哥CR,秘鲁PE,新西兰NZ,智利CL 2.4 瑞士CH 3.6 澳AU 5 巴PK	0 受惠国LD	30	-Other
	73.07	**钢铁管子附件(例如，接头、肘管、管套):**					**Tube or pipe fittings (for example, couplings, elbows, sleeves) , of iron or steel:**
		-铸件:					-Cast fittings:
5389	7307.1100	--无可锻性铸铁制	5	0 澳AU,巴PK,冰岛IS,东盟AS,哥CR,秘鲁PE,瑞士CH,新西兰NZ,智利CL 3 韩国KR	0 受惠国LD	20	--Of non-malleable cast iron
5390	7307.1900	--其他	8	0 冰岛IS,东盟AS,哥CR,秘鲁PE,新西兰NZ,智利CL 4.8 澳AU,韩国KR 5 巴PK 5.6 瑞士CH	0 受惠国LD	20	--Other
		-其他，不锈钢制:					-Other, of stainless steel:
5391	7307.2100	--法兰	8.4	0 冰岛IS,东盟AS,哥CR,秘鲁PE,新西兰NZ,智利CL 3.36 瑞士CH 5 澳AU,巴PK,韩国KR 6.7 亚太AP	0 受惠国LD	20	--Flanges
5392	7307.2200	--螺纹肘管、弯管及管套	8.4	0 冰岛IS,东盟AS,哥CR,秘鲁PE,香港HK,新西兰NZ,智利CL 3.36 瑞士CH 5 澳AU,巴PK,韩国KR	0 受惠国LD	20	--Threaded elbows, bends and sleeves
5393	7307.2300	--对焊件	8.4	0 冰岛IS,东盟AS,哥CR,秘鲁PE,新西兰NZ,智利CL 3.36 瑞士CH 5 澳AU,巴PK,韩国KR	0 受惠国LD	20	--Butt welding fittings

序号 No.	税则号列 Tariff Line	中文货品名称 Article Description in Chinese	最惠国税率 MFN(%)	协定税率 Agreement(%)	特惠税率 SP(%)	普通税率 Gen(%)	英文货品名称 Article Description
5394	7307.2900	--其他	8.4	0 冰岛IS,东盟AS,哥CR,秘鲁PE,香港HK,新西兰NZ,智利CL 5 澳AU,巴PK 5.9 瑞士CH	0 受惠国LD	20	--Other
		-其他:					-Other:
5395	7307.9100	--法兰	7	0 冰岛IS,东盟AS,哥CR,秘鲁PE,新西兰NZ,智利CL 2.8 瑞士CH 4.2 澳AU 5 巴PK 6 韩国KR	0 受惠国LD	20	--Flanges
5396	7307.9200	--螺纹肘管、弯管及管套	4	0 澳AU,巴PK,冰岛IS,东盟AS,哥CR,秘鲁PE,新西兰NZ,智利CL 1.6 瑞士CH 2.4 韩国KR	0 受惠国LD	20	--Threaded elbows, bends and sleeves
5397	7307.9300	--对焊件	7	0 冰岛IS,东盟AS,哥CR,秘鲁PE,新西兰NZ,智利CL 2.8 瑞士CH 4.2 澳AU,韩国KR 5 巴PK	0 受惠国LD	20	--Butt welding fittings
5398	7307.9900	--其他	4	0 澳AU,巴PK,冰岛IS,东盟AS,哥CR,秘鲁PE,新西兰NZ,智利CL 1.6 瑞士CH 2.4 韩国KR	0 受惠国LD	20	--Other
	73.08	**钢铁结构体（税号94.06的活动房屋除外）及其部件（例如，桥梁及桥梁体段、闸门、塔楼、格构杆、屋顶、屋顶框架、门窗及其框架、门槛、百叶窗、栏杆、支柱及立柱）；上述结构体用的已加工钢铁板、杆、角材、型材、异型材、管子及类似品：**					**Structures (excluding prefabricated buildings of heading 9406) and parts of structures (for example, bridges and bridge-sections, lock-gates, towers, lattice masts, roofs, roofing frameworks, doors and windows and their frames and thresholds for doors, shutters, balustrades, pillars and columns) , of iron or steel; plates, rods, angles, shapes, sections, tubes and the like, prepared for use in structures, of iron or steel:**
5399	7308.1000	-桥梁及桥梁体段	8	0 巴PK,冰岛IS,东盟AS,哥CR,秘鲁PE,新西兰NZ,智利CL 3.2 瑞士CH 4.8 澳AU,韩国KR	0 受惠国LD	30	-Bridges and bridge-sections
5400	7308.2000	-塔楼及格构杆	8.4	0 巴PK,冰岛IS,东盟AS,哥CR,秘鲁PE,新西兰NZ,智利CL 3.36 瑞士CH 5 澳AU 6.7 韩国KR	0 受惠国LD	30	-Towers and lattice masts
5401	7308.3000	-门窗及其框架、门槛	10	0 澳门MO,巴PK,冰岛IS,东盟AS,哥CR,秘鲁PE,香港HK,新加坡SG,新西兰NZ,智利CL 4 瑞士CH 6 澳AU 8 韩国KR	0 受惠国LD	50	-Doors, windows and their frames and thresholds for doors
5402	7308.4000	-脚手架、模板或坑道支撑用的支柱及类似设备	8.4	0 巴PK,冰岛IS,东盟AS,哥CR,秘鲁PE,新西兰NZ,智利CL 3.36 瑞士CH 5 澳AU,韩国KR	0 受惠国LD	30	-Equipment for scaffolding, shuttering, propping or pit-propping

序号 No.	税则号列 Tariff Line	中文货品名称 Article Description in Chinese	最惠国税率 MFN(%)	协定税率 Agreement(%)	特惠税率 SP(%)	普通税率 Gen(%)	英文货品名称 Article Description
5403	7308.9000	-其他	4	0 澳AU,巴PK,冰岛IS,东盟AS,哥CR,秘鲁PE,香港HK,新西兰NZ,智利CL 1.6 瑞士CH 2.4 韩国KR	0 受惠国LD	30	-Other
	73.09	**盛装物料用的钢铁囤、柜、罐、桶及类似容器(装压缩气体或液化气体的除外),容积超过300升,不论是否衬里或隔热,但无机械或热力装置**					**Reservoirs, tanks, vats and similar containers for any material (other than compressed or liquefied gas) , of iron or steel, of a capacity exceeding 300L, whether or not lined or heat-insulated, but not fitted with mechanical or thermal equipment**
5404	7309.0000	盛装物料用的钢铁囤、柜、罐、桶及类似容器(装压缩气体或液化气体的除外),容积超过300升,不论是否衬里或隔热,但无机械或热力装置	10.5	0 冰岛IS,东盟AS,哥CR,新加坡SG,新西兰NZ,智利CL 3.2 秘鲁PE 5 巴PK 6.3 澳AU 7.4 瑞士CH 8.4 韩国KR	0 受惠国LD	35	Reservoirs, tanks, vats and similar containers for any material (other than compressed or liquefied gas) , of iron or steel, of a capacity exceeding 300L, whether or not lined or heat-insulated, but not fitted with mechanical or thermal equipment
	73.10	**盛装物料用的钢铁柜、桶、罐、听、盒及类似容器(装压缩气体或液化气体的除外),容积不超过300升,不论是否衬里或隔热,但无机械或热力装置:**					**Tanks, casks, drums, cans, boxes and similar containers, for any material (other than compressed or liquefied gas) , of iron or steel, of a capacity not exceeding 300L, whether or not lined or heat-insulated, but not fitted with mechanical or thermal equipment:**
5405	7310.1000	-容积在50升及以上	10.5	0 冰岛IS,东盟AS,哥CR,香港HK,新加坡SG,新西兰NZ,智利CL 3.2 秘鲁PE 5 巴PK 6.3 澳AU 7.4 瑞士CH 9.4 韩国KR	0 受惠国LD	40	-Of a capacity of 50L or more
		-容积在50升以下:					-Of a capacity of less than 50L:
		--焊边或卷边接合的罐:					--Cans which are to be closed by soldering or crimping:
5406	7310.2110	---易拉罐及罐体	17.5	0 冰岛IS,东盟AS,哥CR,香港HK,新加坡SG,新西兰NZ,智利CL 5.2 秘鲁PE 10.5 澳AU 12.3 瑞士CH 14 巴PK,韩国KR	0 受惠国$_1$LD$_1$	70	---Steel tear tab ends and bodies thereof
5407	7310.2190	---其他	17.5	0 冰岛IS,东盟AS,哥CR,香港HK,新加坡SG,新西兰NZ,智利CL 5.2 秘鲁PE 10.5 澳AU 12.3 瑞士CH 14 巴PK,韩国KR	0 受惠国$_1$LD$_1$	70	---Other
		--其他:					--Other:
5408	7310.2910	---易拉罐及罐体	17.5	0 冰岛IS,东盟AS,哥CR,香港HK,新加坡SG,新西兰NZ,智利CL 5.2 秘鲁PE 10.5 澳AU 13.1 瑞士CH 14 巴PK,韩国KR	0 受惠国LD	70	---Steel tear tab ends and bodies thereof

序号 No.	税则号列 Tariff Line	中文货品名称 Article Description in Chinese	最惠国税率 MFN(%)	协定税率 Agreement(%)	特惠税率 SP(%)	普通税率 Gen(%)	英文货品名称 Article Description
5409	7310.2990	---其他	17.5	0 冰岛IS,东盟AS,哥CR,香港HK,新加坡SG,新西兰NZ,智利CL 5.2 秘鲁PE 10.5 澳AU 13.1 瑞士CH 14 巴PK,韩国KR	0 受惠国LD	70	---Other
	73.11	**装压缩气体或液化气体用的钢铁容器:**					**Containers for compressed or liquefied gas, of iron or steel:**
5410	7311.0010	---零售包装用	17.5	0 冰岛IS,东盟AS,哥CR,香港HK,新加坡SG,新西兰NZ,智利CL 5.2 秘鲁PE 10.5 澳AU 12.3 瑞士CH 14 巴PK,韩国KR	0 受惠国$_1$LD$_1$	70	---For retail packing
5411	7311.0090	---其他	8	0 冰岛IS,东盟AS,哥CR,秘鲁PE,香港HK,新西兰NZ,智利CL 3.2 瑞士CH 4.8 澳AU 5 巴PK 6.9 韩国KR	0 受惠国$_1$LD$_1$	17	---Other
	73.12	**非绝缘的钢铁绞股线、绳、缆、编带、吊索及类似品:**					**Stranded wire, ropes, cables, plaited bands, slings and the like, of iron or steel, not electrically insulated:**
5412	7312.1000	-绞股线、绳、缆	4	0 澳AU,巴PK,冰岛IS,东盟AS,哥CR,秘鲁PE,新西兰NZ,智利CL 1.6 瑞士CH 2.4 韩国KR	0 受惠国$_1$LD$_1$	20	-Stranded wire, ropes and cables
5413	7312.9000	-其他	4	0 澳AU,巴PK,冰岛IS,东盟AS,哥CR,秘鲁PE,新西兰NZ,智利CL 1.6 瑞士CH 2.4 韩国KR	0 受惠国LD	20	-Other
	73.13	**带刺钢铁丝;围篱用的钢铁绞带或单股扁丝(不论是否带刺)及松绞的双股丝**					**Barbed wire of iron or steel; twisted hoop or single flat wire, barbed or not, and loosely twisted double wire, of a kind used for fencing, of iron or steel**
5414	7313.0000	带刺钢铁丝;围篱用的钢铁绞带或单股扁丝(不论是否带刺)及松绞的双股丝	7	0 冰岛IS,东盟AS,哥CR,秘鲁PE,新西兰NZ,智利CL 2.8 瑞士CH 4.2 澳AU,韩国KR 5 巴PK 6.3 亚太AP	0 受惠国LD	70	Barbed wire of iron or steel; twisted hoop or single flat wire, barbed or not, and loosely twisted double wire, of a kind used for fencing, of iron or steel
	73.14	**钢铁丝制的布(包括环形带)、网、篱、格栅;网眼钢铁板:**					**Cloth (including endless bands), grill, netting and fencing, of iron or steel wire; expanded metal of iron or steel:**
		-机织品:					-Woven cloth:
5415	7314.1200	--不锈钢制的机器用环形带	12	0 冰岛IS,东盟AS,哥CR,秘鲁PE,新加坡SG,新西兰NZ,智利CL 6 巴PK 7.2 澳AU 8.6 瑞士CH 9.6 韩国KR	0 受惠国LD	20	--Endless bands for machinery, of stainless steel

序号 No.	税则号列 Tariff Line	中文货品名称 Article Description in Chinese	最惠国税率 MFN(%)	协定税率 Agreement(%)	特惠税率 SP(%)	普通税率 Gen(%)	英文货品名称 Article Description
5416	7314.1400	--不锈钢制的其他机织品	12	0 冰岛IS,东盟AS,哥CR,秘鲁PE,瑞士CH,新加坡SG,新西兰NZ,智利CL 6 巴PK 7.2 澳AU 9.6 韩国KR	0 受惠国LD	20	--Other woven cloth, of stainless steel
5417	7314.1900	--其他	7	0 冰岛IS,东盟AS,哥CR,秘鲁PE,新西兰NZ,智利CL 3.5 巴PK 4.2 澳AU,韩国KR	0 受惠国LD	20	--Other
5418	7314.2000	-交点焊接的网、篱及格栅，其丝的最大截面尺寸在3毫米及以上，网眼尺寸在100平方厘米及以上	7	0 冰岛IS,东盟AS,哥CR,秘鲁PE,香港HK,新西兰NZ,智利CL 2.8 瑞士CH 4.2 澳AU,韩国KR 5 巴PK	0 受惠国LD	70	-Grill, netting and fencing, welded at the intersection, of wire with a maximum cross-sectional dimension of 3mm or more and having a mesh size of $100cm^2$ or more
		-其他交点焊接的网、篱及格栅：					-Other grill, netting and fencing, welded at the intersection:
5419	7314.3100	--镀或涂锌的	7	0 冰岛IS,东盟AS,哥CR,秘鲁PE,香港HK,新西兰NZ,智利CL 2.8 瑞士CH 4.2 澳AU,韩国KR 5 巴PK	0 受惠国LD	70	--Plated or coated with zinc
5420	7314.3900	--其他	7	0 冰岛IS,东盟AS,哥CR,秘鲁PE,香港HK,新西兰NZ,智利CL 2.8 瑞士CH 4.2 澳AU 5 巴PK 5.6 韩国KR	0 受惠国LD	70	--Other
		-其他网、篱及格栅：					-Other cloth, grill, netting and fencing:
5421	7314.4100	--镀或涂锌的	8	0 冰岛IS,东盟AS,哥CR,秘鲁PE,新西兰NZ,智利CL 3.2 瑞士CH 4.8 澳AU,韩国KR 5 巴PK 6 亚太AP	0 受惠国LD	20	--Plated or coated with zinc
5422	7314.4200	--涂塑的	8	0 冰岛IS,东盟AS,哥CR,秘鲁PE,新西兰NZ,智利CL 4.8 澳AU 5 巴PK 5.6 瑞士CH 6.4 韩国KR	0 受惠国LD	20	--Coated whith plastics
5423	7314.4900	--其他	8	0 冰岛IS,东盟AS,哥CR,秘鲁PE,新西兰NZ,智利CL 4.8 澳AU,韩国KR 5 巴PK 5.6 瑞士CH	0 受惠国LD	20	--Other
5424	7314.5000	-网眼钢铁板	8	0 冰岛IS,东盟AS,哥CR,秘鲁PE,香港HK,新西兰NZ,智利CL 3.2 瑞士CH 4.8 澳AU,韩国KR 5 巴PK	0 受惠国LD	70	-Expanded metal
	73.15	**钢铁链及其零件：**					**Chain and parts thereof, of iron or steel:**
		-铰接链及其零件：					-Articulated link chain and parts thereof:
		--滚子链：					--Roller chain:

序号 No.	税则号列 Tariff Line	中文货品名称 Article Description in Chinese	最惠国税率 MFN(%)	协定税率 Agreement(%)	特惠税率 SP(%)	普通税率 Gen(%)	英文货品名称 Article Description
5425	7315.1110	---自行车用	12	0 冰岛IS,东盟AS,哥CR,秘鲁PE,香港HK,新加坡SG,新西兰NZ,智利CL 6 巴PK 7.2 澳AU 8.4 瑞士CH 9.6 韩国KR	0 受惠国$_1$LD$_1$	80	---For bicycles
5426	7315.1120	---摩托车用	12	0 冰岛IS,东盟AS,哥CR,秘鲁PE,香港HK,新加坡SG,新西兰NZ,智利CL 6 巴PK 7.2 澳AU 8.4 瑞士CH 10.4 韩国KR	0 受惠国$_1$LD$_1$	80	---For motorcycles
5427	7315.1190	---其他	12	0 冰岛IS,东盟AS,哥CR,秘鲁PE,香港HK,新加坡SG,新西兰NZ,智利CL 6 巴PK 7.2 澳AU 8.4 瑞士CH 9.6 韩国KR	0 受惠国$_1$LD$_1$	80	---Other
5428	7315.1200	--其他链	12	0 冰岛IS,东盟AS,哥CR,秘鲁PE,新加坡SG,新西兰NZ,智利CL 6 巴PK 7.2 澳AU 8.4 瑞士CH 10.8 韩国KR	0 受惠国$_1$LD$_1$	80	--Other chain
5429	7315.1900	--零件	12	0 冰岛IS,东盟AS,哥CR,秘鲁PE,新加坡SG,新西兰NZ,智利CL 6 巴PK 7.2 澳AU 8.4 瑞士CH 9.6 韩国KR	0 受惠国$_1$LD$_1$	80	--Parts
5430	7315.2000	-防滑链	12	0 冰岛IS,东盟AS,哥CR,秘鲁PE,新加坡SG,新西兰NZ,智利CL 6 巴PK 7.2 澳AU 8.4 瑞士CH 9.6 韩国KR	0 受惠国$_1$LD$_1$	80	-Skid chain
		-其他链:					-Other chain:
5431	7315.8100	--日字环节链	12	0 冰岛IS,东盟AS,哥CR,秘鲁PE,新加坡SG,新西兰NZ,智利CL 6 巴PK 7.2 澳AU 8.4 瑞士CH 9.6 韩国KR	0 受惠国$_1$LD$_1$	80	--Stud-link
5432	7315.8200	--其他焊接链	12	0 冰岛IS,东盟AS,哥CR,秘鲁PE,新加坡SG,新西兰NZ,智利CL 6 巴PK 7.2 澳AU 8.4 瑞士CH 9.6 韩国KR	0 受惠国LD	80	--Other, welded link

序号 No.	税则号列 Tariff Line	中文货品名称 Article Description in Chinese	最惠国税率 MFN(%)	协定税率 Agreement(%)	特惠税率 SP(%)	普通税率 Gen(%)	英文货品名称 Article Description
5433	7315.8900	--其他	12	0 冰岛IS,东盟AS,哥CR,新加坡SG,新西兰NZ,智利CL 3.6 秘鲁PE 6 巴PK 7.2 澳AU 8.4 瑞士CH 9.6 韩国KR	0 受惠国$_1$LD$_1$	80	--Other
5434	7315.9000	-其他零件	10	0 冰岛IS,东盟AS,哥CR,秘鲁PE,新西兰NZ,智利CL 4 瑞士CH 5 巴PK 6 澳AU 8 韩国KR	0 受惠国$_1$LD$_1$	80	-Other parts
	73.16	**钢铁锚、多爪锚及其零件**					**Anchors, grapnels and parts thereof, of iron or steel**
5435	7316.0000	钢铁锚、多爪锚及其零件	10	0 冰岛IS,东盟AS,哥CR,秘鲁PE,新西兰NZ,智利CL 4 瑞士CH 5 巴PK 6 澳AU 8 韩国KR	0 受惠国$_1$LD$_1$	40	Anchors, grapnels and parts thereof, of iron or steel
	73.17	**钢铁制的钉、平头钉、图钉、波纹钉、U形钉（税号83.05的货品除外）及类似品，不论钉头是否用其他材料制成，但不包括铜头钉**					**Nails, tacks, drawing pins, corrugated nails, staples (other than those of heading 8305) and similar articles, of iron or steel, whether or not with heads of other material, but excluding such articles with heads of copper**
5436	7317.0000	钢铁制的钉、平头钉、图钉、波纹钉、U形钉（税号83.05的货品除外）及类似品，不论钉头是否用其他材料制成，但不包括铜头钉	10	0 冰岛IS,东盟AS,哥CR,新西兰NZ,智利CL 3 秘鲁PE 4 瑞士CH 5 巴PK 6 澳AU 8 韩国KR	0 受惠国$_1$LD$_1$	80	Nails, tacks, drawing pins, corrugated nails, staples (other than those of heading No.83.05) and similar articles, of iron or steel, whether or not with heads of other material, but excluding such articles with heads of copper
	73.18	**钢铁制的螺钉、螺栓、螺母、方头螺钉、钩头螺钉、铆钉、销、开尾销、垫圈（包括弹簧垫圈）及类似品：**					**Screws, bolts, nuts, coach screws, screw hooks, rivets, cotters, cotter pins, washers (including spring washers) and similar articles, of iron or steel:**
		-螺纹制品：					-Threaded articles:
5437	7318.1100	--方头螺钉	10	0 冰岛IS,东盟AS,哥CR,新西兰NZ,智利CL 3 秘鲁PE 4 瑞士CH 5 巴PK 6 澳AU	0 受惠国$_1$LD$_1$	80	--Coach screws
5438	7318.1200	--其他木螺钉	10	0 冰岛IS,东盟AS,哥CR,新西兰NZ,智利CL 3 秘鲁PE 4 瑞士CH 5 巴PK 6 澳AU 8 韩国KR	0 受惠国$_1$LD$_1$	80	--Other wood screws
5439	7318.1300	--钩头螺钉及环头螺钉	10	0 冰岛IS,东盟AS,哥CR,秘鲁PE,新西兰NZ,智利CL 4 瑞士CH 5 巴PK 6 澳AU	0 受惠国$_1$LD$_1$	80	--Screw hooks and screw rings

序号 No.	税则号列 Tariff Line	中文货品名称 Article Description in Chinese	最惠国税率 MFN(%)	协定税率 Agreement(%)	特惠税率 SP(%)	普通税率 Gen(%)	英文货品名称 Article Description
5440	7318.1400	--自攻螺钉	10	0 冰岛IS,东盟AS,哥CR,新加坡SG,新西兰NZ,智利CL 3 秘鲁PE 5 巴PK 6 澳AU 7 瑞士CH	0 受惠国$_1$LD$_1$	80	--Self-tapping screws
		--其他螺钉及螺栓，不论是否带有螺母或垫圈：					--Other screws and bolts, whether or not with their nuts or washers:
5441	7318.1510	---抗拉强度在800兆帕及以上的	8	0 巴PK,冰岛IS,东盟AS,哥CR,秘鲁PE,香港HK,新西兰NZ,智利CL 4 亚太AP 4.8 澳AU 5.6 瑞士CH 6.9 韩国KR	0 受惠国LD	80	---Of tensile strength of 800Mpa or more
5442	7318.1590	---其他	8	0 巴PK,冰岛IS,东盟AS,哥CR,秘鲁PE,香港HK,新西兰NZ,智利CL 4 亚太AP 4.8 澳AU 5.6 瑞士CH 6.9 韩国KR	0 受惠国LD	80	---Other
5443	7318.1600	--螺母	8	0 冰岛IS,东盟AS,哥CR,秘鲁PE,新西兰NZ,智利CL 4.8 澳AU 5 巴PK 5.6 瑞士CH	0 受惠国LD	80	--Nuts
5444	7318.1900	--其他	5	0 澳AU,巴PK,冰岛IS,东盟AS,哥CR,秘鲁PE,新西兰NZ,智利CL 2 瑞士CH 3 韩国KR	0 受惠国LD	80	--Other
		-无螺纹制品：					-Non-threaded articles:
5445	7318.2100	--弹簧垫圈及其他防松垫圈	10	0 冰岛IS,东盟AS,哥CR,秘鲁PE,香港HK,新加坡SG,新西兰NZ,智利CL 4 瑞士CH 5 巴PK 6 澳AU	0 受惠国LD	80	--Spring washers and other lock washers
5446	7318.2200	--其他垫圈	10	0 冰岛IS,东盟AS,哥CR,新加坡SG,新西兰NZ,智利CL 3 秘鲁PE 4 瑞士CH 5 巴PK 6 澳AU	0 受惠国LD	80	--Other washers
5447	7318.2300	--铆钉	10	0 冰岛IS,东盟AS,哥CR,秘鲁PE,香港HK,新加坡SG,新西兰NZ,智利CL 4 瑞士CH 5 巴PK 6 澳AU	0 受惠国LD	80	--Rivets
5448	7318.2400	--销及开尾销	10	0 冰岛IS,东盟AS,哥CR,秘鲁PE,新加坡SG,新西兰NZ,智利CL 5 巴PK 6 澳AU 7 瑞士CH 9 韩国KR	0 受惠国LD	80	--Cotters and cotter-pins

序号 No.	税则号列 Tariff Line	中文货品名称 Article Description in Chinese	最惠国税率 MFN(%)	协定税率 Agreement(%)	特惠税率 SP(%)	普通税率 Gen(%)	英文货品名称 Article Description
5449	7318.2900	--其他	10	0 冰岛IS,东盟AS,哥CR,秘鲁PE,新加坡SG,新西兰NZ,智利CL 4 瑞士CH 5 巴PK 6 澳AU	0 受惠国LD	80	--Other
	73.19	**钢铁制的手工缝针、编织针、引针、钩针、刺绣穿孔锥及类似制品;其他税号未列名的钢铁制安全别针及其他别针:**					**Sewing needles, knitting needles, bodkins, crochet hooks, embroidery stilettos and similar articles, for use in the hand, of iron or steel; safety pins and other pins of iron or steel, not elsewhere specified or included:**
		-安全别针及其他别针:					-Safety pins and other pins:
5450	7319.4010	---安全别针	10	0 澳门MO,冰岛IS,东盟AS,哥CR,秘鲁PE,新西兰NZ,智利CL 4 瑞士CH 5 巴PK 6 澳AU 8 韩国KR	0 受惠国LD	90	---Safety pins
5451	7319.4090	---其他别针	10	0 冰岛IS,东盟AS,哥CR,秘鲁PE,新西兰NZ,智利CL 4 瑞士CH 5 巴PK 6 澳AU 8 韩国KR	0 受惠国$_1$LD$_1$	90	---Other pins
5452	7319.9000	-其他	10	0 冰岛IS,东盟AS,哥CR,新西兰NZ,智利CL 3 秘鲁PE 5 巴PK 6 澳AU 7 瑞士CH	0 受惠国LD	80	-Other
	73.20	**钢铁制弹簧及弹簧片:**					**Springs and leaves for springs, of iron or steel:**
		-片簧及簧片:					-Leaf-springs and leaves therefor:
5453	7320.1010	---铁道车辆用	6	0 冰岛IS,东盟AS,哥CR,秘鲁PE,新西兰NZ,智利CL 2.4 瑞士CH 3.6 澳AU,韩国KR 5 巴PK	0 受惠国LD	14	---For railway locomotives and rollingstock
5454	7320.1020	---汽车用	10	0 冰岛IS,东盟AS,哥CR,秘鲁PE,新西兰NZ,智利CL 4 瑞士CH 5 巴PK 6 澳AU 9 韩国KR	0 受惠国LD	14	---For motor vehicles
5455	7320.1090	---其他	10	0 冰岛IS,东盟AS,哥CR,秘鲁PE,新加坡SG,新西兰NZ,智利CL 5 巴PK 6 澳AU 7 瑞士CH	0 受惠国LD	50	---Other
		-螺旋弹簧:					-Helical springs:
5456	7320.2010	---铁道车辆用	6	0 冰岛IS,东盟AS,哥CR,秘鲁PE,新西兰NZ,智利CL 2.4 瑞士CH 3.6 澳AU,韩国KR 5 巴PK	0 受惠国LD	14	---For railway locomotives and rollingstock

序号 No.	税则号列 Tariff Line	中文货品名称 Article Description in Chinese	最惠国税率 MFN(%)	协定税率 Agreement(%)	特惠税率 SP(%)	普通税率 Gen(%)	英文货品名称 Article Description
5457	7320.2090	---其他	10	0 冰岛IS,东盟AS,哥CR,秘鲁PE,新加坡SG,新西兰NZ,智利CL 5 巴PK 6 澳AU 7 瑞士CH 8.5 亚太AP 9 韩国KR	0 受惠国LD	50	---Other
		-其他:					-Other:
5458	7320.9010	---铁道车辆用	6	0 冰岛IS,东盟AS,哥CR,秘鲁PE,新西兰NZ,智利CL 2.4 瑞士CH 3.6 澳AU,韩国KR 5 巴PK	0 受惠国LD	14	---For railway locomotives and rolling-stock
5459	7320.9090	---其他	12	0 冰岛IS,东盟AS,哥CR,秘鲁PE,新加坡SG,新西兰NZ,智利CL 6 巴PK 7.2 澳AU 8.4 瑞士CH	0 受惠国LD	50	---Other
	73.21	**非电热的钢铁制家用炉、灶(包括附有集中供暖用的热水锅的炉)、烤肉架、烤炉、煤气灶、加热板和类似非电热的家用器具及其零件:**					**Stoves, ranges, grates, cookers (including those with subsidiary boilers for central heating), barbecues, braziers, gas rings, plate warmers and similar non-electric domestic appliances, and parts thereof, of iron or steel:**
		-炊事器具及加热板:					-Cooking appliances and plate warmers:
5460	7321.1100	--使用气体燃料或可使用气体燃料及其他燃料的	15	0 冰岛IS,东盟AS,哥CR,新加坡SG,新西兰NZ,智利CL 4.5 秘鲁PE 9 澳AU 10.5 瑞士CH 12 巴PK,韩国KR	0 受惠国$_1$LD$_1$	80	--For gas fuel or for both gas and other fuels
		--使用液体燃料的:					--For liquid fuel:
5461	7321.1210	---煤油炉	21	0 冰岛IS,东盟AS,哥CR,新加坡SG,新西兰NZ,智利CL 6.3 秘鲁PE 12.6 澳AU 14.7 瑞士CH 18.9 韩国KR	0 受惠国$_1$LD$_1$	80	---Kerosene cooking stoves
5462	7321.1290	---其他	21	0 冰岛IS,东盟AS,哥CR,新加坡SG,新西兰NZ,智利CL 6.3 秘鲁PE 12.6 澳AU 14.7 瑞士CH 18.9 韩国KR	0 受惠国$_1$LD$_1$	80	---Other
5463	7321.1900	--其他,包括使用固体燃料的	21	0 冰岛IS,东盟AS,哥CR,新加坡SG,新西兰NZ,智利CL 6.3 秘鲁PE 12.6 澳AU 14.7 瑞士CH 18.9 韩国KR	0 受惠国$_1$LD$_1$	80	--Other, including for solid fuel
		-其他器具:					-Other appliances:

序号 No.	税则号列 Tariff Line	中文货品名称 Article Description in Chinese	最惠国税率 MFN(%)	协定税率 Agreement(%)	特惠税率 SP(%)	普通税率 Gen(%)	英文货品名称 Article Description
5464	7321.8100	--使用气体燃料或可使用气体燃料及其他燃料的	23	0 冰岛IS,东盟AS,哥CR,新加坡SG,新西兰NZ,智利CL 6.9 秘鲁PE 11.5 巴PK 13.8 澳AU,亚太AP 16.1 瑞士CH 20.7 韩国KR	0 受惠国$_1$LD$_1$	80	--For gas fuel or for both gas and other fuels
5465	7321.8200	--使用液体燃料的	21	0 冰岛IS,东盟AS,哥CR,新加坡SG,新西兰NZ,智利CL 6.3 秘鲁PE 12.6 澳AU 14.7 瑞士CH 18.9 韩国KR	0 受惠国$_1$LD$_1$	80	--For liquid fuel
5466	7321.8900	--其他，包括使用固体燃料的	21	0 冰岛IS,东盟AS,哥CR,新加坡SG,新西兰NZ,智利CL 6.3 秘鲁PE 12.6 澳AU 14.7 瑞士CH 18.9 韩国KR	0 受惠国$_1$LD$_1$	80	--Other, including for solid fuel
5467	7321.9000	-零件	12	0 冰岛IS,东盟AS,哥CR,新加坡SG,新西兰NZ,智利CL 3.6 秘鲁PE 5 巴PK 7.2 澳AU 8.4 瑞士CH 9.6 韩国KR,亚太AP	0 受惠国LD	80	-Parts
	73.22	**非电热的钢铁制集中供暖用散热器及其零件;非电热的钢铁制空气加热器、暖气分布器（包括可分布新鲜空气或调节空气的）及其零件，装有电动风扇或鼓风机：**					**Radiators for central heating, not electrically heated, and parts thereof, of iron or steel; air heaters and hot-air distributors (including distributors which can also distribute fresh or conditioned air) , not electrically heated, incorporating a motor-driven fan or blower, and parts thereof, of iron or steel:**
		-散热器及其零件：					-Radiators and parts thereof:
5468	7322.1100	--铸铁制	21	0 冰岛IS,东盟AS,哥CR,新加坡SG,新西兰NZ,智利CL 6.3 秘鲁PE 12.6 澳AU 14.7 瑞士CH 18.9 韩国KR	0 受惠国$_1$LD$_1$	80	--Of cast iron
5469	7322.1900	--其他	21	0 冰岛IS,东盟AS,哥CR,新加坡SG,新西兰NZ,智利CL 6.3 秘鲁PE 12.6 澳AU 14.7 瑞士CH 18.9 韩国KR	0 受惠国$_1$LD$_1$	80	--Other
5470	7322.9000	-其他	20	0 冰岛IS,东盟AS,哥CR,新加坡SG,新西兰NZ,智利CL 6 秘鲁PE 12 澳AU 14 瑞士CH 17.3 韩国KR	0 受惠国LD	80	-Other

序号 No.	税则号列 Tariff Line	中文货品名称 Article Description in Chinese	最惠国税率 MFN(%)	协定税率 Agreement(%)	特惠税率 SP(%)	普通税率 Gen(%)	英文货品名称 Article Description
	73.23	餐桌、厨房或其他家用钢铁器具及其零件;钢铁丝绒;钢铁制擦锅器、洗刷擦光用的块垫、手套及类似品:					**Table, kitchen or other household articles and parts thereof, of iron or steel; iron or steel wool; pot scourers and scouring or polishing pads, gloves and the like, of iron or steel:**
5471	7323.1000	-钢铁丝绒;擦锅器及洗刷擦光用的块垫、手套及类似品	14	0 冰岛IS,东盟AS,哥CR,新加坡SG,新西兰NZ,智利CL 4.2 秘鲁PE 8.4 澳AU 9.8 瑞士CH 11.2 巴PK,韩国KR	0 受惠国$_1$LD$_1$	80	-Iron or steel wool; pot scourers and scouring or polishing pads, gloves and the like
		-其他:					-Other:
5472	7323.9100	--铸铁制，未搪瓷	20Δ10	0 冰岛IS,东盟AS,哥CR,新加坡SG,新西兰NZ,智利CL 6 秘鲁PE 12 澳AU 14 瑞士CH 17.3 韩国KR	0 受惠国$_1$LD$_1$	80	--Of cast iron, not enamelled
5473	7323.9200	--铸铁制，已搪瓷	20Δ10	0 冰岛IS,东盟AS,哥CR,新加坡SG,新西兰NZ,智利CL 6 秘鲁PE 12 澳AU 14 瑞士CH 17.3 韩国KR	0 受惠国$_1$LD$_1$	100	--Of cast iron, enamelled
5474	7323.9300	--不锈钢制	12	0 澳门MO,冰岛IS,东盟AS,哥CR,秘鲁PE,香港HK,新加坡SG,新西兰NZ,智利CL 5 巴PK 7.2 澳AU 8.4 瑞士CH,亚太AP 9.6 韩国KR	0 受惠国LD	80	--Of stainless steel
		--钢铁（铸铁除外）制，已搪瓷:					--Of iron (other than cast iron) or steel, enamelled:
5475	7323.9410	---面盆	20	0 冰岛IS,东盟AS,哥CR,新加坡SG,新西兰NZ,智利CL 6 秘鲁PE 12 澳AU 14 瑞士CH 17.3 韩国KR	0 受惠国$_1$LD$_1$	100	---Basin
5476	7323.9420	---烧锅	20Δ10	0 冰岛IS,东盟AS,哥CR,新加坡SG,新西兰NZ,智利CL 6 秘鲁PE 12 澳AU 14 瑞士CH 17.3 韩国KR	0 受惠国$_1$LD$_1$	100	---Casserole
5477	7323.9490	---其他	20	0 冰岛IS,东盟AS,哥CR,新加坡SG,新西兰NZ,智利CL 6 秘鲁PE 12 澳AU 14 瑞士CH 17.3 韩国KR	0 受惠国$_1$LD$_1$	100	---Other

序号 No.	税则号列 Tariff Line	中文货品名称 Article Description in Chinese	最惠国税率 MFN(%)	协定税率 Agreement(%)	特惠税率 SP(%)	普通税率 Gen(%)	英文货品名称 Article Description
5478	7323.9900	--其他	20	0 冰岛IS,东盟AS,哥CR,新加坡SG,新西兰NZ,智利CL 6 秘鲁PE 12 澳AU 14 瑞士CH 17.3 韩国KR	0 受惠国$_1$LD$_1$	80	--Other
	73.24	钢铁制卫生器具及其零件：					Sanitary ware and parts thereof, of iron or steel:
5479	7324.1000	-不锈钢制洗涤槽及脸盆	18∆10	0 冰岛IS,东盟AS,哥CR,香港HK,新加坡SG,新西兰NZ,智利CL 5.4 秘鲁PE 10.8 澳AU 12.6 瑞士CH 14.4 韩国KR	0 受惠国LD	80	-Sinks and wash basins, of stainless steel
		-浴缸：					-Baths:
5480	7324.2100	--铸铁制，不论是否搪瓷	10	0 冰岛IS,东盟AS,哥CR,新加坡SG,新西兰NZ,智利CL 3 秘鲁PE 4 瑞士CH 5 巴PK 6 澳AU 8 韩国KR	0 受惠国$_1$LD$_1$	100	--Of cast iron, whether or not enamelled
5481	7324.2900	--其他	30∆15	0 冰岛IS,东盟AS,哥CR,新加坡SG,新西兰NZ,智利CL 9 秘鲁PE 18 澳AU 21 瑞士CH 27 韩国KR	0 受惠国$_1$LD$_1$	100	--Other
5482	7324.9000	-其他，包括零件	25∆15	0 冰岛IS,东盟AS,哥CR,新加坡SG,新西兰NZ,智利CL 7.5 秘鲁PE 15 澳AU 17.5 瑞士CH 22.5 韩国KR	0 受惠国$_1$LD$_1$	100	-Other, including parts
	73.25	其他钢铁铸造制品：					Other cast articles of iron or steel:
		-无可锻性铸铁制：					-Of non-malleable cast iron:
5483	7325.1010	---工业用	7	0 东盟AS,哥CR,秘鲁PE,新西兰NZ,智利CL 2.8 瑞士CH 4.2 澳AU 5 巴PK 6 韩国KR	0 受惠国LD	40	---For technical use
5484	7325.1090	---其他	20	0 冰岛IS,东盟AS,哥CR,新加坡SG,新西兰NZ,智利CL 6 秘鲁PE 12 澳AU 14 瑞士CH 17.3 韩国KR	0 受惠国$_1$LD$_1$	90	---Other
		-其他：					-Other:
5485	7325.9100	--研磨机用的研磨球及类似品	10.5	0 冰岛IS,东盟AS,哥CR,新加坡SG,新西兰NZ,智利CL 3.2 秘鲁PE 5 巴PK 6.3 澳AU 7.4 瑞士CH 8.4 韩国KR	0 受惠国$_1$LD$_1$	40	--Grinding balls and similar articles for mills
		--其他：					--Other:

序号 No.	税则号列 Tariff Line	中文货品名称 Article Description in Chinese	最惠国税率 MFN(%)	协定税率 Agreement(%)	特惠税率 SP(%)	普通税率 Gen(%)	英文货品名称 Article Description
5486	7325.9910	---工业用	10.5	0 冰岛IS,东盟AS,哥CR,新加坡SG,新西兰NZ,智利CL 3.2 秘鲁PE 5 巴PK 6.3 澳AU 7.4 瑞士CH 8.4 韩国KR 8.9 亚太AP	0 受惠国$_1$LD$_1$	40	---For technical use
5487	7325.9990	---其他	20	0 冰岛IS,东盟AS,哥CR,新加坡SG,新西兰NZ,智利CL 6 秘鲁PE 10 巴PK 12 澳AU,亚太AP 14 瑞士CH 17.3 韩国KR	0 受惠国$_1$LD$_1$	90	---Other
	73.26	**其他钢铁制品:**					**Other articles of iron or steel:**
		-经锻造或冲压，但未经进一步加工:					-Forged or stamped, but not further worked:
5488	7326.1100	--研磨机用的研磨球及类似品	10.5	0 冰岛IS,东盟AS,哥CR,新加坡SG,新西兰NZ,智利CL 3.2 秘鲁PE 5 巴PK 6.3 澳AU 7.4 瑞士CH 8.4 韩国KR	0 受惠国$_1$LD$_1$	40	--Grinding balls and similar articles for mills
		--其他:					--Other:
5489	7326.1910	---工业用	10.5	0 冰岛IS,东盟AS,哥CR,新加坡SG,新西兰NZ,智利CL 3.2 秘鲁PE 5 巴PK 6.3 澳AU 7.4 瑞士CH	0 受惠国$_1$LD$_1$	40	---For technical use
5490	7326.1990	---其他	20	0 冰岛IS,东盟AS,哥CR,新加坡SG,新西兰NZ,智利CL 6 秘鲁PE 12 澳AU 14 瑞士CH 16 韩国KR	0 受惠国$_1$LD$_1$	90	---Other
		-钢铁丝制品:					-Articles of iron or steel wire:
5491	7326.2010	---工业用	10	0 冰岛IS,东盟AS,哥CR,秘鲁PE,新西兰NZ,智利CL 4 瑞士CH 5 巴PK,亚太AP 6 澳AU 8 韩国KR	0 受惠国$_1$LD$_1$	40	---For technical use
5492	7326.2090	---其他	18	0 冰岛IS,东盟AS,哥CR,新加坡SG,新西兰NZ,智利CL 5.4 秘鲁PE 9 巴PK 10.8 澳AU 12.6 瑞士CH,亚太AP 14.4 韩国KR	0 受惠国$_1$LD$_1$	90	---Other
		-其他:					-Other:
		---工业用:					---For technical use:

序号 No.	税则号列 Tariff Line	中文货品名称 Article Description in Chinese	最惠国税率 MFN(%)	协定税率 Agreement(%)	特惠税率 SP(%)	普通税率 Gen(%)	英文货品名称 Article Description
5493	7326.9011	----钢铁纤维及其制品	10.5	0 冰岛IS,东盟AS,哥CR,香港HK,新加坡SG,新西兰NZ,智利CL 3.2 秘鲁PE 5 巴PK 6.3 澳AU 7.4 瑞士CH 8.4 韩国KR 8.9 亚太AP	0 受惠国LD	40	----Iron or steel fibres and articles thereof
5494	7326.9019	----其他	10.5	0 冰岛IS,东盟AS,哥CR,香港HK,新加坡SG,新西兰NZ,智利CL 3.2 秘鲁PE 5 巴PK 6.3 澳AU 7.4 瑞士CH 8.4 韩国KR 8.9 亚太AP	0 受惠国LD	40	----Other
5495	7326.9090	---其他	8	0 冰岛IS,东盟AS,哥CR,秘鲁PE,香港HK,新加坡SG,新西兰NZ,智利CL 4.8 澳AU,韩国KR 5 巴PK 5.6 瑞士CH 6.8 亚太AP	0 受惠国LD	90	---Other

第七十四章
铜及其制品

注释：

本章所用有关名词解释如下：

一、精炼铜

按重量计含铜量至少为99.85%的金属；或按重量计含铜量至少为97.5%，但其他各种元素的含量不超过下表中规定的限量的金属：

其他元素表

元素		所含重量百分比
Ag	银	0.25
As	砷	0.5
Cd	镉	1.3
Cr	铬	1.4
Mg	镁	0.8
Pb	铅	1.5
S	硫	0.7
Sn	锡	0.8
Te	碲	0.8
Zn	锌	1
Zr	锆	0.3
其他元素*，每种		0.3

*其他元素，例如，铝、铍、钴、铁、锰、镍、硅。

二、铜合金

除未精炼铜以外的金属物质，按重量计含铜量大于其他元素单项含量，但：

1.按重量计至少有一种其他元素的含量超过上表中规定的限量；

2.按重量计其他元素的总含量超过2.5%。

三、铜母合金

含有其他元素，但按重量计含铜量超过10%的合金，该合金无实用可锻性，通常用作生产其他合金的添加剂或用作冶炼有色金属的脱氧剂、脱硫剂及类似用途。但按重量计含磷量超过15%的磷化铜归入税号28.48。

四、条、杆

轧、挤、拔或锻制的实心产品，非成卷的，其全长截面均为圆形、椭圆形、矩形（包括正方形）、等边三角形或规则外凸多边形(包括相对两边为弧拱形，另外两边为等长平行直线的“扁圆形”及“变形矩形”）。对于矩形（包括正方形）、三角形或多边形截面的产品，其全长边角可经磨圆。矩形（包括“变形矩形”）截面的产品，其厚度应大于宽度的十分之一。所述条、杆也包括同样形状及尺寸的铸造或烧结产品。该产品在铸造或烧结后再经加工(简单剪修或去氧化皮的除外)，但不具有其他税号所列制品或产品的特征。

线锭及坯段，已具锥形尾端或经其他简单加工以便送入机器制成盘条或管子等的，仍应作为未锻轧铜归入税号74.03。

Chapter 74
Copper and articles thereof

Notes:

In this Chapter the following expressions have the meanings hereby assigned to them:

1. Refined copper

Metal containing at least 99.85% by weight of copper;or metal containing at least 97.5% by weight of copper, provided that the content by weight of any other element does not exceed the limit specified in the following table:

TABLE-Other elements

Element		Limiting content % by weight
Ag	Silver	0.25
As	Arsenic	0.5
Cd	Cadmium	1.3
Cr	Chromium	1.4
Mg	Magnesium	0.8
Pb	Lead	1.5
S	Sulphur	0.7
Sn	Tin	0.8
Te	Tellurium	0.8
Zn	Zinc	1
Zr	Zirconium	0.3
Other elements*, each		0.3

*Other elements are, for example, Al, Be, Co, Fe, Mn, Ni, Si.

2. Copper alloys

Metallic substances other than unrefined copper in which copper predominates by weight over each of the other elements, provided that:

(1) the content by weight of at least one of the other elements is greater than the limit specified in the foregoing table; or

(2) the total content by weight of such other elements exceeds 2.5%.

3. Master alloys Alloys containing with other elements more than 10% by weight of copper, not usefully malleable and commonly used as an additive in the manufacture of other alloys or as deoxidants, desulphurizing agents or for similar uses in the metallurgy of non-ferrous metals. However, copper phosphide (phosphor copper) containing more than 15% by weight of phosphorus falls in heading No.28.48.

4. Bars and rods

Rolled, extruded, drawn or forged products, not in coils, which have a uniform solid cross-section along their whole length in the shape of circles, ovals, rectangles (including squares), equilateral triangles or regular convex polygons (including "flattened circles" and "modified rectangles", of which two opposite sides are convex arcs, the other two sides being straight, of equal length and parallel). Products, with a rectangular (including square), triangular or polygonal cross-section may have corners rounded along their whole length.The thickness of such products which have a rectangular (including "modified rectangular") cross-section exceeds one-tenth of the width.The expression also covers cast or sintered products, of the same forms and dimensions, which have been subsequently worked after production (otherwise than by simple trimming or de-scaling), provided that they have not thereby assumed the character of articles or products of other headings.

Wire-bars and billets with their ends tapered or otherwise worked simply to facilitate their entry into machines for converting them into, for example, drawing stock (wire-rod) or tubes, are however to be taken to be unwrought copper of heading No.74.03.

五、型材及异型材

轧、挤、拔、锻制的产品或其他成型产品，不论是否成卷，其全长截面相同，但与条、杆、丝、板、片、带、箔、管的定义不相符合。同时也包括同样形状的铸造或烧结产品。该产品在铸造或烧结后再经加工(简单剪修或去氧化皮的除外)，但不具有其他税号所列制品或产品的特征。

5. Profiles

Rolled, extruded, drawn, forged or formed pruducts, coiled or not, of a uniform cross-section along their whole length, which do not conform to any of the definitions of bars, rods, wire, plates, sheets, strip, foil, tubes or pipes.The expression also covers cast or sintered products, of the same forms, which have been subsequently worked after production (otherwise than by simple trimming or descaling), provided that they have not thereby assumed the character of articles or products of other headings.

六、丝

盘卷的轧、挤或拔制实心产品，其全长截面均为圆形、椭圆形、矩形（包括正方形）、等边三角形或规则外凸多边形（包括相对两边为弧拱形，另外两边为等长平行直线的“扁圆形”及“变形矩形”）。对于矩形（包括正方形）、三角形或多边形截面的产品，其全长边角可经磨圆。矩形（包括“变形矩形”）截面的产品，其厚度应大于宽度的十分之一。

6. Wire

Rolled, extruded or drawn products, in coils, which have a uniform solid cross-section along their whole length in the shape of circles, ovals, rectangles (including squares), e-quilateral triangles or regular convex polygons (including “flattened circles”and“modified rectangles”, of which two opposite sides are convex arcs, the other two sides being straight, of equal length and parallel). Products with a rectangular (including square), triangular or polygonal cross-section may have corners rounded along their whole length.The thickness of such products which have a rectangular (including “modified rectangular”) cross-section exceeds one-tenth of the width.

七、板、片、带、箔

成卷或非成卷的平面产品(税号 74.03 的未锻轧产品除外)，截面均为厚度相同的实心矩形(不包括正方形)，不论边角是否磨圆（包括相对两边为弧拱形，另外两边为等长平行直线的“变形矩形”），并且符合以下规格:

1. 矩形(包括正方形)的，厚度不超过宽度的十分之一;

2. 矩形或正方形以外形状的，任何尺寸，但不具有其他税号所列制品或产品的特征。

税号 74.09 及 74.10 还适用于具有花样（例如，凹槽、肋条形、格槽、珠粒及菱形）的板、片、带、箔以及穿孔、抛光、涂层或制成瓦楞形的这类产品，但不具有其他税号所列制品或产品的特征。

7. Plates, sheets, strip and foil

Flat-surfaced products (other than the unwrought products of heading No.74.03), coiled or not, of soild rectangular (other than square) cross-section with or without rounded corners (including “modified rectangles” of which two opposite sides are convex arcs, the other two sides being straight, of equal length and parallel) of a uniform thickness, which are:

-of rectanglular (including square) shape with a thickness not exceeding one-tenth of the width.

-of a shape other than rectangular or square, of any size, provided that they do not assume the character of articles or products of other headings.

Headings Nos.74.09 and 74.10 apply, *inter alia*, to plates, sheets, strip and foil with patterns (for example, grooves, ribs, chequers, tears, buttons, lozenges) and to such products which have been perforated, corrugated, polished or coated, provided that they do not thereby assume the character of articles or products of other headings.

八、管

全长截面及管壁厚度相同并只有一个闭合空间的空心产品，成卷或非成卷的，其截面为圆形、椭圆形、矩形（包括正方形）、等边三角形或规则外凸多边形。对于截面为矩形(包括正方形)、等边三角形或规则外凸多边形的产品，不论全长边角是否磨圆，只要其内外截面为同一圆心并为同样形状及同一轴向，也可视为管子。上述截面的管子可经抛光、涂层、弯曲、攻丝、钻孔、缩腰、胀口、成锥形或装法兰、颈圈或套环。

8.Tubes and pipes

Hollow products, coiled or not, which have a uniform cross-section with only onc enclosed void along their whole length in the shape of circles, ovals, rectangles (including squares), equilateral triangles or regular convex polygons, and which have a uniform wall thickness. Products with a rectangular (including square), equilateral triangular or regular convex polygonal cross-section, which may have corners rounded along their whole length, are also to be taken to be tubes and pipes provided the inner and outer cross-sections are concentric and have the same form and orientation.Tubes and pipes of the foregoing cross-sections may be polished, coated, bent, threaded, drilled, waisted, expanded, cone-shaped or fitted with flanges, collars or rings.

子目注释:

本章所用有关名词解释如下:

一、铜锌合金（黄铜）铜与锌的合金，不论是否含有其他元素。含有其他元素时:

按重量计含锌量应大于其他各种元素的单项含量;

按重量计含镍量应低于 5%[参见铜镍锌合金(德银)];

Subheading Notes:

In this Chapter the following expressions have the meanings hereby assigned to them:

1. opper-zinc base alloys (brasses)

Alloys of copper and zinc, with or without other elements.When other elments are present:

-zinc predominates by weight over each of such other elements;

-any nickel content by weight is less than 5% (seecop-

按重量计含锡量应低于 3%［参见铜锡合金（青铜）］。

二、铜锡合金（青铜）

铜与锡的合金，不论是否含有其他元素。含有其他元素时，按重量计含锡量应大于其他各种元素的单项含量。当按重量计含锡量在 3%及以上时，锌的含量可大于锡的含量，但必须小于 10%。

三、铜镍锌合金（德银）

铜、镍、锌的合金，不论是否含有其他元素，按重量计含镍量在 5%及以上［参见铜锌合金（黄铜）］。

四、铜镍合金

铜与镍的合金，不论是否含有其他元素，但按重量计含锌量不得大于 1%。含有其他元素时，按重量计含镍量应大于其他各种元素的单项含量。

per-nickel-zinc alloys (nickel silvers));

-any tin content by weight is less than 3% (see copper-tinalloys (bronzes)).

2. Copper-tin base alloys (bronzes)

Alloys of copper and tin, with or without other elements. When other elements are present, tin predominates by weight over each of such other elements, except that when the tin content is 3% or more the zinc content by weight may exceed that of tin but must be less than 10%.

3. Copper-nickel-zinc base alloys (nickel silvers)

Alloys of copper, nickel and zinc, with or without other elements. The nickelcontent is 5% or more by weight (see copper- zinc alloys (brasses)).

4. Copper-nickel base alloys

Alloys of copper and nickel, with or without other elements but in any case containing by weight not more than 1% of zinc. When other elements are present, nickel predominates by weight over each of such other elements.

序号 No.	税则号列 Tariff Line	中文货品名称 Article Description in Chinese	最惠国税率 MFN(%)	协定税率 Agreement(%)		特惠税率 SP(%)		普通税率 Gen(%)	英文货品名称 Article Description
	74.01	**铜锍;沉积铜（泥铜）**							**Copper mattes; cement copper (precipitated copper)**
5496	7401.0000	铜锍,沉积铜(泥铜)	2	0	澳AU,巴PK,冰岛IS,东盟AS,哥CR,韩国KR,秘鲁PE,瑞士CH,新西兰NZ,智利CL	0	老挝LA,受惠国LD	11	Copper mattes, cement copper (precipitated copped)
	ex74010000	铜锍	Δ0						Copper mattes
	74.02	**未精炼铜;电解精炼用的铜阳极**							**Unrefined copper; copper anodes for electrolytic refining**
5497	7402.0000	未精炼铜;电解精炼用的铜阳极	2Δ0	0	澳AU,巴PK,冰岛IS,东盟AS,哥CR,韩国KR,瑞士CH,新西兰NZ,智利CL	0	受惠国LD	11	Unrefined copper; copper anodes for electrolytic refining
	74.03	**未锻轧的精炼铜及铜合金:**							**Refined copper and copper alloys, unwrought:**
		-精炼铜:							-Refined copper:
		--阴极及阴极型材:							--Cathodes and sections of cathodes:
		---阴极:							---Cathodes:
5498	7403.1111	----按重量计铜含量超过99. 9935%的	2Δ0	0	澳AU,巴PK,冰岛IS,东盟AS,哥CR,韩国KR,秘鲁PE,瑞士CH,新西兰NZ,智利CL	0	受惠国LD	11	----Containing by weight more than 99.9935% of copper
5499	7403.1119	----其他	2Δ0	0	澳AU,巴PK,冰岛IS,东盟AS,哥CR,韩国KR,秘鲁PE,瑞士CH,新西兰NZ,智利CL	0	受惠国LD	11	----Other
5500	7403.1190	---阴极型材	2Δ0	0	澳AU,巴PK,冰岛IS,东盟AS,哥CR,韩国KR,秘鲁PE,瑞士CH,新西兰NZ,智利CL	0	受惠国LD	11	---Sections of cathodes
5501	7403.1200	--线锭	2Δ0	0 1.4	澳AU,巴PK,冰岛IS,东盟AS,哥CR,韩国KR,秘鲁PE,新西兰NZ,智利CL 瑞士CH	0	受惠国LD	11	--Wire-bars
5502	7403.1300	--坯段	2Δ0	0	澳AU,巴PK,冰岛IS,东盟AS,哥CR,韩国KR,秘鲁PE,瑞士CH,新西兰NZ,智利CL	0	受惠国LD	11	--Billets
5503	7403.1900	--其他	2Δ0	0	澳AU,巴PK,冰岛IS,东盟AS,哥CR,韩国KR,秘鲁PE,瑞士CH,新西兰NZ,智利CL	0	受惠国LD	11	--Other

序号 No.	税则号列 Tariff Line	中文货品名称 Article Description in Chinese	最惠国税率 MFN(%)	协定税率 Agreement(%)		特惠税率 SP(%)		普通税率 Gen(%)	英文货品名称 Article Description
		-铜合金:							-Copper alloys:
5504	7403.2100	--铜锌合金(黄铜)	1	0	澳AU,澳门MO,巴PK,冰岛IS,东盟AS,哥CR,韩国KR,秘鲁PE,瑞士CH,新西兰NZ,智利CL	0	受惠国LD	14	--Copper-zinc base alloys (brass)
5505	7403.2200	--铜锡合金(青铜)	1	0	澳AU,巴PK,冰岛IS,东盟AS,哥CR,韩国KR,秘鲁PE,瑞士CH,新西兰NZ,智利CL	0	受惠国LD	17	--Copper-tin base alloys (bronze)
5506	7403.2900	--其他铜合金(税号74.05的铜母合金除外)	1	0	澳AU,巴PK,冰岛IS,东盟AS,哥CR,韩国KR,秘鲁PE,瑞士CH,新西兰NZ,智利CL	0	受惠国LD	17	--Other copper alloys (other than master alloys of heading No.74.05)
	74.04	**铜废碎料**							**Copper waste and scrap**
5507	7404.0000	铜废碎料	1.5Δ0	0	澳AU,巴PK,冰岛IS,东盟AS,哥CR,韩国KR,瑞士CH,香港HK,新西兰NZ,智利CL	0	老挝LA,受惠国LD	11	Copper waste and scrap
	74.05	**铜母合金**							**Master alloys of copper**
5508	7405.0000	铜母合金	4	0	澳AU,巴PK,冰岛IS,东盟AS,哥CR,韩国KR,秘鲁PE,瑞士CH,香港HK,新西兰NZ,智利CL	0	受惠国$_1$LD$_1$	17	Master alloys of copper
	74.06	**铜粉及片状粉末:**							**Copper powders and flakes:**
		-非片状粉末:							-Powders of non-lamellar structure:
5509	7406.1010	---精炼铜制	3	0	澳AU,巴PK,冰岛IS,东盟AS,哥CR,韩国KR,秘鲁PE,瑞士CH,新西兰NZ,智利CL	0	受惠国LD	14	---Of refined copper
5510	7406.1020	---铜镍合金(白铜)或铜镍锌合金(德银)制	6	0 2.4 3.6 5	冰岛IS,东盟AS,哥CR,秘鲁PE,新西兰NZ,智利CL 瑞士CH 澳AU,韩国KR 巴PK	0	受惠国LD	40	---Of copper-nickel base alloys (cupronickel) or copper-nickel-zinc base alloys (nickel silver)
5511	7406.1030	---铜锌合金(黄铜)制	6	0 2.4 3.6 4.8 5	冰岛IS,东盟AS,哥CR,秘鲁PE,新西兰NZ,智利CL 瑞士CH 澳AU 韩国KR 巴PK	0	受惠国LD	30	---Of copper-zinc base alloys (brass)
5512	7406.1040	---铜锡合金(青铜)制	6	0 2.4 3.6 5	冰岛IS,东盟AS,哥CR,秘鲁PE,新西兰NZ,智利CL 瑞士CH 澳AU,韩国KR 巴PK	0	受惠国LD	30	---Of copper-tin base alloys (bronze)
5513	7406.1090	---其他铜合金制	6	0 2.4 3.6 5	冰岛IS,东盟AS,哥CR,秘鲁PE,新西兰NZ,智利CL 瑞士CH 澳AU,韩国KR 巴PK	0	受惠国LD	30	---Other
		-片状粉末:							-Powders of lamellar structure; flakes:
5514	7406.2010	---精炼铜制	4	0	澳AU,巴PK,冰岛IS,东盟AS,哥CR,韩国KR,秘鲁PE,瑞士CH,新西兰NZ,智利CL	0	受惠国LD	14	---Of refined copper

序号 No.	税则号列 Tariff Line	中文货品名称 Article Description in Chinese	最惠国税率 MFN(%)	协定税率 Agreement(%)	特惠税率 SP(%)	普通税率 Gen(%)	英文货品名称 Article Description
5515	7406.2020	---铜镍合金（白铜）或铜镍锌合金（德银）制	6	0 冰岛IS,东盟AS,哥CR,秘鲁PE,新西兰NZ,智利CL 2.4 瑞士CH 3.6 澳AU,韩国KR 5 巴PK	0 受惠国LD	40	---Of copper-nickel base alloys (cupronickel) or copper-nickel-zinc base alloys (nickel silver)
5516	7406.2090	---其他铜合金制	6	0 冰岛IS,东盟AS,哥CR,秘鲁PE,新西兰NZ,智利CL 2.4 瑞士CH 3.6 澳AU,韩国KR 5 巴PK	0 受惠国LD	30	---Other
	74.07	铜条、杆、型材及异型材:					**Copper bars, rods and profiles:**
		-精炼铜制:					-Of refined copper:
5517	7407.1010	---铬锆铜制	4	0 澳AU,巴PK,冰岛IS,东盟AS,哥CR,韩国KR,秘鲁PE,台湾TW,新西兰NZ,智利CL 1.6 瑞士CH	0 受惠国LD	14	---Of chrominm and zirconium copper
5518	7407.1090	---其他	4	0 澳AU,巴PK,冰岛IS,东盟AS,哥CR,韩国KR,秘鲁PE,台湾TW,新西兰NZ,智利CL 1.6 瑞士CH	0 受惠国LD	14	---Other
		-铜合金制:					-Of copper alloys:
		--铜锌合金（黄铜）:					--Of copper-zinc base alloys (brass) :
		---铜条、杆:					---Copper bars and rods:
5519	7407.2111	----直线度不大于0.5毫米/米	7	0 澳门MO,冰岛IS,东盟AS,哥CR,秘鲁PE,台湾TW,新西兰NZ,智利CL 4.2 澳AU 4.9 瑞士CH 5 巴PK	0 受惠国LD	20	----Of a straightness not exceeding 0.5mm/m
5520	7407.2119	----其他	7	0 澳门MO,冰岛IS,东盟AS,哥CR,秘鲁PE,台湾TW,新西兰NZ,智利CL 4.2 澳AU 4.9 瑞士CH 5 巴PK	0 受惠国LD	20	----Other
5521	7407.2190	---其他	7	0 澳门MO,冰岛IS,东盟AS,哥CR,秘鲁PE,台湾TW,新西兰NZ,智利CL 4.2 澳AU 4.9 瑞士CH 5 巴PK	0 受惠国LD	20	---Other
5522	7407.2900	--其他	7	0 冰岛IS,东盟AS,哥CR,韩国KR,秘鲁PE,台湾TW,新西兰NZ,智利CL 4.2 澳AU 4.9 瑞士CH 5 巴PK	0 受惠国LD	20	--Other
	74.08	**铜丝:**					**Copper wire:**
		-精炼铜制:					-Of refined copper:
5523	7408.1100	--最大截面尺寸超过6毫米	4	0 澳AU,巴PK,冰岛IS,东盟AS,哥CR,韩国KR,瑞士CH,台湾TW,新西兰NZ,智利CL 1.2 秘鲁PE 2.8 亚太AP	0 受惠国LD	14	--Of which the maximum cross-sectional dimension exceeds 6mm
5524	7408.1900	--其他	4	0 澳AU,巴PK,冰岛IS,东盟AS,哥CR,韩国KR,秘鲁PE,台湾TW,香港HK,新西兰NZ,智利CL 1.6 瑞士CH 3.4 亚太AP	0 受惠国LD	14	--Other

序号 No.	税则号列 Tariff Line	中文货品名称 Article Description in Chinese	最惠国税率 MFN(%)	协定税率 Agreement(%)	特惠税率 SP(%)	普通税率 Gen(%)	英文货品名称 Article Description
	ex74081900	其他含氧量小于5PPM的精炼铜丝	Δ2				Other refined copper wire, containing oxygen not more than 5PPM
		-铜合金制:					-Of copper alloys:
5525	7408.2100	--铜锌合金（黄铜）	7	0 冰岛IS,东盟AS,哥CR,秘鲁PE,台湾TW,新西兰NZ,智利CL 2.8 瑞士CH 4.2 澳AU 5 巴PK 6 韩国KR	0 受惠国LD	20	--Of copper-zinc base alloys (brass)
		--铜镍合金（白铜）或铜镍锌合金（德银）:					--Of copper-nickel base alloys (cupro-nickel) or copper-nickel-zinc base alloys (nickel silver) :
5526	7408.2210	---铜镍锌铅合金(加铅德银)	8	0 冰岛IS,东盟AS,哥CR,秘鲁PE,新西兰NZ,智利CL 3.2 瑞士CH 4.8 澳AU,韩国KR 5 巴PK	0 受惠国LD	40	---Of copper-nickel-zinc-lead base alloys (leaded nickel silver)
5527	7408.2290	---其他	8	0 冰岛IS,东盟AS,哥CR,秘鲁PE,新西兰NZ,智利CL 3.2 瑞士CH 4.8 澳AU,韩国KR 5 巴PK	0 受惠国LD	40	---Other
5528	7408.2900	--其他	7	0 冰岛IS,东盟AS,哥CR,秘鲁PE,新西兰NZ,智利CL 2.8 瑞士CH 4.2 澳AU 5 巴PK 5.6 韩国KR	0 受惠国LD	20	--Other
	74.09	**铜板、片及带，厚度超过0.15毫米:**					**Copper plates, sheets and strip, of a thickness exceeding 0.15mm:**
		-精炼铜制:					-Of refined copper:
		--盘卷的:					--In coils:
5529	7409.1110	---氧含量不超过10PPM	4	0 澳AU,巴PK,冰岛IS,东盟AS,哥CR,秘鲁PE,瑞士CH,新西兰NZ,智利CL 2.4 韩国KR	0 受惠国LD	14	---Containing oxygen not more than 10PPM
5530	7409.1190	---其他	4	0 澳AU,巴PK,冰岛IS,东盟AS,哥CR,秘鲁PE,瑞士CH,新西兰NZ,智利CL 2.4 韩国KR	0 受惠国LD	14	---Other
5531	7409.1900	--其他	4	0 澳AU,巴PK,冰岛IS,东盟AS,哥CR,韩国KR,秘鲁PE,台湾TW,新西兰NZ,智利CL 1.6 瑞士CH	0 受惠国LD	14	--Other
		-铜锌合金（黄铜）制:					-Of copper-zinc base alloys (brass) :
5532	7409.2100	--盘卷的	7	0 冰岛IS,东盟AS,哥CR,秘鲁PE,台湾TW,香港HK,新西兰NZ,智利CL 4.2 澳AU 4.9 瑞士CH 5 巴PK 6 韩国KR	0 受惠国LD	20	--In coils

序号 No.	税则号列 Tariff Line	中文货品名称 Article Description in Chinese	最惠国税率 MFN(%)	协定税率 Agreement(%)	特惠税率 SP(%)	普通税率 Gen(%)	英文货品名称 Article Description
5533	7409.2900	--其他	7	0 冰岛IS,东盟AS,哥CR,秘鲁PE,台湾TW,香港HK,新西兰NZ,智利CL 2.8 瑞士CH 4.2 澳AU 5 巴PK 6 韩国KR	0 受惠国LD	20	--Other
		-铜锡合金（青铜）制：					-Of copper-tin base alloys (bronze) :
5534	7409.3100	--盘卷的	7	0 冰岛IS,东盟AS,哥CR,秘鲁PE,台湾TW,新西兰NZ,智利CL 2.8 瑞士CH 4.2 澳AU 5 巴PK 5.6 韩国KR	0 受惠国LD	20	--In coils
5535	7409.3900	--其他	7	0 冰岛IS,东盟AS,哥CR,韩国KR,秘鲁PE,台湾TW,新西兰NZ,智利CL 2.8 瑞士CH 4.2 澳AU 5 巴PK	0 受惠国LD	20	--Other
5536	7409.4000	-铜镍合金（白铜）或铜镍锌合金（德银）制	7	0 冰岛IS,东盟AS,哥CR,韩国KR,秘鲁PE,台湾TW,新西兰NZ,智利CL 2.8 瑞士CH 4.2 澳AU 5 巴PK	0 受惠国LD	40	-Of copper-nickel base alloys (cupronickel) or copper-nickel-zinc base al-loys (nickel silver)
5537	7409.9000	-其他铜合金制	7	0 冰岛IS,东盟AS,哥CR,秘鲁PE,台湾TW,香港HK,新西兰NZ,智利CL 2.8 瑞士CH 4.2 澳AU 5 巴PK 5.6 韩国KR	0 受惠国LD	20	-Of other copper alloys
	74.10	**铜箔（不论是否印花或用纸、纸板、塑料或类似材料衬背），厚度（衬背除外）不超过0.15毫米：**					**Copper foil (whether or not printed or backed with paper, paperboard, plastics or similar backing materials) of a thickness (excluding any backing) not exceeding 0.15mm:**
		-无衬背：					-Not backed:
5538	7410.1100	--精炼铜制	4	0 澳AU,巴PK,冰岛IS,东盟AS,哥CR,韩国KR,秘鲁PE,台湾TW,香港HK,新西兰NZ,智利CL 1.6 瑞士CH 2.8 亚太AP	0 受惠国$_1$LD$_1$	14	--Of refined copper
		--铜合金制：					--Of copper alloys:
5539	7410.1210	---铜镍合金（白铜）或铜镍锌合金（德银）	7	0 冰岛IS,东盟AS,哥CR,韩国KR,秘鲁PE,台湾TW,新西兰NZ,智利CL 2.8 瑞士CH 4.2 澳AU 5 巴PK	0 受惠国$_1$LD$_1$	40	---Of copper-nickel base alloys (cupronickel) or copper-nickel-zinc base alloys (nickel silver)
5540	7410.1290	---其他	7	0 冰岛IS,东盟AS,哥CR,韩国KR,秘鲁PE,台湾TW,新西兰NZ,智利CL 2.8 瑞士CH 4.2 澳AU 5 巴PK	0 受惠国$_1$LD$_1$	20	---Other
		-有衬背：					-Backed:
		--精炼铜制：					--Of refined copper:

序号 No.	税则号列 Tariff Line	中文货品名称 Article Description in Chinese	最惠国税率 MFN(%)	协定税率 Agreement(%)	特惠税率 SP(%)	普通税率 Gen(%)	英文货品名称 Article Description
5541	7410.2110	---印制电路用覆铜板	4	0 澳AU,澳门MO,巴PK,冰岛IS,东盟AS,哥CR,韩国KR,秘鲁PE,瑞士CH,台湾TW,香港HK,新西兰NZ,智利CL 3.4 亚太AP	0 受惠国$_1$LD$_1$	14	---Suitable for manufacturing printed circuit board
5542	7410.2190	---其他	4	0 澳AU,澳门MO,巴PK,冰岛IS,东盟AS,哥CR,韩国KR,秘鲁PE,瑞士CH,台湾TW,香港HK,新西兰NZ,智利CL 3.4 亚太AP	0 受惠国$_1$LD$_1$	14	---Other
		--铜合金制:					--Of copper alloys:
5543	7410.2210	---铜镍合金（白铜）或铜镍锌合金（德银）	7	0 冰岛IS,东盟AS,哥CR,秘鲁PE,新西兰NZ,智利CL 2.8 瑞士CH 4.2 澳AU,韩国KR 5 巴PK	0 受惠国$_1$LD$_1$	40	---Of copper-nickel base alloys (cupronickel) or copper-nickel-zinc base alloys (nickel silver)
5544	7410.2290	---其他	7	0 冰岛IS,东盟AS,哥CR,秘鲁PE,新西兰NZ,智利CL 2.8 瑞士CH 4.2 澳AU,韩国KR 5 巴PK	0 受惠国$_1$LD$_1$	20	---Other
	74.11	**铜管:**					**Copper tubes and pipes:**
		-精炼铜制:					-Of refined copper:
		---外径不超过25毫米的:					---The external diameter not exceeds 25mm:
5545	7411.1011	----带有螺纹或翅片的	4	0 澳AU,巴PK,冰岛IS,东盟AS,哥CR,秘鲁PE,瑞士CH,新西兰NZ,智利CL 2.4 韩国KR 2.8 亚太AP	0 受惠国LD	14	----With screw thread or wing
5546	7411.1019	----其他	4	0 澳AU,巴PK,冰岛IS,东盟AS,哥CR,秘鲁PE,瑞士CH,新西兰NZ,智利CL 2.4 韩国KR 2.8 亚太AP	0 受惠国LD	14	----Other
	ex74111019	其他含氧量小于5PPM，外径不超过25毫米的精炼铜管	Δ2				Other refined copper tubes and pipes with the external diameter not exceeding 25mm, containing oxygen not more than 5PPM
5547	7411.1020	---外径超过70毫米的	4	0 澳AU,巴PK,冰岛IS,东盟AS,哥CR,韩国KR,秘鲁PE,瑞士CH,新西兰NZ,智利CL 2.8 亚太AP	0 受惠国LD	14	---The external diameter exceeds 70mm
5548	7411.1090	---其他	4	0 澳AU,巴PK,冰岛IS,东盟AS,哥CR,韩国KR,秘鲁PE,新西兰NZ,智利CL 2.8 瑞士CH,亚太AP	0 受惠国LD	14	---Other
		-铜合金制:					-Of copper alloys:
		--铜锌合金（黄铜）:					--Of copper-zinc base alloys (brass) :
5549	7411.2110	---盘卷的	7	0 冰岛IS,东盟AS,哥CR,秘鲁PE,香港HK,新西兰NZ,智利CL 2.8 瑞士CH 4.2 澳AU,韩国KR 5 巴PK	0 受惠国LD	20	---Circumvolution

序号 No.	税则号列 Tariff Line	中文货品名称 Article Description in Chinese	最惠国税率 MFN(%)	协定税率 Agreement(%)	特惠税率 SP(%)	普通税率 Gen(%)	英文货品名称 Article Description
5550	7411.2190	---其他	7	0 冰岛IS,东盟AS,哥CR,秘鲁PE,香港HK,新西兰NZ,智利CL 2.8 瑞士CH 4.2 澳AU 5 巴PK 6 韩国KR	0 受惠国LD	20	---Other
5551	7411.2200	--铜镍合金（白铜）或铜镍锌合金（德银）	7	0 冰岛IS,东盟AS,哥CR,秘鲁PE,新西兰NZ,智利CL 2.8 瑞士CH 4.2 澳AU,韩国KR 5 巴PK	0 受惠国LD	40	--Of copper-nickel base alloys (cupronickel) or copper-nickel-zinc base alloys (nickel silver)
5552	7411.2900	--其他	7	0 冰岛IS,东盟AS,哥CR,秘鲁PE,新西兰NZ,智利CL 2.8 瑞士CH 4.2 澳AU,韩国KR 5 巴PK	0 受惠国LD	20	--Other
	74.12	**铜制管子附件（例如，接头、肘管、管套）：**					**Copper tube or pipe fittings (for example, couplings, elbows, sleeves) :**
5553	7412.1000	-精炼铜制	4	0 澳AU,巴PK,冰岛IS,东盟AS,哥CR,秘鲁PE,新西兰NZ,智利CL 2.4 韩国KR 2.8 瑞士CH	0 受惠国LD	14	-Of refined copper
		-铜合金制:					-Of copper alloys:
5554	7412.2010	---铜镍合金（白铜）或铜镍锌合金（德银）	7	0 冰岛IS,东盟AS,哥CR,秘鲁PE,新西兰NZ,智利CL 4.2 澳AU,韩国KR 4.9 瑞士CH 5 巴PK 6 亚太AP	0 受惠国LD	40	---Of coppernickel base alloys (cupron-ickel) or copper-nickel-zinc base alloys (nickel silver)
5555	7412.2090	---其他	7	0 冰岛IS,东盟AS,哥CR,秘鲁PE,新西兰NZ,智利CL 2.8 瑞士CH 4.2 澳AU,韩国KR 5 巴PK 6 亚太AP	0 受惠国LD	20	---Other
	74.13	**非绝缘的铜丝绞股线、缆、编带及类似品**					**Stranded wire, cables, plaited bands and the like, of copper, not electrically insulated**
5556	7413.0000	非绝缘的铜丝绞股线、缆、编带及类似品	5	0 澳AU,巴PK,冰岛IS,东盟AS,哥CR,秘鲁PE,新西兰NZ,智利CL 2 瑞士CH 4.3 韩国KR	0 受惠国LD	14	Stranded wire, cables plaited bands and the like, of copper, not electrically insulated
	74.15	**铜制或钢铁制带铜头的钉、平头钉、图钉、U形钉（税号83.05的货品除外）及类似品;铜制螺钉、螺栓、螺母、钩头螺钉、铆钉、销、开尾销、垫圈（包括弹簧垫圈）及类似品:**					**Nails, tacks, drawing pins, staples (other than those of heading 8305) and similar articles, of copper or of iron or steel with heads of copper; screws, bolts, nuts, screw hooks, rivets, cotters, cotter pins, washers (including spring washers) and similar articles, of copper:**
5557	7415.1000	-钉、平头钉、图钉、U形钉及类似品	8	0 冰岛IS,东盟AS,哥CR,秘鲁PE,新西兰NZ,智利CL 3.2 瑞士CH 4.8 澳AU,韩国KR 5 巴PK	0 受惠国LD	80	-Nails and tacks, drawing pins, staples and similar articles

序号 No.	税则号列 Tariff Line	中文货品名称 Article Description in Chinese	最惠国税率 MFN(%)	协定税率 Agreement(%)	特惠税率 SP(%)	普通税率 Gen(%)	英文货品名称 Article Description
		-其他无螺纹制品：					-Other articles, not threaded:
5558	7415.2100	--垫圈（包括弹簧垫圈）	10	0 冰岛IS,东盟AS,哥CR,秘鲁PE,香港HK,新加坡SG,新西兰NZ,智利CL 4 瑞士CH 5 巴PK 6 澳AU 8 韩国KR	0 受惠国LD	80	--Washers (including spring washers)
5559	7415.2900	--其他	10	0 冰岛IS,东盟AS,哥CR,秘鲁PE,香港HK,新加坡SG,新西兰NZ,智利CL 4 瑞士CH 5 巴PK 6 澳AU 8 韩国KR	0 受惠国LD	80	--Other
		-其他螺纹制品：					-Other threaded articles:
		--螺钉；螺栓及螺母：					--Screws; bolts and nuts:
5560	7415.3310	---木螺钉	8	0 冰岛IS,东盟AS,哥CR,秘鲁PE,香港HK,新西兰NZ,智利CL 3.2 瑞士CH 4.8 澳AU,韩国KR 5 巴PK	0 受惠国LD	80	---Screws for wood
5561	7415.3390	---其他	8	0 冰岛IS,东盟AS,哥CR,秘鲁PE,香港HK,新西兰NZ,智利CL 3.2 瑞士CH 4.8 澳AU,韩国KR 5 巴PK	0 受惠国LD	80	---Other
5562	7415.3900	--其他	10	0 冰岛IS,东盟AS,哥CR,秘鲁PE,香港HK,新西兰NZ,智利CL 4 瑞士CH 5 巴PK 6 澳AU 8 韩国KR	0 受惠国LD	80	--Other
	74.18	**餐桌、厨房或其他家用铜制器具及其零件；铜制擦锅器、洗刷擦光用的块垫、手套及类似品；铜制卫生器具及其零件：**					**Table, kitchen or other household articles and parts thereof, of copper; pot scourers and scouring or polishing pads, gloves and the like, of copper; sanitary ware and parts thereof, of copper:**
		-餐桌、厨房或其他家用器具及其零件；擦锅器及洗刷擦光用的块垫、手套及类似品：					-Table, kitchen or other household articles and parts thereof; pot scourers and scouring or polishing pads, gloves and the like:
5563	7418.1010	---擦锅器及洗刷、擦光用的块垫、手套及类似品	18	0 冰岛IS,东盟AS,哥CR,新加坡SG,新西兰NZ,智利CL 5.4 秘鲁PE 10.8 澳AU 12.6 瑞士CH 14.4 巴PK,韩国KR	0 受惠国LD	80	---Pot scourers and scouring or polishing pads, gloves and the like
5564	7418.1020	---非电热的铜制家用烹饪器具及其零件	20	0 冰岛IS,东盟AS,哥CR,新加坡SG,新西兰NZ,智利CL 6 秘鲁PE 12 澳AU 14 瑞士CH 17.3 韩国KR	0 受惠国$_1$LD$_1$	80	---Cooking or heating apparatus of a kind used for domestic purposes, non-electric, and parts thereof, of copper

序号 No.	税则号列 Tariff Line	中文货品名称 Article Description in Chinese	最惠国税率 MFN(%)	协定税率 Agreement(%)	特惠税率 SP(%)	普通税率 Gen(%)	英文货品名称 Article Description
5565	7418.1090	---其他	18∆10	0 冰岛IS,东盟AS,哥CR,新加坡SG,新西兰NZ,智利CL 5.4 秘鲁PE 10.8 澳AU 12.6 瑞士CH 14.4 巴PK,韩国KR	0 受惠国LD	80	---Other
5566	7418.2000	-卫生器具及其零件	18∆10	0 冰岛IS,东盟AS,哥CR,新加坡SG,新西兰NZ,智利CL 5.4 秘鲁PE 10.8 澳AU 12.6 瑞士CH 14.4 韩国KR	0 受惠国LD	80	-Sanitary ware and parts thereof
	74.19	**其他铜制品：**					**Other articles of copper:**
5567	7419.1000	-链条及其零件	14	0 冰岛IS,东盟AS,哥CR,秘鲁PE,香港HK,新加坡SG,新西兰NZ,智利CL 8.4 澳AU 9.8 瑞士CH 11.2 巴PK,韩国KR	0 受惠国$_1$LD$_1$	80	-Chain and parts thereof
		-其他：					-Other:
		--铸造、模压、冲压或锻造，但未经进一步加工的：					--Cast, moulded, stamped or forged, but not further worked:
5568	7419.9110	---工业用	10	0 东盟AS,哥CR,秘鲁PE,新加坡SG,新西兰NZ,智利CL 4 瑞士CH 5 巴PK,冰岛IS 6 澳AU,韩国KR	0 受惠国LD	40	---For technical use
5569	7419.9190	---其他	20	0 冰岛IS,东盟AS,哥CR,新加坡SG,新西兰NZ,智利CL 6 秘鲁PE 12 澳AU 14 瑞士CH 17.3 韩国KR	0 受惠国$_1$LD$_1$	80	---Other
		--其他：					--Other:
5570	7419.9920	---铜弹簧	10	0 冰岛IS,东盟AS,哥CR,秘鲁PE,新西兰NZ,智利CL 5 巴PK 6 澳AU 7 瑞士CH 8 韩国KR	0 受惠国$_1$LD$_1$	40	---Copper springs
5571	7419.9930	---铜丝制的布（包括环形带）	7	0 冰岛IS,东盟AS,哥CR,秘鲁PE,新西兰NZ,智利CL 2.8 瑞士CH 4.2 澳AU,韩国KR 5.6 巴PK	0 受惠国LD	20	---Cloth (including endless bands) , of copper wire
5572	7419.9940	---铜丝制的网、格栅、网眼铜板	8	0 冰岛IS,东盟AS,哥CR,秘鲁PE,新西兰NZ,智利CL 3.2 瑞士CH 4.8 澳AU 6.4 巴PK,韩国KR	0 受惠国LD	20	---Grill and netting, of copper wire; expanded meta of copper
5573	7419.9950	---非电热的铜制家用供暖器具及其零件	20	0 冰岛IS,东盟AS,哥CR,新加坡SG,新西兰NZ,智利CL 6 秘鲁PE 12 澳AU 14 瑞士CH 17.3 韩国KR	0 受惠国$_1$LD$_1$	80	---Cooking or heating apparatus of a kind used for domestic purposes, non-electric, and parts thereof, of copper

序号 No.	税则号列 Tariff Line	中文货品名称 Article Description in Chinese	最惠国税率 MFN(%)	协定税率 Agreement(%)	特惠税率 SP(%)	普通税率 Gen(%)	英文货品名称 Article Description
		---其他：					---Other:
5574	7419.9991	----工业用	10	0 东盟AS,哥CR,秘鲁PE,新加坡SG,新西兰NZ,智利CL 5 巴PK 6 澳AU,韩国KR 7 瑞士CH 8.5 亚太AP	0 受惠国LD	40	----For technical use
5575	7419.9999	----其他	20	0 冰岛IS,东盟AS,哥CR,新加坡SG,新西兰NZ,智利CL 6 秘鲁PE 12 澳AU 14 瑞士CH 16 巴PK 17 亚太AP 18 韩国KR	0 受惠国LD	80	----Other

第七十五章
镍及其制品

注释:

本章所用有关名词解释如下:

一、条、杆

轧、挤、拔或锻制的实心产品，非成卷的，其全长截面均为圆形、椭圆形、矩形（包括正方形）、等边三角形或规则外凸多边形（包括相对两边为弧拱形，另外两边为等长平行直线的“扁圆形”及“变形矩形”）。对于矩形（包括正方形）、三角形或多边形截面的产品，其全长边角可经磨圆。矩形（包括“变形矩形”）截面的产品，其厚度应大于宽度的十分之一。所述条、杆也包括同样形状及尺寸的铸造或烧结产品。该产品在铸造或烧结后再经加工（简单剪修或去氧化皮的除外），但不具有其他税号所列制品或产品的特征。

二、型材及异型材

轧、挤、拔、锻制的产品或其他成型产品，不论是否成卷，其全长截面相同，但与条、杆、丝、板、片、带、箔、管的定义不相符合。同时也包括同样形状的铸造或烧结产品。该产品在铸造或烧结后再经加工（简单剪修或去氧化皮的除外），但不具有其他税号所列制品或产品的特征。

三、丝

盘卷的轧、挤或拔制实心产品，其全长截面均为圆形、椭圆形、矩形（包括正方形）、等边三角形或规则外凸多边形（包括相对两边为弧拱形，另外两边为等长平行直线的“扁圆形”及“变形矩形”）。对于矩形（包括正方形）、三角形或多边形截面的产品，其全长边角可经磨圆。矩形（包括“变形矩形”）截面的产品，其厚度应大于宽度的十分之一。

Chapter 75
Nickel and articles thereof

Notes:

In this Chapter the following expressions have the meanings hereby assigned to them:

1. Bars and rods

Rolled, extruded, drawn or forged products, not in coils, which have a uniform soild cross-section along their whole length in the shape of circles, ovals, rectangles (including squares), equilateral triangles or regular convex polygons (including “flattened circles” and “modified rectangles”, of which two opposite sides are convex arcs, the other two sides being straight, of equal length and parallel). Products with a rectangular (including square), triangular or polygonal cross-section may have corners rounded along their whole length. The thickness of such products which have a rectangular (including “modified rectangular”) cross-section exceeds one-tenth of the width. The expression also covers cast or sintered products, of the same forms and dimensions, which have been subsequently worked after production (otherwise than by simple trimming or descaling), provided that they have not thereby assumed the character of articles or products of other headings.

2. Profiles

Rolled, extruded, drawn, forged or formed products, coiled or not, of a uniform cross-section along their whole length, which do not conform to any of the definitions of bars, rods, wire, plates, sheets, strip, foil, tubes or pipes. The expression also covers cast or sintered products, of the same forms, which have been subsequently worked after production (otherwise than by simple trimming or descaling), provided that they have not thereby assumed the character of articles or products of other headings.

3. Wire

Rolled, extruded or drawn products, in coils, which have a uniform soild cross-section along their whole length in the shape of circles, ovals, rectangles (including squares), equilateral triangles or regular convex polygons (including “flattened circles” and “modified rectangles”, of which two opposite sides are convex arcs, the other two sides being straight, of equal length and parallel).Products with a rectangular (including square), triangular or polygonal cross-section may have corners rounded along their whole length. The thickness of such products which have a rectangular (including “modified rectangular”) cross-section exceeds one-tenth of the width.

四、板、片、带、箔

成卷或非成卷的平面产品（税号75.02的未锻轧产品除外），截面均为厚度相同的实心矩形（不包括正方形），不论边角是否磨圆（包括相对两边为弧拱形，另外两边为等长平行直线的“变形矩形”），并且符合以下规格:

矩形（包括正方形）的，厚度不超过宽度的十分之一;

矩形或正方形以外形状的，任何尺寸，但不具有其他税号所列制品或产品的特征。

税号75.06还适用于具有花样（例如，凹槽、肋条形、格槽、珠粒及菱形）的板、片、带、箔以及穿孔、抛光、涂层或制成瓦楞形的这类产品，但不具有其他税号所列制品或产品的特征。

4. Plates, sheets, strip and foil

Flat-surfaced products (other than the unwrought products of heading No.75.02), coiled or not, of soild rectangular (other than square) cross-section with or without rounded corners (including “modified rectangles” of which two opposite sides are convex arcs, the other two sides being straight, of equal length and parallel) of a uniform thickness, which are:

-of rectanglular (including square) shape with a thickness not exceeding one-tenth of the width.

-of a shape other than rectangular or square, of any size, provided that they do not assume the character of articles or products of other headings.

Heading No.75.06 applies, *inter alia*, to plates, sheets, strip and foil with patterns (for example, grooves, ribs, chequers, tears, buttons, lozenges) and to such products which have been perforated, corrugated, polished or coated, provided that they do not thereby assume the character of articles or products of other headings.

五、管

全长截面及管壁厚度相同并只有一个闭合空间的空心产品，成卷或非成卷的，其截面为圆形、椭圆形、矩形（包括正方形）、等边三角形或规则外凸多边形。对于截面为矩形（包括正方形）、等边三角形或规则外凸多边形的产品，不论全长边角是否磨圆，只要其内外截面为同一圆心并为同样形状及同一轴向，也可视为管子。上述截面的管子可经抛光、涂层、弯曲、攻丝、钻孔、缩腰、胀口、成锥形或装法兰、颈圈或套环。

5.Tubes and pipes

Hollow products, coiled or not, which have a uniform crosssection with only one enclosed void along their whole length in the shape of circles, ovals, rectangles (including squares), equilateral triangles of regular convex polygons, and which have a uniform wall thickness. Products with a rectangular (including square), equilateral triangular, or regular convex polygonal cross-section, which may have corners rounded along their whole length, are also to be considered as tubes and pipes provided the inner and outer cross-sections are concentric and have the same form and orientation. Tubes and pipes of the foregoing cross-sections may be polished, coated, bent, threaded, drilled, waisted, expanded, cone-shaped or fitted with flanges, collars or rings.

子目注释:

一、本章所用有关名词解释如下:

（一）非合金镍

按重量计镍及钴的含量至少为99%的金属，但:

1.按重量计含钴量不超过1.5%;

2.按重量计其他各种元素的含量不超过下表中规定的限量;

Subheading Notes:

1. In this Chapter the following expressions have the meanings hereby assigned to them:

(a) Nickel, not alloyed

Metal containing by weight at least 99% of nickel plus cobalt, provided that:

(1) the cobalt by weight does not exceed 1.5%; and

(2) the content by weight of any other element does not exceed the limit specified in the following table:

其他元素表

元素		所含重量百分比
Fe	铁	0.5
O	氧	0.4
其他元素，每种		0.3

（二）镍合金

按重量计含镍量大于其他元素单项含量的金属物质，但：

1.按重量计含钴量超过1.5%；

2.按重量计至少有一种其他元素的含量超过上表中规定的限量；

3.除镍及钴以外，按重量计其他元素的总含量超过1%。

二、子目号7508.10所称“丝”，不受本章注释三的限制，仅适用于截面尺寸不超过6毫米的任何截面形状的产品，不论是否盘卷。

TABLE-Other elements

Element		Limiting content % by weight
Fe	Iron	0.5
O	Oxygen	0.4
Other elements, each		0.3

(b) Nickel alloys

Metallic substances in which nickel predominates by weight over each of the other elements provided that:

(1) the content by weight of cobalt exceeds 1.5%;

(2) the content by weight of at least one of the other elements is greater than the limit specified in the foregoing table;or

(3) the total content by weight of elements other than nickel plus cobalt exceeds 1%.

2.Notwithstanding the provisions of Chapter Note3, for the purposes of subheading No.7508.10 the term “wire” applies only to products, whether or not in coils, of any cross-sectional shape, of which no cross-sectional dimension exceeds 6mm.

序号 No.	税则号列 Tariff Line	中文货品名称 Article Description in Chinese	最惠国税率 MFN(%)	协定税率 Agreement(%)	特惠税率 SP(%)	普通税率 Gen(%)	英文货品名称 Article Description
	75.01	**镍锍、氧化镍烧结物及镍冶炼的其他中间产品：**					**Nickel mattes, nickel oxide sinters and other intermediate products of nickel metallurgy:**
5576	7501.1000	-镍锍	3Δ0	0 澳AU,巴PK,冰岛IS,东盟AS,哥CR,韩国KR,秘鲁PE,瑞士CH,新西兰NZ,智利CL	0 受惠国LD	11	-Nickel mattes
		-氧化镍烧结物及镍冶炼的其他中间产品：					-Nickel oxide sinters and other intermediate products of nickel metallurgy:
5577	7501.2010	---镍湿法冶炼中间品	3Δ0	0 澳AU,巴PK,冰岛IS,东盟AS,哥CR,韩国KR,秘鲁PE,瑞士CH,新西兰NZ,智利CL	0 受惠国LD	11	---Nickelintermediate products obtained by hydrometallurgical processing
5578	7501.2090	---其他	3Δ0	0 澳AU,巴PK,冰岛IS,东盟AS,哥CR,韩国KR,秘鲁PE,瑞士CH,新西兰NZ,智利CL	0 受惠国LD	11	---Other
	75.02	**未锻轧镍：**					**Unwrought nickel:**
		-非合金镍：					-Nickel, not alloyed:
5579	7502.1010	---按重量计镍、钴总量在99.99%及以上的，但钴含量不超过0.005%	3Δ1	0 澳AU,巴PK,冰岛IS,东盟AS,哥CR,韩国KR,秘鲁PE,瑞士CH,新西兰NZ,智利CL	0 受惠国LD	11	---Containing by weight no less than 99.99% of copper and cobalt, but no more than 0.005% of cobalt
5580	7502.1090	---其他	3Δ1	0 澳AU,巴PK,冰岛IS,东盟AS,哥CR,韩国KR,秘鲁PE,瑞士CH,新西兰NZ,智利CL	0 受惠国LD	11	---Other
5581	7502.2000	-镍合金	3	0 澳AU,巴PK,冰岛IS,东盟AS,哥CR,秘鲁PE,瑞士CH,新西兰NZ,智利CL 1.8 韩国KR	0 受惠国LD	11	-Nickel alloys
	75.03	**镍废碎料**					**Nickel waste and scrap**
5582	7503.0000	镍废碎料	1.5Δ1	0 澳AU,巴PK,冰岛IS,东盟AS,哥CR,韩国KR,秘鲁PE,瑞士CH,新西兰NZ,智利CL	0 受惠国LD	11	Nickel waste and scrap

序号 No.	税则号列 Tariff Line	中文货品名称 Article Description in Chinese	最惠国税率 MFN(%)	协定税率 Agreement(%)	特惠税率 SP(%)	普通税率 Gen(%)	英文货品名称 Article Description
	75.04	镍粉及片状粉末：					Nickel powders and flakes:
5583	7504.0010	---非合金镍粉及片状粉末	4	0 澳AU,巴PK,冰岛IS,东盟AS,哥CR,韩国KR,秘鲁PE,瑞士CH,新西兰NZ,智利CL	0 受惠国$_1$LD$_1$	17	---Nickel powders and flakes, not alloyed
5584	7504.0020	---合金镍粉及片状粉末	4	0 澳AU,巴PK,冰岛IS,东盟AS,哥CR,韩国KR,秘鲁PE,瑞士CH,新西兰NZ,智利CL	0 受惠国$_1$LD$_1$	17	---Nickel powders and flakes, alloys
	75.05	镍条、杆、型材及异型材或丝：					Nickel bars, rods, profiles and wire:
		-条、杆、型材及异型材：					-Bars, rods and profiles:
5585	7505.1100	--非合金镍制	6	0 冰岛IS,东盟AS,哥CR,秘鲁PE,新西兰NZ,智利CL 2.4 瑞士CH 3.6 澳AU 4.8 韩国KR 5 巴PK	0 受惠国LD	14	--Of nickel, not alloyed
5586	7505.1200	--镍合金制	6	0 冰岛IS,东盟AS,哥CR,秘鲁PE,新西兰NZ,智利CL 2.4 瑞士CH 3.6 澳AU 4.8 韩国KR 5 巴PK	0 受惠国LD	14	--Of nickel alloys
		-丝：					-Wire:
5587	7505.2100	--非合金镍制	6	0 冰岛IS,东盟AS,哥CR,秘鲁PE,新西兰NZ,智利CL 3.6 澳AU,韩国KR 4.2 瑞士CH 5 巴PK	0 受惠国LD	17	--Of nickel, not alloyed
5588	7505.2200	--镍合金制	6	0 冰岛IS,东盟AS,哥CR,秘鲁PE,新西兰NZ,智利CL 2.4 瑞士CH 3.6 澳AU,韩国KR 5 巴PK	0 受惠国LD	17	--Of nickel alloys
	75.06	镍板、片、带、箔：					Nickel plates, sheets, strip and foil:
5589	7506.1000	-非合金镍制	6	0 冰岛IS,东盟AS,哥CR,秘鲁PE,新西兰NZ,智利CL 2.4 瑞士CH 3.6 澳AU 4.8 韩国KR 5 巴PK	0 受惠国$_1$LD$_1$	14	-Of nickel, not alloyed
5590	7506.2000	-镍合金制	6	0 冰岛IS,东盟AS,哥CR,秘鲁PE,香港HK,新西兰NZ,智利CL 2.4 瑞士CH 3.6 澳AU,韩国KR 5 巴PK	0 受惠国$_1$LD$_1$	14	-Of nickel alloys
	75.07	镍管及管子附件（例如，接头、肘管、管套）：					Nickel tubes, pipes and tube or pipe fittings (for example, couplings, elbows, sleeves) :
		-镍管：					-Tubes and pipes:
5591	7507.1100	--非合金镍制	6	0 冰岛IS,东盟AS,哥CR,秘鲁PE,新西兰NZ,智利CL 3.6 澳AU,韩国KR 4.3 瑞士CH 5 巴PK	0 受惠国$_1$LD$_1$	17	--Of nickel, not alloyed

序号 No.	税则号列 Tariff Line	中文货品名称 Article Description in Chinese	最惠国税率 MFN(%)	协定税率 Agreement(%)	特惠税率 SP(%)	普通税率 Gen(%)	英文货品名称 Article Description
5592	7507.1200	--镍合金制	6	0 冰岛IS,东盟AS,哥CR,秘鲁PE,新西兰NZ,智利CL 2.4 瑞士CH 3.6 澳AU 4.8 韩国KR 5 巴PK	0 受惠国$_1$LD$_1$	17	--Of nickel alloys
5593	7507.2000	-管子附件	6	0 冰岛IS,东盟AS,哥CR,秘鲁PE,新西兰NZ,智利CL 2.4 瑞士CH 3.6 澳AU,韩国KR 5 巴PK	0 受惠国$_1$LD$_1$	17	-Tube or pipe fittings
	75.08	**其他镍制品:**					**Other articles of nickel:**
		-镍丝布、网及格栅:					-Cloth, grill and netting, of nickel wire:
5594	7508.1010	---镍丝布	6	0 冰岛IS,东盟AS,哥CR,秘鲁PE,新西兰NZ,智利CL 2.4 瑞士CH 3.6 澳AU,韩国KR 5 巴PK	0 受惠国$_1$LD$_1$	20	---Wire cloth
5595	7508.1080	---其他工业用镍制品	6	0 冰岛IS,东盟AS,哥CR,秘鲁PE,新西兰NZ,智利CL 2.4 瑞士CH 3.6 澳AU,韩国KR 5 巴PK	0 受惠国$_1$LD$_1$	40	---Other articles of nickel, for technical use
5596	7508.1090	---其他	6	0 冰岛IS,东盟AS,哥CR,秘鲁PE,新西兰NZ,智利CL 2.4 瑞士CH 3.6 澳AU,韩国KR 5 巴PK	0 受惠国$_1$LD$_1$	70	---Other
		-其他:					-Other:
5597	7508.9010	---电镀用镍阳极	4	0 澳AU,巴PK,冰岛IS,东盟AS,哥CR,秘鲁PE,瑞士CH,新西兰NZ,智利CL 2.4 韩国KR	0 受惠国$_1$LD$_1$	14	---Electroplating anodes
5598	7508.9080	---其他工业用镍制品	6	0 冰岛IS,东盟AS,哥CR,秘鲁PE,新西兰NZ,智利CL 2.4 瑞士CH 3.6 澳AU,韩国KR 5 巴PK	0 受惠国$_1$LD$_1$	40	---Other articles of nickel, for technical use
5599	7508.9090	---其他	6	0 冰岛IS,东盟AS,哥CR,秘鲁PE,新西兰NZ,智利CL 2.4 瑞士CH 3.6 澳AU,韩国KR 5 巴PK	0 受惠国$_1$LD$_1$	70	---Other

第七十六章
铝及其制品

注释:

本章所用有关名词解释如下:

一、条、杆

轧、挤、拔或锻制的实心产品，非成卷的，其全长截面均为圆形、椭圆形、矩形（包括正方形）、等边三角形或规则外凸多边形（包括相对两边为弧拱形，另外两边为等长平行直线的“扁圆形”及“变形矩形”）。对于矩形（包括正方形）、三角形或多边形截面的产品，其全长边角可经磨圆。矩形（包括“变形矩形”）截面的产品其厚度应大于宽度的十分之一。所述条、杆也包括同样形状及尺寸的铸造或烧结产品。该产品在铸造或烧结后再经加工（简单剪修或去氧化皮的除外），但不具有其他税号所列制品或产品的特征。

二、型材及异型材

轧、挤、拔、锻制的产品或其他成型产品，不论是否成卷，其全长截面相同，但与条、杆、丝、板、片、带、箔、管的定义不相符合。同时也包括同样形状的铸造或烧结产品。该产品在铸造或烧结后再经加工（简单剪修或去氧化皮的除外），但不具有其他税号所列制品或产品的特征。

三、丝

盘卷的轧、挤或拔制实心产品，其全长截面均为圆形、椭圆形、矩形（包括正方形）等边三角形或规则外凸多边形（包括相对两边为弧拱形，另外两边为等长平行直线的“扁圆形”及“变形矩形”）。对于矩形（包括正方形）、三角形或多边形截面的产品，其全长边角可经磨圆。矩形（包括“变形矩形”）截面的产品，其厚度应大于宽度的十分之一。

Chapter 76
Aluminium and articles thereof

Notes:

In this Chapter the following expressions have the meanings hereby assigned to them:

1. Bars and rods

Rolled, extruded, drawn or forged products, not in coils, which have a uniform solid cross-section along their whole length in the shape of circles, ovals, rectangles (including squares) , equilateral triangles or regular convex polygons (including "flattened circles" and "modified rectangles", of which two opposite sides are convex arcs, the other two sides being straight, of equal length and parallel). Products with a rectangular (including square), triangular or polygonal cross-section may have corners rounded along their whole length. The thickness of such products which have a rectangular (including "modified rectangular") cross-section exceeds one-tenth of the width. The expression also covers cast or sintered products, of the same forms and dimensions, which have been subsequently worked after production (otherwise than by simple trimming or descaling), provided that they have not thereby assumed the character of articles or products of other headings.

2. Profiles

Rolled, extruded, drawn, forged or formed products, coiled or not, of a uniform cross-section along their whole length, which do not conform to any of the definitions of bars, rods, wire, plates, sheets, strip, foil, tubes or pipes. The expression also covers cast or sintered products, of the same forms, which have been subsequently worked after production (otherwise than by simple trimming or descaling) , provided that they have not thereby assumed the character of articles or products of other headings.

3. Wire

Rolled, extruded or drawn products, in coils, which have a uniform soild cross-section along their whole length in the shape of circles, ovals, rectangles (including squares) , equilateral triangles or regular convex polygons(including "flattened circles" and "modified rectangles", of which two opposite sides are convex arcs, the other two sides being straight, of equal length and parallel) . Products with a rectangular (including square), triangular or polygonal cross-section may have corners rounded along their whole length. The thickness of such products which have a rectangular (including "modified rectangular") cross-section exceeds one-tenth of the width.

四、板、片、带、箔

成卷或非成卷的平面产品（税号 76.01 的未锻轧产品除外），截面均为厚度相同的实心矩形（不包括正方形），不论边角是否磨圆（包括相对两边为弧拱形，另外两边为等长平行直线的“变形矩形”），并且符合以下规格：

1. 矩形（包括正方形）的，厚度不超过宽度的十分之一；
2. 矩形或正方形以外形状的，任何尺寸，但不具有其他税号所列制品或产品的特征。税号 76.06 和 76.07 还适用于具有花样（例如，凹槽、肋条形、格槽、珠粒及菱形）的板、片、带、箔以及穿孔、抛光、涂层或制成瓦楞形的这类产品，但不具有其他税号所列制品或产品的特征。

五、管

全长截面及管壁厚度相同并只有一个闭合空间的空心产品，成卷或非成卷的，其截面为圆形、椭圆形、矩形（包括正方形）、等边三角形或规则外凸多边形。对于截面为矩形（包括正方形）、等边三角形或规则外凸多边形的产品，不论全长边角是否磨圆，只要其内外截面为同一圆心并为同样形状及同一轴向，也可视为管子。上述截面的管子可经抛光、涂层、弯曲、攻丝、钻孔、缩腰、胀口、成锥形或装法兰、颈圈或套环。

4. Plates, sheets, strip and foil

Flat-surfaced products (other than the unwrought products of heading No.76.01), coiled or not, of solid rectangular (other than square) cross-section with or without rounded corners (including “modified rectangles” of which two opposite sides are convex arcs, the other two sides being straight, of equal length and parallel) of a uniform thick-ness, which are:

-of rectangular (including square) shape with a thickness not exceeding one-tenth of the width;

-of a shape other than rectangular or square, of any size, provided that they do not assume the character of articles or products of other headings. Headings No. 76.06 and 76.07 apply, *inter alia*, to plates, sheets, strip and foil with patterns (for example, grooves, ribs, chequers, tears, buttons, lozenges) and to such products which have been perforated, corrugated, polished or coated, provided that they do not thereby assume the character of articles or products of other headings.

5. Tubes and pipes

Hollow products, coiled or not, which have a uniform cross-section with only one enclosed void along their whole length in the shape of circles, ovals, rectangles(including squares), equilateral triangles or regular convex polygons, and which have a uniform wall thickness. Products with a rectangular (including square), equilateral triangular or regular convex polygonal cross-section, which may have corners rounded along their whole length, are also to be considered as tubes and pipes provided the inner and outer cross-sections are concentric and have the same form and orientation. Tubes and pipes of the foregoing cross-sections may be polished, coated, bent, threaded, drilled, waisted, expanded, cone-shaped or fitted with flanges, collars or rings.

子目注释：

一、本章所用有关名词解释如下：

（一）非合金铝

按重量计含铝量至少为 99%的金属，但其他各种元素的含量不超过下表中规定的限量：

其他元素表

元素	所含重量百分比
Fe+Si（铁+硅）	1
其他元素（1），每种	0.1(2)

（1）其他元素，例如，铬、铜、镁、锰、镍、锌。

Subheading Notes:

1. In this Chapter the following expressions have the meanings hereby assigned to them:

(a) Aluminium, not alloyed

Metal containing by weight at least 99% of aluminium, provided that the content by weight of any other element does not exceed the limit specified in he following table:

TABLE-Other elements

Element	Limiting content % by weight
Fe+Si (iron plus silicon)	1
Other elements (1) ,each	0.1 (2)

(1) Other elements are, for example, Cr, Cu, Mg, Mn, Ni, Zn.

（2）含铜成分可大于0.1%，但不得大于0.2%，且铬和锰的含量均不得超过0.05%。

(2) Copper is permitted in a proportion greater than 0.1% but not more than 0.2%, provided that neither the chromium nor manganese content exceeds 0.05%.

（二）铝合金

按重量计含铝量大于其他元素单项含量的金属物质，但：

1. 按重量计至少有一种其他元素或铁加硅的含量大于上表中规定的限量；

2. 按重量计其他元素的总含量超过1%。

(b) Aluminium alloys

Metallic substances in which aluminium predominates by weight over each of the other elements, provided that:

(1) the content by weight of at least one of the other elements or of iron plus silicon taken together is greater than the limit specified in the foregoing table; or

(2) the total content by weight of such other elements exceeds 1%.

二、子目号7616.91所称“丝”，不受本章注释三的限制，仅适用于截面尺寸不超过6毫米的任何截面形状的产品，不论是否盘卷。

2. Notwithstanding the provisions of Chapter Note1(c), for the purposes of subheading No.7616.91 the term “wire” applies only to products, whether or not in coils, of any crosssectional shape, of which no cross-sectional dimension exceeds 6mm.

序号 No.	税则号列 Tariff Line	中文货品名称 Article Description in Chinese	最惠国税率 MFN(%)	协定税率 Agreement(%)	特惠税率 SP(%)	普通税率 Gen(%)	英文货品名称 Article Description
	76.01	**未锻轧铝：**					**Unwrought aluminium:**
		-非合金铝：					-Aluminium, not alloyed:
5600	7601.1010	---按重量计含铝量在99.95%及以上	5	0 澳AU,巴PK,冰岛IS,东盟AS,哥CR,秘鲁PE,瑞士CH,香港HK,新西兰NZ,智利CL 4 韩国KR	0 受惠国LD	14	---Containing by weight 99.95% or more of aluminium
5601	7601.1090	---其他	5Δ0	0 澳AU,巴PK,冰岛IS,东盟AS,哥CR,韩国KR,秘鲁PE,瑞士CH,香港HK,新西兰NZ,智利CL	0 受惠国LD	14	---Other
5602	7601.2000	-铝合金	7	0 澳门MO,冰岛IS,东盟AS,哥CR,秘鲁PE,新西兰NZ,智利CL 2.8 瑞士CH 4.2 澳AU,韩国KR 5 巴PK 6 亚太AP	0 受惠国LD	14	-Aluminium alloys
	76.02	**铝废碎料**					**Aluminium waste and scrap**
5603	7602.0000	铝废碎料	1.5Δ0	0 澳AU,巴PK,冰岛IS,东盟AS,哥CR,韩国KR,瑞士CH,香港HK,新西兰NZ,智利CL	0 受惠国LD	14	Aluminium waste and scrap
	76.03	**铝粉及片状粉末：**					**Aluminium powders and flakes:**
5604	7603.1000	-非片状粉末	6	0 冰岛IS,东盟AS,哥CR,秘鲁PE,新西兰NZ,智利CL 2.4 瑞士CH 3.6 澳AU,韩国KR 5 巴PK	0 受惠国LD	30	-Powders of non-lamellar structure
5605	7603.2000	-片状粉末	7	0 冰岛IS,东盟AS,哥CR,秘鲁PE,新西兰NZ,智利CL 2.8 瑞士CH 4.2 澳AU,韩国KR 5 巴PK	0 受惠国LD	30	-Powders of lamellar structure; flakes
	76.04	**铝条、杆、型材及异型材：**					**Aluminium bars, rods and profiles:**
		-非合金铝制：					-Of aluminium, not alloyed:

序号 No.	税则号列 Tariff Line	中文货品名称 Article Description in Chinese	最惠国税率 MFN(%)	协定税率 Agreement(%)	特惠税率 SP(%)	普通税率 Gen(%)	英文货品名称 Article Description
5606	7604.1010	---铝条、杆	5	0 澳AU,巴PK,冰岛IS,东盟AS,哥CR,秘鲁PE,瑞士CH,新西兰NZ,智利CL 3 韩国KR	0 受惠国LD	30	---Aluminium bars, rods
5607	7604.1090	---其他	5	0 澳AU,巴PK,冰岛IS,东盟AS,哥CR,秘鲁PE,瑞士CH,新西兰NZ,智利CL 4.3 韩国KR	0 受惠国LD	30	---Other
		-铝合金制:					-Of aluminium alloys:
5608	7604.2100	--空心异型材	5	0 澳AU,巴PK,冰岛IS,东盟AS,哥CR,秘鲁PE,瑞士CH,新西兰NZ,智利CL 4.3 韩国KR	0 受惠国LD	30	--Hollow profiles
		--其他:					--Other:
5609	7604.2910	---铝合金条、杆	5	0 澳AU,巴PK,冰岛IS,东盟AS,哥CR,秘鲁PE,新西兰NZ,智利CL 2 瑞士CH 3.5 亚太AP 4.3 韩国KR	0 受惠国LD	30	---Aluminium alloys bars, rods
5610	7604.2990	---其他	5	0 澳AU,巴PK,冰岛IS,东盟AS,哥CR,秘鲁PE,新西兰NZ,智利CL 2 瑞士CH 3 韩国KR 3.5 亚太AP	0 受惠国LD	30	---Other
	76.05	**铝丝:**					**Aluminium wire:**
		-非合金铝制:					-Of aluminium, not alloyed:
5611	7605.1100	--最大截面尺寸超过7毫米	8	0 冰岛IS,东盟AS,哥CR,秘鲁PE,新西兰NZ,智利CL 3.2 瑞士CH 4.8 澳AU,韩国KR 5 巴PK	0 受惠国$_1$LD$_1$	17	--Of which the maximum cross-sectional dimension exceeding 7mm
5612	7605.1900	--其他	8	0 冰岛IS,东盟AS,哥CR,秘鲁PE,香港HK,新西兰NZ,智利CL 3.2 瑞士CH 4.8 澳AU,韩国KR 5 巴PK 6.8 亚太AP	0 受惠国$_1$LD$_1$	17	--Other
		-铝合金制:					-Of aluminium alloys:
5613	7605.2100	--最大截面尺寸超过7毫米	8	0 冰岛IS,东盟AS,哥CR,秘鲁PE,新西兰NZ,智利CL 3.2 瑞士CH 4.8 澳AU,韩国KR 5 巴PK	0 受惠国$_1$LD$_1$	17	--Of which the maximum cross-sectional dimension exceeding 7mm
5614	7605.2900	--其他	8	0 冰岛IS,东盟AS,哥CR,秘鲁PE,新西兰NZ,智利CL 3.2 瑞士CH 4.8 澳AU,韩国KR 5 巴PK	0 受惠国$_1$LD$_1$	17	--Other
	76.06	**铝板、片及带，厚度超过0.2毫米:**					**Aluminium plates, sheets and strip, of a thickness exceeding 0.2mm:**
		-矩形（包括正方形）:					-Rectangular (including square) :
		--非合金铝制:					--Of aluminium, not alloyed:
		---厚度在0. 30毫米及以上，但不超过0. 36毫米:					---Of a thickness of 0.30mm or more but not exceeding 0.36mm:

序号 No.	税则号列 Tariff Line	中文货品名称 Article Description in Chinese	最惠国税率 MFN(%)	协定税率 Agreement(%)	特惠税率 SP(%)	普通税率 Gen(%)	英文货品名称 Article Description
5615	7606.1121	----铝塑复合的	6	0 巴PK,冰岛IS,东盟AS,哥CR,秘鲁PE,新西兰NZ,智利CL 2.4 瑞士CH 3.6 澳AU,韩国KR 4.2 亚太AP	0 受惠国LD	50	----Of aluminium-plastic composite
5616	7606.1129	----其他	6Δ4	0 巴PK,冰岛IS,东盟AS,哥CR,秘鲁PE,新西兰NZ,智利CL 2.4 瑞士CH 3.6 澳AU 4.2 亚太AP 5.2 韩国KR	0 受惠国LD	50	----Other
		---其他：					---Other:
5617	7606.1191	----铝塑复合的	6	0 巴PK,冰岛IS,东盟AS,哥CR,韩国KR,秘鲁PE,台湾TW,香港HK,新西兰NZ,智利CL 2.4 瑞士CH 3.6 澳AU 4.2 亚太AP	0 受惠国LD	30	----Of aluminium-plastic composite
5618	7606.1199	----其他	6	0 巴PK,冰岛IS,东盟AS,哥CR,秘鲁PE,台湾TW,香港HK,新西兰NZ,智利CL 2.4 瑞士CH 3.6 澳AU 4.2 亚太AP 4.8 韩国KR	0 受惠国LD	30	----Other
		--铝合金制：					--Of aluminium alloys:
5619	7606.1220	---厚度小于0.28毫米	6	0 巴PK,冰岛IS,东盟AS,哥CR,秘鲁PE,台湾TW,香港HK,新西兰NZ,智利CL 2.4 瑞士CH 3.6 澳AU 4.2 亚太AP 5.2 韩国KR	0 受惠国LD	30	---Of a thickness less than 0.28mm
5620	7606.1230	---厚度在0.28毫米及以上，但不超过0.35毫米	6	0 巴PK,冰岛IS,东盟AS,哥CR,秘鲁PE,台湾TW,香港HK,新西兰NZ,智利CL 2.4 瑞士CH 3.6 澳AU 4.2 亚太AP 5.2 韩国KR	0 受惠国LD	30	---Of a thickness of 0.28mm or more but not exceeding 0.35mm
		---厚度在0.35毫米以上，但不超过4毫米：					---Of a thickness of 0.35mm or more but not exceeding 4mm:
5621	7606.1251	----铝塑复合的	6	0 巴PK,冰岛IS,东盟AS,哥CR,秘鲁PE,香港HK,新西兰NZ,智利CL 3.6 澳AU 4.2 瑞士CH,亚太AP 4.8 韩国KR	0 受惠国LD	50	----Of aluminium-plastic composite
5622	7606.1259	----其他	6	0 巴PK,冰岛IS,东盟AS,哥CR,秘鲁PE,香港HK,新西兰NZ,智利CL 3.6 澳AU 4.2 瑞士CH,亚太AP 5.2 韩国KR	0 受惠国LD	50	----Other
5623	7606.1290	---其他	6	0 巴PK,冰岛IS,东盟AS,哥CR,秘鲁PE,香港HK,新西兰NZ,智利CL 3.6 澳AU,韩国KR 4.2 瑞士CH,亚太AP	0 受惠国LD	50	---Other
		-其他：					-Other:

序号 No.	税则号列 Tariff Line	中文货品名称 Article Description in Chinese	最惠国税率 MFN(%)	协定税率 Agreement(%)	特惠税率 SP(%)	普通税率 Gen(%)	英文货品名称 Article Description
5624	7606.9100	--非合金铝制	6	0 冰岛IS,东盟AS,哥CR,秘鲁PE,台湾TW,香港HK,新西兰NZ,智利CL 2.4 瑞士CH 3.6 澳AU 5 巴PK 5.2 韩国KR	0 受惠国LD	30	--Of aluminium, not alloyed
5625	7606.9200	--铝合金制	10	0 冰岛IS,东盟AS,哥CR,秘鲁PE,台湾TW,香港HK,新加坡SG,新西兰NZ,智利CL 4 瑞士CH 5 巴PK 6 澳AU 8.6 韩国KR	0 受惠国LD	30	--Of aluminium alloys
	76.07	**铝箔(不论是否印花或用纸、纸板、塑料或类似材料衬背),厚度(衬背除外)不超过0.2毫米:**					**Aluminium foil (whether or not printed or backed with paper, paperboard, plastics or similar backing materials) of a thickness (excluding any backing) not exceeding 0.2mm:**
		-无衬背:					-Not backed:
		--轧制后未经进一步加工的:					--Rolled but not further worked:
5626	7607.1110	---厚度不超过0.007毫米	6	0 冰岛IS,东盟AS,哥CR,秘鲁PE,新西兰NZ,智利CL 3.6 澳AU 4.2 瑞士CH 5 巴PK 5.2 韩国KR 5.7 亚太AP	0 受惠国$_1$LD$_1$	35	---Of a thickness not exceeding 0.007mm
5627	7607.1120	---厚度大于0.007毫米,但不超过0.01毫米	6	0 冰岛IS,东盟AS,哥CR,秘鲁PE,新西兰NZ,智利CL 2.4 瑞士CH 3.6 澳AU,韩国KR 5 巴PK 5.7 亚太AP	0 受惠国$_1$LD$_1$	35	---Of a thickness exceeding 0.007mm, but not exceeding 0.01mm
5628	7607.1190	---其他	6	0 东盟AS,哥CR,韩国KR,秘鲁PE,台湾TW,新西兰NZ,智利CL 2.4 瑞士CH 3.6 澳AU 5 巴PK 5.7 亚太AP	0 受惠国$_1$LD$_1$	35	---Other
5629	7607.1900	--其他	6	0 东盟AS,哥CR,秘鲁PE,台湾TW,新西兰NZ,智利CL 2.4 瑞士CH 3.6 澳AU 4.8 韩国KR 5 巴PK 5.1 亚太AP	0 受惠国$_1$LD$_1$	35	--Other
	ex76071900	化成箔	Δ3				Formed Al foil
5630	7607.2000	-有衬背	6	0 东盟AS,哥CR,秘鲁PE,台湾TW,香港HK,新西兰NZ,智利CL 3.6 澳AU 4.2 瑞士CH 5 巴PK 5.2 韩国KR	0 受惠国$_1$LD$_1$	35	-Backed
	76.08	**铝管:**					**Aluminium tubes and pipes:**

序号 No.	税则号列 Tariff Line	中文货品名称 Article Description in Chinese	最惠国税率 MFN(%)	协定税率 Agreement(%)	特惠税率 SP(%)	普通税率 Gen(%)	英文货品名称 Article Description
5631	7608.1000	-非合金铝制	8	0 冰岛IS,东盟AS,哥CR,秘鲁PE,新西兰NZ,智利CL 3.2 瑞士CH 4.8 澳AU 5 巴PK 6.9 韩国KR	0 受惠国LD	30	-Of aluminium, not alloyed
		-铝合金制:					-Of aluminium alloys:
5632	7608.2010	---外径不超过10厘米的	8	0 冰岛IS,东盟AS,哥CR,秘鲁PE,新西兰NZ,智利CL 3.2 瑞士CH 4.8 澳AU 5 巴PK 6.9 韩国KR	0 受惠国LD	30	---Having an outside diameter not exceeding 10cm
		---其他:					---Other:
5633	7608.2091	----壁厚不超过25毫米	8	0 冰岛IS,东盟AS,哥CR,秘鲁PE,新西兰NZ,智利CL 3.2 瑞士CH 4.8 澳AU,韩国KR 5 巴PK	0 受惠国LD	30	----Having a wall thickness not exceeding 25mm
5634	7608.2099	----其他	8	0 冰岛IS,东盟AS,哥CR,秘鲁PE,新西兰NZ,智利CL 3.2 瑞士CH 4.8 澳AU,韩国KR 5 巴PK	0 受惠国LD	30	----Other
	76.09	**铝制管子附件(例如,接头、肘管、管套)**					**Aluminium tube or pipe fittings (for example, couplings, elbows, sleeves)**
5635	7609.0000	铝制管子附件(例如,接头、肘管、管套)	8	0 冰岛IS,东盟AS,哥CR,秘鲁PE,新西兰NZ,智利CL 3.2 瑞士CH 4.8 澳AU 5 巴PK 6.4 韩国KR	0 受惠国LD	35	Aluminium tube or pipe fittings (for example, couplings, elbows, sleeves)
	76.10	**铝制结构体(税号94.06的活动房屋除外)及其部件(例如,桥梁及桥梁体段、塔、格构杆、屋顶、屋顶框架、门窗及其框架、门槛、栏杆、支柱及立柱);上述结构体用的已加工铝板、杆、型材、异型材、管子及类似品:**					**Aluminium structures (excluding prefabricated buildings of heading No.94.06) and parts of structures (for example, bridges and bridgesections, towers, lattice masts, roofs, roofing frameworks, doors and windows and their frames and thresholds for doors, balustrades, pillars and columns) ; aluminium plates, rods, profiles, tubes and the like, prepared for use in structures:**
5636	7610.1000	-门窗及其框架、门槛	25	0 澳门MO,冰岛IS,东盟AS,哥CR,新加坡SG,新西兰NZ,智利CL 7.5 秘鲁PE 15 澳AU 17.5 瑞士CH 22.5 韩国KR	0 受惠国$_1$LD$_1$	80	-Doors, windows and their frames and thresholds for doors
5637	7610.9000	-其他	6	0 冰岛IS,东盟AS,哥CR,秘鲁PE,新西兰NZ,智利CL 2.4 瑞士CH 3.6 澳AU,韩国KR 5 巴PK	0 受惠国LD	50	-Other

序号 No.	税则号列 Tariff Line	中文货品名称 Article Description in Chinese	最惠国税率 MFN(%)	协定税率 Agreement(%)	特惠税率 SP(%)	普通税率 Gen(%)	英文货品名称 Article Description
	76.11	**盛装物料用的铝制囤、柜、罐、桶及类似容器(装压缩气体或液化气体的除外),容积超过300升,不论是否衬里或隔热,但无机械或热力装置**					**Aluminium reservoirs, tanks, vats and similar containers, for any material (other than compressed or liquefied gas), of a capacity exceeding 300 litres, whether or not lined or heat-insulated, but not fitted with mechanical or thermal equipment**
5638	7611.0000	盛装物料用的铝制囤、柜、罐、桶及类似容器(装压缩气体或液化气体的除外),容积超过300升,不论是否衬里或隔热,但无机械或热力装置	12	0 冰岛IS,东盟AS,哥CR,秘鲁PE,新加坡SG,新西兰NZ,智利CL 6 巴PK 7.2 澳AU 8.4 瑞士CH 9.6 韩国KR	0 受惠国$_1$LD$_1$	35	Aluminium reservoirs, tanks, vats and similar containers, for any material (other than compressed or liquefied gas), of a capacity exceedIng 300 litres, whether or not lined or heat-insulated, but not fitted with mechanical or thermal equipment
	76.12	**盛装物料用的铝制桶、罐、听、盒及类似容器,包括软管容器及硬管容器(装压缩气体或液化气体的除外),容积不超过300升,不论是否衬里或隔热,但无机械或热力装置:**					**Aluminium casks, drums, cans, boxes and similar containers (including rigid or collapsible tubular containers), for any material (other than compressed or liquefied gas), of a capacity not exceeding 300 litres, whether or not lined or heat-insulated, but not fitted with mechanical or thermal equipment:**
5639	7612.1000	-软管容器	12	0 冰岛IS,东盟AS,哥CR,新加坡SG,新西兰NZ,智利CL 3.6 秘鲁PE 6 巴PK 7.2 澳AU 8.4 瑞士CH 9.6 韩国KR	0 受惠国LD	50	-Collapsible tubular containers
		-其他:					-Other:
5640	7612.9010	---易拉罐及罐体	30	0 冰岛IS,东盟AS,哥CR,新加坡SG,新西兰NZ,智利CL 9 秘鲁PE 18 澳AU 21 瑞士CH	0 受惠国$_1$LD$_1$	100	---Tear tab ends and bodies thereof
5641	7612.9090	---其他	12	0 冰岛IS,东盟AS,哥CR,新加坡SG,新西兰NZ,智利CL 3.6 秘鲁PE 6 巴PK 7.2 澳AU 8.4 瑞士CH 9.6 韩国KR	0 受惠国LD	70	---Other
	76.13	**装压缩气体或液化气体用的铝制容器:**					**Aluminium containers for compressed or liquefied gas:**
5642	7613.0010	---零售包装用	12	0 冰岛IS,东盟AS,哥CR,秘鲁PE,新加坡SG,新西兰NZ,智利CL 6 巴PK 7.2 澳AU 8.6 瑞士CH 9.6 韩国KR	0 受惠国$_1$LD$_1$	70	---For retail packing
5643	7613.0090	---其他	6	0 冰岛IS,东盟AS,哥CR,秘鲁PE,新西兰NZ,智利CL 2.4 瑞士CH 3.6 澳AU,韩国KR 5 巴PK	0 受惠国$_1$LD$_1$	17	---Other

序号 No.	税则号列 Tariff Line	中文货品名称 Article Description in Chinese	最惠国税率 MFN(%)	协定税率 Agreement(%)	特惠税率 SP(%)	普通税率 Gen(%)	英文货品名称 Article Description
	76.14	**非绝缘的铝制绞股线、缆、编带及类似品:**					**Stranded wire, cables, plaited bands and the like, of aluminium, not electrically insulated:**
5644	7614.1000	-带钢芯的	6	0 冰岛IS,东盟AS,哥CR,秘鲁PE,新西兰NZ,智利CL 2.4 瑞士CH 3.6 澳AU,韩国KR 5 巴PK	0 受惠国LD	20	-With steel core
5645	7614.9000	-其他	6	0 冰岛IS,东盟AS,哥CR,秘鲁PE,新西兰NZ,智利CL 2.4 瑞士CH 3.6 澳AU,韩国KR 5 巴PK	0 受惠国LD	20	-Other
	76.15	**餐桌、厨房或其他家用铝制器具及其零件;铝制擦锅器、洗刷擦光用的块垫、手套及类似品;铝制卫生器具及其零件:**					**Table, kitchen or other household articles and parts thereof, of aluminium; pot scourers and scouring or polishing pads, gloves and the like, of aluminium; sanitary ware and parts thereof, of aluminium:**
		-餐桌、厨房或其他家用器具及其零件;擦锅器及洗刷擦光用的块垫、手套及类似品:					-Table, kitchen or other household articles and parts thereof; pot scourers and scouring or polishing pads, gloves and the like:
5646	7615.1010	---擦锅器、洗刷、擦光用的块垫、手套及类似品	18	0 冰岛IS,东盟AS,哥CR,新加坡SG,新西兰NZ,智利CL 5.4 秘鲁PE 10.8 澳AU 12.6 瑞士CH 14.4 巴PK,韩国KR	0 受惠国LD	90	---Pot scourers and scouring or polishing pads, gloves and the like
5647	7615.1090	---其他	15Δ10	0 冰岛IS,东盟AS,哥CR,新加坡SG,新西兰NZ,智利CL 4.5 秘鲁PE 9 澳AU 10.5 瑞士CH 12 巴PK 13.5 韩国KR	0 受惠国LD	90	---Other
5648	7615.2000	-卫生器具及其零件	18	0 冰岛IS,东盟AS,哥CR,新加坡SG,新西兰NZ,智利CL 5.4 秘鲁PE 10.8 澳AU 12.6 瑞士CH 14.4 巴PK,韩国KR	0 受惠国$_1$LD$_1$	90	-Sanitary ware and parts thereof
	76.16	**其他铝制品:**					**Other articles of aluminium:**
5649	7616.1000	-钉、平头钉、U形钉(税号83.05的货品除外)、螺钉、螺栓、螺母、钩头螺钉、铆钉、销、开尾销、垫圈及类似品其他	10	0 冰岛IS,东盟AS,哥CR,秘鲁PE,香港HK,新加坡SG,新西兰NZ,智利CL 4 瑞士CH 5 巴PK 6 澳AU 8 韩国KR 8.5 亚太AP	0 受惠国LD	40	-Nails, tacks, staples (other than those of heading No.83.05), screws, bolts, nuts, screw hooks, rivets, cotters, cotter-pins, washers and similar articles-other
5650	7616.9100	--铝丝制的布、网、篱及格栅	10	0 冰岛IS,东盟AS,哥CR,秘鲁PE,新加坡SG,新西兰NZ,智利CL 4 瑞士CH 6 澳AU 8 韩国KR	0 受惠国LD	40	--Cloth, grill, netting and fencing, of aluminium wire

序号 No.	税则号列 Tariff Line	中文货品名称 Article Description in Chinese	最惠国税率 MFN(%)	协定税率 Agreement(%)	特惠税率 SP(%)	普通税率 Gen(%)	英文货品名称 Article Description
		--其他:					--Other:
5651	7616.9910	---工业用	10	0 冰岛IS,东盟AS,哥CR,新加坡SG,新西兰NZ,智利CL 3 秘鲁PE 5 巴PK 6 澳AU 7 瑞士CH 8.5 亚太AP 9 韩国KR	0 受惠国LD	40	---For technical use
5652	7616.9990	---其他	15	0 冰岛IS,东盟AS,哥CR,新加坡SG,新西兰NZ,智利CL 4.5 秘鲁PE 7.5 巴PK 9 澳AU 10.5 瑞士CH 12 韩国KR 12.8 亚太AP	0 受惠国LD	80	---Other

第七十八章
铅及其制品

注释:

本章所用有关名词解释如下:

一、条、杆

轧、挤、拔或锻制的实心产品，非成卷的，其全长截面均为圆形、椭圆形、矩形（包括正方形）、等边三角形或规则外凸多边形（包括相对两边为弧拱形，另外两边为等长平行直线的“扁圆形”及“变形矩形”）。对于矩形（包括正方形）、三角形或多边形截面的产品，其全长边角可经磨圆。矩形(包括“变形矩形”）截面的产品，其厚度应大于宽度的十分之一。所述条、杆也包括同样形状及尺寸的铸造或烧结产品。该产品在铸造或烧结后再经加工（简单剪修或去氧化皮的除外），但不具有其他税号所列制品或产品的特征。

二、型材及异型材

轧、挤、拔、锻制的产品或其他成型产品，不论是否成卷，其全长截面相同，但与条、杆、丝、板、片、带、箔、管的定义不相符合。同时也包括同样形状的铸造或烧结产品。该产品在铸造或烧结后再经加工（简单剪修或去氧化皮的除外），但不具有其他税号所列制品或产品的特征。

三、丝

盘卷的轧、挤或拔制实心产品，其全长截面均为圆形、椭圆形、矩形（包括正方形）、等边三角形或规则外凸多边形（包括相对两边为弧拱形，另外两边为等长平行直线的“扁圆形”及“变形矩形”）。对于矩形（包括正方形）、三角形或多边形截面的产品，其全长边角可经磨圆。矩形（包括“变形矩形”）截面的产品，其厚度应大于宽度的十分之一。

四、板、片、带、箔

成卷或非成卷的平面产品（税号 78.01 的未锻轧产品除外），截面均为厚度相同的实心矩形（不包括正方形），不论边角是否磨圆（包括相对两边为弧拱形，另外两边为等长平行直线的“变形矩形”），并且符合以下规格:

1. 矩形（包括正方形）的，厚度不超过宽度的十分之一;
2. 矩形或正方形以外形状的，任何尺寸，但不具有其他税号所列制品或产品的特征。

Chapter 78
Lead and articles therof

Notes:

In this Chapter the following expressions have the meanings hereby assigned to them:

1. Bars and rods

Rolled, extruded, drawn or forged products, not in coils, which have a uniform solid cross-section along their whole length in the shape of circles, ovals, rectangles(including squares), equilateral triangles or regular convex polygons (including “flattened circles” and “modified rectangles”, of which two opposite sides are convex arcs, the other two sides being straight, of equal length and parallel).Products with a rectangular (including square), triangular or polygonal cross-section may have corners rounded along their whole length. The thickness of such products which have a rectangular (including “modified rectangular”) cross-section exceeds one-tenth of the width. The expression also covers cast or sintered products, of the same forms and dimensions, which have been subsequently worked after production (otherwise than by simple trimming or de-scaling), provided that they have not thereby assumed the character of articles or products of other headings.

2. Profiles

Rolled, extruded, drawn, forged or formed products, coiled or not, of a uniform cross-section along their whole length, which do not conform to any of the definitions of bars, rods, wire, plates, sheets, strip, foil, tubes or pipes. The expression also covers cast or sintered products, of the same forms, which have been subsequently worked after production (otherwise than by simple trimming of descaling), provided that they have not thereby assumed the character of articles or products of other headings.

3. Wire

Rolled, extruded or drawn products, in coils, which have a uniform soild cross-section along their whole length in the shape of circles, ovals, rectangles (including squares), equilateral triangles or regular convex polygons (including “flattened circles” and “modified rectangles”, of which two opposite sides are convex arcs, the other two sides being straight, of equal length and parallel). Products with a rectangular (including square), triangular or polygonal cross-section may have corners rounded along their whole length. The thickness of such products which have a rectangular (including “modified rectangular”) cross-section exceeds one-tenth of the width.

4. Plates, sheets, strip and foil

Flat-surfaced products (other than the unwrought products of heading No.78.01), coiled or not, of solid rectangular (other than square) cross-section with or without rounded corners (including “modified rectanges” of which two opposite sides are convex arcs, the other two sides being straight, of equal length and parallel) of a uniform thickness, which are:

(1) of rectangular (including square) shape with a thickness not exceeding, one-tenth of the width,

(2) of a shape other than rectangular or square, of any size, proviede that they do not assume the character of

税号78.04还适用于具有花样（例如，凹槽、肋条形、格槽、珠粒及菱形）的板、片、带、箔以及穿孔、抛光、涂层或制成瓦楞形的这类产品，但不具有其他税号所列制品或产品的特征。

五、管

全长截面及管壁厚度相同并只有一个闭合空间的实心产品，成卷或非成卷的，其截面为圆形、椭圆形、矩形（包括正方形）、等边三角形或规则外凸多边形。对于截面为矩形（包括正方形）、等边三角形或规则外凸多边形的产品，不论全长边角是否磨圆，只要其内外截面为同一圆心并为同样形状及同一轴向，也可视为管子。上述截面的管子可经抛光、涂层、弯曲、攻丝、钻孔、缩腰、胀口、成锥形或装法兰、颈圈或套环。

articles or products of other headings.

Heading No.78.04 applies, *inter alia*, to plates, sheets, strip and foil with patterns (for example, grooves, ribs, chequers, tears, buttons, lozenges) and to such products which have been perforated, corrugated, polished or coated, provided that they do not thereby assume the character of articles or products of other headings.

5. Tubes and pipes

Hollow products, coiled or not, which have a uniform cross-section with only one enclosed void along their whole length in the shape of circles, ovals, rectangles (including squares), equilateral triangles or regular convex polygons, and which have a uniform wall thickness. Products with a rectangular (including square), equilateral triangular or regular convex polygonal cross-section, which may have corners rounded along their whole length, are also to be considered as tubes and pipes provided the inner and outer cross-sections are concentric and have the same form and orientation. Tubes and pipes of the foregoing cross-sections may be polished, coated, bent, threaded, drilled, waisted, expanded, cone-shaped or fitted with flanges, collars or rings.

子目注释：

本章所称“精炼铅”，是指：

按重量计含铅量至少为99.9%的金属，但其他各种元素的含量不超过下表中规定的限量：

其他元素表

元　素	所含重量百比
Ag 银	0.02
As 砷	0.005
Bi 铋	0.05
Ca 钙	0.002
Cd 镉	0.002
Cu 铜	0.08
Fe 铁	0.002
S 硫	0.002
Sb 锑	0.005
Sn 锡	0.005
Zn 锌	0.002
其他（例如碲），每种	0.001

Subheading Note:

In this Chapter the expression“refined lead” means:

Metal containing by weight at least 99.9% of lead, provided that the content by weight of any other element does not exceed the limit specified in the following table:

TABLE—Other elements

Element	Limiting conten % by weight
Ag Silver	0.02
As Arsenic	0.005
Bi Bismuth	0.05
Ca Calcium	0.002
Cd Cadmium	0.002
Cu Copper	0.08
Fe Iron	0.002
S Sulphur	0.002
Sb Antimony	0.005
Sn Tin	0.005
Zn Zinc	0.002
Other (for example Te)，each	0.001

序号 No.	税则号列 Tariff Line	中文货品名称 Article Description in Chinese	最惠国税率 MFN(%)	协定税率 Agreement(%)	特惠税率 SP(%)	普通税率 Gen(%)	英文货品名称 Article Description
	78.01	未锻轧铅：					**Unwrought lead:**
5653	7801.1000	-精炼铅	3	0 澳AU,巴PK,冰岛IS,东盟AS,哥CR,秘鲁PE,瑞士CH,新西兰NZ,智利CL 1.8 韩国KR	0 受惠国LD	20	-Refined lead
		-其他：					-Other:
5654	7801.9100	--按重量计所含其他元素是以锑为主的	3	0 澳AU,巴PK,冰岛IS,东盟AS,哥CR,韩国KR,秘鲁PE,瑞士CH,新西兰NZ,智利CL	0 受惠国LD	20	--Containing by weight antimony as the principal other element

序号 No.	税则号列 Tariff Line	中文货品名称 Article Description in Chinese	最惠国税率 MFN(%)	协定税率 Agreement(%)		特惠税率 SP(%)		普通税率 Gen(%)	英文货品名称 Article Description
5655	7801.9900	--其他	3	0 1.8	澳AU,巴PK,冰岛IS,东盟AS,哥CR,秘鲁PE,瑞士CH,新西兰NZ,智利CL 韩国KR	0	受惠国LD	20	--Other
	78.02	**铅废碎料**							**Lead waste and scrap**
5656	7802.0000	铅废碎料	1.5	0	澳AU,巴PK,冰岛IS,东盟AS,哥CR,韩国KR,秘鲁PE,瑞士CH,新西兰NZ,智利CL	0	受惠国$_1$LD$_1$	10	Lead waste and scrap
	78.04	**铅板、片、带、箔;铅粉及片状粉末:**							**Lead plates, sheets, strip and foil; lead powders and flakes:**
		-板、片、带、箔:							-Plates, sheets, strip and foil:
5657	7804.1100	--片、带及厚度(衬背除外)不超过0.2毫米的箔	6	0 2.4 3.6 5	冰岛IS,东盟AS,哥CR,秘鲁PE,新西兰NZ,智利CL 瑞士CH 澳AU,韩国KR 巴PK	0	受惠国LD	30	--Sheets, strip and foil of a thickness (excluding any backing) not exceeding 0.2mm
5658	7804.1900	--其他	6	0 2.4 3.6 5	冰岛IS,东盟AS,哥CR,秘鲁PE,新西兰NZ,智利CL 瑞士CH 澳AU,韩国KR 巴PK	0	受惠国LD	30	--Other
5659	7804.2000	-粉末及片状粉末	6	0 2.4 3.6 5	冰岛IS,东盟AS,哥CR,秘鲁PE,新西兰NZ,智利CL 瑞士CH 澳AU,韩国KR 巴PK	0	受惠国LD	35	-Powders and flakes
	78.06	**其他铅制品:**							**Other articles of lead:**
5660	7806.0010	---铅条、杆、型材及异型材或丝	6	0 2.4 3.6 4.8 5	冰岛IS,东盟AS,哥CR,秘鲁PE,新西兰NZ,智利CL 瑞士CH 澳AU 韩国KR 巴PK	0	受惠国LD	30	---Lead bars, rods, profiles and wire
5661	7806.0090	---其他	6	0 2.4 3.6 5	冰岛IS,东盟AS,哥CR,秘鲁PE,新西兰NZ,智利CL 瑞士CH 澳AU,韩国KR 巴PK	0	受惠国LD	40	---Other

第七十九章
锌及其制品

注释:

本章所用名词解释如下:

一、条、杆

轧、挤、拔或锻制的实心产品，非成卷的，其全长截面均为圆形、椭圆形、矩形（包括正方形）、等边三角形或规则外凸多边形（包括相对两边为弧拱形，另外两边为等长平行直线的“扁圆形”及“变形矩形”）。对于矩形（包括正方形）、三角形或多边形截面的产品，其全长边角可经磨圆。矩形（包括“变形矩形”）截面的产品，其厚度应大于宽度的十分之一。所述条、杆也包括同样形状及尺寸的铸造或烧结产品。该产品在铸造或烧结后再经加工（简单剪修或去氧化皮的除外），但不具有其他税号所列制品或产品的特征。

二、型材及异型材

轧、挤、拔、锻制的产品或其他成型产品，不论是否成卷，其全长截面相同，但与条、杆、丝、板、片、带、箔、管的定义不相符合。同时也包括同样形状的铸造或烧结产品。该产品在铸造或烧结后再经加工（简单剪修或去氧化皮的除外），但不具有其他税号所列制品或产品的特征。

三、丝

盘卷的轧、挤或拔制实心产品，其全长截面均为圆形、椭圆形、矩形（包括正方形）、等边三角形或规则外凸多边形（包括相对两边为弧拱形，另外两边为等长平行直线的“扁圆形”及“变形矩形”）。对于矩形（包括正方形）、三角形或多边形截面的产品，其全长边角可经磨圆。矩形（包括“变形矩形”）截面的产品，其厚度应大于宽度的十分之一。

Chapter 79
Zinc and articles therof

Notes:

In this Chapter the following expressions have the meanings hereby assigned to them:

1. Bars and rods

Rolled, extruded, drawn or forged products, not in coils, which have a uniform solid cross-section along their whole length in the shape of circles, ovals, rectangle (including squares), equilateral triangles or regular convex polygons (including “flattened circles” and “modified rectangles”, of which two opposite sides are convex arcs, the other two sides being straight, of equal length and parallel). Products with a rectangular (including square), triangular or polygonal cross-section may have corners rounded alongtheir whole length. The thickness of such products which have a rectangular (including “modified rectangular”) cross-section exceeds one-tenth of the width. The expression also covers cast or sintered products, of the same forms and dimensions, which have been subsequently worked after production (otherwise than by simple trimming or descaling), provided that they have not thereby assumed the character of articles or products of other headings.

2. Profiles

Rolled, extruded, drawn, forged or formed products, coiled or not, of a uniform cross-section along their whole length, which do not conform to any of the definitions of bars, rods, wire, plates, sheets, strip, foil, tubes or pipes. The expression also covers cast or sintered products, of the same forms, which have been subsequently worked after production (otherwise than by simple trimming or descaling), provided that they have not thereby assumed the character of articles or products of other headings.

3. Wire

Rolled, extruded or drawn products, in coils, which have a uniform soild cross-section along their whole length in the shape of circles, ovals, rectangles (including squares), equilateral triangles or regular convex polygons (including “flattened circles” and “modified rectangles”, of which two opposite sides are convex arcs, the other two sides being straight, of equal length and parallel). Products with a rectangular (including square), triangular or polygonal cross-section may have corners rounded along their whole length. The thickness of such products which have a rectangular (including "modified rectangular") cross-section exceeds one-tenth of the width.

四、板、片、带、箔

成卷或非成卷的平面产品（税号 79.01 的未锻轧产品除外），截面均为厚度相同的实心矩形（不包括正方形），不论边角是否磨圆（包括相对两边为弧拱形，另外两边为等长平行直线的“变形矩形”），并且符合以下规格：

1. 矩形（包括正方形）的，厚度不超过宽度的十分之一；
2. 矩形或正方形以外形状的，任何尺寸，但不具有其他税号所列制品或产品的特征。

税号 79.05 还适用于具有花样（例如，凹槽、肋条形，格槽、珠粒及菱形）的板、片、带、箔以及穿孔、抛光、涂层或制成瓦楞形的这类产品，但不具有其他税号所列制品或产品的特征。

4. Plates, sheets, strip and foil

Flat-surfaced products (other than the unwrought products of heading No.79.01), coiled or not, of solid rectangular (other than square) cross-section with or without rounded corners (including "modified rectangles" of which two opposite sides are convex arcs, the other two sides being straight, of equal length and parallel) of a uniform thickness, which are:

(1) of rcctangular (including square) shape with a thickness not exceeding, one-tenth of the width,

(2) of a shape other than rectangular or square, of any size, provided that they do not assume the character of articles or products of other headings.

Heading No.79.05 applies, *inter alia*, to plates, sheets, strip and foil with patterns (for example, grooves, ribs chequers, tears, buttons, lozenges) and to such products which have been perforated, corrugated, polished or coated, provided that they do not thereby assume the character of articles or products of other headings.

五、管

全长截面及管壁厚度相同并只有一个闭合空间的实心产品，成卷或非成卷的，其截面为圆形、椭圆形、矩形（包括正方形）、等边三角形或规则外凸多边形。对于截面为矩形（包括正方形）、等边三角形或规则外凸多边形的产品，不论全长边角是否磨圆，只要其内外截面为同一圆心并为同样形状及同一轴向，也可视为管子。上述截面的管子可经抛光、涂层、弯曲、攻丝、钻孔、缩腰、胀口、成锥形或装法兰、颈圈或套环。

5. Tubes and pipes

Hollow products, coiled or not, which have a uniform cross-section with only one enclosed void along their whole langth in the shape of circles, ovals, rectangles (including squares), equilateral triangles or regular convex polygons, and which have a uniform wall thickness. Products with a rectangular (including square), equilateral triangular or regular convex polygonal cross-section, which may have corners rounded along their whole length, are also to be considered as tubes and pipes provided the inner and outer cross-sections are concentric and have the same form and orientation. Tubes and pipes of the foregoing cross-sections may be polished, coated, bent, threaded, drilled, waisted, expanded, cone-shaped or fitted with flanges, collars or rings.

子目注释：

本章所用有关名词解释如下：

一、非合金锌

按重量计含锌量至少为 97.5%的金属。

二、锌合金

按重量计含锌量大于其他元素单项含量的金属物质，但

Subheading Notes:

In this Chapter the following expressions have the meanings hereby assigned to them:

1. Zinc, not alloyed

Metal containing by weight at least 97.5% of zinc.

2. Zinc alloys

Metallic substances in which zinc predominates by

按重量计其他元素的总含量超过2.5%。

weight over each of the other elements, provided that the total content by weight of such other elements exceeds 2.5%.

三、锌末

冷凝锌雾所得的锌末。该产品由球形微粒组成，比锌粉更为精细，按重量计至少80%的微粒可以通过孔径为63微米的筛子，而且必须含有按重量计至少为85%的金属锌。

3. Zinc dust

Dust obtained by condensation of zinc vapour, consisting of spherical particles which are finer than zinc powders. At least 80% by weight of the particles pass through a sieve with 63 micrometres (microns) mesh. It must contain at least 85% by weight of metallic zinc.

序号 No.	税则号列 Tariff Line	中文货品名称 Article Description in Chinese	最惠国税率 MFN(%)	协定税率 Agreement(%)	特惠税率 SP(%)	普通税率 Gen(%)	英文货品名称 Article Description
	79.01	**未锻轧锌:**					**Unwrought zinc:**
		-非合金锌:					-Zinc, not alloyed:
		--按重量计含锌量在99.99%及以上:					--Containing by weight 99.99 % or more of zinc:
5662	7901.1110	---按重量计含锌量在99.995%及以上	3Δ1	0 澳AU,巴PK,冰岛IS,东盟AS,哥CR,韩国KR,秘鲁PE,瑞士CH,新西兰NZ,智利CL	0 受惠国LD	20	---Containing by weight 99.995% or more of zinc
5663	7901.1190	---其他	3Δ1	0 澳AU,巴PK,冰岛IS,东盟AS,哥CR,韩国KR,秘鲁PE,瑞士CH,新西兰NZ,智利CL	0 受惠国LD	20	---Other
5664	7901.1200	--按重量计含锌量低于99.99%	3Δ1	0 澳AU,巴PK,冰岛IS,东盟AS,哥CR,秘鲁PE,瑞士CH,新西兰NZ,智利CL 1.8 韩国KR	0 受惠国LD	20	--Containing by weight less than 99.99% of zinc
5665	7901.2000	-锌合金	3Δ1	0 澳AU,巴PK,冰岛IS,东盟AS,哥CR,韩国KR,秘鲁PE,瑞士CH,香港HK,新西兰NZ,智利CL	0 受惠国LD	20	-Zinc alloys
	79.02	**锌废碎料**					**Zinc waste and scrap**
5666	7902.0000	锌废碎料	1.5Δ1	0 澳AU,巴PK,冰岛IS,东盟AS,哥CR,韩国KR,秘鲁PE,瑞士CH,新西兰NZ,智利CL	0 受惠国LD	20	Zinc waste and scrap
	79.03	**锌末、锌粉及片状粉末:**					**Zinc dust, powders and flakes:**
5667	7903.1000	-锌末	6	0 冰岛IS,东盟AS,哥CR,秘鲁PE,新西兰NZ,智利CL 2.4 瑞士CH 3.6 澳AU 4.8 韩国KR 5 巴PK	0 受惠国LD	20	-Zinc dust
5668	7903.9000	-其他	6	0 冰岛IS,东盟AS,哥CR,秘鲁PE,新西兰NZ,智利CL 3.6 澳AU 4.2 瑞士CH 4.8 韩国KR 5 巴PK	0 受惠国LD	20	-Other
	79.04	**锌条、杆、型材及异型材或丝**					**Zinc bars, rods, profiles and wire**
5669	7904.0000	锌条、杆、型材及异型材或丝	6	0 冰岛IS,东盟AS,哥CR,秘鲁PE,新西兰NZ,智利CL 2.4 瑞士CH 3.6 澳AU 5 巴PK 5.2 韩国KR	0 受惠国$_1$LD$_1$	30	Zinc bars, rods, profiles and wire
	79.05	**锌板、片、带、箔**					**Zinc plates, sheets, strip and foil**

序号 No.	税则号列 Tariff Line	中文货品名称 Article Description in Chinese	最惠国税率 MFN(%)	协定税率 Agreement(%)	特惠税率 SP(%)	普通税率 Gen(%)	英文货品名称 Article Description
5670	7905.0000	锌板、片、带、箔	6	0 冰岛IS,东盟AS,哥CR,秘鲁PE,新西兰NZ,智利CL 2.4 瑞士CH 3.6 澳AU,韩国KR 5 巴PK	0 受惠国LD	30	Zinc plates, sheets, strip and foil
	79.07	**其他锌制品：**					**Other articles of zinc:**
5671	7907.0020	---锌管及锌制管子附件（例如，接头、肘管、管套）	6	0 冰岛IS,东盟AS,哥CR,秘鲁PE,新西兰NZ,智利CL 2.4 瑞士CH 3.6 澳AU,韩国KR 5 巴PK	0 受惠国LD	30	---Zinc tubes or pipes and zinc tube or pipe fittings (for example, couplings, elbows, sleeves)
5672	7907.0030	---电池壳体坯料（锌饼）	6	0 冰岛IS,东盟AS,哥CR,新西兰NZ,智利CL 2.4 瑞士CH 3.6 澳AU,韩国KR 3.8 秘鲁PE 5 巴PK	0 受惠国LD	40	---Cellpacking blanks (zinc biscuits)
5673	7907.0090	---其他	6	0 冰岛IS,东盟AS,哥CR,秘鲁PE,新西兰NZ,智利CL 2.4 瑞士CH 3.6 澳AU,韩国KR 5 巴PK	0 受惠国LD	40	---Other

第八十章
锡及其制品

注释:

本章所用有关名词解释如下:

一、条、杆

轧、挤、拔或锻制的实心产品,非成卷的,其全长截面均为圆形、椭圆形、矩形(包括正方形)、等边三角形或规则外凸多边形(包括相对两边为弧拱形,另外两边为等长平行直线的“扁圆形”及“变形矩形”)。对于矩形(包括正方形)、三角形或多边形截面的产品,其全长边角可经磨圆。矩形(包括“变形矩形”)截面的产品,其厚度应大于宽度的十分之一。所述条、杆也包括同样形状及尺寸的铸造或烧结产品。该产品在铸造或烧结后再经加工(简单剪修或去氧化皮的除外),但不具有其他税号所列制品或产品的特征。

二、型材及异型材

轧、挤、拔、锻制的产品或其他成型产品,不论是否成卷,其全长截面相同,但与条、杆、丝、板、片、带、箔、管的定义不相符合。同时也包括同样形状的铸造或烧结产品。该产品在铸造或烧结后再经加工(简单剪修或去氧化皮的除外),但不具有其他税号所列制品或产品的特征。

三、丝

盘卷的轧、挤或拔制实心产品,其全长截面均为圆形、椭圆形、矩形(包括正方形)、等边三角形或规则外凸多边形(包括相对两边为弧拱形,另外两边为等长平行直线的“扁圆形”及“变形矩形”)。对于矩形(包括正方形)、三角形或多边形截面的产品,其全长边角可经磨圆。矩形(包括“变形矩形”)截面的产品,其厚度应大于宽度的十分之一。

四、板、片、带、箔

成卷或非成卷的平面产品(税号 80.01 的未锻轧产品除外),截面均为厚度相同的实心矩形(不包括正方形),不论边角是否磨圆(包括相对两边为弧拱形,另外两边为等长平行直线的“变形矩形”),并且符合以下规格:

1. 矩形(包括正方形)的,厚度不超过宽度的十分之一;
2. 矩形或正方形以外形状的,任何尺寸,但不具有其他税号所列制品或产品的特征。

五、管

全长截面及管壁厚度相同并只有一个闭合空间的实心产品,成卷或非成卷的,其截面为圆形、椭圆形、矩形(包括正方形)、等边三角形或规则外凸多边形。对于截面为矩形(包括正方形)、等边三角形或规则外凸多边形的产品,不论全长边角是否

Chapter 80
Tin and articles therof

Notes:

In this Chapter the following expressions have the meanings hereby assigned to them:

1. Bars and rods

Rolled, extruded, drawn or forged products, not in coils, which have a uniform solid cross-section along their whole length in the shape of circles, ovals, rectangle (including squares), equilateral triangles or regular convex polygons (including "flattened circles" and "modified rectangles", of which two opposite sides are convex arcs, the other two sides being straight, of equal length and parallel). Products with a rectangular (including square), triangular or polygonal cross-section may have corners rounded along their whole length. The thickness of such products which have a rectangular (including "modified rectangular") cross-section exceeds one-tenth of the width. The expression also covers cast or sintered products, of the same forms and dimensions, which have been subsequently worked after production (otherwise than by simple trimming or descaling), provided that they have not thereby assumed the character of articles or products of other headings.

2. Profiles

Rolled, extruded, drawn, forged or formed products, coiled or not, of a uniform cross-section along their whole length, which do not conform to any of the definitions of bars, rods, wire, plates, sheets, strip, foil, tubes or pipes. The expression also covers cast or sintered products, of the same forms, which have been subsequently worked after production (otherwise than by simple trimming or descaling), provided that they have not thereby assumed the character of articles or products of other headings.

3. Wire

Rolled, extruded or drawn products, in coils, which have a uniform solid cross-section along their whole length in the shape of circles, ovals, rectanges (including squares), equilateral triangles or regular convex polygons (including "flattened circles" and "modified rectangles", of which two opposite sides are convex arcs, the other two sides being straight, of equal length and parallel). Products with a rectangular (including square), triangular or polygonal cross-section may have corners rounded along their whole length. The thickness of such products which have a rectangular (including"modified rectangular") cross-section exceeds one-tenth of the width.

4. Plates, sheets, strip and foil

Flat-surfaced products (other than the unwrought products of heading No.80.01), coiled or not, of solid rectangular (other than square) cross-section with or without rounded corners (including "modified rectanges" of which two opposite sides are convex arcs, the other two sides being straight, of equal length and parallel) of a uniform thickness, which are:

-of rectangular (including square) shape with a thickness not exceedingone-tenth of the width;

-of a shape other than rectangular or square, of any size, provided that they do not assume the character of articles or products of other headings.

5. Tubes and pipes

Hollow products, coiled or not, which have a uniform cross-section with only one enclosed void along their whole langth in the shape of circles, ovals, rectangles (including squares), equilateral triangles or regular convex polygons, and which have a uniform wall thickness. Products with a rectangular (including square), equilateral

磨圆，只要其内外截面为同一圆心并为同样形状及同一轴向，也可视为管子。上述截面的管子可经抛光、涂层、弯曲、攻丝、钻孔、缩腰、胀口、成锥形或装法兰、颈圈或套环。

triangular or regular convex polygonal cross-section, which may have corners rounded along their whole length, are also to be considered as tubes and pipes provided the inner and outer cross-sections are concentric and have the same form and orientation. Tubes and pipes of the foregoing cross-sections may be polished, coated, bent, threaded, drilled, waisted, expanded, cone-shaped or fitted with flanges, collars or rings.

子目注释：

本章所用有关名词解释如下：

一、非合金锡

按重量计含锡量至少为99%的金属，但含铋量或含铜量不超过下表中规定的限量：

其他元素表

元素	所含重量百分比
Bi 铋	0.1
Cu 铜	0.4

二、锡合金

按重量计含锡量大于其他元素单项含量的金属物质，但：

（一）按重量计其他元素的总含量超过1%;或

（二）按重量计含铋量或含铜量应等于或大于上表中规定的限量。

Subheading Notes:

In this Chapter the following expressions have the meanings hereby assigned to them:

1. Tin, not alloyed.

Metal containing by weight at least 99% of tin, provided that the content by weight of any bismuth or copper is less than the limit specified in the following table:

TABLEOther elements

Element	Limiting content % by weight
Bi Bismuth	0.1
Cu Copper	0.4

2. Tin alloys

Metallic substances in which tin predominates by weight over each of the other elements, provided that:

(a) the total content by weight of such other elements exceeds1%; or

(b) the content by weight of either bismuth or copper is equal to or greater than the limit specified in the foregoing table.

序号 No.	税则号列 Tariff Line	中文货品名称 Article Description in Chinese	最惠国税率 MFN(%)	协定税率 Agreement(%)	特惠税率 SP(%)	普通税率 Gen(%)	英文货品名称 Article Description
	80.01	**未锻轧锡：**					**Unwrought tin:**
5674	8001.1000	-非合金锡	3	0 澳AU,巴PK,冰岛IS,东盟AS,哥CR,秘鲁PE,瑞士CH,香港HK,新西兰NZ,智利CL 1.8 韩国KR	0 受惠国LD	20	-Tin, not alloyed
		-锡合金：					-Tin alloys:
5675	8001.2010	---锡基巴毕脱合金	3	0 澳AU,巴PK,冰岛IS,东盟AS,哥CR,韩国KR,秘鲁PE,瑞士CH,香港HK,新西兰NZ,智利CL	0 受惠国LD	20	---Babbitt metal
		---焊锡：					---Solder:
5676	8001.2021	----按重量计含铅量在0.1%以下的	3	0 澳AU,澳门MO,巴PK,冰岛IS,东盟AS,哥CR,秘鲁PE,瑞士CH,香港HK,新西兰NZ,智利CL 1.8 韩国KR	0 受惠国LD	30	----Containing by weight less than 0.1% of lead
5677	8001.2029	----其他	3	0 澳AU,澳门MO,巴PK,冰岛IS,东盟AS,哥CR,秘鲁PE,瑞士CH,香港HK,新西兰NZ,智利CL 1.8 韩国KR	0 受惠国LD	30	----Other
5678	8001.2090	---其他	3	0 澳AU,巴PK,冰岛IS,东盟AS,哥CR,秘鲁PE,瑞士CH,香港HK,新西兰NZ,智利CL 1.8 韩国KR	0 受惠国LD	30	---Other
	80.02	**锡废碎料**					**Tin waste and scrap**
5679	8002.0000	锡废碎料	1.5	0 澳AU,巴PK,冰岛IS,东盟AS,哥CR,韩国KR,秘鲁PE,瑞士CH,香港HK,新西兰NZ,智利CL	0 受惠国$_1$LD$_1$	30	Tin waste and scrap
	80.03	**锡条、杆、型材及异型材或丝**					**Tin bars, rods, profiles and wire**

序号 No.	税则号列 Tariff Line	中文货品名称 Article Description in Chinese	最惠国税率 MFN(%)	协定税率 Agreement(%)	特惠税率 SP(%)	普通税率 Gen(%)	英文货品名称 Article Description
5680	8003.0000	锡条、杆、型材及异型材或丝	8	0 冰岛IS,东盟AS,哥CR,秘鲁PE,香港HK,新西兰NZ,智利CL 3.2 瑞士CH 4.8 澳AU 5 巴PK 6.4 韩国KR	0 受惠国LD	40	Tin bars, rods, profiles and wire
	80.07	**其他锡制品:**					**Other articles of tin:**
5681	8007.0020	---锡板、片及带，厚度超过0.2毫米	8	0 冰岛IS,东盟AS,哥CR,秘鲁PE,新西兰NZ,智利CL 3.2 瑞士CH 4.8 澳AU,韩国KR 5 巴PK	0 受惠国$_1$LD$_1$	40	---Tin plates, sheets and strip, of a thickness exceeding 0.2mm
5682	8007.0030	---锡箔（不论是否印花或用纸、纸板、塑料或类似材料衬背），厚度（衬背除外）不超过0.2毫米;锡粉及片状粉末	8	0 冰岛IS,东盟AS,哥CR,秘鲁PE,新西兰NZ,智利CL 3.2 瑞士CH 4.8 澳AU,韩国KR 5 巴PK	0 受惠国$_1$LD$_1$	40	---Tin foil (whether or not printed or backed with paper, paperboard, plastics or similar backing materials) , of a thickness (excluding any backing) not exceeding 0.2mm; tin powders and flakes
5683	8007.0040	---锡管及管子附件（例如，接头、肘管、管套）	8	0 冰岛IS,东盟AS,哥CR,秘鲁PE,新西兰NZ,智利CL 4.8 澳AU,韩国KR 5 巴PK 5.6 瑞士CH	0 受惠国$_1$LD$_1$	45	---Tin tubes, pipes and tube or pipe fittings (for example, couplings, elbows, sleeves)
5684	8007.0090	---其他	8	0 冰岛IS,东盟AS,哥CR,秘鲁PE,香港HK,新西兰NZ,智利CL 3.2 瑞士CH 4.8 澳AU 6.4 巴PK 6.9 韩国KR	0 受惠国$_1$LD$_1$	80	---Other

第八十一章
其他贱金属、金属陶瓷及其制品

Chapter 81
Other base metals; cermets; artiles thereof

子目注释：

第七十四章注释中有关“条、杆”、“型材及异型材”、“丝”及“板、片、带、箔”的规定也适用于本章。

Subheading Note:

Note 1 to Chapter 74, defining “bars and rods”, “profiles”, “wire” and “plates, sheets, strip and foil” applies, *mutatis mutandis*, to this Chapter.

序号 No.	税则号列 Tariff Line	中文货品名称 Article Description in Chinese	最惠国税率 MFN(%)	协定税率 Agreement(%)	特惠税率 SP(%)	普通税率 Gen(%)	英文货品名称 Article Description
	81.01	**钨及其制品，包括废碎料：**					**Tungsten (wolfram) and articles thereof, including waste and scrap:**
5685	8101.1000	-粉末	6	0 冰岛IS,东盟AS,哥CR,秘鲁PE,新西兰NZ,智利CL 2.4 瑞士CH 3.6 澳AU,韩国KR 5 巴PK	0 受惠国$_1$LD$_1$	20	-Powders
		-其他：					-Other:
5686	8101.9400	--未锻轧钨，包括简单烧结而成的条、杆	3	0 澳AU,巴PK,冰岛IS,东盟AS,哥CR,韩国KR,秘鲁PE,新西兰NZ,智利CL 2.1 瑞士CH	0 受惠国$_1$LD$_1$	20	--Unwrought tungsten, including bars and rods obtained simply by sintering
5687	8101.9600	--丝	8	0 冰岛IS,东盟AS,哥CR,秘鲁PE,新西兰NZ,智利CL 3.2 瑞士CH 4.8 澳AU,韩国KR 5 巴PK	0 受惠国$_1$LD$_1$	20	--Wire
5688	8101.9700	--废碎料	3Δ1	0 澳AU,巴PK,冰岛IS,东盟AS,哥CR,韩国KR,秘鲁PE,瑞士CH,新西兰NZ,智利CL	0 受惠国$_1$LD$_1$	20	--Waste and scrap
		--其他：					--Other:
5689	8101.9910	---条、杆，但简单烧结而成的除外；型材及异型材、板、片、带、箔	5	0 澳AU,巴PK,冰岛IS,东盟AS,哥CR,秘鲁PE,新西兰NZ,智利CL 2 瑞士CH 3 韩国KR	0 受惠国$_1$LD$_1$	30	---Bars and rods, other than those obtained simply by sintering, profiles, plates, sheets, strip and foil
5690	8101.9990	---其他	8	0 冰岛IS,东盟AS,哥CR,秘鲁PE,新西兰NZ,智利CL 3.2 瑞士CH 4.8 澳AU,韩国KR 5 巴PK	0 受惠国$_1$LD$_1$	70	---Other
	81.02	**钼及其制品，包括废碎料：**					**Molybdenum and articles thereof, including waste and scrap:**
5691	8102.1000	-粉末	6	0 冰岛IS,东盟AS,哥CR,秘鲁PE,新西兰NZ,智利CL 2.4 瑞士CH 3.6 澳AU,韩国KR 5 巴PK	0 受惠国$_1$LD$_1$	20	-Powders
		-其他：					-Other:
5692	8102.9400	--未锻轧钼，包括简单烧结而成的条、杆	3	0 澳AU,巴PK,冰岛IS,东盟AS,哥CR,韩国KR,秘鲁PE,瑞士CH,新西兰NZ,智利CL	0 受惠国$_1$LD$_1$	20	--Unwrought molybdenum, including bars and rods obtained simply by sintering

序号 No.	税则号列 Tariff Line	中文货品名称 Article Description in Chinese	最惠国税率 MFN(%)	协定税率 Agreement(%)	特惠税率 SP(%)	普通税率 Gen(%)	英文货品名称 Article Description
5693	8102.9500	--条、杆，但简单烧结而成的除外；型材及异型材、板、片、带、箔	8	0 冰岛IS,东盟AS,哥CR,秘鲁PE,新西兰NZ,智利CL 3.2 瑞士CH 4.8 澳AU 5 巴PK 6.4 韩国KR	0 受惠国$_1$LD$_1$	30	--Bars and rods, other than those obtained simply by sintering, profiles, plates, sheets, strip and foil
5694	8102.9600	--丝	8	0 冰岛IS,东盟AS,哥CR,秘鲁PE,新西兰NZ,智利CL 3.2 瑞士CH 4.8 澳AU,韩国KR 5 巴PK	0 受惠国$_1$LD$_1$	20	--Wire
5695	8102.9700	--废碎料	3	0 澳AU,巴PK,冰岛IS,东盟AS,哥CR,韩国KR,秘鲁PE,瑞士CH,新西兰NZ,智利CL	0 受惠国$_1$LD$_1$	20	--Waste and scrap
5696	8102.9900	--其他	8	0 冰岛IS,东盟AS,哥CR,秘鲁PE,新西兰NZ,智利CL 3.2 瑞士CH 4.8 澳AU,韩国KR 5 巴PK	0 受惠国$_1$LD$_1$	70	--Other
	81.03	**钽及其制品，包括废碎料：**					**Tantalum and articles thereof, including waste and scrap:**
		-未锻轧钽，包括简单烧结而成的条、杆；粉末：					-Unwrought tantalum, including bars and rods obtained simply by sintering; powders:
		---钽粉：					---Powder:
5697	8103.2011	----松装密度小于2.2g/cm^3	6	0 冰岛IS,东盟AS,哥CR,秘鲁PE,新西兰NZ,智利CL 2.4 瑞士CH 3.6 澳AU,韩国KR 5 巴PK	0 受惠国$_1$LD$_1$	14	----Loose density less than 2.2g/cm^3
5698	8103.2019	----其他	6	0 冰岛IS,东盟AS,哥CR,秘鲁PE,新西兰NZ,智利CL 2.4 瑞士CH 3.6 澳AU,韩国KR 5 巴PK	0 受惠国$_1$LD$_1$	14	----Other
5699	8103.2090	---其他	6	0 冰岛IS,东盟AS,哥CR,秘鲁PE,新西兰NZ,智利CL 2.4 瑞士CH 3.6 澳AU,韩国KR 5 巴PK	0 受惠国$_1$LD$_1$	14	---Other
5700	8103.3000	-废碎料	6Δ0	0 冰岛IS,东盟AS,哥CR,韩国KR,秘鲁PE,新西兰NZ,智利CL 2.4 瑞士CH 3.6 澳AU 5 巴PK	0 受惠国$_1$LD$_1$	14	-Waste and scrap
		-其他：					-Other:
		---钽丝：					---Wire:
5701	8103.9011	----直径小于0.5毫米	8	0 冰岛IS,东盟AS,哥CR,秘鲁PE,新西兰NZ,智利CL 3.2 瑞士CH 4.8 澳AU,韩国KR 5 巴PK	0 受惠国$_1$LD$_1$	30	----Smaller than 0.5mm in diameter

序号 No.	税则号列 Tariff Line	中文货品名称 Article Description in Chinese	最惠国税率 MFN(%)	协定税率 Agreement(%)	特惠税率 SP(%)	普通税率 Gen(%)	英文货品名称 Article Description
5702	8103.9019	----其他	8	0 冰岛IS,东盟AS,哥CR,秘鲁PE,新西兰NZ,智利CL 3.2 瑞士CH 4.8 澳AU,韩国KR 5 巴PK	0 受惠国$_1$LD$_1$	30	----Other
5703	8103.9090	---其他	8	0 冰岛IS,东盟AS,哥CR,秘鲁PE,新西兰NZ,智利CL 3.2 瑞士CH 4.8 澳AU,韩国KR 5 巴PK	0 受惠国$_1$LD$_1$	30	---Other
	81.04	**镁及其制品，包括废碎料：**					**Magnesium and articles thereof, including waste and scrap:**
		-未锻轧镁：					-Unwrought magnesium:
5704	8104.1100	--按重量计含镁量至少为99.8%	6	0 巴PK,冰岛IS,东盟AS,哥CR,韩国KR,秘鲁PE,新西兰NZ,智利CL 2.4 瑞士CH 3.6 澳AU 4.2 亚太AP	0 受惠国$_1$LD$_1$	20	--Containing at least 99.8% by weight of magnesium
5705	8104.1900	--其他	6	0 冰岛IS,东盟AS,哥CR,秘鲁PE,新西兰NZ,智利CL 2.4 瑞士CH 3.6 澳AU,韩国KR 5 巴PK	0 受惠国$_1$LD$_1$	20	--Other
5706	8104.2000	-废碎料	1.5	0 澳AU,巴PK,冰岛IS,东盟AS,哥CR,韩国KR,秘鲁PE,瑞士CH,新西兰NZ,智利CL	0 受惠国$_1$LD$_1$	20	-Waste and scrap
5707	8104.3000	-锉屑、车屑及颗粒，已按规格分级的;粉末	8	0 冰岛IS,东盟AS,哥CR,秘鲁PE,新西兰NZ,智利CL 3.2 瑞士CH 4.8 澳AU,韩国KR 5 巴PK	0 受惠国$_1$LD$_1$	30	-Raspings, turnings and granules, graded according to size; powders
		-其他：					-Other:
5708	8104.9010	---锻轧镁	8	0 冰岛IS,东盟AS,哥CR,秘鲁PE,新西兰NZ,智利CL 3.2 瑞士CH 4.8 澳AU,韩国KR 5 巴PK	0 受惠国$_1$LD$_1$	30	---Wrought magnesium
5709	8104.9020	---镁制品	8.4	0 冰岛IS,东盟AS,哥CR,秘鲁PE,新西兰NZ,智利CL 3.36 瑞士CH 5 澳AU,巴PK,韩国KR	0 受惠国$_1$LD$_1$	70	---Magnesium articles
	81.05	**钴锍及其他冶炼钴时所得的中间产品;钴及其制品，包括废碎料：**					**Cobalt mattes and other intermediate products of cobalt metallurgy; cobalt and articles thereof, including waste and scrap:**
		-钴锍及其他冶炼钴时所得的中间产品;未锻轧钴;粉末：					-Cobalt mattes and other intermediate products of cobalt metallurgy; unwrought cobalt; powders:
5710	8105.2010	---钴湿法冶炼中间品	4Δ0	0 澳AU,巴PK,冰岛IS,东盟AS,哥CR,韩国KR,秘鲁PE,瑞士CH,新西兰NZ,智利CL	0 受惠国LD	14	---Intermediate products of cobalt wet processing metallurgy
5711	8105.2020	---未锻轧钴	4	0 澳AU,巴PK,冰岛IS,东盟AS,哥CR,韩国KR,秘鲁PE,瑞士CH,新西兰NZ,智利CL	0 受惠国LD	14	---Unwrought cobalt

序号 No.	税则号列 Tariff Line	中文货品名称 Article Description in Chinese	最惠国税率 MFN(%)	协定税率 Agreement(%)		特惠税率 SP(%)		普通税率 Gen(%)	英文货品名称 Article Description
5712	8105.2090	---其他	4	0	澳AU,巴PK,冰岛IS,东盟AS,哥CR,韩国KR,秘鲁PE,瑞士CH,新西兰NZ,智利CL	0	受惠国LD	14	---Other
	ex81052090	钴锍及其他冶炼钴时所得的中间产品	Δ0						Cobalt mattes and other intermediate products of cobalt metallurgy
5713	8105.3000	-废碎料	4	0	澳AU,巴PK,冰岛IS,东盟AS,哥CR,韩国KR,秘鲁PE,瑞士CH,新西兰NZ,智利CL	0	受惠国LD	14	-Waste and scrap
5714	8105.9000	-其他	8	0 3.2 4.8 5 6.4	冰岛IS,东盟AS,哥CR,秘鲁PE,新西兰NZ,智利CL 瑞士CH 澳AU 巴PK 韩国KR	0	受惠国LD	30	-Other
	81.06	**铋及其制品，包括废碎料：**							**Bismuth and articles thereof, including waste and scrap:**
5715	8106.0010	---未锻轧铋;废碎料;粉末	3	0	澳AU,巴PK,冰岛IS,东盟AS,哥CR,韩国KR,秘鲁PE,瑞士CH,新西兰NZ,智利CL	0	受惠国$_1$LD$_1$	20	---Unwroght bismuth; waste and scrap; powders
	ex81060010	未锻轧铋	Δ1						Unwrought bismuth
5716	8106.0090	---其他	8	0 3.2 4.8 5 6.4	冰岛IS,东盟AS,哥CR,秘鲁PE,新西兰NZ,智利CL 瑞士CH 澳AU 巴PK 韩国KR	0	受惠国$_1$LD$_1$	30	---Other
	81.07	**镉及其制品，包括废碎料：**							**Cadmium and articles thereof, including waste and scrap:**
5717	8107.2000	-未锻轧镉;粉末	3	0 1.8	澳AU,巴PK,冰岛IS,东盟AS,哥CR,瑞士CH,新西兰NZ,智利CL 韩国KR	0	受惠国$_1$LD$_1$	14	-Unwrought cadmium; powders
5718	8107.3000	-废碎料	3	0	澳AU,巴PK,冰岛IS,东盟AS,哥CR,韩国KR,秘鲁PE,瑞士CH,新西兰NZ,智利CL	0	受惠国$_1$LD$_1$	14	-Waste and scrap
5719	8107.9000	-其他	8	0 3.2 4.8 5	冰岛IS,东盟AS,哥CR,秘鲁PE,新西兰NZ,智利CL 瑞士CH 澳AU,韩国KR 巴PK	0	受惠国$_1$LD$_1$	30	-Other
	81.08	**钛及其制品，包括废碎料：**							**Titanium and articles thereof, including waste and scrap:**
		-未锻轧钛;粉末：							-Unwrought titanium; powders:
		---未锻轧钛：							---Unwrought tatanium:
5720	8108.2021	----海绵钛	3	0	澳AU,巴PK,冰岛IS,东盟AS,哥CR,韩国KR,秘鲁PE,瑞士CH,新西兰NZ,智利CL	0	受惠国$_1$LD$_1$	14	----Titanium sponge
5721	8108.2029	----其他	3	0 1.8	澳AU,巴PK,冰岛IS,东盟AS,哥CR,秘鲁PE,瑞士CH,新西兰NZ,智利CL 韩国KR	0	受惠国$_1$LD$_1$	14	----Other
5722	8108.2030	---粉末	3	0	澳AU,巴PK,冰岛IS,东盟AS,哥CR,韩国KR,秘鲁PE,瑞士CH,新西兰NZ,智利CL	0	受惠国$_1$LD$_1$	14	---Powders

序号 No.	税则号列 Tariff Line	中文货品名称 Article Description in Chinese	最惠国税率 MFN(%)	协定税率 Agreement(%)	特惠税率 SP(%)	普通税率 Gen(%)	英文货品名称 Article Description
5723	8108.3000	-废碎料	3	0 澳AU,巴PK,冰岛IS,东盟AS,哥CR,韩国KR,秘鲁PE,瑞士CH,新西兰NZ,智利CL	0 受惠国$_1$LD$_1$	14	-Waste and scrap
		-其他:					-Other:
5724	8108.9010	---条、杆、型材及异型材	8	0 冰岛IS,东盟AS,哥CR,秘鲁PE,新西兰NZ,智利CL 3.2 瑞士CH 4.8 澳AU 5 巴PK 6.4 韩国KR	0 受惠国$_1$LD$_1$	30	---Bars、rods、shapes and sections
5725	8108.9020	---丝	8	0 冰岛IS,东盟AS,哥CR,秘鲁PE,新西兰NZ,智利CL 3.2 瑞士CH 4.8 澳AU,韩国KR 5 巴PK	0 受惠国$_1$LD$_1$	30	---Wire
		---板、片、带、箔:					---Plates, sheets, strap, foil:
5726	8108.9031	----厚度不超过0.8毫米	8Δ4	0 冰岛IS,东盟AS,哥CR,秘鲁PE,新西兰NZ,智利CL 3.2 瑞士CH 4.8 澳AU,韩国KR 5 巴PK	0 受惠国$_1$LD$_1$	30	----Of a thickness not more than 0.8mm
5727	8108.9032	----厚度超过0.8毫米	8Δ4	0 冰岛IS,东盟AS,哥CR,秘鲁PE,新西兰NZ,智利CL 3.2 瑞士CH 4.8 澳AU,韩国KR 5 巴PK	0 受惠国$_1$LD$_1$	30	----Of a thickness more than 0.8mm
5728	8108.9040	---管	8	0 冰岛IS,东盟AS,哥CR,秘鲁PE,新西兰NZ,智利CL 3.2 瑞士CH 4.8 澳AU 5 巴PK 6.4 韩国KR	0 受惠国$_1$LD$_1$	30	---Tubes or pipes
5729	8108.9090	---其他	8	0 冰岛IS,东盟AS,哥CR,秘鲁PE,新西兰NZ,智利CL 3.2 瑞士CH 4.8 澳AU,韩国KR 5 巴PK	0 受惠国$_1$LD$_1$	30	---Other
	81.09	**锆及其制品，包括废碎料:**					**Zirconium and articles thereof, including waste and scrap:**
5730	8109.2000	-未锻轧锆;粉末	3	0 澳AU,巴PK,冰岛IS,东盟AS,哥CR,秘鲁PE,瑞士CH,新西兰NZ,智利CL 1.8 韩国KR	0 受惠国$_1$LD$_1$	20	-Unwrought zirconium; powders
5731	8109.3000	-废碎料	3	0 澳AU,巴PK,冰岛IS,东盟AS,哥CR,韩国KR,秘鲁PE,瑞士CH,新西兰NZ,智利CL	0 受惠国$_1$LD$_1$	20	-Waste and scrap
5732	8109.9000	-其他	8	0 冰岛IS,东盟AS,哥CR,秘鲁PE,新西兰NZ,智利CL 3.2 瑞士CH 4.8 澳AU 5 巴PK 6.4 韩国KR	0 受惠国$_1$LD$_1$	30	-Other
	81.10	**锑及其制品，包括废碎料:**					**Antimony and articles thereof, including waste and scrap:**
		-未锻轧锑;粉末:					-Unwrought antimony; powders:

序号 No.	税则号列 Tariff Line	中文货品名称 Article Description in Chinese	最惠国税率 MFN(%)	协定税率 Agreement(%)		特惠税率 SP(%)		普通税率 Gen(%)	英文货品名称 Article Description
5733	8110.1010	---未锻轧锑	3∆1	0	澳AU,巴PK,冰岛IS,东盟AS,哥CR,韩国KR,秘鲁PE,瑞士CH,新西兰NZ,智利CL	0	受惠国$_1$LD$_1$	30	---Unwrought antimony
5734	8110.1020	---粉末	3	0	澳AU,巴PK,冰岛IS,东盟AS,哥CR,韩国KR,秘鲁PE,瑞士CH,新西兰NZ,智利CL	0	受惠国$_1$LD$_1$	30	---Powders
5735	8110.2000	-废碎料	3	0	澳AU,巴PK,冰岛IS,东盟AS,哥CR,韩国KR,秘鲁PE,瑞士CH,新西兰NZ,智利CL	0	受惠国$_1$LD$_1$	30	-Antimony waste and scrap
5736	8110.9000	-其他	8	0	冰岛IS,东盟AS,哥CR,秘鲁PE,新西兰NZ,智利CL	0	受惠国$_1$LD$_1$	40	-Other
				3.2	瑞士CH				
				4.8	澳AU,韩国KR				
				5	巴PK				
	81.11	**锰及其制品，包括废碎料：**							**Manganese and articles thereof, including waste and scrap:**
5737	8111.0010	---未锻轧锰；废碎料；粉末	3	0	澳AU,巴PK,冰岛IS,东盟AS,哥CR,韩国KR,秘鲁PE,瑞士CH,新西兰NZ,智利CL	0	受惠国LD	20	---Unwrought manganese; waste and scrap; powders
5738	8111.0090	---其他	8	0	冰岛IS,东盟AS,哥CR,秘鲁PE,新西兰NZ,智利CL	0	受惠国LD	30	---Other
				3.2	瑞士CH				
				4.8	澳AU,韩国KR				
				5	巴PK				
	81.12	**铍、铬、锗、钒、镓、铪、铟、铼、铌、铊及其制品，包括废碎料：**							**Beryllium, chromium, germanium, vanadium, gallium, hafnium, indium, niobium (columbium) , rhenium and thallium, and articles of these metals, including waste and scrap:**
		-铍：							-Beryllium:
5739	8112.1200	--未锻轧铍；粉末	3	0	澳AU,巴PK,冰岛IS,东盟AS,哥CR,韩国KR,秘鲁PE,瑞士CH,新西兰NZ,智利CL	0	受惠国LD	30	--Unwrought; powders
5740	8112.1300	--废碎料	3	0	澳AU,巴PK,冰岛IS,东盟AS,哥CR,韩国KR,秘鲁PE,瑞士CH,新西兰NZ,智利CL	0	受惠国LD	30	--Waste and scrap
5741	8112.1900	--其他	8	0	冰岛IS,东盟AS,哥CR,秘鲁PE,新西兰NZ,智利CL	0	受惠国LD	30	--Other
				3.2	瑞士CH				
				4.8	澳AU,韩国KR				
				5	巴PK				
		-铬：							-Chromium:
5742	8112.2100	--未锻轧铬；粉末	3	0	澳AU,巴PK,冰岛IS,东盟AS,哥CR,秘鲁PE,瑞士CH,新西兰NZ,智利CL	0	受惠国LD	20	--Unwrought; powders
				1.8	韩国KR				
5743	8112.2200	--废碎料	3	0	澳AU,巴PK,冰岛IS,东盟AS,哥CR,韩国KR,秘鲁PE,瑞士CH,新西兰NZ,智利CL	0	受惠国LD	20	--Waste and Scrap
5744	8112.2900	--其他	3	0	澳AU,巴PK,冰岛IS,东盟AS,哥CR,韩国KR,秘鲁PE,瑞士CH,新西兰NZ,智利CL	0	受惠国LD	20	--Other

序号 No.	税则号列 Tariff Line	中文货品名称 Article Description in Chinese	最惠国税率 MFN(%)	协定税率 Agreement(%)	特惠税率 SP(%)	普通税率 Gen(%)	英文货品名称 Article Description
		-铊:					-Thallium:
5745	8112.5100	--未锻轧铊;粉末	3	0 澳AU,巴PK,冰岛IS,东盟AS,哥CR,韩国KR,秘鲁PE,瑞士CH,新西兰NZ,智利CL	0 受惠国LD	20	--Unwrought; powders
5746	8112.5200	--废碎料	3	0 澳AU,巴PK,冰岛IS,东盟AS,哥CR,韩国KR,秘鲁PE,瑞士CH,新西兰NZ,智利CL	0 受惠国LD	20	--Waste and Scrap
5747	8112.5900	--其他	8	0 冰岛IS,东盟AS,哥CR,秘鲁PE,新西兰NZ,智利CL 3.2 瑞士CH 4.8 澳AU,韩国KR 5 巴PK	0 受惠国LD	30	--Other
		-其他:					-Other:
		--未锻轧;废碎料;粉末:					--Unwrought; waste and scrap; powders:
5748	8112.9210	---锗	3	0 澳AU,巴PK,冰岛IS,东盟AS,哥CR,韩国KR,秘鲁PE,瑞士CH,新西兰NZ,智利CL	0 受惠国LD	20	---Germanium
5749	8112.9220	---钒	3	0 澳AU,巴PK,冰岛IS,东盟AS,哥CR,韩国KR,秘鲁PE,瑞士CH,新西兰NZ,智利CL	0 受惠国LD	20	---Vanadium
	ex81129220	未锻轧、废碎料或粉末状的钒氮合金	Δ0				Vanadic-nitrogen; unwroght, waste and scrape, powder
5750	8112.9230	---铟	3	0 澳AU,巴PK,冰岛IS,东盟AS,哥CR,韩国KR,秘鲁PE,瑞士CH,新西兰NZ,智利CL	0 受惠国LD	20	---Indium
5751	8112.9240	---铌	3Δ1	0 澳AU,巴PK,冰岛IS,东盟AS,哥CR,韩国KR,秘鲁PE,瑞士CH,新西兰NZ,智利CL	0 受惠国LD	20	---Niobium
5752	8112.9290	---其他	3	0 澳AU,巴PK,冰岛IS,东盟AS,哥CR,韩国KR,秘鲁PE,瑞士CH,新西兰NZ,智利CL	0 受惠国LD	20	---Other
		--其他:					--Other:
5753	8112.9910	---锗	3	0 澳AU,巴PK,冰岛IS,东盟AS,哥CR,韩国KR,秘鲁PE,瑞士CH,新西兰NZ,智利CL	0 受惠国LD	20	---Germanium
5754	8112.9920	---钒	3	0 澳AU,巴PK,冰岛IS,东盟AS,哥CR,韩国KR,秘鲁PE,瑞士CH,新西兰NZ,智利CL	0 受惠国LD	20	---Vanadium
	ex81129920	其他钒氮合金	Δ0				Other vanadic-nitrogen
5755	8112.9930	---铟	8	0 冰岛IS,东盟AS,哥CR,秘鲁PE,新西兰NZ,智利CL 3.2 瑞士CH 4.8 澳AU,韩国KR 5 巴PK	0 受惠国LD	20	---Indium
5756	8112.9940	---铌	8	0 冰岛IS,东盟AS,哥CR,秘鲁PE,新西兰NZ,智利CL 3.2 瑞士CH 4.8 澳AU,韩国KR 5 巴PK	0 受惠国LD	20	---Niobium

序号 No.	税则号列 Tariff Line	中文货品名称 Article Description in Chinese	最惠国税率 MFN(%)	协定税率 Agreement(%)	特惠税率 SP(%)	普通税率 Gen(%)	英文货品名称 Article Description
5757	8112.9990	---其他	8	0 巴PK,冰岛IS,东盟AS,哥CR,秘鲁PE,新西兰NZ,智利CL 3.2 瑞士CH 4.8 澳AU,韩国KR	0 受惠国LD	30	---Other
	81.13	**金属陶瓷及其制品，包括废碎料：**					**Cermets and articles thereof, including waste and scrap:**
5758	8113.0010	---颗粒；粉末	8.4	0 冰岛IS,东盟AS,哥CR,秘鲁PE,台湾TW,新西兰NZ,智利CL 3.36 瑞士CH 5 澳AU,巴PK	0 受惠国$_1$LD$_1$	30	---Granules and powders
5759	8113.0090	---其他	8.4	0 冰岛IS,东盟AS,哥CR,秘鲁PE,台湾TW,新西兰NZ,智利CL 3.36 瑞士CH 5 澳AU,巴PK	0 受惠国$_1$LD$_1$	30	---Other

第八十二章
贱金属工具、器具、利口器、餐匙、餐叉及其零件

Chapter 82
Tools, implements, cutlery, spoons and forks, of base metal

注释：

一、除喷灯、轻便锻炉、带支架的砂轮、修指甲和修脚用器具及税号 82.09 的货品外，本章仅包括带有用下列材料制成的刀片、工作刃、工作面或其他工作部件的物品：

（一）贱金属；

（二）硬质合金或金属陶瓷；

（三）装于贱金属、硬质合金或金属陶瓷底座上的宝石或半宝石（天然、合成或再造）；

（四）附于贱金属底座上的磨料，当附上磨料后，所具有的切齿、沟、槽或类似结构仍保持其特性及功能。

二、本章所列物品的贱金属零件，应与该制品归入同一税号，但具体列名的零件及手工工具的工具夹具（税号 84.66）除外。第十五类注释二所述的通用零件，均不归入本章。电动剃须刀及电动毛发推剪的刀头、刀片应归入税号 85.10。

三、由税号 82.11 的一把或多把刀具与税号 82.15 至少数量相同的物品构成的成套货品应归入税号 82.15。

Notes:

1. Apart from blow lamps, portable forges, grinding wheels with frameworks, manicure or pedicure sets, and goods of heading No.82.09, this Chapter covers only articles with a blade, working edge, working surface or other working part of:
   (a) Base metal;
   (b) Metal carbides or cermets;
   (c) Precious or semi-precious stones(natural, synthetic or reconstructed) on a support of base metal, metal carbide or cermet; or
   (d) Abrasive materials on a support of base metal, provided that the articles have cutting teeth, flutes, grooves, or the like, of base metal, which retain their identity and function after the application of the abrasive.
2. Parts of base metal of the articles of this Chapter are to be classified with the articles of which they are parts, except parts separately specified as such and tool-holders for hand tools (heading No.84.66). However, parts of general use as defined in Note2 to Section XV are in all cases excluded from this Chapter. Heads, blades and cutting plates for electric shavers or electric hair clippers are to be classified in heading No.85.10.
3. Sets consisting of one or more knives of heading No.82.11 and at least an equal number of articles of heading No.82.15 are to be classified in heading No.82.15.

序号 No.	税则号列 Tariff Line	中文货品名称 Article Description in Chinese	最惠国税率 MFN(%)	协定税率 Agreement(%)	特惠税率 SP(%)	普通税率 Gen(%)	英文货品名称 Article Description
	82.01	**锹、铲、镐、锄、叉及耙；斧子、钩刀及类似砍伐工具；各种修枝用剪刀；镰刀、秣刀、树篱剪、伐木楔子及其他农业、园艺或林业用手工工具：**					**Hand tools, the following: spades, shovels, mattocks, picks, hoes, forks and rakes; axes, billhooks and similar hewing tools; secateurs and pruners of any kind; scythes, sickles, hay knives, hedge shears, timber wedges and other tools of a kind used in agriculture, horticulture or forestry:**
5760	8201.1000	-锹及铲	8	0 冰岛IS,东盟AS,哥CR,秘鲁PE,新西兰NZ,智利CL 3.2 瑞士CH 4.8 澳AU,韩国KR 5 巴PK	0 受惠国LD	50	-Spades and shovels
5761	8201.3000	-镐、锄及耙	8	0 冰岛IS,东盟AS,哥CR,秘鲁PE,新西兰NZ,智利CL 3.2 瑞士CH 4.8 澳AU,韩国KR 5 巴PK	0 受惠国LD	50	-Mattocks, picks, hoes and rakes
5762	8201.4000	-斧子、钩刀及类似砍伐工具	8	0 冰岛IS,东盟AS,哥CR,秘鲁PE,新西兰NZ,智利CL 3.2 瑞士CH 4.8 澳AU,韩国KR 5 巴PK	0 受惠国LD	50	-Axes, bill hooks and similar hewing tools

序号 No.	税则号列 Tariff Line	中文货品名称 Article Description in Chinese	最惠国税率 MFN(%)	协定税率 Agreement(%)	特惠税率 SP(%)	普通税率 Gen(%)	英文货品名称 Article Description
5763	8201.5000	-修枝剪及类似的单手操作剪刀（包括家禽剪）	8	0 冰岛IS,东盟AS,哥CR,秘鲁PE,新西兰NZ,智利CL 3.2 瑞士CH 4.8 澳AU,韩国KR 5 巴PK	0 受惠国LD	50	-Secateurs and similar one-handed pruners and shears (including poultry shears)
5764	8201.6000	-树篱剪、双手修枝剪及类似的双手操作剪刀	8	0 冰岛IS,东盟AS,哥CR,秘鲁PE,新西兰NZ,智利CL 3.2 瑞士CH 4.8 澳AU,韩国KR 5 巴PK	0 受惠国LD	50	-Hedge shears, two-handed pruning shears and similar two-handed shears
		-用于农业、园艺或林业的其他手工工具：					-Other hand tools of a kind used in agriculture, horticulture or forestry:
5765	8201.9010	---叉	8	0 冰岛IS,东盟AS,哥CR,秘鲁PE,新西兰NZ,智利CL 3.2 瑞士CH 4.8 澳AU,韩国KR 5 巴PK	0 受惠国LD	50	---Forks
5766	8201.9090	---其他	8	0 冰岛IS,东盟AS,哥CR,秘鲁PE,新西兰NZ,智利CL 3.2 瑞士CH 4.8 澳AU 5 巴PK 6.4 韩国KR	0 受惠国LD	50	---Other
	82.02	**手工锯;各种锯的锯片（包括切条、切槽或无齿锯片）:**					**Handsaws; blades for saws of all kinds (including slitting, slotting or toothless saw blades) :**
5767	8202.1000	-手工锯	8.4	0 冰岛IS,东盟AS,哥CR,秘鲁PE,新西兰NZ,智利CL 3.36 瑞士CH 5 澳AU,巴PK 6.7 韩国KR	0 受惠国LD	50	-Hand saws
		-带锯片：					-Band saw blades:
5768	8202.2010	---双金属带锯条	8	0 冰岛IS,东盟AS,哥CR,秘鲁PE,新西兰NZ,智利CL 4.8 澳AU 5 巴PK 5.6 瑞士CH 6.4 韩国KR	0 受惠国LD	20	---Bi-metal band saw blades
5769	8202.2090	---其他	8	0 冰岛IS,东盟AS,哥CR,秘鲁PE,新西兰NZ,智利CL 4.8 澳AU 5 巴PK 5.6 瑞士CH 6.4 韩国KR	0 受惠国LD	20	---Other
		-圆锯片（包括切条或切槽锯片）：					-Circular saw blades (including slitting or slotting saw blades) :
5770	8202.3100	--带有钢制工作部件	8	0 冰岛IS,东盟AS,哥CR,秘鲁PE,新西兰NZ,智利CL 3.2 瑞士CH 4.8 澳AU 5 巴PK 6.4 韩国KR	0 受惠国LD	20	--With working part of steel
		--其他，包括部件：					--Other, including parts:

序号 No.	税则号列 Tariff Line	中文货品名称 Article Description in Chinese	最惠国税率 MFN(%)	协定税率 Agreement(%)	特惠税率 SP(%)	普通税率 Gen(%)	英文货品名称 Article Description
5771	8202.3910	---带有天然或合成金刚石、立方氮化硼制的工作部件	8	0 冰岛IS,东盟AS,哥CR,秘鲁PE,香港HK,新西兰NZ,智利CL 3.2 瑞士CH 4.8 澳AU,韩国KR 5 巴PK	0 受惠国LD	20	---With working part of natural or synthetic diamonds or cubic boron nitride
5772	8202.3990	---其他	8	0 冰岛IS,东盟AS,哥CR,秘鲁PE,香港HK,新西兰NZ,智利CL 3.2 瑞士CH 4.8 澳AU,韩国KR 5 巴PK	0 受惠国LD	20	---Other
5773	8202.4000	-链锯片	8	0 冰岛IS,东盟AS,哥CR,秘鲁PE,新西兰NZ,智利CL 4.8 澳AU,韩国KR 5 巴PK 5.6 瑞士CH	0 受惠国LD	20	-Chain saw blades
		-其他锯片：					-Other saw blades:
		--直锯片，加工金属用：					--Straight saw blades, for working metal:
5774	8202.9110	---机械锯用	8	0 冰岛IS,东盟AS,哥CR,秘鲁PE,新西兰NZ,智利CL 4.8 澳AU 5 巴PK 5.6 瑞士CH 6.4 韩国KR 7 亚太AP	0 受惠国LD	20	---For sawing machines
5775	8202.9190	---其他	8	0 冰岛IS,东盟AS,哥CR,秘鲁PE,新西兰NZ,智利CL 4.8 澳AU,韩国KR 5 巴PK 5.6 瑞士CH	0 受惠国LD	50	---Other
		--其他：					--Other:
5776	8202.9910	---机械锯用	8.4	0 冰岛IS,东盟AS,哥CR,秘鲁PE,新西兰NZ,智利CL 5 澳AU,巴PK 5.9 瑞士CH 6.7 韩国KR	0 受惠国LD	20	---For sawing machines
5777	8202.9990	---其他	10.5	0 冰岛IS,东盟AS,哥CR,秘鲁PE,新加坡SG,新西兰NZ,智利CL 5 巴PK 6.3 澳AU 7.4 瑞士CH 8.4 韩国KR	0 受惠国[1]LD[1]	50	---Other
	82.03	**钢锉、木锉、钳子（包括剪钳）、镊子、白铁剪、切管器、螺栓切头器、打孔冲子及类似手工工具：**					**Files, rasps, pliers (including cutting pliers) , pincers, tweezers, metal-cutting shears, pipe-cutters, bolt croppers, perforating punches and similar hand tools:**
5778	8203.1000	-钢锉、木锉及类似工具	10.5	0 冰岛IS,东盟AS,哥CR,秘鲁PE,新加坡SG,新西兰NZ,智利CL 5 巴PK 6.3 澳AU 7.4 瑞士CH 8.4 韩国KR	0 受惠国LD	50	-Files, rasps and similar tools

序号 No.	税则号列 Tariff Line	中文货品名称 Article Description in Chinese	最惠国税率 MFN(%)	协定税率 Agreement(%)	特惠税率 SP(%)	普通税率 Gen(%)	英文货品名称 Article Description
5779	8203.2000	-钳子（包括剪钳）、镊子及类似工具	10.5	0 澳门MO,冰岛IS,东盟AS,哥CR,秘鲁PE,台湾TW,新加坡SG,新西兰NZ,智利CL 6.3 澳AU 7.4 瑞士CH 8.4 韩国KR	0 受惠国$_1$LD$_1$	50	-Pliers (including cutting pliers) , pincers, tweezers and similar tools
5780	8203.3000	-白铁剪及类似工具	10.5	0 冰岛IS,东盟AS,哥CR,秘鲁PE,新加坡SG,新西兰NZ,智利CL 5 巴PK 6.3 澳AU 7.4 瑞士CH 8.4 韩国KR	0 受惠国$_1$LD$_1$	50	-Metal cutting shears and similar tools
5781	8203.4000	-切管器、螺栓切头器、打孔冲子及类似工具	10.5	0 冰岛IS,东盟AS,哥CR,秘鲁PE,新加坡SG,新西兰NZ,智利CL 5 巴PK 6.3 澳AU 7.4 瑞士CH 8.4 韩国KR	0 受惠国$_1$LD$_1$	50	-Pipe-cutters, bolt croppers, perforat-ing punches and similar tools
	82.04	**手动扳手及扳钳(包括转矩扳手,但不包括丝锥扳手);可互换的扳手套筒,不论是否带手柄:**					**Hand-operated spanners and wrenches (including torque meter wrenches but not including tap wrenches) ; interchangeable spanner sockets, with or without handles:**
		-手动扳手及扳钳:					-Hand-operated spanners and wrenches:
5782	8204.1100	--固定的	10.5	0 冰岛IS,东盟AS,哥CR,秘鲁PE,新加坡SG,新西兰NZ,智利CL 5 巴PK 6.3 澳AU 7.4 瑞士CH 8.4 韩国KR	0 受惠国LD	50	--Non-adjustable
5783	8204.1200	--可调的	10	0 冰岛IS,东盟AS,哥CR,秘鲁PE,台湾TW,新西兰NZ,智利CL 4 瑞士CH 5 巴PK 6 澳AU 8 韩国KR	0 受惠国LD	50	--Adjustable
5784	8204.2000	-可互换的扳手套筒，不论是否带手柄	10	0 冰岛IS,东盟AS,哥CR,秘鲁PE,新西兰NZ,智利CL 4 瑞士CH 5 巴PK 6 澳AU 8 韩国KR	0 受惠国$_1$LD$_1$	50	-Interchangeable spanner sockets, with or without handles
	82.05	**其他税号未列名的手工工具（包括玻璃刀）;喷灯;台钳、夹钳及类似品,但作为机床附件或零件的除外;砧;轻便锻炉;带支架的手摇或脚踏砂轮:**					**Hand tools (including glaziers' diamonds) , not elsewhere specified or included; blowlamps; vices, clamps and the like, other than accessories for and parts of machine tools; anvils; portable forges; hand- or pedal-operated grinding wheels with frameworks:**
5785	8205.1000	-钻孔或攻丝工具	10	0 冰岛IS,东盟AS,哥CR,秘鲁PE,新西兰NZ,智利CL 4 瑞士CH 5 巴PK 6 澳AU 8 韩国KR	0 受惠国$_1$LD$_1$	50	-Drilling, threading or tapping tools

序号 No.	税则号列 Tariff Line	中文货品名称 Article Description in Chinese	最惠国税率 MFN(%)	协定税率 Agreement(%)	特惠税率 SP(%)	普通税率 Gen(%)	英文货品名称 Article Description
5786	8205.2000	-锤子	10	0 冰岛IS,东盟AS,哥CR,秘鲁PE,台湾TW,新西兰NZ,智利CL 4 瑞士CH 5 巴PK 6 澳AU 8 韩国KR	0 受惠国LD	50	-Hammers and sledge hammers
5787	8205.3000	-木工用刨子、凿子及类似切削工具	10.5	0 冰岛IS,东盟AS,哥CR,秘鲁PE,新加坡SG,新西兰NZ,智利CL 5 巴PK 6.3 澳AU 7.4 瑞士CH 8.4 韩国KR	0 受惠国$_1$LD$_1$	50	-Planes, chisels, gouges and similar cutting tools for working wood
5788	8205.4000	-螺丝刀	10.5	0 冰岛IS,东盟AS,哥CR,秘鲁PE,台湾TW,新加坡SG,新西兰NZ,智利CL 5 巴PK 6.3 澳AU 7.4 瑞士CH 8.4 韩国KR	0 受惠国LD	50	-Screwdrivers
		-其他手工工具（包括玻璃刀）:					-Other hand tools (including glaziers' diamonds) :
5789	8205.5100	--家用工具	10.5	0 冰岛IS,东盟AS,哥CR,秘鲁PE,新加坡SG,新西兰NZ,智利CL 5 巴PK 6.3 澳AU 7.4 瑞士CH 8.4 韩国KR	0 受惠国$_1$LD$_1$	50	--Household tools
5790	8205.5900	--其他	10	0 冰岛IS,东盟AS,哥CR,秘鲁PE,台湾TW,新西兰NZ,智利CL 5 巴PK 6 澳AU 7 瑞士CH 8 韩国KR 8.5 亚太AP	0 受惠国$_1$LD$_1$	50	--Other
5791	8205.6000	-喷灯	10	0 冰岛IS,东盟AS,哥CR,秘鲁PE,新西兰NZ,智利CL 5 巴PK 6 澳AU 7 瑞士CH 8 韩国KR	0 受惠国$_1$LD$_1$	50	-Blow lamps
5792	8205.7000	-台钳、夹钳及类似品	10.5	0 冰岛IS,东盟AS,哥CR,秘鲁PE,新加坡SG,新西兰NZ,智利CL 5 巴PK 6.3 澳AU 7.6 瑞士CH 8.4 韩国KR	0 受惠国$_1$LD$_1$	50	-Vices, clamps and the like
5793	8205.9000	-其他，包括由本税目项下两个或多个子目所列物品组成的成套货品	10.5	0 冰岛IS,东盟AS,哥CR,秘鲁PE,新加坡SG,新西兰NZ,智利CL 5 巴PK 6.3 澳AU 7.4 瑞士CH 8.4 韩国KR	0 受惠国$_1$LD$_1$	50	-Other, inculding sets of articles of two or more of subheadings of this heading
	82.06	**由税号82.02至82.05中两个或多个税目所列工具组成的零售包装成套货品**					**Tools of two or more of headings 8202 to 8205, put up in sets for retail sale**

序号 No.	税则号列 Tariff Line	中文货品名称 Article Description in Chinese	最惠国税率 MFN(%)	协定税率 Agreement(%)	特惠税率 SP(%)	普通税率 Gen(%)	英文货品名称 Article Description
5794	8206.0000	由税号82.02至82.05中两个或多个税目所列工具组成的零售包装成套货品	10.5	0 冰岛IS,东盟AS,哥CR,秘鲁PE,新加坡SG,新西兰NZ,智利CL 5 巴PK 6.3 澳AU 7.9 瑞士CH 8.4 韩国KR	0 受惠国$_1$LD$_1$	50	Tools of two or more of the headings Nos.82.02 to 82.05, put up in sets for retail sale
	82.07	**手工工具(不论是否有动力装置)及机床(例如,锻压、冲压、攻丝、钻孔、镗孔、铰孔及铣削、车削或上螺丝用的机器)的可互换工具,包括金属拉拔或挤压用模以及凿岩或钻探工具:**					**Interchangeable tools for hand tools, whether or not power-operated, or for machine tools (for example, for pressing, stamping, punching, tapping, threading, drilling, boring, broaching, milling, turning or screw driving), including dies for drawing or extruding metal, and rock-drilling or earth-boring tools:**
		-凿岩或钻探工具:					-Rock-drilling or earth-boring tools:
5795	8207.1300	--带有金属陶瓷制的工作部件	8	0 冰岛IS,东盟AS,哥CR,秘鲁PE,新西兰NZ,智利CL 3.2 瑞士CH 4.8 澳AU,韩国KR 5 巴PK	0 受惠国LD	20	--With working part of cermets
		--其他,包括部件:					--Other, including parts:
5796	8207.1910	---带有天然或合成金刚石、立方氮化硼制的工作部件	8	0 冰岛IS,东盟AS,哥CR,秘鲁PE,新西兰NZ,智利CL 3.2 瑞士CH 4.8 澳AU,韩国KR 5 巴PK	0 受惠国LD	20	---With working part of natural or synthetic diamonds or cubic boron nitride
5797	8207.1990	---其他	8	0 冰岛IS,东盟AS,哥CR,秘鲁PE,新西兰NZ,智利CL 3.2 瑞士CH 4.8 澳AU 5 巴PK 6.4 韩国KR	0 受惠国LD	20	---Other
		-金属拉拔或挤压用模:					-Dies for drawing or extruding metal:
5798	8207.2010	---带有天然或合成金刚石、立方氮化硼制的工作部件	8	0 冰岛IS,东盟AS,哥CR,秘鲁PE,台湾TW,新西兰NZ,智利CL 3.2 瑞士CH 4.8 澳AU,韩国KR 5 巴PK	0 受惠国LD	20	---With working part of natural or synthetic diamonds or cubic boron nitride
5799	8207.2090	---其他	8	0 冰岛IS,东盟AS,哥CR,秘鲁PE,台湾TW,新西兰NZ,智利CL 4.8 澳AU,韩国KR 5 巴PK 5.6 瑞士CH	0 受惠国LD	20	---Other
5800	8207.3000	-锻压或冲压工具	8	0 冰岛IS,东盟AS,哥CR,秘鲁PE,台湾TW,香港HK,新西兰NZ,智利CL 3.2 瑞士CH 4.8 澳AU 5 巴PK 6.8 亚太AP 6.9 韩国KR	0 受惠国LD	20	-Tools for pressing, stamping or punching

序号 No.	税则号列 Tariff Line	中文货品名称 Article Description in Chinese	最惠国税率 MFN(%)	协定税率 Agreement(%)	特惠税率 SP(%)	普通税率 Gen(%)	英文货品名称 Article Description
	ex82073000	加工小轿车车身冲压件用的4种关键模具（侧围外板模具、翼子板模具、拼接整体侧围内板模具、拼焊整体侧围加强板模具）	Δ6				Four key dies, used for processing stamping parts of car body (side outer panels dies , fender dies, dies for joining the whole side inner panels, dies for joining and welding the whole side-panel reinforcement)
	ex82073000	加工小轿车车身冲压件用的4种特种模具（σb≥980牛顿/平方毫米的冷冲压模具、热成型模具、内高压成型模具和铝板模具）	Δ6				Four special dies, used for processing stamping parts of car body (cold stamping dies with σ b≥980N/mm^2, hot forming dies, inside high pressure forming dies and aluminium panel dies)
5801	8207.4000	-攻丝工具	8	0 冰岛IS,东盟AS,哥CR,秘鲁PE,台湾TW,新西兰NZ,智利CL 3.2 瑞士CH 4.8 澳AU 5 巴PK	0 受惠国LD	20	-Tools for tapping or threading
		-钻孔工具，但凿岩及钻探用的除外：					-Tools for drilling, other than for rock-drilling:
5802	8207.5010	---带有天然或合成金刚石、立方氮化硼制的工作部件	8	0 冰岛IS,东盟AS,哥CR,秘鲁PE,瑞士CH,台湾TW,香港HK,新西兰NZ,智利CL 4.8 澳AU 5 巴PK	0 受惠国LD	20	---With working part of natural or synthetic diamonds or cubic boron nitride
5803	8207.5090	---其他	8	0 冰岛IS,东盟AS,哥CR,秘鲁PE,台湾TW,香港HK,新西兰NZ,智利CL 3.2 瑞士CH 4.8 澳AU 5 巴PK	0 受惠国LD	20	---Other
		-镗孔或铰孔工具：					-Tools for boring or broaching:
5804	8207.6010	---带有天然或合成金刚石、立方氮化硼制的工作部件	8	0 冰岛IS,东盟AS,哥CR,秘鲁PE,台湾TW,新西兰NZ,智利CL 3.2 瑞士CH 4.8 澳AU 5 巴PK	0 受惠国LD	20	---With working part of natural or synthetic diamonds or cubic boron nitride
5805	8207.6090	---其他	8	0 冰岛IS,东盟AS,哥CR,秘鲁PE,新西兰NZ,智利CL 3.2 瑞士CH 4.8 澳AU 5 巴PK 6.9 韩国KR	0 受惠国LD	20	---Other
		-铣削工具：					-Tools for milling:
5806	8207.7010	---带有天然或合成金刚石、立方氮化硼制的工作部件	8	0 冰岛IS,东盟AS,哥CR,秘鲁PE,台湾TW,香港HK,新西兰NZ,智利CL 3.2 瑞士CH 4.8 澳AU 5 巴PK	0 受惠国LD	20	---With working part of natural or synthetic diamonds or cubic boron nitride
5807	8207.7090	---其他	8	0 冰岛IS,东盟AS,哥CR,秘鲁PE,台湾TW,香港HK,新西兰NZ,智利CL 3.2 瑞士CH 4.8 澳AU 5 巴PK	0 受惠国LD	20	---Other
		-车削工具：					-Tools for turning:

序号 No.	税则号列 Tariff Line	中文货品名称 Article Description in Chinese	最惠国税率 MFN(%)	协定税率 Agreement(%)	特惠税率 SP(%)	普通税率 Gen(%)	英文货品名称 Article Description
5808	8207.8010	---带有天然或合成金刚石、立方氮化硼制的工作部件	8	0 冰岛IS,东盟AS,哥CR,秘鲁PE,台湾TW,新西兰NZ,智利CL 3.2 瑞士CH 4.8 澳AU 5 巴PK 6.8 韩国KR,亚太AP	0 受惠国LD	20	---With working part of natural or synthetic diamonds or cubic boron nitride
5809	8207.8090	---其他	8	0 冰岛IS,东盟AS,哥CR,秘鲁PE,台湾TW,新西兰NZ,智利CL 3.2 瑞士CH 4.8 澳AU 5 巴PK 6.8 韩国KR,亚太AP	0 受惠国LD	20	---Other
		-其他可互换工具:					-Other interchangeable tools:
5810	8207.9010	---带有天然或合成金刚石、立方氮化硼制的工作部件	8	0 冰岛IS,东盟AS,哥CR,秘鲁PE,台湾TW,香港HK,新西兰NZ,智利CL 3.2 瑞士CH 4.8 澳AU 5 巴PK 6.8 韩国KR,亚太AP	0 受惠国LD	20	---With working part of natural or synthetic diamonds or cubic boron nitride
5811	8207.9090	---其他	8	0 冰岛IS,东盟AS,哥CR,秘鲁PE,台湾TW,香港HK,新西兰NZ,智利CL 4.8 澳AU 5 巴PK 5.6 瑞士CH 6.8 韩国KR,亚太AP	0 受惠国LD	20	---Other
	82.08	**机器或机械器具的刀及刀片:**					**Knives and cutting blades, for machines or for mechanical appliances:**
		-金属加工用:					-For metalworking:
		---硬质合金制的:					---Of cemented carbide:
5812	8208.1011	----经镀或涂层的	8	0 冰岛IS,东盟AS,哥CR,秘鲁PE,香港HK,新西兰NZ,智利CL 4.8 澳AU 5 巴PK 5.6 瑞士CH 6.9 韩国KR	0 受惠国$_1$LD$_1$	20	----Plated or coated
5813	8208.1019	----其他	8	0 冰岛IS,东盟AS,哥CR,秘鲁PE,香港HK,新西兰NZ,智利CL 4.8 澳AU 5 巴PK 5.6 瑞士CH 6.9 韩国KR	0 受惠国$_1$LD$_1$	20	----Other
5814	8208.1090	---其他	8	0 冰岛IS,东盟AS,哥CR,秘鲁PE,香港HK,新西兰NZ,智利CL 4.8 澳AU 5 巴PK 5.6 瑞士CH 6.9 韩国KR	0 受惠国$_1$LD$_1$	20	---Other
5815	8208.2000	-木器加工用	8	0 冰岛IS,东盟AS,哥CR,秘鲁PE,台湾TW,新西兰NZ,智利CL 3.2 瑞士CH 4.8 澳AU,韩国KR 5 巴PK	0 受惠国LD	20	-For wood working

序号 No.	税则号列 Tariff Line	中文货品名称 Article Description in Chinese	最惠国税率 MFN(%)	协定税率 Agreement(%)	特惠税率 SP(%)	普通税率 Gen(%)	英文货品名称 Article Description
5816	8208.3000	-厨房器具或食品工业机器用	8	0 冰岛IS,东盟AS,哥CR,秘鲁PE,新西兰NZ,智利CL 3.2 瑞士CH 4.8 澳AU 5 巴PK 6.4 韩国KR	0 受惠国LD	20	-For kitchen appliances or for machines used by the food industry
5817	8208.4000	-农业、园艺或林业机器用	8	0 冰岛IS,东盟AS,哥CR,秘鲁PE,台湾TW,新西兰NZ,智利CL 4.8 澳AU,韩国KR 5 巴PK 5.6 瑞士CH	0 受惠国$_{1}$LD$_{1}$	20	-For agricultural, horticultural or forestry machines
5818	8208.9000	-其他	8	0 冰岛IS,东盟AS,哥CR,秘鲁PE,台湾TW,新西兰NZ,智利CL 4.8 澳AU,韩国KR 5 巴PK 5.6 瑞士CH 7.2 亚太AP	0 受惠国$_{1}$LD$_{1}$	20	-Other
	82.09	**未装配的工具用金属陶瓷板、杆、刀头及类似品:**					**Plates, sticks, tips and the like for tools, unmounted, of cermets:**
5819	8209.0010	---板	8	0 冰岛IS,东盟AS,哥CR,秘鲁PE,新西兰NZ,智利CL 3.2 瑞士CH 4.8 澳AU 5 巴PK 6.4 韩国KR 7.2 亚太AP	0 受惠国LD	20	---Plates
		---条、杆:					---Sticks:
5820	8209.0021	----晶粒度小于0.8微米的	8	0 冰岛IS,东盟AS,哥CR,秘鲁PE,新西兰NZ,智利CL 4.8 澳AU,韩国KR 5 巴PK 5.6 瑞士CH 7.2 亚太AP	0 受惠国LD	20	----Of a grain size of less than 0.8 microns
5821	8209.0029	----其他	8	0 冰岛IS,东盟AS,哥CR,秘鲁PE,新西兰NZ,智利CL 4.8 澳AU,韩国KR 5 巴PK 5.6 瑞士CH 7.2 亚太AP	0 受惠国LD	20	----Other
5822	8209.0030	---刀头	8	0 冰岛IS,东盟AS,哥CR,秘鲁PE,新西兰NZ,智利CL 3.2 瑞士CH 4.8 澳AU 5 巴PK 6.9 韩国KR 7.2 亚太AP	0 受惠国LD	20	---Tips
5823	8209.0090	---其他	8	0 冰岛IS,东盟AS,哥CR,秘鲁PE,新西兰NZ,智利CL 3.2 瑞士CH 4.8 澳AU,韩国KR 5 巴PK 7.2 亚太AP	0 受惠国LD	20	---Other
	82.10	**用于加工或调制食品或饮料的手动机械器具,重量不超过10公斤**					**Hand-operated mechanical appliances, weighing 10kg or less, used in the preparation, conditioning or serving of food or drink**

序号 No.	税则号列 Tariff Line	中文货品名称 Article Description in Chinese	最惠国税率 MFN(%)	协定税率 Agreement(%)	特惠税率 SP(%)	普通税率 Gen(%)	英文货品名称 Article Description
5824	8210.0000	用于加工或调制食品或饮料的手动机械器具，重量不超过10公斤	18	0 澳门MO,冰岛IS,东盟AS,哥CR,新加坡SG,新西兰NZ,智利CL 5.4 秘鲁PE 10.8 澳AU 12.6 瑞士CH 14.4 巴PK,韩国KR 16.2 亚太AP	0 受惠国$_1$LD$_1$	80	Hand-operated mechanical appliances, weighing 10kg or less, used in the preparation, conditioning or serving of food or drink
	82.11	**有刃口的刀及其刀片，不论是否有锯齿（包括整枝刀），但税号82.08的刀除外：**					**Knives with cutting blades, serrated or not (including pruning knives) , other than knives of heading 8208, and blades therefor:**
5825	8211.1000	-成套货品	18Δ10	0 巴PK,冰岛IS,东盟AS,哥CR,新加坡SG,新西兰NZ,智利CL 5.4 秘鲁PE 10.8 澳AU 12.6 瑞士CH 14.4 韩国KR	0 受惠国$_1$LD$_1$	80	-Sets of assorted articles
		-其他：					-Other:
5826	8211.9100	--刃面固定的餐刀	18Δ10	0 巴PK,冰岛IS,东盟AS,哥CR,新加坡SG,新西兰NZ,智利CL 5.4 秘鲁PE 10.8 澳AU 12.6 瑞士CH 14.4 韩国KR	0 受惠国$_1$LD$_1$	80	--Table knives having fixed blades
5827	8211.9200	--刃面固定的其他刀	12	0 巴PK,冰岛IS,东盟AS,哥CR,秘鲁PE,新加坡SG,新西兰NZ,智利CL 7.2 澳AU 9 瑞士CH 9.6 韩国KR	0 受惠国LD	80	--Other knives having fixed blades
5828	8211.9300	--刃面不固定的刀	18Δ10	0 巴PK,冰岛IS,东盟AS,哥CR,新加坡SG,新西兰NZ,智利CL 5.4 秘鲁PE 7.2 瑞士CH 10.8 澳AU 14.4 韩国KR	0 受惠国$_1$LD$_1$	80	--Knives having other than fixed blades
5829	8211.9400	--刀片	14	0 巴PK,冰岛IS,东盟AS,哥CR,秘鲁PE,新加坡SG,新西兰NZ,智利CL 8.4 澳AU 9.8 瑞士CH 11.2 韩国KR	0 受惠国$_1$LD$_1$	80	--Blades
5830	8211.9500	--贱金属制的刀柄	12	0 巴PK,冰岛IS,东盟AS,哥CR,秘鲁PE,新加坡SG,新西兰NZ,智利CL 7.2 澳AU 8.6 瑞士CH 9.6 韩国KR	0 受惠国LD	80	--Handles of base metal
	82.12	**剃刀及其刀片（包括未分开的刀片条）：**					**Razors and razor blades (including razor blade blanks in strips) :**
5831	8212.1000	-剃刀	12	0 巴PK,冰岛IS,东盟AS,哥CR,秘鲁PE,新加坡SG,新西兰NZ,智利CL 7.2 澳AU 8.4 瑞士CH 9.6 韩国KR	0 受惠国LD	80	-Razors

序号 No.	税则号列 Tariff Line	中文货品名称 Article Description in Chinese	最惠国税率 MFN(%)	协定税率 Agreement(%)	特惠税率 SP(%)	普通税率 Gen(%)	英文货品名称 Article Description
5832	8212.2000	-安全刀片，包括未分开的刀片条	14	0 巴PK,冰岛IS,东盟AS,哥CR,秘鲁PE,新加坡SG,新西兰NZ,智利CL 8.4 澳AU 9.8 瑞士CH 11.2 韩国KR	0 受惠国$_1$LD$_1$	80	-Safety razor blades, including razor blade blanks in strips
5833	8212.9000	-其他零件	12	0 巴PK,冰岛IS,东盟AS,哥CR,秘鲁PE,新加坡SG,新西兰NZ,智利CL 7.2 澳AU 8.4 瑞士CH 9.6 韩国KR	0 受惠国LD	80	-Other parts
	82.13	**剪刀、裁缝剪刀及类似品、剪刀片**					**Scissors, tailors' shears and similar shears, and blades therefor**
5834	8213.0000	剪刀、裁缝剪刀及类似品、剪刀片	12	0 巴PK,冰岛IS,东盟AS,哥CR,秘鲁PE,新加坡SG,新西兰NZ,智利CL 7.2 澳AU 8.4 瑞士CH 9.6 韩国KR 10.8 亚太AP	0 受惠国LD	80	Scissors, tailors' shears and similar shears, and blades therefor
	82.14	**其他利口器（例如，理发推剪、屠刀、砍骨刀、切肉刀、切菜刀、裁纸刀）；修指甲及修脚用具（包括指甲锉）：**					**Other articles of cutlery (for example, hair clippers, butchers' or kitchen cleavers, choppers and mincing knives, paperknives) ; manicure or pedicure sets and instruments (including nail files) :**
5835	8214.1000	-裁纸刀、开信刀、改错刀、铅笔刀及其刀片	12	0 冰岛IS,东盟AS,哥CR,秘鲁PE,新加坡SG,新西兰NZ,智利CL 5 巴PK 7.2 澳AU 8.4 瑞士CH 9.6 韩国KR 10.8 亚太AP	0 受惠国LD	80	-Paper knives, letter openers, erasing knives, pencil sharpeners and blades therefor
5836	8214.2000	-修指甲及修脚用具（包括指甲锉）	18	0 冰岛IS,东盟AS,哥CR,新加坡SG,新西兰NZ,智利CL 5.4 秘鲁PE 10.8 澳AU 12.6 瑞士CH 14.4 韩国KR 16.2 巴PK,亚太AP	0 受惠国LD	90	-Manicure or pedicure sets and instruments (including nail files)
5837	8214.9000	-其他	18	0 冰岛IS,东盟AS,哥CR,新加坡SG,新西兰NZ,智利CL 5.4 秘鲁PE 10.8 澳AU 12.6 瑞士CH 14.4 韩国KR	0 受惠国$_1$LD$_1$	80	-Other
	82.15	**餐匙、餐叉、长柄勺、漏勺、糕点夹、鱼刀、黄油刀、糖块夹及类似的厨房或餐桌用具：**					**Spoons, forks, ladles, skimmers, cake-servers, fish-knives, butter-knives, sugar tongs and similar kitchen or tableware:**
5838	8215.1000	-成套货品，至少其中一件物品是镀贵金属的	18	0 巴PK,冰岛IS,东盟AS,哥CR,新加坡SG,新西兰NZ,智利CL 5.4 秘鲁PE 10.8 澳AU 12.6 瑞士CH 14.4 韩国KR	0 受惠国$_1$LD$_1$	80	-Sets of assorted articles containing at least one article plated with precious metal

序号 No.	税则号列 Tariff Line	中文货品名称 Article Description in Chinese	最惠国税率 MFN(%)	协定税率 Agreement(%)	特惠税率 SP(%)	普通税率 Gen(%)	英文货品名称 Article Description
5839	8215.2000	-其他成套货品	18	0 巴PK,冰岛IS,东盟AS,哥CR,新加坡SG,新西兰NZ,智利CL 5.4 秘鲁PE 10.8 澳AU 12.6 瑞士CH 14.4 韩国KR	0 受惠国$_1$LD$_1$	80	-Other sets of assorted articles
		-其他：					-Other:
5840	8215.9100	--镀贵金属的	18	0 巴PK,冰岛IS,东盟AS,哥CR,新加坡SG,新西兰NZ,智利CL 5.4 秘鲁PE 10.8 澳AU 12.6 瑞士CH 14.4 韩国KR	0 受惠国$_1$LD$_1$	80	--Plated with precious metal
5841	8215.9900	--其他	18Δ10	0 巴PK,冰岛IS,东盟AS,哥CR,香港HK,新加坡SG,新西兰NZ,智利CL 5.4 秘鲁PE 10.8 澳AU 12.6 瑞士CH 14.4 韩国KR	0 受惠国LD	80	--Other

第八十三章
贱金属杂项制品

注释:

一、在本章，贱金属零件应与制品一同归类。但税号73.12、73.15、73.17、73.18及73.20的钢铁制品或其他贱金属（第七十四章至第七十六章及第七十八章至第八十一章）制的类似物品不应视为本章制品的零件。

二、税号83.02所称“脚轮”，是指直径（对于有胎的，连胎计算在内，下同）不超过75毫米的或直径虽超过75毫米，但所装轮或胎的宽度必须小于30毫米的脚轮。

Chapter 83
Miscellaneous articles of base metal

Notes:

1. For the purposes of this Chapter, parts of base metal are to be classified with their parent artcles. However, articles of iron or steel of heading No.73.12, 73.15, 73.17, 73.18 or 73.20, or similar articles of other base metal (Chapters 74 to 76 and 78 to 81) are not to be taken as parts of articles of this Chapter.
2. For the purposes of heading No.83.02, the word "castors" means those having a diameter (including, where appropriate, tyres) not exceeding75mm, or those having a diameter (including, where appropriatetyres) exceeding 75mm provided that the width of the wheel or tyre fitted thereto is less than 30mm.

序号 No.	税则号列 Tariff Line	中文货品名称 Article Description in Chinese	最惠国税率 MFN(%)	协定税率 Agreement(%)	特惠税率 SP(%)	普通税率 Gen(%)	英文货品名称 Article Description
	83.01	**贱金属制的锁（钥匙锁、数码锁及电动锁）；贱金属制带锁的扣环及扣环框架；上述锁的贱金属制钥匙：**					**Padlocks and locks (key, combination or electrically operated), of base metal; clasps and frames with clasps, incorporating locks, of base metal; keys for any of the foregoing articles, of base metal:**
5842	8301.1000	-挂锁	14	0 冰岛IS,东盟AS,哥CR,秘鲁PE,新加坡SG,新西兰NZ,智利CL 8.4 澳AU 9.8 瑞士CH 11.2 巴PK,韩国KR	0 受惠国$_1$LD$_1$	80	-Padlocks
		-机动车用锁：					-Locks of a kind used for motor vehicles:
5843	8301.2010	---中央控制门锁	10	0 冰岛IS,哥CR,秘鲁PE,新西兰NZ,智利CL 4 瑞士CH 6 澳AU 9 韩国KR	0 受惠国LD	80	---Central control door lock
5844	8301.2090	---其他	10	0 冰岛IS,哥CR,秘鲁PE,新西兰NZ,智利CL 4 瑞士CH 6 澳AU 9 韩国KR	0 受惠国LD	80	---Other
5845	8301.3000	-家具用锁	14	0 冰岛IS,东盟AS,哥CR,秘鲁PE,新加坡SG,新西兰NZ,智利CL 8.4 澳AU 9.8 瑞士CH 11.2 巴PK,韩国KR	0 受惠国LD	80	-Locks of a kind used for furniture
5846	8301.4000	-其他锁	14	0 冰岛IS,东盟AS,哥CR,秘鲁PE,新加坡SG,新西兰NZ,智利CL 8.4 澳AU 9.8 瑞士CH 11.2 巴PK,韩国KR	0 受惠国LD	80	-Other locks
5847	8301.5000	-带锁的扣环及扣环框架	14	0 冰岛IS,东盟AS,哥CR,秘鲁PE,香港HK,新加坡SG,新西兰NZ,智利CL 8.4 澳AU 9.8 瑞士CH 11.2 巴PK,韩国KR	0 受惠国$_1$LD$_1$	80	-Clasps and frames with clasps, incorporating locks

序号 No.	税则号列 Tariff Line	中文货品名称 Article Description in Chinese	最惠国税率 MFN(%)	协定税率 Agreement(%)		特惠税率 SP(%)		普通税率 Gen(%)	英文货品名称 Article Description
5848	8301.6000	-零件	12	0 6 7.2 8.4 9.6	冰岛IS,东盟AS,哥CR,秘鲁PE,新加坡SG,新西兰NZ,智利CL 巴PK 澳AU 瑞士CH 韩国KR	0	受惠国LD	80	-Parts
5849	8301.7000	-钥匙	10	0 4 5 6 8.6	冰岛IS,东盟AS,哥CR,秘鲁PE,新西兰NZ,智利CL 瑞士CH 巴PK 澳AU 韩国KR	0	受惠国LD	80	-Keys presented separately
	83.02	**用于家具、门窗、楼梯、百叶窗、车厢、鞍具、衣箱、盒子及类似品的贱金属附件及架座;贱金属制帽架、帽钩、托架及类似品;用贱金属做支架的小脚轮;贱金属制的自动闭门器:**							**Base metal mountings, fittings and similar articles suitable for furniture, doors, staircases, windows, blinds, coachwork, saddlery, trunks, chests, caskets or the like; base metal hat-racks, hat-pegs, brackets and similar fixtures; castors with mountings of base metal; automatic door closers of base metal:**
5850	8302.1000	-铰链（折叶）	10	0 4 5 6	冰岛IS,东盟AS,哥CR,秘鲁PE,香港HK,新西兰NZ,智利CL 瑞士CH 巴PK 澳AU,韩国KR	0	受惠国LD	80	-Hinges
5851	8302.2000	-小脚轮	12	0 6 7.2 8.4 9.6	冰岛IS,东盟AS,哥CR,秘鲁PE,新加坡SG,新西兰NZ,智利CL 巴PK 澳AU 瑞士CH 韩国KR	0	受惠国LD	80	-Castors
5852	8302.3000	-机动车辆用的其他附件及架座	10	0 4 5 6 8.6	冰岛IS,东盟AS,哥CR,秘鲁PE,新西兰NZ,智利CL 瑞士CH 巴PK 澳AU 韩国KR	0	受惠国LD	80	-Other mountings, fittings and similar articles suitable for motor vehicles
		-其他附件及架座:							-Other mountings, fittings and similar articles:
5853	8302.4100	--建筑用	14	0 8.4 9.8 11.2	冰岛IS,东盟AS,哥CR,秘鲁PE,新加坡SG,新西兰NZ,智利CL 澳AU 瑞士CH 巴PK,韩国KR	0	受惠国$_1$LD$_1$	80	--Suitable for buildings
5854	8302.4200	--其他，家具用	12	0 6 7.2 8.4 9.6	冰岛IS,东盟AS,哥CR,秘鲁PE,新加坡SG,新西兰NZ,智利CL 巴PK 澳AU 瑞士CH 韩国KR	0	受惠国LD	80	--Other, suitable for furniture
5855	8302.4900	--其他	12	0 6 7.2 8.4 9.6	冰岛IS,东盟AS,哥CR,秘鲁PE,新加坡SG,新西兰NZ,智利CL 巴PK 澳AU 瑞士CH 韩国KR	0	受惠国LD	80	--Other

序号 No.	税则号列 Tariff Line	中文货品名称 Article Description in Chinese	最惠国税率 MFN(%)	协定税率 Agreement(%)	特惠税率 SP(%)	普通税率 Gen(%)	英文货品名称 Article Description
5856	8302.5000	-帽架、帽钩、托架及类似品	14	0 冰岛IS,东盟AS,哥CR,秘鲁PE,新加坡SG,新西兰NZ,智利CL 8.4 澳AU 9.8 瑞士CH 11.2 巴PK,韩国KR	0 受惠国$_1$LD$_1$	80	-Hat-racks, hat-pegs, brackets and similar fixtures
5857	8302.6000	-自动闭门器	12	0 冰岛IS,东盟AS,哥CR,秘鲁PE,新加坡SG,新西兰NZ,智利CL 6 巴PK 7.2 澳AU 8.4 瑞士CH 9.6 韩国KR	0 受惠国LD	80	-Automatic door closers
	83.03	**装甲或加强的贱金属制保险箱、保险柜及保险库的门和带锁保险储存橱、钱箱、契约箱及类似品**					**Armoured or reinforced safes, strongboxes and doors and safe deposit lockers for strong-rooms, cash or deed boxes and the like, of base metal**
5858	8303.0000	装甲或加强的贱金属制保险箱、保险柜及保险库的门和带锁保险储存橱、钱箱、契约箱及类似品	14	0 冰岛IS,东盟AS,哥CR,秘鲁PE,新加坡SG,新西兰NZ,智利CL 8.4 澳AU 9.8 瑞士CH 11.2 巴PK,韩国KR	0 受惠国$_1$LD$_1$	50	Armoured or reinforced safes, strong-boxes and doors and safe deposit lockers for strong-rooms, cash or deed boxes and the like, of base metal
	83.04	**贱金属制的档案柜、卡片索引柜、文件盘、文件篮、笔盘、公章架及类似的办公用具，但税号94.03的办公室家具除外**					**Filing cabinets, card-index cabinets, paper trays, paper rests, pen trays, office-stamp stands and similar office or desk equipment, of base metal, other than office furniture of heading 9403**
5859	8304.0000	贱金属制的档案柜、卡片索引柜、文件盘、文件篮、笔盘、公章架及类似的办公用具，但税号94.03的办公室家具除外	10.5	0 冰岛IS,东盟AS,哥CR,秘鲁PE,香港HK,新加坡SG,新西兰NZ,智利CL 5 巴PK 6.3 澳AU 7.4 瑞士CH 8.4 韩国KR	0 受惠国LD	80	Filing cabinets, card-index cabinets, paper trays, paper rests, pen trays, office-stamp stands and similar office or desk equipment, of base metal, other than office furniture of heading No.94.03
	83.05	**活页夹、卷宗夹的贱金属附件，贱金属制的信夹、信角、文件夹、索引标签及类似的办公用品;贱金属制的成条钉书钉（例如，供办公室、室内装饰或包装用）:**					**Fittings for loose-leaf binders or files, letter clips, letter corners, paper clips, indexing tags and similar office articles, of base metal; staples in strips (for example, for offices, upholstery, packaging) , of base metal:**
5860	8305.1000	-活页夹或卷宗夹的附件	10.5	0 冰岛IS,东盟AS,哥CR,秘鲁PE,新加坡SG,新西兰NZ,智利CL 5 巴PK 6.3 澳AU 7.4 瑞士CH 8.4 韩国KR	0 受惠国LD	80	-Fittings for loose-leaf binders of files
5861	8305.2000	-成条钉书钉	10.5	0 冰岛IS,东盟AS,哥CR,秘鲁PE,新加坡SG,新西兰NZ,智利CL 5 巴PK 6.3 澳AU 7.4 瑞士CH 8.4 韩国KR	0 受惠国LD	80	-Staples in strips

序号 No.	税则号列 Tariff Line	中文货品名称 Article Description in Chinese	最惠国税率 MFN(%)	协定税率 Agreement(%)	特惠税率 SP(%)	普通税率 Gen(%)	英文货品名称 Article Description
5862	8305.9000	-其他，包括零件	10.5	0 冰岛IS,东盟AS,哥CR,秘鲁PE,香港HK,新加坡SG,新西兰NZ,智利CL 5 巴PK 6.3 澳AU 7.4 瑞士CH 8.4 韩国KR	0 受惠国LD	80	-Other, including parts
	83.06	**非电动的贱金属铃、钟、锣及类似品;贱金属雕塑像及其他装饰品;贱金属相框或画框及类似框架;贱金属镜子:**					**Bells, gongs and the like, non-electric, of base metal; statuettes and other ornaments, of base metal; photograph, picture or similar frames, of base metal; mirrors of base metal:**
5863	8306.1000	-铃、钟、锣及类似品	8	0 冰岛IS,东盟AS,哥CR,秘鲁PE,新西兰NZ,智利CL 3.2 瑞士CH 4.8 澳AU 5 巴PK 6.4 韩国KR	0 受惠国LD	80	-Bells, gongs and the like
		-雕塑像及其他装饰品:					-Statuettes and other ornaments:
5864	8306.2100	--镀贵金属的	8	0 冰岛IS,东盟AS,哥CR,秘鲁PE,新西兰NZ,智利CL 3.2 瑞士CH 4.8 澳AU,韩国KR 5 巴PK	0 受惠国LD	100	--Plated with precious metal
		--其他:					--Other:
5865	8306.2910	---景泰蓝的	8	0 冰岛IS,东盟AS,哥CR,秘鲁PE,新西兰NZ,智利CL 3.2 瑞士CH 4.8 澳AU,韩国KR 5 巴PK	0 受惠国LD	100	---Cloisonne
5866	8306.2990	---其他	8	0 冰岛IS,东盟AS,哥CR,秘鲁PE,新加坡SG,新西兰NZ,智利CL 3.2 瑞士CH 4.8 澳AU 5 巴PK 6.4 韩国KR	0 受惠国LD	100	---Other
5867	8306.3000	-相框、画框及类似框架;镜子	8	0 冰岛IS,东盟AS,哥CR,秘鲁PE,新西兰NZ,智利CL 3.2 瑞士CH 4.8 澳AU 5 巴PK 6.4 韩国KR	0 受惠国LD	100	-Photograph, picture or similar frames; mirrors
	83.07	**贱金属软管，不论是否有附件:**					**Flexible tubing of base metal, with or without fittings:**
5868	8307.1000	-钢铁制	8.4	0 冰岛IS,东盟AS,哥CR,秘鲁PE,新西兰NZ,智利CL 5 澳AU,巴PK 5.9 瑞士CH 6.7 韩国KR	0 受惠国LD	35	-Of iron or steel
5869	8307.9000	-其他贱金属制	8.4	0 冰岛IS,东盟AS,哥CR,秘鲁PE,香港HK,新西兰NZ,智利CL 3.36 瑞士CH 5 澳AU,巴PK 6.7 韩国KR	0 受惠国LD	35	-Of other base metal

序号 No.	税则号列 Tariff Line	中文货品名称 Article Description in Chinese	最惠国税率 MFN(%)	协定税率 Agreement(%)	特惠税率 SP(%)	普通税率 Gen(%)	英文货品名称 Article Description
	83.08	**贱金属制的扣、钩、环、眼及类似品，用于衣着、鞋靴、天篷、提包、旅行用品或其他制成品;贱金属制的管形铆钉及开口铆钉;贱金属制的珠子及亮晶片：**					**Clasps, frames with clasps, buckles, buckle-clasps, hooks, eyes, eyelets and the like, of base metal, of a kind used for clothing, footwear, awnings, handbags, travel goods or other made-up articles, tubular or bifurcated rivets, of base metal; beads and spangles of base metal:**
5870	8308.1000	-钩、环及眼	10.5	0 冰岛IS,东盟AS,哥CR,秘鲁PE,香港HK,新加坡SG,新西兰NZ,智利CL 5 巴PK 6.3 澳AU 7.4 瑞士CH 9.4 韩国KR	0 受惠国LD	80	-Hooks, eyes and eyelets
5871	8308.2000	-管形铆钉及开口铆钉	10.5	0 冰岛IS,东盟AS,哥CR,秘鲁PE,香港HK,新加坡SG,新西兰NZ,智利CL 5 巴PK 6.3 澳AU 7.4 瑞士CH 8.4 韩国KR	0 受惠国LD	80	-Tubular or bifurcated rivets
5872	8308.9000	-其他，包括零件	10.5	0 冰岛IS,东盟AS,哥CR,秘鲁PE,香港HK,新加坡SG,新西兰NZ,智利CL 5 巴PK 6.3 澳AU 7.4 瑞士CH 9.4 韩国KR	0 受惠国LD	80	-Other, including parts
	83.09	**贱金属制的塞子、盖子（包括冠形瓶塞、螺口盖及倒水塞）、瓶帽、螺口塞、塞子帽、封志及其他包装用附件：**					**Stoppers, caps and lids (including crown corks, screw caps and pouring stoppers), capsules for bottles, threaded bungs, bung covers, seals and other packing accessories, of base metal:**
5873	8309.1000	-冠形瓶塞	18	0 冰岛IS,东盟AS,哥CR,秘鲁PE,香港HK,新加坡SG,新西兰NZ,智利CL 10.8 澳AU 12.6 瑞士CH 14.4 巴PK,韩国KR	0 受惠国$_1$LD$_1$	90	-Crown corks
5874	8309.9000	-其他	12	0 冰岛IS,东盟AS,哥CR,秘鲁PE,香港HK,新加坡SG,新西兰NZ,智利CL 6 巴PK 7.2 澳AU 8.4 瑞士CH 9.6 韩国KR	0 受惠国LD	80	-Other
	83.10	**贱金属制的标志牌、铭牌、地名牌及类似品、号码、字母及类似标志，但税号94.05的货品除外**					**Sign-plates, name-plates, addressplates and similar plates, numbers, letters and other symbols, of base metal, excluding those of heading No.94.05**

序号 No.	税则号列 Tariff Line	中文货品名称 Article Description in Chinese	最惠国税率 MFN(%)	协定税率 Agreement(%)	特惠税率 SP(%)	普通税率 Gen(%)	英文货品名称 Article Description
5875	8310.0000	贱金属制的标志牌、铭牌、地名牌及类似品、号码、字母及类似标志，但税号94.05的货品除外	18	0 冰岛IS,东盟AS,哥CR,新加坡SG,新西兰NZ,智利CL 5.4 秘鲁PE 10.8 澳AU 12.6 瑞士CH 14.4 韩国KR	0 受惠国$_1$LD$_1$	80	Sign-plates, name-plates, address-plates and similar plates, numbers, letters and other symbols, of base metal, excluding those of heading No.94.05
	83.11	**贱金属或硬质合金制的丝、条、管、板、电极及类似品，以焊剂涂面或以焊剂为芯，用于焊接或沉积金属、硬质合金;贱金属粉粘聚而成的丝或条，供金属喷镀用:**					**Wire, rods, tubes, plates, electrodes and similar products, of base metal or of metal carbides, coated or cored with flux material, of a kind used for soldering, brazing, welding or deposition of metal or of metal carbides; wire and rods, of agglomerated base metal powder, used for metal spraying:**
5876	8311.1000	-以焊剂涂面的贱金属制电极，电弧焊用	8	0 冰岛IS,东盟AS,哥CR,秘鲁PE,香港HK,新西兰NZ,智利CL 3.2 瑞士CH 4.8 澳AU,韩国KR 5 巴PK	0 受惠国LD	30	-Coated electrodes of base metal, for electric arc-welding
5877	8311.2000	-以焊剂为芯的贱金属制焊丝，电弧焊用	8	0 冰岛IS,东盟AS,哥CR,秘鲁PE,香港HK,新西兰NZ,智利CL 3.2 瑞士CH 4.8 澳AU 5 巴PK 6.9 韩国KR	0 受惠国LD	30	-Cored wire of base metal, for electric arcwelding
5878	8311.3000	-以焊剂涂面或以焊剂为芯的贱金属条或丝，钎焊或气焊用	8	0 冰岛IS,东盟AS,哥CR,秘鲁PE,香港HK,新西兰NZ,智利CL 3.2 瑞士CH 4.8 澳AU 5 巴PK	0 受惠国LD	30	-Coated rods and cored wire, of base metal, for soldering, brazing or welding by flame
5879	8311.9000	-其他	8	0 冰岛IS,东盟AS,哥CR,秘鲁PE,香港HK,新西兰NZ,智利CL 3.2 瑞士CH 4.8 澳AU,韩国KR 5 巴PK 5.6 亚太AP	0 受惠国LD	30	-Other

第十六类
机器、机械器具、电气设备及其零件；录音机及放声机、电视图像、声音的录制和重放设备及其零件、附件

注释：

一、本类不包括：

(一)第三十九章的塑料或税号 40.10 的硫化橡胶制的传动带、输送带，除硬质橡胶以外的硫化橡胶制的机器、机械器具、电气器具或其他专门技术用途的物品(税号 40.16)；

(二)机器、机械器具或其他专门技术用途的皮革、再生皮革(税号 42.05)或毛皮(税号 43.03)的制品；

(三)各种材料(例如，第三十九章、第四十章、第四十四章、第四十八章及第十五类的材料)制的筒管、卷轴、纡子、锥形筒管、芯子、线轴及类似品；

(四)提花机及类似机器用的穿孔卡片(例如，归入第三十九章、第四十八章或第十五类的)；

(五)纺织材料制的传动带、输送带或带料(税号 59.10)或专门技术用途的其他纺织材料制品(税号 59.11)；

(六)税号 71.02 至 71.04 的宝石或半宝石(天然、合成或再造)或税号 71.16 的完全以宝石或半宝石制成的物品，但已加工未装配的唱针用蓝宝石和钻石除外(税号 85.22)；

(七)第十五类注释二所规定的贱金属制通用零件(第十五类)及塑料制的类似品(第三十九章)；

(八)钻管(税号 73.04)；

(九)金属丝、带制的环形带(第十五类)；

(十)第八十二章或第八十三章的物品；

(十一)第十七类的物品；

(十二)第九十章的物品；

(十三)第九十一章的钟、表及其他物品；

(十四)税号 82.07 的可互换工具及作为机器零件的刷子(税号 96.03)；类似的可互换工具应按其构成工作部件的材料归类(例如，归入第四十章、第四十二章、第四十三章、第四十五章、第五十九章或税号 68.04、69.09)；

(十五)第九十五章的物品；

(十六)打字机色带或类似色带，不论是否装轴或装盒(按其材料属性归类；如已上油或经其他方法处理能着色的，应归入税号 96.12)。

SECTION XVI
MACHINERY AND MECHANICAL APPLIANCES; ELECTRICALEQUIPMENT; PARTS THEREOF; SOUND RECORDERS AND REPRODUCERS, TELEVISION IMAGE AND SOUND RECORDERS AND REPRODUCERS,AND PARTS AND ACCESSORIES OF SUCH ARTICLES

Notes:

1. This Section does not cover:

(a)Transmission or conveyor belts or belting, of plastics of Chapter 39, orofvulcanized rubber (headingNo. 40.10), or other articles of a kind used in machinery or mechanical or electrical appliances or for other technical uses, of vulcanized rubber other than hard rubber (heading No. 40.16);

(b)Articles of leather or of composition leather (heading No. 42.05) or of furskin (heading No. 43.03), of a kind used in machinery or mechanical appliances or for other technical uses;

(c) Bobbins, spools, cops, cones, cores, reels or similar supports of any material (for example, Chapter 39, 40, 44 or 48 or Section XV);

(d)Perforated cards for Jacquard or similar machines (for example, Chapter 39 or 48 Section XV);

(e)Transmission or conveyor belts or belting of textile material (heading No. 59.10) or other articles of textile material for technical uses (heading No. 59.11);

(f)Precious or semi-precious stones (natural, synthetic or reconstructed) of headings Nos. 71.02 to 71.04, or articles wholly of such stones of heading No. 71.16, except unmounted worked sapphires and diamonds for styli (heading No. 85.22);

(g)Parts of general use, as defined in Note 2 to Section XV, of base metal (Section XV), or similar goods of plastics (Chapter 39);

(h)Drill pipe (heading No. 73.04);

(i)Endless belts of metal wire or strip (Section XV);

(j)Articles of Chapter 82 or 83;

(k)Articles of Section XVII;

(l)Articles of Chapter 90;

(m)Clocks, watches or other articles of Chapter 91;

(n)Interchangeable tools of heading No. 82.07 brushes of a kind used as parts of machines (heading No. 96.03), similar interchangable tools are to be classified according to the material of working parts (for example, Chapter 40, 42, 43, 45, 59 or heading No. 68.04 or 69.09);

(o)Articles of Chapter 95;

(p)Typewriter or similar ribbons, whether or not on spools or in cartridges (classified according to their constituent material, or in heading 96.12 if inked or otherwise prepared for

二、除本类注释一、第八十四章注释一及第八十五章注释一另有规定的以外，机器零件(不属于税号 84.84、85.44、85.45、85.46 或 85.47 所列物品的零件)应按下列规定归类:

(一)凡在第八十四章、第八十五章的税号(税号 84.09、84.31、84.48、84.66、84.73、84.87、85.03、85.22、85.29、85.38 及 85.48 除外)列名的货品，均应归入该两章的相应税号;

(二)专用于或主要用于某一种机器或同一税号的多种机器(包括税号 84.79 或 85.43 的机器)的零件，应与该种机器一并归类，或酌情归入税号 84.09、84.31、84.48、84.66、84.73、85.03、85.22、85.29 或 85.38。但能同时主要用于税号 85.17 和 85.25 至 85.28 所列机器的零件，应归入税号 85.17;

(三)所有其他零件应酌情归入税号 84.09、84.31、84.48、84.66、84.73、85.03、85.22、85.29 或 85.38，如不能归入上述税号，则应归入税号 84.87 或 85.48。

三、由两部及两部以上机器装配在一起形成的组合式机器，或具有两种及两种以上互补或交替功能的机器，除条文另有规定的以外，应按具有主要功能的机器归类。

四、由不同独立部件(不论是否分开或由管道、传动装置、电缆或其他装置连接)组成的机器(包括机组)，如果组合后明显具有一种第八十四章或第八十五章某个税号所列功能，则全部机器应按其功能归入有关税号。

五、上述各注释所称“机器”，是指第八十四章或第八十五章各税号所列的各种机器、设备、装置及器具。

第八十四章
核反应堆、锅炉、机器、机械器具及其零件

注释:

一、本章不包括:

(一)第六十八章的石磨、石碾及其他物品;

(二)陶瓷材料制的机器或器具(例如，泵)及供任何材料制的机器或器具用的陶瓷零件(第六十九章);

(三)实验室用玻璃器(税号 70.17);玻璃制的机器、器具或其他专门技术用途的物品及其零件(税号 70.19 或 70.20);

(四)税号 73.21 或 73.22 的物品或其他贱金属制的类似物品(第七十四章至第七十六章或第

giving impressions).

2. Subject to Note1to this Section, Note1to Chapter 84 and Note 1 to Chapter 85, parts of machines (not being parts of the articles of heading No. 84.84, 85.44, 85.45, 85.46 or 85.47) are to be classified according to the following rules:

(a)Parts which aregoods includedin any of theheadings of Chapter 84 or 85 (other thanheadings Nos. 84.09, 84.31, 84.48, 84.66, 84.73, 84.87, 85.03, 85.22, 85.29, 85.38, and 85.48) are in all cases to be classified in their respective headings;

(b)Other parts, if suitable for use solely or principally with a particular kind of machine, or with a number of machines of the same heading (including machines of heading No. 84.79 or 85.43) are to be classified with the machines of that kind or in heading No. 84.09, 84.31, 84.48, 84.66, 84.73, 85.03, 85.22, 85.29 or 85.38 as appropriate.However, parts which are equally suitable for use principally with thegoods of headings Nos.85.17and85.25to85.28are to be classified inheading No.85.17;

(c)All other parts are to be classified in heading No. 84.09, 84.31, 84.48, 84.66, 84.73, 85.03, 85.22, 85.29 or 85.38 as appropriate or, failing that, in heading No.84.87 or 85.48.

3. Unless the context otherwise requires, composite machines consisting of two or more machines fitted together to form a whole and other machines adapted for the purpose of performing two or more complementary or alternative functions are to be classified as if consisting only of that component or as being thatmachine which performs the principal function.

4. Where a machine (including a combination of machines) consists of individual components (whether separate or interconnected by piping, by transmission devices, by electric cables or by other devices) intended to contribute together to a clearly defined function covered by one of the headings in Chapter 84 or Chapter 85, then the whole falls to be classified in the heading appropriate to that function.

5. For the purposes of these Notes, the expression “machine” means any machine, machinery, plant, equipment, apparatus or appliance cited in the headings of Chapter 84 or 85.

Chapter 84
Nuclear reactors, boilers, machinery and mechanical appliances; parts thereof

Notes:

1. This Chapter does not cover:

(a) Millstones, grindstones or other articles of Chapter 68;

(b) Machinery or appliances (for example, pumps) of ceramic material and ceramic parts of machinery or appliances of any material (Chapter 69);

(c) Laboratory glassware(heading No.70.17); machinery, appliances or otherarticles for technical uses or parts thereof, of glass (heading No.70.19 or 70.20);

(d) Articles of heading No.73.21or 73.22or similar articles of other base metals (Chapters 74 to 76 or 78 to 81);

七十八章至第八十一章);

(五)税号 85.08 的真空吸尘器;

(六)税号 85.09 的家用电动器具;或税号 85.25 的数字照相机;

(七)非机动的手工操作地板清扫器(税号 96.03)。

(e) Vacuum cleaners of heading 85.08;

(f) Electro-mechanical domestic appliances of heading No.85.09; or digital cameras of heading85.25;

(g) Hand-operated mechanical floor sweepers, not motorized (heading No.96.03).

二、除第十六类注释三及本章注释九另有规定的以外，如果某种机器或器具既符合税号 84.01 至 84.24 或税目 84.86 中一个或几个税号的规定，又符合税号 84.25 至 84.80 中一个或几个税号的规定，则应归入税号 84.01 至 84.24 或税目 84.86 中的相应税号，而不归入税号 84.25 至 84.80 中的有关税号。

但税号 84.19 不包括:

(一)催芽装置、孵卵器或育雏器(税号 84.36);

(二)谷物调湿机(税号 84.37);

(三)萃取糖汁的浸提装置(税号 84.38);

(四)纱线、织物及纺织制品的热处理机器(税号 84.51);

(五)温度变化(即使必不可少)仅作为辅助功能的机器设备。

税号 84.22 不包括:

(一)缝合袋子或类似品用的缝纫机(税号 84.52);

(二)税号 84.72 的办公室用机器。

税号 84.24 不包括:

(一)喷墨印刷(打印)机器(税号 84.43);

(二)水射流切割机(税号 84.56)。

2. Subject to the operation of Note3to Section XVI and subject to Note 9 to this Chapter, a machine or appliance which answers to a description in oneor more of the headings 84.01 to 84.24, or heading 84.86 and at the same time to a description in one or other of the headings Nos.84.25 to 84.80is to be classified under the appropriate heading of the former group or under heading 84.86, as the case may be, and not the latter.

Heading No.84.19does not, however, cover:

(a) Germination plant, incubators or brooders (heading No.84.36);

(b) Grain dampening machines (heading No.84.37);

(c) Diffusing apparatus for sugar juice extraction (heading No.84.38);

(d) Machinery for the heat-treatment of textile yarns, fabrics or made up textile articles (heading No.84.51); or

(e) Machinery or plant, designed for mechanical operation, in which a change of temperature, even if necessary, is subsidiary.

Heading No.84.22does not cover:

(a) Sewing machines for closing bags or similar containers (heading No.84.52); or

(b) Office machinery of heading No.84.72.

Heading No.84.24does not cover:

(a) Ink-jet printing machines (heading No.84.43); or

(b) Water-jet cutting machines(heading No.84.56).

三、如果用于加工各种材料的某种机床既符合税号 84.56 的规定，又符合税号 84.57、84.58、84.59、84.60、84.61、84.64 或 84.65 的规定，则应归入税号 84.56。

3. A machine-tool for working any material which answers to a description in heading No.84.56and at the same time to a descriptionin heading No.84.57, 84.58, 84.59, 84.60, 84.61, 84.64 or 84.65 is to be classified in heading No.84.56.

四、税号 84.57 仅适用于可以完成下列不同形式机械操作的金属加工机床，但车床(包括车削中心)除外:

(一)按照机械加工程序从刀具库中自动更换刀具(加工中心);

(二)同时或顺序地自动使用不同的动力头对固定不动的工件进行加工(单工位组合机床);

(三)自动将工件送向不同的动力头(多工位组合机床)。

4. Heading No.84.57 applies only to machine-tools for working metal other than lathes (including turning centres), which can carry out different types of machining operations either:

(a) by automatic tool change from a magazine or the like in conformity with a machining programme (machining centres);

(b) by the automatic use, simultaneously or sequentially, of different unitheads working on a fixed position workpiece (unit construction machines, single station), or

(c) by the automatic transfer of the workpiece to different unit heads (multi-station transfer machines).

五、

(一)税号 84.71 所称“自动数据处理设备”，是指具有如下功能的机器:

1、存储处理程序和执行程序直接需要的起码的数据;

2、按照用户的要求随意编辑程序;

5.

(a) For the purposes of heading No.84.71, theexpression “automatic data processing machines”means machines capable of:

(1) storing the processing program or programs and at least the data immediately necessary for the execution of the program;

(2) being freely programmed in accordance with the requirements of the user;

3、按照用户指令进行算术计算；以及

4、在运行过程中，可不需人为干预而通过逻辑判断，执行一个处理程序，这个处理程序可改变计算机指令的执行。

(二)自动数据处理设备可以是一套由若干单独部件所组成的系统。

(三)除本条注释(四)、(五)另有规定的以外，一个部件如果符合下列所有规定，即可视为自动数据处理系统的一部分：

1. 专用于或主要用于自动数据处理系统；

2. 可以直接或通过一个或几个其他部件同中央处理器相联接；

3. 能够以本系统所使用的方式(代码或信号)接收或传送数据。

自动数据处理设备的部件如果单独报验，应归入税号 84.71。

但是,键盘、X—Y 座标输入装置及盘(片)式存储部件，只要符合上述注释(三)2、3 所列的规定,应一律作为税号 84.71 的部件归类。

(四)税目 84.71 不包括单独报验的下述设备，即使该设备符合本条注释五(三)的所有规定：

1.打印机、复印机及传真机，不论是否组合在一起；

2. 发送或接收声音、图像或其他数据的设备，包括无线或有线网络的通信设备(如局域网或广播网)；

3. 扬声器和传声器(麦克风)；

4. 电视摄像机、数字照相机、视频摄录一体机；

5. 监视器和投影机，未装有电视接收装置.

(五)装有自动数据处理装置或与自动数据处理设备连接使用，但却从事数据处理以外的某项专门功能的机器，应按其功能归入相应的税号，对于无法按功能归类的，应归入未列名税号。

六、税号 84.82 还包括最大直径及最小直径与标称直径相差均不超过 1%或 0.05 毫米(以相差数值较小的为准)的抛光钢珠，其他钢珠归入税号 73.26。

七、具有一种以上用途的机器在归类时，其主要用途可作为唯一的用途对待。除本章注释二、第十六类注释三另有规定的以外，凡任何税号都未列明其主要用途的机器，以及没有哪一种用途是主要用途的机器，均应归入税号 84.79。税

(3) performing arthmetical computations specified by the user; and

(4) executing, without human intervention, a processing program which requires them to modify their execution, by logical decision during the processing run.

(b)Automatic data processing machines may be in theform of systems consisting of a variable number of separate units.

(c) Subject to paragraph (d) and (e) below, a unit is to be regarded as being a part of a complete system if it meets all of the following conditions:

(1) It is of a kind solely or principally used in an automatic data processing system;

(2) It is connectable to the central processing unit either directly or through one or more other units;and

(3) It is able to accept or deliver data in a form (codes or signals) whichcan be used by the system.

Separately presented units of an automatic data processing machine are to be classified in heading 84.71.

However, keyboards, X-Y co-ordinate input devices and disk storage units which satisfy the conditions of paragraphs (c) (2) and (c) (3) above, are in all cases to be classified as units of heading No.84.71.

(d)Heading 84.71does not cover the following when presented separately, even if they meet all of the conditions set forth in Note 5(c) above:

(1)Printers, copyingmachines,facsimilemachines, whether or not combined;

(2)Apparatus for the transmission or reception of voice, images or other data,including apparatus for communication in a wired or wireless network (such as a local or wide area network);

(3) Loudspeakers and microphones;

(4)Television cameras, digital cameras and video camera recorders;

(5) Monitors and projectors, not incorporating television reception apparatus.

(e)Machines performing a specific function other than data processing and incorporating or working in conjunction with an automatic data processing machine are to be classified in the headings appropriate to their respective functions or, failing that, in residual headings.

6. Heading No.84.82applies, *inter alia*, to polished steel balls, the maximum and minimum diameters of which do not differ from the nominal diameter by more than 1% or by more than 0.05mm, whichever is less. Other steel balls are to be classified in heading No.73.26.

7. A machine which is used for more than one purpose is, for the purposes of classification, to be treated as if its principal purpose were its sole purpose.Subject to Note 2 to this Chapter and Note 3 to Section XVI, a machine, the principal purpose of which is not described in any heading or for which no one

号 84.79 还包括将金属丝、纺织纱线或其他各种材料以及它们的混合材料制成绳、缆的机器(例如，捻股机、绞扭机、制缆机)。

purpose is the principal purpose, unless the context otherwise requires, is to be classified in heading No.84.79. Heading No.84.79 also covers machines for making rope or cable (for example, stranding, twisting or cabling machines) from metal wire, textile yarn or any other material or from a combination of such materials.

八、税号 84.70 所称“袖珍式”，仅适用于外形尺寸不超过 170 毫米 × 100 毫米 × 45 毫米的机器。

8. For the purposes of heading No.84.70, the term“pocketsize”applies only to machines the dimensions of which do notexceed 170mm×100mm×45mm.

九、

(一)第八十五章注释八(一)、(二)中对“半导体器件”和“集成电路”的相关描述同样适用于本条注释和税目 84.86。本条注释和税目 84.86 的描述中所称“半导体器件”也包括光敏半导体器件和发光二极管。

(二)本条注释和税目 84.86 所称“平板显示器的制造设备”包括将各层基片制造成平板的设备。但不包括玻璃的制造设备、将印刷电路板或其他电子元件装配在平板上的设备。“平板显示”不包括阴极射线管技术。

(三)税目 84.86 也包括下列机器及装置，其专用或主要用于:

1、制造或修补掩膜版及投影掩膜版;

2、组装半导体器件或集成电路;

3、升降、搬运、装卸单晶柱、晶圆、半导体器件、集成电路和平板显示器;

(四)除十六类注释一和第八十四章注释一另有规定的以外，符合税目 84.86 规定的机器及装置应归入该税目而不归入本目录的其他税目。

9.

(a) Notes 8(a) and 8(b) to Chapter 85 also apply with respect to the expressions “semiconductor devices” and “electronic integrated circuits”. However, for the purposes of this Note and of heading No.84.86, the expression “semiconductor devices” also covers photosensitive semiconductor devices and light emitting diodes.

(b)For the purposes of this Note and of heading No.84.86, the expression “manufacture of flat panel displays” covers the fabrication of substrates into a flat panel. It does not cover the or other electronic components onto the flat panel. The expression “flat panel display” does not cover cathode-ray tube technology.

(c)Heading No. 84.86 also includes machines and apparatus solely or principally of a kind used for:

(1)the manufacture or rapair of masks and reticles;

(2)assembling semiconductor devices or electronic integrated circuits;

(3)lifting, handling, loading or unlading of boules, wafers, semiconductor devices, electronic integrated circuits and flat panel displays.

(d)Subject to Note 1 to Section XVI and Note 1 to Chapter 84, machines and apparatus answering to the description in heading No.84.86 are to be classified in that heading and in no other heading of the Nomenclature.

子目注释:

一、子目号 8471.49 所称“系统”，是指各部件符合第八十四章注释五(三)所列条件，并且至少由一个中央处理部件、一个输入部件(例如，键盘或扫描器)及一个输出部件(例如，视频显示器或打印机)组成的自动数据处理设备。

二、子目号 8482.40 仅包括滚柱直径相同，最大不超过 5 毫米，且长度至少是直径三倍的圆滚柱轴承，滚柱的两端可以磨圆。

Subheading Notes:

1. For the purposes of subheading No.8471.49, the term “systems” means automatic data processing machines whose units satisfy the conditions laid down in Note5(c) to Chapter 84 and which comprise at least a central processing unit, one input unit (e.g. a keyboard or a scanner), and one output unit (e.g. a visual display unit or a printer).

2. Subheading No.8482.40 applies only to bearingswith cylindrical rollers of a uniform diameter not exceeding5mm and having a length which is at least three times the diameter. The ends of the rollers may be rounded.

序号 No.	税则号列 Tariff Line	中文货品名称 Article Description in Chinese	最惠国税率 MFN(%)	协定税率 Agreement(%)	特惠税率 SP(%)	普通税率 Gen(%)	英文货品名称 Article Description
	84.01	**核反应堆;核反应堆的未辐照燃料元件（释热元件）;同位素分离机器及装置:**					**Nuclear reactors; fuel elements (cartridges) , non-irradiated, for nuclear reactors; machinery and apparatus for isotopic separation:**
5880	8401.1000	-核反应堆	2	0 澳AU,巴PK,冰岛IS,东盟AS,哥CR,韩国KR,秘鲁PE,瑞士CH,新西兰NZ,智利CL	0 受惠国$_1$LD$_1$	8	-Nuclear reactors
5881	8401.2000	-同位素分离机器、装置及其零件	1	0 澳AU,巴PK,冰岛IS,东盟AS,哥CR,韩国KR,秘鲁PE,瑞士CH,新西兰NZ,智利CL	0 受惠国$_1$LD$_1$	8	-Machinery and apparatus for isotopic separation, and parts thereof
		-未辐照燃料元件（释热元件）:					-Fuel elements (cartridges) , non-irradiated:
5882	8401.3010	---未辐照燃料元件	2	0 澳AU,巴PK,冰岛IS,东盟AS,哥CR,韩国KR,秘鲁PE,瑞士CH,新西兰NZ,智利CL	0 受惠国$_1$LD$_1$	8	---Fuel elements, non-irrdadiated
5883	8401.3090	---未辐照燃料元件的零件	1	0 澳AU,巴PK,冰岛IS,东盟AS,哥CR,韩国KR,秘鲁PE,瑞士CH,新西兰NZ,智利CL	0 受惠国$_1$LD$_1$	8	---Parts for fuel elements non-irradiated
		-核反应堆零件:					-Parts of nuclear reactors:
5884	8401.4010	---未辐照相关组件	1	0 澳AU,巴PK,冰岛IS,东盟AS,哥CR,韩国KR,秘鲁PE,瑞士CH,新西兰NZ,智利CL	0 受惠国$_1$LD$_1$	8	---Non-irradiated Associated Assembly
5885	8401.4020	---堆内构件	1	0 澳AU,巴PK,冰岛IS,东盟AS,哥CR,韩国KR,秘鲁PE,瑞士CH,新西兰NZ,智利CL	0 受惠国$_1$LD$_1$	8	---Reactor internals
5886	8401.4090	---其他	1	0 澳AU,巴PK,冰岛IS,东盟AS,哥CR,韩国KR,秘鲁PE,瑞士CH,新西兰NZ,智利CL	0 受惠国$_1$LD$_1$	8	---Other
	84.02	**蒸汽锅炉（能产生低压水蒸汽的集中供暖用的热水锅炉除外）;过热水锅炉:**					**Steam or other vapour generating boilers (other than central heating hot water boilers capable also of producing low pressure steam) ; superheated water boilers:**
		-蒸汽锅炉:					-Steam or other vapour generating boilers:
		--蒸发量超过45吨/时的水管锅炉:					--Watertube boilers with a steam production exceeding 45 tonnes per hour:
5887	8402.1110	---蒸发量在900吨/时及以上的发电用锅炉	3	0 澳AU,巴PK,冰岛IS,东盟AS,哥CR,韩国KR,秘鲁PE,瑞士CH,新西兰NZ,智利CL 2.5 亚太AP	0 受惠国$_1$LD$_1$	11	---Boilers for generating electricity with a steam production 900t or more per hour
5888	8402.1190	---其他	14	0 冰岛IS,东盟AS,哥CR,秘鲁PE,新加坡SG,新西兰NZ,智利CL 7 巴PK 8.4 澳AU 9.8 瑞士CH 11.2 韩国KR 13.3 亚太AP	0 受惠国$_1$LD$_1$	35	---Other

序号 No.	税则号列 Tariff Line	中文货品名称 Article Description in Chinese	最惠国税率 MFN(%)	协定税率 Agreement(%)	特惠税率 SP(%)	普通税率 Gen(%)	英文货品名称 Article Description
5889	8402.1200	--蒸发量不超过45吨/时的水管锅炉	5	0 澳AU,巴PK,冰岛IS,东盟AS,哥CR,秘鲁PE,瑞士CH,新西兰NZ,智利CL 3.9 亚太AP 4.3 韩国KR	0 受惠国$_1$LD$_1$	35	--Watertube boilers with a steam production not exceeding 45t per hour
5890	8402.1900	--其他蒸汽锅炉, 包括混合式锅炉	5	0 澳AU,巴PK,冰岛IS,东盟AS,哥CR,秘鲁PE,瑞士CH,新西兰NZ,智利CL 4.3 韩国KR	0 受惠国$_1$LD$_1$	35	--Other vapour generating boilers, including hybrid boilers
5891	8402.2000	-过热水锅炉	16	0 冰岛IS,东盟AS,哥CR,新加坡SG,新西兰NZ,智利CL 4.8 秘鲁PE 9.6 澳AU 11.2 瑞士CH 12.8 巴PK,韩国KR	0 受惠国$_1$LD$_1$	35	-Super-heated water boilers
5892	8402.9000	-零件	2	0 澳AU,巴PK,冰岛IS,东盟AS,哥CR,韩国KR,秘鲁PE,瑞士CH,新西兰NZ,智利CL	0 受惠国$_1$LD$_1$	11	-Parts
	84.03	**集中供暖用的热水锅炉,但税号84.02的货品除外:**					**Central heating boilers other than those of heading 8402:**
5893	8403.1010	---家用型	10	0 冰岛IS,东盟AS,哥CR,秘鲁PE,新西兰NZ,智利CL 4 瑞士CH 5 巴PK 6 澳AU 8 韩国KR 9.5 亚太AP	0 受惠国$_1$LD$_1$	80	---Household type
5894	8403.1090	---其他	10	0 冰岛IS,东盟AS,哥CR,秘鲁PE,新西兰NZ,智利CL 4 瑞士CH 5 巴PK 6 澳AU 8 韩国KR 9.5 亚太AP	0 受惠国$_1$LD$_1$	80	---Other
5895	8403.9000	-零件	6	0 冰岛IS,东盟AS,哥CR,秘鲁PE,新西兰NZ,智利CL 2.4 瑞士CH 3.6 澳AU 4.8 韩国KR 5 巴PK	0 受惠国$_1$LD$_1$	80	-Parts
	84.04	**税号84.02或84.03所列锅炉的辅助设备(例如,节热器、过热器、除灰器、气体回收器);水蒸汽或其他蒸汽动力装置的冷凝器:**					**Auxiliary plant for use with boilers of heading 8402 or 8403 (for example, economisers, superheaters, soot removers, gas recoverers) ; condensers for steam or other vapour power units:**
		-税号84. 02或84. 03所列锅炉的辅助设备:					-Auxiliary plant for use with boilers of heading 8402 or 8403:
5896	8404.1010	---税号84. 02所列锅炉的辅助设备	7	0 巴PK,冰岛IS,东盟AS,哥CR,秘鲁PE,新西兰NZ,智利CL 3.5 亚太AP 4.2 澳AU,韩国KR 4.9 瑞士CH	0 受惠国$_1$LD$_1$	35	---For use with boilers of heading No. 84.02
	ex84041010	使用(可再生)生物质燃料的非水管蒸汽锅炉的辅助设备	Δ5				Auxiliary plants of non-water pipe stearm boiler using renewable biomass fuel

序号 No.	税则号列 Tariff Line	中文货品名称 Article Description in Chinese	最惠国税率 MFN(%)	协定税率 Agreement(%)	特惠税率 SP(%)	普通税率 Gen(%)	英文货品名称 Article Description
5897	8404.1020	---税号84.03所列锅炉的辅助设备	10Δ5	0 冰岛IS,东盟AS,哥CR,秘鲁PE,新西兰NZ,智利CL 4 瑞士CH 5 巴PK,亚太AP 6 澳AU 8 韩国KR	0 受惠国$_1$LD$_1$	80	---For use with boilers of heading No. 84.03
5898	8404.2000	-水蒸汽或其他蒸汽动力装置的冷凝器	14Δ5	0 冰岛IS,东盟AS,哥CR,秘鲁PE,新加坡SG,新西兰NZ,智利CL 8.4 澳AU 9.8 瑞士CH 11.2 巴PK,韩国KR	0 受惠国$_1$LD$_1$	35	-Condensers for steam or other vapour power units
		-零件:					-Parts:
5899	8404.9010	---子目号8404.1020所列设备的零件	10Δ5	0 巴PK,冰岛IS,东盟AS,哥CR,秘鲁PE,新西兰NZ,亚太AP,智利CL 4 瑞士CH 6 澳AU,韩国KR	0 受惠国$_1$LD$_1$	80	---Of the auxiliary plant of subheading No. 8404.1020
5900	8404.9090	---其他	7	0 巴PK,冰岛IS,东盟AS,哥CR,韩国KR,秘鲁PE,新西兰NZ,亚太AP,智利CL 2.8 瑞士CH 4.2 澳AU	0 受惠国$_1$LD$_1$	35	---Other
	ex84049090	使用(可再生)生物质燃料的非水管蒸汽锅炉的辅助设备的零件;水蒸汽或其他蒸汽动力装置的冷凝器的零件	Δ5				Parts of auxiliary plants of non-water pipe stearm boiler using renewable biomass fuel.Parts of condensers for steam or other vapour power units
	84.05	**煤气发生器,不论有无净化器;乙炔发生器及类似的水解气体发生器,不论有无净化器:**					**Producer gas or water gas generators, with or without their purifiers; acetylene gas generators and similar water process gas generators, with or without their purifiers:**
5901	8405.1000	-煤气发生器,不论有无净化器;乙炔发生器及类似的水解气体发生器,不论有无净化器	14	0 冰岛IS,东盟AS,哥CR,秘鲁PE,新加坡SG,新西兰NZ,智利CL 8.4 澳AU 9.8 瑞士CH 11.2 巴PK 12.6 韩国KR	0 受惠国$_1$LD$_1$	30	-Producer gas or water gas generators, with or without their purifiers; acetylene gas generators and similar water process gas generators, with or without their purifiers
5902	8405.9000	-零件	8	0 冰岛IS,东盟AS,哥CR,秘鲁PE,新西兰NZ,智利CL 3.2 瑞士CH 4.8 澳AU,韩国KR 5 巴PK	0 受惠国$_1$LD$_1$	30	-Parts
	84.06	**汽轮机:**					**Steam turbines and other vapour turbines:**
5903	8406.1000	-船舶动力用汽轮机	5	0 澳AU,巴PK,冰岛IS,东盟AS,哥CR,秘鲁PE,瑞士CH,新西兰NZ,智利CL 4 韩国KR	0 受惠国LD	35	-Turbines for marine propulsion
		-其他汽轮机:					-Other turbines:
		--输出功率超过40兆瓦的:					--Of an output exceeding 40MW:
5904	8406.8110	---输出功率不超过100兆瓦的	5	0 澳AU,巴PK,冰岛IS,东盟AS,哥CR,秘鲁PE,瑞士CH,新西兰NZ,智利CL 3 韩国KR	0 受惠国LD	35	---Of an output not exceeding 100MW

序号 No.	税则号列 Tariff Line	中文货品名称 Article Description in Chinese	最惠国税率 MFN(%)	协定税率 Agreement(%)	特惠税率 SP(%)	普通税率 Gen(%)	英文货品名称 Article Description
5905	8406.8120	---输出功率超过100兆瓦，但不超过350兆瓦的	5	0 澳AU,巴PK,冰岛IS,东盟AS,哥CR,秘鲁PE,瑞士CH,新西兰NZ,智利CL 3 韩国KR	0 受惠国LD	35	---Of an output exceeding 100MW but not exceeding 350MW
5906	8406.8130	---输出功率超过350兆瓦的	6	0 冰岛IS,东盟AS,哥CR,秘鲁PE,新西兰NZ,智利CL 2.4 瑞士CH 3.6 澳AU,韩国KR 5 巴PK	0 受惠国LD	11	---Of an output exceeding 350MW
5907	8406.8200	--输出功率不超过40兆瓦的	5	0 澳AU,巴PK,冰岛IS,东盟AS,哥CR,秘鲁PE,新西兰NZ,智利CL 3 韩国KR 3.6 瑞士CH	0 受惠国LD	35	--Of an output not exceeding 40MW
5908	8406.9000	-零件	2	0 澳AU,巴PK,冰岛IS,东盟AS,哥CR,韩国KR,秘鲁PE,新西兰NZ,智利CL 1.4 瑞士CH	0 受惠国LD	11	-Parts
	84.07	**点燃往复式或旋转式活塞内燃发动机：**					**Spark-ignition reciprocating or rotary internal combustion piston engines:**
		-航空器发动机：					-Aircraft engines:
5909	8407.1010	---输出功率不超过298千瓦	2	0 澳AU,巴PK,冰岛IS,东盟AS,哥CR,韩国KR,秘鲁PE,瑞士CH,新西兰NZ,智利CL	0 受惠国$_1$LD$_1$	11	---Of an output not exceeding 298KW
5910	8407.1020	---输出功率超过298千瓦	2	0 澳AU,巴PK,冰岛IS,东盟AS,哥CR,韩国KR,秘鲁PE,瑞士CH,新西兰NZ,智利CL	0 受惠国$_1$LD$_1$	11	---Of an output exceeding 298KW
		-船舶发动机：					-Marine propulsion engines:
5911	8407.2100	--舷外发动机	8	0 冰岛IS,东盟AS,哥CR,秘鲁PE,新西兰NZ,智利CL 3.2 瑞士CH 4.8 澳AU 5 巴PK	0 受惠国$_1$LD$_1$	35	--Outboard motors
5912	8407.2900	--其他	8	0 冰岛IS,东盟AS,哥CR,秘鲁PE,新西兰NZ,智利CL 3.2 瑞士CH 4.8 澳AU 5 巴PK	0 受惠国$_1$LD$_1$	20	--Other
		-用于第八十七章所列车辆的往复式活塞发动机：					-Reciprocating piston engines of a kind used for the propulsion of vehicles of Chapter 87:
5913	8407.3100	--气缸容量（排气量）不超过50毫升	10	0 冰岛IS,东盟AS,哥CR,秘鲁PE,新西兰NZ,智利CL 4 瑞士CH 5 巴PK 6 澳AU 9 韩国KR	0 受惠国$_1$LD$_1$	35	--Of a cylinder capacity not exceeding 50cc
5914	8407.3200	--气缸容量（排气量）超过50毫升，但不超过250毫升	10	0 冰岛IS,东盟AS,哥CR,秘鲁PE,新西兰NZ,智利CL 4 瑞士CH 5 巴PK 6 澳AU 9 韩国KR	0 受惠国$_1$LD$_1$	35	--Of a cylinder capacity exceeding 50cc but not exceeding 250cc

序号 No.	税则号列 Tariff Line	中文货品名称 Article Description in Chinese	最惠国税率 MFN(%)	协定税率 Agreement(%)	特惠税率 SP(%)	普通税率 Gen(%)	英文货品名称 Article Description
5915	8407.3300	--气缸容量（排气量）超过250毫升，但不超过1000毫升	10	0 冰岛IS,东盟AS,哥CR,秘鲁PE,香港HK,新加坡SG,新西兰NZ,智利CL 4 瑞士CH 6 澳AU 8 巴PK 9 韩国KR	0 受惠国$_1$LD$_1$	70	--Of a cylinder capacity exceeding 250cc but not exceeding 1000cc
		--气缸容量（排气量）超过1000毫升：					--Of a cylinder capacity exceeding 1000cc:
5916	8407.3410	---气缸容量（排气量）超过1000毫升，但不超过3000毫升	10	0 冰岛IS,哥CR,香港HK,新西兰NZ,智利CL 4 瑞士CH 6 澳AU 7 巴PK,亚太AP 9 韩国KR		70	---Of a cylinder capacity exceeding 1000cc but not exceeding 3000cc
5917	8407.3420	---气缸容量（排气量）超过3000毫升	10	0 冰岛IS,哥CR,香港HK,新西兰NZ,智利CL 4 瑞士CH 6 澳AU 7 巴PK,亚太AP 9 韩国KR	0 受惠国$_2$LD$_2$	35	---Of a cylinder capacity exceeding 3000cc
		-其他发动机：					-Other engines:
5918	8407.9010	---沼气发动机	12	0 冰岛IS,东盟AS,哥CR,秘鲁PE,新加坡SG,新西兰NZ,智利CL 6 巴PK 7.2 澳AU 8.4 瑞士CH 9.6 韩国KR	0 受惠国$_1$LD$_1$	35	---Firedamp engines
5919	8407.9090	---其他	18	0 冰岛IS,东盟AS,哥CR,新加坡SG,新西兰NZ,智利CL 5.4 秘鲁PE 10.8 澳AU 12.6 瑞士CH 15.6 韩国KR	0 受惠国$_1$LD$_1$	35	---Other
	ex84079090	叉车用汽油发动机（800r/min≤转速≤3400r/min）	Δ9				Petrol engines for forklift trucks (800r/min≤rotational speed≤3400r/min)
	ex84079090	立式输出轴汽油发动机	Δ9				Petrol engines with a vertical crankshaft
	84.08	**压燃式活塞内燃发动机（柴油或半柴油发动机）：**					**Compression-ignition internal combustion piston engines (diesel or semi-diesel engines) :**
5920	8408.1000	-船舶发动机	5	0 澳AU,巴PK,冰岛IS,东盟AS,哥CR,秘鲁PE,新加坡SG,新西兰NZ,智利CL 2 瑞士CH 2.5 亚太AP 4 韩国KR	0 受惠国$_1$LD$_1$	11	-Marine propulsion engines
		-用于第八十七章所列车辆的发动机：					-Engines of a kind used for the propulsion of vehicles of Chapter 87:
5921	8408.2010	---输出功率在132.39千瓦（180马力）及以上	9	0 冰岛IS,哥CR,秘鲁PE,香港HK,新西兰NZ,智利CL 3.6 瑞士CH 5.4 澳AU 6.3 巴PK,亚太AP 7.8 韩国KR	0 受惠国$_1$LD$_1$	14	---Of an output power of 132.39KW (180PS) or more
	ex84082010	输出功率在441千瓦（600马力）及以上的柴油发动机	Δ4				Diesel engines with an output power of 441 KW (600HP) or more

序号 No.	税则号列 Tariff Line	中文货品名称 Article Description in Chinese	最惠国税率 MFN(%)	协定税率 Agreement(%)	特惠税率 SP(%)	普通税率 Gen(%)	英文货品名称 Article Description
5922	8408.2090	---其他	25	0 冰岛IS,哥CR,新西兰NZ,智利CL 15 澳AU 17.5 巴PK,亚太AP 20 东盟AS 22.5 韩国KR	0 受惠国$_2$LD$_2$	35	---Other
	ex84082090	升功率≥50千瓦的轿车用柴油发动机	Δ20				Diesel engines for cars, power density ≥ 50 KW
		-其他发动机:					-Other engines:
5923	8408.9010	---机车发动机	6	0 巴PK,冰岛IS,东盟AS,哥CR,秘鲁PE,新西兰NZ,智利CL 2.4 瑞士CH 3.6 澳AU,韩国KR 5.4 亚太AP	0 受惠国$_1$LD$_1$	11	---Locomotive engines
		---其他:					---Other:
5924	8408.9091	----输出功率不超过14千瓦	5	0 澳AU,巴PK,冰岛IS,东盟AS,哥CR,秘鲁PE,瑞士CH,新西兰NZ,智利CL 4.3 韩国KR 4.5 亚太AP	0 受惠国$_1$LD$_1$	35	----Of an output not exceeding14KW
5925	8408.9092	----输出功率超过14千瓦,但小于132.39千瓦（180马力）	8.4	0 冰岛IS,东盟AS,哥CR,秘鲁PE,新西兰NZ,智利CL 3.36 瑞士CH 5 澳AU,巴PK 7.2 韩国KR 7.6 亚太AP	0 受惠国$_1$LD$_1$	35	----Of an output exceeding14KW but not exceeding 132.39KW (180PS)
5926	8408.9093	----输出功率在132.39千瓦（180马力）及以上	5	0 澳AU,巴PK,冰岛IS,东盟AS,哥CR,秘鲁PE,新西兰NZ,智利CL 2 瑞士CH 4.3 韩国KR 4.5 亚太AP	0 受惠国$_1$LD$_1$	14	----Of an output of 132.39KW (180PS) or more
	84.09	**专用于或主要用于税号84.07或84.08所列发动机的零件:**					**Parts suitable for use solely or principally with the engines of heading 8407 or 8408:**
5927	8409.1000	-航空器发动机用	2	0 澳AU,巴PK,冰岛IS,东盟AS,哥CR,韩国KR,秘鲁PE,瑞士CH,新西兰NZ,智利CL	0 受惠国LD	11	-For aircraft engines
		-其他:					-Other:
		--专用于或主要用于点燃式活塞内燃发动机的:					--Suitable for use solely or principally with spark-ignition internal combustion piston engines:
5928	8409.9110	---船舶发动机用	6	0 巴PK,冰岛IS,东盟AS,哥CR,秘鲁PE,新西兰NZ,智利CL 2.4 瑞士CH 3.6 澳AU 4.2 亚太AP 5.1 韩国KR	0 受惠国LD	17	---For marine propulsion engines
		---其他:					---Other:
5929	8409.9191	----电控燃油喷射装置	5	0 澳AU,巴PK,冰岛IS,东盟AS,哥CR,秘鲁PE,瑞士CH,新加坡SG,新西兰NZ,智利CL 3.5 亚太AP 4.3 韩国KR	0 受惠国LD	35	----Electronic fuel injection devices

序号 No.	税则号列 Tariff Line	中文货品名称 Article Description in Chinese	最惠国税率 MFN(%)	协定税率 Agreement(%)	特惠税率 SP(%)	普通税率 Gen(%)	英文货品名称 Article Description
5930	8409.9199	----其他	5	0 澳AU,巴PK,冰岛IS,东盟AS,哥CR,秘鲁PE,新加坡SG,新西兰NZ,智利CL 3.5 瑞士CH,亚太AP 4 韩国KR	0 受惠国LD	35	----Other
		--其他:					--Other:
5931	8409.9910	---船舶发动机用	5	0 澳AU,巴PK,冰岛IS,东盟AS,哥CR,秘鲁PE,新加坡SG,新西兰NZ,智利CL 3.5 瑞士CH 4.3 韩国KR 4.5 亚太AP	0 受惠国LD	11	---For marine propulsion engines
5932	8409.9920	---机车发动机用	2	0 澳AU,巴PK,冰岛IS,东盟AS,哥CR,韩国KR,秘鲁PE,瑞士CH,新西兰NZ,智利CL 1.5 亚太AP	0 受惠国LD	11	---For locomotive engines
		---其他:					---Other:
5933	8409.9991	----输出功率在132.39千瓦（180马力）及以上的发动机用	2	0 澳AU,巴PK,冰岛IS,东盟AS,哥CR,秘鲁PE,瑞士CH,新西兰NZ,智利CL 1.5 亚太AP 1.6 韩国KR	0 受惠国LD	11	----For engines with an output of 132.39KW (180PS) or more
5934	8409.9999	----其他	8.4	0 冰岛IS,东盟AS,哥CR,秘鲁PE,新加坡SG,新西兰NZ,智利CL 3.36 瑞士CH 5 澳AU,巴PK 7.2 韩国KR 8 亚太AP	0 受惠国LD	35	----Other
	ex84099999	电控柴油喷射装置及其零件	Δ5				Electronic diesel oil injection devices and parts
	84.10	**水轮机、水轮及其调节器:**					**Hydraulic turbines, water wheels, and regulators therefor:**
		-水轮机及水轮:					-Hydraulic turbines and water wheels:
5935	8410.1100	--功率不超过1000千瓦	10	0 冰岛IS,东盟AS,哥CR,秘鲁PE,新西兰NZ,智利CL 4 瑞士CH 5 巴PK 6 澳AU 8 韩国KR	0 受惠国$_1$LD$_1$	35	--Of a power not exceeding 1000KW
5936	8410.1200	--功率超过1000千瓦,但不超过10000千瓦	10	0 冰岛IS,东盟AS,哥CR,秘鲁PE,新加坡SG,新西兰NZ,智利CL 4 瑞士CH 5 巴PK 6 澳AU 8 韩国KR	0 受惠国$_1$LD$_1$	35	--Of a power exceeding1000KW but not exceeding 10000KW
		--功率超过10000千瓦:					--Of a power exceeding 10000 kW:
5937	8410.1310	---功率超过30000千瓦的击式水轮机及水轮	10	0 冰岛IS,东盟AS,哥CR,秘鲁PE,新加坡SG,新西兰NZ,智利CL 4 瑞士CH 5 巴PK 6 澳AU 8 韩国KR	0 受惠国$_1$LD$_1$	35	---Impulse hydraulic turbines and water wheels of a power>30000KW

序号 No.	税则号列 Tariff Line	中文货品名称 Article Description in Chinese	最惠国税率 MFN(%)	协定税率 Agreement(%)	特惠税率 SP(%)	普通税率 Gen(%)	英文货品名称 Article Description
5938	8410.1320	---功率超过35000千瓦的贯流式水轮机及水轮	10	0 冰岛IS,东盟AS,哥CR,秘鲁PE,新加坡SG,新西兰NZ,智利CL 4 瑞士CH 5 巴PK 6 澳AU 8 韩国KR	0 受惠国$_1$LD$_1$	35	---Radial hydraulic turbines and water wheels of a power>35000KW
5939	8410.1330	---功率超过200000千瓦的水泵水轮机及水轮	10	0 冰岛IS,东盟AS,哥CR,秘鲁PE,新西兰NZ,智利CL 4 瑞士CH 5 巴PK 6 澳AU 8 韩国KR	0 受惠国$_1$LD$_1$	35	---Pumping hydraulic turbines and water wheels of a power>200000KW
5940	8410.1390	---其他	10	0 冰岛IS,东盟AS,哥CR,秘鲁PE,新西兰NZ,智利CL 4 瑞士CH 5 巴PK 6 澳AU 8 韩国KR	0 受惠国$_1$LD$_1$	35	---Other
		-零件,包括调节器:					-Parts, including regulators:
5941	8410.9010	---调节器	6	0 冰岛IS,东盟AS,哥CR,秘鲁PE,新西兰NZ,智利CL 2.4 瑞士CH 3.6 澳AU,韩国KR 5 巴PK	0 受惠国$_1$LD$_1$	35	---Regulators
5942	8410.9090	---其他	6	0 冰岛IS,东盟AS,哥CR,秘鲁PE,新西兰NZ,智利CL 2.4 瑞士CH 3.6 澳AU 4.8 韩国KR 5 巴PK	0 受惠国$_1$LD$_1$	35	---Other
	84.11	**涡轮喷气发动机,涡轮螺桨发动机及其他燃气轮机:**					**Turbojets, turbopropellers and other gas turbines:**
		-涡轮喷气发动机:					-Turbojets:
		--推力不超过25千牛顿:					--Of a thrust not exceeding 25KN:
5943	8411.1110	---涡轮风扇发动机	1	0 澳AU,巴PK,冰岛IS,东盟AS,哥CR,韩国KR,秘鲁PE,瑞士CH,新西兰NZ,智利CL	0 受惠国LD	11	---Turbofan engines
5944	8411.1190	---其他	1	0 澳AU,巴PK,冰岛IS,东盟AS,哥CR,韩国KR,秘鲁PE,瑞士CH,新西兰NZ,智利CL	0 受惠国LD	11	---Other
		--推力超过25千牛顿:					--Of a thrust exceeding 25 kN:
5945	8411.1210	---涡轮风扇发动机	1	0 澳AU,巴PK,冰岛IS,东盟AS,哥CR,韩国KR,秘鲁PE,瑞士CH,新西兰NZ,亚太AP,智利CL	0 受惠国LD	11	---Turbofan engines
5946	8411.1290	---其他	1	0 澳AU,巴PK,冰岛IS,东盟AS,哥CR,韩国KR,秘鲁PE,瑞士CH,新西兰NZ,智利CL .5 亚太AP	0 受惠国LD	11	---Other
		-涡轮螺桨发动机:					-Turbopropellers:
5947	8411.2100	--功率不超过1100千瓦	2	0 澳AU,巴PK,冰岛IS,东盟AS,哥CR,韩国KR,秘鲁PE,瑞士CH,新西兰NZ,智利CL	0 受惠国LD	11	--Of a power not exceeding 1100KW
		--功率超过1100千瓦:					--Of a power exceeding 1100KW:

序号 No.	税则号列 Tariff Line	中文货品名称 Article Description in Chinese	最惠国税率 MFN(%)	协定税率 Agreement(%)	特惠税率 SP(%)	普通税率 Gen(%)	英文货品名称 Article Description
5948	8411.2210	---功率超过1100千瓦，但不超过2238千瓦	2	0 澳AU,巴PK,冰岛IS,东盟AS,哥CR,韩国KR,秘鲁PE,瑞士CH,新西兰NZ,智利CL	0 受惠国LD	11	---Of a power exceeding 1100KW but not exceeding 2238KW
5949	8411.2220	---功率超过2238千瓦，但不超过3730千瓦	2	0 澳AU,巴PK,冰岛IS,东盟AS,哥CR,韩国KR,秘鲁PE,瑞士CH,新西兰NZ,智利CL	0 受惠国LD	11	---Of a power exceeding 2238KW but not exceeding 3730KW
5950	8411.2230	---功率超过3730千瓦	2	0 澳AU,巴PK,冰岛IS,东盟AS,哥CR,韩国KR,秘鲁PE,瑞士CH,新西兰NZ,智利CL	0 受惠国LD	11	---Of a power exceeding 3730KW
		-其他燃气轮机：					-Other gas turbines:
5951	8411.8100	--功率不超过5000千瓦	15	0 冰岛IS,东盟AS,哥CR,新加坡SG,新西兰NZ,智利CL 4.5 秘鲁PE 9 澳AU 10.5 瑞士CH 12 巴PK,韩国KR	0 受惠国$_1$LD$_1$	35	--Of a power not exceeding 5000KW
	ex84118100	涡轮轴航空发动机	Δ1				Turbo shaft engines for aircraft
5952	8411.8200	--功率超过5000千瓦	3	0 澳AU,巴PK,冰岛IS,东盟AS,哥CR,韩国KR,秘鲁PE,瑞士CH,新西兰NZ,智利CL	0 受惠国LD	35	--Of a power exceeding 5000KW
		-零件：					-Parts:
5953	8411.9100	--涡轮喷气发动机或涡轮螺桨发动机用	1	0 澳AU,巴PK,冰岛IS,东盟AS,哥CR,韩国KR,秘鲁PE,瑞士CH,新西兰NZ,智利CL	0 受惠国LD	11	--Of turbo-jets or turbo-propellers
		--其他：					--Other:
5954	8411.9910	---涡轮轴发动机用	5	0 澳AU,巴PK,冰岛IS,东盟AS,哥CR,韩国KR,秘鲁PE,瑞士CH,新西兰NZ,智利CL	0 受惠国LD	35	---Of turboshaft engines
	ex84119910	涡轮轴航空发动机用零件	Δ1				Parts of turbo shaft engines for aircraft
5955	8411.9990	---其他	5	0 澳AU,巴PK,冰岛IS,东盟AS,哥CR,秘鲁PE,新西兰NZ,智利CL 2 瑞士CH 4 韩国KR	0 受惠国LD	35	---Other
	84.12	**其他发动机及动力装置：**					**Other engines and motors:**
		-喷气发动机，但涡轮喷气发动机除外：					-Reaction engines other than turbojets:
5956	8412.1010	---航空器及航天器用	3	0 澳AU,巴PK,冰岛IS,东盟AS,哥CR,韩国KR,秘鲁PE,瑞士CH,新西兰NZ,智利CL	0 受惠国LD	11	---For aircraft or spacecraft
5957	8412.1090	---其他	10	0 冰岛IS,东盟AS,哥CR,秘鲁PE,新西兰NZ,智利CL 4 瑞士CH 5 巴PK 6 澳AU 8 韩国KR	0 受惠国$_1$LD$_1$	35	---Other
		-液压动力装置：					-Hydraulic power engines and motors:

序号 No.	税则号列 Tariff Line	中文货品名称 Article Description in Chinese	最惠国税率 MFN(%)	协定税率 Agreement(%)	特惠税率 SP(%)	普通税率 Gen(%)	英文货品名称 Article Description
5958	8412.2100	--直线作用（液压缸）的	12	0 冰岛IS,东盟AS,哥CR,台湾TW,香港HK,新加坡SG,新西兰NZ,智利CL 3.6 秘鲁PE 6 巴PK 7.2 澳AU 8.4 瑞士CH 10.8 韩国KR	0 受惠国$_1$LD$_1$	35	--Linear acting (cylinders)
		--其他：					--Other:
5959	8412.2910	---液压马达	10	0 冰岛IS,东盟AS,哥CR,秘鲁PE,新加坡SG,新西兰NZ,智利CL 5 巴PK 6 澳AU 7 瑞士CH 9 韩国KR	0 受惠国$_1$LD$_1$	35	---Hydraulic motors
5960	8412.2990	---其他	14	0 冰岛IS,东盟AS,哥CR,秘鲁PE,新加坡SG,新西兰NZ,智利CL 8.4 澳AU 9.8 瑞士CH 11.2 巴PK 12.1 韩国KR	0 受惠国$_1$LD$_1$	35	---Other
	ex84122990	抓桩器（抱桩器）	Δ7				Skirt Pile Grippers Assembly
		-气压动力装置：					-Pneumatic power engines and motors:
5961	8412.3100	--直线作用（气压缸）的	14	0 冰岛IS,东盟AS,哥CR,秘鲁PE,台湾TW,新加坡SG,新西兰NZ,智利CL 5.6 瑞士CH 7 巴PK 8.4 澳AU,韩国KR 13.3 亚太AP	0 受惠国$_1$LD$_1$	35	--Linear acting (cylinders)
	ex84123100	三坐标测量机用平衡气缸	Δ7				Cylinder balance for coordinate measuring machine of three dimensions
5962	8412.3900	--其他	14	0 冰岛IS,东盟AS,哥CR,秘鲁PE,新加坡SG,新西兰NZ,智利CL 5.6 瑞士CH 8.4 澳AU 11.2 巴PK,韩国KR	0 受惠国$_1$LD$_1$	35	--Other
5963	8412.8000	-其他	10	0 冰岛IS,东盟AS,哥CR,秘鲁PE,新西兰NZ,智利CL 4 瑞士CH 5 巴PK 6 澳AU 8 韩国KR	0 受惠国$_1$LD$_1$	35	-Other
		-零件：					-Parts:
5964	8412.9010	---子目号8412. 1010所列机器的零件	2	0 澳AU,巴PK,冰岛IS,东盟AS,哥CR,韩国KR,秘鲁PE,瑞士CH,新西兰NZ,智利CL	0 受惠国LD	11	---For machines of subheading No. 8412.1010
5965	8412.9090	---其他	8	0 冰岛IS,东盟AS,哥CR,秘鲁PE,新西兰NZ,智利CL 3.2 瑞士CH 4.8 澳AU 5 巴PK 6.9 韩国KR	0 受惠国LD	35	---Other
	ex84129090	风力发动机零件	Δ5				Parts thereof wind turbines.

序号 No.	税则号列 Tariff Line	中文货品名称 Article Description in Chinese	最惠国税率 MFN(%)	协定税率 Agreement(%)	特惠税率 SP(%)	普通税率 Gen(%)	英文货品名称 Article Description
	84.13	**液体泵,不论是否装有计量装置;液体提升机:**					**Pumps for liquids, whether or not fitted with a measuring device; liquid elevators:**
		-装有或可装计量装置的泵:					-Pumps fitted or designed to be fitted with a measuring device:
5966	8413.1100	--分装燃料或润滑油的泵,用于加油站或车库	10Δ6	0 冰岛IS,东盟AS,哥CR,秘鲁PE,新加坡SG,新西兰NZ,智利CL 4 瑞士CH 5 巴PK 6 澳AU 8 韩国KR	0 受惠国LD	30	--Pumps for dispensing fuel or lubricants, of the type used in filling-stations or in garages
5967	8413.1900	--其他	10Δ6	0 冰岛IS,东盟AS,哥CR,秘鲁PE,新加坡SG,新西兰NZ,智利CL 5 巴PK 6 澳AU 7 瑞士CH 9 韩国KR	0 受惠国LD	30	--Other
5968	8413.2000	-手泵,但子目号8413.11或8413.19的货品除外	10	0 冰岛IS,东盟AS,哥CR,秘鲁PE,新加坡SG,新西兰NZ,智利CL 4 瑞士CH 5 巴PK 6 澳AU 8 韩国KR	0 受惠国LD	30	-Hand pumps, other than those of subheading No. 8413.11 or 8413.19
		-活塞式内燃发动机用的燃油泵、润滑油泵或冷却剂泵:					-Fuel, lubricating or cooling medium pumps for internal combustion piston engines:
		---燃油泵:					---Fuel pumps:
5969	8413.3021	----输出功率在132.39千瓦(180马力)及以上的发动机用燃油泵	3	0 澳AU,巴PK,冰岛IS,东盟AS,哥CR,秘鲁PE,瑞士CH,新西兰NZ,智利CL 1.8 韩国KR 2.5 亚太AP	0 受惠国LD	30	----Fuel pumps for engines of an output of 132.39KW (180PS) or more
5970	8413.3029	----其他	3	0 澳AU,巴PK,冰岛IS,东盟AS,哥CR,秘鲁PE,瑞士CH,新西兰NZ,智利CL 1.8 韩国KR	0 受惠国LD	30	----Other
5971	8413.3030	---润滑油泵	3	0 澳AU,巴PK,冰岛IS,东盟AS,哥CR,秘鲁PE,瑞士CH,新西兰NZ,智利CL 1.8 韩国KR	0 受惠国LD	30	---Lubricating oil pumps
5972	8413.3090	---其他	3	0 澳AU,巴PK,冰岛IS,东盟AS,哥CR,秘鲁PE,瑞士CH,新西兰NZ,智利CL 1.8 韩国KR 2.5 亚太AP	0 受惠国LD	30	---Other
5973	8413.4000	-混凝土泵	8	0 冰岛IS,东盟AS,哥CR,秘鲁PE,香港HK,新西兰NZ,智利CL 3.2 瑞士CH 4.8 澳AU 5 巴PK 6.4 韩国KR	0 受惠国LD	30	-Concrete pumps
		-其他往复式排液泵:					-Other reciprocating positive displacement pumps:

序号 No.	税则号列 Tariff Line	中文货品名称 Article Description in Chinese	最惠国税率 MFN(%)	协定税率 Agreement(%)	特惠税率 SP(%)	普通税率 Gen(%)	英文货品名称 Article Description
5974	8413.5010	---气动式	10Δ6	0 冰岛IS,东盟AS,哥CR,秘鲁PE,新加坡SG,新西兰NZ,智利CL 4 瑞士CH 5 巴PK 6 澳AU 8.6 韩国KR	0 受惠国LD	40	---Pneumatic
5975	8413.5020	---电动式	10Δ6	0 冰岛IS,东盟AS,哥CR,秘鲁PE,香港HK,新加坡SG,新西兰NZ,智利CL 5 巴PK 6 澳AU 7.5 瑞士CH 8 韩国KR	0 受惠国LD	40	---Electric
		---液压式:					---Hydraulic:
5976	8413.5031	----柱塞泵	10Δ6	0 冰岛IS,东盟AS,哥CR,秘鲁PE,新加坡SG,新西兰NZ,智利CL 4 瑞士CH 5 巴PK 6 澳AU 9 韩国KR	0 受惠国LD	40	----Plunger pump
5977	8413.5039	----其他	10Δ6	0 冰岛IS,东盟AS,哥CR,秘鲁PE,新加坡SG,新西兰NZ,智利CL 4 瑞士CH 5 巴PK 6 澳AU 8.6 韩国KR	0 受惠国LD	40	----Other
5978	8413.5090	---其他	10Δ6	0 冰岛IS,东盟AS,哥CR,新加坡SG,新西兰NZ,智利CL 3 秘鲁PE 4 瑞士CH 5 巴PK 6 澳AU 9 韩国KR	0 受惠国LD	40	---Other
		-其他回转式排液泵:					-Other rotary positive displacement pumps:
		---齿轮泵:					---Gear pump:
5979	8413.6021	----电动式	10Δ6	0 东盟AS,哥CR,秘鲁PE,新加坡SG,新西兰NZ,智利CL 4 瑞士CH 5 巴PK 6 澳AU 9 韩国KR	0 受惠国LD	40	----Electric
5980	8413.6022	----液压式	10	0 冰岛IS,东盟AS,哥CR,秘鲁PE,新西兰NZ,智利CL 4 瑞士CH 5 巴PK 6 澳AU 8.6 韩国KR	0 受惠国LD	40	----Hydraulic
	ex84136022	回转式液压油泵,输入转速＞2000r/min,输入功率＞190KW,最大流量＞2*280 L/min	Δ3				Rotating hydraulic oil pump, input rotating speed>2000r/min, input power>190KW, maximum flow>2×280 L/min
	ex84136022	其他液压式齿轮回转泵	Δ6				Other hydraulic gear rotating pump

序号 No.	税则号列 Tariff Line	中文货品名称 Article Description in Chinese	最惠国税率 MFN(%)	协定税率 Agreement(%)	特惠税率 SP(%)	普通税率 Gen(%)	英文货品名称 Article Description
5981	8413.6029	-----其他	10Δ6	0 冰岛IS,东盟AS,哥CR,秘鲁PE,新西兰NZ,智利CL 4 瑞士CH 5 巴PK 6 澳AU 8 韩国KR	0 受惠国LD	40	----Other
		---叶片泵:					---Vane pump:
5982	8413.6031	----电动式	10Δ6	0 冰岛IS,东盟AS,哥CR,秘鲁PE,新西兰NZ,智利CL 4 瑞士CH 5 巴PK 6 澳AU 8 韩国KR	0 受惠国LD	40	----Electric
5983	8413.6032	----液压式	10Δ6	0 冰岛IS,东盟AS,哥CR,秘鲁PE,新西兰NZ,智利CL 4 瑞士CH 5 巴PK 6 澳AU 9 韩国KR	0 受惠国LD	40	----Hydraulic
5984	8413.6039	----其他	10Δ6	0 冰岛IS,东盟AS,哥CR,秘鲁PE,新西兰NZ,智利CL 4 瑞士CH 5 巴PK 6 澳AU 9 韩国KR	0 受惠国LD	40	----Other
5985	8413.6040	---螺杆泵	10Δ6	0 冰岛IS,东盟AS,哥CR,秘鲁PE,新西兰NZ,智利CL 4 瑞士CH 5 巴PK 6 澳AU 9 韩国KR	0 受惠国LD	40	---Screw pump
5986	8413.6050	---径向柱塞泵	10Δ6	0 冰岛IS,东盟AS,哥CR,秘鲁PE,新西兰NZ,智利CL 4 瑞士CH 5 巴PK 6 澳AU 9 韩国KR	0 受惠国LD	40	---Radial plunger pump
5987	8413.6060	---轴向柱塞泵	10Δ6	0 冰岛IS,东盟AS,哥CR,秘鲁PE,新西兰NZ,智利CL 4 瑞士CH 5 巴PK 6 澳AU 8.6 韩国KR	0 受惠国LD	40	---Axial plunger pump
5988	8413.6090	---其他	10Δ8	0 冰岛IS,东盟AS,哥CR,秘鲁PE,新加坡SG,新西兰NZ,智利CL 5 巴PK 6 澳AU 7 瑞士CH 8.6 韩国KR	0 受惠国LD	40	---Other
		-其他离心泵:					-Other centrifugal pumps:
5989	8413.7010	---转速在10000转/分及以上	8	0 冰岛IS,东盟AS,哥CR,秘鲁PE,新西兰NZ,智利CL 3.2 瑞士CH 4.8 澳AU,韩国KR 5 巴PK 7.6 亚太AP	0 受惠国LD	40	---Rotational speed no less than10000r/min

序号 No.	税则号列 Tariff Line	中文货品名称 Article Description in Chinese	最惠国税率 MFN(%)	协定税率 Agreement(%)	特惠税率 SP(%)	普通税率 Gen(%)	英文货品名称 Article Description
		---其他:					---Other:
5990	8413.7091	----电动潜油泵及潜水电泵	10Δ8	0 冰岛IS,东盟AS,哥CR,秘鲁PE,新加坡SG,新西兰NZ,智利CL 4 瑞士CH 5 巴PK 6 澳AU 8 韩国KR	0 受惠国LD	40	----Electric submersible oil pumps and electric submersible pumps
5991	8413.7099	----其他	8	0 冰岛IS,东盟AS,哥CR,秘鲁PE,香港HK,新西兰NZ,智利CL 4.8 澳AU,韩国KR 5 巴PK 5.6 瑞士CH 7.6 亚太AP	0 受惠国LD	40	----Other
		-其他泵;液体提升机:					-Other pumps; liquid elevators:
5992	8413.8100	--泵	8	0 巴PK,冰岛IS,东盟AS,哥CR,秘鲁PE,台湾TW,新西兰NZ,智利CL 4 亚太AP 4.8 澳AU,韩国KR 5.6 瑞士CH	0 受惠国LD	40	--Pumps
5993	8413.8200	--液体提升机	8	0 冰岛IS,东盟AS,哥CR,秘鲁PE,新西兰NZ,智利CL 4.8 澳AU 5 巴PK 5.8 瑞士CH 6.4 韩国KR	0 受惠国LD	30	--Liquid elevators
		-零件:					-Parts:
5994	8413.9100	--泵用	5	0 澳AU,巴PK,冰岛IS,东盟AS,哥CR,韩国KR,秘鲁PE,台湾TW,香港HK,新西兰NZ,智利CL 2.5 亚太AP 3.5 瑞士CH	0 受惠国LD	30	--Of pumps
5995	8413.9200	--液体提升机用	6Δ4	0 冰岛IS,东盟AS,哥CR,秘鲁PE,新西兰NZ,智利CL 2.4 瑞士CH 3.6 澳AU,韩国KR 5 巴PK	0 受惠国LD	30	--Of liquid elevators
	84.14	**空气泵或真空泵、空气及其他气体压缩机、风机、风扇;装有风扇的通风罩或循环气罩,不论是否装有过滤器:**					**Air or vacuum pumps, air or other gas compressors and fans; ventilating or recycling hoods incorporating a fan, whether or not fitted with filters:**
5996	8414.1000	-真空泵	8Δ5	0 冰岛IS,东盟AS,哥CR,秘鲁PE,台湾TW,新西兰NZ,智利CL 4.8 澳AU 5 巴PK 5.6 瑞士CH 6.4 韩国KR	0 受惠国$_1$LD$_1$	30	-Vacuum pumps
5997	8414.2000	-手动或脚踏式空气泵	8	0 冰岛IS,东盟AS,哥CR,秘鲁PE,新西兰NZ,智利CL 3.2 瑞士CH 4.8 澳AU,韩国KR 5 巴PK	0 受惠国$_1$LD$_1$	30	-Hand-or foot-operated pumps
		-用于制冷设备的压缩机:					-Compressors of a kind used in refrigerating equipment:
		---电动机驱动的压缩机:					---Driven by a motor:

序号 No.	税则号列 Tariff Line	中文货品名称 Article Description in Chinese	最惠国税率 MFN(%)	协定税率 Agreement(%)	特惠税率 SP(%)	普通税率 Gen(%)	英文货品名称 Article Description
5998	8414.3011	----冷藏箱或冷冻箱用，电动机额定功率不超过0.4千瓦	8	0 冰岛IS,东盟AS,哥CR,秘鲁PE,香港HK,新加坡SG,新西兰NZ,智利CL 3.2 瑞士CH 4.8 澳AU 5 巴PK 5.9 亚太AP 6.9 韩国KR	0 受惠国LD	80	----For refrigerators or freezers, of a motor power not exceeding 0.4KW
5999	8414.3012	----冷藏箱或冷冻箱用，电动机额定功率超过0.4千瓦，但不超过5千瓦	10	0 冰岛IS,东盟AS,哥CR,香港HK,新加坡SG,新西兰NZ,智利CL 3 秘鲁PE 4 瑞士CH 5 巴PK 6 澳AU 8.5 亚太AP 9 韩国KR	0 受惠国LD	80	----For refrigerators or freezers, of a motor power exceeding 0.4KW but not exceeding 5KW
6000	8414.3013	----空气调节器用，电动机额定功率超过0.4千瓦，但不超过5千瓦	10	0 冰岛IS,东盟AS,哥CR,台湾TW,香港HK,新加坡SG,新西兰NZ,智利CL 3 秘鲁PE 4 瑞士CH 5 巴PK 6 澳AU,韩国KR 8.5 亚太AP	0 受惠国LD	80	----For air conditioning machines, of a motor power exceeding 0.4KW but not exceeding 5KW
6001	8414.3014	----空气调节器用，电动机额定功率超过5千瓦	10	0 冰岛IS,东盟AS,哥CR,台湾TW,香港HK,新加坡SG,新西兰NZ,智利CL 3 秘鲁PE 4 瑞士CH 5 巴PK 6 澳AU 8 韩国KR 8.5 亚太AP	0 受惠国LD	80	----For air conditioning machines, of a motor power exceeding 5KW
6002	8414.3015	----冷冻或冷藏设备用，电动机额定功率超过5千瓦	10	0 冰岛IS,东盟AS,哥CR,香港HK,新西兰NZ,智利CL 3 秘鲁PE 4 瑞士CH 5 巴PK 6 澳AU 8 韩国KR 9.2 亚太AP	0 受惠国LD	30	----For refrigerators or freezers, of a motor power exceeding 5KW
6003	8414.3019	----其他	10	0 冰岛IS,东盟AS,哥CR,香港HK,新加坡SG,新西兰NZ,智利CL 3 秘鲁PE 4 瑞士CH 5 巴PK 6 澳AU 9 韩国KR,亚太AP	0 受惠国LD	30	----Other
6004	8414.3090	---非电动机驱动的压缩机	9	0 冰岛IS,东盟AS,哥CR,秘鲁PE,香港HK,新加坡SG,新西兰NZ,智利CL 3.6 瑞士CH 5 巴PK 5.4 澳AU 7.8 韩国KR 8.1 亚太AP	0 受惠国LD	80	---Driven by a non-motor

序号 No.	税则号列 Tariff Line	中文货品名称 Article Description in Chinese	最惠国税率 MFN(%)	协定税率 Agreement(%)	特惠税率 SP(%)	普通税率 Gen(%)	英文货品名称 Article Description
6005	8414.4000	-装在拖车底盘上的空气压缩机	8	0 冰岛IS,东盟AS,哥CR,秘鲁PE,香港HK,新西兰NZ,智利CL 3.2 瑞士CH 4.8 澳AU 5 巴PK 6.4 韩国KR	0 受惠国$_1$LD$_1$	30	-Air compressors mounted on a wheeled chassis for towing
		-风机、风扇：					-Fans:
		--台扇、落地扇、壁扇、换气扇或吊扇，包括风机，本身装有一个输出功率不超过125瓦的电动机：					--Table, floor, wall, window, ceiling or roof fans, with a self-contained electric motor of an output not exceeding 125W:
6006	8414.5110	---吊扇	20	0 冰岛IS,东盟AS,哥CR,新加坡SG,新西兰NZ,智利CL 6 秘鲁PE 12 澳AU 14 瑞士CH 17.3 韩国KR	0 老挝LA,受惠国LD	130	---Ceiling or roof fans
6007	8414.5120	---换气扇	20	0 冰岛IS,东盟AS,哥CR,台湾TW,新加坡SG,新西兰NZ,智利CL 6 秘鲁PE 12 澳AU 14 瑞士CH 17.3 韩国KR	0 老挝LA,受惠国LD	130	---Window fans
6008	8414.5130	---具有旋转导风轮的风扇	12	0 冰岛IS,东盟AS,哥CR,秘鲁PE,新加坡SG,新西兰NZ,智利CL 6 巴PK 7.2 澳AU 8.4 瑞士CH 9.6 韩国KR	0 老挝LA,受惠国LD	130	---Repeating front louver fan
		---其他：					---Other:
6009	8414.5191	----台扇	10	0 冰岛IS,东盟AS,哥CR,秘鲁PE,新西兰NZ,智利CL 4 瑞士CH 5 巴PK 6 澳AU 8 韩国KR	0 老挝LA,受惠国LD	130	----Table fans
6010	8414.5192	----落地扇	10	0 冰岛IS,东盟AS,哥CR,秘鲁PE,新西兰NZ,智利CL 4 瑞士CH 5 巴PK 6 澳AU 8 韩国KR	0 老挝LA,受惠国LD	130	----Floor fans
6011	8414.5193	----壁扇	10	0 冰岛IS,东盟AS,哥CR,秘鲁PE,新西兰NZ,智利CL 4 瑞士CH 5 巴PK 6 澳AU 8 韩国KR	0 老挝LA,受惠国LD	130	----Wall fans
6012	8414.5199	----其他	10	0 冰岛IS,东盟AS,哥CR,秘鲁PE,台湾TW,新加坡SG,新西兰NZ,智利CL 4 瑞士CH 5 巴PK 6 澳AU 8 韩国KR	0 老挝LA,受惠国LD	130	----Other
		--其他：					--Other:

序号 No.	税则号列 Tariff Line	中文货品名称 Article Description in Chinese	最惠国税率 MFN(%)	协定税率 Agreement(%)	特惠税率 SP(%)	普通税率 Gen(%)	英文货品名称 Article Description
6013	8414.5910	---吊扇	8	0 冰岛IS,东盟AS,哥CR,秘鲁PE,新西兰NZ,智利CL 3.2 瑞士CH 4.8 澳AU,韩国KR 5 巴PK 7.2 亚太AP	0 受惠国$_1$LD$_1$	30	---Ceiling or roof fans
6014	8414.5920	---换气扇	8	0 冰岛IS,东盟AS,哥CR,秘鲁PE,新西兰NZ,智利CL 3.2 瑞士CH 4.8 澳AU,韩国KR 5 巴PK 7.2 亚太AP	0 受惠国$_1$LD$_1$	30	---Window fans
6015	8414.5930	---离心通风机	10	0 澳门MO,冰岛IS,东盟AS,哥CR,新加坡SG,新西兰NZ,智利CL 3 秘鲁PE 4 瑞士CH 5 巴PK 6 澳AU,韩国KR 9.5 亚太AP	0 受惠国$_1$LD$_1$	30	---Centrifugal ventilation fans
6016	8414.5990	---其他	8	0 冰岛IS,东盟AS,哥CR,秘鲁PE,台湾TW,新西兰NZ,智利CL 4.8 澳AU,韩国KR 5 巴PK 5.6 瑞士CH 7.2 亚太AP	0 受惠国LD	30	---Other
		-罩的平面最大边长不超过120厘米的通风罩或循环气罩:					-Hoods having a maximum horizontal side not exceeding 120cm:
6017	8414.6010	---抽油烟机	10Δ6	0 冰岛IS,东盟AS,哥CR,秘鲁PE,新西兰NZ,智利CL 4 瑞士CH 5 巴PK 6 澳AU 8 韩国KR	0 老挝LA,受惠国LD	130	---Range hoods
6018	8414.6090	---其他	10	0 冰岛IS,东盟AS,哥CR,秘鲁PE,新加坡SG,新西兰NZ,智利CL 4 瑞士CH 5 巴PK 6 澳AU 8 韩国KR	0 老挝LA,受惠国LD	130	---Other
		-其他:					-Other:
6019	8414.8010	---燃气轮机用的自由活塞式发生器	8	0 冰岛IS,东盟AS,哥CR,秘鲁PE,新西兰NZ,智利CL 3.2 瑞士CH 4.8 澳AU,韩国KR 5 巴PK 5.6 亚太AP	0 受惠国$_1$LD$_1$	50	---Free piston generators for gas turbines
6020	8414.8020	---二氧化碳压缩机	7	0 巴PK,冰岛IS,东盟AS,哥CR,秘鲁PE,新西兰NZ,智利CL 2.8 瑞士CH 4.2 澳AU 4.9 亚太AP 5.6 韩国KR	0 受惠国$_1$LD$_1$	30	---CO_2 compressors

序号 No.	税则号列 Tariff Line	中文货品名称 Article Description in Chinese	最惠国税率 MFN(%)	协定税率 Agreement(%)	特惠税率 SP(%)	普通税率 Gen(%)	英文货品名称 Article Description
6021	8414.8030	---发动机用增压器	7	0 巴PK,冰岛IS,东盟AS,哥CR,新西兰NZ,智利CL 4.2 澳AU 4.9 亚太AP 6 韩国KR	0 受惠国$_2$LD$_2$	30	---Superchargers for engines
	ex84148030	乘用车机械增压器	Δ5				Mechanical superchargers for Passenger cars
6022	8414.8040	---空气及其他气体压缩机	7	0 巴PK,冰岛IS,东盟AS,哥CR,韩国KR,秘鲁PE,台湾TW,香港HK,新西兰NZ,智利CL 4.2 澳AU 4.9 亚太AP 5 瑞士CH	0 受惠国$_1$LD$_1$	30	---Air or other gas compressors
6023	8414.8090	---其他	7	0 巴PK,冰岛IS,东盟AS,哥CR,韩国KR,秘鲁PE,台湾TW,香港HK,新西兰NZ,智利CL 4.2 澳AU 4.9 亚太AP 5 瑞士CH	0 受惠国$_1$LD$_1$	30	---Other
		-零件:					-Parts:
		---子目号8414.3011至8414.3014及8414.3090所列机器的零件:					---Of the machines of subheadings Nos .8414.3011 to 8414.3014 and 8414. 3090:
6024	8414.9011	----压缩机进、排气阀片	8Δ5	0 冰岛IS,东盟AS,哥CR,秘鲁PE,新西兰NZ,智利CL 3.2 瑞士CH 4.8 澳AU,韩国KR 5 巴PK 7.2 亚太AP	0 老挝LA,受惠国LD	80	----In take valve leaf or discharge valve leaf
6025	8414.9019	----其他	8Δ5	0 冰岛IS,东盟AS,哥CR,韩国KR,秘鲁PE,台湾TW,新西兰NZ,智利CL 4.8 澳AU 5 巴PK 5.6 瑞士CH 7.2 亚太AP	0 受惠国$_1$LD$_1$	80	----Other
6026	8414.9020	---子目号8414. 5110至8414. 5199及8414. 6000所列机器的零件	12Δ6	0 冰岛IS,东盟AS,哥CR,台湾TW,新加坡SG,新西兰NZ,智利CL 3.6 秘鲁PE 6 巴PK 7.2 澳AU 8.4 瑞士CH 9.6 韩国KR 11.4 亚太AP	0 受惠国$_1$LD$_1$	130	---Of the machines of subheadings Nos. 8414.5110 to 8414.5199 or 8414.6000
6027	8414.9090	---其他	7Δ4	0 冰岛IS,东盟AS,哥CR,韩国KR,秘鲁PE,台湾TW,香港HK,新西兰NZ,智利CL 4.2 澳AU 5 巴PK,瑞士CH 6.5 亚太AP	0 受惠国$_1$LD$_1$	30	---Other
	84.15	**空气调节器,装有电扇及调温、调湿装置,包括不能单独调湿的空调器:**					**Air-conditioning machines, comprising a motor-driven fan and elements for changing the temperature and humidity, including those machines in which the humidity cannot be separately regulated:**
		-窗式或壁式,独立的或分体的:					-Window or wall types, self-contained or 'split-system':

序号 No.	税则号列 Tariff Line	中文货品名称 Article Description in Chinese	最惠国税率 MFN(%)	协定税率 Agreement(%)	特惠税率 SP(%)	普通税率 Gen(%)	英文货品名称 Article Description
6028	8415.1010	---独立式	15	0 冰岛IS,东盟AS,哥CR,新加坡SG,新西兰NZ,智利CL 4.5 秘鲁PE 7.5 巴PK 9 澳AU 10.5 瑞士CH 12 韩国KR 13.5 亚太AP	0 受惠国$_1$LD$_1$	130	---Self-contained
		---分体式:					---Split-system:
6029	8415.1021	----制冷量不超过4000大卡/时	15	0 冰岛IS,东盟AS,哥CR,新加坡SG,新西兰NZ,智利CL 4.5 秘鲁PE 7.5 巴PK 9 澳AU 10.5 瑞士CH 12 韩国KR 13.5 亚太AP	0 受惠国$_1$LD$_1$	130	----Of a refrigerating effect not exceeding 4000Cal per hour
6030	8415.1022	----制冷量超过4000大卡/时	15	0 冰岛IS,东盟AS,哥CR,新加坡SG,新西兰NZ,智利CL 4.5 秘鲁PE 7.5 巴PK 9 澳AU 10.5 瑞士CH 12 韩国KR 13.5 亚太AP	0 受惠国$_1$LD$_1$	90	----Of a refrigerating effect exceeding 4000Cal per hour
6031	8415.2000	-机动车辆上供人使用的	20△10	0 冰岛IS,哥CR,香港HK,新西兰NZ,智利CL 12 澳AU 14 瑞士CH 18 韩国KR	0 受惠国$_2$LD$_2$	110	-Of a kind used for persons, in motor vehicles
		-其他:					-Other:
		--装有制冷装置及一个冷热循环换向阀的(可逆式热泵):					--Incorporating a refrigerating unit and a valve for reversal of the cooling/heat cycle (reversible heat pumps) :
6032	8415.8110	---制冷量不超过4000大卡/时	15	0 冰岛IS,东盟AS,哥CR,新加坡SG,新西兰NZ,智利CL 4.5 秘鲁PE 9 澳AU 10.5 瑞士CH 12 巴PK,韩国KR	0 受惠国$_1$LD$_1$	130	---Of a refrigerating effect not exceeding 4000Cal per hour
6033	8415.8120	---制冷量超过4000大卡/时	20△12	0 冰岛IS,东盟AS,哥CR,新加坡SG,新西兰NZ,智利CL 6 秘鲁PE 12 澳AU 14 瑞士CH 18 韩国KR	0 受惠国$_1$LD$_1$	90	---Of a refrigerating effect exceeding 4000Cal per hour
		--其他,装有制冷装置的:					--Other, incorporating a refrigerating unit:
6034	8415.8210	---制冷量不超过4000大卡/时	15	0 冰岛IS,东盟AS,哥CR,新加坡SG,新西兰NZ,智利CL 4.5 秘鲁PE 9 澳AU 10.5 瑞士CH 12 巴PK	0 受惠国$_1$LD$_1$	130	---Of a refrigerating effect not exceeding 4000Cal per hour

序号 No.	税则号列 Tariff Line	中文货品名称 Article Description in Chinese	最惠国税率 MFN(%)	协定税率 Agreement(%)	特惠税率 SP(%)	普通税率 Gen(%)	英文货品名称 Article Description
6035	8415.8220	---制冷量超过4000大卡/时	20Δ12	0 冰岛IS,东盟AS,哥CR,新加坡SG,新西兰NZ,智利CL 6 秘鲁PE 12 澳AU 14 瑞士CH	0 受惠国$_1$LD$_1$	90	---Of a refrigerating effect exceeding 4000Cal per hour
6036	8415.8300	--未装有制冷装置的	10	0 冰岛IS,东盟AS,哥CR,秘鲁PE,新加坡SG,新西兰NZ,智利CL 4 瑞士CH 5 巴PK 6 澳AU 8 韩国KR	0 受惠国LD	90	--Not incorporating a refrigerating unit
		-零件:					-Parts:
6037	8415.9010	---子目号8415.1010、8415.1021、8415.8110及8415.8210所列设备的零件	10Δ6	0 冰岛IS,东盟AS,哥CR,秘鲁PE,香港HK,新加坡SG,新西兰NZ,智利CL 4 瑞士CH 5 巴PK 6 澳AU 8 韩国KR,亚太AP	0 受惠国LD	130	---Of the machines of subheading No.8415.1010, 8415.1021, 8415.8110 or 8415.8210
6038	8415.9090	---其他	10Δ6	0 冰岛IS,东盟AS,哥CR,秘鲁PE,台湾TW,香港HK,新加坡SG,新西兰NZ,智利CL 4 瑞士CH 5 巴PK 6 澳AU 8 韩国KR,亚太AP	0 受惠国LD	90	---Other
	84.16	**使用液体燃料、粉状固体燃料或气体燃料的炉用燃烧器;机械加煤机,包括其机械炉篦、机械出灰器及类似装置:**					**Furnace burners for liquid fuel, for pulverised solid fuel or for gas; mechanical stokers, including their mechanical grates, mechanical ash dischargers and similar appliances:**
6039	8416.1000	-使用液体燃料的炉用燃烧器	10	0 冰岛IS,东盟AS,哥CR,秘鲁PE,新加坡SG,新西兰NZ,智利CL 4 瑞士CH 5 巴PK 6 澳AU 8 韩国KR 9.5 亚太AP	0 受惠国$_1$LD$_1$	35	-Furnace burners for liquid fuel
		-其他炉用燃烧器,包括复式燃烧器:					-Other furnace burners, including combination burners:
		---气体的:					---For gas:
6040	8416.2011	----使用天然气的	10.5	0 冰岛IS,东盟AS,哥CR,秘鲁PE,新加坡SG,新西兰NZ,智利CL 5 巴PK 6.3 澳AU 7.4 瑞士CH 8.4 韩国KR	0 受惠国$_1$LD$_1$	35	----Of using natural gas
	ex84162011	溴化锂空调用天然气燃烧机	Δ5				Natural gas burners for lithium bromide air conditioners
6041	8416.2019	----其他	10.5	0 冰岛IS,东盟AS,哥CR,秘鲁PE,新加坡SG,新西兰NZ,智利CL 5 巴PK 6.3 澳AU 7.4 瑞士CH 8.4 韩国KR	0 受惠国$_1$LD$_1$	35	----Other

序号 No.	税则号列 Tariff Line	中文货品名称 Article Description in Chinese	最惠国税率 MFN(%)	协定税率 Agreement(%)	特惠税率 SP(%)	普通税率 Gen(%)	英文货品名称 Article Description
6042	8416.2090	---其他	10.5	0 冰岛IS,东盟AS,哥CR,秘鲁PE,新加坡SG,新西兰NZ,智利CL 4.2 瑞士CH 5 巴PK 6.3 澳AU 8.4 韩国KR	0 受惠国$_1$LD$_1$	35	---Other
	ex84162090	溴化锂空调用复式燃烧机	Δ5				Combination burners for lithium bromide air conditioners
6043	8416.3000	-机械加煤机,包括其机械炉篦、机械出灰器及类似装置	8.4	0 冰岛IS,东盟AS,哥CR,秘鲁PE,新西兰NZ,智利CL 3.36 瑞士CH 5 澳AU,巴PK,韩国KR	0 受惠国$_1$LD$_1$	35	-Mechanical stokers, including their mechanical grates, mechanical ash dis-chargers and similar appliances
6044	8416.9000	-零件	6	0 冰岛IS,东盟AS,哥CR,秘鲁PE,新西兰NZ,智利CL 2.4 瑞士CH 3.6 澳AU,韩国KR 5 巴PK	0 受惠国$_1$LD$_1$	35	-Parts
	84.17	**非电热的工业或实验室用炉及烘箱,包括焚烧炉:**					**Industrial or laboratory furnaces and ovens, including incinerators, non-electric:**
6045	8417.1000	-矿砂、黄铁矿或金属的焙烧、熔化或其他热处理用炉及烘箱	10	0 冰岛IS,东盟AS,哥CR,秘鲁PE,新加坡SG,新西兰NZ,智利CL 4 瑞士CH 5 巴PK 6 澳AU 8 韩国KR	0 受惠国$_1$LD$_1$	35	-Furnaces and ovens for the roasting, melting or other heat-treatment of ores, pyrites or of metals
6046	8417.2000	-面包房用烤炉及烘箱,包括做饼干用的	10	0 冰岛IS,东盟AS,哥CR,秘鲁PE,新西兰NZ,智利CL 4 瑞士CH 5 巴PK 6 澳AU 8 韩国KR	0 受惠国$_1$LD$_1$	35	-Bakery ovens, including biscuit ovens
		-其他:					-Other:
6047	8417.8010	---炼焦炉	10	0 冰岛IS,东盟AS,哥CR,秘鲁PE,新西兰NZ,智利CL 4 瑞士CH 5 巴PK 6 澳AU 8 韩国KR	0 受惠国$_1$LD$_1$	35	---Coke ovens
6048	8417.8020	---放射性废物焚烧炉	5	0 澳AU,巴PK,冰岛IS,东盟AS,哥CR,秘鲁PE,瑞士CH,新西兰NZ,智利CL 3 韩国KR	0 受惠国$_1$LD$_1$	35	---Burn furnaces for radioactive waste
6049	8417.8030	---水泥回转窑	10	0 冰岛IS,东盟AS,哥CR,秘鲁PE,新加坡SG,新西兰NZ,智利CL 4 瑞士CH 5 巴PK 6 澳AU 8 韩国KR	0 受惠国$_1$LD$_1$	35	---Cement rotary kilns
6050	8417.8040	---石灰石分解炉	10	0 冰岛IS,东盟AS,哥CR,秘鲁PE,新西兰NZ,智利CL 4 瑞士CH 5 巴PK 6 澳AU 8 韩国KR	0 受惠国$_1$LD$_1$	35	---Limestone decomposition furnace

序号 No.	税则号列 Tariff Line	中文货品名称 Article Description in Chinese	最惠国税率 MFN(%)	协定税率 Agreement(%)	特惠税率 SP(%)	普通税率 Gen(%)	英文货品名称 Article Description
6051	8417.8050	---垃圾焚烧炉	10Δ5	0 冰岛IS,东盟AS,哥CR,秘鲁PE,台湾TW,新加坡SG,新西兰NZ,智利CL 5 巴PK 6 澳AU 7.5 瑞士CH 9 韩国KR	0 受惠国$_1$LD$_1$	35	---Refuse incinerator
6052	8417.8090	---其他	10	0 冰岛IS,东盟AS,哥CR,秘鲁PE,台湾TW,新加坡SG,新西兰NZ,智利CL 5 巴PK 6 澳AU 7.5 瑞士CH 9 韩国KR	0 受惠国$_1$LD$_1$	35	---Other
		-零件:					-Parts:
6053	8417.9010	---海绵铁回转窑用	7	0 冰岛IS,东盟AS,哥CR,秘鲁PE,新西兰NZ,智利CL 2.8 瑞士CH 4.2 澳AU,韩国KR 5 巴PK	0 受惠国$_1$LD$_1$	35	---For sponge iron rotary kiln
6054	8417.9020	---炼焦炉用	7	0 冰岛IS,东盟AS,哥CR,秘鲁PE,新西兰NZ,智利CL 2.8 瑞士CH 4.2 澳AU,韩国KR 5 巴PK	0 受惠国$_1$LD$_1$	35	---For coke ovens
6055	8417.9090	---其他	7	0 冰岛IS,东盟AS,哥CR,秘鲁PE,新西兰NZ,智利CL 4.2 澳AU,韩国KR 4.9 瑞士CH 5 巴PK	0 受惠国$_1$LD$_1$	35	---Other
	ex84179090	垃圾焚烧炉和放射性废物焚烧炉的零件	Δ5				Parts of Municipal Waste Incinerator, parts of incinerators for radioactive waste
	84.18	**电气或非电气的冷藏箱、冷冻箱及其他制冷设备;热泵,但税号84.15的空气调节器除外:**					**Refrigerators, freezers and other refrigerating or freezing equipment, electric or other; heat pumps other than air-conditioning machines of heading 8415:**
		-冷藏—冷冻组合机,各自装有单独外门的:					-Combined refrigerator-freezers, fitted with separate external doors:
6056	8418.1010	---容积超过500升	10	0 冰岛IS,东盟AS,哥CR,新加坡SG,新西兰NZ,智利CL 3 秘鲁PE 4 瑞士CH 5 巴PK 6 澳AU 9 韩国KR	0 受惠国LD	100	---Of a capacity exceeding 500L
6057	8418.1020	---容积超过200升,但不超过500升	15	0 冰岛IS,东盟AS,哥CR,新加坡SG,新西兰NZ,智利CL 4.5 秘鲁PE 9 澳AU 10.5 瑞士CH 12 巴PK,韩国KR	0 受惠国$_1$LD$_1$	130	---Of a capacity exceeding 200L, not exceeding 500L

序号 No.	税则号列 Tariff Line	中文货品名称 Article Description in Chinese	最惠国税率 MFN(%)	协定税率 Agreement(%)	特惠税率 SP(%)	普通税率 Gen(%)	英文货品名称 Article Description
6058	8418.1030	---容积不超过200升	15	0 冰岛IS,东盟AS,哥CR,新加坡SG,新西兰NZ,智利CL 4.5 秘鲁PE 9 澳AU 10.5 瑞士CH 12 巴PK	0 受惠国$_1$LD$_1$	130	---Of a capacity not exceeding 200L
		-家用型冷藏箱:					-Refrigerators, household type:
		--压缩式:					--Compression-type:
6059	8418.2110	---容积超过150升	10	0 冰岛IS,东盟AS,哥CR,秘鲁PE,新加坡SG,新西兰NZ,智利CL 4 瑞士CH 5 巴PK 6 澳AU 8 韩国KR	0 受惠国LD	130	---Of a capacity exceeding 150L
6060	8418.2120	---容积超过50升,但不超过150升	10	0 冰岛IS,东盟AS,哥CR,秘鲁PE,新加坡SG,新西兰NZ,智利CL 4 瑞士CH 5 巴PK 6 澳AU 8 韩国KR 9 亚太AP	0 受惠国LD	130	---Of a capacity exceeding 50L, not exceeding 150L
6061	8418.2130	---容积不超过50升	10	0 冰岛IS,东盟AS,哥CR,秘鲁PE,新加坡SG,新西兰NZ,智利CL 4 瑞士CH 5 巴PK 6 澳AU 8 韩国KR 9 亚太AP	0 受惠国LD	130	---Of a capacity not exceeding 50L
		--其他:					--Other:
6062	8418.2910	---半导体制冷式	30	0 冰岛IS,东盟AS,哥CR,新加坡SG,新西兰NZ,智利CL 9 秘鲁PE 18 澳AU 21 瑞士CH	0 受惠国$_1$LD$_1$	130	---Semiconductor-type
6063	8418.2920	---电气吸收式	15	0 冰岛IS,东盟AS,哥CR,新加坡SG,新西兰NZ,智利CL 4.5 秘鲁PE 9 澳AU 10.5 瑞士CH 12 巴PK,韩国KR	0 受惠国$_1$LD$_1$	130	---Absorption-type, electrical
6064	8418.2990	---其他	30	0 冰岛IS,东盟AS,哥CR,新加坡SG,新西兰NZ,智利CL 9 秘鲁PE 18 澳AU 21 瑞士CH	0 受惠国$_1$LD$_1$	130	---Other
		-柜式冷冻箱,容积不超过800升:					-Freezers of the chest type, not exceeding 800 litres capacity:
6065	8418.3010	---制冷温度在-40℃及以下	9	0 澳门MO,冰岛IS,东盟AS,哥CR,秘鲁PE,新西兰NZ,智利CL 3.6 瑞士CH 5 巴PK 5.4 澳AU	0 受惠国LD	50	---Of a refrigerating temperature of -40℃or lower
		---制冷温度在-40℃以上:					---Of a refrigerating temperature higher than -40℃:

序号 No.	税则号列 Tariff Line	中文货品名称 Article Description in Chinese	最惠国税率 MFN(%)	协定税率 Agreement(%)	特惠税率 SP(%)	普通税率 Gen(%)	英文货品名称 Article Description
6066	8418.3021	----容积超过500升	23	0 澳门MO,冰岛IS,东盟AS,哥CR,新加坡SG,新西兰NZ,智利CL 6.9 秘鲁PE 13.8 澳AU 16.1 瑞士CH 20.7 韩国KR	0 受惠国$_1$LD$_1$	100	----Of a capacity exceeding 500L
6067	8418.3029	----其他	30	0 澳门MO,冰岛IS,东盟AS,哥CR,新加坡SG,新西兰NZ,智利CL 9 秘鲁PE 18 澳AU 21.6 瑞士CH	0 受惠国$_1$LD$_1$	130	----Other
		-立式冷冻箱,容积不超过900升:					-Freezers of the upright type, not exceeding 900 litres capacity:
6068	8418.4010	---制冷温度在-40℃及以下	9	0 澳门MO,冰岛IS,东盟AS,哥CR,秘鲁PE,新西兰NZ,智利CL 3.6 瑞士CH 5 巴PK 5.4 澳AU	0 受惠国LD	50	---Of a refrigerating temperature of -40℃or lower
		---制冷温度在-40℃以上:					---Of a refrigerating temperature higher than -40℃:
6069	8418.4021	----容积超过500升	15	0 澳门MO,冰岛IS,东盟AS,哥CR,新加坡SG,新西兰NZ,智利CL 4.5 秘鲁PE 9 澳AU 10.5 瑞士CH 12 巴PK	0 受惠国$_1$LD$_1$	100	----Of a capacity exceeding 500L
6070	8418.4029	----其他	30	0 澳门MO,冰岛IS,东盟AS,哥CR,新加坡SG,新西兰NZ,智利CL 9 秘鲁PE 18 澳AU	0 受惠国$_1$LD$_1$	130	----Other
6071	8418.5000	-装有冷藏或冷冻装置的其他设备(柜、箱、展示台、陈列箱及类似品),用于存储及展示	10	0 澳门MO,冰岛IS,东盟AS,哥CR,香港HK,新加坡SG,新西兰NZ,智利CL 3 秘鲁PE 4 瑞士CH 5 巴PK 6 澳AU 8 韩国KR	0 受惠国LD	100	-Other furniture (chests, cabinets, display counters, show-cases and the like) for storage and display, incorporating refrigerating or freezing equipment
		-其他制冷设备;热泵:					-Other refrigerating or freezing equipment; heat pumps:
		--热泵,税目8415的空气调节器除外:					--Heat pumps other than air conditioning machines of heading 8415:
6072	8418.6120	---压缩式	10	0 冰岛IS,东盟AS,哥CR,秘鲁PE,新加坡SG,新西兰NZ,智利CL 4 瑞士CH 5 巴PK 6 澳AU 7 亚太AP 8 韩国KR	0 受惠国LD	90	---Compression type units
6073	8418.6190	---其他	15	0 澳门MO,冰岛IS,东盟AS,哥CR,新加坡SG,新西兰NZ,智利CL 4.5 秘鲁PE 7 巴PK,亚太AP 9 澳AU 10.5 瑞士CH 12 韩国KR	0 受惠国$_1$LD$_1$	130	---Other
		--其他:					--Other:

序号 No.	税则号列 Tariff Line	中文货品名称 Article Description in Chinese	最惠国税率 MFN(%)	协定税率 Agreement(%)	特惠税率 SP(%)	普通税率 Gen(%)	英文货品名称 Article Description
6074	8418.6920	---制冷机组	10	0 澳门MO,冰岛IS,东盟AS,哥CR,秘鲁PE,新加坡SG,新西兰NZ,智利CL 4 瑞士CH 5 巴PK 6 澳AU 7 亚太AP 8 韩国KR	0 受惠国LD	90	---Refrigerating units
6075	8418.6990	---其他	10	0 澳门MO,冰岛IS,东盟AS,哥CR,新加坡SG,新西兰NZ,智利CL 3 秘鲁PE 5 巴PK 6 澳AU 7 瑞士CH,亚太AP 8 韩国KR	0 受惠国LD	130	---Other
		-零件:					-Parts:
6076	8418.9100	--冷藏或冷冻设备专用的特制家具	18	0 冰岛IS,东盟AS,哥CR,新加坡SG,新西兰NZ,智利CL 5.4 秘鲁PE 10.8 澳AU 12.6 瑞士CH 14.4 巴PK,韩国KR 17.1 亚太AP	0 受惠国$_1$LD$_1$	130	--Furniture designed to receive refrigerating or freezing equipment
		--其他:					--Other:
6077	8418.9910	---制冷机组及热泵用	10Δ6	0 冰岛IS,东盟AS,哥CR,新加坡SG,新西兰NZ,智利CL 3 秘鲁PE 4 瑞士CH 5 巴PK 6 澳AU 8 韩国KR	0 受惠国LD	90	---Of refrigerating units and heat pumps
		---其他:					---Other:
6078	8418.9991	----制冷温度在-40℃及以下的冷冻设备用	9.5Δ6	0 澳门MO,冰岛IS,东盟AS,哥CR,秘鲁PE,新西兰NZ,智利CL 3.8 瑞士CH 5 巴PK 5.7 澳AU,韩国KR	0 受惠国LD	50	----Of freezing equipment of a refrigerating temperature of -40℃or lower
6079	8418.9992	----制冷温度在-40℃以上,但容积超过500升的冷藏或冷冻设备用	10Δ6	0 澳门MO,冰岛IS,东盟AS,哥CR,新西兰NZ,智利CL 3 秘鲁PE 4 瑞士CH 5 巴PK 6 澳AU 8 韩国KR	0 受惠国LD	100	----Of refrigerating or freezing equipment of a refrigerating temperature higher than -40℃ and a capacity exceeding 500L
6080	8418.9999	----其他	10Δ6	0 澳门MO,冰岛IS,东盟AS,哥CR,新加坡SG,新西兰NZ,智利CL 3 秘鲁PE 4 瑞士CH 5 巴PK 6 澳AU 8 韩国KR	0 受惠国LD	130	----Other

序号 No.	税则号列 Tariff Line	中文货品名称 Article Description in Chinese	最惠国税率 MFN(%)	协定税率 Agreement(%)	特惠税率 SP(%)	普通税率 Gen(%)	英文货品名称 Article Description
	84.19	**利用温度变化处理材料的机器、装置及类似的实验室设备,例如,加热、烹煮、烘炒、蒸馏、精馏、消毒、灭菌、汽蒸、干燥、蒸发、气化、冷凝、冷却的机器设备,不论是否电热的(不包括税目8514的炉、烘箱及其他设备),但家用的除外;非电热的快速热水器或贮备式热水器:**					**Machinery, plant or laboratory equipment, whether or not electrically heated (excluding furnaces, ovens and other equipment of heading 8514), for the treatment of materials by a process involving a change of temperature such as heating, cooking, roasting, distilling, rectifying, sterilising, pasteurising, steaming, drying, evaporating, vaporising, condensing or cooling, other than machinery or plant of a kind used for domestic purposes; instantaneous or storage water heaters, non-electric:**
		-非电热的快速热水器或贮备式热水器:					-Instantaneous or storage water heaters, non-electric:
6081	8419.1100	--燃气快速热水器	35	0 冰岛IS,东盟AS,哥CR,新加坡SG,新西兰NZ,智利CL 10.5 秘鲁PE 21 澳AU 25.2 瑞士CH 31.5 韩国KR	0 受惠国$_1$LD$_1$	100	--Instantaneous gas water heaters
		--其他:					--Other:
6082	8419.1910	---太阳能热水器	35Δ5	0 冰岛IS,东盟AS,哥CR,台湾TW,新加坡SG,新西兰NZ,智利CL 10.5 秘鲁PE 21 澳AU 24.5 瑞士CH	0 受惠国$_1$LD$_1$	100	---Solar water heaters
6083	8419.1990	---其他	35	0 冰岛IS,东盟AS,哥CR,台湾TW,新加坡SG,新西兰NZ,智利CL 10.5 秘鲁PE 21 澳AU 25.2 瑞士CH	0 受惠国$_1$LD$_1$	100	---Other
6084	8419.2000	-医用或实验室用消毒器具	4	0 澳AU,巴PK,冰岛IS,东盟AS,哥CR,韩国KR,秘鲁PE,新西兰NZ,智利CL 1.6 瑞士CH	0 受惠国$_1$LD$_1$	30	-Medical, surgical or laboratory sterilizers
		-干燥器:					-Dryers:
6085	8419.3100	--农产品干燥用	8	0 冰岛IS,东盟AS,哥CR,秘鲁PE,新西兰NZ,智利CL 3.2 瑞士CH 4.8 澳AU 5 巴PK 6.4 韩国KR	0 老挝LA,受惠国LD	30	--For agricultural products
6086	8419.3200	--木材、纸浆、纸或纸板干燥用	9	0 冰岛IS,东盟AS,哥CR,秘鲁PE,台湾TW,新西兰NZ,智利CL 3.6 瑞士CH 5 巴PK 5.4 澳AU,韩国KR	0 老挝LA,受惠国LD	30	--For wood, paper pulp, paper or pa-perboard
		--其他:					--Other:
6087	8419.3910	---微空气流动陶瓷坯件干燥器	9	0 冰岛IS,东盟AS,哥CR,秘鲁PE,新西兰NZ,智利CL 3.6 瑞士CH 4.5 巴PK,亚太AP 5.4 澳AU,韩国KR	0 受惠国$_1$LD$_1$	30	---Breeze pottery blanks dryers

序号 No.	税则号列 Tariff Line	中文货品名称 Article Description in Chinese	最惠国税率 MFN(%)	协定税率 Agreement(%)	特惠税率 SP(%)	普通税率 Gen(%)	英文货品名称 Article Description
6088	8419.3990	---其他	9	0 冰岛IS,东盟AS,哥CR,秘鲁PE,台湾TW,新西兰NZ,智利CL 3.6 瑞士CH 4.5 巴PK,亚太AP 5.4 澳AU 7.2 韩国KR	0 受惠国$_1$LD$_1$	30	---Other
	ex84193990	生产奶粉用干燥器	Δ4				Dryers for producing powdered milk
	ex84193990	污泥干燥机	Δ5				Sludge driers
		-蒸馏或精馏设备:					-Distilling or rectifying plant:
6089	8419.4010	---提净塔	10	0 冰岛IS,东盟AS,哥CR,秘鲁PE,新加坡SG,新西兰NZ,智利CL 4 瑞士CH 5 巴PK 6 澳AU 8 韩国KR	0 受惠国$_1$LD$_1$	30	---Stripping towers
6090	8419.4020	---精馏塔	10	0 冰岛IS,东盟AS,哥CR,秘鲁PE,新加坡SG,新西兰NZ,智利CL 4 瑞士CH 5 巴PK 6 澳AU 8 韩国KR	0 受惠国$_1$LD$_1$	30	---Rectifying towers
6091	8419.4090	---其他	10	0 冰岛IS,东盟AS,哥CR,秘鲁PE,新加坡SG,新西兰NZ,智利CL 4 瑞士CH 5 巴PK 6 澳AU 8 韩国KR	0 受惠国$_1$LD$_1$	30	---Other
6092	8419.5000	-热交换装置	10	0 冰岛IS,东盟AS,哥CR,台湾TW,香港HK,新加坡SG,新西兰NZ,智利CL 3 秘鲁PE 5 巴PK 6 澳AU,韩国KR 7.5 瑞士CH 9.5 亚太AP	0 老挝LA,受惠国LD	30	-Heat exchange units
		-液化空气或其他气体的机器:					-Machinery for liquefying air or other gases:
		---制氧机:					---Oxygen producers:
6093	8419.6011	----制氧量在15000立方米/小时及以上	12	0 冰岛IS,东盟AS,哥CR,秘鲁PE,香港HK,新加坡SG,新西兰NZ,智利CL 6 巴PK 7.2 澳AU 8.4 瑞士CH 9.6 韩国KR	0 受惠国$_1$LD$_1$	30	----Oxygen preparation volume no less than 15000m^3/h
6094	8419.6019	----其他	13	0 冰岛IS,东盟AS,哥CR,秘鲁PE,香港HK,新加坡SG,新西兰NZ,智利CL 6.5 巴PK 7.8 澳AU 9.1 瑞士CH 10.4 韩国KR	0 受惠国$_1$LD$_1$	30	----Other

序号 No.	税则号列 Tariff Line	中文货品名称 Article Description in Chinese	最惠国税率 MFN(%)	协定税率 Agreement(%)	特惠税率 SP(%)	普通税率 Gen(%)	英文货品名称 Article Description
6095	8419.6090	---其他	10	0 冰岛IS,东盟AS,哥CR,秘鲁PE,香港HK,新加坡SG,新西兰NZ,智利CL 4 瑞士CH 5 巴PK 6 澳AU 8 韩国KR	0 受惠国$_1$LD$_1$	30	---Other
	ex84196090	通过冷凝分离和去除污染物的气体液化设备	Δ5				Machinery of liquefying air or other gases for separation and removal of pollutants through condensation.
		-其他机器设备:					-Other machinery, plant and equipment:
6096	8419.8100	--加工热饮料或烹调、加热食品用	10Δ6	0 澳门MO,冰岛IS,东盟AS,哥CR,瑞士CH,新加坡SG,新西兰NZ,智利CL 3 秘鲁PE 5 巴PK 6 澳AU 8 韩国KR	0 老挝LA,受惠国LD	30	--For making hot drinks of for cooking or heating food
		--其他:					--Other:
6097	8419.8910	---加氢反应器	0		0 老挝LA,受惠国LD	30	---Hydroformer vessels
6098	8419.8990	---其他	0		0 老挝LA,受惠国LD	30	---Other
		-零件:					-Parts:
6099	8419.9010	---热水器用	0		0 受惠国LD	100	---Of water heaters
6100	8419.9090	---其他	4	0 澳AU,巴PK,冰岛IS,东盟AS,哥CR,韩国KR,秘鲁PE,台湾TW,香港HK,新西兰NZ,智利CL 1.6 瑞士CH	0 受惠国$_1$LD$_1$	30	---Other
	84.20	**研光机或其他滚压机器及其滚筒,但加工金属或玻璃用的除外:**					**Calendering or other rolling machines, other than for metals or glass, and cylinders therefor:**
6101	8420.1000	-研光机或其他滚压机器	8.4	0 冰岛IS,东盟AS,哥CR,秘鲁PE,台湾TW,新西兰NZ,智利CL 3.36 瑞士CH 5 澳AU,巴PK,韩国KR	0 受惠国LD	30	-Calendering or other rolling machines
	ex84201000	织物轧光机	Δ6				Woven fabrics calender
		-零件:					-Parts:
6102	8420.9100	--滚筒	8	0 冰岛IS,东盟AS,哥CR,秘鲁PE,新西兰NZ,智利CL 3.2 瑞士CH 4.8 澳AU,韩国KR 5 巴PK	0 受惠国LD	30	--Cylinders
6103	8420.9900	--其他	8	0 冰岛IS,东盟AS,哥CR,秘鲁PE,新西兰NZ,智利CL 3.2 瑞士CH 4.8 澳AU,韩国KR 5 巴PK	0 受惠国LD	30	--Other
	84.21	**离心机,包括离心干燥机;液体或气体的过滤、净化机器及装置:**					**Centrifuges, including centrifugal dryers; filtering or purifying machinery and apparatus, for liquids or gases:**
		-离心机,包括离心干燥机:					-Centrifuges, including centrifugal dryers:

序号 No.	税则号列 Tariff Line	中文货品名称 Article Description in Chinese	最惠国税率 MFN(%)	协定税率 Agreement(%)	特惠税率 SP(%)	普通税率 Gen(%)	英文货品名称 Article Description
6104	8421.1100	--奶油分离器	8.4	0 冰岛IS,东盟AS,哥CR,秘鲁PE,新西兰NZ,智利CL 3.36 瑞士CH 5 澳AU,巴PK,韩国KR	0 受惠国$_1$LD$_1$	30	--Cream separators
		--干衣机:					--Clothes dryers:
6105	8421.1210	---干衣量不超过10公斤	17.5	0 冰岛IS,东盟AS,哥CR,新加坡SG,新西兰NZ,智利CL 5.2 秘鲁PE 10.5 澳AU 12.3 瑞士CH 14 巴PK,韩国KR	0 受惠国$_1$LD$_1$	70	---Of a dry linen capacity not exceeding 10kg
6106	8421.1290	---其他	8	0 冰岛IS,东盟AS,哥CR,秘鲁PE,新西兰NZ,智利CL 3.2 瑞士CH 4.8 澳AU 5 巴PK 6.4 韩国KR	0 受惠国$_1$LD$_1$	30	---Other
		--其他:					--Other:
6107	8421.1910	---脱水机	10Δ6	0 冰岛IS,东盟AS,哥CR,秘鲁PE,新西兰NZ,智利CL 4 瑞士CH 5 巴PK 6 澳AU 8 韩国KR	0 受惠国$_1$LD$_1$	30	---Dewaterers
6108	8421.1920	---固液分离机	10	0 冰岛IS,东盟AS,哥CR,秘鲁PE,新加坡SG,新西兰NZ,智利CL 4 瑞士CH 5 巴PK 6 澳AU 8 韩国KR	0 受惠国$_1$LD$_1$	30	---Solid-liquor separators
6109	8421.1990	---其他	10	0 冰岛IS,东盟AS,哥CR,秘鲁PE,新加坡SG,新西兰NZ,智利CL 5 巴PK 6 澳AU 7 瑞士CH 8 韩国KR	0 受惠国$_1$LD$_1$	30	---Other
		-液体的过滤、净化机器及装置:					-Filtering or purifying machinery and apparatus for liquids:
		--过滤或净化水用:					--For filtering or purifying water:
6110	8421.2110	---家用型	25Δ5	0 澳门MO,冰岛IS,东盟AS,哥CR,香港HK,新加坡SG,新西兰NZ,智利CL 7.5 秘鲁PE 15 澳AU 17.5 巴PK,亚太AP 18 瑞士CH 22.5 韩国KR	0 受惠国$_1$LD$_1$	63	---Of the household type
		---其他:					---Other:
6111	8421.2191	----船舶压载水处理设备	5	0 澳AU,澳门MO,巴PK,冰岛IS,东盟AS,哥CR,秘鲁PE,台湾TW,香港HK,新西兰NZ,智利CL 2 瑞士CH 3.5 亚太AP 4.3 韩国KR	0 受惠国$_1$LD$_1$	50	----Ship ballast water teatment apparatus

序号 No.	税则号列 Tariff Line	中文货品名称 Article Description in Chinese	最惠国税率 MFN(%)	协定税率 Agreement(%)	特惠税率 SP(%)	普通税率 Gen(%)	英文货品名称 Article Description
6112	8421.2199	----其他	5	0 澳AU,澳门MO,巴PK,冰岛IS,东盟AS,哥CR,秘鲁PE,台湾TW,香港HK,新西兰NZ,智利CL 2 瑞士CH 3.5 亚太AP 4.3 韩国KR	0 受惠国$_1$LD$_1$	50	----Other
	ex84212199	喷灌设备用叠式净水过滤器	Δ1				Stackable, filtering or purifying machines for irrigation equipment
	ex84212199	船舶压载水处理设备用过滤器	Δ2				Filters for ship ballast water treatment apparatus
6113	8421.2200	--过滤或净化饮料(水除外)用	12	0 澳门MO,冰岛IS,东盟AS,哥CR,秘鲁PE,新加坡SG,新西兰NZ,智利CL 4.8 瑞士CH 6 巴PK 7.2 澳AU 9.6 韩国KR	0 受惠国$_1$LD$_1$	40	--For filtering or purifying beverages other than water
6114	8421.2300	--内燃发动机的滤油器	10	0 冰岛IS,东盟AS,哥CR,香港HK,新加坡SG,新西兰NZ,智利CL 3 秘鲁PE 4 瑞士CH 5 巴PK 6 澳AU 8 韩国KR	0 受惠国$_1$LD$_1$	40	--Oil or petrol-filters for internal combustion engines
		--其他:					--Other:
6115	8421.2910	---压滤机	5	0 澳AU,巴PK,冰岛IS,东盟AS,哥CR,秘鲁PE,瑞士CH,香港HK,新西兰NZ,智利CL 3.5 亚太AP 4 韩国KR	0 受惠国$_1$LD$_1$	40	---Press filters
6116	8421.2990	---其他	5	0 澳AU,巴PK,冰岛IS,东盟AS,哥CR,韩国KR,秘鲁PE,台湾TW,香港HK,新西兰NZ,智利CL 3.5 瑞士CH,亚太AP	0 受惠国LD	40	---Other
		-气体的过滤、净化机器及装置:					-Filtering or purifying machinery and apparatus for gases:
6117	8421.3100	--内燃发动机的进气过滤器	10	0 冰岛IS,东盟AS,哥CR,香港HK,新西兰NZ,智利CL 3 秘鲁PE 4 瑞士CH 5 巴PK 6 澳AU 9 韩国KR	0 受惠国$_1$LD$_1$	40	--Intake air filters for internal combustion engines
		--其他:					--Other:
6118	8421.3910	---家用型	15Δ5	0 冰岛IS,东盟AS,哥CR,台湾TW,香港HK,新加坡SG,新西兰NZ,智利CL 4.5 秘鲁PE 7.5 巴PK 9 澳AU 10.5 瑞士CH,亚太AP 12.9 韩国KR	0 受惠国$_1$LD$_1$	100	---Of the household type
		---工业用除尘器:					---Dust collectors for industry uses:

序号 No.	税则号列 Tariff Line	中文货品名称 Article Description in Chinese	最惠国税率 MFN(%)	协定税率 Agreement(%)	特惠税率 SP(%)	普通税率 Gen(%)	英文货品名称 Article Description
6119	8421.3921	----静电除尘器	5	0 澳AU,巴PK,冰岛IS,东盟AS,哥CR,韩国KR,秘鲁PE,台湾TW,香港HK,新西兰NZ,智利CL 2 瑞士CH 3.5 亚太AP	0 受惠国$_1$LD$_1$	40	----Electrostatic
6120	8421.3922	----袋式除尘器	5	0 澳AU,巴PK,冰岛IS,东盟AS,哥CR,秘鲁PE,瑞士CH,香港HK,新西兰NZ,智利CL 3 韩国KR 3.5 亚太AP	0 受惠国$_1$LD$_1$	40	----Baghoused
6121	8421.3923	----旋风式除尘器	5	0 澳AU,巴PK,冰岛IS,东盟AS,哥CR,韩国KR,秘鲁PE,台湾TW,香港HK,新西兰NZ,智利CL 2 瑞士CH 3.5 亚太AP	0 受惠国$_1$LD$_1$	40	----Cyclone
6122	8421.3924	----电袋复合除尘器	5	0 澳AU,巴PK,冰岛IS,东盟AS,哥CR,秘鲁PE,瑞士CH,台湾TW,香港HK,新西兰NZ,智利CL 3.5 亚太AP 4.3 韩国KR	0 受惠国$_1$LD$_1$	40	----Electrostatic fabric filter
6123	8421.3929	----其他	5	0 澳AU,澳门MO,巴PK,冰岛IS,东盟AS,哥CR,秘鲁PE,瑞士CH,台湾TW,香港HK,新西兰NZ,智利CL 3.5 亚太AP 4.3 韩国KR	0 受惠国$_1$LD$_1$	40	----Other
6124	8421.3930	---内燃发动机排气过滤及净化装置	5	0 澳AU,巴PK,冰岛IS,东盟AS,哥CR,秘鲁PE,瑞士CH,香港HK,新西兰NZ,智利CL 3.5 亚太AP 4.3 韩国KR	0 受惠国LD	40	---Exhaust-gas filters or purifiers for internal combustion engines
	ex84213930	摩托车发动机排气过滤及净化装置	Δ3				Filtering or purifying machines for motorcycle engine
6125	8421.3940	---烟气脱硫装置	5	0 澳AU,巴PK,冰岛IS,东盟AS,哥CR,韩国KR,秘鲁PE,瑞士CH,台湾TW,香港HK,新西兰NZ,智利CL 3.5 亚太AP	0 受惠国LD	40	---Flue gas desulfurization units
6126	8421.3950	---烟气脱硝装置	5	0 澳AU,巴PK,冰岛IS,东盟AS,哥CR,韩国KR,秘鲁PE,台湾TW,香港HK,新西兰NZ,智利CL 2 瑞士CH 3.5 亚太AP	0 受惠国LD	40	---Flue gas denitrification units
6127	8421.3990	---其他	5	0 澳AU,澳门MO,巴PK,冰岛IS,东盟AS,哥CR,秘鲁PE,台湾TW,香港HK,新西兰NZ,智利CL 2 瑞士CH 3.5 亚太AP 4 韩国KR	0 受惠国LD	40	---Other
		-零件：					-Parts:
		--离心机用，包括离心干燥机用：					--Of centrifuges, including centrifugal dryers:
6128	8421.9110	---干衣量不超过10公斤的干衣机用	0		0 受惠国LD	70	---Of clothes-dryers of a dry linen capacity not exceeding 10kg
6129	8421.9190	---其他	0		0 受惠国LD	30	---Other
		--其他：					--Other:

序号 No.	税则号列 Tariff Line	中文货品名称 Article Description in Chinese	最惠国税率 MFN(%)	协定税率 Agreement(%)	特惠税率 SP(%)	普通税率 Gen(%)	英文货品名称 Article Description
6130	8421.9910	---家用型过滤、净化装置用	10Δ5	0 冰岛IS,东盟AS,哥CR,香港HK,新加坡SG,新西兰NZ,智利CL 3 秘鲁PE 4 瑞士CH 5 巴PK 6 澳AU 8 韩国KR 9 亚太AP	0 受惠国$_1$LD$_1$	100	---Of household-type filtering or purifying machines
6131	8421.9990	---其他	5	0 澳AU,巴PK,冰岛IS,东盟AS,哥CR,韩国KR,秘鲁PE,台湾TW,香港HK,新西兰NZ,智利CL 2 瑞士CH 4.5 亚太AP	0 受惠国LD	40	---Other
	84.22	**洗碟机;瓶子及其他容器的洗涤或干燥机器;瓶、罐、箱、袋或其他容器装填、封口、密封、贴标签的机器;瓶、罐、管、筒或类似容器的包封机器;其他包装或打包机器(包括热缩包装机器);饮料充气机:**					**Dishwashing machines; machinery for cleaning or drying bottles or other containers; machinery for filling, closing, sealing or labelling bottles, cans, boxes, bags or other containers; machinery for capsuling bottles, jars, tubes and similar containers; other packing or wrapping machinery (including heat-shrink wrapping machinery) ; machinery for aerating beverages:**
		-洗碟机:					-Dishwashing machines:
6132	8422.1100	--家用型	10Δ6	0 冰岛IS,东盟AS,哥CR,秘鲁PE,新西兰NZ,智利CL 4 瑞士CH 5 巴PK 6 澳AU	0 受惠国LD	90	--Of the household type
6133	8422.1900	--其他	14	0 冰岛IS,东盟AS,哥CR,秘鲁PE,瑞士CH,新加坡SG,新西兰NZ,智利CL 8.4 澳AU 11.2 巴PK,韩国KR	0 受惠国$_1$LD$_1$	90	--Other
6134	8422.2000	-瓶子或其他容器的洗涤或干燥机器	10	0 澳门MO,冰岛IS,东盟AS,哥CR,新加坡SG,新西兰NZ,智利CL 3 秘鲁PE 4 瑞士CH 5 巴PK 6 澳AU 8 韩国KR	0 受惠国LD	35	-Machinery for cleaning or drying bottles or other containers
		-瓶、罐、箱、袋或其他容器的装填、封口、密封、贴标签的机器;瓶、罐、管、筒或类似容器的包封机器;饮料充气机:					-Machinery for filling, closing, sealing or labelling bottles, cans, boxes, bags or other containers; machinery for capsuling bottles, jars, tubes and similar containers; machinery for aerating beverages:
6135	8422.3010	---饮料及液体食品灌装设备	12	0 冰岛IS,东盟AS,哥CR,秘鲁PE,香港HK,新加坡SG,新西兰NZ,智利CL 5 巴PK 7.2 澳AU 8.4 瑞士CH,亚太AP 9.6 韩国KR	0 受惠国LD	45	---Bottling or canning machinery for beverages or liquid food
	ex84223010	乳品加工用自动化灌装设备	Δ10				Automatic bottling or canning equipment for producing dairy

序号 No.	税则号列 Tariff Line	中文货品名称 Article Description in Chinese	最惠国税率 MFN(%)	协定税率 Agreement(%)	特惠税率 SP(%)	普通税率 Gen(%)	英文货品名称 Article Description
		---水泥包装机：					---Machinery for packing cement:
6136	8422.3021	----全自动灌包机	12	0 冰岛IS,东盟AS,哥CR,香港HK,新加坡SG,新西兰NZ,智利CL 3.6 秘鲁PE 5 巴PK 7.2 澳AU 8.4 瑞士CH,亚太AP 9.6 韩国KR	0 受惠国LD	45	----Automatic filling and sacking machines
6137	8422.3029	----其他	12	0 冰岛IS,东盟AS,哥CR,香港HK,新加坡SG,新西兰NZ,智利CL 3.6 秘鲁PE 5 巴PK 7.2 澳AU 8.4 瑞士CH,亚太AP 9.6 韩国KR	0 受惠国LD	45	----Other
6138	8422.3030	---其他包装机	10	0 冰岛IS,东盟AS,哥CR,香港HK,新加坡SG,新西兰NZ,智利CL 3 秘鲁PE 4 瑞士CH 5 巴PK 6 澳AU,韩国KR 7 亚太AP	0 受惠国LD	35	---Other packing machines
	ex84223030	全自动无菌灌装生产线用包装机,加工速度≥20000只/小时	Δ6				Packing machines of automatic aseptic filling producion line, processing output ≥20000 package/hour
6139	8422.3090	---其他	10	0 冰岛IS,东盟AS,哥CR,瑞士CH,香港HK,新加坡SG,新西兰NZ,智利CL 3 秘鲁PE 5 巴PK 6 澳AU,韩国KR 7 亚太AP	0 受惠国LD	35	---Other
	ex84223090	全自动无菌灌装生产线用贴吸管机,加工速度≥22000只/小时	Δ6				Straw applicators of automatic aseptic filling prodution line, processing output ≥22000 package/hour
6140	8422.4000	-其他包装或打包机器（包括热缩包装机器）	10	0 冰岛IS,东盟AS,哥CR,香港HK,新加坡SG,新西兰NZ,智利CL 3 秘鲁PE 4 瑞士CH 5 巴PK 6 澳AU 8 韩国KR 9.5 亚太AP	0 受惠国LD	35	-Other packing or wrapping machinery (including heat-shrink wrapping machinery)
		-零件：					-Parts:
6141	8422.9010	---洗碟机用	10.5Δ6	0 冰岛IS,东盟AS,哥CR,新加坡SG,新西兰NZ,智利CL 3.2 秘鲁PE 5 巴PK 6.3 澳AU 7.4 瑞士CH 8.4 韩国KR	0 受惠国LD	90	---Of dish washing machines
6142	8422.9020	---饮料及液体食品灌装设备用	8.5	0 冰岛IS,东盟AS,哥CR,秘鲁PE,新西兰NZ,智利CL 3.4 瑞士CH 5 巴PK 5.1 澳AU 6.8 韩国KR	0 受惠国LD	45	---Of bottling or canning machinery for beverages or liquid food

序号 No.	税则号列 Tariff Line	中文货品名称 Article Description in Chinese	最惠国税率 MFN(%)	协定税率 Agreement(%)	特惠税率 SP(%)	普通税率 Gen(%)	英文货品名称 Article Description
6143	8422.9090	---其他	8.5	0 东盟AS,哥CR,秘鲁PE,香港HK,新西兰NZ,智利CL 5 巴PK 5.1 澳AU,韩国KR 6 瑞士CH	0 受惠国LD	35	---Other
	84.23	**衡器(感量为50毫克或更精密的天平除外),包括计数或检验用的衡器;衡器用的各种砝码、秤砣:**					**Weighing machinery (excluding balances of a sensitivity of 5cg or better), including weight-operated counting or checking machines; weighing machine weights of all kinds:**
6144	8423.1000	-体重计,包括婴儿秤;家用秤	10.5	0 澳门MO,冰岛IS,东盟AS,哥CR,秘鲁PE,新加坡SG,新西兰NZ,智利CL 5 巴PK 6.3 澳AU 7.4 瑞士CH 8.4 韩国KR	0 受惠国LD	80	-Personal weighing machines, including baby scales; household scales
		-输送带上连续称货的秤:					-Scales for continuous weighing of goods on conveyors:
6145	8423.2010	---电子皮带秤	10	0 冰岛IS,东盟AS,哥CR,秘鲁PE,新西兰NZ,智利CL 4 瑞士CH 5 巴PK 6 澳AU 8 韩国KR	0 受惠国LD	80	---Electronic belt weighing machines
6146	8423.2090	---其他	10	0 冰岛IS,东盟AS,哥CR,秘鲁PE,新西兰NZ,智利CL 4 瑞士CH 5 巴PK 6 澳AU 8 韩国KR	0 受惠国LD	80	---Other
		-恒定秤、物料定量装袋或装容器用的秤,包括库秤:					-Constant weight scales and scales for discharging a predetermined weight of material into a bag or container, including hopper scales:
6147	8423.3010	---定量包装秤	10.5	0 冰岛IS,东盟AS,哥CR,秘鲁PE,新加坡SG,新西兰NZ,智利CL 5 巴PK 6.3 澳AU 7.4 瑞士CH 8.4 韩国KR	0 受惠国LD	80	---Rationed packing scales
6148	8423.3020	---定量分选秤	10.5	0 冰岛IS,东盟AS,哥CR,秘鲁PE,新加坡SG,新西兰NZ,智利CL 5 巴PK 6.3 澳AU 7.4 瑞士CH 8.4 韩国KR	0 受惠国LD	80	---Rationed sorting scales
6149	8423.3030	---配料秤	10.5	0 冰岛IS,东盟AS,哥CR,秘鲁PE,新加坡SG,新西兰NZ,智利CL 5 巴PK 6.3 澳AU 7.4 瑞士CH 8.4 韩国KR	0 受惠国LD	80	---Proporating scales

序号 No.	税则号列 Tariff Line	中文货品名称 Article Description in Chinese	最惠国税率 MFN(%)	协定税率 Agreement(%)	特惠税率 SP(%)	普通税率 Gen(%)	英文货品名称 Article Description
6150	8423.3090	---其他	10.5	0 冰岛IS,东盟AS,哥CR,秘鲁PE,新加坡SG,新西兰NZ,智利CL 5 巴PK 6.3 澳AU 7.4 瑞士CH 8.4 韩国KR	0 受惠国LD	80	---Other
		-其他衡器:					-Other weighing machinery:
		--最大称量不超过30公斤:					--Having a maximum weighing capacity not exceeding 30kg:
6151	8423.8110	---计价秤	10.5	0 冰岛IS,东盟AS,哥CR,秘鲁PE,新加坡SG,新西兰NZ,智利CL 5 巴PK 6.3 澳AU 7.4 瑞士CH 8.4 韩国KR	0 受惠国LD	80	---Account balances
6152	8423.8120	---弹簧秤	10.5	0 冰岛IS,东盟AS,哥CR,秘鲁PE,新加坡SG,新西兰NZ,智利CL 5 巴PK 6.3 澳AU 7.4 瑞士CH 8.4 韩国KR	0 受惠国LD	80	---Spring balances
6153	8423.8190	---其他	10.5	0 冰岛IS,东盟AS,哥CR,秘鲁PE,新加坡SG,新西兰NZ,智利CL 5 巴PK 6.3 澳AU 8.4 韩国KR 8.6 瑞士CH	0 受惠国LD	80	---Other
		--最大称量超过30公斤,但不超过5000公斤:					--Having a maximum weighing capacity exceeding 30kg but not exceeding 5000kg:
6154	8423.8210	---地中衡	10.5	0 冰岛IS,东盟AS,哥CR,秘鲁PE,新加坡SG,新西兰NZ,智利CL 5 巴PK 6.3 澳AU 7.4 瑞士CH 8.4 韩国KR	0 受惠国LD	80	---Weighbridges
6155	8423.8290	---其他	10.5	0 冰岛IS,东盟AS,哥CR,秘鲁PE,瑞士CH,新加坡SG,新西兰NZ,智利CL 5 巴PK 6.3 澳AU 8.4 韩国KR	0 受惠国LD	80	---Other
		--其他:					--Other:
6156	8423.8910	---地中衡	10	0 冰岛IS,东盟AS,哥CR,新西兰NZ,智利CL 3 秘鲁PE 4 瑞士CH 5 巴PK 6 澳AU 8 韩国KR	0 受惠国LD	80	---Weighbridges
6157	8423.8920	---轨道衡	10	0 冰岛IS,东盟AS,哥CR,新西兰NZ,智利CL 3 秘鲁PE 4 瑞士CH 5 巴PK 6 澳AU 8 韩国KR	0 受惠国LD	80	---Track scales

序号 No.	税则号列 Tariff Line	中文货品名称 Article Description in Chinese	最惠国税率 MFN(%)	协定税率 Agreement(%)	特惠税率 SP(%)	普通税率 Gen(%)	英文货品名称 Article Description
6158	8423.8930	---吊秤	10	0 冰岛IS,东盟AS,哥CR,新西兰NZ,智利CL 3 秘鲁PE 4 瑞士CH 5 巴PK 6 澳AU 8 韩国KR	0 受惠国LD	80	---Hanging scales
6159	8423.8990	---其他	10	0 冰岛IS,东盟AS,哥CR,新西兰NZ,智利CL 3 秘鲁PE 4 瑞士CH 5 巴PK 6 澳AU 8 韩国KR	0 受惠国LD	80	---Other
6160	8423.9000	-衡器用的各种砝码、秤砣;衡器的零件	10	0 冰岛IS,东盟AS,哥CR,秘鲁PE,新加坡SG,新西兰NZ,智利CL 5 巴PK 6 澳AU 7 瑞士CH 8 韩国KR	0 受惠国LD	80	-Weighing machine weights of all kinds; parts of weighing machinery
	84.24	**液体或粉末的喷射、散布或喷雾的机械器具(不论是否手工操作);灭火器,不论是否装药;喷枪及类似器具;喷汽机、喷砂机及类似的喷射机器:**					**Mechanical appliances (whether or not hand-operated) for projecting, dispersing or spraying liquids or powders; fire extinguishers, whether or not charged; spray guns and similar appliances; steam or sandblasting machines and similar jet projecting machines:**
6161	8424.1000	-灭火器,不论是否装药	8.4	0 冰岛IS,东盟AS,哥CR,秘鲁PE,新西兰NZ,智利CL 3.36 瑞士CH 5 澳AU,巴PK 7.2 韩国KR	0 受惠国$_1$LD$_1$	70	-Fire extinguishers, whether or not charged
6162	8424.2000	-喷枪及类似器具	8.4	0 冰岛IS,东盟AS,哥CR,秘鲁PE,新西兰NZ,智利CL 3.36 瑞士CH 5 澳AU,巴PK,韩国KR 8 亚太AP	0 受惠国$_1$LD$_1$	40	-Spray guns and similar appliances
6163	8424.3000	-喷汽机、喷砂机及类似的喷射机器	8.4	0 冰岛IS,东盟AS,哥CR,秘鲁PE,台湾TW,新西兰NZ,智利CL 5 澳AU,巴PK 5.9 瑞士CH 6.7 韩国KR	0 受惠国$_1$LD$_1$	40	-Steam or sand blasting machines and similar jet projecting machines
		-其他器具:					-Other appliances:
6164	8424.8100	--农业或园艺用	8	0 冰岛IS,东盟AS,哥CR,秘鲁PE,香港HK,新西兰NZ,智利CL 3.2 瑞士CH 4.8 澳AU,韩国KR 5 巴PK 7.6 亚太AP	0 受惠国$_1$LD$_1$	30	--Agricultural or horticul tural
		--其他:					--Other:
6165	8424.8910	---家用型	0		0 受惠国LD	80	---Of the household type
6166	8424.8920	---喷涂机器人	0		0 受惠国LD	30	---Spray painting robots
		---其他:					---Other:
6167	8424.8991	----船用洗舱机	0		0 受惠国LD	30	----Marine cabinet washer
6168	8424.8999	----其他	0		0 受惠国LD	30	----Other
		-零件:					-Parts:
6169	8424.9010	---子目号8424.1000所列器具的零件	0		0 受惠国LD	70	---Of the apparatus of subheading No. 8424.1000

序号 No.	税则号列 Tariff Line	中文货品名称 Article Description in Chinese	最惠国税率 MFN(%)	协定税率 Agreement(%)	特惠税率 SP(%)	普通税率 Gen(%)	英文货品名称 Article Description
6170	8424.9020	---子目号8424.8910所列器具的零件	0		0 受惠国LD	80	---Of the apparatus of subheading No. 8424.8910
6171	8424.9090	---其他	0		0 受惠国LD	30	---Other
	84.25	**滑车及提升机,但倒卸式提升机除外;卷扬机及绞盘;千斤顶:**					**Pulley tackle and hoists other than skip hoists; winches and capstans; jacks:**
		-滑车及提升机,但倒卸式提升机及提升车辆用的提升机除外:					-Pulley tackle and hoists other than skip hoists or hoists of a kind used for raising vehicles:
6172	8425.1100	--电动的	6	0 冰岛IS,东盟AS,哥CR,秘鲁PE,新西兰NZ,智利CL 2.4 瑞士CH 3.6 澳AU 5 巴PK 5.2 韩国KR	0 受惠国LD	30	--Powered by electric motor
6173	8425.1900	--其他	5	0 澳AU,巴PK,冰岛IS,东盟AS,哥CR,秘鲁PE,瑞士CH,新西兰NZ,智利CL 4 韩国KR	0 受惠国LD	30	--Other
		-卷扬机;绞盘:					-Winches; capstans:
		--电动的:					--Powered by electric motor:
6174	8425.3110	---矿井口卷扬装置;专为井下使用设计的卷扬机	10	0 冰岛IS,东盟AS,哥CR,秘鲁PE,新西兰NZ,智利CL 4 瑞士CH 5 巴PK 6 澳AU 8 韩国KR	0 受惠国LD	30	---Pit-head winding gear; winches specially designed for use underground
6175	8425.3190	---其他	5	0 澳AU,巴PK,冰岛IS,东盟AS,哥CR,秘鲁PE,新西兰NZ,智利CL 2 瑞士CH 4.3 韩国KR	0 受惠国LD	30	---Other
		--其他:					--Other:
6176	8425.3910	---矿井口卷扬装置;专为井下使用设计的卷扬机	10	0 冰岛IS,东盟AS,哥CR,秘鲁PE,新西兰NZ,智利CL 4 瑞士CH 5 巴PK 6 澳AU 8 韩国KR	0 受惠国LD	30	---Pit-head winding gear; winches specially designed for use underground
6177	8425.3990	---其他	5	0 澳AU,巴PK,冰岛IS,东盟AS,哥CR,秘鲁PE,瑞士CH,香港HK,新西兰NZ,智利CL 4.3 韩国KR	0 受惠国LD	30	---Other
		-千斤顶;提升车辆用的提升机:					-Jacks; hoists of a kind used for raising vehicles:
6178	8425.4100	--车库中使用的固定千斤顶系统	3	0 澳AU,巴PK,冰岛IS,东盟AS,哥CR,韩国KR,秘鲁PE,瑞士CH,新西兰NZ,智利CL 2.5 亚太AP	0 受惠国LD	30	--Built-in jacking systems of a type used in garages
		--其他液压千斤顶及提升机:					--Other jacks and hoists, hydraulic:
6179	8425.4210	---液压千斤顶	3	0 澳AU,巴PK,冰岛IS,东盟AS,哥CR,秘鲁PE,瑞士CH,新西兰NZ,智利CL 1.8 韩国KR	0 受惠国LD	30	---Hydraulic jacks

序号 No.	税则号列 Tariff Line	中文货品名称 Article Description in Chinese	最惠国税率 MFN(%)	协定税率 Agreement(%)	特惠税率 SP(%)	普通税率 Gen(%)	英文货品名称 Article Description
6180	8425.4290	---其他	5	0 澳AU,巴PK,冰岛IS,东盟AS,哥CR,秘鲁PE,瑞士CH,新西兰NZ,智利CL 4.3 韩国KR	0 受惠国LD	30	---Other
		--其他：					--Other:
6181	8425.4910	---其他千斤顶	5	0 澳AU,巴PK,冰岛IS,东盟AS,哥CR,秘鲁PE,新西兰NZ,智利CL 2 瑞士CH 4 韩国KR	0 受惠国LD	30	---Other jacks
6182	8425.4990	---其他	10	0 冰岛IS,东盟AS,哥CR,新西兰NZ,智利CL 3 秘鲁PE 4 瑞士CH 5 巴PK 6 澳AU 8 韩国KR	0 受惠国LD	30	---Other
	84.26	**船用桅杆式起重机;起重机,包括缆式起重机;移动式吊运架、跨运车及装有起重机的工作车：**					**Ships' derricks; cranes, including cable cranes; mobile lifting frames, straddle carriers and works trucks fitted with a crane:**
		-高架移动式起重机、桁架桥式起重机、龙门起重机、桥式起重机、移动式吊运架及跨运车：					-Overhead travelling cranes, transporter cranes, gantry cranes, bridge cranes, mobile lifting frames and straddle carriers:
		--固定支架的高架移动式起重机：					--Overhead travelling cranes on fixed support:
6183	8426.1120	---通用桥式起重机	8	0 冰岛IS,东盟AS,哥CR,秘鲁PE,新西兰NZ,智利CL 3.2 瑞士CH 4.8 澳AU 5 巴PK 6.9 韩国KR	0 受惠国LD	30	---Bridge cranes, all-purpose
6184	8426.1190	---其他	8	0 冰岛IS,东盟AS,哥CR,秘鲁PE,新西兰NZ,智利CL 3.2 瑞士CH 4.8 澳AU 5 巴PK 6.9 韩国KR	0 受惠国LD	30	---Other
6185	8426.1200	--带胶轮的移动式吊运架及跨运车	6	0 冰岛IS,东盟AS,哥CR,秘鲁PE,新西兰NZ,智利CL 2.4 瑞士CH 3.6 澳AU 5 巴PK 5.2 韩国KR	0 受惠国LD	30	--Mobile lifting frames on tyres and straddle carriers
		--其他：					--Other:
6186	8426.1910	---装船机	5	0 澳AU,巴PK,冰岛IS,东盟AS,哥CR,秘鲁PE,瑞士CH,新西兰NZ,智利CL 2.5 亚太AP 4.3 韩国KR	0 受惠国LD	30	---Ship loading cranes
		---卸船机：					---Ship unloading cranes:
6187	8426.1921	----抓斗式	5	0 澳AU,巴PK,冰岛IS,东盟AS,哥CR,秘鲁PE,瑞士CH,新西兰NZ,智利CL 3.5 亚太AP 4.3 韩国KR	0 受惠国LD	30	----Grab ship unloading cranes

序号 No.	税则号列 Tariff Line	中文货品名称 Article Description in Chinese	最惠国税率 MFN(%)	协定税率 Agreement(%)	特惠税率 SP(%)	普通税率 Gen(%)	英文货品名称 Article Description
6188	8426.1929	----其他	5	0 澳AU,巴PK,冰岛IS,东盟AS,哥CR,秘鲁PE,瑞士CH,新西兰NZ,智利CL 3.5 亚太AP 4.3 韩国KR	0 受惠国LD	30	----Other
6189	8426.1930	---龙门式起重机	10	0 冰岛IS,东盟AS,哥CR,秘鲁PE,新西兰NZ,智利CL 4 瑞士CH 5 巴PK 6 澳AU 7 亚太AP 8.6 韩国KR	0 受惠国LD	30	---Gantry cranes
		---装卸桥:					---Loading and unlcading bridges:
6190	8426.1941	----门式装卸桥	10	0 冰岛IS,东盟AS,哥CR,秘鲁PE,新西兰NZ,智利CL 4 瑞士CH 5 巴PK 6 澳AU 7 亚太AP 8.6 韩国KR	0 受惠国LD	30	----Frame loading and unloading bridges
6191	8426.1942	----集装箱装卸桥	10	0 冰岛IS,东盟AS,哥CR,秘鲁PE,新西兰NZ,智利CL 4 瑞士CH 5 巴PK 6 澳AU 7 亚太AP 8.6 韩国KR	0 受惠国LD	30	----Container loading and unloading bridges
6192	8426.1943	----其他动臂式装卸桥	10	0 冰岛IS,东盟AS,哥CR,秘鲁PE,新西兰NZ,智利CL 4 瑞士CH 5 巴PK 6 澳AU 7 亚太AP 9 韩国KR	0 受惠国LD	30	----Derrick loading and unloading bridges
6193	8426.1949	----其他	10	0 冰岛IS,东盟AS,哥CR,秘鲁PE,新西兰NZ,智利CL 4 瑞士CH 5 巴PK 6 澳AU 7 亚太AP 8.6 韩国KR	0 受惠国LD	30	----Other
6194	8426.1990	---其他	10	0 冰岛IS,东盟AS,哥CR,秘鲁PE,新加坡SG,新西兰NZ,智利CL 4 瑞士CH 5 巴PK 6 澳AU 7 亚太AP 9 韩国KR	0 受惠国LD	30	---Other
6195	8426.2000	-塔式起重机	10	0 冰岛IS,东盟AS,哥CR,秘鲁PE,新西兰NZ,智利CL 4 瑞士CH 5 巴PK 6 澳AU 9 韩国KR	0 受惠国LD	30	-Tower cranes

序号 No.	税则号列 Tariff Line	中文货品名称 Article Description in Chinese	最惠国税率 MFN(%)	协定税率 Agreement(%)	特惠税率 SP(%)	普通税率 Gen(%)	英文货品名称 Article Description
6196	8426.3000	-门座式起重机及座式旋臂起重机	6	0 冰岛IS,东盟AS,哥CR,秘鲁PE,新西兰NZ,智利CL 2.4 瑞士CH 3.6 澳AU 5 巴PK 5.2 韩国KR	0 受惠国LD	30	-Portal or pedestal jib cranes
		-其他自推进机械:					-Other machinery, self-propelled:
		--带胶轮的:					--On tyres:
6197	8426.4110	---轮胎式起重机	5	0 澳AU,巴PK,冰岛IS,东盟AS,哥CR,秘鲁PE,瑞士CH,新西兰NZ,智利CL 4.3 韩国KR	0 受惠国LD	30	---Wheel-mounted cranes
6198	8426.4190	---其他	5	0 澳AU,巴PK,冰岛IS,东盟AS,哥CR,秘鲁PE,瑞士CH,新西兰NZ,智利CL 4.3 韩国KR	0 受惠国LD	30	---Other
		--其他:					--Other:
6199	8426.4910	---履带式起重机	8	0 冰岛IS,东盟AS,哥CR,秘鲁PE,香港HK,新西兰NZ,智利CL 3.2 瑞士CH 4.8 澳AU 5 巴PK 6.9 韩国KR	0 受惠国LD	30	---Crawler cranes
6200	8426.4990	---其他	13	0 冰岛IS,东盟AS,哥CR,香港HK,新加坡SG,新西兰NZ,智利CL 3.9 秘鲁PE 6.5 巴PK 7.8 澳AU 9.1 瑞士CH 11.2 韩国KR	0 受惠国[1]LD[1]	30	---Other
		-其他机械:					-Other machinery:
6201	8426.9100	--供装于公路车辆的	10	0 冰岛IS,东盟AS,哥CR,秘鲁PE,新西兰NZ,智利CL 4 瑞士CH 5 巴PK 6 澳AU 9 韩国KR	0 受惠国LD	30	--Designed for mounting on road vehicles
6202	8426.9900	--其他	6	0 冰岛IS,东盟AS,哥CR,秘鲁PE,新西兰NZ,智利CL 2.4 瑞士CH 3.6 澳AU 5 巴PK 5.2 韩国KR	0 受惠国LD	30	--Other
	84.27	**叉车;其他装有升降或搬运装置的工作车:**					**Fork-lift trucks; other works trucks fitted with lifting or handling equipment:**
		-电动机推进的机动车:					-Self-propelled trucks powered by an electric motor:
6203	8427.1010	---有轨巷道堆垛机	9	0 冰岛IS,东盟AS,哥CR,秘鲁PE,新西兰NZ,智利CL 3.6 瑞士CH 5 巴PK 5.4 澳AU,韩国KR	0 受惠国LD	30	---Track alleyway stackers

序号 No.	税则号列 Tariff Line	中文货品名称 Article Description in Chinese	最惠国税率 MFN(%)	协定税率 Agreement(%)	特惠税率 SP(%)	普通税率 Gen(%)	英文货品名称 Article Description
6204	8427.1020	---无轨巷道堆垛机	9	0 冰岛IS,东盟AS,哥CR,秘鲁PE,新西兰NZ,智利CL 3.6 瑞士CH 5 巴PK 5.4 澳AU 7.8 韩国KR	0 受惠国LD	30	---Trackless alleyway stackers
6205	8427.1090	---其他	9	0 冰岛IS,东盟AS,哥CR,秘鲁PE,新西兰NZ,智利CL 3.6 瑞士CH 5 巴PK 5.4 澳AU,韩国KR	0 受惠国LD	30	---Other
		-其他机动车:					-Other self-propelled trucks:
6206	8427.2010	---集装箱叉车	9	0 冰岛IS,东盟AS,哥CR,秘鲁PE,新西兰NZ,智利CL 3.6 瑞士CH 5 巴PK 5.4 澳AU,韩国KR 8.6 亚太AP	0 受惠国LD	30	---Fork-lift trucks cranes
6207	8427.2090	---其他	9	0 冰岛IS,东盟AS,哥CR,秘鲁PE,新西兰NZ,智利CL 3.6 瑞士CH 5 巴PK 5.4 澳AU,韩国KR 8.6 亚太AP	0 受惠国LD	30	---Other
6208	8427.9000	-其他车	9	0 冰岛IS,东盟AS,哥CR,秘鲁PE,新西兰NZ,智利CL 3.6 瑞士CH 5 巴PK 5.4 澳AU,韩国KR	0 受惠国LD	30	-Other trucks
	84.28	**其他升降、搬运、装卸机械（例如,升降机、自动梯、输送机、缆车）:**					**Other lifting, handling, loading or unloading machinery (for example, lifts, escalators, conveyors, teleferics) :**
		-升降机及倒卸式起重机:					-Lifts and skip hoists:
6209	8428.1010	---载客电梯	8	0 澳门MO,冰岛IS,东盟AS,哥CR,秘鲁PE,香港HK,新加坡SG,新西兰NZ,智利CL 4.8 澳AU 5 巴PK 5.6 瑞士CH,亚太AP 6.4 韩国KR	0 受惠国LD	30	---Designed for the transport of persons
	ex84281010	无障碍升降机	Δ4				Lift facilities for the disabled
6210	8428.1090	---其他	6	0 澳门MO,巴PK,冰岛IS,东盟AS,哥CR,韩国KR,秘鲁PE,台湾TW,香港HK,新西兰NZ,智利CL 2.4 瑞士CH 3.6 澳AU 4.2 亚太AP	0 受惠国LD	30	---Other
6211	8428.2000	-气压升降机及输送机	5	0 澳AU,巴PK,冰岛IS,东盟AS,哥CR,秘鲁PE,新西兰NZ,智利CL 2 瑞士CH 4.3 韩国KR	0 受惠国LD	30	-Pneumatic elevators and conveyors
		-其他用于连续运送货物或材料的升降机及输送机:					-Other continuous-action elevators and conveyors, for goods or materials:

序号 No.	税则号列 Tariff Line	中文货品名称 Article Description in Chinese	最惠国税率 MFN(%)	协定税率 Agreement(%)	特惠税率 SP(%)	普通税率 Gen(%)	英文货品名称 Article Description
6212	8428.3100	--地下专用的	5	0 澳AU,巴PK,冰岛IS,东盟AS,哥CR,秘鲁PE,瑞士CH,新西兰NZ,智利CL 3 韩国KR	0 受惠国LD	30	--Specially designed for underground use
6213	8428.3200	--其他,斗式	5	0 澳AU,巴PK,冰岛IS,东盟AS,哥CR,秘鲁PE,香港HK,新西兰NZ,智利CL 4 韩国KR	0 受惠国LD	30	--Other, bucket type
6214	8428.3300	--其他,带式	5	0 澳AU,巴PK,冰岛IS,东盟AS,哥CR,秘鲁PE,台湾TW,香港HK,新西兰NZ,智利CL 2 瑞士CH 4.3 韩国KR,亚太AP	0 受惠国LD	30	--Other, belt type
		--其他:					--Other:
6215	8428.3910	---链式	5	0 澳AU,巴PK,冰岛IS,东盟AS,哥CR,秘鲁PE,瑞士CH,台湾TW,香港HK,新西兰NZ,智利CL 3.5 亚太AP 4.3 韩国KR	0 受惠国LD	30	---Chain type
6216	8428.3920	---辊式	5	0 澳AU,巴PK,冰岛IS,东盟AS,哥CR,秘鲁PE,瑞士CH,台湾TW,香港HK,新西兰NZ,智利CL 3.5 亚太AP 4 韩国KR	0 受惠国LD	30	---Roller type
6217	8428.3990	---其他	5	0 澳AU,巴PK,冰岛IS,东盟AS,哥CR,韩国KR,秘鲁PE,台湾TW,香港HK,新西兰NZ,智利CL 3.5 亚太AP 3.6 瑞士CH	0 受惠国LD	30	---Other
6218	8428.4000	-自动梯及自动人行道	5	0 澳AU,巴PK,冰岛IS,东盟AS,哥CR,秘鲁PE,瑞士CH,新西兰NZ,智利CL 3 韩国KR	0 受惠国LD	30	-Escalators and moving walkways
		-缆车、座式升降机、滑雪拉索、索道用牵引装置:					-Teleferics, chairlifts, ski-draglines; traction mechanisms for funiculars:
6219	8428.6010	---货运架空索道	8	0 冰岛IS,东盟AS,哥CR,秘鲁PE,新西兰NZ,智利CL 3.2 瑞士CH 4.8 澳AU,韩国KR 5 巴PK	0 受惠国LD	30	---Cargo aerial cableways
		---客运架空索道:					---Passanger aerial cableways:
6220	8428.6021	----单线循环式	8	0 冰岛IS,东盟AS,哥CR,秘鲁PE,新西兰NZ,智利CL 3.2 瑞士CH 4.8 澳AU,韩国KR 5 巴PK	0 受惠国LD	30	----Monocable endless
6221	8428.6029	----其他	8	0 冰岛IS,东盟AS,哥CR,秘鲁PE,新西兰NZ,智利CL 3.2 瑞士CH 4.8 澳AU,韩国KR 5 巴PK	0 受惠国LD	30	----Other

序号 No.	税则号列 Tariff Line	中文货品名称 Article Description in Chinese	最惠国税率 MFN(%)	协定税率 Agreement(%)	特惠税率 SP(%)	普通税率 Gen(%)	英文货品名称 Article Description
6222	8428.6090	---其他	8	0 冰岛IS,东盟AS,哥CR,秘鲁PE,新西兰NZ,智利CL 3.2 瑞士CH 4.8 澳AU 5 巴PK 6.4 韩国KR	0 受惠国LD	30	---Other
		-其他机械:					-Other machinery:
6223	8428.9010	---矿车推动机、铁道机车或货车的转车台、货车倾卸装置及类似的铁道货车搬运装置	10	0 冰岛IS,东盟AS,哥CR,秘鲁PE,新西兰NZ,智利CL 4 瑞士CH 5 巴PK 6 澳AU 8 韩国KR	0 受惠国LD	30	---Mine wagon pushers, locmotive or wagon traversers, wagon tippers and similar railway wagon handling equipment
6224	8428.9020	---机械式停车设备	5	0 澳AU,巴PK,冰岛IS,东盟AS,哥CR,秘鲁PE,瑞士CH,香港HK,新西兰NZ,智利CL 4 韩国KR	0 受惠国LD	30	---Mechanical parking equipments
		---其他装卸机械:					---Other loading and unloading machinery:
6225	8428.9031	----堆取料机械	5	0 澳AU,巴PK,冰岛IS,东盟AS,哥CR,秘鲁PE,台湾TW,香港HK,新西兰NZ,智利CL 3.5 瑞士CH 4.3 韩国KR	0 受惠国LD	30	----Stacking and reclaiming machines
6226	8428.9039	----其他	5	0 澳AU,巴PK,冰岛IS,东盟AS,哥CR,秘鲁PE,台湾TW,香港HK,新西兰NZ,智利CL 3.5 瑞士CH 4.3 韩国KR	0 受惠国LD	30	----Other
6227	8428.9040	---搬运机器人	5	0 澳AU,巴PK,冰岛IS,东盟AS,哥CR,秘鲁PE,台湾TW,香港HK,新西兰NZ,智利CL 3.5 瑞士CH 4.3 韩国KR	0 受惠国LD	30	---Transfer robots
6228	8428.9090	---其他	5	0 澳AU,巴PK,冰岛IS,东盟AS,哥CR,秘鲁PE,台湾TW,香港HK,新西兰NZ,智利CL 3.5 瑞士CH 4.3 韩国KR	0 受惠国LD	30	---Other
	84.29	**机动推土机、侧铲推土机、筑路机、平地机、铲运机、机械铲、挖掘机、机铲装载机、捣固机械及压路机:**					**Self-propelled bulldozers, angledozers, graders, levellers, scrapers, mechanical shovels, excavators, shovel loaders, tamping machines and roadrollers:**
		-推土机及侧铲推土机:					-Bulldozers and angledozers:
		--履带式:					--Track laying:
6229	8429.1110	---发动机输出功率超过235.36千瓦(320马力)的	7	0 冰岛IS,东盟AS,哥CR,秘鲁PE,新西兰NZ,智利CL 2.8 瑞士CH 4.2 澳AU,韩国KR 5 巴PK	0 受惠国LD	17	---With an engine of an output exceeding 235.36KW (320PS)
6230	8429.1190	---其他	7	0 冰岛IS,东盟AS,哥CR,秘鲁PE,新西兰NZ,智利CL 2.8 瑞士CH 4.2 澳AU,韩国KR 5 巴PK	0 受惠国LD	30	---Other

序号 No.	税则号列 Tariff Line	中文货品名称 Article Description in Chinese	最惠国税率 MFN(%)	协定税率 Agreement(%)	特惠税率 SP(%)	普通税率 Gen(%)	英文货品名称 Article Description
		--其他:					--Other:
6231	8429.1910	---发动机输出功率超过235.36千瓦（320马力）的	7	0 冰岛IS,东盟AS,哥CR,秘鲁PE,新西兰NZ,智利CL 2.8 瑞士CH 4.2 澳AU,韩国KR 5 巴PK	0 受惠国LD	17	---With an engine of an output exceeding 235.36KW (320PS)
6232	8429.1990	---其他	7	0 冰岛IS,东盟AS,哥CR,秘鲁PE,新西兰NZ,智利CL 2.8 瑞士CH 4.2 澳AU,韩国KR 5 巴PK	0 受惠国LD	30	---Other
		-筑路机及平地机:					-Graders and levellers:
6233	8429.2010	---发动机输出功率超过235.36千瓦（320马力）的	5	0 澳AU,巴PK,冰岛IS,东盟AS,哥CR,秘鲁PE,瑞士CH,新西兰NZ,智利CL 3 韩国KR	0 受惠国LD	17	---With an engine of an output exceeding 235.36KW (320PS)
6234	8429.2090	---其他	5	0 澳AU,巴PK,冰岛IS,东盟AS,哥CR,秘鲁PE,瑞士CH,新西兰NZ,智利CL 3 韩国KR	0 受惠国LD	30	---Other
		-铲运机:					-Scrapers:
6235	8429.3010	---斗容量超过10立方米的	3	0 澳AU,巴PK,冰岛IS,东盟AS,哥CR,韩国KR,秘鲁PE,瑞士CH,新西兰NZ,智利CL	0 受惠国LD	17	---Having a capacity of shovel exceeding $10m^3$
6236	8429.3090	---其他	5	0 澳AU,巴PK,冰岛IS,东盟AS,哥CR,秘鲁PE,瑞士CH,新西兰NZ,智利CL 3 韩国KR	0 受惠国LD	30	---Other
		-捣固机械及压路机:					-Tamping machines and roadrollers:
		---机动压路机:					---Self-propelled road rollers:
6237	8429.4011	----机重18吨及以上的振动压路机	7	0 冰岛IS,东盟AS,哥CR,秘鲁PE,新西兰NZ,智利CL 2.8 瑞士CH 4.2 澳AU,韩国KR 5 巴PK	0 受惠国LD	20	----Vibration type, of a deadweight of 18t or more
6238	8429.4019	----其他	8	0 冰岛IS,东盟AS,哥CR,秘鲁PE,新西兰NZ,智利CL 3.2 瑞士CH 4.8 澳AU,韩国KR 5 巴PK	0 受惠国LD	40	----Other
6239	8429.4090	---其他	6	0 冰岛IS,东盟AS,哥CR,秘鲁PE,新西兰NZ,智利CL 2.4 瑞士CH 3.6 澳AU,韩国KR 5 巴PK	0 受惠国LD	30	---Other
		-机械铲、挖掘机及机铲装载机:					-Mechanical shovels, excavators and shovel loaders:
6240	8429.5100	--前铲装载机	5	0 澳AU,巴PK,冰岛IS,东盟AS,哥CR,秘鲁PE,瑞士CH,新西兰NZ,智利CL 4 韩国KR	0 受惠国LD	30	--Front-end shovel loaders
		--上部结构可旋转360度的机械:					--Machinery with a 360° revolving superstructure:
		---挖掘机:					---Excavators:

序号 No.	税则号列 Tariff Line	中文货品名称 Article Description in Chinese	最惠国税率 MFN(%)	协定税率 Agreement(%)	特惠税率 SP(%)	普通税率 Gen(%)	英文货品名称 Article Description
6241	8429.5211	----轮胎式	8	0 冰岛IS,东盟AS,哥CR,秘鲁PE,新西兰NZ,智利CL 3.2 瑞士CH 4.8 澳AU 5 巴PK 7.2 亚太AP 7.6 韩国KR	0 受惠国LD	30	----Tyre-mounted
6242	8429.5212	----履带式	8	0 冰岛IS,东盟AS,哥CR,秘鲁PE,香港HK,新西兰NZ,智利CL 3.2 瑞士CH 4.8 澳AU 5 巴PK	0 受惠国LD	30	----Track-mounted
6243	8429.5219	----其他	8	0 冰岛IS,东盟AS,哥CR,秘鲁PE,新西兰NZ,智利CL 3.2 瑞士CH 4.8 澳AU 5 巴PK 6.8 韩国KR 7.2 亚太AP	0 受惠国LD	30	----Other
6244	8429.5290	---其他	8	0 冰岛IS,东盟AS,哥CR,秘鲁PE,新西兰NZ,智利CL 3.2 瑞士CH 4.8 澳AU 5 巴PK 6.8 韩国KR 7.2 亚太AP	0 受惠国LD	30	---Other
6245	8429.5900	--其他	8	0 冰岛IS,东盟AS,哥CR,秘鲁PE,新西兰NZ,智利CL 3.2 瑞士CH 4.8 澳AU,韩国KR 5 巴PK	0 受惠国LD	30	--Other
	84.30	**泥土、矿物或矿石的运送、平整、铲运、挖掘、捣固、压实、开采或钻探机械;打桩机及拔桩机;扫雪机及吹雪机:**					**Other moving, grading, levelling, scraping, excavating, tamping, compacting, extracting or boring machinery, for earth, minerals or ores; piledrivers and pile-extractors; snowploughs and snow-blowers:**
6246	8430.1000	-打桩机及拔桩机	10	0 冰岛IS,东盟AS,哥CR,秘鲁PE,新西兰NZ,智利CL 4 瑞士CH 5 巴PK 6 澳AU 8 韩国KR	0 受惠国LD	30	-Pile-drivers and pile-extranctors
6247	8430.2000	-扫雪机及吹雪机	10	0 冰岛IS,东盟AS,哥CR,秘鲁PE,新西兰NZ,智利CL 4 瑞士CH 5 巴PK 6 澳AU 8 韩国KR	0 受惠国LD	30	-Snow-ploughs and snow-blowers
		-截煤机、凿岩机及隧道掘进机:					-Coal or rock cutters and tunnelling machinery:
		--自推进的:					--Self-propelle:

序号 No.	税则号列 Tariff Line	中文货品名称 Article Description in Chinese	最惠国税率 MFN(%)	协定税率 Agreement(%)	特惠税率 SP(%)	普通税率 Gen(%)	英文货品名称 Article Description
6248	8430.3110	---采（截）煤机	10	0 冰岛IS,东盟AS,哥CR,新加坡SG,新西兰NZ,智利CL 3 秘鲁PE 4 瑞士CH 5 巴PK 6 澳AU 8 韩国KR	0 受惠国LD	30	---Coal winning machine
6249	8430.3120	---凿岩机	10	0 冰岛IS,东盟AS,哥CR,新加坡SG,新西兰NZ,智利CL 3 秘鲁PE 4 瑞士CH 5 巴PK 6 澳AU 8 韩国KR	0 受惠国LD	30	---Rock drill machine
6250	8430.3130	---隧道掘进机	10	0 冰岛IS,东盟AS,哥CR,新加坡SG,新西兰NZ,智利CL 3 秘鲁PE 4 瑞士CH 5 巴PK 6 澳AU 8 韩国KR	0 受惠国LD	30	---Tunnel boring machine
6251	8430.3900	--其他	6	0 冰岛IS,东盟AS,哥CR,秘鲁PE,新西兰NZ,智利CL 2.4 瑞士CH 3.6 澳AU 4.8 韩国KR 5 巴PK	0 受惠国LD	30	--Other
		-其他钻探或凿井机械：					-Other boring or sinking machinery:
		--自推进的：					--Self-propelled:
		---石油及天然气钻探机：					---Oil and natural gas drilling machinery:
6252	8430.4111	----钻探深度在6000米及以上的	5	0 澳AU,巴PK,冰岛IS,东盟AS,哥CR,秘鲁PE,瑞士CH,香港HK,新西兰NZ,智利CL 3 韩国KR	0 受惠国LD	11	----Of drilling depth of 6000m or more
6253	8430.4119	----其他	5	0 澳AU,巴PK,冰岛IS,东盟AS,哥CR,秘鲁PE,瑞士CH,香港HK,新西兰NZ,智利CL 3 韩国KR	0 受惠国LD	17	----Other
		---其他钻探机：					---Other drilling machinery:
6254	8430.4121	----钻探深度在6000米及以上的	5	0 澳AU,巴PK,冰岛IS,东盟AS,哥CR,秘鲁PE,瑞士CH,香港HK,新西兰NZ,智利CL 3 韩国KR	0 受惠国LD	11	----Of drilling depth of 6000m or more
6255	8430.4122	----钻探深度在6000米以下的履带式自推进钻机	5	0 澳AU,巴PK,冰岛IS,东盟AS,哥CR,秘鲁PE,瑞士CH,香港HK,新西兰NZ,智利CL 4 韩国KR	0 受惠国LD	17	----Crawler boring machinery of drilling depth<6000m
6256	8430.4129	----钻探深度在6000米以下的其他钻探机	5	0 澳AU,巴PK,冰岛IS,东盟AS,哥CR,秘鲁PE,瑞士CH,香港HK,新西兰NZ,智利CL 3 韩国KR	0 受惠国LD	17	----Other boring machinery of drilling depth<6000m

序号 No.	税则号列 Tariff Line	中文货品名称 Article Description in Chinese	最惠国税率 MFN(%)	协定税率 Agreement(%)	特惠税率 SP(%)	普通税率 Gen(%)	英文货品名称 Article Description
6257	8430.4190	---其他	5	0 澳AU,巴PK,冰岛IS,东盟AS,哥CR,秘鲁PE,瑞士CH,香港HK,新西兰NZ,智利CL 3 韩国KR	0 受惠国LD	30	---Other
6258	8430.4900	--其他	5	0 澳AU,巴PK,冰岛IS,东盟AS,哥CR,秘鲁PE,瑞士CH,新西兰NZ,智利CL 4 韩国KR	0 受惠国LD	30	--Other
		-其他自推进机械:					-Other machinery, self-propelled:
6259	8430.5010	---其他采油机械	3	0 澳AU,巴PK,冰岛IS,东盟AS,哥CR,韩国KR,秘鲁PE,瑞士CH,新西兰NZ,智利CL	0 受惠国LD	17	---For oil production
6260	8430.5020	---矿用电铲	7	0 冰岛IS,东盟AS,哥CR,秘鲁PE,新西兰NZ,智利CL 2.8 瑞士CH 4.2 澳AU,韩国KR 5 巴PK	0 受惠国LD	30	---Mining power shovels
		---采矿钻机:					---Mining drills:
6261	8430.5031	----牙轮直径380毫米及以上	5	0 澳AU,巴PK,冰岛IS,东盟AS,哥CR,秘鲁PE,瑞士CH,新西兰NZ,智利CL 3 韩国KR	0 受惠国LD	30	----Gear wheel diameter more than 380mm
6262	8430.5039	----其他	5	0 澳AU,巴PK,冰岛IS,东盟AS,哥CR,秘鲁PE,瑞士CH,新西兰NZ,智利CL 3 韩国KR	0 受惠国LD	30	----Other
6263	8430.5090	---其他	5	0 澳AU,巴PK,冰岛IS,东盟AS,哥CR,秘鲁PE,瑞士CH,新西兰NZ,智利CL 4.3 韩国KR	0 受惠国LD	30	---Other
		-其他非自推进机械:					-Other machinery, not self-propelled:
6264	8430.6100	--捣固或压实机械	6	0 冰岛IS,东盟AS,哥CR,秘鲁PE,新西兰NZ,智利CL 2.4 瑞士CH 3.6 澳AU,韩国KR 5 巴PK	0 受惠国LD	30	--Tamping or compacting machinery
		--其他:					--Other:
		---工程钻机:					---Engineering drills:
6265	8430.6911	----钻筒直径3米及以上	6	0 冰岛IS,东盟AS,哥CR,秘鲁PE,新西兰NZ,智利CL 2.4 瑞士CH 3.6 澳AU,韩国KR 5 巴PK	0 受惠国LD	30	----Boring casing diameter more than 3m
6266	8430.6919	----其他	6	0 冰岛IS,东盟AS,哥CR,秘鲁PE,新西兰NZ,智利CL 2.4 瑞士CH 3.6 澳AU 4.8 韩国KR 5 巴PK	0 受惠国LD	30	----Other
6267	8430.6920	---铲运机	6	0 冰岛IS,东盟AS,哥CR,秘鲁PE,新西兰NZ,智利CL 2.4 瑞士CH 3.6 澳AU,韩国KR 5 巴PK	0 受惠国LD	30	---Scrapers

序号 No.	税则号列 Tariff Line	中文货品名称 Article Description in Chinese	最惠国税率 MFN(%)	协定税率 Agreement(%)	特惠税率 SP(%)	普通税率 Gen(%)	英文货品名称 Article Description
6268	8430.6990	---其他	6	0 冰岛IS,东盟AS,哥CR,秘鲁PE,新西兰NZ,智利CL 2.4 瑞士CH 3.6 澳AU,韩国KR 5 巴PK	0 受惠国LD	30	---Other
	84.31	**专用于或主要用于税号84.25至84.30所列机械的零件:**					**Parts suitable for use solely or principally with the machinery of headings 8425 to 8430:**
6269	8431.1000	-税号84.25所列机械的零件	3	0 澳AU,巴PK,冰岛IS,东盟AS,哥CR,秘鲁PE,瑞士CH,新西兰NZ,智利CL 1.8 韩国KR	0 受惠国LD	30	-Of machinery of heading No.84.25
		-税号84.27所列机械的零件:					-Of machinery of heading No.84.27:
6270	8431.2010	---装有差速器的驱动桥及其零件,不论是否装有其他传动部件	6	0 巴PK,冰岛IS,东盟AS,哥CR,秘鲁PE,新西兰NZ,智利CL 2.4 瑞士CH 3.6 澳AU 5.2 韩国KR 5.4 亚太AP	0 受惠国LD	30	---Drive-axles with differential, whether or not provided with other transmission components, parts thereof
6271	8431.2090	---其他	6∆3	0 巴PK,冰岛IS,东盟AS,哥CR,秘鲁PE,新西兰NZ,智利CL 2.4 瑞士CH 3.6 澳AU 5.2 韩国KR 5.4 亚太AP	0 受惠国LD	30	---Other
		-税号84.28所列机械的零件:					-Of machinery of heading 8428:
6272	8431.3100	--升降机、倒卸式起重机或自动梯的零件	3	0 澳AU,巴PK,冰岛IS,东盟AS,哥CR,韩国KR,秘鲁PE,瑞士CH,新西兰NZ,智利CL	0 受惠国LD	30	--Of lifts, skip hoists or escalators
	ex84313100	无障碍升降机的零件	∆1				Parts, for Lift facilities for the disabled
6273	8431.3900	--其他	5	0 澳AU,巴PK,冰岛IS,东盟AS,哥CR,秘鲁PE,香港HK,新西兰NZ,智利CL 2 瑞士CH 2.5 亚太AP 4.3 韩国KR	0 受惠国LD	30	--Other
		-税号84.26、84.29、或84.30所列机械的零件:					-Of machinery of heading 8426, 8429 or 8430:
6274	8431.4100	--戽斗、铲斗、抓斗及夹斗	6	0 巴PK,冰岛IS,东盟AS,哥CR,秘鲁PE,新西兰NZ,智利CL 2.4 瑞士CH 3.6 澳AU 4.8 韩国KR 5.4 亚太AP	0 受惠国LD	17	--Buckets, shovels, grabs and grips
6275	8431.4200	--推土机或侧铲推土机用铲	6	0 冰岛IS,东盟AS,哥CR,秘鲁PE,新西兰NZ,智利CL 2.4 瑞士CH 3.6 澳AU,韩国KR 5 巴PK	0 受惠国LD	17	--Bulldozer or angledozer blades
		--子目号8430.41或8430.49所列钻探或凿井机械的零件:					--Parts for boring or sinking machinery of subheading 843041 or 843049:

序号 No.	税则号列 Tariff Line	中文货品名称 Article Description in Chinese	最惠国税率 MFN(%)	协定税率 Agreement(%)	特惠税率 SP(%)	普通税率 Gen(%)	英文货品名称 Article Description
6276	8431.4310	---石油或天然气钻探机用	4	0 澳AU,巴PK,冰岛IS,东盟AS,哥CR,秘鲁PE,瑞士CH,香港HK,新西兰NZ,智利CL 2.4 韩国KR 2.8 亚太AP	0 受惠国LD	11	---Of oil and natural gas drilling machinery
6277	8431.4320	---其他钻探机用	4	0 澳AU,巴PK,冰岛IS,东盟AS,哥CR,韩国KR,秘鲁PE,瑞士CH,香港HK,新西兰NZ,智利CL 2.8 亚太AP	0 受惠国LD	11	---Of other drilling machinery
6278	8431.4390	---其他	5	0 澳AU,巴PK,冰岛IS,东盟AS,哥CR,秘鲁PE,瑞士CH,香港HK,新西兰NZ,智利CL 3.5 亚太AP 4 韩国KR	0 受惠国LD	17	---Other
		--其他:					--Other:
6279	8431.4920	---装有差速器的驱动桥及其零件,不论是否装有其他传动部件	5	0 澳AU,巴PK,冰岛IS,东盟AS,哥CR,秘鲁PE,香港HK,新西兰NZ,智利CL 2 瑞士CH 4.3 韩国KR 4.5 亚太AP	0 受惠国LD	17	---Drive-axles with differential, whether or not provided with other transmission components, parts thereof
		---其他:					---Other:
6280	8431.4991	----矿用电铲用	5	0 澳AU,巴PK,冰岛IS,东盟AS,哥CR,秘鲁PE,瑞士CH,香港HK,新西兰NZ,智利CL 4 韩国KR 4.5 亚太AP	0 受惠国LD	17	----For mining power shovels
6281	8431.4999	----其他	5	0 澳AU,巴PK,冰岛IS,东盟AS,哥CR,秘鲁PE,香港HK,新西兰NZ,智利CL 2 瑞士CH 4.3 韩国KR 4.5 亚太AP	0 受惠国LD	17	----Other
	84.32	**农业、园艺及林业用整地或耕作机械;草坪及运动场地滚压机:**					**Agricultural, horticultural or forestry machinery for soil preparation or cultivation; lawn or sports-ground rollers:**
6282	8432.1000	-犁	5	0 澳AU,巴PK,冰岛IS,东盟AS,哥CR,秘鲁PE,瑞士CH,新西兰NZ,智利CL 4 韩国KR	0 受惠国LD	30	-Ploughs
		-耙、松土机、中耕机、除草机及耕耘机:					-Harrows, scarifiers, cultivators, weeders and hoes:
6283	8432.2100	--圆盘耙	5	0 澳AU,巴PK,冰岛IS,东盟AS,哥CR,秘鲁PE,瑞士CH,新西兰NZ,智利CL 3 韩国KR	0 受惠国LD	30	--Disc harrows
6284	8432.2900	--其他	4	0 澳AU,巴PK,冰岛IS,东盟AS,哥CR,韩国KR,秘鲁PE,瑞士CH,新西兰NZ,智利CL	0 受惠国$_1$LD$_1$	30	--Other
		-播种机、种植机及移植机:					-Seeders, planters and transplanters:
		---播种机:					---Seeders:

序号 No.	税则号列 Tariff Line	中文货品名称 Article Description in Chinese	最惠国税率 MFN(%)	协定税率 Agreement(%)		特惠税率 SP(%)		普通税率 Gen(%)	英文货品名称 Article Description
6285	8432.3011	----谷物播种机	4	0 3.5	澳AU,巴PK,冰岛IS,东盟AS,哥CR,韩国KR,秘鲁PE,瑞士CH,新西兰NZ,智利CL 亚太AP	0	受惠国$_1$LD$_1$	30	----Grain seeders
6286	8432.3019	----其他	4	0 3.2 3.5	澳AU,巴PK,冰岛IS,东盟AS,哥CR,秘鲁PE,瑞士CH,新西兰NZ,智利CL 韩国KR 亚太AP	0	受惠国$_1$LD$_1$	30	----Other
		---种植机:							---Planters:
6287	8432.3021	----马铃薯种植机	4	0 3.5	澳AU,巴PK,冰岛IS,东盟AS,哥CR,韩国KR,秘鲁PE,瑞士CH,新西兰NZ,智利CL 亚太AP	0	受惠国$_1$LD$_1$	30	----Tuber planters
6288	8432.3029	----其他	4	0 3.5	澳AU,巴PK,冰岛IS,东盟AS,哥CR,韩国KR,秘鲁PE,瑞士CH,新西兰NZ,智利CL 亚太AP	0	受惠国$_1$LD$_1$	30	----Other
		---移植机(栽植机):							---Transplanters:
6289	8432.3031	----水稻插秧机	4	0 2.4 3.5	澳AU,巴PK,冰岛IS,东盟AS,哥CR,秘鲁PE,瑞士CH,新西兰NZ,智利CL 韩国KR 亚太AP	0	受惠国$_1$LD$_1$	30	----Rice transplanters
6290	8432.3039	----其他	4	0 3.4 3.5	澳AU,巴PK,冰岛IS,东盟AS,哥CR,秘鲁PE,瑞士CH,新西兰NZ,智利CL 韩国KR 亚太AP	0	受惠国$_1$LD$_1$	30	----Other
6291	8432.4000	-施肥机	4	0	澳AU,巴PK,冰岛IS,东盟AS,哥CR,韩国KR,秘鲁PE,瑞士CH,新西兰NZ,智利CL	0	受惠国$_1$LD$_1$	30	-Manure spreaders and fertilizer distributors
		-其他机械:							-Other machinery:
6292	8432.8010	---草坪及运动场地滚压机	7	0 2.8 4.2 5 6	冰岛IS,东盟AS,哥CR,秘鲁PE,新西兰NZ,智利CL 瑞士CH 澳AU 巴PK 韩国KR	0	受惠国$_1$LD$_1$	40	---Lawn or sports-ground rollers
6293	8432.8090	---其他	4	0	澳AU,巴PK,冰岛IS,东盟AS,哥CR,韩国KR,秘鲁PE,瑞士CH,新西兰NZ,智利CL	0	受惠国$_1$LD$_1$	30	---Other
6294	8432.9000	-零件	4	0 2.4	澳AU,巴PK,冰岛IS,东盟AS,哥CR,秘鲁PE,瑞士CH,新西兰NZ,智利CL 韩国KR	0	受惠国$_1$LD$_1$	17	-Parts
	84.33	**收割机、脱粒机,包括草料打包机;割草机;蛋类、水果或其他农产品的清洁、分选、分级机器,但税号84.37的机器除外:**							**Harvesting or threshing machinery, including straw or fodder balers; grass or hay mowers; machines for cleaning, sorting or grading eggs, fruit or other agricultural produce, other than machinery of heading 8437:**
		-草坪、公园或运动场地用的割草机:							-Mowers for lawns, parks or sports grounds:

序号 No.	税则号列 Tariff Line	中文货品名称 Article Description in Chinese	最惠国税率 MFN(%)	协定税率 Agreement(%)	特惠税率 SP(%)	普通税率 Gen(%)	英文货品名称 Article Description
6295	8433.1100	--机动的，切割装置在同一水平面上旋转的	6	0 冰岛IS,东盟AS,哥CR,秘鲁PE,新西兰NZ,智利CL 2.4 瑞士CH 3.6 澳AU,韩国KR 5 巴PK	0 受惠国$_1$LD$_1$	30	--Powered, with the cutting device rotating in a horizontal plane
6296	8433.1900	--其他	6	0 冰岛IS,东盟AS,哥CR,秘鲁PE,新西兰NZ,智利CL 2.4 瑞士CH 3.6 澳AU,韩国KR 5 巴PK	0 受惠国$_1$LD$_1$	30	--Other
6297	8433.2000	-其他割草机，包括牵引装置用的刀具杆	4	0 澳AU,巴PK,冰岛IS,东盟AS,哥CR,韩国KR,秘鲁PE,瑞士CH,新西兰NZ,智利CL	0 受惠国$_1$LD$_1$	30	-Other mowers, including cutter bars for tractor mounting
6298	8433.3000	-其他干草切割、翻晒机器	5	0 澳AU,巴PK,冰岛IS,东盟AS,哥CR,秘鲁PE,瑞士CH,新西兰NZ,智利CL 3 韩国KR	0 受惠国$_1$LD$_1$	30	-Other haymaking machinery
6299	8433.4000	-草料打包机，包括收集打包机	5	0 澳AU,巴PK,冰岛IS,东盟AS,哥CR,秘鲁PE,瑞士CH,新西兰NZ,智利CL 4.3 韩国KR	0 受惠国$_1$LD$_1$	30	-Straw or fodder balers, including pickup balers
		-其他收割机；脱粒机：					-Other harvesting machinery; threshing machinery:
6300	8433.5100	--联合收割机	8	0 冰岛IS,东盟AS,哥CR,秘鲁PE,新西兰NZ,智利CL 3.2 瑞士CH 4.8 澳AU 5 巴PK 6.9 韩国KR 7.6 亚太AP	0 受惠国$_1$LD$_1$	17	--Combine harvester-threshers
	ex84335100	功率≥160马力的联合收割机	Δ5				Combine harvester-threshers, power not less than 160HP
6301	8433.5200	--其他脱粒机	8	0 冰岛IS,东盟AS,哥CR,秘鲁PE,新西兰NZ,智利CL 3.2 瑞士CH 4.8 澳AU,韩国KR 5 巴PK	0 受惠国$_1$LD$_1$	30	--Other threshing machinery
6302	8433.5300	--根茎或块茎收获机	8	0 冰岛IS,东盟AS,哥CR,秘鲁PE,新西兰NZ,智利CL 3.2 瑞士CH 4.8 澳AU 5 巴PK 6.4 韩国KR	0 受惠国$_1$LD$_1$	30	--Root or tuber harvesting machines
	ex84335300	功率≥160马力的土豆、甜菜收获机	Δ4				Potato or sugar beet harvestors , power no less than 160HP
		--其他：					--Other:
6303	8433.5910	---甘蔗收获机	8	0 冰岛IS,东盟AS,哥CR,秘鲁PE,新西兰NZ,智利CL 3.2 瑞士CH 4.8 澳AU,韩国KR 5 巴PK	0 受惠国$_1$LD$_1$	30	---Sugarcane harvesters
	ex84335910	功率≥160马力的甘蔗收获机	Δ4				Sugarcane harvestors, power no less than 160HP

序号 No.	税则号列 Tariff Line	中文货品名称 Article Description in Chinese	最惠国税率 MFN(%)	协定税率 Agreement(%)	特惠税率 SP(%)	普通税率 Gen(%)	英文货品名称 Article Description
6304	8433.5920	---棉花采摘机	8Δ5	0 冰岛IS,东盟AS,哥CR,秘鲁PE,新西兰NZ,智利CL 3.2 瑞士CH 4.8 澳AU,韩国KR 5 巴PK	0 受惠国$_1$LD$_1$	30	---Cotton picker
6305	8433.5990	---其他	8	0 冰岛IS,东盟AS,哥CR,秘鲁PE,新西兰NZ,智利CL 3.2 瑞士CH 4.8 澳AU,韩国KR 5 巴PK	0 受惠国$_1$LD$_1$	30	---Other
	ex84335990	茶叶采摘机	Δ4				Tea pickers
	ex84335990	自走式青储饲料收获机	Δ5				Mobile silage harvesters
6306	8433.6000	-蛋类、水果或其他农产品的清洁、分选、分级机器	5	0 澳AU,巴PK,冰岛IS,东盟AS,哥CR,秘鲁PE,瑞士CH,新西兰NZ,智利CL 4 韩国KR	0 受惠国$_1$LD$_1$	30	-Machines for cleaning, sorting or grading eggs, fruit or other agricultural product
		-零件:					-Parts:
6307	8433.9010	---联合收割机用	5	0 澳AU,巴PK,冰岛IS,东盟AS,哥CR,秘鲁PE,瑞士CH,新西兰NZ,智利CL 4.3 韩国KR	0 受惠国$_1$LD$_1$	11	---Of combined harvester-thrashers
6308	8433.9090	---其他	3	0 澳AU,巴PK,冰岛IS,东盟AS,哥CR,韩国KR,秘鲁PE,瑞士CH,新西兰NZ,智利CL	0 受惠国LD	17	---Other
	84.34	**挤奶机及乳品加工机器:**					**Milking machines and dairy machinery:**
6309	8434.1000	-挤奶机	10	0 冰岛IS,东盟AS,哥CR,新西兰NZ,智利CL 4 瑞士CH 5 巴PK 6 澳AU 8 韩国KR	0 受惠国$_1$LD$_1$	20	-Milking machines
6310	8434.2000	-乳品加工机器	6Δ2	0 冰岛IS,东盟AS,哥CR,韩国KR,秘鲁PE,新西兰NZ,智利CL 2.4 瑞士CH 3.6 澳AU 5 巴PK	0 受惠国$_1$LD$_1$	30	-Dairy machinery
6311	8434.9000	-零件	5	0 澳AU,巴PK,冰岛IS,东盟AS,哥CR,秘鲁PE,瑞士CH,新西兰NZ,智利CL 3 韩国KR	0 受惠国$_1$LD$_1$	17	-Parts
	84.35	**制酒、制果汁或制类似饮料用的压榨机、轧碎机及类似机器:**					**Presses, crushers and similar machinery used in the manufacture of wine, cider, fruit juices or similar beverages:**
6312	8435.1000	-机器	10	0 澳门MO,冰岛IS,东盟AS,哥CR,秘鲁PE,新西兰NZ,智利CL 4 瑞士CH 5 巴PK 6 澳AU 8 韩国KR	0 受惠国$_1$LD$_1$	30	-Machinery
6313	8435.9000	-零件	6	0 冰岛IS,东盟AS,哥CR,秘鲁PE,新西兰NZ,智利CL 2.4 瑞士CH 3.6 澳AU,韩国KR 5 巴PK	0 受惠国$_1$LD$_1$	30	-Part

序号 No.	税则号列 Tariff Line	中文货品名称 Article Description in Chinese	最惠国税率 MFN(%)	协定税率 Agreement(%)	特惠税率 SP(%)	普通税率 Gen(%)	英文货品名称 Article Description
	84.36	**农业、园艺、林业、家禽饲养业或养蜂业用的其他机器,包括装有机械或热力装置的催芽设备;家禽孵卵器及育雏器:**					**Other agricultural, horticultural, forestry, poultry-keeping or bee-keeping machinery, including germination plant fitted with mechanical or thermal equipment; poultry incubators and brooders:**
6314	8436.1000	-动物饲料配制机	7	0 冰岛IS,东盟AS,哥CR,秘鲁PE,新西兰NZ,智利CL 4.2 澳AU 5 巴PK,瑞士CH 6 韩国KR	0 受惠国$_1$LD$_1$	30	-Machinery for preparing animal feeding stuffs
		-家禽饲养用的机器;家禽孵卵器及育雏器:					-Poultry-keeping machinery; poultry incubators and brooders:
6315	8436.2100	--家禽孵卵器及育雏器	5	0 澳AU,巴PK,冰岛IS,东盟AS,哥CR,秘鲁PE,瑞士CH,新西兰NZ,智利CL 4.3 韩国KR	0 受惠国$_1$LD$_1$	30	--Poultry incubators and brooders
6316	8436.2900	--其他	10	0 冰岛IS,东盟AS,哥CR,秘鲁PE,新西兰NZ,智利CL 4 瑞士CH 5 巴PK 6 澳AU 9 韩国KR	0 受惠国$_1$LD$_1$	30	--Other
6317	8436.8000	-其他机器	10	0 冰岛IS,东盟AS,哥CR,秘鲁PE,新西兰NZ,智利CL 4 瑞士CH 5 巴PK 6 澳AU 8 韩国KR	0 受惠国$_1$LD$_1$	30	-Other machinery
	ex84368000	青储饲料切割上料机	Δ3				Feeder of silage harvesters
	ex84368000	自走式饲料搅拌投喂车	Δ5				Self waking type feed mixing and feeding vehicles
		-零件:					-Parts:
6318	8436.9100	--家禽饲养用机器的零件或家禽孵卵器及育雏器的零件	6	0 冰岛IS,东盟AS,哥CR,秘鲁PE,新西兰NZ,智利CL 2.4 瑞士CH 3.6 澳AU 5 巴PK 5.2 韩国KR	0 受惠国$_1$LD$_1$	17	--Of poultry-keeping machinery or poultry incubators and brooders
6319	8436.9900	--其他	6	0 冰岛IS,东盟AS,哥CR,秘鲁PE,新西兰NZ,智利CL 3.6 澳AU 4.3 瑞士CH 4.8 韩国KR 5 巴PK	0 受惠国$_1$LD$_1$	17	--Other
	84.37	**种子、谷物或干豆的清洁、分选或分级机器;谷物磨粉业加工机器或谷物、干豆加工机器,但农业用机器除外:**					**Machines for cleaning, sorting or grading seed, grain or dried leguminous vegetables; machinery used in the milling industry or for the working of cereals or dried leguminous vegetables, other than farm-type machinery:**
		-种子、谷物或干豆的清洁、分选或分级机器:					-Machines for cleaning, sorting or grading seed, grain or dried leguminous vegetables:

序号 No.	税则号列 Tariff Line	中文货品名称 Article Description in Chinese	最惠国税率 MFN(%)	协定税率 Agreement(%)	特惠税率 SP(%)	普通税率 Gen(%)	英文货品名称 Article Description
6320	8437.1010	---光学色差颗粒选别机（色选机）	10	0 冰岛IS,东盟AS,哥CR,秘鲁PE,新西兰NZ,智利CL 4 瑞士CH 5 巴PK 6 澳AU 8 韩国KR	0 受惠国$_1$LD$_1$	30	---Optical color sorting machines for grains (color sorters)
6321	8437.1090	---其他	10	0 冰岛IS,东盟AS,哥CR,秘鲁PE,新西兰NZ,智利CL 4 瑞士CH 5 巴PK 6 澳AU 9 韩国KR	0 受惠国$_1$LD$_1$	30	---Other
6322	8437.8000	-其他机器	10	0 冰岛IS,东盟AS,哥CR,秘鲁PE,新西兰NZ,智利CL 4 瑞士CH 5 巴PK 6 澳AU 8.5 亚太AP 9 韩国KR	0 受惠国$_1$LD$_1$	30	-Other machinery
6323	8437.9000	-零件	6	0 冰岛IS,东盟AS,哥CR,秘鲁PE,新西兰NZ,智利CL 3.6 澳AU 4.2 瑞士CH 4.8 韩国KR 5 巴PK	0 受惠国$_1$LD$_1$	30	-Parts
	84.38	**本章其他税号未列名的食品、饮料工业用的生产或加工机器,但提取、加工动物油脂或植物固定油脂的机器除外：**					**Machinery, not specified or included elsewhere in this chapter, for the industrial preparation or manufacture of food or drink, other than machinery for the extraction or preparation of animal or fixed vegetable fats or oils:**
6324	8438.1000	-糕点加工机器及生产通心粉、面条或类似产品的机器	7	0 冰岛IS,东盟AS,哥CR,秘鲁PE,新西兰NZ,智利CL 4.2 澳AU 4.9 瑞士CH 5 巴PK 6 韩国KR	0 受惠国LD	30	-Bakery machinery and machinery for the manufacture of macaroni, spaghetti or similar products
6325	8438.2000	-生产糖果、可可粉、巧克力的机器	8	0 冰岛IS,东盟AS,哥CR,秘鲁PE,瑞士CH,新西兰NZ,智利CL 4.8 澳AU,韩国KR 5 巴PK	0 受惠国LD	30	-Machinery for the manufacture of confectionery, cocoa or chocolate
6326	8438.3000	-制糖机器	10	0 冰岛IS,东盟AS,哥CR,秘鲁PE,新西兰NZ,智利CL 5 巴PK 6 澳AU 8 韩国KR	0 受惠国LD	30	-Machinery for sugar manufacture
6327	8438.4000	-酿酒机器	7	0 冰岛IS,东盟AS,哥CR,秘鲁PE,新西兰NZ,智利CL 2.8 瑞士CH 4.2 澳AU 5 巴PK 5.6 韩国KR	0 受惠国LD	30	-Brewery machinery

序号 No.	税则号列 Tariff Line	中文货品名称 Article Description in Chinese	最惠国税率 MFN(%)	协定税率 Agreement(%)	特惠税率 SP(%)	普通税率 Gen(%)	英文货品名称 Article Description
6328	8438.5000	-肉类或家禽加工机器	7	0 冰岛IS,东盟AS,哥CR,秘鲁PE,新西兰NZ,智利CL 2.8 瑞士CH 4.2 澳AU 5 巴PK 5.6 韩国KR	0 受惠国LD	30	-Machinery for the preparation of meat or poultry
6329	8438.6000	-水果、坚果或蔬菜加工机器	10	0 冰岛IS,东盟AS,哥CR,新加坡SG,新西兰NZ,智利CL 3 秘鲁PE 4 瑞士CH 5 巴PK 6 澳AU 8 韩国KR	0 受惠国LD	30	-Machinery for the preparation of fruits, nuts or vegetables
6330	8438.8000	-其他机器	8.5	0 冰岛IS,东盟AS,哥CR,秘鲁PE,台湾TW,新西兰NZ,智利CL 5 巴PK 5.1 澳AU,韩国KR 6 瑞士CH 8.1 亚太AP	0 受惠国LD	30	-Other machinery
6331	8438.9000	-零件	5	0 澳AU,巴PK,冰岛IS,东盟AS,哥CR,秘鲁PE,瑞士CH,新西兰NZ,智利CL 3 韩国KR	0 受惠国LD	30	-Parts
	84.39	**纤维素纸浆、纸及纸板的制造或整理机器:**					**Machinery for making pulp of fibrous cellulosic material or for making or finishing paper or paperboard:**
6332	8439.1000	-制造纤维素纸浆的机器	8.4	0 冰岛IS,东盟AS,哥CR,秘鲁PE,新西兰NZ,智利CL 3.36 瑞士CH 5 澳AU,巴PK 6.7 韩国KR	0 受惠国LD	30	-Machinery for making pulp of fibrous cellulosic material
6333	8439.2000	-纸或纸板的抄造机器	8.4	0 冰岛IS,东盟AS,哥CR,秘鲁PE,台湾TW,新西兰NZ,智利CL 5 澳AU,巴PK,韩国KR 5.9 瑞士CH	0 受惠国LD	30	-Machinery for making paper or paper board
6334	8439.3000	-纸或纸板的整理机器	8.4	0 冰岛IS,东盟AS,哥CR,秘鲁PE,台湾TW,新西兰NZ,智利CL 3.36 瑞士CH 5 澳AU,巴PK,韩国KR	0 受惠国LD	30	-Machinery for finishing paper or paper board
		-零件:					-Parts:
6335	8439.9100	--制造纤维素纸浆的机器用	6	0 冰岛IS,东盟AS,哥CR,秘鲁PE,新西兰NZ,智利CL 2.4 瑞士CH 3.6 澳AU 5 巴PK 5.2 韩国KR	0 受惠国LD	30	--Of machinery for making pulp of fibrous cellulosic material
6336	8439.9900	--其他	6	0 巴PK,冰岛IS,东盟AS,哥CR,秘鲁PE,新西兰NZ,智利CL 3 亚太AP 3.6 澳AU 4.2 瑞士CH 5.2 韩国KR	0 受惠国LD	30	--Other
	84.40	**书本装订机器,包括锁线订书机:**					**Book-binding machinery, including booksewing machines:**
		-机器:					-Machinery:

序号 No.	税则号列 Tariff Line	中文货品名称 Article Description in Chinese	最惠国税率 MFN(%)	协定税率 Agreement(%)	特惠税率 SP(%)	普通税率 Gen(%)	英文货品名称 Article Description
6337	8440.1010	---锁线装订机	10	0 冰岛IS,东盟AS,哥CR,秘鲁PE,新西兰NZ,智利CL 4 瑞士CH 5 巴PK 6 澳AU 8 韩国KR	0 受惠国$_1$LD$_1$	35	---Sewing bookbinders
6338	8440.1020	---胶订机	12	0 冰岛IS,东盟AS,哥CR,秘鲁PE,新加坡SG,新西兰NZ,智利CL 4.8 瑞士CH 6 巴PK 7.2 澳AU 9.6 韩国KR	0 受惠国$_1$LD$_1$	35	---Glueing bookbinders
6339	8440.1090	---其他	12	0 冰岛IS,东盟AS,哥CR,秘鲁PE,瑞士CH,新加坡SG,新西兰NZ,智利CL 6 巴PK 7.2 澳AU 9.6 韩国KR	0 受惠国$_1$LD$_1$	35	---Other
6340	8440.9000	-零件	8	0 冰岛IS,东盟AS,哥CR,秘鲁PE,新西兰NZ,智利CL 4.8 澳AU,韩国KR 5 巴PK 5.6 瑞士CH	0 受惠国$_1$LD$_1$	35	-Parts
	84.41	**其他制造纸浆制品、纸制品或纸板制品的机器,包括各种切纸机:**					**Other machinery for making up paper pulp, paper or paperboard, including cutting machines of all kinds:**
6341	8441.1000	-切纸机	12	0 冰岛IS,东盟AS,哥CR,秘鲁PE,台湾TW,新加坡SG,新西兰NZ,智利CL 6 巴PK 7.2 澳AU 9.6 韩国KR	0 受惠国LD	50	-Cutting machines
6342	8441.2000	-制造包、袋或信封的机器	12	0 冰岛IS,东盟AS,哥CR,新加坡SG,新西兰NZ,智利CL 3.6 秘鲁PE 6 巴PK 7.2 澳AU 8.4 瑞士CH 9.6 韩国KR 11.4 亚太AP	0 受惠国LD	30	-Machines for making bags, sacks or envelopes
		-制造箱、盒、管、桶或类似容器的机器,但模制成型机器除外:					-Machines for making cartons, boxes, cases, tubes, drums or similar containers, other than by moulding:
6343	8441.3010	---制造纸塑铝复合罐的生产设备	13.5	0 冰岛IS,东盟AS,哥CR,新加坡SG,新西兰NZ,智利CL 4 秘鲁PE 6.8 巴PK 8.1 澳AU 9.5 瑞士CH 10.8 韩国KR 12.8 亚太AP	0 受惠国$_1$LD$_1$	30	---Machines for paper, plastic and aluminium composite can manufacture

序号 No.	税则号列 Tariff Line	中文货品名称 Article Description in Chinese	最惠国税率 MFN(%)	协定税率 Agreement(%)	特惠税率 SP(%)	普通税率 Gen(%)	英文货品名称 Article Description
6344	8441.3090	---其他	13.5	0 冰岛IS,东盟AS,哥CR,新加坡SG,新西兰NZ,智利CL 4 秘鲁PE 6.8 巴PK 8.1 澳AU 9.5 瑞士CH 12.1 韩国KR 12.8 亚太AP	0 受惠国$_1$LD$_1$	30	---Other
6345	8441.4000	-纸浆、纸或纸板制品模制成型机器	12	0 冰岛IS,东盟AS,哥CR,秘鲁PE,新加坡SG,新西兰NZ,智利CL 6 巴PK 7.2 澳AU 8.4 瑞士CH 10.8 韩国KR	0 受惠国LD	30	-Machines for moulding articles in paper pulp, paper or paperboard
		-其他机器:					-Other machinery:
6346	8441.8010	---制造纸塑铝软包装的生产设备	12	0 冰岛IS,东盟AS,哥CR,秘鲁PE,新加坡SG,新西兰NZ,智利CL 6 巴PK 7.2 澳AU 8.4 瑞士CH 9.6 韩国KR 11.4 亚太AP	0 受惠国LD	30	---Machines for paper plastic and aluminium flexible packaging manufacture
6347	8441.8090	---其他	12	0 冰岛IS,东盟AS,哥CR,秘鲁PE,台湾TW,新加坡SG,新西兰NZ,智利CL 6 巴PK 7.2 澳AU 8.4 瑞士CH 9.6 韩国KR 11.4 亚太AP	0 受惠国LD	30	---Other
		-零件:					-Parts:
6348	8441.9010	---切纸机用	8	0 冰岛IS,东盟AS,哥CR,秘鲁PE,新西兰NZ,智利CL 3.2 瑞士CH 4.8 澳AU 5 巴PK 6.4 韩国KR	0 受惠国LD	50	---Of cutting machines
	ex84419010	切纸机用横切刀单元	Δ3				Crosscut knife units of cutting machines
	ex84419010	切纸机用弧形辊	Δ4				Curved metal spreader roll of cutting machines
6349	8441.9090	---其他	8.4	0 冰岛IS,东盟AS,哥CR,秘鲁PE,新西兰NZ,智利CL 5 澳AU,巴PK,韩国KR	0 受惠国LD	30	---Other
	84.42	**制版用的机器、器具及设备(税号84.56至84.65的机床除外);印刷用版(片)、滚筒及其他部件;制成供印刷用(例如,刨平、压纹或抛光)的版(片)、滚筒及石板:**					**Machinery, apparatus and equipment (other than the machine tools of headings 8456 to 8465) for preparing or making plates, cylinders or other printing components; plates, cylinders and other printing components; plates, cylinders and lithographic stones, prepared for printing purposes (for example, planed, grained or polished) :**
		-机器、器具及设备:					-Machinery, apparatus and equipment:

序号 No.	税则号列 Tariff Line	中文货品名称 Article Description in Chinese	最惠国税率 MFN(%)	协定税率 Agreement(%)	特惠税率 SP(%)	普通税率 Gen(%)	英文货品名称 Article Description
6350	8442.3010	---铸字机	9	0 冰岛IS,东盟AS,哥CR,秘鲁PE,新西兰NZ,智利CL 3.6 瑞士CH 5 巴PK 5.4 澳AU,韩国KR	0 受惠国LD	35	---Type casters
		---制版机器、器具及设备:					---Other machinery, apparatus and equipment for typesetting:
6351	8442.3021	----计算机直接制版设备	9	0 冰岛IS,东盟AS,哥CR,秘鲁PE,新西兰NZ,智利CL 5 巴PK 5.4 澳AU,韩国KR 6.3 瑞士CH	0 受惠国LD	35	----Computer-to-plate equipments
	ex84423021	凹版式计算机直接制版设备	Δ3				Intaglio Equipments for preparing computer-to-plate plates
	ex84423021	除凹版式以外的其他计算机直接制版设备(CTP)	Δ5				Computer-to-plate equipments excluding intaglio ones
6352	8442.3029	----其他	9	0 冰岛IS,东盟AS,哥CR,秘鲁PE,新西兰NZ,智利CL 3.6 瑞士CH 5 巴PK 5.4 澳AU 7.8 韩国KR	0 受惠国LD	35	----Other
6353	8442.3090	---其他	9	0 冰岛IS,东盟AS,哥CR,秘鲁PE,新西兰NZ,智利CL 3.6 瑞士CH 5 巴PK 5.4 澳AU 7.8 韩国KR	0 受惠国LD	35	---Other
6354	8442.4000	-上述机器、器具及设备的零件	7	0 冰岛IS,东盟AS,哥CR,韩国KR,秘鲁PE,新西兰NZ,智利CL 2.8 瑞士CH 4.2 澳AU 5 巴PK	0 受惠国LD	20	-Parts of the foregoing machinery, apparatus or equipment
	ex84424000	计算机直接制版机器用零件	Δ1				Parts of computer-to-plate equipments
6355	8442.5000	-印刷用版、滚筒及其他印刷部件;制成供印刷用(例如,刨平、压纹或抛光)的版、滚筒及石板	7	0 冰岛IS,东盟AS,哥CR,秘鲁PE,香港HK,新西兰NZ,智利CL 2.8 瑞士CH 4.2 澳AU,韩国KR 5 巴PK	0 受惠国LD	35	-Plates, cylinders and other printing components; plates, cylinders and lithographic stones, prepared for printing purposes (for example, planed, grained or polished)
	84.43	**用于税目84.42的印刷用版(片)、滚筒及其他印刷部件进行印刷的机器;其他打印机、复印机及传真机,不论是否组合式;上述机器的零件及附件:**					**Printing machinery used for printing by means of plates, cylinders and other printing components of heading 8442; other printers, copying machines and facsimile machines, whether or not combined; parts and accessories thereof:**
		-用税目84.42的印刷用版(片)、滚筒及其他印刷部件进行印刷的机器:					-Printing machinery used for printing by means of plates, cylinders and other printing components of heading 8442:
6356	8443.1100	--卷取进料式胶印机	10	0 冰岛IS,东盟AS,哥CR,新西兰NZ,智利CL 3 秘鲁PE 4 瑞士CH 5 巴PK 6 澳AU 7 亚太AP 8 韩国KR	0 受惠国LD	35	--Offset printing machinery, reel-fed

序号 No.	税则号列 Tariff Line	中文货品名称 Article Description in Chinese	最惠国税率 MFN(%)	协定税率 Agreement(%)	特惠税率 SP(%)	普通税率 Gen(%)	英文货品名称 Article Description
6357	8443.1200	--办公室用片取进料式胶印机（展开片尺寸一边长不超过22厘米，另一边长不超过36厘米）	12	0 冰岛IS,东盟AS,哥CR,秘鲁PE,新加坡SG,新西兰NZ,智利CL 6 巴PK 7.2 澳AU 8.4 瑞士CH 9.6 韩国KR	0 受惠国LD	35	--Offset printing machinery, sheet-fed, office type (using sheets with one side not exceeding 22cm and the other side not exceeding 36 cm in the unfolded state)
		--其他胶印机：					--Other offset printing machinery:
		---平张纸进料式：					---Sheet fed:
6358	8443.1311	----单色机	10	0 冰岛IS,东盟AS,哥CR,秘鲁PE,新西兰NZ,智利CL 4 瑞士CH 5 巴PK 6 澳AU 7 亚太AP 8 韩国KR	0 受惠国LD	35	----Single-color printing press
6359	8443.1312	----双色机	10	0 冰岛IS,东盟AS,哥CR,秘鲁PE,新西兰NZ,智利CL 4 瑞士CH 5 巴PK 6 澳AU 7 亚太AP 8 韩国KR	0 受惠国LD	35	----Double-color printing press
6360	8443.1313	----四色机	10	0 冰岛IS,东盟AS,哥CR,秘鲁PE,新西兰NZ,智利CL 4 瑞士CH 5 巴PK 6 澳AU 7 亚太AP 8 韩国KR	0 受惠国LD	35	----Quadruple-color printing press
	ex84431313	四色平张纸胶印机，对开单张纸单面印刷速度≥17000张/小时；对开单张纸双面印刷速度≥13000张/小时；全张或超全张单张纸单面印刷速度≥13000张/小时	Δ7				Four-color sheet-fed offset press, Folio size, maximum out-put of single-sided printing≥17000iph; Folio size, maximum out-put of perfect (double-sided) printing ≥ 13000iph; Full size or super large format, maximum out-put of single-sided printing≥13000iph
6361	8443.1319	----其他	10	0 冰岛IS,东盟AS,哥CR,秘鲁PE,新西兰NZ,智利CL 4 瑞士CH 5 巴PK 6 澳AU 7 亚太AP 8 韩国KR	0 受惠国LD	35	----Other
	ex84431319	五色及以上平张纸胶印机，对开单张纸单面印刷速度≥17000张/小时；对开单张纸双面印刷速度≥13000张/小时；全张或超全张单张纸单面印刷速度≥13000张/小时	Δ7				Five-color and more sheet-fed offset printing machines, Folio size, maximum out-put of single-sided printing≥17000iph; Folio size, maximum out-put of perfect (double-sided) printing≥13000iph; Full size or super large format, maximum out-put of single-sided printing≥13000iph
6362	8443.1390	---其他	10	0 冰岛IS,东盟AS,哥CR,秘鲁PE,新西兰NZ,智利CL 4 瑞士CH 5 巴PK 6 澳AU 7 亚太AP 8 韩国KR	0 受惠国LD	35	---Other

序号 No.	税则号列 Tariff Line	中文货品名称 Article Description in Chinese	最惠国税率 MFN(%)	协定税率 Agreement(%)	特惠税率 SP(%)	普通税率 Gen(%)	英文货品名称 Article Description
6363	8443.1400	--卷取进料式凸版印刷机,但不包括苯胺印刷机	12	0 冰岛IS,东盟AS,哥CR,秘鲁PE,香港HK,新加坡SG,新西兰NZ,智利CL 6 巴PK 7.2 澳AU 8.4 瑞士CH	0 受惠国LD	35	--Letterpress printing machinery, reel fed, excluding flexographic printing
6364	8443.1500	--其他凸版印刷机,但不包括苯胺印刷机	12	0 冰岛IS,东盟AS,哥CR,秘鲁PE,新加坡SG,新西兰NZ,智利CL 6 巴PK 7.2 澳AU 8.4 瑞士CH	0 受惠国LD	35	--Letterpress printing machinery, other than reel fed, excluding flexographic printing
6365	8443.1600	--苯胺印刷机	10	0 冰岛IS,东盟AS,哥CR,秘鲁PE,新西兰NZ,智利CL 4 瑞士CH 5 巴PK 6 澳AU	0 受惠国LD	35	--Flexographic printing machinery
	ex84431600	苯胺印刷机(柔性版印刷机),线速度≥350米/分钟,幅宽≥800毫米	Δ3				Flexographic printing machines, press line speed≥350m/min, web width≥800mm
	ex84431600	具有烫印或全息或丝网印刷功能单元的机组式柔性版印刷机,线速度≥160米/分钟,250毫米≤幅宽<800毫米	Δ5				Multi-functional narrow-web flexographic printing machine with module of stamping or holographic or screen printing, line speed≥160m/min, 250mm≤web width< 800mm
6366	8443.1700	--凹版印刷机	18	0 冰岛IS,东盟AS,哥CR,新加坡SG,新西兰NZ,智利CL 5.4 秘鲁PE 10.8 澳AU 12.6 瑞士CH 14.4 巴PK 15.4 韩国KR 16.2 亚太AP	0 受惠国$_1$LD$_1$	35	--Gravure printing machinery
	ex84431700	凹版印刷机,印刷速度≥350米/分钟	Δ9				Gravure printing machinery, printing speed≥350m/min
		--其他:					--Other:
		---网式印刷机:					---Screen printing machinery:
6367	8443.1921	----圆网印刷机	10	0 冰岛IS,东盟AS,哥CR,秘鲁PE,新西兰NZ,智利CL 4 瑞士CH 5 巴PK 6 澳AU 8 韩国KR 9 亚太AP	0 受惠国LD	35	----Cylinder screen press
	ex84431921	纺织用圆网印花机	Δ6				Cylinder screen woven fabric printing range
6368	8443.1922	----平网印刷机	10	0 冰岛IS,东盟AS,哥CR,秘鲁PE,台湾TW,新西兰NZ,智利CL 5 巴PK 6 澳AU 7 瑞士CH 8.6 韩国KR 9 亚太AP	0 受惠国LD	35	----Platen screen press
	ex84431922	纺织用平网印花机	Δ6				Flate screen woven fabric printing range

序号 No.	税则号列 Tariff Line	中文货品名称 Article Description in Chinese	最惠国税率 MFN(%)	协定税率 Agreement(%)	特惠税率 SP(%)	普通税率 Gen(%)	英文货品名称 Article Description
6369	8443.1929	----其他	10	0 冰岛IS,东盟AS,哥CR,秘鲁PE,台湾TW,新加坡SG,新西兰NZ,智利CL 4 瑞士CH 5 巴PK 6 澳AU 8 韩国KR 9 亚太AP	0 受惠国LD	35	----Other
6370	8443.1980	---其他	8	0 冰岛IS,东盟AS,哥CR,秘鲁PE,台湾TW,香港HK,新西兰NZ,智利CL 3.2 瑞士CH 4.8 澳AU,韩国KR 5 巴PK 7.2 亚太AP	0 受惠国LD	35	---Other
		-其他印刷（打印）机、复印机及传真机，不论是否组合式：					-Other printers, copying machines and facsimile machines, whether or not combined:
		--具有打印、复印或传真中两种及以上功能的机器，可与自动数据处理设备或网络连接：					--Machines which perform two or more of the functions of printing, copying or facsimile transmission, capable of connecting to an automatic data-processing machine or to a network:
6371	8443.3110	---静电感光式	10Δ3	0 冰岛IS,东盟AS,哥CR,秘鲁PE,新加坡SG,新西兰NZ,智利CL 4 瑞士CH 5 巴PK 6 澳AU	0 受惠国LD	70	---Electrostatic photo type
6372	8443.3190	---其他	0		0 受惠国LD	17	---Other
		---其他，可与自动数据处理设备或网络连接：					--Other, capable of connecting to an automatic data-processing machine or to a network:
		---专用于税目8471所列设备的打印机：					---Printer suitable for use solely with the machines of heading No.8471:
6373	8443.3211	----针式打印机	0		0 受惠国LD	14	----Stylus printers
6374	8443.3212	----激光打印机	0		0 受惠国LD	14	----Laser printers
6375	8443.3213	----喷墨打印机	0		0 受惠国LD	14	----Ink-jet printers
6376	8443.3214	----热敏打印机	0		0 受惠国LD	14	----Thermal printers
6377	8443.3219	----其他	0		0 受惠国LD	14	----Other
		---数字式印刷设备：					---Digital printing machines:
6378	8443.3221	----喷墨印刷机	8Δ5	0 冰岛IS,东盟AS,哥CR,秘鲁PE,新加坡SG,新西兰NZ,智利CL 3.2 瑞士CH 4.8 澳AU 5 巴PK 6.4 韩国KR	0 受惠国LD	30	----Ink-jet printing machines
6379	8443.3222	----静电照相印刷机(激光印刷机)	8Δ5	0 冰岛IS,东盟AS,哥CR,秘鲁PE,新西兰NZ,智利CL 3.2 瑞士CH 4.8 澳AU 5 巴PK 6.9 韩国KR 7.2 亚太AP	0 受惠国LD	35	----Electrostatic photographic printing machines (laser printing machines)

序号 No.	税则号列 Tariff Line	中文货品名称 Article Description in Chinese	最惠国税率 MFN(%)	协定税率 Agreement(%)	特惠税率 SP(%)	普通税率 Gen(%)	英文货品名称 Article Description
6380	8443.3229	----其他	8	0 冰岛IS,东盟AS,哥CR,秘鲁PE,新西兰NZ,智利CL 3.2 瑞士CH 4.8 澳AU 5 巴PK 6.4 韩国KR 7.2 亚太AP	0 受惠国LD	30	----Other
6381	8443.3290	---其他	0		0 受惠国LD	17	---Other
		--其他:					--Other:
		---静电感光复印设备:					---Electrostatic photo-copying apparatus:
6382	8443.3911	----将原件直接复印的（直接法）	0		0 受惠国LD	70	----Operating by reproducing the original image directly onto the copy (direct process)
6383	8443.3912	----将原件通过中间体转印的（间接法）	10	0 冰岛IS,东盟AS,哥CR,秘鲁PE,新加坡SG,新西兰NZ,智利CL 4 瑞士CH 5 巴PK 6 澳AU	0 受惠国LD	70	----Operating by reproducing the original image via an intermediate onto the copy (indirect process)
		---其他感光复印设备:					---Other photocopying apparatus:
6384	8443.3921	----带有光学系统的	0		0 受惠国LD	70	----Incorporating an optical system
6385	8443.3922	----接触式的	20	0 冰岛IS,东盟AS,哥CR,新加坡SG,新西兰NZ,智利CL 6 秘鲁PE 12 澳AU,韩国KR 14 瑞士CH	0 受惠国$_1$LD$_1$	70	----Of the contact type
6386	8443.3923	----热敏复印设备	20	0 冰岛IS,东盟AS,哥CR,新加坡SG,新西兰NZ,智利CL 6 秘鲁PE 12 澳AU,韩国KR 14 瑞士CH	0 受惠国$_1$LD$_1$	70	----Heat-sensitive copying apparatus
6387	8443.3924	----热升华复印设备	20	0 冰岛IS,东盟AS,哥CR,新加坡SG,新西兰NZ,智利CL 6 秘鲁PE 12 澳AU,韩国KR 14 瑞士CH	0 受惠国$_1$LD$_1$	70	----Heat-sublimated copying apparatus
		---数字式印刷设备:					---Digital printing machines:
6388	8443.3931	----喷墨印刷机	8	0 冰岛IS,东盟AS,哥CR,秘鲁PE,新加坡SG,新西兰NZ,智利CL 3.2 瑞士CH 4.8 澳AU,韩国KR 5 巴PK	0 受惠国LD	30	----Ink-jet printing machines
6389	8443.3932	----静电照相印刷机（激光印刷机）	8	0 冰岛IS,东盟AS,哥CR,秘鲁PE,新西兰NZ,智利CL 3.2 瑞士CH 4.8 澳AU,韩国KR 5 巴PK 7.2 亚太AP	0 受惠国LD	35	----Electrostatic photographic printing machines (laser printing machines)
6390	8443.3939	----其他	8	0 冰岛IS,东盟AS,哥CR,秘鲁PE,新加坡SG,新西兰NZ,智利CL 3.2 瑞士CH 4.8 澳AU 5 巴PK 6.4 韩国KR 7.2 亚太AP	0 受惠国LD	30	----Other
6391	8443.3990	---其他	0		0 受惠国LD	30	---Other
		-零件及附件:					-Parts and accessories:

序号 No.	税则号列 Tariff Line	中文货品名称 Article Description in Chinese	最惠国税率 MFN(%)	协定税率 Agreement(%)	特惠税率 SP(%)	普通税率 Gen(%)	英文货品名称 Article Description
		--用于税目84.42的印刷用版、滚筒及其他印刷部件进行印刷的机器零件及附件:					--Parts and accessories of printing machinery used for printing by means of plates, cylinders and other printing components of heading 8442:
		---印刷用辅助机器:					---Machines for uses ancillary to printing:
6392	8443.9111	----卷筒料给料机	12	0 冰岛IS,东盟AS,哥CR,秘鲁PE,新加坡SG,新西兰NZ,智利CL 6 巴PK 7.2 澳AU 8.4 瑞士CH 9.6 韩国KR	0 受惠国LD	35	----Splicers of web press
	ex84439111	卷筒料自动给料机，给料线速度≥12米/秒	Δ4				Automatic splicer of web offset press, splicing speed ≥12m/s
6393	8443.9119	----其他	12Δ6	0 冰岛IS,东盟AS,哥CR,秘鲁PE,新加坡SG,新西兰NZ,智利CL 4.8 瑞士CH 6 巴PK 7.2 澳AU 9.6 韩国KR	0 受惠国LD	35	----Other
6394	8443.9190	---其他	6	0 冰岛IS,东盟AS,哥CR,秘鲁PE,新西兰NZ,智利CL 3.6 澳AU 4.2 瑞士CH 4.8 韩国KR 5 巴PK	0 受惠国LD	20	---Other
	ex84439190	胶印机用墨量遥控装置（包括墨色控制装置、墨量调节装置、墨斗体等组成部分）	Δ1				Ink remote control unit for offset printing machinery (including ink coclor control unit and ink adjust device and inking pot)
	ex84439190	传统印刷机用零件及附件(胶印机用墨量遥控装置除外)	Δ3				Parts and accessories of printing machinery (with the exception of ink remote control unit)
		--其他:					--Other:
6395	8443.9910	---数字印刷设备用辅助机器	12	0 冰岛IS,东盟AS,哥CR,秘鲁PE,新加坡SG,新西兰NZ,智利CL 4.8 瑞士CH 6 巴PK 7.2 澳AU 9.6 韩国KR	0 受惠国LD	35	---Machines for uses ancillary to digital printing
		---数字印刷设备的零件:					---Parts of digital printing machinery:
6396	8443.9921	----热敏打印头	6	0 冰岛IS,东盟AS,哥CR,秘鲁PE,新西兰NZ,智利CL 2.4 瑞士CH 3.6 澳AU 4.8 韩国KR 5 巴PK	0 受惠国LD	20	----Thermal printer heads
6397	8443.9929	----其他	6	0 冰岛IS,东盟AS,哥CR,秘鲁PE,新西兰NZ,智利CL 2.4 瑞士CH 3.6 澳AU 4.8 韩国KR 5 巴PK	0 受惠国LD	20	----Other
	ex84439929	压电式喷墨头	Δ3				Piezoelectric inkjet print head
6398	8443.9990	---其他	0		0 受惠国LD	35	---Other
	84.44	**化学纺织纤维挤压、拉伸、变形或切割机器:**					**Machines for extruding, drawing, texturing or cutting man-made textile materials:**

序号 No.	税则号列 Tariff Line	中文货品名称 Article Description in Chinese	最惠国税率 MFN(%)	协定税率 Agreement(%)	特惠税率 SP(%)	普通税率 Gen(%)	英文货品名称 Article Description
6399	8444.0010	---合成纤维长丝纺丝机	10	0 冰岛IS,东盟AS,哥CR,秘鲁PE,台湾TW,新西兰NZ,智利CL 5 巴PK 6 澳AU,韩国KR 7 亚太AP	0 受惠国$_1$LD$_1$	30	---Synthetic filaments spinning jets
6400	8444.0020	---合成纤维短纤纺丝机	10	0 冰岛IS,东盟AS,哥CR,秘鲁PE,新西兰NZ,智利CL 4 瑞士CH 5 巴PK 6 澳AU 7 亚太AP 8 韩国KR	0 受惠国$_1$LD$_1$	30	---Synthetic staple fibres spinning jets
6401	8444.0030	---人造纤维纺丝机	10	0 冰岛IS,东盟AS,哥CR,秘鲁PE,新西兰NZ,智利CL 4 瑞士CH 5 巴PK 6 澳AU 7 亚太AP 8 韩国KR	0 受惠国$_1$LD$_1$	30	---Artificial fibres spinning jets
6402	8444.0040	---化学纤维变形机	10	0 冰岛IS,东盟AS,哥CR,秘鲁PE,新西兰NZ,智利CL 5 巴PK 6 澳AU 7 瑞士CH,亚太AP 8 韩国KR	0 受惠国$_1$LD$_1$	30	---Man-made filaments crimping machinery
6403	8444.0050	---化学纤维切断机	10	0 冰岛IS,东盟AS,哥CR,秘鲁PE,新西兰NZ,智利CL 5 巴PK 6 澳AU 7 瑞士CH,亚太AP 8 韩国KR	0 受惠国$_1$LD$_1$	30	---Manmade filaments cutting machinery
6404	8444.0090	---其他	10	0 冰岛IS,东盟AS,哥CR,秘鲁PE,新西兰NZ,智利CL 5 巴PK 6 澳AU 7 瑞士CH,亚太AP 8 韩国KR	0 受惠国$_1$LD$_1$	30	---Other
	84.45	**纺织纤维的预处理机器;纺纱机、并线机、加捻机及其他生产纺织纱线的机器;摇纱机、络纱机(包括卷纬机)及处理税号84.46或84.47所列机器用的纺织纱线的机器:**					**Machines for preparing textile fibres; spinning, doubling or twisting machines and other machinery for producing textile yarns; textile reeling or winding (including weft-winding) machines and machines for preparing textile yarns for use on the machines of heading 8446 or 8447:**
		-纺织纤维的预处理机器:					-Machines for preparing textile fibres:
		--梳理机:					--Carding machines:
		---棉纤维型:					---For cotton type fibres:
6405	8445.1111	----清梳联合机	10	0 冰岛IS,东盟AS,哥CR,秘鲁PE,新西兰NZ,智利CL 4 瑞士CH 5 巴PK 6 澳AU 8 韩国KR 9 亚太AP	0 受惠国LD	30	----Blowing-carding Machinery

序号 No.	税则号列 Tariff Line	中文货品名称 Article Description in Chinese	最惠国税率 MFN(%)	协定税率 Agreement(%)	特惠税率 SP(%)	普通税率 Gen(%)	英文货品名称 Article Description
6406	8445.1112	----自动抓棉机	10	0 冰岛IS,东盟AS,哥CR,秘鲁PE,新西兰NZ,智利CL 5 巴PK 6 澳AU 8 韩国KR 9 亚太AP	0 受惠国LD	30	----Bale Plucker
6407	8445.1113	----梳棉机	10	0 冰岛IS,东盟AS,哥CR,秘鲁PE,新西兰NZ,智利CL 5 巴PK 6 澳AU 7 瑞士CH 8 韩国KR 9 亚太AP	0 受惠国LD	30	----Card or Carding Mackine
6408	8445.1119	----其他	10	0 冰岛IS,东盟AS,哥CR,秘鲁PE,新西兰NZ,智利CL 4 瑞士CH 5 巴PK 6 澳AU 8 韩国KR 9 亚太AP	0 受惠国LD	30	----Other
6409	8445.1120	---毛纤维型	10	0 冰岛IS,东盟AS,哥CR,秘鲁PE,新西兰NZ,智利CL 4 瑞士CH 5 巴PK 6 澳AU 8 韩国KR 9 亚太AP	0 受惠国LD	30	---For wool type fibres
6410	8445.1190	---其他	10	0 冰岛IS,东盟AS,哥CR,秘鲁PE,新西兰NZ,智利CL 4 瑞士CH 5 巴PK 6 澳AU 9 亚太AP	0 受惠国LD	30	---Other
	ex84451190	宽幅非织造布梳理机,工作幅宽＞3.5米，工作速度＞120米/分钟	Δ6				Nonwoven carding machines, working width>3.5m, working speed>120m/min
		--精梳机:					--Combing machines:
6411	8445.1210	---棉精梳机	10	0 冰岛IS,东盟AS,哥CR,秘鲁PE,新西兰NZ,智利CL 5 巴PK 6 澳AU 8 韩国KR	0 受惠国LD	30	---Cotton Comber
6412	8445.1220	---毛精梳机	10	0 冰岛IS,东盟AS,哥CR,秘鲁PE,新西兰NZ,智利CL 4 瑞士CH 5 巴PK 6 澳AU 8 韩国KR	0 受惠国LD	30	---Worsted Comber
6413	8445.1290	---其他	10	0 冰岛IS,东盟AS,哥CR,秘鲁PE,新西兰NZ,智利CL 4 瑞士CH 5 巴PK 6 澳AU 8 韩国KR	0 受惠国LD	30	---Other
		--拉伸机或粗纱机:					--Drawing or roving machines:

序号 No.	税则号列 Tariff Line	中文货品名称 Article Description in Chinese	最惠国税率 MFN(%)	协定税率 Agreement(%)	特惠税率 SP(%)	普通税率 Gen(%)	英文货品名称 Article Description
6414	8445.1310	---拉伸机	10	0 冰岛IS,东盟AS,哥CR,秘鲁PE,新西兰NZ,智利CL 4 瑞士CH 5 巴PK 6 澳AU 8 韩国KR	0 受惠国LD	30	---Drawing machines
		---粗纱机:					---Roving machines:
6415	8445.1321	----棉纺粗纱机	10	0 冰岛IS,东盟AS,哥CR,秘鲁PE,新西兰NZ,智利CL 5 巴PK 6 澳AU 8 韩国KR	0 受惠国LD	30	----Cotton Roving Frames
6416	8445.1322	----毛纺粗纱机	10	0 冰岛IS,东盟AS,哥CR,秘鲁PE,新西兰NZ,智利CL 4 瑞士CH 5 巴PK 6 澳AU 8 韩国KR	0 受惠国LD	30	----Worsted Roving Machines
6417	8445.1329	----其他	10	0 冰岛IS,东盟AS,哥CR,秘鲁PE,新西兰NZ,智利CL 4 瑞士CH 5 巴PK 6 澳AU 8 韩国KR	0 受惠国LD	30	----Other
6418	8445.1900	--其他	10	0 冰岛IS,东盟AS,哥CR,新西兰NZ,智利CL 3 秘鲁PE 5 巴PK 6 澳AU 9 亚太AP	0 受惠国LD	30	--Other
		-纺纱机:					-Textile spinning machines:
		---自由端纺纱机:					---Open-end spinner:
6419	8445.2031	----转杯纺纱机	10	0 冰岛IS,东盟AS,哥CR,秘鲁PE,新西兰NZ,智利CL 4 瑞士CH 5 巴PK 6 澳AU 8 韩国KR 9 亚太AP	0 受惠国LD	30	----Rotor spinning machine
	ex84452031	全自动转杯纺纱机	Δ5				Automatic rotor spinning machines
6420	8445.2032	----喷气纺纱机	10	0 冰岛IS,东盟AS,哥CR,秘鲁PE,新西兰NZ,智利CL 5 巴PK 6 澳AU 8 韩国KR	0 受惠国LD	30	----Jet spinner
6421	8445.2039	----其他	10	0 冰岛IS,东盟AS,哥CR,秘鲁PE,新西兰NZ,智利CL 4 瑞士CH 5 巴PK 6 澳AU 8 韩国KR	0 受惠国LD	30	----Other
		---环锭细纱机:					---Ring spinning frames:

序号 No.	税则号列 Tariff Line	中文货品名称 Article Description in Chinese	最惠国税率 MFN(%)	协定税率 Agreement(%)	特惠税率 SP(%)	普通税率 Gen(%)	英文货品名称 Article Description
6422	8445.2041	----棉细纱机	10.5	0 冰岛IS,东盟AS,哥CR,秘鲁PE,新加坡SG,新西兰NZ,智利CL 5 巴PK 6.3 澳AU 7.4 瑞士CH 8.4 韩国KR 9.5 亚太AP	0 受惠国LD	40	----Cotton Ring Spinning Frame
6423	8445.2042	----毛细纱机	10	0 冰岛IS,东盟AS,哥CR,秘鲁PE,新西兰NZ,智利CL 4 瑞士CH 5 巴PK 6 澳AU 8 韩国KR	0 受惠国LD	40	----Worsted Ring Spinning Frame
6424	8445.2049	----其他	10	0 冰岛IS,东盟AS,哥CR,秘鲁PE,新西兰NZ,智利CL 4 瑞士CH 5 巴PK 6 澳AU 8 韩国KR	0 受惠国LD	40	----Other
6425	8445.2090	---其他	10	0 冰岛IS,东盟AS,哥CR,秘鲁PE,新西兰NZ,智利CL 5 巴PK 6 澳AU 8 韩国KR 9 亚太AP	0 受惠国LD	30	---Other
6426	8445.3000	-并线机或加捻机	10	0 冰岛IS,东盟AS,哥CR,秘鲁PE,新西兰NZ,智利CL 4 瑞士CH 5 巴PK 6 澳AU 8 韩国KR 9 亚太AP	0 受惠国LD	30	-Textile doubling or twisting machines
		-络纱机（包括卷纬机）或摇纱机：					-Textile winding (including weft-winding) or reeling machines:
6427	8445.4010	---自动络筒机	10	0 冰岛IS,东盟AS,哥CR,新西兰NZ,智利CL 3 秘鲁PE 4 瑞士CH 5 巴PK 6 澳AU 9 韩国KR,亚太AP	0 受惠国LD	30	---Automatic bobbin winders
6428	8445.4090	---其他	10	0 冰岛IS,东盟AS,哥CR,新西兰NZ,智利CL 3 秘鲁PE 4 瑞士CH 5 巴PK 6 澳AU 8.6 韩国KR 9 亚太AP	0 受惠国LD	30	---Other
		-其他：					-Other:
6429	8445.9010	---整经机	10	0 冰岛IS,东盟AS,哥CR,秘鲁PE,新西兰NZ,智利CL 5 巴PK 6 澳AU 8 韩国KR 9 亚太AP	0 受惠国LD	30	---Warping machines

序号 No.	税则号列 Tariff Line	中文货品名称 Article Description in Chinese	最惠国税率 MFN(%)	协定税率 Agreement(%)	特惠税率 SP(%)	普通税率 Gen(%)	英文货品名称 Article Description
6430	8445.9020	---浆纱机	10	0 冰岛IS,东盟AS,哥CR,秘鲁PE,新西兰NZ,智利CL 5 巴PK 6 澳AU 8 韩国KR 9 亚太AP	0 受惠国LD	30	---Sizing machines
6431	8445.9090	---其他	10	0 冰岛IS,东盟AS,哥CR,秘鲁PE,新西兰NZ,智利CL 5 巴PK 6 澳AU 7 瑞士CH 8.6 韩国KR 9 亚太AP	0 受惠国LD	30	---Other
	84.46	**织机:**					**Weaving machines (looms) :**
6432	8446.1000	-所织织物宽度不超过30厘米的织机	8	0 冰岛IS,东盟AS,哥CR,秘鲁PE,新西兰NZ,智利CL 4.8 澳AU 5 巴PK 5.6 瑞士CH 6.4 韩国KR 7.2 亚太AP	0 受惠国$_1$LD$_1$	30	-For weaving fabrics of a width not exceeding 30cm
		-所织织物宽度超过30厘米的梭织机:					-For weaving fabrics of a width exceeding 30cm, shuttle type:
		--动力织机:					--Power looms:
6433	8446.2110	---地毯织机	12	0 冰岛IS,东盟AS,哥CR,新加坡SG,新西兰NZ,智利CL 3.6 秘鲁PE 5 巴PK 7.2 澳AU 8.4 瑞士CH 9.6 韩国KR 10.8 亚太AP	0 受惠国$_1$LD$_1$	35	---For making carpets or rugs
6434	8446.2190	---其他	10	0 冰岛IS,东盟AS,哥CR,新加坡SG,新西兰NZ,智利CL 3 秘鲁PE 5 巴PK 6 澳AU 8 韩国KR 9 亚太AP	0 受惠国$_1$LD$_1$	30	---Other
6435	8446.2900	--其他	10	0 冰岛IS,东盟AS,哥CR,新西兰NZ,智利CL 3 秘鲁PE 4 瑞士CH 5 巴PK 6 澳AU 8 韩国KR	0 受惠国$_1$LD$_1$	30	--Other
		-所织织物宽度超过30厘米的无梭织机:					-For weaving fabrics of a width exceeding 30cm, shuttleless type:
6436	8446.3020	---剑杆织机	8	0 冰岛IS,东盟AS,哥CR,秘鲁PE,新西兰NZ,智利CL 4.8 澳AU 5 巴PK 5.6 瑞士CH 6.4 韩国KR 6.8 亚太AP	0 受惠国$_1$LD$_1$	30	---Rapier looms

序号 No.	税则号列 Tariff Line	中文货品名称 Article Description in Chinese	最惠国税率 MFN(%)	协定税率 Agreement(%)	特惠税率 SP(%)	普通税率 Gen(%)	英文货品名称 Article Description
6437	8446.3030	---片梭织机	8	0 冰岛IS,东盟AS,哥CR,秘鲁PE,新西兰NZ,智利CL 4.8 澳AU,韩国KR 5 巴PK 5.6 亚太AP	0 受惠国$_1$LD$_1$	30	---Carrier looms
6438	8446.3040	---喷水织机	8	0 冰岛IS,东盟AS,哥CR,秘鲁PE,台湾TW,新西兰NZ,智利CL 3.2 瑞士CH 4.8 澳AU,韩国KR 5 巴PK 6.8 亚太AP	0 受惠国$_1$LD$_1$	30	---Water jet looms
6439	8446.3050	---喷气织机	8Δ3	0 冰岛IS,东盟AS,哥CR,秘鲁PE,新西兰NZ,智利CL 3.2 瑞士CH 4.8 澳AU 5 巴PK 6.8 亚太AP 6.9 韩国KR	0 受惠国$_1$LD$_1$	30	---Air jet looms
6440	8446.3090	---其他	8	0 冰岛IS,东盟AS,哥CR,秘鲁PE,新西兰NZ,智利CL 3.2 瑞士CH 4.8 澳AU,韩国KR 5 巴PK 6.8 亚太AP	0 受惠国$_1$LD$_1$	30	---Other
	84.47	**针织机、缝编机及制粗松螺旋花线、网眼薄纱、花边、刺绣品、装饰带、编织带或网的机器及簇绒机:**					**Knitting machines, stitch-bonding machines and machines for making gimped yarn, tulle, lace, embroidery, trimmings, braid or net and machines for tufting:**
		-圆型针织机:					-Circular knitting machines:
6441	8447.1100	--圆筒直径不超过165毫米	8	0 冰岛IS,东盟AS,哥CR,秘鲁PE,台湾TW,新西兰NZ,智利CL 3.2 瑞士CH 4.8 澳AU,韩国KR 5 巴PK 7 亚太AP	0 受惠国LD	30	--With cylinder diameter not exceeding 165mm
6442	8447.1200	--圆筒直径超过165毫米	8	0 冰岛IS,东盟AS,哥CR,秘鲁PE,台湾TW,新西兰NZ,智利CL 3.2 瑞士CH 4.8 澳AU,韩国KR 5 巴PK	0 受惠国LD	30	--With cylinder diameter exceeding 165mm
		-平型针织机;缝编机:					-Flat knitting machines; stitch-bonding machines:
		---经编机:					---Warp knitting machines:
6443	8447.2011	----特里科经编机	8	0 冰岛IS,东盟AS,哥CR,秘鲁PE,新西兰NZ,智利CL 3.2 瑞士CH 4.8 澳AU,韩国KR 5 巴PK 6.8 亚太AP	0 受惠国LD	30	----Tricot warp knitting machines
6444	8447.2012	----拉舍尔经编机	8	0 冰岛IS,东盟AS,哥CR,秘鲁PE,新西兰NZ,智利CL 3.2 瑞士CH 4.8 澳AU 5 巴PK 6.4 韩国KR 6.8 亚太AP	0 受惠国LD	30	----Raschel warp knitting machine

序号 No.	税则号列 Tariff Line	中文货品名称 Article Description in Chinese	最惠国税率 MFN(%)	协定税率 Agreement(%)	特惠税率 SP(%)	普通税率 Gen(%)	英文货品名称 Article Description
6445	8447.2019	----其他	8	0 冰岛IS,东盟AS,哥CR,秘鲁PE,新西兰NZ,智利CL 3.2 瑞士CH 4.8 澳AU 5 巴PK 6.4 韩国KR 6.8 亚太AP	0 受惠国LD	30	----Other
6446	8447.2020	---平型纬编机	8	0 冰岛IS,东盟AS,哥CR,秘鲁PE,台湾TW,新西兰NZ,智利CL 4.8 澳AU,韩国KR 5 巴PK 5.6 瑞士CH 6.8 亚太AP	0 受惠国LD	30	---Flat weft knitting machines
6447	8447.2030	---缝编机	8	0 冰岛IS,东盟AS,哥CR,秘鲁PE,新西兰NZ,智利CL 3.2 瑞士CH 4.8 澳AU,韩国KR 5 巴PK 6.8 亚太AP	0 受惠国LD	30	---Stitch-bonding machines
		-其他:					-Other:
		---簇绒机:					---Tufting machines:
6448	8447.9011	----地毯织机	7	0 巴PK,冰岛IS,东盟AS,哥CR,秘鲁PE,新西兰NZ,智利CL 2.8 瑞士CH 4.2 澳AU,韩国KR 4.9 亚太AP	0 受惠国LD	35	----For making carpets or rugs
6449	8447.9019	----其他	8	0 冰岛IS,东盟AS,哥CR,秘鲁PE,新西兰NZ,智利CL 3.2 瑞士CH 4.8 澳AU,韩国KR 5 巴PK 5.6 亚太AP	0 受惠国LD	30	----Other
6450	8447.9020	---绣花机	8	0 冰岛IS,东盟AS,哥CR,秘鲁PE,新西兰NZ,智利CL 4.8 澳AU 5 巴PK 6.4 韩国KR 6.8 亚太AP	0 受惠国LD	30	---Embroidery machines
6451	8447.9090	---其他	10	0 冰岛IS,东盟AS,哥CR,秘鲁PE,新西兰NZ,智利CL 5 巴PK,亚太AP 6 澳AU 8 韩国KR	0 受惠国LD	30	---Other
	84.48	**税号84.44、84.45、84.46或84.47所列机器的辅助机器(例如,多臂机、提花机、自停装置及换梭装置);专用于或主要用于税号84.44、84.45、84.46或84.47所列机器的零件、附件(例如,锭子、锭壳、钢丝针布、梳、喷丝头、梭子、综丝、综框、针织机用针):**					**Auxiliary machinery for use with machines of heading 8444, 8445, 8446 or 8447 (for example, dobbies, jacquards, automatic stop motions, shuttle changing mechanisms) ; parts and accessories suitable for use solely or principally with the machines of this heading or of heading 8444, 8445, 8446 or 8447 (for example, spindles and spindle flyers, card clothing, combs, extruding nipples, shuttles, healds and heald-frames, hosiery needles) :**

序号 No.	税则号列 Tariff Line	中文货品名称 Article Description in Chinese	最惠国税率 MFN(%)	协定税率 Agreement(%)	特惠税率 SP(%)	普通税率 Gen(%)	英文货品名称 Article Description
		-税号84.44、84.45、84.46或84.47所列机器的辅助机器：					-Auxiliary machinery for machines of heading 8444, 8445, 8446 or 8447:
6452	8448.1100	--多臂机或提花机及其所用的卡片缩小、复制、穿孔或汇编机器	8	0 冰岛IS,东盟AS,哥CR,秘鲁PE,新西兰NZ,智利CL 3.2 瑞士CH 4.8 澳AU 5 巴PK 6.4 韩国KR	0 受惠国LD	20	--Dobbies and Jacquards; card reducing, copying, punching or assembling machines for use therewith
	ex84481100	多臂机或提花机转速指标：500转/分以上	Δ4				Dobbies or Jacquards, rotational speed >500r/min
6453	8448.1900	--其他	8	0 冰岛IS,东盟AS,哥CR,秘鲁PE,新西兰NZ,智利CL 4.8 澳AU 5 巴PK 5.6 瑞士CH 6.4 韩国KR	0 受惠国LD	20	--Other
		-税号84.44所列机器及其辅助机器的零件、附件：					-Parts and accessories of machines of heading 8444 or of their auxiliary machinery:
6454	8448.2020	---喷丝头或喷丝板	6	0 冰岛IS,东盟AS,哥CR,秘鲁PE,新西兰NZ,智利CL 3.6 澳AU 4.2 瑞士CH 4.8 韩国KR 5 巴PK	0 受惠国LD	14	---Extruding nipples or spinnerets
6455	8448.2090	---其他	6	0 冰岛IS,东盟AS,哥CR,秘鲁PE,新西兰NZ,智利CL 3.6 澳AU 4.2 瑞士CH 5 巴PK 5.2 韩国KR	0 受惠国LD	17	---Other
		-税号84.45所列机器及其辅助机器的零件、附件：					-Parts and accessories of machines of heading 8445 or of their auxiliary machinery:
6456	8448.3100	--钢丝针布	6	0 冰岛IS,东盟AS,哥CR,秘鲁PE,新西兰NZ,智利CL 3.6 澳AU 4.8 韩国KR,瑞士CH 5 巴PK	0 受惠国LD	17	--Card clothing
6457	8448.3200	--纺织纤维预处理机器的零件、附件，但钢丝针布除外	6	0 冰岛IS,东盟AS,哥CR,秘鲁PE,新西兰NZ,智利CL 3.6 澳AU 4.2 瑞士CH 5 巴PK 5.2 韩国KR	0 受惠国LD	17	--Of machines for preparing textile fibres, other than card clothing
		--锭子、锭壳、纺丝环、钢丝圈：					--Spindles, spindle flyers, spinning rings and ring travellers:
6458	8448.3310	---络筒锭	6	0 冰岛IS,东盟AS,哥CR,秘鲁PE,新西兰NZ,智利CL 2.4 瑞士CH 3.6 澳AU,韩国KR 5 巴PK	0 受惠国LD	17	---Winding spindle

序号 No.	税则号列 Tariff Line	中文货品名称 Article Description in Chinese	最惠国税率 MFN(%)	协定税率 Agreement(%)	特惠税率 SP(%)	普通税率 Gen(%)	英文货品名称 Article Description
6459	8448.3390	---其他	6	0 冰岛IS,东盟AS,哥CR,秘鲁PE,新西兰NZ,智利CL 3.6 澳AU 4.2 瑞士CH 4.8 韩国KR 5 巴PK	0 受惠国LD	17	---Other
		--其他:					--Other:
6460	8448.3910	---气流杯	6	0 冰岛IS,东盟AS,哥CR,秘鲁PE,新西兰NZ,智利CL 2.4 瑞士CH 3.6 澳AU,韩国KR 5 巴PK	0 受惠国LD	14	---Open-end rotors
6461	8448.3920	---电子清纱器	6Δ3	0 冰岛IS,东盟AS,哥CR,秘鲁PE,新西兰NZ,智利CL 3.6 澳AU,韩国KR 4.8 瑞士CH 5 巴PK	0 受惠国LD	17	---Electronic yarn clearers
6462	8448.3930	---空气捻接器	6Δ3	0 冰岛IS,东盟AS,哥CR,秘鲁PE,新西兰NZ,智利CL 2.4 瑞士CH 3.6 澳AU,韩国KR 5 巴PK	0 受惠国LD	17	---Air twisting devices
6463	8448.3940	---环锭细纱机紧密纺装置	6	0 冰岛IS,东盟AS,哥CR,韩国KR,秘鲁PE,新西兰NZ,智利CL 3.6 澳AU 4.3 瑞士CH 5 巴PK	0 受惠国LD	17	---Compact set of ring spinning frames
6464	8448.3990	---其他	6Δ3	0 冰岛IS,东盟AS,哥CR,秘鲁PE,新西兰NZ,智利CL 3.6 澳AU 4.8 瑞士CH 5 巴PK 5.2 韩国KR	0 受惠国LD	17	---Other
		-织机及其辅助机器的零件、附件:					-Parts and accessories of weaving machines (looms) or of their auxiliary machinery:
6465	8448.4200	--织机用筘、综丝及综框	6	0 冰岛IS,东盟AS,哥CR,秘鲁PE,新西兰NZ,智利CL 3.6 澳AU 4.2 瑞士CH 5 巴PK 5.2 韩国KR	0 受惠国LD	50	--Reeds for looms, healds and heald frames
		--其他:					--Other:
6466	8448.4910	---接、投梭箱	6	0 冰岛IS,东盟AS,哥CR,秘鲁PE,新西兰NZ,智利CL 3.6 澳AU,韩国KR 4.2 瑞士CH 5 巴PK	0 受惠国LD	17	---Catching and throwing shuttle boxes
6467	8448.4920	---引纬、送经装置	6Δ3	0 冰岛IS,东盟AS,哥CR,秘鲁PE,新西兰NZ,智利CL 3.6 澳AU 4.2 瑞士CH 4.8 韩国KR 5 巴PK	0 受惠国LD	17	---Weft insertion and let-off motions

序号 No.	税则号列 Tariff Line	中文货品名称 Article Description in Chinese	最惠国税率 MFN(%)	协定税率 Agreement(%)	特惠税率 SP(%)	普通税率 Gen(%)	英文货品名称 Article Description
6468	8448.4930	---梭子	6	0 冰岛IS,东盟AS,哥CR,秘鲁PE,新西兰NZ,智利CL 2.4 瑞士CH 3.6 澳AU,韩国KR 5 巴PK	0 受惠国LD	50	---Shuttles
6469	8448.4990	---其他	6Δ3	0 冰岛IS,东盟AS,哥CR,秘鲁PE,新西兰NZ,智利CL 3.6 澳AU 4.2 瑞士CH 5 巴PK 5.2 韩国KR	0 受惠国LD	17	---Other
		-税号84.47所列机器及其辅助机器的零件、附件:					-Parts and accessories of machines of heading 8447 or of their auxiliary machinery:
		--沉降片、织针及其他成圈机件:					--Sinkers, needles and other articles used in forming stitches:
6470	8448.5120	---针织机用28号以下的弹簧针、钩针及复合针	6	0 冰岛IS,东盟AS,哥CR,秘鲁PE,新西兰NZ,智利CL 2.4 瑞士CH 3.6 澳AU 4.8 韩国KR 5 巴PK	0 受惠国LD	50	---Barbered needles, crotchet hooks and complex needles for knitting machines, smaler than gauge No.28
6471	8448.5190	---其他	6	0 冰岛IS,东盟AS,哥CR,秘鲁PE,新西兰NZ,智利CL 2.4 瑞士CH 3.6 澳AU 5 巴PK 5.2 韩国KR	0 受惠国LD	17	---Other
6472	8448.5900	--其他	6Δ3	0 冰岛IS,东盟AS,哥CR,韩国KR,秘鲁PE,台湾TW,香港HK,新西兰NZ,智利CL 3.6 澳AU 4.2 瑞士CH 5 巴PK	0 受惠国LD	17	--Other
	84.49	**成匹、成形的毡呢或无纺织物制造或整理机器,包括制毡呢帽机器;帽模:**					**Machinery for the manufacture or finishing of felt or nonwovens in the piece or in shapes, including machinery for making felt hats; blocks for making hats:**
6473	8449.0010	---针刺机	8	0 冰岛IS,东盟AS,哥CR,秘鲁PE,新西兰NZ,智利CL 3.2 瑞士CH 4.8 澳AU 5 巴PK 6.4 韩国KR	0 受惠国$_1$LD$_1$	30	---Needle punching machine
	ex84490010	高速针刺机,针刺频率＞2000次/分钟	Δ6				High speed needle punching machine, punching frequecny＞2000bis/min
6474	8449.0020	---水刺设备	8	0 冰岛IS,东盟AS,哥CR,秘鲁PE,新西兰NZ,智利CL 3.2 瑞士CH 4.8 澳AU,韩国KR 5 巴PK	0 受惠国$_1$LD$_1$	30	---Spunlace equipment
	ex84490020	高速宽幅水刺设备,工作幅宽＞3.5米,工作速度＞250米/分钟,水刺压力≥400帕	Δ6				High speed width spunlace equipment, working width＞3.5m, workding speed＞250m/min,spunlace pressure≥400Pa

序号 No.	税则号列 Tariff Line	中文货品名称 Article Description in Chinese	最惠国税率 MFN(%)	协定税率 Agreement(%)	特惠税率 SP(%)	普通税率 Gen(%)	英文货品名称 Article Description
6475	8449.0090	---其他	8	0 冰岛IS,东盟AS,哥CR,秘鲁PE,新西兰NZ,智利CL 3.2 瑞士CH 4.8 澳AU 5 巴PK 6.9 韩国KR	0 受惠国$_1$LD$_1$	30	---Other
	84.50	家用型或洗衣房用洗衣机,包括洗涤干燥两用机:					**Household or laundry-type washing machines, including machines which both wash and dry:**
		-干衣量不超过10公斤的洗衣机:					-Machines, each of a dry linen capacity not exceeding 10kg:
		--全自动的:					--Fully-automatic machines:
6476	8450.1110	---波轮式	10	0 冰岛IS,东盟AS,哥CR,秘鲁PE,新加坡SG,新西兰NZ,智利CL 4 瑞士CH 5 巴PK 6 澳AU 8 韩国KR 8.7 亚太AP	0 受惠国LD	130	---Of the continuously rotating impeller
6477	8450.1120	---滚筒式	10	0 冰岛IS,东盟AS,哥CR,秘鲁PE,新加坡SG,新西兰NZ,智利CL 4 瑞士CH 5 巴PK 6 澳AU 8.6 韩国KR 8.7 亚太AP	0 受惠国LD	130	---Of the drum type
6478	8450.1190	---其他	10	0 冰岛IS,东盟AS,哥CR,秘鲁PE,新加坡SG,新西兰NZ,智利CL 4 瑞士CH 5 巴PK 6 澳AU 8.7 亚太AP	0 受惠国LD	130	---Other
6479	8450.1200	--其他机器,装有离心甩干机	30	0 冰岛IS,东盟AS,哥CR,新加坡SG,新西兰NZ,智利CL 9 秘鲁PE 18 澳AU 21.6 瑞士CH 24.9 巴PK,亚太AP	0 受惠国$_1$LD$_1$	130	--Other machines, with built-in centrifugal drier
6480	8450.1900	--其他	30	0 冰岛IS,东盟AS,哥CR,新加坡SG,新西兰NZ,智利CL 9 秘鲁PE 18 澳AU 21.6 瑞士CH	0 受惠国$_1$LD$_1$	130	--Other
		-干衣量超过10公斤的洗衣机:					-Machines, each of a dry linen capacity exceeding 10kg:
		---全自动的:					---Fully-automatic machines:
6481	8450.2011	----波轮式	10	0 冰岛IS,东盟AS,哥CR,秘鲁PE,新西兰NZ,智利CL 4 瑞士CH 5 巴PK 6 澳AU	0 受惠国LD	80	----Of the continuously rotating impeller
6482	8450.2012	----滚筒式	10	0 冰岛IS,东盟AS,哥CR,秘鲁PE,新西兰NZ,智利CL 4 瑞士CH 5 巴PK 6 澳AU	0 受惠国LD	80	----Of the drum type

序号 No.	税则号列 Tariff Line	中文货品名称 Article Description in Chinese	最惠国税率 MFN(%)	协定税率 Agreement(%)	特惠税率 SP(%)	普通税率 Gen(%)	英文货品名称 Article Description
6483	8450.2019	----其他	10	0 冰岛IS,东盟AS,哥CR,秘鲁PE,新西兰NZ,智利CL 4 瑞士CH 5 巴PK 6 澳AU	0 受惠国LD	80	----Other
6484	8450.2090	---其他	10	0 冰岛IS,东盟AS,哥CR,秘鲁PE,新西兰NZ,智利CL 4 瑞士CH 5 巴PK 6 澳AU	0 受惠国LD	80	---Other
		-零件:					-Parts:
6485	8450.9010	---干衣量不超过10公斤的洗衣机用	5	0 澳AU,巴PK,冰岛IS,东盟AS,哥CR,秘鲁PE,瑞士CH,新西兰NZ,智利CL 4.2 亚太AP 4.3 韩国KR	0 受惠国LD	130	---Of machines, each of a dry linen capacity not exceeding 10kg
6486	8450.9090	---其他	16∆5	0 冰岛IS,东盟AS,哥CR,新加坡SG,新西兰NZ,智利CL 4.8 秘鲁PE 9.6 澳AU 11.2 瑞士CH 12.8 巴PK,韩国KR 14.4 亚太AP	0 受惠国$_1$LD$_1$	80	---Other
	84.51	**纱线、织物及纺织制品的洗涤、清洁、绞拧、干燥、熨烫、挤压(包括熔压)、漂白、染色、上浆、整理、涂布或浸渍机器(税号84.50的机器除外);列诺伦(亚麻油地毡)及类似铺地制品的布基或其他底布的浆料涂布机器;纺织物的卷绕、退绕、折叠、剪切或剪齿边机器:**					**Machinery (other than machines of heading 8450) for washing, cleaning, wringing, drying, ironing, pressing (including fusing presses) , bleaching, dyeing, dressing, finishing, coating or impregnating textile yarns, fabrics or made-up textile articles and machines for applying the paste to the base fabric or other support used in the manufacture of floor coverings such as linoleum; machines for reeling, unreeling, folding, cutting or pinking textile fabrics:**
6487	8451.1000	-干洗机	21	0 冰岛IS,东盟AS,哥CR,新加坡SG,新西兰NZ,智利CL 6.3 秘鲁PE 12.6 澳AU 14.7 瑞士CH 16 巴PK,亚太AP 18.2 韩国KR	0 受惠国$_1$LD$_1$	80	-Dry-cleaning machines
		-干燥机:					-Drying machines:
6488	8451.2100	--干衣量不超过10公斤	15	0 冰岛IS,东盟AS,哥CR,新加坡SG,新西兰NZ,智利CL 4.5 秘鲁PE 7.5 巴PK 9 澳AU 10.5 瑞士CH 12 韩国KR 13.5 亚太AP	0 受惠国$_1$LD$_1$	80	--Each of a dry linen capacity not exceeding 10kg

序号 No.	税则号列 Tariff Line	中文货品名称 Article Description in Chinese	最惠国税率 MFN(%)	协定税率 Agreement(%)	特惠税率 SP(%)	普通税率 Gen(%)	英文货品名称 Article Description
6489	8451.2900	--其他	8	0 冰岛IS,东盟AS,哥CR,秘鲁PE,新西兰NZ,智利CL 3.2 瑞士CH 4.8 澳AU 5 巴PK 6.4 韩国KR 7.2 亚太AP	0 受惠国LD	30	--Other
6490	8451.3000	-熨烫机及挤压机（包括熔压机）	8	0 冰岛IS,东盟AS,哥CR,秘鲁PE,新加坡SG,新西兰NZ,智利CL 3.2 瑞士CH 4.8 澳AU 5 巴PK 6.4 韩国KR 7.2 亚太AP	0 受惠国LD	30	-Ironing machines and presses (including fusing presses)
6491	8451.4000	-洗涤、漂白或染色机器	8.4	0 澳门MO,冰岛IS,东盟AS,哥CR,秘鲁PE,台湾TW,香港HK,新西兰NZ,智利CL 3.36 瑞士CH 5 澳AU,巴PK,韩国KR 7 亚太AP	0 受惠国LD	20	-Washing, bleaching or dyeing machines
6492	8451.5000	-纺织物的卷绕、退绕、折叠、剪切或剪齿边机器	8	0 冰岛IS,东盟AS,哥CR,秘鲁PE,台湾TW,新西兰NZ,智利CL 3.2 瑞士CH 4.8 澳AU,韩国KR 5 巴PK 7.2 亚太AP	0 受惠国LD	20	-Machines for reeling, unreeling, folding, cutting or pinking textile fabrics
6493	8451.8000	-其他机器	12	0 冰岛IS,东盟AS,哥CR,台湾TW,香港HK,新加坡SG,新西兰NZ,智利CL 3.6 秘鲁PE 5 巴PK 7.2 澳AU 10.8 韩国KR,亚太AP	0 受惠国LD	30	-Other machinery
	ex84518000	涂层机	Δ8				Coating machine
	ex84518000	柔软整理机	Δ10				Supple finishing machine
	ex84518000	磨毛机、丝光机	Δ10				Napping grinder, mercerizing range
	ex84518000	定型机	Δ10				Boarding machine
	ex84518000	罐蒸机、精炼机	Δ10				Potting steamer, refining machine
	ex84518000	剪绒、洗缩联合机	Δ10				Pile shearing and shrinking combine
	ex84518000	预缩机	Δ10				Sanforizer
	ex84518000	服装液氨整理机	Δ10				Dress aqua ammoniae finishing range
	ex84518000	服装定型焙烘炉	Δ10				Dress shaping cabinet
	ex84518000	剪毛联合机	Δ10				Sheepshearing combination machine
6494	8451.9000	-零件	8	0 冰岛IS,东盟AS,哥CR,秘鲁PE,新西兰NZ,智利CL 3.2 瑞士CH 4.8 澳AU 5 巴PK 6.4 韩国KR 7.2 亚太AP	0 受惠国LD	20	-Parts

序号 No.	税则号列 Tariff Line	中文货品名称 Article Description in Chinese	最惠国税率 MFN(%)	协定税率 Agreement(%)	特惠税率 SP(%)	普通税率 Gen(%)	英文货品名称 Article Description
	84.52	**缝纫机,但税号84.40的锁线订书机除外;缝纫机专用的特制家具、底座及罩盖;缝纫机针:**					**Sewing machines, other than book-sewing machines of heading 8440; furniture, bases and covers specially designed for sewing machines; sewing machine needles:**
		-家用型缝纫机:					-Sewing machines of the household type:
6495	8452.1010	---多功能型	21	0 冰岛IS,东盟AS,哥CR,新加坡SG,新西兰NZ,智利CL 6.3 秘鲁PE 12.6 澳AU 14.7 瑞士CH 16.8 巴PK 17 亚太AP 18.2 韩国KR	0 受惠国$_1$LD$_1$	80	---Multifunctional
		---其他:					---Other:
6496	8452.1091	----手动式	21	0 冰岛IS,东盟AS,哥CR,新加坡SG,新西兰NZ,智利CL 6.3 秘鲁PE 12.6 澳AU 14.7 瑞士CH 16.8 巴PK 17 亚太AP 18.2 韩国KR	0 受惠国$_1$LD$_1$	80	----Hand-operated
6497	8452.1099	----其他	21	0 冰岛IS,东盟AS,哥CR,新加坡SG,新西兰NZ,智利CL 6.3 秘鲁PE 12.6 澳AU 14.7 瑞士CH 16.8 巴PK 17 亚太AP 18.2 韩国KR	0 受惠国$_1$LD$_1$	80	----Other
		-其他缝纫机:					-Other sewing machines:
		--自动的:					--Automatic units:
6498	8452.2110	---平缝机	12	0 冰岛IS,东盟AS,哥CR,秘鲁PE,新加坡SG,新西兰NZ,智利CL 5 巴PK 7.2 澳AU 8.4 瑞士CH 9.6 韩国KR 10.7 亚太AP	0 受惠国LD	40	---Flatseam
6499	8452.2120	---包缝机	12	0 冰岛IS,东盟AS,哥CR,秘鲁PE,台湾TW,新加坡SG,新西兰NZ,智利CL 5 巴PK 7.2 澳AU 8.4 瑞士CH 9.6 韩国KR 10.7 亚太AP	0 受惠国LD	40	---Overlock stitch
6500	8452.2130	---绷缝机	12	0 冰岛IS,东盟AS,哥CR,秘鲁PE,台湾TW,新加坡SG,新西兰NZ,智利CL 5 巴PK 7.2 澳AU 8.4 瑞士CH 9.6 韩国KR 10.7 亚太AP	0 受惠国LD	40	---Covering stitch

序号 No.	税则号列 Tariff Line	中文货品名称 Article Description in Chinese	最惠国税率 MFN(%)	协定税率 Agreement(%)	特惠税率 SP(%)	普通税率 Gen(%)	英文货品名称 Article Description
6501	8452.2190	---其他	12	0 冰岛IS,东盟AS,哥CR,秘鲁PE,台湾TW,新加坡SG,新西兰NZ,智利CL 5 巴PK 7.2 澳AU 8.4 瑞士CH 9.6 韩国KR 10.7 亚太AP	0 受惠国LD	40	---Other
6502	8452.2900	--其他	12	0 冰岛IS,东盟AS,哥CR,秘鲁PE,香港HK,新加坡SG,新西兰NZ,智利CL 5 巴PK 7.2 澳AU 8.4 瑞士CH 9.6 韩国KR 10.8 亚太AP	0 受惠国LD	40	--Other
6503	8452.3000	-缝纫机针	14	0 冰岛IS,东盟AS,哥CR,秘鲁PE,新加坡SG,新西兰NZ,智利CL 7 巴PK 8.4 澳AU 9.8 瑞士CH 11.2 韩国KR 12.6 亚太AP	0 受惠国$_1$LD$_1$	100	-Sewing machine needles
		-缝纫机专用的特制家具、底座和罩盖及其零件；缝纫机的其他零件：					-Furniture, bases and covers for sewing machines and parts thereof; other parts of sewing machines:
		---家用型缝纫机用：					---Of sewing machines of the household type:
6504	8452.9011	----旋梭	14	0 冰岛IS,东盟AS,哥CR,秘鲁PE,新加坡SG,新西兰NZ,智利CL 7 巴PK 8.4 澳AU 9.8 瑞士CH,亚太AP 11.2 韩国KR	0 受惠国$_1$LD$_1$	80	----Rotating shuttles
6505	8452.9019	----其他	14	0 冰岛IS,东盟AS,哥CR,秘鲁PE,新加坡SG,新西兰NZ,智利CL 7 巴PK 8.4 澳AU 9.8 瑞士CH,亚太AP 11.2 韩国KR	0 受惠国$_1$LD$_1$	80	----Other
		---其他：					---Other:
6506	8452.9091	----旋梭	14	0 冰岛IS,东盟AS,哥CR,秘鲁PE,新加坡SG,新西兰NZ,智利CL 7 巴PK 8.4 澳AU 9.8 瑞士CH,亚太AP 11.2 韩国KR	0 受惠国LD	80	----Rotating shuttles
6507	8452.9092	----缝纫机专用的特制家具、底座和罩盖及其零件	14	0 冰岛IS,东盟AS,哥CR,秘鲁PE,新加坡SG,新西兰NZ,智利CL 8.4 澳AU 9.8 瑞士CH 11.2 巴PK,韩国KR	0 受惠国$_1$LD$_1$	100	----Furniture, bases and covers for sewing machines and parts thereof

序号 No.	税则号列 Tariff Line	中文货品名称 Article Description in Chinese	最惠国税率 MFN(%)	协定税率 Agreement(%)	特惠税率 SP(%)	普通税率 Gen(%)	英文货品名称 Article Description
6508	8452.9099	----其他	14	0 冰岛IS,东盟AS,哥CR,秘鲁PE,台湾TW,新加坡SG,新西兰NZ,智利CL 7 巴PK 8.4 澳AU 9.8 瑞士CH,亚太AP 11.2 韩国KR	0 受惠国LD	80	----Other
	84.53	**生皮、皮革的处理、鞣制或加工机器,鞋靴、毛皮及其他皮革制品的制作或修理机器,但缝纫机除外:**					**Machinery for preparing, tanning or working hides, skins or leather or for making or repairing footwear or other articles of hides, skins or leather, other than sewing machines:**
6509	8453.1000	-生皮、皮革的处理、鞣制或加工机器	8.4	0 冰岛IS,东盟AS,哥CR,秘鲁PE,新西兰NZ,智利CL 3.36 瑞士CH 5 澳AU,巴PK 6.7 韩国KR 8 亚太AP	0 受惠国$_1$LD$_1$	30	-Machinery for preparing, tanning or working hides, skins or leather
6510	8453.2000	-鞋靴制作或修理机器	8.4	0 冰岛IS,东盟AS,哥CR,秘鲁PE,新西兰NZ,智利CL 3.36 瑞士CH 5 澳AU,巴PK 6.7 韩国KR 8 亚太AP	0 受惠国$_1$LD$_1$	30	-Machinery for making or repairing footwear
6511	8453.8000	-其他机器	8.4	0 冰岛IS,东盟AS,哥CR,秘鲁PE,新西兰NZ,智利CL 3.36 瑞士CH 5 澳AU,巴PK 6.7 韩国KR	0 受惠国$_1$LD$_1$	30	-Other machinery
6512	8453.9000	-零件	8	0 冰岛IS,东盟AS,哥CR,秘鲁PE,新西兰NZ,智利CL 3.2 瑞士CH 4.8 澳AU 5 巴PK 6.4 韩国KR	0 受惠国$_1$LD$_1$	30	-Parts
	84.54	**金属冶炼及铸造用的转炉、浇包、锭模及铸造机:**					**Converters, ladles, ingot moulds and casting machines, of a kind used in metallurgy or in metal foundries:**
6513	8454.1000	-转炉	8.4	0 冰岛IS,东盟AS,哥CR,秘鲁PE,新西兰NZ,智利CL 3.36 瑞士CH 5 澳AU,巴PK,韩国KR	0 受惠国LD	35	-Converters
		-锭模及浇包:					-Ingot moulds and ladles:
6514	8454.2010	---炉外精炼设备	8.4	0 冰岛IS,东盟AS,哥CR,秘鲁PE,新西兰NZ,智利CL 3.36 瑞士CH 5 澳AU,巴PK,韩国KR	0 受惠国LD	35	---Fining equipments, outside of converters
6515	8454.2090	---其他	8.4	0 冰岛IS,东盟AS,哥CR,秘鲁PE,新西兰NZ,智利CL 5 澳AU,巴PK 6.7 韩国KR	0 受惠国LD	35	---Other
		-铸造机:					-Casting machines:

序号 No.	税则号列 Tariff Line	中文货品名称 Article Description in Chinese	最惠国税率 MFN(%)	协定税率 Agreement(%)	特惠税率 SP(%)	普通税率 Gen(%)	英文货品名称 Article Description
6516	8454.3010	---冷室压铸机	12	0 冰岛IS,东盟AS,哥CR,秘鲁PE,新加坡SG,新西兰NZ,智利CL 6 巴PK 7.2 澳AU 8.4 瑞士CH 9.6 韩国KR 11.4 亚太AP	0 受惠国LD	35	---Cold chamber die-casting machines
		---钢坯连铸机:					---Ingot continuous casting machines:
6517	8454.3021	----方坯连铸机	10	0 冰岛IS,东盟AS,哥CR,秘鲁PE,新西兰NZ,智利CL 5 巴PK 6 澳AU 7 瑞士CH 8 韩国KR 9.5 亚太AP	0 受惠国LD	35	----Ingot block
6518	8454.3022	----板坯连铸机	12	0 冰岛IS,东盟AS,哥CR,秘鲁PE,新加坡SG,新西兰NZ,智利CL 6 巴PK 7.2 澳AU 8.4 瑞士CH 9.6 韩国KR 11.4 亚太AP	0 受惠国LD	35	----Ingot slab
6519	8454.3029	----其他	12	0 冰岛IS,东盟AS,哥CR,秘鲁PE,新加坡SG,新西兰NZ,智利CL 6 巴PK 7.2 澳AU 8.4 瑞士CH 9.6 韩国KR 11.4 亚太AP	0 受惠国LD	35	----Other
6520	8454.3090	---其他	12	0 冰岛IS,东盟AS,哥CR,秘鲁PE,新加坡SG,新西兰NZ,智利CL 6 巴PK 7.2 澳AU 8.4 瑞士CH 10.8 韩国KR 11.4 亚太AP	0 受惠国LD	35	---Other
		-零件:					-Parts:
6521	8454.9010	---炉外精炼设备用	8	0 冰岛IS,东盟AS,哥CR,秘鲁PE,新西兰NZ,智利CL 3.2 瑞士CH 4.8 澳AU 5 巴PK 6.4 韩国KR	0 受惠国LD	20	---For the fining equipments outside of converters
		---钢坯连铸机用:					---For ingot continuous casting machines:
6522	8454.9021	----结晶器	8	0 冰岛IS,东盟AS,哥CR,秘鲁PE,新西兰NZ,智利CL 3.2 瑞士CH 4.8 澳AU,韩国KR 5 巴PK	0 受惠国LD	20	----Crystallizers
6523	8454.9022	----振动装置	8	0 冰岛IS,东盟AS,哥CR,秘鲁PE,新西兰NZ,智利CL 3.2 瑞士CH 4.8 澳AU,韩国KR 5 巴PK	0 受惠国LD	20	----Vibrating devices

序号 No.	税则号列 Tariff Line	中文货品名称 Article Description in Chinese	最惠国税率 MFN(%)	协定税率 Agreement(%)	特惠税率 SP(%)	普通税率 Gen(%)	英文货品名称 Article Description
6524	8454.9029	----其他	8	0 冰岛IS,东盟AS,哥CR,秘鲁PE,新西兰NZ,智利CL 4.8 澳AU 5 巴PK 5.6 瑞士CH 6.4 韩国KR	0 受惠国LD	20	----Other
6525	8454.9090	---其他	8	0 冰岛IS,东盟AS,哥CR,秘鲁PE,新西兰NZ,智利CL 4.8 澳AU,韩国KR 5 巴PK 5.6 瑞士CH	0 受惠国LD	20	---Other
	84.55	**金属轧机及其轧辊:**					**Metal-rolling mills and rolls therefor:**
		-轧管机:					-Tube mills:
6526	8455.1010	---热轧管机	12	0 冰岛IS,东盟AS,哥CR,秘鲁PE,新加坡SG,新西兰NZ,智利CL 5 巴PK 7.2 澳AU 8.4 瑞士CH,亚太AP 9.6 韩国KR	0 受惠国LD	35	---Tube mills, for hot-rolled
6527	8455.1020	---冷轧管机	12	0 冰岛IS,东盟AS,哥CR,秘鲁PE,新加坡SG,新西兰NZ,智利CL 5 巴PK 7.2 澳AU 8.4 瑞士CH,亚太AP 9.6 韩国KR	0 受惠国LD	35	---Tube mills for cold-rolled
6528	8455.1030	---定减径轧管机	12	0 冰岛IS,东盟AS,哥CR,秘鲁PE,新加坡SG,新西兰NZ,智利CL 5 巴PK 7.2 澳AU 8.4 瑞士CH,亚太AP 9.6 韩国KR	0 受惠国LD	35	---Fixed and reduced tube mills
6529	8455.1090	---其他	12	0 冰岛IS,东盟AS,哥CR,秘鲁PE,新加坡SG,新西兰NZ,智利CL 5 巴PK 7.2 澳AU 8.4 瑞士CH,亚太AP 9.6 韩国KR	0 受惠国LD	35	---Other
		-其他轧机:					-Other rolling mills:
		--热轧机或冷热联合轧机:					--Hot or combination hot and cold:
6530	8455.2110	---板材热轧机	15	0 冰岛IS,东盟AS,哥CR,新加坡SG,新西兰NZ,智利CL 4.5 秘鲁PE 7.5 巴PK 9 澳AU 10.5 瑞士CH,亚太AP 12 韩国KR	0 受惠国$_1$LD$_1$	35	---Sheet mills, hot-rolled
6531	8455.2120	---型钢轧机	15	0 冰岛IS,东盟AS,哥CR,新加坡SG,新西兰NZ,智利CL 4.5 秘鲁PE 7.5 巴PK 9 澳AU 10.5 瑞士CH,亚太AP 12 韩国KR	0 受惠国$_1$LD$_1$	35	---Rolled-steel section mills

序号 No.	税则号列 Tariff Line	中文货品名称 Article Description in Chinese	最惠国税率 MFN(%)	协定税率 Agreement(%)	特惠税率 SP(%)	普通税率 Gen(%)	英文货品名称 Article Description
6532	8455.2130	---线材轧机	15	0 冰岛IS,东盟AS,哥CR,新加坡SG,新西兰NZ,智利CL 4.5 秘鲁PE 7.5 巴PK 9 澳AU 10.5 瑞士CH,亚太AP 12 韩国KR	0 受惠国$_1$LD$_1$	35	---Wire mills
6533	8455.2190	---其他	15	0 冰岛IS,东盟AS,哥CR,新加坡SG,新西兰NZ,智利CL 4.5 秘鲁PE 7.5 巴PK 9 澳AU 10.5 瑞士CH,亚太AP 12 韩国KR	0 受惠国$_1$LD$_1$	35	---Other
		--冷轧机:					--Cold:
6534	8455.2210	---板材冷轧机	10	0 冰岛IS,东盟AS,哥CR,秘鲁PE,新西兰NZ,智利CL 4 瑞士CH 5 巴PK 6 澳AU 8 韩国KR	0 受惠国$_1$LD$_1$	35	---Sheet mills
6535	8455.2290	---其他	15	0 冰岛IS,东盟AS,哥CR,新加坡SG,新西兰NZ,智利CL 4.5 秘鲁PE 9 澳AU 10.5 瑞士CH 12 巴PK,韩国KR	0 受惠国$_1$LD$_1$	35	---Other
6536	8455.3000	-轧机用轧辊	8.4	0 冰岛IS,东盟AS,哥CR,秘鲁PE,新西兰NZ,智利CL 3.36 瑞士CH 5 澳AU,巴PK,韩国KR	0 受惠国LD	20	-Rolls for rolling mills
6537	8455.9000	-其他零件	8	0 巴PK,冰岛IS,东盟AS,哥CR,秘鲁PE,新西兰NZ,智利CL 3.2 瑞士CH 4 亚太AP 4.8 澳AU,韩国KR	0 受惠国LD	20	-Other parts
	84.56	**用激光、其他光、光子束、超声波、放电、电化学法、电子束、离子束或等离子弧处理各种材料的加工机床；水射流切割机：**					**Machine tools for working any material by removal of material, by laser or other light or photon beam, ultrasonic, electrodischarge, electrochemical, electron beam, ionic-beam or plasma arc processes; water-jet cutting machines:**
6538	8456.1000	-用激光、其他光或光子束处理的	0		0 受惠国LD	30	-Operated by laser or other light or photon beam processes
6539	8456.2000	-用超声波处理的	10	0 冰岛IS,东盟AS,哥CR,秘鲁PE,新加坡SG,新西兰NZ,智利CL 5 巴PK 6 澳AU	0 受惠国$_1$LD$_1$	30	-Operated by ultrasonic processes
		-用放电处理的:					-Operated by electrodischarge processes:
6540	8456.3010	---数控的	9.7	0 冰岛IS,东盟AS,哥CR,秘鲁PE,新西兰NZ,智利CL 5 巴PK 5.8 澳AU	0 受惠国$_1$LD$_1$	30	---Numerically controlled

序号 No.	税则号列 Tariff Line	中文货品名称 Article Description in Chinese	最惠国税率 MFN(%)	协定税率 Agreement(%)	特惠税率 SP(%)	普通税率 Gen(%)	英文货品名称 Article Description
6541	8456.3090	---其他	10	0 冰岛IS,东盟AS,哥CR,秘鲁PE,新加坡SG,新西兰NZ,智利CL 4 瑞士CH 5 巴PK 6 澳AU	0 受惠国$_1$LD$_1$	30	---Other
		-其他:					-Other:
6542	8456.9010	---等离子切割机	0		0 受惠国LD	30	---Cutting machines of plasma arc
6543	8456.9020	---水射流切割机	0		0 受惠国LD	30	---Water-jet cutting machines
6544	8456.9090	---其他	0		0 受惠国LD	30	---Other
	84.57	**加工金属的加工中心、单工位组合机床及多工位组合机床:**					**Machining centres, unit construction machines (single station) and multi-station transfer machines, for working metal:**
		-加工中心:					-Machining centres:
6545	8457.1010	---立式	9.7	0 冰岛IS,东盟AS,哥CR,秘鲁PE,新西兰NZ,智利CL 5 巴PK 5.8 澳AU 6.8 亚太AP 8.5 韩国KR	0 受惠国$_1$LD$_1$	20	---Vertical
6546	8457.1020	---卧式	9.7	0 冰岛IS,东盟AS,哥CR,秘鲁PE,新西兰NZ,智利CL 5 巴PK 5.8 澳AU 8.5 韩国KR 8.8 亚太AP	0 受惠国$_1$LD$_1$	20	---Horizontal
6547	8457.1030	---龙门式	9.7	0 冰岛IS,东盟AS,哥CR,秘鲁PE,新西兰NZ,智利CL 3.9 瑞士CH 5 巴PK 5.8 澳AU 6.8 亚太AP 8.5 韩国KR	0 受惠国$_1$LD$_1$	20	---Plano
		---其他:					---Other:
6548	8457.1091	----铣车复合	9.7	0 冰岛IS,东盟AS,哥CR,秘鲁PE,新西兰NZ,智利CL 5 巴PK 5.8 澳AU 6.8 亚太AP 8.5 韩国KR	0 受惠国$_1$LD$_1$	20	----Turning with milling
6549	8457.1099	----其他	9.7	0 冰岛IS,东盟AS,哥CR,秘鲁PE,新西兰NZ,智利CL 5 巴PK 5.8 澳AU 6.8 亚太AP 8.5 韩国KR	0 受惠国$_1$LD$_1$	20	----Other
6550	8457.2000	-单工位组合机床	8	0 冰岛IS,东盟AS,哥CR,秘鲁PE,新西兰NZ,智利CL 3.2 瑞士CH 4.8 澳AU 5 巴PK 7.2 韩国KR	0 受惠国$_1$LD$_1$	20	-Unit construction machines (single station)
6551	8457.3000	-多工位组合机床	5	0 澳AU,巴PK,冰岛IS,东盟AS,哥CR,秘鲁PE,新西兰NZ,智利CL	0 受惠国$_1$LD$_1$	20	-Multi-station transfer machines
	84.58	**切削金属的车床(包括车削中心):**					**Lathes (including turning centres) for removing metal:**
		-卧式车床:					-Horizontal lathes:

序号 No.	税则号列 Tariff Line	中文货品名称 Article Description in Chinese	最惠国税率 MFN(%)	协定税率 Agreement(%)	特惠税率 SP(%)	普通税率 Gen(%)	英文货品名称 Article Description
6552	8458.1100	--数控的	9.7	0 冰岛IS,东盟AS,哥CR,秘鲁PE,台湾TW,香港HK,新西兰NZ,智利CL 5 巴PK 5.8 澳AU 7 瑞士CH	0 受惠国LD	20	--Numerically controlled
6553	8458.1900	--其他	12	0 冰岛IS,东盟AS,哥CR,秘鲁PE,香港HK,新加坡SG,新西兰NZ,智利CL 6 巴PK 7.2 澳AU 8.4 瑞士CH 10.8 韩国KR	0 受惠国LD	50	--Other
		-其他车床:					-Other lathes:
		--数控的:					--Numerically controlled:
6554	8458.9110	---立式	5	0 澳AU,巴PK,冰岛IS,东盟AS,哥CR,秘鲁PE,台湾TW,新西兰NZ,智利CL 2 瑞士CH	0 受惠国LD	20	---Vertical
6555	8458.9120	---其他	5	0 澳AU,巴PK,冰岛IS,东盟AS,哥CR,秘鲁PE,台湾TW,新西兰NZ,智利CL 2 瑞士CH	0 受惠国LD	20	---Other
6556	8458.9900	--其他	12	0 冰岛IS,东盟AS,哥CR,秘鲁PE,新加坡SG,新西兰NZ,智利CL 6 巴PK 7.2 澳AU 8.4 瑞士CH 10.8 韩国KR	0 受惠国LD	50	--Other
	84.59	**切削金属的钻床、镗床、铣床、攻丝机床(包括直线移动式动力头钻床),但税号84.58的车床(包括车削中心)除外:**					**Machine tools (including way-type unit head machines) for drilling, boring, milling, threading or tapping by removing metal, other than lathes (including turning centres) of heading 8458:**
6557	8459.1000	-直线移动式动力头钻床	15	0 冰岛IS,东盟AS,哥CR,新加坡SG,新西兰NZ,智利CL 4.5 秘鲁PE 9 澳AU 10.5 瑞士CH 12 巴PK 13.5 韩国KR	0 受惠国$_{1}$LD$_{1}$	50	-Way-type unit head machines
		-其他钻床:					-Other drilling machines:
6558	8459.2100	--数控的	9.7	0 冰岛IS,东盟AS,哥CR,秘鲁PE,台湾TW,新西兰NZ,智利CL 3.9 瑞士CH 5 巴PK 5.8 澳AU	0 受惠国LD	20	--Numerically controlled
6559	8459.2900	--其他	15	0 冰岛IS,东盟AS,哥CR,新加坡SG,新西兰NZ,智利CL 4.5 秘鲁PE 9 澳AU 10.5 瑞士CH 12 巴PK 13.5 韩国KR	0 受惠国$_{1}$LD$_{1}$	50	--Other
		-其他镗铣机床:					-Other boring-milling machines:

序号 No.	税则号列 Tariff Line	中文货品名称 Article Description in Chinese	最惠国税率 MFN(%)	协定税率 Agreement(%)	特惠税率 SP(%)	普通税率 Gen(%)	英文货品名称 Article Description
6560	8459.3100	--数控的	9.7	0 冰岛IS,东盟AS,哥CR,秘鲁PE,新西兰NZ,智利CL 5 巴PK 5.8 澳AU 6.8 瑞士CH	0 受惠国LD	20	--Numerically controlled
6561	8459.3900	--其他	10	0 冰岛IS,东盟AS,哥CR,秘鲁PE,新西兰NZ,智利CL 4 瑞士CH 5 巴PK 6 澳AU	0 受惠国LD	50	--Other
		-其他镗床:					-Other boring machines:
6562	8459.4010	---数控的	9.7	0 冰岛IS,东盟AS,哥CR,秘鲁PE,新西兰NZ,智利CL 3.9 瑞士CH 5 巴PK 5.8 澳AU	0 受惠国LD	20	---Numerically controlled
6563	8459.4090	---其他	15	0 冰岛IS,东盟AS,哥CR,新加坡SG,新西兰NZ,智利CL 4.5 秘鲁PE 9 澳AU 10.5 瑞士CH 12 巴PK	0 受惠国$_1$LD$_1$	50	---Other
		-升降台式铣床:					-Milling machines, knee-type:
6564	8459.5100	--数控的	9.7	0 冰岛IS,东盟AS,哥CR,秘鲁PE,新西兰NZ,智利CL 5 巴PK 5.8 澳AU	0 受惠国LD	20	--Numerically controlled
6565	8459.5900	--其他	15	0 冰岛IS,东盟AS,哥CR,新加坡SG,新西兰NZ,智利CL 4.5 秘鲁PE 9 澳AU 10.5 瑞士CH 12 巴PK	0 受惠国$_1$LD$_1$	50	--Other
		-其他铣床:					-Other milling machines:
		--数控的:					--Numerically controlled:
6566	8459.6110	---龙门铣床	5	0 澳AU,巴PK,冰岛IS,东盟AS,哥CR,秘鲁PE,瑞士CH,新西兰NZ,智利CL	0 受惠国LD	20	---Planomilling machines
6567	8459.6190	---其他	5	0 澳AU,巴PK,冰岛IS,东盟AS,哥CR,秘鲁PE,新西兰NZ,智利CL 2 瑞士CH	0 受惠国LD	20	---Other
		--其他:					--Other:
6568	8459.6910	---龙门铣床	12	0 冰岛IS,东盟AS,哥CR,秘鲁PE,新加坡SG,新西兰NZ,智利CL 5 巴PK 7.2 澳AU 8.4 瑞士CH 10 亚太AP	0 受惠国LD	50	---Planomilling machines
6569	8459.6990	---其他	12	0 冰岛IS,东盟AS,哥CR,秘鲁PE,新加坡SG,新西兰NZ,智利CL 6 巴PK 7.2 澳AU 8.4 瑞士CH 11 亚太AP 11.6 韩国KR	0 受惠国LD	50	---Other

序号 No.	税则号列 Tariff Line	中文货品名称 Article Description in Chinese	最惠国税率 MFN(%)	协定税率 Agreement(%)	特惠税率 SP(%)	普通税率 Gen(%)	英文货品名称 Article Description
6570	8459.7000	-其他攻丝机床	12	0 冰岛IS,东盟AS,哥CR,秘鲁PE,新加坡SG,新西兰NZ,智利CL 6 巴PK 7.2 澳AU	0 受惠国LD	50	-Other threading or tapping machines
	84.60	**用磨石、磨料或抛光材料对金属或金属陶瓷进行去毛刺、刃磨、磨削、珩磨、研磨、抛光或其他精加工的机床,但税号84.61的切齿机、齿轮磨床或齿轮精加工机床除外:**					**Machine-tools for deburring, sharpening, grinding, honing, lapping, polishing or otherwise finishing metal or cermets by means of grinding stones, abrasives or polishing products, other than gear cutting, gear grinding or gear finishing machines of heading 84.61:**
		-平面磨床,在任一坐标的定位精度至少是0.01毫米:					-Flat-surface grinding machines, in which the positioning in any one axis can be set up to an accuracy of at least 0.01mm:
6571	8460.1100	--数控的	9.7	0 冰岛IS,东盟AS,哥CR,秘鲁PE,台湾TW,新西兰NZ,智利CL 3.9 瑞士CH 5 巴PK 5.8 澳AU	0 受惠国LD	20	--Numerically controlled
6572	8460.1900	--其他	15	0 冰岛IS,东盟AS,哥CR,新加坡SG,新西兰NZ,智利CL 4.5 秘鲁PE 9 澳AU 10.5 瑞士CH 12 巴PK	0 受惠国$_1$LD$_1$	50	--Other
		-其他磨床,在任一坐标的定位精度至少是0.01毫米:					-Other grinding machines, in which the positioning in any one axis can be set up to an accuracy of at least 0.01mm:
		--数控的:					--Numerically controlled:
		---外圆磨床:					---Cylindrical grinding machines:
6573	8460.2111	----曲轴磨床	9.7	0 冰岛IS,东盟AS,哥CR,秘鲁PE,新西兰NZ,智利CL 5 巴PK 5.8 澳AU	0 受惠国LD	20	----Crankshaft grinding
6574	8460.2119	----其他	9.7	0 冰岛IS,东盟AS,哥CR,秘鲁PE,新西兰NZ,智利CL 5 巴PK 5.8 澳AU	0 受惠国LD	20	----Other
6575	8460.2120	---内圆磨床	9.7	0 冰岛IS,东盟AS,哥CR,秘鲁PE,新西兰NZ,智利CL 5 巴PK 5.8 澳AU	0 受惠国LD	20	---Internal grinding machines
6576	8460.2190	---其他	9.7	0 冰岛IS,东盟AS,哥CR,秘鲁PE,新西兰NZ,智利CL 5 巴PK 5.8 澳AU 7 瑞士CH	0 受惠国LD	20	---Other
		--其他:					--Other:
6577	8460.2910	---外圆磨床	15	0 冰岛IS,东盟AS,哥CR,香港HK,新加坡SG,新西兰NZ,智利CL 4.5 秘鲁PE 9 澳AU 10.5 瑞士CH 12 巴PK	0 受惠国$_1$LD$_1$	50	---Cylindrical grinding machines

序号 No.	税则号列 Tariff Line	中文货品名称 Article Description in Chinese	最惠国税率 MFN(%)	协定税率 Agreement(%)	特惠税率 SP(%)	普通税率 Gen(%)	英文货品名称 Article Description
6578	8460.2920	---内圆磨床	15	0 冰岛IS,东盟AS,哥CR,新加坡SG,新西兰NZ,智利CL 4.5 秘鲁PE 9 澳AU 10.5 瑞士CH 12 巴PK	0 受惠国$_1$LD$_1$	50	---Internal grinding machines
6579	8460.2930	---轧辊磨床	13	0 冰岛IS,东盟AS,哥CR,秘鲁PE,新加坡SG,新西兰NZ,智利CL 6.5 巴PK 7.8 澳AU 9.1 瑞士CH	0 受惠国$_1$LD$_1$	50	---Grinding machines of roll
6580	8460.2990	---其他	13	0 冰岛IS,东盟AS,哥CR,秘鲁PE,新加坡SG,新西兰NZ,智利CL 6.5 巴PK 7.8 澳AU	0 受惠国$_1$LD$_1$	50	---Other
		-刃磨（工具或刀具）机床:					-Sharpening (tool or cutter grinding) machines:
6581	8460.3100	--数控的	9.7	0 冰岛IS,东盟AS,哥CR,秘鲁PE,新西兰NZ,智利CL 5 巴PK 5.8 澳AU	0 受惠国LD	20	--Numerically controlled
6582	8460.3900	--其他	15	0 冰岛IS,东盟AS,哥CR,香港HK,新加坡SG,新西兰NZ,智利CL 4.5 秘鲁PE 9 澳AU 12 巴PK	0 受惠国$_1$LD$_1$	50	--Other
		-珩磨或研磨机床:					-Honing or lapping machines:
6583	8460.4010	---珩磨	13	0 冰岛IS,东盟AS,哥CR,秘鲁PE,新加坡SG,新西兰NZ,智利CL 6.5 巴PK 7.8 澳AU 9.1 瑞士CH	0 受惠国$_1$LD$_1$	50	---Honing
6584	8460.4020	---研磨	13	0 冰岛IS,东盟AS,哥CR,秘鲁PE,台湾TW,新加坡SG,新西兰NZ,智利CL 6.5 巴PK 7.8 澳AU 9.1 瑞士CH	0 受惠国$_1$LD$_1$	50	---Lapping
		-其他:					-Other:
6585	8460.9010	---砂轮机	15	0 冰岛IS,东盟AS,哥CR,台湾TW,新加坡SG,新西兰NZ,智利CL 4.5 秘鲁PE 9 澳AU 10.5 瑞士CH 12 巴PK,韩国KR	0 受惠国$_1$LD$_1$	50	---Grinding wheel machines
6586	8460.9020	---抛光机床	15	0 冰岛IS,东盟AS,哥CR,台湾TW,新加坡SG,新西兰NZ,智利CL 4.5 秘鲁PE 9 澳AU,韩国KR 10.5 瑞士CH 12 巴PK	0 受惠国$_1$LD$_1$	50	---Polishing machines

序号 No.	税则号列 Tariff Line	中文货品名称 Article Description in Chinese	最惠国税率 MFN(%)	协定税率 Agreement(%)	特惠税率 SP(%)	普通税率 Gen(%)	英文货品名称 Article Description
6587	8460.9090	---其他	15	0 冰岛IS,东盟AS,哥CR,新加坡SG,新西兰NZ,智利CL 4.5 秘鲁PE 9 澳AU 10.5 瑞士CH 12 巴PK 13.5 韩国KR	0 受惠国$_1$LD$_1$	50	---Other
	84.61	**切削金属或金属陶瓷的刨床、牛头刨床、插床、拉床、切齿机、齿轮磨床或齿轮精加工机床、锯床、切断机及其他税号未列名的切削机床:**					**Machine tools for planing, shaping, slotting, broaching, gear cutting, gear grinding or gear finishing, sawing, cutting-off and other machine tools working by removing metal or cermets, not elsewhere specified or included:**
		-牛头刨床或插床:					-Shaping or slotting machines:
6588	8461.2010	---牛头刨床	15	0 冰岛IS,东盟AS,哥CR,新加坡SG,新西兰NZ,智利CL 4.5 秘鲁PE 9 澳AU 10.5 瑞士CH 12 巴PK,韩国KR	0 受惠国$_1$LD$_1$	50	---Shaping machines
6589	8461.2020	---插床	15	0 冰岛IS,东盟AS,哥CR,台湾TW,新加坡SG,新西兰NZ,智利CL 4.5 秘鲁PE 9 澳AU 10.5 瑞士CH 12 巴PK,韩国KR	0 受惠国$_1$LD$_1$	50	---Slotting machines
6590	8461.3000	-拉床	12	0 冰岛IS,东盟AS,哥CR,秘鲁PE,台湾TW,新加坡SG,新西兰NZ,智利CL 6 巴PK 7.2 澳AU 8.4 瑞士CH 9.6 韩国KR	0 受惠国$_1$LD$_1$	50	-Broaching machines
		-切齿机、齿轮磨床或齿轮精加工机床:					-Gear-cutting, gear-grinding or gear-finishing machines:
		---数控的:					---Numerically controlled:
6591	8461.4011	----齿轮磨床	9.7	0 冰岛IS,东盟AS,哥CR,秘鲁PE,新西兰NZ,智利CL 5 巴PK 5.8 澳AU	0 受惠国LD	20	----Gear grinding
6592	8461.4019	----其他	9.7	0 冰岛IS,东盟AS,哥CR,秘鲁PE,新西兰NZ,智利CL 5 巴PK 5.8 澳AU	0 受惠国LD	20	----Other
6593	8461.4090	---其他	15	0 冰岛IS,东盟AS,哥CR,新加坡SG,新西兰NZ,智利CL 4.5 秘鲁PE 9 澳AU 12 巴PK	0 受惠国$_1$LD$_1$	50	---Other
6594	8461.5000	-锯床或切断机	12	0 冰岛IS,东盟AS,哥CR,秘鲁PE,台湾TW,新加坡SG,新西兰NZ,智利CL 6 巴PK 7.2 澳AU 8.4 瑞士CH	0 受惠国$_1$LD$_1$	50	-Sawing or cutting-off machines
		-其他:					-Other:

序号 No.	税则号列 Tariff Line	中文货品名称 Article Description in Chinese	最惠国税率 MFN(%)	协定税率 Agreement(%)	特惠税率 SP(%)	普通税率 Gen(%)	英文货品名称 Article Description
		---刨床:					---Planing machines:
6595	8461.9011	----龙门刨床	15	0 冰岛IS,东盟AS,哥CR,台湾TW,新加坡SG,新西兰NZ,智利CL 4.5 秘鲁PE 9 澳AU 10.5 瑞士CH 12 巴PK,韩国KR	0 受惠国$_1$LD$_1$	50	----Double-column (open-side) planing machines
6596	8461.9019	----其他	15	0 冰岛IS,东盟AS,哥CR,台湾TW,新加坡SG,新西兰NZ,智利CL 4.5 秘鲁PE 6 瑞士CH 9 澳AU 12 巴PK,韩国KR	0 受惠国$_1$LD$_1$	50	----Other
6597	8461.9090	---其他	12	0 冰岛IS,东盟AS,哥CR,秘鲁PE,新加坡SG,新西兰NZ,智利CL 6 巴PK 7.2 澳AU 8.4 瑞士CH 10.8 韩国KR	0 受惠国$_1$LD$_1$	50	---Other
	84.62	**加工金属的锻造(包括模锻)或冲压机床;加工金属的弯曲、折叠、矫直、矫平、剪切、冲孔或开槽机床;其他加工金属或硬质合金的压力机:**					**Machine tools (including presses) for working metal by forging, hammering or die-stamping; machine tools (including presses) for working metal by bending, folding, straightening, flattening, shearing, punching or notching; presses for working metal or metal carbides, not specified above:**
		-锻造(包括模锻)或冲压机床及锻锤:					-Forging or die-stamping machines (including presses) and hammers:
6598	8462.1010	---数控的	9.7	0 冰岛IS,东盟AS,哥CR,秘鲁PE,台湾TW,新西兰NZ,智利CL 5 巴PK 5.8 澳AU 6.8 瑞士CH,亚太AP 8.5 韩国KR	0 受惠国LD	20	---Numerically controlled
6599	8462.1090	---其他	12	0 冰岛IS,东盟AS,哥CR,台湾TW,新加坡SG,新西兰NZ,智利CL 3.6 秘鲁PE 5 巴PK 7.2 澳AU 8.4 瑞士CH,亚太AP 10.5 韩国KR	0 受惠国LD	50	---Other
		-弯曲、折叠、矫直或矫平机床:					-Bending, folding, straightening or flattening machines (including presses) :
		--数控的:					--Numerically controlled:
6600	8462.2110	---矫直机	9.7	0 冰岛IS,东盟AS,哥CR,秘鲁PE,新西兰NZ,智利CL 5 巴PK 5.8 澳AU 6.8 瑞士CH	0 受惠国LD	20	---Straightening machines
6601	8462.2190	---其他	9.7	0 冰岛IS,东盟AS,哥CR,秘鲁PE,新西兰NZ,智利CL 5 巴PK 5.8 澳AU 6.8 瑞士CH	0 受惠国LD	20	---Other

序号 No.	税则号列 Tariff Line	中文货品名称 Article Description in Chinese	最惠国税率 MFN(%)	协定税率 Agreement(%)	特惠税率 SP(%)	普通税率 Gen(%)	英文货品名称 Article Description
		--其他:					--Other:
6602	8462.2910	---矫直机	10	0 冰岛IS,东盟AS,哥CR,新西兰NZ,智利CL 3 秘鲁PE 5 巴PK 6 澳AU 7.2 瑞士CH	0 受惠国LD	50	---Straightening machines
6603	8462.2990	---其他	10	0 冰岛IS,东盟AS,哥CR,新加坡SG,新西兰NZ,智利CL 3 秘鲁PE 4 瑞士CH 5 巴PK 6 澳AU	0 受惠国LD	50	---Other
		-剪切机床,但冲剪两用机除外:					-Shearing machines (including presses) , other than combined punching and shearing machines:
		--数控的:					--Numerically controlled:
6604	8462.3110	---板带纵剪机	7	0 冰岛IS,东盟AS,哥CR,秘鲁PE,新西兰NZ,智利CL 2.8 瑞士CH 4.2 澳AU 5 巴PK	0 受惠国LD	20	---Shearing lengthwise
6605	8462.3120	---板带横剪机	7	0 冰岛IS,东盟AS,哥CR,秘鲁PE,新西兰NZ,智利CL 2.8 瑞士CH 4.2 澳AU 5 巴PK	0 受惠国LD	20	---Shearing transverse
6606	8462.3190	---其他	7	0 冰岛IS,东盟AS,哥CR,秘鲁PE,新西兰NZ,智利CL 2.8 瑞士CH 4.2 澳AU 5 巴PK	0 受惠国LD	20	---Other
		--其他:					--Other:
6607	8462.3910	---板带纵剪机	10	0 冰岛IS,东盟AS,哥CR,秘鲁PE,新西兰NZ,智利CL 4 瑞士CH 5 巴PK 6 澳AU 9.5 亚太AP	0 受惠国LD	50	---Shearing lengthwise
6608	8462.3920	---板带横剪机	10	0 冰岛IS,东盟AS,哥CR,秘鲁PE,新西兰NZ,智利CL 4 瑞士CH 5 巴PK 6 澳AU 9.5 亚太AP	0 受惠国LD	50	---Shearing transverse
6609	8462.3990	---其他	10	0 冰岛IS,东盟AS,哥CR,秘鲁PE,新西兰NZ,智利CL 4 瑞士CH 5 巴PK 6 澳AU 9.5 亚太AP	0 受惠国LD	50	---Other
		-冲孔或开槽机床,包括冲剪两用机:					-Punching or notching machines (including presses) , including combined punching and shearing machines:
		--数控的:					--Numerically controlled:
		---冲床:					---Punch press:

序号 No.	税则号列 Tariff Line	中文货品名称 Article Description in Chinese	最惠国税率 MFN(%)	协定税率 Agreement(%)	特惠税率 SP(%)	普通税率 Gen(%)	英文货品名称 Article Description
6610	8462.4111	----自动模式数控步冲压力机	9.7	0 冰岛IS,东盟AS,哥CR,秘鲁PE,新西兰NZ,智利CL 5 巴PK 5.8 澳AU 6.8 瑞士CH	0 受惠国LD	20	----CNC automatic tool change punch press
6611	8462.4119	----其他	9.7	0 冰岛IS,东盟AS,哥CR,秘鲁PE,新西兰NZ,智利CL 3.9 瑞士CH 5 巴PK 5.8 澳AU	0 受惠国LD	20	----Other
6612	8462.4190	---其他	9.7	0 冰岛IS,东盟AS,哥CR,秘鲁PE,新西兰NZ,智利CL 3.9 瑞士CH 5 巴PK 5.8 澳AU	0 受惠国LD	20	---Other
6613	8462.4900	--其他	10	0 冰岛IS,东盟AS,哥CR,秘鲁PE,台湾TW,新加坡SG,新西兰NZ,智利CL 4 瑞士CH 5 巴PK 6 澳AU	0 受惠国LD	50	--Other
		-其他:					-Other:
		--液压压力机:					--Hydraulic presses:
6614	8462.9110	---金属型材挤压机	10	0 冰岛IS,东盟AS,哥CR,秘鲁PE,新西兰NZ,智利CL 4 瑞士CH 5 巴PK 6 澳AU 9.2 亚太AP 9.6 韩国KR	0 受惠国LD	50	---Metal section squeezing machine
6615	8462.9190	---其他	10	0 冰岛IS,东盟AS,哥CR,秘鲁PE,新加坡SG,新西兰NZ,智利CL 5 巴PK 6 澳AU 7 瑞士CH 9.2 亚太AP 9.6 韩国KR	0 受惠国LD	50	---Other
		--其他:					--Other:
6616	8462.9910	---机械压力机	10	0 冰岛IS,东盟AS,哥CR,秘鲁PE,台湾TW,新加坡SG,新西兰NZ,智利CL 4 瑞士CH 5 巴PK 6 澳AU 9.5 亚太AP 9.6 韩国KR	0 受惠国LD	50	---Mechanical presses
6617	8462.9990	---其他	10	0 冰岛IS,东盟AS,哥CR,秘鲁PE,新加坡SG,新西兰NZ,智利CL 4 瑞士CH 5 巴PK 6 澳AU 9.5 亚太AP 9.6 韩国KR	0 受惠国LD	50	---Other
	84.63	**金属或金属陶瓷的其他非切削加工机床:**					**Other machine tools for working metal or cermets, without removing material:**
		-杆、管、型材、异型材、丝及类似品的拉拔机:					-Drawbenches for bars, tubes, profiles, wire or the like:

序号 No.	税则号列 Tariff Line	中文货品名称 Article Description in Chinese	最惠国税率 MFN(%)	协定税率 Agreement(%)	特惠税率 SP(%)	普通税率 Gen(%)	英文货品名称 Article Description
		---冷拔管机:					---Cold-drawing tube benches:
6618	8463.1011	----拉拔力为300吨及以下	10	0 冰岛IS,东盟AS,哥CR,秘鲁PE,新西兰NZ,智利CL 4 瑞士CH 5 巴PK 6 澳AU 9 韩国KR	0 受惠国$_1$LD$_1$	50	----Drawing power≤300t
6619	8463.1019	----其他	10	0 冰岛IS,东盟AS,哥CR,秘鲁PE,台湾TW,新加坡SG,新西兰NZ,智利CL 4 瑞士CH 5 巴PK 6 澳AU	0 受惠国$_1$LD$_1$	50	----Other
6620	8463.1020	---拔丝机	10	0 冰岛IS,东盟AS,哥CR,秘鲁PE,新西兰NZ,智利CL 4 瑞士CH 5 巴PK 6 澳AU	0 受惠国$_1$LD$_1$	50	---Wiredrawing machines
6621	8463.1090	---其他	10	0 冰岛IS,东盟AS,哥CR,秘鲁PE,新西兰NZ,智利CL 4 瑞士CH 5 巴PK 6 澳AU	0 受惠国$_1$LD$_1$	50	---Other
6622	8463.2000	-螺纹滚轧机	15	0 冰岛IS,东盟AS,哥CR,新加坡SG,新西兰NZ,智利CL 4.5 秘鲁PE 9 澳AU 10.5 瑞士CH 12 巴PK	0 受惠国$_1$LD$_1$	50	-Thread rolling machines
6623	8463.3000	-金属丝加工机	10	0 冰岛IS,东盟AS,哥CR,秘鲁PE,新西兰NZ,智利CL 4 瑞士CH 5 巴PK 6 澳AU	0 受惠国$_1$LD$_1$	50	-Machines for working wire
6624	8463.9000	-其他	10	0 冰岛IS,东盟AS,哥CR,新西兰NZ,智利CL 3 秘鲁PE 5 巴PK 6 澳AU 7 瑞士CH	0 受惠国$_1$LD$_1$	50	-Other
	84.64	**石料、陶瓷、混凝土、石棉水泥或类似矿物材料的加工机床、玻璃冷加工机床:**					**Machine tools for working stone, ceramics, concrete, asbestos-cement or like mineral materials or for cold working glass:**
		-锯床:					-Sawing machines:
6625	8464.1010	---圆盘锯	0		0 受惠国LD	30	---Of disk saw
6626	8464.1020	---钢丝锯	0		0 受惠国LD	30	---Of scroll saw
6627	8464.1090	---其他	0		0 受惠国LD	30	---Other
		-研磨或抛光机床:					-Grinding or polishing machines:
6628	8464.2010	---玻璃研磨或抛光机床	0		0 受惠国LD	30	---Machines for grinding or polishing glass or glassware
6629	8464.2090	---其他	0		0 受惠国LD	30	---Other
		-其他:					-Other:
		---玻璃的其他冷加工机床:					---Other machines for cold-working glass or glassware:
6630	8464.9011	----切割机	0		0 受惠国LD	30	----Cutting-off machines
6631	8464.9012	----刻花机	0		0 受惠国LD	30	----Carving machines
6632	8464.9019	----其他	0		0 受惠国LD	30	----Other

序号 No.	税则号列 Tariff Line	中文货品名称 Article Description in Chinese	最惠国税率 MFN(%)	协定税率 Agreement(%)	特惠税率 SP(%)	普通税率 Gen(%)	英文货品名称 Article Description
6633	8464.9090	---其他	0		0 受惠国LD	30	---Other
	84.65	**木材、软木、骨、硬质橡胶、硬质塑料或类似硬质材料的加工机床(包括用打钉或打U形钉、胶粘或其他方法组合前述材料的机器):**					**Machine tools (including machines for nailing, stapling, glueing or otherwise assembling) for working wood, cork, bone, hard rubber, hard plastics or similar hard materials:**
6634	8465.1000	-不需更换工具即可进行不同机械加工的机器	10	0 冰岛IS,东盟AS,哥CR,香港HK,新加坡SG,新西兰NZ,智利CL 3 秘鲁PE 4 瑞士CH 5 巴PK 6 澳AU 9 韩国KR	0 受惠国$_1$LD$_1$	30	-Machines which can carry out different types of machining operations without tool change between such operations
		-其他:					-Other:
6635	8465.9100	--锯床	10	0 冰岛IS,东盟AS,哥CR,香港HK,新西兰NZ,智利CL 3 秘鲁PE 4 瑞士CH 5 巴PK 6 澳AU 9 韩国KR	0 受惠国$_1$LD$_1$	30	--Sawing machines
6636	8465.9200	--刨、铣或切削成形机器	10	0 冰岛IS,东盟AS,哥CR,秘鲁PE,香港HK,新加坡SG,新西兰NZ,智利CL 4 瑞士CH 5 巴PK 6 澳AU 9 韩国KR	0 受惠国$_1$LD$_1$	30	--Planing, milling or moulding (by cut-ting) machines
6637	8465.9300	--研磨、砂磨或抛光机器	10	0 冰岛IS,东盟AS,哥CR,秘鲁PE,香港HK,新西兰NZ,智利CL 4 瑞士CH 5 巴PK 6 澳AU 9 韩国KR	0 受惠国$_1$LD$_1$	30	--Grinding, sanding or polishing machines
6638	8465.9400	--弯曲或装配机器	10	0 冰岛IS,东盟AS,哥CR,秘鲁PE,新加坡SG,新西兰NZ,智利CL 4 瑞士CH 5 巴PK 6 澳AU 9 韩国KR	0 受惠国$_1$LD$_1$	30	--Bending or assembling machines
6639	8465.9500	--钻孔或凿榫机器	10	0 冰岛IS,东盟AS,哥CR,秘鲁PE,香港HK,新加坡SG,新西兰NZ,智利CL 5 巴PK 6 澳AU 7 瑞士CH 9 韩国KR	0 受惠国$_1$LD$_1$	30	--Drilling or mortising machines
6640	8465.9600	--剖开、切片或刮削机器	10	0 冰岛IS,东盟AS,哥CR,秘鲁PE,新加坡SG,新西兰NZ,智利CL 4 瑞士CH 5 巴PK 6 澳AU 9 韩国KR	0 受惠国$_1$LD$_1$	30	--Splitting, slicing or paring machines

序号 No.	税则号列 Tariff Line	中文货品名称 Article Description in Chinese	最惠国税率 MFN(%)	协定税率 Agreement(%)	特惠税率 SP(%)	普通税率 Gen(%)	英文货品名称 Article Description
6641	8465.9900	--其他	10	0 冰岛IS,东盟AS,哥CR,香港HK,新加坡SG,新西兰NZ,智利CL 3 秘鲁PE 4 瑞士CH 5 巴PK 6 澳AU 9 韩国KR	0 受惠国$_1$LD$_1$	30	--Other
	84.66	**专用于或主要用于税号84.56至84.65所列机器的零件、附件,包括工件或工具的夹具、自启板牙切头、分度头及其他专用于机床的附件;各种手提工具的工具夹具:**					**Parts and accessories suitable for use solely or principally with the machines of headings 8456 to 8465, including work or tool holders, self-opening dieheads, dividing heads and other special attachments for machine tools; tool holders for any type of tool for working in the hand:**
6642	8466.1000	-工具夹具及自启板牙切头	7	0 冰岛IS,东盟AS,哥CR,秘鲁PE,新西兰NZ,智利CL 4.2 澳AU 4.9 瑞士CH 5 巴PK 6 韩国KR	0 受惠国LD	17	-Tool holders and self-opening dieheads
6643	8466.2000	-工件夹具	7	0 巴PK,冰岛IS,东盟AS,哥CR,秘鲁PE,台湾TW,新西兰NZ,智利CL 4.2 澳AU 4.9 瑞士CH,亚太AP 5.6 韩国KR	0 受惠国LD	17	-Work holders
6644	8466.3000	-分度头及其他专用于机床的附件	7	0 冰岛IS,东盟AS,哥CR,秘鲁PE,新西兰NZ,智利CL 4.2 澳AU 4.9 瑞士CH 5 巴PK 6 韩国KR	0 受惠国LD	17	-Dividing heads and other special attachments for machine-tools
		-其他:					-Other:
6645	8466.9100	--税号84.64所列机器用	0		0 受惠国LD	17	--For machines of heading No.84.64
6646	8466.9200	--税号84.65所列机器用	6	0 冰岛IS,东盟AS,哥CR,秘鲁PE,香港HK,新西兰NZ,智利CL 2.4 瑞士CH 3.6 澳AU 5 巴PK 5.2 韩国KR	0 受惠国LD	17	--For machines of heading No.84.65
		--税号84.56至84.61所列机器用:					--For machines of headings 8456 to 8461:
6647	8466.9310	---刀库及自动换刀装置	0		0 受惠国LD	17	---Tool magazine & ATC (Automatic Tool Changer)
6648	8466.9390	---其他	0		0 受惠国LD	17	---Other
6649	8466.9400	--税号84.62或84.63所列机器用	6	0 冰岛IS,东盟AS,哥CR,韩国KR,秘鲁PE,台湾TW,新西兰NZ,智利CL 3.6 澳AU 4.2 瑞士CH 5 巴PK	0 受惠国LD	17	--For machines of heading No.84.62 or 84.63
	84.67	**手提式风动或液压工具及本身装有电动或非电动动力装置的手提式工具:**					**Tools for working in the hand, pneumatic, hydraulic or with self-contained electric or non-electric motor:**
		-风动的:					-Pneumatic:

序号 No.	税则号列 Tariff Line	中文货品名称 Article Description in Chinese	最惠国税率 MFN(%)	协定税率 Agreement(%)	特惠税率 SP(%)	普通税率 Gen(%)	英文货品名称 Article Description
6650	8467.1100	--旋转式（包括旋转冲击式的）	8	0 冰岛IS,东盟AS,哥CR,秘鲁PE,新西兰NZ,智利CL 3.2 瑞士CH 4.8 澳AU 5 巴PK 6.9 韩国KR	0 受惠国LD	30	--Rotary type (including combined rotarypercussion)
6651	8467.1900	--其他	8	0 冰岛IS,东盟AS,哥CR,秘鲁PE,新西兰NZ,智利CL 3.2 瑞士CH 4.8 澳AU,韩国KR 5 巴PK	0 受惠国LD	30	--Other
		-本身装有电动动力装置的：					-With self-contained electric motor:
6652	8467.2100	--各种钻	10	0 冰岛IS,东盟AS,哥CR,香港HK,新加坡SG,新西兰NZ,智利CL 3 秘鲁PE 4 瑞士CH 5 巴PK 6 澳AU 8 韩国KR 9 亚太AP	0 受惠国LD	30	--Drills of all kinds
		--锯：					--Saws:
6653	8467.2210	---链锯	10	0 冰岛IS,东盟AS,哥CR,香港HK,新西兰NZ,智利CL 3 秘鲁PE 4 瑞士CH 5 巴PK 6 澳AU 8 韩国KR 9 亚太AP	0 受惠国LD	30	---Chain saws
6654	8467.2290	---其他	10	0 冰岛IS,东盟AS,哥CR,香港HK,新加坡SG,新西兰NZ,智利CL 3 秘鲁PE 4 瑞士CH 5 巴PK 6 澳AU 8 韩国KR 9 亚太AP	0 受惠国LD	30	---Other
		--其他：					--Other:
6655	8467.2910	---砂磨工具（包括磨光机、砂光机、砂轮机等）	10	0 冰岛IS,东盟AS,哥CR,香港HK,新加坡SG,新西兰NZ,智利CL 3 秘鲁PE 5 巴PK 6 澳AU 7.2 瑞士CH 8 韩国KR,亚太AP	0 受惠国LD	30	---Grinding tools (induding burnisher, belt sander, wheel-sander)
6656	8467.2920	---电刨	10	0 冰岛IS,东盟AS,哥CR,香港HK,新西兰NZ,智利CL 3 秘鲁PE 4 瑞士CH 5 巴PK 6 澳AU 8 韩国KR,亚太AP	0 受惠国LD	30	---Planings

序号 No.	税则号列 Tariff Line	中文货品名称 Article Description in Chinese	最惠国税率 MFN(%)	协定税率 Agreement(%)	特惠税率 SP(%)	普通税率 Gen(%)	英文货品名称 Article Description
6657	8467.2990	---其他	10	0 冰岛IS,东盟AS,哥CR,香港HK,新加坡SG,新西兰NZ,智利CL 3 秘鲁PE 4 瑞士CH 5 巴PK 6 澳AU 8 韩国KR,亚太AP	0 受惠国LD	30	---Other
		-其他工具:					-Other tools:
6658	8467.8100	--链锯	8	0 冰岛IS,东盟AS,哥CR,秘鲁PE,新西兰NZ,智利CL 3.2 瑞士CH 4.8 澳AU,韩国KR 5 巴PK	0 受惠国LD	30	--Chain saws
6659	8467.8900	--其他	8	0 冰岛IS,东盟AS,哥CR,秘鲁PE,新西兰NZ,智利CL 3.2 瑞士CH 4.8 澳AU 5 巴PK 6.9 韩国KR	0 受惠国LD	30	--Other
		-零件:					-Parts:
		--链锯用:					--Of chainsaws:
6660	8467.9110	---电动的	6	0 巴PK,冰岛IS,东盟AS,哥CR,秘鲁PE,香港HK,新西兰NZ,智利CL 2.4 瑞士CH 3.6 澳AU,韩国KR 4.8 亚太AP	0 受惠国LD	30	---With self-contained electric motor
6661	8467.9190	---其他	6	0 冰岛IS,东盟AS,哥CR,秘鲁PE,新西兰NZ,智利CL 3.6 澳AU,韩国KR 4.2 瑞士CH 5 巴PK	0 受惠国LD	30	---Other
6662	8467.9200	--风动工具用	6	0 东盟AS,哥CR,秘鲁PE,新西兰NZ,智利CL 2.4 瑞士CH 3.6 澳AU,韩国KR 5 巴PK	0 受惠国LD	30	--Of pneumatic tools
		--其他:					--Other:
6663	8467.9910	---电动工具用	10	0 冰岛IS,东盟AS,哥CR,秘鲁PE,香港HK,新加坡SG,新西兰NZ,智利CL 5 巴PK 6 澳AU 7 瑞士CH 8 韩国KR 9 亚太AP	0 受惠国LD	30	---With self-contained electric motor
6664	8467.9990	---其他	6	0 冰岛IS,东盟AS,哥CR,秘鲁PE,新西兰NZ,智利CL 2.4 瑞士CH 3.6 澳AU 4.8 韩国KR 5 巴PK	0 受惠国LD	30	---Other
	84.68	**焊接机器及装置,不论是否兼有切割功能,但税号85.15的货品除外;气体加温表面回火机器及装置:**					**Machinery and apparatus for soldering, brazing or welding, whether or not capable of cutting, other than those of heading 8515; gas-operated surface tempering machines and appliances:**

序号 No.	税则号列 Tariff Line	中文货品名称 Article Description in Chinese	最惠国税率 MFN(%)	协定税率 Agreement(%)	特惠税率 SP(%)	普通税率 Gen(%)	英文货品名称 Article Description
6665	8468.1000	-手提喷焊器	12	0 冰岛IS,东盟AS,哥CR,秘鲁PE,新加坡SG,新西兰NZ,智利CL 6 巴PK 7.2 澳AU 8.4 瑞士CH 9.6 韩国KR	0 受惠国LD	30	-Hand-held blow pipes
6666	8468.2000	-其他气体焊接或表面回火机器及装置	12	0 冰岛IS,东盟AS,哥CR,秘鲁PE,新加坡SG,新西兰NZ,智利CL 4.8 瑞士CH 6 巴PK 7.2 澳AU 9.6 韩国KR	0 受惠国LD	30	-Other gas-operated machinery and apparatus
6667	8468.8000	-其他机器及装置	12	0 冰岛IS,东盟AS,哥CR,秘鲁PE,新加坡SG,新西兰NZ,智利CL 6 巴PK 7.2 澳AU 8.4 瑞士CH	0 受惠国LD	30	-Other machinery and apparatus
6668	8468.9000	-零件	7Δ3	0 冰岛IS,东盟AS,哥CR,秘鲁PE,新西兰NZ,智利CL 2.8 瑞士CH 4.2 澳AU,韩国KR 5 巴PK	0 受惠国LD	30	-Parts
	84.69	**打字机,但税号84.43的打印机除外;文字处理机:**					**Typewriters other than printers of heading 8443; word-processing machines:**
		---自动打字机及文字处理机:					---Automatic typewriters and word-pro-cessing machines:
6669	8469.0011	----文字处理机	0		0 受惠国LD	40	----Word-processing machines
6670	8469.0012	----自动打字机	12	0 冰岛IS,东盟AS,哥CR,秘鲁PE,新加坡SG,新西兰NZ,智利CL 6 巴PK 7.2 澳AU 8.4 瑞士CH	0 受惠国$_1$LD$_1$	40	----Automatic typewriters
6671	8469.0020	---其他电动打字机	12	0 冰岛IS,东盟AS,哥CR,秘鲁PE,新加坡SG,新西兰NZ,智利CL 5 巴PK 7.2 澳AU 8.4 瑞士CH 10.8 亚太AP	0 受惠国$_1$LD$_1$	40	---Other typewriters, electric
6672	8469.0030	---其他非电动打字机	12	0 冰岛IS,东盟AS,哥CR,秘鲁PE,新加坡SG,新西兰NZ,智利CL 6 巴PK 7.2 澳AU 8.4 瑞士CH 9.6 韩国KR	0 受惠国$_1$LD$_1$	40	---Other typewriters, non-electric
	84.70	**计算机器及具有计算功能的袖珍式数据记录、重现及显示机器;装有计算装置的会计计算机、邮资盖戳机、售票机及类似机器;现金出纳机:**					**Calculating machines and pocket-size data recording, reproducing and displaying machines with calculating functions; accounting machines, postage-franking machines, ticket-issuing machines and similar machines, incorporating a calculating device; cash registers:**

序号 No.	税则号列 Tariff Line	中文货品名称 Article Description in Chinese	最惠国税率 MFN(%)	协定税率 Agreement(%)	特惠税率 SP(%)	普通税率 Gen(%)	英文货品名称 Article Description
6673	8470.1000	-不需外接电源的电子计算器及具有计算功能的袖珍式数据记录、重现及显示机器	0		0 受惠国LD	80	-Electronic calculators capable of operation without an external source of electric power and pocket-size data recording, reproducing and displaying machines with calculating functions
		-其他电子计算器:					-Other electronic calculating machines:
6674	8470.2100	--装有打印装置的	0		0 受惠国LD	80	--Incorporating a printing device
6675	8470.2900	--其他	0		0 受惠国LD	80	--Other
6676	8470.3000	-其他计算机器	0		0 受惠国LD	40	-Other calculating machines
		-现金出纳机:					-Cash registers:
6677	8470.5010	---销售点终端出纳机	0		0 受惠国LD	40	---Terminal registers for market
6678	8470.5090	---其他	0		0 受惠国LD	40	---Other
6679	8470.9000	-其他	0		0 受惠国LD	40	-Other
	84.71	**自动数据处理设备及其部件;其他税号未列名的磁性或光学阅读机、将数据以代码形式转录到数据记录媒体的机器及处理这些数据的机器:**					**Automatic data-processing machines and units thereof; magnetic or optical readers, machines for transcribing data onto data media in coded form and machines for processing such data, not elsewhere specified or included:**
		-重量不超过10公斤的便携自动数据处理设备,至少由一个中央处理部件、一个键盘及一个显示器组成:					-Portable automatic data pro-cessing machines, weighing not more than10kg, consisting of at least a central processing unit, a keyboard and a display:
6680	8471.3010	---平板电脑	0		0 受惠国LD	70	---Tablet computer
6681	8471.3090	---其他	0		0 受惠国LD	70	---Other
		-其他自动数据处理设备:					-Other automatic data-processing machines:
		--同一机壳内至少有一个中央处理部件及一个输入和输出部件,不论是否组合式:					--Comprising in the same housing at least a central processing unit and an input and output unit, whether or not combined:
6682	8471.4110	---巨型机、大型机及中型机	0		0 受惠国LD	14	---Mainframes
6683	8471.4120	---小型机	0		0 受惠国LD	14	---Mini-computers
6684	8471.4140	---微型机	0		0 受惠国LD	70	---Microprocessings
6685	8471.4190	---其他	0		0 受惠国LD	70	---Other
		--其他,以系统形式进口或出口的:					--Other, presented in the form of systems:
6686	8471.4910	---巨型机、大型机及中型机	0		0 受惠国LD	29	---Mainframes
6687	8471.4920	---小型机	0		0 受惠国LD	29	---Mini-computers
6688	8471.4940	---微型机	0		0 受惠国LD	70	---Microprocessings
		---其他:					---Other:
6689	8471.4991	----分散型工业过程控制设备	0		0 受惠国LD	70	----Processing machines for the dis-tributed control system
6690	8471.4999	----其他	0		0 受惠国LD	70	----Other
		-子目号8471.41或8471.49所列以外的处理部件,不论是否在同一机壳内有一个或两个下列部件:存储部件、输入部件、输出部件:					-Processing units other than those of subheading 847141 or 847149, whether or not containing in the same housing one or two of the following types of unit: storage units, input units, output units:
6691	8471.5010	---巨型机、大型机及中型机的	0		0 受惠国LD	14	---Of mainframes
6692	8471.5020	---小型机的	0		0 受惠国LD	14	---Of mini-computers
6693	8471.5040	---微型机的	0		0 受惠国LD	70	---Of microprocessings
6694	8471.5090	---其他	0		0 受惠国LD	70	---Other
		-输入或输出部件,不论是否在同一机壳内有存储部件:					-Input or output units, whether or not containing storage units in the same housing:

序号 No.	税则号列 Tariff Line	中文货品名称 Article Description in Chinese	最惠国税率 MFN(%)	协定税率 Agreement(%)	特惠税率 SP(%)	普通税率 Gen(%)	英文货品名称 Article Description
6695	8471.6040	---巨型机、大型机、中型机及小型机用终端	0		0 受惠国LD	14	---Terminating machines for the huge computers, mainframes and minicomputers
6696	8471.6050	---扫描仪	0		0 受惠国LD	14	---Scanner
6697	8471.6060	---数字化仪	0		0 受惠国LD	14	---Digitizer
		---键盘、鼠标器：					---Keyboards, mouses:
6698	8471.6071	----键盘	0		0 受惠国LD	40	----Keyboards
6699	8471.6072	----鼠标器	0		0 受惠国LD	40	----Mouses
6700	8471.6090	---其他	0		0 受惠国LD	14	---Other
		-存储部件：					-Storage units:
6701	8471.7010	---硬盘驱动器	0		0 受惠国LD	14	---Rigid disk drivers
6702	8471.7020	---软盘驱动器	0		0 受惠国LD	14	---Floppy disk drivers
6703	8471.7030	---光盘驱动器	0		0 受惠国LD	14	---CD drivers
6704	8471.7090	---其他	0		0 受惠国LD	14	---Other
6705	8471.8000	-自动数据处理设备的其他部件	0		0 受惠国LD	40	-Other units automatic data processing machines
6706	8471.9000	-其他	0		0 受惠国LD	40	-Other
	84.72	**其他办公室用机器（例如,胶版复印机、油印机、地址印写机、自动付钞机、硬币分类、计数及包装机、削铅笔机、打洞机或订书机）：**					**Other office machines (for example, hectograph or stencil duplicating machines, addressing machines, automatic banknote dispensers, coin-sorting machines, coin-counting or -wrapping machines, pencil-sharpening machines, perforating or stapling machines) :**
6707	8472.1000	-胶版复印机、油印机	14	0 冰岛IS,东盟AS,哥CR,秘鲁PE,新加坡SG新西兰NZ,智利CL 8.4 澳AU 9.8 瑞士CH 11.2 巴PK,韩国KR	0 受惠国$_1$LD$_1$	40	-Duplicating machines
		-信件分类或折叠机或信件装封机、信件开封或闭封机、粘贴或盖销邮票机：					-Machines for sorting or folding mail or for inserting mail in envelopes or bands, machines for opening, closing or sealing mail and machines for affixing or cancelling postage stamps:
6708	8472.3010	---邮政信件分拣及封装设备	10	0 冰岛IS,东盟AS,哥CR,秘鲁PE,新西兰NZ,智利CL 5 巴PK 6 澳AU 8 韩国KR	0 受惠国LD	40	---Machines for sorting or banding mail
6709	8472.3090	---其他	14	0 冰岛IS,东盟AS,哥CR,秘鲁PE,新加坡SG新西兰NZ,智利CL 5.6 瑞士CH 7 巴PK 8.4 澳AU 11.2 韩国KR	0 受惠国$_1$LD$_1$	40	---Other
		-其他：					-Other:
6710	8472.9010	---自动柜员机	0		0 受惠国LD	40	---Automated teller
		---装订用机器：					---Stapling machines:
6711	8472.9021	----打洞机	0		0 受惠国LD	40	----Perforator
6712	8472.9022	----订书机	0		0 受惠国LD	40	----Stapler
6713	8472.9029	----其他	0		0 受惠国LD	40	----Other
6714	8472.9030	---碎纸机	0		0 受惠国LD	40	---Paper shrudders
6715	8472.9040	---地址印写机及地址铭牌压印机	14	0 冰岛IS,东盟AS,哥CR,秘鲁PE,新加坡SG新西兰NZ,智利CL 8.4 澳AU 9.8 瑞士CH 11.2 巴PK,韩国KR	0 受惠国$_1$LD$_1$	40	---Addressing machines and address plate embossing machines
6716	8472.9090	---其他	0		0 受惠国LD	40	---Other

序号 No.	税则号列 Tariff Line	中文货品名称 Article Description in Chinese	最惠国税率 MFN(%)	协定税率 Agreement(%)	特惠税率 SP(%)	普通税率 Gen(%)	英文货品名称 Article Description
	84.73	**专用于或主要用于税号84.69至84.72所列机器的零件、附件（罩套、提箱及类似品除外）：**					**Parts and accessories (other than covers, carrying cases and the like) suitable for use solely or principally with machines of headings 8469 to 8472:**
6717	8473.1000	-税号84.69所列机器的零件、附件	8	0 冰岛IS,东盟AS,哥CR,秘鲁PE,新西兰NZ,智利CL 3.2 瑞士CH 4.8 澳AU 5 巴PK 6.9 韩国KR	0 受惠国LD	35	-Parts and accessories of the machines of heading No.84.69
		-税号84.70所列机器的零件、附件：					-Parts and accessories of the machines of heading 8470:
6718	8473.2100	--子目号8470.10、8470.21或8470.29所列电子计算器的零件、附件	0		0 受惠国LD	50	--Of the electronic calculating ma-chines of subheading No.8470.10, 8470.21 or 8470.29
6719	8473.2900	--其他	0		0 受惠国LD	35	--Other
		-税号84.71所列机器的零件、附件：					-Parts and accessories of the machines of heading 8471:
6720	8473.3010	---子目号8471.4110、8471.4120、8471.4910、8471.4920、8471.5010、8471.5020、8471.6090、8471.7010、8471.7020、8471.7030及8471.7090所列机器及装置的零件、附件	0		0 受惠国LD	14	---Of the machines of subheading 8471.4110, 8471.4120, 8471.4910, 8471.4920, 8471.5010, 8471.5020, 8471.6090, 8471.7019, 8471.7020, 8471.7030 or 8471.7090
6721	8473.3090	---其他	0		0 受惠国LD	40	---Other
		-税号84.72所列机器的零件、附件：					-Parts and accessories of the machines of heading 8472:
6722	8473.4010	---自动柜员机用出钞器	10.5Δ5	0 冰岛IS,东盟AS,哥CR,秘鲁PE,新加坡SG,新西兰NZ,智利CL 5 巴PK 6.3 澳AU 7.4 瑞士CH 9.4 韩国KR	0 受惠国LD	35	---Banknote dispenser of automated teller
6723	8473.4090	---其他	10.5	0 冰岛IS,东盟AS,哥CR,秘鲁PE,新加坡SG,新西兰NZ,智利CL 5 巴PK 6.3 澳AU 7.4 瑞士CH 8.4 韩国KR	0 受惠国LD	35	---Other
	ex84734090	钞票清分机零附件	Δ3				Parts of banknote processing system
6724	8473.5000	-同样适用于税号84.69至84.72中两个或两个以上税号所列机器的零件、附件	0		0 受惠国LD	35	-Parts and accessories equally suitable for use with machines of two or more of the headings No.84.69 to 84.72

序号 No.	税则号列 Tariff Line	中文货品名称 Article Description in Chinese	最惠国税率 MFN(%)	协定税率 Agreement(%)		特惠税率 SP(%)		普通税率 Gen(%)	英文货品名称 Article Description
	84.74	泥土、石料、矿石或其他固体（包括粉状、浆状）矿物质的分类、筛选、分离、洗涤、破碎、磨粉、混合或搅拌机器;固体矿物燃料、陶瓷坯泥、未硬化水泥、石膏材料或其他粉状、浆状矿产品的粘聚或成形机器;铸造用砂模的成形机器:							**Machinery for sorting, screening, separating, washing, crushing, grinding, mixing or kneading earth, stone, ores or other mineral substances, in solid (including powder or paste) form; machinery for agglomerating, shaping or moulding solid mineral fuels, ceramic paste, unhardened cements, plastering materials or other mineral products in powder or paste form; machines for forming foundry moulds of sand:**
6725	8474.1000	-分类、筛选、分离或洗涤机器	5	0 2 4	澳AU,巴PK,冰岛IS,东盟AS,哥CR,秘鲁PE,新西兰NZ,智利CL 瑞士CH 韩国KR	0	受惠国LD	30	-Sorting, screening, separating or washing machines
		-破碎或磨粉机器:							-Crushing or grinding machines:
6726	8474.2010	---齿辊式	5	0 4	澳AU,巴PK,冰岛IS,东盟AS,哥CR,秘鲁PE,瑞士CH,新西兰NZ,智利CL 韩国KR	0	受惠国LD	30	---Toothing roller type
6727	8474.2020	---球磨式	5	0 2 4.3	澳AU,巴PK,冰岛IS,东盟AS,哥CR,秘鲁PE,新西兰NZ,智利CL 瑞士CH 韩国KR	0	受惠国LD	30	---Em-Peters type
6728	8474.2090	---其他	5	0 2 4	澳AU,巴PK,冰岛IS,东盟AS,哥CR,秘鲁PE,新西兰NZ,智利CL 瑞士CH 韩国KR	0	受惠国LD	30	---Other
		-混合或搅拌机器:							-Mixing or kneading machines:
6729	8474.3100	--混凝土或砂浆混合机器	7	0 2.8 4.2 5 5.6	冰岛IS,东盟AS,哥CR,秘鲁PE,新西兰NZ,智利CL 瑞士CH 澳AU 巴PK 韩国KR	0	受惠国LD	30	--Concrete or mortar mixers
6730	8474.3200	--矿物与沥青的混合机器	7	0 4.2 5 5.6	冰岛IS,东盟AS,哥CR,秘鲁PE,新西兰NZ,智利CL 澳AU 巴PK 韩国KR	0	受惠国LD	30	--Machines for mixing mineral substances with bitumen
6731	8474.3900	--其他	5	0 3.6 4	澳AU,巴PK,冰岛IS,东盟AS,哥CR,秘鲁PE,新西兰NZ,智利CL 瑞士CH 韩国KR	0	受惠国LD	30	--Other
		-其他机器:							-Other machinery:
6732	8474.8010	---辊压成型机	5	0 4 4.5	澳AU,巴PK,冰岛IS,东盟AS,哥CR,秘鲁PE,瑞士CH,新西兰NZ,智利CL 韩国KR 亚太AP	0	受惠国LD	30	---Rolling forming machines

序号 No.	税则号列 Tariff Line	中文货品名称 Article Description in Chinese	最惠国税率 MFN(%)	协定税率 Agreement(%)	特惠税率 SP(%)	普通税率 Gen(%)	英文货品名称 Article Description
6733	8474.8020	---模压成型机	5	0 澳AU,巴PK,冰岛IS,东盟AS,哥CR,秘鲁PE,瑞士CH,新西兰NZ,智利CL 4.3 韩国KR 4.5 亚太AP	0 受惠国LD	30	---Mould pressing machines
6734	8474.8090	---其他	5	0 澳AU,巴PK,冰岛IS,东盟AS,哥CR,秘鲁PE,瑞士CH,新西兰NZ,智利CL 4 韩国KR 4.5 亚太AP	0 受惠国LD	30	---Other
6735	8474.9000	-零件	5	0 澳AU,巴PK,冰岛IS,东盟AS,哥CR,秘鲁PE,新西兰NZ,智利CL 3.5 瑞士CH 4 韩国KR	0 受惠国LD	30	-Parts
	84.75	**白炽灯泡、灯管、放电灯管、电子管、闪光灯泡及类似品的封装机器;玻璃或玻璃制品的制造或热加工机器:**					**Machines for assembling electric or electronic lamps, tubes or valves or flashbulbs, in glass envelopes; machines for manufacturing or hot working glass or glassware:**
6736	8475.1000	-白炽灯泡、灯管、放电灯管、电子管、闪光灯泡及类似品的封装机器	8	0 冰岛IS,东盟AS,哥CR,秘鲁PE,新西兰NZ,智利CL 3.2 瑞士CH 4.8 澳AU 5 巴PK 6.4 韩国KR	0 受惠国LD	30	-Machines for assembling electric or electronic lamps, tubes or valves or flashbulbs, in glass envelopes
		-玻璃或玻璃制品的制造或热加工机器:					-Machines for manufacturing or hot working glass or glassware:
6737	8475.2100	--制造光导纤维及其预制棒的机器	10	0 冰岛IS,东盟AS,哥CR,秘鲁PE,新加坡SG新西兰NZ,智利CL 4 瑞士CH 5 巴PK 6 澳AU 8 韩国KR	0 受惠国LD	30	--Machines for making optical fibres and preforms thereof
		--其他:					--Other:
		---玻璃的热加工设备:					---Equipments for hot working glass or glasswares:
6738	8475.2911	----连续式玻璃热弯炉	10	0 冰岛IS,东盟AS,哥CR,秘鲁PE,新西兰NZ,智利CL 4 瑞士CH 5 巴PK 6 澳AU 8 韩国KR	0 受惠国LD	30	----Continuous hot bending furnaces
6739	8475.2912	----玻璃纤维拉丝机(光纤拉丝机除外)	10	0 冰岛IS,东盟AS,哥CR,秘鲁PE,新西兰NZ,智利CL 4 瑞士CH 5 巴PK 6 澳AU 8 韩国KR	0 受惠国LD	30	----Fiber glass winder (excluding Opti-caefiber winder)
6740	8475.2919	----其他	10	0 冰岛IS,东盟AS,哥CR,秘鲁PE,新加坡SG新西兰NZ,智利CL 4 瑞士CH 5 巴PK 6 澳AU 8 韩国KR	0 受惠国LD	30	----Other

序号 No.	税则号列 Tariff Line	中文货品名称 Article Description in Chinese	最惠国税率 MFN(%)	协定税率 Agreement(%)	特惠税率 SP(%)	普通税率 Gen(%)	英文货品名称 Article Description
6741	8475.2990	---其他	10	0 冰岛IS,东盟AS,哥CR,秘鲁PE,新西兰NZ,智利CL 4 瑞士CH 5 巴PK 6 澳AU 8 韩国KR	0 受惠国LD	30	---Other
6742	8475.9000	-零件	8	0 冰岛IS,东盟AS,哥CR,秘鲁PE,新西兰NZ,智利CL 3.2 瑞士CH 4.8 澳AU 5 巴PK 6.4 韩国KR	0 受惠国LD	30	-Parts
	84.76	自动售货机（例如,出售邮票、香烟、食品或饮料的机器）,包括钱币兑换机:					**Automatic goods-vending machines (for example, postage stamp, cigarette, food or beverage machines) , including money-changing machines:**
		-饮料自动销售机:					-Automatic beverage-vending machines:
6743	8476.2100	--装有加热或制冷装置的	14	0 冰岛IS,东盟AS,哥CR,秘鲁PE,新加坡SG,新西兰NZ,智利CL 8.4 澳AU 9.8 瑞士CH 11.2 巴PK,韩国KR	0 受惠国$_1$LD$_1$	50	--Incorporating heating or refrigerating devices
6744	8476.2900	--其他	15	0 冰岛IS,东盟AS,哥CR,新加坡SG,新西兰NZ,智利CL 4.5 秘鲁PE 9 澳AU 10.5 瑞士CH 12 巴PK,韩国KR	0 受惠国$_1$LD$_1$	50	--Other
		-其他机器:					-Other machines:
6745	8476.8100	--装有加热或制冷装置的	14	0 冰岛IS,东盟AS,哥CR,秘鲁PE,新加坡SG,新西兰NZ,智利CL 7 巴PK 8.4 澳AU 9.8 瑞士CH 11.2 韩国KR	0 受惠国$_1$LD$_1$	50	--Incorporating heating or refrigerating devices
6746	8476.8900	--其他	15	0 冰岛IS,东盟AS,哥CR,新加坡SG,新西兰NZ,智利CL 4.5 秘鲁PE 6 瑞士CH 9 澳AU 12 巴PK,韩国KR	0 受惠国$_1$LD$_1$	50	--Other
6747	8476.9000	-零件	10	0 冰岛IS,东盟AS,哥CR,秘鲁PE,瑞士CH,新西兰NZ,智利CL 5 巴PK 6 澳AU 8 韩国KR	0 受惠国LD	50	-Parts
	84.77	本章其他税号未列名的橡胶或塑料及其产品的加工机器:					**Machinery for working rubber or plastics or for the manufacture of products from these materials, not specified or included elsewhere in this chapter:**
		-注射机:					-Injection-moulding machines:
6748	8477.1010	---注塑机	0		0 受惠国LD	45	---For working plastics
6749	8477.1090	---其他	0		0 受惠国LD	30	---Other
		-挤出机:					-Extruders:

序号 No.	税则号列 Tariff Line	中文货品名称 Article Description in Chinese	最惠国税率 MFN(%)	协定税率 Agreement(%)	特惠税率 SP(%)	普通税率 Gen(%)	英文货品名称 Article Description
6750	8477.2010	---塑料造粒机	5	0 澳AU,巴PK,冰岛IS,东盟AS,哥CR,韩国KR,秘鲁PE,瑞士CH,台湾TW,香港HK,新西兰NZ,智利CL 4.5 亚太AP	0 受惠国LD	30	---Plastic pelletizers
6751	8477.2090	---其他	5	0 澳AU,巴PK,冰岛IS,东盟AS,哥CR,韩国KR,秘鲁PE,台湾TW,香港HK,新西兰NZ,智利CL 3.6 瑞士CH 4.5 亚太AP	0 受惠国LD	30	---Other
		-吹塑机:					-Blow-moulding machines:
6752	8477.3010	---挤出吹塑机	5	0 澳AU,巴PK,冰岛IS,东盟AS,哥CR,秘鲁PE,香港HK,新西兰NZ,智利CL 2 瑞士CH 4 韩国KR	0 受惠国LD	30	---Extruding blow molding machines
6753	8477.3020	---注射吹塑机	5	0 澳AU,巴PK,冰岛IS,东盟AS,哥CR,秘鲁PE,香港HK,新西兰NZ,智利CL 2 瑞士CH 3 韩国KR	0 受惠国LD	30	---Injecting blow molding machines
6754	8477.3090	---其他	5	0 澳AU,巴PK,冰岛IS,东盟AS,哥CR,秘鲁PE,香港HK,新西兰NZ,智利CL 2 瑞士CH 4 韩国KR	0 受惠国LD	30	---Other
		-真空模塑机器及其他热成型机器:					-Vacuum-moulding machines and other thermoforming machines:
6755	8477.4010	---塑料中空成型机	5	0 澳AU,巴PK,冰岛IS,东盟AS,哥CR,韩国KR,秘鲁PE,台湾TW,新西兰NZ,智利CL 4.5 亚太AP	0 受惠国LD	30	---Plastics brideg-die-forming machines
6756	8477.4020	---塑料压延成型机	5	0 澳AU,巴PK,冰岛IS,东盟AS,哥CR,韩国KR,秘鲁PE,台湾TW,新西兰NZ,智利CL 3.5 瑞士CH 4.5 亚太AP	0 受惠国LD	30	---Plastics calender-forming machines
6757	8477.4090	---其他	5	0 澳AU,巴PK,冰岛IS,东盟AS,哥CR,韩国KR,秘鲁PE,台湾TW,新西兰NZ,智利CL 3.6 瑞士CH 4.5 亚太AP	0 受惠国LD	30	---Other
		-其他模塑或成型机器:					-Other machinery for moulding or otherwise forming:
6758	8477.5100	--用于充气轮胎模塑或翻新的机器及内胎模塑或用其他方法成型的机器	5	0 澳AU,巴PK,冰岛IS,东盟AS,哥CR,秘鲁PE,瑞士CH,新西兰NZ,智利CL 4 韩国KR	0 受惠国LD	30	--For moulding or retreading pneumat-ic tyres or for moulding or otherwise forming inner tubes
		--其他:					--Other:
6759	8477.5910	---三维打印机（3D打印机）	5	0 澳AU,巴PK,冰岛IS,东盟AS,哥CR,秘鲁PE,台湾TW,香港HK,新西兰NZ,智利CL 2 瑞士CH 3.5 亚太AP 4.3 韩国KR	0 受惠国LD	30	---3D printers

序号 No.	税则号列 Tariff Line	中文货品名称 Article Description in Chinese	最惠国税率 MFN(%)	协定税率 Agreement(%)	特惠税率 SP(%)	普通税率 Gen(%)	英文货品名称 Article Description
6760	8477.5990	---其他	5	0 澳AU,巴PK,冰岛IS,东盟AS,哥CR,秘鲁PE,台湾TW,香港HK,新西兰NZ,智利CL 2 瑞士CH 3.5 亚太AP 4.3 韩国KR	0 受惠国LD	30	---Other
6761	8477.8000	-其他机器	5	0 澳AU,巴PK,冰岛IS,东盟AS,哥CR,韩国KR,秘鲁PE,台湾TW,香港HK,新西兰NZ,智利CL 3.6 瑞士CH 4.5 亚太AP	0 受惠国LD	30	-Other machinery
6762	8477.9000	-零件	0		0 受惠国LD	30	-Parts
	84.78	**本章其他税号未列名的烟草加工及制作机器：**					**Machinery for preparing or making up tobacco, not specified or included elsewhere in this chapter:**
6763	8478.1000	-机器	5	0 巴PK,冰岛IS,东盟AS,哥CR,秘鲁PE,瑞士CH,新西兰NZ,智利CL 2.5 亚太AP	0 受惠国$_1$LD$_1$	30	-Machinery
6764	8478.9000	-零件	10Δ5	0 冰岛IS,东盟AS,哥CR,秘鲁PE,新西兰NZ,智利CL 4 瑞士CH 5 巴PK	0 受惠国$_1$LD$_1$	30	-Parts
	84.79	**本章其他税号未列名的具有独立功能的机器及机械器具：**					**Machines and mechanical appliances having individual functions, not specified or included elsewhere in this chapter:**
		-公共工程用机器：					-Machinery for public works, building or the like:
		---摊铺机：					---Spreading machines:
6765	8479.1021	----沥青混凝土摊铺机	8	0 冰岛IS,东盟AS,哥CR,秘鲁PE,新西兰NZ,智利CL 3.2 瑞士CH 4.8 澳AU,韩国KR 5 巴PK 5.6 亚太AP	0 受惠国LD	30	----Machines for spreading bituminous concrete
6766	8479.1022	----稳定土摊铺机	8	0 冰岛IS,东盟AS,哥CR,秘鲁PE,新西兰NZ,智利CL 3.2 瑞士CH 4.8 澳AU,韩国KR 5 巴PK 5.6 亚太AP	0 受惠国LD	30	----Stabilizer spreading machines
6767	8479.1029	----其他	8	0 冰岛IS,东盟AS,哥CR,秘鲁PE,新西兰NZ,智利CL 3.2 瑞士CH 4.8 澳AU,韩国KR 5 巴PK 5.6 亚太AP	0 受惠国LD	30	----Other
6768	8479.1090	---其他	8	0 冰岛IS,东盟AS,哥CR,秘鲁PE,新西兰NZ,智利CL 3.2 瑞士CH 4.8 澳AU 5 巴PK 5.6 亚太AP 6.4 韩国KR	0 受惠国LD	30	---Other

序号 No.	税则号列 Tariff Line	中文货品名称 Article Description in Chinese	最惠国税率 MFN(%)	协定税率 Agreement(%)	特惠税率 SP(%)	普通税率 Gen(%)	英文货品名称 Article Description
6769	8479.2000	-提取、加工动物油脂或植物固定油脂的机器	10	0 冰岛IS,东盟AS,哥CR,秘鲁PE,新加坡SG,新西兰NZ,智利CL 4 瑞士CH 5 巴PK 6 澳AU 8 韩国KR	0 受惠国LD	30	-Machinery for the extraction or preparation of animal or fixed vegetable fats or oils
6770	8479.3000	-木碎料板或木纤维板的挤压机及其他木材或软木处理机	10	0 冰岛IS,东盟AS,哥CR,秘鲁PE,新西兰NZ,智利CL 4 瑞士CH 5 巴PK 6 澳AU 8 韩国KR	0 受惠国LD	30	-Presses for the manufacture of particle board or fibre building board or wood or other ligneous materials and other machinery for treating wood or cork
6771	8479.4000	-绳或缆的制造机器	7Δ5	0 冰岛IS,东盟AS,哥CR,秘鲁PE,新西兰NZ,智利CL 2.8 瑞士CH 4.2 澳AU,韩国KR 5 巴PK	0 受惠国LD	30	-Rope or cable-making machines
		-未列名工业机器人:					-Industrial robots, not elsewhere specified or included:
6772	8479.5010	---多功能工业机器人	0		0 受惠国LD	20	---Industrial robots for multiple functions
6773	8479.5090	---其他	0		0 受惠国LD	30	---Other
6774	8479.6000	-蒸发式空气冷却器	10	0 冰岛IS,东盟AS,哥CR,秘鲁PE,新西兰NZ,智利CL 4 瑞士CH 5 巴PK 6 澳AU 8 韩国KR 9 亚太AP	0 受惠国LD	30	-Evaporative air coolers
		-旅客登机船(桥):					-Passenger boarding bridges:
6775	8479.7100	--用于机场的	0		0 受惠国LD	30	--Used in airports
6776	8479.7900	--其他	0		0 受惠国LD	30	--Other
		-其他机器及机械器具:					-Other machines and mechanical appliances:
		--处理金属的机械,包括线圈绕线机:					--For treating metal, including electric wire coil-winders:
6777	8479.8110	---绕线机	9.5	0 冰岛IS,东盟AS,哥CR,秘鲁PE,台湾TW,香港HK,新西兰NZ,智利CL 5 巴PK 5.7 澳AU 6.7 瑞士CH 7.6 韩国KR 9 亚太AP	0 受惠国LD	30	---Filament winding machines
6778	8479.8190	---其他	9.5	0 冰岛IS,东盟AS,哥CR,秘鲁PE,台湾TW,香港HK,新西兰NZ,智利CL 5 巴PK 5.7 澳AU 6.7 瑞士CH 7.6 韩国KR 9 亚太AP	0 受惠国LD	30	---Other
6779	8479.8200	--混合、搅拌、轧碎、研磨、筛选、均化或乳化机器	7	0 巴PK,冰岛IS,东盟AS,哥CR,韩国KR,秘鲁PE,台湾TW,新西兰NZ,智利CL 4.2 澳AU 4.9 亚太AP	0 受惠国LD	30	--Mixing, kneading, crushing, grinding, screening, sifting, homogenizing, emulsifying or stirring machines
	ex84798200	用于废物和废水处理的混合、搅拌、轧碎、研磨、筛选、均化或乳化机器	Δ5				Devices for waste and wastewater mixing, stirring , crushing, grinding, screeing, homogenising and emulsifying devices.

序号 No.	税则号列 Tariff Line	中文货品名称 Article Description in Chinese	最惠国税率 MFN(%)	协定税率 Agreement(%)	特惠税率 SP(%)	普通税率 Gen(%)	英文货品名称 Article Description
		--其他:					--Other:
6780	8479.8910	---船舶用舵机及陀螺稳定器	0		0 受惠国LD	14	---Steering and rudder equipment or gyroscopic stabilizers for ships
6781	8479.8920	---空气增湿器及减湿器	0		0 受惠国LD	70	---Air humidifiers or dehumidifiers
6782	8479.8940	---邮政用包裹、印刷品分拣设备	0		0 受惠国LD	30	---Bundle and printed matter sorting machines used in post offices
6783	8479.8950	---放射性废物压实机	0		0 受惠国LD	30	---Presses for radioactive waste material
		---在印刷电路电路板上装配元器件的机器:					---Machines for assemblying elements on printed circuit boards:
6784	8479.8961	----自动插件机	0		0 受惠国LD	30	----Automatic plugin machines
6785	8479.8962	----自动贴片机	0		0 受惠国LD	30	----Automatic coreslice adhering machines
6786	8479.8969	----其他	0		0 受惠国LD	30	----Other
		---其他:					---Other:
6787	8479.8992	----自动化立体仓储设备	0		0 受惠国LD	30	----Automated high-rise warehouse
6788	8479.8999	----其他	0		0 受惠国LD	30	----Other
		-零件:					-Parts:
6789	8479.9010	---船舶用舵机及陀螺稳定器用	0		0 受惠国LD	14	---Of the machines of subheading No.8479.8910
6790	8479.9020	---空气增湿器及减湿器用	0		0 受惠国LD	70	---Of the machines of subheading No.8479.8920
6791	8479.9090	---其他	0		0 受惠国LD	20	---Other
	84.80	**金属铸造用型箱;型模底板;阳模;金属用型模(锭模除外)、硬质合金、玻璃、矿物材料、橡胶或塑料用型模:**					**Moulding boxes for metal foundry; mould bases; moulding patterns; moulds for metal (other than ingot moulds), metal carbides, glass, mineral materials, rubber or plastics:**
6792	8480.1000	-金属铸造用型箱	10	0 冰岛IS,东盟AS,哥CR,秘鲁PE,新西兰NZ,智利CL 4 瑞士CH 5 巴PK 6 澳AU 8 韩国KR	0 受惠国LD	20	-Moulding boxes for metal foundry
6793	8480.2000	-型模底板	8	0 冰岛IS,东盟AS,哥CR,秘鲁PE,新西兰NZ,智利CL 3.2 瑞士CH 4.8 澳AU 5 巴PK 6.4 韩国KR	0 受惠国LD	20	-Mould bases
6794	8480.3000	-阳模	10	0 冰岛IS,东盟AS,哥CR,秘鲁PE,新加坡SG,新西兰NZ,智利CL 4 瑞士CH 5 巴PK 6 澳AU 8 韩国KR	0 受惠国LD	20	-Moulding patterns
		-金属、硬质合金用型模:					-Moulds for metal or metal carbides:
		--注模或压模:					--Injection or compression types:
6795	8480.4110	---压铸模	8	0 冰岛IS,东盟AS,哥CR,秘鲁PE,台湾TW,香港HK,新西兰NZ,智利CL 3.2 瑞士CH 4.8 澳AU 5 巴PK 5.6 亚太AP 6.9 韩国KR	0 受惠国LD	20	---Die casting moulds

序号 No.	税则号列 Tariff Line	中文货品名称 Article Description in Chinese	最惠国税率 MFN(%)	协定税率 Agreement(%)	特惠税率 SP(%)	普通税率 Gen(%)	英文货品名称 Article Description
6796	8480.4120	---粉末冶金用压模	8	0 冰岛IS,东盟AS,哥CR,秘鲁PE,台湾TW,香港HK,新西兰NZ,智利CL 3.2 瑞士CH 4.8 澳AU 5 巴PK 5.6 亚太AP 6.9 韩国KR	0 受惠国LD	20	---Compression moulds for power metallurgy
6797	8480.4190	---其他	8	0 冰岛IS,东盟AS,哥CR,秘鲁PE,台湾TW,香港HK,新西兰NZ,智利CL 3.2 瑞士CH 4.8 澳AU 5 巴PK 5.6 亚太AP 6.9 韩国KR	0 受惠国LD	20	---Other
6798	8480.4900	--其他	8	0 冰岛IS,东盟AS,哥CR,秘鲁PE,新西兰NZ,智利CL 3.2 瑞士CH 4.8 澳AU 5 巴PK 5.6 亚太AP 6.9 韩国KR	0 受惠国LD	20	--Other
6799	8480.5000	-玻璃用型模	8.4	0 冰岛IS,东盟AS,哥CR,秘鲁PE,新西兰NZ,智利CL 3.36 瑞士CH 5 澳AU,巴PK 7.2 韩国KR	0 受惠国LD	20	-Moulds for glass
6800	8480.6000	-矿物材料用型模	8.4	0 冰岛IS,东盟AS,哥CR,秘鲁PE,新西兰NZ,智利CL 3.36 瑞士CH 5 澳AU,巴PK 6.7 韩国KR	0 受惠国LD	20	-Moulds for mineral materials
		-塑料或橡胶用型模:					-Moulds for rubber or plastics:
		注模或压模:					--Injection or compression types:
6801	8480.7110	---硫化轮胎用囊式型模	0		0 受惠国LD	20	---"Bladder" moulds for vulcanising tyres
6802	8480.7190	---其他	0		0 受惠国LD	20	---Other
6803	8480.7900	--其他	5	0 澳AU,巴PK,东盟AS,哥CR,韩国KR,秘鲁PE,台湾TW,香港HK,新西兰NZ,智利CL 2 瑞士CH 3.5 亚太AP	0 受惠国LD	20	--Other
	84.81	**用于管道、锅炉、罐、桶或类似品的龙头、旋塞、阀门及类似装置,包括减压阀及恒温控制阀:**					**Taps, cocks, valves and similar appliances for pipes, boiler shells, tanks, vats or the like, including pressure-reducing valves and thermostatically controlled valves:**
6804	8481.1000	-减压阀	5	0 澳AU,巴PK,冰岛IS,东盟AS,哥CR,秘鲁PE,新西兰NZ,智利CL 3.5 瑞士CH 4.3 韩国KR	0 受惠国LD	30	-Pressure-reducing valves
	ex84811000	喷灌设备用减压阀	Δ2				Pressure reducing valves for sprinkler equipment
		-油压或气压传动阀:					-Valves for oleohydraulic or pneumatic transmissions:

序号 No.	税则号列 Tariff Line	中文货品名称 Article Description in Chinese	最惠国税率 MFN(%)	协定税率 Agreement(%)	特惠税率 SP(%)	普通税率 Gen(%)	英文货品名称 Article Description
6805	8481.2010	---油压的	5	0 澳AU,巴PK,冰岛IS,东盟AS,哥CR,秘鲁PE,台湾TW,新西兰NZ,智利CL 3.5 瑞士CH 4.3 韩国KR	0 受惠国LD	30	---For oleohydraulic transmissions
6806	8481.2020	---气压的	5	0 澳AU,巴PK,冰岛IS,东盟AS,哥CR,秘鲁PE,新西兰NZ,智利CL 3.5 瑞士CH 4.3 韩国KR	0 受惠国LD	30	---For pneumatic transmissions
6807	8481.3000	-止回阀	5	0 澳AU,巴PK,冰岛IS,东盟AS,哥CR,秘鲁PE,台湾TW,新西兰NZ,智利CL 3.5 瑞士CH 4.3 韩国KR	0 受惠国LD	30	-Check (nonreturn) valves
6808	8481.4000	-安全阀或溢流阀	5	0 澳AU,巴PK,冰岛IS,东盟AS,哥CR,秘鲁PE,台湾TW,新西兰NZ,智利CL 2 瑞士CH 4.3 韩国KR	0 受惠国LD	30	-Safety or relief valves
		-其他器具：					-Other appliances:
		---换向阀：					---Directional control valves:
6809	8481.8021	----电磁式	7	0 巴PK,冰岛IS,东盟AS,哥CR,秘鲁PE,台湾TW,香港HK,新西兰NZ,智利CL 4.2 澳AU 4.9 瑞士CH,亚太AP 6 韩国KR	0 受惠国LD	30	----Electromagnetical operated
6810	8481.8029	----其他	7	0 巴PK,冰岛IS,东盟AS,哥CR,秘鲁PE,台湾TW,香港HK,新西兰NZ,智利CL 4.2 澳AU 4.9 瑞士CH,亚太AP 6 韩国KR	0 受惠国LD	30	----Other
		---流量阀：					---Flow valves:
6811	8481.8031	----电子膨胀阀	7	0 巴PK,冰岛IS,东盟AS,哥CR,秘鲁PE,台湾TW,香港HK,新西兰NZ,智利CL 2.8 瑞士CH 4.2 澳AU 4.9 亚太AP 6 韩国KR	0 受惠国LD	30	----Electronic expansion valves
6812	8481.8039	----其他	7	0 巴PK,冰岛IS,东盟AS,哥CR,秘鲁PE,台湾TW,香港HK,新西兰NZ,智利CL 4.2 澳AU 4.9 瑞士CH,亚太AP 6 韩国KR	0 受惠国LD	30	----Other
6813	8481.8040	---其他阀门	7Δ5	0 巴PK,冰岛IS,东盟AS,哥CR,韩国KR,秘鲁PE,台湾TW,香港HK,新西兰NZ,智利CL 4.2 澳AU 4.9 瑞士CH,亚太AP	0 受惠国LD	30	---Other valves

序号 No.	税则号列 Tariff Line	中文货品名称 Article Description in Chinese	最惠国税率 MFN(%)	协定税率 Agreement(%)	特惠税率 SP(%)	普通税率 Gen(%)	英文货品名称 Article Description
6814	8481.8090	---其他	5	0 澳AU,巴PK,冰岛IS,东盟AS,哥CR,秘鲁PE,香港HK,新西兰NZ,智利CL 2 瑞士CH 3 韩国KR	0 受惠国LD	50	---Other
		-零件:					-Parts:
6815	8481.9010	---阀门用	8Δ4	0 冰岛IS,东盟AS,哥CR,韩国KR,秘鲁PE,台湾TW,新西兰NZ,智利CL 4.8 澳AU 5 巴PK 5.6 瑞士CH	0 受惠国LD	30	---Of valves
6816	8481.9090	---其他	8	0 冰岛IS,东盟AS,哥CR,秘鲁PE,台湾TW,新西兰NZ,智利CL 3.2 瑞士CH 4.8 澳AU,韩国KR 5 巴PK	0 受惠国LD	50	---Other
	84.82	**滚动轴承:**					**Ball or roller bearings:**
		-滚珠轴承:					-Ball bearings:
6817	8482.1010	---调心球轴承	8	0 冰岛IS,东盟AS,哥CR,秘鲁PE,香港HK,新加坡SG,新西兰NZ,智利CL 3.2 瑞士CH 4.8 澳AU,韩国KR 5 巴PK 7.6 亚太AP	0 受惠国LD	20	---Self-aligning ball bearing
6818	8482.1020	---深沟球轴承	8	0 冰岛IS,东盟AS,哥CR,秘鲁PE,香港HK,新加坡SG,新西兰NZ,智利CL 3.2 瑞士CH 4.8 澳AU,韩国KR 5 巴PK 7.6 亚太AP	0 受惠国LD	20	---Deep groove ball bearing
6819	8482.1030	---角接触轴承	8	0 冰岛IS,东盟AS,哥CR,秘鲁PE,香港HK,新加坡SG,新西兰NZ,智利CL 3.2 瑞士CH 4.8 澳AU,韩国KR 5 巴PK 7.6 亚太AP	0 受惠国LD	20	---Angular contact ball bearing
6820	8482.1040	---推力球轴承	8	0 冰岛IS,东盟AS,哥CR,秘鲁PE,香港HK,新加坡SG,新西兰NZ,智利CL 3.2 瑞士CH 4.8 澳AU,韩国KR 5 巴PK 7.6 亚太AP	0 受惠国LD	20	---Thrust ball bearing
6821	8482.1090	---其他	8	0 冰岛IS,东盟AS,哥CR,秘鲁PE,香港HK,新加坡SG,新西兰NZ,智利CL 4.8 澳AU,韩国KR 5 巴PK 5.6 瑞士CH 7.6 亚太AP	0 受惠国LD	20	---Other

序号 No.	税则号列 Tariff Line	中文货品名称 Article Description in Chinese	最惠国税率 MFN(%)	协定税率 Agreement(%)	特惠税率 SP(%)	普通税率 Gen(%)	英文货品名称 Article Description
6822	8482.2000	-锥形滚子轴承,包括锥形滚子组件	8	0 冰岛IS,东盟AS,哥CR,秘鲁PE,新西兰NZ,智利CL 3.2 瑞士CH 4.8 澳AU,韩国KR 5 巴PK	0 受惠国LD	20	-Tapered roller bearings, including cone and tapered roller assemblies
6823	8482.3000	-鼓形滚子轴承	8Δ6	0 冰岛IS,东盟AS,哥CR,秘鲁PE,新西兰NZ,智利CL 3.2 瑞士CH 4.8 澳AU,韩国KR 5 巴PK	0 受惠国LD	20	-Spherical roller bearings
6824	8482.4000	-滚针轴承	8Δ6	0 东盟AS,哥CR,秘鲁PE,台湾TW,新西兰NZ,智利CL 3.2 瑞士CH 4.8 澳AU,韩国KR 5 巴PK	0 受惠国LD	20	-Needle roller bearings
6825	8482.5000	-其他圆柱形滚子轴承	8	0 冰岛IS,东盟AS,哥CR,秘鲁PE,新加坡SG,新西兰NZ,智利CL 4.8 澳AU 5 巴PK 5.6 瑞士CH 6.9 韩国KR	0 受惠国LD	20	-Other cylindrical roller bearings
	ex84825000	三环、二环偏心滚动轴承	Δ4				Eccentric 3-ring or 2-ring roller bearing
6826	8482.8000	-其他,包括球、柱混合轴承	8	0 冰岛IS,东盟AS,哥CR,秘鲁PE,新西兰NZ,智利CL 4.8 澳AU 5 巴PK 5.6 瑞士CH,亚太AP 6.9 韩国KR	0 受惠国LD	20	-Other, including combined ball/roller bearings
		-零件:					-Parts:
6827	8482.9100	--滚珠、滚针及滚柱	8Δ6	0 冰岛IS,东盟AS,哥CR,秘鲁PE,新西兰NZ,智利CL 3.2 瑞士CH 4.8 澳AU,韩国KR 5 巴PK	0 受惠国LD	20	--Balls, needles and rollers
6828	8482.9900	--其他	6Δ3	0 冰岛IS,东盟AS,哥CR,韩国KR,秘鲁PE,台湾TW,新西兰NZ,智利CL 3.6 澳AU 4.2 瑞士CH 5 巴PK	0 受惠国LD	20	--Other
	84.83	**传动轴(包括凸轮轴及曲柄轴)及曲柄;轴承座及滑动轴承;齿轮及齿轮传动装置;滚珠或滚子螺杆传动装置;齿轮箱及其他变速装置,包括扭矩变换器;飞轮及滑轮,包括滑轮组;离合器及联轴器(包括万向节):**					**Transmission shafts (including cam shafts and crank shafts) and cranks; bearing housings and plain shaft bearings; gears and gearing; ball or roller screws; gear boxes and other speed changers, including torque converters; flywheels and pulleys, including pulley blocks; clutches and shaft couplings (including universal joints) :**
		-传动轴(包括凸轮轴及曲柄轴)及曲柄:					-Transmission shafts (including cam shafts and crank shafts) and cranks:
		---船舶用传动轴:					---Transmission shafts for ships:

序号 No.	税则号列 Tariff Line	中文货品名称 Article Description in Chinese	最惠国税率 MFN(%)	协定税率 Agreement(%)	特惠税率 SP(%)	普通税率 Gen(%)	英文货品名称 Article Description
6829	8483.1011	----柴油机曲轴	6	0 澳门MO,冰岛IS,东盟AS,哥CR,秘鲁PE,香港HK,新西兰NZ,智利CL 2.4 瑞士CH 3.6 澳AU 5 巴PK 5.1 韩国KR,亚太AP	0 受惠国LD	14	----Diesel engine crankshaft
6830	8483.1019	----其他	6	0 澳门MO,冰岛IS,东盟AS,哥CR,秘鲁PE,香港HK,新西兰NZ,智利CL 2.4 瑞士CH 3.6 澳AU 5 巴PK 5.1 亚太AP 5.2 韩国KR	0 受惠国LD	14	----Other
6831	8483.1090	---其他	6	0 澳门MO,冰岛IS,东盟AS,哥CR,秘鲁PE,香港HK,新西兰NZ,智利CL 3.6 澳AU 4.2 瑞士CH 5 巴PK 5.2 韩国KR 5.4 亚太AP	0 受惠国LD	30	---Other
6832	8483.2000	-装有滚珠或滚子轴承的轴承座	6	0 澳门MO,冰岛IS,东盟AS,哥CR,秘鲁PE,新西兰NZ,智利CL 3.6 澳AU,韩国KR 4.2 瑞士CH 5 巴PK	0 受惠国LD	30	-Bearing housings, incorporating ball or roller bearings
6833	8483.3000	-未装有滚珠或滚子轴承的轴承座;滑动轴承	6Δ4	0 澳门MO,冰岛IS,东盟AS,哥CR,秘鲁PE,新西兰NZ,智利CL 3.6 澳AU,韩国KR 4.2 瑞士CH 5 巴PK	0 受惠国LD	30	-Bearing housings, not incorporating ball or roller bearings; plain shaft bearings
		-齿轮及齿轮传动装置,但单独进口或出口的带齿的轮、链轮及其他传动元件除外;滚珠或滚子螺杆传动装置;齿轮箱及其他变速装置,包括扭矩变换器:					-Gears and gearing, other than toothed wheels, chain sprockets and other transmission elements presented separately; ball or roller screws; gear boxes and other speed changers, including torque converters:
6834	8483.4010	---滚子螺杆传动装置	8	0 澳门MO,冰岛IS,东盟AS,哥CR,秘鲁PE,台湾TW,香港HK,新西兰NZ,智利CL 4.8 澳AU,韩国KR 5 巴PK 5.6 瑞士CH,亚太AP	0 受惠国LD	30	---Roller Screws
6835	8483.4020	---行星齿轮减速器	8	0 澳门MO,冰岛IS,东盟AS,哥CR,秘鲁PE,香港HK,新西兰NZ,智利CL 4.8 澳AU 5 巴PK 5.6 瑞士CH,亚太AP 6.8 韩国KR	0 受惠国LD	30	---Planet decelerators
6836	8483.4090	---其他	8	0 澳门MO,冰岛IS,东盟AS,哥CR,秘鲁PE,台湾TW,香港HK,新西兰NZ,智利CL 4.8 澳AU 5 巴PK 5.6 瑞士CH,亚太AP 6.9 韩国KR	0 受惠国LD	30	---Other

序号 No.	税则号列 Tariff Line	中文货品名称 Article Description in Chinese	最惠国税率 MFN(%)	协定税率 Agreement(%)	特惠税率 SP(%)	普通税率 Gen(%)	英文货品名称 Article Description
6837	8483.5000	-飞轮及滑轮，包括滑轮组	8	0 澳门MO,冰岛IS,东盟AS,哥CR,秘鲁PE,新西兰NZ,智利CL 4.8 澳AU 5 巴PK 5.6 瑞士CH 6.4 韩国KR	0 受惠国LD	30	-Flywheels and pulleys, including pulley blocks
6838	8483.6000	-离合器及联轴器（包括万向节）	8	0 澳门MO,冰岛IS,东盟AS,哥CR,秘鲁PE,新西兰NZ,智利CL 4.8 澳AU 5 巴PK 5.6 瑞士CH 6.9 韩国KR	0 受惠国LD	30	-Clutches and shaft couplings (including universal joints)
	ex84836000	压力机用组合式湿式离合/制动器,离合扭距为60KNM~300KNM,制动扭距为30KNM~100KNM	Δ4				Hydraulic actuated clutch/brake, for press machinery, 60KNM≤clutch torque≤300KNM, 30KNM≤braking torque ≤100KNM
6839	8483.9000	-单独报验的带齿的轮、链轮及其他传动元件；零件	8	0 澳门MO,冰岛IS,东盟AS,哥CR,秘鲁PE,台湾TW,香港HK,新西兰NZ,智利CL 4.8 澳AU,韩国KR 5 巴PK 5.6 瑞士CH	0 受惠国LD	30	-Toothed wheels, chain sprockets and other transmission elements presented separately; parts
	ex84839000	车用凸轮轴相位调节器	Δ4				Camshaft phase adjuster for vehicle
	84.84	**密封垫或类似接合衬垫,用金属片与其他材料制成或用双层或多层金属片制成;成套或各种不同材料的密封垫或类似接合衬垫,装于袋、套或类似包装内;机械密封件:**					**Gaskets and similar joints of metal sheeting combined with other material or of two or more layers of metal; sets or assortments of gaskets and similar joints, dissimilar in composition, put up in pouches, envelopes or similar packings; mechanical seals:**
6840	8484.1000	-密封垫或类似接合衬垫，用金属片与其他材料制成或用双层或多层金属片制成	8Δ5	0 冰岛IS,东盟AS,哥CR,秘鲁PE,台湾TW,新西兰NZ,智利CL 4.8 澳AU 5 巴PK 5.6 瑞士CH 6.9 韩国KR	0 受惠国LD	30	-Gaskets and similar joints of metal sheeting combined with other material or of two or more layers of metal
6841	8484.2000	-机械密封件	8Δ5	0 冰岛IS,东盟AS,哥CR,秘鲁PE,新西兰NZ,智利CL 4.8 澳AU 5 巴PK 5.6 瑞士CH 6.9 韩国KR	0 受惠国LD	30	-Mechanical seals
6842	8484.9000	-其他	8Δ5	0 冰岛IS,东盟AS,哥CR,秘鲁PE,新西兰NZ,智利CL 3.2 瑞士CH 4.8 澳AU 5 巴PK 6.9 韩国KR	0 受惠国LD	30	-Other

序号 No.	税则号列 Tariff Line	中文货品名称 Article Description in Chinese	最惠国税率 MFN(%)	协定税率 Agreement(%)	特惠税率 SP(%)	普通税率 Gen(%)	英文货品名称 Article Description
	84.86	专用于或主要用于制造半导体单晶柱或晶圆、半导体器件、集成电路或平板显示器的机器及装置；本章注释九（三）规定的机器及装置；零件及附件：					**Machines and apparatus of a kind used solely or principally for the manufacture of semiconductor boules or wafers, semiconductor devices, electronic integrated circuits or flat panel displays; machines and apparatus specified in note 9 (C) to this chapter; parts and accessories:**
		-制造单晶柱或晶圆用的机器及装置：					-Machines and apparatus for the manufacture of boules or wafers:
6843	8486.1010	---利用温度变化处理单晶硅的机器及装置	0		0 老挝LA,受惠国LD	30	---Machines and apparatus for the manufacture of boules by aprocess involving a change of temperature
6844	8486.1020	---研磨设备	0		0 受惠国LD	30	---Grinding machines
6845	8486.1030	---切割设备	0		0 受惠国LD	30	---Sawing or cutting-off machines
6846	8486.1040	---化学机械抛光设备（CMP）	0		0 受惠国LD	30	---Chemical mechanical polishers (CMP)
6847	8486.1090	---其他	0		0 受惠国LD	30	---Other
		-制造半导体器件或集成电路用的机器及装置：					-Machines and apparatus for the manufacture of semiconductor devices or of electronic integrated circuits:
6848	8486.2010	---氧化、扩散、退火及其他热处理设备	0		0 老挝LA,受惠国LD	30	---Diffusion, oxidation or annealing furnaces, ovens and other heating equipments
		---薄膜沉积设备：					---Film deposition equipments:
6849	8486.2021	----化学气相沉积装置（CVD）	0		0 受惠国LD	30	----Chemical Vapour Deposition (CVD) equipment
6850	8486.2022	----物理气相沉积装置（PVD）	0		0 受惠国LD	30	----Physical Vapour Deposition (PVD) equipment
6851	8486.2029	----其他	0		0 受惠国LD	30	----Other
		---将电路图投影或绘制到感光半导体材料上的装置：					---Apparatus for the projection or drawing of circuit patterns on sensitized semiconductor materials:
6852	8486.2031	----分步重复光刻机（步进光刻机）	0		0 受惠国LD	100	----Step and repeat aligners
6853	8486.2039	----其他	0		0 受惠国LD	100	----Other
		---刻蚀及剥离设备：					---Etching and stripping equipments:
6854	8486.2041	----等离子体干法刻蚀机	0		0 受惠国LD	30	----Dry plasma etching
6855	8486.2049	----其他	0		0 受惠国LD	30	----Other
6856	8486.2050	---离子注入机	0		0 受惠国LD	11	---Ion Implanters for doping
6857	8486.2090	---其他	0		0 受惠国LD	30	---Other
		-制造平板显示器用的机器及装置：					-Machines and apparatus for the manufacture of flat panel displays:
6858	8486.3010	---扩散、氧化、退火及其他热处理设备	0		0 老挝LA,受惠国LD	30	---Diffusion, oxidation or annealing furnaces, ovens and other heating equipments
		---薄膜沉积设备：					---Film deposition equipments:
6859	8486.3021	----化学气相沉积设备（CVD）	0		0 受惠国LD	30	----Chemical Vapour Deposition (CVD) equipment
6860	8486.3022	----物理气相沉积设备（PVD）	0		0 受惠国LD	30	----Physical Vapour Deposition (PVD) equipment
6861	8486.3029	----其他	0		0 受惠国LD	30	----Other
		---将电路图投影或绘制到感光半导体材料上的装置：					---Apparatus for the projection or drawing of circuit patterns on sensitized semiconductor materials:
6862	8486.3031	----分布重复光刻机	0		0 受惠国LD	100	----Step and repeat aligners
6863	8486.3039	----其他	0		0 受惠国LD	100	----Other

序号 No.	税则号列 Tariff Line	中文货品名称 Article Description in Chinese	最惠国税率 MFN(%)	协定税率 Agreement(%)	特惠税率 SP(%)	普通税率 Gen(%)	英文货品名称 Article Description
		---湿法蚀刻、显影、剥离、清洗装置：					---Apparatus for wet-etching, developing, stripping or cleaning:
6864	8486.3041	----超声波清洗装置	10Δ5	0 冰岛IS,东盟AS,哥CR,秘鲁PE,新加坡SG,新西兰NZ,智利CL 4 瑞士CH 5 巴PK 6 澳AU	0 受惠国LD	30	----Cleaning apparatus operated by ultrasonic processes
6865	8486.3049	----其他	0		0 受惠国LD	30	----Other
6866	8486.3090	---其他	0		0 受惠国LD	30	---Other
		-本章注释九（三）规定的机器及装置：					-Machines and apparatus specified in note 9 (C) to this chapter:
6867	8486.4010	---主要用于或专用于制作和修复掩膜版或投影掩膜版的装置	0		0 受惠国LD	70	---Machines and apparatus solely or principally of a kind used for the manufacture or repair of masks and reticles
		---主要用于或专用于装配与封装半导体器件或集成电路的设备：					---Machines and apparatus solely or principally of a kind used for assembling semiconductor devices or electronic integrated circuits:
6868	8486.4021	----塑封机	5	0 澳AU,巴PK,冰岛IS,东盟AS,哥CR,秘鲁PE,瑞士CH,新西兰NZ,智利CL 4.5 亚太AP 4.8 韩国KR	0 受惠国LD	30	----Encapsulation equipment for making the plastic casings
6869	8486.4022	----引线键合装置	8	0 冰岛IS,东盟AS,哥CR,秘鲁PE,香港HK,新西兰NZ,智利CL 4.8 澳AU 5 巴PK 5.6 瑞士CH 7.6 亚太AP	0 受惠国LD	30	----Wire bonders
	ex84864022	全自动铝丝焊接机	Δ6				Automatic aluminum wire bonders
	ex84864022	全自动铜丝焊接机	Δ6				Automatic copper wire bonders
	ex84864022	全自动金丝焊接机	Δ6				Automatic gold wire bonders
6870	8486.4029	----其他	0		0 受惠国LD	17	----Other
		---主要用于或专用于升降、装卸、搬运单晶柱、晶圆、半导体器件、集成电路或平板显示器的装置：					---Machines and apparatus solely or principally of a kind used for lifting, handling, loading or unloading of boules, wafers, semiconductor devices, electronic integrated circuits and flat panel displays:
6871	8486.4031	----集成电路工厂专用的自动搬运机器人	0		0 受惠国LD	20	----Automated material handling robots solely of a kind used for transport in electronic integrated circuits industry
6872	8486.4039	----其他	5	0 澳AU,巴PK,冰岛IS,东盟AS,哥CR,秘鲁PE,新西兰NZ,智利CL 2 瑞士CH 3.5 亚太AP 4.4 韩国KR	0 受惠国LD	30	----Other
		-零件及附件：					-Parts and accessories:
6873	8486.9010	---升降、搬运、装卸机器用(自动搬运设备用除外)	5	0 澳AU,巴PK,冰岛IS,东盟AS,哥CR,秘鲁PE,新西兰NZ,智利CL 2 瑞士CH 2.5 亚太AP 3 韩国KR	0 受惠国LD	30	---Of machines and apparatus for lifting, handling, loading or unloading (excluding automated material handling machines)

序号 No.	税则号列 Tariff Line	中文货品名称 Article Description in Chinese	最惠国税率 MFN(%)	协定税率 Agreement(%)	特惠税率 SP(%)	普通税率 Gen(%)	英文货品名称 Article Description
6874	8486.9020	---引线键合装置用	6	0 冰岛IS,东盟AS,哥CR,秘鲁PE,新西兰NZ,智利CL 2.4 瑞士CH 3.6 澳AU,韩国KR 5 巴PK 5.7 亚太AP	0 受惠国LD	30	---Of wire bonders
		---其他:					---Other:
6875	8486.9091	----带背板的溅射靶材组件	0		0 受惠国LD	17	----Sputtering targets modules with backing plate
6876	8486.9099	----其他	0		0 受惠国LD	17	----Other
	84.87	**本章其他税号未列名的机器零件,不具有电气接插件、绝缘体、线圈、触点或其他电气器材特征的:**					**Machinery parts, not containing electrical connectors, insulators, coils, contacts or other electrical features, not specified or included elsewhere in this chapter:**
6877	8487.1000	-船用推进器及桨叶	6	0 冰岛IS,东盟AS,哥CR,秘鲁PE,新西兰NZ,智利CL 2.4 瑞士CH 3.6 澳AU 5 巴PK 5.2 韩国KR	0 受惠国LD	14	-Ships' or boats' propellers and blades
6878	8487.9000	-其他	8	0 冰岛IS,东盟AS,哥CR,秘鲁PE,台湾TW,香港HK,新西兰NZ,智利CL 4.8 澳AU 5 巴PK 5.6 瑞士CH 6.4 韩国KR	0 受惠国LD	30	-Other

第八十五章
电机、电气设备及其零件；录音机及放声机、电视图像、声音的录制和重放设备及其零件、附件

注释：

一、本章不包括：

（一）电暖的毯子、褥子、足套及类似品，电暖的衣服、靴、鞋、耳套或其他供人穿戴的电暖物品；

（二）税号 70.11 的玻璃制品；

（三）税目 84.86 的机器及装置；

（四）用于医疗、外科、牙科或兽医的真空设备（税号 90.18）；

（五）第九十四章的电热家具。

二、税号 85.01 至 85.04 不适用于税号 85.11、85.12、85.40、85.41 或 85.42 的货品，但金属槽汞弧整流器仍归入税号 85.04。

三、税号 85.09 仅包括通常供家用的下列电动器具：

（一）任何重量的地板打蜡机、食品研磨机及食品搅拌器，水果或蔬菜的榨汁器；

（二）重量不超过 20 公斤的其他机器。

但该税号不适用于风机、风扇或装有风扇的通风罩及循环气罩（不论是否装有过滤器）（税号 84.14）、离心干衣机（税号 84.21）、洗碟机（税号 84.22）、家用洗衣机（税号 84.50）、滚筒式或其他形式的熨烫机器（税号 84.20 或 84.51）、缝纫机（税号 84.52）、电剪子（税号 84.67）或电热器具（税号 85.16）。

四、税目 85.23 所称：

（一）“固态、非易失性存储器件”（例如，“闪存卡”或“电子闪存卡”）是指带有接口的存储器件，其在同一壳体内包含一块或多块闪存（FLASH E^2 PROM），以集成电路的形式装配在一块印刷电路板上。它们可以包括一个集成电路形式的控制器及分立无源元件，例如，电容器及电阻器；

Chapter 85
Electrical machinery and equipment and parts thereof; sound recorders and reproducers, television image and sound recorders and reproducers, and parts and accessories of such articles

Notes:

1. This Chapter does not cover:

(a) Electrically warmed blankets, bed pads, foot-muffs or the like; electrically warmed clothing, footwear or ear pads or other electrically warmed articles worn on or about the person;

(b) Articles of glass of heading No.70.11;

(c) Machines and apparatus of heading 84.86;

(d) Vacuum apparatus of a kind used in medical, surgical, dental or veterinary sciences (heading 90.18); or

(e) Electrically heated furniture of Chapter 94.

2. Headings No.85.01 to 85.04 do not apply to goods described in heading No.85.11, 85.12, 85.40, 85.41 or 85.42.However, metal tank mercury arc rectifiers remain classified in heading No.85.04.

3. Heading No.85.09covers only the following electro mechanical machines of the kind commonly used for domestic purposes:

(a) Floor polishers, food grinders and mixers, and fruit or vegetable juice extractors, of any weight;

(b) Other machines provided the weight of such machines does not exceed 20kg.

The heading does not, however, apply to fans or ventilating or recycling hoods incorporating a fan, whether or not fitted with filters (heading No.84.14), centrifugal clothes-dryers (heading No.84.21), dish washing machines (heading No.84.22), household washing machines (heading No.84.50) , roller or other ironing machines (heading No.84.20 or 84.51), sewing machines (heading No.84.52), electric scissors (heading No.84.67) or to electrochemical appliances (heading No.85.16) .

4. For the purposes of heading 85.23 :

(a) “Solid-state non-volatile storage devices” (for example, “flash memory cards” or “flash electronic storage cards”) are storage devices with a connecting socket, comprising in the same housing one or more flash memories (for example, “FLASH E^2PROM”) in the form of integrated circuits mounted on a printed circuit board. They may include a controller in the form of an integrated circuit and discrete passive components, such as capacitors and resistors;

（二）所称“智能卡”，是指装有一块或多块集成电路(微处理器、随机存取存储器（RAM）或只读存储器（ROM）)芯片的卡。这些卡可带有触点、磁条或嵌入式天线，但不包含任何其他有源或无源电路元件。

(b) The term “smart cards” means cards which have embedded in them one or more electronic integrated circuits (a microprocessor, random access memory (RAM) or read-only memory (ROM)) in the form of chips. These cards may contain contacts, a magnetic stripe or an embedded antenna but do not contain any other active or passive circuit elements.

五、税号 85.34 所称“印刷电路”，是指采用各种印制方法（例如，压印、覆镀、腐蚀）或采用“膜电路”工艺，将导线、接点或其他印制元件（例如，电感器、电阻器、电容器）按预定的图形单独或互相连接地印制在绝缘基片上的电路，但能够产生、整流、调制或放大电信号的元件（例如，半导体元件）除外。

5. For the purposes of heading No.85.34 “printed circuits” are circuits obtained by forming on an insulating base, by any printing process (for example, embossing, plating up, etching) or by the “film circuit” technique, conductor elements, contacts or other printed components (for example, inductances, resistors, capacitors) alone or interconnected according to a preestablished pattern, other than elements which can produce, rectify, modulate or amplify an electrical signal (for example, semiconductor elements).

所称“印刷电路”，不包括装有非印制元件的电路，也不包括单个的分立式电阻器、电容器及电感器。但印刷电路可配有非经印刷的连接元件。

The expression “printed circuits” does not cover circuits combined with elements other than those obtained during the printing process, nor does it cover individual, discrete resistors, capacitors or inductances.

用同样工艺制得的无源元件及有源元件组成的薄膜电路或厚膜电路应归入税号 85.42。

Thinor thick-film circuits comprising passive and active elements obtained during the same technological process are to be classified in heading No.85.42.

六、税目 85.36 所称“光导纤维、光导纤维束或光缆用连接器”，是指在有线数字通讯设备中，简单机械地把光纤端部相连成一线的连接器。它们不具备诸如对信号进行放大、再生或修正等其它功能。

6. For the purpose of heading 85.36, “connectors for optical fibres, optical fibre bundles or cables” means connectors that simply mechanically align optical fibres end to end in a digital line system. They perform no other function, such as the amplification, regeneration or modification of a signal.

七、税目 85.37 不包括电视接收机或其他电气设备用的无绳红外遥控器（税目 85.43）。

7. Heading 85.37 does not include cordless infrared devices for the remote control of television receivers or other electrical equipment (heading 85.43).

八、税号 85.41 及 85.42 所称:

8. For the purposes of headings Nos.85.41 and 85.42:

（一）“二极管、晶体管及类似的半导体器件”，是指那些依靠外加电场引起电阻率的变化而进行工作的半导体器件。

(a) “Diodes, transistors and similar semiconductor devices” are semiconductor devices the operation of which depends on variations in resistivity on the application of an electric field;

（二）“集成电路”，是指:

(b) “Electronic integrated circuits” are:

1. 单片集成电路，即电路元件（二极管、晶体管、

(1) Monolithic integrated circuits in which the circuit

电阻器、电容器、电感器等）主要整体制作在一片半导体材料或化合物半导体材料（例如掺杂硅、砷化镓、硅锗或磷化铟）基片的表面，并不可分割地连接在一起的电路；

elements, (diodes, transistors, resistors, capacitors, inductances, etc.) are created in the mass (essentially) and on the surface of a semiconductor or compound semiconductor material (for example, doped silicon, gallium arsenide, silicon germanium, indium phosphide) and are inseparably associated;

2. 混合集成电路，即通过薄膜或厚膜工艺制得的无源元件（电阻器、电容器、电感器等）和通过半导体工艺制得的有源元件（二极管、晶体管、单片集成电路等）用互连或连接线不可分割地组合在同一绝缘基片（玻璃、陶瓷等）上的电路。这种电路也可包括分立元件；

(2) Hybrid integrated circuits in which passive elements (resistors, capacitors, inductances, etc.), obtained by thin-or thick-film technology, and active elements (diodes, transistors, monolithic integrated circuits, etc.), obtained by semiconductor technology, are combined to all intents and purposes indivisibly, by interconnections or interconnecting cables, on a single insulating substrate (glass, ceramic, etc.). These circuits may also include discrete components;

3. 多芯片集成电路是由两个或多个单片集成电路不可分割地组合在一片或多片绝缘基片上构成的电路，不论是否带有引线框架，但不带有其他有源或无源的电路元件。

(3) Multichip integrated circuits consisting of two or more interconnected monolithic integrated circuits combined to all intents and purposes indivisibly, whether or not on one or more insulating substrates, with or without leadframes, but with no other active or passive circuit elements.

本注释所述物品在归类时，即使本目录其他税号涉及上述的物品，尤其是物品的功能，仍应优先考虑归入税号 85.41 及 85.42。

For the classification of the articles defined in this Note, headings 85.41 and 85.42 shall take precedence over any other heading in the Nomenclature which might cover them by reference to, in particular, their function.

九、税号 85.48 所称“废原电池、废原电池组及废蓄电池”，是指因破损、拆解、耗尽或其他原因而不能再使用，也不能再充电的电池。

9. For the purposes of heading No.85.48, spent primary cells, “spent primary batteries and spent electric accumulators” are those which are neither usable as such because of breakage, cutting-up, wear or other reasons, nor capable of being recharged.

子目注释：

子目号 8527.12 仅包括有内置放大器但无内置扬声器的盒式磁带放声机，不需外接电源即能工作，且外形尺寸不超过 170 毫米×100 毫米×45 毫米。

Subheading Note:

1. Subheadings 8527.12 covers only cassetteplayers with built-in amplifier, without built-in loudspeaker, capable of operating without an external source of electric power and the dimensions of which do not exceed170mm×100mm×45mm.

序号 No.	税则号列 Tariff Line	中文货品名称 Article Description in Chinese	最惠国税率 MFN(%)	协定税率 Agreement(%)	特惠税率 SP(%)	普通税率 Gen(%)	英文货品名称 Article Description
	85.01	电动机及发电机（不包括发电机组）：					**Electric motors and generators (excluding generating sets) :**
		-输出功率不超过37.5瓦的电动机：					-Motors of an output not exceeding 37.5 W:

序号 No.	税则号列 Tariff Line	中文货品名称 Article Description in Chinese	最惠国税率 MFN(%)	协定税率 Agreement(%)	特惠税率 SP(%)	普通税率 Gen(%)	英文货品名称 Article Description
6879	8501.1010	---玩具用	24.5	0 冰岛IS,东盟AS,哥CR,台湾TW,香港HK,新加坡SG,新西兰NZ,智利CL 7.4 秘鲁PE 14.7 澳AU 17.2 瑞士CH 22 韩国KR 23.3 巴PK,亚太AP	0 受惠国$_1$LD$_1$	80	---For use in toys
		---其他:					---Other:
6880	8501.1091	----微电机，机座尺寸在20毫米及以上，但不超过39毫米	9	0 冰岛IS,东盟AS,哥CR,秘鲁PE,香港HK,新加坡SG,新西兰NZ,智利CL 5 巴PK 5.4 澳AU 6.3 瑞士CH 7.8 韩国KR 8.6 亚太AP	0 受惠国LD	70	----Micromotors with a housing size of 20mm or more but not exceeding 39mm
	ex85011091	激光视盘机机芯精密微型电机（1瓦≤功率≤18瓦，20毫米≤直径≤30毫米）	Δ5				Minitype precise motor for mechanism of laser disc player (1W≤power≤18W, 20mm≤diameter≤30mm)
	ex85011091	摄像机、摄录一体机用精密微型电机(0.5瓦≤功率≤10瓦，20毫米≤直径≤39毫米）	Δ5				Minitype precise motor for mechanism of video cameras or camera recorders (0.5W≤power≤10W, 20mm≤diameter≤39mm)
6881	8501.1099	----其他	9	0 冰岛IS,东盟AS,哥CR,秘鲁PE,台湾TW,香港HK,新加坡SG,新西兰NZ,智利CL 5 巴PK 5.4 澳AU 6.3 瑞士CH 7.8 韩国KR 8.6 亚太AP	0 受惠国LD	35	----Other
	ex85011099	功率不大于0.5瓦(圆柱型:直径不大于6毫米,高不大于25毫米;扁圆型:直径不大于15毫米,厚不大于5毫米)非用于激光视盘机机芯的微型电机	Δ5				Micromotors with a cylindrical housing diameter not exceeding 6mm and height not exceeding 25mm or a oblatecylindrical housing diameter not exceeding 15mm and thickness not exceeding 5mm (power≤0.5W) , excluding minitype motor for mechanism of laser disc player
	ex85011099	激光视盘机机芯用精密微型电机(0.5瓦≤功率≤2瓦，5毫米≤直径<20毫米）	Δ5				Minitype precise motor for mechanism of laser disc player (0.5W≤power≤2W, 5mm≤diameter<20mm)
	ex85011099	摄像机、摄录一体机用精密微型电机(0.5瓦≤功率≤10瓦，5毫米≤直径<20毫米或39毫米<直径≤40毫米）	Δ5				Minitype precise motor for mechanism of video cameras or camera recorders (0.5W≤power≤10W, 5mm≤diameter<20mm or 39mm<diameter≤40mm)
6882	8501.2000	-交直流两用电动机，输出功率超过37. 5瓦	12	0 冰岛IS,东盟AS,哥CR,新加坡SG,新西兰NZ,智利CL 3.6 秘鲁PE 6 巴PK 7.2 澳AU 8.4 瑞士CH 9.6 韩国KR	0 受惠国LD	35	-Universal AC/DC motors of an output exceeding 37.5W
		-其他直流电动机;直流发电机:					-Other DC motors; DC generators:

序号 No.	税则号列 Tariff Line	中文货品名称 Article Description in Chinese	最惠国税率 MFN(%)	协定税率 Agreement(%)	特惠税率 SP(%)	普通税率 Gen(%)	英文货品名称 Article Description
6883	8501.3100	--输出功率不超过750瓦	12	0 澳门MO,冰岛IS,东盟AS,哥CR,秘鲁PE,台湾TW,香港HK,新加坡SG,新西兰NZ,智利CL 4.8 瑞士CH 6 巴PK 7.2 澳AU 10.3 韩国KR 11 亚太AP	0 受惠国LD	35	--Of an output not exceeding 750W
6884	8501.3200	--输出功率超过750瓦，但不超过75千瓦	10	0 冰岛IS,东盟AS,哥CR,秘鲁PE,新加坡SG,新西兰NZ,智利CL 4 瑞士CH 5 巴PK 6 澳AU 8 韩国KR	0 受惠国LD	35	--Of an output exceeding 750W but not exceeding 75KW
6885	8501.3300	--输出功率超过75千瓦，但不超过375千瓦	5	0 澳AU,巴PK,冰岛IS,东盟AS,哥CR,秘鲁PE,瑞士CH,新西兰NZ,智利CL 3 韩国KR	0 受惠国LD	35	--Of an output exceeding 75KW but not exceeding 375KW
6886	8501.3400	--输出功率超过375千瓦	12	0 冰岛IS,东盟AS,哥CR,秘鲁PE,新加坡SG,新西兰NZ,智利CL 6 巴PK 7.2 澳AU 8.4 瑞士CH 10.8 韩国KR	0 受惠国LD	35	--Of an output exceeding 375KW
6887	8501.4000	-其他单相交流电动机	12	0 冰岛IS,东盟AS,哥CR,新加坡SG,新西兰NZ,智利CL 3.6 秘鲁PE 6 巴PK 7.2 澳AU 8.4 瑞士CH 10.4 韩国KR	0 受惠国LD	35	-Other AC motors, single-phase
		-其他多相交流电动机：					-Other AC motors, multi-phase:
6888	8501.5100	--输出功率不超过750瓦	5	0 澳AU,巴PK,冰岛IS,东盟AS,哥CR,秘鲁PE,新西兰NZ,智利CL 2 瑞士CH	0 受惠国LD	35	--Of an output not exceeding 750W
6889	8501.5200	--输出功率超过750瓦，但不超过75千瓦	10	0 冰岛IS,东盟AS,哥CR,秘鲁PE,新加坡SG,新西兰NZ,智利CL 5 巴PK 6 澳AU 7 瑞士CH 9 韩国KR	0 受惠国LD	35	--Of an output exceeding 750W but not exceeding 75KW
6890	8501.5300	--输出功率超过75千瓦	12	0 冰岛IS,东盟AS,哥CR,秘鲁PE,新加坡SG,新西兰NZ,智利CL 6 巴PK 7.2 澳AU 8.4 瑞士CH 10.4 韩国KR 11.4 亚太AP	0 受惠国LD	35	--Of an output exceeding 75KW
	ex85015300	高速(200千米/时及以上)电力机车的交流异步牵引电动机	Δ3				AC asyncronous traction motor for high speed electric locomotive (speed≥200km/h)
		-交流发电机：					-AC generators (alternators) :
6891	8501.6100	--输出功率不超过75千伏安	5	0 澳AU,巴PK,冰岛IS,东盟AS,哥CR,秘鲁PE,瑞士CH,新西兰NZ,智利CL 4 韩国KR	0 受惠国LD	30	--Of an output not exceeding 75KVA

序号 No.	税则号列 Tariff Line	中文货品名称 Article Description in Chinese	最惠国税率 MFN(%)	协定税率 Agreement(%)	特惠税率 SP(%)	普通税率 Gen(%)	英文货品名称 Article Description
6892	8501.6200	--输出功率超过75千伏安，但不超过375千伏安	12	0 冰岛IS,东盟AS,哥CR,新加坡SG,新西兰NZ,智利CL 3.6 秘鲁PE 6 巴PK 7.2 澳AU 8.4 瑞士CH 10.8 韩国KR	0 受惠国LD	30	--Of an output exceeding 75KVA but not exceeding 375KVA
6893	8501.6300	--输出功率超过375千伏安，但不超过750千伏安	12	0 冰岛IS,东盟AS,哥CR,新加坡SG,新西兰NZ,智利CL 3.6 秘鲁PE 6 巴PK 7.2 澳AU 8.4 瑞士CH 10.8 韩国KR	0 受惠国LD	30	--Of an output exceeding 375KVA but not exceeding 750KVA
		--输出功率超过750千伏安：					--Of an output exceeding 750KVA:
6894	8501.6410	---输出功率超过750千伏安，但不超过350兆伏安	10	0 冰岛IS,东盟AS,哥CR,新加坡SG,新西兰NZ,智利CL 3 秘鲁PE 4 瑞士CH 5 巴PK 6 澳AU 9 韩国KR	0 受惠国LD	30	---Of an output exceeding 750KVA but not exceeding 350MVA
	ex85016410	由使用可再生燃料锅炉和涡轮机组驱动的交流发电机，750千伏安＜输出功率≤350兆伏安	Δ5				AC generators of an output exceeding 750KVA but not exceeding 350MVA, used in conjunction with boiler and turbines to generate electricity from renewable fuels
6895	8501.6420	---输出功率超过350兆伏安，但不超过665兆伏安	5.8	0 冰岛IS,东盟AS,哥CR,秘鲁PE,新西兰NZ,智利CL 2.3 瑞士CH 3.4 韩国KR 3.5 澳AU 5 巴PK	0 受惠国LD	14	---Of an output exceeding 350 MVA but not exceeding 665 MVA
	ex85016420	由使用可再生燃料锅炉和涡轮机组驱动的交流发电机，350兆伏安＜输出功率≤665兆伏安	Δ5				AC generators of an output exceeding 350MVA but not exceeding 665MVA, used in conjunction with boiler and turbines to generate electricity from renewable fuels
6896	8501.6430	---输出功率超过665兆伏安	6	0 冰岛IS,东盟AS,哥CR,秘鲁PE,新西兰NZ,智利CL 2.4 瑞士CH 3.6 澳AU,韩国KR 5 巴PK	0 受惠国LD	11	---Of an output exceeding 665MVA
	ex85016430	由使用可再生燃料锅炉和涡轮机组驱动的交流发电机，输出功率＞665兆伏安	Δ5				AC generators of an output exceeding 665MVA, used in conjunction with boiler and turbines to generate electricity from renewable fuels
	85.02	**发电机组及旋转式变流机：**					**Electric generating sets and rotary converters:**
		-装有压燃式活塞内燃发动机（柴油或半柴油发动机）的发电机组：					-Generating sets with compression-ignition internal combustion piston engines (diesel or semi-diesel engines) :

序号 No.	税则号列 Tariff Line	中文货品名称 Article Description in Chinese	最惠国税率 MFN(%)	协定税率 Agreement(%)	特惠税率 SP(%)	普通税率 Gen(%)	英文货品名称 Article Description
6897	8502.1100	--输出功率不超过75千伏安	10	0 冰岛IS,东盟AS,哥CR,秘鲁PE,香港HK,新加坡SG,新西兰NZ,智利CL 4 瑞士CH 5 巴PK 6 澳AU 8 韩国KR	0 受惠国LD	45	--Of an output not exceeding 75KVA
6898	8502.1200	--输出功率超过75千伏安，但不超过375千伏安	10	0 冰岛IS,东盟AS,哥CR,香港HK,新加坡SG,新西兰NZ,智利CL 3 秘鲁PE 4 瑞士CH 5 巴PK 6 澳AU 8.6 韩国KR	0 受惠国LD	45	--Of an output exceeding 75KVA but not exceeding 375KVA
		--输出功率超过375千伏安:					--Of an output exceeding 375KVA:
6899	8502.1310	---输出功率超过375千伏安，但不超过2兆伏安	10	0 冰岛IS,东盟AS,哥CR,秘鲁PE,香港HK,新加坡SG,新西兰NZ,智利CL 4 瑞士CH 5 巴PK 6 澳AU 7 亚太AP 9 韩国KR	0 受惠国LD	45	---Of an output exceeding 375KVA but not exceeding 2MVA
6900	8502.1320	---输出功率超过2兆安	10	0 冰岛IS,东盟AS,哥CR,秘鲁PE,香港HK,新加坡SG,新西兰NZ,智利CL 4 瑞士CH 5 巴PK 6 澳AU 7 亚太AP 9 韩国KR	0 受惠国LD	30	---Of an output exceeding 2MVA
6901	8502.2000	-装有点燃式活塞内燃发动机的发电机组	10	0 冰岛IS,东盟AS,哥CR,秘鲁PE,新加坡SG,新西兰NZ,智利CL 4 瑞士CH 5 巴PK 6 澳AU 8 韩国KR	0 受惠国LD	45	-Generating sets with spark-ignition internal combustion piston engines
		-其他发电机组:					-Other generating sets:
6902	8502.3100	--风力驱动的	8Δ5	0 冰岛IS,东盟AS,哥CR,秘鲁PE,新西兰NZ,智利CL 3.2 瑞士CH 4.8 澳AU 5 巴PK 6.9 韩国KR	0 受惠国LD	30	--Wind-powered
6903	8502.3900	--其他	10	0 冰岛IS,东盟AS,哥CR,秘鲁PE,新西兰NZ,智利CL 4 瑞士CH 5 巴PK 6 澳AU 8.6 韩国KR	0 受惠国LD	30	--Other
	ex85023900	依靠可再生能源（太阳能、小水电、潮汐、沼气、地热能、生物质/余热驱动的汽轮机）生产电力的发电机组	Δ5				Electric generating sets by using renewable energy (e.g. solar power, Small hydro, Wave power, biogas, geothermal, and gas turbines for biomass plants and for waste heat applications)

序号 No.	税则号列 Tariff Line	中文货品名称 Article Description in Chinese	最惠国税率 MFN(%)	协定税率 Agreement(%)	特惠税率 SP(%)	普通税率 Gen(%)	英文货品名称 Article Description
6904	8502.4000	-旋转式变流机	10	0 冰岛IS,东盟AS,哥CR,秘鲁PE,新西兰NZ,智利CL 4 瑞士CH 5 巴PK 6 澳AU 8 韩国KR	0 受惠国LD	30	-Electric rotary converters
	85.03	**专用于或主要用于税号85.01或85.02所列机器的零件:**					**Parts suitable for use solely or principally with the machines of heading 8501 or 8502:**
6905	8503.0010	---子目号8501. 1010及8501. 1091所列电动机用	12	0 冰岛IS,东盟AS,哥CR,台湾TW,香港HK,新加坡SG,新西兰NZ,智利CL 3.6 秘鲁PE 6 巴PK 7.2 澳AU 8.4 瑞士CH 10.3 韩国KR 11.4 亚太AP	0 受惠国LD	70	---Of the motors of subheading No. 8501.1010 or 8501.1091
6906	8503.0020	---子目号8501. 6420及8501. 6430所列发电机用	3	0 澳AU,巴PK,冰岛IS,东盟AS,哥CR,韩国KR,秘鲁PE,香港HK,新西兰NZ,智利CL 2.1 瑞士CH 2.5 亚太AP	0 受惠国LD	11	---Of the generators of subheading No.8501.6420 or 8501.6430
6907	8503.0030	---子目号8502. 3100所列发电机组用	3Δ1	0 澳AU,巴PK,冰岛IS,东盟AS,哥CR,韩国KR,秘鲁PE,瑞士CH,香港HK,新西兰NZ,智利CL 2.5 亚太AP	0 受惠国LD	30	---Of the generating sets of subheading No.8502.3100
6908	8503.0090	---其他	8	0 东盟AS,哥CR,秘鲁PE,台湾TW,香港HK,新西兰NZ,智利CL 4.8 澳AU,韩国KR 5 巴PK 5.6 瑞士CH 7.6 亚太AP	0 受惠国LD	30	---Other
	ex85030090	由使用可再生燃料锅炉和涡轮机组驱动的输出功率超过750千伏安的交流发电机的零件;依靠可再生能源(太阳能、小水电、潮汐、沼气、地热能、生物质/余热驱动的汽轮机)生产电力的发电机组的零件	Δ5				Parts of AC generators of an output exceeding 750KVA, used in conjunction with boiler and turbines to generate electricity from renewable fuels;Parts of electric generating sets by using renewable energy (e.g. solar power, Small hydro,Wave power, biogas, geothermal, and gas turbines for biomass plants and for waste heat applications)
	85.04	**变压器、静止式变流器(例如整流器)及电感器:**					**Electrical transformers, static converters (for example, rectifiers) and inductors:**
		-放电灯或放电管用镇流器:					-Ballasts for discharge lamps or tubes:
6909	8504.1010	---电子镇流器	10	0 澳门MO,冰岛IS,东盟AS,哥CR,新加坡SG,新西兰NZ,智利CL 3 秘鲁PE 4 瑞士CH 5 巴PK 6 澳AU 8 韩国KR	0 受惠国LD	35	---Electronic ballats

序号 No.	税则号列 Tariff Line	中文货品名称 Article Description in Chinese	最惠国税率 MFN(%)	协定税率 Agreement(%)	特惠税率 SP(%)	普通税率 Gen(%)	英文货品名称 Article Description
6910	8504.1090	---其他	10	0 澳门MO,冰岛IS,东盟AS,哥CR,新西兰NZ,智利CL 3 秘鲁PE 4 瑞士CH 5 巴PK 6 澳AU 8 韩国KR	0 受惠国LD	35	---Other
		-液体介质变压器:					-Liquid dielectric transformers:
6911	8504.2100	--额定容量不超过650千伏安	10.5	0 冰岛IS,东盟AS,哥CR,新加坡SG,新西兰NZ,智利CL 3.2 秘鲁PE 5 巴PK 6.3 澳AU 7.4 瑞士CH 8.4 韩国KR	0 受惠国LD	50	--Having a power handling capacity not exceeding 650KVA
6912	8504.2200	--额定容量超过650千伏安，但不超过10兆伏安	12.6	0 冰岛IS,东盟AS,哥CR,新加坡SG,新西兰NZ,智利CL 3.8 秘鲁PE 6.3 巴PK 7.6 澳AU 8.8 瑞士CH 10 韩国KR	0 受惠国LD	50	--Having a power handling capacity exceeding 650KVA but not exceeding 10MVA
		--额定容量超过10兆伏安:					--Having a power handling capacity exceeding 10MVA:
		---额定容量超过10兆伏安，但小于400兆伏安:					---Having a power handling capacity exceeding 10MVA but less than 400MVA:
6913	8504.2311	----额定容量超过10兆伏安，但小于220兆伏安	10	0 冰岛IS,东盟AS,哥CR,秘鲁PE,新西兰NZ,智利CL 5 巴PK 6 澳AU 7 亚太AP 8.6 韩国KR	0 受惠国LD	50	----Having a power handing capacity exceeding 10MVA but less than 220MVA
6914	8504.2312	----额定容量在220兆伏安及以上，但小于330兆伏安	10	0 冰岛IS,东盟AS,哥CR,秘鲁PE,新西兰NZ,智利CL 4 瑞士CH 5 巴PK 6 澳AU 7 亚太AP 8 韩国KR	0 受惠国LD	50	----Having a power handling capacity exceeding 220MVA but less than 330MVA
6915	8504.2313	----额定容量在330兆伏安及以上，但小于400兆伏安	10	0 冰岛IS,东盟AS,哥CR,秘鲁PE,新西兰NZ,智利CL 4 瑞士CH 5 巴PK 6 澳AU 7 亚太AP 8 韩国KR	0 受惠国LD	50	----Having a power handling capacity exceeding 330MVA but less than 400MVA
		---额定容量在400兆伏安及以上:					---Having a power handling capacity of 400MVA or more:
6916	8504.2321	----额定容量在400兆伏安及以上，但小于500兆伏安	6	0 巴PK,冰岛IS,东盟AS,哥CR,秘鲁PE,新西兰NZ,智利CL 2.4 瑞士CH 3.6 澳AU,韩国KR 4.2 亚太AP	0 受惠国LD	11	----Having a power handling capacity exceeding 400MVA but less than 500MVA

序号 No.	税则号列 Tariff Line	中文货品名称 Article Description in Chinese	最惠国税率 MFN(%)	协定税率 Agreement(%)	特惠税率 SP(%)	普通税率 Gen(%)	英文货品名称 Article Description
6917	8504.2329	----其他	6	0 巴PK,冰岛IS,东盟AS,哥CR,秘鲁PE,新西兰NZ,智利CL 2.4 瑞士CH 3.6 澳AU,韩国KR 4.2 亚太AP	0 受惠国LD	11	----Other
		-其他变压器:					-Other transformers:
		--额定容量不超过1千伏安:					--Having a power handling capacity not exceeding 1KVA:
6918	8504.3110	---互感器	5	0 澳AU,澳门MO,巴PK,冰岛IS,东盟AS,哥CR,韩国KR,秘鲁PE,台湾TW,新西兰NZ,智利CL 2 瑞士CH 4.3 亚太AP	0 受惠国LD	50	---Mutual inductor
6919	8504.3190	---其他	5	0 澳AU,澳门MO,巴PK,冰岛IS,东盟AS,哥CR,韩国KR,秘鲁PE,台湾TW,香港HK,新加坡SG,新西兰NZ,智利CL 2 瑞士CH 4.3 亚太AP	0 受惠国LD	50	---Other
		--额定容量超过1千伏安，但不超过16千伏安:					--Having a power handling capacity exceeding 1KVA but not exceeding 16KVA:
6920	8504.3210	---互感器	5	0 澳AU,澳门MO,巴PK,冰岛IS,东盟AS,哥CR,秘鲁PE,瑞士CH,新西兰NZ,智利CL 4.3 韩国KR	0 受惠国LD	50	---Mutual inductor
6921	8504.3290	---其他	5	0 澳AU,澳门MO,巴PK,冰岛IS,东盟AS,哥CR,秘鲁PE,新西兰NZ,智利CL 2 瑞士CH 3 韩国KR	0 受惠国LD	50	---Other
		--额定容量超过16千伏安，但不超过500千伏安:					--Having a power handling capacity exceeding 16KVA but not exceeding 500KVA:
6922	8504.3310	---互感器	5	0 澳AU,澳门MO,巴PK,冰岛IS,东盟AS,哥CR,秘鲁PE,新西兰NZ,智利CL 2 瑞士CH 4.3 韩国KR	0 受惠国LD	50	---Mutual inductor
6923	8504.3390	---其他	5	0 澳AU,澳门MO,巴PK,冰岛IS,东盟AS,哥CR,秘鲁PE,新西兰NZ,智利CL 2 瑞士CH 4.3 韩国KR	0 受惠国LD	50	---Other
		--额定容量超过500千伏安:					--Having a power handling capacity exceeding 500KVA:
6924	8504.3410	---互感器	14	0 澳门MO,冰岛IS,东盟AS,哥CR,秘鲁PE,新加坡SG,新西兰NZ,智利CL 5.6 瑞士CH 8.4 澳AU 11.2 巴PK 12.1 韩国KR	0 受惠国$_1$LD$_1$	50	---Mutual inductor

序号 No.	税则号列 Tariff Line	中文货品名称 Article Description in Chinese	最惠国税率 MFN(%)	协定税率 Agreement(%)	特惠税率 SP(%)	普通税率 Gen(%)	英文货品名称 Article Description
6925	8504.3490	---其他	14	0 澳门MO,冰岛IS,东盟AS,哥CR,秘鲁PE,新加坡SG,新西兰NZ,智利CL 5.6 瑞士CH 8.4 澳AU 11.2 巴PK 12.1 韩国KR	0 受惠国$_1$LD$_1$	50	---Other
		-静止式变流器:					-Static converters:
		---稳压电源:					---Voltage-stabilized suppliers:
6926	8504.4013	----税号84.71所列机器用	0		0 受惠国LD	40	----Of the machines of heading No.84.71
6927	8504.4014	----其他直流稳压电源，功率小于1千瓦，精度低于万分之一	7Δ3	0 冰岛IS,东盟AS,哥CR,秘鲁PE,新西兰NZ,智利CL 4.2 澳AU 4.9 瑞士CH 5 巴PK 5.6 亚太AP 6 韩国KR	0 受惠国LD	80	----Other DC Voltage-stabilized suppliers, of a power of less than 1KW and an accuracy of not better than 0.0001
6928	8504.4015	----其他交流稳压电源，功率小于10千瓦，精度低于千分之一	0		0 受惠国LD	80	----Other AC voltage-stabilized suppliers, of a power of less than 10KW and an accuracy of not better than 0.001
6929	8504.4019	----其他	0		0 受惠国LD	50	----Other
6930	8504.4020	---不间断供电电源	10	0 冰岛IS,东盟AS,哥CR,秘鲁PE,香港HK,新加坡SG,新西兰NZ,智利CL 5 巴PK 6 澳AU 8.5 亚太AP 8.6 韩国KR	0 受惠国LD	50	---Uninterrupted power suppliers
6931	8504.4030	---逆变器	10	0 澳门MO,冰岛IS,东盟AS,哥CR,香港HK,新加坡SG,新西兰NZ,智利CL 3 秘鲁PE 5 巴PK 6 澳AU 7 瑞士CH 8.6 韩国KR	0 受惠国LD	30	---Inverters
	ex85044030	纯电动或混合动力汽车用逆变器模块，功率密度≥8千瓦/升	Δ6				Inverter module for electric vehicles or hybrid electric vehicles, power density≥8000W/L
		---其他:					---Other:
6932	8504.4091	----具有变流功能的半导体模块	10Δ3	0 澳门MO,冰岛IS,东盟AS,哥CR,香港HK,新加坡SG,新西兰NZ,智利CL 3 秘鲁PE 5 巴PK 6 澳AU,韩国KR 7 瑞士CH	0 受惠国LD	30	----Semiconductor modules with converting function
	ex85044091	自动数据处理设备机器及组件、电讯设备用的具有变流动能的半导体模块	0				Semicondutor modules with converting function for automatic data processing machines and units thereof, and telecommunication apparatus

序号 No.	税则号列 Tariff Line	中文货品名称 Article Description in Chinese	最惠国税率 MFN(%)	协定税率 Agreement(%)	特惠税率 SP(%)	普通税率 Gen(%)	英文货品名称 Article Description
6933	8504.4099	----其他	10	0 澳门MO,冰岛IS,东盟AS,哥CR,香港HK,新加坡SG,新西兰NZ,智利CL 3 秘鲁PE 5 巴PK 6 澳AU 7 瑞士CH 8.6 韩国KR	0 受惠国LD	30	----Other
	ex85044099	自动数据处理设备机器及组件、电讯设备用的其他静止变流器;ITA产品用的印刷电路组件，包括外接组件，如符合PCMCIA标准的卡	0				Other stastic converters for automatic data processing machines and units thereof, and telecommunication apparatus; Printed Circuit Assemblies for products falling within the ITA, including such assemblies for external connections such as cards that conform to the PCMCIA standard
	ex85044099	高速(200千米/时及以上)电力机车的牵引变流器	Δ3				Traction converter for high speed electric locomotive (speed ≥ 200km/h)
	ex85044099	纯电动汽车或混合动力汽车用电机控制器	Δ4				Motor controller for blade electric vehicles or hybrid electric vehicles
	ex85044099	汽车冲压线用压力机变频调速装置	Δ5				Frequency conversion speed regulation set for punch press machine for manufacture automobiles
	ex85044099	纯电动汽车或插电式混合动力汽车用车载充电机	Δ6				On-board charger for blade electric vehicles or plug-in hybrid electric vehicles
6934	8504.5000	-其他电感器	0		0 受惠国LD	35	-Other inductors
		-零件:					-Parts:
		---变压器用:					---Of transformers:
6935	8504.9011	----子目号8504. 2321，8504. 2329所列变压器用	5	0 澳AU,巴PK,冰岛IS,东盟AS,哥CR,秘鲁PE,香港HK,新西兰NZ,智利CL 3.5 瑞士CH 4.3 韩国KR 4.5 亚太AP	0 受惠国LD	11	----Of the transformers of subheading No.8504.2321, 8504.2329
6936	8504.9019	----其他	8	0 冰岛IS,东盟AS,哥CR,秘鲁PE,台湾TW,香港HK,新西兰NZ,智利CL 4.5 巴PK,亚太AP 4.8 澳AU 5.6 瑞士CH 6.9 韩国KR	0 受惠国LD	50	----Other
6937	8504.9020	---稳压电源及不间断供电电源用	8	0 澳门MO,冰岛IS,东盟AS,哥CR,秘鲁PE,台湾TW,香港HK,新西兰NZ,智利CL 4.8 澳AU 5 巴PK 5.6 瑞士CH,亚太AP 6.9 韩国KR	0 受惠国LD	50	---Of voltage-stabilized suppliers and uninterrupted power suppliers
6938	8504.9090	---其他	8	0 澳门MO,冰岛IS,东盟AS,哥CR,秘鲁PE,台湾TW,香港HK,新西兰NZ,智利CL 4.8 澳AU 5 巴PK 5.6 瑞士CH,亚太AP 6.9 韩国KR	0 受惠国LD	30	---Other

序号 No.	税则号列 Tariff Line	中文货品名称 Article Description in Chinese	最惠国税率 MFN(%)	协定税率 Agreement(%)	特惠税率 SP(%)	普通税率 Gen(%)	英文货品名称 Article Description
	ex85049090	用于将可再生能源发电机组输出的直流电转换成交流电的逆变器的零件	Δ5				Parts of the static converters which are used to convert DC current from renewable energy generating sets into conventional AC electricity
	85.05	**电磁铁;永磁铁及磁化后准备制永磁铁的物品;电磁铁或永磁铁卡盘、夹具及类似的工件夹具;电磁联轴节、离合器及制动器;电磁起重吸盘:**					**Electromagnets; permanent magnets and articles intended to become permanent magnets after magnetisation; electromagnetic or permanent magnet chucks, clamps and similar holding devices; electromagnetic couplings, clutches and brakes; electromagnetic lifting heads:**
		-永磁铁及磁化后准备制永磁铁的物品:					-Permanent magnets and articles intended to become permanent magnets after magnetisation:
		--金属的:					--Of metal:
6939	8505.1110	---稀土永磁体	7	0 冰岛IS,东盟AS,哥CR,韩国KR,秘鲁PE,台湾TW,新西兰NZ,智利CL 2.8 瑞士CH 4.2 澳AU 5 巴PK	0 受惠国LD	20	---Of rare-earth metals
6940	8505.1190	---其他	7	0 冰岛IS,东盟AS,哥CR,韩国KR,秘鲁PE,台湾TW,香港HK,新西兰NZ,智利CL 2.8 瑞士CH 4.2 澳AU 5 巴PK	0 受惠国LD	20	---Other
6941	8505.1900	--其他	7	0 冰岛IS,东盟AS,哥CR,秘鲁PE,香港HK,新西兰NZ,智利CL 2.8 瑞士CH 4.2 澳AU 5 巴PK 5.6 韩国KR 6.7 亚太AP	0 受惠国LD	20	--Other
6942	8505.2000	-电磁联轴节、离合器及制动器	8	0 冰岛IS,东盟AS,哥CR,秘鲁PE,新西兰NZ,智利CL 3.2 瑞士CH 4.8 澳AU 5 巴PK 6.9 韩国KR 7.6 亚太AP	0 受惠国LD	20	-Electro-magnetic couplings, clutches and brakes
		-其他，包括零件:					-Other, including parts:
6943	8505.9010	---电磁起重吸盘	8	0 冰岛IS,东盟AS,哥CR,秘鲁PE,新西兰NZ,智利CL 3.2 瑞士CH 4.8 澳AU,韩国KR 5 巴PK	0 受惠国LD	20	---Electro-magnetic lifting heads
6944	8505.9090	---其他	8	0 冰岛IS,东盟AS,哥CR,秘鲁PE,新西兰NZ,智利CL 4.8 澳AU,韩国KR 5 巴PK 5.6 瑞士CH 7.6 亚太AP	0 受惠国LD	20	---Other
	85.06	**原电池及原电池组:**					**Primary cells and primary batteries:**
		-二氧化锰的:					-Manganese dioxide:

序号 No.	税则号列 Tariff Line	中文货品名称 Article Description in Chinese	最惠国税率 MFN(%)	协定税率 Agreement(%)	特惠税率 SP(%)	普通税率 Gen(%)	英文货品名称 Article Description
		---碱性锌锰的：					---Alkaline zinc-manganese dioxide:
6945	8506.1011	----扣式	20	0 冰岛IS,东盟AS,哥CR,香港HK,新加坡SG,新西兰NZ,智利CL 6 秘鲁PE 12 澳AU 14 瑞士CH 18 韩国KR	0 受惠国$_1$LD$_1$	80	----Button type
6946	8506.1012	----圆柱式	20	0 冰岛IS,东盟AS,哥CR,香港HK,新加坡SG,新西兰NZ,智利CL 6 秘鲁PE 12 澳AU 14 瑞士CH 18 韩国KR	0 受惠国$_1$LD$_1$	80	----Cylinder type
6947	8506.1019	----其他	20	0 冰岛IS,东盟AS,哥CR,香港HK,新加坡SG,新西兰NZ,智利CL 6 秘鲁PE 12 澳AU 14 瑞士CH	0 受惠国$_1$LD$_1$	80	----Other
6948	8506.1090	---其他	20	0 冰岛IS,东盟AS,哥CR,香港HK,新加坡SG,新西兰NZ,智利CL 6 秘鲁PE 12 澳AU 14 瑞士CH 18 韩国KR	0 受惠国$_1$LD$_1$	80	---Other
6949	8506.3000	-氧化汞的	14	0 冰岛IS,东盟AS,哥CR,秘鲁PE,新加坡SG,新西兰NZ,智利CL 8.4 澳AU 9.8 瑞士CH 11.2 巴PK,韩国KR	0 受惠国$_1$LD$_1$	40	-Mercuric oxide
6950	8506.4000	-氧化银的	14	0 冰岛IS,东盟AS,哥CR,秘鲁PE,新加坡SG,新西兰NZ,智利CL 8.4 澳AU 9.8 瑞士CH 11.2 巴PK,韩国KR	0 受惠国$_1$LD$_1$	40	-Silver oxide
6951	8506.5000	-锂的	14	0 冰岛IS,东盟AS,哥CR,秘鲁PE,新加坡SG,新西兰NZ,智利CL 8.4 澳AU 9.8 瑞士CH 11.2 巴PK	0 受惠国$_1$LD$_1$	40	-Lithium
6952	8506.6000	-锌空气的	14	0 冰岛IS,东盟AS,哥CR,秘鲁PE,新加坡SG,新西兰NZ,智利CL 8.4 澳AU 11.2 巴PK,韩国KR	0 受惠国$_1$LD$_1$	40	-Air-zinc
6953	8506.8000	-其他原电池及原电池组	14	0 冰岛IS,东盟AS,哥CR,秘鲁PE,香港HK,新加坡SG,新西兰NZ,智利CL 8.4 澳AU 9.8 瑞士CH 11.2 巴PK,韩国KR	0 受惠国LD	40	-Other primary cells and primary batteries
		-零件：					-Parts:
6954	8506.9010	---子目号8506. 1000所列电池用	14	0 冰岛IS,东盟AS,哥CR,秘鲁PE,新加坡SG,新西兰NZ,智利CL 8.4 澳AU 9.8 瑞士CH 11.2 巴PK	0 受惠国$_1$LD$_1$	80	---Of the cells of subheading No. 8506.1000

序号 No.	税则号列 Tariff Line	中文货品名称 Article Description in Chinese	最惠国税率 MFN(%)	协定税率 Agreement(%)	特惠税率 SP(%)	普通税率 Gen(%)	英文货品名称 Article Description
6955	8506.9090	---其他	10	0 冰岛IS,东盟AS,哥CR,秘鲁PE,新加坡SG,新西兰NZ,智利CL 4 瑞士CH 5 巴PK 6 澳AU 9 韩国KR	0 受惠国$_1$LD$_1$	40	---Other
	85.07	**蓄电池，包括隔板，不论是否矩形(包括正方形)：**					**Electric accumulators, including separators therefor, whether or not rectangular (including square) :**
6956	8507.1000	-铅酸蓄电池，用于起动活塞式发动机	10	0 澳门MO,冰岛IS,东盟AS,哥CR,新加坡SG,新西兰NZ,智利CL 3 秘鲁PE 4 瑞士CH 5 巴PK 6 澳AU 6.9 亚太AP 9 韩国KR	0 受惠国$_1$LD$_1$	90	-Lead-acid, of a kind used for starting piston engines
6957	8507.2000	-其他铅酸蓄电池	10	0 澳门MO,冰岛IS,东盟AS,哥CR,秘鲁PE,新加坡SG,新西兰NZ,智利CL 4 瑞士CH 5 巴PK 6 澳AU 6.9 亚太AP 8 韩国KR	0 受惠国$_1$LD$_1$	90	-Other lead-acid accumulators
6958	8507.3000	-镍镉蓄电池	10	0 冰岛IS,东盟AS,哥CR,秘鲁PE,香港HK,新加坡SG,新西兰NZ,智利CL 4 瑞士CH 5 巴PK 6 澳AU 8 韩国KR,亚太AP	0 受惠国$_1$LD$_1$	40	-Nickel-cadmium
6959	8507.4000	-镍铁蓄电池	12	0 冰岛IS,东盟AS,哥CR,秘鲁PE,新加坡SG,新西兰NZ,智利CL 5 巴PK 7.2 澳AU 8.4 瑞士CH 9.6 韩国KR,亚太AP	0 受惠国$_1$LD$_1$	40	-Nickel-iron
6960	8507.5000	-镍氢蓄电池	12	0 冰岛IS,东盟AS,哥CR,秘鲁PE,香港HK,新加坡SG,新西兰NZ,智利CL 5 巴PK 7.2 澳AU 8.4 瑞士CH 9.6 韩国KR,亚太AP	0 受惠国$_1$LD$_1$	40	-Nickel-hydrogen
6961	8507.6000	-锂离子蓄电池	12	0 冰岛IS,东盟AS,哥CR,秘鲁PE,台湾TW,香港HK,新加坡SG,新西兰NZ,智利CL 5 巴PK 7.2 澳AU 8.4 瑞士CH 9.6 亚太AP 11 韩国KR	0 受惠国$_1$LD$_1$	40	-Lithium ion
	ex85076000	纯电动汽车或插电式混合动力汽车用锂离子蓄电池单体，容量≥10安时，比能量≥110瓦时/千克	Δ8				Lithium ion accumulators cell for blade electric vehicles or plug-in hybrid electric vehicles, capacity ≥10Ah and energy density≥ 110Wh/kg

序号 No.	税则号列 Tariff Line	中文货品名称 Article Description in Chinese	最惠国税率 MFN(%)	协定税率 Agreement(%)	特惠税率 SP(%)	普通税率 Gen(%)	英文货品名称 Article Description
	ex85076000	纯电动汽车或插电式混合动力汽车用锂离子蓄电池系统（包含蓄电池模块、容器、盖、冷却系统、管理系统等），比能量≥80瓦时/千克	Δ10				Lithium ion accumulators system for blade electric vehicles or plug-in hybrid electric vehicles, energy density≥80Wh/kg
		-其他蓄电池：					-Other accumulators:
6962	8507.8030	---全钒液流电池	12	0 冰岛IS,东盟AS,哥CR,秘鲁PE,香港HK,新加坡SG,新西兰NZ,智利CL 5 巴PK 7.2 澳AU 8.4 瑞士CH 9 亚太AP 9.6 韩国KR	0 受惠国$_1$LD$_1$	40	---All-vanadium redox flow batteries
6963	8507.8090	---其他	12	0 冰岛IS,东盟AS,哥CR,秘鲁PE,香港HK,新加坡SG,新西兰NZ,智利CL 5 巴PK 7.2 澳AU 8.4 瑞士CH 9 亚太AP 9.6 韩国KR	0 受惠国$_1$LD$_1$	40	---Other
		-零件：					-Parts:
6964	8507.9010	---铅酸蓄电池用	10	0 冰岛IS,东盟AS,哥CR,秘鲁PE,香港HK,新西兰NZ,智利CL 4 瑞士CH 5 巴PK 6 澳AU 8 韩国KR	0 受惠国$_1$LD$_1$ 5 亚太AP	90	---Of lead-acid accumulators
	ex85079010	铅酸蓄电池电极（仅保留电极）	Δ5				Electrodes of lead-acid accumulators (only including Electrodes)
6965	8507.9090	---其他	8Δ5	0 冰岛IS,东盟AS,哥CR,秘鲁PE,香港HK,新西兰NZ,智利CL 3.2 瑞士CH 4.8 澳AU 5 巴PK 6.9 韩国KR	0 受惠国LD 4 亚太AP	40	---Other
	85.08	**真空吸尘器：**					**Vacuum cleaners:**
		-电动的：					-With self-contained electric motor:
6966	8508.1100	--功率不超过1500瓦，且带有容积不超过20升的集尘袋或其他集尘容器	10	0 冰岛IS,东盟AS,哥CR,秘鲁PE,台湾TW,香港HK,新加坡SG,新西兰NZ,智利CL 4 瑞士CH 5 巴PK 6 澳AU 8 韩国KR 8.2 亚太AP	0 受惠国LD	130	--Of a power not exceeding 1500W and having a dust bag or other receptacle capacity not exceeding 20L
6967	8508.1900	--其他	0		0 受惠国LD	30	--Other
6968	8508.6000	-其他真空吸尘器	0		0 受惠国LD	30	-Other vacuum cleaners
		-零件：					-Parts:
6969	8508.7010	---子目8508. 1100所列吸尘器用	12	0 冰岛IS,东盟AS,哥CR,秘鲁PE,香港HK,新加坡SG,新西兰NZ,智利CL 6 巴PK 7.2 澳AU 8.4 瑞士CH 9.6 韩国KR	0 受惠国$_1$LD$_1$	100	---For the goods of heading No.8508.1100

序号 No.	税则号列 Tariff Line	中文货品名称 Article Description in Chinese	最惠国税率 MFN(%)	协定税率 Agreement(%)	特惠税率 SP(%)	普通税率 Gen(%)	英文货品名称 Article Description
6970	8508.7090	---其他	0		0 受惠国LD	20	---Other
	85.09	**家用电动器具，税目85.08的真空吸尘器除外：**					**Electromechanical domestic appliances, with self-contained electric motor, other than vacuum cleaners of heading 8508:**
		-食品研磨机及搅拌器；水果或蔬菜的榨汁机：					-Food grinders and mixers; fruit or vegetable juice extractors:
6971	8509.4010	---水果或蔬菜的榨汁机	10Δ6	0 澳门MO,冰岛IS,东盟AS,哥CR,秘鲁PE,新加坡SG,新西兰NZ,智利CL 4 瑞士CH 5 巴PK 6 澳AU 9 韩国KR	0 受惠国$_1$LD$_1$	100	---Fruit or vegetable juice extractors
6972	8509.4090	---其他	10Δ6	0 冰岛IS,东盟AS,哥CR,秘鲁PE,瑞士CH,台湾TW,新加坡SG,新西兰NZ,智利CL 5 巴PK 6 澳AU 8 韩国KR	0 受惠国$_1$LD$_1$	100	---Other
		-其他器具：					-Other appliances:
6973	8509.8010	---地板打蜡机	30	0 冰岛IS,东盟AS,哥CR,新加坡SG,新西兰NZ,智利CL 9 秘鲁PE 18 澳AU 21.6 瑞士CH	0 受惠国$_1$LD$_1$	100	---Floor polishers
6974	8509.8020	---厨房废物处理器	20	0 冰岛IS,东盟AS,哥CR,新加坡SG,新西兰NZ,智利CL 6 秘鲁PE 12 澳AU 14 瑞士CH 18 韩国KR	0 受惠国$_1$LD$_1$	100	---Kitchen waste disposers
6975	8509.8090	---其他	30Δ15	0 冰岛IS,东盟AS,哥CR,新加坡SG,新西兰NZ,智利CL 9 秘鲁PE 18 澳AU	0 受惠国$_1$LD$_1$	100	---Other
6976	8509.9000	-零件	12Δ6	0 冰岛IS,东盟AS,哥CR,秘鲁PE,香港HK,新加坡SG,新西兰NZ,智利CL 6 巴PK 7.2 澳AU 8.4 瑞士CH 9.6 韩国KR	0 受惠国$_1$LD$_1$	100	-Parts
	85.10	**电动剃须刀、电动毛发推剪及电动脱毛器：**					**Shavers, hair clippers and hair-removing appliances, with self-contained electric motor:**
6977	8510.1000	-剃须刀	30Δ15	0 东盟AS,哥CR,新加坡SG,新西兰NZ,智利CL 9 秘鲁PE 18 澳AU 21.6 瑞士CH	0 受惠国$_1$LD$_1$	100	-Shavers
6978	8510.2000	-毛发推剪	30	0 冰岛IS,东盟AS,哥CR,香港HK,新加坡SG,新西兰NZ,智利CL 9 秘鲁PE 18 澳AU 21.6 瑞士CH	0 受惠国$_1$LD$_1$	100	-Hair clippers

序号 No.	税则号列 Tariff Line	中文货品名称 Article Description in Chinese	最惠国税率 MFN(%)	协定税率 Agreement(%)	特惠税率 SP(%)	普通税率 Gen(%)	英文货品名称 Article Description
6979	8510.3000	-脱毛器	20	0 澳门MO,冰岛IS,东盟AS,哥CR,新加坡SG,新西兰NZ,智利CL 6 秘鲁PE 12 澳AU 14 瑞士CH 17.3 韩国KR	0 受惠国$_1$LD$_1$	100	-Hair-removing appliances
6980	8510.9000	-零件	24.5Δ12	0 冰岛IS,东盟AS,哥CR,新加坡SG,新西兰NZ,智利CL 7.4 秘鲁PE 14.7 澳AU 17.2 瑞士CH 22 韩国KR	0 受惠国$_1$LD$_1$	100	-Parts
	85.11	**点燃式或压燃式内燃发动机用的电点火及电起动装置(例如，点火磁电机、永磁直流发电机、点火线圈、火花塞、电热塞及起动电机);附属于上述内燃发动机的发电机(例如，直流发电机、交流发电机)及断流器:**					**Electrical ignition or starting equipment of a kind used for spark-ignition or compression-ignition internal combustion engines (for example, ignition magnetos, magneto-dynamos, ignition coils, sparking plugs and glow plugs, starter motors) ; generators (for example, dynamos, alternators) and cut-outs of a kind used in conjunction with such engines:**
6981	8511.1000	-火花塞	10	0 冰岛IS,东盟AS,哥CR,新加坡SG,新西兰NZ,智利CL 3 秘鲁PE 4 瑞士CH 5 巴PK 6 澳AU 8 韩国KR	0 受惠国$_1$LD$_1$	30	-Sparking plugs
		-点火磁电机;永磁直流发电机;磁飞轮:					-Ignition magnetos; magneto-dynamos; magnetic flywheels:
6982	8511.2010	---机车、航空器及船舶用	5	0 澳AU,巴PK,冰岛IS,东盟AS,哥CR,秘鲁PE,瑞士CH,新西兰NZ,智利CL 3 韩国KR	0 受惠国LD	11	---For locomotives, aircraft or ships
6983	8511.2090	---其他	10	0 冰岛IS,东盟AS,哥CR,秘鲁PE,新西兰NZ,智利CL 4 瑞士CH 5 巴PK 6 澳AU 8 韩国KR	0 受惠国LD	30	---Other
		-分电器;点火线圈:					-Distributors; ignition coils:
6984	8511.3010	---机车、航空器及船舶用	5	0 澳AU,巴PK,冰岛IS,东盟AS,哥CR,秘鲁PE,瑞士CH,新西兰NZ,智利CL 3 韩国KR	0 受惠国LD	11	---For locomotives, aircraft or ships
6985	8511.3090	---其他	8.4	0 冰岛IS,东盟AS,哥CR,秘鲁PE,新西兰NZ,智利CL 3.36 瑞士CH 5 澳AU,巴PK 7.2 韩国KR	0 受惠国LD	30	---Other
		-起动电机及两用启动发电机:					-Starter motors and dual purpose starter-generators:

序号 No.	税则号列 Tariff Line	中文货品名称 Article Description in Chinese	最惠国税率 MFN(%)	协定税率 Agreement(%)	特惠税率 SP(%)	普通税率 Gen(%)	英文货品名称 Article Description
6986	8511.4010	---机车、航空器及船舶用	5	0 澳AU,巴PK,冰岛IS,东盟AS,哥CR,秘鲁PE,瑞士CH,新西兰NZ,智利CL 4 韩国KR	0 受惠国LD	11	---For locomotives, aircraft or ships
		---其他:					---Other:
6987	8511.4091	----输出功率在132.39千瓦（180马力）及以上的发动机用启动电机	8.4	0 冰岛IS,东盟AS,哥CR,秘鲁PE,新西兰NZ,智利CL 3.36 瑞士CH 5 澳AU,巴PK 6.7 韩国KR	0 受惠国LD	30	----Starter motors for engines of an output of 132.39KW (180HP) or more
6988	8511.4099	----其他	8.4	0 冰岛IS,东盟AS,哥CR,秘鲁PE,新西兰NZ,智利CL 3.36 瑞士CH 5 澳AU,巴PK 7.2 韩国KR	0 受惠国LD	30	----Other
		-其他发电机:					-Other generators:
6989	8511.5010	---机车、航空器及船舶用	5	0 澳AU,巴PK,冰岛IS,东盟AS,哥CR,秘鲁PE,瑞士CH,新西兰NZ,智利CL 4 韩国KR	0 受惠国LD	11	---For locomotives, aircraft or ships
6990	8511.5090	---其他	8.4	0 冰岛IS,东盟AS,哥CR,秘鲁PE,新西兰NZ,智利CL 3.36 瑞士CH 5 澳AU,巴PK	0 受惠国LD	30	---Other
6991	8511.8000	-其他装置	8.4	0 冰岛IS,东盟AS,哥CR,秘鲁PE,新西兰NZ,智利CL 3.36 瑞士CH 5 澳AU,巴PK 6.7 韩国KR	0 受惠国LD	30	-Other equipment
		-零件:					-Parts:
6992	8511.9010	---本税号所列供机车、航空器及船舶用的各种装置的零件	4.5	0 澳AU,巴PK,冰岛IS,东盟AS,哥CR,秘鲁PE,瑞士CH,新西兰NZ,智利CL	0 受惠国LD	11	---Of the equipment of heading No.85.11used for locomotives, aircraft or ships
6993	8511.9090	---其他	5	0 澳AU,巴PK,冰岛IS,东盟AS,哥CR,秘鲁PE,瑞士CH,新西兰NZ,智利CL 4 韩国KR	0 受惠国LD	30	---Other
	85.12	**自行车或机动车辆用的电气照明或信号装置（税号85.39的物品除外）、风挡刮水器、除霜器及去雾器:**					**Electrical lighting or signalling equipment (excluding articles of heading 8539) , windscreen wipers, defrosters and demisters, of a kind used for cycles or motor vehicles:**
6994	8512.1000	-自行车用照明或视觉信号装置	10.5	0 冰岛IS,东盟AS,哥CR,秘鲁PE,新加坡SG,新西兰NZ,智利CL 5 巴PK 6.3 澳AU 7.4 瑞士CH 8.4 韩国KR	0 受惠国LD	45	-Lighting or visual signalling equipment of a kind used on bicycles
		-其他照明或视觉信号装置:					-Other lighting or visual signalling equipment:
6995	8512.2010	---机动车辆用照明装置	10	0 冰岛IS,哥CR,秘鲁PE,台湾TW,新西兰NZ,智利CL 4 瑞士CH 6 澳AU 9 韩国KR	0 受惠国LD	45	---Lighting equipment of a kind used for motor vehicles

序号 No.	税则号列 Tariff Line	中文货品名称 Article Description in Chinese	最惠国税率 MFN(%)	协定税率 Agreement(%)	特惠税率 SP(%)	普通税率 Gen(%)	英文货品名称 Article Description
6996	8512.2090	---其他	10	0 冰岛IS,哥CR,秘鲁PE,新西兰NZ,智利CL 4 瑞士CH 6 澳AU 9 韩国KR	0 受惠国LD	45	---Other
		-音响信号装置:					-Sound signalling equipment:
		---机动车辆用:					---For motor Vehicles:
6997	8512.3011	----喇叭、蜂鸣器	10	0 冰岛IS,哥CR,秘鲁PE,新西兰NZ,智利CL 4 瑞士CH 6 澳AU 8.5 巴PK,亚太AP 8.6 韩国KR	0 受惠国LD	45	----Loudspeaker, buzzers
6998	8512.3012	----防盗报警器	10	0 冰岛IS,东盟AS,哥CR,秘鲁PE,新西兰NZ,智利CL 4 瑞士CH 5 巴PK 6 澳AU 8.6 韩国KR 9 亚太AP	0 受惠国LD	40	----Burglar alarms
6999	8512.3019	----其他	10	0 冰岛IS,哥CR,秘鲁PE,新西兰NZ,智利CL 4 瑞士CH 6 澳AU 8.5 巴PK,亚太AP 8.6 韩国KR	0 受惠国LD	45	----Other
7000	8512.3090	---其他	10	0 冰岛IS,哥CR,秘鲁PE,新西兰NZ,智利CL 4 瑞士CH 6 澳AU 8.5 巴PK,亚太AP	0 受惠国LD	45	---Other
7001	8512.4000	-风挡刮水器、除霜器及去雾器	10	0 冰岛IS,哥CR,秘鲁PE,新西兰NZ,智利CL 4 瑞士CH 6 澳AU	0 受惠国LD	45	-Windscreen wipers, defrosters and demisters
7002	8512.9000	-零件	8	0 冰岛IS,东盟AS,哥CR,秘鲁PE,台湾TW,新西兰NZ,智利CL 3.2 瑞士CH 4.8 澳AU 5 巴PK 6.4 韩国KR	0 受惠国LD	45	-Parts
	85.13	**自供能源(例如,使用干电池、蓄电池、永磁发电机)的手提式电灯,但税号85.12的照明装置除外:**					**Portable electric lamps designed to function by their own source of energy (for example, dry batteries, accumulators, magnetos), other than lighting equipment of heading 8512:**
		-灯:					-Lamps:
7003	8513.1010	---手电筒	15	0 澳门MO,冰岛IS,东盟AS,哥CR,新加坡SG,新西兰NZ,智利CL 4.5 秘鲁PE 7.5 巴PK 9 澳AU 10.5 瑞士CH 12 韩国KR 13.2 亚太AP	0 受惠国LD	100	---Portable electric torches designed to function by dry batteries
7004	8513.1090	---其他	17.5	0 澳门MO,冰岛IS,东盟AS,哥CR,新加坡SG,新西兰NZ,智利CL 5.2 秘鲁PE 10.5 澳AU 12.3 瑞士CH 14 巴PK,韩国KR	0 受惠国$_1$LD$_1$	70	---Other

序号 No.	税则号列 Tariff Line	中文货品名称 Article Description in Chinese	最惠国税率 MFN(%)	协定税率 Agreement(%)	特惠税率 SP(%)	普通税率 Gen(%)	英文货品名称 Article Description
		-零件:					-Parts:
7005	8513.9010	---手电筒用	14	0 澳门MO,冰岛IS,东盟AS,哥CR,秘鲁PE,香港HK,新加坡SG,新西兰NZ,智利CL 8.4 澳AU 9.8 瑞士CH 11.2 巴PK,韩国KR	0 受惠国LD	100	---Of the torches of subheading No.8513.1010
7006	8513.9090	---其他	14	0 澳门MO,冰岛IS,东盟AS,哥CR,秘鲁PE,香港HK,新加坡SG,新西兰NZ,智利CL 8.4 澳AU 9.8 瑞士CH 11.2 巴PK,韩国KR	0 受惠国$_1$LD$_1$	70	---Other
	85.14	**工业或实验室用电炉及电烘箱(包括通过感应或介质损耗工作的);工业或实验室用其他通过感应或介质损耗对材料进行热处理的设备:**					**Industrial or laboratory electric furnaces and ovens (including those functioning by induction or dielectric loss) ; other industrial or laboratory equipment for the heat treatment of materials by induction or dielectric loss:**
		-电阻加热的炉及烘箱:					-Resistance heated furnaces and ovens:
7007	8514.1010	---可控气氛热处理炉	0		0 受惠国LD	30	---Furnaces for heat treatment, atmosphere controllable
7008	8514.1090	---其他	0		0 受惠国LD	30	---Other
7009	8514.2000	-通过感应或介质损耗工作的炉及烘箱	0		0 受惠国LD	30	-Furnaces and ovens functioning by induction or dielectric loss
7010	8514.3000	-其他炉及烘箱	0		0 受惠国LD	30	-Other furnaces and ovens
7011	8514.4000	-其他通过感应或介质损耗对材料进行热处理的设备	10	0 冰岛IS,东盟AS,哥CR,秘鲁PE,新加坡SG,新西兰NZ,智利CL 4 瑞士CH 5 巴PK 6 澳AU,韩国KR	0 受惠国LD	30	-Other equipment for the heat treatment of materials by induction or dielectric loss
	ex85144000	焊缝中频退火装置	Δ7				Intermediate frequency annealing device for weld
		-零件:					-Parts:
7012	8514.9010	---炼钢电炉用	8	0 冰岛IS,东盟AS,哥CR,秘鲁PE,新西兰NZ,智利CL 3.2 瑞士CH 4.8 澳AU,韩国KR 5 巴PK	0 受惠国LD	30	---Of steel making electric furnaces
7013	8514.9090	---其他	0		0 受惠国LD	30	---Other
	85.15	**电气(包括电热气体)、激光、其他光、光子束、超声波、电子束、磁脉冲或等离子弧焊接机器及装置,不论是否兼有切割功能;用于热喷金属或金属陶瓷的电气机器及装置:**					**Electric (including electrically heated gas) , laser or other light or photon beam, ultrasonic, electron beam, magnetic pulse or plasma arc soldering, brazing or welding machines and apparatus, whether or not capable of cutting; electric machines and apparatus for hot spraying of metals or cermets:**
		-钎焊机器及装置:					-Brazing or soldering machines and apparatus:
7014	8515.1100	--烙铁及焊枪	10	0 冰岛IS,东盟AS,哥CR,秘鲁PE,新加坡SG,新西兰NZ,智利CL 4 瑞士CH 5 巴PK 6 澳AU 8 韩国KR	0 受惠国LD	30	--Soldering irons and guns

序号 No.	税则号列 Tariff Line	中文货品名称 Article Description in Chinese	最惠国税率 MFN(%)	协定税率 Agreement(%)	特惠税率 SP(%)	普通税率 Gen(%)	英文货品名称 Article Description
7015	8515.1900	--其他	10	0 冰岛IS,东盟AS,哥CR,秘鲁PE,新加坡SG,新西兰NZ,智利CL 5 巴PK 6 澳AU 8 瑞士CH	0 受惠国LD	30	--Other
		-电阻焊接机器及装置:					-Machines and apparatus for resistance welding of metal:
		--全自动或半自动的:					--Fully or partly automatic:
7016	8515.2120	---机器人	10	0 冰岛IS,东盟AS,哥CR,秘鲁PE,香港HK,新加坡SG,新西兰NZ,智利CL 5 巴PK 6 澳AU 9 韩国KR	0 受惠国LD	30	---Robots
	ex85152120	汽车生产线电阻焊接机器人	Δ5				Resistance welding robots, used for automobile production line
		---其他:					---Other:
7017	8515.2191	----直缝焊管机	10	0 冰岛IS,东盟AS,哥CR,秘鲁PE,香港HK,新西兰NZ,智利CL 4 瑞士CH 5 巴PK 6 澳AU 9 韩国KR	0 受惠国LD	30	----Aligning tube welding machines
7018	8515.2199	----其他	10	0 冰岛IS,东盟AS,哥CR,秘鲁PE,香港HK,新加坡SG,新西兰NZ,智利CL 5 巴PK 6 澳AU 9 韩国KR	0 受惠国LD	30	----Other
7019	8515.2900	--其他	10	0 冰岛IS,东盟AS,哥CR,秘鲁PE,新加坡SG,新西兰NZ,智利CL 4 瑞士CH 5 巴PK 6 澳AU 9 韩国KR 9.5 亚太AP	0 受惠国LD	30	--Other
		-电弧(包括等离子弧)焊接机器及装置:					-Machines and apparatus for arc (including plasma arc) welding of metals:
		--全自动或半自动的:					--Fully or partly automatic:
7020	8515.3120	---机器人	10	0 冰岛IS,哥CR,秘鲁PE,新西兰NZ,智利CL 4 瑞士CH 6 澳AU 9 韩国KR	0 受惠国LD	30	---Robots
		---其他:					---Other:
7021	8515.3191	----螺旋焊管机	10	0 冰岛IS,东盟AS,哥CR,秘鲁PE,新西兰NZ,智利CL 4 瑞士CH 5 巴PK 6 澳AU 8 韩国KR	0 受惠国LD	30	----Spiralling tube welding machines
7022	8515.3199	----其他	10	0 冰岛IS,哥CR,秘鲁PE,新西兰NZ,智利CL 4 瑞士CH 6 澳AU 9 韩国KR	0 受惠国LD	30	----Other

序号 No.	税则号列 Tariff Line	中文货品名称 Article Description in Chinese	最惠国税率 MFN(%)	协定税率 Agreement(%)		特惠税率 SP(%)	普通税率 Gen(%)	英文货品名称 Article Description
7023	8515.3900	--其他	10	0 4 5 6 8	冰岛IS,东盟AS,哥CR,秘鲁PE,新西兰NZ,智利CL 瑞士CH 巴PK 澳AU 韩国KR	0 受惠国LD	30	--Other
		-其他机器及装置:						-Other machines and apparatus:
7024	8515.8010	---激光焊接机器人	8	0 4.8 5 6.4 7.6	冰岛IS,东盟AS,哥CR,秘鲁PE,台湾TW,香港HK,新西兰NZ,智利CL 澳AU,韩国KR 巴PK 瑞士CH 亚太AP	0 受惠国LD	30	---Laser-welding robots
	ex85158010	汽车生产线激光焊接机器人	Δ5					Laser welding robots, used for automobile production line
7025	8515.8090	---其他	8	0 4.8 5 6.4 7.6	冰岛IS,东盟AS,哥CR,秘鲁PE,台湾TW,香港HK,新西兰NZ,智利CL 澳AU,韩国KR 巴PK 瑞士CH 亚太AP	0 受惠国LD	30	---Other
7026	8515.9000	-零件	6Δ3	0 3.6 4.2 5 5.7	冰岛IS,东盟AS,哥CR,秘鲁PE,香港HK,新西兰NZ,智利CL 澳AU,韩国KR 瑞士CH 巴PK 亚太AP	0 受惠国LD	30	-Parts
	85.16	**电热的快速热水器、储存式热水器、浸入式液体加热器;电气空间加热器及土壤加热器;电热的理发器具(例如,电吹风机、电卷发器、电热发钳)及干手器;电熨斗;其他家用电热器具;加热电阻器,但税号85.45的货品除外:**						**Electric instantaneous or storage water heaters and immersion heaters; electric space-heating apparatus and soil-heating apparatus; electrothermic hairdressing apparatus (for example, hairdryers, hair curlers, curling tong heaters) and hand dryers; electric smoothing irons; other electrothermic appliances of a kind used for domestic purposes; electric heating resistors, other than those of heading 8545:**
		-电热的快速热水器、储存式热水器、浸入式液体加热器:						-Electric instantaneous or storage water heaters and immersion heaters:
7027	8516.1010	---储存式电热水器	10	0 4 5 6 8	冰岛IS,东盟AS,哥CR,秘鲁PE,新加坡SG,新西兰NZ,智利CL 瑞士CH 巴PK 澳AU 韩国KR	0 受惠国LD	100	---Electrical storage water heaters
7028	8516.1020	---即热式电热水器	10	0 4 5 6 8	冰岛IS,东盟AS,哥CR,秘鲁PE,新加坡SG,新西兰NZ,智利CL 瑞士CH 巴PK 澳AU 韩国KR	0 受惠国LD	100	---Electrical geysers

序号 No.	税则号列 Tariff Line	中文货品名称 Article Description in Chinese	最惠国税率 MFN(%)	协定税率 Agreement(%)	特惠税率 SP(%)	普通税率 Gen(%)	英文货品名称 Article Description
7029	8516.1090	---其他	10	0 冰岛IS,东盟AS,哥CR,秘鲁PE,新加坡SG,新西兰NZ,智利CL 4 瑞士CH 5 巴PK 6 澳AU	0 受惠国LD	100	---Other
		-电气空间加热器及土壤加热器：					-Electric space-heating apparatus and electric soil-heating apparatus:
7030	8516.2100	--储存式散热器	35	0 澳门MO,冰岛IS,东盟AS,哥CR,台湾TW,新加坡SG,新西兰NZ,智利CL 10.5 秘鲁PE 21 澳AU 25.2 瑞士CH	0 受惠国$_1$LD$_1$	100	--Storage heating radiators
		--其他：					--Other:
7031	8516.2910	---土壤加热器	10	0 澳门MO,冰岛IS,东盟AS,哥CR,秘鲁PE,香港HK,新西兰NZ,智利CL 4 瑞士CH 5 巴PK 6 澳AU 8 韩国KR	0 受惠国LD	40	---Electric soil heating apparatus
7032	8516.2920	---辐射式空间加热器	10	0 澳门MO,冰岛IS,东盟AS,哥CR,秘鲁PE,香港HK,新加坡SG,新西兰NZ,智利CL 4 瑞士CH 5 巴PK 6 澳AU 8 韩国KR	0 受惠国LD	100	---Radiation space heaters
		---对流式空间加热器：					---Convection space heaters:
7033	8516.2931	----风扇式	10	0 澳门MO,冰岛IS,东盟AS,哥CR,秘鲁PE,香港HK,新加坡SG,新西兰NZ,智利CL 4 瑞士CH 5 巴PK 6 澳AU 8 韩国KR	0 受惠国LD	100	----Fan heaters
7034	8516.2932	----充液式	10	0 澳门MO,冰岛IS,东盟AS,哥CR,秘鲁PE,香港HK,新加坡SG,新西兰NZ,智利CL 4 瑞士CH 5 巴PK 6 澳AU 8 韩国KR	0 受惠国LD	100	----Liquid filled heaters
7035	8516.2939	----其他	10	0 澳门MO,冰岛IS,东盟AS,哥CR,秘鲁PE,香港HK,新加坡SG,新西兰NZ,智利CL 4 瑞士CH 5 巴PK 6 澳AU 8 韩国KR	0 受惠国LD	100	----Others
7036	8516.2990	---其他	10	0 澳门MO,冰岛IS,东盟AS,哥CR,秘鲁PE,香港HK,新加坡SG,新西兰NZ,智利CL 4 瑞士CH 5 巴PK 6 澳AU 8 韩国KR	0 受惠国LD	100	---Other

序号 No.	税则号列 Tariff Line	中文货品名称 Article Description in Chinese	最惠国税率 MFN(%)	协定税率 Agreement(%)	特惠税率 SP(%)	普通税率 Gen(%)	英文货品名称 Article Description
		-电热的理发器具及干手器:					-Electrothermic hairdressing or hand-drying apparatus:
7037	8516.3100	--吹风机	10	0 澳门MO,冰岛IS,东盟AS,哥CR,秘鲁PE,新加坡SG,新西兰NZ,智利CL 5 巴PK 6 澳AU 7 瑞士CH 8 韩国KR	0 受惠国LD	100	--Hair dryers
7038	8516.3200	--其他理发器具	35	0 澳门MO,冰岛IS,东盟AS,哥CR,新加坡SG,新西兰NZ,智利CL 10.5 秘鲁PE 21 澳AU 25.2 瑞士CH 31.5 韩国KR	0 受惠国$_1$LD$_1$	100	--Other hair-dressing apparatus
7039	8516.3300	--干手器	35	0 澳门MO,冰岛IS,东盟AS,哥CR,新加坡SG,新西兰NZ,智利CL 10.5 秘鲁PE 21 澳AU 25.2 瑞士CH	0 受惠国$_1$LD$_1$	100	--Hand-drying apparatus
7040	8516.4000	-电熨斗	35Δ17	0 澳门MO,冰岛IS,东盟AS,哥CR,台湾TW,新加坡SG,新西兰NZ,智利CL 10.5 秘鲁PE 21 澳AU 24.5 瑞士CH	0 受惠国$_1$LD$_1$	100	-Electric smoothing irons
7041	8516.5000	-微波炉	15Δ8	0 冰岛IS,东盟AS,哥CR,新加坡SG,新西兰NZ,智利CL 4.5 秘鲁PE 7.5 巴PK 9 澳AU 10.5 瑞士CH 12 韩国KR 13.5 亚太AP	0 受惠国$_1$LD$_1$	130	-Microwave ovens
		-其他炉;电锅、电热板、加热环、烧烤炉及烘烤器:					-Other ovens; cookers, cooking plates, boiling rings; grillers and roasters:
7042	8516.6010	---电磁炉	15	0 澳门MO,冰岛IS,东盟AS,哥CR,新加坡SG,新西兰NZ,智利CL 4.5 秘鲁PE 9 澳AU 10.5 瑞士CH 12 巴PK,韩国KR	0 受惠国$_1$LD$_1$	130	---Electromagnetic ovens
7043	8516.6030	---电饭锅	15Δ8	0 澳门MO,冰岛IS,东盟AS,哥CR,台湾TW,新加坡SG,新西兰NZ,智利CL 4.5 秘鲁PE 9 澳AU 10.5 瑞士CH 12 巴PK,韩国KR	0 受惠国$_1$LD$_1$	130	---Electric rice cookers
7044	8516.6040	---电炒锅	15	0 澳门MO,冰岛IS,东盟AS,哥CR,新加坡SG,新西兰NZ,智利CL 4.5 秘鲁PE 9 澳AU 10.5 瑞士CH 12 巴PK,韩国KR	0 受惠国$_1$LD$_1$	130	---Electric frying pans

序号 No.	税则号列 Tariff Line	中文货品名称 Article Description in Chinese	最惠国税率 MFN(%)	协定税率 Agreement(%)	特惠税率 SP(%)	普通税率 Gen(%)	英文货品名称 Article Description
7045	8516.6050	---电烤箱	15∆8	0 澳门MO,冰岛IS,东盟AS,哥CR,台湾TW,新西兰NZ,智利CL 4.5 秘鲁PE 9 澳AU 10.5 瑞士CH 12 巴PK,韩国KR	0 受惠国$_1$LD$_1$	130	---Electric roasters
7046	8516.6090	---其他	15∆10	0 澳门MO,冰岛IS,东盟AS,哥CR,新加坡SG,新西兰NZ,智利CL 4.5 秘鲁PE 9 澳AU 10.5 瑞士CH 12 巴PK,韩国KR	0 受惠国$_1$LD$_1$	130	---Other
		-其他电热器具:					-Other electrothermic appliances:
		--咖啡壶或茶壶:					--Coffee or tea makers:
7047	8516.7110	---滴液式咖啡机	32∆16	0 澳门MO,东盟AS,哥CR,新加坡SG,新西兰NZ,智利CL 9.6 秘鲁PE 12.8 瑞士CH 19.2 澳AU	0 受惠国$_1$LD$_1$	130	---Drip coffee makers
7048	8516.7120	---蒸馏渗滤式咖啡机	32∆16	0 澳门MO,东盟AS,哥CR,新加坡SG,新西兰NZ,智利CL 9.6 秘鲁PE 12.8 瑞士CH 19.2 澳AU	0 受惠国$_1$LD$_1$	130	---Steam espresso makers
7049	8516.7130	---泵压式咖啡机	32∆16	0 澳门MO,冰岛IS,东盟AS,哥CR,新加坡SG,新西兰NZ,智利CL 9.6 秘鲁PE 12.8 瑞士CH 19.2 澳AU	0 受惠国$_1$LD$_1$	130	---Pump espresso makers
7050	8516.7190	---其他	32∆16	0 澳门MO,冰岛IS,东盟AS,哥CR,新加坡SG,新西兰NZ,智利CL 9.6 秘鲁PE 12.8 瑞士CH 19.2 澳AU	0 受惠国$_1$LD$_1$	130	---Other
		--烤面包器:					--Toasters:
7051	8516.7210	---家用自动面包机	32	0 澳门MO,东盟AS,哥CR,台湾TW,新加坡SG,新西兰NZ,智利CL 9.6 秘鲁PE 19.2 澳AU 23 瑞士CH	0 受惠国$_1$LD$_1$	130	---Automatic bread makers
7052	8516.7220	---片式烤面包机(多士炉)	32	0 澳门MO,东盟AS,哥CR,新加坡SG,新西兰NZ,智利CL 9.6 秘鲁PE 19.2 澳AU 23 瑞士CH	0 受惠国$_1$LD$_1$	130	---Slice pop-up toasters
7053	8516.7290	---其他	32	0 澳门MO,东盟AS,哥CR,新加坡SG,新西兰NZ,智利CL 9.6 秘鲁PE 19.2 澳AU 23 瑞士CH	0 受惠国$_1$LD$_1$	130	---Other
		--其他:					--Other:
7054	8516.7910	---电热饮水机	32	0 澳门MO,东盟AS,哥CR,新加坡SG,新西兰NZ,智利CL 9.6 秘鲁PE 19.2 澳AU 22.4 瑞士CH	0 受惠国$_1$LD$_1$	100	---Electro-thermic water dispensers

序号 No.	税则号列 Tariff Line	中文货品名称 Article Description in Chinese	最惠国税率 MFN(%)	协定税率 Agreement(%)	特惠税率 SP(%)	普通税率 Gen(%)	英文货品名称 Article Description
7055	8516.7990	---其他	32Δ16	0 澳门MO,东盟AS,哥CR,香港HK,新加坡SG,新西兰NZ,智利CL 9.6 秘鲁PE 19.2 澳AU	0 受惠国[1]LD[1]	100	---Other
7056	8516.8000	-加热电阻器	10	0 冰岛IS,东盟AS,哥CR,秘鲁PE,新加坡SG,新西兰NZ,智利CL 5 巴PK 6 澳AU 7 瑞士CH 8 韩国KR	0 受惠国LD	40	-Electric heating resistors
		-零件:					-Parts:
7057	8516.9010	---土壤加热器及加热电阻器用	8	0 冰岛IS,东盟AS,哥CR,秘鲁PE,香港HK,新西兰NZ,智利CL 3.2 瑞士CH 4.8 澳AU 5 巴PK 6.4 韩国KR	0 受惠国LD	40	---Of apparatus of subheading No. 8516.2910 or 8516.8000
7058	8516.9090	---其他	12Δ8	0 冰岛IS,东盟AS,哥CR,秘鲁PE,香港HK,新加坡SG,新西兰NZ,智利CL 4.8 瑞士CH 6 巴PK 7.2 澳AU 9.6 韩国KR	0 受惠国LD	100	---Other
	85.17	**电话机，包括用于蜂窝网络或其他无线网络的电话机；其他发送或接收声音、图像或其他数据用的设备，包括有线或无线网络（例如，局域网或广域网）的通信设备，税目84.43、85.25、85.27或85.28的发送或接收设备除外：**					**Telephone sets, including telephones for cellular networks or for other wireless networks; other apparatus for the transmission or reception of voice, images or other data, including apparatus for communication in a wired or wireless network (such as a local or wide area network), other than transmission or reception apparatus of heading 8443, 8525, 8527 or 8528:**
		-电话机，包括蜂窝网络或其他无线网络用电话机：					-Telephone sets, including telephones for cellular networks or for other wireless networks:
7059	8517.1100	--无绳电话机	0		0 受惠国LD	30	--Line telephone sets with cordless handsets
		--用于蜂窝网络或其他无线网络的电话机：					--Telephones for cellular networks or for other wireless networks:
7060	8517.1210	---手持（包括车载）式无线电话机	0		0 受惠国LD	20	---Radio telephone handsets (including vehicle installed)
7061	8517.1220	---对讲机	0		0 受惠国LD	17	---Walkie-talkie
7062	8517.1290	---其他	0		0 受惠国LD	14	---Other
7063	8517.1800	--其他	0		0 受惠国LD	30	--Other
		-其他发送或接收声音、图像或其他数据用的设备，包括有线或无线网络（例如，局域网或广域网）的通信设备：					-Other apparatus for the transmission or reception of voice, images or other data, including apparatus for communication in a wired or wireless network (such as a local or wide area network):
		--基站：					--Base stations:
7064	8517.6110	---移动通信基站	0		0 受惠国LD	14	---Mobile communication base station
7065	8517.6190	---其他	0		0 受惠国LD	14	---Other

序号 No.	税则号列 Tariff Line	中文货品名称 Article Description in Chinese	最惠国税率 MFN(%)	协定税率 Agreement(%)	特惠税率 SP(%)	普通税率 Gen(%)	英文货品名称 Article Description
		--接收、转换并且发送或再生声音、图像或其他数据用的设备，包括交换及路由设备：					--Machines for the reception, conversion and transmission or regeneration of voice, images or other data, including switching and routing apparatus:
		---数字式程控电话或电报交换机：					---Digital program-controlled switching systems:
7066	8517.6211	----局用电话交换机；长途电话交换机；电报交换机	0		0 受惠国LD	17	----Public telephonic switching systems, toll telephonic or telegraphic switching systems
7067	8517.6212	----移动通信交换机	0		0 受惠国LD	40	----Mobile communication switching systems
7068	8517.6219	----其他电话交换机	0		0 受惠国LD	40	----Other telephonic switching system
		---光通讯设备：					---Optical communication equipments:
7069	8517.6221	----光端机及脉冲编码调制设备（PCM）	0		0 受惠国LD	17	----Optical line terminal equipments and pulse code modulation mutilexers
7070	8517.6222	----波分复用光传输设备	0		0 受惠国LD	30	----Optical transmission equipments for wave-division multiplexing
7071	8517.6229	----其他	0		0 受惠国LD	30	----Other
		---其他有线数字通信设备：					---Other telecommunication apparatus for digit line system:
7072	8517.6231	----通信网络时钟同步设备	0		0 受惠国LD	30	----Communication network synchronizing equipments
7073	8517.6232	----以太网络交换机	0		0 受惠国LD	30	----Ethernet exchangers
7074	8517.6233	----IP电话信号转换设备	0		0 受惠国LD	30	----IP telephone signal converters
7075	8517.6234	----调制解调器	0		0 受惠国LD	30	----Modem
7076	8517.6235	----集线器	0		0 受惠国LD	40	----Network concentrators
7077	8517.6236	----路由器	0		0 受惠国LD	40	----Network path-control devices
7078	8517.6237	----有线网络接口卡	0		0 受惠国LD	30	----Wired network interface card
7079	8517.6239	----其他	0		0 受惠国LD	30	----Thermograph recording heads
		---其他：					---Other:
7080	8517.6292	----无线网络接口卡	0		0 受惠国LD	14	----Wireless network interface card
7081	8517.6293	----无线接入固定台	0		0 受惠国LD	14	----Fixed wireless communicating terminal
7082	8517.6294	----无线耳机	0		0 受惠国LD	14	----Wireless headset
7083	8517.6299	----其他	0		0 受惠国LD	14	----Other
		--其他：					--Other:
7084	8517.6910	---其他无线设备	9	0 巴PK,冰岛IS,东盟AS,哥CR,秘鲁PE,新西兰NZ,智利CL 3.6 瑞士CH 5.4 澳AU,韩国KR	0 受惠国LD	14	---Other apparatus for communication in a wireless network
	ex85176910	用于呼叫、提示和寻呼的便携式接收器	0				Portable receivers for calling, alerting or paging
7085	8517.6990	---其他有线设备	0		0 受惠国LD	30	---Other apparatus for communication in a wired network
		-零件：					-Parts:
7086	8517.7010	---数字式程控电话或电报交换机用	0		0 受惠国LD	14	---Of digital program-controlled switching apparatus
7087	8517.7020	---光端机及脉冲编码调制设备（PCM）用	0		0 受惠国LD	14	---Of the equipment of subheading No.8517.6221
7088	8517.7030	---手持式无线电话机用（天线除外）	0		0 受惠国LD	17	---Of radio telephone handsets (other than aerials)

序号 No.	税则号列 Tariff Line	中文货品名称 Article Description in Chinese	最惠国税率 MFN(%)	协定税率 Agreement(%)	特惠税率 SP(%)	普通税率 Gen(%)	英文货品名称 Article Description
7089	8517.7040	---对讲机用(天线除外)	8	0 冰岛IS,东盟AS,哥CR,秘鲁PE,香港HK,新西兰NZ,智利CL 3.2 瑞士CH 4.8 澳AU 5 巴PK 5.6 亚太AP 6.4 韩国KR	0 受惠国LD	20	---Of walkie-talkie (other than aerials)
7090	8517.7060	---光通信设备的激光收发模块	0		0 受惠国LD	30	---Laser transmitting and receiving unit of laser communication equipment
7091	8517.7070	---税号8517所列设备用天线及其零件	2	0 澳AU,巴PK,冰岛IS,东盟AS,哥CR,秘鲁PE,瑞士CH,新西兰NZ,智利CL 1.2 韩国KR	0 受惠国LD	20	---Aerials or parts thereof for use with the apparatus of No.8517
	ex85177070	无线电话电报装置的天线	0				Aerials or antennae of a kind used with apparatus for radio-telephony and radio-telegraphy
7092	8517.7090	---其他	0		0 受惠国LD	20	---Other
	85.18	**传声器（麦克风）及其座架;扬声器，不论是否装成音箱;耳机、耳塞机，不论是否装有传声器，由传声器及一个或多个扬声器组成的组合机;音频扩大器;电气扩音机组:**					**Microphones and stands therefor; loudspeakers, whether or not mounted in their enclosures; headphones and earphones, whether or not combined with a microphone, and sets consisting of a microphone and one or more loudspeakers; audio-frequency electric amplifiers; electric sound amplifier sets:**
7093	8518.1000	-传声器（麦克风）及其座架	10	0 冰岛IS,东盟AS,哥CR,秘鲁PE,台湾TW,香港HK,新加坡SG,新西兰NZ,智利CL 4 瑞士CH 5 巴PK 6 澳AU,韩国KR	0 受惠国LD	40	-Microphones and stands therefor
	ex85181000	电讯用麦克风，频率范围在300赫兹到3.4千赫之间，直径不超过10毫米，高度不超过3毫米	0				Microphones having a frequency range of 300Hz to 3.4kHz with a diameter of not exceeding10mm and a height not exceeding 3mm, for telecommunication use
	ex85181000	传声器(麦克风)及其座架(列入ITA的电讯用麦克风除外)	Δ6				Microphones and stands therefor (not inculding microphones for telecom-communicaiton use within ITA)
		-扬声器，不论是否装成音箱:					-Loudspeakers, whether or not mounted in their enclosures:
7094	8518.2100	--单喇叭音箱	10Δ6	0 冰岛IS,东盟AS,哥CR,秘鲁PE,香港HK,新加坡SG,新西兰NZ,智利CL 4 瑞士CH 5 巴PK 6 澳AU 8 韩国KR	0 受惠国LD	40	--Single loudspeakers, mounted in their enclosures
7095	8518.2200	--多喇叭音箱	10Δ6	0 冰岛IS,东盟AS,哥CR,香港HK,新加坡SG,新西兰NZ,智利CL 3 秘鲁PE 4 瑞士CH 5 巴PK 6 澳AU 8 韩国KR	0 受惠国LD	40	--Multiple loudspeakers, mounted in the same enclosure
7096	8518.2900	--其他	0		0 受惠国LD	40	--Other

序号 No.	税则号列 Tariff Line	中文货品名称 Article Description in Chinese	最惠国税率 MFN(%)	协定税率 Agreement(%)	特惠税率 SP(%)	普通税率 Gen(%)	英文货品名称 Article Description
7097	8518.3000	-耳机、耳塞机，不论是否装有传声器，由传声器及一个或多个扬声器组成的组合机	0		0 受惠国LD	40	-Headphones and earphones, whether or not combined with a microphone, and sets consisting of a microphone and one or more loudspeakers
7098	8518.4000	-音频扩大器	12	0 冰岛IS,东盟AS,哥CR,台湾TW,香港HK,新加坡SG,新西兰NZ,智利CL 3.6 秘鲁PE 4.8 瑞士CH 6 巴PK 7.2 澳AU 9.6 韩国KR	0 受惠国LD	40	-Audio-frequency electric amplifiers
	ex85184000	列入ITA的有线电话重复器用的电器扩音器	0				Electric amplifiers when used as repeaters in line telephony products falling within the ITA
7099	8518.5000	-电气扩音机组	10	0 冰岛IS,东盟AS,哥CR,秘鲁PE,新加坡SG,新西兰NZ,智利CL 4 瑞士CH 5 巴PK 6 澳AU 9 韩国KR	0 受惠国LD	40	-Electric sound amplifier sets
7100	8518.9000	-零件	10.5	0 冰岛IS,东盟AS,哥CR,秘鲁PE,台湾TW,香港HK,新加坡SG,新西兰NZ,智利CL 5 巴PK 6.3 澳AU 7.4 瑞士CH 9.6 韩国KR	0 受惠国LD	40	-Parts
	ex85189000	列入ITA的有线电话重复器用的电器扩音器的零件	0				Parts of electric amplifiers when used as repeaters in line telephony products falling within the ITA
	85.19	**声音录制或重放设备：**					**Sound recording or sound reproducing apparatus:**
7101	8519.2000	-用硬币、钞票、银行卡、代币或其他支付方式使其工作的设备	20	0 冰岛IS,东盟AS,哥CR,新加坡SG,新西兰NZ,智利CL 6 秘鲁PE 12 澳AU 14 瑞士CH 16.4 巴PK,亚太AP 17.3 韩国KR	0 受惠国$_1$LD$_1$	80	-Apparatus operated by coins, banknotes, bank cards, tokens or by other means of payment
7102	8519.3000	-转盘（唱机唱盘）	30	0 冰岛IS,东盟AS,哥CR,新加坡SG,新西兰NZ,智利CL 9 秘鲁PE 18 澳AU 21.6 瑞士CH	0 受惠国$_1$LD$_1$	130	-Turntables (record-decks)
7103	8519.5000	-电话应答机	0		0 受惠国LD	80	-Telephone answering machines
		-其他设备：					-Other apparatus:
		--使用磁性、光学或半导体媒体的：					--Using magnetic, optical or semiconductor media:
		---使用磁性媒体的：					---Using magnetic media:
7104	8519.8111	----未装有声音录制装置的盒式磁带型声音重放装置，编辑节目用放声机除外	17	0 冰岛IS,东盟AS,哥CR,新加坡SG,新西兰NZ,智利CL 5.1 秘鲁PE 10.2 澳AU 11.9 瑞士CH 13.6 巴PK,韩国KR	0 受惠国$_1$LD$_1$	130	----Cassette-players, not incorporating a sound recording device, not including transcribing machines

序号 No.	税则号列 Tariff Line	中文货品名称 Article Description in Chinese	最惠国税率 MFN(%)	协定税率 Agreement(%)	特惠税率 SP(%)	普通税率 Gen(%)	英文货品名称 Article Description
7105	8519.8112	----装有声音重放装置的盒式磁带型录音机	30	0 冰岛IS,东盟AS,哥CR,新加坡SG,新西兰NZ,智利CL 9 秘鲁PE 18 澳AU 21.6 瑞士CH 27 韩国KR	0 受惠国$_1$LD$_1$	130	----Cassette-type magnetic tape recorders incorporating sound reproducing apparatus
7106	8519.8119	----其他	20	0 冰岛IS,东盟AS,哥CR,新加坡SG,新西兰NZ,智利CL 6 秘鲁PE 12 澳AU 14 瑞士CH 16.4 巴PK,亚太AP 17.3 韩国KR	0 受惠国$_1$LD$_1$	80	----Other
		---使用光学媒体的：					---Using optical media:
7107	8519.8121	----激光唱机，未装有声音录制装置	30	0 冰岛IS,东盟AS,哥CR,新加坡SG,新西兰NZ,智利CL 9 秘鲁PE 18 澳AU 21.6 瑞士CH 26 巴PK,亚太AP 27 韩国KR	0 受惠国$_1$LD$_1$	80	----Compact disc players, not incorporating a sound recording devices
7108	8519.8129	----其他	20	0 冰岛IS,东盟AS,哥CR,新加坡SG,新西兰NZ,智利CL 6 秘鲁PE 12 澳AU 14 瑞士CH 16 巴PK 16.4 亚太AP 17.3 韩国KR	0 受惠国$_1$LD$_1$	80	----Other
		---使用半导体媒体的：					---Using semiconductor media:
7109	8519.8131	----装有声音重放装置的闪速存储器型声音录制设备	20Δ12	0 冰岛IS,东盟AS,哥CR,新加坡SG,新西兰NZ,智利CL 6 秘鲁PE 12 澳AU 14 瑞士CH 18 韩国KR	0 受惠国$_1$LD$_1$	80	----Flash memory recorders incorporating sound reproducing apparatus
7110	8519.8139	----其他	20Δ12	0 冰岛IS,东盟AS,哥CR,新加坡SG,新西兰NZ,智利CL 6 秘鲁PE 12 澳AU 14 瑞士CH 16.4 巴PK,亚太AP 17.3 韩国KR	0 受惠国$_1$LD$_1$	80	----Other
		--其他：					--Other:
7111	8519.8910	---不带录制装置的其他唱机，不论是否带有扬声器	30	0 冰岛IS,东盟AS,哥CR,新加坡SG,新西兰NZ,智利CL 9 秘鲁PE 18 澳AU 21.6 瑞士CH 27 韩国KR	0 受惠国$_1$LD$_1$	130	---Record-players, not incorporating a sound recording device

序号 No.	税则号列 Tariff Line	中文货品名称 Article Description in Chinese	最惠国税率 MFN(%)	协定税率 Agreement(%)	特惠税率 SP(%)	普通税率 Gen(%)	英文货品名称 Article Description
7112	8519.8990	---其他声音录制或重放设备	20Δ12	0 冰岛IS,东盟AS,哥CR,新加坡SG,新西兰NZ,智利CL 6 秘鲁PE 12 澳AU 14 瑞士CH 16 巴PK 16.4 亚太AP 17.3 韩国KR	0 受惠国$_1$LD$_1$	80	---Other
	85.21	**视频信号录制或重放设备，不论是否装有高频调谐器：**					**Video recording or reproducing apparatus, whether or not incorporating a video tuner:**
		-磁带型：					-Magnetic tape-type:
		---录像机：					---Video tape recorders:
7113	8521.1011	----广播级	①	0 冰岛IS,东盟AS,哥CR,新加坡SG,新西兰NZ,智利CL 9 秘鲁PE 18 澳AU 21.6 瑞士CH ③ 巴PK,亚太AP ④ 韩国KR	0 受惠国$_1$LD$_1$	②	----Broadcast quality
7114	8521.1019	----其他	⑤	0 冰岛IS,东盟AS,哥CR,新加坡SG,新西兰NZ,智利CL 9 秘鲁PE 18 澳AU 21.6 瑞士CH ⑦ 巴PK,亚太AP ⑧ 韩国KR	0 受惠国$_1$LD$_1$	⑥	----Other

①**最惠国税率**：完税价格≤2000 美元/台:30%；完税价格>2000 美元/台:3%+3283 元/台
MFN Tariff: Price≤2000$/Set:30%; Price>2000$/Set:3%+3283¥/Set
暂定最惠国税率：完税价格≤5000 美元/台:15%；完税价格>5000 美元/台:3%+3648 元/台
Interim MFN Tariff: Price≤5000$/Set:15%; Price>5000$/Set:3%+3648¥/Set
②**普通税率**：完税价格≤2000 美元/台:130%；完税价格>2000 美元/台:6%+20600 元/台
General Duty: Price≤2000$/Set:130%; Price>2000$/Set:6%+20600¥/Set
③**协定税率**：完税价格≤2000 美元/台:16%；完税价格>2000 美元/台:3%+1581 元/台
Agreement Import Tariff: Price≤2000$/Set:16%; Price>2000$/Set:3%+1581¥/Set
④**协定税率**：价格≤2000 美元/台:27%；价格>2000 美元/台:2.7%+3936.6 元/台
Agreement Import Tariff: Price≤2000$/Set:27%; Price>2000$/Set:2.7%+3936.6¥/Set
⑤**最惠国税率**：完税价格≤2000 美元/台:30%；完税价格>2000 美元/台:3%+3283 元/台
MFN Tariff: Price≤2000$/Set:30%; Price>2000$/Set:3%+3283¥/Set
⑥**普通税率**：完税价格≤2000 美元/台:130%；完税价格>2000 美元/台:6%+20600 元/台
General Duty: Price≤2000$/Set:130%; Price>2000$/Set:6%+20600¥/Set
⑦**协定税率**：完税价格≤2000 美元/台:24.5%；完税价格>2000 美元/台:3%+2614 元/台
Agreement Import Tariff: Price≤2000$/Set:24.5%; Price>2000$/Set:3%+2614¥/Set
⑧**协定税率**：价格≤2000 美元/台:27%；价格>2000 美元/台:2.7%+3936.6 元/台
Agreement Import Tariff: Price≤2000$/Set:27%; Price>2000$/Set:2.7%+3936.6¥/Set

序号 No.	税则号列 Tariff Line	中文货品名称 Article Description in Chinese	最惠国税率 MFN(%)	协定税率 Agreement(%)	特惠税率 SP(%)	普通税率 Gen(%)	英文货品名称 Article Description
7115	8521.1020	---放像机	①	0 冰岛IS,东盟AS,哥CR,新加坡SG,新西兰NZ,智利CL 9 秘鲁PE 18 澳AU 21.6 瑞士CH ③ 巴PK ④ 亚太AP ⑤ 韩国KR	0 受惠国$_1$LD$_1$	②	---Video tape reproducers
		-其他:					-Other:
		---激光视盘机:					---Laser video compact disk player:
7116	8521.9011	----视频高密光盘(VCD)播放机	20	0 冰岛IS,东盟AS,哥CR,新加坡SG,新西兰NZ,智利CL 6 秘鲁PE 12 澳AU 14 瑞士CH 16 巴PK,亚太AP 17.3 韩国KR	0 受惠国$_1$LD$_1$	130	----Video Compact Disc player
7117	8521.9012	----数字化视频光盘(DVD)播放机	20	0 冰岛IS,东盟AS,哥CR,新加坡SG,新西兰NZ,智利CL 6 秘鲁PE 12 澳AU 14 瑞士CH 16 巴PK,亚太AP 18 韩国KR	0 受惠国$_1$LD$_1$	130	----Digital Video Disc player
7118	8521.9019	----其他	20	0 冰岛IS,东盟AS,哥CR,新加坡SG,新西兰NZ,智利CL 6 秘鲁PE 12 澳AU 14 瑞士CH 16 巴PK,亚太AP 17.3 韩国KR	0 受惠国$_1$LD$_1$	130	----Other
7119	8521.9090	---其他	20	0 冰岛IS,东盟AS,哥CR,香港HK,新加坡SG,新西兰NZ,智利CL 6 秘鲁PE 12 澳AU 14 瑞士CH 16 巴PK,亚太AP 18 韩国KR	0 受惠国$_1$LD$_1$	130	---Other
	ex85219090	光盘型广播级录像机	⑥				CD-type video recorder, broadcast quality
	85.22	**专用于或主要用于税号85.19或85.21所列设备的零件、附件:**					**Parts and accessories suitable for use solely or principally with the apparatus of heading 8519 or 8521:**

①**最惠国税率**: 完税价格≤2000 美元/台:30%; 完税价格>2000 美元/台:3%+3283 元/台
MFN Tariff: Price≤2000$/Set:30%; Price>2000$/Set:3%+3283¥/Set

②**普通税率**: 完税价格≤2000 美元/台:130%; 完税价格>2000 美元/台:6%+20600 元/台
General Duty: Price≤2000$/Set:130%; Price>2000$/Set:6%+20600¥/Set

③**协定税率**: 完税价格≤2000 美元/台:18%; 完税价格>2000 美元/台:3%+1824 元/台
Agreement Import Tariff: Price≤2000$/Set:18%; Price>2000$/Set:3%+1824¥/Set

④**协定税率**: 完税价格≤2000 美元/台:18%; 完税价格>2000 美元/台:3%+1824 元/台
Agreement Import Tariff: Price≤2000$/Set:18%; Price>2000$/Set:3%+1824¥/Set

⑤**协定税率**: 价格≤2000 美元/台:27%; 价格>2000 美元/台:2.7%+3936.6 元/台
Agreement Import Tariff: Price≤2000$/Set:27%; Price>2000$/Set:2.7%+3936.6¥/Set

⑥**暂定最惠国税率**: 完税价格≤7000 美元/台:15%; 完税价格>7000 美元/台:5%+4256 元/台
Interim MFN Tariff: Price≤7000$/Set:15%; Price>7000$/Set:5%+4256¥/Set

序号 No.	税则号列 Tariff Line	中文货品名称 Article Description in Chinese	最惠国税率 MFN(%)	协定税率 Agreement(%)	特惠税率 SP(%)	普通税率 Gen(%)	英文货品名称 Article Description
7120	8522.1000	-拾音头	35	0 冰岛IS,东盟AS,哥CR,香港HK,新加坡SG,新西兰NZ,智利CL 10.5 秘鲁PE 21 澳AU 25.2 瑞士CH	0 受惠国$_1$LD$_1$	130	-Pick up cartridges
		-其他:					-Other:
7121	8522.9010	---转盘或唱机用	25	0 冰岛IS,东盟AS,哥CR,香港HK,新加坡SG,新西兰NZ,智利CL 7.5 秘鲁PE 15 澳AU 18 瑞士CH 20 巴PK,亚太AP 21.6 韩国KR	0 受惠国$_1$LD$_1$	130	---Of turntables (record decks) or recordplayers
		---盒式磁带录音机或放声机用:					---Of cassette magnetic tape recorders or reproducers:
7122	8522.9021	----走带机构（机芯），不论是否装有磁头	25	0 冰岛IS,东盟AS,哥CR,香港HK,新加坡SG,新西兰NZ,智利CL 7.5 秘鲁PE 15 澳AU 18 瑞士CH 21.6 韩国KR 22.5 巴PK,亚太AP	0 受惠国$_1$LD$_1$	100	----Transport mechanisms, whether or not incorporating a magnetic head
7123	8522.9022	----磁头	25	0 冰岛IS,东盟AS,哥CR,香港HK,新加坡SG,新西兰NZ,智利CL 7.5 秘鲁PE 15 澳AU 18 瑞士CH 21.5 韩国KR 22.5 巴PK,亚太AP	0 受惠国$_1$LD$_1$	100	----Magnetic heads
7124	8522.9023	----磁头零件	20	0 冰岛IS,东盟AS,哥CR,香港HK,新加坡SG,新西兰NZ,智利CL 6 秘鲁PE 12 澳AU 14 瑞士CH 17.3 韩国KR 18 巴PK,亚太AP	0 受惠国$_1$LD$_1$	100	----Parts of magnetic heads
7125	8522.9029	----其他	30	0 冰岛IS,东盟AS,哥CR,香港HK,新加坡SG,新西兰NZ,智利CL 9 秘鲁PE 18 澳AU 21.6 瑞士CH 25.8 韩国KR 27 巴PK,亚太AP	0 受惠国$_1$LD$_1$	100	----Other
		---视频信号录制或重放设备用:					---Of video recording or reproducing apparatus:
7126	8522.9031	----激光视盘机的机芯	30	0 冰岛IS,东盟AS,哥CR,香港HK,新加坡SG,新西兰NZ,智利CL 9 秘鲁PE 18 澳AU 21 巴PK,亚太AP 21.6 瑞士CH 25.8 韩国KR	0 受惠国$_1$LD$_1$	100	----Movements for Laser video compact disk player
	ex85229031	车载导航仪视频播放机机芯	Δ17				Movements for video players in the navigation system in vehicle

序号 No.	税则号列 Tariff Line	中文货品名称 Article Description in Chinese	最惠国税率 MFN(%)	协定税率 Agreement(%)	特惠税率 SP(%)	普通税率 Gen(%)	英文货品名称 Article Description
7127	8522.9039	----其他	30△15	0 冰岛IS,东盟AS,哥CR,香港HK,新加坡SG,新西兰NZ,智利CL 9 秘鲁PE 18 澳AU 21 巴PK,亚太AP 25.8 韩国KR	0 受惠国$_1$LD$_1$	100	----Other
		---其他:					---Other:
7128	8522.9091	----车载音频转播器或发射器	20	0 冰岛IS,东盟AS,哥CR,香港HK,新加坡SG,新西兰NZ,智利CL 6 秘鲁PE 12 澳AU 14 瑞士CH 16 巴PK,亚太AP 17.3 韩国KR	0 受惠国LD	80	----Car audio frequency relays ware or FM car transmitter
7129	8522.9099	----其他	20△10	0 冰岛IS,东盟AS,哥CR,香港HK,新加坡SG,新西兰NZ,智利CL 6 秘鲁PE 12 澳AU 14 瑞士CH 16 巴PK,亚太AP 17.3 韩国KR	0 受惠国LD	80	----Other
	85.23	**录制声音或其他信息用的圆盘、磁带、固态非易失性数据存储器件、“智能卡”及其他媒体，不论是否已录制，包括供复制圆盘用的母片及母带，但不包括第三十七章的产品：**					**Discs, tapes, solid-state non-volatile storage devices, 'smart cards' and other media for the recording of sound or of other phenomena, whether or not recorded, including matrices and masters for the production of discs, but excluding products of Chapter 37:**
		-磁性媒体：					-Magnetic media:
		--磁条卡：					--Cards incorporating a magnetic stripe:
7130	8523.2110	---未录制	17.5	0 澳门MO,冰岛IS,东盟AS,哥CR,香港HK,新加坡SG,新西兰NZ,智利CL 5.2 秘鲁PE 10.5 澳AU 12.3 瑞士CH 14 巴PK,韩国KR	0 受惠国$_1$LD$_1$	70	---Prepared unrecorded
7131	8523.2120	---已录制	15	0 澳门MO,冰岛IS,东盟AS,哥CR,香港HK,新加坡SG,新西兰NZ,智利CL 4.5 秘鲁PE 9 澳AU 10.5 瑞士CH 12 巴PK,韩国KR	0 受惠国$_1$LD$_1$	130	---Recorded
		--其他：					--Other:
		---磁盘：					---Magnetic discs:
7132	8523.2911	----未录制	0		0 受惠国LD	14	----Prepared unrecorded
7133	8523.2919	----其他	0		0 受惠国LD	14	----Other
		---磁带：					---Magnetic tapes:
7134	8523.2921	----未录制的宽度不超过4毫米磁带	0		0 受惠国LD	130	----Prepared unrecorded, of a width not exceeding 4mm
7135	8523.2922	----未录制的宽度超过4毫米，但不超过6. 5毫米的磁带	0		0 受惠国LD	130	----Prepared unrecorded, of a width exceeding 4mm but not exceeding 6.5mm
7136	8523.2923	----未录制的宽度超过6. 5毫米的磁带	0		0 受惠国LD	20	----Prepared unrecorded, of a width exceeding 6.5mm

序号 No.	税则号列 Tariff Line	中文货品名称 Article Description in Chinese	最惠国税率 MFN(%)	协定税率 Agreement(%)	特惠税率 SP(%)	普通税率 Gen(%)	英文货品名称 Article Description
7137	8523.2928	----重放声音或图像信息的磁带	10Δ6	0 冰岛IS,东盟AS,哥CR,秘鲁PE,香港HK,新加坡SG,新西兰NZ,智利CL 4 瑞士CH 5 巴PK 6 澳AU 8.6 韩国KR	0 受惠国LD	130	----For reproducing sound or image
7138	8523.2929	----已录制的其他磁带	0		0 受惠国LD	14	----Other, recorded
7139	8523.2990	---其他	0		0 受惠国LD	14	---Other
		-光学媒体:					-Optical media:
7140	8523.4100	--未录制	0		0 受惠国LD	14	--Prepared unrecorded
		--其他:					--Other:
7141	8523.4910	---仅用于重放声音信息的已录制光盘	10Δ6	0 澳门MO,冰岛IS,东盟AS,哥CR,秘鲁PE,香港HK,新西兰NZ,智利CL 4 瑞士CH 5 巴PK 6 澳AU 8 韩国KR	0 受惠国$_1$LD$_1$	130	---For reproducing sound only, recorded
7142	8523.4920	---用于重放声音、图像以外信息的，税号84.71所列机器用	0		0 受惠国LD	14	---For the machines of heading No.84.71 reproducing phenomena other than sound or image
7143	8523.4990	---其他	0		0 受惠国LD	14	---Other
		-半导体媒体:					-Semiconductor media:
		--固态非易失性存储器件（闪速存储器）:					--Solid-state non-volatile storage devices:
7144	8523.5110	---未录制	0		0 受惠国LD	70	---Prepared unrecorded
7145	8523.5120	---已录制	0		0 受惠国LD	14	---Recorded
		--“智能卡”:					--' Smart cards' :
7146	8523.5210	---未录制	0		0 受惠国LD	21	---Prepared unrecorded
7147	8523.5290	---其他	0		0 受惠国LD	21	---Other
		--其他:					--Other:
7148	8523.5910	---未录制	0		0 受惠国LD	70	---Prepared unrecorded
7149	8523.5920	---已录制	0		0 受惠国LD	14	---Recorded
		-其他:					-Other:
		---唱片:					---Gramophone records:
7150	8523.8011	----已录制唱片	15	0 澳门MO,冰岛IS,东盟AS,哥CR,新加坡SG,新西兰NZ,智利CL 4.5 秘鲁PE 9 澳AU 10.5 瑞士CH 12 巴PK,韩国KR	0 受惠国$_1$LD$_1$	130	----Prepared recorded
7151	8523.8019	----其他	0		0 受惠国LD	70	----Other
		---税号84.71所列机器用:					---For the machines of heading No.84.71:
7152	8523.8021	----未录制	0		0 受惠国LD	14	----Prepared unrecorded
7153	8523.8029	----其他	0		0 受惠国LD	14	----Other
		---其他:					---Other:
7154	8523.8091	----未录制	0		0 受惠国LD	14	----Prepared unrecorded
7155	8523.8099	----其他	0		0 受惠国LD	14	----Other
	85.25	**无线电广播、电视发送设备，不论是否装有接收装置或声音的录制、重放装置;电视摄像机、数字照相机及视频摄录一体机:**					**Transmission apparatus for radio-broadcasting or television, whether or not incorporating reception apparatus or sound recording or reproducing apparatus; television cameras, digital cameras and video camera recorders:**
7156	8525.5000	-发送设备	0		0 受惠国LD	30	-Transmission apparatus
		-装有接收装置的发送设备:					-Transmission apparatus incorporating reception apparatus:
7157	8525.6010	---卫星地面站设备	0		0 受惠国LD	14	---Satellite earth station
7158	8525.6090	---其他	0		0 受惠国LD	30	---Other

序号 No.	税则号列 Tariff Line	中文货品名称 Article Description in Chinese	最惠国税率 MFN(%)	协定税率 Agreement(%)	特惠税率 SP(%)	普通税率 Gen(%)	英文货品名称 Article Description
		-电视摄像机、数字照相机及视频摄录一体机:					-Television cameras, digital cameras and video camera recorders:
		---电视摄像机:					---Television cameras:
7159	8525.8011	----特种用途的	10	0 冰岛IS,东盟AS,哥CR,秘鲁PE,新加坡SG,新西兰NZ,智利CL 4 瑞士CH 5 巴PK 6 澳AU 9 亚太AP	0 受惠国$_1$LD$_1$	17	----For special purposes
7160	8525.8012	----非特种用途的，广播级	①	0 冰岛IS,东盟AS,哥CR,新加坡SG,新西兰NZ,智利CL 10.5 秘鲁PE 21 澳AU 28 瑞士CH ③ 巴PK,亚太AP	0 受惠国$_1$LD$_1$	②	----Other, broadcast quality
7161	8525.8013	----非特种用途的，其他类型	④	0 澳门MO,冰岛IS,东盟AS,哥CR,台湾TW,香港HK,新加坡SG,新西兰NZ,智利CL 10.5 秘鲁PE 21 澳AU 28.7 瑞士CH ⑥ 巴PK,亚太AP ⑦ 韩国KR	0 受惠国$_1$LD$_1$	⑤	----Other
	ex85258013	手机用摄像组件（由镜头+CCD/CMOS+数字信号处理电路三部分构成）	Δ4				Camera subassembly used for mobile telephone made up of lens, CCD/CMOS sensor and digital signal processing circuit, not broadcast quality
	ex85258013	高清摄像头（必须满足以下三个条件：（1）镜头元件必须使用5层及以上玻璃镜头；（2）使用USB2.0及以上高速接口；（3）硬件传感器像素达到130万及以上）	Δ10				High definition video cameras (must satisfy the 3 points below: (1)lens unit must use 5 and more lenses; (2)using connectors not less than USB2.0; (3)the pixels of imager must be over 1.3 million)
		---数字照相机:					---Digital cameras:
7162	8525.8021	----特种用途的	0		0 受惠国LD	17	----For special purposes
7163	8525.8022	----非特种用途的，单镜头反光型	0		0 受惠国LD	⑧	----Other, single lens reflex
7164	8525.8025	----非特种用途的，其他可换镜头的	0		0 受惠国LD	⑨	----Other, lens interchangeable

①**最惠国税率**：完税价格≤5000 美元/台:35%；完税价格>5000 美元/台:3%+9728 元/台
MFN Tariff: Price≤5000$/Set:35%; Price>5000$/Set:3%+9728¥/Set

②**普通税率**：完税价格≤5000 美元/台:130%；完税价格>5000 美元/台:6%+51500 元/台
General Duty: Price≤5000$/Set:130%; Price>5000$/Set:6%+51500¥/Set

③**协定税率**：完税价格≤5000 美元/台:29.8%；完税价格>5000 美元/台:3%+8147 元/台
Agreement Import Tariff: Price≤5000$/Set:29.8%; Price>5000$/Set:3%+8147¥/Set

④**最惠国税率**：完税价格≤5000 美元/台:35%；完税价格>5000 美元/台:3%+9728 元/台
MFN Tariff: Price≤5000$/Set:35%; Price>5000$/Set:3%+9728¥/Set

⑤**普通税率**：完税价格≤5000 美元/台:130%；完税价格>5000 美元/台:6%+51500 元/台
General Duty: Price≤5000$/Set:130%; Price>5000$/Set:6%+51500¥/Set

⑥**协定税率**：完税价格≤5000 美元/台:29.8%；完税价格>5000 美元/台:3%+8147 元/台
Agreement Import Tariff: Price≤5000$/Set:29.8%; Price>5000$/Set:3%+8147¥/Set

⑦**协定税率**：价格≤5000 美元/台:31.5%；价格>5000 美元/台:2.7%+11664 元/台
Agreement Import Tariff: Price≤5000$/Set:31.5%; Price>5000$/Set:2.7%+11664¥/Set

⑧**普通税率**：完税价格≤5000 美元/台:130%；完税价格>5000 美元/台:6%+51500 元/台
General Duty: Price≤5000$/Set:130%; Price>5000$/Set:6%+51500¥/Set

⑨**普通税率**：完税价格≤5000 美元/台:130%；完税价格>5000 美元/台:6%+51500 元/台
General Duty: Price≤5000$/Set:130%; Price>5000$/Set:6%+51500¥/Set

序号 No.	税则号列 Tariff Line	中文货品名称 Article Description in Chinese	最惠国税率 MFN(%)	协定税率 Agreement(%)		特惠税率 SP(%)		普通税率 Gen(%)	英文货品名称 Article Description
7165	8525.8029	----非特种用途的，其他类型	0			0	受惠国LD	①	----Other
		---视频摄录一体机：							---Video camera recorders:
7166	8525.8031	----特种用途的	0			0	受惠国LD	17	----For special purposes
7167	8525.8032	----非特种用途的，广播极	0			0	受惠国LD	②	----Other, broadcast quality
7168	8525.8033	----非特种用途的，家用型	0			0	受惠国LD	130	----Other, household
7169	8525.8039	----非特种用途的，其他类型	0			0	受惠国LD	③	----Other
	85.26	**雷达设备、无线电导航设备及无线电遥控设备：**							**Radar apparatus, radio navigational aid apparatus and radio remote control apparatus:**
		-雷达设备：							-Radar apparatus:
7170	8526.1010	---导航用	2	0 1.7	澳AU,巴PK,冰岛IS,东盟AS,哥CR,秘鲁PE,瑞士CH,新西兰NZ,智利CL 韩国KR	0	受惠国$_1$LD$_1$	8	---For navigational aid
7171	8526.1090	---其他	5	0 4.3	澳AU,巴PK,冰岛IS,东盟AS,哥CR,秘鲁PE,瑞士CH,新西兰NZ,智利CL 韩国KR	0	受惠国$_1$LD$_1$	14	---Other
	ex85261090	飞机机载雷达（包括气象雷达、地形雷达和空中交通管制应答系统）	Δ1						Airborne radars (including aero-radars, terrain-following radars and air-traffic- control-interrogator-responder systems)
	ex85261090	雷达生命探测仪	Δ2						Radar life detectors
		-其他：							-Other:
		--无线电导航设备：							--Radio navigational aid apparatus:
7172	8526.9110	---机动车辆用	2	0	澳AU,巴PK,冰岛IS,东盟AS,哥CR,韩国KR,秘鲁PE,瑞士CH,新西兰NZ,智利CL	0	受惠国$_1$LD$_1$	8	---For motor vehicles
7173	8526.9190	---其他	2	0 1.4 1.6	澳AU,巴PK,冰岛IS,东盟AS,哥CR,秘鲁PE,新西兰NZ,智利CL 瑞士CH 韩国KR	0	受惠国$_1$LD$_1$	8	---Other
7174	8526.9200	--无线电遥控设备	5	0 4	澳AU,巴PK,冰岛IS,东盟AS,哥CR,秘鲁PE,瑞士CH,新西兰NZ,智利CL 韩国KR	0	受惠国$_1$LD$_1$	14	--Radio remote control apparatus
	85.27	**无线电广播接收设备，不论是否与声音的录制、重放装置或时钟组合在同一机壳内：**							**Reception apparatus for radio-broadcasting, whether or not combined, in the same housing, with sound recording or reproducing apparatus or a clock:**
		-不需外接电源的无线电收音机：							-Radio-broadcast receivers capable of operating without an external source of power:

①**普通税率**：完税价格≤5000 美元/台:130%；完税价格>5000 美元/台:6%+51500 元/台
General Duty: Price≤5000$/Set:130%; Price>5000$/Set:6%+51500¥/Set

②**普通税率**：完税价格≤5000 美元/台:130%；完税价格>5000 美元/台:6%+51500 元/台
General Duty: Price≤5000$/Set:130%; Price>5000$/Set:6%+51500¥/Set

③**普通税率**：完税价格≤5000 美元/台:130%；完税价格>5000 美元/台:6%+51500 元/台
General Duty: Price≤5000$/Set:130%; Price>5000$/Set:6%+51500¥/Set

序号 No.	税则号列 Tariff Line	中文货品名称 Article Description in Chinese	最惠国税率 MFN(%)	协定税率 Agreement(%)	特惠税率 SP(%)	普通税率 Gen(%)	英文货品名称 Article Description
7175	8527.1200	--袖珍盒式磁带收放机	20	0 冰岛IS,东盟AS,哥CR,新加坡SG,新西兰NZ,智利CL 6 秘鲁PE 12 澳AU 14 瑞士CH 17.3 韩国KR	0 受惠国$_1$LD$_1$	130	--Pocket-size radio cassette-players
7176	8527.1300	--其他收录（放）音组合机	15	0 冰岛IS,东盟AS,哥CR,新加坡SG,新西兰NZ,智利CL 4.5 秘鲁PE 9 澳AU 10.5 瑞士CH 12 巴PK,韩国KR	0 受惠国$_1$LD$_1$	130	--Other apparatus combined with sound recording or reproducing apparatus
7177	8527.1900	--其他	15	0 冰岛IS,东盟AS,哥CR,新加坡SG,新西兰NZ,智利CL 4.5 秘鲁PE 9 澳AU 10.5 瑞士CH 12 巴PK 13 韩国KR	0 受惠国$_1$LD$_1$	130	--Other
		-需外接电源的汽车用无线电收音机：					-Radio-broadcast receivers not capable of operating without an external source of power, of a kind used in motor vehicles:
7178	8527.2100	--收录（放）音组合机	15	0 冰岛IS,东盟AS,哥CR,新加坡SG,新西兰NZ,智利CL 4.5 秘鲁PE 9 澳AU 10.5 瑞士CH 12 巴PK 13 韩国KR	0 受惠国$_1$LD$_1$	130	--Combined with sound recording or reproducing apparatus
7179	8527.2900	--其他	15	0 冰岛IS,东盟AS,哥CR,新加坡SG,新西兰NZ,智利CL 4.5 秘鲁PE 9 澳AU 10.5 瑞士CH 12 巴PK 13 韩国KR	0 受惠国$_1$LD$_1$	130	--Other
		-其他：					-Other:
7180	8527.9100	--收录（放）音组合机	15	0 冰岛IS,东盟AS,哥CR,新加坡SG,新西兰NZ,智利CL 4.5 秘鲁PE 9 澳AU 10.5 瑞士CH 12 巴PK,韩国KR	0 受惠国$_1$LD$_1$	130	--Combined with sound recording or reproducing apparatus
7181	8527.9200	--带时钟的收音机	15	0 冰岛IS,东盟AS,哥CR,新加坡SG,新西兰NZ,智利CL 4.5 秘鲁PE 9 澳AU 10.5 瑞士CH 12 巴PK,韩国KR	0 受惠国$_1$LD$_1$	130	--Not combined with sound recording or reproducing apparatus but combined with a clock
7182	8527.9900	--其他	27	0 冰岛IS,东盟AS,哥CR,新加坡SG,新西兰NZ,智利CL 8.1 秘鲁PE 16.2 澳AU 19.4 瑞士CH 24.3 韩国KR	0 受惠国$_1$LD$_1$	130	--Other

序号 No.	税则号列 Tariff Line	中文货品名称 Article Description in Chinese	最惠国税率 MFN(%)	协定税率 Agreement(%)	特惠税率 SP(%)	普通税率 Gen(%)	英文货品名称 Article Description
	85.28	**监视器及投影机，未装电视接收装置；电视接收装置，不论是否装有无线电收音装置或声音、图像的录制或重放装置：**					**Monitors and projectors, not incorporating television reception apparatus; reception apparatus for television, whether or not incorporating radio-broadcast receivers or sound or video recording or reproducing apparatus:**
		-阴极射线管监视器：					-Cathode-ray tube monitors:
7183	8528.4100	--专用于或主要用于税目84.71的自动数据处理系统的	0		0 受惠国LD	40	--Of a kind solely or principally used in an automatic data processing system of heading 8471
		--其他：					--Other:
7184	8528.4910	---彩色的	30	0 澳门MO,冰岛IS,东盟AS,哥CR,新加坡SG,新西兰NZ,智利CL 9 秘鲁PE 18 澳AU 21 瑞士CH 26 巴PK,亚太AP 27 韩国KR	0 受惠国$_1$LD$_1$	130	---Colour
7185	8528.4990	---单色的	19	0 澳门MO,冰岛IS,东盟AS,哥CR,新加坡SG,新西兰NZ,智利CL 5.7 秘鲁PE 11.4 澳AU 13.3 瑞士CH 15.2 巴PK,韩国KR,亚太AP	0 受惠国$_1$LD$_1$	100	---Monochrome
		-其他监视器：					-Other monitors:
		--专用于或主要用于税目84.71的自动数据处理系统的：					--Of a kind solely or principally used in an automatic data-processing system of heading 8471:
7186	8528.5110	---液晶显示器的	0		0 受惠国LD	40	---With liquid crystal display
7187	8528.5190	---其他	0		0 受惠国LD	40	---Other
		--其他：					--Other:
7188	8528.5910	---彩色的	30	0 澳门MO,冰岛IS,东盟AS,香港HK,新加坡SG,新西兰NZ,智利CL 9 秘鲁PE 18 澳AU 25.8 韩国KR 26 巴PK,亚太AP	0 受惠国$_1$LD$_1$	130	---Colour
	ex85285910	专用于车载导航仪的液晶监视器	Δ15				Liquid crystal display monitors for use solely with car navigation instruments
7189	8528.5990	---单色的	19	0 澳门MO,冰岛IS,东盟AS,哥CR,香港HK,新加坡SG,新西兰NZ,智利CL 5.7 秘鲁PE 11.4 澳AU 13.3 瑞士CH 15.2 巴PK,亚太AP	0 受惠国$_1$LD$_1$	100	---Monochrome
		-投影机：					-Projectors:
7190	8528.6100	--专用于或主要用于税目84.71的自动数据处理系统的	0		0 受惠国LD	14	--Of a kind solely or principally used in an automatic data processing system of heading 8471
		--其他：					--Other:

序号 No.	税则号列 Tariff Line	中文货品名称 Article Description in Chinese	最惠国税率 MFN(%)	协定税率 Agreement(%)	特惠税率 SP(%)	普通税率 Gen(%)	英文货品名称 Article Description
7191	8528.6910	---彩色的	30	0 澳门MO,冰岛IS,东盟AS,哥CR,香港HK,新加坡SG,新西兰NZ,智利CL 9 秘鲁PE 18 澳AU 25.5 巴PK,亚太AP 25.8 韩国KR	0 受惠国$_1$LD$_1$	130	---Colour
7192	8528.6990	---单色的	15	0 澳门MO,冰岛IS,东盟AS,哥CR,新加坡SG,新西兰NZ,智利CL 4.5 秘鲁PE 9 澳AU 10.5 瑞士CH 12 巴PK	0 受惠国$_1$LD$_1$	100	---Monochrome
		-电视接收装置，不论是否装有无线电收音装置或声音、图像的录制或重放装置：					-Reception apparatus for television, whether or not incorporating radio-broadcast receivers or sound or video recording or reproducing apparatus:
		--在设计上不带有视频显示器或屏幕的：					--Not designed to incorporate a video display or screen:
7193	8528.7110	---彩色卫星电视接收机	30	0 冰岛IS,哥CR,新西兰NZ,智利CL 18 澳AU 24 巴PK,亚太AP	0 受惠国$_2$LD$_2$	130	---Satellite television receivers
7194	8528.7180	---其他彩色的	30	0 冰岛IS,东盟AS,哥CR,新加坡SG,新西兰NZ,智利CL 18 澳AU 21 巴PK,亚太AP	0 受惠国$_2$LD$_2$	130	---Other, colour
7195	8528.7190	---单色的	15	0 澳门MO,冰岛IS,东盟AS,哥CR,新加坡SG,新西兰NZ,智利CL 4.5 秘鲁PE 9 澳AU 10.5 瑞士CH 12 巴PK,韩国KR	0 受惠国$_1$LD$_1$	100	---Monochrome
		--其他，彩色的：					--Other, colour:
		---阴极射线显像管的：					---Cathode-ray tube monitors:
7196	8528.7211	----模拟电视接收机	30	0 冰岛IS,哥CR,新西兰NZ,智利CL 18 澳AU 21 巴PK,亚太AP 21.6 瑞士CH	0 受惠国$_2$LD$_2$	130	----Analog television
7197	8528.7212	----数字电视接收机	30	0 冰岛IS,哥CR,新西兰NZ,智利CL 21 巴PK,亚太AP 21.6 瑞士CH 26 澳AU	0 受惠国$_2$LD$_2$	130	----Digital television
7198	8528.7219	----其他	30	0 冰岛IS,哥CR,新西兰NZ,智利CL 18 澳AU 21 巴PK,亚太AP 21.6 瑞士CH	0 受惠国$_2$LD$_2$	130	----Other
		---液晶显示器的：					---With liquid crystal display:
7199	8528.7221	----模拟电视接收机	30	0 澳门MO,冰岛IS,新西兰NZ,智利CL 18 澳AU 20 东盟AS 21 巴PK,亚太AP	0 受惠国$_2$LD$_2$	130	----Analog television

序号 No.	税则号列 Tariff Line	中文货品名称 Article Description in Chinese	最惠国税率 MFN(%)	协定税率 Agreement(%)	特惠税率 SP(%)	普通税率 Gen(%)	英文货品名称 Article Description
7200	8528.7222	----数字电视接收机	30	0 冰岛IS,新西兰NZ,智利CL 20 东盟AS 21 巴PK,亚太AP 26 澳AU 26.4 韩国KR	0 受惠国$_2$LD$_2$	130	----Digital television
7201	8528.7229	----其他	30	0 澳门MO,冰岛IS,新西兰NZ,智利CL 18 澳AU 20 东盟AS 21 巴PK,亚太AP	0 受惠国$_2$LD$_2$	130	----Other
		---等离子显示器的:					---With plasma display Panels:
7202	8528.7231	----模拟电视接收机	30	0 澳门MO,冰岛IS,新西兰NZ,智利CL 18 澳AU 20 东盟AS 21 巴PK,亚太AP	0 受惠国$_2$LD$_2$	130	----Analog television
7203	8528.7232	----数字电视接收机	30	0 冰岛IS,新西兰NZ,智利CL 20 东盟AS 21 巴PK,亚太AP 26 澳AU	0 受惠国$_2$LD$_2$	130	----Digital television
7204	8528.7239	----其他	30	0 澳门MO,冰岛IS,新西兰NZ,智利CL 18 澳AU 20 东盟AS 21 巴PK,亚太AP 26.4 韩国KR	0 受惠国$_2$LD$_2$	130	----Other
		---其他:					---Other:
7205	8528.7291	----模拟电视接收机	30	0 冰岛IS,哥CR,新西兰NZ,智利CL 9 秘鲁PE 18 澳AU 20 东盟AS 21 巴PK,亚太AP	0 受惠国$_1$LD$_1$	130	----Analog television
7206	8528.7292	----数字电视接收机	30	0 冰岛IS,新西兰NZ,智利CL 20 东盟AS 21 巴PK,亚太AP 26 澳AU	0 受惠国$_2$LD$_2$	130	----Digital television
7207	8528.7299	----其他	30	0 冰岛IS,哥CR,新西兰NZ,智利CL 18 澳AU 20 东盟AS 21 巴PK,亚太AP	0 受惠国$_2$LD$_2$	130	----Other
7208	8528.7300	--其他，单色的	15	0 澳门MO,冰岛IS,东盟AS,哥CR,新加坡SG,新西兰NZ,智利CL 4.5 秘鲁PE 9 澳AU 10.5 瑞士CH 12 巴PK,韩国KR	0 受惠国$_1$LD$_1$	100	--Other, monochrome
	85.29	**专用于或主要用于税号85.25至85.28所列装置或设备的零件：**					**Parts suitable for use solely or principally with the apparatus of headings 8525 to 8528:**
		-各种天线或天线反射器及其零件：					-Aerials and aerial reflectors of all kinds; parts suitable for use therewith:
7209	8529.1010	---雷达设备及无线电导航设备用	1.5	0 澳AU,巴PK,冰岛IS,东盟AS,哥CR,秘鲁PE,瑞士CH,香港HK,新西兰NZ,智利CL 1.2 韩国KR	0 受惠国$_1$LD$_1$	8	---For radar apparatus and radio navigational aid apparatus
7210	8529.1020	---无线电收音机及其组合机、电视接收机用	0		0 受惠国LD	90	---For radio-broadcast receivers and their combinations, television receivers

序号 No.	税则号列 Tariff Line	中文货品名称 Article Description in Chinese	最惠国税率 MFN(%)	协定税率 Agreement(%)	特惠税率 SP(%)	普通税率 Gen(%)	英文货品名称 Article Description
7211	8529.1090	---其他	2	0 澳AU,巴PK,冰岛IS,东盟AS,哥CR,韩国KR,秘鲁PE,瑞士CH,新西兰NZ,智利CL	0 受惠国$_1$LD$_1$	20	---Other
		-其他:					-Other:
7212	8529.9010	---电视发送、差转设备及卫星电视地面接收转播设备用	0		0 受惠国LD	30	---Of television transmission or translation apparatus, satellite television ground receiving and relaying apparatus
		---电视摄像机、视频摄录一体机、数字照相机用:					---Of television cameras, video camera recorders and digital cameras:
7213	8529.9041	----特种用途的	8	0 冰岛IS,东盟AS,哥CR,秘鲁PE,香港HK,新西兰NZ,智利CL 3.2 瑞士CH 4.8 澳AU 5 巴PK 6.8 韩国KR,亚太AP	0 受惠国$_1$LD$_1$	17	----Of special purpose
7214	8529.9042	----非特种用途的取像模块	12	0 冰岛IS,东盟AS,哥CR,台湾TW,香港HK,新加坡SG,新西兰NZ,智利CL 3.6 秘鲁PE 5 巴PK 7.2 澳AU 8.4 瑞士CH 9.6 韩国KR 10.8 亚太AP	0 受惠国$_1$LD$_1$	100	----Camera modules without special purpose
	ex85299042	电视摄像机、摄录一体机、数码相机用取像模块	Δ3				Camera modules for television cameras, video camera recorders, digital cameras
	ex85299042	手机、平板电脑用取像模块	Δ4				Camera modules for mobile telephones and tablet computers
7215	8529.9049	----其他	12Δ2	0 冰岛IS,东盟AS,哥CR,秘鲁PE,台湾TW,香港HK,新加坡SG,新西兰NZ,智利CL 5 巴PK 7.2 澳AU 8.4 瑞士CH 10.4 韩国KR 10.8 亚太AP	0 受惠国$_1$LD$_1$	100	----Other
7216	8529.9050	---雷达设备及无线电导航设备用	1.5	0 澳AU,巴PK,冰岛IS,东盟AS,哥CR,秘鲁PE,瑞士CH,新西兰NZ,智利CL 1.2 韩国KR 1.4 亚太AP	0 受惠国$_1$LD$_1$	8	---Of radar apparatus and radio navigational aid apparatus
7217	8529.9060	---无线电收音机及其组合机用	15Δ7	0 冰岛IS,东盟AS,哥CR,香港HK,新加坡SG,新西兰NZ,智利CL 4.5 秘鲁PE 7.5 巴PK 9 澳AU 10.5 瑞士CH 12 韩国KR,亚太AP	0 受惠国LD	130	---Of radio-broadcast receivers and their combinations
		---电视接收机用(高频调谐器除外):					---Of television receivers (Other than H.F. turners) :
7218	8529.9081	----彩色电视接收机用(等离子显像组件及其零件除外)	15Δ6	0 冰岛IS,东盟AS,新加坡SG,新西兰NZ,智利CL 4.5 秘鲁PE 7.5 巴PK 9 澳AU 10.5 瑞士CH 12 亚太AP	0 受惠国$_1$LD$_1$	80	----Of colour television receivers (Other than plasma display modules or parts thereof)

序号 No.	税则号列 Tariff Line	中文货品名称 Article Description in Chinese	最惠国税率 MFN(%)	协定税率 Agreement(%)	特惠税率 SP(%)	普通税率 Gen(%)	英文货品名称 Article Description
7219	8529.9082	----等离子显像组件及其零件	15Δ5	0 冰岛IS,东盟AS,新西兰NZ,智利CL 7.5 巴PK 9 澳AU 10.5 瑞士CH 12 亚太AP 13.8 韩国KR		80	----Plasma display modules and part thereof
7220	8529.9083	----有机发光二极管显示屏	15Δ5	0 冰岛IS,东盟AS,新加坡SG,新西兰NZ,智利CL 4.5 秘鲁PE 7.5 巴PK 10.5 瑞士CH 12 亚太AP	0 受惠国$_1$LD$_1$	80	----Of colour television receiver (Other than plasma display modules of parts thereof, oled panel)
7221	8529.9089	----其他	0		0 受惠国LD	50	----Other
7222	8529.9090	---其他	0		0 受惠国LD	57	---Other
	85.30	**铁道、电车道、道路或内河航道、停车场、港口或机场用的电气信号、安全或交通管理设备（税号86.08的货品除外）：**					**Electrical signaling, safety or traffic control equipment for railways, tram-ways, roads, inland waterways, parking facilities, port installations or airfields (other than those of heading No. 86.08) :**
7223	8530.1000	-铁道或电车道用的设备	10	0 冰岛IS,东盟AS,哥CR,秘鲁PE,新西兰NZ,智利CL 4 瑞士CH 5 巴PK 6 澳AU 8 韩国KR	0 受惠国$_1$LD$_1$	20	-Equipment for railways or tramways
7224	8530.8000	-其他设备	8	0 冰岛IS,东盟AS,哥CR,秘鲁PE,新西兰NZ,智利CL 3.2 瑞士CH 4.8 澳AU 5 巴PK 6.4 韩国KR	0 受惠国LD	20	-Other equipment
7225	8530.9000	-零件	8	0 冰岛IS,东盟AS,哥CR,秘鲁PE,新西兰NZ,智利CL 3.2 瑞士CH 4.8 澳AU 5 巴PK 6.4 韩国KR	0 受惠国LD	20	-Parts
	85.31	**电气音响或视觉信号装置（例如，电铃、电笛、显示板、防盗或防火报警器），但税号85.12或85.30的货品除外：**					**Electric sound or visual signalling apparatus (for example, bells, sirens, indicator panels, burglar or fire alarms), other than those of heading 8512 or 8530:**
7226	8531.1000	-防盗或防火报警器及类似装置	10	0 冰岛IS,东盟AS,哥CR,秘鲁PE,香港HK,新加坡SG,新西兰NZ,智利CL 4 瑞士CH 5 巴PK 6 澳AU 8 韩国KR	0 受惠国LD	40	-Burglar or fire alarms and similar apparatus
7227	8531.2000	-装有液晶装置（LCD）或发光二极管（LED）的显示板	0		0 受惠国LD	70	-Indicator panels incorporating liquid crystal devices (LCD) or light emitting diodes (LED)
		-其他装置：					-Other apparatus:

序号 No.	税则号列 Tariff Line	中文货品名称 Article Description in Chinese	最惠国税率 MFN(%)	协定税率 Agreement(%)	特惠税率 SP(%)	普通税率 Gen(%)	英文货品名称 Article Description
7228	8531.8010	---蜂鸣器	15	0 冰岛IS,东盟AS,哥CR,香港HK,新加坡SG,新西兰NZ,智利CL 4.5 秘鲁PE 9 澳AU 10.5 瑞士CH 12 巴PK,韩国KR	0 受惠国$_1$LD$_1$	70	---Buzzers
	ex85318010	音量不超过110dB的小型蜂鸣器	Δ7.5				Minitype electric buzzers, maximum volume not exceeding110dB
7229	8531.8090	---其他	10	0 冰岛IS,东盟AS,哥CR,秘鲁PE,香港HK,新加坡SG,新西兰NZ,智利CL 4 瑞士CH 5 巴PK 6 澳AU 8 韩国KR	0 受惠国$_1$LD$_1$	70	---Other
		-零件:					-Parts:
7230	8531.9010	---防盗或防火报警器及类似装置用	0		0 受惠国LD	40	---Of burglar or fire alarms and similar apparatus
7231	8531.9090	---其他	0		0 受惠国LD	70	---Other
	85.32	**固定、可变或可调(微调)电容器:**					**Electrical capacitors, fixed, variable or adjustable (pre-set) :**
7232	8532.1000	-固定电容器,用于50/60赫兹电路,其额定无功功率不低于0.5千乏(电力电容器)	0		0 受惠国LD	20	-Fixed capacitors designed for use in 50/60 Hz circuits and having a reactive power handling capacity of not less than0.5kVar (power capacitors)
		-其他固定电容器:					-Other fixed capacitors:
		--钽电容器:					--Tantalum:
7233	8532.2110	---片式	0		0 受惠国LD	35	---Laminate
7234	8532.2190	---其他	0		0 受惠国LD	35	---Other
		--铝电解电容器:					--Aluminium electrolytic:
7235	8532.2210	---片式	0		0 受惠国LD	35	---Laminate
7236	8532.2290	---其他	0		0 受惠国LD	35	---Other
7237	8532.2300	--单层瓷介电容器	0		0 受惠国LD	35	--Ceramic dielectric, single layer
		--多层瓷介电容器:					--Ceramic dielectric, multilayer:
7238	8532.2410	---片式	0		0 受惠国LD	35	---Laminate
7239	8532.2490	---其他	0		0 受惠国LD	35	---Other
		--纸介质或塑料介质电容器:					--Dielectric of paper or plastics:
7240	8532.2510	---片式	0		0 受惠国LD	35	---Laminate
7241	8532.2590	---其他	0		0 受惠国LD	35	---Other
7242	8532.2900	--其他	0		0 受惠国LD	35	--Other
7243	8532.3000	-可变或可调(微调)电容器	0		0 受惠国LD	35	-Variable or adjustable (pre-set) capacitors
		-零件:					-Parts:
7244	8532.9010	---子目号8532.1000所列电容器用	0		0 受惠国LD	20	---Of the capacitors of subheading No.8532.1000
7245	8532.9090	---其他	0		0 受惠国LD	35	---Other
	85.33	**电阻器(包括变阻器及电位器),但加热电阻器除外:**					**Electrical resistors (including rheostats and potentiometers) , other than heating resistors:**
7246	8533.1000	-固定碳质电阻器,合成或薄膜式	0		0 受惠国LD	50	-Fixed carbon resistors, composition or film types
		-其他固定电阻器:					-Other fixed resistors:
		--额定功率不超过20瓦:					--For a power handling capacity not exceeding 20W:
7247	8533.2110	---片式	0		0 受惠国LD	50	---Laminate
7248	8533.2190	---其他	0		0 受惠国LD	50	---Other
7249	8533.2900	--其他	0		0 受惠国LD	50	--Other
		-线绕可变电阻器,包括变阻器及电位器:					-Wirewound variable resistors, including rheostats and potentiometers:

序号 No.	税则号列 Tariff Line	中文货品名称 Article Description in Chinese	最惠国税率 MFN(%)	协定税率 Agreement(%)	特惠税率 SP(%)	普通税率 Gen(%)	英文货品名称 Article Description
7250	8533.3100	--额定功率不超过20瓦	0		0 受惠国LD	50	--For a power handling capacity not exceeding 20W
7251	8533.3900	--其他	0		0 受惠国LD	50	--Other
7252	8533.4000	-其他可变电阻器，包括变阻器及电位器	0		0 受惠国LD	50	-Other variable resistors, including rheostats and potentiometers
7253	8533.9000	-零件	0		0 受惠国LD	50	-Parts
	85.34	**印刷电路：**					**Printed circuits:**
7254	8534.0010	---4层以上的	0		0 受惠国LD	35	---Of more than 4 layers
7255	8534.0090	---其他	0		0 受惠国LD	50	---Other
	85.35	**电路的开关、保护或连接用的电气装置（例如，开关、熔断器、避雷器、电压限幅器、电涌抑制器、插头及其他连接器、接线盒），用于电压超过1000伏的线路：**					**Electrical apparatus for switching or protecting electrical circuits, or for making connections to or in electrical circuits (for example, switches, fuses, lightning arresters, voltage limiters, surge suppressors, plugs and other connectors, junction boxes) , for a voltage exceeding 1000 V:**
7256	8535.1000	-熔断器	14	0 冰岛IS,东盟AS,哥CR,秘鲁PE,新加坡SG,新西兰NZ,智利CL 8.4 澳AU 9.8 瑞士CH 11.2 巴PK,韩国KR	0 受惠国$_1$LD$_1$	50	-Fuses
		-自动断路器：					-Automatic circuit breakers:
7257	8535.2100	--用于电压低于72.5千伏的线路	14	0 冰岛IS,东盟AS,哥CR,秘鲁PE,新加坡SG,新西兰NZ,智利CL 5.6 瑞士CH 8.4 澳AU 11.2 巴PK,韩国KR	0 受惠国$_1$LD$_1$	50	--For a voltage of less than 72.5KV
		--其他：					--Other:
7258	8535.2910	---用于电压在72.5千伏及以上，但不高于220千伏的线路	10	0 冰岛IS,东盟AS,哥CR,秘鲁PE,新西兰NZ,智利CL 4 瑞士CH 5 巴PK 6 澳AU 11.2 韩国KR	0 受惠国LD	50	---For a voltage of 72.5KV or more, but not exceeding 220KV
7259	8535.2920	---用于电压高于220千伏，但不高于750千伏的线路	10	0 冰岛IS,东盟AS,哥CR,秘鲁PE,新西兰NZ,智利CL 4 瑞士CH 5 巴PK 6 澳AU 11.2 韩国KR	0 受惠国LD	50	---For a voltage exceeding 220KV, but not exceeding 750KV
7260	8535.2990	---其他	10	0 冰岛IS,东盟AS,哥CR,秘鲁PE,新西兰NZ,智利CL 4 瑞士CH 5 巴PK 6 澳AU 8 韩国KR	0 受惠国LD	50	---Other
		-隔离开关及断续开关：					-Isolating switches and make-and-break switches:
7261	8535.3010	---用于电压在72.5千伏及以上，但不高于220千伏的线路	10	0 冰岛IS,东盟AS,哥CR,秘鲁PE,新西兰NZ,智利CL 5 巴PK 6 澳AU 7.5 瑞士CH 8 韩国KR	0 受惠国LD	50	---For a voltage of 72.5KV or more, but not exceeding 220KV

序号 No.	税则号列 Tariff Line	中文货品名称 Article Description in Chinese	最惠国税率 MFN(%)	协定税率 Agreement(%)	特惠税率 SP(%)	普通税率 Gen(%)	英文货品名称 Article Description
7262	8535.3020	---用于电压高于220千伏，但不高于750千伏的线路	10	0 冰岛IS,东盟AS,哥CR,秘鲁PE,新西兰NZ,智利CL 5 巴PK 6 澳AU 7.5 瑞士CH 8 韩国KR	0 受惠国LD	50	---For a voltage exceeding 220KV, but not exceeding 750KV
7263	8535.3090	---其他	10	0 冰岛IS,东盟AS,哥CR,秘鲁PE,新西兰NZ,智利CL 5 巴PK 6 澳AU 7.5 瑞士CH 8 韩国KR	0 受惠国LD	50	---Other
7264	8535.4000	-避雷器、电压限幅器及电涌抑制器	18	0 冰岛IS,东盟AS,哥CR,香港HK,新加坡SG,新西兰NZ,智利CL 5.4 秘鲁PE 10.8 澳AU 12.6 瑞士CH 14.4 韩国KR	0 受惠国$_1$LD$_1$	50	-Lightning arresters, voltage limiters and surge suppressors
7265	8535.9000	-其他	10	0 冰岛IS,东盟AS,哥CR,香港HK,新加坡SG,新西兰NZ,智利CL 3 秘鲁PE 5 巴PK 6 澳AU 7 瑞士CH 9 韩国KR 9.5 亚太AP	0 受惠国LD	50	-Other
	85.36	**电路的开关、保护或连接用的电器装置（例如，开关、继电器、熔断器、电涌抑制器、插头、插座、灯座及其他连接器、接线盒），用于电压不超过1000伏的线路；光导纤维、光导纤维束或光缆用连接器：**					**Electrical apparatus for switching or protecting electrical circuits, or for making connections to or in electrical circuits (for example, switches, relays, fuses, surge suppressors, plugs, sockets, lamp holders and other connectors, junction boxes) , for a voltage not exceeding 1000V; connectors for optical fibres, optical fibre bundles or cables:**
7266	8536.1000	-熔断器	10	0 冰岛IS,东盟AS,哥CR,秘鲁PE,台湾TW,香港HK,新加坡SG,新西兰NZ,智利CL 5 巴PK 6 澳AU 7 瑞士CH	0 受惠国LD	50	-Fuses
7267	8536.2000	-自动断路器	9	0 冰岛IS,东盟AS,哥CR,秘鲁PE,香港HK,新西兰NZ,智利CL 5 巴PK 5.4 澳AU,韩国KR 6.3 瑞士CH	0 受惠国LD	50	-Automatic circuit breakers
7268	8536.3000	-其他电路保护装置	9	0 冰岛IS,东盟AS,哥CR,秘鲁PE,香港HK,新西兰NZ,智利CL 3.6 瑞士CH 5 巴PK 5.4 澳AU 7.8 韩国KR	0 受惠国LD	50	-Other apparatus for protecting electrical circuits
		-继电器：					-Relays:
		--用于电压不超过60伏的线路：					--For a voltage not exceeding 60V:

序号 No.	税则号列 Tariff Line	中文货品名称 Article Description in Chinese	最惠国税率 MFN(%)	协定税率 Agreement(%)	特惠税率 SP(%)	普通税率 Gen(%)	英文货品名称 Article Description
7269	8536.4110	---用于电压不超过36伏的线路	10	0 冰岛IS,东盟AS,哥CR,秘鲁PE,新加坡SG,新西兰NZ,智利CL 4 瑞士CH 5 巴PK 6 澳AU 8.6 韩国KR	0 受惠国LD	50	---For a voltage not exceeding 36V
7270	8536.4190	---其他	10	0 冰岛IS,东盟AS,哥CR,秘鲁PE,新加坡SG,新西兰NZ,智利CL 4 瑞士CH 5 巴PK 6 澳AU 9 韩国KR	0 受惠国LD	50	---Other
7271	8536.4900	--其他	10	0 冰岛IS,东盟AS,哥CR,香港HK,新加坡SG,新西兰NZ,智利CL 3 秘鲁PE 4 瑞士CH 5 巴PK 6 澳AU 8.6 韩国KR	0 受惠国LD	50	--Other
7272	8536.5000	-其他开关	0		0 受惠国LD	50	-Other switches
		-灯座、插头及插座:					-Lamp holders, plugs and sockets:
7273	8536.6100	--灯座	10	0 冰岛IS,东盟AS,哥CR,秘鲁PE,新加坡SG,新西兰NZ,智利CL 4 瑞士CH 5 巴PK 6 澳AU 8.6 韩国KR	0 受惠国LD	50	--Lamp-holders
7274	8536.6900	--其他	0		0 受惠国LD	50	--Other
7275	8536.7000	-光导纤维、光导纤维束或光缆用连接器	8	0 澳门MO,冰岛IS,东盟AS,哥CR,秘鲁PE,香港HK,新西兰NZ,智利CL 4.8 澳AU 5 巴PK 5.6 瑞士CH	0 受惠国LD	30	-Connectors for optical fibres, optical fibre bundles or cables
		-其他装置:					-Other apparatus:
		---接插件:					---Connector:
7276	8536.9011	----工作电压不超过36伏的	0		0 受惠国LD	50	----For a voltage not exceeding 36V
7277	8536.9019	----其他	0		0 受惠国LD	50	----Other
7278	8536.9090	---其他	0		0 受惠国LD	50	---Other
	85.37	**用于电气控制或电力分配的盘、板、台、柜及其他基座，装有两个或多个税号85.35或85.36所列的装置，包括装有第九十章所列的仪器或装置，以及数控装置，但税号85.17的交换机除外:**					**Boards, panels, consoles, desks, cabinets and other bases, equipped with two or more apparatus of heading 8535 or 8536, for electric control or the distribution of electricity, including those incorporating instruments or apparatus of Chapter 90, and numerical control apparatus, other than switching apparatus of heading 8517:**
		-用于电压不超过1000伏的线路:					-For a voltage not exceeding 1000V:
		---数控装置:					---Numerical control panels:
7279	8537.1011	----可编程序控制器	5	0 澳AU,巴PK,冰岛IS,东盟AS,哥CR,秘鲁PE,台湾TW,香港HK,新西兰NZ,智利CL 2.5 亚太AP 3.5 瑞士CH 4 韩国KR	0 受惠国LD	14	----Programmable controuers

序号 No.	税则号列 Tariff Line	中文货品名称 Article Description in Chinese	最惠国税率 MFN(%)	协定税率 Agreement(%)	特惠税率 SP(%)	普通税率 Gen(%)	英文货品名称 Article Description
	ex85371011	机床用可编程序控制器（PLC）	Δ3				Programmable logic controllers (PLC) for machine tools
7280	8537.1019	----其他	5	0 澳AU,巴PK,冰岛IS,东盟AS,哥CR,秘鲁PE,台湾TW,香港HK,新西兰NZ,智利CL 2.5 亚太AP 3.6 瑞士CH 4 韩国KR	0 受惠国LD	14	----Other
	ex85371019	机床用数控单元（包括单独进口的CNC操作单元）	Δ3				Numerical control equipment for machine tools (including CNC unit imported separately)
7281	8537.1090	---其他	8.4	0 澳门MO,巴PK,冰岛IS,东盟AS,哥CR,秘鲁PE,香港HK,新西兰NZ,智利CL 4.2 亚太AP 5 澳AU 6 瑞士CH 7.2 韩国KR	0 受惠国LD	50	---Other
	ex85371090	电梯用控制柜及控制柜专用印刷电路板	Δ4				Control cabinets for elevator and printed circuits solely used for control cabinets
		-用于电压超过1000伏的线路：					-For a voltage exceeding 1000V:
7282	8537.2010	---全封闭组合式高压开关装置，用于电压在500千伏及以上的线路	8.4	0 巴PK,冰岛IS,东盟AS,哥CR,秘鲁PE,新西兰NZ,智利CL 4.2 亚太AP 5 澳AU 6.3 瑞士CH 7.2 韩国KR	0 受惠国LD	30	---Gas insulated switchgear, for a voltage of 500KV or more
7283	8537.2090	---其他	8.4	0 巴PK,冰岛IS,东盟AS,哥CR,秘鲁PE,香港HK,新西兰NZ,智利CL 3.36 瑞士CH 4.2 亚太AP 5 澳AU 7.2 韩国KR	0 受惠国LD	50	---Other
	85.38	**专用于或主要用于税号85.35、85.36或85.37所列装置的零件：**					**Parts suitable for use solely or principally with the apparatus of heading 8535, 8536 or 8537:**
		-税号85.37所列货品用的盘、板、台、柜及其他基座，但未装有关装置：					-Boards, panels, consoles, desks, cabinets and other bases for the goods of heading 8537, not equipped with their apparatus:
7284	8538.1010	---税号8537.2010所列货品用	8.4	0 巴PK,冰岛IS,东盟AS,哥CR,秘鲁PE,新西兰NZ,智利CL 3.36 瑞士CH 4.2 亚太AP 5 澳AU 6.7 韩国KR	0 受惠国LD	50	---For the goods of heading No.8537.2010
7285	8538.1090	---其他	7	0 巴PK,冰岛IS,东盟AS,哥CR,秘鲁PE,新西兰NZ,智利CL 3.5 亚太AP 4.2 澳AU 4.9 瑞士CH 5.6 韩国KR	0 受惠国LD	50	---Other

序号 No.	税则号列 Tariff Line	中文货品名称 Article Description in Chinese	最惠国税率 MFN(%)	协定税率 Agreement(%)	特惠税率 SP(%)	普通税率 Gen(%)	英文货品名称 Article Description
7286	8538.9000	-其他	7	0 冰岛IS,东盟AS,哥CR,韩国KR,秘鲁PE,台湾TW,香港HK,新西兰NZ,智利CL 4.2 澳AU 5 巴PK 5.6 瑞士CH	0 受惠国LD	50	-Other
	85.39	**白炽灯泡、放电灯管，包括封闭式聚光灯及紫外线灯管或红外线灯泡;弧光灯：**					**Electric filament or discharge lamps, including sealed beam lamp units and ultraviolet or infra-red lamps; arc lamps:**
7287	8539.1000	-封闭式聚光灯	10	0 冰岛IS,东盟AS,哥CR,秘鲁PE,新西兰NZ,智利CL 4 瑞士CH 5 巴PK 6 澳AU 8 韩国KR	0 受惠国LD	45	-Sealed beam lamp units
		-其他白炽灯泡，但不包括紫外线灯管或红外线灯泡：					-Other filament lamps, excluding ultraviolet or infra-red lamps:
		--卤钨灯：					--Tungsten halogen:
7288	8539.2110	---科研、医疗专用	8	0 冰岛IS,东盟AS,哥CR,秘鲁PE,新西兰NZ,智利CL 3.2 瑞士CH 4.8 澳AU,韩国KR 5 巴PK	0 受惠国LD	20	---For scientific or medical uses only
7289	8539.2120	---火车、航空器及船舶用	8	0 冰岛IS,东盟AS,哥CR,秘鲁PE,新西兰NZ,智利CL 3.2 瑞士CH 4.8 澳AU 5 巴PK 6.4 韩国KR	0 受惠国LD	20	---For locomotives and rolling-stock, aircraft or ships
7290	8539.2130	---机动车辆用	10	0 冰岛IS,东盟AS,哥CR,秘鲁PE,新西兰NZ,智利CL 4 瑞士CH 5 巴PK 6 澳AU 9 韩国KR	0 受惠国LD	45	---For motor vehicles
7291	8539.2190	---其他	10.5	0 冰岛IS,东盟AS,哥CR,秘鲁PE,新加坡SG,新西兰NZ,智利CL 6.3 澳AU 7.4 瑞士CH 8.4 韩国KR	0 受惠国LD	70	---Other
		--其他灯，功率不超过200瓦，但额定电压超过100伏：					--Other, of a power not exceeding 200W and for a voltage exceeding 100V:
7292	8539.2210	---科研、医疗专用	10.5	0 冰岛IS,东盟AS,哥CR,秘鲁PE,新加坡SG,新西兰NZ,智利CL 5 巴PK 6.3 澳AU 7.4 瑞士CH	0 受惠国LD	20	---For scientific or medical uses only
7293	8539.2290	---其他	5	0 澳AU,巴PK,冰岛IS,东盟AS,哥CR,秘鲁PE,瑞士CH,新西兰NZ,智利CL 3 韩国KR	0 受惠国LD	70	---Other
		--其他：					--Other:

序号 No.	税则号列 Tariff Line	中文货品名称 Article Description in Chinese	最惠国税率 MFN(%)	协定税率 Agreement(%)	特惠税率 SP(%)	普通税率 Gen(%)	英文货品名称 Article Description
7294	8539.2910	---科研、医疗专用	5	0 澳AU,巴PK,冰岛IS,东盟AS,哥CR,秘鲁PE,瑞士CH,新西兰NZ,智利CL 3 韩国KR	0 受惠国LD	20	---For scientific or medical uses only
7295	8539.2920	---火车、航空器及船舶用	10.5	0 冰岛IS,东盟AS,哥CR,秘鲁PE,新加坡SG,新西兰NZ,智利CL 5 巴PK 6.3 澳AU 7.4 瑞士CH 8.4 韩国KR	0 受惠国LD	20	---For locomotives and rolling-stock, aircraft or ships
7296	8539.2930	---机动车辆用	5	0 澳AU,巴PK,冰岛IS,东盟AS,哥CR,秘鲁PE,瑞士CH,新西兰NZ,智利CL 4.3 韩国KR	0 受惠国LD	45	---For motor vehicles
		---其他:					---Other:
7297	8539.2991	----12伏及以下的	12	0 冰岛IS,东盟AS,哥CR,秘鲁PE,香港HK,新加坡SG,新西兰NZ,智利CL 6 巴PK 7.2 澳AU 8.4 瑞士CH 9.6 韩国KR	0 受惠国LD	70	----Of a voltage 12V or less
7298	8539.2999	----其他	12	0 冰岛IS,东盟AS,哥CR,秘鲁PE,新加坡SG,新西兰NZ,智利CL 6 巴PK 7.2 澳AU 8.4 瑞士CH 9.6 韩国KR	0 受惠国LD	70	----Other
		-放电灯管，但紫外线灯管除外:					-Discharge lamps, other than ultraviolet lamps:
		--热阴极荧光灯:					--Fluorescent, hot cathode:
7299	8539.3110	---科研、医疗专用	8	0 冰岛IS,东盟AS,哥CR,秘鲁PE,新西兰NZ,智利CL 3.2 瑞士CH 4.8 澳AU 5 巴PK	0 受惠国LD	20	---For scientific or medical uses only
7300	8539.3120	---火车、航空器及船舶用	8	0 冰岛IS,东盟AS,哥CR,秘鲁PE,新西兰NZ,智利CL 3.2 瑞士CH 4.8 澳AU 5 巴PK	0 受惠国LD	20	---For locomotives and rolling-stock, aircraft or ships
		---其他:					---Other:
7301	8539.3191	----紧凑型	8	0 冰岛IS,东盟AS,哥CR,秘鲁PE,新西兰NZ,智利CL 3.2 瑞士CH 4.8 澳AU,韩国KR 5 巴PK	0 受惠国LD	70	----Compact fluorescent lamp
7302	8539.3199	----其他	8	0 冰岛IS,东盟AS,哥CR,秘鲁PE,新西兰NZ,智利CL 3.2 瑞士CH 4.8 澳AU,韩国KR 5 巴PK	0 受惠国LD	70	----Other
		--汞或钠蒸汽灯;金属卤化物灯:					--Mercury or sodium vapour lamps; metal halide lamps:

序号 No.	税则号列 Tariff Line	中文货品名称 Article Description in Chinese	最惠国税率 MFN(%)	协定税率 Agreement(%)	特惠税率 SP(%)	普通税率 Gen(%)	英文货品名称 Article Description
7303	8539.3230	---钠蒸气灯	8	0 冰岛IS,东盟AS,哥CR,秘鲁PE,新西兰NZ,智利CL 3.2 瑞士CH 4.8 澳AU 5 巴PK 6.4 韩国KR	0 受惠国LD	20	---Sodium-vapour lamps
7304	8539.3240	---汞蒸气灯	8	0 冰岛IS,东盟AS,哥CR,秘鲁PE,新西兰NZ,智利CL 3.2 瑞士CH 4.8 澳AU 5 巴PK 6.4 韩国KR	0 受惠国LD	20	---Mercury-vapour lamps
	ex85393240	彩色投影机的照明光源	Δ3				Illumiation light source of colour projectors
7305	8539.3290	---其他	8	0 冰岛IS,东盟AS,哥CR,秘鲁PE,新西兰NZ,智利CL 3.2 瑞士CH 4.8 澳AU,韩国KR 5 巴PK	0 受惠国LD	70	---Other
		--其他:					--Other:
7306	8539.3910	---科研、医疗专用	8	0 冰岛IS,东盟AS,哥CR,秘鲁PE,新西兰NZ,智利CL 3.2 瑞士CH 4.8 澳AU 5 巴PK	0 受惠国LD	20	---For scientific or medical uses only
7307	8539.3920	---火车、航空器及船舶用	8	0 冰岛IS,东盟AS,哥CR,秘鲁PE,新西兰NZ,智利CL 3.2 瑞士CH 4.8 澳AU 5 巴PK	0 受惠国LD	20	---For locomotives and rolling-stock, aircraft or ships
7308	8539.3990	---其他	8	0 澳门MO,冰岛IS,东盟AS,哥CR,秘鲁PE,台湾TW,新西兰NZ,智利CL 3.2 瑞士CH 4.8 澳AU 5 巴PK 6.9 韩国KR	0 受惠国LD	70	---Other
		-紫外线灯管或红外线灯泡;弧光灯:					-Ultraviolet or infra-red lamps; arc lamps:
7309	8539.4100	--弧光灯	8	0 冰岛IS,东盟AS,哥CR,秘鲁PE,新西兰NZ,智利CL 3.2 瑞士CH 4.8 澳AU 5 巴PK	0 受惠国LD	20	--Arc-lamps
7310	8539.4900	--其他	8	0 冰岛IS,东盟AS,哥CR,秘鲁PE,新西兰NZ,智利CL 3.2 瑞士CH 4.8 澳AU 5 巴PK	0 受惠国LD	20	--Other
7311	8539.9000	-零件	8	0 冰岛IS,东盟AS,哥CR,秘鲁PE,台湾TW,新西兰NZ,智利CL 3.2 瑞士CH 4.8 澳AU 5 巴PK	0 受惠国LD	20	-Parts

序号 No.	税则号列 Tariff Line	中文货品名称 Article Description in Chinese	最惠国税率 MFN(%)	协定税率 Agreement(%)	特惠税率 SP(%)	普通税率 Gen(%)	英文货品名称 Article Description
	85.40	热电子管、冷阴极管或光阴极管（例如，真空管或充气管、汞弧整流管、阴极射线管、电视摄像管）：					**Thermionic, cold cathode or photocathode valves and tubes (for example, vacuum or vapour or gas filled valves and tubes, mercury arc rectifying valves and tubes, cathoderay tubes, television camera tubes) :**
		-阴极射线电视显像管，包括视频监视器用阴极射线管：					-Cathode ray television picture tubes, including video monitor cathode ray tubes:
7312	8540.1100	--彩色的	12	0 冰岛IS,东盟AS,哥CR,秘鲁PE,新加坡SG,新西兰NZ,智利CL 6 巴PK 7.2 澳AU 8.4 瑞士CH 10.4 韩国KR	0 受惠国$_1$LD$_1$	40	--Colour
7313	8540.1200	--单色的	15	0 冰岛IS,东盟AS,哥CR,新加坡SG,新西兰NZ,智利CL 4.5 秘鲁PE 9 澳AU 10.5 瑞士CH 12 巴PK,韩国KR	0 受惠国$_1$LD$_1$	40	--Monochrome
		-电视摄像管；变像管及图像增强管；其他光阴极管：					-Television camera tubes; image converters and intensifiers; other photocathode tubes:
7314	8540.2010	---电视摄像管	12	0 冰岛IS,东盟AS,哥CR,秘鲁PE,新加坡SG,新西兰NZ,智利CL 6 巴PK 7.2 澳AU 8.4 瑞士CH 9.6 韩国KR	0 受惠国$_1$LD$_1$	35	---Television camera tubes
7315	8540.2090	---其他	8	0 冰岛IS,东盟AS,哥CR,秘鲁PE,新西兰NZ,智利CL 3.2 瑞士CH 4.8 澳AU,韩国KR 5 巴PK	0 受惠国LD	17	---Other
		-单色的数据/图形显示管；彩色的数据/图形显示管，屏幕荧光点间距小于0. 4毫米：					-Data/graphic display tubes, monochrome; data/graphic display tubes, colour, with a phosphor dot screen pitch smaller than 0.4mm:
7316	8540.4010	---彩色的数据/图形显示管，屏幕荧光点间距小于0. 4毫米	8	0 冰岛IS,东盟AS,哥CR,秘鲁PE,香港HK,新西兰NZ,智利CL 3.2 瑞士CH 4.8 澳AU,韩国KR 5 巴PK	0 受惠国LD	17	---Data/graphic display tubes, colour, with a phosphor dot screen pitch less than 0.4mm
7317	8540.4020	---单色的数据/图形显示管	8	0 冰岛IS,东盟AS,哥CR,秘鲁PE,新西兰NZ,智利CL 3.2 瑞士CH 4.8 澳AU,韩国KR 5 巴PK	0 受惠国LD	17	---Data/graphic display tubes, black and white or other monochrome
		-其他阴极射线管：					-Other cathode ray tubes:
7318	8540.6010	---雷达显示管	6	0 冰岛IS,东盟AS,哥CR,秘鲁PE,新西兰NZ,智利CL 2.4 瑞士CH 3.6 澳AU,韩国KR 5 巴PK	0 受惠国LD	14	---Radar display tubes

序号 No.	税则号列 Tariff Line	中文货品名称 Article Description in Chinese	最惠国税率 MFN(%)	协定税率 Agreement(%)	特惠税率 SP(%)	普通税率 Gen(%)	英文货品名称 Article Description
7319	8540.6090	---其他	8	0 冰岛IS,东盟AS,哥CR,秘鲁PE,新西兰NZ,智利CL 3.2 瑞士CH 4.8 澳AU,韩国KR 5 巴PK	0 受惠国LD	17	---Other
		-微波管（例如，磁控管、速调管、行波管、返波管），但不包括栅控管：					-Microwave tubes (for example, magnetrons, klystrons, travelling wave tubes, carcinotrons) , excluding grid-controlled tubes:
7320	8540.7100	--磁控管	8	0 冰岛IS,东盟AS,哥CR,秘鲁PE,新西兰NZ,智利CL 3.2 瑞士CH 4.8 澳AU 5 巴PK 6.9 韩国KR	0 受惠国LD	17	--Magnetrons
		--其他：					--Other:
7321	8540.7910	---速调管	8	0 冰岛IS,东盟AS,哥CR,秘鲁PE,新西兰NZ,智利CL 3.2 瑞士CH 4.8 澳AU,韩国KR 5 巴PK	0 受惠国LD	17	---Klystrons
7322	8540.7990	---其他	8	0 冰岛IS,东盟AS,哥CR,秘鲁PE,新西兰NZ,智利CL 3.2 瑞士CH 4.8 澳AU,韩国KR 5 巴PK	0 受惠国LD	17	---Other
		-其他管：					-Other valves and tubes:
7323	8540.8100	--接收管或放大管	8	0 冰岛IS,东盟AS,哥CR,秘鲁PE,新西兰NZ,智利CL 3.2 瑞士CH 4.8 澳AU 5 巴PK	0 受惠国LD	17	--Receiver or amplifier valves and tubes
7324	8540.8900	--其他	8	0 冰岛IS,东盟AS,哥CR,秘鲁PE,台湾TW,新西兰NZ,智利CL 3.2 瑞士CH 4.8 澳AU,韩国KR 5 巴PK	0 受惠国LD	17	--Other
		-零件：					-Parts:
		--阴极射线管用：					--Of cathode ray tubes:
7325	8540.9110	---电视显像管用	6	0 冰岛IS,东盟AS,哥CR,秘鲁PE,新西兰NZ,智利CL 2.4 瑞士CH 3.6 澳AU,韩国KR 5 巴PK	0 受惠国LD	40	---Of television picture tubes
7326	8540.9120	---雷达显示管用	5	0 澳AU,巴PK,冰岛IS,东盟AS,哥CR,秘鲁PE,瑞士CH,新西兰NZ,智利CL 3 韩国KR	0 受惠国LD	14	---Of radar display tubes
7327	8540.9190	---其他	8Δ4	0 冰岛IS,东盟AS,哥CR,秘鲁PE,新西兰NZ,智利CL 3.2 瑞士CH 4.8 澳AU 5 巴PK	0 受惠国LD	17	---Other
		--其他：					--Other:

序号 No.	税则号列 Tariff Line	中文货品名称 Article Description in Chinese	最惠国税率 MFN(%)	协定税率 Agreement(%)	特惠税率 SP(%)	普通税率 Gen(%)	英文货品名称 Article Description
7328	8540.9910	---电视摄像管用	8	0 冰岛IS,东盟AS,哥CR,秘鲁PE,新西兰NZ,智利CL 3.2 瑞士CH 4.8 澳AU,韩国KR 5 巴PK	0 受惠国LD	35	---Of television camera tubes
7329	8540.9990	---其他	8	0 冰岛IS,东盟AS,哥CR,秘鲁PE,新西兰NZ,智利CL 3.2 瑞士CH 4.8 澳AU 5 巴PK	0 受惠国LD	17	---Other
	85.41	**二极管、晶体管及类似的半导体器件;光敏半导体器件,包括不论是否装在组件内或组装成块的光电池;发光二极管;已装配的压电晶体:**					**Diodes, transistors and similar semiconductor devices; photosensitive semiconductor devices, including photovoltaic cells whether or not assembled in modules or made up into panels; light-emitting diodes; mounted piezoelectric crystals:**
7330	8541.1000	-二极管，但光敏二极管或发光二极管除外	0		0 受惠国LD	30	-Diodes, other than photosensitive or light emitting diodes
		-晶体管，但光敏晶体管除外:					-Transistors, other than photosensitive transistors:
7331	8541.2100	--耗散功率小于1瓦的	0		0 受惠国LD	30	--With a dissipation rate of less than 1W
7332	8541.2900	--其他	0		0 受惠国LD	30	--Other
7333	8541.3000	-半导体开关元件、两端交流开关元件及三端双向可控硅开关元件，但光敏器件除外	0		0 受惠国LD	30	-Thyristors, diacs and triacs, other than photosensitive devices
		-光敏半导体器件，包括不论是否装在组件内或组装成块的光电池;发光二极管:					-Photosensitive semiconductor devices, including photovoltaic cells whether or not assembled in modules or made up into panels; light-emitting diodes:
7334	8541.4010	---发光二极管	0		0 受惠国LD	30	---Light emitting diodes
7335	8541.4020	---太阳能电池	0		0 受惠国LD	30	---Solar cells
7336	8541.4090	---其他	0		0 受惠国LD	30	---Other
7337	8541.5000	-其他半导体器件	0		0 受惠国LD	30	-Other semiconductor devices
7338	8541.6000	-已装配的压电晶体	0		0 受惠国LD	30	-Mounted piezoelectric crystals
7339	8541.9000	-零件	0		0 受惠国LD	30	-Parts
	85.42	**集成电路:**					**Electronic integrated circuits:**
		-集成电路:					-Electronic integrated circuits:
7340	8542.3100	--处理器及控制器，不论是否带有存储器、转换器、逻辑电路、放大器、时钟及时序电路或其他电路	0		0 受惠国LD	24	--Processors and controllers, whether or not combined with memories, converters, logic circuits, amplifiers, clock and timing circuits, or other circuits
7341	8542.3200	--存储器	0		0 受惠国LD	24	--Memories
7342	8542.3300	--放大器	0		0 受惠国LD	24	--Amplifiers
7343	8542.3900	--其他	0		0 受惠国LD	24	--Other
7344	8542.9000	-零件	0		0 受惠国LD	30	-Parts
	85.43	**本章其他税号未列名的具有独立功能的电气设备及装置:**					**Electrical machines and apparatus, having individual functions, not specified or included elsewhere in this chapter:**
7345	8543.1000	-粒子加速器	5	0 澳AU,巴PK,冰岛IS,东盟AS,哥CR,秘鲁PE,瑞士CH,新西兰NZ,智利CL 4 韩国KR	0 受惠国LD	11	-Particle accelerators
		-信号发生器:					-Signal generators:

序号 No.	税则号列 Tariff Line	中文货品名称 Article Description in Chinese	最惠国税率 MFN(%)	协定税率 Agreement(%)	特惠税率 SP(%)	普通税率 Gen(%)	英文货品名称 Article Description
7346	8543.2010	---输出信号频率在1500兆赫兹以下的通用信号发生器	15	0 冰岛IS,东盟AS,哥CR,台湾TW,新加坡SG,新西兰NZ,智利CL 4.5 秘鲁PE 9 澳AU 10.5 瑞士CH 12 巴PK	0 受惠国$_1$LD$_1$	80	---Universal signal generators, with a frequency range of less than 1500MHz
7347	8543.2090	---其他	8	0 冰岛IS,东盟AS,哥CR,秘鲁PE,台湾TW,新西兰NZ,智利CL 3.2 瑞士CH 4.8 澳AU,韩国KR 5 巴PK	0 受惠国LD	20	---Other
7348	8543.3000	-电镀、电解或电泳设备及装置	0		0 受惠国LD	35	-Machines and apparatus for electro-plating, electrolysis or electrophoresis
		---其他设备及装置:					---Other machines and apparatus:
7349	8543.7091	----金属、矿藏探测器	0		0 受惠国LD	17	----Metal or mine detectors
7350	8543.7092	----高、中频放大器	0		0 受惠国LD	17	----High or intermediate frequency amplifiers
7351	8543.7093	----电篱网激发器	10	0 冰岛IS,东盟AS,哥CR,秘鲁PE,新加坡SG,新西兰NZ,智利CL 4 瑞士CH 5 巴PK 6 澳AU 8 韩国KR	0 受惠国LD	35	----Electric fence energizers
7352	8543.7099	----其他	0		0 受惠国LD	35	----Other
		-零件:					-Parts:
7353	8543.9010	---粒子加速器用	0		0 受惠国LD	11	---Of particle accelerators
		---信号发生器用:					---Of signal generators:
7354	8543.9021	----输出信号频率在1500兆赫兹以下的通用信号发生器用	0		0 受惠国LD	80	----Of the generators of subheading No.8543.2010
7355	8543.9029	----其他	0		0 受惠国LD	20	----Other
7356	8543.9030	---金属、矿藏探测器用	0		0 受惠国LD	17	---Of metal or mine detectors
7357	8543.9040	---高、中频放大器用	0		0 受惠国LD	17	---Of high or intermediate frequency amplifiers
7358	8543.9090	---其他	0		0 受惠国LD	35	---Other
	85.44	**绝缘(包括漆包或阳极化处理)电线、电缆(包括同轴电缆)及其他绝缘电导体,不论是否有接头;由每根被覆光纤组成的光缆,不论是否与电导体装配或装有接头:**					**Insulated (including enamelled or anodised) wire, cable (including coaxial cable) and other insulated electric conductors, whether or not fitted with connectors; optical fibre cables, made up of individually sheathed fibres, whether or not assembled with electric conductors or fitted with connectors:**
		-绕组电线:					-Winding wire:
7359	8544.1100	--铜制	10△6	0 澳门MO,冰岛IS,东盟AS,哥CR,秘鲁PE,台湾TW,香港HK,新加坡SG,新西兰NZ,智利CL 5 巴PK 6 澳AU 7 瑞士CH,亚太AP 8.6 韩国KR	0 受惠国LD	70	--Of copper
7360	8544.1900	--其他	20	0 冰岛IS,东盟AS,哥CR,新加坡SG,新西兰NZ,智利CL 6 秘鲁PE 12 澳AU 14 瑞士CH 18 韩国KR	0 受惠国$_1$LD$_1$	70	--Other

序号 No.	税则号列 Tariff Line	中文货品名称 Article Description in Chinese	最惠国税率 MFN(%)	协定税率 Agreement(%)	特惠税率 SP(%)	普通税率 Gen(%)	英文货品名称 Article Description
7361	8544.2000	-同轴电缆及其他同轴电导体	10	0 冰岛IS,东盟AS,哥CR,台湾TW,新加坡SG,新西兰NZ,智利CL 3 秘鲁PE 5 巴PK 6 澳AU 8 韩国KR,瑞士CH 9 亚太AP	0 受惠国LD	20	-Co-axial cable and other co-axial electric conductors
		-车辆、航空器、船舶用点火布线组及其他布线组:					-Ignition wiring sets and other wiring sets of a kind used in vehicles, aircraft or ships:
7362	8544.3020	---机动车辆用	10	0 冰岛IS,哥CR,秘鲁PE,新西兰NZ,智利CL 4 瑞士CH 6 澳AU 8.6 韩国KR	0 受惠国LD	20	---For motor vehicles
	ex85443020	车辆用电控柴油机的线束	Δ5				Wiring harness of electric diesel engines used for vehicles
7363	8544.3090	---其他	5	0 澳AU,冰岛IS,哥CR,秘鲁PE,新西兰NZ,智利CL 2 瑞士CH 4.3 韩国KR	0 受惠国LD	70	---Other
		-其他电导体，额定电压不超过1000伏:					-Other electric conductors, for a voltage not exceeding 1000V:
		--有接头:					--Fitted with connectors:
		---额定电压不超过80伏:					---For a voltage not exceeding 80V:
7364	8544.4211	----电缆	0		0 受惠国LD	20	----Electric cable
7365	8544.4219	----其他	0		0 受惠国LD	70	----Other
		---额定电压超过80伏，但不超过1000伏:					---Other electric conductors, for a voltage exceeding 80V but not exceeding 1000V:
7366	8544.4221	----电缆	0		0 受惠国LD	20	----Electric cable
7367	8544.4229	----其他	0		0 受惠国LD	70	----Other
		--其他:					--Other:
		---额定电压不超过80伏:					---For a voltage not exceeding 80V:
7368	8544.4911	----电缆	0		0 受惠国LD	20	----Electric cable
7369	8544.4919	----其他	0		0 受惠国LD	70	----Other
		---额定电压超过80伏，但不超过1000伏:					---Other electric conductors, for a voltage exceeding 80V but not exceeding 1000V:
7370	8544.4921	----电缆	6	0 巴PK,冰岛IS,东盟AS,哥CR,秘鲁PE,香港HK,新西兰NZ,智利CL 3.6 澳AU 4.2 瑞士CH,亚太AP 5.1 韩国KR	0 受惠国LD	20	----Electric cable
7371	8544.4929	----其他	12	0 澳门MO,冰岛IS,东盟AS,哥CR,秘鲁PE,台湾TW,香港HK,新加坡SG,新西兰NZ,智利CL 5 巴PK 7.2 澳AU,韩国KR 8.4 瑞士CH,亚太AP	0 受惠国LD	70	----Other
		-其他电导体，额定电压超过1000伏:					-Other electric conductors, for a voltage exceeding 1000V:
		---电缆:					---Electric cable:

序号 No.	税则号列 Tariff Line	中文货品名称 Article Description in Chinese	最惠国税率 MFN(%)	协定税率 Agreement(%)	特惠税率 SP(%)	普通税率 Gen(%)	英文货品名称 Article Description
7372	8544.6012	----额定电压不超过35千伏	10	0 冰岛IS,东盟AS,哥CR,秘鲁PE,香港HK,新加坡SG,新西兰NZ,智利CL 5 巴PK 6 澳AU 7 瑞士CH 8 韩国KR 8.9 亚太AP	0 受惠国LD	50	----For a voltage not exceeding 35KV
7373	8544.6013	----额定电压超过35千伏，但不超过110千伏	8.4	0 冰岛IS,东盟AS,哥CR,秘鲁PE,香港HK,新西兰NZ,智利CL 3.36 瑞士CH 5 澳AU,巴PK 6.7 韩国KR 8 亚太AP	0 受惠国LD	20	----For a voltage exceeding 35KV but not exceeding 110KV
7374	8544.6014	----额定电压超过110千伏，但不超过220千伏	8.4	0 冰岛IS,东盟AS,哥CR,秘鲁PE,香港HK,新西兰NZ,智利CL 3.36 瑞士CH 5 澳AU,巴PK,韩国KR 8 亚太AP	0 受惠国LD	20	----For a voltage exceeding 110KV but not exceeding 220KV
7375	8544.6019	----其他	8.4	0 冰岛IS,东盟AS,哥CR,秘鲁PE,香港HK,新西兰NZ,智利CL 5 澳AU,巴PK 7.2 韩国KR 8 亚太AP	0 受惠国LD	20	----Other
7376	8544.6090	---其他	21	0 冰岛IS,东盟AS,哥CR,香港HK,新加坡SG,新西兰NZ,智利CL 6.3 秘鲁PE 8.4 瑞士CH 12.6 澳AU 18.9 韩国KR 20 巴PK,亚太AP	0 受惠国1LD1	70	---Other
	ex85446090	额定电压为500千伏及以上的气体绝缘金属封闭输电线	Δ10				Gas insulated metal enclosed transmission line, for a voltage of 500KV or more
7377	8544.7000	-光缆	0		0 受惠国LD	20	-Optical fibre cables
	85.45	**碳电极、碳刷、灯碳棒、电池碳棒及电气设备用的其他石墨或碳精制品，不论是否带金属：**					**Carbon electrodes, carbon brushes, lamp carbons, battery carbons and other articles of graphite or other carbon, with or without metal, of a kind used for electrical purposes:**
		-碳电极：					-Electrodes:
7378	8545.1100	--炉用	8	0 冰岛IS,东盟AS,哥CR,秘鲁PE,新西兰NZ,智利CL 3.2 瑞士CH 4.8 澳AU 5 巴PK 6.4 韩国KR	0 受惠国LD	35	--Of a kind used for furnaces
7379	8545.1900	--其他	10.5	0 冰岛IS,东盟AS,哥CR,秘鲁PE,新加坡SG,新西兰NZ,智利CL 5 巴PK 6.3 澳AU 7.4 瑞士CH 8.4 韩国KR	0 受惠国LD	35	--Other

序号 No.	税则号列 Tariff Line	中文货品名称 Article Description in Chinese	最惠国税率 MFN(%)	协定税率 Agreement(%)	特惠税率 SP(%)	普通税率 Gen(%)	英文货品名称 Article Description
7380	8545.2000	-碳刷	10.5	0 冰岛IS,东盟AS,哥CR,秘鲁PE,新加坡SG,新西兰NZ,智利CL 5 巴PK 6.3 澳AU 7.4 瑞士CH 8.4 韩国KR	0 受惠国LD	35	-Brushes
7381	8545.9000	-其他	10.5	0 冰岛IS,东盟AS,哥CR,秘鲁PE,新加坡SG,新西兰NZ,智利CL 5 巴PK 6.3 澳AU 7.4 瑞士CH 8.4 韩国KR	0 受惠国LD	35	-Other
	85.46	**各种材料制的绝缘子：**					**Electrical insulators of any material:**
7382	8546.1000	-玻璃制	10.5	0 冰岛IS,东盟AS,哥CR,秘鲁PE,新加坡SG,新西兰NZ,智利CL 5 巴PK 6.3 澳AU 7.4 瑞士CH 8.4 韩国KR	0 受惠国LD	35	-Of glass
		-陶瓷制：					-Of ceramics:
7383	8546.2010	---输变电线路绝缘瓷套管	6	0 冰岛IS,东盟AS,哥CR,秘鲁PE,新西兰NZ,智利CL 3.6 澳AU 4.2 瑞士CH 4.8 韩国KR 5 巴PK	0 受惠国LD	35	---Power transmission and converting ceramic bushings
7384	8546.2090	---其他	12	0 冰岛IS,东盟AS,哥CR,新加坡SG,新西兰NZ,智利CL 3.6 秘鲁PE 6 巴PK 7.2 澳AU 8.4 瑞士CH 9.6 韩国KR	0 受惠国LD	35	---Other
	ex85462090	输变电架空线路用长棒形瓷绝缘子瓷件(单支长度为1~2米,实芯)	Δ3				Long solid rod ceramic insulator body for power overhead transmission and converting lines (each rod is 1~2 meters in length)
7385	8546.9000	-其他	10	0 冰岛IS,东盟AS,哥CR,秘鲁PE,新加坡SG,新西兰NZ,智利CL 5 巴PK 6 澳AU 7 瑞士CH 8 韩国KR	0 受惠国LD	35	-Other
	85.47	**电气机器、器具或设备用的绝缘零件，除了为装配需要而在模制时装入的小金属零件（例如螺纹孔）以外，全部用绝缘材料制成，但税号85.46的绝缘子除外;内衬绝缘材料的贱金属制线路导管及其接头：**					**Insulating fittings for electrical machines, appliances or equipment, being fittings wholly of insulating material apart from any minor components of metal (for example, threaded sockets) incorporated during moulding solely for purposes of assembly, other than insulators of heading 8546; electrical conduit tubing and joints therefor, of base metal lined with insulating material:**

序号 No.	税则号列 Tariff Line	中文货品名称 Article Description in Chinese	最惠国税率 MFN(%)	协定税率 Agreement(%)	特惠税率 SP(%)	普通税率 Gen(%)	英文货品名称 Article Description
7386	8547.1000	-陶瓷制绝缘零件	8	0 冰岛IS,东盟AS,哥CR,秘鲁PE,新西兰NZ,智利CL 4.8 澳AU 5 巴PK 5.6 瑞士CH 6.9 韩国KR	0 受惠国LD	35	-Insulating fittings of ceramics
7387	8547.2000	-塑料制绝缘零件	8	0 冰岛IS,东盟AS,哥CR,秘鲁PE,香港HK,新西兰NZ,智利CL 4.8 澳AU 5 巴PK 5.6 瑞士CH 6.9 韩国KR	0 受惠国LD	35	-Insulating fittings of plastics
		-其他:					-Other:
7388	8547.9010	---内衬绝缘材料的贱金属制线路导管及其接头	10	0 冰岛IS,东盟AS,哥CR,秘鲁PE,瑞士CH,新加坡SG,新西兰NZ,智利CL 5 巴PK 6 澳AU 8 韩国KR	0 受惠国LD	50	---Electrical conduit tubing and joints therefor, of base metal lined with insulating material
7389	8547.9090	---其他	8	0 冰岛IS,东盟AS,哥CR,秘鲁PE,瑞士CH,新西兰NZ,智利CL 4.8 澳AU,韩国KR 5 巴PK	0 受惠国LD	35	---Other
	85.48	**原电池、原电池组及蓄电池的废碎料;废原电池、废原电池组及废蓄电池;机器或设备的本章其他税号未列名的电气零件:**					**Waste and scrap of primary cells, primary batteries and electric accumulators; spent primary cells, spent primary batteries and spent electric accumulators; electrical parts of machinery or apparatus, not specified or included elsewhere in this chapter:**
7390	8548.1000	-原电池、原电池组及蓄电池的废碎料;废原电池、废原电池组及废蓄电池	8	0 冰岛IS,东盟AS,哥CR,秘鲁PE,新西兰NZ,智利CL 3.2 瑞士CH 4.8 澳AU,韩国KR 5 巴PK	0 受惠国$_1$LD$_1$ 4 亚太AP	36	-Waste and scrap of primary cells, primary batteries and electric accumulators; spent primary cells, spent primary batteries and spent electric accumulators
7391	8548.9000	其他	12	0 冰岛IS,东盟AS,哥CR,秘鲁PE,新加坡SG,新西兰NZ,智利CL 6 巴PK 7.2 澳AU 8.4 瑞士CH 10.8 韩国KR	0 受惠国$_1$LD$_1$	40	-Other
	ex85489000	电磁干扰滤波器	Δ3				Electromagnetic interference filters
	ex85489000	非电磁干扰滤波器	Δ6				Non electromagnetic interference filters

第十七类
车辆、航空器、船舶及有关运输设备

注释:

一、本类不包括税号 95.03 或 95.08 的物品以及税号 95.06 的长雪橇、平底雪橇及类似品。

二、本类所称“零件”及“零件、附件”，不适用于下列货品，不论其是否确定为供本类货品使用:

(一)各种材料制的接头、垫圈或类似品(按其构成材料归类或归入税号 84.84)或硫化橡胶(硬质橡胶除外)的其他制品(税号 40.16);

(二)第十五类注释二所规定的贱金属制通用零件(第十五类)或塑料制的类似品(第三十九章);

(三)第八十二章的物品(工具);

(四)税号 83.06 的物品;

(五)税号 84.01 至 84.79 的机器或装置及其零件;税号 84.81 或 84.82 的物品及税号 84.83 的物品(这些物品是构成发动机或其他动力装置所必需的);

(六)电机或电气设备(第八十五章);

(七)第九十章的物品;

(八)第九十一章的物品;

(九)武器(第九十三章);

(十)税号 94.05 的灯具或照明装置;

(十一)作为车辆零件的刷子(税号 96.03)。

三、第八十六章至第八十八章所称“零件”或“附件”，不适用于那些非专用于或非主要用于这几章所列物品的零件、附件。同时符合这几章内两个或两个以上税号规定的零件、附件，应按其主要用途归入相应的税号。

四、在本类中:

(一)既可在道路上又可在轨道上行驶的特殊构造的车辆，应归入第八十七章的相应税号;

(二)水陆两用的机动车辆，应归入第八十七章的相应税号;

(三)可兼作地面车辆使用的特殊构造的航空器，应归入第八十八章的相应税号。

五、气垫运输工具应按本类最相似的运输工具归类，其规定如下:

SECTION XVII
VEHICLES, AIRCRAFT, VESSELS AND ASSOCIATED TRANSPORT EQUIPMENT

Notes:

1. This Section does not cover articles of heading No.95.03 or 95.08, or bobsleighs, toboggans or the like of heading No.95.06.

2. The expressions “parts” and “parts and accessories” do not apply to the following articles, whether or not they are identifiable as for the goods of this Section:

(a) Joints, washers or the like of any material (classified according to their constituent material or in heading No.84.84)or other articles of vulcanized rubber other than hard rubber(heading No.40.16);

(b) Parts of general use, as defined in Note2to Section XV, of base metal(Section XV), or similar goods of plastics(Chapter39);

(c) Articles of Chapter82(tools);

(d) Articles of heading No.83.06;

(e) Machines or apparatus of headings Nos.84.01 to 84.79, or parts thereof; articles of heading No.84.81 or 84.82 or, provided they constitute integral parts of engines or motors, articles of heading No.84.83;

(f) Electrical machinery or equipment (Chapter 85);

(g) Articles of Chapter 90;

(h) Articles of Chapter 91;

(i) Arms(Chapter 93);

(j) Lamps or lighting fittings of heading No.94.05; or

(k) Brushes of a kind used as parts of vehicles (heading No.96.03).

3. References in Chapters 86 to 88 to “parts” or “accessories” do not apply to parts or accessories which are not suitable for use solely or principally with the articles of those Chapters. A part or accessory which answers to a description in two or more of the headings of those Chapters is to be classified under that heading which corresponds to the principal use of that part or accessory.

4. For the purposes of this Section:

(a) Vehicles specially constructed to travel on both road and rail are classified under the appropriate heading of Chapter 87;

(b) Amphibious motor vehicles are classified under the appropriate heading of Chapter 87;

(c) Aircraft specially constructed so that they can also be used as road vehicles are classified under the appropriate heading of Chapter 88.

5. Air cushion vehicles are to be classified within this Section with the vehicles to which they are most akin as follows:

（一）在导轨上运行的（气垫火车），归入第八十六章;

（二）在陆地行驶或水陆两用的，归入第八十七章;

（三）在水上航行的，不论能否在海滩或浮码头登陆及能否在冰上行驶，一律归入第八十九章。

气垫运输工具的零件、附件，应按照上述规定，与最相类似的运输工具的零件、附件一并归类。

气垫火车的导轨固定装置及附件应与铁道轨道固定装置及附件一并归类。气垫火车运行系统的信号、安全或交通管理设备应与铁路的信号、安全或交通管理设备一并归类。

第八十六章
铁道及电车道机车、车辆及其零件；铁道及电车道轨道固定装置及其零件、附件；各种机械（包括电动机械）交通信号设备

注释：

一、本章不包括：

（一）木制或混凝土制的铁道或电车道轨枕及气垫火车用的混凝土导轨（税号44.06或68.10）;

（二）税号73.02的铁道及电车道铺轨用钢铁材料;

（三）税号85.30的电气信号、安全或交通管理设备。

二、税号86.07主要适用于：

（一）轴、轮、行走机构、金属轮箍、轮圈、毂及轮子的其他零件;

（二）车架、底架、转向架;

（三）轴箱；制动装置;

（四）车辆缓冲器；钩或其他联结器及车厢走廊联结装置;

（五）车身。

三、除上述注释一另有规定的以外，税号86.08包括：

（一）已装配的轨道、转车台、站台缓冲器、量载规;

（二）铁道及电车道、道路、内河航道、停车场、港口或机场用的臂板信号机、机械信号盘、平交道口控制器、信号及道岔控制器及其他机械（包括电动机械）信号、安全或交通管理设备，不论是否装有电力照明装置。

(a) In Chapter 86 if designed to travel on a guide-track (hovertrains);

(b) In Chapter 87 if designed to travel over land or over both land and water;

(c) In Chapter 89 if designed to travel over water, whether or not able to land on beaches or landingstages or also able to travel over ice.

Parts and accessories of air-cushion vehicles are to be classified in the same way as those of vehicles of the heading in which the air-cushion vehicles are classified under the above provisions.

Hovertrain track fixtures and fittings are to be classified as railway track fixtures and fittings, and signalling, safety or traffic control equipment for hovertrain transport systems as signalling, safety or traffic control equipment for railways.

Chapter 86
Railway or tramway locomotives, rolling-stock and parts thereof; railway or tramway track fixtures and fittings and parts thereof; mechanical (including electro-mechanical)traffic signaling equipment of all kinds

Notes:

1. This Chapter does not cover:

(a) Railway or tramway sleepers of wood or of concrete, or concrete guide-track sections for hovertrain (heading No. 44.06 or 68.10);

(b) Railway or tramway track construction material of iron or steel of heading No. 73.02; or

(c) Electrical signalling, safety of traffic control equipment of heading No.85.30.

2. Heading No.86.07 applies, *inter alia*, to:

(a) Axles, wheels, wheel sets (running gear), metal tyres, hoops and hubs and other parts of wheels;

(b) Frames, underframes, bogies and bissel-bogies;

(c) Axle boxes; brake gear;

(d) Buffers for rolling-stock; hooks and other coupling gear and corridor connections;

(e) Coachwork.

3. Subject to the provisions of Note 1 above, heading No. 86.08 applies, *inter alia*, to:

(a) Assembled track, turntables, platform buffers, loading gauges;

(b) Semaphores, mechanical signal discs, level crossing control gear, signal and point controls, and other mechanical (including electro-mechanical) signalling, safety or traffic control equipment, whether or not fitted with electric lighting, for railways, tramways, roads, inland waterways, parking facilities, port installations or airfields.

序号 No.	税则号列 Tariff Line	中文货品名称 Article Description in Chinese	最惠国税率 MFN(%)	协定税率 Agreement(%)	特惠税率 SP(%)	普通税率 Gen(%)	英文货品名称 Article Description
	86.01	**铁道电力机车，由外部电力或蓄电池驱动：**					**Rail locomotives powered from an external source of electricity or by electric accumulators:**
		-由外部电力驱动：					-Powered from an external source of electricity:
		---直流电机驱动的：					---Drived by DC motors:
7392	8601.1011	----微型机控制的	3	0 澳AU,巴PK,冰岛IS,东盟AS,哥CR,韩国KR,秘鲁PE,瑞士CH,新西兰NZ,智利CL	0 受惠国LD	11	----Controlled by microprocessings
7393	8601.1019	----其他	3	0 澳AU,巴PK,冰岛IS,东盟AS,哥CR,韩国KR,秘鲁PE,瑞士CH,新西兰NZ,智利CL	0 受惠国LD	11	----Other
7394	8601.1020	---交流电机驱动的	3	0 澳AU,巴PK,冰岛IS,东盟AS,哥CR,韩国KR,秘鲁PE,瑞士CH,新西兰NZ,智利CL	0 受惠国LD	11	---Drived by AC motors
7395	8601.1090	---其他	3	0 澳AU,巴PK,冰岛IS,东盟AS,哥CR,韩国KR,秘鲁PE,瑞士CH,新西兰NZ,智利CL	0 受惠国LD	11	---Other
7396	8601.2000	-由蓄电池驱动	3	0 澳AU,巴PK,冰岛IS,东盟AS,哥CR,韩国KR,秘鲁PE,瑞士CH,新西兰NZ,智利CL	0 受惠国LD	11	-Powered by electric accumulators
	86.02	**其他铁道机车;机车煤水车：**					**Other rail locomotives; locomotive tenders:**
		-柴油电力机车：					-Diesel-electric locomotives:
7397	8602.1010	---微型机控制的	3	0 澳AU,巴PK,冰岛IS,东盟AS,哥CR,韩国KR,秘鲁PE,瑞士CH,新西兰NZ,智利CL	0 受惠国LD	11	---Controled by microprocessings
7398	8602.1090	---其他	3	0 澳AU,巴PK,冰岛IS,东盟AS,哥CR,韩国KR,秘鲁PE,瑞士CH,新西兰NZ,智利CL	0 受惠国LD	11	---Other
7399	8602.9000	-其他	3	0 澳AU,巴PK,冰岛IS,东盟AS,哥CR,韩国KR,秘鲁PE,瑞士CH,新西兰NZ,智利CL	0 受惠国LD	11	-Other
	86.03	**铁道及电车道用的机动客车、货车、敞车，但税号86.04的货品除外：**					**Self-propelled railway or tramway coaches, vans and trucks, other than those of heading 8604:**
7400	8603.1000	-由外部电力驱动	3	0 澳AU,巴PK,冰岛IS,东盟AS,哥CR,韩国KR,秘鲁PE,瑞士CH,新西兰NZ,智利CL	0 受惠国LD	11	-Powered from an external source of electricity
7401	8603.9000	-其他	3	0 澳AU,巴PK,冰岛IS,东盟AS,哥CR,韩国KR,秘鲁PE,瑞士CH,新西兰NZ,智利CL	0 受惠国LD	11	-Other
	86.04	**铁道及电车道用的维修或服务车，不论是否机动（例如，工场车、起重机车、道碴捣固车、轨道校正车、检验车及查道车）：**					**Railway or tramway maintenance or service vehicles, whether or not self-propelled (for example, workshops, cranes, ballast tampers, trackliners, testing coaches and track inspection vehicles) :**
		---检验车及查道车：					---Testing coaches and track inspection vehicles:
7402	8604.0011	----隧道限界检查车	3	0 澳AU,巴PK,冰岛IS,东盟AS,哥CR,韩国KR,秘鲁PE,瑞士CH,新西兰NZ,智利CL	0 受惠国LD	14	----Inspection vehicles for tunnel learance

序号 No.	税则号列 Tariff Line	中文货品名称 Article Description in Chinese	最惠国税率 MFN(%)	协定税率 Agreement(%)	特惠税率 SP(%)	普通税率 Gen(%)	英文货品名称 Article Description
7403	8604.0012	-----钢轨在线打磨列车	3	0 澳AU,巴PK,冰岛IS,东盟AS,哥CR,韩国KR,秘鲁PE,瑞士CH,新西兰NZ,智利CL	0 受惠国LD	14	----Sanding vehicles for on-line rails
7404	8604.0019	-----其他	5	0 澳AU,巴PK,冰岛IS,东盟AS,哥CR,秘鲁PE,瑞士CH,新西兰NZ,智利CL 3 韩国KR	0 受惠国LD	14	----Other
		----其他:					---Other:
7405	8604.0091	-----电气化接触网架线机（轨行式）	5	0 澳AU,巴PK,冰岛IS,东盟AS,哥CR,秘鲁PE,瑞士CH,新西兰NZ,智利CL 3 韩国KR	0 受惠国LD	20	----Installing vehicles for suspension of contact wire (running on rails)
7406	8604.0099	-----其他	7	0 冰岛IS,东盟AS,哥CR,秘鲁PE,新西兰NZ,智利CL 2.8 瑞士CH 4.2 澳AU,韩国KR 5 巴PK	0 受惠国LD	20	----Other
	86.05	**铁道及电车道用的非机动客车;行李车、邮政车和其他铁道及电车道用的非机动特殊用途车辆（税号86.04的货品除外）:**					**Railway or tramway passenger coaches, not self-propelled; luggage vans, post office coaches and other special purpose railway or tramway coaches, not self-propelled (excluding those of heading 8604) :**
7407	8605.0010	---铁道客车	5	0 澳AU,巴PK,冰岛IS,东盟AS,哥CR,秘鲁PE,瑞士CH,新西兰NZ,智利CL 3 韩国KR	0 受惠国LD	14	---Railway passenger coaches
7408	8605.0090	---其他	5	0 澳AU,巴PK,冰岛IS,东盟AS,哥CR,秘鲁PE,瑞士CH,新西兰NZ,智利CL 3 韩国KR	0 受惠国LD	14	---Other
	86.06	**铁道及电车道用的非机动有篷及无篷货车:**					**Railway or tramway goods vans and wagons, not self-propelled:**
7409	8606.1000	-油罐货车及类似车	5	0 澳AU,巴PK,冰岛IS,东盟AS,哥CR,秘鲁PE,瑞士CH,新西兰NZ,智利CL 3 韩国KR	0 受惠国LD	14	-Tank wagons and the like
7410	8606.3000	-自卸货车，但子目号8606. 1000或8606. 2000的货品除外	5	0 澳AU,巴PK,冰岛IS,东盟AS,哥CR,秘鲁PE,瑞士CH,新西兰NZ,智利CL 3 韩国KR	0 受惠国LD	14	-Self-discharging vans and wagons, other than those of subheading No. 8606.1000 or 8606.2000
		-其他:					-Other:
7411	8606.9100	--带篷及封闭的	5	0 澳AU,巴PK,冰岛IS,东盟AS,哥CR,秘鲁PE,瑞士CH,新西兰NZ,智利CL 3 韩国KR	0 受惠国LD	14	--Covered and closed
7412	8606.9200	--敞篷的，厢壁固定且高度超过60厘米	5	0 澳AU,巴PK,冰岛IS,东盟AS,哥CR,秘鲁PE,瑞士CH,新西兰NZ,智利CL 3 韩国KR	0 受惠国LD	14	--Open, with non-removable sides of a height exceeding 60cm
7413	8606.9900	--其他	5	0 澳AU,巴PK,冰岛IS,东盟AS,哥CR,秘鲁PE,瑞士CH,新西兰NZ,智利CL 3 韩国KR	0 受惠国LD	14	--Other

序号 No.	税则号列 Tariff Line	中文货品名称 Article Description in Chinese	最惠国税率 MFN(%)	协定税率 Agreement(%)		特惠税率 SP(%)		普通税率 Gen(%)	英文货品名称 Article Description
	86.07	铁道及电车道机车或其他车辆的零件：							**Parts of railway or tramway locomotives or rolling stock:**
		-转向架、轴、轮及其零件：							-Bogies, bissel-bogies, axles and wheels, and parts thereof:
7414	8607.1100	--驾驶转向架	3	0	澳AU,巴PK,冰岛IS,东盟AS,哥CR,韩国KR,秘鲁PE,瑞士CH,新西兰NZ,智利CL	0	受惠国LD	11	--Driving bogies and bissel-bogies
7415	8607.1200	--其他转向架	3	0	澳AU,巴PK,冰岛IS,东盟AS,哥CR,韩国KR,秘鲁PE,瑞士CH,新西兰NZ,智利CL	0	受惠国LD	11	--Other bogies and bissel-bogies
		--其他，包括零件：							--Other, including parts:
7416	8607.1910	---轴	3	0	澳AU,巴PK,冰岛IS,东盟AS,哥CR,韩国KR,秘鲁PE,瑞士CH,新西兰NZ,智利CL	0	受惠国LD	11	---Axles
7417	8607.1990	---其他	3	0	澳AU,巴PK,冰岛IS,东盟AS,哥CR,韩国KR,秘鲁PE,瑞士CH,新西兰NZ,智利CL	0	受惠国LD	11	---Other
		-制动装置及其零件：							-Brakes and parts thereof:
7418	8607.2100	--空气制动器及其零件	3	0	澳AU,巴PK,冰岛IS,东盟AS,哥CR,韩国KR,秘鲁PE,瑞士CH,新西兰NZ,智利CL	0	受惠国LD	11	--Air brakes and parts thereof
7419	8607.2900	--其他	3	0	澳AU,巴PK,冰岛IS,东盟AS,哥CR,韩国KR,秘鲁PE,瑞士CH,新西兰NZ,智利CL	0	受惠国LD	11	--Other
7420	8607.3000	-钩、其他联结器、缓冲器及其零件	3	0	澳AU,巴PK,冰岛IS,东盟AS,哥CR,韩国KR,秘鲁PE,瑞士CH,新西兰NZ,智利CL	0	受惠国LD	11	-Hooks and other coupling devices, buffers, and parts thereof
		-其他：							-Other:
7421	8607.9100	--机车用	3	0 1.8	澳AU,巴PK,冰岛IS,东盟AS,哥CR,秘鲁PE,瑞士CH,新西兰NZ,智利CL 韩国KR	0	受惠国LD	11	--Of locomotives
7422	8607.9900	--其他	3	0 2.1	澳AU,巴PK,冰岛IS,东盟AS,哥CR,韩国KR,秘鲁PE,新西兰NZ,智利CL 瑞士CH	0	受惠国LD	11	--Other
	86.08	铁道及电车道轨道固定装置及附件;供铁道、电车道、道路、内河航道、停车场、港口或机场用的机械（包括电动机械）信号、安全或交通管理设备;上述货品的零件：							**Railway or tramway track fixtures and fittings; mechanical (including electromechanical) signalling, safety or traffic control equipment for railways, tramways, roads, inland waterways, parking facilities, port installations or airfields; parts of the foregoing:**
7423	8608.0010	---轨道自动计轴设备	3	0	澳AU,巴PK,冰岛IS,东盟AS,哥CR,韩国KR,秘鲁PE,瑞士CH,新西兰NZ,智利CL	0	受惠国LD	20	---Rail automatic axle counting equipments
7424	8608.0090	---其他	4	0 1.6	澳AU,巴PK,冰岛IS,东盟AS,哥CR,韩国KR,秘鲁PE,新西兰NZ,智利CL 瑞士CH	0	受惠国LD	20	---Other

序号 No.	税则号列 Tariff Line	中文货品名称 Article Description in Chinese	最惠国税率 MFN(%)	协定税率 Agreement(%)		特惠税率 SP(%)		普通税率 Gen(%)	英文货品名称 Article Description
	86.09	集装箱(包括运输液体的集装箱),经特殊设计、装备适用于各种运输方式:							**Containers (including containers for the transport of fluids) specially designed and equipped for carriage by one or more modes of transport:**
		---20英尺的:							---Of 20 feet:
7425	8609.0011	----保温式	10.5	0 5 6.3 7.4 8.4	冰岛IS,东盟AS,哥CR,秘鲁PE,新加坡SG,新西兰NZ,智利CL 巴PK 澳AU 瑞士CH 韩国KR	0	受惠国LD	35	----Thermal
7426	8609.0012	----罐式	10.5	0 5 6.3 7.4 8.4	冰岛IS,东盟AS,哥CR,秘鲁PE,新加坡SG,新西兰NZ,智利CL 巴PK 澳AU 瑞士CH 韩国KR	0	受惠国LD	35	----Tank
7427	8609.0019	----其他	10.5	0 5 6.3 7.4 8.4	冰岛IS,东盟AS,哥CR,秘鲁PE,新加坡SG,新西兰NZ,智利CL 巴PK 澳AU 瑞士CH 韩国KR	0	受惠国LD	35	----Other
		---40英尺的:							---Of 40 feet:
7428	8609.0021	----保温式	10.5	0 5 6.3 7.4 8.4	冰岛IS,东盟AS,哥CR,秘鲁PE,新加坡SG,新西兰NZ,智利CL 巴PK 澳AU 瑞士CH 韩国KR	0	受惠国LD	35	----Thermal
7429	8609.0022	----罐式	10.5	0 5 6.3 7.4 8.4	冰岛IS,东盟AS,哥CR,秘鲁PE,新加坡SG,新西兰NZ,智利CL 巴PK 澳AU 瑞士CH 韩国KR	0	受惠国LD	35	----Tank
7430	8609.0029	----其他	10.5	0 5 6.3 7.4 8.4	冰岛IS,东盟AS,哥CR,秘鲁PE,新加坡SG,新西兰NZ,智利CL 巴PK 澳AU 瑞士CH 韩国KR	0	受惠国LD	35	----Other
7431	8609.0030	---45、48、53英尺的	10.5	0 5 6.3 7.4 8.4	冰岛IS,东盟AS,哥CR,秘鲁PE,新加坡SG,新西兰NZ,智利CL 巴PK 澳AU 瑞士CH 韩国KR	0	受惠国LD	35	---Of 45, 48, 53 feet
7432	8609.0090	---其他	10.5	0 5 6.3 7.4 8.4	冰岛IS,东盟AS,哥CR,秘鲁PE,新加坡SG,新西兰NZ,智利CL 巴PK 澳AU 瑞士CH 韩国KR	0	受惠国LD	35	---Other

第八十七章
车辆及其零件、附件，
但铁道及电车道车辆除外

Chapter 87
Vehicles other than railway or tramway rolling-stock, and parts and accessories thereof

注释：

一、本章不包括仅可在钢轨上运行的铁道及电车道车辆。

二、本章所称“牵引车、拖拉机”，是指主要为牵引或推动其他车辆、器具或重物的车辆。除了上述主要用途以外，不论其是否还具有装运工具、种子、肥料或其他货品的辅助装置。

用于安装在税号 87.01 的牵引车或拖拉机上，作为可替换设备的机器或作业工具，即使与牵引车或拖拉机一同进口或出口，不论其是否已安装在车（机）上，仍应归入其各自相应的税号。

三、装有驾驶室的机动车辆底盘，应归入税号 87.02 至 87.04，而不归入税号 87.06。

四、税号 87.12 包括所有儿童两轮车，其他儿童脚踏车归入税号 95.03。

Notes:

1. This Chapter does not cover railway or tramway rolling-stock designed solely for running on rails.

2. For the purposes of this Chapter, “tractors” means vehicles constructed essentially for hauling or pushing another vehicle, appliance or load, whether or not they contain subsidiary provision for the transport, in connection with the main use of the tractor, of tools, seeds, fertilizers or other goods.

Machines and working tools designed for fitting to tractors of heading No.87.01as interchangeable equipment remain classified in their respective headings even if presented with the tractor, and whether or not mounted on it.

3. Motor chassis fitted with cabs fall in headings Nos.87.02 to 87.04, and not in heading No.87.06.

4. Heading No.87.12 includes all children’s bicycles. Other children’s cycles fall in heading No.95.03.

序号 No.	税则号列 Tariff Line	中文货品名称 Article Description in Chinese	最惠国税率 MFN(%)	协定税率 Agreement(%)	特惠税率 SP(%)	普通税率 Gen(%)	英文货品名称 Article Description
	87.01	牵引车、拖拉机（税号87.09的牵引车除外）：					**Tractors (other than tractors of heading 8709) :**
7433	8701.1000	-手扶拖拉机	9	0 冰岛IS,东盟AS,哥CR,秘鲁PE,新西兰NZ,智利CL 3.6 瑞士CH 5 巴PK 5.4 澳AU 7.2 韩国KR	0 受惠国$_1$LD$_1$	20	-Pedestrian controlled tractors
7434	8701.2000	-半挂车用的公路牵引车	6	0 冰岛IS,哥CR,新西兰NZ,智利CL 2.4 瑞士CH 3.6 澳AU 5.2 韩国KR	0 受惠国$_2$LD$_2$	20	-Road tractors for semi-trailers
7435	8701.3000	-履带式牵引车、拖拉机	6	0 冰岛IS,东盟AS,哥CR,秘鲁PE,新西兰NZ,智利CL 2.4 瑞士CH 3.6 澳AU,韩国KR 5 巴PK	0 受惠国$_1$LD$_1$	20	-Track-laying tractors
		-其他：					-Other:
		---拖拉机：					---Tractors:
7436	8701.9011	----轮式	8	0 冰岛IS,东盟AS,哥CR,秘鲁PE,新西兰NZ,智利CL 3.2 瑞士CH 4.8 澳AU,韩国KR 5 巴PK	0 受惠国$_1$LD$_1$	20	----Wheeled
	ex87019011	功率大于150马力的轮式拖拉机	Δ5				Wheeled tractors with power more than 150HP

序号 No.	税则号列 Tariff Line	中文货品名称 Article Description in Chinese	最惠国税率 MFN(%)	协定税率 Agreement(%)	特惠税率 SP(%)	普通税率 Gen(%)	英文货品名称 Article Description
7437	8701.9019	----其他	8	0 冰岛IS,东盟AS,哥CR,秘鲁PE,新西兰NZ,智利CL 3.2 瑞士CH 4.8 澳AU,韩国KR 5 巴PK	0 受惠国$_1$LD$_1$	20	----Other
	ex87019019	功率大于150马力的其他拖拉机	Δ5				Other tractors with power more than 150HP
7438	8701.9090	---其他	8	0 冰岛IS,东盟AS,哥CR,秘鲁PE,新西兰NZ,智利CL 3.2 瑞士CH 4.8 澳AU,韩国KR 5 巴PK	0 受惠国$_1$LD$_1$	20	---Other
	87.02	**客运机动车辆，10座及以上（包括驾驶座）：**					**Motor vehicles for the transport of ten or more persons, including the driver:**
		-装有压燃式活塞内燃发动机（柴油或半柴油发动机）的车辆：					-With compression-ignition internal combustion piston engine (diesel or semi-diesel) :
7439	8702.1020	---机坪客车	4	0 澳AU,巴PK,冰岛IS,东盟AS,哥CR,秘鲁PE,瑞士CH,新西兰NZ,智利CL 3.4 韩国KR	0 受惠国$_1$LD$_1$	90	---Buses for transport passengers at airport
		---其他：					---Other:
7440	8702.1091	----30座及以上（大型客车）	25	0 冰岛IS,哥CR,新西兰NZ,智利CL 15 澳AU 22.5 韩国KR	0 受惠国$_2$LD$_2$	90	----With 30 seats or more
7441	8702.1092	----20座及以上，但不超过29座	25	0 冰岛IS,哥CR,新西兰NZ,智利CL 15 澳AU 22.5 韩国KR	0 受惠国$_2$LD$_2$	230	----With 20 seats or more, but not exceeding 29 seats
7442	8702.1093	----10座及以上，但不超过19座	25	0 冰岛IS,哥CR,新西兰NZ,智利CL 15 澳AU 22.5 韩国KR	0 受惠国$_2$LD$_2$	230	----With 10 seats or more, but not exceeding 19 seats
		-其他：					-Other:
7443	8702.9010	---30座及以上（大型客车）	25	0 冰岛IS,哥CR,新西兰NZ,智利CL 15 澳AU 20 东盟AS 22.5 韩国KR	0 受惠国$_2$LD$_2$	90	---With 30 seats or more
7444	8702.9020	---20座及以上，但不超过29座	25	0 冰岛IS,哥CR,新西兰NZ,智利CL 15 澳AU 20 东盟AS 22.5 韩国KR	0 受惠国$_2$LD$_2$	230	---With 20 seats or more, but not exceeding 29 seats
7445	8702.9030	---10座及以上，但不超过19座	25	0 冰岛IS,哥CR,新西兰NZ,智利CL 7.5 秘鲁PE 15 澳AU 20 东盟AS 22.5 韩国KR	0 受惠国$_1$LD$_1$	230	---With 10 seats or more, but not exceeding 19 seats
	87.03	**主要用于载人的机动车辆（税号87.02的货品除外），包括旅行小客车及赛车：**					**Motor cars and other motor vehicles principally designed for the transport of persons (other than those of heading 8702) , including station wagons and racing cars:**
		-雪地行走专用车；高尔夫球车及类似车辆：					-Vehicles specially designed for travelling on snow; golf cars and similar vehicles:
		---高尔夫球车及类似车辆：					---Golf cars and similar vehicles:

序号 No.	税则号列 Tariff Line	中文货品名称 Article Description in Chinese	最惠国税率 MFN(%)	协定税率 Agreement(%)	特惠税率 SP(%)	普通税率 Gen(%)	英文货品名称 Article Description
7446	8703.1011	----全地形车	25	0 冰岛IS,东盟AS,哥CR,新加坡SG,新西兰NZ,智利CL 7.5 秘鲁PE 15 澳AU 22.5 韩国KR	0 受惠国$_1$LD$_1$	150	----All Terrain Vehicles
7447	8703.1019	----其他	25	0 冰岛IS,东盟AS,哥CR,新加坡SG,新西兰NZ,智利CL 7.5 秘鲁PE 15 澳AU	0 受惠国$_1$LD$_1$	150	----Other
7448	8703.1090	---其他	25	0 冰岛IS,东盟AS,哥CR,新加坡SG,新西兰NZ,智利CL 7.5 秘鲁PE 15 澳AU	0 受惠国$_1$LD$_1$	150	---Other
		-装有点燃往复式活塞内燃发动机的其他车辆:					-Other vehicles, with spark-ignition internal combustion reciprocating piston engine:
		--气缸容量(排气量)不超过1000毫升:					--Of a cylinder capacity not exceeding 1000cm^3:
7449	8703.2130	---小轿车	25	0 冰岛IS,哥CR,新西兰NZ,智利CL 15 澳AU 22.5 巴PK,亚太AP		230	---Saloon cars
7450	8703.2140	---越野车(4轮驱动)	25	0 冰岛IS,哥CR,新西兰NZ,智利CL 15 澳AU 22.5 巴PK,亚太AP		230	---Cross-country Cars (4WD)
7451	8703.2150	---9座及以下的小客车	25	0 冰岛IS,哥CR,新西兰NZ,智利CL 15 澳AU 22.5 巴PK,亚太AP		230	---Station Wagons (with 9 seats or less)
7452	8703.2190	---其他	25	0 冰岛IS,哥CR,新西兰NZ,智利CL 15 澳AU 22.5 巴PK,亚太AP		230	---Other
		--气缸容量(排气量)超过1000毫升,但不超过1500毫升:					--Of a cylinder capacity exceeding 1000cm^3 but not exceeding 1500cm^3:
7453	8703.2230	---小轿车	25	0 冰岛IS,哥CR,新西兰NZ,智利CL 15 澳AU 22.5 巴PK,亚太AP 24 韩国KR		230	---Saloon cars
7454	8703.2240	---越野车(4轮驱动)	25	0 冰岛IS,哥CR,新西兰NZ,智利CL 15 澳AU 22.5 巴PK,亚太AP		230	---Cross-country cars (4WD)
7455	8703.2250	---9座及以下的小客车	25	0 冰岛IS,哥CR,新西兰NZ,智利CL 15 澳AU 22.5 巴PK,亚太AP		230	---Station wagons (with 9 seats or less)
7456	8703.2290	---其他	25	0 冰岛IS,哥CR,新西兰NZ,智利CL 15 澳AU 22.5 巴PK,亚太AP		230	---Other
		---气缸容量(排气量)超过1500毫升,但不超过2000毫升:					---Of a cylinder capacity exceeding 1500cc but not exceeding 2000cc:
7457	8703.2341	----小轿车	25	0 冰岛IS,哥CR,新西兰NZ,智利CL 20 澳AU 22.5 巴PK,亚太AP 24 韩国KR		230	----Saloon Cars

序号 No.	税则号列 Tariff Line	中文货品名称 Article Description in Chinese	最惠国税率 MFN(%)	协定税率 Agreement(%)	特惠税率 SP(%)	普通税率 Gen(%)	英文货品名称 Article Description
7458	8703.2342	----越野车（4轮驱动）	25	0 冰岛IS,哥CR,新西兰NZ,智利CL 20 澳AU 22.5 巴PK,亚太AP 24 韩国KR		230	----Cross-country Cars (4WD)
7459	8703.2343	----9座及以下的小客车	25	0 冰岛IS,哥CR,新西兰NZ,智利CL 20 澳AU 22.5 巴PK,亚太AP 24 韩国KR		230	----Station Wagons (with 9 seats or less)
7460	8703.2349	----其他	25	0 冰岛IS,哥CR,新西兰NZ,智利CL 20 澳AU 22.5 巴PK,亚太AP		230	----Other
		---气缸容量（排气量）超过2000毫升，但不超过2500毫升：					---Of a cylinder capacity exceeding 2000cc but not exceeding 2500cc:
7461	8703.2351	----小轿车	25	0 冰岛IS,哥CR,新西兰NZ,智利CL 20 澳AU 22.5 巴PK,亚太AP 24 韩国KR		230	----Saloon Cars
7462	8703.2352	----越野车（4轮驱动）	25	0 冰岛IS,哥CR,新西兰NZ,智利CL 20 澳AU 22.5 巴PK,亚太AP 24 韩国KR		230	----Cross-country Cars (4WD)
7463	8703.2353	----9座及以下的小客车	25	0 冰岛IS,哥CR,新西兰NZ,智利CL 20 澳AU 22.5 巴PK,亚太AP 24 韩国KR		230	----Station Wagons (with 9 seats or less)
7464	8703.2359	----其他	25	0 冰岛IS,哥CR,新西兰NZ,智利CL 20 澳AU 22.5 巴PK,亚太AP		230	----Other
		---气缸容量（排气量）超过2500毫升，但不超过3000毫升：					---Of a cylinder capacity exceeding 2500cc but not exceeding 3000cc:
7465	8703.2361	----小轿车	25	0 冰岛IS,哥CR,新西兰NZ,智利CL 20 澳AU 22.5 巴PK,亚太AP 24 韩国KR		270	----Saloon Cars
7466	8703.2362	----越野车（4轮驱动）	25	0 冰岛IS,东盟AS,哥CR,新加坡SG,新西兰NZ,智利CL 20 澳AU 22.5 巴PK,亚太AP		270	----Cross-country Cars (4WD)
7467	8703.2363	----9座及以下的小客车	25	0 冰岛IS,东盟AS,哥CR,新加坡SG,新西兰NZ,智利CL 20 澳AU 22.5 巴PK,亚太AP 24 韩国KR		270	----Station Wagons (with 9 seats or less)
7468	8703.2369	----其他	25	0 冰岛IS,东盟AS,哥CR,新加坡SG,新西兰NZ,智利CL 20 澳AU 22.5 巴PK,亚太AP		270	----Other
		---气缸容量（排气量）超过3000毫升，但不超过4000毫升：					---Of a cylinder capacity exceeding 3000cc but not exceeding 4000cc:

序号 No.	税则号列 Tariff Line	中文货品名称 Article Description in Chinese	最惠国税率 MFN(%)	协定税率 Agreement(%)	特惠税率 SP(%)	普通税率 Gen(%)	英文货品名称 Article Description
7469	8703.2411	----小轿车	25	0 冰岛IS,哥CR,新西兰NZ,智利CL 20 澳AU 22.5 巴PK,亚太AP 24 韩国KR	0 受惠国$_2$LD$_2$	270	----Saloon cars
7470	8703.2412	----越野车（4轮驱动）	25	0 冰岛IS,哥CR,新西兰NZ,智利CL 20 澳AU 22.5 巴PK,亚太AP 24 韩国KR	0 受惠国$_2$LD$_2$	270	----Cross-country cars (4WD)
7471	8703.2413	----9座及以下的小客车	25	0 冰岛IS,哥CR,新西兰NZ,智利CL 20 澳AU 22.5 巴PK,亚太AP	0 受惠国$_2$LD$_2$	270	----Station wagons (with 9 seats or less)
7472	8703.2419	----其他	25	0 冰岛IS,哥CR,新西兰NZ,智利CL 20 澳AU 22.5 巴PK,亚太AP	0 受惠国$_2$LD$_2$	270	----Other
		---气缸容量（排气量）超过4000毫升：					---Of a cylinder capacity exceeding 4000cc:
7473	8703.2421	----小轿车	25	0 冰岛IS,哥CR,新西兰NZ,智利CL 20 澳AU 22.5 巴PK,亚太AP 24 韩国KR	0 受惠国$_2$LD$_2$	270	----Saloon Cars
7474	8703.2422	----越野车（4轮驱动）	25	0 冰岛IS,哥CR,新西兰NZ,智利CL 20 澳AU 22.5 巴PK,亚太AP	0 受惠国$_2$LD$_2$	270	----Cross-country Cars (4WD)
7475	8703.2423	----9座及以下的小客车	25	0 冰岛IS,哥CR,新西兰NZ,智利CL 20 澳AU 22.5 巴PK,亚太AP	0 受惠国$_2$LD$_2$	270	----Station Wagons (with 9 seats or less)
7476	8703.2429	----其他	25	0 冰岛IS,哥CR,新西兰NZ,智利CL 20 澳AU 22.5 巴PK,亚太AP	0 受惠国$_2$LD$_2$	270	----Other
		--装有压燃式活塞内燃发动机（柴油或半柴油发动机）的其他车辆：					--Of a cylinder capacity not exceeding 1500cm^3:
		---气缸容量（排气量）不超过1000毫升：					---Of a cylinder capacity not exceeding 1000cc:
7477	8703.3111	----小轿车	25	0 冰岛IS,哥CR,新西兰NZ,智利CL 20 澳AU	0 受惠国$_2$LD$_2$	230	----Saloon cars
7478	8703.3119	----其他	25	0 冰岛IS,东盟AS,哥CR,新加坡SG,新西兰NZ,智利CL 7.5 秘鲁PE 20 澳AU	0 受惠国$_1$LD$_1$	230	----Cross-country cars (4WD)
		---气缸容量（排气量）超过1000毫升，但不超过1500毫升：					---Of a cylinder capacity exceeding 1000cc but not exceeding 1500cc:
7479	8703.3121	----小轿车	25	0 冰岛IS,哥CR,新西兰NZ,智利CL 20 澳AU		230	----Saloon cars
7480	8703.3122	----越野车（4轮驱动）	25	0 冰岛IS,哥CR,新西兰NZ,智利CL 20 澳AU		230	----Cross-country cars (4WD)
7481	8703.3123	----9座及以下的小客车	25	0 冰岛IS,哥CR,新西兰NZ,智利CL 20 澳AU		230	----Station wagons (with 9 seats or less)

序号 No.	税则号列 Tariff Line	中文货品名称 Article Description in Chinese	最惠国税率 MFN(%)	协定税率 Agreement(%)	特惠税率 SP(%)	普通税率 Gen(%)	英文货品名称 Article Description
7482	8703.3129	----其他	25	0 冰岛IS,东盟AS,哥CR,新加坡SG,新西兰NZ,智利CL 7.5 秘鲁PE 20 澳AU	0 受惠国$_1$LD$_1$	230	----Other
		---气缸容量（排气量）超过1500毫升，但不超过2000毫升：					---Of a cylinder capacity exceeding 1500cc but not exceeding 2000cc:
7483	8703.3211	----小轿车	25	0 冰岛IS,哥CR,新西兰NZ,智利CL 20 澳AU 22.5 巴PK,亚太AP		230	----Saloon Cars
7484	8703.3212	----越野车（4轮驱动）	25	0 冰岛IS,哥CR,新西兰NZ,智利CL 20 澳AU 22.5 巴PK,亚太AP 24 韩国KR		230	----Cross-country Cars (4WD)
7485	8703.3213	----9座及以下的小客车	25	0 冰岛IS,哥CR,新西兰NZ,智利CL 20 澳AU 22.5 巴PK,亚太AP 24 韩国KR		230	----Station Wagons (with 9 seats or less)
7486	8703.3219	----其他	25	0 冰岛IS,哥CR,新西兰NZ,智利CL 20 澳AU 22.5 巴PK,亚太AP		230	----Other
		---气缸容量（排气量）超过2000毫升，但不超过2500毫升：					---Of a cylinder capacity exceeding 2000cc but not exceeding 2500cc:
7487	8703.3221	----小轿车	25	0 冰岛IS,哥CR,新西兰NZ,智利CL 20 澳AU 22.5 巴PK,亚太AP		230	----Saloon Cars
7488	8703.3222	----越野车（4轮驱动）	25	0 冰岛IS,哥CR,新西兰NZ,智利CL 20 澳AU 22.5 巴PK,亚太AP		230	----Cross-country Cars (4WD)
7489	8703.3223	----9座及以下的小客车	25	0 冰岛IS,哥CR,新西兰NZ,智利CL 20 澳AU 22.5 巴PK,亚太AP 24 韩国KR		230	----Station Wagons (with 9 seats or less)
7490	8703.3229	----其他	25	0 冰岛IS,哥CR,新西兰NZ,智利CL 20 澳AU 22.5 巴PK,亚太AP		230	----Other
		---气缸容量（排气量）超过2500毫升，但不超过3000毫升：					---Of a cylinder capacity exceeding 2500cc but not exceeding 3000cc:
7491	8703.3311	----小轿车	25	0 冰岛IS,东盟AS,哥CR,新加坡SG,新西兰NZ,智利CL 20 澳AU 22.5 巴PK,亚太AP		270	----Saloon Cars
7492	8703.3312	----越野车（4轮驱动）	25	0 冰岛IS,东盟AS,哥CR,新加坡SG,新西兰NZ,智利CL 20 澳AU 22.5 巴PK,亚太AP 24 韩国KR		270	----Cross-country Cars (4WD)
7493	8703.3313	----9座及以下的小客车	25	0 冰岛IS,东盟AS,哥CR,新加坡SG,新西兰NZ,智利CL 20 澳AU 22.5 巴PK,亚太AP		270	----Station Wagons (with 9 seats or less)

序号 No.	税则号列 Tariff Line	中文货品名称 Article Description in Chinese	最惠国税率 MFN(%)	协定税率 Agreement(%)	特惠税率 SP(%)	普通税率 Gen(%)	英文货品名称 Article Description
7494	8703.3319	----其他	25	0 冰岛IS,东盟AS,哥CR,新加坡SG,新西兰NZ,智利CL 20 澳AU 22.5 巴PK,亚太AP		270	----Other
		---气缸容量（排气量）超过3000毫升，但不超过4000毫升：					---Of a cylinder capacity exceeding 3000cc but not exceeding 4000cc:
7495	8703.3321	----小轿车	25	0 冰岛IS,东盟AS,哥CR,新加坡SG,新西兰NZ,智利CL 20 澳AU 22.5 巴PK,亚太AP	0 受惠国$_2$LD$_2$	270	----Saloon Cars
7496	8703.3322	----越野车（4轮驱动）	25	0 冰岛IS,东盟AS,哥CR,新加坡SG,新西兰NZ,智利CL 20 澳AU 22.5 巴PK,亚太AP	0 受惠国$_2$LD$_2$	270	----Cross-country Cars (4WD)
7497	8703.3323	----9座及以下的小客车	25	0 冰岛IS,东盟AS,哥CR,新加坡SG,新西兰NZ,智利CL 20 澳AU 22.5 巴PK,亚太AP	0 受惠国$_2$LD$_2$	270	----Station Wagons (with 9 seats or less)
7498	8703.3329	----其他	25	0 冰岛IS,东盟AS,哥CR,新加坡SG,新西兰NZ,智利CL 20 澳AU 22.5 巴PK,亚太AP	0 受惠国$_2$LD$_2$	270	----Other
		---气缸容量（排气量）超过4000毫升：					---Of a cylinder capacity exceeding 4000cc:
7499	8703.3361	----小轿车	25	0 冰岛IS,东盟AS,哥CR,新加坡SG,新西兰NZ,智利CL 15 澳AU 22.5 巴PK,亚太AP	0 受惠国$_2$LD$_2$	270	----Saloon Cars
7500	8703.3362	----越野车（4轮驱动）	25	0 冰岛IS,东盟AS,哥CR,新加坡SG,新西兰NZ,智利CL 15 澳AU 22.5 巴PK,亚太AP	0 受惠国$_2$LD$_2$	270	----Cross-country Cars (4WD)
7501	8703.3363	----9座及以下的小客车	25	0 冰岛IS,东盟AS,哥CR,新加坡SG,新西兰NZ,智利CL 15 澳AU 22.5 巴PK,亚太AP	0 受惠国$_2$LD$_2$	270	----Station Wagons (with 9 seats or less)
7502	8703.3369	----其他	25	0 冰岛IS,东盟AS,哥CR,新加坡SG,新西兰NZ,智利CL 15 澳AU 22.5 巴PK,亚太AP	0 受惠国$_2$LD$_2$	270	----Other
7503	8703.9000	-其他	25	0 冰岛IS,东盟AS,哥CR,新加坡SG,新西兰NZ,智利CL 7.5 秘鲁PE 15 澳AU 22.5 巴PK,亚太AP 24 韩国KR	0 受惠国$_1$LD$_1$	270	-Other
	87.04	货运机动车辆：					**Motor vehicles for the transport of goods:**
		-非公路用自卸车：					-Dumpers designed for off-highway use:

序号 No.	税则号列 Tariff Line	中文货品名称 Article Description in Chinese	最惠国税率 MFN(%)	协定税率 Agreement(%)	特惠税率 SP(%)	普通税率 Gen(%)	英文货品名称 Article Description
7504	8704.1030	---电动轮货运自卸车	6	0 冰岛IS,东盟AS,哥CR,秘鲁PE,新西兰NZ,智利CL 2.4 瑞士CH 3.6 澳AU,韩国KR 5 巴PK	0 受惠国LD	20	---Electric-wheel dumpers for the transport of goods
7505	8704.1090	---其他	6	0 冰岛IS,东盟AS,哥CR,秘鲁PE,新西兰NZ,智利CL 2.4 瑞士CH 3.6 澳AU,韩国KR 5 巴PK	0 受惠国LD	20	---Other
		-装有压燃式活塞内燃发动机（柴油或半柴油发动机）的其他货车：					-Other, with compression-ignition internal combustion piston engine (diesel or semi-diesel) :
7506	8704.2100	--车辆总重量不超过5吨	25	0 冰岛IS,哥CR,新西兰NZ,智利CL 15 澳AU 22.5 韩国KR	0 受惠国$_2$LD$_2$	70	--G.V.W. not exceeding 5 tons
		--车辆总重量超过5吨，但不超过20吨：					--Of a gross vehicle weight exceeding 5 tonnes but not exceeding 20 tonnes:
7507	8704.2230	---车辆总重量超过5吨，但小于14吨	20	0 冰岛IS,哥CR,新西兰NZ,智利CL 6 秘鲁PE 12 澳AU 14 瑞士CH 17.3 韩国KR 18 巴PK,亚太AP	0 受惠国$_1$LD$_1$	70	---G.V.W. exceeding 5 tons but not exceeding 14 tons
7508	8704.2240	---车辆总重量在14吨及以上，但不超过20吨	20	0 冰岛IS,哥CR,新西兰NZ,智利CL 6 秘鲁PE 12 澳AU 14 瑞士CH 17.3 韩国KR 18 巴PK,亚太AP	0 受惠国$_1$LD$_1$	40	---G.V.W. of 14 tons or more but not exceeding 20 tons
7509	8704.2300	--车辆总重量超过20吨	15	0 冰岛IS,哥CR,新西兰NZ,智利CL 9 澳AU 10.5 瑞士CH 13 韩国KR	0 受惠国$_2$LD$_2$	40	--G.V.W. exceeding 20 tons
	ex87042300	起重55吨及以上的汽车起重机用底盘	Δ8				Chassis (incoraporating cabs) of crane lorries, eifting capacity≥55t
	ex87042300	装有驾驶室的固井水泥车、压裂车、混砂车、连续油管车、液氮泵车用底盘（车辆总重量>35吨，装驾驶室）	Δ10				Chassis (incoraporating cabs) of cementing unit trucks, fractruring unit trucks , coil unit trucks, liquid nitrogen trucks, and mixing sand trucks (G.V.W exceeding 35t)
	ex87042300	车辆总重量≥31吨清障车专用底盘	Δ10				Special chassis for the wrecker of G.V.W≥31t
		-装有点燃式活塞内燃发动机的其他货车：					-Other, with spark-ignition internal combustion piston engine:
7510	8704.3100	--车辆总重量不超过5吨	25	0 冰岛IS,哥CR,新西兰NZ,智利CL 15 澳AU 20 东盟AS 22.5 韩国KR	0 受惠国$_2$LD$_2$	70	--G.V.W. not exceeding 5 tons
		--车辆总重量超过5吨：					--Of a gross vehicle weight exceeding 5 tonnes:
7511	8704.3230	---车辆总重量超过5吨，但不超过8吨	20	0 冰岛IS,哥CR,新西兰NZ,智利CL 6 秘鲁PE 12 澳AU 14 瑞士CH 17.3 韩国KR	0 受惠国$_1$LD$_1$	70	---G.V.W. exceeding 5 tons, but not exceeding 8 tons

序号 No.	税则号列 Tariff Line	中文货品名称 Article Description in Chinese	最惠国税率 MFN(%)	协定税率 Agreement(%)	特惠税率 SP(%)	普通税率 Gen(%)	英文货品名称 Article Description
7512	8704.3240	---车辆总重量超过8吨	20	0 冰岛IS,哥CR,新西兰NZ,智利CL 6 秘鲁PE 12 澳AU 14 瑞士CH 17.3 韩国KR	0 受惠国$_1$LD$_1$	70	---G.V.W. exceeding 8 tons
7513	8704.9000	-其他	25	0 冰岛IS,东盟AS,哥CR,新加坡SG,新西兰NZ,智利CL 7.5 秘鲁PE 15 澳AU 22.5 韩国KR	0 受惠国$_1$LD$_1$	70	-Other
	87.05	**特殊用途的机动车辆(例如,抢修车、起重车、救火车、混凝土搅拌车、道路清洁车、喷洒车、流动工场车及流动放射线检查车),但主要用于载人或运货的车辆除外:**					**Special purpose motor vehicles, other than those principally designed for the transport of persons or goods (for example, breakdown lorries, crane lorries, fire fighting vehicles, concrete-mixer lorries, road sweeper lorries, spraying lorries, mobile workshops, mobile radiological units) :**
		-起重车:					-Crane lorries:
		---全路面起重车:					---All-road crane lorries:
7514	8705.1021	----最大起重重量不超过50吨	15	0 冰岛IS,东盟AS,哥CR,新加坡SG,新西兰NZ,智利CL 4.5 秘鲁PE 9 澳AU 10.5 瑞士CH 12 巴PK 13 韩国KR	0 受惠国$_1$LD$_1$	30	----Of maximum hoisting capacity not more than 50 tons
7515	8705.1022	----最大起重重量超过50吨,但不超过100吨	10	0 冰岛IS,东盟AS,哥CR,秘鲁PE,新加坡SG,新西兰NZ,智利CL 4 瑞士CH 5 巴PK 6 澳AU 8.6 韩国KR	0 受惠国LD	30	----Of a maximum hoisting capacity exceeding 50 tons but not exceeding 100 tons
7516	8705.1023	----最大起重重量超过100吨	10	0 冰岛IS,东盟AS,哥CR,秘鲁PE,新加坡SG,新西兰NZ,智利CL 4 瑞士CH 5 巴PK 6 澳AU 8.6 韩国KR	0 受惠国LD	30	----Of a maximum hoisting capacity exceeding 100 tons
		---其他:					---Other:
7517	8705.1091	----最大起重重量不超过50吨	15	0 冰岛IS,东盟AS,哥CR,新加坡SG,新西兰NZ,智利CL 4.5 秘鲁PE 9 澳AU 10.5 瑞士CH 12 巴PK 13 韩国KR	0 受惠国$_1$LD$_1$	30	----Of maximum hoisting capacity not more than 50 tons
7518	8705.1092	----最大起重重量超过50吨,但不超过100吨	10	0 冰岛IS,东盟AS,哥CR,秘鲁PE,新加坡SG,新西兰NZ,智利CL 4 瑞士CH 5 巴PK 6 澳AU 8.6 韩国KR	0 受惠国LD	30	----Of a maximum hoisting capacity exceeding 50 tons but not exceeding 100 tons

序号 No.	税则号列 Tariff Line	中文货品名称 Article Description in Chinese	最惠国税率 MFN(%)	协定税率 Agreement(%)	特惠税率 SP(%)	普通税率 Gen(%)	英文货品名称 Article Description
7519	8705.1093	----最大起重重量超过100吨	10	0 冰岛IS,东盟AS,哥CR,秘鲁PE,新加坡SG,新西兰NZ,智利CL 4 瑞士CH 5 巴PK 6 澳AU 8.6 韩国KR	0 受惠国LD	30	----Of a maximum hoisting capacity exceeding 100 tons
7520	8705.2000	-钻探车	12	0 冰岛IS,东盟AS,哥CR,秘鲁PE,新加坡SG,新西兰NZ,智利CL 6 巴PK 7.2 澳AU 8.4 瑞士CH 10.4 韩国KR	0 受惠国LD	17	-Mobile drilling derricks
		-救火车:					-Fire fighting vehicles:
7521	8705.3010	---装有云梯的救火车	3	0 澳AU,巴PK,冰岛IS,东盟AS,哥CR,秘鲁PE,瑞士CH,新西兰NZ,智利CL 2.6 韩国KR	0 受惠国LD	8	---Mounted with scaling ladder
7522	8705.3090	---其他	3	0 澳AU,巴PK,冰岛IS,东盟AS,哥CR,秘鲁PE,瑞士CH,新西兰NZ,智利CL 2.6 韩国KR	0 受惠国LD	8	---Other
7523	8705.4000	-混凝土搅拌车	15	0 冰岛IS,东盟AS,哥CR,新加坡SG,新西兰NZ,智利CL 4.5 秘鲁PE 7.5 巴PK 9 澳AU 10.5 瑞士CH 13 韩国KR 13.5 亚太AP	0 受惠国$_1$LD$_1$	35	-Concrete-mixer lorries
		-其他:					-Other:
7524	8705.9010	---无线电通信车	9	0 冰岛IS,东盟AS,哥CR,秘鲁PE,新加坡SG,新西兰NZ,智利CL 3.6 瑞士CH 5 巴PK 5.4 澳AU 7.8 韩国KR 8.1 亚太AP	0 受惠国LD	35	---Radio communication vans
7525	8705.9020	---放射线检查车	9	0 冰岛IS,东盟AS,哥CR,秘鲁PE,新西兰NZ,智利CL 3.6 瑞士CH 5 巴PK 5.4 澳AU 7.8 韩国KR 8.1 亚太AP	0 受惠国LD	14	---Mobile radiological units
7526	8705.9030	---环境监测车	12	0 冰岛IS,东盟AS,哥CR,秘鲁PE,新加坡SG,新西兰NZ,智利CL 5 巴PK 7.2 澳AU 8.4 瑞士CH 10.4 韩国KR 10.8 亚太AP	0 受惠国$_1$LD$_1$	20	---Mobile environmental monitoring units
7527	8705.9040	---医疗车	12	0 冰岛IS,东盟AS,哥CR,秘鲁PE,新加坡SG,新西兰NZ,智利CL 5 巴PK 7.2 澳AU 8.4 瑞士CH 10.8 韩国KR,亚太AP	0 受惠国$_1$LD$_1$	30	---Mobile clinics

序号 No.	税则号列 Tariff Line	中文货品名称 Article Description in Chinese	最惠国税率 MFN(%)	协定税率 Agreement(%)	特惠税率 SP(%)	普通税率 Gen(%)	英文货品名称 Article Description
		---电源车：					---Mobile electric generator sets:
7528	8705.9051	----航空电源车（频率为400赫兹）	12	0 冰岛IS,东盟AS,哥CR,秘鲁PE,新加坡SG,新西兰NZ,智利CL 5 巴PK 7.2 澳AU 8.4 瑞士CH 10.4 韩国KR 10.8 亚太AP	0 受惠国$_1$LD$_1$	30	----Airplane charging vehicles (frequency 400 Hz)
7529	8705.9059	----其他	12	0 冰岛IS,东盟AS,哥CR,秘鲁PE,新加坡SG,新西兰NZ,智利CL 5 巴PK 7.2 澳AU 8.4 瑞士CH 10.4 韩国KR 10.8 亚太AP	0 受惠国$_1$LD$_1$	30	----Other
7530	8705.9060	---飞机加油车、调温车、除冰车	12	0 冰岛IS,东盟AS,哥CR,秘鲁PE,新加坡SG,新西兰NZ,智利CL 5 巴PK 7.2 澳AU 8.4 瑞士CH 10.4 韩国KR 10.8 亚太AP	0 受惠国$_1$LD$_1$	35	---Mobile vehicles for aircraft refuelling, air-conditioning or deicing
7531	8705.9070	---道路（包括跑道）扫雪车	12	0 冰岛IS,东盟AS,哥CR,秘鲁PE,新加坡SG,新西兰NZ,智利CL 5 巴PK 7.2 澳AU 8.4 瑞士CH 10.4 韩国KR 10.8 亚太AP	0 受惠国$_1$LD$_1$	35	---Snow sweepers vehicles for cleansing streets or airfield runways
7532	8705.9080	---石油测井车、压裂车、混沙车	12	0 冰岛IS,东盟AS,哥CR,秘鲁PE,新加坡SG,新西兰NZ,智利CL 5 巴PK 7.2 澳AU 8.4 瑞士CH 10.4 韩国KR 10.8 亚太AP	0 受惠国$_1$LD$_1$	35	---Petroleum well logging trucks, fracturing unit trucks and mixing sand trucks
		---其他：					---Other:
7533	8705.9091	----混凝土泵车	12	0 冰岛IS,东盟AS,哥CR,秘鲁PE,新加坡SG,新西兰NZ,智利CL 5 巴PK 7.2 澳AU 8.4 瑞士CH 10.4 韩国KR 10.8 亚太AP	0 受惠国$_1$LD$_1$	35	----Concrete pump truck
7534	8705.9099	----其他	12	0 冰岛IS,东盟AS,哥CR,秘鲁PE,新加坡SG,新西兰NZ,智利CL 5 巴PK 7.2 澳AU 8.4 瑞士CH 10.4 韩国KR 10.8 亚太AP	0 受惠国$_1$LD$_1$	35	----Other
	ex87059099	跑道除冰车	Δ10				Runway deicing trucks
	87.06	**装有发动机的机动车辆底盘，税号87.01至87.05所列车辆用：**					**Chassis fitted with engines, for the motor vehicles of headings 8701 to 8705:**

序号 No.	税则号列 Tariff Line	中文货品名称 Article Description in Chinese	最惠国税率 MFN(%)	协定税率 Agreement(%)	特惠税率 SP(%)	普通税率 Gen(%)	英文货品名称 Article Description
7535	8706.0010	---非公路用自卸车底盘	8	0 冰岛IS,东盟AS,哥CR,秘鲁PE,新西兰NZ,智利CL 3.2 瑞士CH 4.8 澳AU 5 巴PK 6.9 韩国KR	0 受惠国$_1$LD$_1$	14	---For the vehicles of subheading No. 8704.1030 or 8704.1090
		---货车底盘:					---For the vehicles of subheading Nos. 8704.2100 to 8704.9000:
7536	8706.0021	----车辆总重量在14吨及以上的	10	0 冰岛IS,哥CR,新西兰NZ,智利CL 4 瑞士CH 6 澳AU 8.6 韩国KR	0 受惠国$_2$LD$_2$	30	----For vehicles G.V.W of 14 tons or more
7537	8706.0022	----车辆总重量在14吨以下的	10	0 冰岛IS,哥CR,秘鲁PE,新西兰NZ,智利CL 4 瑞士CH 6 澳AU 8.6 韩国KR	0 受惠国$_1$LD$_1$	45	----For vehicles G.V.W less than 14 tons
7538	8706.0030	---大型客车底盘	20	0 冰岛IS,东盟AS,哥CR,新加坡SG,新西兰NZ,智利CL 12 澳AU 14 瑞士CH 17.3 韩国KR	0 受惠国$_2$LD$_2$	70	---For passenger motor vehicles with 30 seats or more
7539	8706.0040	---汽车起重机底盘	20	0 冰岛IS,东盟AS,哥CR,新加坡SG,新西兰NZ,智利CL 6 秘鲁PE 12 澳AU 14 瑞士CH 17.3 韩国KR	0 受惠国$_1$LD$_1$	100	---For crane trucks
7540	8706.0090	---其他	10	0 冰岛IS,东盟AS,哥CR,秘鲁PE,新加坡SG,新西兰NZ,智利CL 4 瑞士CH 6 澳AU 8.6 韩国KR	0 受惠国$_1$LD$_1$	100	---Other
	87.07	**机动车辆的车身(包括驾驶室),税号87.01至87.05所列车辆用:**					**Bodies (including cabs), for the motor vehicles of headings 8701 to 8705:**
7541	8707.1000	-税号87.03所列车辆用	10	0 冰岛IS,东盟AS,哥CR,秘鲁PE,新加坡SG,新西兰NZ,智利CL 4 瑞士CH 6 澳AU 8.6 韩国KR	0 受惠国$_1$LD$_1$	100	-For the vehicles of heading No.87.03
		-其他:					-Other:
7542	8707.9010	---税号8702.1092、8702.1093、8702.9020及8702.9030所列车辆用	10	0 冰岛IS,东盟AS,哥CR,秘鲁PE,新加坡SG,新西兰NZ,智利CL 4 瑞士CH 5 巴PK 6 澳AU 8.6 韩国KR 9 亚太AP	0 受惠国$_1$LD$_1$	70	---For the vehicles of subheading No.8702.1092、8702.1093、8702.9020 or 8702.9030
7543	8707.9090	---其他	10	0 冰岛IS,东盟AS,哥CR,秘鲁PE,新加坡SG,新西兰NZ,智利CL 4 瑞士CH 5 巴PK 6 澳AU 8.6 韩国KR 9 亚太AP	0 受惠国$_1$LD$_1$	70	---Other

序号 No.	税则号列 Tariff Line	中文货品名称 Article Description in Chinese	最惠国税率 MFN(%)	协定税率 Agreement(%)	特惠税率 SP(%)	普通税率 Gen(%)	英文货品名称 Article Description
	87.08	机动车辆的零件、附件，税号87.01至87.05所列车辆用：					**Parts and accessories of the motor vehicles of headings 8701 to 8705:**
7544	8708.1000	-缓冲器（保险杠）及其零件	10	0 冰岛IS,东盟AS,哥CR,秘鲁PE,台湾TW,新加坡SG,新西兰NZ,智利CL 4 瑞士CH 5 巴PK 6 澳AU 9 韩国KR 9.6 亚太AP	0 受惠国LD	100	-Bumpers and parts thereof
		-车身（包括驾驶室）的其他零件、附件：					-Other parts and accessories of bodies (including cabs) :
7545	8708.2100	--座椅安全带	10	0 澳门MO,冰岛IS,东盟AS,哥CR,秘鲁PE,新加坡SG,新西兰NZ,智利CL 4 瑞士CH 5 巴PK 6 澳AU 8.6 韩国KR	0 受惠国LD	100	--Safety seat belts
		--其他：					--Other:
7546	8708.2930	---车窗玻璃升降器	10	0 冰岛IS,哥CR,秘鲁PE,台湾TW,香港HK,新西兰NZ,智利CL 4 瑞士CH 6 澳AU 8.6 韩国KR 9 巴PK,亚太AP	0 受惠国LD	100	---Windowpane raiser
		---天窗：					---Sunroofs:
7547	8708.2941	----电动的	10	0 冰岛IS,东盟AS,哥CR,秘鲁PE,台湾TW,香港HK,新加坡SG,新西兰NZ,智利CL 4 瑞士CH 5 巴PK 6 澳AU 9 亚太AP 9.6 韩国KR	0 受惠国LD	100	----Electric
7548	8708.2942	----手动的	10	0 冰岛IS,东盟AS,哥CR,秘鲁PE,台湾TW,香港HK,新加坡SG,新西兰NZ,智利CL 4 瑞士CH 5 巴PK 6 澳AU 8.6 韩国KR 9 亚太AP	0 受惠国LD	100	----Manual
		---其他车身覆盖件：					---Other body Coverings:
7549	8708.2951	----侧围	10	0 冰岛IS,东盟AS,哥CR,秘鲁PE,台湾TW,新加坡SG,新西兰NZ,智利CL 4 瑞士CH 5 巴PK 6 澳AU 9 韩国KR,亚太AP	0 受惠国LD	100	----Side panels
7550	8708.2952	----车门	10	0 冰岛IS,东盟AS,哥CR,秘鲁PE,台湾TW,新加坡SG,新西兰NZ,智利CL 4 瑞士CH 5 巴PK 6 澳AU 9 韩国KR,亚太AP	0 受惠国LD	100	----Car doors

序号 No.	税则号列 Tariff Line	中文货品名称 Article Description in Chinese	最惠国税率 MFN(%)	协定税率 Agreement(%)	特惠税率 SP(%)	普通税率 Gen(%)	英文货品名称 Article Description
7551	8708.2953	----发动机罩盖	10	0 冰岛IS,东盟AS,哥CR,秘鲁PE,台湾TW,新加坡SG,新西兰NZ,智利CL 4 瑞士CH 5 巴PK 6 澳AU 9 韩国KR,亚太AP	0 受惠国LD	100	----Engine hood
7552	8708.2954	----前围	10	0 冰岛IS,东盟AS,哥CR,秘鲁PE,台湾TW,新加坡SG,新西兰NZ,智利CL 4 瑞士CH 5 巴PK 6 澳AU 9 韩国KR,亚太AP	0 受惠国LD	100	----Front wall
7553	8708.2955	----行李箱盖（或背门）	10	0 冰岛IS,东盟AS,哥CR,秘鲁PE,台湾TW,新加坡SG,新西兰NZ,智利CL 4 瑞士CH 5 巴PK 6 澳AU 9 韩国KR,亚太AP	0 受惠国LD	100	----Baggage compartment lids (or back door)
7554	8708.2956	----后围	10	0 冰岛IS,东盟AS,哥CR,秘鲁PE,台湾TW,新加坡SG,新西兰NZ,智利CL 4 瑞士CH 5 巴PK 6 澳AU 9 韩国KR,亚太AP	0 受惠国LD	100	----Rear wall
7555	8708.2957	----翼子板（或叶子板）	10	0 冰岛IS,东盟AS,哥CR,秘鲁PE,台湾TW,新加坡SG,新西兰NZ,智利CL 4 瑞士CH 5 巴PK 6 澳AU 9 韩国KR,亚太AP	0 受惠国LD	100	----Fender
7556	8708.2959	----其他	10	0 冰岛IS,东盟AS,哥CR,秘鲁PE,台湾TW,新加坡SG,新西兰NZ,智利CL 4 瑞士CH 5 巴PK 6 澳AU 9 韩国KR,亚太AP	0 受惠国LD	100	----Other
7557	8708.2990	---其他	10	0 冰岛IS,东盟AS,哥CR,秘鲁PE,台湾TW,新加坡SG,新西兰NZ,智利CL 5 巴PK 6 澳AU 7 瑞士CH 9 亚太AP 9.6 韩国KR	0 受惠国LD	100	---Other
		-制动器、助力制动器及其零件：					-Brakes and servo-brakes; parts thereof:

序号 No.	税则号列 Tariff Line	中文货品名称 Article Description in Chinese	最惠国税率 MFN(%)	协定税率 Agreement(%)	特惠税率 SP(%)	普通税率 Gen(%)	英文货品名称 Article Description
7558	8708.3010	---装在蹄片上的制动摩擦片	10	0 冰岛IS,东盟AS,哥CR,新加坡SG,新西兰NZ,智利CL 3 秘鲁PE 4 瑞士CH 5 巴PK 6 澳AU 8 韩国KR	0 受惠国LD	100	---Mounted brake linings
		---防抱死制动系统:					---Anti-skid brake system:
7559	8708.3021	----子目号87.01、8704.1030及8704.1090所列车辆用	6	0 巴PK,冰岛IS,东盟AS,哥CR,秘鲁PE,新西兰NZ,智利CL 2.4 瑞士CH 3.6 澳AU 5.2 韩国KR 5.4 亚太AP	0 受惠国LD	11	----Of the vehicles of subheading No.87.01, 8704.1030 or 8704.1090
7560	8708.3029	----其他	10	0 冰岛IS,哥CR,秘鲁PE,新西兰NZ,智利CL 4 瑞士CH 6 澳AU 9 巴PK,亚太AP 9.6 韩国KR	0 受惠国LD	100	----Other
		---其他:					---Other:
7561	8708.3091	----税号87.01所列车辆用	6	0 巴PK,冰岛IS,东盟AS,哥CR,秘鲁PE,新西兰NZ,智利CL 2.4 瑞士CH 3.6 澳AU 5.2 韩国KR 5.4 亚太AP	0 受惠国LD	14	----Of the vehicles of heading No.87.01
7562	8708.3092	----子目号8702.1091及8702.9010所列车辆用	10	0 冰岛IS,哥CR,秘鲁PE,新西兰NZ,智利CL 4 瑞士CH 6 澳AU 9 巴PK,韩国KR,亚太AP	0 受惠国LD	70	----Of the vehicles of subheading No.8702.1091 or 8702.9010
7563	8708.3093	----子目号8704.1030及8704.1090所列车辆用	6	0 巴PK,冰岛IS,东盟AS,哥CR,秘鲁PE,新西兰NZ,智利CL 2.4 瑞士CH 3.6 澳AU 5.2 韩国KR 5.4 亚太AP	0 受惠国LD	11	----Of the vehicles of subheading No.8704.1030 or 8704.1090
7564	8708.3094	----子目号8704.2100、8704.2230、8704.3100及8704.3230所列车辆用	10	0 冰岛IS,哥CR,秘鲁PE,新西兰NZ,智利CL 4 瑞士CH 6 澳AU 9 巴PK,韩国KR,亚太AP	0 受惠国LD	45	----Of the vehicles of subheading No.8704.2100, 8704.2230, 8704.3100 or 8704.3230
7565	8708.3095	----子目号8704.2240、8704.2300及8704.3240所列车辆用	10	0 冰岛IS,东盟AS,哥CR,秘鲁PE,新加坡SG,新西兰NZ,智利CL 4 瑞士CH 5 巴PK 6 澳AU 8 韩国KR 9 亚太AP	0 受惠国LD	30	----Of the vehicles of subheading No.8704.2240, 8704.2300 or 8704.3240
7566	8708.3096	----税号87.05所列车辆用	10	0 冰岛IS,东盟AS,哥CR,秘鲁PE,新加坡SG,新西兰NZ,智利CL 4 瑞士CH 5 巴PK 6 澳AU 8.6 韩国KR 9 亚太AP	0 受惠国LD	100	----Of the vehicles of heading No.87.05

序号 No.	税则号列 Tariff Line	中文货品名称 Article Description in Chinese	最惠国税率 MFN(%)	协定税率 Agreement(%)	特惠税率 SP(%)	普通税率 Gen(%)	英文货品名称 Article Description
7567	8708.3099	-----其他	10	0 冰岛IS,哥CR,秘鲁PE,新西兰NZ,智利CL 6 澳AU 7 瑞士CH 9 巴PK,韩国KR,亚太AP	0 受惠国LD	100	----Other
	ex87083099	纯电动或混合动力汽车用电动制动器(由制动器电子控制单元、踏板行程模拟器、制动执行器等组成)	Δ5				Electrically operated brake for electric vehicle or hybrid electric vehicles (composed of Electronic control unit, Pedal travel simulator, Brake actuator etc.)
		-变速箱及其零件:					-Gear boxes and parts thereof:
7568	8708.4010	---税号87.01所列车辆用	6	0 冰岛IS,东盟AS,哥CR,秘鲁PE,台湾TW,新西兰NZ,智利CL 2.4 瑞士CH 3.6 澳AU 5 巴PK	0 受惠国LD	14	---Of the vehicles of heading No.87.01
7569	8708.4020	---子目号8702.1091及8702.9010所列车辆用	10	0 冰岛IS,哥CR,台湾TW,新西兰NZ,智利CL 4 瑞士CH 6 澳AU	0 受惠国$_2$LD$_2$	70	---Of the vehicles of subheading No.8702.1091 or 8702.9010
7570	8708.4030	---子目号8704.1030及8704.1090所列车辆用	6	0 冰岛IS,东盟AS,哥CR,台湾TW,新西兰NZ,智利CL 2.4 瑞士CH 3.6 澳AU 5 巴PK 5.5 韩国KR	0 受惠国$_2$LD$_2$	11	---Of the vehicles of subheading No. 8704.1030 or 8704.1090
	ex87084030	扭矩>1500Nm非公路自卸车用变速箱	Δ3				Gear boxes of dumpers designed for off-highway use, torque>1500Nm
7571	8708.4040	---子目号8704.2100、8704.2230、8704.3100及8704.3230所列车辆用	10	0 冰岛IS,哥CR,台湾TW,新西兰NZ,智利CL 4 瑞士CH 6 澳AU	0 受惠国$_2$LD$_2$	45	---Of the vehicles of subheading No. 8704.2100, 8704.2230, 8704.3100 or 8704.3230
7572	8708.4050	---子目号8704.2240、8704.2300及8704.3240所列车辆用	10	0 冰岛IS,哥CR,台湾TW,新西兰NZ,智利CL 4 瑞士CH 6 澳AU	0 受惠国$_2$LD$_2$	30	---Of the vehicles of subheading No. 8704.2240, 8704.2300 or 8704.3240
7573	8708.4060	---税号87.05所列车辆用	10	0 冰岛IS,东盟AS,哥CR,秘鲁PE,台湾TW,新加坡SG,新西兰NZ,智利CL 4 瑞士CH 5 巴PK 6 澳AU	0 受惠国LD	100	---Of the vehicles of heading No.87.05
		---其他:					---Other:
7574	8708.4091	----小轿车用自动换档变速箱及其零件	10	0 冰岛IS,哥CR,新西兰NZ,智利CL 4 瑞士CH 6 澳AU 9.2 韩国KR	0 受惠国$_2$LD$_2$	100	----Automatic transmission for saloon cars and parts thereof
	ex87084091	小轿车用自动换档变速箱及其零件(6档及6档以上)	Δ6.5				Automatic transmission and parts thereof for saloon cars (6-speed and above)
7575	8708.4099	----其他	10	0 冰岛IS,东盟AS,哥CR,台湾TW,新加坡SG,新西兰NZ,智利CL 4 瑞士CH 6 澳AU	0 受惠国$_2$LD$_2$	100	----Other
		-装有差速器的驱动桥及其零件，不论是否装有其他传动部件；非驱动桥及其零件:					-Drive-axles with differential, whether or not provided with other transmission components, and non-driving axles; parts thereof:

序号 No.	税则号列 Tariff Line	中文货品名称 Article Description in Chinese	最惠国税率 MFN(%)	协定税率 Agreement(%)	特惠税率 SP(%)	普通税率 Gen(%)	英文货品名称 Article Description
		---装有差速器的驱动桥及其零件，不论是否装有其他传动部件：					---Drive-axles with differential, whether or not provided with other transmission components, parts thereof:
7576	8708.5071	----税号87.01所列车辆用	6	0 巴PK,冰岛IS,东盟AS,哥CR,秘鲁PE,新西兰NZ,智利CL 2.4 瑞士CH 3.6 澳AU 5.2 韩国KR 5.4 亚太AP	0 受惠国LD	14	----Of the vehicles of heading No.87.01
7577	8708.5072	----子目号8702.1091及8702.9010所列车辆用	10	0 冰岛IS,哥CR,秘鲁PE,新西兰NZ,智利CL 4 瑞士CH 6 澳AU 9 巴PK,亚太AP 9.6 韩国KR	0 受惠国LD	70	----Of the vehicles of subheading No. 8702.1091 or 8702.9010
	ex87085072	轴荷≥10t的中后驱动桥的零件	Δ8				Parts of middle and rear drive-axles, axle capacity≥10t
7578	8708.5073	----子目号8704.1030及8704.1090所列车辆用	6	0 巴PK,冰岛IS,东盟AS,哥CR,秘鲁PE,新西兰NZ,智利CL 2.4 瑞士CH 3.6 澳AU 5.2 韩国KR 5.4 亚太AP	0 受惠国LD	11	----Of the vehicles of subheading No. 8704.1030 or 8704.1090
7579	8708.5074	----子目号8704.2100、8704.2230、8704.3100及8704.3230所列车辆用	10	0 冰岛IS,哥CR,秘鲁PE,新西兰NZ,智利CL 4 瑞士CH 6 澳AU 9 巴PK,韩国KR,亚太AP	0 受惠国LD	45	----Of the vehicles of subheading No. 8704.2100, 8704.2230, 8704.3100 or 8704.3230
7580	8708.5075	----子目号8704.2240、8704.2300及8704.3240所列车辆用	10	0 冰岛IS,哥CR,秘鲁PE,新西兰NZ,智利CL 4 瑞士CH 6 澳AU 9 巴PK,韩国KR,亚太AP	0 受惠国LD	30	----Of the vehicles of subheading No. 8704.2240, 8704.2300 or 8704.3240
7581	8708.5076	----税号87.05所列车辆用	10	0 冰岛IS,东盟AS,哥CR,秘鲁PE,新加坡SG,新西兰NZ,智利CL 4 瑞士CH 5 巴PK 6 澳AU 8.6 韩国KR 9 亚太AP	0 受惠国LD	100	----Of the vehicles of heading No.87.05
7582	8708.5079	----其他	10	0 冰岛IS,哥CR,秘鲁PE,新西兰NZ,智利CL 6 澳AU 8 瑞士CH 9 巴PK,亚太AP 9.6 韩国KR	0 受惠国LD	100	----Other
		---非驱动的桥及其零件：					---Non-driving axles and parts thereof:
7583	8708.5081	----税号87.01所列车辆用	6	0 冰岛IS,东盟AS,哥CR,秘鲁PE,新西兰NZ,智利CL 2.4 瑞士CH 3.6 澳AU 5 巴PK 5.2 韩国KR	0 受惠国LD	14	----Of the vehicles of heading No.87.01

序号 No.	税则号列 Tariff Line	中文货品名称 Article Description in Chinese	最惠国税率 MFN(%)	协定税率 Agreement(%)	特惠税率 SP(%)	普通税率 Gen(%)	英文货品名称 Article Description
7584	8708.5082	----子目号8702.1091及8702.9010所列车辆用	15	0 冰岛IS,东盟AS,哥CR,新加坡SG,新西兰NZ,智利CL 4.5 秘鲁PE 9 澳AU 9.7 巴PK 10.5 瑞士CH 13.5 韩国KR	0 受惠国$_1$LD$_1$	70	----Of the vehicles of subheading No. 8702.1091 or 8702.9010
7585	8708.5083	----子目号8704.1030及8704.1090所列车辆用	6	0 冰岛IS,东盟AS,哥CR,秘鲁PE,新西兰NZ,智利CL 2.4 瑞士CH 3.6 澳AU 5 巴PK 5.2 韩国KR	0 受惠国LD	11	----Of the vehicles of subheading No. 8704.1030 or 8704.1090
7586	8708.5084	----子目号8704.2100、8704.2230、8704.3100及8704.3230所列车辆用	10	0 冰岛IS,东盟AS,哥CR,秘鲁PE,新加坡SG,新西兰NZ,智利CL 4 瑞士CH 5 巴PK 6 澳AU 8.6 韩国KR	0 受惠国LD	45	----Of the vehicles of subheading No. 8704.2100, 8704.2230, 8704.3100 or 8704.3230
7587	8708.5085	----子目号8704.2240、8704.2300及8704.3240所列车辆用	10	0 冰岛IS,东盟AS,哥CR,秘鲁PE,新加坡SG,新西兰NZ,智利CL 4 瑞士CH 5 巴PK 6 澳AU 8.6 韩国KR	0 受惠国LD	30	----Of the vehicles of subheading No.8704.2240, 8704.2300 or 8704.3240
7588	8708.5086	----税号87.05所列车辆用	10	0 冰岛IS,东盟AS,哥CR,秘鲁PE,新加坡SG,新西兰NZ,智利CL 4 瑞士CH 5 巴PK 6 澳AU 8.6 韩国KR	0 受惠国LD	100	----Of the vehicles of heading No.87.05
7589	8708.5089	----其他	10	0 冰岛IS,东盟AS,哥CR,秘鲁PE,新加坡SG,新西兰NZ,智利CL 4 瑞士CH 5 巴PK 6 澳AU	0 受惠国LD	100	----Other
		-车轮及其零件、附件：					-Road wheels and parts and accessories thereof:
7590	8708.7010	---子目号87.01所列车辆用	6	0 冰岛IS,东盟AS,哥CR,秘鲁PE,台湾TW,新西兰NZ,智利CL 2.4 瑞士CH 3.6 澳AU 5 巴PK 5.2 韩国KR	0 受惠国LD	14	---Of the vehicles of heading No.87.01
7591	8708.7020	---子目号8702.1091及8702.9010所列车辆用	10	0 冰岛IS,东盟AS,哥CR,秘鲁PE,台湾TW,新加坡SG,新西兰NZ,智利CL 4 瑞士CH 5 巴PK 6 澳AU 8.6 韩国KR	0 受惠国LD	70	---Of the vehicles of subheading No.8702.1091 or 8702.9010
7592	8708.7030	---子目号8704.1030及8704.1090所列车辆用	6	0 冰岛IS,东盟AS,哥CR,秘鲁PE,台湾TW,新西兰NZ,智利CL 2.4 瑞士CH 3.6 澳AU 5 巴PK 5.2 韩国KR	0 受惠国LD	11	---Of the vehicles of subheading No.8704.1030 or 8704.1090

序号 No.	税则号列 Tariff Line	中文货品名称 Article Description in Chinese	最惠国税率 MFN(%)	协定税率 Agreement(%)	特惠税率 SP(%)	普通税率 Gen(%)	英文货品名称 Article Description
7593	8708.7040	---子目号8704.2100、8704.2230、8704.3100及8704.3230所列车辆用	10	0 冰岛IS,东盟AS,哥CR,秘鲁PE,台湾TW,新加坡SG,新西兰NZ,智利CL 4 瑞士CH 5 巴PK 6 澳AU 8 韩国KR	0 受惠国LD	45	---Of the vehicles of subheading No.8704.2100, 8704.2230, 8704.3100 or 8704.3230
7594	8708.7050	---子目号8704.2240、8704.2300及8704.3240所列车辆用	10	0 冰岛IS,东盟AS,哥CR,秘鲁PE,台湾TW,新加坡SG,新西兰NZ,智利CL 4 瑞士CH 5 巴PK 6 澳AU 8.6 韩国KR	0 受惠国LD	30	---Of the vehicles of subheading No.8704.2240, 8704.2300 or 8704.3240
7595	8708.7060	---税号87.05所列车辆用	10	0 冰岛IS,东盟AS,哥CR,秘鲁PE,台湾TW,新加坡SG,新西兰NZ,智利CL 4 瑞士CH 5 巴PK 6 澳AU 8.6 韩国KR	0 受惠国LD	100	---Of the vehicles of heading No.87.05
		---其他:					---Other:
7596	8708.7091	----铝合金制的	10	0 冰岛IS,东盟AS,哥CR,秘鲁PE,台湾TW,新加坡SG,新西兰NZ,智利CL 4 瑞士CH 5 巴PK 6 澳AU	0 受惠国LD	100	----Of Aluminium alloy
7597	8708.7099	----其他	10	0 冰岛IS,东盟AS,哥CR,秘鲁PE,台湾TW,新加坡SG,新西兰NZ,智利CL 4 瑞士CH 5 巴PK 6 澳AU	0 受惠国LD	100	----Other
		-悬挂系统及其零件(包括减震器):					-Suspension systems and parts thereof (including shock-absorbers) :
7598	8708.8010	---税号87.03所列车辆用	10	0 冰岛IS,东盟AS,哥CR,秘鲁PE,新加坡SG,新西兰NZ,智利CL 4 瑞士CH 5 巴PK 6 澳AU 8 韩国KR 9 亚太AP	0 受惠国LD	100	---Of the vehicles of heading No.87.03
7599	8708.8090	---其他	10	0 冰岛IS,东盟AS,哥CR,秘鲁PE,新加坡SG,新西兰NZ,智利CL 4 瑞士CH 5 巴PK 6 澳AU 8 韩国KR 9 亚太AP	0 受惠国LD	100	---Other
		-其他零件、附件:					-Other parts and accessories:
		--散热器及其零件:					--Radiators and parts thereof:

序号 No.	税则号列 Tariff Line	中文货品名称 Article Description in Chinese	最惠国税率 MFN(%)	协定税率 Agreement(%)	特惠税率 SP(%)	普通税率 Gen(%)	英文货品名称 Article Description
7600	8708.9110	---水箱散热器	10	0 冰岛IS,东盟AS,哥CR,秘鲁PE,新加坡SG,新西兰NZ,智利CL 4 瑞士CH 5 巴PK 6 澳AU 8.6 韩国KR	0 受惠国LD	100	---Radiator
7601	8708.9120	---机油冷却器	10	0 冰岛IS,东盟AS,哥CR,秘鲁PE,新加坡SG,新西兰NZ,智利CL 4 瑞士CH 5 巴PK 6 澳AU 8.6 韩国KR	0 受惠国LD	100	---Oil Coolor
7602	8708.9190	---其他	10	0 冰岛IS,东盟AS,哥CR,秘鲁PE,新加坡SG,新西兰NZ,智利CL 4 瑞士CH 5 巴PK 6 澳AU 8.6 韩国KR	0 受惠国LD	100	---Other
7603	8708.9200	--消声器（消音器）、排气管及其零件	10	0 冰岛IS,东盟AS,哥CR,秘鲁PE,新加坡SG,新西兰NZ,智利CL 4 瑞士CH 5 巴PK 6 澳AU	0 受惠国LD	100	--Silencers (mufflers) and exhaust pipes; parts thereof
		--离合器及其零件：					--Clutches and parts thereof:
7604	8708.9310	---税号87.01所列车辆用	6	0 冰岛IS,东盟AS,哥CR,秘鲁PE,新西兰NZ,智利CL 2.4 瑞士CH 3.6 澳AU 5 巴PK 5.2 韩国KR	0 受惠国LD	14	---Of the vehicles of heading No.87.01
7605	8708.9320	---子目号8702.1091及8702.9010所列车辆用	10	0 冰岛IS,东盟AS,哥CR,秘鲁PE,新加坡SG,新西兰NZ,智利CL 4 瑞士CH 5 巴PK 6 澳AU 9 韩国KR	0 受惠国LD	70	---Of the vehicles of subheading No. 8702.1091 or 8702.9010
7606	8708.9330	---子目号8704.1030及8704.1090所列车辆用	6	0 冰岛IS,东盟AS,哥CR,秘鲁PE,新西兰NZ,智利CL 2.4 瑞士CH 3.6 澳AU 5 巴PK 5.2 韩国KR	0 受惠国LD	11	---Of the vehicles of subheading No.8704.1030 or 8704.1090
7607	8708.9340	---子目号8704.2100、8704.2230、8704.3100及8704.3230所列车辆用	10	0 冰岛IS,东盟AS,哥CR,秘鲁PE,新加坡SG,新西兰NZ,智利CL 4 瑞士CH 5 巴PK 6 澳AU 8.6 韩国KR	0 受惠国LD	45	---Of the vehicles of subheading No.8704.2100, 8704.2230, 8704.3100 or 8704.3230
7608	8708.9350	---子目号8704.2240、8704.2300及8704.3240所列车辆用	10	0 冰岛IS,东盟AS,哥CR,秘鲁PE,新加坡SG,新西兰NZ,智利CL 4 瑞士CH 5 巴PK 6 澳AU 9 韩国KR	0 受惠国LD	30	---Of the vehicles of subheading No.8704.2240, 8704.2300 or 8704.3240

序号 No.	税则号列 Tariff Line	中文货品名称 Article Description in Chinese	最惠国税率 MFN(%)	协定税率 Agreement(%)	特惠税率 SP(%)	普通税率 Gen(%)	英文货品名称 Article Description
7609	8708.9360	---税号87.05所列车辆用	10	0 冰岛IS,东盟AS,哥CR,秘鲁PE,新加坡SG,新西兰NZ,智利CL 4 瑞士CH 5 巴PK 6 澳AU 9 韩国KR	0 受惠国LD	100	---Of the vehicles of heading No.87.05
7610	8708.9390	---其他	10	0 冰岛IS,东盟AS,哥CR,秘鲁PE,新加坡SG,新西兰NZ,智利CL 4 瑞士CH 5 巴PK 6 澳AU	0 受惠国LD	100	---Other
		--转向盘、转向柱及转向器及其零件:					--Steering wheels, steering columns and steering boxes; parts thereof:
7611	8708.9410	---税号87.01所列车辆用	6	0 冰岛IS,东盟AS,哥CR,秘鲁PE,新西兰NZ,智利CL 2.4 瑞士CH 3.6 澳AU 5 巴PK 5.2 韩国KR	0 受惠国LD	14	---Of the vehicles of heading No.87.01
7612	8708.9420	---子目号8702.1091及8702.9010所列车辆用	10	0 冰岛IS,东盟AS,哥CR,秘鲁PE,新加坡SG,新西兰NZ,智利CL 4 瑞士CH 5 巴PK 6 澳AU 8.6 韩国KR	0 受惠国LD	70	---Of the vehicles of subheading No.8702.1091 or 8702.9010
	ex87089420	30座及以上客车用转向器的零件	Δ8				Parts of steering boxes of buses with 30 seats of more
7613	8708.9430	---子目号8704.1030及8704.1090所列车辆用	6	0 冰岛IS,东盟AS,哥CR,秘鲁PE,新西兰NZ,智利CL 2.4 瑞士CH 3.6 澳AU 5 巴PK 5.2 韩国KR	0 受惠国LD	11	---Of the vehicles of subheading No.8704.1030 or 8704.1090
7614	8708.9440	---子目号8704.2100、8704.2230、8704.3100及8704.3230所列车辆用	10	0 冰岛IS,东盟AS,哥CR,秘鲁PE,新加坡SG,新西兰NZ,智利CL 4 瑞士CH 5 巴PK 6 澳AU 8.6 韩国KR	0 受惠国LD	45	---Of the vehicles of subheading No.8704.2100, 8704.2230, 8704.3100 or 8704.3230
7615	8708.9450	---子目号8704.2240、8704.2300及8704.3240所列车辆用	10	0 冰岛IS,东盟AS,哥CR,秘鲁PE,新加坡SG,新西兰NZ,智利CL 4 瑞士CH 5 巴PK 6 澳AU 8.6 韩国KR	0 受惠国LD	30	---Of the vehicles of subheading No.8704.2240, 8704.2300 or 8704.3240
	ex87089450	总重≥14吨柴油型货车转向器的零件	Δ8				Parts of steering boxes for diesel trucks of G.V.W≥14t
7616	8708.9460	---税号87.05所列车辆用	10	0 冰岛IS,东盟AS,哥CR,秘鲁PE,新加坡SG,新西兰NZ,智利CL 4 瑞士CH 5 巴PK 6 澳AU 8.6 韩国KR	0 受惠国LD	100	---Of the vehicles of heading No.87.05

序号 No.	税则号列 Tariff Line	中文货品名称 Article Description in Chinese	最惠国税率 MFN(%)	协定税率 Agreement(%)	特惠税率 SP(%)	普通税率 Gen(%)	英文货品名称 Article Description
7617	8708.9490	---其他	10	0 冰岛IS,东盟AS,哥CR,秘鲁PE,新加坡SG,新西兰NZ,智利CL 5 巴PK 6 澳AU 8 瑞士CH	0 受惠国LD	100	---Other
	ex87089490	采用电动转向系统的转向盘、转向柱及转向器及其零件	Δ8				Steering wheels, steering columns, steering gears with electric powder steering and their parts
7618	8708.9500	--带充气系统的安全气囊及其零件	10	0 冰岛IS,哥CR,香港HK,新西兰NZ,智利CL 4 瑞士CH 6 澳AU 9 巴PK,亚太AP 9.6 韩国KR	0 受惠国$_2$LD$_2$	100	--Safety airbags with inflater system; parts thereof
		--其他:					--Other:
7619	8708.9910	---税号87.01所列车辆用	6	0 冰岛IS,东盟AS,哥CR,秘鲁PE,新西兰NZ,智利CL 2.4 瑞士CH 3.6 澳AU 4.8 韩国KR 5 巴PK	0 受惠国LD	14	---Of the vehicles of heading No.87.01
		---子目号8702.1091及8702.9010所列车辆用:					---Of the vehicles of subheading No.8702.1091 or 8702.9010:
7620	8708.9921	----车架	25	0 冰岛IS,东盟AS,哥CR,新加坡SG,新西兰NZ,智利CL 7.5 秘鲁PE 15 澳AU 22.5 韩国KR	0 受惠国$_1$LD$_1$	70	----Frames
7621	8708.9929	----其他	25	0 冰岛IS,东盟AS,哥CR,新加坡SG,新西兰NZ,智利CL 7.5 秘鲁PE 15 澳AU 22.5 韩国KR	0 受惠国$_1$LD$_1$	70	----Other
		---子目号8704.1030及8704.1090所列车辆用:					---Of the vehicles of subheading No.8704.1030 or 8704.1090:
7622	8708.9931	----车架	6	0 冰岛IS,东盟AS,哥CR,秘鲁PE,新西兰NZ,智利CL 2.4 瑞士CH 3.6 澳AU 5 巴PK 5.2 韩国KR	0 受惠国LD	11	----Frames
7623	8708.9939	----其他	6Δ3	0 冰岛IS,东盟AS,哥CR,秘鲁PE,新西兰NZ,智利CL 2.4 瑞士CH 3.6 澳AU 5 巴PK 5.2 韩国KR	0 受惠国LD	11	----Other
		---子目号8704.2100、8704.2230、8704.3100及8704.3230所列车辆用:					---Of the vehicles of subheading No.8704.2100, 8704.2230, 8704.3100 or 8704.3230:
7624	8708.9941	----车架	25	0 冰岛IS,东盟AS,哥CR,新加坡SG,新西兰NZ,智利CL 7.5 秘鲁PE 15 澳AU 22.5 韩国KR	0 受惠国$_1$LD$_1$	45	----Frames

序号 No.	税则号列 Tariff Line	中文货品名称 Article Description in Chinese	最惠国税率 MFN(%)	协定税率 Agreement(%)	特惠税率 SP(%)	普通税率 Gen(%)	英文货品名称 Article Description
7625	8708.9949	----其他	25	0 冰岛IS,东盟AS,哥CR,新加坡SG,新西兰NZ,智利CL 7.5 秘鲁PE 15 澳AU 22.5 韩国KR	0 受惠国$_1$LD$_1$	45	----Other
		---子目号8704.2240、8704.2300及8704.3240所列车辆用:					---Of the vehicles of subheading No. 8704.2240, 8704.2300 or 8704.3240:
7626	8708.9951	----车架	10	0 冰岛IS,东盟AS,哥CR,秘鲁PE,新加坡SG,新西兰NZ,智利CL 4 瑞士CH 5 巴PK 6 澳AU 8.6 韩国KR	0 受惠国LD	30	----Frames
7627	8708.9959	----其他	10	0 冰岛IS,东盟AS,哥CR,秘鲁PE,新加坡SG,新西兰NZ,智利CL 4 瑞士CH 5 巴PK 6 澳AU 8.6 韩国KR	0 受惠国LD	30	----Other
7628	8708.9960	---税号87.05所列车辆用	15	0 冰岛IS,东盟AS,哥CR,新加坡SG,新西兰NZ,智利CL 4.5 秘鲁PE 9 澳AU 10.5 瑞士CH 12 巴PK,韩国KR	0 受惠国$_1$LD$_1$	100	---Of the vehicles of heading No.87.05
		---其他:					---Other:
7629	8708.9991	----车架	10	0 冰岛IS,东盟AS,哥CR,秘鲁PE,台湾TW,新加坡SG,新西兰NZ,智利CL 4 瑞士CH 5 巴PK 6 澳AU 8.6 韩国KR	0 受惠国LD	100	----Frames
7630	8708.9992	----传动轴	10	0 冰岛IS,东盟AS,哥CR,秘鲁PE,台湾TW,新加坡SG,新西兰NZ,智利CL 4 瑞士CH 5 巴PK 6 澳AU 8.6 韩国KR	0 受惠国LD	100	----Driving shafts
7631	8708.9999	----其他	10	0 冰岛IS,东盟AS,哥CR,秘鲁PE,台湾TW,新加坡SG,新西兰NZ,智利CL 4 瑞士CH 5 巴PK 6 澳AU 8.6 韩国KR	0 受惠国LD	100	----Other
	ex87089999	混合动力汽车动力传动装置(由发电机、电动机和动力分配装置等组成)及其零件	Δ6				Hybird vehicle transimission unit, composed of generator, motor, power delivery unit, including parts

序号 No.	税则号列 Tariff Line	中文货品名称 Article Description in Chinese	最惠国税率 MFN(%)	协定税率 Agreement(%)	特惠税率 SP(%)	普通税率 Gen(%)	英文货品名称 Article Description
	87.09	**短距离运输货物的机动车辆，未装有提升或搬运设备，用于工厂、仓库、码头或机场;火车站台上用的牵引车;上述车辆的零件：**					**Works trucks, self-propelled, not fitted with lifting or handling equipment, of the type used in factories, warehouses, dock areas or airports for short distance transport of goods; tractors of the type used on railway station platforms; parts of the foregoing vehicles:**
		-车辆：					-Vehicles:
		--电动的：					--Electrical:
7632	8709.1110	---牵引车	10	0 冰岛IS,东盟AS,哥CR,秘鲁PE,新加坡SG,新西兰NZ,智利CL 4 瑞士CH 5 巴PK 6 澳AU 8 韩国KR	0 受惠国LD	30	---Tractors
7633	8709.1190	---其他	10	0 冰岛IS,东盟AS,哥CR,秘鲁PE,新加坡SG,新西兰NZ,智利CL 4 瑞士CH 5 巴PK 6 澳AU 8 韩国KR	0 受惠国LD	30	---Other
		--其他：					--Other:
7634	8709.1910	---牵引车	10.5	0 冰岛IS,东盟AS,哥CR,秘鲁PE,新加坡SG,新西兰NZ,智利CL 5 巴PK 6.3 澳AU 7.4 瑞士CH 9.1 韩国KR	0 受惠国LD	30	---Tractors
7635	8709.1990	---其他	10.5	0 冰岛IS,东盟AS,哥CR,秘鲁PE,新加坡SG,新西兰NZ,智利CL 5 巴PK 6.3 澳AU 7.4 瑞士CH 9.1 韩国KR	0 受惠国LD	30	---Other
7636	8709.9000	-零件	8.4	0 冰岛IS,东盟AS,哥CR,秘鲁PE,新西兰NZ,智利CL 3.36 瑞士CH 5 澳AU,巴PK 6.7 韩国KR	0 受惠国LD	17	-Parts
	87.10	**坦克及其他机动装甲战斗车辆，不论是否装有武器;上述车辆的零件：**					**Tanks and other armoured fighting vehicles, motorized, whether or not fitted with weapons, and parts of such vehicles:**
7637	8710.0010	---整车	15	0 冰岛IS,东盟AS,哥CR,新加坡SG,新西兰NZ,智利CL 4.5 秘鲁PE 9 澳AU 10.5 瑞士CH 12 巴PK,韩国KR	0 受惠国$_1$LD$_1$	100	---Assembled
7638	8710.0090	---零件	15	0 冰岛IS,东盟AS,哥CR,新加坡SG,新西兰NZ,智利CL 4.5 秘鲁PE 9 澳AU 10.5 瑞士CH 12 巴PK,韩国KR	0 受惠国$_1$LD$_1$	100	---Parts and accessories

序号 No.	税则号列 Tariff Line	中文货品名称 Article Description in Chinese	最惠国税率 MFN(%)	协定税率 Agreement(%)	特惠税率 SP(%)	普通税率 Gen(%)	英文货品名称 Article Description
	87.11	**摩托车(包括机器脚踏两用车)及装有辅助发动机的脚踏车，不论有无边车;边车:**					**Motorcycles (including mopeds) and cycles fitted with an auxiliary motor, with or without side-cars; side-cars:**
7639	8711.1000	-装有往复式活塞内燃发动机，气缸容量（排气量）不超过50毫升	45	0 冰岛IS,东盟AS,哥CR,新加坡SG,新西兰NZ,智利CL 13.5 秘鲁PE 27 澳AU 32.4 瑞士CH 40.5 韩国KR	0 受惠国$_1$LD$_1$	150	-With reciprocating internal combustion piston engine of a cylinder capacity not exceeding 50cc
		-装有往复式活塞内燃发动机，气缸容量（排气量）超过50毫升，但不超过250毫升:					-With reciprocating internal combustion piston engine of a cylinder capacity exceeding 50cm^3 but not exceeding 250cm^3:
7640	8711.2010	---气缸容量超过50毫升，但不超过100毫升	45	0 冰岛IS,东盟AS,哥CR,新加坡SG,新西兰NZ,智利CL 13.5 秘鲁PE 27 澳AU 32.4 瑞士CH 40.5 韩国KR	0 受惠国$_1$LD$_1$	150	---Of a cylinder capacity exceeding 50cc but not exceeding 100cc
7641	8711.2020	---气缸容量超过100毫升，但不超过125毫升	45	0 冰岛IS,东盟AS,哥CR,新加坡SG,新西兰NZ,智利CL 13.5 秘鲁PE 27 澳AU 32.4 瑞士CH 40.5 韩国KR	0 受惠国$_1$LD$_1$	150	---Of a cylinder capacity exceeding 100cc but not exceeding 125cc
7642	8711.2030	---气缸容量超过125毫升，但不超过150毫升	45	0 冰岛IS,东盟AS,哥CR,新加坡SG,新西兰NZ,智利CL 13.5 秘鲁PE 27 澳AU 32.4 瑞士CH 40.5 韩国KR	0 受惠国$_1$LD$_1$	150	---Of a cylinder capacity exceeding 125cc but not exceeding 150cc
7643	8711.2040	---气缸容量超过150毫升，但不超过200毫升	45	0 冰岛IS,东盟AS,哥CR,新加坡SG,新西兰NZ,智利CL 27 澳AU 32.4 瑞士CH 40.5 韩国KR	0 受惠国$_2$LD$_2$	150	---Of a cylinder capacity exceeding 150cc but not exceeding 200cc
7644	8711.2050	---气缸容量超过200毫升，但不超过250毫升	45	0 冰岛IS,东盟AS,哥CR,新加坡SG,新西兰NZ,智利CL 27 澳AU 32.4 瑞士CH 40.5 韩国KR	0 受惠国$_2$LD$_2$	150	---Of a cylinder capacity exceeding 200cc but not exceeding 250cc
		-装有往复式活塞内燃发动机，气缸容量（排气量）超过250毫升，但不超过500毫升:					-With reciprocating internal combustion piston engine of a cylinder capacity exceeding 250cm^3 but not exceeding 500cm^3:
7645	8711.3010	---气缸容量超过250毫升，但不超过400毫升	45	0 冰岛IS,东盟AS,哥CR,新加坡SG,新西兰NZ,智利CL 27 澳AU 32.8 巴PK,亚太AP 40.5 韩国KR	0 受惠国$_2$LD$_2$	150	---Of a cylinder capacity exceeding 250cc but not exceeding 400cc
7646	8711.3020	---气缸容量超过400毫升，但不超过500毫升	45	0 冰岛IS,东盟AS,哥CR,新加坡SG,新西兰NZ,智利CL 27 澳AU 32.8 巴PK,亚太AP 40.5 韩国KR	0 受惠国$_2$LD$_2$	150	---Of a cylinder capacity exceeding 400cc but not exceeding 500cc

序号 No.	税则号列 Tariff Line	中文货品名称 Article Description in Chinese	最惠国税率 MFN(%)	协定税率 Agreement(%)	特惠税率 SP(%)	普通税率 Gen(%)	英文货品名称 Article Description
7647	8711.4000	-装有往复式活塞内燃发动机，气缸容量（排气量）超过500毫升，但不超过800毫升	40	0 冰岛IS,东盟AS,哥CR,新加坡SG,新西兰NZ,智利CL 24 澳AU 36 韩国KR	0 受惠国$_2$LD$_2$	150	-With reciprocating internal combustion piston engine of a cylinder capacity exceeding 500cc but not exceeding 800cc
7648	8711.5000	-装有往复式活塞内燃发动机，气缸容量（排气量）超过800毫升	30	0 冰岛IS,东盟AS,哥CR,新加坡SG,新西兰NZ,智利CL 18 澳AU 27 韩国KR	0 受惠国$_2$LD$_2$	150	-With reciprocating internal combustion piston engine of a cylinder capacity exceeding 800cc
		-其他：					-Other:
7649	8711.9010	---电动及电动助力的	45	0 冰岛IS,东盟AS,哥CR,新加坡SG,新西兰NZ,智利CL 27 澳AU	0 受惠国$_2$LD$_2$	150	---Electric and electric auxiliary
7650	8711.9090	---其他	45	0 冰岛IS,东盟AS,哥CR,新加坡SG,新西兰NZ,智利CL 27 澳AU	0 受惠国$_2$LD$_2$	150	---Other
	87.12	**自行车及其他非机动脚踏车(包括运货三轮脚踏车)：**					**Bicycles and other cycles (including delivery tricycles), not motorised:**
7651	8712.0020	---竞赛型自行车	13	0 冰岛IS,东盟AS,哥CR,秘鲁PE,台湾TW,新加坡SG,新西兰NZ,智利CL 5 巴PK 7.8 澳AU 9.1 瑞士CH,亚太AP 10.4 韩国KR	0 受惠国$_1$LD$_1$	130	---Racing bicycle
7652	8712.0030	---山地自行车	13	0 冰岛IS,东盟AS,哥CR,秘鲁PE,台湾TW,新加坡SG,新西兰NZ,智利CL 5 巴PK 7.8 澳AU 9.1 瑞士CH,亚太AP 10.4 韩国KR	0 受惠国$_1$LD$_1$	130	---Mountain bicycle
		---越野自行车：					---Cross-country bicycles:
7653	8712.0041	----16、18及20英寸	13	0 冰岛IS,东盟AS,哥CR,秘鲁PE,台湾TW,新加坡SG,新西兰NZ,智利CL 5 巴PK 7.8 澳AU 9.1 瑞士CH,亚太AP 10.4 韩国KR	0 受惠国LD	130	----16″, 18″ or 20″
7654	8712.0049	----其他	13	0 冰岛IS,东盟AS,哥CR,秘鲁PE,台湾TW,新加坡SG,新西兰NZ,智利CL 5 巴PK 7.8 澳AU 9.1 瑞士CH,亚太AP 10.4 韩国KR	0 受惠国$_1$LD$_1$	130	----Other
		---其他自行车：					---Other cycles:
7655	8712.0081	----16英寸及以下	13	0 澳门MO,冰岛IS,东盟AS,哥CR,秘鲁PE,台湾TW,新加坡SG,新西兰NZ,智利CL 5 巴PK 7.8 澳AU 9.1 瑞士CH,亚太AP 10.4 韩国KR	0 受惠国$_1$LD$_1$	130	----Not larger than16″

序号 No.	税则号列 Tariff Line	中文货品名称 Article Description in Chinese	最惠国税率 MFN(%)	协定税率 Agreement(%)		特惠税率 SP(%)	普通税率 Gen(%)	英文货品名称 Article Description
7656	8712.0089	----其他	13	0 5 7.8 9.1 10.4	澳门MO,冰岛IS,东盟AS,哥CR,秘鲁PE,台湾TW,新加坡SG,新西兰NZ,智利CL 巴PK 澳AU 瑞士CH,亚太AP 韩国KR	0 受惠国$_1$LD$_1$	130	----Other
7657	8712.0090	---其他	23	0 6.9 13.8 16.1	澳门MO,冰岛IS,东盟AS,哥CR,台湾TW,新加坡SG,新西兰NZ,智利CL 秘鲁PE 澳AU 巴PK,瑞士CH,亚太AP	0 受惠国$_1$LD$_1$	130	---Other
	87.13	**残疾人用车，不论是否机动或其他机械驱动：**						**Carriages for disabled persons, whether or not motorised or otherwise mechanically propelled:**
7658	8713.1000	-非机械驱动	6	0 2.4 3.6 5	冰岛IS,东盟AS,哥CR,秘鲁PE,新西兰NZ,智利CL 瑞士CH 澳AU,韩国KR 巴PK	0 受惠国$_1$LD$_1$	20	-Not mechanically propelled
7659	8713.9000	-其他	4	0 3.2	澳AU,巴PK,冰岛IS,东盟AS,哥CR,秘鲁PE,瑞士CH,新西兰NZ,智利CL 韩国KR	0 受惠国$_1$LD$_1$	20	-Other
	87.14	**零件、附件、税号87.11至87.13所列车辆用：**						**Parts and accessories of vehicles of headings 8711 to 8713:**
7660	8714.1000	-摩托车（包括机器脚踏两用车）用	30	0 9 18 27	冰岛IS,东盟AS,哥CR,新加坡SG,新西兰NZ,智利CL 秘鲁PE 澳AU 韩国KR	0 受惠国$_1$LD$_1$	100	-Of motorcycles (including mopeds)
	ex87141000	星型轮及碟刹件	Δ10					Planetary gears and Plate brake
7661	8714.2000	-残疾人车辆用	5	0 3	澳AU,巴PK,冰岛IS,东盟AS,哥CR,秘鲁PE,瑞士CH,新西兰NZ,智利CL 韩国KR	0 受惠国LD	17	-Of carriages for disabled persons
		-其他：						-Other:
7662	8714.9100	--车架、轮叉及其零件	12	0 6 7.2 8.4 9.6	冰岛IS,东盟AS,哥CR,秘鲁PE,台湾TW,新加坡SG,新西兰NZ,智利CL 巴PK 澳AU 瑞士CH 韩国KR	0 受惠国$_1$LD$_1$	80	--Frames and forks, and parts thereof
		--轮圈及辐条：						--Wheel rims and spokes:
7663	8714.9210	---轮圈	12	0 6 7.2 8.4 9.6	冰岛IS,东盟AS,哥CR,秘鲁PE,台湾TW,新加坡SG,新西兰NZ,智利CL 巴PK 澳AU 瑞士CH 韩国KR	0 受惠国$_1$LD$_1$	80	---Wheel rims

序号 No.	税则号列 Tariff Line	中文货品名称 Article Description in Chinese	最惠国税率 MFN(%)	协定税率 Agreement(%)	特惠税率 SP(%)	普通税率 Gen(%)	英文货品名称 Article Description
7664	8714.9290	---辐条	12	0 冰岛IS,东盟AS,哥CR,秘鲁PE,台湾TW,新加坡SG,新西兰NZ,智利CL 6 巴PK 7.2 澳AU 8.4 瑞士CH 9.6 韩国KR	0 受惠国$_1$LD$_1$	80	---Spokes
		--轮毂(倒轮制动毂及毂闸除外);飞轮、链轮:					--Hubs, other than coaster braking hubs and hub brakes, and free-wheel sprocket-wheels:
7665	8714.9310	---轮毂	12	0 冰岛IS,东盟AS,哥CR,秘鲁PE,台湾TW,新加坡SG,新西兰NZ,智利CL 6 巴PK 7.2 澳AU 8.4 瑞士CH 9.6 韩国KR	0 受惠国$_1$LD$_1$	80	---Hubs
7666	8714.9320	---飞轮	12	0 冰岛IS,东盟AS,哥CR,秘鲁PE,台湾TW,新加坡SG,新西兰NZ,智利CL 6 巴PK 7.2 澳AU 8.4 瑞士CH 9.6 韩国KR	0 受惠国$_1$LD$_1$	80	---Free wheel
7667	8714.9390	---其他	12	0 冰岛IS,东盟AS,哥CR,秘鲁PE,台湾TW,新加坡SG,新西兰NZ,智利CL 6 巴PK 7.2 澳AU 8.4 瑞士CH 9.6 韩国KR	0 受惠国$_1$LD$_1$	80	---Other
7668	8714.9400	--制动器(包括倒轮制动毂及毂闸)及其零件	12	0 冰岛IS,东盟AS,哥CR,秘鲁PE,台湾TW,新加坡SG,新西兰NZ,智利CL 6 巴PK 7.2 澳AU 8.4 瑞士CH 9.6 韩国KR	0 受惠国$_1$LD$_1$	80	--Brakes, including coaster braking hubs and hub brakes, and parts thereof
7669	8714.9500	--鞍座	12	0 冰岛IS,东盟AS,哥CR,秘鲁PE,台湾TW,新加坡SG,新西兰NZ,智利CL 6 巴PK 7.2 澳AU 8.4 瑞士CH 9.6 韩国KR	0 受惠国$_1$LD$_1$	80	--Saddles
		--脚蹬、曲柄链轮及其零件:					--Pedals and crank-gear, and parts thereof:
7670	8714.9610	---脚蹬及其零件	12	0 冰岛IS,东盟AS,哥CR,秘鲁PE,台湾TW,新加坡SG,新西兰NZ,智利CL 6 巴PK 7.2 澳AU 8.4 瑞士CH 9.6 韩国KR	0 受惠国$_1$LD$_1$	80	---Pedals and parts thereof

序号 No.	税则号列 Tariff Line	中文货品名称 Article Description in Chinese	最惠国税率 MFN(%)	协定税率 Agreement(%)	特惠税率 SP(%)	普通税率 Gen(%)	英文货品名称 Article Description
7671	8714.9620	---曲柄链轮及其零件	12	0 冰岛IS,东盟AS,哥CR,秘鲁PE,台湾TW,新加坡SG,新西兰NZ,智利CL 6 巴PK 7.2 澳AU 8.4 瑞士CH 9.6 韩国KR	0 受惠国$_1$LD$_1$	80	---Crank-gear and parts thereof
7672	8714.9900	--其他	12	0 冰岛IS,东盟AS,哥CR,秘鲁PE,台湾TW,新加坡SG,新西兰NZ,智利CL 5 巴PK 7.2 澳AU 8.4 瑞士CH,亚太AP 9.6 韩国KR	0 受惠国$_1$LD$_1$	80	--Other
	87.15	**婴孩车及其零件**					**Baby carriages and parts thereof**
7673	8715.0000	婴孩车及其零件	20	0 澳门MO,冰岛IS,东盟AS,哥CR,新加坡SG,新西兰NZ,智利CL 6 秘鲁PE 12 澳AU 14 瑞士CH 17.3 韩国KR	0 受惠国$_1$LD$_1$	80	Baby carriages and parts thereof
	87.16	**挂车及半挂车或其他非机械驱动车辆及其零件:**					**Trailers and semi-trailers; other vehicles, not mechanically propelled; parts thereof:**
7674	8716.1000	-供居住或野营用厢式挂车及半挂车	10	0 冰岛IS,东盟AS,哥CR,秘鲁PE,新加坡SG,新西兰NZ,智利CL 4 瑞士CH 5 巴PK 6 澳AU 8.6 韩国KR	0 受惠国$_1$LD$_1$	35	-Trailers and semi-trailers of the caravan type, for housing or camping
7675	8716.2000	-农用自装或自卸式挂车及半挂车	10	0 冰岛IS,东盟AS,哥CR,秘鲁PE,新西兰NZ,智利CL 4 瑞士CH 5 巴PK 6 澳AU 8.6 韩国KR	0 受惠国$_1$LD$_1$	35	-Self-loading or self-unloading trailers and semi-trailers for agricultural purposes
		-其他货运挂车及半挂车:					-Other trailers and semi-trailers for the transport of goods:
		--罐式挂车及半挂车:					--Tanker trailers and tanker semi-trailers:
7676	8716.3110	---油罐挂车及半挂车	10	0 冰岛IS,东盟AS,哥CR,秘鲁PE,新加坡SG,新西兰NZ,智利CL 4 瑞士CH 5 巴PK 6 澳AU 8.6 韩国KR	0 受惠国$_1$LD$_1$	20	---Oil tanker trailers and semi-trailers
7677	8716.3190	---其他	10	0 冰岛IS,东盟AS,哥CR,秘鲁PE,新西兰NZ,智利CL 4 瑞士CH 5 巴PK 6 澳AU 8 韩国KR	0 受惠国$_1$LD$_1$	35	---Other
		--其他:					--Other:

序号 No.	税则号列 Tariff Line	中文货品名称 Article Description in Chinese	最惠国税率 MFN(%)	协定税率 Agreement(%)	特惠税率 SP(%)	普通税率 Gen(%)	英文货品名称 Article Description
7678	8716.3910	---货柜挂车及半挂车	10	0 冰岛IS,东盟AS,哥CR,秘鲁PE,新西兰NZ,智利CL 4 瑞士CH 5 巴PK 6 澳AU 8 韩国KR	0 受惠国$_1$LD$_1$	20	---Van trailers and semi-trailers
7679	8716.3990	---其他	10	0 冰岛IS,东盟AS,哥CR,秘鲁PE,新西兰NZ,智利CL 4 瑞士CH 5 巴PK 6 澳AU 8 韩国KR	0 受惠国$_1$LD$_1$	35	---Other
7680	8716.4000	-其他挂车及半挂车	10	0 冰岛IS,东盟AS,哥CR,秘鲁PE,新西兰NZ,智利CL 4 瑞士CH 5 巴PK 6 澳AU 8 韩国KR	0 受惠国$_1$LD$_1$	35	-Other trailers and semi-trailers
7681	8716.8000	-其他车辆	10	0 澳门MO,冰岛IS,东盟AS,哥CR,秘鲁PE,新加坡SG,新西兰NZ,智利CL 4 瑞士CH 5 巴PK 6 澳AU 8 韩国KR	0 受惠国$_1$LD$_1$	80	-Other vehicles
7682	8716.9000	-零件	10	0 冰岛IS,东盟AS,哥CR,秘鲁PE,新加坡SG,新西兰NZ,智利CL 4 瑞士CH 5 巴PK 6 澳AU 8 韩国KR	0 受惠国LD	35	-Parts

第八十八章

航空器、航天器及其零件

Chapter 88

Aircraft, spacecraft and parts thereof

子目注释:

子目号8802.11至8802.40所称“空载重量”，是指航空器在正常飞行状态下，除去机组人员、燃料及非永久性安装设备后的重量。

Note:

For the purposes of subheadings Nos. 8802.11 to 8802.40, the expression “unladen weight” means the weight of the machine in normal flying order, excluding the weight of the crew and of fuel and equipment other than permanently fitted items of equipment.

序号 No.	税则号列 Tariff Line	中文货品名称 Article Description in Chinese	最惠国税率 MFN(%)	协定税率 Agreement(%)	特惠税率 SP(%)	普通税率 Gen(%)	英文货品名称 Article Description
	88.01	**气球及飞艇;滑翔机、悬挂滑翔机及其他无动力航空器:**					**Balloons and dirigibles; gliders, hang gliders and other non-powered aircraft:**
7683	8801.0010	---滑翔机及悬挂滑翔机	3	0 澳AU,巴PK,冰岛IS,东盟AS,哥CR,韩国KR,秘鲁PE,瑞士CH,新西兰NZ,智利CL	0 受惠国LD	11	---Gliders and hang gliders
7684	8801.0090	---其他	3	0 澳AU,巴PK,冰岛IS,东盟AS,哥CR,韩国KR,秘鲁PE,瑞士CH,新西兰NZ,智利CL	0 受惠国LD	11	---Other
	88.02	**其他航空器（例如，直升机、飞机）;航天器（包括卫星）及其运载工具、亚轨道运载工具:**					**Other aircraft (for example, helicopters, aeroplanes) ; spacecraft (including satellites) and suborbital and spacecraft launch vehicles:**
		-直升机:					-Helicopters:
7685	8802.1100	--空载重量不超过2000公斤	2	0 澳AU,巴PK,冰岛IS,东盟AS,哥CR,韩国KR,秘鲁PE,瑞士CH,新西兰NZ,智利CL	0 受惠国LD	11	--Of an unladen weight not exceeding 2000kg
		--空载重量超过2000公斤:					--Of an unladen weight exceeding 2000kg:
7686	8802.1210	---空载重量超过2000公斤，但不超过7000公斤	2	0 澳AU,巴PK,冰岛IS,东盟AS,哥CR,韩国KR,秘鲁PE,瑞士CH,新西兰NZ,智利CL	0 受惠国LD	11	---Of an unladen weight exceeding 2000kg but not exceeding 7000kg
7687	8802.1220	---空载重量超过7000公斤	2	0 澳AU,巴PK,冰岛IS,东盟AS,哥CR,韩国KR,秘鲁PE,瑞士CH,新西兰NZ,智利CL	0 受惠国LD	11	---Of an unladen weight exceeding 7000kg
7688	8802.2000	-飞机及其他航空器，空载重量不超过2000公斤	5	0 澳AU,巴PK,冰岛IS,东盟AS,哥CR,秘鲁PE,瑞士CH,新西兰NZ,智利CL 4 韩国KR	0 受惠国LD	11	-Aeroplanes and other aircraft, of an unladen weight not exceeding 2000kg
7689	8802.3000	-飞机及其他航空器，空载重量超过2000公斤，但不超过15000公斤	4	0 澳AU,巴PK,冰岛IS,东盟AS,哥CR,韩国KR,秘鲁PE,瑞士CH,新西兰NZ,智利CL	0 受惠国LD	11	-Aeroplanes and other aircraft, of an unladen weight exceeding 2000kg but not exceeding 15000kg
		-飞机及其他航空器，空载重量超过15000公斤:					-Aeroplanes and other aircraft, of an unladen weight exceeding 15000kg:
7690	8802.4010	---空载重量超过15000公斤，但不超过45000公斤	5	0 澳AU,巴PK,冰岛IS,东盟AS,哥CR,韩国KR,秘鲁PE,瑞士CH,新西兰NZ,智利CL 3.5 亚太AP	0 受惠国LD	11	---Of an unladen weight exceeding 15000kg but not exceeding 45000kg

序号 No.	税则号列 Tariff Line	中文货品名称 Article Description in Chinese	最惠国税率 MFN(%)	协定税率 Agreement(%)		特惠税率 SP(%)		普通税率 Gen(%)	英文货品名称 Article Description
7691	8802.4020	---空载重量超过45000公斤	1	0 .7	澳AU,巴PK,冰岛IS,东盟AS,哥CR,韩国KR,秘鲁PE,瑞士CH,新西兰NZ,智利CL 亚太AP	0	受惠国LD	11	---Of an unladen weight exceeding 45000kg
7692	8802.6000	-航天器（包括卫星）及其运载工具、亚轨道运载工具	2	0	澳AU,巴PK,冰岛IS,东盟AS,哥CR,韩国KR,秘鲁PE,瑞士CH,新西兰NZ,智利CL	0	受惠国LD	11	-Spacecraft (including satellites) and suborbital and spacecraft launch vehicles
	88.03	**税号88.01或88.02所列货品的零件：**							**Parts of goods of heading 8801 or 8802:**
7693	8803.1000	-推进器、水平旋翼及其零件	1	0	澳AU,巴PK,冰岛IS,东盟AS,哥CR,韩国KR,秘鲁PE,瑞士CH,新西兰NZ,智利CL	0	受惠国LD	11	-Propellers and rotors and parts thereof
7694	8803.2000	-起落架及其零件	1	0	澳AU,巴PK,冰岛IS,东盟AS,哥CR,韩国KR,秘鲁PE,瑞士CH,新西兰NZ,智利CL	0	受惠国LD	11	-Under-carriages and parts thereof
7695	8803.3000	-飞机及直升机的其他零件	1	0	澳AU,巴PK,冰岛IS,东盟AS,哥CR,韩国KR,秘鲁PE,瑞士CH,新西兰NZ,智利CL	0	受惠国$_1$LD$_1$	11	-Other parts of aeroplanes or helicopters
7696	8803.9000	-其他	0			0	受惠国LD	11	-Other
	88.04	**降落伞（包括可操纵降落伞及滑翔伞）、旋翼降落伞及其零件、附件**							**Parachutes (including dirigible parachutes and paragliders) and rotochutes; parts thereof and accessories thereto**
7697	8804.0000	降落伞（包括可操纵降落伞及滑翔伞）、旋翼降落伞及其零件、附件	2	0	澳AU,巴PK,冰岛IS,东盟AS,哥CR,韩国KR,秘鲁PE,瑞士CH,新西兰NZ,智利CL	0	受惠国LD	11	Parachutes (including dirigible parachutes and paragliders) and rotochutes; parts thereof and accessories thereto
	88.05	**航空器的发射装置、甲板停机装置或类似装置和地面飞行训练器及其零件：**							**Aircraft launching gear; deck-arrestor or similar gear; ground flying trainers; parts of the foregoing articles:**
7698	8805.1000	-航空器的发射装置及其零件；甲板停机装置或类似装置及其零件	1.5	0	澳AU,巴PK,冰岛IS,东盟AS,哥CR,韩国KR,秘鲁PE,瑞士CH,新西兰NZ,智利CL	0	受惠国LD	11	-Aircraft launching gear and parts thereof; deck-arrestor or similar gear and parts thereof
		-地面飞行训练器及其零件：							-Ground flying trainers and parts thereof:
7699	8805.2100	--空战模拟器及其零件	1.5	0	澳AU,巴PK,冰岛IS,东盟AS,哥CR,韩国KR,秘鲁PE,瑞士CH,新西兰NZ,智利CL	0	受惠国$_1$LD$_1$	11	--Air combat simulators and parts thereof
7700	8805.2900	--其他	1.5	0	澳AU,巴PK,冰岛IS,东盟AS,哥CR,韩国KR,秘鲁PE,瑞士CH,新西兰NZ,智利CL	0	受惠国LD	11	--Other

第八十九章 船舶及浮动结构体

Chapter 89 Ships, boats and floating structures

注释:

已装配、未装配或已拆卸的船体、未完工或不完整的船舶以及未装配或已拆卸的完整船舶，如果不具有某种船舶的基本特征，应归入税号 89.06。

Notes:

A hull, an unfinished or incomplete vessel, assembled, unassembled or disassembled, or a complete vessel unassembled or disassembled, is to be classified in heading No.89.06 if it does not have the essential character of a vessel of a particular kind.

序号 No.	税则号列 Tariff Line	中文货品名称 Article Description in Chinese	最惠国税率 MFN(%)	协定税率 Agreement(%)	特惠税率 SP(%)	普通税率 Gen(%)	英文货品名称 Article Description
	89.01	**巡航船、游览船、渡船、货船、驳船及类似的客运或货运船舶:**					**Cruise ships, excursion boats, ferry-boats, cargo ships, barges and similar vessels for the transport of persons or goods:**
		-巡航船、游览船及主要用于客运的类似船舶；各式渡船:					-Cruise ships, excursion boats and similar vessels principally designed for the transport of persons; ferry-boats of all kinds:
7701	8901.1010	---机动船舶	5	0 澳AU,巴PK,冰岛IS,东盟AS,哥CR,秘鲁PE,瑞士CH,香港HK,新加坡SG,新西兰NZ,智利CL 4.3 韩国KR	0 受惠国$_1$LD$_1$	14	---Motor vessels
7702	8901.1090	---非机动船舶	8	0 冰岛IS,东盟AS,哥CR,秘鲁PE,新西兰NZ,智利CL 3.2 瑞士CH 4.8 澳AU 5 巴PK 6.9 韩国KR	0 受惠国$_1$LD$_1$	30	---Other
		-液货船:					-Tankers:
		---成品油船:					---Finished oil tankers:
7703	8901.2011	----载重量不超过10万吨	9	0 冰岛IS,哥CR,秘鲁PE,新西兰NZ,智利CL 3.6 瑞士CH 5.4 澳AU 7.8 韩国KR	0 受惠国$_1$LD$_1$	14	----Loading not exceeding 100000t
7704	8901.2012	----载重量超过10万吨，但不超过30万吨	9	0 冰岛IS,哥CR,秘鲁PE,新西兰NZ,智利CL 3.6 瑞士CH 5.4 澳AU 7.8 韩国KR	0 受惠国$_1$LD$_1$	14	----Loading exceeding 100000t, but not exceeding 300000t
7705	8901.2013	----载重量超过30万吨	6	0 冰岛IS,哥CR,秘鲁PE,新西兰NZ,智利CL 2.4 瑞士CH 3.6 澳AU 5.2 韩国KR	0 受惠国$_1$LD$_1$	14	----Loading exceeding 300000t
		---原油船:					---Crude oil tankers:
7706	8901.2021	----载重量不超过15万吨	9	0 冰岛IS,哥CR,秘鲁PE,新西兰NZ,智利CL 3.6 瑞士CH 5.4 澳AU 7.8 韩国KR	0 受惠国$_1$LD$_1$	14	----Loading not exceeding 150000t
7707	8901.2022	----载重量超过15万吨，但不超过30万吨	9	0 冰岛IS,哥CR,秘鲁PE,新西兰NZ,智利CL 3.6 瑞士CH 5.4 澳AU 7.8 韩国KR	0 受惠国$_1$LD$_1$	14	----Loading exceeding 150000t, but not exceeding 300000t

序号 No.	税则号列 Tariff Line	中文货品名称 Article Description in Chinese	最惠国税率 MFN(%)	协定税率 Agreement(%)	特惠税率 SP(%)	普通税率 Gen(%)	英文货品名称 Article Description
7708	8901.2023	----载重量超过30万吨	6	0 冰岛IS,哥CR,秘鲁PE,新西兰NZ,智利CL 2.4 瑞士CH 3.6 澳AU 5.2 韩国KR	0 受惠国$_1$LD$_1$	14	----Loading exceeding 300000t
		---液化石油气船:					---Liquified petroleum gas carriers:
7709	8901.2031	----容积在20000立方米及以下	9	0 冰岛IS,哥CR,秘鲁PE,新西兰NZ,智利CL 3.6 瑞士CH 5.4 澳AU 7.8 韩国KR	0 受惠国$_1$LD$_1$	14	----Volume with 20000m^3 or less
7710	8901.2032	----容积在20000立方米以上	6	0 冰岛IS,哥CR,秘鲁PE,新西兰NZ,智利CL 2.4 瑞士CH 3.6 澳AU 5.2 韩国KR	0 受惠国$_1$LD$_1$	14	----Volume more than 20000m^3
		---液化天然气船:					---Liquified natural gas carriers:
7711	8901.2041	----容积在20000立方米及以下	9	0 冰岛IS,哥CR,秘鲁PE,新西兰NZ,智利CL 3.6 瑞士CH 5.4 澳AU 7.8 韩国KR	0 受惠国$_1$LD$_1$	14	----Volume with 20000m^3 or less
7712	8901.2042	----容积在20000立方米以上	6	0 冰岛IS,哥CR,秘鲁PE,新西兰NZ,智利CL 2.4 瑞士CH 3.6 澳AU 5.2 韩国KR	0 受惠国$_1$LD$_1$	14	----Volume more than 20000m^3
7713	8901.2090	---其他	9	0 冰岛IS,哥CR,秘鲁PE,新西兰NZ,智利CL 3.6 瑞士CH 5.4 澳AU 7.8 韩国KR	0 受惠国$_1$LD$_1$	14	---Other
7714	8901.3000	-冷藏船，但子目号8901.20的船舶除外	9	0 冰岛IS,东盟AS,哥CR,秘鲁PE,新加坡SG,新西兰NZ,智利CL 3.6 瑞士CH 5 巴PK 5.4 澳AU 7.8 韩国KR	0 受惠国$_1$LD$_1$	14	-Refrigerated vessels, other than those of subheading No.8901.20
		-其他货运船舶及其他客货兼运船舶:					-Other vessels for the transport of goods and other vessels for the transport of both persons and goods:
		---机动集装箱船:					---Motor container vessels:
7715	8901.9021	----可载标准集装箱在6000箱及以下	9	0 冰岛IS,哥CR,秘鲁PE,新西兰NZ,智利CL 3.6 瑞士CH 5.4 澳AU 7.8 韩国KR	0 受惠国$_1$LD$_1$	14	----Capable loading standard containers with 6000 or less
7716	8901.9022	----可载标准集装箱在6000箱以上	6	0 冰岛IS,哥CR,秘鲁PE,新西兰NZ,智利CL 2.4 瑞士CH 3.6 澳AU 5.2 韩国KR	0 受惠国$_1$LD$_1$	14	----Capable loading standard containers more than 6000
		---机动滚装船:					---Motor Ro-Ro carriers:
7717	8901.9031	----载重量在2万吨及以下	9	0 冰岛IS,哥CR,秘鲁PE,新西兰NZ,智利CL 3.6 瑞士CH 5.4 澳AU 7.8 韩国KR	0 受惠国$_1$LD$_1$	14	----Loading with 20000t or less
7718	8901.9032	----载重量在2万吨以上	6	0 冰岛IS,哥CR,秘鲁PE,新西兰NZ,智利CL 2.4 瑞士CH 3.6 澳AU 5.2 韩国KR	0 受惠国$_1$LD$_1$	14	----Loading more than 20000t

序号 No.	税则号列 Tariff Line	中文货品名称 Article Description in Chinese	最惠国税率 MFN(%)	协定税率 Agreement(%)	特惠税率 SP(%)	普通税率 Gen(%)	英文货品名称 Article Description
		---机动散货船:					---Motor bulk carriers:
7719	8901.9041	----载重量不超过15万吨	9	0 冰岛IS,哥CR,秘鲁PE,新西兰NZ,智利CL 3.6 瑞士CH 5.4 澳AU 7.8 韩国KR	0 受惠国$_1$LD$_1$	14	----Loading not exceeding 150000t
7720	8901.9042	----载重量超过15万吨，但不超过30万吨	9	0 冰岛IS,哥CR,秘鲁PE,新西兰NZ,智利CL 3.6 瑞士CH 5.4 澳AU 7.8 韩国KR	0 受惠国$_1$LD$_1$	14	----Loading exceeding 150000t, not exceeding 300000t
7721	8901.9043	----载重量超过30万吨	9	0 冰岛IS,哥CR,秘鲁PE,新西兰NZ,智利CL 3.6 瑞士CH 5.4 澳AU 7.8 韩国KR	0 受惠国$_1$LD$_1$	14	----Loading exceeding 300000t
7722	8901.9050	---机动多用途船	9	0 冰岛IS,哥CR,秘鲁PE,新西兰NZ,智利CL 3.6 瑞士CH 5.4 澳AU 7.8 韩国KR	0 受惠国$_1$LD$_1$	14	---Multi-purposes motor vessels
7723	8901.9080	---其他，机动的	9	0 冰岛IS,东盟AS,哥CR,秘鲁PE,新加坡SG,新西兰NZ,智利CL 3.6 瑞士CH 5 巴PK 5.4 澳AU 7.8 韩国KR	0 受惠国$_1$LD$_1$	14	---Other motor vessels
7724	8901.9090	---非机动的	8	0 冰岛IS,东盟AS,哥CR,秘鲁PE,新加坡SG,新西兰NZ,智利CL 3.2 瑞士CH 4.8 澳AU 5 巴PK 6.9 韩国KR	0 受惠国$_1$LD$_1$	30	---Other non-motor vessels
	89.02	**捕鱼船;加工船及其他加工保藏鱼类产品的船舶:**					**Fishing vessels; factory ships and other vessels for processing or preserving fishery products:**
7725	8902.0010	---机动船舶	7	0 冰岛IS,东盟AS,哥CR,秘鲁PE,新加坡SG,新西兰NZ,智利CL 2.8 瑞士CH 4.2 澳AU 5 巴PK 6 韩国KR	0 受惠国$_1$LD$_1$	14	---Motor vessels
7726	8902.0090	---非机动船舶	8	0 冰岛IS,东盟AS,哥CR,秘鲁PE,新西兰NZ,智利CL 3.2 瑞士CH 4.8 澳AU 5 巴PK 6.9 韩国KR	0 受惠国$_1$LD$_1$	30	---Other
	89.03	**娱乐或运动用快艇及其他船舶;划艇及轻舟:**					**Yachts and other vessels for pleasure or sports; rowing boats and canoes:**
7727	8903.1000	-充气的	10	0 冰岛IS,东盟AS,哥CR,秘鲁PE,新西兰NZ,智利CL 4 瑞士CH 5 巴PK 6 澳AU 8.6 韩国KR	0 受惠国LD	30	-Inflatable
		-其他:					-Other:

序号 No.	税则号列 Tariff Line	中文货品名称 Article Description in Chinese	最惠国税率 MFN(%)	协定税率 Agreement(%)	特惠税率 SP(%)	普通税率 Gen(%)	英文货品名称 Article Description
7728	8903.9100	--帆船，不论是否装有辅助发动机	8	0 冰岛IS,东盟AS,哥CR,秘鲁PE,新西兰NZ,智利CL 3.2 瑞士CH 4.8 澳AU 5 巴PK 6.9 韩国KR	0 受惠国LD	30	--Sailboats, with or without auxiliary motor
7729	8903.9200	--汽艇，但装有舷外发动机的除外	10.5	0 冰岛IS,东盟AS,哥CR,香港HK,新加坡SG,新西兰NZ,智利CL 3.2 秘鲁PE 5 巴PK 6.3 澳AU 7.4 瑞士CH 9.1 韩国KR	0 受惠国LD	30	--Motorboats, other than outboard motorboats
7730	8903.9900	--其他	10	0 冰岛IS,东盟AS,哥CR,秘鲁PE,新西兰NZ,智利CL 4 瑞士CH 5 巴PK 6 澳AU	0 受惠国LD	30	--Other
	89.04	**拖轮及顶推船**					**Tugs and pusher craft**
7731	8904.0000	拖轮及顶推船	9	0 冰岛IS,东盟AS,哥CR,秘鲁PE,新加坡SG,新西兰NZ,智利CL 3.6 瑞士CH 5 巴PK 5.4 澳AU 7.8 韩国KR	0 受惠国LD	14	Tugs and pusher craft
	89.05	**灯船、消防船、挖泥船、起重船及其他不以航行为主要功能的船舶;浮船坞;浮动或潜水式钻探或生产平台:**					**Light-vessels, fire-floats, dredgers, floating cranes, and other vessels the navigability of which is subsidiary to their main function; floating docks; floating or submersible drilling or production platforms:**
7732	8905.1000	-挖泥船	3	0 澳AU,巴PK,冰岛IS,东盟AS,哥CR,秘鲁PE,瑞士CH,新西兰NZ,智利CL 2.6 韩国KR	0 受惠国LD	11	-Dredgers
7733	8905.2000	-浮动或潜水式钻探或生产平台	6	0 冰岛IS,东盟AS,哥CR,秘鲁PE,新西兰NZ,智利CL 2.4 瑞士CH 3.6 澳AU 5 巴PK 5.2 韩国KR	0 受惠国LD	11	-Floating or submersible drilling or production platforms
		-其他:					-Other:
7734	8905.9010	---浮船坞	8	0 冰岛IS,哥CR,秘鲁PE,新西兰NZ,智利CL 3.2 瑞士CH 4.8 澳AU 6.9 韩国KR	0 受惠国LD	30	---Floating docks
7735	8905.9090	---其他	3	0 澳AU,巴PK,冰岛IS,东盟AS,哥CR,秘鲁PE,瑞士CH,新西兰NZ,智利CL 2.6 韩国KR	0 受惠国LD	11	---Other
	89.06	**其他船舶，包括军舰及救生船，但划艇除外:**					**Other vessels, including warships and lifeboats other than rowing boats:**

序号 No.	税则号列 Tariff Line	中文货品名称 Article Description in Chinese	最惠国税率 MFN(%)	协定税率 Agreement(%)	特惠税率 SP(%)	普通税率 Gen(%)	英文货品名称 Article Description
7736	8906.1000	-军舰	5	0 澳AU,巴PK,冰岛IS,东盟AS,哥CR,秘鲁PE,瑞士CH,新西兰NZ,智利CL 4.3 韩国KR	0 受惠国$_1$LD$_1$	14	-Warships
		-其他:					-Other:
7737	8906.9010	---机动船舶	5	0 澳AU,巴PK,冰岛IS,东盟AS,哥CR,秘鲁PE,瑞士CH,新西兰NZ,智利CL	0 受惠国LD	14	---Motor vessels
7738	8906.9020	---非机动船舶	8	0 冰岛IS,东盟AS,哥CR,秘鲁PE,新西兰NZ,智利CL 3.2 瑞士CH 4.8 澳AU 5 巴PK 6.9 韩国KR	0 受惠国LD	30	---Non-motor vessels
7739	8906.9030	---未制成或不完整的船舶, 包括船舶分段	8	0 冰岛IS,东盟AS,哥CR,秘鲁PE,新西兰NZ,智利CL 3.2 瑞士CH 4.8 澳AU 5 巴PK 6.9 韩国KR	0 受惠国LD	30	---Incomplete or unfinished vessels, including subsections of vessels
	89.07	**其他浮动结构体（例如，筏、柜、潜水箱、浮码头、浮筒及航标）:**					**Other floating structures (for example, rafts, tanks, coffer-dams, landing stages, buoys and beacons) :**
7740	8907.1000	-充气筏	8	0 冰岛IS,东盟AS,哥CR,秘鲁PE,新西兰NZ,智利CL 3.2 瑞士CH 4.8 澳AU 5 巴PK 6.9 韩国KR	0 受惠国LD	30	-Inflatable rafts
7741	8907.9000	-其他	8	0 冰岛IS,东盟AS,哥CR,秘鲁PE,新西兰NZ,智利CL 3.2 瑞士CH 4.8 澳AU 5 巴PK 6.9 韩国KR	0 受惠国LD	30	-Other
	89.08	**供拆卸的船舶及其他浮动结构体**					**Vessels and other floating structures for breaking up**
7742	8908.0000	供拆卸的船舶及其他浮动结构体	3Δ1	0 澳AU,巴PK,冰岛IS,东盟AS,哥CR,秘鲁PE,瑞士CH,新西兰NZ,智利CL 2.6 韩国KR	0 受惠国LD	11	Vessels and other floating structures for breaking up

第十八类

光学、照相、电影、计量、检验、医疗或外科用仪器及设备、精密仪器及设备；钟表；乐器；上述物品的零件、附件

第九十章
光学、照相、电影、计量、检验、医疗或外科用仪器及设备、精密仪器及设备；上述物品的零件、附件

注释：

一、本章不包括：

（一）机器、设备或其他专门技术用途的硫化橡胶（硬质橡胶除外）制品（税号 40.16）、皮革或再生皮革制品（税号 42.04）或纺织材料制品（税号 59.11）；

（二）纺织材料制的承托带及其他承托物品，其承托器官的作用仅依靠自身的弹性（例如，孕妇用的承托带，用于胸部、腹部、关节或肌肉的承托绷带）（第十一类）；

（三）税号 69.03 的耐火材料制品；税号 69.09 的实验室、化学或其他专门技术用途的陶瓷器；

（四）税号 70.09 的未经光学加工的玻璃镜及税号 83.06 或第七十一章的非光学元件的贱金属或贵金属制的镜子；

（五）税号 70.07、70.08、70.11、70.14、70.15 或 70.17 的货品；

（六）第十五类注释二所规定的贱金属制通用零件（第十五类）或塑料制的类似品（第三十九章）；

（七）税号 84.13 的装有计量装置的泵；计数和检验用的衡器或单独进口或出口的天平砝码（税号 84.23）；升降、起重及搬运机械（税号 84.25 至 84.28）；纸张或纸板的各种切割机器（税号 84.41）；税号 84.66 的用于机床上调整工件或工具的附件，包括具有读度用的光学装置的附件（例如，“光学”分度头），但其本身主要是光学仪器的除外（例如校直望远镜）；计算机器（税号 84.70）；税号 84.81 的阀门及其他装置；税目 84.86 的机器及装置（包括将电路图投影或绘制到感光半导体材料上的装置）；

SECTION XVIII

OPTICAL, PHOTOGRAPHIC, CINEMATOGRAPHIC, MEASURING, CHECKING, PRECISION, MEDICAL OR SURGICAL INSTRUMENTS AND APPARATUS;CLOCKS AND WATCHES; MUSICAL INSTRUMENTS;PARTS AND ACCESSORIES THEREOF

Chapter 90
Optical, photographic, cinematographic, measuring, checking, precision, medical or surgical instruments and apparatus; parts and accessories thereof

Notes:

1. This Chapter does not cover:

(a) Articles of a kind used in machines, appliances or for other technical uses, of vulcanized rubber other than hard rubber (heading No.40.16), of leather or of composition leather (heading No.42.04) or of textile material (heading No.59.11);

(b) Supporting belts or other support articles of textile material, whose intended effect on the organ to be-supported or held derives solely from their elasticity (for example, maternity belts, thoracic support bandages, abdominal support bandages, supports for joints or muscles) (SectionXI);

(c) Refractory goods of heading No.69.03; ceramic wares for laboratory, chemical or other technical uses, of heading No.69.09;

(d) Glass mirrors, not optically worked, of heading No.70.09, or mirrors of base metal or of precious metal, not being optical elements (headingNo.83.06 or Chapter71);

(e) Goods of heading No.70.07, 70.08, 70.11, 70.14, 70.15 or 70.17;

(f) Parts of general use, as defined in Note2to Section XV, of base metal (Section XV) or similar goods of plastics(Chapter39);

(g) Pumps incorporating measuring devices, of heading No.84.13; weight-operated counting or checking machinery, or separatelypresented weights for balances (heading No.84.23); lifting or handling machinery (headings Nos.84.25 to 84.28); paper or paperboard cutting machines of all kinds(heading No.84.41); fittings for adjusting work or tools on machine-tools, of heading No.84.66, including fittings with optical devices for reading the scale (for example, "optical" dividing heads) but not those which are in themselves essentially optical instruments (for example, alignment telescopes); calculating machines (heading No.84.70); valves or other appliances of heading No.84.81; machines and apparatus (including apparatus for the projection or drawing of circuit pattern on sensitized semiconductor materials) of heading 84.86;

（八）自行车或机动车辆用探照灯或聚光灯（税号 85.12）；税号 85.13 的手提式电灯；电影录音机、还音机及转录机（税号 85.19）；拾音头或录音头（税号 85.22）；电视摄像机、数字照相机及视频摄录一体机(税目 85.25)；雷达设备、无线电导航设备或无线电遥控设备（税目 85.26）；光导纤维、光导纤维束或光缆用连接器（税目 85.36）；税目 85.37 的数控装置；税号 85.39 的封闭式聚光灯；税号 85.44 的光缆；

(h) Searchlights or spotlights of a kind used for cycles or motor vehicles (heading 85.12); portable electric lamps of heading 85.13;cinematographic sound recording， reproducing or re-recording apparatus (heading 85.19); sound-heads (heading 85.22); television cameras, digital cameras and video camera recorders (heading 85.25); andradar apparatus，radio navigational aid apparatus or radio remote control apparatus (heading 85.26); connectors for optical fibres, optical fibre bundles or cables (heading 85.36); numerical control apparatus of heading 85.37; sealed beam lamp units of heading 85.39; optical fibre cables of heading 85.44;

（九）税号 94.05 的探照灯及聚光灯；

(i) Searchlights or spotlights of heading No.94.05;

（十）第九十五章的物品；

(j) Articles of Chapter 95;

（十一）容量的计量器具（按其构成的材料归类）；

(k) Capacity measures，which are to be classified according to their constituent material; or

（十二）卷轴、线轴及类似芯子（按其构成材料归类，例如，归入税号 39.23 或第十五类）。

(l) Spools，reels or similar supports (which are to be classified according to their constituent material，for example，in heading No.39.23 or Section XV).

二、除上述注释一另有规定的以外，本章各税号所列机器、设备、仪器或器具的零件、附件，应按下列规定归类：

2. Subject to Note1above，parts and accessories for machines，apparatus，instruments or articles of this Chapter are to be classified according to the following rules:

（一）凡零件、附件本身已构成本章或第八十四章、第八十五章或第九十一章各税号（税号 84.87、84.85、85.48 或 90.33 除外）所包括的货品，应一律归入其相应的税号；

(a) Parts and accessories which are goods included in any of the headings of this Chapter or of Chapter 84, 85 or 91 (other than heading 84.87, 84.85, 85.48 or 90.33) are in all cases to be classified in their respective headings;

（二）其他零件、附件，如果专用于或主要用于某种或同一税号项下的多种机器、仪器或器具（包括税号 90.10、90.13 或 90.31 的机器、仪器或器具），应归入相应机器、仪器或器具的税号；

(b) Other parts and accessories，if suitable for use solely or principally with a particular kind of machine，instrument or apparatus，or with a number of machines, instruments or apparatus of the same heading (including a machine，instrument or apparatus of heading No.90.10，90.13 or 90.31) are to be classified with the machines，instruments or apparatus of that kind;

（三）所有其他零件、附件均应归入税号 90.33。

(c) All other parts and accessories are to be classified in heading No.90.33.

三、第十六类的注释三、四也适用于本章。

3. The provisions of Note 3 and 4 to Section XVI applyalsoto this Chapter.

四、税号 90.05 不包括武器用望远镜瞄准具、潜艇或坦克上的潜望镜式望远镜及本章或第十六类的机器、设备、仪器或器具用的望远镜；这类望远镜瞄准具及望远镜应归入税号 90.13。

4. Heading No.90.05 does not apply to telescopic sights for fitting to arms，periscopic telescopes for fitting to submarines or tanks，or to telescopes for machines，appliances，instruments or apparatus of this Chapter of Section XVI; such telescopic sights and elescopes are to be classified in heading No.90.13.

五、计量或检验用的光学仪器、器具或机器，如果既可归入税号 90.13，又可归入税号 90.31，则应归入税号 90.31。

5. Measuring or checking optical instruments，appliances or machines which，but for this Note，could be classified both in heading No.90.13 and in heading No.90.31 are to be classified in heading No.90.31.

六、税目 90.21 所称“矫形器具”，是指下列用途的器具：

预防或矫正人体畸变；

生病、手术或受伤后人体部位支撑或固定；

矫形器具包括用于矫正畸形的鞋及特种鞋垫，但需符合下列任一条件：

（一）定制的；

6. For the purposes of heading 90.21，the expression “orthopaedic appliances” means appliances for:

-Preventing or correcting bodily deformities; or

-Supporting or holding parts of the body following an illness，operation or injury.

Orthopaedic appliances include footwear and special insoles designed to correct orthopaedic conditions，provided that they are either:

(1) made to measure; or

（二）成批生产的、单独报验、且不成双的、设计为左右两脚同样适用。

(2) mass-produced，presented singly.

七、税号90.32仅适用于：

（一）液体或气体的流量、液位、压力或其他变化量的自动控制仪器及装置或温度自动控制装置，不论其是否依靠要被自控的因素所发生的电现象来进行工作，这些仪器或装置将被自控因素调到并保持在一设定值上，通过持续或定期测量实际值来保持稳定，修正偏差；

（二）电量自动调节器及自动控制非电量的仪器或装置，依靠要被控制的因素所发生的电现象来进行工作，这些仪器或装置将被控制的因素调到并保持在一设定值上，通过持续或定期测量实际来保持稳定，修正偏差。

7. Heading90.32applies only to:

(a) Instruments and apparatus for automatically controlling the flow, level, pressure or other variables of liquids or gases, or for automatically controlling temperature, whether or not their operation depends on an electrical phenomenon which varies according to the factor to be automatically controlled，which are designed to bring this factor to, and maintain it at, a desired value, stabilised against disturbances, by constantly or periodically measuring its actual value; and

(b) Automatic regulators of electrical quantities, and instruments or apparatus for automatically controlling non-electrical quantities the operation of which depends on an electrical phenomenon varying according to the factor to be controlled，which are designed to bring this factor to, and maintain it at, a desired value, stabilised against disturbances, by constantly or periodically measuring its actual value.

序号 No.	税则号列 Tariff Line	中文货品名称 Article Description in Chinese	最惠国税率 MFN(%)	协定税率 Agreement(%)	特惠税率 SP(%)	普通税率 Gen(%)	英文货品名称 Article Description
	90.01	**光导纤维及光导纤维束；光缆，但税号85.44的货品除外；偏振材料制的片及板；未装配的各种材料制透镜（包括隐形眼镜片）、棱镜、反射镜及其他光学元件，但未经光学加工的玻璃制上述元件除外：**					**Optical fibres and optical fibre bundles; optical fibre cables other than those of heading 8544; sheets and plates of polarising material; lenses (including contact lenses) , prisms, mirrors and other optical elements, of any material, unmounted, other than such elements of glass not optically worked:**
7743	9001.1000	-光导纤维、光导纤维束及光缆	5	0 澳AU,巴PK,冰岛IS,东盟AS,哥CR,秘鲁PE,香港HK,新西兰NZ,智利CL 2 瑞士CH 4.5 亚太AP 4.8 韩国KR	0 受惠国LD	20	-Optical fibres, optical fibre bundles and cables
7744	9001.2000	-偏振材料制的片及板	8	0 冰岛IS,东盟AS,哥CR,秘鲁PE,香港HK,新西兰NZ,智利CL 3.2 瑞士CH 4.8 澳AU 5 巴PK 6.4 韩国KR 7.6 亚太AP	0 受惠国LD	20	-Sheets and plates of polarizing material
	ex90012000	液晶投影仪用偏光板	Δ6				Polarizing Plate or sheet for liquid-crystal projectors
	ex90012000	数字电影放映机用偏光板	Δ6				Polarizing plates or sheets for digital cinema projector
7745	9001.3000	-隐形眼镜片	10Δ6	0 冰岛IS,东盟AS,哥CR,秘鲁PE,香港HK,新加坡SG,新西兰NZ,智利CL 4 瑞士CH 5 巴PK 6 澳AU 9 韩国KR	0 受惠国LD	70	-Contact lenses
		-玻璃制眼镜片：					-Spectacle lenses of glass:

序号 No.	税则号列 Tariff Line	中文货品名称 Article Description in Chinese	最惠国税率 MFN(%)	协定税率 Agreement(%)	特惠税率 SP(%)	普通税率 Gen(%)	英文货品名称 Article Description
7746	9001.4010	---变色镜片	20Δ15	0 冰岛IS,东盟AS,哥CR,香港HK,新加坡SG,新西兰NZ,智利CL 6 秘鲁PE 12 澳AU 14 瑞士CH 17.3 韩国KR	0 受惠国$_1$LD$_1$	90	---Photochromic
		---其他:					---Other:
7747	9001.4091	----太阳镜片	20	0 冰岛IS,东盟AS,哥CR,香港HK,新加坡SG,新西兰NZ,智利CL 6 秘鲁PE 12 澳AU 14 瑞士CH 17.3 韩国KR	0 受惠国$_1$LD$_1$	90	----For sunglasses
7748	9001.4099	----其他	20	0 冰岛IS,东盟AS,哥CR,香港HK,新加坡SG,新西兰NZ,智利CL 6 秘鲁PE 12 澳AU 14 瑞士CH 17.3 韩国KR	0 受惠国$_1$LD$_1$	70	----Other
		-其他材料制眼镜片:					-Spectacle lenses of other materials:
7749	9001.5010	---变色镜片	20Δ15	0 冰岛IS,东盟AS,哥CR,香港HK,新加坡SG,新西兰NZ,智利CL 6 秘鲁PE 12 澳AU 14 瑞士CH 17.3 韩国KR	0 受惠国$_1$LD$_1$	90	---Photochromic
		---其他:					---Other:
7750	9001.5091	----太阳镜片	20	0 冰岛IS,东盟AS,哥CR,香港HK,新加坡SG,新西兰NZ,智利CL 6 秘鲁PE 12 澳AU 14 瑞士CH 17.3 韩国KR	0 受惠国$_1$LD$_1$	90	----For sunglasses
7751	9001.5099	----其他	20Δ12	0 冰岛IS,东盟AS,哥CR,香港HK,新加坡SG,新西兰NZ,智利CL 6 秘鲁PE 12 澳AU 14 瑞士CH 16 韩国KR	0 受惠国$_1$LD$_1$	70	----Other
		-其他:					-Other:
7752	9001.9010	---彩色滤光片	8	0 冰岛IS,东盟AS,哥CR,秘鲁PE,香港HK,新西兰NZ,智利CL 3.2 瑞士CH 4.8 澳AU 5 巴PK 6.9 韩国KR 7.6 亚太AP	0 受惠国LD	20	---Color filter
7753	9001.9090	---其他	8	0 冰岛IS,东盟AS,哥CR,秘鲁PE,香港HK,新西兰NZ,智利CL 4.8 澳AU 5 巴PK 5.6 瑞士CH 6.4 韩国KR 7.6 亚太AP	0 受惠国LD	20	---Other

序号 No.	税则号列 Tariff Line	中文货品名称 Article Description in Chinese	最惠国税率 MFN(%)	协定税率 Agreement(%)	特惠税率 SP(%)	普通税率 Gen(%)	英文货品名称 Article Description
	ex90019090	光通信用微光组件的光学元件（包括工作波长为800nm～1700nm的薄膜滤光片、自聚焦透镜、法拉第旋转片）	Δ1				Micro-optic component for optical communication (including thin film filter, gradient index lens and faraday Rotator, with working wavelength between 800nm and 1700nm)
	ex90019090	液晶显示屏背光模组的光学元件(包括导光板、反射板、扩散片、增亮片)	Δ2				Optical elements for backlight module of liquid crystal display (including light guide, reflect sheet, diffuser, prism sheet to enhance brightness)
	ex90019090	激光视盘机激光收发装置用的微型镜片	Δ3				Mini lens use for with laser transmitting and receving device of laser disc player
	ex90019090	非涅耳透镜投影屏（屏幕对角线≥80英寸，投射比≤0.26，增益比≥0.8，镜头间距≤100微米）	Δ6				Fresnel lens porojection screen (the length of diagoncal screen≥80 inch, Projection ratio≤0.26, ratio of gains≥0.8, lens spacing≤100 microns)
	ex90019090	液晶投影仪用偏光元件	Δ6				Polarizer for liquid-crystal projectors
	ex90019090	数字电影放映机用偏光元件	Δ6				Polarizer for digital cinema projector
	90.02	**已装配的各种材料制透镜、棱镜、反射镜及其他光学元件，作为仪器或装置的零件、配件，但未经光学加工的玻璃制上述元件除外：**					**Lenses, prisms, mirrors and other optical elements, of any material, mounted, being parts of or fittings for instruments or apparatus, other than such elements of glass not optically worked:**
		-物镜：					-Objective lenses:
		--照相机、投影仪、照片放大机及缩片机用：					--For cameras, projectors or photographic enlargers or reducers:
7754	9002.1110	---子目号9006. 1010至9006. 3000所列照相机用	8	0 冰岛IS,东盟AS,哥CR,秘鲁PE,新西兰NZ,智利CL 3.2 瑞士CH 4.8 澳AU,韩国KR 5 巴PK	0 受惠国LD	14	---For the photographic cameras of subheadings Nos. 9006.1010 to 9006.3000
7755	9002.1120	---缩微阅读机用	8	0 冰岛IS,东盟AS,哥CR,秘鲁PE,新西兰NZ,智利CL 3.2 瑞士CH 4.8 澳AU,韩国KR 5 巴PK	0 受惠国LD	14	---For microfilm, microfiche or other microform readers
		---其他照相机用：					---For other photographic cameras:
7756	9002.1131	----单反相机镜头	15Δ3	0 冰岛IS,东盟AS,哥CR,新加坡SG,新西兰NZ,智利CL 4.5 秘鲁PE 9 澳AU 10.5 瑞士CH 12 巴PK	0 受惠国$_1$LD$_1$	80	----For single lens reflex cameras
7757	9002.1139	----其他	15Δ3	0 冰岛IS,东盟AS,哥CR,新加坡SG,新西兰NZ,智利CL 4.5 秘鲁PE 9 澳AU 10.5 瑞士CH 12 巴PK,韩国KR	0 受惠国LD	80	----Other

序号 No.	税则号列 Tariff Line	中文货品名称 Article Description in Chinese	最惠国税率 MFN(%)	协定税率 Agreement(%)	特惠税率 SP(%)	普通税率 Gen(%)	英文货品名称 Article Description
7758	9002.1190	---其他	15	0 冰岛IS,东盟AS,哥CR,台湾TW,新加坡SG,新西兰NZ,智利CL 4.5 秘鲁PE 9 澳AU 10.5 瑞士CH 12 巴PK 13 韩国KR	0 受惠国LD	80	---Other
	ex90021190	彩色投影机和数字光处理器的镜头及镜头组件	Δ3				Lens and lens assembly of colour projectors or digital light proceesors
		--其他:					--Other:
7759	9002.1910	---摄影机或放映机用	15	0 冰岛IS,东盟AS,哥CR,新加坡SG,新西兰NZ,智利CL 4.5 秘鲁PE 9 澳AU 10.5 瑞士CH 12 巴PK,韩国KR	0 受惠国$_1$LD$_1$	40	---For cinematographic cameras or projectors
7760	9002.1990	---其他	15	0 冰岛IS,东盟AS,哥CR,台湾TW,香港HK,新加坡SG,新西兰NZ,智利CL 4.5 秘鲁PE 9 澳AU 10.5 瑞士CH 12 巴PK 13 韩国KR	0 受惠国LD	50	---Other
	ex90021990	摄像机、摄录一体机的镜头	Δ3				Lens for video cameras or camcorders
	ex90021990	手机、平板电脑用物镜（800万像素及以上）	Δ6				Objective lens for mobile telephones and tablet computers (pixels≥8 million)
		-滤色镜:					-Filters:
7761	9002.2010	---照相机用	15	0 冰岛IS,东盟AS,哥CR,新加坡SG,新西兰NZ,智利CL 4.5 秘鲁PE 9 澳AU 10.5 瑞士CH 12 巴PK 13 韩国KR 14.3 亚太AP	0 受惠国$_1$LD$_1$	80	---For cameras
7762	9002.2090	---其他	15	0 冰岛IS,东盟AS,哥CR,新加坡SG,新西兰NZ,智利CL 4.5 秘鲁PE 9 澳AU 10.5 瑞士CH 12 巴PK 13 韩国KR 14.3 亚太AP	0 受惠国$_1$LD$_1$	40	---Other
		-其他:					-Other:
7763	9002.9010	---照相机用	15	0 冰岛IS,东盟AS,哥CR,台湾TW,香港HK,新加坡SG,新西兰NZ,智利CL 4.5 秘鲁PE 9 澳AU 10.5 瑞士CH 12 巴PK 13 韩国KR	0 受惠国$_1$LD$_1$	80	---For cameras
	ex90029010	照相机用带屈光度调节装置的目镜	Δ10				Eyepieces with diopter adjustment devices for cameras

序号 No.	税则号列 Tariff Line	中文货品名称 Article Description in Chinese	最惠国税率 MFN(%)	协定税率 Agreement(%)	特惠税率 SP(%)	普通税率 Gen(%)	英文货品名称 Article Description
7764	9002.9090	---其他	15	0 冰岛IS,东盟AS,哥CR,台湾TW,香港HK,新加坡SG,新西兰NZ,智利CL 4.5 秘鲁PE 9 澳AU 10.5 瑞士CH 12 巴PK 13 韩国KR	0 受惠国LD	40	---Other
	ex90029090	其他带屈光度调节装置的目镜	Δ10				Other eyepieces with diopter adjustment devices
	ex90029090	掩膜版	Δ10				Photo masks
	90.03	**眼镜架及其零件：**					**Frames and mountings for spectacles, goggles or the like, and parts thereof:**
		-眼镜架：					-Frames and mountings:
7765	9003.1100	--塑料制	18Δ12	0 澳门MO,冰岛IS,东盟AS,哥CR,香港HK,新加坡SG,新西兰NZ,智利CL 5.4 秘鲁PE 10.8 澳AU 12.6 瑞士CH 14.4 韩国KR	0 受惠国$_1$LD$_1$	70	--Of plastics
		--其他材料制：					--Of other materials:
7766	9003.1910	---金属材料制	10Δ6	0 澳门MO,冰岛IS,东盟AS,哥CR,秘鲁PE,香港HK,新西兰NZ,智利CL 4 瑞士CH 5 巴PK 6 澳AU 8 韩国KR	0 受惠国$_1$LD$_1$	70	---Of metal materials
7767	9003.1920	---天然材料制	10	0 澳门MO,冰岛IS,东盟AS,哥CR,秘鲁PE,香港HK,新西兰NZ,智利CL 4 瑞士CH 5 巴PK 6 澳AU 8 韩国KR	0 受惠国$_1$LD$_1$	70	---Of narural materials
7768	9003.1990	---其他	10	0 澳门MO,冰岛IS,东盟AS,哥CR,秘鲁PE,香港HK,新西兰NZ,智利CL 4 瑞士CH 5 巴PK 6 澳AU 8 韩国KR	0 受惠国$_1$LD$_1$	70	---Other
7769	9003.9000	-零件	10Δ6	0 冰岛IS,东盟AS,哥CR,秘鲁PE,香港HK,新西兰NZ,智利CL 4 瑞士CH 5 巴PK 6 澳AU 8 韩国KR	0 受惠国$_1$LD$_1$	70	-Parts
	90.04	**矫正视力、保护眼睛或其他用途的眼镜、挡风镜及类似品：**					**Spectacles, goggles and the like, corrective, protective or other:**
7770	9004.1000	-太阳镜	20Δ6	0 澳门MO,冰岛IS,东盟AS,哥CR,香港HK,新加坡SG,新西兰NZ,智利CL 6 秘鲁PE 12 澳AU 14 瑞士CH 17.3 韩国KR	0 受惠国$_1$LD$_1$	100	-Sunglasses
		-其他：					-Other:

序号 No.	税则号列 Tariff Line	中文货品名称 Article Description in Chinese	最惠国税率 MFN(%)	协定税率 Agreement(%)	特惠税率 SP(%)	普通税率 Gen(%)	英文货品名称 Article Description
7771	9004.9010	---变色镜	16	0 澳门MO,冰岛IS,东盟AS,哥CR,香港HK,新加坡SG,新西兰NZ,智利CL 4.8 秘鲁PE 9.6 澳AU 11.2 瑞士CH 12.8 巴PK,韩国KR	0 受惠国$_1$LD$_1$	100	---Photochromic spectacles
7772	9004.9090	---其他	20Δ12	0 澳门MO,冰岛IS,东盟AS,哥CR,香港HK,新加坡SG,新西兰NZ,智利CL 6 秘鲁PE 12 澳AU 14 瑞士CH 16 韩国KR	0 受惠国$_1$LD$_1$	90	---Other
	90.05	**双筒望远镜、单筒望远镜、其他光学望远镜及其座架;其他天文仪器及其座架,但不包括射电天文仪器:**					**Binoculars, monoculars, other optical telescopes, and mountings therefor; other astronomical instruments and mountings therefor, but not including instruments for radio-astronomy:**
7773	9005.1000	-双筒望远镜	15	0 冰岛IS,东盟AS,哥CR,新加坡SG,新西兰NZ,智利CL 4.5 秘鲁PE 9 澳AU 10.5 瑞士CH 12 巴PK,韩国KR	0 受惠国$_1$LD$_1$	50	-Binoculars
		-其他仪器:					-Other instruments:
7774	9005.8010	---天文望远镜及其他天文仪器	3	0 澳AU,巴PK,冰岛IS,东盟AS,哥CR,韩国KR,秘鲁PE,瑞士CH,新西兰NZ,智利CL	0 受惠国LD	8	---Astronomical telescopes and other astronomical instruments
7775	9005.8090	---其他	12	0 冰岛IS,东盟AS,哥CR,秘鲁PE,新加坡SG,新西兰NZ,智利CL 6 巴PK 7.2 澳AU 8.4 瑞士CH 9.6 韩国KR	0 受惠国LD	50	---Other
		-零件、附件(包括座架):					-Parts and accessories (including mountings) :
7776	9005.9010	---天文望远镜及其他天文仪器用	2	0 澳AU,巴PK,冰岛IS,东盟AS,哥CR,韩国KR,秘鲁PE,瑞士CH,新西兰NZ,智利CL	0 受惠国LD	8	---Of instruments of subheading No. 9005.8010
7777	9005.9090	---其他	8	0 冰岛IS,东盟AS,哥CR,秘鲁PE,新西兰NZ,智利CL 3.2 瑞士CH 4.8 澳AU,韩国KR 5 巴PK	0 受惠国LD	30	---Other
	90.06	**照相机(电影摄影机除外);照相闪光灯装置及闪光灯泡,但税号85.39的放电灯泡除外:**					**Photographic (other than cinematographic) cameras; photographic flashlight apparatus and flashbulbs other than discharge lamps of heading 8539:**
		-制版照相机:					-Cameras of a kind used for preparing printing plates or cylinders:

序号 No.	税则号列 Tariff Line	中文货品名称 Article Description in Chinese	最惠国税率 MFN(%)	协定税率 Agreement(%)	特惠税率 SP(%)	普通税率 Gen(%)	英文货品名称 Article Description
7778	9006.1010	---电子分色机	12	0 冰岛IS,东盟AS,哥CR,秘鲁PE,新加坡SG,新西兰NZ,智利CL 6 巴PK 7.2 澳AU 8.4 瑞士CH 9.6 韩国KR	0 受惠国LD	20	---Electronic colour scanners
7779	9006.1090	---其他	10	0 冰岛IS,东盟AS,哥CR,秘鲁PE,新西兰NZ,智利CL 4 瑞士CH 5 巴PK 6 澳AU 8 韩国KR	0 受惠国LD	20	---Other
7780	9006.3000	-水下、航空测量或体内器官检查用的特种照相机;法庭或犯罪学用的比较照相机	9	0 冰岛IS,东盟AS,哥CR,秘鲁PE,新西兰NZ,智利CL 3.6 瑞士CH 5 巴PK 5.4 澳AU	0 受惠国LD	17	-Cameras specially designed for underwater use, for aerial survey or for medical or surgical examination of internal organs; comparison cameras for forensic or criminological purposes
7781	9006.4000	-一次成像照相机	5	0 澳AU,巴PK,冰岛IS,东盟AS,哥CR,秘鲁PE,瑞士CH,新西兰NZ,智利CL 4 韩国KR	0 受惠国LD	70	-Instant print cameras
		-其他照相机:					-Other cameras:
7782	9006.5100	--通过镜头取景(单镜头反光式(SLR)),使用胶片宽度不超过35毫米	25	0 冰岛IS,东盟AS,哥CR,新加坡SG,新西兰NZ,智利CL 15 澳AU 18 瑞士CH 22.5 韩国KR	0 受惠国$_2$LD$_2$	100	--With a through-the-lens viewfinder (single lens reflex (SLR)), for roll film of a width not exceeding 35mm
		--其他,使用胶片宽度小于35毫米:					--Other, for roll film of a width less than 35mm:
7783	9006.5210	---缩微照相机,使用缩微胶卷、胶片或其他缩微品的	9	0 冰岛IS,东盟AS,哥CR,秘鲁PE,新西兰NZ,智利CL 3.6 瑞士CH 5 巴PK 5.4 澳AU,韩国KR	0 受惠国LD	17	---Cameras of a kind used for recording documents on microfilm, microfiche or other microforms
7784	9006.5290	---其他	25	0 东盟AS,哥CR,新加坡SG,新西兰NZ,智利CL 15 澳AU 18 瑞士CH 22.5 韩国KR	0 受惠国$_2$LD$_2$	100	---Other
7785	9006.5300	--其他,使用胶片宽度为35毫米	20	0 冰岛IS,东盟AS,哥CR,新加坡SG,新西兰NZ,智利CL 6 秘鲁PE 12 澳AU 14 瑞士CH 17.3 韩国KR	0 受惠国$_1$LD$_1$	100	--Other, for roll film of a width of 35mm
		--其他:					--Other:
7786	9006.5910	---激光照相排版设备	9	0 冰岛IS,东盟AS,哥CR,秘鲁PE,新加坡SG,新西兰NZ,智利CL 3.6 瑞士CH 5 巴PK 5.4 澳AU 7.8 韩国KR	0 受惠国LD	35	---Laser photo typesetting equipments
7787	9006.5990	---其他	25	0 冰岛IS,东盟AS,哥CR,新加坡SG,新西兰NZ,智利CL 15 澳AU 22.5 韩国KR	0 受惠国$_2$LD$_2$	100	---Other

序号 No.	税则号列 Tariff Line	中文货品名称 Article Description in Chinese	最惠国税率 MFN(%)	协定税率 Agreement(%)	特惠税率 SP(%)	普通税率 Gen(%)	英文货品名称 Article Description
		-照相闪光灯装置及闪光灯泡:					-Photographic flashlight apparatus and flashbulbs:
7788	9006.6100	--放电式（电子式）闪光灯装置	18	0 冰岛IS,东盟AS,哥CR,新加坡SG,新西兰NZ,智利CL 5.4 秘鲁PE 10.8 澳AU 12.6 瑞士CH 14.4 韩国KR	0 受惠国$_1$LD$_1$	80	--Discharge lamp (“electronic”) flashlight apparatus
	ex90066100	照相手机用闪光灯组件	Δ4				Flashlight modules for mobile telephones with camera function
	ex90066100	照相机外置式电子闪光灯(闪光指数GN≥30,具有无线闪光功能,支持自动变焦)	Δ15				External flashlights for cameras (Flash guide number≥30, with wireless flash and automatic focusing function)
		--其他:					--Other:
7789	9006.6910	---闪光灯泡	18	0 冰岛IS,东盟AS,哥CR,新加坡SG,新西兰NZ,智利CL 5.4 秘鲁PE 10.8 澳AU 12.6 瑞士CH 14.4 巴PK 16.2 韩国KR	0 受惠国$_1$LD$_1$	80	---Flashbulbs
7790	9006.6990	---其他	18	0 冰岛IS,东盟AS,哥CR,新加坡SG,新西兰NZ,智利CL 5.4 秘鲁PE 10.8 澳AU 12.6 瑞士CH 14.4 巴PK,韩国KR	0 受惠国$_1$LD$_1$	80	---Other
		-零件、附件:					-Parts and accessories:
		--照相机用:					--For cameras:
7791	9006.9110	---子目号9006. 1010至9006. 3000所列相机用	8	0 冰岛IS,东盟AS,哥CR,秘鲁PE,香港HK,新西兰NZ,智利CL 3.2 瑞士CH 4.8 澳AU 5 巴PK 5.6 亚太AP 6.4 韩国KR	0 受惠国LD,亚太AP	17	---For cameras of subheadings No.9006.1010 to 9006.3000
7792	9006.9120	---一次成像照相机用	5	0 澳AU,巴PK,冰岛IS,东盟AS,哥CR,秘鲁PE,瑞士CH,香港HK,新西兰NZ,智利CL 3 韩国KR 3.5 亚太AP	0 受惠国LD,亚太AP	100	---For instant print cameras
		---其他:					---Other:
7793	9006.9191	----自动调焦组件	10Δ6	0 冰岛IS,东盟AS,哥CR,秘鲁PE,香港HK,新加坡SG,新西兰NZ,智利CL 4 瑞士CH 5 巴PK 6 澳AU 7 亚太AP 8 韩国KR	0 受惠国LD,亚太AP	100	----Automatic focal setting units
7794	9006.9192	----快门组件	10Δ6	0 冰岛IS,东盟AS,哥CR,秘鲁PE,香港HK,新加坡SG,新西兰NZ,智利CL 4 瑞士CH 5 巴PK 6 澳AU 7 亚太AP 8 韩国KR	0 受惠国LD,亚太AP	100	----Shutter units

序号 No.	税则号列 Tariff Line	中文货品名称 Article Description in Chinese	最惠国税率 MFN(%)	协定税率 Agreement(%)	特惠税率 SP(%)	普通税率 Gen(%)	英文货品名称 Article Description
7795	9006.9199	----其他	10Δ6	0 冰岛IS,东盟AS,哥CR,秘鲁PE,香港HK,新加坡SG,新西兰NZ,智利CL 4 瑞士CH 5 巴PK 6 澳AU 7 亚太AP 8 韩国KR	0 受惠国LD,亚太AP	100	----Other
7796	9006.9900	--其他	12	0 冰岛IS,东盟AS,哥CR,秘鲁PE,新加坡SG,新西兰NZ,智利CL 6 巴PK 7.2 澳AU 8.4 瑞士CH 9.6 韩国KR	0 受惠国LD	80	--Other
	90.07	**电影摄影机、放映机，不论是否带有声音的录制或重放装置：**					**Cinematographic cameras and projectors, whether or not incorporating sound recording or reproducing apparatus:**
		-摄影机：					-Cameras:
7797	9007.1010	---高速摄影机	14	0 冰岛IS,东盟AS,哥CR,秘鲁PE,新加坡SG,新西兰NZ,智利CL 7 巴PK 8.4 澳AU 9.8 瑞士CH 11.2 韩国KR	0 受惠国$_1$LD$_1$	40	---High speed cameras
7798	9007.1090	---其他	14	0 冰岛IS,东盟AS,哥CR,秘鲁PE,新加坡SG,新西兰NZ,智利CL 8.4 澳AU 9.8 瑞士CH 11.2 巴PK,韩国KR	0 受惠国$_1$LD$_1$	40	---Other
		-放映机：					-Projectors:
7799	9007.2010	---数字式	14	0 冰岛IS,东盟AS,哥CR,秘鲁PE,香港HK,新加坡SG,新西兰NZ,智利CL 8.4 澳AU 9.8 瑞士CH 11.2 巴PK,韩国KR	0 受惠国$_1$LD$_1$	40	---Digital
	ex90072010	2K及以上分辨率的硬盘式数字电影放映机	Δ8				Digital cinematographs with magnetic discs, resolving power≥2k
7800	9007.2090	---其他	14	0 冰岛IS,东盟AS,哥CR,秘鲁PE,新加坡SG,新西兰NZ,智利CL 8.4 澳AU 9.8 瑞士CH 11.2 巴PK,韩国KR	0 受惠国$_1$LD$_1$	40	---Other
		-零件、附件：					-Parts and accessories:
7801	9007.9100	--摄影机用	8.4Δ5	0 冰岛IS,东盟AS,哥CR,秘鲁PE,新西兰NZ,智利CL 3.36 瑞士CH 5 澳AU,巴PK 6.7 韩国KR	0 受惠国$_1$LD$_1$	40	--For cameras
7802	9007.9200	--放映机用	8.4Δ5	0 冰岛IS,东盟AS,哥CR,秘鲁PE,新西兰NZ,智利CL 3.36 瑞士CH 5 澳AU,巴PK,韩国KR	0 受惠国$_1$LD$_1$	40	--For projectors

序号 No.	税则号列 Tariff Line	中文货品名称 Article Description in Chinese	最惠国税率 MFN(%)	协定税率 Agreement(%)	特惠税率 SP(%)	普通税率 Gen(%)	英文货品名称 Article Description
	90.08	**影像投影仪，但电影用除外;照片（电影片除外）放大机及缩片机:**					**Image projectors, other than cinematographic; photographic (other than cinematographic) enlargers and reducers:**
		-投影仪、放大机及缩片机:					-Projectors, enlargers and reducers:
7803	9008.5010	---幻灯机	14	0 冰岛IS,东盟AS,哥CR,秘鲁PE,新加坡SG,新西兰NZ,智利CL 7 巴PK 8.4 澳AU 9.8 瑞士CH 11.2 韩国KR	0 受惠国$_1$LD$_1$	40	---Slide projectors
7804	9008.5020	---缩微胶卷、缩微胶片或其他缩微品的阅读机，不论是否可以进行复制	10	0 冰岛IS,东盟AS,哥CR,秘鲁PE,新西兰NZ,智利CL 4 瑞士CH 5 巴PK 6 澳AU 8 韩国KR	0 受惠国$_1$LD$_1$	40	---Microfilm, microfiche or other microform readers, whether or not capable of producing copies
		---其他影像投影仪:					---Other image projectors:
7805	9008.5031	----正射投影仪	18	0 冰岛IS,东盟AS,哥CR,新加坡SG,新西兰NZ,智利CL 5.4 秘鲁PE 10.8 澳AU 12.6 瑞士CH	0 受惠国$_1$LD$_1$	40	----Orthographical projectors
7806	9008.5039	----其他	18	0 冰岛IS,东盟AS,哥CR,新加坡SG,新西兰NZ,智利CL 5.4 秘鲁PE 10.8 澳AU 12.6 瑞士CH	0 受惠国$_1$LD$_1$	40	----Other
7807	9008.5040	---照片（电影片除外）放大机及缩片机	20	0 冰岛IS,东盟AS,哥CR,新加坡SG,新西兰NZ,智利CL 6 秘鲁PE 12 澳AU 14 瑞士CH 17.3 韩国KR	0 受惠国$_1$LD$_1$	80	---Photographic (other than cinematographic) enlargers and reducers
		-零件、附件:					-Parts and accessories:
7808	9008.9010	---缩微阅读机用	8	0 冰岛IS,东盟AS,哥CR,秘鲁PE,新西兰NZ,智利CL 3.2 瑞士CH 4.8 澳AU,韩国KR 5 巴PK	0 受惠国$_1$LD$_1$	17	---Of microfilm, microfiche or other microform readers
7809	9008.9020	---照片放大机及缩片机用	14	0 冰岛IS,东盟AS,哥CR,秘鲁PE,新加坡SG,新西兰NZ,智利CL 7 巴PK 8.4 澳AU 9.8 瑞士CH 11.2 韩国KR	0 受惠国$_1$LD$_1$	80	---Of photographic enlargers and reducers
7810	9008.9090	---其他	14	0 冰岛IS,东盟AS,哥CR,秘鲁PE,新加坡SG,新西兰NZ,智利CL 8.4 澳AU 9.8 瑞士CH 11.2 巴PK,韩国KR	0 受惠国$_1$LD$_1$	40	---Other

序号 No.	税则号列 Tariff Line	中文货品名称 Article Description in Chinese	最惠国税率 MFN(%)	协定税率 Agreement(%)	特惠税率 SP(%)	普通税率 Gen(%)	英文货品名称 Article Description
	90.10	**本章其他税号未列名的照相（包括电影）洗印用装置及设备;负片显示器;银幕及其他投影屏幕:**					**Apparatus and equipment for photographic (including cinematographic) laboratories, not specified or included elsewhere in this Chapter; negatoscopes; projection screens:**
		-照相（包括电影）胶卷或成卷感光纸的自动显影装置及设备或将已冲洗胶卷自动曝光到成卷感光纸上的装置及设备:					-Apparatus and equipment for automatically developing photographic (including cinematographic) film or paper in rolls or for automatically exposing developed film to rolls of photographic paper:
7811	9010.1010	---电影用	14	0 冰岛IS,东盟AS,哥CR,秘鲁PE,香港HK,新加坡SG,新西兰NZ,智利CL 7 巴PK 8.4 澳AU 9.8 瑞士CH 11.2 韩国KR	0 受惠国$_1$LD$_1$	40	---Of a kind used in cinematographic film
7812	9010.1020	---特种照相用	8.4	0 冰岛IS,东盟AS,哥CR,秘鲁PE,香港HK,新西兰NZ,智利CL 3.36 瑞士CH 5 澳AU,巴PK,韩国KR	0 受惠国LD	20	---Of a kind used in special photographic film or paper
		---其他:					---Other:
7813	9010.1091	----彩色胶卷用	25	0 冰岛IS,东盟AS,哥CR,香港HK,新加坡SG,新西兰NZ,智利CL 7.5 秘鲁PE 15 澳AU 18 瑞士CH 22.5 韩国KR	0 受惠国$_1$LD$_1$	100	----For the colour photographic film in rolls
7814	9010.1099	----其他	15	0 冰岛IS,东盟AS,哥CR,香港HK,新加坡SG,新西兰NZ,智利CL 4.5 秘鲁PE 9 澳AU 10.5 瑞士CH 12 巴PK 13.5 韩国KR	0 受惠国$_1$LD$_1$	100	----Other
		-照相（包括电影）洗印用其他装置及设备;负片显示器:					-Other apparatus and equipment for photographic (including cinematographic) laboratories; negatoscopes:
7815	9010.5010	---负片显示器	14	0 冰岛IS,东盟AS,哥CR,秘鲁PE,新加坡SG,新西兰NZ,智利CL 7 巴PK 8.4 澳AU 9.8 瑞士CH 11.2 韩国KR	0 受惠国$_1$LD$_1$	50	---Negatoscopes
		---其他:					---Other:
7816	9010.5021	----电影用	14	0 冰岛IS,东盟AS,哥CR,秘鲁PE,新加坡SG,新西兰NZ,智利CL 8.4 澳AU 9.8 瑞士CH 11.2 巴PK,韩国KR	0 受惠国$_1$LD$_1$	40	----Of a kind used in cinematographic film

序号 No.	税则号列 Tariff Line	中文货品名称 Article Description in Chinese	最惠国税率 MFN(%)	协定税率 Agreement(%)	特惠税率 SP(%)	普通税率 Gen(%)	英文货品名称 Article Description
7817	9010.5022	----特种照相用	8.4	0 冰岛IS,东盟AS,哥CR,秘鲁PE,新西兰NZ,智利CL 3.36 瑞士CH 5 澳AU,巴PK 6.7 韩国KR	0 受惠国LD	20	----Of a kind used in special photo-graphic film or paper
7818	9010.5029	----其他	17	0 冰岛IS,东盟AS,哥CR,新加坡SG,新西兰NZ,智利CL 5.1 秘鲁PE 10.2 澳AU 11.9 瑞士CH 13.6 巴PK,韩国KR	0 受惠国$_1$LD$_1$	100	----Other
7819	9010.6000	-银幕及其他投影屏幕	14	0 冰岛IS,东盟AS,哥CR,秘鲁PE,新加坡SG,新西兰NZ,智利CL 8.4 澳AU 9.8 瑞士CH 11.2 巴PK,韩国KR	0 受惠国$_1$LD$_1$	50	-Projection screens
		-零件、附件:					-Parts and accessories:
7820	9010.9010	---电影用	0		0 受惠国LD	40	---Of a kind used in cinematographic film
7821	9010.9020	---特种照相用	0		0 受惠国LD	20	---Of a kind used in special photographic film or paper
7822	9010.9090	---其他	0		0 受惠国LD	100	---Other
	90.11	**复式光学显微镜，包括用于缩微照相、显微电影摄影及显微投影的:**					**Compound optical microscopes, including those for photomicrography, cinephotomicrography or microprojection:**
7823	9011.1000	-立体显微镜	0		0 受惠国LD	14	-Stereoscopic microscopes
7824	9011.2000	-缩微照相、显微电影摄影及显微投影用的其他显微镜	0		0 受惠国LD	14	-Other microscopes, for photomicrography, cinephotomi-crography or microprojection
7825	9011.8000	-其他显微镜	7	0 冰岛IS,东盟AS,哥CR,秘鲁PE,新西兰NZ,智利CL 4.2 澳AU 4.9 瑞士CH 5 巴PK 5.6 韩国KR	0 受惠国$_1$LD$_1$	14	-Other microscopes
	ex90118000	高倍测量显微镜，放大倍数≥1000倍，分辨率≤0.08微米	Δ3				high power microscope , enlargment ratio≥1000, resolution ration≤0.08mm
7826	9011.9000	-零件、附件	0		0 受惠国LD	14	-Parts and accessories
	90.12	**显微镜，但光学显微镜除外;衍射设备:**					**Microscopes other than optical microscopes; diffraction apparatus:**
7827	9012.1000	-显微镜，但光学显微镜除外;衍射设备	0		0 受惠国LD	14	-Microscopes other than optical microscopes; and diffraction apparatus
7828	9012.9000	-零件、附件	0		0 受惠国LD	14	-Parts and accessories
	90.13	**其他税号未列名的液晶装置;激光器，但激光二极管除外;本章其他税号未列名的光学仪器及器具:**					**Liquid crystal devices not constituting articles provided for more specifically in other headings; lasers, other than laser diodes; other optical appliances and instruments, not specified or included elsewhere in this chapter:**

序号 No.	税则号列 Tariff Line	中文货品名称 Article Description in Chinese	最惠国税率 MFN(%)	协定税率 Agreement(%)	特惠税率 SP(%)	普通税率 Gen(%)	英文货品名称 Article Description
7829	9013.1000	-武器用望远镜瞄准具；潜望镜式望远镜；作为本章或第十六类的机器、设备、仪器或器具部件的望远镜	8	0 冰岛IS,东盟AS,哥CR,秘鲁PE,新西兰NZ,智利CL 3.2 瑞士CH 4.8 澳AU,韩国KR 5 巴PK	0 受惠国$_1$LD$_1$	14	-Telescopic sights for fitting to arms; periscopes; telescopes designed to formparts of machines, appliances, instruments or apparatus of this Chapter or Section XVI
7830	9013.2000	-激光器，但激光二极管除外	6	0 澳门MO,冰岛IS,东盟AS,哥CR,秘鲁PE,新西兰NZ,智利CL 3.6 澳AU 4.2 瑞士CH 4.8 韩国KR 5 巴PK	0 受惠国$_1$LD$_1$	11	-Lasers, other than laser diodes
	ex90132000	用于2.5GB/s及以上SDH、波分复用光传输设备的980纳米、1480纳米的泵浦激光器	Δ3				980nm or 1480nm pump laster of SDH≥2.5GB/s, for optical transmission equipment for wave divison mulitiplexing
	ex90132000	激光切割机用气体激光发生器,切割功率≥2千瓦	Δ3				Gas laser oscillators for laser cutting machines, cutting powr≥2kW
	ex90132000	用于2.5GB/s及以上光通信设备的850纳米、1260~1625纳米，且功率≤200毫瓦的激光器（泵浦激光器除外）	Δ3				850nm or 1260-1625nm laster of SDH≥2.5GB/s, for optical transmission equipment (excluding pump laster)
		-其他装置、仪器及器具：					-Other devices, appliances and instruments:
7831	9013.8010	---放大镜	12	0 澳门MO,冰岛IS,东盟AS,哥CR,秘鲁PE,香港HK,新加坡SG,新西兰NZ,智利CL 5 巴PK 7.2 澳AU 8.4 瑞士CH,亚太AP 9.6 韩国KR	0 受惠国$_1$LD$_1$	50	---Hand magnifying glasses
7832	9013.8020	---光学门眼	12	0 冰岛IS,东盟AS,哥CR,秘鲁PE,新加坡SG,新西兰NZ,智利CL 5 巴PK 7.2 澳AU 8.4 瑞士CH,亚太AP 9.6 韩国KR	0 受惠国$_1$LD$_1$	50	---Door eyes
7833	9013.8030	---液晶显示板	5	0 澳门MO,巴PK,冰岛IS,东盟AS,香港HK,新西兰NZ,智利CL 4.3 澳AU 5 韩国KR		50	---Liquid crystal display panel
7834	9013.8090	---其他	5	0 澳AU,澳门MO,巴PK,冰岛IS,东盟AS,哥CR,秘鲁PE,香港HK,新西兰NZ,智利CL 2 瑞士CH	0 受惠国$_1$LD$_1$	17	---Other
		-零件、附件：					-Parts and accessories:
7835	9013.9010	---子目录9013. 1000及9013. 2000所列货品用	6	0 澳门MO,冰岛IS,东盟AS,哥CR,秘鲁PE,香港HK,新西兰NZ,智利CL 2.4 瑞士CH 3.6 澳AU 4.8 韩国KR 5 巴PK	0 受惠国$_1$LD$_1$	11	---For goods of subheading No. 9013.1000 or 9013.2000

序号 No.	税则号列 Tariff Line	中文货品名称 Article Description in Chinese	最惠国税率 MFN(%)	协定税率 Agreement(%)		特惠税率 SP(%)		普通税率 Gen(%)	英文货品名称 Article Description
7836	9013.9020	---子目录9013.8030所列货品用	8	0 3.2 4.8 5 6.9	澳门MO,冰岛IS,东盟AS,哥CR,秘鲁PE,香港HK,新西兰NZ,智利CL 瑞士CH 澳AU 巴PK 韩国KR	0	受惠国$_1$LD$_1$	17	---For goods of subheading No.9013.8030
7837	9013.9090	---其他	8	0 3.2 4.8 5 8	澳门MO,冰岛IS,东盟AS,哥CR,秘鲁PE,香港HK,新西兰NZ,智利CL 瑞士CH 澳AU 巴PK 韩国KR	0	受惠国$_1$LD$_1$	17	---Other
	ex90139090	太阳能定日镜的零件	Δ5						Parts of solar heliostats
	90.14	**定向罗盘;其他导航仪器及装置:**							**Direction finding compasses; other navigational instruments and appliances:**
7838	9014.1000	-定向罗盘	2	0 1.7	澳AU,巴PK,冰岛IS,东盟AS,哥CR,秘鲁PE,瑞士CH,新西兰NZ,智利CL 韩国KR	0	受惠国LD	8	-Direction finding compasses
		-航空或航天导航仪器及装置（罗盘除外）:							-Instruments and appliances for aeronautical or space navigation (other than compasses) :
7839	9014.2010	---自动驾驶仪	2Δ1	0 1.7	澳AU,巴PK,冰岛IS,东盟AS,哥CR,秘鲁PE,瑞士CH,新西兰NZ,智利CL 韩国KR	0	受惠国LD	8	---Automatic pilot
7840	9014.2090	---其他	2	0	澳AU,巴PK,冰岛IS,东盟AS,哥CR,韩国KR,秘鲁PE,瑞士CH,新西兰NZ,智利CL	0	受惠国LD	8	---Other
	ex90142090	航空惯性导航仪	Δ1						Aviation inetial navigator
7841	9014.8000	-其他仪器及装置	2	0 1.2	澳AU,巴PK,冰岛IS,东盟AS,哥CR,秘鲁PE,瑞士CH,新西兰NZ,智利CL 韩国KR	0	受惠国LD	8	-Other instruments and appliances
		-零件、附件:							-Parts and accessories:
7842	9014.9010	---自动驾驶仪用	1.5Δ1	0	澳AU,巴PK,冰岛IS,东盟AS,哥CR,韩国KR,秘鲁PE,瑞士CH,新西兰NZ,智利CL	0	受惠国LD	8	---For automatic pilot
7843	9014.9090	---其他	1.5	0	澳AU,巴PK,冰岛IS,东盟AS,哥CR,韩国KR,秘鲁PE,瑞士CH,新西兰NZ,智利CL	0	受惠国$_1$LD$_1$	8	---Other
	90.15	**大地测量（包括摄影测量）、水道测量、海洋、水文、气象或地球物理用仪器及装置，不包括罗盘;测距仪:**							**Surveying (including photogrammetrical surveying) , hydrographic, oceanographic, hydrological, meteorological or geophysical instruments and appliances, excluding compasses; rangefinders:**
7844	9015.1000	-测距仪	9	0 5 5.4 6.8 7.2	冰岛IS,东盟AS,哥CR,秘鲁PE,新西兰NZ,智利CL 巴PK 澳AU 瑞士CH 韩国KR	0	受惠国LD	14	-Rangefinders

序号 No.	税则号列 Tariff Line	中文货品名称 Article Description in Chinese	最惠国税率 MFN(%)	协定税率 Agreement(%)	特惠税率 SP(%)	普通税率 Gen(%)	英文货品名称 Article Description
7845	9015.2000	-经纬仪及视距仪	9	0 冰岛IS,东盟AS,哥CR,秘鲁PE,新西兰NZ,智利CL 3.6 瑞士CH 5 巴PK 5.4 澳AU,韩国KR	0 受惠国LD	14	-Theodolites and tachymeters (tacheometers)
7846	9015.3000	-水平仪	9	0 冰岛IS,东盟AS,哥CR,秘鲁PE,新西兰NZ,智利CL 3.6 瑞士CH 5 巴PK 5.4 澳AU 7.2 韩国KR	0 受惠国LD	14	-Levels
7847	9015.4000	-摄影测量用仪器及装置	9	0 冰岛IS,东盟AS,哥CR,秘鲁PE,新西兰NZ,智利CL 3.6 瑞士CH 5 巴PK 5.4 澳AU,韩国KR	0 受惠国LD	14	-Photogrammetrical surveying instruments and appliances
7848	9015.8000	-其他仪器及装置	5	0 澳AU,巴PK,冰岛IS,东盟AS,哥CR,秘鲁PE,新西兰NZ,智利CL 3.5 亚太AP 4 韩国KR	0 受惠国LD	14	-Other instruments and appliances
7849	9015.9000	-零件、附件	5	0 澳AU,巴PK,冰岛IS,东盟AS,哥CR,秘鲁PE,新西兰NZ,智利CL 2 瑞士CH 4 韩国KR	0 受惠国LD	14	-Parts and accessories
	90.16	**感量为50毫克或更精密的天平，不论是否带有砝码：**					**Balances of a sensitivity of 5cg or better, with or without weights:**
7850	9016.0010	---感量为0.1毫克或更精密的天平	9	0 冰岛IS,东盟AS,哥CR,秘鲁PE,新西兰NZ,智利CL 5 巴PK 5.4 澳AU 7.2 韩国KR	0 受惠国LD	14	---Of a sensitivity of 0.1mg or better
7851	9016.0090	---其他	10.5	0 冰岛IS,东盟AS,哥CR,秘鲁PE,新加坡SG,新西兰NZ,智利CL 4.2 瑞士CH 5 巴PK 6.3 澳AU 8.4 韩国KR	0 受惠国LD	30	---Other
	90.17	**绘图、划线或数学计算仪器及器具（例如，绘图机、比例缩放仪、分度规、绘图工具、计算尺及盘式计算器）；本章其他税号未列名的手用测量长度的器具（例如，量尺、量带、千分尺及卡尺）：**					**Drawing, marking-out or mathematical calculating instruments (for example, drafting machines, pantographs, protractors, drawing sets, slide rules, disc calculators) ; instruments for measuring length, for use in the hand (for example, measuring rods and tapes, micrometers, callipers) , not specified or included elsewhere in this chapter:**
7852	9017.1000	-绘图台及绘图机，不论是否自动	8	0 冰岛IS,东盟AS,哥CR,秘鲁PE,新西兰NZ,智利CL 3.2 瑞士CH 4.8 澳AU 5 巴PK 6.4 韩国KR	0 受惠国LD	20	-Drafting tables and machines, whether or not automatic

序号 No.	税则号列 Tariff Line	中文货品名称 Article Description in Chinese	最惠国税率 MFN(%)	协定税率 Agreement(%)		特惠税率 SP(%)		普通税率 Gen(%)	英文货品名称 Article Description
7853	9017.2000	-其他绘图、划线或数学计算器具	0			0	受惠国LD	70	-Other drawing, marking-out or mathematical calculating instruments
7854	9017.3000	-千分尺、卡尺及量规	8	0 4.8 5 5.6 6.4	冰岛IS,东盟AS,哥CR,秘鲁PE,新西兰NZ,智利CL 澳AU 巴PK 瑞士CH 韩国KR	0	受惠国LD	20	-Micrometers, callipers and gauges
7855	9017.8000	-其他仪器及器具	8	0 4.8 5 5.6	冰岛IS,东盟AS,哥CR,秘鲁PE,新西兰NZ,智利CL 澳AU,韩国KR 巴PK 瑞士CH	0	受惠国LD	20	-Other instruments
7856	9017.9000	-零件、附件	0			0	受惠国LD	20	-Parts and accessories
	90.18	**医疗、外科、牙科或兽医用仪器及器具,包括闪烁扫描装置、其他电气医疗装置及视力检查仪器:**							**Instruments and appliances used in medical, surgical, dental or veterinary sciences, including scintigraphic apparatus, other electromedical apparatus and sight-testing instruments:**
		-电气诊断装置(包括功能检查或生理参数检查用装置):							-Electrodiagnostic apparatus (including apparatus for functional exploratory examination or for checking physiological parameters) :
7857	9018.1100	--心电图记录仪	5	0 2 3	澳AU,巴PK,冰岛IS,东盟AS,哥CR,秘鲁PE,新西兰NZ,智利CL 瑞士CH 韩国KR	0	受惠国LD	17	--Electro-cardiographs
		--超声波扫描装置:							--Ultrasonic scanning apparatus:
7858	9018.1210	---B型超声波诊断仪	7	0 2.8 3.5 4.2 6	巴PK,东盟AS,哥CR,秘鲁PE,新西兰NZ,智利CL 瑞士CH 冰岛IS 澳AU 韩国KR,亚太AP	0	受惠国LD	35	---B-ultrasonic diagnostic equipment
		---其他:							---Other:
7859	9018.1291	----彩色超声波诊断仪	5	0 4.5 4.8	澳AU,巴PK,冰岛IS,东盟AS,哥CR,秘鲁PE,瑞士CH,新西兰NZ,智利CL 亚太AP 韩国KR	0	受惠国LD	17	----Chromoscope ultrasonic diagnostic equipment
7860	9018.1299	----其他	5	0 4.5 4.8	澳AU,巴PK,冰岛IS,东盟AS,哥CR,秘鲁PE,瑞士CH,新西兰NZ,智利CL 亚太AP 韩国KR	0	受惠国LD	17	----Other
		--核磁共振成像装置:							--Magnetic resonance imaging apparatus:
7861	9018.1310	---成套装置	4	0 1.6 3.4	澳AU,巴PK,冰岛IS,东盟AS,哥CR,秘鲁PE,香港HK,新西兰NZ,智利CL 瑞士CH 韩国KR	0	受惠国LD	17	---Complete set of appartus

序号 No.	税则号列 Tariff Line	中文货品名称 Article Description in Chinese	最惠国税率 MFN(%)	协定税率 Agreement(%)	特惠税率 SP(%)	普通税率 Gen(%)	英文货品名称 Article Description
7862	9018.1390	---零件	4	0 澳AU,巴PK,冰岛IS,东盟AS,哥CR,秘鲁PE,香港HK,新西兰NZ,智利CL 1.6 瑞士CH 3.4 韩国KR	0 受惠国LD	17	---Parts
7863	9018.1400	--闪烁摄影装置	5	0 澳AU,巴PK,冰岛IS,东盟AS,哥CR,秘鲁PE,瑞士CH,新西兰NZ,智利CL 4.3 韩国KR	0 受惠国LD	17	--Scintigraphic apparatus
		--其他:					--Other:
7864	9018.1930	---病员监护仪	4	0 澳AU,巴PK,冰岛IS,东盟AS,哥CR,秘鲁PE,新西兰NZ,智利CL 1.6 瑞士CH 2.4 韩国KR 3.5 亚太AP	0 受惠国LD	17	---Patient monitors
		---听力诊断装置:					---Audio-diagnostic apparatus:
7865	9018.1941	----听力计	4	0 澳AU,巴PK,冰岛IS,东盟AS,哥CR,韩国KR,秘鲁PE,瑞士CH,新西兰NZ,智利CL 3.5 亚太AP	0 受惠国LD	17	----Audiometer
7866	9018.1949	----其他	4	0 澳AU,巴PK,冰岛IS,东盟AS,哥CR,秘鲁PE,瑞士CH,新西兰NZ,智利CL 3.5 亚太AP	0 受惠国LD	17	----Other
7867	9018.1990	---其他	4	0 澳AU,巴PK,冰岛IS,东盟AS,哥CR,韩国KR,秘鲁PE,新西兰NZ,智利CL 1.6 瑞士CH 3.5 亚太AP	0 受惠国LD	17	---Other
7868	9018.2000	-紫外线及红外线装置	4	0 澳AU,巴PK,冰岛IS,东盟AS,哥CR,秘鲁PE,瑞士CH,新西兰NZ,智利CL 2.4 韩国KR	0 受惠国LD	17	-Ultra-violet or infra-red ray apparatus
		-注射器、针、导管、插管及类似品:					-Syringes, needles, catheters, cannulae and the like:
7869	9018.3100	--注射器,不论是否装有针头	8	0 巴PK,冰岛IS,东盟AS,哥CR,秘鲁PE,新西兰NZ,智利CL 4.8 澳AU 5.6 瑞士CH 6.4 韩国KR 7.6 亚太AP	0 受惠国LD	50	--Syringes, with or without needles
		--管状金属针头及缝合用针:					--Tubular metal needles and needles for sutures:
7870	9018.3210	---管状金属针头	8	0 巴PK,冰岛IS,东盟AS,哥CR,秘鲁PE,新西兰NZ,智利CL 3.2 瑞士CH 4.8 澳AU 6.4 韩国KR 7 亚太AP	0 受惠国LD	50	---Tubular metal needles
7871	9018.3220	---缝合用针	4	0 澳AU,巴PK,冰岛IS,东盟AS,哥CR,韩国KR,秘鲁PE,瑞士CH,新西兰NZ,智利CL 3.5 亚太AP	0 受惠国LD	17	---Needles for sutures

序号 No.	税则号列 Tariff Line	中文货品名称 Article Description in Chinese	最惠国税率 MFN(%)	协定税率 Agreement(%)	特惠税率 SP(%)	普通税率 Gen(%)	英文货品名称 Article Description
7872	9018.3900	--其他	4	0 澳AU,巴PK,东盟AS,哥CR,秘鲁PE,新西兰NZ,智利CL 2 冰岛IS 2.4 韩国KR 2.8 瑞士CH	0 受惠国LD	17	--Other
		-牙科用其他仪器及器具:					-Other instruments and appliances, used in dental sciences:
7873	9018.4100	--牙钻机，不论是否与其他牙科设备组装在同一底座上	4	0 澳AU,巴PK,冰岛IS,东盟AS,哥CR,韩国KR,秘鲁PE,新西兰NZ,智利CL 1.6 瑞士CH	0 受惠国LD	17	--Dental drill engines, whether or not combined on a single base with other dental equipment
		--其他:					--Other:
7874	9018.4910	---装有牙科设备的牙科用椅	4	0 澳AU,巴PK,冰岛IS,东盟AS,哥CR,秘鲁PE,新西兰NZ,智利CL 2.8 瑞士CH 3.2 韩国KR	0 受惠国LD	17	---Dentists chairs incorporating dental equipment
7875	9018.4990	---其他	4	0 澳AU,巴PK,冰岛IS,东盟AS,哥CR,秘鲁PE,新西兰NZ,智利CL 2.4 韩国KR 2.8 瑞士CH	0 受惠国LD	17	---Other
7876	9018.5000	-眼科用其他仪器及器具	4	0 澳AU,巴PK,冰岛IS,东盟AS,哥CR,秘鲁PE,新西兰NZ,智利CL 2.8 瑞士CH 3.4 韩国KR 3.5 亚太AP	0 受惠国LD	17	-Other ophthalmic instruments and appliances
		-其他仪器及器具:					-Other instruments and appliances:
7877	9018.9010	---听诊器	4	0 澳AU,巴PK,冰岛IS,东盟AS,哥CR,韩国KR,秘鲁PE,瑞士CH,香港HK,新西兰NZ,智利CL 3.5 亚太AP	0 受惠国LD	17	---Stethoscopes
7878	9018.9020	---血压测量仪器及器具	4	0 澳AU,巴PK,冰岛IS,东盟AS,哥CR,韩国KR,秘鲁PE,瑞士CH,香港HK,新西兰NZ,智利CL 3.5 亚太AP	0 受惠国LD	17	---Sphygmomanometers
7879	9018.9030	---内窥镜	4	0 澳AU,巴PK,冰岛IS,东盟AS,哥CR,韩国KR,秘鲁PE,香港HK,新西兰NZ,智利CL 1.6 瑞士CH 3.5 亚太AP	0 受惠国LD	17	---Endoscopes
7880	9018.9040	---肾脏透析设备（人工肾）	4	0 澳AU,巴PK,冰岛IS,东盟AS,哥CR,韩国KR,秘鲁PE,香港HK,新西兰NZ,智利CL 1.6 瑞士CH 3.5 亚太AP	0 受惠国LD	17	---Artificial kidney (dialysis) apparatus
7881	9018.9050	---透热疗法设备	4	0 澳AU,巴PK,冰岛IS,东盟AS,哥CR,韩国KR,秘鲁PE,瑞士CH,香港HK,新西兰NZ,智利CL 3.5 亚太AP	0 受惠国LD	17	---Diathermy apparatus
7882	9018.9060	---输血设备	4	0 澳AU,巴PK,冰岛IS,东盟AS,哥CR,韩国KR,秘鲁PE,香港HK,新西兰NZ,智利CL 2.8 瑞士CH 3.5 亚太AP	0 受惠国LD	17	---Blood transfusion apparatus

序号 No.	税则号列 Tariff Line	中文货品名称 Article Description in Chinese	最惠国税率 MFN(%)	协定税率 Agreement(%)	特惠税率 SP(%)	普通税率 Gen(%)	英文货品名称 Article Description
7883	9018.9070	---麻醉设备	4	0 澳AU,巴PK,冰岛IS,东盟AS,哥CR,秘鲁PE,瑞士CH,香港HK,新西兰NZ,智利CL 2.4 韩国KR 3.5 亚太AP	0 受惠国LD	17	---Anaesthetic apparatus and instruments
7884	9018.9080	---宫内节育器	4	0 澳AU,巴PK,冰岛IS,东盟AS,哥CR,韩国KR,秘鲁PE,瑞士CH,香港HK,新西兰NZ,智利CL 2 亚太AP	0 受惠国LD	17	---Intrauterine contraceptive device
7885	9018.9090	---其他	4	0 澳AU,澳门MO,巴PK,冰岛IS,东盟AS,哥CR,秘鲁PE,香港HK,新西兰NZ,智利CL 2.4 韩国KR 2.8 瑞士CH 3.5 亚太AP	0 受惠国LD	17	---Other
	90.19	**机械疗法器具;按摩器具;心理功能测验装置;臭氧治疗器;氧气治疗器、喷雾治疗器、人工呼吸器及其他治疗用呼吸器具:**					**Mechano-therapy appliances; massage apparatus; psychological aptitude-testing apparatus; ozone therapy, oxygen therapy, aerosol therapy, artificial respiration or other therapeutic respiration apparatus:**
		-机械疗法器具;按摩器具;心理功能测验装置:					-Mechano-therapy appliances; massage apparatus; psychological aptitude-testing apparatus:
7886	9019.1010	---按摩器具	15	0 冰岛IS,东盟AS,哥CR,香港HK,新加坡SG,新西兰NZ,智利CL 4.5 秘鲁PE 9 澳AU 10.5 瑞士CH 12 巴PK,韩国KR	0 受惠国$_1$LD$_1$	40	---Massage apparatus
7887	9019.1090	---其他	4	0 澳AU,巴PK,东盟AS,哥CR,秘鲁PE,香港HK,新西兰NZ,智利CL 2 冰岛IS 2.4 韩国KR 2.8 瑞士CH	0 受惠国LD	30	---Other
7888	9019.2000	-臭氧治疗器、氧气治疗器、喷雾治疗器、人工呼吸器及其他治疗用呼吸器具	4	0 澳AU,澳门MO,巴PK,冰岛IS,东盟AS,哥CR,秘鲁PE,新西兰NZ,智利CL 2.8 瑞士CH 3.4 韩国KR	0 受惠国LD	17	-Ozone therapy, oxygen therapy, aerosol therapy, artificial respiration or other therapeutic respiration apparatus
	90.20	**其他呼吸器具及防毒面具,但不包括既无机械零件又无可互换过滤器的防护面具**					**Other breathing appliances and gas masks, excluding protective masks having neither mechanical parts nor replaceable filters**
7889	9020.0000	其他呼吸器具及防毒面具,但不包括既无机械零件又无可互换过滤器的防护面具	8Δ4	0 澳门MO,冰岛IS,东盟AS,哥CR,秘鲁PE,香港HK,新西兰NZ,智利CL 3.2 瑞士CH 4.8 澳AU 5 巴PK 6.4 韩国KR	0 受惠国LD	30	Other breathing appliances and gas masks, excluding protective masks having neither mechanical parts nor replaceable filters

序号 No.	税则号列 Tariff Line	中文货品名称 Article Description in Chinese	最惠国税率 MFN(%)	协定税率 Agreement(%)	特惠税率 SP(%)	普通税率 Gen(%)	英文货品名称 Article Description
	90.21	矫形器具，包括支具、外科手术带、疝气带;夹板及其他骨折用具;人造的人体部分;助听器及为弥补生理缺陷或残疾而穿戴、携带或植入人体内的其他器具：					**Orthopaedic appliances, including crutches, surgical belts and trusses; splints and other fracture appliances; artificial parts of the body; hearing aids and other appliances which are worn or carried, or implanted in the body, to compensate for a defect or disability:**
7890	9021.1000	-矫形或骨折用器具	4	0 澳AU,巴PK,冰岛IS,东盟AS,哥CR,秘鲁PE,新西兰NZ,智利CL 2.9 瑞士CH 3.4 韩国KR	0 受惠国LD	17	-Orthopaedic or fracture appliances
		-假牙及牙齿固定件：					-Artificial teeth and dental fittings:
7891	9021.2100	--假牙	4	0 澳AU,巴PK,冰岛IS,东盟AS,哥CR,韩国KR,秘鲁PE,瑞士CH,香港HK,新西兰NZ,智利CL	0 受惠国LD	17	--Artificial teeth
7892	9021.2900	--其他	4	0 澳AU,巴PK,冰岛IS,东盟AS,哥CR,秘鲁PE,新西兰NZ,智利CL 2.4 韩国KR 2.8 瑞士CH	0 受惠国LD	17	--Other
		-其他人造的人体部分：					-Other artificial parts of the body:
7893	9021.3100	--人造关节	4	0 澳AU,巴PK,冰岛IS,东盟AS,哥CR,韩国KR,秘鲁PE,台湾TW,新西兰NZ,智利CL 2.8 瑞士CH	0 受惠国LD	17	--Artificial joints
7894	9021.3900	--其他	4	0 澳AU,巴PK,冰岛IS,东盟AS,哥CR,秘鲁PE,新西兰NZ,智利CL 1.6 瑞士CH 3.2 韩国KR	0 受惠国LD	17	--Other
7895	9021.4000	-助听器，不包括零件、附件	4	0 澳AU,巴PK,冰岛IS,东盟AS,哥CR,韩国KR,秘鲁PE,香港HK,新西兰NZ,智利CL 2.8 瑞士CH	0 受惠国LD	17	-Hearing aids, excluding parts and accessories
7896	9021.5000	-心脏起搏器，不包括零件、附件	4Δ2	0 澳AU,巴PK,冰岛IS,东盟AS,哥CR,韩国KR,秘鲁PE,新西兰NZ,智利CL 2.8 瑞士CH	0 受惠国LD	17	-Pacemakers for stimulating heart muscles, excluding parts and accessories
		-其他：					-Other:
		---支架：					---Stents:
7897	9021.9011	----血管支架	4Δ2	0 澳AU,巴PK,冰岛IS,东盟AS,哥CR,韩国KR,秘鲁PE,新西兰NZ,智利CL 2.8 瑞士CH	0 受惠国LD	17	----Intravascular stents
7898	9021.9019	----其他	4Δ2	0 澳AU,巴PK,冰岛IS,东盟AS,哥CR,秘鲁PE,新西兰NZ,智利CL 2.8 瑞士CH 3.2 韩国KR	0 受惠国LD	17	----Other
7899	9021.9090	---其他	4	0 澳AU,巴PK,东盟AS,哥CR,秘鲁PE,新西兰NZ,智利CL 2 冰岛IS 2.4 韩国KR 2.8 瑞士CH	0 受惠国LD	17	---Other
	ex90219090	人工耳蜗植入装置	Δ0				Artificial cochlear implant appliances

序号 No.	税则号列 Tariff Line	中文货品名称 Article Description in Chinese	最惠国税率 MFN(%)	协定税率 Agreement(%)	特惠税率 SP(%)	普通税率 Gen(%)	英文货品名称 Article Description
	90.22	**X射线或α射线、β射线、γ射线的应用设备，不论是否用于医疗、外科、牙科或兽医，包括射线照相及射线治疗设备，X射线管及其他X射线发生器、高压发生器、控制板及控制台、荧光屏、检查或治疗用的桌、椅及类似品：**					**Apparatus based on the use of X-rays or of alpha, beta or gamma radiations, whether or not for medical, surgical, dental or veterinary uses, including radiography or radiotherapy apparatus, X-ray tubes and other X-ray generators, high tension generators, control panels and desks, screens, examination or treatment tables, chairs and the like:**
		-X射线的应用设备，不论是否用于医疗、外科、牙科或兽医，包括射线照相或射线治疗设备：					-Apparatus based on the use of X-rays, whether or not for medical, surgical, dental or veterinary uses, including radiography or radiotherapy apparatus:
7900	9022.1200	--X射线断层检查仪	4	0 澳AU,巴PK,冰岛IS,东盟AS,哥CR,秘鲁PE,瑞士CH,新西兰NZ,智利CL 2.8 亚太AP 3.4 韩国KR	0 受惠国LD	11	--Computed tomography apparatus
7901	9022.1300	--其他，牙科用	4	0 澳AU,巴PK,冰岛IS,东盟AS,哥CR,秘鲁PE,瑞士CH,新西兰NZ,智利CL 2.4 韩国KR	0 受惠国LD	11	--Other, for dental uses
7902	9022.1400	--其他，医疗、外科或兽医用	4	0 澳AU,巴PK,冰岛IS,东盟AS,哥CR,秘鲁PE,新西兰NZ,智利CL 1.6 瑞士CH 2.4 韩国KR	0 受惠国LD	11	--Other, for medical, surgical or veterinary uses
		--其他：					--For other uses:
7903	9022.1910	---低剂量X射线安全检查设备	4	0 澳AU,巴PK,冰岛IS,东盟AS,哥CR,秘鲁PE,瑞士CH,新西兰NZ,智利CL 3.4 韩国KR	0 受惠国LD	11	---Low dosage X-ray security inspecting equipment
7904	9022.1920	---X射线无损探伤检测仪	4	0 澳AU,巴PK,冰岛IS,东盟AS,哥CR,秘鲁PE,香港HK,新西兰NZ,智利CL 2.8 瑞士CH	0 受惠国LD	11	---X-ray Non-destructive testing instruments
7905	9022.1990	---其他	4	0 澳AU,巴PK,冰岛IS,东盟AS,哥CR,秘鲁PE,香港HK,新西兰NZ,智利CL 2.8 瑞士CH	0 受惠国LD	11	---Other
		-α射线、β射线、γ射线的应用设备，不论是否用于医疗、外科、牙科或兽医，包括射线照相或射线治疗设备：					-Apparatus based on the use of alpha, beta or gamma radiations, whether or not for medical, surgical, dental or veterinary uses, including radiography or radiotherapy apparatus:
7906	9022.2100	--医疗、外科、牙科或兽医用	4	0 澳AU,巴PK,冰岛IS,东盟AS,哥CR,韩国KR,秘鲁PE,瑞士CH,新西兰NZ,智利CL	0 受惠国LD	11	--For medical, surgical, dental or veterinary uses
		--其他：					--For other uses:

序号 No.	税则号列 Tariff Line	中文货品名称 Article Description in Chinese	最惠国税率 MFN(%)	协定税率 Agreement(%)		特惠税率 SP(%)	普通税率 Gen(%)	英文货品名称 Article Description
7907	9022.2910	---γ 射线无损探伤检测仪	6	0	冰岛IS,东盟AS,哥CR,秘鲁PE,新西兰NZ,智利CL	0 受惠国LD	11	---Γ-ray Non-destructive testing instruments
				2.4	瑞士CH			
				3.6	澳AU,韩国KR			
				5	巴PK			
7908	9022.2990	---其他	6	0	冰岛IS,东盟AS,哥CR,秘鲁PE,新西兰NZ,智利CL	0 受惠国LD	11	---Other
				2.4	瑞士CH			
				3.6	澳AU,韩国KR			
				5	巴PK			
7909	9022.3000	-X射线管	2	0	澳AU,巴PK,冰岛IS,东盟AS,哥CR,秘鲁PE,瑞士CH,新西兰NZ,智利CL	0 受惠国LD	11	-X-ray tubes
				1.6	韩国KR			
		-其他，包括零件、附件：						-Other, including parts and accessories:
7910	9022.9010	---X射线影像增强器	6	0	冰岛IS,东盟AS,哥CR,秘鲁PE,新西兰NZ,智利CL	0 受惠国LD	11	---X-ray intensifiers
				2.4	瑞士CH			
				3.6	澳AU			
				5	巴PK			
				5.2	韩国KR			
7911	9022.9090	---其他	6	0	东盟AS,哥CR,秘鲁PE,新西兰NZ,智利CL	0 受惠国LD	11	---Other
				3	冰岛IS			
				3.6	澳AU			
				4.2	瑞士CH			
				5	巴PK			
				5.2	韩国KR			
	ex90229090	射线发生器的零部件	Δ1					Parts of ray generators
	90.23	**专供示范（例如，教学或展览）而无其他用途的仪器、装置及模型：**						**Instruments, apparatus and models, designed for demonstrational purposes (for example, in education or exhibitions), unsuitable for other uses:**
7912	9023.0010	---教习头	7	0	冰岛IS,东盟AS,哥CR,秘鲁PE,新西兰NZ,智利CL	0 受惠国LD	20	---Human hair training mannequin head
				4.2	澳AU,韩国KR			
				4.9	瑞士CH			
				5	巴PK			
7913	9023.0090	---其他	7	0	冰岛IS,东盟AS,哥CR,秘鲁PE,新西兰NZ,智利CL	0 受惠国LD	20	---Other
				4.2	澳AU,韩国KR			
				4.9	瑞士CH			
				5	巴PK			
	90.24	**各种材料（例如，金属、木材、纺织材料、纸张、塑料）的硬度、强度、压缩性、弹性或其他机械性能的试验机器及器具：**						**Machines and appliances for testing the hardness, strength, compressibility, elasticity or other mechanical properties of materials (for example, metals, wood, textiles, paper, plastics) :**
		-金属材料的试验用机器及器具：						-Machines and appliances for testing metals:

序号 No.	税则号列 Tariff Line	中文货品名称 Article Description in Chinese	最惠国税率 MFN(%)	协定税率 Agreement(%)	特惠税率 SP(%)	普通税率 Gen(%)	英文货品名称 Article Description
7914	9024.1010	---电子万能试验机	7	0 冰岛IS,东盟AS,哥CR,秘鲁PE,新西兰NZ,智利CL 2.8 瑞士CH 4.2 澳AU 5 巴PK 5.6 韩国KR 6.5 亚太AP	0 受惠国LD	20	---Electronic universal testing machine
7915	9024.1020	---硬度计	7	0 冰岛IS,东盟AS,哥CR,秘鲁PE,新西兰NZ,智利CL 4.2 澳AU 4.9 瑞士CH 5 巴PK 5.6 韩国KR 6.5 亚太AP	0 受惠国LD	20	---Sclerometer
7916	9024.1090	---其他	7	0 冰岛IS,东盟AS,哥CR,秘鲁PE,新西兰NZ,智利CL 2.8 瑞士CH 4.2 澳AU 5 巴PK 6 韩国KR 6.5 亚太AP	0 受惠国LD	20	---Other
7917	9024.8000	-其他机器及器具	5	0 澳AU,巴PK,冰岛IS,东盟AS,哥CR,秘鲁PE,新西兰NZ,智利CL 2 瑞士CH 4.3 韩国KR	0 受惠国LD	20	-Other machines and appliances
7918	9024.9000	-零件、附件	6	0 冰岛IS,东盟AS,哥CR,秘鲁PE,新西兰NZ,智利CL 3.6 澳AU 4.2 瑞士CH 5 巴PK	0 受惠国LD	20	-Parts and accessories
	90.25	**记录式或非记录式的液体比重计及类似的浮子式仪器、温度计、高温计、气压计、温度计、干湿球温度计及其组合装置:**					**Hydrometers and similar floating instruments, thermometers, pyrometers, barometers, hygrometers and psychrometers, recording or not, and any combination of these instruments:**
		-温度计及高温计，未与其他仪器组合:					-Thermometers and pyrometers, not combined with other instruments:
7919	9025.1100	--液体温度计，可直接读数	4	0 澳AU,澳门MO,巴PK,冰岛IS,东盟AS,哥CR,韩国KR,秘鲁PE,新西兰NZ,智利CL 1.6 瑞士CH	0 受惠国LD	40	--Liquid-filled, for direct reading
		--其他:					--Other:
7920	9025.1910	---工业用	8.4	0 冰岛IS,东盟AS,哥CR,秘鲁PE,新西兰NZ,智利CL 3.36 瑞士CH 5 澳AU,巴PK,韩国KR 8 亚太AP	0 受惠国LD	20	---For technical use
7921	9025.1990	---其他	8.4	0 澳门MO,冰岛IS,东盟AS,哥CR,秘鲁PE,新西兰NZ,智利CL 3.36 瑞士CH 5 澳AU,巴PK,韩国KR 8 亚太AP	0 受惠国LD	80	---Other
	ex90251990	红外线人体测温仪	Δ4				Body temperature measuring apparatus by infrared ray

序号 No.	税则号列 Tariff Line	中文货品名称 Article Description in Chinese	最惠国税率 MFN(%)	协定税率 Agreement(%)	特惠税率 SP(%)	普通税率 Gen(%)	英文货品名称 Article Description
7922	9025.8000	-其他仪器	11	0 冰岛IS,东盟AS,哥CR,新加坡SG,新西兰NZ,智利CL 3.3 秘鲁PE 5 巴PK 6.6 澳AU 7.7 瑞士CH 9.9 韩国KR	0 受惠国$_1$LD$_1$	30	-Other instruments
7923	9025.9000	-零件、附件	8	0 冰岛IS,东盟AS,哥CR,秘鲁PE,新西兰NZ,智利CL 4.8 澳AU,韩国KR 5 巴PK 5.6 瑞士CH 7.6 亚太AP	0 受惠国LD	20	-Parts and accessories
	ex90259000	红外线测温仪传感器元件	Δ3				Sensors of infrared temperature measuring apparatus
	90.26	**液体或气体的流量、液位、压力或其他变化量的测量或检验仪器及装置（例如，流量计、液位计、压力表、热量计），但不包括税号90.14、90.15、90.28或90.32的仪器及装置：**					**Instruments and apparatus for measuring or checking the flow, level, pressure or other variables of liquids or gases (for example, flow meters, level gauges, manometers, heat meters) , excluding instruments and apparatus of heading 9014, 9015, 9028 or 9032:**
7924	9026.1000	-测量、检验液体流量或液位的仪器及装置	0		0 受惠国LD	17	-For measuring or checking the flow or level of liquids
		-测量、检验压力的仪器及装置：					-For measuring or checking pressure:
7925	9026.2010	---压力/差压变送器	0		0 受惠国LD	17	---Pressure/differential pressure transmitters
7926	9026.2090	---其他	0		0 受惠国LD	17	---Other
		-其他仪器及装置：					-Other instruments or apparatus:
7927	9026.8010	---测量气体流量的仪器及装置	0		0 受惠国LD	17	---Instruments and apparatus for measuring the flow of gas
7928	9026.8090	---其他	0		0 受惠国LD	17	---Other
7929	9026.9000	-零件、附件	0		0 受惠国LD	17	-Parts and accessories
	90.27	**理化分析仪器及装置（例如，偏振仪、折光仪、分光仪、气体或烟雾分析仪）；测量或检验粘性、多孔性、膨胀性、表面张力及类似性能的仪器及装置；测量或检验热量、声量或光量的仪器及装置（包括曝光表）；检镜切片机：**					**Instruments and apparatus for physical or chemical analysis (for example, polarimeters, refractometers, spectrometers, gas or smoke analysis apparatus) ; instruments and apparatus for measuring or checking viscosity, porosity, expansion, surface tension or the like; instruments and apparatus for measuring or checking quantities of heat, sound or light (including exposure meters) ; microtomes:**
7930	9027.1000	-气体或烟雾分析仪	7Δ5	0 冰岛IS,东盟AS,哥CR,秘鲁PE,香港HK,新西兰NZ,智利CL 4.2 澳AU 4.9 瑞士CH 5 巴PK 6 韩国KR	0 受惠国LD	17	-Gas or smoke analysis apparatus
		-色谱仪及电泳仪：					-Chromatographs and electrophoresis instruments:
		---色谱仪：					---Chromatographs instruments:
7931	9027.2011	----气相色谱仪	0		0 受惠国LD	17	----Gas-chromatrographs instruments
7932	9027.2012	----液相色谱仪	0		0 受惠国LD	17	----Liquid-chromatrographs instruments

序号 No.	税则号列 Tariff Line	中文货品名称 Article Description in Chinese	最惠国税率 MFN(%)	协定税率 Agreement(%)	特惠税率 SP(%)	普通税率 Gen(%)	英文货品名称 Article Description
7933	9027.2019	----其他	0		0 受惠国LD	17	----Other
7934	9027.2020	---电泳仪	0		0 受惠国LD	17	---Electrophoresis instruments
7935	9027.3000	-使用光学射线（紫外线、可见光、红外线）的分光仪、分光光度计及摄谱仪	0		0 受惠国LD	17	-Spectrometers, spectrophotometers and spectrographs using optical radiations (UV, visible, IR)
7936	9027.5000	-使用光学射线（紫外线、可见光、红外线）的其他仪器及装置	0		0 受惠国LD	17	-Other instruments and apparatus using optical radiations (UV, visible, IR)
		-其他仪器及装置：					-Other instruments and apparatus:
		---质谱仪：					---Mass spectrograph:
7937	9027.8011	----集成电路生产用氦质谱检漏台	0		0 受惠国LD	17	----Integrated circuit belium spectra leak detectors
7938	9027.8012	----质谱联用仪	0		0 受惠国LD	17	----Combined instruments or apparatus utilized mass spectrograph
7939	9027.8019	----其他	0		0 受惠国LD	17	----Other
		---其他：					---Other:
7940	9027.8091	----曝光表	14	0 冰岛IS,东盟AS,哥CR,秘鲁PE,新加坡SG,新西兰NZ,智利CL 8.4 澳AU 9.8 瑞士CH 11.2 巴PK,韩国KR	0 受惠国$_1$LD$_1$	70	----Exposure meters
7941	9027.8099	----其他	0		0 受惠国LD	17	----Other
7942	9027.9000	-检镜切片机；零件、附件	0		0 受惠国LD	17	-Microtomes; parts and accessories
	90.28	**生产或供应气体、液体及电力用的计量仪表，包括它们的校准仪表：**					**Gas, liquid or electricity supply or production meters, including calibrating meters therefor:**
		-气量计：					-Gas meters:
7943	9028.1010	---煤气表	10	0 冰岛IS,东盟AS,哥CR,秘鲁PE,新西兰NZ,智利CL 4 瑞士CH 5 巴PK 6 澳AU 8 韩国KR	0 受惠国$_1$LD$_1$	30	---Coal gas meters
7944	9028.1090	---其他	10	0 冰岛IS,东盟AS,哥CR,秘鲁PE,新加坡SG,新西兰NZ,智利CL 4 瑞士CH 5 巴PK 6 澳AU 8 韩国KR	0 受惠国$_1$LD$_1$	30	---Other
		-液量计：					-Liquid meters:
7945	9028.2010	---水表	10	0 冰岛IS,东盟AS,哥CR,秘鲁PE,新加坡SG,新西兰NZ,智利CL 4 瑞士CH 5 巴PK 6 澳AU 8 韩国KR	0 受惠国$_1$LD$_1$	30	---Water meters
7946	9028.2090	---其他	10	0 冰岛IS,东盟AS,哥CR,新加坡SG,新西兰NZ,智利CL 3 秘鲁PE 4 瑞士CH 5 巴PK 6 澳AU	0 受惠国$_1$LD$_1$	30	---Other
		-电量计：					-Electricity meters:
		---电度表：					---Watt-hour meter:

序号 No.	税则号列 Tariff Line	中文货品名称 Article Description in Chinese	最惠国税率 MFN(%)	协定税率 Agreement(%)	特惠税率 SP(%)	普通税率 Gen(%)	英文货品名称 Article Description
7947	9028.3011	----单相感应式	10	0 冰岛IS,东盟AS,哥CR,秘鲁PE,香港HK,新西兰NZ,智利CL 4 瑞士CH 5 巴PK 6 澳AU 8 韩国KR	0 受惠国$_1$LD$_1$	30	----Single-phase induction
7948	9028.3012	----三相感应式	10	0 冰岛IS,东盟AS,哥CR,秘鲁PE,香港HK,新西兰NZ,智利CL 4 瑞士CH 5 巴PK 6 澳AU 8 韩国KR	0 受惠国$_1$LD$_1$	30	----Triple-phase induction
7949	9028.3013	----单相电子式(静止式)	10	0 冰岛IS,东盟AS,哥CR,秘鲁PE,香港HK,新西兰NZ,智利CL 4 瑞士CH 5 巴PK 6 澳AU 8 韩国KR	0 受惠国$_1$LD$_1$	30	----Single-phase static
7950	9028.3014	----三相电子式(静止式)	10	0 冰岛IS,东盟AS,哥CR,秘鲁PE,香港HK,新西兰NZ,智利CL 5 巴PK 6 澳AU 8 韩国KR	0 受惠国$_1$LD$_1$	30	----Triple-phase static
7951	9028.3019	----其他	10	0 冰岛IS,东盟AS,哥CR,秘鲁PE,香港HK,新西兰NZ,智利CL 4 瑞士CH 5 巴PK 6 澳AU 9 韩国KR	0 受惠国$_1$LD$_1$	30	----Other
7952	9028.3090	---其他	10	0 冰岛IS,东盟AS,哥CR,秘鲁PE,香港HK,新加坡SG,新西兰NZ,智利CL 4 瑞士CH 5 巴PK 6 澳AU 8 韩国KR	0 受惠国$_1$LD$_1$	30	---Other
		-零件、附件:					-Parts and accessories:
7953	9028.9010	---工业用	8.4	0 冰岛IS,东盟AS,哥CR,秘鲁PE,新西兰NZ,智利CL 3.36 瑞士CH 5 澳AU,巴PK 6.7 韩国KR	0 受惠国LD	30	---For technical use
7954	9028.9090	---其他	8.4	0 冰岛IS,东盟AS,哥CR,秘鲁PE,新西兰NZ,智利CL 3.36 瑞士CH 5 澳AU,巴PK,韩国KR	0 受惠国LD	50	---Other
	90.29	**转数计、产量计数器、车费计、里程计、步数计及类似仪表;速度计及转速表,税号90.14及90.15的仪表除外;频闪观测仪:**					**Revolution counters, production counters, taximeters, milometers, pedometers and the like; speed indicators and tachometers, other than those of heading 9014 or 9015; stroboscopes:**
		-转数计、产量计数器、车费计、里程计、步数计及类似仪表:					-Revolution counters, production counters, taximeters, milometers, pedometers and the like:

序号 No.	税则号列 Tariff Line	中文货品名称 Article Description in Chinese	最惠国税率 MFN(%)	协定税率 Agreement(%)	特惠税率 SP(%)	普通税率 Gen(%)	英文货品名称 Article Description
7955	9029.1010	---转数计	15	0 冰岛IS,东盟AS,哥CR,新加坡SG,新西兰NZ,智利CL 4.5 秘鲁PE 9 澳AU 12 巴PK,韩国KR,瑞士CH	0 受惠国$_1$LD$_1$	50	---Revolution counters
7956	9029.1020	---车费计、里程计	15	0 冰岛IS,东盟AS,哥CR,新加坡SG,新西兰NZ,智利CL 4.5 秘鲁PE 9 澳AU 10.5 瑞士CH 12 巴PK	0 受惠国$_1$LD$_1$	35	---Taximeters and mileometers
7957	9029.1090	---其他	15	0 冰岛IS,东盟AS,哥CR,新加坡SG,新西兰NZ,智利CL 4.5 秘鲁PE 9 澳AU 10.5 瑞士CH 12 巴PK	0 受惠国$_1$LD$_1$	35	---Other
		-速度计及转速表，频闪观测仪：					-Speed indicators and tachometers; stroboscopes:
7958	9029.2010	---车辆用速度计	10	0 冰岛IS,东盟AS,哥CR,秘鲁PE,新西兰NZ,智利CL 4 瑞士CH 5 巴PK 6 澳AU 9 韩国KR	0 受惠国$_1$LD$_1$	35	---Speed indicators for motor vehicles
7959	9029.2090	---其他	10	0 冰岛IS,东盟AS,哥CR,秘鲁PE,新西兰NZ,智利CL 4 瑞士CH 5 巴PK 6 澳AU 8 韩国KR	0 受惠国$_1$LD$_1$	35	---Other
7960	9029.9000	-零件、附件	6	0 冰岛IS,东盟AS,哥CR,秘鲁PE,新西兰NZ,智利CL 3.6 澳AU 4.2 瑞士CH 5 巴PK	0 受惠国LD	35	-Parts and accessories
	90.30	**示波器、频谱分析仪及其他用于电量测量或检验的仪器和装置，但不包括税号90.28的各种仪表；α射线、β射线、γ射线、X射线、宇宙射线或其他离子射线的测量或检验仪器及装置：**					**Oscilloscopes, spectrum analysers and other instruments and apparatus for measuring or checking eclectrical quantities, excluding meters of heading No.90.28; instruments and apparatus for measuring or detecting alpha, beta, gamma, X-ray, cosmic or other ionizing radiations:**
7961	9030.1000	-离子射线的测量或检验仪器及装置	5	0 澳AU,巴PK,冰岛IS,东盟AS,哥CR,秘鲁PE,瑞士CH,新西兰NZ,智利CL	0 受惠国LD	20	-Instruments and apparatus for measuring or detecting ionizing radiations
		-示波器：					-Oscilloscopes and oscillographs:
7962	9030.2010	---测试频率在300兆赫兹以下的通用示波器	8	0 冰岛IS,东盟AS,哥CR,秘鲁PE,新加坡SG,新西兰NZ,智利CL 3.2 瑞士CH 4.8 澳AU 5 巴PK 6.4 韩国KR	0 受惠国LD	80	---For general use, of test frequency less than 300MHz

序号 No.	税则号列 Tariff Line	中文货品名称 Article Description in Chinese	最惠国税率 MFN(%)	协定税率 Agreement(%)	特惠税率 SP(%)	普通税率 Gen(%)	英文货品名称 Article Description
7963	9030.2090	---其他	5	0 澳AU,巴PK,冰岛IS,东盟AS,哥CR,秘鲁PE,新西兰NZ,智利CL 2 瑞士CH 4 韩国KR	0 受惠国LD	20	---Other
		-检测电压、电流、电阻或功率的其他仪器及装置：					-Other instruments and apparatus, for measuring or checking voltage, current, resistance or power:
		--万用表，不带记录装置：					--Multimeters, without a recording device:
7964	9030.3110	---量程在五位半及以下的数字万用表	15	0 澳门MO,冰岛IS,东盟AS,哥CR,新加坡SG,新西兰NZ,智利CL 4.5 秘鲁PE 9 澳AU 10.5 瑞士CH 12 巴PK,韩国KR	0 受惠国$_1$LD$_1$	130	---Digital, of measuring range of 5 1/2 or less
7965	9030.3190	---其他	5	0 澳AU,巴PK,冰岛IS,东盟AS,哥CR,秘鲁PE,瑞士CH,新西兰NZ,智利CL 4.3 韩国KR	0 受惠国LD	20	---Other
7966	9030.3200	--万用表，带记录装置	8	0 冰岛IS,东盟AS,哥CR,秘鲁PE,新西兰NZ,智利CL 3.2 瑞士CH 4.8 澳AU 5 巴PK 6.4 韩国KR	0 受惠国LD	20	--Multimeters with a recording device
		--其他，不带记录装置：					--Other, without a recording device:
7967	9030.3310	---量程在五位半及以下的数字电流表、电压表	15	0 冰岛IS,东盟AS,哥CR,香港HK,新加坡SG,新西兰NZ,智利CL 4.5 秘鲁PE 9 澳AU 10.5 瑞士CH 12 巴PK,韩国KR	0 受惠国$_1$LD$_1$	130	---Digital ammeters or voltmeters, of measuring rang of 5 1/2 or less
7968	9030.3320	---电阻测试仪	14	0 冰岛IS,东盟AS,哥CR,秘鲁PE,香港HK,新加坡SG,新西兰NZ,智利CL 8.4 澳AU 9.8 瑞士CH 11.2 巴PK	0 受惠国$_1$LD$_1$	80	---Resistance measuring instruments
7969	9030.3390	---其他	9	0 冰岛IS,东盟AS,哥CR,秘鲁PE,香港HK,新西兰NZ,智利CL 5 巴PK 5.4 澳AU 6.3 瑞士CH	0 受惠国LD	20	---Other
7970	9030.3900	--其他，带记录装置	8	0 冰岛IS,东盟AS,哥CR,秘鲁PE,新西兰NZ,智利CL 4.8 澳AU 5 巴PK 5.6 瑞士CH	0 受惠国LD	20	--Other, with a recording device
		-通信专用的其他仪器及装置（例如，串音测试器、增益测量仪、失真度表、噪声计）：					-Other instruments and apparatus, specially designed for telecommunications (for example, cross-talk meters, gain measuring instruments, distortion factor meters, psophometers) :

序号 No.	税则号列 Tariff Line	中文货品名称 Article Description in Chinese	最惠国税率 MFN(%)	协定税率 Agreement(%)	特惠税率 SP(%)	普通税率 Gen(%)	英文货品名称 Article Description
7971	9030.4010	---测试频率在12.4千兆赫兹以下的数字式频率计	0		0 受惠国LD	80	---Digital frequency meters, of test frequency less than 12.4GHz
7972	9030.4090	---其他	0		0 受惠国LD	20	---Other
		-其他仪器及装置:					-Other instruments and apparatus:
7973	9030.8200	--测试或检验半导体晶片或器件用	0		0 受惠国LD	20	--For measuring or checking semiconductor wafers or devices
		--其他，带记录装置的:					--Other, with a recording device:
7974	9030.8410	---电感及电容测试仪	10	0 冰岛IS,东盟AS,哥CR,秘鲁PE,新加坡SG,新西兰NZ,智利CL 4 瑞士CH 5 巴PK 6 澳AU	0 受惠国$_1$LD$_1$	80	---For measuring inductances or capacitances
7975	9030.8490	---其他	8	0 冰岛IS,东盟AS,哥CR,秘鲁PE,新西兰NZ,智利CL 4.8 澳AU 5 巴PK 5.6 瑞士CH 6.9 韩国KR	0 受惠国LD	20	---Other
		--其他:					--Other:
7976	9030.8910	---电感及电容测试仪	14	0 冰岛IS,东盟AS,哥CR,秘鲁PE,新加坡SG,新西兰NZ,智利CL 8.4 澳AU 9.8 瑞士CH 11.2 巴PK	0 受惠国$_1$LD$_1$	80	---For measuring inductances or capacitances
7977	9030.8990	---其他	8	0 冰岛IS,东盟AS,哥CR,秘鲁PE,新西兰NZ,智利CL 3.2 瑞士CH 4.8 澳AU 5 巴PK	0 受惠国LD	20	---Other
7978	9030.9000	-零件、附件	7	0 冰岛IS,东盟AS,哥CR,秘鲁PE,香港HK,新西兰NZ,智利CL 4.2 澳AU 4.9 瑞士CH 5 巴PK 5.6 韩国KR	0 受惠国LD	17	-Parts and accessories
	ex90309000	用于检测半导体晶片及器件的仪器的零件和附件;ITA产品用的印刷电路组件，包括外接组件，如符合PCMCIA标准的卡	0				Parts and accessories of instruments and apparatus for measuring or checking semiconductor wafers or devices; Printed Circuit Assemblies for products falling within the ITA, including such assemblies for external connections such as cards that conform to the PCMCIA standard.
	90.31	**本章其他税号未列名的测量或检验仪器、器具及机器;轮廓投影仪:**					**Measuring or checking instruments, appliances and machines, not specified or included elsewhere in this chapter; profile projectors:**
7979	9031.1000	-机械零件平衡试验机	7	0 冰岛IS,东盟AS,哥CR,秘鲁PE,新西兰NZ,智利CL 2.8 瑞士CH 4.2 澳AU,韩国KR 5 巴PK 6.5 亚太AP	0 受惠国LD	17	-Machines for balancing mechanical parts

序号 No.	税则号列 Tariff Line	中文货品名称 Article Description in Chinese	最惠国税率 MFN(%)	协定税率 Agreement(%)		特惠税率 SP(%)		普通税率 Gen(%)	英文货品名称 Article Description
7980	9031.2000	-试验台	7	0 4.2 5 6	冰岛IS,东盟AS,哥CR,秘鲁PE,新西兰NZ,智利CL 澳AU 巴PK,瑞士CH 韩国KR	0	受惠国LD	17	-Test benches
		-其他光学仪器及器具:							-Other optical instruments and appliances:
7981	9031.4100	--制造半导体器件时检验半导体晶片、器件或检测光掩模或光栅用	0			0	受惠国LD	17	--For inspecting semiconductor wafers or devices or for inspecting photomasks or reticles used in manufacturing semiconductor devices
		--其他:							--Other:
7982	9031.4910	---轮廓投影仪	10∆5	0 4 5 6 8.6	冰岛IS,东盟AS,哥CR,秘鲁PE,新西兰NZ,智利CL 瑞士CH 巴PK 澳AU 韩国KR	0	受惠国LD	20	---Profile projectors
7983	9031.4920	---光栅测量装置	0			0	受惠国LD	17	---Grating measuring instrument
7984	9031.4990	---其他	0			0	受惠国LD	17	---Other
		-其他仪器、器具及机器:							-Other instruments, appliances and machines:
7985	9031.8010	---光纤通信及光纤性能测试仪	5	0 4 4.3	澳AU,巴PK,冰岛IS,东盟AS,哥CR,秘鲁PE,瑞士CH,香港HK,新西兰NZ,智利CL 亚太AP 韩国KR	0	受惠国LD	17	---Optical telecommunication and optical fibre performance testing instruments
7986	9031.8020	---坐标测量仪	5	0 2 4.3	澳AU,巴PK,冰岛IS,东盟AS,哥CR,秘鲁PE,香港HK,新西兰NZ,智利CL 瑞士CH 韩国KR	0	受惠国LD	17	---Coordinate measuring machine
		---无损探伤检测仪器(射线探伤仪除外):							---Instrument for nondestructive testing (other than instruments using radiations) :
7987	9031.8031	----超声波探伤检测仪	5	0 4 4.3	澳AU,巴PK,冰岛IS,东盟AS,哥CR,秘鲁PE,瑞士CH,香港HK,新西兰NZ,智利CL 亚太AP 韩国KR	0	受惠国LD	17	----Ultrasonic inspection instrument
7988	9031.8032	----磁粉探伤检测仪	5	0 4 4.3	澳AU,巴PK,冰岛IS,东盟AS,哥CR,秘鲁PE,瑞士CH,香港HK,新西兰NZ,智利CL 亚太AP 韩国KR	0	受惠国LD	17	----Inspection instrument for magnetic particle testing
7989	9031.8033	----涡流探伤检测仪	5∆3	0 4 4.3	澳AU,巴PK,冰岛IS,东盟AS,哥CR,秘鲁PE,瑞士CH,香港HK,新西兰NZ,智利CL 亚太AP 韩国KR	0	受惠国LD	17	----Inspection instrument for eddy current testing
7990	9031.8039	----其他	5	0 4	澳AU,巴PK,冰岛IS,东盟AS,哥CR,秘鲁PE,瑞士CH,香港HK,新西兰NZ,智利CL 亚太AP	0	受惠国LD	17	----Other

序号 No.	税则号列 Tariff Line	中文货品名称 Article Description in Chinese	最惠国税率 MFN(%)	协定税率 Agreement(%)	特惠税率 SP(%)	普通税率 Gen(%)	英文货品名称 Article Description
7991	9031.8090	---其他	5	0 澳AU,巴PK,东盟AS,哥CR,秘鲁PE,台湾TW,香港HK,新西兰NZ,智利CL 3.6 瑞士CH 4 韩国KR,亚太AP	0 受惠国LD	17	---Other
	ex90318090	音频生命探测仪	Δ2				Audio life detectors
	ex90318090	音视频生命探测仪	Δ2				Audio and video life detectors
	ex90318090	跑道摩擦系数测试仪	Δ3				Runway friction coefficient tester
7992	9031.9000	-零件、附件	0		0 受惠国LD	17	-Parts and accessories
	90.32	**自动调节或控制仪器及装置:**					**Automatic regulating or controlling instruments and apparatus:**
7993	9032.1000	-恒温器	7	0 冰岛IS,东盟AS,哥CR,秘鲁PE,香港HK,新西兰NZ,智利CL 4.2 澳AU,韩国KR 4.9 瑞士CH 5 巴PK	0 受惠国LD	17	-Thermostats
7994	9032.2000	-恒压器	7	0 冰岛IS,东盟AS,哥CR,秘鲁PE,香港HK,新西兰NZ,智利CL 2.8 瑞士CH 4.2 澳AU 5 巴PK 5.6 韩国KR	0 受惠国LD	17	-Manostats
		-其他仪器及装置:					-Other instruments and apparatus:
7995	9032.8100	--液压或气压的	7	0 冰岛IS,东盟AS,哥CR,秘鲁PE,香港HK,新西兰NZ,智利CL 4.2 澳AU 4.9 瑞士CH 5 巴PK 6 韩国KR 6.5 亚太AP	0 受惠国LD	17	--Hydraulic or pneumatic
		--其他:					--Other:
		---列车自动控制系统(ATC)车载设备:					---On-board equipments of automatic train Control system:
7996	9032.8911	----列车自动防护系统(ATP)车载设备	7	0 冰岛IS,东盟AS,哥CR,秘鲁PE,香港HK,新西兰NZ,智利CL 4.2 澳AU 5 巴PK 6 韩国KR	0 受惠国LD	17	----On-board equipments of automatic train Protection
7997	9032.8912	----列车自动运行系统(ATO)车载设备	7	0 冰岛IS,东盟AS,哥CR,秘鲁PE,香港HK,新西兰NZ,智利CL 4.2 澳AU 5 巴PK 6 韩国KR	0 受惠国LD	17	----On-board equipments of automatic train Operation
7998	9032.8919	----其他	7	0 冰岛IS,东盟AS,哥CR,秘鲁PE,香港HK,新西兰NZ,智利CL 4.2 澳AU 5 巴PK 6 韩国KR	0 受惠国LD	17	----Other
7999	9032.8990	---其他	7	0 冰岛IS,东盟AS,哥CR,秘鲁PE,香港HK,新西兰NZ,智利CL 4.2 澳AU 5 巴PK 6 韩国KR	0 受惠国LD	17	---Other

序号 No.	税则号列 Tariff Line	中文货品名称 Article Description in Chinese	最惠国税率 MFN(%)	协定税率 Agreement(%)	特惠税率 SP(%)	普通税率 Gen(%)	英文货品名称 Article Description
	ex90328990	飞机自动驾驶系统（包括自动驾驶、电子控制飞行、自动故障分析、警告系统配平系统及推力监控设备及其相关仪表）	Δ1				Parts of automatic pilotting systems for aircraft (including automatic pilotting, electronic flight contral, automatic failure analysis, warning systems, trimming systems, thrust monitoring equipments and the meters thereof)
	ex90328990	电喷点火程序控制单元	Δ3				Program controlling units for electric ignition
	ex90328990	机床用成套数控伺服装置（包括CNC操作单元，带有配套的伺服放大器和伺服电机）	Δ3				Numerical control servomechanism for machine tools (including CNC unit, with servo amplifier and servomotor)
	ex90328990	印刷机用成套数控伺服传动装置（包括运动控制器或可编程序自动控制器、人机界面单元，带有配套的伺服驱动器和伺服电机）	Δ3				Complete set of CNC servo devices used for printers (including PAC and HMI units, servo drivers and sero motoers)
	ex90328990	三坐标测量机用自动控制柜	Δ3				Automatic controller for coordinate measuring machine of three dimensions
	ex90328990	纯电动或混合动力汽车用电机控制器总成	Δ4				Motor controller assembly for blade electric vehicles or hybrid electric vehicles
	ex90328990	具有可再生能源和智能电网应用的自动电压和电流调节器；非液压或气压的自动调控流量、液位和湿度的仪器	Δ5				Automatic voltage and current regulators which have renewable energy and smart grid applications; process control instruments and apparatus for flow, level and humidity, excluding hydraulic or pneumatic
8000	9032.9000	-零件、附件	5	0 澳AU,巴PK,冰岛IS,东盟AS,哥CR,秘鲁PE,新西兰NZ,智利CL 3.5 瑞士CH 4.3 韩国KR	0 受惠国LD	17	-Parts and accessories
	ex90329000	飞机自动驾驶系统（包括自动驾驶、电子控制飞行、自动故障分析、警告系统配平系统及推力监控设备及其相关仪表）的零件	Δ1				Parts of automatic pilotting systems for aircraft (including automatic pilotting, electronic flight contral, automatic failure analysis, warning systems, trimming systems, thrust monitoring equipments and the meters therof)
	90.33	**第九十章所列机器、器具、仪器或装置用的本章其他税号未列名的零件、附件**					**Parts and accessories (not specified or included elsewhere in this chapter) for machines, appliances, instruments or apparatus of Chapter 90**
8001	9033.0000	第九十章所列机器、器具、仪器或装置用的本章其他税号未列名的零件、附件	6	0 冰岛IS,东盟AS,哥CR,秘鲁PE,新西兰NZ,智利CL 3.6 澳AU,韩国KR 4.2 瑞士CH 5 巴PK	0 受惠国LD	17	Parts and accessories (not specified or in cluded elsewhere in this Chapter) for machines, appliances, instruments or apparatus of Chapter 90

序号 No.	税则号列 Tariff Line	中文货品名称 Article Description in Chinese	最惠国税率 MFN(%)	协定税率 Agreement(%)	特惠税率 SP(%)	普通税率 Gen(%)	英文货品名称 Article Description
	ex90330000	用于90章下列环境产品，包括太阳能定日镜、其他测量海洋、水文、气象或地球物理用仪器及设备，测量，检验液体流量或液位的仪器，测量、检验压力的仪器及装置，9026其他税号未列名的液体或气体测量仪器及装置，气体或烟雾分析仪，色谱仪和电泳仪，使用光学射线（紫外线，可见光，红外线）的分光仪、分光光度计及摄谱仪以及其他理化分析仪器及装置，用于测量、记录、分析和评估环境样品或对环境的影响的理化分析仪器及装置，检镜切片机，轮廓投影仪，光栅测量装置，其他光学测量或检验仪器和器具，测振仪，手振动仪，具有可再生能源和智能电网应用的自动电压和电流调节器，自动调控流量、液位和湿度的仪器,且在其他税目未列名的零附件	Δ5				Parts of the CH 90 following environment products, including solar heliostats, other surveying oceanographic, hydrological, meteorological or geophysical instruments and appliances, instruments for measuring or checking the flow or level of liquids, instruments/apparatus for measuring or checking pressure, other Instruments/Apparatus for measuring or checking variables of liquids and gases of heading 9026, nesoi, gas or smoke analysis apparatus, chromatographs and electrophoresis instruments, spectrometers, spectrophotometers and spectrographs and other instruments and apparatus for physical and chemical analysis using optical radiations (ultraviolet, visible, infrared) , instruments and apparatus for physical or chemical analysis used to measure, record, analyse and assess environmental samples or environmental influences, microtomes, profile projectors, optical Grating Measuring insruments, other optical measuring and checking instruments and appliances, vibrometers, hand vibration meters, automatic voltage and current regulators which have renewable energy and smart grid applications; process control instruments and apparatus for flow, level and humidity, not elsewhere specified

第九十一章
钟表及其零件

注释:

一、本章不包括:

（一）钟表玻璃及钟锤（按其构成材料归类）;

（二）表链(根据不同情况,归入税号71.13或71.17);

（三）第十五类注释二所规定的贱金属制通用零件（第十五类）、塑料制的类似品（第三十九章）及贵金属或包贵金属制的类似品（一般归入税号71.15）;但钟、表发条则应作为钟、表的零件归类（税号91.14）;

（四）轴承滚珠（根据不同情况，归入税号73.26或84.82）;

（五）税号84.12的物品，不需擒纵器可以工作的;

（六）滚珠轴承（税号84.82）;

（七）第八十五章的物品，本身未组装在或未与其他零件组装在钟、表机芯内，也未组装成专用于或主要用于钟、表机芯零件的（第八十五章）。

二、税号91.01仅包括表壳完全以贵金属或包贵金属制的表，以及用贵金属或包贵金属与税号71.01至71.04的天然、养殖珍珠或宝石、半宝石（天然、合成或再造）合制的表。用贱金属上镶嵌贵金属制成表壳的表应归入税号91.02。

三、本章所称"表芯"，是指由摆轮及游丝、石英晶体或其他能确定时间间隔的装置来进行调节的机构，并带有显示器或可装机械指示器的系统。表芯的厚度不超过12毫米，长、宽或直径不超过50毫米。

四、除注释一另有规定的以外，钟、表的机芯及其他零件，既适用于钟或表，又适用于其他物品(例如精密仪器)的，均应归入本章。

Chapter 91
Clocks and watches and parts thereof

Notes:

1. This Chapter does not cover:

(a) Clock or watch glasses or weights (classified according to their constituent material) ;

(b) Watch chains (heading No.71.13 or 71.17， as the case may be);

(c) Parts of general use defined in Note 2 to Section XV，of base metal (Section XV)，or similar goods of plastics (Chapter 39) or of precious metal or metal clad with precious metal (generally heading No. 71.15); clock or watch springs are, however, to be classified as clock or watch parts (heading No.91.14);

(d) Bearing balls (heading No. 73.26 or 84.82， as the case may be) ;

(e) Articles of heading No. 84.12 constructed to work without an escapement;

(f) Ball bearings (heading No.84.82); or

(g) Articles of Chapter 85，not yet assembled together or with other components into watch or clock movements or into articles suitable for use solely or principally as parts of such movements (Chapter 85) .

2. Heading No. 91.01 covers only watches with case wholly of precious metal or of metal clad with precious metal, or of the same materials combined with natural or cultured pearls, or precious or semiprecious stones (natural, synthetic or reconstructed) of headings No.71.01 to 71.04. Watches with case of base metal inlaid with precious metal fall in heading No. 91.02.

3. For the purposes of this Chapter, the expression "watch move ments" means devices regulated by a balance-wheel and hairspring, quartz crystal or any other system capable of determining intevals of time, with a display or a system to which a mechanical display can be incorporated. Such watch movements shall not exceed 12mm in thickness and 50mm in width，length or diameter.

4. Except as provided in Note 1，movements and other parts suitable for use both in clocks or watches and in other articles (for example, precision instruments) are to be classified in this Chapter.

序号 No.	税则号列 Tariff Line	中文货品名称 Article Description in Chinese	最惠国税率 MFN(%)	协定税率 Agreement(%)	特惠税率 SP(%)	普通税率 Gen(%)	英文货品名称 Article Description
	91.01	手表、怀表及其他表，包括秒表，表壳用贵金属或包贵金属制成的：					**Wristwatches, pocket-watches and other watches, including stopwatches, with case of precious metal or of metal clad with precious metal:**
		-电力驱动的手表，不论是否附有秒表装置：					-Wristwatches, electrically operated, whether or not incorporating a stopwatch facility:
8002	9101.1100	--仅有机械指示器的	11	0 冰岛IS,东盟AS,哥CR,秘鲁PE,新加坡SG,新西兰NZ,智利CL 5 巴PK 6.6 澳AU 7.9 瑞士CH 8.8 韩国KR 9.9 亚太AP	0 受惠国$_1$LD$_1$	100	--With mechanical display only
		--其他：					--Other:
8003	9101.1910	---仅有光电显示器的	16	0 冰岛IS,东盟AS,哥CR,新加坡SG,新西兰NZ,智利CL 4.8 秘鲁PE 9.6 澳AU 11.2 瑞士CH 12.8 巴PK,韩国KR	0 受惠国$_1$LD$_1$	100	---With opto-electronic display only
8004	9101.1990	---其他	15	0 冰岛IS,东盟AS,哥CR,新加坡SG,新西兰NZ,智利CL 4.5 秘鲁PE 9 澳AU 10.8 瑞士CH 12 巴PK,韩国KR	0 受惠国$_1$LD$_1$	100	---Other
		-其他手表，不论是否附有秒表装置：					-Other wristwatches, whether or not incorporating a stopwatch facility:
8005	9101.2100	--自动上弦的	11	0 冰岛IS,东盟AS,哥CR,秘鲁PE,新加坡SG,新西兰NZ,智利CL 5 巴PK 6.6 澳AU 7.9 瑞士CH 8.8 韩国KR	0 受惠国$_1$LD$_1$	80	--Automatic winding
8006	9101.2900	--其他	15	0 冰岛IS,东盟AS,哥CR,新加坡SG,新西兰NZ,智利CL 4.5 秘鲁PE 9 澳AU 10.8 瑞士CH 12 巴PK,韩国KR	0 受惠国$_1$LD$_1$	80	--Other
		-其他：					-Other:
8007	9101.9100	--电力驱动的	15	0 冰岛IS,东盟AS,哥CR,新加坡SG,新西兰NZ,智利CL 4.5 秘鲁PE 9 澳AU 10.5 瑞士CH 12 巴PK,韩国KR	0 受惠国$_1$LD$_1$	100	--Electrically operated
8008	9101.9900	--其他	20	0 冰岛IS,东盟AS,哥CR,新加坡SG,新西兰NZ,智利CL 6 秘鲁PE 12 澳AU 14.4 瑞士CH 17.3 韩国KR	0 受惠国$_1$LD$_1$	80	--Other

序号 No.	税则号列 Tariff Line	中文货品名称 Article Description in Chinese	最惠国税率 MFN(%)	协定税率 Agreement(%)	特惠税率 SP(%)	普通税率 Gen(%)	英文货品名称 Article Description
	91.02	**手表、怀表及其他表，包括秒表，但税号91.01的货品除外：**					**Wristwatches, pocket-watches and other watches, including stopwatches, other than those of heading 9101:**
		-电力驱动的手表，不论是否附有秒表装置：					-Wristwatches, electrically operated, whether or not incorporating a stopwatch facility:
8009	9102.1100	--仅有机械指示器的	12.5	0 澳门MO,冰岛IS,东盟AS,哥CR,秘鲁PE,香港HK,新加坡SG,新西兰NZ,智利CL 6.2 巴PK 7.5 澳AU 9 瑞士CH 10 韩国KR 11.1 亚太AP	0 受惠国$_1$LD$_1$	100	--With mechanical display only
8010	9102.1200	--仅有光电显示器的	23	0 澳门MO,冰岛IS,东盟AS,哥CR,香港HK,新加坡SG,新西兰NZ,智利CL 6.9 秘鲁PE 13.8 澳AU 16.1 瑞士CH 20.7 韩国KR	0 受惠国$_1$LD$_1$	100	--With opto-electronic display only
8011	9102.1900	--其他	15	0 冰岛IS,东盟AS,哥CR,新加坡SG,新西兰NZ,智利CL 4.5 秘鲁PE 9 澳AU 10.5 瑞士CH 12 巴PK,韩国KR	0 受惠国$_1$LD$_1$	100	--Other
		-其他手表，不论是否装有秒表装置：					-Other wristwatches, whether or not incorporating a stopwatch facility:
8012	9102.2100	--自动上弦的	11	0 冰岛IS,东盟AS,哥CR,秘鲁PE,香港HK,新加坡SG,新西兰NZ,智利CL 5 巴PK 6.6 澳AU 7.9 瑞士CH 8.8 韩国KR	0 受惠国$_1$LD$_1$	80	--Automatic winding
8013	9102.2900	--其他	15	0 冰岛IS,东盟AS,哥CR,香港HK,新加坡SG,新西兰NZ,智利CL 4.5 秘鲁PE 9 澳AU 10.8 瑞士CH 12 巴PK,韩国KR	0 受惠国$_1$LD$_1$	80	--Other
		-其他：					-Other:
8014	9102.9100	--电力驱动的	15	0 冰岛IS,东盟AS,哥CR,新加坡SG,新西兰NZ,智利CL 4.5 秘鲁PE 9 澳AU 10.8 瑞士CH 12 巴PK,韩国KR	0 受惠国$_1$LD$_1$	100	--Electrically operated
8015	9102.9900	--其他	20	0 冰岛IS,东盟AS,哥CR,新加坡SG,新西兰NZ,智利CL 6 秘鲁PE 12 澳AU 14.4 瑞士CH 17.3 韩国KR	0 受惠国$_1$LD$_1$	80	--Other

序号 No.	税则号列 Tariff Line	中文货品名称 Article Description in Chinese	最惠国税率 MFN(%)	协定税率 Agreement(%)	特惠税率 SP(%)	普通税率 Gen(%)	英文货品名称 Article Description
	91.03	**以表芯装成的钟，但不包括税号91.04的钟：**					**Clocks with watch movements, excluding clocks of heading 9104:**
8016	9103.1000	-电力驱动的	23	0 澳门MO,冰岛IS,东盟AS,哥CR,香港HK,新加坡SG,新西兰NZ,智利CL 6.9 秘鲁PE 13.8 澳AU 16.6 瑞士CH 20.7 韩国KR	0 受惠国$_{1}$LD$_{1}$	100	-Electrically operated
8017	9103.9000	-其他	20	0 冰岛IS,东盟AS,哥CR,新加坡SG,新西兰NZ,智利CL 6 秘鲁PE 12 澳AU 14.4 瑞士CH 17.3 韩国KR	0 受惠国$_{1}$LD$_{1}$	100	-Other
	91.04	**仪表板钟及车辆、航空器、航天器或船舶用的类似钟**					**Instrument panel clocks and clocks of a similar type for vehicles, aircraft, spacecraft or vessels**
8018	9104.0000	仪表板钟及车辆、航空器、航天器或船舶用的类似钟	10	0 冰岛IS,东盟AS,哥CR,秘鲁PE,新西兰NZ,智利CL 4 瑞士CH 5 巴PK 6 澳AU 8 韩国KR	0 受惠国$_{1}$LD$_{1}$	100	Instrument panel clocks and clocks of a similar type for vehicles, aircraft, spacecraft or vessels
	91.05	**其他钟：**					**Other clocks:**
		-闹钟：					-Alarm clocks:
8019	9105.1100	--电力驱动的	23	0 澳门MO,冰岛IS,东盟AS,哥CR,香港HK,新加坡SG,新西兰NZ,智利CL 6.9 秘鲁PE 13.8 澳AU 16.6 瑞士CH 20.7 韩国KR	0 受惠国LD	100	--Electrically operated
8020	9105.1900	--其他	20	0 冰岛IS,东盟AS,哥CR,新加坡SG,新西兰NZ,智利CL 6 秘鲁PE 12 澳AU 14 瑞士CH 17.3 韩国KR	0 受惠国$_{1}$LD$_{1}$	100	--Other
		-挂钟：					-Wall clocks:
8021	9105.2100	--电力驱动的	23	0 冰岛IS,东盟AS,哥CR,新加坡SG,新西兰NZ,智利CL 6.9 秘鲁PE 13.8 澳AU 16.1 瑞士CH 20.7 韩国KR	0 受惠国$_{1}$LD$_{1}$	100	--Electrically operated
8022	9105.2900	--其他	20	0 冰岛IS,东盟AS,哥CR,新加坡SG,新西兰NZ,智利CL 6 秘鲁PE 12 澳AU 14 瑞士CH 17.3 韩国KR	0 受惠国$_{1}$LD$_{1}$	100	--Other
		-其他：					-Other:
		--电力驱动的：					--Electrically operated:

序号 No.	税则号列 Tariff Line	中文货品名称 Article Description in Chinese	最惠国税率 MFN(%)	协定税率 Agreement(%)	特惠税率 SP(%)	普通税率 Gen(%)	英文货品名称 Article Description
8023	9105.9110	---天文钟	3	0 澳AU,巴PK,冰岛IS,东盟AS,哥CR,韩国KR,秘鲁PE,新西兰NZ,智利CL 2.1 瑞士CH	0 受惠国LD	8	---Astronomical chronometer
8024	9105.9190	---其他	23	0 冰岛IS,东盟AS,哥CR,新加坡SG,新西兰NZ,智利CL 6.9 秘鲁PE 13.8 澳AU 16.1 瑞士CH 20.7 韩国KR	0 受惠国$_1$LD$_1$	100	---Other
8025	9105.9900	--其他	16	0 冰岛IS,东盟AS,哥CR,新加坡SG,新西兰NZ,智利CL 4.8 秘鲁PE 9.6 澳AU 11.5 瑞士CH 12.8 巴PK,韩国KR	0 受惠国$_1$LD$_1$	100	--Other
	91.06	**时间记录器以及测量、记录或指示时间间隔的装置，装有钟、表机芯或同步电动机的（例如，考勤钟、时刻记录器）：**					**Time of day recording apparatus and apparatus for measuring, recording or otherwise indicating intervals of time, with clock or watch movement or with synchronous motor (for example, time-registers, time-recorders) :**
8026	9106.1000	-考勤钟、时刻记录器	16	0 冰岛IS,东盟AS,哥CR,新加坡SG,新西兰NZ,智利CL 4.8 秘鲁PE 9.6 澳AU 11.2 瑞士CH 12.8 巴PK,韩国KR	0 受惠国$_1$LD$_1$	50	-Time-registers; time-recorders
8027	9106.9000	-其他	16	0 冰岛IS,东盟AS,哥CR,新加坡SG,新西兰NZ,智利CL 4.8 秘鲁PE 9.6 澳AU 11.5 瑞士CH 12.8 巴PK,韩国KR	0 受惠国$_1$LD$_1$	50	-Other
	91.07	**装有钟、表机芯或同步电动机的定时开关**					**Time switches, with clock or watch movement or with synchronous motor**
8028	9107.0000	装有钟、表机芯或同步电动机的定时开关	12	0 冰岛IS,东盟AS,哥CR,秘鲁PE,新加坡SG,新西兰NZ,智利CL 6 巴PK 7.2 澳AU 8.4 瑞士CH 9.6 韩国KR	0 受惠国$_1$LD$_1$	50	Time switches with clock or watch movement or with synchronous motor
	91.08	**已组装的完整表芯：**					**Watch movements, complete and assembled:**
		-电力驱动的：					-Electrically operated:
8029	9108.1100	--仅有机械指示器或有可装机械指示器的装置的	16Δ10	0 澳门MO,冰岛IS,东盟AS,哥CR,香港HK,新加坡SG,新西兰NZ,智利CL 4.8 秘鲁PE 9.6 澳AU 11.2 瑞士CH 12.8 巴PK,韩国KR	0 受惠国$_1$LD$_1$	80	--With mechanical display only or with a device to which a mechanical display can be incorporated

序号 No.	税则号列 Tariff Line	中文货品名称 Article Description in Chinese	最惠国税率 MFN(%)	协定税率 Agreement(%)	特惠税率 SP(%)	普通税率 Gen(%)	英文货品名称 Article Description
8030	9108.1200	--仅有光电显示器的	16	0 澳门MO,冰岛IS,东盟AS,哥CR,香港HK,新加坡SG,新西兰NZ,智利CL 4.8 秘鲁PE 9.6 澳AU 11.5 瑞士CH 12.8 巴PK,韩国KR	0 受惠国$_1$LD$_1$	80	--With opto-electronic display only
8031	9108.1900	--其他	16	0 澳门MO,冰岛IS,东盟AS,哥CR,香港HK,新加坡SG,新西兰NZ,智利CL 4.8 秘鲁PE 8 巴PK 9.6 澳AU 11.5 瑞士CH 12 亚太AP 12.8 韩国KR	0 受惠国$_1$LD$_1$	80	--Other
8032	9108.2000	-自动上弦的	16	0 冰岛IS,东盟AS,哥CR,新加坡SG,新西兰NZ,智利CL 4.8 秘鲁PE 9.6 澳AU 11.5 瑞士CH 12.8 巴PK,韩国KR	0 受惠国$_1$LD$_1$	80	-Automatic winding
		-其他:					-Other:
8033	9108.9010	---表面尺寸在33.8毫米及以下	16	0 冰岛IS,东盟AS,哥CR,新加坡SG,新西兰NZ,智利CL 4.8 秘鲁PE 9.6 澳AU 11.5 瑞士CH 12.8 巴PK,韩国KR	0 受惠国$_1$LD$_1$	80	---Measuring 33.8mm or less
8034	9108.9090	---其他	16	0 澳门MO,冰岛IS,东盟AS,哥CR,香港HK,新加坡SG,新西兰NZ,智利CL 4.8 秘鲁PE 9.6 澳AU 11.5 瑞士CH 12.8 巴PK,韩国KR	0 受惠国$_1$LD$_1$	80	---Other
	91.09	**已组装的完整钟芯:**					**Clock movements, complete and assembled:**
8035	9109.1000	-电力驱动的	16	0 冰岛IS,东盟AS,哥CR,新加坡SG,新西兰NZ,智利CL 4.8 秘鲁PE 9.6 澳AU 11.2 瑞士CH 12.8 巴PK,韩国KR	0 受惠国$_1$LD$_1$	100	-Eletrically operated
8036	9109.9000	-其他	16	0 冰岛IS,东盟AS,哥CR,新加坡SG,新西兰NZ,智利CL 4.8 秘鲁PE 9.6 澳AU 11.2 瑞士CH 12.8 巴PK,韩国KR	0 受惠国$_1$LD$_1$	100	-Other
	91.10	**未组装或部分组装的完整钟、表机芯(机芯套装件);已组装的不完整钟、表机芯;未组装的不完整钟、表机芯:**					**Complete watch or clock movements, unassembled or partly assembled (mo-vement sets) ; incomplete watch or clock movements, assembled; rough watch or clock movements:**
		-表的:					-Of watches:

序号 No.	税则号列 Tariff Line	中文货品名称 Article Description in Chinese	最惠国税率 MFN(%)	协定税率 Agreement(%)	特惠税率 SP(%)	普通税率 Gen(%)	英文货品名称 Article Description
8037	9110.1100	--未组装或部分组装的完整机芯（机芯套装件）	16	0 冰岛IS,东盟AS,哥CR,新加坡SG,新西兰NZ,智利CL 4.8 秘鲁PE 9.6 澳AU 11.5 瑞士CH 12.8 巴PK,韩国KR	0 受惠国$_1$LD$_1$	80	--Complete movements, unassembled or partly assembled (movement sets)
8038	9110.1200	--已组装的不完整机芯	16	0 冰岛IS,东盟AS,哥CR,新加坡SG,新西兰NZ,智利CL 4.8 秘鲁PE 9.6 澳AU 11.2 瑞士CH 12.8 巴PK,韩国KR	0 受惠国$_1$LD$_1$	70	--Incomplete movements, assembled
8039	9110.1900	--未组装的不完整机芯	16	0 冰岛IS,东盟AS,哥CR,新加坡SG,新西兰NZ,智利CL 4.8 秘鲁PE 9.6 澳AU 11.2 瑞士CH 12.8 巴PK,韩国KR	0 受惠国$_1$LD$_1$	70	--Rough movements
		-其他:					-Other:
8040	9110.9010	---未组装或部分组装的完整机芯	16	0 冰岛IS,东盟AS,哥CR,新加坡SG,新西兰NZ,智利CL 4.8 秘鲁PE 9.6 澳AU 11.2 瑞士CH 12.8 巴PK,韩国KR	0 受惠国$_1$LD$_1$	100	---Complete movements, unassembled or partly assembled
8041	9110.9090	---其他	16	0 冰岛IS,东盟AS,哥CR,新加坡SG,新西兰NZ,智利CL 4.8 秘鲁PE 9.6 澳AU 11.2 瑞士CH 12.8 巴PK,韩国KR	0 受惠国$_1$LD$_1$	80	---Other
	91.11	**表壳及其零件:**					**Watch cases and parts thereof:**
8042	9111.1000	-贵金属表壳或包贵金属表壳	14	0 冰岛IS,东盟AS,哥CR,秘鲁PE,新加坡SG,新西兰NZ,智利CL 8.4 澳AU 10 瑞士CH 11.2 巴PK,韩国KR	0 受惠国$_1$LD$_1$	80	-Cases of precious metal or of metal clad with precious metal
8043	9111.2000	-贱金属表壳，不论是否镀金或镀银	14	0 澳门MO,冰岛IS,东盟AS,哥CR,秘鲁PE,香港HK,新加坡SG,新西兰NZ,智利CL 7 巴PK 8.4 澳AU 9.8 瑞士CH 10 亚太AP 11.2 韩国KR	0 受惠国$_1$LD$_1$	80	-Cases of base metal, whether or not gold or silver-plated
8044	9111.8000	-其他表壳	14	0 冰岛IS,东盟AS,哥CR,秘鲁PE,新加坡SG,新西兰NZ,智利CL 8.4 澳AU 9.8 瑞士CH 11.2 巴PK,韩国KR	0 受惠国$_1$LD$_1$	80	-Other cases
8045	9111.9000	-零件	14	0 冰岛IS,东盟AS,哥CR,秘鲁PE,新加坡SG,新西兰NZ,智利CL 8.4 澳AU 9.8 瑞士CH 11.2 巴PK,韩国KR	0 受惠国$_1$LD$_1$	80	-Parts

序号 No.	税则号列 Tariff Line	中文货品名称 Article Description in Chinese	最惠国税率 MFN(%)	协定税率 Agreement(%)	特惠税率 SP(%)	普通税率 Gen(%)	英文货品名称 Article Description
	91.12	钟壳和本章所列其他货品的类似外壳及其零件：					**Clock cases and cases of a similar type for other goods of this chapter, and parts thereof:**
8046	9112.2000	-壳	14	0 冰岛IS,东盟AS,哥CR,秘鲁PE,新加坡SG,新西兰NZ,智利CL 8.4 澳AU 9.8 瑞士CH 11.2 巴PK,韩国KR	0 受惠国$_1$LD$_1$	80	-Cases
8047	9112.9000	-零件	12	0 冰岛IS,东盟AS,哥CR,秘鲁PE,新加坡SG,新西兰NZ,智利CL 6 巴PK 7.2 澳AU 8.4 瑞士CH 9.6 韩国KR	0 受惠国$_1$LD$_1$	80	-Parts
	91.13	表带及其零件：					**Watch straps, watch bands and watch bracelets, and parts thereof:**
8048	9113.1000	-贵金属或包贵金属制	20	0 冰岛IS,东盟AS,哥CR,新加坡SG,新西兰NZ,智利CL 6 秘鲁PE 12 澳AU 17.3 韩国KR	0 受惠国$_1$LD$_1$	130	-Of precious metal or of metal clad with precious metal
8049	9113.2000	-贱金属制，不论是否镀金或镀银	14	0 澳门MO,冰岛IS,东盟AS,哥CR,秘鲁PE,香港HK,新加坡SG,新西兰NZ,智利CL 8.4 澳AU 9.8 瑞士CH 11.2 巴PK,韩国KR	0 受惠国$_1$LD$_1$	100	-Of base metal, whether or not gold-or silver-plated
8050	9113.9000	-其他	14	0 冰岛IS,东盟AS,哥CR,秘鲁PE,香港HK,新加坡SG,新西兰NZ,智利CL 8.4 澳AU 9.8 瑞士CH 11.2 巴PK,韩国KR	0 受惠国LD	100	-Other
	91.14	钟、表的其他零件：					**Other clock or watch parts:**
8051	9114.1000	-发条，包括游丝	14	0 冰岛IS,东盟AS,哥CR,秘鲁PE,新加坡SG,新西兰NZ,智利CL 7 巴PK 8.4 澳AU 9.8 瑞士CH 11.2 韩国KR	0 受惠国$_1$LD$_1$	50	-Springs, including hair-springs
8052	9114.3000	-钟面或表面	14	0 冰岛IS,东盟AS,哥CR,秘鲁PE,新加坡SG,新西兰NZ,智利CL 8.4 澳AU 10 瑞士CH 11.2 巴PK,韩国KR	0 受惠国$_1$LD$_1$	50	-Dials
8053	9114.4000	-夹板及横担（过桥）	14	0 冰岛IS,东盟AS,哥CR,秘鲁PE,新加坡SG,新西兰NZ,智利CL 8.4 澳AU 9.8 瑞士CH 11.2 巴PK,韩国KR	0 受惠国$_1$LD$_1$	50	-Plates and bridges
		-其他：					-Other:

序号 No.	税则号列 Tariff Line	中文货品名称 Article Description in Chinese	最惠国税率 MFN(%)	协定税率 Agreement(%)	特惠税率 SP(%)	普通税率 Gen(%)	英文货品名称 Article Description
8054	9114.9010	---宝石轴承	14	0 冰岛IS,东盟AS,哥CR,秘鲁PE,新加坡SG,新西兰NZ,智利CL 7 巴PK 8.4 澳AU 9.8 瑞士CH 11.2 韩国KR	0 受惠国$_1$LD$_1$	50	---Jewel bearings
8055	9114.9090	---其他	14	0 澳门MO,冰岛IS,东盟AS,哥CR,秘鲁PE,香港HK,新加坡SG,新西兰NZ,智利CL 8.4 澳AU 10 瑞士CH 11.2 巴PK,韩国KR	0 受惠国$_1$LD$_1$	70	---Other

第九十二章

乐器及其零件、附件

注释：

一、本章不包括：

（一）第十五类注释二所规定的贱金属制通用零件（第十五类）或塑料制的类似品（第三十九章）；

（二）第八十五章或第九十章的传声器、扩大器、扬声器、耳机、开关、频闪观测仪及其他附属仪器、器具或设备，虽用于本章物品但未与该物品组成一体或安装在同一机壳内；

（三）玩具乐器或器具（税号95.03）；

（四）清洁乐器用的刷子（税号96.03）；

（五）收藏品或古物（税号97.05或97.06）。

二、用于演奏税号92.02、92.06所列乐器的弓、槌及类似品，如果与该乐器一同进口或出口，数量合理，用途明确，应归入有关乐器的相应税号。

税号92.09的卡片、盘或卷，即使与乐器一同进口或出口，也不视为该乐器的组成部分，而应作为单独进口或出口的物品对待。

Chapter 92

Musical instruments; parts and accessories of such articles

Notes:

1. This Chapter does not cover:

(a) Parts of general use，as defined in Note 2 to Section XV, of base metal (Section XV), or similar goods of plastics (Chapter 39);

(b) Microphones，amplifiers，loudspeakers，headphones，switches, stroboscopes or other accessory instruments, apparatus or equipment of Chapter 85 or 90, for use with but not incorporated in or housed in the same cabinet as instruments of this Chapter;

(c) Toy instruments or apparatus (heading No.95.03);

(d) Brushes for cleaning musical instruments (heading No.96.03); or

(c) Collectors' pieces or antiques (heading No.97.05 or 97.06).

2. Bows and sticks and similar devices used in playing the musical instruments of heading No.92.02 or 92.06 presented with such instruments in numbers normal thereto and clearly intended for use therewith, are to be classified in the same heading as the relative instruments.

Cards, discs and rolls of heading No.92.09 presented with an instrument are to be treated as separate articles and not as forming a part of such instrument.

序号 No.	税则号列 Tariff Line	中文货品名称 Article Description in Chinese	最惠国税率 MFN(%)	协定税率 Agreement(%)	特惠税率 SP(%)	普通税率 Gen(%)	英文货品名称 Article Description
	92.01	**钢琴，包括自动钢琴、拨弦古钢琴及其他键盘弦乐器：**					**Pianos, including automatic pianos; harpsichords and other keyboard stringed instruments:**
8056	9201.1000	-竖式钢琴	17.5	0 澳门MO,冰岛IS,东盟AS,哥CR,新加坡SG,新西兰NZ,智利CL 5.2 秘鲁PE 10.5 澳AU 12.3 瑞士CH 14 巴PK,韩国KR	0 受惠国$_1$LD$_1$	70	-Upright pianos
8057	9201.2000	-大钢琴	17.5	0 冰岛IS,东盟AS,哥CR,新加坡SG,新西兰NZ,智利CL 5.2 秘鲁PE 10.5 澳AU 12.3 瑞士CH 14 巴PK,韩国KR	0 受惠国$_1$LD$_1$	70	-Grand pianos
	ex92012000	完税价格50000美元及以上的大钢琴	Δ1				Grand pianos, the duty-paying value≥50000USD

序号 No.	税则号列 Tariff Line	中文货品名称 Article Description in Chinese	最惠国税率 MFN(%)	协定税率 Agreement(%)	特惠税率 SP(%)	普通税率 Gen(%)	英文货品名称 Article Description
8058	9201.9000	-其他	17.5	0 冰岛IS,东盟AS,哥CR,新加坡SG,新西兰NZ,智利CL 5.2 秘鲁PE 10.5 澳AU 12.3 瑞士CH 14 巴PK,韩国KR	0 受惠国$_1$LD$_1$	70	-Other
	92.02	**其他弦乐器(例如,吉他、小提琴、竖琴):**					**Other string musical instruments (for example, guitars, violins, harps) :**
8059	9202.1000	-弓弦乐器	17.5	0 冰岛IS,东盟AS,哥CR,新加坡SG,新西兰NZ,智利CL 5.2 秘鲁PE 10.5 澳AU,韩国KR 12.3 瑞士CH 14 巴PK	0 受惠国LD	70	-Played with a bow
	ex92021000	完税价格15000美元及以上的弓弦乐器	Δ1				Played with a bow, the duty-paying value≥15000USD
8060	9202.9000	-其他	17.5	0 冰岛IS,东盟AS,哥CR,新加坡SG,新西兰NZ,智利CL 5.2 秘鲁PE 10.5 澳AU 12.3 瑞士CH 14 巴PK,韩国KR	0 受惠国LD	70	-Other
	92.05	**管乐器(例如,键盘管风琴、手风琴、单簧管、小号、风笛),但游艺场风琴及手摇风琴除外:**					**Wind musical instruments (for example, keyboard pipe organs, accordions, clarinets, trumpets, bagpipes) , other than fairground organs and mechanical street organs:**
8061	9205.1000	-铜管乐器	17.5	0 冰岛IS,东盟AS,哥CR,新加坡SG,新西兰NZ,智利CL 5.2 秘鲁PE 10.5 澳AU,韩国KR 12.3 瑞士CH 14 巴PK	0 受惠国LD	70	-Brass-wind instruments
	ex92051000	完税价格2000美元及以上的铜管乐器	Δ1				Brass-wind instruments, the duty-paying value≥2000USD
		-其他:					-Other:
8062	9205.9010	---键盘管风琴;簧风琴及类似的游离金属簧片键盘乐器	20	0 冰岛IS,东盟AS,哥CR,新加坡SG,新西兰NZ,智利CL 6 秘鲁PE 12 澳AU 14 瑞士CH 17.3 韩国KR	0 受惠国$_1$LD$_1$	80	---Keyboard pipe organs; harmoniums and similar keyboard instruments with free metal reeds
8063	9205.9020	---手风琴及类似乐器	21	0 冰岛IS,东盟AS,哥CR,新加坡SG,新西兰NZ,智利CL 6.3 秘鲁PE 12.6 澳AU 14.7 瑞士CH 18.2 韩国KR	0 受惠国$_1$LD$_1$	80	---Accordions and similar instruments
8064	9205.9030	---口琴	21	0 冰岛IS,东盟AS,哥CR,新加坡SG,新西兰NZ,智利CL 6.3 秘鲁PE 12.6 澳AU 14.7 瑞士CH 18.2 韩国KR	0 受惠国$_1$LD$_1$	80	---Mouth organs

序号 No.	税则号列 Tariff Line	中文货品名称 Article Description in Chinese	最惠国税率 MFN(%)	协定税率 Agreement(%)	特惠税率 SP(%)	普通税率 Gen(%)	英文货品名称 Article Description
8065	9205.9090	---其他	17.5	0 冰岛IS,东盟AS,哥CR,新加坡SG,新西兰NZ,智利CL 5.2 秘鲁PE 10.5 澳AU,韩国KR 12.3 瑞士CH 14 巴PK	0 受惠国$_1$LD$_1$	70	---Other
	ex92059090	完税价格10000美元及以上的其他管乐器	Δ1				Other wind musical instruments, the duty-paying value≥ 10000USD
	92.06	**打击乐器（例如，鼓、木琴、铙、钹、响板、响葫芦）**					**Percussion musical instruments (for example, drums, xylophones, cymbals, castanets, maracas)**
8066	9206.0000	打击乐器（例如，鼓、木琴、铙、钹、响板、响葫芦）	17.5	0 冰岛IS,东盟AS,哥CR,秘鲁PE,新加坡SG,新西兰NZ,智利CL 10.5 澳AU 12.3 瑞士CH 14 巴PK,韩国KR	0 受惠国LD	70	Percussion musical instruments (for example, drums, xylophones, cymbals, castanets, maracas)
	92.07	**通过电产生或扩大声音的乐器（例如，电风琴、电吉他、电手风琴）：**					**Musical instruments, the sound of which is produced, or must be amplified, electrically (for example, organs, guitars, accordions) :**
8067	9207.1000	-键盘乐器，但手风琴除外	30Δ15	0 冰岛IS,东盟AS,哥CR,新加坡SG,新西兰NZ,智利CL 9 秘鲁PE 18 澳AU 21.6 瑞士CH	0 受惠国$_1$LD$_1$	100	-Keyboard instruments, other than accordions
8068	9207.9000	-其他	30	0 冰岛IS,东盟AS,哥CR,新加坡SG,新西兰NZ,智利CL 9 秘鲁PE 18 澳AU 21.6 瑞士CH	0 受惠国$_1$LD$_1$	100	-Other
	92.08	**百音盒、游艺场风琴、手摇风琴、机械鸣禽、乐锯及本章其他税号未列名的其他乐器;各种媒诱音响器、哨子、号角、口吹音响信号器:**					**Musical boxes, fairground organs, mechanical street organs, mechanical singing birds, musical saws and other musical instruments not falling within any other heading of this chapter; decoy calls of all kinds; whistles, call horns and other mouth-blown sound signalling instruments:**
8069	9208.1000	-百音盒	22	0 冰岛IS,东盟AS,哥CR,新加坡SG,新西兰NZ,智利CL 6.6 秘鲁PE 13.2 澳AU 15.4 瑞士CH 19.8 韩国KR	0 受惠国$_1$LD$_1$	80	-Musical boxes
8070	9208.9000	-其他	22	0 冰岛IS,东盟AS,哥CR,新加坡SG,新西兰NZ,智利CL 6.6 秘鲁PE 13.2 澳AU 15.4 瑞士CH 19.8 韩国KR	0 受惠国$_1$LD$_1$	80	-Other

序号 No.	税则号列 Tariff Line	中文货品名称 Article Description in Chinese	最惠国税率 MFN(%)	协定税率 Agreement(%)	特惠税率 SP(%)	普通税率 Gen(%)	英文货品名称 Article Description
	92.09	乐器的零件（例如百音盒的机械装置）、附件（例如，机械乐器用的卡片、盘及带卷），节拍器、音叉及各种定音管：					**Parts (for example, mechanisms for musical boxes) and accessories (for example, cards, discs and rolls for mechanical instruments) of musical instruments; metronomes, tuning forks and pitch pipes of all kinds:**
8071	9209.3000	-乐器用的弦	17.5	0 冰岛IS,东盟AS,哥CR,新加坡SG,新西兰NZ,智利CL 5.2 秘鲁PE 10.5 澳AU 12.3 瑞士CH 14 巴PK,韩国KR	0 受惠国$_1$LD$_1$	70	-Musical instrument strings
		-其他：					-Other:
8072	9209.9100	--钢琴的零件、附件	17.5	0 冰岛IS,东盟AS,哥CR,新加坡SG,新西兰NZ,智利CL 5.2 秘鲁PE 10.5 澳AU 12.3 瑞士CH 14 巴PK,韩国KR	0 受惠国$_1$LD$_1$	70	--Parts and accessories for pianos
8073	9209.9200	--税号92.02所列乐器的零件、附件	17.5	0 冰岛IS,东盟AS,哥CR,新加坡SG,新西兰NZ,智利CL 5.2 秘鲁PE 10.5 澳AU 12.3 瑞士CH 14 巴PK,韩国KR	0 受惠国LD	70	--Parts and accessories for the musical instruments of heading No.92.02
8074	9209.9400	--税号92.07所列乐器的零件、附件	17.5Δ10	0 冰岛IS,东盟AS,哥CR,新加坡SG,新西兰NZ,智利CL 5.2 秘鲁PE 10.5 澳AU 12.3 瑞士CH 14 巴PK 15.1 韩国KR	0 受惠国$_1$LD$_1$	70	--Parts and accessories for the musical instruments of heading No.92.07
		--其他：					--Other:
8075	9209.9910	---节拍器、音叉及定音管	17.5	0 冰岛IS,东盟AS,哥CR,新加坡SG,新西兰NZ,智利CL 5.2 秘鲁PE 10.5 澳AU 12.3 瑞士CH 14 巴PK,韩国KR	0 受惠国$_1$LD$_1$	70	---Metronomes, tuning forks and pitch pipes
8076	9209.9920	---百音盒的机械装置	17.5	0 冰岛IS,东盟AS,哥CR,新加坡SG,新西兰NZ,智利CL 5.2 秘鲁PE 10.5 澳AU 12.3 瑞士CH 14 巴PK,韩国KR	0 受惠国$_1$LD$_1$	70	---Mechanisms for musical boxes
8077	9209.9990	---其他	17.5	0 冰岛IS,东盟AS,哥CR,新加坡SG,新西兰NZ,智利CL 5.2 秘鲁PE 10.5 澳AU 12.3 瑞士CH 14 巴PK,韩国KR	0 受惠国LD	70	---Other

第十九类

武器、弹药及其零件、附件

第九十三章
武器、弹药及其零件、附件

注释:

一、本章不包括:

（一）第三十六章的货品（例如，火帽、雷管、信号弹）;

（二）第十五类注释二所规定的贱金属制通用零件（第十五类）或塑料制的类似品（第三十九章）;

（三）装甲战斗车辆（税号87.10）;

（四）武器用的望远镜瞄准具及其他光学装置（第九十章），但安装在武器上或与武器一同进口或出口以备安装在该武器上的除外;

（五）弓、箭、钝头击剑或玩具（第九十五章）;

（六）收藏品及古物（税号97.05或97.06）。

二、税号93.06所称“零件”，不包括税号85.26的无线电设备及雷达设备。

SECTION XIX

ARMS AND AMMUNITION; PARTS AND ACCESSORIES THEREOF

Chapter 93
Arms and ammunition; parts and accessories thereof

Notes:

1. This Chapter does not cover:

(a) Goods of Chapter 36 (for example, percussion caps, detonators, signalling flares);

(b) Parts of general use, as defined in Note 2 to Section XV, of base metal (Section XV), or similar goods of plastics (Chapter 39);

(c) Armoured fighting vehicles (heading No.87.10);

(d) Telescopic sights or other optical devices suitable for use with arms, unless mounted on a firearm or presented with the firearm on which they are designed to be mounted (Chapter 90);

(e) Bows, arrows, fencing foils or toys (Chapter 95); or

(f) Collectors' pieces or antiques (heading No.97.05 or 97.06).

2.In heading No.93.06, the reference to “parts thereof” does not include radio or radar apparatus of heading No.85.26.

序号 No.	税则号列 Tariff Line	中文货品名称 Article Description in Chinese	最惠国税率 MFN(%)	协定税率 Agreement(%)	特惠税率 SP(%)	普通税率 Gen(%)	英文货品名称 Article Description
	93.01	军用武器，但左轮手枪、其他手枪及税目93.07的兵器除外:					Military weapons, other than revolvers, pistols and the arms of heading 9307:
		-火炮武器（例如，榴弹炮及迫击炮）:					-Artillery weapons (for example, guns, howitzers and mortars) :
8078	9301.1010	---自推进的	13	0 冰岛IS,东盟AS,哥CR,秘鲁PE,新加坡SG,新西兰NZ,智利CL 6.5 巴PK 7.8 澳AU 9.1 瑞士CH 10.4 韩国KR	0 受惠国$_1$LD$_1$	80	---Self-propelled
8079	9301.1090	---其他	13	0 冰岛IS,东盟AS,哥CR,秘鲁PE,新加坡SG,新西兰NZ,智利CL 6.5 巴PK 7.8 澳AU 9.1 瑞士CH 10.4 韩国KR	0 受惠国$_1$LD$_1$	80	---Other
8080	9301.2000	-火箭发射装置;火焰喷射器;手榴弹发射器;鱼雷发射管及类似发射装置自推进的	13	0 冰岛IS,东盟AS,哥CR,秘鲁PE,新加坡SG,新西兰NZ,智利CL 6.5 巴PK 7.8 澳AU 9.1 瑞士CH 10.4 韩国KR	0 受惠国$_1$LD$_1$	80	-Rocket launchers; flamethrowers; gren-ade launchers; torpedo tubes and similar projectors

序号 No.	税则号列 Tariff Line	中文货品名称 Article Description in Chinese	最惠国税率 MFN(%)	协定税率 Agreement(%)	特惠税率 SP(%)	普通税率 Gen(%)	英文货品名称 Article Description
8081	9301.9000	-其他	13	0 冰岛IS,东盟AS,哥CR,秘鲁PE,新加坡SG,新西兰NZ,智利CL 6.5 巴PK 7.8 澳AU 9.1 瑞士CH 10.4 韩国KR	0 受惠国$_1$LD$_1$	80	-Other
	93.02	**左轮手枪及其他手枪，但税号93.03或93.04的货品除外**					**Revolvers and pistols, other than those of heading 9303 or 9304**
8082	9302.0000	左轮手枪及其他手枪，但税号93.03或93.04的货品除外	13	0 冰岛IS,东盟AS,哥CR,秘鲁PE,新加坡SG,新西兰NZ,智利CL 6.5 巴PK 7.8 澳AU 9.1 瑞士CH 10.4 韩国KR	0 受惠国$_1$LD$_1$	80	Revolvers and pistols, other than those of heading No.93.03 or 93.04
	93.03	**靠爆炸药发射的其他火器及类似装置（例如，运动用猎枪及步枪、前装枪、维利式信号枪及其他专为发射信号弹的装置、发射空包弹的左轮手枪和其他手枪、弩枪式无痛捕杀器、抛缆枪）：**					**Other firearms and similar devices which operate by the firing of an explosive charge (for example, sporting shotguns and rifles, muzzle-loading firearms, Very pistols and other devices designed to project only signal flares, pistols and revolvers for firing blank ammunition, captive-bolt humane killers, line-throwing guns) :**
8083	9303.1000	-前装枪	13	0 冰岛IS,东盟AS,哥CR,秘鲁PE,新加坡SG,新西兰NZ,智利CL 6.5 巴PK 7.8 澳AU 9.1 瑞士CH 10.4 韩国KR	0 受惠国$_1$LD$_1$	80	-Muzzle-loading firearms
8084	9303.2000	-其他运动、狩猎或打靶用猎枪，包括组合式滑膛来复枪	13	0 冰岛IS,东盟AS,哥CR,秘鲁PE,新加坡SG,新西兰NZ,智利CL 6.5 巴PK 7.8 澳AU 9.4 瑞士CH 10.4 韩国KR	0 受惠国$_1$LD$_1$	80	-Other sporting, hunting or target shooting shotguns, including combination shotgunrifles
8085	9303.3000	-其他运动、狩猎或打靶用步枪	13	0 冰岛IS,东盟AS,哥CR,秘鲁PE,新加坡SG,新西兰NZ,智利CL 6.5 巴PK 7.8 澳AU 9.1 瑞士CH 10.4 韩国KR	0 受惠国$_1$LD$_1$	80	-Other sporting, hunting or target shooting rifles
8086	9303.9000	-其他	13	0 冰岛IS,东盟AS,哥CR,秘鲁PE,新加坡SG,新西兰NZ,智利CL 6.5 巴PK 7.8 澳AU 9.1 瑞士CH 10.4 韩国KR	0 受惠国$_1$LD$_1$	80	-Other
	93.04	**其他武器(例如，弹簧枪、气枪、气手枪、警棍)，但不包括税号93.07的货品**					**Other arms (for example, spring, air or gas guns and pistols, truncheons) , excluding those of heading 9307**
8087	9304.0000	其他武器(例如，弹簧枪、气枪、气手枪、警棍)，但不包括税号93.07的货品	13	0 冰岛IS,东盟AS,哥CR,秘鲁PE,新加坡SG,新西兰NZ,智利CL 6.5 巴PK 7.8 澳AU 10.4 韩国KR	0 受惠国$_1$LD$_1$	80	Other arms (for example, spring, air or gas guns and pistols, truncheons) excluding those of heading No.93.07

序号 No.	税则号列 Tariff Line	中文货品名称 Article Description in Chinese	最惠国税率 MFN(%)	协定税率 Agreement(%)	特惠税率 SP(%)	普通税率 Gen(%)	英文货品名称 Article Description
	93.05	**税号93.01至93.04所列物品的零件、附件：**					**Parts and accessories of articles of headings 9301 to 9304:**
8088	9305.1000	-左轮手枪或其他手枪用	13	0 冰岛IS,东盟AS,哥CR,秘鲁PE,新加坡SG,新西兰NZ,智利CL 6.5 巴PK 7.8 澳AU 9.1 瑞士CH 10.4 韩国KR	0 受惠国$_1$LD$_1$	80	-Of revolvers or pistols
8089	9305.2000	-税号93.03的猎枪或步枪用	13	0 冰岛IS,东盟AS,哥CR,秘鲁PE,新加坡SG,新西兰NZ,智利CL 6.5 巴PK 7.8 澳AU 9.1 瑞士CH 10.4 韩国KR	0 受惠国$_1$LD$_1$	80	-Of shotguns or rifles of heading No.93.03
		-其他：					-Other:
8090	9305.9100	--税目93.01的军用武器用	13	0 冰岛IS,东盟AS,哥CR,秘鲁PE,新加坡SG,新西兰NZ,智利CL 6.5 巴PK 7.8 澳AU 9.1 瑞士CH 10.4 韩国KR	0 受惠国$_1$LD$_1$	80	--Of military weapons of heading 93.01
8091	9305.9900	--其他	13	0 冰岛IS,东盟AS,哥CR,秘鲁PE,新加坡SG,新西兰NZ,智利CL 6.5 巴PK 7.8 澳AU 9.1 瑞士CH 10.4 韩国KR	0 受惠国$_1$LD$_1$	80	--Other
	93.06	**炸弹、手榴弹、鱼雷、地雷、水雷、导弹及类似武器及其零件;子弹、其他弹药和射弹及其零件,包括弹丸及弹垫：**					**Bombs, grenades, torpedoes, mines, missiles and similar munitions of war and parts thereof; cartridges and other ammunition and projectiles and parts thereof, including shot and cartridge wads:**
		-猎枪子弹及其零件;气枪弹丸：					-Shotgun cartridges and parts thereof; air gun pellets:
8092	9306.2100	--猎枪子弹	13	0 冰岛IS,东盟AS,哥CR,秘鲁PE,新加坡SG,新西兰NZ,智利CL 6.5 巴PK 7.8 澳AU 9.1 瑞士CH 10.4 韩国KR	0 受惠国$_1$LD$_1$	80	--Cartridges
8093	9306.2900	--其他	13	0 冰岛IS,东盟AS,哥CR,秘鲁PE,新加坡SG,新西兰NZ,智利CL 6.5 巴PK 7.8 澳AU 9.1 瑞士CH 10.4 韩国KR	0 受惠国$_1$LD$_1$	80	--Other
		-其他子弹及其零件：					-Other cartridges and parts thereof:
8094	9306.3080	---铆接机或类似工具用及弩枪式无痛捕杀器用子弹及其零件	13	0 冰岛IS,东盟AS,哥CR,秘鲁PE,新加坡SG,新西兰NZ,智利CL 6.5 巴PK 7.8 澳AU 9.1 瑞士CH 10.4 韩国KR	0 受惠国$_1$LD$_1$	80	---Cartridges for riveting or similar tools or for captivebolt humane killers and parts thereof

序号 No.	税则号列 Tariff Line	中文货品名称 Article Description in Chinese	最惠国税率 MFN(%)	协定税率 Agreement(%)	特惠税率 SP(%)	普通税率 Gen(%)	英文货品名称 Article Description
8095	9306.3090	---其他子弹及其零件	13	0 冰岛IS,东盟AS,哥CR,秘鲁PE,新加坡SG,新西兰NZ,智利CL 6.5 巴PK 7.8 澳AU 9.1 瑞士CH 10.4 韩国KR	0 受惠国$_1$LD$_1$	80	---Other cartridges and parts thereof
8096	9306.9000	-其他	13	0 冰岛IS,东盟AS,哥CR,秘鲁PE,新加坡SG,新西兰NZ,智利CL 6.5 巴PK 7.8 澳AU 9.1 瑞士CH 10.4 韩国KR	0 受惠国$_1$LD$_1$	80	-Other
	93.07	**剑、短弯刀、刺刀、长矛和类似的武器及其零件;刀鞘、剑鞘:**					**Swords, cutlasses, bayonets, lances and similar arms and parts thereof and scabbards and sheaths therefor:**
8097	9307.0010	---军用	13	0 冰岛IS,东盟AS,哥CR,秘鲁PE,新加坡SG,新西兰NZ,智利CL 6.5 巴PK 7.8 澳AU 9.1 瑞士CH 10.4 韩国KR	0 受惠国LD	80	---Military
8098	9307.0090	---其他	13	0 冰岛IS,东盟AS,哥CR,秘鲁PE,新加坡SG,新西兰NZ,智利CL 6.5 巴PK 7.8 澳AU 9.1 瑞士CH 10.4 韩国KR	0 受惠国LD	80	---Other

第二十类

杂项制品

SECTION XX
MISCELLANEOUS MANUFACTURED ARTICLES

第九十四章
家具；寝具、褥垫、弹簧床垫、软座垫及类似的填充制品；未列名灯具及照明装置；发光标志、发光铭牌及类似品；活动房屋

注释：

一、本章不包括：

（一）第三十九章、第四十章或第六十三章的充气或充水的褥垫、枕头及座垫；

（二）落地镜〔例如税号 70.09 的试衣镜（旋转镜）〕；

（三）第七十一章的物品；

（四）第十五类注释二所规定的贱金属制通用零件（第十五类）、塑料制的类似品（第三十九章）或税号 83.03 的保险箱；

（五）冷藏或冷冻设备专用的特制家具（税号 84.18）；缝纫机专用的特制家具（税号 84.52）；

（六）第八十五章的灯具及照明装置；

（七）税目 85.18、85.19、85.21 或税目 85.25 至 85.28 所列装置专用的特制家具（应分别归入税目 85.18、85.22 或 85.29）；

（八）税号 87.14 的物品；

（九）装有税号 90.18 所列牙科用器具或漱口盂的牙科用椅（税号 90.18）；

（十）第九十一章的物品（例如，钟及钟壳）；

（十一）玩具家具、玩具灯或玩具照明装置（税号 95.03）、台球桌或其他供游戏用的特制家具（税号 95.04）、魔术用的特制家具或中国灯笼及类似的装饰品（电气彩灯串除外）（税号 95.05）。

二、税号 94.01 至 94.03 的物品（零件除外），只适用于落地式的物品。

对下列物品，即使是悬挂的、固定在墙壁上的或叠摞的，仍归入上述各税号：

（一）碗橱、书柜、架式家具及组合家具；

（二）座具及床。

Chapter 94
Furniture; bedding, mattresses, mattress supports, cushions and similar stuffed furnishings; lamps and lighting fittings, not elsewhere specified or included; illuminated signs, illuminated name-plates and the like; prefabricated buildings

Notes:

1. This Chapter does not cover:

(a) Pneumatic or water mattresses, pillows or cushions, of Chapter 39, 40 or 63;

(b) Mirrors designed for placing on the floor or ground (for example, cheval-glasses (swing- mirrors) of heading No.70.09);

(c) Articles of Chapter 71;

(d) Parts of general use as defined in Note 2 to Section XV, of base metal (Section XV), or similar goods of plastics(Chapter 39), or safes of heading No.83.03;

(e) Furniture specially designed as parts of refrigerating or freezing equipment of heading No.84.18; furniture specially designed for sewing machines (heading No.84.52);

(f) Lamps or lighting fittings of Chapter 85;

(g) Furniture specially designed as parts of apparatus of heading No.85.18 (heading No.85.18), of headings No.85.19 or 85.21 (heading No.85.22) or of headings No.85.25 to 85.28 (heading No.85.29);

(h) Articles of heading No.87.14;

(ij) Dentists' chairs incorporating dental appliances of heading No.90.18 or dentists' spittoons (heading No.90.18);

(k) Articles of Chapter 91 (for example, clocks and clock cases);or

(l) Toy furniture or toy lamps or lighting fittings (heading No.95.03), billiard tables or other furniture specially constructed for games (heading No.95.04), furniture for conjuring tricks or decorations (other than electric garlands) such as Chinese lanterns (heading No.95.05).

2. The articles (other than parts) referred to in headings No.94.01 to 94.03 are to be classified in those headings only if they are designed for placing on the floor or ground.

The following are, however, to be classified in the abovementioned headings even if they are designed to be hung, to be fixed to the wall or to stand one on the other:

(a) Cupboards, bookcases, other shelved furniture and unit furniture;

(b) Seats and beds.

三、

（一）税号94.01至94.03所列货品的零件，不包括玻璃（包括镜子）、大理石或其他石料以及第六十八章及第六十九章所列任何其他材料的片、块（不论是否切割成形，但未与其他零件组装）。

（二）税号94.04的货品，如果单独进口或出口，不能作为税号94.01、94.02或94.03所列货品的零件归类。

四、税号94.06所称"活动房屋"，是指在工厂制成成品或制成部件并一同进口或出口，供以后在有关地点上组装的房屋，例如，工地用房、办公室、学校、店铺、工作棚、车房或类似的建筑物。

3.

(a) In headings No.94.01 to 94.03references to parts of goods do not include references to sheets or slabs (whether or not cut to shape but not combined with other parts) of glass (including mirrors), marble or other stone or of any other material referred to in Chapter 68 or 69.

(b) Goods described in heading No.94.04, presented separately, are not to be classified in heading No.94.01, 94.02 or 94.03 as parts of goods.

4.For the purposes of heading No.94.06, the expression' "prefabricated buildings" means buildings which are finished in the factory or put up as elements, presented together, to be assembled on site, such as housing or worksite accommodation, offices, schools, shops, sheds, garages or similar buildings.

序号 No.	税则号列 Tariff Line	中文货品名称 Article Description in Chinese	最惠国税率 MFN(%)	协定税率 Agreement(%)	特惠税率 SP(%)	普通税率 Gen(%)	英文货品名称 Article Description
	94.01	**座具（包括能作床用的两用椅，但税号94.02的货品除外）及其零件：**					**Seats (other than those of heading 9402) , whether or not convertible into beds, and parts thereof:**
8099	9401.1000	-飞机用座具	0		0 受惠国LD	100	-Seats of a kind used for aircraft
		-机动车辆用座具：					-Seats of a kind used for motor vehicles:
8100	9401.2010	---皮革或再生皮革面的	10	0 澳门MO,冰岛IS,哥CR,秘鲁PE,新西兰NZ,智利CL 4 瑞士CH 6 澳AU 9 韩国KR	0 受惠国$_1$LD$_1$	100	---With outer surface of leather or composition leather
8101	9401.2090	---其他	10	0 澳门MO,冰岛IS,哥CR,秘鲁PE,新西兰NZ,智利CL 4 瑞士CH 6 澳AU 8.6 韩国KR	0 受惠国$_1$LD$_1$	100	---Other
8102	9401.3000	-可调高度的转动座具	0		0 受惠国LD	100	-Swivel seats with variable height adjustment
		-能作床用的两用椅，但庭园座具或野营设备除外：					-Seats other than garden seats or camping equipment, convertible into beds:
8103	9401.4010	---皮革或再生皮革面的	0		0 受惠国LD	100	---With outer surface of leather or composition leather
8104	9401.4090	---其他	0		0 受惠国LD	100	---Other
		-藤、柳条、竹及类似材料制的座具：					-Seats of cane, osier, bamboo or similar materials:
8105	9401.5100	--竹制或藤制的	0		0 老挝LA,受惠国LD	100	--Of bamboo or rattan
8106	9401.5900	--其他	0		0 老挝LA,受惠国LD	100	--Other
		-木框架的其他座具：					-Other seats, with wooden frames:
		--装软垫的：					--Upholstered:

序号 No.	税则号列 Tariff Line	中文货品名称 Article Description in Chinese	最惠国税率 MFN(%)	协定税率 Agreement(%)	特惠税率 SP(%)	普通税率 Gen(%)	英文货品名称 Article Description
8107	9401.6110	---皮革或再生皮革面的	0		0 受惠国LD	100	---With outer surface of leather or composition leather
8108	9401.6190	---其他	0		0 受惠国LD	100	---Other
8109	9401.6900	--其他	0		0 受惠国LD	100	--Other
		-金属框架的其他座具:					-Other seats, with metal frames:
		--装软垫的:					--Upholstered:
8110	9401.7110	---皮革或再生皮革面的	0		0 受惠国LD	100	---With outer surface of leather or composition leather
8111	9401.7190	---其他	0		0 受惠国LD	100	---Other
8112	9401.7900	--其他	0		0 受惠国LD	100	--Other
		-其他座具:					-Other seats:
8113	9401.8010	---石制的	0		0 受惠国LD	100	---Of stone
8114	9401.8090	---其他	0		0 受惠国LD	100	---Other
		-零件:					-Parts:
		---机动车辆用:					---Of the motor Vehicles:
8115	9401.9011	----座椅调角器	10	0 冰岛IS,哥CR,香港HK,新西兰NZ,智利CL 3 秘鲁PE 4 瑞士CH 6 澳AU	0 受惠国LD	100	----Seat angle regulating devices
8116	9401.9019	----其他	0		0 受惠国LD	100	----Other
8117	9401.9090	---其他	0		0 受惠国LD	100	---Other
	94.02	**医疗、外科、牙科或兽医用家具(例如,手术台、检查台、带机械装置的病床、牙科用椅);有旋转、倾斜、升降装置的理发用椅及类似椅;上述物品的零件:**					**Medical, surgical, dental or veterinary furniture (for example, operating tables, examination tables, hospital beds with mechanical fittings, dentists' chairs) ; barbers' chairs and similar chairs, having rotating as well as both reclining and elevating movements; parts of the foregoing articles:**
		-牙科、理发及类似用途的椅及其零件:					-Dentists' , barbers' or similar chairs and parts thereof:
8118	9402.1010	---理发用椅及其零件	0		0 受惠国LD	100	---Barbers chair and parts thereof
8119	9402.1090	---其他	0		0 受惠国LD	30	---Other
8120	9402.9000	-其他	0		0 受惠国LD	30	-Other
	94.03	**其他家具及其零件:**					**Other furniture and parts thereof:**
8121	9403.1000	-办公室用金属家具	0		0 受惠国LD	100	-Metal furniture of a kind used in offices
8122	9403.2000	-其他金属家具	0		0 受惠国LD	100	-Other metal furniture
8123	9403.3000	-办公室用木家具	0		0 柬埔寨KH,老挝LA,受惠国LD	100	-Wooden furniture of a kind used in offices
8124	9403.4000	-厨房用木家具	0		0 柬埔寨KH,受惠国LD	100	-Wooden furniture of a kind used in the kitchen
		-卧室用木家具:					-Wooden furniture of a kind used in the bedroom:
8125	9403.5010	---红木制	0		0 柬埔寨KH,受惠国LD	100	---Of rose wood
		---其他:					---Other:
8126	9403.5091	----漆木家具	0		0 柬埔寨KH,受惠国LD	100	----Of lacquered wood
8127	9403.5099	----其他	0		0 柬埔寨KH,受惠国LD	100	----Other
		-其他木家具:					-Other wooden furniture:
8128	9403.6010	---红木制	0		0 柬埔寨KH,受惠国LD	100	---Of rose wood
		---其他:					---Other:
8129	9403.6091	----漆木家具	0		0 柬埔寨KH,受惠国LD	100	----Of lacquered wood
8130	9403.6099	----其他	0		0 柬埔寨KH,受惠国LD	100	----Other
8131	9403.7000	-塑料家具	0		0 受惠国LD	100	-Furniture of plastics

序号 No.	税则号列 Tariff Line	中文货品名称 Article Description in Chinese	最惠国税率 MFN(%)	协定税率 Agreement(%)	特惠税率 SP(%)	普通税率 Gen(%)	英文货品名称 Article Description
		-其他材料制的家具，包括藤、柳条、竹或类似材料制的：					-Furniture of other materials, including cane, osier, bamboo or similar materials:
8132	9403.8100	--竹制或藤制的	0		0 柬埔寨KH,受惠国LD	100	--Of bamboo or rattan
		--其他：					--Other:
8133	9403.8910	---柳条及类似材料制	0		0 柬埔寨KH,受惠国LD	100	---Of osier, or similar materials
8134	9403.8920	---石制的	0		0 受惠国LD	100	---Of stone
8135	9403.8990	---其他	0		0 受惠国LD	100	---Other
8136	9403.9000	-零件	0		0 受惠国LD	100	-Parts
	94.04	**弹簧床垫;寝具及类似用品，装有弹簧、内部用任何材料填充、衬垫或用海绵橡胶、泡沫塑料制成，不论是否包面（例如，褥垫、棉被、羽绒被、靠垫、座垫及枕头）：**					**Mattress supports; articles of bedding and similar furnishing (for example, mattresses, quilts, eiderdowns, cushions, pouffes and pillows) fitted with springs or stuffed or internally fitted with any material or of cellular rubber or plastics, whether or not covered:**
8137	9404.1000	-弹簧床垫	20Δ10	0 冰岛IS,东盟AS,哥CR,新加坡SG,新西兰NZ,智利CL 6 秘鲁PE 12 澳AU 14 瑞士CH 17.3 韩国KR	0 受惠国[1]LD[1]	100	-Mattress supports
		-褥垫：					-Mattresses:
8138	9404.2100	--海绵橡胶或泡沫塑料制，不论是否包面	20Δ10	0 澳门MO,冰岛IS,东盟AS,哥CR,香港HK,新加坡SG,新西兰NZ,智利CL 6 秘鲁PE 12 澳AU 14 瑞士CH 17.3 韩国KR	0 受惠国LD	100	--Of cellular rubber or plastics, whether or not covered
8139	9404.2900	--其他材料制	20Δ10	0 澳门MO,冰岛IS,东盟AS,哥CR,香港HK,新加坡SG,新西兰NZ,智利CL 6 秘鲁PE 12 澳AU 14 巴PK,瑞士CH,亚太AP 17.3 韩国KR	0 受惠国LD	100	--Of other materials
		-睡袋：					-Sleeping bags:
8140	9404.3010	---羽毛或羽绒填充的	20Δ10	0 澳门MO,冰岛IS,东盟AS,哥CR,新加坡SG,新西兰NZ,智利CL 6 秘鲁PE 12 澳AU 14 瑞士CH 17.3 韩国KR	0 受惠国LD	130	---Stuffed with feathers or down
8141	9404.3090	---其他	20Δ10	0 澳门MO,冰岛IS,东盟AS,哥CR,新加坡SG,新西兰NZ,智利CL 6 秘鲁PE 12 澳AU 14 瑞士CH 17.3 韩国KR	0 受惠国LD	100	---Other
		-其他：					-Other:

序号 No.	税则号列 Tariff Line	中文货品名称 Article Description in Chinese	最惠国税率 MFN(%)	协定税率 Agreement(%)	特惠税率 SP(%)	普通税率 Gen(%)	英文货品名称 Article Description
8142	9404.9010	---羽毛或羽绒填充的	20∆10	0 澳门MO,东盟AS,哥CR,香港HK,新加坡SG,新西兰NZ,智利CL 6 秘鲁PE 12 澳AU 14 瑞士CH 17.3 韩国KR	0 受惠国LD	130	---Stuffed with feathers or down
8143	9404.9020	---兽毛填充的	20∆10	0 澳门MO,冰岛IS,东盟AS,哥CR,香港HK,新加坡SG,新西兰NZ,智利CL 6 秘鲁PE 12 澳AU 14 瑞士CH 17.3 韩国KR	0 受惠国LD	130	---Stuffed with animal hair
8144	9404.9030	---丝棉填充的	20∆10	0 澳门MO,冰岛IS,东盟AS,哥CR,香港HK,新加坡SG,新西兰NZ,智利CL 6 秘鲁PE 12 澳AU 14 瑞士CH 17.3 韩国KR	0 受惠国LD	130	---Stuffed with silk wadding
8145	9404.9040	---化纤棉填充的	20∆10	0 澳门MO,冰岛IS,东盟AS,哥CR,香港HK,新加坡SG,新西兰NZ,智利CL 6 秘鲁PE 12 澳AU 14 瑞士CH 17.3 韩国KR	0 受惠国LD	130	---Stuffed with man-made fibres
8146	9404.9090	---其他	20∆10	0 澳门MO,冰岛IS,东盟AS,哥CR,香港HK,新加坡SG,新西兰NZ,智利CL 6 秘鲁PE 12 澳AU 14 瑞士CH 17.3 韩国KR	0 受惠国LD	130	---Other
	94.05	**其他税号未列名的灯具及照明装置，包括探照灯、聚光灯及其零件;装有固定光源的发光标志、发光铭牌及类似品，以及其他税号未列名的这些货品的零件:**					**Lamps and lighting fittings including searchlights and spotlights and parts thereof, not elsewhere specified or included; illuminated signs, illuminated nameplates and the like, having a permanently fixed light source, and parts thereof not elsewhere specified or included:**
8147	9405.1000	-枝形吊灯及天花板或墙壁上的其他电气照明装置，但不包括公共露天场所或街道上的电气照明装置	10	0 冰岛IS,东盟AS,哥CR,秘鲁PE,新西兰NZ,智利CL 4 瑞士CH 5 巴PK 6 澳AU 8 韩国KR	0 受惠国LD	80	-Chandeliers and other electric ceiling or wall lighting fittings, excluding those of a kind used for lighting public open spaces or thorough-fares
8148	9405.2000	-电气的台灯、床头灯或落地灯	20	0 冰岛IS,东盟AS,哥CR,新加坡SG,新西兰NZ,智利CL 6 秘鲁PE 12 澳AU 14 瑞士CH 18 韩国KR	0 受惠国LD	80	-Electric table, desk, bedside or floor-standing lamps

序号 No.	税则号列 Tariff Line	中文货品名称 Article Description in Chinese	最惠国税率 MFN(%)	协定税率 Agreement(%)	特惠税率 SP(%)	普通税率 Gen(%)	英文货品名称 Article Description
8149	9405.3000	-圣诞树用的成套灯具	16	0 冰岛IS,东盟AS,哥CR,新加坡SG,新西兰NZ,智利CL 4.8 秘鲁PE 9.6 澳AU 11.2 瑞士CH 12.8 巴PK,韩国KR	0 受惠国LD	100	-Lighting sets of a kind used for Christmas trees
		-其他电灯及照明装置:					-Other electric lamps and lighting fittings:
8150	9405.4010	---探照灯	17.5	0 澳门MO,冰岛IS,东盟AS,哥CR,新加坡SG,新西兰NZ,智利CL 5.2 秘鲁PE 10.5 澳AU 12.3 瑞士CH 14 巴PK,韩国KR	0 受惠国LD	70	---Searchlights
8151	9405.4020	---聚光灯	17.5	0 澳门MO,冰岛IS,东盟AS,哥CR,新加坡SG,新西兰NZ,智利CL 5.2 秘鲁PE 10.5 澳AU 12.3 瑞士CH 14 巴PK,韩国KR	0 受惠国LD	70	---Spotlights
8152	9405.4090	---其他	10	0 澳门MO,冰岛IS,东盟AS,哥CR,秘鲁PE,香港HK,新加坡SG,新西兰NZ,智利CL 4 瑞士CH 5 巴PK 6 澳AU,韩国KR	0 受惠国LD	80	---Other
8153	9405.5000	-非电气的灯具及照明装置	20	0 冰岛IS,东盟AS,哥CR,新加坡SG,新西兰NZ,智利CL 6 秘鲁PE 12 澳AU 14 瑞士CH 18 韩国KR	0 受惠国$_1$LD$_1$	80	-Non-electrical lamps and lighting fittings
8154	9405.6000	-发光标志、发光铭牌及类似品	20	0 冰岛IS,东盟AS,哥CR,香港HK,新加坡SG,新西兰NZ,智利CL 6 秘鲁PE 12 澳AU 14 瑞士CH 17.3 韩国KR	0 受惠国$_1$LD$_1$	80	-Illuminated signs, illuminated name plates and the like
		-零件:					-Parts:
8155	9405.9100	--玻璃制	20	0 冰岛IS,东盟AS,哥CR,新加坡SG,新西兰NZ,智利CL 6 秘鲁PE 12 澳AU 14 瑞士CH 18 韩国KR	0 受惠国$_1$LD$_1$	70	--Of glass
8156	9405.9200	--塑料制	20	0 澳门MO,冰岛IS,东盟AS,哥CR,新加坡SG,新西兰NZ,智利CL 6 秘鲁PE 12 澳AU 14 瑞士CH 17.3 韩国KR	0 受惠国$_1$LD$_1$	70	--Of plastics
8157	9405.9900	--其他	20	0 澳门MO,冰岛IS,东盟AS,哥CR,新加坡SG,新西兰NZ,智利CL 6 秘鲁PE 12 澳AU 14 瑞士CH 17.3 韩国KR	0 受惠国LD	70	--Other

序号 No.	税则号列 Tariff Line	中文货品名称 Article Description in Chinese	最惠国税率 MFN(%)	协定税率 Agreement(%)	特惠税率 SP(%)	普通税率 Gen(%)	英文货品名称 Article Description
	94.06	活动房屋					**Prefabricated buildings**
8158	9406.0000	活动房屋	10	0 澳门MO,冰岛IS,东盟AS,哥CR,新加坡SG,新西兰NZ,智利CL 3 秘鲁PE 4 瑞士CH 5 巴PK 6 澳AU 7 亚太AP 8 韩国KR	0 受惠国LD	70	Prefabricated buildings

第九十五章
玩具、游戏品、运动用品及其零件、附件

Chapter 95
Toys, games and sports requisites; parts and accessories thereof

注释：

一、本章不包括：

（一）蜡烛（税号34.06）；

（二）税号36.04的烟花、爆竹或其他烟火制品；

（三）已切成一定长度但未制成钓鱼线的纱线、单丝、绳、肠线及类似品（第三十九章、税号42.06或第十一类）；

（四）税号42.02、43.03或43.04的运动用袋或其他容器；

（五）第六十一章或第六十二章的纺织品制的运动服或化妆舞会服装；

（六）第六十三章的纺织品制的旗帜及帆板或滑行车用帆；

（七）第六十四章的运动鞋靴（装有冰刀或滑轮的溜冰鞋除外）或第六十五章的运动用帽；

（八）手杖、鞭子、马鞭或类似品（税号66.02）及其零件（税号66.03）；

（九）税号70.18的未装配的玩偶或其他玩具用的玻璃假眼；

（十）第十五类注释二所规定的贱金属制通用零件（第十五类）或塑料制的类似货品（第三十九章）；

（十一）税号83.06的铃、钟、锣及类似品；

（十二）液体泵（税号84.13）、液体或气体的过滤、净化机器及装置（税号84.21）、电动机（税号85.01）、变压器（税号85.04）或无线电遥控设备（税号85.26）；

（十三）第十七类的运动用车辆（长雪橇、平底雪橇及类似品除外）；

（十四）儿童两轮车（税号87.12）；

（十五）运动用船艇，例如，轻舟、赛艇（第八十九章）及其桨、橹和类似品（木制的归入第四十四章）；

（十六）运动及户外游戏用的眼镜、护目镜及类似品（税号90.04）；

（十七）媒诱音响器及哨子（税号92.08）；

Notes:

1. This Chapter does not cover:

(a) Candles (heading No.34.06);

(b) Fireworks or other pyrotechnic articles of heading No.36.04;

(c) Yarns, monofilament, cords or gut or the like for fishing, cut to length but not made up into fishing lines, of Chapter 39, heading No.42.46 or Section XI;

(d) Sports bags or other containers of heading No.42.02, 43.03 or 43.04;

(e) Sports clothing or fancy dress, of textiles, of Chapter 61 or 62;

(f) Textile flags or bunting, or sails for boats, sailboards or land craft, of Chapter 63;

(g) Sports footwear (other than skating boots with ice or roller skates attached) of Chapter 64, or sports head-gear of Chapter 65;

(h) Walking-sticks, whips, riding-crops or the like (heading No.66.02), or parts thereof (heading No.66.03);

(i) Unmounted glass eyes for dolls or other toys, of heading No.70.18;

(j) Parts of general use, as defined in Note2 to Section XV, of base metal(Section XV), or similar goods of plastics (Chapter 39);

(k) Bells, gongs or the like of heading No.83.06;

(l) Pumps for liquids(heading No.84.13), filtering or purifying machinery and apparatus for liquids or gases (heading No.84.21), electric motors (heading No.85.01), electric transformers (heading No.85.04) or radio remote control apparatus (heading No.85.26);

(m) Sports vehicles (other than bobsleighs, toboggans and the like) of Section XVII;

(n) Children's bicycles(heading No.87.12);

(o) Sports craft such as canoes and skiffs (Chapter 89), or their means of propulsion (Chapter 44 for such articles made of wood);

(p) Spectacles, goggles or the like, for sports or outdoor games (heading No.90.04);

(q) Decoy calls or whistles (heading No.92.08);

（十八）第九十三章的武器及其他物品;

（十九）各种电气彩灯串（税号 94.05）;

（二十）球拍线、帐篷或类似的野营用品、手套、棒球手套和露指手套（按其构成材料归类）; 或

（二十一）餐具、厨房用具、盥洗用品、地毯及纺织材料制的其他铺地制品、服装、床上及餐桌用织物制品、盥洗及厨房用织物制品及具有实用功能的类似货品（按其构成材料归类）。

二、本章包括天然或养殖珍珠、宝石或半宝石（天然、合成或再造）、贵金属或包贵金属只作为小零件的物品。

三、除上述注释一另有规定的以外，凡专用于或主要用于本章各税号所列物品的零件、附件，应与有关物品一并归类。

四、除上述注释一另有规定的以外，税目 95.03 特别适用于该税目物品与一项或多项其他货品组合而成的物品，只要这些物品为零售包装，且组合后具有玩具的基本特征。这些组合物品不能视为归类总规则三（二）所指的成套货品，如果单独报验，应归入其他税目。

五、税目 95.03 不包括因其设计、形状或构成材料可确认为专供动物使用的物品，例如"宠物玩具"归入其相应的税目。

六、子目 9504.50 包括:

（一）在电视机、监视器或其他外部屏幕或表面上重放图像的视频游戏控制器; 或

（二）自带显示屏的视频游戏设备，不论是否便携式。

本子目不包括用硬币、钞票、银行卡、代币或任何其他支付方式使其工作的视频游戏控制器或设备（子目 9504.30）。

(r) Arms or other articles of Chapter 93;

(s) Electric garlands of all kinds(heading No.94.05);

(t) Racket strings, tents or other camping goods, or gloves, mittens and mitts (classified according to their constituent material); or

(u) Tableware, kitchenware, toilet articles, carpets and other textilefloor coverings, apparel, bed linen, table linen, toilet linen, kitchenlinen and similar articles having a utilitarian function (classifiedaccording to their constituent material).

2. This Chapter includes articles in which natural or cultured pearls, precious or semi-precious stones (natural, synthetic or reconstructed), precious metal or metal clad with precious metal constitute only minor consistuents.

3. Subject to Note 1 above, parts and accessories which are suitable for use solely or principally with articles of this Chapter are to be classified with those articles.

4. Subject to the provisions of Note 1 above, heading 95.03 applies,*inter alia*, to articles of this heading combined with one or moreitems, which cannot be considered as sets under the terms of General Interpretative Rule 3(b), and which, if presentedseparately, would be classified in other headings, provided thearticles are put up together for retail sale and the combinationshave the essential character of toys.

5. Heading No.95.03 does not cover articles which, on account of their design, shape or constituent material, are identifiable as intended exclusively for animals, for example, "pet toys" (classification in their own appropriate heading).

6. Subheading 9504.50 covers :

(a) Video game consoles from which the image is reproduced on atelevision receiver, a monitor or other external screen or surface; or

(b) Video game machines having a self-contained video screen, whetheror not portable.

This subheading does not cover video game consoles or machines operated by coins, banknotes, bank cards, tokens or by any other means of payment (subheading 9504.30)."

序号 No.	税则号列 Tariff Line	中文货品名称 Article Description in Chinese	最惠国税率 MFN(%)	协定税率 Agreement(%)	特惠税率 SP(%)	普通税率 Gen(%)	英文货品名称 Article Description
	95.03	**三轮车、踏板车、踏板汽车和类似的带轮玩具；玩偶车；玩偶；其他玩具；缩小（按比例缩小）的模型及类似的娱乐用模型，不论是否活动；各种智力玩具：**					**Tricycles, scooters, pedal cars and similar wheeled toys; dolls' carriages; dolls; other toys; reduced-size (' scale') models and similar recreational models, working or not; puzzles of all kinds:**
8159	9503.0010	---供儿童乘骑的带轮玩具（例如，三轮车、踏板车、踏板汽车）；玩偶车	0		0 受惠国LD	80	---Wheeled toys designed to be ridden by children (for example, tricycles, scooters, pedal cars) ; doll' s carriages
		---玩偶，不论是否着装；玩具动物：					---Dolls, whether or not dressed; Toys representing animals or non-human creatures:
8160	9503.0021	----动物	0		0 受惠国LD	80	----Toys representing animals or non-human creatures
8161	9503.0029	----其他	0		0 受惠国LD	80	----Other
		---缩小（按比例缩小）的全套模型组件，不论是否活动：					---Reduced-size (“scale”) model assembly kits, whether or not working:
8162	9503.0031	----电动火车	0		0 受惠国LD	80	----Electric trains
8163	9503.0039	----其他	0		0 受惠国LD	80	----Other
8164	9503.0040	---其他建筑套件及建筑玩具	0		0 受惠国LD	80	---Other construction sets and constructional toys
8165	9503.0050	---玩具乐器	0		0 受惠国LD	80	---Toy musical instruments and apparatus
8166	9503.0060	---智力玩具	0		0 受惠国LD	80	---Puzzles
		---其他玩具：					---Other toys:
8167	9503.0081	----组装成套或全套的	0		0 受惠国LD	80	----Put up in sets or outfits
8168	9503.0082	----其他带动力装置的玩具及模型	0		0 受惠国LD	80	----Other, incorporating a motor
8169	9503.0089	----其他	0		0 受惠国LD	80	----Other
8170	9503.0090	---零件、附件	0		0 受惠国LD	80	---Parts and accessories
	95.04	**视频游戏控制器及设备、游艺场所、桌上或室内游戏用品，包括弹球机、台球、娱乐专用桌及保龄球自动球道设备：**					**Video game consoles and machines, articles for funfair, table or parlour games, including pintables, billiards, special tables for casino games and automatic bowling alley equipment:**
8171	9504.2000	-台球用品及附件	0		0 受惠国LD	80	-Articles and accessories for billiards of all kinds
		-使用硬币、钞票、银行卡、代币或任何其他支付方式使其工作的其他游戏用品，但保龄球自动球道设备除外：					-Other games, operated by coins, banknotes, bank cards, tokens or by any other means of payment, other than automatic bowling alley equipment:
8172	9504.3010	---电子游戏机	0		0 受惠国LD	130	---Video games
8173	9504.3090	---其他	0		0 受惠国LD	80	---Other
8174	9504.4000	-扑克牌	0		0 受惠国LD	80	-Playing cards
		-视频游戏控制器及设备，但子目9504.30的货品除外：					-Video game consoles and machines, other than those of subheading 950430:
		---与电视接收机配套使用的：					---Used with a television receiver:
8175	9504.5011	----零件及附件	0		0 受惠国LD	130	----Parts and accessories
8176	9504.5019	----其他	0		0 受惠国LD	130	----Other
		---其他：					---Other:
8177	9504.5091	----零件及附件	0		0 受惠国LD	130	----Parts and accessories
8178	9504.5099	----其他	0		0 受惠国LD	130	----Other
		-其他：					-Other:
8179	9504.9010	---其他电子游戏机	0		0 受惠国LD	130	---Other video games
		---保龄球自动球道设备及器具：					---Automatic bowling alley equipments and appliances:
8180	9504.9021	----保龄球自动分瓶机	0		0 受惠国LD	80	----Automatic bowling pin distributing machines

序号 No.	税则号列 Tariff Line	中文货品名称 Article Description in Chinese	最惠国税率 MFN(%)	协定税率 Agreement(%)	特惠税率 SP(%)	普通税率 Gen(%)	英文货品名称 Article Description
8181	9504.9022	-----保龄球	0		0 受惠国LD	80	----Bowling balls
8182	9504.9023	-----保龄球瓶	0		0 受惠国LD	80	----Bowling pins
8183	9504.9029	-----其他	0		0 受惠国LD	80	----Other
8184	9504.9030	---中国象棋、国际象棋、跳棋等棋类用品	0		0 受惠国LD	80	---Chess and other board games, including Chinese chess, international chess, Chinese cherkers and draughts
8185	9504.9040	---麻将及类似桌上游戏用品	0		0 受惠国LD	80	---Mahjong and similar table games
8186	9504.9090	---其他	0		0 受惠国LD	80	---Other
	95.05	**节日（包括狂欢节）用品或其他娱乐用品，包括魔术道具及嬉戏品：**					**Festive, carnival or other entertainment articles, including conjuring tricks and novelty jokes:**
8187	9505.1000	-圣诞节用品	0		0 受惠国LD	100	-Articles for Christmas festivities
8188	9505.9000	-其他	0		0 受惠国LD	100	-Other
	95.06	**一般的体育活动、体操、竞技及其他运动（包括乒乓球运动）或户外游戏用的本章其他税号未列名用品及设备；游泳池或戏水池：**					**Articles and equipment for general physical exercise, gymnastics, athletics, other sports (including table tennis) or outdoor games, not specified or included elsewhere in this chapter; swimming pools and paddling pools:**
		-滑雪屐及其他滑雪用具：					-Snow-skis and other snow-ski equipment:
8189	9506.1100	--滑雪屐	14	0 巴PK,东盟AS,哥CR,秘鲁PE,新加坡SG,新西兰NZ,智利CL 8.4 澳AU 9.8 瑞士CH 11.2 韩国KR	0 受惠国$_1$LD$_1$	50	--Skis
8190	9506.1200	--滑雪屐扣件（滑雪屐带）	14	0 巴PK,冰岛IS,东盟AS,哥CR,秘鲁PE,新加坡SG,新西兰NZ,智利CL 8.4 澳AU 9.8 瑞士CH 11.2 韩国KR	0 受惠国$_1$LD$_1$	50	--Ski-fastenings (ski-bindings)
8191	9506.1900	--其他	14	0 巴PK,冰岛IS,东盟AS,哥CR,秘鲁PE,新加坡SG,新西兰NZ,智利CL 8.4 澳AU 9.8 瑞士CH 11.2 韩国KR	0 受惠国$_1$LD$_1$	50	--Other
		-滑水板、冲浪板、帆板及其他水上运动用具：					-Water-skis, surf-boards, sailboards and other water-sport equipment:
8192	9506.2100	--帆板	12	0 巴PK,冰岛IS,东盟AS,哥CR,秘鲁PE,新加坡SG,新西兰NZ,智利CL 7.2 澳AU 8.4 瑞士CH 9.6 韩国KR	0 受惠国$_1$LD$_1$	50	--Sailboards
8193	9506.2900	--其他	14	0 巴PK,冰岛IS,东盟AS,哥CR,秘鲁PE,香港HK,新加坡SG,新西兰NZ,智利CL 8.4 澳AU 9.8 瑞士CH 11.2 韩国KR	0 受惠国$_1$LD$_1$	50	--Other
		-高尔夫球棍及其他高尔夫球用具：					-Golf clubs and other golf equipment:

序号 No.	税则号列 Tariff Line	中文货品名称 Article Description in Chinese	最惠国税率 MFN(%)	协定税率 Agreement(%)	特惠税率 SP(%)	普通税率 Gen(%)	英文货品名称 Article Description
8194	9506.3100	--棍，全套	14	0 巴PK,东盟AS,哥CR,秘鲁PE,新加坡SG,新西兰NZ,智利CL 8.4 澳AU 9.8 瑞士CH 11.2 韩国KR	0 受惠国LD	50	--Clubs, complete
8195	9506.3200	--球	12	0 巴PK,冰岛IS,东盟AS,哥CR,秘鲁PE,新加坡SG,新西兰NZ,智利CL 7.2 澳AU 8.4 瑞士CH 9.6 韩国KR	0 受惠国$_1$LD$_1$	50	--Balls
8196	9506.3900	--其他	14	0 巴PK,东盟AS,哥CR,秘鲁PE,台湾TW,新加坡SG,新西兰NZ,智利CL 8.4 澳AU 9.8 瑞士CH 11.2 韩国KR	0 受惠国LD	50	--Other
		-乒乓球运动用品及器械：					-Articles and equipment for table tennis:
8197	9506.4010	---乒乓球	12	0 巴PK,冰岛IS,东盟AS,哥CR,秘鲁PE,新加坡SG,新西兰NZ,智利CL 7.2 澳AU 8.4 瑞士CH 9.6 韩国KR	0 受惠国$_1$LD$_1$	50	---Table-tennis balls
8198	9506.4090	---其他	14Δ7	0 巴PK,冰岛IS,东盟AS,哥CR,秘鲁PE,新加坡SG,新西兰NZ,智利CL 8.4 澳AU 9.8 瑞士CH 11.2 韩国KR	0 受惠国$_1$LD$_1$	50	---Other
		-网球拍、羽毛球拍或类似的球拍，不论是否装弦：					-Tennis, badminton or similar rackets, whether or not strung:
8199	9506.5100	--草地网球拍，不论是否装弦	14	0 巴PK,冰岛IS,东盟AS,哥CR,秘鲁PE,新加坡SG,新西兰NZ,智利CL 8.4 澳AU 9.8 瑞士CH 11.2 韩国KR	0 受惠国$_1$LD$_1$	50	--Lawn-tennis rackets, whether or not strung
8200	9506.5900	--其他	14	0 巴PK,冰岛IS,东盟AS,哥CR,秘鲁PE,新加坡SG,新西兰NZ,智利CL 8.4 澳AU 9.8 瑞士CH 11.2 韩国KR	0 受惠国$_1$LD$_1$	50	--Other
		-球，但高尔夫球及乒乓球除外：					-Balls, other than golf balls and table-tennis balls:
8201	9506.6100	--草地网球	12	0 巴PK,冰岛IS,东盟AS,哥CR,秘鲁PE,新加坡SG,新西兰NZ,智利CL 7.2 澳AU 8.4 瑞士CH 9.6 韩国KR	0 受惠国$_1$LD$_1$	50	--Lawn-tennis balls
		--可充气的球：					--Inflatable:
8202	9506.6210	---篮球、足球、排球	12Δ6	0 巴PK,冰岛IS,东盟AS,哥CR,秘鲁PE,新加坡SG,新西兰NZ,智利CL 7.2 澳AU 8.4 瑞士CH 9.6 韩国KR	0 受惠国$_1$LD$_1$	50	---Basketballs, footballs or volley balls

序号 No.	税则号列 Tariff Line	中文货品名称 Article Description in Chinese	最惠国税率 MFN(%)	协定税率 Agreement(%)	特惠税率 SP(%)	普通税率 Gen(%)	英文货品名称 Article Description
8203	9506.6290	---其他	12	0 巴PK,冰岛IS,东盟AS,哥CR,秘鲁PE,新加坡SG,新西兰NZ,智利CL 7.2 澳AU 8.4 瑞士CH 9.6 韩国KR	0 受惠国$_1$LD$_1$	50	---Other
8204	9506.6900	--其他	12	0 巴PK,冰岛IS,东盟AS,哥CR,秘鲁PE,新加坡SG,新西兰NZ,智利CL 7.2 澳AU 8.4 瑞士CH 9.6 韩国KR	0 受惠国$_1$LD$_1$	50	--Other
		-溜冰鞋及旱冰鞋，包括装有冰刀的溜冰靴：					-Ice skates and roller skates, including skating boots with skates attached:
8205	9506.7010	---溜冰鞋	14	0 巴PK,冰岛IS,东盟AS,哥CR,秘鲁PE,新加坡SG,新西兰NZ,智利CL 8.4 澳AU 9.8 瑞士CH 11.2 韩国KR 12 亚太AP	0 受惠国$_1$LD$_1$	50	---Ice skates
8206	9506.7020	---旱冰鞋	14	0 巴PK,冰岛IS,东盟AS,哥CR,秘鲁PE,新加坡SG,新西兰NZ,智利CL 8.4 澳AU 9.8 瑞士CH 11.2 韩国KR 12 亚太AP	0 受惠国$_1$LD$_1$	50	---Roller skates
		-其他：					-Other:
		--一般的体育活动、体操或竞技用品及设备：					--Articles and equipment for general physical exercise, gymnastics or athletics:
		---健身及康复器械：					---Equipment for exercise and recovery:
8207	9506.9111	----跑步机	12Δ6	0 巴PK,冰岛IS,东盟AS,哥CR,秘鲁PE,台湾TW,香港HK,新加坡SG,新西兰NZ,智利CL 7.2 澳AU 8.4 瑞士CH 9.6 韩国KR	0 受惠国$_1$LD$_1$	50	----Treadmill
8208	9506.9119	----其他	12Δ6	0 巴PK,冰岛IS,东盟AS,哥CR,秘鲁PE,台湾TW,香港HK,新加坡SG,新西兰NZ,智利CL 7.2 澳AU 8.4 瑞士CH 9.6 韩国KR	0 受惠国$_1$LD$_1$	50	----Other
8209	9506.9120	---滑板	12Δ6	0 巴PK,冰岛IS,东盟AS,哥CR,秘鲁PE,香港HK,新加坡SG,新西兰NZ,智利CL 7.2 澳AU 8.4 瑞士CH 9.6 韩国KR	0 受惠国$_1$LD$_1$	50	---Skateboards
8210	9506.9190	---其他	12Δ6	0 澳门MO,巴PK,冰岛IS,东盟AS,哥CR,秘鲁PE,香港HK,新加坡SG,新西兰NZ,智利CL 7.2 澳AU 8.4 瑞士CH 9.6 韩国KR	0 受惠国LD	50	---Other

序号 No.	税则号列 Tariff Line	中文货品名称 Article Description in Chinese	最惠国税率 MFN(%)	协定税率 Agreement(%)	特惠税率 SP(%)	普通税率 Gen(%)	英文货品名称 Article Description
8211	9506.9900	--其他	12	0 澳门MO,巴PK,冰岛IS,东盟AS,哥CR,秘鲁PE,香港HK,新加坡SG,新西兰NZ,智利CL 4.8 瑞士CH 7.2 澳AU 9.6 韩国KR	0 受惠国$_1$LD$_1$	50	--Other
	95.07	**钓鱼竿、钓鱼钩及其他钓鱼用品;捞鱼网、捕蝶网及类似网;化子"鸟"(税号92.08或97.05的货品除外)以及类似的狩猎用品:**					**Fishing rods, fish-hooks and other line fishing tackle; fish landing nets, butterfly nets and similar nets; decoy ' birds' (other than those of heading 9208 or 9705) and similar hunting or shooting requisites:**
8212	9507.1000	-钓鱼竿	21	0 东盟AS,哥CR,新加坡SG,新西兰NZ,智利CL 6.3 秘鲁PE 12.6 澳AU 14.7 瑞士CH	0 受惠国$_1$LD$_1$	80	-Fishing rods
8213	9507.2000	-钓鱼钩，不论有无系钓丝	21	0 东盟AS,哥CR,新加坡SG,新西兰NZ,智利CL 6.3 秘鲁PE 12.6 澳AU 14.7 瑞士CH 18.9 韩国KR	0 受惠国LD	80	-Fish-hooks, whether or not snelled
8214	9507.3000	-钓线轮	21	0 东盟AS,哥CR,新加坡SG,新西兰NZ,智利CL 6.3 秘鲁PE 12.6 澳AU 14.7 瑞士CH 18.9 韩国KR	0 受惠国$_1$LD$_1$	80	-Fishing reels
8215	9507.9000	-其他	21	0 冰岛IS,东盟AS,哥CR,新加坡SG,新西兰NZ,智利CL 6.3 秘鲁PE 12.6 澳AU 14.7 瑞士CH 18.9 巴PK,韩国KR,亚太AP	0 受惠国$_1$LD$_1$	80	-Other
	95.08	**旋转木马、秋千、射击用靶及其他游乐场的娱乐设备;流动马戏团及流动动物园;流动剧团:**					**Roundabouts, swings, shooting galleries and other fairground amusements; travelling circuses and travelling menageries; travelling theatres:**
8216	9508.1000	-流动马戏团及流动动物园	15	0 冰岛IS,东盟AS,哥CR,新加坡SG,新西兰NZ,智利CL 4.5 秘鲁PE 9 澳AU 10.5 瑞士CH 12 巴PK,韩国KR	0 受惠国$_1$LD$_1$	100	-Travelling circuses and travelling menageries
8217	9508.9000	-其他	15	0 冰岛IS,东盟AS,哥CR,新加坡SG,新西兰NZ,智利CL 4.5 秘鲁PE 9 澳AU 10.5 瑞士CH 12 巴PK,韩国KR	0 受惠国$_1$LD$_1$	100	-Other

第九十六章
杂项制品

Chapter 96
Miscellaneous manufactured articles

注释:

一、本章不包括:

（一）化妆盥洗用笔（第三十三章）；

（二）第六十六章的制品（例如，伞或手杖的零件）；

（三）仿首饰（税号 71.17）；

（四）第十五类注释二所规定的贱金属制通用零件（第十五类）或塑料制的类似品（第三十九章）；

（五）第八十二章的利口器及其他物品，其柄或其他零件是雕刻或模塑材料制的；但税号 96.01 或 96.02 适用于单独进口或出口的上述物品的柄或其他零件；

（六）第九十章的物品，例如，眼镜架（税号 90.03）、数学绘图笔（税号 90.17）、各种牙科、医疗、外科或兽医专用刷子（税号 90.18）；

（七）第九十一章的物品（例如，钟壳或表壳）；

（八）乐器及其零件、附件（第九十二章），

（九）第九十三章的物品（武器及其零件）；

（十）第九十四章的物品（例如，家具、灯具及照明装置）；

（十一）第九十五章的物品（玩具、游戏品、运动用品）；

（十二）艺术品、收藏品及古物（第九十七章）。

二、税号 96.02 所称“植物质或矿物质雕刻材料”，是指:

（一）用于雕刻的硬种子、硬果核、硬果壳、坚果及类似植物材料（例如，象牙果及棕榈子）；

Notes:

1. This Chapter does not cover:

(a) Pencils for cosmetic or toilet uses(Chapter 33);

(b) Articles of Chapter 66 (for example, parts of umbrellas or walking-sticks);

(c)Imitation jewellery (heading No.71.17);

(d) Parts of general use, as defined in Note2to Section XV, of base metal (Section XV), or similar goods of plastics (Chapter 39);

(e) Cutlery or other articles of Chapter 82 with handles or other parts of carving or moulding materials; heading No.96.01 or 96.02 applies, however, to separately presented handles or other parts of such articles;

(f) Articles of Chapter 90, for example, spectacle frames (heading No.90.03), mathematical drawing pens (heading No.90.17), brushes of a kind specialized for use in dentistry or for medical, surgical or veterinary purposes (heading No.90.18);

(g) Articles of Chapter 91 (for example, clock or watch cases);

(h) Musical instruments or parts or accessories thereof (Chapter 92);

(i) Articles of Chapter 93 (arms and parts thereof);

(j) Articles of Chapter 94 (for example, furniture, lamps and lighting fittings);

(k) Articles of Chapter 95 (toys, games, sports requisites); or

(l) Works of art, collectors' pieces or antiques (Chapter 97).

2.In heading No.96.02 the expression "vegetable or mineral carving material" means:

(a) Hard seeds, pips, hulls and nuts and similar vegetable materials of a kind used for carving (for example, corozo and dom);

（二）琥珀、海泡石、粘聚琥珀、粘聚海泡石、黑玉及其矿物代用品。

(b) Amber, meerschaum, agglomerated amber and agglomerated meerschaum, jet and mineral substitutes for jet.

三、税号 96.03 所称“制帚、制刷用成束、成簇的材料”，仅指未装配的成束、成簇的兽毛、植物纤维或其他材料。这些成束、成簇的材料无需分开即可安装在帚、刷之上，或只需经过简单加工（例如将顶端修剪成形）即可安装的。

3.In heading No.96.03 the expression “prepared knots and tufts for broom or brush making” applies only to unmounted knots and tufts of animal hair, vegetable fibre or other material, which are ready for incorporation without division in brooms or brushes, or which require only such further minor processes as trimming to shape at the top, to render them ready for such incorporation.

四、除税号 96.01 至 96.06 或 96.15 的货品以外，本章的物品还包括全部或部分用贵金属、包贵金属、天然或养殖珍珠、宝石或半宝石（天然、合成或再造）制成的物品。而且，税号 96.01 至 96.06 及 96.15 包括天然或养殖珍珠、宝石或半宝石（天然、合成或再造）、贵金属或包贵金属只作为小零件的物品。

4. Articles of this Chapter, other than those of headings No.96.01 to 96.06 or 96.15, remain classified in the Chapter whether or not composed wholly or partly of precious metal or metal clad with precious metal, of natural or cultured pearls, or precious or semi-precious stones (natural, synthetic or reconstructed). However, headings No.96.01 to 96.06 and 96.15 include articles in which natural or cultured pearls, precious or semi-precious stones (natural, synthetic or reconstructed), precious metal or metal clad with precious metal constitute only minor constituents.

序号 No.	税则号列 Tariff Line	中文货品名称 Article Description in Chinese	最惠国税率 MFN(%)	协定税率 Agreement(%)	特惠税率 SP(%)	普通税率 Gen(%)	英文货品名称 Article Description
	96.01	**已加工的兽牙、骨、玳瑁壳、角、鹿角、珊瑚、珍珠母及其他动物质雕刻材料及其制品（包括模塑制品）：**					**Worked ivory, bone, tortoiseshell, horn, antlers, coral, mother-of-pearl and other animal carving material, and articles of these materials (including articles obtained by moulding) :**
8218	9601.1000	-已加工的兽牙及其制品	20	0 冰岛IS,东盟AS,哥CR,新加坡SG,新西兰NZ,智利CL 6 秘鲁PE 12 澳AU 14 瑞士CH 17.3 韩国KR	0 受惠国[1]LD[1]	100	-Worked ivory and articles of ivory
8219	9601.9000	-其他	20	0 冰岛IS,东盟AS,哥CR,新加坡SG,新西兰NZ,智利CL 6 秘鲁PE 12 澳AU 14 瑞士CH 17.3 韩国KR	0 受惠国LD	100	-Other

序号 No.	税则号列 Tariff Line	中文货品名称 Article Description in Chinese	最惠国税率 MFN(%)	协定税率 Agreement(%)	特惠税率 SP(%)	普通税率 Gen(%)	英文货品名称 Article Description
	96.02	已加工的植物质或矿物质雕刻材料及其制品;蜡、硬脂、天然树胶、天然树脂或塑型膏制成的模塑或雕刻制品以及其他税号未列名的模塑或雕刻制品;已加工的未硬化明胶(税号35.03的明胶除外)及未硬化明胶制品:					**Worked vegetable or mineral carving material and articles of these materials; moulded or carved articles of wax, of stearin, of natural gums or natural resins or of modelling pastes, and other moulded or carved articles, not elsewhere specified or included; worked, unhardened gelatin (except gelatin of heading 3503) and articles of unhardened gelatin:**
8220	9602.0010	---装药用胶囊	10.5	0 冰岛IS,东盟AS,哥CR,秘鲁PE,新加坡SG,新西兰NZ,智利CL 5 巴PK 6.3 澳AU 7.4 瑞士CH 8.4 韩国KR	0 受惠国$_1$LD$_1$	40	---Pharmaceutical capsules
8221	9602.0090	---其他	25	0 冰岛IS,东盟AS,哥CR,新加坡SG,新西兰NZ,智利CL 7.5 秘鲁PE 15 澳AU 17.5 瑞士CH 22.5 韩国KR	0 受惠国LD	100	---Other
	96.03	帚、刷(包括作为机器、器具、车辆零件的刷)、非机动的手工操作地板清扫器、拖把及毛掸;供制帚、刷用的成束或成簇的材料;油漆块垫及滚筒;橡皮扫帚(橡皮辊除外):					**Brooms, brushes (including brushes constituting parts of machines, appliances or vehicles) , hand-operated mechanical floor sweepers, not motorised, mops and feather dusters; prepared knots and tufts for broom or brush making; paint pads and rollers; squeegees (other than roller squeegees) :**
8222	9603.1000	-用枝条或其他植物材料捆扎而成的帚及刷,不论是否有把	25	0 澳门MO,冰岛IS,东盟AS,哥CR,新加坡SG,新西兰NZ,智利CL 7.5 秘鲁PE 15 澳AU 17.5 瑞士CH 22.5 韩国KR	0 受惠国$_1$LD$_1$	100	-Brooms and brushes, consisting of twigs or other vegetable materials bound together, with or without handles
		-牙刷、剃须刷、发刷、指甲刷、睫毛刷及其他人体化妆用刷,包括作为器具零件的上述刷:					-Toothbrushes, shaving brushes, hairbrushes, nail brushes, eyelash brushes and other toilet brushes for use on the person, including such brushes constituting parts of appliances:
8223	9603.2100	--牙刷,包括齿板刷	25Δ10	0 澳门MO,冰岛IS,东盟AS,哥CR,香港HK,新加坡SG,新西兰NZ,智利CL 7.5 秘鲁PE 15 澳AU 17.5 瑞士CH 22.5 韩国KR	0 受惠国$_1$LD$_1$	100	--Tooth brushes, including dental-plate brushes

序号 No.	税则号列 Tariff Line	中文货品名称 Article Description in Chinese	最惠国税率 MFN(%)	协定税率 Agreement(%)	特惠税率 SP(%)	普通税率 Gen(%)	英文货品名称 Article Description
8224	9603.2900	--其他	15	0 澳门MO,冰岛IS,东盟AS,哥CR,新加坡SG,新西兰NZ,智利CL 4.5 秘鲁PE 7.5 巴PK 9 澳AU 10.5 瑞士CH 12 韩国KR 13.5 亚太AP	0 受惠国LD	100	--Other
		-画笔、毛笔及化妆用的类似笔:					-Artists' brushes, writing brushes and similar brushes for the application of cosmetics:
8225	9603.3010	---画笔	25	0 冰岛IS,东盟AS,哥CR,新加坡SG,新西兰NZ,智利CL 7.5 秘鲁PE 15 澳AU,巴PK,亚太AP 17.5 瑞士CH 22.5 韩国KR	0 受惠国$_1$LD$_1$	100	---Artists' brushes
8226	9603.3020	---毛笔	20	0 冰岛IS,东盟AS,哥CR,新加坡SG,新西兰NZ,智利CL 6 秘鲁PE 12 澳AU 14 瑞士CH 17.3 韩国KR 18 巴PK,亚太AP	0 受惠国$_1$LD$_1$	100	---Writing brushes
8227	9603.3090	---其他	25	0 冰岛IS,东盟AS,哥CR,新加坡SG,新西兰NZ,智利CL 7.5 秘鲁PE 15 澳AU 17.5 瑞士CH 22.5 巴PK,韩国KR,亚太AP	0 受惠国$_1$LD$_1$	100	---Other
		-油漆刷、涂料刷、清漆刷及类似的刷（子目号9603.30的货品除外）；油漆块垫及滚筒:					-Paint, distemper, varnish or similar brushes (other than brushes of subheading 960330) ; paint pads and rollers:
		---漆刷及类似刷:					---Paint, distemper, varnish or similar brushes:
8228	9603.4011	----猪鬃制	20	0 冰岛IS,东盟AS,哥CR,新加坡SG,新西兰NZ,智利CL 6 秘鲁PE 12 澳AU 14 瑞士CH 17.3 韩国KR	0 受惠国$_1$LD$_1$	100	----Of pigs' , hogs' or boars' bristle
8229	9603.4019	----其他	23	0 冰岛IS,东盟AS,哥CR,新加坡SG,新西兰NZ,智利CL 6.9 秘鲁PE 13.8 澳AU 16.1 瑞士CH 20.7 韩国KR	0 受惠国$_1$LD$_1$	100	----Other
8230	9603.4020	---油漆块垫及滚筒	23	0 冰岛IS,东盟AS,哥CR,新加坡SG,新西兰NZ,智利CL 6.9 秘鲁PE 13.8 澳AU 16.1 瑞士CH 20.7 韩国KR	0 受惠国$_1$LD$_1$	100	---Paint pads and rollers
		-作为机器、器具、车辆零件的刷:					-Other brushes constituting parts of machines, appliances or vehicles:
		---金属丝刷:					---Brushes of metal wire:

序号 No.	税则号列 Tariff Line	中文货品名称 Article Description in Chinese	最惠国税率 MFN(%)	协定税率 Agreement(%)	特惠税率 SP(%)	普通税率 Gen(%)	英文货品名称 Article Description
8231	9603.5011	----作为机器、器具零件的刷	14	0 冰岛IS,东盟AS,哥CR,秘鲁PE,新加坡SG,新西兰NZ,智利CL 8.4 澳AU 9.8 瑞士CH 11.2 巴PK,韩国KR	0 受惠国$_1$LD$_1$	50	----Constituting parts of machines or ap-pliances
8232	9603.5019	----其他	14	0 冰岛IS,东盟AS,哥CR,秘鲁PE,新加坡SG,新西兰NZ,智利CL 7 巴PK 8.4 澳AU 10 瑞士CH 11.2 韩国KR	0 受惠国$_1$LD$_1$	100	----Other
		---其他:					---Other:
8233	9603.5091	----作为机器、器具零件的刷	14	0 冰岛IS,东盟AS,哥CR,秘鲁PE,新加坡SG,新西兰NZ,智利CL 8.4 澳AU 9.8 瑞士CH 11.2 巴PK,韩国KR	0 受惠国$_1$LD$_1$	50	----Constituting parts of machines or appliances
8234	9603.5099	----其他	14	0 冰岛IS,东盟AS,哥CR,秘鲁PE,新加坡SG,新西兰NZ,智利CL 7 巴PK 8.4 澳AU 9.8 瑞士CH 11.2 韩国KR	0 受惠国$_1$LD$_1$	100	----Other
		-其他:					-Other:
8235	9603.9010	---羽毛掸	21	0 冰岛IS,东盟AS,哥CR,新加坡SG,新西兰NZ,智利CL 6.3 秘鲁PE 12.6 澳AU 14.7 瑞士CH 18.2 韩国KR 18.9 巴PK,亚太AP	0 受惠国$_1$LD$_1$	130	---Feather dusters
8236	9603.9090	---其他	15	0 冰岛IS,东盟AS,哥CR,新加坡SG,新西兰NZ,智利CL 4.5 秘鲁PE 9 澳AU 10.5 瑞士CH 12 韩国KR	0 受惠国$_1$LD$_1$	100	---Other
	96.04	**手用粗筛、细筛**					**Hand sieves and hand riddles**
8237	9604.0000	手用粗筛、细筛	21	0 冰岛IS,东盟AS,哥CR,新加坡SG,新西兰NZ,智利CL 6.3 秘鲁PE 12.6 澳AU 14.7 瑞士CH 18.9 韩国KR	0 受惠国$_1$LD$_1$	100	Hand sieves and hand riddles
	96.05	**个人梳妆、缝纫或清洁鞋靴、衣服用的成套旅行用具**					**Travel sets for personal toilet, sewing or shoe or clothes cleaning**
8238	9605.0000	个人梳妆、缝纫或清洁鞋靴、衣服用的成套旅行用具	15	0 冰岛IS,东盟AS,哥CR,新加坡SG,新西兰NZ,智利CL 4.5 秘鲁PE 9 澳AU 10.5 瑞士CH 12 巴PK,韩国KR	0 受惠国$_1$LD$_1$	100	Travel sets for personal toilet, sewing or shoe or clothes cleaning
	96.06	**钮扣、揿扣、钮扣芯及钮扣和揿扣的其他零件;钮扣坯:**					**Buttons, press-fasteners, snap-fasteners and press studs, button moulds and other parts of these articles; button blanks:**

序号 No.	税则号列 Tariff Line	中文货品名称 Article Description in Chinese	最惠国税率 MFN(%)	协定税率 Agreement(%)	特惠税率 SP(%)	普通税率 Gen(%)	英文货品名称 Article Description
8239	9606.1000	-揿扣及其零件	21	0 冰岛IS,东盟AS,哥CR,新加坡SG,新西兰NZ,智利CL 6.3 秘鲁PE 12.6 澳AU 14.7 瑞士CH 18.9 韩国KR	0 受惠国$_1$LD$_1$	100	-Press-fasteners, snap-fasteners and pre ss-studs and parts therefor
		-钮扣:					-Buttons:
8240	9606.2100	--塑料制，未用纺织材料包裹	21	0 冰岛IS,东盟AS,哥CR,台湾TW,新加坡SG,新西兰NZ,智利CL 6.3 秘鲁PE 12.6 澳AU 14.7 瑞士CH 18.9 韩国KR	0 受惠国LD	100	--Of plastics, not covered with textile material
8241	9606.2200	--贱金属制，未用纺织材料包裹	15	0 澳门MO,冰岛IS,东盟AS,哥CR,台湾TW,香港HK,新加坡SG,新西兰NZ,智利CL 4.5 秘鲁PE 9 澳AU 10.5 瑞士CH 12 巴PK,韩国KR	0 受惠国LD	100	--Of base mental, not covered with textile material
8242	9606.2900	--其他	15	0 冰岛IS,东盟AS,哥CR,香港HK,新加坡SG,新西兰NZ,智利CL 4.5 秘鲁PE 9 澳AU 10.5 瑞士CH 12 巴PK,韩国KR	0 受惠国LD	100	--Other
8243	9606.3000	-钮扣芯及钮扣的其他零件；钮扣坯	15	0 冰岛IS,东盟AS,哥CR,香港HK,新加坡SG,新西兰NZ,智利CL 4.5 秘鲁PE 9 澳AU 10.5 瑞士CH 12 巴PK,韩国KR	0 受惠国LD	100	-Button moulds and other parts of buttons; button blanks
	96.07	**拉链及其零件:**					**Slide fasteners and parts thereof:**
		-拉链:					-Slide fasteners:
8244	9607.1100	--装有贱金属制咪牙齿的	21	0 澳门MO,冰岛IS,东盟AS,哥CR,香港HK,新加坡SG,新西兰NZ,智利CL 6.3 秘鲁PE 12.6 澳AU 14.7 瑞士CH 18.9 韩国KR	0 受惠国LD	130	--Fitted with chain scoops of base metal
8245	9607.1900	--其他	21	0 澳门MO,冰岛IS,东盟AS,哥CR,香港HK,新加坡SG,新西兰NZ,智利CL 6.3 秘鲁PE 12.6 澳AU 14.7 巴PK,瑞士CH,亚太AP 18.9 韩国KR	0 受惠国$_1$LD$_1$	130	--Other
8246	9607.2000	-零件	21	0 冰岛IS,东盟AS,哥CR,新加坡SG,新西兰NZ,智利CL 6.3 秘鲁PE 12.6 澳AU 14.7 瑞士CH 18.9 韩国KR	0 受惠国$_1$LD$_1$	130	-Parts

序号 No.	税则号列 Tariff Line	中文货品名称 Article Description in Chinese	最惠国税率 MFN(%)	协定税率 Agreement(%)	特惠税率 SP(%)	普通税率 Gen(%)	英文货品名称 Article Description
	96.08	**圆珠笔;毡尖和其他渗水式笔尖笔及唛头笔;自来水笔、铁笔型自来水笔及其他钢笔;蜡纸铁笔;活动铅笔;钢笔杆、铅笔套及类似的笔套;上述物品的零件（包括帽、夹），但税号96.09的货品除外：**					**Ballpoint pens; felt-tipped and other porous-tipped pens and markers; fountain pens, stylograph pens and other pens; duplicating stylos; propelling or sliding pencils; pen-holders, pencil-holders and similar holders; parts (including caps and clips) of the foregoing articles, other than those of heading 9609:**
8247	9608.1000	-圆珠笔	15	0 冰岛IS,东盟AS,哥CR,新加坡SG,新西兰NZ,智利CL 4.5 秘鲁PE 7.5 巴PK 9 澳AU 10.5 瑞士CH 12 韩国KR 13.5 亚太AP	0 受惠国LD	80	-Ball point pens
8248	9608.2000	-毡尖和其他渗水式笔尖笔及唛头笔	21	0 冰岛IS,东盟AS,哥CR,新加坡SG,新西兰NZ,智利CL 6.3 秘鲁PE 12.6 澳AU 14.7 瑞士CH 18.9 韩国KR	0 受惠国$_1$LD$_1$	80	-Felt tipped and other porous tipped pens and markers
		-自来水笔、铁笔型自来水笔及其他钢笔：					-Fountain pens, stylograph pens and other pens:
8249	9608.3010	---墨汁画笔	21	0 冰岛IS,东盟AS,哥CR,新加坡SG,新西兰NZ,智利CL 6.3 秘鲁PE 12.6 澳AU 14.7 瑞士CH 18.2 韩国KR	0 受惠国$_1$LD$_1$	80	---Indian ink drawing pens
8250	9608.3020	---自来水笔	21	0 冰岛IS,东盟AS,哥CR,新加坡SG,新西兰NZ,智利CL 6.3 秘鲁PE 12.6 澳AU 14.7 瑞士CH 18.9 韩国KR	0 受惠国LD	80	---Fountain pens
8251	9608.3090	---其他	21	0 冰岛IS,东盟AS,哥CR,新加坡SG,新西兰NZ,智利CL 6.3 秘鲁PE 12.6 澳AU 14.7 瑞士CH 18.9 韩国KR	0 受惠国LD	80	---Other
8252	9608.4000	-活动铅笔	21	0 冰岛IS,东盟AS,哥CR,新加坡SG,新西兰NZ,智利CL 6.3 秘鲁PE 12.6 澳AU 14.7 瑞士CH 18.9 韩国KR	0 受惠国$_1$LD$_1$	80	-Propelling or sliding pencils
8253	9608.5000	-由上述两个或多个子目所列物品组成的成套货品	21	0 冰岛IS,东盟AS,哥CR,新加坡SG,新西兰NZ,智利CL 6.3 秘鲁PE 12.6 澳AU 14.7 瑞士CH 18.9 韩国KR	0 受惠国$_1$LD$_1$	80	-Sets of articles from two or more of the foregoing subheadings

序号 No.	税则号列 Tariff Line	中文货品名称 Article Description in Chinese	最惠国税率 MFN(%)	协定税率 Agreement(%)	特惠税率 SP(%)	普通税率 Gen(%)	英文货品名称 Article Description
8254	9608.6000	-圆珠笔芯，由圆珠笔头和墨芯构成	21	0 澳门MO,冰岛IS,东盟AS,哥CR,香港HK,新加坡SG,新西兰NZ,智利CL 6.3 秘鲁PE 12.6 澳AU 14.7 瑞士CH 18.9 韩国KR	0 受惠国$_1$LD$_1$	80	-Refills for ball point pens, comprising the ball point and ink-reservoir
		-其他：					-Other:
8255	9608.9100	--钢笔头及笔尖粒	12	0 澳门MO,冰岛IS,东盟AS,哥CR,秘鲁PE,香港HK,新加坡SG,新西兰NZ,智利CL 6 巴PK 7.2 澳AU 8.4 瑞士CH 9.6 韩国KR	0 受惠国$_1$LD$_1$	70	--Pen nibs and nib points
		--其他：					--Other:
8256	9608.9910	---机器、仪器用笔	17.5	0 冰岛IS,东盟AS,哥CR,香港HK,新加坡SG,新西兰NZ,智利CL 5.2 秘鲁PE 10.5 澳AU 12.3 瑞士CH 14 巴PK,韩国KR	0 受惠国$_1$LD$_1$	40	---Of a kind used on machines or instruments
8257	9608.9920	---蜡纸铁笔；钢笔杆、铅笔杆及类似的笔杆	21	0 澳门MO,冰岛IS,东盟AS,哥CR,香港HK,新加坡SG,新西兰NZ,智利CL 6.3 秘鲁PE 12.6 澳AU 14.7 瑞士CH 18.9 韩国KR	0 受惠国$_1$LD$_1$	80	---Duplicating stylos; pen-holders, pencil-holders and similar holders
8258	9608.9990	---其他	21	0 澳门MO,冰岛IS,东盟AS,哥CR,瑞士CH,香港HK,新加坡SG,新西兰NZ,智利CL 6.3 秘鲁PE 12.6 澳AU 18.9 韩国KR	0 受惠国$_1$LD$_1$	80	---Other
	96.09	**铅笔（税号96.08的铅笔除外）、颜色铅笔、铅笔芯、蜡笔、图画碳笔、书写或绘画用粉笔及裁缝划粉：**					**Pencils (other than pencils of heading 9608) , crayons, pencil leads, pastels, drawing charcoals, writing or drawing chalks and tailors' chalks:**
		-铅笔及颜色铅笔：					-Pencils and crayons, with leads encased in a rigid sheath:
8259	9609.1010	---铅笔	21	0 冰岛IS,东盟AS,哥CR,新加坡SG,新西兰NZ,智利CL 6.3 秘鲁PE 12.6 澳AU 14.7 瑞士CH 18.9 韩国KR	0 受惠国LD	80	---Pencils
8260	9609.1020	---颜色铅笔	21	0 冰岛IS,东盟AS,哥CR,新加坡SG,新西兰NZ,智利CL 6.3 秘鲁PE 12.6 澳AU 14.7 瑞士CH 18.9 韩国KR	0 受惠国$_1$LD$_1$	80	---Crayons

序号 No.	税则号列 Tariff Line	中文货品名称 Article Description in Chinese	最惠国税率 MFN(%)	协定税率 Agreement(%)	特惠税率 SP(%)	普通税率 Gen(%)	英文货品名称 Article Description
8261	9609.2000	-铅笔芯，黑的或其他颜色的	21	0 冰岛IS,东盟AS,哥CR,新加坡SG,新西兰NZ,智利CL 6.3 秘鲁PE 12.6 澳AU 14.7 瑞士CH 18.9 韩国KR	0 受惠国$_1$LD$_1$	80	-Pencil leads, black or coloured
8262	9609.9000	-其他	15	0 冰岛IS,东盟AS,哥CR,新加坡SG,新西兰NZ,智利CL 4.5 秘鲁PE 9 澳AU 10.5 瑞士CH 12 巴PK,韩国KR	0 受惠国$_1$LD$_1$	80	-Other
	96.10	**具有书写或绘画面的石板、黑板及类似板，不论是否镶框**					**Slates and boards, with writing or drawing surfaces, whether or not framed**
8263	9610.0000	具有书写或绘画面的石板、黑板及类似板，不论是否镶框	15	0 冰岛IS,东盟AS,哥CR,新加坡SG,新西兰NZ,智利CL 4.5 秘鲁PE 9 澳AU 10.5 瑞士CH 12 巴PK,韩国KR	0 受惠国$_1$LD$_1$	80	Slates and boards, with writing or drawing surfaces, whether or not framed
	96.11	**手用日期戳、封缄戳、编号戳及类似印戳（包括标签压印器）;手工操作的排字盘及带有排字盘的手印器**					**Date, sealing or numbering stamps, and the like (including devices for printing or embossing labels) , designed for operating in the hand; hand-operated composing sticks and hand printing sets incorporating such composing sticks**
8264	9611.0000	手用日期戳、封缄戳、编号戳及类似印戳（包括标签压印器）;手工操作的排字盘及带有排字盘的手印器	21	0 冰岛IS,东盟AS,哥CR,新加坡SG,新西兰NZ,智利CL 6.3 秘鲁PE 12.6 澳AU 14.7 瑞士CH 18.9 韩国KR	0 受惠国$_1$LD$_1$	80	Date, sealing or numbering stamps, and the like (including devices for printing or embossing labels) , designed for operating in the hand; and operated composing sticks and hand printing sets incorporating such composing sticks
	96.12	**打字机色带或类似色带，已上油或经其他方法处理能着色的，不论是否装轴或装盒;印台，不论是否已加印油或带盒子：**					**Typewriter or similar ribbons, inked or otherwise prepared for giving impressions, whether or not on spools or in cartridges; ink-pads, whether or not inked, with or without boxes:**
8265	9612.1000	-色带	10.5	0 澳门MO,冰岛IS,东盟AS,哥CR,秘鲁PE,新加坡SG,新西兰NZ,智利CL 5 巴PK 6.3 澳AU 7.4 瑞士CH 9.1 韩国KR	0 受惠国LD	35	-Inked ribbons
8266	9612.2000	-印台	25	0 冰岛IS,东盟AS,哥CR,新加坡SG,新西兰NZ,智利CL 7.5 秘鲁PE 15 澳AU 17.5 瑞士CH 22.5 韩国KR	0 受惠国$_1$LD$_1$	100	-Ink-pads

序号 No.	税则号列 Tariff Line	中文货品名称 Article Description in Chinese	最惠国税率 MFN(%)	协定税率 Agreement(%)	特惠税率 SP(%)	普通税率 Gen(%)	英文货品名称 Article Description
	96.13	**香烟打火机和其他打火器（不论是机械的，还是电气的）及其零件，但打火石及打火机芯除外：**					**Cigarette lighters and other lighters, whether or not mechanical or electrical, and parts thereof other than flints and wicks:**
8267	9613.1000	-袖珍气体打火机，一次性的	25	0 冰岛IS,东盟AS,哥CR,新加坡SG,新西兰NZ,智利CL 7.5 秘鲁PE 15 澳AU 17.5 瑞士CH 22.5 韩国KR	0 受惠国$_1$LD$_1$	130	-Pocket lighters, gas fuelled, non refillable
8268	9613.2000	-袖珍气体打火机，可充气的	25	0 冰岛IS,东盟AS,哥CR,新加坡SG,新西兰NZ,智利CL 7.5 秘鲁PE 15 澳AU 17.5 瑞士CH 22.5 韩国KR	0 受惠国$_1$LD$_1$	130	-Pocket lighters, gas fuelled, refillable
8269	9613.8000	-其他打火器	25	0 冰岛IS,东盟AS,哥CR,新加坡SG,新西兰NZ,智利CL 7.5 秘鲁PE 15 澳AU 17.5 瑞士CH 22.5 韩国KR	0 受惠国$_1$LD$_1$	130	-Other lighters
8270	9613.9000	-零件	25	0 冰岛IS,东盟AS,哥CR,新加坡SG,新西兰NZ,智利CL 7.5 秘鲁PE 15 澳AU 17.5 瑞士CH 22.5 韩国KR	0 受惠国$_1$LD$_1$	130	-Parts
	96.14	**烟斗（包括烟斗头）和烟嘴及其零件：**					**Smoking pipes (including pipe bowls) and cigar or cigarette holders, and parts thereof:**
8271	9614.0010	---烟斗及烟斗头	25	0 冰岛IS,东盟AS,哥CR,新加坡SG,新西兰NZ,智利CL 7.5 秘鲁PE 15 澳AU 17.5 瑞士CH	0 受惠国$_1$LD$_1$	130	---Pipes and pipe bowls
8272	9614.0090	---其他	25	0 冰岛IS,东盟AS,哥CR,新加坡SG,新西兰NZ,智利CL 7.5 秘鲁PE 15 澳AU 17.5 瑞士CH	0 受惠国$_1$LD$_1$	130	---Other
	96.15	**梳子、发夹及类似品;发卡、卷发夹、卷发器或类似品及其零件，但税号85.16的货品除外：**					**Combs, hair-slides and the like; hairpins, curling pins, curling grips, hair-curlers and the like, other than those of heading 8516, and parts thereof:**
		-梳子、发夹及类似品：					-Combs, hair-slides and the like:
8273	9615.1100	--硬质橡胶或塑料制	18	0 冰岛IS,东盟AS,哥CR,新加坡SG,新西兰NZ,智利CL 5.4 秘鲁PE 10.8 澳AU 12.6 瑞士CH 14.4 巴PK,韩国KR 16.2 亚太AP	0 受惠国LD	130	--Of hard rubber or plastics

序号 No.	税则号列 Tariff Line	中文货品名称 Article Description in Chinese	最惠国税率 MFN(%)	协定税率 Agreement(%)	特惠税率 SP(%)	普通税率 Gen(%)	英文货品名称 Article Description
8274	9615.1900	--其他	18	0 冰岛IS,东盟AS,哥CR,新加坡SG,新西兰NZ,智利CL 5.4 秘鲁PE 10.8 澳AU 12.6 瑞士CH 14.4 韩国KR	0 受惠国LD	130	--Other
8275	9615.9000	-其他	18	0 冰岛IS,东盟AS,哥CR,新加坡SG,新西兰NZ,智利CL 5.4 秘鲁PE 10.8 澳AU 12.6 瑞士CH 14.4 巴PK,韩国KR 16.2 亚太AP	0 受惠国LD	130	-Other
	96.16	**香水喷雾器或类似的化妆用喷雾器及其座架、喷头;粉扑及粉拍,施敷脂粉或化妆品用:**					**Scent sprays and similar toilet sprays, and mounts and heads therefor; powder-puffs and pads for the application of cosmetics or toilet preparations:**
8276	9616.1000	-香水喷雾器或类似的化妆用喷雾器及其座架、喷头	18	0 冰岛IS,东盟AS,哥CR,新加坡SG,新西兰NZ,智利CL 5.4 秘鲁PE 10.8 澳AU 12.6 瑞士CH 14.4 巴PK,韩国KR 16.2 亚太AP	0 受惠国$_1$LD$_1$	130	-Scent sprays and similar toilet sprays, and mounts and heads therefor
8277	9616.2000	-粉扑及粉拍,施敷脂粉或化妆品用	18	0 冰岛IS,东盟AS,哥CR,新加坡SG,新西兰NZ,智利CL 5.4 秘鲁PE 10.8 澳AU 12.6 瑞士CH 14.4 巴PK,韩国KR 16.2 亚太AP	0 受惠国$_1$LD$_1$	130	-Powder-puffs and pads for the applic-ation of cosmetics or toilet preparations
	96.17	**带壳的保温瓶和其他真空容器及其零件,但玻璃瓶胆除外:**					**Vacuum flasks and other vacuum vessels, complete with cases; parts thereof other than glass inners:**
		---保温瓶:					---Vacuum flasks:
8278	9617.0011	----玻璃内胆制	24	0 冰岛IS,东盟AS,哥CR,香港HK,新加坡SG,新西兰NZ,智利CL 7.2 秘鲁PE 14.4 澳AU 16.8 瑞士CH 21.6 韩国KR	0 受惠国$_1$LD$_1$	130	----Of glass inners
8279	9617.0019	----其他	24	0 冰岛IS,东盟AS,哥CR,香港HK,新加坡SG,新西兰NZ,智利CL 7.2 秘鲁PE 14.4 澳AU 16.8 瑞士CH 21.6 韩国KR	0 受惠国$_1$LD$_1$	130	----Other
	ex96170019	真空保温杯	Δ12				Vacuum keep-warm cup
8280	9617.0090	---其他	18	0 冰岛IS,东盟AS,哥CR,香港HK,新加坡SG,新西兰NZ,智利CL 5.4 秘鲁PE 10.8 澳AU 12.6 瑞士CH 14.4 韩国KR	0 受惠国$_1$LD$_1$	130	---Other

序号 No.	税则号列 Tariff Line	中文货品名称 Article Description in Chinese	最惠国税率 MFN(%)	协定税率 Agreement(%)	特惠税率 SP(%)	普通税率 Gen(%)	英文货品名称 Article Description
	96.18	裁缝用人体模型及其他人体活动模型;橱窗装饰用的自动模型及其他活动陈列品					**Tailors' dummies and other lay figures; automata and other animated displays used for shop window dressing**
8281	9618.0000	裁缝用人体模型及其他人体活动模型;橱窗装饰用的自动模型及其他活动陈列品	21	0 冰岛IS,东盟AS,哥CR,新加坡SG,新西兰NZ,智利CL 6.3 秘鲁PE 12.6 澳AU 14.7 瑞士CH 18.9 韩国KR	0 受惠国$_1$LD$_1$	80	Tailors' dummies and other lay figures; automata and other animated displays used for shop window dressing
	96.19	任何材料制的卫生巾(护垫)及止血塞、婴儿尿布及尿布衬里和类似品:					**Sanitary towels (pads) and tampons, napkins and napkin liners for babies, and similar articles, of any material:**
8282	9619.0010	---尿裤及尿布	7.5Δ2	0 澳门MO,东盟AS,哥CR,秘鲁PE,台湾TW,香港HK,新西兰NZ,智利CL 4.5 澳AU	0 受惠国LD	80	---Diapers and napkins
8283	9619.0020	---卫生巾(护垫)及止血塞	10	0 澳门MO,冰岛IS,东盟AS,哥CR,秘鲁PE,台湾TW,香港HK,新西兰NZ,智利CL 4 瑞士CH 6 澳AU 7.5 巴PK 8 韩国KR	0 受惠国LD	80	---Sanitary towels (pads) and tampons
8284	9619.0090	---其他	14	0 澳门MO,冰岛IS,东盟AS,哥CR,台湾TW,香港HK,新加坡SG,新西兰NZ,智利CL 4.8 秘鲁PE 7.5 巴PK 8.4 澳AU 9.3 亚太AP 11.2 韩国KR 11.5 瑞士CH	0 受惠国LD	80	---Other

第二十一类
艺术品、收藏品及古物

SECTION XXI
WORKS OF ART, COLLECTORS' PIECES AND ANTIQUES

第九十七章
艺术品、收藏品及古物

Chapter 97
Works of art, collectors' pieces and antiques

注释:

一、本章不包括:

（一）在指运国流通或新发行的未经使用的邮票、印花税票、邮政信笺（印有邮票的纸品）及类似的票证（第四十九章）;

（二）作舞台、摄影的布景及类似用途的已绘制画布（税号 59.07），但可归入税号 97.06 的除外;

（三）天然或养殖珍珠、宝石或半宝石（税号 71.01 至 71.03）。

二、税号 97.02 所称“雕版画、印制画、石印画的原本”，是指以艺术家完全手工制作的单块或数块印版直接印制出来的黑白或彩色原本，不论艺术家使用何种方法或材料，但不包括使用机器或照相制版方法制作的。

三、税号 97.03 不适用于成批生产的复制品及具有商业性质的传统手工艺品，即使这些物品是艺术家设计或创造的。

四、

（一）除上述注释一至三另有规定的以外，可归入本章各税号的物品，均应归入本章的相应税号而不归入本目录的其他税号;

（二）税号 97.06 不适用于可以归入本章其他各税号的物品。

五、已装框的油画、粉画及其他绘画、版画、拼贴画及类似装饰板，如果框架的种类及价值与作品相称，应与作品一并归类。如果框架的种类及价值与作品不相称，应分别归类。

Notes:

1. This Chapter does not cover:

(a) Unused postage or revenue stamps, postal stationery (stamped paper) or the like, of heading 49.07;

(b) Theatrical scenery, studio back-cloths or the like, of painted canvas (heading No.59.07) except if they may be classified in heading No.97.06; or

(c) Pearls, natural or cultured, or precious or semi-precious stones (headings No.71.01 to 71.03).

2. For the purposes of heading No.97.02, the expression “original engravings, prints and lithographs” means impressions produced directly, in black and white or in colour, of one or of several plates wholly executed by hand by the artist, irrespective of the process or of the material employed by him, but not including any mechanical or photomechanical process.

3. Heading No.97.03 does not apply to mass-produced reproductions or works of conventional craftsmanship of a commercial character, even if these articles are designed or created by artists.

4.

(a) Subject to Notes 1 to 3 above, articles of this Chapter are to be classified in this Chapter and not in any other Chapter of the Nomenclature;

(b) Heading No.97.06 does not apply to articles of the preceding headings of this Chapter.

5. Frames around paintings, drawings, pastels, collages or similar decorative plaques, engravings, prints or lithographs are to be classified with those articles, provided they are of a kind and of a value normal to those articles. Frames which are not of a kind or of a value normal to the articles referred to in this Note are to be classified separately.

序号 No.	税则号列 Tariff Line	中文货品名称 Article Description in Chinese	最惠国税率 MFN(%)	协定税率 Agreement(%)	特惠税率 SP(%)	普通税率 Gen(%)	英文货品名称 Article Description
	97.01	**油画、粉画及其他手绘画，但带有手工绘制及手工描饰的制品或税号49.06的图纸除外；拼贴画及类似装饰板：**					**Paintings, drawings and pastels, executed entirely by hand, other than drawings of heading 4906 and other than hand-painted or hand-decorated manufactured articles; collages and similar decorative plaques:**
		-油画、粉画及其他手绘画：					-Paintings, drawings and pastels:
		---原件：					---The originals:
8285	9701.1011	----唐卡	12	0 冰岛IS,东盟AS,哥CR,新加坡SG,新西兰NZ,智利CL 3.6 秘鲁PE 6 巴PK 7.2 澳AU 8.4 瑞士CH 9.6 韩国KR	0 受惠国LD	50	----Tangka
8286	9701.1019	----其他	12Δ6	0 冰岛IS,东盟AS,哥CR,新加坡SG,新西兰NZ,智利CL 3.6 秘鲁PE 6 巴PK 7.2 澳AU 8.4 瑞士CH 9.6 韩国KR	0 受惠国LD	50	----Other
8287	9701.1020	---复制品	14	0 冰岛IS,东盟AS,哥CR,秘鲁PE,新加坡SG,新西兰NZ,智利CL 8.4 澳AU 9.8 瑞士CH 11.2 巴PK,韩国KR	0 受惠国LD	50	---Reproductions
8288	9701.9000	-其他	14	0 冰岛IS,东盟AS,哥CR,秘鲁PE,新加坡SG,新西兰NZ,智利CL 8.4 澳AU 9.8 瑞士CH 11.2 巴PK,韩国KR	0 受惠国LD	50	-Other
	97.02	**雕版画、印制画、石印画的原本**					**Original engravings, prints and lithographs**
8289	9702.0000	雕版画、印制画、石印画的原本	12Δ6	0 冰岛IS,东盟AS,哥CR,新加坡SG,新西兰NZ,智利CL 3.6 秘鲁PE 6 巴PK 7.2 澳AU 8.4 瑞士CH 9.6 韩国KR	0 受惠国$_1$LD$_1$	50	Original engravings, prints and lithographs
	97.03	**各种材料制的雕塑品原件**					**Original sculptures and statuary, in any material**
8290	9703.0000	各种材料制的雕塑品原件	12Δ6	0 冰岛IS,东盟AS,哥CR,秘鲁PE,新加坡SG,新西兰NZ,智利CL 6 巴PK 7.2 澳AU 8.4 瑞士CH 9.6 韩国KR	0 受惠国LD	50	Original sculptures and statuary, in any material
	97.04	**使用过或未使用过的邮票、印花税票、邮戳印记、首日封、邮政信笺（印有邮票的纸品）及类似品，但税目49.07的货品除外：**					**Postage or revenue stamps, stamp-postmarks, first-day covers, postal stationery (stamped paper), and the like, used or unused, other than those of heading 4907:**

序号 No.	税则号列 Tariff Line	中文货品名称 Article Description in Chinese	最惠国税率 MFN(%)	协定税率 Agreement(%)	特惠税率 SP(%)	普通税率 Gen(%)	英文货品名称 Article Description
8291	9704.0010	---邮票	8	0 澳门MO,冰岛IS,东盟AS,哥CR,秘鲁PE,香港HK,新西兰NZ,智利CL 3.2 瑞士CH 4.8 澳AU,韩国KR 5 巴PK	0 受惠国LD	50	---Postage
8292	9704.0090	---其他	14	0 澳门MO,冰岛IS,东盟AS,哥CR,秘鲁PE,香港HK,新加坡SG,新西兰NZ,智利CL 7 巴PK 8.4 澳AU 9.8 瑞士CH 11.2 韩国KR	0 受惠国$_1$LD$_1$	50	---Other
	97.05	**具有动物学、植物学、矿物学、解剖学、历史学、考古学、古生物学、人种学或钱币学意义的收集品及珍藏品**					**Collections and collectors' pieces of zoological, botanical, mineralogical, anatomical, historical, archaeological, palaeontological, ethnographic or numismatic interest**
8293	9705.0000	具有动物学、植物学、矿物学、解剖学、历史学、考古学、古生物学、人种学或钱币学意义的收集品及珍藏品	0		0 受惠国LD	0	Collections and collectors pieces of zoological, botanical, mineralogical, anatomical, historical, archaeological, palaeontological, ethnographic or numis-matic interest
	97.06	**超过一百年的古物**					**Antiques of an age exceeding 100years**
8294	9706.0000	超过一百年的古物	0		0 受惠国LD	0	Antiques of an age exceeding one hundred years

中华人民共和国出口税则

（2016 年 1 月 1 日起实施）

Customs Tariff of Export of the People’s Republic of China

（Enforced from January 1，2016）

序号 No.	税则号列 Tariff Item	货 品 名 称	出口税率(%) Export Duty Rate	Article Description
	03.01			
1	03019210	鳗鱼苗	20	Live eels fry
	05.06			
2	05061000	经酸处理的骨胶原及骨	40	Ossein and bones treated with acid
3	05069011	含牛羊成分的骨粉及骨废料	40	Power and waste bones, containing bovine composition or sheep and goat's thereof
4	05069019	其他骨粉及骨废料	40	Other powder and waste of bones
5	05069090	其他骨及角柱	40	Bones and horn-cores, unworked, defatted, simply prepared, not cut to shape, nes
	26.07			
6	26070000	铅矿砂及其精矿	30	Lead ores & concentrates
	26.08			
7	26080000	锌矿砂及其精矿	30	Zinc ores & concentrates
	26.09			
8	26090000	锡矿砂及其精矿	50	Tin ores & concentrates
	26.11			
9	26110000	钨矿砂及其精矿	20	Tungsten ores & concentrates
	26.15			
10	26159010	水合钽铌原料（钽铌富集物）	30	Hydrated Tantalum/Niobium materials or enriched materials from Tantalum/Niobium ore
11	26159090	其他铌钽矿砂及其精矿	30	Niobium, tantalum & vanadium ores & concentrates, others
	26.17			
12	26171010	生锑（锑精矿，选矿产品）	20	Crude antimony (Antimony concentrates which are mineral products)
	28.04			
13	28047010	黄磷(白磷)	20	Yellow phosphorus (white phosphorus)
14	28047090	其他磷	20	Phosphorus, nes
	28.26			
15	ex28269090	氟钽酸钾	30	Potassium fluotantalate
	29.02			
16	29022000	苯	40	Benzene
	41.03			
17	41039011	经退鞣处理的山羊板皮	20	Raw hides and skins of goats，have undergone a reversible tanning process
18	41039019	山羊板皮，经退鞣处理的除外	20	Raw hides and skins of goats，nes
	72.01			
19	72011000	非合金生铁，含磷量小于或等于 0.5%	20	Non-alloy pig iron, by wt.≤0.5% of phosphorus in primary forms
20	72012000	非合金生铁，含磷量大于 0.5%	20	Non-alloy pig iron, by wt.>0.5% of phosphorus in primary forms

序号 No.	税则号列 Tariff Item	货 品 名 称	出口税率(%) Export Duty Rate	Article Description
21	72015000	合金生铁	20	Alloy pig iron; spiegeleisen
	72.02			
22	72021100	锰铁，含碳量＞2%	20	Ferro-manganese, containing by weight more than 2% of carbon
23	72021900	锰铁，含碳量≤2%	20	Ferro-manganese, nes
24	72022100	硅铁，含硅量＞55%	25	Ferro-silicon, containing by weight more than 55% of silicon
25	72022900	硅铁，含硅量≤55%	25	Ferro-silicon, nes
26	72023000	硅锰铁	20	Ferro-silico-manganese
27	72024100	铬铁，含碳量＞4%	40	Ferro-chromium containing by weight more than 4% of carbon
28	72024900	铬铁，含碳量≤4%	40	Ferro-chromium, nes
	72.04			
29	72041000	铸铁废碎料	40	Waste & scrap, cast iron
30	72042100	不锈钢废碎料	40	Waste & scrap, stainless steel
31	72042900	其他合金钢废碎料	40	Waste & scrap, of alloy steel, other than stainless
32	72043000	镀锡钢铁废碎料	40	Waste & scrap, of tinned iron or steel
33	72044100	机械加工中产生的废料	40	Ferrous waste & scrap, i/s, from the mechanical working of mtl, nes
34	72044900	其他钢铁废碎料	40	Ferrous waste & scrap, iron or steel, nes
35	72045000	供再熔的碎料钢铁锭	40	Remelting scrap ingots, of iron or steel
	74.02			
36	74020000	未精炼铜，电解精炼用的铜阳极	30	Cu unrefined, Cu anodes for electrolytic refining
	74.03			
37	74031111	按重量计铜含量超过99.9935％的精炼铜阴极	30	Cu cathodes containing more than 99.9935% Cu by weight, unwrought
38	74031119	其他精炼铜阴极	30	Cu cathodes, unwrought, nes
39	74031190	精炼铜阴极型材	30	sections of Cu cathodes unwrought
40	74031200	精炼铜的线锭	30	Wire bars, Cu, unwrought
41	74031300	精炼铜的坯段	30	Billets, Cu, unwrought
42	74031900	其他未锻轧的精炼铜	30	Refined Cu products, unwrought, nes
43	74032100	未锻轧的铜锌合金(黄铜)	30	Cu-zinc base alloys, unwrought
44	74032200	未锻轧的铜锡合金(青铜)	30	Cu-tin base alloys, unwrought
45	74032900	未锻轧的其他铜合金	30	Cu alloys, unwrought (other than master alloys of heading No 74.05)
	74.04			
46	74040000	铜废碎料	30	Waste & scrap, Copper
	74.07			
47	74071010	铬锆铜制条、杆及型材及异型材	30	Bars, rods & profiles of chromium and zirconium copper
48	74071090	其他精炼铜条、杆及型材及异型材	30	Other bars, rods & profiles of other refined Cu

序号 No.	税则号列 Tariff Item	货 品 名 称	出口税率(%) Export Duty Rate	Article Description
49	74072111	直线度不大于 0.5 毫米/米铜锌合金条、杆	30	Copper-zinc base alloys (brass) bars and rods, of a straightness not exceeding 0.5mm/m
50	74072119	其他铜锌合金条、杆	30	Other bars, rods of copper-zinc base alloys(brass)
51	74072190	其他铜锌合金型材及异型材	30	Profiles of Cu-Zn base alloys
52	74072900	其他铜合金条杆、型材及异型材	30	Bars, rods & profiles, Cu alloy nes
	74.08			
53	74081100	最大截面尺寸＞6 毫米的精炼铜丝	30	Wire of refined Cu of which the max cross sectional dimension＞6mm
54	74081900	其他精炼铜丝	30	Wire of refined Cu of which the max cross sectional dimension≤6mm
55	74082100	铜锌合金丝	30	Wire, Cu-zinc base alloy
56	74082210	铜镍锌铅合金（加铅德银）丝	30	Wire, of copper-nickel-zinc-lead base alloys(leaded nickel silver)
57	74082290	其他白铜或德银丝	30	Other wire, of Copper-Ni base alloy or Copper-Ni-zinc base alloy
58	74082900	其他铜合金丝	30	Wire, Cu alloy, nes
	74.09			
59	74091110	含氧量不超过 10PPM 盘卷的精炼铜板、片、带	30	Plate, sheet & strip of refined Cu, in coil, containing Oxygen no more than 10PPM
60	74091190	其他成卷精炼铜板、片、带	30	Plate, sheet & strip of refined Cu, in coil, nes
61	74091900	其他精炼铜板、片、带	30	Plate, sheet & strip of refined Cu, not in coil
62	74092100	成卷的铜锌合金板、片、带	30	Plate, sheet & strip of Cu-Zn base alloys, in coil
63	74092900	其他铜锌合金板、片、带	30	Plate, sheet & strip of Cu-Zn base alloys, not in coil
64	74093100	成卷的铜锡合金板、片、带	30	Plate, sheet & strip of Cu-tin base alloys, in coil
65	74093900	其他铜锡合金板、片、带	30	Plate, sheet & strip of Cu-tin base alloys, not in coil
66	74094000	铜镍合金或铜镍锌合金板、片、带	30	Plate, sheet & strip of Cu-Ni' Cu-Ni-Zn base alloy
67	74099000	其他铜合金板、片、带	30	Plate, sheet & strip of Cu alloy, nes
	75.02			
68	75021010	按重量计镍、钴总量在 99.99%及以上的，但含钴量不超过 0.005%的未锻轧非合金镍	40	Ni contain more than 99.99% Ni and Co, and Co less than 0.005% by weight, unwrought, not alloyed
69	75021090	其他未锻轧非合金镍	40	Ni unwrought, not alloyed, nes
70	75022000	未锻轧镍合金	40	Ni unwrought, alloyed
	75.08			
71	75089010	电镀用镍阳极	40	Electroplating anodes of Ni
	76.01			
72	76011010	按重量计含铝量在 99.95%及以上的非合金铝	30	Containing by weight 99.95% or more of aluminium unwrought aluminium, not alloyed
73	76011090	按重量计含铝量在 99.95%以下的非合金铝	30	Al unwrought, not alloyed, nes
74	76012000	未锻轧铝合金	30	Al unwrought, alloyed

序号 No.	税则号列 Tariff Item	货品名称	出口税率(%) Export Duty Rate	Article Description
	76.02			
75	76020000	铝废碎料	30	Waste & scrap, Al
	76.04			
76	76041010	非合金铝条、杆	20	Bars, rods, Al, not alloyed
77	76041090	非合金型材及异型材	20	Profiles, Al, not alloyed
78	76042100	铝合金制空心异型材	20	Profiles, hollow, Al, alloyed
79	76042910	铝合金制条、杆	20	Bars, rods, Al alloyed
80	76042990	铝合金制其他型材及异型材	20	Other profiles, Al alloyed
	76.05			
81	76051100	最大截面尺寸超过7毫米的非合金铝丝	20	Wire, Al, not alloyed, with a max cross sectional dimension exceeding 7mm
82	76051900	其他非合金铝丝	20	Wire, Al, not alloyed, with a max cross sectional dimension not exceeding 7mm
83	76052100	最大截面尺寸超过7毫米的铝合金丝	20	Wire, Al alloy, with a max cross sectional dimension exceeding 7mm
84	76052900	其他铝合金丝	20	Wire, Al alloy, with a max cross sectional dimension not exceeding 7mm
	76.06			
85	76061121	0.3 毫米≤厚度<0.36 毫米的非合金铝与塑料复合的矩形板、片及带	20	Rectangular plates, sheets and strip, of not alloyed aluminium-plastic composite, 0.3mm≤thickness<0.36mm
86	76061129	其他 0.3 毫米≤厚度<0.36 毫米的非合金铝制矩形铝板、片及带	20	Other rectangular plates, sheets and strip, of not alloyed aluminium-plastic composite, 0.3mm ≤ thickness<0.36mm
87	76061191	其他非合金铝与塑料复合的矩形板、片及带	20	Rectangular plates, sheets and strip, of not alloyed aluminium-plastic composite, nes
88	76061199	纯铝制矩形的其他板、片及带	20	Other rectangular plates, sheets and strip, of not alloyed aluminium-plastic composite, nes
89	76061220	厚度<0.28 毫米的铝合金制矩形铝板、片及带	20	Plate, sheet & strip, Al alloy, rectangular (including square), of a thickness exceeding 0.2mm, but less than 0.28mm
90	76061230	0.28 毫米≤厚度≤0.35 毫米的铝合金制矩形铝板、片及带	20	Plate, sheet & strip, Al alloy, rectangular (including square), of a thickness 0.28mm or more but not exceeding 0.35mm
91	76061251	0.35 毫米<厚度≤0.4 毫米的铝合金与塑料复合的矩形板、片及带	20	Rectangular plates, sheets and strip of aluminium alloys-plastic composite, of a thickness of 0.35mm or more but not exceeding 0.4mm
92	76061259	其他 0.35 毫米<厚度≤0.4 毫米的铝合金制矩形铝板、片及带	20	Other rectangular plates, sheets and strip of aluminium alloys, of a thickness of 0.35mm or more but not exceeding 0.4mm
93	76061290	厚度>0.4 毫米的铝合金制矩形铝板、片及带	20	Rectangular plates, sheets and strip of aluminium alloys, of a thickness exceeding 0.4mm
94	76069100	非合金铝制非矩形的板、片及带	20	Plate, sheet & strip, Al, not alloyed, of a thickness exceeding 0.2mm, nes

序号 No.	税则号列 Tariff Item	货 品 名 称	出口税率(%) Export Duty Rate	Article Description
95	76069200	铝合金制非矩形的板、片及带	20	Plate, sheet & strip, Al alloy, of a thickness exceeding 0.2mm, nes
	79.01			
96	79011110	含锌量≥99.995%的未锻轧锌	20	Unwrought zinc, not alloyed, containing by weight 99.995% or more of zinc
97	79011190	99.99%≤含锌量＜99.995%的未锻轧锌	20	Unwrought zinc, not alloyed, containing by weight 99.99% or more, but less than 99.995% of zinc
98	79011200	含锌量＜99.99%的未锻轧锌	20	Unwrought zinc, not alloyed, containing by weight less than 99.99% of zinc
99	79012000	未锻轧锌合金	20	Zinc alloys unwrought
	81.10			
100	81101010	未锻轧锑	20	Antimony unwrought
101	81101020	锑粉末	20	Antimony powders
102	81102000	锑废碎料	20	Antimony waste & scrap

出口商品暂定税率表

Interim Duty Rate on Exported Goods

序号 No	EX	税则号列 Tariff Item	货品名称	出口税率 (%) Export Duty Rate	暂定税率 (%) Interim Duty Rate	Article Description
1		03019210	鳗鱼苗	20		Live eels fry
2		05061000	经酸处理的骨胶原及骨	40		Ossein and bones treated with acid
3		05069011	含牛羊成分的骨粉及骨废料	40		Power and waste bones, containing bovine composition or sheep and goat's thereof
4		05069019	其他骨粉及骨废料	40		Other powder and waste of bones
5	ex	05069090	其他骨及角柱(已脱胶骨、角柱除外)	40		Bones and horn-cores, unworked, defatted, simply prepared, not cut to shape, nes
6	ex	05069090	已脱胶骨、角柱	40	0	Degelantinized bones
7		25041010	鳞片状天然石墨		20	Natural graphite in flakes
8		25041099	其他粉末状天然石墨		20	Other natural graphite in powder
9		25049000	其他天然石墨		20	Other natural graphite (excl. in powder or in flakes)
10		25085000	红柱石、蓝晶石及硅线石，不论是否煅烧		10	Andalusite, kyanite & sillimanite, whether or not calcined
11		25086000	富铝红柱石		10	Mullite
12		25101010	未碾磨磷灰石		20	Unground apatites
13		25101090	未碾磨天然磷酸钙、天然磷酸铝钙及磷酸盐白垩，磷灰石除外		20	Unground natural calcium phosphates, natural aluminium calcium phosphates and phosphatic chalk, excl. apatites
14		25102010	已碾磨磷灰石		20	Ground apatites
15		25102090	已碾磨天然磷酸钙、天然磷酸铝钙及磷酸盐白垩，磷灰石除外		20	Ground natural calcium phosphates, natural aluminium calcium phosphates and phosphatic chalk, excl. apatites
16		25112000	天然碳酸钡(毒重石)，不论是否煅烧		10	Natural barium carbonate (whitherite), whether or not calcined
17		25191000	天然碳酸镁（菱镁矿）		5	Natural magnesium carbonate (magnesite)
18		25199010	熔凝镁氧矿		10	Fused magnesia
19		25199020	烧结镁氧矿（重烧镁）		10	Dead-burned (sintered) magnesia
20		25199030	碱烧镁（轻烧镁）		5	Light-burned magnesia
21		25199099	非纯氧化镁		5	Magnesium oxide, excl. chemically pure
22		25261020	未破碎及未研粉的滑石,不论是否粗加修整或切割成矩形板块		10	Talc, not crushed, not powdered, whether or not roughly trimmed or merely cut into blocks or slabs of a rectangular (incl. square) shape
23	ex	25262020	已破碎或已研粉的天然滑石（体积百分比 90%及以上的产品粒度小于等于 18 微米的滑石粉除外）		10	Talc, crushed or powdered,except for talc powder containing at least 90% by volume with granulatity size ≤18μm
24		25301010	未膨胀的绿泥石		10	Chlorites, unexpanded
25	ex	25309099	其他氧化镁含量在 70%(含 70%)以上的矿产品		5	Other mineral substances containing by weight not less than 70% of magnesium oxide

序号 No	EX	税则号列 Tariff Item	货 品 名 称	出口税率 (%) Export Duty Rate	暂定税率 (%) Interim Duty Rate	Article Description
26		26011110	平均粒径小于 0.8 毫米的未煅烧铁矿砂及其精矿；但焙烧黄铁矿除外		10	Of a granularity less than 0.8mm, non-agglomerated iron ores and concentrates, other than roasted iron pyrites
27		26011120	平均粒径不小于 0.8 毫米，但不大于 6.3 毫米的未煅烧铁矿砂及其精矿；但焙烧黄铁矿除外		10	Of a granularity of 0.8mm or more, but not exceeding 6.3mm, non-agglomerated iron ores and concentrates, other than roasted iron pyrites
28		26011190	平均粒径大于 6.3 毫米的未烧结铁矿砂及其精矿，但焙烧黄铁矿除外		10	Of a granularity exceeding 6.3mm, non-agglomerated iron ores and concentrates, other than roasted iron pyrites
29		26011200	已烧结铁矿砂及其精矿		10	Agglomerated iron ores & concentrates, other than roasted iron pyrites
30		26012000	焙烧黄铁矿		10	Roasted iron pyrites
31		26030000	铜矿砂及其精矿		10	Copper ores & concentrates
32		26040000	镍矿砂及其精矿		15	Nickel ores & concentrates
33		26050000	钴矿砂及其精矿		15	Cobalt ores & concentrates
34		26070000	铅矿砂及其精矿	30		Lead ores & concentrates
35	ex	26080000	锌矿砂及其精矿（氧化锌含量大于80%的灰色饲料氧化锌除外）	30		Zinc ores & concentrates，except for Gray feed grade zinc oxide (containing by weight more than 80% of ZnO)
36	ex	26080000	灰色饲料氧化锌（氧化锌 ZnO 含量大于 80%）	30	0	Gray feed grade zinc oxide (containing by weight more than 80% of ZnO)
37		26090000	锡矿砂及其精矿	50	20	Tin ores & concentrates
38		26100000	铬矿砂及其精矿		15	Chromium ores & concentrates
39		26110000	钨矿砂及其精矿	20		Tungsten ores & concentrates
40		26121000	铀矿砂及其精矿		10	Uranium ores & concentrates
41		26140000	钛矿砂及其精矿		10	Titanium ores & concentrates
42		26151000	锆矿砂及其精矿		10	Zirconium ores & concentrates
43		26159010	水合钽铌原料（钽铌富集物）	30		Hydrated Tantalum/Niobium materials or enriched materials from Tantalum/Niobium ore
44		26159090	其他铌钽矿砂及其精矿	30		Niobium, tantalum & vanadium ores & concentrates ,others
45		26161000	银矿砂及其精矿		10	Silver ores & concentrates
46		26169000	其他贵金属矿砂及其精矿		10	Precious metal (excl. silver) ores & concentrates
47		26171010	生锑（锑精矿，选矿产品）	20		Crude antimony(Antimony concentrates which are mineral products)
48		26171090	其他锑矿砂及其精矿		10	Antimony ores & concentrates (excl.crude)
49		26179010	朱砂(辰砂)		10	Cinnabar
50		26179090	其他矿砂及其精矿		10	Ores & concentrates, nes
51		26180010	冶炼钢铁产生的锰渣		10	Granulated slag mainly containing manganese (slag sand) from the manufacture of iron or steel
52		26180090	冶炼钢铁产生的其他粒状熔渣(熔渣砂)		10	Granulated slag (slag sand) from the manufacture of iron or steel

序号 No	EX	税则号列 Tariff Item	货 品 名 称	出口税率 (%) Export Duty Rate	暂定税率 (%) Interim Duty Rate	Article Description
53		26190000	冶炼钢铁产生的熔渣、浮渣、氧化皮及其他废料		10	Slag, dross (other than granulated slag & slag sand), scaling and other from manufacture of iron or steel
54		26202100	含铅汽油的淤渣及含铅抗震化合物的淤渣		10	Leaded gasoline sludge and leaded anti-knock compound sludge
55		26202900	其他主要含铅的矿灰及残渣		10	Ash & residues containing mainly lead & compound thereof, nes
56		26203000	主要含铜的矿灰及残渣		10	Ash & residues containing mainly copper & compound thereof
57		26206000	含砷、汞、铊及其混合物，用于提取或生产砷、汞、铊及其化合物的矿灰及残渣		10	Ash & residues containing arsenic, mercopperry, thallium or their mixtures, of a kind used for the extraction of arsenic or those metals or for the manufacture of their chemical compound
58		26209100	含锑、铍、镉、铬及其混合物的矿灰及残渣		10	Ash & residues containing antimony, beryllium, cadmium, chromium or their mixture
59		26209990	含其他金属及化合物的矿灰及残渣		10	Ash & residues containing metals & compound thereof, nes
60		27011100	未制成型的无烟煤，不论是否粉化		3	Anthracite, not agglomerated, whether or not pulverized
61		27011210	未制成型的炼焦烟煤，不论是否粉化		3	Bituminous coking coal, not agglomerated, whether or not pulverized
62		27011290	未制成型的其他烟煤，不论是否粉化		3	Other bituminous coal, other than coking coal, not agglomerated, whether or not pulverized
63		27011900	未制成型的其他煤，不论是否粉化		3	Coal nes, not agglomerated, whether or not pulverized
64		27012000	煤砖、煤球及类似用煤制固体燃料		3	Briquettes, ovoids & similar solid fuels manufactured from coal
65		27021000	褐煤		3	Lignite, not agglomerated, whether or not pulverized
66		27022000	制成型的褐煤		3	Agglomerated lignite
67		27030000	泥煤(包括肥料用泥煤) 不论是否成型		3	Peat (incl. peat litter), whether or not agglomerated
68	ex	27060000	从煤、褐煤、或泥煤蒸馏所得的焦油及矿物焦油，不论是否脱水或部分蒸馏，包括再造焦油（含蒽油≥50%及沥青≥40%的"炭黑油"除外）		15	Tar distilled from coal, lignite or peat & other mineral tars, whether or not dehydrated or partially distilled, incl. reconstituted tars
69		27071000	粗苯		10	Benzole
70		27090000	石油原油及从沥青矿物提取的原油		5	Petroleum oils & oils obtained from bituminous minerals, crude
71		28047010	黄磷(白磷)	20		Yellow phosphorus (white phosphorus)
72		28047090	其他磷	20	10	Phosphorus, nes
73	ex	28269090	氟钽酸钾	30		Potassium fluotantalate
74		28271010	肥料用氯化铵		5	Ammonium chloride, use as fertilizer

序号 No	EX	税则号列 Tariff Item	货 品 名 称	出口税率 (%) Export Duty Rate	暂定税率 (%) Interim Duty Rate	Article Description
75		28342110	肥料用硝酸钾		5	Nitrates of potassium, use as fertilizer
76		29022000	苯	40	0	Benzene
77		31021000	尿素		80 元/吨	Urea，whether or not in aqueous solution
78		31029090	其他矿物氮肥及化学氮肥，包括上述子目未列名的混合物		5	Other mineral or chemical fertilizers, nitrogenous, including mixtures not specified in the foregoing subheadings
79		31031010	重过磷酸钙		5	Triple superphosphates
80		31031090	其他过磷酸钙		5	Other superphosphates
81		31039000	其他矿物磷肥或化学磷肥		5	Mineral or chemical fertilizers, phosphatic, nes
82		31042090	其他氯化钾		600 元/吨	Potassium chloride, nes
83		31043000	硫酸钾		600 元/吨	Potassium sulphate
84		31049010	光卤石、钾盐及其他天然粗钾盐		30	Carnallite, sylvite and other crude natural potassium salts
85		31049090	其他矿物钾肥及化学钾肥		30	Mineral or chemical fertilizers, potassic, other than potassium chloride and potassium sulphate and other crude natural potassium salts
86		31051000	制成片状及类似形状或每包毛重不超过 10 公斤的 31 章各货品		5	Goods of Chapter 31 in tables or similar forms or in packages of a gross weight ≤10kg
87		31052000	三元复合肥		30	Mineral or chemical fertilizers containing the three fertilizing elements nitrogen, phosphorus & potassium
88		31053000	磷酸氢二铵		100 元/吨	Diammonium hydrogenorthophosphate (diammonium phosphate)
89		31054000	磷酸二氢铵及磷酸二氢铵与磷酸氢二铵的混合物		100 元/吨	Ammonium dihydrogenorthophosphate (monoammonium phosphate) and mixtures thereof with diammonium hydrogenorthophosphate (diammonium phosphate)
90		31055100	含有硝酸盐及磷酸盐的肥料		5	Mineral or chemical fertilizers containing nitrates & phosphates
91		31055900	其他含氮磷两种肥效元素的矿物肥料或化学肥料		5	Mineral or chemical fertilizers containing the two fertilizing elements nitrogen & phosphorus, nes
92		31056000	含磷钾两种元素的肥料		5	Mineral or chemical fertilizers with phosphorus & potassium, nes
93		31059000	其他肥料		5	Mineral or chemical fertilizers, nes
94		38249091	含滑石 50%以上的混合物		10	Mixture containing more than 50% talc by weight
95		41039011	经退鞣处理的山羊板皮	20		Dried hides and skins of goats, have undergone a reversible tanning process
96		41039019	山羊板皮，经退鞣处理的除外	20		Dried hides and skins of goats other than those have undergone a reversible tanning process
97		44012100	针叶木木片或木粒		15	Coniferous wood in chips or particles

序号 No	EX	税则号列 Tariff Item	货 品 名 称	出口税率 (%) Export Duty Rate	暂定税率 (%) Interim Duty Rate	Article Description
98		44012200	非针叶木木片或木粒		15	Non-coniferous wood in chips or articles
99		44091010	针叶木地板条（块）		10	Floor board strips of Coniferous
100		44092910	其他非针叶木地板条		10	Floor board strips of non-coniferous other than those of bamboo
101		44190031	木制一次性筷子		10	One-time chopsticks, of wood
102		44219021	木制圆签、圆棒、冰果棒、压舌片及类似一次性制品		10	Round picks and sticks, sticks for icesucker, spatulas and similar one-time articles, of wood
103		47010000	机械木浆		10	Mechanical wood pulp
104		47020000	化学木浆，溶解级		10	Chemical wood pulp, dissolving grades
105		47031100	未漂白针叶木碱木浆或硫酸盐木浆		10	Unbleached coniferous chemical wood pulp, soda or sulphite, other than dissolving grades
106		47031900	未漂白非针叶木碱木浆或硫酸盐木浆		10	Unbleached non-coniferous chemical wood pulp, soda or sulphite, other than dissolving grades
107		47032100	漂白针叶木碱木浆或硫酸盐木浆		10	Semi-bleached or bleached coniferous chemical wood pulp, soda or sulphite, other than dissolving grades
108		47032900	漂白非针叶木碱木浆或硫酸盐木浆		10	Semi-bleached or bleached non- coniferous chemical wood pulp, soda or sulphite, other than dissolving grades
109		47041100	未漂白的针叶木亚硫酸盐木浆		10	Unbleached coniferous chemical wood pulp, sulphite, other than dissolving grades
110		47041900	未漂白的非针叶木亚硫酸盐木浆		10	Unbleached non-coniferous chemical wood pulp, sulphite, other than dissolving grades
111		47042100	漂白的针叶木亚硫酸盐木浆		10	Semi-bleached or bleached coniferous chemical wood pulp, sulphite, other than dissolving grades
112		47042900	漂白的非针叶木亚硫酸盐木浆		10	Semi-bleached or bleached non-coniferous chemical wood pulp, sulphite, other than dissolving grades
113		47050000	半化学木浆		10	Semi-chemical wood pulp
114		47062000	从回收纸或纸板提取的纤维浆		10	Pulp of fibres derived from recovered (waste and scrap) paper or paperboard
115		47063000	竹浆		10	Pulps of bamboo
116		47069100	其他纤维状纤维素机械浆		10	Mechanical pulp of fibrous cellulosic material, nes
117		47069200	其他纤维状纤维素化学浆		10	Chemical pulp of fibrous cellulosic material, nes
118		47069300	其他纤维状纤维素半化学浆		10	Semi-chemical pulp of fibrous cellulosic material, nes
119	ex	72011000	非合金生铁，含磷量小于或等于0.5%(含锰量＜0.08%，含磷量＜0.03%,含硫量＜0.02%,含钛量＜0.03%的高纯生铁除外)	20		Non-alloy pig iron, containing by weight 0.5% or less of phosphorus in primary forms, other than high purity pig iron in which containing by weight less than 0.08% of manganese, less than 0.03% of phosphorus, less than 0.02% of sulphur , less than 0.03% of titanium

序号 No	EX	税则号列 Tariff Item	货品名称	出口税率 (%) Export Duty Rate	暂定税率 (%) Interim Duty Rate	Article Description
120	ex	72011000	高纯生铁(含锰量<0.08%, 含磷量<0.03%,含硫量<0.02%,含钛量<0.03%)	20	10	high purity pig iron, containing by weight less than 0.08% of manganese, less than 0.03% of phosphorus, less than 0.02% of sulphur ,less than 0.03% of titanium
121		72012000	非合金生铁，含磷量大于 0.5%	20		Non-alloy pig iron, containing by weight more than 0.5% of phosphorus in primary forms
122		72015000	合金生铁	20		Alloy pig iron; spiegeleisen
123		72021100	锰铁,含碳量>2%	20		Ferro-manganese, containing by weight more than 2% of carbon
124		72021900	锰铁,含碳量≤2%	20		Ferro-manganese,containing by weight 2% or less of carbon
125		72022100	硅铁,含硅量>55%	25		Ferro-silicon, containing by weight more than 55% of silicon
126		72022900	硅铁,含硅量≤55%	25		Ferro-silicon, nes
127		72023000	硅锰铁	20		Ferro-silico-manganese
128		72024100	铬铁,含碳量>4%	40	20	Ferro-chromium containing by weight more than 4% of carbon
129		72024900	铬铁,含碳量≤4%	40	20	Ferro-chromium containing by weight no more than 4% of carbon
130		72025000	硅铬铁		20	Ferro-silico-chromium
131		72026000	镍铁		20	Ferro-nickel
132		72029100	钛铁及硅钛铁		20	Ferro-titanium & ferro-silico-titanium
133		72029290	其他钒铁		20	Ferro-vanadium containing by weight no more than 75% of vanadium
134		72029300	铌铁		20	Ferro-niobium
135		72031000	直接从铁矿还原的铁产品		20	Ferrous products obtained by direct reduction of iron ore
136		72039000	其他铁，海绵铁,产品纯度>99.94%		20	Spongy ferrous products / iron having a minimum purity by weight of 99.94%
137		72041000	铸铁废碎料	40		Waste & scrap, cast iron
138		72042100	不锈钢废碎料	40		Waste & scrap, stainless steel
139		72042900	其他合金钢废碎料	40		Waste & scrap, of alloy steel, other than stainless
140		72043000	镀锡钢铁废碎料	40		Waste & scrap, of tinned iron or steel
141		72044100	机械加工中产生的废料	40		Ferrous waste & scrap,i/s,from the mechanical working of mtl,nes
142		72044900	其他钢铁废碎料	40		Ferrous waste & scrap, iron or steel, nes
143		72045000	供再熔的碎料钢铁锭	40		Remelting scrap ingots, of iron or steel
144		72061000	铁及非合金钢锭		20	Iron and non-alloy steel in ingots
145		72069000	其他初级形状的铁及非合金钢		20	Iron and non-alloy steel in other primary forms
146		72071100	宽度<厚度两倍的矩形截面钢坯, C<0.25%		20	Semi-finished product, of iron or non-alloy steel, of rectangular (including square) cross-section, containing by weight less than 0.25% of carbon, the width measuring less than twice the thickness

序号 No	EX	税则号列 Tariff Item	货 品 名 称	出口税率 (%) Export Duty Rate	暂定税率 (%) Interim Duty Rate	Article Description
147		72071200	其他矩形截面钢坯,C＜0.25%		20	Semi-finished product, of iron or non- alloy steel, of rectangular (other than square) cross-section, containing by weight less than 0.25% of carbon
148		72071900	其他含碳量＜0.25%的钢坯		20	Other semi-finished product, of iron or non-alloy steel, containing by weight less than 0.25% of carbon
149		72072000	含碳量≥0.25%的钢坯		20	Semi-finished product, of iron or non- alloy steel, containing by weight 0.25% or more of carbon
150		72131000	带有轧制花纹的热轧盘条		15	Bars & rods, of iron or non-alloy steel, hot-rolled, in irregularly wound coils, containing indent, ribs, etc produced during process
151		72132000	其他易切削钢制热轧盘条		15	Bars & rods, of iron or non-alloy steel, hot-rolled, in irregularly wound coils, of free coppertting steel
152		72139100	直径＜14mm 圆截面的其他热轧盘条		15	Bars & rods, of iron or non-alloy steel, hot-rolled, in irregularly wound coils, of circopperlar cross-section, measuring less than 14mm in diameter
153		72139900	其他热轧盘条		15	Bars & rods, of iron or non-alloy steel, hot-rolled, in irregularly wound coils, of circopperlar cross-section, nes
154		72142000	热加工带有轧制花纹的条、杆		15	Bars & rods, of iron or non-alloy steel, forged, hot-rolled, hot-drawn or hot-extended, containing indentations, ribs, etc, produced during the process
155		72143000	热加工易切削钢的条、杆		15	Bars & rods, of iron or non-alloy steel, forged, hot-rolled, hot-drawn or hot-extended, of free coppertting steel, nes
156		72149100	热加工其他矩形截面的条杆		15	Bars & rods, of iron or non-alloy steel, forged, hot-rolled, hot-drawn or hot-extended, of rectangular cross section
157		72149900	热加工其他条、杆		15	Bars & rods, of iron or non-alloy steel, forged, hot-rolled, hot-drawn or hot-extended, nes
158		72151000	冷加工其他易切削钢制条、杆		15	Bars & rods, of iron or non-alloy steel, not further worked than cold formed or finished, of free coppertting steel
159		72155000	冷加工或冷成形的其他条、杆		15	Bars & rods, of iron or non-alloy steel, not further worked than cold formed or finished
160		72159000	铁及非合金钢的其他条、杆		15	Bars & rods, of iron or non-alloy steel, nes
161		72181000	不锈钢锭及其他初级形状产品		15	Ingots & other primary forms of stainless steel
162	EX	72189100	矩形截面的不锈钢半制成品		15	Semi-finished products of stainless steel, rectangular cross-section

序号 No	EX	税则号列 Tariff Item	货 品 名 称	出口税率 (%) Export Duty Rate	暂定税率 (%) Interim Duty Rate	Article Description
163		72189900	其他不锈钢半制成品		15	Other semi-finished products of stainless steel
164		72191312	厚度在3毫米及以上，但小于4.75毫米的未经酸洗的按重量计含锰量在5.5%及以上的铬锰系不锈钢卷板		10	Ferro-chromiam-manganese stainless steel, in coil, not acid pickled，of a thickness of 3mm or more but less than 4.75mm, containing by weight more than 5.5% of manganese
165		72191322	厚度在3毫米及以上，但小于4.75毫米的经酸洗的按重量计含锰量在5.5%及以上的铬锰系不锈钢卷板		10	Ferro-chromiam-manganese stainless steel, in coil, acid pickled，of a thickness of 3mm or more but less than 4.75mm, containing by weight more than 5.5% of manganese
166		72191412	厚度小于3毫米的未经酸洗的按重量计含锰量在5.5%及以上的铬锰系不锈钢卷板		10	Ferro-chromiam-manganese stainless steel, in coil, not acid pickled, of a thickness less than 3mm , containing by weight more than 5.5% of manganese
167		72191422	厚度小于3毫米的经酸洗的按重量计含锰量在5.5%及以上的铬锰系不锈钢卷板		10	Ferro-chromiam-manganese stainless steel, in coil, acid pickled, of a thickness less than 3mm, containing by weight more than 5.5% of manganese
168		72241000	合金钢锭及其他初级形状合金钢		15	Ingots & other primary forms of alloy steel, other than stainless
169		72249010	单重≥10吨的粗铸锻件坯		15	Raw casting forging stocks, of alloy steel other than stainless, individual piece weight of 10t or more
170		72249090	其他合金钢坯		15	Semi-finished products of alloy steel other than stainless, nes
171		74010000	铜锍、沉积铜（泥铜）		15	Copper mattes; cement copper (precipitated copper)
172		74020000	未精炼铜，电解精炼用的铜阳极	30	15	Copper unrefined, Copper anodes for electrolytic refining
173	ex	74031111	高纯阴极铜（铜含量不低于99.9999%）	30	0	Copper cathodes containing by weight no less than 99.9999% of copper, unwrought
174	ex	74031111	高纯阴极铜（铜含量高于99.9935%，但低于99.9999%）	30	5	Copper cathodes containing by weight more than 99.9935% but less than 99.9999% of copper , unwrought
175		74031119	其他阴极精炼铜	30	10	Other Copper cathodes, unwrought
176		74031190	其他精炼铜的阴极型材	30	10	Copper sections of cathodes, unwrought
177		74031200	精炼铜的线锭	30	10	Wire bars, Copper, unwrought
178		74031300	精炼铜的坯段	30	10	Billets, Copper, unwrought
179		74031900	其他未锻轧的精炼铜	30	10	Refined Copper products, unwrought, nes
180		74032100	未锻轧的铜锌合金(黄铜)	30	5	Copper-zinc base alloys, unwrought
181		74032200	未锻轧的铜锡合金(青铜)	30	5	Copper-tin base alloys, unwrought
182		74032900	未锻轧的其他铜合金	30	5	Copper alloys, unwrought (other than master alloys of heading No 74.05)
183		74040000	铜废碎料	30	15	Waste & scrap, Copper
184		74050000	铜母合金		10	Master alloys of Copper

序号 No	EX	税则号列 Tariff Item	货品名称	出口税率 (%) Export Duty Rate	暂定税率 (%) Interim Duty Rate	Article Description
185		74071010	铬锆铜制条、杆及型材及异型材	30	0	Bars, rods & profiles of chrominm and zirconium copper
186		74071090	其他精炼铜制条、杆及型材及异型材	30	0	Other bars, rods & profiles of other refined Cu
187		74072111	直线度不大于 0.5 毫米/米铜锌合金条、杆	30	0	Copper-zinc base alloys(brass) bars and rods, of a straightness not exceeding 0.5mm/m
188		74072119	其他铜锌合金条、杆	30	0	Other bars, rods of copper-zinc base alloys (brass)
189		74072190	其他铜锌合金型材及异型材	30	0	Profiles of Cu-Zn base alloys
190		74072900	其他铜合金条杆、型材及异型材	30	0	Bars, rods & profiles, of Copper alloy, nes
191		74081100	最大截面尺寸＞6mm 的精炼铜丝	30	0	Wire of refined Copper of which the max cross-sectional dimension exceeds 6mm
192		74081900	其他精炼铜丝	30	0	Wire of refined Copper of which the max cross-sectional dimension not exceeds 6mm
193		74082100	铜锌合金丝	30	0	Wire, of Copper-zinc base alloy
194		74082210	铜镍锌铅合金（加铅德银）丝	30	0	Wire, of copper-nickel-zinc-lead base alloys (leaded nickel silver)
195		74082290	其他白铜或德银丝	30	0	Other wire, of Copper-Ni base alloy or Copper- Ni-zinc base alloy
196		74082900	其他铜合金丝	30	0	Wire, of Copper alloy, nes
197		74091110	含氧量不超过 10PPM 的成卷的精炼铜板、片、带	30	0	Plate, sheet & strip of refined Copper, in coil, of a thickness exceeding 0.15mm, containing Oxygen no more than 10PPM
198		74091190	其他成卷的精炼铜板、片、带	30	0	Plate, sheet & strip of refined Copper, in coil, of a thickness exceeding 0.15mm, nes
199		74091900	其他精炼铜板、片、带	30	0	Plate, sheet & strip of refined Copper, not in coil, of a thickness exceeding 0.15mm
200		74092100	成卷的铜锌合金板、片、带	30	0	Plate, sheet & strip of Copper-Zn base alloys, in coil, of a thickness exceeding 0.15mm
201		74092900	其他铜锌合金板、片、带	30	0	Plate, sheet & strip of Copper-Zn base alloys, not in coil, of a thickness exceeding 0.15mm
202		74093100	成卷的铜锡合金板、片、带	30	0	Plate, sheet & strip of Copper-tin base alloys, in coil, of a thickness exceeding 0.15mm
203		74093900	其他铜锡合金板、片、带	30	0	Plate, sheet & strip of Copper-tin base alloys, not in coil, of a thickness exceeding 0.15mm
204		74094000	铜镍合金或铜镍锌合金板、片、带	30	0	Plate, sheet & strip of Copper-Ni or Copper-Ni-Zn base alloy, of a thickness exceeding 0.15mm
205		74099000	其他铜合金板、片、带	30	0	Plate, sheet & strip of Copper alloy, of a thickness exceeding 0.15mm, nes
206		75021010	高纯镍（镍含量大于 99.99%，钴含量不大于 0.005%)，	40	5	Ni, containing Ni more than 99.99%, and Co less than 0.005% by weight, unwrought, not alloyed

序号 No	EX	税则号列 Tariff Item	货 品 名 称	出口税率 (%) Export Duty Rate	暂定税率 (%) Interim Duty Rate	Article Description
207		75021090	未锻轧的非合金镍	40	15	Ni unwrought, not alloyed
208		75022000	未锻轧镍合金	40	15	Ni unwrought, alloyed
209		75030000	镍废碎料		10	Waste & scrap, Ni
210		75089010	电镀用镍阳极	40	15	Electroplating anodes of Ni
211		76011010	按重量计含铝量在99.95%及以上的非合金铝	30	0	Containing by weight 99.95% or more of aluminium unwrought aluminium, not alloyed
212		76011090	按重量计含铝量在99.95%以下的非合金铝	30	15	Al unwrought, not alloyed, nes
213	ex	76012000	碱金属含量（Na+K+Ca）＜10ppm，氢含量＜0.12ml/100gAl的低碱精炼铝合金	30	0	low-alkaline, refined alloyed Al, unwrought, in which containing alkalis (Na+K+Ca)＜10ppm, hydrogen＜0.12ml/100gAl
214	ex	76012000	其他未锻轧铝合金	30	15	Other Al unwrought, alloyed
215		76020000	铝废碎料	30	15	Waste & scrap of Al
216		76041010	非合金铝条、杆	20	0	Bars, rods, of Al, not alloyed
217		76041090	非合金铝型材及异型材	20	0	Bars, rods & profiles, of Al, not alloyed
218		76042100	铝合金制空心异型材	20	0	Profiles, hollow, of Al, alloyed
219	ex	76042910	截面周长大于等于 210 毫米的铝合金制条、杆	20	0	Al alloyed bars and rods of perimeter of cross-section of 210mm or more
220	ex	76042910	截面周长小于 210 毫米的铝合金条杆	20	0	Al alloyed bars and rods of perimeter of cross-section less than 210mm
221		76042990	铝合金制其他型材及异型材	20	0	Bars, rods & other profiles, Al alloyed
222		76051100	最大截面尺寸超过 7mm 的非合金铝丝	20	0	Wire, Al, not alloyed, with a max cross sectional dimension exceeding 7mm
223		76051900	其他非合金铝丝	20	0	Wire, Al, not alloyed, with a max cross sectional dimension not exceeding 7mm
224		76052100	最大截面尺寸超过 7mm 的铝合金丝	20	0	Wire, Al alloy, with a max cross sectional dimension exceeding 7mm
225		76052900	其他铝合金丝	20	0	Wire, Al alloy, with a max cross sectional dimension not exceeding 7mm
226		76061121	厚度在 0.3mm 及以上，但不超过 0.36mm 的非合金铝与塑料复合的矩形铝板片带	20	0	Rectangular plates, sheets and strip, of not alloyed aluminium-plastic composite, 0.3mm≤thickness<0.36mm
227		76061129	厚度在 0.3mm 及以上，但不超过 0.36mm 的其他非合金铝制矩形铝板片带	20	0	Other rectangular plates, sheets and strip, of not alloyed aluminium-plastic composite, 0.3mm≤thickness<0.36mm
228		76061191	非合金铝与塑料复合的矩形的其他板、片及带	20	0	Rectangular plates, sheets and strip, of not alloyed aluminium-plastic composite, nes
229		76061199	非合金铝制矩形的其他板、片及带	20	0	Other rectangular plates, sheets and strip, of not alloyed aluminium-plastic composite, nes
230		76061220	厚度小于 0.28mm 的铝合金制矩形铝板片带	20	0	Plate, sheet & strip, Al alloy, rectangular (including square), of a thickness exceeding 0.2mm, but less than 0.28mm

序号 No	EX	税则号列 Tariff Item	货 品 名 称	出口税率 (%) Export Duty Rate	暂定税率 (%) Interim Duty Rate	Article Description
231		76061230	厚度在 0.28mm 及以上，但不超过 0.35mm 的铝合金制矩形铝板片带	20	0	Plate, sheet & strip, Al alloy, rectangular (including square), of a thickness 0.28mm or more but not exceeding 0.35mm
232		76061251	厚度在 0.35mm 以上,但不超过 4mm 的铝合金与塑料复合的矩形铝板片带	20	0	Rectangular plates, sheets and strip of aluminium alloys-plastic composite, of a thickness of 0.35mm or more but not exceeding 4mm
233		76061259	厚度在 0.35mm 以上,但不超过 4mm 的其他铝合金制矩形铝板片带	20	0	Other rectangular plates, sheets and strip of aluminium alloys, of a thickness of 0.35mm or more but not exceeding 4mm
234		76061290	厚度>4mm 的铝合金制矩形铝板片带	20	0	Rectangular plates, sheets and strip of aluminium alloys, of a thickness exceeding 0.4mm
235		76069100	非合金铝制非矩形的板、片及带	20	0	Plate, sheet & strip, Al, not alloyed, of a thickness exceeding 0.2mm, nes
236		76069200	铝合金制非矩形的板、片及带	20	0	Plate, sheet & strip, Al alloy, of a thickness exceeding 0.2mm, nes
237		78011000	未锻轧精炼铅		10	Lead refined unwrought
238		78020000	铅废碎料		10	Lead waste & scrap
239		79011110	按重量计含锌量在 99.995%及以上的未锻轧锌	20	0	Unwrought zinc, not alloyed, containing by weight 99.995% or more of zinc
240		79011190	99.99≤含锌量<99.995%的未锻轧锌	20	5	Unwrought zinc, not alloyed, containing by weight 99.99% or more, but less than 99.995% of zinc
241		79011200	含锌量＜99.99%的未锻轧锌	20	15	Unwrought zinc, not alloyed, containing by weight less than 99.99% of zinc
242		79012000	未锻轧锌合金	20	0	Zinc alloys unwrought
243		80011000	非合金锡		10	Tin not alloyed unwrought
244		80020000	锡废碎料		10	Tin waste, scrap
245		81033000	钽废碎料		10	Molybdenum waste and scrap
246		81101010	未锻轧锑	20	5	Antimony unwrought
247		81101020	锑粉末	20		Antimony powders
248		81102000	锑废碎料	20		Antimony waste, scrap
249		81122100	未锻轧铬、铬粉末		15	Chromium unwrought; powders
250		81122200	铬废碎料		15	Chromium waste, scrap

部分本国子目注释

Domestic Heading Explanation Notes

子目 0304.6211	斑点叉尾鮰鱼亦称沟鲶，属于鲇形目、鮰科、叉尾鮰属。体形较长，体前部宽于后部，头较小，吻稍尖，口亚端位，体表光滑无鳞，粘液丰富，侧线完全，皮肤上有明显的侧线孔。体两侧背部淡灰色，腹部乳白色。头部上下颌具有深灰色触须 4 对，其中鼻须 1 对，颌须 1 对，颐须 2 对，长短各异，以颌须为最长，末端超过胸鳍基部，鼻须最短。鳃孔较大，鳃膜不连于峡部，颐部有较明显而不规则的斑点，成年鱼斑点逐步消失。具有脂鳍一个，尾鳍分叉较深，各鳍均为深灰色。冻鱼片呈乳白色，色泽自然，肉质细嫩，冰衣均匀。
子目 0603.1500	百合花是百合科百合属多年生草本球根植物，花着生于茎杆顶端，单生、簇生或呈总状花序，花色因品种不同而色彩多样，也有一朵花具多种色彩的。
子目 0704.9010	学名结球甘蓝，又名圆白菜、洋白菜，属十字花科芸苔属甘蓝变种。外观近圆形，结球紧实个头大，层层包裹成球状体，重量 1~2 公斤，颜色绿，芯白或淡黄色。其嫩叶可供食用。
子目 0704.9020	西兰花，又称青花菜、绿菜花，属十字花科芸苔属甘蓝变种。花球紧实鲜嫩，无现蕾现象，色泽浓绿，成熟度适中。其食用部分为绿色幼嫩花茎和花蕾。
子目 0714.4000	芋头又称芋艿，为天南星科芋属植物。块茎粗大，常为卵形或长椭圆形，褐色，有纤毛。其地下肉质球茎（母芋）和侧生子芋可供食用。按其需水量的不同，分为旱芋和水芋两种。
子目 1517.9010	起酥油是指动、植物油脂的食用氢化油、高级精制油或上述油脂的混合物，经过速冷捏和制造的固状油脂，或不经速冷捏和制造的固状、半固体状或流动状的具有良好起酥性能的油脂制品。
子目 1604.1931	斑点叉尾鮰鱼亦称沟鲶，属于鲇形目、鮰科、叉尾鮰属。体形较长，体前部宽于后部，头较小，吻稍尖，口亚端位，体表光滑无鳞，粘液丰富，侧线完全，皮肤上有明显的侧线孔。体两侧背部淡灰色，腹部乳白色。头部上下颌具有深灰色触须 4 对，其中鼻须 1 对，颌须 1 对，颐须 2 对，长短各异，以颌须为最长，末端超过胸鳍基部，鼻须最短。鳃孔较大，鳃膜不连于峡部，颐部有较明显而不规则的斑点，成年鱼斑点逐步消失。具有脂鳍一个，尾鳍分叉较深，各鳍均为深灰色。
子目 2206.0010	黄酒是指以稻米、黍米、玉米、小米、小麦等为主要原料，经蒸煮、加曲、糖化、发酵、压榨、过滤、煎酒、贮存、勾兑而成的酿造酒。
子目 2208.9020	白酒是指以高粱等谷物为主要原料，以大曲、小曲或麸曲及酒母等为糖化发酵剂，经蒸煮、糖化、发酵、蒸馏、陈酿、勾兑而制成的蒸馏酒。
子目 2504.1091	球化石墨是天然石墨经过球化加工，将微观结构从原来的鳞片状变为球形或半球形后，分级得到的产品，直径在 120 微米以下。
子目 2809.2011	食品级磷酸的具体技术指标参考 GB3149-2004。
子目 2826.1210	无水氟化铝是无水氟化氢气体与氢氧化铝经气固反应生产的氟化铝产品,其主要技术指标为:氟质量分数≥61%,铝质量分数≥31.5%,烧减量≤0.5%,松装密度≥1.5 克/立方厘米。

子目 2917.3611	白色针状结晶或粉末，密度 1.510，约在 300℃ 升华。能溶于碱溶液，稍溶于热乙醇，不溶于乙醚、冰醋酸和氯仿。用于制造合成树脂、合成纤维和增塑剂等。主要技术指标为 4-羧基苯甲醛（4-CBA）≤25PPM。
子目 3104.2020	本税目所指“纯氯化钾”，按重量计氯化钾含量不小于 99.5%
子目 3802.1010	木质活性炭以锯末、树皮、木屑、竹子等为原料生产，广泛用于医药、果汁、饮料等领域，其干品填充密度小于 0.5 克/立方厘米（粉状，200 目晒余物 20%以内）。
子目 3808.9112	生物杀虫剂是指以多杀霉素、除虫菊素、苦参碱、鱼藤酮、乙蒜素、诱虫烯中的一种或多种为有效成分的杀虫剂。
子目 3824.9093	该产品主要用于电池正极，通常由镍盐与碱反应制备，并按需要掺杂一定比例的碳，以及进行表面覆钴加工。
子目 4802.1010	宣纸是采用产自安徽省泾县境内及周边地区的青檀皮和沙田稻草，不掺杂其他原材料，并利用泾县独有的山泉水，按照传统工艺经过特殊的传统工艺配方，在严密的技术监控下，在安徽省泾县内以传统工 艺生产的，具有润墨和耐久等独特性能，供书画、裱拓、水印等用途的高级艺术用纸。
子目 4811.5191	纸塑铝复合材料是以原纸、聚乙烯及铝箔经专用设备一次性复合生产而成。主要生产环节包括印刷、复合等工艺，可在食品罐装机上成型—罐装—封合，无须再经其他复杂加工。主要用于牛奶、饮料等液体食品包装，实现在常温状态下长距离运输及保存。
子目 5003.0011	下茧、茧衣、长吐、滞头是指不适合缫丝的下茧、茧衣、长吐、滞头等缫丝副产品按一定的比例混合后的产品，该产品是重要的绢纺原料。该产品需符合《中华人民共和国纺织行业标准——桑蚕绢纺原料》（FZ/T41001-94）。
子目 5003.0012	回收纤维是指将碎绸布或其他丝绸织物及制品的废碎料拉松成纤维状的废丝。
子目 5003.0091	绵球是指不能缫丝的下茧、茧衣、长吐、滞头等缫丝副产品经精练、脱胶、干燥处理后既成为白色的精干绵，再经梳理后制成无杂质的绵球（包括绵条、绵片）等。
子目 5402.1110、5503.1110、5506.1011	聚间苯二甲酰间苯二胺纤维，属芳香族聚酰胺，因其高分子链上的酰胺键位于苯环的 1、3 位，所以又称之为芳纶 1313，或间位芳纶。
子目 5402.1120、5503.1120、5506.1012	聚对苯二甲酰对苯二胺纤维，属芳香族聚酰胺纤维，因其高分子链上的酰胺键位于苯环的 1、4 位，又称之为芳纶 1414，或对位芳纶。
子目 5402.4910、5402.5920	这种纱线是由分子量在 100 万及以上，500 万以下的线形聚乙烯制得的长丝纱线，断裂强度大于等于 22cN/dtex,且初始模量大于等于 750cN/dtex。
子目 5504.1021	阻燃粘胶纤维是通过添加无机阻燃剂制成的,氧指数应在 28%以上,回潮率应在 13%及以下。
子目 6404.1910	拖鞋，指没有后帮（带），露趾或不露趾的、日常穿用的鞋

子目 6404.2010	拖鞋，指没有后帮（带），露趾或不露趾的、日常穿用的鞋
子目 6802.9311	墓碑石用天然石材加工成的立在坟墓前面或后面的石碑套件，一般由墓碑和外栅组成，上面刻有相关文字图案和造型。
子目 6815.9932	碳纤维预浸料是碳纤维在环氧树脂等基体树脂中浸渍而成的材料。
子目 6815.9940	玄武岩纤维是以玄武岩为原料经高温熔融后拉制而成的无机纤维（国标 GB/T25045-2010）。
子目 7020.0013	该产品是以天然水晶、优质硅石或四氯化硅为主要原料经过电熔、气熔等不同工艺生产的由二氧化硅单一组分构成的特种工业玻璃。
子目 7103.9920	根据中华人民共和国国家标准 GB/T 16552-2010《珠宝玉石—名称》，水晶的矿物名称为石英，品种包括紫晶、黄晶、烟晶、绿水晶、芙蓉石、发晶。
子目 7103.9930	根据中华人民共和国国家标准 GB/T 16552-2010《珠宝玉石—名称》，碧玺的矿物名称为电气石。
子目 7103.9940	根据中华人民共和国国家标准 GB/T 16552-2010《珠宝玉石—名称》，软玉的主要组成矿物为透闪石、阳起石，品种包括和田玉、白玉、青白玉、青玉、碧玉、墨玉、糖玉。
子目 7202.9911	以稀土金属（主要为钕）、纯铁、硼铁等初级产品为原料，经真空高温熔融、速凝成晶、破碎、热处理制成的薄片状合金。其组成成分为稀土（钕、镨、镝、铽）25%～39%，硼 0.8%～1.3%，其他为铁及少量铜、钴、铝、锆、镓等添加元素。形状为不规则薄片，厚度 0.1%～0.8 毫米。经加工后，充磁制成永磁体，应用于计算机、通讯产品、电子设备等高科技领域。
子目 7202.9912	钕铁硼磁粉是以铁合金、钕和其他金属等初级产品为原料，经高温二次重熔、快淬、破碎、退火制成的粉末，其组成成分为钕 20%~32%，钴 0%~16%，硼 0.8%~1.3%，铌 0%~2.5%,其他为铁。钕铁硼磁粉主要应用于计算机、通讯产品电子设备等高科技领域。
子目 7225.4010	除不锈钢、高速钢以外的合金钢，按重量计，成份含量范围符合下列任一条款，不论是否含有其他元素：碳含量大于 1.2%，同时铬含量大于 10.5%的；或者碳含量大于等于 0.3%，同时铬含量大于等于 1.25%，且小于 10.5%的；或者铬含量大于等于 0.9%，且小于等于 1.2%，同时钼含量大于等于 0.9%，且小于等于 1.4%的；或者含碳量大于等于 0.5%，同时钼含量大于等于 3.5%的；或者碳含量大于等于 0.5%，同时钨含量大于等于 5.5%的。
子目 7326.9011	本税目所指的钢铁纤维，是单根直径为 40 纳米至 40 微米的多功能合金纤维，主要材质为不锈钢、铁铬铝合金等。钢铁纤维主要通过表面处理（在原料不锈钢或铁铬铝合金表面电化学涂覆金属或物理涂覆非金属隔离层，制得复合丝）、封装集束复合材料（采用封装材料封装被嵌入基体的不锈钢或铁铬铝合金复合丝，形成一种复合材料）、细晶强化（压实封装之后的复合材料，然后经过多次减径拉拔和退火成为成品复合线）、选择性分离（将成品复合线采用电化学分离的方式，除去封装及基体材料，最终获得钢铁纤维）等工艺流程制备。钢铁纤维及其制品的主要用途包括汽车尾气颗粒捕集、高温气体、熔体过滤，化纤行业过滤，汽车玻璃膜布，电磁屏蔽材料、防静电导电材料等。

子目 7407.1010	铬锆铜的主要成分为铜、铬、锆，按重量计铬含量 0.6%~1.4%，锆含量 0.05%~0.3%。
子目 7408.2210	铜、镍、锌、铅的合金，是在锌白铜的基础上添加微量的易切削元素铅,形成的易切削的白铜。按重量计含铜量 40%~65%，含镍量 9%~16%，含铅量 1.0%~2.5%，含锰量 0.05%~6.5%。锌为余量，且铁、磷、硫、锡等杂质元素总和不大于 0.9%。
子目 7411.1011	一般用作空调、冰箱及其他系统的热交换管材，整根管的内或外表面具有一定数量、一定规则螺纹或翅片。
子目 8103.2011	主要用于电容器生产，松装密度可用“振动漏斗法”（GB/T5061-1998）测定。
子目 8202.2010	双金属带锯条主要用于金属切割，其齿部材料为高速钢或高性能高速钢或硬质合金，锯条体的材料是低合金弹簧钢。齿部硬度不低于 62HRC（766HV），锯条体经过热处理后硬度不低于 436HV（45HRC）。
子目 8413.5031	柱塞泵的工作原理与活塞泵相同，由泵缸、柱塞、吸入阀、排出阀和驱动机构，区别在于柱塞是穿过装在泵缸上的固定填料密封件在缸体内运动，其密封性较活塞的好。
子目 8413.6040	螺杆泵由相互啮合的螺杆和泵体内包括螺杆的泵套组成。螺杆泵按螺杆根数分为单螺杆泵、双螺杆泵、三螺杆泵和五螺杆泵。
子目 8413.6050	径向柱塞泵由壳体、油缸主体、配液轴、若干个柱塞和弹簧等组成。配液轴偏心固定在壳体上，当它转动时，柱塞在缸筒内做径向往返运动，进行吸液和注液。
子目 8413.6060	轴向柱塞泵按其结构特征可分为直轴式（斜盘式）和斜轴式（摆缸式）两大类。斜盘式柱塞泵由壳体、转子（驱动轴、缸筒、柱塞）和斜盘组成。壳体端面配有配液盘；缸筒体内安装着若干个柱塞，沿圆周方向均布在缸筒体内，并能在其中滑动。斜盘固定在壳体上，并与转动轴线的垂线成一定的夹角，斜盘不随转子转动。但转子转动时，驱动轴带动缸筒体转动，柱塞也随之转动，同时柱塞在缸筒内作轴向的往返运动，进行吸液和注液，柱塞端部始终紧靠在斜盘上。摆缸式轴向柱塞泵的特点是：转子轴线与传动轴轴线之间成一个角度；转子及其各钢筒体内的柱塞分别用带万向接头的连杆与传动轴相连。转子转动时，传动轴带动缸筒体和柱塞一起旋转，同时柱塞在缸筒内作轴向的往返运动，进行吸液和注液。
子目 8414.8040	该类压缩机主要用于石化、煤化工、天然气等行业，输送介质是指氮气、氧气、氯气、乙烯、丙烯等气体(二氧化碳除外)。可分为离心式、轴流式、喷射式等速度式压缩机和螺杆式、涡旋式、滑片式、罗茨式、活塞式、隔膜式等容积式压缩机。
子目 8417.8050	垃圾焚烧炉由垃圾前处理系统、焚烧系统、烟气净化系统及煤气发生炉等组成，具有自动送料、分筛、烘干、焚烧、除尘、控制等功能。可用于处理城市生活垃圾、危险废弃物(含医用垃圾)、一般工业垃圾，分为机械炉排焚烧炉、流化床焚烧炉、回转式焚烧炉、CAO 焚烧炉等类型。
子目 8419.1910	太阳能热水器是利用太阳能将水从低温加热到高温的装置，由全玻璃真空集热管、储水箱、支架及相关附件组成，主要依靠玻璃真空集热管把太阳能转换成热能，使水产生微循环而达到所需热水。

子目 8421.2191	船舶压载水处理设备主要是为了有效控制和防止船舶压载水传播有害水生物和病原体。该设备通常采用电解海水制氯技术对压载水进行杀菌，并采用中和技术除去压载水中的余氯，从而达到压载水排放标准。
子目 8421.3924	电袋复合除尘器由前级电场除尘、后级布袋除尘、检测系统、保护系统、电气控制系统等组成。烟气从进口喇叭进入前级电除尘区，烟尘在电场电晕电流作用下荷电，大部分被电场收集下来，少量未被捕集粉尘随烟气进入后级布袋除尘区，经滤袋过滤后达到烟气净化目的。
子目 8421.3940	烟气脱硫设备主要用于火电厂烟气脱硫和重要工业领域（如烧结机脱硫），主导的烟气脱硫工艺为石灰石/石灰—石膏脱硫（设备）与烟气循环硫化床法脱硫（设备）。脱硫设备一般包括烟气脱硫反应器、循环浆液泵、水力旋流分离器、脱硫增压风机、除雾器、烟气挡板门、搅拌器等部分。
子目 8421.3950	烟气脱硝装置主要用于火电站、有色金属冶炼等工业领域，主要利用还原剂与氮氧化物（NOX）发生化学反应生成氮气和气态水，降低烟气中氮氧化物排放量。主流装置为选择催化还原法（SCR）脱硝技术，该装置主要包括 SCR 反应器、氨存储与供应系统、测试与控制系统等组成。
子目 8424.8920	本税目所指喷涂机器人是指专用于自动喷漆或喷涂其他涂料的工业机器人，由机器人本体、减速器、控制系统、伺服系统、喷具和涂料输供系统等部分组成。主要应用于汽车、船舶、仪表、电器、搪瓷等工艺生产部门。
子目 8428.9020	机械式停车设备是通过机械方式搬运、停放车辆的机械设备。此类设备大多采用自动控制、计算机管理等手段，综合应用机、电、声、光、自动化等技术，达到存取储放车辆的高效率、高可靠性和高安全性。此类设备分为升降横移类、垂直循环类、水平循环类、多层循环类、平面移动类、巷道堆垛类、垂直升降类和简易升降类等多种型式。主要由钢结构件、传动系统、控制系统等部分组成。
子目 8428.9031	堆取料机械是大型料场专用设备，一般分为臂式斗轮堆取料机、桥门式斗轮堆取料机和刮板式取料机三类。臂式一般由取料机构（堆料机无取料机构）、输送机构、回转、俯仰、行走机构、金属结构、电气控制设备等组成。桥门式和刮板式结构形式不同，但工作原理基本类似。
子目 8428.9040	本税目所指搬运机器人是指专用于自动化搬运作业的工业机器人，由机器人本体、减速器、控制系统和伺服系统等部分组成。主要应用于机械、电子、食品、医疗等行业的搬运、传输。
子目 8430.3110	采煤机（含截煤机、割煤机），由装有风镐的棒条或圆盘组成，按装在自推进的轮式或履带式底盘上，以旋转工作机劈开或击碎煤层，并将其装入输送机或其他运输设备。
子目 8430.3120	凿岩机是用来直接开采石料的工具，由一环形切割链环绕一金属臂运作，切割平面和角度均可调节，一般与工程车、液压挖掘机等配套使用。
子目 8430.3130	隧道掘进机是用机械破碎岩石、出碴和支护实行连续作业的一种综合设备，利用回转刀具开挖，破碎洞内围岩及掘进，形成整个隧道断面。一般由刀盘、主驱动、盾体、推进系统、输送机、注浆系统、液压系统、控制系统、导向测量系统、管片拼装系统、润滑系统等组成。
子目 8431.2010	税号 84.27 所列机械用驱动桥是传动系统组成部分，由主减速器、差速器、半轴、轮边减速器、桥壳等构成，主要功能是增大由传动轴或变速器产生的转矩，并将动力合理分配给左右驱动轮。

子目 8431.4920	税号 84.26、84.29 或 84.30 所列机械用驱动桥是传动系统组成部分，由主减速器、差速器、半轴、轮边减速器、桥壳等构成，主要功能是增大由传动轴或变速器产生的转矩，并将动力合理分配给左右驱动轮。
子目 8432.3011	按规定播量和行距在田间播种谷物种子的农业机具，主要完成开沟、排种、覆土和镇压等作业，按排种方式的不同，排种器分为槽轮式、磨盘式等，我国生产的谷物播种机大都有播种时同时施肥的功能。
子目 8432.3021	按一定行距、种薯间距和栽种深度栽植马铃薯的机具。能一次完成开沟、施肥、栽种薯块和覆土等作业。
子目 8432.3031	按一定的行距、株距、秧苗数和栽植深度将水稻秧苗栽植于水田的机具。由秧箱、送秧机构、分插秧机构、动力驱动、行走装置等部件组成。
子目 8433.5920	棉花采摘机的基本机构：除驾驶室、发动机、行走机构外，主要工作部件还有采棉滚筒、气流输送装置、集棉箱等。在棉花采摘机前进时，扶导器压缩棉株，并把棉株引入由采棉滚筒及固定护板组成的工作室（采棉区），棉株宽度被积压成 8~9 厘米，旋转着的采棉滚筒有规律地把摘锭送入采棉区，旋转的摘锭伸出栅板，插入被挤压的棉株，同开裂棉铃相遇，其钩齿抓住籽棉，把棉絮从开裂的棉铃中拉出，缠绕在摘锭上。然后摘锭进入脱棉区，高速旋转的橡胶圆盘式脱棉器将摘锭上的籽棉脱下，落入集棉室，有气流管道送入集棉箱。摘锭从湿润器下边通过时，表面涂上一层水，清除掉绿色汁液和泥土垢（以利于采棉和脱棉）重新进入采棉区。
子目 8437.1010	光学色差颗粒选别机（色选机）是运用特定的光学方法，凸显被选物料与正常物料的颜色或形状差异，这些差异被电子视觉系统检测，经控制系统处理产生输出信号，控制执行机构剔除被选物料，得到品质一致的物料。该设备广泛应用于粮食及食品的精深加工领域，同时还适用于工业领域（塑料、矿石等）的分选。
子目 8443.3214	热敏打印机采用加热显色技术实现打印输出。该产品的结构相对比较简单，仅包括热敏打印头、进纸胶辊及进纸电机等，不需要各种复杂的辅助机构。热敏打印机可作为模块嵌入到各种终端设备中使用。热敏打印机广泛应用于条码、标签、收据、日志等专业打印领域。
子目 8443.9111	卷筒料给料机按更换料卷方式分为高速接料和零速接料两类。高速自动给料机是指机器在全速或略微降速的运行过程中，在料卷运行状态下完成粘结料卷、更换料卷的自动接料装置。零速接料是指料卷在静止状态下完成粘接，而印刷机仍在正常高速运行，在此期间是由给料机的料卷储存装置——储料器向印刷机供给输送料带。
子目 8443.9921	热敏头组件由小型电加热器和逻辑电路组成，小型加热器排成方阵，由逻辑电路控制加热器工作。同时也控制进纸，当加热器被驱动时在介质上就会产生一个与加热元素相对应的图形，从而完成输出图像的任务。热敏打印的介质是热敏纸，热敏纸上覆有一层透明膜，将膜加热一段时间以后纸会变成深色（蓝或黑），热敏打印就是利用热敏纸的这种特性，通过热敏打印头将打印介质上的热敏材料加热、熔化、变色，生成所需要的文字和图形。
子目 8447.2011	特里科经编机织物相对于织针平面近似成直角状牵拉，织物张力由织针承担。在成圈配置以及编织方面的特点如下：(1) 沉降片上纱线接触点为 2 个。(2) 经轴一般放在机器后面或者放在机器的上面。(3) 织针可以从机前更换。(4) 老式特里科经编机导纱梳栉编号从机后到机前(从 2001 年 1 月开始，编号从机前到机后)。 (5) 目前最多使用 5 把梳栉。(6) 使用复合针。(7) 没有牵拉就可以起头编织。(8) 光编链组织不能编织(编链衬纬可以编织)。(9) 纱线与坯布牵拉成 90°，织针受力较大。

子目 8447.2012	拉舍尔经编机织物相对于织针平面近似成平行状牵拉，织物张力对织针不大起作用。在成圈配置以及编织方面的特点如下：(1) 沉降片纱线接触点为 3 个。(2) 经轴一般放在机器的顶部。(3) 织针必须从机后更换。(4) 导纱梳栉的编号从机前到机后。(5) 最多使用 78 把梳栉。(6) 使用复合针和舌针。(7) 没有牵拉不能起头编织。(8) 光编链线圈也能编织。(9) 纱线与坯布牵拉成 170°，织针受力较小。
子目 8448.3940	紧密纺装置是在环锭细纱机设备的基础上,突破传统纺纱工艺,在牵引部分增加集聚、吸风和气流导向装置，通过对加捻点的纺纱三角区中纤维的控制，纺出了高质量的紧密纱线。该纱具有纺纱强力高、毛羽少、条干好等特点，可适应纺多种纤维。
子目 8449.0010	针刺法是一种机械加固方法,其基本原理是用截面为三角形（或其他形状）且棱边带有钩刺的针，对蓬松的纤网进行反复针刺，将纤网加工成具有一定厚度和强度的针刺法非织造布。针刺机按加工纤网的状态可分为预针刺机和主针刺机；按结构可分为单针梁式和双针梁式；按传动形式可分为上传动式和下传动式。针刺机的机构由以下几部分组成：送网机构、针刺机构、牵拉机构、花纹机构（仅花纹针刺机由此机构）、传动机构、附属机构、机架等。
子目 8449.0020	水刺法又称射流喷射网法、力缠结法、喷水成布法，采用高速高压的水流促使纤维相互缠结抱合，达到加固纤网，制成水刺非织造布。水刺设备主要由水刺装置（水刺头）、输送网帘和水循环装置组成。水刺装置是由内部带有通水孔的集流腔体与水针板组成，采用耐腐蚀和耐高压材料制成。水针板是一个长条薄型不锈钢板，根据工艺要求，在针板上开有单排孔、双排孔或三排孔。一般水刺装置的配置为四上四下，可以水平排列，也可以圆周排列。水刺设备一般是将两组或多组水刺装置串联使用。
子目 8450.2011	波轮式全自动洗衣机主要结构由箱体、洗涤桶、外桶（盛水桶）、电机、传动部件以及全自动程序控制器、传感器等电控系统组成，电机等洗涤系统轴向垂直设置。其工作原理为：通过各种器件组成的控制电路来控制电机、进水阀、排水阀，使洗衣机实现程序运转；依靠装在洗衣桶底部的波轮正、反旋转形成水流，带动衣物上、下、左、右翻转，使衣物在洗涤液中进行柔和地摩擦，在洗涤剂的作用下实现去污清洗，洗涤过程全自动控制。
子目 8450.2012	滚筒式全自动洗衣机主要结构由箱体、洗涤桶、外桶（盛水桶）、电机、传动部件、平衡块以及全自动程序控制器、传感器等电控系统组成，电机等洗涤系统轴向水平设置。其工作原理为：通过各种器件组成的控制电路来控制电机、进水阀、排水阀，使洗衣机实现程序运转；模仿棒锤击打衣物原理设计，利用电动机的机械做功使滚筒旋转，带动衣物在滚筒中不断地被提升摔下，再提升再摔下，做重复运动，加上洗涤剂与水的共同作用使衣物洗涤干净，洗涤过程全自动控制。
子目 8452.1091	手动式小缝纫机又称为缝纫器，产品体积通常小于 15*10*15 厘米，重量轻于 2 公斤，可随身携带，手握按压式动力，作单线链式线迹缝纫，能够轻松自如地缝纫悬挂着的窗帘、壁挂、手帕、围裙、枕套等，也可缝制小衣物等。
子目 8452.2120	包缝机是由针线和弯针线，通过机器的运动循环穿套在缝料边缘形成包缝链式线迹（500 类包缝链式线迹），将缝料包边并缝合的工业缝纫机。自动包缝机采用微型计算机控制，具有自动剪线、定针位、抬压脚等自动功能。机器由机壳、传动机构、针杆机构、勾线机构、送料机构、压脚机构、切刀机构以及机架、台板、控制系统、驱动电机等机构与部件组成，产品主要用于服装的包边、包缝、镶边等，能有效防止缝料边缘脱散，广泛应用于印染、服装、地毯等行业。

子目 8452.2130	绷缝机是利用针、梭两种缝线自连、互连、交织，在缝料底面形成单面覆盖链式线迹，或在缝料正面再增加覆盖线形成双面覆盖链式线迹（400 类多线链式线迹），将两层或多层缝料缝合的工业用缝纫机。自动绷缝机采用微型计算机控制，具有自动剪线、拔线、倒缝、定针位及抬压脚等自动功能，产品主要由机壳、刺料机构、主轴传动机构、上轴传动及挑线机构、勾线机构、绷针机构、送料机构、输回油机构以及机架、台板、控制系统、驱动电机等组成，主要应用于针织服装厂缝制棉毛衫、汗衫及类似的化纤织物的搭缝连接、针织服装的滚领、滚边、折边、拼接缝等作业。
子目 8457.1091	数控铣车复合加工中心是在车床基础上复合了铣车功能,利用刀具移动或旋转和工件旋转的合成运动实现对工件表面的切削加工的设备。工件主轴为水平或垂直状态，并配有自动换刀装置（刀库机械手），主要用于工序多、形状复杂的回转体零件的加工。与车削中心相比,增加了一个旋转轴和自动换刀装置(刀库机械手)。
子目 8458.9110	数控立式车床主要由床身、立柱、刀架、卡盘（或工作盘）、X/Z 轴进给等组成，其主轴处于垂直位置，主要有两种结构形式：(1)主轴和工作台位于下方的床身上，刀架在立柱上，适于加工大型和重型零件，通常称为数控立式(正置)车床；(2)主轴和卡盘位于立柱上，刀架则位于下方床身上，适于加工中小型盘、盖类零件，自动化程度高，通常称为数控立式倒置车床。
子目 8460.2111	数控曲轴磨床是曲轴精加工设备,一般由基础部分（床身、工作台）、支承部分（头架、尾架、卡盘、中心架等）、砂轮架、进给机构、数控系统、液压系统、对刀测量装置等组成的。主要用于磨削汽车、拖拉机、机车内燃机、柴油机及船用发动机用曲轴。
子目 8461.4011	数控齿轮磨床是利用磨具对齿轮表面进行磨削加工的精加工设备，一般由主轴部件、床具、进给单元、辅助单元等组成。按齿轮型式分为渐开线圆柱齿轮磨床和锥齿轮磨床。
子目 8466.9310	刀库是存放待换工具的装置，自动换刀装置则是能自动更换加工中所用工具的装置。刀库系统是提供自动化加工过程中所需储刀及换刀需求的一种装置，由自动换刀机构及可以储放多把刀具的刀库构成。该装置由电脑程序控制，可完成各种不同的加工需求，如铣削、钻孔、镗孔、攻牙等，大幅缩短加工时程，降低生产成本。刀库可分为斗笠式、圆盘式、链条式，自动换刀装置则可分为油压机构、气压机构、电气凸轮机构三类。目前电气凸轮机构因设计简单使用操作可靠被广泛采用。
子目 8471.3010	平板电脑是指输入输出部件集成在一起、以触摸屏为基本输入设备的便携式电脑（通常屏幕大于等于 7 英寸）。
子目 8477.3010	挤出吹塑机是挤出机和合模机构的组合体,由挤出机及型坯模头、吹胀装置、合模机构、型坯厚度控制系统和传动机构组成。
子目 8477.3020	注射吹塑机是注塑机与吹塑机构的组合体，包括塑化机构、液压系统、控制电器及其他机械部件。注射吹塑机生产的塑料容器尺寸精确，无需二次加工，但模具费用较高。
子目 8477.3090	其他吹塑机包括特殊结构的吹塑机，这些吹塑机是用片材、熔融材和冷坯为型坯吹塑具有特殊形状和用途的空心体的吹塑机。
子目 8477.5910	本税目所指三维打印机（3D 打印机）是以数字模型文件为基础，加工材质以塑料或橡胶及其制品为主，通过逐层打印的方式实现固态物体成型，属于增材技术的重要应用。一般由打印头、控制组件、机械组件、耗材和介质等组成，主要应用于模具制造、工业设计等领域。

子目 8479.8991	机场用旅客登机桥是供旅客上、下飞机通行的、联接飞机与机场航站楼之间的活动封闭式通道。按结构可分为轮式登机桥、柱座式登机桥和其他形式登机桥，其中轮式又分为旋转式和旋转伸缩式。按传动方式可分为液压式、机电式和液压机电混合式。外观侧壁材料可由波纹板、钢板或玻璃板构成。旅客登机桥整桥由旋转平台、活动通道、升降机构、接机平台、接机口、行走机构、服务梯、立柱及固定通道等组成。旅客登机桥采用 PLC 可编程序控制，具有终端控制、自动预靠、自动退桥等功能。
子目 8480.4110	压铸模一般是由两个互补冷硬铸模组成，其型腔与所需铸件两面的形状形同，合模后将融熔状态的金属液体注入模腔，经加压、保压、冷却、开模，生产出各种压铸件。
子目 8480.4120	粉末冶金用压模用于压制各种粉末冶金件。将模具组装到压力机上，调试，在开模状态下装入金属粉末（钢粉、铜粉、不锈钢及各种合金粉等）压力机动作，加压、模具压紧，经过烧结的金属粉末在高压下成型为零件。
子目 8480.7110	硫化轮胎用囊式型模由两个可调节的金属冷硬铸模组成，用蒸汽或电加热，内有环状的充气袋或热水袋，以将胎坯牢牢地压向型模的内壁。
子目 8481.8021	电磁换向阀是利用电磁铁的推力来驱动阀芯运动以变换流体流动方向的控制阀，简称电磁阀。电磁换向阀有滑阀和球阀两种结构。通常所说的电磁换向阀为滑阀结构，球状或锥状阀芯的电磁换向阀被称为电磁换向座阀，也称电磁球阀。电磁换向阀的品种繁多，按其工作位置数和通路数可分为二位二通、二位三通、二位四通、三位四通等；按其复位和定位形式可分为弹簧复位式、钢球定位式、无复位弹簧式；按其阀体与电磁铁的连接形式可分为法兰连接和螺纹连接；按其配电磁铁的结构形式可分为干式和湿式。
子目 8481.8031	电子膨胀阀主要用于变频制冷系统中，实现对系统制冷流量的自动调节，使系统始终保持在最佳的工况下运行。电子膨胀阀由阀体和线圈两部分组成，阀体由阀座部件、转子部件和止动器三个部件组成，线圈由缠绕在骨架上的上下绕组、导磁体和引出电缆等组成。线圈与阀体内永磁转子组成永磁步进电机，通过控制线圈的脉冲输入信号可以实现阀体内转子部件的正反向旋转。转子的转动通过丝杆和螺母的螺纹传动，将转子部件的旋转运动转化为阀针轴向移动，从而调节阀口通流面积的大小，实现系统制冷流量大小的自动调节。电子膨胀阀是采用步进电机驱动的电力驱动阀门。
子目 8482.1010	调心轴承的滚道是球面形的,能够适应两滚道轴心线间的角偏差及角运动的轴承。
子目 8482.1020	深沟球轴承属于径向接触的向心轴承，主要用于承受径向载荷，其公称接触角为 0°。
子目 8482.1030	角接触轴承是指角接触向心轴承，也是主要用于承受径向载荷，0°＜其公称接触角≤45°。该税目不包括角接触推力球轴承。
子目 8482.1040	推力球轴承是指主要用于承受轴向载荷的球轴承，45°＜其公称接触角≤90°。按公称接触角的不同，又分为：轴向接触轴承——公称接触角为 90°的推力球轴承；角接触推力轴承——公称接触角为 45°但小于 90°的推力球轴承。
子目 8483.1011	曲轴是船用柴油机的重要组成部分，主要作用是与连杆配合将活塞上的气体压力转变为传动轴（包括曲轴）的旋转动力，曲轴一般由主轴颈、连杆轴颈、曲柄、平衡块、前端和后段等组成。大功率低速船用曲轴的结构比较复杂，在工作过程中受到各种冲击力、扭距、磨损、应力等作用，因此对曲轴的材质和加工工艺要求比较高。

子目 8486.9091	溅射靶材组件由裸靶和支撑背板两部分组成，背板与裸靶通过焊接连接为一体。裸靶原材料通常为高纯金属或金属合金，通过特殊的热机械处理和精密机械加工制造而成，背板通常带有与溅射机配合的连接孔、定位突起或卡环、卡口等结构。单金属裸靶无背板结构按原材料归类。
子目 8504.4030	逆变器是一种将直流电变成交流电的装置，它由逆变桥、控制逻辑和滤波电路组成。逆变器根据发电源的不同，分为煤电逆变器、太阳能发电逆变器、风能发电逆变器、水能发电逆变器以及柴油机发电逆变器等；根据用途不同，分为独立控制逆变器和并网逆变器；按照输出波形，分为正弦波逆变器和方波逆变器。
子目 8507.8030	全钒液流电池是一种高效电化学储能设备。由电堆单元、能量存储部分及控制部分组成。钒电解质溶液在循环泵的推动下流经电堆，实现电能的存储与释放。全钒液流电池系统因其突出的寿命长、可深度充放电、安全环保等优势，是解决太阳能、风能等可再生能源发电并网瓶颈，构建智能电网的首选储能技术之一。
子目 8512.3012	该品目包括所有机动车辆用防盗报警器,无论其是否带有视觉信号报警装置。
子目 8515.2120	本税目所指机器人是指利用电阻热进行自动焊接的工业机器人，由机器人本体、控制系统、传感器、焊钳、电阻焊机及控制器等部分组成。主要应用于汽车制造、电工电子等领域。
子目 8515.3120	本税目所指机器人是指专门用于电弧（包括等离子弧）焊接的工业机器人，由机器人本体、控制系统、传感器、焊枪、焊机、自动送丝装置等部分组成。主要应用于汽车、工程机械、摩托车、船舶、运动器材、航空、航天、锅炉等领域。
子目 8515.8010	本税目所指激光焊接机器人是指以激光器为焊接源的焊接机器人，由机器人本体、控制系统、传感器、激光头、激光系统等部分组成。主要应用于汽车、电子、冶金等行业。
子目 8516.1010	储存式电热水器是将水加热的固定式容器，它可以长期临时储存非饮用热水，并装有控制或限制水温的装置。这种热水器为配有浸入式加热元件的保温水箱，水可在其中逐渐得到加热。
子目 8516.1020	即热式电热水器又称快速热水器，指没有储存容器，可用电即时加热非饮用水的固定式容器。水流过此类热水器时即可加热。
子目 8516.2920	产品结构以发热管、辐射板、控制部分等构成。其中辐射板通常是抛物柱面的反射镜。发热管通常是卤素管或石英管等。
子目 8516.2931	风扇式加热器又称强制对流式加热器，利用风扇鼓动空气流经电热元件，再将暖风送出。通常分为离心式、轴流式、贯流式、涡轮式等型式，基本结构包括电热元件、风扇、温度控制器和外壳构成。
子目 8516.2932	充液式加热器又称充液式散热器、电热油汀，封闭的装置中充有导热油或导热液作为传热媒介，电气元件将传热媒介加热，然后把热量散发到周围的空气中。根据不同的功率大小，充液式加热器分为板式和多片式等结构。

子目 8516.6050	电烤箱(Roaster Oven)是用于烘烤鸡、肉、汉堡包等食物的厨房炊事器具（家用烤面包机除外），其结构由箱体、门、发热器（单个或上下双势）、烤盘、控制系统等组成，靠热风加热或靠电热管加热事物，根据不同容积分别设有一层或两层烤盘，按容积分为 9 升、12 升、16 升、22 升不等，功率为 600W~1200W。电烤箱与多士炉、三明治炉最大的不同是，前者是将生鲜食材经加热制成熟食，内部结构更为复杂。
子目 8516.7110	滴液式咖啡机占据了咖啡机市场的主要销售份额,主要结构由水箱、加热器、过滤器、保温盘、咖啡壶、微电脑控制部件和附件等七部分构成。其工作原理为：将咖啡粉放入过滤器内，水箱内加满水，开启咖啡机。加热器将对进入加热器内的水进行加热，并将热水从过滤器上部洒下。对过滤器内的咖啡粉进行充分浸泡，利用水的自重将咖啡粉内的咖啡精华通过过滤网滤出。滤出的咖啡液流到下部的咖啡壶内，即完成咖啡的制作。
子目 8516.7120	蒸馏渗滤式咖啡机：主要结构由水罐（含加热功能）、漏斗、微电脑控制部件和附件等四部分构成。其工作原理为：制作咖啡的水放入水罐内，加热后产生高温高压的水蒸气，利用虹吸原理将高温高压的水蒸汽通过水罐中心的水管引流到装有咖啡粉的漏斗内。让水蒸气瞬间穿过咖啡粉的细胞壁，将咖啡的内在精华萃取出来制作咖啡。
子目 8516.7130	泵压式咖啡机主要结构由水箱、水泵、加热器、漏斗、微电脑控制部件和附件等六大部分组成。水箱与水泵连接，通过微电脑控制部件控制水泵从水箱抽水至加热器，水通过加热器加热后，由于水泵提供的压力使热水流至加热器下部的压力过滤漏斗内，热水从而将压力过滤漏斗内的咖啡粉的精华过滤出来。同时通过过滤网内的小孔作用产生丰富的泡沫。
子目 8516.7210	家用自动面包机是通过微电脑控制搅面、发酵、醒面和焙烤来制作各种特色面包蛋糕的家电产品，只要将面粉，水，糖，酵母等所有配料放入面包桶后, 启动机器就能自动完成面包制作的全过程。
子目 8516.7220	多士炉主要功能是烘烤面包片、面包圈、法式面包、华夫饼、酥皮馅饼，可烤制出不同焦硬度，口感和烧色图案。有 2 片、3 片和 4 片多士炉。多士炉由炉身组件、炉胆组件、发热板组件、滑动机构组件、电子板控制组件、电磁铁组件和炉底组件构成。使用时将面包放入面包槽腔内，压下提手，滑动组件向下运动，网架将整片面包夹持归中，并沉入烘烤腔内，电子板工作，发热板开始发热，进行烘烤；电子板组件控制线圈的通断电时间，从而控制磁吸片的吸合时间，到达设定的时间后，电子板组件控制线圈断电，磁铁吸力消失，滑动组件弹起，同时发热板断电不再加热，托架将烤好的面包托至炉胆上端，方便用户取出，完成烘烤过程。
子目 8517.6237	网卡是物理上连接自动数据处理设备或其他网络设备终端与网络的一种数字式适配器。有线网卡是指网卡连接网络设备和终端设备的两个端口都是以有线形式实现的。其设备端接口常见的有 PCI 接口和 USB 接口；其网络端接口常见的有 PJ-45 接口、BNC 接口和光纤接口。
子目 8517.6292	无线网卡，通常其设备端接口以有线方式实现，常见的有 PCMCIA 接口和 USB 接口，而其网络端接口以无线方式通过天线和基站连接，常见的无线局域网使用的接入标准包括 IEEE802.11a、IEEE802.11b、IEEE802.11g 三种。无线网络接入卡的结构主要由主板（基带+射频+电源管理+外围器件+PCB 板）、射频天线、MD 结构件等组成。
子目 8517.6293	无线接入固定台是一种采用无线通信技术体制的无线终端接入设备，这种产品具备语音通信功能，有的还可具备收发短信、手机模式上网等功能。能在无线网络覆盖的范围内,将无线网络信号转化为普通固定电话模拟信号,适用于固定电话不易布线地区,可直接代替固定电话。该设备可以是一部无线固定电话机，也可以是一部无线接入系统多用户固定台。可以为多个用户提供服务并具有内部交换功能，多个用户共用若干个无线信道。该设备一般包括天馈线、电源模块、接口单元、主控单元和模块化的射频单元。对于带传真功能的产品还会有传真模块。

子目 8522.9091	车载音频转播器或发射器通常包括三个部分：一个液晶显示屏，一个控制器，一个输入输出终端。多数产品可以通过 FM 发射和汽车的收音模块相接，通过汽车或者家中的 FM 立体声接收机来收听（iPod、MP3、MP4、CD 唱机）中的音乐。有些产品还可以用音频线与汽车音箱直接相连。
子目 8529.9083	有机发光二极管显示屏是利用有机半导体发光材料将电能直接转换成光能的显示器件。电视用 OLED 显示屏还包括背板、驱动电路相关部件。
子目 8536.9011	接插件是指连接两个器件的连接器，用于传输电流或信号(光缆用连接器除外),工作电压不超过 36 伏。
子目 8539.3191	紧凑型荧光灯(又称节能灯,国外简称 CFL 灯)，具有体积小、省电、发光效率高、光线柔和等特点。紧凑型荧光灯与普通荧光灯相比，最主要的特点在于灯管的结构是紧凑型的，通常被弯成 H 形、U 形、双 n 形、螺旋形等；多数紧凑型荧光灯的灯管、电子镇流器部件和灯头部件通常是有机地结合成一体的，在不损坏其中部件的情况下一般是可拆卸的。紧凑型节能灯节能主要是通过节能灯管的节能和电子镇流器低功耗的体现。
子目 8539.3230	钠灯是利用钠蒸气放电产生可见光的电光源。钠灯又分低压钠灯和高压钠灯。低压钠灯的工作蒸气压不超过几个帕。低压钠灯的放电辐射集中在 589.0 纳米和 589.6 纳米的两条双 D 谱线上，其发光效率极高，目前已达到 200 流每瓦（lm / W），成为各种电光源中发光效率最高的节能型光源。高压钠灯的工作蒸气压大于 0.01 兆帕。高压钠灯是由半透明的多晶氧化铝（PCA）陶瓷电弧管，外泡壳，金属支架，消气剂和灯头组成。电弧管为核心元件，内充汞，钠和惰性气体。放电时，内部的钠蒸气压力为 10~100kPa。高压钠灯具有发光效率高，耗电少，寿命长，透雾强和不诱虫等特点。主要有普通型，高显色型，高光效型，低汞型，农用型等。
子目 8539.3240	汞灯是利用汞放电时产生汞蒸气获得可见光的电光源。汞灯可分为低压汞灯、高压汞灯和超高压汞灯三种。低压汞灯点燃时汞蒸气压小于一个大气压，此时汞原子主要辐射波长为 253.7nm 的紫外线。这类灯又称灭菌灯、冷阴极和热阴极灯。低压汞灯光强低，光固化速度慢，但发热量小，不需冷却就可使用，在印刷制版上用得较多。也可用作杀菌灯。高压汞灯的工作汞蒸气压为 0.2~1 兆帕。其发光效率可达 35~50 流 / 瓦(lm / W)，广泛用于环境温度为-20~40℃的街道、广场、高大建筑物、交通运输场所作为室内外照明光源。超高压汞灯的工作汞蒸气压为 1 兆帕以上。该灯从长波紫外到可见光都有很强的辐射，电弧亮度极高。超高压汞灯有短弧超高压汞灯和毛细管超高压汞灯两种。短弧超高压汞灯是辐射极强的长波紫外光和可见光的点光源。广泛用于荧光显微镜、紫外分光仪、全息照相等光学仪器，也用于集成电路光刻制版工艺。毛细管超高压汞灯主要用于照相制版和彩色显像管涂荧光屏制版工艺。
子目 8541.4010	发光二极管或电发光二极管是一种可把电能变成可见光线、红外线或紫外线的半导体器件。本品目包括有机发光二极管（OLED）和聚合物发光二极管（PLED）。有机发光二极管（OLED）的基本结构是由一层薄而透明具半导体特征的铟锡氧化物（ITO）与电力的正极相连，再加上另一个金属阴极，包成如三明治的结构。整个结构由阴极、电子输运层、发光层、空穴输运层和阳极组成。当电力供应到适当电压时，电子从阴极注入到电子输运层，同时，空穴由阳极注入到空穴输运层，它们在发光层重新结合而发光。
子目 8541.4020	太阳能电池是一种硅阻挡层光电池，可直接把太阳光变成电能。太阳能电池通常成组作为电源使用。例如，用于探索太空的火箭及人造卫星；山区呼救送话器。本税号也包括不论是否装在组件内或组装成块的太阳电池。但本税号不包括配有元件，直接为电动机、电解槽等供电的电池板及电池组件，不论所配元件如何简单（例如，用于控制电流方向的二极管）（税号 85.01）。
子目 8609.0011	保温集装箱是指安装有制冷设备，用于运输易腐食物或者货物的集装箱。

子目 8609.0012	罐式集装箱是指圆筒型罐式结构，配有支撑架使其可固定于车辆或船舶，用于运输液体、气体或其他特种货物的集装箱。
子目 9001.9010	彩色滤光片通常是作为液晶显示器的关键部件使用,液晶显示器依靠彩色滤光片实现图像的彩色。彩色滤光片是镀有 BM、R、G、B、ITO 镀层的有色玻璃。彩色滤光片的制备方法有四种,包括颜料分散法、染色法、印刷法和电沉积法（该税目不包括等离子显示器用滤光片,等离子显示器用滤光片带有电磁屏蔽夹层,不属于纯粹的光学元件,应按专用零件归类，不在该税目项下）。
子目 9003.1910	用于眼镜架的金属材料有铜合金、镍合金和贵金属三大类，要求具有一定的硬度、柔软性、弹性、耐磨性、耐腐蚀性、重量轻、有光泽和色泽好等。因此，用于制作眼镜架的金属材料几乎都是合金或在金属表面加工处理后使用。
子目 9003.1920	用于制作眼镜架的天然材料有玳瑁、特殊木材和动物头角等。一般木质眼镜架和牛角架很少见，常见的是玳瑁眼镜架。
子目 9014.2010	自动驾驶仪用于暂时替代驾驶员,保持稳定飞机以及使飞机按给定参数(高度、航向等)飞行的装置，主要由直接操作或伺服马达控制机构（通常为替代驾驶员动作的液压马达）以及调整仪表读数和伺服机构动作的自动感应装置（高速陀螺仪）构成。
子目 9018.1310	核磁共振成像成套装置由电磁体、梯度系统、频射发生器以及用于进行数据分析的自动数据处理主机、接口控制器、外部控制器、外部设备、软件等部分组成。其中外部设备包括外部存储设备、成像仪、图像处理器、测量控制系统、操作台等设备，这些设备由应用软件提供数据。软件部分包括操作系统和应用软件。该税目不包括单独进口的零部件。
子目 9021.9011	血管支架由支架和导管输送系统组成。通过导管输送器将支架输送至病变部位，植入支架以达到支撑狭窄闭塞段血管，保持管壁血流通畅的目的。血管支架主要分为冠脉支架、脑血管支架、肾动脉支架、大动脉支架等。支架通常由金属材料、覆膜材料或生物材料制成，部分支架表面涂覆治疗药物。支架按照在血管内展开的方式可分为自展式和球囊扩张式两种。
子目 9022.1920	利用 X 射线的电磁辐射检测物体内部缺陷的装置。X 射线能够使胶片感光或激发某些材料发出荧光，射线在穿透物体过程中按一定的规律衰减，利用衰减程度与射线感光或激发荧光的关系可检查物体内部的缺陷。X 射线是由 X 射线管加高压电激发而成，可以通过所加电压、电流来调节 X 射线的强度。射线穿过材料到达底片，会使底片感光；如果遇到裂缝、洞孔以及气泡和夹渣等缺陷，将会在底片上显示出暗影区来。这种方法能检测出缺陷的大小和形状，还能测定材料的厚度。
子目 9022.2910	利用γ 射线的电磁辐射检测物体内部缺陷的装置。γ 射线是由放射性元素激发，强度不能调节，只随时间呈指数倍减少。不同厚度的物体需要用不同能量的射线来穿透。
子目 9023.0010	用胶头皮、色发等制成的供美容、美发使用的教具。
子目 9024.1010	电子万能试验机适用于各种金属、非金属、复合村料的拉伸（δ su，δ sl，δ 0.2，δ b，E）压缩、弯曲、剪切、剥离撕裂及金属簿板塑性应变比 r 值，拉伸硬化指数 n 值等多项试验,但其主要功能是测金属材料的性能。
子目 9024.1020	硬度是衡量金属材料软硬程度的一项重要的性能指标，是材料弹性、塑性、强度和韧性等力学性能的综合指标。硬度试验根据其测试方法的不同可分为静压法（如布氏硬度、洛氏硬度、维氏硬度等）、划痕法（如莫氏硬度）、回跳法（如肖氏硬度）及里氏硬度（电磁原理，硬度值是冲击回跳速度与冲击速度之比表示）显微硬度、高温硬度等多种方法。利用上述方法测量金属材料硬度的仪器分别称为布氏硬度计、洛氏硬度计、维氏硬度计、里氏硬度计等。

子目 9026.8010	用不同原理和方法测量管道中气体的瞬时流量和累计流量的仪器及装置。
子目 9027.8012	质谱联用仪主要包括色谱质谱联用仪、光谱质谱联用仪、磁质谱联用仪等，质谱联用仪将色谱、光谱、磁场等对混合物出色的分离技术和质谱对单一物质精准的检测分析能力相结合，可以使样品的分离、定性及定量一次完成，其中质谱仪起到主要作用。
子目 9028.3011	单相感应式电度表主要用于居民用电的计量、计费。感应式电度表采用电磁感应的原理把电压、电流、相位转变为磁力矩，推动铝制圆盘转动，圆盘的轴（蜗杆）带动齿轮驱动计度器的鼓轮转动，转动的过程即是时间量累积的过程。感应式电度表有很多种类，它们的基本结构一般都由驱动元件、转动元件、制动元件、机架、轴承、计度器、铭牌、端钮盒、表盖等构成。
子目 9028.3012	三相感应式电度表是主要用于工商业等大用户的用电计量、计费。结构基本原理同上。
子目 9028.3013	电子式（静止式）电能表是采用固态（电子）器件测量电能及相关被测量的电度表。一般由锰铜分流器或电流互感器、电阻分压网络或电压互感器、电能测量芯片、机电计度器或液晶显示器、接口及电源电路等构成。由于运用数字技术，分时记费电度表、预付费电度表、多用户电度表、多功能电度表等。载波电度表利用电力载波技术，用于远程自动集中抄表，属于电子式电度表。
子目 9028.3014	三相电子式(静止式)电度表主要用于电厂、变电站、大用户及电网间的关口计量，是电力系统计量管理的关键设备，结构基本原理同上。
子目 9031.4920	光栅测量装置是利用光栅的光学原理工作的测量装置,主要由标尺光栅、光电读数头和数显表组成,通常标尺光栅固定在机床活动部件上,光栅读数头固定在机床固定部件上,指示光栅装在光栅读数头中。光栅测量装置经常应用于机床和加工中心等方面，可用作直线位移和角位移的检测。
子目 9031.8031	运用超声检测的方法来检测的仪器称之为超声波探伤仪。它的原理是：超声波在被检测材料中传播时,材料的声学特性和内部组织的变化对超声波的传播产生一定的影响，通过对超声波受影响程度和状况的探测了解材料性能和结构变化的技术称为超声检测。超声检测方法通常有穿透法、脉冲反射法、串列法等。
子目 9031.8032	磁粉探伤是检测铁磁性材料表面及近表面缺陷的一种无损检测方法,运用该方法来检测的仪器称之为磁粉探伤仪。磁粉探伤原理是:有表面和近表面缺陷的工件磁化后，当缺陷方向和磁场方向成一定角度时，由于缺陷处的磁导率的变化使磁力线逸出工件表面，产生漏磁场，可以吸附磁粉而产生磁痕显示。
子目 9031.8033	涡流检测法利用的是电磁感应原理,运用该方法来检测的仪器称之为涡流探伤仪。涡流检测法适用于检测导电材料。检测线圈通以交变电流，线圈子内交变电流的流动将在线圈子周围产生一个交变磁场，这种磁场称为“原磁场”。把一导体置于原磁场中时，在导体内将产生感应电流，这种电流叫做涡流。导体中的电特性（如电阻、磁导率等）变化时，将引起涡流的变化。利用涡流的变化检测工件中的不连续性的方法称为涡流检测原理。
子目 9032.8911	主要功能：防止列车相撞，保证列车运行的安全。工作原理：自动检测列车实际运行位置，自动确定列车最大安全运行速度，连续不断地实行速度监督，实现超速防护，自动监测列车运行间隔，以保证实现规定地行车间隔。ATP 是整个 ATC 系统的基础，ATO 和 ATS 子系统都依托于 ATP 子系统的工作。

子目 9032.8912	主要功能保证列车正常的运行和行车调整的优化。作用：代替司机来自动驾驶，包括平滑加速、调速和车站程序定点停车。ATO 辅助 ATP 工作，接受 ATP 的信息，其中有 ATP 速度指令、列车实际速度和列车走行距离。此外还从 ATS 子系统和地面标志线圈接受列车运行等级等信息。根据以上信息，ATO 通过牵引/制动线控制列车，使其维持在一个参考速度上运行，并在设有屏蔽门的站台准确停车。
子目 9307.0010	军用刀是指刺刀、多用途刀具、伞兵刀、飞行员刀等纳入军品出口管理清单的军用刀具。
子目 9506.9111	跑步机是具有单方向运动表面,在该运动面上可进行漫步或跑步,脚可以自由地离开运动表面的训练器械。一般由跑步表面、跑步板、防滑面、紧急停止装置、前把手、侧扶手、前护罩、后滚筒及护罩、脚踏平台以及显示器等组成。

附　　录

Appendix

附录一

关税配额商品税目税率表
Tariff Quota Rate on Imported Goods

序号 No.	货品类别 Article Description	税则号列 Tariff Item	普通税率 General(%)	最惠国税率 M.F.N.(%)	关税配额税率 In Quota Duty Rate(%)	国别关税配额税率 Country-Specific Quota Duty Rate	
						中国—新西兰自贸区(China-New Zealand FTA)(%)	中国—澳大利亚自贸区(China-Australia FTA)(%)
1	小麦 Wheat	10011100	180	65	1		
		10011900	180	65	1		
		10019100	180	65	1		
		10019900	180	65	1		
		11010000	130	65	6		
		11031100	130	65	9		
		11032010	180	65	10		
2	玉米 Corn	10051000	180	20	1		
		10059000	180	65	1		
		11022000	130	40	9		
		11031300	130	65	9		
		11042300	180	65	10		
3	稻谷和大米 Rice, whether or not husked	10061011	180	65	1		
		10061019	180	65	1		
		10061091	180	65	1		
		10061099	180	65	1		
		10062010	180	65	1		
		10062090	180	65	1		
		10063010	180	65	1		
		10063090	180	65	1		
		10064010	180	65	1		
		10064090	180	65	1		
		11029011	130	40	9		
		11029019	130	40	9		
		11031921	70	10	9		
		11031929	70	10	9		
4	糖 Sugar	17011200	125	50	15		
		17011300	125	50	15		
		17011400	125	50	15		
		17019100	125	50	15		
		17019910	125	50	15		
		17019920	125	50	15		
		17019990	125	50	15		
5	羊毛 Wool	51011100	50	38	1	0	0
		51011900	50	38	1	0	0
		51012100	50	38	1	0	0
		51012900	50	38	1	0	0
		51013000	50	38	1	0	0
		51031010	50	38	1	0	0

序号 No.	货品类别 Article Description	税则号列 Tariff Item	普通税率 General(%)	最惠国税率 M.F.N.(%)	关税配额税率 In Quota Duty Rate(%)	国别关税配额税率 Country-Specific Quota Duty Rate	
						中国—新西兰自贸区(China-New Zealand FTA)(%)	中国—澳大利亚自贸区(China-Australia FTA)(%)
6	毛条 Wool tops	51051000	50	38	3	0	
		51052100	50	38	3	0	
		51052900	50	38	3	0	
7	棉花 Cotton	52010000	125	40[①]	1		
		52030000	125	40	1		
8	化肥 Chemical fertilizer	31021000	150	50	4[②]		
		31052000	150	50	4[②]		
		31053000	150	50	4[②]		

[①]对配额外进口的一定数量棉花，适用滑准税形式暂定关税，具体方式如下：

(1) 当进口棉花完税价格高于或等于 15.000 元/千克时，按 0.570 元/千克计征从量税；

(2) 当进口棉花完税价格低于 15.000 元/千克时，暂定从价税率按下式计算：

$Ri=9.337/Pi+2.77\%\times Pi-1$

对上式计算结果四舍五入保留 3 位小数。其中 Ri 为暂定从价税率，当按上式计算值高于 40%时，Ri 取值 40%；Pi 为关税完税价格，单位为元/千克。

[②]暂定税率为 1%。

附录二

进口商品暂定税率表

Interim Duty Rate on Imported Goods

序号 No	EX	税则号列 Tariff Item	货品名称	最惠国税率 (%) M.F.N.	暂定税率 (%) Interim Duty Rate	Article Description
1		01061211	改良种用鲸、海豚和鼠海豚；改良种用海牛及儒艮	10	0	Whales, dolphins and porpoises, for pure- bred breading manatees and dugongs, for pure-bred breeding
2		03033110	冻格陵兰庸鲽鱼	10	5	Frozen Greenland halibut
		03033200	冻鲽鱼，但鱼肝及鱼卵除外	12	2	Frozen plaice, excluding livers and roes
4		03035100	冻鲱鱼，但鱼肝及鱼卵除外	10	2	Frozen herrings, excluding livers and roes
5		03036300	冻鳕鱼，但鱼肝及鱼卵除外	10	2	Frozen cod, excluding livers and roes
6		03038910	冻带鱼	10	5	Frozen scabber fish (trichurius), excluding livers and roes
7		03062190	未冻的其他岩礁虾和其他龙虾	15	10	Not frozen rock lobster and other sea crawfish, nes
8		03062290	未冻的其他螯龙虾	15	10	Unfrozen lobsters other than for cultivation
9	ex	03079190	活、鲜或冷的象拔蚌	14	10	Panopea abrupta,live, fresh or chilled
10		04041000	乳清及改性乳清	6	2	Whey and modified whey
11		05051000	填充用羽毛;羽绒	10	2	Raw feathers for stuffing; down
12		05119111	受精鱼卵	12	0	Fertilized fish eggs
13		08013100	鲜或干的未去壳腰果	20	10	Walnuts in shell
14		08021100	鲜或干的未去壳扁桃仁	24	10	Almonds in shell, fresh or dried
15		08024190	鲜或干的未去壳栗子(板栗除外)	25	20	Other chestnuts in shell, fresh or dried
16		08024290	鲜或干的去壳栗子(板栗除外)	25	20	Other chestnuts, shelled, fresh or dried
17		08025100	鲜或干的未去壳阿月浑子果(开心果)	10	5	Pistachios in shell, fresh or dried
18		08025200	鲜或干的去壳阿月浑子果(开心果)	10	5	Pistachios, shelled, fresh or dried
19		08026190	未去壳非种用马卡达姆坚果（夏威夷果）	24	19	Macadamia nuts, in shell, not for cultivation
20		08026200	去壳马卡达姆坚果（夏威夷果）	24	19	Shelled Macadamia nuts
21		08029020	鲜或干的白果	25	20	Gingko nuts, fresh or dried
22	ex	08029090	碧根果	24	10	Pecan
23		08044000	鲜或干鳄梨	25	10	Avocados, fresh or dried
24		12119036	甘草	6	0	Liquorice roots
25		12122190	其他适合供人食用的海草及藻类	15	2	Other edible seaweeds and algae
26		12122910	马尾藻	15	2	Sargassum

序号 No	EX	税则号列 Tariff Item	货品名称	最惠国税率 (%) M.F.N.	暂定税率 (%) Interim Duty Rate	Article Description
27		12122990	其他海草及藻类	15	2	Other seaweeds and algae
28	ex	12149000	其他紫苜蓿（粗粉及团粒除外）	9	7	Other lucerne (alfalfa), excluding meal and pellets
29	ex	12149000	以除紫苜蓿外的禾本科和豆科为主的多种混合天然饲草	9	4	Mixed non-artificial forage grass majorly composed of poaceae and fabaceae other than lucerne
30		13021200	甘草汁液及浸膏	6	0	Saps and extracts of liquorice
31		15021000	牛羊油脂	8	2	Tallow
32		15029000	其他牛羊脂肪	8	4	Other fats of bovine animals, sheep or goats
33	ex	15119020	固态棕榈硬脂（50 度≤熔点≤56 度）	8	2	Solid palm stearin (melting point no less than 50 centigrade and no more than 56 centigrade)
34		15200000	粗甘油；甘油水及甘油碱液	20	6	Glycerol, crude; glycerol waters and glycerol lyes
35		18010000	整颗或破碎的可可豆，生的或焙炒的	8	2	Cocoa beans, whole or broken, raw or roasted
36		19011010	供婴幼儿食用的零售包装配方奶粉	15	5	Formula milk powder for infant use, put up for retail sale
37		19011090	其他供婴幼儿食用的零售包装食品	15	5	Other preparations for infant use, put up for retail sale
38		19019000	麦精以及细粉、粗粉、粗粒、淀粉或麦精制的其他未列名食品	10	5	Other food preparations of flour, etc.
39		21031000	酱油	28	15	Soya sauce
40	ex	21069090	乳蛋白部分水解配方、乳蛋白深度水解配方、氨基酸配方、无乳糖配方特殊婴幼儿奶粉	20	5	Partial hydrolyzed,extensively hydrolyzed milk protein, amino acid based, and lactose-free inftant formula milk powder
41		22072000	任何浓度的改性乙醇及其他酒精	30	5	Ethyl alcohol & other denatured spirits of any strength
42		22090000	醋及醋酸制得的醋代用品	20	15	Vinegar and substitutes for vinegar obtained from acetic acid
43		23099090	其他配制的动物饲料	6.5	4	Other preparations of a kind used in animal feeding
44	ex	24039100	再造烟草	57	40	Reconstituted tobacco
45		25020000	未焙烧的黄铁矿	3	1	Unroasted iron pyrites
46		25030000	硫磺	3	1	Sulphur
47		25041010	鳞片石墨	3	1	Natural graphite in flakes
48		25051000	硅砂及石英砂，不论是否着色	3	1	Silica sands & quartz sands, whether or not coloured
49		25059000	其他天然砂，不论是否着色	3	1	Natural sands, whether or not coloured
50		25061000	石英	3	1	Quartz

序号 No	EX	税则号列 Tariff Item	货品名称	最惠国税率 (%) M.F.N.	暂定税率 (%) Interim Duty Rate	Article Description
51		25062000	石英岩，不论是否切割成矩形板、块	3	1	Quartzite, wether or not by sawing into blocks or slabs of a rectangular shape
52		25070010	高岭土	3	1	Kaolin
53		25070090	高岭土的类似土	3	1	Other kaolinic clays
54		25083000	耐火粘土,不论是否煅烧	3	1	Fire-clay, whether or not calcined
55		25101010	未碾磨的磷灰石	3	0	Unground apatites
56		25102010	已碾磨的磷灰石	3	0	Ground apatites
57		25151100	原状或粗加修正的大理石	4	0	Marble & travertine crude or roughly trimmed
58		25151200	矩形大理石及石灰华	4	0	Marble & travertine merely cut into a square or rectangular shape
59		25152000	其他石灰质碑用或建筑用石；蜡石，不论是否粗加修整或切割成矩形板块	3	0	Ecaussine and other calcarcous monumental or building stone; alabaster, whether or not roughly trimmed or cut into blocks or slabs of a rectangular (incl. square) shape
60		25161100	原状或粗加修正的花岗石	4	0	Granite, crude or roughly trimmed
61		25161200	矩形或正方形的花岗岩	4	0	Granite, merely cut into blocks or slabs of a rectangular (incl. square) shape
62		25162000	原状或粗加修正的砂岩	3	0	Sandstone, crude or roughly trimmed
63		25169000	其他碑用或建筑用石	3	0	Other monumental or building stones
64		25181000	未煅烧或烧结的白云石	3	0	Dolomite, not calcined or sintered
65		25182000	已煅烧或烧结的白云石	3	0	Dolomite, calcined or sintered
66		25183000	夯混白云石	3	0	Dolomite ramming mix
67		25191000	天然碳酸镁（菱镁矿）	3	1	Natural magnesium carbonate (magnesite)
68		25199010	熔凝镁氧矿（电熔镁，包括喷补料）	3	1	Fused magnesia
69		25199020	烧结镁氧矿（重烧镁，包括喷补料）	3	1	Dead-burned (sintered) magnesia
70		25199030	碱烧镁（轻烧镁）	3	1	Light-burned magnesia
71	ex	25199099	其它氧化镁含量在 70%（含 70%）以上的矿产品	3	1	Other mineral substances,containing MgO 70% or more
72		25251000	原状云母或破开的云母片	5	1	Crude mica and mica rifted into sheets or splittings
73		25261020	未破碎及未研粉的滑石	3	1	Talc, not crushed, not powdered
74		25262020	已破碎或已研粉的其他天然滑石	3	1	Talc, powdered
75		25280010	天然硼砂及其精矿	3	0	Natural sodium borates and concentrates thereof (calcined or not)
76		25280090	天然粗硼酸,含硼酸干重不超过 85%	5	0	Natural sodium borates and concentrates thereof (calcined or not)
77		25291000	长石	3	1	Felspar
78	ex	25309099	天青石	3	1	Celesite

序号 No	EX	税则号列 Tariff Item	货品名称	最惠国税率 (%) M.F.N.	暂定税率 (%) Interim Duty Rate	Article Description
79	ex	25309099	锂辉石矿	3	0	Spodumene
80	ex	25309099	废镁砖	3	1	Waste magnesia brick
81	ex	25309099	未煅烧的水镁石	3	1	Brucite
82	ex	26180010	冶炼钢铁产生的锰渣，含锰量大于25%	4	1	Granulated slag from the manufacture of iron or steel,containing manganese more than 25%
83	ex	26190000	冶炼钢铁产生的熔渣、浮渣、氧化皮及其他废料，五氧化二钒含量大于20%	4	1	Slag, dross scalings and other from manufacture of iron or steel, containing V_2O_5>20%
84	ex	26209990	含其他金属及化合物的矿灰及残渣，五氧化二钒含量大于20%	4	1	Ash and residues containing V_2O_5>20%
85		27040010	煤制焦炭及半焦炭不论是否成型	5	0	Lignite
86		27040090	甑炭	5	0	Agglomerated lignite
87		27050000	煤气、水煤气、炉煤气及类似气体，石油气及其他烃类气除外	5	1	Coal, water, producer gas & similar gases, other than petroleum gases & gaseous hydrocarbons
88		27060000	从煤、褐煤、或泥煤蒸馏所得的焦油及矿物焦油，不论是否脱水或部分蒸馏，包括再造焦油	6	1	Tar distilled from coal, lignite or peat & other mineral tars, whether or not dehydrated or partially distilled, incl. reconstituted tars
89		27073000	粗二甲苯	6	2	Xylole
90	ex	27082000	针状沥青焦	6	3	Needle Pitch coke
91		27101210	车用汽油及航空汽油	5	1	Motor gasoline & aviation gasoline
92		27101220	石脑油	6	0	Naphtha
93	ex	27101291	壬烯(碳九混合异构体含量高于90%)	9	4	Nonene (C9 >90%)
94	ex	27101299	异戊烯同分异构体混合物	9	5	ISOpentene
95		27101911	航空煤油	9	0	Aviation kerosene
96	ex	27101919	正构烷烃(C9～C13)	6	2	n-Alkanes (C9～C13)
97		27101922	5~7 号燃料油	6	1	Fuel oil No.5 to No.7 (National Code)
98		27101923	柴油	6	1	Diesel oil
99	ex	27101929	350 度以下馏出物体积百分比小于20%，550 度以下馏出物体积百分比大于 80%的蜡油	6	0	Paraffin oils: 350°C distillage<20%, 550°C distillage>80%
100		27111200	液化丙烷	5	1	Propane, liquefied
101		27111390	其他液化丁烷	5	1	Liquefied butanes, nes
102		27149010	天然沥青	8	4	Natural bitumen and asphalt
103		28013020	溴	5.5	1	Bromine
104		28020000	升华硫磺、沉淀硫磺、胶态硫磺	5.5	1	Sulphur, sublimed or precipitated; colloidal sulphur
105	ex	28045000	碲	5.5	0	Polysilicon

序号 No	EX	税则号列 Tariff Item	货品名称	最惠国税率 (%) M.F.N.	暂定税率 (%) Interim Duty Rate	Article Description
106		28049090	其他硒	5.5	0	Selenium nes
107		28051200	钙	5.5	1	Calcium
108		28051910	锂	5.5	1	Lithium
109		28051990	其他碱金属及碱土金属	5.5	1	Alkali or alkaline-earth metals (excl. sodium and calcium)
110		28053011	钕	5.5	0	Neodymium
111		28053012	镝	5.5	0	Dysprosium
112		28053013	铽	5.5	0	Terbium
113		28053014	镧	5.5	0	Lanthanum
114		28053015	铈	5.5	0	Cerium
115		28053016	镨	5.5	0	Praseodymium
116		28053017	钇	5.5	0	Yttrium
117		28053019	其他未相互混合或熔合的稀土金属、钪及钇	5.5	0	Rare-earth metals nes, scandium and yttrium, not intermixed or interalloyed
118		28053021	已相互混合或熔合的稀土金属、钪及钇，电池级	5.5	0	Rare-earth metals, scandium and yttrium, intermixed or interalloyed, battery quality
119		28053029	其他已相互混合或熔合的稀土金属、钪及钇	5.5	0	Rare-earth metals, scandium and yttrium, intermixed or interalloyed, other than battery quality
120		28070000	硫酸、发烟硫酸	5.5	1	Sulphuric acid; oleum
121		28121010	氯化亚砜	5.5	2	Sulphoxide chloride
122		28141000	氨	5.5	0	Anhydrous ammonia
123		28142000	氨水	5.5	0	Ammonia in aqueous solution
124		28164000	锶或钡的氧化物、氢氧化物及过氧化物	5.5	2	Oxide, hydroxide and peroxide of strontium or of barium
125		28182000	氧化铝，但人造刚玉除外	8	0	Aluminium oxide, other than artificial corundum
126		28220010	四氧化三钴	5.5	2	Cobalt tetroxide
127		28220090	其他钴的氧化物和氢氧化物	5.5	2	Other Cobalt oxides and hydroxides
128		28254000	镍的氧化物和氢氧化物	5.5	2	Nickel oxides and hydroxides
129		28342110	肥料用硝酸钾	4	1	Nitrates of potassium, use as fertilizer
130	ex	28342990	硝酸钡	5.5	2	Barium nitrate
131		28366000	碳酸钡	5.5	1	Barium carbonate
132		28369100	锂的碳酸盐	5.5	2	Lithium curbonates
133		28369200	锶的碳酸盐	5.5	2	Strontium carbonate
134		28369930	碳酸钴	5.5	2	Cobaltous carbonate
135	ex	28399000	锆的硅酸盐	5.5	2	Ziconium silicate

序号 No	EX	税则号列 Tariff Item	货品名称	最惠国税率 (%) M.F.N.	暂定税率 (%) Interim Duty Rate	Article Description
136		28401100	无水四硼酸钠	5.5	2	Anhydrous disodium tetraborate
137		28401900	其他四硼酸钠	5.5	2	Disodium tetraborate,other than anhydrous
138	ex	28419000	钴酸锂	5.5	2	Lithium cobaltate
139	ex	28419000	铼酸盐	5.5	0	Rhenate
140	ex	28441000	天然铀及其化合物	5.5	0	Nature uranium and its compounds
141	ex	28442000	含铀 235 浓度低于 5%的低浓铀及其化合物	5.5	0	Uranium (including enriched U_{235} less than 5%) and its compounds
142		28461010	氧化铈	5.5	0	Cerium oxide
143		28461020	氢氧化铈	5.5	0	Cerium hydroxide
144		28461030	碳酸铈	5.5	0	Cerium carbonate
145		28461090	铈的其他化合物	5.5	0	Cerium compounds, nes
146		28469011	氧化钇	5.5	0	Yttrium oxide
147		28469012	氧化镧	5.5	0	Lanthanum oxide
148		28469013	氧化钕	5.5	0	Neodymium oxide
149		28469014	氧化铕	5.5	0	Europium oxide
150		28469015	氧化镝	5.5	0	Dysprosium oxide
151		28469016	氧化铽	5.5	0	Terbium oxide
152		28469017	氧化镨	5.5	0	Praseodymium oxide
153		28469019	其他氧化稀土	5.5	0	Other Rare-earth oxides
154		28469021	氯化铽	5.5	0	Other Rare-earth chlorinates,mixed
155		28469022	氯化镝	5.5	0	Terbium chlorinates
156		28469023	氯化镧	5.5	0	Dysprosium chlorinates
157		28469024	氯化钕	5.5	0	Neodymium chlorinates
158		28469025	氯化镨	5.5	0	Praseodymium chlorinates
159		28469026	氯化钇	5.5	0	Yttrium chlorinates
160		28469028	混合氯化稀土	5.5	0	Rare-earth chlorinates other than of cerium, mixed
161		28469029	未混合氯化稀土	5.5	0	Other Rare-earth chlorinates, unmixed
162		28469031	氟化铽	5.5	0	Other Rare-earth fluorides
163		28469032	氟化镝	5.5	0	Dysprosium fluorides
164		28469033	氟化镧	5.5	0	Lanthanum fluorides
165		28469034	氟化钕	5.5	0	Neodymium fluorides
166		28469035	氟化镨	5.5	0	Praseodymium fluorides
167		28469036	氟化钇	5.5	0	Yttrium fluorides
168		28469039	其他氟化稀土	5.5	0	Rare-earth fluorides,nes

序号 No	EX	税则号列 Tariff Item	货 品 名 称	最惠国税率 (%) M.F.N.	暂定税率 (%) Interim Duty Rate	Article Description
169		28469041	碳酸镧	5.5	0	Lanthanum carbonates
170		28469042	碳酸铽	5.5	0	Terbium carbonates
171		28469043	碳酸镝	5.5	0	Dysprosium carbonates
172		28469044	碳酸钕	5.5	0	Neodymium carbonates
173		28469045	碳酸镨	5.5	0	Praseodymium carbonates
174		28469046	碳酸钇	5.5	0	Yttrium carbonates
175		28469048	混合碳酸稀土	5.5	0	Rare-earth carbonates other than of cerium, mixed
176		28469049	未混合碳酸稀土	5.5	0	Rare-earth carbonates other than of cerium, unmixed
177		28469091	镧的其他化合物	5.5	0	Compounds of Lanthanum
178		28469092	钕的其他化合物	5.5	0	Compounds of Neodymium
179		28469093	铽的其他化合物	5.5	0	Compounds of Terbium
180		28469094	镝的其他化合物	5.5	0	Compounds of Dysprosium
181		28469095	镨的其他化合物	5.5	0	Compounds of Praseodymium
182		28469096	钇的其他化合物	5.5	0	Compounds of Yttrium
183		28469099	稀土金属、钇、钪的其他化合物	5.5	0	Other compounds of rare-earth, yttrium or scandium
184		29012100	乙烯	2	1	Ethylene
185		29012200	丙烯	2	1	Propene (propylene)
186		29031500	1,2-二氯乙烷(ISO)	5.5	1	1,2-Dichloroethane (ISO) (ethylene dichloride)
187		29032100	氯乙烯	5.5	1	chloroethylene
188		29051210	正丙醇	5.5	3	Propan-l-ol(propyl alcohol)
189		29053200	1，2—丙二醇	5.5	3	1,2-dihydroxypropare
190	ex	29053990	1，3—丙二醇	5.5	3	1,3-dihydroxypropare
191		29054500	丙三醇（甘油）	14	3	Glycerol
192		29061310	固醇	5.5	3	Sterols, and their halogenated, sulphonated, nitrated or nitrosated derivatives
193		29071211	间甲酚	5.5	3	m-Cresols
194		29071212	邻甲酚	5.5	3	o-Cresols
195		29071910	邻仲丁基酚、邻异丙基酚	4	2	o-Sec-butyl phenol,o-Isopropyl phenol
196		29094100	二甘醇	5.5	3	2,2-Oxydiethanol (diethylene glycol,digol)
197	ex	29121900	乙二醛	5.5	3	Glyoxal(Ethanedial)
198		29155010	丙酸	5.5	3	Propionic acid
199	ex	29209090	碳酸二苯酯	6.5	2	Diphenyl carbonate
200		29211920	异丙胺	6.5	2	Isopropyl amine

序号 No	EX	税则号列 Tariff Item	货品名称	最惠国税率 (%) M.F.N.	暂定税率 (%) Interim Duty Rate	Article Description
201		29224190	赖氨酸盐及其酯	6	5	Lysine esters and salts
202		29224210	谷氨酸	10	5	Glutamic acid
203	ex	29225090	苏氨酸	6.5	5	Threonine
204		29261000	丙烯腈	6.5	3	Acrylonitrile
205	ex	29269090	己二腈	6.5	1	Hexanedinitrile
206		29304000	蛋氨酸	6.5	5	Methionine
207	ex	29339900	阿托伐他汀钙	6.5	4	Atorvatatin calcium
208		30021000	抗血清、其他血份及修饰免疫制品(不论是否通过生物工艺加工制得)	3	0	Antisera & other blood fractions & modified immunological products, whether or not obtained by means of biotechnological processes
209		30022000	人用疫苗	3	0	Vaccines for human medicine
210		30029040	遗传物质和基因修饰生物体	3	0	Genetics material and Gene modified organism
211		30029090	人血；治病、防病或诊断用动物血制品；其他毒素、培养微生物（不包括酵母）及类似产品	3	0	Human blood; animal blood prepared for therapeutic, prophylactic or diagnostic uses; other toxins, cultures of micro-organisms (excl. yeasts) and similar products, nes
212		31031010	重过磷酸钙	4	1	Triple superphosphates
213		31031090	其他过磷酸钙	4	1	Other superphosphates
214		31039000	其他矿物磷肥或化学磷肥	4	1	Mineral or chemical fertilizers, phosphatic, nes
215		31042090	其他氯化钾	3	1	Potassium chloride, nes
216		31043000	硫酸钾	3	1	Potassium sulphate
217		31049010	光卤石、钾盐及其他天然粗钾盐	3	1	Carnallite, sylvite & other crude natural potassium salts
218		31049090	其他矿物钾肥及化学钾肥	3	1	Mineral or chemical fertilizers, potassic, nes
219		31051000	制成片状及类似形状或每包毛重不超过 10 公斤的 31 章各货品	4	1	Goods of Chapter 31 in tables or similar forms or in packages of a gross weight≤10kg
220		31054000	磷酸二氢铵及磷酸二氢铵与磷酸氢二铵的混合物	4	1	Ammonium dihydrogenorthophosphate (monoammonium phosphate) and mixtures thereof with diammonium hydrogenorthophosphate (diammonium phosphate)
221		31055100	含有硝酸盐及磷酸盐的肥料	4	1	Mineral or chemical fertilizers containing nitrates & phosphates
222		31055900	其他含氮、磷两种肥效元素的矿物肥料或化学肥料	4	1	Mineral or chemical fertilizers containing the two fertilizing elements nitrogen & phosphorus, nes
223		31056000	含磷、钾两种元素的肥料	4	1	Mineral or chemical fertilizers with phosphorus & potassium, nes
224		31059000	其他肥料	4	1	Mineral or chemical fertilizers, nes

序号 No	EX	税则号列 Tariff Item	货品名称	最惠国税率 (%) M.F.N.	暂定税率 (%) Interim Duty Rate	Article Description
225	ex	32029000	无铬鞣剂	6.5	3	Tanning agent,with out chromium
226	ex	32082010	分散于或溶于非水介质的光导纤维用涂料（主要成分为聚胺酯丙烯酸酯类化合物）	10	6	Paint for optial fibers (based on polyaminate acrylate resin polymers), dispersed or dissolved in a nonaqueous medium
227	ex	32089010	光导纤维用涂料（主要成分为聚胺酯丙烯酸酯类化合物）	10	6	Paint for optial fibers (based on polyaminate acrylate resin polymers)
228	ex	32100000	光导纤维用涂料	10	6	Paint for optial fibers
229		33012500	其他薄荷油	15	5	Other oils of mints (incl. concretes & absolutes), nes
230	ex	33012999	黄樟油	15	7	Sassafras oil
231		33013010	鸢尾凝脂（香膏类）	20	10	Balsam of irises
232		33043000	指(趾)甲化妆品	15	10	Manicure or pedicure preparations
233	ex	33049900	护肤品	6.5	2	Skin care products
234		33052000	烫发剂	15	10	Preparations for permanent waving or straightening
235		33053000	定型剂	15	10	Hair lacquers
236		34011990	其他用肥皂及有机表面活性产品，条、块状或模制形状的，以及用肥皂或洗涤剂浸渍、涂面或包覆的纸、絮胎、毡呢及无纺织物	15	10	Other soap and organic surface-active products & preparations for use as soap,in bars, cakes , moulded pieces or shapes; paper, wadding , felt & nonwovens, impregnated ,coated or covered with soap or detergent
237		34012000	其他形状的肥皂	15	10	Soap in other forms
238	ex	34029000	十二烷基苯磺酸钙甲醇溶液(十二烷基苯磺酸钙含量应高于 70%)	9	7	Calcium dodecyl benzosulfonate methanol solution (Calcium dodecyl benzosulfonate content>70%)
239		34031100	用于纺织、皮革、毛皮或其他材料油脂处理的制剂	10	8	Preparations for the oil or grease treatment of textile, materials , leathers , furskins or other materials
240		34031900	其他含有石油或从沥青矿物提取的油类	10	8	Lubricating preparations, containing petroleum oils or oils obtained from bituminous minerals
241		34039100	处理纺织材料、皮革、毛皮或其他材料的制剂	10	8	Preparations for the oil or grease treatment of textiles, materials, leathers, furskins or other materials
242	ex	35030010	明胶	12	5	Gelatin
243		35051000	糊精及其他改性淀粉	12	6	Dextrins & other modified starches
244		37011000	X 光片	20	10	Photographic plates & film for X-ray, in the flat, sensitized, unexposed, of any material other than paper, paperboard or textiles
245	ex	37013025	柔性印刷版（厚度小于 3 毫米的）	10	5	Flexographic plate (Thickness<3mm)
246	ex	37019920	石英玻璃基质的未曝光感光硬片	10	5	Photographic plates and film, unexposed, quartz based

序号 No	EX	税则号列 Tariff Item	货品名称	最惠国税率 (%) M.F.N.	暂定税率 (%) Interim Duty Rate	Article Description
247	ex	37024292	红色或红外激光胶片，宽度>80 厘米，长度大于 1000 米	2.4 元/平方米	1.05 元/平方米	Red or infra-red laser film width>80cm, length>1000m
248	ex	37071000	感光乳剂（不含银的）	8	4	Sensitizing emulsions(without silver component)
249		37079020	复印机用化学制剂	10	8	Chemical preparations, unmixed products for photographic uses , for photo-copying machines
250		38011000	人造石墨	6.5	3	Artificial graphite
251		38151200	以贵金属及其化合物为活性物的载体催化剂	6.5	4	Supported catalysts with precious metal or its compounds as the active substances
252		38231200	油酸	16	8	Industrial oleic acid
253	ex	38231900	植物酸性油	16	5	Botanic acid oil
254		38237000	工业用脂肪醇	13	9	Aliphatic alcohols for Industrial uses
255	ex	38249099	高钛渣（二氧化钛质量百分含量大于 70%的）	6.5	0	The Ag electrode paste, dieletric paste, barrier ribs paste phosphor paste used for the plasma display panel production
256	ex	38249099	按重量计氧化锌含量在 50%及以上的混合物	6.5	3	Mixture containing ZnO 50% or more
257	ex	39011000	比重小于 0.94 的聚乙烯（进口 CIF 价高于 3800 美元/吨）	6.5	3	Polyethylene, gravity < 0.94, (import CIF ≥3800usd/t)
258	ex	39012000	比重在 0.94 及以上的聚乙烯（进口 CIF 价高于 3800 美元/吨）	6.5	3	Polyethylene, gravity≥0.94, (import CIF ≥3800usd/t)
259	ex	39021000	电工级初级形状聚丙烯树脂(灰分含量不大于 30ppm)	6.5	3	Electrotechonical polypropylene resin in primary forms (Ash content not more than 30ppm)
260	ex	39069090	丙烯酸钠聚合物	6.5	3	Sodium acrylate polymer
261		39072010	聚四亚甲基醚二醇	6.5	3	Polvtetramethylene Ether Glycol
262	ex	39073000	溴的质量百分含量在 18%及以上或进口 CIF 价格高于 3800 美元/吨的环氧树脂（如溶于溶剂，以纯环氧树脂折算溴的百分含量）	6.5	4	Epoxyresins containing by weight more than 18% Bromine or import CIF>3800usd/t (base on pure epoxyresins if dissolved in solvent)
263		39074000	初级形状的聚碳酸酯	6.5	3	Polycarbonates, in primary forms
264		39077000	初级形状的聚乳酸	6.5	3	Poly (lactic acid)
265	ex	39119000	偏苯三酸酐和异氰酸预缩聚物	6.5	3	Precondensed polymer of modified trihydroxy acetate
266	ex	39119000	芳基酸与芳基胺预缩聚物	6.5	3	Precondensed polymer of modified trihydroxy acetate
267	ex	39119000	改性三羟乙基脲酸酯类预缩聚物	6.5	3	Precondensed polymer of modified trihydroxy acetate
268		39201010	乙烯聚合物制电池隔膜	6.5	3	Battery separator, of polymers of ethylene
269	ex	39209100	聚乙烯醇缩丁醛膜（厚度不超过 3 毫米）	6.5	3	Polyvinyl butyral membrane (Thickness ≤3mm)

序号 No	EX	税则号列 Tariff Item	货品名称	最惠国税率 (%) M.F.N.	暂定税率 (%) Interim Duty Rate	Article Description
270	ex	39209990	聚酰亚胺膜（厚度不超过 0.03 毫米）	6.5	3	Membrane of polyimide(thickness≤0.03mm)
271	ex	39219090	离子交换膜	6.5	5	Ion exchange membrane
272		40011000	天然胶乳	20	10%或900元/吨，两者从低	Natural rubber latex
273		40012100	烟胶片	20	20%或1500元/吨，两者从低	Smoked sheets of natural rubber
274		40012200	技术分类天然橡胶	20	20%或1500元/吨，两者从低	Technically specified natural rubber, in primary forms or in plates, sheets or strip
275	ex	40112000	断面宽度 30 英寸及以上的轮胎	10	8	Tyres, having a fracture surface of a width of 30 inches or more
276	ex	40116100	断面宽度 24 英寸及以上的轮胎	17.5	8	Tyres,having a fracture surface of a width of 24 inches or more
277	ex	40116300	断面宽度 24 英寸及以上的轮胎	17.5	8	Tyres,having a fracture surface of a width of 24 inches or more
278	ex	40116900	断面宽度 30 英寸及以上的轮胎	17.5	8	Tyres, having a fracture surface of a width of 30 inches or more
279	ex	40119400	断面宽度 24 英寸及以上的轮胎	25	8	Tyres,having a fracture surface of a width of 24 inches or more
280	ex	40119900	断面宽度 30 英寸及以上的轮胎	25	8	Tyres, having a fracture surface of a width of 30 inches or more
281		40121300	航空器用翻新轮胎	20	4	Retreaded tyres of rubber, of a kind used on aircraft
282	ex	40169500	液压隔离式蓄能器用胶囊	18	9	Hydraulic pressure-insulation type accumulator bladder
283	ex	40169910	奶衬	8	4	Liner
284	ex	40169990	动车组用胶囊、外风挡板	10	5	Locomotive fording intercar barrier, gangway bellows
285		41041111	全粒面未剖层或粒面剖层蓝湿牛皮	7	3	Chrome-tanned bovine leather (wet blue skin leather), full grain, unsplit, or grain splits, not further prepared
286		41041911	其他蓝湿牛皮	6	3	Wet blue bovine leather, not further prepared, nes
287		41041920	其他湿马皮	7	5	Equine leather, wet state, not further prepared, nes
288		41044100	全粒面未剖层革 粒面剖层革的牛干革（坯革）	5	3	Bovine or equine leather, without hair on, dry state (crust), full grains, unsplit, or grain splits, not further prepared

序号 No	EX	税则号列 Tariff Item	货 品 名 称	最惠国税率 (%) M.F.N.	暂定税率 (%) Interim Duty Rate	Article Description
289		41051010	蓝湿绵羊、羔羊皮	14	10	Wet-blue sheep or lamb skin leather, without wool on, but not further prepared, whether or not split
290	ex	41062100	蓝湿山羊皮	14	10	Goat skin leather, in the wet-blue state, without hair on, but not further prepared, whether or not split
291		41063110	蓝湿猪皮	14	10	Wet-blue swine leather, without hair on, but not further prepared, whether or not split
292		41071210	已鞣粒面剖层整张牛皮革	8	6	Leather further prepared after tanning or crusting, including parchment-dressed leather, of bovine (including buffalo) animals, without hair on, other than leather of heading 41.14, whole hides and skins, grain splits
293		42021110	以皮革、再生皮革作面的衣箱	15	10	Trunks and suitcases with outer surface of leather, of composition leather or of patent leather
294		42021210	以塑料或纺织材料作面的衣箱	20	10	Trunks and suitcases with outer surface of plastics or textile materials
295		42022900	以钢纸或纸板作面的手提包	20	10	Handbags, whether or not with shoulder strap, incl. those without handle, nes (for example, with outer surface of vulcanized fibre or of paperboard)
296		43011000	整张水貂皮，不论是否带头、尾、爪	15	10	Raw furskins of mink, whole, with or without head, tail or paws
297		43016000	整张狐皮，不论是否带头、尾、爪	20	15	Raw furskins of fox, whole, with or without head, tail or paws
298		43031010	毛皮衣服	23	10	Articles of apparel of furskin
299		44089012	温带非针叶木制饰面用单板	3	1	Wood nes veneer sheets, whether or not planed, sanded or finger-jointed, of a thickness not exceeding 6mm, of temperate non-coniferous wood
300	ex	44089019	家具饰面单板	3	1	Veneer sheets for furniture
301	ex	44089029	胶合板用旋切单板	3	1	Peeled sheets for plywood
302		45011000	未经加工或简单加工的天然软木	6	1	Natural cork, raw or simply prepared
303		48022010	照相原纸	7.5	5	Photo paper base
304		48064000	高光泽透明或半透明纸	7.5	5	Glassine and other glazed transparent or translucent papers
305		48070000	成卷或成张的复合纸及纸板，未经表面涂布或未浸渍	7.5	5	Composite paper and paperboard (made by sticking flat layers of paper or paperboard together with an adhesive), not surface- coated or impregnated, whether or not internally reinforced, in rolls or sheets

序号 No	EX	税则号列 Tariff Item	货品名称	最惠国税率 (%) M.F.N.	暂定税率 (%) Interim Duty Rate	Article Description
306		48115110	彩色相纸用双面涂塑纸，每平方米重量超过 150 克	7.5	1	Paper coated on both sides with plastics (excl. adhesives) for color photography, bleached, weighing＞150g/m^2, in rolls or sheets
307	ex	49070090	特许权使用凭证（包括软件升级许可证、软件用户许可证等。但游戏软件升级许可证、游戏软件用户许可证除外）	7.5	0	Certificate of Franchise license inculding software upgrade license, software user license, etc. Excluding game software upgrade license, software user license
308		52101100	与化纤混纺未漂白轻质平纹棉布	12	6	Unbleached plain cotton weave, mixed mainly or solely with man-made fibres, with less than 85% by weight of cotton, weighting ≤200g/m^2
309		52101990	与化纤混纺未漂白轻质其他棉布	12	6	Other unbleached fabrics of cotton, mixed mainly or solely with man-made fibres, with less than 85% by weight of cotton, weighting ≤200g/m^2
310		52111100	与化纤混纺未漂白重质平纹棉布	12	6	Unbleached plain cotton weave, mixed mainly or solely with man-made fibres, with less than 85% by weight of cotton, weighting ＞200g/m^2
311		52111200	化纤混纺未漂白重质三线或四线斜纹棉布	12	6	Unbleached woven fabrics, 3-thread or 4-thread twill, including cross twill, mixed mainly or solely with man-made fibres, with less than 85% by weight of cotton, weighting ＞200g/m^2
312		52122100	未漂白的其他混纺重质棉布	12	6	Other unbleached woven fabrics of cotton, weighting ＞200g/m^2
313		53012100	破开的麻或打成的麻	6	1	Broken or scutched flax
314		53013000	亚麻短纤及废麻	6	1	Flax tow and waste (incl. yarn waste & garnetted stock)
315		53062000	亚麻多股纱线或缆线	10	5	Multiple (folded) or cabled flax yarn
316	ex	56013000	由两种或两种以上有机聚合物纺制的纤维（横截面为皮芯结构或并列结构或海岛结构），长度不超过 5 毫米	10	5	of two or more kinds of polymers (with cross section of skin-core or juxtapose or island structure), length not more than 5mm
317	ex	56039110	乙烯聚合物制电池隔膜基布	10	5	Base cloth for battery separator, of polymers of ethylene
318	ex	56039210	乙烯聚合物制电池隔膜基布	10	5	Base cloth for battery separator, of polymers of ethylene
319	ex	56039310	乙烯聚合物制电池隔膜基布	10	5	Base cloth for battery separator, of polymers of ethylene
320		61019010	毛制针织或钩编男式大衣、防风衣	25	13	Men's or boys' overcoats, etc, of wool or fine animal hair, knitted or crocheted
321		61021000	毛制针织或钩编女式大衣、防风衣	25	13	Woman's or girls' overcoats, etc, of wool or fine animal hair, knitted or crocheted

序号 No	EX	税则号列 Tariff Item	货 品 名 称	最惠国税率 (%) M.F.N.	暂定税率 (%) Interim Duty Rate	Article Description
322		61101200	喀什米尔山羊细毛制针织或钩编套头衫等	14	7	Jerseys, pullovers, etc, of cashmere, knitted or crocheted
323		62011100	毛制男式大衣、斗篷及类似品	16	8	Men's or boys' overcoats, etc, of wool or fine animal hair
324		62011290	棉制男式大衣、斗篷及类似品	16	8	Men's or boys' overcoats, etc, of cotton, nes
325		62021100	毛制女式大衣、斗篷及类似品	16	8	Woman's or girls' overcoats, etc, of wool or fine animal hair
326		62021290	棉制女式大衣、斗篷及类似品	16	8	Woman's or girls' overcoats, etc, of cotton, nes
327		62031100	毛制男式西服套装	17.5	10	Men's or boys' suits of wool or fine animal hair
328		62033100	毛制男式上衣	16	8	Men's or boys' jackets & blazers of wool or fine animal hair
329		62041100	毛制女式西服套装	17.5	10	Women's or girls' suits of wool or fine animal hair
330		62043100	毛制女式上衣	16	8	Women's or girls' jackets & blazers of wool or fine animal hair
331		62141000	丝制披巾、头巾、围巾及类似品	14	8	Shawls, scarves, mufflers, mantillas, veils, etc, of silk/silk waste
332		62142010	羊毛制披巾、领巾、围巾、披纱、面纱及类似品	14	8	Shawls, scarves, mufflers, mantillas, veils, etc, of wool
333		62142020	山羊绒制披巾、领巾、围巾、披纱、面纱及类似品	14	8	Shawls, scarves, mufflers, mantillas, veils, etc, of cashmere
334		63012000	毛制毯子及旅行毯	16	8	Blankets (excl. electric blankets) & travelling rugs, of wool or fine animal hair
335		64029100	其他橡胶、塑料短统靴(过踝)	24	12	Footwear, nes, covering the ankle of rubber or plastics
336		64029910	橡胶制鞋面的其他橡胶、塑料鞋靴	24	12	Footwear, nes, with rubber uppers, not covering the ankle, of rubber or plastics
337		64041100	纺织材料制鞋面的运动鞋靴	24	12	Sports footwear,with rubber or plastic soles & textile uppers
338		64051010	橡胶、塑料、皮革及再生皮革制外底的皮革或再生皮革制面的其他鞋靴	24	12	Footwear, nes, with leather or composition leather uppers and rubber, plastics, leather or composition leather outer soles
339		64051090	其他材料制外底的皮革或再生皮革制面的其他鞋靴	24	12	Footwear, nes, with leather or composition leather uppers and other material outer soles
340		64052000	纺织材料制面的其他鞋靴	22	12	Footwear, nes, with textile uppers
341	ex	68061090	矿物纤维，渣球含量小于 5%	10.5	5	Mineral fiber, of a shot content less than 5%
342		69051000	陶瓷制屋顶瓦	24.5	15	Roofing tiles, ceramic
343		69060000	陶瓷套管、导管、槽管及管子配件	15	10	Ceramic pipes, conduits, guttering & pipe fittings
344		69099000	农业用、运输或盛装货物用陶瓷容器	21	15	Ceramic troughs, tubes etc used in agriculture, ceramic pots etc

序号 No	EX	税则号列 Tariff Item	货品名称	最惠国税率 (%) M.F.N.	暂定税率 (%) Interim Duty Rate	Article Description
345		69111011	骨瓷餐具	12	8	Bone porcelain tableware
346		69111019	其他瓷餐具	12	8	Other tableware of porcelain or china
347		69111021	瓷刀具	15	10	Knife of porcelain or china
348		69111029	其他瓷厨房器具	15	10	Other kitchenware of porcelain or china
349		69120010	陶餐具	15	10	Ceramic tableware
350		69120090	陶制厨房器具	15	10	Ceramic kitchenware and other household or toilet articles nes
351		70023110	光导纤维用波导级石英玻璃管	5	1	Tubes of fused quartz, of waveguide-level, for optical fibre use
352	ex	70023900	光通信用微光组件的玻璃毛细管、定位管（外径小于 3 毫米）	12	3	Micro capillary and galass tube for optical communication (out diameter < 3 mm)
353	ex	70031900	液晶或有机发光二极管（OLED）显示屏用原板玻璃，包括保护屏用含碱玻璃	17.5	3	Bare glass for liquid crystal or organic light emitting diode display,inculding the protective glass containing alkali
354	ex	70049000	光学平板玻璃，厚度 0.7 毫米以下	17.5	9	Optical flat glass, of a thickness less than 0.7mm
355	ex	70052900	液晶或有机发光二极管（OLED）显示屏用原板玻璃，包括保护屏用含碱玻璃	15	3	Float glass, for liquid crystal or organic light emitting diode display,inculding the protective glass containing alkali
356	ex	70060000	液晶玻璃基板,6 代(1850 毫米×1500 毫米）以上，不含 6 代	15	4	Glass parts for liquid crystal display, above the 6 generation (1850mm×1500mm)
357	ex	70060000	液晶玻璃基板,6 代(1850 毫米×1500 毫米）及以下	15	6	Glass parts for liquid crystal display,the 6 generation (1850mm×1500mm) and below
358	ex	70071110	空载重量 25 吨及以上飞机的挡风玻璃	2	1	Windshield for airplane unloaden weight ≥25t
359	ex	70099100	槽式太阳能抛物面反射镜	21	10	Parabolic trough in Solar Energy Generating Systems (SEGS)
360	ex	70112090	显示管玻壳及其零件	10	6	Glass envelopes and parts thereof for display tubes
361		70132200	铅晶质高脚杯	24.5	15	Stemware drinking glasses of lead crystal
362		70133300	其他铅晶质玻璃杯	24.5	15	Other drinking glasses, of lead crystal, other than of glass-ceramics
363		70134100	铅晶质玻璃制餐桌、厨房用器皿	24.5	15	Glassware of a kind used for table kitchen, etc, of lead crystal
364	ex	70140090	带有抗红外和防反射薄膜的滤波玻璃	17.5	9	Wave-filter galss with anti-IR and anti-reflection film
365	ex	70182000	熔融球形二氧化硅微粉，直径小于等于 100μm	20	5.5	Fused spherical SiO_2, diameter not exceeding 100 micron
366		70189000	玻璃假眼；灯工方法制的玻璃塑像及玻璃饰品	20	10	Glass eyes, statuetts and oth ornaments of lamp-workd glass

序号 No	EX	税则号列 Tariff Item	货品名称	最惠国税率 (%) M.F.N.	暂定税率 (%) Interim Duty Rate	Article Description
367	ex	70195200	覆铜板用玻璃纤维长丝平纹布，开纤或每平方米重不超过 180 克	12	10	Glass fiber colth, covered with copper foil, open filament fabric or weighting less than or equal to 180g/m^2
368		70200011	导电玻璃	10.5	7	Conductive glass
369	ex	70200099	石英玻璃，平整度小于等于 1 微米	15	4	Quartz glass, of a flatness less than or equal to 1μm
370		71011011	天然黑珍珠	21	0	Tahitian pearls
371		71011091	天然黑珍珠	21	0	Tahitian pearls
372	ex	71012110	养殖黑珍珠	21	0	Cultured tahitian pearls
373	ex	71012190	养殖黑珍珠	21	0	Cultured tahitian pearls
374	ex	71012210	养殖黑珍珠	21	0	Cultured tahitian pearls
375	ex	71012290	养殖黑珍珠	21	0	Cultured tahitian pearls
376	ex	71049012	蓝宝石衬底（由人造刚玉加工而成，厚度小于 0.5 毫米）	6	1	Sapphire substrate (made of synthetic corundum, with thickness less than 0.5mm)
377	ex	71129220	铂含量在 3%以上的其他含铂或铂化合物的废碎料	6	0	Waste and scrap with plutinum containing by weight more than 3% plutinum
378		71159010	工业或试验室用贵或包金属制品	3	0	Other articles of precious metal, for technical or lab use
379		72024100	铬铁，含碳量>4%	2	0	Ferro-chromium containing by weight more than 4% of carbon
380		72024900	铬铁，含碳量≤4%	2	1	Ferro-chromium, nes
381		72026000	镍铁	2	0	Ferro-nickel
382		72027000	钼铁	2	1	Ferro-molybdenum
383		72028010	钨铁	2	1	Ferro-tungsten
384		72029300	铌铁	2	1	Ferro-niobium
385	ex	72031000	热压铁块	2	0	Hot Briguetted Iron (HBI)
386		72041000	铸铁废碎料	2	0	Waste and scrap, cast iron
387		72043000	镀锡钢铁废碎料	2	0	Waste and scrap, of tinned iron or steel
388		72044100	机械加工中产生的钢铁废料	2	0	Ferrous waste and scrap, of iron or steel, from the mechanical working of metal, nes
389		72091810	厚度小于 0.3 毫米的冷轧卷材，宽大于或等于 600 毫米	6	4	Flat-rolled products of iron or non-alloy steel, in coils, not further worked than cold-rolled, of a width of 600mm or more and a thickness less than 0.3mm
390	ex	72269990	铁镍合金带材（生产集成电路框架用），宽度小于 600 毫米	7	4	Fe-Ni alloy strip (production of the frame for electronic integrated circuits), of a width less than 600mm
391		73239100	餐桌、厨房等家用铸铁制器具	20	10	Table, kitchen and other household articles and parts thereof, of cast iron, not enamelled

序号 No	EX	税则号列 Tariff Item	货 品 名 称	最惠国税率 (%) M.F.N.	暂定税率 (%) Interim Duty Rate	Article Description
392		73239200	餐桌、厨房等家用铸铁制搪瓷器	20	10	Table, kitchen and other household articles and parts, of cast iron, enamelled
393		73239420	钢铁制搪瓷烧锅	20	10	Casserole of iron or steel, enamelled
394		73241000	不锈钢制洗涤槽及脸盆	18	10	Sinks and wash basins, stainless steel
395		73242900	其他钢铁制浴缸	30	15	Other iron baths
396		73249000	其他钢铁制卫生器具及零件	25	15	Sanitary ware & parts thereof, of iron or steel nes, for example bedpans, douche cans
397	ex	74010000	铜锍	2	0	Copper mattes
398		74020000	未精炼铜、电解精炼用铜阳极	2	0	Unrefined copper, copper anodes for electrolytic refining
399		74031111	精炼铜阴极，按重量计铜含量超过99.9935%的	2	0	Unrefined copper cathodes containing by weight more than 99.9935% of copper
400		74031119	其他精炼铜阴极	2	0	Other unrefined copper cathodes
401		74031190	精炼铜阴极型材	2	0	Unrefined copper sections of cathodes
402		74031200	精炼铜线锭	2	0	Unrefined copper wire-bars
403		74031300	精炼铜坯段	2	0	Unrefined copper billets
404		74031900	其他未锻轧精炼铜	2	0	Other unrefined copper
405		74040000	铜废碎料	1.5	0	Copper waste and scrap
406	ex	74081900	其他含氧量小于5PPM的精炼铜丝	4	2	Other refined copper wire, containing oxygen not more than 5PPM
407	ex	74111019	其他含氧量小于5PPM，外径不超过25毫米的精炼铜管	4	2	Other refined copper tubes and pipes with the external diameter not exceeding 25mm, containing oxygen not more than 5PPM
408		74181090	餐桌厨房等家用铜制器具及其零件	18	10	Table kitchen or other household articles and parts thereof, of copper
409		74182000	铜制卫生器具及其零件	18	10	Sanitary ware & parts thereof of Cu
410		75011000	镍锍	3	0	Nickel matte
411		75012010	镍湿法冶炼中间品	3	0	Nickel intermediate products obtained by hydrometallurgical processing
412		75012090	其他冶炼镍时所得的中间品	3	0	Ni oxide sinters & other intermediate products of Ni metallurgy
413		75021010	按重量计镍、钴总量在99.99%及以上的，但钴含量不超过0.005%的非合金镍	3	1	Nickel, contain more than 99.99% Nickel and Cobalt, and Cobalt less than 0.005% by weight
414		75021090	其他非合金镍	3	1	Other unwrought nickel
415		75030000	镍废碎料	1.5	1	Nickel waste and scrap
416		76011090	电解铝	5	0	Al unwrought, not alloyed, nes
417		76020000	铝废碎料	1.5	0	Aluminium waste and scrap

序号 No	EX	税则号列 Tariff Item	货品名称	最惠国税率 (%) M.F.N.	暂定税率 (%) Interim Duty Rate	Article Description
418		76061129	厚度在 0.3 毫米及以上,但不超过 0.36 毫米的其他非合金铝制矩形板、片、带	6	4	Aluminium plates, of a thickness of 0.3mm or more but not exceeding 0.36mm
419	ex	76071900	化成箔	6	3	Formed Al foil
420		76151090	餐桌厨房等家用铝制器具及其零件	15	10	Table kitchen or other household articles and parts thereof, of aluminium
421		79011110	按重量计含锌量在 99.995%及以上的未锻轧锌	3	1	Unerought zinc, not alloyed, containing by weight 99.995% or more of zinc
422		79011190	含锌量不小于 99.99％，并小于 99.995％的未锻轧锌	3	1	Unerought zinc, not alloyed, containing by weight 99.99% or more and less than 99.995% of zinc
423		79011200	含锌量＜99.99%的未锻轧锌	3	1	Unerought zinc, not alloyed, containing by weight less than 99.99% of zinc
424		79012000	未锻轧锌合金	3	1	Unwrought zinc alloys
425		79020000	锌废碎料	1.5	1	Zinc waste and scrap
426		81019700	钨废碎料	3	1	Tungsten waste and scrap
427		81033000	钽废碎料	6	0	Tantalum waste and scrap
428		81052010	钴湿法冶炼中间品	4	0	Cobalt intermediate products obtained by hydrometallurgical processing
429	ex	81052090	钴锍及其他冶炼钴时所得的中间产品	4	0	Cobalt mattes and other inter-mediate products of cobalt metallurgy
430	ex	81060010	未锻轧铋	3	1	Unwrought bismuth
431		81089031	厚度≤0.8 毫米钛板、片、带、箔	8	4	Titanium plates, sheets, strip, foil, of a thickness not more than 0.8mm
432		81089032	厚度＞0.8 毫米钛板、片、带、箔	8	4	Titanium plates, sheets, strip, foil, of a thickness more than 0.8mm
433		81101010	未锻轧锑	3	1	Unwrought antimony
434	ex	81129220	未锻轧、废碎料或粉末状的钒氮合金	3	0	Vanadic-nitrogen; unwroght, waste and scrape, powder
435		81129240	未锻轧铌；铌废碎料；铌粉末	3	1	Niobium; unwrought, waste and scrap, powders
436	ex	81129920	其他钒氮合金	3	0	Other vanadic-nitrogen
437	ex	82073000	加工小轿车车身冲压件用的4种关键模具（侧围外板模具、翼子板模具、拼接整体侧围内板模具、拼焊整体侧围加强板模具）	8	6	Four key dies, used for processing stamping parts of car body (side outer panels dies , fender dies, dies for joining the whole side inner panels, dies for joining and welding the whole side-panel reinforcement)
438	ex	82073000	加工小轿车车身冲压件用的4种特种模具（σb≥980 牛顿/平方毫米的冷冲压模具、热成型模具、内高压成型模具和铝板模具）	8	6	Four special dies, used for processing stamping parts of car body (cold stamping dies with σb≥980N/mm^2, hot forming dies, inside high pressure forming dies and aluminium panel dies)

序号 No	EX	税则号列 Tariff Item	货 品 名 称	最惠国税率 (%) M.F.N.	暂定税率 (%) Interim Duty Rate	Article Description
439		82111000	以刀为主的成套货品	18	10	Sets of assorted knives
440		82119100	刃面固定的餐刀	18	10	Table knives having fixed blades
441		82119300	可换刃面刀	18	10	Knives having other than fixed blades
442		82159900	其他非成套的厨房或餐桌用具	18	10	Other kitchen or tableware articles not in sets (not plated with precious metal)
443	ex	84041010	使用（可再生）生物质燃料的非水管蒸汽锅炉的辅助设备	7	5	Auxiliary plants of non-water pipe stearm boiler using renewable biomass fuel
444		84041020	税目 84.03 所列锅炉的辅助设备	10	5	Auxiliary plant for use with boilers of heading 8403
445		84042000	水蒸汽或其他蒸汽动力装置的冷凝器	14	5	condensers for steam or other vapour power units.
446		84049010	集中供暖热水锅炉辅助设备的零件	10	5	Parts of auxiliary plant for central boiler
447	ex	84049090	使用（可再生）生物质燃料的非水管蒸汽锅炉的辅助设备的零件；水蒸汽或其他蒸汽动力装置的冷凝器的零件	7	5	Parts of auxiliary plants of non-water pipe stearm boiler using renewable biomass fuel.Parts of condensers for steam or other vapour power units
448	ex	84079090	叉车用汽油发动机（800r/min≤转速≤3400r/min）	18	9	Petrol engines for forklift trucks (800r/min ≤rotational speed≤3400r/min)
449	ex	84079090	立式输出轴汽油发动机	18	9	Petrol engines with a vertical crankshaft
450	ex	84082010	输出功率在 441 千瓦（600 马力）及以上的柴油发动机	9	4	Diesel engines with an output power of 441KW (600HP) or more
451	ex	84082090	升功率≥50 千瓦的轿车用柴油发动机	25	20	Diesel engines for cars, power density ≥50KW
452	ex	84099999	电控柴油喷射装置及其零件	8.4	5	Electronic diesel oil injection devices and parts
453	ex	84118100	涡轮轴航空发动机	15	1	Turbo shaft engines for aircraft
454	ex	84119910	涡轮轴航空发动机用零件	5	1	Parts of turbo shaft engines for aircraft
455	ex	84122990	抓桩器（抱桩器）	14	7	Skirt Pile Grippers Assembly
456	ex	84123100	三坐标测量机用平衡气缸	14	7	Cylinder balance for coordinate measuring machine of three dimensions
457	ex	84129090	风力发动机零件	8	5	Parts thereof wind turbines.
458		84131100	分装燃料或润滑油的泵	10	6	Pumps for dispersing fuel or lubricants used in fillng-stations or in garage
459		84131900	其他装有或可装计量装置的泵	10	6	Pumps fitted or designed to be fitted with a measuring device
460		84135010	气动式往复式排液泵	10	6	Pneumatic reciprocating positive displacement pumps
461		84135020	电动式往复式排液泵	10	6	Electric reciprocating positive displacement pumps
462		84135031	液压式往复式柱塞泵	10	6	Plunger pump

序号 No	EX	税则号列 Tariff Item	货品名称	最惠国税率 (%) M.F.N.	暂定税率 (%) Interim Duty Rate	Article Description
463		84135039	液压式往复式排液泵	10	6	Hydraulic reciprocating positive displacement pumps
464		84135090	其他往复式排液泵	10	6	Other reciprocating positive displacement pumps
465		84136021	电动式齿轮回转泵	10	6	Electric gear rotary pump
466	ex	84136022	回转式液压油泵，输入转速＞2000r/min，输入功率＞190KW，最大流量＞2×280 L/min	10	3	Rotating hydraulic oil pump,input rotating speed＞2000r/min, input power＞190KW, maximum flow＞2×280 L/min
467	ex	84136022	其他液压式齿轮回转泵	10	6	Other hydraulic gear rotating pump
468		84136029	其他齿轮回转泵	10	6	Other gear rotary pump
469		84136031	电动式叶片回转泵	10	6	Electric vane rotary pump
470		84136032	液压式叶片回转泵	10	6	Hydraulic vane rotary pump
471		84136039	其他叶片回转泵	10	6	Other vane rotary pump
472		84136040	螺杆回转泵	10	6	Screw rotary pump
473		84136050	径向柱塞泵	10	6	Radial plunger pump
474		84136060	轴向柱塞泵	10	6	Axial plunger pump
475		84136090	其他回转式排液泵	10	8	Other rotary positive displacement pumps
476		84137091	电动潜油泵及潜水电泵	10	8	Submersible oil pump and submersible pump
477		84139200	液体提升机用零件	6	4	Parts of liquid elevators
478		84141000	真空泵	8	5	Vacuum pumps
479		84146010	抽油烟机	10	6	Range hoods
480	ex	84148030	乘用车机械增压器	7	5	Mechanical superchargers for Passenger cars
481		84149011	用于制冷设备的压缩机进、排气阀片	8	5	Air inlet on discharge valve plates for compressoors for refrigerating equipment
482		84149019	其他用于制冷设备的压缩机零件	8	5	Other parts of compressors for refrigerating equipment
483		84149020	风机、风扇、通风罩及循环气罩零件	12	6	Parts of machines of ventilators, fan,ventilating or recycling hoods
484		84149090	税号 84.14 其他所列机器零件	7	4	Parts of of machines of other subheadings of 84.14
485		84152000	机动车辆上供人使用的空气调节器	20	10	Air conditioning machines used for persons in motor vehicles
486		84158120	制冷量＞4 千大卡/时热泵式空调器	20	12	Air-conditioner, with refrigerating unit of a refrigerating effect＞4000 Kcal/h and a valve for reversal of cooling/heat cycle
487		84158220	制冷量＞4 千大卡/时的其他空调器	20	12	Other air-conditioner, with refrigerating unit of a refrigerating effect＞4000 Kcal/h
488		84159010	制冷量≤4 千大卡/时等空调的零件	10	6	Parts of air conditners with rerefrigerating unit of a refrigerating effect≤4000 Kcal/h

序号 No	EX	税则号列 Tariff Item	货品名称	最惠国税率 (%) M.F.N.	暂定税率 (%) Interim Duty Rate	Article Description
489		84159090	制冷量＞4 千大卡/时等空调的零件	10	6	Parts of air conditioners with refrigerating unit of a refrigerating effect>4000 Kcal/h
490	ex	84162011	溴化锂空调用天然气燃烧机	10.5	5	Natural gas burners for lithium bromide air conditioners
491	ex	84162090	溴化锂空调用复式燃烧机	10.5	5	Combination burners for lithium bromide air conditioners
492		84178050	垃圾焚烧炉	10	5	Municipal Waste Incinerator
493	ex	84179090	垃圾焚烧炉和放射性废物焚烧炉的零件	7	5	Parts of Municipal Waste Incinerator,parts of incinerators for radioactive waste
494		84189910	制冷机组及热泵用零件	10	6	Parts of refrigerating units and heat pumps
495		84189991	制冷温度≤-40℃冷冻设备零件	9.5	6	Parts of freezing equipment of refrigeration temperature≤-40℃
496		84189992	制冷温度＞-40℃，容积＞500L 冷藏设备零件	10	6	Parts of refrigerating or freezing equip of refrigeration temperature ＞-40℃, capacity ＞500L
497		84189999	税号 84.18 其他制冷设备用零件	10	6	Parts of other refrigerating or freezing equipment of subheading 84.18
498		84191910	太阳能热水器	35	5	Solar water heater
499	ex	84193990	生产奶粉用干燥器	9	4	Dryers for producing powdered milk
500	ex	84193990	污泥干燥机	9	5	Sludge driers
501	ex	84196090	通过冷凝分离和去除污染物的气体液化设备	10	5	Machinery of liquefying air or other gases for separation and removal of pollutants through condensation.
502		84198100	加工热饮料、烹调、加热食品的机器	10	6	Machinery for making hot drinks or for cooking or heating food, non domestic
503	ex	84201000	织物轧光机	8.4	6	Woven fabrics calender
504		84211910	脱水机	10	6	Dehydrators
505		84212110	家用型过滤或净化水的机器及装置	25	5	Filtering or purifying machines for water, household type
506	ex	84212199	船舶压载水处理设备用过滤器	5	2	Filters for ship ballast water treatment apparatus
507	ex	84212199	喷灌设备用叠式净水过滤器	5	1	Stackable, filtering or purifying machines for irrigation equipment
508		84213910	家用型气体过滤、净化机器及装置	15	5	Filtering or purifying machines for gases , household type
509	ex	84213930	摩托车发动机排气过滤及净化装置	5	3	Filtering or purifying machines for motorcycle engine
510		84219910	家用型过滤、净化装置用零件	10	5	Filtering or purifying machines for water, household type
511		84221100	家用型洗碟机	10	6	Dish washing machines of the home type

序号 No	EX	税则号列 Tariff Item	货 品 名 称	最惠国税率 (%) M.F.N.	暂定税率 (%) Interim Duty Rate	Article Description
512	ex	84223010	乳品加工用自动化灌装设备	12	10	Automatic bottling or canning equipment for producing dairy
513	ex	84223030	全自动无菌灌装生产线用包装机,加工速度≥20000 只/小时	10	6	Packing machines of automatic aseptic filling producion line, processing output ≥20000 package/hour
514	ex	84223090	全自动无菌灌装生产线用贴吸管机,加工速度≥22000 只/小时	10	6	Straw applicators of automatic aseptic filling prodution line, processing output ≥22000 package/hour
515		84229010	洗碟机用零件	10.5	6	Parts of dish washing machines
516	ex	84281010	无障碍升降机	8	4	Lift facilities for the disabled
517		84312090	叉车及装有升降或搬运装置的工作车用其他零件	6	3	Parts suitable for Fork-lift trucks; other works trucks fitted with lifting or handling equipment.
518	ex	84313100	无障碍升降机的零件	3	1	Parts, for Lift facilities for the disabled
519	ex	84335100	功率≥160 马力的联合收割机	8	5	Combine harvester-threshers, power not less than 160HP
520	ex	84335300	功率≥160 马力的土豆、甜菜收获机	8	4	Potato or sugar beet harvestors , power no less than 160 HP
521	ex	84335910	功率≥160 马力的甘蔗收获机	8	4	Sugarcane harvestors, power no less than 160 HP
522		84335920	棉花采摘机	8	5	Cotton pickers
523	ex	84335990	茶叶采摘机	8	4	Tea pickers
524	ex	84335990	自走式青储饲料收获机	8	5	Mobile silage harvesters
525		84342000	乳品加工机器	6	2	Dairy machinery
526	ex	84368000	自走式饲料搅拌投喂车	10	5	Self waking type feed mixing and feeding vehicles
527	ex	84368000	青储饲料切割上料机	10	3	Feeder of silage harvesters
528	ex	84419010	切纸机用弧形辊	8	4	Curved metal spreader roll of cutting machines
529	ex	84419010	切纸机用横切刀单元	8	3	Crosscut knife units of cutting machines
530	ex	84423021	凹版式计算机直接制版设备	9	3	Intaglio Equipments for preparing computer-to-plate plates
531	ex	84423021	除凹版式以外的其他计算机直接制版设备(CTP)	9	5	Computer-to-plate equipments excluding intaglio ones
532	ex	84424000	计算机直接制版机器用零件	7	1	Parts of computer-to-plate equipments
533	ex	84431313	四色平张纸胶印机，对开单张纸单面印刷速度≥17000 张/小时；对开单张纸双面印刷速度≥13000 张/小时；全张或超全张单张纸单面印刷速度≥13000 张/小时	10	7	Four-color sheet-fed offset press,Folio size, maximum out-put of single-sided printing ≥17000 iph；Folio size, maximum out-put of perfect (double-sided) printing ≥13000 iph；Full size or super large format, maximum out-put of single-sided printing ≥13000iph

序号 No	EX	税则号列 Tariff Item	货品名称	最惠国税率 (%) M.F.N.	暂定税率 (%) Interim Duty Rate	Article Description
534	ex	84431319	五色及以上平张纸胶印机，对开单张纸单面印刷速度≥17000 张/小时；对开单张纸双面印刷速度≥13000 张/小时；全张或超全张单张纸单面印刷速度≥13000 张/小时	10	7	Five-color and more sheet-fed offset printing machines, Folio size, maximum out-put of single-sided printing≥17000 iph; Folio size, maximum out-put of perfect (double-sided) printing≥13000 iph; Full size or super large format, maximum out-put of single-sided printing≥13000iph
535	ex	84431600	苯胺印刷机（柔性版印刷机），线速度≥350 米/分钟，幅宽≥800 毫米	10	3	Flexographic printing machines, press line speed≥350m/min, web width≥800mm
536	ex	84431600	具有烫印或全息或丝网印刷功能单元的机组式柔性版印刷机,线速度≥160 米/分钟，250 毫米≤幅宽<800 毫米	10	5	Multi-functional narrow-web flexographic printing machine with module of stamping or holographic or screen printing，line speed ≥160m/min, 250mm≤web width< 800mm
537	ex	84431700	凹版印刷机,印刷速度≥350 米/分钟	18	9	Gravure printing machinery, printing speed≥350m/min
538	ex	84431921	纺织用圆网印花机	10	6	Cylinder screen woven fabric printing range
539	ex	84431922	纺织用平网印花机	10	6	Flate screen woven fabric printing range
540		84433110	静电感光式多功能一体机	10	3	Electrostatic photo type multifunctional machines
541		84433221	可与网络或自动数据处理设备连接的喷墨印刷机	8	5	Ink-jet printing machines, capable of connecting to an automatic data processing machine or to a network
542		84433222	可与网络或自动数据处理设备连接的静电照相印刷设备（激光印刷机）	8	5	Electrostatic photographic printing machines (laser printing machines), capable of connecting to an automatic data processing machine or to a network
543	ex	84439111	卷筒料自动给料机，给料线速度≥12 米/秒	12	4	Automatic splicer of web offset press, splicing speed ≥12m/s
544		84439119	其他传统印刷机用辅助机器	12	6	Other general accessory machines
545	ex	84439190	胶印机用墨量遥控装置（包括墨色控制装置、墨量调节装置、墨斗体等组成部分）	6	1	Ink remote control unit for offset printing machinery (including ink coclor control unit and ink adjust device and inking pot)
546	ex	84439190	传统印刷机用零件及附件(胶印机用墨量遥控装置除外)	6	3	Parts and accessories of printing machinery (with the exception of ink remote control unit)
547	ex	84439929	压电式喷墨头	6	3	Piezoelectric inkjet print head
548	ex	84451190	宽幅非织造布梳理机,工作幅宽＞3.5 米，工作速度＞120 米/分钟	10	6	Nonwoven carding machines,working width＞3.5m, working speed＞120m/min
549	ex	84452031	全自动转杯纺纱机	10	5	Automatic rotor spinning machines
550		84463050	喷气织机	8	3	Air jet looms
551	ex	84481100	多臂机或提花机　转速指标：500 转/分以上	8	4	Dobbies or Jacquards, rotational speed >500r/min
552		84483920	电子清纱器	6	3	Electronic yarn cleaner

序号 No	EX	税则号列 Tariff Item	货品名称	最惠国税率 (%) M.F.N.	暂定税率 (%) Interim Duty Rate	Article Description
553		84483930	空气捻接器	6	3	Air twisting devices
554		84483990	税号 84.45 所列机器用的其他零附件	6	3	Other parts or accessories of machines of 84.45 or of their auxiliary machinery
555		84484920	引纬、送经装置	6	3	Weft insertion and let-off motions
556		84484990	织机及其辅助机器用其他零附件	6	3	Other parts and accessories of weaving mches or of their auxiliary machinery
557		84485900	税号 84.47 机器用的其他零附件	6	3	Other parts and accessories of machns of 84.47 or of their auxiliary machinery
558	ex	84490010	高速针刺机，针刺频率＞2000 次/分钟	8	6	High speed needle punching machine, punching frequecny＞2000bis/min
559	ex	84490020	高速宽幅水刺设备，工作幅宽＞3.5 米，工作速度＞250 米/分钟，水刺压力≥400 帕	8	6	High speed width spunlace equipment, working width ＞ 3.5m, workding speed ＞ 250m/min, spunlace pressure≥400Pa
560		84509090	干衣量＞10kg 的洗衣机零件	16	5	Parts of washing machines, dry linen capacity>10kg
561	ex	84518000	柔软整理机	12	10	Supple finishing machine
562	ex	84518000	磨毛机、丝光机	12	10	Napping grinder, mercerizing range
563	ex	84518000	定型机	12	10	Boarding machine
564	ex	84518000	涂层机	12	8	Coating machine
565	ex	84518000	罐蒸机、精炼机	12	10	Potting steamer, refining machine
566	ex	84518000	剪绒、洗缩联合机	12	10	Pile shearing and shrinking combine
567	ex	84518000	预缩机	12	10	Sanforizer
568	ex	84518000	服装液氨整理机	12	10	Dress aqua ammoniae finishing range
569	ex	84518000	服装定型焙烘炉	12	10	Dress shaping cabinet
570	ex	84518000	剪毛联合机	12	10	Sheepshearing combination machine
571		84689000	焊接机器用零件	7	3	Welding machinery parts
572		84734010	自动柜员机出钞器和循环出钞器	10.5	5	Banknote dispenser and cycling banknote dispenser of automated teller
573	ex	84734090	钞票清分机零附件	10.5	3	Parts of banknote processing system
574		84789000	烟草加工及制作机器的零件	10	5	Parts of machinery for preparing or making up tobacco
575		84794000	绳或缆的制造机器	7	5	Rope or cable-making machines
576	ex	84798200	用于废物和废水处理的混合、搅拌、轧碎、研磨、筛选、均化或乳化机器	7	5	Devices for waste and wastewater mixing, stirring, crushing, grinding, screeing, homogenising and emulsifying devices
577	ex	84811000	喷灌设备用减压阀	5	2	Pressure reducing valves for sprinkler equipment
578		84818040	其他阀门	7	5	Other valves

序号 No	EX	税则号列 Tariff Item	货 品 名 称	最惠国税率 (%) M.F.N.	暂定税率 (%) Interim Duty Rate	Article Description
579		84819010	阀门用零件	8	4	Parts of valves
580		84823000	鼓形滚子轴承	8	6	Bearings, spherical roller
581		84824000	滚针轴承	8	6	Bearings, needle roller
582	ex	84825000	三环、二环偏心滚动轴承	8	4	Eccentric 3-ring or 2-ring roller bearing
583		84829100	滚珠、滚针及滚柱	8	6	Balls, needles and rollers for bearings
584		84829900	滚动轴承的其他零件	6	3	Other parts of bearings
585		84833000	未装滚珠或滚子轴承的轴承座；滑动轴承	6	4	Bearing housings,not incorporating ball or roller bearing; plain shaft bearing
586	ex	84836000	压力机用组合式湿式离合/制动器,离合扭距为 60KNM~300KNM,制动扭距为 30KNM~100KNM	8	4	Hydraulic actuated clutch/brake, for press machinery, 60KNM≤clutch torque≤300KNM, 30KNM≤braking torque ≤100KNM
587	ex	84839000	车用凸轮轴相位调节器	8	4	Camshaft phase adjuster for vehicle
588		84841000	金属片密封垫或类似接合衬垫	8	5	Gaskets of metal sheeting combined with other material
589		84842000	机械密封件	8	5	Mechnical seals
590		84849000	其他材料制密封垫及类似接合衬垫	8	5	Gasket sets consisting of gaskets of different materials
591		84863041	制造平板显示器用超声波清洗装置	10	5	Cleaning apparatus opparatus operated by ultrasonic process, for the manufacture of flat panel displays
592	ex	84864022	全自动铝丝焊接机	8	6	Automatic aluminum wire bonders
593	ex	84864022	全自动铜丝焊接机	8	6	Automatic copper wire bonders
594	ex	84864022	全自动金丝焊接机	8	6	Automatic gold wire bonders
595	ex	85011091	激光视盘机机芯精密微型电机（1 瓦≤功率≤18 瓦，20 毫米≤直径≤30 毫米）	9	5	Minitype precise motor for mechanism of laser disc player (1W≤power≤18W, 20mm ≤diameter≤30mm)
596	ex	85011091	摄像机、摄录一体机用精密微型电机(0.5 瓦≤功率≤10 瓦，20 毫米≤直径≤39 毫米)	9	5	Minitype precise motor for mechanism of video cameras or camera recorders (0.5W≤power≤10W, 20mm≤diameter ≤39mm)
597	ex	85011099	功率不大于 0.5 瓦(圆柱型:直径不大于 6 毫米,高不大于 25 毫米;扁圆型:直径不大于 15 毫米,厚不大于 5 毫米)非用于激光视盘机机芯的微型电机	9	5	Micromotors with a cylindrical housing diameter not exceeding 6mm and height not exceeding 25mm or a oblatecylindrical housing diameter not exceeding 15mm and thickness not exceeding 5mm (power≤0.5W), excluding minitype motor for mechanism of laser disc player
598	ex	85011099	激光视盘机机芯用精密微型电机(0.5 瓦≤功率≤2 瓦，5 毫米≤直径<20 毫米)	9	5	Minitype precise motor for mechanism of laser disc player (0.5W≤power≤2W, 5mm≤diameter <20mm)

序号 No	EX	税则号列 Tariff Item	货品名称	最惠国税率 (%) M.F.N.	暂定税率 (%) Interim Duty Rate	Article Description
599	ex	85011099	摄像机、摄录一体机用精密微型电机(0.5 瓦≤功率≤10 瓦，5 毫米≤直径＜20 毫米或 39 毫米＜直径≤40 毫米）	9	5	Minitype precise motor for mechanism of video cameras or camera recorders (0.5W≤power≤10W, 5mm≤diameter<20mm or 39mm<diameter≤40mm)
600	ex	85015300	高速(200km/h 及以上)电力机车的交流异步牵引电动机	12	3	AC asyncronous traction motor for high speed electric locomotive（speed≥200km/h）
601	ex	85016410	由使用可再生燃料锅炉和涡轮机组驱动的交流发电机，750 千伏安＜输出功率≤350 兆伏安	10	5	AC generators of an output exceeding 750 KVA but not exceeding 350MVA, used in conjunction with boiler and turbines to generate electricity from renewable fuels
602	ex	85016420	由使用可再生燃料锅炉和涡轮机组驱动的交流发电机，350 兆伏安＜输出功率≤665 兆伏安	5.8	5	AC generators of an output exceeding 350 MVA but not exceeding 665MVA, used in conjunction with boiler and turbines to generate electricity from renewable fuels
603	ex	85016430	由使用可再生燃料锅炉和涡轮机组驱动的交流发电机，输出功率＞665MVA	6	5	AC generators of an output exceeding 665 MVA, used in conjunction with boiler and turbines to generate electricity from renewable fuels
604		85023100	风力驱动的发电机组	8	5	Wind-powered electric generating sets
605	ex	85023900	依靠可再生能源(太阳能、小水电、潮汐、沼气、地热能、生物质/余热驱动的汽轮机）生产电力的发电机组	10	5	Electric generating sets by using renewable energy (e.g. solar power, Small hydro,Wave power, biogas, geothermal, and gas turbines for biomass plants and for waste heat applications)
606		85030030	风力发电设备的零件	3	1	Parts of windmill generating sets
607	ex	85030090	由使用可再生燃料锅炉和涡轮机组驱动的输出功率超过 750 千伏安的交流发电机的零件；依靠可再生能源（太阳能、小水电、潮汐、沼气、地热能、生物质/余热驱动的汽轮机）生产电力的发电机组的零件	8	5	Parts of AC generators of an output exceeding 750 KVA, used in conjunction with boiler and turbines to generate electricity from renewable fuels;Parts of electric generating sets by using renewable energy (e.g. solar power, Small hydro,Wave power, biogas, geothermal, and gas turbines for biomass plants and for waste heat applications)
608		85044014	功率小于 1 千瓦,稳压系数低于万分之一的直流稳压电源(税号 84.71 所列机器用除外)	7	3	DC voltage-stabilized suppliers of a power of less than 1KW and an accuracy of not better than 0.0001 (excluding those used for the machines of heading No.84.71)
609	ex	85044030	纯电动或混合动力汽车用逆变器模块，功率密度≥8 千瓦/升	10	6	Inverter module for electric vehicles or hybrid electric vehicles,power density≥8000W/L
610		85044091	具有变流功能的半导体模块	10	3	Semiconductor modules with converting function
611	ex	85044099	高速(200 千米/时及以上)电力机车的牵引变流器	10	3	Traction converter for high speed electric locomotive（speed ≥200km/h）
612	ex	85044099	汽车冲压线用压力机变频调速装置	10	5	Frequency conversion speed regulation set for punch press machine for manufacture automobiles

序号 No	EX	税则号列 Tariff Item	货品名称	最惠国税率 (%) M.F.N.	暂定税率 (%) Interim Duty Rate	Article Description
613	ex	85044099	纯电动汽车或混合动力汽车用电机控制器	10	4	Motor controller for blade electric vehicles or hybrid electric vehicles
614	ex	85044099	纯电动汽车或插电式混合动力汽车用车载充电机	10	6	On-board charger for blade electric vehicles or plug-in hybrid electric vehicles
615	ex	85049090	用于将可再生能源发电机组输出的直流电转换成交流电的逆变器的零件	8	5	Parts of the static converters which are used to convert DC current from renewable energy generating sets into conventional AC electricity
616	ex	85076000	纯电动汽车或插电式混合动力汽车用锂离子蓄电池单体，容量≥10安时，比能量≥110 瓦时/千克	12	8	Lithium ion accumulators cell for blade electric vehicles or plug-in hybrid electric vehicles,capacity≥10Ah and energy density≥110Wh/kg
617	ex	85076000	纯电动汽车或插电式混合动力汽车用锂离子蓄电池系统（包含蓄电池模块、容器、盖、冷却系统、管理系统等），比能量≥80 瓦时/千克	12	10	Lithium ion accumulators system for blade electric vehicles or plug-in hybrid electric vehicles,energy density≥80Wh/kg
618	ex	85079010	铅酸蓄电池电极（仅保留电极）	10	5	Electrodes of lead-acid accumulators (only including Electrodes)
619		85079090	其他蓄电池(铅酸蓄电池除外)用零件	8	5	Parts of other electric accumulators, nes
620		85094010	水果或蔬菜榨汁机	10	6	Fruit or vegetable juice extractors
621		85094090	食品研磨机及搅拌器	10	6	Other domestic food grinders and mixers; fruit or veg juice extractors
622		85098090	其他家用电动器具	30	15	Other electro-mechanical domestic appliances
623		85099000	家用电动器具用零件	12	6	Parts of electro-mechanical domestic appliances with electric motor
624		85101000	电动剃须刀	30	15	Shavers, with self-contained electric motor
625		85109000	税号 85.10 所列货品的零件	24.5	12	Parts of headings No. 85.10
626	ex	85144000	焊缝中频退火装置	10	7	Intermediate frequency annealing device for weld
627	ex	85152120	汽车生产线电阻焊接机器人	10	5	Resistance welding robots, used for automobile production line
628	ex	85158010	汽车生产线激光焊接机器人	10	5	Laser welding robots, used for automobile production line
629		85159000	电气等焊接机器及装置零件	6	3	Parts of electric machine for weld/cut metal
630		85164000	电熨斗	35	17	Electric smoothing irons
631		85165000	微波炉	15	8	Microwave ovens
632		85166030	电饭锅	15	8	Electric cookers
633		85166050	电烤箱	15	8	Electric oven
634		85166090	其他电热炉	15	10	Other electric ovens
635		85167110	滴液式咖啡机	32	16	Drip coffee makers

序号 No	EX	税则号列 Tariff Item	货 品 名 称	最惠国税率 (%) M.F.N.	暂定税率 (%) Interim Duty Rate	Article Description
636		85167120	蒸馏渗滤式咖啡机	32	16	Steam espresso makers
637		85167130	泵压式咖啡机	32	16	Pump espresso makers
638		85167190	其他电热咖啡壶或茶壶	32	16	Other electric-thermic coffee or tea makers
639		85167990	其他电热器具	32	16	Other electro-thermic appliances
640		85169090	税号 85.16 所列货品的其他零件	12	8	Parts of ofther apparatus of heading No. 85.16
641	ex	85181000	传声器(麦克风)及其座架(列入ITA 的电讯用麦克风除外)	10	6	Microphones and stands therefor (not inculding microphones for telecom-communicaiton use within ITA)
642		85182100	单喇叭音箱	10	6	Single loudspeakers, mounted in the same enclosure
643		85182200	多喇叭音箱	10	6	Multiple loudspeakers, mounted in the same enclosure
644		85198131	闪速存储器型声音录放机	20	12	Flash memory recorders incorporating sound reproducing apparatus
645		85198139	使用半导体媒体的其他声音录放装置	20	12	Other sound recording or reproducing apparatus, using semiconductor media
646		85198990	其他声音录制或重放设备	20	12	Other sound recording or reproducing apparatus
647		85211011	磁带型广播级录像机	完税价格不超过 2000 美元/台：30%；完税价格高于 2000 美元/台：3%+3283 元/台	完税价格不超过 5000 美元/台：15%；完税价格高于 5000 美元/台：3%+3648 元/台	Magnetic video tape recorders,broadcast quality
648	ex	85219090	光盘型广播级录像机	20	完税价格不超过 7000 美元/台：15%；完税价格高于 7000 美元/台：5%+4256 元/台	CD-type video recorder,broadcast quality
649	ex	85219091	光盘型广播级录像机	21	完税价格不超过 7000 美元/台：15%；完税价格高于 7000 美元/台：5%+4257 元/台	CD-type video recorder,broadcast quality
650		85229039	其他视频信号录制或重放设备的零件	30	15	Other parts / accessories of video recording or reproducing apparatus
651		85229099	声音录制或重放设备用其他零件	20	10	Other parts/accessories for sound recorder or playback equipment

序号 No	EX	税则号列 Tariff Item	货品名称	最惠国税率 (%) M.F.N.	暂定税率 (%) Interim Duty Rate	Article Description
652		85232928	重放声音或图像信息的磁带	10	6	Tapes for reproducing sound or image
653		85234910	仅用于重放声音信息的已录制光盘	10	6	Recorded optical media, for reproducing sound only
654	ex	85258013	手机用摄像组件（由镜头+CCD/CMOS+数字信号处理电路三部分构成）	完税价格不超过 5000 美元/台：35%;完税价格高于 5000 美元/台：3%+9728 元/台	4	Camera subassembly used for mobile telephone made up of lens, CCD/CMOS sensor and digital signal processing circuit, not broadcast quality
655	ex	85258013	高清摄像头（必须满足以下三个条件：（1）镜头元件必须使用 5 层及以上玻璃镜头;（2）使用 USB2.0 及以上高速接口；（3）硬件传感器像素达到 130 万及以上）	完税价格不超过 5000 美元/台：35%;完税价格高于 5000 美元/台：3%+9728 元/台	10	High definition video cameras (must satisfy the 3 points below: (1)lens unit must use 5 and more lenses; (2)using connectors not less than USB2.0; (3)the pixels of imager must be over 1.3 million)
656	ex	85261090	飞机机载雷达（包括气象雷达、地形雷达和空中交通管制应答系统）	5	1	Airborne radars（including aero- radars，terrain-following radars and air-traffic-control-interrogator-responder systems）
657	ex	85261090	雷达生命探测仪	5	2	Radar life detectors
658	ex	85285910	专用于车载导航仪的液晶监视器	30	15	Liquid crystal display monitors for use solely with car navigation instruments
659	ex	85299042	电视摄像机、摄录一体机、数码相机用取像模块	12	3	Camera modules for television cameras, video camera recorders, digital cameras
660	ex	85299042	手机、平板电脑用取像模块	12	4	Camera modules for mobile telephones and tablet computers
661		85299049	摄像机、摄录一体机、数码相机的其他零件	12	2	Parts for video cameras or camera recorders or digital cameras
662		85299060	无线电收音机及其组合机用零件	15	7	Parts for radio broacast receivers and their combinations
663		85299081	彩色电视机零件(等离子组件及其零件、有机发光二极管显示屏除外)	15	6	Parts for colour TV receivers (with the exception of Plasma display modules and parts)
664		85299082	等离子显像组件及其零件（含滤光片）	15	5	Plasma display modules and parts thereof（including filter glass）
665		85299083	彩色电视机的有机发光二极管显示屏	15	5	Oled panel for colour television receivers
666	ex	85318010	音量不超过 110dB 的小型蜂鸣器	15	7.5	Minitype electric buzzers, maximum volume not exceeding110dB
667	ex	85371011	机床用可编程序控制器（PLC）	5	3	Programmable logic controllers (PLC) for machine tools

序号 No	EX	税则号列 Tariff Item	货品名称	最惠国税率 (%) M.F.N.	暂定税率 (%) Interim Duty Rate	Article Description
668	ex	85371019	机床用数控单元（包括单独进口的CNC 操作单元）	5	3	Numerical control equipment for machine tools (including CNC unit imported separately)
669	ex	85371090	电梯用控制柜及控制柜专用印刷电路板	8.4	4	Control cabinets for elevator and printed circuits solely used for control cabinets
670	ex	85393240	彩色投影机的照明光源	8	3	Illumiation light source of colour projectors
671		85409190	其他阴极射线管零件	8	4	Other parts of cathode-ray tubes
672		85441100	铜制绕组电线	10	6	Insulated winding wire of copper
673	ex	85443020	车辆用电控柴油机的线束	10	5	Wiring harness of electric diesel engines used for vehicles
674	ex	85446090	额定电压为500千伏及以上的气体绝缘金属封闭输电线	21	10	Gas insulated metal enclosed transmission line,for a voltage of 500KV or more
675	ex	85462090	输变电架空线路用长棒形瓷绝缘子瓷件(单支长度为 1~2 米,实芯)	12	3	Long solid rod ceramic insulator body for power overhead transmission and converting lines (each rod is 1~2 meters in length)
676	ex	85489000	电磁干扰滤波器	12	3	Electromagnetic interference filters
677	ex	85489000	非电磁干扰滤波器	12	6	Non electromagnetic interference filters
678	ex	87019011	功率大于 150 马力的轮式拖拉机	8	5	Wheeled tractors with power more than 150H.P.
679	ex	87019019	功率大于 150 马力的其他拖拉机	8	5	Other tractors with power more than 150H.P.
680	ex	87042300	装有驾驶室的固井水泥车、压裂车、混砂车、连续油管车、液氮泵车用底盘（车辆总重量>35 吨，装驾驶室）	15	10	Chassis (incoraporating cabs) of cementing unit trucks, fractruring unit trucks ,coil unit trucks,liquid nitrogen trucks,and mixing sand trucks (G.V.W exceeding 35t)
681	ex	87042300	起重 55 吨及以上的汽车起重机用底盘	15	8	Chassis (incoraporating cabs) of crane lorries, eifting capacity≥55t
682	ex	87042300	车辆总重量≥31 吨清障车专用底盘	15	10	Special chassis for the wrecker of G.V.W ≥31t
683	ex	87059099	跑道除冰车	12	10	Runway deicing trucks
684	ex	87083099	纯电动或混合动力汽车用电动制动器(由制动器电子控制单元、踏板行程模拟器、制动执行器等组成）	10	5	Electrically operated brake for electric vehicle or hybrid electric vehicles(composed of Electronic control unit,Pedal travel simulator,Brake actuator etc.)
685	ex	87084030	扭矩>1500Nm 非公路自卸车用变速箱	6	3	Gear boxes of dumpers designed for off-highway use, torque＞1500Nm
686	ex	87084091	小轿车用自动换档变速箱及其零件（6 档及 6 档以上）	10	6.5	Automatic transmission and parts thereof for saloon cars (6-speed and above)
687	ex	87085072	轴荷≥10t 的中后驱动桥的零件	10	8	Parts of middle and rear drive-axles, axle capacity≥10t
688	ex	87089420	30 座及以上客车用转向器的零件	10	8	Parts of steering boxes of buses with 30 seats of more
689	ex	87089450	总重≥14 吨柴油型货车转向器的零件	10	8	Parts of steering boxes for diesel trucks of G.V.W≥14t

序号 No	EX	税则号列 Tariff Item	货 品 名 称	最惠国税率 (%) M.F.N.	暂定税率 (%) Interim Duty Rate	Article Description
690	ex	87089490	采用电动转向系统的转向盘、转向柱及转向器及其零件	10	8	Steering wheels, steering columns, steering gears with electric powder steering and their parts
691		87089939	非公路用自卸车未列名零部件	6	3	Not specified parts of dumpers designed for off-highway use
692	ex	87089999	混合动力汽车动力传动装置（由发电机、电动机和动力分配装置等组成）及其零件	10	6	Hybird vehicle transimission unit, composed of generator, motor, power delivery unit,including parts
693	ex	87141000	星型轮及碟刹件	30	10	Planetary gears and Plate brake
694		89080000	供拆卸的船舶及其他浮动结构体	3	1	Vessels and other floating structures for breaking up
695	ex	90012000	液晶投影仪用偏光板	8	6	Polarizing Plate or sheet for liquid-crystal projectors
696	ex	90012000	数字电影放映机用偏光板	8	6	Polarizing plates or sheets for digital cinema projector
697		90013000	隐形眼镜片	10	6	Contact lenses
698		90014010	玻璃制变色镜片	20	15	Photochromic spectacle lenses of glass
699		90015010	非玻璃制变色镜片	20	15	Photochromic spectacle lenses of other materials
700		90015099	非玻璃材料制其他眼镜片	20	12	Spectacle lenses of other materials, not photochromic
701	ex	90019090	非涅耳透镜投影屏（屏幕对角线≥80 英寸，投射比≤0.26，增益比≥0.8，镜头间距≤100 微米）	8	6	Fresnel lens porojection screen (the length of diagonal screen≥80 inch,Projection ratio≤0.26,ratio of gains ≥0.8,lens spacing ≤100 microns)
702	ex	90019090	光通信用微光组件的光学元件（包括工作波长为 800nm～1700nm 的薄膜滤光片、自聚焦透镜、法拉第旋转片）	8	1	Micro-optic component for optical communication (including thin film filter, gradient index lens and faraday Rotator, with working wavelength between 800nm and 1700nm)
703	ex	90019090	激光视盘机激光收发装置用的微型镜片	8	3	Mini lens use for with laser transmitting and receving device of laser disc player
704	ex	90019090	液晶显示屏背光模组的光学元件(包括导光板、反射板、扩散片、增亮片)	8	2	Optical elements for backlight module of liquid crystal display (including light guide, reflect sheet, diffuser,prism sheet to enhance brightness)
705	ex	90019090	液晶投影仪用偏光元件	8	6	Polarizer for liquid-crystal projectors
706	ex	90019090	数字电影放映机用偏光元件	8	6	Polarizer for digital cinema projector
707		90021131	单反相机的镜头	15	3	Lens of digital single lens reflex camera
708		90021139	普通相机(单反相机除外)的镜头	15	3	Lens of digital camera (exception to digital single lens reflex camera)
709	ex	90021190	彩色投影机和数字光处理器的镜头及镜头组件	15	3	Lens and lens assembly of colour projectors or digital light proceesors

序号 No	EX	税则号列 Tariff Item	货品名称	最惠国税率 (%) M.F.N.	暂定税率 (%) Interim Duty Rate	Article Description
710	ex	90021990	摄像机、摄录一体机的镜头	15	3	Lens for video cameras or camcorders
711	ex	90021990	手机、平板电脑用物镜（800 万像素及以上）	15	6	Objective lens for mobile telephones and tablet computers (pixels≥8 million)
712	ex	90029010	照相机用带屈光度调节装置的目镜	15	10	Eyepieces with diopter adjustment devices for cameras
713	ex	90029090	其他带屈光度调节装置的目镜	15	10	Other eyepieces with diopter adjustment devices
714	ex	90029090	掩膜版	15	10	Photo masks
715		90031100	塑料制眼镜架	18	12	Frames and mountings for spectacles, goggles or the like, of plastic
716		90031910	金属材料制眼镜架	10	6	Frames and mountings of metal materials
717		90039000	眼镜架零件	10	6	Parts for frames and mountings for spectacles, goggles or the like
718		90041000	太阳镜	20	6	Sunglasses
719		90049090	其他眼镜	20	12	Other spectacles, goggles
720	ex	90066100	照相手机用闪光灯组件	18	4	Flashlight modules for mobile telephones with camera function
721	ex	90066100	照相机外置式电子闪光灯(闪光指数 GN≥30,具有无线闪光功能,支持自动变焦)	18	15	External flashlights for cameras (Flash guide number≥30, with wireless flash and automatic focusing function)
722		90069191	照相机自动调焦组件	10	6	Automatic focal setting units of photo cameras
723		90069192	其他照相机的快门组件	10	6	Shutter units of photo cameras
724		90069199	其他照相机的其他零附件	10	6	Parts and accessories nes of other photo cameras
725	ex	90072010	2K 及以上分辨率的硬盘式数字电影放映机	14	8	Digital cinematographs with magnetic discs, resolving power≥2k
726		90079100	电影摄影机用零附件	8.4	5	Parts and accessories for cinematographic cameras
727		90079200	电影放映机用零附件	8.4	5	Parts and accessories for cinematographic projectors
728	ex	90118000	高倍测量显微镜，放大倍数≥1000 倍，分辨率≤0.08 微米	7	3	high power microscope , enlargment ratio≥1000, resolution ration≤0.08mm
729	ex	90132000	用于 2.5GB/s 及以上 SDH、波分复用光传输设备的 980 纳米、1480 纳米的泵浦激光器	6	3	980nm or 1480nm pump laster of SDH≥2.5GB/s, for optical transmission equipment for wave divison mulitiplexing
730	ex	90132000	激光切割机用气体激光发生器,切割功率≥2 千瓦	6	3	Gas laser oscillators for laser cutting machines, cutting powr≥2KW
731	ex	90132000	用于 2.5GB/s 及以上光通信设备的 850 纳米、1260~1625 纳米，且功率≤200 毫瓦的激光器（泵浦激光器除外）	6	3	850nm or 1260~1625nm laster of SDH≥2.5GB/s, for optical transmission equipment(excluding pump laster)

序号 No	EX	税则号列 Tariff Item	货品名称	最惠国税率 (%) M.F.N.	暂定税率 (%) Interim Duty Rate	Article Description
732	ex	90139090	太阳能定日镜的零件	8	5	Parts of solar heliostats
733		90142010	自动驾驶仪	2	1	Automatic pilot
734	ex	90142090	航空惯性导航仪	2	1	Aviation inetial navigator
735		90149010	自动驾驶仪的零件、附件	1.5	1	Parts/accessories for automatic pilot
736		90200000	其他呼吸器具及防毒面具	8	4	Other breathing applicances and gas masks
737		90215000	心脏起搏器，不包括零件、附件	4	2	Pacemakers for stimulating heart muscles, excluding parts and accessories
738		90219011	血管支架	4	2	Intravascular stents
739		90219019	其他支架	4	2	Other stents
740	ex	90219090	人工耳蜗植入装置	4	0	Artificial cochlear implant appliances
741	ex	90229090	射线发生器的零部件	6	1	Parts of ray generators
742	ex	90251990	红外线人体测温仪	8.4	4	Body temperature measuring apparatus by infrared ray
743	ex	90259000	红外线测温仪传感器元件	8	3	Sensors of infrared temperature measuring apparatus
744		90271000	气体或烟雾分析仪	7	5	Gas or smoke analysis apparatus
745		90314910	轮廓投影仪	10	5	Profile projectors
746		90318033	涡流探伤仪	5	3	Inspection instrument for eddy current testing
747	ex	90318090	音频生命探测仪	5	2	Audio life detectors
748	ex	90318090	音视频生命探测仪	5	2	Audio and video life detectors
749	ex	90318090	跑道摩擦系数测试仪	5	3	Runway friction coefficient tester
750	ex	90328990	电喷点火程序控制单元	5	3	Program controlling units for electric ignition
751	ex	90328990	机床用成套数控伺服装置（包括CNC 操作单元，带有配套的伺服放大器和伺服电机）	7	3	Numerical control servomechanism for machine tools (including CNC unit, with servo amplifier and servomotor)
752	ex	90328990	印刷机用成套数控伺服传动装置（包括运动控制器或可编程序自动控制器、人机界面单元，带有配套的伺服驱动器和伺服电机）	7	3	Complete set of CNC servo devices used for printers (including PAC and HMI units, servo drivers and sero motoers)
753	ex	90328990	三坐标测量机用自动控制柜	7	3	Automatic controller for coordinate measuring machine of three dimensions
754	ex	90328990	纯电动或混合动力汽车用电机控制器总成	7	4	Motor controller assembly for blade electric vehicles or hybrid electric vehicles
755	ex	90328990	飞机自动驾驶系统（包括自动驾驶、电子控制飞行、自动故障分析、警告系统配平系统及推力监控设备及其相关仪表）	7	1	Parts of automatic pilotting systems for aircraft (including automatic pilotting, electronic flight contral, automatic failure analysis, warning systems, trimming systems, thrust monitoring equipments and the meters thereof)
756	ex	90328990	具有可再生能源和智能电网应用的自动电压和电流调节器；非液压或气压的自动调控流量、液位和湿度的仪器	7	5	Automatic voltage and current regulators which have renewable energy and smart grid applications;process control instruments and apparatus for flow, level and humidity , excluding hydraulic or pneumatic

序号 No	EX	税则号列 Tariff Item	货品名称	最惠国税率 (%) M.F.N.	暂定税率 (%) Interim Duty Rate	Article Description
757	ex	90329000	飞机自动驾驶系统（包括自动驾驶、电子控制飞行、自动故障分析、警告系统配平系统及推力监控设备及其相关仪表）的零件	5	1	Parts of automatic pilotting systems for aircraft (including automatic pilotting, electronic flight contral, automatic failure analysis, warning systems, trimming systems, thrust monitoring equipments and the meters therof)
758	ex	90330000	用于 90 章下列环境产品，包括太阳能定日镜、其他测量海洋、水文、气象或地球物理用仪器及设备，测量、检验液体流量或液位的仪器，测量、检验压力的仪器及装置，90.26 其他税号未列名的液体或气体测量仪器及装置，气体或烟雾分析仪，色谱仪和电泳仪，使用光学射线（紫外线、可见光、红外线）的分光仪、分光光度计及摄谱仪以及其他理化分析仪器及装置，用于测量、记录、分析和评估环境样品或对环境的影响的理化分析仪器及装置，检镜切片机，轮廓投影仪，光栅测量装置，其他光学测量或检验仪器和器具，测振仪，手振动仪，具有可再生能源和智能电网应用的自动电压和电流调节器，自动调控流量、液位和湿度的仪器,且在其他税目未列名的零附件	6	5	Parts of the Chapter 90 following environment products, including solar heliostats,other surveying oceanographic, hydrological, meteorological or geophysical instruments and appliances, instruments for measuring or checking the flow or level of liquids, instruments/apparatus for measuring or checking pressure,other Instruments/Apparatus for measuring or checking variables of liquids and gases of heading 9026, nesoi, gas or smoke analysis apparatus,chromatographs and electrophoresis instruments, spectrometers, spectrophotometers and spectrographs and other instruments and apparatus for physical and chemical analysis using optical radiations (ultraviolet, visible, infrared), instruments and apparatus for physical or chemical analysis used to measure, record, analyse and assess environmental samples or environmental influences, microtomes, profile projectors, optical Grating Measuring insruments, other optical measuring and checking instruments and appliances, vibrometers, hand vibration meters, automatic voltage and current regulators which have renewable energy and smart grid applications; process control instruments and apparatus for flow, level and humidity, not elsewhere specified
759		91081100	已组装的机械指示式完整电子表芯	16	10	Electric atch movements, assembled, with mechnical display
760	ex	92012000	完税价格 50000 美元及以上的大钢琴	17.5	1	Grand pianos, the duty-paying value≥50000USD
761	ex	92021000	完税价格 15000 美元及以上的弓弦乐器	17.5	1	Played with a bow, the duty-paying value≥15000USD
762	ex	92051000	完税价格 2000 美元及以上的铜管乐器	17.5	1	Brass-wind instruments, the duty- paying value≥2000USD
763	ex	92059090	完税价格 10000 美元及以上的其他管乐器	17.5	1	Other wind musical instruments, the duty-paying value≥10000USD
764		92071000	通过电产生或扩大声音的键盘乐器	30	15	Electric keyboard instruments other than accordions
765		92099400	税号 92.07 所列乐器的零附件	17.5	10	Parts & accessories for musical instruments of heading 92.07

序号 No	EX	税则号列 Tariff Item	货品名称	最惠国税率 (%) M.F.N.	暂定税率 (%) Interim Duty Rate	Article Description
766		94041000	弹簧床垫	20	10	Mattress supports
767		94042100	海绵橡胶或泡沫塑料制褥垫	20	10	Mattresses of cellular rubber or plastics
768		94042900	其他材料制褥垫	20	10	Mattresses fitted with springs or stuffed with any material
769		94043010	羽毛或羽绒填充的睡袋	20	10	Sleeping bags, feather or down stuffed
770		94043090	其他睡袋	20	10	Other sleeping bags, nes
771		94049010	羽绒或羽毛填充的寝具及类似品	20	10	Articles of bedding/furnishing nes, feather or down stuffed
772		94049020	兽毛填充的寝具及类似品	20	10	Articles of bedding/furnishing nes, animal hair stuffed
773		94049030	丝棉填充的寝具及类似品	20	10	Articles of bedding/furnishing nes, silk wadding stuffed
774		94049040	化纤棉填充的寝具及类似品	20	10	Articles of bedding/furnishing nes, man-made fibre stuffed
775		94049090	其他材料制的寝具及类似品	20	10	Articles of bedding/furnishing nes, stuffed, nes
776		95064090	其他乒乓球运动用品及器械	14	7	Articles & equipment for table-tennis, excl balls
777		95066210	篮球、足球、排球	12	6	Basketballs, footballs and volleyballs
778		95069111	跑步机	12	6	Treadmill
779		95069119	其他健身及康复器械	12	6	Gymnasium or recovered equipment
780		95069120	滑板	12	6	Skateboards
781		95069190	一般的体育活动、体操或竞技用品	12	6	General physica exercise / gymnastics/ athlctics articl/equipment
782		96032100	牙刷，包括齿板刷	25	10	Tooth brushes, including dental-plate brushes
783	ex	96170019	真空保温杯	24	12	Vacuum keep-warm cup
784		96190010	尿裤及尿布	7.5	2	Diapers and napkins
785		97011019	油画、粉画及其他手绘画原件	12	6	Original paintings, drawings and pastels
786		97020000	雕版画、印制画、石印画的原本	12	6	Original engravings, prints and lithographs
787		97030000	各种材料制的雕塑品原件	12	6	Original sculptures and statuary, in any material

附录三

进口商品从量税、复合税税目税率表
Specific and Compound Duty Rate on Imported Goods

序号 No.	税则号列 Tariff Item	货品名称	普通税率 Gen.	最惠国税率 M.F.N.	Article Description
1	02071200	冻的整只鸡	5.6 元/千克	1.3 元/千克	Frozen whole chickens, not cut in pieces
2	02071411	冻的带骨鸡块（包括鸡胸脯、鸡大腿等）	4.2 元/千克	0.6 元/千克	Frozen chicken cuts, breasts, legs, with bone in
3	02071419	冻的不带骨鸡块（包括鸡胸脯、鸡大腿等）	9.5 元/千克	0.7 元/千克	Frozen boneless chicken cuts, breasts, legs
4	02071421	冻的鸡翼（不包括翼尖）	8.1 元/千克	0.8 元/千克	Frozen wing of chicken (other than wingtips)
5	02071422	冻的鸡爪	3.2 元/千克	1 元/千克	Frozen claw of chicken
6	02071429	冻的其他鸡杂碎（包括鸡翼尖、鸡肝等）	3.2 元/千克	0.5 元/千克	Frozen offal of chicken, nes
7	05040021	冷、冻的鸡肫（即鸡胃）	7.7 元/千克	1.3 元/千克	Cold, frozen broiler gizzard
8	22030000	麦芽酿造的啤酒	7.5 元/升	0	Beer made from malt
9	27090000	石油原油（包括从沥青矿物提取的原油）	85 元/吨	0	Petroleum oils & oils obtained from bituminous minerals, crude
10	37023190	其他未曝光无齿孔彩色窄胶卷（窄胶卷指宽度≤105毫米，彩色摄影用）	433 元/平方米	56 元/平方米	Other photographic film rolls, unexposed, without perforations, for colour photography, of any material other than paper, paperboard or textiles, width≤105mm
11	37023220	照相制版涂卤化银液无齿孔窄胶卷（成卷未曝光感光胶片， 窄胶卷指宽度≤105 毫米）	104 元/平方米	4.5 元/平方米	Photographic film rolls, unexposed, without perforations, with silver halide emulsion, for preparing printing plates or cylinders, of any material other than paper, paperboard or textiles, width≤105mm
12	37023290	其他涂卤化银乳液无齿孔窄胶卷（成卷未曝光感光胶片，窄胶卷指宽度≤105毫米）	202 元/平方米	21 元/平方米	Photographic film rolls, unexposed, without perforations, with silver halide emulsion, of any material other than paper, paperboard or textiles, width≤105mm, nes
13	37023920	照相制版用其他无齿孔窄感光胶卷（成卷未曝光感光胶片，窄胶卷指宽度≤105 毫米）	104 元/平方米	12 元/平方米	Photographic film rolls, unexposed, without perforations and silver halide emulsion, of any material other than paper, paperboard or textiles, width ≤ 105mm, for preparing printing plates or cylinders
14	37023990	其他用无齿孔窄感光胶卷（成卷未曝光感光胶片，窄胶卷指宽度≤105 毫米）	202 元/平方米	24 元/平方米	Photographic film rolls, unexposed, without perforations and silver halide emulsion, of any material other than paper, paperboard or textiles, width≤105mm, nes

序号 No.	税则号列 Tariff Item	货 品 名 称	普通税率 Gen.	最惠国税率 M.F.N.	Article Description
15	37024100	未曝光无齿孔宽长彩色胶卷（宽长胶卷指宽度＞610毫米， 长度＞200米）	202元/平方米	7.1元/平方米	Film rolls, for colour photography, unexposed, without perforations, of any material other than paper, paperboard or textiles, width >610mm, length>200m
16	37024221	印刷电路板制造用光致抗蚀干膜（指宽度＞610毫米， 长度＞200米）	110元/平方米	0.6元/平方米	Wide anticorrosive photographic plate for printed circuit processing, unexposed, without perforations, of any material other than paper, paperboard or textiles, width >610mm, length>200m
17	37024229	照相制版其他未曝光无齿宽长胶卷(宽长指宽度＞610毫米， 长度＞200米)	110元/平方米	1.6元/平方米	Film rolls for preparing printing plates or cylinders, unexposed, without perforations, of any material other than paper, paperboard or textiles, width >610mm, length >200m, excl. wide anticorrosive photographic plate for printed circuit processing
18	37024292	红色或红外激光胶片	213元/平方米	2.4元/平方米	Infra-red or red laser film,unexposed, without perforations, of any material other than paper, paperboard or textiles, width＞610mm, length＞200m, excl. wide anticorrosive photographic plate for printed circuit processing
19	37024299	黑白其他未曝光无齿孔宽长胶卷（宽长胶卷指宽度＞610毫米,长度＞200米)	213元/平方米	7元/平方米	Unexposed monochrome phtotgraphic film in rolls, without perforations, width >610mm, length>200m
20	37024329	其他照相制版用未曝光无齿孔胶卷(指宽度＞610毫米， 长度≤200米)	104元/平方米	3.7元/平方米	Film rolls for preparing printing plates or cylinders, unexposed, without perforations, width >610mm, length≤200m, of any material other than paper, paperboard or textile, excl. laser phototypesetting film
21	37024390	彩色或黑白其他用未曝光无齿孔中长胶卷（中长胶卷指宽度＞610毫米， 长度≤200米）	202元/平方米	17元/平方米	Film rolls, unexposed, without perforations, width>610mm, length ≤200m, of any material other than paper, paperboard or textiles, nes
22	37024421	照相制版用未曝光激光照排片(宽度＞105毫米，≤610毫米)	115元/平方米	2元/平方米	Laser phototypesetting film, unexposed, without perforations, 105mm＜width≤610mm, of any material other than paper, paperboard or textiles
23	37024422	印刷电路板制造用光致抗蚀干膜（宽度＞105毫米，≤610毫米）	115元/平方米	5元/平方米	Narrow anticorrosive photographic plate for printed circuit processing, unexposed, without perforations, 105mm＜width≤610mm, of any material other than paper,

序号 No.	税则号列 Tariff Item	货 品 名 称	普通税率 Gen.	最惠国税率 M.F.N.	Article Description
					paperboard or textiles
24	37024429	其他照相制版用无齿孔未曝光胶卷（宽度＞105 毫米，≤610 毫米）	115 元/平方米	2.9 元/平方米	Film rolls for preparing printing plates or cylinders, unexposed, without perforations, 105mm <width ≤610mm, of any material other than paper, paperboard or textiles
25	37024490	彩色或黑白其他用无齿孔未曝光中宽胶卷（中宽胶卷指宽度>105 毫米，但≤610 毫米）	202 元/平方米	27 元/平方米	Film rolls, unexposed, without perforations, 105mm<width ≤ 610mm, of any material other than paper, paperboard or textiles, nes
26	37025200	彩色摄影用未曝光彩色胶卷，宽度小于 16 毫米	433 元/平方米	95 元/平方米	Film for colour photography (polychrome), of a width not exceeding 16mm
27	37025300	幻灯片用未曝光彩色摄影胶卷（宽度＞16 毫米，但≤35 毫米，长度≤30 米）	433 元/平方米	128 元/平方米	Slide film rolls for colour photography, unexposed, 16mm <width≤ 35mm, length<30m, of any material other than paper, paperboard or textiles
28	37025410	非幻灯片用彩色摄影胶卷（宽度=35 毫米，长度≤2 米）	433 元/平方米	18 元/平方米	Film rolls for colour photography other than for slides, unexposed, width=35mm and length≤2m, of any material other than paper, paperboard or textiles
29	37025490	其他非幻灯片用彩色摄影胶卷（宽度＞16 毫米，但≤35 毫米，长度≤30 米）	433 元/平方米	24 元/平方米	Film rolls for colour photography other than for slides, unexposed, 16mm＜width＜35mm, length≤ 30m, of any material other than paper, paperboard or textiles
30	37025520	未曝光的窄长彩色电影胶卷（窄长胶卷指宽度＞16 毫米，但≤35 毫米，长度＞30 米）	232 元/平方米	9 元/平方米	Colour cinematographic film rolls, unexposed, 16mm ＜ width ≤ 35mm, length ＞ 30m, of any material other than paper, paperboard or textiles
31	37025590	其他未曝光窄长彩色胶卷（窄长胶卷指宽度＞16 毫米，但≤35 毫米，长度＞30 米）	433 元/平方米	27 元/平方米	Colour film rolls for colour photography, unexposed, 16mm <width ≤ 35mm, length >30m, excl. cinematographic film
32	37025620	未曝光的中宽彩色电影胶卷（中宽胶卷指宽度＞35 毫米）	232 元/平方米	13 元/平方米	Colour cinematographic film rolls, unexposed, width >35mm, of any material other than paper, paperboard or textiles
33	37025690	其他未曝光的中宽彩色胶卷（中宽胶卷指宽度＞35 毫米）	433 元/平方米	74 元/平方米	Film in rolls for colour photography, unexposed, width >35mm, of any material other than paper, paperboard or textiles, excl. cinematographic film
34	37029600	未曝光非彩色胶卷（宽度≤35 毫米，长度≤30 米）	210 元/平方米	21 元/平方米	Film rolls of neutral colour, unexposed, of any material other than paper, paperboard or textiles, of a width not exceeding 35mm and of a length not exceeding 30m

序号 No.	税则号列 Tariff Item	货 品 名 称	普通税率 Gen.	最惠国税率 M.F.N.	Article Description
35	37029700	未曝光非彩色胶卷（宽度≤35毫米， 长度>30米）	210元/平方米	9元/平方米	Film rolls of neutral colour, unexposed, of any material other than paper, paperboard or textiles, of a width not exceeding 35mm and of a length exceeding 30m
36	37029800	未曝光非彩色胶卷，宽度>35毫米	210元/平方米	10元/平方米	Film rolls of neutral colour, unexposed, of any material other than paper, paperboard or textiles, of a width exceeding 35mm
37	85211011	广播级磁带录像机	完税价格小于2000美元： 130%；完税价格大于2000美元：6%+20600元/台	完税价格小于2000美元： 30%；完税价格大于2000美元：3%+3283元/台	Broadcast quality, magnetic video tape recorders
38	85211019	其他磁带录像机	完税价格不高于2000美元：130%；完税价格高于2000美元：6%+20600元/台	完税价格不高于2000美元：30%；完税价格高于2000美元：3%+3283元/台	Other magnetic video tape recorders
39	85211020	磁带放像机	完税价格不高于2000美元：130%；完税价格高于2000美元：6%+20600元/台	完税价格不高于2000美元：30%；完税价格高于2000美元： 3%+3283元/台	Magnetic video tape reproducers
40	85258012	非特种用途的广播级电视摄像机	完税价格不高于5000美元：130%；完税价格高于5000美元：6%+51500元/台	完税价格不高于5000美元：35%；完税价格高于5000美元：3%+9728元/台	Other broadcast quality, television cameras, not for special purposes
41	85258013	非特种用途的其他电视摄像机	完税价格不高于5000美元：130%；完税价格高于5000美元：6%+51500元/台	完税价格不高于5000美元：35%；完税价格高于5000美元：3%+9728元/台	Other television cameras, not for special purposes
42	85258022	非特种用途的单镜头反光型数字照相机	完税价格不高于5000美元：130%；完税价格高于5000美元：6%+51500元/台	0	Other single lens reflex digital cameras, not for special purposes
43	85258025	非特种用途的其他可换镜头的数字照相机	完税价格不高于5000美元/台：130%；完税价格高于5000美元/台：6％+51500元	0	Other lens interchangeable digital cameras, not for special purposes
44	85258029	非特种用途的其他数字照相机	每台完税价格不高于5000美元：130%；每台完税价格高于5000美元：6%+51500元/台	0	Other digital cameras
45	85258032	非特种用途的广播级视频摄录一体机	每台完税价格不高于5000美元：130%；每台完税价格高于5000美元：6%+51500元/台	0	Other broadcast quality, video camera recorders
46	85258039	非特种用途的其他视频摄录一体机（家用型摄录一体机除外）	每台完税价格不高于5000美元：130%；每台完税价格高于5000美元：6%+51500元/台	0	Other video camera recorders, other than household video camera recorders

附录四

中华人民共和国进境物品进口税率表

Duty Rate on Inward Articles of the People's Republic of China

序号 No.	物品名称	税率(%) Duty	Article Description
1	书报、刊物、教育专用电影片、幻灯片、原版录音带、录相带； 金、银及其制品； 计算机、视频摄录一体机、数字照相机等信息技术产品、照相机； 食品、饮料； 本表2、3、4税号及备注中所不包含的其他商品	10	Book，newspaper，journal，movie copy for education，slide，cassette，video cassette，gold，silver or article，computer，video camera recorder，digital camera and other IT products，photographic camera，food，beverage，articles other than item 2, 3, 4
2	纺织品及其制成品； 电视摄像机及其他电器用具、自行车、手表、钟表（含配件、附件）	20	Textile product，television camera and other electric products，bicycles，watch，clock
3	高尔夫球及球具、高档手表	30	Golf ball and other golf equipment, luxury watch
4	烟、酒、化妆品	50	Tobacco product，spirits，wine，beer，cosmetic

注：避孕用具和避孕药品，超过海关规定的自用合理数量部分按有关规定予以退运或按货物进口程序办理报关及验放手续。

Note: About contraceptive instruments and contraceptive medicines，the extra amount of which exceeding the reasonable self-using level set by customs regulations should be backtrack，or apply for customs registration and examination as required by goods－importing procedures.

附录五

中华人民共和国进出口关税条例

（国务院总理温家宝2003年11月23日签署第392号国务院令，发布《中华人民共和国进出口关税条例》，自2004年1月1日起施行。）

第一章 总 则

第一条 为了贯彻对外开放政策，促进对外经济贸易和国民经济的发展，根据《中华人民共和国海关法》（以下简称《海关法》）的有关规定，制定本条例。

第二条 中华人民共和国准许进出口的货物、进境物品，除法律、行政法规另有规定外，海关依照本条例规定征收进出口关税。

第三条 国务院制定《中华人民共和国进出口税则》（以下简称《税则》）、《中华人民共和国进境物品进口税税率表》（以下简称《进境物品进口税税率表》），规定关税的税目、税则号列和税率，作为本条例的组成部分。

第四条 国务院设立关税税则委员会，负责《税则》和《进境物品进口税税率表》的税目、税则号列和税率的调整和解释，报国务院批准后执行；决定实行暂定税率的货物、税率和期限；决定关税配额税率；决定征收反倾销税、反补贴税、保障措施关税、报复性关税以及决定实施其他关税措施；决定特殊情况下税率的适用，以及履行国务院规定的其他职责。

第五条 进口货物的收货人、出口货物的发货人、进境物品的所有人，是关税的纳税义务人。

第六条 海关及其工作人员应当依照法定职权和法定程序履行关税征管职责，维护国家利益，保护纳税人合法权益，依法接受监督。

第七条 纳税义务人有权要求海关对其商业秘密予以保密，海关应当依法为纳税义务人保密。

Regulations of the People's Republic of China on Import and Export Duties

(Adopted at the 26th Executive Meeting of the State Council on 29 October 2003, promulgated by Decree No. 392 of the State Council of the People's Republic of China on 23 November 2003, and effective as of 1 January 2004.)

Chapter I General Provisions

Article 1 These Regulations are formulated in accordance with the relevant provisions of the Customs Law of the People's Republic of China (hereinafter referred to as the Customs Law) for the purposes of implementing the policy of opening to the outside world and promoting the development of foreign economic relations and foreign trade and the national economy.

Article 2 Unless otherwise provided for by laws or administrative regulations, the Customs shall, in accordance with these Regulations, collect import or export duties on all goods permitted by the People's Republic of China to be imported into or exported out of the Customs territory and all inward articles.

Article 3 The State Council shall formulate the Customs Import and Export Tariff of the People's Republic of China (hereinafter referred to as the Tariff) and the Flat Duty Rates on Inward Articles of the People's Republic of China (hereinafter referred to as the Flat Duty Rates on Inward Articles), providing for tariff items, tariff headings and duty rates, which constitute component parts of these Regulations.

Article 4 The State Council shall establish the Tariff Commission, which is responsible for making adjustment to and interpretation of tariff items, tariff headings and duty rates in the Tariff and the Flat Duty Rates on Inward Articles and implementing such adjustment and interpretation after they are submitted to and approved by the State Council; determining the goods subject to temporary duty rates and the rates and duration thereof; determining tariff quota rates; determining the imposition of anti-dumping duty, countervailing duty, safeguard duty, retaliatory duty or other tariff measures; determining the application of duty rates under special circumstances; and performing other functions and responsibilities prescribed by the State Council.

Article 5 The consignee of import goods, the consignor of export goods and the owner of inward articles are duty payers.

Article 6 The Customs and staff members thereof shall fulfil the responsibility of duty collection in accordance with the statutory authority and procedure, safeguard State interests, protect lawful rights and interests of duty payers, and receive supervision according to law.

Article 7 A duty payer has the right to request the Customs to keep confidential its commercial secrets, and the Customs shall keep confidential such secrets for the duty payer according to law.

第八条 海关对检举或者协助查获违反本条例行为的单位和个人，应当按照规定给予奖励，并负责保密。

Article 8 The Customs shall, in accordance with the relevant provisions, reward units and individuals that inform against violations of these Regulations or provide assistance in investigating such violations, and be responsible for keeping secrets concerned.

第二章 进出口货物关税税率的设置和适用

Chapter II Composition and Application of Duty Rates on Import and Export Goods

第九条 进口关税设置最惠国税率、协定税率、特惠税率、普通税率、关税配额税率等税率。对进口货物在一定期限内可以实行暂定税率。

Article 9 Duty rates on import goods are composed of most-favoured-nation duty rates, conventional duty rates, special preferential duty rates, general duty rates, tariff quota duty rates, etc. Temporary duty rates may apply to import goods within a specific time limit.

出口关税设置出口税率。对出口货物在一定期限内可以实行暂定税率。

Duty rates on export goods are designed to collect export duty. Temporary duty rates may apply to export goods within a specific time limit.

第十条 原产于共同适用最惠国待遇条款的世界贸易组织成员的进口货物，原产于与中华人民共和国签订含有相互给予最惠国待遇条款的双边贸易协定的国家或者地区的进口货物，以及原产于中华人民共和国境内的进口货物，适用最惠国税率。

Article 10 The most-favoured-nation duty rates shall apply to import goods originated from members of the World Trade Organization that are subject to the common application of the most-favoured-nation clause, import goods originated from countries or regions with which the People's Republic of China has concluded a bilateral trade agreement for reciprocally granting of most-favoured-nation treatment, and import goods originated from the Customs territory of the People's Republic of China.

原产于与中华人民共和国签订含有关税优惠条款的区域性贸易协定的国家或者地区的进口货物，适用协定税率。

The conventional duty rates shall apply to import goods originated from countries or regions with which the People's Republic of China has concluded a regional trade agreement that comprises preferential duty clauses.

原产于与中华人民共和国签订含有特殊关税优惠条款的贸易协定的国家或者地区的进口货物，适用特惠税率。

The special preferential duty rates shall apply to import goods originated from countries or regions with which the People's Republic of China has concluded a trade agreement that comprises special preferential duty clauses.

原产于本条第一款、第二款和第三款所列以外国家或者地区的进口货物，以及原产地不明的进口货物，适用普通税率。

The general duty rates shall apply to import goods originated from countries or regions other than those specified in Paragraphs 1, 2 and 3 of this Article or to the import goods of undetermined origins.

第十一条 适用最惠国税率的进口货物有暂定税率的，应当适用暂定税率；适用协定税率、特惠税率的进口货物有暂定税率的，应当从低适用税率；适用普通税率的进口货物，不适用暂定税率。

Article 11 Where there are temporary duty rates on import goods to which the most-favoured-nation duty rates are applicable, such temporary duty rates shall apply; where there are temporary duty rates on import goods to which the conventional duty rates or preferential duty rates are applicable, the lower duty rates shall apply; temporary duty rates shall not apply to import goods to which the general duty rates are applicable.

适用出口税率的出口货物有暂定税率的，应当适用暂定税率。

Where there are temporary duty rates on export goods to which the export duty rates are applicable, such temporary duty rates shall apply.

第十二条 按照国家规定实行关税配额管理的进口货物，关税配额内的，适用关税配额税率；关税配额外的，其税率的适用按照本条例第十条、第十一条的规定执行。

Article 12 Where the quantity of import goods that are subject to tariff quota administration in accordance with the provisions of the State is within the tariff quota, the tariff quota duty rates shall apply; if such quantity exceeds the tariff quota, the application of the duty rates shall be governed by the provisions of Article 10 or 11 of these Regulations.

第十三条 按照有关法律、行政法规的规定对进口货物采取反倾销、反补贴、保障措施的，其税率的适用按照《中华人民共和国反倾销条例》、《中华人民共和国反补贴条例》和《中华人民共和国保障措施条例》的有关规定执行。

Article 13 Where anti-dumping, countervailing or safeguard measures are adopted on import goods in accordance with the provisions of the relevant laws or administrative regulations, the application of duty rates of such import goods shall be governed by the relevant provisions of the Regulations of the People's Republic of China on Anti-Dumping, the Regulations of the People's Republic of China on Countervailing Measures, and the Regulations of the People's Republic of China on Safeguards.

第十四条 任何国家或者地区违反与中华人民共和国签订或者共同参加的贸易协定及相关协定，对中华人民共和国在贸易方面采取禁止、限制、加征关税或者其他影响正常贸易的措施的，对原产于该国家或者地区的进口货物可以征收报复性关税，适用报复性关税税率。

Article 14 Where any country or region, in violation of the trade agreements or other relevant agreements that it concludes or accedes to with the People's Republic of China, unilaterally adopts measures affecting normal trade such as imposition of prohibition or restriction or surcharge of duties in the trade with the People's Republic of China, retaliatory duty may be imposed on import goods originated from such country or region and retaliatory duty rates may apply.

征收报复性关税的货物、适用国别、税率、期限和征收办法，由国务院关税税则委员会决定并公布。

The goods and countries subject to retaliatory duty, as well as the rates, duration and collection measures of retaliatory duty shall bc determined and published by the Tariff Commission of the State Council.

第十五条 进出口货物，应当适用海关接受该货物申报进口或者出口之日实施的税率。

Article 15 For any import or export goods, the duty rates implemented on the date when the Customs accepts the declaration for import or export of such goods shall apply.

进口货物到达前，经海关核准先行申报的，应当适用装载该货物的运输工具申报进境之日实施的税率。

Where, upon verification and approval of the Customs, the declaration is made prior to entry of import goods, the duty rates implemented on the date of declaration of the means of transport carrying such goods for entry shall apply.

转关运输货物税率的适用日期，由海关总署另行规定。

The date for application of the duty rates on goods for the transport under Customs transit shall be separately provided for by the General Administration of Customs.

第十六条 有下列情形之一，需缴纳税款的，应当适用海关接受申报办理纳税手续之日实施的税率：

Article 16 Where duty needs to be paid under any of the following circumstances, the duty rates implemented on the date when the Customs accepts the declaration for duty payment shall apply:

（一）保税货物经批准不复运出境的；

(1)where bonded goods are, with approval, not to be re-transported out of the Customs territory;

（二）减免税货物经批准转让或者移作他用的；

(2)where goods subject to duty reduction or exemption are, with approval, to be transferred or diverted to other purposes;

（三）暂准进境货物经批准不复运出境，以及暂准出境货物经批准不复运进境的；

(3)where goods permitted to temporarily enter or leave the Customs territory are, with approval, not to be re-transported out of or into the Customs territory;

（四）租赁进口货物，分期缴纳税款的。

(4)where the duty on import goods on lease is to be paid by instalments.

第十七条 补征和退还进出口货物关税，应当按照本条例第十五条或者第十六条的规定确定适用的税率。

Article 17 In the recovery or refund of duties on import or export goods, the duty rates to apply shall be determined in accordance with the provisions of Article 15 or 16 of these Regulations.

因纳税义务人违反规定需要追征税款的，应当适用该行为发生之日实施的税率；行为发生之日不能确定的，适用海关发现该行为之日实施的税率。

Where there is a need to pursue the payment of duties unpaid due to the duty payer's violation of relevant provisions, the duty rates implemented on the date when such violation occurs shall apply; if it is impossible to ascertain the date when such violation occurs, the duty rates implemented on the date when the Customs finds such violation shall apply.

第三章 进出口货物完税价格的确定

Chapter III Determination of Customs Value of Import and Export Goods

第十八条 进口货物的完税价格由海关以符合本条第三款所列条件的成交价格以及该货物运抵中华人民共和国境内输入地点起卸前的运输及其相关费用、保险费为基础审查确定。

Article 18 The customs value of import goods shall be determined by the Customs on the basis of the transaction value which complies with the conditions specified in Paragraph 3 of this Article, as well as the costs of transport, charges associated with transport, and the cost of insurance incurred prior to unloading of such goods at the port or place of entry within the Customs territory of the People's Republic of China.

进口货物的成交价格，是指卖方向中华人民共和国境内销售该货物时买方为进口该货物向卖方实付、应付的，并按照本条例第十九条、第二十条规定调整后的价款总额，包括直接支付的价款和间接支付的价款。

The transaction value of import goods is the price actually paid or payable for the import goods by the buyer when sold by the seller for export to the Customs territory of the People's Republic of China, adjusted in accordance with the provisions of Articles 19 and 20 of these Regulations, including the price paid directly and indirectly.

进口货物的成交价格应当符合下列条件：

The transaction value of import goods shall comply with the following conditions:

（一）对买方处置或者使用该货物不予限制，但法律、行政法规规定实施的限制、对货物转售地域的限制和对货物价格无实质性影响的限制除外；

(1)there are no restrictions as to the disposition or use of the goods by the buyer other than restrictions which are imposed by laws or administrative regulations, restrictions which limit the geographical area in which the goods may be resold, or restrictions which do not substantially affect the value of the goods;

（二）该货物的成交价格没有因搭售或者其他因素的影响而无法确定；

(2)the transaction value of such goods is not subject to some condition or consideration such as tie-in sale for which a value cannot be determined with respect to the goods being valued;

（三）卖方不得从买方直接或者间接获得因该货物进口后转售、处置或者使用而产生的任何收益，或者虽有收益但能够按照本条例第十九条、第二十条的规定进行调整；

(3)no part of the proceeds of any subsequent resale, disposal or use of the import goods by the buyer will accrue directly or indirectly to the seller, or appropriate adjustment can be made to the proceeds, if any, in accordance with the provisions of Articles 19 and 20 of these Regulations;

（四）买卖双方没有特殊关系，或者虽有特殊关系但未对成交价格产生影响。

(4)the buyer and seller are not related or, although the buyer and seller are related, such relationship does not affect the transaction value.

第十九条 进口货物的下列费用应当计入完税价格：

Article 19 The following costs shall be added to the customs value of import goods:

（一）由买方负担的购货佣金以外的佣金和经纪费；

(1)commissions and brokerage incurred by the buyer, except buying commissions;

（二）由买方负担的在审查确定完税价格时与该货物视为一体的容器的费用；

(2)the cost of containers treated as being one for customs purposes with the goods in question, which is incurred by the buyer;

（三）由买方负担的包装材料费用和包装劳务费用；

(3)the cost of packing incurred by the buyer, whether for labour or materials;

（四）与该货物的生产和向中华人民共和国境内销售有关的，由买方以免费或者以低于成本的方式提供并可以按适当比例分摊的料件、工具、模具、消耗材料及类似货物的价款，以及在境外开发、设计等相关服务的费用；

(4)the value, apportioned as appropriate, of such goods as materials, components, parts, tools, dies, moulds, consumed materials and similar items, and such services as development, design and associated services undertaken elsewhere than in the Customs territory of the People's Republic of China where supplied by the buyer free of charge or at reduced cost for use in connection with the production and sale for export of the import goods to the Customs territory of the People's Republic of China;

（五）作为该货物向中华人民共和国境内销售的条件，买方必须支付的、与该货物有关的特许权使用费；

(5)royalties and license fees related to the import goods that the buyer must pay, as a condition for sale of such goods to the Customs territory of the People's Republic of China;

（六）卖方直接或者间接从买方获得的该货物进口后转售、处置或者使用的收益。

(6)the value of any part of the proceeds of any subsequent resale, disposal or use of the goods that accrues directly or indirectly to the seller.

第二十条 进口时在货物的价款中列明的下列税收、费用，不计入该货物的完税价格：

Article 20 The customs value of import goods shall not include the following taxes and charges that are specified in the price of such import goods at the time of importation:

（一）厂房、机械、设备等货物进口后进行建设、安装、装配、维修和技术服务的费用；

(1)charges for construction, erection, assembly, maintenance, or technical assistance, undertaken after importation on import goods such as industrial plant, machinery or equipment;

（二）进口货物运抵境内输入地点起卸后的运输及其相关费用、保险费；

(2)the costs of transport, charges associated with transport, and the cost of insurance incurred after unloading of import goods at the port or place of entry within the Customs territory;

（三）进口关税及国内税收。

(3)import duty and other internal taxes.

第二十一条 进口货物的成交价格不符合本条例第十八条第三款规定条件的，或者成交价格不能确定的，海关经了解有关情况，并与纳税义务人进行价格磋商后，依次以下列价格估定该货物的完税价格：

Article 21 Where the transaction value of import goods does not comply with the conditions prescribed in Paragraph 3 of Article 18 of these Regulations, or it is impossible to determine the transaction value, the Customs shall, after acquainting itself with the relevant information and consulting over price with the duty payer, determine the customs value of the import goods in accordance with the following values in their given order:

（一）与该货物同时或者大约同时向中华人民共和国境内销售的相同货物的成交价格；

(1)the transaction value of identical goods sold for export to the Customs territory of the People's Republic of China and exported at or about the same time as the goods being valued;

（二）与该货物同时或者大约同时向中华人民共和国境内销售的类似货物的成交价格；

(2)the transaction value of similar goods sold for export to the Customs territory of the People's Republic of China and exported at or about the same time as the goods being valued;.

（三）与该货物进口的同时或者大约同时，将该进口货物、相同或者类似进口货物在第一级销售环节销售给无特殊关系买方最大销售总量的单位价格，但应当扣除本条例第二十二条规定的项目；

(3)the unit price at which the import goods or identical or similar import goods are sold in the greatest aggregate quantity, at or about the time of importation of the goods being valued, to an unrelated buyer in the first sale, with all items specified in Article 22 of these Regulations deducted;

（四）按照下列各项总和计算的价格：生产该货物所使用的料件成本和加工费用，向中华人民共和国境内销售同等级或者同种类货物通常的利润和一般费用，该货物运抵境内输入地点起卸前的运输及其相关费用、保险费；

(4)the computed value which consists of the total sum of the following items: the cost or value of materials, components and parts, and fabrication or other processing employed in producing the import goods; an amount for profit and general expenses equal to that usually reflected in sales of goods of the same class or kind as the import goods being valued to the Customs territory of the People's Republic of China; the costs of transport, charges associated with transport, and the cost of insurance incurred prior to unloading of import goods at the port or place of entry within the Customs territory;

（五）以合理方法估定的价格。

(5)the value determined on a reasonable basis.

纳税义务人向海关提供有关资料后，可以提出申请，颠倒前款第（三）项和第（四）项的适用次序。

The duty payer may, after providing relevant information or data to the Customs, make a request to reverse the order of the application of items (3) and (4) of the preceding paragraph.

第二十二条 按照本条例第二十一条第一款第（三）项规定估定完税价格，应当扣除的项目是指：

Article 22 In determining the customs value of import goods in accordance with item (3) of Paragraph 1 of Article 21 of these Regulations, the items that shall be deducted are as follows:

（一）同等级或者同种类货物在中华人民共和国境内第一级销售环节销售时通常的利润和一般费用以及通常支付的佣金；

(1)either profit and general expenses or commissions usually paid in the first sale of import goods of the same class or kind within the Customs territory of the People's Republic of China;

（二）进口货物运抵境内输入地点起卸后的运输及其相关费用、保险费；

(2)the costs of transport, charges associated with transport, and the cost of insurance incurred after unloading of import goods at the port or place of entry within the Customs territory;

（三）进口关税及国内税收。

(3)import duty and internal taxes.

第二十三条 以租赁方式进口的货物，以海关审查确定的该货物的租金作为完税价格。

Article 23 The customs value of import goods on lease shall be the rental determined by the Customs.

纳税义务人要求一次性缴纳税款的，纳税义务人可以选择按照本条例第二十一条的规定估定完税价格，或者按照海关审查确定的租金总额作为完税价格。

Where the duty payer requests to pay the duties in a lump sum, it may choose to have the customs value determined in accordance with the provisions of Article 21 of these Regulations or take total rental determined by the Customs as the customs value.

第二十四条 运往境外加工的货物，出境时已向海关报明并在海关规定的期限内复运进境的，应当以境外加工费和料件费以及复运进境的运输及其相关费用和保险费审查确定完税价格。

Article 24 The customs value of goods which are transported out of the Customs territory for processing with the declaration thereof made to the Customs at the time of departure and re-transported into the Customs territory within the time limit set by the Customs shall be determined on the basis of the charges on overseas processing, the cost of materials, components and parts, the costs of the re-transport, charges associated with re-transport, and the cost of insurance for the re-transport.

第二十五条 运往境外修理的机械器具、运输工具或者其他货物，出境时已向海关报明并在海关规定的期限内复运进境的，应当以境外修理费和料件费审查确定完税价格。

Article 25 The customs value for mechanic appliances, means of transport or any other goods which are transported out of the Customs territory for repairs with the declaration thereof made to the Customs at the time of departure and re-transported into the Customs territory within the time limit set by the Customs shall be determined on the basis of the charges on the repairs and the cost of materials, components and parts used for the repairs.

第二十六条 出口货物的完税价格由海关以该货物的成交价格以及该货物运至中华人民共和国境内输出地点装载前的运输及其相关费用、保险费为基础审查确定。

Article 26 The customs value of export goods shall be determined by the Customs on the basis of the transaction value thereof and the costs of transport, charges associated with transport, and the cost of insurance incurred prior to loading of such goods at the port or place of departure within the Customs territory of the People's Republic of China.

出口货物的成交价格，是指该货物出口时卖方为出口该货物应当向买方直接收取和间接收取的价款总额。

The transaction value of export goods is the total amount of the price that shall be charged by the seller, directly or indirectly, from the buyer for the goods sold for export.

出口关税不计入完税价格。

The export duty shall not be added to the customs value of export goods.

第二十七条 出口货物的成交价格不能确定的，海关经了解有关情况，并与纳税义务人进行价格磋商后，依次以下列价格估定该货物的完税价格：

Article 27 Where it is impossible to determine the transaction value of export goods, the Customs shall, after acquainting itself with the relevant information and consulting over price with the duty payer, determine the customs value of export goods in accordance with the following values in their given order:

（一）与该货物同时或者大约同时向同一国家或者地区出口的相同货物的成交价格；

(1)the transaction value of identical goods sold for export to the same country or region of importation and exported at or about the same time as the goods being valued;

（二）与该货物同时或者大约同时向同一国家或者地区出口的类似货物的成交价格；

(2)the transaction value of similar goods sold for export to the same country or region of importation and exported at or about the same time as the goods being valued;

（三）按照下列各项总和计算的价格：境内生产相同或者类似货物的料件成本、加工费用，通常的利润和一般费用，境内发生的运输及其相关费用、保险费；

(3)the computed value which consists of the total sum of the following items: the cost or value of materials, components and parts and fabrication or other processing employed in producing the identical or similar goods within the Customs territory; normal profit and general expenses; the costs of transport, charges associated with transport, and the cost of insurance incurred within the Customs territory;

（四）以合理方法估定的价格。

(4)the value determined on a reasonable basis.

第二十八条 按照本条例规定计入或者不计入完税价格的成本、费用、税收，应当以客观、可量化的数据为依据。

Article 28 The additions or deductions of costs, charges or taxes to or from the customs value in accordance with the provisions of these Regulations shall be made on the basis of objective and quantifiable data.

第四章 进出口货物关税的征收

Chapter IV Duty Collection on Import and Export Goods

第二十九条 进口货物的纳税义务人应当自运输工具申报进境之日起14日内，出口货物的纳税义务人除海关特准的外，应当在货物运抵海关监管区后、装货的24小时以前，向货物的进出境地海关申报。进出口货物转关运输的，按照海关总署的规定执行。

Article 29 Declaration of import goods shall be made to the Customs at the port or place of entry by the duty payer within 14 days from the date of declaration of entry of the means of transport; declaration of export goods shall, unless otherwise specially approved by the Customs, be made to the Customs at the port or place of departure by the duty payer after the arrival of the goods at the Customs Surveillance Zone and 24 hours prior to loading thereof. Import or export goods in transit shall be dealt with in accordance with the provisions of the General Administration of Customs.

进口货物到达前，纳税义务人经海关核准可以先行申报。具体办法由海关总署另行规定。

An advance declaration may be made by the duty payer with the approval of the Customs before the arrival of import goods. The specific measures therefore shall be separately formulated by the General Administration of Customs.

第三十条 纳税义务人应当依法如实向海关申报，并按照海关的规定提供有关确定完税价格、进行商品归类、确定原产地以及采取反倾销、反补贴或者保障措施等所需的资料；必要时，海关可以要求纳税义务人补充申报。

Article 30 The duty payer shall make a truthful declaration to the Customs in accordance with the law and provide, as required by the Customs, the relevant information or data needed for determination of customs value, classification of goods, determination of origin, or adoption of antidumping, countervailing, or safeguard measures. When necessary, the Customs may require the duty payer to make a supplementary declaration.

第三十一条 纳税义务人应当按照《税则》规定的目录条文和归类总规则、类注、章注、子目注释以及其他归类注释，对其申报的进出口货物进行商品归类，并归入相应的税则号列；海关应当依法审核确定该货物的商品归类。

Article 31 The duty payer shall classify the declared import or export goods into the corresponding tariff headings in accordance with the terms of the headings, the general rules for the classification, and the notes to sections, chapters or sub-headings as well as other explanatory notes to classification, which are prescribed in the Tariff. The Customs shall verify and determine the goods classification according to law.

第三十二条 海关可以要求纳税义务人提供确定商品归类所需的有关资料；必要时，海关可以组织化验、检验，并将海关认定的化验、检验结果作为商品归类的依据。

Article 32 The Customs may require the duty payer to provide the information or data needed for goods classification and, when necessary, organize laboratory analysis or inspection. The results of the analysis or inspection shall, after being confirmed by the Customs, be taken as the grounds for goods classification.

第三十三条 海关为审查申报价格的真实性和准确性，可以查阅、复制与进出口货物有关的合同、发票、账册、结付汇凭证、单据、业务函电、录音录像制品和其他反映买卖双方关系及交易活动的资料。

Article 33 The Customs may, in order to verify the truth and accuracy of the declared value, examine or copy the contracts, invoices, accounts, certificates for foreign exchange payment and settlement, bills, records, documents, business correspondences, audio and visual products related to import and export goods and other materials reflecting the relationship and transaction between the buyer and the seller.

海关对纳税义务人申报的价格有怀疑并且所涉关税数额较大的，经直属海关关长或者其授权的隶属海关关长批准，凭海关总署统一格式的协助查询账户通知书及有关工作人员的工作证件，可以查询纳税义务人在银行或者其他金融机构开立的单位账户的资金往来情况，并向银行业监督管理机构通报有关情况。

Where the Customs has doubts about the value declared by the duty payer and the duties involved are of a large amount, the Customs may, upon the approval of the director of the Customs office directly under the General Administration of Customs or the director of a Customs office subordinate to and authorized by the former and on the strength of the Notice for Assistance in Account Inquiry with the format unified by the General Administration of Customs and credentials of relevant staff members, inquire about the fund transactions through the unit accounts opened at banks or other financial institutions by the duty payer, and inform the banking regulatory agency of relevant information.

第三十四条 海关对纳税义务人申报的价格有怀疑的，应当将怀疑的理由书面告知纳税义务人，要求其在规定的期限内书面作出说明、提供有关资料。

Article 34 Where the Customs has doubts about the value declared by the duty payer, the Customs shall inform the duty payer in writing of the grounds for such doubts and require the duty payer to provide a written explanation and the relevant information and data within a specified time limit.

纳税义务人在规定的期限内未作说明、未提供有关资料的，或者海关仍有理由怀疑申报价格的真实性和准确性的，海关可以不接受纳税义务人申报的价格，并按照本条例第三章的规定估定完税价格。

If the duty payer fails to provide explanation and relevant information and data within the specified time limit or the Customs still has reasonable doubts about the truth or accuracy of the declared value, the Customs may refuse to accept the declared value and determine the customs value in accordance with the provisions of Chapter III of these Regulations.

第三十五条 海关审查确定进出口货物的完税价格后，纳税义务人可以以书面形式要求海关就如何确定其进出口货物的完税价格作出书面说明，海关应当向纳税义务人作出书面说明。

Article 35 Upon determination of the customs value of import or export goods by the Customs, the duty payer may request the Customs in writing to provide a written explanation as to how the customs value of import or export goods is determined. The Customs shall provide the written explanation to the duty payer accordingly.

第三十六条 进出口货物关税，以从价计征、从量计征或者国家规定的其他方式征收。

Article 36 The duty on import or export goods shall be collected in the form of *ad valorem* duty, specific duty, or other forms prescribed by the State.

从价计征的计算公式为：

应纳税额=完税价格×关税税率

The calculation formula for *ad valorem* duty is:

Duty Payable=Customs Value × Duty Rate

从量计征的计算公式为：

应纳税额=货物数量×单位税额

The calculation formula for specific duty is:

Duty Payable = Quantity of Goods × Unit Duty

第三十七条 纳税义务人应当自海关填发税款缴款书之日起 15 日内向指定银行缴纳税款。纳税义务人未按期缴纳税款的，从滞纳税款之日起，按日加收滞纳税款万分之五的滞纳金。

Article 37 The duty payer shall pay the duties at a designated bank within 15 days after the date of issuance of the memorandum of duty payment by the Customs. In case of any payment in arrears, 0.05% of the total amount of the overdue duties shall be charged as a fine for late payment per day from the date when the delayed payment occurs.

海关可以对纳税义务人欠缴税款的情况予以公告。

The Customs may publish the information about the arrearages on duties by duty payers.

海关征收关税、滞纳金等，应当制发缴款凭证，缴款凭证格式由海关总署规定。

The Customs shall issue a duty-memo for duties collected or receipt for fines for late payment. The format of the duty-memo or receipt shall be prescribed by the General Administration of Customs.

第三十八条 海关征收关税、滞纳金等，应当按人民币计征。

Article 38 The Customs shall collect duties and fines for late payment in terms of RMB.

进出口货物的成交价格以及有关费用以外币计价的，以中国人民银行公布的基准汇率折合为人民币计算完税价

Where the transaction value of import or export goods and associated costs are computed in a foreign currency, such

格；以基准汇率币种以外的外币计价的，按照国家有关规定套算为人民币计算完税价格。适用汇率的日期由海关总署规定。

foreign currency shall be converted into RMB at the basic exchange rate published by the People's Bank of China for the calculation of customs value. Where such basic exchange rate is not available for the foreign currency in question, the customs value shall be converted into RMB in accordance with the relevant provisions of the State. The date when the exchange rate applies shall be prescribed by the General Administration of Customs.

第三十九条 纳税义务人因不可抗力或者在国家税收政策调整的情形下，不能按期缴纳税款的，经海关总署批准，可以延期缴纳税款，但是最长不得超过6个月。

Article 39 Where the duty payer cannot pay duties within the time limit due to force majeure or adjustments to the State's taxation policy, such time limit may be extended upon the approval of the General Administration of Customs, but in any case the extension shall not exceed six months.

第四十条 进出口货物的纳税义务人在规定的纳税期限内有明显的转移、藏匿其应税货物以及其他财产迹象的，海关可以责令纳税义务人提供担保；纳税义务人不能提供担保的，海关可以按照《海关法》第六十一条的规定采取税收保全措施。

Article 40 Where there is an obvious indication that the duty payer of import or export goods is transferring or concealing the dutiable goods or other property in the specified time limit for duty payment, the Customs may order the duty payer to provide a bond; if the duty payer fails to do so, the Customs may take protective measures for duty collection in accordance with the provisions of Article 61 of the Customs Law.

纳税义务人、担保人自缴纳税款期限届满之日起超过3个月仍未缴纳税款的，海关可以按照《海关法》第六十条的规定采取强制措施。

Where the duty payer or the guarantor thereof fails to pay the duties within three months from the date of expiration of the time limit for duty payment, the Customs may take compulsory measures in accordance with the provisions of Article 60 of the Customs Law.

第四十一条 加工贸易的进口料件按照国家规定保税进口的，其制成品或者进口料件未在规定的期限内出口的，海关按照规定征收进口关税。

Article 41 Where the materials, components and parts for processing trade are imported in bond in accordance with the provisions of the State, but such import materials, components and parts or the finished products made thereof are not exported within the specified time limit, the Customs shall collect import duties in accordance with the relevant provisions.

加工贸易的进口料件进境时按照国家规定征收进口关税的，其制成品或者进口料件在规定的期限内出口的，海关按照有关规定退还进境时已征收的关税税款。

Where the import duty has been collected on materials, components and parts for processing trade upon entry in accordance with the provisions of the State and such materials, components and parts or the finished products made thereof are exported within the specified time limit, the Customs shall refund the duties previously collected in accordance with the relevant provisions.

第四十二条 经海关批准暂时进境或者暂时出境的下列货物，在进境或者出境时纳税义务人向海关缴纳相当于应纳税款的保证金或者提供其他担保的，可以暂不缴纳关税，并应当自进境或者出境之日起6个月内复运出境或者复运进境；经纳税义务人申请，海关可以根据海关总署的规定延长复运出境或者复运进境的期限：

Article 42 Where the following goods are permitted by the Customs to temporarily enter or leave the Customs territory and a cash deposit of an amount equivalent to that of the duties payable or a bond in another form has been provided to the Customs by the duty payer upon entry or departure, the duties of such goods may be temporarily exempted, on the condition that such goods shall be re-transported out of or into the Customs territory within six months from the date of entry or departure. Upon the request of the duty payer, the Customs may extend the time limit for re-transportation out of or into the Customs territory in accordance with the provisions of the General Administration of Customs:

（一）在展览会、交易会、会议及类似活动中展示或者使用的货物；

(1)goods for display or use at exhibitions, fairs, meetings or similar events;

（二）文化、体育交流活动中使用的表演、比赛用品；

(2)items for performance or contest in cultural or sports exchange;

（三）进行新闻报道或者摄制电影、电视节目使用的仪器、设备及用品；

(3)apparatus, equipment or items for press, cinematography or television programs;

（四）开展科研、教学、医疗活动使用的仪器、设备及用品；

(4)apparatus, equipment or items for scientific research, pedagogical or medical activities;

（五）在本款第（一）项至第（四）项所列活动中使用的交通工具及特种车辆；

(5)means of transport and special purpose motor vehicles for functions specified in Items (1) through (4) of this Paragraph;

（六）货样；

(6)samples;

（七）供安装、调试、检测设备时使用的仪器、工具；

(7)apparatus and tools for installation, adjustment or test of equipment;

（八）盛装货物的容器；

(8)containers of goods;

（九）其他用于非商业目的的货物。

(9)other goods intended for non-commercial purposes.

第一款所列暂准进境货物在规定的期限内未复运出境的，或者暂准出境货物在规定的期限内未复运进境的，海关应当依法征收关税。

Where the goods permitted to temporarily enter or leave the Customs territory in Paragraph 1 are not re-transported out of or into the Customs territory within the specified time limit, the Customs shall collect duties according to law.

第一款所列可以暂时免征关税范围以外的其他暂准进境货物，应当按照该货物的完税价格和其在境内滞留时间与折旧时间的比例计算征收进口关税。具体办法由海关总署规定。

Import duty on the goods permitted to temporarily enter the Customs territory other than those that are temporarily exempted from duties as prescribed by Paragraph 1 shall be computed on the basis of the customs value of such goods and the proportion of the time when such goods remain inside the Customs territory to the time of depreciation. The specific measures therefore shall be provided for by the General Administration of Customs.

第四十三条 因品质或者规格原因，出口货物自出口之日起 1 年内原状复运进境的，不征收进口关税。

Article 43 No import duty shall be collected on export goods re-transported into the Customs territory in the same state within one year from the date of exportation due to problems with quality or specifications.

因品质或者规格原因，进口货物自进口之日起 1 年内原状复运出境的，不征收出口关税。

No export duty shall be collected on import goods re-transported out of the Customs territory in the same state within one year from the date of importation due to problems with quality or specifications.

第四十四条 因残损、短少、品质不良或者规格不符原因，由进出口货物的发货人、承运人或者保险公司免费补偿或者更换的相同货物，进出口时不征收关税。被免费更换的原进口货物不退运出境或者原出口货物不退运进境的，海关应当对原进出口货物重新按照规定征收关税。

Article 44 Where, due to damage, shortage, poor quality or unconformity to specifications of import or export goods, the consignor or carrier of such goods or the insurance company provides, free of charge, identical import or export goods as compensation or replacement, no duties shall be collected on such identical goods. Where the original import or export goods that are replaced free of charge are not re-transported out of or into the Customs territory, the Customs shall re-collect duties thereon in accordance with the relevant provisions.

第四十五条 下列进出口货物，免征关税：

Article 45 The following import and export goods shall be exempted from duties:

（一）关税税额在人民币 50 元以下的一票货物；

(1)goods of a single consignment on which the duties are estimated to be not more than RMB 50 yuan;

（二）无商业价值的广告品和货样；

(2)advertising matter and samples, which are of no commercial value;

（三）外国政府、国际组织无偿赠送的物资；

(3)goods and materials, which are rendered gratis by international organizations or foreign governments;

（四）在海关放行前损失的货物；

（五）进出境运输工具装载的途中必需的燃料、物料和饮食用品。

(4)goods lost prior to Customs release;

(5)fuels, stores, beverages and provisions for use en route loaded on any means of transport, which is in transit across the frontier.

在海关放行前遭受损坏的货物，可以根据海关认定的受损程度减征关税。

The duties on goods damaged prior to Customs release may be deducted in accordance with the degree of damage confirmed by the Customs.

法律规定的其他免征或者减征关税的货物，海关根据规定予以免征或者减征。

The Customs shall, in accordance with the relevant provisions, grant duty reduction or exemption to other goods that are subject to duty reduction or exemption prescribed by law.

第四十六条 特定地区、特定企业或者有特定用途的进出口货物减征或者免征关税，以及临时减征或者免征关税，按照国务院的有关规定执行。

Article 46 Duty reduction or exemption granted to import and export goods of special areas or special enterprises or for special uses, as well as temporary duty reduction or exemption, shall be governed by the relevant provisions of the State Council.

第四十七条 进口货物减征或者免征进口环节海关代征税，按照有关法律、行政法规的规定执行。

Article 47 Any reduction or exemption of taxes collected on import goods by the Customs on behalf of other government departments shall be governed by the provisions of relevant laws and administrative regulations.

第四十八条 纳税义务人进出口减免税货物的，除另有规定外，应当在进出口该货物之前，按照规定持有关文件向海关办理减免税审批手续。经海关审查符合规定的，予以减征或者免征关税。

Article 48 Where the duty payer is to import or export goods granted duty reduction or exemption, the duty payer shall, unless otherwise prescribed, go through the formalities with the Customs for approval of duty reduction or exemption by presenting relevant documents as required before such goods are imported or exported. The duty reduction or exemption shall be granted if the Customs confirms such goods as qualified through examination.

第四十九条 需由海关监管使用的减免税进口货物，在监管年限内转让或者移作他用需要补税的，海关应当根据该货物进口时间折旧估价，补征进口关税。

Article 49 Where the import goods which are granted duty reduction or exemption and the use of which are under the Customs control are diverted to other purposes within the duration of Customs control and therefore the recovery of duties is needed, the import duty shall be recovered by the Customs on the basis of the value of import goods depreciated according to the time after importation.

特定减免税进口货物的监管年限由海关总署规定。

The duration of the Customs control over import goods granted special duty reduction or exemption shall be prescribed by the General Administration of Customs.

第五十条 有下列情形之一的，纳税义务人自缴纳税款之日起 1 年内，可以申请退还关税，并应当以书面形式向海关说明理由，提供原缴款凭证及相关资料：

Article 50 Under any of the following circumstances, the duty payer may, within one year from the date of duty payment, apply for a refund of duties by stating the reasons therefore in writing to the Customs and providing the original duty-memo and the relevant information and data:

（一）已征进口关税的货物，因品质或者规格原因，原状退货复运出境的；

(1)where any goods, on which the import duty has been collected, are re-transported out of the Customs territory in the original state due to problems with quality or specifications;

（二）已征出口关税的货物，因品质或者规划原因，原状退货复运进境，并已重新缴纳因出口而退还的国内环节有关税收的；

(2)where any goods, on which the export duty has been collected, are re-transported into the Customs territory in the original state due to problems with quality or specifications and all internal taxes refunded for export have been repaid;

（三）已征出口关税的货物，因故未装运出口，申报退关的。

(3)Where any goods, on which the export duty has been paid, are re-declared to the Customs as shut-out cargo because they are not loaded for export due to certain reasons.

海关应当自受理退税申请之日起 30 日内查实并通知纳税义务人办理退还手续。纳税义务人应当自收到通知之日起 3 个月内办理有关退税手续。

The Customs shall, within 30 days from the date of accepting an application for duty refund, ascertain the relevant facts and notify the duty payer to go through the refund formalities. The duty payer shall go through the refund formalities within three months from the date of receipt of the notification.

按照其他有关法律、行政法规规定应当退还关税的，海关应当按照有关法律、行政法规的规定退税。

Where duties shall be refunded in accordance with the provisions of other relevant laws and administrative regulations, the Customs shall refund duties accordingly.

第五十一条 进出口货物放行后，海关发现少征或者漏征税款的，应当自缴纳税款或者货物放行之日起 1 年内，向纳税义务人补征税款。但因纳税义务人违反规定造成少征或者漏征税款的，海关可以自缴纳税款或者货物放行之日起 3 年内追征税款，并从缴纳税款或者货物放行之日起按日加收少征或者漏征税款万分之五的滞纳金。

Article 51 Where the Customs finds that duties are short-collected or not collected on a consignment of import or export goods after the release, the Customs shall recover the duties payable from the duty payer within one year from the date of the duty payment or the release. If the short-collected or non-collected duties are attributable to the duty payer's violation of the provisions, the Customs may pursue the payment of the unpaid duties within three years from the date of the duty payment or the release, and impose a fine for late payment of 0.05% of the short-collected or non-collected duties per day from the date of the duty payment or the release.

海关发现海关监管货物因纳税义务人违反规定造成少征或者漏征税款的，应当自纳税义务人应缴纳税款之日起 3 年内追征税款，并从应缴纳税款之日起按日加收少征或者漏征税款万分之五的滞纳金。

Where the Customs finds that the short-collection or non-collection of duties on goods under Customs control is attributable to the duty payer's violation of the provisions, the Customs shall pursue the payment of the unpaid duties within three years from the date of the duty payment or the release, and impose a fine for late payment of 0.05% of the short-collected or non-collected duties per day from the date of the duty payment or the release.

第五十二条 海关发现多征税款的，应当立即通知纳税义务人办理退还手续。

Article 52 Upon finding any over-collection of duties, the Customs shall immediately notify the duty payer to go through the refund formalities.

纳税义务人发现多缴税款的，自缴纳税款之日起 1 年内，可以以书面形式要求海关退还多缴的税款并加算银行同期活期存款利息；海关应当自受理退税申请之日起 30 日内查实并通知纳税义务人办理退还手续。

Upon finding any over-collection of duties, the duty payer may, within one year from the date of duty payment, request in writing the Customs to refund the over-collected duties together with the interest for the corresponding period computed at the current deposit interest rate of the bank. The Customs shall, within 30 days from the date of accepting the application for duty refund, ascertain the relevant facts and notify the duty payer to go through the refund formalities.

纳税义务人应当自收到通知之日起 3 个月内办理有关退税手续。

The duty payer shall go through the refund formalities within three months from the date of receipt of the notification.

第五十三条 按照本条例第五十条、第五十二条的规定退还税款、利息涉及从国库中退库的，按照法律、行政法规有关国库管理的规定执行。

Article 53 Where the refund of duties or interest incurred therefrom under Articles 50 and 52 of these Regulations involves refund from the State treasury, such refund shall be governed by the provisions of the laws and administrative regulations on administration of the State treasury.

第五十四条 报关企业接受纳税义务人的委托，以纳税义务人的名义办理报关纳税手续，因报关企业违反规定而造成海关少征、漏征税款的，报关企业对少征或者漏征的税款、滞纳金与纳税义务人承担纳税的连带责任。

Article 54 Where a Customs broker that is commissioned by a duty payer to go through the formalities for declaration and duty payment in the name of the duty payer violates the relevant provisions and thus causes the short-collection or non-collection of duties, the Customs broker shall bear the joint and several liability with the duty payer for payment of the short-collected or non-collected duties and fines for late payment.

报关企业接受纳税义务人的委托，以报关企业的名义办理报关纳税手续的，报关企业与纳税义务人承担纳税的连带责任。

Where a Customs broker is commissioned by a duty payer to go through the formalities for declaration and duty payment in the name of the Customs broker, the Customs broker shall bear the joint and several liability with the duty payer for duty payment.

除不可抗力外，在保管海关监管货物期间，海关监管货物损毁或者灭失的，对海关监管货物负有保管义务的人应当承担相应的纳税责任。

Where, except due to force majeure, goods under Customs control are damaged, destroyed or irrecoverably lost during the period of Customs control, the person who is obliged to keep such goods shall bear the corresponding liability for duty payment.

第五十五条 欠税的纳税义务人，有合并、分立情形的，在合并、分立前，应当向海关报告，依法缴清税款。纳税义务人合并时未缴清税款的，由合并后的法人或者其他组织继续履行未履行的纳税义务；纳税义务人分立时未缴清税款的，分立后的法人或者其他组织对未履行的纳税义务承担连带责任。

Article 55 Where a duty payer that is in arrears with duty payment comes under circumstances such as merger or division, the duty payer shall, prior to the merger or division, notify the Customs and pay off the duties. If the duty payer fails to pay off the duties when it is merged, the legal person or other organization that results from the merger shall continue to fulfil the duty payment obligation that has not been fulfilled. If the duty payer fails to pay off the duties when it is divided, the legal person or other organization that results from the division shall bear the joint and several liability for fulfilling the duty payment obligation that has not been fulfilled.

纳税义务人在减免税货物、保税货物监管期间，有合并、分立或者其他资产重组情形的，应当向海关报告。按照规定需要缴税的，应当依法缴清税款；按照规定可以继续享受减免税、保税待遇的，应当到海关办理变更纳税义务人的手续。

Where a duty payer, during the period of Customs control over goods granted duty reduction or exemption or bonded goods, comes under circumstances such as merger, division or any other form of asset restructuring, the duty payer shall make a report thereon to the Customs. Those that need to pay duties in accordance with the relevant provisions shall pay off the duties according to law. Those that may continue to enjoy duty reduction or exemption or bond treatment in accordance with the relevant provisions shall go through the formalities for change of the duty payer with the Customs.

纳税义务人欠税或者在减免税货物、保税货物监管期间，有撤销、解散、破产或者其他依法终止经营情形的，应当在清算前向海关报告。海关应当依法对纳税义务人的应缴税款予以清缴。

Where a duty payer is in arrears with the payment of duties or, during the period of Customs control over goods granted duty reduction or exemption or bonded goods, comes under circumstances such as dissolution, disbandment, bankruptcy or any other statutory form of termination, the duty payer shall make a report thereon to the Customs prior to the liquidation. The Customs shall collect all the duties payable from the duty payer according to law.

第五章 进境物品进口税的征收

Chapter V Collection of Flat Duty on Inward Articles

第五十六条 进境物品的关税以及进口环节海关代征税合并为进口税，由海关依法征收。

Article 56 The import duty on inward articles and taxes collected by the Customs on behalf of other government departments for importation of such articles are amalgamated into the flat duty, which shall be collected by the Customs according to law.

第五十七条 海关总署规定数额以内的个人自用进境物品，免征进口税。

Article 57 Inward articles for personal use the aggregate value or quantity of which is within the quota prescribed by the General Administration of Customs shall be exempted from flat duty.

超过海关总署规定数额但仍在合理数量以内的个人自用进境物品，由进境物品的纳税义务人在进境物品放行前按照规定缴纳进口税。

The flat duty on inward articles for personal use that exceed the quota prescribed by the General Administration of Customs but are still within a reasonable quantity shall be paid by the duty payer of such inward articles in accordance with the relevant provisions prior to the release.

超过合理、自用数量的进境物品应当按照进口货物依法办理相关手续。

Where inward articles exceed the reasonable quantity for personal use, the relevant formalities shall be gone through in accordance with that of import goods.

国务院关税税则委员会规定按货物征税的进境物品，按照本条例第二章至第四章的规定征收关税。

The duty on inward articles that are deemed as import goods by the Tariff Commission of the State Council for duty collection shall be collected in accordance with the provisions of the Chapters II through IV of these Regulations.

第五十八条 进境物品的纳税义务人是指，携带物品进境的入境人员、进境邮递物品的收件人以及以其他方式进口物品的收件人。

Article 58 The duty payer of inward articles refers to the person who carries articles into the Customs territory, the addressee of inward postal items, or the recipient of articles imported in any other ways.

第五十九条 进境物品的纳税义务人可以自行办理纳税手续，也可以委托他人办理纳税手续。接受委托的人应当遵守本章对纳税义务人的各项规定。

Article 59 The duty payer of inward articles may go through the formalities for duty payment on its own or commission an agent to go through such formalities. The agent commissioned shall abide by all the provisions of this Chapter on the duty payer.

第六十条 进口税从价计征。

Article 60 Flat duty shall be collected in terms of *ad valorem* duty.

进口税的计算公式为：

进口税税额=完税价格×进口税税率

The calculation formula of flat duty is:

Flat Duty Payable= Customs Value ×Flat Duty Rate

第六十一条 海关应当按照《进境物品进口税税率表》及海关总署制定的《中华人民共和国进境物品归类表》、《中华人民共和国进境物品完税价格表》对进境物品进行归类、确定完税价格和确定适用税率。

Article 61 The Customs shall determine the classification, customs value and applicable duty rate of inward articles in accordance with the Flat Duty Rates on Inward Articles, and the Classification Table of Inward Articles of the People's Republic of China and Customs Value Table of Inward Articles of the People's Republic of China that are formulated by the General Administration of Customs.

第六十二条 进境物品，适用海关填发税款缴款书之日实施的税率和完税价格。

Article 62 The flat duty rate and customs value implemented on the date when the Customs issues the memorandum of duty payment shall apply to inward articles.

第六十三条 进口税的减征、免征、补征、追征、退还以及对暂准进境物品征收进口税参照本条例对货物征收进口关税的有关规定执行。

Article 63 The reduction, exemption, recovery, pursuit and refund of flat duty and the collection of flat duty on inward articles permitted to be temporarily transported into the Customs territory shall be governed by the relevant provisions of these Regulations on collection of import duty on goods.

第六章 附 则

Chapter VI Supplementary Provisions

第六十四条 纳税义务人、担保人对海关确定纳税义务人、确定完税价格、商品归类、确定原产地、适用税率或者汇率、减征或者免征税款、补税、退税、征收滞纳金、确定计征方式以及确定纳税地点有异议的，应当缴纳税款，并可以依法向上一级海关申请复议。对复议决定不服的，可以依法向人民法院提起诉讼。

Article 64 Where the duty payer or guarantor has objections to the Customs' determination of the duty payer or customs value; goods classification; determination of origin, applicable duty rates or exchange rates; duty reduction, exemption, recovery or refund; collection of fines for late payment; or determination of the manner and place of duty collection; it shall pay the duties and may apply to the Customs at the next higher level for administrative reconsideration according to law; if the duty payer or guarantor refuses to accept the decision of administrative reconsideration, it may lodge a lawsuit to the people's court according to law.

第六十五条 进口环节海关代征税的征收管理，适用关税征收管理的规定。

Article 65 Tax collection by the Customs on behalf of other government departments for importation shall be governed in accordance with the provisions on administration of duty collection.

第六十六条 有违反本条例规定行为的，按照《海关法》、

Article 66 The penalty for violation of the provisions of these

《中华人民共和国海关法行政处罚实施细则》和其他有关法律、行政法规的规定处罚。

Regulations shall be imposed in accordance with the provisions of the Customs Law, the Rules for the Implementation of Administrative Penalty under the Customs Law of the People's Republic of China and other relevant laws and administrative regulations.

第六十七条 本条例自2004年1月1日起施行。1992年3月18日国务院修订发布的《中华人民共和国进出口关税条例》同时废止。

Article 67 These Regulations shall be effective as of 1 January 2004. The Regulations of the People's Republic of China on Import and Export Duties revised and promulgated by the State Council on March 18, 1992 shall be simultaneously repealed.